ISSAC 2016

Proceedings of the 2016 ACM International Symposium on Symbolic and Algebraic Computation

Markus Rosenkranz
Editor

WILFRID LAURIER UNIVERSITY
LAURIER
Inspiring Lives.

July 20-22
2016
Tutorials:
July 19th

Wilfrid Laurier University
Waterloo
Ontario

www.issac-symposium.org/2016

Association for Computing Machinery

Association for
Computing Machinery

Advancing Computing as a Science & Profession

The Association for Computing Machinery
2 Penn Plaza, Suite 701
New York, New York 10121-0701

ISBN: 978-1-4503-4380-0

Additional copies may be ordered prepaid from:

ACM Order Department
PO Box 30777
New York, NY 10087-0777, USA

Phone: 1-800-342-6626 (USA and Canada)
+1-212-626-0500 (Global)
Fax: +1-212-944-1318
E-mail: acmhelp@acm.org
Hours of Operation: 8:30 am – 4:30 pm ET

Printed in the USA

Foreword

The 2016 International Symposium on Symbolic and Algebraic Computation (ISSAC 2016) is the premier conference for research in symbolic computation and computer algebra. ISSAC 2016, held at Wilfrid Laurier University, Canada, is the 41st meeting in the series. ISSAC was directly preceded by a series of conferences with the names SYMSAC, EUROCAL, EUROSAM and EUROCAM, initiated by the seminal ACM Symposium on Symbolic and Algebraic Manipulation (SYMSAM-1966) held 50 years ago.

The ISSAC conference is a showcase for original research contributions on all aspects of computer algebra and symbolic mathematical computation, including:

Algorithmic aspects:

- Exact and symbolic linear, polynomial and differential algebra
- Symbolic-numeric, homotopy, perturbation and series methods
- Computational algebraic geometry, group theory and number theory
- Computer arithmetic
- Summation, recurrence equations, integration, solution of ODEs and PDEs
- Symbolic methods in other areas of pure and applied mathematics
- Complexity of algebraic algorithms

Software aspects:

- Design of symbolic computation packages and systems
- Language design and type systems for symbolic computation
- Data representation
- Consideration for modern hardware
- Algorithm implementation and performance tuning
- Mathematical user interfaces

Application aspects:

- Applications stretching the current limits of computer algebra algorithms or systems, use computer algebra in new areas or new ways, or apply it in situations with broad impact.

The ISSAC Program Committee adhered to the highest standards and practices in the evaluation of submitted papers, and we are very pleased with the quality of the papers appearing at the conference. All papers submitted to ISSAC 2016 were judged, and accepted or rejected, solely according to their scientific novelty and excellence. Each submitted paper was assigned to three members of the Program Committee, and a minimum of three referee reports were obtained for each submission. Ultimately 50 papers were accepted for presentation and publication in the proceedings. The authors of accepted papers are from 17 countries.

In addition to the contributed research presentations, the program of ISSAC 2016 features 3 invited talks given by Ioannis Z. Emiris, J. Ian Munro, and Carsten Schneider, 3 tutorials given by Clemens G. Raab, Daniel Robertz, and Georg Regensburger, 2 satellite workshops: "Milestones in Computer Algebra" and "The Waterloo Workshop on Computer Algebra," as well as a poster session and a software exhibits session.

We gratefully acknowledge the thorough and important work of the Program Committee Members and external reviewers, whose names appear on the following pages, and thank all the authors and speakers for their contribution.

The success of a conference depends on the dedicated work of numerous volunteers, many of whom are listed on the following pages. To them, and to the rest of the community who contributed in various ways to the success of ISSAC 2016, we extend our thanks. We are grateful to the sponsors of the conference, who are also listed on these pages. Finally, we thank all the members of the local organization team at the Wilfrid Laurier University, our host institution.

We anticipate an exciting scientific event and an impressive demonstration of the vigorous community of symbolic and algebraic computation devoted to the 50th anniversary of ISSAC.

Sergei Abramov *(General co- Chair)*

Eugene Zima *(General co- Chair)*

Xiao-Shan Gao *(Program Committee Chair)*

Markus Rosenkranz *(Proceedings Editor)*

Table of Contents

ISSAC 2016 Symposium Organization

General Chairs:	Sergei Abramov *(Russian Academy of Sciences, Russia)* Eugene Zima *(Wilfrid Laurier University, Canada)*
Program Committee Chair:	Xiao-Shan Gao *(Chinese Academy of Sciences, China)*
Local Arrangements Chair:	Eugene Zima *(Wilfrid Laurier University, Canada)*
Treasurer:	Jacques Carette *(McMaster University, Canada)*
Proceedings Editor:	Markus Rosenkranz *(Johannes Kepler University, Austria)*
Tutorial Chair:	Moulay Barkatou *(University of Limoges, France)*
Poster Chair:	Shaoshi Chen *(Chinese Academy of Sciences, China)*
Software Presentations Chair:	Roman Pearce *(Simon Fraser University, Canada)*
Publicity Chair / Webmaster:	Albert Heinle *(University of Waterloo, Canada)*
Program Committee:	Alin Bostan *(INRIA, France)* Russell Bradford *(University of Bath, UK)* Carlos D'Andrea *(University of Barcelona, Spain)* Jean-Guillaume Dumas *(Université de Grenoble Alpes, France)* Ruyong Feng *(Chinese Academy of Sciences, China)* Xiao-Shan Gao *(Chinese Academy of Sciences, China)* Jonathan Hauenstein *(University of Notre Dame, USA)* Hoon Hong *(North Carolina State University, USA)* Deepak Kapur *(University of New Mexico, USA)* George Labahn *(University of Waterloo, Canada)* Wen-shin Lee *(University of Antwerp, Belgium)* Ernst W. Mayr *(Technische Universität München, Germany)* Scott McCallum *(Macquarie University, Australia)* Teo Mora *(Università di Genova, Italy)* Michael Monagan *(Simon Fraser University, Canada)* Daniel Panario *(Carleton University, Canada)* Ludovic Perret *(Université Pierre et Marie Curie, France)* Michael Sagraloff *(Max-Planck-Institut für Informatik, Germany)* Franz Winkler *(Johannes Kepler University, Austria)* Kazuhiro Yokoyama *(Rikkyo University, Japan)*
Poster Presentation Committee:	Shaoshi Chen *(Chinese Academy of Sciences, China)* Ryoya Fukasaku *(Tokyo University of Science, Japan)* Gregor Kemper *(Technische Universität München, Germany)* Christoph Koutschan *(Austrian Academy of Sciences, Austria)* Romain Lebreton *(Université Montpellier 2, France)* Wei Li *(Chinese Academy of Sciences, China)*

Additional Reviewers (continued):

Samuel Lundqvist
Gennadi Malaschonok
Thomas Markwig
Guillermo Matera
Marc Moreno Maza
Stephen Melczer
Andrey Minchenko
Guillaume Moroz
Chenqi Mou
Christophe Mouilleron
Hirokazu Murao
Katsusuke Nabeshima
Simone Naldi
Vincent Neiger
Winfried Neun
L.X.Chau Ngo
Johan S. R. Nielsen
Sebastian Pauli
Roman Pearce
Robin Pemantle
Clément Pernet
Gerhard Pfister
Veronika Pillwein
Marc Pouget
John Power
Guenael Renault
Bruce Reznick
Cordian Riener
Daniel Roche
David Roe
Margherita Roggero
Julien Roques
Fabrice Rouillier
Mohab Safey El Din
Massimiliano Sala
Bruno Salvy
B. David Saunders
David Saunders
Dmytro Savchuk
Nitin Saxena
Carsten Scherer
Stefan Schirra
Éric Schost
Igor Semaev
J.Rafael Sendra
Fatma Senguler Ciftci
Jeffrey Shallit
Vikram Sharma
Zhikun She
Ekaterina Shemyakova
Liyong Shen
Takafumi Shibuta
Igor Shparlinski
Michael Singer
William Sit
Allan Steel
Arne Storjohann
Adam Strzeboński
Thomas Sturm
Agnes Szanto
Akira Terui
Emmanuel Thomé
Stefan Toman
Elias Tsigaridas
William Turner
William Unger
Tristan Vaccon
Brigitte Vallee
Marc Van Barel
Joop Van De Pol
Joris van der Hoeven
Jan Verschelde
Gilles Villard
Alfredo Viola
Joachim von Zur Gathen
Michael Walter
Daqing Wan
Dingkang Wang
Qiang Wang
Volker Weispfenning
Thomas Wolf
Min Wu
Bican Xia
Dianyan Xiao
Zhengfeng Yang
Chee Yap
Masaya Yasuda
Josephine Yu
Chunming Yuan
Alessandro Zaccagnini
Guangxing Zeng
Lihong Zhi
Meng Zhou

Sponsors: ACM Special Interest Group on Symbolic and Algebraic Computation

Wilfrid Laurier University

Maplesoft

Interdisciplinary Research Institute MS2Discovery, Wilfrid Laurier University

The Fields Institute for Research in Mathematical Sciences, University of Toronto

Institute for Quantum Computing University of Waterloo

Perimeter Institute for Theoretical Physics

Faculty of Science Wilfrid Laurier University

Centre for Women in Science Wilfrid Laurier University

Fachgruppe Computeralgebra

Compact Formulae in Sparse Elimination

[Extended Abstract]

Ioannis Z. Emiris*
National and Kapodistrian University of Athens, and "Athena" Research Center, Greece
emiris@di.uoa.gr

ABSTRACT

It has by now become a standard approach to use the theory of sparse (or toric) elimination, based on the Newton polytope of a polynomial, in order to reveal and exploit the structure of algebraic systems. This talk surveys compact formulae, including older and recent results, in sparse elimination.

We start with root bounds and juxtapose two recent formulae: a generating function of the m-Bézout bound and a closed-form expression for the mixed volume by means of a matrix permanent. For the sparse resultant, a bevy of results have established determinantal or rational formulae for a large class of systems, starting with Macaulay. The discriminant is closely related to the resultant but admits no compact formula except for very simple cases. We offer a new determinantal formula for the discriminant of a sparse multilinear system arising in computing Nash equilibria. We introduce an alternative notion of compact formula, namely the Newton polytope of the unknown polynomial. It is possible to compute it efficiently for sparse resultants, discriminants, as well as the implicit equation of a parameterized variety. This leads us to consider implicit matrix representations of geometric objects.

Categories and Subject Descriptors

I.1.2 [**Computing Methodologies**]: Symbolic and Algebraic Manipulation—*Algebraic Algorithms*

Keywords

Sparse elimination; permanent; generating function; resultant matrix; discriminant; matrix representation

*Member of AROMATH, a joint team between INRIA Sophia-Antipolis, France, and NKU Athens. Partially supported by H2020 Marie Skłodowska Curie European Training Network ARCADES (Algebraic Representations for Computer-Aided Design of complEx Shapes), 2016-2019, project number: 675789.

ISSAC'16, July 19–22, 2016, Waterloo, ON, Canada

ISBN 978-1-4503-4380-0/16/07...$15.00

DOI: http://dx.doi.org/10.1145/2930889.2930943

1. INTRODUCTION

It is today a standard approach to use the theory of sparse (or toric) elimination, based on the Newton polytope of a polynomial, in order to reveal and exploit the structure of algebraic systems. Consider Laurent polynomials in N variables:

$$f_i = \sum_{j=1}^{k_i} c_{ij} x^{a_{ij}}, \quad c_{ij} \neq 0,$$

where $x = (x_1, \ldots, x_N)$, $x^e = \prod_i x_i^{e_i}$, and $\{a_{i1}, \ldots, a_{ik_i}\} \subset \mathbb{Z}^N$ is the *support* of f_i. Let Q_i be the *Newton polytope* of f_i defined as the convex hull of the support.

A more constrained form of structure corresponds to multihomogeneous systems, which are defined on a product

$$\mathbb{P}^{n_1} \times \mathbb{P}^{n_2} \times \cdots \times \mathbb{P}^{n_S} \tag{1}$$

of projective spaces: the variables are partitioned into S subsets, or blocks, so that each equation is homogeneous in each block of $n_j + 1$ homogeneous variables. In contrast, semi-mixed systems are those whose polynomials can be partitioned into subsets, or blocks, with fixed monomial support. In sparse elimination, each subset of polynomials has the same Newton polytope. In the case of semi-mixed multihomogeneous systems, the polynomials in each block are homogeneous of the same degree per block of variables.

An interesting example of a semi-mixed multihomogeneous system appears in game theory and was studied in [20, 26]. Consider a game of S players, each with m_i options or strategies. The j-th player plays a totally mixed strategy when the corresponding strategy is chosen randomly with nonzero probabilities $p_1^{(j)}, \ldots, p_{m_j}^{(j)}$. A totally mixed Nash equilibrium (TMNE) is a combination of such strategies so that no player can improve his payoff by unilaterally choosing other (pure or mixed) strategy. We express payoff P_j of the j-th player choosing the i-th strategy by the polynomial

$$\sum_{k_1,\ldots,k_{j-1},k_{j+1},\ldots,k_S} a^{(j)}_{\ldots,k_{j-1},i,k_{j+1},\ldots} p^{(1)}_{k_1} \cdots p^{(j-1)}_{k_{j-1}} p^{(j+1)}_{k_{j+1}} \cdots p^{(S)}_{k_S}. \tag{2}$$

Here $a^{(j)}_{k_1,k_2,\ldots,k_S}$ denotes the predefined payoff of the player, assuming each player chooses the pure option $k_\ell \in \{1, \ldots, m_\ell\}$. The equations imply that the payoff P_j does not depend on own strategy i, as long as other players do not change their strategies. Eliminating the P_j's leads to a multilinear system with $n_j = m_j - 1$ in space (1). Actual probabilities are determined from the normalizing conditions $\sum_{i=1}^{m_j} p_i^{(j)} = 1$, for $j \in \{1, \ldots, S\}$.

2. ROOT BOUNDS

Bounds on the number of common roots of an algebraic system admit different types of compact formulae. We start with classic bounds named after Bézout, tight for (multi)homogeneous systems. The most general such bound is the following m-Bézout bound, stated for dehomogenized system.

THEOREM 2.1 (M-BÉZOUT BOUND). *Consider a system of N equations in N affine variables, partitioned into S subsets so that the j-th subset includes n_j affine variables, and $N = n_1 + \cdots + n_S$. Let d_{ij} be the degree of the i-th equation in the j-th variable subset, for $i = 1, \ldots, N$ and $j = 1, \ldots, S$. If the system has finitely many complex roots in space (1), the coefficient of $x_1^{n_1} \cdots x_S^{n_S}$ in*

$$\prod_{i=1}^{N}(d_{i1}x_1 + \cdots + d_{iS}x_S) \tag{3}$$

bounds the number of roots. For generic coefficients this bound is tight.

We shall give a generating function for the m-Bézout number by extending results in [26, 27, 32]. MacMahon's Master theorem [25] is a powerful combinatorial result.

THEOREM 2.2 (MACMAHON'S MASTER THEOREM). [25] *Let $A = (a_{ij})$ be a complex $S \times S$ matrix, $x_1, \ldots, x_S$ be formal variables, and V denote the diagonal matrix with nonzero entries $x_1, \ldots, x_S$. The coefficient of $x_1^{n_1} \cdots x_S^{n_S}$ in*

$$\prod_{j=1}^{S}(a_{j1}x_1 + \cdots + a_{jS}x_S)^{n_j} \tag{4}$$

equals the coefficient of $x_1^{n_1} \cdots x_S^{n_S}$ in the multivariate Taylor expansion of

$$f(x_1, \ldots, x_S) = \frac{1}{\det(I - VA)} \tag{5}$$

around $(x_1, \ldots, x_S) = (0, 0, \ldots, 0)$.

Let us consider semi-mixed multihomogeneous systems, where the number of equation blocks equals the number S of variable blocks, and we have a varying number of equations per block; more importantly, the degree per block is arbitrary. Generically, this system has a finite number of solutions. MacMahon's Theorem yields a multivariate generating function for the m-Bézout bound of these systems, which could be helpful when one seeks root counts for a family of systems.

THEOREM 2.3. [20] *Consider a multihomogeneous system on space (1) of $N = n_1 + \cdots + n_S$ equations, where the equations are partitioned into S subsets of exactly $n_1, \ldots, n_S$ equations. We assume that for any $i, j \in \{1, 2, \ldots, S\}$, the polynomial equations in the i-th subset have degree a_{ij} in the variables of the j-th variable subset. Let A be the $S \times S$ matrix defined by the a_{ij}'s. Then the m-Bézout bound for the multihomogeneous system equals the coefficient of $x_1^{n_1} \cdots x_S^{n_S}$ in the multivariate Taylor expansion of*

$$1/\det(I - VA)$$

around $(x_1, \ldots, x_S) = (0, 0, \ldots, 0)$.

For TMNE system (2), we have $a_{ii} = 0$, and $a_{ij} = 1$ for $i \neq j$. Then

$$I - VA = \begin{bmatrix} 1 & -x_1 & -x_1 & \cdots & -x_1 \\ -x_2 & 1 & -x_2 & \cdots & -x_2 \\ \vdots & \vdots & \ddots & \ddots & \vdots \\ -x_S & -x_S & \cdots & -x_S & 1 \end{bmatrix},$$

and

$$1/\det(I - VA) = \frac{1}{1 - \sigma_2 - 2\sigma_3 - \cdots - (S-1)\sigma_S},$$

where σ_j (for $j = 2, \ldots, S$) denotes the j-th elementary symmetric polynomial in $x_1, \ldots, x_S$.

Now we pass to the most general root bound in sparse elimination theory, namely mixed volume: there are efficient algorithms but, in certain cases, the mixed volume computation is reduced to a matrix permanent. The toric root bound is named after Bernstein, Khovanskii, and Kushnirenko (BKK) [1]:

THEOREM 2.4. *For $f_1, \ldots f_N \in \mathbb{C}[x_1^{\pm 1}, \ldots, x_N^{\pm 1}]$ with Newton polytopes $Q_1, \ldots, Q_N$, the number of common isolated solutions, multiplicities counted, in the corresponding toric variety, which contains $(\mathbb{C}^*)^N$ as a dense subset, does not exceed $\mathrm{MV}(Q_1, \ldots, Q_N)$, independently of the toric variety's dimension.*

It is known that mixed volume is related to the permanent. In fact, by reduction to the latter one shows that mixed volume is #P-complete. For a multihomogeneous system on space (1) of $N = n_1 + \cdots + n_S$ equations, assume the i-th equation has degree a_{ij} in the j-th variable block. Let $A = (a_{ij})$ be an $N \times N$ matrix with the columns repeated n_j times for each $j \in \{1, 2, \ldots, S\}$. Then the mixed volume equals [27, Thm 2]

$$\frac{1}{n_1! \cdots n_S!} \operatorname{perm} A.$$

A generalization to arbitrary (non-homogeneous) systems follows. For each block of variables there is a n_j-dimensional polytope Γ_j, each in a separate complementary space, $1 \leq j \leq S$. Assume the Newton polytopes are direct products of scalar multiples (by a_{ij}) of the Γ_j's. We obtain an algebraic system on the product of toric varieties corresponding to Γ_j, of dimension n_j.

THEOREM 2.5. [20] *Let A be the matrix of a_{ij}'s with columns repeated n_j times. If there are $N = \sum_{j=1}^{S} n_j$ equations, then*

$$\mathrm{MV}(Q_1, \ldots, Q_N) = \operatorname{perm} A \prod_{j=1}^{S} \mathrm{vol}(\Gamma_j), \quad Q_i = \prod_{j=1}^{S} a_{ij}\Gamma_j.$$

3. RESULTANT FORMULAE

For the sparse resultant, a bevy of results have established matrix and, more particularly, determinantal formulae for a large class of systems. An introductory survey can be found in [28].

Resultants provide efficient ways for studying and solving polynomial systems by means of matrices whose determinant is a non-trivial multiple of the resultant. They are most efficiently expressed by a generically non-singular matrix, whose determinant is the resultant polynomial or, when this is impossible, by also specifying a minor M' of resultant matrix M which divides the determinant of the latter so as to yield a rational formula for the resultant R:

$$R = \det M \;/\; \det M'.$$

Macaulay's classical result [24] establishes such rational formula for arbitrary dense systems, and D'Andrea, 100 years later [7], for arbitrary systems in the context of sparse elimination. His recursive construction has been simplified in certain cases [17].

For two univariate polynomials there are matrix formulae named after Sylvester and Bézout, whose determinant is equal to the resultant; we refer to them as determinantal formulae. The largest family admitting determinantal formulae is a class of multihomogeneous systems studied in [31, 33], see also [21, Sect.13.2], where, each block of variables contains a single dehomogenized variable or is of linear total degree. These systems are moreover unmixed, in other words all polynomials have the same Newton polytope; they are called multigraded.

The multigraded resultant matrices were made explicit in [10, 18], which offered determinantal formulae of Sylvester, Bézout and hybrid types, the latter containing blocks of both Sylvester and Bézout types. In [10], it is shown that there exists a determinantal pure Bézout-type resultant formula if and only if there exists such a Sylvester-type formula. The Bézout-type matrices generalize those identified in [6]. In [18] was proven the existence of determinantal formulae for systems whose Newton polytopes are scaled copies of one polytope.

In [8], hybrid formulae were proposed in the mixed homogeneous case. The most complete study of hybrid formulae is [12] where resultants are given as a matrix determinant or a Pfaffian, i.e. a determinant square root, for unmixed systems of 3 dense polynomials, for up to 5 polynomials of degree up to 4, 6, or 8, and for 6 quadratic polynomials.

Some studies have focused on three polynomials. In the unmixed case a determinantal formula is established in [23], more direct than [12] and generalizing the Macaulay-style formula obtained for the dense case in [22], where the numerator matrix has one row corresponding to the affine Jacobian. For Newton polygons which are scaled copies of a single one, the smallest Sylvester-type matrices are obtained by using a row containing the coefficients of the toric Jacobian [9]. In [34] they construct determinantal Sylvester-type formulae for unmixed systems whose Newton polygon is a rectangle from which smaller rectangles have been removed at the corners.

4. DISCRIMINANT FORMULAE

Discriminants are crucial in studying well-constrained algebraic systems, the system's zero set, its singularities, and other properties of the system. The discriminant is closely related to the resultant but admits no compact formula except for very simple cases. Below we offer a new determinantal formula for a specific system. Recent work has shed light on the degree of mixed discriminants [5, 11] as a function of the Newton polytopes of the corresponding polynomials. An important open question is to obtain an explicit formula for multilinear systems [30].

In the context of sparse elimination the discriminant is defined for a set of polynomials F_i with fixed supports A_i, hence it is denoted $\Delta_{A_1,\ldots,A_n}(F_1,\ldots,F_n)$ or $\Delta(F_1,\ldots,F_n)$.

Definition 4.1. *The mixed discriminant $\Delta(F_1,\ldots,F_n)$ of n polynomials in n variables with fixed supports $A_1,\ldots,A_n$ in $\mathbb{Z}^n$ is the irreducible polynomial (with integer coprime coefficients, defined up to sign) in the coefficients of the F_i which vanishes whenever the system $F_1 = \cdots = F_n = 0$ has a multiple root (i.e., a root which is not simple) with nonzero coordinates, provided his discriminantal variety is a hypersurface; otherwise, the mixed discriminant is equal to the constant 1.*

Clearly, the zero locus of the mixed discriminant is the variety of ill-posed systems, i.e., systems with at least one multiple root.

We focus on systems over $\mathbb{P}^1\times\mathbb{P}^1\times\mathbb{P}^1$ where each equation is missing one variable, motivated by the study of TMNE in games of 3 players with 2 pure strategies each, see polynomials (2). The bilinear system is as follows:

$$\begin{aligned}
F_1: &\quad a_0y_1z_1 + a_1y_1z_0 + a_2y_0z_1 + a_4y_0x_0 = 0,\\
F_2: &\quad b_0x_1z_1 + b_1x_1z_0 + b_3x_0z_1 + b_4x_0z_0 = 0,\\
F_3: &\quad c_0x_1y_1 + c_2x_1y_0 + c_3x_0y_1 + c_4x_0y_0 = 0.
\end{aligned}$$

The projective coordinates $(x_1:x_0)$, $(y_1:y_0)$, $(z_1:z_0)$ represent the unknown probability ratios for the two options of each player; the coefficients a_i equal the differences in the given payoffs (between the two options) of the first player, for the 4 combinations of pure choices of the other two players; similarly, b_i, c_i equal the differences in the given payoffs (between their two options) of the other two players.

The following theorem gives a 6×6 determinantal expression for the discriminant. The formula is of Sylvester-type because the matrix entries are either zero or equal to a polynomial coefficient.

Theorem 4.2. [19] *The discriminant $\Delta(F_1,F_2,F_3)$ equals*

$$\det\begin{bmatrix}
0 & 0 & c_0 & c_1 & b_0 & b_1\\
0 & 0 & c_2 & c_4 & b_3 & b_4\\
c_0 & c_2 & 0 & 0 & a_0 & a_2\\
c_1 & c_4 & 0 & 0 & a_3 & a_4\\
b_0 & b_3 & a_0 & a_3 & 0 & 0\\
b_1 & b_4 & a_2 & a_4 & 0 & 0
\end{bmatrix}.$$

5. SPARSE IMPLICITIZATION

We argue that in sparse elimination it makes sense to consider an alternative notion of compact formula, namely the Newton polytope of the unknown polynomial. It typically allows computation of the polynomial by interpolation of the coefficients. It is possible to compute it efficiently for sparse resultants [13], discriminants, as well as the implicit equation of a parameterized variety.

This section focuses on the latter case. Given (a superset of) the Newton polytope of the implicit equation, one constructs an interpolation matrix, which allows for various geometric operations to be efficiently computed on this matrix without need of developing the monomial representation of the implicit equation. The representation by interpolation matrices has been developed for parametric plane curves, surfaces, and hypersurfaces in the context of sparse elimination [15, 16]. It generalizes to space curves and, generally, objects of codimension higher than 1 by means of the Chow form, which is a generalization of resultants to N-variate systems with more than $N+1$ polynomials [14].

Another powerful matrix representation of geometric objects is based on syzygies. The corresponding theory, including μ-bases, has been developed for parametric models [3, 4, 29]. The computation of syzygies can exploit the sparse elimination setting [2] and, moreover, can be achieved for point cloud models [14]. Roughly, syzygies of a sufficiently high degree define moving curves or surfaces that "follow" the parametric object. One forms the matrix expressing these moving curves and/or surfaces, which represents the geometric object because its rank at some point p drops if and only if p belongs to the algebraic closure of the image of the parameterization [3].

6. REFERENCES

[1] D. Bernstein. The number of roots of a system of equations. *Funct. Anal. and Appl.*, 9(2):183–185, 1975.

[2] N. Botbol and A. Dickenstein. Implicitization of rational hypersurfaces via linear syzygies: A practical overview. *J. Symbolic Computation*, 74:493–512, 2016.

[3] L. Busé and T. Luu Ba. Matrix-based implicit representations of rational algebraic curves and applications. *Computer-Aided Geometric Design*, 27(9):681–699, 2010.

[4] L. Busé, D. Cox, and C. D'Andrea. Implicitization of surfaces in P^3 in the presence of base points, *J. Algebra Appl.*, 2(2):189-214, 2003.

[5] E. Cattani, M. Cueto, A. Dickenstein, S. Di Rocco, and B. Sturmfels. Mixed discriminants. *Math. Z.*, 274:761–778, 2013.

[6] A. Chtcherba and D. Kapur. Conditions for exact resultants using the Dixon formulation. In *Proc. ACM Intern. Symp. on Symbolic & Algebraic Comput.*, pages 62–70, 2000.

[7] C. D'Andrea. Macaulay-style formulas for the sparse resultant. *Trans. AMS*, 354:2595–2629, 2002.

[8] C. D'Andrea and A. Dickenstein. Explicit formulas for the multivariate resultant. *J. Pure & Applied Algebra*, 164(1-2):59–86, 2001.

[9] C. D'Andrea and I. Emiris. Hybrid sparse resultant matrices for bivariate polynomials. *J. Symbolic Computation, Special Issue*, 33(5):587–608, 2002.

[10] A. Dickenstein and I. Emiris. Multihomogeneous resultant formulae by means of complexes. *J. Symbolic Computation, Special issue*, 36(3-4):317–342, 2003.

[11] A. Dickenstein, I. Emiris, and A. Karasoulou. Plane mixed discriminants and toric jacobians. In *SAGA: Advances in ShApes, Geometry, and Algebra*, volume 10 of *Geometry and Computing*, pages 105–121. Springer, 2014.

[12] D. Eisenbud and F.-O. Schreyer. Resultants and Chow forms via exterior syzygies. *J. AMS*, 16:534–579, 2003.

[13] I. Emiris, V. Fisikopoulos, C. Konaxis, and L. Peñaranda. An oracle-based, output-sensitive algorithm for projections of resultant polytopes. *Intern. J. Computational Geom. Appl., Special Issue*, 23:397–423, 2014.

[14] I. Emiris, K. Gavriil, and C. Konaxis. Matrix representations by means of interpolation. Manuscript, 2016.

[15] I. Emiris, T. Kalinka, and C. Konaxis. Geometric operations using sparse interpolation matrices. *Graphical Models*, 82:99–109, Nov. 2015.

[16] I. Emiris, T. Kalinka, C. Konaxis, and T. Luu Ba. Sparse implicitization by interpolation: Characterizing non-exactness, and an application to computing discriminants. *Computer-Aided Design, Special Issue*, 45:252–261, 2013.

[17] I. Emiris and C. Konaxis. Single-lifting Macaulay-type formulae of generalized unmixed sparse resultants. *J. Symbolic Computation*, 46(8):919–942, 2011.

[18] I. Emiris and A. Mantzaflaris. Multihomogeneous resultant matrices for systems with scaled support. In *Proc. ACM Intern. Symp. on Symbolic & Algebraic Comput.*, pages 143–150, 2009.

[19] I. Emiris and R. Vidunas. Discriminants of multilinear systems. Manuscript, 2015.

[20] I. Emiris and R. Vidunas. Root counts of semi-mixed systems, and an application to counting Nash equilibria. In *Proc. ACM Intern. Symp. on Symbolic & Algebraic Comput.*, pages 154–161, Kobe, Japan, 2014.

[21] I. Gelfand, M. Kapranov, and A. Zelevinsky. *Discriminants, Resultants and Multidimensional Determinants.* Birkhäuser, Boston, 1994.

[22] J.-P. Jouanolou. Formes d'inertie et résultant : Un formulaire. *Adv. in Math.*, 126:119–250, 1997.

[23] A. Khetan. The resultant of an unmixed bivariate system. *J. Symbolic Computation*, 36:425–442, 2003.

[24] F. Macaulay. Some formulae in elimination. *Proc. London Math. Soc.*, 1(33):3–27, 1902.

[25] P. MacMahon. *Combinatory analysis.* Cambridge Univ. Press, 1916.

[26] R. McKelvey and A. McLennan. The maximal number of regular totally mixed Nash equilibria. *J. Economic Theory*, 72:411–425, 1997.

[27] A. McLennan. The maximum number of real roots of a multihomogeneous system of polynomial equations. *Beitrage zur Algebra und Geom.*, 40:343–350, 1999.

[28] A. Morozov and S. Shakirov. New and old results in resultant theory. *Theoretical & Math. Physics*, 163(2):587–617, 2010.

[29] T. Sederberg and F. Chen. Implicitization using moving curves and surfaces. In R. Cook, editor, *Proc. SIGGRAPH*, pages 301–308. Addison Wesley, 1995.

[30] B. Sturmfels. The Hurwitz form of a projective variety. Presented at MEGA 2015. Submitted to journal, 2016.

[31] B. Sturmfels and A. Zelevinsky. Multigraded resultants of Sylvester type. *J. Algebra*, 163(1):115–127, 1994.

[32] R. Vidunas. Counting derangements and Nash equilibria. arxiv.org/1401.5400, 2014.

[33] J. Weyman and A. Zelevinsky. Multigraded formulae for multigraded resultants. *J. Algebr. Geometry*, 3(4):569–597, 1994.

[34] M. Zhang and R. Goldman. Rectangular corner cutting and Sylvester A-resultants. In *Proc. ACM Intern. Symp. on Symbolic & Algebraic Comput.*, pages 301–308, 2000.

Succinct Data Structures ... Potential for Symbolic Computation?

J. Ian Munro *
Cheriton School of Computer Science
University of Waterloo
Waterloo, ON, Canada
imunro@uwaterloo.ca

Keywords

data structures; space efficiency; information theory; succinct data structures

ABSTRACT

We focus on *succinct data structures*, that is on time and space efficient representations of trees and other combinatorial objects that dominate the memory requirements of most sophisticated programs and systems.

1. SUCCINCT DATA STRUCTURES, WHAT ARE THEY?

This paper deals with space efficient data structures, and their potential for application in Symbolic Computation. In particular we focus on *succinct data structures*, which are best thought of as representations of combinatorial objects, such as trees, in a number of bits close to the information theoretic minimum, that support performing the "natural" operations (for trees, that would include finding parent, first child, next child, subtree size, etc.) quickly, ideally in time independent of the size of the structure. Such representations can have a dramatic effect on the space, and indeed time requirements, of common computational problems. Consider, for example, the representation of a binary tree on four billion nodes. The number of trees on n nodes is the nth Catalan number, $C_n = \binom{2n}{n} = 4^n/(\pi n^{3/2})$, so the information theoretic bound on the space to represent this is the lg (or logarithm base 2) of this number, i.e. $2n - O(lg\, n)$ bits. Succinct structures can get away withabout $2n + n\, lg\, lg\, n/lg\, n$ bits. If n is four billion, the lower bound is about 8 billion bits, or a gigabyte, and succinct structures use somewhat under 9 gigabits. Using a standard representation of $lg\, n$ bits for a pointer, and requiring references to *leftchild*, *rightchild*, *parent* and *leftmost descendent* (useful especially in text indexing), as well as the size of the subtree rooted at each node, we would need $5\, n\, lg\, n$ bits. For $n = 4$ billion, this is 640 gigabits, 70 times that of the succinct representation. Space differences such as this can change the level of memory on which much of a structure is stored, and hence the time required.

This paper is intended to give the reader a brief and informal overview and pointers to papers on a variety of aspects of the subject. It is definitely the personal perspective of the author. The forthcoming book, *Compact Data Structures: A Practical Approach* by Gonzalo Navarro [30], is an excellent source on the topic. He uses the title in as a somewhat more general term than "succinct data structures", to mean structures using dramatically less storage than conventional implementations. As his title suggests, it also focuses on techniques appropriate for use on today's machines and problem sizes, rather than asymptotics as such. The surveys noted [27, 29] also provide readable summaries of the highlights. Most of the work, especially the work on which we will focus, has been on static objects, as the methods are simpler. There has, however, been substantial work of dynamic structures. We will comment briefly on this (mostly by giving a few references) in the appropriate sections.

2. THE BASICS

The term "succinct data structure" first appears as the title of Guy Jacobson's Ph.D. thesis [20]. Most of the key results of that work also appear in [19], which, curiously, does not use the term "succinct". The easiest tree representation, through which to get a feel for the topic, is probably that for binary trees. (Note in this example the nodes are "named" by the encoding mechanism. This is generally the case with succinct data structures.) Recall the heap structure of Williams [36], whereby one thinks of an array $A[1..n]$ as a complete binary tree, i.e. all levels, except possibly the last, are full, and the nodes on the bottom level occupy the leftmost positions. One can then see that the left child of node i is node $2i$, the right child is node $2i+1$, and the parent is $\lfloor i/2 \rfloor$. Given this starting point, Jacobson suggests a representation of an arbitrary binary tree. We add $n+1$ external nodes, annotating each internal node with a 1 and each external node with a 0. The tree is represented by the bits string of length $2n+1$, reading these annotations level by level, from left to right. The parent-child relation is a twist on William's technique for the special case, in which "all the 1's precede all the 0's." We require two operations on bit strings: $rank(i)$, which is the number of $1'$s up to and including position i and $select(i)$, which gives the position of the ith 1. Children and parents are then a simple twist

*This research was supported by NSERC and the Canada Research Chairs Programme.

ISSAC '16, July 19-22, 2016, Waterloo, ON, Canada
© 2016 ACM. ISBN 978-1-4503-4380-0/16/07...$15.00
DOI: http://dx.doi.org/10.1145/2930889.2930944

on Williams' formulae: *leftchild(i)* is $2\,rank(i)$, *rightchild* is one more and *parent(i)* is *select*($\lfloor i/2 \rfloor$. The issue now is to create auxiliary structures, for which we assume we are working on a random access machine with words of $lg\,n$ bits. For *rank* this is fairly easy: corresponding to each $(lg\,n)^2$ position in the bit string, store the number of 1's up to that position, so $lg\,n$ bits each. For each $lg\,n^{th}$ position, store the number of 1's since the last $(lg\,n)^2$ marker, so $lg\,lg\,n$ bits each. Rank is now found by looking at one element in each of these structures plus a small table to examine the final $lg\,n$ or fewer bits. The *select* operation is similar, though a bit trickier. Indeed Jacobson's approach for *select* involved looking at $lg\,n$ bits, though more than a constant number of $lg\,n$ bit words. Perhaps this is why it took more than five years until the approach was utilized (and a modified form implemented) for text search. Munro [25] and Clark and Munro [6] report a constant time technique for *select* as well as *rank*. Full details are in David Clark's Ph.D. thesis [5], and several further refinements have been made though the extra memory can be shown to be within a constant factor of minimum if one requires constant time responses [12, 31, 32]. The rank and select operations can be generalized to arbitrary alphabets through wavelet trees [15]. The problem of maintaining indices for rank and select on dynamic compressed strings has also been addressed [14, 33]

One can get minor time-space tradeoffs in the details of these. One can also intersperse the indices with the basic bit strings to reduce cache misses to produce a very effective index.

Over the past thirty years great strides have been made in many aspects of succinct data structures, most notably on space efficient indexing. There are (at least) two major packages. The oldest was developed by Gonzalo Navarro of the University of Chile and Paulo Ferragina of the University of Pisa [11]. This is "of course" known as the *Pizza & Chili Corpus*. It contains not only a variety of text indexing and search procedures, based heavily on succinct representation of suffix trees and suffix arrays, but also a collection of texts, large enough to demonstrate the space efficiency of the methods, which one can use in performing experiments. The second is Simon Gog's *Succinct Data Structure Library* [34].

3. TEXT SEARCH

By far the most fertile application of succinct data structures (thus far) has been in full text search. By this we mean exact match of the full query phrase, so very applicable in bioinformatics applications [16] as well as large corpora of natural language text. Indeed both packages noted above have been used primarily in this domain. The fundamental structures for full text search are suffix arrays and suffix trees. These structures were first proposed by Weiner in 1973 [35], though heavy use of the technique did not occur for another 15 years. A *suffix array*, of a text of length n, is an array containing the positions in the text ordered lexicographically by the string (suffix) starting at that point. A *suffix tree* is a (probably binary) search tree which (like a PATRICIA tree [24]) permits search for any of these suffices up to the point where they become unique and skipping tests (and nodes) where there is no branching. This permits search for (references to) all instances of any query string in a number of steps at most the length of the query (in binary or the alphabet size). The problem with conventional implementations of suffix trees is that space costs become huge. Indeed, it was the abandonment of suffix trees in a project to develop software tools for creating and using the (New) Oxford English Dictionary [13] that ultimately led the author to the area of succinct data structures. The software developed in the OED project was based on doing binary searches over the suffix array. This approach was soon being used for DNA matching applications [16]. The suffix array still requires $n\,lg\,n$ bits, in addition to the text, though Makinen and Navarro [23] have demonstrated that even this can be avoided. The last decade, in particular, has been marked by an enormous number of advances in compact text search and working with compressed data [30]. Specific work on dynamic sequences include [4] and [18]

4. GRAPHS AND TREES

A graph is typically represented by either an adjacency matrix ($\frac{1}{2}n^2$ bits) or an adjacency list ($m\,lg\,n$ bits, where m is the number of edges). In terms of space, the former is ideal for dense graphs, while the latter is for sparse graphs. In between, both are less than ideal. In terms of time, the adjacency matrix is perfect for determining whether an edge is present, while the list structure suits scanning through the edges incident with a given node (if we double the space). It turns out that an "ideal" structure is impossible. Under the cell probe model (i.e. essentially no restrictions on operations on a $lg\,n$ bit word) one cannot come within a lower order term of the information theoretic lower bound (and support navigation in constant time) unless the graph is sparse ($m = o(n^{\delta})$ for arbitrary constant $\delta > 0$), or very dense ($m = \omega(n^{2-\delta})$. However, the space bound can be achieved [9], with constant time operations, in the exceptions noted, and one can come within a factor of $1+\epsilon$ in all other cases. ("Clearly" the constant time for operations depends on ϵ.) Here we are asking about simple adjacency. Connectivity in a graph is the same thing as an equivalence class, and discussed below. But suppose we want transitivity in a digraph. This too can be supported in minimum space and constant time [26].

As noted earlier, succinct representations of trees have been very heavily studied, perhaps because Computer Science is rather arborphilic. The general goal has been to support as many (useful) operations as possible on both "cardinal" (children fit in to set positions of their parents, e.g. binary trees) or "ordinal" (children of a node are ordered, but in no particular "position") e.g.[3]. One easily quoted result deals with representing special types of either kind of tree [10]. Consider a class of (rooted) tree with the property that the subtree rooted at any node is a member of the class. For instance, consider either AVL trees or ordinal trees where nodes have at most two children (i.e. binary trees in which we do not distinguish between a node with just a left child and one with only a right child). Such trees can be encoded in space equal to the information theoretic lower bound plus a lower order term and support the natural navigation operations in constant time. This holds even if we do not know the space bound.

Tree representations are an area in which updates to the trees have been considered in more than a cursory manner. If one adds a leaf in a tree, one increments the number of descendants of all along the path to the root. Issues of this sort have encouraged an update model in which one crawl around a tree following edges and updating along the way. One can get close to optimal space bounds, in poly-log time per node insertion or deletion, though the methods are complex and not yet ready for inclusion in systems, but show great hope for the future [2, 28, 8, 33]

5. MORE COMBINATORIAL OBJECTS

Other combinatorial objects have also been the object of succinct representations, for example, groups and equivalence classes. These are prime examples of naming objects, essentially to the point that almost nothing be explicitly stored. With appropriate, non-unique, naming of the elements of an abelian group of order n, the operations of multiplication, inverse and equivalence can be performed in constant time. The method uses about $6\,lg\,n$ bits to represent each element, so the name space is certainly not tight and it does bring in the issue of non-unique names. The method also relies on the operation of reversing a $lg\,n$ bit word in constant time, but needs only a constant number of such words to represent the group. This is an example of increasing the name space to reduce the space necessary to work with a combinatorial object. (It is certainly not the first such example; [1] ánd [21] are much better candidates.)

Representing equivalence classes, where the algorithm can choose the names of the objects, is a topic in which one sees an interesting name space - extra memory trade-off. Giving the elements names 1 through $n\,ln\,n$ (i.e. $lg\,n + lg\,lg\,n + O(1)$ bits) permits the support of equivalence classes on n elements with no extra storage [21, 22]. If the label space is restricted to 1 through n, all the information must be stored separately, hence the logarithm of the Hardy-Ramanujan number [17] is a lower bound , i.e. we need at least $\pi\sqrt{2n/3}\,lg\,e - lg\,n + O(1)$ bits. Near constant time queries can be achieved with $O(n^{1/2})$ extra bits [22]. If this name space is increased to cn $(c > 1)$, only $O(lg\,n)$ extra bits are needed to support queries in constant time [7].

It is natural to ask what other algebraic and combinatorial structures can be succinctly represented and worked with efficiently; and of course there is work on making updates easier as well as more efficient.

6. REFERENCES

[1] S. Alstrup, P. Bille, and T. Rauhe. Labeling schemes for small distances in trees. In *Proceedings of the Fourteenth Annual ACM-SIAM Symposium on Discrete Algorithms, January 12-14, 2003, Baltimore, Maryland, USA.*, pages 689–698. ACM/SIAM, 2003.

[2] D. Arroyuelo, P. Davoodi, and S. R. Satti. Succinct dynamic cardinal trees. *Algorithmica*, 74(2):742–777, 2016.

[3] D. Benoit, E. D. Demaine, J. I. Munro, R. Raman, V. Raman, and S. S. Rao. Representing trees of higher degree. *Algorithmica*, 43(4):275–292, 2005.

[4] H. Chan, W. Hon, T. W. Lam, and K. Sadakane. Compressed indexes for dynamic text collections. *ACM Trans. Algorithms*, 3(2), 2007.

[5] D. R. Clark. *Compact Pat Trees*. University of Waterloo, 1996.

[6] D. R. Clark and J. I. Munro. Efficient suffix trees on secondary storage (extended abstract). In É. Tardos, editor, *Proceedings of the Seventh Annual ACM-SIAM Symposium on Discrete Algorithms, 28-30 January 1996, Atlanta, Georgia.*, pages 383–391. ACM/SIAM, 1996.

[7] H. El-Zein, J. I. Munro, and S. Yang. On the succinct representation of unlabeled permutations. In K. M. Elbassioni and K. Makino, editors, *Algorithms and Computation - 26th International Symposium, ISAAC 2015, Nagoya, Japan, December 9-11, 2015, Proceedings*, volume 9472 of *Lecture Notes in Computer Science*, pages 49–59. Springer, 2015.

[8] A. Farzan and J. I. Munro. Succinct representation of dynamic trees. *Theor. Comput. Sci.*, 412(24):2668–2678, 2011.

[9] A. Farzan and J. I. Munro. Succinct encoding of arbitrary graphs. *Theor. Comput. Sci.*, 513:38–52, 2013.

[10] A. Farzan and J. I. Munro. A uniform paradigm to succinctly encode various families of trees. *Algorithmica*, 68(1):16–40, 2014.

[11] P. Ferragina and G. Navarro. Pizza & chili corpus compressed indexes and their testbeds, Sept. 2005.

[12] A. Golynski. Optimal lower bounds for rank and select indexes. *Theor. Comput. Sci.*, 387(3):348–359, 2007.

[13] G. H. Gonnet, R. A. Baeza-Yates, and T. Snider. New indices for text: Pat trees and pat arrays. In *Information Retrieval: Data Structures & Algorithms*, pages 66–82. 1992.

[14] R. González and G. Navarro. Rank/select on dynamic compressed sequences and applications. *Theor. Comput. Sci.*, 410(43):4414–4422, 2009.

[15] R. Grossi, A. Gupta, and J. S. Vitter. High-order entropy-compressed text indexes. In *Proceedings of the Fourteenth Annual ACM-SIAM Symposium on Discrete Algorithms*, SODA '03, pages 841–850, Philadelphia, PA, USA, 2003. Society for Industrial and Applied Mathematics.

[16] D. Gusfield. *Algorithms on Strings, Trees, and Sequences - Computer Science and Computational Biology*. Cambridge University Press, 1997.

[17] G. H. Hardy and S. Ramanujan. Asymptotic formulae in combinatory analysis. *Proceedings of the London Mathematical Society*, 2(1):75–115, 1918.

[18] M. He and J. I. Munro. Succinct representations of dynamic strings. In E. Chávez and S. Lonardi, editors, *String Processing and Information Retrieval - 17th International Symposium, SPIRE 2010, Los Cabos, Mexico, October 11-13, 2010. Proceedings*, volume 6393 of *Lecture Notes in Computer Science*, pages 334–346. Springer, 2010.

[19] G. Jacobson. Space-efficient static trees and graphs. In *30th Annual Symposium on Foundations of Computer Science, Research Triangle Park, North Carolina, USA, 30 October - 1 November 1989*, pages 549–554. IEEE Computer Society, 1989.

[20] G. Jacobson. *Succinct Data Structures*. Carnegie Melon University, 1989.

[21] M. Katz, N. A. Katz, A. Korman, and D. Peleg. Labeling schemes for flow and connectivity. *SIAM J. Comput.*, 34(1):23–40, 2004.

[22] M. Lewenstein, J. I. Munro, and V. Raman. Succinct data structures for representing equivalence classes. In L. Cai, S. Cheng, and T. W. Lam, editors, *Algorithms*

and Computation - 24th International Symposium, ISAAC 2013, Hong Kong, China, December 16-18, 2013, Proceedings, volume 8283 of *Lecture Notes in Computer Science*, pages 502–512. Springer, 2013.

[23] V. Mäkinen and G. Navarro. Compressed compact suffix arrays. In S. C. Sahinalp, S. Muthukrishnan, and U. Dogrusöz, editors, *Combinatorial Pattern Matching, 15th Annual Symposium, CPM 2004, Istanbul, Turkey, July 5-7, 2004, Proceedings*, volume 3109 of *Lecture Notes in Computer Science*, pages 420–433. Springer, 2004.

[24] D. R. Morrison. Patricia - practical algorithm to retrieve information coded in alphanumeric. *J. ACM*, 15(4):514–534, Oct. 1968.

[25] J. I. Munro. Tables. In V. Chandru and V. Vinay, editors, *Foundations of Software Technology and Theoretical Computer Science, 16th Conference, Hyderabad, India, December 18-20, 1996, Proceedings*, volume 1180 of *Lecture Notes in Computer Science*, pages 37–42. Springer, 1996.

[26] J. I. Munro and P. K. Nicholson. Succinct posets. In L. Epstein and P. Ferragina, editors, *Algorithms - ESA 2012 - 20th Annual European Symposium, Ljubljana, Slovenia, September 10-12, 2012. Proceedings*, volume 7501 of *Lecture Notes in Computer Science*, pages 743–754. Springer, 2012.

[27] J. I. Munro and P. K. Nicholson. Compressed representations of graphs. In *Encyclopedia of Algorithms*, pages 382–386. 2016.

[28] J. I. Munro, V. Raman, and A. J. Storm. Representing dynamic binary trees succinctly. In S. R. Kosaraju, editor, *Proceedings of the Twelfth Annual Symposium on Discrete Algorithms, January 7-9, 2001, Washington, DC, USA.*, pages 529–536. ACM/SIAM, 2001.

[29] J. I. Munro and S. S. Rao. Succinct representation of data structures. In D. P. Mehta and S. Sahni, editors, *Handbook of Data Structures and Applications.* Chapman and Hall/CRC, 2004.

[30] G. Navarro. *Compact Data Structures: A Practical Approach.* Cambridge University Press, 2016, forthcoming.

[31] M. Patrascu. Succincter. In *49th Annual IEEE Symposium on Foundations of Computer Science, FOCS 2008, October 25-28, 2008, Philadelphia, PA, USA*, pages 305–313. IEEE Computer Society, 2008.

[32] M. Patrascu. A lower bound for succinct rank queries. *CoRR*, abs/0907.1103, 2009.

[33] R. Raman and S. S. Rao. Succinct dynamic dictionaries and trees. In J. C. M. Baeten, J. K. Lenstra, J. Parrow, and G. J. Woeginger, editors, *Automata, Languages and Programming, 30th International Colloquium, ICALP 2003, Eindhoven, The Netherlands, June 30 - July 4, 2003. Proceedings*, volume 2719 of *Lecture Notes in Computer Science*, pages 357–368. Springer, 2003.

[34] T. B. Simon Gog, J. Bader and M. Petri. Succinct data structure library 2.0, Mar. 2016.

[35] P. Weiner. Linear pattern matching algorithms. In *14th Annual Symposium on Switching and Automata Theory, Iowa City, Iowa, USA, October 15-17, 1973*, pages 1–11. IEEE Computer Society, 1973.

[36] J. W. J. Williams. Algorithm 232 (heapsort). *Commun. ACM*, 7(6):347–349, June 1964.

Symbolic Summation in Difference Rings and Applications

Carsten Schneider
Research Institute for Symbolic Computation (RISC)
Johannes Kepler University Linz
4040 Linz
Carsten.Schneider@risc.jku.at

Keywords

Difference rings, (creative) telescoping, recurrence solving, nested sums, hypergeometric products

Symbolic summation started with Abramov [1] for rational expressions and has been pushed forward by Gosper [7], Zeilberger [31], Petkovšek [16] and Paule [15] to tackle sums for hypergeometric expressions. In the last decade the class of input sums has been extended significantly and covers, for instance, hypergeometric multi-sums [30, 4], holonomic sequences [6, 14], unspecified sequences [12], radical expressions [13] or Stirling numbers [10].

We will focus on a new difference ring approach. The foundation was led by Karr's summation algorithm [8, 9], which enables one to rephrase indefinite nested sums and products in the setting of difference fields.

Definition. Let $\mathbb{F}$ be a field with characteristic 0 and let σ be a field automorphism of $\mathbb{F}$. Then $(\mathbb{F},\sigma)$ is called a *difference field*; the *constant field* of $\mathbb{F}$ is defined by $\mathbb{K}=\text{const}(\mathbb{F},\sigma)=\{f\in\mathbb{F}\mid\sigma(f)=f\}$. A difference field $(\mathbb{F},\sigma)$ with constant field $\mathbb{K}$ is called a *$\Pi\Sigma^*$-field* if

$$\mathbb{K}=\mathbb{F}_0\leq\mathbb{F}_1\leq\cdots\leq\mathbb{F}_e=\mathbb{F}$$

is a tower of field extensions where for all $1\leq i\leq e$ each $\mathbb{F}_i=\mathbb{F}_{i-1}(t_i)$ is a transcendental field extension of $\mathbb{F}_{i-1}$ and for σ one of the following holds[1]:

- $\frac{\sigma(t_i)}{t_i}\in(\mathbb{F}_{i-1})^*$ *(Π-field extension)*;
- $\sigma(t_i)-t_i\in\mathbb{F}_{i-1}$ *(Σ^*-field extension)*.

Many new ideas have been incorporated into a strong summation theory, see e.g., [5, 18, 5, 17, 21, 19, 20, 23, 24, 26] which led to new algorithms for the summation paradigms of telescoping, creative telescoping and recurrence solving [22]. However, this elegant difference field approach has one central drawback. Alternating signs cannot be represented in such a field: zero-divisors like

$$(1+(-1)^k)(1-(-1)^k)=0$$

are introduced which can be formulated only within a ring. We will present a class of difference rings in which one can represent algorithmically indefinite nested sums and products together with the alternating sign, and more generally products over primitive roots of unity [27].

Definition. Let $\mathbb{A}$ be a ring with characteristic 0 and let σ be a ring automorphism of $\mathbb{A}$. Then $(\mathbb{A},\sigma)$ is called a *difference ring*; the *constant ring* of $\mathbb{A}$ is defined by $\text{const}(\mathbb{A},\sigma)=\{f\in\mathbb{A}\mid\sigma(f)=f\}$. A difference ring $(\mathbb{A},\sigma)$ is called an *$R\Pi\Sigma^*$-extension* of a difference field $(\mathbb{F},\sigma)$ if the constants remain unchanged, i.e., $\text{const}(\mathbb{A},\sigma)=\text{const}(\mathbb{F},\sigma)$ and if

$$\mathbb{F}=\mathbb{A}_0\leq\mathbb{A}_1\leq\cdots\leq\mathbb{A}_e=\mathbb{A}$$

is a tower of ring extensions where for all $1\leq i\leq e$ one of the following holds:

- $\mathbb{A}_i=\mathbb{A}_{i-1}[t_i]$ is a ring extension subject to the relation $t_i^n=1$ for some $n>1$ where $\frac{\sigma(t_i)}{t_i}\in(\mathbb{A}_{i-1})^*$ is a primitive nth root of unity *(R-extension)*;
- $\mathbb{A}_i=\mathbb{A}_{i-1}[t_i,t_i^{-1}]$ is a Laurent polynomial ring extension with $\frac{\sigma(t_i)}{t_i}\in(\mathbb{A}_{i-1})^*$ *(Π-extension)*;
- $\mathbb{A}_i=\mathbb{A}_{i-1}[t_i]$ is a polynomial ring extension with $\sigma(t_i)-t_i\in\mathbb{A}_{i-1}$ *(Σ^*-extension)*.

Representation of nested sums in $R\Pi\Sigma^*$-rings

We will restrict ourselves to basic $R\Pi\Sigma^*$-extensions [28]: for R-extensions we require that $\frac{\sigma(t_i)}{t_i}\in\text{const}(\mathbb{F},\sigma)^*$ holds and for Π-extensions we assume that $\frac{\sigma(t_i)}{t_i}\in\mathbb{F}^*$ holds. Together with an appropriate difference field $(\mathbb{F},\sigma)$ one can represent in this setting expressions (and in particular sequences produced by these expressions) in terms of indefinite nested sums defined over hypergeometric, q-hypergeometric or q-mixed hypergeometric products [28]. In the following we consider the hypergeometric case only. Let $f(k)$ be an expression in a variable k that evaluates at non-negative integers (from a certain point on) to elements of a field $\mathbb{K}$. Then $f(k)$ is called a *nested sum expression over hypergeometric products* w.r.t $\mathbb{K}$ and k if it is composed recursively by

- elements from the rational function field $\mathbb{K}(k)$;
- hypergeometric products of the form $\prod_{j=l}^{k}h(j)$ with $l\in\mathbb{N}=\{0,1,\dots\}$ and a rational function $h(j)\in\mathbb{K}(j)^*$, where $h(\nu)$ has no pole and is non-zero for all $\nu\in\mathbb{N}$ with $\nu\geq l$;
- the three operations $+$, $-$ and $\cdot$;

[1] For a ring or field $\mathbb{A}$ we denote by $\mathbb{A}^*$ the set of units.

ISSAC '16, July 19 - 22, 2016, Waterloo, ON, Canada

ISBN 978-1-4503-4380-0/16/07...$15.00
DOI: http://dx.doi.org/10.1145/2930889.2930945

- sums of the form $\sum_{j=l}^{k} h(j)$ with $l \in \mathbb{N}$ and with $h(j)$ being a nested sum expression over hypergeometric products w.r.t. $\mathbb{K}$ and j and being free of k; here l is chosen big enough such that $h(j)|_{j\mapsto\nu}$ does not introduce poles for all $\nu \geq l$. $\sum_{j=l}^{k} h(j)$ is also called a nested sum over hypergeometric products w.r.t. $\mathbb{K}$ and k.

Example. Consider the sum

$$S(k) = \sum_{j=2}^{k} F(j) = \sum_{j=2}^{k} \frac{(-1)^j - \sum_{i=1}^{j} \frac{(-1)^i}{i}}{(-1+j)j}$$

which belongs to the class of nested sum expressions over hypergeometric products w.r.t. $\mathbb{Q}$ and k. As a consequence it follows that any shifted version of the objects within $S(k)$ can be expressed again by the non-shifted versions: we have

$$(-1)^{k+1} = -(-1)^k, \tag{1}$$

$$\sum_{i=1}^{k+1} \frac{(-1)^i}{i} = \sum_{i=1}^{k} \frac{(-1)^i}{i} + \frac{-(-1)^k}{k+1} \tag{2}$$

and $S(k+1) = S(k) + F(k+1)$ with

$$F(k+1) = -\frac{1}{(k+1)^2}(-1)^k - \frac{1}{k(k+1)} \sum_{i=1}^{k} \frac{(-1)^i}{i}; \tag{3}$$

note that the equalities on the expression level are justified since both sides agree for any evaluation $k \mapsto \nu$ with $\nu \in \mathbb{N}$. In the following we will construct a difference ring composed by a tower of $R\Pi\Sigma^*$-extensions in which the objects $(-1)^k$, $\sum_{i=1}^{k} \frac{(-1)^i}{i}$ and $S(k)$ with their explicitly given shift-behaviors are represented accordingly. Starting with the difference field $(\mathbb{Q}(x), \sigma)$ with $\sigma(x) = x+1$ and constant field $\mathbb{Q}$ (which is a $\Pi\Sigma^*$-field) we proceed as follows:

(1) We take the ring extension $\mathbb{Q}(x)[y]$ subject to the relation $y^2 = 1$. Further, we extend σ to a ring automorphism of $\mathbb{Q}(x)[y]$ with $\sigma(y) = -y$. In this way, we can model $(-1)^k$ with $((-1)^k)^2 = 1$ and (1) by y. By [28, Prop 2.20] we conclude that $\text{const}(\mathbb{Q}(x)[y], \sigma) = \text{const}(\mathbb{Q}(x), \sigma)$ holds, i.e., that $(\mathbb{Q}(x)[y], \sigma)$ forms an $R\Pi\Sigma^*$-extension of $(\mathbb{Q}(x), \sigma)$.

(2) Next, we want to model $\sum_{i=1}^{k} \frac{(-1)^i}{i}$ with (2). First, we check if this is possible in our given difference ring. To be more precise, we test if there is a $g \in \mathbb{Q}(x)[y]$ with $\sigma(g) = g + \frac{-y}{x+1}$. Our telescoping algorithms [27] (see also below) show that such a solution is not possible. Therefore we take the polynomial ring extension $\mathbb{Q}(x)[y][s]$ and extend σ to a ring automorphism of $\mathbb{Q}(x)[y][s]$ with $\sigma(s) = s + \frac{-y}{x+1}$. Using [27, Theorem 2.12] the non-existence of a solution $g \in \mathbb{Q}(x)[y]$ of $\sigma(g) = g + \frac{-y}{x+1}$ implies that

$$\text{const}(\mathbb{Q}(x)[y][s], \sigma) = \text{const}(\mathbb{Q}(x)[y], \sigma) = \text{const}(\mathbb{Q}(x), \sigma)$$

holds, Hence the constructed difference ring $(\mathbb{Q}(x)[y][s], \sigma)$ forms an $R\Pi\Sigma^*$-extension of $(\mathbb{Q}(x), \sigma)$ in which we can represent the sum $\sum_{i=1}^{k} \frac{(-1)^i}{i}$ by s.

(3) Finally, we want to model $S(k) = \sum_{j=2}^{k} F(j)$ with (3). As above, we check if this is possible in the given difference ring $(\mathbb{Q}(x)[y][s], \sigma)$. By our earlier construction we can rephrase $F(k+1)$ with $f = -\frac{yx+(x+1)s}{x(x+1)^2}$. Thus we check if there exists a $g \in \mathbb{Q}(x)[y][s]$ such that $\sigma(g) = g + f$ holds. This time our telescoping algorithms produce $g = \frac{s}{x}$. We conclude that for $G(k) = \frac{1}{k}\sum_{i=1}^{k} \frac{(-1)^i}{i} + c$ with $c \in \mathbb{Q}$ we obtain $G(\nu+1) = G(\nu) + F(\nu+1)$ for all $\nu \in \mathbb{N}$. Choosing $c = 1$ we get $G(1) = S(1) = 0$. Together with $S(\nu+1) = S(\nu) + F(\nu+1)$ for all $\nu \in \mathbb{N}$ we get

$$S(k) = \frac{1}{k} \sum_{i=1}^{k} \frac{(-1)^i}{i} + 1. \tag{4}$$

This means that both sides agree whenever we evaluate k at positive integers. Hence $S(k)$ can be represented by $g+1 = \frac{s}{x} + 1$ in $(\mathbb{Q}(x)[y][s], \sigma)$. Internally, we used the map

$$\text{expr}_k(a) = a|_{x\mapsto k, y\mapsto(-1)^k, s\mapsto\sum_{i=1}^{k}\frac{(-1)^i}{i}}$$

for $a \in \mathbb{Q}(x)[y][s]$ that links our difference ring elements to our nested sum expressions. E.g., $\text{expr}_k(f)$ and $\text{expr}_k(g+1)$ are precisely the right hand sides of (3) and (4), respectively.

In general, given an $R\Pi\Sigma^*$-extension over a $\Pi\Sigma^*$-field $(\mathbb{K}(x), \sigma)$ with $\sigma(x) = x+1$ such a map expr_k is canonically induced by the action of σ and is uniquely determined up to choice of the lower summation/multiplication bounds and of additive constants (for sums) or multiplicative constants (for products) from $\mathbb{K}$. We are now ready to introduce the following problem which has been solved in [28, Subsec. 7.1].

Problem RNS: Representation of Nested Sums. Given a nested sum expression over hypergeometric products $A(k)$, find a nested sum expression over hypergeometric products $B(k)$ and a δ with the following properties:

(1) $A(\nu) = B(\nu)$ for all $\nu \in \mathbb{N}$ with $\nu \geq \delta$;

(2) the nested sums and hypergeometric products in $B(k)$ (except products of the form α^k with α being a root of unity) are algebraically independent among each other.

Our solution. We start with the $\Pi\Sigma^*$-field $(\mathbb{K}(x), \sigma)$ with $\sigma(x) = x+1$. Then we compute a basic $R\Pi\Sigma^*$-extension $(\mathbb{K}(x)[y][p_1, p_1^{-1}]\dots[p_r, p_r^{-1}][s_1]\dots[s_e], \sigma)$ of $(\mathbb{K}(x), \sigma)$ with an element $a \in \mathbb{A}$ and a $\delta \in \mathbb{N}$ such that property (1) of Problem RNS holds with $B(k) := \text{expr}_k(a)$; for details see the above example (for the product case see [25, 11]). By the explicitly given map expr_k it follows that $B(k)$ is given in terms of one root of unity product $R(k) = \text{expr}_k(y) = \alpha^k$ (note that one R-extension is sufficient by [28, Lemma 2.22]), hypergeometric products $P_i(k) := \text{expr}_k(p_i)$ with $1 \leq i \leq r$ and nested sums $S_i(k) = \text{expr}_k(s_i)$ with $1 \leq i \leq e$.
Now consider the ring of sequences $\mathbb{K}^{\mathbb{N}}$ with component-wise addition and multiplication, and define $\text{ev}\colon \mathbb{K}(x) \to \mathbb{K}^{\mathbb{N}}$ by

$$\text{ev}(\tfrac{p}{q}, k) = \begin{cases} 0 & \text{if } q(k) = 0 \\ \frac{p(k)}{q(k)} & \text{if } q(k) \neq 0 \end{cases}$$

where $p, q \in \mathbb{K}[x]$, $q \neq 0$ are co-prime. Then $\tau\colon \mathbb{K}(x) \to \mathbb{K}^{\mathbb{N}}$ with $\tau(a) = \langle \text{ev}(a,k)\rangle_{k\geq 0}$ for $a \in \mathbb{K}(x)$ establishes a ring monomorphism. Thus the field $\mathbb{K}(x)$ and the field of rational sequences $F := \tau(\mathbb{K}(x))$ are isomorphic. Further, difference ring theory[2] [28] (see also [29]) implies that

$$S[\langle P_1(\nu)\rangle_{\nu\geq 0}, \langle \tfrac{1}{P_1(\nu)}\rangle_{\nu\geq 0}]\dots[\langle P_r(\nu)\rangle_{\nu\geq 0}, \langle \tfrac{1}{P_r(\nu)}\rangle_{\nu\geq 0}]$$
$$[\langle S_1(\nu)\rangle_{\nu\geq 0}]\dots[\langle S_e(\nu)\rangle_{\nu\geq 0}]$$

forms a (Laurent) polynomial ring extension over the ring

$$S = F[\langle R(\nu)\rangle_{\nu\geq 0}] = \tau(\mathbb{K}(x))[\langle \alpha^\nu\rangle_{\nu\geq 0}]$$

of rational sequences adjoined with $\langle \alpha^\nu\rangle_{\nu\geq 0}$. In conclusion, the arising sums and products in $B(k)$ (except $R(k) = \alpha^k$) are algebraically independent among each other. □

[2] Internally, one works within the difference ring of sequences: there two sequences are considered to be equal if they agree from a certain point on.

Among many interesting features we emphasize that our solution of Problem RNS contains the zero-recognition problem: the input $A(k)$ evaluates to zero from a certain point on if and only if the output $B(k)$ is the zero-expression.

Summation paradigms in difference rings

As illustrated in the above example, our solution of Problem RNS relies on algorithms that decide if a telescoping equation has a solution within the already constructed difference ring. More generally, we can use efficient algorithms that solve the so-called parameterized telescoping problem.

Let $(\mathbb{A},\sigma)$ be a difference ring with constant field $\mathbb{K}$, and take the elements $f_0,\dots,f_d \in \mathbb{A}$. Then we are interested in finding all solutions $g \in \mathbb{A}$ and $c_0,\dots,c_d \in \mathbb{K}$ such that

$$\sigma(g) - g = c_0\, f_0 + \cdots + c_d\, f_d \qquad (5)$$

holds. Since the set of solutions

$$\{(c_0,\dots,c_d,g) \in \mathbb{K}^{d+1} \times \mathbb{A} \mid \text{(5) holds}\} \qquad (6)$$

forms a $\mathbb{K}$-vector space of dimension $\le d+2$, we can formulate this task as follows.

Problem PT: Parameterized Telescoping.
Given a difference ring $(\mathbb{A},\sigma)$ with constant field $\mathbb{K}$ and given $f_0,\dots,f_d \in \mathbb{A}$; find a basis of (6).

General algorithms for this task are worked out in [27, 28] relying on algorithms from [8]. In particular, we can solve this problem if we take a $\Pi\Sigma^*$-field $(\mathbb{F},\sigma)$ over a constant field $\mathbb{K}$ and choose any basic $R\Pi\Sigma^*$-extension $(\mathbb{A},\sigma)$ on top of $(\mathbb{F},\sigma)$; by definition we have $\mathbb{K} = \text{const}(\mathbb{F},\sigma) = \text{const}(\mathbb{A},\sigma)$.

The special case $d = 0$ of Problem PT is nothing else than the telescoping problem in the setting of difference rings and is applied iteratively to solve Problem RNS. At this point we emphasize that refined telescoping algorithms can be exploited which leads to improved versions of Problem RNS: e.g., the sums in $B(k)$ are minimal nested [18, 20, 23, 26].

Creative telescoping. Problem PT and our algorithms cover as special case Zeilberger's celebrated summation paradigm of creative telescoping. In its simplest form it can be formulated as follows.
Given $d \in \mathbb{N}$ and a nested sum expression $F(n,k)$ over hypergeometric products w.r.t. $\mathbb{K}$ and k where $F(n,k)$ depends on an extra parameter n; here $\mathbb{K} = \mathbb{K}'(n)$ is supposed to be a rational function field over a subfield $\mathbb{K}'$.
Find constants $c_0,\dots,c_d$, free of k, and a nested sum expression $G(n,k)$ w.r.t. $\mathbb{K}$ and k, which depends only on the sums and products given in $F(n,k)$, such that the creative telescoping equation

$$G(n,\nu+1) - G(n,\nu) = c_0\, F(n,\nu) + \cdots + c_d F(n+d,\nu) \qquad (7)$$

holds for all evaluations $\nu \in \mathbb{N}$ with $\nu \ge \lambda$ for some $\lambda \in \mathbb{N}$.
We can tackle this problem as follows: We take the difference field $(\mathbb{K}(x),\sigma)$ with $\sigma(x) = x+1$ and construct an $R\Pi\Sigma^*$-extension $(\mathbb{A},\sigma)$ of $(\mathbb{K}(x),\sigma)$ with $f_0,\dots,f_d \in \mathbb{A}$ and a $\delta \in \mathbb{N}$ such that for $0 \le i \le d$ the evaluations of $\text{expr}_k(f_i)$ and $F(n+i,k)$ with $k \mapsto \nu$ agree for all non-negative integers $\nu \ge \delta$ (compare Problem RNS). If we fail to find a solution $c_0,\dots,c_d \in \mathbb{K}$ (not all c_i being non-zero) and $g \in \mathbb{A}$ for (5), then we conclude that the desired solution of (7) does not exist; in this case we can either increase d or we can use our enhanced algorithms [18, 20, 23, 26] for Problem PT. Otherwise, if we find such a solution, we obtain the desired $G(n,k) := \text{expr}_k(g)$ and a $\lambda \in \mathbb{N}$ with $\lambda \ge \delta$ such that (7) holds all $\nu \in \mathbb{N}$ with $\nu \ge \lambda$.
Given such a solution, we can sum (7) over k and get

$$G(n,a+1) - G(n,\lambda) = c_0\, S(n,a) + \cdots + c_d\, S(n+d,a)$$

for the sum $S(n,a) = \sum_{k=\lambda}^{a} F(n,k)$. This means that both sides of the obtained recurrence in terms of nested sums over hypergeometric products agree for any evaluation $a \mapsto \nu$ with $\nu \in \mathbb{N}$ and $\nu \ge \lambda$. Further, we can specialize a, e.g., to n which yields a recurrence for the definite sum $\sum_{k=\lambda}^{n} F(n,k)$.
Recurrence solving. Finally, we can look for solutions of a given recurrence relation

$$a_0(k)S(k) + a_1(k)S(k+1) + \cdots + a_d(k)S(k+d) = b(k) \quad (8)$$

where $a_i(k)$ are polynomials in $\mathbb{K}[k]$ and $b(k)$ is a nested sum expression over hypergeometric products w.r.t. $\mathbb{K}$ and k. More precisely, we find the so-called d'Alembertian solutions [2, 3]. This means that we find all solutions of (8) that are expressible in terms of nested sums over hypergeometric products. Internally, the expression $b(k)$ is rephrased to a difference ring composed by a tower of $R\Pi\Sigma^*$-extensions and variants of the algorithms from [16, 5, 17, 21, 19] are used to compute these solutions. We remark that the produced solutions are highly nested. As a consequence, the simplification of these solutions with our telescoping algorithms for Problem RNS is a crucial and highly challenging task.

Applications

Combining this toolbox of computing recurrences and solving them in terms of nested sums over hypergeometric, q-hypergeometric or q-mixed hypergeometric products, we obtain an efficient summation machinery that has been built into the Mathematica package Sigma [22].

```
In[1]:= << Sigma.m
```

Sigma - A summation package by Carsten Schneider © RISC-Linz

For instance, after entering the definite sum

```
In[2]:= mySum = SigmaSum[(1 - (-1)^k)SigmaBinomial[n, k]
            SigmaSum[SigmaPower[-1, i]/i, {i, 1, k}], {k, 0, n}]
```

Out[2]= $\sum_{k=0}^{n}(1-(-1)^k)\binom{n}{k}\sum_{i=1}^{k}\frac{(-1)^i}{i}$

one can calculate a linear recurrence by the function call

```
In[3]:= rec = GenerateRecurrence[mySum]
```

Out[3]= $-4n\text{SUM}[n] + 4(n+1)\text{SUM}[n+1] + (-n-2)\text{SUM}[n+2] = \frac{-2n}{n+1}$

Internally, one activates the parameterized telescoping algorithms mentioned above. Next, we solve the computed recurrence in terms of nested sums over hypergeometric products by executing the function call

```
In[4]:= recSol = SolveRecurrence[rec[[1]], SUM[n]]
```

Out[4]= $\{\{0,-2^n\}\{0,-\frac{2^n}{n}\},\{1,\frac{1}{n}-2^n\sum_{i=1}^{n}\frac{2^{-i}}{i}\}\}$

This means that $h_1(n) = -2^n$ and $h_2(n) = -\frac{2^n}{n}$ are two linearly independent solutions of the homogeneous version of the input recurrence and $p(n) = \frac{1}{n} - 2^n\sum_{i=1}^{n}\frac{2^{-i}}{i}$ is a particular solution of the recurrence itself. In a nutshell, we obtain the full solution set

$$\{c_1\, h_1(n) + c_2\, h(n) + p(n) \mid c_1, c_2 \in \mathbb{Q}\}. \qquad (9)$$

In particular, the arising sums and products are algebraically independent among each other. Finally, we determine c_1, c_2 such that (9) equals to $S(n)$ for $n = 1, 2$:

In[5]:= **sol = FindLinearCombination[recSol, mySum, n, 2]**

$$\text{Out[5]=}\quad -2^{n}\sum_{i=1}^{n}\frac{2^{-i}}{i}+\frac{1-2^{n}}{n}$$

Since this expression and $S(n)$ are both a solution of the same recurrence of order 2, they must agree for all $n \in \mathbb{N}$.

In this talk we exploit this summation machinery of `Sigma` and demonstrate challenging problems coming from combinatorics and particle physics; in the latter case see, e.g., [28] and references therein.

Acknowledgments

I am grateful to the organizers and the program committee who gave me the possibility to present this work at the ISSAC 2016. This work has been supported by the Austrian Science Fund (FWF) grant SFB F50 (F5009-N15)

1. REFERENCES

[1] S. A. Abramov. On the summation of rational functions. *Zh. vychisl. mat. Fiz.*, 11:1071–1074, 1971.

[2] S. A. Abramov and M. Petkovšek. D'Alembertian solutions of linear differential and difference equations. In *Proc. ISSAC'94*, pages 169–174. ACM Press, 1994.

[3] S. A. Abramov and E. V. Zima. D'Alembertian solutions of inhomogeneous linear equations (differential, difference, and some other). In *Proc. ISSAC'96*, pages 232–240. ACM Press, 1996.

[4] M. Apagodu and D. Zeilberger. Multi-variable Zeilberger and Almkvist-Zeilberger algorithms and the sharpening of Wilf-Zeilberger theory. *Adv. Appl. Math.*, 37:139–152, 2006.

[5] M. Bronstein. On solutions of linear ordinary difference equations in their coefficient field. *J. Symbolic Comput.*, 29(6):841–877, 2000.

[6] F. Chyzak. An extension of Zeilberger's fast algorithm to general holonomic functions. *Discrete Math.*, 217:115–134, 2000.

[7] R. W. Gosper. Decision procedures for indefinite hypergeometric summation. *Proc. Nat. Acad. Sci. U.S.A.*, 75:40–42, 1978.

[8] M. Karr. Summation in finite terms. *J. ACM*, 28:305–350, 1981.

[9] M. Karr. Theory of summation in finite terms. *J. Symbolic Comput.*, 1:303–315, 1985.

[10] M. Kauers. Summation Algorithms for Stirling Number Identities. *Journal of Symbolic Computation*, 42(10):948–970, 2007.

[11] E. Doe Ocansey and C. Schneider. Representation of (q–)hypergeometric products and mixed versions in difference rings. In preparation, 2016.

[12] M. Kauers and C. Schneider. Application of unspecified sequences in symbolic summation. In *Proc. ISSAC'06.*, pages 177–183. ACM Press, 2006.

[13] M. Kauers and C. Schneider. Symbolic summation with radical expressions. In *Proc. ISSAC'07*, pages 219–226, 2007.

[14] C. Koutschan. Creative telescoping for holonomic functions. In *Computer Algebra in Quantum Field Theory: Integration, Summation and Special Functions*, Texts and Monographs in Symbolic Computation, pages 171–194. Springer, 2013. arXiv:1307.4554 [cs.SC].

[15] P. Paule. Greatest factorial factorization and symbolic summation. *J. Symbolic Comput.*, 20(3):235–268, 1995.

[16] M. Petkovšek. Hypergeometric solutions of linear recurrences with polynomial coefficients. *J. Symbolic Comput.*, 14(2-3):243–264, 1992.

[17] C. Schneider. A collection of denominator bounds to solve parameterized linear difference equations in $\Pi\Sigma$-extensions. *An. Univ. Timişoara Ser. Mat.-Inform.*, 42(2):163–179, 2004. Extended version of Proc. SYNASC'04.

[18] C. Schneider. Symbolic summation with single-nested sum extensions. In *Proc. ISSAC'04*, pages 282–289. ACM Press, 2004.

[19] C. Schneider. Degree bounds to find polynomial solutions of parameterized linear difference equations in $\Pi\Sigma$-fields. *Appl. Algebra Engrg. Comm. Comput.*, 16(1):1–32, 2005.

[20] C. Schneider. Finding telescopers with minimal depth for indefinite nested sum and product expressions. In *Proc. ISSAC'05*, pages 285–292. ACM, 2005.

[21] C. Schneider. Solving parameterized linear difference equations in terms of indefinite nested sums and products. *J. Differ. Equations Appl.*, 11(9):799–821, 2005.

[22] C. Schneider. Symbolic summation assists combinatorics. *Sém. Lothar. Combin.*, 56:1–36, 2007. Article B56b.

[23] C. Schneider. A refined difference field theory for symbolic summation. *J. Symbolic Comput.*, 43(9):611–644, 2008. [arXiv:0808.2543v1].

[24] C. Schneider. Structural theorems for symbolic summation. *Appl. Algebra Engrg. Comm. Comput.*, 21(1):1–32, 2010.

[25] C. Schneider. A streamlined difference ring theory: Indefinite nested sums, the alternating sign and the parameterized telescoping problem. In *Symbolic and Numeric Algorithms for Scientific Computing (SYNASC)*, pages 26–33. IEEE Computer Society, 2014. arXiv:1412.2782v1 [cs.SC].

[26] C. Schneider. Fast algorithms for refined parameterized telescoping in difference fields. In *Computer Algebra and Polynomials*, number 8942 in Lecture Notes in Computer Science (LNCS), pages 157–191. Springer, 2015. arXiv:1307.7887 [cs.SC].

[27] C. Schneider. A difference ring theory for symbolic summation. *J. Symb. Comput.*, 72:82–127, 2016. arXiv:1408.2776 [cs.SC].

[28] C. Schneider. Summation Theory II: Characterizations of $R\Pi\Sigma$-extensions and algorithmic aspects. pages 1–54, 2016. arXiv:1603.04285 [cs.SC].

[29] M. van der Put and M. Singer. *Galois theory of difference equations*, volume 1666 of *Lecture Notes in Mathematics*. Springer-Verlag, Berlin, 1997.

[30] H. Wilf and D. Zeilberger. An algorithmic proof theory for hypergeometric (ordinary and "q") multisum/integral identities. *Invent. Math.*, 108:575–633, 1992.

[31] D. Zeilberger. The method of creative telescoping. *J. Symbolic Comput.*, 11:195–204, 1991.

Symbolic Computation of Parameter Integrals

Clemens G. Raab*
Johann Radon Institute for Computational and Applied Mathematics (RICAM)
Austrian Academy of Sciences
4040 Linz, Austria
clemens.raab@ricam.oeaw.ac.at

ABSTRACT

Integrals are important to many applications ranging from physics over engineering to statistics. While systematic methods for symbolic computation of integrals have a long history, computer algebra tools for computation of parameter integrals are a more recent topic. For computing (definite) parameter integrals, one does not necessarily need to know an explicit antiderivative of the integrand, such computations often rely on techniques like differentiation under the integral sign instead.

Keywords

Symbolic integration; definite integrals; parameter integrals; creative telescoping; Risch algorithm

1. INTRODUCTION

Parameter integrals are integrals where the integrand, and possibly also the integration bounds, depend on one or more discrete parameters $\vec{n}$ and/or continuous parameters $\vec{y}$.

$$F(\vec{n}, \vec{y}) = \int_{a(\vec{n},\vec{y})}^{b(\vec{n},\vec{y})} f(\vec{n}, \vec{y}, x)\, dx$$

Computing $F(\vec{n}, \vec{y})$ commonly refers to finding a closed form representation for it. Which representations are considered to be in closed form depends on the application context and on the algorithmic tools used.

Indefinite integration aims at finding an explicit antiderivative $g(x)$ for a given integrand $f(x)$, i.e. $f(x) = \frac{d}{dx}g(x)$. Then the definite integral can, at least in principle, be computed via the well-known fundamental theorem of calculus $\int_a^b f(x)\, dx = g(b) - g(a)$. If an antiderivative of the integrand is not available in closed form, then other methods need to be used for computing the parameter integral.

In applications, parameter integrals often arise from integral transforms or convolution of functions, where it is sometimes possible to exploit properties of the integral transform in order to reduce the parameter integral to known cases. For many parameter integrals, regardless of their origin, it is possible to systematically derive linear relations they satisfy. These can then be used for obtaining more information on the parameter integral, even closed form evaluations. Development of computer algebra tools for algorithmic evaluation of parameter integrals along these lines, related to differentiation under the integral sign, started around 1990 [1, 15, 24, 27].

For obtaining linear relations of integrals, one can distinguish two closely related problems: *parametric integration*, sometimes also referred to as parameterized integration, and *creative telescoping*, see Section 2. Originally, creative telescoping was a method to compute linear recurrences for sums [18, 28], but the name soon was used in other contexts as well [14]. Also parametric integration has a summation analog: *parameterized telescoping*, see [22] and references therein. For recent surveys on the paradigm of creative telescoping see [16, 12].

In 1969 Risch [20] gave an algorithm for computing indefinite integrals of elementary functions, which received much attention. Ever since, his algorithm has been improved and generalized in various ways, see e.g. [17, 23, 5, 6] and many more. The tutorial presentation gives an introduction to a variant [19] of the algorithm that solves parametric integration and can deal with several types of special functions occurring in the integrand. In the following, instead, we briefly provide some background relating the majority of algorithms in the context of parametric integration and creative telescoping without going much into detail.

2. LINEAR RELATIONS OF INTEGRALS

2.1 Parametric integration

Parametric integration generalizes indefinite integration in the sense that several integrands $f_1(x), \ldots, f_m(x)$ are given at once and the task is to find coefficients $c_1, \ldots, c_m$ (not depending on x) and a function $g(x)$ such that

$$\sum_{i=1}^{m} c_i f_i(x) = \frac{d}{dx} g(x). \tag{1}$$

Having such an identity, integration from a to b yields the linear relation of integrals

$$\sum_{i=1}^{m} c_i \int_a^b f_i(x)\, dx = g(b) - g(a), \tag{2}$$

since the coefficients do not depend on x. Lifting a relation

*Supported by Austrian Science Fund (FWF): P27229

ISSAC '16 July 19-22, 2016, Waterloo, ON, Canada

ACM ISBN 978-1-4503-4380-0/16/07.
DOI: http://dx.doi.org/10.1145/2930889.2930940

of integrands (1) to a relation of corresponding integrals (2) may require additional justification if some integrand $f_i(x)$ has a singularity in the integration interval.

In contrast to creative telescoping below, parametric integration neither relies on the presence of extra parameters in the integrands $f_i(x)$ nor on a specific way of how the $f_i(x)$ are related to each other, c.f. the ansatz for the operators L below.

2.2 Creative telescoping

In creative telescoping, usually only one integrand $f(x)$ depending on extra parameters is considered and the goal is to find a linear operator L (acting on the parameters in $f(x)$ and commuting with $\frac{d}{dx}$) and a function $g(x)$ such that

$$Lf(x) = \frac{d}{dx}g(x). \tag{3}$$

The operator L is then called a *telescoper*. Similar to above, such an identity gives rise to the linear equation

$$L(F) = g(b) - g(a) \tag{4}$$

satisfied by the integral $F = \int_a^b f(x)\,dx$. Again, inferring (4) from $\int_a^b Lf(x)\,dx = g(b) - g(a)$ may require additional justification. Moreover, if also a or b depends on some of the parameters, additional boundary terms have to be taken into account.

Of course, in order to algorithmically find solutions of (3), more structure needs to be imposed on L and g. In applications, the operator L often is a differential operator or recurrence operator and the equation (4) obtained is a differential equation or a recurrence for the definite integral. Many algorithms for creative telescoping actually proceed by solving parametric integration problems. For example, if the integrand $f(y, x)$ depends on a parameter y in a differentiable way, the ansatz

$$L = \sum_{i=0}^{k} c_i(y)\partial_y^i$$

for the differential operator leads to parametric integration for the $k + 1$ integrands $f(y, x), \partial_y f(y, x), \dots, \partial_y^k f(y, x)$. A solution $c_0(y), \dots, c_k(y)$, $g(y, x)$ of that parametric integration problem gives rise to the kth-order differential equation

$$c_k(y)F^{(k)}(y) + \dots + c_1(y)F'(y) + c_0(y)F(y) = g(y, b) - g(y, a)$$

for the integral, assuming that the integration bounds a and b do not depend on the parameter y for simplicity of presentation. A similar ansatz can be used for recurrence operators, partial differential operators, mixed difference-differential operators, and other types of operators L. If (4) can be solved explicitly, then an evaluation of the parameter integral can be determined based on side conditions (e.g. initial values, asymptotic behaviour, etc.) that make the solution of the equation (4) unique. It can also happen that several equations of that form are available if the integral depends on more than one parameter.

2.3 Certificates

The correctness of an indefinite integral usually can be verified easily by differentiating the antiderivative. How to verify that a definite (parameter) integral was evaluated correctly is not so clear in general. However, solutions $g(x)$ of (1) or (3) can be verified rather easily again. So, given an integral relation of the form (2) or (4) along with the corresponding *certificate* $g(x)$, we can verify its correctness by first plugging $g(x)$ into the corresponding relation on the integrand-level (1) or (3). The left hand side of that relation can be read off easily from the integral relation. Then it remains to verify that the right hand side of the integral relation is indeed obtained by evaluation of $g(x)$.

3. ALGORITHMS

One can interpret parametric integration (1) also as determining those values of $c_1, \dots, c_m$ such that an antiderivative of the integrand $f(x) = \sum c_i f_i(x)$ can be found explicitly. So it seems natural to augment indefinite integration algorithms to also find appropriate choices for $c_1, \dots, c_m$. Many of the algorithms mentioned in the following can be understood that way.

The multitude of algorithms in the literature for treating parametric integration or creative telescoping largely is due to the many ways one can make the somewhat vague problem formulations above precise. In particular, one needs to specify a class of functions, which the integrands should belong to, as well as a way of representing the integrands. In addition, also the allowed form of the antiderivative has to be specified (relative to the integrands). Even for the same problem specification there is often more than one algorithmic approach.

Most general algorithms rely on one of the following two representations of integrands. Either a class of differential fields (or differential rings) is fixed and integrands are elements of a particular field from that class, or a class of operator algebras is fixed and integrands are implicitly described by an ideal of annihilating operators in a particular operator algebra.

3.1 Differential field approach

Given integrands from some differential field K, the antiderivative $g(x)$ can either be required to be from the same field or one can allow field extensions of certain type in order to construct the antiderivative. For parametric integration, only elementary extensions of K can be handled so far by relying on Liouville's theorem [21], see [23, Appendix] and [19]. The main result of Risch's paper [20] is a decision algorithm for indefinite integration in elementary extensions of K, but as a sub-algorithm he also describes a procedure that can be used for parametric integration without extending the field K. A similar statement can be made about [6]. For indefinite integration, algorithms treating more general field extensions of K have been obtained, e.g. [9, 10], relying on generalizations of Liouville's theorem like [23]. There are still many algorithmic challenges in this direction.

The algorithms for parametric integration mentioned so far vary greatly in the conditions they impose on the field K. They cover integrands being (certain cases of) elementary functions [20], Liouvillian functions [23, Appendix], and more general functions [6, 19]. All of them disallow algebraic relations among the generators of K, which excludes algebraic functions as integrands, for instance. A notable exception is [8], providing creative telescoping for algebraic functions without extending the field K. Indefinite integration in the presence of algebraic relations has been considered in [25, 26, 5, 3], for instance.

For an algorithmic solution of integration problems in differential fields, the generators of the field K are either considered recursively one by one, as most of the above algorithms do, or all in parallel, see e.g. [17], [6, Chap. 10], and [3]. The parallel approach typically results in rather fast algorithms which to a large extent have remained heuristic.

3.2 Holonomic systems approach

When integrands are given implicitly by an ideal of annihilating operators in some algebra A of (linear) operators, algorithms typically construct the antiderivative $g(x)$ by applying an operator from A to the integrand, i.e. $g(x)$ is contained in the A-module generated by the integrand. In such a setting the integrand is necessarily considered as a whole and cannot be broken down into smaller pieces like it is possible in terms of the generators of differential fields above. On the other hand, one only needs to compute with operators in A, not with the possibly complicated functions themselves. Those operators usually are defined with rational function coefficients.

Regarding the class of integrands, most integration algorithms of this type are designed either for hyperexponential functions, i.e. $\frac{d}{dx}f(x)$ can be written as $f(x)$ multiplied by a rational function, or for ∂-finite functions defined in [14] such that the A-module generated by the integrand is finite dimensional over the rational functions. The first general algorithm to obtain differential equations for parameter integrals was given in [1] for hyperexponential integrands. Other algorithms for creative telescoping of hyperexponential functions include [2, 4]. Important practical algorithms for creative telescoping of ∂-finite functions are [11, 7], the seminal paper being [27]. Also the algorithm [24] mentioned in the beginning works with ∂-finite functions. Even non-∂-finite functions are considered [13]. New algorithms are still being developed for increased efficiency. Note that general algorithms for ∂-finite functions typically are not restricted to integration but also can be used for summation.

4. REFERENCES

[1] G. E. T. Almkvist and D. Zeilberger. The method of differentiating under the integral sign. *J. Symb. Comput.*, 10:571–591, 1990.

[2] M. Apagodu and D. Zeilberger. Multi-variable Zeilberger and Almkvist-Zeilberger algorithms and the sharpening of Wilf-Zeilberger theory. *Adv. Appl. Math.*, 37:139–152, 2006.

[3] S. T. Boettner, *Mixed Transcendental and Algebraic Extensions for the Risch-Norman Algorithm*, PhD Thesis, Tulane Univ., New Orleans, USA, 2010.

[4] A. Bostan, S. Chen, F. Chyzak, Z. Li, and G. Xin. Hermite Reduction and Creative Telescoping for Hyperexponential Functions. In *Proc. ISSAC 2013*, pp. 77–84, 2013.

[5] M. Bronstein. Integration of Elementary Functions. *J. Symb. Comput.*, 9:117–173, 1990.

[6] M. Bronstein. *Symbolic Integration I — Transcendental Functions.* 2nd ed., Springer, 2005.

[7] S. Chen, M. Kauers, and C. Koutschan. A Generalized Apagodu-Zeilberger Algorithm. In *Proc. ISSAC 2014*, pp. 107–114, 2014.

[8] S. Chen, M. Kauers, and M. F. Singer. Telescopers for Rational and Algebraic Functions via Residues. In *Proc. ISSAC 2012*, pp. 130–137, 2012.

[9] G. W. Cherry. Integration in Finite Terms with Special Functions: the Error Function. *J. Symb. Comput.*, 1:283–302, 1985.

[10] G. W. Cherry. Integration in finite terms with special functions: the logarithmic integral. *SIAM J. Comput.*, 15:1–21, 1986.

[11] F. Chyzak. An extension of Zeilberger's fast algorithm to general holonomic functions. *Discrete Math.*, 217:115–134, 2000.

[12] F. Chyzak. *The ABC of Creative Telescoping — Algorithms, Bounds, Complexity.* Habilitation à diriger des recherches (HDR), Univ. Paris-Sud 11, France, 2014. http://specfun.inria.fr/chyzak/Chyzak-2014-ABC.pdf

[13] F. Chyzak, M. Kauers, and B. Salvy. A Non-Holonomic Systems Approach to Special Function Identities. In *Proc. ISSAC 2009*, pp. 111–118, 2009.

[14] F. Chyzak and B. Salvy. Non-commutative elimination in Ore algebras proves multivariate identities. *J. Symb. Comput.*, 26:187–227, 1998.

[15] K. O. Geddes, M. L. Glasser, R. A. Moore, T. C. Scott. Evaluation of Classes of Definite Integrals Involving Elementary Functions via Differentiation of Special Functions. *Appl. Alg. Eng. Comm. Comp.*, 1:149–165, 1990.

[16] C. Koutschan. Creative Telescoping for Holonomic Functions. In *Computer Algebra in Quantum Field Theory*, pp. 171–194, Springer, 2013.

[17] A. C. Norman and P. M. A. Moore. Implementing the new Risch Integration algorithm. In *Proc. 4th International Colloquium on Advanced Computing Methods in Theoretical Physics*, pp. 99–110, 1977.

[18] A. van der Poorten. A Proof that Euler Missed... Apéry's Proof of the Irrationality of $\zeta(3)$ — An Informal Report. *Math. Intelligencer*, 1:195–203, 1979.

[19] C. G. Raab. *Definite Integration in Differential Fields.* PhD Thesis, Johannes Kepler Univ. Linz, Austria, 2012. http://www.risc.jku.at/publications/download/risc_4583/PhD_CGR.pdf

[20] R. H. Risch. The problem of integration in finite terms. *Trans. Amer. Math. Soc.*, 139:167–189, 1969.

[21] M. Rosenlicht. Liouville's theorem on functions with elementary integrals. *Pacific J. Math.*, 24:153–161, 1968.

[22] C. Schneider. A difference ring theory for symbolic summation. *J. Symb. Comput.*, 72:82–127, 2016.

[23] M. F. Singer, B. D. Saunders, and B. F. Caviness. An Extension of Liouville's Theorem on Integration in Finite Terms. *SIAM J. Comput.*, 14:966–990, 1985.

[24] N. Takayama. An algorithm of constructing the integral of a module — an infinite dimensional analog of Gröbner basis. In *Proc. ISSAC'90*, pp. 206–211, 1990.

[25] B. M. Trager. Integration of simple radical extensions. In *Proc. EUROSAM'79*, pp. 408–414, 1979.

[26] B. M. Trager. *Integration of algebraic functions.* PhD Thesis, MIT, USA, 1984.

[27] D. Zeilberger. A holonomic systems approach to special functions identities. *J. Comp. Appl. Math.*, 32:321–368, 1990.

[28] D. Zeilberger. The Method of Creative Telescoping. *J. Symb. Comput.*, 11:195–204, 1991.

Symbolic Computation with Integro-Differential Operators

Georg Regensburger*
Johann Radon Institute for Computational and Applied Mathematics (RICAM)
Austrian Academy of Sciences
4040 Linz, Austria
georg.regensburger@ricam.oeaw.ac.at

ABSTRACT

The algebraic and algorithmic study of integro-differential algebras and operators has only started in the past decade. Integro-differential operators allow us in particular to study initial value and boundary problems for linear ODEs from an algebraic point of view. Differential operators already provide a rich algebraic structure with a wealth of results and algorithmic methods. Adding integral operators and evaluations, many new phenomena appear, including zero devisors and non-finitely generated ideals.

In this tutorial, we give an introduction to symbolic methods for integro-differential operators and boundary problems developed over the last years. In particular, we discuss normal forms, basic algebraic properties, and the computation of polynomial solutions for ordinary integro-differential equations with polynomial coefficients. We will also outline methods for manipulating and solving linear boundary problems and illustrate them with an implementation.

Keywords

integro-differential operators; integro-differential algebra; linear boundary problem; integro-differential equations; polynomial solutions

1. OVERVIEW

Boundary (value) problems and integro-differential equations are ubiquitous in science, engineering, and applied mathematics; see, e.g., [2, 11, 34]. While algebraic structures and computer algebra for differential equations per se are very well developed, the investigation of their integro-differential counterparts has started only recently. For studying linear differential equations, the basic algebraic structure is the noncommutative ring of differential operators over a differential algebra. More generally, skew polynomials are used for an algebraic and algorithmic treatment of many common operator algebras; see, e.g., [22, 9, 35, 8] and the survey [14] describing also implementations in computer algebra systems. However, if we add an integral operator, the resulting algebra cannot be modeled that way.

The basic algebraic identities between the derivation and the integral operator are the fundamental theorem of calculus and integration by parts. Based on these identities, a new operator approach for symbolic computation with linear ordinary boundary problems was introduced in [26, 27] and generalized to a differential algebra setting in [31, 30]. For further references and an implementation in Theorema, see [32]. We refer to [29, 19, 17, 20, 13, 33, 28, 12, 18] for recent developments including partial differential equations, generalized Green's operators and functions, free integro-differential algebras, singular coefficients, and a finite tensor reduction system for integro-differential operators.

The notion of integro-differential algebras combines a differential algebra with an integral operator and the corresponding multiplicative evaluation. The associated integro-differential operators over an ordinary integro-differential algebra allow to express and compute with boundary problems (differential equation plus boundary conditions) and their solution (Green's) operators in a single algebraic structure. For the related notion of differential Rota-Baxter algebras, we refer to [16] and to [17] for a detailed comparison. A Rota-Baxter algebra is an algebra with one linear operator that generalizes the algebra of continuous functions with the integral operator; see [15] and the references therein.

The simplest integro-differential algebra is given by the univariate polynomials over a field of characteristic zero with the usual derivation and integration. However, integro-differential operators with polynomial coefficients reflect many aspects and properties of the general constructions, and we focus in the tutorial on this case. We will discuss a parametrized noncommutative Gröbner basis of the defining relations, the corresponding normal forms, and basic algebraic properties in comparison with the Weyl algebra [10]. In particular, the algebra of integro-differential operators contains zero-divisors and is non-Noetherian. Polynomial coefficients also allow for some special constructions, for example, as a factor algebra of a skew polynomial ring [25]. Using generalized Weyl algebras [4], numerous important results on integro-differential operators with polynomial coefficients are shown in [5, 6].

Computing polynomial solutions of ordinary differential equations is well-studied in symbolic computation; see, e.g., [1, 3, 7]. Building on these methods, we describe an approach [23] for computing polynomial solutions for a class of algorithmic Fredholm operators that includes also integro-

*Supported by the Austrian Science Fund (FWF): P27229.

ISSAC '16 July 19-22, 2016, Waterloo, ON, Canada

ACM ISBN 978-1-4503-4380-0/16/07.

DOI: http://dx.doi.org/10.1145/2930889.2930942

differential operators. Using the Maple package `IntDiffOp` [21], we also illustrate how to compute Green's operators and to factor boundary problems [24] into lower order problems along a factorization of the differential operator.

2. REFERENCES

[1] S. A. Abramov, M. Bronstein, and M. Petkovšek. On polynomial solutions of linear operator equations. In *Proceedings of ISSAC '95*, pages 290–296, New York, NY, USA, 1995. ACM.

[2] R. P. Agarwal. *Boundary value problems for higher order differential equations*. World Scientific Publishing Co. Inc., Teaneck, NJ, 1986.

[3] M. A. Barkatou. On rational solutions of systems of linear differential equations. *J. Symbolic Comput.*, 28:547–567, 1999.

[4] V. V. Bavula. Generalized Weyl algebras and their representations. *Algebra i Analiz*, 4:75–97, 1992.

[5] V. V. Bavula. The algebra of integro-differential operators on a polynomial algebra. *J. Lond. Math. Soc. (2)*, 83:517–543, 2011.

[6] V. V. Bavula. The algebra of integro-differential operators on an affine line and its modules. *J. Pure Appl. Algebra*, 217:495–529, 2013.

[7] A. Bostan, T. Cluzeau, and B. Salvy. Fast algorithms for polynomial solutions of linear differential equations. In *Proceedings of ISSAC '05*, pages 45–52, New York, NY, USA, 2005. ACM.

[8] F. Chyzak, A. Quadrat, and D. Robertz. Effective algorithms for parametrizing linear control systems over Ore algebras. *Appl. Algebra Engrg. Comm. Comput.*, 16:319–376, 2005.

[9] F. Chyzak and B. Salvy. Non-commutative elimination in Ore algebras proves multivariate identities. *J. Symbolic Comput.*, 26:187–227, 1998.

[10] S. C. Coutinho. *A primer of algebraic D-modules*. Cambridge University Press, Cambridge, 1995.

[11] D. G. Duffy. *Green's functions with applications*. Chapman & Hall/CRC, Boca Raton, FL, 2001.

[12] X. Gao, L. Guo, and M. Rosenkranz. Free integro-differential algebras and Gröbner-Shirshov bases. *J. Algebra*, 442:354–396, 2015.

[13] X. Gao, L. Guo, and S. Zheng. Construction of free commutative integro-differential algebras by the method of Gröbner-Shirshov bases. *J. Algebra Appl.*, 13:1350160, 38, 2014.

[14] J. Gómez-Torrecillas. Basic module theory over non-commutative rings with computational aspects of operator algebras. In *AADIOS 2012*, volume 8372 of *LNCS*, pages 23–82. Springer, 2014. With an appendix by V. Levandovskyy.

[15] L. Guo. *An introduction to Rota-Baxter algebra*. International Press, Somerville, MA, 2012.

[16] L. Guo and W. Keigher. On differential Rota-Baxter algebras. *J. Pure Appl. Algebra*, 212:522–540, 2008.

[17] L. Guo, G. Regensburger, and M. Rosenkranz. On integro-differential algebras. *J. Pure Appl. Algebra*, 218:456–473, 2014.

[18] J. Hossein Poor, C. G. Raab, and G. Regensburger. Algorithmic operator algebras via normal forms for tensors. In *Proceedings of ISSAC '16*, this volume, New York, NY, USA, 2016. ACM.

[19] A. Korporal and G. Regensburger. Composing and factoring generalized Green's operators and ordinary boundary problems. In *AADIOS 2012*, volume 8372 of *LNCS*, pages 116–134. Springer, 2014.

[20] A. Korporal and G. Regensburger. On the product of projectors and generalized inverses. *Linear Multilinear Algebra*, 62:1567–1582, 2014.

[21] A. Korporal, G. Regensburger, and M. Rosenkranz. Symbolic computation for ordinary boundary problems in Maple. *ACM Commun. Comput. Algebra*, 46:154–156, 2012. Software demonstration ISSAC '12.

[22] Ø. Ore. Theory of non-commutative polynomials. *Ann. Math.*, 34:480–508, 1933.

[23] A. Quadrat and G. Regensburger. Polynomial solutions and annihilators of ordinary integro-differential operators. In *Proceedings of SSSC 2013*, pages 308–313. IFAC, 2013.

[24] G. Regensburger and M. Rosenkranz. An algebraic foundation for factoring linear boundary problems. *Ann. Mat. Pura Appl. (4)*, 188:123–151, 2009.

[25] G. Regensburger, M. Rosenkranz, and J. Middeke. A skew polynomial approach to integro-differential operators. In *Proceedings of ISSAC '09*, pages 287–294, New York, NY, USA, 2009. ACM.

[26] M. Rosenkranz. *The Green's Algebra: A Polynomial Approach to Boundary Value Problems*. PhD thesis, RISC, Johannes Kepler University Linz, 2003.

[27] M. Rosenkranz. A new symbolic method for solving linear two-point boundary value problems on the level of operators. *J. Symbolic Comput.*, 39:171–199, 2005.

[28] M. Rosenkranz, J. Liu, A. Maletzky, and B. Buchberger. Two-point boundary problems with one mild singularity and an application to graded Kirchhoff plates. In *Proceedings of CASC 2015*, volume 9301 of *LNCS*, pages 406–423. Springer, 2015.

[29] M. Rosenkranz and N. Phisanbut. A symbolic approach to boundary problems for linear partial differential equations. In *Proceedings of CASC 2013*, volume 8136 of *LNCS*, pages 301–314. Springer, 2013.

[30] M. Rosenkranz and G. Regensburger. Integro-differential polynomials and operators. In *Proceedings of ISSAC '08*, pages 261–268, New York, NY, USA, 2008. ACM.

[31] M. Rosenkranz and G. Regensburger. Solving and factoring boundary problems for linear ordinary differential equations in differential algebras. *J. Symbolic Comput.*, 43:515–544, 2008.

[32] M. Rosenkranz, G. Regensburger, L. Tec, and B. Buchberger. Symbolic analysis for boundary problems: From rewriting to parametrized Gröbner bases. In *Numerical and Symbolic Scientific Computing: Progress and Prospects*, pages 273–331. Springer Vienna, 2012.

[33] M. Rosenkranz and N. Serwa. Green's functions for Stieltjes boundary problems. In *Proceedings of ISSAC '15*, pages 315–321, New York, NY, USA, 2015. ACM.

[34] I. Stakgold. *Green's functions and boundary value problems*. John Wiley & Sons, New York, 1979.

[35] M. van der Put and M. F. Singer. *Galois theory of linear differential equations*. Springer-Verlag, 2003.

Formal Algorithmic Elimination for PDEs

Daniel Robertz
School of Computing, Electronics and Mathematics
Plymouth University
Plymouth PL4 8AA, United Kingdom
daniel.robertz@plymouth.ac.uk

ABSTRACT

Similarly to the correspondence between radical ideals of a polynomial ring and varieties in algebraic geometry, a correspondence between radical differential ideals and their analytic solution sets has been established in differential algebra. This tutorial discusses aspects of this correspondence involving symbolic computation. In particular, an introduction to the Thomas decomposition method is given. It splits a system of polynomially nonlinear partial differential equations into finitely many so-called simple differential systems whose solution sets form a partition of the original solution set. The power series solutions of each simple system can be determined in a straightforward way. Conversely, certain sets of analytic functions admit an implicit description in terms of partial differential equations and inequations. Strategies for solving related differential elimination problems and applications to symbolic solving of differential equations are presented. A Maple implementation of the Thomas decomposition method is freely available.

Keywords

Thomas decomposition; differential eliminiation; nonlinear PDEs; analytic functions

1. INTRODUCTION

This tutorial gives an introduction to differential elimination methods and to the Thomas decomposition method in particular [23], [24], [8], [15], [4], [5]. The motivation is given by the question whether certain families of complex analytic functions admit an implicit description in terms of differential equations [20]. Related problems or special cases of this question were considered, e.g., in [7], [17], [21], [26]. Interesting families of analytic functions can often be characterized as solutions to determinantal equations and inequations (cf. also [18]). One aim of this project is to improve methods for solving systems of differential equations symbolically. Alternative approaches which serve a similar purpose as the Thomas decomposition method are, e.g., given in [1], [6], [10], [11], [13], [19], [22], [25].

ISSAC '16 July 19-22, 2016, Waterloo, ON, Canada

ACM ISBN 978-1-4503-4380-0/16/07.
DOI: http://dx.doi.org/10.1145/2930889.2930941

2. ALGEBRAIC SYSTEMS

Let K be a field of characteristic zero, $R = K[x_1, \ldots, x_n]$ the polynomial algebra over K with variables $x_1, \ldots, x_n$. A *system of algebraic equations and inequations* is given by

$$\begin{cases} p_1 = 0, \quad p_2 = 0, \quad \ldots, \quad p_s = 0, \\ q_1 \neq 0, \quad q_2 \neq 0, \quad \ldots, \quad q_t \neq 0 \end{cases} \qquad (s, t \in \mathbb{Z}_{\geq 0}),$$

where $p_1, \ldots, p_s, q_1, \ldots, q_t \in R$. The *solution set* of this algebraic system S in $\overline{K}^n$, where $\overline{K}$ is an algebraic closure of K, is

$$\mathrm{Sol}_{\overline{K}}(S) := \{\, a \in \overline{K}^n \mid p_1(a) = p_2(a) = \ldots = p_s(a) = 0, \\ q_1(a) \neq 0,\, q_2(a) \neq 0,\, \ldots,\, q_t(a) \neq 0 \,\},$$

which is (an open subset of) a variety.

We assume that a total ordering $>$ on $\{x_1, \ldots, x_n\}$ is fixed. Then for any non-constant polynomial $p \in R$ the greatest variable with respect to $>$ which effectively occurs in p is referred to as the *leader* of p. Every non-constant polynomial in R has a recursive representation as univariate polynomial in its leader with coefficients that are again considered as univariate polynomials in their leaders (if not constant) and so on. The *initial* of $p \in R \setminus K$ is the coefficient of the highest power of the leader in p. We may choose

$$x_1 > x_2 > \ldots > x_n.$$

Geometrically this choice corresponds to the projections

$$\begin{aligned} \pi_1 &: \overline{K}^n \to \overline{K}^{n-1} : (a_1, a_2, \ldots, a_n) \mapsto (a_2, a_3, a_4, \ldots, a_n), \\ \pi_2 &: \overline{K}^n \to \overline{K}^{n-2} : (a_1, a_2, \ldots, a_n) \mapsto (a_3, a_4, \ldots, a_n), \\ &\vdots \\ \pi_{n-1} &: \overline{K}^n \to \overline{K} : (a_1, a_2, \ldots, a_n) \mapsto a_n. \end{aligned}$$

A Thomas decomposition of S (or of $\mathrm{Sol}_{\overline{K}}(S)$) determines a partition $\mathrm{Sol}_{\overline{K}}(S_1)$, $\mathrm{Sol}_{\overline{K}}(S_2)$, ..., $\mathrm{Sol}_{\overline{K}}(S_r)$ of $\mathrm{Sol}_{\overline{K}}(S)$, where $S_1, S_2, \ldots, S_r$ are algebraic systems as above, such that for every $i = 1, \ldots, r$ and every $k = 1, \ldots, n-1$ the cardinality $|\pi_{k-1}^{-1}(\{a\})|$ is independent of $a \in \pi_k(\mathrm{Sol}_{\overline{K}}(S_i))$.

Definition 1. An algebraic system S as above is said to be *simple* (w.r.t. $>$) if the following three conditions hold.

a) $p_i \notin K$ and $q_j \notin K$ for all $i = 1, \ldots, s$, $j = 1, \ldots, t$.

b) The leaders of all p_i and q_j are pairwise distinct.

c) For every $r \in \{p_1, \ldots, p_s, q_1, \ldots, q_t\}$, if the leader of r is x_k, then neither the coefficient of the highest power of x_k in r nor the discriminant of r with respect to x_k has a root $(a_{k+1}, a_{k+2}, \ldots, a_n)$ in $\pi_k(\mathrm{Sol}_{\overline{K}}(S))$.

Definition 2. A *Thomas decomposition* of an algebraic system S (or $\mathrm{Sol}_{\overline{K}}(S)$) is a finite collection of simple algebraic systems $S_1, \ldots, S_r$ such that $\mathrm{Sol}_{\overline{K}}(S)$ is the disjoint union of the solution sets $\mathrm{Sol}_{\overline{K}}(S_1), \ldots, \mathrm{Sol}_{\overline{K}}(S_r)$.

THEOREM 1. *Let S be a simple algebraic system as above, E the ideal of R which is generated by $p_1, \ldots, p_s$, and q the product of the initials of all p_i. Then the elements of*

$$E : q^\infty := \{\, p \in R \mid q^r \cdot p \in E \text{ for some } r \in \mathbb{Z}_{\geq 0} \,\}$$

are all polynomials which vanish on $\mathrm{Sol}_{\overline{K}}(S)$. Hence, $E : q^\infty$ is a radical ideal. We have $p \in E : q^\infty$ if and only if (pseudo-) polynomial division of p modulo $p_1, \ldots, p_s$ yields zero.

An implementation of the Thomas decomposition method for algebraic systems in Maple was developed in [3, 2].

3. DIFFERENTIAL SYSTEMS

Let K be the differential field of meromorphic functions on a connected open subset Ω of $\mathbb{C}^n$. The derivations on K are given by the partial differential operators with respect to the coordinates of $\mathbb{C}^n$. Moreover, let $R = K\{u_1, \ldots, u_m\}$ be the differential polynomial ring in the differential indeterminates $u_1, \ldots, u_m$. These indeterminates give rise to symbols $(u_k)_J$, where $J \in (\mathbb{Z}_{\geq 0})^n$, which represent the partial derivatives of m infinitely differentiable functions. A *differential system* S is given by

$$\left\{ \begin{array}{llll} p_1 = 0, & p_2 = 0, & \ldots, & p_s = 0, \\ q_1 \neq 0, & q_2 \neq 0, & \ldots, & q_t \neq 0 \end{array} \right. \qquad (s, t \in \mathbb{Z}_{\geq 0}),$$

where $p_1, \ldots, p_s, q_1, \ldots, q_t \in R$. The *solution set* of S is

$$\mathrm{Sol}_\Omega(S) := \{\, f = (f_1, \ldots, f_m) \mid f_k : \Omega \to \mathbb{C} \text{ analytic}, \\ p_1(f) = \ldots = p_s(f) = 0,\, q_1(f) \neq 0, \ldots, q_t(f) \neq 0 \,\}.$$

(An appropriate choice of Ω can often only be made after the application of the Thomas decomposition method.)

A *ranking* $>$ on R is a total ordering on the set

$$\{\, (u_k)_J \mid k \in \{1, \ldots, m\},\, J \in (\mathbb{Z}_{\geq 0})^n \,\}$$

such that $(u_{k_1})_{J_1} > (u_{k_2})_{J_2} \Rightarrow (u_{k_1})_{J_1 + 1_j} > (u_{k_2})_{J_2 + 1_j}$ and $(u_k)_{1_j} > u_k$ hold, where 1_j is the j-th standard basis vector of $\mathbb{Z}^n$. Similarly to the algebraic case, a ranking identifies the *leader* of any differential polynomial $p \in R \backslash K$, its *initial* and *separant*, which is the initial of any derivative of p.

Definition 3. A differential system S as above is said to be *simple* (w.r.t. $>$) if the following three conditions hold.

a) S is simple as an algebraic system (in the finitely many variables $(u_i)_J$ which occur in the equations and inequations of S, totally ordered by $>$).

b) $\{p_1 = 0, \ldots, p_s = 0\}$ is formally integrable, i.e., the cross-derivative of each pair of distinct equations whose leaders involve the same differential indeterminate reduces to zero modulo $p_1, \ldots, p_s$ and their derivatives.

c) $q_1, \ldots, q_t$ are reduced modulo $p_1, \ldots, p_s$ and their derivatives.

Definition 4. A *Thomas decomposition* of a differential system S (or $\mathrm{Sol}_\Omega(S)$) is a finite collection of simple differential systems $S_1, \ldots, S_r$ such that $\mathrm{Sol}_\Omega(S)$ is the disjoint union of the solution sets $\mathrm{Sol}_\Omega(S_1), \ldots, \mathrm{Sol}_\Omega(S_r)$.

THEOREM 2. *Let S be a simple differential system of the above form, E the differential ideal of R which is generated by $p_1, \ldots, p_s$, and q the product of the initials and separants of all p_i. Then $E : q^\infty$ is a radical differential ideal. We have $p \in E : q^\infty$ if and only if (pseudo-) polynomial division of p modulo $p_1, \ldots, p_s$ and their derivatives yields zero.*

An implementation of the Thomas decomposition method for differential systems in Maple was developed in [3, 12].

4. IMPLICITIZATION PROBLEM

Let Ω be a connected open subset of $\mathbb{C}^n$ with coordinates $z = (z_1, \ldots, z_n)$. The ring $\mathcal{O}$ of analytic functions on Ω is an integral domain. Let $k \in \mathbb{N}$, $\alpha_i : \Omega \to \mathbb{C}^{\nu(i)}$, $i = 1, \ldots, k$, be analytic functions and $p \in \mathcal{O}[F_1, \ldots, F_k]$ a polynomial in which each F_i occurs at most to the first power. We consider the family $S(p; \alpha_1, \ldots, \alpha_k)$ of analytic functions of the form

$$p(f_1(\alpha_1(z)), \ldots, f_k(\alpha_k(z))), \qquad (1)$$

where $f_i : \alpha_i(\Omega) \to \mathbb{C}$, $i = 1, \ldots, k$, are arbitrary functions such that each $f_i \circ \alpha_i$ is analytic. (If $\nu(i) = 0$, then f_i is understood as an arbitrary constant.)

The aim is to find, if possible, an implicit description of $S(p; \alpha_1, \ldots, \alpha_k)$ in terms of PDEs (and inequations).

Example 1. Let w, x, y, z be coordinates of $\mathbb{C}^4$ and consider the family of analytic functions of the form

$$u(w, x, y, z) = f_1(w) \cdot f_2(x) + f_3(y) \cdot f_4(z).$$

A partition of this family of functions into four sets is given by the sets of analytic solutions of the systems of differential equations and inequations defined by the combinations $((\Sigma_0), (\Sigma_1))$, $((\Sigma_0), (\Sigma_2))$, $((\Sigma_0), (\Sigma_3))$, and $((\Sigma_0), (\Sigma_4))$:

$$u_{w,y} = u_{w,z} = u_{x,y} = u_{x,z} = 0 \qquad (\Sigma_0)$$

$$u_w\, u_x = 0, \quad u_y\, u_z = 0 \qquad (\Sigma_1)$$

$$\left. \begin{array}{c} u_{y,z} \neq 0, \quad u_w\, u_x = 0, \\ \begin{vmatrix} u_y & u_{y,y} \\ u_{y,z} & u_{y,y,z} \end{vmatrix} = 0, \quad \begin{vmatrix} u_z & u_{y,z} \\ u_{z,z} & u_{y,z,z} \end{vmatrix} = 0 \end{array} \right\} \qquad (\Sigma_2)$$

$$\left. \begin{array}{c} u_{w,x} \neq 0, \quad u_y\, u_z = 0, \\ \begin{vmatrix} u_w & u_{w,w} \\ u_{w,x} & u_{w,w,x} \end{vmatrix} = 0, \quad \begin{vmatrix} u_x & u_{w,x} \\ u_{x,x} & u_{w,x,x} \end{vmatrix} = 0 \end{array} \right\} \qquad (\Sigma_3)$$

$$u_{w,x} \neq 0, \quad u_{y,z} \neq 0, \quad \begin{vmatrix} u & u_w & u_y \\ u_x & u_{w,x} & 0 \\ u_z & 0 & u_{y,z} \end{vmatrix} = 0 \qquad (\Sigma_4)$$

The closure of $S(p; \alpha_1, \ldots, \alpha_k)$ with respect to the Kolchin topology is irreducible in the following sense.

PROPOSITION 1. *Let K be the field of fractions of $\mathcal{O}$. The ideal $\mathcal{I}_{K\{u\}}(S(p; \alpha_1, \ldots, \alpha_k))$ of $K\{u\}$ of all differential polynomials which vanish under substitution of (1) for u is prime and finitely generated as a radical differential ideal.*

5. DIFFERENTIAL ELIMINATION

Elimination methods of different generality can be applied to compute generators of the vanishing ideal of the family $S(p;\alpha_1,\ldots,\alpha_k)$ in $K\{u\}$ (cf. Proposition 1).

a) For each $i=1,\ldots,k$, the vanishing ideal Z_i in $K\{F_i\}$ of the family of analytic functions of the form $f_i\circ\alpha_i$ is generated by linear differential polynomials of order 1. Therefore, the differential ideal Z of $K\{F_1,\ldots,F_k\}$ generated by $Z_1,\ldots,Z_k$ is prime. Let I be the differential ideal of $(K\{F_1,\ldots,F_k\}/Z)\{u\}$ which is generated by $u-(p+Z)$. Then we have

$$\mathcal{I}_{K\{u\}}(S(p;\alpha_1,\ldots,\alpha_k)) = I\cap K\{u\}.$$

This intersection can be determined by computing a Thomas decomposition of the radical differential ideal of $K\{F_1,\ldots,F_k,u\}$ generated by $u-p(F_1,\ldots,F_k)$ and $Z_1,\ldots,Z_k$ with respect to a ranking which ranks every derivative of any F_i higher than every derivative of u.

b) Since the previous elimination task is computationally very difficult in general, one may decide to postpone differentiation in the elimination procedure, consider the ideal of $K\{u\}_{\le\omega} = K[\,u_J \mid J\in(\mathbb{Z}_{\ge 0})^n,\ |J|\le\omega]$ generated by the derivatives of $u-p(F_1,\ldots,F_k)$ up to some order ω and compute

$$\mathcal{I}_{K\{u\}}(S(p;\alpha_1,\ldots,\alpha_k))\cap K\{u\}_{\le\omega}$$

using methods from commutative algebra (e.g., [16]).

c) If $p\in\mathbb{C}[F_1,\ldots,F_k]$ and all components of each α_i are homogeneous polynomials of degree one, then the vanishing ideal is generated as a radical differential ideal of $\mathbb{C}\{u\}$ by finitely many homogeneous differential polynomials, each comprising of terms with the same total number ω of differentiations. Since for fixed degree and fixed ω the subset of such polynomials in $\mathbb{C}\{u\}$ is a finite-dimensional $\mathbb{C}$-vector space, methods of linear algebra can be applied to compute generators.

In cases b) and c) knowledge about the parametrized family of functions is required to verify whether a generating set for $\mathcal{I}_{K\{u\}}(S(p;\alpha_1,\ldots,\alpha_k))$ is complete [20].

6. APPLICATIONS

Example 2. Let us consider the Korteweg-de Vries (KdV) equation, which is used to describe shallow water waves:

$$\frac{\partial u}{\partial t} - 6\,u\,\frac{\partial u}{\partial x} + \frac{\partial^3 u}{\partial x^3} = 0. \tag{2}$$

The command `pdsolve` in Maple 2015 returns solutions

$$u(t,x) = 2\,c_3^2\,(\tanh(c_3\,x + c_2\,t + c_1))^2 + \frac{c_2 - 8\,c_3^3}{6\,c_3}, \tag{3}$$

where c_1, c_2, $c_3\in\mathbb{R}$. We compute solutions of the form

$$u(t,x) = f(t)\,g(x), \tag{4}$$

which is reminiscent of separation of variables. Substitution of (4) into (2) gives no hint how to obtain more information about f or g. But the family of analytic functions of the form (4) admits an implicit description as solution set of

$$\begin{vmatrix} u & u_x \\ u_t & u_{t,x}\end{vmatrix} = 0. \tag{5}$$

A Thomas decomposition of the differential system

$$\{\,u_t - 6\,u\,u_x + u_{x,x,x} = 0,\ u\,u_{t,x} - u_t\,u_x = 0\,\} \tag{6}$$

is given in Figure 1. It is a straightforward task to determine the analytic solutions of the second and the third simple system. In the former case we obtain

$$u(t,x) = c \qquad \text{or} \qquad u(t,x) = \frac{x+c_1}{-6\,t+c_2}, \tag{7}$$

where $c\in\mathbb{R}\setminus\{0\}$, c_1, $c_2\in\mathbb{R}$. In the latter case $u=u(x)$ does not depend on t and we obtain

$$x = \pm\int_{u(0)}^{u(x)} \frac{dz}{\sqrt{2\,z^3 + a\,z + b}}, \qquad a,b,c\in\mathbb{R}.$$

Some solutions of the third simple system are

$$u(t,x) = 2\,c_1^2\,(\tanh(c_1\,x + c_2))^2 - \frac{4\,c_1^2}{3},\ \ c_1\in\mathbb{R}\setminus\{0\},\ c_2\in\mathbb{R}.$$

Most of the solutions in (7) have been omitted by `pdsolve`.

Example 3. We consider the Navier-Stokes equations, i.e., the equations of motion of a viscous fluid:

$$\left\{\begin{array}{rcl} \dfrac{\partial v}{\partial t} + (v\cdot\nabla)\,v &=& -\dfrac{1}{\rho}\,\mathrm{grad}(p) + \dfrac{\eta}{\rho}\,\Delta v, \\ \nabla\cdot v &=& 0. \end{array}\right. \tag{8}$$

We assume that the flow is incompressible, i.e., that the fluid density ρ is constant, and thus $\nu := \eta/\rho$ is constant.

In order to find exact solutions to (8) of a certain form, say in cylindrical coordinates r, φ, z, we add an implicit description of the family of analytic functions of this form in terms of polynomial partial differential equations to (8) and compute a Thomas decomposition of the combined system. Here we choose the assumption that each component of the velocity field is a product of a function of r, a function of φ, and a function of z, without any assumption on the dependence of t. An implicit description of functions of this type is given by the nine PDEs for $u\in\{v_1,v_2,v_3\}$:

$$\begin{vmatrix} u & u_z \\ u_r & u_{r,z}\end{vmatrix} = 0, \quad \begin{vmatrix} u & u_\varphi \\ u_r & u_{r,\varphi}\end{vmatrix} = 0, \quad \begin{vmatrix} u & u_z \\ u_\varphi & u_{\varphi,z}\end{vmatrix} = 0.$$

By applying the Maple package `DifferentialThomas` [3] and the command `pdsolve`, from one of the many simple differential systems arising from the combined system we obtain the following family of exact solutions of (8):

$$\left\{\begin{array}{rcl} v_1(t,r,\varphi,z) &=& -\dfrac{(t+c_1)\,F_1(t)}{r} - \dfrac{r}{2\,(t+c_1)}, \\ v_2(t,r,\varphi,z) &=& \dfrac{(\varphi+c_2)\,r}{t+c_1}, \\ v_3(t,r,\varphi,z) &=& 0, \\ p(t,r,\varphi,z) &=& (t+c_1)\ln(r)\,\dfrac{dF_1(t)}{dt} - \dfrac{(t+c_1)^2\,F_1(t)^2}{2\,r^2} \\ && +\,(\ln(r) + (\varphi+c_2)^2)\,F_1(t) + F_2(t) \\ && -\,\dfrac{2\,\nu\ln(r)}{t+c_1} + \dfrac{((\varphi+c_2)^2 - \frac{3}{4})\,r^2}{2\,(t+c_1)^2}, \end{array}\right.$$

where c_1, $c_2\in\mathbb{R}$ and F_1, F_2 are arbitrary analytic functions of t (and no assumption is made about the constant ν).

$$\begin{array}{rcl} u & = & 0 \end{array}$$

$$\begin{array}{rcl} u_t - 6\,u\,u_x & = & 0 \\ u_{x,x} & = & 0 \\ u & \neq & 0 \end{array}$$

$$\begin{array}{rcl} u_t & = & 0 \\ u_{x,x,x} - 6\,u\,u_x & = & 0 \\ u_{x,x} & \neq & 0 \\ u & \neq & 0 \end{array}$$

Figure 1: Thomas decomposition of the differential system (6)

7. REFERENCES

[1] P. Aubry, D. Lazard, and M. Moreno Maza. On the theories of triangular sets. *J. Symb. Comput.*, 28(1-2):105–124 (1999).

[2] T. Bächler. Counting Solutions of Algebraic Systems via Triangular Decomposition. Ph.D. thesis, RWTH Aachen University, Germany (2014). Available online at `http://publications.rwth-aachen.de/record/444946?ln=en`.

[3] T. Bächler and M. Lange-Hegermann. `AlgebraicThomas` and `DifferentialThomas`: Thomas decomposition of algebraic and differential systems. Available online at `http://wwwb.math.rwth-aachen.de/thomasdecomposition`.

[4] T. Bächler, V. P. Gerdt, M. Lange-Hegermann, and D. Robertz. Thomas Decomposition of Algebraic and Differential Systems. In: V. P. Gerdt, W. Koepf, E. W. Mayr, and E. H. Vorozhtsov, editors, *Computer Algebra in Scientific Computing, 12th International Workshop, CASC 2010, Tsakhkadzor, Armenia*, Vol. 6244 of Lecture Notes in Computer Science, pp. 31–54. Springer, 2010.

[5] T. Bächler, V. P. Gerdt, M. Lange-Hegermann, and D. Robertz. Algorithmic Thomas Decomposition of Algebraic and Differential Systems. *J. Symb. Comput.*, 47(10):1233–1266 (2012).

[6] F. Boulier, D. Lazard, F. Ollivier, and M. Petitot. Computing representations for radicals of finitely generated differential ideals. *Appl. Algebra Engrg. Comm. Comput.*, 20(1):73–121 (2009).

[7] X. S. Gao. Implicitization of differential rational parametric equations. *J. Symb. Comput.*, 36(5):811–824 (2003).

[8] V. P. Gerdt. On decomposition of algebraic PDE systems into simple subsystems. *Acta Appl. Math.*, 101(1-3):39–51 (2008).

[9] V. P. Gerdt and D. Robertz. Lagrangian Constraints and Differential Thomas Decomposition. *Adv. in Appl. Math.*, 72:113–138 (2016).

[10] E. Hubert. Notes on triangular sets and triangulation-decomposition algorithms. I. Polynomial systems. II. Differential systems. In: F. Winkler and U. Langer, editors, Symbolic and numerical scientific computation (Hagenberg, 2001), pp. 1–39 resp. 40–87, Vol. 2630 of Lecture Notes in Computer Science, Springer, Berlin, 2003.

[11] E. R. Kolchin. *Differential algebra and algebraic groups.* Vol. 54 of Pure and Applied Mathematics. Academic Press, New York-London, 1973.

[12] M. Lange-Hegermann. Counting Solutions of Differential Equations. Ph.D. thesis, RWTH Aachen University, Germany (2014). Available online at `http://publications.rwth-aachen.de/record/229056?ln=en`.

[13] F. Lemaire, M. Moreno Maza, and Y. Xie. The `RegularChains` library in MAPLE. SIGSAM Bull., 39:96–97, September 2005.

[14] P. J. Olver and P. Rosenau. The construction of special solutions to partial differential equations. *Phys. Lett. A*, 114(3):107–112 (1986).

[15] W. Plesken. Counting solutions of polynomial systems via iterated fibrations. *Arch. Math. (Basel)*, 92(1):44–56 (2009).

[16] W. Plesken and D. Robertz. Elimination for coefficients of special characteristic polynomials. *Experiment. Math.*, 17(4):499–510 (2008).

[17] W. Plesken and D. Robertz. Linear differential elimination for analytic functions. *Math. Comput. Sci.*, 4(2–3):231–242 (2010).

[18] T. M. Rassias and J. Šimša. *Finite sums decompositions in mathematical analysis.* Pure and Applied Mathematics (New York). John Wiley & Sons, Chichester, 1995.

[19] J. F. Ritt. Differential Algebra. Vol. XXXIII of American Mathematical Society Colloquium Publications. American Mathematical Society, New York, N. Y., 1950.

[20] D. Robertz. *Formal Algorithmic Elimination for PDEs.* Vol. 2121 of Lecture Notes in Mathematics, Springer, Cham, 2014.

[21] S. L. Rueda and J. R. Sendra. Linear complete differential resultants and the implicitization of linear DPPEs. *J. Symb. Comput.*, 45(3):324–341 (2010).

[22] A. Seidenberg. An elimination theory for differential algebra. Univ. California Publ. Math. (N.S.) 3, 31–65 (1956).

[23] J. M. Thomas. *Differential Systems.* Vol. XXI of American Mathematical Society Colloquium Publications. American Mathematical Society, New York, N. Y., 1937.

[24] D. Wang. Decomposing polynomial systems into simple systems. *J. Symb. Comput.*, 25(3):295–314 (1998).

[25] D. Wang. *Elimination methods.* Texts and Monographs in Symbolic Computation. Springer-Verlag, Vienna, 2001.

[26] T. Wolf, A. Brand, and M. Mohammadzadeh. Computer algebra algorithms and routines for the computation of conservation laws and fixing of gauge in differential expressions. *J. Symb. Comput.*, 27(2):221–238 (1999).

Detecting Similarities Of Rational Space Curves

Juan Gerardo Alcázar
Departamento de Física y Matemáticas, Universidad de Alcalá,
E-28871 Madrid, Spain
juange.alcazar@uah.es

Carlos Hermoso
Departamento de Física y Matemáticas, Universidad de Alcalá,
E-28871 Madrid, Spain
carlos.hermoso@uah.es

Georg Muntingh
SINTEF ICT,
PO Box 124, Blindern
0314 Oslo, Norway
georg.muntingh@sintef.no

ABSTRACT

We provide an algorithm to check whether two rational space curves are related by a *similarity*, i.e., whether they are equal up to position, orientation and scale. The algorithm exploits the relationship between the curvatures and torsions of two similar curves, which is formulated in a computer algebra setting. Helical curves, where curvature and torsion are proportional, need to be distinguished as a special case. The algorithm is easy to implement, as it involves only standard computer algebra techniques, such as greatest common divisors and resultants, and Gröbner bases for the special case of helical curves.

Keywords

similarity detection; rational space curves; 3D shape; pattern recognition

1. INTRODUCTION

Two objects are *similar* when one of them is the result of applying an isometry and scaling to the other. Therefore, two similar objects have the same shape, although their position, orientation, or size can be different. Because of this, recognizing similar objects is important in the field of Pattern Recognition, where one typically has a database of objects and wants to compare, *up to a similarity*, a given object with all the elements in the database.

Three-dimensional similarity detection is also important in Computer Graphics and Computer Vision, and therefore it has been addressed in a long list of papers. Following the introduction of [8], the methods proposed in these papers can roughly be grouped into two different categories: *shape-based* and *topology-based*. In the first category, one picks *feature descriptors* for the objects to be checked, giving rise to feature vectors that are later compared using appropriate metrics; see for instance the survey [7] or the papers [6, 14, 15]. In the second category, which has gained attention in recent years, a "skeleton" is computed from each object, which is later used for comparison purposes; see [13, 18].

ISSAC '16, July 19 - 22, 2016, Waterloo, ON, Canada

ISBN 978-1-4503-4380-0/16/07...$15.00

DOI: http://dx.doi.org/10.1145/2930889.2930892

The aforementioned papers, and others that can be found in their bibliographies, focus on surfaces, upon which (almost) no structure is assumed. At most, some of these papers require the objects to be modeled by means of polyhedra, so that they are considered to be meshings of perhaps more complex shapes. Additionally, in these references similarity detection is considered only up to a certain tolerance, so that the criteria are approximate.

Our approach is different. First, we deal with exact one-dimensional objects with a strong structure, namely space curves defined by rational parametrizations. Furthermore, we exploit the structure of the space curves to check, in a deterministic fashion, whether they are similar, and to explicitly compute the similarities between both curves in the affirmative case. In order to do this, we build on previous work on similarities of plane curves [2] and symmetries of plane and space curves [3, 4]. As in these papers, since the curves are rational, we reduce the problem to the parameter space. Analogously to the algorithm in [4], the algorithm in this paper is based on comparing curvatures and torsions. However, similarity has the additional substantial difficulty of determining the scaling. Interestingly, this forces us to distinguish as a special case the *helical curves*, i.e., space curves with proportional curvature and torsion.

The basic steps in the algorithm are as follows. If the two given rational space curves are similar, then there exists a rational function relating the corresponding parameter spaces. Under the hypothesis that the parametrizations of the curves are proper (birational), this rational function is a Möbius transformation. In our algorithm one first computes candidates for the scaling constants and then candidates for the Möbius transformations. After this, the similarities between the curves can be computed. If the input curves are non-helical, then we have two independent conditions involving the curvatures and torsions of the curves, and from these conditions the scaling constant can be found. If the input curves are helical, these two conditions are no longer independent, and a different approach based on a procedure in [4] is provided.

The algorithm has been implemented and tested in the computer algebra system Maple 18. Because of space limitations, details on timings and performance are not provided here, but instead can be found in an extended version of the paper [5].

2. BACKGROUND

2.1 Similarities of Euclidean space

A *similarity* of Euclidean space is a linear affine map from the space to itself that preserves ratios of distances. Equivalently, a map $f : \mathbb{R}^3 \longrightarrow \mathbb{R}^3$ is a similarity if

$$\begin{aligned} f(\mathbf{x}) = \lambda \boldsymbol{Q}\mathbf{x} + \boldsymbol{b}, \qquad 0 \neq \lambda \in \mathbb{R}, \qquad \boldsymbol{b} \in \mathbb{R}^3, \\ \boldsymbol{Q} \in \mathbb{R}^{3\times 3}, \quad \boldsymbol{Q}^{\mathrm{T}}\boldsymbol{Q} = \boldsymbol{I}, \quad \det(\boldsymbol{Q}) = 1, \end{aligned} \tag{1}$$

where the latter two conditions mean that $\boldsymbol{Q}$ is a *special orthogonal matrix*, i.e., a rotation about a line. Equivalently, with $\|\mathbf{x}\|$ the Euclidean norm of $\mathbf{x}$ and $d(\mathbf{x}, \mathbf{y}) := \|\mathbf{x} - \mathbf{y}\|$ the Euclidean distance between $\mathbf{x}$ and $\mathbf{y}$,

$$d\big(f(\mathbf{x}), f(\mathbf{y})\big) = |\lambda| \cdot d(\mathbf{x}, \mathbf{y}), \qquad \mathbf{x}, \mathbf{y} \in \mathbb{C}^3. \tag{2}$$

We refer to λ as the *(signed) ratio* of the similarity. A similarity is said to *preserve* the orientation if $\lambda > 0$, and *reverse* the orientation if $\lambda < 0$. The identity map $f(\mathbf{x}) = \mathbf{x}$ is called the *trivial similarity*.

If $|\lambda| = 1$ then f is an *(affine) isometry*, i.e., f preserves distances. The classification of nontrivial isometries includes reflections (in a plane), rotations (about an axis), and translations, and these combine in commutative pairs to form twists, glide reflections, and rotatory reflections. A composition of three reflections in mutually perpendicular planes through a point $\mathbf{x}$ yields a *central inversion* (with respect to the point $\mathbf{x}$). The particular case of rotation by an angle π is of special interest, and it is called a *half-turn*.

If λ^{-1} is not an eigenvalue of $\boldsymbol{Q}$, then f has a unique fixed point $\boldsymbol{c} := (\boldsymbol{I}-\lambda\boldsymbol{Q})^{-1}\boldsymbol{b}$, called the *center* of the similarity. In particular any similarity that is not an isometry has a center, because $\boldsymbol{Q}$, being orthogonal, has eigenvalues of modulus equal to 1. A *dilatation* is a special type of similarity, defined as a map that sends any line to a parallel line (which could be the original line). Any dilatation that is not a translation sends any point $\mathbf{x}$ to $\mathbf{c}+\lambda(\mathbf{x}-\mathbf{c})$ and therefore takes the form $f(\mathbf{x}) = \lambda \boldsymbol{I}\mathbf{x} + (1 - \lambda)\mathbf{c}$. A *dilative rotation* is a composition of a dilatation with center $\mathbf{c}$ with a rotation $\boldsymbol{Q}$ about a line ℓ containing $\mathbf{c}$, which takes the form

$$f(\boldsymbol{Q}\mathbf{x}) = \boldsymbol{Q}f(\mathbf{x}) = \lambda\boldsymbol{Q}\mathbf{x} + (1 - \lambda)\mathbf{c}, \qquad \boldsymbol{Q}\mathbf{c} = \mathbf{c}. \tag{3}$$

We recall the following characterization of similarities from [10, p. 103].

Theorem 1. *Any similarity is either an isometry or a dilative rotation.*

Similarities form a group under composition, and isometries form a subgroup of this group.

2.2 Similarities of rational space curves

Theoretical aspects of the equivalence problem for space curves can be traced back to Élie Cartan [9]. Here we consider this problem for two rational space curves $\mathcal{C}_1, \mathcal{C}_2 \subset \mathbb{R}^3$, assumed to be nonplanar unless specified otherwise. Such curves are irreducible and can be parametrized by rational maps

$$\boldsymbol{x}_j : \mathbb{R} \dashrightarrow \mathcal{C}_j \subset \mathbb{R}^3, \qquad \boldsymbol{x}_j(t) = \big(x_j(t), y_j(t), z_j(t)\big), \tag{4}$$

where $j = 1, 2$. The components x_j, y_j, z_j of $\boldsymbol{x}_j$ are rational functions of t with real coefficients, therefore defined for all but a finite number of values of t. We assume that the parametrizations (4) are *proper*, i.e., birational. This can be assumed without loss of generality, since any rational curve can quickly be properly reparametrized [17], [1, §3.1]. We also assume that the numerators and denominators of the components of $\boldsymbol{x}_j$ are relatively prime.

This paper concerns algebraic space curves (4) that are *similar*, i.e., one is the image of the other under a similarity. Two curves $\mathcal{C}_1$ and $\mathcal{C}_2$ are *related by a similarity* f when $f(\mathcal{C}_1) = \mathcal{C}_2$. If in addition $\mathcal{C}_1 = \mathcal{C}_2$, then this curve is *invariant* under f. We first establish some basic properties.

Lemma 2 (See [4, Lemma 1]). *A rational space curve different from a line cannot be invariant under a translation, glide reflection, or twist.*

Therefore, reflections, rotations, and their combinations are the only isometries that leave a rational space curve different from a line invariant.

Lemma 3. *Let f be a nontrivial similarity that is not an isometry, leaving an algebraic space curve $\mathcal{C}$ invariant. Then its center $\mathbf{c} \in \mathcal{C}$.*

Proof. Since f is not an isometry, $|\lambda| \neq 1$. If $|\lambda| > 1$ then f^{-1} is a similarity with ratio λ^{-1} satisfying $|\lambda^{-1}| < 1$, also leaving $\mathcal{C}$ invariant. Therefore we can and will assume $|\lambda| < 1$. Let $\mathbf{x} \in \mathcal{C}$. Since $f(\mathcal{C}) = \mathcal{C}$, the entire orbit $\{\mathbf{x}, f(\mathbf{x}), f^2(\mathbf{x}), \ldots\} \subset \mathcal{C}$. Using (2), $|\lambda| < 1$, and $f(\mathbf{c}) = \mathbf{c}$, we have

$$\lim_{k\to\infty} d\big(\mathbf{c}, f^k(\mathbf{x})\big) = \lim_{k\to\infty} |\lambda|^k d(\mathbf{c}, \mathbf{x}) = 0,$$

and $f^k(\mathbf{x})$ approaches $\mathbf{c}$. Since $\mathcal{C} \subset \mathbb{R}^3$ is closed, this limit $\mathbf{c} \in \mathcal{C}$. □

In addition, note that $\mathbf{c}$ is not an isolated point, since it is the limit of a sequence of points of $\mathcal{C}$.

Lemma 4. *Let f be a similarity that is not an isometry. Then for any positive integer n, the n-fold composition f^n is not an isometry either.*

Proof. By (1), f^n is a similarity of ratio λ^n, and $|\lambda| \neq 1$ implies $|\lambda^n| \neq 1$. □

Lemma 5. *Let f be a similarity such that there exist distinct vectors $\mathbf{x}, \mathbf{y}$ with $d\big(f(\mathbf{x}), f(\mathbf{y})\big) = d(\mathbf{x}, \mathbf{y})$. Then f is an isometry.*

Proof. $d\big(f(\mathbf{x}), f(\mathbf{y})\big) = d(\mathbf{x}, \mathbf{y}) \neq 0$ and (2) yield $|\lambda| = 1$. □

Analogous to [2, Proposition 2] for algebraic plane curves, the following theorem states that a self-similarity of an algebraic space curve is an isometry.

Theorem 6. *Let f be a similarity that leaves an algebraic space curve $\mathcal{C}$, which is not a union of (possibly complex) concurrent lines, invariant. Then f is an isometry.*

Proof. Suppose f is not an isometry. By Theorem 1, the similarity is a dilative rotation $f(\mathbf{x}) = \lambda\boldsymbol{Q}\mathbf{x} + (1 - \lambda)\mathbf{c}$, with $|\lambda| \neq 1$ and $\boldsymbol{Q}$ a rotation about a line ℓ containing $\mathbf{c}$. Let Π be the plane through $\mathbf{c}$ normal to ℓ.

Since f maps lines through $\mathbf{c}$ to each other, we can assume without loss of generality that $\mathcal{C}$ has no such components. First consider the case that $\mathcal{C}$ has one or more planar irreducible components that are not a real or complex line.

Since a similarity maps planes to planes, one of these components $\mathcal{C}' \subset \mathcal{C}$ satisfies $f^n(\mathcal{C}') = \mathcal{C}'$ for some integer $n \geq 1$. Since $\mathcal{C}'$ is not a line, it spans a plane Π' and f^n restricts to a plane similarity $f' := f^n|_{\Pi'}$ with $f'(\mathcal{C}') = \mathcal{C}'$, which is an isometry by [2, Proposition 2]. Hence f^n is an isometry by Lemma 5 and f is an isometry by Lemma 4.

It remains to show the case where $\mathcal{C}$ does not have any planar irreducible components besides lines. Supposing f is not an isometry, $\mathcal{C}$ cannot contain a line L parallel to ℓ, because then it would also contain any parallel line $f^n(L), n \in \mathbb{N}$, of which there are infinitely many since each has a different distance to ℓ. Therefore the image $\mathcal{C}^\perp$ of the orthogonal projection $p : \mathcal{C} \longrightarrow \Pi$ is a plane curve. Since $\mathcal{C}$ does not have any planar components, $\mathcal{C}^\perp$ does not have any lines. Moreover,

$$f(\mathcal{C}^\perp) = f \circ p(\mathcal{C}) = p \circ f(\mathcal{C}) = p \circ \mathcal{C} = \mathcal{C}^\perp,$$

showing that the restriction $f|_\Pi$ is a plane similarity that leaves $\mathcal{C}^\perp$ invariant. It follows that $f|_\Pi$ is an isometry by [2, Proposition 2] and that f is an isometry by Lemma 5. □

Proposition 7. *Let $\mathcal{C}_1, \mathcal{C}_2$ be algebraic space curves, neither a union of (possibly complex) concurrent lines, for which there exist similarities $f_i(\mathbf{x}) = \lambda_i \boldsymbol{Q}_i \mathbf{x} + \boldsymbol{b}_i$ such that $f_i(\mathcal{C}_1) = \mathcal{C}_2$, with $i = 1, 2$. Then $|\lambda_1| = |\lambda_2|$.*

Proof. One has $f_2^{-1}(\mathbf{x}) = \lambda_2^{-1} \boldsymbol{Q}_2^{-1}(\mathbf{x} - \boldsymbol{b}_2)$. Then $(f_2^{-1} \circ f_1)(\mathbf{x}) = \lambda \boldsymbol{Q} \mathbf{x} + \boldsymbol{b}$, with

$$\lambda := \frac{\lambda_1}{\lambda_2}, \qquad \boldsymbol{Q} := \boldsymbol{Q}_2^{\mathrm{T}} \boldsymbol{Q}_1, \qquad \boldsymbol{b} := \frac{1}{\lambda_2} \boldsymbol{Q}_2^{\mathrm{T}} (\boldsymbol{b}_1 - \boldsymbol{b}_2),$$

a similarity since $0 \neq \lambda \in \mathbb{R}$, $\det(\boldsymbol{Q}) = 1$, and

$$\boldsymbol{Q}^{\mathrm{T}} \boldsymbol{Q} = \boldsymbol{Q}_1^{\mathrm{T}} \boldsymbol{Q}_2 \boldsymbol{Q}_2^{\mathrm{T}} \boldsymbol{Q}_1 = \boldsymbol{Q}_1^{\mathrm{T}} \boldsymbol{I} \boldsymbol{Q}_1 = \boldsymbol{I}.$$

Since $f_2^{-1} \circ f_1$ leaves $\mathcal{C}_1$ invariant, Theorem 6 implies that $f_2^{-1} \circ f_1$ is an isometry, implying $|\lambda_1/\lambda_2| = 1$ and therefore $|\lambda_1| = |\lambda_2|$. □

It is well known that the birational functions on the line are the *Möbius transformations* [17], i.e., rational functions

$$\varphi : \mathbb{R} \dashrightarrow \mathbb{R}, \quad \varphi(t) = \frac{at + b}{ct + d}, \qquad \Delta := ad - bc \neq 0. \tag{5}$$

The following result relates the similarity in space to a Möbius transformation on the line. In [2] a proof was given for the case of plane curves, which generalizes *mutatis mutandis* to the case of space curves.

Theorem 8. *Let $\mathcal{C}_1, \mathcal{C}_2 \subset \mathbb{R}^3$ be rational space curves with proper parametrizations $\boldsymbol{x}_1, \boldsymbol{x}_2 : \mathbb{R} \dashrightarrow \mathbb{R}^3$. Then $\mathcal{C}_1$, $\mathcal{C}_2$ are similar if and only if there exists a similarity f and a Möbius transformation φ for which we have a commutative diagram*

$$\begin{array}{ccc} \mathcal{C}_1 & \xrightarrow{\ f\ } & \mathcal{C}_2 \\ \uparrow & & \uparrow \\ \boldsymbol{x}_1 \,| & & |\, \boldsymbol{x}_2 \\ | & & | \\ \mathbb{R} & \underset{\varphi}{\dashrightarrow} & \mathbb{R} \end{array} \tag{6}$$

Moreover, if $\mathcal{C}_1, \mathcal{C}_2$ are related by a similarity f, then there exists a unique Möbius transformation φ that makes the above diagram commutative.

Since the Möbius transformation φ maps the real line to itself, its coefficients can always be assumed to be real by dividing by a common complex number if necessary [4, Lemma 3]. Notice that $s = \varphi(t)$ provides the s-value generating the image, in $\mathcal{C}_2$, under the similarity f, of the point generated by t in $\mathcal{C}_1$.

Corollary 9. *Consider proper parametrizations $\boldsymbol{x}_j$, $j = 1, 2$, as in (4), a similarity f as in (1), and a Möbius transformation φ, related by (6). Then*

$$|\lambda| \cdot \|\boldsymbol{x}_1'(t)\| - \|(\boldsymbol{x}_2 \circ \varphi)'(t)\| = 0. \tag{7}$$

Proof. The commutative diagram (6) has the corresponding equation

$$\lambda \boldsymbol{Q} \boldsymbol{x}_1(t) + \boldsymbol{b} = (\boldsymbol{x}_2 \circ \varphi)(t).$$

Differentiating and taking norms yields $\|\lambda \boldsymbol{Q} \boldsymbol{x}_1'(t)\| = \|(\boldsymbol{x}_2 \circ \varphi)'(t)\|$, which, using the orthogonality of $\boldsymbol{Q}$, yields (7). □

2.3 Differential invariants

Next we consider the effect of a similarity and Möbius transformation on the *curvature* κ and *torsion* τ of a parametric curve $\boldsymbol{x}$, which are defined by

$$\kappa = \kappa_{\boldsymbol{x}} := \frac{\|\boldsymbol{x}' \times \boldsymbol{x}''\|}{\|\boldsymbol{x}'\|^3}, \qquad \tau = \tau_{\boldsymbol{x}} := \frac{\langle \boldsymbol{x}' \times \boldsymbol{x}'', \boldsymbol{x}''' \rangle}{\|\boldsymbol{x}' \times \boldsymbol{x}''\|^2}. \tag{8}$$

Notice in particular that $\kappa \geq 0$, while τ can be positive, negative, or zero. Moreover, although τ and κ^2 are rational functions for any rational map $\boldsymbol{x}$, the curvature κ is in general not rational.

Lemma 10. *For a parametrization $\boldsymbol{x}$ as in (4) and a similarity $f(\mathbf{x}) = \lambda \boldsymbol{Q} \mathbf{x} + \boldsymbol{b}$,*

$$|\lambda| \cdot \kappa_{f \circ \boldsymbol{x}} = \kappa_{\boldsymbol{x}}, \qquad \lambda \cdot \tau_{f \circ \boldsymbol{x}} = \tau_{\boldsymbol{x}}.$$

Proof. A straightforward calculation yields, for any invertible matrix $\boldsymbol{M} \in \mathbb{R}^{3,3}$ and vectors $\boldsymbol{u}, \boldsymbol{v} \in \mathbb{R}^3$, the identity

$$(\boldsymbol{M}\boldsymbol{u}) \times (\boldsymbol{M}\boldsymbol{v}) = \det(\boldsymbol{M}) \boldsymbol{M}^{-\mathrm{T}} (\boldsymbol{u} \times \boldsymbol{v}). \tag{9}$$

Using $(f \circ \boldsymbol{x})^{(n)} = \lambda \boldsymbol{Q} \boldsymbol{x}^{(n)}$ for $n = 1, 2, 3$ and $\det(\boldsymbol{Q}) = 1$ with $\boldsymbol{Q}$ orthogonal, the result follows. □

Next we recall a lemma from [4], which describes the behavior of the curvature and torsion under reparametrization, for instance by a Möbius transformation.

Lemma 11. *Let $\boldsymbol{x}$ be a rational parametrization (4) and let $\phi \in C^3(U)$, with $U \subset \mathbb{R}$ open. Then*

$$\kappa_{\boldsymbol{x} \circ \phi} = \kappa_{\boldsymbol{x}} \circ \phi, \qquad \tau_{\boldsymbol{x} \circ \phi} = \tau_{\boldsymbol{x}} \circ \phi,$$

whenever both sides are defined.

The following lemma relates the curvatures and torsions of similar curves.

Lemma 12. *Suppose $\boldsymbol{x}_1, \boldsymbol{x}_2$ define curves $\mathcal{C}_1, \mathcal{C}_2$ with $f(\mathcal{C}_1) = \mathcal{C}_2$ for a similarity f with ratio λ. Then there is a Möbius transformation φ such that*

$$\begin{aligned} \kappa_{\boldsymbol{x}_2} \circ \varphi &= \kappa_{\boldsymbol{x}_2 \circ \varphi} = \kappa_{f \circ \boldsymbol{x}_1} = \frac{1}{|\lambda|} \kappa_{\boldsymbol{x}_1}, \\ \tau_{\boldsymbol{x}_2} \circ \varphi &= \tau_{\boldsymbol{x}_2 \circ \varphi} = \tau_{f \circ \boldsymbol{x}_1} = \frac{1}{\lambda} \tau_{\boldsymbol{x}_1}. \end{aligned} \tag{10}$$

Proof. By Theorem 8, there exist a Möbius transformation φ such that $f \circ \boldsymbol{x}_1 = \boldsymbol{x}_2 \circ \varphi$. The statement follows from Lemmas 10 and 11. □

2.4 Helical curves

Consider parametrizations $\boldsymbol{x}_1, \boldsymbol{x}_2$ as in (4) defining nonplanar curves. Then the corresponding torsions $\tau_{\boldsymbol{x}_1}, \tau_{\boldsymbol{x}_2}$ are not identically zero, and we can consider the ratio

$$\mu_i := \frac{\kappa_{\boldsymbol{x}_i}}{\tau_{\boldsymbol{x}_i}}, \qquad i = 1, 2.$$

We say that a space curve is *helical*, if the above ratio is constant. In that case, we refer to this ratio as the *proportionality constant.* The interested reader can consult [12, Chapter 23] or [16] for further information on helical curves.

Proposition 13. *Suppose $\boldsymbol{x}_1, \boldsymbol{x}_2$ define helical curves $\mathcal{C}_1, \mathcal{C}_2$ with proportionality constants μ_1, μ_2 satisfying $f(\mathcal{C}_1) = \mathcal{C}_2$ for a similarity f with ratio λ. Then $\mu_2 = \operatorname{sgn}(\lambda) \cdot \mu_1$.*

Proof. Taking the quotient in (10) yields

$$\mu_2 = \frac{\kappa_{\boldsymbol{x}_2}}{\tau_{\boldsymbol{x}_2}} \circ \varphi = \frac{\kappa_{\boldsymbol{x}_2} \circ \varphi}{\tau_{\boldsymbol{x}_2} \circ \varphi} = \frac{\frac{1}{|\lambda|}}{\frac{1}{\lambda}} \cdot \frac{\kappa_{\boldsymbol{x}_1}}{\tau_{\boldsymbol{x}_1}} = \operatorname{sgn}(\lambda) \cdot \mu_1. \quad \square$$

This proposition provides a necessary condition for similarity of helical curves. The following example shows that the converse does not hold in general.

Example 1. *The helical quintics $\mathcal{C}_1, \mathcal{C}_2$ parametrized by*

$$\boldsymbol{x}_1(t) = \left(\frac{3}{4}t^5 + \frac{3}{8}t^4 + \frac{1}{4}t^3, \frac{4}{5}t^5 + t^4, -\frac{3}{5}t^5 + \frac{1}{2}t^4 + \frac{1}{3}t^3\right),$$

$$\boldsymbol{x}_2(t) = \left(\frac{3}{2}t^5 + \frac{3}{4}t^4 + t^3, \frac{6}{5}t^5 + 3t^4, -\frac{8}{5}t^5 + t^4 + \frac{4}{3}t^3\right)$$

have proportionality constants $\mu_1 = \mu_2 = -4/3$. However, by applying Algorithm `Similar3D` *in Section 3, one can show that $\mathcal{C}_1$ and $\mathcal{C}_2$ are not similar.*

In order to check whether the condition in Proposition 13 is sufficient, we tried first several examples of helical cubics, following the method for constructing these curves presented in [12]. Interestingly, we could not find any counterexample with helical cubics, leaving us to conjecture that the converse of Proposition 13 holds for helical cubics.

Conjecture 14. *Any two cubic rational helical space curves with proportionality constants of equal modulus are similar.*

3. DETECTING AND FINDING SIMILARITIES OF RATIONAL SPACE CURVES

Let $\mathcal{C}_1, \mathcal{C}_2$ be curves with parametrizations $\boldsymbol{x}_1, \boldsymbol{x}_2$ as in (4). In this section we first present a criterion for whether $f(\mathcal{C}_1) = \mathcal{C}_2$ for a similarity f with a given ratio λ_0. Next, to determine the potential ratios λ_0, we develop separate methods for helical and non-helical curves. The section concludes with a method for finding the similarities with a given ratio λ_0. If $\mathcal{C}_1, \mathcal{C}_2$ are neither lines nor circles, there are finitely many similarities relating $\mathcal{C}_1, \mathcal{C}_2$. In fact, the similarity is unique precisely when $\mathcal{C}_1, \mathcal{C}_2$ are not symmetric; see [5, Corollary 7].

We will use the following standard notions for multivariate polynomials $p \in \mathbb{R}[x_1, \ldots, x_n]$, viewed as a polynomial in x_n with coefficients in $\mathbb{R}[x_1, \ldots, x_{n-1}]$. The *leading term* of p with respect to x_n is the monomial of p with highest degree in x_n, and its coefficient is called the *leading coefficient.* Moreover, the *content* of p with respect to x_n is the greatest common divisor of its coefficients, viewed as elements of $\mathbb{R}[x_1, \ldots, x_{n-1}]$.

3.1 An algorithm for detecting similarity

Since $\kappa^2_{\boldsymbol{x}_i}$ and $\tau_{\boldsymbol{x}_i}$, with $i = 1, 2$, are rational, we can write

$$\kappa^2_{\boldsymbol{x}_i}(t) =: \frac{A_i(t)}{B_i(t)}, \qquad \tau_{\boldsymbol{x}_i}(t) =: \frac{C_i(t)}{D_i(t)}, \qquad i = 1, 2,$$

for coprime pairs (A_i, B_i) and (C_i, D_i), $i = 1, 2$, of polynomials. Let

$$\begin{aligned} K_\lambda(t, s) &:= A_1(t)B_2(s) - \lambda^2 \cdot A_2(s)B_1(t), \\ T_\lambda(t, s) &:= C_1(t)D_2(s) - \lambda \cdot C_2(s)D_1(t) \end{aligned} \tag{11}$$

be the result of clearing denominators in the expressions $\kappa^2_{\boldsymbol{x}_1}(t) - \lambda^2 \kappa^2_{\boldsymbol{x}_2}(s) = 0$ and $\tau_{\boldsymbol{x}_1}(t) - \lambda \tau_{\boldsymbol{x}_2}(s) = 0$. Note that $K_{-\lambda} = K_\lambda$. For a fixed λ_0, we consider the bivariate greatest common divisor and s-resultant

$$G_{\lambda_0} := \gcd(K_{\lambda_0}, T_{\lambda_0}), \quad R_{\lambda_0} := \operatorname{Res}_s(K_{\lambda_0}, T_{\lambda_0}). \tag{12}$$

of the specialized polynomials $K_{\lambda_0}, T_{\lambda_0}$.

To any Möbius transformation φ as in (5), associate the *Möbius-like* polynomial

$$F(t, s) := (ct + d)s - (at + b), \qquad ad - bc \neq 0, \tag{13}$$

as the result of clearing denominators in $s - \varphi(t) = 0$. Note that F is irreducible since $ad - bc \neq 0$.

The following theorem provides a criterion for similarity of $\mathcal{C}_1$ and $\mathcal{C}_2$ with a given ratio.

Theorem 15. *Let $\boldsymbol{x}_1, \boldsymbol{x}_2$ as in (4) define curves $\mathcal{C}_1, \mathcal{C}_2$. There exists a similarity $f(\mathbf{x}) = \lambda_0 \boldsymbol{Q}\mathbf{x} + \boldsymbol{b}$ such that $f(\mathcal{C}_1) = \mathcal{C}_2$ if and only if there exists a polynomial F of type (13) dividing G_{λ_0}, associated with a Möbius transformation φ satisfying (7) with $\lambda = \lambda_0$.*

Proof. "$\Longrightarrow$": If $f(\mathcal{C}_1) = \mathcal{C}_2$ for some similarity $f(\mathbf{x}) = \lambda_0 \boldsymbol{Q}\mathbf{x} + \boldsymbol{b}$, by Theorem 8 there exists a Möbius transformation φ such that $f \circ \boldsymbol{x}_1 = \boldsymbol{x}_2 \circ \varphi$. Let F be the Möbius-like polynomial associated with φ. The points (t, s) for which $K_{\lambda_0}(t, s) = T_{\lambda_0}(t, s) = 0$ are the points satisfying $\kappa_{\boldsymbol{x}_1}(t) = |\lambda_0| \kappa_{\boldsymbol{x}_2}(s)$ and $\tau_{\boldsymbol{x}_1}(t) = \lambda_0 \tau_{\boldsymbol{x}_2}(s)$. By Lemma 10, this includes the zeroset $\{(t, s) : s = \varphi(t)\}$ of $F(t, s)$. Since F is irreducible, Bézout's theorem implies that F divides K_{λ_0} and T_{λ_0}, and therefore G_{λ_0} as well. Moreover, since $\boldsymbol{Q}$ is orthogonal,

$$\|(\boldsymbol{x}_2 \circ \varphi)'\| = \|(f \circ \boldsymbol{x}_1)'\| = \|\lambda_0 \boldsymbol{Q} \boldsymbol{x}_1'\| = |\lambda_0| \cdot \|\boldsymbol{x}_1'\|.$$

"$\Longleftarrow$": Let φ be the transformation associated to F. Let $t_0 \in I \subset \mathbb{R}$ be such that $\boldsymbol{x}_1(t)$ is a regular point on $\mathcal{C}_1$ for every $t \in I$, and consider the arc length function

$$s = s(t) := \int_{t_0}^{t} \|\boldsymbol{x}_1'(t)\| \mathrm{d}t, \qquad t \in I,$$

which (locally) has an infinitely differentiable inverse $t = t(s)$. For $\tilde{\boldsymbol{x}}_2 := \lambda_0^{-1} \boldsymbol{x}_2$,

$$\begin{aligned} \left\| \frac{\mathrm{d}}{\mathrm{d}s}(\boldsymbol{x}_1 \circ t) \right\| &= \left\| \frac{\mathrm{d}\boldsymbol{x}_1}{\mathrm{d}t} \frac{\mathrm{d}t}{\mathrm{d}s} \right\| = 1 \\ &= \frac{1}{|\lambda_0|} \left\| \frac{\mathrm{d}}{\mathrm{d}t}(\boldsymbol{x}_2 \circ \varphi) \frac{\mathrm{d}t}{\mathrm{d}s} \right\| = \left\| \frac{\mathrm{d}}{\mathrm{d}s}(\tilde{\boldsymbol{x}}_2 \circ \varphi \circ t) \right\|, \end{aligned}$$

by (7), so that both $\boldsymbol{x}_1 \circ t$ and $\tilde{\boldsymbol{x}}_2 \circ \varphi \circ t$ are parametrized by arc length.

Since F divides G_{λ_0}, any zero $\big(t, \varphi(t)\big)$ of F is also a zero of K_{λ_0} and T_{λ_0}, implying that $\kappa_{\boldsymbol{x}_1} = |\lambda_0| \cdot \kappa_{\boldsymbol{x}_2} \circ \varphi$ and

$\tau_{\boldsymbol{x}_1} = \lambda_0 \cdot \tau_{\boldsymbol{x}_2} \circ \varphi$. Together with Lemmas 10 and 11, this yields

$$\kappa_{\boldsymbol{x}_1 \circ t} = \kappa_{\boldsymbol{x}_1} \circ t = |\lambda_0| \cdot \kappa_{\boldsymbol{x}_2} \circ \varphi \circ t = \kappa_{\tilde{\boldsymbol{x}}_2} \circ \varphi \circ t = \kappa_{\tilde{\boldsymbol{x}}_2 \circ \varphi \circ t},$$

$$\tau_{\boldsymbol{x}_1 \circ t} = \tau_{\boldsymbol{x}_1} \circ t = \lambda_0 \cdot \tau_{\boldsymbol{x}_2} \circ \varphi \circ t = \tau_{\tilde{\boldsymbol{x}}_2} \circ \varphi \circ t = \tau_{\tilde{\boldsymbol{x}}_2 \circ \varphi \circ t}.$$

The fundamental theorem of space curves (see [11, p. 19]) then implies that there exists an isometry $\tilde{f}(\mathbf{x}) = \boldsymbol{Q}\mathbf{x} + \boldsymbol{b}$, with $\det(\boldsymbol{Q}) = 1$, such that $\tilde{f} \circ \boldsymbol{x}_1 \circ t = \tilde{\boldsymbol{x}}_2 \circ \varphi \circ t$ on $s(I)$. In terms of the similarity $f(\mathbf{x}) := \lambda_0 \tilde{f}(\mathbf{x})$, it follows that

$$f(\boldsymbol{x}_1(t)) = \lambda_0 \tilde{f}(\boldsymbol{x}_1(t)) = \lambda_0 \tilde{\boldsymbol{x}}_2(\varphi(t)) = \boldsymbol{x}_2(\varphi(t)), \quad t \in I.$$

Therefore the irreducible algebraic curves $f(\mathcal{C}_1)$ and $\mathcal{C}_2$ have infinitely many points in common, implying $f(\mathcal{C}_1) = \mathcal{C}_2$. □

If some tentative values for λ_0 are known, similarity of curves can be quickly detected with this criterion, by checking if G_{λ_0} has a non-trivial Möbius-like factor. In order to do this, and since λ_0 is in general an algebraic number, we can use efficient techniques for factoring bivariate polynomials with coefficients in an algebraic number field. For instance, the command `AFactor` in Maple 18 computes the factorization of bivariate polynomials over the algebraic numbers of moderately high degree in a fraction of a second. Thus we arrive at Algorithm `Similar3D` for checking whether $\mathcal{C}_1$ and $\mathcal{C}_2$ are similar.

Note that by Theorem 6, any 'self-similarity' of an irreducible algebraic space curve that is not a line is a symmetry. Therefore, for $\boldsymbol{x}_1 = \boldsymbol{x}_2$ one has $|\lambda| = 1$, and Algorithm `Similar3D` reduces to the algorithm presented in [4] for detecting symmetries of algebraic space curves.

It remains to compute sets $\mathcal{S}_0, \mathcal{S}_1, \mathcal{S}_2$ of tentative values for λ_0 in the next two sections, where it is necessary to distinguish between helical and non-helical curves.

3.2 Finding the ratio for non-helical curves

Assume $\boldsymbol{x}_1, \boldsymbol{x}_2$ define non-helical curves. By the following proposition, there are only finitely many λ for which the resultant R_λ is identically zero.

Proposition 16. *The resultant R_λ is identically zero if and only if $\mathcal{C}_1$, $\mathcal{C}_2$ are helical curves with proportionality constants μ_1, μ_2 satisfying $|\mu_1| = |\mu_2|$.*

Proof. "$\Longleftarrow$": Since the proportionality constants have the same absolute value $\mu := |\mu_1| = |\mu_2|$,

$$\frac{A_i(t)}{B_i(t)} = \kappa^2_{\boldsymbol{x}_i}(t) = \mu^2 \cdot \tau^2_{\boldsymbol{x}_i}(t) = \mu^2 \cdot \frac{C_i^2(t)}{D_i^2(t)},$$

with $\mu \neq 0$. Therefore

$$\begin{aligned} K_\lambda(t,s) &= \mu^2 \cdot \big(C_1^2(t)D_2^2(s) - \lambda^2 C_2^2(s)D_1^2(t)\big) \\ &= \mu^2 \cdot \big(C_1(t)D_2(s) - \lambda C_2(s)D_1(t)\big) \\ &\quad \cdot \big(C_1(t)D_2(s) + \lambda C_2(s)D_1(t)\big) \\ &= \mu^2 \cdot T_\lambda(t,s) \cdot T_{-\lambda}(t,s). \end{aligned}$$

Hence K_λ has a non-trivial factor, depending on s, in common with both T_λ or $T_{-\lambda}$, since $K_\lambda = K_{-\lambda}$. It follows that R_λ is identically zero.

"$\Longrightarrow$": If R_λ is identically zero then K_λ, T_λ have nontrivial greatest common divisor G_λ. Suppose T_λ has a factor S not depending on λ. Then S divides both T_λ and $T_0(t,s) = C_1(t)D_2(s)$, and therefore also $C_2(s)D_1(t)$, contradicting that C_1, D_1 and C_2, D_2 are coprime. A similar argument shows that any nonconstant factor of K_λ depends on λ. It follows that G_λ is a linear polynomial in λ in constant proportion with T_λ. Since $G_\lambda, G_{-\lambda}$ both divide $K_\lambda = K_{-\lambda}$, which is a quadratic polynomial in λ, it follows that

$$K_\lambda = \nu \cdot T_\lambda \cdot T_{-\lambda}$$

for some nonzero constant ν. Comparing coefficients yields

$$A_1(t)B_2(s) = \nu \cdot C_1^2(t)D_2^2(s), \quad A_2(s)B_1(t) = \nu \cdot C_2^2(s)D_1^2(t).$$

Dividing these equations yields

$$\frac{\kappa^2_{\boldsymbol{x}_1}(t)}{\kappa^2_{\boldsymbol{x}_2}(s)} = \frac{A_1(t)B_2(s)}{B_1(t)A_2(s)} = \frac{C_1^2(t)D_2^2(s)}{D_1^2(t)C_2^2(s)} = \frac{\tau^2_{\boldsymbol{x}_1}(t)}{\tau^2_{\boldsymbol{x}_2}(s)},$$

or equivalently

$$\frac{\kappa^2_{\boldsymbol{x}_1}(t)}{\tau^2_{\boldsymbol{x}_1}(t)} = \frac{\kappa^2_{\boldsymbol{x}_2}(s)}{\tau^2_{\boldsymbol{x}_2}(s)},$$

which must be constant. After taking square roots the statement follows. □

Algorithm `Similar3D`

Require: Two proper parametrizations $\boldsymbol{x}_1, \boldsymbol{x}_2$ of two non-planar space curves $\mathcal{C}_1, \mathcal{C}_2$.

Ensure: Whether there exists a similarity $f(\mathbf{x}) = \lambda \boldsymbol{Q}\mathbf{x} + \boldsymbol{b}$ with $f(\mathcal{C}_1) = \mathcal{C}_2$.

1: Find the curvatures $\kappa_{\boldsymbol{x}_1}, \kappa_{\boldsymbol{x}_2}$ and torsions $\tau_{\boldsymbol{x}_1}, \tau_{\boldsymbol{x}_2}$ from (8).

2: Find the polynomials K_λ and T_λ from (11).

3: Find $\mu_1 := \kappa_{\boldsymbol{x}_1}/\tau_{\boldsymbol{x}_1}$ and $\mu_2 := \kappa_{\boldsymbol{x}_2}/\tau_{\boldsymbol{x}_2}$.

4: If precisely one of μ_1, μ_2 is constant, return `FALSE`.

5: If μ_1, μ_2 are both constant (*helical case*):

- 5.1 If $|\mu_1| \neq |\mu_2|$ return `False`. Otherwise:
- 5.2 Let $G_\lambda := T_\lambda$.
- 5.3 Choose $t_0 \in \mathbb{Q}$ such that the leading coefficient of $G_\lambda(t,s)$ with respect to s does not vanish at $t = t_0$.
- 5.4 Find the sets $\mathcal{S}_0, \mathcal{S}_1, \mathcal{S}_2$ of tentative λ using the method in Section 3.3.
- 5.5 For each $\lambda \in \mathcal{S}_0 \cup \mathcal{S}_1 \cup \mathcal{S}_2$, check whether G_λ contains a Möbius-like factor F for which the associated Möbius transformation φ satisfies (7).
- 5.6 If some λ succeeds, return `True`, otherwise return `False`.

6: If μ_1, μ_2 are not constant (*non-helical case*):

- 6.1 Find the resultant $R_\lambda = \mathrm{Res}_s(K_\lambda, T_\lambda)$.
- 6.2 Find the set $\mathcal{S}_0$ of tentative λ using the method in Section 3.2.
- 6.3 For each $\lambda \in \mathcal{S}_0$, check whether G_λ contains a Möbius-like factor F for which the associated Möbius transformation φ satisfies (7).
- 6.4 In the affirmative case, return `True`, otherwise return `False`.

Let $\Lambda^\star(\lambda)$ be the content of the resultant $\mathrm{Res}_s(K_\lambda, T_\lambda)$, viewed as a polynomial in t with coefficients depending on λ. Let $\mathrm{lc}_s(K_\lambda)$, $\mathrm{lc}_s(T_\lambda)$ be the leading coefficients with respect to s of K_λ, T_λ. Whenever $\mathrm{lc}_s(K_\lambda)$, $\mathrm{lc}_s(T_\lambda)$ do not vanish identically and simultaneously for $\lambda = \lambda_0$, the resultant R_{λ_0} of the specialized polynomials $K_{\lambda_0}, T_{\lambda_0}$ is the result of specializing $\mathrm{Res}_s(K_\lambda, T_\lambda)$ at $\lambda = \lambda_0$ (see Lemma 4.3.1 of [19]). Let $\Lambda(\lambda)$ be the product of $\Lambda^\star(\lambda)$ and the content of $\gcd(\mathrm{lc}_s(K_\lambda), \mathrm{lc}_s(T_\lambda))$ with respect to t. Let $\mathcal{S}_0$ be the set of nonzero real roots of $\Lambda(\lambda)$.

Proposition 17. *Let $\boldsymbol{x}_1, \boldsymbol{x}_2$ define non-helical curves $\mathcal{C}_1, \mathcal{C}_2$ satisfying $f(\mathcal{C}_1) = \mathcal{C}_2$ for some similarity $f(\mathbf{x}) = \lambda_0 \boldsymbol{Q}\mathbf{x} + \boldsymbol{b}$. Then $\lambda_0 \in \mathcal{S}_0$.*

Proof. By Lemma 12, there exists a Möbius transformation φ such that $K_{\lambda_0}(t, \varphi(t)) = T_{\lambda_0}(t, \varphi(t)) = 0$, and therefore $G_{\lambda_0}(t, \varphi(t)) = 0$, hold identically. Hence the Möbius-like polynomial F associated to φ divides G_{λ_0}. Since the polynomial ring $\mathbb{R}[t]$ is an integral domain, the bivariate polynomial G_{λ_0} is non-constant precisely when the resultant R_{λ_0} is identically zero, which implies $\Lambda(\lambda_0) = 0$. □

Proposition 17 provides tentative values of λ_0, which must be tested afterwards using Theorem 15.

Example 2. *Let $\mathcal{C}_1$ be the crunode parametrized by*

$$\boldsymbol{x}_1(t) = \left(\frac{t}{t^4+1}, \frac{t^2}{t^4+1}, \frac{t^3}{t^4+1} \right).$$

Based on the reparametrization $\phi(t) = t + 1$ and similarity $f(\mathbf{x}) = \lambda \boldsymbol{Q}\mathbf{x} + \boldsymbol{b}$, with $\lambda = 2$ and

$$\boldsymbol{Q} = \begin{bmatrix} 3/5 & 4/5 & 0 \\ -4/5 & 3/5 & 0 \\ 0 & 0 & 1 \end{bmatrix}, \qquad \boldsymbol{b} = \begin{bmatrix} 0 \\ 0 \\ 2 \end{bmatrix},$$

we define another crunode $\mathcal{C}_2 := f(\mathcal{C}_1)$ parametrized by $\boldsymbol{x}_2 = f \circ \boldsymbol{x}_1 \circ \phi$, i.e., $\boldsymbol{x}_2(t)$ is

$$\left(\frac{2}{5}\frac{(t+1)(4t+7)}{(t+1)^4+1}, \frac{2}{5}\frac{(t+1)(3t-1)}{(t+1)^4+1}, \frac{2(t+1)^3}{(t+1)^4+1} + 2 \right).$$

The curves $\mathcal{C}_1$ and $\mathcal{C}_2$ are shown in Figure 1a, together with the invariant sets of their symmetries, i.e., two planes of reflection and an axis of rotation.

One verifies that $\kappa^2_{\boldsymbol{x}_1}, \kappa^2_{\boldsymbol{x}_2}$ are rational functions where the numerators and denominators have degree 36. Furthermore, the numerator and denominator of $\tau_{\boldsymbol{x}_1}, \tau_{\boldsymbol{x}_2}$ have degree 8. Therefore $K_\lambda(t,s)$ has bidegree $(36, 36)$ and $T_\lambda(t,s)$ has bidegree $(8,8)$. After computing $R_\lambda = \mathrm{Res}_s(K_\lambda, T_\lambda)$, we get $\Lambda(\lambda) = \Lambda^\star(\lambda) = \lambda^2 - 4$, so $\mathcal{S}_0 = \{-2, 2\}$ contains the tentative values for λ. For $\lambda_0 = 2$ we obtain $G_2(t,s) = (s+t+1)(s-t+1)$ and two corresponding Möbius transformations satisfying (7), namely $\varphi_1(t) = -t-1$ and $\varphi_2(t) = t-1$. For $\lambda_0 = -2$ we obtain $G_{-2}(t,s) = (st+t+1)(st+t-1)$ and two corresponding Möbius transformations satisfying (7), namely $\varphi_3(t) = -(t+1)/t$ and $\varphi_4(t) = (-t+1)/t$. Therefore $\mathcal{C}_1$ and $\mathcal{C}_2$ are related by four similarities.

3.3 Finding the ratio for helical curves

Assume that $\mathcal{C}_1, \mathcal{C}_2$ are similar helical curves. Then their proportionality constants are equal up to a sign by Proposition 13, and $\gcd(K_\lambda, T_\lambda) = T_\lambda$ for any λ by the proof of Proposition 16. Therefore $R_\lambda \equiv 0$, and we cannot use the method in Section 3.2 to find the potential ratios λ. However, since $G_\lambda = T_\lambda$ is known, we can directly apply Theorem 15 to find the λ values for which G_λ has a Möbius-like factor. In order to do this, we adapt the method in [4, §3.2], where the problem of directly computing the Möbius-like factors of a bivariate polynomial is solved. The idea is that, if λ_0 is the ratio we are seeking, the Möbius transformation φ corresponding to the similarity is implicitly defined by G_{λ_0}, so that it can be reconstructed from its local data.

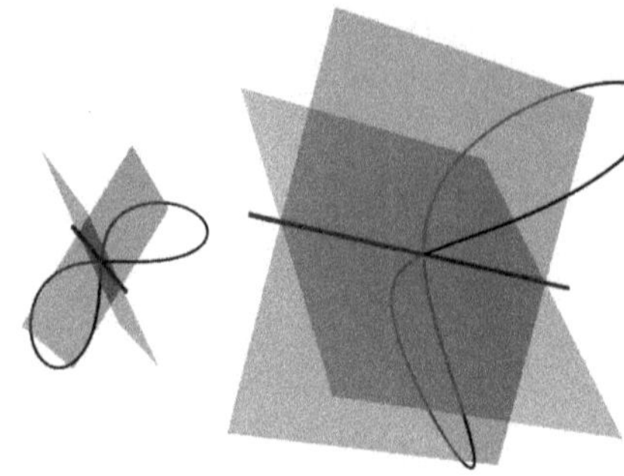

(a)

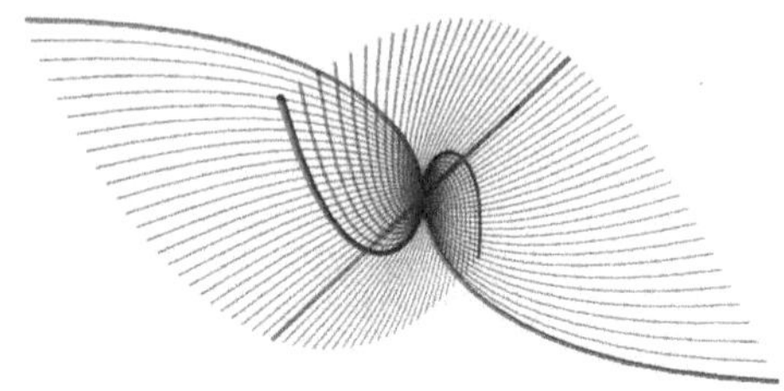

(b)

Figure 1: Top: The similar crunode curves from Example 2. Bottom: The family of helical curves $\mathcal{C}_\alpha$, with $-1 \le \alpha \le 1$, from Example 3, with the curves $\mathcal{C}_{-1}, \mathcal{C}_0, \mathcal{C}_1$ emphasized.

Lemma 18. *Let either $c = 0$ or $t_0 \neq -d/c$, and consider the Taylor expansion*

$$\varphi(t) = \frac{at+b}{ct+d} = s_0 + s_0'(t-t_0) + \frac{1}{2}s_0''(t-t_0)^2 + \cdots \quad (14)$$

Then, as homogeneous coordinates, $[a : b : c : d]$ is equal to

$$[2(s_0')^2 - s_0 s_0'' : 2s_0 s_0' + t_0 s_0 s_0'' - 2t_0(s_0')^2 : -s_0'' : 2s_0' + t_0 s_0''] \quad (15)$$

Proof. Differentiating (14) and evaluating at $t = t_0$ yields

$$s_0 = \varphi(t_0) = \frac{at_0+b}{ct_0+d},$$
$$s_0' = \varphi'(t_0) = \frac{\Delta}{(ct_0+d)^2},$$
$$s_0'' = \varphi''(t_0) = \frac{-2c\Delta}{(ct_0+d)^3}.$$

The statement follows by a straightforward calculation. □

Let $t_0 \in \mathbb{Q}$ be such that $\mathrm{lc}_s(G_\lambda(t,s))$ evaluated at $t = t_0$ is not *identically* zero. In order to detect Möbius-like factors of G_λ using the implicit function theorem, we need to exclude any λ from $\mathcal{S}_1 \cup \mathcal{S}_2$, with $\mathcal{S}_1 := \{0 \neq \lambda \in \mathbb{R} : \mathrm{lc}_s(G_\lambda(t_0, s)) = 0\}$ and

$$\mathcal{S}_2 := \left\{ 0 \neq \lambda \in \mathbb{R} \,\middle|\, \exists s \in \mathbb{C} : G_\lambda(t_0, s) = 0,\ \frac{\partial G_\lambda}{\partial s}(t_0, s) = 0 \right\}$$

The elements of $\mathcal{S}_2$ can be found by eliminating the variable s from the bivariate polynomial system $G_\lambda(t_0, s) = \frac{\partial G_\lambda}{\partial s}(t_0, s) = 0$ in λ, s, for instance using the Sylvester resultant.

Suppose $\lambda \notin \mathcal{S}_1 \cup \mathcal{S}_2$. With the dependency on the variable λ understood, write $G = G_\lambda$ and $G_t, G_s, G_{tt}, G_{ts}, G_{ss}$ for the first and second order partial derivatives of G. Suppose G has a Möbius-like factor F, and let s_0 be a variable required to satisfy $F(t_0, s_0) = 0$. Since $G(t_0, s_0) = 0$ and $G_s(t_0, s_0) \neq 0$ one has $\frac{\partial F}{\partial s}(t_0, s_0) \neq 0$, and the equation $F(t, s) = 0$ implicitly defines a function $s = \varphi(t)$ in a neighborhood of t_0 with $s_0 = \varphi(t_0)$ as in (14).

In order to determine F, we find expressions for s_0', s_0'' in terms of s_0, λ, using that $\varphi(t)$ is also implicitly defined by $G(t, s) = 0$, because F divides G and $G_s(t_0, s_0) \neq 0$. Differentiating once and twice the identity $G\big(t, \varphi(t)\big) = 0$ with respect to t, solving for φ', φ'', and evaluating at t_0 expresses

$$s_0' = \varphi'(t_0) = -\frac{G_t}{G_s}(t_0, s_0), \tag{16}$$

$$s_0'' = \varphi''(t_0) = -\frac{G_s^2 G_{tt} - 2G_t G_s G_{ts} + G_t^2 G_{ss}}{G_s^3}(t_0, s_0) \tag{17}$$

in terms of the unknown s_0. Substituting these expressions into (15) and multiplying by $-G_s^3(t_0, s_0)$ yields polynomial expressions for the coefficients of φ in terms of s_0,

$$\begin{aligned}
a(s_0, \lambda) &= -\ \big(G_s^2 G_{tt} - 2G_t G_s G_{ts} + G_t^2 G_{ss}\big) s_0 - 2G_t^2 G_s, \\
b(s_0, \lambda) &= +\ \big(G_s^2 G_{tt} - 2G_t G_s G_{ts} + G_t^2 G_{ss}\big) t_0 s_0 \\
&\quad + 2 s_0 G_t G_s^2 + 2 t_0 G_t^2 G_s, \\
c(s_0, \lambda) &= -\ \big(G_s^2 G_{tt} - 2G_t G_s G_{ts} + G_t^2 G_{ss}\big), \\
d(s_0, \lambda) &= +\ \big(G_s^2 G_{tt} - 2G_t G_s G_{ts} + G_t^2 G_{ss}\big) t_0 + 2G_t G_s^2,
\end{aligned} \tag{18}$$

where these expressions are understood to be evaluated at (t_0, s_0).

The polynomial F divides G if and only if the resultant $\mathrm{Res}_s(F, G)$ is identically zero, or equivalently precisely when

$$0 = G\big(t, \varphi(t)\big) = G\left(t, \frac{a(s_0, \lambda)t + b(s_0, \lambda)}{c(s_0, \lambda)t + d(s_0, \lambda)}\right) \tag{19}$$

holds identically. Clearing denominators yields a polynomial $P(t)$, whose coefficients are polynomials $P_i(s_0, \lambda)$. Then F divides G if and only if there exist $s_0 \in \mathbb{R}$ and $0 \neq \lambda \in \mathbb{R}$ for which the P_i are simultaneously zero, i.e., when there is such a point (s_0, λ) on the real variety generated by the ideal $\langle P_i \rangle_i \subset \mathbb{R}[s, \lambda]$. Using Gröbner bases, one eliminates the variable s from this ideal, resulting in a principal ideal $\langle \Lambda \rangle \subset \mathbb{R}[\lambda]$. Let $\mathcal{S}_0 := \{0 \neq \lambda \in \mathbb{R} : \Lambda(\lambda) = 0\}$. We have shown:

Theorem 19. *Suppose $f(\mathcal{C}_1) = \mathcal{C}_2$ for a similarity f with ratio λ. Let t_0 be such that $lc_s(G_\lambda(t, s))$ evaluated at $t = t_0$ is not identically zero. Then $\lambda \in \mathcal{S}_0 \cup \mathcal{S}_1 \cup \mathcal{S}_2$.*

Therefore, $f(\mathcal{C}_1) = \mathcal{C}_2$ for a similarity f with ratio λ_0 if and only if

(i) $\lambda_0 \in \mathcal{S}_1 \cup \mathcal{S}_2$ and G_{λ_0} has a Möbius-like factor, or

(ii) $\lambda_0 \in \mathcal{S}_0$ and the polynomials P_i, after substituting λ_0, have a common real root s_0,

for which, in either case, the corresponding Möbius transformation satisfies (7).

Example 3. *Consider the family of curves $\{\mathcal{C}_\alpha\}_\alpha$ defined by the parametrizations*

$$\boldsymbol{x}_\alpha(t) = \left(-\frac{1}{3}t^3 + \alpha^2 t, \frac{2}{3}t^3 + \alpha t^2, \frac{2}{3}t^3 - \alpha t^2\right), \quad \alpha \in \mathbb{R}.$$

These curves are shown in Figure 1b for parameters $-1 \leq \alpha \leq 1$, with the curves $\mathcal{C}_{-1}, \mathcal{C}_0, \mathcal{C}_1$ emphasized. Except for the line $\mathcal{C}_0$, each curve $\mathcal{C}_\alpha$ is a cubic helical curve with proportionality constant μ_α satisfying $|\mu_\alpha| = \sqrt{2}$, since

$$\kappa_{\boldsymbol{x}_\alpha} = \frac{2|\alpha|\sqrt{2}}{(\alpha^2 + 3t^2)^2}, \qquad \tau_{\boldsymbol{x}_\alpha} = \frac{2\alpha}{(\alpha^2 + 3t^2)^2}.$$

In order to determine if the curves $\mathcal{C}_1, \mathcal{C}_{-1}$ are similar, we compute

$$G_\lambda(t, s) = 9\lambda t^4 + 9s^4 + 6\lambda t^2 + 6s^2 + \lambda + 1.$$

Letting $t_0 = 1$, one has $G_\lambda(t_0, s) = 9s^4 + 6s^2 + 16\lambda + 1$ with constant leading coefficient $lc_s(G_\lambda(t_0, s)) = 9$, implying $\mathcal{S}_1 = \emptyset$. Moreover, $\frac{\partial G_\lambda}{\partial s}(t_0, s) = 36s^3 + 12s$, so $\mathcal{S}_2 = \{-1/16\}$. Since

$$s_0' = \frac{-4\lambda}{s_0(3s_0^2 + 1)}, \quad s_0'' = \frac{2\lambda(45s_0^6 + 30s_0^4 + 72\lambda s_0^2 + 5s_0^2 + 8\lambda)}{-s_0^3(3s_0^2 + 1)^3}$$

we have, after scaling by a common factor,

$$\begin{aligned}
a(s_0, \lambda) &= -s_0(45s_0^6 + 30s_0^4 + 120\lambda s_0^2 + 5s_0^2 + 24\lambda), \\
b(s_0, \lambda) &= 3s_0(27s_0^6 + 18s_0^4 + 40\lambda s_0^2 + 3s_0^2 + 8\lambda), \\
c(s_0, \lambda) &= -(45s_0^6 + 30s_0^4 + 72\lambda s_0^2 + 5s_0^2 + 8\lambda), \\
d(s_0, \lambda) &= 81s_0^6 + 54s_0^4 + 72\lambda s_0^2 + 9s_0^2 + 8\lambda.
\end{aligned} \tag{20}$$

Substituting (20) into (19) and clearing denominators, we get a polynomial $P(t)$ with polynomial coefficients $P_i(s_0, \lambda)$. Eliminating the variable s_0 from the ideal $\langle P_i \rangle_i$, we obtain the generator $\Lambda(\lambda) = \lambda^5(\lambda + 1)$ and $\mathcal{S}_0 = \{-1\}$. Then

$$G_{-1}(t, s) = 3(s - t)(s + t)(3s^2 + 3t^2 + 2),$$

and the corresponding Möbius transformations $\varphi_1(t) = t$ and $\varphi_2(t) = -t$ satisfy (7). Since $\lambda = -1$ succeeds, one does not need to try $\lambda = -1/16 \in \mathcal{S}_2$ by Proposition 7. We conclude that $\mathcal{C}_1$ and $\mathcal{C}_{-1}$ are related by two similarities.

3.4 Finding the similarities

Suppose that using Algorithm `Similar3D` we have determined that $f(\mathcal{C}_1) = \mathcal{C}_2$ for a similarity $f(\mathbf{x}) = \lambda_0 \boldsymbol{Q}\mathbf{x} + \boldsymbol{b}$. Then we have computed the associated Möbius transformation φ and the ratio λ_0, and we would like to find $\boldsymbol{Q}$ and $\boldsymbol{b}$. For this purpose, we adapt to our problem the discussion in [4, §4]. By Theorem 8,

$$\lambda_0 \cdot \boldsymbol{Q}\boldsymbol{x}_1(t) + \boldsymbol{b} = \boldsymbol{x}_2\big(\varphi(t)\big). \tag{21}$$

Without loss of generality, we assume that $\boldsymbol{x}_1(t)$, and therefore any of its derivatives, are well defined at $t = 0$ and that $\boldsymbol{x}_1'(0), \boldsymbol{x}_1''(0)$ are well defined, nonzero, and not parallel. This is equivalent to requiring that the curvature $\kappa_{\boldsymbol{x}_1}(0)$ is well defined and nonzero, which can always be achieved by a reparametrization of type $t \longmapsto t + \alpha$.

Once $\boldsymbol{Q}$ is determined, one finds $\boldsymbol{b}$ by evaluating (21) at $t = 0$. To determine $\boldsymbol{Q}$, we must consider separately the cases when the coefficient d of the Möbius transformation φ satisfies $d \neq 0$ or $d = 0$. Here we address the case $d \neq 0$; the case $d = 0$ is easier and has been addressed in [5, §3.4]. Differentiating (21) once and twice, yields

$$\lambda_0 \cdot \boldsymbol{Q}\boldsymbol{x}_1'(t) = \boldsymbol{x}_2'\left(\frac{at+b}{ct+d}\right)\frac{\Delta}{(ct+d)^2}, \tag{22}$$

$$\lambda_0 \cdot \boldsymbol{Q}\boldsymbol{x}_1''(t) = \boldsymbol{x}_2''\left(\frac{at+b}{ct+d}\right)\frac{\Delta^2}{(ct+d)^4} - 2\boldsymbol{x}_2'\left(\frac{at+b}{ct+d}\right)\frac{c\cdot\Delta}{(ct+d)^3}, \tag{23}$$

where $\Delta = ad - bc$. Evaluating (22) and (23) at $t = 0$ yields

$$\lambda_0 \cdot \boldsymbol{Q}\boldsymbol{x}_1'(0) = \boldsymbol{x}_2'(b/d)\cdot\Delta/d^2, \tag{24}$$

$$\lambda_0 \cdot \boldsymbol{Q}\boldsymbol{x}_1''(0) = \boldsymbol{x}_2''(b/d)\cdot\Delta^2/d^4 - 2\boldsymbol{x}_2'(b/d)\cdot c\cdot\Delta/d^3. \tag{25}$$

Taking the cross product and using (9) with $\boldsymbol{M} = \boldsymbol{Q}$ orthogonal yields

$$\lambda_0^2\cdot\boldsymbol{Q}\big(\boldsymbol{x}_1'(0)\times\boldsymbol{x}_1''(0)\big) = (\Delta^3/d^6)\cdot\big(\boldsymbol{x}_2'(b/d)\times\boldsymbol{x}_2''(b/d)\big). \tag{26}$$

Since λ_0 and φ are known, the matrix $\boldsymbol{Q}$ can be determined from its action on $\boldsymbol{x}_1'(0), \boldsymbol{x}_1''(0)$, and $\boldsymbol{x}_1'(0)\times\boldsymbol{x}_1''(0)$, which is given by (24)–(26). In more detail, let

$$\boldsymbol{B} := [\lambda_0\cdot\boldsymbol{x}_1'(0), \lambda_0\cdot\boldsymbol{x}_1''(0), \lambda_0^2\cdot\boldsymbol{x}_1'(0)\times\boldsymbol{x}_1''(0)], \tag{27}$$

and let $\boldsymbol{C}$ be the matrix whose columns are the right hand sides of (24)–(26). Then $\boldsymbol{Q} = \boldsymbol{C}\boldsymbol{B}^{-1}$.

Example 4. *In Example 2, let us find the similarity corresponding to $\lambda_0 = 2$ and $\varphi(t) = t - 1$ relating the crunode curves $\mathcal{C}_1, \mathcal{C}_2$. Then φ has coefficients $a = 1$, $b = -1$, $c = 0$, $d = 1$, and therefore $\Delta = 1$. One obtains*

$$\boldsymbol{B} = \begin{bmatrix} 2 & 0 & 0 \\ 0 & 4 & 0 \\ 0 & 0 & 8 \end{bmatrix}, \quad \boldsymbol{C} = \begin{bmatrix} 6/5 & 16/5 & 0 \\ -8/5 & 12/5 & 0 \\ 0 & 0 & 8 \end{bmatrix},$$

and then

$$\boldsymbol{Q} = \boldsymbol{C}\boldsymbol{B}^{-1} = \begin{bmatrix} 3/5 & 4/5 & 0 \\ -4/5 & 3/5 & 0 \\ 0 & 0 & 1 \end{bmatrix}.$$

Substituting $t = 0$ in (21) yields $\boldsymbol{b} = \boldsymbol{x}_2(-1) - 2\boldsymbol{Q}\boldsymbol{x}_1(0) = [0, 0, 2]^T$, consistent with Example 2.

4. ACKNOWLEDGMENTS

We are grateful to the referees for providing detailed feedback, which helped improve the quality of the paper. Juan Gerardo Alcázar is supported by the Spanish "Ministerio de Ciencia e Innovacion" under the Project MTM2014-54141-P, and is also a member of the Research Group ASYNACS (Ref. CCEE2011/R34).

5. REFERENCES

[1] Juan Gerardo Alcázar, *Computing the shapes arising in a family of space rational curves depending on one parameter*, Comput. Aided Geom. Design **29** (2012), no. 6, 315–331.

[2] Juan Gerardo Alcázar, Carlos Hermoso, and Georg Muntingh, *Detecting similarity of rational plane curves*, J. Comput. Appl. Math. **269** (2014), 1–13.

[3] ———, *Detecting symmetries of rational plane and space curves*, Comput. Aided Geom. Design **31** (2014), no. 3-4, 199–209.

[4] ———, *Symmetry detection of rational space curves from their curvature and torsion*, Comput. Aided Geom. Design **33** (2015), 51–65.

[5] ———, *Detecting similarities of rational space curves*, arXiv:1512.02620.

[6] Mihael Ankerst, Gabi Kastenmüller, Hans-Peter Kriegel, and Thomas Seidl, *3D shape histograms for similarity search and classification in spatial databases*, 6th International Symposium on Spatial Databases (SSD 99) (Hong Kong, July 1999), Advances in Spatial Databases, Lecture Notes in Computer Science, vol. 1651, Springer, 1999, pp. 207–226.

[7] Benjamin Bustos, Daniel A. Keim, Dietmar Saupe, Tobias Schreck, and Dejan V. Vranić, *Feature-based Similarity Search in 3D Object Databases*, ACM Comput. Surv. **37** (December 2005), no. 4, 345–387.

[8] Ding-Yun Chen, Xiao-Pei Tian, Yu-Te Shen, and Ming Ouhyoung, *On Visual Similarity Based 3D Model Retrieval*, Computer Graphics Forum **22** (2003), no. 3, 223–232.

[9] É. Cartan, *La méthode de repére mobile, la théorie des groupes continus et les espaces généralisées*, Exposés de geéométrie, 5; Actualités scientifiques et industrielles, No. 194, Hermann et Cie, editeurs, Paris, 1935.

[10] Harold S.M. Coxeter, *Introduction to geometry*, 2nd ed., John Wiley & Sons, Inc., New York-London-Sydney, 1969.

[11] Manfredo P. do Carmo, *Differential geometry of curves and surfaces*, Prentice-Hall, Inc., Englewood Cliffs, N.J., 1976. Translated from the Portuguese.

[12] Rida T. Farouki, *Pythagorean-hodograph curves: algebra and geometry inseparable*, Geometry and Computing, vol. 1, Springer, Berlin, 2008.

[13] Masaki Hilaga, Yoshihisa Shinagawa, Taku Kohmura, and Tosiyasu L. Kunii, *Topology Matching for Fully Automatic Similarity Estimation of 3D Shapes*, Proceedings of the 28th Annual Conference on Computer Graphics and Interactive Techniques, SIGGRAPH '01, ACM, 2001, pp. 203–212.

[14] Marcel Körtgen, Marcin Novotni, and Reinhard Klein, *3D shape matching with 3D shape contexts*, The 7th Central European Seminar on Computer Graphics (April 2003), pp. 5–17.

[15] Robert Osada, Thomas Funkhouser, Bernard Chazelle, and David Dobkin, *Matching 3D models with shape distributions*, International Conference on Shape Modeling and Applications (May 2001), Shape Modeling and Applications, 2001, pp. 154–166.

[16] Fatma Şengüler-Çiftçi, *Geometry of rational helices and its applications* (2014), available at http://arxiv.org/abs/1306.3689.

[17] J. Rafael Sendra, Franz Winkler, and Sonia Pérez-Díaz, *Rational algebraic curves*, Algorithms and Computation in Mathematics, vol. 22, Springer, Berlin, 2008.

[18] H. Sundar, D. Silver, N. Gagvani, and S. Dickinson, *Skeleton Based Shape Matching and Retrieval*, Proceedings of the Shape Modeling International 2003, SMI '03, IEEE Computer Society, Washington, DC, USA, 2003, pp. 130–139.

[19] F. Winkler, *Polynomial algorithms in computer algebra*, Texts and Monographs in Symbolic Computation, Springer-Verlag, Vienna, 1996.

Solving Generic Nonarchimedean Semidefinite Programs Using Stochastic Game Algorithms

Xavier Allamigeon* Stéphane Gaubert* Mateusz Skomra*,†

INRIA and CMAP, École polytechnique, CNRS
firstname.lastname@inria.fr

ABSTRACT

A general issue in computational optimization is to develop combinatorial algorithms for semidefinite programming. We address this issue when the base field is *nonarchimedean*. We provide a solution for a class of semidefinite feasibility problems given by generic matrices with a Metzler-type sign pattern. Our approach is based on tropical geometry. We define tropical spectrahedra as the images by the valuation of nonarchimedean spectrahedra, and provide an explicit description of the tropical spectrahedra arising from the aforementioned class of problems. We deduce that the tropical semidefinite feasibility problems obtained in this way are equivalent to stochastic mean payoff games, which have been well studied in algorithmic game theory. This allows us to solve nonarchimedean semidefinite feasibility problems using algorithms for stochastic games. These algorithms are of a combinatorial nature and work for large instances.

1. INTRODUCTION

Semidefinite programming consists in optimizing a linear function over a spectrahedron. The latter is a subset of $\mathbb{R}^n$ defined by linear matrix inequalities, i.e., a set of the form

$$\mathcal{S} = \{x \in \mathbb{R}^n : Q^{(0)} + x_1 Q^{(1)} + \cdots + x_n Q^{(n)} \succcurlyeq 0\}$$

where the $Q^{(k)}$ are symmetric matrices of order m, and $\succcurlyeq$ denotes the Loewner order on the space of symmetric matrices. By definition, $X \succcurlyeq Y$ if and only if $X - Y$ is positive semidefinite.

Semidefinite programming is a fundamental tool in convex optimization. It is used to solve various applications from engineering sciences, and also to obtain approximate solutions or bounds for hard problems arising in combinatorial optimization and semialgebraic optimization. We refer the reader to [7, 12] for information.

Semidefinite programs are usually solved via interior point methods. The latter provide an approximate solution in a polynomial number of iterations, provided that a strictly feasible initial solution, i.e., a point belonging to the interior of the set $\mathcal{S}$, is known. We refer the reader to [9] for a detailed analysis of the complexity in the bit model of interior point methods for semidefinite programming, and for a discussion of earlier complexity results based on the ellipsoid method.

Semidefinite programming becomes a much harder matter if one requires an exact solution. The feasibility problem (deciding the emptiness of the set $\mathcal{S}$) belongs to $\text{NP}_{\mathbb{R}} \cap \text{coNP}_{\mathbb{R}}$, where the subscript $\mathbb{R}$ refers to the BSS model of computation [22]. It is not known to be in NP in the bit model. A difficulty here is that all feasible points may have entries of absolute value doubly exponential in the size of the input. Also, there may be no rational solution [23]. Beyond their theoretical interest, exact semidefinite algorithms may be useful to address problems of formal proofs, which sometimes lead to challenging (degenerate) instances [20]. Known exact methods rely either on general purpose semialgebraic techniques (like cylindrical decomposition) or on dedicated methods based on the computation of critical points, see the recent work [15] and the references therein.

Semidefinite programing is meaningful in any real closed field, and in particular in *nonarchimedean* (real closed) fields like the field of Puiseux series with real coefficients. Nonarchimedean semidefinite programming arises when considering *parametric* semidefinite programming problems over the reals, or structured problems in which the entries of the matrices have different orders of magnitudes. They are also of an intrinsic interest, since, by analogy with linear programming [19], shifting to the nonarchimedean case is expected to shed light on the complexity of the classical problem over the reals. We note that the fields of Puiseux series are representative of the general nonarchimedean situation, since any nonarchimedean ordered field can be embedded in a field of generalized (Hahn) series [24, Th. 5.2.20].

Description of Main Results

In this paper, we address semidefinite programming in the *nonarchimedean* case, to which methods from tropical geometry can be applied. These methods are expected to allow one, in generic situations, to reduce semialgebraic problems to combinatorial problems, involving only the nonarchimedean valuations (leading exponents) of the coefficients of the input. We exploit the tropical approach by considering trop-

*Partially supported by the ANR projects CAFEIN (ANR-12-INSE-0007) and MALTHY (ANR-13-INSE-0003), and by the PGMO program of EDF and Fondation Mathématique Jacques Hadamard.

†Funded by a grant from Région Ile-de-France.

ISSAC '16, July 19 - 22, 2016, Waterloo, ON, Canada

ISBN 978-1-4503-4380-0/16/07...$15.00

DOI: http://dx.doi.org/10.1145/2930889.2930935

ical spectrahedra, defined as the images by the valuation of nonarchimedean spectrahedra.

We first give a combinatorial description (Theorems 3.3 and 3.5) of tropical spectrahedra arising as the images of generic nonarchimedean spectrahedra determined by symmetric matrices that satisfy a Metzler-type sign condition (nonpositivity of off-diagonal entries). The subclass of inputs under consideration already covers known hard examples of semidefinite feasibility problems, involving for instance cascades of quadratic inequalities, as in [22]. The genericity assumption involves valuations. Assumptions of this nature are familiar in tropical geometry.

Then, we show (Corollaries 4.5 and 4.6) that the tropical semidefinite feasibility problem for the aforementioned class is equivalent to solving stochastic mean payoff games. The latter are a well-studied class of combinatorial zero-sum games with perfect information. The complexity of these games is a long-standing open problem. They belong to the class NP $\cap$ coNP, but they are not known to be polynomial.

This allows us to apply stochastic game algorithms to solve nonarchimedean semidefinite feasibility problems (Section 4.3). We obtain in this way both theoretical bounds and a practicable method solving some large scale instances.

The proofs of most statements can be found in the extended version of the present paper available as [4].

Related Work

It is a general principle in tropical geometry that some information on the solutions of polynomial systems can be obtained by combinatorial reasoning about valuations. Early incarnations of this idea are the patchworking method of Viro to construct real curves with a prescribed topology [26] and its extension by Sturmfels [25] to complete intersections of hypersurfaces. See also the more recent work by Bihan [6]. Our characterization of tropical spectrahedra is obtained by applying the same kind of ideas to a class of *semialgebraic* systems which arise from semidefinite feasibility problems.

Yu [27] showed that the image by the valuation of the cone of nonarchimedean positive semidefinite matrices is described only by tropical minors of order 2. Our characterization of tropical Metzler spectrahedra can be thought of as an extension of her theorem to the case of spectrahedra.

This work also originates from the equivalence between tropical polyhedral feasibility problems and deterministic zero-sum games with mean payoff, established by Akian, Gaubert, and Guterman [2]. The novelty here is the handling of nonlinear semialgebraic convex problems, and the proof that the well-known class of *stochastic* mean payoff games correspond precisely to semidefinite feasibility problems with a Metzler structure, therefore relating two classes of problems which both have an unsettled complexity.

Finally, as mentioned above, the computation of exact solutions of semidefinite programming problems is of current interest. In particular, Nie, Ranestad, and Sturmfels [21] provided complexity measures based on the notion of algebraic degree, and dedicated algorithms have been developed by Henrion, Naldi, and Safey El Din [15].

2. STATEMENT OF THE PROBLEM AND ILLUSTRATION OF OUR APPROACH

The nonarchimedean structure which we use in this paper is the *field* $\mathbb{K}$ *of (formal generalized real) Puiseux series*,

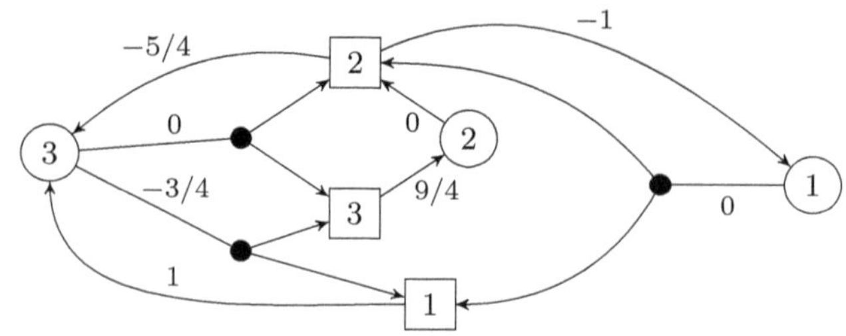

Figure 1: Stochastic game associated with the spectrahedron considered in Section 2.

which is composed of formal series of the form

$$\boldsymbol{x} = \sum_{i=1}^{\infty} c_{\lambda_i} t^{\lambda_i} , \tag{1}$$

where t is a formal parameter, $(\lambda_i)_{i \geqslant 1}$ is a strictly decreasing sequence of real numbers that is either finite or unbounded, and $c_{\lambda_i} \in \mathbb{R} \setminus \{0\}$ for all λ_i. There is also a special, empty series, which is denoted by 0. We denote by $\mathsf{lc}(\boldsymbol{x})$ the coefficient c_{λ_1} of the leading term in the series $\boldsymbol{x}$, with the convention that $\mathsf{lc}(0) = 0$. The addition and multiplication in $\mathbb{K}$ are defined in a natural way. Moreover, $\mathbb{K}$ can be endowed with a linear order $\geqslant$, which is defined as $\boldsymbol{x} \geqslant \boldsymbol{y}$ if $\mathsf{lc}(\boldsymbol{x} - \boldsymbol{y}) \geqslant 0$. We denote $\mathbb{K}_{\geqslant 0}$ the set of nonnegative series $\boldsymbol{x}$, i.e., satisfying $\boldsymbol{x} \geqslant 0$. The *valuation* of an element $\boldsymbol{x} \in \mathbb{K}$ as in (1) is defined as the greatest exponent λ_1 occurring in the series. It is known that $\mathbb{K}$ is a real closed field (see [18] for instance).

In this paper, we consider a homogeneous variant of the semidefinite feasibility problem over the field $\mathbb{K}$. More precisely, given symmetric matrices $\boldsymbol{Q}^{(1)}, \dots, \boldsymbol{Q}^{(n)} \in \mathbb{K}^{m \times m}$, the problem which we study consists in determining whether or not the following spectrahedral cone

$$\{\boldsymbol{x} \in \mathbb{K}^n_{\geqslant 0} \colon \boldsymbol{x}_1 \boldsymbol{Q}_1 + \dots + \boldsymbol{x}_n \boldsymbol{Q}_n \succcurlyeq 0\}$$

is *trivial*, meaning that it is reduced to the identically null point of $\mathbb{K}^n_{\geqslant 0}$. The linear map $\boldsymbol{x} \mapsto \boldsymbol{x}_1 \boldsymbol{Q}_1 + \dots + \boldsymbol{x}_n \boldsymbol{Q}_n$ is a *matrix pencil*, which we denote by $\boldsymbol{Q}(\boldsymbol{x})$ for more brevity. The latter decision problem is in fact equivalent to the nontriviality problem of general spectrahedral cones in which the nonnegativity condition $\boldsymbol{x} \in \mathbb{K}^n_{\geqslant 0}$ is relaxed. Indeed, given a pencil $\boldsymbol{Q}(\boldsymbol{x})$ of symmetric matrices, the spectrahedron $\{\boldsymbol{x} \in \mathbb{K}^n \colon \boldsymbol{Q}(\boldsymbol{x}) \succcurlyeq 0\}$ is trivial if and only if the spectrahedron $\{(\boldsymbol{y}, \boldsymbol{z}) \in \mathbb{K}^{2n}_{\geqslant 0} \colon (\boldsymbol{y}_1 - \boldsymbol{z}_1)\boldsymbol{Q}_1 + \dots + (\boldsymbol{y}_n - \boldsymbol{z}_n)\boldsymbol{Q}_n \succcurlyeq 0\}$ is trivial. Even if the instances arising in this way are unlikely to be generic in the sense we define later in Section 3, we consider that the decision problem which we focus on already retains much of the complexity of the semidefinite feasibility problem over the field of Puiseux series.

Our approach applies to the case where the off-diagonal entries of the matrices $\boldsymbol{Q}^{(1)}, \dots, \boldsymbol{Q}^{(n)}$ are nonpositive. Then, we associate to these matrices the following zero-sum game. There are two players, Player Min and Player Max, who control disjoint sets of states. The states of Player Min can be identified to the variables $\boldsymbol{x}_1, \dots, \boldsymbol{x}_n$. The states of Player Max can be identified to the row (or column) indices of the matrices, i.e., to the elements of $\{1, \dots, m\}$. In state $\boldsymbol{x}_k$, Player Min choses a subset $\{i, j\} \subset \{1, \dots, m\}$ such that the entry $\boldsymbol{Q}^{(k)}_{ij}$ is negative. Next, Player Min pays to Player

Max the opposite of the valuation of $Q_{ij}^{(k)}$. Then, Nature selects one element among i or j at random, with uniform probabilities (i.e., i or j is drawn with probability $1/2$).[1] If i is drawn, meaning that the current state is now i, Player Max chooses a variable $\boldsymbol{x}_l$ such that $Q_{ii}^{(l)}$ has a positive sign. He receives the valuation of $Q_{ii}^{(l)}$ from Player Min, and the next state becomes $\boldsymbol{x}_l$. If j is drawn, the rule of move and the payment are identical, up to the replacement of i by j. A (stationary) policy of one player is a map which associates to a state of the player an admissible move. We are interested in infinite plays, with an infinite number of turns. Player Max looks for a policy which maximizes the mean payment received from Player Min per time unit, while Player Min looks for a policy which minimizes it.

We can think informally of this construction as follows: Player Min wishes to show that the semidefinite programming problem is infeasible, whereas Player Max wishes to show that it is feasible.

Let us now illustrate our approach on an example in dimension 3. We consider the following pencil of symmetric matrices

$$Q(\boldsymbol{x}) := \begin{bmatrix} t\boldsymbol{x}_3 & -\boldsymbol{x}_1 & -t^{3/4}\boldsymbol{x}_3 \\ -\boldsymbol{x}_1 & t^{-1}\boldsymbol{x}_1 + t^{-5/4}\boldsymbol{x}_3 - \boldsymbol{x}_2 & -\boldsymbol{x}_3 \\ -t^{3/4}\boldsymbol{x}_3 & -\boldsymbol{x}_3 & t^{9/4}\boldsymbol{x}_2 \end{bmatrix},$$

and we aim at checking whether or not the spectrahedron $\{\boldsymbol{x} \in \mathbb{K}^3_{\geqslant 0} : Q(\boldsymbol{x}) \succcurlyeq 0\}$ is trivial. The associated game is depicted on Figure 1. The states of Player Min are depicted by circles. The states of Player Max are depicted by squares. The states in which Nature plays are depicted by full dots. The admissible moves of the game are represented by the edges between the states. The corresponding payments received by Player Max are indicated on these edges.

Observe that both players in this game have only two policies: at state $\boxed{2}$ Player Max can move to ① or to ③, whereas at state ③ Player Min can choose the move $\{\boxed{1}, \boxed{3}\}$ or the move $\{\boxed{2}, \boxed{3}\}$.

Suppose that Player Max chooses the policy which goes to state ① from state $\boxed{2}$. If Player Min plays using the move $\{\boxed{1}, \boxed{3}\}$ at state ③, then a standard computation on Markov chain shows that the long-term average payoff of Player Max is equal to $3/40$. Similarly, if Player Min chooses the move $\{\boxed{2}, \boxed{3}\}$ instead, then the payoff of Player Max is equal to $1/56$. Therefore, Player Max has a policy which guarantees him to win the game, i.e., to obtain a nonnegative payoff. The main theorem of this paper states that this fact is equivalent to the nontriviality of the spectrahedron $\{\boldsymbol{x} \in \mathbb{K}^3_{\geqslant 0} : Q(\boldsymbol{x}) \succcurlyeq 0\}$. In this way, a winning policy of Player Max (resp. Min) will be seen to provide a feasibility (resp. infeasibility) certificate. The mean payoff represents a feasibility/infeasibility margin.

3. TROPICAL SPECTRAHEDRA

3.1 Tropical Algebra

In this section, we briefly introduce the basic concepts of tropical algebra and its connection with the nonarchimedean field of Puiseux series.

[1]We allow the case $i = j$. In other words, Player Min can choose a subset $\{i\} \subset \{1, \dots, m\}$ such that $Q_{ii}^{(k)}$ is negative. In this case, Nature selects i.

We denote by $\mathsf{val} \colon \mathbb{K} \to \mathbb{R} \cup \{-\infty\}$ the map which associates a Puiseux series $\boldsymbol{x} \in \mathbb{K}$ to its valuation. We use the convention $\mathsf{val}(0) = -\infty$. It is immediate to see that the map val satisfies the following properties

$$\mathsf{val}(\boldsymbol{x} + \boldsymbol{y}) \leqslant \max(\mathsf{val}(\boldsymbol{x}), \mathsf{val}(\boldsymbol{y})) \tag{2}$$

$$\mathsf{val}(\boldsymbol{x}\boldsymbol{y}) = \mathsf{val}(\boldsymbol{x}) + \mathsf{val}(\boldsymbol{y}) \tag{3}$$

meaning that val is a *nonarchimedean valuation*. Moreover, the equality holds in (2) if the leading terms of $\boldsymbol{x}$ and $\boldsymbol{y}$ do not cancel, which is the case if $\mathsf{val}(\boldsymbol{x}) \neq \mathsf{val}(\boldsymbol{y})$ or if $\boldsymbol{x}, \boldsymbol{y} \geqslant 0$.

Loosely speaking, the *tropical semifield* $\mathbb{T}$ can be thought of as the image of $\mathbb{K}$ by the nonarchimedean valuation. The base set of $\mathbb{T}$ is defined to be $\mathbb{R} \cup \{-\infty\}$. It is endowed with the addition $x \oplus y := \max(x, y)$ and the multiplication $x \odot y := x + y$. The term semifield refers to the fact that the addition does not have an opposite law. We use the notation $\bigoplus_{i=1}^n a_i = a_1 \oplus \dots \oplus a_n$ and $a^{\odot n} = a \odot \dots \odot a$ (n times). We also endow $\mathbb{T}$ with the standard order $\leqslant$. The map val yields an order-preserving morphism of semifields from $\mathbb{K}_{\geqslant 0}$ to $\mathbb{T}$. This follows from (3) and from the equality case in (2). We refer the reader to [8, 17] for more information on the tropical semifield.

It is convenient to keep track not only of the valuation of a series but also of its sign. To this end, we introduce the *signed valuation*, denoted by sval, which associates to a series $\boldsymbol{x} \in \mathbb{K}$ the couple $(\mathsf{sign}(\boldsymbol{x}), \mathsf{val}(\boldsymbol{x}))$, where $\mathsf{sign}(\boldsymbol{x}) \in \{0, \pm 1\}$ denotes the *sign* of $\boldsymbol{x}$, which is equal to $+1$ if $\boldsymbol{x} > 0$, -1 if $\boldsymbol{x} < 0$, and 0 otherwise. We denote by $\mathbb{T}_\pm$ the image of $\mathbb{K}$ by sval. We call it the set of *signed tropical numbers*. For brevity, we denote an element of the form (ϵ, a) by a if $\epsilon = 1$, $\ominus a$ if $\epsilon = -1$, and $-\infty$ if $\epsilon = 0$. Here, $\ominus$ is a formal symbol. We call the elements of the first and second kind the *positive* and *negative* tropical numbers, respectively. We denote by $\mathbb{T}_+$ and $\mathbb{T}_-$ the corresponding sets. In this way, (-2) is tropically positive, but $\ominus(-2)$ is tropically negative. Also, $\mathbb{T}$ is embedded in $\mathbb{T}_\pm$, i.e., $\mathbb{T} = \mathbb{T}_+ \cup \{-\infty\}$.

In $\mathbb{T}_\pm$, we define a *modulus* function, $|\cdot| \colon \mathbb{T}_\pm \to \mathbb{T}$, as $|-\infty| = -\infty$ and $|a| = |\ominus a| = a$ for all $a \in \mathbb{T}_+$. We point out that $\odot$ straightforwardly extends to $\mathbb{T}_\pm$ using the standard rules for the sign, for instance $2 \odot (\ominus 3) = \ominus 5$. In contrast, we only partially extend the tropical addition $\oplus$ to elements of $\mathbb{T}_\pm$ of identical sign, e.g., $2 \oplus 3 = 3$ and $(\ominus 2) \oplus (\ominus 3) = \ominus 3$.

We shall extend the valuation maps val and sval to vectors and matrices in a coordinate-wise manner.

Finally, we use the notion of tropical polynomials. A *tropical (signed) polynomial* over the variables $X_1, \dots, X_n$ is a formal expression of the form

$$P(X) = \bigoplus_{\alpha \in A} a_\alpha \odot X_1^{\odot \alpha_1} \odot \dots \odot X_n^{\odot \alpha_n}, \tag{4}$$

where $A \subset \{0, 1, 2, \dots\}^n$, and $a_\alpha \in \mathbb{T}_\pm \setminus \{-\infty\}$ for all $\alpha \in A$. We say that the tropical polynomial P *vanishes* on the point $x \in \mathbb{T}_\pm^n$ if the terms $a_\alpha \odot x_1^{\odot \alpha_1} \odot \dots \odot x_n^{\odot \alpha_n}$ which have the greatest modulus do not have the same sign. If P does not vanish on x, we define $P(x)$ as the tropical sum of the terms which have the greatest modulus. As an example, if $P(X) = 2 \odot X_1^{\odot 3} \odot X_2^{\odot 4} \oplus (\ominus 0) X_2$, then $P(1, \ominus 5) = 25$, $P(1, -5) = \ominus(-5)$, whereas P vanishes on $(1, -5/3)$. These definitions are motivated by the following immediate lemma, which shows that the structure laws of $\mathbb{T}_\pm$ are essentially the images of the ones of $\mathbb{K}$.

LEMMA 3.1. *Let*

$$\boldsymbol{P}(X) = \sum_{\alpha \in \Lambda} \boldsymbol{a}_\alpha X_1^{\alpha_1} \dots X_n^{\alpha_n} \in \mathbb{K}[X_1, \dots, X_n]$$

and let P *be defined as in* (4) *with* $a_\alpha := \mathsf{sval}(\boldsymbol{a}_\alpha)$. *Then, for all* $\boldsymbol{x} \in \mathbb{K}^n$,

$$\mathsf{sval}(\boldsymbol{P}(\boldsymbol{x})) = P(\mathsf{sval}(\boldsymbol{x})) ,$$

provided that P *does not vanish on* $\mathsf{sval}(\boldsymbol{x})$. □

Given a polynomial $\boldsymbol{P}$ as in Lemma 3.1, we denote by $\boldsymbol{P}^+$ the polynomial formed by the terms $\boldsymbol{a}_\alpha X_1^{\alpha_1} \dots X_n^{\alpha_n}$ such that $\boldsymbol{a}_\alpha > 0$. Similarly, $\boldsymbol{P}^-$ refers to the polynomial consisting of the terms $-\boldsymbol{a}_\alpha X_1^{\alpha_1} \dots X_n^{\alpha_n}$ verifying $\boldsymbol{a}_\alpha < 0$. In this way, $\boldsymbol{P} = \boldsymbol{P}^+ - \boldsymbol{P}^-$. We also use the analogues of these polynomials in the tropical setting. If P is the tropical polynomial given in (4), we define P^+ (resp. P^-) as the tropical polynomial generated by the terms $|a_\alpha| \odot X_1^{\odot \alpha_1} \odot \dots \odot X_n^{\odot \alpha_n}$ where $a_\alpha \in \mathbb{T}_+$ (resp. $\mathbb{T}_-$). Observe that the quantities $P^+(x)$ and $P^-(x)$ are well defined for all $x \in \mathbb{T}^n$, since the tropical polynomials P^+ and P^- only involve tropically positive coefficients.

Throughout the paper, we denote the set $\{1, \dots, k\}$ by $[k]$.

3.2 Tropicalization of Nonarchimedean Spectrahedra

We now introduce the notion of tropical spectrahedra.

DEFINITION 3.2. *A set* $\mathcal{S} \subset \mathbb{T}^n$ *is said to be a* tropical spectrahedron *if there exists a spectrahedron* $\boldsymbol{\mathcal{S}} \subset \mathbb{K}^n_{\geqslant 0}$ *such that* $\mathcal{S} = \mathsf{val}(\boldsymbol{\mathcal{S}})$.

If $\mathcal{S} = \mathsf{val}(\boldsymbol{\mathcal{S}})$, then we refer to $\mathcal{S}$ as the *tropicalization* of the spectrahedron $\boldsymbol{\mathcal{S}}$, and $\boldsymbol{\mathcal{S}}$ is said to be a *lift (over the field* $\mathbb{K}$*)* of $\mathcal{S}$. Our approach to the problem of checking the triviality of a spectrahedron $\boldsymbol{\mathcal{S}} \subset \mathbb{K}^n_{\geqslant 0}$ consists in determining whether or not the corresponding tropical spectrahedron $\mathcal{S} = \mathsf{val}(\boldsymbol{\mathcal{S}})$ is *trivial*, i.e., is reduced to the singleton $\{(-\infty, \dots, -\infty)\}$. To this purpose, it is convenient to exploit some explicit description of the set $\mathcal{S}$. Recall that a symmetric matrix with entries in a real closed field is positive semidefinite if and only if every principal minor of the matrix is nonnegative. This property provides a description of $\boldsymbol{\mathcal{S}}$ by a system of polynomial inequalities of the form $\det \boldsymbol{Q}_{I \times I}(\boldsymbol{x}) \geqslant 0$, where I is a nonempty subset of $[m]$, and $\det \boldsymbol{Q}_{I \times I}(\boldsymbol{x})$ corresponds to the $(I \times I)$-minor of the matrix $\boldsymbol{Q}(\boldsymbol{x}) = \boldsymbol{x}_1 \boldsymbol{Q}^{(1)} + \dots + \boldsymbol{x}_n \boldsymbol{Q}^{(n)}$. Following this, we obtain that the tropical spectrahedron $\mathcal{S}$ is included in the intersection of the images of the sets $\{\boldsymbol{x} \in \mathbb{K}^n_{\geqslant 0} \colon \det \boldsymbol{Q}_{I \times I}(\boldsymbol{x}) \geqslant 0\}$ under the valuation map. Unfortunately, this inclusion may be strict, see [3, Example 15] for an example in which $\mathcal{S}$ is a polyhedron.

Section 3.2.1 deals with a class of tropical spectrahedra for which we overcome this difficulty, and obtain an explicit description. It turns out that this description only involves the tropical counterpart of the nonnegativity constraints on minors of order 1 and 2. In Section 3.2.2, we show that this kind of description is valid for the tropicalization of a large class of spectrahedra, for which the valuation of the coefficients of the matrices $\boldsymbol{Q}^{(k)}$ satisfy a genericity condition. Section 3.2.2 also provides an illustration of these results on the spectrahedron introduced in Section 2.

3.2.1 Tropical Metzler Spectrahedra

Recall that a matrix A is called *(negated) Metzler matrix* if its off-diagonal coefficients are nonpositive. Similarly, we say that a matrix $M \in \mathbb{T}_\pm^{m \times m}$ is a *tropical Metzler matrix* if $M_{ij} \in \mathbb{T}_- \cup \{-\infty\}$ for all $i \neq j$. Let $Q^{(1)}, \dots, Q^{(n)} \in \mathbb{T}_\pm^{m \times m}$ be symmetric tropical Metzler matrices. Given $i, j \in [m]$, we refer to $Q_{ij}(X)$ as the tropical polynomial:

$$Q_{ij}(X) := Q_{ij}^{(1)} \odot X_1 \oplus \dots \oplus Q_{ij}^{(n)} \odot X_n .$$

We define the *tropical Metzler spectrahedron* associated with $Q^{(1)}, \dots, Q^{(n)}$ as the set $\mathcal{S}$ of the points $x \in \mathbb{T}^n$ that fulfill the following two conditions:

- for all $i \in [m]$, $Q_{ii}^+(x) \geqslant Q_{ii}^-(x)$;
- for all $i, j \in [m]$, $i < j$, $Q_{ii}^+(x) \odot Q_{jj}^+(x) \geqslant (Q_{ij}(x))^{\odot 2}$.

Observe that the term $Q_{ij}(x)$ $(i \neq j)$ is well defined for any $x \in \mathbb{T}^n$ thanks to the Metzler property of the matrices $Q^{(k)}$.

With standard notation, the constraints defining the set $\mathcal{S}$ respectively read: for all $i \in [m]$,

$$\max_{Q_{ii}^{(k)} \in \mathbb{T}_+} (Q_{ii}^{(k)} + x_k) \geqslant \max_{Q_{ii}^{(l)} \in \mathbb{T}_-} (|Q_{ii}^{(l)}| + x_l) , \tag{5}$$

and for all $i, j \in [m]$ such that $i < j$,

$$\max_{Q_{ii}^{(k)} \in \mathbb{T}_+} (Q_{ii}^{(k)} + x_k) + \max_{Q_{jj}^{(k')} \in \mathbb{T}_+} (Q_{jj}^{(k')} + x_{k'}) \geqslant 2 \max_{l \in [n]} (|Q_{ij}^{(l)}| + x_l) . \tag{6}$$

The next theorem ensures that $\mathcal{S}$ is indeed a tropical spectrahedron. To this purpose, we explicitly construct a spectrahedron $\boldsymbol{\mathcal{S}} \subset \mathbb{K}^n_{\geqslant 0}$ verifying $\mathsf{val}(\boldsymbol{\mathcal{S}}) = \mathcal{S}$.

THEOREM 3.3. *The set* $\mathcal{S}$ *is a tropical spectrahedron.*

We next sketch the proof of this theorem. We define the matrices $\boldsymbol{Q}^{(1)}, \dots, \boldsymbol{Q}^{(n)} \in \mathbb{K}^{m \times m}$ as follows:

- if $Q_{ij}^{(k)} \in \mathbb{T}_-$, then we set $\boldsymbol{Q}_{ij}^{(k)} := -t^{|Q_{ij}^{(k)}|}$;
- if $Q_{ij}^{(k)} \in \mathbb{T}_+$ (which, under our assumptions, can happen only if $i = j$), then $\boldsymbol{Q}_{ij}^{(k)} := mnt^{Q_{ij}^{(k)}}$;
- if $Q_{ij}^{(k)} = -\infty$, then $\boldsymbol{Q}_{ij}^{(k)} := 0$.

We consider the spectrahedron $\boldsymbol{\mathcal{S}} := \{\boldsymbol{x} \in \mathbb{K}^n_{\geqslant 0} \colon \boldsymbol{Q}(\boldsymbol{x}) \succcurlyeq 0\}$. It is easy to see that $\mathsf{val}(\boldsymbol{\mathcal{S}}) \subset \mathcal{S}$. To show the opposite inclusion, we introduce the following set

$$\boldsymbol{\mathcal{S}}' = \Big\{\boldsymbol{x} \in \mathbb{K}^n_{\geqslant 0} \colon \forall i, \boldsymbol{Q}(\boldsymbol{x})_{ii} \geqslant 0 , \\ \forall i \neq j, \boldsymbol{Q}(\boldsymbol{x})_{ii} \boldsymbol{Q}(\boldsymbol{x})_{jj} \geqslant (m-1)^2 (\boldsymbol{Q}(\boldsymbol{x})_{ij})^2 \Big\}$$

and show that $\mathcal{S} \subset \mathsf{val}(\boldsymbol{\mathcal{S}}')$. The following elementary lemma implies that $\boldsymbol{\mathcal{S}}' \subset \boldsymbol{\mathcal{S}}$.

LEMMA 3.4. *Let* $\boldsymbol{A} \in \mathbb{K}^{m \times m}$ *be a symmetric matrix. Suppose that* $\boldsymbol{A}$ *has nonnegative entries on its diagonal and that the inequality* $\boldsymbol{A}_{ii} \boldsymbol{A}_{jj} \geqslant (m-1)^2 \boldsymbol{A}_{ij}^2$ *holds for all pairs* (i, j) *such that* $i \neq j$. *Then* $\boldsymbol{A}$ *is positive semidefinite.*

3.2.2 Tropicalization of Nonarchimedean Spectrahedra in the Generic Case

Theorem 3.3 and its proof exhibits a construction of a lift $\boldsymbol{\mathcal{S}} = \{\boldsymbol{x} \in \mathbb{K}^n_{\geqslant 0} \colon \boldsymbol{Q}(\boldsymbol{x}) \succcurlyeq 0\}$. This lift is obtained by taking matrices $\boldsymbol{Q}^{(k)}$ such that $\mathsf{sval}(\boldsymbol{Q}^{(k)}) = Q^{(k)}$. However, we have chosen the entries of these matrices in a careful way to ensure that $\mathsf{val}(\boldsymbol{\mathcal{S}}) = \mathcal{S}$. It is natural to ask if the latter relation still holds for other choices of the coefficients $\boldsymbol{Q}_{ij}^{(k)}$. Said in a different way, we aim at identifying a larger class of spectrahedra $\boldsymbol{\mathcal{S}}$ whose tropicalization is described by the constraints (5) and (6) defining $\mathcal{S}$. The next theorem states that if the entries $Q_{ij}^{(k)}$ of the tropical matrices satisfy a certain genericity condition, then the tropicalization of *any* spectrahedron $\boldsymbol{\mathcal{S}} = \{\boldsymbol{x} \in \mathbb{K}_{\geqslant 0}^n : \boldsymbol{Q}(\boldsymbol{x}) \succcurlyeq 0\}$ satisfying $\mathsf{sval}(\boldsymbol{Q}^{(k)}) = Q^{(k)}$ is given by the set $\mathcal{S}$. Our genericity condition has two components: first, we assume that each matrix $Q^{(k)}$ has *nondegenerate tropical minors of order two*. In other words, we suppose that $Q_{ii}^{(k)} + Q_{jj}^{(k)} \neq 2|Q_{ij}^{(k)}|$ for every $i \neq j$ such that $Q_{ii}^{(k)}$ and $Q_{jj}^{(k)}$ belong to $\mathbb{T}_+$. This ensures that the closure of the interior of $\mathcal{S} \cap \mathbb{R}^n$ lies inside $\mathsf{val}(\boldsymbol{\mathcal{S}} \cap \mathbb{K}_{>0}^n)$. Therefore, the claim is true if we further assume that *every stratum of $\mathcal{S}$ is regular*, i.e., that for every nonempty set $K \subset [n]$, the tropical Metzler spectrahedron associated with $(Q^{(k)})_{k \in K}$, denoted $\mathcal{S}_K$, fulfills the equality $\mathcal{S}_K \cap \mathbb{R}^{|K|} = \mathrm{cl}(\mathrm{int}(\mathcal{S}_K \cap \mathbb{R}^{|K|}))$. This is generically true and constitutes the second part of our condition.

THEOREM 3.5. *Suppose that for every k the matrix $Q^{(k)}$ has nondegenerate tropical minors of order two. Moreover, suppose that every stratum of $\mathcal{S}$ is regular. Then $\mathsf{val}(\boldsymbol{\mathcal{S}}) = \mathcal{S}$ for every spectrahedron $\boldsymbol{\mathcal{S}} = \{\boldsymbol{x} \in \mathbb{K}_{\geqslant 0}^n : \boldsymbol{Q}(\boldsymbol{x}) \succcurlyeq 0\}$ such that $\mathsf{sval}(\boldsymbol{Q}^{(k)}) = Q^{(k)}$.*

LEMMA 3.6. *Let $d = nm(m+1)/2$. There exists a finite set of hyperplanes in $\mathbb{R}^d$ such that, if the vector with entries $|Q_{ij}^{(k)}|$ (for $i \leqslant j$) is in $\mathbb{R}^d$ and belongs to none of these hyperplanes, then the assumptions of Theorem 3.5 are fulfilled.*

Let us illustrate the results of this section on the spectrahedron defined in Section 2. The corresponding tropical matrices $Q^{(1)}, Q^{(2)}, Q^{(3)} \in \mathbb{T}^{3\times 3}$ are of Metzler type, and the associated tropical Metzler spectrahedron $\mathcal{S}$ is defined by the constraints:

$$\begin{aligned} \max(-1 + x_1, -5/4 + x_3) &\geqslant x_2 \\ \max(x_1 + x_3, -1/4 + 2x_3) &\geqslant 2x_1 \\ x_2 &\geqslant -7/4 + x_3 \\ \max(5/4 + x_1 + x_2, 1 + x_2 + x_3) &\geqslant 2x_3 \end{aligned}$$

The first inequality comes from (5) with $i = 2$, and the last three constraints from (6).[2] The intersection of $\mathcal{S}$ with the hyperplane $x_3 = 0$ is depicted on Figure 2. It can be checked that $\mathcal{S}$ fulfills the conditions of Theorem 3.5, so that the tropicalization of the spectrahedron of Section 2 is precisely described by the four inequalities given above.

4. TROPICAL SPECTRAHEDRA AND STOCHASTIC GAMES

4.1 Stochastic Mean Payoff Games

In this section, we present the class of games which is related to nonarchimedean semidefinite feasibility problems. For simplicity, we refer to them as stochastic mean payoff games, although as we shall see, this terminology usually corresponds to a larger class of games. This abuse of language is justified by the fact that the associated decision problems are poly-time equivalent, as discussed below.

[2]The constraints of the form (5) with $i = 1, 3$ are trivial.

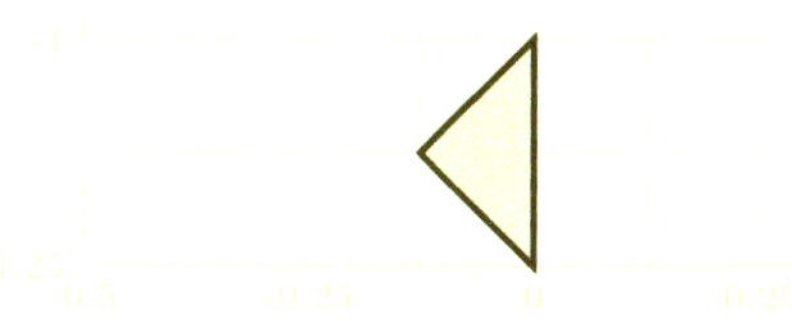

Figure 2: The tropicalization of the spectrahedron of Section 2.

In our setting, a *stochastic mean payoff game* involves two players, Max and Min, which control disjoint sets of states. The states owned by Max and Min are respectively indexed by elements of $[m]$ and $[n]$. We will use the symbols i, j to refer to states of Player Max, and k, l to states of Player Min. Both players alternatively move a pawn over these states as follows. When the pawn is on a state $k \in [n]$, Player Min chooses an action $a \in A^{(k)}$, which is defined as a subset of states of Max of cardinality 1 or 2: if $a = \{i\}$, then the pawn is moved to the state i, while if $a = \{i, j\}$ with $i \neq j$, it is moved to the state i (resp. j) with probability 1/2. In both cases, Player Max receives from Player Min a reward denoted by r_k^a. Once the pawn is on a state $i \in [m]$, Player Max picks an action $b \in B^{(i)}$, where b is a subset of states of Min of cardinality 1. Then, Player Max moves the pawn to the state l such that $b = \{l\}$, and Player Min pays him a payment denoted by r_i^b.

We suppose that Player Min starts the game and that players can always make the next move, i.e., that $A^{(k)} \neq \emptyset$ and $B^{(i)} \neq \emptyset$ for all $i \in [m]$ and $k \in [n]$.

A *policy for Player Min* is a function mapping every state $k \in [n]$ to an action $\sigma(k)$ in $A^{(k)}$. Analogously, a *policy for Player Max* is a function τ such that $\tau(i) \in B^{(i)}$ for all $i \in [m]$. Suppose that the game starts from a state k^* of Player Min. When players play according to a couple (σ, τ) of policies, the movement of the pawn is described by a Markov chain. The average payoff of Player Max in the long-term is then defined as:

$$g_{k^*}(\sigma, \tau) = \lim_{N \to \infty} \mathbb{E}_{\sigma,\tau}\Big(\frac{1}{2N}\sum_{p=1}^{N}\big(r_{k_p}^{\sigma(k_p)} + r_{i_p}^{\tau(i_p)}\big)\Big)\,, \quad (7)$$

where the expectation $\mathbb{E}_{\sigma,\tau}$ is taken over all the trajectories $k_1, i_1, k_2, \ldots, i_p$ starting from $k_1 = k^*$ in the Markov chain.[3] The goal of Player Max is to find a policy which maximizes his average payoff, while Player Min aims at minimizing this quantity. The basic theorem of stochastic mean payoff games is the existence of "optimal" policies for both players. This was first proven by Liggett and Lippman [16].

THEOREM 4.1. *There exists a pair of policies $(\bar{\sigma}, \bar{\tau})$ and a unique vector $\chi \in \mathbb{R}^n$ such that for all initial states $k \in [n]$, the following two conditions are satisfied:*

- *for each policy σ of Player Min, $\chi_k \leqslant g_k(\sigma, \bar{\tau})$;*
- *for each policy τ of Player Max, $\chi_k \geqslant g_k(\bar{\sigma}, \tau)$.*

The vector χ in Theorem 4.1 is referred to as the *value* of the game. Note that for every k, the quantity χ_k coincides with

[3]The limit in (7) can be shown to exist by the ergodic theorem.

average payoff $g_k(\bar\sigma, \bar\tau)$ associated with the couple of policies $(\bar\sigma, \bar\tau)$. The first condition in Theorem 4.1 states that, by playing according to the policy $\bar\tau$, Player Max is certain to get an average payoff greater than or equal to the value χ_k associated with the initial state. Symmetrically, Player Min is ensured to limit her average loss to the quantity χ_k by following the policy $\bar\sigma$.

A state $k \in [n]$ is said to be *winning (for Player Max)* if the value χ_k of the game starting from the initial state k is nonnegative. We denote by SMPG the following decision problem: "given a stochastic mean payoff game, does there exist an initial state which is winning for Player Max?" It can be shown that if a policy of one player is fixed, then the remaining 1-player game can be solved in polynomial time by linear programming [11, Section 2.9]. This readily implies that SMPG is in NP $\cap$ coNP. However, as discussed in the introduction, the question whether there exists a poly-time algorithm to solve this problem is open.

REMARK 4.2. In the literature, stochastic mean payoff games correspond to a larger class of problems [5]. These general games admit a value and optimal policies as well. It turns out that the associated decision problem is poly-time equivalent to the problem SMPG defined above. Moreover, these decision problems are poly-time equivalent to the problem of computing the value and a pair of optimal policies.

One of the possible approaches to analyze stochastic mean payoff games is to introduce the associated *Shapley operator*, which is a map F from $\mathbb{R}^n$ to itself defined as:

$$(F(x))_k = \min_{\substack{a \in A^{(k)} \\ a=\{i,j\}}} \Big(r_k^a + \frac{1}{2}\big(\max_{\substack{b\in B^{(i)} \\ b=\{l\}}} (r_i^b + x_l) + \max_{\substack{b\in B^{(j)} \\ b=\{l\}}} (r_j^b + x_l)\big)\Big) ,$$

where we use the convention that $i = j$ when $a \in A^{(i)}$ is the singleton $\{i\}$. This map naturally extends to a self-map of $\mathbb{T}^n$, by setting $\frac{1}{2}(-\infty) = -\infty$.

The vectors x such that $x \leqslant F(x)$ may be thought of as nonlinear analogues of subharmonic functions. The existence of such a nontrivial vector x was shown in [2] to be equivalent to the property that the mean payoff game has at least one winning state, in the case of deterministic games. The approach of [2] is based in particular on a nonlinear fixed point theorem (Collatz-Wielandt theorem). The same arguments lead to the following result in the case of stochastic games.

THEOREM 4.3. *Player Max has at least one winning initial state if and only if the set $\{x \in \mathbb{T}^n : x \leqslant F(x)\}$ is nontrivial (i.e., contains a point different than $(-\infty, \dots, -\infty)$).*

4.2 Equivalence between Stochastic Games and Tropical Metzler Spectrahedra

We now describe the connection between tropical spectrahedra and stochastic mean payoff games. Let us consider a tropical Metzler spectrahedron $\mathcal{S}$ associated with the matrices $Q^{(1)}, \dots, Q^{(n)} \in \mathbb{T}_\pm^{m\times m}$. We construct a stochastic mean payoff game Γ consisting of m states of Max and n states of Min. For each state $k \in [n]$ of Player Min, the set $A^{(k)}$ consists of:

- the actions $\{i\}$ with payment $-|Q_{ii}^{(k)}|$ for all $i \in [m]$ such that $Q_{ii}^{(k)} \in \mathbb{T}_-$;
- the actions $\{i,j\}$ with payment $-|Q_{ij}^{(k)}|$ for all $i < j$ such that $Q_{ij}^{(k)} \in \mathbb{T}_-$.

For every state $i \in [m]$ of Player Max, the set $B^{(i)}$ is formed by the actions $\{k\}$ with payment $Q_{ii}^{(k)}$ for all states $k \in [n]$ satisfying $Q_{ii}^{(k)} \in \mathbb{T}_+$.

Recall that in the games which we consider, every state has to be equipped with at least one action, i.e., the sets $A^{(k)}$ and $B^{(i)}$ must be nonempty. In consequence, our construction is valid provided that the following assumption on the matrices $Q^{(k)}$ is satisfied:

ASSUMPTION A. *(a) For all $k \in [n]$, the matrix $Q^{(k)}$ has at least one coefficient in $\mathbb{T}_-$.*
(b) For all $i \in [m]$, there exists $k \in [n]$ such that the diagonal coefficient $Q_{ii}^{(k)}$ belongs to $\mathbb{T}_+$.

Concerning the nontriviality of tropical spectrahedra, Assumption A can be made without loss of generality, up to extracting submatrices from $Q^{(k)}$ or eliminating some of them.

The relationship between the tropical spectrahedron $\mathcal{S}$ and the game Γ is given by the following lemma:

LEMMA 4.4. *Let $F\colon \mathbb{T}^n \to \mathbb{T}^n$ be the Shapley operator associated with Γ. Then, $\mathcal{S} = \{x \in \mathbb{T}^n : x \leqslant F(x)\}$.*

PROOF. By construction of the game Γ, a vector $x \in \mathbb{T}^n$ satisfies $x \leqslant F(x)$ if and only if for all $k \in [n]$,

$$x_k \leqslant \min_{Q_{ij}^{(k)} \in \mathbb{T}_-} \Big(-|Q_{ij}^{(k)}| + \frac{1}{2}\big(\max_{Q_{ii}^{(l)} \in \mathbb{T}_+} (Q_{ii}^{(l)} + x_l) + \max_{Q_{jj}^{(l)} \in \mathbb{T}_+} (Q_{jj}^{(l)} + x_l)\big)\Big) ,$$

or, equivalently, for all $i, j \in [m]$,

$$2\big(\max_{Q_{ij}^{(k)} \in \mathbb{T}_-} (|Q_{ij}^{(k)}| + x_k)\big) \leqslant \max_{Q_{ii}^{(l)} \in \mathbb{T}_+} (Q_{ii}^{(l)} + x_l) + \max_{Q_{jj}^{(l)} \in \mathbb{T}_+} (Q_{jj}^{(l)} + x_l) .$$

By distinguishing whether i and j are equal in these inequalities, we recover the constraints given in (5) and (6). □

Then, from Theorem 4.3 and Lemma 4.4, we obtain:

COROLLARY 4.5. *The tropical spectrahedron $\mathcal{S}$ is nontrivial if and only if the stochastic game Γ has at least one winning initial state.*

Along the same lines, we can reciprocally associate a tropical spectrahedron with any stochastic game. In more details, starting from a stochastic game Γ specified as in Section 4.1, we construct symmetric Metzler matrices $Q^{(1)}, \dots, Q^{(n)} \in \mathbb{T}_\pm^{m\times m}$ from the actions of the players. We define $Q_{ij}^{(k)} = Q_{ji}^{(k)} := \ominus(-r_k^a)$ for all $k \in [n]$ and $i, j \in [m]$ such that $i \neq j$ and $a = \{i, j\}$ is an available action of Player Min at the state k. Diagonal coefficients of the matrices $Q^{(k)}$ are defined according to whether the actions $a := \{i\}$ and $b := \{k\}$ are available from the states k and i respectively:

- if $a \in A^{(k)}$ and $b \notin B^{(i)}$, we set $Q_{ii}^{(k)} := \ominus(-r_k^a)$, while if $b \in B^{(i)}$ and $a \notin A^{(k)}$, we define $Q_{ii}^{(k)} := r_i^b$;
- if both actions a and b occur simultaneously, we set $Q_{ii}^{(k)}$ to $\ominus(-r_k^a)$ if $(-r_k^a) > r_i^b$, and to r_i^b if $r_i^b \geqslant (-r_k^a)$.

Finally, all the other entries of the matrices $Q^{(k)}$ are set to $-\infty$. With this construction, it can be verified that Lemma 4.4 and, subsequently, Corollary 4.5 are still valid.

We denote by TMSDFP the tropical Metzler semidefinite feasibility problem: "given symmetric tropical Metzler matrices $Q^{(1)}, \dots, Q^{(n)} \in \mathbb{T}_{\pm}^{m\times m}$ satisfying Assumption A, is the associated tropical Metzler spectrahedron trivial?" As a consequence of Corollary 4.5, we obtain the equivalence between the two decision problems SMPG and TMSDFP. This equivalence can be refined thanks to the fact that SMPG restricted to games with payments equal to 0 or ± 1 is poly-time equivalent to SMPG for arbitrary payments. This yields the following result:

COROLLARY 4.6. *The problems* SMPG *and* TMSDFP *are poly-time equivalent. Furthermore, if either of these problems can be solved in pseudopolynomial time, then both of them can be solved in polynomial time.*

4.3 Algorithms for Tropical Metzler Semidefinite Feasibility Problem

In this section, we discuss algorithms that can solve TMSDFP thanks to the equivalence with SMPG established in Corollary 4.6. Let L denote the maximal number of bits needed to encode an entry from matrices $Q^{(1)}, \dots, Q^{(n)}$. An exponential bound for TMSDFP is achieved by a naive algorithm that enumerates all policies of one player and uses linear programming to solve the remaining 1-player game.

THEOREM 4.7. *There is an algorithm that solves* TMSDFP *in* $\min\{n^m, m^{2n}\}\mathrm{Poly}(n, m, L)$ *arithmetic operations.*

The best currently known bound for TMSDFP can be derived from the randomized subexponential algorithm of Halman [14]. The distinctive feature of this algorithm is that it works in *strongly* subexponential time, i.e., its arithmetic complexity does not depend on L.

THEOREM 4.8. *There exists a randomized algorithm that solves* TMSDFP *in expected* $\exp(O(\sqrt{(m+n)}\log(m+n)))$ *arithmetic operations.*

We next illustrate our approach by benchmarks. We rely here on an algorithm with poorer theoretical bounds, but which is well adapted practically to some large scale instances: value iteration. This algorithm may be thought of as a nonlinear analogue of the power algorithm to compute the dominant eigenvalue of a matrix. Its advantage lies in scalability. This leads to a procedure called CHECKFEASIBILITY, provided in Figure 3 and which checks the triviality of a tropical spectrahedron. We next establish the validity of this algorithm in a special situation.

PROPOSITION 4.9. *Assume that* $Q^{(1)}, \dots, Q^{(n)}$ *have finite entries. Then, the mean payoff of the associated game* Γ *is independent of the initial state. Suppose in addition that this mean payoff differs from* 0. *Then, for all choices of* $\varepsilon > 0$, *the procedure* CHECKFEASIBILITY *terminates and is correct.*

Note that the situation in which the mean payoff is zero is degenerate: then, an infinitesimal perturbation of the entries can make the spectrahedron trivial or nontrivial. Value iteration cannot naturally handle such degenerate situations, which can be solved by different methods like the policy iteration algorithm of [1] (with an implementation in exact arithmetics). Every iteration (while loop) of the procedure CHECKFEASIBILITY takes a time $O(nm^2)$, which is *linear* in the size of the input. The number of iterations can only be bounded by an exponential in the size of the input. However, our benchmarks indicate that the algorithm is fast when the instance is "far from being degenerate".

procedure CHECKFEASIBILITY($Q^{(1)}, \dots, Q^{(n)}$, ε)
 ▷ $Q^{(1)}, \dots, Q^{(n)} \in \mathbb{T}_{\pm}^{m\times m}$, *Metzler matrices satisfying Assumption A,* $\varepsilon > 0$ *a numerical precision.*
 $u := 0 \in \mathbb{R}^n$, $v := 0 \in \mathbb{R}^n$
 while $\max_k u_k > -\varepsilon$ and $\min_k u_k < \varepsilon$ **do**
  $v := \max(v, u)$, $u := F(u)$
  ▷ *F is the Shapley operator of the game Γ associated to* $Q^{(1)}, \dots, Q^{(n)}$. *The operation max on vectors is understood entrywise.*
 done
 if $\max_k u_k \leqslant -\varepsilon$ **then**
  The tropical spectrahedron is trivial.
 else
  The vector v belongs to the tropical spectrahedron.
 end
end

Figure 3: Checking the feasibility of a tropical semidefinite problem by value iteration.

(n,m)	$(50,10)$	$(50,40)$	$(50,50)$	$(50,100)$	$(50,1000)$
time	0.000065	0.000049	0.000077	0.000279	0.026802
(n,m)	$(100,10)$	$(100,15)$	$(100,80)$	$(100,100)$	$(100,1000)$
time	0.000025	0.000270	0.000366	0.000656	0.053944
(n,m)	$(1000,10)$	$(1000,50)$	$(1000,100)$	$(1000,200)$	$(1000,500)$
time	0.000233	0.073544	0.015305	0.027762	0.148714
(n,m)	$(2000,10)$	$(2000,70)$	$(2000,100)$	$(10000,150)$	$(10000,400)$
time	0.000487	1.852221	0.087536	19.919844	2.309174

Table 1: Execution time (in sec.) of Procedure CHECKFEASIBILITY **on random instances.**

EXAMPLE 4.10. *Procedure* CHECKFEASIBILITY *applied to the nonarchimedean spectrahedron of Section 2, with* $\varepsilon = 10^{-8}$, *terminates in 20 iterations. It returns a vector*

$$v = (1.05612\dots, 0.0204082\dots, 1.12755\dots)$$

which lies in the interior of the tropical spectrahedron shown in Figure 2. The rounded vector $(1.06, 0.02, 1.13)$ *is also in the interior, and* $\boldsymbol{x} := (t^{1.06}, t^{0.02}, t^{1.13})$ *fulfills* $\boldsymbol{Q}(\boldsymbol{x}) \succcurlyeq 0$.

We report in Table 1 experimental results for different values of (n,m). We chose all the $|Q_{ij}^{(k)}|$, for $i \leqslant j$, to be independent random variables uniformly distributed on $[0,1]$. Moreover, the diagonal coefficients $Q_{ii}^{(k)}$ were chosen to have a positive tropical sign. We took $\varepsilon = 10^{-8}$ (the performance was similar for $\varepsilon = 10^{-6}$ or $\varepsilon = 10^{-10}$). Our experiments were obtained using a C program, distributed as an ancillary file attached to the arXiv preprint [4] for reproducibility purposes. This program was compiled under Linux with gcc -O3, and executed on a single core of an Intel(R) i7-4600U CPU at 2.10GHz with 16GB RAM. We report the average execution time over 10 samples for every value of (n,m). The number of iterations did not exceed 731 on this benchmark, and, for most (n,m), it was limited to a few units. Indeed, random instances exhibit experimentally a phase transition: for a given (n,m), the system is either feasible with overwhelming probability, or infeasible with overwhelming probability, unless (n,m) lies in a tiny region of the parameter space. Value iteration quickly decides feasibility, except in regions close to the phase transition. As a result, the execution time does not increase monotonically with (n,m).

REMARK 4.11. By Theorem 3.5, the procedure CHECK-FEASIBILITY allows us to verify the feasibility of a Metzler nonarchimedean spectrahedron if the *genericity* condition of this theorem is satisfied. However, even when this genericity condition is not satisfied, the same procedure can be shown to check correctly the feasibility of the nonarchimedean problem assuming that the value of the mean payoff game Γ *differs from zero.*

5. CONCLUDING REMARKS

In this paper, we have shown that under a genericity condition on the valuations, solving feasibility semidefinite problems over the field of Puiseux series, in which the input matrices have a Metzler sign pattern, reduces to a well studied class of zero-sum stochastic games. This leads both to complexity bounds and to algorithms capable experimentally to solve large scale nonarchimedean instances. The interest is also to relate two different problems with unsettled complexities. This is the first exposition of this approach. Let us now point some limitations of our current results, together with possible developments of this work.

First, the present approach can be extended to handle non-Metzler sign patterns. However, the description of tropical spectrahedra is more involved in this case.

Moreover, it would be interesting to provide a characterization of all (not necessarily generic) tropical spectrahedra. Such a characterization is known for tropical polyhedra, and is given by the tropical Minkowski-Weyl theorem (see [10, Prop. 2.1] and [13, Th. 2]). Unfortunately, the proof relies on the classical Minkowski-Weyl theorem, which has no known analogue for spectrahedra. Currently, we are unable to give a full characterization of tropical spectrahedra.

Finally, an interesting question is to use the present approach to deal with the real case, i.e., to see t as a deformation parameter and use the fact that the semidefinite feasibility problem is easily solvable for a large parameter t, to infer the solvability for smaller values of t. However, we expect exponential bounds on the bit size of t to guarantee that the deformed feasibility problem and the nonarchimedean feasibility problem have the same answer.

6. ACKNOWLEDGMENTS

We thank the referees for their detailed comments.

7. REFERENCES

[1] M. Akian, J. Cochet-Terrasson, S. Detournay, and S. Gaubert. Solving multichain stochastic games with mean payoff by policy iteration. In *IEEE 52nd Annual Conference on Decision and Control (CDC)*, 2013.

[2] M. Akian, S. Gaubert, and A. Guterman. Tropical polyhedra are equivalent to mean payoff games. *Int. J. Algebra Comput.*, 22(1), 2012.

[3] X. Allamigeon, P. Benchimol, S. Gaubert, and M. Joswig. Tropicalizing the simplex algorithm. *SIAM Journal on Discrete Mathematics*, 29(2), 2015.

[4] X. Allamigeon, S. Gaubert, and M. Skomra. Solving generic nonarchimedean semidefinite programs using stochastic game algorithms. arXiv:1603.06916, Extended version of the present paper, 2016.

[5] D. Andersson and P. Miltersen. The complexity of solving stochastic games on graphs. In *Proceedings of ISAAC'09*, number 5878 in LNCS. Springer, 2009.

[6] F. Bihan. Viro method for the construction of real complete intersections. *Adv. Math.*, 169(2), 2002.

[7] G. Blekherman, P. Parrilo, and T. Rekha. *Semidefinite Optimization and Convex Algebraic Geometry.* MOS-SIAM Series on Optimization. SIAM, 2013.

[8] P. Butkovič. *Max-linear systems: theory and algorithms.* Springer Monographs in Mathematics. Springer-Verlag London, Ltd., London, 2010.

[9] E. de Klerk and F. Vallentin. On the Turing model complexity of interior point methods for semidefinite programming. arXiv:1507.03549, 2015.

[10] M. Develin and J. Yu. Tropical polytopes and cellular resolutions. *Experimental Mathematics*, 16(3), 2007.

[11] J. Filar and K. Vrieze. *Competitive Markov Decision Processes.* Springer, 2007.

[12] B. Gärtner and J. Matoušek. *Approximation algorithms and semidefinite programming.* Springer, 2012.

[13] S. Gaubert and R. Katz. Minimal half-spaces and external representation of tropical polyhedra. *Journal of Algebraic Combinatorics*, 33(3):325–348, 2011.

[14] N. Halman. Simple stochastic games, parity games, mean payoff games and discounted payoff games are all LP-type problems. *Algorithmica*, 49(1):37–50, 2007.

[15] D. Henrion, S. Naldi, and M. Safey El Din. Exact algorithms for linear matrix inequalities. arXiv:1508.03715, 2015.

[16] T. Liggett and S. Lippman. Stochastic games with perfect information and time average payoff. *SIAM Review*, 11(4):604–607, 1969.

[17] D. Maclagan and B. Sturmfels. *Introduction to tropical geometry*, volume 161 of *Graduate Studies in Mathematics.* American Mathematical Society, 2015.

[18] T. Markwig. A field of generalized Puiseux series for tropical geometry. *Rendiconti del Seminario Matematico, Università e Politecnico di Torino*, 68(1):79–92, 2010.

[19] N. Megiddo. On the complexity of linear programming. In *Advances in economic theory*, volume 12 of *Econom. Soc. Monogr.* CUP, 1989.

[20] D. Monniaux and P. Corbineau. On the generation of Positivstellensatz witnesses in degenerate cases. In *Proceedings of ITP'11*, pages 249–264, 2011.

[21] J. Nie, K. Ranestad, and B. Sturmfels. The algebraic degree of semidefinite programming. *Math. Program.*, 122(2, Ser. A):379–405, 2010.

[22] M. Ramana. An exact duality theory for semidefinite programming and its complexity implications. *Mathematical Programming*, 77(1):129–162, 1997.

[23] C. Scheiderer. Sums of squares of polynomials with rational coefficients. *J. European Math. Soc.*, 2013.

[24] S. A. Steinberg. *Lattice-ordered rings and modules.* Springer, New York, 2010.

[25] B. Sturmfels. Viro's theorem for complete intersections. *Ann. Scuola Norm. Sup. Pisa Cl. Sci. (4)*, 21(3):377–386, 1994.

[26] O. Y. Viro. Real plane algebraic curves: constructions with controlled topology. *Algebra i Analiz*, 1(5), 1989.

[27] J. Yu. Tropicalizing the positive semidefinite cone. *Proc. Amer. Math. Soc*, 143(5):1891–1895, 2015.

Computing Limits of Real Multivariate Rational Functions

Parisa Alvandi
ORCCA, University of Western Ontario, London, Ontario, Canada
palvandi@uwo.ca

Mahsa Kazemi
Isfahan University of Technology, Isfahan, Iran
mahsa.kazemi@math.iut.ac.ir

Marc Moreno Maza
ORCCA, University of Western Ontario, London, Ontario, Canada
moreno@csd.uwo.ca

ABSTRACT

We present an algorithm for determining the existence of the limit of a real multivariate rational function q at a given point which is an isolated zero of the denominator of q. When the limit exists, the algorithm computes it, without making any assumption on the number of variables.

A process, which extends the work of Cadavid, Molina and Vélez, reduces the multivariate setting to computing limits of bivariate rational functions. By using regular chain theory and triangular decomposition of semi-algebraic systems, we avoid the computation of singular loci and the decomposition of algebraic sets into irreducible components.

Keywords

Limits of multivariate rational functions; regular chains; real algebraic sets

1. INTRODUCTION

Computing limits of functions is a basic task in multivariate calculus and many fundamental mathematical concepts are defined in terms of such limits. The case of univariate functions, including transcendental ones, has been well studied [7, 8, 12] and the corresponding algorithms are available in popular computer algebra systems. Surprisingly, the case of multivariate rational functions (i.e. quotients of polynomials) is still an active research area. Undergraduate students learn heuristics, like the adaptation of *L'hospital's rule* presented in [9] by G.R. Lawlor, but no general procedures for handling limits of multivariate rational functions.

Two recent papers have revitalized the search for such general procedures. In [15] S.J. Xiao and G.X. Zeng propose a first algorithm that, given a multivariate rational function $q \in \mathbb{Q}(X_1, \ldots, X_n)$, decides whether $\lim_{(x_1,\ldots,x_n)\to(0,\ldots,0)} q$ is zero or not. The "not-case" includes the situation where $\lim_{(x_1,\ldots,x_n)\to(0,\ldots,0)} q$ does not exist as well as the case where it exists but it is not zero. Their algorithm is based on the observation that the posed question can be phrased as a quantifier elimination problem, that the authors solve using triangular decomposition of algebraic systems, rational univariate representation as well as adjoining infinitesimal elements to the base field. A second algorithm and a result in the paper reduce the question of deciding whether $\lim_{(x_1,\ldots,x_n)\to(0,\ldots,0)} q$ exists or not (and computing it, when it exists) to calling the first algorithm.

In [2], C. Cadavid, S. Molina and J.D. Vélez propose an algorithm, now available in MAPLE as the `limit/multi` command, for determining the existence and possible value of limits of the form $\lim_{(x,y)\to(0,0)} q$, where q is a bivariate rational function, and such that $(0,0)$ is an isolated zero of the real algebraic set defined by the denominator of q. In a follow-up preprint [14], J.D. Vélez, P. Hernández and C. Cadavid extend the method of [2] to rational functions in three variables, still assuming that the origin is an isolated zero of the denominator. Both papers [2] and [14] rely on the key observation that, for determining the existence and possible value of limits of the form $\lim_{(x,y)\to(0,0)} q$ and $\lim_{(x,y,z)\to(0,0,0)} q$, it is sufficient to study *limits along a real algebraic set* $\chi(q)$, that is, limits of the form $\lim_{(x,y)\to(0,0),(x,y)\in\chi(q)} q$ and $\lim_{(x,y,z)\to(0,0,0),(x,y,z)\in\chi(q)} q$. This latter notion is defined in Section 3 of the present paper. In the three variable case, the method of [14] requires to compute the singular locus of $\chi(q)$ and the irreducible components of the algebraic set over $\mathbb{C}$ associated with $\chi(q)$.

The method of S.J. Xiao and G.X. Zeng [15] has the advantage of not making any assumptions on the number of variables nor the zero set of the denominator. Meanwhile, the works of C. Cadavid, S. Molina, J.D. Vélez and P. Hernández avoid the use of infinitesimal elements and rely on a deeper geometrical insight, through a notion of *discriminant variety*, see Notation 1; unfortunately, the recourse to singular loci and irreducible decomposition is a limitation in view of an implementation.

In this paper, we propose an algorithm for determining the existence and possible value of $\lim_{(x_1,\ldots,x_n)\to(0,\ldots,0)} q$, for an arbitrary number n of variables. As in [2] and [14], we assume that the origin is an isolated zero of the denominator of the rational function q. However, we avoid the computation of singular loci and decompositions into irreducible components of the real and complex algebraic sets involved in the method. Instead, we take advantage of the theory of regular chains and the RealTriangularize algorithm [4, 3] for decomposing semi-algebraic systems. The experimental results reported in Section 6 suggest that our algorithm can solve more problems than the algorithm of S.J. Xiao and G.X. Zeng, in particular when the number n of variables

ISSAC '16, July 19-22, 2016, Waterloo, ON, Canada

DOI: http://dx.doi.org/10.1145/2930889.2930938

increases. We illustrate our algorithm with two examples.

EXAMPLE 1. *Let* $q \in \mathbb{Q}(x,y,z,w)$ *be the rational function defined by* $q(x,y,z,w) = \frac{z\,w + x^2 + y^2}{x^2+y^2+z^2+w^2}$. *We aim at computing* $\lim_{(x,y,z,w)\to(0,0,0,0)} q$. *A first step of the procedure consists in calculating the real algebraic set* $\chi(q)$ *such that our limit problem reduces to compute* $\lim_{(x,y,z,w)\to(0,0,0,0),(x,y,z,w)\in\chi(q)} q$. *The set* $\chi(q)$*, defined in Notation 1, is obtained by the method of Lagrange multipliers, see Section 2.1 and the proof of Lemma 1. The* RealTriangularize *algorithm yields the following decomposition:* $\chi(q) = Z_{\mathbb{R}}(R_1) \cup Z_{\mathbb{R}}(R_2) \cup Z_{\mathbb{R}}(R_3) \cup Z_{\mathbb{R}}(R_4)$*, where* R_1, R_2, R_3, R_4 *are respectively given by the* regular semi-algebraic systems *(see Section 2.4 for this term):*

$$\left\{\begin{array}{l} x=0\\ y=0\\ z=0\\ w=0\end{array}\right., \left\{\begin{array}{l} z=0\\ w=0\end{array}\right., \left\{\begin{array}{l} x=0\\ y=0\\ z+w=0\end{array}\right. \text{ and } \left\{\begin{array}{l} x=0\\ y=0\\ z-w=0\end{array}\right. .$$

For our purpose of limit computation, only R_2, R_3, R_4 *are interesting, since they define either a curve or a surface passing through the origin, whereas* R_1 *is simply the origin.*

Computing the limit of q *along each of the curves* $Z_{\mathbb{R}}(R_3)$ *and* $Z_{\mathbb{R}}(R_4)$ *is achieved by a specific procedure presented in Section 5, based on Puiseux series. This procedure extends to the real case a technique presented in [1] for the complex case. On this particular example, evaluating* $q(x,y,z,w)$ *at* $Z_{\mathbb{R}}(R_3)$ *and* $Z_{\mathbb{R}}(R_4)$*, immediately yields the value of the limit in each case, which are* $-\frac{1}{2}$ *and* $\frac{1}{2}$*, respectively.*

Now we focus on R_2 *which consists simply of a regular chain, namely* $T := \{t_1, t_2\}$ *with* $t_1 = z$ *and* $t_2 = w$*. In order to compute the limit of* $q(x,y,z,w)$ *along* $Z_{\mathbb{R}}(R_2)$*, we apply again the method of Lagrange multipliers. More precisely, we wish to optimize* $q(x,y,z,w)$ *along* $t_1(x,y,z,w) = t_2(x,y,z,w) = 0$ *intercepted with a family of ellipsoids* $E_r(x,y,z,w) = 0$ *with* $E_r := A_1\,x^2 + A_2\,y^2 + A_3 z^2 + A_4\,w^2 - r^2$*, where* A_1, A_2, A_3, A_4 *are positive values to be determined.*

By definition of $\chi(q)$*, the gradient* $\nabla_{x,y,z,w} q$ *is proportional to* (x,y,z,w) *along* $\chi(q)$*. Hence, in order to apply the Lagrange multipliers method, we need to check that the vectors* $\nabla_{x,y,z,w} t_1$*,* $\nabla_{x,y,z,w} t_2$ *and* (x,y,z,w) *are linearly independent almost everywhere on* $Z_{\mathbb{R}}(R_2)$*. By considering the following Jacobian matrix*

$$\begin{bmatrix} x & y & z & w\\ \frac{\partial t_1}{\partial x} & \frac{\partial t_1}{\partial y} & \frac{\partial t_1}{\partial z} & \frac{\partial t_1}{\partial w}\\ \frac{\partial t_2}{\partial x} & \frac{\partial t_2}{\partial y} & \frac{\partial t_2}{\partial z} & \frac{\partial t_2}{\partial w}\end{bmatrix} = \begin{bmatrix} x & y & z & w\\ 0 & 0 & 1 & 0\\ 0 & 0 & 0 & 1\end{bmatrix}$$

we see that the vectors $\nabla_{x,y,z,w} t_1$*,* $\nabla_{x,y,z,w} t_2$ *and* (x,y,z,w) *are linearly independent as long as* $x \neq 0$ *or* $y \neq 0$ *holds. We choose to impose the constraint* $y \neq 0$*; using the incremental version of* RealTriangularize*, we compute the intersection* $Z_{\mathbb{R}}(R_2) \cap \{y \neq 0\}$ *and obtain* $Z_{\mathbb{R}}(R_5)$ *where* $R_5 := \{z = 0, w = 0, y \neq 0\}$*. Now we choose* $(A_1, A_2, A_3, A_4) = (3,1,2,3)$ *such that*

$$\begin{bmatrix} A_1 x & A_2 y & A_3 z & A_4 w\\ x & y & z & w\end{bmatrix}$$

is full rank. We are ready to apply the method of Lagrange multipliers, considering the following matrix

$$\begin{bmatrix} A_1 x & A_2 y & A_3 z & A_4 w\\ x & y & z & w\\ \frac{\partial t_1}{\partial x} & \frac{\partial t_1}{\partial y} & \frac{\partial t_1}{\partial z} & \frac{\partial t_1}{\partial w}\\ \frac{\partial t_2}{\partial x} & \frac{\partial t_2}{\partial y} & \frac{\partial t_2}{\partial z} & \frac{\partial t_2}{\partial w}\end{bmatrix} = \begin{bmatrix} 3x & 1y & 2z & 3w\\ x & y & z & w\\ 0 & 0 & 1 & 0\\ 0 & 0 & 0 & 1\end{bmatrix}$$

which has a single non-zero minor, namely $m = 4xy$*. Using again the incremental version of* RealTriangularize*, we compute* $Z_{\mathbb{R}}(R_5) \cap Z_{\mathbb{R}}(m = 0)$ *and obtain* $Z_{\mathbb{R}}(R_6)$*, where* $R_6 := \{x = 0, z = 0, w = 0, y \neq 0\}$*. We are now in dimension one. Using the procedure of Section 5 (or, on this particular example, using substitution and elementary calculations) yields* 1 *as the limit along* $Z_{\mathbb{R}}(R_6)$*.*

Putting everything together, we have three different values for the limit of $q(x,y,z,w)$ *along the three curves* $Z_{\mathbb{R}}(R_3)$*,* $Z_{\mathbb{R}}(R_4)$ *and* $Z_{\mathbb{R}}(R_6)$*. The corresponding values are* $-\frac{1}{2}, \frac{1}{2}, 1$*, which shows that the limit of* q *at the origin does not exist.*

EXAMPLE 2. *Let* $q \in \mathbb{Q}(x,y,z)$ *be the rational function defined by* $q(x,y,z) = \frac{x^2 y z^2}{x^4+z^4+y^4}$*. Here again, we aim at computing* $\lim_{(x,y,z)\to(0,0,0)} q$*.* RealTriangularize *produces the following decomposition of the real algebraic set* $\chi(q)$*:* $\chi(q) = Z_{\mathbb{R}}(R_1) \cup Z_{\mathbb{R}}(R_2) \cup Z_{\mathbb{R}}(R_3) \cup Z_{\mathbb{R}}(R_4)$*, where* R_1, R_2, R_3, R_4 *are respectively given by the regular semi-algebraic systems:*

$$\{\; x=0\;, \{\; z=0\;, \left\{\begin{array}{l} x^2 - z^2 = 0\\ y^6 + 3\,y^4\,z^2 - 2\,z^6 = 0\\ z \neq 0\end{array}\right. \text{ and } \left\{\begin{array}{l} x=0\\ y=0\\ z=0\end{array}\right. .$$

The system R_4 *can be discarded and the system* R_3 *has dimension one, hence the limit of* q *along* $Z_{\mathbb{R}}(R_3)$ *is handled by the procedure of Section 5, which yields* 0*.*

We focus on R_1 *and* R_2*. Similarly to the previous example, we consider the non-linear program consisting of optimizing* $q(x,y,z)$ *subject to* $(x,y,z) \in Z_{\mathbb{R}}(R_1)$ *(resp.* $(x,y,z) \in Z_{\mathbb{R}}(R_2)$*) and* $E_r(x,y,z) = 0$ *with* $E_r := A_1\,x^2 + A_2\,y^2 + A_3 z^2 - r^2$*, where* A_1, A_2, A_3 *are positive values to be determined.*

Let $T := \{t_1\} = \{x\}$ *be the regular chain part of* R_1*. Recall that* $\nabla_{x,y,z} q$ *is proportional to* (x,y,z) *along* $\chi(q)$*. Hence, we first determine when the following matrix*

$$\begin{bmatrix} x & y & z\\ \frac{\partial t_1}{\partial x} & \frac{\partial t_1}{\partial y} & \frac{\partial t_1}{\partial z}\end{bmatrix} = \begin{bmatrix} x & y & z\\ 1 & 0 & 0\end{bmatrix}$$

is full rank. The set of its 2-by-2 minors is $\{y, z, 0\}$*; hence this matrix is full rank whenever* $y \neq 0$ *or* $z \neq 0$ *holds. Since* $Z_{\mathbb{R}}(R_1) \notin Z_{\mathbb{R}}(y)$ *holds, we impose the constraint* $y \neq 0$ *and compute* $Z_{\mathbb{R}}(R_1) \cap \{y \neq 0\}$ *yielding* $Z_{\mathbb{R}}(R_5)$ *with* $R_5 := \{x = 0, y \neq 0\}$*. Next, we let* $(A_1, A_2, A_3) = (9, 10, 2)$ *such that*

$$\begin{bmatrix} A_1 x & A_2 y & A_3 z\\ x & y & z\end{bmatrix}$$

has at least one non-zero minor. Putting the three gradient vectors together, we form the following matrix

$$\begin{bmatrix} A_1 x & A_2 y & A_3 z\\ x & y & z\\ \frac{\partial t_1}{\partial x} & \frac{\partial t_1}{\partial y} & \frac{\partial t_1}{\partial z}\end{bmatrix} = \begin{bmatrix} 9x & 10y & 2z\\ x & y & z\\ 1 & 0 & 0\end{bmatrix}.$$

Its determinant is $8yz$ *and we compute* $Z_{\mathbb{R}}(R_5) \cap \{yz = 0\}$ *yielding* $Z_{\mathbb{R}}(R_6)$ *with* $R_6 := \{x = 0, z = 0, y \neq 0\}$*. The regular semi-algebraic system* R_6 *represents a space curve and the procedure of Section 5 computes the limit of* q *at the origin along* $Z_{\mathbb{R}}(R_6)$*, yielding* 0*. We proceed similarly with* R_2*. In this case, the non-linear programming trick yields the following space curve* $\{y = 0, z = 0, x \neq 0\}$ *along which the limit of* q *at the origin is also* 0*. Finally, the limit of* q *at origin exists and is equal to* 0*.*

The paper is organized as follows. In Section 2, we review different mathematical concepts and techniques used throughout the paper. Regular chains (Section 2.2) and regular semi-algebraic systems (Section 2.4) are the key concepts. They have rich properties. A regular semi-algebraic system R can be seen as a parametrization of its zero $Z_{\mathbb{R}}(R)$. Therefore, the fundamental properties of parametric polynomial systems (Section 2.3) are essential to take full advantage of the theory of regular semi-algebraic systems.

Section 3 gathers lemmas which together with the proportions of Section 2, support the correctness and termination of our algorithm, which is presented in Sections 4 and 5. Sections 6 and 7 offer experimental results and conclusions.

2. PRELIMINARIES

2.1 Non-linear programming

Lagrange multipliers. Let Ω be an open set of $\mathbb{R}^n$, let $f, g_1, \ldots, g_m : \Omega \to \mathbb{R}$ be C^1 functions, let $b = (b_1, \ldots, b_m) \in \mathbb{R}^m$ and let $x^\star$ be a point of Ω. Define $\Sigma_b := \{y \in \mathbb{R}^n : g_1(y) = b_1, \ldots, g_m(y) = b_m\}$. The point $x^\star$ is called a *local conditional extremal point of f under the constraints* $g_1 = \cdots = g_m = 0$, whenever there exists a neighbourhood U of $x^\star$ such that $f(x)$ takes an extremal value (maximum or minimum) at $x = x^\star$ on $\Sigma_b \cap U$. When this holds, the gradients $\nabla f(x^\star), \nabla g_1(x^\star), \ldots, \nabla g_m(x^\star)$ are linearly dependent. The above theorem is, in fact, usually stated when $m < n$ holds and $\nabla g_1(x^\star), \ldots, \nabla g_m(x^\star)$ are linearly independent, i.e. when $g(x^\star)$ is a regular value of the function $g = (g_1, \ldots, g_m)$ (at least if we restrict g to some neighbourhood V of $x^\star$). Then, the necessary condition of the theorem can be translated into the identity

$$\nabla f(x^\star) = \lambda_1^\star \nabla g_1(x^\star) + \ldots + \lambda_m^\star \nabla g_m(x^\star), \qquad (1)$$

for some real numbers $\lambda_1^\star, \ldots, \lambda_m^\star$ called *Lagrange multipliers*. Observe that, if we define the *Lagrange function* $F(x, \lambda) = f(x) + \sum_{i=1}^m \lambda_i (b_i - g_i(x))$, then the conditions (1) and $x^\star \in \Sigma_b$, for some neighbourhood U of $x^\star$ are equivalent to the fact that $(x^\star, \lambda^\star)$ is a critical point of F.

2.2 Regular chain theory

This section is a brief summary of concepts and algorithms for which details can be found in [5]. Throughout this paper, $\mathbb{K}$ is a field of characteristic 0 and $\overline{\mathbb{K}}$ is its algebraic closure. Let $\mathbb{K}[\underline{X}]$ be the polynomial ring over $\mathbb{K}$ and with ordered variables $\underline{X} = X_1 < \cdots < X_n$. Let $p \in \mathbb{K}[\underline{X}]$. Assume that $p \notin \mathbb{K}$. Denote by $\mathrm{mvar}(p)$ and $\mathrm{init}(p)$ the greatest variable appearing in p (called the *main variable* of p) and the leading coefficient of p w.r.t. $\mathrm{mvar}(p)$ (called the *initial* of p). For $F \subset \mathbb{K}[\underline{X}]$, we denote by $\langle F \rangle$ and $V(F)$ the ideal generated by F in $\mathbb{K}[\underline{X}]$ and the algebraic set of $\overline{\mathbb{K}}^n$ consisting of the common roots of the polynomials of F.

Triangular set. Let $T \subset \mathbb{K}[\underline{X}]$ be a *triangular set*, that is, a set of non-constant polynomials with pairwise distinct main variables. Denote by $\mathrm{mvar}(T)$ the set of main variables of the polynomials in T. A variable $v \in \underline{X}$ is called *algebraic* w.r.t. T if $v \in \mathrm{mvar}(T)$, otherwise it is said *free* w.r.t. T. If no confusion is possible, we shall always denote by $\underline{U} = U_1, \ldots, U_d$ and $\underline{Y} = Y_1, \ldots, Y_m$ the free and the main variables of T, respectively. We let $d = 0$ whenever T has no free variables. For $v \in \mathrm{mvar}(T)$, we denote by T_v and T_v^- the polynomial $f \in T$ with $\mathrm{mvar}(f) = v$ and the polynomials $f \in T$ with $\mathrm{mvar}(f) < v$, respectively. Let h_T be the product of the initials of the polynomials in T. We denote by $\mathrm{sat}(T)$ the *saturated ideal* of T: if T is the empty triangular set, then $\mathrm{sat}(T)$ is defined as the trivial ideal $\langle 0 \rangle$, otherwise it is the ideal $\langle T \rangle : h_T^\infty$. The *quasi-component* $W(T)$ of T is defined as $V(T) \setminus V(h_T)$. The Zariski closure of $W(T)$ in $\overline{\mathbb{K}}^n$, denoted by $\overline{W(T)}$, is the intersection of all algebraic sets $V \subseteq \overline{\mathbb{K}}^n$ such that $W(T) \subseteq V$ holds. For $f \in \mathbb{K}[\underline{X}]$, we denote by $\mathrm{res}(f, T)$ the *iterated resultant* of f w.r.t. T, that is, f itself, if f is constant, or $\mathrm{res}(\mathrm{res}(f, T_v, v), T_v^-)$ if $v \in \mathrm{mvar}(T)$ and $v = \mathrm{mvar}(f)$ hold, or $\mathrm{res}(f, T_v^-)$ otherwise.

Regular chain. A triangular set $T \subset \mathbb{K}[\underline{X}]$ is a *regular chain* if either T is empty, or letting v be the largest variable occurring in T, T_v^- is a regular chain, and the initial of T_v is regular (that is, neither zero nor zero divisor) modulo $\mathrm{sat}(T_v^-)$. Let $H \subset \mathbb{K}[\underline{X}]$. The pair $[T, H]$ is a *regular system* if each polynomial in H is regular modulo $\mathrm{sat}(T)$. A regular chain T, or a regular system $[T, H]$, is *square-free* if for all $t \in T$, the polynomial $\mathrm{der}(t)$ is regular w.r.t. $\mathrm{sat}(T)$, where $\mathrm{der}(t) = \frac{\partial t}{\partial v}$ and $v = \mathrm{mvar}(t)$. By $[T, H_{\neq}]$, we denote the algebraic system consisting of the equations $f = 0$ for all $f \in T$ and the inequations $h \neq 0$ for $h \in H \cup \{h_T\}$.

Good specialization. Let $[T, H]$ be a square-free regular system of $\mathbb{K}[\underline{X}]$. Recall that $\underline{Y}$ and $\underline{U} = U_1, \ldots, U_d$ stand respectively for $\mathrm{mvar}(T)$ and $\underline{X} \setminus \underline{Y}$. Let $a = (a_1, \ldots, a_d)$ be a point of $\overline{\mathbb{K}}^d$. We say that $[T, H]$ *specializes well* at a if: (i) for each $t \in T$ the polynomial $\mathrm{init}(t)$ is not zero modulo the ideal $\langle U_1 - a_1, \ldots, U_d - a_d \rangle$; (ii) the image of $[T, H]$ modulo $\langle U_1 - a_1, \ldots, U_d - a_d \rangle$ is a square-free regular system.

Border polynomial [16]. Let $[T, H]$ be a square-free regular system of $\mathbb{K}[\underline{X}]$. Let *bp* be the primitive and square free part of the product of all $\mathrm{res}(\mathrm{der}(t), T)$ and all $\mathrm{res}(h, T)$ for $h \in H$ and $t \in T$. We call *bp* the *border polynomial* of $[T, H]$.

Proposition 1. *The system $[T, H]$ specializes well at $a \in \overline{\mathbb{K}}^d$ if and only if the border polynomial $bp(a) \neq 0$.*

2.3 Parametric polynomial systems

The following is based on [10] and [11]. From now, the field $\mathbb{K}$ is either $\mathbb{R}$ or $\mathbb{C}$. Let $f_1, \ldots, f_s, p_1, \ldots, p_r \in \mathbb{Q}[\underline{X}]$, with, as before $\underline{X} = X_1 < \cdots < X_n$. Consider the constructible set $\mathcal{C} = \{x \in \mathbb{C}^n : f_1(x) = \cdots = f_s(x) = 0, p_1(x) \neq 0, \ldots, p_r(x) \neq 0\}$ and the semi-algebraic set $\mathcal{S} = \{x \in \mathbb{R}^n : f_1(x) = \cdots = f_s(x) = 0, p_1(x) > 0, \ldots, p_r(x) > 0\}$. Let $1 \leq d < n$. We view the variables $X_1, \ldots, X_d$ as *parameters* and we rename them as $\underline{U} = U_1, \ldots, U_d$. We denote by $\Pi_{\underline{U}}$ the canonical projection on the parameter space.

Discriminant variety in the complex case. Let δ be the dimension of $\overline{\Pi_{\underline{U}}(\mathcal{C})} = \Pi_{\underline{U}}(\overline{\mathcal{C}})$. An algebraic set $W \subset \mathbb{C}^n$ is a *discriminant variety* of $\mathcal{C}$ w.r.t. $\Pi_{\underline{U}}$ if the following four conditions hold: (1) $W \subseteq \overline{\Pi_{\underline{U}}(\mathcal{C})}$ holds, (2) $W = \overline{\Pi_{\underline{U}}(\mathcal{C})}$ holds if and only if $\Pi_{\underline{U}}^{-1}(u) \cap \mathcal{C}$ is infinite for almost all $u \in \overline{\Pi_{\underline{U}}(\mathcal{C})}$, (3) the connected components $\mathcal{U}_1, \ldots, \mathcal{U}_k$ of $\overline{\Pi_{\underline{U}}(\mathcal{C})} \setminus W$ are analytic submanifolds (i.e. non-singular) of dimension δ, (4) for all $1 \leq i \leq k$, the pair $(\Pi_{\underline{U}}^{-1}(\mathcal{U}_i), \Pi_{\underline{U}})$ is an analytic covering of $\mathcal{U}_i$. This latter condition implies that there exists finitely many disjoint connected subsets $\mathcal{C}_1, \ldots, \mathcal{C}_{i_k}$ of $\mathbb{C}^n$ such that their union equals $\Pi_{\underline{U}}^{-1}(\mathcal{U}_i) \cap \mathcal{C}$ and $\Pi_{\underline{U}}$ is a local diffeomorphism from $\mathcal{C}_j$ onto $\mathcal{U}_i$, for $1 \leq j \leq i_k$ and $1 \leq i \leq k$. Moreover, W contains the union of the critical values of the restriction of $\Pi_{\underline{U}}$ to the regular locus of $\mathcal{C}$, as well as the projection of the singular locus of $\mathcal{C}$.

PROPOSITION 2. *Let $[T, H]$ be a square-free regular system of $\mathbb{K}[\underline{X}]$ and bp its border polynomial. Then, the zero set of bp in $\mathbb{K}^d$ is the $\subseteq$-minimal discriminant variety of $[T, H_{\neq}]$ regarded as a parametric polynomial system, for which the parameters are the free variables of T.*

The real case. In practice, studying the parametric semi-algebraic system $\mathcal{S}$ can be done by

1. computing a discriminant variety W of the parametric constructible set $\mathcal{C}$, and
2. applying the following proposition.

PROPOSITION 3. *Assume that $W \neq \overline{\Pi_{\underline{U}}(\mathcal{C})}$ holds. Then, $(\overline{\Pi_{\underline{U}}(\mathcal{C})} \setminus W) \cap \mathbb{R}^d$ has finitely many connected components, $\mathcal{U}_1, \ldots, \mathcal{U}_e$, which are real analytic manifolds. Moreover, for each $i = 1, \ldots, e$, the number of points of $\mathcal{S}$ over $\mathcal{U}_i$ is constant, and if $\Pi_{\underline{U}}^{-1}(\mathcal{U}_i) \cap \mathcal{S}$ is not empty, then $(\Pi_{\underline{U}}^{-1}(\mathcal{U}_i) \cap \mathcal{S}, \Pi_{\underline{U}})$ is a real analytic covering of $\mathcal{U}_i$.*

2.4 Triangular decomposition of semi-algebraic sets

In this section, we recall that any semi-algebraic system decomposes into finitely many *regular semi-algebraic systems*. Since this material supports software implementation, we restrict the base field of polynomial coefficients to be $\mathbb{Q}$ instead of $\mathbb{R}$. See [3] for details.

Semi-algebraic system. Let us consider four finite polynomial subsets $F = \{f_1, \ldots, f_s\}$, $N = \{n_1, \ldots, n_t\}$, $P = \{p_1, \ldots, p_r\}$ and $H = \{h_1, \ldots, h_\ell\}$ of $\mathbb{Q}[\underline{X}]$, where, as before, $\underline{X}$ stands for n ordered variables $X_1 < \cdots < X_n$. Let $N_{\geq}$ denote the set of the inequalities $\{n_1 \geq 0, \ldots, n_t \geq 0\}$. Let $P_{>}$ denote the set of the inequalities $\{p_1 > 0, \ldots, p_r > 0\}$. Let $H_{\neq}$ denote the set of inequations $\{h_1 \neq 0, \ldots, h_\ell \neq 0\}$. We will denote by $[F, P_{>}]$ the *basic semi-algebraic system* $\{f_1 = 0, \ldots, f_s = 0, p_1 > 0, \ldots, p_r > 0\}$ and by $S := [F, N_{\geq}, P_{>}, H_{\neq}]$ the semi-algebraic system (SAS) which is the conjunction of the following conditions: $f_1 = 0, \ldots, f_s = 0$, $n_1 \geq 0, \ldots, n_t \geq 0$, $p_1 > 0, \ldots, p_r > 0$ and $h_1 \neq 0, \ldots, h_\ell \neq 0$. The algebraic set consisting of the zeros of S in $\mathbb{R}^n$ is denoted by $Z_{\mathbb{R}}(S)$ while the constructible set consisting of the zeros of $[F, N_{\geq}]$ in $\mathbb{C}^n$ is denoted by $Z_{\mathbb{C}}([F, N_{\geq}])$; if $N_{\geq}$ is empty we simply write $V(F)$ instead of $Z_{\mathbb{C}}([F, N_{\geq}])$. For an algebraic set $W \subseteq \mathbb{C}^n$, we denote by $W \cap \mathbb{R}^n$ the subset of $\mathbb{R}^n$ consisting of the points of W with real coordinates.

DEFINITION 1. *Let $T \subset \mathbb{Q}[\underline{X}]$ be a square-free regular chain. As before, let $\underline{U} = U_1, \ldots, U_d$ and $\underline{Y} = Y_1, \ldots, Y_{n-d}$ designate respectively the variables of $\underline{X}$ that are free and algebraic w.r.t. T. With $P \subset \mathbb{Q}[\underline{X}]$ as above, assume that each polynomial in P is regular w.r.t. sat(T). Let $\mathcal{Q}$ be a quantifier-free formula over $\mathbb{Q}[\underline{X}]$ involving only the $\underline{U}$ variables. Let $\mathcal{O}$ be the semi-algebraic subset of $\mathbb{R}^d$ defined by $\mathcal{Q}$. We say that $R := [\mathcal{Q}, T, P_{>}]$ is a* regular semi-algebraic system *if either $d = 0$ and the semi-algebraic system $[T, P_{>}]$ admits real solutions, or $d > 0$ and the following conditions hold:*

(i) $\mathcal{O}$ is a non-empty open subset in $\mathbb{R}^d$,
(ii) the regular system $[T, P]$ specializes well at every point a of $\mathcal{O}$,
(iii) at each point a of $\mathcal{O}$, the specialized system $[T(a), P(a)_{>}]$ admits real solutions.

The zero set *of R, denoted by $Z_{\mathbb{R}}(R)$, is the set of points $(a, \zeta) \in \mathbb{R}^d \times \mathbb{R}^{n-d}$ such that $\mathcal{Q}(a)$ holds, and $t(a, \zeta) = 0$, $p(a, \zeta) > 0$ both hold for all $t \in T$ and all $p \in P$.*

Using the notations of Definition 1, let $R = [\mathcal{Q}, T, P_{>}]$ be a regular semi-algebraic system. Since $\mathcal{O}$ is open, each connected component C of $\mathcal{O}$ in $\mathbb{R}^d$ is locally homeomorphic to the hyper-cube $(0,1)^d$. From Property *(ii)*, the zero set $Z_{\mathbb{R}}(R)$ consists of disjoint graphs of continuous semi-algebraic functions defined on each such C. Moreover, from Property *(iii)*, there is at least one such graph. For these reasons, the regular semi-algebraic system R can be understood as a parameterization of the set $Z_{\mathbb{R}}(R)$. Clearly, the dimension of $Z_{\mathbb{R}}(R)$ is d.

PROPOSITION 4. *As above, let $S := [F, N_{\geq}, P_{>}, H_{\neq}]$ be a semi-algebraic system. Then, there exists a finite family of regular semi-algebraic systems $R_1, \ldots, R_e$ such that $Z_{\mathbb{R}}(S)$ equals the union of $Z_{\mathbb{R}}(R_1), \ldots, Z_{\mathbb{R}}(R_e)$. We call $R_1, \ldots, R_e$ a* triangular decomposition *of S and we denote by* RealTriangularize *an algorithm computing such a decomposition.*

3. BASIC LEMMAS

Fix a real number $\rho > 0$ and let D_ρ^* be the punctured ball

$$D_\rho^* = \{(x_1, \ldots, x_n) \in \mathbb{R}^n \mid 0 < \sqrt{x_1^2 + \cdots + x_n^2} < \rho\}.$$

Let $q : \mathbb{R}^n \longrightarrow \mathbb{R}$ be a rational function defined on D_ρ^*.

NOTATION 1. *Let $\chi(q)$ be the subset of $\mathbb{R}^n$ (regarded as an affine space) where the gradient $\nabla_{x_1,\ldots,x_n} q$ of q at $(x_1, \ldots, x_n)$ and the vector $(x_1, \ldots, x_n)$ of $\mathbb{R}^n$ (regarded as a vector space) are co-linear. For $n = 2$, we have*

$$\chi(q) = \{(x, y) \in \mathbb{R}^2 \mid y\frac{\partial q}{\partial x} - x\frac{\partial q}{\partial y} = 0\}.$$

In higher dimension, using McCoy theorem, the real algebraic set $\chi(q)$ is the vanishing locus of all 2-by-2 minors of the 2-by-n matrix which rows are $\nabla_{x_1,\ldots,x_n} q$ and $(x_1, \ldots, x_n)$.

DEFINITION 2. *Let S be a semi-algebraic set of dimension at least 1 and such that the origin of $\mathbb{R}^n$ belongs to the closure $\overline{Z_{\mathbb{R}}(S)}$ of $Z_{\mathbb{R}}(S)$ in the Euclidean topology. Let $L \in \mathbb{R}$. We say that, when $(x_1, \ldots, x_n) \in \mathbb{R}^n$ approaches the origin along S, the limit of the rational function $q(x_1, \ldots, x_n)$ exists and equals L, whenever for all $\varepsilon > 0$, there exists $0 < \delta$ such that for all $(x_1, \ldots, x_n) \in S \cap D_\delta^*$ the inequality $|q(x_1, \ldots, x_n) - L| < \varepsilon$ holds. When this holds, we write*

$$\lim_{\substack{(x_1, \ldots, x_n) \to (0, \ldots, 0) \\ (x_1, \ldots, x_n) \in S}} q = L$$

Lemma 1 is a direct generalization of Proposition 1 in [2] and Lemma 3 is a less direct generalization of one of the properties established in Proposition 17 of [2]. We provide proofs for those results since they are essential for understanding the algorithm presented in Section 4. Meanwhile, Lemma 2 follows from Lemma 1 and elementary reasoning about limits; hence we omit its proof.

LEMMA 1. *For all $L \in \mathbb{R}$ the following two assertions are equivalent:*

(i) $\lim_{(x_1,\ldots,x_n)\to(0,\ldots,0)} q$ exists and equals L,
(ii) $\lim_{\substack{(x_1, \ldots, x_n) \to (0, \ldots, 0) \\ (x_1, \ldots, x_n) \in \chi(q)}} q$ exists and equals L.

Proof. Clearly the first assertion implies the second one. Next, we assume that the second one holds and we prove that the first one holds as well. Hence, we assume that for all $\varepsilon > 0$, there exists $0 < \delta < \rho$ such that for all $(x_1, \ldots, x_n) \in \chi(q) \cap D_\delta^*$ the inequality $|q(x_1, \ldots, x_n) - L| < \varepsilon$ holds. We fix $\varepsilon > 0$. For every $r > 0$, we define $C_r = \{(x_1, \ldots, x_n) \in \mathbb{R}^n \mid \sqrt{x_1^2 + \cdots + x_n^2} = r\}$. For all $0 < r < \rho$, we choose $t_1(r)$ (resp. $t_2(r)$) minimizing (resp. maximizing) q on C_r. Applying the method of Lagrange multipliers, we have $t_1(r), t_2(r) \in \chi(q)$, for all $0 < r < \rho$. Observe that for all $(x_1, \ldots, x_n) \in \mathbb{R}^n$, with $r := \sqrt{x_1^2 + \cdots + x_n^2} < \rho$, we have $q(t_1(r)) - L \leq q(x_1, \ldots, x_n) - L \leq q(t_2(r)) - L$. From the assumption and the definitions of $t_1(r), t_2(r)$, there exists $0 < \delta < \rho$ such that, for all $r < \delta$, we have $-\varepsilon < q(t_1(r)) - L$ and $q(t_2(r)) - L < \varepsilon$. Therefore, there exists $0 < \delta < \rho$ such that for all $(x_1, \ldots, x_n) \in D_\delta^*$ the inequality $|q(x_1, \ldots, x_n) - L| < \varepsilon$ holds. □

LEMMA 2. *Let $R_1, \ldots, R_e$ be regular semi-algebraic systems forming a triangular decomposition of $\chi(q)$ in the sense of Proposition 4. Then, for all $L \in \mathbb{R}$ the following two assertions are equivalent:*

(i) $\lim_{\substack{(x_1,\ldots,x_n)\to(0,\ldots,0)\\ (x_1,\ldots,x_n)\in\chi(q)}} q$ exists and equals L.

(ii) for all $i \in \{1, \ldots, e\}$ such that $\overline{Z_{\mathbb{R}}(R_i)}$ has dimension at least 1 and the origin belongs to $\overline{Z_{\mathbb{R}}(R_i)}$, we have $\lim_{\substack{(x_1,\ldots,x_n)\to(0,\ldots,0)\\ (x_1,\ldots,x_n)\in Z_{\mathbb{R}}(R_i)}} q$ exists and equals L.

LEMMA 3. *Assume $n \geq 3$. Let $S = [\mathcal{Q}, \{t_n\}, P_>]$ be a regular semi-algebraic system of $\mathbb{Q}[X_1, \ldots, X_n]$ such that $Z_{\mathbb{R}}(S)$ has dimension $d := n-1$, and the closure $\overline{Z_{\mathbb{R}}(S)}$ contains the origin. W.l.o.g. we assume that $mvar(t_n) = X_n$ holds. Let $\mathcal{M}$ be the $2 \times n$ matrix with the vector $(X_1, \ldots, X_n)$ as first row and the gradient vector $\nabla t_n = \left(\frac{\partial t_n}{\partial X_1} \cdots \frac{\partial t_n}{\partial X_n}\right)$ as second row. Then, there exists a non-empty set $\mathcal{O} \subset D_\rho^* \cap Z_{\mathbb{R}}(S)$, which is open relatively to $Z_{\mathbb{R}}(S)$, such that $\mathcal{M}$ is full rank at any point of $\mathcal{O}$, and the origin is in the closure of $\mathcal{O}$.*

Proof. Assume that there exists $0 < r < \rho$ such that $\mathcal{M}$ is not full rank at any point of $D_r^* \cap Z_{\mathbb{R}}(S)$. Then, the system of partial differential equations (PDEs) $X_j \frac{\partial t_n}{\partial X_i} - X_i \frac{\partial t_n}{\partial X_j} = 0$, for $1 \leq i < j \leq n$ holds at any point of $D_r^* \cap Z_{\mathbb{R}}(S)$. This implies that $t_n = u(X_1^2 + \cdots + X_n^2)$ where u is a univariate polynomial. Let $0 < r' < r$ and $S_{r'}$ be the sphere centred at the origin, with radius r'. Our hypotheses and the previous PDE argument imply that $Z_{\mathbb{R}}(S)$ contains a non-empty set $V_{r'} \subset S_{r'}$ which is an open set in the Euclidean topology induced on $S_{r'}$. The fact that this holds for all r', with $0 < r' < r$, contradicts the fact that $Z_{\mathbb{R}}(S)$ is a semi-algebraic set of dimension less than n.

Therefore, for all $r > 0$ small enough, the set $D_r^* \cap Z_{\mathbb{R}}(S)$ contains a point p_r, as well as a neighbourhood N_r of p_r (due to the full rank characterization in terms of minors) such that N_r is open relatively to $Z_{\mathbb{R}}(S)$ and $\mathcal{M}$ is full rank at any point of N_r. From there, the desired conclusion follows. □

4. MAIN ALGORITHM

We describe in this section our procedure for determining the existence and the possible value of limits of the form $\lim_{(x_1,\ldots,x_n)\to(0,\ldots,0)} q(x_1, \ldots, x_n)$. Recall that q is a rational function in the n ordered variables $X_1 < \cdots < X_n$ and with rational number coefficients. We assume that the origin is an isolated zero of the denominator. The pseudo-code for this procedure is stated in Algorithms 2, 1, 3 and 4.

Algorithm 1 Limit of rational function $q \in \mathbb{Q}(X_1, \ldots, X_n)$ at origin along zero set of regular semi-algebraic system S

```
procedure LimitInner(q, S)
    if dim(Z_R(S)) = 1 then
        return (LimitAlongCurve(q, S), S);
    end if
    let [Q, T, P_>] := S;
    M := [ X_1 ... X_n ; ∇t, t ∈ T ];
    state := search_first_minor;
    for m ∈ Minors(M) do
        if Z_R(S) ⊆ Z_R(m) then
            next;
        end if
        J := ∅;
        for S' ∈ Intersect(S, {m ≠ 0}) do
            if o ∉ closure(Z_R(S')) or dim(Z_R(S')) = 0 then
                next;
            end if
            (A_1, ..., A_n, r) := RandomEllipse(n);
            let E_r := Σ_{i=1}^n A_i X_i^2 − r^2;
            M' := [ ∂E_r/∂X_1 ... ∂E_r/∂X_n ; X_1 ... X_n ; ∇t, t ∈ T ];
            let [Q', T', P_>'] := S';
            state := search_second_minor;
            for m' ∈ Minors(M') do
                if res(m', T') = 0 then
                    next;
                end if
                I := ∅;
                for C ∈ Intersect(S', m' = 0) do
                    if o ∉ closure(Z_R(C)) or dim(Z_R(C)) = 0 then
                        next;
                    end if
                    L := LimitInner(q, C);
                    if L = backtrack then
                        state := backtrack;
                        break;
                    else
                        I := I ∪ {L};
                    end if
                end for
                if I ≠ ∅ and state ≠ backtrack then
                    J := J ∪ I;
                    state := found_second_minor;
                    break;
                end if
            end for
            if state ≠ found_second_minor then
                state := backtrack;
                break;
            end if
        end for
        if state ≠ backtrack then
            state := found_first_minor;
            break;
        end if
    end for
    if state = found_first_minor then
        return J;
    else
        return backtrack;
    end if
end procedure
```

PROPOSITION 5. *Algorithm 2 terminates and returns finitely many pairs $(L_1, S_1), \dots, (L_e, S_e)$ where each of $L_1, \dots, L_e$ is either a real number, or the flag* `no_limit`, *and $S_1, \dots, S_e$ are all regular semi-algebraic systems such that each of the sets $Z_{\mathbb{R}}(S_1), \dots, Z_{\mathbb{R}}(S_e)$ has dimension one and contains the origin in its closure. Moreover, if $L_i \in \mathbb{R}$, then L_i is the limit of q at the origin along the $Z_{\mathbb{R}}(S_i)$ for all $i = 1, \dots, e$. In addition, the rational function q admits a finite limit at the origin if and only if $L_1, \dots, L_e$ are all real and equal; if this holds, then this common value is the limit of q at the origin.*

Proof. Algorithm 2 applies Lemma 1 as follows. It computes the real algebraic set $\chi(q)$ defined in Notation 1 and computes a triangular decomposition $\mathcal{D}$ of $\chi(q)$ as defined in Proposition 4. Following Lemma 2, each regular semi-algebraic system $S \in \mathcal{D}$ which is zero-dimensional, or such that the origin is not contained in the closure of $Z_{\mathbb{R}}(S)$, can be discarded. For all the other regular semi-algebraic systems (RSASs), one runs $\mathsf{LimitInner}(q, S)$, that is, makes a call to Algorithm 1. We note that computing the dimension of $Z_{\mathbb{R}}(S)$ is trivial, since it is equal to the dimension of the saturated ideal of the regular chain, which is part of S. We also observe that testing whether the origin $\underline{o}$ belongs to $\overline{Z_{\mathbb{R}}(R)}$ can be done via quantifier elimination; in our code we use the QuantifierElimination algorithm [6] implemented in the **RegularChains** library in MAPLE.

Algorithm 1 is the core routine. It first checks whether $Z_{\mathbb{R}}(S)$ has dimension one or not. If $\dim(Z_{\mathbb{R}}(S)) = 1$ holds, one runs $\mathsf{LimitAlongCurve}(q, S)$, that is, Algorithm 4. Applying Algorithm 1 with RSASs of dimension one can be seen as the *base case* of that recursive routine while the rest of that routine reduces computation with RSASs of dimension higher than one to the one-dimensional case.

This reduction is performed by repeated applications of the Lagrange multipliers trick, as in the proof of Lemma 1. It follows from Lemma 3 that there exists a minor $m \in \mathsf{Minors}(\mathcal{M})$ (where $\mathcal{M}$ is defined at Line (6) of Algorithm 1) such that we have $Z_{\mathbb{R}}(S) \notin Z_{\mathbb{R}}(m)$. Note that we know that the Jacobian of T (that is, the matrix formed with the ∇t, for $t \in T$) is full rank. This follows from Proposition 3 and explains why we do not need to compute any singular loci.

Once such a minor $m \in \mathsf{Minors}(\mathcal{M})$ is found, we compute $Z_{\mathbb{R}}(S) \cap Z_{\mathbb{R}}(\{m \neq 0\})$ using the incremental version of the RealTriangularize[1] algorithm [4]; this is done at Line (13). The resulting triangular decomposition consists of RSAS with the same dimension as S. The goal of Line (14) is to remove any RSAS S' such that $\overline{Z_{\mathbb{R}}(S')}$ does not contain the origin.

At Lines (17) to (20), we prepare for applying the Lagrange multipliers trick: since $\nabla_{(X_1,\dots,X_n)} q$ is proportional to $(X_1, \dots, X_n)$ along $\chi(q)$ we cannot re-use the family of circles C_r as in the proof of Lemma 1; instead, we use a family of ellipsoids, given by E_r; this idea was introduced in [14]. In particular, at Line (17), we determine values for the coefficients $A_1, \dots, A_n$ of the polynomial E_r such that at least one minor of $\mathcal{M}'$ is not zero. This task is delegated to Algorithm 3: in practice, choosing $A_1, \dots, A_n$ all positive at random works; if this would not work, $A_1, \dots, A_n$ would be determined by solving polynomial systems.

[1]the function $\mathsf{Intersect}(S_1, S_2)$ computes the intersection of the real zero sets of two regular semi-algebraic systems S_1 and RS_2; it is the core routine in the incremental version of RealTriangularize presented in [4]. Note that S_2 can be a constraint of the form $f = 0$ or $f > 0$ with $f \in \mathbb{Q}[X_1, \dots, X_n]$.

The for-loop located between Lines (22) and (44) runs until we find a minor m' of the matrix $\mathcal{M}'$ (where $\mathcal{M}'$ is defined at Line (19) of Algorithm 1) such that the dimension of $Z_{\mathbb{R}}(S) \cap Z_{\mathbb{R}}(\{m' = 0\})$ is less than that of $Z_{\mathbb{R}}(S)$. This search is expected to be *successful* because the non-linear programs consisting of minimizing/maximizing $q(x_1, \dots, x_n)$ under the constraints $(x_1, \dots, x_n) \in Z_{\mathbb{R}}(S) \cap \{E_r = 0\}$ have solutions, necessarily. However, this search depends on the minor m, as well. In fact, what the previous non-linear optimization argument guarantees is the existence of a pair of minors (m, m') such that $\mathcal{M}$ is full rank for $m \neq 0$ while $\mathcal{M}'$ is not full rank for $m' = 0$. For this reason, for certain m, the search for m', or the recursive call at Line (31), may fail. Such a situation leads the algorithm to try the next m from $\mathsf{Minors}(\mathcal{M})$. It follows that Algorithm 1 must implement a *backtracking* mechanism.

This backtracking feature is achieved by enhancing the algorithm with a *state machine*. Note that at Lines (7), (21), (33), (41), (46), and (51) a variable called state is assigned in order to record the *new* state of the algorithm. Observe that, if the variable state never receives the value `backtrack` during the execution of Algorithm 1, then only the first minor $m \in \mathsf{Minors}(\mathcal{M})$ and the first minor $m' \in \mathsf{Minors}(\mathcal{M}')$ are considered by the algorithm.

Observe that, during one iteration of the for-loop located between Lines (22) and (44), if the variable L receives the value `backtrack` , or the variable $\mathcal{I}$ remains empty, then this iteration failed to find a minor m'; as a consequence either this for-loop goes for another iteration, or, if all iterations have been executed, the variable state will receive the value `backtrack` implying that the current value of the minor m cannot lead to find a minor m' with the desired properties.

Finally, observe that the execution of the for-loop located between Lines (8) and (55) terminates either with state reaching the value `found_second_minor` (implying that a pair of minors (m, m') with the desired properties has been found) or with state having the value `backtrack` (implying that no such pair was found).

It follows from the above discussion that Algorithm 1 always terminates and so does Algorithm 2. Moreover, and as mentioned above, since the non-linear programs consisting of minimizing/maximizing q under the constraints $(x_1, \dots, x_n) \in Z_{\mathbb{R}}(S) \cap \{E_r = 0\}$ necessarily have solutions (where q and S are the input of Algorithm 1), the calls that Algorithm 2 makes to Algorithm 1 will ultimately produce an answer of the form $(L_1, S_1), \dots, (L_e, S_e)$ with the desired properties. □

Algorithm 2 Limit of rational function $q \in \mathbb{Q}(X_1, \dots, X_n)$ at origin

procedure LIMIT(q)
  $\mathcal{A} := \mathsf{Minors}(\begin{bmatrix} X_1 & \cdots & X_n \\ \frac{\partial q}{\partial X_1} & \cdots & \frac{\partial q}{\partial X_n} \end{bmatrix});$
  $\mathcal{D} := \mathsf{RealTriangularize}(\mathcal{A});$
  $\mathcal{L} := \varnothing;$
  for $S \in \mathcal{D}$ **do**
    if $\underline{o} \in \overline{Z_{\mathbb{R}}(S)}$ and $\dim(Z_{\mathbb{R}}(S)) > 0$ **then**
      $\mathcal{L} := \mathcal{L} \cup \{\mathsf{LimitInner}(q, S)\};$
    end if
  end for
  return $\mathcal{L}$;
end procedure

Algorithm 3 Ellipse in $\mathbb{R}^n$ randomly generated

> **procedure** RANDOMELLIPSE(n)
>   **repeat**
>   choose $A_1, \ldots, A_n, r$ randomly with $r > 0$;
>   let $E_r := \sum_{i=1}^{n} A_i X_i^2 - r^2$;
> $\mathcal{S} := \begin{bmatrix} \frac{\partial E_r}{\partial X_1} & \cdots & \frac{\partial E_r}{\partial X_n} \\ X_1 & \cdots & X_n \end{bmatrix}$;
>   **until** $\mathcal{S}$ has at least one non-zero minor
>   **return** $(A_1, \ldots, A_n, r)$;
> **end procedure**

Algorithm 4 Limit of rational function $q \in \mathbb{Q}(X_1, \ldots, X_n)$ at origin along real curve C given by a RSAS $[\mathcal{Q}, T, P_>]$

> **procedure** LIMITALONGCURVE(q, C)
>   Let f, g be the numerator and denominator of q;
>   Let $R := \{gX_{n+1} - f\} \cup T$ with X_{n+1} a new variable; ▷ R is a regular chain for $X_1 < \cdots < X_{n+1}$;
>   Compute the limit points of $Z_{\mathbb{R}}(R) \setminus Z_{\mathbb{R}}(h_R)$ in $\mathbb{R}^n$ for the Euclidean topology; see Section 5;
>   If there is only one such limit point $(x_1, \ldots, x_n, x_{n+1})$ with $x_1 = \cdots = x_n = 0$, then x_{n+1} is the desired limit of q;
>   Otherwise return `no_limit` since q has no limit along C at the origin;
> **end procedure**

5. REAL LIMIT POINTS

Let $T \subset \mathbb{Q}[X_1, \ldots, X_n]$ be a one-dimensional regular chain; we denote by U its free variable. In [1], an algorithm is proposed for computing the non-trivial limit points of the quasi-component $W(T)$, that is, $\overline{W(T)} \setminus W(T)$ (where $\overline{W(T)}$ is the Zariski closure of $W(T)$). In Algorithm 4, a similar, but different, computation is needed. In this case, we need the non-trivial limit points of $W_{\mathbb{R}}(T) := Z_{\mathbb{R}}(T) \setminus Z_{\mathbb{R}}(h_T)$, that is, $\overline{W_{\mathbb{R}}(T)} \setminus W_{\mathbb{R}}(T)$, in $\mathbb{R}^n$ endowed with the Euclidean topology. Unfortunately, it is not true that the non-trivial limit points of $W_{\mathbb{R}}(T)$ are the non-trivial limit points of $W(T)$ that have real coordinates. We shall see that in Example 3. However, the algorithm of [1], which is based on Puiseux series, can be adapted in order to compute the non-trivial limit points of $W_{\mathbb{R}}(T)$. This adaptation is explained hereafter. Note that the LimitPoints command of the `RegularChains` library in MAPLE handles both cases, $W(T)$ and $W_{\mathbb{R}}(T)$.

The *Puiseux parametrizations* of the regular chain T (see [1], Definition 2) encode all the branches of $V(\mathrm{sat}(T))$ when the free variable U approaches zero. It is proved in [1] that the non-trivial limit points of $W(T)$ are obtained by letting U be zero in all the Puiseux parametrizations of T.

EXAMPLE 3. *Let* $T := \{X_1^4 X_3 + X_2^3 - X_2^2, X_2^4 - 2X_2^3 + X_2^2 + X_1^5\} \subseteq \mathbb{Q}[X_1 < X_2 < X_3]$ *be a regular chain. Then the Puiseux parametrizations of* T *at* $U = 0$ *are as follow:*

- $\left(X_1 = U^2, X_2 = U^5\left(-U^5 + \sqrt{-1}\right),\right.$ $\left.X_3 = -U^2\left(-U^{20} + 3\sqrt{-1}U^{15} + 2U^{10} + \sqrt{-1}U^5 + 1\right)\right)$,
- $\left(X_1 = U^2, X_2 = -U^5\left(U^5 + \sqrt{-1}\right),\right.$ $\left.X_3 = U^2\left(U^{20} + 3\sqrt{-1}U^{15} - 2U^{10} + \sqrt{-1}U^5 - 1\right)\right)$.

$W(T)$ *has one non-trivial limit point, namely* $\{(X_1 = 0, X_2 = 0, X_3 = 0)\}$, *which coordinates are real. However, none of the branches of the space curve defined by* $W(T)$ *is real. Hence,* $W_{\mathbb{R}}(T)$ *has no non-trivial limit points!*

Thus, in order to compute the non-trivial limit points of $Z_{\mathbb{R}}(T)$, one needs to compute the real Puiseux parametrizations of $Z_{\mathbb{R}}(T)$ about $\underline{o}$, which are the parametrizations with coefficients in $\mathbb{R}$. To do so, it is enough to have a method for detecting the real Puiseux expansions of a single polynomial.

As it is explained in [2], for the bivariate case, one way of separating the real Puiseux expansions from the complex ones is to detect for which initial factors of the method of computing the Puiseux expansions, complex coefficients will appear in the computations.

PROPOSITION 6. *Let* $f(U, Y) \in \mathbb{Q}\langle U\rangle[Y]$ *be square-free, monic w.r.t* Y *and of degree* $s > 0$ *in* Y. *Then, for each* $\ell = 1, \ldots, s$, *one can compute a positive integer* σ_ℓ *as well as algebraic numbers* $\Theta_\ell^1, \ldots, \Theta_\ell^{\sigma_\ell}$ *over* $\mathbb{Q}$ *such that*

1. *for* $i = 1, \ldots, \sigma_\ell$, *the algebraic number* Θ_ℓ^i *has a minimal polynomial of the form* $h_\ell^i(Y) \in \mathbb{Q}[\Theta_\ell^1, \ldots, \Theta_\ell^{i-1}][Y]$,
2. $f(U, Y)$ *factorizes as* $(Y - \chi_1(U)) \cdots (Y - \chi_s(U))$ *where* $\chi_\ell(U) \in \mathbb{Q}((U^*))[\Theta_\ell^1, \ldots, \Theta_\ell^{\sigma_\ell}]$ *holds.*

Note that $\mathbb{Q}((U^*))$ *is the field of Puiseux series over* $\mathbb{Q}$.

Proposition 6 is derived from the *extended Hensel construction* method described in [13], in particular Theorem 3 of that paper. In fact, Proposition 6 gives a characterization of all the Puiseux expansions of polynomial f. This proposition shows that there is a finite extension of $\mathbb{Q}$ for which $f(U, Y)$ can be written as $(Y - \chi_1(U)) \cdots (Y - \chi_s(U))$, and therefore all the coefficients of the Puiseux expansions of f are determined. It is worth mentioning that determining whether or not $\chi_\ell(U)$ is a real Puiseux expansion is equivalent to the fact that each Θ_ℓ^{i-1} is a real algebraic number over $\mathbb{Q}[\Theta_\ell^1, \ldots, \Theta_\ell^{i-1}]$, for $i = 1, \ldots, \sigma_\ell$.

Each solution tuple of the polynomials $h_\ell^1(Y), \ldots, h_\ell^{\sigma_\ell}(Y)$ will result in a different Puiseux expansion for $f(U, Y)$. Determining if one Puiseux expansion $\chi_\ell(U)$ is real or not requires to factorize the corresponding minimal polynomials $h_\ell^1(Y), \ldots, h_\ell^{\sigma_\ell}(Y)$ into linear factors, which is done in our implementation with the command `Splits` of MAPLE. From this representation of $h_\ell^1(Y), \ldots, h_\ell^{\sigma_\ell}(Y)$, one determines whether there is a sequence $\Theta_\ell^1, \ldots, \Theta_\ell^{\sigma_\ell}$ of algebraic numbers that are all real; we do this with RealTriangularize.

6. EXPERIMENTATION

This section is devoted to an experimental comparison of various MAPLE's codes for computing limits of multivariate rational functions: MAPLE's built-in command `limit`, the `TestLimit` command presented in [15] and our implementation of the algorithm of Section 4 within the `RationalFunctionLimit` command of the `RegularChains` library. We used more than 50 test-examples[2] and a representative subset of them is provided in Table 1. The abbreviations LM, TL, and RFL stand for `limit`, `TestLimit`, and `RationalFunctionLimit` commands. Further, NV, TD and LV represent the number of variables, the maximum total degree between numerator and denominator, and the value of the limit, respectively. The timings in columns LM, TL, RFL are in seconds.

For bivariate rational functions (examples 1-5), both LM and TL run faster than RFL, except on example 2. Recall that LM applies to bivariate rational functions only.

[2] The list of the examples and the timings corresponding to Table 1 can be found at www.regularchains.org/RationalLimit/RationalFunctionLimit.zip and www.regularchains.org/RationalLimit/Report, respectively.

Out of the 25 examples in 3 variables or more, TL and RFL solve respectively 9 and 24 examples within the prescribed resource limits of 2 GB of memory and 1800 sec of CPU time. Moreover, out of those 25 examples, TL fails on 8 of them due to a division-by-zero error. For the 17 examples in 3 variables or more, for which TL does not hit such an error, RFL runs faster than TL on 10 examples.

Taking into account the 30 examples: (1) TL and RFL solve respectively 13 and 29 examples, (2) for the 21 examples for which TL does not hit an error, RFL runs faster than TL 11 times, and (3) for the 13 examples for which TL computes the answer, TL is faster than RFL on 10 times.

These experimental results were obtained on an Ubuntu desktop (3.33GHz Intel Core i5 CPU, 3.7Gb total mem.).

Ex	NV	TD	LM	TL	RFL	LV
1	2	4	0.061	0.097	0.134	-1
2	2	4	0.056	wrong answer	0.126	-1
3	2	2	0.015	0.002	0.074	undefined
4	2	4	0.096	0.001	0.906	undefined
5	2	4	0.064	0.089	0.127	-1
6	3	5	N/A	0.508	5.278	0
7	3	8	N/A	> *2GB*	> *2GB*	0
8	3	18	N/A	10.422	0.166	0
9	3	18	N/A	0.502	0.128	0
10	4	4	N/A	0.002	1.498	undefined
11	4	2	N/A	0.003	0.205	undefined
12	4	4	N/A	0.002	1.495	undefined
13	4	5	N/A	> *2GB*	1.991	0
14	4	21	N/A	> *2GB*	0.545	0
15	4	6	N/A	> *2GB*	0.526	0
16	5	19	N/A	> *2GB*	0.376	0
17	5	4	N/A	2.705	1.205	0
18	6	6	N/A	Error	1.228	0
19	6	6	N/A	Error	1.399	undefined
20	6	18	N/A	Error	0.391	0
21	6	10	N/A	> *2GB*	0.627	0
22	6	10	N/A	> *2GB*	1.143	0
23	6	6	N/A	Error	3.497	0
24	7	6	N/A	0.002	0.012	undefined
25	8	5	N/A	> *2GB*	5.445	0
26	8	9	N/A	Error	19.747	undefined
27	9	4	N/A	0.003	3.628	undefined
28	9	10	N/A	Error	36.959	0
29	9	5	N/A	Error	1.193	0
30	10	10	N/A	Error	7.093	0

Table 1

7. CONCLUSION

We have presented a procedure for determining the existence and possible value of limits of n-variate rational function over $\mathbb{Q}$. Our work extends the articles [2] and [14] dedicated to $n = 2$ and $n = 3$, respectively. We rely on the theory of regular chains, which allows us to avoid computing singular loci and decompositions into irreducible components. Our main tool is the RealTriangularize algorithm. We have implemented our procedure within the RegularChains library and our code is available at www.regularchains.org.

Experimental results show that our code solves more test cases than the implementation of [15], in particular as variable number or total degree increases. Nevertheless, our code is still under development and many optimizations are planned, including borrowing techniques used in [15].

Acknowledgements

We are grateful to the reviewers for their comments as well as to S.J. Xiao and G.X. Zeng [15] for making their code available.

References

[1] P. Alvandi, C. Chen, and M. Moreno Maza. Computing the limit points of the quasi-component of a regular chain in dimension one. In *Proc. of CASC'13*, volume 8136 of *Lect. Notes Comput. Sci.*, pages 30–45, 2013.

[2] C. Cadavid, S. Molina, and J. D. Vélez. Limits of quotients of bivariate real analytic functions. *J. Symb. Comput.*, 50:197–207, 2013.

[3] C. Chen, J. H. Davenport, J. P. May, M. Moreno Maza, B. Xia, and R. Xiao. Triangular decomposition of semi-algebraic systems. *J. Symb. Comput.*, 49:3–26, 2013.

[4] C. Chen, J. H. Davenport, M. Moreno Maza, B. Xia, and R. Xiao. Computing with semi-algebraic sets: Relaxation techniques and effective boundaries. *J. Symb. Comput.*, 52:72–96, 2013.

[5] C. Chen and M. Moreno Maza. Algorithms for computing triangular decomposition of polynomial systems. *J. Symb. Comput.*, 47(6):610–642, 2012.

[6] C. Chen and M. Moreno Maza. Quantifier elimination by cylindrical algebraic decomposition based on regular chains. In *ISSAC'14*, pages 91–98. ACM, 2014.

[7] D. Gruntz. A new algorithm for computing asymptotic series. In *ISSAC'93*, pages 239–244. ACM, 1993.

[8] D. Gruntz. *On computing limits in a symbolic manipulation system.* PhD thesis, ETZ Zurich, 1996.

[9] G. R. Lawlor. A L'hospital's rule for multivariable functions. *ArXiv e-prints*, August 2012.

[10] D. Lazard and F. Rouillier. Solving parametric polynomial systems. *J. Symb. Comput.*, 42(6):636–667, 2007.

[11] M. Moreno Maza, B. Xia, and R. Xiao. On solving parametric polynomial systems. *Mathematics in Computer Science*, 6(4):457–473, 2012.

[12] B. Salvy and J. Shackell. Symbolic asymptotics: Multiseries of inverse functions. *J. Symb. Comput.*, 27(6):543–563, 1999.

[13] T. Sasaki and F. Kako. Solving multivariate algebraic equation by hensel construction. *Japan Journal of Industrial and Applied Mathematics*, 1999.

[14] J. D. Vélez, J. P. Hernández, and C. A. Cadavid. Limits of quotients of real polynomial functions of three variables. *ArXiv e-prints*, May 2015.

[15] S.J. Xiao and G.X. Zeng. Determination of the limits for multivariate rational functions. *Science China Mathematics*, 57(2):397–416, 2014.

[16] L. Yang, X. Hou, and B. Xia. A complete algorithm for automated discovering of a class of inequality-type theorems. *Science in China Series F: Information Sciences*, 44(1):33–49, 2001.

Infinitely Many Carmichael Numbers for a Modified Miller-Rabin Prime Test

Eric Bach and Rex Fernando
Dept. of Computer Sciences
University of Wisconsin – Madison
Madison, WI, USA
bach@cs.wisc.edu, rex@cs.wisc.edu

ABSTRACT

We study a variant of the Miller-Rabin primality test, which only looks at the last $z+1$ powers of the base. This test is between Miller-Rabin and Fermat in terms of strength. For $z=1$ the test can be thought of as a variant of the Solovay-Strassen test. We show that for every $z \geq 0$ this test has infinitely many "Carmichael" numbers. We also give empirical results on the rate of growth of the test's "Carmichael" numbers, noting that the growth rate decreases geometrically with increasing z. We provide some heuristic evidence for this pattern. We also extend our existence result to some generalizations of Miller-Rabin that use b-th powers instead of squares.

Keywords

Primality testing, Carmichael numbers, computational number theory.

1. INTRODUCTION

Primality testing is an important ingredient in many cryptographic protocols. Although it was shown by [AKS04] that primality is in **P**, the majority of tests in practical use are probabilistic. Two important examples of probabilistic primality tests are Solovay and Strassen's test [SS77], and Rabin's modification [Rab80] of a test by Miller [Mil76], commonly called the Miller-Rabin test. The Solovay-Strassen test has historical significance because it was proposed as the test to be used as part of the RSA cryptosystem in [RSA78], arguably one of the most important applications of primality testing. Miller-Rabin is the more widely used of the two tests, because it is more reliable than Solovay-Strassen. This holds in a strong sense; for example, every Miller-Rabin liar is also a Solovay-Strassen liar [PSW80]. A notable example of Miller-Rabin's usage is in the popular OpenSSL secure communication library [ope].

*Research supported by NSF: CCF-1420750

ISSAC '16, July 19–22, 2016, Waterloo, ON, Canada.
© 2016 ACM. ISBN 978-1-4503-4380-0/16/07...$15.00
DOI: http://dx.doi.org/10.1145/2930889.2930911

We explore the relationship between these two tests and the much older Fermat test. Both tests can be thought of as building upon the Fermat test; indeed, all three algorithms have a very similar structure, but the Fermat test has a fatal weakness which the two more modern tests fix: as Alford, Granville and Pomerance proved in [AGP94], there is an infinite set of composite numbers which in effect fool the Fermat test. In the case where a number from this set is given as input, the test performs no better than randomly guessing a non-unit for the number. These numbers are called *Carmichael numbers*, after the discoverer of the first example of such a number [Car10]. (A. Korselt found an important characterization of Carmichael numbers ten years earlier [Kor99], but did not find an actual example.)

We now describe the three algorithms. All three take an odd number $n \in \mathbb{Z}$ to be tested for primality, and start by choosing a random $a \in \mathbb{Z}$, where $2 \leq a \leq n-1$. The Fermat test, the simplest of the three, checks whether $a^{n-1} \equiv 1 \pmod{n}$. If so, it returns "Probably Prime", and if not it returns "Composite". The Solovay-Strassen test computes the Jacobi symbol $\left(\frac{a}{n}\right)$, and returns "Composite" if $\left(\frac{a}{n}\right) = 0$ or $a^{(n-1)/2} \not\equiv \left(\frac{a}{n}\right) \pmod{n}$. Otherwise it returns "Probably prime". Let $n-1 = 2^r \cdot d$ with d odd. The Miller-Rabin test considers the sequence

$$a^d, a^{2d}, \ldots, a^{2^{r-1}d}, a^{2^r d}; \tag{1}$$

if 1 does not appear in the sequence, or if it first appears directly after a number that is not -1, then the test returns "Composite"; otherwise it returns "Probably Prime".

We can think of the two newer algorithms as being more specific versions of the Fermat test. Both essentially fall back to the Fermat test in the case of non-Carmichael numbers. In this paper we explore the gap between these two tests and Fermat.

In particular, we study the following variant of the Miller-Rabin test. Fix some constant z, which we call the depth. Instead of checking the whole sequence (1), only check the last $z+1$ numbers. If $z=1$, the test can be thought of as the following variant of Solovay-Strassen: after generating a, check whether $a^{(n-1)/2} \equiv \pm 1 \pmod{n}$. These two variants form intermediate steps between Fermat and the respective tests they are based on. The main result of this paper shows that these variants behave more like the Fermat test than the Miller-Rabin and Solovay-Strassen tests from which they are derived: namely, there are infinitely many "Carmichael" numbers for both tests. In other words, these tests are strictly weaker than Miller-Rabin and Solovay-Strassen. We also provide heuristic evidence that as z increases, the number of "Carmichael" numbers for the corresponding test decreases geometrically.

Note that these tests are no faster than the original Miller-Rabin, since the usual computation of a^{n-1} would produce the entire sequence (1) anyway. Therefore, we study the tests not for their runtime efficiency but for their interesting theoretical properties, which may prove useful in other contexts.

Let $C_z(X)$ count the "Carmichael" numbers less than X for our variant of Miller-Rabin with parameter z. We call these z-deep Carmichael numbers. The contributions of this paper are:

1. A lower bound on $C_z(X)$, of the same strength as Alford, Granville and Pomerance's lower bound on the number of Carmichael numbers and based on their work.
2. A generalization of this result for some modifications of Miller-Rabin which use b-th powers instead of squares.
3. An empirical comparison of $C_z(X)$ to $C(X)$, the number of Carmichael numbers less than X.
4. Two heuristic arguments suggesting that the ratio $C_z(X)/C(X)$ decays geometrically with increasing z.

Although not stated explicitly, the results in [AGP94] imply that there is an infinite sequence of Carmichaels n, for which the probability of "accidental factorization" (by guessing a base a not coprime to n) is asymptotically less than the inverse of any polynomial in $\log n$. The same holds for the specialized Carmichaels we discuss.

The organization of this paper is as follows. Section 2 contains relevant preliminaries. Section 3 contains the main result and generalization to other tests, and Section 4 contains the upper bound discussion and empirical results.

1.1 Acknowledgements

The authors would like to thank Carl Pomerance for pointing out the generalization in Section 3.3 and an alternative proof of the lower bound result. We would also like to thank Nigel Boston for some helpful suggestions, and Andrew Shallue for providing detailed comments on an early draft of the paper. Finally we would like to thank the anonymous reviewers for their many helpful suggestions.

2. OVERVIEW OF ALFORD, GRANVILLE, AND POMERANCE'S ORIGINAL ARGUMENT

We describe the argument used in [AGP94] to prove there are infinitely many Carmichael numbers.

By Korselt's criterion [Kor99] a positive composite integer $n > 1$ is a Carmichael number iff it is odd and squarefree and for all primes p dividing n, $n \equiv 1 \pmod{p-1}$. The approach of [AGP94] uses this criterion and exploits following theorem, proved by multiple independent parties (see the discussion in [AGP94]).

THEOREM 1 (2 IN [AGP94]). *If G is a finite abelian group in which the maximal order of an element is m, then in any sequence of at least $m(1+\log(|G|/m))$ (not necessarily distinct) elements of G, there is a nonempty subsequence whose product is the identity.*

Given this theorem, assume we have some integer M where the corresponding m is small in $(\mathbb{Z}/M\mathbb{Z})^*$. Assume we can find many primes p where $p-1$ divides M. If there are enough such primes, some of them must multiply to equal the identity in $(\mathbb{Z}/M\mathbb{Z})^*$. The product of those primes is then a Carmichael number, by Korselt's criterion. This strategy was suggested by Erdös [Erd56] as a way to prove there are infinitely many Carmichael numbers, although he did not know Theorem 1 and simply guessed that there might be a way to exhibit many products that produce the identity. [AGP94] successfully implemented a modified version of this strategy. We state the main theorem in [AGP94] before continuing. Here $\mathcal{E}$ is a set of positive number-theoretic constants related to smooth values of shifted primes, useful in finding integers where the multiplicative group has small m. $\mathcal{B}$ is another set of constants related to finding primes in arithmetic progressions, useful in finding the set of primes p to construct Carmichael numbers from. Let $C(X)$ be the number of Carmichael numbers less than X.

THEOREM 2 (1 IN [AGP94]). *For each $E \in \mathcal{E}$ and $B \in \mathcal{B}$ there is a number $X_0 = X_0(E, B)$ such that $C(X) \geq X^{EB}$ for all $X \geq X_0$.*

At the time the best results for $\mathcal{E}$ and $\mathcal{B}$ allowed the exponent to be $2/7$. The exponent has since been improved slightly; see [Har05, Har08].

To prove Theorem 2, [AGP94] show there is an L (parameterized by X) where $n((\mathbb{Z}/L\mathbb{Z})^*)$ is relatively small compared to L. (We denote by $n(G)$ the largest number of elements of G which does not have a subsequence that multiplies to the identity.) They then use a theorem by Prachar [Pra55] which shows there is some $k < L^c$ for some constant $c < 1$ where there are many primes p that satisfy $p-1|kL$. This is a departure from Erdos's original heuristic. and at first seems problematic: now the group in question is $G = (\mathbb{Z}/kL\mathbb{Z})^*$, whose largest order m is not necessarily small. [AGP94] gets around this by modifying Prachar's theorem to guarantee that $(k, L) = 1$ and for each p, p is $1 \pmod{k}$. The primes chosen are in the subgroup of $(\mathbb{Z}/kL\mathbb{Z})^*$ of residue classes that are $1 \mod k$, which is isomorphic to $(\mathbb{Z}/L\mathbb{Z})^*$, thus fixing the problem. They use a simple counting argument based on Theorem 1 to show the existence of enough products of primes chosen from the set of p to satisfy the lower bound claimed.

3. HIGHER DEPTH TESTS

Our variant of the Miller-Rabin test follows the same procedure as the original Miller-Rabin test (described in the introduction), but only considers the last $z+1$ numbers in the sequence (1). (If there are fewer than $z+1$ numbers in the sequence it looks at all of them.) Hereafter we refer to this test as the *z-deep Miller-Rabin test* (with parameter z). Note that the 0-deep Miller-Rabin test is simply the Fermat test.

We define a *z-deep Carmichael number* to be a composite number n which fools the z-deep Miller-Rabin test for all $a \in \mathbb{Z}_n^*$. Such an n must satisfy a strong divisibility condition:

PROPOSITION 1. *A positive integer n is a z-deep Carmichael number iff it is odd and squarefree and for all $p \mid n$, $(p-1) \mid \frac{n-1}{2^z}$.*

PROOF. The proposition follows from (i) and (ii) below. Let us write n_z for $(n-1)/2^z$.

(i) Let $n > 1$ be composite. Then $a^{n_z} \equiv 1 \pmod{n}$ for all $a \in (\mathbb{Z}/n\mathbb{Z})^*$ if and only if n is odd and squarefree and for all primes $p \mid n$, we have $p - 1 \mid n_z$.

(ii) Let $n > 1$ be composite. There is an $a \in (\mathbb{Z}/n\mathbb{Z})^*$ with $a^{n_z} \not\equiv 1 \pmod{n}$ if and only if the z-deep Miller-Rabin test reports n is composite for some base $a \in (\mathbb{Z}/n\mathbb{Z})^*$.

(i) is proved the same way as Korselt's criterion (Thm. 3.4.6 in [CP05]). Let us prove (ii). If n is a prime power, then both parts hold. We therefore assume n is not a prime power.

First, the forward direction: if $a^{n_z} \equiv 1 \pmod{n}$ then either the test with base a reports "composite" or $a^{n_y} \equiv -1 \pmod{n}$ for some $y \le z$. Let a map to $(a_1, a_2, \ldots, a_r)$ under the Chinese remainder isomorphism. Then the z-deep Miller-Rabin test reports "composite" on base $a' = (1, a_2, \ldots, a_r)$.

For the reverse direction: if the z-deep Miller-Rabin test reports "composite" upon choosing a then $a^{n_z} \not\equiv 1 \pmod{n}$. □

As before, $C_z(X)$ is the number of z-deep Carmichael numbers less than X. Our goal is to prove the following theorem.

THEOREM 3. *Choose any constant $z \in \mathbb{Z}^+$. For each $E \in \mathcal{E}, B \in \mathcal{B}$ and $\epsilon > 0$, there is a number $X_1(E, B, \epsilon)$, such that whenever $X \ge X_1(E, B, \epsilon)$, we have $C_z(X) \ge X^{EB-\epsilon}$.*

We now introduce our modification of the argument in [AGP94]. Intuitively, we want to constrain the Carmichael numbers constructed in [AGP94] to additionally be 1 modulo a high power of 2 which is sufficiently higher than the largest power of two which divides any $p - 1$. If we can do this, then we should get z-deep Carmichael numbers. Banks and Pomerance [BP10] show how to modifiy the method in [AGP94] to constrain the constructed Carmichael numbers to be 1 modulo some given constant number. (This is a simple subcase of their general result.) We modify [AGP94]'s argument further to constrain the highest power of 2 which divides any $p - 1$ to be constant. We then can use the modification from [BP10] to construct Carmichael numbers which are 1 modulo a higher power of 2 (how much higher depending on z) which gives us Theorem 3.

Carmichael numbers are constructed in [AGP94] from sequences of primes which are of the form $p = dk + 1$ where $d \mid L$ and for some $k \le L^c$, $c < 1$. (These are the primes provided by Prachar's theorem, as explained in the previous section.) An artifact of [AGP94]'s proof which turns out to be convenient for us is that L is always chosen to be odd; this means that the entire power of 2 which divides $p - 1$ is in k. Let $k = 2^\nu l$, with $\nu \ge 1, l$ odd. In Section 3.1 we show that k can be constrained so that ν is bounded above by a constant. In Section 3.2 we show how to tie everything together to get a proof of Theorem 3.

3.1 Constraining k

[AGP94] choose k during their proof of the modified Prachar's Theorem, which we now state. Recall that B is one of the two number-theoretic constants which [AGP94] relies on throughout their paper. Here x is a parameter which ends up being polylog(X).

THEOREM 4 (3.1 IN [AGP94]). *There exists a number $x_2(B)$ such that if $x \ge x_2(B)$ and L is a squarefree integer not divisible by any prime exceeding $x^{(1-B)/2}$ and for which $\sum_{prime\ q|L} 1/q \le (1-B)/32$, then there is a positive integer $k \le x^{1-B}$ with $(k, L) = 1$ such that*

$$\#\{d \mid L : dk+1 \le x, dk+1 \text{ is prime}\} \ge \frac{2^{-D_B-2}}{\log x} \#\{d \mid L : 1 \le d \le x^B\}.$$

We sketch [AGP94]'s proof. It involves showing that for each divisor $d < x^B$ of L (excluding some troublesome divisors) the number of primes $p \le dx^{1-B}$ with $p \equiv 1 \pmod{d}$ and $((p-1)/d, L) = 1$ is large, and then by choosing k to be the $(p-1)/d$ that shows up the most. The lower bound on the number of such primes p is achieved by taking the number of primes $p \le dx^{1-B}$ with $p \equiv 1 \pmod{d}$, and then subtracting the number of primes less than dx^{1-B} that are $1 \pmod{dq}$ for any prime $q \mid L$:

$$\pi(dx^{1-B}; d, 1) - \sum_{\text{prime } q|L} \pi(dx^{1-B}; dq, 1).$$

[AGP94] use a lower bound which they derive to show

$$\pi(dx^{1-B}; d, 1) \ge \frac{dx^{1-B}}{2\phi(d)\log x},$$

and the Brun-Titchmarsh upper bound [MV73] to show

$$\pi(dx^{1-B}; dq, 1) \le \frac{8}{q(1-B)} \frac{dx^{1-B}}{\phi(d)\log x}.$$

It then follows that

$$\pi(dx^{1-B}; d, 1) - \sum_{\text{prime } q|L} \pi(dx^{1-B}; dq, 1)$$
$$\ge \left(\frac{1}{2} - \frac{8}{1-B} \sum_{\text{prime } q|L} \frac{1}{q}\right) \frac{dx^{1-B}}{\phi(d)\log x} \ge \frac{x^{1-B}}{4\log x},$$

the last bound following from the assumption that $\sum_{\text{prime } q|L} 1/q \le (1-B)/32$. This concludes our sketch.

Our goal is to get the same result with the added guarantee that the largest power of 2 that divides k is small. We add the additional condition that $p \not\equiv 1 \pmod{2^{\nu_0} d}$, where $\nu_0 \in \mathbb{Z}^+$ is a constant chosen so that $\frac{1-B}{32} > \frac{1}{2^{\nu_0}}$. So the number of such primes p becomes

$$\pi(dx^{1-B}; d, 1) - \sum_{\text{prime } q|L} \pi(dx^{1-B}; dq, 1) - \pi(dx^{1-b}; 2^{\nu_0} d, 1).$$

By the same bound as before,

$$\pi(dx^{1-B}; 2^{\nu_0} d, 1) \le \frac{8}{2^{\nu_0}(1-B)} \frac{dx^{1-B}}{\phi(d)\log x},$$

thus

$$\pi(dx^{1-B}; d, 1) - \sum_{\text{prime } q|L} \pi(dx^{1-B}; dq, 1) - \pi(dx^{1-b}; 2^{\nu_0} d, 1)$$
$$\ge \left(\frac{1}{2} - \frac{8}{1-B}\left(\sum_{\text{prime } q|L} \frac{1}{q} + \frac{1}{2^{\nu_0}}\right)\right) \frac{dx^{1-B}}{\phi(d)\log x}.$$

This requires $\sum_{\text{prime } q|L} \frac{1}{q} \le \frac{1-B}{32} - \frac{1}{2^{\nu_0}}$ in order to result in the same lower bound of $\frac{x^{1-B}}{4\log x}$, which is a stronger assumption than before; but this turns out not to be a problem (explained later). The result of all the above is our modified version of [AGP94]'s Theorem 3.1:

THEOREM 5. *Choose any* $\nu_0 \in \mathbb{Z}^+$ *so that* $\frac{1-B}{32} > 1/2^{\nu_0}$. *Then there exists a number* $x_3(B)$ *such that if* $x \geq x_3(B)$ *and* L *is a squarefree integer not divisible by any prime exceeding* $x^{(1-B)/2}$ *and for which* $\sum_{prime\ q|L} 1/q \leq (1-B)/32 - 1/2^{\nu_0}$*, then there is a positive integer* $k \leq x^{1-B}$ *with* $(k, L) = 1$ *and* $2^{\nu_0} \nmid k$ *such that*

$$\#\{d\,|\,L{:}dk{+}1{\leq}x{,}dk{+}1 \text{ is prime}\} \geq \frac{2^{-D_B-2}}{\log x}\#\{d\,|\,L{:}1{\leq}d{\leq}x^B\}.$$

3.2 The Modified Proof

We follow the [AGP94] method using our new result above (Theorem 5). Recall [AGP94] works in the group $G = (\mathbb{Z}/L\mathbb{Z})^*$ in order to get products which are 1 (mod L) and hence are Carmichael numbers. We follow the strategy in [BP10], choosing a new G with the aim of also forcing the product to also be 1 (mod 2^{ν_0+z}).

Let $G = (\mathbb{Z}/2^{\nu_0+z}L\mathbb{Z})^*$. If there is a sequence whose product is the identity in G, then the product is indeed both 1 (mod L) and 1 (mod 2^{ν_0+z}). We plug in this new G and Theorem 5 into the proof of Theorem 4.1 in [AGP94]; a careful analysis of the argument in [AGP94] shows our changes do not cause any problems, and do not even affect the asympotic lower bound achieved. A lack of space prevents us from including the entire modified argument of Theorem 4.1 in detail, but we present two key points here.

First is that the choice of G does not change the upper bound on $n(G)$ given in [AGP94]'s original argument. [AGP94] parameterizes the proof of Theorem 4.1 on some y sufficiently large, and calculates both L and the outwardly visible parameter X based on y. The upper bound on $n(G)$ parameterized by y, given originally in equation (4.4) in [AGP94], becomes

$$n(G) < 2^{\nu_0+z}\lambda(L)(1 + \log 2^{\nu_0+z}L) \leq e^{3\theta y},$$

with the right hand side not changing.

Second is the issue mentioned in the previous section, that $\sum_{\text{prime } q|L} \frac{1}{q}$ must be less than $\frac{1-B}{32} - \frac{1}{2^{\nu_0}}$ instead of just $\frac{1-B}{32}$. The reason why this is not a problem is that AGP shows $\sum_{\text{prime } q|L} \frac{1}{q} \leq 2\frac{\log\log y}{\theta \log y}$, which is actually asymptotically less than any constant.

The changes we have made have only affected the minimum choice of X for which the proof will work; the other logic of the proof is not affected. So for large enough X we get the same fraction of sequences whose products are 1 in G. Since any product of such a sequence $\prod(S)$ is 1 (mod L) it follows that the product is 1 (mod kL) and thus a Carmichael number. Any prime number $p \in S$ is of the form $dk + 1$ with d odd, $k = 2^{\nu}l$, and $2^{\nu+z} \mid \prod(S) - 1$, so $p - 1 = dk|\frac{\prod(S)-1}{2^z}$. Hence, we have a proof of Theorem 3.

3.3 Generalization and Alternate Proof

In correspondence with the authors, Carl Pomerance suggested a generalization of the notion of depth to numbers other than powers of 2. He also pointed out an alternate proof of the main result of the last section, that there are infinitely many z-deep Carmichaels. With his permission, we present his ideas here. The alternate proof is advantageous because it does not require modification of Theorem 4. The z-deep Carmichaels we construct with the aid of Theorem 5, on the other hand, are composed of primes p for which $\nu_2(p-1)$, the number of 2's in $p-1$, is not too large. Since there are algorithms with complexity dependent on this number, such as the Tonelli-Shanks square root algorithm [Sha72], this constraint might be useful in future work.

Fix a number $m \geq 1$. Let $n > 1$ be odd, and congruent to 1 mod m. We will call n an m-Carmichael number if $a^{(n-1)/m} \equiv 1$ for all $a \in (\mathbb{Z}/n\mathbb{Z})^*$. Thus, a 1-Carmichael number is just a Carmichael number, and 2^z-Carmichael numbers are just z-deep Carmichaels.

We now select θ and, from it, L, as in the proof of [AGP94]'s Theorem 4.1. (L also depends on a parameter y which we imagine to be "sufficiently large.") Let the integer $k > 1$, prime to L, be as is guaranteed to exist by Theorem 4. Now, we deviate from [AGP94] choosing G as the subgroup of $(\mathbb{Z}/mkL\mathbb{Z})^*$ consisting of residues that are 1 mod k. There is a relatively prime factorization $m = m_1m_2$ where the primes in m_1 divide k and the primes in m_2 do not. Since $(k, L) = 1$, we have $(m_1k, m_2L) = 1$, and therefore

$$(\mathbb{Z}/mkL\mathbb{Z})^* \cong (\mathbb{Z}/m_1k\mathbb{Z})^* \times (\mathbb{Z}/m_2L\mathbb{Z})^*.$$

So,

$$G \cong (\mathbb{Z}/m_1\mathbb{Z})^+ \times (\mathbb{Z}/m_2L\mathbb{Z})^*.$$

(To prove this, apply the result $(\mathbb{Z}/q^e\mathbb{Z})^* \cong (\mathbb{Z}/q\mathbb{Z})^* \times (\mathbb{Z}/q^{e-1}\mathbb{Z})^+$ for each maximal prime-power factor q^e of m_1k.) We can bound the exponent of G independently of k; since $(k, L) = 1$ this exponent is $m_1\lambda(m_2L) \leq m_1m_2\lambda(L) \leq m\lambda(L)$. (Here $\lambda(n)$ is the maximum order of any element in $(\mathbb{Z}/n\mathbb{Z})^*$.) Therefore, $n(G) \leq m\lambda(L)[1+\log mL] \leq e^{3\theta y}$, where the last inequality holds for all sufficiently large y.

Suppose that S is a sequence of primes $p \in G$ for which $n := \prod_{p\in S} p \equiv 1 \pmod{mkL}$. Then, since $p = dk+1$ where $d \mid L$, we have

$$p - 1 = dk \mid kL = \frac{mkL}{m} \mid \frac{n-1}{m}.$$

This shows (by an extension of the Korselt criterion) that n is m-Carmichael. The argument in [AGP94] shows that there are many such sequences, in fact, enough to produce infinitely many m-Carmichaels.

Theorem 5 guarantees that there is an auxiliary modulus k that is not "too even." With the same sort of modification used to prove this result, we could guarantee that, for each prime $l|k$, $\nu_l(k)$ is not too large. This would provide infinitely many m-Carmichaels with a potentially useful further constraint on their prime factors.

If the Miller-Rabin test is modified appropriately, the successive squarings it does can be replaced by repeated computation of b-th powers, for some fixed b. Berrizbeitia and Berry [BB00] have studied such generalizations. For simplicity, we restrict to the case where b is prime. Suppose that $n > 1$ is composite, and all prime factors of n are 1 mod b. Then $n \equiv 1$ mod b, and $(\mathbb{Z}/n\mathbb{Z})^*$ has a primitive b-th root of unity ω. (We could find ω by factoring $X^b - 1$ mod n, using a Las Vegas method such as the Cantor-Zassenhaus algorithm. It will either work or show n is not prime.) With such a number in hand, we can run the following b-test: Let $n-1 = b^rd$, where $(b, d) = 1$. Choose a base a, and compute

$$a^d, a^{bd}, a^{b^2d}, \ldots, a^{b^rd} = a^{n-1}.$$

modulo n. When n is prime, the sequence must end in 1, and the predecessor of the first 1 in the sequence, if there is any, must be a power of ω. If this is not observed we declare n composite (with certainty); if it is, we say that n is probably prime.

When $b = 2$ this b-test is just Miller-Rabin. Many of the known results about Miller-Rabin, including error bounds and a version valid under ERH, have been generalized to the b-test; see e.g. [BO08]. By the work of Banks and Pomerance [BP10], there are infinitely many Carmichaels that fool the b-test. By the results of this section, we can state the following generalization: suppose we modify the b-test by only observing the last z elements of the sequence, where z is a constant. Any b^z-Carmichael will fool this test, and by the results of this section, we know there are infinitely many of them.

4. GROWTH BASED ON DEPTH

From the OEIS' list of the first 10,000 Carmichael numbers [Slo], we tallied the numbers which are z-deep Carmichaels for $z = 1$ to 14, the maximum depth observed. We also separated the counts by the number of prime factors up to 8, the maximum number observed. The results are in Table 1.

Observe that $C_z(x)$ is about $1/2^z$ of $C(x)$. We now discuss two points of evidence that this pattern might hold globally. First is an observation about the proof of the latest upper bound for $C(x)$, given in [PSW80] and improved in [Pom81]. We observe that the dominant term in the proof of the upper bound follows the pattern in the table. Second is a heuristic idea which models the prime factors of Carmichael numbers as 2-adic integers. Although it is far from rigorous, it does allow for some quantitative predictions.

4.1 The Dominant Term in the Carmichaels Upper Bound

Let $\ln_k x$ denote the k-fold iteration of ln. In 1980 [PSW80] proved the following:

THEOREM 6 (6 IN [PSW80]). *For each $\epsilon > 0$, there is an $X_0(\epsilon)$ such that for all $X \geq X_0(\epsilon)$, we have $C(X) \leq X \exp(-(1-\epsilon)\ln X \cdot \ln_3 X/\ln_2 X)$*

[Pom81] later sharpened one of the terms in this proof, which resulted in a slightly stronger result. To the authors' knowledge, this is the best known upper bound for $C(X)$. We present our observation in terms of the 1980 result, and discuss [Pom81] briefly later.

We outline their proof here. Let $\delta > 0$. Divide the Carmichael numbers $n \leq X$ into three classes:

$N_1 = \#$ of Carmichaels $n \leq X^{1-\delta}$

$N_2 = \#$ of Carmichaels $X^{1-\delta} < n \leq X$ where n has a prime factor $p \geq X^{\delta}$

$N_3 = \#$ of Carmichaels $X^{1-\delta} < n \leq X$ where all prime factors of n are below X^{δ}

We get that $N_1 \leq X^{1-\delta}$ trivially, and $N_2 < 2X^{1-\delta}$ (see [PSW80] for details).

It is shown in [PSW80] that

$$N_3 \leq X^{1-\delta} + \sum_{X^{1-2\delta} < k \leq X^{1-\delta}} X/kf(k), \qquad (2)$$

where $f(k)$ is the least common multiple of $p-1$ for all $p \mid k$. The sum in (2) is the dominating term in the sum $N_1 + N_2 + N_3 = C(X)$. We show how to strengthen this term for $C_z(X)$.

PROPOSITION 2. *Let $k \geq 2$. The number of z-deep Carmichael numbers $n \leq X$ divisible by k is at most $1 + X/2^z kf(k)$.*

PROOF. Any such n is 0 (mod k) and 1 (mod $2^z f(k)$). The latter congruence is because $n \equiv 1 \pmod{f(k)}$ and $n \equiv 1 \pmod{2^{z+y}}$, where y is the largest number such that $2^y \mid p-1$ for some $p \mid n$ prime. So $2^z f(k)$ and k are coprime, and the result follows by the Chinese Remainder Theorem. □

With this lemma, and the observation that any n in the third class has a $k \mid n$ where $X^{1-2\delta} < k \leq X^{1-\delta}$, we have that

$$N_3 \leq X^{1-\delta} + \frac{1}{2^z} \sum_{X^{1-2\delta} < k \leq X^{1-\delta}} X/kf(k).$$

It is possible to also derive similar bounds for N_1 and N_2, in order to show that

$$C_z(X) < \frac{1}{2^z} X \exp(-(1-\epsilon)\ln X \cdot \ln_3 X/\ln_2 X).$$

This does not improve the bound asymptotically, though, since if $\epsilon_1 < \epsilon_2$ then

$$X \exp(-(1-\epsilon_1)\ln X \cdot \ln_3 X/\ln_2 X) < \frac{1}{2^z} X \exp(-(1-\epsilon_2)\ln X \cdot \ln_3 X/\ln_2 X)$$

asymptotically for any z. Nevertheless, we still find this interesting. Pomerance [Pom81] sharpens the estimate for the sum in (2) to get a slightly better upper bound for $C(X)$, and conjectures that this upper bound is tight. Assuming this is the case, the sum in (2) is the most important term in determining the growth of $C(X)$. Additionally, Proposition 2 fits almost perfectly with the data in Table 1.

4.2 The Local Korselt Criterion

Proposition 1 shows that the depth of a Carmichael number is determined by a local condition, at the prime 2. Accordingly, if we want a heuristic explanation for the observed thinning of Carmichaels by depth, we should base it on 2-adic analysis. In the next two subsections we pursue this idea in detail.

Let n be a composite number. If p is prime, we say that n is *p-Korselt* if $\nu_p(\lambda(n)) \leq \nu_p(n-1)$. For example, 33 is 2-Korselt but 15 is not. This is a local version of the Korselt criterion. Indeed, n is a Carmichael number iff it is p-Korselt for every p, and satisfies a global property (squarefree with at least 3 prime factors).

Let $n = p_1 p_2 ... p_r$ be a Carmichael number. Then

$$\nu_2(n-1) - \max_i \{\nu_2(p_i - 1)\} \geq 0.$$

We say n has exact depth z if this difference is z. By Proposition 1, then, "depth z" is the same as "exact depth $\geq z$."

To study this situation, we shall model $p_1, p_2, \ldots, p_r$ by i.i.d. random elements of $(\mathbb{Z}_2)^*$ (invertible 2-adic integers). In binary notation, such numbers are written

$$\cdots b_4 b_3 b_2 b_1 1.$$

# Prime factors:	3	4	5	6	7	8	All
$z = 0$	1166	2390	3807	2233	388	16	10000
1	498	1244	1834	1090	204	8	4878
2	239	586	916	553	99	6	2399
3	110	297	462	298	48	3	1218
4	52	139	232	142	23	1	589
5	26	76	108	75	13	1	299
6	12	39	49	40	6		146
7	10	20	21	21			72
8	2	12	10	11			35
9		8	2	5			15
10		4	1	3			8
11		3	1	2			6
12		2		2			4
13		2		1			3
14				1			1

Table 1: The number of depth-z Carmichael numbers up to 1713045574801 (the 10000th Carmichael number), filtered by number of prime factors.

Here $b_i \in \{0, 1\}$ for $i \geq 1$. Our model amounts to imagining that these bits are chosen by independent flips of a fair coin.

Let $\nu_i = \nu_2(p_i - 1)$, for $i = 1, \ldots, r$, with $\mu = \min\{\nu_i\}$ and $\nu = \max\{\nu_i\}$. The *exponent vector* is $(\nu_1, \ldots, \nu_r)$ Finally, we let

$$p_i = 1 + 2^{\nu_i} + u_i 2^{\nu_i + 1}, \qquad i = 1, \ldots, r. \tag{3}$$

If μ occurs s times in the exponent vector, we have

$$p_1 p_2 \cdots p_r \equiv 1 + s2^{\mu} \pmod{2^{\mu+1}}. \tag{4}$$

It is an interesting fact that the 2-Korselt property constrains the exponent vector. In particular, unless the exponents are equal, the minimum exponent μ must occur an even number of times, as follows from (4). This holds for Carmichael numbers as well. We have not seen this observation in the literature, although it is known for $\mu = 1$. (We thank Andrew Shallue for informing us about this.) Another consequence of (4) is that $p_1, \ldots, p_r$ is 2-Korselt whenever the exponents are equal.

We now establish the probability that an r-tuple is 2-Korselt in our model.

LEMMA 1. *Let $X_1, \ldots, X_n$ be i.i.d. random variables having a geometric distribution with parameter 1/2. (So X_i is 1 with probability 1/2, 2 with probability 1/4, and so on.) Let $Z = \max_i\{X_i\}$. Then*

$$W(n) := \sum_{k \geq 1} \Pr[Z = k] \cdot \frac{1}{2^{k-1}} = \sum_{j=0}^{n} (-1)^j \binom{n}{j} \frac{1}{2^{j+1} - 1}.$$

PROOF. Let $P_n(k) = \Pr[Z \leq k] = (1 - 2^{-k})^n$. Applying partial summation,

$$W(n) = \sum_{k \geq 1} \frac{1}{2^{k-1}} \left[P_n(k) - P_n(k+1)\right] = \sum_{k \geq 1} \frac{1}{2^k}(1 - 2^{-k})^n.$$

To obtain the result, expand the n-th powers by the binomial theorem, interchange the order of summation, and sum the resulting geometric series. □

THEOREM 7. *Let $p_1, \ldots, p_r$ be random elements of $(\mathbb{Z}_2)^*$, with $r \geq 1$. Then $p_1, p_2, \ldots, p_r$ is 2-Korselt with probability*

$$\frac{1}{2^r - 1}\left[1 + \sum_{\substack{2 \leq s < r \\ s \text{ even}}} \binom{r}{s} \sum_{j=0}^{r-s} (-1)^j \binom{r-s}{j} \frac{1}{2^{j+1} - 1}\right].$$

PROOF. We will exploit the principle of deferred decisions, which was popularized by Donald Knuth. Also, we will assume $r \geq 2$, since no proof is needed for $r = 1$.

Imagine that we reveal bits of the $(p_i - 1)$'s in parallel (taking blocks of r at a time), until the minimal exponent μ is known. Then, the p_i's might look like this:

$$\begin{array}{c} \cdots * *10 \cdots 001. \\ \cdots * *00 \cdots 001. \\ \vdots \\ \cdots * *10 \cdots 001. \\ \longleftarrow \text{ time} \end{array}$$

In this picture, the *'s stand for bits that are not yet revealed. Note that the bits immediately to their right mark the earliest appearance of a nonzero block. Suppose there are s 1's and $r - s$ 0's in that block. The probability of obtaining such a block is $\binom{r}{s}/(2^r - 1)$, since there are $\binom{r}{s}$ binary tuples with Hamming weight s, and $2^r - 1$ blocks that force a stop.

Given this information, what is the probability that $p_1, p_2, \ldots, p_r$ is 2-Korselt? It is 1 when $s = r$ (regardless of parity), and it is 0 when s is odd with $s < r$.

The remaining case (s even, $s < r$) can be analyzed as follows. We continue the process, revealing only enough bits to determine $\nu_{s+1}, \ldots, \nu_r$. Whether or not the 2-Korselt property holds is determined solely by the unseen bits. Order the p_i's so that p_1 and p_2 have the minimum exponent, and now reveal all of $p_3, \ldots, p_r$. Writing t_i for $1 + 2u_i$, we see that $p_1 p_2 \ldots p_r \equiv 1 \pmod{2^\nu}$ iff

$$t_1(1 + 2^{\mu} t_2) + t_2 \equiv \frac{(p_3 \cdots p_r)^{-1} - 1}{2^{\mu}} \pmod{2^{\nu - \mu}}.$$

The right hand side is integral, and even because the p_i with exponent μ come in pairs. The coefficient of t_1 is odd.

1	2	3	4	5	6	7	8	9	10
1	$\frac{1}{3}$	$\frac{3}{7}$	$\frac{9}{35}$	$\frac{167}{651}$	$\frac{43}{217}$	$\frac{725}{3937}$	$\frac{95339}{602361}$	$\frac{24834279}{171003595}$	$\frac{49160655}{376207909}$
1.000	0.333	0.429	0.257	0.257	0.198	0.184	0.158	0.145	0.131

Table 2: Exact 2-Korselt probabilities.

Therefore, for each possible t_2 (odd), there is exactly one way to choose t_1 (odd) mod $2^{\nu-\mu}$ so as to make the above congruence true. Since $\nu - \mu - 1$ bits of t_1 are now forced, we have (for these s)

$$\Pr\left[p_1, p_2, \ldots, p_r \text{ is 2-Korselt} \mid \mu, \nu\right] = \frac{1}{2^{\nu-\mu-1}}.$$

Let A be the event that $p_1, p_2, \cdots p_r$ is 2-Korselt. To summarize,

$$\Pr\left[A \mid \nu_1, \ldots, \nu_r\right] = \begin{cases} 1, & \text{if } s = r; \\ 0, & \text{if } 1 \leq s < r \text{ and } s \text{ is odd}; \\ \frac{1}{2^{\nu-\mu-1}}, & \text{if } 2 \leq s < r \text{ and } s \text{ is even}. \end{cases}$$

(Note that s, μ, ν are all functions of $\nu_1, \ldots, \nu_r$.) When $s < r$ is even, the random variable $\nu - \mu$, necessarily 1 or greater, has the same distribution as Z in Lemma 1, but with $n = r - s$. Therefore,

$$\Pr\left[A \mid s\right] = \begin{cases} 1, & \text{if } s = r; \\ 0, & \text{if } 1 \leq s < r \text{ and } s \text{ is odd}; \\ W(r-s), & \text{if } 2 \leq s < r \text{ and } s \text{ is even}. \end{cases}$$

The theorem now follows from Lemma 1 and the conditional probability formula $\Pr[A] = E[\Pr[A|s]]$. □

Exact values of the probabilities, which are rational, can be readily computed from Theorem 7. We list a few of them in Table 2. They seem to decay slowly with r, and the results below make that precise.

THEOREM 8. $\Pr[\, p_1, \ldots, p_r$ *is 2-Korselt* $] = \Omega(r^{-1})$.

PROOF. Let Z be as in the lemma. It can be shown that

$$\frac{H_n}{\log 2} \leq E[Z] \leq \frac{H_n}{\log 2} + 1.$$

Also, from comparison with the integral, $H_n \leq \log n + 1$. Therefore, by Jensen's inequality, $E[2^{-Z}] \geq 1/(4n)$. Therefore, the probability in question is at least

$$\frac{1}{2^r} + \frac{1}{2^r} \sum_{\substack{2 \leq s < r \\ s \text{ even}}} \binom{r}{s} \frac{1}{4(r-s)}.$$

The first term is exponentially small and can be neglected. Since $\binom{r}{s} = \binom{r}{s'}$ when $s' = r - s$, we can rewrite the second term as

$$\frac{1}{4} \sum_{s' \in B} \binom{r}{s'} \frac{2^{-r}}{s'},$$

where $B = \{s' : 1 \leq s' \leq r - 2 \text{ and } s' \equiv r(2)\}$. The sum above equals $E[(s')^{-1}|B] \Pr[B]$, with $s' \sim \text{binomial}(r, 1/2)$. By Jensen's inequality

$$E[(s')^{-1}|B] \geq \frac{1}{E[s'|B]} \geq \frac{\Pr[B]}{E[s']} = \frac{2\Pr[B]}{r}.$$

The claimed result now follows, since $\Pr[B] = 1/2 + o(1)$. □

THEOREM 9. $\Pr[\, p_1, \ldots, p_r$ *is 2-Korselt* $] = O(r^{-1})$.

PROOF. Consider $f(t) = e^{-t}(1 - e^{-t})^n$. This vanishes at 0 and $+\infty$, and is nonnegative when $t \geq 0$. Moreover, since

$$f'(t) = e^{-t}(1 - e^{-t})^{n-1}\left[(n+1)e^{-t} - 1\right],$$

f is unimodal (increases, then decreases) and is maximized when $e^t = (n+1)$. Its maximum value is $\leq 1/(n+1)$. Let $\alpha = \log 2$. Then,

$$W(n) = \sum_{k \geq 1} 2^{-k}(1 - 2^{-k})^n = \sum_{k \geq 1} f(\alpha k)$$

$$\leq \int_0^\infty f(\alpha t) dt + 2\max\{f(\alpha t)\} = \frac{1}{\alpha(n+1)} + \frac{2}{n+1} \leq \frac{4}{n+1}.$$

Using symmetry as before, and including omitted terms (they are all positive), we get

$$\Pr[A] \leq \frac{1}{2^r + 1} + \frac{4}{2^r + 1} \sum_{s' \geq 1} \binom{r}{s'} \frac{1}{s' + 1}.$$

Only the second term matters, and it equals

$$\frac{2^{r+3}}{(2^r + 1)(r + 1)} \sum_{s' \geq 2} \binom{r+1}{s'} 2^{-(r+1)} = O(r^{-1}),$$

since binomial probabilities sum to 1. □

4.3 A Depth Distribution Conjecture

Having analyzed our local model in detail, we can now draw some conclusions from it.

THEOREM 10. *Let $p_1, \ldots, p_r$ be randomly chosen odd 2-adic integers, with $r \geq 3$. Let $z \geq 1$. Under the condition that $p_1, \ldots, p_r$ is 2-Korselt,*

$$\Pr[\text{ depth} = z\ ] = \begin{cases} 0 & \text{if } r \text{ is odd and all } \nu_i \text{ are equal} \\ 1/2^{z-1} & \text{if } r \text{ is even and all } \nu_i \text{ are equal} \\ 1/2^z & \text{otherwise} \end{cases}$$

PROOF. The first case follows from (4).

For the second case, if r is even then the exact depth is ≥ 1, again by (4). By expanding p_r, we see that $p_1 \ldots p_r \equiv 1 \pmod{2^{\nu+z}}$ iff

$$\frac{p_1 \ldots p_{r-1}(1 + 2^\nu) - 1}{2^{\nu+1}} + p_1 \ldots p_{r-1} u_r \equiv 0 \pmod{2^{z-1}}.$$

This determines u_r mod 2^{z-1}, making the probability of exact depth $\geq z$ equal to $1/2^{z-1}$, for $z \geq 1$.

For the third case (unequal exponents), we write

$$p_i = 1 + 2x_i + y_i 2^\nu, \; i = 1, \ldots r,$$

where $0 \leq x_1, \ldots, x_r < 2^{\nu-1}$, and (rearrange if necessary) $x_1 = 0$ and $x_r \neq 0$. Whether 2-Korselt holds depends entirely on the x_i's. If it does, we have $p_1 \ldots p_r \equiv 1 \pmod{2^{\nu+z}}$ iff

$$\frac{p_1 \cdots p_{r-1}(1+2x_r)-1}{2^\nu} + p_1 \cdots p_{r-1} y_r \equiv 0 \pmod{2^z}$$

The coefficient of y_r is odd, so there is one solution to this congruence, and the claimed result follows. □

Observe that the fraction of tuples $p_1, ..., p_r$ for which all ν_i are equal is $2^{-r} + 2^{-2r} + 2^{-3r} + \cdots = 1/(2^r - 1)$. Since the fraction of 2-Korselt r-tuples is $\Theta(1/r)$, we can draw the following conclusion about the local model: Ignoring the equal-exponent case, whose frequency diminishes with increasing r, the fraction of 2-Korselt r-tuples with depth z (that is, exact depth $\geq z$) decreases geometrically, with multiplier 1/2.

We conjecture, therefore, that for every $z \geq 1$,

$$\lim_{X\to\infty} C_z(X)/C(X) = 1/2^z.$$

Also, if $C_z^{(r)}(X)$ and $C^{(r)}(X)$ denote similar counts for Carmichaels with r prime factors, there is a constant $c_r^{(z)}$ such that

$$\lim_{X\to\infty} C_z^{(r)}(X)/C^{(r)}(X) = c_r^{(z)},$$

and $c_r^{(z)} \to 2^{-z}$ as r increases.

Let us look at Table 1 in this light. The prediction seems accurate for overall counts, but becomes less so when z and r are small. For example, the local model predicts that 1/3 of the 2-Korselt numbers for $r = 3$ will have depth 1 (this was checked by simulation). However, the actual fraction in our population of Carmichaels is $498/1166 = 0.427101....$

We do not have an explanation for this, but we can point out two weaknesses of the local model. First, it ignores the odd primes. Second, it assumes that the p_i are independent, when in fact they interact. For example, $\sum_{i=1}^{r} \nu_i \leq \log_2 n$, and the odd prime divisors of the $(p_i - 1)$'s are related, since they all divide $n - 1$.

What would it take to make the heuristic argument rigorous? First, we would need to know that the prime number theorem for arithmetic progressions still held, when the primes were restricted to those appearing in Carmichael numbers. Second, we would need a precise understanding of the deviation from independence for primes appearing together in a Carmichael number. That there are such deviations is clear, from the discussion following (4).

5. REFERENCES

[AGP94] W. R. Alford, A. Granville, and C. Pomerance. There are infinitely many Carmichael numbers. *Ann. Math.*, 139(3):703–722, 1994.

[AKS04] M. Agrawal, N. Kayal, and N. Saxena. PRIMES is in P. *Ann. Math.*, 160(2):781–793, 2004.

[BB00] P. Berrizbeitia and T. G. Berry. Generalized strong pseudoprime tests and applications. *J. Symb. Comput.*, 30:151–160, 2000.

[BO08] P. Berrizbeitia and A. Olivieri. A generalization of Miller's primality theorem. *Proc. American Math. Soc.*, 136:3095–3104, 2008.

[BP10] W. D. Banks and C. Pomerance. On Carmichael numbers in arithmetic progressions. *J. Australian Math. Soc.*, 88(3):313–321, 2010.

[Car10] R. D. Carmichael. Note on a new number theory function. *Bull. American Math. Soc.*, 16(5):232–238, 1910.

[CP05] R. Crandall and C. Pomerance. *Prime Numbers: a Computational Perspective.* Springer-Verlag, 2nd edition, 2005.

[Erd56] P. Erdös. On pseudoprimes and Carmichael numbers. *Publ. Math. Debrecen*, 4:201–206, 1956.

[Har05] G. Harman. On the number of Carmichael numbers up to x. *Bull. London Math. Soc.*, 37(5):641–650, 2005.

[Har08] G. Harman. Watt's mean value theorem and Carmichael numbers. *Int. J. Number Theory*, 4(2):241–248, 2008.

[Kor99] A. Korselt. Probleme chinois. *L'intermédiaire des Mathématiciens*, 6:143–143, 1899.

[Mil76] G. L. Miller. Riemann's hypothesis and tests for primality. *J. Computer and System Sciences*, 13(3):300–317, 1976.

[MV73] H. L. Montgomery and R. C. Vaughan. The large sieve. *Mathematika*, 20(02):119–134, 1973.

[ope] Openssl source code. https://github.com/openssl/openssl/blob/master/include/openssl/bn.h.

[Pom81] C. Pomerance. On the distribution of pseudoprimes. *Math. Comp.*, 37(156):587–593, 1981.

[Pra55] K. Prachar. Über die Anzahl der Teiler einer natürlichen Zahl, welche die Form $p - 1$ haben. *Monatshefte für Mathematik*, 59(2):91–97, 1955.

[PSW80] C. Pomerance, J. L. Selfridge, and S. S. Wagstaff. The pseudoprimes to $25 \cdot 10^9$. *Math. Comp.*, 35(151):1003–1026, 1980.

[Rab80] M. O. Rabin. Probabilistic algorithm for testing primality. *J. Number Theory*, 12(1):128–138, 1980.

[RSA78] R. L. Rivest, A. Shamir, and L. Adleman. A method for obtaining digital signatures and public-key cryptosystems. *Commun. ACM*, 21(2):120–126, 1978.

[Sha72] D. Shanks. Five number-theoretic algorithms. In *Proc. 2nd Southeastern Conf. on Combinatorics, Graph Theory, and Computing*, pages 51–70, 1972.

[Slo] N. J. A. Sloane. The On-Line Encyclopedia of Integer Sequences. http://oeis.org. Sequence A002997.

[SS77] R. Solovay and V. Strassen. A fast Monte-Carlo test for primality. *SIAM J. Comput.*, 6(1):84–85, 1977.

Baby-Step Giant-Step Algorithms for the Symmetric Group

Eric Bach*
bach@cs.wisc.edu

Bryce Sandlund*
sandlund@cs.wisc.edu

University of Wisconsin - Madison
1210 W Dayton St.
Madison, WI 53706

ABSTRACT

We study discrete logarithms in the setting of group actions. Suppose that G is a group that acts on a set S. When $r, s \in S$, a solution $g \in G$ to $r^g = s$ can be thought of as a kind of logarithm. In this paper, we study the case where $G = S_n$, and develop analogs to the Shanks baby-step / giant-step procedure for ordinary discrete logarithms. Specifically, we compute two sets $A, B \subseteq S_n$ such that every $\sigma \in S_n$ can be written as a product ab of elements $a \in A$ and $b \in B$. Our deterministic procedure is close to optimal, in the sense that A and B can be computed efficiently and $|A|$ and $|B|$ are not too far from $\sqrt{n!}$ in size. We also analyze randomized "collision" algorithms for the same problem.

Keywords

Symmetric group, group actions, discrete logarithm, collision algorithm, computational group theory.

1. INTRODUCTION

Collision algorithms have been used to obtain polynomial (typically square root) speedups since the advent of computer science. Indeed, there are even collision "algorithms" in the world of analog measurement [9]. Most collision algorithms exploit time-space tradeoffs, arriving at a quicker algorithm by storing part of the search space in memory and utilizing an efficient lookup scheme. One of the most famous of these collision-style methods is Shanks's baby-step giant-step procedure for the discrete logarithm problem [17].

Traditionally, the discrete logarithm problem is the problem of finding an integer k such that $b^k = g$, where b and g are elements of a finite cyclic group of order n and b is a generator (has order n). Then there is exactly one $k \in \{1, \ldots, n\}$ such that $b^k = g$. Shanks's baby-step giant-step algorithm then writes $k = im + j$ with $m = \lceil \sqrt{n} \rceil$ and $0 \leq i, j \leq m$ and looks for a collision in the equation:

$$g(b^{-m})^i = b^j.$$

*Research supported by NSF: CCF-1420750

ISSAC '16, July 19–22, 2016, Waterloo, ON, Canada

DOI: http://dx.doi.org/10.1145/2930889.2930930

By precomputing values of b^j (or b^{-mi}) and storing them in a hash table, a collision can be found in $O(\sqrt{n})$ time and $O(\sqrt{n})$ space, recovering the solution k.

Various extensions of the baby-step giant-step algorithm have been developed, mostly focusing on discrete logarithm problems in groups that are important to cryptography. For the classic problem, Pollard [14] contributed two elegant methods that also exploit collision, but use very little space. (They have yet to be rigorously analyzed, in their original form.) For more information about these algorithms, and more efficient methods that apply to specific groups of an arithmetic nature, we refer to surveys by McCurley [11] and Teske [18].

Ideas similar to the baby-step giant-step algorithm have been used on 0-1 integer programming problems. (This seems to be folklore.) Suppose we want to solve $Ax = b$, where x is a 0-1 column vector. If we let x_1 and x_2 be half-length column vectors, and split A down the central column into A_1 and A_2, we can use collision to solve $A_1x_1 = b - A_2x_2$. (Here, we exploit not a group structure, but rather, the associative law for matrix-vector multiplication.) For a recent application, see [5].

In this paper, we focus on a different discrete log generalization that can be stated as follows.

Definition 1.1. *Suppose that G is a finite group that acts on a set S. Denote by r^g the action of $g \in G$ on $r \in S$. Then, given elements $r, s \in S$, the group action discrete logarithm problem is the problem of finding a g such that $r^g = s$.*

The first step beyond brute force search for this problem is to design an analog to the Shanks method. We will find appropriate splitting sets $A, B \subseteq G$ so that for any s in the orbit $r^G = \{r^g : g \in G\}$, we have $r^{ab} = s$ for some $a \in A$ and $b \in B$. A match in the two sets

$$\{r^a : a \in A\} \text{ and } \{s^{b^{-1}} : b \in B\}$$

recovers the solution $g = ab$.

In this work, we treat two situations. The first is one of maximum generality: we know almost nothing about the structure of G, and can only work with it by applying it to elements of S. The second is maximally specific: G is the symmetric group S_n. In neither case do we assume any particular knowledge about the orbit of r or s.

For general groups (the first case), we analyze randomized methods that achieve square root speedups when compared to the naive approach of exhaustive search. For the important second case, we develop deterministic algorithms that utilize the structure of S_n. These algorithms have close to square root complexity.

To motivate our model and concentration on S_n, we give several applications that fit into our framework.

2. APPLICATIONS

We first show how group actions lead to an unconventional algorithm for the graph isomorphism problem (GI). Let S be the set of adjacency matrices for graphs on n vertices. The symmetric group S_n acts on S, via $M^g = P_g M P_g^{-1}$. (P_g is just the permutation matrix for g.) In this case, the group action discrete logarithm problem is exactly graph isomorphism: given adjacency matrices M and N, find $g \in S_n$ to make $M^g = N$. Using our results, we arrive at a deterministic graph isomorphism procedure with run time about $\sqrt{n!}$.

Although there are much faster algorithms than this, they are either conceptually involved [1, 2], cannot guarantee efficient performance in all cases [3], or both [12]. The baby-step giant-step algorithm, on the other hand, gives an immediate proof that exhaustive search through permutations is not the best method for graph isomorphism.

There are a variety of other GI-related problems that also fit in the discrete log symmetric group action framework. In particular, hypergraph isomorphism and equivalence of permutation groups via conjugation can both be formulated as symmetric group actions. Furthermore, the latter problem has no known moderately exponential ($\exp(n^{1-c})$ for $c > 0$) algorithm [2].

We further note that in cryptography, the solution of iterated block ciphers [10] is closely related to a group-action discrete logarithm problem in a symmetric group. Our approach may also be useful in computational Galois theory, specifically, in computing the splitting field of a polynomial [13].

Because our approach is orbit-oblivious, our framework is very general. In some problems, however, algorithms aware of orbit restrictions may benefit significantly by reducing the number of $g \in G$ to consider. This is true, for example, in the graph isomorphism problem. An orbit-sensitive GI algorithm can utilize the fact that a vertex can only be mapped to another vertex of the same degree, whereas our approach will test every permutation.

On the other hand, there seem to be problems where one cannot exploit such orbit restrictions. We will now develop such an example.

Our problem will rely on the existence of fully homomorphic encryption schemes. Such schemes were only recently discovered, and utilize the presumed difficulty of the learning with errors problem [6]. We can explain the basic idea of homomorphic encryption as follows.

Denote by $\mathcal{E}(x)$ the result of encrypting bitstring x into ciphertext. Then in a fully homomorphic encryption scheme, we may convert any function f to a function f' on ciphertext, such that $\mathcal{E}(f(x)) = f'(\mathcal{E}(x))$. This leads to the following problem:

DEFINITION 2.1. *Let G be a finite group that acts on a set S. Then G acts on $\{\mathcal{E}(s) : s \in S\}$ via the induced action $\mathcal{E}(r)^g = \mathcal{E}(r^g)$. Then, given $\mathcal{E}(r)$ and $\mathcal{E}(s)$, the obfuscated group action discrete logarithm problem is the problem of finding a $g \in G$ such that $\mathcal{E}(r)^g = \mathcal{E}(s)$.*

The obfuscated group action discrete log problem is a special case of the general version. In this problem, we are not given the decryption keys, r, s, or S. We may only work with the ciphertexts of S and the action of G on these ciphertexts. Thus, we must utilize orbit-oblivious approaches.

Furthermore, observe that this problem can be applied to any group G. In particular, this suggests there are actions over the symmetric group such that there is no easily discernible relation between the action of S_n on $\{1, 2, \ldots, n\}$ and the set S.

It is worth noting that in the above setting, no backtrack search or other heuristical approaches will yield an efficient solution in practice. In the case where backtracking can yield an efficient solution, however, the worst case running time of such backtrack approaches is typically exponential. Additionally, their performance can vary from instance to instance and is often hard to predict. Although there are Monte Carlo procedures that can be used to estimate the runtime on a particular instance, such methods exhibit large variance. It is therefore of interest to develop techniques with provable running times.

For the algorithm designer, realization of such a baby-step giant-step algorithm for group actions reduces to efficient construction of the sets A and B. In the remainder of this paper, we discuss various methods for this.

3. A RANDOMIZED APPROACH

In this section our approach is general enough to work over any group G where random elements can be generated efficiently. In this setting, an obvious idea is to simply pick k random elements of G for the set A and k random elements of G for the set B. Then the probability a particular $g \in G$ is present in AB will depend on the value of k. For ease of notation, let $m = |G|$. We have:

PROPOSITION 3.1. *Suppose we pick k random elements of G **without** replacement for the set A and likewise for B. Then the probability a particular $g \in G$ is present in AB satisfies:*

$$Pr[g \in AB] \geq 1 - e^{-k^2/m}.$$

PROOF. Observe that $g \notin AB$ precisely when each $b \in B$ avoids the set $\{a^{-1}g : a \in A\}$. The probability of this event is

$$\left(1 - \frac{k}{m}\right)\left(1 - \frac{k}{m-1}\right)\cdots\left(1 - \frac{k}{m-k+1}\right),$$

which is at most $(1 - k/m)^k$. Rewriting the exponent and utilizing that $(1 - x/n)^n \leq e^{-x}$ gives us

$$\Pr[g \notin AB] \leq \left(\left(1 - \frac{k}{m}\right)^m\right)^{k/m} \leq e^{-k^2/m},$$

from which the claim follows. □

By setting $k = \Theta(\sqrt{m})$, we can make the probability that g is present in AB constant. Our analysis, however, assumed sampling without replacement. If we simply sample with replacement and redraw when a duplicate is found, it is not hard to see that as long as we are sampling $o(m)$ elements, the number of extra draws is $O(1)$ in expectation.

Note that with this approach, there will always be a nonzero probability that some group elements are missing in AB, which will lead to one-sided error in our algorithm.

Namely, if no g is found where $r^g = s$, the randomized procedure only gives probabilistic evidence that no g exists. Furthermore, checking for missing elements of G in AB takes $O(|G|)$ time. While this would only need to be done once and work for any set G acts on, it is prohibitively expensive.

This leads us to ask for a deterministic algorithm to construct the sets A and B. This question inherently asks about structure of the group G that can be exploited, similarly to the original Shanks method for the traditional discrete logarithm. Therefore, we will focus on the special case when $G = S_n$.

4. BACKGROUND ON GROUPS

Our deterministic algorithm will rely on some elementary group theory. For this, we state a few necessary results and definitions.

All groups in this paper will be finite. If K is a subgroup of G, we write $K \le G$, and $K < G$ if the containment is proper. We do not assume that K is normal in G.

When $K \le G$, its left cosets are the $|G|/|K|$ sets gK with $g \in G$. Right cosets are defined similarly.

Note that the set of left (or right) cosets of K in G forms a partition of G. Thus if we have a subgroup K of G, we can take $B = K$ and A to be a set of elements of G such that each left coset of K in G is represented in A. Then every element of G will be present in AB.

In group theory, a minimal perfect set A of this kind is called a transversal.

DEFINITION 4.1 (TRANSVERSAL). *A left (right) transversal T of a subgroup K of G is a set of elements of G such that each left (right) coset of K in G has exactly one representative in T. Thus, T is a minimal set of coset representatives of K in G.*

To make this definition clear, we give the following:

EXAMPLE 4.2. *Let $G = \mathbb{Z}_{n^2}$ and let K be the unique subgroup of G with n elements. Then $|G : K| = n$. If $G = \{0, \dots, n^2 - 1\}$, $K = \{0, n, 2n, \dots, (n-1)n\}$. One transversal of K in G is $T = \{0, 1, 2, \dots, n-1\}$.*

For this example, K and T are exactly the sets of giant steps and baby steps that the Shanks algorithm would use. However, transversals are not unique; for example, we could have taken T to be any complete set of representatives modulo n.

Combinatorially, a subgroup B and its left transversal A form a perfect splitting set for G, in the sense that every $g \in G$ is uniquely of the form ab, for $a \in A$ and $b \in B$. Perfect splitting sets need not be subgroups, as we could always replace A by Ax and B by $x^{-1}B$, choosing $x \in G$ at will.

Ideally, these splitting sets have cardinality exactly $\sqrt{|G|}$. However, $n!$ is never a square for $n > 1$, so such perfect splitting sets cannot exist for $G = S_n$. Therefore, we will either have to tolerate duplicated products (as we did in the last section), or look for set sizes close to, but not exactly matching, $\sqrt{n!}$.

We now give some concepts that provide a "data structure" for working with permutation groups:

DEFINITION 4.3 (BASE). *Let G act on Ω. A base B for G is an ordered subset of Ω (i.e. a list) with the following property: the only element of G that stabilizes everything in B is the identity.*

For our purposes $G = S_n$, which stabilizes no element of $\Omega = \{1, \dots, n\}$. So, we will use $B := [1, 2, \dots, n]$; that is, $B = \Omega$ with the natural ordering of the integers. We could choose to not include any single integer from B, since the action of a permutation on the missing integer can be inferred via its action on the other elements; however, it will be easier to describe the transversal algorithm with a more complete base, and no loss of efficiency will be incurred. A base provides a convenient form to represent elements of G:

DEFINITION 4.4 (BASE IMAGE). *If $g \in G$ and $B = [\beta_1, \beta_2, \dots, \beta_k]$ is a base for G, then $B^g := [\beta_1^g, \dots, \beta_k^g]$ is called the base image of g (relative to B).*

Recall that β_i^g means the result of applying the group element g to the object $\beta_i \in \Omega$.

With the base $B := [1, 2, \dots, n]$, the base image gives the typical vector notation of a permutation. The base image B^g uniquely determines the element $g \in G$.

5. BIDIRECTIONAL COLLISIONS

In recent work [15], David Rosenbaum described a general framework for applying collision algorithms to isomorphism problems. Potential isomorphisms are represented by paths in a tree. Given objects X and Y, we choose one set of paths that exhaust all levels halfway down (the remainder can be chosen arbitrarily), and apply these to X. Similarly, for Y, we choose one path that goes halfway down, extend it in all possible ways, and then apply each of these to Y. If we denote the set of transformations applied to X as C and to Y as D, then, borrowing the group action notation, this framework finds some $c \in C$ and $d \in D$ so that

$$X^c = Y^d$$

whenever there exists some g such that

$$X^g = Y.$$

Thus by taking $A = C$ and $B = D^{-1}$, where by D^{-1} we denote the set of inverses of all elements of D, this approach produces sets A and B with $AB = G$.

To split the search space for permutations, we choose a k with $1 \le k \le n$. The set C will consist of $(n)_k$ (n pick k) permutations. Each permutation sends $1, 2, \dots, k$ to all possible k-tuples in $\{1, 2, \dots, n\}$. We can choose arbitrarily where to send $k+1, \dots, n$.

To make D, choose an image tuple for the first k elements arbitrarily (not moving them at all will do) and then extend with all $(n-k)!$ possible suffixes.

Since $|C| = (n)_k$ and $|D| = (n-k)!$, the counting functions for these two sets are not interchangable. However, we can try to balance the values of $(n)_k$ and $(n-k)!$. Since $(n)_k \cdot (n-k)! = n!$, finding a k such that $(n)_k \approx (n-k)!$ will, at least approximately, minimize $(n)_k + (n-k)!$, the cost of the collision algorithm. We will show that the "right" value of k is roughly, but not exactly, $n/2$. Surprisingly, the performance of the algorithm is very sensitive to k.

PROPOSITION 5.1. *The method presented above finds $A, B \subset S_n$ such that $AB = S_n$ and $\max(|A|, |B|) = O(n^{1/2}\sqrt{n!})$.*

PROOF. Let x be the positive real solution to $x! = \sqrt{n!}$ (we use $x!$ as an abbreviation for $\Gamma(x+1)$). Stirling's approximation says that

$$n! \sim \sqrt{2\pi n}\left(\frac{n}{e}\right)^n.$$

Use this on both variables in the defining relation for x, and then take logarithms of both sides. We can then apply "bootstrapping" [7] and show that

$$x = \frac{n}{2}\left(1 + O\left(\frac{1}{\log n}\right)\right).$$

Since $x!$ increases for $x \geq 1$, there is an integer m such that

$$(m-1)! \leq x! = \sqrt{n!} \leq m!.$$

Choose k so that $n-k$ (either m or $m-1$) is the closest integer to x. This will cause one of our sets to be larger than its "ideal" value $\sqrt{n!}$, and we must estimate this disparity. Let

$$n - k = x + \alpha, \qquad \text{with } |\alpha| \leq 1/2.$$

Recall that $(x+\alpha)! \sim x!x^\alpha$ as $x \to \infty$, in the sense that the limiting ratio is 1. Using this, and our asymptotic expression for x, we have

$$(n-k)! = (x+\alpha)! \sim x!x^\alpha \sim \sqrt{n!}\left(\frac{n}{2}\right)^\alpha.$$

Similarly,

$$(n)_k = \frac{n!}{(n-k)!} \sim \frac{n!}{\sqrt{n!}(n/2)^\alpha} = \sqrt{n!}(n/2)^{-\alpha}.$$

The bound on $|\alpha|$ gives

$$\max(|A|,|B|) = \max((n)_k,(n-k)!) = O\left(n^{1/2}\sqrt{n!}\right).$$

□

Probably, the factor $n^{1/2}$ is best possible. Examination of numerical data shows that α varies irregularly within the interval $(-1/2, 1/2)$, and we see no reason why this behavior should not continue. In particular, there is likely to be an infinite sequence of n's on which α's limiting value is 1/2.

It is also interesting to compare our procedure to one that splits the permutation vectors exactly in half, as Rosenbaum initially recommends [15, p. 193]. This splitting amounts to taking $k = n/2$, and as a consequence of Stirling's formula,

$$(n)_{n/2} = \Theta(n^{-1/4}2^{n/2}\sqrt{n!})$$

when n is even. Therefore, the "overhead" for exact splitting is exponential in n. It is not hard to see this intuitively, by considering a decision tree for generating permutations. Each of the "large" branching factors $n-i$, $0 \leq i < n/2$, is roughly twice as large as its "small" counterpart $n/2 - i$. By choosing the best splitting fraction for each n, we have reduced this overhead to a small power of n.

Finally, we note that this approach indeed employs a subgroup and a corresponding transversal of that subgroup. The set D fixes the first k elements and permutes the remaining $n-k$ elements amongst themselves in all possible ways. So D is simply S_{n-k}. Because of this, $D^{-1} = D$. Then, since $CD^{-1} = CD = S_n$, C is a left transversal of S_{n-k} in S_n.

6. A BETTER SUBGROUP

We can improve the results of the last section by using a different subgroup and its corresponding transversal. Intuitively, we can expect to get better results for the following reason: in bidirectional collision detection, we start with a fixed-length code for group elements and seek a good "halfway" point in the code words. This approach provides only n subgroups to choose from. To improve it, we can select our subgroup from a larger set.

A better choice of subgroup is the centralizer of a product of $\lfloor n/2 \rfloor$ disjoint two-cycles. Recall that the centralizer of an element $h \in G$ is the set $\{g \in G \mid gh = hg\}$, and is always a subgroup [4]. We have:

LEMMA 6.1. *The centralizer of a product of $\lfloor n/2 \rfloor$ disjoint two-cycles, denoted H, is a subgroup of S_n. We have*

$$|H| = \Theta(n^{1/4}\sqrt{n!})$$

if n is even and

$$|H| = \Theta(n^{-1/4}\sqrt{n!})$$

if n is odd. When n is odd, H is the same subgroup as it would be for $n-1$. When n is even, write $a = (1\ 2)(3\ 4)\ldots(n-1\ n)$, and so $H = C_{S_n}(a) = \{g \in S_n \mid ga = ag\}$.

PROOF. When n is odd, no permutation σ that moves the integer n can commute with a, because $a\sigma$ and σa will always move n in different directions. Therefore, when n is odd, the group is the same as for $n-1$.

Now, the centralizer of a in S_n, $C_{S_n}(a)$, has order:

$$|C_{S_n}(a)| = \frac{|S_n|}{\text{Size of conjugacy class of } a}.$$

See [4] for a proof. The size of the conjugacy class of a is determined by its cycle type [4]. The number of possible permutations with $\lfloor n/2 \rfloor$ disjoint two-cycles is given by:

$$\text{Size of conjugacy class of } a = \frac{n!}{2^{\lfloor n/2 \rfloor}\lfloor n/2 \rfloor !}.$$

This can be explained as follows. First, take all possible permutations on n items. Then, since the ordering of pairs within two-cycles does not matter, we can divide by $2^{\lfloor n/2 \rfloor}$. Furthermore, how the two-cycles are arranged does not matter, so we can further divide by $\lfloor n/2 \rfloor!$. Then:

$$|C_{S_n}(a)| = 2^{\lfloor n/2 \rfloor}\lfloor n/2 \rfloor!\,.$$

We can transform this into the desired result. We will show the algebra for the case that n is even, and then make a small change for when n is odd.

When n is even we have (by Stirling's approximation):

$$2^{n/2}(n/2)! \sim \sqrt{\pi n}\left(\frac{n}{e}\right)^{n/2},$$

$$\sqrt{n!} \sim \sqrt[4]{2\pi n}\left(\frac{n}{e}\right)^{n/2},$$

so

$$|C_{S_n}(a)| = 2^{n/2}(n/2)! \sim \sqrt[4]{\frac{\pi}{2}}n^{1/4}\sqrt{n!}.$$

When n is odd, a similar argument yields

$$|C_{S_n}(a)| = 2^{(n-1)/2}((n-1)/2)! \sim \sqrt[4]{\frac{\pi}{2}}n^{-1/4}\sqrt{n!}.$$

We therefore see when n is even, $|H|$ is $\Theta(n^{1/4}\sqrt{n!})$, and when n is odd, $|H|$ is $\Theta(n^{-1/4}\sqrt{n!})$. $\Box$

The subgroup H gives an improvement on bidirectional collision detection by a factor of $\Theta(n^{1/4})$. However, we also must have that H is efficiently enumerable. By Lemma 6.1, when n is odd, the group is the same as for $n-1$. Thus we need only concern ourselves with the even case:

LEMMA 6.2. *Let n be even. The centralizer of $a = (1\ 2)(3\ 4)\ldots(n-1\ n)$ in S_n, denoted H, is generated by:*

$$H = \langle(1\ 2), (1\ 3)(2\ 4), (1\ 3\ldots\ n-1)(2\ 4\ldots\ n)\rangle.$$

PROOF. Any products of the disjoint two-cycles of a will commute with a. The two-cycle $(1\ 2)$ is present in the generating set, and by conjugating $(1\ 2)$ by powers of $(1\ 2\ldots\ n-1)(2\ 4\ldots\ n)$, we may obtain the two-cycles $(3\ 4), (5\ 6), \ldots, (n-1\ n)$.

Furthermore, we may permute any of the disjoint two-cycles themselves by composing them with an appropriate transformation permutation.

We give the following homomorphism $\varphi : S_{n/2} \to S_n$: For each of the disjoint cycles of $\sigma \in S_{n/2}$, map $(\tau_1\ \tau_2\ldots\ \tau_k)$ to

$$(2\tau_1 - 1\ 2\tau_2 - 1\ldots\ 2\tau_k - 1)(2\tau_1\ 2\tau_2\ldots\ 2\tau_k).$$

This map is clearly a homomorphism because all we have done is replaced each cycle with two cycles, one of which maps τ_i to $2\tau_i - 1$ and the other τ_i to $2\tau_i$. Since the two cycles will never share the same integers (one contains odd integers, the other even), we have effectively only relabeled σ, and thus the group operations are preserved under φ.

Furthermore, φ represents the necessary mapping to permute the two-cycles of a, since it is swapping both integers within a cycle with another cycle. Then, since

$$S_{n/2} = \langle(1\ 2), (1\ 2\ldots\ n/2)\rangle,$$

the transformations that permute the two-cycles of a are generated by

$$\langle\varphi((1\ 2)), \varphi((1\ 2\ldots\ n/2))\rangle,$$

which equals

$$\langle(1\ 3)(2\ 4), (1\ 3\ldots\ n-1)(2\ 4\ldots\ n)\rangle.$$

Note that any of the products of the disjoint two-cycles of a can be composed with any of the permutations of the disjoint two-cycles of a to form a new element in the centralizer. Thus the transformations described amount to $2^{n/2}(n/2)!$ unique elements. This is the size of the centralizer, so we know we have accounted for every element. $\Box$

With generators, we can run a closure algorithm to produce all the elements of H. This would achieve an $O(n|H|)$ time enumeration, but is slightly wasteful, because for each element of H, we must compose it with all generators before we can ensure all elements have been constructed. We can avoid this factor of 3 overhead by explicitly generating the elements of H themselves.

Note that the proof of Lemma 6.2 shows that H is isomorphic to the wreath product $C_2 \wr S_{n/2}$, and gives an explicit way to construct H given this property. We utilize this in the following algorithm:

Algorithm 1 Enumeration of the elements of H

1. Generate all possible products of the disjoint two-cycles of $a = (1\ 2)(3\ 4)\ldots(n-1\ n)$; call the set X.
2. Generate all elements of $S_{n/2}$; call the set Y.
3. Apply the homomorphism φ described in the proof of Lemma 6.2 to each element of Y, resulting in a new set, Y'.
4. Compose every element of X with every element of Y' and return this set.

Before analyzing the algorithm, we make a few statements regarding our model of computation. For the purposes of this paper, we will charge $O(1)$ space for each integer and $O(1)$ time for accessing elements of an array. This hides logarithmic factors in runtime and space bounds. We will additionally charge space for output, though a note on this will be made after the proof of Lemma 7.4.

In this model of computation, a permutation can be represented in vector (base image) form using space $O(n)$ and two permutations can be composed in $O(n)$ time. Further note that we may choose to represent permutations as lists of arrays representing cycle notation, and in section 7, we will represent them as "partial base images" in a linked list or array. All representations can be converted to and from each other in $O(n)$ time.

We then have:

LEMMA 6.3. *Algorithm 1 correctly enumerates the elements of H in time $O(n|H|)$ and space $O(n|H|)$.*

PROOF. For correctness, Lemma 6.2 shows that the product set $XY' = H$.

For runtime, observe that a backtracking procedure can enumerate through all binary strings on $n/2$ bits in time $O(n2^{n/2})$. In practice, this can be done particularly efficiently by incrementing an integer and accessing its binary representation. Then for each binary string, we can concatenate the corresponding two-cycle of a for every set bit. If we represent elements in cycle notation, this concatenation can be done in $O(1)$ time. Thus we can construct the set X in $O(n2^{n/2})$ time.

To construct the set Y, note that a backtracking procedure can also enumerate every permutation of $S_{n/2}$ in time $O(n(n/2)!)$ (see [8] for the simple procedure). Applying the homomorphism φ can then be done in $O(n)$ time per element, producing all of Y' in overall $O(n(n/2)!)$ time.

There are $2^{n/2}(n/2)!$ elements in the product set XY', and each can be computed by composing an element of X with an element of Y' in $O(n)$ time per element. Thus the elements of H can be enumerated in $O(n|H|)$ time.

Regarding space, note that the most space used is in representing the output. We represent each $h \in H$ in $O(n)$ space, and so the space complexity is $O(n|H|)$. $\Box$

7. CONSTRUCTING TRANSVERSALS

We now consider finding a transversal of H in S_n. Although finding transversals can be complicated and require backtrack search through the parent group G [8], we can take advantage of having $G = S_n$.

We first give the following definition:

DEFINITION 7.1. *Let $B = [\beta_1, \ldots, \beta_k]$ be a base. Define a partial ordering $\prec$ on elements of Ω by taking $\beta_i \prec \beta_{i+1}$ for all $1 \leq i < k$, and $\beta_i \prec \alpha$, for every $\alpha \in \Omega$ not present in B. We extend this to base images by saying that for $g, h \in G$, $B^g \prec B^h$ if g precedes h in the lexicographic ordering on the base vectors.*

For our purposes, this is the natural ordering of the integers in B. Furthermore, this defines lexicographical ordering in the typical manner for base images B^g and B^h, $g, h \in G$.

Our transversal construction will exploit the following lemma.

LEMMA 7.2. *Let $K < G \leq S_n$ and let $B = [\beta_1, \ldots, \beta_k]$ be a base of G. Then $g \in G$ is the $\prec$-least element of its coset gK if and only if β_j^g is the $\prec$-least element of its orbit in $K_{\beta_1^g,\ldots,\beta_{j-1}^g}$ for $1 \leq j \leq k$.*

In this lemma, $K_{\beta_1^g,\ldots,\beta_{j-1}^g}$ denotes the subgroup of K consisting of the elements that fix each of the elements listed as subscripts. (When $j = 1$, this subgroup is just K.)

Although the result has been known since the work of Charles Sims, we present a proof in the interest of being self-contained. This lemma can be found (without proof) in [8, p. 115].

PROOF. Suppose that g satisfies the property given in Lemma 7.2. We must show g is $\prec$-least in gK. Write:

$$g = [\alpha_1, \alpha_2, \ldots, \alpha_k].$$

Now suppose there exists some $h \in gK$ such that $h \prec g$. Write:

$$h = [\gamma_1, \gamma_2, \ldots, \gamma_k].$$

Since $h \in gK$, we can write $h = gk$ for some $k \in K$. Therefore we can think of h as applying some element k to g. Now, since $h \prec g$, there must be a first index j such that $\gamma_j \prec \alpha_j$; so $\gamma_i = \alpha_i$ for all $1 \leq i < j$. Then k must stabilize $\alpha_1, \ldots, \alpha_{j-1}$. Since $\gamma_j \prec \alpha_j$, k must map α_j to γ_j, therefore γ_j and α_j are in the same orbit in $K_{\alpha_1,\ldots,\alpha_{j-1}}$. But by assumption, α_j is the $\prec$-least such element in its orbit in $K_{\alpha_1,\ldots,\alpha_{j-1}}$. Therefore the element h cannot exist and so g is minimal in gK.

In the other direction, suppose g does not satisfy the property in Lemma 7.2. Let j be the first index such that α_j is not $\prec$-least in its orbit in $K_{\alpha_1,\ldots,\alpha_{j-1}}$. Then there must be some $k \in K$ that stabilizes $\alpha_1, \ldots, \alpha_{j-1}$ and maps α_j to some η such that $\eta \prec \alpha_j$. Then $gk \prec g$. □

We can apply Lemma 7.2 to find base images that satisfy the property required to be $\prec$-least elements in their respective cosets. However, these base images might not necessarily correspond to elements of G if G is an arbitrary permutation group. Here we take advantage of the fact $G = S_n$. Every base image that satisfies Lemma 7.2 corresponds to some permutation on $\{1, 2, \ldots, n\}$, which is necessarily an element of S_n. Thus if it easy enough to find orbits after stabilizing in H, a transversal of H in S_n can be calculated efficiently. Below we have a useful fact about the structure of H.

LEMMA 7.3. *Denote by H_n our subgroup H for $G = S_n$. When n is even, we have that $(H_n)_{(\beta)} \cong H_{n-2}$. That is, H_n stabilized by any $\beta \in \Omega$ is isomorphic to H_{n-2}. When n is odd, $H_n = H_{n-1}$, so the result carries through for any $\beta \in \Omega$, $\beta \neq n$. If $\beta = n$, then $(H_n)_{(\beta)} = H_n$.*

PROOF. For odd n, the proof of Lemma 6.1 shows that H_n already stabilizes the integer n. Now, assume n is even. It should be clear that H is symmetric around any $\beta \in \Omega$, both because H is the centralizer of $a = (1\ 2)(3\ 4)\ldots(n-1\ n)$, where each $\beta \in \Omega$ plays the same role, and also by the proof of Lemma 6.2. We therefore can assume without loss of generality that $\beta = 1$.

Now, again observing the proof of Lemma 6.2, we can look at permutations σ that do not move 1 and have the property that $a\sigma = \sigma a$. Clearly we cannot use $(1\ 2)$ as a product in any such σ, and additionally permuting the first cycle will require that 1 is not stabilized in σ. It is then clear that:

$$\begin{aligned} &C_{S_n}((1\ 2)(3\ 4)\ldots(n-1\ n))_{(1)} \\ = \ &C_{S_n}((3\ 4)(5\ 6)\ldots(n-1\ n)). \end{aligned}$$

Again, by the symmetry in H, we have for even n and any $\beta \in \Omega$, $(H_n)_{(\beta)} \cong H_{n-2}$. □

This leads to the following algorithm to compute a transversal of H in $G = S_n$:

Algorithm 2 Transversal of H in $G = S_n$

If n is even:

1. Recursively obtain a transversal for $n-2$. As a base case, if $n = 2$, let $T = \{[1, 2]\}$.
2. Increase every integer in the base images returned for $n-2$ by 2.
3. Prepend 1 to the base images.
4. Put 2 in all possible locations after 1 in each base image, increasing the number of base images by a factor of $n-1$, and return this set.

If n is odd:

1. Obtain a transversal for $n-1$.
2. Put n in all possible locations in each base image returned for $n-1$, increasing the number of base images by a factor of n, and return this set.

By design, the algorithm finds the transversal consisting of the $\prec$-least element in each coset. We then have:

LEMMA 7.4. *Algorithm 2 correctly computes a transversal of H in $G = S_n$ in time $O(n|G : H|)$ and space $O(n|G : H|)$.*

PROOF. We first prove correctness. We use Lemma 7.2 to find the $\prec$-least element of each coset of H in G. From the list of generators, it is clear that if n is even, all objects of Ω are in the same orbit in H, and if n is odd, the two orbits of Ω are $\{1, 2, \ldots, n-1\}$ and $\{n\}$. Focusing on the even case, the first base element of every transversal base image will be 1, since it is the $\prec$-least of $\{1, 2, \ldots, n\}$. Furthermore, when we stabilize 1, by Lemma 7.3, we are left with a smaller instance of the same problem, with one caveat; the base element 2 is in its own orbit, and so can exist in any position after 1. We then see we can compute the transversal efficiently by recursively computing a solution to the smaller problem and then inserting 2 in all possible positions after 1. As a base case we have $H_2 = S_2$, so the transversal is $T = \{[1, 2]\}$. For the odd case, we now must simply place n in every possible location within the entire base image of every transversal element for $n-1$.

We now prove runtime. Ignoring the recursion, in the even case the algorithm must add 2 to each integer of the base images and place 2 in all possible locations after 1. In the odd case the algorithm must do similarly but with n. Both cases must also copy the new transversal elements into the updated list T. With appropriate data structures, this can easily be accomplished in time $O(n \cdot \textit{number of transversal elements})$. Since the number of transversal elements is $|G:H| = \frac{|G|}{|H|}$, we then have the following recurrence for the runtime, when n is even:

$$T(n) = T(n-2) + O(n^{3/4}\sqrt{n!}).$$

This implies

$$\begin{aligned} T(n) &= O(n^{3/4}\sqrt{n!}) + O\left(\sum_{\substack{2 \le i \le n-2 \\ i \text{ even}}} i^{3/4}\sqrt{i!}\right) \\ &\le O(n^{3/4}\sqrt{n!}) + O\left(n^{7/4}\sqrt{(n-2)!}\right) \\ &= O(n^{3/4}\sqrt{n!}). \end{aligned}$$

When n is odd, we can first compute the transversal for $n-1$ in time $O((n-1)^{3/4}\sqrt{(n-1)!}) = O(n^{1/4}\sqrt{n!})$. We can then add n in the necessary locations and produce output in time $O(n \cdot n^{1/4}\sqrt{n!}) = O(n^{5/4}\sqrt{n!})$. So the runtime when n is odd is $O(n^{5/4}\sqrt{n!})$. Both of these runtimes are $O(n|G:H|)$.

Regarding space, note that the most space used is in representing the final output. Representing each permutation takes $O(n)$ space, so the space cost is $O(n|G:H|)$. □

As a further remark, we note the $O(n|G:H|)$ runtime can be improved by a factor of $O(n)$ if instead of writing the output, it is iterated. By iterating, we mean cycling through the transversal, rather than writing each element of the transversal to a list. In this same model, we can make the space bound as little as $O(n)$.

Let us consider the even n case, and the same logic applies to the case of odd n. Assume we can cycle through the output at the level of recursion for $n-2$. For each output given by $n-2$, prepending 1 and inserting 2 in all positions after 1 can be done in $O(1)$ time per insertion if the base images are represented as integers in a linked list. Furthermore, we must only maintain $O(1)$ bits of information per level. Therefore, since there are $O(n)$ levels of recursion, we do amortized constant amount of work per element of the transversal, resulting in a runtime that is improved by a factor of $O(n)$ and a space bound that is simply $O(n)$.

This same logic applies to enumerating the elements of H, though we omit the argument for brevity. In general, the collision framework for our discrete logarithm problem will have each $s \in S$ taking at least $O(n)$ space and $O(n)$ time to hash into a dictionary, so this observation will only bring a slight improvement in the space bound for our problem in certain cases.

Finally, we note that the property exploited in computing the transversal was that every base image found directly via stabilizers and orbits is necessarily an element of the parent group G if $G = S_n$. This observation can be combined with black-box orbit, stabilizer, and base changing methods as discussed in [8] to compute a transversal of an arbitrary permutation group $K < S_n$ efficiently. We will not discuss the details here, nor give exact asymptotic guarantees. For more information, consult the transversal algorithms discussed in Holt's book.

8. THE MAIN RESULT

We have the following theorem:

THEOREM 8.1. *We can compute sets A and B such that $AB = S_n$ with $\max(|A|, |B|) = O(n^{1/4}\sqrt{n!})$. The computation can be done deterministically in time and space $O(n^{5/4}\sqrt{n!})$.*

PROOF. Let H be the subgroup of S_n specified in Lemma 6.1. It has size $O(n^{1/4}\sqrt{n!})$ when n is even and $O(n^{-1/4}\sqrt{n!})$ when n is odd. Using Algorithm 1, it can be enumerated deterministically in time and space $O(n|H|)$. Furthermore, by employing Algorithm 2, its transversal can be found and enumerated deterministically in time and space $O(n^{3/4}\sqrt{n!})$ when n is even and $O(n^{5/4}\sqrt{n!})$ when n is odd. This means we can find sets of permutations A and B deterministically such that every $\sigma \in S_n$ can be represented as a product ab, $a \in A$ and $b \in B$ in time $O(n^{5/4}\sqrt{n!})$. □

This lemma implies that the group action discrete logarithm problem in the symmetric group can be solved deterministically in roughly $O(n^{5/4}\sqrt{n!})$ time. The specifics depend on the ability to hash or compare elements of S generated for the collision procedure. We note that while randomization may be used in the analysis of such hashing functions, the algorithm itself will always produce correct results.

In comparison, the computation of sets A and B by the randomized approach will take time $O(n\sqrt{n!})$ and by bidirectional collision detection time $O(n^{1.5}\sqrt{n!})$. In this sense, our result shows the difference between randomized and deterministic algorithms for this problem can be made as little as $O(n^{1/4})$. It is unclear if this can be eliminated entirely, but $O(n^{1/4})$ is so small when compared to $O(\sqrt{n!})$ that the improvement would be very minor. In particular, since $3^4 = 81$ and $\sqrt{81!} \doteq 2.4 \times 10^{60}$, for practical values of n, $n^{1/4}$ will not exceed 3.

Furthermore, in computing (an upper bound of) the expected number of permutations needed to achieve various reliability percentages, we note that our deterministic approach uses fewer permutations for reliability $> 80\%$ for $n < 12$, and $> 90\%$ for all other reasonable values of n. Thus due to the simplicity of Algorithm 1 and Algorithm 2, we consider our approach a viable practical alternative to the randomized one.

9. ACKNOWLEDGEMENTS

We thank Derek Holt, Gene Cooperman, and László Babai for correspondence on computing transversals in permutation groups. We additionally thank the stackexchange community for their input on subgroup choices and the anonymous reviewers for their constructive feedback.

10. REFERENCES

[1] L. Babai, W. M. Kantor, E. M. Luks. Computational complexity and the classification of finite simple groups. In *Proc. 24th Ann. Symp. Found. Comp. Sci.*, 1983, pp. 162-171.

[2] L. Babai. Graph isomorphism in quasipolynomial time. Manuscript, 2016. http://arxiv.org/pdf/1512.03547v2.pdf.

[3] J. Cai, M. Fürer, N. Immerman. An optimal lower bound on the number of variables for graph identification. *Combinatorica*, v. 12, 1992, pp. 389-410.

[4] D. Dummit, R. Foote. *Abstract Algebra.* Wiley, 2004.

[5] C. J. Etherington, M. W. Anderson, E. Bach, J. T. Butler, and P. Stănică. A parallel approach in computing correlation immunity up to six variables. *Int. J. Found. Comp. Sci.*, to appear.

[6] C. Gentry. Fully homomorphic encryption using ideal lattices. In *Proc. 41st ACM Symp. on Theory of Computing.* 41, 2009, pp. 169-178.

[7] D. H. Greene and D. E. Knuth. *Mathematics for the Analysis of Algorithms.* Birkhäuser, 1982.

[8] D. Holt. *Handbook of Computational Group Theory.* Chapman & Hall, 2005.

[9] A. Kwan. Vernier scales and other early devices for precision measurement. *American J. Physics*, v. 79, 2011, pp. 368-373.

[10] R. C. Merkle and M. E. Hellman, On the security of multiple encryption. *Comm. ACM*, v. 24, 1981, pp. 465-467.

[11] K. S. McCurley, The discrete logarithm problem. *Proc. Symp. Appl. Math.*, v. 42, 1990, pp. 49-73.

[12] B. McKay, A. Piperno. Practical graph isomorphism, II. *J. Symb. Comp.*, v. 60, 2014, pp. 94-112.

[13] S. Orange, G. Renault, K. Yokoyama. Computation schemes for splitting fields of polynomials. In *Proc. 2009 Int. Symp. on Symbolic and Algebraic Computation*, 2009, pp. 279-286.

[14] J. M. Pollard. Monte Carlo methods for index computation (mod p). *Math. Comp.*, v. 32, 1978, pp. 918-924.

[15] D. Rosenbaum. *Quantum Computation and Isomorphism Testing.* Dissertation, U. Washington, 2015.

[16] A. Seress. *Permutation Group Algorithms.* Cambridge Univ. Press, 2003.

[17] D. Shanks. Class number, a theory of factorization and genera. *Proc. Symp. Pure Math.*, v. 20, 1969, pp. 415-440.

[18] E. Teske, Square-root algorithms for the discrete logarithm problem (a survey). In *Public Key Cryptography and Computational Number Theory*, de Gruyter, 2001, pp. 283-301.

Computing the Lie Algebra of the Differential Galois Group of a Linear Differential System

Moulay Barkatou, Thomas Cluzeau, Jacques-Arthur Weil
Univ. de Limoges, CNRS ; XLIM UMR 7252
123 av. Albert Thomas, 87 060 Limoges, France
forename.surname@unilim.fr

Lucia Di Vizio
Univ. de Versailles Saint-Quentin-En-Yvelines
Laboratoire de Mathématiques ; UMR 8100
45 av. des États-Unis, 78035 Versailles, France
divizio@math.cnrs.fr

ABSTRACT

We consider a linear differential system $[A] : \mathbf{y}' = A\,\mathbf{y}$ with coefficients in $\mathbb{C}(x)$. The differential Galois group G of $[A]$ is a linear algebraic group which measures the algebraic relations among solutions. Although there exist general algorithms to compute G, none of them is either practical or implemented. This paper proposes an algorithm to compute the Lie algebra $\mathfrak{g}$ of G when $[A]$ is absolutely irreducible. The algorithm is implemented in MAPLE.

Keywords

Computer algebra; Algorithms; Linear differential systems; Differential Galois theory; Lie algebras; Grothendieck-Katz p-curvature conjecture; Eigenrings; Reduced forms

1. INTRODUCTION

Consider a linear differential system $[A] : \mathbf{y}' = A\,\mathbf{y}$ with $A \in \mathbb{M}_n(\mathbb{C}(x))$ and $n > 1$. Its differential Galois group G measures everything that algebra can tell about the solutions, see [25]. For example, it measures solvability (with applications to integrability of dynamical systems, see references in [3, 1]), reducibility, transcendance properties for number theory, and so on. In theory, there exist general algorithms for computing differential Galois groups. Compoint and Singer gave such an algorithm in [12] in the case of reductive groups. Hrushovski gave a general algorithm in [19] which was recently clarified and improved by Feng in [16]. A symbolic-numeric algorithm is proposed by van der Hoeven in [24], based on the Schlesinger-Ramis density theorems. However, although these are wonderful decision procedures, none of them are either practical or implemented.

For a large class of problems, it is sufficient to compute the Lie algebra $\mathfrak{g}$ of G (which amounts to computing the connected component of the identity G°) instead of the differential Galois group G itself. See, for instance, Morales-Ramis-Simó integrability theory ([3]) or the work by Nguyen and van der Put in [22] where they study when a given differential system can be solved in terms of systems of lower order. The purpose of the present paper is to use a similar philosophy for computing $\mathfrak{g}$. Our starting point is the theory of Katz ([21]). Let $\mathcal{M}$ be the differential module associated with $[A]$. There is a theoretical identification (tannakian correspondence) between $\mathfrak{g}$ and a submodule $\mathcal{W}$ of $\mathrm{End}(\mathcal{M})$. Our main contribution is to make this identification algorithmic and provide an effective algorithm to compute $\mathfrak{g}$ when $\mathcal{M}$ is *absolutely irreducible*.

To achieve this, we proceed in four main steps. The first step (Section 3) consists in computing a maximal decomposition of $\mathrm{End}(\mathcal{M})$. Using eigenring techniques, this requires to compute rational solutions ([4]) of a structured system of dimension n^4. By exploiting the structure of the system, we reduce this problem to computing rational solutions of systems of lower dimensions which significantly improves the complexity of this step. In Section 4, to find a candidate for the submodule $\mathcal{W}$ (corresponding to $\mathfrak{g}$), we use a modular approach based on Grothendieck-Katz conjecture (see Conjecture 4.1). We choose a prime p, compute the p-curvature χ_p ([10]) and identify the smallest submodule of $\mathrm{End}(\mathcal{M})$ whose reduction modulo p contains χ_p. This provides a guess for $\mathcal{W}$ which is given by a basis $M_1, \ldots, M_d$ of matrices in $\mathbb{M}_n(\mathbb{C}(x))$. The next steps (Section 5) rely on the fact that $\mathfrak{g}$ can also be directly read off from a reduced form of $[A]$ (see Theorem 5.1). Using recent results from [2], we then prove that computing a reduction matrix amounts to computing a conjugation matrix between two semisimple Lie subalgebras of $\mathfrak{gl}_n(\mathbb{C}(x))$ respectively generated by the M_i and their evaluations $M_i(x_0)$ at some ordinary point x_0 of $[A]$. For the third step of our algorithm, we use a method for computing conjugation matrices based on results on semisimple Lie algebras ([20, 14]). In our last step, we find a reduction matrix among the conjugation matrices. If our guess for $\mathcal{W}$ is not correct, then the third and fourth steps may fail. In this case, we go back to the second step and restart with another prime.

The resulting algorithm is deterministic, assuming the veracity of the Grothendieck-Katz conjecture. We also give a less fancy algorithm which works independently of the Grothendieck-Katz conjecture. Note that a reduced form is obtained as a byproduct of our algorithm.

We have a prototype implementation of our algorithm in MAPLE. We have applied it to many examples and it turns out that the most costly step is the decomposition of $\mathrm{End}(\mathcal{M})$. This step has a polynomial complexity in n ([7]) compared to the exponential (several levels) complexity in n of the existing algorithms for computing G ([16]).

ISSAC '16, July 19-22, 2016, Waterloo, ON, Canada
© 2016 ACM. ISBN 978-1-4503-4380-0/16/07...$15.00
DOI: http://dx.doi.org/10.1145/2930889.2930932

Notations.

Throughout this paper, $k \triangleq \mathbb{C}(x)$ denotes the differential field of rational functions in the (complex) variable x with the derivation $' \triangleq \frac{d}{dx}$. For the actual calculations in our algorithms, $\mathbb{C}$ is replaced by a computable subfield of $\overline{\mathbb{Q}}$. If $u_1, \ldots, u_n$ are elements of some vector space E, we denote by $\mathbf{u}$ in bold the column vector $\mathbf{u} = (u_1 \ldots u_n)^T \in E^n$. For a square matrix $U \in \mathbb{M}_n(k)$ of size n with entries in k, we denote $U_{i\bullet}$ (resp. $U_{\bullet i}$) the ith row (resp. column) of U, and $\mathrm{Vect}(U) \triangleq (U_{1\bullet}, \ldots, U_{n\bullet})^T \in k^{n^2}$ is the vector obtained by stacking the vectors $U_{i\bullet}^T$ successively. Conversely, for a vector $\mathbf{v} \in k^{n^2}$, we note $\mathrm{Mat}(\mathbf{v})$ the matrix in $\mathbb{M}_n(k)$ obtained by the reverse operation. The *Kronecker product* $A \otimes B$ of $A \in \mathbb{M}_{n\times p}(k)$ and $B \in \mathbb{M}_{q\times r}(k)$ is the matrix defined by:

$$A \otimes B \triangleq \begin{pmatrix} a_{1,1}\,B & \ldots & a_{1,p}\,B \\ \vdots & \vdots & \vdots \\ a_{n,1}\,B & \ldots & a_{n,p}\,B \end{pmatrix} \in \mathbb{M}_{nq\times pr}(k).$$

If $A \in \mathbb{M}_n(k)$, we denote $[A]$ the linear differential system $[A] : \mathbf{y}' = A\,\mathbf{y}$, where $\mathbf{y}$ is a column vector of n unknown functions. A change of variables also called *gauge transformation* $\mathbf{y} = P\,\mathbf{z}$ with $P \in \mathrm{GL}_n(k)$ yields $\mathbf{z}' = P[A]\,\mathbf{z}$, where $P[A] \triangleq P^{-1}(A\,P - P')$. The linear differential systems $[A]$ and $[P[A]]$ are then said to be *(gauge) equivalent* over k.

Acknowledgements.

We warmly thank the referees for their suggestions which enhanced the clarity of this paper.

2. PRELIMINARIES

We recall here some definitions and facts concerning differential modules, linear differential systems, differential Galois groups and their Lie algebras. See, e.g., [25] for more details.

2.1 Differential modules and systems

A *differential module* $\mathcal{M}$ over k is a finite-dimensional k-vector space equipped with an additive map $\partial : \mathcal{M} \to \mathcal{M}$ satisfying $\partial(f\,m) = f'\,m + f\,\partial(m)$, for all $f \in k$ and for all $m \in \mathcal{M}$. A *differential submodule* of $\mathcal{M}$ is then a vector subspace of $\mathcal{M}$ which is stable under the action of ∂.

A differential module $\mathcal{M}$ is *irreducible* if it has no non-trivial submodules. Otherwise it is *reducible*. $\mathcal{M}$ is *absolutely irreducible* if $\overline{k} \otimes_k \mathcal{M}$ is irreducible. $\mathcal{M}$ is *decomposable* if there exist two non-trivial differential submodules $\mathcal{M}_1$ and $\mathcal{M}_2$ of $\mathcal{M}$ such that we have the direct sum decomposition $\mathcal{M} = \mathcal{M}_1 \oplus \mathcal{M}_2$. Otherwise $\mathcal{M}$ is *indecomposable*. $\mathcal{M}$ is *completely reducible* if it is a direct sum of *irreducible* modules.

REMARK 2.1. *Every differential module $\mathcal{M}$ can be written as $\mathcal{M} = \mathcal{M}_1 \oplus \mathcal{M}_2 \oplus \cdots \oplus \mathcal{M}_r$, where the $\mathcal{M}_i$'s are indecomposable differential submodules of $\mathcal{M}$. If we have another decomposition $\mathcal{M} = \mathcal{N}_1 \oplus \mathcal{N}_2 \oplus \cdots \oplus \mathcal{N}_s$, then $s = r$ and there is a permutation σ such that $\mathcal{M}_i \simeq \mathcal{N}_{\sigma(i)}$ (Krull-Schmidt theorem). In the sequel, such a decomposition is called a* maximal decomposition *of $\mathcal{M}$. If $\mathcal{M}$ is completely reducible, then in such a maximal decomposition, the differential submodules $\mathcal{M}_i$ are irreducible.*

Let $\mathcal{M}$ be a differential module of dimension n. Choosing a basis $e_1, \ldots, e_n$, $\mathcal{M}$ is associated with the linear differential system $[A]$, where $A = (a_{i,j})_{1\le i,j\le n} \in \mathbb{M}_n(k)$ is defined by the relations $\partial(e_i) \triangleq -\sum_{j=1}^n a_{j,i}\,e_j$, $i = 1, \ldots, n$. A change of basis $\overline{\mathbf{e}}^T = \mathbf{e}^T\,P$ with $P \in \mathrm{GL}_n(k)$ in $\mathcal{M}$, corresponds to a gauge transformation $\mathbf{y} = P\,\mathbf{z}$ in $[A]$. The fact that $\mathcal{M}$ is a reducible, decomposable or completely reducible differential module then corresponds to the fact that $[A]$ is equivalent to a linear differential system $[B]$ with $B = P[A]$ block triangular, block diagonal or block diagonal with irreducible diagonal blocks. A maximal decomposition corresponds to a block diagonal form with indecomposable diagonal blocks.

Let $\mathcal{M}$ be a differential module of dimension n over k. We fix a basis $e_1, \ldots, e_n$ of $\mathcal{M}$ and we denote by $[A]$ the associated linear differential system. The module $\mathcal{M}$ is called *trivial* when $[A]$ has a full space of rational solutions, i.e, if there exists a basis $\tilde{e}_1, \ldots, \tilde{e}_n$ such that $\partial(\tilde{e}_i) = 0$ for all i. The *dual of the differential module* $\mathcal{M}$ is the differential module $\mathcal{M}^\star$ of dimension n over k defined by $\mathcal{M}^\star \triangleq \mathrm{Hom}_k(\mathcal{M}, \mathbb{1}_k)$, where $\mathbb{1}_k$ is the trivial differential module of dimension 1 over k. The dual $\mathcal{M}^\star$ is endowed with the map $\partial^\star$ given by $(\partial^\star(\phi))(m) \triangleq -\phi(\partial(m)) + \partial_{\mathbb{1}_k}(\phi(m))$, for $\phi \in \mathcal{M}^\star$ and $m \in \mathcal{M}$. The linear differential system associated with $\mathcal{M}^\star$ with respect to the dual basis $e_1^\star, \ldots, e_n^\star$ defined by $e_i^\star(e_j) = 1$, if $i = j$ and 0 otherwise, is then $[-A^T]$.

Let $\mathcal{M}_1$ and $\mathcal{M}_2$ be two differential modules over k endowed respectively with the maps ∂_1 and ∂_2. The *tensor product* of $\mathcal{M}_1$ and $\mathcal{M}_2$ is the differential module $\mathcal{M}_1 \otimes_k \mathcal{M}_2$ endowed with the map ∂ defined by $\partial(m_1 \otimes m_2) \triangleq \partial_1(m_1) \otimes m_2 + m_1 \otimes \partial_2(m_2)$, for all $m_1 \in \mathcal{M}_1$ and for all $m_2 \in \mathcal{M}_2$.

Let us now consider the differential module $\mathcal{M} \otimes_k \mathcal{M}^\star$. With respect to the basis $e_i \otimes e_j^\star$, $i, j = 1, \ldots, n$, the elements of $\mathcal{M} \otimes_k \mathcal{M}^\star$ can be identified with matrices in $\mathbb{M}_n(k)$, namely, if $m = \mathbf{x}^T\,\mathbf{e} \in \mathcal{M}$ and $\phi = \mathbf{y}^T\,\mathbf{e}^\star \in \mathcal{M}^\star$, then $m \otimes \phi$ is identified with the Kronecker product $\mathbf{x}^T \otimes \mathbf{y}$. The matrix differential system associated with $\mathcal{M} \otimes_k \mathcal{M}^\star$ is then

$$F' = [A, F] \triangleq A\,F - F\,A. \qquad (1)$$

If A, B and C are three matrices of appropriate dimensions, then we have the relation $\mathrm{Vect}(A\,B\,C) = (A \otimes C^T)\,\mathrm{Vect}(B)$ so that (1) can be written as the linear differential system

$$\mathrm{Vect}(F)' = \left(A \otimes I_n - I_n \otimes A^T\right)\,\mathrm{Vect}(F). \qquad (2)$$

Finally, from [25, Ex. 2.38(3)], if $\mathcal{M}$ is an irreducible differential module, then $\mathcal{M} \otimes_k \mathcal{M}^\star$ is completely reducible so that all its submodules can be read off from a maximal decomposition as in remark 2.1.

2.2 Decomposition of differential modules

The problem of computing a decomposition of a differential module $\mathcal{M}$ has been studied in the literature of computer algebra: see [23, 5], [25, §4.2] and references therein.

Decomposing $\mathcal{M}$ (over k) is equivalent to finding a gauge transformation $P \in \mathrm{GL}_n(k)$ such that $P[A]$ is a block diagonal matrix and such a gauge transformation can be found by calculating the so-called *eigenring* $\mathcal{E}(A)$ of $[A]$ defined by $\mathcal{E}(A) \triangleq \{F \in \mathbb{M}_n(k) \mid F' = [A, F] = A\,F - F\,A\}$. In practice, computing $\mathcal{E}(A)$ reduces to computing the rational solutions of the matrix differential system (1) or equivalently of the linear differential system (2). The MAPLE package INTEGRABLECONNECTIONS ([6]) based on ISOLDE ([8]) provides a procedure for computing the eigenring using the algorithm in [4] for computing rational solutions.

If $\mathcal{M} = \mathcal{M}_1 \oplus \cdots \oplus \mathcal{M}_r$ is a decomposition of $\mathcal{M}$ into submodules $\mathcal{M}_i$ of dimension n_i, then $\mathcal{E}(A)$ contains an element similar to $\mathrm{diag}(\lambda_1 I_{n_1}, \dots, \lambda_r I_{n_r})$, where $\lambda_i \in \mathbb{C}$. Given $F \in \mathcal{E}(A)$ and $T \in \mathrm{GL}_n(k)$ such that $T^{-1} F T = \mathrm{diag}(F_1, \dots, F_r)$, for constant[1] matrices $F_1, \dots, F_r$ having distinct eigenvalues in $\mathbb{C}$ (e.g., Jordan blocks of F), we have $T[A] = \mathrm{diag}(A_1, \dots, A_r)$ for some matrices $A_i \in \mathbb{M}_{n_i}(k)$. Bases of the submodules $\mathcal{M}_i$ in the corresponding decomposition $\mathcal{M} = \mathcal{M}_1 \oplus \cdots \oplus \mathcal{M}_r$ are given by the columns of the matrix T, namely, a basis of $\mathcal{M}_i$ is given by the columns $T_{\bullet j}$ of T for $j = (n_1 + \cdots + n_{i-1} + 1), \dots, (n_1 + \cdots + n_{i-1} + n_i)$. Note finally that a *maximal* decomposition is in general obtained by taking a random element in the eigenring. We refer to [5] for more details.

2.3 Differential Galois group and Lie algebra

Let $\mathcal{M}$ be a differential module of dimension n over k. We fix a basis of $\mathcal{M}$ and we denote by $[A]$ the associated linear differential system.

There exists a differential field extension K of k called *Picard-Vessiot extension* for $\mathcal{M}$ (equivalently for $[A]$) which is such that K has the same constants as k (namely, the elements of $\mathbb{C}$), $[A]$ admits a *fundamental matrix of solutions* $U \in \mathrm{GL}_n(K)$ and K is the differential field generated over k by the entries of U (see [25, §1.3, Prop. 1.22]).

The *differential Galois group* G of $\mathcal{M}$ (equivalently of $[A]$), is the group $\mathrm{Aut}_\partial(K/k)$ of differential automorphisms of the k-algebra K, *i.e.*, for every $g \in G$ and every $f \in K$, we have $g(f') = g(f)'$ and, if $f \in k$, then $g(f) = f$. The *differential Galois correspondence* shows that we have $K^G = k$, where $K^G = \{f \in K \mid \forall g \in G,\ g(f) = f\}$.

The group G acts on vectors or matrices with entries in K componentwise. If $g \in G$ and $U \in \mathrm{GL}_n(K)$ is a fundamental matrix of solutions of $[A]$, then $g(U)$ is also a fundamental matrix of solutions of $[A]$ so that there exists $C_g \in \mathrm{GL}_n(\mathbb{C})$ such that $g(U) = U\, C_g$. Hence choosing a fundamental matrix of solutions yields a faithful representation of G in $\mathrm{GL}_n(\mathbb{C})$, *i.e.*, the map $\rho : G \to \mathrm{GL}_n(\mathbb{C})$, $g \mapsto C_g$, is an injective group homomorphism.

The group G viewed as a subgroup of $\mathrm{GL}_n(\mathbb{C})$ is a *linear algebraic group* (see [25, Thm 1.27]). Indeed, there exists a polynomial ideal $\mathcal{I} \subset \mathbb{C}[X_{1,1}, X_{1,2}, \dots, X_{n,n}, \det^{-1}]$, where $\det^{-1}$ is the inverse of $\det((X_{i,j})_{1 \le i,j \le n})$, such that

$$G \cong \{M = (m_{i,j})_{1 \le i,j \le n} \in \mathrm{GL}_n(\mathbb{C}) \mid \forall P \in \mathcal{I},\ P(m_{i,j}) = 0\}.$$

Let $\mathfrak{g}$ denote the *Lie algebra of the differential Galois group* G, namely, the tangent space of G at the identity. The Lie algebra $\mathfrak{g}$ can be represented as a Lie subalgebra of the Lie algebra $\mathfrak{gl}_n(\mathbb{C})$ of $n \times n$ matrices with entries in $\mathbb{C}$ and endowed with the natural Lie bracket $[\cdot,\cdot]$ of matrices:

$$\mathfrak{g} \cong \{N \in \mathbb{M}_n(\mathbb{C}) \mid I_n + \epsilon N \in G(\mathbb{C}[\epsilon]) \text{ with } \epsilon \neq 0 \text{ and } \epsilon^2 = 0\},$$

where $G(\mathbb{C}[\epsilon])$ is the set of $\mathbb{C}[\epsilon]$-points of G, i.e., the set of matrices with entries in $\mathbb{C}[\epsilon]$ satisfying the equations of the polynomial ideal $\mathcal{I}$ defined above.

For $g \in G$ and $h \in \mathfrak{g}$, we have $g\,(\mathrm{id} + \epsilon\, h)\, g^{-1} = \mathrm{id} + \epsilon(g\,h\,g^{-1}) \in G(\mathbb{C}[\epsilon])$. Thus $g\,h\,g^{-1} \in \mathfrak{g}$ and G acts on $\mathfrak{g}$ via the *adjoint action*: $G \times \mathfrak{g} \to \mathfrak{g}$, $(g, h) \mapsto g\,h\,g^{-1}$. In terms of matrices, the adjoint action Ad is given by $(M, N) \mapsto M\,N\,M^{-1}$.

Let V denote the $\mathbb{C}$-vector space of solutions of $[A]$ in K^n and $\mathrm{End}(V)$ the set of endomorphisms of V, *i.e.*, the set of linear maps from V to V. The set $\mathrm{End}(V)$ is naturally endowed with a Lie algebra structure denoted by $\mathfrak{gl}(V)$. As V is a finite-dimensional $\mathbb{C}$-vector space of dimension n, $\mathfrak{gl}(V)$ can be identified with $\mathfrak{gl}_n(\mathbb{C})$. Now, we have the following classical isomorphism of finite-dimensional k-vector spaces: $V \otimes V^\star \to \mathrm{End}(V)$, $v \otimes \varphi \mapsto (w \in V \mapsto \varphi(w)\, v)$. Consequently *the Lie algebra $\mathfrak{g}$ can be viewed as a vector subspace of $V \otimes V^\star$ which is stable under the adjoint action Ad of G.*

With the previous notation, the *tannakian correspondence* ([25, Thm 2.33, Cor. 2.35]) provides a one-to-one correspondence between vector subspaces of V stable under the action of G and differential submodules of $\mathcal{M}$. More precisely, to a vector subspace W of V stable under the action of G corresponds the differential submodule $(K \otimes_{\mathbb{C}} W)^G$ of $\mathcal{M}$, [25, Rmk 2.34]. This correspondence is compatible with all constructions of linear algebra (see Definition 5.2 below) and the fact of taking subspaces or quotients, so that there is a one-to-one correspondence between vector subspaces of $V \otimes V^\star$ stable under the action of G and differential submodules of $\mathcal{M} \otimes \mathcal{M}^\star$. With the previous notation, this yields:

PROPOSITION 2.1. *The Lie algebra $\mathfrak{g}$, viewed as a G-module under the adjoint action of G on $\mathrm{End}(V)$, corresponds to the differential submodule $\mathfrak{g}^k \triangleq (K \otimes_{\mathbb{C}} \mathfrak{g})^G$ of $\mathcal{M} \otimes \mathcal{M}^\star$.*

We shall denote by $\mathfrak{g}^k$ this *k-Lie algebra* $(K \otimes_{\mathbb{C}} \mathfrak{g})^G$ included in $\mathfrak{gl}_n(k)$. Note that $\mathfrak{g}^k$ corresponds to the Lie algebra considered by Katz in [21, Conj. 9.2]. For expository reasons, we assume in this paper that $\mathcal{M}$ is an *absolutely irreducible* differential module (which can be effectively tested, see [13]). The case of a completely reducible module $\mathcal{M}$ is quite similar and will appear in a forthcoming paper.

REMARK 2.2. *The assumption that $\mathcal{M}$ is absolutely irreducible means that $\mathfrak{g}$ acts* irreducibly *on V. If we further assume, w.l.o.g. [12, Thm. 4.1], that $\mathfrak{g} \subseteq \mathfrak{sl}_n(\mathbb{C})$, then the Lie algebras $\mathfrak{g}$ and $\mathfrak{g}^k$ are* semisimple *([20, Prop. 19.1]).*

Thanks to Proposition 2.1, the k-Lie algebra $\mathfrak{g}^k$ can be investigated by studying differential submodules of $\mathcal{M} \otimes \mathcal{M}^\star$.

3. DECOMPOSITION OF $\mathcal{M} \otimes \mathcal{M}^\star$

In the sequel, $\mathcal{M}$ is an absolutely irreducible differential module of dimension $n > 1$ over k. We fix a basis of $\mathcal{M}$ and we denote by $[A]$ the associated linear differential system.

Our algorithm requires to compute a maximal decomposition of the differential module $\mathcal{M} \otimes \mathcal{M}^\star$ associated to the linear differential system $\mathbf{y}' = \left(A \otimes I_n - I_n \otimes A^T\right) \mathbf{y}$. If we denote $\mathcal{A} \triangleq A \otimes I_n - I_n \otimes A^T$, then such a decomposition can be obtained by computing the eigenring $\mathcal{E}(\mathcal{A})$ of $[\mathcal{A}]$, as shown in Subsection 2.2. However, starting from a differential module of dimension n, this method would then require to compute the rational solutions of a linear differential system of size n^4 so that the dependency on n in the arithmetic complexity estimate for computing rational solutions of such a linear differential system would roughly be in n^{20} (see [7, Cor. 1]). Consequently, to obtain a more practicable algorithm, we will take into account the specific form of the differential module $\mathcal{M} \otimes \mathcal{M}^\star$/the particular structure of the linear differential system $[A \otimes I_n - I_n \otimes A^T]$.

3.1 Adapting the general method

The algorithm in [4] for computing rational solutions of a linear differential system is divided into two steps: the first one consists in computing local datas (considering one by one each singularity of the system) in order to construct

[1]the eigenvalues of any element of $\mathcal{E}(A)$ are constants in $\mathbb{C}$.

a universal denominator for the rational solutions and the second one consists in computing polynomial solutions of an auxiliary linear differential system. Here, the linear differential system that we consider has a specific structure, namely, its matrix is given by $\overline{\mathcal{A}} \triangleq \mathcal{A} \otimes I_{n^2} - I_{n^2} \otimes \mathcal{A}^T$ with the previous notation $\mathcal{A} = A \otimes I_n - I_n \otimes A^T$. Consequently, the specific techniques developed in [9] for computing rational solutions of $[\mathcal{A}]$ can be adapted and reused here. This implies that all the local datas needed for computing rational solutions of $[\overline{\mathcal{A}}]$ can be deduced from the local datas needed for computing rational solutions of $[A]$. For instance, the local exponential parts of $[\mathcal{A}]$ (resp. of $[\overline{\mathcal{A}}]$) are the differences (resp. the differences of the differences) between the local exponential parts of $[A]$. The first step of the algorithm can thus be performed by considering only the matrix A of size n instead of $\overline{\mathcal{A}}$ of size n^4 which leads to a real gain. Note that the ideas in [9] to accelerate the second step of the algorithm can also be adapted to be used here.

3.2 Using structural decompositions

With the previous notation, we are interested in computing the rational solutions of the linear differential system $[\overline{\mathcal{A}}]$ which is associated with the differential module

$$\mathrm{End}(\mathrm{End}(\mathcal{M})) \triangleq (\mathcal{M} \otimes \mathcal{M}^\star) \otimes (\mathcal{M} \otimes \mathcal{M}^\star)^\star.$$

We shall now prove that the problem can be reduced to computing the rational solutions of linear differential systems of size smaller than n^4. To do that, we shall first use the isomorphism $(\mathcal{M} \otimes \mathcal{M}^\star)^\star \cong (\mathcal{M} \otimes \mathcal{M}^\star)$ which leads to

$$\mathrm{End}(\mathrm{End}(\mathcal{M})) \cong (\mathcal{M} \otimes \mathcal{M}^\star) \otimes (\mathcal{M} \otimes \mathcal{M}^\star). \tag{3}$$

Let us provide explicit matrix formulas for (3):

LEMMA 3.1. *The matrix $\mathcal{A} = A \otimes I_n - I_n \otimes A^T$ satisfies*

$$-\mathcal{A}^T = \mathcal{J}\,\mathcal{A}\,\mathcal{J}, \qquad \mathcal{J} \triangleq \sum_{i=1}^{n}\sum_{j=1}^{n} E_{i,j}(n) \otimes E_{i,j}(n)^T,$$

where $E_{i,j}(n)$ denotes the elementary $n \times n$ matrix having 1 at position (i,j) and 0 elsewhere. In particular, the matrix $\mathcal{J}$ is orthogonal and further satisfies $\mathcal{J}^T = \mathcal{J}^{-1} = \mathcal{J}$.

PROOF. A result about the Kronecker product asserts that given two square matrices M and N of size n, we have $N \otimes M = \mathcal{J}\,(M \otimes N)\,\mathcal{J}$, where $\mathcal{J}$ is the matrix defined in Lemma 3.1 (see [17, §2.5]). Therefore, we get $-\mathcal{A}^T = I_n \otimes A - A^T \otimes I_n = \mathcal{J}\,(A \otimes I_n - I_n \otimes A^T)\,\mathcal{J} = \mathcal{J}\,\mathcal{A}\,\mathcal{J}$. □

Lemma 3.1 implies $\mathcal{J}[\mathcal{A}] = -\mathcal{A}^T$ so that the isomorphism $(\mathcal{M} \otimes \mathcal{M}^\star) \cong (\mathcal{M} \otimes \mathcal{M}^\star)^\star$ is explicitly given by:

$$\mathcal{M} \otimes \mathcal{M}^\star \to (\mathcal{M} \otimes \mathcal{M}^\star)^\star, \quad U \mapsto \mathrm{Mat}(\mathcal{J}\,\mathrm{Vect}(U)).$$

With the previous notation, a rational solution of the linear differential system associated with the differential module $(\mathcal{M}\otimes\mathcal{M}^\star)\otimes(\mathcal{M}\otimes\mathcal{M}^\star)$ is then sent to a rational solution of $[\overline{\mathcal{A}}]$ by multiplication by $I_{n^2} \otimes \mathcal{J}$.

For any differential module $\mathcal{N}$ of dimension n, we have the classical explicit isomorphism $\mathcal{N} \otimes \mathcal{N} \cong \mathrm{Sym}^2(\mathcal{N}) \oplus \Lambda^2(\mathcal{N})$, where $\mathrm{Sym}^2(\mathcal{N})$ (resp. $\Lambda^2(\mathcal{N})$) denotes the symmetric (resp. exterior) square of the differential module $\mathcal{N}$ which is of dimension $\frac{n\,(n+1)}{2}$ (resp. $\frac{n\,(n-1)}{2}$). From (3), we thus have:

$$\mathrm{End}(\mathrm{End}(\mathcal{M})) \cong \mathrm{Sym}^2(\mathcal{M} \otimes \mathcal{M}^\star) \oplus \Lambda^2(\mathcal{M} \otimes \mathcal{M}^\star). \tag{4}$$

Now, due to its specific structure the differential module $\mathcal{M} \otimes \mathcal{M}^\star$ can always be decomposed which allows us to go further in the decomposition of the right-hand side of (4).

LEMMA 3.2. *With the previous notation, the matrix defined by $\mathcal{T} \triangleq \mathrm{Vect}(I_n)^T \otimes \mathrm{Vect}(I_n) \in \mathbb{M}_{n^2}(\mathbb{C})$ belongs to the eigenring $\mathcal{E}(\mathcal{A})$ and provides the decomposition*

$$\mathcal{M} \otimes \mathcal{M}^\star = \mathbb{1}_k \oplus \mathcal{W}, \tag{5}$$

where $\mathcal{W}$ is a submodule of $\mathcal{M} \otimes \mathcal{M}^\star$ of dimension $n^2 - 1$.

PROOF. The fact that $\mathcal{T} \in \mathcal{E}(\mathcal{A})$ is straightforward since $\mathrm{Vect}(I_n)$ is a trivial rational solution of both $\mathbf{y}' = \mathcal{A}\mathbf{y}$ and $\mathbf{y}' = -\mathcal{A}^T\mathbf{y}$. The result then follows from the explanations in Subsection 2.2 because $\mathcal{T}$ is the block matrix $(E_{i,j}(n))_{1 \le i,j \le n}$ which admits two distinct eigenvalues, namely n of multiplicity 1 and 0 of multiplicity $n^2 - 1$. □

THEOREM 3.1. *With the previous notation, we have:*

$$\mathrm{End}(\mathrm{End}(\mathcal{M})) \cong \mathbb{1}_k \oplus \mathcal{W} \oplus \mathrm{Sym}^2(\mathcal{W}) \oplus \mathcal{W} \oplus \Lambda^2(\mathcal{W}). \tag{6}$$

PROOF. From Lemma 3.2 and the isomorphism (4), we obtain $\mathrm{End}(\mathrm{End}(\mathcal{M})) \cong \mathrm{Sym}^2(\mathbb{1}_k \oplus \mathcal{W}) \oplus \Lambda^2(\mathbb{1}_k \oplus \mathcal{W})$. If we denote e the basis element of $\mathbb{1}_k$ and e_i, $i = 1, \ldots, n^2 - 1$ a basis of $\mathcal{W}$, then a basis of $\mathrm{Sym}^2(\mathbb{1}_k \oplus \mathcal{W})$ is given by $e.e$, $e.e_i$, $i = 1, \ldots, n^2 - 1$ and $e_i.e_j$ for $i, j = 1, \ldots, n^2 - 1$ and $i \le j$. This basis yields the isomorphism $\mathrm{Sym}^2(\mathbb{1}_k \oplus \mathcal{W}) \cong \mathbb{1}_k \oplus \mathcal{W} \oplus \mathrm{Sym}^2(\mathcal{W})$. Moreover, a basis of $\Lambda^2(\mathbb{1}_k \oplus \mathcal{W})$ is given by $e \wedge e_i$, $i = 1, \ldots, n^2 - 1$ and $e_i \wedge e_j$ for $i, j = 1, \ldots, n^2 - 1$ and $i < j$ so that $\Lambda^2(\mathbb{1}_k \oplus \mathcal{W}) \cong \mathcal{W} \oplus \Lambda^2(\mathcal{W})$. The isomorphisms of k-vector spaces explicitly given above are isomorphisms of differential modules which ends the proof. □

Let us explain how to use decomposition (6) of Theorem 3.1 for computing effectively the rational solutions of $[\overline{\mathcal{A}}]$:

① Let $\mathbf{u} \in k^m$ with $m = \frac{(n^2-1)\,n^2}{2}$ be a rational solution of $\mathbf{u}' = \mathrm{sym}^2(W)\,\mathbf{u}$, where $[W]$ (resp. $[\mathrm{sym}^2(W)]$) is the differential system associated with $\mathcal{W}$ (resp. $\mathrm{Sym}^2(\mathcal{W})$);

② Construct the associated matrix U in $\mathrm{Sym}^2(\mathbb{1}_k \oplus \mathcal{W})$ (see the proof of Theorem 3.1) which can also be viewed as an element of $(\mathbb{1}_k \oplus \mathcal{W}) \otimes (\mathbb{1}_k \oplus \mathcal{W})$;

③ Computing $(P \otimes P)\mathrm{Vect}(U)$, where P denotes the gauge transformation yielding (5), we then obtain an element of $(\mathcal{M} \otimes \mathcal{M}^\star) \otimes (\mathcal{M} \otimes \mathcal{M}^\star)$;

④ Finally, using the isomorphism (3), we then get the rational solution $(P \otimes \mathcal{J}\,P)\,\mathrm{Vect}(U)$ of $[\overline{\mathcal{A}}]$.

Note that the matrix P appearing in the above process is formed by eigenvectors of the diagonalizable matrix $\mathcal{T}$ of Lemma 3.2 and can be given explicitly. A similar constructive process can be applied from a rational solution of the differential system $[\mathrm{ext}^2(W)]$ associated with $\Lambda^2(\mathcal{W})$.

PROPOSITION 3.1. *With the previous notation, the eigenring $\mathcal{E}(\mathcal{A})$ can be computed from the rational solutions of two linear differential systems $[\mathrm{sym}^2(W)]$ and $[\mathrm{ext}^2(W)]$ of respective sizes $\frac{(n^2-1)\,n^2}{2}$ and $\frac{(n^2-1)\,(n^2-2)}{2}$.*

PROOF. This is straightforward from Theorem 3.1 and the assumption that $\mathcal{M}$ is irreducible since a rational solution of $[W]$ would lead to a decomposition of $\mathcal{M}$. □

Note that, in practice, this has a real gain since already for $n = 3$, we have $\frac{(n^2-1)\,n^2}{2} = 36$ and $\frac{(n^2-1)\,(n^2-2)}{2} = 28$

compared to $n^4 = 81$. Moreover, one can speed up the computation of rational solutions since the systems under considerations are symmetric (resp. exterior) squares so that the techniques in [1, §5] can be applied to obtain the local datas by considering smaller systems.

We now provide another isomorphism as (6). We have $\mathrm{End}(\mathrm{End}(\mathcal{M})) \cong (\mathcal{M}\otimes\mathcal{M})\otimes(\mathcal{M}\otimes\mathcal{M})^\star$ which can be written as $\mathrm{End}(\mathrm{End}(\mathcal{M})) \cong \mathrm{End}(\mathcal{M}\otimes\mathcal{M})$ so that we obtain $\mathrm{End}(\mathrm{End}(\mathcal{M})) \cong \mathrm{End}(\mathrm{S}^2 \oplus \Lambda^2)$, where, for the purposes of notation, we denote $\mathrm{S}^2 \triangleq \mathrm{Sym}^2(\mathcal{M})$, $\Lambda^2 \triangleq \Lambda^2(\mathcal{M})$. We then get: $\mathrm{End}(\mathrm{End}(\mathcal{M})) \cong \mathrm{End}(\mathrm{S}^2) \oplus \mathrm{End}(\Lambda^2) \oplus \mathrm{Hom}(\mathrm{S}^2, \Lambda^2) \oplus \mathrm{Hom}(\Lambda^2, \mathrm{S}^2)$. Finally, using the decompositions $\mathrm{End}(\mathrm{S}^2) = \mathbb{1}_k \oplus \mathcal{N}_{\mathrm{S}^2}$ and $\mathrm{End}(\Lambda^2) = \mathbb{1}_k \oplus \mathcal{N}_{\Lambda^2}$ for some differential modules $\mathcal{N}_{\mathrm{S}^2}$ and $\mathcal{N}_{\Lambda^2}$ of respective dimensions $\frac{n^2\,(n+1)^2}{4} - 1$ and $\frac{n^2\,(n-1)^2}{4} - 1$, we have proved:

THEOREM 3.2. *The module* $\mathrm{End}(\mathrm{End}(\mathcal{M}))$ *decomposes as*

$$\mathrm{End}(\mathrm{End}(\mathcal{M})) \cong \mathbb{1}_k \oplus \mathcal{N}_{\mathrm{S}^2} \oplus \mathbb{1}_k \oplus \mathcal{N}_{\Lambda^2} \oplus \mathrm{Hom}(\mathrm{S}^2, \Lambda^2) \oplus \mathrm{Hom}(\Lambda^2, \mathrm{S}^2). \quad (7)$$

The decomposition (7) can be used exactly as (6) for our purposes and we get:

PROPOSITION 3.2. *With the previous notation, the eigenring $\mathcal{E}(\mathcal{A})$ can be computed from the rational solutions of four linear differential systems of respective sizes* $\frac{n^2\,(n+1)^2}{4} - 1$, $\frac{n^2\,(n-1)^2}{4} - 1$, $\frac{n^2\,(n^2-1)}{4}$, *and* $\frac{n^2\,(n^2-1)}{4}$.

Note that for $n = 3$, we would then have to compute the rational solutions of four linear differential systems of respective size 35, 8, 18 and 18. The systems corresponding to (7) have specific structures so that existing techniques (e.g., adapting the ones developed in [9, 1]) can be used here to speed up the computation.

4. CANDIDATE FOR THE LIE ALGEBRA

Let $\mathcal{M}$ be an absolutely irreducible differential module. From Proposition 2.1, the representation of the Lie algebra $\mathfrak{g}$ in $\mathrm{End}(V)$ corresponds to the submodule $\mathfrak{g}^k$ of $\mathcal{M}\otimes\mathcal{M}^\star$. Section 3 provides a maximal decomposition of the completely reducible module $\mathcal{M}\otimes\mathcal{M}^\star$ which yields all its submodules. We now develop a modular method for identifying $\mathfrak{g}^k$ as a submodule of $\mathcal{M}\otimes\mathcal{M}^\star$.

The approach that we propose relies on the reduction modulo a prime number p of the linear differential system $[A]$ or equivalently of the differential module $\mathcal{M}$. Here, the constant field $\mathbb{C}$ of k is replaced by a computable subfield of $\overline{\mathbb{Q}}$. For almost all primes p, the coefficients of the matrix $A \in \mathbb{M}_n(k)$ can be reduced modulo p and we obtain a matrix $A_p \in \mathbb{M}_n(\mathbb{F}_q(x))$, for $q = p^r$, corresponding to a linear differential system $[A_p]$ over the differential field $\mathbb{F}_q(x) = \oplus_{i=0}^{p-1}\mathbb{F}_q(x^p)\,x^i$ of characteristic p. As in characteristic zero, a differential module $\mathcal{M}_p$ over $\mathbb{F}_q(x)$ endowed with an action ∂ is associated with $[A_p]$. We refer to [25, §13] and references therein or [21] for details on differential modules and differential systems in characteristic p. A central object for the study of differential modules/systems in characteristic p is the so-called *p-curvature* defined as the operator $\chi_p \triangleq \partial^p$ acting on $\mathcal{M}_p$ or equivalently $\chi_p \triangleq \left(\frac{d}{dx} - A_p\right)^p$. In terms of matrices, the p-curvature χ_p corresponds to the p-th iterate of the sequence of matrices $(\chi_i)_{i\geq 1}$ defined by $\chi_1 = A_p$ and, for $i > 1$, $\chi_{i+1} = \frac{d}{dx}\chi_i - A_p\,\chi_i$, so that it can be effectively computed (see [21, 11] or [25, §13]). For a fast algorithm and complexity analyses, we refer to the recent work [10].

The following *Grothendieck-Katz p-curvature conjecture* ([21, Conj. 9.2 & 10.1]) links the reductions modulo p of the Lie algebra $\mathfrak{g}^k$ and the p-curvature of the reduction modulo p of the differential system/module.

CONJECTURE 4.1. *The k-Lie algebra $\mathfrak{g}^k$ is the smallest (algebraic) Lie subalgebra of $\mathfrak{gl}_n(k)$ whose reduction modulo p contains the p-curvature for almost all p.*

One inclusion of the conjecture, namely, the fact that the reduction modulo p of $\mathfrak{g}^k$ contains the p-curvature for all but finitely many primes p, has been proved (see [21, Prop. 9.3]). We refer to [21] for more details.

Let $\mathcal{M}\otimes\mathcal{M}^\star = \bigoplus_{i=1}^r \mathcal{W}_i$ be a maximal decomposition given by a gauge transformation $T \in \mathrm{GL}_{n^2}(k)$ (see Subsection 2.2) so that the $\mathrm{Mat}(T_{\bullet j})$'s provide bases of the submodules $\mathcal{W}_i$. We can then obtain a guess $\mathfrak{g}^s$ for the k-Lie algebra $\mathfrak{g}^k$ by using the following procedure:

MODULARSELECTION

1. Choose a prime number p such that A can be reduced modulo p and $\det(T)$ does not vanish modulo p. Reducing the maximal decomposition $\bigoplus_{i=1}^r \mathcal{W}_i$ modulo p we get a decomposition $\bigoplus_{i=1}^r \mathcal{W}_{i,p}$ which is given by the reduction T_p of T modulo p;
2. Compute the p-curvature χ_p of $[A_p]$;
3. Compute $T_p^{-1}\,\mathrm{Vect}(\chi_p)$ and let $\mathcal{S}$ be the set containing the indices of its non-zero entries which correspond to the columns of T_p involved in the writing of $\mathrm{Vect}(\chi_p)$;
4. Return the Lie algebra generated by the $\mathrm{Mat}(T_{\bullet j})$'s for $j \in \mathcal{S}$, which form then a basis of the submodule of the maximal decomposition $\bigoplus_{i=1}^r \mathcal{W}_i$ whose reduction modulo p contains χ_p.

This method yields a submodule $\mathfrak{g}^s$ of $\mathcal{M}\otimes\mathcal{M}^\star$ which according to the above Grothendieck-Katz conjecture 4.1 can be used as a guess for the k-Lie algebra $\mathfrak{g}^k$. However, MODULARSELECTION may select either a bigger or a smaller submodule of $\mathcal{M}\otimes\mathcal{M}^\star$ than $\mathfrak{g}^k$ (see explanations in Section 6). The next section will use the notion of *reduced form* to check whether or not our guess is correct. In practice, we can (and will) perform the above (fast) modular guessing for several prime numbers in order to refine our guess.

5. VALIDATION OF THE CANDIDATE

In this section, we check whether the guessed Lie algebra $\mathfrak{g}^s$ is the desired k-Lie algebra $\mathfrak{g}^k$ from Proposition 2.1.

5.1 Reduced Form and conjugation problem

Let $\mathcal{M}$ be a differential module and $[A]$, $A \in \mathbb{M}_n(k)$, an associated linear differential system. We denote by V the $\mathbb{C}$-vector space of solutions of $\mathcal{M}$ in a Picard-Vessiot extension K of k, G the differential Galois group of $\mathcal{M}$, and $\mathfrak{g}$ the Lie algebra of G. Let $N_1, \ldots, N_d \in \mathbb{M}_n(\mathbb{C})$ denote a basis of $\mathfrak{g}$.

One can associate another Lie algebra to $[A]$ by considering a *Wei-Norman decomposition* [2] of the matrix A, namely, $A = \sum_{i=1}^m \alpha_i\,A_i$ where $\alpha_1, \ldots, \alpha_m$ is a basis of the $\mathbb{C}$-vector space generated by the entries of A, and $A_i \in \mathbb{M}_n(\mathbb{C})$. We then define $\mathrm{Lie}(A)$ as the smallest algebraic Lie algebra containing the matrices A_i. The Lie algebra $\mathfrak{g}$ is always contained in $\mathrm{Lie}(A)$, [25, Prop. 1.31], hence $\mathfrak{g} \subset \mathrm{Lie}(P[A])$ for any matrix $P \in \mathrm{GL}_n(\overline{k})$. The *reduced form* corresponds to the case where we have $\mathrm{Lie}(A) = \mathfrak{g}$.

DEFINITION 5.1. *Let $[A]$ with $A \in \mathbb{M}_n(k)$ be a linear differential system. A matrix $B \in \mathbb{M}_n(\overline{k})$ is a* reduced form *of $[A]$ if $B \in \overline{k} \otimes \mathfrak{g}$ and there exists $P \in \mathrm{GL}_n(\overline{k})$ such that $B = P[A]$.*

The linear differential system $[A]$ is thus in reduced form iff there exist $f_1, \ldots, f_d$ in $\overline{k}$ such that $A = f_1 N_1 + \cdots + f_d N_d$. The following result due to Kolchin and Kovacic proves the existence of a reduced form: see [25, Prop. 1.31 & Cor. 1.32] and [2, Prop. 3 & Cor. 4].

THEOREM 5.1. *Let $[A]$ with $A \in \mathbb{M}_n(k)$ be a linear differential system. There exists a matrix $P \in \mathrm{GL}_n(\overline{k})$ such that $[P[A]]$ is in reduced form.*

A matrix P as in Theorem 5.1 is called a *reduction matrix* for $[A]$. We shall now recall a useful result of [2] concerning invariants and reduced forms.

DEFINITION 5.2. *A* (tensor) construction $\mathrm{Const}(V)$ *on the G-module V is a vector space obtained from V by finite iterations of tensor products $\otimes$, direct sums $\oplus$, taking the dual $\star$, symmetric powers Sym^m, and exterior powers Λ^r. To a constructor* Const *corresponds naturally a "Lie algebra" constructor* $\mathfrak{Const}$. *An* invariant *of $[A]$ is a rational solution of a linear differential system $[\mathfrak{Const}(A)]$.*

Let $P \in \mathrm{GL}_n(k_0)$ with $k \subseteq k_0 \subset \overline{k}$. A change of variables $\mathbf{y} = P\mathbf{z}$ in $[A]$ induces an action on the elements of constructions. If $\mathbf{f}$ is an invariant of $\mathcal{M}$ given as a rational solution of $[\mathfrak{Const}(A)]$, then we say that P *sends* $\mathbf{f}$ *to* $\mathbf{g}$ if $\mathbf{f} = \mathrm{Const}(P)\,\mathbf{g}$ ($\mathbf{g}$ is then a rational solution of $[\mathfrak{Const}(P[A])]$). Theorems 1 and 2 of [2] show that when a system is in reduced form, all its invariants have *constant* coefficients in $\mathbb{C}$ and we have:

LEMMA 5.1 ([2], THM. 3). *Let $[A]$ with $A \in \mathbb{M}_n(k)$ be a linear differential system. For any ordinary point $x_0 \in \mathbb{C}$ of $[A]$, there exists a reduction matrix $P \in \mathrm{GL}_n(\overline{k})$ for $[A]$ that sends every invariant $\mathbf{f}$ of $[A]$ to its evaluation at x_0, namely* $\mathrm{Const}(P)\,\mathbf{f} = \mathbf{f}(x_0)$.

In Section 4, we found a candidate $\mathfrak{g}^s$ for the Lie algebra $\mathfrak{g}^k$ as a submodule of $\mathcal{M} \otimes \mathcal{M}^\star$. Let $F \in \mathbb{M}_{n^2}(k)$ denote the element of $\mathcal{E}(\mathcal{A})$ from which we obtained this maximal decomposition of $\mathcal{M} \otimes \mathcal{M}^\star$; let $T \in \mathrm{GL}_{n^2}(k)$ denote the gauge transformation which provides the maximal decomposition, namely, $T^{-1}\,F\,T = J$ is the Jordan form of F. Note that $J \in \mathbb{M}_{n^2}(\mathbb{C})$ and T is formed by generalized eigenvectors of F so that it can be chosen as a polynomial matrix.

Following the terminology in [18], we introduce the notion of *conjugated Lie algebras.*

DEFINITION 5.3. *Two Lie subalgebras $\mathfrak{g}_1$ and $\mathfrak{g}_2$ of $\mathfrak{gl}_n(k)$ are said to be* conjugated (over $\overline{k}$) *if there exists $P \in \mathrm{GL}_n(\overline{k})$ such that $\mathfrak{g}_2 = P^{-1}\,\mathfrak{g}_1\,P$. Such a matrix P is then a* conjugation matrix *between $\mathfrak{g}_1$ and $\mathfrak{g}_2$.*

THEOREM 5.2. *Let $M_i \triangleq \mathrm{Mat}(T_{\bullet i})$, $i = 1, \ldots, d$, be a basis of the Lie algebra $\mathfrak{g}^s$ and let x_0 be an ordinary point of $[A]$ such that $\det(T(x_0)) \neq 0$. Let $\mathfrak{g}^t$ denote the Lie subalgebra of $\mathfrak{gl}_n(\mathbb{C})$ with basis $M_1(x_0), \ldots, M_d(x_0)$. If $\mathfrak{g}^s = \mathfrak{g}^k$, then there exists a gauge transformation $P \in \mathrm{GL}_n(\overline{k})$ that is a conjugation matrix between $\mathfrak{g}^s$ and $\mathfrak{g}^t$ and for which $\mathrm{Lie}(P[A]) = \mathfrak{g}^t$.*

PROOF. The matrix $F \in \mathcal{E}(\mathcal{A})$ is an invariant of $[A]$ so that Lemma 5.1 implies that there exists a reduction matrix P that sends F to its evaluation $F(x_0)$. Now we have $T(x_0)^{-1}\,F(x_0)\,T(x_0) = J$ so that if we perform the change of variables defined by P in $\mathcal{M}$, a new basis of $\mathfrak{g}^s$ will be given by the $M_i(x_0) \triangleq \mathrm{Mat}(T(x_0)_{\bullet i})$. On the other hand, M_i belongs to the construction $\mathcal{M} \otimes \mathcal{M}^\star$ so that after a change of variables given by P, M_i is transformed to $P^{-1}\,M_i\,P$. Consequently, P is a conjugation matrix between $\mathfrak{g}^s$ and $\mathfrak{g}^t$. ☐

If $\mathfrak{g}^s = \mathfrak{g}^k$, Theorem 5.2 suggests to find a reduction matrix among conjugation matrices between the "target" Lie algebra $\mathfrak{g}^t$ with basis $M_i(x_0)$ and the "source" Lie algebra $\mathfrak{g}^s$ with basis M_i. Conversely, if we find a conjugation matrix P between $\mathfrak{g}^s$ and $\mathfrak{g}^t$ such that $\mathrm{Lie}(P[A]) = \mathfrak{g}^t$, then $\mathfrak{g} \subseteq \mathfrak{g}^t$ so that $\mathfrak{g}^k \subseteq \mathfrak{g}^s$.

5.2 Step 1: computing conjugation matrices

Let $\mathcal{M}$ be an absolutely irreducible module and recall that if we assume, w.l.o.g., that $\mathfrak{g} \subseteq \mathfrak{sl}_n(\mathbb{C})$, then $\mathfrak{g}^t$ and $\mathfrak{g}^s$ are semisimple Lie algebras (otherwise, the guess $\mathfrak{g}^s$ is wrong). See Remark 2.2.

DEFINITION 5.4. *Let $\mathfrak{g}$ be a semisimple Lie algebra of dimension d and rank r. Let $\mathfrak{h}$ be a Cartan subalgebra of $\mathfrak{g}$, Φ a root system associated with $\mathfrak{h}$ and $\Delta = \{\alpha_1, \ldots, \alpha_r\}$ a simple system of Φ. Then a* set of canonical generators *of $\mathfrak{g}$ is a set of $3r$ non-zero matrices $H_1, \ldots, H_r$, $X_1, \ldots, X_r$, $Y_1, \ldots, Y_r$ such that, for $i = 1, \ldots, r$, $H_i \in \mathfrak{h}$, $X_i \in L_{\alpha_i}$, the root space associated with α_i and $Y_i \in L_{-\alpha_i}$ and which satisfies, for all $i, j \in \{1, \ldots, r\}$, the relations*

$$\begin{cases} [H_i, H_j] = 0, \quad [X_i, Y_j] = \delta_{i,j}\,H_i, \\ [H_i, X_j] = c_{j,i}\,X_j, \quad [H_i, Y_j] = -c_{j,i}\,Y_j, \quad c_{i,i} = 2. \end{cases} \tag{8}$$

where $\delta_{i,j} = 1$ if $i = j$ and 0 otherwise.
The matrix $C = (c_{i,j})_{1 \le i,j \le r}$ is called a Cartan matrix *of $\mathfrak{g}$.*

The sets of canonical generators (and their completion into *Chevalley bases*) are central objects in the study of semisimple Lie algebras. We refer to [20] and [14] for more details. Moreover algorithms for computing sets of canonical generators and Chevalley bases are given in [14].

Conjugation matrices between $\mathfrak{g}^t$ and $\mathfrak{g}^s$ can be computed using the following[2] procedure:

CONJUGATIONMATRICES (between $\mathfrak{g}^s$ and $\mathfrak{g}^t$)

① Compute canonical generators $\{H_i^t, X_i^t, Y_i^t\}_{i=1,\ldots,r}$ of $\mathfrak{g}^t$;

② Compute generators $\tilde{H}_i^s$ of a split Cartan subalgebra $\mathfrak{h}^s$ of $\mathfrak{g}^s$ such that we have $\chi(\tilde{H}_i^s) = \chi(H_i^t)$, $i = 1, \ldots, r$, where $\chi(M)$ denotes the characteristic polynomial of a matrix M. This can be done by taking an ansatz $\tilde{H}_i^s = \sum_{j=1}^{d} a_{i,j}\,M_j$ in $\mathfrak{g}^s$ and solving the algebraic equations in the $a_{i,j}$'s provided by the relation $\chi(\tilde{H}_i^s) = \chi(H_i^t)$;

③ From $\mathfrak{h}^s$ generated by the $\tilde{H}_i^s$, compute a set of canonical generators $\{H_i^s, X_i^s, Y_i^s\}_{i=1,\ldots,r}$ of $\mathfrak{g}^s$ having the same Cartan matrix as $\{H_i^t, X_i^t, Y_i^t\}_{i=1,\ldots,r}$;

④ Compute the matrices $P \in \mathrm{GL}_n(\overline{k})$ such that for $i = 1, \ldots, r$, $P\,X_i^t = X_i^s\,P$ and $P\,Y_i^t = Y_i^s\,P$. This amounts

[2]This is probably known but we have not found a reference.

to solving a linear system of $2rn^2$ equations for the n^2 unknown entries of P in $\bar{k}$.

Proposition 5.1. ConjugationMatrices *computes the conjugation matrices between the semisimple Lie algebras $\mathfrak{g}^t$ and $\mathfrak{g}^s$. If $\mathfrak{g}^t$ is (or contains) a representation of $\mathfrak{g}$ in $\mathfrak{gl}_n(\mathbb{C})$, e.g., if we have made the correct guess for $\mathfrak{g}^s$, then all the conjugation matrices found are of the form $P = c\tilde{P}$, with $\tilde{P} \in \mathrm{GL}_n(\bar{k})$ given and c an arbitrary element of $\bar{k}$.*

Proof. The correctness of ConjugationMatrices follows essentially from material in the book of W. de Graaf [14], in particular, Cor. 5.11.5 (see also [20]). The split Cartan subalgebra $\mathfrak{h}^s$ in Step ② exists because we know that $\mathfrak{g}^t$ and $\mathfrak{g}^s$ are conjugated (see Theorem 5.2). In Step ②, the matrices H_i^t (resp. $\tilde{H}_i^s$) are simultaneously diagonalizable ([20, Cor. 15.3, p.80]) so that there exists $P \in \mathrm{GL}_n(\bar{k})$ such that $P\,H_i^t = \tilde{H}_i^s\,P$, for $i = 1, \ldots, r$. The feasability of Step ③ is ensured by the fact that we know from Theorem 5.2 that the Lie algebras $\mathfrak{g}^t$ and $\mathfrak{g}^s$ are conjugated and a conjugation matrix sends a set of canonical generators of $\mathfrak{g}^t$ to a set of canonical generators of $\mathfrak{g}^s$ having the same Cartan matrix. In Step ④, the conjugation of the H_i^t and H_i^s is automatic because of the second relation of (8).
If P and $\tilde{P}$ are two conjugation matrices in Step ④, then $P\,\tilde{P}^{-1} \in \mathrm{GL}_n(\bar{k})$ commutes with all matrices in $\mathfrak{g}^t \otimes \bar{k}$ which contains $\mathfrak{g} \otimes \bar{k}$. As $\mathfrak{g}$ acts irreducibly on V (Remark 2.2), the only such matrices are scalar multiples of the identity (Schur's lemma) so $P = c\,\tilde{P}$ with $c \in \bar{k}$. □

In the procedure CheckGuess below, we say that "ConjugationMatrices fails" if the set of the matrices P computed in Step ④ is not of the form $P = c\,\tilde{P}$ given in Proposition 5.1. This implies that our guess $\mathfrak{g}^s$ was not correct.

5.3 Step 2: computing a reduction matrix

In the previous subsection, we found the conjugation matrices between the Lie algebras $\mathfrak{g}^t$ and $\mathfrak{g}^s$. If our guess $\mathfrak{g}^s$ equals $\mathfrak{g}^k$, then we know that among these conjugation matrices there exists a gauge transformation P such that $\mathrm{Lie}(P[A]) = \mathfrak{g}^t$. The last step then consists in finding this P which, if it succeeds, will partially validate our choice for the Lie algebra $\mathfrak{g}^s$ (i.e., $\mathfrak{g}^s = \mathfrak{g}^k$ or $\mathfrak{g}^k \subset \mathfrak{g}^s$). Let $P = c\,\tilde{P}$ be as in Proposition 5.1 and let $(N_i^t)_{i=1,\ldots,d}$ be a Chevalley basis of $\mathfrak{g}^t$. See [14] for an algorithm to complete our set of canonical generators of $\mathfrak{g}^t$ into a Chevalley basis. If $\mathrm{Lie}(P[A]) = \mathfrak{g}^t$, then there exist $c \in \bar{k}$ and $f_i \in \bar{k}$ such that $P[A] = \sum_{i=1}^d f_i\,N_i^t$. The latter relation then yields

$$\tilde{P}^{-1}\,A\,\tilde{P} - \frac{c'}{c}\,I_n - \tilde{P}^{-1}\,\tilde{P}' = \sum_{i=1}^{d} f_i\,N_i^t. \qquad (9)$$

Taking the trace Tr(.) of the matrices in (9) we obtain

$$\mathrm{Tr}(A) - n\,\frac{c'}{c} - \frac{\det(\tilde{P})'}{\det(\tilde{P})} = \sum_{i=1}^{d} f_i\,\mathrm{Tr}(N_i^t).$$

As we can assume, w.l.o.g., that $\mathfrak{g} \subseteq \mathfrak{sl}_n(\mathbb{C})$ (see Remark 2.2), we have $\mathrm{Tr}(N_i^t) = 0$ and $\mathrm{Tr}(A) = w'/w$, for some $w \in k$, so that we get $c = \left(w/\det(\tilde{P})\right)^{1/n}$. The following procedure checks if there exists a gauge transformation $P = c\,\tilde{P}$ such that $\mathrm{Lie}(P[A]) = \mathfrak{g}^t$:

PartialReductionMatrix

① Let $c = \left(w/\det(\tilde{P})\right)^{1/n}$ and set $P = c\,\tilde{P}$;

② Check if there exist $f_1, \ldots, f_d$ in $\bar{k}$ such that $P[A] = \sum_{i=1}^d f_i\,N_i^t$. If it succeeds, Return P, Else Return "Fail".

6. ALGORITHM AND IMPLEMENTATION

6.1 Full algorithm

Let $A \in \mathbb{M}_n(k)$ be such that $[A]$ is an absolutely irreducible linear differential system. Let G be its differential Galois group and $\mathfrak{g}$ be the Lie algebra of G. We first design an algorithm which, given a submodule $\mathfrak{g}^s$ of $\mathcal{M} \otimes \mathcal{M}^\star$, returns "Yes" when $\mathfrak{g}^s = \mathfrak{g}^k$ (or $\mathfrak{g}^s \supset \mathfrak{g}^k$) and "Fail" if $\mathfrak{g}^k \not\subseteq \mathfrak{g}^s$.

CheckGuess

① Given a basis $M_1, \ldots, M_d$ of $\mathfrak{g}^s$, pick an ordinary point x_0 and let $\mathfrak{g}^t$ be generated by $M_1(x_0), \ldots, M_d(x_0)$;

② Apply ConjugationMatrices to $\mathfrak{g}^s$ and $\mathfrak{g}^t$. If it fails, Return "Fail";

③ Complete the set of canonical generators of $\mathfrak{g}^t$ into a Chevalley basis $(N_i^t)_{i=1,\ldots,d}$ of $\mathfrak{g}^t$;

④ Apply PartialReductionMatrix. If it fails, Return "Fail"; Else Return "Yes".

Correctness of CheckGuess follows from Theorem 5.2 and Proposition 5.1: if it returns "Yes" then $\mathfrak{g}^k \subset \mathfrak{g}^s$; it surely returns "Yes" when $\mathfrak{g}^s = \mathfrak{g}^k$. This provides a first algorithm for computing $\mathfrak{g}$. Apply CheckGuess to each (isomorphism class of) submodule of $\mathcal{M} \otimes \mathcal{M}^\star$: $\mathfrak{g}^k$ is the only one for which CheckGuess replies "Yes" while it replies "Fail" to each of its proper submodules.
We now give our (better) full algorithm[3] for computing $\mathfrak{g}$.

Algorithm 1 (Computing the Lie Algebra $\mathfrak{g}$).

① *Compute a maximal decomposition of $\mathcal{M} \otimes \mathcal{M}^\star$. Let $\mathcal{G} := \{0\}$.*

② *Apply* ModularSelection *to get a guess for $\mathfrak{g}^s$. Let $\mathcal{G} := \mathcal{G} + \mathfrak{g}^s$.*

③ *Apply* CheckGuess *to $\mathcal{G}$. If it fails, pick next prime p, go to Step ②. Repeat until* CheckGuess *replies "Yes".*

④ *Apply* CheckGuess *to all (finitely many isomorphism classes of) proper submodules of $\mathcal{G}$. If the answer is "Fail" for all of them, then $\mathfrak{g}^k = \mathcal{G}$. Otherwise, $\mathfrak{g}^k$ is the smallest submodule for which the answer is "Yes".*

In Step ②, Algorithm 1 applies calculations modulo a prime number p to make a guess $\mathfrak{g}^s$ for the Lie algebra $\mathfrak{g}^k$ based on the Grothendieck-Katz conjecture 4.1. This guess may, for some primes, pick a $\mathfrak{g}^s$ which is "too small" (e.g., the p-curvature may be accidentally zero); this is a "Fail" case of Step ③. If we choose *successive* primes, the Grothendieck-Katz conjecture 4.1 implies that, after a finite number of primes, the sum $\mathcal{G}$ of guessed modules will contain $\mathfrak{g}^k$.
For a finite number of primes, the guess in Step ② may pick a "bigger" $\mathfrak{g}^s$, i.e. $\mathfrak{g}^s \supsetneq \mathfrak{g}^k$ and this will not be tested by CheckGuess, hence the necessity of Step ④. This situation may also occur when we have two isomorphic $L \oplus L$ in the maximal decomposition of $\mathcal{M} \otimes \mathcal{M}^\star$: ModularSelec-

[3]Note that we get a reduced form of $[A]$ as a byproduct.

TION may select the sum when only one summand appears in the true $\mathfrak{g}^k$, hence Step ④.

REMARK 6.1. *In Algorithm 1, Step ② is cheap. It often fastens calculations to apply Step ② to several p and deduce from this a "reasonable" guess before applying the next step.*

Note that each step of Algorithm 1 can be performed in an arithmetic complexity which is polynomial in n except (maybe) in Step 2 of the procedure CONJUGATIONMATRICES where we need to solve algebraic systems. This makes a significant difference compared to the exponential (several levels) complexity obtained in [16] for the computation of the differential Galois group G.

6.2 Implementation and example

We have a prototype implementation of Algorithm 1 in MAPLE. We use the package INTEGRABLECONNECTIONS ([6]) based on ISOLDE ([8]) for computing the maximal decomposition of $\mathcal{M} \otimes \mathcal{M}^\star$ and the package LIEALGEBRAS for computing a set of canonical generators (and a Chevalley basis) of $\mathfrak{g}^t$. The other steps are based on linear algebra calculations and solving linear and algebraic systems. We have applied our implementation to many examples up to $n = 7$. It turns out that in practice the most costly step is the decomposition of $\mathrm{End}(\mathcal{M})$. For lack of space, we only give a small example here.

EXAMPLE 6.1. *We consider the absolutely irreducible differential module $\mathcal{M}$ associated via a choice of basis with $[A]$ given by:*

$$A := \begin{bmatrix} \frac{x-1}{x} & x & -1 \\ -x^3+1 & 0 & -1 \\ \frac{x-1}{x} + x^2 & x+1 & -1 \end{bmatrix}.$$

The Lie algebra $\mathrm{Lie}(A)$ *of the matrix A is of dimension 9. Computing a maximal decomposition of $\mathcal{M} \otimes \mathcal{M}^\star$, we find that $\mathcal{M} \otimes \mathcal{M}^\star = \mathbb{1}_k \oplus \mathcal{W}_1 \oplus \mathcal{W}_2$ where $\mathcal{W}_1$ (resp. $\mathcal{W}_2$) is of dimension 3 (resp. 5). Computing the p-curvature of $[A]$ for a random prime p, we find that a candidate for the Lie algebra $\mathfrak{g}^s$ is the irreducible differential submodule $\mathcal{W}_1$ of $\mathcal{M} \otimes \mathcal{M}^\star$ which admits the basis M_1, M_2, M_3 given by:*

$$\begin{bmatrix} -1 & 0 & 1 \\ 0 & 0 & 0 \\ -x^2-1 & 0 & 1 \end{bmatrix}, \begin{bmatrix} 0 & 1 & 0 \\ -x^2 & 0 & 0 \\ 0 & 1 & 0 \end{bmatrix}, \begin{bmatrix} 0 & 1 & 0 \\ -x^2-1 & 0 & 1 \\ 0 & 0 & 0 \end{bmatrix}.$$

The point $x_0 = 1$ is an ordinary point for $[A]$ and a set of canonical generators H^t, X^t, Y^t for the Lie algebra $\mathfrak{g}^t$ generated by $M_1(x_0), M_2(x_0), M_3(x_0)$ is given by:

$$\begin{bmatrix} 2i & 0 & -2i \\ 0 & 0 & 0 \\ 4i & 0 & -2i \end{bmatrix}, \begin{bmatrix} 0 & -i & 0 \\ 1+i & 0 & -1 \\ 0 & 1-i & 0 \end{bmatrix}, \begin{bmatrix} 0 & -i & 0 \\ -1+i & 0 & 1 \\ 0 & -1-i & 0 \end{bmatrix}.$$

Computing an "aligned" set of canonical generators H^s, X^s, Y^s for $\mathfrak{g}^s$, we find:

$$\begin{bmatrix} \frac{-2i}{x} & 0 & \frac{2i}{x} \\ 0 & 0 & 0 \\ \frac{-2i\left(x^2+1\right)}{x} & 0 & \frac{2i}{x} \end{bmatrix}, \begin{bmatrix} 0 & \frac{i}{x} & 0 \\ -ix+1 & 0 & -1 \\ 0 & \frac{i+x}{x} & 0 \end{bmatrix}, \begin{bmatrix} 0 & \frac{i}{x} & 0 \\ -ix-1 & 0 & 1 \\ 0 & \frac{i-x}{x} & 0 \end{bmatrix}.$$

The conjugation matrices $P \in \mathrm{GL}_n(k)$ such that we have simultaneously $X^t P = P X^s$ and $Y^t P = P Y^s$ are then given by the matrices $P = c\tilde{P}$, where $c \in \overline{k}$ and

$$\tilde{P} = \begin{bmatrix} 1 & 0 & 0 \\ 0 & -x & 0 \\ x+1 & 0 & -x \end{bmatrix}.$$

Next, we find $c = a/x$ for an arbitrary constant $a \in \mathbb{C}^*$ so that $P = (a/x)\tilde{P}$ and $f_1, f_2, f_3 \in \overline{k}$ given by

$$\left\{ f_1 = \frac{i}{2x},\ f_2 = -\frac{i}{2}(x^2+i),\ f_3 = \frac{i}{2}(-x^2+i) \right\},$$

satisfy $P[A] = f_1 H^t + f_2 X^t + f_3 Y^t$.

We can then conclude that the Lie algebra $\mathfrak{g}$ viewed as a Lie subalgebra of $\mathfrak{gl}_3(\mathbb{C})$ admits the basis H^t, X^t, Y^t and $R = P[A]$ is in reduced form where:

$$P = \begin{bmatrix} \frac{a}{x} & 0 & 0 \\ 0 & -a & 0 \\ \frac{(x+1)a}{x} & 0 & -a \end{bmatrix}, \quad R = \begin{bmatrix} -x & -x^2 & x \\ x^2+1 & 0 & -1 \\ -2x & -x^2+1 & x \end{bmatrix}.$$

7. CONCLUSION

We have provided an algorithm for computing the Lie algebra of the differential Galois group of an absolutely irreducible differential system. The case of a completely reducible system is not handled here only for lack of space but can be tackled by a slightly modified algorithm. It will appear in a future paper. Finally, the case of a reducible system is treated in the forthcoming paper [15].

8. REFERENCES

[1] A. Aparicio Monforte, M. A. Barkatou, S. Simon, and J.-A. Weil. Formal first integrals along solutions of differential systems I. In *ISSAC'11*, pages 19–26. ACM Press, 2011.

[2] A. Aparicio Monforte, E. Compoint, and J.-A. Weil. A characterization of reduced forms of linear differential systems. *Journal of Pure and Applied Algebra*, 217(8):1504–1516, 2013.

[3] A. Aparicio-Monforte, T. Dreyfus, and J.-A. Weil. Liouville integrability: an effective Morales–Ramis–Simó theorem. *J. Symbolic Comput.*, 74:537 – 560, 2016.

[4] M. A. Barkatou. On rational solutions of systems of linear differential equations. *J. Symbolic Comput.*, 28:547–567, 1999.

[5] M. A. Barkatou. Factoring systems of linear functional equations using eigenrings. *Latest Advances in Symbolic Algorithms, Proc. of the Waterloo Workshop, Ontario, Canada (10-12/04/06)*, I. Kotsireas and E. Zima (Eds.), World Scientific:22–42, 2007.

[6] M. A. Barkatou, T. Cluzeau, C. El Bacha, and J.-A. Weil. INTEGRABLECONNECTIONS, http://www.unilim.fr/pages_perso/thomas.cluzeau/PDS.html.

[7] M. A. Barkatou, T. Cluzeau, C. El Bacha, and J.-A. Weil. Computing closed-form solutions of integrable connections. In *ISSAC'12*, pages 43–50. ACM, 2012.

[8] M. A. Barkatou and E. Pfluegel. ISOLDE (Integration of Systems of Ordinary Linear Differential Equations) project, http://isolde.sourceforge.net/.

[9] M. A. Barkatou and E. Pfluegel. On the equivalence problem of linear differential systems and its application for factoring completely reducible systems. In *ISSAC'98*, pages 268–275. ACM Press, 1998.

[10] A. Bostan, X. Caruso, and É. Schost. A fast algorithm for computing the p-curvature. In *ISSAC'15*, pages 69–76. ACM Press, 2015.

[11] T. Cluzeau. Factorization of differential systems in characteristic p. In *ISSAC'03*, pages 58–65. ACM Press, 2003.

[12] E. Compoint and M. F. Singer. Computing Galois groups of completely reducible differential equations. *J. Symbolic Comput.*, 28(4-5):473–494, 1999.

[13] E. Compoint and J.-A. Weil. Absolute reducibility of differential operators and Galois groups. *J. Algebra*, 275(1):77–105, 2004.

[14] W. de Graaf. Lie Algebras: Theory and Algorithms. volume 56 of *North-Holland Mathematical Library*. Elsevier, 2000.

[15] T. Dreyfus and J.-A. Weil. Computing the Lie algebra of the differential Galois group: the reducible case. Preprint, February 2016.

[16] R. Feng. Hrushovski's algorithm for computing the Galois group of a linear differential equation. *Advances in Applied Mathematics*, 65:1 – 37, 2015.

[17] M. A. Graham. *Kronecker Products and Matrix Calculus with Applications*. E. Horwood Series in Math. and its Appl. Wiley & Sons, 1981.

[18] J. A. Grochow. Matrix Lie algebra isomorphism. In *IEEE Conference on Computational Complexity (CCC12)*, pages 203–213, 2012.

[19] E. Hrushovski. Computing the Galois group of a linear differential equation. In *Differential Galois theory (Bedlewo, 2001)*, volume 58 of *Banach Center Publ.*, pages 97–138. Polish Acad. Sci., Warsaw, 2002.

[20] J. E. Humphreys. *Introduction to Lie Algebras and Representation Theory*, volume 9 of *Graduate Texts in Mathematics*. Springer-Verlag, 1972.

[21] N. M. Katz. A conjecture in the arithmetic theory of differential equations. *Bull. Soc. Math. France*, 110(2):203–239, 1982.

[22] K. A. Nguyen and M. van der Put. Solving linear differential equations. *Journal of Pure Appl. Math.*, Q. 6, no. 1, Special Issue: In honor of John Tate. Part 2:173–208, 2010.

[23] M. F. Singer. Testing reducibility of linear differential operators: a group theoretic perspective. *Appl. Alg. in Engrg. Comm. Comput.*, 7(2):77–104, 1996.

[24] J. van der Hoeven. Around the numeric-symbolic computation of differential Galois groups. *J. Symbolic Comput.*, 42(1-2):236–264, 2007.

[25] M. van der Put and M. F. Singer. *Galois theory of linear differential equations*, volume 328 of *Grundlehren der Mathematischen Wissenschaften [Fundamental Principles of Mathematical Sciences]*. Springer-Verlag, Berlin, 2003.

Complexity Analysis of Root Clustering for a Complex Polynomial

Ruben Becker[*]
MPI for Informatics,
Saarbrücken Graduate School of Computer Science
Saarbrücken, Germany
ruben@mpi-inf.mpg.de

Michael Sagraloff[†]
MPI for Informatics
Saarbrücken, Germany
msagralo@mpi-inf.mpg.de

Vikram Sharma[†]
Institute of Mathematical Sciences
Chennai, India
vikram@imsc.res.in

Juan Xu[‡]
Courant Institute of Mathematical Sciences
NYU, New York, USA
jx732@nyu.edu

Chee Yap[§]
Courant Institute of Mathematical Sciences
NYU, New York, USA
yap@cs.nyu.edu

ABSTRACT

Let $F(z)$ be an arbitrary complex polynomial. We introduce the **local root clustering problem**, to compute a set of natural ε-clusters of roots of $F(z)$ in some box region B_0 in the complex plane. This may be viewed as an extension of the classical root isolation problem. Our contribution is two-fold: we provide an efficient certified subdivision algorithm for this problem, and we provide a bit-complexity analysis based on the local geometry of the root clusters.

Our computational model assumes that arbitrarily good approximations of the coefficients of F are provided by means of an oracle at the cost of reading the coefficients. Our algorithmic techniques come from a companion paper [3] and are based on the Pellet test, Graeffe and Newton iterations, and are independent of Schönhage's splitting circle method. Our algorithm is relatively simple and promises to be efficient in practice.

1. INTRODUCTION

The problem of computing the roots of a univariate polynomial F has a venerable history that dates back to antiquity. With the advent of modern computing, the subject received several newfound aspects [17, 20]; in particular, the introduction of algorithmic rigor and complexity analysis has been extremely fruitful. This development is usually traced to Schönhage's 1982 landmark paper, "*Fundamental Theorem of Algebra in Terms of Computational Complexity*" [28]. Algorithms in this tradition are usually described as "exact and efficient". Schönhage considers the problem of approximate polynomial factorization, that is, the computation of approximations $\tilde{z}_i$ of the roots z_i of F such that $\|F - \widetilde{F}\|_1 < 2^{-b} \cdot \|F\|_1$, where $\widetilde{F}(z) := \operatorname{lcf}(F) \cdot \prod_{i=1}^{n}(z - \tilde{z}_i)$ and b is a given positive integer. The sharpest result for this problem is given by Pan [22, Theorem 2.1.1], [20, p.196]. Hereafter, we refer to the underlying algorithm in this theorem as "Pan's algorithm". Under some mild assumption on F (i.e., $|z_i| \leq 1$ and $b \geq n \log n$), Pan's algorithm uses only $\tilde{O}(n \log b)$ arithmetic operations with a precision bounded by $\tilde{O}(b)$, and thus $\tilde{O}(nb)$ bit operations. This result further implies that the complexity of approximating all z_i's to any specified b/n bits, with $b > n \log n$, is also $\widetilde{O}(nb)$ [22, Corollary 2.1.2]. Here, $\widetilde{O}$ means we ignore logarithmic factors in the displayed parameters. In a model of computation, where it is assumed that the coefficients of F are complex numbers for which approximations are given up to a demanded precision, the above bound is tight (up to polylogarithmic factors) for polynomial factorization as well as for root approximation.

In parallel, a major focus of exact and efficient root approximation research has been to determine the complexity of *isolating* all the roots of an *integer* polynomial $F(z)$ of degree n with L-bit coefficients. We call this the **benchmark problem** [27] since this case is the main theoretical tool for comparing root isolation algorithms. Although this paper addresses complex root isolation, we will also refer to the related **real benchmark problem** which concerns real roots for integer polynomials.

The problem of isolating the roots of a polynomial can be reduced to approximate polynomial factorization. Schönhage showed that, for a square-free polynomial, it suffices to choose a b of size $\Omega(n(\log n + L))$ to ensure that the distance between the approximations $\tilde{z}_i$ and the actual roots z_i is small enough to directly deduce isolating regions of

*Supported by the Max Planck Center for Visual Computing and Communication.
†Supported by IMPECS (Indo-German Max Planck Center for Computer Science).
‡Supported by China Scholarship Council, No.201506020005.
§Supported by NSF Grant #CCF-1423228.

ISSAC '16, July 19-22, 2016, Waterloo, ON, Canada
© 2016 ACM. ISBN 978-1-4503-4380-0/16/07...$15.00
DOI: http://dx.doi.org/10.1145/2930889.2930939

the z_i's. Together with Pan's result on approximate polynomial factorization, this yields a complexity of $\widetilde{O}(n^2L)$ for the benchmark problem. Interestingly, the latter bound was not explicitly stated until recently ([11, Theorem 3.1]).

Mehlhorn et al. [18] extend the latter result to (not necessarily square-free) polynomials F with arbitrary complex coefficients for which the number of distinct roots is given as an additional input. That is, Pan's algorithm is used as a blackbox with successively increasing precision b to isolate the roots of F. For the benchmark problem, this yields the bound $\widetilde{O}(n^3 + n^2L)$; however, the actual cost adapts to the geometry of the roots, and for most input polynomials, the complexity is considerably lower than the worst case bound.

We further remark that it seems likely that the bound $\widetilde{O}(n^2L)$ is also near-optimal for the benchmark problem because it is generally believed that Pan's algorithm is near-optimal for the problem of approximately factorizing a polynomial with complex coefficients. However, rigorous arguments for such claims are missing.

It had been widely assumed that near-optimal bounds need the kind of "muscular" divide and conquer techniques such as the splitting circle method of Schönhage (which underlies Pan's algorithm and most of the fast algorithms in the complexity literature). These algorithms are far from practical (see below). So, also the bound $\widetilde{O}(n^2(n+L))$ achieved by Mehlhorn et al. [18] is mainly of theoretical interest as the algorithm uses Pan's method as a blackbox.

This paper is interested in subdivision methods. The classical example here is root isolation based on Sturm sequences. Two types of subdivision algorithms are actively investigated currently: the **Descartes Method** [7, 15, 24, 28, 25, 26] and the **Evaluation Method** [5, 4, 29, 2, 27, 13, 21]. See [27] for a comparison of Descartes and Evaluation (or Bolzano) methods.

The development of certain tools, such as the Mahler-Davenport root bounds [8, 9], have been useful in deriving tight bounds on the subdivision tree size for certain subdivision algorithms [10, 4, 29]. Moreover, most of these analyses can be unified under the "continuous amortization" framework [5, 6] which can even incorporate bit-complexity. However, these algorithms only use bisection in their subdivision, which seems destined to lag behind the above "near optimal bounds" by a factor of n. To overcome this, we need to combine Newton iteration with bisection, an old idea that goes back to Dekker and Brent in the 1960s. In recent years, a formulation of Newton iteration due to Abbott [1] and Sagraloff [25] has proven especially useful. This has been adapted to achieve the recent near-optimal algorithms of Sagraloff and Mehlhorn [25, 26] for real roots, and [3] for complex roots.

The Root Clustering Problem. In this paper, we are interested in root clustering. The requirements of root clustering represents a simultaneous strengthening of root approximation (i.e., the output discs must be disjoint) and weakening of root isolation (i.e., the output discs can have more than one root). Hereafter, "root finding" refers generally to any of the tasks of approximating, isolating or clustering roots.

For an analytic function $F : \mathbb{C} \to \mathbb{C}$ and a complex disc $\Delta \subseteq \mathbb{C}$, let $\mathcal{Z}(\Delta; F)$ denote the multiset of roots of F in Δ and $\#(\Delta; F)$ counts the size of this multiset. We write $\mathcal{Z}(\Delta)$ and $\#(\Delta)$ since F is usually supplied by the context. Any non-empty set of roots of the form $\mathcal{Z}(\Delta)$ is called a **cluster**. The disc Δ is called an **isolator** for F if $\#(\Delta) = \#(3\Delta) > 0$. Here, $k\Delta = k \cdot \Delta$ denotes the centrally scaled version of Δ by a factor $k \geq 0$. The set $\mathcal{Z}(\Delta)$ is called a **natural cluster** when Δ is an isolator. A set of n roots could contain $\Theta(n^3)$ clusters, but at most $2n - 1$ of these are natural. This follows from the fact that any two natural clusters are either disjoint or have a containment relationship. The benchmark problem is a global problem because it concerns *all* roots of the polynomial $F(z)$; we now address local problems where we are interested in finding only *some* roots of $F(z)$. For instance, Yakoubson [30] gave a method to test if Newton iteration from a given point will converge to a cluster. In [31], we introduced the following **local root clustering problem**: *given $F(z)$, a box $B_0 \subseteq \mathbb{C}$ and $\varepsilon > 0$, to compute a set $\{(\Delta_i, m_i) : i \in I\}$ where the Δ_i's are pairwise disjoint isolators, each of radius $\leq \varepsilon$ and $m_i = \#(\Delta_i) \geq 1$, such that*

$$\mathcal{Z}(B_0) \subseteq \bigcup_{i \in I} \mathcal{Z}(\Delta_i) \subseteq \mathcal{Z}(2B_0).$$

We call the set $S = \{\Delta_i : i \in I\}$ (omitting the m_i's) a **solution** for the local root clustering instance $(F(z), B_0, \varepsilon)$. The roots in $2B_0 \setminus B_0$ are said to be **adventitious** because we are really only interested in roots in B_0. Suppose S and $\widehat{S}$ are both solutions for an instance $(F(z), B_0, \varepsilon)$. If $S \subseteq \widehat{S}$, then we call $\widehat{S}$ an augmentation of S. Thus any $\Delta \in \widehat{S} \setminus S$ contains only adventitious roots.

We solved the local root clustering problem in [31] for any analytic function F, provided an upper on $\#(2B_0)$ is known, but no complexity analysis was given. Let us see why our formulation is reasonable. It is easy to modify our algorithm so that the adventitious roots in the output are contained in $(1 + \delta)B_0$ for any fixed $\delta > 0$. We choose $\delta = 1$ for convenience. Some $\delta > 0$ is necessary because in our computational model where only approximate coefficients of F are available, we cannot decide the implicit "Zero Problem" [33] necessary to decide if the input has a root on the boundary of B_0, or to decide whether Δ contains a root of multiplicity $k > 1$. Thus, root clustering is the best one can hope for.

1.1 Main Result

In this paper, we describe a local root clustering algorithm and provide an analysis of its bit-complexity. Standard complexity bounds for root isolation are based on **synthetic parameters** such as degree n and bitsize L of the input polynomial. But our computational model for $F(z)$ has no notion of bit size. Moreover, to address "local" complexity of roots, we must invoke **geometric parameters** such as root separation [25, 26]. We will now introduce new geometric parameters arising from cluster considerations.

Assume $F(z)$ has m distinct complex roots $z_1, \ldots, z_m$ where z_j has multiplicity $n_j \geq 1$, the degree of $F(z)$ is $n = \sum_{j=1}^{m} n_j$, and the leading coefficient of F has magnitude $\geq 1/4$. Let k be the number of roots counted with multiplicities in $2B_0$. An input instance $(F(z), B_0, \varepsilon)$ is called **normal** if $k \geq 1$ and $\varepsilon \leq \min\{1, \frac{w_0}{96n}\}$ with w_0 the width of B_0. For any set $U \subseteq \mathbb{C}$, let $\overline{\log}(U) := \max(1, \log \sup(|z| : z \in U))$.

Our algorithm outputs a set of discs, each one contains a natural cluster. We provide a bit complexity bound of the algorithm in terms of the output.

Theorem A *Let S be the solution computed by our algorithm for a normal instance $(F(z), B_0, \varepsilon)$. Then there is an augmentation $\widehat{S} = \{D_i : i \in I\}$ of S such that the bit* *complexity of the algorithm is*

$$\widetilde{O}\Big(n^2\,\overline{\log}(B_0) + n\sum\nolimits_{D\in\widehat{S}} L_D\Big) \qquad (1)$$

with

$$\begin{aligned} L_D =& \widetilde{O}\Big(\tau_F + n\cdot\overline{\log}(\xi_D) + k_D\cdot(k+\overline{\log}(\varepsilon^{-1})) \\ &+ \overline{\log}(\prod\nolimits_{z_j\notin D}|\xi_D - z_j|^{-n_j})\Big) \end{aligned} \qquad (2)$$

where $k_D = \#(D)$, and ξ_D is an arbitrary root in D. Moreover, an L_D^*-bit approximation of the coefficients of F is required with $L_D^* := \max_{D\in\widehat{S}} L_D$.

The solution $\widehat{S}$ in this theorem is called the **augmented solution** for input $(F(z), B_0, \varepsilon)$. Each natural ε-cluster $D\in\widehat{S}$ is an isolator of radius $\le\varepsilon$. From (1), we deduce:

Corollary to Theorem A
The bit complexity of the algorithm is bounded by

$$\widetilde{O}\Big(n^2(\tau_F + k + m) + nk\,\overline{\log}(\varepsilon^{-1}) + n\,\overline{\log}\,|\operatorname{GenDisc}(F_\varepsilon)|^{-1}\Big). \quad (3)$$

In case F is an integer polynomial, this bound becomes

$$\widetilde{O}\Big(n^2(\tau_F + k + m) + nk\,\overline{\log}(\varepsilon^{-1})\Big). \qquad (4)$$

The bound (4) is the sum of two terms: the first is essentially the near-optimal root bound, the second is linear in k, n and $\overline{\log}(\varepsilon^{-1})$. This suggests that Theorem A is quite sharp.

On strong ε-clusters. Actually, the natural ε-clusters in the $\widehat{S}$ have some intrinsic property captured by the following definition. Two roots z, z' of F are **ε-equivalent**, written $z \overset{\varepsilon}{\sim} z'$, if there exists a disk $\Delta = \Delta(r, m)$ containing z and z' such that $r \le \frac{\varepsilon}{12}$ and $\#(\Delta) = \#(114\cdot\Delta)$. Clearly Δ is an isolator; from this, we see that ε-equivalence is an equivalence relationship. We define a **strong ε-cluster** to be any such ε-equivalence class. Unlike natural clusters, any two strong ε-clusters must be disjoint.

Theorem B
Each natural cluster $D\in\widehat{S}$ is a union of strong ε-clusters.

This implies that our algorithm will never split any strong ε-cluster. It might appear surprising that our "soft" techniques can avoid accidentally splitting a strong ε-cluster.

1.2 What is New

Our algorithm and analysis is noteworthy for its wide applicability: (1) We do not require square-free polynomials. This is important because we cannot compute the square-free part of $F(z)$ in our computational model where the coefficients of $F(z)$ are only arbitrarily approximated. Most of the recent fast subdivision algorithms for real roots [25, 26] require square-free polynomials. (2) We address the local root problem and provide a complexity analysis based on the local geometry of roots. Many practical applications (e.g., computational geometry) can exploit locality. The companion paper [3] also gives a local analysis. However, it is under the condition that the initial box is not too large or is centered at the origin, and an additional preprocessing step is needed for the latter case. But our result does not depend on any assumptions on B_0 nor require any preprocessing. (3) Our complexity bound is based on cluster geometry instead of individual roots. To see its benefits, recall that the bit complexity in [3] involves a term $\overline{\log}\,\sigma(z_i)^{-1}$ where $\sigma(z_i)$ is the distance to the nearest root of $F(z)$. If z_i is a multiple root, $\sigma(z_i) = 0$. If square-freeness is not assumed, we must replace $\sigma(z_i)$ by the distance $\sigma^*(z_i)$ to the closest root $\ne z_i$ (so $\sigma^*(z_i) > 0$). But in fact, our bound in (1) involves $T_D := \overline{\log}\prod_{z_j\notin D}|\xi_i - z_j|^{-n_j}$ which depends only on the inverse distance from a root within a cluster D to the other roots outside of D, which is smaller than $\overline{\log}\,\sigma^*(z_i)^{-1}$. So the closeness of roots within D has no consequence on T_D.

Why can't we just run the algorithm in [3] by changing the stopping criteria so that it terminates as soon as a component C is verified to be a natural ε-cluster? Yes, indeed one can. But our previous method of charging the work associated with a box B to a root $\phi(B)$ may now cause a cluster of multiplicity k to be charged a total of $\Omega(k)$ times, instead of $\widetilde{O}(1)$ times. Cf. Lemma 11 below where $\phi(B)$ is directly charged to a cluster.

1.3 Practical Significance

Our algorithm is not only theoretically efficient, but has many potential applications. Local root isolation is useful in applications where the roots of interest lie in a known locality, and this local complexity can be much smaller than that of finding all roots. From this perspective, focusing on the benchmark problem is misleading for such applications.

We believe our algorithm is practical, and plan to implement it. Many recent subdivision algorithms were implemented, with promising results: Rouillier and Zimmermann [24] engineered a very efficient Descartes method algorithm which is widely used in the Computer Algebra community, through Maple. The `CEVAL` algorithm in [27] was implemented in [12, 13]. Kobel, Rouillier and Sagraloff[1] implemented the `ANewDsc` algorithm from [26]. Becker [2] gave a Maple implementation of the `REVAL` algorithm for isolating real roots of a square-free real polynomial.

In contrast, none of the divide-and-conquer algorithms [23, 19, 14] have been implemented. Pan notes [22, p. 703]: "*Our algorithms are quite involved, and their implementation would require a non-trivial work, incorporating numerous known implementation techniques and tricks.*" Further [22, p. 705] "*since Schönhage (1982b) already has 72 pages and Kirrinnis (1998) has 67 pages, this ruled out a self-contained presentation of our root-finding algorithm*". But our paper [3] is self-contained with over 50 pages, and explicit precision requirements for all numerical primitives.

2. PRELIMINARY

We review the basic tools from [3]. The coefficients of F are viewed as an oracle from which we can request approximations to any desired absolute precision. Approximate complex numbers are represented by a pair of dyadic numbers, where the set of dyadic numbers (or BigFloats) may be denoted $\mathbb{Z}[\frac{1}{2}] := \{n2^m : n, m\in\mathbb{Z}\}$. We formalize[2] this as follows: a complex number $z\in\mathbb{C}$ is an **oracular number** if it is represented by an **oracle function** $\widetilde{z}:\mathbb{N}\to\mathbb{Z}[\frac{1}{2}]$ with some $\tau\ge 0$ such that for all $L\in\mathbb{N}$, $|\widetilde{z}(L) - z|\le 2^{-L}$ and $\widetilde{z}(L)$ has $O(\tau + L)$ bits. The oracular number is said to

[1] Private communication.

[2] This is essentially the "bit-stream model", but the term is unfortunate because it suggests that we are getting successive bits of an infinite binary representation of a real number. We know from Computable Analysis that this representation of real numbers is not robust.

be **τ-regular** in this case. In our computational model, the algorithm is charged the cost to read these $O(\tau + L)$ bits. This cost model is reasonable when z is an algebraic number because in this case, $\widetilde{z}(L)$ can be computed in time $\widetilde{O}(\tau+L)$ on a Turing machine. Following [3, 31], we can construct a procedure $\texttt{SoftCompare}(z_\ell, z_r)$ that takes two non-negative real oracular numbers z_ℓ and z_r with $z_\ell+z_r > 0$, that returns a value in $\{+1, 0, -1\}$ such that if $\texttt{SoftCompare}(z_\ell, z_r)$ returns 0 then $\frac{2}{3}z_\ell < z_r < \frac{3}{2}z_\ell$; otherwise $\texttt{SoftCompare}(z_\ell, z_r)$ returns $\texttt{sign}(z_\ell - z_r) \in \{+1, -1\}$. Note that SoftCompare is non-deterministic since its output depends on the underlying oracular functions used.

LEMMA 1 (see [3, Lemma 4] and [31]).
In evaluating $\texttt{SoftCompare}(z_\ell, z_r)$*:*
(a) The absolute precision requested from the oracular numbers z_ℓ and z_r is at most $L = 2(\overline{\log}(\max(z_\ell, z_r)^{-1}) + 4)$.
(b) The time complexity of the evaluation is $\widetilde{O}(\tau+L)$ where z_ℓ, z_r are τ-regular.

The critical predicate for our algorithm is a test from Pellet (1881) (see [16]). Let $\Delta = \Delta(m, r)$ denote a disc with radius $r > 0$ centered at $m \in \mathbb{C}$. For $k = 0, 1, \ldots, n$ and $K \geq 1$, define the **Pellet test** $T_k(\Delta, K) = T_k(\Delta, K; F)$ as the predicate

$$|F_k(m)|r^k > K \cdot \sum_{i=0, i\neq k}^{n} |F_i(m)|r^i$$

Here $F_i(m)$ is defined as the Taylor coefficient $\frac{F^{(i)}(m)}{i!}$. Call the test $T_k(\Delta, K)$ a **success** if the predicate holds; else a **failure**. Pellet's theorem says that for $K \geq 1$, a success implies $\#(\Delta) = k$. Following [31, 3], we define the "soft version" of Pellet test $\widetilde{T}_k(\Delta)$ to mean that $\texttt{SoftCompare}(z_\ell, z_r) > 0$ where $z_\ell = |F_k(m)|r^k$ and $z_r = \sum_{i=0,i\neq k}^{n} |F_i(m)|r^i$. We need to derive quantitative information in case the soft Pellet test fails. Contra-positively, what quantitative information ensures that the soft Pellet test will succeed? Roughly, it is that $\#(\Delta) = \#(r\Delta) = k$ for a suitably large $r > 1$, as captured by the following theorem:

THEOREM 2.
Let k be an integer with $0 \leq k \leq n = \deg(F)$ and $K \geq 1$.
Let $c_1 = 7kK$, and $\lambda_1 = 3K(n-k) \cdot \max\{1, \{4k(n-k)\}\}$.
If $\#(\Delta) = \#(c_1\lambda_1\Delta) = k$, then

$$T_k(c_1\Delta, K, F) \quad \textit{holds.}$$

The factor $c_1\lambda_1$ is $O(n^4)$ in this theorem, an improvement from $O(n^5)$ in [3]. A proof is given in Appendix A. In application, we choose $K = \frac{3}{2}$ and thus $c_1 \cdot \lambda_1 \leq (7Kn) \cdot (12Kn^3) = 189n^4$. The preceding theorem implies that if $\#(\Delta) = \#(189n^4\Delta)$ then $T_k(\frac{21}{2}n\Delta, \frac{3}{2}, F)$ holds. This translates into the main form for our application:

COROLLARY
If $k = \#(\frac{1}{11}n\Delta) = \#(18n^3\Delta)$ then $T_k(\Delta, \frac{3}{2}; F)$ holds.

In other words, under the hypothesis of this Corollary, $\widetilde{T}_k(\Delta)$ succeeds. We need one final extension: instead of applying $\widetilde{T}_k(\Delta)$ directly on F, we apply $\widetilde{T}_k(\Delta(0,1))$ to the Nth Graeffe iterations of $F_\Delta(z) := F(m + rz)$. Here, $\Delta = \Delta(m, r)$ and $N = \lceil \log(1 + \log n) \rceil + 4 = O(\log\log n)$. The result is called the **Graeffe-Pellet test**, denoted $\widetilde{T}_k^G(\Delta) = \widetilde{T}_k^G(\Delta; F)$. As in [3] we combine $\widetilde{T}_k^G(\Delta)$ for all $k = 0, 1, \ldots, n$ to obtain

$$\widetilde{T}_*^G(\Delta)$$

which returns the unique $k \in \{0, \ldots, n\}$ such that $\widetilde{T}_k^G(\Delta)$ succeeds, or else returns -1. We say that the test $\widetilde{T}_*^G(\Delta)$ **succeeds** iff $T_*^G(\Delta, K) \geq 0$.

The key property of $\widetilde{T}_i^G(\Delta)$ is [3, Lemma 6]:

LEMMA 3 (Soft Graeffe-Pellet Test).
Let $\rho_1 = \frac{2\sqrt{2}}{3} \simeq 0.943$ and $\rho_2 = \frac{4}{3}$.
(a) If $\widetilde{T}_k^G(\Delta)$ succeeds then $\#(\Delta) = k$.
(b) If $\widetilde{T}_*^G(\Delta)$ fails then $\#(\rho_2\Delta) > \#(\rho_1\Delta)$.

The bit complexity of the combined test $\widetilde{T}_*^G(\Delta)$ is asymptotically the same as any individual test [3, Lemma 7]:

LEMMA 4. *Let*

$$L(\Delta, F) := 2 \cdot (4 + \overline{\log}(\|F_\Delta\|_\infty^{-1})).$$

(a) To evaluate $\widetilde{T}_k^G(\Delta)$, it is sufficient to have an M-bit approximation of each coefficient of F where $M = \widetilde{O}(n\,\overline{\log}(m, r) + \tau_F + L(\Delta, F))$.
(b) The total bit-complexity of computing $\widetilde{T}_*^G(\Delta)$ is $\widetilde{O}(nM)$.

2.1 Box Subdivision

Let $A, B \subseteq \mathbb{C}$. Their **separation** is $\text{Sep}(A, B) := \inf\{|a - b| : a \in A, b \in B\}$, and $\text{rad}(A)$, the **radius** of A, is the smallest radius of a disc containing A. Also, ∂A denotes the boundary of A.

We use the terminology of subdivision trees (quadtrees) [3]. All boxes are closed subsets of $\mathbb{C}$ with square shape and axes-aligned. Let $B(m, w')$ denote the axes-aligned box centered at m of width $w(B) := w'$. As for discs, if $k \geq 0$ and $B = B(m, w')$, then kB denotes the box $B(m, kw')$. The smallest covering disc of $B(m, w')$ is $\Delta(m, \frac{1}{\sqrt{2}}w')$. If $B = B(m, w')$ then we define $\Delta(B)$ as the disc $\Delta(m, \frac{3}{4}w')$. Thus $\Delta(m, \frac{1}{\sqrt{2}}w')$ is properly contained in $\Delta(B)$. Any collection $\mathcal{S}$ of boxes is called a (box) **subdivision** if the interior of any two boxes in $\mathcal{S}$ are disjoint. The union $\bigcup\mathcal{S}$ of these boxes is called the **support** of S. Two boxes B, B' are **adjacent** if $B \cup B'$ is a connected set, equivalently, $B \cap B' \neq \emptyset$. A subdivision $\mathcal{S}$ is said to be **connected** if its support is connected. A **component** C is the support of some connected subdivision $\mathcal{S}$, i.e., $C = \bigcup\mathcal{S}$.

The **split** operation on a box B creates a subdivision $\texttt{Split}(B) = \{B_1, \ldots, B_4\}$ of B comprising four congruent subboxes. Each B_i is a **child** of B, denoted $B \to B_i$. Therefore, starting from any box B_0, we may split B_0 and recursively split zero or more of its children. After a finite number of such splits, we obtain a **subdivision tree** rooted at B_0, denoted $\mathcal{T}_{subdiv}(B_0)$.

The **exclusion test** for a box $B(m, w')$ is $\widetilde{T}_0^G(\Delta(m, \frac{3w'}{4})) = \widetilde{T}_0^G(\Delta(B))$. We say that $B(m, w')$ is **excluded** if this test succeeds, and **included** if it fails. The key fact we use is a consequence of Lemma 3 for the test $\widetilde{T}_0^G(\Delta)$:

COROLLARY 5. *Consider any box $B = B(m, w')$.*
(a) If B is excluded, then $\#(\Delta(m, \frac{3w'}{4})) = 0$, so $\#(B) = 0$.
(b) If B is included, then $\#(\Delta(m, w')) > 0$, so $\#(2B) > 0$.

2.2 Component Tree

In traditional subdivision algorithms, we focus on the complexity analysis on the subdivision tree $\mathcal{T}_{subdiv}(B_0)$. But for our algorithm, it is more natural to work with a tree whose nodes are higher level entities called components above.

Typical of subdivision algorithms, our algorithm consists of several while loops, but for now, we only consider the main loop. This loop is controlled by the **active queue** Q_1. At the start of each loop iteration, there is a set of included boxes. The maximally connected sets in the union of these boxes constitute our (current) components. And the boxes in the subdivision of a component C are called the **constituent boxes** of C. While Q_1 is non-empty, we remove a component C from Q_1 for processing. There are 3 dispositions for C: We try to put C to the **output queue** Q_{out}. Failing this, we try a **Newton Step**. If successful, it produces a single new component $C' \subset C$ which is placed in Q_1. If Newton Step fails, we apply a **Bisection Step**. In this step, we split each constituent box of C, and apply the exclusion test to each of its four children. The set of included children are again organized into maximally connected sets $C_1, \ldots, C_t$ $(t \geq 1)$. Each subcomponent C_i is either placed in Q_1 or Q_{dis}, depending on whether C_i intersects the initial box B_0. The components in Q_{dis} are viewed as **discarded** because we do not process them further (but our analysis need to ensure that other components are sufficiently separated from them in the main loop). We will use the notation $C \to C'$ or $C \to C_i$ to indicate the parent-child relationship. The **component tree** is defined by this parent-child relationship, and denoted $\mathcal{T}_{comp}$. In [3], the root of the component tree is B_0; we take $\frac{5}{4}B_0$ as the root to address boundary issues. So we write $\mathcal{T}_{comp} = \mathcal{T}_{comp}(\frac{5}{4}B_0)$ to indicate that $\frac{5}{4}B_0$ is the root. The leaves of $\mathcal{T}_{comp}$ are either discarded (adventitious) or output.

For efficiency, the set of boxes in the subdivision of a component C must maintain links to adjacent boxes within the subdivision; such links are easy to maintain because all the boxes in a component have the same width.

3. COMPONENT PROPERTIES

Before providing details about the algorithm, we discuss some critical data associated with each component C. Such data is subscripted by C. We also describe some qualitative properties so that the algorithm can be intuitively understood. Figure 1 may be an aid in the following description.

Figure 1: Three components C_1, C_2, C_3: blue dots indicate roots of F, pink boxes are constituent boxes, and the non-pink parts of each B_C is colored cyan. Only C_3 is confined.

(C1) All the constituent boxes of a component share a common width, denoted by w_C.

(C2) Our algorithm never discards any box B if B contains a root in B_0; it follows that all the roots in B_0 are contained in $\bigcup_C C$ where C ranges over components in $Q_0 \cup Q_1 \cup Q_{out}$ (at any moment during our algorithm).

(C3) Recall that a zero ζ of $F(z)$ in $2B_0 \setminus B_0$ is called adventitious. A component C is **adventitious** if $C \cap B_0$ is empty (placed in Q_{dis}). We say a component C is **confined** if $C \cap \partial(\frac{5}{4}B_0)$ is empty; otherwise it is non-confined. Figure 2 shows these different kinds of components. Note that after the preprocessing step, all components are confined.

(C4) If C, C' are distinct active components, then their separation $\mathrm{Sep}(C, C')$ is at least $\max\{w_C, w_{C'}\}$. If C is an adventitious component, then $\mathrm{Sep}(C, B_0) \geq w_C$. If C is a confined component, then $\mathrm{Sep}(C, \partial(\frac{5}{4}B_0)) \geq w_C$.

(C5) Let C^+ be the **extended component** defined as the set $\bigcup_{B \in S_C} 2B$. If C and C' are distinct components, then C^+ and C'^+ are disjoint. Moreover, if C is confined, then $\#(C) = \#(C^+)$ (see Appendix B).

(C6) Define the **component box** B_C to be any smallest square containing C subject to $B_C \subseteq (5/4)B_0$. Define W_C as the width of B_C and the disc $\Delta_C = \Delta(B_C)$. Define R_C as the radius of Δ_C; note that $R_C = \frac{3}{4}W_C$.

(C7) Each component is associated with a "Newton speed" denoted by N_C with $N_C \geq 4$. A key idea in the Abbot-Sagraloff technique for Newton-Bisection is to automatically update N_C: if Newton fails, the children of C have speed $\max\{4, \sqrt{N_C}\}$ else they have speed N_C^2.

(C8) Let $k_C = \#(\Delta_C)$, the number of roots of $\mathcal{Z}(\Delta_C)$, *counted with multiplicity*. Note that k_C is not always available, but it is needed for the Newton step. We try to determine k_C before the Newton Step in the main loop.

(C9) A component C is **compact** if $W_C \leq 3w_C$. Such components have many nice properties, and we will require output components to be compact.

In recap, each component C is associated with the data:

$$w_C, W_C, M_C, B_C, \Delta_C, R_C, k_C, N_C.$$

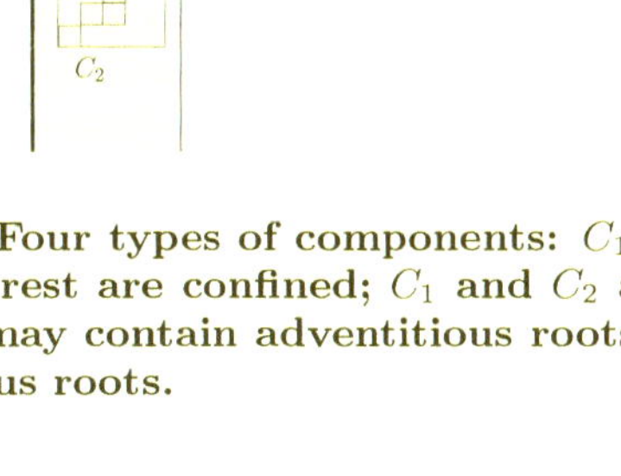

Figure 2: Four types of components: C_1 is not confined, the rest are confined; C_1 and C_2 are adventitious; C_3 may contain adventitious roots; C_4 has no adventitious roots.

4. THE CLUSTERING ALGORITHM

As outlined above, our clustering algorithm is a process for constructing and maintaining components, globally controlled by queues containing components. Each component C represents a non-empty set of roots. In addition to the queues Q_1, Q_{out}, Q_{dis} above, we also need a **preprocessing queue** Q_0. Furthermore, Q_1 is a priority queue such that the operation $C \leftarrow Q_1.pop()$ returns the component with the largest width W_C.

We first provide a high level description of the two main subroutines.

The **Newton Step** $Newton(C)$ is directly taken from [3]. This procedure takes several arguments, $Newton(C, N_C, k_C, x_C)$. The intent is to perform an order k_C Newton step:

$$x'_C \leftarrow x_C - k_C \frac{F(x_C)}{F'(x_C)}.$$

We then check whether $\mathcal{Z}(C)$ is actually contained in the small disc $\Delta' := \Delta(x'_C, r')$ where

$$r' := \max\{\varepsilon, w_C/(8N_C)\}. \quad (5)$$

This amounts to checking whether $\widetilde{T}^G_{k_C}(\Delta')$ succeeds. If it does, Newton test succeeds, and we return a new component C' that contains $\Delta' \cap C$ with speed $N_{C'} := (N_C)^2$ and constituent width $w_{C'} := \frac{w_C}{2N_C}$. The new component C' consist of at most 4 boxes and $W_{C'} \leq 2w_{C'}$. In the original paper [3], r' was simply set to $\frac{w_C}{8N_C}$; but (5) ensures that $r' \geq \varepsilon$. This avoids the overshot of Newton Step and simplifies our complexity analysis. If $\widetilde{T}^G_{k_C}(\Delta')$ fails, then Newton test fails, and it returns an empty set. In the following context, we simply denote this routine as "$Newton(C)$".

The **Bisection Step** $Bisect(C)$ returns a set of components. Since it is different from that in [3], we list the modified bisection algorithm in Figure 3.

We list the clustering algorithm in Figure 4.

Remarks on Root Clustering Algorithm:

1. In the preprocessing stage, for each component C, $w_C \geq \frac{w(B_0)}{48n}$ (see Appendix B). Thus depth of C in $\mathcal{T}_{comp}$ is $O(\log n)$.
2. In the main stage, each component C is confined. Moreover, the separation of $\partial((5/4)B_0)$ from $\partial(2B_0)$ is $\frac{3}{8}w(B_0)$. It follows that $2B_C \subseteq 2B_0$ (using the fact that $W_C \leq w(B_0)/2$ from preprocessing).
3. The steps in this algorithm should appear well-motivated (after [3]). The only non-obvious step is the test "$W_C \leq 3w_C$" (colored in red). This part is only needed for the analysis; the correctness of the algorithm is not impacted if we simply replace this test by the Boolean constant `true` (i.e., allowing the output components to have $W_C > 3w_C$).
4. We ensure that $W_C \geq \varepsilon$ before we attempt to do the Newton Step. This is not essential, but simplifies the analysis.

Based on the stated properties, we prove the correctness of our algorithm (see Appendix B).

THEOREM 6 (Correctness). *The Root Clustering Algorithm halts and outputs a collection $\{(\Delta_C, k_C) : C \in Q_{out}\}$ of pairwise disjoint ε-isolators such that $\mathcal{Z}(B_0) \subseteq \bigcup_{C \in Q_{out}} \mathcal{Z}(\Delta_C) \subseteq \mathcal{Z}(2B_0)$.*

5. BOUND ON NUMBER OF BOXES

In this section, we bound the number of boxes produced by our algorithm. All the proofs for this section are found in Appendix B.

```
Bisect(C)
  OUTPUT: a set of components containing all
      the non-adventitious roots in C
      (but possibly some adventitious ones)
  Initialize a Union-Find data structure U
      for boxes.
  For each constituent box B of C
     For each child B' of B
        If (T~_0^G(Δ(B')) fails)
           U.add(B')
           For each box B'' ∈ U adjacent to B'
              U.union(B', B'')
  Initialize Q to be empty.
  specialFlag ← true
  If (U has only one connected component)
     specialFlag ← false
  For each connected component C' of U
     If (C' intersects B0) // C' ≠ adventitious
        If (specialFlag)    N_C' = 4
        Else     N_C' = max{4, √N_C}
        Q.add(C')
     Else Q_dis.add(C')
  Return Q
```

Figure 3: Bisection Step

The goal is to bound the number of all the constituent boxes of the components in $\mathcal{T}_{comp}$. But, in anticipation of the following complexity analysis, we want to consider an **augmented component tree** $\widehat{\mathcal{T}}_{comp}$ instead of $\mathcal{T}_{comp}$.

Let $\widehat{\mathcal{T}}_{comp}$ be the extension of $\mathcal{T}_{comp}$ in which, for each confined adventitious components in $\mathcal{T}_{comp}$, we (conceptually) continue to run our algorithm until they finally produce output components, i.e., leaves of $\widehat{\mathcal{T}}_{comp}$. As before, these leaves have at most 9 constituent boxes.

Since $C' \to C$ denote the parent-child relation, a path in $\mathcal{T}_{comp}$ may be written

$$P = (C_1 \to C_2 \to \cdots \to C_s). \quad (6)$$

We write w_i, R_i, N_i, etc, instead of $w_{C_i}, R_{C_i}, N_{C_i}$, etc.

A component C is **special** if C is the root or a leaf of $\widehat{\mathcal{T}}_{comp}$, or if $\#(C) < \#(C')$ with C' the parent of C in $\widehat{\mathcal{T}}_{comp}$; otherwise it is **non-special**. This is a slight variant of [3].

We call P a **non-special path led by** C_1, if each C_i ($i = 2, \ldots, s$) is non-special, i.e., $\#(C_i) = \#(C_{i-1})$. The **special component tree** $\mathcal{T}^*_{comp}$ is obtained from $\widehat{\mathcal{T}}_{comp}$ by eliminating any non-special components while preserving the descendent/ancestor relationship among special nodes.

Define $s_{\max}$ to be the maximum length of a non-special path in $\widehat{\mathcal{T}}_{comp}$.

LEMMA 7.

$$s_{\max} = O\Big(\log n + \log\log \frac{w(B_0)}{\varepsilon}\Big).$$

Charging function $\phi_0(B)$**.** For each component C, define the **root radius** of C to be $r_C := \mathrm{rad}(\mathcal{Z}(C))$, that is the radius of the smallest disc enclosing all the roots in C. We are ready to define a charging function ϕ_0 for each box B in the components of $\widehat{\mathcal{T}}_{comp}$: Let $C_B \in \widehat{\mathcal{T}}_{comp}$ be the component of which B is a constituent box. Let ξ_B be any root

```
ROOT CLUSTERING ALGORITHM
Input:  Polynomial F(z), box B_0 ⊆ ℂ and ε > 0
Output:  Components in Q_out representing
      natural ε-clusters of F(z) in 2B_0.
   ▷ Initialization
   Q_out ← Q_1 ← Q_dis ← ∅.
   Q_0 ← {(5/4)B_0} // initial component
   ▷ Preprocessing
   While Q_0 is non-empty
      C ← Q_0.pop()
      If (C is confined and W_C ≤ w(B_0)/2)
            Q_1.add(C)
      Else  Q_0.add(Bisect(C))
   ▷ Main Loop
   While Q_1 is non-empty
      C ← Q_1.pop() // C has the largest W_C in Q_1
      If (4Δ_C ∩ C' = ∅ for all C' ∈ Q_1 ∪ Q_dis)
         k_C ← T̃^G_*(Δ_C)
         If (k_C > 0) // Note:  k_C ≠ 0.
            If (W_C ≥ ε)
               C' ← Newton(C)
               If (C' ≠ ∅)
                  Q_1.add(C');  Continue
            Else if (W_C ≤ 3w_C) // C is compact
               Q_out.add(C);  Continue
      Q_1.add(Bisect(C))
   Return Q_out
```

Figure 4: Clustering Algorithm

in $2B$. There are two cases: (i) If C_B is a confined component, there is a unique maximum path in $\widehat{\mathcal{T}}_{comp}$ from C_B to a confined leaf E_B in $\widehat{\mathcal{T}}_{comp}$ containing ξ_B. Define $\phi_0(B)$ to be the first special component C along this path such that

$$r_C < 3w_B. \qquad (7)$$

where w_B is the width of B. (ii) If C_B is not confined, it means that C is a component in the preprocessing stage. In this case, define $\phi_0(B)$ to be the largest natural ε-cluster containing ξ_B. Notice that $\phi_0(B)$ is a special component in (i) but a cluster in (ii).

LEMMA 8. *The map ϕ_0 is well-defined.*

Using this map, we can now bound the number of boxes.

LEMMA 9. *The total number of boxes in all the components in $\widehat{\mathcal{T}}_{comp}$ is*

$$O(t \cdot s_{\max}) = O(\#(2B_0) \cdot s_{\max})$$

with $t = |\{\phi_0(B) : B \text{ is any box in } \widehat{\mathcal{T}}_{comp}\}|$.

This improves the bound in [3] by a factor of $\log n$.

6. BIT COMPLEXITY

Our goal is to prove the bit-complexity theorem stated in the Introduction. All proofs are found in Appendix C.

The road map is as follows: we will charge the work of each box B (resp., component C) to some natural ε-cluster denoted $\phi(X)$ (resp., $\phi(C)$). We show that each cluster $\phi(X)$ (X is a box or a component) is charged $\widetilde{O}(1)$ times. Summing up over these clusters, we obtain our bound.

We may assume $\overline{\log}(B_0) = O(\tau_F)$ since Cauchy's root bound implies that any root z_i satisfies $|z_i| \le 1 + 4 \cdot 2^\tau$, thus we can replace B_0 by $B_0 \cap B(0, 2 + 8 \cdot 2^\tau)$.

Cost of $\widetilde{T}^G$-tests and Charging function $\phi(X)$: Our algorithm performs 3 kinds of $\widetilde{T}^G$-tests:

$$\widetilde{T}^G_*(\Delta_C), \quad \widetilde{T}^G_{k_C}(\Delta'), \quad \widetilde{T}^G_0(\Delta(B)) \qquad (8)$$

respectively appearing in the main loop, the Newton Step and the Bisection Step. We define the **cost** of processing component C to be the costs in doing the first 2 tests in (8), and the **cost** of processing a box B to be the cost of doing the last test. Note that the first 2 tests do not apply to the non-confined components (which appear in the preprocessing stage only), so there is no corresponding cost.

We next "charge" the above costs to natural ε-clusters. More precisely, if X is a confined component or any box produced in the algorithm, we will charge its cost to a natural ε-cluster denoted $\phi(X)$: (a) For a special component C, let $\phi(C)$ be the natural ε-cluster $\mathcal{Z}(C')$ where C' is the confined leaf of $\mathcal{T}^*_{comp}$ below C which minimizes the length of path from C to C' in $\mathcal{T}^*_{comp}$. (b) For a non-special component C, we define $\phi(C)$ to be equal to $\phi(C')$ where C' is the first special component below C. (c) For a box B, we had previously defined $\phi_0(B)$ (see Section 5). There are two possibilities: If $\phi_0(B)$ is defined as a special component, then $\phi(\phi_0(B))$ was already defined in (a) above, so we let $\phi(B) = \phi(\phi_0(B))$. Otherwise, $\phi_0(B)$ is defined as a natural ε-cluster, and we let $\phi(B) = \phi_0(B)$.

LEMMA 10. *The map ϕ is well-defined.*

Define $\widehat{S}$ to be the range of ϕ, so it is a set of natural ε-clusters. The clusters in $\widehat{S}$ are of two types: those defined by the confined leaves of $\widehat{\mathcal{T}}_{comp}$, and those largest ε-clusters of the form $\phi(B)$ with B in non-confined components.

LEMMA 11. *Each natural ε-cluster in $\widehat{S}$ is charged $O(s_{\max} \log n)$ times, i.e., $\widetilde{O}(1)$ times.*

We are almost ready to prove the theorems announced in Section 1.1. Theorem A is easier to prove if we assume that the initial box B_0 is **nice** in the following sense:

$$\max_{z \in 2B_0} \overline{\log}(z) = O(\min_{z \in 2B_0} \overline{\log}(z)). \qquad (9)$$

Then the following lemma bounds the cost of processing X where X is a box or a component.

LEMMA 12. *If the initial box is nice, the cost of processing X (where X is a box or a component) is bounded by*

$$\widetilde{O}(n \cdot L_D)$$

bit operations with $D = \phi(X)$ and with L_D defined in (2). Moreover, an L_D-bit approximation of F is required.

Using this lemma, we could prove Theorem A of Section 1.1 under the assumption that B_0 is nice. The appendix will prove Theorem A holds even if B_0 is not nice; the proof of Theorems B is also found in the appendix. In [3], the complexity bound for global root isolation is reduced to the case where B_0 is centered at the origin. This requires a global pre-processing step. It is unclear that we can adapt that pre-processing to our local complexity analysis.

7. CONCLUSION

This paper initiates the investigation of the local complexity of root clustering. It modifies the basic analysis and techniques of [3] to achieve this. Moreover, it solves a problem left open in [3], which is to show that our complexity bounds can be achieved without adding a preprocessing step to search for "nice boxes" containing roots.

We mention some open problems. Our Theorem A expresses the complexity in terms of local geometric parameters; how tight is this? Another challenge is to extend our complexity analysis to analytic root clustering [31].

8. REFERENCES

[1] J. Abbott. Quadratic interval refinement for real roots. *Communications in Computer Algebra*, 28:3–12, 2014. Poster at the ISSAC 2006.

[2] R. Becker. The Bolzano Method to isolate the real roots of a bitstream polynomial. Bachelor Thesis, Uni. Saarland, Saarbruecken, Germany, May 2012.

[3] R. Becker, M. Sagraloff, V. Sharma, and C. Yap. A simple near-optimal subdivision algorithm for complex root isolation based on Pellet test and Newton iteration. *arXiv:1509.06231v3 [cs.NA]*, Sept. 2015. 51 Pages. Submitted to Journal.

[4] M. Burr and F. Krahmer. SqFreeEVAL: An (almost) optimal real-root isolation algorithm. *J. Symbolic Computation*, 47(2):153–166, 2012.

[5] M. Burr, F. Krahmer, and C. Yap. Continuous amortization: A non-probabilistic adaptive analysis technique. ECCC, TR09(136), Dec 2009.

[6] M. A. Burr. Continuous amortization and extensions: With applications to bisection-based root isolation. *J. Symbolic Computation*, 77:78–126, 2016.

[7] G. E. Collins and A. G. Akritas. Polynomial real root isolation using Descartes' rule of signs. In R. D. Jenks, editor, *Proc. 1976 ACM Symp. on Symbolic and Algebraic Comp.*, pp. 272–275. ACM Press, 1976.

[8] J. H. Davenport. Computer algebra for cylindrical algebraic decomposition. Tech. Rep., The Royal Inst. of Technology, Dept. of Numerical Analysis and Comput. Sci., S-100 44, Stockholm, Sweden, 1985.

[9] Z. Du, V. Sharma, and C. Yap. Amortized bounds for root isolation via Sturm sequences. In D. Wang and L. Zhi, eds., *Symbolic-Numeric Computation*, Trends in Mathematics, pp. 113–130. Birkhäuser, 2007.

[10] A. Eigenwillig, V. Sharma, and C. Yap. Almost tight complexity bounds for the Descartes method. In *31st ISSAC*, pp. 71–78.

[11] I. Z. Emiris, V. Y. Pan, and E. P. Tsigaridas. Algebraic algorithms. In *Computing Handbook, 3rd Edition: Computer Science and Software Engineering*, pages 10: 1–30. Chapman and Hall/CRC, 2014.

[12] N. Kamath. Subdivision algorithms for complex root isolation: Empirical comparisons. MSc thesis, Oxford University, Oxford Computing Lab, Aug. 2010.

[13] N. Kamath, I. Voiculescu, and C. Yap. Empirical study of an evaluation-based subdivision algorithm for complex root isolation. In *4th SNC Workshop*, pp. 155–164, 2011.

[14] P. Kirrinnis. Polynomial factorization and partial fraction decomposition by simultaneous Newton's iteration. *J. of Complexity*, 14:378–444, 1998.

[15] J. M. Lane and R. F. Riesenfeld. Bounds on a polynomial. *BIT*, 21:112–117, 1981.

[16] M. Marden. *The Geometry of Zeros of a Polynomial in a Complex Variable.* Amer. Math. Soc., 1949.

[17] J. McNamee and V. Pan. *Numerical Methods for Roots of Polynomials, Part 2.* Elsevier, Amsterdam, 2013.

[18] K. Mehlhorn, M. Sagraloff, and P. Wang. From approximate factorization to root isolation with application to cylindrical algebraic decomposition. *J. Symbolic Computation*, 66:34–69, 2015.

[19] C. A. Neff and J. H. Reif. An efficient algorithm for the complex roots problem. *J. of Complexity*, 12:81–115, 1996.

[20] V. Y. Pan. Solving a polynomial equation: some history and recent progress. *SIAM Review*, 39(2):187–220, 1997.

[21] V. Y. Pan. Approximating polynomial zeros: Modified quadtree (Weyl's) construction and improved Newton's iteration. *J.Complexity*, 16(1):213–264, 2000.

[22] V. Y. Pan. Univariate polynomials: Nearly optimal algorithms for numerical factorization and root-finding. *J. Symb. Comput.*, 33(5):701–733, 2002.

[23] J. Renegar. On the worst-case arithmetic complexity of approximating zeros of polynomials. *Journal of Complexity*, 3:90–113, 1987.

[24] F. Rouillier and P. Zimmermann. Efficient isolation of [a] polynomial's real roots. *J. Computational and Applied Mathematics*, 162:33–50, 2004.

[25] M. Sagraloff. When Newton meets Descartes: A simple and fast algorithm to isolate the real roots of a polynomial. In *37th ISSAC*, pages 297–304, 2012.

[26] M. Sagraloff and K. Mehlhorn. Computing real roots of real polynomials. *J. Symbolic Computation*, 2015.

[27] M. Sagraloff and C. K. Yap. A simple but exact and efficient algorithm for complex root isolation. In *36th ISSAC*, pages 353–360, 2011.

[28] A. Schönhage. The fundamental theorem of algebra in terms of computational complexity, 1982. Manuscript, Department of Mathematics, University of Tübingen. 2004 Update with typo corrections and an appendix.

[29] V. Sharma and C. Yap. Near optimal tree size bounds on a simple real root isolation algorithm. In *37th ISSAC*, pp. 319 – 326, 2012.

[30] J.-C. Yakoubsohn. Finding a cluster of zeros of univariate polynomials. *Journal of Complexity*, 16(3):603–638, 2000.

[31] C. Yap, M. Sagraloff, and V. Sharma. Analytic root clustering: A complete algorithm using soft zero tests. In *Computability in Europe (CiE2013)*, LNCS vol. 7921, pages 434–444, Heidelberg, 2013. Springer.

[32] C. K. Yap. *Fundamental Problems of Algorithmic Algebra.* Oxford University Press, 2000.

[33] C. K. Yap. In praise of numerical computation. In *Efficient Algorithms*, volume 5760 of *Lect. Notes in C.S.*, pp. 308–407. Springer-Verlag, 2009.

APPENDIX

We have omitted the three appendices which may be found in our full paper: Appendix A contain proofs for Section 2. Similarly, Appendix B and C are for Sections 5 and 6.

A Superfast Randomized Algorithm to Decompose Binary Forms

Matías R. Bender
matias.bender@inria.fr

Jean-Charles Faugère
jean-charles.faugere@inria.fr

Ludovic Perret
ludovic.perret@lip6.fr

Elias Tsigaridas
elias.tsigaridas@inria.fr

Sorbonne Universités, UPMC Univ Paris 06, CNRS, INRIA,
Laboratoire d'Informatique de Paris 6 (LIP6), Équipe PolSys, 4 place Jussieu, 75252 Paris Cedex 05, France

ABSTRACT

Symmetric Tensor Decomposition is a major problem that arises in areas such as signal processing, statistics, data analysis and computational neuroscience. It is equivalent to write a homogeneous polynomial in n variables of degree D as a sum of D-th powers of linear forms, using the minimal number of summands. This minimal number is called the *rank* of the polynomial/tensor. We consider the decomposition of binary forms, that corresponds to the decomposition of symmetric tensors of dimension 2 and order D. This problem has its roots in Invariant Theory, where the decompositions are known as canonical forms. As part of that theory, different algorithms were proposed for the binary forms. In recent years, those algorithms were extended for the general symmetric tensor decomposition problem.

We present a new randomized algorithm that enhances the previous approaches with results from *structured linear algebra* and techniques from *linear recurrent sequences*. It achieves a *softly linear* arithmetic complexity bound. To the best of our knowledge, the previously known algorithms have quadratic complexity bounds. We compute a symbolic minimal decomposition in $O(\mathtt{M}(D)\log(D))$ arithmetic operations, where $\mathtt{M}(D)$ is the complexity of multiplying two polynomials of degree D. We approximate the terms of the decomposition with an error of $2^{-\varepsilon}$, in $O\big(D\log^2(D)\big(\log^2(D)+\log(\varepsilon)\big)\big)$ arithmetic operations. To bound the size of the representation of the coefficients involved in the decomposition, we bound the algebraic degree of the problem by $\min(rank, D-rank+1)$. When the input polynomial has integer coefficients, our algorithm performs, up to poly-logarithmic factors, $\widetilde{O}_B(D\ell+D^4+D^3\tau)$ bit operations, where τ is the maximum bitsize of the coefficients and $2^{-\ell}$ is the relative error of the terms in the decomposition.

Keywords

Binary Form Decomposition; Superfast Algorithm; Hankel Matrix; Complexity; Algebraic Degree; Canonical Form; Waring's problem

1. INTRODUCTION

The Symmetric Tensor Decomposition problem (STD) consists in writing a symmetric tensor of dimension n and order D as a sum of rank-1 symmetric tensors, using the minimal number of summands. The length of the shortest sum is known as the rank of the symmetric tensor. A symmetric tensor is said to have rank 1 when it is, roughly speaking, the k-th outer-product of a vector. This definition of rank is also called symmetric rank [8]. Under different formulations, STD appears in many various areas like signal processing, computer vision, statistics, psychometrics, chemometrics, data mining, computational neuroscience. For an up-to-date introduction of the state-of-the-art in STD, we refer to e.g. [6, 20].

We can express STD in terms of homogeneous polynomials, e.g. [8]: given a homogeneous polynomial in n variables of degree D, we want to write it as a sum of D-th powers of linear forms, using the minimal numbers of summands. The rank of the polynomial, and equivalently of the tensor, is this minimal number.

Under this formulation, STD dates back to the origin of modern linear algebra, as it was studied in Invariant Theory. There, the decompositions are known as the canonical forms [11, 34, 35]. This problem, and the related theory of apolarity, were important for this classical theory, because they give information on the behavior of the polynomials under a linear change of variables [19]. It was also studied as a polynomial version of Waring's problem [8, 13].

Binary Form Decomposition (BFD). We consider the decomposition of symmetric tensors of order D and dimension 2. In terms of polynomials, given a binary form

$$f(x,y) := \textstyle\sum_{i=0}^{D}\binom{D}{i}a_i x^i y^{D-i}, \tag{1}$$

with $a_i \in \mathbb{F} \subset \mathbb{C}$ and $\mathbb{F}$ some field of characteristic zero, we want to compute a decomposition

$$f(x,y) = \textstyle\sum_{j=1}^{r}(\alpha_j x + \beta_j y)^D \tag{2}$$

where $\alpha_1,\dots,\alpha_r,\beta_1,\dots,\beta_r \in \overline{\mathbb{F}}$ (the algebraic closure of $\mathbb{F}$) and r is minimal. A decomposition is said to be *unique* when for all the decompositions, the set of points $\{(\alpha_j,\beta_j) : 1 \leq j \leq r\} \subset \mathbb{P}(\overline{\mathbb{F}})$ is unique, where $\mathbb{P}(\overline{\mathbb{F}})$ is the projective space of $\overline{\mathbb{F}}$ [32].

Previous work. The decomposition problem of Eq. (2) has been extensively studied for $\mathbb{F} = \mathbb{C}$. The classical work of Sylvester [34, 35] described the necessary and sufficient conditions for a decomposition to exist (see Sec. 2.1). He showed how the decompositions are linked to Hankel matrices. He proved that the vectors, of dimension $r+1$, in the kernel of these matrices are related to decompositions of rank r. For a modern approach of this topic, we refer to [14, 18, 19, 32]. Sylvester's work can be extended to a more general kind of polynomial decompositions [11, 14, 31].

Sylvester's ideas lead straightforwardly to Sylvester's algorithm (Alg. 1) of [7, Sec. 3.4.3]. In addition, several algorithms were proposed to decompose binary forms, but with complexity at least quadratic in the degree of the binary form. For binary forms of

ISSAC '16, July 19-22, 2016, Waterloo, ON, Canada

DOI: http://dx.doi.org/10.1145/2930889.2930896

odd degree we can modify Berlekamp-Massey algorithm [2, 22] to compute the decompositions [9]. When the decomposition is unique, the Catalectican algorithm, which also works for symmetric tensors of bigger dimension [14, 26], improves Alg. 1. For an arbitrary binary form, Helmke [13] presented a randomized algorithm based on Padé approximates and continued fractions and described the different possible decompositions.

Besides of BFD, the subproblems of estimating the rank and deciding the uniqueness of the decompositions were considered [3, 5, 13, 34, 35]. Sylvester considered them [34, 35] for generic binary forms; that is for binary forms with coefficients belonging to a dense algebraic open subset of $\overline{\mathbb{F}}^{D+1}$ [7, Sec. 3]. He proved that when the degree is $2k$ or $2k+1$, the rank is $k+1$ and that the minimal decomposition is unique only when the degree is odd. In the non-generic case, the rank is related with the kernel of a Hankel matrix [5, 13, 14]. Moreover, the decomposition of a binary form of degree $2k$ or $2k-1$ and rank r, is unique if and only if $r \leq k$. Different algorithms were proposed to compute only the rank [3, 5, 8]. They do not provide complexity estimates, but using recent superfast algorithms for Hankel matrices [27], we can deduce a nearly-optimal arithmetic complexity bound for [5].

For the general STD problem, Sylvester's work was successfully extended to cases where the decomposition is unique [4, 26].

Formulation of the problem. To control the algebraic degree [1, 24] of the terms in the decompositions, we consider an equivalent problem. Instead of decomposing the polynomials as in Eq. (2), we compute $\lambda_1 \dots \lambda_r$, $\alpha_1 \dots \alpha_r$, $\beta_1 \dots \beta_r \in \overline{\mathbb{F}}$, where r is minimal, such that,

$$f(x,y) = \sum_{j=1}^{r} \lambda_j(\alpha_j x + \beta_j y)^D. \quad (3)$$

Since $\lambda_j \in \overline{\mathbb{F}}$, the problems are equivalent. However, if $\lambda_j, \alpha_j, \beta_j \in \mathbb{F}$, then the task is not the same. We do not study this problem, and we refer to [8, 13, 33], for $\mathbb{F} = \mathbb{R}$, and to [31, 32], $\mathbb{F} \subset \mathbb{C}$.

Main results and organization of the paper. We extend Sylvester's algorithm to achieve a nearly-optimal complexity bound in the degree of the binary form. Exploiting the relation between the kernel of the Hankel matrices and the decompositions, we bound the possible values of the rank of the decomposition, and we identify when the decomposition is unique. We build upon [13] and we use Berlekamp-Massey algorithm to provide a better complexity bound than what is currently known. As Sylvester's algorithm does, our approach decomposes successfully any binary form.

We present a superfast randomized algorithm to compute a *symbolic decomposition* in $O(\mathtt{M}(D)\log(D))$, where $\mathtt{M}(D)$ is the arithmetic complexity of polynomial multiplication. Such a decomposition refers to a representation of the decomposition as a sum of a rational function evaluated at the roots of a univariate polynomial. Using this representation, we can approximate the terms in the decomposition, with a relative error of $2^{-\varepsilon}$, in $O\big(D\log^2(D)\big(\log^2(D)+\log(\varepsilon)\big)\big)$ arithmetic operations [23, 28]. From the symbolic decomposition, we can deduce for free the rank and the border rank of the tensor (see [5, Sec. 1]). The algorithm is randomized because it performs a random linear change of variables to fulfill some genericity assumptions. We stress that we can check if the genericity assumptions hold in $O(\mathtt{M}(D)\log(D))$.

Using results from Kaltofen and Yagati [17], we bound the algebraic degree of the decompositions by $\min(r, D-r+1)$. For polynomials with integer coefficients, we bound the bit complexity, up to poly-logarithmic factors, by $\widetilde{O}_B(D\ell + D^4 + D^3\tau)$, where τ is the maximum bitsize of the coefficients of the binary form and $2^{-\ell}$ is the error of the terms in the decomposition.

The rest of the paper is organized as follows. First we present the notation. In Sec. 2 we present the preliminaries needed by the algorithm. Sec. 3 contains the main algorithm and its proof of correctness. In Sec. 4, we study the algebraic degree of the problem and the arithmetic and bit complexity of our algorithm

Notation. We denote by O, resp. O_B, the arithmetic, resp. bit, complexity and we use $\widetilde{O}$, resp. $\widetilde{O}_B$, to ignore (poly-)logarithmic factors. $\mathtt{M}(n)$ is the arithmetic complexity of multiplying two polynomial of degree n. Let $\mathbb{F}$ be a subfield of $\mathbb{C}$, and $\overline{\mathbb{F}}$ its algebraic closure. If $v = (v_0, \dots, v_n)^\top$ then $P_v = P_{(v_0,\dots,v_n)} := \sum_{i=0}^{n} v_i x^i y^{n-i}$. Given a binary form $f(x,y)$, we refer as $f(x)$ to the univariate polynomial $f(x) := f(x,1)$. By $f'(x)$ we denote the derivative with respect to x. For a matrix M, we refer as $\mathtt{rk}(M)$ and $\mathtt{Ker}(M)$ to the rank and the kernel of M.

Algorithm 1 IncrDecomp [7, Fig. 1]

1. $r := 1$
2. Get a random $c \in \mathtt{Ker}(H^r)$
3. If P_c is not square-free, $r := r+1$ and GO TO 2
4. Write P_c as $\prod_{j=1}^{r}(\beta_j x - \alpha_j y)$
5. Solve the Vandermonde transposed system:

$$\begin{pmatrix} \beta_1^D & \cdots & \beta_r^D \\ \beta_1^{D-1}\alpha_1 & \cdots & \beta_r^{D-1}\alpha_r \\ \vdots & \ddots & \vdots \\ \alpha_1^D & \cdots & \alpha_r^D \end{pmatrix} \begin{pmatrix} \lambda_1 \\ \vdots \\ \lambda_r \end{pmatrix} = \begin{pmatrix} a_0 \\ \vdots \\ a_D \end{pmatrix} \quad (5)$$

6. Return $\sum_{j=1}^{r} \lambda_j(\alpha_j x + \beta_j y)^D$

2. PRELIMINARIES

2.1 An algorithm based on Sylvester's theorem

Sylvester's theorem (Thm. 2.2) relates the minimal decomposition of a binary form to the kernel of a Hankel matrix. Moreover, it implies an (incremental) algorithm for computing the minimal decomposition. The version that we present in Alg. 1 comes from Common and Mourrain [7, Sec. 3.2].

Definition 2.1 *Given a vector $a = (a_0, \dots, a_D)^\top$, we denote by $\{H_a^k\}_{1 \leq k \leq D}$ the family of Hankel matrices indexed by k, where $H_a^k \in \mathbb{F}^{(D-k+1)\times(k+1)}$ and*

$$H_a^k := \begin{pmatrix} a_0 & a_1 & \cdots & a_{k-1} & a_k \\ a_1 & a_2 & \cdots & a_k & a_{k+1} \\ \vdots & \vdots & \ddots & \vdots & \vdots \\ a_{D-k-1} & a_{D-k} & \cdots & a_{D-2} & a_{D-1} \\ a_{D-k} & a_{D-k+1} & \cdots & a_{D-1} & a_D \end{pmatrix}. \quad (4)$$

We may omit the a in H_a^k when it is clear from the context.

Theorem 2.2 (Sylvester, 1851) *Let $f = \sum_{i=0}^{D} \binom{D}{i} a_i x^i y^{D-i}$ with $a_i \in \mathbb{F} \subseteq \mathbb{C}$. Also, consider $c = (c_0, \dots, c_r)^\top \in \mathbb{F}^{r+1}$ non-zero, such that the polynomial*

$$P_c = \sum_{i=0}^{r} c_i x^i y^{r-i} = \prod_{j=1}^{r} (\beta_j x - \alpha_j y)$$

is square-free and $\alpha_i, \beta_i \in \overline{\mathbb{F}}$. Then, there are $\lambda_1, \dots \lambda_r \in \overline{\mathbb{F}}$ such that $f(x,y) = \sum_{j=1}^{r} \lambda_j(\alpha_j x + \beta_j y)^D$, iff $(c_0, \dots, c_r)^\top \in \mathtt{Ker}(H_a^r)$.

For a proof of Thm. 2.2 we refer to the work of Reznick [32, Thm. 2.1 & Cor. 2.2]. His proof is of interest to us because it relates the decomposition with linear recurrent sequences (Sec. 2.3).

Thm. 2.2 implies Alg. 1. This algorithm will loop as many times as the rank. In the i-th loop it will compute the kernel of H^i. The dimension of this kernel is $\leq i$, and each vector in the kernel has $i+1$ coordinates. As the rank of the binary form can be as big as the degree of the binary form, a straightforward bound for the arithmetic complexity of Alg. 1 is at least cubic in the degree.

We can improve the complexity of Alg. 1 by a factor of D by noticing that the rank of the binary form is either $\mathtt{rk}(H^{\lceil \frac{D}{2} \rceil})$ or $D - \mathtt{rk}(H^{\lceil \frac{D}{2} \rceil}) + 2$ [5, Sec. 3][13, Thm. B]. Another way to compute the rank is by using the minors [3, Alg. 2].

The bottleneck of the previous approaches is that they have to compute the kernel of a Hankel matrix. However, even if we know that the rank of the binary form is r, the dimension of the kernel of H^r, as well as the dimension of the vectors in the kernel, can be as big as $O(D)$. Hence, the complexity is lower bounded by $O(D^2)$.

Our approach avoids the incremental construction. We exploit the structure of the kernel of the Hankel matrices and we prove that the rank has just two possible values (Lem. 3.1). Moreover, we use a compact representation of the vectors in the kernel. We describe them as a combination of two polynomials of degree $O(D)$.

2.2 Kernel of the Hankel matrices

The Hankel matrices are one of the most well known structured matrices [27]. We present results about the structure of their kernel. For details, we refer to Heinig and Rost [12, Ch. 5].

Consider a family of Hankel matrices $\{H_a^k\}_{1 \leq k \leq D}$ (Def. 2.1). There is a formula for the dimension of the kernel of each matrix in the family, involving two numbers, N_1^a and N_2^a.

Proposition 2.3 *For a family of Hankel matrices $\{H_a^k\}_{1 \leq k \leq D}$ there are two constants, N_1^a and N_2^a, such that*

1. $0 \leq N_1^a \leq N_2^a \leq D$,
2. $(\forall k : 1 \leq k \leq D)$
   $\mathtt{dim}(\mathtt{Ker}(H_a^k)) = \max(0; k - N_1^a) + \max(0; k - N_2^a)$, *and*
3. $N_1^a + N_2^a = D$.

We may skip a in N_1^a, N_2^a when it is clear from the context.

Fig. 1 illustrates Prop. 2.3. The dimension of the kernels is a piecewise-linear and increasing function. If $N_1 = N_2$, then the curve degenerates to two line segments, one of slope 0, from 1 to N_1, and one of slope 2, from N_1 to D. The elements of the kernel of the matrices in $\{H^k\}$ are related. To express this relation from a linear algebra point of view, we to introduce the **U-chains**.

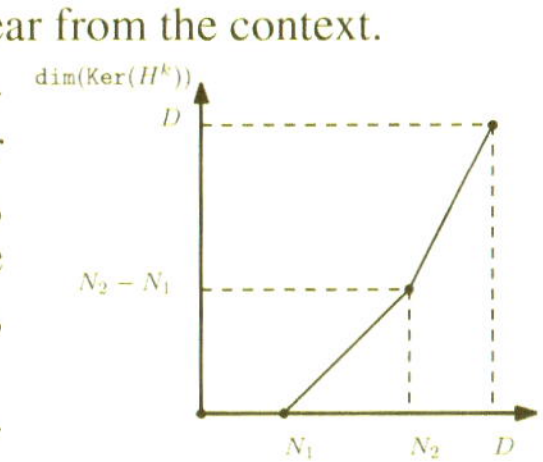

Figure 1: Dimension of the kernel of H^k

Definition 2.4 ([12, Def. 5.1]) *A **U-chain** of length k of a vector $v = (v_0, \ldots, v_n)^\intercal \in \mathbb{F}^{n+1}$ is a set of vectors $\{U_k^0 v, U_k^1 v, \ldots, U_k^{k-1} v\} \subset \mathbb{F}^{n+k}$.*
The i-th element, $0 \leq i \leq k-1$, is

$$U_k^i v = (\underbrace{0 \ldots 0}_{i}, \underbrace{v_0 \ldots v_n}_{n+1}, \underbrace{0 \ldots 0}_{k-1-i})$$

where U_k^i is a $(n+k) \times (n+1)$ i-shifting matrix [12, Page 11].

If v is not zero, then all the elements in a U-chain of v are linearly independent. The following theorem uses the U-chains to relate the vectors of the kernels in a family of Hankel matrices.

Proposition 2.5 (Vectors v and w) *Given a family of Hankel matrices $\{H^k\}_{1 \leq k \leq D}$, let N_1 and N_2 be the constants of Prop. 2.3. There are two vectors, $v \in \mathbb{F}^{N_1+1}$ and $w \in \mathbb{F}^{N_2+1}$, such that,*

- *If $0 \leq k \leq N_1$, then $\mathtt{Ker}(H^k) = \{0\}$.*
- *If $N_1 < k \leq N_2$, then the U-chain of v of length $(k - N_1)$ is a basis of $\mathtt{Ker}(H^k)$, that is*
  $$\mathtt{Ker}(H^k) = \langle U_{k-N_1}^0 v, \ldots, U_{k-N_1}^{k-N_1-1} v \rangle.$$
- *If $N_2 < k \leq D$, the U-chain of v of length $k - N_1$ together with the U-chain of w of length $k - N_2$ is a basis of $\mathtt{Ker}(H^k)$, that is*
  $$\mathtt{Ker}(H^k) = \langle U_{k-N_1}^0 v \ldots U_{k-N_1}^{k-N_1-1} v, U_{k-N_2}^0 w \ldots U_{k-N_2}^{k-N_2-1} w \rangle.$$

The vectors v and w of Prop. 2.5 are not unique. Vector v could be any vector in $\mathtt{Ker}(H^{N_1+1})$. Vector w could be any vector in $\mathtt{Ker}(H^{N_2+1})$ that does not belong to the vector space generated by the U-chain of v of length $N_2 - N_1 + 1$. From now on, given a family of Hankel matrices, we refer to v and w as the vectors of Prop. 2.5.

Let u be a vector in the kernel of H^k and P_u the corresponding polynomial (see Notation). We call P_u a **kernel polynomial**.

As $P_{U_k^j v} = x^j y^{k-1-j} P_v$, we write any kernel polynomial of a family of Hankel matrices as a combination of P_v and P_w [12, Prop. 5.1 & 5.5]. Moreover, P_v and P_w are relative prime.

Proposition 2.6 *Consider the family of Hankel matrices $\{H^k\}_{1 \leq k \leq D}$. The kernel polynomials P_v and P_w are relative prime. The set of kernel polynomials of the matrix H^k are*

- *If $0 < k \leq N_1$, then it is $\{0\}$.*
- *If $N_1 < k \leq N_2$, then $\{P_\mu \cdot P_v : \mu \in \mathbb{F}^{k-N_1}\}$.*
- *If $N_2 < k \leq D$, $\{P_\mu \cdot P_v + P_\rho \cdot P_w : \mu \in \mathbb{F}^{k-N_1}, \rho \in \mathbb{F}^{k-N_2}\}$.*

2.3 Linear recurrent sequences

Linear recurrent sequences are related to kernels of Hankel matrices. Essentially, their generating sequences generate these kernels.

Definition 2.7 *A sequence S (finite or not) is **linearly recurrent** when there is a finite sequence $(u_0, \ldots, u_n)$, known as the **generating sequence**, such that: $S_{n+1+i} = \sum_{k=0}^{n} u_k \cdot S_{i+k}$, $(0 \leq i)$.*

*A **minimal generating sequence (m.g.s.)** of S is a generating sequence whose length is the shortest with respect to the length of all the generating sequences of S.*

Berlekamp-Massey algorithm computes a minimal generating sequence [2, 22]. Moreover, Massey [22, Thm. 3] showed that a m.g.s. is unique, if and only if, its length is at most half of the length of the recurrent sequence. He also proposed to use rational function reconstruction to compute the m.g.s., when it is unique.

When the m.g.s. is unique, we compute it in softly-linear time [10, Sec. 12.3]. When it is not unique, to the best of our knowledge, the fastest deterministic algorithm to compute it has quadratic complexity , with well-known constants [25].

The Hankel matrices are related to the Berlekamp-Massey algorithm [15, 16]. In particular, we have Prop. 2.8.

Proposition 2.8 *The sequence $(u_0, \ldots, u_k)$ is a generating sequence of $a = (a_0, \ldots, a_D)$ iff $(u_0, \ldots, u_k, -1)^\intercal \in \mathtt{Ker}(H_a^{k+1})$.*

2.4 Linear change of variables

Instead of working with the input binary form, we perform a linear change of variables to ensure that we only compute unique m.g.s. A linear change of variables L_M, in our case, is associated to an invertible matrix $M := \left(\begin{smallmatrix} a & b \\ c & d \end{smallmatrix}\right)$, where

$$L_M(f)(x,y) := f(M \cdot \left(\begin{smallmatrix} x \\ y \end{smallmatrix}\right)) = f\big((ax+by),(cx+dy)\big).$$

This transformation preserves the rank of the binary form.

Lemma 2.9 *Let M be a non-singular 2×2 matrix. Given f and a minimal decomposition $f(x,y) = \sum_{j=1}^{r} \lambda_j (\alpha_j x + \beta_j y)^D$, a minimal decomposition for $L_M(f)$ is $\sum_{j=1}^{r} \lambda_j ((\alpha_j, \beta_j) \cdot M \cdot \left(\begin{smallmatrix} x \\ y \end{smallmatrix}\right))^D$.*

We compute any linear change of variables in $O(\mathtt{M}(D) \cdot \log(D))$ using multi-point evaluation and interpolation algorithms for univariate polynomials [10, Ch. 10].

For a 2×2 non-singular matrix, it holds $f = L_{M^{-1}}(L_M(f))$.

We want to perform a linear change of variables so that the matrices of the transformed polynomial have generic rank profile.

Definition 2.10 *A matrix has **Generic Rank Profile** if its leading principal minors of dimension less or equal to its rank are not zero.*

Proposition 2.11 ([21, Cor. 2.9]) *Let $M(t) := \binom{1\ t}{0\ 1}$. Given the binary form f associated to the family of Hankel matrices $\{H_a^k\}_k$, there are at most $\sum_{i=1}^{N_1+1} i(D-2i)$ values for t such that the Hankel matrices related to $L_{M(t)}(f)$ do not have generic rank profile.*

3. THE ALGORITHM

One of the drawbacks of Alg. 1, and its variants, is that they rely on the computation of the kernels of many Hankel matrices, and they ignore the particular structure that is present. Using Lem. 3.1, we can skip many calculations by computing only two vectors, v and w (Prop. 2.5). This is the main idea behind Alg. 2 that leads to a softly-linear arithmetic complexity (Sec. 4.2).

Alg. 2 performs as follows: First, (step 1) it performs a linear change of variables to ensure that the Hankel matrices have generic rank profile (see Sec. 2.4). Next, in step 2 computes two vectors, which are intended to be v and w from Prop. 2.5, to obtain the kernel of the Hankel matrices (see Sec. 3.1). Step 3 checks if the vectors computed are in fact the v and w of Prop. 2.5 (see Lem. 3.7). If they are not, this means that the linear change of variables was not appropriate. The algorithm goes back to the first step to perform a new linear change of variables. If the vectors are the correct ones, step 4 computes a square-free kernel polynomial of the minimum degree r (see Sec. 3.2). Next, step 5 computes the coefficients $\lambda_1, \ldots, \lambda_r$ (see Sec. 4.1.2). Finally, step 6 recovers a decomposition for the original binary form.

Let f be a binary form as in Eq. (1) and let $\{H^k\}_{1 \le k \le D}$ be its corresponding family of Hankel matrices (see Def. 2.1).

The next lemma establishes the rank of f.

Lemma 3.1 *Assume f, $\{H^k\}_k$, N_1 and N_2 of Prop. 2.3, and v and w of Prop. 2.5. If P_v (Prop. 2.6) is square-free then the rank of f is N_1+1, else, it is N_2+1.*

PROOF. By Prop. 2.3, for $k < N_1+1$, the kernel of H^k is trivial. Hence, by Sylvester's theorem (Thm. 2.2), there is no decomposition with a rank smaller than N_1+1. Recall that $v \in \mathtt{Ker}(H^{N_1+1})$. So, if P_v is square-free, by Sylvester's theorem, there is a decomposition of rank N_1+1.

Assume P_v is not square-free. For $N_1+1 \le k \le N_2$, P_v divides all the kernel polynomials of the matrices H^k (Prop. 2.6). Therefore, none of them is square-free, and so the rank is at least N_2+1. By Prop. 2.6, P_v and P_w do not share a root. So, there is a polynomial P_μ of degree N_2-N_1 such that $Q_\mu := P_v \cdot P_\mu + P_w$ is square-free. A formal proof of this appears in Thm. 3.8. By Prop. 2.6, Q_μ is a square-free kernel polynomial of degree N_2+1. Consequently, by Sylvester's theorem, there is a decomposition with rank N_2+1. □

Link with the classical theory. To relate Lem. 3.1 with the theory of BFD, we recall that the decompositions are identified with the square-free polynomials in the annihilator of f [19][14, Chp. 1]. All the kernel polynomials of $\{H_k\}_k$ belong to the annihilator of f, which is an ideal. If f is a binary form of degree $D=2k$ or $2k+1$, then this ideal is generated by two binary forms of degrees $\mathtt{rk}(H^k)$ and $D+2-\mathtt{rk}(H^k)$, with no common zeros [14, Thm. 1.44]. These are the polynomials P_v and P_w. Using this interpretation, Alg. 1, and its variants, computes a (redundant) generating set of the annihilator, while Alg. 2 computes a basis.

3.1 Computing the vectors v and w

We use Prop. 2.8 to compute the vectors v and w as minimal generating sequences (m.g.s.) in Alg. 3.

Algorithm 2 FASTDECOMP

Input: A binary form $\hat{f}(x,y)$ of degree D
Output: A decomposition for $\hat{f}(x,y)$ of rank r.

1. **Perform a random linear change of variables**
   We choose a 2×2 random matrix M, and we take
   $$f(x,y) := L_M(\hat{f})(x,y) = \sum_{i=0}^{D} \binom{D}{i} a_i x^i y^{D-i}$$
2. **Compute v and w of $\{\mathbf{H}_a^k\}_k$**
   We use Alg. 3 with $a := (a_0, \ldots, a_D)^\mathsf{T}$.
3. **Test if Step 2 computed v and w.** If not, GO TO Step 1.
   Check if the preconditions of Alg. 3 hold (Lem. 3.7).
4. **IF $P_v(x,y)$ is square-free,** $Q \longleftarrow P_v$
   ELSE Compute a square-free binary form Q
   We compute a vector μ of length $(N_2 - N_1 + 1)$, such that $(P_\mu \cdot P_v + P_w)$ is square-free (Sec. 4.1.1).
   $Q \longleftarrow P_\mu \cdot P_v + P_w$
5. **Compute the coefficients** $\lambda_1, \ldots, \lambda_r$ by solving the system of Eq. (5) where $Q(x,y) = \prod_{j=1}^{r}(\beta_j x - \alpha_j y)$.
   For details and the representation of λ_j, see Sec. 4.1.2.
6. **Return** $\hat{f}(x,y) = \sum_{j=1}^{r} \lambda_j ((\alpha_j, \beta_j) M^{-1} \binom{x}{y})^D$

There are different variants of the Berlekamp-Massey algorithm to compute m.g.s. (see Sec. 2.3). The algorithm with no preconditions on the uniqueness of the m.g.s., as Berlekamp's iterative algorithm [22, Sec. 3], returns two polynomials which are, essentially, P_v and P_w of our Prop. 2.6. It is not known to us if there is a variant with softly-linear complexity in this case. Therefore, we propose a randomized alternative that uses the variant of the Berlekamp-Massey algorithm for sequences with a unique m.g.s.; The arithmetic complexity of such variant is softly-linear [10, Sec. 12.3].

We only consider families of Hankel matrices that have generic rank profile (see Def. 2.10). We prove that this property implies that v is related to a m.g.s. of a, and w is related to the unique m.g.s. of the first $2N_1^a$ elements of a, where N_1^a is defined by Prop. 2.3. This approach guarantees a softly-linear complexity bound (Sec. 4.2).

The assumption on the generic rank profile is not restrictive. As Prop. 2.11 indicates, we can achieve this property by applying a generic linear change of variables to f.

Lemma 3.2 *If $\{H_a^k\}_k$ has generic rank profile, then there is a vector $(v_0, \ldots, v_{N_1^a}, -1)^\mathsf{T}$ in the kernel of $H_a^{N_1^a+1}$.*

PROOF. We skip the index a to simplify the notation.

If $N_1 \neq N_2$, then the kernel of $H^{N_1+1} \in \mathbb{F}^{(N_2)\times(N_1+2)}$ has dimension 1 (Prop. 2.3). Hence, by the Rank-Nullity theorem, the rank of the matrix H^{N_1+1} is N_1+1.

The matrix $H^{N_1+1} \in \mathbb{F}^{(N_2)\times(N_1+2)}$ has generic rank profile (Def. 2.10) and $N_2 \ge N_1+1$, hence its $(N_1+1)\times(N_1+1)$ leading principal submatrix of H^{N_1+1} is invertible. Let $(u_0, \ldots, u_{N_1}, 0)^\mathsf{T}$ be a vector in $\mathtt{Ker}(H^{N_1+1})$. Therefore $(u_0, \ldots, u_{N_1})^\mathsf{T}$ must be in the kernel of its $(N_1+1)\times(N_1+1)$ leading principal submatrix. Hence, $(u_0, \ldots, u_{N_1})^\mathsf{T}$ is the 0 vector. As the dimension of the kernel of H^{N_1+1} is one, there exists a vector $(v_0, \ldots, v_{N_1}, v_{N_1+1})^\mathsf{T}$ in this kernel such that $v_{N_1+1} \neq 0$. After normalization, we take a vector in this kernel such that $v_{N_1+1} = -1$.

If $N_1 = N_2$, the dimension of the kernel $H^{N_1+1} \in \mathbb{F}^{(N_1)\times(N_1+2)}$ is 2 (Prop. 2.3) and its rank is N_1 (Rank-Nullity theorem). As it has generic rank profile, its $N_1 \times N_1$ leading principal submatrix is invertible. Hence, as in the previous paragraph, there are two vectors $(w_0, \ldots, w_{N_2-1}, -1, 0)$ and $(v_0, \ldots, v_{N_1-1}, 0, -1)$ in $\mathtt{Ker}(H^{N_1+1})$. □

Algorithm 3 COMPUTE_V_AND_W

Input: Hankel matrices $\{H_a^k\}_{1 \leq k \leq D}$ with **Generic Rank Profile**.
Output: Vectors v and w as Prop. 2.5

1. $(v_0, \ldots, v_{N_1}) \leftarrow$ Min. gen. seq. of $(a_0, \ldots, a_D)$
2. $v \leftarrow (v_0 \ldots v_{N_1}, -1)^\mathsf{T}$
3. $(w_0, \ldots, w_{N_1-1}) \leftarrow$ Min. gen. seq. of $(a_0, \ldots, a_{2N_1-1})$
4. $w \leftarrow (w_0, \ldots, w_{N_1-1}, -1, \underbrace{0, \ldots, 0}_{N_2-N_1+1})^\mathsf{T}$
5. **Return** v and w

Lemma 3.3 *If $(v_0, \ldots, v_{N_1^a}, -1)^\mathsf{T} \in \mathtt{Ker}(H_a^{N_1^a+1})$, for a sequence a, then $(v_0, \ldots, v_{N_1^a})$ is a m.g.s. of a.*

PROOF. By Prop. 2.8, every generating sequence of a, of length k, is related to a non-zero vector in the kernel of H_a^k. By Prop. 2.3, the kernel of the matrices $\{H_a^k\}_{1 \leq k \leq N_1^a}$ is trivial. Thus, there is no generating sequence of length smaller than $N_1^a + 1$. Since $(v_0, \ldots, v_{N_1^a}, -1)^\mathsf{T} \in \mathtt{Ker}(H_a^{N_1^a+1})$, $(v_0, \ldots, v_{N_1^a})$ is a m.g.s. of a. □

Lemma 3.4 *Alg. 3 computes v of Prop. 2.5.*

PROOF. When the corresponding Hankel matrices have generic rank profile, by Lem. 3.2, there is vector $(v_0, \ldots, v_{N_1^a}, -1)^\mathsf{T} \in \mathtt{Ker}(H_a^{N_1^a+1})$. Hence, by Lem. 3.3, $(v_0, \ldots, v_{N_1^a})$ is a m.g.s. of a, and so the length of the m.g.s. of a is $N_1^a + 1$. Given a m.g.s. $(\hat{v}_0, \ldots, \hat{v}_{N_1^a})$ of a, by Prop. 2.8, $(\hat{v}_0, \ldots, \hat{v}_{N_1^a}, -1)^\mathsf{T} \in \mathtt{Ker}(H_a^{N_1^a})$. Hence, we can take $v = (\hat{v}_0, \ldots, \hat{v}_{N_1^a}, -1)^\mathsf{T}$, as the algorithm does. □

Lemma 3.5 *Given a family of Hankel matrices $\{H_a^k\}_k$ with generic rank profile, there is a vector $w \in \mathtt{Ker}(H^{N_2+1})$ linearly independent to all the elements in the U-chain of v of length $N_2 - N_1 + 1$. It is of the form $w = (w_0 \ldots w_{N_1-1}, -1, 0, \ldots, 0)^\mathsf{T}$, where $(w_0, \ldots, w_{N_1-1})$ is the unique m.g.s. of $(a_0, \ldots, a_{2N_1-1})$, its number of tailing 0's is $N_2 - N_1 + 1$, and v is from step 2 of Alg. 3.*

PROOF. By step 2 of Alg. 3, $v_{N_1+1} \neq 0$. Hence, none of the vectors in the vector space generated by the elements in the U-chain of v of length $N_2 - N_1 + 1$ has its last $N_2 - N_1 + 1$ positions equal to zero. As this property holds for the candidate vector for w, it cannot belong to this space.

The dimension of the kernel of $H^{N_2+1} \in \mathbb{F}^{(D-N_2)\times(N_2+2)}$ is $N_2 - N_1 + 2$ (Prop. 2.3). As $N_1 = D - N_2$ and we assumed having generic rank profile, the $N_1 \times N_1$ leading principal submatrix of H^{N_2+1} is invertible. Hence, the following system has a unique solution,

$$\begin{pmatrix} a_0 & \cdots & a_{N_1-1} \\ \vdots & \ddots & \vdots \\ a_{N_1-1} & \cdots & a_{2N_1-2} \end{pmatrix} \cdot \begin{pmatrix} w_0 \\ \vdots \\ w_{N_1-1} \end{pmatrix} = \begin{pmatrix} a_{N_1} \\ \vdots \\ a_{2N_1-1} \end{pmatrix} \tag{6}$$

So, the vector $w = (w_0 \ldots w_{N_1-1}, -1, 0 \ldots 0)^\mathsf{T}$ is in $\mathtt{Ker}(H^{N_2+1})$.

As there is a unique solution to the system of Eq. (6), by Prop. 2.8, $(w_0 \ldots w_{N_1-1})$ is the unique generating sequence of $(a_0, \ldots, a_{2N_1-1})$ with length N_1. Note that if $(u_0, \ldots, u_n)$ is a generating sequence, then for any ρ, $(\rho(u_0, \ldots, u_n, -1) + (0, u_0, \ldots, u_n))$ is a generating sequence too. Hence, it is the unique m.g.s. of $(a_0, \ldots, a_{2N_1-1})$. □

Lemmas 3.2, 3.3 and 3.5 imply the correctness of Alg. 3.

Theorem 3.6 *Given the Hankel matrices $\{H_a^k\}_{(1 \leq k \leq D)}$ with generic rank profile, Alg. 3 computes the vectors v and w of Prop. 2.5.*

Alg. 3 outputs vectors v and w of 2.5 when then input family of Hankel matrices have generic rank profile. The following lemma allows to check when two vectors are the vectors of Prop. 2.5. Recall that those vectors are not unique.

Lemma 3.7 *Given a sequence a of length $D + 1$ and two non-zero vectors $u_1 := (v_0, \ldots, v_{\hat{N}_1+1})^\mathsf{T}$ and $u_2 := (w_0, \ldots, w_{\hat{N}_2+1})^\mathsf{T}$, they are the vectors v and w of Prop. 2.5 if and only if $u_1 \in \mathtt{Ker}(H_a^{\hat{N}_1+1})$, $u_2 \in \mathtt{Ker}(H_a^{\hat{N}_2+1})$, $\hat{N}_1 + \hat{N}_2 = D$ and P_{u_1} and P_{u_2} are relative prime.*

PROOF. With out loss of generality, let $\hat{N}_1 \leq \hat{N}_2$. Clearly, if u_1 and u_2 are v and w, all the conditions hold (see Sec. 2.2).

For the other direction, if $u_1 \in \mathtt{Ker}(H_a^{\hat{N}_1+1})$, the kernel of $\mathtt{Ker}(H_a^{\hat{N}_1+1})$ is not trivial. Hence, by definition of N_1^a (Prop. 2.3), $N_1^a \leq \hat{N}_1$. If $u_2 \in \mathtt{Ker}(H_a^{\hat{N}_2+1})$ and $\hat{N}_2 < N_2^a$, by Prop. 2.6, P_{u_1} and P_{u_2} should be divisible by P_v. But, as P_{u_1} and P_{u_2} are relative prime, this cannot happen. Hence, $u_2 \in \mathtt{Ker}(H_a^{\hat{N}_2+1})$ and $N_2^a \leq \hat{N}_2$. By Prop. 2.3, $N_1^a + N_2^a = D$ and $N_1^a \leq N_2^a$. At the same time we assumed $D = \hat{N}_1 + \hat{N}_2$ and $\hat{N}_1 \leq \hat{N}_2$. Therefore, $N_1^a = \hat{N}_1$ and $N_2^a = \hat{N}_2$. So, $u_1 \in \mathtt{Ker}(H_a^{N_1^a+1})$ and $u_2 \in \mathtt{Ker}(H_a^{N_2^a+1})$. Hence, u_1 is the vector v.

By Prop. 2.5, all the kernel polynomials spanned by the elements in the U-chain of u_1 are divisible by P_{u_1}. As P_{u_1} and P_{u_2} are relative primes, the vector u_2 that does not belong to the vector space generated by the elements in the U-chain of u_1 of length $(N_2^a - N_1^a + 1)$. This implies that u_2 is the vector w. □

3.2 Computing a square-free polynomial Q

We can compute Q at step 4 of Alg. 2 in different ways. If P_v is square-free, then we set Q equal to P_v. If P_v is not square-free, by Lem. 3.1, we need to find a vector $\mu \in \mathbb{F}^{(N_2-N_1+1)}$ such that $Q_\mu := P_\mu \cdot P_v + P_w$ is square-free. By Prop. 2.6, P_v and P_w are relative prime. Thus, if we take a random vector μ, generically, Q_μ would be square-free. For this to hold, we have to prove that the discriminant of Q_μ is not identically zero. To simplify notation, in the following theorem we dehomogenize the polynomials.

Theorem 3.8 *Given two relative prime univariate polynomials $P_v(x)$ and $P_w(x)$ of degrees $N_1 + 1$ and $N_2 + 1$ respectively, let $Q_\mu(x) := P_\mu \cdot P_v + P_w \in \mathbb{F}[\mu_0, \ldots, \mu_{N_2-N_1}][x]$. The discriminant of $Q_\mu(x)$ with respect to x is a non-zero polynomial.*

PROOF. The zeros in $\mathbb{F}$ of the discriminant of $Q_\mu(x)$ with respect to x, considering it a polynomial in μ, is the set $\{\mu \in \mathbb{F}^{N_2-N_1+1} : Q_\mu \text{ has double roots}\}$.

A univariate polynomial is square-free if and only if it does share any root with its derivative. Hence, $(\mu_0, \ldots, \mu_{N_2-N_1})^\mathsf{T} \in \{\mu \in \mathbb{F}^{N_2-N_1+1} : Q_\mu \text{ has double roots}\}$ if and only if, there is $(\mu_0, \ldots, \mu_{N_2-N_1}, \alpha) \in \mathbb{F}^{N_2-N_1+1} \times \overline{\mathbb{F}}$ such that it is a solution of

$$\begin{cases} (P_\mu \cdot P_v + P_w)(x) = 0 \\ (P_\mu \cdot P_v' + P_\mu' \cdot P_v + P_w')(x) = 0. \end{cases} \tag{7}$$

We can rewrite P_μ as $\mu_0 + xP_{\hat{\mu}}$, where $\hat{\mu} := (\mu_1, \ldots, \mu_{N_2-N_1})^\mathsf{T}$. From Eq. (7), we can eliminate μ_0 to obtain the equation $(P_v(P_{\hat{\mu}} \cdot P_v + P_w)' - P_v'(P_{\hat{\mu}} \cdot P_v + P_w))(x) = 0$. As P_v and P_w are relative prime, this polynomial is not identically 0. Hence, for each $\hat{\mu}$, there is a finite number of solutions for this equation, bounded by the degree of the polynomial. Moreover, as the polynomials of Eq. (7) are linear in μ_0, each solution of the deduced equation is extensible to a finite number of solutions of Eq. (7). Therefore, there is a $\mu \in \mathbb{F}^{N_2-N_1+1}$, such that Q_μ is square-free. For this reason, the discriminant of $Q_\mu(x)$ is not identically zero. □

Corollary 3.9 *For every vector $(\mu_1, \ldots, \mu_{N_2-N_1})^\mathsf{T} \in \mathbb{F}^{N_2-N_1}$, there are at most $D + 1$ different values for $\mu_0 \in \mathbb{F}$ such that the polynomial $Q_\mu(x, y)$ is not square-free, where $\mu = (\mu_0, \ldots, \mu_{N_2-N_1})^\mathsf{T}$.*

3.3 Correctness of Algorithm 2

For computing a decomposition for a binary form f, we need to compute the kernel of a Hankel matrix (Thm. 2.2). Alg. 3 computes correctly the vectors v and w that characterize the kernels of the family of Hankel matrices associated to f, if they have generic rank profile. To ensure this precondition, in step 1, we perform a linear change of variables using a random non-singular matrix M. We will decompose $L_M(f)$ to recover a decomposition for f (Lem. 2.9).

By Lem. 3.7, step 3 tests if the output of Alg. 3 is correct. By definition of Alg. 3, the algorithm computes v and w if the input Hankel matrices, associated to $L_M(f)$, have generic rank profile (Thm. 3.6). Therefore, if the output is not correct, then the Hankel matrices do not have generic rank profile. Hence, we perform a new random change of variables and try again. There is a bounded number of "bad" changes of variables (Prop. 2.11), so we can always obtain a family of Hankel matrices with generic rank profile.

Once we obtain the vectors v and w, step 4 (see Cor. 3.9) and step 5 computes the coefficients $\alpha_j, \beta_j, \lambda_j$ of the decomposition. Hence, we have a decomposition for $L_M(f)$. As $L_{M^{-1}}(L_M(f)) = f$, by Lem. 2.9, a minimal decomposition of f is, $f(x,y) = \sum_{j=1}^{r} \lambda_j \cdot ((\alpha,\beta)\cdot M^{-1} \cdot \binom{x}{y})^D$.

Example. Consider $f(x,y) = y^4 + 8xy^3 + 18x^2y^2 + 16x^3y + 5x^4$. The Hankel matrices associated to f are related to the vector $(1,2,3,4,5)^\mathsf{T}$. Those matrices have generic rank profile. We apply Alg. 3 to compute v and w. The m.g.s. of $(1,2,3,4,5)$ is $(-1,2)$. Therefore, $v = (-1,2,-1)^\mathsf{T}$, $N_1 = 1$ and $N_2 = 3$. The m.g.s. of $(1,2)$ is (2), then $w = (2,-1,0,0,0)^\mathsf{T}$.

As $P_v = -(y-x)^2$, the rank of f is $N_2 + 1 = 4$ and we need to get a square-free kernel polynomial of degree 4. We consider the square-free kernel polynomial $(\frac{28}{5}y^2 - \frac{4}{5}xy - x^2)P_v + \frac{36}{5}P_w = \frac{36}{5}Q_{(\frac{7}{9},-\frac{1}{9},-\frac{5}{36})^\mathsf{T}} = (x - \frac{11}{5}y)(x-2y)(x+2y)(x+y)$. Solving the system of Eq. (5), we obtain the decomposition $f(x,y) = -\frac{625}{336}(\frac{11}{5}x+y)^4 + 3(2x+y)^4 + \frac{1}{21}(-2x+y)^4 - \frac{3}{16}(-x+y)^4$.

4. COMPLEXITY

In this section we study the complexity of Alg. 2.

4.1 Algebraic degree of the problem

4.1.1 The complexity of computing Q

Following the discussion of Sec. 3.2, we prove that, when the rank of the binary form is $N_2 + 1$, we can compute a square-free kernel polynomial Q of this degree such that the largest degree of its irreducible factors is N_1. Moreover, we prove that for almost all the choices of $(N_2 - N_1 + 1)$ pairwise linearly independent linear forms in $\mathbb{F}[x,y]$ there is a square-free kernel polynomial of H^{N_2+1} divisible by these forms.

Lemma 4.1 *Let f be a binary form of rank N_2+1. Given $(N_2 - N_1 + 1)$ pairwise linearly independent linear forms $(\beta_i x - \alpha_i y)$ such that none of them divides P_v, then there is a unique binary form P_μ of degree $N_2 - N_1$, such that the kernel polynomial $Q_\mu := P_\mu \cdot P_v + P_w$ is divisible by $\prod_i(\beta_i x - \alpha_i y)$.*

PROOF. Without loss of generality, we assume $\beta_i = 1$. By Prop. 2.6, for any polynomial P_μ of degree $N_2 - N_1$, Q_μ is a kernel polynomial. Since $\prod_i(x - \alpha_i y)$ divides $Q_\mu(x,y)$, it holds that for every α_i, $Q_\mu(\alpha_i, 1) = 0$. Hence, we can interpolate P_μ by noticing that $P_\mu(\alpha_j) = -\frac{P_w(\alpha_j)}{P_v(\alpha_j)}$.

The degree of P_μ is $(N_2 - N_1)$ and we interpolate it at $(N_2 - N_1 + 1)$ different points. Hence there is a unique interpolation polynomial P_μ. So, Q_μ is the unique kernel polynomial of H^{N_2+1} divisible by all those linear forms. □

Example (cont.) For the example of Sec. 3.3, we obtained the square-free kernel polynomial by choosing the factors $(x-2y)$, $(x+2y)$ and $(x+y)$. If we choose other factors such that Q_μ is square-free, we will obtain a different decomposition. Hence, f does not have a unique decomposition. This holds in general.

Corollary 4.2 *A decomposition is not unique iff the rank is $N_2 + 1$.*

Theorem 4.3 *Let the rank of f be $N_2 + 1$. There is a square-free kernel polynomial Q such that the largest degree of its irreducible factors is at most N_1.*

PROOF. Assume $\mathbb{F} = \mathbb{C}$. If the rank of f is N_2+1, then for each set of $N_2 - N_1 + 1$ linear forms $(x - \alpha_i y)$, following the assumptions of Lem. 4.1, there is a unique kernel polynomial. There is a rational map that realizes this relation (see the proof of Lem. 4.1). Let this map be $Q_{[\overline{\alpha}]}$, where $\overline{\alpha} = (\alpha_0, \dots, \alpha_{N_2-N_1})$. The image of the map is contained in $\{P_\mu \cdot P_v + P_w : \mu \in \mathbb{F}^{N_2-N_1+1}\}$. This set and the domain of the rational map have the same dimension, $N_2 - N_1 + 1$.

Given a kernel polynomial $\hat{Q}(x,y)$, there is a finite number of distinct linear forms $(x - \alpha_i y)$ that divides it, because $\hat{Q}(x)$ is a non-zero univariate polynomial. Hence, the pre-image of an element in the image of $Q_{[\overline{\alpha}]}$ is a finite set. Therefore, the dimension of the image and the dimension of the domain are the same.

By Thm. 3.8, the non-square-free kernel polynomials form a hypersurface in the space of kernel polynomials of the shape $P_\mu \cdot P_v + P_w$. If we consider the pre-image of the intersection between this hypersurface and the image of the rational map, then its dimension is smaller than $N_2 - N_1 + 1$.

Therefore, generically, for $N_2 - N_1 + 1$ linear forms, the map $Q_{[\overline{\alpha}]}(x,y)$ results a square-free kernel polynomial.

If $\mathbb{F} \subset \mathbb{C}$, this proof can be adapted taking into consideration that $\mathbb{F}$ is a dense algebraic open subset of $\mathbb{C}$. □

Corollary 4.4 *Given a binary form f of rank r and degree D, there is a square-free kernel polynomial of degree r such that the biggest degree of its irreducible factors is $\min(r, D-r+1)$.*

PROOF. If the rank is $r = N_2 + 1$, then $\min(r, D-r+1) = N_1$. By Thm. 4.3, such a square-free kernel polynomial exists. If the rank is $r = N_1 + 1$ and $N_1 < N_2$, by Lem. 3.1, there is a square-free kernel polynomial of degree $\min(r, D-r+1) = N_1 + 1$. □

The previous result is related to the decomposition of tensors of the same border rank [5, Thm. 2][3, Thm. 23].

4.1.2 Complexity of computing λ

We compute the coefficients λ_j of the decomposition by solving a linear system involving a transposed Vandermonde matrix (Step 5 of Alg. 2). We follow Kaltofen and Yagati [17] to write the solution of Eq. (5) as the evaluation of a rational function over the roots of a univariate polynomial.

Definition 4.5 *Given a polynomial $P(x) := \sum_{i=0}^{n} a_i x^i$ and $0 < k \le n$, let $Quo(P,k)(x) := \sum_{i=k}^{n} a_i x^{i-k}$.*

Proposition 4.6 ([17, Sec. 5]) *If $\alpha_j \neq \alpha_i$, for all $i \neq j$, then there is a unique solution to the system of Eq. (8). Moreover, if the solution is $\lambda = (\lambda_1, \dots, \lambda_r)^\mathsf{T}$ then, $\lambda_j = \frac{T}{Q'}(\alpha_j)$*

$$\begin{pmatrix} 1 & 1 & \cdots & 1 \\ \alpha_1 & \alpha_2 & \cdots & \alpha_r \\ \vdots & \vdots & \ddots & \vdots \\ \alpha_1^{r-1} & \alpha_2^{r-1} & \cdots & \alpha_r^{r-1} \end{pmatrix} \lambda = \begin{pmatrix} a_0 \\ a_1 \\ \vdots \\ a_r \end{pmatrix} \tag{8}$$

where $Q'(x)$ is the derivative of $Q(x) := \prod_{i=1}^{r}(x - \alpha_i)$, $R(x) := \sum_{i=1}^{r} a_{r-i} x^{i-1}$ and $T(x) := Quo(Q(x) \cdot R(x), r)$.

Lemma 4.7 *Given a binary form $f(x,y) := \sum_{i=0}^{D} \binom{D}{i} a_i x^i y^{D-i}$, let Q be a square-free kernel polynomial of degree r, obtained after step 5 of Alg. 2. Assume that y does not divide Q. Let α_j be the j-th roots of $Q(x)$, $Q'(x)$ be the derivative of $Q(x)$ and the polynomial $T(x) := Quo(Q(x) \cdot R(x), r)$, with $R(x) := \sum_{i=1}^{r} a_{r-i} x^{i-1}$. Then, each λ_j from step 5 in Alg. 3 can be written as $\lambda_j = \frac{T}{Q'}(\alpha_j)$.*

PROOF. As y does not divide Q, we can write it as $Q(x,y) = \prod_i (x - \alpha_i y)$, where all the α_i are different. Hence, as the $r \times r$ leading principal submatrix of Eq. (5) is invertible, we can restrict the problem to solve that $r \times r$ leading principal subsystem. This system is Eq. (8). Therefore, the proof follows from Prop. 4.6. □

Corollary 4.8 *Let Q be a square-free kernel polynomial related to a minimal decomposition of a binary form f of degree D, such that y does not divide Q. In this case, we can write f as $f(x,y) = \sum_{\{\alpha \in \overline{\mathbb{F}} | Q(\alpha)=0\}} \frac{T}{Q'}(\alpha) \cdot (\alpha x + y)^D$.*

If the square-free kernel polynomial related to a decomposition of rank r is divisible by y, we can compute $\{\lambda_j\}_{j<r}$ of Eq. (5) as in Lem. 4.7, by taking $\frac{Q}{y}$ as the kernel polynomial. It is wlog to consider $Q = P_{(u_0,\dots,-1,0)^\top}$, because Q is square-free, and so y^2 can not divide it. Hence, $\lambda_r = a_D - \sum_{i=0}^{r-2} u_i a_{D-r+i+1}$ [32, Eq. 2.12].

To summarize the section, given a binary form f of rank r and a generic non-singular 2×2 matrix M, there is a square-free kernel polynomial Q of the degree r, such that the largest degree of its irreducible factors is bounded by $\min(r, D-r+1)$ (Cor. 4.8). If $Q(x,y)$ is not divisible by y, the decomposition is

$$f(x,y) = \sum_{\{\alpha \in \overline{\mathbb{F}} | Q(\alpha)=0\}} \frac{T}{Q'}(\alpha) \cdot ((\alpha, 1) \cdot M^{-1} \cdot \binom{x}{y})^D,$$

where T and Q' are polynomials whose coefficients belong to $\mathbb{F}$ and whose degrees are bounded by r, defined in Lem. 4.7. When y divides Q, the form is similar.

4.2 Arithmetic complexity

Lemma 4.9 (Complexity of Alg. 3) *Given a binary form f of degree D, if its Hankel matrices $\{H_a^k\}_{(1 \le k \le D)}$ has generic rank profile, Alg. 3 computes v and w in $O(\mathtt{M}(D) \cdot \log(D))$.*

PROOF. Alg. 3 computes v and w of Prop. 2.5 as minimal generating sequences (m.g.s.). The superfast version of Berlekamp-Massey (BM) algorithm computes a m.g.s. in $O(\mathtt{M}(D) \cdot \log(D))$ when it is unique [10, Sec. 12.3].

We consider the computation of v (step 1 of Alg. 3). The m.g.s. of $a = (a_0, \dots, a_D)$ has always length $N_1 + 1$ (Lem. 3.4). But, it is not always unique. The length of a is $D+1$ and $N_1 + N_2 = D$. Therefore $N_1 < N_2$ if and only if $2(N_1 + 1) \le D + 1$. Massey [22] states that the m.g.s. is unique if and only if its length is less or equal to half of the length of the recurrent sequence. Hence, if $N_1 \neq N_2$, the m.g.s. is unique and so we can compute it superfast.

We consider the case where $N_1 = N_2$. As $N_1 + N_2 = D$, it holds that $N_1 = \frac{D}{2}$. Thus, the matrix $H_a^{N_1}$ is square and has a trivial kernel (Prop. 2.3). Hence, it is invertible and the system $H_a^{N_1} \cdot u = \hat{a}$ has always a solution; where u is a vector of unknowns, $\hat{a} = (a_{N_1^a+1}, \dots, a_D, c)^\top$, and c is arbitrary.

By Prop. 2.8, for each c, the solution of the system is a generating sequence of $(a_0, \dots, a_D, c)$ of length $N_1^a + 1$. Reasoning as in the proof of Lem. 3.5, since this generating sequence of length $N_1^a + 1$ is unique, it has to be the unique m.g.s. of $(a_0, \dots, a_D, c)$. In addition it is also a generating sequence of $(a_0, \dots, a_D)$. As it has the length, $N_1^a + 1$, of the m.g.s. of $(a_0, \dots, a_D)$, it is minimal. We compute it superfast as an m.g.s. of $(a_0, \dots, a_D, c)$ for any c.

It remains to identify when $N_1 = N_2$. We adopt a try and error approach. For an input $a = (a_0, \dots, a_d)$ we run the superfast version of BM. The algorithm terminates and outputs a sequence u in $O(\mathtt{M}(D) \cdot \log(D))$, independently of the uniqueness of m.g.s. [10, Sec. 12.3]. We verify the correctness of the output.

First we check if u is a generating sequence of a. By Prop. 2.8 this is equivalent to test if u belongs to the kernel of certain Hankel matrix; it corresponds to polynomial multiplication [27, Sec. 2.4].

If u is not a generating sequence of a, then the m.g.s. of a is not unique, and so $N_1 = N_2$. If u is a generating sequence of a, then we proceed as follows: Let L be the length of u. We compare $2L$ and $D+1$. If $2L \le D+1$ then m.g.s. of a is unique and $N_1 \neq N_2$. If L_m is the length of m.g.s., then $L_m \le L$ and $2L_m \le D+1$. Hence, by Massey's uniqueness argument [22], the m.g.s. is unique. In this case the m.g.s. of a is u. If $2L > D+1$, then the m.g.s. of a is not unique and $N_1 = N_2$. To see this notice that if the m.g.s. of a is unique then u has to be the unique m.g.s., by the correctness of BM. And so by Massey's uniqueness argument [22] it holds $2L \le D+1$ and $N_1 \neq N_2$. Therefore, we identify when $N_1 = N_2$ in $O(\mathtt{M}(D))$.

The vector w always corresponds to a unique m.g.s (Lem. 3.5). Therefore, we can always compute it efficiently. □

Lemma 4.10 (Complexity of computing Q) *Given the vectors v and w from Alg. 3, we compute a square-free polynomial $Q_\mu := P_\mu \cdot P_v + P_w$ with the algebraic degree of Cor. 4.4 in $O(\mathtt{M}(D) \cdot \log(D))$.*

PROOF. To compute the vector μ, we choose randomly $N_2 - N_1 + 1$ linear forms and we proceed as in Lem. 4.1. The complexity bound is due to multi-point evaluation and interpolation of a univariate polynomial [10, Ch. 10]. □

Theorem 4.11 *Alg. 2 computes a symbolic decomposition (see Introduction) of a binary form in $O(\mathtt{M}(D) \cdot \log(D))$.*

PROOF. The complexity of performing the random linear change of variables of step 1 is bounded by $O(\mathtt{M}(D) \cdot \log(D))$ (Sec. 2.4). In step 2, we call Alg. 3. It computes the candidate vectors v and w of Prop. 2.5 in $O(\mathtt{M}(D) \cdot \log(D))$ (Lem. 4.9). At step 3 we check if the candidates are valid using Lem. 3.7 in $O(\mathtt{M}(D) \cdot \log(D))$. After random linear change of variables at step 1, they are correct with probability 1. Using the vectors v and w, step 4 computes a square-free polynomial (Thm. 4.3) in $O(\mathtt{M}(D) \cdot \log(D))$ (Cor. 4.4). In step 5 we compute the rational function that describes the solution of the system in Eq. (5), in $O(\mathtt{M}(D) \cdot \log(D))$ [17]. Finally, step 6 returns the decomposition. □

Remark 4.12 *To output an approximation of the terms of the minimal decomposition, with a relative error of $2^{-\varepsilon}$, we use Pan's algorithm [28] [23, Thm. 15.1.1] to approximate the roots of Q. In this case the complexity becomes $O\big(D \log^2(D) \big(\log^2(D) + \log(\varepsilon)\big)\big)$.*

4.3 Bit complexity

Let $f \in \mathbb{Z}[x,y]$ be a binary form as in Eq. (1), of degree D and let τ be the maximum bitsize of the coefficients a_i. We study the bit complexity of computing suitable approximations of the α_j's, β_j's, and λ_j's of Eq. (3), say $\widetilde{\alpha}_j$, $\widetilde{\beta}_j$ and $\widetilde{\lambda}_j$ respectively, that induce an approximate decomposition correct up to ℓ bits. That is a decomposition such that $\|f - \sum_j \widetilde{\lambda}_j (\widetilde{\alpha}_j x + \widetilde{\beta}_j y)^D\|_\infty \le 2^{-\ell}$. We need to estimate an upper bound on the number of bits that are necessary to perform all the operations of the algorithm.

Initially the algorithm performs a linear change of variables, according to the discussion in Sec. 2.4. The element t of the matrix $M = \left(\begin{smallmatrix} 1 & t \\ 0 & 1 \end{smallmatrix}\right)$ that we use for the linear change of variables has less than D^3 forbidden values. Therefore, at least one of the first D^3

integers is valid to perform the transformation. Hence, in the worst case, t has bitsize $O(\log(D))$. After the transformation we obtain a new polynomial, F, of the same degree as f and of maximum coefficient bitsize $O(D\lg(D)+\tau)=\widetilde{O}(D+\tau)$.

It is wlog to consider $y=1$, because we have already performed the linear change of variables, and the degree of the binary form does not change with this substitution.

In the sequel, the algorithm computes the vectors v and w and, through them, the polynomial Q. This costs $\widetilde{O}(D)$. The degree of Q is $\leq D$ and its maximum coefficient bitsize is $\widetilde{O}(D^2+D\tau)=\sigma$ as it is the Bézout coefficient of an EGCD computation [10, Sec. 12.3]. Let α_j be the roots of Q. We isolate them in $\widetilde{O}_B(D^2\sigma)$ [28]. For the (aggregate) separation bound of the roots it holds that $-\lg\prod_j\Delta(\alpha_j)=O(D\sigma+D\lg(D))$. We approximate all the roots up to accuracy $2^{-\ell_1}$ in $\widetilde{O}_B(D^2\sigma+D\ell_1)$ [29]. That is, we compute absolute approximations of α_j, say $\widetilde{\alpha}_j$, such that $|\alpha_j-\widetilde{\alpha}_j|\leq 2^{-\ell_1}$.

The next step consists in solving the (transposed) Vandermonde system, $V(\widetilde{\alpha})^\top\lambda=a$, where $V(\widetilde{\alpha})$ is the Vandermonde matrix we construct with the roots of Q, λ is a vector contains the coefficients of decomposition, and a is a vector containing the coefficients of F, see also Eq. (5). We know the entries of $V(\widetilde{\alpha})$ up to ℓ_1 bits. Therefore, we can compute the elements of the solution vector λ with an absolute approximation correct up to $\ell_2=\ell_1-O(D\lg(D)\sigma-\lg\prod_j\Delta(\alpha_j))=\ell_1-O(D\lg(D)\sigma)$ bits [30, Thm. 29]. That is, we compute $\widetilde{\lambda}_j$'s such that $|\lambda_j-\widetilde{\lambda}_j|\leq 2^{-\ell_2}$.

At this point we have obtained the approximate decomposition $\sum_{j=1}^r\widetilde{\lambda}_j(\widetilde{\alpha}_jx+1)^D$; it corresponds to a polynomial $\widetilde{F}$. We apply the inverse transformation, $M^{-1}=\left(\begin{smallmatrix}1&-t\\0&1\end{smallmatrix}\right)$, to obtain an approximate decomposition, say $\widetilde{f}$, for f, which is

$$\widetilde{f}(x,y)=\sum_{j=1}^r\widetilde{\lambda}_j(\widetilde{\alpha}_jx+(1-\widetilde{\alpha}_jt)y)^D.$$

To estimate the accuracy of $\widetilde{f}$ we need to expand the approximate decomposition and consider it as a polynomial in x. We do not actually perform this operation; we only estimate the accuracy as if we were. First, we expand each $(\widetilde{\alpha}_jx+(1-\widetilde{\alpha}_jt)y)^D$. This results polynomials with coefficients correct up $\ell_3=\ell_2-O(D\sigma)=\ell_1-O(D\lg(D)\sigma)-O(D\sigma)=\ell_1-O(D\lg(D)\sigma)$ bits [30, Lemma 19]. Next, we multiply each such polynomial with $\widetilde{\lambda}_i$, and we collect the coefficients for the various powers of x. Each coefficient is the sum of $r\leq D$ terms. The last two operations do not affect, asymptotically, the precision. Therefore, the polynomial $\widetilde{f}=\sum_{j=1}^r\widetilde{\lambda}_j(\widetilde{\alpha}_jx+(1-\widetilde{\alpha}_jt)y)^D$ that corresponds to the approximate decomposition has an absolute approximation such that $\|f-\widetilde{f}\|\leq 2^{-\ell_1+O(D\lg(D)\sigma)}$. To achieve an accuracy of $2^{-\ell}$ in the decomposition, such that $\|f-\widetilde{f}\|\leq 2^{-\ell}$, we should choose $\ell_1=\ell+O(D\lg(D)\sigma)$. Thus, all the computations should be performed with precision of $\ell+O(D\lg(D)\sigma)$ bits. The bit complexity of computing the decomposition of f up to ℓ bits is dominated by the solving and refining process and it is $\widetilde{O}_B(D\ell+D^2\sigma)$. If we substitute the value for σ, then we arrive at the complexity bound of $\widetilde{O}_B(D\ell+D^4+D^3\tau)$.

Theorem 4.13 *Let $f\in\mathbb{Z}[x,y]$ be of degree D and maximum coefficient bitsize τ. We compute an approximate decomposition of accuracy $2^{-\ell}$ in $\widetilde{O}_B(D\ell+D^4+D^3\tau)$.*

Acknowledgments

The authors thank the anonymous reviewers for their helpful comments. Matías Bender thanks Joos Heintz for supervising his Master's thesis. The authors were partially supported by French ANR-11-BS02-0013 HPAC project. Elias Tsigaridas was partially supported by an FP7 Marie Curie Career Integration Grant.

References

[1] C. Bajaj. The algebraic degree of geometric optimization problems. *Discrete & Computational Geometry*, 3(1):177–191, 1988.

[2] E. R. Berlekamp. *Nonbinary BCH decoding*. University of North Carolina, 1966.

[3] A. Bernardi, A. Gimigliano, and M. Ida. Computing symmetric rank for symmetric tensors. *J. Symbolic Comput.*, 46(1):34–53, 2011.

[4] J. Brachat, P. Comon, B. Mourrain, and E. Tsigaridas. Symmetric tensor decomposition. *Linear Algebra and its Applications*, 433(11):1851–1872, 2010.

[5] G. Comas and M. Seiguer. On the rank of a binary form. *Foundations of Computational Mathematics*, 11(1):65–78, 2011.

[6] P. Comon. Tensors: a brief introduction. *IEEE Signal Processing Magazine*, 31 (3):44–53, 2014.

[7] P. Comon and B. Mourrain. Decomposition of quantics in sums of powers of linear forms. *Signal Processing*, 53(2):93–107, 1996.

[8] P. Comon, G. Golub, L.-H. Lim, and B. Mourrain. Symmetric tensors and symmetric tensor rank. *SIAM J. on Matrix Analysis & Apps*, 30(3):1254–1279, 2008.

[9] A. Dür. On computing the canonical form for a binary form of odd degree. *J. Symbolic Comput.*, 8(4):327–333, Oct 1989. .

[10] J. v. z. Gathen and J. Gerhard. *Modern computer algebra*. Cambridge University Press, Cambridge, 2013.

[11] S. Gundelfinger. Zur theorie der binären formen. *Journal für die reine und angewandte Mathematik*, 100:413–424, 1887.

[12] G. Heinig and K. Rost. *Algebraic methods for Toeplitz-like matrices and operators*. Springer, 1984.

[13] U. Helmke. Waring's problem for binary forms. *Journal of pure and applied algebra*, 80(1):29–45, 1992.

[14] A. Iarrobino and V. Kanev. *Power sums, Gorenstein algebras, and determinantal loci*. Springer, 1999.

[15] K. Imamura and W. Yoshida. A simple derivation of the berlekamp-massey algorithm and some applications. *IEEE Transactions on Information Theory*, 33(1):146–150, 1987.

[16] E. Jonckheere and C. Ma. A simple Hankel interpretation of the Berlekamp-Massey algorithm. *Linear Algebra and its Applications*, 125:65–76, 1989.

[17] E. Kaltofen and L. Yagati. Improved sparse multivariate polynomial interpolation algorithms. In *Symbolic and Algebraic Computation*, pages 467–474. Springer, 1989.

[18] J. P. Kung. Canonical forms of binary forms: variations on a theme of Sylvester. *Institute for Mathematics and Its Applications*, 19:46, 1990.

[19] J. P. Kung and G.-C. Rota. The invariant theory of binary forms. *Bull. Amer. Math. Soc.*, 10(1):27–85, 1984.

[20] J. M. Landsberg. *Tensors: geometry and applications*. AMS, 2012.

[21] W. Manthey, U. Helmke, and D. Hinrichsen. Topological aspects of the partial realization problem. *Math. of Control, Signals and Systems*, 5(2):117–149, 1992.

[22] J. L. Massey. Shift-register synthesis and bch decoding. *Information Theory, IEEE Transactions on*, 15(1):122–127, 1969.

[23] J. M. McNamee and V. Y. Pan. *Numerical methods for roots of polynomials (II)*, chapter 15. Elsevier, 2013.

[24] J. Nie, K. Ranestad, and B. Sturmfels. The algebraic degree of semidefinite programming. *Mathematical Programming*, 122(2):379–405, 2010.

[25] G. Norton. On the minimal realizations of a finite sequence. *J. Symbolic Comput.*, 20(1):93–115, Jul 1995.

[26] L. Oeding and G. Ottaviani. Eigenvectors of tensors and algorithms for waring decomposition. *J. Symbolic Comput.*, 54:9–35, 2013.

[27] V. Pan. *Structured matrices and polynomials: unified superfast algorithms*. Springer, 2001.

[28] V. Y. Pan. Univariate polynomials: Nearly optimal algorithms for numerical factorization and root-finding. *J. Symbolic Comput.*, 33(5):701 – 733, 2002.

[29] V. Y. Pan and E. Tsigaridas. Accelerated Approximation of the Complex Roots and Factors of a Univariate Polynomial. *Theor. Comput. Sci.*, 2016. URL https://hal.inria.fr/hal-01105267. (To appear).

[30] V. Y. Pan and E. Tsigaridas. Nearly optimal computations with structured matrices. *Theor. Comput. Sci.*, 2016. URL https://hal.inria.fr/hal-01105263.

[31] B. Reznick. Homogeneous polynomial solutions to constant coefficient pde's. *advances in mathematics*, 117(2):179–192, 1996.

[32] B. Reznick. On the length of binary forms. In *Quadratic and Higher Degree Forms*, pages 207–232. Springer, 2013.

[33] B. A. Reznick. *Sums of even powers of real linear forms*, volume 463. American Mathematical Soc., 1992.

[34] J. Sylvester. An essay on canonical forms, supplement to a sketch of a memoir on elimination, transformation and canonical forms. In *The collected papers of JJ Sylvester*, volume 1, pages 203–216. Cambridge University Press, 1904.

[35] J. Sylvester. On a remarkable discovery in the theory of canonical forms and of hyperdeterminants. In *The collected papers of JJ Sylvester*, volume 1, pages 265–283. Cambridge University Press, 1904.

Analysis of the Brun Gcd Algorithm

Valérie Berthé
IRIF (CNRS and Université Paris Diderot), France
berthe@liafa.univ-paris-diderot.fr

Loïck Lhote
GREYC (CNRS, ENSICAEN, and Université of Caen), France
loick.lhote@ensicaen.fr

Brigitte Vallée
GREYC (CNRS, ENSICAEN, and Université of Caen), France
brigitte.vallee@unicaen.fr

ABSTRACT

We introduce and study a multiple gcd algorithm that is a natural extension of the usual Euclid algorithm, and coincides with it for two entries; it performs Euclidean divisions, between the largest entry and the second largest entry, and then re-orderings. This is the discrete version of a multidimensional continued fraction algorithm due to Brun. We perform the average-case analysis of this algorithm, and prove that the mean number of steps is linear with respect to the size of the entry. The method relies on dynamical analysis, and is based on the study of the underlying Brun dynamical system. The dominant constant of the analysis is related to the entropy of the system. We also compare this algorithm to another extension of the Euclid algorithm, proposed by Knuth, and already analyzed by the authors.

Keywords

GCD algorithms; Brun continued fractions; average-case analysis; analytic combinatorics; Dirichlet generating functions; dynamical analysis; transfer operators; Tauberian theorems

Acknowledgments. Thanks to the ANR DynA3S (ANR-13-BS02-0003) and AleaEnAmSud AmSud-STIC Project.

1. INTRODUCTION.

General Context. We study a multiple gcd algorithm that is a natural extension of the usual Euclid algorithm for $(d+1)$ integers, and coincides with it for $d = 1$. This is a discrete version of a multidimensional continued fraction algorithm, that is itself based on a dynamical system, the Brun dynamical system, described for instance in [6, 12]. The Brun continued fraction algorithm admits various descriptions and appears under various names; it is closely related to the Podsypanin modified Jacobi–Perron algorithm, it is also called the d-dimensional Gauss transformation or the ordered Jacobi–Perron algorithm [7].

This dynamical system belongs to the class of multidimensional unimodular continued fraction algorithms, described in [12], which produce simultaneous diophantine approximations of a real vector. Then, the literature, for instance in [9, 5], mainly focuses on the convergence of these approximations, closely related to the Lyapunov exponents of the underlying dynamical systems. These algorithms have also important applications to discrete geometry [3].

With each multidimensional continued fraction algorithm, a gcd algorithm may be of course associated. However, the analysis of such a class of gcd algorithms has not been yet considered. This is our general project, and we begin by the `BrunGcd` Algorithm, as it is one of the most "natural" algorithms of this class, and shares many important properties with the Euclid dynamical system based on the Gauss map.

Main results. We perform the probabilistic analysis of the BrunGcd algorithm. We first focus on the total number of steps and prove that it is on average linear in the size of the entries. The dominant constant equals $(d+1)/\mathcal{E}_d$ where $\mathcal{E}_d$ is the entropy of the Brun dynamical system. This entropy is not precisely studied in the literature, but there exists a conjecture in [7] that states that $\mathcal{E}_d$ is $\Theta(1)$ for $d \to \infty$. However, we show that $\mathcal{E}_d$ is $\sim \log d$ for $d \to \infty$, so that the dominant constant for the number of steps grows as $d/\log d$.

We then compare the `BrunGcd` with another multiple gcd algorithm, the `PlainGcd` algorithm, described in Knuth's book [8], which deals with the classical one-dimensional Euclid dynamical system. The authors have already analyzed this algorithm in [4], and prove that the mean number of steps is also linear in the size of the entries. However, the dominant constant is independent of the dimension d and equals $2/\mathcal{E}_1$, where $\mathcal{E}_1$ is the entropy of the Euclid dynamical system. We conclude that the `PlainGcd` algorithm is much more efficient than the `BrunGcd` algorithm, in particular for large d.

We finally explain the inefficiency of the BrunGcd algorithm when d is large: almost all divisions deal with a quotient equal to 1. Then the main operation performed is not a division but... a plain subtraction. This is reinforced by the comparison with the subtractive version of the algorithm, whose number of steps is proven to be also of linear complexity. This exhibits two strong differences with the classical Gcd algorithm (case $d = 1$).

Methods. We use here the methods of *dynamical analysis* such as developed in [2, 10, 13]: a gcd algorithm is viewed as a dynamical system, with each iterative step being a linear fractional transformation. Costs of interest are then described with Dirichlet generating functions that are algebraically related to transfer operators of the system. The main analytical property of these series is the existence of a dominant pole, which is itself closely related to the existence

ISSAC '16, July 19–22, 2016, Waterloo, ON, Canada.

DOI: http://dx.doi.org/10.1145/2930889.2930899

of a spectral gap for the corresponding transfer operators. The asymptotic extraction of coefficients is then achieved by means of Tauberian theorems.

Plan of the paper. We first introduce the algorithm in Section 2 and state the main results. Then, we study in Section 3 the underlying dynamical system, closely related to the Brun dynamical system, and we provide a characterization of its rational trajectories. The following two sections perform the dynamical analysis of the algorithm, with its two steps, the combinatorial step (Section 4) and the analytic step (Section 5). The paper ends with open problems.

2. THE BRUN GCD ALGORITHM.

We describe the `BrunGcd` algorithm, state the main complexity results, and compare it with the `PlainGcd` algorithm.

2.1 General description.

The algorithm $\texttt{BrunGcd}(d)$ computes the gcd of $(d+1)$ positive integers. It deals with the input set $\Omega_{(d)}$ which gathers the *ordered* $(d+1)$-uples $\boldsymbol{u}$ formed with *positive* and *distinct* integer numbers

$$\Omega_{(d)} := \{\boldsymbol{u} = (u_0, u_1, \ldots, u_d) \mid u_0 > u_1 > u_2 > \ldots > u_d > 0\}.$$

During the execution of the algorithm, some components "disappear" and the algorithm deals with the *disjoint union*

$$\Gamma_{(d)} = \bigoplus_{\ell=0}^{d-1} \Omega_{(d-\ell)}\,.$$

The algorithm $\texttt{BrunGcd}(d)$ performs a sequence of steps, and each step deals with the pair (u_0, u_1) (that contains the two largest entries of $\boldsymbol{u}$) and the list $\texttt{End}\,\boldsymbol{u}$ which gathers all the components of $\boldsymbol{u}$ except u_0; it divides the first component u_0 by the second component u_1, and creates a remainder v_0

$$v_0 := u_0 - m u_1, \qquad m := \left\lfloor \frac{u_0}{u_1} \right\rfloor.$$

Then, the procedure $\texttt{InsDis}\,(v_0, \texttt{End}\,\boldsymbol{u})$ inserts $v_0 \geq 0$ at a suitable position inside the list $\texttt{End}\,\boldsymbol{u}$, so that the result remains an ordered uple of distinct positive values: the second component u_1 becomes the largest one, and there are three possible cases for the insertion (or not) of v_0:

- (G) (Generic case) if v_0 is not present in the list $\texttt{End}\,\boldsymbol{u}$, this is a usual insertion;
- (Z) (Zero case) if $v_0 = 0$, we *do not* insert v_0;
- (E) (Equality case) if $v_0 \neq 0$ is already present in the list $\texttt{End}\,\boldsymbol{u}$ at position i, we *do not* insert v_0.

In each of the cases (Z) or (E), we do not insert v_0, but we memorize the potential insertion position (in case (E), we would have inserted v_0 "in front of" u_i). Finally, each *step* of the algorithm $\texttt{BrunGcd}(d)$ is described by the map $U_{(d)} : \Gamma_{(d)} \to \Gamma_{(d)}$ which associates with $\boldsymbol{u}$

$$U_{(d)}(\boldsymbol{u}) = \texttt{InsDis}\,(u_0 \bmod u_1, \texttt{End}\,\boldsymbol{u})\,. \qquad (1)$$

The algorithm $\texttt{BrunGcd}(d)$ described in the following figure decomposes into d *phases*, labelled from $\ell = 0$ to $\ell = d-1$. During each phase, a component is "lost", and the ℓ-th phase, denoted by $\texttt{BrunGcd}_{(d,\ell)}$, transforms an element of $\Omega_{(d-\ell)}$ into an element of $\Omega_{(d-\ell-1)}$. The phase ends as soon as it meets case (Z), or[1] case (E), where it looses a component. The algorithm stops at the end of the $(d-1)$-th phase with an element of $\Omega_{(0)}$ which equals the gcd.

[1]The $(d-1)$-th phase always ends with the case (Z).

$\texttt{BrunGcd}(d)$
Input : $\boldsymbol{u} \in \Omega_{(d)}$
Ouput: $\boldsymbol{u} \in \mathbb{N}$
For $\ell = 0$ to $d-1$ **do** $\boldsymbol{u} := \texttt{Gcd}_{(d,\ell)}(\boldsymbol{u})$;

$\texttt{BrunGcd}_{(d,\ell)}$
Input : $\boldsymbol{u} \in \Omega_{(d-\ell)}$
Repeat $\boldsymbol{u} := U_{(d)}(\boldsymbol{u})$ **until** $u \in \Omega_{(d-\ell-1)}$.

2.2 Worst-case behavior.

As will be shown in the long version paper, the worst-case of the `BrunGcd` algorithm arises when the quotients are the smallest possible (all equal to 1, except the last one, equal to 2), and the insertion positions the largest possible. Then, the best worst-case bound involves an algebraic number τ_d which extends to general dimensions the inverse of the Golden ratio.

PROPOSITION 1. *For any fixed positive integer d, consider the smallest real root $\tau_d \in]0,1[$ of the polynomial $z^{d+1}+z-1$, and, for any integer N, the set of inputs*

$$\Omega_{(d,N)} := \{\boldsymbol{u} \in \Omega_{(d)} \mid u_0 \leq N\}. \qquad (2)$$

Then the maximum number $Q_{(d,N)}$ of steps of the `BrunGcd` *Algorithm on $\Omega_{(d,N)}$ satisfies*

$$Q_{(d,N)} \sim \frac{1}{|\log \tau_d|} \log N \qquad (N \to \infty).$$

When $d \to \infty$, the real τ_d satisfies $1/|\log \tau_d| \sim (d+1)/\log d$.

2.3 Probabilistic behavior.

We now describe the precise probabilistic behavior of the algorithm $\texttt{BrunGcd}(d)$ on the set $\Omega_{(d,N)}$ defined in (2).

THEOREM 1. *When the algorithm* `BrunGcd` *acts on the set $\Omega_{(d,N)}$ endowed with the uniform distribution, the following holds when d is fixed and N tends to ∞:*

- (a) *The total number L_d of steps and the number M_d of steps performed during the first phase satisfies*

  $$\mathbb{E}_N[L_d] \sim \mathbb{E}_N[M_d] \sim \frac{d+1}{\mathcal{E}_d} \cdot \log N$$

  and involves the entropy $\mathcal{E}_d$ of the underlying Brun dynamical system in dimension d.
  When $d \to \infty$, the entropy $\mathcal{E}_d$ satisfies $\mathcal{E}_d \sim \log d$.
  The number R_d of steps performed during the remainder of the execution (after the first phase) has a mean value that is asymptotic to a constant r_d.
- (b) *Let O_d be the number of quotients equal to 1 during the first phase. The ratio between the means $\mathbb{E}_N[O_d]$ and $\mathbb{E}_N[M_d]$ is asymptotic to a constant $\rho_d < 1$, that tends to 1 for $d \to \infty$ with a speed $O(2^{-d/\log d})$.*
  Let Σ_d be the number of steps of the subtractive version of `BrunGcd` *during the first phase. The ratio between $\mathbb{E}_N[\Sigma_d]$ and $\mathbb{E}_N[M_d]$ is asymptotic to a constant ${\sigma_d}^2$.*

[2]We conjecture the asymptotics $\sigma_d \sim \zeta(d/\log d)$ for $d \to \infty$.

In (a), the total number of steps L_d is proven to remain on average linear in the size $\log N$. Moreover, (a) exhibits a strong difference between the first phase, where most of the work is done, and the remainder of the execution, where the total number of steps R_d is on average asymptotically constant. The PlainGcd algorithm exhibits exactly the same phenomena, as it is shown in [4].

The following figure compares the number of steps of the BrunGcd and the PlainGcd algorithms, as a function of dimension d, when the binary size is fixed to $\log_2 N = 5000$. The complexity of BrunGcd algorithm appears to be sublinear with respect to d (see Section 5), whereas the complexity of the PlainGcd algorithm appears to be independent of d.

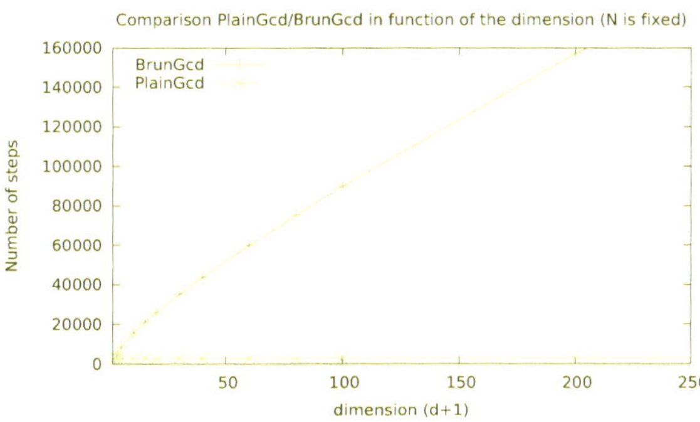

The two dominant constants, the ratio $(d+1)/\mathcal{E}_d$ which involves the entropy and intervenes in the average case, and the ratio $1/|\log \tau_d|$ which arises in the worst-case, both behave as $d/\log d$ for $d \to \infty$. This indicates the same behavior for the algorithm in the average-case and in the worst-case. As the worst-case is reached when the quotients are all equal to 1, this seems to indicate that the BrunGcd Algorithm deals with quotients which are very often equal to 1.

This is indeed the case, described in (b), and also illustrated in the following figure, that exhibits the proportion of quotients equal to 1 during the first phase as a function of the dimension d. This proportion tends quickly to 1: when $d = 16$, more than 99% of the Euclidean divisions are in fact subtractions and for $d = 50$, the proportion is 99.99%.

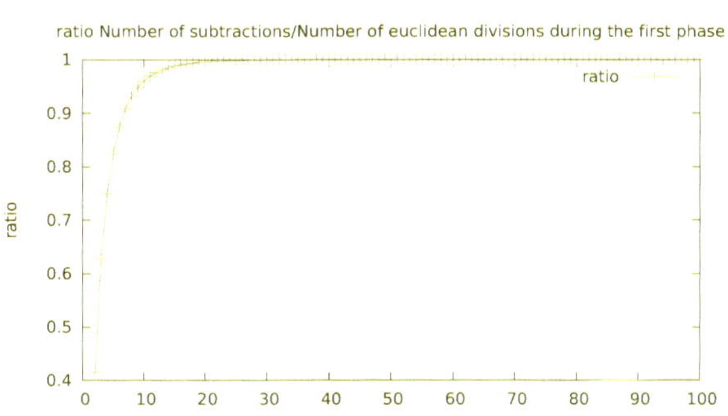

3. THE UNDERLYING DYNAMICAL SYSTEM.

We first describe a continuous extension of the algorithm, relate it with the Brun dynamical system, and provide an exact characterization of the trajectories that are related to the execution of the algorithm.

3.1 Continuous extension of the Gcd algorithm.

We now extend the BrunGcd(d) algorithm into a continuous process. We use the projection π defined on $\Gamma_{(d)} \setminus \{0\}$ as

$$\pi(\boldsymbol{u}) = \frac{1}{u_0}\texttt{End}\,\boldsymbol{u}\,,$$

and the closure of the image $\pi(\Gamma_d)$ is exactly the disjoint union $\mathcal{I}_{(d)}$ of simplexes $\mathcal{J}_{(d-\ell)}$, defined as

$$\mathcal{J}_{(d-\ell)} := \{\boldsymbol{x} = (x_1, \ldots, x_{d-\ell}) \mid 1 \geq x_1 \geq \ldots \geq x_{d-\ell} \geq 0\}\,,$$

and is written as $\mathcal{I}_{(d)} := \bigoplus_{\ell=0}^{d-1} \mathcal{J}_{(d-\ell)}$. Now, the map $V_{(d)} : \mathcal{I}_{(d)} \to \mathcal{I}_{(d)}$ is defined on each $\mathcal{J}_{(d-\ell)}$ by $V_{(d)}(\mathbf{0}^{d-\ell}) = \mathbf{0}^{d-\ell}$,

$$\text{and} \quad V_{(d)}(\boldsymbol{x}) = \texttt{InsDis}\left(\left\{\frac{1}{x_1}\right\}, \frac{1}{x_1}\texttt{End}\,\boldsymbol{x}\right) \quad \text{for } \boldsymbol{x} \neq \mathbf{0}^{d-\ell}\,,$$

where $\texttt{InsDis}(y_0, \boldsymbol{y})$ is now extended to $\mathcal{I}_{(d)}$. The map $V_{(d)}$ provides the extension of the conjugate with the projection π of the map $U_{(d)}$ defined in (1) and used in the BrunGcd(d) algorithm. Indeed, the equality $V_{(d)} \circ \pi(\boldsymbol{u}) = \pi \circ U_{(d)}(\boldsymbol{u})$ leads to the definition of $V_{(d)}$ on the set $\pi(\Gamma_d)$ which is further extended to $\mathcal{I}_{(d)}$ "by continuity".

The dynamical system $(V_d, \mathcal{I}_{(d)})$ is closely related to the usual Brun dynamical system defined on the simplex $\mathcal{J}_{(d)}$ with the transformation $T_{(d)}$ defined by $T_{(d)}(\mathbf{0}^d) = \mathbf{0}^d$, and

$$T_{(d)}(\boldsymbol{x}) = \texttt{Ins}\left(\left\{\frac{1}{x_1}\right\}, \frac{1}{x_1}\texttt{End}\,\boldsymbol{x}\right) \quad \text{for } \boldsymbol{x} \neq \mathbf{0}^d\,, \qquad (3)$$

where now the map $\texttt{Ins}(y_0, \boldsymbol{y})$ is the usual insertion "in front of": it performs as InsDis, *without* removing zeroes and equal components, and the cases (Z) and (E) may be gathered into a unique case (ZE). There are now only two cases:

(G) if y_0 is not present in the list $\boldsymbol{y}$, this is an usual insertion;

(ZE) if y_0 is already present in the list $\boldsymbol{y}$, we insert y_0 *in front of the block* of components equal to y_0.

It is clear that $V_{(d)}(\boldsymbol{x}) = T_{(d)}(\boldsymbol{x})$ except in case (ZE). Then, the two dynamical systems coincide "almost everywhere" and the trajectories which do not meet case (ZE) will be the same for the two systems. But we are mainly interested in rational trajectories, and the rational trajectories may meet case (ZE) and differ in the two systems. For instance, the two trajectories of the input $\pi(4,3,2,1) = (3/4, 2/4, 1/4)$ are (the inserted component is in bold):

for $V_{(d)}$: $(3/4, 2/4, 1/4) \to (2/3, 1/3) \to (1/2, 1/3) \to$
$(1/3) \to (0)$

for $T_{(d)}$: $(3/4, 2/4, 1/4) \to (2/3, \mathbf{1/3}, 1/3) \to$
$(\mathbf{1/2}, 1/2, 1/2) \to (1, 1, \mathbf{0}) \to (1, \mathbf{0}, 0) \to (\mathbf{0}, 0, 0)\,.$

However, we will prove in Section 3.3 that a rational trajectory under $V_{(d)}$ –which exactly describes an execution of the BrunGcd(d) algorithm– mainly decomposes into rational trajectories under $T_{(d-\ell)}$. Indeed, except possibly at the end of each phase, it uses Ins and not InsDis. This is why the BrunGcd algorithm will use, except at the end of each phase, the Brun dynamical system, which we now describe.

3.2 The Brun dynamical system.

The pair $(T_{(d)}, \mathcal{J}_{(d)})$ defines a dynamical system denoted as $\mathcal{D}_{(d)}$. For any $\boldsymbol{x} \in \mathcal{J}_{(d)}$, the map $T_{(d)}$ defined in (3) uses *digit* (m, j) formed with a quotient $m(\boldsymbol{x}) \geq 1$ and an insertion index $j(\boldsymbol{x}) \in [1..d]$. The set of digits is thus $\mathcal{A}_{(d)} := \mathbb{N}^* \times [1..d]$. We associate with (m, j) the subset

$$\mathcal{K}_{(d,m,j)} := \{\boldsymbol{x} \in \mathcal{J}_{(d)} \mid m(\boldsymbol{x}) = m, \quad j(\boldsymbol{x}) = j\}.$$

When (m, j) varies in $\mathcal{A}_{(d)}$, the subsets $\mathcal{K}_{(d,m,j)}$ form a topological partition of $\mathcal{J}_{(d)}$, and the restriction $T_{(d,m,j)}$ of $T_{(d)}$ to $\mathcal{K}_{(d,m,j)}$ is a bijection from $\mathcal{K}_{(d,m,j)}$ onto $\mathcal{J}_{(d)}$, written as

$$T_{(d,m,j)}(x_1, x_2, \ldots, x_d) = \left(\frac{x_2}{x_1}, \ldots, \frac{x_{j-1}}{x_1}, \frac{1}{x_1} - m, \frac{x_{j+1}}{x_1}, \ldots, \frac{x_d}{x_1}\right).$$

Its inverse is a bijection from $\mathcal{J}_{(d)}$ onto $\mathcal{K}_{(d,m,j)}$ written as

$$h_{(d,m,j)}(y_1, \ldots, y_d) = \left(\frac{1}{m+y_j}, \frac{y_1}{m+y_j}, \ldots, \frac{y_{j-1}}{m+y_j}, \frac{y_{j+1}}{m+y_j}, \ldots, \frac{y_d}{m+y_j}\right). \quad (4)$$

Any inverse branch of the map $T_{(d)}$ is called an *elementary inverse branch* (or an *inverse branch of depth one*) and the set of the elementary inverse branches is then

$$\mathcal{H}_{(d)} := \{h_{(d,m,j)} \mid (m, j) \in \mathcal{A}_{(d)}\}, \quad (5)$$

whereas the inverse branches of the map $T^k_{(d)}$ are said to be of *depth* k and belong to the set $\mathcal{H}^k_{(d)}$. We thus define

$$\mathcal{H}^\star_{(d-\ell)} := \bigoplus_{k \geq 0} \mathcal{H}^k_{(d-\ell)}.$$

3.3 Return to the Gcd Algorithm

On an input $\boldsymbol{u} \in \Omega_{(d)}$, the execution of the $\texttt{BrunGcd}(d)$ algorithm is described by the trajectory of $\boldsymbol{u}$ under the map $U_{(d)}$ which ends at $\gcd(\boldsymbol{u})$. It proves useful to consider one more step, and now, the trajectory of $\boldsymbol{u}$ under the map $U_{(d)}$ ends at 0. It gives rise to the rational trajectory of the vector $\boldsymbol{x} := \pi(\boldsymbol{u})$ under $V_{(d)}$, that also ends at 0. This trajectory uses at each step a branch of the map $V_{(d)}$. And we wish to precisely describe the set $\mathcal{B}_{(d)}$ of compositions of inverse branches of the map $V_{(d)}$ which are possibly used by such particular trajectories. Then the equality $\pi(\boldsymbol{u}) = h(0)$ (for $h \in \mathcal{B}_{(d)}$) gives rise to a bijection between $\pi(\Omega_{(d)})$ and $\mathcal{B}_{(d)}$. Moreover, there is also a bijection between $\pi(\Omega_{(d)})$ and the set of coprime inputs

$$\underline{\Omega}_{(d)} := \{u \in \Omega_{(d)} \mid \gcd(\boldsymbol{u}) = 1\}, \quad (6)$$

and thus a bijection between $\mathcal{B}_{(d)}$ and $\underline{\Omega}_{(d)}$.

We now describe $\mathcal{B}_{(d)}$, and first focus, for each $\ell \in [0..d-1]$, on the set $\mathcal{P}_{(d-\ell)}$ used by the part of the trajectory associated with the ℓ-th phase, when the iterates of $\boldsymbol{u}$ under $U_{(d)}$ belong to $\Omega_{(d-\ell)}$. Then, the iterates of $\boldsymbol{x}$ under $V_{(d)}$ belong to the simplex $\mathcal{J}_{(d-\ell)}$. We study in a separate way

(a) the steps of the ℓ-phase, which are not the last one,

(b) and the last step of the ℓ-phase.

Consider first (a). In this case, such a step does not loose a component, and only involves a step of type (G). Then, the trajectory uses branches of the map $T_{(d-\ell)}$, and each step uses possibly any inverse branch in the set $\mathcal{H}_{(d-\ell)}$ defined in (5). Hence, the set of the inverse branches used during the ℓ-phase, except in the final step, is the set $\mathcal{H}^\star_{(d-\ell)}$.

Consider (b). Now, a component is lost since the insertion is not done, and there are two possible cases.

Case (Z). The quotient $1/x_1$ is equal to an integer $m \geq 2$, the position of potential insertion is $j = d - \ell$. The equality $V_{(d)}(\boldsymbol{x}) = m \cdot \texttt{End}\, \boldsymbol{x}$ holds and the inverse branch associates with the $(d-\ell-1)$-uple $\boldsymbol{y}$ the $(d-\ell)$-uple

$$z_{(d-\ell,m)}(\boldsymbol{y}) = \frac{1}{m}(1, \boldsymbol{y}). \quad (7)$$

The set $\mathcal{Z}_{(d-\ell)}$ of inverse branches used in case (Z) is thus

$$\mathcal{Z}_{(d-\ell)} = \{z_{(d-\ell,m)} \mid m \geq 2\}.$$

Case (E). An equality of the form $(1/x_1) - m = x_i/x_1$ holds with a quotient $m \geq 1$ and a potential insertion position[3] $j = i-1 < d-\ell$. Then, Case (E) cannot occur for $\ell = d-1$. The equality $V_{(d)}(\boldsymbol{x}) = (\texttt{End}\, \boldsymbol{x})/(1-x_i)$ holds and the inverse branch associates with the $(d-\ell-1)$-uple $\boldsymbol{y}$ the $(d-\ell)$-uple

$$s_{(d-\ell,m,j)}(\boldsymbol{y}) = \frac{1}{m+y_j}(1, \boldsymbol{y}). \quad (8)$$

The set of inverse branches $\mathcal{S}_{(d-\ell)}$ used in case (E) is thus the empty set for $\ell = d-1$ and

$$\mathcal{S}_{(d-\ell)} = \{s_{(d-\ell,m,j)} \mid m \geq 1, j < d-\ell\} \quad (\text{for } \ell < d-1).$$

In summary, the set of possible inverse branches used during the last step of the ℓ-th phase is $\mathcal{F}_{(d-\ell)} = \mathcal{S}_{(d-\ell)} \cup \mathcal{Z}_{(d-\ell)}$.

Finally, we have proven the following.

PROPOSITION 2. *The* $\texttt{BrunGcd}(d)$ *algorithm builds a bijection between the set* $\underline{\Omega}_{(d)}$ *of coprime inputs of* $\Omega_{(d)}$ *and the set* $\mathcal{B}_{(d)}$ *of inverse branches possibly used by the rational trajectories of the shift* $V_{(d)}$. *This set is written as*

$$\mathcal{B}_{(d)} = \mathcal{P}_{(d)} \circ \mathcal{P}_{(d-1)} \circ \ldots \circ \mathcal{P}_{(1)} = \mathcal{P}_{(d)} \circ \mathcal{B}_{(d-1)}$$

and involves the sets $\mathcal{P}_{(d-\ell)}$ *of inverse branches used by the* $\texttt{BrunGcd}_{(d,\ell)}$, *characterized as*

$$\mathcal{P}_{(d-\ell)} = \mathcal{H}^\star_{(d-\ell)} \circ \mathcal{F}_{(d-\ell)}.$$

3.4 Why InsDis rather than Ins ?

We have decided to deal with the set $\Gamma_{(d)}$. We are then led to use $\texttt{InsDis}$ to stay inside $\Gamma_{(d)}$. But there is a natural question: why not dealing with the set $\Gamma_{(=,d)}$ with possible blocks of equal non-zero components? Then, we could use $\texttt{Ins}$ and stay inside $\Gamma_{(=,d)}$. This defines another algorithm, the $\texttt{BrunGcd}_=(d)$ algorithm, whose continuous extension directly leads to the Brun dynamical system. Even though the whole path seems more natural, we have to memorize the position of each block of equal components, and this leads to a quite involved analogue set $\mathcal{B}_{(=,d)}$ that describes the rational trajectories of the $\texttt{BrunGcd}_=(d)$ algorithm.

4. DYNAMICAL ANALYSIS (I).

We now begin the analysis of the algorithm, and introduce the main objects: the class of costs of interest, the (Dirichlet) generating functions, the generating operators. The main result of this section (Theorem 2) relates generating functions and generating operators.

4.1 Additive costs

We consider here costs that are said to be additive. One begins with a nonnegative *elementary* cost c defined on each inverse branch in $\mathcal{B}_{(d)}$ of depth one. Such a cost is then extended in an additive way on $\mathcal{B}_{(d)}$, namely

$$c(h_1 \circ h_2 \circ \cdots \circ h_p) := \textstyle\sum_{i=1}^p c(h_i).$$

[3]We recall that we would have inserted "in front of".

Now, a cost C defined on $\Omega_{(d)}$ is said to be *additive* if it is associated with such a cost c, and satisfies

$$C(\boldsymbol{u}) := c(h) \qquad \text{when } \pi(\boldsymbol{u}) = h(0).$$

Then $C(\boldsymbol{u})$ equals the total cost of c of the trajectory of $\pi(\boldsymbol{u})$ and satisfies $C(\boldsymbol{u}) = C(\lambda \boldsymbol{u})$ for any integer $\lambda \neq 0$. There are three main additive costs of interest here.

(*i*) The total number $C_{d,\ell}$ of steps during the ℓ-th phase (except the final step), associated with the characteristic function c of the set $\mathcal{H}_{(d-\ell)}$; with the family $C_{d,\ell}$, we return to the number of steps mentioned in Theorem 1, as the following relations hold: $L_d = M_d + R_d$

$$M_d = 1 + C_{d,0}, \qquad R_d = (d-1) + \sum_{\ell=1}^{d-1} C_{d,\ell}. \quad (9)$$

(*ii*) The number O_d of steps of the first phase with a quotient equal to 1, associated with the characteristic function c of the subset $\mathcal{H}^{(1)}_{(d)}$ with quotients equal to 1.

(*iii*) The number Σ_d of steps of the subtractive algorithm during the first phase, associated with the cost c which associates with an inverse branch h of the first phase its quotient m.

The associated elementary costs deal with a specific phase[4]: the ℓ-phase for $C_{d,\ell}$ and the first phase $\ell = 0$ for M_d, O_d, R_d. The cost C is said to *be concentrated* on this phase. inverse,

4.2 Dirichlet generating functions.

The (basic) Dirichlet generating function $S_{(d)}(s)$, of the input set $\Omega_{(d)}$ relative to the length $||\boldsymbol{u}|| := u_0$, is defined as

$$S_{(d)}(s) := \sum_{\boldsymbol{u} \in \Omega_d} \frac{1}{||\boldsymbol{u}||^s}. \quad (10)$$

In the same vein, with a cost $C : \Omega_{(d)} \to \mathbb{N}$, we associate the cumulative generating function of the cost

$$\widehat{S}_{(d,C)}(s) := \sum_{\boldsymbol{u} \in \Omega_d} \frac{C(\boldsymbol{u})}{||\boldsymbol{u}||^s} = \sum_{n \geq 1} n^{-s} \sum_{||\boldsymbol{u}|| = n} C(\boldsymbol{u}). \quad (11)$$

When $\Omega_{(d,N)}$ is endowed with the uniform distribution, the mean $\mathbb{E}_N[C]$ of cost C on $\Omega_{(d,N)}$ is expressed with the coefficients of the cumulative generating function, as

$$\mathbb{E}_N[C] = \frac{1}{\Phi_N\left[S_{(d)}\right]} \Phi_N\left[\widehat{S}_{(d,C)}\right], \quad (12)$$

where $\Phi_N[f]$ is defined as

$$\Phi_N[f] = \sum_{n \leq N} a_n \quad \text{when} \quad f(s) = \sum_{n \geq 1} \frac{a_n}{n^s}. \quad (13)$$

Here, singularity analysis uses the Delange Tauberian Theorem (stated in Section 5) which relates the asymptotics of the coefficients of a generating function to the nature and the position of its dominant singularity. Then, we need an alternative expression of the series which highlights the singularities. Such an expression exists for the series $S_{(d)}(s)$,

$$S_{(d)}(s) = \frac{1}{d!} \sum_{n \geq d+1} \frac{1}{n^s}(n-1)(n-2)\ldots(n-d).$$

[4] except with its final step

As its "dominant" series is $(1/d!)\zeta(s-d)$, the series $S_{(d)}(s)$ has a dominant simple pole at $s = d+1$ with residue $1/d!$.

However, such a "dominant" behavior is not known for the other Dirichlet series. The remaining of the paper is devoted to this task and is based on the dynamical analysis approach where generating functions are expressed with generating transfer operators. For this aim, we introduce an intermediate tool, the Dirichlet (bivariate) generating function,

$$S_{(d,C)}(s, w) := \sum_{\boldsymbol{u} \in \Omega_d} \frac{w^{C(\boldsymbol{u})}}{||\boldsymbol{u}||^s}. \quad (14)$$

whose derivative is related to the cumulative generating function: the relation $\widehat{S}_{(d,C)} = \Delta[S_{(d,C)}]$ holds and involves the functional Δ defined as

$$\Delta[A](s) := \frac{\partial}{\partial w} A(s, w)\Big|_{w=1}. \quad (15)$$

As we wish to use the bijection described in Proposition 2, we also introduce the three underlined series that are the exact counterparts of series defined in (10), (11), (14), now with respect to the set $\underline{\Omega}_{(d)}$ of coprime inputs. As C is an additive cost, the non-underlined series are related to their underlined conterparts as

$$\frac{S_{(d)}(s)}{\underline{S}_{(d)}(s)} = \frac{S_{(d,C)}(s, w)}{\underline{S}_{(d,C)}(s, w)} = \frac{\widehat{S}_{(d,C)}(s)}{\widehat{\underline{S}}_{(d,C)}(s)} = \zeta(s). \quad (16)$$

4.3 Generating operators

Let $\mathcal{G}$ be a set of inverse branches; we say that h is a *factor* of $\mathcal{G}$ if h is a factor of an element of $\mathcal{G}$, and we denote this situation as $h \propto \mathcal{G}$. In the same vein, a set $\mathcal{H}$ is said to be a factor of $\mathcal{G}$ if each element of $\mathcal{H}$ is a factor of $\mathcal{G}$, and this will be denoted as $\mathcal{H} \propto \mathcal{G}$. We will consider in the sequel factors of $\mathcal{B}_{(d)}$. The following easy result is central in this work.

LEMMA 1. *Any inverse branch $h \propto \mathcal{B}_{(d)}$ is a linear fractional transformation (LFT), and any factor of $\mathcal{P}_{(d-\ell)}$ can be written as* $h = \frac{1}{D[h]}\Big(N_1[h], N_2[h], \ldots, N_{d-\ell}[h]\Big)$,

where the denominator $D[h]$ and the numerators $N_i[h]$ are co-prime affine functions. When $h \in \mathcal{H}_{(d-\ell)}$, its Jacobian $J[h]$ is related to the denominator $D[h]$ as

$$J[h] = |D[h]|^{-(d-\ell+1)}. \quad (17)$$

The proof (by recurrence on the depth of h) begins with the expression of the branches of depth 1 given in (4),(7),(8).

Transfer operators are central tools for studying probabilistic properties of trajectories in dynamical systems; see e.g. [2, 10, 13]. Here, we adapt these tools to our needs, strongly use the fact that inverse branches are LFT, and also consider an additive cost c. It proves useful to deal with two parameters s and w, and we define the *generating operator* $\mathbf{G}_{s,w,[c],\langle h \rangle}$ of the inverse branch $h \propto \mathcal{B}_{(d)}$ as

$$\mathbf{G}_{s,w,[c],\langle h \rangle}[f](\boldsymbol{x}) := |D[h](\boldsymbol{x})|^{-s} w^{c(h)} f \circ h(\boldsymbol{x}).$$

Then, the operator may be extended for a subset $\mathcal{G} \propto \mathcal{B}_{(d)}$, via the equality $\mathbf{G}_{s,w,[c],\langle \mathcal{G} \rangle} := \sum_{h \in \mathcal{G}} \mathbf{G}_{s,w,[c],\langle h \rangle}$,

and the following relation is valid for disjoint factors of $\mathcal{B}_{(d)}$:

$$\mathbf{G}_{s,w,[c],\langle\mathcal{G}_1+\mathcal{G}_2\rangle} = \mathbf{G}_{s,w,[c],\langle\mathcal{G}_1\rangle} + \mathbf{G}_{s,w,[c],\langle\mathcal{G}_2\rangle} \, .$$

If now $\mathcal{G}_1$ and $\mathcal{G}_2$ may be composed and satisfy $(\mathcal{G}_1 \circ \mathcal{G}_2) \propto \mathcal{B}_{(d)}$, multiplicative properties of the denominator, together with additive properties of the cost, entail the equality

$$\mathbf{G}_{s,w,[c],\langle\mathcal{G}_1\circ\mathcal{G}_2\rangle} = \mathbf{G}_{s,w,[c],\langle\mathcal{G}_2\rangle} \circ \mathbf{G}_{s,w,[c],\langle\mathcal{G}_1\rangle} \, .$$

Then, there exists a "dynamical" dictionary similar to the analytic combinatorics dictionary. In particular, when $\mathcal{G}^\star \propto \mathcal{B}_{(d)}$, the generating operator of $\mathcal{G}^\star$ is the quasi-inverse

$$\mathbf{G}_{s,w,[c],\langle\mathcal{G}^\star\rangle} = \left(\mathbf{I} - \mathbf{G}_{s,w,[c],\langle\mathcal{G}\rangle}\right)^{-1}.$$

When $\mathcal{G}$ coincides with the set $\mathcal{H}_{(d-\ell)} \propto \mathcal{B}_{(d)}$ of inverse branches of the Brun dynamical system $\mathcal{D}_{(d-\ell)}$, then the generating operator $\mathbf{G}_{s,w,[c],\langle\mathcal{H}_{(d-\ell)}\rangle}$ is closely related to the (usual) weighted transfer operator $\mathbf{H}_{s,w,[c],(d-\ell)}$ of the Brun dynamical system $\mathcal{D}_{(d-\ell)}$ defined by

$$\mathbf{H}_{s,w,[c],(d-\ell)}[f](\boldsymbol{x}) := \sum_{h\in\mathcal{H}_{(d-\ell)}} J[h](\boldsymbol{x})^s \, w^{c(h)} f\circ h(\boldsymbol{x}) \, , \quad (18)$$

and, with the scale change of (17), we will obtain (19). With Proposition 2, this yields the following characterization of the generating operator of the set $\mathcal{B}_{(d)}$ used by the $\texttt{BrunGcd}(d)$ algorithm.

PROPOSITION 3. *Let c be an additive cost on the set $\mathcal{B}_{(d)}$. (a) The generating operator $\mathbf{B}_{s,w,[c],(d)}$ of the set $\mathcal{B}_{(d)}$ used by the $\texttt{BrunGcd}(d)$ algorithm decomposes as*

$$\mathbf{B}_{s,w,[c],(d)} = \mathbf{P}_{s,w,[c],(1)} \circ \mathbf{P}_{s,w,[c],(2)} \circ \cdots \circ \mathbf{P}_{s,w,[c],(d)} \, ,$$

and involves the sequence of generating operators $\mathbf{P}_{s,w,[c],(d-\ell)}$ of the set $\mathcal{P}_{(d-\ell)}$ used by the $\texttt{BrunGcd}_{(d,\ell)}$ algorithm. It then satisfies the recurrence relation

$$\mathbf{B}_{s,w,[c],(d)} = \mathbf{B}_{s,w,[c],(d-1)} \circ \mathbf{P}_{s,w,[c],(d)} .$$

(b) Each operator $\mathbf{P}_{s,w,[c],(d-\ell)}$ involves the quasi-inverse of the generating operator $\mathbf{G}_{s,w,[c],(d-\ell)}$ of the set $\mathcal{H}_{(d-\ell)}$ and the generating operator $\mathbf{F}_{s,w,[c],(d-\ell)}$ associated with the final set $\mathcal{F}_{(d-\ell)}$ of the ℓ-th phase, and is equal to

$$\mathbf{P}_{s,w,[c],(d-\ell)} = \mathbf{F}_{s,w,[c],(d-\ell)} \circ \left(I - \mathbf{G}_{s,w,[c],(d-\ell)}\right)^{-1}.$$

(c) The generating operator $\mathbf{G}_{s,w,[c],(d-\ell)}$ of the set $\mathcal{H}_{(d-\ell)}$ is closely related to the (weighted) transfer operator $\mathbf{H}_{s,w,[c],(d-\ell)}$ of the dynamical system $\mathcal{D}_{(d-\ell)}$ defined in (18) via the change of scale $s \mapsto s/(d-\ell+1)$, namely

$$\mathbf{G}_{s,w,[c],(d-\ell)} = \mathbf{H}_{s/(d-\ell+1),w,[c],(d-\ell)} \, . \quad (19)$$

Remark. It proves also useful to deal with the plain (unweighted) operator $\mathbf{G}_{s,\langle\mathcal{G}\rangle}$, and the cumulative operator $\widehat{\mathbf{G}}_{s,\langle\mathcal{G}\rangle}$ defined in an analogue way as for series as

$$\mathbf{G}_{s,\langle\mathcal{G}\rangle} = \sum_{h\in\mathcal{G}} \mathbf{G}_{s,\langle h\rangle} \qquad \widehat{\mathbf{G}}_{s,\langle\mathcal{G}\rangle} = \sum_{h\in\mathcal{G}} c(h)\mathbf{G}_{s,\langle h\rangle}, \quad (20)$$

with $\mathbf{G}_{s,\langle h\rangle}[f](\boldsymbol{x}) := |D[h](\boldsymbol{x})|^{-s} f \circ h(\boldsymbol{x})$.

These two operators are related to the weighted operator relative to any cost c via the equality

$$\mathbf{G}_{s,\langle\mathcal{G}\rangle} = \mathbf{G}_{s,1,[c],\langle\mathcal{G}\rangle}, \qquad \widehat{\mathbf{G}}_{s,[c],\langle\mathcal{G}\rangle} = \Delta[w \mapsto \mathbf{G}_{s,w,[c],\langle\mathcal{G}\rangle}] \, .$$

4.4 Useful expressions for generating functions.

The following result is one of the key ingredients of the paper. It is typical in dynamical analysis as it relates generating functions and generating operators.

THEOREM 2. *Consider the $\texttt{BrunGcd}(d)$ algorithm acting on the set $\Omega_{(d)}$, together with an additive cost C, related to some elementary cost c. Then, the three following relations hold between*

(i) the three generating functions relative to cost C, defined in (10),(11),(14),

(ii) the three analogous generating operators of the set $\mathcal{B}_d$, i.e., the bivariate one defined in Proposition 3 and the other two defined in (20)

$$S_{(d,C)}(s,w) = \zeta(s) \cdot \mathbf{B}_{s,w,[c],(d)}[1](0) \, ,$$
$$S_{(d)}(s) = \zeta(s) \cdot \mathbf{B}_{s,1,[c],(d)}[1](0) \, ,$$
$$\widehat{S}_{(d,C)}(s) = \zeta(s) \cdot \widehat{\mathbf{B}}_{s,[c],(d)}[1](0) \, .$$

The proof is indeed quite short. Let $h \in \mathcal{B}_{(d)}$. The equalitiy

$$\pi(\boldsymbol{u}) = \left(\frac{u_1}{u_0}, \frac{u_2}{u_0}, \ldots, \frac{u_d}{u_0}\right) = h(0)$$

together with $\gcd(\boldsymbol{u}) = 1$ proves that the denominator of the LFT h satisfies $|D[h](0)| = u_0$. Moreover, as C is an additive cost associated with cost c, the equality $C(\boldsymbol{u}) = c(h)$ holds. Now, the bijection between $\underline{\Omega}_{(d)}$ and the set $\mathcal{B}_{(d)}$, together with Eq. (16), entail the relations

$$S_{(d,C)}(s,w) = \zeta(s) \cdot \underline{S}_{(d,C)}(s) = \zeta(s) \cdot \sum_{\boldsymbol{u}\in\underline{\Omega}_{(d)}} \frac{w^{C(\boldsymbol{u})}}{u_0^s}$$
$$= \zeta(s) \cdot \sum_{h\in\mathcal{B}_{(d)}} w^{c(h)} \, |D[h](0)|^{-s} = \zeta(s) \cdot \mathbf{B}_{s,w,[c],d}[1](0) \, .$$

4.5 Derivatives of quasi-inverses.

When the cost C is concentrated on the phase ℓ, the functional Δ defined in (15) is applied to the quasi-inverse $(I - \mathbf{G}_{s,w,[c],(k)})^{-1}$ with $k = d - \ell$. This produces two (plain) quasi-inverses and a middle operator (which depends on the cost c). Now, via (19), we return to the operator $\mathbf{H}$ defined in (18), with the scale-change $t = s/(k+1)$, and obtain

$$\Delta[w \mapsto (I - \mathbf{G}_{s,w,[c],(k)})^{-1}]$$
$$= (I - \mathbf{H}_{t,(k)})^{-1} \circ \mathbf{H}^{(c)}_{t,(k)} \circ (I - \mathbf{H}_{t,(k)})^{-1} \, ,$$

where the "middle" operator is a weighted operator

$$\mathbf{H}^{(c)}_{t,(k)}[f] := \sum_{h\in\mathcal{H}_{(k)}} c(h) \cdot J[h]^t \cdot f \circ h \, .$$

The (plain) quasi-inverses will play a central role in the analysis, whereas the middle operators[5] and the end-of-phase operators will only play a secondary role. We will now focus on the quasi-inverses of the transfer operators and denote

$$\mathbf{Q}_{(k)}(t) := (I - \mathbf{H}_{t,(k)})^{-1}. \quad (21)$$

The plain Dirichlet series involves one quasi-inverse for each phase, whereas the cumulative Dirichlet series relative to a cost C concentrated on the ℓ-th phase involves two quasi-inverses for the ℓ-th phase, and only one for each other phase. This is now precisely stated:

PROPOSITION 4. *Associate with $\ell \in [0..d-1]$ the scale change $t_\ell : s \mapsto s/(d-\ell+1)$. Then the following holds:*

[5]except for $d = 1$

(a) *The plain Dirichlet series* $S_{(d)}(s)$ *involves a unique quasi-inverse* $\mathbf{Q}_{(d-\ell)}(t_\ell)$ *for each phase of index* $\ell \in [0..d-1]$.

(b) *If* C *is* ℓ*-concentrated, the cumulative series* $\widehat{S}_{(d,C)}$ *of cost* C *involves one quasi-inverse* $\mathbf{Q}_{(d-k)}(t_{d-k})$ *for each phase of index* $k \neq \ell$ *and a "double" quasi-inverse* $\mathbf{Q}^2_{(d-\ell)}(t_{d-\ell})$ *for the* ℓ*-th phase.*

This ends the first part of our analysis, of a combinatorial nature. We now begin the second part of our analysis, of an analytic nature.

5. DYNAMICAL ANALYSIS (II)

We now return to the proof of Theorem 1. With (12) and (13), we know that the mean values of interest are related to coefficients of Dirichlet series, plain or cumulative ones. With the Delange Tauberian theorem, stated in Section 5.3, we know how to relate the asymptotic behavior of coefficients with singularities of the Dirichlet series. We then have now to study the Dirichlet series, from an analytic point of view, and discover their singularities. With Proposition 4, their singularities are brought by quasi-inverses. This is why we begin by studying the quasi-inverse in Section 5.1, and then apply this study to the Dirichlet series in Section 5.2.

5.1 Properties of quasi-inverses.

Consider an index $k \in [1..d]$. The transfer operator $\mathbf{H}_{t,(k)}$ acts on the space $\mathcal{C}^1(\mathcal{J}_{(k)})$. It is *quasi-compact* and the dominant part of its spectrum is discrete. Furthermore, as the operator $\mathbf{H}_{t,(k)}$ is the density transformer of the system for $t=1$, the value 1 belongs to the spectrum, and as the system is ergodic [12], this is its unique dominant eigenvalue. The dominant eigenfunction is explicitly known (see [1])

$$\psi_k(\boldsymbol{x}) = \sum_{\sigma\in\mathfrak{S}_k}\prod_{i=1}^{k}\frac{1}{1+x_{\sigma(1)}+x_{\sigma(2)}+\ldots+x_{\sigma(i)}}; \qquad (22)$$

and involves the set $\mathfrak{S}_k$ of permutations on $[1..k]$. The quasi-compacity of the operator together with perturbation theory entails the existence of a spectral decomposition

$$\mathbf{H}_{t,(k)} = \lambda_{(k)}(t)\mathbf{A}_{t,(k)} + \mathbf{K}_{t,(k)},$$

on a neighborhood of $t=1$ that involves the dominant eigenvalue $\lambda_{(k)}(t)$, the projection $\mathbf{A}_{t,(k)}$ on the dominant eigenspace, and a "remainder" operator $\mathbf{K}_{s,(k)}$ whose spectral radius is strictly smaller than $|\lambda_{(k)}(t)|$. Then, the relation $\mathbf{A}_{t,(k)}\circ\mathbf{K}_{t,(k)} = \mathbf{K}_{t,(k)}\circ\mathbf{A}_{t,(k)} = 0$ leads to the spectral decomposition for the quasi-inverse

$$\mathbf{Q}_{(k)}(t) = \frac{\lambda_{(k)}(t)}{1-\lambda_{(k)}(t)}\mathbf{A}_{t,(k)} + (\mathbf{I}-\mathbf{K}_{t,(k)})^{-1}.$$

Thus, the quasi-inverse has a pole at $t=1$, with a residue which involves in particular the entropy $\mathcal{E}_k = -\lambda'_{(k)}(1)$. Furthermore, as the inverse branches are LFT's, there is an *aperiodicity* property that entails that $t\mapsto\mathbf{Q}_{(k)}(t)$ is analytic on the punctured vertical line $\{\Re t = 1,\ t\neq 1\}$.

Letting now $k := d-\ell$, and using for each phase of index ℓ the scale change $t_\ell = s/(d-\ell+1)$, we describe the behavior of the quasi inverse $s\mapsto\mathbf{Q}_{(d-\ell)}(t_\ell)$.

PROPOSITION 5. *Consider for* $\ell\in[0..d-1]$ *the scale change* $s\mapsto s/(d-\ell+1)$. *Then, the quasi-inverse* $s\mapsto\mathbf{Q}_{(d-\ell)}(t_\ell)$ *relative to the* ℓ*-th phase is analytic on the punctured half-plane* $\{\Re s\geq d-\ell+1, s\neq d-\ell+1\}$ *and admits a simple pole at* $s=d-\ell+1$, *with a residue* $\mathbf{T}_{(d-\ell)}$ *defined as*

$$\mathbf{T}_{(d-\ell)}[f] = \frac{d-\ell+1}{\mathcal{E}_{d-\ell}}\,I_{d-\ell}[f]\,\frac{\psi_{d-\ell}}{\kappa_{d-\ell}}, \qquad (23)$$

which involves the entropy $\mathcal{E}_k$, *the integral* I_k *on the simplex* $\mathcal{J}_{(k)}$ *and the constant* $\kappa_k := I[\psi_k]$.

5.2 Analytic properties of Dirichlet series.

We now return to the number of steps that the `BrunGcd` algorithm performs during its various phases. With Theorem 2, Propositions 4, 5, and Eq. (9), we describe the analytic properties of the Dirichlet series of interest.

PROPOSITION 6. *Consider the* `BrunGcd` *algorithm when acting on* $\Omega_{(d)}$, *together with the total number* L_d *of steps, the number* M_d *of steps in the first phase, the number* O_d *of quotients equal to 1 during the first phase, the number* Σ_d *of subtractive steps during the first phase and the number* R_d *of steps in the following phases. Associate the six Dirichlet generating functions of interest, namely, the plain series and the five cumulative series relative with number of steps* $L_d, M_d, O_d, \Sigma_d, R_d$. *The following holds:*

(a) *The six series are analytic in the punctured half-plane* $\{\Re s\geq d+1, s\neq d+1\}$.

(b) *The plain series and the cumulative series relative to* R_d *admit a simple pole at* $s=d+1$. *Their residues are denoted as* T_d *and* r_dT_d, *with* $T_d = \mathbf{T}_{(d)}[1](0)$.

(c) *The cumulative series relative to* M_d, O_d, Σ_d *and* L_d *admit a pole of order 2 at* $s=d+1$, *and their dominant constants* Dom *are expressed with the residue* T_d *and three other constants* a_d, ρ_d, σ_d. *One has:*

$$\mathtt{Dom}[L_d] = \mathtt{Dom}[M_d] = a_d\,T_d,$$
$$\mathtt{Dom}[O_d] = a_d\,\rho_d\,T_d, \quad \mathtt{Dom}[\Sigma_d] = a_d\,\sigma_d\,T_d.$$

The constants a_d, ρ_d *and* σ_d *involve the entropy* $\mathcal{E}_d$ *and the constant* $\kappa_d(y)$, *defined in* (24),

$$a_d = \frac{d+1}{\mathcal{E}_d}, \quad \rho_d = 1-\frac{\kappa_d(1/2)}{\kappa_d}, \quad \sigma_d = \frac{1}{\kappa_d}\sum_{m\geq 1}\kappa_d\left(\frac{1}{m}\right).$$

5.3 Extraction of coefficients.

It remains to relate the asymptotics of the coefficients of the Dirichlet series and their dominant singularities, and this is done via the Delange Tauberian Theorem.

THEOREM 3 (DELANGE). *For* $\sigma>0$, *consider a Dirichlet series* $S(s)$ *with non-negative coefficients which converges for* $\Re s>\sigma$. *Assume that the following holds:*
(i) $S(s)$ *is analytic on* $\Re s=\sigma, s\neq\sigma$;
(ii) *near* σ, $S(s)$ *satisfies* $S(s) = A(s)/(s-\sigma)^{\gamma+1}$ *where* A *is analytic in* σ, $A(\sigma)\neq 0$ *and* $\gamma\geq 0$.
Then as $N\to\infty$, *the following asymptotics holds*

$$\Phi_N[S] \sim \frac{A(\sigma)}{\sigma\Gamma(\gamma+1)}N^\sigma(\log N)^\gamma, \qquad \textit{for } \Phi_N \textit{ defined in } (13).$$

With Proposition 6, all the Dirichlet series of interest satisfy the hypotheses of the Delange Tauberian Theorem with $\sigma=d+1$, the series of (b) with $\gamma=0$ and the series of (c)

with $\gamma = 1$. With Eq. (12), the mean value of any cost C of interest equals a ratio whose numerator and denominator can be estimated with the Delange Tauberian Theorem. This concludes the proof of Theorem 1, and the main constants involved are constants $r_d, a_d, \rho_d, \sigma_d$. We do not know much about the asymptotics of r_d, but we now focus on the asymptotics of the other constants a_d, ρ_d, σ_d for $d \to \infty$.

5.4 The main constants of the analysis.

Except for $d = 1$ and $d = 2$, the values of the volume constant κ_d and the entropy $\mathcal{E}_d$ are not known, as well as their dependency with respect to dimension d. We deal with the simplex $y\mathcal{J}_{(d)}$, for $y \in [0, 1]$, and introduce the function

$$\kappa_d(y) := \int_{y\mathcal{J}_{(d)}} \psi_d(\boldsymbol{x})d\boldsymbol{x} = \int_{[0,y]^d} \varphi_d(\boldsymbol{x})d\boldsymbol{x} \qquad (24)$$

$$\text{with} \quad \varphi_d(\boldsymbol{x}) = \frac{1}{1+x_1} \cdots \frac{1}{1+x_1+x_2+\cdots+x_d}.$$

Note that $\kappa_d = \kappa_d(1)$. The ratio $\kappa_d(y)/\kappa_d$ is central, because it coincides with the limit probability that a quotient m of the Brun system in dimension d be larger than $1/y$.

The following result provides two new (and important) estimates: the first one contradicts a conjecture of Hardcastle and Khanin [7] which states that the entropy is asymptotically constant. The second one describes (for $d \to \infty$) the limit distribution of the quotients in the Brun system.

PROPOSITION 7. *The constant $\kappa_d(y)$ and the entropy $\mathcal{E}_d$ are expressed as one-dimensional integrals:*

$$\kappa_d(y) = \frac{1}{d!}\int_0^\infty e^{-u}\beta(uy)^d du, \quad \beta(u) := \int_0^u \frac{1-e^{-v}}{v}dv,$$

$$\mathcal{E}_d = (d+1)\int_0^1 \frac{1}{y}\frac{\kappa_d(y)}{\kappa_d}dy = \frac{d+1}{d!\,\kappa_d}\int_0^\infty \frac{e^{-u}}{u}\beta(u)^d du.$$

The following estimates hold for $d \to \infty$ and $y \in]0, 1]$ fixed:

$$\mathcal{E}_d \sim \log d, \qquad \frac{\kappa_d(y)}{\kappa_d} = y^{(1-\epsilon)d/\log d} \quad \text{for } d > d_\epsilon. \qquad (25)$$

The complete proof will be given in the long version paper. We describe here the main ideas. The integral expression for $\kappa_d(y)$ is obtained via the Laplace transform. The expression of the entropy is obtained via the Rohlin formula. As each integral expression involves a large power of the function β, a method of Laplace type asymptotically compares such an integral to the maximum value of the integrand.

The following figure compares the theoretical curve $\mathcal{E}_d = \log d$ with experimental values of $\mathcal{E}_d$ which are obtained via the number of steps during the first phase.

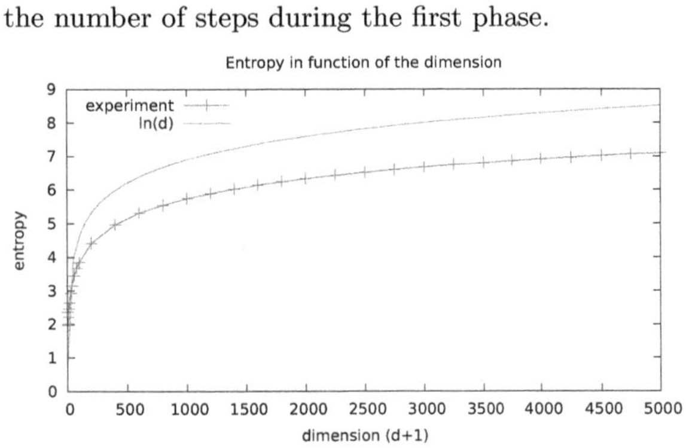

6. CONCLUSION AND OPEN PROBLEMS

We have precisely used the Brun underlying dynamical system to describe the probabilistic behaviour of the `BrunGcd` algorithm. We have studied the asymptotics (for $d \to \infty$) of the main constants that intervene in the analysis and also confirmed with experiments the main results of the analysis. We conclude that the `BrunGcd` algorithm is not efficient. This is probably the case for all the gcd algorithms which are based on multidimensional continued fraction algorithms.

Nevertheless, it would be interesting to study other costs such as the bit-complexity as in [10] or perform a distributional analysis; in this case, we need to extend to higher dimensions the approach that was conducted in [2] for $d = 1$.

We also wish to use our good knowledge of the Brun rational trajectories obtained through dynamical analysis, in order to study simultaneous approximations associated with rational vectors, which corresponds to the real algorithmic situation.

Finally, it would be interesting to analyze the extended gcd algorithm based on the LLL algorithm and described in [11], even if its underlying system is quite complex to deal with.

7. REFERENCES

[1] P. Arnoux and A. Nogueira. Mesures de Gauss pour des algorithmes de fractions continues multidimensionnelles. *Ann. Sci. Ecole Norm. Sup.*, 26:645–664, 1993.

[2] V. Baladi and B. Vallée. Euclidean algorithms are Gaussian. *Journal Number Theory*, 110:331–386, 2006.

[3] V. Berthé, J. Bourdon, T. Jolivet, and A. Siegel. Generating discrete planes with substitutions. In *Combinatorics on words*, volume 8079 of *LNCS*, pages 58–70. Springer, 2013.

[4] V. Berthé, L. Lhote, and B. Vallée. Probabilistic analyses of the plain multiple gcd algorithm. *Journal of Symbolic Computation*, 74:425–474, 2016.

[5] A. Broise-Alamichel and Y. Guivarc'h. Exposants caractéristiques de l'algorithme de Jacobi-Perron et de la transformation associée. *Annales de l'Institut Fourier*, 51(3):565–686, 2001.

[6] V. Brun. Algorithmes euclidiens pour trois et quatre nombres. In *13e congrès des mathématiciens scandinaves, Helsinki 1957*, pages 45–64.

[7] D. M. Hardcastle and K. Khanin. On almost everywhere strong convergence of multi-dimensional continued fraction algorithms. *Ergodic Theory Dynam. Systems*, 20(6):1711–1733, 2000.

[8] D. E. Knuth. *Seminumerical Algorithms*, volume 2 of *The Art of Computer Programming*. Addison-Wesley, 3rd edition, 1998.

[9] J. Lagarias. The quality of the diophantine approximations found by the Jacobi-Perron algorithm, and related algorithms. *Mh. Math*, 115:299–328, 1993.

[10] L. Lhote and B. Vallée. Gaussian laws for the main parameters of the Euclid algorithms. *Algorithmica*, 50(4):497–554, 2008.

[11] B. S. Majewski and G. Havas. A solution to the extended GCD problem. In *ISSAC95*, pages 248–253.

[12] F. Schweiger. *Multidimensional continued fractions.* Oxford University Press, 2000.

[13] B. Vallée. Euclidean dynamics. *Discrete and Continuous Dynamical Systems*, 1(15):281–352, 2006.

Guessing Linear Recurrence Relations of Sequence Tuples and P-recursive Sequences with Linear Algebra

Jérémy Berthomieu
jeremy.berthomieu@lip6.fr

Jean-Charles Faugère
jean-charles.faugere@inria.fr

Sorbonne Universités, UPMC Univ Paris 06, CNRS, INRIA,
Laboratoire d'Informatique de Paris 6 (LIP6), Équipe PolSys, 4 place Jussieu, 75252 Paris Cedex 05, France

ABSTRACT

Given several n-dimensional sequences, we first present an algorithm for computing the Gröbner basis of their module of linear recurrence relations.

A P-recursive sequence $(u_{\mathbf{i}})_{\mathbf{i}\in\mathbb{N}^n}$ satisfies linear recurrence relations with polynomial coefficients in $\mathbf{i}$, as defined by Stanley in 1980. Calling directly the aforementioned algorithm on the tuple of sequences $\left((\mathbf{i}^{\mathbf{j}}\,u_{\mathbf{i}})_{\mathbf{i}\in\mathbb{N}^n}\right)_{\mathbf{j}}$ for retrieving the relations yields redundant relations. Since the module of relations of a P-recursive sequence also has an extra structure of a 0-dimensional right ideal of an Ore algebra, we design a more efficient algorithm that takes advantage of this extra structure for computing the relations.

Finally, we show how to incorporate Gröbner bases computations in an Ore algebra $\mathbb{K}\langle t_1,\dots,t_n,x_1,\dots,x_n\rangle$, with commutators $x_k\,x_\ell - x_\ell\,x_k = t_k\,t_\ell - t_\ell\,t_k = t_k\,x_\ell - x_\ell\,t_k = 0$ for $k\neq\ell$ and $t_k\,x_k - x_k\,t_k = x_k$, into the algorithm designed for P-recursive sequences. This allows us to compute faster the Gröbner basis of the ideal spanned by the first relations, such as in 2D/3D-space walks examples.

CCS Concepts

•Comput. method. → Symbolic calculus algorithms;

Keywords

Gröbner bases, P-recursive sequences, FGLM algorithm

1. INTRODUCTION

Computing linear recurrence relations of multi-dimensional sequences is a fundamental problem in Computer Science. As this is the core of the paper, we start with an example. The binomial sequence $\mathbf{b} = \left(i_1!/(i_2!\,(i_1-i_2)!)\right)_{(i_1,i_2)\in\mathbb{N}^2}$ satisfies Pascal's rule, a linear recurrence relation:

$$\forall\,(i_1,i_2)\in\mathbb{N}^2,\qquad b_{i_1+1,i_2+1} = b_{i_1,i_2+1} + b_{i_1,i_2}. \quad (1)$$

It has constant coefficients. But this sequence also satisfies relations with polynomial coefficients in (i_1,i_2):

$$\forall\,(i_1,i_2)\in\mathbb{N}^2,\ (i_1-i_2+1)\,b_{i_1+1,i_2} = (i_1+1)\,b_{i_1,i_2}, \quad (2a)$$

$$(i_2+1)\,b_{i_1,i_2+1} = (i_1-i_2)\,b_{i_1,i_2}. \quad (2b)$$

ISSAC '16 July 19–22, 2016, Waterloo, ON, Canada

© 2016 ACM. ISBN 978-1-4503-4380-0/16/07...$15.00

DOI: http://dx.doi.org/10.1145/2930889.2930926

Thanks to equations (2a) and (2b), we can compute any term of $\mathbf{b}$ starting with $b_{0,0}=1$. This makes $\mathbf{b}$ P-recursive.

Deciding if a sequence is P-recursive, as defined by Stanley [28] finds applications for instance in Combinatorics and in Computer algebra [27]. We refer the reader to the series of papers on planar [10, 11, 12] and 3D-space walks [7, 8].

The generating series $\sum_{i_1,\dots,i_n\in\mathbb{N}} u_{i_1,\dots,i_n}\,x_1^{i_1}\cdots x_n^{i_n}$ of a P-recursive sequence $(u_{i_1,\dots,i_n})_{(i_1,\dots,i_n)\in\mathbb{N}^n}$ is a D-finite function in $x_1,\dots,x_n$, see [19, Theorem 3.7]. A D-finite function is such that the dimension of the vector space spanned by all its derivatives is finite over $\mathbb{K}(x_1,\dots,x_n)$, this allows one to characterize such functions with initial conditions and differential equations. For instance, the Dynamical Dictionary of Mathematical Functions [3] generates dynamically and automatically web pages on elementary and special functions thanks to the equations they satisfy. Likewise, a P-recursive sequence is uniquely defined by the linear recurrence relations with polynomial coefficients it satisfies and a finite number of initial terms.

1.1 Related work

For one-dimensional sequences, *C-relations* (linear recurrence relations with constant coefficients) can be guessed with Berlekamp – Massey algorithm [4, 20], while for multi-dimensional sequences, they can be guessed with Berlekamp – Massey – Sakata algorithm [24, 26] or Scalar-FGLM [5, 6]. All these algorithms only *guess* and check that the relations are valid for a finite number of terms of the sequence. Then, usually, one need to *prove* that they are satisfied for all the terms of the sequence. In this paper, a *table* shall denote a finite subset of terms of a sequence: it is one of the input parameter of the algorithms since one cannot handle an infinite sequence.

Likewise, for one-dimensional sequences, *P-relations* (linear recurrence relations with polynomial coefficients) can be guessed with Beckermann – Labahn algorithm [2] for computing Hermite-Padé approximants.

When computing parameterized sums of multivariate sequences, or integrals of multivariate functions, in general, it is hopeless to obtain a closed form. Indeed, even for elementary univariate function we may not have closed forms when computing their integral on some domain. This motivated Zeilberger in 1990 [29] to introduce the so-called *creative telescoping* method. It is now one of the most efficient ways to do so and has been a tremendously active research topic. We refer the reader to the up-to-date nice survey on the state of the art in creative telescoping in [13] and the references therein.

Although sequences can satisfy some linear recurrence relations with constant or polynomial coefficients, they still may be neither C-recursive nor P-recursive. Given a subset $\mathcal{S}$ of steps in $\{0,\pm1\}^2$, one can define the sequence $\mathbf{u} = (u_{n,i,j})_{(n,i,j)\in\mathbb{N}^3}$ of the number of planar walks of length n ending at (i,j) with steps in $\mathcal{S}$. Determining if $\mathbf{u}$ is P-recursive has applications in lattice path enumeration [1, 11, 12]. Likewise, now 3D-space walks are investigated. In [7], the authors use several different methods to prove that somes sequences of walks are P-recursive among which: the algebraic kernel method, the reduction to smaller dimensions and the guessing and proving method.

1.2 Contributions

We start by recalling the definitions of *C-recursive* (linear recursive with constant coefficients) sequences and define C-recursive tuples of sequences. This framework allows us to transform a P-recursive sequence into a tuple of sequences.

In Section 3, we extends SCALAR-FGLM [5, 6] for guessing the module of C-relations satisfied by a tuple of tables up to a degree bound d. The algorithm returns a $(d+1)$-truncated Gröbner basis of their module of relations. The main idea of this algorithm is the same as SCALAR-FGLM's: extracting a full-rank submatrix of maximal rank.

P-relations with coefficients of degree at most δ satisfied by a sequence $\mathbf{u} = (u_{i_1,\dots,i_n})_{(i_1,\dots,i_n)\in\mathbb{N}^n}$ are C-relations satisfied by the tuple of sequences $(i_1^{j_1}\cdots i_n^{j_n}\,u_{i_1,\dots,i_n})_{(i_1,\dots,i_n)\in\mathbb{N}^n}$, with $j_1,\dots,j_n \geq 0$ and $j_1+\cdots+j_n \leq \delta$. Hence, a first idea is to compute them with the extended SCALAR-FGLM for instance. However, this strategy is not optimal because the sequences are not independent: the module of relations has an additional structure, see also [21].

This is why, in Section 4, we design algorithm P-RECURSIVE-FGLM to take advantage of this particular structure. This algorithm input is a P-recursive table, a degree bound on the order of the relations and a degree bound on the polynomial coefficients. It returns a Gröbner basis of the right ideal of relations in a skew-polynomial ring $\mathbb{K}\langle t_1,\dots,t_n,x_1\dots,x_n\rangle$ with commutation rules $x_k\,x_\ell - x_\ell\,x_k = t_k\,t_\ell - t_\ell\,t_k = t_k\,x_\ell - x_\ell\,t_k = 0$ for $k\neq\ell$ and $t_k\,x_k - x_k\,t_k = x_k$. P-RECURSIVE-FGLM uses an extra criterion *à la* FGLM: if relation (2b) is only known to be valid for a given pair (i_1,i_2), then we still know that for any $j_1,j_2\geq 0$, $i_1^{j_1}\,i_2^{j_2}\,(i_2+1)\,b_{i_1,i_2+1} = i_1^{j_1}\,i_2^{j_2}\,(i_1-i_2)\,b_{i_1,i_2}$. This makes the extracted matrix smaller.

Sometimes an estimate of the Gröbner basis staircase size is known. To optimize the number of table queries, we present an output sensitive probabilistic algorithm in Section 4.2.

The relations computed by P-RECURSIVE-FGLM can be output one after the other. When several relations are found, it seems profitable not to look for any relation in the ideal they span. In Section 5, we use a mixed approach by computing truncated Gröbner bases in the aforementioned skew-polynomial ring to determine "needed redundant relations". On the one hand, they are redundant for they are deduced from previously found relations. On the other hand, they are computed faster since this approach does not require any extra queries to the table. Furthermore, these relations can help us to close the staircase in order to guess prematurely the P-recursiveness of the table for a given degree. We illustrate this with Examples 6 and 7

In Section 6, we show that the matrices handled by MULTI-SCALAR-FGLM and P-RECURSIVE-FGLM are heavily structured. When the monomial ordering is LEX, we can make use of the quasi-Hankel structure to improve the complexity of the linear system solving [9]. We also investigate the number of table queries performed by the algorithms.

2. DEFINITIONS AND NOTATION

We recall the classical definitions of a C-recursive sequence and of a P-recursive sequence. We shall also see how to deal with C-relations between terms of multiple sequences and see that from a P-recursive sequence, we can create a tuple of sequences satisfying C-relations.

In all the paper, we shall use standard notation with bolded letters corresponding to vectors and sequences: for $n\in\mathbb{N}^*$, $\mathbf{i} = (i_1,\dots,i_n)$ and $\mathbf{x} = (x_1,\dots,x_n)$. As usual, $\mathbf{x}^{\mathbf{i}}$ denotes $x_1^{i_1}\cdots x_n^{i_n}$ and $|\mathbf{i}| = i_1+\cdots+i_n$. Finally, $\mathbf{u} = (u_{\mathbf{i}})_{\mathbf{i}\in\mathbb{N}^n}$ is an n-dimensional sequence over a field $\mathbb{K}$.

For $\mathbf{i}\in\mathbb{N}^n$, we let $[\mathbf{x}^{\mathbf{i}}]_{\mathbf{u}} = u_{\mathbf{i}} = [\mathbf{x}^{\mathbf{i}}]$, if no ambiguity on $\mathbf{u}$ shall arise. We extend linearly this $[\,]$ operator to $\mathbb{K}[\mathbf{x}]$.

C-relations are straightforwardly extended to n-dimensional sequences [23, Definition 21]: let $\mathcal{S}$ be a finite subset of $\mathbb{N}^n$, let $\boldsymbol{\alpha} = (\alpha_{\mathbf{s}})_{\mathbf{s}\in\mathcal{S}}$ be nonzero, then $\mathbf{u} = (u_{\mathbf{i}})_{\mathbf{i}\in\mathbb{N}^n}$ satisfies the linear relation defined by $\boldsymbol{\alpha}$ if for all $\mathbf{i}\in\mathbb{N}^n$,

$$\left[\sum\nolimits_{\mathbf{s}\in\mathcal{S}}\alpha_{\mathbf{s}}\,\mathbf{x}^{\mathbf{i}+\mathbf{s}}\right] = \sum\nolimits_{\mathbf{s}\in\mathcal{S}}\alpha_{\mathbf{s}}\,u_{\mathbf{i}+\mathbf{s}} = 0. \qquad (3)$$

Operator $[\,]$ allows us to make a one-to-one correspondence between C-relations satisfied by $\mathbf{u}$ and polynomials in $\mathbb{K}[\mathbf{x}]$: relation $\sum_{\mathbf{s}\in\mathcal{S}}\alpha_{\mathbf{s}}\,u_{\mathbf{s}} = 0$ is *associated* to polynomial $\sum_{\mathbf{s}\in\mathcal{S}}\alpha_{\mathbf{s}}\,x^{\mathbf{s}}$.

According to Sakata [24] and to Fitzpatrick and Norton [17], a C-recursive sequence is defined as follows.

Definition 1. An n-dimensional sequence $\mathbf{u} = (u_{\mathbf{i}})_{\mathbf{i}\in\mathbb{N}^n}$ is *C-recursive* if from a nonzero finite number of initial terms $u_{\mathbf{s}}, \mathbf{s}\in\mathcal{S}$, and a finite number of C-relations, without any contradiction, one can compute any term of the sequence.

From the polynomial viewpoint, Definition 1 can be restated as sequence $\mathbf{u}$ is *C-recursive* if and only if set $I = \{P\in\mathbb{K}[\mathbf{x}],\ \forall\,\mathbf{i}\in\mathbb{N}^n, [P\,\mathbf{x}^{\mathbf{i}}] = 0\}$ is a zero-dimensional ideal.

A Gröbner basis of this ideal can be computed using the so-called BMS [25] and SCALAR-FGLM [5, Algorithm 3] algorithms, see also [6] for an extended version of [5].

C-recursive sequences are also exactly the only sequences such that their generating series $\sum_{\mathbf{i}\in\mathbb{N}^n} u_{\mathbf{i}}\,\mathbf{x}^{\mathbf{i}}$ is a rational fraction in $\mathbf{x}$ whose denominator factors into univariate polynomials, see for instance [6, Propostion 19]

For a sequence $\mathbf{u}$ not C-recursive, both algorithms, called on the table of terms $u_{\mathbf{i}}$, $|\mathbf{i}|\leq d$, return a $(d+1)$-truncated Gröbner basis. Sequences such as the binomial one $\mathbf{b} = \left(\binom{i_1}{i_2}\right)_{\mathbf{i}\in\mathbb{N}^2}$ may satisfy a C-relation but not be C-recursive. For instance, $\mathbf{b}$ satisfies equation (1), Pascal's rule, while its generating series is the rational fraction $1/(1-x_1-x_1\,x_2)$ whose denominator is irreducible.

The greater class of P-recursive sequences satisfy *P-relations* (linear recurrence relations with polynomials coefficients). These relations are analogous to relations as equation (3) but with $\alpha_{\mathbf{s}}$ a polynomial in $\mathbf{i}$. For instance, both equations (2a) and (2b) satisfied by $\mathbf{b}$ are P-relations.

Definition 2. An n-dimensional sequence $\mathbf{u} = (u_{\mathbf{i}})_{\mathbf{i}\in\mathbb{N}^n}$ is *P-recursive* if from a nonzero finite number of initial terms $u_{\mathbf{i}}, \mathbf{i}\in\mathcal{S}$, and a finite number of P-relations with polynomials coefficients, without any contradiction, one can compute any term of the sequence.

2.1 Tuple of sequences

In this section, we aim to deal with multiple sequences $\mathbf{u}^{(1)}, \ldots, \mathbf{u}^{(m)}$ all n-dimensional over a common field $\mathbb{K}$. In particular, we shall ask them to satisfy C-relations, of type $[P_1]_{\mathbf{u}^{(1)}} + \cdots + [P_m]_{\mathbf{u}^{(m)}} = 0$.

We extend the operator $[]$ to vector of polynomials: for all $\mathbf{P} = (P_1, \ldots, P_m) \in \mathbb{K}[\mathbf{x}]^m$, $[\mathbf{P}] = \sum_{\ell=1}^m [P_\ell]_{\mathbf{u}^{(\ell)}}$. This yields a one-to-one correspondence between vectors of polynomials in $\mathbb{K}[\mathbf{x}]^m$ and linear relations. We now aim to find the $\mathbb{K}[\mathbf{x}]$-submodule $I = \{(P_1, \ldots, P_m) \in \mathbb{K}[\mathbf{x}]^m, \forall\, \mathbf{i} \in \mathbb{N}^n, [P_1\, \mathbf{x}^{\mathbf{i}}]_{\mathbf{u}^{(1)}} + \cdots + [P_m\, \mathbf{x}^{\mathbf{i}}]_{\mathbf{u}^{(m)}} = 0\}$ of $\mathbb{K}[\mathbf{x}]^m$. We shall denote $(e_1, \ldots, e_m)$ the canonical basis of $\mathbb{K}[\mathbf{x}]^m$.

Let $\mathbf{u}^{(1)} = (3^{i_1})_{\mathbf{i} \in \mathbb{N}^2}$ and $\mathbf{u}^{(2)} = (3^{i_1} + 2^{i_2})$. The ideal of relations of $\mathbf{u}^{(1)}$ is $\langle x_2 - 1, x_1 - 3\rangle$, while this of $\mathbf{u}^{(2)}$ is $\langle x_2^2 - 3\,x_2 + 2, x_1 + 2\,x_2 - 5\rangle$. Therefore, we need to know $u_{0,0}^{(1)}, u_{0,0}^{(2)}, u_{0,1}^{(2)}$ to compute any term of both sequences.

Yet, the module of relations satisfied by $(\mathbf{u}^{(1)}, \mathbf{u}^{(2)})$ is spanned by $\{(x_2 - 1, 0), (x_1 - 3, 0), (1, x_2 - 2), (-2, x_1 - 1)\}$ and we only need to know $u_{0,0}^{(1)}, u_{0,0}^{(2)}$ to compute any term.

2.2 P-recursive sequences

For P-recursive sequences, we can naturally create several auxiliary sequences such that they satisfy C-relations. For instance, with sequence $\mathbf{b}$, we introduce the three auxiliary sequences: $\mathbf{b}^{(0)} = \mathbf{b}$, $\mathbf{b}^{(1)} = \left(i_1 \binom{i_1}{i_2}\right)_{\mathbf{i} \in \mathbb{N}}$ and $\mathbf{b}^{(2)} = \left(i_2 \binom{i_1}{i_2}\right)_{\mathbf{i} \in \mathbb{N}}$. Equation (1) is still satisfied by $\mathbf{b}^{(0)}$ and both equations (2a) and (2b) can be restated as C-relations satisfied by these 3 auxiliary sequences:

$$\forall\, \mathbf{i} \in \mathbb{N}^2, \quad b_{i_1+1,i_2}^{(1)} + b_{i_1+1,i_2}^{(2)} = b_{i_1,i_2}^{(1)} + b_{i_1,i_2}^{(0)}, \tag{4a}$$

$$b_{i_1,i_2+1}^{(2)} = b_{i_1,i_2}^{(1)} - b_{i_1,i_2}^{(2)}. \tag{4b}$$

Hence, their module of relations contains $\operatorname{Span}\{(x_1\, x_2 - x_2 - 1, 0, 0), (1, 1 - x_1, x_1), (0, -1, x_2 + 1)\} \subseteq \mathbb{K}[\mathbf{x}]^3$. More generally, for any P-recursive sequence, one would have to introduce as many auxiliary sequences as needed depending on the number of indices and the allowed degree for the polynomial coefficients.

Usually a new set of variables $\mathbf{t} = (t_1, \ldots, t_n)$ is introduced, such that $[t_k\, \mathbf{x}^{\mathbf{i}}] = i_k\, u_{\mathbf{i}}$, and thus $[\mathbf{t}^{\mathbf{j}}\, \mathbf{x}^{\mathbf{i}}] = \mathbf{i}^{\mathbf{j}}\, u_{\mathbf{i}}$. This yields commutation rules $t_k\, x_k = x_k\, (t_k + 1)$ and $t_k\, x_\ell = x_\ell\, t_k$ for $k \neq \ell$. We denote by $\mathbb{K}\langle \mathbf{t}, \mathbf{x}\rangle$ the skew-polynomial ring with these commutation rules. We also let $\mathbb{K}(\mathbf{t})\langle \mathbf{x}\rangle$ be the ring of skew-polynomials in $\mathbf{x}$ whose coefficients are rational fractions in $\mathbf{t}$.

In this setting, P-relations are in a one-to-one correspondence with polynomials in $\mathbb{K}\langle \mathbf{t}, \mathbf{x}\rangle$ and a P-recursive sequence is a sequence such that the set of relations $I = \{P \in \mathbb{K}(\mathbf{t})\langle \mathbf{x}\rangle, \forall\, \mathbf{i}, \mathbf{j} \in \mathbb{N}^n, [P\, \mathbf{t}^{\mathbf{j}}\, \mathbf{x}^{\mathbf{i}}] = 0\}$ is a 0-dimensional right ideal, i.e. for all k, $1 \leq k \leq n$, $I \cap \mathbb{K}(\mathbf{t})\langle x_k\rangle \neq \{0\}$. For $\mathbf{b}$, this yields the right ideal spanned by $\langle (t_1 - t_2)\, x_1 - (t_1 + 1), t_2\, x_2 + t_2 - t_1\rangle \subseteq \mathbb{K}(\mathbf{t})\langle \mathbf{x}\rangle$.

In general, if one considers the right ideal $I' = \{P \in \mathbb{K}\langle \mathbf{t}, \mathbf{x}\rangle, \forall\, \mathbf{i}, \mathbf{j} \in \mathbb{N}^n, [P\, \mathbf{t}^{\mathbf{j}}\, \mathbf{x}^{\mathbf{i}}] = 0\}$, then for all k, there exists $d > 0$ and $\mathbf{j}$ such that $\mathbf{t}^{\mathbf{j}}\, x_k^d$ is the leading monomial of a polynomial in the ideal.

2.3 Lattice-based relations

We now deal with sequences satisfying C-relations when evaluated in points $\mathbf{i} \in \Lambda$, a sublattice of $\mathbb{N}^n$.

The one-dimensional sequence $\mathbf{u} = (u_i)_{i \in \mathbb{N}}$ defined by for all $i \in \mathbb{N}$, $u_{2i} = u_i^{(0)} = i!$ and $u_{2i+1} = u_i^{(1)} = i! + 1$ satisfies for all $i \in \mathbb{N}$

$$u_{2i+3} - u_{2i+2} - u_{2i+1} + u_{2i} = u_{i+1}^{(1)} - u_{i+1}^{(0)} - u_i^{(1)} + u_i^{(0)} = 0. \tag{5}$$

but not $u_{i+3} - u_{i+2} - u_{i+1} + u_i = 0$ for odd i. Nonetheless, computing equation 5 is of interest since with $(u_{2i})_{i \in \mathbb{N}}$ and u_1, it allows us to compute all the odd-indexed terms of $\mathbf{u}$.

As in Section 2.1, we can write equation 5:

$$u_{i+1}^{(1)} - u_{i+1}^{(0)} - u_i^{(1)} + u_i^{(0)} = [(x + 1)\,(e_2 - e_1)\, x^i] = 0.$$

More generally, let $(\lambda_1, \ldots, \lambda_n)$ be a basis of Λ, $\mathcal{S}$ be a finite subset of $\mathbb{N}^n$ such that sequence $\mathbf{u} = (u_{\mathbf{i}})_{\mathbf{i} \in \mathbb{N}^n}$ satisfies

$$\sum\nolimits_{\mathbf{s} \in \mathcal{S}} \alpha_{\mathbf{s}}\, u_{\mathbf{i}+\mathbf{s}} = 0, \quad \forall\, \mathbf{i} \in \Lambda. \tag{6}$$

Then, one can create auxiliary sequences $\mathbf{u}^{(\mathbf{f})} = (u_{\mathbf{i}+\mathbf{f}})_{\mathbf{i} \in \Lambda}$ for all $\mathbf{f} \in \mathcal{F}$, the fundamental domain of Λ to find the relation of equation 6.

Mimicking the P-recursive case, we introduce a new variable t such that for all $\mathbf{i} \in \mathbb{N}^n$, $t\, \mathbf{x}^{\mathbf{i}} = \mathbf{x}^{i_1\, \lambda_1} \cdots \mathbf{x}^{i_n\, \lambda_n}\, t$ and $[t\, \mathbf{x}^{\mathbf{i}}] = u_{i_1\, \lambda_1 + \cdots + i_n\, \lambda_n}$, we can extend these relations to $\mathbb{K}\langle t, \mathbf{x}\rangle$ by linearity. For $\mathbf{i} \in \Lambda$, we let $\mathbf{i} = c_1\, \lambda_1 + \cdots + c_n\, \lambda_n$, therefore $\mathbf{x}^{\mathbf{i}} = t\, x_1^{c_1} \cdots x_n^{c_n}$. Then, one obtains relation

$$\left[\sum\nolimits_{\mathbf{s} \in \mathcal{S}} \alpha_{\mathbf{s}}\, \mathbf{x}^{\mathbf{i}+\mathbf{s}}\right] = \left[\sum\nolimits_{\mathbf{s} \in \mathcal{S}} \alpha_{\mathbf{s}}\, \mathbf{x}^{\mathbf{s}}\, t\, x_1^{c_1} \cdots x_n^{c_n}\right] = 0.$$

3. GUESSING RELATIONS FOR TUPLES OF SEQUENCES

This section is devoted to the design of an FGLM-like algorithm in the module $\mathbb{K}[\mathbf{x}]^m$ to compute the Gröbner basis of the submodule of relations of n-dimensional tables $\mathbf{u}^{(1)}, \ldots, \mathbf{u}^{(m)}$ defined over a common field $\mathbb{K}$.

For the paper to be self-contained, we recall the notation and definitions of [5]. We fix an admissible order $\prec$ on $\mathbf{x}$, $\mathcal{T}$ is the ordered set of terms made from $\mathbf{x}$. We extend $\prec$ to monomial vectors of type $\mathbf{x}^{\mathbf{i}}\, e_\ell, \mathbf{x}^{\mathbf{i}'}\, e_{\ell'}$ with $\mathbf{x}^{\mathbf{i}}\, e_\ell \preceq \mathbf{x}^{\mathbf{i}'}\, e_{\ell'}$ if $\mathbf{x}^{\mathbf{i}} \prec \mathbf{x}^{\mathbf{i}'}$ or if $\mathbf{x}^{\mathbf{i}} = \mathbf{x}^{\mathbf{i}'}$ and $\ell \leq \ell'$.

For $\mathbf{P} \in \mathbb{K}[\mathbf{x}]^m$, we denote by $\mathcal{T}(\mathbf{P})$ the set of terms appearing in $\mathbf{P}$ and by $\operatorname{LT}(\mathbf{P})$ the maximum of $\mathcal{T}(\mathbf{P})$ for $\prec$.

As we try to design an algorithm, we cannot expect to check that a relation is satisfied for all indices $\mathbf{i} \in \mathbb{N}^n$. During the execution of the algorithm, we shall deal with a finite subset of indices $\mathcal{U} \subset \mathbb{N}^n$, and we aim to find relations valid for those indices: $\forall\, \mathbf{i} \in \mathcal{U}$, $\sum_{\ell=1}^m \sum_{\mathbf{s} \in \mathcal{S}} \alpha_{\ell,\mathbf{s}}\, u_{\mathbf{i}+\mathbf{s}}^{(\ell)} = 0$.

From the polynomial viewpoint, this translates to $\forall\, \mathbf{i} \in \mathcal{U}$,

$$\left[\sum_{\ell=1}^{m} \sum_{\mathbf{s} \in \mathcal{S}} \alpha_{\ell,\mathbf{s}}\, \mathbf{x}^{\mathbf{i}+\mathbf{s}}\, e_\ell\right] = 0.$$

Definition 3. Let $\mathcal{U}$ be a finite subset of $\mathbb{N}^n$. We say that a vector of polynomials $\mathbf{P} = (P_1, \ldots, P_m) \in \mathbb{K}[\mathbf{x}]^m$ is valid up to $\mathcal{U}$ if $[\mathbf{P}\, \mathbf{x}^{\mathbf{i}}] = \sum_{\ell=1}^m [P_\ell\, \mathbf{x}^{\mathbf{i}}]_{\mathbf{u}^{(\ell)}} = 0$ for all $\mathbf{i} \in \mathcal{U}$.

3.1 Staircases

Since we want to generate minimal relations, it is mandatory to determine a set of terms in $\mathcal{T}$ for which there is no C-relations. *Useful staircases* were defined for C-recursive tables in [5, Definition 6]. The following definitions extends it for multiple tables.

Definition 4. Let $T_1,\ldots,T_m,U$ be finite subsets of $\mathcal{T}$ such that $T_1,\ldots,T_m \subseteq U$ and $\# U = \sum_{\ell=1}^{m} \# T_\ell$. We say that a set $S = S_1\, e_1 \cup \cdots \cup S_m\, e_m$, with $S_1 \subseteq T_1,\ldots,S_m \subseteq T_m$, is a *useful staircase* with $V \subseteq U$ wrt. $\mathbf{u}^{(1)},\ldots,\mathbf{u}^{(m)}$, $T = T_1\, e_1 \cup \cdots \cup T_m\, e_m, U$, and $\prec$ if $\# V = \# S$ and

$$\sum_{1\leq \ell\leq m} \sum_{s\in S_\ell} \beta_{\ell,s}\, [s\, v\, e_\ell] = 0,\ \forall v \in V$$

implies that $\beta_{\ell,s} = 0$ for all ℓ, s, sets $S_1,\ldots,S_m,V$ are maximal for the inclusion and minimal for $\prec$. We compare two ordered sets for $\prec$ by seeing them as tuples of their elements and then comparing them lexicographically.

As we are in a more general case, useful staircases still fail in general to be true staircases in $\mathbb{K}[\mathbf{x}]^m$, see [5, Example 3]. However, this problem is easily solved by stabilizing the staircase, i.e. adding to each set of the tuple all the divisors of its elements.

3.2 Algorithm for finding the relations

We design an algorithm for checking that a finite subset $S \subseteq T$ is a useful staircase with $V \subseteq U$ wrt. $\mathbf{u}^{(1)},\ldots,\mathbf{u}^{(m)}$, T, U and $\prec$. In the following example, we compute the useful staircase for two univariate tables.

Example 1. Let us consider $\mathbf{u}^{(1)} = (3^{i_1})_{\mathbf{i}\in\mathbb{N}^2}$ and $\mathbf{u}^{(2)} = (3^{i_1}+2^{i_2})_{\mathbf{i}\in\mathbb{N}^2}$. Let $T_1 = T_2 = \{1, x_2\}$ and $U = \{1, x_2, x_1, x_2^2\}$, then we have the following potential relations

$$\begin{array}{c} \\ 1 \\ x_2 \\ x_1 \\ x_2^2 \end{array} \begin{array}{c} \begin{array}{cccc} e_1 & e_2 & x_2\,e_1 & x_2\,e_2 \end{array} \\ \begin{pmatrix} 1 & 2 & 1 & 3 \\ 1 & 3 & 1 & 5 \\ 3 & 4 & 3 & 5 \\ 1 & 5 & 1 & 9 \end{pmatrix} \end{array} \begin{pmatrix} \alpha_1 \\ \beta_1 \\ \alpha_{x_2} \\ \beta_{x_2} \end{pmatrix} = 0.$$

From the matrix viewpoint, a useful staircase is a set of independent columns with as many low-labeled columns as possible wrt. independent rows with as many low-labeled rows as possible. This matrix has rank 2: the first two columns (resp. the first two rows) are independent. Therefore, $S = \{e_1, e_2\}$ is the useful staircase with $V = \{1, x_2\}$.

Thus, we can find relations $(-\alpha_1 + x_2)\, e_1 - \beta_1\, e_2$ and $-\alpha_1'\, e_1 + (-\beta_1' + x_2)\, e_2$ with a linear system:

$$\begin{pmatrix} 1 & 2 \\ 1 & 3 \end{pmatrix} \begin{pmatrix} \alpha_1 & \alpha_1' \\ \beta_1 & \beta_1' \end{pmatrix} = \begin{pmatrix} 1 & 3 \\ 1 & 5 \end{pmatrix}.$$

This yields $(x_2 - 1)\, e_1 = e_1 + (x_2 - 2)\, e_2 = 0$.

We are now in a position to define the structured matrix associated to lists of terms $T_1,\ldots,T_m \subseteq U \subseteq \mathcal{T}$.

Definition 5. Let $T_1,\ldots,T_m,U$ be finite lists of terms such that $T_1,\ldots,T_m \subseteq U \subseteq \mathcal{T}$ and $\# U = \sum_{\ell=1}^{m} \# T_\ell$. The *multi-Hankel* matrix $H_{U,T}$ has the same columns and rows as the concatenation of matrices $H_{U,T_1},\ldots,H_{U,T_m}$, where each H_{U,T_ℓ} is a multi-Hankel matrix for table $\mathbf{u}^{(\ell)}$ as defined in [5, Definition 7]:

$$\begin{array}{c} \\ \vdots \\ v\in U \\ \vdots \end{array} \begin{array}{c} \begin{array}{ccccccccc} \cdots & s\in T_1 & \cdots & & \cdots & & \cdots & s\in T_m & \cdots \end{array} \\ \left(\begin{array}{ccc|c|ccc} \ddots & \vdots & \iddots & \cdots & \ddots & \vdots & \iddots \\ \cdots & [s\,v]_{\mathbf{u}^{(1)}} & \cdots & \cdots & \cdots & [s\,v]_{\mathbf{u}^{(m)}} & \cdots \\ \iddots & \vdots & \ddots & \cdots & \iddots & \vdots & \ddots \end{array}\right) \end{array}.$$

If each $S_\ell \subseteq T_\ell, V \subseteq U$, $\# V = \sum_{\ell=1}^{m} \# S_\ell$ and $H_{V,S}$ has full rank, then $\bigcup_{\ell=1}^{m} S_\ell\, e_\ell$ is a useful staircase with V.

Furthermore, finding a *monic* polynomial vector $\mathbf{P}$ of a given support such that $[\mathbf{P}\, \mathbf{x}^{\mathbf{i}}] = 0$, for all $\mathbf{x}^{\mathbf{i}} \in U$ is equivalent to solving a linear system $H_{U,T}\, \boldsymbol{\alpha} + H_{U,\mathrm{LT}(\mathbf{P})} = 0$, where T is the support of $\mathbf{P}$ without its leading term.

Proposition 1. *Let $T_1,\ldots,T_m,U$ be finite subsets of $\mathcal{T}$. If the finite sets $S_1,\ldots,S_m,V$ are such that $S = \bigcup_{\ell=1}^{m} S_\ell\, e_\ell$ is a useful staircase with V wrt. $\mathbf{u}^{(1)},\ldots,\mathbf{u}^{(m)}, T, U$ and $\prec$, then* $\det H_{V,S} \neq 0$, $\operatorname{rank} H_{V,S} = \operatorname{rank} H_{U,T}$.

If $S_1' \subseteq S_1,\ldots,S_m' \subseteq S_m, V' \subseteq V$ are finite sets of terms, then $\operatorname{rank} H_{V',S'} \leq \operatorname{rank} H_{V,S}$.

3.3 Extension of Scalar-FGLM

As presented in [5, 6], Scalar-FGLM is an algorithm whose input is a table $\mathbf{u}$, an integer d and a monomial order $\prec$ refined by the total degree. If $\mathbf{u}$ is C-recursive of order less than d, then the algorithm returns a Gröbner basis of the ideal of relations of $\mathbf{u}$. Otherwise it returns a $(d+1)$-truncated Gröbner basis of an ideal such that the relations induced by the Gröbner basis are only valid up to degree d. This extension is natural: the input shall be a vector of n-dimensional tables $(\mathbf{u}^{(1)},\ldots,\mathbf{u}^{(m)})$, a vector of integers $(d_1,\ldots,d_m)$ and a monomial order $\prec$ on $\mathbb{K}[\mathbf{x}]$ which we extend to $\mathbb{K}[\mathbf{x}]^m$ as specified earlier.

Algorithm 1, Multi-Scalar-FGLM, computes the module of relations of a list of tables $\mathbf{u}^{(1)},\ldots,\mathbf{u}^{(m)}$ up to degrees $d_1,\ldots,d_m$.

Algorithm 1: Multi-Scalar-FGLM.

Input: Tables $\mathbf{u}^{(1)},\ldots,\mathbf{u}^{(m)}$ over $\mathbb{K}$ of dimension n, $(d_1,\ldots,d_m)$ given bounds and $\prec$ a monomial order.
Output: A reduced $(d_1+1,\ldots,d_m+1)$-truncated Gröbner basis wrt. $\prec$ of their module of relations.

Let $T = \mathcal{T}_{d_1}\, e_1 \cup \cdots \cup \mathcal{T}_{d_m}\, e_m$ where $\mathcal{T}_d$ is the ordered list of monomials of degree at most d.
Let U be the ordered list of the first $\# T$ monomials in $\mathbf{x}$.
Build the matrix $H_{U,T}$.
Extract a submatrix of maximal rank by finding $S = S_1\, e_1 \cup \cdots \cup S_m\, e_m$ and V such that S is the useful staircase for V, i.e. s.t. $\operatorname{rank} H_{U,T} = \operatorname{rank} H_{V,S}$.
$S' :=$ Stabilize(S).
$L := \{\mathcal{T}_{d_1+1} \setminus S_1',\ldots,\mathcal{T}_{d_m+1} \setminus S_m'\}$. `// list of next terms`
$G := \{\}$. `// the future Gröbner basis`
For ℓ **from** 1 **to** m **do**
  While $L[\ell] \neq \varnothing$ **do**
    $\tau := \min_\prec(L[\ell])$ and remove τ from $L[\ell]$.
    Find $\boldsymbol{\alpha}$ s.t. $H_{V,S}\, \boldsymbol{\alpha} + H_{V,\{\tau\, e_\ell\}} = 0$.
    $G := G \cup \{\tau\, e_\ell + \sum_{s\in S} \alpha_s\, s\}$.
    Sort $L[\ell]$ by increasing order (wrt. $\prec$) and remove multiples of $\mathrm{LT}(G)$.
Return G.

Example 2. Let us unroll the algorithm on a modified version of Example 1, with tables $\mathbf{u}^{(1)} = (3^{i_1})_{\mathbf{i}\in\mathbb{N}^2}$, $\mathbf{u}^{(2)} = (3^{i_1}+2^{i_2})_{\mathbf{i}\in\mathbb{N}^2}$ and $(d_1, d_2) = (1, 1)$.

First, $T = \{1, x_2, x_1\}\, e_1 \cup \{1, x_2, x_1\}\, e_2$, so that $U = \{1, x_2, x_1, x_2^2, x_1\, x_2, x_1^2\}$ and matrix $H_{U,T}$ is

$$\begin{array}{c} \\ 1 \\ x_2 \\ x_1 \\ x_2^2 \\ x_1\,x_2 \\ x_1^2 \end{array} \begin{array}{c} \begin{array}{cccccc} e_1 & e_2 & x_2\,e_1 & x_2\,e_2 & x_1\,e_1 & x_1\,e_2 \end{array} \\ \begin{pmatrix} 1 & 2 & 1 & 3 & 3 & 4 \\ 1 & 3 & 1 & 5 & 3 & 5 \\ 3 & 4 & 3 & 5 & 9 & 10 \\ 1 & 5 & 1 & 9 & 3 & 7 \\ 3 & 5 & 3 & 7 & 9 & 11 \\ 9 & 10 & 9 & 11 & 27 & 20 \end{pmatrix} \end{array}.$$

The first two independent columns are e_1, e_2 while the first two independent rows are $1, x_2$. This means that the useful staircase is $S = \{e_1, e_2\}$ with $V = \{1, x_2\}$. The true staircase is then $S' = S$ and we initialize L with $\{x_2, x_1, x_2^2, x_1\,x_2, x_1^2\}\,e_1 \cup \{x_2, x_1, x_2^2, x_1\,x_2, x_1^2\}\,e_2$.

For $\ell = 1$, we set $\tau = x_2$, solve the system $H_{V,S}\,\boldsymbol{\alpha} + \binom{1}{1}$ yielding $\mathbf{P} = (x_2 - 1)\,e_1$ and update L to $\{x_1, x_1^2\}\,e_1 \cup \{x_2, x_1, x_2^2, x_1\,x_2, x_1^2\}\,e_2$.

Then, we set $\tau = x_1$, solve the system $H_{V,S}\,\boldsymbol{\alpha} + \binom{3}{3}$ yielding $\mathbf{P}' = (x_1 - 3)\,e_1$ and update L to $\{x_2, x_1, x_2^2, x_1\,x_2, x_1^2\}\,e_2$.

For $\ell = 2$, we set $\tau = x_2$, solve the system $H_{V,S}\,\boldsymbol{\alpha} + \binom{3}{5}$ yielding $\mathbf{P}'' = e_1 + (x_2 - 2)\,e_2$ and update L to $\{x_1, x_1^2\}\,e_2$.

Then, we set $\tau = x_1$, solve the system $H_{V,S}\,\boldsymbol{\alpha} + \binom{4}{5}$ yielding $\mathbf{P}''' = -2\,e_1 + (x_1 - 1)\,e_2$ and update L to $\varnothing$.

The algorithm returns $\{\mathbf{P}, \mathbf{P}', \mathbf{P}'', \mathbf{P}'''\}$.

4. GUESSING RELATIONS FOR P-RECURSIVE SEQUENCES

As stated in Section 2.2, one could use Algorithm 1 to deal with P-recursive tables. For instance, if one suspects a sequence $\mathbf{u}$ to satisfy relations of type $\sum_{\mathbf{s}\in\mathcal{S}} \alpha_{\mathbf{s}}(\mathbf{i}+\mathbf{s})\,u_{\mathbf{i}+\mathbf{s}} = 0$ with $\alpha_{\mathbf{s}} \in \mathbb{K}[\mathbf{i}]$ of degree at most δ, then one would just need to call the algorithm with all the $\mathbf{u}^{(\mathbf{j})} = (\mathbf{i}^{\mathbf{j}}\,u_{\mathbf{i}})_{\mathbf{i}\in\mathbb{N}}$, s.t. $|\mathbf{j}| \le \delta$, as input tables.

4.1 A criterion for P-recursive sequences

The main drawback of this strategy is the output of the algorithm: there are polynomials representing redundant relations if the sequence is P-recursive but not C-recursive. For instance, Algorithm 1 called on $\mathbf{b}^{(0)}, \mathbf{b}^{(1)}, \mathbf{b}^{(2)}$, of Section 2.2, with degree bounds $(1, 1, 1)$ in $\mathbf{x}$ returns both relations (4a) and (4b) together with six extra relations.

Yet, the first two are enough to compute every term of the sequence starting from $\binom{0}{0} = 1$.

These superfluous relations come from the fact that we forget the extra structure of the module of relations, i.e. it is also a right ideal of $\mathbb{K}\langle\mathbf{t},\mathbf{x}\rangle$ for $\mathbf{t} = (t_1, \ldots, t_n)$, $t_k\,x_\ell = x_\ell\,t_k$ if $k \ne \ell$ and $t_k\,x_k = x_k(t_k + 1)$.

Therefore, it is possible to extend MULTI-SCALAR-FGLM to take into account this structure. Whenever a relation

$$\left[\mathbf{t}^{\mathbf{j}+\boldsymbol{\delta}}\,\mathbf{x}^{\mathbf{i}+\mathbf{d}}\right] = \left[\sum_{\mathbf{r}\in\mathcal{R},\mathbf{s}\in\mathcal{S}} \alpha_{\mathbf{r},\mathbf{s}}\,\mathbf{t}^{\mathbf{j}+\mathbf{r}}\,\mathbf{x}^{\mathbf{i}+\mathbf{s}}\right]$$

$$(\mathbf{i}+\mathbf{d})^{\mathbf{j}+\boldsymbol{\delta}}\,u_{\mathbf{i}+\mathbf{d}} = \sum_{\mathbf{r}\in\mathcal{R},\mathbf{s}\in\mathcal{S}} \alpha_{\mathbf{r},\mathbf{s}}\,(\mathbf{i}+\mathbf{s})^{\mathbf{j}+\mathbf{r}}\,u_{\mathbf{i}+\mathbf{s}}$$

is true up to a certain threshold for $\mathbf{i}$, then its multiples by $i_k + d_k$ are also true up to the same threshold.

PROPOSITION 2. *Let $\mathbf{u}$ be a P-recursive table over $\mathbb{K}$. Let T (resp. U) be a finite subset of monomials in $\mathbb{K}\langle\mathbf{t},\mathbf{x}\rangle$ (resp. in $\mathbb{K}[\mathbf{x}]$). If $\mathbf{t}^{\mathbf{j}}\,\mathbf{x}^{\mathbf{i}}$ is not in the useful staircase of matrix $\left(\left[\mathbf{t}^{\mathbf{j}}\,\mathbf{x}^{\mathbf{i}+\mathbf{i}'}\right]\right)_{\mathbf{t}^{\mathbf{j}}\mathbf{x}^{\mathbf{i}}\in T,\mathbf{x}^{\mathbf{i}'}\in U}$ then neither is any multiple $\mathbf{t}^{\mathbf{j}+\mathbf{j}'}\,\mathbf{x}^{\mathbf{i}}$.*

PROOF. If $\mathbf{t}^{\mathbf{j}}\,\mathbf{x}^{\mathbf{i}}$ is not in the useful staircase, a relation starting with $u_{\mathbf{i}+\mathbf{k}}$ exists. Multiplying it by $i_k + d_k$ yields a new relation whose associated polynomial has a leading term $t_k\,\mathbf{t}^{\mathbf{j}}\,\mathbf{x}^{\mathbf{i}}$, hence column $t_k\,\mathbf{t}^{\mathbf{j}}\,\mathbf{x}^{\mathbf{i}}$ can also be removed. □

Let us notice that this is analogous to the behavior of FGLM for polynomial ideals in $\mathbb{K}[\mathbf{x}]$ [16]: whenever a relation $\mathbf{x}^{\mathbf{d}} = \sum_{\mathbf{s}\prec\mathbf{d}} \alpha_{\mathbf{s}}\,\mathbf{x}^{\mathbf{s}}$ is found, then automatically for all $\mathbf{i} \in \mathbb{N}^n$, $\mathbf{x}^{\mathbf{i}+\mathbf{d}} = \sum_{\mathbf{s}\prec\mathbf{d}} \alpha_{\mathbf{s}}\,\mathbf{x}^{\mathbf{i}+\mathbf{s}}$. This is also analogous to Buchberger – Möller algorithms wherein the finitely many points can be interpreted as the finitely many table terms we have. We illustrate this criterion.

Example 3. We consider $\mathbf{u} = (i!)_{i\in\mathbb{N}}$ and skew-polynomial ring $\mathbb{K}\langle t, x\rangle$. Columns will be labeled by $T = \{1, t, x, t\,x\}$ and rows by $U = \{1, x, x^2, x^3\}$. This yield the rank 3 matrix

$$H_{U,T} = \begin{array}{c} \\ 1 \\ x \\ x^2 \\ x^3 \end{array}\!\!\begin{array}{c} \begin{array}{cccc} 1 & t & x & t\,x \end{array} \\ \begin{pmatrix} 1 & 0 & 1 & 1 \\ 1 & 1 & 2 & 4 \\ 2 & 4 & 6 & 18 \\ 6 & 18 & 24 & 96 \end{pmatrix} \end{array}.$$

Column labeled x is the first dependent one meaning we find relations $[x^{i+1} - (t+1)\,x^i] = u_{i+1} - (i+1)\,u_i = 0$ for all $i \in \{0, \ldots, 3\}$. This leads us to determine that $(i+1)\,u_{i+1} + (i^2 + 2\,i + 1)\,u_i = 0 = [t\,x^{i+1} + (t^2 + 2\,t + 1)\,x^i]$ for all $i \in \{0, \ldots, 3\}$ without computing $[t^2], [t^2\,x], [t^2\,x^2], [t^2\,x^3]$, i.e. column t^2. Therefore, column $t\,x$ is independent from the previous ones but is not in the useful staircase.

In this context, a *useful staircase* is the maximal subset $S \subseteq T$ such that columns of $H_{U,S}$ are all linearly independent and for all $\mathbf{t}^{\mathbf{j}}\,\mathbf{x}^{\mathbf{i}} \in T \setminus S$ and $\mathbf{j}' \in \mathbb{N}^n$, $\mathbf{t}^{\mathbf{j}+\mathbf{j}'}\,\mathbf{x}^{\mathbf{i}} \notin S$.

To compare monomials in $\mathbb{K}\langle\mathbf{t},\mathbf{x}\rangle$ in order to build our matrix, we proceed as follows. We let $\prec$ be a monomial ordering refined by the total degree on $\mathbf{t}$ and $\mathbf{x}$ with the convention that for any k, ℓ, $t_k \prec x_\ell$.

The following algorithm, P-RECURSIVE-FGLM, computes the linear recurrence relations with polynomial coefficients of an input P-recursive table. Thanks to the criterion given in Proposition 2, the linear systems that we solve at the end are smaller than in Algorithm 1.

Algorithm 2: P-RECURSIVE-FGLM.

Input: A table $\mathbf{u} = (u_{\mathbf{i}})_{\mathbf{i}\in\mathbb{N}^n}$ with coefficients in $\mathbb{K}$, (δ, d) given bounds and $\prec$ a monomial ordering.
Output: A reduced (δ, d)-truncated Gröbner basis wrt. $\prec$ of the ideal of relations of $\mathbf{u}$ in $\mathbb{K}\langle\mathbf{t},\mathbf{x}\rangle$.
Let T be the ordered list of monomials in $\mathbf{t}, \mathbf{x}$ of bidegree at most (δ, d).
Let U be the ordered list of the first $\#T$ monomials in $\mathbf{x}$.
Build the matrix $H_{U,T}$.
Find S the useful staircase.
Find V the set of first linearly independent rows of $H_{U,S}$.
$S' :=$ Stabilize(S).
$L := T \setminus S'$. // list of next terms to study
$G := \{\}$. // the future Gröbner basis
While $L \ne \varnothing$ **do**
  $\tau := \min_\prec(L)$.
  Find $\boldsymbol{\alpha}$ s.t. $H_{V,S}\,\boldsymbol{\alpha} + H_{V,\{\tau\}} = 0$.
  $G := G \cup \{\tau + \sum_{s\in S} \alpha_s\,s\}$.
  Sort L by increasing order (wrt. $\prec$) and remove multiples of LT(G).
Return G.

Example 4. Let us unroll Algorithm 2 on table $(i_1!/i_2!)_{\mathbf{i}\in\mathbb{N}^2}$ with $\delta = d = 1$ and ordering DRL($t_2 \prec t_1 \prec x_2 \prec x_1$).

We have $T = \{1, t_2, t_1, x_2, x_1, t_2\,x_2, t_2\,x_1, t_1\,x_2, t_1\,x_1\}$ and we let $U = \{1, x_2, x_1, x_2^2, x_1\,x_2, x_1^2, x_2^3, x_1\,x_2^2, x_1^2\,x_2\}$. This yields matrix $H_{U,T}$ described in equation 7.

The first linearly independent columns are $1, t_2, t_1, x_2, t_2\,x_1, t_1\,x_2, t_1\,x_1$. As x_1 is not in this set, we need to remove both $t_2\,x_1$ and $t_1\,x_1$ by Proposition 2. Hence the useful staircase is $S = \{1, t_2, t_1, x_2, t_1\,x_2\}$. The set of the first 5 independent rows is $V = \{1, x_2, x_1, x_2^2, x_1\,x_2\}$.

$$
\begin{array}{c} \\ 1 \\ x_2 \\ x_1 \\ x_2^2 \\ x_1 x_2 \\ x_1^2 \\ x_2^3 \\ x_1 x_2^2 \\ x_1^2 x_2 \end{array}
\begin{array}{c}
\begin{array}{ccccccccc} 1 & t_2 & t_1 & x_2 & x_1 & t_2 x_2 & t_2 x_1 & t_1 x_2 & t_1 x_1 \end{array} \\
\left(\begin{array}{ccccccccc}
1 & 0 & 0 & 1 & 1 & 1 & 0 & 0 & 1 \\
1 & 1 & 0 & 1/2 & 1 & 1 & 1 & 0 & 1 \\
1 & 0 & 1 & 1 & 2 & 1 & 0 & 1 & 4 \\
1/2 & 1 & 0 & 1/6 & 1/2 & 1/2 & 1 & 0 & 1/2 \\
1 & 1 & 1 & 1/2 & 2 & 1 & 2 & 1/2 & 4 \\
2 & 0 & 4 & 2 & 6 & 2 & 0 & 4 & 18 \\
1/6 & 1/2 & 0 & 1/24 & 1/6 & 1/6 & 1/2 & 0 & 1/6 \\
1/2 & 1 & 1/2 & 1/6 & 1 & 1/2 & 2 & 1/6 & 2 \\
2 & 2 & 4 & 1 & 6 & 2 & 6 & 2 & 18
\end{array}\right)
\end{array}
\qquad (7)
$$

We set $L = \{x_1, t_2 x_2, t_2 x_1, t_1 x_1\}$ and let $\tau = x_1$. We then find $G = \{x_1 - t_1 - 1\}$ and L is updated to $\{t_2 x_2\}$.

We set $\tau = t_2 x_2$, find $G = \{x_1 - t_1 - 1, t_2 x_2 - 1\}$ and update L to $\varnothing$.

REMARK 3. *It is sometimes more convenient to obtain the ideal of relations, not in $\mathbb{K}\langle \mathbf{t}, \mathbf{x}\rangle$ but in $\mathbb{K}(\mathbf{t})\langle \mathbf{x}\rangle$, the ring of skew-polynomials in $\mathbf{x}$ with rational fractions in $\mathbf{t}$ coefficients. In this setting, we can mimic* SCALAR-FGLM *algorithm by setting L to the set of all monomials in $\mathbf{t}, \mathbf{x}$ of bidegree at most $(\delta, d+1)$ which are not in S'. In a way, this would ensure that the staircase of the Gröbner basis obtained at the end is closed. Then, we need to change also how to update L: since now each t_k is invertible, whenever $\tau = \mathbf{t}^{\mathbf{j}}\,\mathbf{x}^{\mathbf{i}}$, we remove every monomial $\mathbf{t}^{\mathbf{j}'}\,\mathbf{x}^{\mathbf{i}+\mathbf{i}'}$.*

Example 5. Algorithm 2 on the binomial table $\mathbf{b}$ returns the three relations (1), (2a) and (2b) as $\{t_2 x_2 - (t_1 - t_2), (t_1 - t_2) x_1 - (t_1 + 1), x_1 x_2 - x_2 - 1\}$ for degree bounds at least $(1, 2)$ in $\mathbf{t}$ and $\mathbf{x}$ and ordering $\mathrm{DRL}(t_2 \prec t_1 \prec x_2 \prec x_1)$. Therefore during the execution of the algorithm, the least monomials of list L were $t_2 x_2, t_1 x_1$ and $x_1 x_2$.

Over $\mathbb{K}(\mathbf{t})\langle \mathbf{x}\rangle$, we would have to consider that $x_1 x_2$ is a multiple of $t_2 x_2$, when updating L. Therefore, Pascal's rule is never computed. This is consistent with the fact that $g_1 = t_2 x_2 - t_1 + t_2$ and $g_2 = (t_1 - t_2) x_1 - (t_1 + 1)$ form a Gröbner basis in $\mathbb{K}\langle \mathbf{t}, \mathbf{x}\rangle$, that $(x_1 x_2 - x_2 - 1) \notin I = \langle g_1, g_2\rangle$ but that $g_1 + g_2 x_2 = (t_1 - t_2)(x_1 x_2 - x_2 - 1) \in I$. Hence, $x_1 x_2 - x_2 - 1$ is a member of the ideal $I\,\mathbb{K}(\mathbf{t})\langle \mathbf{x}\rangle$.

4.2 Adaptive algorithm

If one is concerned about the number of queries to table $\mathbf{u}$, it is necessary not to visit monomials yielding relations which are multiple of already computed relations. Therefore, we need to have an adaptive approach of the algorithm: we shall discover the staircase term by term, see also ADAPTIVE SCALAR-FGLM [5, Section 5]. As in Remark 3, we assume that we look for a Gröbner basis of the ideal in $\mathbb{K}(\mathbf{t})\langle \mathbf{x}\rangle$.

We start from $S = \varnothing, V = \varnothing$ and try to increase them both: if $H_{V \cup \{\mathbf{x}^{\mathbf{i}'}\}, S \cup \{\mathbf{t}^{\mathbf{j}}\,\mathbf{x}^{\mathbf{i}}\}}$ has a greater rank than $H_{V,S}$, then S and V are updated accordingly. Otherwise, we have found a new relation whose leading term is $\mathbf{t}^{\mathbf{j}}\,\mathbf{x}^{\mathbf{i}}$. Therefore, we do not update S nor V and shall never suggest any multiple of $\mathbf{x}^{\mathbf{i}}$ (resp. $\mathbf{x}^{\mathbf{i}'}$) as a new term in S (resp. V). This yields Algorithm 3.

5. MIXED APPROACH WITH GRÖBNER BASES COMPUTATIONS

When dealing with a sequence $\mathbf{u} = (u_{\mathbf{i}})_{\mathbf{i} \in \mathbb{N}^n}$, not all its ideal of relations I in $\mathbb{K}\langle \mathbf{t}, \mathbf{x}\rangle$ is necessarily interesting. For instance, whenever one wants to know if $\mathbf{u}$ is P-recursive, it is enough to compute for all k, $1 \le k \le n$, a polynomial

Algorithm 3: ADAPTIVE P-RECURSIVE-FGLM.

Input: A table $\mathbf{u} = (u_{\mathbf{i}})_{\mathbf{i} \in \mathbb{N}^n}$ with coefficients in $\mathbb{K}$, (δ, d) given bounds and $\prec$ a monomial ordering.

Output: A reduced Gröbner basis of a zero-dimensional ideal of degree $\ge d$.

$L := \{1\}, M := \{1\}$. `// list of next terms to study`

$S := \{\}, V := \{\}$. `// S is a useful staircase for V`

$G' := \{\}$. `// leading terms of the Gröbner basis`

$H' := \{\}$. `// deleted rows`

While $L \neq \varnothing$ *and* $M \neq \varnothing$ **do**

- $\tau := \min_{\prec} L, \chi := \min_{\prec} M$.
- **If** $H_{V \cup \{\chi\}, S \cup \{\tau\}}$ *is full rank* **then**
  - $S := S \cup \{\tau\}, V := V \cup \{\chi\}$,
  - $L := L \cup \{t_1\,\tau, \ldots, t_n\,\tau, x_1\,\tau, \ldots, x_n\,\tau \mid \deg_{\mathbf{t}} t_i\,\tau \le \delta\}$
  - $M := M \cup \{x_1\,\chi, \ldots, x_n\,\chi\}$
  - Sort L (resp. M) by increasing order (wrt. $\prec$) and remove duplicates and multiples of G' (resp. H').
  - **If** $\# S \ge d$ **then** `// early termination`
    - $G := \{\}$ and $G' := \mathrm{MinGBasis}\,(G' \cup L \cup T \setminus S)$, with T the set of monomials in $\mathbf{t}, \mathbf{x}$ of bidegree at most $(\deg_{\mathbf{t}} \tau, \deg_{\mathbf{x}} \tau + 1)$.
    - **For all** $\tau' \in G'$ **do**
      - $G := G \cup \{\tau' + \sum_{s \in S} \alpha_s\, s\}$ with $H_{V,S}\,\boldsymbol{\alpha} + H_{V,\{\tau'\}} = 0$.
    - **Return** S, V and G.
- **Else**
  - $G' := G' \cup \{\tau\}, H' := H' \cup \{\chi\}$ and remove multiples of τ in L and of χ in M.

Error "Run Algorithm 2".

in I whose leading monomial is $\mathbf{t}^{\mathbf{j}}\,x_k^d$ with $\mathbf{j}$ any and $d > 0$. We recall that this ensures that $I\,\mathbb{K}(\mathbf{t})\langle \mathbf{x}\rangle$ is 0-dimensional. Therefore, only a subideal of I may be needed to certify that $\mathbf{u}$ is P-recursive.

In ADAPTIVE P-RECURSIVE-FGLM algorithm, as soon as a polynomial P_1 with leading monomial $\mathrm{LT}(P_1)$ is found, all the $\mathbf{t}^{\mathbf{j}}\,\mathbf{x}^{\mathbf{i}}\,\mathrm{LT}(P_1)$ are discarded so that the multiples of P_1 are not computed. Therefore, whenever polynomials $P_2, \ldots, P_r$ are found, we can discard all the right-linear combinations of $P_1, \ldots, P_r$, hence the ideal they span. In this algorithm, if $P_1, \ldots, P_r$ are exactly the first output polynomials, then we know that they are in the final Gröbner basis and that their leading monomials are the least first. By computing the Gröbner basis of $J = \langle P_1, \ldots, P_r\rangle \subseteq \mathbb{K}\langle \mathbf{t}, \mathbf{x}\rangle$, we can expect to be able to find polynomials with leading monomials not in $\langle \mathrm{LT}(P_1), \ldots, \mathrm{LT}(P_r)\rangle$. On the one hand, these polynomials are redundant since they are deduced from $P_1, \ldots, P_r$, i.e. the relations they represent are deduced by those induced by $P_1, \ldots, P_r$. On the other hand, we may find polynomials ensuring that J is zero-dimensional and thus that I is.

Let us assume that when computing the Gröbner basis of J, we find another polynomial P_{r+1}. Let us assume furthermore that, seen as monomials in $\mathbf{x}$, $\mathrm{LT}(P_1), \ldots, \mathrm{LT}(P_r) \prec \mathrm{LT}(P_{r+1})$ and that P_{r+1} is also in the Gröbner basis of I. Then, we computed P_{r+1} without new queries to the table.

REMARK 4. *The Gröbner basis computation can be done either in $\mathbb{K}\langle \mathbf{t}, \mathbf{x}\rangle$ or in $\mathbb{K}(\mathbf{t})\langle \mathbf{x}\rangle$. In the latter case, as soon as a relation with leading monomial $\mathbf{x}^{\mathbf{i}}$ is found, no relation with leading monomial $\mathbf{x}^{\mathbf{i}+\mathbf{i}'}$ shall be computed. However, in the former case, it is possible that we find new relations with leading monomials $\mathbf{x}^{\mathbf{i}+\mathbf{i}'}$, hence with higher degrees in $\mathbf{x}$, but with also lower degrees in $\mathbf{t}$.*

In the *black-box* model, this approach can be very beneficial, since the computation of even one element of $\mathbf{u}$ can be costly. Therefore, we can modify ADAPTIVE P-RECURSIVE-

FGLM so that it takes these Gröbner bases computations into account: first we compute the polynomials as soon as they are found, instead of just storing their leading monomials in G'. Then, whenever $\# G$ is big enough, we replace G by the true Gröbner basis of the ideal spanned by G and we remove all the multiples of $\mathrm{LT}(g)$, for $g \in G$, in L.

Computation of Gröbner bases in an Ore algebra can be done with the adaptations of Buchberger and F4 [14] algorithms in computer algebra systems [18], such as MAPLE or PLURAL the noncommutative extension of SINGULAR.

Let us illustrate this behavior with an example.

Example 6. We consider Gessel's walks and sequence $\mathbf{g} = (g_{n,i,j})_{(n,i,j)\in\mathbb{N}^3}$ denoting the number of walks of length n ending at (i, j), with steps in $\{(-1,0),(-1,-1),(1,0),(1,1)\}$. The kernel method, see [7] for instance, ensures that $\mathbf{g}$ is P-recursive if and only if so are both $\mathbf{g}' = (g_{n,0,j})_{(n,j)\in\mathbb{N}^2}$ and $\mathbf{g}'' = (g_{n,i,0})_{(n,i)\in\mathbb{N}^2}$.

We apply this mixed approach to find a 0-dimensional subideal of relations of table $\mathbf{g}'$ up to degrees $(5,5)$. Variables t_0, x_0 shall be associated with n, while t_2, x_2 shall be associated with j. The first computed polynomial has leading monomial $t_0\, t_2^3\, x_0^2\, x_2^3$. Then, four polynomials with leading monomials $t_0^4\, t_2\, x_0^4\, x_2, t_0^3\, t_2^2\, x_0^4\, x_2, t_0^3\, t_2^2\, x_0^2\, x_2^3, t_0^4\, x_0^4\, x_2$.

Calling a Gröbner basis computation on these polynomials in $\mathbb{K}\langle \mathbf{t}, \mathbf{x}\rangle$ allows us to determine polynomials with leading monomials $t_0^5\, t_2^2\, x_0^4, t_0^5\, x_0^6, t_0^3\, t_2^4\, x_2^4, t_0^3\, t_2^3\, x_2^5$. We can notice that the first (resp. last) two are purely in $\mathbf{t}$ and x_0 (resp. x_2). Hence we can suspect that $\mathbf{g}'$ is P-recursive.

Given a 3D-space walk sequence $\mathbf{w} = (w_{n,i,j,k})_{(n,i,j,k)\in\mathbb{N}^3}$ counting the number of walks of length n ending at (i, j, k), the kernel method still applies. Thanks to the C-relation satisfied by said walk, one can prove, see [7, Section 4.3] that the generating series $W(\mathbf{x}) = \sum_{n,i,j,k\geq 0} w_{n,i,j,k}\, x_0^n\, x_1^i\, x_2^j\, x_3^k$ is a $\mathbb{K}(\mathbf{x})$-linear combination of $W_1 = W(x_0, 0, x_2, x_3), W_2, W_3, W_{12} = W(x_0, 0, 0, x_3), W_{13}, W_{23}, W_{123} = W(x_0, 0, 0, 0)$ and 1. That is, there is a C-relation between $\mathbf{w}, (w_{n,0,j,k})_{(n,j,k)\in\mathbb{N}^3}, \ldots, (w_{n,0,0,k})_{(n,k)\in\mathbb{N}^2}, \ldots, (w_{n,0,0,0})_{n\in\mathbb{N}}$.

In the next example, we deal with the 3D-space walk $\mathbf{w}$ whose steps are in $\{(-1,-1,-1),(-1,-1,1),(-1,-1,0),(1,0,0)\}$, see [7, Proposition 6].

Example 7. We use the same notation as in Example 6 with the extra convention that t_1, x_1 (resp. t_3, x_3) are associated with i (resp. k).

Running MULTI-SCALAR-FGLM on $\mathbf{w}$ and all seven tables obtained from it when possibly setting parameters i, j, k to 0 yields the kernel equation

$$\begin{aligned}(x_0\, x_1^2\, x_2\, x_3 + x_0\, x_2^2\, x_3 + x_0\, x_3^2 - x_1\, x_2\, x_3 + x_0)\, W\\ = (x_0\, x_2^2\, x_3 + x_0\, x_3^2 + x_0)\, W_1 + (x_0\, x_3^2 + x_0)\, W_2 + x_0\, W_3\\ - (x_0\, x_3^2 + x_0)\, W_{12} - x_0\, (W_{13} + W_{23} - W_{123}) - x_1\, x_2\, x_3.\end{aligned}$$

Now, let us see why we can guess that W_3 is D-finite, i.e. $(w_{n,i,j,0})_{(n,i,j)\in\mathbb{N}^3}$ is P-recursive [19, Theorem 3.7]. The least relation for this table, $t_0\, t_1\, x_0\, x_1 + t_1^2\, x_0\, x_1 + 2\, t_1\, x_0\, x_1 - 2\, t_0\, t_1 - 4\, t_0 - 2\, t_1 - 4$, is found in degree $(\delta, d) = (2,2)$.

Increasing gradually to column degree $(2,4)$ and row degree 30, we obtain a 1448×350 matrix and 8 leading terms. A Gröbner basis computation yields 25 leading terms including $t_0\, t_1\, t_2\, x_1^2$. This closes the staircase on the x_1 side.

We increase now the column degree to $(3,4)$ and the row degree to 40, obtain a 2959×600 matrix and find an extra 25 relations. Unfortunately this does not close the staircase on either side.

A Gröbner basis computation, ideally truncated in total degree 9, returns 127 relations. Among which, there are leading monomials $t_0^3\, t_2\, t_3^2\, x_0^4$ and $t_0\, t_1^2\, t_2\, x_2^4$. In total, 19 monomials are purely in $\mathbf{t}$ and one of the x_i. Hence, the staircase is closed in $\mathbb{K}(\mathbf{t})\langle \mathbf{x}\rangle$.

In Table 1, we detail the linear algebra part for W_3. These computations have been integated in and done with FGB [15].

Degree	Matrix		Rank	
$(2,2)$	270×100	$0.57\,s$	98	$0.00\,s$
$(2,3)$	766×200	$0.60\,s$	181	$0.00\,s$
$(3,3)$	766×368	$0.64\,s$	98	$0.01\,s$

Table 1: Results and timings of Example 7.

6. COMPLEXITY ANALYSIS

This section is devoted to the study of the complexity of both MULTI-SCALAR-FGLM and P-RECURSIVE-FGLM algorithms. This comes down to the study of the structure of the multi-Hankel matrix.

6.1 Algorithm for tuples of tables

For the MULTI-SCALAR-FGLM algorithm, the multi-Hankel matrix $H_{U,T}$ is the concatenation of m multi-Hankel matrices H_{U,T_ℓ}. From [6, Section 6], we know that for an n-dimensional table and $\mathrm{LEX}(x_1 \prec \cdots \prec x_n)$ ordering, if the leading monomials are $x_1^{d_1}, \ldots, x_2^{d_2}, \ldots, x_n^{d_n}$, then the multi-Hankel matrix created by SCALAR-FGLM is a submatrix of a *multilevel block Hankel matrix of depth* n, or n*-multiblock Hankel* matrix which is heavily structured.

Definition 6. A *multilevel block Hankel matrix of depth* 0 is a scalar. For any $n \in \mathbb{N}$, a *multilevel block Hankel matrix of depth* $n+1$ is a block Hankel matrix whose blocks are multilevel block Hankel matrices of depth n.

By construction in Algorithm 1, each T_ℓ of $T = T_1\, e_1 \cup \cdots \cup T_n\, e_n$ is a subset of U, therefore $H_{T_\ell, T_\ell\, e_\ell}$ is a submatrix of the generalized multi-Hankel matrix handled by the algorithm. Let $S = S_1\, e_1 \cup \cdots \cup S_m\, e_m$ and V be such that S is a useful staircase with V. A necessary condition for a monomial s to be in S_ℓ is that column $s\, e_\ell$ is linearly independent from the previous ones in $H_{T_\ell, T_\ell\, e_\ell}$. Thus, row $s\, e_\ell$ is also independent from the previous ones in $H_{U,T}$. Hence, $s \in S_\ell$ implies that $s \in V$ and each S_ℓ is a subset of V.

Let $\Sigma = \bigcup_{\ell=1}^m S_\ell$, then $\Sigma \subseteq V$. Let M be the least integer such that $V \subseteq W = \Sigma \cup \bigcup_{k=2}^M w_k\, \Sigma$. Now, $H_{V,S}$ is a submatrix of $H_{W,\Sigma\, e_1 \cup\cdots\cup \Sigma\, e_m}$ and $H_{W,\Sigma\, e_1\cup\cdots\cup\Sigma\, e_m}$ is a block matrix whose blocks $H_{w_k\, \Sigma, \Sigma}$ are all n-multiblock:

$$H_{W,\Sigma\, e_1\cup\cdots\cup\Sigma\, e_m} = \begin{pmatrix} H_{\Sigma,\Sigma}(\mathbf{u}^{(1)}) & \cdots & H_{\Sigma,\Sigma}(\mathbf{u}^{(m)})\\ \vdots & & \vdots\\ H_{w_M\,\Sigma,\Sigma}(\mathbf{u}^{(1)}) & \cdots & H_{w_M\,\Sigma,\Sigma}(\mathbf{u}^{(m)})\end{pmatrix}.$$

PROPOSITION 5. *Given a tuple of m tables. Let μ be the number of polynomials in the Gröbner basis output by* MULTI-SCALAR-FGLM. *For $1 \leq k \leq n$, let d_k be the greatest powers in x_k appearing in the Gröbner basis. Let M be the number of blocks of size $d_1 \cdots d_n$ appearing on each column of the computed matrix by the algorithm. Then the* *number of operations in the base field to compute the Gröbner basis is no more than*

$$O\left(\mu\,(M\,m\,d_2\,\cdots\,d_n)^{\omega-1}\mathsf{M}(d_1\cdots d_n)\,\log(d_1\,\cdots\,d_n)\right).$$

PROOF. Applying Hankel displacement operator makes each block $H_{w_k\,\Sigma,\Sigma}$ have displacement rank $d_2\,\cdots\,d_n$, see [6, Proposition 17]. Therefore, $H_{W,\Sigma\,e_1\cup\cdots\cup\Sigma\,e_m}$ have displacement rank $M\,m\,d_2\,\cdots\,d_n$. Thanks to [9], solving a linear system with this matrix can be done in $O\big((M\,m\,d_1\,\cdots\,d_n)^{\omega-1}$ $\mathsf{M}(d_1\,\cdots\,d_n)\,\log(d_1\,\cdots\,d_n)\big)$. Finally, we solve μ systems. □

6.2 Algorithms for P-recursive tables

For $\mathbf{j}\in\mathbb{N}^n$, let $\Sigma_{\mathbf{j}}$ be the set of all monomials $\mathbf{t}^{\mathbf{j}}\,\mathbf{x}^{\mathbf{i}}$ in the useful staircase. By the column removal criterion of Proposition 2, we know that $\Sigma_{\mathbf{j}+\mathbf{j}'}\subseteq\Sigma_{\mathbf{j}}$ for any $\mathbf{j}'\in\mathbb{N}^n$. Hence for all $\mathbf{j}$, $\Sigma_{\mathbf{j}}\subseteq\Sigma_{\mathbf{0}}=\Sigma$.

The remaining part of the analysis is the same as for MULTI-SCALAR-FGLM called on $m=\binom{n+\delta}{\delta}=O(n^\delta)$ tables. This yields the following corollary.

COROLLARY 6. *Let δ be the maximal degree in $\mathbf{t}$ allowed to compute the relations of a table. Let μ be the number of polynomials in the Gröbner basis output by* P-RECURSIVE-FGLM. *For $1\le k\le n$, let d_k be the greatest powers in x_k appearing in the Gröbner basis. Let M be the number of blocks of size $d_1\,\cdots\,d_n$ appearing on each column of the computed matrix by the algorithm. Then the number of operations in the base field to compute the Gröbner basis is no more than*

$$O\left(\mu\,(M\,n^\delta\,d_2\,\cdots\,d_n)^{\omega-1}\mathsf{M}(d_1\cdots d_n)\,\log(d_1\,\cdots\,d_n)\right).$$

Concerning the number of table queries, Algorithm 2, P-RECURSIVE-FGLM, can reach elements of $\mathbf{u}$ far away from the useful staircase whenever the degree bound in $\mathbf{x}$ is too big. In Algorithm 3, ADAPTIVE P-RECURSIVE-FGLM, the matrix elements are $[\mathbf{t}^{\mathbf{j}}\,\mathbf{x}^{\mathbf{i}+\mathbf{i}'}]=(\mathbf{i}+\mathbf{i}')^{\mathbf{j}}\,u_{\mathbf{i}+\mathbf{i}'}$ with $\mathbf{t}^{\mathbf{j}}\,\mathbf{x}^{\mathbf{i}}\in S,\mathbf{x}^{\mathbf{i}}\in\Sigma$ and $\mathbf{x}^{\mathbf{i}'}\in V$. Hence, the number of table queries is the cardinal of $\Sigma\,V=\{\tau\,\chi\mid\tau\in\Sigma,\chi\in V\}$.

Embedding V into $\Sigma\cup\bigcup_{k=2}^M w_k\,\Sigma$ ensures that $\Sigma\,V\subseteq(2\,\Sigma)\cup\bigcup_{k=2}^M w_k\,(2\,\Sigma)$, where $2\,\Sigma=\{\tau\,\tau'\mid\tau,\tau'\in\Sigma\}$. Hence, $\#\,(\Sigma\,V)\le M\,\#\,(2\,\Sigma)\le M\,(\#\,\Sigma)^2/2$ in the worst case.

Whenever Σ is included in a parallelotope of size $C\,\#\,\Sigma$, then Ruzsa's Theorem [22, Theorem 1.1] ensures that there exists c such that $\#\,(2\,\Sigma)\le c\,\#\,\Sigma$, hence $\#\,(\Sigma\,V)\le c\,M\,\#\,\Sigma$.

Acknowledgments

We thank the anonymous referees for their careful reading and their helpful comments, C. Banderier, A. Bostan, F. Chyzak and B. Salvy for valuable discussions. This work has been partly supported by the French National Research Agency ANR-11-BS02-0013 HPAC project.

7. REFERENCES

[1] C. Banderier and P. Flajolet. Basic analytic combinatorics of directed lattice paths. *Theoret. Comput. Sci.*, 281(1–2):37–80, 2002. Selected Papers in honour of Maurice Nivat.

[2] B. Beckermann and G. Labahn. A uniform approach for the fast computation of matrix-type pade approximants. *SIAM J. Matrix Anal. Appl.*, 15(3):804–823, 1994.

[3] A. Benoit, F. Chyzak, A. Darrasse, S. Gerhold, M. Mezzarobba, and B. Salvy. The Dynamic Dictionary of Mathematical Functions (DDMF). In K. Fukuda, J. v. d. Hoeven, M. Joswig, and N. Takayama, editors, *Mathematical Software – ICMS 2010*, pages 35–41, Berlin, Heidelberg, 2010. Springer.

[4] E. Berlekamp. Nonbinary BCH decoding. *IEEE Trans. Inform. Theory*, 14(2):242–242, 1968.

[5] J. Berthomieu, B. Boyer, and J.-Ch. Faugère. Linear Algebra for Computing Gröbner Bases of Linear Recursive Multidimensional Sequences. In *Proc. of the 40th ISSAC*, pages 61–68, Bath, UK, 2015.

[6] J. Berthomieu, B. Boyer, and J.-Ch. Faugère. Linear Algebra for Computing Gröbner Bases of Linear Recursive Multidimensional Sequences. Extended version, preprint available at https://hal.inria.fr/hal-01253934, Dec. 2015.

[7] A. Bostan, M. Bousquet-Mélou, M. Kauers, and S. Melczer. On 3-dimensional lattice walks confined to the positive octant. To appear in Annals of Combinatorics, 2014.

[8] A. Bostan, F. Chyzak, M. van Hoeij, and L. Pech. Explicit formula for the generating series of diagonal 3D rook paths. *Séminaire Lotharingien de Combinatoire*, B66a, 2011.

[9] A. Bostan, C.-P. Jeannerod, and É. Schost. Solving Toeplitz- and Vandermonde-like Linear Systems with Large Displacement Rank. In C. W. Brown, editor, *Proc. of the 32nd ISSAC*, pages 33–40. ACM Press, 2007.

[10] A. Bostan, K. Raschel, and B. Salvy. Non-D-finite excursions in the quarter plane. *J. Combin. Theory Ser. A*, 121:45–63, 2014.

[11] M. Bousquet-Mélou and M. Mishna. Walks with small steps in the quarter plane. In *Algorithmic probability and combinatorics*, volume 520 of *Contemp. Math.*, pages 1–39. Amer. Math. Soc., Providence, RI, 2010.

[12] M. Bousquet-Mélou and M. Petkovšek. Walks confined in a quadrant are not always d-finite. *Theoret. Comput. Sci.*, 307(2):257–276, 2003. Random Generation of Combinatorial Objects and Bijective Combinatorics.

[13] F. Chyzak. *The ABC of Creative Telescoping — Algorithms, Bounds, Complexity*. Accreditation to supervise research, École polytechnique X, 2014.

[14] J.-Ch. Faugère. A new efficient algorithm for computing Gröbner bases (F4). *J. Pure Appl. Algebra*, 139(1–3):61–88, 1999.

[15] J.-Ch. Faugère. FGb: A Library for Computing Gröbner Bases. In K. Fukuda, J. v. d. Hoeven, M. Joswig, and N. Takayama, editors, *Mathematical Software - ICMS 2010*, pages 84–87, Berlin, Heidelberg, 2010. Springer.

[16] J.-Ch. Faugère, P. Gianni, D. Lazard, and T. Mora. Efficient Computation of Zero-dimensional Gröbner Bases by Change of Ordering. *J. Symbolic Comput.*, 16(4):329–344, 1993.

[17] P. Fitzpatrick and G. Norton. Finding a basis for the characteristic ideal of an n-dimensional linear recurring sequence. *Information Theory, IEEE Transactions on*, 36(6):1480–1487, 1990.

[18] V. Levandovskyy. *Non-commutative Computer Algebra for polynomial algebras: Gröbner bases, applications and implementation.* PhD thesis, Technische Universität Kaiserslautern, 2005.

[19] L. Lipshitz. D-finite power series. *Journal of Algebra*, 122(2):353 – 373, 1989.

[20] J. L. Massey. Shift-register synthesis and BCH decoding. *IEEE Trans. Inform. Theory*, IT-15:122–127, 1969.

[21] A. Quadrat and D. Robertz. A constructive study of the module structure of rings of partial differential operators. *Acta Applicandae Mathematicae*, 133(1):187–234, 2014.

[22] I. Z. Ruzsa. Generalized arithmetical progressions and sumsets. *Acta Math. Hungar.*, 65(4):379–388, 1994.

[23] K. Saints and C. Heegard. Algebraic-geometric codes and multi-dimensional cyclic codes: Theory and algorithms for decoding using Gröbner bases. *IEEE Trans. Inform. Theory*, 41(6):1733–1751, 1995.

[24] S. Sakata. Finding a minimal set of linear recurring relations capable of generating a given finite two-dimensional array. *J. Symbolic Comput.*, 5(3):321–337, 1988.

[25] S. Sakata. Extension of the Berlekamp-Massey algorithm to N Dimensions. *Inform. and Comput.*, 84(2):207–239, 1990.

[26] S. Sakata. The BMS algorithm. In M. Sala, T. Mora, L. Perret, S. Sakata, and C. Traverso, editors, *Gröbner Bases, Coding, and Cryptography*, pages 143–163. Springer Berlin, 2009.

[27] B. Salvy. D-finiteness: Algorithms and applications. In *Proc. of the 30th ISSAC*, pages 2–3, New York, NY, USA, 2005. ACM.

[28] R. Stanley. Differentiably finite power series. *European J. Combin.*, 1(2):175–188, 1980.

[29] D. Zeilberger. A holonomic systems approach to special functions identities. *J. Comput. Appl. Math.*, 32(3):321–368, 1990.

Determinantal Sets, Singularities and Application to Optimal Control in Medical Imagery

Bernard Bonnard[be]
Bernard.Bonnard@u-bourgogne.fr

Jean-Charles Faugère[dac]
Jean-Charles.Faugere@inria.fr

Alain Jacquemard[dbac]
Alain.Jacquemard@u-bourgogne.fr

Mohab Safey El Din[acd]
Mohab.Safey@lip6.fr

Thibaut Verron[acd]
Thibaut.Verron@lip6.fr

[a]Sorbonne Universités, UPMC Univ Paris 06, UMR 7606, LIP6, F-75005, Paris, France
[b]Institut de Mathématiques de Bourgogne, UMR CNRS 5584, Dijon F-21078, France
[c]CNRS, UMR 7606, LIP6, F-75005, Paris, France
[d]Inria, Paris Center, PolSys Project
[e]Inria, Sophia Antipolis, McTao Project

ABSTRACT

Control theory has recently been involved in the field of nuclear magnetic resonance imagery. The goal is to control the magnetic field optimally in order to improve the contrast between two biological matters on the pictures.

Geometric optimal control leads us here to analyze meromorphic vector fields depending upon physical parameters, and having their singularities defined by a determinantal variety. The involved matrix has polynomial entries with respect to both the state variables and the parameters. Taking into account the physical constraints of the problem, one needs to classify, with respect to the parameters, the number of real singularities lying in some prescribed semi-algebraic set.

We develop a dedicated algorithm for real root classification of the singularities of the rank defects of a polynomial matrix, cut with a given semi-algebraic set. The algorithm works under some genericity assumptions which are easy to check. These assumptions are not so restrictive and are satisfied in the aforementioned application. As more general strategies for real root classification do, our algorithm needs to compute the critical loci of some maps, intersections with the boundary of the semi-algebraic domain, etc. In order to compute these objects, the determinantal structure is exploited through a stratification by the rank of the polynomial matrix. This speeds up the computations by a factor 100. Furthermore, our implementation is able to solve the application in medical imagery, which was out of reach of more general algorithms for real root classification. For instance, computational results show that the contrast problem where one of the matters is water is partitioned into three distinct classes.

Keywords

Polynomial system solving; Real geometry; Applications

ISSAC '16, July 19-22, 2016, Waterloo, ON, Canada

DOI: http://dx.doi.org/10.1145/2930889.2930916

1. INTRODUCTION

Motivations and problem description. Nuclear Magnetic Resonance (NMR) is a powerful tool in medical imagery. In order to distinguish two biological matters on a picture, it is required to optimize the contrast between the two matters. Because of its importance in medical sciences, this contrast imaging problem has received a lot of attention. The pioneering work of [3] has established geometric optimal control techniques as a major tool for designing optimal control strategies for the problem of improving the contrast.

These strategies depend on the biological matters under study. In NMR imagery the main physical parameters involved are the longitudinal and transversal relaxation times of each matter. This approach is formalized in [2]. It requires us to solve the following real root classification problem.

Consider a $k \times k$ matrix M whose coefficients are polynomials in $\mathbb{Q}[X_1, \ldots, X_n, G_1, \ldots, G_t]$, and assume that $n = (k-r+1)^2$ with $r \in \{1, \ldots, k-1\}$. Let $\pi : \mathbb{C}^n \times \mathbb{C}^t \to \mathbb{C}^t$ be the canonical projection. Let $V_r \subset \mathbb{C}^n \times \mathbb{C}^t$ be the set of points at which M has rank r, and let V be the union of the singular locus of V_r and of the critical points of π restricted to V_r. Generically, this variety has dimension $n+t-(k-r+1)^2 = t$. Also consider a semi-algebraic set B in $\mathbb{R}^n \times \mathbb{R}^t$. Assume that B has non-empty interior and that there exists a Zariski-open set $\mathcal{O} \subset \mathbb{C}^t$ such that $V \cap \pi^{-1}(\mathbf{g})$ is a non-empty finite set for $\mathbf{g} \in \mathcal{O}$. Further assume that the projection π restricted to $V \cap B$ is proper ([10, Def. 2.10.1]). We aim at describing connected open sets $C_1, \ldots, C_\ell \subset \mathbb{R}^t$ such that $\bigcup_{i=1}^{\ell} C_i$ is dense in $\mathbb{R}^t$ (for the Euclidean topology) and the cardinality of $V \cap \pi^{-1}(\mathbf{g})$ inside $B \cap \pi^{-1}(\mathbf{g})$ is invariant when $\mathbf{g}$ ranges over C_i.

For our application, the size of the matrix is 4, and the target rank is $k-1 = 3$. The number of variables and parameters are $n = 4$ and $t = 4$ for the general case. Since the system is homogeneous in the parameters, we may set one of the parameters to 1, reducing the problem to $t = 3$. An important particular case is when one of the matters is water; then the corresponding relaxation times are 1, and the number of parameters is $t = 2$.

Such a determinantal structure is general enough to design dedicated algorithms. We also mention that the optimal control problems in [6] lead to algebraic classification problems with similar structures.

State-of-the-art. The modeling through an optimal control problem is introduced in [2]. The so-called Bloch modeling and saturation method for tackling this problem is developed therein.

In [2], four experimental important cases are studied (all parameters of the classification problem are fixed). Among other properties, it has been observed there that the number of singularities is constant when water is involved. This led to the following questions:

1. Is this number of singularities preserved for any choice of a second matter, the first one being water?
2. If not, how many different classes of pairs of matters can we distinguish through the analysis of those singularities?

Answering these questions leads to the real root classification problem described above. Symbolic computation techniques are good candidates to solve them.

Properties of Cylindrical Algebraic Decomposition (CAD) adapted to a given polynomial family allow to solve real root classification problems. Hence the CAD algorithm [7] can be used in our context. However, the complexity of computing a CAD is doubly exponential in the number of variables ([4, 9]); its implementations are usually limited to non-trivial problems involving 4 variables and cannot tackle our application.

The complexity of computing a CAD can be much improved when taking into account equational constraints (see e.g. [22]). In the context of real root classification problems, this leads us to take advantage of the presence of equations to compute closed sets in the parameter space ($\mathbb{R}^t$ using our notation) containing the boundaries of the regions $C_1, \ldots, C_\ell$, hence substituting the recursive (doubly exponential) projection steps of CAD with more involved projection techniques. In the past ten years, several works have focused on this problem [20, 26] using various computer algebra tools such as Gröbner bases, regular chains, etc. We also mention [24] which uses evaluation/interpolation techniques to compute those closed sets in the parameters space.

While the implementation of [26] is able to solve our classification problem for the case of water, none of the implementations were able to classify the singular locus of V in the general case (the number of parameters is 3).

Our strategy is not as general as the ones in [26] or [20]. It exploits properties of sets defined by minors of matrices with polynomial entries. Such structures have been used for computing sample points in each connected component of the real trace of determinantal varieties [16, 17, 18] or for solving linear matrix inequalities [15]. These works are based on dedicated strategies for computing critical loci of some projections restricted to determinantal varieties. Such computations are naturally related to real root classification problems and real quantifier elimination (see e.g. [19]). Finally, our computations rely on Gröbner bases. Several works have shown some connection between Gröbner bases and determinantal ideals [14] and critical point computation [13, 25].

Main results. Our main results are twofold:

- an algorithm solving the special real root classification problem described above and which exploits the determinantal structure of the input data arising in contrast imaging problems;
- its successful use for solving the challenging application to the contrast problem in the general case;
- answers to the questions raised by the experimental data involving water: the answer to question 1. is *no*, and the answer to question 2. is that there are 3 classes of second matters that we can separate, depending on whether there are 1, 2 or 3 singularities.

We start by describing our algorithmic contribution. Recall that we are given a matrix, denoted by M, with polynomial entries. As in [15, 16, 17, 18], it is based on splitting computations according to the rank of M.

More precisely, in order to solve our real root classification problem, we need to identify where the number of real solutions inside B of the determinantal system describing V changes depending on the values of the parameters. The real root classification problem we want to solve involves inequalities defining a semi-algebraic set with non-empty interior. In this context, we use standard tools from real geometry, such as Thom's first isotopy lemma, which reduce our classification problem to computing the singular points of V, the critical points of the projection of the parameter space restricted to V, and the intersection of V with the boundary of the semi-algebraic set B.

This computation may be difficult because generically, the variety V_r has singularities corresponding to points where $\mathrm{rank}(M) < r$: this is proved using Bertini's theorem and [5, Prop. 1.1], as in [16, Prop. 2]). Hence, observe that the variety V is naturally split according to the rank of M. This is the very basic idea on which our algorithm relies: we compute critical loci of the projection on the parameter space restricted to the variety V by distinguishing those points at which M has rank less than r from those at which M has rank exactly r. Incidentally, it raises the question of how these higher rank deficiencies should be interpreted from the application viewpoint. To the best of our knowledge, this question was never raised in the optimal control community.

Our algorithms need to compute projection of algebraic sets, which is done using elimination algorithms such as Gröbner bases or triangular sets for example. We have performed experiments for both these tools, using the package FGb [12] in Maple and an implementation of F5 [11] for Gröbner bases, and using the package RegularChains [21] in Maple for triangular sets.

Regarding the contrast imaging problem, we illustrate the behaviour of our algorithm in the case of water, giving the whole classification. Using Gröbner bases to perform the eliminations, the computation takes 10 s on an 2 GHz Intel Xeon CPU. The RealRootClassification command of the Maple RegularChain library needs 1600 s to find this classification.

We also ran our algorithm on the general case. While none of the available implementation is able to tackle this classification problem directly, ours can find the polynomials separating the open sets C_i within 4 h using FGb, or 2 min using F5, and the projection step of the CAD can be done in 4 h. We see similar speed-ups when using triangular sets to perform the elimination.

This illustrates how our dedicated algorithms take advantage of the special structure of the problem, to achieve speed-ups when compared with more general techniques.

Conclusion. We propose an algorithmic strategy refining general roots classification strategies for the case of singularities of a determinantal variety, under genericity hypotheses. We give an overview of the results for the application at the end of the paper[1]. We were able to give a full classification in the case of water, answering the questions raised by the experiments. For the general case, the separating polynomials were found, it remains to perform the analysis of the subdivisions in order to obtain the full classification. This work also raised questions concerning the interpretation of higher rank deficiencies from the viewpoint of control theory.

Structure of the paper. In Section 2, we present the mathematical background around NMR imagery and the contrast problem. Sec-

[1]The full results and the source code which produced them are available at http://mercurey.gforge.inria.fr/

tion 3 deals with the dedicated classification algorithm. Finally, in Section 4, we report on experimental results obtained when solving the application to the contrast imaging problem.

We acknowledge the support from the ANR-DFG research program Explosys (Grant No.ANR-14-CE35-0013-01; GL203/9-1). Mohab Safey El Din is member of and supported by Institut Universitaire de France.

2. MODELING THE DYNAMICS

The model we describe below has been introduced in [3] in order to apply techniques from geometric optimal control theory to the control of the spin dynamics by NMR. Up to some normalization, each spin $1/2$ particle is governed by the Bloch equation

$$\begin{cases} \dot{x} &= -\Gamma x + u_y z \\ \dot{y} &= -\Gamma y - u_x z \\ \dot{z} &= \gamma(1-z) + u_x y - u_y x. \end{cases}$$

where the *state variable* $q = (x, y, z)$ represents the magnetization vector which must lie in the *Bloch ball* defined by $|q| \leq 1$, and the *parameters* (Γ, γ) are related to the physical relaxation times. The parameters must also satisfy $2\Gamma \geq \gamma > 0$. The *control* $u = (u_x, u_y)$ represents the magnetic field whose magnitude is bounded by a maximum value μ.

In the context of the contrast imaging problem, this leads to the simultaneous control of two non-interacting spins with different relaxation time parameters. The *contrast by saturation method* consists in bringing the magnetization vector of the first spin toward the center of the Bloch ball while maximizing the modulus of the magnetization vector of the other matter. The matter with a zero magnetization is black on the picture, while the other matter with a maximum modulus of the magnetization vector is bright.

Using the symmetry of revolution [2] which allows to eliminate one state variable for each matter, we obtain the system

$$\begin{cases} \dot{y_1} &= -\Gamma_1 y_1 - u_x z_1 \\ \dot{z_1} &= \gamma_1 (1-z_1) + u_x y_1 \\ \dot{y_2} &= -\Gamma_2 y_2 - u_x z_2 \\ \dot{z_2} &= \gamma_2 (1-z_2) + u_x y_2, \end{cases} \qquad |u| \leq \mu \tag{1}$$

and the optimal control problem is: starting from the equilibrium point $N = ((0,1),(0,1))$, saturate the first spin, that is $q_1(T) = 0$, where T is the transfer time while maximizing $|q_2(T)|^2$, where $|q_2(T)|$ represents the final contrast. It is a standard Mayer problem in optimal control, studied in [3] through the analysis of the Hamiltonian dynamics given by the Pontryagin Maximum Principle [23]. We summarize this analysis below.

Writing (1) as $\dot{q} = F(q) + uG(q)$, $\quad |u| \leq \mu$, the optimality conditions associated with the Maximum Principle lead us to construct the optimal solution as a concatenation of *bang-arcs* where the control is $u = \pm\mu$, and *singular arcs* solutions of $X_e = F + u_s G$ where the control u_s is the rational fraction $-D'/D$ with

$$D = \det(F, G, [G,F], [[G,F],G])$$
$$D' = \det(F, G, [G,F], [[G,F],F]),$$

where $[\ ,\ ]$ denotes the Lie bracket of vector fields. Explicitly, with $d_i = \gamma_i - \Gamma_i$ ($i \in \{1,2\}$),

$$D = \det \begin{bmatrix} -\Gamma_1 y_1 & -z_1 - 1 & d_1 z_1 - \Gamma_1 & 2d_1 y_1 \\ -\gamma_1 z_1 & y_1 & d_1 y_1 & -2d_1 z_1 + \Gamma_1 - d_1 \\ -\Gamma_2 y_2 & -z_2 - 1 & d_2 z_2 - \Gamma_2 & 2d_2 y_2 \\ -\gamma_2 z_2 & y_2 & d_2 y_2 & -2d_2 z_2 + \Gamma_2 - d_2 \end{bmatrix}.$$

The localization of the singularities of $\{D = 0\}$ inside the Bloch ball is important to understand the geometry of the hypersurface, as well as the dynamics of the vector field X_e which is closely linked to the presence of such singularities. Indeed, generically when approaching the surface $D = 0$ along a singular arc, the control $u = -D'/D$ is such that $|u| > \mu$. Hence the control policy switches from singular to bang. Therefore this surface is related to the complexity of the optimal law, as a concatenation of singular and bang arcs. See [3] for numerical simulations related to this phenomenon.

3. ALGORITHM

3.1 Classification strategy

We consider the polynomial algebra $\mathbb{Q}[\mathbf{X}, \mathbf{G}]$ with variables $\mathbf{X} = (X_1, \ldots, X_n)$ and parameters $\mathbf{G} = (G_1, \ldots, G_t)$. Let F and H be families of polynomials in $\mathbb{Q}[\mathbf{X}, \mathbf{G}]$. Let $V_{\mathbb{R}} = V_{\mathbb{R}}(F)$, $V = V_{\mathbb{C}}(F)$ be respectively the set of zeroes of F in $\mathbb{R}^{n+t}$ and in $\mathbb{C}^{n+t}$. Let B be the closed semi-algebraic set defined by H:

$$B = \{(\mathbf{x}, \mathbf{g}) \in \mathbb{R}^{n+t} \mid \forall h \in H, h(\mathbf{x}, \mathbf{g}) \leq 0\},$$

and let $B_0 = \bigcup_{h \in H} V_{\mathbb{C}}(h)$. Let $\pi : \mathbb{C}^{n+t} \to \mathbb{C}^t$ be the projection onto the affine space with coordinates $\mathbf{G}$. Let $\mathrm{sing}(V)$ be the singular locus of V, $\mathrm{crit}(\pi, V)$ be the set of critical points of π restricted to V, and $K(\pi, V) = \pi(\mathrm{sing}(V) \cup \mathrm{crit}(\pi, V)) \cap \mathbb{R}^t$.

Given a subset A of a real or complex affine space, $\overline{A}$ and ∂A are used to denote the closure and the boundary of A for the Euclidean topology respectively.

Assume that the following hypotheses are satisfied:

$\mathcal{H}1$ There exists a nonempty Zariski-open subset $\mathcal{O}_1$ of $\mathbb{C}^t$ such that for all $\mathbf{g} \in \mathcal{O}_1$, the fiber $V \cap \pi^{-1}(\mathbf{g})$ is a nonempty finite subset of $\mathbb{C}^{n+t}$;

$\mathcal{H}2$ The restriction of the projection π to B is proper ([10, Def. 2.10.1]);

$\mathcal{H}3$ The intersection $V \cap B_0$ has dimension at most $t-1$ in $\mathbb{C}^{n+t}$;

$\mathcal{H}4$ The variety V is equidimensional of dimension t.

We want to find a non-zero polynomial $P \in \mathbb{Q}[\mathbf{G}]$ such that, on each connected component U of $\mathbb{R}^t \setminus V_{\mathbb{R}}(P)$, for $\mathbf{g} \in U$, the cardinality of $V \cap B \cap \pi^{-1}(\mathbf{g})$ does not depend on $\mathbf{g}$.

In Lemma 1, we describe a well-known strategy for computing these objects (see for example [20, 26]).

LEMMA 1. *Let F and H be polynomial systems satisfying hypotheses $\mathcal{H}1$, $\mathcal{H}2$, $\mathcal{H}3$ and $\mathcal{H}4$. Let $C_B = \pi(V \cap B_0)$, U a non-empty connected open subset of $\mathbb{R}^t$ which does not meet $C_B \cup K(\pi, V)$, and $\mathbf{g} \in U$. Then $V \cap \pi^{-1}(\mathbf{g})$ is finite, and $\forall \mathbf{g}' \in U$, $\#(V \cap \pi^{-1}(\mathbf{g}')) = \#(V \cap \pi^{-1}(\mathbf{g}))$.*

PROOF. We will construct a Whitney stratification of $V \cap B$ ([1, Def. 9.7.1]) with certain properties. First note that since V is t-equidimensional by $\mathcal{H}4$, V has real dimension at most t ([1, Prop. 2.8.2]). Let $\mathcal{S}_{=t}$ be the intersection of the points where $V_{\mathbb{R}}$ has local dimension t and of the interior of B. There exists a Whitney stratification $(\mathcal{S}_i)$ of the semi-algebraic set $V \cap B$ such that $\mathcal{S}_{=t}$ is the union of strata of dimension t ([1, Th. 9.7.11]). Let $\mathcal{S}_{<t}$ be the union of the other strata, they all have real dimension less than t. By construction, this is a semi-algebraic set which is the union of $(V \cap \partial B) \subset (V \cap B_0)$ and of the singular locus of $V \cap B$, and it has dimension less than t (by $\mathcal{H}3$ for $V \cap B_0$). Its image through π has dimension less than t, and so it has codimension at least 1.

Now consider $\mathcal{S}_{=t}$. By Hyp. $\mathcal{H}1$, for any $\mathbf{g} \in \mathcal{O}_1$, $\pi^{-1}(g) \cap V$ is non-empty, hence $\pi(V)$ contains the non-empty Zariski-open set $\mathcal{O}_1 \subset \mathbb{C}^t$. The intersection $\mathcal{O}_1 \cap \mathbb{R}^t$ is a non-empty Zariski-open set of $\mathbb{R}^t$, contained in $\pi(V)$, hence $\pi(V) \cap \mathbb{R}^t$ has real dimension t. Let U_0 be its interior. The subset $\mathcal{S}_{=t} \cap \pi^{-1}(U_0)$ is a locally closed semi-algebraic set. If it is empty, then there is nothing to prove. Otherwise, by construction it has dimension t; and the projection π restricted to this subspace is proper, by Hyp. $\mathcal{H}2$. Thom's isotopy lemma ([8]) states that for any nonempty connected open set U of $\mathbb{R}^t$ not meeting $K(\pi,V)$, and for any $\mathbf{g} \in U$, there exists a semi-algebraic diffeomorphism $h = (h_0, \pi) : V \cap B \cap \pi^{-1}(U) \xrightarrow{\sim} \pi^{-1}(\mathbf{g}) \times U$. By Hyp. $\mathcal{H}1$, if U is nonempty, $\pi^{-1}(\mathbf{g})$ is finite, and the cardinality of the fibers is constant on U. $\square$

So computing the wanted decomposition of the parameter space is equivalent to computing a polynomial $P \in \mathbb{Q}[\mathbf{G}]$ such that $V(P)$ covers $\pi(V \cap B_0)$ and $K(\pi,V)$.

3.2 The determinantal problem

Let k be an integer greater than 1, $r_0 \in \{1,\dots,k-1\}$, and $n = (k-r_0+1)^2$. Let $t \in \mathbb{N}$, and let $M(\mathbf{X},\mathbf{G})$ be a $k \times k$ matrix with polynomial entries in n variables $\mathbf{X} = (X_1,\dots,X_n)$ and t parameters $\mathbf{G} = (G_1,\dots,G_t)$. As before, let $\pi : \mathbb{C}^{n+t} \to \mathbb{C}^t$ be the projection onto the affine space with coordinates $\mathbf{G}$.

Let $\{h(\mathbf{X},\mathbf{G}) \le 0 \mid h \in H\}$ be a system of inequalities, with $H \subset \mathbb{Q}[\mathbf{X},\mathbf{G}]$. Let $V_{-1} = \emptyset$ by convention, and for any $r \in \{0,\dots,k\}$, we define the variety

$$V_r = \{(\mathbf{x},\mathbf{g}) \in \mathbb{C}^{n+t} \mid \mathrm{rank}(M(\mathbf{x},\mathbf{g})) \le r\}$$

and the constructible set $V_{=r} = V_r \setminus V_{r-1}$, that is the set of points at which the matrix M has rank exactly r.

Let V be the union of the singular locus of V_{r_0} and of the set of critical points of π restricted to V_{r_0}. We want to classify the cardinality of the real fibers by π of the semi-algebraic set $V \cap \{(\mathbf{x},\mathbf{g}) \mid \forall h \in H, h(\mathbf{x},\mathbf{g}) \le 0\}$.

Assume that V and H satisfy hypotheses $\mathcal{H}1$, $\mathcal{H}2$, $\mathcal{H}3$ and $\mathcal{H}4$. Further assume that:

- $\mathcal{H}5$ There exists a non-empty Zariski-open subset $\mathcal{O}_2 \subset \mathbb{C}^t$ such that $V \cap \pi^{-1}(\mathcal{O}_2) = V_{r_0-1} \cap \pi^{-1}(\mathcal{O}_2)$;
- $\mathcal{H}6$ For any $r \in \{0,\dots,k-1\}$, the ideal defined by the $(r+1)$-minors of M is radical;
- $\mathcal{H}7$ For any $r \in \{0,\dots,k-1\}$, the variety V_r is equidimensional with dimension $n+t-(k-r+1)^2$.

These properties are generic ([16, Prop. 2]).

LEMMA 2. *Assuming Hyp. $\mathcal{H}6$, for any $r \in \{1,\dots,k\}$, $V_{r-1} \subset \mathrm{sing}(V_r)$.*

PROOF. We will prove the following stronger statement: let $(\mathbf{x},\mathbf{g}) \in V_{r-1}$, then all partial derivatives of all $(r+1)$-minors of M vanish at $(\mathbf{x},\mathbf{g})$. This will prove that the Jacobian of V_r at $(\mathbf{x},\mathbf{g})$ is the zero matrix , and in particular has rank 0. By Hyp. $\mathcal{H}6$ the ideal of all $(r+1)$-minors of M is radical, so we can use the Jacobian criterion to characterize $\mathrm{sing}(V)$, so $(\mathbf{x},\mathbf{g}) \in \mathrm{sing}(V_r)$.

Let $(\mathbf{x},\mathbf{g}) \in V_{r-1}$. For any $(r+1)\times(r+1)$-submatrix of M, the result we want to prove depends only on the coefficients of the submatrix. So *w.l.o.g.*, we may assume that $r = k-1$. Let $(\mathbf{x},\mathbf{g}) \in V_{k-2}$, this means that all $(k-1)$-minors of M vanish at $(\mathbf{x},\mathbf{g})$. Consider a matrix of polynomial indeterminates $\mathbf{U}$:

$$\tilde{M} = \begin{bmatrix} U_{1,1} & \dots & U_{1,k} \\ \vdots & & \vdots \\ U_{k,1} & \dots & U_{k,k} \end{bmatrix}$$

and let $\tilde{D}$ be its determinant. Then for any $i,j \in \{1,\dots,k\}$, $\frac{\partial \tilde{D}}{\partial U_{i,j}} = (-1)^{i+j} \cdot \tilde{\mathcal{M}}_{i,j}(\mathbf{U})$ where $\tilde{\mathcal{M}}_{i,j}$ is the $(k-1)$-minor of $\tilde{M}$ obtained by removing row i and column j.

For any $i,j \in \{1,\dots,k\}$, let $m_{i,j}$ (*resp.* $\mathcal{M}_{i,j}$) be the coefficient at row i and column j of the matrix M (*resp.* the minor obtained by removing row i and column j from M). By the derivation chain rule, for any $v \in \{X_1,\dots,X_n,G_1,\dots,G_t\}$, $\frac{\partial D}{\partial v} = \sum_{i,j=1}^{k} (-1)^{i+j} \frac{\partial m_{i,j}}{\partial v} \cdot \tilde{\mathcal{M}}_{i,j}(\mathbf{m})$, which equals $\sum_{i,j=1}^{k} (-1)^{i+j} \frac{\partial m_{i,j}}{\partial v} \cdot \mathcal{M}_{i,j}(\mathbf{X})$. Since by hypothesis all $(k-1)$ minors of M vanish at $(\mathbf{x},\mathbf{g})$, all partial derivatives $\frac{\partial D}{\partial v}$ vanish at $(\mathbf{x},\mathbf{g})$. $\square$

In the following subsections, we will describe two algorithms DeterminantCritVals and DeterminantBoundary, which, given such a matrix M, a target rank r_0 and inequalities H, compute a polynomial whose zeroes cover $K(\pi,V)$, and a polynomial whose zeroes cover $\pi(V \cap B_0)$ respectively. By Lemma 1, the zeroes of the product of these polynomials will subdivide the parameter space into connected components where the cardinality of real fibers is constant. These algorithms are probabilistic, because they will rely on the choice of generic linear forms to ensure linear independence. However, the algorithms could be made deterministic by testing that these linear forms are generic enough for our purpose, and repeating the random draw otherwise.

The algorithms will also need to compute the projection of algebraic sets onto coordinate subspaces. For this purpose, we assume that we are given a routine Elimination, which, given a system of polynomials
$F \subset \mathbb{Q}[V_1,\dots,V_N]$ and a set of variables $\mathbf{V}' \subset \{V_1,\dots,V_N\}$, computes a system of generators of $\langle F \rangle \cap \mathbb{Q}[\mathbf{V}']$. Such a routine can be implemented using Gröbner bases or regular chains, for example.

3.3 Incidence varieties

We decompose the problem depending on the rank of the matrix. The classical technique that we use to model properties on the rank relies on incidence varieties.

DEFINITION 3. *Let $r \in \{0,\dots,k-1\}$. The* incidence variety *of* rank r *associated with M is the variety $\mathcal{V}_r \subset \mathbb{C}^{n+t} \times (\mathbb{P}^{k-1}(\mathbb{C}))^{k-r}$ defined by:*

$$M \cdot \begin{bmatrix} y_{1,1} & \dots & y_{1,k-r} \\ \vdots & & \vdots \\ y_{k,1} & \dots & y_{k,k-r} \end{bmatrix} = \begin{bmatrix} 0 & \dots & 0 \\ \vdots & & \vdots \\ 0 & \dots & 0 \end{bmatrix} \quad (2)$$

with the additional condition that the matrix $(y_{i,j})$ has rank $k-r$.

The projection of $\mathcal{V}_r$ onto the affine space with coordinates $(\mathbf{X},\mathbf{G})$ is V_r. Let $(u_{1,1},\dots,u_{k-r,k}) \in \mathbb{C}^{k(k-r)}$, we define the variety $\mathcal{V}'_{r,\mathbf{u}}$ as the intersection of $\mathcal{V}_r$ and the complex solutions of

$$\begin{bmatrix} u_{1,1} & \dots & u_{1,k} \\ \vdots & & \vdots \\ u_{k-r,1} & \dots & u_{k-r,k} \end{bmatrix} \cdot \begin{bmatrix} y_{1,1} & \dots & y_{1,k-r} \\ \vdots & & \vdots \\ y_{k,1} & \dots & y_{k,k-r} \end{bmatrix} = \mathrm{Id}_{k-r} \quad (3)$$

In the rest of Section 3, $\mathcal{F}_{r,\mathbf{u}}$ denotes the union of Equations (2) and (3).

LEMMA 4. *For any $r \in \{0,\dots,k-1\}$, the varieties V_r and $\mathcal{V}'_{r,\mathbf{u}}$ are birational ([1, Sec. 3.4]).*

PROOF. We need to define a morphism $f : W \to \mathcal{V}'_{r,\mathbf{u}}$ with W a non-empty Zariski-open subset of V_r, and such that f is inverse to the projection $\mathcal{V}'_{r,\mathbf{u}} \to V_r$ onto the affine space with coordinates $(\mathbf{X},\mathbf{G})$. Let W be the open subset of V_r defined as the non-vanishing locus of the top-left r-minor of M. Consider the block decompositions, where A, $Y_{(1)}$ and $U_{(1)}$ are $r \times r$ matrices:

$$M = \begin{bmatrix} A & B \\ C & D \end{bmatrix} \quad Y = \begin{bmatrix} Y_{(1)} \\ Y_{(2)} \end{bmatrix} \quad U = \begin{bmatrix} U_{(1)} & U_{(2)} \end{bmatrix}$$

Over W, A is invertible, let $\Delta = \det(A)$. Let M/A be the Schur complement of A in M, Equations (2) and (3) can be rewritten

$$\begin{bmatrix} \Delta \mathrm{Id}_r & A^{-1}B \\ 0 & M/A \\ U_{(1)} & U_{(2)} \end{bmatrix} \cdot \begin{bmatrix} Y_{(1)} \\ Y_{(2)} \end{bmatrix} = \begin{bmatrix} 0 \\ 0 \\ \mathrm{Id}_r \end{bmatrix}$$

We may restrict to the open subset of $\mathcal{V}'_{r,\mathbf{u}}$ where $Y_{(2)}$ is invertible, then eliminating $Y_{(1)}$ yields that

$$\begin{cases} Y_{(2)} = (U_{(2)} - U_{(1)}A^{-1}B)^{-1} \\ Y_{(1)} = \frac{-1}{\Delta}A^{-1}BY_{(2)} \end{cases}$$

which defines the wanted morphism $W \to \mathcal{V}'_{r,\mathbf{u}}$. □

PROPOSITION 5. *Let $r_1 = r_0 - 1$. Let $\varphi : \mathcal{V}'_{r_1,\mathbf{u}} \to \mathbb{C}^t$ be the projection onto the affine space with coordinates* $\mathbf{G}$. *Assuming that hypotheses $\mathcal{H}1$ to $\mathcal{H}7$ hold, there exists a Zariski-open subset $\mathcal{U} \subset \mathbb{C}^{k(k-r_1)}$ such that if $\mathbf{u} \in \mathcal{U} \cap \mathbb{Q}^{k(k-r_1)}$, $K(\pi, V_{r_1}) = K(\varphi, \mathcal{V}'_{r_1,\mathbf{u}})$.*

PROOF. Let $P = (\mathbf{x},\mathbf{g},\mathbf{y}) \in \mathcal{V}'_{r_1,\mathbf{u}}$.

If $M(\mathbf{x},\mathbf{g})$ has rank less than r_1, then by Lemma 2, $(\mathbf{x},\mathbf{g}) \in \mathrm{sing}(V_{r_1})$, hence $\mathbf{g} \in K(\pi, V_{r_1})$.

Since $M(\mathbf{x},\mathbf{g})$ has rank less than r_1, its kernel L_1 has dimension at least $k - r_1 + 1$. Equations (3) encode that the vectors $\mathbf{y}_i$ given by the columns of matrix $(y_{i,j})$ generate a r_1-dimensional vector space L_2. So there exists $\mathbf{y}_0 \in L_1 \cap L_2$, and for all $a \in \mathbb{C}$, $(\mathbf{x},\mathbf{g},\mathbf{y}_1 + a\mathbf{y}_0,\mathbf{y}_2)$ belongs to the fiber above $(\mathbf{x},\mathbf{g})$ in $\mathcal{V}_{r_1}$. So this fiber has dimension at least 1, while the generic fiber has dimension 0 by hypothesis $\mathcal{H}1$. So $(\mathbf{x},\mathbf{g})$ is a critical value of the projection of $\mathcal{V}_{r_1}$ onto $\mathbb{R}^{n+t}$, hence $(\mathbf{g}) \in K(\varphi, \mathcal{V}'_{r_1,\mathbf{u}})$.

So we may assume that $M(\mathbf{x},\mathbf{g})$ has rank exactly r_1. There is a $r_1 \times r_1$ submatrix A of $M(\mathbf{x},\mathbf{g})$ which is invertible, without loss of generality we may assume that it is the top-left $r_1 \times r_1$ submatrix. In an open neighborhood of $(\mathbf{x},\mathbf{g})$, $V_{=r_1}$ is described by the vanishing of the entries of M/A, that is the determinants of the $(r_1+1) \times (r_1+1)$ submatrices containing A. The same computations as in the proof of Lemma 4 give the following equations describing $\mathcal{V}'_{r_1,\mathbf{u}}$ in the open neighborhood of $(\mathbf{x},\mathbf{g},\mathbf{y})$ where $\Delta = \det(A)$ does not vanish:

$$\begin{cases} M/A = 0 \\ Y_{(2)} = (U_{(2)} - U_{(1)}A^{-1}B)^{-1} \\ Y_{(1)} = \frac{-1}{\Delta}A^{-1}BY_{(2)} \end{cases} \tag{4}$$

and the truncated Jacobian matrix in $(\mathbf{X},\mathbf{Y})$ of this system can be written

$$\begin{bmatrix} \mathrm{Jac}_{\mathbf{X}}(M/A) & 0 & 0 \\ \star & \mathrm{Id}_{r_1(k-r_1)} & \star \\ \star & 0 & \mathrm{Id}_{r_1(k-r_1)} \end{bmatrix}$$

where $\mathrm{Jac}_{\mathbf{X}}(M/A)$ is the truncated Jacobian matrix in $\mathbf{X}$ of the $(k-r_1)^2$ entries of M/A, which define $V_{r_1} \setminus \{(\mathbf{x},\mathbf{g} \mid \Delta = 0)\}$ in $\mathbb{C}^{n+t}$. By hypothesis $\mathcal{H}6$, the ideal defined by the entries of M/A, which is a subideal of the ideal of all (r_1+1)-minors of M, is radical. Since the Schur complement appears by multiplication with invertible matrices with entries in the localized ring $\mathbb{Q}[\mathbf{X},\mathbf{g}]_\Delta$ (using the same notations as in the proof of Lemma 4):

$$\begin{bmatrix} \mathrm{Id}_{r_1} & 0 \\ -C & \mathrm{Id}_{k-r_1} \end{bmatrix} \cdot \begin{bmatrix} A^{-1} & 0 \\ 0 & \mathrm{Id}_{k-r_1} \end{bmatrix} \cdot M = \begin{bmatrix} \mathrm{Id}_{r_1} & A^{-1}B \\ 0 & M/A \end{bmatrix}.$$

Equations (4) describe the localization of $\langle \mathcal{F}_{r_1,\mathbf{u}} \rangle$ in $\mathbb{Q}[\mathbf{X},\mathbf{g}]_\Delta$, so this ideal is radical as well. So we can use the Jacobian criterion on V_{r_1} near $(\mathbf{x},\mathbf{g})$ and on $\mathcal{V}'_{r_1,\mathbf{u}}$ near $(\mathbf{x},\mathbf{g},\mathbf{y})$. Both Jacobians matrices have the same rank and both varieties have the same local codimension $(k-r_1)^2$ (by Lemma 4 and hypothesis $\mathcal{H}7$), so

$$K(\pi, V_{=r_1}) \cap \varphi(\mathcal{V}'_{r_1,\mathbf{u}}) = K(\varphi, \mathcal{V}'_{r_1,\mathbf{u}}) \cap \pi(V_{=r_1})$$

The image $\varphi(\mathcal{V}'_{r_1,\mathbf{u}}) \cap \pi(V_{=r_1})$ is a Zariski-open subset $\mathcal{O}_\mathbf{u}$ of $\pi(V_{=r_1})$. It remains to prove that if $\mathbf{u}$ is sufficiently generic, then all irreducible components of $K(\pi, V_{=r_1})$ meet this open subset.

Let $\mathcal{C}_1, \ldots, \mathcal{C}_a$ be these irreducible components, and let $(\mathbf{x}_1,\mathbf{g}_1) \in \pi^{-1}(\mathcal{C}_1), \ldots, (\mathbf{x}_a,\mathbf{g}_a) \in \pi^{-1}(\mathcal{C}_a)$. For any $(\mathbf{x},\mathbf{g}) \in V_{=r_1}$, the proof of [16, Prop. 4, Sec. 6] shows that there exists a non-empty Zariski-open subset $\mathcal{U}_{(\mathbf{x},\mathbf{g})} \subset \mathbb{C}^{k(k-r_1)}$ such that if $\mathbf{u} \in \mathcal{U}_{(\mathbf{x},\mathbf{g})} \cap \mathbb{Q}^{k(k-r_1)}$, then $(\mathbf{x},\mathbf{g}) \in \mathcal{O}_\mathbf{u}$; namely, $\mathcal{U}$ is the set of $\mathbf{u}$ such that $\mathrm{rank}\begin{bmatrix} M(\mathbf{x},\mathbf{g}) \\ (u_{i,j}) \end{bmatrix} = k$. Taking the finite intersection of the non-empty Zariski-open subsets $\mathcal{U}_{(\mathbf{x}_i,\mathbf{g}_i)}$ for $i \in \{1,\ldots,a\}$ yields the wanted subset $\mathcal{U}$. □

3.4 Locus of rank exactly r_0

Recall that by $\mathcal{H}5$, $\pi(V \cap V_{=r_0})$ has codimension at least 1, and that we want to compute a polynomial whose zeroes cover $K(\pi,V)$ and $\pi(V \cap B_0)$. So we may multiply the result by the equation of one hypersurface covering $\pi(V \cap V_{=r_0})$, it will naturally cover $\pi(V \cap V_{=r_0}) \cap K(\pi,V)$ and $\pi(V \cap V_{=r_0}) \cap \pi(V \cap B_0)$.

Algorithm RankExactly:

Input $M \subset \mathbb{Q}[\mathbf{X},\mathbf{G}]^{k\times k}$, $r_0 \in \{1,\ldots,k-1\}$

Output $P_1 \in \mathbb{Q}[\mathbf{G}] \setminus \{0\}$ *s.t.* $\pi(V \cap V_{=r_0}) \subset V(P_1)$

Procedure

res ← 1
$F_{V,0} \leftarrow \{(r_0+1)\text{-minors of } M\}$
$J \leftarrow \mathrm{Jac}_{\mathbf{X}}(F_{V,0})$
$F_{V,1} \leftarrow F_{V,0} \cup \{(k-r_0)^2\text{-minors of } J\}$
Pick at random $u_1,\ldots,u_{k(k-r_0)} = \mathbf{u} \in \mathbb{Q}^{k(k-r_0)}$
$F_0 \leftarrow \mathcal{F}_{k-r_0,\mathbf{u}}$
$\{\mathcal{M}_1,\ldots,\mathcal{M}_N\} \leftarrow \{r_0\text{-minors of } M\}$
For i in $\{1,\ldots,N\}$ do
  $F_1 \leftarrow F_0 \cup \mathcal{F}_{V,1} \cup \{\mathcal{M}_1,\ldots,\mathcal{M}_{i-1}, u \cdot \mathcal{M}_i - 1\}$
  $G \leftarrow$ Elimination$(F_1, \{u,\mathbf{X},\mathbf{Y}\})$
  Multiply res by 1 polynomial from G
End for
Return res

3.5 Singularities

Algorithm DeterminantCritVals:

Input $M \subset \mathbb{Q}[\mathbf{X},\mathbf{G}]^{k\times k}$, $r_0 \in \{1,\ldots,k-1\}$

Output $P_c \in \mathbb{Q}[\mathbf{G}] \setminus \{0\}$ *s.t.* $K(\pi,V) \subset V(P_c)$

Procedure

res ← RankExactly(M, r_0)
Pick at random $u_1,\ldots,u_{k(k-r_0+1)} = \mathbf{u} \in \mathbb{Q}^{k(k-r_0+1)}$
$F_0 \leftarrow \mathcal{F}_{r_0-1,\mathbf{u}}$
$J \leftarrow \mathrm{Jac}_{\mathbf{X},\mathbf{Y}}(F_0)$
$F_1 \leftarrow F_0 \cup \{k(k-r_0+1) + (k-r_0+1)^2\text{-minors of } J\}$
$G \leftarrow$ Elimination$(F_1, \{\mathbf{X},\mathbf{Y}\})$
Multiply res by 1 polynomial from G
Return res

PROPOSITION 6. *Algorithm* DeterminantCritVals *is correct.*

PROOF. By definition, $V \subset V_{r_0}$. Using the decomposition $V_{r_0} = V_{=r_0} \cup V_{r_0-1}$, we decompose the variety V as $V = (V \cap V_{=r_0}) \cup (V \cap V_{r_0-1})$.

The subspace $\pi(V \cap V_{=r_0})$ is covered by the output of RankExactly, so we may restrict to $V \cap V_{r_0-1}$, which is the whole variety V_{r_0-1} by Lemma 2. Recall that by hypothesis $\mathcal{H}7$, V_{r_0-1} is t-equidimensional.

By Prop. 5, in order to compute $K(\pi, V_{r_0-1})$, we can compute polynomials whose zeroes cover $K(\varphi, \mathcal{V}'_{r_0-1,\mathbf{u}})$ with $\mathbf{u}$ sufficiently generic instead.

By hypotheses $\mathcal{H}6$, $\mathcal{H}7$ and the proof of Prop. 5, $\mathcal{V}'_{r_0-1,\mathbf{u}}$ is t-equidimensional and $\mathcal{F}_{r_0-1,\mathbf{u}}$ is a set of generators of its ideal, so we can use the Jacobian criterion to compute equations defining $K(\varphi, \mathcal{V}'_{r_0-1,\mathbf{u}})$. □

3.6 Boundary

Algorithm DeterminantBoundary:

Input

- $M \subset \mathbb{Q}[\mathbf{X},\mathbf{G}]^{k\times k}$

- $r_0 \in \{1,\dots,k-1\}$
- $H \subset \mathbb{Q}[\mathbf{X},\mathbf{G}]$ (set of constraints on the variables)

Output $P_b \in \mathbb{Q}[\mathbf{G}] \setminus \{0\}$ *s.t.* $\pi(V \cap B_0) \subset V(P_b)$

Procedure

1. res $\leftarrow$ RankExactly(M, r_0)
2. Pick at random $u_1,\dots,u_{k(k-r_0+1)} = \mathbf{u} \in \mathbb{Q}^{k(k-r_0+1)}$
3. $F_0 \leftarrow \mathcal{F}_{r_0-1,\mathbf{u}}$
4. For h in H do
5. $F_1 \leftarrow F_0 \cup \{h\}$
6. $G \leftarrow$ Elimination$(F, \{\mathbf{X},\mathbf{Y}\})$
7.   Multiply res by 1 polynomial from G
8. End for
9. Return res

PROPOSITION 7. *Algorithm* DeterminantBoundary *is correct.*

PROOF. As in Section 3.5, we write: $V = (V \cap V_{=r_0}) \cup (V \cap V_{r_0-1})$. Since $B_0 = \bigcup_{h\in H} V(h)$, the intersection $V \cap \partial B$ is contained in the union of the varieties $V(\langle F\rangle + \langle h\rangle)$ for h ranging over H, and the equation of the projections can be obtained with polynomial elimination. □

REMARK 8. *For the real root classification problem, the subdivision is given by the product of the outputs of* DeterminantCritVals *and* DeterminantBoundary. *In order to avoid repeating computations, we may skip the call to* RankExactly *in either subroutine (but not both), and initialize* res *to* 1 *instead.*

4. THE CONTRAST PROBLEM

4.1 The case of water

With the notations of Section 2, the variety V is the complex algebraic variety defined by

$$D = \frac{\partial D}{\partial y_1} = \frac{\partial D}{\partial y_2} = \frac{\partial D}{\partial z_1} = \frac{\partial D}{\partial z_2} = 0.$$

With the notations of Section 3, we want to classify the singularities of the set of points where M has rank at most $r_0 = 3$. Our semi-algebraic constraints are that the solutions are within the Bloch ball, that is

$$\mathcal{B} : \begin{cases} h_1 = y_1^2 + (z_1+1)^2 \le 1 \\ h_2 = y_2^2 + (z_2+1)^2 \le 1. \end{cases}$$

Since the equations are homogeneous in $\Gamma_1, \Gamma_2, \gamma_1, \gamma_2$, and the parameters are supposed to be non-zero, we may normalize by setting $\gamma_1 = 1$. In the case where the first matter is water, we further simplify by setting $\Gamma_1 = \gamma_1 = 1$, leaving free the two parameters Γ_2, γ_2 corresponding to the second matter. We recall that we also assume that $2\Gamma_2 \ge \gamma_2$ and that $(\gamma_2,\Gamma_2) \ne (1,1) = (\gamma_1,\Gamma_1)$ (that is, the second matter is not water).

THEOREM 9. *Consider the 9 polynomials:*

$$f_1 = \Gamma_2 - 1,\ f_2 = 3\Gamma_2 - 2\gamma_2 - 1,$$
$$f_3 = 3\Gamma_2^2 - 5\Gamma_2\gamma_2 + \gamma_2^2 + 2\Gamma_2 - 2\gamma_2 + 1,$$
$$f_4 = 2\Gamma_2^2 - 5\Gamma_2\gamma_2 + 2\gamma_2^2 - 2\Gamma_2 + 3\gamma_2,$$
$$f_5 = 2\gamma_2^3 - (3\Gamma_2 + 11)\gamma_2^2 + (9\Gamma_2 + 6 - 3\Gamma_2^2)\gamma_2 + 2\Gamma_2(\Gamma_2+2)(\Gamma_2-1),$$
$$f_6 = \Gamma_2 - 2\gamma_2 + 1,\ f_7 = 2\Gamma_2 - \gamma_2 - 1,$$
$$f_8 = \gamma_2 - 2 + \Gamma_2,\ f_9 = 2\Gamma_2^2 - 5\Gamma_2\gamma_2 + 2\gamma_2^2 + 1.$$

The zeroes of their product divide the subset of $\mathbb{R}^2$ *defined by* $2\Gamma_2 > \gamma_2 > 0$ *into connected components where the cardinality of* $V_{\mathbb{R}} \cap \pi^{-1}(\gamma_2,\Gamma_2)$ *is constant.*

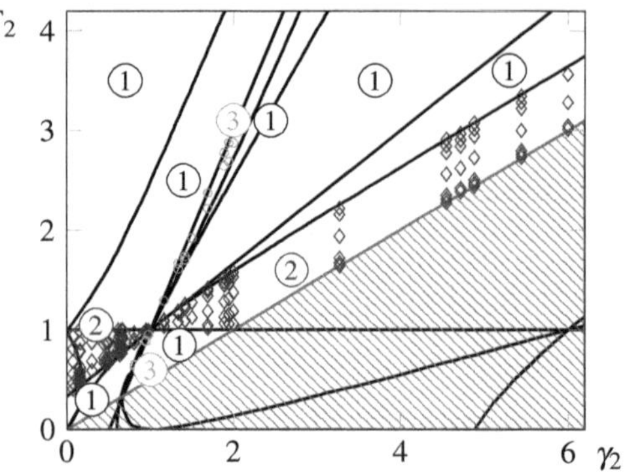

Figure 1: Curves involved in the definition of the semi-algebraic set $\mathcal{G}$. The blue (*resp.* green) sample points correspond to points in $\mathcal{G}_1^- \cup \mathcal{G}_1^+$ (*resp.* $\mathcal{G}_2^- \cup \mathcal{G}_2^+$). The circled numbers in each area correspond to the number of singularities in B for parameters in the area. Parameters in the red area are physically irrelevant.

Let $\psi : (y_1,z_1,y_2,z_2) \mapsto (-y_1,z_1,-y_2,z_2)$ be the symmetry fixing $\Pi = \{y_1 = y_2 = 0\}$, and let us consider the semi-algebraic sets (see Fig. 1):

$$\mathcal{G}_1^- = \{0 < \gamma_2 < 2\Gamma_2, \Gamma_2 < 1, f_2 > 0\},$$
$$\mathcal{G}_1^+ = \{0 < \gamma_2 < 2\Gamma_2, \Gamma_2 > 1, f_2 < 0, f_4 > 0\},$$
$$\mathcal{G}_2^- = \{0 < \Gamma_2 < 1, f_6 > 0, f_3 < 0\},$$
$$\mathcal{G}_2^+ = \{\Gamma_2 > 1, f_6 < 0, f_5 > 0\},$$
$$\mathcal{G} = \mathcal{G}_1^- \cup \mathcal{G}_1^+ \cup \mathcal{G}_2^- \cup \mathcal{G}_2^+.$$

THEOREM 10. *For all* (γ_2,Γ_2) *such that* $2\Gamma_2 > \gamma_2 > 0$, *the center* O *of the Bloch ball* $\mathcal{B}$ *is a singularity of* $\{D = 0\}$. *And provided* $(\gamma_2,\Gamma_2) \in \mathcal{G}$, *there exist at most two other singularities:*

1. *provided* $(\gamma_2,\Gamma_2) \in \mathcal{G}_1^- \cup \mathcal{G}_1^+$ *there is one other singularity lying on* $\Pi \cap \mathcal{B}$;
2. *provided* $(\gamma_2,\Gamma_2) \in \mathcal{G}_2^- \cup \mathcal{G}_2^+$ *there are two other singularities in* $\mathcal{B}$, ψ*-symmetric, outside* Π.

The configuration is illustrated in Figs. 1 and 2. Observe that the number of singularities inside $\mathcal{B}$ is an invariant of the contrast problem. Two of the pairs of biological matters studied in [2], water-cerebrospinal fluid (normalized parameters $[\gamma_2 = \frac{5}{4}, \Gamma_2 = \frac{25}{3}]$) and water-fat (normalized parameters $[\gamma_2 = \frac{25}{2}, \Gamma_2 = 25]$) correspond to points outside $\mathcal{G}$, and their invariant is 1 in both cases (see Fig. 2). But our results give answers to our guiding questions: there exist pairs of matters for which this algebraic invariant can differ; and any pair (water, matter) belongs to one of 3 classes, depending on whether the number of singularities inside $\mathcal{B}$ is 1, 2 or 3.

PROOF OF THEOREM 9. Let $V_{=3} = \{p \in \mathbb{C}^4 \times \mathbb{R}^2 \mid \mathrm{rank}(M) = 3\}$ and $V_2 = \{p \in \mathbb{C}^4 \times \mathbb{R}^2 \mid \mathrm{rank}(M) < 3\}$, where $p = (y_1,y_2,z_1,z_2,\gamma_2,\Gamma_2)$. We apply the strategies described in Section 3.

We study the generic case $V_2 \cap V$ first. This set does cover a dense subset of $\mathbb{R}^2$. Its intersection with the boundary of $\mathcal{B}$ is given by the vanishing of either h_1 or h_2. The projection on (Γ_2,γ_2) of the set of points of $V_2 \cap V$ such that $h_1 = 0$ is described by $0 = \gamma_2 f_1^2 f_2 f_3$ which gives us polynomials f_1, f_2 and f_3.

The projection on (Γ_2,γ_2) of the set of points of $V_2 \cap V$ such that $h_2 = 0$ is described by $0 = (2\Gamma_2 - \gamma_2) f_1^2 f_4 f_5$ which gives us new polynomials f_4 and f_5.

Next, we consider the incidence variety $\mathcal{V}_2$ associated with the matrix M:

System	RegularChain (direct)	Gröbner (direct)	RegularChain (new algo.)	FGb (new algo.)	F5 (new algo.)	CAD
Water	1600 s	100 s		10 s	1 s	50 s
General	>24 h	>24 h	90×200 s	46×200 s	110 s	4 h (projection step)

Table 1: Timings

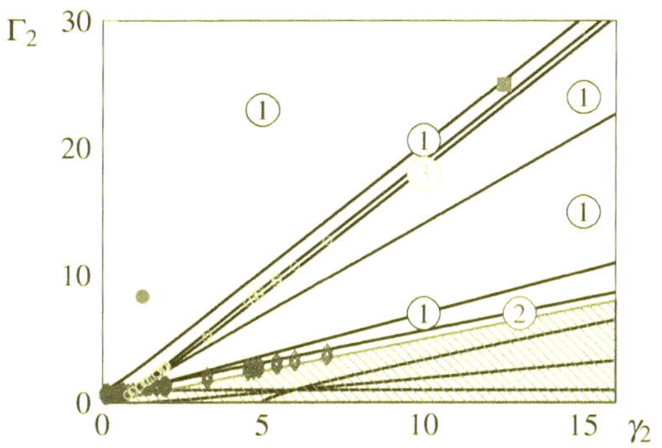

Figure 2: Positions of the parameters corresponding to the pairs water-cerebrospinal fluid (red circle) and water-fat (red square) and the set $\mathcal{G}$ (with the same conventions as in Fig. 1). For both these pairs, there is only 1 singularity in $\mathcal{B}$.

$$M \cdot \begin{pmatrix} \lambda_{1,1} & \lambda_{1,2} \\ \lambda_{2,1} & \lambda_{2,2} \\ \lambda_{3,1} & \lambda_{3,2} \\ \lambda_{4,1} & \lambda_{4,2} \end{pmatrix} = \begin{pmatrix} 0 & 0 \\ 0 & 0 \\ 0 & 0 \\ 0 & 0 \end{pmatrix}$$

with random linear equations ensuring that the matrix $(\lambda_{i,j})$ has rank 2.

Out of the surface $\gamma_2 = 0$, this affine variety is a complete intersection (it has dimension 2 and it is given by 9 equations in 11 variables, including the saturation by γ_2). The set of critical values of π is described by $0 = (2\Gamma_2 - \gamma_2)(\Gamma_2 + 1) f_1^2 f_6^2 f_7^2$ which gives us new polynomials f_6 and f_7 ($\Gamma_2 + 1$ has no solutions within our constraint range).

This completes the study of $V \cap V_2$. We now move on to the study of $V \cap V_{=3}$. As described in the algorithm, we define the incidence variety of rank 3 of M, and we saturate successively by the 3-minors of M. Only the first of these subcases is nonempty, and it is described by $0 = (2\Gamma_2 - \gamma_2) f_8 f_9$ which gives us f_8 and f_9. □

PROOF OF THEOREM 10. Observe first by means of a trivial evaluation that O is a singularity of $\{D = 0\}$. We now focus on singularities in $\mathcal{B}^* = \mathcal{B} \setminus \{O\}$. Theorem 9 provides a list of 9 polynomials to which we add our constraints $2\Gamma_2 \geq \gamma_2 > 0$. Let $\xi = \gamma_2 \Gamma_2 (\gamma_2 - 2\Gamma_2) \prod_{i=1}^{9} f_i$. The complementary of $\{\xi = 0\}$ is the union of a sequence of connected open semi-algebraic sets where the number of singularities is constant. The routine CylindricalAlgebraicDecompose of the Maple package RegularChains[SemiAlgebraicSetTools] provides 1533 sample points. Excluding those at which ξ vanishes and those outside our physical constraints domain, remains a set K_c of 570 points. At each point of K_c we locate the singularities by computing a Gröbner basis.

We get 187 points of K_c such that there exists at least one singularity in $\mathcal{B}^*$. We have a set K_s of 31 points, each of them corresponding to a couple of ψ-symmetric singularities outside the symmetry plane Π, and a set K_p of 156 points corresponding to a unique singularity on $\Pi \cap \mathcal{B}^*$. For parameters at which ξ does not vanish, the number of singularities in $\mathcal{B}^*$ is at most two.

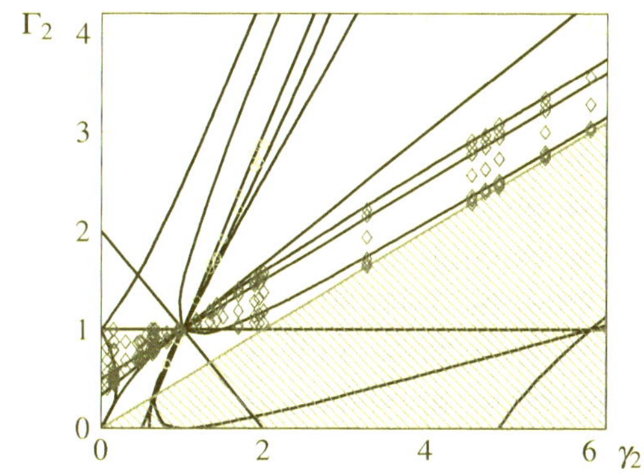

Figure 3: The curves involved in the decomposition of the parameter space (with the same conventions as in Fig. 1).

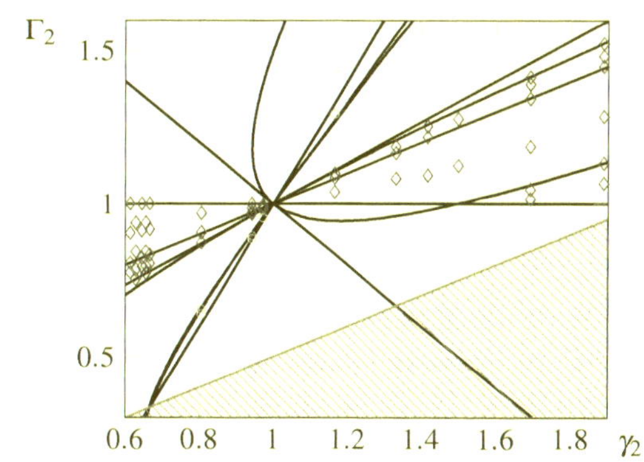

Figure 4: Magnification of Fig. 3 near $(1, 1)$.

Points of K_s (*resp.* K_p) are represented in green (*resp.* blue) in Figs. 1, 3 and 4. Let us evaluate on K_c the condition ($\Gamma_2 < 1$, $f_2 > 0$, $f_4 < 0$) or ($\Gamma_2 > 1$, $f_2 < 0$, $f_4 > 0$). Indeed the set of points of K_c satisfying this condition coincides with K_p. This proves item 1). The proof of item 2) is similar. □

4.2 The general case

The variety V and the semi-algebraic set $\mathcal{B}$ are defined as in the previous section. We normalize again by $\gamma_1 = 1$, we assume that $2\Gamma_1 \geq 1, 2\Gamma_2 \geq \gamma_2 > 0, (\gamma_2, \Gamma_2) \neq (1, \Gamma_1)$, and that $\Gamma_1 \neq 1, \Gamma_2 \neq \gamma_2$ (case of water).

THEOREM 11. *Splitting the subset of $\mathbb{R}^3$ defined by $2\Gamma_2 > \gamma_2 > 0$ and $2\Gamma_1 > 1$ into open subsets where the number of real singularities of V in the fibers is constant, can be done by cutting out 12 irreducible surfaces, consisting of 5 planes, 3 quadrics, two surfaces of degree 9 and one of degree 14.*

These polynomials were obtained by applying the algorithms from Section 3 to our system. The elimination steps were done using both Gröbner bases with FGb or with F5, and with triangular sets with RegularChains. Table 1 presents some timings for these methods (for computations done with interpolation, we give the results as $a \times b$ where a is the interpolation degree and b the time taken for each specialized computation). It shows that our algorithm, implemented with either Gröbner bases or regular chains, is more efficient than the direct (general) approach, and it allows to deal with the previously untractable general case. Furthermore, the implementation using Gröbner bases appears to be faster.

5. REFERENCES

[1] J. Bochnak, M. Coste, and M.-F. Roy. *Real algebraic geometry*, volume 36 of *Ergebnisse der Mathematik und ihrer Grenzgebiete (3) [Results in Mathematics and Related Areas (3)]*. Springer-Verlag, Berlin, 1998. Translated from the 1987 French original, Revised by the authors.

[2] B. Bonnard, M. Chyba, A. Jacquemard, and J. Marriott. Algebraic geometric classification of the singular flow in the contrast imaging problem in nuclear magnetic resonance. *Math. Control Relat. Fields*, 3(4):397–432, 2013.

[3] B. Bonnard, O. Cots, S.J. Glaser, M. Lapert, D. Sugny, and Y. Zhang. Geometric optimal control of the contrast imaging problem in nuclear magnetic resonance. *IEEE Trans. Automat. Control*, 57(8):1957–1969, 2012.

[4] C. W. Brown and J. H. Davenport. The complexity of quantifier elimination and cylindrical algebraic decomposition. In *ISSAC 2007*, pages 54–60. ACM, New York, 2007.

[5] W. Bruns and U. Vetter. *Determinantal Rings*. Springer, 2014.

[6] M. Chyba, J-M. Coron, P. Gabriel, A. Jacquemard, G. Patterson, G. Picot, and P. Shang. Optimal geometric control applied to the protein misfolding cyclic amplification process. *Acta Applicandae Mathematicae*, 135(1):145–173, 2015.

[7] G. E. Collins. Quantifier elimination for real closed fields by cylindrical algebraic decomposition. In *Automata theory and formal languages (Second GI Conf., Kaiserslautern, 1975)*, pages 134–183. Lecture Notes in Comput. Sci., Vol. 33. Springer, Berlin, 1975.

[8] M. Coste and M. Shiota. Thom's first isotopy lemma: a semialgebraic version, with uniform bound. In *Real analytic and algebraic geometry (Trento, 1992)*, pages 83–101. de Gruyter, Berlin, 1995.

[9] J. H. Davenport and J. Heintz. Real quantifier elimination is doubly exponential. *J. Symbolic Comput.*, 5(1-2):29–35, 1988.

[10] M. Demazure. *Bifurcations and catastrophes*. Universitext. Springer-Verlag, Berlin, 2000. Geometry of solutions to nonlinear problems, Translated from the 1989 French original by D. Chillingworth.

[11] J.-C. Faugère. A new efficient algorithm for computing Gröbner bases without reduction to zero (F_5). In *Proceedings of the 2002 International Symposium on Symbolic and Algebraic Computation*, pages 75–83 (electronic), New York, 2002. ACM.

[12] J.-C. Faugère. FGb: A Library for Computing Gröbner Bases. In Komei Fukuda, Joris Hoeven, Michael Joswig, and Nobuki Takayama, editors, *Mathematical Software - ICMS 2010*, volume 6327 of *Lecture Notes in Computer Science*, pages 84–87, Berlin, Heidelberg, September 2010. Springer Berlin / Heidelberg.

[13] J.-C. Faugère, M. Safey El Din, and P.-J. Spaenlehauer. Critical points and Gröbner bases: the unmixed case. In *Proceedings of the 2012 International Symposium on Symbolic and Algebraic Computation (ISSAC 2012)*, pages 162–169, 2012.

[14] J.-C. Faugère, M. Safey El Din, and P.-J. Spaenlehauer. On the complexity of the Generalized MinRank Problem. *Journal of Symbolic Computation*, 55:30–58, 2013.

[15] D. Henrion, S. Naldi, and M. Safey El Din. Exact algorithms for linear matrix inequalities. Submitted., August 2015.

[16] D. Henrion, S. Naldi, and M. Safey El Din. Real root finding for low rank linear matrices. Submitted., June 2015.

[17] D. Henrion, S. Naldi, and M. Safey El Din. Real root finding for rank defects in linear Hankel matrices. In *Proceedings of the 2015 ACM on International Symposium on Symbolic and Algebraic Computation*, page 26p., Bath, United Kingdom, July 2015.

[18] D. Henrion, S. Naldi, and M. Safey El Din. Real root finding for determinants of linear matrices. *Journal of Symbolic Computation*, 74:205 – 238, 2016.

[19] H. Hong and M. Safey El Din. Variant quantifier elimination. *Journal of Symbolic Computation*, 47(7):883 – 901, 2012. International Symposium on Symbolic and Algebraic Computation (ISSAC 2009).

[20] D. Lazard and F. Rouillier. Solving parametric polynomial systems. *Journal of Symbolic Computation*, 42(6):636–667, 2007.

[21] F. Lemaire, M. Moreno Maza, and Y. Xie. The regularchains library. In *Maple conference*, volume 5, pages 355–368, 2005.

[22] S. McCallum. On projection in CAD-based quantifier elimination with equational constraint. In *Proceedings of the 1999 International Symposium on Symbolic and Algebraic Computation (Vancouver, BC)*, pages 145–149 (electronic). ACM, New York, 1999.

[23] L. S. Pontryagin, V. G. Boltyanskii, R. V. Gamkrelidze, and E. F. Mishchenko. *The mathematical theory of optimal processes*. Translated from the Russian by K. N. Trirogoff; edited by L. W. Neustadt. Interscience Publishers John Wiley & Sons, Inc. New York-London, 1962.

[24] J. I. Rodriguez and X. Tang. Data-discriminants of likelihood equations. In *Proceedings of the 2015 ACM on International Symposium on Symbolic and Algebraic Computation*, ISSAC '15, pages 307–314, New York, NY, USA, 2015. ACM.

[25] P.-J. Spaenlehauer. On the complexity of computing critical points with Gröbner bases. *SIAM Journal on Optimization*, 24(3):1382–1401, 2014.

[26] L. Yang, X. Hou, and B. Xia. A complete algorithm for automated discovering of a class of inequality-type theorems. *Sci. China Ser. F*, 44(1):33–49, 2001.

Computation of the Similarity Class of the p-Curvature*

Alin Bostan
Inria (France)
alin.bostan@inria.fr

Xavier Caruso
Université Rennes 1 (France)
xavier.caruso@normalesup.org

Éric Schost
Univ. of Waterloo (Canada)
eschost@uwaterloo.ca

ABSTRACT

The p-curvature of a system of linear differential equations in positive characteristic p is a matrix that measures how far the system is from having a basis of polynomial solutions. We show that the similarity class of the p-curvature can be determined without computing the p-curvature itself. More precisely, we design an algorithm that computes the invariant factors of the p-curvature in time quasi-linear in $\sqrt{p}$. This is much less than the size of the p-curvature, which is generally linear in p. The new algorithm allows to answer a question originating from the study of the Ising model in statistical physics.

CCS Concepts

•Computing methodologies → Algebraic algorithms;

Keywords

differential equations; p-curvature; algebraic complexity

1. INTRODUCTION

Differential equations in positive characteristic p are important and well-studied objects in mathematics [22, 32, 33]. The main reason is arguably one of Grothendieck's (still unsolved) conjectures [26, 27, 1], stating that a linear differential equation with coefficients in $\mathbb{Q}(x)$ admits a basis of algebraic solutions if and only if its reductions modulo (almost) all primes p admit a basis of polynomial solutions modulo p. Another motivation stems from the fact that the reductions modulo prime numbers yield useful information about the factorization of differential operators in characteristic zero.

To a linear differential equation in fixed characteristic p, or more generally to a system of such equations, is attached a simple yet very useful object, the *p-curvature*. Let $\mathbb{F}_q$ be the finite field with $q = p^a$ elements. The p-curvature of a system of linear differential equations with coefficients in $\mathbb{F}_q(x)$ is a matrix with entries in $\mathbb{F}_q(x)$ that measures the obstructions for the given system to possess a fundamental matrix of polynomial solutions in $\mathbb{F}_q[x]$. Its definition is remarkably simple, especially at a higher level of generality: the p-curvature of a differential module (M, ∂) of dimension r over $\mathbb{F}_q(x)$ is the "differential-Frobenius-map" $\partial^p = \partial \circ \cdots \circ \partial$ (p times). When applied to the differential module canonically attached with the system $Y' = A(x)Y$, the p-curvature materializes into the p-th iterate ∂_A^p of the map $\partial_A : \mathbb{F}_q(x)^r \to \mathbb{F}_q(x)^r$ that sends v to $v' - Av$, or more concretely, into the matrix $A_p(x)$ of this map with respect to the canonical basis of $\mathbb{F}_q(x)^r$. It is given as the term A_p of the sequence $(A_i)_i$ of matrices in $M_r(\mathbb{F}_q(x))$ defined by

$$A_1 = -A \quad \text{and} \quad A_{i+1} = A_i' - A \cdot A_i \quad \text{for} \quad i \geq 1.$$

From a computer algebra perspective, many effectivity questions naturally arise. They primarily concern the algorithmic complexity of various operations and properties related to the p-curvature: How fast can one compute A_p? How fast can one decide its nullity? How fast can one determine its minimal and characteristic polynomial? Apart the fundamental nature of these questions from the algebraic complexity theory viewpoint, there are concrete motivations for the efficient computation of the p-curvature, coming from various applications, notably in enumerative combinatorics and statistical physics [7, 8, 2].

We pursue the algorithmic study of the p-curvature, initiated in [9, 3, 4]. In those articles, several questions were answered satisfactorily, but a few other problems were left open. In summary, the current state of affairs is as follows. First, the p-curvature A_p can be computed in time $O(\log p)$ when $r = 1$ and $O\tilde{~}(p)$ when $r > 1$. The soft-O notation $O\tilde{~}(\,)$ indicates that polylogarithmic factors in the argument of $O(\,)$ are deliberately not displayed. These complexities match, up to polylogarithmic factors, the generic size of A_p. Secondly, one can decide the nullity of A_p in time $O\tilde{~}(p)$ and compute its characteristic polynomial in time $O\tilde{~}(\sqrt{p})$. It is not known whether the exponent $1/2$ is optimal for the last problem. In all these estimates, the complexity ("time") measure is the number of arithmetic operations ($\pm, \times, \div$) in the ground field $\mathbb{F}_q$, and the dependence is expressed in the main parameter p only. Nevertheless, precise estimates are also available in terms of the other parameters of the input.

In the present work, we focus on the computation of all the invariant factors of the p-curvature, and show that they can also be determined in time $O\tilde{~}(\sqrt{p})$. Previously, this was unknown even for the minimal polynomial of A_p or for testing the nullity of A_p. The fact that a sublinear cost could in principle be achievable, although A_p itself has a

*We warmly thank the referees for their very helpful comments, and for pointing out a mistake in an earlier version of the article. We thank M. Giesbrecht, G. Labahn and A. Storjohann for useful discussions. The third author is supported by NSERC.

ISSAC '16, July 19–22, 2016, Waterloo, ON, Canada.

ACM ISBN 978-1-4503-4380-0/16/07...$15.00.

DOI: http://dx.doi.org/10.1145/2930889.2930897

total arithmetic size linear in p, comes from the observation that the coefficients of the invariant factors of A_p lie in the subfield $\mathbb{F}_q(x^p)$ of $\mathbb{F}_q(x)$, in other words they are very sparse.

To achieve our objective, we blend the methods used in our previous works [3] and [4]. The first key ingredient is the construction, for any point a in the algebraic closure of $\mathbb{F}_q$ that is not a pole of $A(x)$, of a matrix Y_a with entries in $\ell = \mathbb{F}_q(a)$ which is similar to the evaluation $A_p(a)$ of the p-curvature at the point a. This construction comes from [4] and ultimately relies on the existence of a well-suited ring, of so-called *Hurwitz series in* $x-a$, for which an analogue of the Cauchy–Lipschitz theorem holds for the system $Y' = A(x)Y$ around the (ordinary) point $x = a$. The matrix Y_a is the p-th coefficient of the fundamental matrix of Hurwitz series solutions of $Y' = A(x)Y$ at $x = a$.

The second key ingredient is a baby step / giant step algorithm that computes Y_a in $\tilde{O}(\sqrt{p})$ operations in ℓ via fast matrix factorials. Finally, we recover the invariant factors of A_p from those of the matrices Y_a, for a suitable number of values a. The main difficulty in this interpolation process is that there exist badly behaved points a for which the invariant factors of $A_p(a)$ are not the evaluations at a of the invariant factors of $A_p(x)$. The remaining task is then to bound the number of unlucky evaluation points a. The key feature allowing a good control on these points, independent of p, is the fact that the invariant factors of $A_p(x)$ have coefficients in $\mathbb{F}_q(x^p)$.

Relationship to previous work. There exists a large body of work concerning the computation of so-called Frobenius forms of matrices (that is, the list of their invariant factors, possibly with corresponding transformation matrices), and the related problem of Smith forms of polynomial matrices. The specificities of our problem prevent us from applying these methods directly; however, our work is related to several of these previous results.

Let ω be a feasible exponent for matrix multiplication. The best deterministic algorithm known so far for the computation of the Frobenius form of an $n \times n$ matrix over a field k is due to Storjohann [30]. This algorithm has running time $O(n^\omega \log(n) \log\log(n))$ operations in k. We will use it to compute the invariant factors of the matrices Y_a above. Las Vegas algorithms were given by Giesbrecht [19], Eberly [14] and Pernet and Storjohann [28], the latter having expected running time $O(n^\omega)$ over sufficiently large fields.

The case of matrices with integer or rational entries has attracted a lot of attention; this situation is close to ours, with the bit size of integers playing a role similar to the degree of the entries in the p-curvature. Early work goes back to algorithms of Kaltofen *et al.* [23, 24] for the Smith form of matrices over $\mathbb{Q}[x]$, which introduced techniques used in several further algorithms, such as the Las Vegas algorithm by Storjohann and Labahn [31]. Giesbrecht's PhD thesis [18] gives a Las Vegas algorithm with expected cost $\tilde{O}(n^{\omega+2}d)$ for the Frobenius normal form of an $n\times n$ matrix with integer entries of bit size d; Storjohann and Giesbrecht substantially improved this result in [20], with an algorithm of expected cost $\tilde{O}(n^4 d + n^3 d^2)$. The best Monte Carlo running time known to us is $\tilde{O}(n^{2.698}d)$, by Kaltofen and Villard [25].

In the latter case of matrices with integer coefficients, a common technique relies on reduction modulo primes, and a main source of difficulty is to control the number of "unlucky" reductions. We pointed out above that this is the case in our algorithm as well. In general, the number of unlucky primes is showed to be $\tilde{O}(n^2 d)$ in [18]; in our case, the degree d of the entries grows linearly with p, but as we said above, we can alleviate this issue by exploiting the properties of the p-curvature. Storjohann and Giesbrecht proved in [20] that a candidate for the Frobenius form of an integer matrix can be verified using only $\tilde{O}(nd)$ primes; it would be most interesting to adapt this idea to our situation.

Structure of the paper. In Section 2, we recall the main theoretical properties of the invariant factors of a polynomial matrix, and study their behavior under specialization. We obtain bounds on bad evaluation points, and use them to design (deterministic and probabilistic) evaluation-interpolation algorithms for computing the invariant factors of a polynomial matrix. Section 3 is devoted to the design of our main algorithms for the similarity class of the p-curvature, with deterministic and probabilistic versions for both the system case and the scalar case. Finally, Section 4 presents an application of our algorithm, that allows to answer a question coming from theoretical physics.

Complexity basics. We use standard complexity notation, such as ω for the exponent of matrix multiplication. The best known upper bound is $\omega < 2.3729$ from [15]. Many arithmetic operations on univariate polynomials of degree d in $k[x]$ can be performed in $\tilde{O}(d)$ operations in the field k: addition, multiplication, shift, interpolation, *etc*, the key to these results being fast polynomial multiplication [29, 11, 21]. A general reference for these questions in [17].

2. COMPUTING INVARIANT FACTORS OF SPECIAL POLYNOMIAL MATRICES

2.1 Definition and classical facts

We recall here some basic facts about invariant factors of matrices defined over a field. We fix for now a field K, and a matrix $M \in M_n(K)$. For a monic polynomial $P = T^d - \sum_{i=0}^{d-1} a_i T^i \in K[T]$, let M_P denote its companion matrix:

$$M_P = \begin{pmatrix} & & & a_0 \\ 1 & & & a_1 \\ & \ddots & & \vdots \\ & & 1 & a_{d-1} \end{pmatrix}.$$

A well-known theorem [16, Th. 9, Ch. VII] asserts that there exist a unique sequence of monic polynomials $I_1, \ldots, I_n$ for which I_j divides I_{j+1} for all j and M is similar to a block diagonal matrix whose diagonal entries are $M_{I_1}, \ldots, M_{I_n}$. The I_j's are called the *invariant factors* of M. We emphasize that, with our convention, there are always n invariant factors but some of them may be equal to 1, in which case the corresponding companion matrix is the empty one. Under this normalization, the j-th invariant factor I_j can be obtained as $I_j = G_j / G_{j-1}$, where G_j is the gcd of the minors of size j of the matrix $T\mathrm{I}_n - M$, where I_n stands for the identity matrix of size n. The invariant factors are closely related to the characteristic polynomial; indeed, we have

$$I_1 \cdot I_2 \cdots I_n = G_n = \det(T\mathrm{I}_n - M). \quad (1)$$

Given some irreducible polynomial P in $K[T]$, we consider the sequence (of integers):

$$e \mapsto d_{P,e} = \frac{\dim_K \ker P^e(M)}{\deg P}. \quad (2)$$

It turns out that this sequence completely determines the P-adic valuation of the invariant factors. Indeed, denoting by v_j the P-adic valuation of I_j, we have the relations:

$$d_{P,e} = \sum_{j=1}^{n} \min(e, v_j), \tag{3}$$

$$d_{P,e} - d_{P,e-1} = \mathrm{Card}\{j \mid v_j \geq e\} \tag{4}$$

from which the v_j's can be recovered without ambiguity since they form a nondecreasing sequence. It also follows from the above formula that the sequence $e \mapsto d_{P,e}$ is concave and eventually constant. Its final value is the dimension of the characteristic subspace associated to P and it is reached as soon as e is greater than or equal to v_n.

2.2 Behaviour under specialization

Let k be a perfect field of characteristic p. We consider a matrix $M(x)$ with coefficients in $k[x]$. For an element a lying in a finite extension ℓ of k, we denote by $M(a)$ the image of $M(x)$ under the mapping $k[x] \to \ell$, $x \mapsto a$. Our aim is to compare the invariant factors of $M(x)$ and those of $M(a)$.

We introduce some notation. Let $I_1(x,T), \ldots, I_n(x,T)$ be the invariant factors of $M(x)$. It follows from the relation (1) that they all lie in $k[x,T]$. We can therefore evaluate them at $x = a$ for each element $a \in \ell$ as above and get this way univariate polynomials with coefficients in ℓ. Let $I_1(a,T), \ldots, I_n(a,T)$ be these evaluations. We also consider the invariant factors of $M(a)$ and call them $I_{1,a}(T), \ldots, I_{n,a}(T)$. We furthemore define

$$G_j(x,T) = I_1(x,T) \cdot I_2(x,T) \cdots I_j(x,T)$$
$$\text{and} \quad G_{j,a}(T) = I_{1,a}(T) \cdot I_{2,a}(T) \cdots I_{j,a}(T).$$

The characterization of the G_j's in term of minors yields:

LEMMA 2.1. *For all $a \in \ell$ and all $j \in \{1, \ldots, n\}$, the polynomial $G_j(a,T)$ divides $G_{j,a}(T)$ in $\ell[T]$.*

Let $P_1(x,T), \ldots, P_s(x,T)$ be the irreducible factors of the characteristic polynomial $\chi(x,T)$ of $M(x)$, and let us write $\chi^{\mathrm{sep}}(x,T)$ for $P_1(x,T) \cdots P_s(x,T)$. For all $1 \leq i \leq s$ and $1 \leq j \leq n$, let $e_{i,j}$ be the multiplicity of $P_i(x,T)$ in $I_j(x,T)$.

PROPOSITION 2.2. *We assume $\chi^{\mathrm{sep}}(a,T)$ is separable and*

$$\dim_{k(x)} \ker P_i(x, M(x))^{e_{i,j}+1} = \dim_\ell \ker P_i(a, M(a))^{e_{i,j}+1}$$

for all i and for all $j < n$. Then $I_j(a,T) = I_{j,a}(T)$ for all j.

PROOF. The equality of dimensions is also true for $j = n$, since their sum on both sides is equal to n (using separability) and these dimensions can only increase by specialization. Let $d_{P_i,e}$ be the sequence defined by Eq. (2) with respect to the irreducible polynomial $P_i(x,T)$ and the matrix $M(x)$. We define similarly for each irreducible factor $P(T)$ of $P_i(a,T)$ the sequence $d_{P,e}$ corresponding to the polynomial $P(T)$ and the matrix $M(a)$. We claim that it is enough to prove that $d_{P_i,e} = d_{P,e}$ for all e, i and all irreducible divisors $P(T)$ of $P_i(a,T)$. Indeed, by Eq. (4), such an equality would imply:

$$v_{P(T)}(I_{j,a}(T)) = e_{i,j} \tag{5}$$

provided that $P(T)$ is an irreducible divisor of $P_i(a,T)$, and where $v_{P(T)}$ denotes the $P(T)$-adic valuation. On the other hand, still assuming that $P(T)$ is an irreducible divisor of $P_i(a,T)$, it follows from the definition of the $e_{i,j}$'s that:

$$v_{P(T)}(I_j(a,T)) \geq e_{i,j} \tag{6}$$

and that the equality holds if and only if $P(T)$ does not divide any of the $P_{i'}(a,T)$ for $i' \neq i$. Comparing characteristic polynomials, we know moreover that $\sum_{j=1}^{n} v_{P(T)}(I_{j,a}(T)) = \sum_{j=1}^{n} v_{P(T)}(I_j(a,T))$. Combining this with (5) and (6), we find that the $P_i(a,T)$'s are pairwise coprime and finally get $I_j(a,T) = I_{j,a}(T)$ for $1 \leq j \leq n$, as wanted.

Until the end of the proof, we fix the index i and reserve the letter P to denote an irreducible divisor of $P_i(a,T)$. For a fixed integer e, denote by j_0 the greatest index j for which $v_{P(T)}(I_{j,a}(T)) < e$ and observe that Eq. (3) can be rewritten $d_{P,e} = e \cdot \big(n - j_0\big) + v_{P(T)}\big(G_{j_0,a}(T)\big)$. Using Lemma 2.1, we derive $d_{P,e} \geq e \cdot \big(n - j_0\big) + v_{P(T)}\big(G_{j_0}(a,T)\big) \geq d_{P_i,e}$ for all P and e. Eq. (4) now implies that the indices e for which $d_{P_i,e} - d_{P_i,e-1} > d_{P_i,e+1} - d_{P_i,e}$ are exactly the $e_{i,j}$'s $(1 \leq j \leq n)$. Using concavity, we then observe that it is enough to check that $d_{P_i,e} = d_{P,e}$ for indices e of the form $e_{i,j} + 1$. For those e, we have by assumption:

$$\begin{aligned} \textstyle\sum_P \deg P \cdot d_{P,e} &= \dim_\ell \ker P_i(a, M(a))^e \\ &= \dim_{k(x)} \ker P_i(x, M(x))^e \\ &= \deg_T P_i \cdot d_{P_i,e} = \textstyle\sum_P \deg P \cdot d_{P_i,e} \end{aligned}$$

and thus $d_{P,e} = d_{P_i,e}$ for all P because the inequalities $d_{P,e} \geq d_{P_i,e}$ are already known. □

2.3 A bound on bad evaluation points

Let $M(x)$ be a square matrix of size n with coefficients in $k[x]$. We set $X = x^p$ and assume that:

(i) the entries of $M(x)$ have degree at most pm (for a $m \in \mathbb{N}$),
(ii) $M(x)$ is similar to a matrix with coefficients in $k(X)$.

We are going to bound the number of values of a for which the invariant factors of $M(x)$ do not specialize correctly at $x = a$. Similar discussions appear is Section 4 of Giesbrecht's thesis [18] in the (more complicated) case of integer matrices. Our treatment is nevertheless rather different in many places.

The basic bound. By assumption (ii), the characteristic polynomial $\chi(x,T)$ lies in the subring $k[X,T]$ of $k[x,T]$.

LEMMA 2.3. *The invariant factors $I_j(x,T)$ all belong to $k[X,T]$. Their degree with respect to X is at most mn.*

PROOF. By assumption (i), $\chi(x,T)$ is a polynomial in x of degree at most pmn. It then follows from Eq. (1) that the $I_j(x,T)$'s are polynomials in x of degree at most pmn as well. Now, the assumption (ii) ensures that the $I_j(x,T)$'s actually lie in $k(X)[T]$. This completes the proof. □

LEMMA 2.4. *We assume that $p > n$. There are at most $\deg_X \chi(x,T) \cdot (2n-1)$ points $a \in k$ such that at least one of the $P_i(a,T)$'s is not separable.*

PROOF. We have that $\deg_X \chi^{\mathrm{sep}}(x,T) \leq \deg_X \chi(x,T)$ and $\deg_T \chi^{\mathrm{sep}}(x,T) \leq n$, since χ^{sep} divides χ. Denote by $D(x)$ the discriminant of $\chi^{\mathrm{sep}}(x,T)$ with respect to T. Its degree in X is at most $\deg_X \chi(x,T) \cdot (2n-1)$, and the assumption $p > n$ implies that $D(x)$ is not identically zero. For any $a \in k$ such that $D(a^p) \neq 0$, the polynomial $\chi^{\mathrm{sep}}(a^p, T)$ is separable, and the same holds for the $P_i(a^p,T)$'s. Noting that k is perfect, the conclusion holds. □

PROPOSITION 2.5. *We assume $p > n$. Let $a_1, \ldots, a_N$ be elements in a separable closure of k which are pairwise non* *conjugate over k. We assume that for each $i \in \{1,\dots,N\}$, there exists $j \in \{1,\dots,n\}$ with $I_j(a_i,T) \neq I_{a_i,j}(T)$. Then:*

$$\sum_{i=1}^{N} \deg(a_i) \leq 4mn\cdot(n-1) + mn\cdot(2n-1)$$

where $\deg(a_i)$ denotes the algebraicity degree of a_i over k.

PROOF. We use the criteria of Proposition 2.2. We start by putting away the values of a for which at least one of the $P_i(a,T)$'s is not separable. By Lemma 2.4, there are at most $mn\cdot(2n-1)$ such values. We then have to bound from above the values of a such that the equalities:

$$\dim_{k(x)} \ker P_i(x, M(x))^e = \dim_\ell \ker P_i(a, M(a))^e$$

may fail for some i and some exponent $e = e_{i,j}+1$ for some j.

Let us fix such a pair (i,e). Set $N(x) = P_i(x, M(x))^e$ for simplicity. By assumption (i), the entries of $N(x)$ have degree at most $pm_{i,e}$ with $m_{i,e} = e\cdot\big(m \deg_T P_i + \deg_X P_i\big)$. On the other hand, we deduce from assumption (ii) that the $P_i(x,T)$'s all lie in $k[X,T]$ and, as a consequence, that $N(x)$ is similar to a matrix with coefficients in $k(X)$. Define $d = \dim_{k(x)} \ker N(x)$. The equality $\dim_\ell \ker N(a) = d$ then fails if and only if the minors of $N(x)$ of size $n-d$ all vanish at $x = a$, i.e., if and only if the gcd $\Delta(x)$ of these minors is divisible by the minimal polynomial of a over k, say $\pi_a(x)$. Noting that $\Delta(x) \in k[X]$, the latter condition is also equivalent to the fact that $\pi_a(x)^p$ divides $\Delta(x)$ in the ring $k[X]$. This can be possible for at most $\deg_X \Delta(x) \leq (n-d)m_{i,e} \leq (n-1)m_{i,e}$ values of a.

Therefore, if $a_1,\dots,a_N$ are pairwise non-conjugate "unlucky values" of a, the sum appearing in the statement of the proposition is bounded from above by:

$$(n-1)\textstyle\sum_{i,e} m_{i,e} = m(n-1)\sum_{i,e} e \deg_T P_i + (n-1)\sum_{i,e} e \deg_X P_i.$$

We notice that, when i remains fixed, the number of exponents of the form $e_{i,j}+1$ $(1 \leq j < n)$ is bounded from above by $e_{i,n}+1$. The sum of these exponents is then at most:

$$\big(\textstyle\sum_{j=1}^{n-1} e_{i,j}\big) + e_{i,n} + 1 = e_i + 1 \leq 2e_i,$$

where e_i denotes the multiplicity of the factor $P_i(x,T)$ in the characteristic polynomial $\chi(x,T)$. Our bound then becomes $2m(n-1)\deg_T \chi + 2(n-1)\deg_X \chi$. Using $\deg_T \chi = n$ and $\deg_X \chi \leq mn$ yields the bound. □

A refinement. For the applications we have in mind, we shall need a refinement of Proposition 2.5 under the following hypothesis depending on a parameter $\mu \in \mathbb{N}$:

$(\mathbf{H}_\mu)$: the polynomial χ has degree at most $p\mu$ w.r.t x.

We observe that $(\mathbf{H}_\mu)$ is fulfilled when $M(x)$ is a companion matrix whose entries are polynomials of degree at most $p\mu$.

PROPOSITION 2.6. *Under the assumptions of Prop. 2.5 and the additional hypothesis $(\mathbf{H}_\mu)$, we have:*

$$\sum_{i=1}^{N} \deg(a_i) \leq 2\mu\cdot(2n-1) + \mu\cdot(2n-1).$$

PROOF. Let $P(x,T)$ be any bivariate polynomial with coefficients in k. Set $N(x) = P(x, M(x))$ and let $\delta(x)$ denote the gcd of the minors of size s (for some integer s) of $N(x)$. We claim that:

$$\deg_x \delta(x) \leq p\mu\cdot\deg_T P + s\cdot\deg_x P \qquad (7)$$

To prove the claim, we consider the Frobenius normal form $\tilde{M}(x)$ of $M(x)$ and set $\tilde{N}(x) = P(x, \tilde{N}(x))$. Observe that any minor of $\tilde{M}(x)$ vanishes or has the shape $\pm c_1(x)\cdots c_n(x)$ where $c_j(x)$ is a coefficient of $I_j(x,T)$ for all j. Noting that $\deg_x I_1 + \cdots + \deg_x I_n = \deg_x \chi \leq p\mu$, we derive that *all* the minors of $\tilde{M}(x)$ have degree at most $p\mu$. Now write $P(x,T) = \sum_{j=0}^{\deg_T P} a_j(x)T^j$ where the $a_i(x)$'s lie in $k[x]$. Let $\tilde{f}$ denote the $k[x]$-linear endomorphism of $k[x]^n$ attached to the matrix $\tilde{M}(x)$. Set $\tilde{g} = P(x, \tilde{f})$; it clearly corresponds to $\tilde{N}(x)$. Given a vector space E and s linear endomorphisms $u_1,\dots,u_s$ of E, let us agree to define $u_1\wedge\cdots\wedge u_s$ as

$$\begin{array}{rcl} E^{\otimes s} & \to & \bigwedge^s E \\ x_1\otimes\cdots\otimes x_s & \mapsto & u_1(x_1)\wedge\cdots\wedge u_s(x_s). \end{array}$$

where $\bigwedge^s E$ is here defined as a quotient of $E^{\otimes s}$. Expanding the exterior product $\bigwedge^s \tilde{g}$, we get:

$$\bigwedge^s \tilde{g} = \sum_{i_1,\dots,i_s=0}^{\deg_T P} a_{i_1}(x)\cdots a_{i_s}(x)\cdot \tilde{f}^{i_1}\wedge\cdots\wedge\tilde{f}^{i_s}. \qquad (8)$$

Moreover, assuming for simplicity that $i_1 \leq i_2 \leq \cdots \leq i_s$ and letting $i_0 = 0$ by convention, we can write:

$$\tilde{f}^{i_1}\otimes\cdots\otimes\tilde{f}^{i_s} = \bigcirc_{j=0}^{s}\big[(\textstyle\bigotimes^j \mathrm{id})\otimes(\bigotimes^{s-j}\tilde{f})^{i_j-i_{j-1}}\big],$$

where $\bigcirc$ denotes the composition of the above (pairwise commuting) maps. We get that the entries of the matrix (in the canonical basis) of $\tilde{f}^{i_1}\wedge\cdots\wedge\tilde{f}^{i_s}$ all have degree at most $p\mu\cdot i_s$. The same argument demonstrates that the degrees of the entries of the above matrix are not greater than:

$$p\mu\cdot\max(i_1,\dots,i_s) \leq p\mu\cdot\deg_T P$$

when we no longer assume that the i_j's are sorted by nondecreasing order. Therefore, back to Eq. (8), we find that the entries of $\bigwedge^s \tilde{N}(x)$ have degree at most $p\mu\cdot\deg_T P + s\cdot\deg_x P$. It is then also the case of its trace, which is the same as the trace of $\bigwedge^s N(x)$ since $N(x)$ and $\tilde{N}(x)$ are similar. This finally implies the claimed inequality (7) because $\delta(x)$ has to divide this trace.

The Proposition now follows by inserting the above input in the proof of Proposition 2.5. □

2.4 Algorithms

We keep the matrix $M(x)$ satisfying the assumptions (i) and (ii) of §2.3. From now on, we assume that the only access we have to the matrix $M(x)$ passes through a black box $\texttt{invariant\_factors\_at}_{M(x)}$ that takes as input an element a lying in a finite extension ℓ of k and outputs instantly the invariant factors $I_{j,a}(T)$ of the matrix $M(a)$. Our aim is to compute the invariant factors of $M(x)$. We will propose two possible approaches: the first one is deterministic but rather slow although the second one is faster but probabilistic and comes up with a Monte-Carlo algorithm which may sometimes output wrong answers.

Throughout this section, the letter D refers to *a priori* upper bound on the X-degree of the characteristic polynomial of $M(x)$. One can of course always take $D = mn$ but better bounds might be available in particular cases. Similarly we reserve the letter F for an upper bound on the sum of degrees of "unlucky evaluation points". Proposition 2.5 tells us that $mn(6n-5)$ is always an acceptable value for F. Remember however that this value can be lowered to $3\mu(2n-1)$ under the hypothesis $(\mathbf{H}_\mu)$ thanks to Proposition 2.6. We will always assume that $F \geq D$.

For simplicity of exposition, we assume from now on that $k = \mathbb{F}_q$ is a finite field of cardinality q (it is more difficult and the case of most interest for us).

Deterministic. The discussion of §2.3 suggests the following algorithm whose correctness follows directly from the definition of F together with the assumption $F \geq D$.

Algorithm `invariant_factors_deterministic`
Input: $M(x)$ satisfying (i) and (ii), D, F with $F \geq D$
Output: The invariant factors of $M(x)$

1. Construct an extension ℓ of $\mathbb{F}_q$ of degree $F+1$ and pick an element $a \in \ell$ such that $\ell = \mathbb{F}_q[a]$
   Cost: $O\tilde{}(F)$ operations in $\mathbb{F}_q$
2. $I_{1,a}(T), \ldots, I_{n,a}(T) =$ `invariant_factors_at`$_{M(x)}(a)$
3. **for** $j = 1, \ldots, n$
4. Find $I_j(x,T)$ of degree $\leq D$ s.t. $I_j(a,T) = I_{j,a}(T)$
5. **return** $I_1(x,T), \ldots, I_n(x,T)$

Proposition 2.7. *The algorithm above requires only one call to the black box* `invariant_factors_at`$_{M(x)}$ *with an input of degree exactly* $F+1$.

Probabilistic. We now present a Monte-Carlo algorithm:

Algorithm `invariant_factors_montecarlo`
Input: $M(x)$ s.t. (i) and (ii), $\varepsilon \in (0,1)$, D, F with $F \geq D$
Output: The invariant factors of $M(x)$

1. Find the smallest integer s such that:
$$2 \cdot \frac{(D+s+1)^2}{s(q^s - 2F)} + \frac{1}{2} \cdot \left(\frac{4F}{q^s}\right)^{(D-2)/s} \leq \varepsilon \qquad (9)$$
   and set $K = \lceil \frac{3D}{s} \rceil$ and $k = \lceil \frac{D+1}{s} \rceil$.
2. **for** $i = 1, \ldots, K$
3. pick at random $a_i \in \mathbb{F}_{q^s}$ s.t. $\mathbb{F}_{q^s} = \mathbb{F}_q[a_i]$
   Cost: $O\tilde{}(s)$ operations in $\mathbb{F}_q$
4. $I_{1,i}(T), \ldots, I_{n,i}(T) =$ `invariant_factors_at`$_{M(x)}(a_i)$
5. **for** $j = 1, \ldots, n$
6. $d_j = \max_i \deg(I_{1,i}(T) \cdot I_{2,i}(T) \cdots I_{j,i}(T))$
7. select $I \subset \{1, \ldots, K\}$ of cardinality k s.t.
   (i) $\deg(I_{1,i}(T) \cdot I_{2,i}(T) \cdots I_{j,i}(T)) = d_j$ for all $i \in I$
   (ii) the a_i are pairwise non conjugate for $i \in I$
   Remark: if such I does not exist, raise an error
8. compute $I_j \in \mathbb{F}_q[X,T]$ of X-degree $\leq D$ s.t.
   $I_j(a_i, T) = I_{j,i}(T)$ for all $i \in I$
   Cost: $O\tilde{}(D)$ operations in $\mathbb{F}_q$
9. **return** $I_1(x,T), \ldots, I_n(x,T)$

Proposition 2.8. *We have* $s \in O(\log \frac{FD}{\varepsilon})$. *Moreover:*

- Correctness: *Algorithm* `invariant_factors_montecarlo` *fails or returns a wrong answer with probability at most* ε.
- Complexity: *It performs* $\lceil \frac{3D}{s} \rceil$ *calls to the black box with inputs of degree* s *and* $O\tilde{}(n(D + \log \frac{F}{\varepsilon}))$ *operations in* $\mathbb{F}_q$.

Proof. The first assertion is left to the reader. Let $\mathcal{A}$ be the set of elements a of $\mathbb{F}_{q^s}$ such that $\mathbb{F}_q[a] = \mathbb{F}_{q^s}$. It is an easy exercise to prove that $\mathcal{A}$ has at least $\frac{q^s}{2}$ elements (the bound is not sharp). Let $\mathcal{C}_1, \ldots, \mathcal{C}_C$ be the conjugacy classes (under the Galois action) in $\mathcal{A}$. Remark that each $\mathcal{C}_i$ has by definition s elements, so that $C \geq \frac{q^s}{2s}$. We say that a conjugacy class is *bad* if it contains one element a for which $I_j(a,T) \neq I_{a,j}(T)$ for some j. Otherwise, we say that it is *good*. Let B (resp. G) be the number of bad (resp. good) classes. We have $B + G = C$ and $B \leq \frac{F}{s}$ by definition of F.

The algorithm `invariant_factors_montecarlo` succeeds if there exist at least k indices i for which the corresponding a_i's lie in pairwise distinct good classes. This happens with probability at least:

$$\frac{1}{C^K} \cdot \sum_{j=k}^{K} \binom{K}{j} \cdot G(G-1)\cdots(G-k+1) \cdot G^{j-k} \cdot B^{K-j}.$$

(The above formula gives the probability that the *first* k good classes are pairwise distinct, which is actually stronger than what we need.) The above quantity is at least equal to

$$\left(1 - \frac{k}{G}\right)^k \cdot \left(1 - \sum_{j=0}^{k-1} \binom{K}{j} \cdot \left(\frac{G}{C}\right)^j \cdot \left(\frac{B}{C}\right)^{K-j}\right).$$

Moreover for $j \leq k-1$, we have:

$$\left(\frac{G}{C}\right)^j \cdot \left(\frac{B}{C}\right)^{K-j} \leq \left(\frac{BG}{C^2}\right)^j \cdot \left(\frac{B}{C}\right)^{K-2j} \leq \frac{1}{2^{2j}} \cdot \left(\frac{2F}{q^s}\right)^{K-2j}$$
$$\leq \frac{1}{2^K} \cdot \left(\frac{4F}{q^s}\right)^{K-2j} \leq \frac{1}{2^K} \cdot \left(\frac{4F}{q^s}\right)^{(D-2)/s}.$$

Therefore the probability of success is at least:

$$\left(1 - \frac{k}{G}\right)^k \cdot \left(1 - \frac{1}{2} \cdot \left(\frac{4F}{q^s}\right)^{(D-2)/s}\right).$$

Using $k \leq \frac{D+s+1}{s}$ and $G \geq \frac{q^2 - 2F}{2s}$, we find that the probability of failure is at most the LHS of Eq. (9). The correctness is proved. As for the complexity, the results are obvious. □

3. COMPUTING INVARIANT FACTORS OF THE P-CURVATURE

Throughout this section, we fix a finite field $k = \mathbb{F}_q$ of cardinality q and characteristic p. We endow the field of rational functions $k(x)$ with the natural derivation $f \mapsto f'$.

3.1 The case of differential modules

We recall that a differential module over $k(x)$ is $k(x)$-vector space M endowed with an additive map $\partial : M \to M$ satisfying the following Leibniz rule:

$$\forall f \in k(x), \forall m \in M, \quad \partial(fm) = f' \cdot m + f \cdot \partial(m).$$

The *p-curvature* of a differential module M is the mapping $\partial^p = \partial \circ \cdots \circ \partial$ (p times). Using the fact that the p-th derivative of any $f \in k(x)$ vanishes, we derive from the Leibniz relation above that ∂^p is $k(x)$-linear endomorphism of M. It follows moreover from [4, Remark 4.5] that ∂^p is defined over $k(x^p)$, in the sense that there exists a $k(x)$-basis of M in which the matrix of ∂^p has coefficients in $k(x^p)$. In particular, all the invariant factors of the p-curvature have their coefficients in $k(x^p)$.

Statement of the main Theorem. From now on, we fix a differential module (M, ∂). We assume that M is finite dimensional over $k(x)$ and let r denote its dimension. We pick $(e_1, \ldots, e_r)$ a basis of M and let A denote the matrix of ∂ with respect to this basis. We write $A = \frac{1}{f_A}\tilde{A}$ where f_A and the entries of $\tilde{A}$ all lie in $k[x]$. Let d be an upper bound on the degrees of all these polynomials. The aim of this section is to design fast deterministic and probabilistic algorithms for computing the invariant factors of the p-curvature of (M, ∂). The following Theorem summarizes our results.

THEOREM 3.1. *We assume $p > r$.*

1. There exists a deterministic algorithm that computes the invariant factors of the p-curvature of (M, ∂) within

$$O\tilde{~}\big(d^{\omega+\frac{3}{2}} r^{\omega+2} \sqrt{p}\big)$$

operations in $k = \mathbb{F}_q$.

2. Let $\varepsilon \in (0,1)$. There exists a Monte-Carlo algorithm that computes the invariant factors of the p-curvature of (M, ∂) in

$$O\tilde{~}\big(d^{\omega+\frac{1}{2}} r^{\omega} \cdot (dr - \log \varepsilon) \cdot \sqrt{p}\big)$$

operations in $k = \mathbb{F}_q$. This algorithm returns a wrong answer with probability at most ε.

In what follows, we will use the notation $A_p(x)$ for the matrix of the p-curvature of (M, ∂) with respect to the distinguished basis $(e_1, \ldots, e_r)$. Given an element a lying in a finite extension ℓ of k, we denote by $A_p(a) \in M_r(\ell)$ the matrix deduced from A_p by evaluating it at $x = a$.

The similarity class of $A_p(a)$. Let S be an irreducible polynomial over k. Set $\ell = k[u]/S$ and let a denote the image of the variable u in ℓ. We assume that S does not divide f_A, i.e., $f_A(a) \neq 0$. The first ingredient we need is the construction of an auxiliary matrix which is similar to $A_p(a)$. This construction comes from our previous paper [4]. Let us recall it briefly. We define the ring $\ell[[t]]^{\mathrm{dp}}$ of Hurwitz series whose elements are formal infinite sums of the shape:

$$a_0 + a_1\gamma_1(t) + a_2\gamma_2(t) + \cdots + a_n\gamma_n(t) + \cdots \qquad (10)$$

and on which the addition is straightforward and the multiplication is governed by the rule $\gamma_i(t) \cdot \gamma_j(t) = \binom{i+j}{i}\gamma_{i+j}(t)$. (The symbol $\gamma_i(t)$ should be thought of as $\frac{t^i}{i!}$.) We moreover endow $\ell[[t]]^{\mathrm{dp}}$ with the derivation defined by $\gamma_i(t)' = \gamma_{i-1}(t)$ (with the convention that $\gamma_0(t) = 1$) and the projection map $\mathrm{pr} : \ell[[t]]^{\mathrm{dp}} \to \ell$ sending the series given by Eq. (10) to its constant coefficient a_0. We shall often use the alternative notation $f(0)$ for $\mathrm{pr}(f)$. If $f \in \ell[[t]]^{\mathrm{dp}}$ is given by the series (10), we then have $a_n = f^{(n)}(0)$ for all nonnegative integers n. We have a homomorphism of rings:

$$\psi_S : k[x][\tfrac{1}{f_A}] \to \ell[[t]]^{\mathrm{dp}}, \quad f(x) \mapsto \sum_{i=0}^{p-1} f^{(i)}(a)\gamma_i(t).$$

It is easily checked that ψ_S commutes with the derivation. We can then consider the differential module over $\ell[[t]]^{\mathrm{dp}}$ obtained from (M, ∂) by scalar extension. By definition, it corresponds to the differential system $Y' = \psi_S(A) \cdot Y$.

The benefit of working over $\ell[[t]]^{\mathrm{dp}}$ is the existence of an analogue of the well-known Cauchy–Lipschitz Theorem [4, Proposition 3.4]. This notably implies the existence of a fundamental matrix of solutions, i.e., an $r \times r$ matrix Y_S with entries in $\ell[[t]]^{\mathrm{dp}}$, and satisfying:

$$Y_S' = \psi_S(A) \cdot Y_S \quad \text{and} \quad Y_S(0) = \mathrm{I}_r \qquad (11)$$

with I_r the identity matrix of size r. Moreover, as explained in more details later, the construction of Y_S is effective.

For any integer $n \geq 0$, we let $Y_S^{(n)}$ denote the matrix obtained from Y_S by taking the n-th derivative entry-wise. The next proposition is a consequence of [4, Proposition 4.4].

PROPOSITION 3.2. *The matrices $A_p(a)$ and $-Y_S^{(p)}(0)$ are similar over ℓ.*

Fast computation of $Y_S^{(p)}(0)$. We recall that Y_S is defined as the solution of the system (11). Remembering that we have written $A = \frac{1}{f_A}\tilde{A}$, we obtain the relation:

$$\psi_S(f_A) \cdot Y_S' = \psi_S(\tilde{A}) \cdot Y_S. \qquad (12)$$

Write $f_A = \sum_{i=0}^{d} f_i \cdot (x-a)^i$ and $\tilde{A} = \sum_{i=0}^{d} \tilde{A}_i \cdot (x-a)^i$ where the f_i's lie in ℓ and the A_i's are square matrices of size r with entries in ℓ. Remark that f_0 does not vanish because it is equal to $f_A(a)$. Note moreover that the f_i's can be computed for a cost of $O\tilde{~}(d)$ operations in k using divide-and-conquer techniques. Given a fixed pair of indices (i', j'), the same discussion applies to the collection of the (i', j')-entries of the A_i's. The total cost for computing the decompositions of f_A and $\tilde{A}$ is then $O\tilde{~}(dr^2)$. Now, coming back to the definitions, we find that $\psi_S(f_A) = \sum_{i=0}^{d} i! f_i \cdot \gamma_i(t)$ and $\psi_S(\tilde{A}) = \sum_{i=0}^{d} i! \tilde{A}_i \cdot \gamma_i(t)$. Eq. (12) yields the recurrence:

$$Y_S^{(n+1)}(0) = \sum_{i=0}^{\min(n,d)} B_i(n) \cdot Y_S^{(n-i)}(0) \qquad (13)$$

where the $B_i \in M_r(\ell[u])$ are defined by:

$$f_0 B_i = u(u-1)\cdots(u-i+1) \cdot \big(\tilde{A}_i - (u-i) f_{i+1} \cdot \mathrm{I}_r\big) \qquad (14)$$

with the convention that $f_{d+1} = 0$. Now setting:

$$Z_n = \begin{pmatrix} Y_S^{(n-d)}(0) \\ Y_S^{(n-d+1)}(0) \\ \vdots \\ Y_S^{(n)}(0) \end{pmatrix}, \quad B = \begin{pmatrix} & \mathrm{I}_r & & & \\ & & \mathrm{I}_r & & \\ & & & \ddots & \\ & & & & \mathrm{I}_r \\ B_d & \cdots & \cdots & \cdots & B_0 \end{pmatrix}$$

(with the convention $Y_S^{(i)}(0) = 0$ when $i < 0$), the recurrence (13) becomes $Z_{n+1} = B(n) \cdot Z_n$. Hence, we obtain $Z_p = B(p-1) \cdot B(p-2) \cdots B(0) \cdot Z_0$ from what we finally get that $Y_S^{(p)}(0)$ is the $(r \times r)$-matrix located at the bottom right corner of $B(p-1) \cdot B(p-2) \cdots B(0)$. The computation of the former matrix factorial can be performed efficiently using a variation of the Chudnovskys' algorithm [12, 6]. Combining this with Proposition 3.2, we end up with the following.

PROPOSITION 3.3. *The invariant factors of $A_p(a)$ can be computed in $O\tilde{~}(d^\omega r^\omega \sqrt{dp})$ operations in the field ℓ.*

PROOF. Note that B is a square matrix of size $(d+1)r$. Moreover coming back to (14), we observe that the entries of B all have degree at most d. By [5, Theorem 2] the matrix factorial $-B(p-1) \cdot B(p-2) \cdots B(0)$ can then be computed for the cost of $O\tilde{~}(d^\omega r^\omega \sqrt{dp})$ operations in ℓ. By [30], the invariant factors of its submatrix $-Y_S^{(p)}(0)$ can be obtained for an extra cost of $O\tilde{~}(r^\omega)$ operations in ℓ (which is negligible compared to the previous one). Using Proposition 3.2 these invariant factors are also those of $A_p(a)$, and we are done. □

Conclusion. Proposition 3.3 yields an acceptable primitive `invariant_factors_at`$_{A_p(x)}$. Plugging it in the algorithm `invariant_factors_deterministic` and using the parameters $D = dr$ and $F = 6dr(r-1)$, we end up with an algorithm that computes the invariant factors of $A_p(x)$ for the cost of one unique call to `invariant_factors_at`$_{A_p(x)}$ with an input lying in an extension ℓ/k of degree $F+1$ (cf. Proposition 2.7). By Proposition 3.3, we find that the total complexity of the obtained algorithm is $O\tilde{}\big(d^{\omega+\frac{3}{2}} r^{\omega+2} \sqrt{p}\big)$ operations in $\mathbb{F}_q$. The first part of Theorem 3.1 is then established. The second part is obtained in a similar fashion using the algorithm `invariant_factors_montecarlo` together with Proposition 2.8 for correctness and complexity results.

3.2 The case of differential operators

The ring of differential operators $k(x)\langle\partial\rangle$ is the ring of usual polynomials over $k(x)$ in the variable ∂ except that the multiplication is ruled by the relation $\partial \cdot f = f \cdot \partial + f'$. We define similarly the ring $k[x]\langle\partial\rangle$. We say that $L \in k[x]\langle\partial\rangle$ has bidegree (d, r) if it has degree d with respect to x and degree r with respect to ∂.

If L is a differential operator in $k(x)\langle\partial\rangle$, one easily checks that the set $k(x)\langle\partial\rangle\, L$ of left multiples of L is a left ideal of $k(x)\langle\partial\rangle$. The quotient $M_L = k(x)\langle\partial\rangle / k(x)\langle\partial\rangle\, L$ is then a vector space over $k(x)$. It is moreover endowed with a map $\partial : M_L \to M_L$ given by the left multiplication by ∂. This map turns M_L into a differential module.

We shall prove in this section that the complexities announced in Theorem 3.1 can be improved in the case of differential modules coming from differential operators. Below is the statement of our precise result.

THEOREM 3.4. *Let $L \in k[x]\langle\partial\rangle$ be a differential operator of bidegree (d, r). We assume $p > r$.*

1. There exists a deterministic algorithm that computes the invariant factors of the p-curvature of M_L within

$$O\tilde{}\big((d+r)^{\omega+1} d^{\frac{1}{2}} r \cdot \sqrt{p}\big)$$

operations in $k = \mathbb{F}_q$.

2. Let $\varepsilon \in (0,1)$. There exists a Monte-Carlo algorithm that computes the invariant factors of the p-curvature of M_L in

$$O\tilde{}\big((d+r)^{\omega} d^{\frac{1}{2}} \cdot (d - \log\varepsilon) \cdot \sqrt{p}\big)$$

operations in $k = \mathbb{F}_q$. This algorithm returns a wrong answer with probability at most ε.

Better bounds. From now on, we fix a differential operator $L \in k(x)\langle\partial\rangle$ of bidegree (d, r). We denote by $A_p(x)$ the matrix of the p-curvature of M_L with respect to the canonical basis $(1, \partial, \dots, \partial^{r-1})$. If $a_r(x)$ is the leading coefficient of L (with respect to ∂), it follows from [13, Proposition 3.2] that $A_p(x)$ has the form $A_p(x) = \frac{1}{a_r(x)^p} \cdot \tilde{A}_p(x)$ where $\tilde{A}_p(x)$ is a matrix with polynomial entries of degree at most pd.

PROPOSITION 3.5. *The matrix $\tilde{A}_p(x)$ satisfies the hypothesis ($\boldsymbol{H}_{r+d}$) (introduced just before Proposition 2.6).*

PROOF. This is a direct consequence of Lemma 3.9 and Theorem 3.11 of [3]. □

The similarity class of $A_p(a)$. We now revisit Proposition 3.3 when the differential module comes from the differential operator L. We fix an irreducible polynomial $S \in k[x]$ and assume that S is coprime with the leading coefficient $a_r(x)$ of L. We set $\ell = k[x]/S$ and let a denote the image of x is ℓ. We define $t = x - a \in \ell[x]$ and consider the ring of differential operators $\ell[x]\langle\partial\rangle$. The latter acts on $\ell[[t]]^{\mathrm{dp}}$ by letting ∂ act as the derivation. Let Y_S be the fundamental system of solutions of the equation $Y_S' = \psi_S(A) \cdot Y_S$ where A is the companion matrix which gives the action of ∂ on M_L. It takes the form:

$$Y_S = \begin{pmatrix} y_0 & y_1 & \cdots & y_{r-1} \\ y_0' & y_1' & \cdots & y_{r-1}' \\ \vdots & \vdots & & \vdots \\ y_0^{(r-1)} & y_1^{(r-1)} & \cdots & y_{r-1}^{(r-1)} \end{pmatrix}$$

where $y_j \in \ell[[t]]^{\mathrm{dp}}$ is the unique solution of the differential equation $Ly_j = 0$ with initial conditions $y_j^{(n)}(0) = \delta_{j,n}$ (where $\delta_{\cdot,\cdot}$ is the Kronecker symbol) for $0 \leq n < r$.

We introduce the Euler operator $\theta = t \cdot \partial \in \ell[x]\langle\partial\rangle$. Using the techniques of [3, Section 4.1], one can write $L \cdot \partial^d = \sum_{i=0}^{d+r} b_i(\theta)\partial^i$ within $O\tilde{}((r+d)d)$ operations in ℓ. Here the b_i's are polynomials with coefficients in ℓ of degree at most d. One can check moreover that the polynomial b_{d+r} is constant equal to $a_r(a)$; in particular, it does not vanish thanks to our assumption on S. For all j, define $z_j = \sum_{n=0}^{\infty} y_j^{(n)}(0)\gamma_{n+d}(t)$. Clearly $\partial^d z_j = y_j$, so that we have $\left(\sum_{i=0}^{d+r} b_i(\theta)\partial^i\right) \cdot z_i = 0$ for all i. Noting that θ acts on $\gamma_n(t)$ by multiplication by n, we get the recurrence relation:

$$\forall n \geq 0, \quad \sum_{i=0}^{d+r} b_i(n) \cdot y_j^{(n+i-d)}(0) = 0$$

with the convention that $y_j^{(n)} = 0$ when $n < 0$. Letting:

$$Z_n = \begin{pmatrix} y_0^{(n-d)}(0) & \cdots & y_{r-1}^{(n-d)}(0) \\ y_0^{(n-d+1)}(0) & \cdots & y_{r-1}^{(n-d+1)}(0) \\ \vdots & & \vdots \\ Y_0^{(n+r-1)}(0) & \cdots & y_{r-1}^{(n+r-1)}(0) \end{pmatrix} \in M_{d+r,r}(\ell)$$

$$\text{and} \quad B = \frac{-1}{a_r(a)} \cdot \begin{pmatrix} & 1 & & \\ & & \ddots & \\ & & & 1 \\ b_0 & b_1 & \cdots & b_{d+r-1} \end{pmatrix} \in M_{d+r,d+r}(\ell)$$

the above recurrence rewrites $Z_{n+1} = B(n)Z_n$. Solving the recurrence, we get $Z_p = B(p-1) \cdots B(0) \cdot Z_0$, and we derive that $Y_S^{(p)}(0)$ is the $(r \times r)$ matrix located at the bottom right corner of $B(p-1) \cdot B(p-2) \cdots B(0)$. Using Proposition 3.2 and [5, Theorem 2], we end up with the following proposition (compare with Proposition 3.3).

PROPOSITION 3.6. *The invariant factors of $A_p(a)$ can be computed in $O\tilde{}((d+r)^{\omega}\sqrt{dp})$ operations in the field ℓ.*

Conclusion. The final discussion is now similar to the one we had in the case of differential modules. Proposition 3.6 provides the primitive `invariant_factors_at`$_{A_p(x)}$. Using it in the algorithms `invariant_factors_deterministic` and `invariant_factors_montecarlo` with the parameters $D = d$ and $F = 3d(2r-1)$ (coming from the combination of Propositions 2.6 and 3.5), we respectively end up with deterministic and Monte-Carlo algorithms whose complexities agree with the ones announced in Theorem 3.4.

It is instructive to compare the methods and results of this section with those of our previous paper [3]. We remark that the matrix factorial considered above is nothing but the specialization at $\theta = 0$ of the matrix factorial in [3]. Although the theoretical approaches of the two papers are definitively different, they lead to very similar computations. However, each of them has its own advantages and disadvantages. On the one hand, the methods of [3] only deal with characteristic polynomials and cannot see invariant factors. On the other hand, they do not require the assumption $a_r(a) \neq 0$ (that is why we always took $a = 0$ in [3]) and can handle at the same time the local computations at the point a and *around* it, i.e., they provide roughly speaking a framework which allows to work modulo $(x-a)^{pn}$ for some integer n fixed in advance (not just $n = 1$) without increasing the complexity with respect to p. The practical consequence is that the methods of the current paper end up with algorithms whose complexity is weakened by a factor $\sqrt{d}$ compared to what we might have expected at first. It would be very interesting to find a general theoretical setting unifying the two approaches discussed above and allowing the benefits of both of them.

4. SOLVING A PHYSICAL APPLICATION

In [10], a globally nilpotent differential operator $\phi_H^{(6)}$ was introduced in order to model the 6-particle contribution to the square lattice Ising model. As shown in *loc. cit.*, this operator factors as a product of differential operators of smaller orders. The factor which is the least understood is called L_{23} and has order 23. Actually L_{23} has not been computed so far because its size is too large. Nevertheless there exists a multiple of L_{23} which has a more reasonable size: its bidegree is $(140, 77)$. It turns out that this multiple, say L_{77}, has been determined modulo several prime numbers. Based on this computation and using the strategy developed in this paper, we were able to study a bit further the factorization of L_{23}, answering a question of the authors of [10].

PROPOSITION 4.1. *The operator L_{23} cannot be factorized as a product $L_{21} \cdot L_2$ where L_2 is an operator of order 2, and L_{21} is an operator of order 21 whose differential module is isomorphic to a symmetric product $\mathrm{Sym}^n M$ for an integer $n > 1$ and a differential module M.*

PROOF. We argue by contradiction by assuming that such a factorization exists. This would imply that, for all p the matrix $A_{23,p}$ of the p-curvature of L_{23} mod p decomposes:

$$A_{23,p} = \begin{pmatrix} A_{2,p} & \star \\ 0 & A_{21,p} \end{pmatrix} \qquad (15)$$

where $A_{2,p}$ (resp. $A_{21,p}$) is the square matrix of size 2 (resp. 21) and $A_{21,p}$ is similar to a symmetric product of a $d \times d$ matrix $A_{d,p}$. We now pick $p = 32647$ for which L_{77} mod p is known. Using Proposition 3.3, we were able to determine the invariant factors of the p-curvature of $A_{77,p}(15)$. The computation ran actually rather fast: just a few minutes. We observed that the generalized eigenspace of $A_{77,p}(15)$ for the eigenvalue 0 has dimension 23. Combining this with that fact that L_{23} is a factor of L_{77} whose p-curvature is nilpotent, we deduce that the restriction of $A_{77,p}(15)$ to this characteristic space is similar to $A_{23,p}(15)$. Arguing similarly, we determine the Jordan type of $A_{23,p}(15)$:

m	0	1	2	3	4	≥ 5
$\mathrm{rank}(A_{23,p}(15)^m)$	23	17	11	6	3	0

Moreover the writing (15) would imply that for all m:

$$0 \leq \mathrm{rank}\big(A_{23,p}(15)^m\big) - \mathrm{rank}\big(A_{21,p}(15)^m\big) \leq 2$$
$$\text{and} \quad \mathrm{rank}\big(A_{21,p}(15)^m\big) = \binom{n - 1 + \mathrm{rank}\big(A_{d,p}(15)^m\big)}{n}.$$

There is only one way to satisfy these numerical constraints which consists in taking $n = 2$ and:

m	0	1	2	3	4	≥ 5
$\mathrm{rank}(A_{d,p}(15)^m)$	6	5	4	3	2	0

Since the sequence $\mathrm{rank}\big(A_{d,p}(15)^m\big) - \mathrm{rank}\big(A_{d,p}(15)^{m+1}\big)$ has to be non-increasing, this is impossible. ☐

5. REFERENCES

[1] Y. André. Sur la conjecture des p-courbures de Grothendieck-Katz et un problème de Dwork. In *Geometric aspects of Dwork theory. Vol. I, II*, pages 55–112. Walter de Gruyter GmbH & Co. KG, Berlin, 2004.

[2] A. Bostan, S. Boukraa, S. Hassani, J.-M. Maillard, J.-A. Weil, and N. Zenine. Globally nilpotent differential operators and the square Ising model. *J. Phys. A*, 42(12):125206, 50, 2009.

[3] A. Bostan, X. Caruso, and E. Schost. A fast algorithm for computing the characteristic polynomial of the p-curvature. In *ISSAC'14*, pages 59–66. ACM, New York, 2014.

[4] A. Bostan, X. Caruso, and E. Schost. A fast algorithm for computing the p-curvature. In *ISSAC'15*, pages 69–76. ACM, New York, 2015.

[5] A. Bostan, T. Cluzeau, and B. Salvy. Fast algorithms for polynomial solutions of linear differential equations. In *ISSAC'05*, pages 45–52. ACM Press, 2005.

[6] A. Bostan, P. Gaudry, and É. Schost. Linear recurrences with polynomial coefficients and application to integer factorization and Cartier-Manin operator. *SIAM Journal on Computing*, 36(6):1777–1806, 2007.

[7] A. Bostan and M. Kauers. Automatic classification of restricted lattice walks. In *FPSAC'09*, DMTCS Proc., AK, pages 201–215. 2009.

[8] A. Bostan and M. Kauers. The complete generating function for Gessel walks is algebraic. *Proc. Amer. Math. Soc.*, 138(9):3063–3078, 2010. With an appendix by Mark van Hoeij.

[9] A. Bostan and É. Schost. Fast algorithms for differential equations in positive characteristic. In *ISSAC'09*, pages 47–54. ACM, New York, 2009.

[10] S. Boukraa, S. Hassani, I. Jensen, J.-M. Maillard, and N. Zenine. High-order Fuchsian equations for the square lattice Ising model: $\chi^{(6)}$. *J. Phys. A*, 43(11):115201, 22, 2010.

[11] D. G. Cantor and E. Kaltofen. On fast multiplication of polynomials over arbitrary algebras. *Acta Inform.*, 28(7):693–701, 1991.

[12] D. V. Chudnovsky and G. V. Chudnovsky. Approximations and complex multiplication according to Ramanujan. In *Ramanujan revisited (Urbana-Champaign, 1987)*, pages 375–472. Academic Press, Boston, 1988.

[13] T. Cluzeau. Factorization of differential systems in characteristic p. In *ISSAC'03*, pages 58–65. ACM Press, 2003.

[14] W. Eberly. Asymptotically efficient algorithms for the Frobenius form. Technical report, 2000.

[15] F. L. Gall. Powers of tensors and fast matrix multiplication. In *ISSAC'14*, pages 296–303, 2014.

[16] F. R. Gantmacher. *The theory of matrices. Vols. 1, 2*. Translated by K. A. Hirsch. Chelsea Publishing Co., New York, 1959.

[17] J. von zur Gathen and J. Gerhard. *Modern Computer Algebra*. Cambridge University Press, second edition, 2003.

[18] M. Giesbrecht. *Nearly optimal algorithms for canonical matrix forms*. PhD thesis, University of Toronto, 1993.

[19] M. Giesbrecht. Nearly optimal algorithms for canonical matrix forms. *SIAM Journal on Computing*, 24(5):948–969, 10 1995.

[20] M. Giesbrecht and A. Storjohann. Computing rational forms of integer matrices. *Journal of Symbolic Computation*, 34(3):157–172, 2002.

[21] D. Harvey, J. van der Hoeven, and G. Lecerf. Faster polynomial multiplication over finite fields. http://arxiv.org/abs/1407.3361, 2014.

[22] T. Honda. Algebraic differential equations. In *Symposia Mathematica, Vol. XXIV*, pages 169–204. Academic Press, London, 1981.

[23] E. Kaltofen, M. S. Krishnamoorthy, and B. D. Saunders. Fast parallel computation of Hermite and Smith forms of polynomial matrices. *SIAM Journal on Matrix Analysis and Applications*, 8(4):683–690, 1987.

[24] E. Kaltofen, M. S. Krishnamoorthy, and B. D. Saunders. Parallel algorithms for matrix normal forms. *Linear Algebra and its Applications*, 136:189–208, 1990.

[25] E. Kaltofen and G. Villard. On the complexity of computing determinants. *Comput. Complexity*, 13(3-4):91–130, 2004.

[26] N. M. Katz. Algebraic solutions of differential equations (p-curvature and the Hodge filtration). *Invent. Math.*, 18:1–118, 1972.

[27] N. M. Katz. A conjecture in the arithmetic theory of differential equations. *Bull. Soc. Math. France*, (110):203–239, 1982.

[28] C. Pernet and A. Storjohann. Frobenius form in expected matrix multiplication time over sufficiently large fields, 2007.

[29] A. Schönhage. Schnelle Multiplikation von Polynomen über Körpern der Charakteristik 2. *Acta Informatica*, 7:395–398, 1977.

[30] A. Storjohann. Deterministic computation of the Frobenius form. In *FOCS'01*, pages 368–377. IEEE Computer Society Press, 2001.

[31] A. Storjohann and G. Labahn. A fast Las Vegas algorithm for computing the Smith normal form of a polynomial matrix. *Linear Algebra and its Applications*, 253(1–3):155–173, 1997.

[32] M. van der Put. Differential equations in characteristic p. *Compositio Mathematica*, 97:227–251, 1995.

[33] M. van der Put. Reduction modulo p of differential equations. *Indag. Mathem.*, 7(3):367–387, 1996.

Fast Computation of the Nth Term of an Algebraic Series over a Finite Prime Field*

Alin Bostan
Inria (France)
alin.bostan@inria.fr

Gilles Christol
IMJ (France)
gilles.christol@imj-prg.fr

Philippe Dumas
Inria (France)
philippe.dumas@inria.fr

ABSTRACT

We address the question of computing one selected term of an algebraic power series. In characteristic zero, the best algorithm currently known for computing the Nth coefficient of an algebraic series uses differential equations and has arithmetic complexity quasi-linear in $\sqrt{N}$. We show that over a prime field of positive characteristic p, the complexity can be lowered to $O(\log N)$. The mathematical basis for this dramatic improvement is a classical theorem stating that a formal power series with coefficients in a finite field is algebraic if and only if the sequence of its coefficients can be generated by an automaton. We revisit and enhance two constructive proofs of this result for finite prime fields. The first proof uses Mahler equations, whose sizes appear to be prohibitively large. The second proof relies on diagonals of rational functions; we turn it into an efficient algorithm, of complexity linear in $\log N$ and quasi-linear in p.

Keywords

algebraic series; finite fields; Mahler equations; diagonals; p-rational series; section operators; algebraic complexity

1. INTRODUCTION

One of the most difficult questions in modular computations is the complexity of computations mod p *for a large prime* p *of coefficients in the expansion of an algebraic function.*

D.V. Chudnovsky & G.V. Chudnovsky, 1990 [11].

Context. Algebraic functions are ubiquitous in all branches of pure and applied mathematics, notably in algebraic geometry, combinatorics and number theory. They also arise at the confluence of several fields in computer science: functional equations, automatic sequences, complexity theory. From a computer algebra perspective, a fundamental question is the efficient computation of power series expansions of algebraic functions. We focus on the particular question of computing *one selected term* of an *algebraic power series* f whose coefficients belong to a *field of positive characteristic* p. Beyond its relevance to complexity theory, this problem is important in applications to integer factorization and point-counting [4].

Setting. More precisely, we assume in this article that the ground field is the prime field $\mathbb{F}_p$ and that the power series f is (implicitly) given as the unique solution in $\mathbb{F}_p[[x]]$ of

$$E(x, f(x)) = 0, \qquad f(0) = 0,$$

where E is a polynomial in $\mathbb{F}_p[x, y]$ that satisfies

$$E(0, 0) = 0 \quad \text{and} \quad E_y(0, 0) \neq 0.$$

(Here, and hereafter, E_y stands for the partial derivative $\frac{\partial E}{\partial y}$.)

Given as input the polynomial E and an integer $N > 0$, our algorithmic problem is to efficiently compute the Nth coefficient f_N of $f = \sum_i f_i x^i$. The efficiency is measured in terms of number of arithmetic operations ($\pm, \times, \div$) in the field $\mathbb{F}_p$, the main parameters being the index N, the prime p and the bidegree (h, d) of E with respect to (x, y).

In the particular case $d = 1$, the algebraic function f is actually a rational function, and thus the Nth coefficient of its series expansion can be computed in $O(\log N)$ operations in $\mathbb{F}_p$, using standard binary powering techniques [20, 14].

Therefore, it will be assumed in all that follows that $d > 1$.

Previous work and contribution. The most straightforward method for computing the coefficient f_N of the algebraic power series f proceeds by undetermined coefficients. Its arithmetic complexity is $O(N^d)$. Kung and Traub [19] showed that the formal Newton iteration can accelerate this to $\tilde{O}(dN)$. (The soft-O notation $\tilde{O}(\cdot)$ indicates that polylogarithmic factors are omitted.) Both methods work in arbitrary characteristic and compute f_N together with all $f_i, i < N$.

In characteristic zero, it is possible to compute the coefficient f_N faster, without computing all the previous ones. This result is due to the Chudnovsky brothers [10] and is based on the classical fact that the coefficient sequence $(f_n)_{n \geq 0}$ satisfies a linear recurrence with polynomial coefficients [12, 9, 3]. Combined with baby steps/giant steps techniques, this leads to an algorithm of complexity quasi-linear in $\sqrt{N}$. Except for the very particular case of rational functions ($d = 1$), no faster method is currently known.

Under restrictive assumptions, the baby step/giant step algorithm can be adapted to the case of positive characteristic [4]. The main obstacle is the fact that the linear recurrence satisfied by the sequence $(f_n)_{n \geq 0}$ has a leading coefficient that may vanish at various indices. In the spirit of [4, §8], p-adic lifting techniques could in principle be used, but we are not aware of any sharp analysis of the sufficient p-adic precision in the general case. Anyways, the best that can be expected from this method is a cost quasi-linear in $\sqrt{N}$.

---

*We warmly thank the referees for their very helpful comments.

ISSAC '16, July 19–22, 2016, Waterloo, ON, Canada.

ACM ISBN 978-1-4503-4380-0/16/07...$15.00.

DOI: http://dx.doi.org/10.1145/2930889.2930904

We attack the problem from a different angle. Our starting point is a theorem due to the second author in the late 1970s [2, Th. 12.2.5]. It states that a formal power series with coefficients in a finite field is algebraic if and only if the sequence $(f_n)_{n\geq 0}$ of its coefficients can be generated by a p-automaton, i.e., f_N is the output of a finite-state machine taking as input the digits of N in base p. This implicitly contains the roots of a $\log N$-method for computing f_N, but the size of the p-automaton is at least $p^{(d+h)^2}$, see e.g. [22].

In its original version [7] the theorem was stated for $\mathbb{F}_2$, but the proof extends *mutatis mutandis* to any finite field. A different proof was given by Christol, Kamae, Mendès-France and Rauzy [8, §7]. Although constructive in essence, these proofs do not focus on computational complexity aspects.

Inspired by [1] and [13], we show that each of them leads to an algorithm of arithmetic complexity $O(\log N)$ for the computation of f_N, after a precomputation that may be costly for p large. On the one hand, the proof in [8] relies on the fact that the sequence $(f_n)_{n\geq 0}$ satisfies a divide-and-conquer recurrence. However, we show (Sec. 2) that the size of the recurrence is polynomial in p^d, making the algorithm uninteresting even for very moderate values of p. On the other hand, the key of the proof in [7] is to represent f as the diagonal of a bivariate rational function. We turn it (Sections 3–4) into an efficient algorithm that has complexity $O(\log N)$ after a precomputation whose cost is $\tilde{O}(p)$ only. To our knowledge, the only previous explicit occurrence of a $\log N$-type complexity for this problem appears in [11, p. 121], which announces the bound $O(p \cdot \log N)$ but without proof.

Structure of the paper. In Sec. 2, we propose an algorithm that computes the Nth coefficient f_N using Mahler equations and divide-and-conquer recurrences. Sec. 3 is devoted to the study of a different algorithm, based on the concept of diagonals of rational functions. We conclude in Sec. 4 with the design of our main algorithm.

Cost measures. We use standard complexity notation. The real number $\omega > 2$ denotes a feasible exponent for matrix multiplication i.e., there exists an algorithm for multiplying $n \times n$ matrices with entries in $\mathbb{F}_p$ in $O(n^\omega)$ operations in $\mathbb{F}_p$. The best bound currently known is $\omega < 2.3729$ from [16]. We use the fact that many arithmetic operations in $\mathbb{F}_p[x]_d$, the set of polynomials of degree at most d in $\mathbb{F}_p[x]$, can be performed in $\tilde{O}(d)$ operations: addition, multiplication, division, *etc.* The key to these results is a divide-and-conquer approach combined with fast polynomial multiplication [23, 5, 18]. A general reference on fast algebraic algorithms is [17].

2. USING MAHLER EQUATIONS

We revisit, from an algorithmic point of view, the proof in [8, §7] of the fact that the coefficients of an algebraic power series $f \in \mathbb{F}_p[[x]]$ can be recognized by a p-automaton. Starting from an algebraic equation for $f = \sum_n f_n x^n$, we first compute a Mahler equation satisfied by f, then we derive an appropriate divide-and-conquer recurrence for its coefficient sequence $(f_n)_n$, and use it to compute f_N efficiently. We will show that, although the complexity of this method is very good (i.e., logarithmic) with respect to the index N, the computation cost of the recurrence, and actually its mere size, are extremely high (i.e., exponential) with respect to the algebraicity degree d.

2.1 From algebraic equations to Mahler equations and DAC recurrences

Mahler equations are functional equations which use the Mahler operator M_p, or M for short, acting on formal power series by substitution: $Mg(x) = g(x^p)$. Their power series solutions are called *Mahler series*. In characteristic 0, there is no a priori link between algebraic equations and Mahler equations; moreover, a series which is at the same time algebraic and Mahler is a rational function [21, §1.3].

By contrast, over $\mathbb{F}_p$, a Mahler equation is nothing but an algebraic equation, because of the Frobenius endomorphism that permits writing $g(x^p) = g(x)^p$ for any $g \in \mathbb{F}_p[[x]]$. Hence a Mahler series in $\mathbb{F}_p[[x]]$ is an algebraic series. Conversely, an algebraic series is Mahler, since if f is algebraic of degree d then the $(d+1)$ power series f, $Mf = f^p$, …, $M^d f = f^{p^d}$ are linearly dependent over $\mathbb{F}_p(x)$.

Concretely, the successive powers f^{p^k} $(0 \leq k \leq d)$ are expressed as linear combinations of $1, f, \ldots, f^{d-1}$ over $\mathbb{F}_p(x)$, and any dependence relation between them delivers a nontrivial Mahler equation with polynomial coefficients

$$c_0(x)f(x) + c_1(x)f(x^p) + \cdots + c_K(x)f(x^{p^K}) = 0, \qquad (1)$$

whose order K is at most d.

EXAMPLE 1 (A TOY EXAMPLE). Consider $E = x + y - y^3$ in $\mathbb{F}_5[x,y]$. Let $f = -x - x^3 + 2x^5 - 2x^7 + 2x^{11} + \cdots$ be the unique solution in $x\,\mathbb{F}_5[[x]]$ of $E(x, f(x)) = 0$. The expressions of f, f^5, f^{25}, f^{125} as linear combinations of 1, f, f^2 with coefficients in $\mathbb{F}_5(x)$ give the columns of the matrix

$$\begin{bmatrix} 0 & x & -2\,x^7 + x^5 + x & x^{41} - x^{37} + \cdots \\ 1 & 1 & x^8 - x^6 + 1 & x^{40} - 2\,x^{38} + \cdots \\ 0 & x & -2\,x^7 + x^5 + x & x^{41} - x^{37} + \cdots \end{bmatrix}.$$

The first three columns are linearly dependent and lead to the Mahler equation

$$x^4(1 - x^2 - x^4)f(x) - (1 + x^4 - 2x^6)f(x^5) + f(x^{25}) = 0. \quad (2)$$

A Mahler equation instantly translates into a recurrence of divide-and-conquer type, in short a DAC recurrence. Such a recurrence links the value of the index-n coefficient f_n with some values for the indices n/p, $n/p^2 \ldots$, and some shifted indices. The translation is absolutely simple: a term $x^s f(x)$ in equation (1) translates into f_{n-s}; more generally, a term $x^s f(x^q)$ becomes $f_{(n-s)/q}$, with the convention that a coefficient f_ν is zero if ν is not a nonnegative integer.

EXAMPLE 2 (A BINOMIAL CASE). Let $p > 2$ be a prime number and let $f = x + x^2 + \cdots$ be the algebraic series in $x\,\mathbb{F}_p[[x]]$ solution of $E(x,y) = x + (1+y)^{p-1} - 1$. The rewriting

$$x + (1+f)^{p-1} - 1 = x + \frac{1+f^p}{1+f} - 1 = \frac{(x-1)(1+f) + (1+f^p)}{1+f}$$

yields $f^p = -x + (1-x)f$ and $f^{p^2} = -x^p + (1-x^p)f^p$; hence $f^{p^2} = (1-x)^{p+1} - 1 + (1-x)^{p+1} f$. The situation is highly non-generic, since all powers f^{p^k} are expressible as linear combinations of 1 and f only. This delivers the second-order Mahler equation

$$(x^{p-1} - x^p)\, f(x) - (1 + x^{p-1} - x^p)\, f(x^p) + f(x^{p^2}) = 0,$$

which translates into a recurrence on the coefficients sequence

$$f_{n-p+1} - f_{n-p} - f_{\frac{n}{p}} - f_{\frac{n-p+1}{p}} + f_{\frac{n-p}{p}} + f_{\frac{n}{p^2}} = 0. \quad (3)$$

It is possible to make the recurrence more explicit by considering the p^2 cases according to the value of the residue of n modulo p^2.

2.2 Nth coefficient via a DAC recurrence

The DAC recurrence relation attached to the Mahler equation (1), together with enough initial conditions, can be used to compute the Nth coefficient f_N of the algebraic series f. The complexity of the resulting algorithm is linear with respect to N. The reason is that the coefficient $c_0(x)$ in (1) generally has more than one monomial, and as a consequence, all the coefficients f_i, $i < N$ are needed to compute f_N.

EXAMPLE 3 (A BINOMIAL CASE, CONT.). We specialize Ex. 2 by taking $p = 7$ and compute f_N with $N = 100$. Applying (3) to $n = 106$, we need to know the value for $n = 99$, next for $n = 98$, $n = 15$, $n = 14$, and also for $n = 97$, …, $n = 91$, $n = 14$, $n = 13$, $n = 2$. In the end, it appears that all values of f_n for the indices n smaller than $N = 100$ are needed to compute f_N.

It is possible to decrease dramatically the cost of the computation of f_N, from linear in N to logarithmic in N. The idea is to derive from (1) another Mahler equation with the additional feature that its trailing coefficient $c_0(x)$ is 1. To do so, it suffices to perform a change of unknown series. Putting $f(x) = c_0(x)g(x)$, we obtain the Mahler equation

$$g(x) + c_1(x)c_0(x)^{p-2}g(x^p) + \cdots \\ + c_K(x)c_0(x)^{p^K-2}g(x^{p^K}) = 0. \quad (4)$$

Obviously this approach assumes that c_0 is not zero. But, as proved in [2, Lemma 12.2.3], this is the case if (1) is assumed to be a *minimal-order* Mahler equation satisfied by f.

The series $g(x)$ is no longer a power series, but a Laurent series in $\mathbb{F}_p((x))$. We cut it into two parts, its negative part $g_-(x)$ in $\mathbb{F}_p[x^{-1}]$ and its nonnegative part $h(x)$ in $\mathbb{F}_p[[x]]$:

$$g_-(x) = \sum_{n<0} g_n x^n, \qquad h(x) = \sum_{n\geq 0} g_n x^n.$$

Let us rewrite Eq. (4) in the compact form $L(x, M)g(x) = 0$, where $L(x, M)$ is a skew polynomial in the variable x and in the Mahler operator M. Plugging $g(x) = g_-(x)+h(x)$ in it yields three terms. The first is the power series $L(x, M)h(x)$. The second is the nonnegative part $-b(x)$ of $L(x, M)g_-(x)$, in $\mathbb{F}_p[x]$. The third is the negative part of $L(x, M)g_-(x)$, and it is zero because it is the only one which belongs to $x^{-1}\mathbb{F}_p[x^{-1}]$. Eq. (4) is rewritten as a new (inhomogeneous) Mahler equation $L(x, M)h(x) = b(x)$, namely

$$h(x) + c_1(x)c_0(x)^{p-2}h(x^p) + \cdots \\ + c_K(x)c_0(x)^{p^K-2}h(x^{p^K}) = b(x). \quad (5)$$

EXAMPLE 4 (A TOY EXAMPLE, CONT.). The change of series $f(x) = x^4(1 - x^2 - x^4)h(x)$ in (2) gives the new equation

$$h(x) - x^{12}(1-x)(1+x)(1+x^2+2x^4)(1-x^2-x^4)^3h(x^5) \\ + x^{92}(1-x^2-x^4)^{23}h(x^{25}) = \\ -x - x^5 + x^7 + 2\,x^9 + \cdots + x^{149} - x^{157} - 2\,x^{159}$$

and a recurrence

$$h_n = h_{\frac{n-12}{5}} + 2h_{\frac{n-14}{5}} + \cdots - h_{\frac{n-92}{25}} + \cdots,$$

while f_n is given by $f_n = h_{n-4} - h_{n-6} - h_{n-8}$ for $n \geq 8$.

The right-hand side $b(x)$ of this new inhomogeneous equation is obtained as the nonnegative part of $-(c_1c_0^3g_-^5 + c_2c_0^{23}g_-^{25})$, where $c_0 = x^4(1-x^2-x^4)$, $c_1 = 2x^6 - x^4 - 1$, $c_2 = 1$ are the coefficients of Eq. (2), and where $g_- = -2x^{-1} - x^{-3}$, the negative part of f/c_0, can be determined starting from (f mod x^4).

To compute the coefficient f_N for $N = 1251$, this approach only requires the computation of thirteen terms of the sequence h_n, namely for $n \in \{0, 3, 5, 7, 43, 45, 47, 243, 245, 247, 1243, 1245, 1247\}$. This number of terms behaves like $3\log_p N$, and compares well to the use of a recurrence like (3), which requires N terms.

At this point, it is intuitively plausible that the Nth coefficient f_N can be computed in arithmetic complexity $O(\log N)$: to obtain f_N, we need a few values h_N and these ones are essentially obtained from a bounded number of $h_{N/p}$, h_{N/p^2} … .

2.3 Nth coefficient via the section operators

This plausibility can be strengthened and made clearer with the introduction of the *section operators* (sometimes called *Cartier operators*, or *decimation operators*) and the concept of *p-rational series*.

DEFINITION 1. *The section operators $S_0, \dots, S_{p-1}$, with respect to the radix p, are defined by*

$$S_r \sum_{n\geq 0} f_n x^n = \sum_{k\geq 0} f_{pk+r}x^k, \qquad \text{for } 0 \leq r < p. \quad (6)$$

In other words, there is a section operator for each digit of the radix-p numeration system and the rth section operator extracts from a given series its part associated with the indices congruent to the digit r modulo p. These operators are linear and well-behaved with respect to the product:

$$S_r[f(x)g(x)] = \sum_{s+t\equiv r \bmod p} x^{\lfloor \frac{s+t}{p} \rfloor} S_s f(x) S_t g(x).$$

In particular, for $g(x) = h(x^p)$ the previous formula becomes

$$S_r[f(x)h(x^p)] = S_r[f(x)] \times h(x), \quad (7)$$

because of the obvious relationships with the Mahler operator $S_0 M = \mathrm{I}_{\mathbb{F}_p[[x]]}$, $S_r M = 0$ for $r > 0$. The action of the section operators can be extended to the field $\mathbb{F}_p((x))$ of formal Laurent series and the same properties apply to the extended operators, which we denote in the same way.

The section operators permit to express the coefficient h_N of a formal power series $h(x)$ using the radix-p digits of N.

LEMMA 2. *Let h be in $\mathbb{F}_p[[x]]$ and let $N = (N_\ell \cdots N_1 N_0)_p$ be the radix-p expansion of N. Then*

$$h_N = (S_{N_\ell} \cdots S_{N_1} S_{N_0} h)(0). \quad (8)$$

PROOF. We first apply the section operator S_{N_0} to the series $h(x)$ associated with the least significant digit of N, that is we start from N_0 and we pick every pth coefficient of $h(x)$. This gives $S_{N_0}h(x) = h_{N_0} + h_{N_0+p}x + h_{N_0+2p}x^2 + \cdots$. Iterating this process with each digit produces the series

$$S_{N_\ell} \cdots S_{N_1} S_{N_0} h(x) = h_N + h_{N+p^{\ell+1}}x + \cdots,$$

whose constant coefficient is h_N. □

2.4 Linear representation

Let us return to the algebraic series $f(x)$ and its relative $h(x)$. The Mahler equation (5) can be rewritten

$$h(x) = b(x) + a_1(x)h(x^p) + \cdots + a_K(x)h(x^{p^K}). \quad (9)$$

The coefficients $b(x)$ and $a_k(x)$, $1 \leq k \leq K$, are polynomials of degrees at most D, say. As a matter of fact, the vector space $\mathcal{W}$ of linear combinations

$$s(x) = a(x) + b_0(x)h(x) + b_1(x)h(x^p) + \cdots + b_K(x)h(x^{p^K})$$

with $a(x)$ and all $b_k(x)$ in $\mathbb{F}_p[x]_D$ is stable under the action of the section operators. Indeed, from

$$s(x) = (a(x) + b_0(x)b(x)) + (b_0(x)a_1(x) + b_1(x))h(x^p) + \cdots + (b_0(x)a_K(x) + b_K(x))h(x^{p^K})$$

we deduce

$$\begin{aligned} S_r s(x) = {} & S_r\,(a(x) + b_0(x)b(x)) \\ & + S_r\,(b_0(x)a_1(x) + b_1(x))\,h(x) + \cdots \\ & + S_r\,(b_0(x)a_K(x) + b_K(x))\,h(x^{p^{K-1}}), \end{aligned} \quad (10)$$

and the polynomials $S_r(a+b_0b)$ and $S_r(b_0a_k+b_k)$, $1 \le k \le K$, have degrees not greater than $2D/p \le D$.

The important consequence of this observation is that we have produced a finite dimensional $\mathbb{F}_p$-vector space $\mathcal{W}$ that contains $h(x)$ and that is stable under the sections $(S_r)_{0 \le r < p}$. This will enable us to effectively compute the coefficient h_N using formula (8), by performing matrix computations.

The vector space $\mathcal{W}$ is spanned over $\mathbb{F}_p$ by the family $\mathcal{F} = \{x^i, 0 \le i \le D\} \cup \{x^j h(x^{p^k}), 0 \le j \le D, 0 \le k \le K\}$. Let A_r be a matrix of S_r with respect to $\mathcal{F}$, let C be the column vector containing only zero entries except an entry equal to 1 at index $(j,k) = (0,0)$, and L be the row matrix of the evaluations at 0 of the elements of $\mathcal{F}$.

With these notation, Eq. (8) rewrites in matrix terms:

$$h_N = LA_{N_\ell} \cdots A_{N_1} A_{N_0} C. \quad (11)$$

Definition 3. *The family of matrices* $(L, (A_r)_{0 \le r < p}, C)$ *is a* linear representation *of the series* $h(x)$. *A power series that admits a linear representation is said to be* p-rational.

As it was pointed out in [1, p. 178], an immediate consequence of Eq. (11) is that the coefficient h_N can be computed using only $O(\log N)$ matrix-vector products in size $(D+1)(K+1)$, therefore in arithmetic complexity $O((DK)^2 \log N)$.

Actually, the matrices A_r are structured, and their product by a vector can be done faster than quadratically. Indeed, Eq. (10) shows that one can perform a matrix-vector product by the matrix A_r using K polynomial products in $\mathbb{F}_p[x]_D$, thus in quasi-linear complexity $\tilde{O}(DK)$. We deduce:

Proposition 4. *The* N*th coefficient* h_N *of the solution* h *of* (9) *can be computed in time* $\tilde{O}((DK)\log N)$.

2.5 Nth coefficient using Mahler equations

We are ready to prove the main result of this section.

Theorem 5. *Let* E *be a polynomial in* $\mathbb{F}_p[x,y]_{h,d}$ *such that* $E(0,0) = 0$ *and* $E_y(0,0) \ne 0$, *and let* $f \in \mathbb{F}_p[[x]]$ *be its unique root with* $f(0) = 0$. *Algorithm 1 computes the* N*th coefficient* f_N *of* f *using* $\tilde{O}(d^3h^2p^{3d}\log N)$ *operations in* $\mathbb{F}_p$.

To do this, we first need a preliminary result that will also be useful in Sec. 4. It provides size and complexity bounds for the remainder of the Euclidean division of a monomial in y by a polynomial in y with coefficients in $\mathbb{F}_p[x]$.

Lemma 6. *Let* $E = \sum_i e_i(x)y^i$ *be a polynomial in* $\mathbb{F}_p[x][y]$ *of degree* d *in* y *and at most* h *in* x. *Then, for* $D \ge d$,

$$y^D \bmod E = \frac{1}{e_d^{D-d+1}}\left(r_0(x) + \cdots + r_{d-1}(x)y^{d-1}\right),$$

where the r_i*'s are in* $\mathbb{F}_p[x]$ *of degree at most* $h(D-d+1)$.
One can compute the r_i*'s using* $\tilde{O}(hdD)$ *operations in* $\mathbb{F}_p$.

Algorithm **Nth coefficient via Mahler equations**

Input A polynomial $E(x,y) \in \mathbb{F}_p[x,y]$ with $E(0,0) = 0$ and $E_y(0,0) \ne 0$, and an integer $N \ge 0$.
Output The Nth coefficient f_N of the unique formal power series $f \in \mathbb{F}_p[[x]]$ solution of $E(x, f(x)) = 0$, $f(0) = 0$.

1. Use Algorithm 2 to compute a minimal-order Mahler equation (with $c_0 = c_{0,v_0}x^{v_0} + \cdots + c_{0,d_0}x^{d_0}$, $c_{0,v_0} \ne 0$):
   $L(x,M)f(x) = c_0(x)f(x) + \cdots + c_K(x)f(x^{p^K}) = 0.$
2. Deduce an equation $L'(x,M)g(x) = 0$ (4), with $c_0' = 1$, satisfied by $g(x) = f(x)/c_0(x)$.
3. Compute $f(x) \bmod x^{v_0}$ by Newton iteration, and deduce the negative part $g_-(x)$ of $f(x)/c_0(x)$.
4. Compute the nonnegative part $b(x)$ of $-L'(x,M)g_-(x)$
   ▷ The nonnegative part $h(x)$ of $f(x)/c_0(x)$ satisfies the equation $L'(x,M)h(x) = b(x)$ (5).
5. Get a linear representation $(L, (A_r)_{0 \le r < p}, C)$ for $h(x)$.
6. **for** N' in $\{N - d_0, \ldots, N - v_0\}$
   write $N' = (N'_\ell \ldots N'_0)_p$ and
   compute $h_{N'} = LA_{N'_\ell} \cdots A_{N'_0}C$;
7. **return** $f_N = c_{0,v_0}h_{N-v_0} + \cdots + c_{0,d_0}h_{N-d_0}$.

Algorithm 1. Nth coefficient via Mahler equations.

Proof. The degree bounds are proved by induction on D. The computation of $y^D \bmod E$ can be performed by binary powering. The last step dominates the cost of the whole process. It amounts to first computing the product of two polynomials in $\mathbb{F}_p[x,y]$ of degree at most $d-1$ in y and of degree $O(hD)$ in x, then reducing the result modulo E. Both steps have complexity $\tilde{O}(hdD)$: the multiplication is done via Kronecker's substitution [17, Cor. 8.28], the reduction via an adaptation of the Newton iteration used for the fast division of univariate polynomials [17, Th. 9.6]. □

The first step of Algorithm 1 is the computation of a Mahler equation for the algebraic series f. We begin by analyzing the sizes of this equation, and the cost of its computation.

Theorem 7. *Let* E *be a polynomial in* $\mathbb{F}_p[x,y]_{h,d}$ *such that* $E(0,0) = 0$ *and* $E_y(0,0) \ne 0$, *and let* $f \in \mathbb{F}_p[[x]]$ *be its unique root with* $f(0) = 0$. *Algorithm 2 computes a Mahler equation of minimal-order satisfied by* f *using* $\tilde{O}(d^\omega hp^d)$ *operations in* $\mathbb{F}_p$. *The output equation has order at most* d *and polynomial coefficients in* $\mathbb{F}_p[x]$ *of degree at most* dhp^d.

Proof. We first prove the correctness part. Since the R_i's all live in the vector space generated by $1, f, \ldots, f^{d-1}$ over $\mathbb{F}_p(x)$, the algorithm terminates and returns a Mahler operator of order K at most d.

At step s we have $R_s = y^{p^s} \bmod E$, thus $R_s(x,f) = f^{p^s}$. Since $\sum_{k=0}^K c_kR_k = 0$, this yields $L(f) = \sum_{k=0}^K c_kf^{p^k} = 0$, so L is a Mahler operator for f. It has minimal order, because otherwise $R_0, \ldots, R_{K-1}$ would be linearly dependent over $\mathbb{F}_p(x)$. Therefore, the algorithm is correct.

By Lemma 6, $e_d^{p^s-d+1}R_s$ is in $\mathbb{F}_p[x,y]$ of degree in y at most $d-1$ and degree in x at most $h(p^s - d + 1)$. Moreover, $R_0, \ldots, R_K$ can be computed in time $\tilde{O}(hdp^K)$.

By Cramer's rule, the degrees of the c_k's are bounded by $dhp^K \le dhp^d$. Testing the rank condition, and solving for the c_k's amounts to polynomial linear algebra in size at most $d \times (d+1)$ and degree at most hp^d. This can be done in complexity $\tilde{O}(d^\omega hp^d)$, using Storjohann's algorithm [24]. □

Algorithm **AlgeqToMahler**

Input $E(x, y) \in \mathbb{F}_p[x, y]$ with $E(0,0) = 0$ and $E_y(0,0) \neq 0$.
Output A minimal-order monic Mahler operator for the unique $f \in \mathbb{F}_p[[x]]$ with $E(x, f(x)) = 0$ and $f(0) = 0$.

$R_0 = y$;
for $s = 1, 2, \ldots$ **do**
  $R_s = R_{s-1}^p \bmod E$ $\triangleright$ $R_s = y^{p^s} \bmod E$
  if $\operatorname{rank}_{\mathbb{F}_p(x)}(R_0, R_1, \ldots, R_s) < s + 1$ **then**
    Solve $\sum_{k=0}^{s-1} \frac{c_k}{c_s} R_k = -R_s$ for $c_0, \ldots, c_s$ in $\mathbb{F}_p[x]$
    return $\sum_{k=0}^{s} c_k M^k$

Algorithm 2. From algebraic equations to Mahler equations.

We are now ready to prove Theorem 5.

Proof of Theorem 5. The correctness of Algorithm 1 follows from the discussion in Sec. 2.4. By Theorem 7, the output of Step 1 is a Mahler equation of order $K \leq d$ and coefficients c_j of maximum degree $H \leq dhp^K$. In particular, $d_0 \leq dhp^d$. The cost of Step 1 is $\tilde{O}(d^\omega hp^d)$. Step 2 consists in computing the coefficients $c'_j = c_j c_0^{p^j - 2}$ for $1 \leq j \leq K$, of maximum degree $D \leq Hp^K$. It can be performed in time $\tilde{O}(KHp^K) = \tilde{O}(d^2 hp^{2d})$. Step 3 has negligible complexity $\tilde{O}(dv_0) = \tilde{O}(d^2 hp^d)$ using the Kung-Traub algorithm [19]. Step 4 requires $\tilde{O}(KHp^K) = \tilde{O}(d^2 hp^{2d})$ operations. By Proposition 4 the last steps of the algorithm can be done using $\tilde{O}((DK) \log N) = \tilde{O}((d^2 hp^{2d}) \log N)$ for each N', thus for a total cost of $\tilde{O}((d^3 h^2 p^{3d}) \log N)$. This dominates the whole computation. □

Generically, the size bounds in Theorem 5 are quite tight. This is illustrated by the following example.

Example 5 (A cubic equation). Let us consider the algebraic equation $E(x, y) = x - (1 + x)y + x^2 y^2 + (1 + x)y^3 = 0$ in $\mathbb{F}_3[x, y]$. The assumption $E_y(0, 0) = -1 \neq 0$ is fulfilled. We find a Mahler equation of order 3, whose coefficients $c_0 = x^{10} - x^{11} + \cdots - x^{40} + x^{45}$, c_1, c_2, c_3 have respectively heights 45, 47, 50, 32. We compute within precision $O(x^{10})$ the solution $f(x) = x - x^2 - x^3 + x^5 + \cdots - x^{44} + \cdots$, and the negative part $g_-(x) = x^{-9} + x^{-7} + x^{-6} - x^{-4} - x^{-2}$ of $g = f/c_0$. We find a new operator $L'(x, M)$ by computing the product $L(x, M)c_0(x)$ in $\mathbb{F}_3[x, M]$ and next a new equation $L'(x, M)y(x) = b(x)$ for the nonnegative part $h(x)$ of $g(x)$ by computing the polynomial $b(x) = L'(x, M)g_-(x)$. It appears that the coefficients $c'_0 = 1$, c'_1, c'_2, c'_3 and the right-hand side $b(x)$ have respectively heights 0, 92, 365, 1157, and 1103. We arrive at a linear representation with size $(1 + 3 + 1) \times (1 + 1157) = 5790$ for $p = 3$. If we increase the prime number p, we successively find sizes 155190 for $p = 5$, and 1342725 for $p = 7$. We do not pursue further because it is clear that such sizes make the computation unfeasible.

3. USING DIAGONALS

To improve the arithmetic complexity with respect to the prime number p, we need a different way to represent the algebraic series f. It is given by Furstenberg's theorem, and relies on the concept of *diagonal of rational functions.*

$$
\begin{array}{llllllll}
\multicolumn{8}{l}{\dfrac{y-(2-x)y^2-3y^3+(4-2x^2)y^4+4xy^5}{(1-x)-(1-x)y-y^2+(1-x^2)y^3+xy^4} =} \\
+\,y & +\,xy & +\,x^2y & +\,x^3y & +\,x^4y & +\,x^5y & +\,x^6y & +\,x^7y \\
-\,y^2 & & & & & & & \\
-\,3y^3 & -\,xy^3 & & +\,x^3y^3 & +\,2x^4y^3 & +\,3x^5y^3 & +\,4x^6y^3 & +\,5x^7y^3 \\
-\,y^4 & & -\,x^2y^4 & & +\,x^4y^4 & +\,2x^5y^4 & +\,3x^6y^4 & +\,4x^7y^4 \\
-\,3y^5 & & -\,3x^2y^5 & -\,2x^3y^5 & & +\,3x^5y^5 & -\,4x^6y^5 & +\,x^7y^5 \\
-\,y^6 & +\,4xy^6 & -\,3x^2y^6 & -\,4x^3y^6 & -\,3x^4y^6 & & +\,5x^6y^6 & +\,x^7y^6 \\
-\,3y^7 & +\,5xy^7 & -\,4x^2y^7 & +\,4x^3y^7 & +\,2x^4y^7 & +\,4x^5y^7 & & +\,2x^7y^7 \\
 & & & & & & & +\cdots
\end{array}
$$

Figure 1. A diagonal of a bivariate rational series (see Ex. 6).

3.1 From algebraic equation to diagonal

Furstenberg's theorem [15] tells us that every algebraic series is the diagonal of a bivariate rational function

$$f(x) = D\frac{a(x, y)}{b(x, y)}, \qquad b(0, 0) \neq 0. \tag{12}$$

This means that $f(x) = \sum_i c_{i,i} x^i$, where $a/b = \sum_{i,j} c_{i,j} x^i y^j$.

Moreover, under the working assumption $E_y(0, 0) \neq 0$, the rational function a/b is explicit in terms of E:

$$a(x, y) = yE_y(xy, y), \qquad b(x, y) = E(xy, y)/y.$$

(Notice that $b(0, 0) = E_y(0, 0) \neq 0$.) If the polynomial $E(x, y)$ has degree d and height h, then the partial degrees of a and b are bounded as follows

$$d_x = \max(\deg_x a, \deg_x b) \leq h,$$
$$d_y = \max(\deg_y a, \deg_y b) \leq d + h. \tag{13}$$

Example 6 (A quartic equation). Consider

$$f(x) = x + x^3 + x^4 + 3x^5 + 5x^6 + 2x^7 + 4x^8 - x^9 - x^{10} - 2x^{11} + \cdots,$$

the unique solution in $x\mathbb{F}_{11}[[x]]$ of the algebraic equation

$$E(x, y) = -x + (1 + x)y - (1 + x^2)y^2 - y^3 + (1 + x)y^4 = 0.$$

Then f is the diagonal of the rational function a/b with

$$a = y - (2 - x)y^2 - 3y^3 + (4 - 2x^2)y^4 + 4xy^5,$$

$$b = (1 - x) - (1 - x)y - y^2 + (1 - x^2)y^3 + xy^4.$$

Fig. 1 shows pictorially that $f(x)$ is the diagonal of a/b.

We will follow the path drawn in [6], and compute the Nth coefficient f_N using a/b as intermediate data structure.

3.2 Nth coefficient via diagonals

Bivariate section operators can be defined by mimicking (6). Although they depend on two residues modulo p, we will always use them with the same residue for both variables; thus we will simply denote them by S_r for $0 \leq r < p$. A nice feature is that they commute with the diagonal operator,

$$S_r D = DS_r.$$

Together with (12), this property translates the action of the section operators from the algebraic series f to the rational function a/b. Moreover, property (7) extends to bivariate section operators and justifies the following computation

$$S_r \frac{a(x, y)}{b(x, y)} = S_r \frac{a(x, y)b(x, y)^{p-1}}{b(x, y)^p}$$
$$= S_r \frac{a(x, y)b(x, y)^{p-1}}{b(x^p, y^p)} = \frac{S_r a(x, y)b(x, y)^{p-1}}{b(x, y)}.$$

Algorithm **Nth coefficient via diagonals**

Input A polynomial $E(x,y) \in \mathbb{F}_p[x,y]$ with $E(0,0)=0$ and $E_y(0,0) \neq 0$, and an integer $N \geq 0$.
Output The Nth coefficient f_N of the unique formal power series $f \in \mathbb{F}_p[[x]]$ solution of $E(x,f(x))=0$, $f(0)=0$.

1. Compute $a(x,y) = yE_y(xy,y), b(x,y) = E(xy,y)/y$.
   ▷ At this point $f = D(a/b)$.
2. Set $d_x = \max(\deg_x a, \deg_x b)$, $d_y = \max(\deg_y a, \deg_y b)$, $L = [1,0,\cdots,0]$, and C the column vector expressing $a(x,y)$ in the canonical basis of $\mathbb{F}_p[x,y]_{d_x,d_y}$.
3. Compute $B = b^{p-1}$.
4. **for** r from 0 to $p-1$
   compute the image of the canonical basis
   $T_r x^i y^j = \sum_{n,m} A_{r;i,j;n,m} x^n y^m$
   and store the result in the matrix A_r
5. **return** $f_N = LA_{N_\ell} \cdots A_{N_0} \frac{C}{b(0,0)}$ for $N = (N_\ell \dots N_0)_p$.

Algorithm 3. Nth coefficient, via diagonals.

To put it plainly

$$S_r \frac{a}{b} = \frac{S_r a b^{p-1}}{b}.$$

This yields an action on bivariate polynomials v of what we may call pseudo-section operators, defined by

$$T_r v = S_r v b^{p-1}, \qquad 0 \leq r < p,$$

hence

$$(S_{r_1} \cdots S_{r_k}) \left(\frac{a}{b}\right) = \frac{(T_{r_1} \cdots T_{r_k})(a)}{b}, \qquad 0 \leq r_i < p.$$

At this point, it is not difficult to see that the vector subspace $\mathbb{F}_p[x,y]_{d_x,d_y}$, where d_x and d_y are the maximal partial degrees of a and b defined in (13), is stable under the pseudo-section operators. The supports of b and of polynomials v in $\mathbb{F}_p[x,y]_{d_x,d_y}$ belong to a small rectangle $[0,d_x] \times [0,d_y]$. Raising b to the power $p-1$ enlarges the rectangle by a factor $p-1$ and the product by v results in a rectangle p times larger than the small rectangle. The pseudo-section operators, essentially based on a Euclidean division by p, send the large rectangle back into the small rectangle.

As a consequence we have at our disposal a new linear representation $\big(L, (A_r)_{0 \leq r < p}, C\big)$, this time based on the vector space $\mathbb{F}_p[x,y]_{d_x,d_y}$, and on its canonical basis. The row vector L has all its components equal to 0 except the first one, equal to 1, because all monomials of the canonical basis take the value 0 at $x=0$, $y=0$, except the monomial 1. The family $(A_r)_{0 \leq r < p}$ of matrices of size $(1+d_x)(1+d_y)$ expresses the pseudo-section operators T_r. The column vector C contains the coordinates of the polynomial a.

The crucial difference with the linear representation in Sec. 2.2 is that the dimension of the new one is much smaller.

It remains to compute f_N by using the rational nature with respect to the radix p of the power series $f(x)$. The process is summarized in Algorithm 3. Anew we conclude that the arithmetic complexity for the computing of f_N is $O(\log N)$. More precisely, since the linear representation has size $(1+d_x)(1+d_y)$, the computation of f_N is of order $O(d_x^2 d_y^2 \log N)$.

Example 7 (A cubic equation, cont.). We return to Ex. 5 with $p=7$. We find $a = -y - xy^2 + 3y^3 + 3xy^4 + 2x^2y^4$ and $b = -1 + x - xy + y^2 + xy^3 + x^2y^3$, hence $d_x = 2$, $d_y = 4$. Next we compute $B = b^{p-1}$ and we build the linear representation. The main point is the size of the representation, namely $(1+d_x)(1+d_y) = 15$. This is ridiculously small as compared to the value obtained in Ex. 5. Even more importantly, the size remains the same if we change the prime number.

$$\begin{bmatrix}
\begin{bmatrix} 6 & 1 & \cdot & \cdot & \cdot \\ 5 & 6 & 4 & 6 & 3 \\ \cdot & \cdot & 6 & \cdot & 6 \\ \cdot & \cdot & \cdot & \cdot & \cdot \\ \cdot & \cdot & \cdot & \cdot & \cdot \end{bmatrix} &
\begin{bmatrix} \cdot & 1 & \cdot & \cdot & \cdot \\ 1 & \cdot & 1 & \cdot & 1 \\ \cdot & \cdot & \cdot & 1 & \cdot \\ \cdot & \cdot & \cdot & \cdot & \cdot \\ \cdot & \cdot & \cdot & \cdot & \cdot \end{bmatrix} &
\begin{bmatrix} \cdot & \cdot & \cdot & \cdot & \cdot \\ \cdot & \cdot & \cdot & \cdot & \cdot \\ \cdot & \cdot & \cdot & \cdot & \cdot \\ \cdot & \cdot & \cdot & \cdot & \cdot \\ \cdot & \cdot & \cdot & \cdot & \cdot \end{bmatrix} \\
\begin{bmatrix} \cdot & \cdot & \cdot & \cdot & \cdot \\ 6 & 3 & 1 & \cdot & \cdot \\ 6 & 5 & \cdot & 1 & 5 \\ \cdot & \cdot & \cdot & \cdot & 1 \\ \cdot & \cdot & \cdot & \cdot & \cdot \end{bmatrix} &
\begin{bmatrix} \cdot & \cdot & \cdot & \cdot & \cdot \\ 5 & 6 & 1 & 4 & 5 \\ \cdot & 4 & 6 & 4 & \cdot \\ \cdot & \cdot & \cdot & \cdot & 6 \\ \cdot & \cdot & \cdot & \cdot & \cdot \end{bmatrix} &
\begin{bmatrix} 1 & 1 & \cdot & \cdot & \cdot \\ 5 & 6 & 3 & 2 & \cdot \\ 2 & 6 & 5 & 6 & 6 \\ \cdot & \cdot & \cdot & \cdot & 1 \\ \cdot & \cdot & \cdot & \cdot & \cdot \end{bmatrix} \\
\begin{bmatrix} \cdot & \cdot & \cdot & \cdot & \cdot \\ \cdot & \cdot & \cdot & \cdot & \cdot \\ \cdot & \cdot & \cdot & \cdot & \cdot \\ \cdot & \cdot & \cdot & \cdot & \cdot \\ \cdot & \cdot & \cdot & \cdot & \cdot \end{bmatrix} &
\begin{bmatrix} \cdot & \cdot & \cdot & \cdot & \cdot \\ \cdot & \cdot & \cdot & \cdot & \cdot \\ \cdot & \cdot & \cdot & \cdot & \cdot \\ \cdot & \cdot & \cdot & \cdot & \cdot \\ \cdot & \cdot & \cdot & \cdot & \cdot \end{bmatrix} &
\begin{bmatrix} \cdot & \cdot & \cdot & \cdot & \cdot \\ \cdot & \cdot & \cdot & \cdot & \cdot \\ \cdot & \cdot & \cdot & \cdot & \cdot \\ \cdot & \cdot & \cdot & \cdot & \cdot \\ \cdot & \cdot & \cdot & \cdot & \cdot \end{bmatrix}
\end{bmatrix}$$

Figure 2. The matrix A_1 in Ex. 7.

Although it is not necessary that we see the linear representation with our human eyes, it is quite normal that we watch it if only to control the computations. The matrices A_r, whose size is $(1+d_x)(1+d_y)$, have indices which are pairs of pairs. We can view them as square matrices of size $1+d_x$ whose elements are square blocks of size $1+d_y$. The coordinates over x^iy^j of the image $T_r x^n y^m$ is in the block with indices (i,n) at place (j,m).

We only display the matrix A_1 (the zero coefficients are replaced by dots), in Fig. 2. It gives us for example the value of $T_1 xy^2$. Because the exponent of x is 1, we look at the column of blocks number 1 (the second one) and because the exponent of y is 2 we look at the column number 2 (the third one) in the matrices of this column (red column). In the first block, which corresponds to x^0, we see a coefficient 1 in row number 1, hence a term $x^0y^1 = y$. In the second block, we see a coefficient 1 in row number 1 hence a term $x^1y^1 = xy$ and a coefficient 6 in row number 2 hence a term $6x^1y^2 = 6xy^2$. We conclude $T_1 xy^2 = y + xy + 6xy^2$.

3.3 Precomputation

All the needed information to build the linear representation is contained in the polynomial $B = b^{p-1}$. Indeed, when we compute the image of an element x^iy^j of the canonical basis by the pseudo-section operator T_r, we first multiply B by x^iy^j; this transformation is merely a translation of the exponents, that requires no arithmetic operation. Next, we extract the monomials whose exponents are congruent to r modulo p, again without any computation in $\mathbb{F}_p$. The conclusion is that, apart the final computation to obtain the value f_N, the cost comes from the computation of $B = b^{p-1}$. This can be done using binary powering and Kronecker's substitution. Since B has partial degrees at most pd_x in x and at most pd_y in y, the arithmetic complexity is $\tilde{O}(p^2 d_x d_y)$.

Gathering the study of the computation and the precomputation, and using Eq. (13), we obtain the following result.

Theorem 8. *Let E be in $\mathbb{F}_p[x,y]_{h,d}$ such that $E(0,0)=0$ and $E_y(0,0) \neq 0$, and let $f \in \mathbb{F}_p[[x]]$ be its unique root with $f(0)=0$. Algorithm 3 computes the Nth coefficient f_N of f in $O(h^2(d+h)^2 \log N) + \tilde{O}(p^2 h(d+h))$ operations in $\mathbb{F}_p$.*

The striking points are the decreasing of the exponent of p

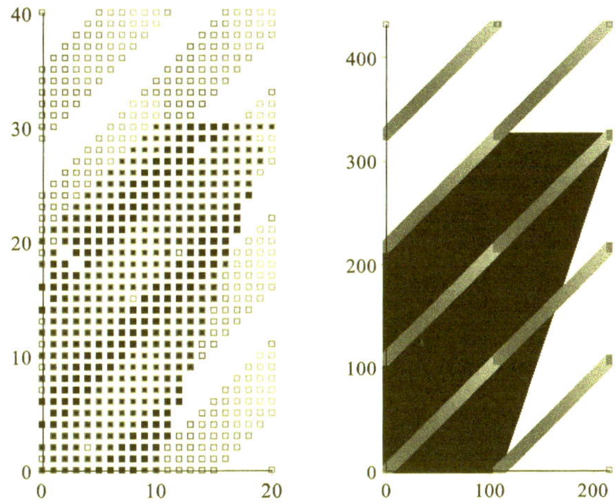

Figure 3. The useful coefficients of $B = b^{p-1}$ are located in the diagonal strips. See Ex. 8 for explanations.

from $3d$ to 2, and the replacement of the *multiplicative* complexity $p^{3d} \times \log N$ of Theorem 5 by the *additive* complexity $p^2 + \log N$. This is already a tremendous improvement. In the next section, we will present a further improvement.

4. A FASTER ALGORITHM

We will improve the algorithm of the previous section in order to decrease the exponent of the prime p from 2 to 1.

4.1 A small part of the large power is enough

As pointed out in Sec. 3.3, all the information needed to build the square matrices $A_0, \ldots, A_{p-1}$ of the linear representation is contained in the large power $B = b^{p-1}$. However building the A_i's does not require the whole polynomial B.

To see this, assume $0 \le \alpha \le (p-1)d_x$ and $0 \le \beta \le (p-1)d_y$ are such that the monomial $x^\alpha y^\beta$ of B contributes to one of the matrices A_r. Since $A_{r;i,j;n,m}$ is the coefficient of $x^n y^m$ in $T_r(x^i y^j) = S_r(x^i y^j B)$, this means that $i + \alpha \equiv j + \beta \bmod p$ for some $0 \le i \le d_x$ and $0 \le j \le d_y$. As a consequence, the difference exponent $\delta = \beta - \alpha$ necessarily belongs to $[-d_y, d_x] + p\mathbb{Z}$. For large p, this means that only a fraction $1/p$ of B is useful. The aim of this section is to take an algorithmic advantage of this remark.

Example 8 (A cubic equation, cont.). The previous phenomenon is exemplified in Fig. 3 for the equation $E(x,y) = x - (1+x)y + x^2y^2 + (1+x)y^3 = 0$, already encountered in Ex. 5 and 7. We use $p = 11$ on the left-hand side, and $p = 109$ on the right-hand side. The polynomial B is represented by its monomial support (in black). Besides, the points (α, β) defined by $\alpha = pk + r - i$, $\beta = p\ell + r - j$, with $0 \le i \le d_x$, $0 \le j \le d_y$ are colored, with a color which goes from blue to red when r goes from 0 to $p-1$ (but the pieces overlap). This generates strips with slope 1: only monomials in these strips contribute to the linear representation. For p small ($p = 11$), the strips cover almost the whole rectangle, but for p moderately large ($p = 109$) the proportion of useful coefficients in B becomes much smaller.

To emphasize the difference exponent $\delta = \beta - \alpha$, we perform a change of variables $x := x/t$, $y := t$, which produces Laurent polynomials with respect to t, namely $b(x/t, t)$ and

$$B(x/t,t) = b(x/t,t)^{p-1} = \sum_\delta \pi_\delta(x) t^\delta.$$

By construction, the coefficient $\pi_\delta(x)$ is a polynomial, namely the δ-diagonal $\sum_i B_{i,i+\delta} x^i$ of $B(x,y) = \sum_{i,j} B_{i,j} x^i y^j$.

Let δ_- be the opposite of the lowest degree with respect to t of $b(x/t,t)$, and δ_+ be the degree with respect to t of $b(x/t,t)$. An immediate bound is $\delta_- \le d_x$ and $\delta_+ \le d_y$.

By the previous discussion, all the information needed to build up the matrices of the linear representation is contained in the polynomials $\pi_\delta(x)$, for δ in

$$\Delta := ([-d_y, d_x] + p\mathbb{Z}) \cap [(1-p)\delta_-, (p-1)\delta_+].$$

This set is a union of small intervals of length $d_x + d_y + 1$ regularly spaced by p and within $[(1-p)d_x, (p-1)d_y]$.

4.2 Partial bivariate powering

Our aim is to show that the collection of $\pi_\delta(x)$ for $\delta \in \Delta$ can be computed in complexity quasi-linear in p. The starting point is to write

$$B(x/t,t) = \frac{b(x/t,t)^p}{b(x/t,t)} = \frac{b(x^p/t^p, t^p)}{b(x/t,t)}.$$

Here $b(x^p/t^p, t^p)$ is obtained by a mere rewriting of $b(x/t,t)$, hence at no cost, while $1/b(x/t,t)$ is a rational function. To be more concrete, we denote

$$b(x/t,t) = \sum_{v=-\delta_-}^{\delta_+} b_v(x) t^v, \qquad \frac{1}{b(x/t,t)} = \sum_{u \ge \delta_-} c_u(x) t^u,$$

where the coefficients $b_v(x)$ are polynomials in x and the coefficients $c_v(x)$ are rational functions in x.

Now, the polynomial $\pi_\delta(x)$ is expressed by a convolution

$$\pi_\delta(x) = \sum_{u+pv=\delta} c_u(x) b_v(x^p). \tag{14}$$

The constraint $u + pv = \delta$ implies $u \equiv \delta \bmod p$. Therefore, it is sufficient to compute the $c_\delta(x)$ for all $\delta \in \Delta' = p\delta_- + \Delta$.

To do this efficiently, we will exploit the fact that the sequence of rational functions $(c_u(x))_u$ satisfies a linear recurrence with coefficients in $\mathbb{F}_p[x]$. The coefficients of the recurrence relation are those of the polynomial $t^{\delta_-} b(x/t,t)$.

We are facing the following issue: since we need the values of $c_\delta(x)$ for indices of order $\delta = \Theta(p)$, we can not unroll the recurrence relation directly, otherwise the complexity (and actually the mere arithmetic size of the rational functions $c_i(x), i < u$, computed along the way) becomes quadratic in p. Fortunately, one can compute the Nth term of a recurrent sequence without computing all the previous coefficients. The key is the following lemma.

Lemma 9. [14] *Let R be a commutative ring and $a(t)/b(t)$ be a rational function in $R(t)$ with $b(0)$ invertible in R. Let d be the degree of $b(t)$ and $b^*(t) = t^d b(1/t)$ be its reciprocal. For any integer $N \ge 0$, the coefficients $c_N, c_{N+1}, \ldots, c_{N+d-1}$ of the formal power series expansion of $a(t)/b(t) = \sum_{n \ge 0} c_n t^n$ are the coefficients of $t^{2d-2}, \ldots, t^d, t^{d-1}$ in the product*

$$(t^N \bmod b^*(x)) \times (c_{2d-2} + \cdots + c_0 t^{2d-2}).$$

Fiduccia's algorithm [14] relies on Lemma 9 and computes $t^N \bmod b^*(t)$ by binary powering. As a consequence, the Nth term of a linear recurrent sequence of order d is computed in $\tilde{O}(d \log N)$ operations in R. In our setting, we use Fiduccia's algorithm for $R = \mathbb{F}_p(x)$.

Theorem 10. *Let b be in $\mathbb{F}_p[x,y]_{d_x,d_y}$ and let $\delta \in \mathbb{Z}$. Algorithm 4 computes the δ-diagonal $\pi_\delta(x) = \sum_i B_{i,i+\delta} x^i$ of $B = b^{p-1}$ in $\tilde{O}(d_x(d_x+d_y)^3 p)$ operations in $\mathbb{F}_p$.*

PROOF. By (14), to compute π_δ it is sufficient to have the coefficients $c_{\delta-pv}$ for $-d_x \le v \le d_y$. The coefficient c_N has the form $p(x)/q(x)^{N+1}$, where $\deg p = O(Nd_x)$, $\deg q \le d_x$. The most expensive step in Fiduccia's algorithm for c_N is computing t^N modulo a polynomial in $\mathbb{F}_p[x,y]_{d_x, d_x+d_y}$. By Lemma 6, this can be done in time $T_N = \tilde{O}(Nd_x(d_x+d_y))$. Summing the costs T_N over all N's of the form $\delta - pv$ with $-d_x \le v \le d_y$ concludes the proof. □

Algorithm **PartialPowering**

Input A polynomial b in $\mathbb{F}_p[x,y]$ and $\delta \in \mathbb{Z}$.
Output The δ-diagonal of $B = b^{p-1}$, that is $\sum_i B_{i,i+\delta} x^i$.

for v from $\mathrm{val}_t\, b(x/t,t)$ to $\deg_t b(x/t,t)$ **do**
  Compute $c_{\delta-pv}(x) = [t^{\delta-pv}]\frac{1}{b(x/t,t)}$ via Fiduccia's algo
return $\pi_\delta(x) = \sum_{u+pv=\delta} c_u(x) b_v(x^p)$

Algorithm 4. δ-diagonal of a bivariate polynomial power.

4.3 Faster precomputation

We finally combine the results in Sections 4.1 and 4.2 with the ones of Sec. 3, and modify Algorithm 3 accordingly, by replacing its Step 3 with the partial powering routine (Algorithm 4). This yields our main result.

THEOREM 11. *Let E be in $\mathbb{F}_p[x,y]_{h,d}$ satisfy $E(0,0)=0$ and $E_y(0,0) \neq 0$, and let $f \in \mathbb{F}_p[[x]]$ be its unique root with $f(0)=0$. One can compute the coefficient f_N of f in $O(h^2(d+h)^2 \log N) + \tilde{O}(h(d+h)^5 p)$ operations in $\mathbb{F}_p$.*

PROOF. Only the cost of the precomputation changes. Instead of computing the whole power $B = b^{p-1}$, we only compute its δ-diagonals $\pi_\delta(x)$, for $\delta \in \Delta'$. Since $|\Delta'| = |\Delta| \le (d_x+d_y+1)^2$, we conclude using Theorem 10. □

EXAMPLE 9 (CATALAN). Let $E(x,y) = y - x - y^2$ be in $\mathbb{F}_p[x,y]$, with root $f = \sum_{n\ge 0} C_n x^{n+1}$, where C_n is $\frac{1}{n+1}\binom{2n}{n}$. Then f is the diagonal of a/b with $a = y(1-2y)$ and $b = 1-x-y$. Thus $d_x = 1, d_y = 2$, and the linear representation has size 6. The needed information to compute the 6×6 matrices $A_0,\dots,A_{p-1}$ consists in the δ-diagonals of $B = b^{p-1}$ for $\delta \in \Delta := ([-2,1] + p\mathbb{Z}) \cap [1-p, p-1] = \{1-p, -2, -1, 0, 1, p-2, p-1\}$. Writing $B(x/t,t) = (1-x/t-t)^{p-1} = \sum_{\delta=1-p}^{p-1} \pi_\delta(x) t^\delta$, the goal is to compute the polynomials $\pi_\delta(x)$ for $\delta \in \Delta$. This is done via the formula $B(x/t,t) = (1 - x^p/t^p - t^p)/(1-x/t-t)$ which gives $\pi_\delta(x) = -c_{\delta+p}(x)x^p + c_\delta(x) - c_{\delta-p}(x)$. Therefore, it is sufficient to compute the rational functions $c_\delta(x)$ for all $\delta \in \Delta' = \Delta + p$. This is done using Fiduccia's algorithm, which exploits the fact that the c_δ's satisfy the recurrence $xc_{k+2}(x) = c_{k+1}(x) - c_k(x)$.
For instance, $\pi_0(x) = -x^p c_p(x)$, where $c_p(x)$ is obtained as the coefficient of t^2 in the product $(-1/x^2 - t/x)\cdot(t^p \bmod -xt^2+t-1)$. This is done by binary powering. Checking that the algorithm correctly computes $\pi_0(x)$ amounts to checking the amusing identity:

$$[t^1]\ \left(t^p \bmod -xt^2+t-1\right) = \sum_{\ell=0}^{p-1} \binom{2\ell}{\ell} x^{\ell+1-p} \quad \text{in } \mathbb{F}_p[x].$$

4.4 Practical issues and future work

We have implemented the algorithms described in this section in Maple. Our prototype is available at the url
http://specfun.inria.fr/dumas/Research/AlgModp/.
The implementation permits getting an idea of the feasibility of the approach using diagonals. For instance, in the case of the quartic equation in Ex. 6, with $p = 9001$ instead of $p = 11$, the algorithm spends 142 seconds on the precomputation, then computes the N-th coefficient for $N = 10^{10,000}$, resp. $10^{100,000}$, resp. $10^{1,000,000}$ in: 3, resp. 25, resp. 344 seconds. (Timings on a personal laptop, Intel Core i5, 2.8 GHz, 3MB.)
In a forthcoming article, we plan to extend our algorithms to all finite fields, and to improve the complexity results.

5. REFERENCES

[1] J.-P. Allouche and J. Shallit. The ring of k-regular sequences. *Theoret. Comput. Sci.*, 98(2):163–197, 1992.
[2] J.-P. Allouche and J. Shallit. *Automatic sequences.* Cambridge University Press, 2003. Theory, applications, generalizations.
[3] A. Bostan, F. Chyzak, G. Lecerf, B. Salvy, and É. Schost. Differential equations for algebraic functions. In *ISSAC'07*, pages 25–32. ACM Press, 2007.
[4] A. Bostan, P. Gaudry, and É. Schost. Linear recurrences with polynomial coefficients and application to integer factorization and Cartier-Manin operator. *SIAM Journal on Computing*, 36(6):1777–1806, 2007.
[5] D. G. Cantor and E. Kaltofen. On fast multiplication of polynomials over arbitrary algebras. *Acta Inform.*, 28(7):693–701, 1991.
[6] G. Christol. Éléments algébriques. In *Groupe de travail d'Analyse Ultra-métrique (1ère année : 1973/74)*, number 14, 10 pp. Secrétariat Mathématique, Paris, 1974.
[7] G. Christol. Ensembles presque periodiques k-reconnaissables. *Theoret. Comput. Sci.*, 9(1):141–145, 1979.
[8] G. Christol, T. Kamae, M. Mendès France, and G. Rauzy. Suites algébriques, automates et substitutions. *Bull. Soc. Math. France*, 108(4):401–419, 1980.
[9] D. V. Chudnovsky and G. V. Chudnovsky. On expansion of algebraic functions in power and Puiseux series. I. *J. Complexity*, 2(4):271–294, 1986.
[10] D. V. Chudnovsky and G. V. Chudnovsky. Approximations and complex multiplication according to Ramanujan. In *Ramanujan revisited (Urbana-Champaign, 1987)*, pages 375–472. 1988.
[11] D. V. Chudnovsky and G. V. Chudnovsky. Computer algebra in the service of mathematical physics and number theory. In *Computers in mathematics (Stanford, 1986)*, volume 125 of *Lecture Notes in Pure and Appl. Math.*, pages 109–232. 1990.
[12] L. Comtet. Calcul pratique des coefficients de Taylor d'une fonction algébrique. *Enseignemen Math.*, 10:267–270, 1964.
[13] P. Dumas. *Récurrences mahlériennes, suites automatiques, études asymptotiques.* PhD thesis, Univ. Bordeaux I, 1993. Available at https://tel.archives-ouvertes.fr/tel-00614660.
[14] C. M. Fiduccia. An efficient formula for linear recurrences. *SIAM J. Comput.*, 14(1):106–112, 1985.
[15] H. Furstenberg. Algebraic functions over finite fields. *J. Algebra*, 7:271–277, 1967.
[16] F. L. Gall. Powers of tensors and fast matrix multiplication. In *ISSAC'14*, pages 296–303, 2014.
[17] J. von zur Gathen and J. Gerhard. *Modern computer algebra.* Cambridge University Press, third edition, 2013.
[18] D. Harvey, J. van der Hoeven, and G. Lecerf. Faster polynomial multiplication over finite fields. http://arxiv.org/abs/1407.3361, 2014.
[19] H. T. Kung and J. F. Traub. All algebraic functions can be computed fast. *J. Assoc. Comput. Mach.*, 25(2):245–260, 1978.
[20] J. C. P. Miller and D. J. Spencer Brown. An algorithm for evaluation of remote terms in a linear recurrence sequence. *Computer Journal*, 9:188–190, 1966.
[21] K. Nishioka. *Mahler Functions and Transcendence.* Number 1631 in Lecture Notes in Mathematics. Springer, Berlin, 1996.
[22] E. Rowland and R. Yassawi. Automatic congruences for diagonals of rational functions. *J. Théor. Nombres Bordeaux*, 27(1):245–288, 2015.
[23] A. Schönhage. Schnelle Multiplikation von Polynomen über Körpern der Charakteristik 2. *Acta Informat.*, 7:395–398, 1977.
[24] A. Storjohann. High-order lifting and integrality certification. *J. Symb. Comp.*, 36(3-4):613–648, 2003.

Efficient Algorithms for Mixed Creative Telescoping

Alin Bostan
Inria
France
Alin.Bostan@inria.fr

Louis Dumont
Inria
France
Louis.Dumont@inria.fr

Bruno Salvy
Inria, Laboratoire LIP
(U. Lyon, CNRS, ENS Lyon, UCBL)
France
Bruno.Salvy@inria.fr

ABSTRACT

Creative telescoping is a powerful computer algebra paradigm –initiated by Doron Zeilberger in the 90's– for dealing with definite integrals and sums with parameters. We address the mixed continuous–discrete case, and focus on the integration of bivariate hypergeometric-hyperexponential terms. We design a new creative telescoping algorithm operating on this class of inputs, based on a Hermite-like reduction procedure. The new algorithm has two nice features: it is efficient and it delivers, for a suitable representation of the input, a minimal-order telescoper. Its analysis reveals tight bounds on the sizes of the telescoper it produces.

CCS Concepts

•**Computing methodologies → Algebraic algorithms;**

Keywords

symbolic integration; creative telescoping; hypergeometric-hyperexponential term; Hermite reduction

1. INTRODUCTION

Context. *Creative telescoping* is an algorithmic approach introduced in computer algebra by Zeilberger [23, 24, 21] to address definite summation and integration for a large class of functions and sequences involving parameters.

In this article, we focus on the mixed continuous–discrete case. Given a term $F_n(x)$ that is both hypergeometric (i.e., $F_{n+1}(x)/F_n(x)$ is a rational function) and hyperexponential (i.e., $F'_n(x)/F_n(x)$ is a rational function), the question is to find a linear recurrence relation satisfied by the sequence of integrals $I_n = \int_\gamma F_n(x)dx$ over a domain γ where $F_n(x)$ is integrable. To do this, the method of creative telescoping looks for polynomials $c_0(n), \dots, c_r(n)$, not all zero, and for a rational function $Q(n,x)$ such that $G_n(x) = Q(n,x)F_n(x)$ satisfies the telescoping relation

$$L(F_n(x)) \stackrel{\text{def}}{=} \sum_{i=0}^{r} c_i(n)F_{n+i}(x) = G'_n(x). \tag{1}$$

The recurrence operator $L = \sum_{i=0}^{r} c_i(n)S_n^i$ in the shift operator S_n is called a *telescoper* for $F_n(x)$, and the rational function $Q(n,x)$ is called a *certificate* for the telescoper L. The integer r is the *order* of L and $\max_j \deg c_j$ is its *degree*.

Throughout the article, the ground field, denoted by $\mathbf{k}$, is assumed to be of characteristic zero. Under suitable additional assumptions, $L(I_n) = 0$ is a recurrence relation satisfied by the sequence of integrals $I_n = \int_\gamma F_n(x)dx$.
A subtle point is that not all hypergeometric-hyperexponential terms admit telescopers. A criterion for deciding when this is the case has been given only recently [7, Section 6]: a hypergeometric-hyperexponential term is telescopable if and only if it can be written as the sum of a derivative and of a *proper term*. In our context, proper terms are of the form

$$P(n,x) \cdot H(x)^n \cdot \exp\Bigl(\int \frac{S(x)}{T(x)}\Bigr) \cdot \Upsilon(n), \tag{2}$$

for $P \in \mathbf{k}[n,x]$, $H \in \mathbf{k}(x)$, $S, T \in \mathbf{k}[x]$ and Υ hypergeometric.

Several methods are known for computing a telescoper L and the corresponding certificate Q, even in much greater generality [1, 21, 11, 20, 2, 15]. Despite a very rich research activity during the last decade, not much is known about the complexity of creative telescoping methods when applied to an input of the type (2). In particular, few estimates are available in the literature on the order and degree of the minimal-order telescoper.

If $\Upsilon(n) \neq 1$, one can compute a telescoper of the form (1) for the rest and then multiply the coefficient $c_i(n)$ by the rational function $\Upsilon(n)/\Upsilon(n+i)$; this process does not affect the minimality of the telescoper. Thus we focus on the case

$$F_n(x) = P(n,x) \cdot H(x)^n \cdot \exp\Bigl(\int \frac{S(x)}{T(x)}\Bigr). \tag{3}$$

Previous work. Among the various classes of creative telescoping methods, three different approaches allow to obtain bounds on the sizes of the telescoper and the certificate, and to control the algorithmic complexity. The first approach is based on elimination techniques [23, 21, 22]; it generally yields pessimistic bounds, not very efficient algorithms and telescopers of non-minimal order. The second approach, initiated by Apagodu and Zeilberger [2], provides sharp bounds on the order and degree of telescopers, more efficient algorithms, but does not provide information on telescopers of minimal

ISSAC'16, July 19–22, 2016, Waterloo, ON, Canada

ACM ISBN 978-1-4503-4380-0/16/07...$15.00.

DOI: http://dx.doi.org/10.1145/2930889.2930907

order and works under a restrictive genericity assumption. It was successfully applied by Kauers and co-authors [10, 9, 14] to (bivariate) hyperexponential terms and hypergeometric terms. The third approach, based on Hermite-like reduction, is the only one that computes telescopers of minimal order, while guaranteeing a good control on sizes and complexity. It has been introduced by Bostan *et alii* for the integration of bivariate rational functions [3], then extended to bivariate hyperexponential functions [4], multivariate rational functions [5, 17] and recently adapted to summation [8] for bivariate hypergeometric terms. The present work is part of the on-going effort in this direction.

Contributions. We present the first Hermite-style algorithm in the mixed (continuous–discrete) setting. Our approach is inspired by the proof of Manivel's lemma [12, §2.3], originally designed in connection with the so-called *polynomial rigidity conjecture.*

Our algorithm works on terms of the form (3). Its input is $F_n(x) = P(n,x)\Phi(n,x)$, given by

$$P(n,x), \quad \frac{\Phi'}{\Phi}(n,x) = \frac{A(n,x)}{B(x)} = n\frac{H'(x)}{H(x)} + \frac{S(x)}{T(x)}, \qquad (\star)$$

i.e., a polynomial in $\mathbf{k}[n,x]$ and a rational function in $\mathbf{k}(n,x)$ of a special form given either in lowest terms (A/B with $\gcd(A,B)=1$ and $\deg_n B = 0$) or decomposed as the sum of the logarithmic derivative of a rational function $H \in \mathbf{k}(x)$ multiplied by n and another rational function $S/T \in \mathbf{k}(x)$. Note that, for a given term, several choices are available for P and Φ. If we further assume that Φ'/Φ has no positive integer residue, they become unique and we call them the *minimal decomposition* of $F_n(x)$.

Our main results consist in bounds on the order and degree of telescopers for $F_n(x)$, that are summarized in Theorem 1 below (see Theorems 6 and 15 for more precise statements). A complexity analysis of the algorithms leading to these bounds is conducted in section 4 (see in particular Theorem 21).

In the statement of the following theorem, $\deg_x H$ and $\deg_n P$ denote the maximum of the degrees of their numerator and denominator, and d_H is the degree of H at infinity.

Theorem 1 *Given a decomposition as in* ($\star$), $F_n(x)$ *admits a telescoper of order* r *bounded by* δ, *where*

$$\delta := \max(\deg_x A, \deg_x B - 1), \qquad (4)$$

and degree bounded by

$$r(\deg_x H + \deg_n P) + \deg_x P.$$

Moreover, if the decomposition is minimal then these bounds apply to a minimal-order telescoper for $F_n(x)$.

Algorithm MixedCT *(§2.3) produces a telescoper with these properties. If* d *denotes an upper bound on the degrees of the numerator and denominator of* H, *and of all the polynomials in* ($\star$), *and if all these polynomials are square-free, then the telescoper has arithmetic size* $O(d^3)$ *and* MixedCT *computes it using at most*

$$\begin{cases} \tilde{O}(d^{\omega+1}) & \text{if } d_H < 0, \\ \tilde{O}(d^5) & \text{if } d_H \geqslant 0 \end{cases}$$

arithmetic operations in $\mathbf{k}$, *where* ω *denotes a feasible matrix multiplication exponent for* $\mathbf{k}$.

Note that one can always choose the decomposition of $F_n(x)$ in ($\star$) to be minimal. Indeed, we may write $\Phi = Q\tilde{\Phi}$ where Q is a polynomial and $\tilde{\Phi}'/\tilde{\Phi}$ has no positive integer residue. We then have a minimal decomposition $F_n(x) = (PQ)\tilde{\Phi}$.

The proof of Theorem 1 is achieved through two main ingredients: *confinement* and *Hermite reduction*. Confinement is the property that given Φ, any polynomial P can be reduced modulo derivatives to a polynomial R of degree at most $\delta - 1$: $P\Phi = R\Phi + \Gamma'$ for some Γ. It gives a finite dimensional vector space over $\mathbf{k}(n)$, where the computation will be confined. Hermite reduction is more classical. In this context, it consists in an algorithm that performs a reduction $P\Phi(n+1,x) = R\Phi(n,x) + \Gamma'$ for some Γ. By iterated application of both these operations, all $P(n+i,x)\Phi(n+i,x)$ for $i = 0,\dots,\delta$ can be rewritten in a vector space of dimension δ over $\mathbf{k}(n)$. Thus by (polynomial) linear algebra there exists a non-trivial linear relation between them, i.e., a telescoper. A more careful study of the increase of the degrees in n during these rewritings gives the degree bound.

Notation. In all that follows, $\mathbf{k}$ and $\mathbb{K}$ will denote fields of characteristic 0. In our applications we will often set $\mathbb{K} = \mathbf{k}(n)$. We denote by $\mathbb{K}[x]_d$ the set of polynomials in $\mathbb{K}[x]$ of degree less than d.

Rational functions are always written in reduced form, with monic denominator. Thus the numerator and denominator are defined without ambiguity. If k is the degree of the numerator and ℓ the degree of the denominator of a rational function F, we say that F has *rational degree* (k,ℓ), that we denote $\mathrm{Rdeg}(F) = [k]/[\ell]$. We also define the *regular degree* $\deg(F)$ of F as $\deg(F) = \max(k,\ell)$. Finally, the *degree at infinity* of F is defined as $\deg^\infty(F) = k - \ell$. The variable with respect to which the degree is taken will be indicated as a subscript when there is an ambiguity.

A polynomial is called *square-free* when its gcd with its derivative is trivial. The *square-free decomposition* of a monic polynomial $Q \in \mathbb{K}[x]$ is a factorization $Q = Q_1^1 \cdots Q_m^m$, with $Q_i \in \mathbb{K}[x]$ monic and square-free, the Q_i's pairwise coprime and $\deg_x(Q_m) > 0$. The *square-free part* of Q is the polynomial $Q^\star = Q_1 \cdots Q_m$.

Structure of the article. Section 2 gives the main properties of the confinement and of the mixed Hermite-like reduction, leading to the bound on the order of the telescoper. Section 3 gives a bound on the degree of the telescoper and analyzes the evolution of the degrees during the reductions, preparing the complexity analyses in Section 4. We conclude the article in Section 5 with a few applications of our implementation and experiments on the actual growth of the minimal-order telescopers.

2. ALGORITHMS AND ORDER BOUND

In this section, we introduce the algorithms with just enough information to prove their correctness and to obtain a bound on the order of the telescoper they compute. A more thorough analysis of the degrees is in the next section.

2.1 Confinement

In terms of integrals, the operation of confinement writes

$$\int_\gamma P(n,x)\Phi(n,x)\,dx = \int_\gamma R(n,x)\Phi(n,x)\,dx,$$

with R a polynomial of degree smaller than δ from Eq (4). This transformation is based on the following lemma.

Lemma 2 *Let Φ, A and B be as in Eq. (*), and δ as in Eq. (4). Then for any polynomial $P \in \mathbb{K}[x]$, there exist unique polynomials R and Q in $\mathbb{K}[x]$ with $\deg R \leqslant \delta - 1$ and $\deg Q \leqslant \deg P - \delta$ such that*

$$P\Phi = R\Phi + (QB\Phi)'. \tag{5}$$

Thus all polynomial multiples of Φ can be written modulo derivatives on a vector space of dimension δ.

Proof. Equation (5) rewrites

$$QA + (QB)' = P - R. \tag{6}$$

Denote $d = \deg(P) - \delta$, and consider the linear map

$$f \ : \ \mathbb{K}[x]_{d+1} \to \mathbb{K}[x]_{d+1} \quad Q \mapsto (QA + (QB)') \operatorname{div} x^{\delta},$$

where $u \operatorname{div} v$ denotes the quotient in the Euclidean division of u by v. For $m \leqslant d$, $f(x^m)$ has degree at most m. Its coefficient of degree m equals either $\operatorname{lc} A \neq 0$ if $\delta = \deg A > \deg B - 1$, or $m + \delta + 1 \neq 0$ if $\delta = \deg B - 1 > \deg A$, or $\operatorname{lc} A + m + \delta + 1$ if $\deg A = \deg B - 1$. For this case to occur, it is necessary that $\deg S < \deg T$. In that case, write $H'/H = U/V$ with U, V polynomials such that $\deg U = \deg V - 1$. Then $A/B = (nUT + VS)/(VT)$, and

$$\deg(VS) \leqslant \deg V + \deg T - 1 = \deg(UT).$$

From this we see that $\operatorname{lc}(A)$ depends on n and we deduce that $f(x^m)$ has degree exactly m in all cases.

Thus f is an isomorphism. It follows that Equation (6) is equivalent to Q being the unique polynomial such that $f(Q) = P \operatorname{div} x^{\delta}$, and then R is $P - QA - (QB)'$. The degrees of Q and R directly follow from the construction. □

Algorithm Confinement implements the proof of Lemma 2. Its correctness follows from the fact that the relation used in the loop is obtained by extracting the coefficient of $x^{i+\delta}$ in Eq. (6).

The key to the minimality in Theorem 1 is the following property of the confinement.

Proposition 3 *With the notation of (*), further assume that Φ'/Φ has no positive integer residue. Then, for any polynomial $R \in \mathbb{K}[x]$ such that $\deg_x R < \delta$*

$$\exists K \in \mathbb{K}(x) \ R\Phi = (K\Phi)' \Leftrightarrow R = 0.$$

Proof. Only the direct implication is not obvious. If such a K exists, the equation rewrites

$$R = K' + K\frac{A}{B}.$$

If K is a polynomial, this equality can only be satisfied if B divides K, in which case the result is a direct consequence of the uniqueness in Lemma 2. Now assume that K has a pole x_0 of order $v > 0$. Then the equation shows that A/B must have a simple pole at x_0 with residue v, which contradicts the assumption on the residues of Φ'/Φ. □

2.2 Hermite Reduction

In terms of integrals, our Algorithm HermiteReduction lets one change H^{n+1} into H^n in the integral, writing

$$\int_{\gamma} P(n,x)H(x)\Phi(n,x)\,dx = \int_{\gamma} \tilde{P}(n,x)\Phi(n,x)\,dx,$$

for some polynomial $\tilde{P}$. It relies on a sequence of elementary steps (BasicReduction) based on the following lemma.

Algorithm Confinement(P,F)

Input A polynomial $P \in \mathbb{K}[x]$, a rational function $F = A/B$ with $\gcd(A, B) = 1$.
Output A polynomial $R \in \mathbb{K}[x]$ of degree less than $\max(\deg(A), \deg(B) - 1)$ such that $P = R + (QB)' + QA$ for some $Q \in \mathbb{K}[x]$.

$\delta \leftarrow \max(\deg(A), \deg(B) - 1)$;
$d \leftarrow \deg(P) - \delta$;
Write $A = \sum_i a_i x^i$, $B = \sum_i b_i x^i$, $P = \sum_i p_i x^i$;
for $i \leftarrow d$ to 0 by -1 **do**
  $c \leftarrow a_{\delta} + (\delta + i + 1) b_{\delta+1}$;
  $q_i \leftarrow \frac{1}{c}\Big(p_{\delta+i} - \sum_{j=1}^{\delta} q_{i+j} a_{\delta-j}$
   $-(\delta + i + 1)\sum_{j=1}^{\delta+1} q_{i+j} b_{\delta+1-j}\Big)$;
$Q \leftarrow \sum_{i=0}^{d} q_i x^i$;
return $P - (QB)' - QA$.

Lemma 4 *Let Φ, A and B be as in Eq. (*). Then for any G dividing B and satisfying $\gcd(G, A + B') = 1$, there exist polynomials Q and R in $\mathbb{K}[x]$ such that*

$$P\Phi = RG\Phi + (QB\Phi)'. \tag{7}$$

Proof. The hypothesis $\gcd(G, A + B') = 1$ implies the existence of polynomials $U, Q \in \mathbb{K}[x]$ such that $P = UG + Q(A + B')$. Then the derivative $(QB\Phi)'$ expands as

$$\frac{(QB\Phi)'}{\Phi} = Q'B + Q(A + B') = (Q'B/G - U)G + P,$$

which has exactly the form of Equation (7). □

The crucial condition $\gcd(G, A + B') = 1$ required to apply this lemma does not hold for arbitrary A and B and divisor G of B, but when G is square-free, it is a consequence of the presence of n in Eq. (*), as shown in the following.

Lemma 5 *Let Φ, A and B be as in Eq. (*). Then for any square-free polynomial G in $\mathbf{k}[x]$ dividing the denominator of H, $\gcd(G, A + B') = 1$. This is also true if A/B is replaced by the reduced form of $A/B + iG'/G$ for some $i \in \mathbb{Z}$.*

Proof. If $H' = 0$ then the denominator of H is 1 and then $G = 1$ and the property holds.

Otherwise, let first G be an irreducible factor of the denominator of H, so that there exist an integer k and polynomials

---

Algorithm BasicReduction(P,F,G,k)

Input A polynomial $P \in \mathbb{K}[x]$, a rational function $F = A/B \in \mathbb{K}(x)$, a square-free factor G of B s.t. $\gcd(G, A + B' + iBG'/G) = 1$ for all $i \in \mathbb{Z}$, a positive integer k.
Output A polynomial $R \in \mathbb{K}[x]$ such that $P = G^k(R + q' + Fq)$ for some $q \in \mathbb{K}[x][G^{-1}]$.

$R \leftarrow P$;
for $i \leftarrow 1$ to k **do**
  $C \leftarrow A + (i - k - 1)BG'/G + B'$;
  Write $R = QC + VG$ with $\deg Q < \deg G$;
  $R \leftarrow (R - Q'B - QC)/G$; ▷ $\frac{P}{G^k}\Phi = \frac{R}{G^{k-i}}\Phi + (q\Phi)'$
return R.

Algorithm HermiteReduction(P,H,S/T)

Input A polynomial $P \in \mathbf{k}(n)[x]$,
two rational functions H and S/T in $\mathbf{k}(x)$.
Output A polynomial $R \in \mathbf{k}(n)[x]$ such that
$P = R/H + nQH'/H + QS/T + Q'$ for some
$Q \in \mathbf{k}(n,x)$.

Compute the square-free decomposition of the denominator of H: $g = g_1 g_2^2 \dots g_m^m$;
Compute the corresponding partial fraction decomposition: $H = U + \sum_{k=1}^m U_k/g_k^k$;
$R \leftarrow PU$;
$K \leftarrow S/T + (n-1)H'/H$;
for $k \leftarrow 1$ to m **do**
  $r_k \leftarrow$ BasicReduction(PU_k, K, g_k, k);
return $R + r_1 + \dots + r_m$.

$H_1, H_2 \in \mathbf{k}[x]$ such that

$$\frac{A}{B} = nk\frac{G'}{G} + n\frac{H_1}{H_2} + \frac{S}{T},$$

with $\gcd(G, H_2) = 1$ and $B = \operatorname{lcm}(G, H_2, T)$. Write $B = G^\nu \tilde{B}$ with $\gcd(G, \tilde{B}) = 1$. Then

$$A = nkG'G^{\nu-1}\tilde{B} + nH_1G^\nu(\tilde{B}/H_2) + S(G^\nu\tilde{B}/T).$$

Reducing $A + B'$ modulo G then yields

$$A + B' \equiv (nk+\nu)G'G^{\nu-1}\tilde{B} + S(G^\nu\tilde{B}/T) \bmod G. \quad (8)$$

Since G does not depend on n, $G \mid A + B'$ would imply that both $G \mid G'G^{\nu-1}\tilde{B}$ and $G \mid SG^\nu\tilde{B}/T$. The first condition implies $\nu > 1$, which forces that $G^\nu \mid T$, making $G \mid S$ necessary too, a contradiction. This reasoning also proves the result when adding integer multiples of G'/G to the fraction A/B, which adds an integer to $nk + \nu$ in Eq. (8).

If G is only assumed to be a square-free divisor of the denominator of H, then the property holds for each of its irreducible factors, and thus $A + B'$ is invertible modulo their product G by the Chinese remainder theorem. □

Correctness of BasicReduction and HermiteReduction. Algorithm HermiteReduction treats each square-free factor of the denominator of H separately, while the second part of the lemma is used in Algorithm BasicReduction to deal with multiplicities. If G is a square-free factor of multiplicity k, then Lemma 4 is used successively with A/B the reduced form of the logarithmic derivatives of $\Phi/G^k, \Phi/G^{k-1}, \dots, \Phi/G$, thus rewriting $P\Phi/G^k$ as $R\Phi$ up to a derivative.

2.3 Mixed Creative Telescoping

Combining confinement and Hermite reduction gives the final result.

Theorem 6 *Let P be a polynomial in $\mathbf{k}[n,x]$ and Φ, A and B as in Eq. ($\star$) and δ as in Eq. (4). Then, $F_n = P(n,x)\Phi$ admits a telescoper of order bounded by δ.*

Proof. By Lemma 4, Algorithm HermiteReduction can be used to rewrite all the shifts $F_n, F_{n+1}, F_{n+2}, \dots$ under the form $R\Phi$ modulo derivatives, with $R \in \mathbf{k}(n)[x]$. The necessary condition to apply the algorithm is satisfied at each step thanks to Lemma 5. By Lemma 2, $F_n, F_{n+1}, \dots, F_{n+\delta}$ are linearly dependent modulo derivatives. A linear relation between them provides a telescoper of order at most δ. □

Algorithm MixedCT($P, H, S/T$)

Input A polynomial $P \in \mathbf{k}[n,x]$,
two rational functions H and S/T in $\mathbf{k}(x)$.
Output A r-tuple $(c_0, \dots, c_{r-1})$ such that
$P(n+r,x)H^r - \sum_{i=0}^{r-1} c_i P(n+i,x)H^i =$
$nQH'/H + QS/T + Q'$ for some $Q \in \mathbf{k}(n,x)$.

$F \leftarrow S/T + (n-1)H'/H$;
$R_0 \leftarrow$ Confinement($P \mid_{n \mapsto n-1}, F$);
for $k \leftarrow 0, \dots$ **do**
  if $\operatorname{rank}_{\mathbf{k}(n)}(R_0, R_1, \dots, R_k) < k+1$ **then**
    Solve $\sum_{i=0}^{k-1} c_i R_i = R_k$ for $c_0, \dots, c_{k-1}$ in $\mathbf{k}(n)$;
    return $(c_0, \dots, c_{k-1})$.
  $P \leftarrow R_k \mid_{n \mapsto n+1}$;
  $P \leftarrow$ HermiteReduction($P, H, S/T$);
  $R_{k+1} \leftarrow$ Confinement(P, F);

Algorithm MixedCT implements that proof. In practice, for efficiency purposes, the reduction of F_{n+i} is obtained by applying HermiteReduction to the shift of the confined reduction of F_{n+i-1}.

Theorem 7 *With the notation of Theorem 6, further assume that Φ'/Φ does not have any positive integer residue. Then Algorithm MixedCT(P,H,S/T) computes a minimal-order telescoper for $P\Phi$.*

Proof. Consider the minimal-order monic telescoper

$$L(n, S_n) = S_n^r - \sum_{i=0}^{r-1} c_i(n) S_n^i$$

of $P\Phi$ and its certificate $C \in \mathbf{k}(n,x)$ such that

$$L(n, S_n) \cdot (P\Phi) = (C\Phi)'.$$

By Lemma 2, there exist R and K satisfying

$$L(n, S_n) \cdot (P\Phi) = R\Phi + (K\Phi)',$$

where $K \in \mathbf{k}(n,x)$ and

$$R = R_r - \sum_{i=0}^{r-1} c_i(n) R_i$$

is a linear combination of the R_i's of Algorithm MixedCT. It follows that $R\Phi = ((C-K)\Phi)'$ and Proposition 3 then implies that $R = 0$. Thus, this linear combination is detected by the algorithm, producing the output $(c_0, \dots, c_{r-1})$. □

Certificates. Algorithm MixedCT as given here computes the certificate, although not in a normalized form. We chose to only output the telescoper, but it would be possible to return the certificate as well (and normalize it or not).

3. DEGREE BOUNDS

We now review more precisely the algorithms and obtain bounds on the degrees at each step. The first part of this section consists of technical results that are needed for the complexity analysis in the next section. Then, at the end of section 3.3, we give a bound on the degree of the telescoper produced by Algorithm MixedCT.

3.1 Confinement

Lemma 8 *Let A and B be as in Eq. (*) and let P be a polynomial in $\mathbf{k}(n)[x]$. Let R be the polynomial returned by Algorithm* Confinement. *Then* $\operatorname{Rdeg}_n R - \operatorname{Rdeg}_n P$ *is at most*

$$\begin{cases} (\deg_x P - \deg_x A + 1)\frac{[1]}{[1]}, & \text{if } \deg_x B \leqslant \deg_x A + 1, \\ \left[\left\lfloor \frac{\deg_x P - \deg_x B + 1}{\deg_x B - \deg_x A - 1} \right\rfloor + 1\right]/[0] & \text{otherwise.} \end{cases}$$

PROOF. The proof is a case by case analysis of Algorithm Confinement; we use its notation.

When $\delta = \deg_x A$, the recurrence for q_i has a summand $a_{\delta-1}q_{i+1}$ except when $i = d$, while c has a_δ for summand. Thus by induction, the degree in n of the numerator and denominator of q_{d-i} increase by 1 at each step. Since there are $d+1$ steps, $\operatorname{Rdeg}_n Q - \operatorname{Rdeg}_n P$ is bounded by $[d]/[d+1]$. The result for R then follows from Equation (6).

When $\delta = \deg_x B - 1$, the coefficients $a_{\delta-j}$ are zero for $j < \delta - \deg_x A$ and c has degree 0 in n. By induction on i, q_{d-i} has degree that changes (by increases of 1) only when $i \equiv 0 \mod \delta - \deg_x A$. More explicitly, $\operatorname{Rdeg}_n q_{d-i} - \operatorname{Rdeg}_n P$ is bounded by $[\lfloor i/(\delta - \deg_x A)\rfloor]/[0]$. Again, the conclusion for R follows from Equation (6). □

3.2 Hermite Reduction

In order to track the degrees in n of the polynomials involved in Algorithms BasicReduction and HermiteReduction, we need to look deeper into the modular inversions involved. This is done in the next lemma, using the same notation as in the discussion preceding Lemma 5.

Lemma 9 *Let A, B and H be as in Eq. (*). Let G be an irreducible factor of the denominator of H, and ν the G-adic valuation of B. Let P be in $\mathbf{k}(n)[x]$ and let Q be the polynomial such that $\deg_x Q < \deg_x(G)$ and $P \equiv Q(A + B') \bmod G$. Then $\operatorname{Rdeg}_n Q - \operatorname{Rdeg}_n P$ is bounded by*

$$\begin{cases} [0]/[0], & \text{if } \nu > 1; \\ [0]/[1], & \text{if } \nu = 1 \text{ and } G \nmid T; \\ [\deg_x(G) - 1]/[\deg_x(G)], & \text{if } \nu = 1 \text{ and } G \mid T. \end{cases}$$

PROOF. The existence of Q follows from Lemma 5. Notice first that $\operatorname{Rdeg}_n Q - \operatorname{Rdeg}_n P = \operatorname{Rdeg}_n(A + B')^{-1}$ (where $(A + B)^{-1}$ denotes an inverse mod G). Indeed, writing $p(n)P = P_0(x) + \cdots + P_d(x)n^d$ with $p(n)$ the denominator of P, we see that $p(n)Q = (A + B')^{-1}(P_0 \bmod G) + \cdots + (A + B')^{-1}n^d(P_d \bmod G)$ has rational degree in n at most $[d]/[0] + \operatorname{Rdeg}_n(A + B')^{-1}$.

Thus we just need to bound $\operatorname{Rdeg}_n(A + B')^{-1}$. To do so, we take a closer look at Equation (8). If $\nu > 1$, the equation becomes

$$A + B' \equiv S\frac{\tilde{B}}{T/G^\nu} \bmod G,$$

so that $(A + B')^{-1}$ does not depend on n in this case.

If $\nu = 1$ and $G \nmid T$, the equation becomes

$$A + B' \equiv (nk + 1)G'\tilde{B}.$$

Then, $(A + B')^{-1} \equiv (G'\tilde{B})^{-1}/(nk + \nu)$ has rational degree $[0]/[1]$. Finally, if $\nu = 1$ and $G \mid T$, the result follows from Lemma 10 below. □

Lemma 10 *Let A, B, C be polynomials in $\mathbf{k}[x]$ such that C is relatively prime with at least one of A or B. Let $U, V \in \mathbf{k}(n)[x]$ be such that*

$$1 = U(An + B) + VC, \quad \text{with} \quad \deg_x U < \deg C. \qquad (9)$$

Then $\operatorname{Rdeg}_n U$ is bounded by $[\deg C - 1]/[\deg C]$.

PROOF. Let $R(n) \neq 0$ denote the resultant with respect to x of C and $An + B$. Then $R = S(An + B) + TC$ for some S, T in $\mathbf{k}[n, x]$ with $\deg_x S < \deg C$. Moreover, by Cramer's rule applied to the Sylvester matrix of C and $An + B$, we have $\deg R \leq \deg C$ and $\deg_n S < \deg C$.

Now denote by $q(n)$ the monic denominator of U, and by $\tilde{U} \in \mathbf{k}[n, x]$ its numerator. We need to prove that $\deg q \leq \deg C$ and $\deg_n \tilde{U} < \deg C$. Equalities

$$1 = U(An + B) + VC, \quad 1 = S/R(An + B) + (T/R)C$$

imply by subtraction that C divides $(An + B)(U - S/R)$ in $\mathbf{k}(n)[x]$. Since C is coprime with $An + B$, this implies that C divides $U - S/R$. As $\deg C < \deg_x(U - S/R)$, this shows that $U = S/R$. In particular, q divides R. It follows that $\deg q \leq \deg R \leq \deg C$ and $\deg_n \tilde{U} = \deg_y(qS/R) \leq \deg_n S < \deg C$, which concludes the proof. □

Lemma 11 *With the same notation as in Lemma 9, and assuming that G has multiplicity k in the denominator of H, the output R of* BasicReduction$(P, A/B, G, k)$ *satisfies*

$$\deg_x R \leqslant \max(\deg_x P - k\deg_x G, \deg_x A - 1, \deg_x B - 2),$$

and $\operatorname{Rdeg}_n R - \operatorname{Rdeg}_n P$ is bounded by

$$\begin{cases} k[1]/[0], & \text{if } \nu > 1; \\ k[1]/[1], & \text{if } \nu = 1 \text{ and } G \nmid T; \\ k\deg_x(G)[1]/[1], & \text{if } \nu = 1 \text{ and } G \mid T. \end{cases}$$

PROOF. Both bounds follow from Lemma 9. For the degree in n, the polynomial Q of the algorithm is obtained from a modular inverse as above, that is multiplied by R, and then by C that has rational degree $[1]/[0]$ in n. The bound directly follows in the first and third cases since the condition on ν and G is preserved at each step. In the second case, the condition $G \nmid T$ is not preserved, but writing $J = iG'/G + S/T$ at each step shows that the degree in n still increases by $[1]/[1]$ only. For the degree in x, the bound is obtained by bounding each term in the expression of R that is used in the algorithm. □

Lemma 12 *With the same notation, write the denominator g of H as $g = efh$, where*

$$e = \gcd(g, T, T'), \quad f = \gcd(g/e, T).$$

Also denote m the highest multiplicity of the roots of g, and let $e = e_1e_2^2\cdots e_m^m$ and $h = h_1h_2^2\cdots h_m^m$ be the square-free decompositions of e and h.

Then, the result of Algorithm HermiteReduction$(P, H, S/T)$ *is a polynomial in x of degree at most*

$$\max(\deg_x P + \deg_x^\infty H, \deg_x P - 1, \deg_x A - 1, \deg_x B - 2).$$

Seen as a rational function in n, it has degree at most

$$\operatorname{Rdeg}_n P + \frac{[\max_{e_k \neq 1} k + \sum_{h_k \neq 1} k + \deg_x f]}{[\sum_{h_k \neq 1} k + \deg_x f]}.$$

Moreover, the certificate Q in the algorithm satisfies $Q = qB/(gH)$ for some polynomial q such that $\deg_x q < \deg_x g$.

PROOF. Following the notation of Algorithm HermiteReduction, the partial fraction decomposition of H produces U with $\deg_x U \leqslant \deg_x^\infty H$ and U_k with $\deg_x U_k < \deg_x g_k$. PU obviously satisfies the bounds. Now write the square-free decomposition $f = f_1 f_2^2 \cdots f_m^m$. By Lemma 11, $\mathrm{Rdeg}_n r_k \leqslant \mathrm{Rdeg}_n P + [k(\mathbf{1}_{e_k \neq 1} + \mathbf{1}_{h_k \neq 1} + \deg_x f_k)]/[k(\mathbf{1}_{h_k \neq 1} + \deg_x f_k)]$. Normalizing $R + r_1 + r_2 + \cdots + r_m$ then yields the result. The bound for the degree in x is obtained by bounding separately each term using Lemma 11. The form of Q follows from the fact that the certificate of the k-th call to BasicReduction has the form $q_k B/(g_k^k H)$ with $\deg_x q_k < \deg_x(g_k^k)$. □

3.3 Mixed Creative Telescoping

Lemma 13 *With the notation of Eq. (⋆), Eq. (4), Algorithm* MixedCT*, and $d_H = \deg_x^\infty H$, for all i in $\{1, 2, \ldots, \delta\}$ we have*

$$\mathrm{Rdeg}_n R_i \leqslant \deg_n P \cdot \frac{[1]}{[0]} + \alpha + i(\beta + \gamma)$$

where

$$\alpha = \begin{cases} \max(\deg_x P - \delta + 1, 0) \cdot \frac{[1]}{[1]} & \text{if } \delta = \deg_x A, \\ \left[\max\left(\left\lfloor \frac{\deg_x P - \delta}{\delta - \deg_x A} \right\rfloor + 1, 0\right)\right]/[0] & \text{otherwise.} \end{cases}$$

$$\beta = \frac{[\max_{e_k \neq 1} k + \sum_{h_k \neq 1} k + \deg_x f]}{[\sum_{h_k \neq 1} k + \deg_x f]}$$

$$\gamma = \begin{cases} (d_H + 1) \cdot \frac{[1]}{[1]} & \text{if } d_H \geqslant 0 \text{ and } \delta = \deg_x A, \\ \left[\left\lfloor \frac{d_H}{\delta - \deg_x A} \right\rfloor + 1\right]/[0] & \text{if } d_H \geqslant 0 \text{ and } \delta = \deg_x B - 1, \\ 0 & \text{otherwise.} \end{cases}$$

PROOF. By Lemma 8, the initial confinement increases $\mathrm{Rdeg}_n P$ by α. HermiteReduction is then always used with an input polynomial of degree less than δ. By Lemma 12 each call to HermiteReduction increases $\mathrm{Rdeg}_n P$ by at most β, and produces an output of degree at most δ if $d_H < 0$ or $\delta + d_H$ if $d_H \geqslant 0$. Thus the confinement is only necessary in the latter case. Plugging this bound into Lemma 8 shows that each call to Confinement increases $\mathrm{Rdeg}_n P$ by at most γ. □

3.4 Degree bound on the telescoper

Lemma 14 *With the notation of (⋆), let $(c_0, \ldots, c_{r-1})$ be the output of* MixedCT*(P,H,S/T) and write $H = f/g$ with $\gcd(f, g) = 1$.*

Then there exists a polynomial $Q \in \mathbf{k}(n)[x]$ such that

$$\left(S_n^r - \sum_{i=0}^{r-1} c_i S_n^i\right)(P\Phi) = \left(\frac{Q}{g^r} B\Phi\right)',$$

with $\deg_x Q \leqslant r \deg_x H + \max(\deg_x P - \delta, 0) - 1$.

PROOF. Tracking the certificates of the various rewritings in MixedCT, it suffices to show that for all $i \in \{0, \ldots, r\}$

$$P(n + i - 1, x) H^i \frac{\Phi}{H} = R_i \frac{\Phi}{H} + \left(\frac{Q_i}{g^i} B \frac{\Phi}{H}\right)'$$

for some polynomial Q_i such that

$$\deg_x Q_i \leqslant \max(\deg_x P - \delta, 0) + i \deg_x H - 1.$$

This is obvious for $i = 0$ (initial confinement). Assume this is true for $i - 1$, then the next Hermite reduction writes

$$R_{i-1}(n + 1, x)\Phi = \tilde{R}_i \frac{\Phi}{H} + \left(\frac{\tilde{Q}_i}{g} B \frac{\Phi}{H}\right)'$$

with $\deg_x \tilde{Q}_i < \deg_x g$ and $\deg_x \tilde{R}_i \leqslant \delta - 1 + \delta_H$, where $\delta_H = \max(\deg_x^\infty H, 0)$ (see Lemma 12). As for the confinement,

$$\tilde{R}_i \frac{\Phi}{H} = R_i \frac{\Phi}{H} + \left(\overline{Q}_i B \frac{\Phi}{H}\right)',$$

with $\deg_x \overline{Q}_i \leqslant \delta_H - 1$ by Lemma 2. Thus, the property is satisfied for i with

$$Q_i = f Q_{i-1}(n + 1, x) + \tilde{Q}_i g^{i-1} + \overline{Q}_i g^i,$$

from which follows the bound on the degree of Q_i. □

Theorem 15 *With the notation of (⋆), the telescoper L produced by Algorithm* MixedCT*(P,H,S/T) satisfies*

$$\deg_n L \leqslant r(\deg_n P + \deg_x H) + \max(\deg_x P - \delta, 0),$$

where r is the order of L.

PROOF. Write $H = f/g$ with $\gcd(f, g) = 1$. Rewriting Lemma 14 in terms of polynomials yields

$$P(n + r) f^r - \sum_{i=0}^{r-1} c_i P(n + i) f^i g^{r-i} = (QB)' - rQ \frac{Bg'}{g} + QA$$

for some $Q = \sum_{i=0}^{s} q_i x^i$ with $s = \max(\deg_x P - \delta, 0) + r \deg_x H - 1$. This equation is a linear system with two blocks of unknowns: $c_0, \ldots, c_{r-1}$ with coefficients of degree bounded by $\deg_n P$ and $q_0, \ldots, q_s$ with coefficients of degree 1, which by Hadamard's bound yields $\deg_n c_i \leqslant r \deg_n P + s + 1$, whence the theorem. □

4. COMPLEXITY

We will rely on some classical complexity results for the basic operations on polynomials and rational functions. Standard references for these questions are the books [13] and [6]. We will also use the fact that linear systems with polynomial coefficients can be solved efficiently using Storjohann and Villard's algorithm [19]. The needed results are summarized in the following lemma.

Lemma 16 *Addition, product and differentiation of rational functions in $\mathbb{K}(x)$ of regular degree less than d, as well as extended gcd and square-free decomposition in $\mathbb{K}[x]_d$ can be performed using $\tilde{O}(d)$ operations in $\mathbb{K}$.*

The kernel of a $s \times (s + 1)$ matrix with polynomial entries in $\mathbf{k}[x]_d$ can be solved using $\tilde{O}(s^\omega d)$ operations in $\mathbf{k}$.

4.1 Confinement

Lemma 17 *With $P \in \mathbb{K}[x]$, $A/B \in \mathbb{K}(x)$ as input, and $\delta = \max(\deg_x A, \deg_x B - 1)$,* Confinement *performs at most*

$$O(\delta \deg_x P)$$

operations in $\mathbb{K}$.

PROOF. Each iteration of the loop performs $O(\delta)$ operations in $\mathbb{K}$ and the loop is executed $\deg_x P - \delta + 1$ times. The computation of R then needs $\tilde{O}(\deg_x P)$ operations in $\mathbb{K}$. □

4.2 Hermite Reduction

Lemma 18 *With the same notation as in the preceding lemma, G a square-free factor of B and k a positive integer,* BasicReduction*$(P,\ A/B,\ G,\ k)$ performs at most*

$$\tilde{O}(k(\deg_x P + \delta))$$

operations in $\mathbb{K}$.

Proof. The costly steps are the gcd computations, which according to Lemma 16 can be performed using $\tilde{O}(\deg_x P+\delta)$ operations in $\mathbb{K}$. The result then follows since there are k gcd computations. □

Lemma 19 *With the same notation as in Lemma 12, set $\epsilon = \sum_{g_k \neq 1} k$. Then* HermiteReduction*$(P,H,S/T)$ performs at most*

$$\tilde{O}(\max(\epsilon \deg_x P, d_H) + \deg_x g + \epsilon\delta)$$

operations in $\mathbb{K} = \mathbf{k}(n)$.

Proof. By Lemma 16, the square-free decomposition of g can be computed in $\tilde{O}(\deg_x g)$ operations and the product PU is computed at a cost $\tilde{O}(\max(\deg_x P, \deg_x^\infty H))$. By the preceding lemma, the k-th call to BasicReduction uses $\tilde{O}(k(\deg_x P+\deg_x g_k+\delta))$ operations. The announced bound is then obtained by summation. □

4.3 Mixed creative telescoping

For the sake of simplicity, Algorithm MixedCT searches for telescopers for all the possible orders, starting from 0. In practice, a more efficient variant consists in carrying a dichotomic search of the order between 0 and δ. This way the complexity is that of the last step up to a logarithmic factor. Here, we analyze this variant.

Lemma 20 *With the same notation as in Section 3.3, and $\epsilon = \sum_{g_k \neq 1} k$, the number of operations in $\mathbb{K} = \mathbf{k}(n)$ performed by* MixedCT*$(P,H,S/T)$ is*

1. *$\tilde{O}(\delta \max(\epsilon \deg_x P, d_H) + \delta \deg_x g + \epsilon\delta^2 + \delta^\omega)$ if $d_H < 0$;*
2. *$\tilde{O}(\delta \max(\epsilon \deg_x P, \delta d_H) + \delta \deg_x g + \epsilon\delta^2 + \delta^3)$ if $d_H \geqslant 0$.*

Proof. When $d_H < 0$, by Lemma 12 there are no confinement steps and the construction of the system to solve amounts to δ Hermite reductions. The algorithm then computes a vector in the kernel of a $\delta \times (\delta + 1)$ matrix, which by Lemma 16 can be performed in $\tilde{O}(\delta^\omega)$ operations in $\mathbb{K}$, hence the complexity.

When $d_H \geqslant 0$, we have to add the cost of the confinement steps, which by Lemma 12 are performed on polynomials of degree at most $\delta + d_H$. There are at most $\delta + 1$ calls to confinement, so the result follows from Lemma 17. □

Theorem 21 *With the same notation, set $\mu = \max(a, b)$ where $\deg_n P \cdot [1]/[0] + \alpha + \delta(\beta + \gamma) = [a]/[b]$, the number of operations in $\mathbf{k}$ performed by Algorithm* MixedCT *is*

$$\tilde{O}(\mu(\epsilon\delta \deg_x P + \delta \deg_x g + \epsilon\delta^2 + \delta^\omega)),$$

if $d_H < 0$, or

$$\tilde{O}(\mu(\epsilon\delta \deg_x P + \delta \deg_x g + \epsilon\delta^2 + \delta^3 + \delta^2 d_H))$$

if $d_H \geqslant 0$.

Proof. The result follows directly from the preceding lemma and the fact that all the elements of $\mathbb{K} = \mathbf{k}(n)$ appearing in the construction of the linear system have numerator and denominator of degree in n bounded by μ. The cost of solving is then $\tilde{O}(\delta^\omega \mu)$ operations in $\mathbf{k}$ by Lemma 16. □

The complexity result from Theorem 1 follows directly.

5. EXPERIMENTS AND APPLICATIONS

5.1 Various Integrals

Example 1. The Jacobi polynomials have the following integral representation, up to a factor that does not depend on n:

$$\oint \left(\frac{z^2 - 1}{2(z - x)}\right)^n (1 - z)^\alpha (1 + z)^\beta \frac{dz}{z - x},$$

with a contour enclosing $z = x$ once in the positive sense [18, 18.10.8]. It is well-known that the Jacobi polynomials satisfy a recurrence of order 2. Theorem 6 is tight in that case: it predicts a bound 2 on the order of the telescoper, since the logarithmic derivative of the integrand has numerator of degree 2 and denominator of degree 3.

Note however that in such an example, a more direct and efficient way to obtain a recurrence is to change the variable z into $x + u$ making the integral that of the extraction of the n-th coefficient in a hyperexponential term. That is achieved easily by translating the first order linear differential equation it satisfies into a linear recurrence. The only difference is that our method guarantees the minimality of the telescoper.

Example 2. A typical example where several of the difficulties are met at once is the term

$$\left(1 + \tfrac{x}{n^2+1}\right) \left(\tfrac{(x+1)^2}{(x-4)(x-3)^2(x^2-5)^3}\right)^n \sqrt{x^2 - 5}\, e^{\frac{x^3+1}{x(x-3)(x-4)^2}}.$$

Our code[1] finds a telescoper of order 9 and degree 90 in 1.4 sec. The only other code we are aware of that can perform this computation is Koutschan's `HolonomicFunctions` package [16], which takes more than 3 min. This is by no means a criticism of this excellent and very versatile package but rather to indicate the advantage of implementing specialized algorithms like ours for this class.

5.2 Inversion of rational functions

Here is a generalization of Manivel's lemma [12], which led us to this work. It gives an efficient way to compute the recurrence satisfied by the coefficients of the compositional inverse of a rational function. The starting point is Lagrange inversion. Let $f \in \mathbb{Q}(x)$ be a rational function such that $f(0) = 0$, and denote by $f^{(-1)}$ its compositional inverse. By Cauchy's formula, the n-th coefficient u_n of $f^{(-1)}$ is given by

$$u_n = \frac{1}{2\pi i} \oint f^{(-1)}(x) \frac{\mathrm{d}x}{x^{n+1}},$$

where the contour is a small circle around the origin. Integrating by parts and then using the change of variables

[1]The code and Maple worksheet for these examples can be found at http://mixedct.gforge.inria.fr.

$x = f(u)$ yields

$$u_n = \frac{1}{2\pi i n} \oint \frac{f^{(-1)'}(x)\mathrm{d}x}{x^n} = \frac{1}{2\pi i n} \oint \frac{\mathrm{d}u}{f(u)^n}.$$

Thus a recurrence for u_n can be computed with Algorithm MixedCT. Theorem 6 and Theorem 15 then provide bounds for the order and degree of this recurrence.

Theorem 22 *Let $f \in \mathbb{Q}(x)$ be a rational function such that $f(0) = 0$. Write $f = P/Q$ and denote $P = P_1 P_2^2 \cdots P_m^m$ the square-free decomposition of P. Also denote $p, p^\star, q, q^\star$ the degrees of $P, P^\star, Q, Q^\star$ respectively. Then the Taylor coefficients of $f^{(-1)}$ satisfy a recurrence of order at most*

$$q^\star + p^\star - 1$$

and of rational degree in n at most

$$\frac{(q^\star + p^\star)(q^\star + p^\star + 1)}{2}(\max(q - p, 0) + \sum_{P_k \neq 1} k) \cdot \frac{[1]}{[1]}.$$

k	order	degree	coeffs	time
5	10	61	1759	2.49
6	12	88	2440	4.64
7	14	120	3778	13.36
8	16	157	4666	33.89
9	18	199	6192	88.34
10	20	246	8364	260.59
11	22	298	10146	628.21
12	24	355	11802	1451.54

Table 1. Order, degree, bit size and timings for Example 3

Example 3. Experimental results on the family of rational functions $f_k = xP_k(x)^2/Q_k(x)$ with P_k and Q_k two dense polynomials of degree k and integer coefficients of absolute value bounded by 100 are presented in Table 1. The first column gives the index k. The second one is the order of the minimal-order telescopers, which is as predicted by Theorem 22. The next one gives the degree of the telescoper; it displays a quadratic growth, as predicted by Theorem 22. The column "coeffs" gives the bit size of the largest coefficient of the telescoper, whose growth seems slightly more than quadratic. Finally, the time (in seconds) taken by our implementation is given in the last column.

Acknowledgements. We are grateful to the referees for their thorough work and helpful comments. This work has been supported in part by FastRelax ANR-14-CE25-0018-01.

6. REFERENCES

[1] G. Almkvist and D. Zeilberger. The method of differentiating under the integral sign. *J. Symbolic Comput.*, 10(6):571–591, 1990.

[2] M. Apagodu and D. Zeilberger. Multi-variable Zeilberger and Almkvist-Zeilberger algorithms and the sharpening of Wilf-Zeilberger theory. *Adv. in Appl. Math.*, 37(2):139–152, 2006.

[3] A. Bostan, S. Chen, F. Chyzak, and Z. Li. Complexity of creative telescoping for bivariate rational functions. In *ISSAC'10*, pages 203–210. ACM, New York, 2010.

[4] A. Bostan, S. Chen, F. Chyzak, Z. Li, and G. Xin. Hermite reduction and creative telescoping for hyperexponential functions. In *ISSAC'13*, pages 77–84. ACM, New York, 2013.

[5] A. Bostan, P. Lairez, and B. Salvy. Creative telescoping for rational functions using the Griffiths-Dwork method. In *ISSAC'13*, pages 93–100. ACM, New York, 2013.

[6] P. Bürgisser, M. Clausen, and M. A. Shokrollahi. *Algebraic complexity theory*, volume 315 of *Grundlehren der Mathematischen Wissenschaften*. Springer, 1997.

[7] S. Chen, F. Chyzak, R. Feng, G. Fu, and Z. Li. On the existence of telescopers for mixed hypergeometric terms. *J. Symbolic Comput.*, 68:1–26, 2015.

[8] S. Chen, H. Huang, M. Kauers, and Z. Li. A modified Abramov-Petkovšek reduction and creative telescoping for hypergeometric terms. In *ISSAC'15*, pages 117–124. ACM, New York, 2015.

[9] S. Chen and M. Kauers. Order-degree curves for hypergeometric creative telescoping. In *ISSAC'12*, pages 122–129. ACM, New York, 2012.

[10] S. Chen and M. Kauers. Trading order for degree in creative telescoping. *J. Symbolic Comput.*, 47(8):968–995, 2012.

[11] F. Chyzak. An extension of Zeilberger's fast algorithm to general holonomic functions. *Discrete Math.*, 217(1-3):115–134, 2000.

[12] J.-P. Furter. Polynomial composition rigidity and plane polynomial automorphisms. *J. Lond. Math. Soc. (2)*, 91(1):180–202, 2015.

[13] J. von zur Gathen and J. Gerhard. *Modern Computer Algebra*. Cambridge Univ. Press, second edition, 2003.

[14] M. Kauers and L. Yen. On the length of integers in telescopers for proper hypergeometric terms. *J. Symbolic Comput.*, 66:21–33, 2015.

[15] C. Koutschan. Creative telescoping for holonomic functions. In C. Schneider and J. Blümlein, editors, *Computer Algebra in Quantum Field Theory: Integration, Summation and Special Functions*, Texts & Monographs in Symbolic Computation, pages 171–194. Springer, Wien, 2013.

[16] C. Koutschan. Holonomic Functions in Mathematica. *ACM Commun. Comput. Algebra*, 47(3/4):179–182, Jan. 2014.

[17] P. Lairez. Computing periods of rational integrals. *Math. Comp.*, 85(300):1719–1752.

[18] F. W. J. Olver, D. W. Lozier, R. F. Boisvert, and C. W. Clark, editors. *NIST Handbook of Mathematical Functions*. Cambridge University Press, 2010.

[19] A. Storjohann and G. Villard. Computing the rank and a small nullspace basis of a polynomial matrix. In *ISSAC'05*, pages 309–316. ACM, New York, 2005.

[20] A. Tefera. MultInt, a MAPLE package for multiple integration by the WZ method. *J. Symbolic Comput.*, 34(5):329–353, 2002.

[21] H. S. Wilf and D. Zeilberger. An algorithmic proof theory for hypergeometric (ordinary and "q") multisum/integral identities. *Invent. Math.*, 108(3):575–633, 1992.

[22] L. Yen. *Contributions to the proof theory of hypergeometric identities*. ProQuest LLC, Ann Arbor, MI, 1993. Thesis (Ph.D.)–University of Pennsylvania.

[23] D. Zeilberger. A holonomic systems approach to special functions identities. *J. Comput. Appl. Math.*, 32(3):321–368, 1990.

[24] D. Zeilberger. The method of creative telescoping. *J. Symbolic Comput.*, 11(3):195–204, 1991.

GBLA – Gröbner Basis Linear Algebra Package

Brice Boyer
Sorbonne Universités, UPMC
Univ Paris 06, CNRS, INRIA,
Laboratoire d'Informatique de
Paris 6 (LIP6), Équipe PolSys,
4 place Jussieu, 75252 Paris
Cedex 05, France
brice.boyer@lip6.fr

Christian Eder
University of Kaiserslautern
Department of Mathematics
PO box 3049
D-67653 Kaiserslautern
ederc@mathematik.uni-kl.de

Jean-Charles Faugère
Sorbonne Universités, UPMC
Univ Paris 06, CNRS, INRIA,
Laboratoire d'Informatique de
Paris 6 (LIP6), Équipe PolSys,
4 place Jussieu, 75252 Paris
Cedex 05, France
jean-charles.faugere@inria.fr

Sylvian Lachartre
Thalès
sylvain.lachartre@thales
group.com

Fayssal Martani
martani.net@gmail.com

ABSTRACT

This is a system paper about a new GPLv2 open source C library GBLA implementing and improving the idea [8] of Faugère and Lachartre (GB reduction). We further exploit underlying structures in matrices generated during Gröbner basis computations in algorithms like F4 or F5 taking advantage of block patterns by using a special data structure called *multilines*. Moreover, we discuss a new order of operations for the reduction process. In various different experimental results we show that GBLA performs better than GB reduction or Magma in sequential computations (up to 40% faster) and scales much better than GB reduction for a higher number of cores: On 32 cores we reach a scaling of up to 26. GBLA is up to 7 times faster than GB reduction. Further, we compare different parallel schedulers GBLA can be used with. We also developed a new advanced storage format that exploits the fact that our matrices are coming from Gröbner basis computations, shrinking storage by a factor of up to 4. A huge database of our matrices is freely available with GBLA.

Keywords

Gröbner bases, specialized linear algebra, parallel computations

1. INTRODUCTION

In [12, 8], Faugère and Lachartre presented a specialized linear algebra for Gröbner basis computation (GB reduction). The benefit of their approach is due to the very special structure the corresponding matrices have. Using algorithms like F4 the tasks of *searching for reducers* and *reducing the input elements* are isolated. In the so-called *symbolic preprocessing* (see [7]) all possible reducers for all terms of a predefined subset of currently available S-polynomials are collected. Out of this data a matrix M is generated whose rows correspond to the coefficients of the polynomials whereas the columns represent all appearing monomials sorted by the given monomial order on the polynomial ring. New elements for the ongoing Gröbner basis computation are computed via Gaussian elimination of M, *i.e.* the reduction process of several S-polynomials at once. M always has a structure like presented in Figure 1, where black dots correspond to nonzero coefficients of the associated polynomials. Faugère and Lachartre's idea is to take advantage of M's structure nearly being in triangular shape, already before starting the reduction process.

Figure 1: F4 Matrix of degree 6 for homogeneous KATSURA-12

This is a system paper introducing in detail our new open source plain C parallel library GBLA. We have chosen C to enable easy comparisons with BLAS and LAPACK implementations (written in C resp. FORTRAN), to avoid the overhead of virtual function calls as well as to keep compile time at a minimum. GBLA includes efficient implementations not only of the GB reduction but also new algorithmic improvements. It is implemented for prime fields with special optimizations for 16-bit primes, but can also be used for floating point coefficient representations or even 32-bit unsigned integeres. Here we present new ways of exploiting the underlying structure of the matrices, introducing new matrix storage formats and various attempts to improve the reduction process, especially for parallel computations. We discuss different experimental results showing the benefits of our new attempt.

The paper is structured as follows: In Section 2 we give an overview of the structure of our library. Section 3 discusses the special matrix structure and presents a new efficient storage for-

ISSAC '16, July 19-22, 2016, Waterloo, ON, Canada

DOI: http://dx.doi.org/10.1145/2930889.2930914

Folder	Files	Description
src	types.*	general data types
	matrix.*	matrix and multiline vector types; conversion routines for sparse, hybrid, block, multiline matrices
	mapping.*	splicing of input matrix (Step 1 in GB reduction); different routines for usual block and multiline vector submatrix representations
	elimination.*	elimination routines including Steps $2-4$ of GB reduction as well as adjusted routines for new order of operations (see Section 4.3)
cli	io.*	input and output routines
	gbla.*	main routines for GB reduction
tools	dump_matrix.*	routines for dumping matrices; especially towards MatrixMarket or Magma formats
	converter.c	converting matrices from format 1 to format 2 (see Section 3.2)

Table 1: Description of GBLA's structure

mat. This is important for testing and benchmarking purposes. We also recall the general process used for reducing these matrices. In Section 4 we first review the main steps of the GB reduction. Afterwards we propose improvements to the sequential algorithm by further exploiting patterns in the matrices. This is implemented in our new library by specialized data structures and a rearrangement of the order of steps of the GB reduction. Section 5 is dedicated to ideas for efficient parallelization of our library that also takes into account the improvements discussed beforehand. In Section 6 we show GBLA's efficiency by giving experimental results comparing it to several other specialized linear algebra implementations for Gröbner basis computations.

2. LIBRARY & MATRICES

Our library is called GBLA (Gröbner basis linear algebra) and is the first plain *C* open source package available for specialized linear algebra in Gröbner basis-like computations. It is based on a first *C++* implementation of Fayssal Martani in LELA, which is a fork of LinBox [6] and which is no longer actively developed.

The sources of our library can be found at: http://hpac.imag.fr/gbla/. Under this website a database of our input matrices in different formats (see Section 3) is available as well as the routines for converting matrices in our special format.

The general structure of the library is presented in Table 1.

Input can come from files on disk or the standard input. The latter is especially useful because we can use a pipe form `zcat` and never uncompress the matrices to the disk. Uncompressed, our library of matrices would represent hundreds of gigabytes of data.

GBLA supports the following data representations:

1. The code is optimized for prime fields $\mathbb{F}_p$ with $p < 2^{16}$ using SIMD vectorization [3] and storing coefficients as `uint16`.
2. The library also supports a coefficient representation using `float` such that we can use optimized SIMD instructions for floating point arithmetic. In this way 32-bit floating points can be used for exact computations over $\mathbb{F}_p$ with $p < 2^{23}$.
3. There is also a version for 32-bit field characteristic using `uint32` data types that needs further optimization in terms of delayed modulus and SIMD operations.

Note that whereas it is true that vectorization in CPUs is faster for floating point arithmetic compared to exact arithmetic we show in Section 6 that for 16-bit computations memory usage can become a bottleneck: Representing data via `uint16` can make matrices manageable that are not feasible when using `float` data type.

For parallelization GBLA is based on OpenMP. As current versions of XKAAPI can interpret OpenMP macros one can also easily use GBLA with XKAAPI as scheduler.

In order to assure cache locality we use blocks, all of them of dimension 256×256 by default. The matrix is thus represented by an array of small submatrices of size 256×256 each. The user has the freedom to set this to any power of 2, but in all of our experiments the preset size is advantageous due to L1 cache size limitations.

At the moment we have two different types of implementations of the usual GB reduction (see Section 1) and the new order of operations for rank computations (see Section 4.3) each:

1. The first type of implementations is completely based on the multiline data structure, denoted GBLA-v0.1.
2. The second type is nearly always faster and denoted GBLA-v0.2 in this paper. There we use multilines only in a very specific block situation where we can nearly guarantee in advance that they give a speedup due to cache locality. Otherwise we use usual sparse resp. dense row representations that are advantageous when sorting rows by pivots.

Note that GBLA-v0.2 is able to reduce matrices that GBLA-v0.1 cannot due to its smaller memory footprint not introducing too many zeroes in multilines (see also Section 6).

3. FILE FORMATS AND FL MATRICES

Input matrices in the GB reduction have some nearly-triangular structure and patterns in the coefficients that we take advantage of. We describe GB matrices and an efficient way to store them.

3.1 Description of FL matrices

Matrices coming from Gröbner basis computations represent a set of polynomials in a polynomial ring w.r.t. to some given monomial order. This order sorts the columns of the matrix, each column represents a monomial. Each row represents a polynomial whereas the entries are just the coefficients of the polynomial for the corresponding monomial in the appropriate column. Due to this, GB matrices are sparse. We can assume that the matrix has been sorted by weight (number of non zero elements) with row 0 the heaviest[1]. Pivoting the rows corresponds to reordering of the polynomials; permuting non pivot columns is allowed once before the GB reduction and re-done after the elimination steps.

The first non zero element on each row is a 1 (each polynomial is monic), and this element will be called *pivoting candidate*. Every such pivoting candidate lies below the main diagonal. Columns whose last non zero element is not a pivoting candidate can be permuted in order to separate them from the pivot ones.

Now, the first n_{piv} columns contain pivoting candidates, called *pivot columns*. Among the pivoting candidates of a given column, one row is selected, the *pivot row*. This selection tries to keep A (a $n_{\text{piv}} \times n_{\text{piv}}$ matrix, see Section 4.1) as sparse as possible.

3.2 Compressed binary format

In standard Matrix Market[2] file format, GB matrices are huge (hundreds of Gb) and slow to read. We compress them to a CSR-like (Compressed Storage Row) format and store them in *binary* format (*i.e.* streams of bytes rather than a text file). We propose two different formats , see Table 2. The files consist of consecutive sequences of elements of type *size* repeated *length* times.

[1]Throughout this paper, indexing is zero-based.

[2]http://math.nist.gov/MatrixMarket/

Format 1			Format 2		
Size	Length	Data	Size	Length	Data
			uint32_t	1	b
uint32_t	1	m	uint32_t	1	m
uint32_t	1	n	uint32_t	1	n
uint32_t	1	p	uint64_t	1	p
uint64_t	1	nnz	uint64_t	1	nnz
uint16_t	nnz	data	uint32_t	m	rows
uint32_t	nnz	cols	uint32_t	m	polmap
uint32_t	m	rows	uint64_t	1	k
			uint64_t	k	colid
			uint32_t	1	pnb
			uint64_t	1	pnnz
			uint32_t	pnb	prow
			xinty_t	pnnz	pdata

Table 2: Structure of the binary matrix formats.

In Format 1, m, n, p, nnz resp. represent the number of rows, columns, modulus and the number of non zeros in the sparse matrix. rows[i] represents the length of the ith row. If j is the sum row[0] $+\cdots+$ row[i-1], then on row i, there is an element at column cols[j+r] with value data[j+r] for all r in $\{0,\ldots,$row[i]$-1\}$.

In Format 2, we separate the location of the non zero entries and the data. We store the data of the polynomials separately since there is redundancy: many lines will be of the form $m_i f_j$ where m_i is some monomial and f_j is a polynomial in the intermediate Gröbner basis. Hence the coefficients in all lines of this type correspond to the same polynomial f_j and represent the same data, only the location on the basis changes. We allow to store the data on different machine types to adapt to the size of p. Data is blocked, so we utilize the fact that several non zero elements on a row may be adjacents, allowing compression of their consecutive column numbers. In this format matrices must have less than 2^{31} rows.

First, the lowest 3 bits of the first element b represent the value of x and y in xinty_t, namely $b=$ u OR (v « 1) where u is 1 iff the type is signed and y corresponds to a type on $8\cdot 2^{v}$ bits (for instance $\overline{011}^2=$ 1 OR (1 « 1) represents uint16_t type. On the highest bits a mask is used to store a file format version.

The ith row has rows[i] elements. We prefer storing the row length since it fits on 32 bits while pointers (the accumulated row length) would fit on 64 bits.

We compress the column indices: If $s>1$ several non zero elements are consecutive on a row and if f is the first one, then we store f s in the format. If $s=1$ then we use a mask and store f AND (1 « 31). Here we lose a bit for the number of rows.

So far, we have stored the locations of the non zero elements. The polynomial data on a row is stored in pdata in the following fashion. prow[i] gives the ith polynomial number of elements (its support). There are pnb polynomials. $j=$ polmap[i] maps the polynomial number j on row i. The polynomial data is laid out contiguously in pdata, polynomial 0 finishes at pdata+prow[0], polynomial 1 finishes at pdata+prow[0]+prow[1], and so on.

In table 3 we show the raw size (in gigabits) of a few sparse matrices in their binary format, compressed with gzip[3] (default options) and the time it takes (in seconds). Compressing format 2 yields an 8 time improvement on the original uncompressed binary format 1 storage and over 4 times better than compressed format 1, in a much shorter time. The compressed format 2 is hence much faster to load and it makes it easier to perform tests on.

[3]http://www.gzip.org/

Matrix	Format 1			Format 2		
	Size	Compressed	Time	Size	Compressed	Time
F4-kat14-mat9	2.3Gb	1.2Gb	230s	0.74Gb	0.29Gb	66s
F5-kat17-mat10	43Gb	24Gb	4419s	12Gb	5.3Gb	883s

Table 3: Storage and time efficiency of the new format

Submatrix	Dimensions	approx. density
A	$n_{\text{piv}}\times n_{\text{piv}}$	$<2\%$
B	$n_{\text{piv}}\times(n-n_{\text{piv}})$	12%
C	$(m-n_{\text{piv}})\times n_{\text{piv}}$	15%
D	$(m-n_{\text{piv}}\times n-n_{\text{piv}})$	35%

Table 4: Characteristics of submatrices in GB reduction

4. GRÖBNER BASES REDUCTION

In this section we present new developments in the implementation of the GB reduction that can be found in our library (see Section 2). Section 4.2 presents ideas to exploit the structure of the input GB matrix M further with dedicated data structures, and Section 4.3 gives an alternative ordering of the steps of the GB reduction if a non-reduced row echelon form of M is sufficient.

4.1 The reduction by Faugère and Lachartre

There are 4 main steps in the GB reduction:

1. The input matrix M already reveals a lot of its pivots even before the Gaussian elimination starts. For exploiting this fact we rearrange the rows and the columns: we reach a cutting of M into $\begin{pmatrix}A & B\\ C & D\end{pmatrix}$. After this rearrangement one can see 4 different parts of M: A very sparse, upper triangular unit matrix on the top left (A) representing the already known pivots. A denser, but still sparse top right part (B) of the same number of rows. Moreover, there are two bottom parts, a left one which is still rather sparse (C) and a right one, which tends to be denser (D). Whereas A represents already known leading terms in the intermediate Gröbner basis, D corresponds to the new polynomials added to the basis after the reduction step. If M is of dimensions $m\times n$ and if n_{piv} denotes the number of known pivots the characteristics of the four submatrices of M are given in Table 4. In general, $n_{\text{piv}}\gg m-n_{\text{piv}}$ and $n_{\text{piv}}\gg n-n_{\text{piv}}$.
2. In the second step of the GB reduction the known pivot rows are reduced with each other, we perform an TRSM[4]. Algebraically, this is equivalent to computing $B\leftarrow A^{-1}\times B$. A is invertible due to being upper triangular with 1s on the diagonal. From an implementational point of view one only reads A and writes to B. After this step, we receive a representation of M in the format $\begin{pmatrix}\mathrm{Id}_{n_{\text{piv}}} & A^{-1}\times B\\ C & D\end{pmatrix}$.
3. In the third step, we reduce C to zero using the identity matrix $\mathrm{Id}_{n_{\text{piv}}}$ performing AXPY[5]. Doing this we also have to carry out the corresponding operations induced by B on D. We get
$$\begin{pmatrix}\mathrm{Id}_{n_{\text{piv}}} & A^{-1}\times B\\ 0 & D-C\times\left(A^{-1}\times B\right)\end{pmatrix}.$$
4. The fourth step now reveals the data we are searching for: Via computing a Gaussian Elimination on $D-C\times\left(A^{-1}\times B\right)$ we receive new pivots reaching an upper triangular matrix

[4]Solves a triangular matrix equation.

[5]Computes a vector scalar product and adds the result to a vector: $y:=ax+y$.

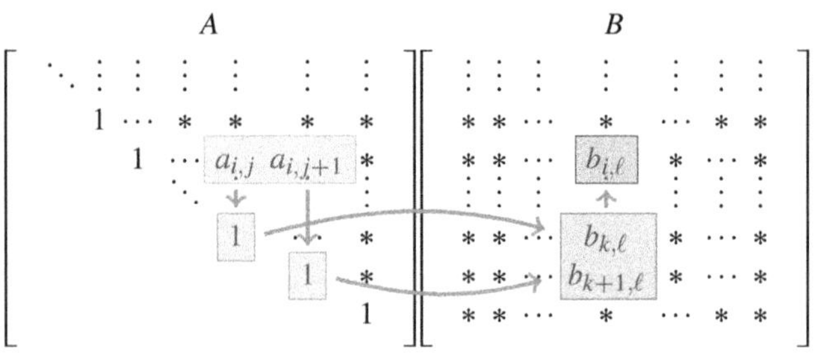

Figure 2: Exploiting horizontal and vertical patterns in the TRSM step.

D'. Those new pivots correspond to new leading terms in our Gröbner basis, thus the corresponding rows represent new polynomials to be added to the basis. On the other hand, rows reducing to zero correspond to zero reductions in the Gröbner basis computation.

5. As the last step we rearrange the columns of the echelon form of M and read off polynomials whose monomials are sorted correctly w.r.t. the monomial order.

If one is interested in a reduced row echelon form of M we have to perform the GB reduction a second time, but only on the right part $\begin{pmatrix} A^{-1} \times B \\ D' \end{pmatrix}$. From the Gröbner basis point of view a fully reduced row echelon form has the advantage that also the multiples of polynomials already in the basis, *i.e.* elements representing the rows $\begin{pmatrix} A & B \end{pmatrix}$ are reduced. Thus, reusing them in later reduction steps of the Gröbner basis computation can be beneficial; we refer to Section 2.4 in [7] discussing the `Simplify` procedure.

4.2 Multiline data structure

As already seen in Section 4.1, matrices coming from Gröbner basis computations are structured in a way that can be exploited for a specialized Gaussian Elimination. Furthermore, there are even more patterns in such matrices that we use in order to speed up the computations. In Figure 1 we can see that the nonzero entries are, in general, grouped in blocks. In other words, if there is a nonzero element $m_{i,j}$ at position j in row i then also $m_{i,j+1}$ (horizontal pattern) and $m_{i+1,j}$ (vertical pattern) tend to be nonzero, too. This fact can be used, for example, to optimize the AXPYresp. TRSM computations in the second step of the GB reduction as illustrated in Figure 2: Assuming that $a_{i,j}$ and $a_{i+1,j}$ are both not zero (horizontal pattern), element $b_{i,\ell}$ is updated by both nonzero elements $b_{k,\ell}$ and $b_{k+1,\ell}$ (vertical pattern). Whereas the horizontal patterns are canonically taken care ofstoring blocks row-wise, we have to pack the vertical pattern in a dedicated data structure.

DEFINITION 1. *An n-*multiline vector `ml` *is a data structure consisting of two vectors in a sparse representation:*

1. *A position vector* `pos` *of column indices such that at each index at least one of n rows of elements has a nonzero element.*
2. *A value vector* `val` *of entries of M. The entries of all n rows in column* `pos`$[i]$ *are stored consecutively, afterwards the n entries at position* `pos`$[i+1]$ *are stored. Note that* `val` *may have zero elements.*

If `pos` *has a length ℓ,* `val` *has length $n \cdot \ell$. In this situation we say that* `ml` *has length ℓ. For a 2-multiline vector we use the shorthand notation* multiline vector.

EXAMPLE 1. *Consider the following two rows:*

$$r_1 = [\ 2\ 0\ 0\ 1\ 0\ 0\ 5\ ],$$
$$r_2 = [\ 1\ 7\ 0\ 0\ 0\ 1\ 0\ ].$$

A sparse representation is given by v_i (values) and p_i (positions):

$$v_1 = [\ 2\ 1\ 5\ ] \quad v_2 = [\ 1\ 7\ 1\ ],$$
$$p_1 = [\ 0\ 3\ 6\ ] \quad p_2 = [\ 0\ 1\ 5\ ].$$

A 2-multiline vector representation of r_1 and r_2 is given by

$$\texttt{ml.val} = [\ 2\ 1\ 0\ 7\ 1\ 0\ 0\ 1\ 5\ 0\ ],$$
$$\texttt{ml.pos} = [\ 0\ 1\ 3\ 5\ 6\ ].$$

Four zero values are added to `ml.val`*, two from r_1 and r_2 resp. We do not add column 2 since there both, r_1 and r_2 have zero entries.*

Multiline vectors are especially useful when performing AXPY. In the following we use multiline vectors to illustrate the reduction of two temporarily dense rows dense_1 and dense_2 with one multiline vector `ml` of length ℓ. For the entries in `ml.val` two situations are possible: Either there is only one of `ml.val`$[2i]$ and `ml.val`$[2i+1]$ nonzero, or both are nonzero. Due to the vertical pattern of GB matrices very often both entries are nonzero. We can perform a specialized **AXPY** operation on dense_1 and dense_2 with scalars $\lambda_{1,1}, \lambda_{1,2}$ coming from column j and $\lambda_{2,1}, \lambda_{2,2}$ from column $j+1$ where j is the loop step in the corresponding **TRSM** operation:

Algorithm 1 **AXPY** of two dense rows of length ℓ with a multiline vector.

Require: $\text{dense}_1, \text{dense}_2, \lambda_{1,1}, \lambda_{1,2}, \lambda_{2,1}, \lambda_{2,2}$, `ml`.

```
v1, v2, i, k
for (i = 0; i < ℓ; i ← i + 1) do
    k ← ml.pos[i]
    v1 ← ml.val[2i]
    v2 ← ml.val[2i + 1]
    dense1[k] ← λ1,1 v1 + λ1,2 v2
    dense2[k] ← λ2,1 v1 + λ2,2 v2
```

The benefit of Algorithm 1 is clear: We perform 4 reductions (each dense row is reduced by two rows) in one step. On the other hand, if the horizontal pattern does not lead to two successive nonzero entries (for example if $a_{i,j+1}$ is zero in Figure 2), then Algorithm 1 would not use `ml.val`$[2i+1]$. This would introduce an disadvantage due to using only every other element of `ml.val`. In our implementation we take care of this situation and have a specialized **AXPY** implementation for that. Still, we are performing two reductions (each dense row is reduced by one row) in one step.

Assuming general n-multiline vectors the problem of introducing useless operations on zero elements appears. For multiline vectors, *i.e.* $n = 2$, we can perform lightweight tests before the actual loop to ensure execution only on nonzero $\lambda_{1,1}, \lambda_{1,2}$ (for single **AXPY**) resp. $\lambda_{1,1}, \lambda_{1,2}, \lambda_{2,1}, \lambda_{2,2}$ (for Algorithm 1). For general n we cannot predict every possible configuration of the n^2 scalars $\lambda_{1,1}, \ldots, \lambda_{n,n}$. Moreover, for n-multiline vectors the memory overhead can get problematic, too. For $n = 2$ we can lose at most `sizeof`(entry) bytes per column index, but for arbitrary n this increases to $(n-1) \cdot$ `sizeof`(entry) bytes. All in all, we note the following fact that is also based on practical experimental results.

REMARK 1. *Based on cache efficiency as well as memory overhead due to adding zero entries to the* `val` *vector 2-multiline vector data structures are the most efficient.*

As already mentioned in [10], representing the matrices A, B, C and D in blocks has several benefits: Firstly, we can pack data in small blocks that fit into cache and thus we increase spatial and temporal locality. Secondly, separating the data into column blocks we can perform operations on B and D rather naturally in parallel. Thus we are combining the multiline vector data structure with a block representation in our implementation. In the following, presented pseudo code is independent of the corresponding row resp. block representation, standard row representation is used. Multiline representations impede the readability of the algorithms, if there is an impact on switching to multilines, we point this out in the text.

Using multilines is useful in situations where we can predict horizontal *and* vertical patterns with a high probability, in order to see advantages and drawbacks we have two different implementations, GBLA-v0.1 and GBLA-v0.2, which use multilines in different ways (see also Section 2).

4.3 New order of operations

If the number of initially known pivots (*i.e.* the number of rows of A and B) is large compared to the number of rows of C and D, then most work of the GB reduction is spent in reducing A, the `TRSM` step $A^{-1}B$. For the Gröbner basis the new information for updating the basis is strictly in D. Thus, if we are not required to compute a reduced echelon form of the input matrix M, but if we are only interested in the reduction of D resp. the rank of M we can omit the `TRSM` step. Whereas in [10] the original GB reduction removes nonzero entries above ($A^{-1}B$) and below (deleting C) the known pivots, it is enough to reduce elements below the pivots.

Thus, after splicing the input matrix M of dimension $m \times n$ we can directly reduce C with A while reflecting the corresponding operations with B on D with the following steps.

Algorithm 2 Reduction of C and D

Require: submatrices $A\left(n_{\text{piv}} \times n_{\text{piv}}\right)$, $B\left(n_{\text{piv}} \times (n-n_{\text{piv}})\right)$, $C\left((m-n_{\text{piv}}) \times n_{\text{piv}}\right)$, $D\left((m-n_{\text{piv}}) \times (n-n_{\text{piv}})\right)$.

```
dense_C, dense_D, i, j
for (i = 0; i < m − n_piv; i ← i + 1) do
    dense_C ← copy_sparse_row_to_dense(C[i, *])
    dense_D ← copy_sparse_row_to_dense(D[i, *])
    for (j = 0; j < n_piv; j ← j + 1) do
        if (dense_C[j] ≠ 0) then
            AXPY(dense_C, dense_C[j], A[j, *])
            AXPY(dense_D, dense_C[j], B[j, *])
    D[i, *] ← copy_dense_row_to_sparse(dense_D)
```

Whereas Algorithm 2 describes the idea of reducing C and D from a mathematical point of view, in practice one would want to use a block representation for the data in order to improve cache locality and also parallelization. Strangely, it turned out that this is not optimal for efficient computations: In fact, in the implememtion we do not reduce C by A to zero, but store the corresponding multiples needed to update D by B later on. In order for a block representation to make sense one needs to completely reduce all rows resp. multilines in a given block before reducing the next block. That is not a problem for B and D since their blocks do not depend on the columns, but it is disadvantageous for A and C. Assuming an operation on a lefthand side block of C due to a reduction from a block from A, any row operation on C must be carried out through all blocks on the right. Even worse, whenever we would try to handle C per row resp. multiline and D per block at the same time this would introduce a lot of writing to D. Thus, in our implementation we found the most efficient solution to be the following:

1. Store A and C in multiline representation and B and D in block multiline representation as defined in Section 4.2.
2. Carry out the reduction of C by A, but store the corresponding coefficients needed for the reduction of D by B later on.
3. Transform C to block multiline representation C'.
4. Reduce D by B using thecoefficients stored in C'.

Thus we have an optimal reduction of C and an optimal reduction of D. The only overhead we have to pay for this is the transformation from C to C'. But copying C into block format is negligible compared to the reduction operations done in C and D.

In Section 6 we see that this new order of operations is faster than the standard GB reduction for full rank matrices from F5. The density of the row echelon form of M does not vary too much from M's initial density which leads in less memory footprint.

4.4 Modified structured Gaussian Elimination

Computing the row echelon form of D the original FL Implementation used a sequential structured Gaussian Elimination. Here we use a modified variant that can be easily parallelized.

Algorithm 3 Modified structured Gaussian Elimination of D

Require: submatrix $D\left((m-n_{\text{piv}}) \times (n-n_{\text{piv}})\right)$.
Ensure: rank_D, rank of D

```
dense_D, i, j
rank_D ← 0
for (i = 0; i < m − n_piv; i ← i + 1) do
    normalize(D[i, *])
    dense_D ← copy_sparse_row_to_dense(D[i, *])
    for (j = 0; j < i − 1; j ← j + 1) do
        if (head(dense_D) = head(D[j, *])) then
            AXPY(dense_D, head(dense_D), D[j, *])
    D[i, *] ← copy_dense_row_to_sparse(dense_D)
    normalize(D[i, *])
    if (not_empty(D[i, *])) then
        rank_D ← rank_D + 1
return rank_D
```

In Algorithm 3 we do a structured Gaussian Elimination on the rows of D. Note that the rows of D have to be normalized and inverted afterwards in order to be correctly reconverted to polynomials for a Gröbner basis algorithm.. At the very end the rank of D is returned. The modification lies mainly in the fact that once we have found a new pivot row, we do not sort the list of known pivot rows, but just add the new one. This is due to the usage of multilines in our implementation. Storing two (or more) rows in this packed format it is inefficient to sort pivots by column index. Possibly we would need to open a multiline row and move the second row to another position. For this, all intermediate multiline rows need to be recalculated. Thus we decided to relinquish the sorting at this point of the computation and sort later on when reconstructing the row echelon form of the initial matrix M. Note that whereas we use multilines everywhere in GBLA-v0.1, in GBLA-v0.2 (see Section 6) we restrict the usage of multilines to specific block situations and no longer use them for the dense Gaussian Elimination of D. Thus we are able to perform a sorting of the pivots.

5. PARALLELIZATION

In this section we discuss improvements concerning parallelizing the GB reduction taking the new ideas presented in the last section into account. For this we have experimented with different parallel schedulers such as OpenMP, XKAAPI and pthreads. Moreover, whereas the initial implementation of Faugère and Lachartre used a sequential Gaussian Elimination of D we are now able to use a parallel version of Algorithm 3.

5.1 Parallelization of the modified structured Gaussian Elimination

As already discussed in Section 4.4 we use a modified structured Gaussian Elimination for multilines which omits sorting the list of known pivots, postponed to the reconstruction of the echelon form of the input matrix M. In our library GBLA there is also a non-multiline version with sorting, see Section 6 for more information.

Assuming that we have already found k pivots in Algorithm 3, we are able to reduce several rows of index $> k$ in parallel. The k pivots are already in their normalized form, they are readonly, thus we can easily update $D[\ell,*] \leftarrow D[\ell,*] + \sum_{i=0}^{k} \lambda_i D[i,*]$for all $k < \ell < m - n_{\text{piv}}$ and corresponding multiples λ_i. Clearly, this introduces some bookkeeping: Whereas in the above situation $D[k+1,*]$ is fully reduced with the k known pivots, the rows $D[k+j,*]$ for $j > 1$ are not. Thus we can add $D[k+1,*]$ to the list of known pivots, but not $D[k+j,*]$. We handle this by using a global waiting list W which keeps the rows not fully reduced and the indices of the last pivot row up to which we have already updated the corresponding row. Different threads share a global variable `lp`: the last known pivot. Each thread performs the following operations:

1. Fetch the next available row $D[j,*]$ which was not updated up to this point or which is already in the waiting list W.
2. Reduce it with all pivots not applied until now, up to `lp`.
3. If $j = \texttt{lp}+1$, $D[j,*]$ is a new pivot and `lp` is incremented.
4. If $j \neq \texttt{lp}+1$, $D[j,*]$ is added to W keeping track that `lp` is the index of the last row $D[j,*]$ is already reduced with.

Naturally, the above description leaves some freedom for the decision which row to fetch and reduce next in Step 1. We found the following choice to be the most efficient for a wide range of examples: When a thread fetches a row to be further reduced it prefers a row that was already previously reduced. This often leads to a faster recognition of new known pivots in Step 3. Synchronization is needed in Steps 3 and 4, besides this the threads can work independent of each other. We handle the communication between the threads using spin locks whose implementation w.r.t. a given used different parallel scheduler (see Section 5.2) might differ slightly.

Talking about load balancing it can happen that one thread gets stuck in reducing already earlier reduced rows further, whereas other threads fetch pristine rows and fill up W more and more. In order to avoid this we use the following techniques:

- If a thread has just fully reduced a row r and thus adds a new known pivot, this thread prefers to take an already reduced row from W possibly waiting for r to become a known pivot.
- If a thread has added t new rows to W consecutively, it is triggered to further reduce elements from W instead of starting with until now untouched rows from D.

For efficiency reasons we do not directly start with the discussed parallel elimination, but we do a sequential elimination on the first k rows resp. multiline rows of D. In this way we can avoid high increasing on the waiting list W at the beginning, which would lead to tasks too small to benefit from the available number of cores executing in parallel. Thus k depends on the number of threads used, in practice we found that $k = 2 \times$ (number of threads) is a good choice. Clearly, the efficiency of this choice depends on how many of the first k rows resp. multiline rows of D reduce to zero in this step. This is not a problem for full rank matrices coming from F5 Gröbner basis computations.

5.2 Different parallel schedulers

We did some research on which parallel schedulers to be used in our library. For this we tested not only well known schedulers like OpenMP [4] and Intel TBB [13] but also XKAAPI [11] and StarPU [1]. We also did experiments with pthreads and own implementations for scheduling. Most of the schedulers have advantages and disadvantages in different situations like depending on sparsity, blocksizes or relying on locking for the structured Gaussian Elimination. Moreover, all those packages are actively developed and further improved, thus we realized different behavoiour for different versions of the same scheduler. In the end we decided to choose OpenMP for the current state of the library.

1. It is in different situations usually not the fastest scheduler, but often tends to be the fastest for the overall computation.
2. Our library should be plain C as much as possible, thus we discarded the usage of Intel TBB which is based on high-level C++ features for optimal usage.
3. Current versions of XKAAPI are able to interpret OpenMP pragmas. Thus one can use our library together with XKAAPI by changing the linker call: instead of `libgomp` one has to link against `libkomp` (see also Section 6).
4. Using pthreads natively is error-prone and leads to code that is not portable (it is not trivial to get them efficiently work on Windows machines). OpenMP's locking mechanism boils down to pthreads on UNIX and their pendants on Windows without having to deal with different implementations.
5. StarPU's performance depends highly on the used data structures. Since the representation of our data is special (see Sections 3 and 4) we need further investigations on how to get data and scheduler playing together efficiently. Moreover, the fact that StarPU can be used for task scheduling even on heterogeneous multicore architectures like CPU/GPU combinations makes it a good candidate for further experiments.

6. EXPERIMENTAL RESULTS

The following experiments were performed on http://hpac.imag.fr/ which is a NUMA architecture of 4x8 processors. Each of the 32 non hyper-threaded Intel(R) Xeon(R) CPUs cores clocks at 2.20GHz (maximal turbo frequency on single core 2.60GHz). Each of the 4 nodes has 96Gb of memory, so we have 384Gb of RAM in total. The compiler is `gcc-4.9.2`. The timings do not include the time spent on reading the files from disk. We state matrix characteristics of our example set in Table 5.

We use various example sets: There are well known benchmarks like `Katsura`, `Eco` and `Cyclic`[6]. Moreover, we use matrices from minrank problems arising in cryptography. Furthermore we have random dense systems `randx-d2-y-mat*` in `x` variables, all input polynomials are of degree 2. Then we deleted `y` polynomials to achieve higher-dimensional benchmarks. All examples are done over the biggest 16-bit prime field, $\mathbb{F}_{65521}$. We use the `uint16` coefficient representation in GBLA. If not otherwise stated GBLA's timings are done using OpenMP as parallel scheduler.

6.1 Behaviour on F5 matrices

We show in Table 6 a comparison with Faugère and Lachartre's FL Implementation from [10] and GBLA. Timings are in seconds, using 1, 16 or 32 threads. This is done for F5 matrices, thus we can use GBLA's new order of operations (see Section 4.3) to compute a Echelon form and to verify that the matrices have full rank.

Usually GBLA-v0.1 is faster even on one core than FL Implementation, GBLA-v0.2 is even faster than GBLA-v0.1. Both GBLA implementations have a much better scaling than FL Implementation, where GBLA-v0.2 preforms better than GBLA-v0.1, even scaling rather good for smaller examples, where the overhead of scheduling different threads starts to become a bottleneck. The only example where FL Implementation is faster than GBLA is `mr-9-10-7-mat3`, a very dense (35.5%) matrix. This good behaviour for FL Implementation might be triggered from the fact that FL Implementation allocates all the memory needed for the computation in advance. Usually the user does not know how much memory the computation might need, so this approach is a bit error-prone. Still, FL Implementation is faster than GBLA only on one core, starting to use several CPU cores the better scaling of GBLA

[6]Also including a version where we have applied the symmetry of the cyclic group action of degree 1, see [9].

Matrix			Rows $\times 10^3$	Columns $\times 10^3$	Nonzeros $\times 10^6$	Density %
F4	kat12	mat9	18.8	22.3	17.1	4.07
	kat13	mat2	4.68	6.53	1.45	4.74
		mat3	12.1	14.6	7.78	4.35
		mat5	35.4	38.2	63.7	4.13
		mat9	43.5	49.2	75.3	3.52
	kat14	mat8	100	103	352	3.39
	kat15	mat7	168	178	832	2.77
		mat8	197	210	1,060	2.55
		mat9	228	234	1,521	2.84
	eco14	mat24	105	107	91.1	0.81
	eco16	mat13	157	141	293	1.32
	mr-9-8-8-5	mat7	26.0	34.1	236	26.6
		mat8	22.1	34.6	189	25.5
	rand16-d2-2	mat5	67.1	106	199	2.80
		mat6	146	217	689	2.19
	rand16-d2-3	mat8	587	874	4,328	0.84
		mat9	980	1,428	8,378	0.60
		mat10	1,544	2,199	14,440	0.43
		mat11	2,287	3,226	23,823	0.32
	rand18-d2-9	mat5	430	1,028	1,048	0.24
		mat6	1,212	2,674	3,879	0.12
F5	kat13	mat5	28.4	35.5	26.8	2.66
		mat6	34.5	42.3	35.9	2.46
	kat14	mat7	69.6	84.5	118	2.01
		mat8	81.0	96.9	156	1.98
	kat15	mat7	139	167	383	1.63
		mat8	168	199	507	1.51
		mat9	187	219	640	1.56
		mat10	195	227	725	1.63
	kat16	mat5	83.8	110	139	1.50
		mat6	168	208	485	1.38
		mat9	393	456	2,234	1.25
	cyc10	mat19	192	256	1,182	2.40
		mat20	303	378	2,239	1.95
	cyc10-sym1	mat17	29.8	43.3	114	0.09
	mr-9-10-7	mat3	20.1	74.5	532	35.5
		mat7	88.5	192	4,055	23.8
	rand16-d2-2	mat11	1,368	1,856	15,134	0.60
		mat12	1,806	2,425	22,385	0.51
		mat13	2,310	3,076	31,247	0.44
	rand16-d2-3	mat8	578	871	3,140	0.62
		mat9	973	1,426	6,839	0.49
		mat10	1,532	2,198	13,222	0.39
		mat11	2,286	3,226	23,221	0.31
		mat12	3.266	4,550	37,796	0.25
	rand18-d2-9	mat5	429	1,027	9,65	0.22
		mat7	3,096	6,414	12,594	0.06
		mat11	1,368	1,856	15,135	0.60

Table 5: Some matrix characteristics

Implementation	FL Implementation			GBLA-v0.1			GBLA-v0.2		
F5 Matrix / # Threads	1	16	32	1	16	32	1	16	32
kat13-mat5	16.7	2.7	2.3	**14.5**	2.02	1.87	**14.5**	**1.73**	**1.61**
kat13-mat6	27.3	4.15	4.0	**23.9**	3.08	2.65	25.9	**3.03**	**2.28**
kat14-mat7	139	17.4	16.6	142	13.4	10.6	**122**	**11.2**	**8.64**
kat14-mat8	181	24.95	23.1	177	16.9	12.7	**158**	**14.7**	**10.5**
kat15-mat7	629	61.8	55.6	633	55.1	38.2	**553**	**46.3**	**30.7**
kat16-mat6	1,203	110	83.3	1,147	98.7	69.9	**988**	**73.9**	**49.0**
mr-9-10-7-mat3	**591**	70.8	71.3	733	57.3	37.9	747	**52.8**	**33.2**
mr-9-10-7-mat7	15,787	1,632	1,565	**15,416**	1,103	793	15,602	**1,057**	**591**
cyc10-mat19	7,482	693	492	1,291	135	103	**1,030**	**80.3**	**62.9**
cyc10-mat20	17,853	1,644	1,180	2,589	274	209	**2,074**	**171**	**152**
cyc10-sym1-mat17	11,083	1,982	1,705	2,463	465	405	**2,391**	**275**	**245**
rand16-d2-2-mat11	mem	mem	mem	**2,568**	946	883	4,553	**425**	**360**
rand16-d2-2-mat12	mem	mem	mem	**5,751**	1,252	1,219	6,758	**632**	**527**
rand16-d2-2-mat13	mem	mem	mem	mem	mem	mem	**8,435**	**816**	**721**
rand16-d2-3-mat8	2,084	500	472	2,243	339	282	**1,654**	**144**	**106**
rand16-d2-3-mat9	bug	bug	bug	2,938	827	781	**2,308**	**236**	**227**
rand16-d2-3-mat10	mem	mem	mem	**2,528**	922	940	4,518	**427**	**372**
rand16-d2-3-mat11	mem	mem	mem	mem	mem	mem	**11,254**	**931**	**696**
rand16-d2-3-mat12	mem	mem	mem	mem	mem	mem	**15,817**	**1,369**	**1,150**
rand18-d2-9-mat5	1,469	287	250	350	297	306	**340**	**52.9**	**50.3**
rand18-d2-9-mat7	mem	mem	mem	mem	mem	mem	**8,752**	**1,112**	**1,098**
rand18-d2-9-mat11	bug	bug	bug	**2,540**	923	882	4,600	**415**	**363**

Table 6: GB reduction vs. GBLA (time in seconds)

Implementation	Magma	GBLA-v0.1			GBLA-v0.2		
F4 Matrix / # Threads	1	1	16	32	1	16	32
kat12-mat9	**11.2**	11.4	1.46	1.60	11.3	1.40	1.40
kat13-mat2	**0.94**	1.18	0.38	0.61	1.11	0.26	0.33
kat13-mat3	9.33	11.0	1.70	3.10	**8.51**	1.07	1.13
kat13-mat9	168	165	16.0	11.8	**114**	9.74	6.83
kat14-mat8	2,747	2,545	207	165	**1,338**	104	65.8
kat15-mat7	10,345	9,514	742	537	**4,198**	298	195
kat15-mat8	13,936	12,547	961	604	**6,508**	470	283
kat15-mat9	24,393	22,247	1,709	1,256	**10,923**	779	450
eco14-mat24	524	169	22.2	21.9	**146**	16.2	16.5
eco16-mat13	6,239	1,537	184	176	**1,346**	104	72.9
mr-9-8-8-5-mat7	1,073	1,080	88.5	57.9	**550**	41.6	24.7
mr-9-8-8-5-mat8	454	600	48.5	30.3	**318**	25.6	14.9
rand16-d2-2-mat5	740	778	62.2	40.8	**589**	43.6	28.6
rand16-d2-2-mat6	4,083	4,092	375	219	**3,054**	224	133
rand16-d2-3-mat8	55,439	48,008	3,473	2,119	**26,533**	1,782	1,027
rand16-d2-3-mat9	91,595	65,126	4,869	2,983	**39,108**	2,614	1,372
rand16-d2-3-mat10	mem	-	9,691	6,223	-	3,820	1,972
rand16-d2-3-mat11	mem	mem	mem	mem	-	5,399	2,385
rand18-d2-9-mat5	2,020	1,892	414	388	**630**	63.1	61.8
rand18-d2-9-mat6	4,915	6,120	981	941	**1,736**	220	218

Table 7: Magma vs. GBLA (time in seconds)

wins (already at 2 cores the timings are nearly identical). Moreover, for dense matrices like the minrank ones we can see a benefit of the multiline structure, at least for fewer cores. Once the number of cores increases the better scaling of GBLA-v0.2 is favourable.

For cyc10-sym1-mat17 the speedup between 16 and 32 is quite small. Due to the applied symmetry the matrix is already nearly reduced, so the scheduling overhead has a higher impact than the gain during reduction for anything greater than 16 cores.

For the higher-dimensional random examples the row dimension of C and D is very small (< 300). Our new order of operations (Section 4.3) enables GBLA to reduce matrices the FL Implementation is not able to handle. For rand18-d2-9-mat7 even GBLA-v0.2 reaches the memory limit of the machine, but it is still able to reduce the matrix. Memory overhead due to multilines hinders GBLA-v0.1 to compute rand16-d2-3-mat11, but is more efficient on rand16-d2-3-mat10 for one core.

6.2 Behaviour on F4 matrices

In Table 7 we compare Magma-2.19 [2] to GBLA. Since there is no F5 implementation in Magma we can only compare matrices coming from F4 computations. Since Magma is closed source we are not able to access the specialized linear algebra for Gröbner basis computations directly. Thus, we are comparing the same problem sets with the same degrees running Magma's F4 implementation. Note that Magma generates matrices that are, for the same problem and same degree, slightly larger, usually 5 to 10%. Note that we use only Magma's CPU implementation of F4, but not the rather new GPU one. We think that it is not really useful to compare GPU and CPU parallelized code. Furthermore, most of our examples are too big to fit into the RAM of a GPU, so data copying between CPU and GPU might be problematic for an accurate comparison.

For small examples Magma, not splicing the matrices, has an advantage. But already for examples in the range of 10 seconds GBLA, especially GBLA-v0.2 gets faster on single core. The dif-

Implementation	GBLA-v0.1				GBLA-v0.2			
# Threads	16		32		16		32	
Matrix / Scheduler	OMP	XK	OMP	XK	OMP	XK	OMP	XK
`F4-kat15-mat8`	961	**916**	**604**	1,223	470	**463**	283	**277**
`F4-kat15-mat9`	1,709	**1,679**	**1,256**	2,122	779	**774**	450	**431**
`F4-rand16-d2-3-mat8`	3,4732	**3,447**	2,119	**1,964**	**1,782**	1,818	1,027	**1,017**
`F4-rand16-d2-3-mat9`	**6,956**	7,073	4,470	**3,783**	3,214	**3,141**	**1,776**	1,785
`F5-kat16-mat6`	**98.7**	105	69.9	**67.2**	**73.9**	75.3	**49.0**	**49.0**
`F5-mr-9-10-7-mat3`	**57.3**	59.6	**37.9**	38.8	**52.8**	54.8	**33.2**	34.7
`F5-cyc10-mat19`	**135**	140	103	**101**	**80.3**	86.7	62.9	**60.9**
`F5-cyc10-mat20`	**274**	292	209	**206**	**171**	203	152	**141**
`F5-cyc10-sym1-mat17`	**465**	496	**405**	406	275	**272**	245	**217**

Table 8: OpenMP vs. XKAAPI (time in seconds)

ference between Magma and GBLA-v0.1 is rather small, whereas GBLA-v0.2 becomes more than twice as fast. Moreover, GBLA-v0.1 and GBLA-v0.2 scale very well on 16 and 32 cores. Due to lack of space we do not state timings for the FL Implementation. It behaves in nearly all examples like expected: Due to preallocation of all memory it is very fast on sequential computations (nearly as fast as GBLA-v0.2), but it scales rather bad. For example, for `kat14-mat8` FL Implementation runs in 1,571s, 861s and 868s for 1, 16 and 32 cores, respectively. Also note that FL Implementation's memory consumption is higher than GBLA's.

For the random, higher dimensional examples Magma cannot reduce matrices starting from `rand16-d2-3-mat9` due to the `float` representation of the matrix entries and resulting higher memory usage on the given machine. For `rand16-d2-3-mat11` even GBLA-v0.1 consumes too much memory by using multilines and thus introducing too many zeros (see Section 4.2). Even GBLA-v0.2 comes to the limit of our chosen compute server, but it can still reduce the matrix: At the end of the computation the process consumed 98% of the machine's RAM.

6.3 Comparing OpenMP (OMP) and XKAAPI (XK)

We compare the different behaviour of the parallel schedulers that can be used in GBLA (see also Section 5.2): The default scheduler in GBLA is OMP, here we use the latest stable version 4.0. XK can interpret OMP pragmas, too, so we are able to run GBLA with XK by just changing the linker call from `libgomp` to `libkomp`. The latest stable version of XK we use is 3.0. In Table 8 we compare both schedulers on representative benchmarks in GBLA-v0.1 and GBLA-v0.2 on 16 and 32 cores. The timings show that in many examples both schedulers are on par. XK tends to be a bit more efficient on 32 cores, but that is not always the case. `F4-kat15-mat8` and `F4-kat15-mat9` are cases where XK has problems on 32 cores for GBLA-v0.1. This comes from the last step, the structured Gaussian Elimination of D where GBLA-v0.1, using multilines, cannot sort the pivots which seems to become a bottleneck for XK's scheduling. For the same examples in GBLA-v0.2 (now with sorting of pivots) we see that XK is even a bit faster than OMP. All in all, in our setting both schedulers behave nearly equal.

7. CONCLUSION

We presented the first open-source, plain C library for linear algebra specialized for matrices coming from Gröbner basis computations including various new ideas exploiting underlying structures. This led to more efficient ways of performing the GB reduction and improved parallel scaling. Moreover, the library uses a new compressed file format that enables us to generate matrices not feasible beforehand. Corresponding routines for dumping and converting own matrices are included such that researchers are able to use their own data in our new format in GBLA.

Also the time needed to reduce D during GB reduction is in general very small compared to the overall reduction, we plan to investigate our parallel structured Gaussian elimination implementation in the future. For this we may again copy D' first to a different data representation and use external libraries for fast exact linear algebra such as FFLAS-FFPACK [5] in given situations.

8. ACKNOWLEDGMENTS

This work is partly funded by the HPAC project of the French Agence Nationale de la Recherche (ANR 11 BS02 013).

9. REFERENCES

[1] C. Augonnet, S. Thibault, R. Namyst, and P.-A. Wacrenier. Starpu: A unified platform for task scheduling on heterogeneous multicore architectures. *Concurr. Comput. : Pract. Exper.*, 23(2):187–198, Feb. 2011.

[2] Bosma, W., Cannon, J., and Playoust, C. The Magma algebra system. I. The user language. *Journal of Symbolic Computation*, 24(3-4):235–265, 1997. http://magma.maths.usyd.edu.au/magma/.

[3] B. Boyer, J.-G. Dumas, P. Giorgi, C. Pernet, and B. Saunders. Elements of design for containers and solutions in the linbox library. In H. Hong and C. Yap, editors, *Mathematical Software ICMS 2014*, volume 8592 of *Lecture Notes in Computer Science*, pages 654–662. Springer Berlin Heidelberg, 2014.

[4] L. Dagum and R. Menon. Openmp: an industry standard api for shared-memory programming. *Computational Science & Engineering, IEEE*, 5(1):46–55, 1998.

[5] J. Dumas, T. Gautier, C. Pernet, and Z. Sultan. Parallel computation of echelon forms. In F. M. A. Silva, I. de Castro Dutra, and V. S. Costa, editors, *Euro-Par 2014 Parallel Processing - 20th International Conference, Porto, Portugal, August 25-29, 2014. Proceedings*, volume 8632 of *Lecture Notes in Computer Science*, pages 499–510. Springer, 2014.

[6] J.-G. Dumas, T. Gautier, M. Giesbrecht, P. Giorgi, B. Hovinen, E. L. Kaltofen, B. D. Saunders, W. J. Turner, and G. Villard. LinBox: A generic library for exact linear algebra. In *Proceedings of the 2002 International Congress of Mathematical Software, Beijing, China*. World Scientific Pub, Aug. 2002.

[7] J.-C. Faugère. A new efficient algorithm for computing Gröbner bases (F4). *Journal of Pure and Applied Algebra*, 139(1–3):61–88, June 1999.

[8] J.-C. Faugère and S. Lachartre. Parallel Gaussian Elimination for Gröbner bases computations in finite fields. In M. Moreno-Maza and J. L. Roch, editors, *Proceedings of the 4th International Workshop on Parallel and Symbolic Computation*, PASCO '10, pages 89–97, New York, NY, USA, July 2010. ACM.

[9] Faugère, J.-C. and Svartz, J. Gröbner Bases of ideals invariant under a Commutative group : the Non-modular Case. In *Proceedings of the 38th international symposium on International symposium on symbolic and algebraic computation*, ISSAC '13, pages 347–354, New York, NY, USA, 2013. ACM.

[10] J.-C. Faugère and S. Lachartre. Parallel Gaussian Elimination for Gröbner bases computations in finite fields. In M. Moreno-Maza and J. L. Roch, editors, *Proceedings of the 4th International Workshop on Parallel and Symbolic Computation*, PASCO '10, pages 89–97, New York, NY, USA, July 2010. ACM.

[11] T. Gautier, X. Besseron, and L. Pigeon. Kaapi: A thread scheduling runtime system for data flow computations on cluster of multi-processors. In *Proceedings of the 2007 International Workshop on Parallel Symbolic Computation*, PASCO '07, pages 15–23, New York, NY, USA, 2007. ACM.

[12] S. Lachartre. *Algèbre linéaire dans la résolution de systèmes polynomiaux Applications en cryptologie*. PhD thesis, Université Paris 6, 2008.

[13] J. Reinders. *Intel Threading Building Blocks*. O'Reilly & Associates, Inc., Sebastopol, CA, USA, first edition, 2007.

Validating the Completeness of the Real Solution Set of a System of Polynomial Equations

Daniel A. Brake*
University of Notre Dame
dbrake@nd.edu

Jonathan D. Hauenstein*
University of Notre Dame
hauenstein@nd.edu

Alan C. Liddell, Jr.*
University of Notre Dame
aliddel1@nd.edu

ABSTRACT

Computing the real solutions to a system of polynomial equations is a challenging problem, particularly verifying that all solutions have been computed. We describe an approach that combines numerical algebraic geometry and sums of squares programming to test whether a given set is "complete" with respect to the real solution set. Specifically, we test whether the Zariski closure of that set is indeed equal to the solution set of the real radical of the ideal generated by the given polynomials. Examples with finitely and infinitely many real solutions are provided, along with an example having polynomial inequalities.

1. INTRODUCTION

Local solving methods, such as using Newton's method, local optimization approaches, and critical point methods as highlighted in Section 5, allow one to compute real solutions to system of equations. The typical drawback of using such local methods is the inability to verify that all real solutions have been computed. This article uses sums of squares programming to validate that a *complete* real solution set has been computed, that is, the Zariski closure of the given set is equal to the Zariski closure of the set of all real solutions. The method follows in the footsteps of work combining numerical and symbolic methods, particularly [4, 18].

A typical situation where one may need to test the completeness of a real solution set is computing critical points. For example, § 8.6 considers computing the critical points of a potential energy landscape. In such situations, local numerical methods, e.g., [20, 51], exist for locating real critical points. Our approach provides a global stopping criterion for validating that all real solutions have been identified.

A related situation is the computation of the real critical points of a projection of a solution set used in the numerical decomposition of real curves and surfaces [3, 11, 14, 47]. The failure to correctly compute the set of real solutions leads to a failure in the decomposition of the real component. Hence, correct and complete computation of sets of real solutions is paramount to correctly computing the decomposition.

One approach for certifying the existence of real solutions is based on the local analysis of Newton's method using Smale's α-theory [60] developed in [33]. Building on α-theory, there are methods for certifying smooth continuous paths for Newton homotopies [29, 30] and general homotopies [10]. For example, if a smooth path is defined by a real system of equations which has a real starting point, then the endpoint of the path must also be real.

From an algebraic viewpoint, the radical of an ideal generated by a given collection of polynomials consists of all polynomials that vanish on the solution set of the given polynomials. There are several algorithms for computing the radical of a zero-dimensional ideal – some numerical, e.g., [35, 42, 43] and some symbolic, e.g., [9, 22]. When there are infinitely many solutions, one can reduce to the zero-dimensional case, for example, via [22, 39].

The *real* radical of an ideal generated by a given collection of polynomials with real coefficients consists of all polynomials that vanish on the *real* solution set of the given polynomials. There have been several proposed methods for computing the real radical of an ideal. Some are symbolic, e.g., [8] based on the primary decomposition (see also [54, 64, 66, 67]). Others are numerical, based on moment matrices when the number of real solutions is finite, e.g., [40, 41, 42, 43, 44]. A promising approach for computing the real radical when there are infinitely many real solutions was developed in [49] providing a stopping criterion for verifying that a Pommaret basis has been computed. Other methods for computing real solutions include computing a point on each semi-algebraically connected component of the real solution set, e.g., [1, 2, 27, 57],

As discussed in [49], one key issue related to computing the real radical using semidefinite programming with moment matrices is knowing when the generated polynomials form a basis for the real radical. In our approach, we first compute a set S which is a subset of the Zariski closure of the real solution set. Then, we compute polynomials that vanish on S. Finally, for each of the computed polynomials, we use sums of squares programming to verify that it is indeed in the real radical. Since the polynomials can be validated independently, one could easily parallelize this part of the computation. Since S is contained in the Zariski closure of the real solution set, every polynomial contained in the real radical vanishes on S. Conversely, if every polynomial

*Research partially supported by NSF grant ACI-1460032, Army Young Investigator Program (YIP), and Sloan Research Fellowship.

ISSAC '16, July 19-22, 2016, Waterloo, ON, Canada
© 2016 ACM. ISBN 978-1-4503-4380-0/16/07...$15.00
DOI: http://dx.doi.org/10.1145/2930889.2930910

that vanishes on S is contained in the real radical, we know that a generating set for the real radical has been computed. Hence, S is complete since the Zariski closure of S is equal to the Zariski closure of the real solution set of the original system of equations, i.e., the solution set of the real radical.

One of the pitfalls of using purely symbolic methods to compute real radicals is the typical computation of field extensions. As an illustrative example, consider the polynomial $f(x) = x^3 - 2$ having rational coefficients, i.e., $f \in \mathbb{Q}[x]$. Since $f = 0$ has one real solution, namely $x = \sqrt[3]{2}$, the real radical of the ideal generated by f is $\langle x - \sqrt[3]{2}\rangle$ which is generated by a polynomial not in $\mathbb{Q}[x]$.

By working over $\mathbb{R}$, one avoids the use of field extensions for computing the generators of the real radical. Thus, the theoretical results for our approach assume an exact computational model over $\mathbb{R}$ as in [12]. The drawback is that the computations in practice are performed using floating-point arithmetic. In the examples, we approximate the computational model by utilizing adaptive precision floating-point computations where each point in the subset S of the solution set is described via a numerical approximation and an algorithm that can be used to approximate it efficiently to arbitrary precision as in [28]. For example, α-theory [60] verifies that a numerical approximation is in the quadratic convergence basin of Newton's method and thus Newton's method can be used to efficiently refine the numerical approximation. One could then use exactness recovery methods, e.g., [5], with the refinability of numerical approximations to determine exact results.

The remainder of the article is as follows. Section 2 focuses on radicals, irreducible decomposition, and Zariski closures. Real radicals, sums of squares, and semidefinite programming are discussed in Section 3. In Section 4, we present the criterion for showing that a set S is complete with respect to the real radical. This approach depends on the ability to compute such an S, which is highlighted in Section 5, and the ideal of S, which is discussed in Section 6. Section 7 considers the real solution set for collection of equations and inequalities. Several examples are presented in Section 8 with a discussion of the limitations of our approach in Section 9. We conclude in Section 10.

Acknowledgments

The authors thank Mohab Safey El Din, Charles Wampler, and Lihong Zhi for discussions related to real solution sets, as well as the reviewers for their helpful comments.

2. ZARISKI CLOSURE AND RADICALS

Let $f_1, \ldots, f_k \in \mathbb{C}[x_1, \ldots, x_n]$ and consider the ideal generated by these polynomials, namely $I = \langle f_1, \ldots, f_k\rangle$. The polynomials $f = \{f_1, \ldots, f_k\}$ and the corresponding ideal $I = \langle f\rangle$ define the same solution set in $\mathbb{C}^n$, namely

$$\mathcal{V}_{\mathbb{C}}(f) = \mathcal{V}_{\mathbb{C}}(I) = \{x \in \mathbb{C}^n \mid f_i(x) = 0 \text{ for } i = 1, \ldots, k\}$$

A set $A \subset \mathbb{C}^n$ is called an *algebraic set* if there is a collection of polynomials $g \subset \mathbb{C}[x_1, \ldots, x_n]$ such that $A = \mathcal{V}_{\mathbb{C}}(g)$. The algebraic set A is *irreducible* if there does not exist algebraic sets $A_1, A_2 \subsetneq A$ with $A = A_1 \cup A_2$. Given an algebraic set A, there exists a unique collection (up to relabeling) of irreducible algebraic sets $X_1, \ldots, X_\ell$ such that

$$A = \bigcup_{i=1}^{\ell} X_i \text{ and } X_j \not\subset \bigcup_{i \neq j} X_i.$$

Each X_i is called an *irreducible component* of A.

In numerical algebraic geometry, an irreducible algebraic set is represented by a *witness set*, see, e.g., [63, Chap. 13]. A *numerical irreducible decomposition* for an algebraic set A is a collection of witness sets for the irreducible components of A. Such a decomposition can be computed using various algorithms, e.g., [6, 32, 61, 62].

For any subset $T \subset \mathbb{C}^n$, the ideal defined by T is

$$I(T) = \{f \in \mathbb{C}[x_1, \ldots, x_n] \mid f(t) = 0 \text{ for all } t \in T\}.$$

The *Zariski closure* of T is the algebraic set $\overline{T} = \mathcal{V}_{\mathbb{C}}(I(T))$, which is the intersection of all algebraic sets that contain T.

For an ideal I, the *radical* of I is

$$\sqrt{I} = \{p \in \mathbb{C}[x_1, \ldots, x_n] \mid p^\alpha \in I \text{ for some } \alpha \in \mathbb{Z}_{>0}\}$$

with $\sqrt{I} = I(\mathcal{V}_{\mathbb{C}}(I))$ following Hilbert's Nullstellensatz.

3. REAL RADICAL & SUMS OF SQUARES

Many of the topics from § 2 have analogous statements over $\mathbb{R}$. Let $f_1, \ldots, f_k \in \mathbb{R}[x_1, \ldots, x_n]$ with $f = \{f_1, \ldots, f_k\}$ and $I = \langle f\rangle$. The set of solutions in $\mathbb{R}^n$ is

$$\mathcal{V}_{\mathbb{R}}(f) = \mathcal{V}_{\mathbb{R}}(I) = \{x \in \mathbb{R}^n \mid f_i(x) = 0 \text{ for } i = 1, \ldots, k\} = \mathcal{V}_{\mathbb{C}}(I) \cap \mathbb{R}^n.$$

The *real radical* of I is

$$\sqrt[\mathbb{R}]{I} = \left\{ p \in \mathbb{R}[x] \;\middle|\; \begin{array}{c} p^{2\alpha} + \sum_{j=1}^{\ell} g_j^2 \in I \\ \text{for some } \alpha \in \mathbb{Z}_{>0}, g_j \in \mathbb{R}[x] \end{array} \right\}, \quad (1)$$

with $\sqrt[\mathbb{R}]{I} = I(\mathcal{V}_{\mathbb{R}}(I))$ following the real Nullstellensatz, e.g., see [13, Chap. 4].

EXAMPLE 1. *For $f(x) = x^3 - 2$ and $I = \langle f\rangle$, we have:*

- $\mathcal{V}_{\mathbb{C}}(I) = \{\sqrt[3]{2}, \omega\sqrt[3]{2}, \omega^2\sqrt[3]{2}\}$ *and* $\mathcal{V}_{\mathbb{R}}(I) = \{\sqrt[3]{2}\}$,
- $\sqrt{I} = I$, *and*
- $\sqrt[\mathbb{R}]{I} = \langle x - \sqrt[3]{2}\rangle$

where ω is the primitive cube root of unity. In particular,

$$(x - \sqrt[3]{2})^4 + (\sqrt{3}x^2 - \sqrt{3}\sqrt[3]{4})^2 = 4(x^3 - 2)(x - \sqrt[3]{2}) \in I.$$

The algebraic description of the real radical $\sqrt[\mathbb{R}]{I}$ presented in (1) shows that this definition depends on *sums of squares*. A polynomial $s \in \mathbb{R}[x_1, \ldots, x_k]$ is called a sum of squares if $s = \sum_{j=1}^{\ell} g_j^2$ for some $g_1, \ldots, g_\ell \in \mathbb{R}[x_1, \ldots, x_k]$. Clearly, every polynomial that is a sum of squares has even degree.

The polynomials of even degree that are sums of squares are characterized by *positive semidefinite* matrices. A symmetric matrix $M \in \mathbb{R}^{m\times m}$ is positive semidefinite if, for all $y \in \mathbb{R}^m$, $y^T My \geq 0$. This condition is equivalent to all eigenvalues of M being nonnegative. We will write $M \succeq 0$ if M is positive semidefinite.

Let $s \in \mathbb{R}[x_1, \ldots, x_k]$ be a polynomial of degree $2d$ and X_d be the vector of all monomials in $x_1, \ldots, x_n$ of degree at most d. Hence, there exists a symmetric matrix C such that

$$s(x) = X_d^T \cdot C \cdot X_d. \quad (2)$$

The polynomial s is a sum of squares if and only if there is a positive semidefinite matrix C such that (2) holds, e.g., [16].

EXAMPLE 2. *As shown in Ex. 1, the quartic polynomial $s(x) = 4(x^3 - 2)(x - \sqrt[3]{2})$ is a sum of squares. Let*

$$X_2 = \begin{bmatrix} 1 \\ x \\ x^2 \end{bmatrix} \text{ and } C = \begin{bmatrix} 8\sqrt[3]{2} & -4 & -2\sqrt[3]{4} \\ -4 & 4\sqrt[3]{4} & -2\sqrt[3]{2} \\ -2\sqrt[3]{4} & -2\sqrt[3]{2} & 4 \end{bmatrix}.$$

It is easy to verify that $C \succeq 0$ and $s(x) = X_2^T \cdot C \cdot X_2$.

For a given polynomial s of degree $2d$, the set of symmetric matrices C such that (2) holds is a linear space. Hence, testing that a polynomial is a sum of squares can be accomplished by solving a semidefinite feasibility problem.

EXAMPLE 3. *Continuing with* $s(x) = 4(x^3 - 2)(x - \sqrt[3]{2})$ *from Ex. 2, consider the linear space*

$$\mathcal{L} = \left\{ \begin{bmatrix} s_{00} & s_{01} & s_{02} \\ s_{01} & s_{11} & s_{12} \\ s_{02} & s_{12} & s_{22} \end{bmatrix} \middle| \begin{array}{rcl} s_{00} & = & 8\sqrt[3]{2} \\ 2s_{01} & = & -8 \\ 2s_{02} + s_{11} & = & 0 \\ 2s_{12} & = & -4\sqrt[3]{2} \\ s_{22} & = & 4 \end{array} \right\}.$$

Since $s(x) = X_2^T \cdot C \cdot X_2$ *if and only if* $C \in \mathcal{L}$, *it follows that* s *is a sum of squares if and only if there exists* $C \in \mathcal{L}$ *such that* $C \succeq 0$, *which is a semidefinite feasibility problem.*

To facilitate the task of converting between sums of squares problems and semidefinite programming problems in the examples, we utilize the software package SOSTOOLS [55].

Given a polynomial $p \in \mathbb{R}[x_1, \ldots, x_n]$, we can decide if $p \in \sqrt[\mathbb{R}]{I}$ using (1). That is, $p \in \sqrt[\mathbb{R}]{I}$ if and only if there exists $\alpha \in \mathbb{Z}_{>0}$ and $h_1, \ldots, h_k, g_1, \ldots, g_\ell \in \mathbb{R}[x_1, \ldots, x_n]$ such that

$$p^{2\alpha} + \sum_{j=1}^{\ell} g_j^2 = \sum_{i=1}^{k} h_i f_i$$

which is equivalent to requiring that

$$-p^{2\alpha} + \sum_{i=1}^{k} h_i f_i \text{ is a sum of squares.} \qquad (3)$$

Thus, given a polynomial $p \in \mathbb{R}[x_1, \ldots, x_n]$, one can test if $p \in \sqrt[\mathbb{R}]{I}$ by solving a semidefinite feasibility problem. We use this observation in our method, which is described next.

4. VALIDATION

Given an ideal $I \subset \mathbb{R}[x_1, \ldots, x_n]$, $S \subset \overline{\mathcal{V}_\mathbb{R}(I)} = \mathcal{V}_\mathbb{C}(\sqrt[\mathbb{R}]{I})$, and $I(S) = \langle g_1, \ldots, g_\ell \rangle$, we describe an approach for validating that S is complete, i.e., $S = \overline{\mathcal{V}_\mathbb{R}(I)}$ which occurs if and only if $\sqrt[\mathbb{R}]{I} = \langle g_1, \ldots, g_\ell \rangle = I(S)$.

Procedure 1 Validating Real Solution Sets

Input: Polynomials $f = \{f_1, \ldots, f_k\} \subset \mathbb{R}[x_1, \ldots, x_n]$, a set $S \subset \overline{\mathcal{V}_\mathbb{R}(I)}$ with $I(S) = \langle g_1, \ldots, g_\ell \rangle$, integer $\alpha_{\max} \in \mathbb{Z}_{\geq 0}$.
Output: A boolean which is TRUE if $I(S) = \sqrt[\mathbb{R}]{I(f)}$ can be validated up to $\alpha_{\max}$, otherwise FALSE.

(Optional) Replace f with a Gröbner basis for $\sqrt{I(f)}$.
for $m = 1, \ldots, \ell$ **do**
  Initialize $\alpha := 1$ and *success* := FALSE.
  while *success* = FALSE **do**
    if there exists $h_i \in \mathbb{R}[x_1, \ldots, x_n]$ such that the polynomial $q = -g_m^{2\alpha} + \sum_i h_i f_i$ is a sum of squares **then**
      Set *success* := TRUE.
    else
      Increment $\alpha := \alpha + 1$.
      if $\alpha > \alpha_{\max}$ **then**
        return (S,FALSE)
return (S,TRUE)

THEOREM 4. *Procedure 1 is a correct algorithm.*

PROOF. Let $I = \langle f_1, \ldots, f_k \rangle$. Since $\mathcal{V}_\mathbb{R}(I) = \mathcal{V}_\mathbb{R}(\sqrt{I})$, replacing f by a Gröbner basis for $\sqrt{I}$ does not impact the set of real solutions.

For a given $p \in \mathbb{R}[x_1, \ldots, x_n]$, we know $p \in \sqrt[\mathbb{R}]{I}$ if and only if there exists $\alpha \in \mathbb{Z}_{>0}$ and $h_1, \ldots, h_k \in \mathbb{R}[x_1, \ldots, x_n]$ such that (3) holds. In particular, since $S \subset \overline{\mathcal{V}_\mathbb{R}(I)}$, we know $\sqrt[\mathbb{R}]{I} \subset I(S) = \langle g_1, \ldots, g_\ell \rangle$ so that $\sqrt[\mathbb{R}]{I} = I(S)$ if and only if (3) holds for each $p = g_i$. If all of the corresponding α's for each g_i are at most $\alpha_{\max}$, then Procedure 1 will correctly determine $I(S) = \sqrt[\mathbb{R}]{I}$.

If $p \notin \sqrt[\mathbb{R}]{I}$, then, for every $\alpha \in \mathbb{Z}_{>0}$, (3) does not hold. In Procedure 1, we use the upper bound $\alpha_{\max}$ so that Procedure 1 always terminates. □

If one could compute an *a priori* upper bound on the largest possible value for α, then we could replace $\alpha_{\max}$ with this bound. However, without such a bound, we simply keep searching for new points to add to S, which is described next. If $p \notin \sqrt[\mathbb{R}]{I}$, then there must exist a point $x \in \mathcal{V}_\mathbb{R}(I)$ such that $p(x) \neq 0$. In fact, there is an irreducible component $X \subset \overline{\mathcal{V}_\mathbb{R}(I)} = \mathcal{V}_\mathbb{C}(\sqrt[\mathbb{R}]{I})$ such that $p(x) \neq 0$ for every x in a dense open subset of X.

We have implemented this procedure using floating-point arithmetic computations for several example systems [1] while a full general-purpose implementation is left for future work.

5. GENERATING A CANDIDATE SET

Input for Procedure 1 is a set S and generators for $I(S)$. Hence, in this section we provide techniques for generating S with the next focusing on computing $I(S)$.

5.1 Approaches for locating real solutions

A classical approach for attempting to find a real solution is to use Newton's method or related variants, see, e.g., [38]. For a polynomial system with real coefficients, if the initial point is real, then every solution obtained from Newton's method is also real. Of course, there are many challenges associated with finding real solutions using Newton's method, particularly when $\mathcal{V}_\mathbb{C}(f)$ is not a complete intersection or the real solutions are singular with respect to f. That is, problems can occur with Newton's method, e.g., divergence, if the dimension of the solution set is less than dimension of the null space of the Jacobian at the solution [23, 24]. Nonetheless, heuristic techniques such as damping methods, reusing Jacobians for several iterations, or using chord or secant methods can be utilized [38].

Another approach for computing real solutions is to utilize numerical optimization techniques. Standard iterative techniques include those based on nonlinear least squares approaches such as the Levenberg-Marquardt algorithm and alternating least squares [37]. Other standard methods in optimization include the worker bees method, genetic algorithms, and the Nelder-Mead method, see, e.g., [17].

Critical point methods combine optimization and polynomial system solving techniques. For example, Seidenberg [58] considered the critical points of the distance function between the set of real solutions and a given real point y^* that was not a solution. The set of all such critical points contains a point on every connected component of the real solution set [1, 56, 58]. By utilizing homotopy continuation, one can compute a finite subset of critical points containing

[1]Available at www.nd.edu/~aliddel1/validate-reals

a point on every connected component [27]. Moreover, one can then sample more real points by moving y^*.

Rather than compute all critical points, one can attempt to compute the closest critical point to the given y^*. This can be accomplished using a classical optimization approach such as the gradient descent method or a homotopy-based approach called gradient-descent homotopy [25]. By testing at many values of y^*, one aims to quickly generate many real solutions, e.g., as shown in [25, Fig. 3].

Other so-called "local" solving methods exist for finding real solutions, which have been used in various disciplines. Some examples include techniques in theoretical chemistry, e.g., [20, 51, 52] and solving power-flow equations in electrical engineering, e.g., [45, 48].

5.2 Real solutions and isosingular sets

After a real solution has been located, one can now try to extract additional information about the geometry of the solution set near this point. One approach is to compute a local irreducible decomposition using local witness sets [15] to see if local structure provides insight into the components of the real solution set passing through the computed real point. Another approach is to utilize *isosingular sets* [34], which may also help in improving the numerical stability of interpolation, described in the next section.

Let $f_1, \ldots, f_k$ be polynomials and $z \in \mathcal{V}_{\mathbb{C}}(f)$. Let $Jf(z)$ be the Jacobian matrix of f evaluated at z. For an integer ℓ, let $\det_\ell Jf(z)$ be the collection of all $(\ell+1) \times (\ell+1)$ minors of $Jf(z)$. Thus, $\det_\ell Jf(z) = 0$ if and only if rank $Jf(z) \leq \ell$. For a polynomial system g, let $\operatorname{dnull}(g, z) = \dim \operatorname{null} Jg(z)$. The *deflation sequence* of z with respect to f is defined by

$$d_i(f, z) = \operatorname{dnull}(\mathcal{D}^i(f, z), z) \text{ for } i \in \mathbb{Z}_{\geq 0}$$

where $\mathcal{D}^0(f, z) = f$ and

$$\mathcal{D}^i(f, z) = \begin{bmatrix} \mathcal{D}^{i-1}(f, z) \\ \det_{d_{i-1}(f,z)} J\mathcal{D}^{i-1}(f, z) \end{bmatrix}.$$

The deflation sequence is a nonincreasing sequence of nonnegative integers and thus has a limit, say $d_\infty(f, z) \geq 0$, called the *isosingular local dimension* of z with respect to f.

Due to potential issues with using minors, e.g., the total number of them and the potential for each to have very high degree, there are alternative approaches. For example, a so-called strong deflation approach based on the null space method of [19, 46] was presented in [34], and a variant involving polynomial many new functions proposed in [31].

If $X(f, z)$ is the Zariski closure of all points in $\mathcal{V}_{\mathbb{C}}(f)$ which have the same deflation sequence with respect to f as z, then [34, Lemma 5.14] yields that there is a unique irreducible component of $X(f, z)$ which contains z, denoted $\operatorname{Iso}_f(z)$, called the *isosingular set* of z with respect to f. In particular, $d_\infty(f, z) = \dim \operatorname{Iso}_f(z)$.

Suppose that $z \in \mathcal{V}_{\mathbb{R}}(f) \subset \mathbb{R}^n$. Since z is a smooth point on the irreducible set $\operatorname{Iso}_f(z)$, we have $\operatorname{Iso}_f(z) \cap \mathbb{R}^n \subset \mathcal{V}_{\mathbb{R}}(f)$ and $\operatorname{Iso}_f(z) = \overline{\operatorname{Iso}_f(z) \cap \mathbb{R}^n} \subset \overline{\mathcal{V}_{\mathbb{R}}(f)}$. That is, if $I = \langle f \rangle$,

$$\operatorname{Iso}_f(z) \subset \mathcal{V}_{\mathbb{C}}(\sqrt[\mathbb{R}]{I}) \text{ and } \sqrt[\mathbb{R}]{I} \subset I(\operatorname{Iso}_f(z)).$$

The isosingular local dimension is a lower bound on the local real dimension at z, which is sharp if z is a smooth point on a unique irreducible component of $\mathcal{V}_{\mathbb{C}}(\sqrt[\mathbb{R}]{I})$. Moreover, if $d_\infty(f, z) > 0$, we can use standard sampling techniques in numerical algebraic geometry, see, e.g., [7, § 8.3], applied to $\operatorname{Iso}_f(z)$ to produce an arbitrary number of additional points for which polynomials in $\sqrt[\mathbb{R}]{I}$ must vanish.

Additionally, by using isosingular sets and numerical algebraic geometry, we can utilize standard membership tests, see, e.g., [7, § 8.4], to determine if a newly found point $x \in \mathcal{V}_{\mathbb{R}}(I)$ is already contained in the set S.

6. INTERPOLATION

From the set $S \subset \overline{\mathcal{V}_{\mathbb{R}}(I)}$ constructed in § 5, the next task is to compute a collection of polynomials which vanish on S with Procedure 1 testing whether $I(S)$ is equal to $\sqrt[\mathbb{R}]{I}$.

Suppose that $T \subset \mathbb{C}^n$ is a finite set such that $I(T)$ is generated by real polynomials and $d \geq 1$. Let $\mathcal{B}$ form a basis for the finite-dimensional vector space of all polynomials in n variables with real coefficients of degree at most d, namely $\mathbb{R}[x_1, \ldots, x_n]_{\leq d}$. The linear space of polynomials of degree at most d in $I(T)$, denoted $I(T)_{\leq d}$, is (isomorphic to) the null space of matrix M where $M_{ij} = \beta_j(t_i)$, i.e., the evaluation of the jth basis element $\beta_j \in \mathcal{B}$ at the ith point $t_i \in T$. If S is a finite set, then we simply take $T = S$. Otherwise, one can take T to be a finite set consisting of sufficiently many points on each irreducible component described by S. The number of sample points needed on each component can be *a priori* bounded based on the dimension of $\mathbb{R}[x_1, \ldots, x_n]_{\leq d}$. One can also algorithmically bound the number of sample points needed per component simply by continuing to add sample points from each component to T until the rank of the associated matrix M stabilizes.

As shown in [26], one can rescale each row independently to improve the conditioning of interpolation. Moreover, for positive-dimensional components, sampling points that are spread out over the component using numerical algebraic geometry as in § 5.2 also helps to improve conditioning.

EXAMPLE 5. *The solution set of the polynomial system*

$$f = \{x^2 + y^2 + z^2 - 1,\ x^2 + y^2 + z - 1,\ x\} \tag{4}$$

consists of the three points

$$\mathcal{V}_{\mathbb{C}}(f) = \mathcal{V}_{\mathbb{R}}(f) = \{(0, 1, 0), (0, -1, 0), (0, 0, 1)\}$$

where the point $(0, 0, 1)$ *has multiplicity two with respect to* f.

To illustrate, for $d = 2$, *we choose the monomial basis*

$$\mathcal{B} = \{1, x, y, z, x^2, xy, xz, y^2, yz, z^2\}$$

for $\mathbb{R}[x, y, z]_{\leq 2}$ *with* $S = T = \mathcal{V}_{\mathbb{R}}(f)$ *where* M *is*

	1	x	y	z	x^2	xy	xz	y^2	yz	z^2
$(0,1,0)$	1	0	1	0	0	0	0	1	0	0
$(0,-1,0)$	1	0	−1	0	0	0	0	1	0	0
$(0,0,1)$	1	0	0	1	0	0	0	0	0	1

A basis for null M *is given by the columns of the matrix*

$$\begin{bmatrix} 0 & 0 & 0 & 0 & -1 & 0 & 0 \\ 1 & 0 & 0 & 0 & 0 & 0 & 0 \\ 0 & 0 & 0 & 0 & 0 & 0 & 0 \\ 0 & 0 & 0 & 0 & 1 & 0 & -1 \\ 0 & 1 & 0 & 0 & 0 & 0 & 0 \\ 0 & 0 & 1 & 0 & 0 & 0 & 0 \\ 0 & 0 & 0 & 1 & 0 & 0 & 0 \\ 0 & 0 & 0 & 0 & 1 & 0 & 0 \\ 0 & 0 & 0 & 0 & 0 & 1 & 0 \\ 0 & 0 & 0 & 0 & 0 & 0 & 1 \end{bmatrix}$$

corresponding to the polynomials

$$x,\ x^2,\ xy,\ xz,\ y^2 + z - 1,\ yz,\ z^2 - z$$

which form a basis for the linear space $(\sqrt[\mathbb{R}]{I})_{\leq 2}$. Note that since each polynomial f_i has degree at most 2, each f_i is contained in the linear span of these polynomials.

For illustrative purposes, we selected a monomial basis. In practice, the choice of basis should be made based on numerical conditioning.

For $d \gg 0$, we know $I(S) = \langle I(S)_{\leq d}\rangle$. If S is a finite set, then one can determine an upper bound on d such that $I(S)$ is generated by $I(S)_{\leq d}$. In particular, the function

$$c \mapsto \dim \mathbb{R}[x_1, \ldots, x_n]_{\leq c} - \dim I(S)_{\leq c}$$

is the Hilbert function of $I(S)$. If r is the minimum such that $|S| = \dim \mathbb{R}[x_1, \ldots, x_n]_{\leq r} - \dim I(S)_{\leq r}$, i.e., the index of regularity, then one knows that $I(S)$ is either generated by $I(S)_{\leq r}$ or $I(S)_{\leq r+1}$. In fact, $I(S)_{\leq r}$ generates $I(S)$ if and only if $\langle I(S)_{\leq r}\rangle_{\leq r+1} = I(S)_{\leq r+1}$, i.e., the Hilbert function of $J = \langle I(S)_{\leq r}\rangle$ in degree $r+1$ is also equal to $|S|$.

EXAMPLE 6. *Continuing with Ex. 5, since*

$$\dim \mathbb{R}[x, y, z]_{\leq 2} - \dim I(S)_{\leq 2} = 10 - 7 = 3 = |S|,$$

one can easily verify that $I(S)$ is generated by $I(S)_{\leq 2}$, i.e.,

$$\sqrt[\mathbb{R}]{I} = \langle x, y^2 + z - 1, yz, z^2 - z\rangle.$$

EXAMPLE 7. *The Hilbert function for the ideal $I(S)$ where $S = \{(0,0), (0,1), (1,0)\}$ is $1, 3, 3, \ldots$ so that $I(S)$ is either generated by $I(S)_{\leq 1}$ or $I(S)_{\leq 2}$. Since $I(S)_{\leq 1} = \{0\}$, we know that $I(S)_{\leq 2}$ must generate $I(S)$.*

When S is infinite, we aim to reduce our computations to standard computations performed over $\mathbb{C}$ as summarized in § 2. In particular, by using isosingular sets as discussed in § 5.2, we can actually assume that $S = \overline{S}$ and that we have a numerical irreducible decomposition of S. Hence, we simply need to compute d large enough so that S and $\mathcal{V}_{\mathbb{C}}(I(S)_{\leq d})$ have the same irreducible components so that $S = \mathcal{V}_{\mathbb{C}}(I(S)_{\leq d})$. Hence, $I(S) = \sqrt{\langle I(S)_{\leq d}\rangle}$.

7. EQUALITIES AND INEQUALITIES

One can naturally generalize from real radicals of systems of polynomial equations to $\mathcal{A}$-radicals of systems of polynomial equations and inequalities. In particular, let $f_1, \ldots, f_k, r_1, \ldots, r_s \in \mathbb{R}[x_1, \ldots, x_n]$ with

$$I = \langle f_1, \ldots, f_k\rangle \text{ and } \mathcal{A} = \{x \in \mathbb{R}^n \mid r_i(x) \geq 0 \text{ for all } i = 1, \ldots, s\}.$$

The $\mathcal{A}$-radical of I is $\sqrt[\mathcal{A}]{I} = I(\mathcal{V}_{\mathbb{R}}(I) \cap \mathcal{A})$. Algebraically, one can characterize $\sqrt[\mathcal{A}]{I}$ using sums of squares [50, 65]:

$$\sqrt[\mathcal{A}]{I} = \left\{ p \in \mathbb{R}[x] \;\middle|\; \begin{array}{c} p^{2\alpha} + \sum\limits_{\nu \in \{0,1\}^s} \sigma_\nu \cdot \prod\limits_{j=1}^{s} r_j^{\nu_j} \in I \\ \text{for some } \alpha \in \mathbb{Z}_{>0}, \\ \text{sum of squares } \sigma_\nu \in \mathbb{R}[x] \end{array} \right\}. \quad (5)$$

Rather than try to locate sample points that satisfy equalities and inequalities, we will instead reduce to equations by introducing "slack" variables. That is, we consider the ideal

$$J = \langle f_1(x), \ldots, f_k(x), r_1(x) - y_1^2, \ldots, r_s(x) - y_s^2\rangle.$$

Since $\mathcal{V}_{\mathbb{R}}(I) \cap \mathcal{A} = \pi(\mathcal{V}_{\mathbb{R}}(J))$ where $\pi(x, y) = x$, we know

$$\sqrt[\mathcal{A}]{I} = \sqrt[\mathbb{R}]{J} \cap \mathbb{R}[x_1, \ldots, x_n]. \quad (6)$$

Thus, we compute $S \subset \mathcal{V}_{\mathbb{R}}(J)$ but only perform interpolation on $\pi(S)$. If $\langle g_1, \ldots, g_\ell\rangle = I(\pi(S)) \subset \mathbb{R}[x_1, \ldots, x_n]$ and each $g_i \in \sqrt[\mathbb{R}]{J}$, then $I(\pi(S)) = \sqrt[\mathcal{A}]{I}$ by (6).

8. EXAMPLES

As mentioned in the Introduction, the following examples were computed using floating-point arithmetic operations. By using approaches described in Section 5, each numerical approximation of a solution naturally comes with an algorithm which can be used to refine the approximation to arbitrary accuracy. The scripts needed to run these examples are available at www.nd.edu/~aliddell/validate-reals.

8.1 An illustrative example

To illustrate our approach, we consider the intersection of a circle and a bivariate cubic, namely

$$f = \{x^2 + y^2 - 2,\ 2xy^2 - x + 1\}.$$

The system $f = 0$ has six solutions, all of which are real:

$$\mathcal{V}_{\mathbb{R}}(f) = \{(-1, \pm 1), (1.366, \pm 0.366), (-0.366, \pm 1.366)\}.$$

In our first test, we simply take $S = \mathcal{V}_{\mathbb{R}}(f)$. Since the Hilbert function of $I(S)$ is $1, 3, 5, 6, 6, \ldots$, we can show that $I(S)$ is generated by $I(S)_{\leq 3}$. A basis for the linear space $I(S)_{\leq 3}$, computed as in § 6, is:

$$G = \left\{ \begin{array}{l} y^3 + x^2 y - 2y,\ xy^2 - x/2 + 1/2, \\ x^3 - 3x/2 - 1/2,\ x^2 + y^2 - 2 \end{array} \right\}.$$

Using either f or a Gröbner basis for $\langle f\rangle$, e.g.,

$$\{x^2 + y^2 - 2,\ 2xy^2 - x + 1,\ 2y^4 - 5y^2 - x + 2\}, \quad (7)$$

every $g \in G$ was found to be in $\sqrt[\mathbb{R}]{\langle f\rangle}$ showing that S is indeed equal to $\mathcal{V}_{\mathbb{R}}(f)$.

Incomplete solution set

Suppose that we take $R = \mathcal{V}_{\mathbb{R}}(f) \cap \{y \geq 0\}$. Since the Hilbert function of $I(R)$ is $1, 3, 3, \ldots$ and $I(R)_{\leq 1} = \{0\}$, we know that $I(R)$ is generated by three quadratics, approximately

$$G = \left\{ \begin{array}{l} y^2 - 2.049y - 0.18301x + 0.86603, \\ xy - 0.18301y - 0.68301x + 1/2 \\ x^2 + 0.18301x + 2.049y - 2.866 \end{array} \right\}. \quad (8)$$

Using $\alpha_{\max} = 5$, we were unable to validate that any of the polynomials in G where in $\sqrt[\mathbb{R}]{\langle f\rangle}$. In fact, we can show that this is indeed correct since each polynomial in G is nonzero at each of the three points in $\mathcal{V}_{\mathbb{R}}(f) \setminus R$.

Semialgebraic condition

We now validate that $R = \mathcal{V}_{\mathbb{R}}(f) \cap \{y \geq 0\}$ is the complete solution set for the $\mathcal{A}$-radical of $\langle f\rangle$ where $\mathcal{A} = \{y \geq 0\}$. To that end, we add a slack variable z and consider the system

$$F = \{x^2 + y^2 - 2,\ 2xy^2 - x + 1,\ y - z^2\}.$$

As described in § 7, we just need to show that each polynomial in G from (8) is contained in $\sqrt[\mathbb{R}]{\langle F\rangle}$. Using either F or a Gröbner basis for $\langle F\rangle$, namely (7) together with $y - z^2$, we validated that $G \subset \sqrt[\mathbb{R}]{\langle F\rangle}$ showing that R is indeed equal to $\mathcal{V}_{\mathbb{R}}(f) \cap \{y \geq 0\}$, i.e., $\sqrt[\mathcal{A}]{\langle f\rangle} = I(R)$.

8.2 Positive-dimensional components

To illustrate the approach on a system such that the real radical ideal is positive-dimensional, consider the system

$$f = \{xyz,\ z(x^2 + y^2 + z^2 + y),\ y(y + z)\}.$$

The set $\mathcal{V}_{\mathbb{C}}(f)$ consists of three lines, two of which are complex conjugates of each other that intersect at the origin and the other is a double line with respect to f, and an isolated point. In particular, $\mathcal{V}_{\mathbb{R}}(f)$ is the line $y = z = 0$ and the isolated point $(0, -1/2, 1/2)$. So, we take

$$S = \{(x, 0, 0) \mid x \in \mathbb{C}\} \cup \{(0, -1/2, 1/2)\} \subset \overline{\mathcal{V}_{\mathbb{R}}(f)}.$$

To simplify the real computations later, we first replace f with a Gröbner basis for the radical $\sqrt{\langle f \rangle}$, namely

$$f = \{2yz - y,\ 2y^2 + y,\ xy,\ 4x^2z + 4z^3 + y\}.$$

With the isolated solution, sampling 3 points on the line is enough to compute a basis for $I(S)_{\leq 2}$ which generates $I(S)$:

$$G = \{z^2 + y/2,\ yz - y/2,\ y^2 + y/2,\ xz,\ xy,\ y + z\}.$$

Each element in G was shown to belong to $\sqrt[\mathbb{R}]{\langle f \rangle}$ with $\alpha \leq 2$.

8.3 Katsura-5 system

As an illustration of our approach on a problem which was solved using the semidefinite characterization of the real radical in [41], we consider the Katsura-5 system as in [41, Ex. 5.4]. The system consists of a linear, say f_1, and five quadratics, say $f_2, \ldots, f_6$, in six variables, namely

$$f = \left\{ \begin{array}{c} x_1 + 2(x_2 + x_3 + x_4 + x_5 + x_6) - 1, \\ x_1^2 + 2(x_2^2 + x_3^2 + x_4^2 + x_5^2 + x_6^2) - x_1, \\ 2(x_1x_2 + x_2x_3 + x_3x_4) + x_4x_5 + x_5x_6 - x_2, \\ x_2^2 + 2(x_1x_3 + x_2x_4 + x_3x_5 + x_4x_6) - x_3, \\ 2(x_1x_4 + x_2x_3 + x_2x_5 + x_3x_6) - x_4, \\ x_3^2 + 2(x_1x_4 + x_1x_5 + x_1x_6) - x_5 \end{array} \right\}.$$

The set $\mathcal{V}_{\mathbb{C}}(f)$ consists of 32 points, 12 of which lie in $\mathbb{R}^6$. The set of real solutions, say S, is readily computed using homotopy continuation.

The Hilbert function is $1, 6, 12, 12, \ldots$ with $I(S)$ being generated by $I(S)_{\leq 2}$. In particular, $I(S)_{\leq 2}$ is a linear space spanned by the linear f_1 and 15 quadratics[2].

Trivially, $f_1 \in \sqrt[\mathbb{R}]{\langle f_1, \ldots, f_6 \rangle}$ and the quadratics are shown to be in the real radical using $\alpha \leq 2$. This computation validates that $\mathcal{V}_{\mathbb{R}}(f)$ consists of 12 points. Moreover, this data matches that displayed in [41, Table 4].

8.4 High degree

Our next example was also presented in [41] which was modeled after a system originally from [36, Sec 4.3]:

$$f = \left\{ \begin{array}{c} 5x_1^9 - 6x_1^5x_2 + x_1x_2^4 + 2x_1x_3 \\ -2x_1^6x_2 + 2x_1^2x_2^3 + 2x_2x_3 \\ x_1^2 + x_2^2 - 0.265625 \end{array} \right\}.$$

We note that the original system in [36] had the term $-6x_1^5x_2^2$ while the system from [41] has the term $-6x_1^5x_2$. The system $f = 0$ has 8 real solutions among the 20 complex solutions. Our computations produce a generating set consisting of 2 quadratics and 10 cubic polynomials for the ideal defined the 8 real solutions which are shown to be in the real radical using $\alpha \leq 2$.

8.5 Seiler system

As an illustration of our approach on a problem considered in [49, Ex. 5], namely the Seiler system [59]

$$f = \left\{ \begin{array}{c} x_3^2 + x_2x_3 - x_1^2, \\ x_1x_3 + x_1x_2 - x_3, \\ x_2x_3 + x_2^2 + x_1^2 - x_1 \end{array} \right\}.$$

[2]Available at www.nd.edu/~aliddel1/validate-reals.

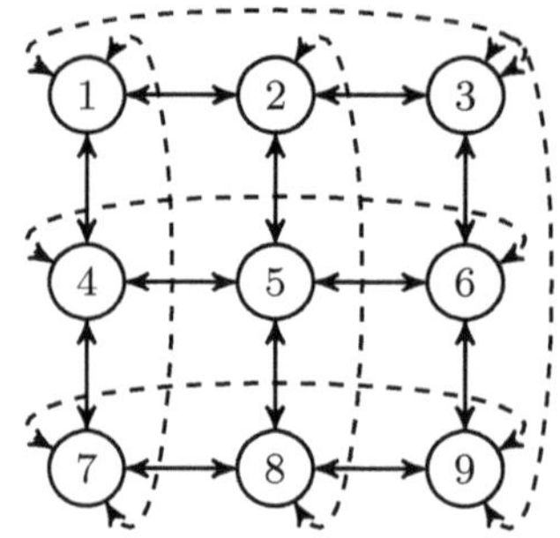

Figure 1: Nearest-neighbor coupling for a 3×3 grid of nodes.

This system does not have a Pommaret basis with respect to the total degree ordering defined by $x_1 < x_2 < x_3$ [59]. Thus, [49] uses a change of coordinates to overcome this.

Even though f consists of 3 polynomials in 3 variables, $\mathcal{V}_{\mathbb{C}}(f)$ is actually a curve. In particular, $I = \langle f \rangle$ is a one-dimensional prime ideal, i.e., $I = \sqrt{I}$ and $\mathcal{V}_{\mathbb{C}}(I)$ is an irreducible curve. Hence, we know that $I = \sqrt[\mathbb{R}]{I}$ if we can compute a real point $x \in \mathcal{V}_{\mathbb{R}}(I)$ which is smooth with respect to f, i.e., the rank of $Jf(x)$ is 2.

To that end, we utilize a gradient-descent homotopy [25]. We took $y = (1, -3/2, 3/4)$ and considered the homotopy

$$H(x, \lambda, t) = \left[\begin{array}{c} f(x) - t \cdot f(y) \\ \lambda_0(x - y) + \lambda_1 \nabla f_1(x) + \lambda_2 \nabla f_2(x) + \lambda_3 \nabla f_3(x) \end{array} \right]$$

where $\lambda \in \mathbb{P}^3$. Starting at $x = y$ and $\lambda = [1, 0, 0, 0] \in \mathbb{P}^3$ when $t = 1$, we obtain a point, which is approximately $(0.7009, -0.2504, -0.5868)$, that lies on $\mathcal{V}_{\mathbb{R}}(f)$ and is indeed a smooth point on $\mathcal{V}_{\mathbb{C}}(f)$. Hence, the isosingular set of this point with respect to f is $\mathcal{V}_{\mathbb{C}}(f)$ showing that $I = \sqrt[\mathbb{R}]{I}$.

8.6 An energy landscape

Our last example aims to compute the real critical points of the energy landscape of the two-dimensional nearest-neighbor ϕ^4 model on a 3×3 grid as in [21, 53]. We label the nodes $1, \ldots, 9$ with Figure 1 showing the coupling between the nodes. Let $N(i)$ denote the four nearest neighbors of node i, e.g., $N(1) = \{2, 3, 4, 7\}$. After selecting various parameters for this model, we consider the potential energy

$$V(x) = \sum_{i=1}^{9} \left[\frac{1}{40} x_i^4 - x_i^2 + \frac{1}{4} \sum_{j \in N(i)} (x_i - x_j)^2 \right].$$

The system defining the critical points is $f = \nabla V$ so that

$$f_i = \frac{1}{10} x_i^3 - 2x_i + \sum_{j \in N(i)} (x_i - x_j)$$

The system f is a Gröbner basis and the set $\mathcal{V}_{\mathbb{C}}(f)$ consists of $3^9 = 19{,}683$ points. However, when searching for real stationary points, one only obtains 3 points, namely

$$S = \{(0, 0, 0, 0, 0, 0, 0, 0, 0),\ \pm(w, w, w, w, w, w, w, w, w)\}$$

where $w = \sqrt{20} \approx 4.4721$. Hence, $I(S)$ is generated by

$$G = \{x_1(x_1^2 - 20), x_2 - x_1, \ldots, x_9 - x_1\}.$$

All nine basis elements were found to be in $\sqrt[\mathbb{R}]{\langle f \rangle}$ with $\alpha = 1, 2, 2, \ldots, 2$, respectively. Therefore, $S = \mathcal{V}_{\mathbb{R}}(f)$, i.e., the energy landscape V has exactly three real critical points.

9. KNOWN LIMITATIONS

As a theoretical approach to computing real radicals using sums of squares, the major practical limitation is based on the value of α needed in (3). To prevent prevent arbitrarily long runtimes, Procedure 1 uses an upper bound $\alpha_{\max}$ which we hope will be replaced in the future by an *a priori* upper bound based on the input system f.

When using floating-point computations as in the examples above, one needs to be cognizant of the effects of round-off error and conditioning in the computations. We can aim to control this using adaptive precision computations with numerical approximations of solutions that can be refined to arbitrary accuracy.

Systems phrased with numerical approximations of exact numbers can present problems in practice. Fundamentally, these systems violate the model of computation as exact numbers should be input exactly. Hence, representing $1/3$ as 0.3333 means that the user is solving a different system from using $1/3$. Nonetheless, the robustness and aspects of conditioning of this approach will be explored in future work.

10. CONCLUSION

By combining numerical algebraic geometry with sums of squares programming, we have produced a method for certifying that a set of polynomials generate the real radical. The set of polynomials arises from the generators of a set S which is contained in the Zariski closure of the set of real solutions. As considered in [18], combining numerical algebraic geometry and semidefinite programming can potentially improve the efficiency of computations and produce new approaches, in particular for computing and analyzing the set of real solutions of a system of polynomial equations.

11. REFERENCES

[1] P. Aubry, F. Rouillier, and M. Safey El Din. Real solving for positive dimensional systems. *J. Symbolic Comput.*, 34(6):543–560, 2002.

[2] B. Bank, M. Giusti, J. Heintz, and G.M. Mbakop. Polar varieties and efficient real elimination. *Mathematische Zeitschrift*, 238(1):115–144, 2001.

[3] D.J. Bates, D.A. Brake, J.D. Hauenstein, A.J. Sommese, and C.W. Wampler. On computing a cell decomposition of a real surface containing infinitely many singularities. In *Mathematical Software – ICMS 2014*, volume 8592 of *Lecture Notes in Computer Science*, pages 246–252. Springer, 2014.

[4] D.J. Bates, W. Decker, J.D. Hauenstein, C. Peterson, G. Pfister, F.-O. Schreyer, A.J. Sommese, and C.W. Wampler. Comparison of probabilistic algorithms for analyzing the components of an affine algebraic variety. *Appl. Math. Comput.*, 231:619–633, 2014.

[5] D.J. Bates, J.D. Hauenstein, T.M. McCoy, C. Peterson, and A.J. Sommese. Recovering exact results from inexact numerical data in algebraic geometry. *Experimental Mathematics*, 22(1):38–50, 2013.

[6] D.J. Bates, J.D. Hauenstein, C. Peterson, and A.J. Sommese. A numerical local dimension test for points on the solution set of a system of polynomial equations. *SIAM Journal on Numerical Analysis*, 47(5):3608–3623, 2009.

[7] D.J. Bates, J.D. Hauenstein, A.J. Sommese, and C.W. Wampler. *Numerically solving polynomial systems with Bertini*, volume 25. SIAM, 2013.

[8] E. Becker and R. Neuhaus. Computation of real radicals of polynomial ideals. In *Computational algebraic geometry*, pages 1–20. Springer, 1993.

[9] E. Becker and T. Wörmann. Radical computations of zero-dimensional ideals and real root counting. *Mathematics and Computers in Simulation*, 42(4):561–569, 1996.

[10] C. Beltrán and A. Leykin. Robust certified numerical homotopy tracking. *Found. Comput. Math.*, 13(2):253–295, 2013.

[11] G.M. Besana, S. DiRocco, J.D. Hauenstein, A.J. Sommese, and C.W. Wampler. Cell decomposition of almost smooth real algebraic surfaces. *Numerical Algorithms*, 63(4):645–678, 2013.

[12] L. Blum, M. Shub, and S. Smale. On a theory of computation and complexity over the real numbers: np-completeness, recursive functions and universal machines. *Bulletin (New Series) of the American Mathematical Society*, 21(1):1–46, 1989.

[13] J. Bochnak, M. Coste, and M.-F. Roy. *Real algebraic geometry*, volume 36 of *Ergebnisse der Mathematik und ihrer Grenzgebiete (3) [Results in Mathematics and Related Areas (3)]*. Springer-Verlag, Berlin, 1998. Translated from the 1987 French original, Revised by the authors.

[14] D.A. Brake, D.J. Bates, W. Hao, J.D. Hauenstein, A.J. Sommese, and C.W. Wampler. Bertini_real: Software for one-and two-dimensional real algebraic sets. In *Mathematical Software–ICMS 2014*, pages 175–182. Springer, 2014.

[15] D.A. Brake, J.D. Hauenstein, and A.J. Sommese. Numerical local irreducible decomposition. To appear in *LNCS*.

[16] M.-D. Choi, T.Y. Lam, and B. Reznick. Sums of squares of real polynomials. In *Proceedings of Symposia in Pure mathematics*, volume 58, pages 103–126. American Mathematical Society, 1995.

[17] E.K.P. Chong and S.H. Zak. *An introduction to optimization*, volume 76. John Wiley & Sons, 2013.

[18] D. Cifuentes and P.A. Parrilo. Sampling algebraic varieties for sum of squares programs. arXiv:1511.06751, 2015.

[19] B.H. Dayton and Z. Zeng. Computing the multiplicity structure in solving polynomial systems. In *ISSAC'05*, pages 116–123 (electronic). ACM, New York, 2005.

[20] J.P.K. Doye and D.J. Wales. Saddle points and dynamics of lennard-jones clusters, solids, and supercooled liquids. *The Journal of Chemical Physics*, 116(9):3777–3788, 2002.

[21] R. Franzosi, L. Casetti, L. Spinelli, and M. Pettini. Topological aspects of geometrical signatures of phase transitions. *Phys. Rev. E*, 60:R5009–R5012, Nov 1999.

[22] P. Gianni, B. Trager, and G. Zacharias. Gröbner bases and primary decomposition of polynomial ideals. *Journal of Symbolic Computation*, 6(2):149–167, 1988.

[23] A. Griewank and M. R. Osborne. Newton's method for singular problems when the dimension of the null space is > 1. *SIAM J. Numer. Anal.*, 18(1):145–149, 1981.

[24] A. Griewank and M. R. Osborne. Analysis of Newton's method at irregular singularities. *SIAM J. Numer. Anal.*, 20(4):747–773, 1983.

[25] Z.A. Griffin and J.D. Hauenstein. Real solutions to systems of polynomial equations and parameter continuation. *Adv. Geom.*, 15(2):173–187, 2015.

[26] Z.A. Griffin, J.D. Hauenstein, C. Peterson, and A.J. Sommese. Numerical computation of the Hilbert function and regularity of a zero dimensional scheme. In *Connections between algebra, combinatorics, and geometry*, volume 76 of *Springer Proc. Math. Stat.*, pages 235–250. Springer, New York, 2014.

[27] J.D. Hauenstein. Numerically computing real points on algebraic sets. *Acta applicandae mathematicae*, 125(1):105–119, 2013.

[28] J.D. Hauenstein and Sommese A.J. What is numerical algebraic geometry? J. Symb. Comput., To appear.

[29] J.D. Hauenstein, I. Haywood, and A.C. Liddell, Jr. An a posteriori certification algorithm for newton homotopies. In *Proceedings of the 39th International Symposium on Symbolic and Algebraic Computation*, ISSAC '14, pages 248–255, New York, NY, USA, 2014. ACM.

[30] J.D. Hauenstein and A.C. Liddell Jr. Certified predictor-corrector tracking for newton homotopies. *Journal of Symbolic Computation*, 74:239 – 254, 2016.

[31] J.D. Hauenstein, B. Mourrain, and A. Szanto. Certifying isolated singular points and their multiplicity structure. In *ISSAC'15—Proceedings of the 2015 ACM International Symposium on Symbolic and Algebraic Computation*, pages 213–220. ACM, New York, 2015.

[32] J.D. Hauenstein, A.J. Sommese, and C.W. Wampler. Regenerative cascade homotopies for solving polynomial systems. *Appl. Math. Comput.*, 218(4):1240–1246, 2011.

[33] J.D. Hauenstein and F. Sottile. Algorithm 921: alphaCertified: certifying solutions to polynomial systems. *ACM Transactions on Mathematical Software (TOMS)*, 38(4):28, 2012.

[34] J.D. Hauenstein and C.W. Wampler. Isosingular sets and deflation. *Found. Comput. Math.*, 13(3):371–403, 2013.

[35] I. Janovitz-Freireich, B. Mourrain, L. Rónyai, and Á. Szántó. On the computation of matrices of traces and radicals of ideals. *Journal of Symbolic Computation*, 47(1):102–122, 2012.

[36] R.B. Kearfott. Some tests of generalized bisection. *ACM Transactions on Mathematical Software (TOMS)*, 13(3):197–220, 1987.

[37] C.T. Kelley. *Iterative methods for optimization*, volume 18 of *Frontiers in Applied Mathematics*. Society for Industrial and Applied Mathematics (SIAM), Philadelphia, PA, 1999.

[38] C.T. Kelley. *Solving nonlinear equations with Newton's method*. SIAM, Philadelphia, 2003.

[39] T. Krick and A. Logar. An algorithm for the computation of the radical of an ideal in the ring of polynomials. In *Applied algebra, algebraic algorithms and error-correcting codes*, pages 195–205. Springer, 1991.

[40] J.B. Lasserre, M. Laurent, B. Mourrain, P. Rostalski, and P. Trébuchet. Moment matrices, border bases and real radical computation. *Journal of Symbolic Computation*, 51:63–85, 2013.

[41] J.B. Lasserre, M. Laurent, and P. Rostalski. Semidefinite characterization and computation of zero-dimensional real radical ideals. *Foundations of Computational Mathematics*, 8(5):607–647, 2008.

[42] J.B. Lasserre, M. Laurent, and P. Rostalski. A prolongation–projection algorithm for computing the finite real variety of an ideal. *Theoretical Computer Science*, 410(27):2685–2700, 2009.

[43] J.B. Lasserre, M. Laurent, and P. Rostalski. A unified approach to computing real and complex zeros of zero-dimensional ideals. In *Emerging applications of algebraic geometry*, pages 125–155. Springer, 2009.

[44] M. Laurent and P. Rostalski. The approach of moments for polynomial equations. In *Handbook on Semidefinite, Conic and Polynomial Optimization*, pages 25–60. Springer, 2012.

[45] B. Lesieutre and D. Wu. An efficient method to locate all the load flow solutions – revisited. In *53rd Annual Allerton Conf. Commun., Control, and Comput.*, Sept. 29 - Oct. 2 2015.

[46] A. Leykin, J. Verschelde, and A. Zhao. Newton's method with deflation for isolated singularities of polynomial systems. *Theoret. Comput. Sci.*, 359(1-3):111–122, 2006.

[47] Y. Lu, D.J. Bates, A.J. Sommese, and C.W. Wampler. Finding all real points of a complex curve. In *Algebra, Geometry and their Interactions*, volume 448 of *Contemporary Mathematics*, pages 183–205, 2007.

[48] W. Ma and J.S. Thorp. An efficient algorithm to locate all the load flow solutions. *IEEE Transactions on Power Systems*, 8(3):1077–1083, Aug 1993.

[49] Y. Ma, C. Wang, and L. Zhi. A certificate for semidefinite relaxations in computing positive-dimensional real radical ideals. *Journal of Symbolic Computation*, 2014.

[50] M. Marshall. *Positive polynomials and sums of squares*, volume 146 of *Mathematical Surveys and Monographs*. American Mathematical Society, Providence, RI, 2008.

[51] D. Mehta, T. Chen, J.D. Hauenstein, and D.J. Wales. Communication: Newton homotopies for sampling stationary points of potential energy landscapes. *The Journal of Chemical Physics*, 141(12):121104, 2014.

[52] D. Mehta, T. Chen, J.W.R Morgan, and D.J. Wales. Exploring the potential energy landscape of the Thomson problem via Newton homotopies. *The Journal of Chemical Physics*, 142(19):194113, 2015.

[53] D. Mehta, J.D. Hauenstein, and M. Kastner. Energy-landscape analysis of the two-dimensional nearest-neighbor φ^4 model. *Phys. Rev. E*, 85:061103, Jun 2012.

[54] R. Neuhaus. Computation of real radicals of polynomial ideals – ii. *Journal of Pure and Applied Algebra*, 124(1):261–280, 1998.

[55] A. Papachristodoulou, J. Anderson, G. Valmorbida, S. Prajna, P. Seiler, and P.A. Parrilo. *SOSTOOLS: Sum of squares optimization toolbox for MATLAB*. `http://arxiv.org/abs/1310.4716`, 2013. Available from `http://www.eng.ox.ac.uk/control/sostools`, `http://www.cds.caltech.edu/sostools` and `http://www.mit.edu/~parrilo/sostools`.

[56] F. Rouillier, M.-F. Roy, and M. Safey El Din. Finding at least one point in each connected component of a real algebraic set defined by a single equation. *J. Complexity*, 16(4):716–750, 2000.

[57] M. Safey El Din and É. Schost. Polar varieties and computation of one point in each connected component of a smooth real algebraic set. In *Proceedings of the 2003 international symposium on Symbolic and algebraic computation*, pages 224–231. ACM, 2003.

[58] A. Seidenberg. A new decision method for elementary algebra. *Ann. of Math. (2)*, 60:365–374, 1954.

[59] W. Seiler. Involution – the formal theory of differential equations and its applications in computer algebra and numerical analysis. Habilitation thesis. University of Mannheim, 2002.

[60] S. Smale. *Newton's method estimates from data at one point*. Springer, 1986.

[61] A.J. Sommese and J. Verschelde. Numerical homotopies to compute generic points on positive dimensional algebraic sets. *J. Complexity*, 16(3):572–602, 2000. Complexity theory, real machines, and homotopy (Oxford, 1999).

[62] A.J. Sommese and C.W. Wampler. Numerical algebraic geometry. In *The mathematics of numerical analysis (Park City, UT, 1995)*, volume 32 of *Lectures in Appl. Math.*, pages 749–763. Amer. Math. Soc., Providence, RI, 1996.

[63] A.J. Sommese and C.W. Wampler, II. *The numerical solution of systems of polynomials arising in engineering and science*. World Scientific Publishing Co. Pte. Ltd., Hackensack, NJ, 2005.

[64] S.J. Spang. *On the computation of the real radical*. PhD thesis, Thesis, Technische Universität Kaiserslautern, 2007.

[65] G. Stengle. A nullstellensatz and a positivstellensatz in semialgebraic geometry. *Math. Ann.*, 207:87–97, 1974.

[66] B. Xia and L. Yang. An algorithm for isolating the real solutions of semi-algebraic systems. *Journal of Symbolic Computation*, 34(5):461–477, 2002.

[67] G. Zeng. Computation of generalized real radicals of polynomial ideals. *Science in China Series A: Mathematics*, 42(3):272–280, 1999.

On the Complexity of Solving Zero-Dimensional Polynomial Systems via Projection

Cornelius Brand*
Saarland University
Cluster of Excellence (MMCI)
Campus E1 7
66123 Saarbrücken, Germany
cbrand@mmci.uni-saarland.de

Michael Sagraloff
Max-Planck-Institut für Informatik
Campus E1 4
66123 Saarbrücken, Germany
msagralo@mpi-inf.mpg.de

ABSTRACT

Given a zero-dimensional polynomial system consisting of n integer polynomials in n variables, we propose a certified and complete method to compute all complex solutions of the system as well as a corresponding separating linear form l with coefficients of small bit size. For computing l, we need to project the solutions into one dimension along $\mathcal{O}(n)$ distinct directions but no further algebraic manipulations. The solutions are then directly reconstructed from the considered projections. The first step is deterministic, whereas the second step uses randomization, thus being Las-Vegas.

The theoretical analysis of our approach shows that the overall cost for the two problems considered above is dominated by the cost of carrying out the projections. We also give bounds on the bit complexity of our algorithms that are exclusively stated in terms of the number of variables, the total degree and the bitsize of the input polynomials.

Keywords

polynomial system solving; bit complexity; certified algorithms; resultant computation; separating form

1. INTRODUCTION

Let $f_i \in \mathbb{Z}[x_1, \ldots, x_n]$, with $i = 1, \ldots, n$, be polynomials of total degree d_i and with integer coefficients of bitsize at most τ, i.e., f_i has *magnitude* (d_i, τ). We further assume that the system

$$f_1(x_1, \ldots, x_n) = \cdots = f_n(x_1, \ldots, x_n) = 0, \qquad (1)$$

has only finitely many solutions (also "at infinity").

There is an extensive literature describing numerous approaches to compute the set $\mathcal{S}$ of complex solutions of (1), and any attempt to provide a comprehensive overview would go far beyond the scope of this work. Instead, we refer the reader to one of the excellent textbooks [9, 29, 8]. A well-studied approach based on elimination techniques such as multivariate resultants or Gröbner Bases first projects the solutions into one dimension and then recovers them from the projections. That is, given a linear form $l = \sum_{i=1}^{n} l_i x_i$ with integer coefficients l_i, we may ask for the image of $\mathcal{S}$ under the mapping $\pi_l : \mathbb{C}^n \mapsto \mathbb{C}$ that sends a point $(x_1, \ldots, x_n) \in \mathbb{C}^n$ to the value $\sum_{i=1}^{n} l_i x_i \in \mathbb{C}$. Using elimination techniques, we can compute a univariate polynomial $E^l \in \mathbb{Z}[x]$, which we call an *elimination polynomial along* l, such that the set $V(E^l) = \{z \in \mathbb{C} : E^l(z) = 0\}$ of roots of E^l contains the image $\mathcal{S}^l := \pi_l(\mathcal{S})$ of $\mathcal{S}$ under π_l. When reconstructing the solutions from the roots of E^l, several problems may arise: The set $V(E^l)$ may contain projections of solutions at infinity, so that $V(E^l) \neq \mathcal{S}^l$. This can be resolved by considering a suitable change of coordinates that transforms the corresponding homogeneous polynomial system into a system with only finite solutions. What is even worse, l may be *non-separating* for $\mathcal{S}$, that is, there exist two solutions that map to the same point. In this case, π_l does not define a bijective mapping between $\mathcal{S}$ and $V(E^l)$, and thus $\mathcal{S}$ cannot be recovered directly from $V(E^l)$. In contrast, if the linear form is known to be separating, then efficient methods exist (e.g. by means of computing a univariate rational representation [27, 1]) to obtain the solutions from the projections.

One possible way [27] of computing a *separating linear form* (SLF for short) is to consider a large enough set $\mathcal{L}$ of linear forms, which is known to contain at least one SLF, and to carry out projections along each $l \in \mathcal{L}$ (i.e. we compute E^l and its roots). Then, each linear form $l \in \mathcal{L}$ that maximizes the number of distinct roots of E^l must be separating. For instance, the approach in [27] considers the set

$$\mathcal{L} := \{x_1 + i \cdot x_2 + \cdots + i^{n-1} x_n : 0 \leq i \leq (n-1)d^n(d^n-1)/2\},$$

where d is an upper bound on the degree of all f_i. Hence, we need to employ $\Omega(nd^{2n})$ projections along linear forms of bitsize $\mathcal{O}(n^2 \log d)$ to compute an SLF, which renders the approach impractical. Our work is driven by the question whether it is possible to compute an SLF using a considerably smaller number of projections. Since two solutions might share $n-1$ coordinates, a reasonable lower bound for the needed number of projections seems to be n. Here, we show that $2n-1$ projections along linear forms of bitsize $\mathcal{O}(n \log d)$ are sufficient, and that the cost for computing an SLF is dominated by the cost for the projections. In addition, the computed linear form has bitsize $\mathcal{O}(n \log d)$, thus being a

*Part of this work was done while visiting the Simons Institute for the Theory of Computing.

ISSAC '16, July 19 - 22, 2016, Waterloo, ON, Canada

ISBN 978-1-4503-4380-0/16/07...$15.00

DOI: http://dx.doi.org/10.1145/2930889.2930934

factor n smaller than what can be obtained with the approach above.

The main tool underlying our approach is a fast method for the computation of a linear form $l = x + sy$, with $s \in \mathbb{Z}$, that is separating for a two-dimensional grid $G := X \times Y \subset \mathbb{C}^2$, where X and Y are the sets consisting of the distinct roots of univariate integer polynomials f and g of magnitude (D, L), respectively. In Section 3, we show how to compute such an $s \in \{1, \ldots, D^4\}$, using $\tilde{O}(D^3 + D^2 L)$ bit operations. This bound is noteworthy as it matches the best bound [23, 25, 2] known for isolating all complex roots of f and g, and thus for computing X and Y. Notice that using the above result, we may immediately derive the current record bound [19, 3] of $\tilde{O}(d^6 + d^5\tau)$ operations for computing an SLF for the solutions of a bivariate system defined by two polynomials of magnitude (d, τ). Indeed, using resultant computation we may first project the solutions of this system on both coordinates. Then, the grid G defined as the product of the roots of the two corresponding resultant polynomials (of magnitude $(d^2, \tilde{O}(d\tau))$) contains all solutions of the system, and thus an SLF for G also constitutes an SLF for the solutions.

We extend this approach to compute an SLF for the solutions of a general n-dimensional system as given in (1): We first project the solutions on each of the coordinate axes, which yields sets X_1 to X_n in $\mathbb{C}$. Then, the n-dimensional grid $G := X_1 \times \cdots \times X_n$ contains all solutions. However, instead of computing an SLF for G, we recursively compute SLFs $l' = l[i_1, \ldots, i_k]$ for the canonical embeddings of $\mathcal{S}$ into proper sub-products $X_{i_1} \times \cdots \times X_{i_k}$ of G until we eventually obtain an SLF l for $\mathcal{S}$. This can be achieved by means of a divide-and-conquer strategy, which uses projections along the linear forms l' and our fast method for the computation of an SLF for a two-dimensional grid. Our method can be combined with any elimination technique that allows to carry out projections of the solutions along linear forms. The worst case bit complexity of our method is then bounded by

$$\tilde{O}(n \cdot (D^3 + D^2 L) + n \cdot \Pi), \qquad (2)$$

where Π bounds the cost of computing an elimination polynomial for (1) along a linear form of bitsize $\mathcal{O}(n \log d)$, and D and L constitute bounds on the degrees and the bitsizes of the produced elimination polynomials. If a deterministic method is used to compute the elimination polynomials, our method is deterministic as well. Using the Las-Vegas algorithm from [13, 28] to compute the hidden-variable resultant, we have $D \leq d^n$, $L = \tilde{O}((nd)^{n-1}(nd + \tau))$, and[1] $\Pi = \tilde{O}(n^{(n-1)(\omega+1)}(d + \tau)d^{(\omega+2)n-\omega-1})$. Then, (2) writes as

$$\tilde{O}(n^{(n-1)(\omega+1)+1}(nd + \tau)d^{(\omega+2)n-\omega-1}), \qquad (3)$$

which bounds the number of bit operations that our algorithm uses in expectation. Indeed, within the same complexity, we can even compute $(nd)^{\mathcal{O}(1)}$ different SLFs for the solutions of (1). With high probability, we may then choose an SLF l in a certified manner such that each root of the corresponding elimination polynomial E^l lifts to a solution of the system.

[1] Here, ω denotes the exponent in the complexity of matrix multiplication. In the general case, where each of the considered hidden variable resultants $R(x)$ are obtained from the formula $R(x) = \det M(x)/\det S$ with a non-singular matrix S, the bound for Π improves by a factor $(nd)^{n-1}$. In this case, the bound in (3) also improves by a factor $(nd)^{n-1}$; see Section 2 for more details.

Using the (intermediate) separating forms $l' = l[i_1, \ldots, i_k]$ from the computation in the first step, we can finally recover all solutions from the projections along l. The total cost for this step is also bounded by (3).

The complexity of all steps in our algorithm, except for the computation of the elimination polynomials, is within the best known bound for the computation of the roots of the occurring elimination polynomials. Since the latter bound is suspected to be near-optimal and since any elimination based approach has to compute certain elimination polynomials of comparable magnitude as well as the roots of such polynomials at some point, there is some evidence that our method may perform near-optimal (at least for elimination approaches). Note that the bound in (3) is dominated by the bound for the computation of the hidden variable resultant. In particular, for fixed n, the cost for the latter task (approximately) scales like[1] $d^{(\omega+2)n}\tau$, whereas the cost for all other steps (approximately) scales like $d^{3n}\tau$. Hence, any improvement on the complexity of computing elimination polynomials yields an improvement of the bound in (3).

How does our bound compare to the complexity results stated in the literature? There has been extensive research [14, 21, 18, 20, 22, 27] in the 80s and 90s showing that the computation of multivariate resultants or Gröbner Bases as well as the computation of the solutions of a zero-dimensional polynomial systems has (arithmetic) complexity bounded by $d^{\mathcal{O}(n)}$, thus being polynomial in the size of the dense input representation; see also [17] for a more comprehensive overview. There also exist more specific bounds [24, 6, 26] yielding an arithmetic complexity for computing the solutions of size approximately $\tilde{O}(d^{3n})$. However, we are not aware of any general bound on the bit complexity that is comparable to ours, even not for lower-dimensional polynomial system with 3 or 4 variables, whereas remarkably, within the last two decades, the thorough investigation [16, 10, 11, 19, 3] of the (bit) complexity of solving bivariate systems eventually yielded bounds (i.e. $\tilde{O}(d^6 + d^5\tau)$) for the computation of an SLF and of all solutions) that are likely to be near-optimal and comparable to our result. The method from [7] for solving zero-dimensional system shares some similarities with our approach. There, it is proposed to recursively compute SLFs $l_k = \sum_{i=1}^{k} l_i x_i$ for the "solutions" of the elimination ideals $\mathcal{I}_k := \mathcal{I} \cap \mathbb{Q}[x_1, \ldots, x_k]$, where $k = 1, \ldots, n$ and $\mathcal{I} := (f_i)_{i=1,\ldots,n}$ is the ideal defined by the polynomials f_i. The crux is that this is done so that all solutions (ξ, x_{k+1}) of $\mathcal{I}_{k+1}$ obtained from lifting a specific solution ξ of $\mathcal{I}_k$ project via l_{k+1} into a small neighborhood of $l_k(\xi)$. Following this approach, the solutions of $\mathcal{I}$ can be represented as linear combinations of the roots of univariate polynomials. The method seems to perform well in practice as the actual separation bounds for the roots of the considered elimination polynomials is small compared to the worst-case. However, no complexity analysis is given, and we suspect that the method is not very well suited for a worst-case analysis as it considers the computation of elimination polynomials along linear forms of a very large bitsize (at least in theory).

2. PRELIMINARIES

We consider a zero-dimensional polynomial system as in (1). Then, the homogenized system

$$F_1(x_1, \ldots, x_{n+1}) = \cdots = F_n(x_1, \ldots, x_{n+1}) = 0, \qquad (4)$$

with $F_i(x_1, \ldots, x_{n+1}) \in \mathbb{Z}[x_1, \ldots, x_n]$ a homogenous polynomial of degree d_i and $F_i(x_1, \ldots, x_n, 1) = f_i(x_1, \ldots, x_n)$, has only finitely many solutions in the complex projective n-space $\mathbb{P}^n$. Then, Bézout's Theorem says that the total number of solutions in $\mathbb{P}^n$ is upper bounded by $B := d_1 \cdots d_n \leq d^n$. A solution of the form $(x_1, \ldots, x_n, 1) \in \mathbb{P}^n$ is called *finite*, whereas each solution of the form $(x_1, \ldots, x_n, 0)$ is called *infinite*. The solution $x_1 = \cdots = x_{n+1} = 0$ is called *trivial*. Let $\mathcal{S} \subset \mathbb{C}^n$ be the set of all complex solutions of (1). Then, the finite solutions $(x_1, \ldots, x_n, 1)$ of (4) exactly correspond to the solutions $(x_1, \ldots, x_n) \in \mathcal{S}$ of (1), whereas the solutions at infinity exactly correspond to the solutions in $\mathbb{P}^{n-1}$ of the (homogeneous) system $\bar{F}_1(x_1, \ldots, x_n) = \cdots = \bar{F}_n(x_1, \ldots, x_n) = 0$, with $\bar{F}_i := F_i|_{x_{n+1}=0}$.

We now briefly review the *hidden variable* approach based on resultant computation, which allows us to project the solutions of (1) on one of the coordinates; for more details, see [8, 15]. We may assume that x_1 is the coordinate onto which we project. For a fixed value $x_1 = \xi \in \mathbb{C}$, (1) transforms into

$$f_1'(x_2, \ldots, x_n) = \cdots = f_n'(x_2, \ldots, x_n) = 0, \qquad (5)$$

with $f_i' := f_i|_{x_1=\xi}$ of generic[2] degree $d_i' \leq d_i$. Let $F_i' \in \mathbb{C}[x_2, \ldots, x_n, x_{n+1}]$ be the corresponding homogenized polynomial of degree d_i', then

$$F_1'(x_2, \ldots, x_{n+1}) = \cdots = F_n'(x_2, \ldots, x_{n+1}) = 0 \qquad (6)$$

defines a system of n homogeneous polynomials in n variables. It is a well-known fact that there exists a homogeneous polynomial of total degree $D' := \sum_{i=1}^n \prod_{j \neq i} d_i' \leq nd^{n-1}$ in the coefficients of the polynomials F_i', the so-called *resultant* $\mathrm{Res}(F_1', \ldots, F_n')$ of the polynomials F_i', which vanishes if and only if the system (6) has a non-trivial solution in $\mathbb{P}^{n-1}$. The resultant is a factor of the determinant of an $m \times m$-matrix M, the so-called *Macaulay matrix*, whose entries are given in terms of the coefficients of the polynomials F_i'; here, $N := \sum_{i=1}^n (d_i' - 1) + 1 < nd$ and $m = \binom{N+(n-1)}{n-1} < (nd)^{n-1}$. Since f_i' has the same coefficients as F_i', one usually defines $\mathrm{Res}(f_1', \ldots, f_n') := \mathrm{Res}(F_1', \ldots, F_n')$.

In order to compute the projections of the solutions $\mathcal{S}$ of (1) onto the first coordinate, we consider f_i as elements of $\mathbb{Z}[x_1][x_2, \ldots, x_n]$ with coefficients in $\mathbb{Z}[x_1]$ of magnitude (d_i, τ). Hence, x_1 is treated as a constant (also "hidden variable"). The *hidden variable resultant* $R^{x_1} = \mathrm{Res}^{x_1}(f_1, \ldots, f_n)$ is a univariate integer polynomial of degree V in x_1, with $V \leq B$, that vanishes at $x_1 = \xi$ if and only if (6) has a non-trivial solution in $\mathbb{P}^{n-1}$. In particular, each solution $(x_1, \ldots, x_n) \in \mathcal{S}$ yields a root x_1 of R^{x_1}. Hence, the set $V(R^{x_1})$ contains the set $\mathcal{S}^{x_1} = \pi_{x_1}(\mathcal{S})$ of projections of all solutions onto the first coordinate. In general, it is wrong that each root of R^{x_1} also extends to a solution of (1). However, under certain assumptions, this can be ensured; see [4] for a proof of the following Lemma.

LEMMA 1. *Suppose that (4) has no infinite solution and that each f_i contains a term of total degree d_i that does not depend on x_1. Then, for all $\xi \in \mathbb{C}$, the specialized system (6) has no infinite solution. In addition, $V(R^{x_1}) = \mathcal{S}^{x_1}$.*

[2]For finitely many ξ, the degree of f_i' can be smaller than d_i', however, for all other values of ξ, each f_i' has degree d_i', which is the degree of f_i considered as a polynomial in the variables $x_2, \ldots, x_n$ with coefficients in $\mathbb{Z}[x_1]$.

In general, R^{x_1} can be written as $\det M(x_1)/\det S$, where $M(x_1)$ is the Macaulay matrix with entries in $\mathbb{Z}[x_1]$ and S a non-singular square sub-matrix of $M(x_1)$ that does not depend on x_1. In the special case, where S is singular, we may use Canny's approach [5],[8, §4] (known as *Generalized Characteristic Polynomial*) to compute R^{x_1} as the quotient of the trailing coefficients of the (non-zero) characteristic polynomials of the matrices $M(x_1)$ and S. From the bounds on m and V, it thus follows that R^{x_1} is of magnitude $(B, \tilde{O}((nd)^{n-1}\tau))$. Emiris and Pan [13] give a Las-Vegas algorithm to compute R^{x_1}. The main idea underlying their approach is to compute the value of R^{x_1} at $V = \mathcal{O}(B)$ many distinct integer points $x_1 = \xi \in \mathbb{Z}$ (each of bit size $\mu = \mathcal{O}(\log B)$), and then to interpolate R^{x_1} from these values. For computing $R^{x_1}(\xi) \in \mathbb{Z}$, one evaluates the determinants of $M(\xi)$ and S modulo p for a sufficiently large set of primes (of near-constant bitsize) followed by a Chinese Remaindering step to recover $R^{x_1}(\xi)$. Exploiting that M is quasi-Toeplitz, the determinants can be computed with $\mathcal{O}(m^2)$ arithmetic operations, which yields the bound $\tilde{O}(m^2nVD'(d+\tau)) = \tilde{O}((d+\tau)n^{2n}d^{4n-3})$ on the expected costs of computing R^{x_1}. There also exist more adaptive bounds (e.g. [12, 13]) for the magnitude as well as for the complexity of computing the (sparse) resultant that take into account the actual support of the coefficients of the input polynomials (e.g. the *mixed volume*). So for sparse systems, the above bounds constitute significant overestimations. When focusing on general systems, a slightly better bound (with respect to the exponent of d) can be derived: Using an asymptotically fast Las-Vegas method [28] to compute the determinant of an $m \times m$ matrix with integer entries of bitsize L at expected cost $\tilde{O}(m^\omega L)$, we obtain the following result. For details, see [4].

PROPOSITION 1. *There is a Las-Vegas algorithm to compute $\det M(x_1)$ and $\det(S)$ in an expected number of*

$$\tilde{O}(m^\omega(d+\tau)B) = \tilde{O}(n^{(n-1)\omega}(d+\tau)d^{(\omega+1)n-\omega})$$

bit operations. If $\det(S) \neq 0$, $\mathrm{Res}^{x_1}_{d_1,\ldots,d_n}(f_1, \ldots, f_n)$ can be computed within the same complexity. Otherwise, it can be computed in an expected number of bit operations bounded by

$$\tilde{O}(m^{\omega+1}(d+\tau)B) = \tilde{O}(n^{(n-1)(\omega+1)}(d+\tau)d^{(\omega+2)n-\omega-1}).$$

Once R^{x_1} is computed, we can use a fast univariate root finder [23, 25, 2] to compute arbitrary small isolating disks for all complex roots of R^{x_1}.

PROPOSITION 2 ([23, THMS. 4, 5]). *Let $f \in \mathbb{Z}[x]$ be a polynomial of magnitude (d, τ), and let ρ be an arbitrary positive integer. Then, using $\tilde{O}(d^3 + d^2\tau + d\rho)$ bit operations, we can compute a sorted list of isolating disks, each of radius less than $2^{-\rho}$, for all complex roots of f.*

To generalize this to projecting solutions along arbitrary directions, let $l := l_1 \cdot x_1 + \cdots + l_n \cdot x_n$ be a linear form with integers l_i of bit size less than μ, and let $\pi_l : \mathbb{C}^n \to \mathbb{C}$ be the corresponding mapping. We say that $\mathcal{S}^l = \pi_l(\mathcal{S})$ is the *projection (of the solutions $\mathcal{S}$) along l*. Suppose that $l_1 = 1$, then, for computing $\mathcal{S}^l$, we first replace x_1 by $x_1 - l_2x_2 - \cdots - l_nx_n$, yielding

$$f_1^*(x_1, \ldots, x_n) = \cdots = f_n^*(x_1, \ldots, x_n) = 0, \qquad (7)$$

with $f_i^* := f_i(x_1 - l_2x_2 - \cdots - l_nx_n, x_2, \ldots, x_n)$. Then, each f_i is an integer polynomial of magnitude $(d, \mathcal{O}(d\mu + \tau))$. Let

$R^l := \mathrm{Res}^{x_1}(f_1^*, \dots, f_n^*)$. Then, $\mathcal{S}^l \subset V(R^l)$. This crucial property of R^l deserves the following definition:

Definition 1. Let l be a linear form as above, then we call $R \in \mathbb{Z}[x]$ an *elimination polynomial for (1) along l* if $\deg R \leq B$ and $\mathcal{S}^l \subset V(R)$. We call R *strong* if $\mathcal{S}^l = V(R)$.

Notice that R^l is a strong elimination polynomial for (1) along l if both conditions from Lemma 1 are fulfilled for the transformed system (7). Lemma 2 shows that, in the case where the linear form

$$l(\lambda) = x_1 + l_2(\lambda)x_2 + \cdots + l_n(\lambda)x_n, \text{ with}$$
$$l_j := a_{j0} + a_{j1} \cdot \lambda \in \mathbb{Z}[\lambda] \text{ and } a_{k1} \neq 0 \text{ for some } k \in \{2, \dots, n\},$$

depends on a parameter λ, we can always choose λ such that (7) fulfills the second requirement from Lemma 1. We sketch the proof of the following Lemma and refer to [4] for details.

LEMMA 2. *Let $l(\lambda)$ be a linear form as above, let $\Lambda \subset \mathbb{Z}$ be an arbitrary set of size $|\Lambda| \geq 2nd$, and let μ be a bound on the bitsize of all l_j and the integers contained in Λ.*

There exists a Las Vegas algorithm with expected bit complexity $\tilde{O}(d^3(d\mu+\tau)(2d)^n)$ that computes an integer $\lambda^* \in \Lambda$ as well as the transformed polynomials $f_i^* = f_i(x_1 - l_2(\lambda^*)x_2 - \cdots - l_n(\lambda^*)x_n, x_2, \dots, x_n)$, such that each f_i^* contains a term of degree d_i that does not depend on x_1.

PROOF. A straightforward calculation shows that, for each f_i, there is at least one term as desired, the coefficient of which is a non-zero polynomial in λ of degree at most d_i. The polynomials f_i^* can be computed in the stated number of bit operations using Kronecker substitution (e.g. see [30, Chapter 8]) for multiplying multivariate polynomials. □

Putting everything together, we obtain the following result:

COROLLARY 1. *Let $l(\lambda)$ and Λ be defined as in Lemma 2.*

(a) There is a Las-Vegas algorithm that computes $R^{l(\lambda)}$ in an expected number of bit operations that is bounded by $\tilde{O}(\Pi(d, \tau, n, \mu))$, where we define

$$\Pi(d, \tau, n, \mu) := n^{(n-1)\omega}(d\mu + \tau)d^{(\omega+2)n-\omega-1}.$$

(b) Suppose that $R^{l(\lambda)}$ is given. Then, for any $\lambda \in \Lambda$ and $\rho \in \mathbb{N}$, we can compute isolating disks of size less than $2^{-\rho}$ for all roots of $R^{l(\lambda)}$ in

$$\tilde{O}(n^{n-1}d^{3n-1}(d\mu + \tau) + d^n\rho) \qquad (8)$$

bit operations.

(c) For each $(x_1, \dots, x_n) \in \mathcal{S}$, we have $2^{-\Gamma} < \max_i |x_i| < 2^{\Gamma}$ with $\Gamma := \max_i \log(1 + \|R^{x_i}\|_\infty) = \tilde{O}((nd)^{n-1}\tau)$.

PROOF. (a) follows from Proposition 1 and the fact that the polynomials f_i^* have bitsize $\tilde{O}(d\mu + \tau)$. For (b), we use Proposition 2 and note that $R^{l(\lambda)}$ has magnitude $(d^n, \tilde{O}((nd)^{n-1}(d\mu + \tau)))$. (c) follows from Cauchy's root bound applied to R^{x_i}. □

By flipping x_1 and x_i, the results from the above corollary apply to any linear form $l(\lambda) = x_i + \sum_{j \neq i} l_j(\lambda) \cdot x_j \not\equiv x_i$ with $l_j = a_{j0} + a_{j1} \cdot \lambda$.

3. TWO-DIMENSIONAL GRIDS

Let $f, g \in \mathbb{Z}[x]$ be two (not necessarily square-free) polynomials of magnitude (d, τ), and let $X = V(f) = \{x_1, \dots, x_{d'}\}$ and $Y = V(g) = \{y_1, \dots, y_{d''}\}$ be the corresponding sets of *distinct* complex roots of f and g. We further define $G := X \times Y \subset \mathbb{C}^2$, which is a two-dimensional grid of $d' \cdot d'' \leq d^2$ many points. For $s \in \mathbb{C}$, let $l_s : \mathbb{C} \times \mathbb{C} \to \mathbb{C}$, $(x, y) \mapsto x + sy$. We call l_s (or simply s) *separating for a set* $M \subset \mathbb{C}$ if l_s restricted to M is injective, and *non-separating* otherwise. Our goal in this section is to show that we can compute an integer (or even a whole sequence of integers) s of bit size $\mathcal{O}(\log n)$ that is separating for G at a cost that is comparable to the computation of the roots of f and g.

THEOREM 1. *Let c be a positive integer of size $d^{\mathcal{O}(1)}$. There is an algorithm using $\tilde{O}(d^3 + d^2\tau)$ bit operations that outputs $s^* \in S := \{1, \dots, (d^4 - 1)c\}$ such that l_s is separating for $G = X \times Y$ for all $s \in S^* = \{s^*, \dots, s^* + c - 1\}$. Additionally, it holds that*

$$|(x + sy) - (x' + sy')| \geq \frac{1}{4} \cdot |y - y'|$$

for any two distinct elements $(x, y) \in G$ and $(x', y') \in G$.

In Section 3.1, we fix some definitions and recall well-known (amortized) bounds on the separations and absolute values of the roots of an integer polynomial. Then, in Section 3.2, we prove the above Theorem. In Section 3.3, we show that if s is separating for G and if a subset G' of G maps via l_s one-to-one onto a subset Z of $V(h)$, where $h \in \mathbb{Z}[x]$ is of magnitude (d, τ), then we can recover G' from Z using $\tilde{O}(d^3 + d^2\tau)$ bit operations.

3.1 Definitions and Bounds

Let X and Y be defined as above. For $i, j, k, l \in \{1, \dots, d\}$, with $i < j$ and $k < l$, we define $\nu_{ij} := |x_i - x_j|$ and $\delta_{kl} := |y_k - y_l|$. Let N, Δ be the sets of all ν_{kl}, δ_{ij}, respectively. Furthermore, let $\mathcal{F} := \{\frac{\nu}{\delta} : \nu \in \mathrm{N} \text{ and } \delta \in \Delta\}$. Notice that, for the proof of Theorem 1, it suffices to compute a positive integer $s^* \leq d^4c - c$ with $|s - \frac{\nu}{\delta}| \geq \frac{1}{4}$ for all $s \in \{s^*, \dots, s^* + c - 1\}$.

For $x \in \mathbb{C}$ and some $\rho \in \mathbb{N}$, we say that $\tilde{x} \in \mathbb{C}$ is an *approximation of absolute (relative) error* $\varepsilon = 2^{-\rho}$ if $|x - \tilde{x}| < \varepsilon$ ($(1 - \varepsilon)x < \tilde{x} < (1 + \varepsilon)x$). In this case, ρ is called the *absolute (relative) approximation quality* of $\tilde{x}$. Furthermore, for $x > 0$, we define $B_x := \log \max\{1, x\} + \log \max\{1, 1/x\}$.

We now recall some well-known results on the separations and the absolute values of the roots of an integer polynomial; proofs can be found in [23, 19].

PROPOSITION 3. *Let $P \in \mathbb{Z}[x]$ be a polynomial of magnitude (d, τ) with distinct complex roots z_1 to $z_{d'}$ of respective multiplicities $m_i := \mathrm{mult}(z_i, P)$. Let* $\mathrm{Mea}(P) := |\mathrm{lcf}(P)| \cdot \prod_{i=1}^{d'} \max(1, |z_i|)^{m_i}$ *be the* Mahler measure *of P, and let* $\sigma_i := \mathrm{sep}(z_i, P) := \min_{j \neq i} |z_i - z_j|$ *be the* separation *of z_i. Then, it holds:*

(a) $\mathrm{Mea}(P) \leq \|P\|_2 \leq (n + 1) \cdot 2^\tau$.

(b) $\sum_{i,j:i \neq j} \log \max(|z_i - z_j|, |z_i - z_j|^{-1}) = \tilde{O}(d^2 + d\tau)$.

(c) $\sum_i m_i \log \mathrm{sep}(z_i, P) = \tilde{O}(d^2 + d\tau)$.

Part (b) of the above proposition implies that

$$\sum_{\nu \in \mathrm{N}} B_\nu + \sum_{\delta \in \Delta} B_\delta = \tilde{O}(d^2 + d\tau). \qquad (9)$$

3.2 Separating Forms

To compute an integer s^* with the properties from Theorem 1, we do not directly work with the set $\mathcal{F}$ of exact fractions but consider instead a set $\tilde{\mathcal{F}}$ of corresponding sufficiently good approximations. We start with the following Lemma:

LEMMA 3. *One can compute approximations of relative quality ρ of Δ and N using $\tilde{\mathcal{O}}(d^3 + d^2\tau + d^2\rho)$ bit operations.*

PROOF. This follows from Propositions 2 and 3 as any approximation $\tilde{\nu}$ of $\nu \in N$ of absolute error $2^{-B_\nu - \rho}$ constitutes an approximation of ν of relative error $2^{-\rho}$. □

In the following, let $\tilde{\mathrm{N}}$ and $\tilde{\Delta}$ be the sets obtained from running the algorithm from Lemma 3 with $\rho := \log(64d^4 \cdot c)$, where c is a fixed positive integer of size $d^{\mathcal{O}(1)}$. From the construction of $\tilde{\mathrm{N}}$, it follows that $B_{\tilde{\nu}} = B_\nu + \mathcal{O}(\log d)$. In addition, each $\tilde{\nu} \in \tilde{\mathrm{N}}$ is a dyadic number that can be represented by at most $\mathcal{O}(B_\nu + \log d)$ many bits, where ν is the corresponding exact value contained in N. A corresponding statement also holds for Δ. For deriving an SLF for G, we employ a kind of binary search on the approximations of the fractions in $\mathcal{F}$. For this, we sort $\tilde{\mathrm{N}}$ using a variant of merge sort. We actually need to modify the classical merge sort algorithm as, in our model of computation, comparisons are not of unit cost, but of cost linear in the bitsize of the operands. This poses a problem if the list to be sorted is composed of two halves of size $\Omega(d^2)$ each, say L and L', such that for all $\ell \in L$ and $\ell' \in L'$, $\ell < \ell'$. In this case, once L and L' are sorted by the respective recursive instance of the sorting procedure, the algorithm continues to compare the largest elements of these sublists with each other. By assumption, no element in L will ever be larger than any element in L', leading to $\Omega(d^2)$ comparisons of the elements in L with the largest element in L'. Notice that the largest element in L' might be of bitsize $\Omega(d\tau)$, so comparing it $\Omega(d^2)$ times requires $\Omega(d^3\tau)$ bit operations, which would exceed our claimed complexity bound. We sketch our variant of merge sort and refer to [4] for details.

LEMMA 4. *There is an algorithm sorting $\tilde{\mathrm{N}}$ in $\tilde{\mathcal{O}}(d^2 + d\tau)$ bit operations.*

PROOF. When merging two sorted sublists, instead of linearly inserting the elements in order, perform a binary search on the respective sublist and then insert the maximal prefix of that list into the merged list.
A simple analysis of this procedure reveals that every element can participate in at most $\mathcal{O}(\log d)$ many comparisons in each merge stage. Applying Proposition 3 and using (9) then yields the claim. □

By definition, $\mathcal{F}$ is the image of $\mathrm{N} \times \Delta$ under the mapping $(\nu, \delta) \mapsto \nu/\delta$. In a similar vein, we will now define a set $\tilde{\mathcal{F}} \subset \mathbb{R} \cup \{+\infty\}$ as the image of $\tilde{\mathrm{N}} \times \tilde{\Delta}$ under a slightly modified mapping $[\cdot]$, which differs from the initial mapping in the way that a pair $\tilde{\phi} = (\tilde{\nu}, \tilde{\delta})$ is either mapped to 0 or $+\infty$ if $\tilde{\nu} \ll \tilde{\delta}$ or $\tilde{\nu} \gg \tilde{\delta}$, respectively. More precisely, let $e_1, e_2 \in \mathbb{Z}$ be such that $2^{e_1} \leq \tilde{\nu} \leq 2^{e_1+1}$ and $2^{e_2} \leq \tilde{\delta} \leq 2^{e_2+1}$. If $e_1 + 4 - e_2 \leq 0$, in which case $\tilde{\nu}/\tilde{\delta} \leq 1/8$, we define $[\tilde{\phi}] := 0$. If $2^{e_1 - e_2 - 1} \geq 8d^4c$, then $\tilde{\nu}/\tilde{\delta} \geq 8d^4c$, and we define $[\tilde{\phi}] := +\infty$. If neither is the case, that is, if $1 < 2^{e_1+4-e_2}$ and $2^{e_1 - e_2 - 1} < 8d^4c$, then this implies that $\tilde{\nu}/\tilde{\delta} \in (1/32, 32d^4c)$. In this case, we define $[\tilde{\phi}]$ to be the nearest integer to $\tilde{\nu}/\tilde{\delta}$; we break ties by rounding to the smaller one. We now collect some properties of this mapping.

LEMMA 5. *Let $\phi := (\nu, \delta) \in \mathrm{N} \times \Delta$ and $\tilde{\phi} = (\tilde{\nu}, \tilde{\delta})$ be the corresponding approximation in $\tilde{\mathrm{N}} \times \tilde{\Delta}$. Then*

(a) $[\tilde{\phi}]$ can be computed using $\tilde{\mathcal{O}}(\min\{B_\delta, B_\nu\} + \log d)$ bit operations.

(b) If $\nu/\delta \in \{1, \ldots, 2d^4c\}$, then $[\tilde{\phi}] = \nu/\delta$

(c) Let $s \in \mathbb{N} \cup \{+\infty\}$, and let $\tilde{\nu}, \tilde{\nu}' \in \tilde{\mathrm{N}}$, $\tilde{\delta} \in \tilde{\Delta}$ with $\tilde{\nu}/\tilde{\delta} < \tilde{\nu}'/\tilde{\delta}$. Then, $[(\tilde{\nu}, \tilde{\delta})] \geq s$ implies $[(\tilde{\nu}', \tilde{\delta})] \geq s$.

PROOF. For any $m \in \mathbb{Z}$, computing the sign of $e_1 - e_2 - m$ can be done using $\tilde{\mathcal{O}}(\min\{|e_1|, |e_2|\} + |m|)$ bit operations as we need not compute the actual values of $e_1 - e_2 - m$, but only compare e_1 with $e_2 + m$ by counting digits until the outcome of the comparison is clear, which happens after $2\min\{|e_1|, |e_2|\} + |m|$ steps. Hence, we can already determine whether $[\tilde{\phi}] \in \{0, \infty\}$ in $\mathcal{O}(\log d + \min\{B_{\tilde{\nu}}, B_{\tilde{\delta}}\})$ bit operations. For the remaining case, we have ensured that $B_{\tilde{\delta}}$ and $B_{\tilde{\nu}}$ differ by at most $\mathcal{O}(\log d)$, and so the division $\tilde{\nu}/\tilde{\delta}$ can be performed in time $\tilde{\mathcal{O}}(\log d + \min\{B_{\tilde{\delta}}, B_{\tilde{\nu}}\})$. Computing the nearest integer to this fraction is at most as expensive. This yields the first claim.

For the second claim, notice that the relative error in $\tilde{\mathrm{N}}$ and $\tilde{\Delta}$ (compared to N and Δ) is bounded by $1/(64d^4c)$ by the choice of ρ. Hence, $\tilde{\nu}/\tilde{\delta}$ is an approximation of ν/δ with relative error of at most $1/(16d^4c)$. In particular, if $\nu/\delta \in [1, 4d^4 \cdot c]$, then $\tilde{\nu}/\tilde{\delta}$ is an approximation with *absolute* error of at most 1/4. So, if $\nu/\delta \in \{1, \ldots, 2d^4c\}$, then the ball of radius 1/4 with center $\tilde{\nu}/\tilde{\delta}$ will contain exactly one integer, namely ν/δ. Since $3/4 \leq \tilde{\nu}/\tilde{\delta} \leq 2d^4c + 1/4$, we have $[\tilde{\phi}] \notin \{\pm\infty\}$, and thus $[\tilde{\phi}]$ must be equal to ν/δ. The third claim follows directly from the definition of $[\cdot]$. □

LEMMA 6. *For $s, s' \in \{1, \ldots, d^4 \cdot c\}$ with $s \leq s'$, the cardinality of the preimage $P := P(s, s') \subset \tilde{\mathrm{N}} \times \tilde{\Delta}$ of $\{s, \ldots, s'\}$ under $[\cdot]$ can be computed using $\tilde{\mathcal{O}}(d^2 + d\tau)$ bit operations.*

PROOF. By Lemma 4, we may assume $\tilde{\mathrm{N}}$ to be sorted. For each $\tilde{\delta} \in \tilde{\Delta}$, the cardinality of $P \cap (\tilde{\mathrm{N}} \times \{\tilde{\delta}\})$ can be computed using $\tilde{\mathcal{O}}((\log d)(B_\delta + \log d))$ bit operations: Use two binary searches on $\tilde{\mathrm{N}}$ to find the maximal and minimal elements $\nu^*, \nu_* \in \tilde{\mathrm{N}}$ with $[(\nu_*, \tilde{\delta})] < s \leq s' < [(\nu^*, \tilde{\delta})]$. The cardinality of $P \cap (\tilde{\mathrm{N}} \times \{\tilde{\delta}\})$ is then the number of elements strictly between ν_* and ν^*. Lemma 5 implies correctness and a bound of $\tilde{\mathcal{O}}((\log d)(B_\delta + \log d))$ bit operations for the binary searches. Summing over all $\tilde{\delta} \in \tilde{\Delta}$ yields the bound. □

We can now prove Theorem 1: By Lemmas 3 and 4, we may already assume that N and Δ are approximated by corresponding sets $\tilde{\mathrm{N}}$ and $\tilde{\Delta}$, and that $\tilde{\mathrm{N}}$ is sorted. As $s \in S = \{1, \ldots, d^4 \cdot c\}$ is non-separating for $G = X \times Y$ if and only if $s \in \mathcal{F}$, the task can be reformulated as follows. We need to find $s^* \in S$ such that $\{s^*, \ldots, s^* + c\} \cap \mathcal{F} = \emptyset$. So, instead of working with $\mathcal{F}$ directly, we may replace $\mathcal{F}$ with $\tilde{\mathcal{F}}$ as $S \cap \mathcal{F} \subset S \cap \tilde{\mathcal{F}}$ according to part (b) of Lemma 5. Using the definition of $\tilde{\mathcal{F}}$, the goal becomes to find $s^* \in S$ such that, for all $\tilde{\phi} \in \tilde{\mathrm{N}} \times \tilde{\Delta}$, we have $[\tilde{\phi}] \notin \{s^*, \ldots, s^* + c - 1\}$, or equivalently, $|P(s^*, s^* + c - 1)| = 0$. To do so, we use a bisection procedure, where we may assume d^4 and c to be powers of two, say $2^k = d^4$ and $2^{k'} = c$. Initially, let $s_0 := 1$ and $s'_0 := d^4c$. Inductively, choose $(s_{i+1}, s'_{i+1}) \in \{(s_i, \theta_i), (\theta_i + 1, s'_i)\}$ such that $|P(s_{i+1}, s'_{i+1})|$ is minimized, where $\theta_i := (s_i + s'_i - 1)/2$ is the center of the set $S_i := \{s_i, \ldots, s'_i\}$.

By definition, the set S_i contains exactly $d^4c/2^i$ elements for $i = 0, \ldots, k$, and hence $S_k = (s_k, s_k + c - 1)$. Moreover, for $i = 0, \ldots, k-1$, it holds that $P(s_i, s'_i) = P(s_i, \theta_i) \cup P(\theta_i + 1, s'_i)$, which is a disjoint union. This implies that $|P(s_i, s'_i)| \leq |P(s_{i-1}, s'_{i-1})|/2$ for $i = 1, \ldots, k$. Since $|P(s_0, s'_0)|$ contains at most $\binom{d^2}{2} < d^4$ elements, we conclude that $P(s_k, \ldots, s_k + c - 1)$ is empty, and thus each $s \in S^* := \{s^*, \ldots, s^* - c + 1\}$, with $s^* := s_k$, is separating.

For the bit complexity, notice that there are $k = \mathcal{O}(\log d)$ recursive steps involved in the above approach, so the total bound follows from Lemma 6.

The claim on the distance to all fractions in $\mathcal{F}$ follows from the fact that $[\cdot]$ maps an element $\tilde{\phi} = (\tilde{\nu}, \tilde{\delta}) \in \tilde{\mathcal{F}}$ to the nearest integer to $\tilde{\nu}/\tilde{\delta}$ if $1/8 < \tilde{\nu}/\tilde{\delta} < 8d^4c$. For these elements, the corresponding exact fraction ν/δ differs from $\tilde{\nu}/\tilde{\delta}$ by at most $1/4$, and thus $|s - \nu/\delta| > 1/4$. For all other $\tilde{\phi}$, we either have $\nu/\delta \leq 1/2$ or $\nu/\delta \geq 2d^4c$ as $\tilde{\nu}/\tilde{\delta}$ approximates ν/δ with relative error at most $1/4$. Hence, also in this case, $|s - \nu/\delta| > 1/4$ for all $s \in S^*$.

3.3 Lifting Projections

LEMMA 7. *Let $G = X \times Y$ and $s \in \{1, \ldots, d^4c\}$ be separating for G as given in Theorem 1. Let $h \in \mathbb{Z}[x]$ be a polynomial of magnitude (d, τ) and let $Z = \{z_1, \ldots, z_{d^*}\} \subset V(h)$. Suppose that, for each $z \in Z$, there exists a pair $(x_z, y_z) \in X \times Y$ such that $l_s(x_z, y_z) = x_z + sy_z = z$. Then, we can compute approximations $(\tilde{x}_z, \tilde{y}_z)$ for all pairs (x_z, y_z) of absolute quality ρ using $\tilde{\mathcal{O}}(d^3 + d^2\tau + d\rho)$ bit operations.*

PROOF. Let i_k, j_k be such that $x_{i_k} + sy_{j_k} = z_k$. By assumption, this uniquely defines i_k, j_k for all k. Fix some $k \in \{1, \ldots, d\}$, let $i \geq 0$ and define $L_i := 2^i$. Then, approximating $z_k \in Z$ and each $y_j \in Y$ with absolute quality $L_i + \mathcal{O}(\log d)$ yields approximations $z_k^{(i)}$ and $y_j^{(i)}$ such that $|z_k^{(i)} - sy_j^{(i)} - (z_k - sy_j)| < 2^{-L_i - 1}$. Further suppose that $x^{(i)}$ is an approximation of $x \in X$ to an absolute error of 2^{-L_i-1}, and define $X_j^{(i)} := \{x \in X : |z_k^{(i)} + sy_j^{(i)} - x^{(i)}| < 2^{-L_i}\}$. Furthermore, let $M_0 := Y$ and $M_{i+1} := M_i \cap \{y_j \mid X_j^{(i+1)} \neq \emptyset\}$.

We first show that $X_j^{(i)} = \emptyset$ if $L_i > B_{y_j - y_{j_k}} + 2$ and $j \neq j_k$. Indeed, in this case, Theorem 1 implies that $|z_k - sy_i - x_i| \geq \frac{|y_j - y_{j_k}|}{4}$. Thus, $L_i > B_{y_j - y_{j_k}} + 2$ implies that $x \notin X_j^{(i)}$. If $j = j_k$, then $z_k - sy_j - x_l = x_{l_k} - x_l$, and therefore, when $L_i > B_{x_{l_k} - x_l}$ for all l, we have that $X_{j_k}^{(i)} = \{x_{l_k}\}$.

Together, this shows that for an L_i that satisfies both bounds, M_i contains exactly y_{j_k}, and $X_{j_k}^{(i)}$ contains exactly x_{l_k}. By definition, this is the preimage of z_k under l_s.

This discussion suggests the following procedure: For all pairs (k, j), compute M_i and $X_j^{(i)}$ (for increasing i) until both contain exactly one element. From Proposition 3 (c), we conclude that $i = \mathcal{O}(\log d + \log \tau)$ for any pair (j, k).

For the bit complexity of this approach, observe that the values $B_{y_j - y_{j_k}}$ and $B_{x_{l_k} - x_l}$ are bounded by $\tilde{\mathcal{O}}(d^2 + d\tau)$, so we can approximate X, Y, Z with absolute precision L_i using $\tilde{\mathcal{O}}(d^3 + d^2\tau)$ bit operations by Proposition 2, and this will suffice for all L_i that are considered before the procedure terminates, by the bound on i. Computing $X_j^{(i)}$ can be done using binary search on the approximations of X, hence requiring $\mathcal{O}(L_i \log d)$ bit operations. As we double L_i in every step, M_i has the desired form after $\log(d) \cdot \tilde{\mathcal{O}}(B_{y_j - y_{j_k}} + B_{\mathrm{sep}(x_{l_k})})$ bit operations.

For all pairs (k, j), this yields a number of bit operations bounded by $\log(d) \cdot \tilde{\mathcal{O}}(\sum_k \sum_{j \neq j_k} B_{y_j - y_{j_k}} + \sum_k B_{\mathrm{sep}(x_{l_k}, f)})$. By part (b) of Proposition 3, the first sum is bounded by $\tilde{\mathcal{O}}(d^2 + d\tau)$, and since $B_{\mathrm{sep}(x_{l_k}, f)} = \tilde{\mathcal{O}}(d^2 + d\tau)$ for each k, the total sum is bounded by $\tilde{\mathcal{O}}(d^3 + d^2\tau)$. Now, approximating X and Y with precision $2^{-\rho}$ using Proposition 2 yields the final claim. □

4. POLYNOMIAL SYSTEMS

4.1 Computation of a Separating Form

In what follows, we consider a polynomial system as in (1), with $f_i \in \mathbb{Z}[x_1, \ldots, x_n]$ polynomials of magnitude (d, τ). Let $\mathcal{S} \subset \mathbb{C}^n$ be the set of all complex solutions of this system.

Our model of computation will be augmented with an oracle for elimination polynomials as follows: Given a linear form $l = x_j + l_{j+1}x_{j+1} + \cdots + l_nx_n$ with integer coefficients, the oracle returns an elimination polynomial $E^l \in \mathbb{Z}[x]$ for the system (1) along l. We further denote Π as an upper bound on the bit complexity of calling the oracle for a linear form of bitsize $\mathcal{O}(n \log d)$. In Section 2, we have already seen how to realize an oracle for elimination polynomials by means of resultant computation, where $E^l = R^l$ is the hidden variable resultant of the polynomials f_i^* obtained after the coordinate transformation $x_j \mapsto x_j - \sum_{i \neq j} l_i x_i$. However, since there exist also other ways to compute elimination polynomials (e.g. using Gröbner Basis), we decided to keep the following considerations as general as possible.

When calling our oracle for $l = x_i$, we obtain the set $X_i := V(E^{x_i})$, which contains the projections of the solutions in $\mathcal{S}$ on the i-th coordinate. Thus, we have $\mathcal{S} \subseteq \mathcal{G} := X_1 \times \ldots \times X_n$. For $I = \{i_1, \ldots, i_j\}$, with $1 \leq i_1 < \ldots < i_j \leq n$ and $1 \leq j \leq n$, let $\pi_I : \mathbb{C}^n \mapsto \mathbb{C}^j$ be the projection on the coordinates $I = \{i_1, \ldots, i_j\}$. In addition, for any linear form $l : \mathbb{C}^j \to \mathbb{C}$, we define $l^I := l \circ \pi_I$. That is, if $l = l_1x_1 + \cdots + l_jx_j$, then $l^I = l_1 \cdot x_{i_1} + \cdots + l_j \cdot x_{i_j}$. In analogous manner to the two-dimensional case, we say that a linear form $l : \mathbb{C}^j \to \mathbb{C}$ is separating for a set $M \subset \mathbb{C}^j$ if l restricted to M is injective.

LEMMA 8. *Let l_1, l_2 be SLFs for $\pi_I(\mathcal{S})$ and $\pi_J(\mathcal{S})$, respectively, where I and J are disjoint subsets of $\{1, \ldots, n\}$. Let s be separating for $Y_1 \times Y_2 := V(E^{l_1^I}) \times V(E^{l_2^J})$, with $E^{l_1^I}$ and $E^{l_2^J}$ elimination polynomials along l_1^I and l_2^J, respectively. Then, the linear form $l_1^I + s \cdot l_2^J$ is separating for $\pi_{I \cup J}(\mathcal{S})$.*

PROOF. This follows directly from the definitions and the choice of l and s. □

Following a divide and conquer strategy, we can now recursively compute an SLF for $\mathcal{S}$ starting with the projections of $\mathcal{S}$ on each of the coordinates x_i. We give details: For simplicity, suppose that n is a power of two. Write $X[i, j] := \pi_{\{i, \ldots, j\}}(\mathcal{S})$ and consider the complete binary tree with root $X[1, n]$, and each node $X[i, j]$ with $|i - j| \geq 1$ having children $X[i, (i + j - 1)/2], X[(i + j + 1)/2, j]$. We aim to compute SLFs for the set at the respective node without actually computing this set. First, for each $i = 1, \ldots, n$, we compute $X_i = V(E^{x_i}) \supset X[i]$ by querying the oracle for E^{x_i}, and then computing its roots. Then, for $i = 1, \ldots, n/2$, Theorem 1 yields an SLF $x + s_i y$, with $s_i \leq d^{4n}$, for $X_{2i-1} \times X_{2i}$, and thus also for $X[2i-1, 2i]$. For the inductive step, assume we can compute SLFs for the sets at all nodes in the levels 1 to j of the tree, and consider some node on level $j+1$, say w.l.o.g $X[1, 2^j]$ with children $X[1, 2^{j-1}]$ and $X[2^{j-1}+1, 2^j]$. Let $l_1 = \sum_{i=1}^{2^{j-1}} l'_i x_i$ and $l_2 = \sum_{i=1}^{2^{j-1}} l''_i x_i$ be SLFs for these sets, respectively, and suppose their coefficients have absolute values bounded by $d^{4n(j-1)}$. We obtain $E^{l_1^I}$ and $E^{l_2^J}$ by calling the oracle twice, where $I = \{1, \ldots, 2^{j-1}\}$ and $J = \{2^{j-1}+1, \ldots, 2^j\}$. Again, Theorem 1 yields a separating form $x + sy$ for $V(E^{l_1^I}) \times V(E^{l_2^J})$. By Lemma 8, the linear form $l = \sum_{i=1}^{2^{j-1}} l'_i x_i + s \cdot \sum_{i=1}^{2^{j-1}} l''_i x_{2^{j-1}+i}$ is separating for $X[1, 2^j]$. Since the absolute values of the coefficients increase by a factor of at most d^{4n}, l has coefficients of absolute value at most d^{4nj}. Hence, after $\log n$ recursive steps, we obtain am SLF for $\mathcal{S} = X[1, n]$ with coefficients of absolute value $d^{4n \log n}$ or less.

THEOREM 2. *The above algorithm computes an SLF for $\mathcal{S}$ with integer coefficients bounded by $d^{4n \log n}$ using*

$$\tilde{O}(n(D^3 + D^2 L) + n \cdot \Pi),$$

bit operations, where (D, L) is an upper bound on the magnitude of all elimination polynomials produced by the algorithm, and Π is an upper bound on the bit complexity of calling the oracle for a linear form l of bitsize $\mathcal{O}(n \log d)$. The algorithm is deterministic if the oracle is deterministic.

If we use the Las Vegas method from Section 2 for resultant computation to realize the oracle, then the above bound transforms into the bound (3) from the introduction.

PROOF. The oracle is called $2n-1$ times, and Theorem 1 is invoked $n-1$ times. For the second claim, suppose that the oracle is realized by means of a resultant computation as proposed in Section 2. Then, using Corollary 1 (a), we see that each computation of an elimination polynomial E^l needs $\Pi = \tilde{O}(n^{(n-1)(\omega+1)}(nd+\tau)d^{(\omega+2)n-\omega-1})$ bit operations in expectation as l has bitsize $\mathcal{O}(n \log d)$. In addition, the magnitude of each elimination polynomial is bounded by $(d^n, \tilde{O}((nd)^{n-1}(nd+\tau)))$, which shows the second claim. □

We can also slightly modify the above algorithm to compute a sufficiently large set of SLFs from which we can then choose a linear form such that R^l is a strong elimination polynomial. For this, we assume that the oracle is realized by means of resultant computation, that is, we have $E^l = R^l$. Now, suppose that SLFs $l_1 = \sum_{i=1}^{n/2} l'_i x_i$ and $l_2 = \sum_{i=1}^{n/2} l''_i x_i$ for the sets $X[1, n/2]$ and $X[n/2+1, n]$ are computed as above. In addition, let $E^{l_1^I}$ and $E^{l_2^J}$ be the elimination polynomials along l_1^I and l_2^J, with $I = \{1, \ldots, n/2\}$ and $J = \{n/2+1, \ldots, n\}$. By Theorem 1, we can compute a set $S^* := \{s^*, \ldots, s^* + 2nd\} \subset \{1, \ldots, 2nd \cdot d^{4n}\}$ such that $x + sy$ is separating for $V(E^{l_1^I}) \times V(E^{l_2^J})$ for all $s \in S^*$. This costs at most $\tilde{O}(d^{3n} + d^{2n}(nd)^{n-1}(nd+\tau))$ bit operations, and the linear form $l(s) = \sum_{i=1}^{2^{j-1}} l'_i x_i + s \cdot \sum_{i=1}^{2^{j-1}} l''_i x_{2^{j-1}+i}$ is separating for $\mathcal{S}$ for each $s \in S^*$. We conclude:

THEOREM 3. *There is a Las Vegas algorithm with expected bit complexity* (3) *to compute a set $S^* := \{s^*, \ldots, s^* + 2nd\} \subset \{1, \ldots, 2nd \cdot d^{4n}\}$ and a linear form $l(s) = \sum_{i=1}^{n}(a_{0i} + a_{1i}s) \cdot x_i \in \mathbb{Z}[s]$ of bitsize $\tilde{O}(n \log d)$, such that $l(s)$ is separating for all $s \in S^*$.*

Combining Lemma 1 and Lemma 2 directly yields the following result:

COROLLARY 2. *Suppose that the system (1) has no solution at infinity. Then, there is a Las Vegas algorithm with expected bit complexity (3) to compute an SLF l with coefficients of bitsize $\mathcal{O}(n \log d)$ and the corresponding hidden-variable resultant R^l, such that $V(R^l) = \mathcal{S}^l$.*

4.2 Computing the Solutions

We first consider the case where (1) has no solution at infinity. By the last subsection, we may assume that, for $j = 1, \ldots, \log n$ and $k = 0, \ldots, n/2^j - 1$, we have already computed SLFs $l_{j,k} = \sum_{i=1}^{2^j} l_i^{(j,k)} x_i$ for the sets $X[k \cdot 2^j + 1, (k+1) \cdot 2^j]$, respectively. We may further assume that $l = l_{\log n, 0}$ is separating for the solutions of our system and that R^l is a strong elimination polynomial. Notice that $l_1^{(j,k)} = 1$ for all (j,k) and each coefficient $l_i^{(j,k)}$ is an integer of bit size $\tilde{O}(n \log d)$. Due to the construction of the $l_{j,k}$'s, it holds that

$$l_{j,k}(\mathbf{x}, \mathbf{y}) = l_{j-1,2k+1}(\mathbf{x}) + s_{j,k} \cdot l_{j-1,2k+2}(\mathbf{y}). \qquad (10)$$

with integers $s_{j,k}$ of bitsize $\tilde{O}(n \log d)$, $\mathbf{x} = (x_1, \ldots, x_{2^{j-1}})$ and $\mathbf{y} = (y_1, \ldots, y_{2^{j-1}})$. Let

$$\phi_{j,k} : (x_1, \ldots, x_n) \mapsto \sum_{i=1}^{2^j} l_i^{(j,k)} x_{2^j \cdot k + i}$$

be the mapping induced by the linear form $l_{j,k}$, that is, $\phi_{j,k}$ only operates on the variables $x_{2^j k+1}$ to $x_{2^{j+1}}$. We further define $\phi_{0,k} : (x_1, \ldots, x_n) \mapsto x_{k+1}$ as the projection onto the $k+1$-th coordinate for all k, and

$$\phi_j := \phi_{j,0} \times \cdots \times \phi_{j,n/2^j-1}$$

as the cartesian product of all $\phi_{j,k}$ for a fixed j.

Now, we recursively apply Lemma 7 to compute the image $\Phi_j := \phi_j(\mathcal{S})$ of $\mathcal{S}$ under ϕ_j. Notice that $\mathcal{G} = \Phi_0$ and $V(R^l) = \mathcal{S}^l = \Phi_{\log n}$ as R^l is a strong elimination polynomial. Suppose that Φ_j is already computed for some j, in particular, we know the image $\Phi_{j,k} = \phi_{j,k}(\mathcal{S})$ of $\mathcal{S}$ under the mapping $\phi_{j,k}$. Further notice that the mapping $\phi : (x, y) \mapsto x + s_{j,k} y$ is injective on the product $\Phi_{j-1,2k+1} \times \Phi_{j-1,2k+2}$, and that it maps the image of $\mathcal{S}$ under $\phi_{j-1,2k+1} \times \phi_{j-1,2k+2}$ one-to-one onto $\Phi_{j,k}$. Hence, using Lemma 7, we may compute the inverse of each point in $\Phi_{j,k}$ under the mapping ϕ, which yields $(\phi_{j-1,2k+1} \times \phi_{j-1,2k+2})(\mathcal{S})$. Thus, after $\log n$ recursive steps, we obtain $\mathcal{S}$.

THEOREM 4. *If the system* (1) *has no solutions at infinity, then the above algorithm computes approximations (in terms of isolating regions) of absolute quality ρ of $\mathcal{S}$ using*

$$\tilde{O}(n^{(n-1)(\omega+1)+1}(nd+\tau)d^{(\omega+2)n-\omega-1} + nd^n \rho)$$

bit operations in expectation.

PROOF. There are $\log n$ levels to be considered, so we employ Lemma 7 at most n times. The involved polynomials are elimination polynomials along the linear forms $l_{j,k}$, which are of magnitude $(d^n, \tilde{O}((nd)^{n-1}(nd+\tau)))$. This yields the bound from (3) for reconstructing all solutions of the given system. We can now compute absolute approximations of quality ρ of these solutions by computing corresponding approximations of the roots of the polynomials R^{x_i}. Hence, the claimed bound follows directly from Corollary 1 (b). □

We now remove the condition on the input system to have no infinite solution. We can easily check whether this condition is fulfilled. Namely, (4) has no infinite solution if and only if $\mathrm{Res}(\bar{F}_1, \ldots, \bar{F}_n) \neq 0$. The following Lemma shows that this can be achieved, with probability at least 1/2, by means of a coordinate transformation, see [4] for a proof.

LEMMA 9. *Let λ_1 to λ_n be a randomly chosen non-negative integers with $\lambda_i \leq 2d^n$ for all i. Then, with probability at least 1/2, the transformed system*

$$F_1^*(x_1, \ldots, x_{n+1}) = \cdots = F_n^*(x_1, \ldots, x_{n+1}) = 0, \quad (11)$$

with $F_i^*(x_1, \ldots, x_{n+1}) = F_i(x_1, \ldots, x_n, x_{n+1}+\lambda_1 x_1+\cdots \lambda_n x_n)$, has no solution at infinity. There is a Las-Vegas algorithm to compute such λ_i's and the polynomials F_i^* with expected bit complexity bounded by (3).

Using this Lemma, we can first transform (1) into a system (11) without roots at infinity. Then, we can compute all solutions of (11) and recover the solutions of (1) via the backward transformation $x_{n+1} \mapsto x_{n+1} - \sum_{i=1}^n \lambda_i \cdot x_i$. That is, each solution $\mathbf{x}^* = (x_1^*, \ldots, x_n^*, 1) \in \mathcal{S}^*$ of (11) maps to a solution $\mathbf{x} = (x_1, \ldots, x_n, x_{n+1}) = (x_1^*, \ldots, x_n^*, x_{n+1}^* - \sum_{i=1}^n \lambda_i x_i^*)$ of the initial system. Using only approximate computation, we cannot directly show that $x_{n+1} = x_{n+1}^* - \sum_{i=1}^n \lambda_i x_i^*$ is equal to zero, and thus a solution $\mathbf{x}$ at infinity cannot directly be verified as such. However, by increasing the precision, we either obtain that $x_n \neq 0$ or we may conclude that $|x_i/x_n|$ is larger than the bound from Corollary 1 (b) on the absolute value of a solution of our system. In the first case, $\mathbf{x}$ is a finite solution, whereas in the second case, $\mathbf{x}$ is an infinite solution. A simple analysis of this approach yields the following result; see [4] for details.

THEOREM 5. *There exists a Las-Vegas algorithm to compute isolating regions of all solutions of (1) whose cost in expectation is bounded by (3).*

5. REFERENCES

[1] M.-E. Alonso, E. Becker, M. F. Roy, and T. Wörmann. *Algorithms in Algebraic Geometry and Applications*, chapter Zeros, multiplicities, and idempotents for zero-dimensional systems, pages 1–15. Birkhäuser Basel, Basel, 1996.

[2] R. Becker, M. Sagraloff, V. Sharma, and C. Yap. A simple near-optimal subdivision algorithm for complex root isolation based on the pellet test and newton iteration. *CoRR*, abs/1509.06231, 2015.

[3] Y. Bouzidi, S. Lazard, G. Moroz, M. Pouget, F. Rouillier, and M. Sagraloff. Improved algorithms for solving bivariate systems via Rational Univariate Representations. Research report, Inria, June 2015.

[4] C. Brand and M. Sagraloff. On the complexity of solving zero-dimensional polynomial systems via projection. *CoRR*, abs/1604.08944, 2016.

[5] J. F. Canny. Generalised characteristic polynomials. *J. Symb. Comput.*, 9(3):241–250, 1990.

[6] J. F. Canny, E. Kaltofen, and L. Yagati. Solving systems of nonlinear polynomial equations faster. In *ISSAC*, pages 121–128, 1989.

[7] J. Cheng, X. Gao, and L. Guo. Root isolation of zero-dimensional polynomial systems with linear univariate representation. *J. Symb. Comput.*, 47(7):843–858, 2012.

[8] D. Cox, J. Little, and D. O'Shea. *Using Algebraic Geometry*. Graduate Texts in Mathematics. Springer New York, 2005.

[9] A. Dickenstein and I. Z. Emiris. *Solving Polynomial Equations: Foundations, Algorithms, and Applications.* Springer Publishing Company, Incorporated, 1st edition, 2010.

[10] D. I. Diochnos, I. Z. Emiris, and E. P. Tsigaridas. On the asymptotic and practical complexity of solving bivariate systems over the reals. *J. Symb. Comput.*, 44(7):818–835, 2009.

[11] P. Emeliyanenko and M. Sagraloff. On the complexity of solving a bivariate polynomial system. In *ISSAC*, pages 154–161, 2012.

[12] I. Z. Emiris, B. Mourrain, and E. P. Tsigaridas. The DMM bound: multivariate (aggregate) separation bounds. In *ISSAC*, pages 243–250, 2010.

[13] I. Z. Emiris and V. Y. Pan. Improved algorithms for computing determinants and resultants. *J. Complexity*, 21(1):43–71, 2005.

[14] J. Faugère, P. Gianni, D. Lazard, and T. Mora. Efficient computation of zero-dimensional gröbner bases by change of ordering. *J. Symb. Comput.*, 16(4):329 – 344, 1993.

[15] I. Gelfand, M. Kapranov, and A. Zelevinsky. *Discriminants, Resultants, and Multidimensional Determinants.* Modern Birkhäuser Classics. Birkhäuser Boston, 2009.

[16] L. González-Vega et al. An improved upper complexity bound for the topology computation of a real algebraic plane curve. *J. Complexity*, 12(4):527–544, 1996.

[17] A. Hashemi and D. Lazard. Sharper complexity bounds for zero-dimensional gröbner bases and polynomial system solving. *International Journal of Algebra and Computation*, 21(05):703–713, 2011.

[18] J. Heintz. Definability and fast quantifier elimination in algebraically closed fields. *Theor. Comput. Sci.*, 24(3):239 – 277, 1983.

[19] A. Kobel and M. Sagraloff. On the complexity of computing with planar algebraic curves. *J. Complexity*, 31(2):206–236, 2015.

[20] Y. N. Lakshman. *Effective Methods in Algebraic Geometry*, chapter A Single Exponential Bound on the Complexity of Computing Gröbner Bases of Zero Dimensional Ideals, pages 227–234. Birkhäuser Boston, Boston, MA, 1991.

[21] D. Lazard. Resolution des systemes d'equations algebriques. *Theor. Comput. Sci.*, 15(1):77 – 110, 1981.

[22] D. Lazard. Gröbner-bases, gaussian elimination and resolution of systems of algebraic equations. In *EUROCAL*, pages 146–156, 1983.

[23] K. Mehlhorn, M. Sagraloff, and P. Wang. From approximate factorization to root isolation with application to cylindrical algebraic decomposition. *J. Symb. Comput.*, 66:34 – 69, 2015.

[24] B. Mourrain, V. Y. Pan, and O. Ruatta. Accelerated solution of multivariate polynomial systems of equations. *SIAM J. Comput.*, 32(2):435–454, 2003.

[25] V. Y. Pan. Univariate polynomials: Nearly optimal algorithms for numerical factorization and root-finding. *J. Symb. Comput.*, 33(5):701–733, 2002.

[26] J. Renegar. On the worst-case arithmetic complexity of approximating zeros of systems of polynomials. *SIAM J. Comput.*, 18(2):350–370, 1989.

[27] F. Rouillier. Solving zero-dimensional systems through the rational univariate representation. *Applicable Algebra in Engineering, Communication and Computing*, 9(5):433–461.

[28] A. Storjohann. The shifted number system for fast linear algebra on integer matrices. *J. Complexity*, 21(4):609–650, 2005.

[29] B. Sturmfels. *Solving systems of polynomial equations.* Number 97. American Mathematical Soc., 2002.

[30] J. von zur Gathen and J. Gerhard. *Modern Computer Algebra.* Cambridge University Press, Cambridge, UK, 3rd edition, 2013.

Division and Slope Factorization of p-Adic Polynomials

Xavier Caruso
Université Rennes 1
xavier.caruso@normalesup.org

David Roe
University of Pittsburgh
roed.math@gmail.com

Tristan Vaccon
JSPS–Rikkyo University
vaccon@rikkyo.ac.jp

ABSTRACT

We study two important operations on polynomials defined over complete discrete valuation fields: Euclidean division and factorization. In particular, we design a simple and efficient algorithm for computing slope factorizations, based on Newton iteration. One of its main features is that we avoid working with fractional exponents. We pay particular attention to stability, and analyze the behavior of the algorithm using several precision models.

Keywords

Algorithms, p-adic precision, Newton polygon, factorization

1. INTRODUCTION

Polynomial factorization is a fundamental problem in computational algebra. The algorithms used to solve it depend on the ring of coefficients, with finite fields, local fields, number fields and rings of integers of particular interest to number theorists. In this article, we focus on a task that forms a building block for factorization algorithms over complete discrete valuation fields: the decomposition into factors based on the slopes of the Newton polygon.

The Newton polygon of a polynomial $f(X) = \sum a_i X^i$ over such a field is given by the convex hull of the points $(i, \mathrm{val}(a_i))$ and the point $(0, +\infty)$. The lower boundary of this polygon consists of line segments $(x_j, y_j) - (x_{j+1}, y_{j+1})$ of slope s_j. The slope factorization of $f(X)$ expresses $f(X)$ as a product of polynomials $g_j(X)$ with degree $x_{j+1} - x_j$ whose roots all have valuation $-s_j$. Our main result is a new algorithm for computing these $g_j(X)$.

Polynomial factorization over local fields has seen a great deal of progress recently [7–10] following an algorithm of Montes. Slope factorization provides a subroutine in such algorithms [10, Section 2]. Note that our algorithm lifts a *slope factor* corresponding to a segment of the Newton polygon, rather than the irreducible factor found by single factor lifting [8]. The slope factors are easier to find; as a consequence our iteration is less involved. We also remark that the methods introduced in this paper extend partially to the non-commutative setting and appear this way as an essential building block in several decomposition algorithms of p-adic Galois representations and p-adic differential equations [3].

Any p-adic computation must work with approximations modulo finite powers of p and include an analysis of how the precision of the variables evolve over the computation. We work with precision models developed by the same authors [4, Section 4.2], focusing on the lattice and Newton models. As part of the analysis of the slope factorization algorithm, we describe how the precision of the quotient and remainder depend on the input polynomials in Euclidean division.

Main Results. Suppose that the Newton polygon of $P(X) = \sum_{i=0}^{n} a_i X^i$ has an extremal point at abscissa d. Set $A_0 = \sum_{i=0}^{d} a_i X^i$, $V_0 = 1$ and

$$A_{i+1} = A_i + (V_i P \,\%\, A_i)$$
$$B_{i+1} = P \,/\!/\, A_{i+1}$$
$$V_{i+1} = (2V_i - V_i^2 B_{i+1}) \,\%\, A_{i+1}.$$

where $S \,/\!/\, T$ and $S \,\%\, T$ denotes the quotient and the remainder in the Euclidean division of S by T respectively. Our main result is Theorem 4.4, which states that the sequence (A_i) converges quadratically to a divisor of P. This provides a quasi-optimal simple-to-implement algorithm for computing slope factorizations. We moreover carry out a careful study of the precision and, applying a strategy coming from [4], we end up with an algorithm that outputs optimal results regarding to accuracy.

In order to prove Theorem 4.4, we also determine the precision of the quotient and remainder in Euclidean division, which may be of independent interest. These results are found in Section 3.2.

Organization of the paper. After setting notation, in Section 2 we recall various models for tracking precision in polynomial arithmetic. We give some background on Newton polygons and explain how using lattices to store precision can allow for extra *diffuse* p-adic digits that are not localized on any single coefficient.

In Section 3, we consider Euclidean division. We describe in Theorem 3.2 how the Newton polygons of the quotient and remainder depend on numerator and denominator. We use this result to describe in Proposition 3.3 the precision evolution in Euclidean division using the Newton precision model. We then compare the precision performance of Euclidean division in the jagged, Newton and lattice models experimentally, finding different behavior depending on the modulus.

ISSAC '16, July 19–22, 2016, Waterloo, ON, Canada

ISBN 978-1-4503-4380-0/16/07...$15.00

DOI: https://dx.doi.org/10.1145/2930889.2930897

Finally, in Section 4 we describe our slope factorization algorithm, which is based on a Newton iteration. Unlike other algorithms for slope factorization, ours does not require working with fractional exponents (compare for instance with [13, § 6]). In Theorem 4.1 we define a sequence of polynomials that will converge to the factors determined by an extremal point in the Newton polygon. We then discuss the precision behavior of the algorithm.

Notations. Throughout this paper, we fix a complete discrete valuation field K; we denote by $\mathrm{val} : K \to \mathbb{Z} \cup \{+\infty\}$ the valuation on it and by W its ring of integers (*i.e.* the set of elements with nonnegative valuation). We assume that val is normalized so that it is surjective and denote by π a uniformizer of K, that is an element of valuation 1. Denoting by $S \subset W$ a fixed set of representatives of the classes modulo π and assuming $0 \in S$, one can prove that each element in $x \in K$ can be represented uniquely as a convergent series:

$$x = \sum_{i=\mathrm{val}(x)}^{+\infty} a_i \pi^i \quad \text{with} \quad a_i \in S. \tag{1}$$

The two most important examples are the field of p-adic numbers $K = \mathbb{Q}_p$ and the field of Laurent series $K = k((t))$ over a field k. The valuation on them are the p-adic valuation and the usual valuation of a Laurent series respectively. Their ring of integers are therefore $\mathbb{Z}_p$ and $k[[t]]$ respectively. A distinguished uniformizer is p and t whereas a possible set S is $\{0, \ldots, p-1\}$ and k respectively. The reader who is not familiar with complete discrete valuation fields may assume (without sacrifying too much to the generality) that K is one of the two aforementioned examples.

In what follows, the notation $K[X]$ refers to the ring of univariate polynomials with coefficients in K. The subspace of polynomials of degree at most n (resp. exactly n) is denoted by $K_{\leq n}[X]$ (resp. $K_n[X]$).

2. PRECISION DATA

Elements in K (and *a fortiori* in $K[X]$) carry an infinite amount of information. They thus cannot be stored entirely in the memory of a computer and have to be truncated. Elements of K are usually represented by truncating Eq.(1) as follows:

$$x = \sum_{i=v}^{N-1} a_i \pi^i + O(\pi^N) \tag{2}$$

where N is an integer called the *absolute precision* and the notation $O(\pi^N)$ means that the coefficients a_i for $i \geq N$ are discarded. If $N > v$ and $a_v \neq 0$, the integer v is the valuation of x and the difference $N - v$ is called the *relative precision*. Alternatively, one may think that the writing (2) represents a subset of K which consists of all elements in K for which the a_i's in the range $[v, N-1]$ are those specified. From the metric point of view, this is a ball (centered at any point inside it).

It is worth noting that tracking precision using this representation is rather easy. For example, if x and y are known with absolute (resp. relative) precision N_x and N_y respectively, one can compute the sum $x+y$ (resp. the product xy) at absolute (resp. relative) precision $\min(N_x, N_y)$. Computations with p-adic and Laurent series are often handled this way on symbolic computation softwares.

2.1 Precision for polynomials

The situation is much more subtle when we are working with a collection of elements of K (*e.g.* a polynomial) and not just a single one. Indeed, several precision data may be considered and, as we shall see later, each of them has its own interest. Below we detail three models of precision for the special case of polynomials.

Flat precision. The simplest method for tracking the precision of a polynomial is to record each coefficient modulo a fixed power of π. While easy to analyze and implement, this method suffers when applied to polynomials whose Newton polygons are far from flat.

Jagged precision. The next obvious approach is to record the precision of each coefficient individually, a method that we will refer to as *jagged* precision. Jagged precision is commonly implemented in computer algebra systems, since standard polynomial algorithms can be written for generic coefficient rings. However, these generic implementations often have suboptimal precision behavior, since combining intermediate expressions into a final answer may lose precision. Moreover, when compared to the Newton precision model, extra precision in the middle coefficients, above the Newton polygon of the remaining terms, will have no effect on any of the values of that polynomial.

Newton precision. We now move to *Newton precision* data. They can be actually seen as particular instances of jagged precision but there exist for them better representations and better algorithms.

Definition 2.1. A *Newton function of degree n* is a convex function $\varphi : [0, n] \to \mathbb{R} \cup \{+\infty\}$ which is piecewise affine, which takes a finite value at n and whose epigraph[1] $\mathrm{Epi}(\varphi)$ have extremal points with integral abscissa.

Remark 2.2. The datum of φ is equivalent to that of $\mathrm{Epi}(\varphi)$ and they can easily be represented and manipulated on a computer.

We recall that one can attach a Newton function to each polynomial. If $P(X) = \sum_{i=0}^{n} a_i X^i \in K_n[X]$, we define its Newton polygon $\mathrm{NP}(P)$ as the convex hull of the points $(i, \mathrm{val}(a_i))$ $(1 \leq i \leq n)$ together with the point at infinity $(0, +\infty)$ and then its Newton function $\mathrm{NF}(P) : [0, n] \to \mathbb{R}$ as the unique function whose epigraph is $\mathrm{NP}(P)$. It is well known [6, Section 1.6] that:

$$\mathrm{NP}(P+Q) \subset \mathrm{Conv}\big(\mathrm{NP}(P) \cup \mathrm{NP}(Q)\big)$$
$$\mathrm{NP}(PQ) = \mathrm{NP}(P) + \mathrm{NP}(Q)$$

where Conv denotes the convex hull and the plus sign stands for the Minkowski sum. This translates to:

$$\mathrm{NF}(P+Q) \geq \mathrm{NF}(P) \oplus \mathrm{NF}(Q)$$
$$\mathrm{NF}(PQ) = \mathrm{NF}(P) \otimes \mathrm{NF}(Q)$$

where the operations $\oplus$ and $\otimes$ are defined accordingly. There exist classical algorithms for computing these two operations whose complexity is quasi-linear with respect to the degree.

In a similar fashion, Newton functions can be used to model precision: given a Newton function φ of degree n, we agree that a polynomial of degree at most n is given at

[1] Recall that the epigraph is the region above the graph.

precision $O(\varphi)$ when, for all i, its i-th coefficient is given at precision $O(\pi^{\lceil \varphi(i) \rceil})$ (where $\lceil \cdot \rceil$ is the ceiling function). In the sequel, we shall write $O(\varphi) = \sum_{i=0}^{n} O(\pi^{\lceil \varphi(i) \rceil}) \cdot X^i$ and use the notation $\sum_{i=0}^{n} a_i X^i + O(\varphi)$ (where the coefficients a_i are given by truncated series) to refer to a polynomial given at precision $O(\varphi)$.

It is easily checked that if P and Q are two polynomials known at precision $O(\varphi_P)$ and $O(\varphi_Q)$ respectively, then $P+Q$ is known at precision $O(\varphi_P \oplus \varphi_Q)$ and PQ is known at precision $O\big((\varphi_P \otimes \mathrm{NF}(Q)) \oplus (\mathrm{NF}(P) \otimes \varphi_Q)\big)$.

Definition 2.3. Let $P = P_{\mathrm{app}} + O(\varphi_P)$. We say that the Newton precision $O(\varphi_P)$ of P is *nondegenerate* if $\varphi_P \geq \mathrm{NF}(P_{\mathrm{app}})$ and $\varphi_P(x) > y$ for all extremal point (x, y) of $\mathrm{NP}(P_{\mathrm{app}})$.

We notice that, under the conditions of the above definition, the Newton polygon of P is well defined. Indeed, if δP is any polynomial whose Newton function is not less than φ_P, we have $\mathrm{NP}(P_{\mathrm{app}} + \delta P) = \mathrm{NP}(P_{\mathrm{app}})$.

Lattice precision. The notion of *lattice precision* was developed in [4]. It encompasses the two previous models and has the decisive advantage of precision optimality. As a counterpart, it might be very space-consuming and time-consuming for polynomials of large degree.

Definition 2.4. Let V be a finite dimensional vector space over K. A lattice in V is a sub-W-module of V generated by a K-basis of V.

We fix an integer n. A lattice precision datum for a polynomial of degree n is a lattice H lying in the vector space $K_{\leq n}[X]$. We shall sometimes denote it $O(H)$ in order to emphasize that it should be considered as a precision datum. The notation $P_{\mathrm{app}}(X) + O(H)$ then refers to any polynomial in the W-affine space $P_{\mathrm{app}}(X) + H$. Tracking lattice precision can be done using differentials as shown in [4, Lemma 3.4 and Proposition 3.12]: if $f : K_{\leq n}[X] \to K_{\leq m}[X]$ denotes any strictly differentiable function with surjective differential, under mild assumption on H, we have:

$$f(P_{\mathrm{app}}(X) + H) = f(P_{\mathrm{app}}(X)) + f'(P_{\mathrm{app}}(X))(H)$$

where $f'(P_{\mathrm{app}}(X))$ denotes the differential of f at $P_{\mathrm{app}}(X)$. The equality sign reflets the optimality of the method.

As already mentioned, the jagged precision model is a particular case of the lattice precision. Indeed, a precision of the shape $\sum_{i=0}^{n} O(\pi^{N_i}) X^i$ corresponds to the lattice generated by the elements $\pi^{N_i} X^i$ $(0 \leq i \leq n)$. This remark is the origin of the notion of *diffused digits of precision* introduced in [5, Definition 2.3]. We shall use it repeatedly in the sequel in order to compare the behaviour of the three aforementioned precision data in concrete situations.

3. EUCLIDEAN DIVISION

Euclidean division provides a building block for many algorithms associated to polynomials in one variable. In order to analyze the precision behavior of such algorithms, we need to first understand the precision attached to the quotient and remainder when dividing two polynomials. In the sequel, we use the notation $A \,/\!\!/\, B$ and $A \,\%\, B$ for the polynomials satisfying $A = (A \,/\!\!/\, B) \cdot B + (A \,\%\, B)$ and $\deg(A \,\%\, B) < \deg(B)$.

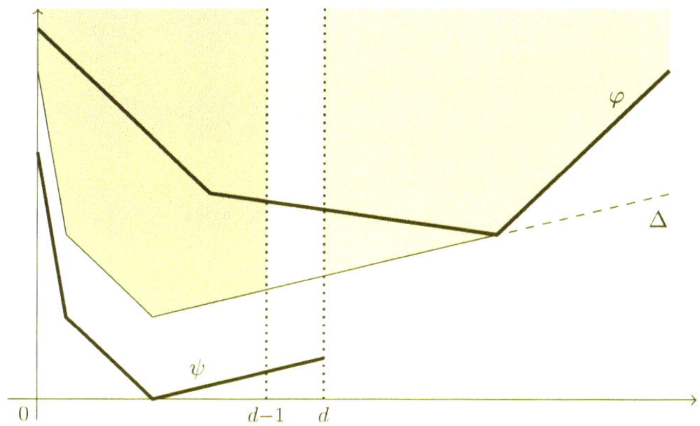

Figure 1: Euclidean division of Newton functions

3.1 Euclidean division of Newton functions

Definition 3.1. Let φ and ψ be two Newton functions of degree n and d respectively. Set $\lambda = \psi(d) - \psi(d-1)$. Letting Δ be the greatest affine function of slope λ with $\Delta \leq \varphi_{|[d,n]}$ and $\delta = \Delta(d) - \psi(d)$, we define:

$$\begin{aligned} \varphi \,\%\, \psi &= \varphi_{|[0,d-1]} \oplus \big(\psi_{|[0,d-1]} + \delta\big) \\ \varphi \,/\!\!/\, \psi :\ [0, n-d] &\to \mathbb{R} \cup \{+\infty\} \\ x &\mapsto \inf_{h \geq 0} \varphi(x + d + h) - \lambda h. \end{aligned}$$

Figure 1 illustrates the definition: if φ and ψ are the functions represented on the diagram, the epigraph of $\varphi \,\%\, \psi$ is the blue area whereas that of $\varphi \,/\!\!/\, \psi$ is the green area translated by $(-d, 0)$. It is an easy exercise (left to the reader) to design quasi-linear algorithms for computing $\varphi \,\%\, \psi$ and $\varphi \,/\!\!/\, \psi$.

Theorem 3.2. *Given $A, B \in K[X]$ with $B \neq 0$, we have:*

$$NF(A \,\%\, B) \geq NF(A) \,\%\, NF(B) \tag{3}$$

$$\text{and} \quad NF(A \,/\!\!/\, B) \geq NF(A) \,/\!\!/\, NF(B) \tag{4}$$

Proof. Write $A = A_{<d} + A_{\geq d}$ where $A_{<d}$ (resp. $A_{\geq d}$) consists of monomials of A of degree less than d (resp. at least d). Noting that:

$$A \,\%\, B = A_{<d} + (A_{\geq d} \,\%\, B) \quad \text{and} \quad A \,/\!\!/\, B = A_{\geq d} \,/\!\!/\, B$$

we may assume that $A = A_{\geq d}$.

Let us now prove Eq. (3). Replacing B by $c^{-1} B$ where c denotes the leading coefficient of B, we may assume that B is monic. Using linearity, we may further assume that A is a monomial. Set $R_n = X^n \,\%\, B$. The relation we have to prove is:

$$\mathrm{NF}(R_n)(x) \geq \mathrm{NF}(B)(x) - \lambda(n - d) \quad \text{for } n \geq d.$$

We proceed by induction. The initialisation is clear because R_d agrees with $(-B)$ up to degree $d-1$. We have the relation $R_{n+1} = X R_n - c_n B$ where c_n is the coefficient in X^{d-1} of R_n. Thanks to the induction hypothesis, we have:

$$\begin{aligned} \mathrm{val}(c_n) \geq \mathrm{NF}(R_n)(d-1) &\geq \mathrm{NF}(B)(d-1) - \lambda(n-d) \\ &= -\lambda(n+1-d) \end{aligned}$$

since $\lambda = -\mathrm{NF}(B)(d-1)$ because B is monic. Therefore $\mathrm{NF}(c_n B)(x) \geq \mathrm{NF}(B)(x) - \lambda(n+1-d)$ for all x. On the other hand, for all x, we have:

$$\mathrm{NF}(X R_n)(x) = \mathrm{NF}(R_n)(x-1) \geq \mathrm{NF}(R_n)(x) - \lambda$$

from what we get $\mathrm{NF}(XR_n)(x) \geq \mathrm{NF}(B)(x) - \lambda(n+1-d)$. As a consequence $\mathrm{NF}(R_{n+1})(x) \geq \mathrm{NF}(B)(x) - \lambda(n+1-d)$ and the induction follows. Eq. (4) is now derived from:

$$\mathrm{NF}(A \,/\!/\, B) \otimes \mathrm{NF}(B) \geq \mathrm{NF}(A) \oplus \mathrm{NF}(A \,\%\, B)$$

using the estimation on $\mathrm{NF}(A \,\%\, B)$ we have just proved (see Figure 1). □

3.2 Tracking precision

Newton precision. We first analyze the precision behavior of Euclidean division in the Newton model. Concretely, we pick $A, B \in K[X]$ two polynomials which are known at precision $O(\varphi_A)$ and $O(\varphi_B)$ respectively:

$$A = A_{\mathrm{app}} + O(\varphi_A) \quad \text{and} \quad B = B_{\mathrm{app}} + O(\varphi_B)$$

Here A_{app} and B_{app} are some approximations of A and B respectively and φ_A and φ_B denotes two Newton functions of degree $\deg A$ and $\deg B$ respectively. We are interested in determining the precision of $A \,\%\, B$ and $A \,/\!/\, B$. The following proposition gives a theoretical answer under mild assumptions.

Proposition 3.3. *We keep the above notations and assume that the Newton precisions $O(\varphi_A)$ and $O(\varphi_B)$ on A and B respectively are both nondegenerate* (cf *Definition* 2.3). *Then, setting:*

$$\varphi = \varphi_A \oplus \left[\varphi_B \otimes \left(NF(A) \oslash NF(B)\right)\right]$$

the polynomials $A \,/\!/\, B$ and $A \,\%\, B$ are known at precision $O(\varphi \oslash NF(B))$ and $O(\varphi \circledast NF(B))$ respectively.

Proof. Let δA (resp. δB) be a polynomial whose Newton function is not less than φ_A (resp. φ_B) and define δQ and δR by:

$$Q_{\mathrm{app}} + \delta Q = (A_{\mathrm{app}} + \delta A) \,/\!/\, (B_{\mathrm{app}} + \delta B)$$
$$R_{\mathrm{app}} + \delta R = (A_{\mathrm{app}} + \delta A) \,\%\, (B_{\mathrm{app}} + \delta B)$$

where $Q_{\mathrm{app}} = A_{\mathrm{app}} \,/\!/\, B_{\mathrm{app}}$ and $R_{\mathrm{app}} = A_{\mathrm{app}} \,\%\, B_{\mathrm{app}}$. We have to show that $\mathrm{NF}(\delta Q) \geq \varphi \oslash \mathrm{NF}(B)$ and $\mathrm{NF}(\delta R) \geq \varphi \circledast \mathrm{NF}(B)$. Set $\delta X = \delta A - Q_{\mathrm{app}} \delta B$. Using Theorem 3.2, we obtain $\mathrm{NF}(Q_{\mathrm{app}}) \geq \mathrm{NF}(A) \oslash \mathrm{NF}(B)$ and consequently $\mathrm{NF}(\delta X) \geq \varphi$. On the other hand, an easy computation yields

$$\delta X = (B + \delta B) \cdot \delta Q + \delta R$$

so that $\delta Q = \delta X \,/\!/\, (B + \delta B)$ and $\delta R = \delta X \,\%\, (B + \delta B)$. Using again Theorem 3.2, we get the desired result. □

With this result in hand, we may split the computation of Euclidean division into two pieces, first computing approximations Q_{app} and R_{app} and separately computing δQ and δR. Both the approximations and the precision can be computing in time that is quasi-linear in the degree.

Lattice precision. We now move to lattice precision. We pick A and B two polynomials of respective degree n and d and assume that they are known at precision $O(H_A)$ and $O(H_B)$ respectively:

$$A = A_{\mathrm{app}} + O(H_A) \quad \text{and} \quad B = B_{\mathrm{app}} + O(H_B).$$

where $H_A \in K_{\leq n}[X]$ and $H_B \in K_{\leq d}[X]$ are lattices. According to the results of [4], in order to determine the precision of $A \,/\!/\, B$ and $A \,\%\, B$, we need to compute the differential of the mappings $(X, Y) \mapsto X \,/\!/\, Y$ and $(X, Y) \mapsto X \,\%\, Y$ at the point $(A_{\mathrm{app}}, B_{\mathrm{app}})$. Writing $Q_{\mathrm{app}} = A_{\mathrm{app}} \,/\!/\, B_{\mathrm{app}}$ and $R_{\mathrm{app}} = A_{\mathrm{app}} \,\%\, B_{\mathrm{app}}$, this can be done by expanding the relation:

$$A_{\mathrm{app}} + dA = (B_{\mathrm{app}} + dB)(Q_{\mathrm{app}} + dQ) + (R_{\mathrm{app}} + dR)$$

and neglecting the terms of order ≥ 2. We get this way $dA = B_{\mathrm{app}} dQ + Q_{\mathrm{app}} dB + dR$ meaning that dQ and dR appears respectively as the quotient and the remainder of the Euclidean division of $dX = dA - Q_{\mathrm{app}} dB$ by B_{app}.

Once this has been done, the strategy is quite similar to that explained for Newton precision: compute approximations and precision lattices separately for quotient and remainder.

3.3 An example: modular multiplication

For this example, we work over $W = \mathbb{Z}_2$ and fix a monic polynomial $M \in \mathbb{Z}[X]$ (known exactly) of degree 5. Our aim is to compare the numerical stability of the multiplication in the quotient $\mathbb{Z}_2[X]/M$ depending on the precision model we are using. In order to do so, we pick n random polynomials $P_1, \ldots, P_n$ in $\mathbb{Z}_2[X]/M(X)$ (according to the Haar measure) whose coefficients are all known at precision $O(2^N)$ for some large integer N. We then compute the product of the P_i's using the following quite naive algorithm.

---

1. **set** $P = 1$
2. **for** $i = 1, \ldots, n$ **do compute** $P = (P \cdot P_i) \,\%\, M$
3. **return** P

The table of Figure 2 reports the average gain of *absolute* precision G which is observed while executing the algorithm above for various modulus and n. The average is taken on a sample of 1000 random inputs. We recall that G is defined as follows:

• in the case of jagged and Newton precision, the precision of the output may be written into the form $\sum_{i=0}^{4} O(2^{N_i})\, X^i$ and $G = \sum_{i=0}^{4} (N_i - N)$;

• in the case of lattice precision, the precision of the output is a lattice H and G is the index of H in $2^N \mathcal{L}$ where $\mathcal{L} = \mathbb{Z}_2[X]/M$ is the standard lattice; in that case, we write G as a sum $G_{\mathrm{nd}} + G_{\mathrm{d}}$ where G_{d} is the index of H in the largest lattice H_0 contained in H which can be generated by elements of the shape $2^{N_i} X^i$ $(0 \leq i \leq 4)$. (The term G_d corresponds to diffused digits according to [5, Definition 2.3].)

We observe several interesting properties. First of all, the gains for Newton precision and jagged precision always agree though one may have thought at first that Newton precision is weaker. Since performing precision computations in the Newton framework is cheaper, it seems (at least on this example) that using the jagged precision model is not relevant.

On the other hand, the lattice precision may end up with better results. Nevertheless this strongly depends on the modulus M. For instance, when M is irreducible modulo $p = 2$ or Eiseistein, there is apparently no benefit to using the lattice precision model. We emphasize that these two particular cases correspond to modulus that are usually used to define (unramified and totally ramified respectively) extensions of $\mathbb{Q}_2$.

For other moduli, the situation is quite different and the benefit of using the lattice precision model becomes more apparent. The comparison between the gain of precision in the jagged model and the number of not diffused digits in

Modulus M	n	Gain of precision		
		Jagged	Newton	Lattice (not dif. + dif.)
X^5+X^2+1 (Irred. mod 2)	10	0.2	0.2	0.2 + 0.0
	50	4.2	4.2	4.2 + 0.0
	100	11.2	11.2	11.2 + 0.0
X^5+1 (Sep. mod 2)	10	0.4	0.4	0.9 + 6.0
	50	5.6	5.6	11.1 + 42.0
	100	13.6	13.6	27.0 + 87.0
X^5+2 (Eisenstein)	10	6.2	6.2	6.2 + 0.0
	50	44.0	44.0	44.0 + 0.0
	100	92.5	92.5	92.5 + 0.0
$(X+1)^5+2$ (Shift Eisenstein)	10	0.6	0.6	4.7 + 1.4
	50	7.1	7.1	42.6 + 1.4
	100	15.1	15.1	91.8 + 1.4
X^5+X+2 (Two slopes)	10	1.7	1.7	7.9 + 9.8
	50	8.1	8.1	70.7 + 59.8
	100	16.1	16.1	152.6 + 125.9

Figure 2: Precision for modular multiplication

the lattice model makes sense: indeed the latter appears as a theoretical upper bound of the former and the difference between them quantifies the quality of the way we track precision in the jagged (or the Newton) precision model. We observe that this difference is usually not negligible (*cf* notably the case of $M(X) = (X+1)^5+2$) meaning that this quality is not very good in general. As for diffused digits, they correspond to digits that cannot be "seen" in the jagged precision model. Their number then measures the intrinsic limitations of this model. We observe that it can be very important as well in several cases.

The modulus $(X+1)^5+2$ shows the advantage of working with lattice precision in intermediate computations. Indeed, the precision behavior using the lattice model closely parallels that of X^5+2, since the lattices are related by a change of variables. But this structure is not detected in the Newton or jagged models.

4. SLOPE FACTORIZATION

A well-known theorem [6, Theorem 6.1] asserts that each extremal point M in the Newton polygon $\mathrm{NP}(P)$ of a polynomial $P \in K[X]$ corresponds to a factorization $P = AB$ where the Newton polygon of A (resp. B) is given by the part of $\mathrm{NP}(P)$ located at the left (resp. the right) of M. Such a factorization is often called a *slope factorization*.

The aim of this section is to design efficient and stable algorithms for computing these factorizations. Precisely the algorithm we obtain has a quasi-optimal complexity (compared to the size of the input polynomial) and outputs a result whose precision is (close to be) optimal. Two of its important additional features are simplicity and flexibility.

4.1 A Newton iteration

The factor A defined above is usually obtained *via* a Newton iteration after having prepared our polynomial by flattening the first slope using a change of variables involving possibly rational exponents. We introduce here a variant of this iteration which does not require the flattening step and is entirely defined over $K[X]$.

Theorem 4.1. *Let $P(X) = \sum_{i=0}^{n} a_i X^i$ be a polynomial of degree n with coefficients in K. We assume that $\mathrm{NP}(P)$ has an extremal point whose abscissa is d. We define the sequences $(A_i)_{i\geq 0}$ and $(V_i)_{i\geq 0}$ recursively by:*

$$A_0 = \sum_{i=0}^{d} a_i X^i, \quad V_0 = 1$$
$$A_{i+1} = A_i + (V_i P \,\%\, A_i),$$
$$V_{i+1} = (2V_i - V_i^2 B_{i+1}) \,\%\, A_{i+1}$$
$$\text{where } B_{i+1} = P \,/\!/\, A_{i+1}.$$

Then the sequence (A_i) converges to a divisor A_∞ of P of degree d whose leading coefficient is a_d and whose Newton function agrees with $NF(P)$ on $[0,d]$. Moreover, setting:

$$\kappa = NF(P)(d{+}1) + NF(P)(d{-}1) - 2 \cdot NF(P)(d)$$

(with $NF(P)(-1) = NF(P)(n{+}1) = +\infty$ if necessary), we have $\kappa > 0$ and the following rate of convergence:

$$\forall i \geq 0, \quad NF(A_\infty - A_i) \geq NF(P)_{|[0,d-1]} + 2^i \kappa. \tag{5}$$

Remark 4.2. The iteration formulae of the above theorem already appeared in [2, § 3.1]; nevertheless, as far as we know, the result of Theorem 4.1 is new.

Remark 4.3. The divisor A is uniquely determined by the conditions of Theorem 4.1. Indeed, consider two divisors A and A' of P such that $\mathrm{NF}(A) = \mathrm{NF}(A') = \mathrm{NF}(P)_{|[0,d]}$. Then $L = \mathrm{lcm}(A, A')$ is a divisor of P as well and the slopes of its Newton polygon are all at most $\lambda_0 = \mathrm{NF}(P)(d) - \mathrm{NF}(P)(d{-}1)$. Therefore $\deg L = d$ and L differs from A and A' by a multiplicative nonzero constant. Then, if A and A' share in addition the same leading coefficient, they must coincide.

The rest of this subsection is devoted to the proof of the theorem. If $d = n$ (resp. $d = 0$), the sequence A_i is constant equal to P (resp. to the constant coefficient of P) and theorem is clear. We then assume $0 < d < n$. We set:

$$\lambda_0 = \mathrm{NF}(P)(d) - \mathrm{NF}(P)(d{-}1)$$
$$\lambda_1 = \mathrm{NF}(P)(d{+}1) - \mathrm{NF}(P)(d),$$

so that $\kappa = \lambda_1 - \lambda_0$. The existence of an extremal point of $\mathrm{NP}(P)$ located at abscissa d ensures that $\lambda_1 > \lambda_0$, *i.e.* $\kappa > 0$. For all indices i, we define:

$$Q_i = V_i P \,/\!/\, A_i, \quad R_i = V_i P \,\%\, A_i = A_{i+1} - A_i,$$
$$S_i = P \,\%\, A_i, \quad T_i = (1 - V_i B_i) \,\%\, A_i$$

and when $\square$ is some letter, we put $\Delta\square_i = \square_{i+1} - \square_i$.

Lemma 4.4. *The following relations hold:*

$$\Delta B_i = -(R_i B_{i+1}) \,/\!/\, A_i, \tag{6}$$
$$\Delta S_i = -(R_i B_{i+1}) \,\%\, A_i, \tag{7}$$
$$S_i = (B_i R_i + T_i S_{i-1} + T_i\, \Delta S_{i-1}) \,\%\, A_i, \tag{8}$$
$$\Delta V_i = (V_i T_i - V_i^2\, \Delta B_i) \,\%\, A_i, \tag{9}$$
$$1 - Q_i = T_i - (V_i S_i) \,/\!/\, A_i, \tag{10}$$
$$R_{i+1} = (\Delta V_i\, S_{i+1} + (1{-}Q_i) R_i) \,\%\, A_{i+1}, \tag{11}$$
$$T_{i+1} = (T_i + V_i\, \Delta B_i)^2 \,\%\, A_{i+1}. \tag{12}$$

Proof. From $P = A_i B_i + S_i = A_{i+1} B_{i+1} + S_{i+1}$, we get $-R_i B_{i+1} = \Delta B_i \cdot A_i + \Delta S_i$. Hence, by consideration of degree, we obtain (6) and (7). On the other hand, from $V_i P = A_i Q_i + R_i = V_i(A_i B_i + S_i)$, we derive

$$(V_i B_i - Q_i) \cdot A_i = R_i - V_i S_i. \tag{13}$$

Thus $R_i = V_i S_i \,\%\, A_i$. Hence $B_i R_i = (S_i - S_i T_i) \,\%\, A_i$ and $S_i = B_i R_i + S_i T_i \,\%\, A_i$, from which (8) follows directly By definition of V_i, we get $\Delta V_i = V_i(1 - V_i B_{i+1}) \,\%\, A_{i+1}$ and consequently (9). We now write $1 - Q_i = T_i + (V_i B_i - Q_i)$. Using (13) and noting that $\deg R_i < \deg A_i = d$, we get (10).

We have $V_i P = A_i Q_i + R_i = (A_{i+1} - R_i) Q_i + R_i$ and $V_{i+1} P = A_{i+1} Q_{i+1} + R_{i+1}$. Thus:

$$\begin{aligned} R_{i+1} &= \Delta V_i \, P + (1 - Q_i) R_i \\ &= (\Delta V_i \, S_{i+1} + (1 - Q_i) R_i) \,\%\, A_{i+1}, \end{aligned}$$

and (11) is proved. Finally

$$\begin{aligned} T_{i+1} &\equiv 1 - 2 V_i B_{i+1} + V_i^2 B_{i+1}^2 \pmod{A_{i+1}} \\ &\equiv (1 - V_i B_{i+1})^2 \pmod{A_{i+1}} \\ &\equiv (T_i + V_i \, \Delta B_i)^2 \pmod{A_{i+1}} \end{aligned}$$

which concludes the proof. □

If $\lambda_0 = -\infty$ or $\lambda_1 = +\infty$, the sequence (A_i) is constant and the theorem follows, so assume that λ_0 and λ_1 are finite.

We define the function $\varphi : \mathbb{R}^+ \to \mathbb{R} \cup \{+\infty\}$ by:

$$\varphi(x) = \begin{cases} \mathrm{NF}(P)(x) & \text{if } x \le d \\ \lambda_0(x - d) + \mathrm{NF}(P)(d) & \text{if } x > d \end{cases} \tag{14}$$

For nonzero c in a finite extension of K, note that the theorem holds for P if and only if it holds for cP, since the A_i's change to cA_i's while the B_i's and the V_i's remained unchanged. We may thus assume that P is normalized so that $\mathrm{NF}(P)(d) = d\lambda_0$, *i.e.* $\varphi(x) = \lambda_0 x$ for $x > d$. For a polynomial $Q \in K[X]$ of degree n, we further define:

$$b_\varphi(Q) = \min_{x \in [0,n]} \mathrm{NF}(Q)(x) - \varphi(x) \tag{15}$$

$$\text{and} \quad b_i(Q) = \min_{x \in [0,n]} \mathrm{NF}(Q)(x) - \lambda_i x \quad \text{for } i \in \{0,1\}. \tag{16}$$

Set also $b_\varphi(0) = b_0(0) = b_1(0) = +\infty$ by convention. With the normalization of P we chose above, we have $b_0(P) = b_\varphi(P) = 0$ and $b_\varphi(Q) \le b_0(Q)$ for all polynomial Q. Similarly $b_1(Q) \le b_0(Q)$ for all Q.

Lemma 4.5. *Let $b \in \{b_\varphi, b_0, b_1\}$. For $Q_1, Q_2 \in K[X]$:*

a) $b(Q_1 + Q_2) \ge \min\big(b(Q_1), b(Q_2)\big)$

b) $b(Q_1 Q_2) \ge \min b(Q_1) + b(Q_2)$

c) $b_\varphi(Q_1 Q_2) \ge b_\varphi(Q_1) + b_0(Q_2)$

For $Q, A \in K[X]$ with $\deg A = d$ and $NF(A) = NF(P)_{|[0,d]}$:

d) $b(Q \,\%\, A) \ge b(Q)$

e) $b_0(Q \,/\!/\, A) \ge b_\varphi(Q)$.

PROOF. *a)* is clear.

We skip the proof of *b)* which is similar to that of *c)*.

Let t_1 (resp. t_2) be the translation of vector $(0, b_\varphi(Q_1))$ (resp. $(0, b_0(Q_2))$. It follows from the definition of b_φ that $\mathrm{NP}(Q_1)$ is a subset of $t_1(\mathrm{Epi}(\varphi))$ where $\mathrm{Epi}(\varphi)$ denotes the epigraph of φ. Similarly $\mathrm{NP}(Q_2) \subset t_2(C)$ where C is the convex cone generated by the vectors starting from $(0,0)$ to $(0,1)$ and $(1, \lambda_0)$. Thus

$$\mathrm{NP}(Q_1 Q_2) \subset t_2 \circ t_1\big(\mathrm{Epi}(\varphi) + C\big) = t_2 \circ t_1\big(\mathrm{Epi}(\varphi)\big)$$

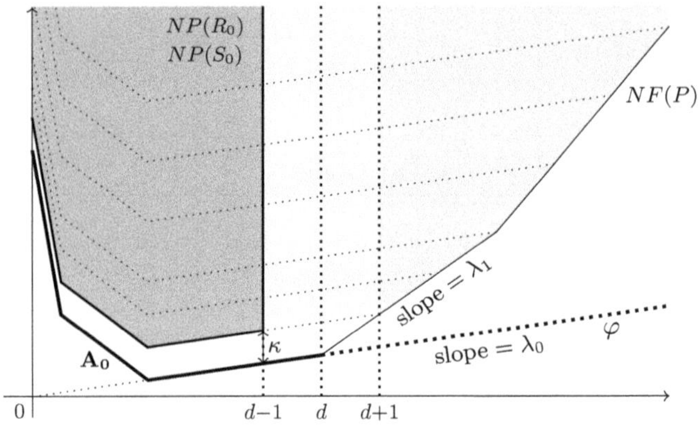

Figure 3: Bound on $\mathbf{NF}(R_0)$ and $\mathbf{NF}(S_0)$

and *c)* follows.

Finally *d)* and *e)* follows from Theorem 3.2. □

We are now going to prove by induction on i the conjonction of all equalities and inequalities below:

$$\begin{gathered} \mathrm{NF}(A_i) = \varphi_{|[0,d]}, \\ b_1(V_i) \ge 0, \quad b_\varphi(R_i) \ge 2^i \kappa \\ b_\varphi(S_i) \ge 0, \quad b_0(T_i) \ge 2^i \kappa. \end{gathered} \tag{17}$$

Noting that A_0 and P agree up to degree d and that $\mathrm{NP}(P)$ has an extremal point at abscissa d, we get $\mathrm{NF}(A_0) = \varphi_{|[0,d]}$. Clearly $b_1(V_0) \ge 0$ since $V_0 = 1$. It follows from the definitions that $R_0 = S_0 = P \,\%\, A_0 = (P - A_0) \,\%\, A_0$. We remark that $P - A_0 = \sum_{i=d+1}^{n} a_i X^i$. Using Theorem 3.2, we obtain that $b_\varphi(P - A_0) \ge \kappa$ and then $b_\varphi(R_0) = b_\varphi(S_0) \ge \kappa$ (see Figure 3). Finally observe that:

$$T_0 = (1 - B_0) \,\%\, A_0 = \big((A_0 - P) \,/\!/\, A_0\big) \,\%\, A_0.$$

Therefore $b_0(T_0) \ge \kappa$ results from $b_\varphi(A_0 - P) \ge \kappa$ thanks to Lemma 4.5. We have then established (17) when $i = 0$.

We now assume (17) for the index i. From $A_{i+1} = A_i + R_i$ and the estimation $b_\varphi(R_i) \ge 2^i \kappa > 0$, we derive $\mathrm{NF}(A_{i+1}) = \varphi_{|[0,d]}$. Therefore, Lemma 4.5 applies with $A = A_i$ and $A = A_{i+1}$. Now coming back to the the definition of B_{i+1} and using Theorem 3.2, we get $b_0(B_{i+1}) \ge b_1(B_{i+1}) \ge 0$. As a consequence:

$$b_\varphi(R_i B_{i+1}) \ge b_\varphi(R_i) + b_0(B_{i+1}) \ge 2^i \kappa$$

by Lemma 4.5 and the induction hypothesis. Using again Lemma 4.5, we then derive from (6) and (7) that $b_0(\Delta B_i) \ge 2^i \kappa$ and $b_\varphi(\Delta S_i) \ge 2^i \kappa$. Similarly, using (8) and the estimations we already know, we obtain $b_\varphi(S_i) \ge 2^i \kappa$. Combining this with $b_\varphi(\Delta S_i) \ge 2^i \kappa$, we find $b_\varphi(S_{i+1}) \ge 2^i \kappa$ as well. Applying again and again the same strategy, we deduce successively $b_0(\Delta V_i) \ge 2^i \kappa$ using (9), $b_0(1 - Q_i) \ge 2^i \kappa$ using (10), $b_\varphi(R_{i+1}) \ge 2^{i+1} \kappa$ using (11), and then $b_0(T_{i+1}) \ge 2^{i+1} \kappa$ using (12). Finally, coming back to the recurrence defining V_{i+1} and remembering that $b_1(V_i)$ and $b_1(B_{i+1})$ are both nonnegative, we find $b_1(V_{i+1}) \ge 0$. The equalities and inequalities of Eq. (17) have then all been established for the index $i + 1$ and the induction goes.

From the inequalities $b_\varphi(R_i) \ge 2^i \kappa$, we deduce that the sequence (A_i) is Cauchy and therefore converges. Its limit A_∞ certainly satisfies $\mathrm{NF}(A_\infty) = \varphi_{|[0,d]}$ because all the A_i's do. Moreover we know that $b_\varphi(S_i) \ge 2^i \kappa$ from what we derive that the sequence (S_i) goes to 0. Coming back to the definition of S_i, we find $P \,\%\, A_\infty = 0$, *i.e.* A_∞ divides P. Finally, Eq. (5) giving the rate of convergence follows from the writing $A_\infty - A_i = \sum_{j=i}^{\infty} R_j$ together with the facts that $b_\varphi(R_j) \geq 2^i \kappa$ and $\deg R_j \leq d-1$ for all $j \geq i$.

Remark 4.6. From the proof above, the sequence $(V_i)_{i \geq 0}$ converges as well. Its limit V_∞ is an inverse of $B_\infty = P \,/\!/\, A_\infty$ modulo A_∞ and it satisfies in addition $b_1(V_\infty) \geq 0$.

Moreover, the conclusion of Theorem 4.1 is still correct if A_0 is any polynomial of degree d with leading coefficient a_d and V_0 is any polynomial as soon as they satisfy:

$$b_\varphi(V_0 P \,\%\, A_0) > 0 \quad \text{and} \quad b_0\big((1 - V_0 B_0) \,\%\, A_0\big) > 0$$

except that the constant κ giving the rate of convergence should be now $\kappa = \min\big(b_\varphi(V_0 P \,\%\, A_0),\, b_0((1 - V_0 B_0) \,\%\, A_0)\big)$.

4.2 A slope factorization algorithm

Let $P \in K_n[X]$ and d be the abscissa of an extremal point of $\mathrm{NP}(P)$. Previously (*cf* Theorem 4.1), we have defined a sequence (A_i, V_i) converging to (A, V) where A is a factor of P whose Newton function is $\mathrm{NF}(P)_{|[0,d]}$ and V is the inverse of $B = P/A$ modulo A. We now assume that P is known up to some finite precision: $P = P_{\mathrm{app}} + O(\cdots)$ where the object inside the O depends on the chosen precision model. We address the two following questions: (1) what is the precision of the factor A, and (2) how can one compute in practice A at this precision?

In the sequel, it will be convenient to use a different normalization on A and B: if a_d is the coefficient of P of degree d, we set $A^{(1)} = a_d^{-1} A$ and $B^{(1)} = a_d B$ so that $A^{(1)}$ is monic and $P = A^{(1)} B^{(1)}$. We also assume the leading coefficient of P is *exactly* 1; the precision datum on P then only concerns the coefficients up to degree $n-1$. Similarly, $A^{(1)}$ and $B^{(1)}$ only carry precision up to degree $d-1$ and $n-d-1$ respectively.

Newton precision. We assume that the precision of the input P has the shape $O(\varphi_P)$ where φ_P is a Newton function of degree $n-1$. From now on, we assume that the precision $O(\varphi_P)$ is nondegenerate in the sense of Definition 2.3. This ensures in particular that the Newton polygon of P is well defined. We import the notations φ, b_φ and b_0 from §4.1 and refer to Eqs. (14)–(16) for the definitions.

Proposition 4.7. *We keep all the above notations and assumptions. We set:*

$$\delta = \min_{x \in [0, n-1]} \varphi_P(x) - \varphi(x)$$

and assume that $\delta > 0$. Then the factor $A^{(1)}$ is known with precision at least $O(\varphi_{A^{(1)}})$ with $\varphi_{A^{(1)}} = \varphi_{|[0,d-1]} - \varphi(d) + \delta$.

Proof. Let $\delta_P \in K[X]$ be such that $\mathrm{NP}(\delta_P) \geq \varphi_P$. Let $A^{(1)}_{\mathrm{app}}$ and $A^{(1)}$ be the monic factors of P_{app} and $P_{\mathrm{app}} + \delta P$ respectively whose Newton functions are $\varphi_{|[0,d]} - \varphi(d)$.

We define the sequences (A_i) and (V_i) by the recurrence:

$$A_0 = A_{\mathrm{app}}, \qquad V_0 = V_{\mathrm{app}}$$

$$A_{i+1} = A_i + \big(V_i(P_{\mathrm{app}} + \delta_P) \,\%\, A_i\big),$$

$$V_{i+1} = (2V_i - V_i^2 B_{i+1}) \,\%\, A_{i+1}$$

$$\text{where } B_{i+1} = (P_{\mathrm{app}} + \delta_P) \,/\!/\, A_{i+1}.$$

where A_{app} and V_{app} are those related to P_{app}. Note that $A_{\mathrm{app}} = a_d \cdot A^{(1)}_{\mathrm{app}}$ if a_d denotes the coefficient of X^d in P_{app}.

By Remark 4.6, we know that the sequence (A_i) converges to $A = a_d \cdot A^{(1)}$ and furthermore:

$$\mathrm{NP}(A - A_{\mathrm{app}}) \geq \varphi_{|[0,d-1]} + b_\varphi\big((V_{\mathrm{app}} \cdot \delta P) \,\%\, A_{\mathrm{app}}\big)$$

since $(V_{\mathrm{app}} P_{\mathrm{app}}) \,\%\, A_{\mathrm{app}} = (1 - V_{\mathrm{app}} B_{\mathrm{app}}) \,\%\, A_{\mathrm{app}} = 0$. Using repeatedly Lemma 4.5, we obtain:

$$b_\varphi\big((V_{\mathrm{app}} \cdot \delta P) \,\%\, A_{\mathrm{app}}\big) \geq b_0(V_{\mathrm{app}}) + b_\varphi(\delta P) \geq b_\varphi(\delta P) \geq \delta.$$

Thus $\mathrm{NP}(A - A_{\mathrm{app}}) \geq \varphi_{[0,d-1]} + \delta$. Dividing by a_d, we find $\mathrm{NP}(A^{(1)} - A^{(1)}_{\mathrm{app}}) \geq \varphi_{A^{(1)}}$ and we are done. □

Remark 4.8. Under the hypothesis **(H)** introduced below, a correct precision on $A^{(1)}$ is also $O(\psi_{A^{(1)}})$ where:

$$\psi_{A^{(1)}} = \big(\varphi_P \otimes (\mathrm{NF}(V_{\mathrm{app}}) - \mathrm{NF}(P)(d))\big) \oslash \mathrm{NF}(P)_{|[0,d]}.$$

This follows from Proposition 4.10 using $V^{(1)}_{\mathrm{app}} = a_d^{-1} V_{\mathrm{app}}$. It follows in addition from Remark 4.6 that $\mathrm{NF}(V_{\mathrm{app}})$ is bounded from below by $x \mapsto \lambda_1 x$. This yields the bound $\psi_{A^{(1)}} \geq (\varphi_P \otimes \psi) \oslash \mathrm{NF}(P)_{|[0,d]}$ where $\psi : [0, d-1] \to \mathbb{R}$ is the affine function mapping x to $\lambda_1 x - \mathrm{NF}(P)(d)$.

We can now move to the second question we have raised before, *i.e.* the design of an algorithm for computing $A^{(1)}$ with the precision given by Proposition 4.7. Our strategy consists in computing first the precision and then applying the Newton iteration until the expected precision is reached.

Algorithm `slope_factorisation_Newton`
Input: a monic polynomial $P + O(\varphi_P) \in K_n[X]$,
a break point d of $\mathrm{NP}(P)$
Output: the factor A described above

1. Compute the functions $\mathrm{NF}(P)$ and φ
2. Compute $\varphi_A = \varphi_{|[0,d-1]} - \varphi(d) + \min_{x \in [0,n]} \varphi_P(x) - \varphi(x)$
3. Compute $\kappa = \mathrm{NP}(P)(d+1) + \mathrm{NF}(P)(d-1) - 2 \cdot \mathrm{NF}(P)(d)$
4. Set $i = 0$, $A_0 = \sum_{i=0}^{d} a_i X^i$ (a_i = coeffs of P), $V_0 = 1$
5. **repeat until** $\varphi_{|[0,d-1]} + 2^i \kappa \geq \varphi_A$
6. lift A_i, V_i and P at enough precision
7. compute
   - $A_{i+1} = A_i + (P V_i \,\%\, A_i)$ at precision $O(\varphi_{|[0,d-1]} + 2^{i+1}\kappa)$
   - $V_{i+1} = (2V_i - V_i^2 \cdot (P \,/\!/\, A_{i+1})) \,\%\, A_{i+1}$ at precision $O(x \mapsto \lambda_1 x + 2^{i+1}\kappa)$
8. set $i = i + 1$
9. **return** $A_i + O(\varphi_A)$

Remark 4.9. The precision needed at line 6 is of course governed by the computation performed at line 7. Note that it can be either computed *a priori* by using Proposition 3.3 or dynamically by using relaxed algorithms from [1, 11, 12]. In both cases, it is in $O(\pi^{N_i})$ with $N_i = O(2^i \kappa + \min \mathrm{NF}(P))$.

It follows from Theorem 4.1, Remark 4.6 and Proposition 4.7 that Algorithm `slope_factorisation_Newton` is correct and stable. Using the standard soft-O notation $\tilde{O}(\cdot)$ for hiding logarithmic factor, our algorithm performs at most $\tilde{O}(n)$ combinatorial operations and $\tilde{O}(n)$ operations in K at precision $O(\pi^N)$ with $N = O(\max \varphi_P - \min \mathrm{NF}(P))$ if one uses quasi-optimal algorithms for multiplication and Euclidean division of polynomials.

Lattice precision. The precision datum is given here by a lattice H_P in $K_{\le n-1}[X]$; we shall then write $P = P_{\text{app}} + O(H_P)$ where P_{app} is a *monic* approximation of the inexact polynomial P we want to factor. We assume from now that H_P is sufficiently small so that the Newton polygon of P is well defined. We then can define the function:

$$F = (F_A, F_B) : P_{\text{app}} + H_P \to K_{=d}[X] \times K_{=n-d}[X]$$

mapping a polynomial P to the pair $(A^{(1)}, B^{(1)})$ obtained from it. We set $(A^{(1)}_{\text{app}}, B^{(1)}_{\text{app}}) = F(P_{\text{app}})$.

We make the following hypothesis **(H)**:

The lattice H_P is a first order lattice at every point of $P_{\text{app}} + H_P$ in the sense of [4, Definition 3.3], *i.e.* for all $P \in P_{\text{app}} + H_P$:

$$F(P + H_P) = F(P) + F'(P)(H_P).$$

Obviously **(H)** gives an answer to the first question we have raised above: the precision of $A^{(1)}$ is the lattice $H_{A^{(1)}}$ defined as projection on the first component of $F'(P_{\text{app}})(H_P)$. It turns out that it can be computed explicitely as shown by the next proposition.

Proposition 4.10. *The map $F_A : P \mapsto A^{(1)}$ is of class C^1 on $P_{app} + H_P$ and its differential at some point P is the linear mapping*

$$dP \mapsto dA^{(1)} = (V^{(1)}\, dP) \,\%\, A^{(1)}$$

where $(A^{(1)}, B^{(1)}) = F(P)$ and $V^{(1)}$ is the inverse of $B^{(1)}$ modulo $A^{(1)}$.

Proof. The function F is injective and a left inverse of it is $G : (A^{(1)}, B^{(1)}) \mapsto A^{(1)}B^{(1)}$. Clearly G is of class C^1 and its differential is given by

$$(dA^{(1)}, dB^{(1)}) \mapsto dP = A^{(1)}\, dB^{(1)} + B^{(1)}\, dA^{(1)}. \qquad (18)$$

Thanks to Bézout Theorem, it is invertible as soon as $A^{(1)}$ and $B^{(1)}$ are coprime, which is true because $\text{NP}(A^{(1)})$ and $\text{NP}(B^{(1)})$ do not shape a common slope. As a consequence F is of class C^1 and its differential is obtained by inverting Eq. (18). Reducing modulo $A^{(1)}$, we get $dP \equiv B^{(1)}\, dA^{(1)} \pmod{A^{(1)}}$. The claimed result follows after having noticed that $dA^{(1)}$ has degree at most $d-1$. □

A remarkable Corollary of Proposition 4.10 asserts the optimality of Proposition 4.7 in a particular case.

Corollary 4.11. *We assume **(H)**. Let $\delta \in \mathbb{R}$. When the precision of P is given by $O(NF(P)_{|[0,d-1]} + \delta)$, the precision of $A^{(1)}$ given by Proposition 4.7 is optimal.*

Proof. First remark that the δ defined in the statement of Proposition 4.7 coincide with the δ introduced in the Corollary. Define $\varphi_{A^{(1)}} = \varphi_{|[0,d-1]} - \varphi(d) + \delta$. Let H_P (resp. $H_{A^{(1)}}$) be the lattice consisting of polynomials of degree at most $n-1$ (resp. at most $d-1$) whose Newton function is not less that $\varphi_P = \text{NF}(P)_{|[0,d-1]} + \delta$ (resp. $\varphi_{A^{(1)}}$). We have to show that $F'_A(P_{\text{app}})(H_P) = H_{A^{(1)}}$. According to Proposition 4.10 the mapping $G : K_{\le d-1}[X] \to K_{\le n-1}[X]$, $dA^{(1)} \mapsto (B^{(1)}_{\text{app}}\, dA^{(1)}) \,\%\, A^{(1)}_{\text{app}}$ is a right inverse of $F'_A(P_{\text{app}})$. It is then enough to prove that G takes $H_{A^{(1)}}$ to H_P, which can be done easily using Theorem 3.2. □

To compute $A^{(1)}$ in practice, we give a stopping criterion.

Proposition 4.12. *We assume **(H)**.*

(i) Let $\tilde{A}^{(1)} \in K_{=d}[X]$ such that $\tilde{A}^{(1)}\tilde{B}^{(1)} \in P_{app} + O(H_P)$ with $\tilde{B}^{(1)} = P_{app} \,/\!/\, \tilde{A}^{(1)}$. Then $\tilde{A}^{(1)} \in A^{(1)}_{app} + H_{A^{(1)}}$.

(ii) Let in addition $\tilde{V}^{(1)} \in K_{\le d-1}[X]$ such that:

$$\big(\tilde{B}^{(1)}\tilde{V}^{(1)} \cdot H_P\big) \,\%\, \tilde{A}^{(1)} = H_P \,\%\, \tilde{A}^{(1)}.$$

Then $H_{A^{(1)}} = \big(\tilde{V}^{(1)} \cdot H_P\big) \,\%\, \tilde{A}^{(1)}$.

Proof. *(i)* Set $\tilde{P} = \tilde{A}^{(1)}\tilde{B}^{(1)}$. We know by assumption that $\tilde{P} = P_{\text{app}} + O(H_P)$. Thus $F(\tilde{P})$ is well defined. The unicity of the slope factorization (*cf* Remark 4.3) further implies that $F(\tilde{P}) = (\tilde{A}^{(1)}, \tilde{B}^{(1)})$. The claimed result now follows from the hypothesis **(H)**.

(ii) By applying **(H)** with $P = \tilde{P}$ and replacing $F'(\tilde{P})$ by its expression given by Proposition 4.10, we find:

$$H_{A^{(1)}} = \big((\tilde{B}^{(1)})^{-1} \cdot H_P\big) \,\%\, \tilde{A}^{(1)}.$$

Dividing $\big(\tilde{B}^{(1)}\tilde{V}^{(1)}H_P\big) \,\%\, \tilde{A}^{(1)} = H_P \,\%\, \tilde{A}^{(1)}$ by $\tilde{B}^{(1)}$ modulo $\tilde{A}^{(1)}$, we get $H_{A^{(1)}} = \big(\tilde{V}^{(1)} \cdot H_P\big) \,\%\, \tilde{A}^{(1)}$ as expected. □

As a conclusion, the algorithm we propose consists in computing the Newton sequences (A_i) and (V_i) (following the strategy of Algorithm `slope_factorisation_Newton` regarding to precision) until we find a pair $(\tilde{A}^{(1)}, \tilde{V}^{(1)})$ satisfying the requirements (i) and (ii) of Proposition 4.12. Once this pair has been found, one may safely output $\tilde{A}^{(1)} + O\big((\tilde{V}^{(1)} \cdot H_P) \,\%\, \tilde{A}^{(1)}\big)$ under **(H)**. The resulting algorithm has quasi-optimal running time and optimal stability.

References

[1] Jérémy Berthomieu, Joris van der Hoeven, and Grégoire Lecerf, *Relaxed algorithms for p-adic numbers*, J. Théorie des Nombres des Bordeaux **23** (2011), no. 3, 541–577.

[2] Jérémy Berthomieu, Grégoire Lecerf, and Guillaume Quintin, *Polynomial root finding over local rings and application to error correcting codes*, Applicable Algebra in Engineering, Communication and Computing **24** (2013), no. 6, 413–443, DOI 10.1007/s00200-013-0200-5.

[3] Xavier Caruso, *Slope factorization of ore polynomials*, 2016. in preparation.

[4] Xavier Caruso, Tristan Vaccon, and David Roe, *Tracking p-adic precision*, LMS Journal of Computation and Mathematics **17 (Special issue A)** (2014), 274–294.

[5] ———, *p-adic stability in linear algebra*, Proceedings of the 2015 acm on international symposium on symbolic and algebraic computation, 2015, pp. 101–108.

[6] Bernard Dwork, Giovanni Gerotto, and Francis Sullivan, *An introduction to G-functions*, Princeton U.P., Princeton, 1994.

[7] Jordi Guàrdia, Jesús Montes, and Enric Nart, *Newton polygons of higher order in algebraic number theory*, Transactions of the AMS **364** (2012), no. 1, 361–416.

[8] Jordi Guàrdia, Enric Nart, and Sebastian Pauli, *Single-factor lifting and factorization of polynomials over local fields*, Journal of Symbolic Computation **47** (2012), no. 11, 1318 –1346.

[9] Jesús Montes, *Polígonos de newton de orden superior y aplicaciones aritméticas*, Ph.D. Thesis, 1999.

[10] Sebastian Pauli, *Factoring polynomials over local fields II*, Algorithmic number theory, 9th international symposium (Guillaume Hanrot, Franccois Morain, and Emmanuel Thomé, eds.), 2010.

[11] Joris van der Hoeven, *Relax, but don't be too lazy*, J. Symbolic Comput. **34** (2002), no. 6, 479–542.

[12] ———, *New algorithms for relaxed multiplication*, J. Symbolic Comput. **42** (2007), no. 8, 792–802.

[13] Adrien Poteaux and Marc Rybowicz, *Improving Complexity Bounds for the Computation of Puiseux Series over Finite Fields*, ISSAC'15, 2015, pp. 299–306.

Existence Problem of Telescopers: Beyond the Bivariate Case *

Shaoshi Chen[1,2], Qing-Hu Hou[3], George Labahn[2], Rong-Hua Wang[4]
[1]KLMM, AMSS, Chinese Academy of Sciences, Beijing, 100190, (China)
[2]Symbolic Computation Group, University of Waterloo, Ontario, N2L3G1, (Canada)
[3]Center for Applied Mathematics, Tianjin University, Tianjin, 300072, (China)
[4]Center for Combinatorics, Nankai University, Tianjin, 300071, (China)
schen@amss.ac.cn, qh_hou@tju.edu.cn
glabahn@uwaterloo.ca, wangwang@mail.nankai.edu.cn

ABSTRACT

In this paper, we solve the existence problem of telescopers for rational functions in three discrete variables. We reduce the problem to that of deciding the summability of bivariate rational functions, a problem which has recently been solved. This existence criteria is used, for example, for detecting the termination of Zeilberger's algorithm to the function classes studied in this paper.

Categories and Subject Descriptors

I.1.2 [**Computing Methodologies**]: Symbolic and Algebraic Manipulation—*Algebraic Algorithms*

Keywords

Rational function, Telescoper, Summability, Reduction

1. INTRODUCTION

The method of creative telescoping is an algorithmic tool in the symbolic evaluation of parameterized definite sums and integrals. In order to evaluate a multiple sum of a given summand $f(x, y_1, \ldots, y_n)$ with respect to $y_1, \ldots, y_n$ with x a discrete parameter, the key step of creative telescoping is to find a nonzero linear recurrence operator L in x such that

$$L(f) = \Delta_{y_1}(g_1) + \cdots + \Delta_{y_n}(g_n),$$

where Δ_{y_i} denotes the difference operator in y_i and the g_i's belong to the same class of functions as f. The operator L is then called a *telescoper* for f, and the g_i's are called the *certificates* of L. In order to be useful in applications, one needs to address two problems: (1) determine whether such an operator L exists for a given function f and (2) if telescopers exist, then design an algorithm for computing them along with their certificates. In this paper we focus on the problem of existence of a telescoper for a given f.

The existence of telescopers is closely related to the termination of Zeilberger's algorithm for computing telescopers. Since the 1990's, extensive work has been done around the existence problem. A sufficient condition was first given by Zeilberger [29] where it was shown that telescopers exist for all holonomic functions. Later Wilf and Zeilberger in [27], using a linear algebra approach proved that telescopers always exist for proper hypergeometric terms. However, being holonomic or proper are only sufficient conditions. That is, there are cases in which the input functions are not holonomic (proper) but telescopers still exist, see [16]. The first necessary and sufficient conditions for the existence of telescopers was given by Abramov and Le [5] for rational functions in two discrete variables. This was later extended to the hypergeometric case by Abramov [3] and to the q-hypergeometric case by Chen et al. in [14]. Recently, the remaining six cases of the existence problem of telescopers for bivariate mixed hypergeometric terms have been solved in [12]. To our knowledge, all the previous work has only focussed on the problem for bivariate functions of a special class. Our long-term goal is to determine necessary and sufficient conditions for the existence problem for general multivariate functions. In this paper, we solve the problem for the starting case, that is, the case of rational functions in three discrete variables.

The previously mentioned existence criteria are all based on reduction algorithms which decompose an input function into the sum of a summable function and a non-summable one. The existence is then detected by checking whether the non-summable part is of a special form (the so-called proper terms). The reduction algorithms can also be used to decide the summabilty of univariate functions. Recently, the reduction algorithms for univariate rational functions were extended to the bivariate case in [13, 21]. The generalized reduction is also the main ingredient for solving the existence

*S. Chen was supported by the NSFC grants 11501552, 11371143 and by the President Fund of the Academy of Mathematics and Systems Science, CAS (2014-cjrwlzx-chshsh). This work was also supported by the Fields Institute's 2015 Thematic Program on Computer Algebra in Toronto, Canada. Q. Hou and R. Wang were supported by the 973 Project, the PCSIRT Project of the Ministry of Education and the National Science Foundation of China. G. Labahn was supported by a grant from the National Science and Engineering Research Council of Canada (NSERC).

ISSAC '16, July 19 - 22, 2016, Waterloo, ON, Canada

ISBN 978-1-4503-4380-0/16/07...$15.00
DOI: http://dx.doi.org/10.1145/2930889.2930895

problem for rational functions of three variables. However, the existence problem in the trivariate case is considerably more involved. As an example, the rational function $1/(x+y+z^2)$ is not proper (even after the reduction). However, it does have a telescoper (see Example 6.4), a phenomenon which does not happen in the bivariate case.

The remainder of this paper is organized as follows. The basic notations and concepts of telescopers are given in Section 2. In Sections 3 and 4, we review the previous work on solving the summability problem for bivariate rational functions and present special properties of linear recurrence operators. The existence problem for general rational functions is reduced to one with simpler rational functions in Section 5 with the existence criteria for these special rational functions presented in Section 6. The paper ends with a conclusion along with topics for future research.

2. PRELIMINARIES

Let $\mathbb{K}$ be a field of characteristic zero and let $\mathbb{E} = \mathbb{K}(x, y, z)$ be the field of rational functions in x, y, z over $\mathbb{K}$. For $f \in \mathbb{E}$ define the shift operators $\sigma_x, \sigma_y, \sigma_z$ on $\mathbb{E}$ by $\sigma_x(f) = f(x+1, y, z), \sigma_y(f) = f(x, y+1, z)$, and $\sigma_z(f) = f(x, y, z+1)$, respectively. Let $\mathcal{R} := \mathbb{E}[S_x, S_y, S_z]$ denote the ring of linear recurrence operators over $\mathbb{E}$, in which S_x, S_y, S_z commute and $S_v \cdot f = \sigma_v(f) \cdot S_v$ for any $f \in \mathbb{E}$ and $v \in \{x, y, z\}$. The action of an operator $P = \sum_{i,j,k} p_{i,j,k} S_x^i S_y^j S_z^k$ in $\mathcal{R}$ on a rational function $f \in \mathbb{E}$ is then given by

$$P(f) = \sum_{i,j,k} p_{i,j,k} f(x+i, y+j, z+k).$$

The *difference operators* Δ_x, Δ_y and Δ_z with respect to x, y and z are defined by

$$\Delta_x = S_x - 1,\ \Delta_y = S_y - 1,\ \text{and}\ \Delta_z = S_z - 1.$$

A rational function $f \in \mathbb{E}$ is said to be *(σ_y, σ_z)-summable* in $\mathbb{E}$ if $f = \Delta_y(g) + \Delta_z(h)$ for some $g, h \in \mathbb{E}$. We also just say summable if the meaning is clear. For brevity, we sometimes just write $f \equiv_{y,z} 0$ if f is (σ_y, σ_z)-summable.

Definition 2.1. *A nonzero linear recurrence operator $L \in \mathbb{K}(x)[S_x]$ is called a* telescoper *for a rational function $f \in \mathbb{E}$ if $L(f)$ is (σ_y, σ_z)-summable in $\mathbb{E}$, that is, there exist $g, h \in \mathbb{E}$ such that*

$$L(f) = \Delta_y(g) + \Delta_z(h).$$

Then the central problem to be solved in this paper is:

Problem 2.2. *Given $f \in \mathbb{E}$, decide whether f has a telescoper in $\mathbb{K}(x)[S_x]$.*

An operator $L \in \mathbb{K}(x)[S_x]$ is called a *common left multiple* of operators $L_1, \ldots, L_m \in \mathbb{K}(x)[S_x]$ if there exist operators $L'_1, \ldots, L'_m \in \mathbb{K}(x)[S_x]$ such that $L = L'_1 L_1 = \cdots = L'_m L_m$. Since $\mathbb{K}(x)[S_x]$ is a left Euclidean domain, such an L always exists. Amongst all of them, the one of smallest degree in S_x is called the least common left multiple (LCLM). When the field $\mathbb{K}$ is computable, e.g., $\mathbb{K} = \mathbb{Q}$, many efficient algorithms for computing LCLM have been developed [11, 6].

Remark 2.3. *Let $f = f_1 + \cdots + f_m$ with all $f_i \in \mathbb{E}$. If each f_i has a telescoper L_i for $i = 1, \ldots, m$, then the LCLM of the L_i is a telescoper for f. This fact follows from the definition of LCLM along with the commutativity between operators in $\mathbb{K}(x)[S_x]$ and the difference operators Δ_y, Δ_z.*

Let $G = \langle \sigma_x, \sigma_y, \sigma_z \rangle$ be the free Abelian multiplicative group generated by $\sigma_x, \sigma_y, \sigma_z$. Let $f \in \mathbb{E}$ and H be a subgroup of G. We call $[f]_H := \{\sigma(f) \mid \sigma \in H\}$ the H-orbit at f. Two elements $f, g \in \mathbb{E}$ are said to be H-equivalent if $[f]_H = [g]_H$, denoted by $f \sim_H g$. The relation $\sim_H$ is an equivalence relation. Typically, we will take $H = G$ or $H = \langle \sigma_y, \sigma_z \rangle$ in the rest of this paper.

Example 2.4. *Let $f = y^2+x+2z$ and $g = y^2+x-4y+2z+7$. Then f and g are G-equivalent since $g = \sigma_x \sigma_y^{-2} \sigma_z(f)$. However they are not $\langle \sigma_y, \sigma_z \rangle$-equivalent. Indeed, if $g = \sigma_y^n \sigma_z^k(f)$ for some $n, k \in \mathbb{Z}$ then equating the coefficients leads to the linear system $\{2n = -4, n^2 + 2k = 7\}$. But this implies that $n = -2$ and $k = 3/2$, a contradiction.*

3. SUMMABILITY

The first necessary step for solving the existence problem of telescopers is to decide whether a given multivariate function $f(x_1, \ldots, x_n)$ in a specific class of functions is equal to $\Delta_{x_1}(g_1) + \cdots + \Delta_{x_n}(g_n)$ for some $g_1, \ldots, g_n$ in the same class as f. For univariate rational functions the summability problem was first solved by Abramov [1, 2], with alternative methods later presented in [24, 25]. The Gosper algorithm [18] solves the problem for univariate hypergeometric terms. This was then used by Zeilberger [28] to design a fast algorithm to construct telescopers for bivariate hypergeometric terms. The Gosper algorithm was extended further to the D-finite case by Abramov and van Hoeij in [8, 4], and to a more general difference-field setting by Karr [22, 23] and Schneider [26]. A significant step in the path towards the multivariate case was taken by Chen et al. in [15], which gave some necessary conditions for the summability of bivariate hypergeometric terms. Chen and Singer [13] then presented the first necessary and sufficient condition for the summability of bivariate rational functions. Based on the theoretical criterion in [13], Hou and Wang [21] then gave a practical algorithm for deciding the summability in the bivariate rational case.

In this section, we will recall the summability criterion for bivariate rational functions from [21]. Let $\mathbb{F} := \mathbb{K}(x)$ and $f \in \mathbb{F}(y, z)$. The key idea is to decompose f into the following form

$$f = \Delta_y(g) + \Delta_z(h) + r,$$

where $g, h \in \mathbb{F}(y, z)$ and r is of the form

$$r = \sum_{i=1}^{n} \sum_{j=1}^{m_i} \frac{a_{i,j}}{d_i^j} \tag{3.1}$$

with $a_{i,j} \in \mathbb{F}(y)[z]$, $\deg_z(a_{i,j}) < \deg_z(d_i)$, $d_i \in \mathbb{F}[y, z]$ are irreducible polynomials, and d_i, $d_{i'}$ are not $\langle \sigma_y, \sigma_z \rangle$-equivalent for any $i \neq i'$. The existence of such decompositions has been shown in [21, Lemma 3.1]. Then f is (σ_y, σ_z)-summable if and only if r is (σ_y, σ_z)-summable. Since shift operators preserve the multiplicities of the fractions $a_{i,j}/d_i^j$, we have r is (σ_y, σ_z)-summable if and only if $\sum_{i=1}^n a_{i,j}/d_i^j$ is (σ_y, σ_z)-summable for each j. Furthermore, Lemma 3.2 in [21] shows that $\sum_{i=1}^n a_{i,j}/d_i^j$ is (σ_y, σ_z)-summable if and only if $a_{i,j}/d_i^j$ is (σ_y, σ_z)-summable for all i with $1 \leq i \leq n$. Thus, the summability problem for general rational functions in $\mathbb{F}(y, z)$ is reduced to the summability problem for simple fractions of the special form a/d^j. The following theorem [21, Theorem 3.3] then gives a criterion for deciding the summability of such special fractions.

Theorem 3.1. *Let $f = a/d^j \in \mathbb{F}(y,z)$ with $d \in \mathbb{F}[y,z]$ being irreducible, $a \in \mathbb{F}(y)[z] \setminus \{0\}$ and $\deg_z(a) < \deg_z(d)$. Then f is (σ_y, σ_z)-summable if and only if*

(1) there exist integers t, ℓ with $t \neq 0$ such that

$$\sigma_y^t(d) = \sigma_z^\ell(d), \tag{3.2}$$

(2) for the smallest positive integer t such that (3.2) holds, we have $a = \sigma_y^t \sigma_z^{-\ell}(p) - p$ for some $p \in \mathbb{F}(y)[z]$ with $\deg_z(p) < \deg_z(d)$.

Definition 3.2. *For a rational function $f \in \mathbb{F}(y,z)$, we call the triple $(g,h,r) \in \mathbb{F}(y,z)^3$ an* additive decomposition *of f with respect to y and z if $f = \Delta_y(g) + \Delta_z(h) + r$, where r is of the form (3.1) and none of the fractions $a_{i,j}/d_i^j$ is (σ_y, σ_z)-summable.*

Remark 3.3. *From the decision procedure for summability given above, additive decompositions always exist for rational functions in $\mathbb{F}(y,z)$. However, we remark that such decompositions may not be unique.*

4. EXPONENT SEPARATION

In this section, we will present some special properties of linear recurrence operators having to do with separating exponents. This separation of exponents of an operator will be used in the next section for separating orbits of shift operators and will help in simplifying the existence problem.

Let $m \in \mathbb{N}$ and L be a nonzero operator in $\mathbb{K}(x)[S_x]$. Then we can always decompose L into the form

$$L = L_0 + L_1 + \cdots + L_{m-1}, \tag{4.1}$$

where $L_i = \sum_{j=0}^{r_i} \ell_{i,j} S_x^{jm+i}$ for $i = 0, 1, \ldots, m-1$. We call such a decomposition an *m-exponent separation* of L. It is clear that $L = 0$ if and only if $L_i = 0$ for all i. Denote

$$\mathcal{L}_m = \begin{bmatrix} L_0 & L_{m-1} & L_{m-2} & \cdots & L_1 \\ L_1 & L_0 & L_{m-1} & \cdots & L_2 \\ L_2 & L_1 & L_0 & \cdots & L_3 \\ \vdots & \vdots & \vdots & & \vdots \\ L_{m-1} & L_{m-2} & L_{m-3} & \cdots & L_0 \end{bmatrix}. \tag{4.2}$$

The next lemma and proposition will show that the m rows of $\mathcal{L}_m$ are linearly independent over the ring $\mathbb{K}(x)[S_x]$.

Lemma 4.1. *Suppose*

$$[T_0, \ldots, T_{m-1}] \cdot \mathcal{L}_m = 0 \tag{4.3}$$

with each $T_k \in \mathbb{K}(x)[S_x]$. Then $T_0 + \cdots + T_{m-1} = 0$.

Proof. Note that $\mathcal{L}_m \cdot [1, \ldots, 1]^T = [L, \ldots, L]^T$. Hence any solution of (4.3) implies that

$$(T_0 + \cdots + T_{m-1}) \cdot L = 0.$$

Since L is nonzero and $\mathbb{K}(x)[S_x]$ is a left Euclidean domain we have $T_0 + \cdots + T_{m-1} = 0$. ∎

In fact our goal is to show that the left kernel of $\mathcal{L}_m$ is trivial, and so need to show that each component T_k of (4.3) is zero. In order to do this we do an m-exponent separation of each T_k and look at the resulting decomposition. Suppose

$$[T_0, \ldots, T_{m-1}] \cdot \mathcal{L}_m = [R_0, \ldots, R_{m-1}]$$

and that for each k

$$\begin{aligned} T_k &= T_{k,0} + T_{k,1} + \cdots + T_{k,m-1} \\ R_k &= R_{k,0} + R_{k,1} + \cdots + R_{k,m-1} \end{aligned}$$

are the m-exponent separations for T_k and R_k, respectively. Let $\mathcal{T}$ and $\mathcal{R}$ be the $m \times m$ matrices defined as

$$\mathcal{T} = \begin{bmatrix} T_{0,0} & T_{1,m-1} & T_{2,m-2} & \cdots & T_{m-1,1} \\ T_{0,1} & T_{1,0} & T_{2,m-1} & \cdots & T_{m-1,2} \\ T_{0,2} & T_{1,1} & T_{2,0} & \cdots & T_{m-1,3} \\ \vdots & \vdots & \vdots & & \vdots \\ T_{0,m-1} & T_{1,m-2} & T_{2,m-3} & \cdots & T_{m-1,0} \end{bmatrix} \tag{4.4}$$

and

$$\mathcal{R} = \begin{bmatrix} R_{0,0} & R_{1,m-1} & R_{2,m-2} & \cdots & R_{m-1,1} \\ R_{0,1} & R_{1,0} & R_{2,m-1} & \cdots & R_{m-1,2} \\ R_{0,2} & R_{1,1} & R_{2,0} & \cdots & R_{m-1,3} \\ \vdots & \vdots & \vdots & & \vdots \\ R_{0,m-1} & R_{1,m-2} & R_{2,m-3} & \cdots & R_{m-1,0} \end{bmatrix}.$$

Then it is straightforward to show that

$$\mathcal{T} \cdot \mathcal{L}_m = \mathcal{R}. \tag{4.5}$$

Proposition 4.2. *Suppose*

$$[T_0, \ldots, T_{m-1}] \cdot \mathcal{L}_m = 0 \tag{4.6}$$

with each $T_k \in \mathbb{K}(x)[S_x]$. Then $T_k = 0$ for each k.

Proof. From (4.5) and (4.6) we have that each $R_k = 0$ and hence also that each $R_{k,j} = 0$. Thus $\mathcal{T} \cdot \mathcal{L}_m = 0$ and so for each $j = 1, 2, \ldots, m$ we have

$$[T_{0,j-1}, \ldots, T_{j-1,0}, T_{j,m-1}, \ldots, T_{m-1,j}] \cdot \mathcal{L}_m = 0.$$

From Lemma 4.1 we get for each j

$$T_{0,j-1} + \cdots + T_{j-1,0} + T_{j,m-1} + \cdots + T_{m-1,j} = 0.$$

This implies that each $T_{k,j} = 0$ and hence also that $T_k = 0$ for all k. ∎

We will also later need to use the following:

Proposition 4.3. *There is a matrix $\mathcal{M} \in \mathbb{K}(x)[S_x]^{m \times m}$ such that*

$$\mathcal{M} \cdot \mathcal{L}_m = diagonal(T_0, T_1, \cdots, T_{m-1}) \tag{4.7}$$

with nonzero $T_i \in \mathbb{K}(x)[S_x]$.

Proof. From the definition of LCLM, we know that for any nonzero $A, B \in \mathbb{K}(x)[S_x]$, there always exist nonzero $A', B' \in \mathbb{K}(x)[S_x]$ such that $A'A + B'B = 0$. Hence similar to the use of the division-free Gaussian elimination over a Euclidean domain, we can find $\mathcal{M} \in \mathbb{K}(x)[S_x]^{m \times m}$ satisfying (4.7) (c.f. [10]). Note that row reductions preserve the linear independency and all rows of $\mathcal{L}_m$ are linearly independent by Proposition 4.2. Then all rows of $\mathcal{M} \cdot \mathcal{L}_m$ are linearly independent. In particular, each diagonal element of $\mathcal{M} \cdot \mathcal{L}_m$ is nonzero, since $\mathcal{M} \cdot \mathcal{L}_m$ is of triangular form. ∎

5. REDUCTION TO SIMPLE FRACTIONS

In this section, we will reduce the existence problem of telescopers for rational functions in $\mathbb{E}$ into the same problem but for simpler rational functions.

Let $f \in \mathbb{E}$ be nonzero with $f = \Delta_y(g) + \Delta_z(h) + r$ with (g, h, r) an additive decomposition of f with respect to y and z. Then f has a telescoper in $\mathbb{K}(x)[S_x]$ if and only if r has a telescoper in $\mathbb{K}(x)[S_x]$. As such, we need only to study the existence problem for rational functions of the form in Theorem 3.1.

For any $\sigma \in \langle \sigma_x, \sigma_y, \sigma_z \rangle$ and $a, b \in \mathbb{E}$, we have

$$\frac{a}{\sigma^n(b)} = \sigma(g) - g + \frac{\sigma^{-n}(a)}{b}, \tag{5.1}$$

where g is equal to $\sum_{i=0}^{n-1} \frac{\sigma^{i-n}(a)}{\sigma^i(b)}$ if $n \geq 0$, and equal to $-\sum_{i=0}^{-n-1} \frac{\sigma^i(a)}{\sigma^{n+i}(b)}$ if $n < 0$. We now simplify the fractions in the form (3.1) using the the formula (5.1). Suppose that $d_{i'} = \sigma_x^m \sigma_y^n \sigma_z^k d_i$ for some index $i \neq i'$ and $m, n, k \in \mathbb{Z}$ with $m \geq 0$. Applying the formula (5.1) repeatedly yields

$$\frac{a_{i',j}}{d_{i'}^j} = \Delta_y(u) + \Delta_z(v) + \frac{\sigma_y^{-n}\sigma_z^{-k}(a_{i',j})}{\sigma_x^m d_i^j}$$

for some $u, v \in \mathbb{E}$. With this reduction, we can always decompose r of the form (3.1) into the form

$$r = \sum_{i=1}^{I} \sum_{j=1}^{J_i} \sum_{\ell=0}^{\ell_{i,j}} \frac{b_{i,j,\ell}}{\sigma_x^\ell d_i^j} \tag{5.2}$$

with $b_{i,j,\ell} \in \mathbb{K}(x,y)[z]$, $d_i \in \mathbb{K}[x,y,z]$, $\deg_z(b_{i,j,\ell}) < \deg_z(d_i)$, and d_i are irreducible polynomials with d_i and $d_{i'}$ being in distinct $\langle \sigma_x, \sigma_y, \sigma_z \rangle$-orbits for any $1 \leq i \neq i' \leq m$.

Let $\mathcal{O} = \{p/q \in \mathbb{E} \mid \deg_z(p) < \deg_z(q)\}$ and V_m be the set of all rational functions of the form $\sum_{i=1}^{I} a_i/b_i^m$, where $a_i, b_i, \in \mathbb{K}(x,y)[z]$, $\deg_z(a_i) < \deg_z(b_i)$ and b_i's are distinct irreducible polynomials in the ring $\mathbb{K}(x,y)[z]$. By definition, the set V_m forms a subspace of $\mathcal{O}$ viewed as vector spaces over $\mathbb{K}(x,y)$. By the irreducible partial fraction decomposition, any $f \in \mathcal{O}$ can be uniquely decomposed into $f = f_1 + \cdots + f_n$ with $f_i \in V_i$ and so $\mathcal{O} = \bigoplus_{i=1}^{\infty} V_i$. The following lemma shows that the space V_m is invariant under certain linear recurrence operators.

Lemma 5.1. *Let $f \in V_m$ and $P \in \mathbb{K}(x,y)[S_x, S_y, S_z]$. Then $P(f) \in V_m$.*

Proof. Let $f = \sum_{t=1}^{n} a_t/b_t^m$ and $P = \sum_{i,j,k} p_{i,j,k} S_x^i S_y^j S_z^k$. For any $\sigma = \sigma_x^i \sigma_y^j \sigma_y^k$ with $i, j, k \in \mathbb{Z}$, $\sigma(b_t)$ is irreducible and $\deg_z(\sigma(a_t)) < \deg_z(\sigma(b_t))$. Then all of the simple fractions $\frac{p_{i,j,k} S_x^i S_y^j S_z^k(a_t)}{S_x^i S_y^j S_z^k(b_t)}$ appearing in $P(f)$ are proper in z and have irreducible denominators. If some of denominators are the same, we can simplify them by adding the numerators to get a simple fraction. After this simplification, we see that $P(f)$ can be written in the same form as f, so it is in V_m. ∎

Lemma 5.2. *Let $r \in \mathbb{E}$ be of the form (5.2). Then r has a telescoper if and only if the summand $\sum_{\ell=0}^{\ell_{i,j}} \frac{b_{i,j,\ell}}{\sigma_x^\ell d_i^j}$ has a telescoper for all i, j with $1 \leq i \leq I$ and $1 \leq j \leq J_i$.*

Proof. From Lemma 5.1 we see that any r as in (5.2) has a telescoper if and only if $\sum_{i=1}^{I} \sum_{\ell=0}^{\ell_{i,j}} \frac{b_{i,j,\ell}}{\sigma_x^\ell d_i^j}$ has a telescoper for all different multiplicities j. Also, from Lemma 3.2 in [21] we have that $\sum_{i=1}^{I} \sum_{\ell=0}^{\ell_{i,j}} \frac{b_{i,j,\ell}}{\sigma_x^\ell d_i^j}$ has a telescoper if and only if $\sum_{\ell=0}^{\ell_{i,j}} \frac{b_{i,j,l}}{\sigma_x^\ell d_i^j}$ has a telescoper for all i with $1 \leq i \leq I$. ∎

At this stage we have reduced the existence of telescopers problem for general rational functions to those having the simple form $r = \sum_{\ell=0}^{\ell_{i,j}} \frac{b_{i,j,\ell}}{\sigma_x^\ell d_i^j}$. If $\sigma_x^{\ell'} d_i = \sigma_x^\ell \sigma_y^n \sigma_z^k d_i$ for some $\ell \neq \ell'$ and $n, k \in \mathbb{Z}$, then applying the formula (5.1), we get

$$\frac{b_{i,j,\ell'}}{\sigma_x^{\ell'} d_i^j} = \frac{b_{i,j,\ell'}}{\sigma_x^\ell \sigma_y^n \sigma_z^k d_i^j} = \Delta_y(u_{i,j}) + \Delta_z(v_{i,j}) + \frac{\sigma_y^{-n}\sigma_z^{-k} b_{i,j,\ell'}}{\sigma_x^\ell d_i^j}$$

for some $u_{i,j}, v_{i,j} \in \mathbb{K}(x,y,z)$. Repeating the above transformation gives a decomposition

$$r = \Delta_y(u) + \Delta_z(v) + \sum_{\ell=0}^{I'} \frac{b'_\ell}{\sigma_x^\ell d_i^j}, \tag{5.3}$$

where $u, v \in \mathbb{K}(x,y,z)$ and $\sigma_x^\ell(d_i)$ and $\sigma_x^{\ell'}(d_i)$ are not $\langle \sigma_y, \sigma_z \rangle$-equivalent for $0 \leq \ell \neq \ell' \leq I'$.

The lemma below reduces the existence problem for rational functions into one whose denominators have distinct orbits.

Lemma 5.3. *Let $r = \sum_{i=0}^{I} \frac{b_i}{\sigma_x^i d^j}$ with $b_i \in \mathbb{K}(x,y)[z], d \in \mathbb{K}[x,y,z]$. Suppose b_i, d are irreducible, $\deg_z(b_i) < \deg_z(d)$ with $\sigma_x^i d$ and $\sigma_x^{i'} d$ in distinct $\langle \sigma_y, \sigma_z \rangle$-orbits, for $0 \leq i \neq i' \leq I$. Then r has a telescoper if and only if each simple fraction $\frac{b_i}{\sigma_x^i d^j}$ has a telescoper for $0 \leq i \leq I$.*

Proof. Sufficiency follows from Remark 2.3. For the other direction assume that $L = \sum_{i=0}^{\rho} \ell_i S_x^i$ (with $\ell_0 \neq 0$) is a telescoper for r. There are two cases to be considered according to whether there exists a positive integer m such that $\sigma_x^m d = \sigma_y^n \sigma_z^k d$ for some integers n, k.

Case 1. There is no positive integer m such that

$$\sigma_x^m d = \sigma_y^n \sigma_z^k d \quad \text{for some } n, k \in \mathbb{Z}.$$

In this case, $\sigma_x^i d$ and $\sigma_x^{i'} d$ are in distinct $\langle \sigma_y, \sigma_z \rangle$-orbits for any $i \neq i'$. We claim that $\frac{b_i}{\sigma_x^i d^j}$ is (σ_y, σ_z)-summable for $0 \leq i \leq I$. Since

$$L(r) = \sum_{i=0}^{\rho} \sum_{t=0}^{I} \ell_i \sigma_x^i (\frac{b_t}{\sigma_x^t d^j}) = \sum_{p=0}^{\rho+I} \sum_{i=0}^{p} \ell_i \sigma_x^i (\frac{b_{p-i}}{\sigma_x^{p-i} d^j})$$

is (σ_y, σ_z)-summable, according to Lemma 3.2 in [21], we get that for any $0 \leq p \leq \rho + I$, there exist $u_p, v_p \in \mathbb{K}(x,y)$ such that

$$\sum_{i=0}^{p} \ell_i \sigma_x^i \left(\frac{b_{p-i}}{\sigma_x^{p-i} d^j} \right) = \Delta_y(u_p) + \Delta_z(v_p). \tag{5.4}$$

We prove the claim by induction. The result is true for $p = 0$ in (5.4) since then $\frac{b_0}{d^j} = \Delta_y(\frac{u_0}{\ell_0}) + \Delta_z(\frac{v_0}{\ell_0})$. Suppose we have shown that $\frac{b_i}{\sigma_x^i d^j}$ is (σ_y, σ_z)-summable for $i = 0, 1, \ldots, k-1$ with $k \leq I$. Letting $p = k$ in (5.4), we get

$$\sum_{i=0}^{k} \ell_i \sigma_x^i \left(\frac{b_{k-i}}{\sigma_x^{k-i} d^j} \right) = \Delta_y(u_k) + \Delta_z(v_k).$$

As $\frac{b_{k-i}}{\sigma_x^{k-i} d^j}$ is (σ_y, σ_z)-summable for all $1 \le i \le k$, it is easy to check that $\sum_{i=1}^k \ell_i \sigma_x^i (\frac{b_{k-i}}{\sigma_x^{k-i} d^j})$ is also (σ_y, σ_z)-summable. Thus $\frac{b_k}{\sigma_x^k d^j}$ is (σ_y, σ_z)-summable.

Case 2. Suppose $\sigma_x^m d = \sigma_y^n \sigma_z^k d$ for m a positive integer and n, k some integers. Let m_0 be the smallest such integer with $\sigma_x^{m_0} d = \sigma_y^{n_0} \sigma_z^{k_0} d$ for some integers n_0, k_0. Since $\sigma_x^i d$ and $\sigma_x^{i'} d$ are in distinct (σ_y, σ_z)-orbits, we can assume $r = \sum_{i=0}^{m_0-1} \frac{b_i}{\sigma_x^i d^j}$. Suppose the m_0-exponent separation of L is

$$L = L_0 + L_1 + \cdots + L_{m_0-1}.$$

According to Lemma 3.1 and Lemma 3.2 in [21], we have

$$\begin{cases} L_0 \dfrac{b_0}{d^j} + L_{m_0-1} \dfrac{b_1}{\sigma_x d^j} + \cdots + L_1 \dfrac{b_{m_0-1}}{\sigma_x^{m_0-1} d^j} \equiv_{y,z} 0 \\ L_1 \dfrac{b_0}{d^j} + L_0 \dfrac{b_1}{\sigma_x d^j} + \cdots + L_2 \dfrac{b_{m_0-1}}{\sigma_x^{m_0-1} d^j} \equiv_{y,z} 0 \\ \cdots \\ L_{m_0-1} \dfrac{b_0}{d^j} + L_{m_0-2} \dfrac{b_1}{\sigma_x d^j} + \cdots + L_0 \dfrac{b_{m_0-1}}{\sigma_x^{m_0-1} d^j} \equiv_{y,z} 0. \end{cases}$$

If we let

$$\mathcal{V} = \left[\frac{b_0}{d^j}, \frac{b_1}{\sigma_x d^j}, \ldots, \frac{b_{m_0-1}}{\sigma_x^{m_0-1} d^j} \right]$$

then we can write this as

$$\mathcal{L}_{m_0} \cdot \mathcal{V}^T \equiv_{y,z} 0,$$

with $\mathcal{L}_{m_0}$ from (4.2). From Proposition 4.3 there exists $T_0, \ldots, T_{m_0-1}$ and a matrix $\mathcal{M}$ having entries from $\mathbb{K}(x)[S_x]$ such that

$$\mathcal{M} \cdot \mathcal{L}_{m_0} = \text{diagonal}(T_0, \ldots, T_{m_0-1}).$$

By the commutativity between operators in $\mathbb{K}(x)[\sigma_x]$ and the difference operators Δ_y, Δ_z, we know T_i is a telescoper for $\frac{b_i}{\sigma_x^i d^j}$ for $0 \le i \le m_0 - 1$. ∎

6. EXISTENCE CRITERIA

Lemma 5.3 from the previous section implies that the telescoper existence problem for rational functions is reduced to the case of a rational function of the form

$$f = \frac{b(x, y, z)}{c(x, y) d(x, y, z)^\lambda} \tag{6.1}$$

where $\lambda \in \mathbb{N}$, $c \in \mathbb{K}[x, y]$, $b, d \in \mathbb{K}[x, y, z]$ with $\deg_z(b) < \deg_z(d)$. In this section, we will give a criterion for deciding the existence of telescopers for rational functions of the above form. If b and c are not primitive, i.e., their contents are not 1, then we can write $b = b_0(x) b_1(x, y, z)$ and $c = c_0(x) c_1(x, y)$, where b_1, c_1 are primitive in y, z. Similarly to the proof of Lemma 7.4 in [12], $\frac{b}{cd^j}$ has a telescoper if and only if $\frac{b_1}{c_1 d^j}$ has a telescoper. As such we can assume in form (6.1) that b, c, d are all primitive in y, z.

As we did in the proof of Lemma 5.3 we will proceed by case distinction according to whether or not certain polynomials $p \in \mathbb{K}[x, y, z]$ and $q \in \mathbb{K}[x, y]$ satisfy the following conditions:

- there exists a positive integer m such that
$$\sigma_x^m(p) = \sigma_y^n \sigma_z^k(p) \quad \text{for some } n, k \in \mathbb{Z}; \tag{6.2}$$
- there exist $n_1, k_1 \in \mathbb{Z}$ with $n_1 > 0$ such that
$$\sigma_y^{n_1}(p) = \sigma_z^{k_1}(p); \tag{6.3}$$
- for (m, n) as in (6.2), there exists a positive integer t such that
$$\sigma_x^{tm}(q) = \sigma_y^{tn}(q); \tag{6.4}$$
- there exist $n_2, k_2 \in \mathbb{Z}$ with $n_2 > 0$ such that
$$\sigma_x^{n_2}(q) = \sigma_y^{k_2}(q). \tag{6.5}$$

To test the existence of telescopers for a simple fraction, we will need to test the conditions as above for polynomials. This amounts to solving the following problem:

Problem 6.1 (Integer Shift Equivalence Testing Problem). *Let $\mathbb{K}$ be any computable field of characteristic zero and σ_i be the shift operator w.r.t. x_i on $\mathbb{K}[x_1, ..., x_n]$. Given $p \in \mathbb{K}[x_1, ..., x_n]$, decide whether there exist integers $m_1, ..., m_n$ with $m_1 > 0$ such that $\sigma_1^{m_1} \cdots \sigma_n^{m_n}(p) = p$.*

This problem is a special case of the problem proposed and solved by Grigoriev in [19, 20] and more recently by Dvir et al. in [17].

First, we consider the case that the polynomial d in (6.1) does not satisfy the condition (6.2). In this case, the existence problem is reduced to the summability problem.

Lemma 6.2. *Let $f = b/(cd^\lambda) \in \mathbb{E}$ be of the form (6.1), with d not satisfying condition (6.2). Then f has a telescoper if and only if f is (σ_y, σ_z)-summable.*

Proof. The sufficiency is obvious. For the necessity, we assume that $L = \sum_{i=0}^I \ell_i S_x^i \in \mathbb{K}(x)[S_x]$ with $\ell_0, \ell_I \neq 0$ is a telescoper for f. Then

$$L(f) = \sum_{i=0}^I \frac{\ell_i \sigma_x^i(b)}{\sigma_x^i(c) \sigma_x^i(d^\lambda)} = \Delta_y(g) + \Delta_z(h)$$

for some $g, h \in \mathbb{E}$. Since $\sigma_x^m(d) \neq \sigma_y^n \sigma_z^k(d)$ for any positive integer m and $n, k \in \mathbb{Z}$, we have $\sigma_x^i(d)$ and $\sigma_x^{i'}(d)$ are in distinct (σ_y, σ_z)-orbits for any $i \neq i'$. By Lemma 3.2 in [21], the summands $\frac{\ell_i \sigma_x^i(b)}{\sigma_x^i(c) \sigma_x^i(d^\lambda)}$ of $L(f)$ are all (σ_y, σ_z)-summable. In particular, $\ell_0 f$ is (σ_y, σ_z)-summable. As $\ell_0 \in \mathbb{K}(x) \setminus \{0\}$, f is (σ_y, σ_z)-summable. ∎

The second case where (6.2) holds for d is considerably more involved. Let $\overline{\mathbb{K}}$ be the algebraic closure of $\mathbb{K}$. An irreducible polynomial $q \in \overline{\mathbb{K}}$ is said to be *integer-linear* in x, y and z over $\overline{\mathbb{K}}$ if it is of the form $\alpha_i x + \beta_j y + \gamma_i z + \delta_i$, where $\alpha_i, \beta_i, \gamma_i \in \mathbb{Z}$ and $\delta_i \in \overline{\mathbb{K}}$. A rational function $f \in \mathbb{E}$ is said to be *proper* if it can be written in the form $f = \frac{p}{\prod_{i=1}^I q_i}$, where $p, q_i \in \mathbb{K}[x, y, z]$ and all q_i are integer-linear in x, y and z over $\overline{\mathbb{K}}$. By the fundamental theorem in [27, p. 590], any proper rational function has a telescoper.

The following lemma describes some necessary conditions for the existence of telescopers.

Lemma 6.3. *Let $f = b/(cd^\lambda) \in \mathbb{E}$ be of the form (6.1), and let d satisfy the condition (6.2). Then f has a telescoper if one of the following conditions is also satisfied:*

(i) c and d satisfy the conditions (6.5) and (6.3), resp.;

(ii) c satisfies the condition (6.4).

Proof. Suppose that the polynomials c and d satisfy the conditions (6.2) and (*i*). By Lemma 3 in [7], the equalities $\sigma_x^{n_2}(c) = \sigma_y^{k_2}(c)$ and $\sigma_x^m(d) = \sigma_y^n\sigma_z^k(d)$ imply that there exist $p \in \mathbb{K}[z]$ and $q \in \mathbb{K}[z_1, z_2]$ such that

$$c = p(y + \frac{k_2}{n_2}x) \quad \text{and} \quad d = q(y + \frac{n}{m}x, z + \frac{k}{m}x).$$

Furthermore, the equality $\sigma_y^{n_1}(d) = \sigma_z^{k_1}(d)$ implies that there exists $h \in \mathbb{K}[z]$ such that

$$d = h(z + \frac{k}{m}x + \frac{k_1}{n_1}(y + \frac{n}{m}x)).$$

Thus both c and d factor into products of integer-linear polynomials in x, y, and z over $\overline{\mathbb{K}}$. Therefore f is a proper rational function, and hence it has a telescoper.

Suppose that c satisfies the condition (*ii*). Set

$$L = \sum_{i=0}^{\rho} \ell_i S_x^{itm},$$

where $\rho \in \mathbb{N}$ and $\ell_i \in \mathbb{K}(x)$ are to be determined. Applying the reduction formula (5.1) yields

$$L(f) = \sum_{i=0}^{\rho} \frac{\ell_i \sigma_x^{itm}(b)}{\sigma_x^{itm}(cd^\lambda)} = \sum_{i=0}^{\rho} \frac{\ell_i \sigma_x^{itm}(b)}{\sigma_y^{itn}(c)\sigma_y^{itn}\sigma_z^{itk}(d^\lambda)}$$

$$= \Delta_y(u) + \Delta_z(v) + \frac{1}{cd^\lambda}\sum_{i=0}^{\rho} \ell_i \sigma_x^{itm}\sigma_y^{-itn}\sigma_z^{-itk}(b)$$

for some $u, v \in \mathbb{K}(x, y)$. Note that the degrees of the polynomials $\sigma_x^{itm}\sigma_y^{-itn}\sigma_z^{-itk}(b)$ in y or z are the same as that of b. Thus all shifts of b lie in a finite dimensional linear space over $\mathbb{K}(x)$. If ρ is large enough, then there always exists $\ell_i \in \mathbb{K}(x)$, not all zero, such that

$$\sum_{i=0}^{\rho} \ell_i \sigma_x^{itm}\sigma_y^{-itn}\sigma_z^{-itk}(b) = 0.$$

As a result $L = \sum_{i=0}^{\rho} \ell_i S_x^{itm}$ is a telescoper for f. ∎

Example 6.4. *Let $f = 1/d$ with $d = x + y + z^2$. Since $\sigma_x(d) = \sigma_y(d)$ and $c = 1$, f has a telescoper by Lemma 6.3.*

Using partial fraction decomposition, we can decompose the rational function $f = \frac{b}{cd^\lambda}$ into the form

$$f = \frac{1}{d^\lambda}\left(p + \frac{B_1}{C_1} + \frac{B_2}{C_2} + \sum_{i=1}^{I}\sum_{\ell=1}^{m_i} \frac{b_{i,\ell}}{c_i^\ell}\right), \tag{6.6}$$

where $p \in \mathbb{K}(x)[y, z]$, $B_1, B_2, b_{i,\ell} \in \mathbb{K}[x, y, z]$, $C_1, C_2, c_i \in \mathbb{K}[x, y]$, $\deg_y(B_2) < \deg_y(C_2)$, $\deg_y(b_{i,\ell}) < \deg_y(c_i)$, all irreducible factors of C_1 satisfy the condition (6.4), but not any factor of C_2 and the c_i's, and the condition (6.5) holds for all irreducible factors of C_2, but not for any of the c_i's. By Lemma 6.3, $(p + B_1/C_1)/d^\lambda$ has a telescoper and so for the existence problem of telescopers we need only to consider

$$r = \frac{1}{d^\lambda}\left(\frac{B_2}{C_2} + \sum_{i=1}^{I}\sum_{\ell=1}^{m_i} \frac{b_{i,\ell}}{c_i^\ell}\right). \tag{6.7}$$

From now on, we always assume that d satisfies the condition (6.2). As before we consider two distinct cases according to whether or not d satisfies the condition (6.3).

Theorem 6.5. *Let $r = \sum_{i=1}^{I}\sum_{\ell=1}^{m_i} \frac{b_{i,\ell}}{c_i^\ell d^\lambda} \in \mathbb{E}$ where none of the c_i's satisfies the condition (6.4). Suppose that d satisfies the condition (6.2) but not the condition (6.3). Then r has a telescoper if and only if $r = 0$.*

Proof. The sufficiency is clear. For the necessity, we assume that $L = \sum_{i=0}^{\rho} \ell_i S_x^i \in \mathbb{K}(x)[S_x]$ with $\ell_0, \ell_\rho \neq 0$ is a telescoper for r. Let m be the smallest positive integer such that $\sigma_x^m(d) = \sigma_y^n\sigma_z^k(d)$ for some $n, k \in \mathbb{Z}$. Then $\sigma_x^i(d)$ and $\sigma_x^j(d)$ are in distinct $\langle\sigma_y, \sigma_z\rangle$-orbits if $m \nmid (i - j)$. Let $L = L_0 + \ldots + L_{m-1}$ be the m-exponent separation of L. Since the denominators of $L_i(r)$ are in distinct $\langle\sigma_y, \sigma_z\rangle$-orbits, Lemma 3.2 in [21] implies that $L_i(r)$ is (σ_y, σ_z)-summable for all i with $0 \leq i \leq m - 1$. Then $L_0 \neq 0$ is a telescoper for r. Write $L_0 = \sum_{t=0}^{T} a_t S_x^{tm}$. Then

$$L_0(r) = \sum_{t=0}^{T}\sum_{i=1}^{I}\sum_{\ell=1}^{m_i} \frac{a_t\sigma_x^{tm}(b_{i,\ell})}{\sigma_x^{tm}(c_i^\ell)\sigma_x^{tm}(d^\lambda)}$$

$$= \sum_{t=0}^{T}\sum_{i=1}^{I}\sum_{\ell=1}^{m_i} \frac{a_t\sigma_x^{tm}(b_{i,\ell})}{\sigma_x^{tm}(c_i^\ell)\sigma_y^{tn}\sigma_z^{tk}(d^\lambda)}$$

$$= \Delta_y(u) + \Delta_z(v) + \frac{1}{d^\lambda}h$$

for some $u, v \in \mathbb{K}(x, y)$ and

$$h = \sum_{t=0}^{T}\sum_{i=1}^{I}\sum_{\ell=1}^{m_i} \frac{a_t\sigma_x^{tm}\sigma_y^{-tn}\sigma_z^{-tk}(b_{i,\ell})}{\sigma_x^{tm}\sigma_y^{-tn}(c_i^\ell)}.$$

Since $L_0(r)$ is (σ_y, σ_z)-summable but d does not satisfy condition (6.3), Theorem 3.1 implies that $h = 0$. By Lemma 5.1, for each multiplicity ℓ, we have

$$h_\ell = \sum_{t=0}^{T}\sum_{i=1}^{I} \frac{a_t\sigma_x^{tm}\sigma_y^{-tn}\sigma_z^{-tk}(b_{i,\ell})}{\sigma_x^{tm}\sigma_y^{-tn}(c_i^\ell)} = 0.$$

We first claim that there exists a polynomial $p \in \Omega := \{c_i \mid 1 \leq i \leq I\}$ such that $p \neq \sigma_x^{\nu m}\sigma_y^{-\nu n}(q)$ for any $q \in \Omega$ and $\nu \in \mathbb{N}$. We prove this claim by contradiction. Suppose that for any $p_1 \in \Omega$, there always exists $p_2 \in \Omega$ such that $p_1 = \sigma_x^{\nu_1 m}\sigma_y^{-\nu_1 n}(p_2)$ for some positive integer ν_1. If $p_1 = p_2$, then we get a contradiction with the assumption on the c_i's in (6.7). If $p_1 \neq p_2$, then there exists $p_3 \in \Omega$ such that $p_2 = \sigma_x^{\nu_2 m}\sigma_y^{-\nu_2 n}(p_3)$ for some positive integer ν_2. Continuing this process, we get a sequence of polynomials $p_1, p_2, \ldots \in \Omega$. Since Ω is a finite set, $p_i = p_j$ for some $i < j$ in this sequence. Then $p_i = \sigma_x^{\nu m}\sigma_y^{-\nu n}(p_i)$ with $\nu = \nu_i + \cdots \nu_{j-1} > 0$, a contradiction. This completes the proof of the claim.

Suppose now that c_1 is an element in Ω such that $c_1 \neq \sigma_x^{\nu m}\sigma_y^{-\nu n}(q)$ for any $q \in \Omega$ and $\nu \in \mathbb{N}$. Then the fraction $\frac{a_0 b_{1,\ell}}{c_1^\ell}$ has a different irreducible denominator from the other fractions in h_ℓ which implies that $a_0 b_{1,\ell} = 0$. Since $a_0 \neq 0$ we have that $b_{1,\ell} = 0$ for all ℓ. We can now repeat the argument for the set $\Omega \setminus \{c_1\}$ to get $b_{i,\ell} = 0$ for all $i = 2, \ldots, n$ and all ℓ. Thus, $r = 0$. ∎

Example 6.6. *Let*

$$f = \frac{xy + xz + y^2 + yz + 1}{(x + y)((x + y)^2 + z^2)}.$$

We first rewrite f into

$$f = \left(y + z + \frac{1}{x+y} \right) \cdot \frac{1}{(x+y)^2 + z^2}.$$

Letting $d = (x+y)^2 + z^2$ one has $\sigma_x d = \sigma_y d$ and hence from Remark 2.3 and Lemma 6.3 we see that f has a telescoper. In fact, following the proof of Lemma 6.3, we can see that

$$L_1 = S_x^2 - 2S_x + 1 = (S_x - 1)^2 \quad \textit{and} \quad L_2 = S_x - 1$$

are telescopers for $\frac{y+z}{d}$ and for $\frac{1}{(x+y)d}$, respectively. Thus $L = (S_x - 1)^2$ is a telescoper for f.

We now study the case when d satisfies the condition (6.3). Assume that n_1 is the smallest positive integer such that $\sigma_y^{n_1}(d) = \sigma_z^{k_1}(d)$ for some $k_1 \in \mathbb{Z}$. By Lemma 6.3, the fraction $\frac{B_2}{C_2 d^\lambda}$ in (6.7) has a telescoper. It remains to study the existence of telescopers for rational functions of the form

$$r = \sum_{i=1}^{I} \sum_{\ell=1}^{m_i} \frac{b_{i,\ell}}{c_i^\ell d^\lambda}, \tag{6.8}$$

where $b_{i,\ell} \in \mathbb{K}[x,y,z], c_i \in \mathbb{K}[x,y], \deg_y(b_{i,\ell}) < \deg_y(c_i)$, and the c_i's are irreducible polynomials such that condition (6.5) is not satisfied.

Theorem 6.7. *Let r be of the form (6.8) with d satisfying conditions (6.2) and (6.3) and where c_i's do not satisfy the condition (6.5). Then r has a telescoper if and only if*

$$r_\ell := \sum_{i=1}^{I} \frac{b_{i,\ell}}{c_i^\ell d^\lambda}$$

is (σ_y, σ_z)-summable for all ℓ.

Proof. The sufficiency follows from Remark 2.3. For the necessity, we assume that L is a telescoper for r. By the same argument as in the proof of Theorem 6.5, we may always assume that $L = \sum_{t=0}^{T} a_t S_x^{tm}$ with $a_0 \neq 0$. The same calculation as in the proof of Theorem 6.5 then yields

$$L(r) = \Delta_y(u) + \Delta_z(v) + \frac{1}{d^\lambda} h,$$

where $u, v \in \mathbb{K}(x,y,z)$ and $h := Q(\sum_{i=1}^{I} \sum_{\ell=1}^{m_i} b_{i,\ell}/c_i^\ell)$ with

$$Q = \sum_{t=0}^{T} a_t S_x^{tm} S_y^{-tn} S_z^{-tk} \in \mathbb{K}(x)[S_x, S_y, S_z].$$

Since $L(r)$ is (σ_y, σ_z)-summable but d satisfies the condition (6.3), Theorem 3.1 implies that $h = \sigma_y^{n_1} \sigma_z^{-k_1}(p) - p$, where $p \in \mathbb{K}(x,y)[z]$ with $\deg_z(p) < \deg_z(d)$. By Lemma 5.1, for each multiplicity ℓ, we have

$$h_\ell = Q\left(\sum_{i=1}^{I} \frac{b_{i,\ell}}{c_i^\ell} \right) = \sigma_y^{n_1} \sigma_z^{-k_1}(p_\ell) - p_\ell.$$

Let $\triangle := \{c_i \mid 1 \le i \le I\}$. As in the argument for the proof of Theorem 6.5, we may assume $c_1 \in \triangle$ satisfying $c_1 \neq \sigma_x^m \sigma_y^n c_i$ for any $c_i \in \triangle$, when $m, n \in \mathbb{Z}$ with $m > 0$. Note that there may exist some $c_i \in \triangle \setminus \{c_1\}$ such that $c_1 = \sigma_y^n c_i$ for some $n \in \mathbb{Z}$, and we will let

$$\triangle_1 = \{i \mid 1 \le i \le I, c_i = \sigma_y^n c_1 \text{ for some } n \in \mathbb{Z}\}.$$

Continuing now with $\triangle \setminus \triangle_1$, we will find $c_1, c_2, \ldots, c_M \in \triangle$ and $\triangle_1, \triangle_2, \ldots, \triangle_M$ such that for $1 \le i < i' \le M$, we have $c_i \neq \sigma_x^m \sigma_y^n c_{i'}$, when $m, n \in \mathbb{Z}$, $m > 0$ and $\{1, 2, \ldots, I\} = \bigcup_{i=1}^{M} \triangle_i$. We can therefore rewrite h_ℓ as

$$Q\left(\sum_{j=1}^{M} \sum_{i \in \triangle_j} \frac{b_{i,\ell}}{c_i^\ell} \right) = \sigma_y^{n_1} \sigma_z^{-k_1}(p_\ell) - p_\ell. \tag{6.9}$$

Since $p_\ell \in \mathbb{Q}(x,y)[z]$, we can decompose it into

$$p_\ell = \sum_{j=1}^{M} \sum_{t=\alpha_j}^{\beta_j} \frac{u_{j,t}}{\sigma_y^t(c_j^\ell)} + q_\ell,$$

where $\alpha_i, \beta_i \in \mathbb{Z}$ and q_ℓ contains no term of the form $\frac{u_{j,t}}{\sigma_y^t(c_j^\ell)}$ in its irreducible partial fraction decomposition with respect to y. According to Equation (6.9) and the uniqueness of irreducible partial fraction decomposition along with the fact that $a_0 \in \mathbb{K}(x) \setminus \{0\}$, we derive that

$$\sum_{i \in \triangle_1} \frac{b_{i,\ell}}{c_i^\ell} = \sigma_y^{n_1} \sigma_z^{-k_1}(h_{1,\ell}) - h_{1,\ell},$$

where $h_{1,\ell} = \frac{1}{a_0} \sum_{t=\alpha_1}^{\beta_1} \frac{u_{1,t}}{\sigma_y^t(c_1^\ell)}$. Collecting all the terms with the denominator $\langle \sigma_x, \sigma_y \rangle$-equivalent to c_1 in Equation (6.9), we obtain

$$Q\left(\sum_{i \in \triangle_1} \frac{b_{i,\ell}}{c_i^\ell} \right) = Q\left(\sigma_y^{n_1} \sigma_k^{-k_1}(h_{1,\ell}) - h_{1,\ell} \right) \tag{6.10}$$

$$= \sigma_y^{n_1} \sigma_k^{-k_1}(p_{1,\ell}) - p_{1,\ell} \tag{6.11}$$

with $p_{1,\ell} = Q(h_{1,\ell})$. Subtracting Equation (6.11) from Equation (6.9), we obtain

$$Q\left(\sum_{j=2}^{M} \sum_{i \in \triangle_j} \frac{b_{i,\ell}}{c_i^\ell} \right) = \sigma_y^{n_1} \sigma_z^{-k_1}(p_\ell^\star) - p_\ell^\star \tag{6.12}$$

with $p_\ell^\star = p_\ell - p_{1,\ell}$. Now we can repeat the arguments for the set $\Delta \setminus \Delta_1$ and Equation (6.12) to get

$$\sum_{i \in \triangle_j} \frac{b_{i,\ell}}{c_i^\ell} = \sigma_y^{n_1} \sigma_z^{-k_1}(h_{j,\ell}) - h_{j,\ell}$$

for all $j = 1, \ldots, M$ and all ℓ. Then $\sum_{i \in \triangle_j} \frac{b_{i,\ell}}{c_i^\ell d^\lambda}$ is (σ_y, σ_z)-summable by Theorem 3.1 and thus $\sum_{i=1}^{I} \frac{b_{i,\ell}}{c_i^\ell d^\lambda}$ is (σ_y, σ_z)-summable for all ℓ. This completes the proof. ∎

Combining Lemmas 6.2, 6.3 and Theorems 6.5, 6.7, we now present an algorithm for testing the existence of telescopers for simple fractions in Figure 1.

Remark 6.8. *For testing the existence of telescopers for a general rational function $f \in \mathbb{K}(x,y,z)$, we first apply the algorithm in [21] to compute the additive decomposition $f = \Delta_y(g) + \Delta_z(h) + r$, where $g, h, r \in \mathbb{K}(x,y,z)$ and r is of the form (5.2) with the d_i's satisfying the condition (5.3). By Lemmas 5.2 and 5.3, the existence of telescoper for f can be determined by applying Algorithm* ExistenceTelescoperSimple *to each simple fraction of r.*

Example 6.9. *Let*

$$f = \frac{x^4 + 2x^2y^2 + y^4 + x^3 + 3yx^2 + y^3 - xy^2 + x^2 - xy}{(x+y)(x^2+y^2+2y+1)(x^2+y^2)(x+y+z)^2}.$$

Algorithm ExistenceTelescoperSimple

INPUT: $f = b/cd^\lambda$ as in (6.1).

OUTPUT: true if f has a telescoper; false otherwise.

1. Using partial fraction decomposition, decompose f into the form (6.6);
2. If d does not satisfy the condition (6.2), return true if f is summable (checked by the algorithm in [21]) and false otherwise; Else
   (a) if d does not satisfy the condition (6.3), return true if $B_2 = 0$ and $b_{i,\ell} = 0$ for all i, ℓ and false otherwise; Else
      i. return true if $r_\ell := \sum_{i=1}^{I} \frac{b_{i,\ell}}{c_i^\ell d^\lambda}$ is summable for all ℓ, and false otherwise.

Figure 1: Testing the existence of telescopers for simple fractions.

First decompose f as

$$f = \left(\frac{1}{x+y} + \frac{y+1}{x^2+y^2+2y+1} - \frac{y}{x^2+y^2}\right) \cdot \frac{1}{(x+y+z)^2}.$$

Letting $d = x+y+z$, we have $\sigma_x d = \sigma_y d$ and $\sigma_y d = \sigma_z d$. As in the proof of Lemma 6.3, we get that $L = S_x - 1$ is a telescoper for $\frac{1}{(x+y)(x+y+z)^2}$. Theorem 3.1 then guarantees

$$\left(\frac{y+1}{x^2+y^2+2y+1} - \frac{y}{x^2+y^2}\right) \cdot \frac{1}{(x+y+z)^2}.$$

is (σ_y, σ_z)-summable, so $L = S_x - 1$ is a telescoper for f.

7. CONCLUSION

In this paper, we solve the existence problem of telescopers for rational functions in three discrete variables. We give a procedure which reduces the problem to a special shift equivalence testing problem and the summability problem of bivariate rational functions. Those problems have recently been solved.

In terms of future research, the first direction is to solve the existence problem of telescopers for multivariate rational functions or a more general class of functions, for example, hypergeometric terms. This would include both efficient algorithms and implementations. A crucial step is to solve the summability problem for these functions. This is also a challenging problem in symbolic summation as noted in [9].

Acknowledgement. The authors would like to thank the anonymous referees for their constructive and helpful comments, which have significantly improved the presentation of this paper.

8. REFERENCES

[1] S. A. Abramov. The rational component of the solution of a first order linear recurrence relation with rational right hand side. *Ž. Vyčisl. Mat. i Mat. Fiz.*, 15(4):1035–1039, 1090, 1975.

[2] S. A. Abramov. Indefinite sums of rational functions. In *Proc. of ISSAC '95*, ACM Press, 303–308, 1995.

[3] S. A. Abramov. When does Zeilberger's algorithm succeed? *Adv. in Appl. Math.*, 30(3):424–441, 2003.

[4] S. A. Abramov and Mark Van Hoeij. Integration of solutions of linear functional equations. *Integral Transforms and Special Functions*, 8(1-2):3–12, 1999.

[5] S. A. Abramov and Ha Quang Le. A criterion for the applicability of Zeilberger's algorithm to rational functions. *Discrete Math.*, 259(1-3):1–17, 2002.

[6] S. A. Abramov, Ha Quang Le, and Ziming Li. Univariate Ore polynomial rings in computer algebra. *Journal of Math. Sci.*, 131(5):5885–5903, 2005.

[7] S. A. Abramov and Marko Petkovšek. On the structure of multivariate hypergeometric terms. *Adv. Appl. Math.*, 29(3):386–411, 2002.

[8] S. A. Abramov and Mark van Hoeij. A method for the integration of solutions of Ore equations. In *Proceedings of ISSAC '97*, ACM Press, 172–175, 1997.

[9] G. E. Andrews and P. Paule. Some questions concerning computer-generated proofs of a binomial double-sum identity. *J. Symbolic Comput.*, 16(2):147–151, August 1993.

[10] B. Beckermann, H. Cheng and G. Labahn, Fraction-free Row Reduction of Matrices of Skew Polynomials, *Proceedings of ISSAC'02*, ACM Press, 8-15, 2002.

[11] M. Bronstein and M. Petkovšek. An introduction to pseudo-linear algebra. *Theoret. Comput. Sci.*, 157:3–33, 1996.

[12] S. Chen, F. Chyzak, R. Feng, G. Fu, and Z. Li. On the existence of telescopers for mixed hypergeometric terms. *J. Symbolic Comput.*, 68:1–26, 2015.

[13] S. Chen and M. F. Singer. On the summability of bivariate rational functions. *Journal of Algebra*, 409:320 – 343, 2014.

[14] W. Y. C. Chen, Q. Hou, and Y. Mu. Applicability of the q-analogue of Zeilberger's algorithm. *J. Symbolic Comput.*, 39(2):155–170, 2005.

[15] W. Y. C. Chen, Q. Hou, and Y. Mu. A telescoping method for double summations. *J. Comput. Appl. Math.*, 196(2):553–566, 2006.

[16] F. Chyzak, M. Kauers, and B. Salvy. A non-holonomic systems approach to special function identities. In *Proceedings of ISSAC'09*, ACM Press, 111–118, 2009.

[17] Z. Dvir, R. Mendes de Oliveira, and A. Shpilka. Testing equivalence of polynomials under shifts. In *Automata, languages, and programming. Part I*, volume 8572 of *LNCS*, pages 417–428. Springer, 2014.

[18] R. W. Gosper, Jr. Decision procedure for indefinite hypergeometric summation. *Proc. Nat. Acad. Sci. U.S.A.*, 75(1):40–42, 1978.

[19] D. Grigoriev. Testing shift-equivalence of polynomials using quantum machines. In *Proc. of ISSAC'96*, ACM Press, 49–54, 1996.

[20] D. Grigoriev. Testing shift-equivalence of polynomials by deterministic, probabilistic and quantum machines. *Theoret. Comput. Sci.*, 180(1-2):217–228, 1997.

[21] Q. Hou and R. Wang. An algorithm for deciding the summability of bivariate rational functions. *Adv. in Appl. Math.*, 64:31 – 49, 2015.

[22] M. Karr. Summation in finite terms. *J. Assoc. Comput. Mach.*, 28(2):305–350, 1981.

[23] M. Karr. Theory of summation in finite terms. *J. Symbolic Comput.*, 1(3):303–315, 1985.

[24] P. Paule. Greatest factorial factorization and symbolic summation. *J. Symbolic Comput.*, 20(3):235–268, 1995.

[25] R. Pirastu. Algorithms for indefinite summation of rational functions in Maple. In *MapleTech*, pages 29–38, 1995.

[26] C. Schneider. *Symbolic Summation in Difference Fields.* PhD thesis, J. Kepler University Linz, 2001.

[27] H. S. Wilf and D. Zeilberger. An algorithmic proof theory for hypergeometric (ordinary and "q") multisum/integral identities. *Invent. Math.*, 108(3):575–633, 1992.

[28] D. Zeilberger. A fast algorithm for proving terminating hypergeometric identities. *Discrete Math.*, 80(2):207–211, 1990.

[29] D. Zeilberger. A holonomic systems approach to special functions identities. *J. Comput. Appl. Math.*, 32:321–368, 1990.

Reduction-Based Creative Telescoping for Algebraic Functions*

Shaoshi Chen[1,2], Manuel Kauers[3], Christoph Koutschan[4]

[1]KLMM, AMSS, Chinese Academy of Sciences, Beijing, 100190, (China)

[2]Symbolic Computation Group, University of Waterloo, Ontario, N2L3G1, (Canada)

[3]Institute for Algebra, Johannes Kepler University, Altenberger Straße 69, A-4040 Linz, (Austria)

[4]RICAM, Austrian Academy of Sciences, Altenberger Straße 69, A-4040 Linz, (Austria)

schen@amss.ac.cn, manuel.kauers@jku.at

christoph.koutschan@ricam.oeaw.ac.at

ABSTRACT

Continuing a series of articles in the past few years on creative telescoping using reductions, we develop a new algorithm to construct minimal telescopers for algebraic functions. This algorithm is based on Trager's Hermite reduction and on polynomial reduction, which was originally designed for hyperexponential functions and extended to the algebraic case in this paper.

Keywords

Algebraic function, Integral basis, Trager's Reduction, Telescoper

1. INTRODUCTION

The classical question in symbolic integration is whether the integral of a given function can be written in "closed form". In its most restricted form, the question is whether for a given function f belonging to some domain D there exists another function g, also belonging to D, such that $f = g'$. For example, if D is the field of rational functions, then for $f = 1/x^2$ we can find $g = -1/x$, while for $f = 1/x$ no suitable g exists. When no g exists in D, there are several other questions we may ask. One possibility is to ask whether there is some extension E of D such that in E there exists some g with $g' = f$. For example, in the case of elementary functions, Liouville's principle restricts the possible extensions E, and there are algorithms which construct such extensions whenever possible. Another possibility is to ask whether for some modification $\tilde{f} \in D$ of f there exists a $g \in D$ such that $\tilde{f} = g'$. Creative telescoping is a question of this type. Here we are dealing with domains D containing functions in several variables, say x and t, and the question is whether there is a linear differential operator P, nonzero and free of x, such that there exists a $g \in D$ with $P \cdot f = g'$, where g' denotes the derivative of g with respect to x. Typically, g itself has the form $Q \cdot f$ for some operator Q (which may be zero and need not be free of x). In this case, we call P a telescoper for f, and Q a certificate for P.

Creative telescoping is the backbone of definite integration, because $P \cdot f = (Q \cdot f)'$ implies, for instance, $P \cdot \int_0^1 f(x,t)dx = (Q \cdot f)(1) - (Q \cdot f)(0)$. A telescoper P for f thus gives rise to an annihilating operator for the definite integral $F(t) = \int_0^1 f(x,t)dx$.

Example 1 (Manin [20]). *The algebraic function*

$$f(x,t) = \frac{1}{\sqrt{x(x-1)(x-t)}}$$

does not admit an elementary integral with respect to x. However, we have $P \cdot f = (Q \cdot f)'$ for

$$P = 4(t-1)t\,D_t^2 + 4(2t-1)D_t + 1, \quad Q = \frac{2x(x-1)}{t-x}.$$

This implies

$$P \cdot \int_0^1 f(x,t)dx = \left[\frac{2x(x-1)}{t-x} f(x,t)\right]_{x=0}^{x=1},$$

so the integral $F(t) = \int_0^1 \frac{1}{\sqrt{x(x-1)(x-t)}}dx$ satisfies the differential equation

$$4(t-1)t\,F''(t) + 4(2t-1)F'(t) + F(t) = 0.$$

In the common case when the right hand side collapses to zero, we say that the integral has "natural boundaries". Readers not familiar with creative telescoping are referred to the literature [21, 25, 27, 26, 18, 16] for additional motivation, theory, algorithms, implementations, and applications.

There are several ways to find telescopers for a given $f \in D$. In recent years, an approach has become popular

*S. Chen was supported by the NSFC grant 11501552 and by the President Fund of the Academy of Mathematics and Systems Science, CAS (2014-cjrwlzx-chshsh). This work was also supported by the Fields Institute's 2015 Thematic Program on Computer Algebra in Toronto, Canada.
M. Kauers was supported by the Austrian Science Fund (FWF): F50-04 and Y464-N18.
C. Koutschan was supported by the Austrian Science Fund (FWF): W1214.

ISSAC '16, July 19 - 22, 2016, Waterloo, ON, Canada

ISBN 978-1-4503-4380-0/16/07...$15.00

DOI: http://dx.doi.org/10.1145/2930889.2930901

which has the feature that it can find a telescoper without also constructing the corresponding certificate. This is interesting because certificates tend to be much larger than telescopers, and in some applications, for instance when an integral has natural boundaries, only the telescoper is of interest. This approach was first formulated for rational functions $f \in C(t,x)$ in [1] and later generalized to rational functions in several variables [3, 19], to hyperexponential functions [2] and, for the shift case, to hypergeometric terms [7, 14] and binomial sums [4]. In the present paper, we will extend the approach to algebraic functions.

The basic principle of the general approach is as follows. Assume that the x-constants $\mathrm{Const}_x(D) = \{ c \in D : c' = 0 \}$ form a field and that D is a vector space over the field of x-constants. Assume further that there is some $\mathrm{Const}_x(D)$-linear map $[\cdot]\colon D \to D$ such that for every $f \in D$ there exists a $g \in D$ with $f - [f] = g'$. Such a map is called a *reduction*. For example, in $D = C(t,x)$ Hermite reduction [13] produces for every $f \in D$ some $g \in D$ such that $f - g'$ is either zero or a rational function with a square-free denominator. In this case, we can take $[f] = f - g'$. In order to find a telescoper, we can compute $[f]$, $[\partial_t \cdot f]$, $[\partial_t^2 \cdot f]$, …, until we find that they are linearly dependent over $\mathrm{Const}_x(D)$. Once we find a relation $p_0[f] + \cdots + p_r[\partial_t^r \cdot f] = 0$, then, by linearity, $[p_0 f + \cdots + p_r \partial_t^r \cdot f] = 0$, and then, by definition of $[\cdot]$, there exists a $g \in D$ such that $(p_0 + \cdots + p_r\partial_t^r) \cdot f = g'$. In other words, $P = p_0 + \cdots + p_r \partial_t^r$ is a telescoper.

There are two ways to guarantee that this method terminates. The first requires that we already know for other reasons that a telescoper exists. The idea is then to show that the reduction $[\cdot]$ has the property that when $f \in D$ is such that there exists a $g \in D$ with $g' = f$, then $[f] = 0$. If this is the case and $P = p_0 + \cdots + p_r \partial_t^r$ is a telescoper for f, then $P \cdot f$ is integrable in D, so $[P \cdot f] = 0$, and by linearity $[f]$, …, $[\partial_t^r \cdot f]$ are linearly dependent over $\mathrm{Const}_x(D)$. This means that the method won't miss any telescoper. In particular, this argument has the nice feature that we are guaranteed to find a telescoper of smallest possible order r. This approach was taken in [7]. The second way consists in showing that the $\mathrm{Const}_x(D)$-vector space generated by $\{ [\partial_t^i \cdot f] : i \in \mathbb{N} \}$ has finite dimension. This approach was taken in [1, 2]. It has the nice additional feature that every bound for the dimension of this vector space gives rise to a bound for the order of the telescoper. In particular, it implies the existence of a telescoper.

In this paper, we show that Trager's Hermite reduction for algebraic functions directly gives rise to a reduction-based creative telescoping algorithm via the first approach (Section 4). We will combine Trager's Hermite reduction with a second reduction, called polynomial reduction (Section 5), to obtain a reduction-based creative telescoping algorithm for algebraic functions via the second approach (Section 6). This gives a new bound for the order of the telescopers, and in particular an independent proof for their existence.

A few years ago, Chen et al. [9] have already considered the problem of creative telescoping for algebraic functions. They have pointed out that by canceling residues of the integrand, a given creative telescoping problem can be reduced to a creative telescoping problem for a function with no residues, which may be much smaller than the original function. For this smaller function, however, they still need to construct a certificate. With some regularity assumption on certificates, Bostan et al. [3] gave a telescoping algorithm for multivariate rational functions using Griffiths-Dwork reduction, which then leads to a reduction-based telescoping algorithm for algebraic functions by Theorem 6 of [9]. The algorithms presented in the present paper can find minimal telescopers for bivariate algebraic functions without any regularity assumption on certificates. Our results also translate into a certificate-free creative telescoping algorithm for rational functions in three variables.

2. ALGEBRAIC FUNCTIONS

Throughout the paper, let C be a field of characteristic zero, $K = C(t)$, and $\bar{K}$ the algebraic closure of K. We consider algebraic functions over K. For some absolutely irreducible polynomial $m \in K[x,y]$, we consider the field $A = K(x)[y]/\langle m \rangle$. If $n = \deg_y m$, then every element of A can be written uniquely in the form $f = f_0 + f_1 y + \cdots + f_{n-1}y^{n-1}$ for some $f_0, \ldots, f_{n-1} \in K(x)$.

The element $y \in A$ is a solution of the equation $m = 0$, because in A we have $m = 0$ by construction. The polynomial m also admits n distinct solutions in the field

$$\bar{K}\langle\langle x-a \rangle\rangle := \bigcup_{r \in \mathbb{N}\setminus\{0\}} \bar{K}((\ (x-a)^{1/r}\ ))$$

of formal Puiseux series around $a \in \bar{K}$. There are also n distinct solutions in the field

$$\bar{K}\langle\langle x^{-1} \rangle\rangle := \bigcup_{r \in \mathbb{N}\setminus\{0\}} \bar{K}((x^{-1/r}))$$

of formal Puiseux series around ∞. Since $\bar{K}\langle\langle x^{-1}\rangle\rangle$ and the $\bar{K}\langle\langle x-a\rangle\rangle$ are fields, we can associate to every $f \in A$ and every $a \in \bar{K} \cup \{\infty\}$ in a natural way n distinct series objects with fractional exponents, by plugging any of the n distinct series solutions of m into the representation $f = f_0 + \cdots + f_{n-1}y^{n-1}$. In other words, for every $a \in \bar{K} \cup \{\infty\}$ there are n distinct natural ring homomorphisms from A to $K\langle\langle x-a\rangle\rangle$ or $K\langle\langle x^{-1}\rangle\rangle$, respectively.

In the field A as well as the fields $\bar{K}\langle\langle x-a\rangle\rangle$ and $\bar{K}\langle\langle x^{-1}\rangle\rangle$, we have natural differentiations with respect to x. For a series, differentiation is defined termwise using the usual rules $\left((x-a)^{\nu+n}\right)' = (\nu+n)(x-a)^{\nu+n-1}$ and $\left((x^{-1})^{\nu+n}\right)' = -(\nu+n)(x^{-1})^{\nu+n+1}$. For the elements of A, note first that $m(x,y) = 0$ implies

$$m(x,y)' = (\frac{d}{dx}m)(x,y) + (\frac{d}{dy}m)(x,y)y' = 0, \qquad (1)$$

so $y' = -(\frac{d}{dx}m)(x,y)/(\frac{d}{dy}m)(x,y)$. Regarding m as element of $K(x)[y]$ and observing that $0 < \deg_y \frac{d}{dy}m < n$, we have $\gcd(m, \frac{d}{dy}m) = 1$ in $K(x)[y]$, so $\frac{d}{dy}m$ is invertible in $A = K(x)[y]/\langle m\rangle$. Note that we have $x' = 1$ and $c' = 0$ for all $c \in K = C(t)$, in particular also $t' = 0$. The derivative of an arbitrary element $f \in A$, say $f = p(x,y)$ for some $p \in K(x)[y]$ of degree less than n, is

$$f' = (\frac{d}{dx}p)(x,y) + (\frac{d}{dy}p)(x,y)y'.$$

Thus we have an action of the algebra $K(x)[\partial_x]$ of differential operators on A.

The derivations on A and on the series domains are compatible in the sense that for every $f \in A$, the series associated to f' are precisely the derivatives of the series associated to f.

In the context of creative telescoping, we will also need to differentiate with respect to t. The action of $K(x)[\partial_x]$ on A and on the series domains is extended to an action of $K(x)[\partial_x, \partial_t]$ on A and on the series domains. On A, the action of ∂_t is defined as the unique derivation with $\partial_t \cdot t = 1$ and $\partial_t \cdot x = 0$, analogously to the construction above. For the series domains, ∂_t acts on the coefficients (which are elements of $\bar{K}$) in the natural way, and does not affect x. Since each particular element $c \in \bar{K}$ belongs to a finite algebraic extension of K, the result $\partial_t \cdot c$ is uniquely determined. The actions of the larger operator algebra $K(x)[\partial_x, \partial_t]$ on A and on the series domains are compatible to each other.

In this paper, the notation f' will always refer to the derivative $\partial_x \cdot f$ with respect to x, not with respect to t.

Trager's Hermite reduction for algebraic functions rests on the notion of integral bases. Let us recall the relevant definitions and properties. Although the elements of a Puiseux series ring $\bar{K}\langle\langle x-a\rangle\rangle$ are formal objects, the series notation suggests certain analogies with complex functions. Terms $(x-a)^\alpha$ or $(\frac{1}{x})^\alpha$ are called *integral* if $\alpha \geq 0$. A series in $\bar{K}\langle\langle x-a\rangle\rangle$ or $\bar{K}\langle\langle x^{-1}\rangle\rangle$ is called integral if it only contains integral terms. A non-integral series is said to have a *pole* at the reference point. Note that in this terminology also $1/\sqrt{x}$ has a pole at 0. Note also that the terminology only refers to x but not to t.

Integrality at $a \in \bar{K}$ is not preserved by differentiation, but if f is integral at a, then so is $(x-a)f'$. On the other hand, integrality at infinity is preserved by differentiation, we even have the stronger property that when f is integral at infinity, then not only f' but also $xf' = (x^{-1})^{-1}f'$ is integral at infinity.

An element $f \in A = K(x)[y]/\langle m\rangle$ is called (locally) integral at $a \in \bar{K} \cup \{\infty\}$ if for every series associated to y the corresponding series for f is integral. The element f is called (globally) integral if it is locally integral at every $a \in \bar{K}$ ("at all finite places"). This is the case if and only if the minimal polynomial of f in $K[x, y]$ is monic with respect to y. Because of Chevalley's theorem [10, page 9, Corollary 3], any non-constant algebraic function has at least one pole. Equivalently, an element f is integral at all $a \in \bar{K} \cup \{\infty\}$ if and only if it is constant.

For an element $f \in A$ to have a "pole" at $a \in \bar{K} \cup \{\infty\}$ means that f is not locally integral at a; to have a "double pole" at a means that $(x-a)f$ (or $\frac{1}{x}f$ if $a = \infty$) is not integral; to have a "double root" at a means that $f/(x-a)^2$ (or $f/(\frac{1}{x})^2 = x^2 f$ if $a = \infty$) is integral, and so on.

The set of all globally integral elements $f \in A$ forms a $K[x]$-submodule of A. A basis $\{\omega_1, \dots, \omega_n\}$ of this module is called an *integral basis* for A. Such bases exist, and algorithms are known for computing them [21, 22, 15]. For a fixed $a \in \bar{K}$, let $\bar{K}(x)_a$ be the ring of rational functions p/q with $q(a) \neq 0$, and write $\bar{K}(x)_\infty$ for the ring of all rational functions p/q with $\deg_x(p) \leq \deg_x(q)$. Then the set of all $f \in A$ which are locally integral at some fixed $a \in \bar{K} \cup \{\infty\}$ forms a $\bar{K}(x)_a$-module. A basis of this module is called a *local integral basis* at a for A. Also local integral bases can be computed.

An integral basis $\{\omega_1, \dots, \omega_n\}$ is always also a $K(x)$-vector space basis of A. A key feature of integral bases is that they make poles explicit. Writing an element $f \in A$ as a linear combination $f = \sum_{i=1}^n f_i \omega_i$ for some $f_i \in K(x)$, we have that f has a pole at $a \in \bar{K}$ if and only if at least one of the f_i has a pole there.

Lemma 2. *Let $\{\omega_1, \dots, \omega_n\}$ be a local integral basis of A at $a \in \bar{K} \cup \{\infty\}$. Let $f \in A$ and $f_1, \dots, f_n \in K(x)$ be such that $f = \sum_{i=1}^n f_i \omega_i$. Then f is integral at a if and only if each $f_i \omega_i$ is integral at a.*

Proof. The direction "$\Leftarrow$" is obvious. To show "$\Rightarrow$", suppose that f is integral at a. Then there exist $w_1, \dots, w_n \in \bar{K}(x)_a$ such that $f = \sum_{i=1}^n w_i \omega_i$. Thus $\sum_{i=1}^n (w_i - f_i)\omega_i = 0$, and then $w_i = f_i$ for all i, because $\omega_1, \dots, \omega_n$ is a vector space basis of A. As elements of $\bar{K}(x)_a$, the f_i are integral at a, and hence also all the $f_i \omega_i$ are integral at a. ∎

The lemma says in particular that poles of the f_i in a linear combination $\sum_{i=1}^n f_i \omega_i$ cannot cancel each other.

Lemma 3. *Let $\{\omega_1, \dots, \omega_n\}$ be an integral basis of A. Let $e \in K[x]$ and $M = ((m_{i,j}))_{i,j=1}^n \in K[x]^{n \times n}$ be such that*

$$e\,\omega_i' = \sum_{j=1}^n m_{i,j}\omega_j$$

for $i = 1, \dots, n$ and $\gcd(e, m_{1,1}, \dots, m_{n,n}) = 1$. Then e is squarefree.

Proof. Let $a \in \bar{K}$ be a root of e. We show that a is not a multiple root. Since ω_i is integral, it is in particular locally integral at a. Therefore $(x-a)\omega_i'$ is locally integral at a. Since $\omega_1, \dots, \omega_n$ is an integral basis, it follows that $(x-a)m_{i,j}/e \in \bar{K}(x)_a$ for all i, j. Because of $\gcd(e, m_{1,1}, \dots, m_{n,n}) = 1$, no factor $x-a$ of e can be canceled by all the $m_{i,j}$. Therefore the factor $x-a$ can appear in e only once. ∎

Lemma 4. *Let $\{\omega_1, \dots, \omega_n\}$ be a local integral basis at infinity of A. Let $e \in K[x]$ and $M = ((m_{i,j}))_{i,j=1}^n \in K[x]^{n \times n}$ be defined as in Lemma 3. Then $\deg_x(m_{i,j}) < \deg_x(e)$ for all i, j.*

Proof. Since every ω_i is locally integral at infinity, so is every $x\omega_i'$. Since $\omega_1, \dots, \omega_n$ is an integral basis at infinity, it follows that $xm_{i,j}/e \in \bar{K}(x)_\infty$ for all i, j. This means that $1 + \deg_x(m_{i,j}) \leq \deg_x(e)$ for all i, j, and therefore $\deg_x(m_{i,j}) < \deg_x(e)$, as claimed. ∎

A $K(x)$-vector space basis $\{\omega_1, \dots, \omega_n\}$ of A is called *normal* at $a \in \bar{K} \cup \{\infty\}$ if there exist $r_1, \dots, r_n \in K(x)$ such that $\{r_1\omega_1, \dots, r_n\omega_n\}$ is a local integral basis at a. Trager shows how to construct an integral basis which is normal at infinity from a given integral basis and a given local integral basis at infinity [24].

Although normality is a somewhat weaker condition on a basis than integrality, it also excludes the possibility that poles in the terms of a linear combination of basis elements can cancel:

Lemma 5. *Let $\{\omega_1, \dots, \omega_n\}$ be a basis of A which is normal at some $a \in \bar{K} \cup \{\infty\}$. Let $f = \sum_{i=1}^n f_i \omega_i$ for some $f_1, \dots, f_n \in K(x)$. Then f has a pole at a if and only if there is some i such that $f_i \omega_i$ has a pole at a.*

Proof. Let $r_1, \dots, r_n \in K(x)$ be such that $r_1\omega_1, \dots, r_n\omega_n$ is a local integral basis at a. By $f = \sum_{i=1}^n (f_i r_i^{-1})(r_i \omega_i)$ and by Lemma 2, f is integral at a iff all $f_i r_i^{-1} r_i \omega_i = f_i \omega_i$ are integral at a. ∎

3. HERMITE REDUCTION

We now recall the Hermite reduction for algebraic functions [24, 12, 6]. Let $\{\omega_1, \ldots, \omega_n\}$ be an integral basis for A. Further let $e, m_{i,j} \in K[x]$ $(1 \leq i, j \leq n)$ be such that $e\omega_i' = \sum_{j=1}^n m_{i,j}\omega_i$ and $\gcd(e, m_{1,1}, m_{1,2}, \ldots, m_{n,n}) = 1$. For describing the Hermite reduction we fix an integrand $f \in A$ and represent it in the integral basis, i.e., $f = \sum_{i=1}^n (f_i/D)\,\omega_i$ with $D, f_1, \ldots, f_n \in K[x]$. The purpose is to find $g, h \in A$ such that $f = g' + h$ and $h = \sum_{i=1}^n (h_i/D^*)\,\omega_i$ with $h_1, \ldots, h_n \in K[x]$ and D^* denoting the squarefree part of D. As differentiating the ω_i can introduce denominators, namely the factors of e, it is convenient to consider those denominators from the very beginning on, which means that we shall assume $e \mid D$. Note that $\gcd(D, f_1, \ldots, f_n)$ can then be nontrivial. Let $v \in K[x]$ be a nontrivial squarefree factor of D of multiplicity $\mu > 1$. Then $D = uv^\mu$ for some $u \in K[x]$ with $\gcd(u, v) = 1$ and $\gcd(v, v') = 1$. One step of the Hermite reduction is as follows:

$$\sum_{i=1}^n \frac{f_i}{uv^\mu}\omega_i = \left(\sum_{i=1}^n \frac{g_i}{v^{\mu-1}}\omega_i\right)' + \sum_{i=1}^n \frac{h_i}{uv^{\mu-1}}\omega_i, \qquad (2)$$

where $g_i, h_i \in K[x]$ and $\deg_x(g_i) < \deg_x(v)$. The existence of such g_i's and h_i's follows from the crucial fact that the elements $s_i := uv^\mu(v^{1-\mu}\omega_i)'$ with $i \in \{1, \ldots, n\}$ form a local integral basis at each root of v [24, page 46]. By a repeated application of such reduction steps, one can decompose any $f \in A$ as $f = g' + h$ where the denominators of the coefficients of h are squarefree and the coefficients of g are proper rational functions (i.e., their numerators have smaller degree than their denominators).

It was observed that Hermite reduction itself often takes less time than the construction of an integral basis. If Hermite reduction is applied to some other basis, for instance the standard basis $\{1, y, \ldots, y^{n-1}\}$, it either succeeds or it runs into a division by zero. Bronstein [5] noticed that when a division by zero occurs, then the basis can be replaced by some other basis that is a little closer to an integral basis, just as much as is needed to avoid this particular division by zero. After finitely many such basis changes, the Hermite reduction will come to an end and produce a correct output. This variant is known as lazy Hermite reduction.

4. TELESCOPING VIA REDUCTIONS: FIRST APPROACH

Recall from the introduction that reduction-based creative telescoping requires some K-linear map $[\cdot]\colon A \to A$ with the property that $f - [f]$ is integrable in A for every $f \in A$. This is sufficient for the correctness of the method, but additional properties are needed in order to ensure that the method terminates.

As also explained already in the introduction, one possibility consists in showing that $[f] = 0$ whenever f is integrable. Trager showed that his Hermite reduction has this property [24, page 50, Theorem 1]. As this result was never published elsewhere, and for the sake of completeness, we reproduce his proof here.

Lemma 6. *Let $W = \{\omega_1, \ldots, \omega_n\}$ be an integral basis for A that is normal at infinity. Let $g = \sum_{i=1}^n g_i\omega_i \in A$ be such that all its coefficients $g_i \in K(x)$ are proper rational functions. If an integral element $f \in A$ has a pole at infinity, then also $f + g$ has a pole at infinity.*

Proof. Since f is assumed to be integral we can write it as $f = f_1\omega_1 + \cdots + f_n\omega_n$ with $f_i \in K[x]$. If f has a pole at infinity, there is at least one index i such that $f_i\omega_i$ has a pole at infinity. There are two cases why this can happen.

(a) The polynomial f_i has positive degree. This means that $f_i + g_i$ has a pole at infinity, because the g_i are proper rational functions. Thus $(f_i + g_i)\omega_i$ has a pole at infinity, because ω_i has no poles at finite places and therefore no root at infinity.

(b) The integral basis element ω_i is not constant and f_i is not zero. Hence ω_i has a pole at infinity, and this also implies that $(f_i + g_i)\omega_i$ has a pole at infinity, again employing the fact that g_i is a proper rational function.

In both cases, therefore, $f + g = \sum_{i=1}^n (f_i + g_i)\omega_i$ has a pole at infinity by Lemma 5. ∎

Theorem 7. *Suppose that $f \in A$ has at least a double root at infinity (i.e., every series in $\bar{K}\langle\langle x^{-1}\rangle\rangle$ associated to f only contains monomials $(1/x)^\alpha$ with $\alpha \geq 2$). Let $W = \{\omega_1, \ldots, \omega_n\}$ be an integral basis for A that is normal at infinity. If $f = g' + h$ is the result of the Hermite reduction with respect to W, then $h = 0$ if and only if f is integrable in A.*

Proof. The direction "⇒" is trivial. To show the implication "⇐" assume that f is integrable in A. From $f = g' + h$ it follows that then also h is integrable in A; let $H \in A$ be such that $H' = h$. In order to show that $h = 0$, we show that H is constant. To this end, it suffices to show that it has neither finite poles nor a pole at infinity; the claim then follows from Chevalley's theorem.

It is clear that H has no finite poles because h has at most simple poles (i.e., all series associated to h have only exponents ≥ -1). This follows from the facts that the ω_i are integral and that the coefficients of h have squarefree denominators.

If H has a pole at infinity, then by Lemma 6 also $g + H$ must have a pole at infinity, because Hermite reduction produces $g = \sum_i g_i\omega_i$ with proper rational functions g_i. On the other hand, since $f = g' + h = (g + H)'$ has at least a double root at infinity by assumption, $g + H$ must have at least a single root at infinity. This is a contradiction. ∎

Note that the condition in Theorem 7 that f has a double root at infinity is not a restriction at all, as it can always be achieved by a suitable change of variables. Let $a \in C$ be a regular point; this means that all series in $\bar{K}\langle\langle x - a\rangle\rangle$ associated to f are formal power series. By the substitution $x \to a + 1/x$ the regular point a is moved to infinity. From

$$\int f(x)\,\mathrm{d}x = \int f\left(\frac{1}{x} + a\right)\left(-\frac{1}{x^2}\right)\mathrm{d}x$$

we see that the new integrand has a double root at infinity.

Moreover, since the action of ∂_t on series domains is defined coefficient-wise, it follows that when f has at least a double root at infinity (with respect to x), then this is also true for $\partial_t \cdot f, \partial_t^2 \cdot f, \partial_t^3 \cdot f, \ldots$, and then also for every K-linear combination $p_0 f + p_1\partial_t \cdot f + \cdots + p_r\partial_t^r \cdot f$. Thus Theorem 7 implies that $p_0 + p_1\partial_t + \cdots + p_r\partial_t^r$ is a telescoper for f if *and only if* $[p_0 f + p_1\partial_t \cdot f + \cdots + p_r\partial_t^r \cdot f] = 0$.

We already know for other reasons [26, 11, 9] that telescopers for algebraic functions exist, and therefore the reduction-based creative telescoping procedure with Hermite reduction with respect to an integral basis that is normal at infinity as reduction function succeeds when applied to an integrand $f \in A$ that has a double root at infinity. In particular, the method finds a telescoper of smallest possible order. Again, if f has no double root at infinity, we can produce one by a change of variables. Note that a change of variables $x \to a + 1/x$ with $a \in C$ has no effect on the telescoper.

Example 8. *We consider the algebraic function $f = y/x^2$ where y is a solution of the third-degree polynomial equation $m(x,y) = y^3 + y + x + t = 0$. An integral basis for $A = K(x)[y]/\langle m\rangle$ that is normal at infinity is given by $\omega_1 = 1$, $\omega_2 = y$, $\omega_3 = y^2$. (This means that employing lazy Hermite reduction avoids completely the computation of an integral basis in this example.)*

By solving Equation (1) for y' we obtain

$$y' = \frac{-6y^2 + 9(t+x)y - 4}{27x^2 + 54tx + 27t^2 + 4}.$$

Then for the differentiation matrix $\frac{1}{e}M$, a simple calculation yields

$$\begin{pmatrix}\omega_1'\\ \omega_2'\\ \omega_3'\end{pmatrix} = \frac{1}{e}\begin{pmatrix} 0 & 0 & 0\\ -4 & 9(t+x) & -6\\ 12(t+x) & 4 & 18(t+x)\end{pmatrix}\begin{pmatrix}\omega_1\\ \omega_2\\ \omega_3\end{pmatrix}$$

with $e = 27x^2 + 54xt + 27t^2 + 4$. Thus we write $f = \sum_{i=1}^{3}(f_i/D)\omega_i$ with $f_1 = f_3 = 0$, $f_2 = e$, and $D = x^2 e$. After a single step the Hermite reduction delivers the result

$$f = \underbrace{\Big(-\frac{y}{x}\Big)'}_{=g_0} + \underbrace{\frac{-6y^2 + 9(x+t)y - 4}{x(27x^2 + 54xt + 27t^2 + 4)}}_{=h_0}.$$

As the Hermite remainder h_0 is nonzero, Theorem 7 tells us that f is not integrable in A. Hence we continue by applying Hermite reduction to

$$\partial_t \cdot f = \frac{-6y^2 + 9(x+t)y - 4}{x^2(27x^2 + 54xt + 27t^2 + 4)}.$$

Note that we could as well take $\partial_t \cdot h_0$ instead of $\partial_t \cdot f$, which in general should result in a faster algorithm. Again after a single reduction step, the decomposition $\partial_t \cdot f = g_1' + h_1$ is obtained, where

$$g_1 = \frac{6y^2 - 9ty + 4}{x(27t^2 + 4)}$$
$$h_1 = \frac{6\big((9x + 27t)y^2 - (27xt + 27t^2 - 2)y + 6x + 18t\big)}{x(27t^2 + 4)(27x^2 + 54xt + 27t^2 + 4)}.$$

Since h_0 and h_1 are linearly independent over $K = C(t)$, we continue with $\partial_t^2 \cdot f$. This time however, it is preferable to start the Hermite reduction with $\partial_t \cdot h_1$, which is given by

$$\frac{1}{x(27t^2 + 4)^2(27x^2 + 54xt + 27t^2 + 4)^2}.$$

Setting $v = 27x^2 + 54xt + 27t^2 + 4 = e$ and doing one reduction step, the Hermite remainder h_2 is found to be

$$\big(6\big((-729xt - 1539t^2 + 96)y^2 + (1215xt^2 - 144x + 1215t^3 - 306t)y - 486xt - 1026t^2 + 64\big)\big) \;/\; \big(x(27t^2 + 4)^2 e\big).$$

The corresponding integrable part g_2 is not displayed here for space reasons.

Now one can find a linear dependence between h_0, h_1, h_2 that gives rise to the telescoper $(27t^2 + 4)\partial_t^2 + 81t\partial_t + 24$, which is indeed the minimal one for this example.

5. POLYNOMIAL REDUCTION

Recall that instead of requesting that $[f] = 0$ if and only if f is integrable (first approach), we can also justify the termination of reduction-based creative telescoping by showing that the K-vector space generated by $\{\,[\partial_t^i f] : i \in \mathbb{N}\,\}$ has finite dimension (second approach). If $[\cdot]$ is just the Hermite reduction, we do not necessarily have this property. We therefore introduce below an additional reduction, called *polynomial reduction*, which we apply after Hermite reduction. We then show that the combined reduction (Hermite reduction followed by polynomial reduction) has the desired dimension property for the space of remainders. As a result, we obtain a new bound on the order of the telescoper, which is similar to those in [9, 8].

In this approach, we use two integral bases. First we use a global integral basis in order to perform Hermite reduction. Then we write the remainder h with respect to some local integral basis at infinity and perform the polynomial reduction on this representation.

Throughout this section let $W = (\omega_1, \ldots, \omega_n)^T \in A^n$ be such that $\{\omega_1, \ldots, \omega_n\}$ is a global integral basis of A, and let $e \in K[x]$ and $M = (m_{i,j}) \in K[x]^{n\times n}$ be such that $eW' = MW$ and $\gcd(e, m_{1,1}, m_{1,2}, \ldots, m_{n,n}) = 1$. The Hermite reduction described in Section 3 decomposes an input element $f \in A$ into the form

$$f = g' + h = g' + \sum_{i=1}^{n}\frac{h_i}{de}\omega_i, \qquad g, h \in A,$$

with $h_i, d \in K[x]$ such that $\gcd(d, e) = \gcd(h_i, de) = 1$ and d is squarefree.

Lemma 9. *If h is integrable in A, then d is in K.*

Proof. Suppose that h is integrable in A, i.e., there exist $a, b_i \in K[x]$ such that $h = \big(\frac{1}{a}\sum_{i=1}^{n} b_i\omega_i\big)'$. Then

$$h = \sum_{i=1}^{n}\frac{h_i}{de}\omega_i = \sum_{i=1}^{n}\left(\Big(\frac{b_i}{a}\Big)'\omega_i + \frac{b_i}{ae}\sum_{j=1}^{n} m_{i,j}\omega_j\right).$$

We show that a is constant. Otherwise, for any irreducible factor p of a, we would have that h has a pole of multiplicity greater than 1 at the roots of p. This contradicts the fact that d, e are squarefree. Thus, d is a constant. ■

By the extended Euclidean algorithm, we compute $u_i, v_i \in K[x]$ such that $h_i = u_i d + v_i e$ and $\deg_x(v_i) < \deg_x(d)$. Then the Hermite remainder h decomposes as

$$\sum_{i=1}^{n}\frac{h_i}{de}\omega_i = \sum_{i=1}^{n}\frac{u_i}{e}\omega_i + \sum_{i=1}^{n}\frac{v_i}{d}\omega_i. \tag{3}$$

We now introduce the *polynomial reduction* whose goal is to confine the u_i to a finite-dimensional vector space over K. Similar reductions have been introduced and used in creative telescoping for hyperexponential functions [2] and hypergeometric terms [7]. Let $V = (\nu_1, \ldots, \nu_n)^T \in A^n$ be such that its entries form a $K(x)$-basis of A, and let $a \in K[x]$

and $B = (b_{i,j}) \in K[x]^{n\times n}$ be such that $aV' = BV$ and $\gcd(a, b_{1,1}, b_{1,2}, \ldots, b_{n,n}) = 1$. Let $p = (p_1, \ldots, p_n) \in K[x]^n$. Then

$$(pV)' = \sum_{i=1}^{n} (p_i \nu_i)' = \frac{ap' + pB}{a} V. \qquad (4)$$

This motivates us to introduce the following definition.

Definition 10. *Let the map $\phi_V \colon K[x]^n \to K[x]^n$ be defined by $\phi_V(p) = ap' + pB$ for any $p \in K[x]^n$. We call ϕ_V the* map for polynomial reduction *with respect to V, and call the subspace $\operatorname{im}(\phi_V) = \{\phi_V(p) \mid p \in K[x]^n\}$ the* subspace for polynomial reduction *with respect to V.*

Note that, by construction and because of Lemma 9, $q \in K[x]^n$ is in $\operatorname{im}(\phi_V)$ if and only if $\frac{q}{a}V$ is integrable in A.

We can always view an element of $K[x]^n$ (resp. $K[x]^{n\times n}$) as a polynomial in x with coefficients in K^n (resp. $K^{n\times n}$). In this sense we use the notation $\operatorname{lc}(\cdot)$ for the leading coefficient and $\operatorname{lt}(\cdot)$ for the leading term of a vector (resp. matrix). For example, if $p \in K[x]^n$ is of the form

$$p = p^{(r)}x^r + \cdots + p^{(1)}x + p^{(0)}, \quad p^{(i)} \in K^n,$$

then $\deg_x(p) = r$, $\operatorname{lc}(p) = p^{(r)}$, and $\operatorname{lt}(p) = p^{(r)}x^r$. Let $\{e_1, \ldots, e_n\}$ be the standard basis of K^n. Then the module $K[x]^n$ viewed as a K-vector space is generated by

$$\mathcal{S} := \{e_i x^j \mid 1 \le i \le n,\ j \in \mathbb{N}\}.$$

We define $K[x]^n_\mu := \{p \in K[x]^n \mid \deg_x(p) \le \mu\}$; as a K-vector space it is generated by

$$\mathcal{S}_\mu := \{e_i x^j \mid 1 \le i \le n,\ 0 \le j \le \mu\}.$$

Any element $p \in K[x]^n_\mu$ can be expressed in the basis $\mathcal{S}_\mu$ as a vector $\vec{p} \in K^{n(\mu+1)}$ (in the following the decoration $\vec{\cdot}$ always indicates such a typecast).

Definition 11. *Let N_V be the K-subspace of $K[x]^n$ generated by*

$$\{t \in \mathcal{S} \mid t \ne \operatorname{lt}(p) \text{ for all } p \in \operatorname{im}(\phi_V)\}.$$

Then $K[x]^n = \operatorname{im}(\phi_V) \oplus N_V$. We call N_V the standard complement *of $\operatorname{im}(\phi_V)$. For any $p \in K[x]^n$, there exist $p_1 \in K[x]^n$ and $p_2 \in N_V$ such that*

$$\frac{p}{a}V = (p_1V)' + \frac{p_2}{a}V.$$

This decomposition is called the polynomial reduction *of p with respect to V.*

Proposition 12. *Let $a \in K[x]$ and $B \in K[x]^{n\times n}$ be such that $aV' = BV$, as before. If $\deg_x(B) \le \deg_x(a) - 1$, then N_V is a finite-dimensional K-vector space.*

Proof. In addition to the proof of the assertion, we also explain how to determine the dimension and a basis for N_V, for later use. For brevity, let $\mu := \deg_x(a) - 1$. We distinguish two cases.

Case 1. Assume that $\deg_x(B) < \mu$. For any $p \in K[x]^n$ of degree $s > 0$, we have

$$\operatorname{lt}(\phi_V(p)) = s \operatorname{lc}(a) \operatorname{lc}(p) x^{s+\mu}.$$

Thus all monomials $e_i x^j \in \mathcal{S}$ with $1 \le i \le n$ and $j \ge \mu + 1$ are not in N_V. Let $\vec{B}_1, \ldots, \vec{B}_n$ be the columns of B, expressed in the basis $\mathcal{S}_\mu$. Let $C(B)$ be the K-subspace of $K[x]^n_\mu$ generated by these column vectors. If $q \in \operatorname{im}(\phi_V)$, then $q = \phi_V(p) = pB$ for some $p \in K^n$, which implies that $\vec{q}$ is a linear combination of $\vec{B}_i$'s. Then $K[x]^n_\mu = C(B) \oplus N_V$. So $\dim_K(N_V) = (\mu + 1)n - \dim_K(C(B))$ and a basis of N_V can be computed by looking at the echelon form of the matrix $(\vec{B}_1, \ldots, \vec{B}_n)$.

Case 2. Assume that $\deg_x(B) = \mu$. For any $p \in K[x]^n$ of degree s, we have

$$\operatorname{lt}(\phi_V(p)) = \operatorname{lc}(p)(s \operatorname{lc}(a) I_n + \operatorname{lc}(B)) x^{s+\mu}.$$

Let ℓ be the largest nonnegative integer such that $-\ell \operatorname{lc}(a)$ is an eigenvalue of $\operatorname{lc}(B) \in K^{n\times n}$. Then for any $s > \ell$, the matrix $J_s = s \operatorname{lc}(a) I_n + \operatorname{lc}(B)$ is invertible. So any monomial $e_i x^j$ with $j > \ell + \mu$ is not in N_V for any $i = 1, \ldots, n$. Let $p = \sum_{i=1}^{n} \sum_{j=0}^{\ell} p_{i,j} e_i x^j$. Then $\phi_V(p)$ belongs to $K[x]^n_{\ell+\mu}$. In the basis $\mathcal{S}_{\ell+\mu}$, we can express $\phi_V(p)$ as a vector of length $n(\ell + \mu + 1)$ with entries linear in the $p_{i,j}$'s. This vector can be written in the form $M_\ell \vec{P}$, where $\vec{P} = (p_{1,0}, p_{2,0}, \ldots, p_{n,\ell})^T$ and $M_\ell \in K^{n(\ell+\mu+1)\times n(\ell+1)}$. Every $q \in K[x]^n_{\ell+\mu}$ can be expressed as a vector $\vec{q} \in K^{n(\ell+\mu+1)}$. Then $q \in \operatorname{im}(\phi_v)$ if and only if $\vec{q}$ is in the column space of M_ℓ. Therefore,

$$K[x]^n_{\ell+\mu} = C(M_\ell) \oplus N_V.$$

This implies that $\dim_K(N_V) = n(\ell+\mu+1) - \operatorname{rank}(M_\ell)$, and a basis of N_V can be computed by looking at the echelon form of the matrix M_ℓ. ∎

In general, the condition $\deg_x(B) \le \deg_x(a) - 1$ may not hold for an arbitrary basis V of A. The following lemma shows that we can perform a simple change of basis to make the condition hold.

Lemma 13. *Let $W = \{\omega_1, \ldots, \omega_n\}$ be an integral basis of A such that it is also normal at infinity. Then there exist nonnegative integers $\tau_1, \ldots, \tau_n$ such that*

$$V := \{\nu_1, \ldots, \nu_n\} \quad \text{with } \nu_i = x^{-\tau_i}\omega_i$$

is a basis of A which is normal at 0 and integral at all other places (including infinity).

Proof. It is clear that such a basis V will be normal at zero, because multiplying the generators by the rational functions x^{τ_i} brings it back to a global integral basis, which is in particular a local integral basis at zero. It is also clear that such a basis will be integral at every other point $a \in \bar{K} \setminus \{0\}$, because the multipliers $x^{-\tau_i}$ are locally units at such a. Finally, since the original basis is normal at infinity, there exist rational functions $u_1, \ldots, u_n$ such that $\{u_1\omega_1, \ldots, u_n\omega_n\}$ is a local integral basis at infinity. Since u_i can be written as $u_i = x^{-\tau_i}\tilde{u}_i$ with $\tau_i \in \mathbb{Z}$ and $\tilde{u}_i$ being a unit in $\bar{C}(x)_\infty$, we see that also V is a local integral basis at infinity. The integers τ_i can only be nonnegative because the ω_i's have no finite poles and therefore each of them is either constant or has a pole at infinity by Chevalley's theorem. ∎

Combining the Hermite reduction and polynomial reduction, we get the following theorem.

Theorem 14. *Let W be an integral basis of A that is normal at infinity. Let $T := \operatorname{diag}(x^{-\tau_1}, \ldots, x^{-\tau_n}) \in K(x)^{n\times n}$ be such that $V = TW$ is integral at infinity. Let $e \in K[x]$,*

$\lambda \in \mathbb{N}$, *and* $B, M \in K[x]^{n\times n}$ *be such that* $eW' = MW$ *and* $x^\lambda eV' = BV$. *Then any element* $f \in A$ *can be decomposed into*

$$f = g' + \frac{1}{d}PW + \frac{1}{x^\lambda e}QV, \tag{5}$$

where $g \in A$, $d \in K[x]$ *is squarefree and* $\gcd(d, e) = 1$, $P, Q \in K[x]^n$ *with* $\deg_x(P) < \deg_x(d)$ *and* $Q \in N_V$, *which is a finite-dimensional* K*-vector space. Moreover,* P, Q *are zero if and only if* f *is integrable in* A.

Proof. After performing the Hermite reduction on f, we get

$$f = \tilde{g}' + \frac{1}{d}PW + \frac{1}{e}UW,$$

where $P = (v_1, \ldots, v_n) \in K[x]^n$ and $U = (u_1, \ldots, u_n) \in K[x]^n$ with u_i, v_i introduced in (3). By Lemma 13, there exists $T := \operatorname{diag}(x^{-\tau_1}, \ldots, x^{-\tau_n}) \in K(x)^{n\times n}$ such that $V = TW$ is integral at infinity. By the same lemma it follows that V is also normal at 0 and integral at all other places. Note that we can choose T as the identity matrix if $\deg_x(M) \leq \deg_x(e) - 1$. By taking derivatives, we get

$$V' = \left(T' + T\frac{M}{e}\right)T^{-1}V = \frac{B}{a}V,$$

where $a = x^\lambda e$ for some $\lambda \in \mathbb{N}$ and $B \in K[x]^{n\times n}$. Since V is locally integral at infinity, $\deg_x(B) \leq \deg_x(a) - 1$ by Lemma 4. By expanding in terms of the new basis V, we get

$$\frac{1}{e}UW = \frac{1}{a}\tilde{U}V,$$

where $\tilde{U} = x^\lambda UT^{-1} \in K[x]^n$. Next, we decompose $\tilde{U}$ into $\tilde{U} = \phi_V(\tilde{U}_1) + \tilde{U}_2$ with $\tilde{U}_1, \tilde{U}_2 \in K[x]^n$ and $\tilde{U}_2 \in N_V$. Then we get

$$\frac{1}{e}UW = (\tilde{U}_1V)' + \frac{1}{a}\tilde{U}_2V.$$

We then get the decomposition (5) by setting $g = \tilde{g} + \tilde{U}_1V$ and $Q = U_2$.

Assume that f is integrable. Then Lemma 9 implies that $d \in K$. Since $\deg_x(P) < \deg_x(d)$, we have $P = 0$. Then

$$\frac{1}{x^\lambda e}QV = \sum_{i=1}^{n}(a_i\nu_i)'$$

for some $a_i \in K[x]$. So $Q \in \operatorname{im}(\phi_V)$. Since $\operatorname{im}(\phi_V) \cap N_V = \{0\}$, it follows that $Q = 0$. ∎

The decomposition in (5) is called an *additive decomposition* of f with respect to x.

6. TELESCOPING VIA REDUCTIONS: SECOND APPROACH

We now discuss how to compute telescopers for algebraic functions via Hermite reduction and polynomial reduction.

Let W, V, e, λ, M, B be as in Theorem 14. To construct a telescoper for $f \in A$, we first consider the additive decompositions of the successive derivatives $\partial_t^i \cdot f$ for $i \in \mathbb{N}$. Assume that

$$\partial_t \cdot W = \frac{1}{\tilde{e}}\tilde{M}W \quad \text{and} \quad \partial_t \cdot V = \frac{1}{x^{\tilde{\lambda}}\tilde{e}}\tilde{B}V,$$

where $\tilde{e} \in K[x]$, $\tilde{M}, \tilde{B} \in K[x]^{n\times n}$, and $\tilde{\lambda} \in \mathbb{N}$. Since ∂_t and ∂_x commute, Proposition 7 in [8] implies that $\tilde{e} \mid e$ and $x^{\tilde{\lambda}}\tilde{e} \mid x^\lambda e$, as polynomials in $K[x]$. So we can just take $\tilde{e} = e$ and $\tilde{\lambda} = \lambda$ by multiplying $\tilde{M}, \tilde{B}$ by some factors of $x^\lambda e$. A direct calculation yields $\partial_t \cdot f = (\partial_t \cdot g)' + h$, where

$$h = \left(\partial_t \cdot \frac{P}{d} + \frac{P\tilde{M}}{de}\right)W + \left(\partial_t \cdot \frac{Q}{x^\lambda e} + \frac{Q\tilde{B}}{x^{2\lambda}e^2}\right)V.$$

This implies that the squarefree part of the denominator of h divides xde. Applying Hermite reduction and polynomial reduction to h yields

$$h = \tilde{g}_1' + \frac{1}{d}P_1W + \frac{1}{x^\lambda e}Q_1V,$$

where $P_1, Q_1 \in K[x]^n$ with $\deg_x(P_1) < \deg_x(d)$ and $Q_1 \in N_V$. Repeating this discussion, we get the following lemma.

Lemma 15. *For any* $i \in \mathbb{N}$, *the derivative* $\partial_t^i \cdot f$ *has an additive decomposition of the form*

$$\partial_t^i \cdot f = g_i' + \frac{1}{d}P_iW + \frac{1}{x^\lambda e}Q_iV,$$

where $g_i \in A$, $P_i, Q_i \in K[x]^n$ *with* $\deg_x(P_i) < \deg_x(d)$ *and* $Q_i \in N_V$.

As application of the above lemma, we can compute the minimal telescoper for f by finding the first linear dependence among the (P_i, Q_i) over K. We also obtain an upper bound for the order of telescopers.

Corollary 16. *Every* $f \in A$ *has a telescoper of order at most* $n\deg_x(d) + \dim_K(N_V)$.

Example 17. *We continue with Example 8, by applying the polynomial reduction to the Hermite remainders* h_0, h_1, h_2. *The matrix* M *computed before satisfies the degree condition of Proposition 12, so no change of basis is needed. First we compute polynomials* $u_i, v_i \in K[x, y]$ *such that for* $i = 0, 1, 2$ *we have*

$$h_i = \frac{u_i}{e} + \frac{v_i}{d} = \frac{u_i}{27x^2 + 54xt + 27t^2 + 4} + \frac{v_i}{x}.$$

By noting that $\deg_x(u_i) = 1$ *and* $\deg_x(e) = 2$, *we see that the map for the polynomial reduction* $\phi(p) = ep' + pM$ *can only be applied for* $p \in K^n$ *so that it turns into* $\phi(p) = pM$. *This means that we reduce* xy^2 *using the third row of* M *and* xy *using its second row. A straightforward calculation reveals that* h_0, h_1, *and* h_2 *all reduce to* 0. *Hence we are left with finding a* K*-linear combination among the* v_i:

$$v_0 = \frac{-6y^2 + 9yt - 4}{27t^2 + 4},$$
$$v_1 = \frac{6\big(27y^2t - (27t^2 - 2)y + 18t\big)}{(27t^2 + 4)^2},$$
$$v_2 = \frac{6\big((96 - 1539t^2)y^2 + (1215t^3 - 306t)y - 1026t^2 + 64\big)}{(27t^2 + 4)^3}.$$

As expected, we obtain the same telescoper as in Example 8.

7. THE D-FINITE CASE

With algebraic functions being settled, it is natural to wonder about a possible reduction-based creative telescoping algorithm for D-finite functions. Recall that in this setting we consider an operator $L \in K(x)[\partial_x]$ instead of a minimal polynomial $m \in K[x, y]$ and instead of an algebraic field extension $K(x)[y]/\langle m\rangle$ we consider the $K(x)[\partial_x]$-left-module $A = K(x)[\partial_x]/\langle L\rangle$. Then the element $1 \in A$ is a solution of L because $L \cdot 1 = L = 0$ in A by construction. If $n = \deg_{\partial_x} L$, then the general element of A has the form $f = f_0 + f_1\partial_x + \cdots + f_{n-1}\partial_x^{n-1}$ for some $f_0, \ldots, f_{n-1} \in K(x)$. Very much as in the algebraic case, there is a natural way to associate certain series objects to the elements of A. Based on these series objects, a notion of integrality was proposed last year [17], and an algorithm for computing integral bases has been given for so-called Fuchsian operators L.

It turns out that the Hermite reduction of Section 3 also works in this setting, if we say that a term $(x-a)^\alpha \log(x)^\beta$ in a generalized series solution is integral if and only if $\alpha \geq 0$. Note that then $\log(x)$ will be considered integral at zero, despite the singularity of the complex function at this point. This has the somewhat counterintuitive consequence that $\log(x)$ is integral at every $a \in \bar{K} \cup \{\infty\}$ although it does not have a pole anywhere. For algebraic functions, this is not possible by Chevalley's theorem, and this fact enters in an essential way in the proofs of Sections 4 and 5. The lack of Chevalley's theorem is not an artefact of a (possibly wrong) treatment of logarithmic terms. Because of the Fuchs relation [23, p. 241] there exist operators $L \in K(x)[\partial_x]$ whose series solutions at any point $a \in \bar{K} \cup \{\infty\}$ have no logarithmic terms, only nonnegative exponents, and which are nevertheless not constant.

For the time being, the existence of such operators is a severe obstruction to a possible generalization of the termination arguments for reduction-based creative telescoping from algebraic functions to Fuchsian D-finite functions. We hope to explore this topic further in the future.

Acknowledgements

We would like to thank Ruyong Feng and Michael F. Singer for helpful discussions, and the anonymous referees for their constructive and helpful comments.

8. REFERENCES

[1] A. Bostan, S. Chen, F. Chyzak, and Z. Li. Complexity of creative telescoping for bivariate rational functions. In *Proceedings of ISSAC'10*, pages 203–210, 2010.

[2] A. Bostan, S. Chen, F. Chyzak, Z. Li, and G. Xin. Hermite reduction and creative telescoping for hyperexponential functions. In *Proceedings of ISSAC'13*, pages 77–84, 2013.

[3] A. Bostan, P. Lairez, and B. Salvy. Creative telescoping for rational functions using the Griffiths-Dwork method. In *Proceedings of ISSAC'13*, pages 93–100, 2013.

[4] A. Bostan, P. Lairez, and B. Salvy. Multiple binomial sums. To appear in Journal of Symbolic Computation, 2016.

[5] M. Bronstein. The lazy Hermite reduction. Technical Report 3562, INRIA, 1998.

[6] M. Bronstein. Symbolic integration tutorial. ISSAC'98, 1998.

[7] S. Chen, H. Huang, M. Kauers, and Z. Li. A modified Abramov-Petkovšek reduction and creative telescoping for hypergeometric terms. In *Proceedings of ISSAC'15*, pages 117–124, 2015.

[8] S. Chen, M. Kauers, and C. Koutschan. A generalized Apagodu-Zeilberger algorithm. In *Proceedings of ISSAC'14*, pages 107–114, 2014.

[9] S. Chen, M. Kauers, and M. F. Singer. Telescopers for rational and algebraic functions via residues. In *Proceedings of ISSAC'12*, pages 130–137, 2012.

[10] C. Chevalley. *Introduction to the Theory of Agebraic Functions of One Variable*, volume VI of *Mathematical Surveys*. Amerian Mathematical Society, N.Y., 1951.

[11] F. Chyzak. An extension of Zeilberger's fast algorithm to general holonomic functions. *Discrete Mathematics*, 217:115–134, 2000.

[12] K. O. Geddes, S. R. Czapor, and G. Labahn. *Algorithms for Computer Algebra*. Kluwer Academic Publishers, Boston, MA, 1992.

[13] C. Hermite. Sur l'intégration des fractions rationnelles. *Ann. Sci. École Norm. Sup. (2)*, 1:215–218, 1872.

[14] H. Huang. New Bounds for Hypergeometric Creative Telescoping. In this volume.

[15] M. van Hoeij. An algorithm for computing an integral basis in an algebraic function field. *Journal of Symbolic Computation*, 18(4):353–363, 1994.

[16] M. Kauers and P. Paule. *The Concrete Tetrahedron*. Springer. 2011.

[17] M. Kauers and C. Koutschan. Integral D-finite functions. In *Proceedings of ISSAC'15*, pages 251–258, 2015.

[18] W. Koepf. *Hypergeometric Summation*. Advanced Lectures in Mathematics. Friedr. Vieweg & Sohn, Braunschweig, 1998. An algorithmic approach to summation and special function identities.

[19] P. Lairez. Computing periods of rational integrals. *Mathematics of Computation*, 85:1719-1752, 2016.

[20] Yu. I. Manin Algebraic curves over fields with differentiation. *Izv. Akad. Nauk SSSR Ser. Mat.*, 22(6): 737–756, 1958.

[21] M. Petkovšek, H. S. Wilf, and D. Zeilberger. *A = B*. A. K. Peters Ltd., Wellesley, MA, 1996.

[22] M. Rybowicz. An algorithms for computing integral bases of an algebraic function field. In *Proceedings of ISSAC 1991*, pages 157–166, 1991.

[23] L. Schlesinger. *Handbuch der Theorie der linearen Differentialgleichungen*, volume 1. Teubner, 1895.

[24] B. M. Trager. *On the Integration of Algebraic Functions*. PhD thesis, MIT, 1984.

[25] D. Zeilberger. A fast algorithm for proving terminating hypergeometric identities. *Discrete Mathematics*, 80(2):207–211, 1990.

[26] D. Zeilberger. A holonomic systems approach to special functions identities. *Journal of Computational and Applied Mathematics*, 32(3):321–368, 1990.

[27] D. Zeilberger. The method of creative telescoping. *Journal of Symbolic Computation*, 11(3):195–204, 1991.

Critical Point Computations on Smooth Varieties: Degree and Complexity Bounds

Mohab Safey El Din
Sorbonne Universités, UPMC Univ Paris 06, 7606, LIP6, F-75005, Paris, France
CNRS, UMR 7606, LIP6, F-75005, Paris, France
Inria, Paris Center, PolSys Project
mohab.safey@lip6.fr

Pierre-Jean Spaenlehauer
Inria, CNRS, Université de Lorraine
Nancy, France
pierre-jean.spaenlehauer@inria.fr

ABSTRACT

Let $V \subset \mathbb{C}^n$ be an equidimensional algebraic set and g be an n-variate polynomial with rational coefficients. Computing the critical points of the map that evaluates g at the points of V is a cornerstone of several algorithms in real algebraic geometry and optimization. Under the assumption that the critical locus is finite and that the projective closure of V is smooth, we provide sharp upper bounds on the degree of the critical locus which depend only on $\deg(g)$ and the degrees of the generic polar varieties associated to V. Hence, in some special cases where the degrees of the generic polar varieties do not reach the worst-case bounds, this implies that the number of critical points of the evaluation map of g is less than the currently known degree bounds. We show that, given a lifting fiber of V, a slight variant of an algorithm due to Bank, Giusti, Heintz, Lecerf, Matera and Solernó computes these critical points in time which is quadratic in this bound up to logarithmic factors, linear in the complexity of evaluating the input system and polynomial in the number of variables and the maximum degree of the input polynomials.

Keywords

Critical points, real geometry, complexity

1. INTRODUCTION

Problem statement. Let $\mathbf{f} = (f_1, \dots, f_p) \subset \mathbb{Q}[X_1, \dots, X_n]$ be a polynomial system defining a smooth and equidimensional algebraic set $V \subset \mathbb{C}^n$ of dimension d and $g \in \mathbb{Q}[X_1, \dots, X_n]$ be a polynomial of degree D. We focus on the complexity of computing the critical points of the map evaluating g at the points of V. These critical points are defined by $f_1 = \cdots = f_p = 0$ and by the simultaneous vanishing of the $(n-d+1)$-minors of the jacobian matrix $\mathrm{jac}(\mathbf{f}, g)$

$$\begin{bmatrix} \frac{\partial f_1}{\partial X_1} & \cdots & \frac{\partial f_1}{\partial X_n} \\ \vdots & & \vdots \\ \frac{\partial f_p}{\partial X_1} & \cdots & \frac{\partial f_p}{\partial X_n} \\ \frac{\partial g}{\partial X_1} & \cdots & \frac{\partial g}{\partial X_n} \end{bmatrix}.$$

Usually, in symbolic computation, when the critical locus is finite, we aim at computing a rational parametrization of it, which is the data $((q, v_1, \dots, v_n), \lambda)$ where q and the v_i's lie in $\mathbb{Q}[T]$ (T is a new variable) and λ is a linear form in $X_1, \dots, X_n$ with q squarefree, $\deg(v_i) < \deg(q)$, $\lambda(v_1, \dots, v_n) = T\frac{\partial q}{\partial T} \mod q$ and the set defined by

$$q(\tau) = 0, \qquad X_i = \frac{v_i}{\partial q / \partial T}(\tau) \quad 1 \le i \le n$$

coincides with the critical locus under consideration. Observe that the degree of q coincides with the number of critical points and the number of rational numbers required in such a rational parametrization is $O(n \deg(q))$.

Assuming again the critical locus to be finite, several bounds on its cardinality have been established (see [26] and references therein). These bounds depend on n, p and the degrees of $f_1, \dots, f_p$ and g. However, it has been remarked that when V is not a complete intersection, or when it has some special properties, the cardinality of the critical locus may be far less than these bounds and sometimes depends only on D and on some quantities attached to geometric objects. These latter objects are *polar varieties* (see [3, 1]); they may be understood as the critical loci of the restriction to V of projections on generic linear subspaces ; we define them further precisely.

Assuming the smoothness of the projective closure of V and the finiteness of the critical locus under study, this paper adresses the following topical questions.

- Provide a bound on the number of complex critical points depending on D and on the degrees of the generic polar varieties associated to V.
- Find an algorithm computing a rational parametrization of this critical locus within an arithmetic complexity which is essentially *quadratic* in the obtained bound and polynomial in p, n, the complexity of evaluating $\mathbf{f}, g$ and $\max_{1 \le i \le p}(\deg(f_i))$.

Motivations and prior works. Since local extrema of the evaluation map of g are reached at critical points, computing critical points is a basic and useful task for polynomial optimization (see *e.g.* [19, 18, 30]). Because of their topological properties related to Morse theory, computing critical points is also a subroutine for many modern algorithms in real algebraic geometry yielding asymptotically optimal complexities (see *e.g.* [20, 29, 21] and [6] for a textbook reference on this family of algorithms). Polar varieties have been introduced in [3] for computing sample points in each connected component of a real algebraic set and this technique has been developed in [31, 4]; they are also used for computing roadmaps for deciding connectivity queries [32, 33, 8, 7], for computing the real dimension of a real algebraic set (see [5] and references therein) or for variant quantifier elimination [23].

Some bounds on the cardinality of the critical locus under consideration are given in [26] when $f_1, \dots, f_p$ is a regular sequence. These bounds depend on the degrees of the f_i's, D, n and p.

Since polynomial systems appearing in applications arise most of

ISSAC '16, July 19-22, 2016, Waterloo, ON, Canada
© 2016 ACM. ISBN 978-1-4503-4380-0/16/07...$15.00
DOI: http://dx.doi.org/10.1145/2930889.2930929

the time with a special structure, a natural question to ask for is to identify situations where the cardinality of the considered critical locus is less than what the worst case bounds predicted in [26]. Such situations have been exhibited in [9] where critical points are used in computational statistics via the notion of ML degree. When $\deg(g) = 2$ the cardinality of the critical locus is bounded by the *generic ED degree* of V which depends only on the degrees of the generic polar varieties associated to V [10]. These bounds do not require any smoothness assumption. The results on polar varieties in [28, 22] play a central role in this setting.

On the algorithmic side, many recent works have focused on the complexity of computing critical loci. The results in [14, 35] provide complexity bounds for computing critical points using Gröbner bases under genericity assumptions on the input polynomials $\mathbf{f}$. The obtained complexity bounds are not quadratic in the generic number of critical points and the genericity assumptions are not well-suited to the situations we are willing to consider. The results in [2] provide complexity bounds for a probabilistic algorithm computing degeneracy loci in time quadratic in an intrinsic quantity called the *system degree*. This work is strongly related to the algorithmic framework of the solver proposed in [17] and to computational aspects of polar varieties which have been deeply investigated in the last decades, see [3, 4, 1] and references therein. We will use a slight variant of [2] for our algorithmic contribution.

Main results. Under some smoothness assumptions which are precised below, we prove a bound on the number of complex critical points of the map $x \in V \to g(x)$ depending on the degree of g and integers $\delta_1(V), \dots, \delta_{d+1}(V)$. The number $\delta_{i+1}(V)$ is the degree of the polar variety of V associated to a generic linear projection on $\mathbb{C}^{i+1}$. In the sequel, given $a = (a_1, \dots, a_i) \subset \mathbb{C}^{ni}$, we denote by $W((g,a),V)$ the critical locus of the map $x \in V \to (g(x), a_1 \cdot x, \dots, a_i \cdot x)$. We also denote by $\mathbb{C}[X_1, \dots, X_n]_{\leq D}$ the set of polynomials in $\mathbb{C}[X_1, \dots, X_n]$ of total degree $\leq D$.

THEOREM 1. *Let $V \subset \mathbb{C}^n$ be a d-equidimensional algebraic set whose projective closure is smooth and $D \geq 1$ and $i \in \{0, \dots, d\}$. There exists a Zariski dense subset $\Omega_i \subset \mathbb{C}[X_1, \dots, X_n]_{\leq D} \times \mathbb{C}^{i \times n}$ such that for any $(g, a) \in \Omega$, the degree of $W((g,a),V) \subset \mathbb{C}^n$ is bounded by*

$$\deg(W((g,a),V)) \leq \begin{cases} \delta_{i+1}(V) \text{ if } D = 1 \\ \sum_{j=i}^{d} \delta_{j+1}(V)(D-1)^{j-i} \text{ otherwise.} \end{cases}$$

One of the central ingredient of the proof is an algebraic version of Thom's weak transversality Theorem. We use a formalism and notation similar to [33, Sec 4.2] which provides a proof of this result using charts and atlases. We also show that this degree bound holds under milder assumptions on g: it is sufficient to assume that the evaluation map of g has finitely many critical points on V. Let us see how such a bound behaves on an example.

EXAMPLE 2. *Let $V \subset \mathbb{C}^8$ be the set of points $(x_1, \dots, x_8)$ where the matrix*

$$\begin{bmatrix} 1 & x_1 & x_2 \\ x_3 & x_4 & x_5 \\ x_6 & x_7 & x_8 \end{bmatrix}$$

has rank 1. This variety has dimension 4, degree 6 and $(\delta_1, \dots, \delta_5) = (1, 4, 10, 12, 6)$. Consider $g = \sum_{i=1}^{8} i x_i^3$. Representing an open subset of V as the zero locus of a reduced regular sequence of quadratic polynomials $f_1, \dots, f_4$, bounds depending on the degrees of $f_1, \dots, f_4, g$ (see e.g. *[26, Thm. 2.2]) would give the upper bound 2608 for the number of complex critical points. Theorem 1 and its variant for non-generic objective functions (see Prop. 12 below) yield the bound $241 = \delta_1 + 2\delta_2 + 4\delta_3 + 8\delta_4 + 16\delta_5$. Computations show that the evaluation map of g restricted to V has actually exactly 241 complex critical points on V.*

A convenient representation of an equidimensional variety V of dimension d is a *lifting fiber* for V (see [17]). Roughly speaking, this lifting fiber consists in a rational parametrization of the (finite) set of points in a section of V by a $(n-d)$-dimensional affine plane, together with a *lifting system* which allows to reconstruct a curve in the variety by symbolic Newton-Hensel iteration. Assuming that a lifting fiber of V has been precomputed and that $\deg(g) \geq 2$, we use the algorithm proposed in [2] to compute the critical points. Since this algorithm handles the more general case of quasi-affine varieties, so does the proposed variant. However, our main complexity results hold only under the assumption that the projective closure of V is smooth and that the evaluation map of g has finitely many critical points on V. Our second main result is a proof that the arithmetic complexity is quadratic up to logarithmic factors in the degree bound from Theorem 1, polynomial in n, the maximum of the degrees of the lifting system, $\deg(g)$, and the complexity of evaluating the lifting system and g.

Organization of the paper. Section 2 describes notation and preliminary results used throughout this paper. Section 3 is devoted to the proof of Theorem 1. It relies on a transversality result which is proved in Section 4. Section 5 deals with nongeneric objective functions. Finally, Section 6 discusses algorithmic aspects and complexity bounds.

Acknowledgments. Mohab Safey El Din is member of and supported by Institut Universitaire de France.

2. PRELIMINARIES

2.1 Notation and basic definitions

We refer to [34] and [12] for basic definitions about algebraic sets and polynomial ideals. Given an algebraic set $V \subset \mathbb{C}^n$, we denote by $I(V)$ the ideal associated to V. Given $\mathbf{f} = (f_1, \dots, f_p)$ in $\mathbb{Q}[X_1, \dots, X_n]$, the set of their common solutions in $\mathbb{C}^n$ is denoted by $Z(\mathbf{f})$ and the ideal generated by $\mathbf{f}$ is denoted by $\langle \mathbf{f} \rangle$. We say that $\mathbf{f} = (f_1, \dots, f_p)$ is a reduced sequence when the ideal $\langle \mathbf{f} \rangle$ generated by $\mathbf{f}$ is radical.

Tangent spaces, regular and singular points. Let $V \subset \mathbb{C}^n$ be an algebraic set. For $x \in V$, the tangent space $T_x V$ at x to V is the vector space defined by $\sum_{i=1}^{n} \frac{\partial f}{\partial X_i}(x) Y_i = 0$ for any $f \in I(V)$. Also, given a finite set of generators $\mathbf{f} = (f_1, \dots, f_p)$ of $I(V)$, $T_x V$ is the kernel of the jacobian matrix $\text{jac}(\mathbf{f}) = \left(\frac{\partial f_i}{\partial X_j}\right)_{\substack{1 \leq i \leq p \\ 1 \leq i \leq n}}$. We denote by $N_x V$ the orthogonal complement to $T_x V$.

Assume now that V is d-equidimensional. The set of points $x \in V$ where $\dim(T_x V) = d$ is the set of regular points of V; we denote it by $\text{reg}(V)$. The subset of singular points $\text{sing}(V)$ is the complement of $\text{reg}(V)$ in V; it has dimension less than d. Observe that given a finite set of generators $\mathbf{f}$ of $I(V)$, $\text{jac}(\mathbf{f})$ has rank $n - d$ at all $x \in \text{reg}(V)$. Also, $N_x V$ is generated by the gradient vectors of the polynomials in $\mathbf{f}$ evaluated at x. An equidimensional algebraic set V is said to be smooth when $\text{sing}(V)$ is empty.

Zariski topology. The Zariski topology over $\mathbb{C}^n$ is the topology for which the closed sets are the algebraic sets of $\mathbb{C}^n$. Let $f \in \mathbb{C}[X_1, \dots, X_n]$; we denote by $\mathcal{O}(f) \subset \mathbb{C}^n$ the subset defined by $f \neq 0$; it is a Zariski open set, which is non-empty when f is not identically 0. Further, we will prove some properties depending on parameters that are generically chosen. That means that, in the parameter space, there exists a non-empty Zariski open set such that the property is satisfied for any choice of the parameter values in this set.

Projective varieties. We will consider algebraic sets in the projective space $\mathbb{P}^n(\mathbb{C})$ defined by homogeneous polynomials. In the sequel, we use the shorthand $\mathbb{P}^n$ for $\mathbb{P}^n(\mathbb{C})$.

Let $V \subset \mathbb{P}^n$ be a projective variety. Notions of dimension, tangent space and regular (resp. singular) spaces extend to projective varieties. We denote by $\mathsf{aff}(V) \subset \mathbb{C}^{n+1}$ the Zariski closure of the set $\{(x_0, \dots, x_n) \subset \mathbb{C}^{n+1} \mid (x_0 : \dots : x_n) \in V\}$. The variety $\mathsf{aff}(V)$ is an *affine cone* (for all $x \in \mathsf{aff}(V)$, $\lambda \in \mathbb{C}$ we have $\lambda x \in \mathsf{aff}(V)$). By a slight abuse of notation, when V is an algebraic set of $\mathbb{C}^n$, we also denote by $\mathsf{aff}(V)$ the affine cone of the projective closure of V. Let now $V' \subset \mathbb{C}^{n+1}$ be an affine cone. Observe that the map $\mathsf{proj} : (x_0, \dots, x_n) \in V' \setminus \{\mathbf{0}\} \to (x_0 : \dots : x_n) \in \mathbb{P}^n$ sends $V' \setminus \{\mathbf{0}\}$ to a projective set. Besides, for a projective variety $V \subset \mathbb{P}^n$, $\mathsf{proj}(\mathsf{aff}(V)) = V$. We also consider bi-projective varieties lying in $\mathbb{P}^n \times \mathbb{P}^n$. The above constructions extend similarly: to any variety $V \subset \mathbb{P}^n \times \mathbb{P}^n$ can be associated a cone $\mathsf{aff}(V) \subset \mathbb{C}^{n+1} \times \mathbb{C}^{n+1}$ which is the Zariski closure of the set of points $(x_0, \dots, x_n, y_0, \dots, y_n)$ such that $((x_0 : \dots : x_n), (y_0 : \dots : y_n)) \in V$. The map proj is extended in the following way: $\mathsf{proj} : (x, y) \in (\mathbb{C}^{n+1} \setminus \{\mathbf{0}\}) \times (\mathbb{C}^{n+1} \setminus \{\mathbf{0}\}) \to (x, y) \in \mathbb{P}^n \times \mathbb{P}^n$.

2.2 Atlases and transversality

Let $V \subset \mathbb{C}^n$ be a d-equidimensional algebraic set of codimension c and $S \subset V$ be a subset. Following the terminology in [33, Chap. 5], an atlas for (V, S) is a finite sequence $\psi = ((\mathbf{h}_j, m_j))_{1 \le j \le \ell}$, with $\mathbf{h}_j = (h_{j,1}, \dots, h_{j,c}) \subset \mathbb{C}[X_1, \dots, X_n]$ and $m_j \in \mathbb{C}[X_1, \dots, X_n]$ such that for all $1 \le j \le \ell$ the following holds:

- P_1 $\mathcal{O}(m_j) \cap (V \setminus S) = \mathcal{O}(m_j) \cap (Z(\mathbf{h}_j) \setminus S)$;
- P_2 $\mathcal{O}(m_j) \cap (V \setminus S)$ is not empty;
- P_3 for all $x \in \mathcal{O}(m_j) \cap V \setminus S$, $\mathrm{jac}(\mathbf{h}_j)$ has full rank c at x;
- P_4 the open sets $\mathcal{O}(m_j)$ cover $V \setminus S$.

We say that $\mathbf{h}_j$ is a set of local equations over $\mathcal{O}(m_j)$. [33, Lemma 5.2.4] establishes that there exists an atlas for $(V, \mathrm{sing}(V))$. Also, observe that $\mathrm{sing}(V) \subset Z(m_1 \cdots m_\ell)$.

Further, we use the notion of transverse intersection for algebraic sets and projective varieties. Let V and W be equidimensional algebraic sets in $\mathbb{C}^n$. As in [13, pp. 21], we say that V and W intersect transversely at x if $x \in \mathrm{reg}(V) \cap \mathrm{reg}(W)$ and $T_xV + T_xW = \mathbb{C}^n$. They intersect generically transversely if they meet transversely at a generic point of each irreducible component of $V \cap W$. This definition is naturally extended to projective varieties. We say that two sets V and W intersect transversely over an open set U if V and W intersect tranversely at any point of $V \cap W \cap U$.

LEMMA 3. *Let V_1 and V_2 be equidimensional algebraic sets of codimensions c_1 and c_2. Consider atlases $\boldsymbol{\alpha}_1 = ((\mathbf{h}_j, m_j))_{1 \le j \le \ell}$ and $\boldsymbol{\alpha}_2 = ((\mathbf{g}_j, n_j))_{1 \le j \le k}$ for $(V_1, \mathrm{sing}(V_1))$ and $(V_2, \mathrm{sing}(V_2))$. Assume that $V_1 \cap V_2$ is either empty or that for any irreducible component Z of $V_1 \cap V_2$, there exist $r \in \{1, \dots, \ell\}$ and $s \in \{1, \dots, k\}$ such that*

- T_1 *$Z \cap \mathcal{O}(m_r n_s)$ is not empty;*
- T_2 *At any point of $\mathrm{reg}(Z) \cap \mathcal{O}(m_r n_s)$, the matrix $\mathrm{jac}(\mathbf{h}_r, \mathbf{g}_s)$ has rank $c_1 + c_2$;*

Then V_1 and V_2 intersect generically transversely.

PROOF. The equality $\mathrm{rank}(\mathrm{jac}(\mathbf{h}_r, \mathbf{g}_s)) = \mathrm{rank}(\mathrm{jac}(\mathbf{h}_r)) + \mathrm{rank}(\mathrm{jac}(\mathbf{g}_s))$ implies that at any point $x \in \mathrm{reg}(Z) \cap \mathcal{O}(m_r n_s)$, $N_xV_1 \cap N_xV_2 = 0$. Consequently, $T_xV_1 + T_xV_2 = (N_xV_1 \cap N_xV_2)^\perp = \mathbb{C}^n$. Finally, noticing that $\mathrm{reg}(Z) \cap \mathcal{O}(m_r n_s)$ is dense in $Z \cap \mathcal{O}(m_r n_s)$, which is dense in Z (by T_1) concludes the proof. □

We also need to prove that the intersection of bi-projective varieties is transverse. This is done via their associated affine cones. In the sequel, the set $\{(x, y) \mid x = \mathbf{0}\} \subset \mathbb{C}^{n+1} \times \mathbb{C}^{n+1}$ is denoted by $\mathscr{X}$ and the set $\{(x, y) \mid y = \mathbf{0}\} \subset \mathbb{C}^{n+1} \times \mathbb{C}^{n+1}$ is denoted by $\mathscr{Y}$.

LEMMA 4. *Let V_1 and V_2 be projective varieties in $\mathbb{P}^n \times \mathbb{P}^n$. Then V_1 and V_2 intersect transversely at every point $(x, y) = ((x_0 : \dots : x_n), (y_0 : \dots : y_n)) \in \mathbb{P}^n \times \mathbb{P}^n$ iff $\mathsf{aff}(V_1)$ and $\mathsf{aff}(V_2)$ intersect transversely over $\mathbb{C}^{n+1} \times \mathbb{C}^{n+1} \setminus (\mathscr{X} \cup \mathscr{Y})$.*

PROOF. Let i, j be such that $x_i \neq 0$ and $y_j \neq 0$. W.l.o.g., we assume that $i = j = 0$. Consider the affine chart $U \subset \mathbb{P}^n \times \mathbb{P}^n$ defined by $x_0 \neq 0, y_0 \neq 0$. Let $H_1 \subset \mathbb{C}^{n+1} \times \mathbb{C}^{n+1}$ (resp. H_2) be the hyperplane defined by $x_0 = 1$ (resp. $y_0 = 1$). For $\ell \in \{1, 2\}$, the variety $V_\ell \cap U$ can be identified to $\mathsf{aff}(V_\ell) \cap H_1 \cap H_2$. By definition of transversality, the varieties V_1 and V_2 intersect transversely at $(x, y) \in \mathbb{P}^n \times \mathbb{P}^n$ if and only if so do $V_1 \cap U$ and $V_2 \cap U$. By the previous identification, this is equivalent to saying that $\mathsf{aff}(V_1) \cap H_1 \cap H_2$ and $\mathsf{aff}(V_2) \cap H_1 \cap H_2$ intersect transversely at $(1, x_1, \dots, x_n, 1, y_1, \dots, y_n)$. Finally, direct tangent space computations show that for z_1, z_2 in $\mathbb{C} \setminus \{0\}$ and for $\ell \in \{1, 2\}$, $T_{(z_1, z_1x_1, \dots, z_1x_n, z_2, z_2y_1, \dots, z_2y_n)}\mathsf{aff}(V_\ell) = T_{(1, x_1, \dots, x_n, 1, y_1, \dots y_n)}\mathsf{aff}(V_\ell)$. □

2.3 Critical points and modified polar varieties

Let $V \subset \mathbb{C}^n$ be an equidimensional algebraic set of codimension c and $g \in \mathbb{Q}[X_1, \dots, X_n]$. Consider the evaluation map $\varphi_g : x \in V \to g(x)$. We denote by $w(\varphi_g, V)$ the set $\{x \in \mathrm{reg}(V) \mid \mathrm{rank}(\mathrm{jac}_x(\mathbf{f}, g)) < c + 1\}$. This is a locally closed constructible set and it coincides with the critical locus of the map φ_g. Its Zariski closure is denoted by $W(\varphi_g, V)$. This construction can be generalized as follows.

Let $a_1, \dots, a_n$ be linearly independent vectors in $\mathbb{C}^n$ and for $1 \le i \le n$, set $\mathbf{a}_i = (a_1, \dots, a_i) \in \mathbb{C}^{i \times n}$. Then, for $1 \le i \le n$, let $W((g, \mathbf{a}_i), V)$ denote the algebraic set

$$\{x \in V \mid \mathrm{rank}(\mathrm{jac}_x(\mathbf{f}, g, \varphi_{\mathbf{a}_i})) < c + i + 1\},$$

where $\mathbf{f}$ is a set of generators of $I(V)$, and $\varphi_{\mathbf{a}_i}$ is the set of linear forms $(a_j \cdot X)_{j \in \{1, \dots, i\}}$ (with $X = (X_1, \dots, X_n)$). Reusing the terminology of [19], we call these sets *modified polar varieties* associated to g and V, the i-th one being $W((g, \mathbf{a}_i), V)$. We let $W(\mathbf{a}_i, V)$ be the classical polar variety $\{x \in V \mid \mathrm{rank}(\mathrm{jac}_x(\mathbf{f}, \varphi_{\mathbf{a}_i}) < c + i\}$, reusing the letter W for the sake of simplicity.

PROPOSITION 5. *Let V be a d-equidimensional algebraic set, and $i \in \{1, \dots, d\}$. There exists a Zariski dense subset $\mathscr{O} \subset \mathbb{C}^{in}$ and an integer integer numbers δ_i such that for any $a \in \mathscr{O}$, the following holds:*

- *$W(a, V)$ is either empty or equidimensional of dimension $i - 1$;*
- *$W(a, V)$ has degree at most δ_i.*

PROOF. The first statement follows directly from [2, Prop.3]. For the second statement, we refer to the definition of $\delta_{classic}$ in [1, Sec. 4]. □

The integers δ_i are denoted by $\delta_i(V)$ in the sequel. By convention, we set $\delta_{d+1} = \deg(V)$. These numbers are also called *projective characters* of V (see [16, Example 14.3.3]).

3. PROOF OF THEOREM 1

We start by introducing some objects which play a central role in the proof. As before, V is a d-equidimensional algebraic set and $\mathsf{aff}(V)$ denotes the affine cone over the projective closure of V.

Let $\mathcal{N}_V \subset \mathbb{C}^{n+1} \times \mathbb{C}^{n+1}$ be the Zariski closure of the set

$$\{(x, y) \in \mathbb{C}^{n+1} \times \mathbb{C}^{n+1} \mid x \in \mathsf{aff}(V) \setminus \{\mathbf{0}\},\ y \in N_x\mathsf{aff}(V) \setminus \{\mathbf{0}\}\}.$$

It is called the conormal variety of $\mathsf{aff}(V)$. Consider $a = (a_1, \dots, a_i) \in \mathbb{C}^{(n+1)i}$, a homogeneous polynomial $g \in \mathbb{C}[X_0, X_1, \dots, X_n]$ of degree D and the matrix

$$\Sigma_i(g, a) = \begin{bmatrix} Y_0 & \cdots & Y_n \\ \partial g/\partial X_0 & \cdots & \partial g/\partial X_n \\ \hline & a_1 & \\ \hline & \vdots & \\ \hline & a_i & \end{bmatrix}.$$

Let $S_i(g,a) \subset \mathbb{C}^{n+1} \times \mathbb{C}^{n+1}$ be the variety defined by the rank condition $\mathrm{rank}(\Sigma_i(g,a)) \leq i+1$. Let Π be the projection

$$\Pi: \quad (x,y) \in \mathbb{C}^{n+1} \times \mathbb{C}^{n+1} \quad \to \quad x \in \mathbb{C}^{n+1}. \tag{3.1}$$

If a is generic, then $\mathcal{N}_V \cap S_i(g,a)$ is the Zariski closure of set of points (x,y) such that $y \in N_x\mathsf{aff}(V)$, and $(y_0,\ldots,y_n) \in \mathrm{Span}(a) + \nabla_x g$. In other words, $(x_0,x_1,\ldots,x_n)$ is a critical point of the map $(X_0,\ldots,X_n) \mapsto (g(X), a_1 \cdot X, \ldots, a_i \cdot X)$. Let $a = (a'_1,\ldots,a'_{i-1}) \in \mathbb{C}^{n(i-1)}$ be a basis of the vector space $\{(u_1,\ldots,u_n) \in \mathbb{C}^n \mid (0,u_1,\ldots,u_n) \in \mathrm{Span}(a_1,\ldots,a_i)\}$. Therefore, if the first coordinate of a_1 is nonzero, then the restriction of $\Pi(\mathcal{N}_V \cap S_i(g,a))$ to the chart $x_0 = 1$ is the modified polar variety $W((g_{|x_0=1},a'),V)$. The set of homogeneous polynomials in $\mathbb{C}[X_0,\ldots,X_n]$ of degree D is a finite dimensional vector space; we denote by N its dimension and identify those homogeneous polynomials to points in $\mathbb{C}^N$. Assume for the moment the following result which is proved in Section 4.

PROPOSITION 6. *Let $V \subset \mathbb{C}^n$ be a d-equidimensional algebraic set such that its projective closure is smooth and $i \in \{0,\ldots,d\}$. There exists a non-empty Zariski open set $\mathscr{O} \subset \mathbb{C}^{(n+1)i} \times \mathbb{C}^N$ such that for any $(g,a) \in \mathscr{O}$, $\mathcal{N}_V$ and $S_i(g,a)$ meet generically transversely over $(\mathbb{C}^{n+1} \setminus \{\mathbf{0}\}) \times (\mathbb{C}^{n+1} \setminus \{\mathbf{0}\})$.*

One can associate to any equidimensional variety $Z \subset \mathbb{P}^n \times \mathbb{P}^n$ of codimension c a bivariate homogenous polynomial $\mathrm{bideg}(Z) \in \mathbb{N}[T,U]$ of degree c, called the bidegree of Z [36, 37]. The coefficient of T^kU^{c-k} in $\mathrm{bideg}(Z)$ is the number of points (counted with multiplicity) of $Z \cap (H_1 \times \mathbb{P}^n) \cap (\mathbb{P}^n \times H_2)$ where H_1 (resp. H_2) is a generic linear space of dimension $n-k$ (resp. $n-c+k$). By [10, Sec. 5], the bidegree of $\mathcal{N}_V$ is $\sum_{k=0}^{d} \delta_{k+1}(V)T^{n-k}U^{k+1}$. We focus now on the bidegree of $S_i(g,a)$.

LEMMA 7. *There exists a non-empty Zariski open set $\mathscr{O}' \subset \mathbb{C}^N \times \mathbb{C}^{(n+1)i}$ such that for $(g,a) \in \mathscr{O}'$, $S_i(g,a) \subset \mathbb{C}^{n+1} \times \mathbb{C}^{n+1}$ has codimension $n-i$ and its bidegree is $\sum_{k=0}^{n-i}(D-1)^kT^kU^{n-k-i}$. Moreover, $\mathrm{reg}(S_i(g,a))$ coincides with the set of points where the matrix $\Sigma_i(g,a)$ has rank $i+1$.*

PROOF. $S_i(g,a)$ is the variety of $(x,y) \in \mathbb{C}^{n+1} \times \mathbb{C}^{n+1}$ where the evaluation of $\Sigma_i(g,a)$ is rank defective. There exists a Zariski dense subset $\mathscr{O}_1 \subset \mathbb{C}^{(n+1)i}$ such that for all $a \in \mathscr{O}_1$, the top-left $i \times i$ submatrix of A is invertible, where A is the matrix with rows $a_1,\ldots,a_i$. For $a \in \mathscr{O}_1$, let $B = (b_{i,j})$ be an invertible $(n+1) \times (n+1)$ matrix such that $A \cdot B = [\mathbf{0} \mid I_i]$. The rank condition on $A \cdot B$ shows that $S_i(g,a)$ is the set of points $(x,y) \in \mathbb{C}^{n+1} \times \mathbb{C}^{n+1}$ where the rank of

$$M = \begin{bmatrix} \sum_{j=1}^{n+1} b_{j,1}Y_j & \cdots & \sum_{j=1}^{n+1} b_{j,n+1-i}Y_j \\ \sum_{j=1}^{n+1} b_{j,1}\partial g/\partial X_j & \cdots & \sum_{j=1}^{n+1} b_{j,n+1-i}\partial g/\partial X_j \end{bmatrix}$$

is at most 1, where $Y_1,\ldots,Y_{n+1-1}$ are new variables. Next, let $S'_i \subset \mathbb{P}^{n-i} \times \mathbb{P}^{n-i}$ denote the determinantal variety of rank-defective matrices

$$\begin{bmatrix} \mathfrak{u}_{1,0} & \cdots & \mathfrak{u}_{1,n-i} \\ \mathfrak{u}_{2,0} & \cdots & \mathfrak{u}_{2,n-i} \end{bmatrix},$$

together with the grading given by $\deg(\mathfrak{u}_{1,j}) = 1$, $\deg(\mathfrak{u}_{2,j}) = D-1$ for all $j \in \{0,\ldots,n-i\}$. Setting $\mathbf{s} = 0$, $\deg(t_1) = D-1$, $\deg(t_2) = 1$, in [25, Example 15.39], the multidegree of S'_i is $\sum_{k=0}^{n-i}(D-1)^kT^kU^{n-k-i}$, where T (resp. U) corresponds to the class of a hyperplane in the first (resp. second) operand in the product $\mathbb{P}^{n-1} \times \mathbb{P}^{n-1}$. Let $\mathbb{C}[X_0,\ldots,X_n]_{D-1}$ denote the set of homogeneous polynomials of degree $D-1$. Since determinantal varieties are Cohen-Macaulay [27, Thm. 11], by the same argument as in [15, Sec. 4], there exists a Zariski dense subset $\mathcal{O}_2 \subset \mathbb{C}[X_0,\ldots,X_n]_{D-1}^{n+1} \times \mathbb{C}^{(n+1)i}$ such that for any $(h_0,\ldots,h_n,a) \in \mathscr{O}_2$, the bidegree of the variety defined by $\mathrm{rank}(M) \leq 1$ also has bidegree $\sum_{k=0}^{n-i}(D-1)^kT^kU^{n-k-i}$. Note that the set of $(h_0,\ldots,h_n)$ which are of the form $(\partial g/\partial X_0,\ldots,\partial g/\partial X_n)$ is a linear subspace of $\mathbb{C}[X_0,\ldots,X_n]$. It remains to prove that the restriction of $\mathscr{O}_2$ to this subspace is nonempty. This is done by considering $(h_0,\ldots,h_n) = (X_0^{D-1},\ldots,X_n^{D-1})$ (which comes from the derivatives of $g = (X_0^D + \cdots + X_n^D)/D$) and $a_{i,j} = 1$ if $i = j$ and 0 otherwise. Direct computations show that the corresponding variety has the expected bidegree. Therefore the open set $\mathcal{O}'$ of pairs (g,a) such that $(\partial g/\partial X_0,\ldots,\partial g/\partial X_n, a) \in \mathscr{O}_2$ satisfies the desired properties. Writing the equations defining the variety of $S_i(g,a)$ from the rank of the matrix M shows that $(x,y) \in \mathrm{sing}(S_i(g,a))$ iff the evaluation of the first row of M is zero, which is equivalent to saying that $(Y_0,\ldots,Y_n)$ lies in $\mathrm{Span}(a)$. This implies that the regular locus of S_i is the set of points where $\Sigma_i(g,a)$ has rank $i+1$. $\square$

By Proposition 6, there exists a non-empty Zariski open set $\mathscr{O} \subset \mathbb{C}^N \times \mathbb{C}^{(n+1)(i+1)}$ such that for g, a' in $\mathscr{O}$, $\mathcal{N}_V$ and $S_{i+1}(g,a')$ meet generically transversely outside the set $\mathscr{X} \cup \mathscr{Y}$ introduced before Lemma 4. Consider the map proj introduced in Section 2 (paragraph on projective varieties). We deduce that for $(g,a') \in \mathscr{O}_2$, $\mathcal{N}'_V = \mathsf{proj}(\mathcal{N}_V)$ and $S'_i(g,a') = \mathsf{proj}(S_i(g,a'))$ meet generically transversely (Lemma 4). Below, we take $(g,a) \in \mathscr{O} \cap \mathscr{O}'$ (where $\mathscr{O}'$ is the non-empty Zariski open set defined in Lemma 7). Intersection theory [13, Theorem Definition 1.7] states that if two subvarieties Z_1 and Z_2 of $\mathbb{P}^n \times \mathbb{P}^n$ intersect generically transversely, then

$\mathrm{bideg}(Z_1 \cap Z_2) = \mathrm{bideg}(Z_1) \cdot \mathrm{bideg}(Z_2) \bmod \langle T^{n+1}, U^{n+1} \rangle$.

We deduce that $\mathrm{bideg}(\mathcal{N}'_V \cap S'_i(g,a))$ equals

$$\left(\sum_{k=0}^{d} \delta_{k+1}(V)T^{n-k}U^{k+1}\right)\left(\sum_{k=0}^{n-i-1} (D-1)^kT^kU^{n-k-i-1}\right) \bmod \langle T^{n+1}, U^{n+1} \rangle.$$

Note that the degree of the image of $S'_{i+1}(g,a') \cap \mathcal{N}'_V$ by the projection $\pi_1 : (x,y) \mapsto x$ is the coefficient of $T^{n-i-1}U^n$ in its bidegree. Direct computations show that it equals

$$\begin{cases} \delta_{i+1}(V) \text{ if } d = 1 \\ \sum_{j=i}^{d} \delta_{j+1}(V)(D-1)^{j-i} \text{ otherwise.} \end{cases}$$

For $j \in \{1,\ldots,i+1\}$, let ν_j be the first coefficient of a'_j and let $\mathcal{U}$ be the set of $a' \in \mathbb{C}^{(n+1)(i+1)}$ such that $\nu_1 \neq 0$. Set $\tilde{\mathscr{O}} = \{(g,a') \in \mathscr{O} \cap \mathscr{O}' \mid a' \in \mathcal{U}\}$. For $a' \in \mathcal{U}$, let χ be the map sending a' to $(a'_2 - \nu_2 a'_1/\nu_1, \ldots, a'_i - \nu_i a'_1/\nu_1)$. The image of $\mathcal{U}$ by χ is a dense open subset $\mathcal{U}' \subset \mathbb{C}^{ni}$. Finally, we write Ω for the set $(g_{|X_0=1},a) \in \mathbb{C}[X_1,\ldots,X_n]_{\leq D} \times \mathbb{C}^{ni}$ such that there exists $(g,a') \in \tilde{\mathscr{O}}$ with $\chi(a') = a$. For $(g_{|X_0=1},a) \in \Omega$, $S'_{i+1}(g,a')$ and $\mathcal{N}'_V$ intersect generically transversely. Moreover, its image by the projection Π (see (3.1)) restricted to the chart $x_0 = 1$, $y_0 = 1$ is $W(g_{|X_0=1},a)$. Consequently,

$$\begin{aligned} \deg(W(g_{|X_0=1},a)) &\leq \deg(\Pi(S'_{i+1}(g^h,a') \cap \mathcal{N}'_V)) \\ &= \begin{cases} \delta_{i+1}(V) & \text{if } d = 1 \\ \sum_{j=i}^{d} \delta_{j+1}(V)(D-1)^{j-i} & \text{otherwise.} \end{cases} \end{aligned}$$

4. PROOF OF PROPOSITION 6

Our proof relies on applying Lemma 3 with $V_1 = \mathcal{N}_V$ and $V_2 = S_i(g,a)$ for a generic choice of (a,g). It simply consists in proving that properties T_1 and T_2 defined in Lemma 3 hold. This leads us to define atlases and local equations for $\mathcal{N}_V$. Next, we define an atlas (and hence local equations) for a set related to $S_i(g,a)$. We will apply an algebraic version of Thom's weak transversality

Theorem to a well chosen map constructed using these local equations, establishing that this map is regular at the origin. Finally, we will use these results in the last paragraph of this Section to prove properties T_1 and T_2 under some genericity assumption on (g, a).

4.1 Local equations for $\mathcal{N}_V$

By assumption, V is d-equidimensional and smooth as is its projective closure; we denote by c its codimension. This implies that the affine cone $\mathsf{aff}(V)$ of the projective closure of V is also equidimensional of codimension c. Besides, if $(x, y) \in \mathsf{aff}(V)$ with $x \neq 0$ then x is a regular point of $\mathsf{aff}(V)$. By [33, Lemma 5.2.4], there exists an atlas $\psi = ((\mathbf{h}_j, m_j))_{1 \leq j \leq J}$ for $(\mathsf{aff}(V), \mathrm{sing}(\mathsf{aff}(V)))$ (see Subsection 2.2). This leads us to define the set

$$U_j = \{(x, y) \mid x \in \mathsf{aff}(V) \cap \mathcal{O}(m_j), y \perp T_x\mathsf{aff}(V) \setminus \{\mathbf{0}\}\}.$$

Since the open sets $\mathcal{O}(m_j)$ cover $\mathsf{aff}(V) \setminus \mathrm{sing}(\mathsf{aff}(V))$ (property P_4), the sets U_j cover $\mathcal{N}_V \setminus \mathscr{X} \cup \mathscr{Y}$.

Let $m'_{j,1}, \ldots, m'_{j,L_j}$ be the $c \times c$ minors of $\mathrm{jac}(\mathbf{h}_j)$ such that $\mathcal{O}(m_j m'_{j,k}) \cap V \neq \emptyset$ for $1 \leq k \leq L_j$. For $1 \leq r \leq n - c$, we denote by $M_{r,k}(m'_{j,k})$ the minor of the $(c + 1, c + 1)$ minors of the $(c + 1, c + 1)$ submatrix of

$$J = \begin{bmatrix} \mathrm{jac}(\mathbf{h}_j) \\ Y_0 \cdots Y_n \end{bmatrix}$$

whose upper left $(c \times c)$ minor is $m'_{j,k}$ and adding the missing row and column. In the sequel, we denote by $\mathbf{H}_{j,k}$ the sequence $\mathbf{h}_j, M_{1,k}(m'_{j,k}), \ldots, M_{n-c,k}(m'_{j,k})$.

LEMMA 8. *Under the above notation and assumptions, the sequence of couples $(\mathbf{H}_{j,k}, m_j m'_{j,k})$ for $1 \leq j \leq J$ and $1 \leq k \leq L_j$ is an atlas for $(\mathcal{N}_V, \mathrm{sing}(\mathcal{N}_V) \cup \mathscr{X} \cup \mathscr{Y})$.*

PROOF. Recall that we are given an atlas $\psi = ((\mathbf{h}_j, m_j))_{1 \leq j \leq J}$ for $(\mathsf{aff}(V), \mathrm{sing}(\mathsf{aff}(V)))$. Let $(x, y) \in \mathcal{N}_V \setminus (\mathrm{sing}(\mathcal{N}_V) \cup \mathscr{X} \cup \mathscr{Y})$. Then, $x \in \mathrm{reg}(\mathsf{aff}(V))$ (because $x \neq \mathbf{0}$ and the projective closure of V is assumed to be smooth) and there exists $1 \leq j \leq J$ such that $x \in \mathsf{aff}(V) \cap \mathcal{O}(m_j)$. Besides note that $\mathsf{aff}(V) \cap \mathcal{O}(m_j)$ coincides with $Z(\mathbf{h}_j) \cap \mathcal{O}(m_j)$ (property P_1) and that $\mathrm{jac}(\mathbf{h}_j)$ has maximal rank at x (property P_3). We let $m'_{j,k}$ be a $(c \times c)$-minor of $\mathrm{jac}(\mathbf{h}_j)$ which does not vanish at x.

Since $(x, y) \in \mathcal{N}_V$, we have $y \perp T_x\mathsf{aff}(V)$. Using property P_1 and P_3, we deduce that $T_x\mathsf{aff}(V)$ is the kernel of $\mathrm{jac}(\mathbf{h}_j)$. We deduce by elementary linear algebra that the matrix J introduced above is rank defective at (x, y). Besides, elementary linear algebra (e.g. using a Schur complement) shows that over $\mathcal{O}(m_j m'_{j,k})$, the variety defined by $\mathbf{h}_j(x) = 0$ and $\mathsf{rank}(J(x, y)) \leq c$ is defined by $\mathbf{H}_{j,k}$. We have established properties P_1 and P_2. Establishing the fact that the sets $\mathcal{O}(m_j m'_k)$ cover $\mathcal{N}_V \setminus (\mathrm{sing}(\mathcal{N}_V) \cup \mathscr{X} \cup \mathscr{Y})$ (property P_4) is immediate from the above discussion. It remains to prove that $\mathrm{jac}(\mathbf{H}_{j,k})$ has maximal rank at (x, y) (property P_3). Without loss of generality, assume that $m'_{j,k}$ is the upper left minor of $\mathrm{jac}(\mathbf{h}_j)$. Observe that the minors $M_{1,k}(m'_{j,k}), \ldots, M_{n-c,k}(m'_{j,k})$ can be written as $Y_{c+\ell} m'_{j,k} + \rho_\ell$ where $\rho_\ell \subset \mathbb{Q}[X_1, \ldots, X_n, Y_1, \ldots, Y_c]$. Extracting from $\mathrm{jac}(\mathbf{H}_{j,k})$ the columns of $\mathrm{jac}(\mathbf{h}_j)$ corresponding to $m'_{j,k}$ and those corresponding to the partial derivatives w.r.t $Y_{c+\ell}$ for $1 \leq \ell \leq n - c$ yields a submatrix which is not rank defective over $Z(\mathbf{h}_j) \cap \mathcal{O}(m_j m'_{j,k})$ which ends the proof. □

4.2 Local equations for $S_i(g, a)$

In this section, we build an atlas for $S_i(g, a)$ for generic (g, a). To do that, we see (g, a) as in point in the space $\mathbb{C}^N \times \mathbb{C}^{(n+1)i}$ (recall that N is the dimension of the vector space of homogeneous polynomials in $\mathbb{C}[X_0, \ldots, X_n]$) and see the entries of a and the coefficients of g as variables.

Formally, for $1 \leq r \leq i$, let $A_r = (A_{0,r}, \ldots, A_{n,r})$ be a vector of indeterminates. Let also $\mathcal{M} = \{(\alpha_0, \ldots, \alpha_n) \in \mathbb{N}^{n+1} \mid \sum_{j=0}^n \alpha_j = D\}$ and $G = (G_\alpha, \alpha \in \mathcal{M})$ be a vector of indeterminates. By abuse of notation, we also denote by G the polynomial $\sum_{\alpha \in \mathcal{M}} G_\alpha X^\alpha$; it lies in $\mathbb{Q}(G)[X_0, \ldots, X_n]$.

We consider now the matrix

$$\Sigma_i = \begin{bmatrix} Y_0 & \cdots & Y_n \\ \partial G/\partial X_0 & \cdots & \partial G/\partial X_n \\ \text{———} & A_1 & \text{———} \\ & \vdots & \\ \text{———} & A_i & \text{———} \end{bmatrix}$$

and the algebraic set $\mathscr{S}_i \subset \mathbb{C}^{n+1} \times \mathbb{C}^{n+1} \times \mathbb{C}^N \times \mathbb{C}^{(n+1)i}$ defined by $\mathrm{rank}(\Sigma_i) \leq i + 1$.

Let $\sigma_1, \ldots, \sigma_L$ be the sequence of $(i + 1, i + 1)$-minors of the submatrix Σ_i obtained by removing the line containing partial derivatives of G or the line A_j for $1 \leq j \leq L$ such that $\mathscr{S}_i \cap \mathcal{O}(\sigma_\ell) \neq \emptyset$. For $1 \leq \ell \leq L$, we denote by $S_{1,\ell}, \ldots, S_{n-i-1,\ell}$ the $(i+2, i+2)$-minors of Σ_i obtained by selecting the rows and columns used to compute σ_ℓ and adding the missing row and column from Σ_i. We denote by $\mathbf{S}_\ell$ the sequence $S_{1,\ell}, \ldots, S_{n-i-1,\ell}$.

Finally, we define the set $\mathscr{T} \subset \mathbb{C}^N \times \mathbb{C}^{(n+1)i}$ as the complementary of the set of points $(g, a = (a_1, \ldots, a_i)) \in \mathbb{C}^N \times \mathbb{C}^{(n+1)i}$ such that

- the coefficients of $X_r X_s^{D-1}$ in G for $1 \leq r, s \leq n$ with $r \neq s$ are not zero;
- (g, a) lies in the non-empty open set $\mathscr{O}$ defined in Lemma 7;
- $\mathrm{Span}(a_1, \ldots, a_i)$ has dimension i and none of the entries of A_r is 0 (for $1 \leq r \leq i$).

Note that $\mathscr{T}$ is Zariski closed in $\mathbb{C}^N \times \mathbb{C}^{(n+1)i}$. Finally, we denote by $\mathscr{S}'$ the union of $\mathrm{sing}(\mathscr{S}_i)$, the set $\mathbb{C}^{n+1} \times \mathbb{C}^{n+1} \times \mathscr{T}$ and the subset of points $\mathscr{S}_i$ such that their Y-coordinates are all 0.

Up to renumbering the sequence of couples $(\mathbf{S}_\ell, \sigma_\ell)_{1 \leq \ell \leq L}$ we assume that the set of indices ℓ such that $(\mathscr{S}_i \setminus \mathscr{S}') \cap \mathcal{O}(\sigma_\ell) \neq \emptyset$ is $\{1, \ldots, L'\}$ (for $L' \leq L$).

LEMMA 9. *The sequence $(\mathbf{S}_\ell, \sigma_\ell)_{1 \leq \ell \leq L'}$ is an atlas for the couple $(\mathscr{S}_i, \mathscr{S}')$. Besides, the truncated Jacobian matrix of $\mathbf{S}_\ell$ obtained by considering the partial derivatives w.r.t the entries of $A_1, \ldots, A_i$ and the coefficients of G has full rank over $\mathcal{O}(\sigma_\ell)$. Moreover, there exists a non-empty Zariski open set $\mathscr{O}''$ such that for all $(g, a) \in \mathscr{O}''$, $(\mathbf{S}_\ell, \sigma_\ell)_{1 \leq \ell \leq L'}$ is an atlas of the couple $(S_i(g, a), \mathrm{sing}(S_i(g, a)))$.*

PROOF. Take (x, y, g, a) in $\mathscr{S}_i \setminus \mathscr{S}'$. Since $(g, a) \notin \mathscr{S}$, $(g, a) \notin \mathscr{O}$ and $(x, y) \notin \mathrm{sing}(S_i(g, a))$. We deduce that Σ_i has rank $i + 1$ at (x, y, g, a). Then, either $\dim(\mathrm{Span}(a_1, \ldots, a_i, y)) = i + 1$ or $y \in \mathrm{Span}(a_1, \ldots, a_i)$ while $\nabla_{x,y,a,g}(G) \notin \mathrm{Span}(a_1, \ldots, a_i)$ (because Σ_i has rank $i + 1$ at (x, y, g, a)). Since $(y_0, \ldots, y_n) \neq 0$ (because $(x, y, g, a) \notin \mathscr{S}$), we deduce that there exists $1 \leq r \leq i$ such that $\mathrm{Span}(a_1, \ldots, a_{r-1}, a_{r+1}, \ldots, a_i, y) = \mathrm{Span}(a_1, \ldots, a_i)$ and we deduce that

$$\dim(\mathrm{Span}(a_1, \ldots, a_{r-1}, a_{r+1}, \ldots, a_i, \nabla_x(g), y)) = i + 1.$$

This implies that one of the $(i + 1, i + 1)$-minor σ_ℓ of Σ_i does not vanish at (x, y, g, a). Elementary linear algebra shows that $\mathscr{S}_i \cap \mathcal{O}(\sigma_\ell) \setminus \mathscr{S}'$ coincides with $Z(\mathbf{S}_\ell)$ over $\mathcal{O}(\sigma_\ell) \setminus \mathscr{S}'$. Thus, we have established properties P_1 and P_2. The covering property P_4 is immediate and follows also from the above discussion.

It remains to prove property P_3, i.e. $\mathrm{jac}(\mathbf{S}_\ell)$ has maximal rank at any point of $\mathscr{S}_i \cap \mathcal{O}(\sigma_\ell) \setminus \mathscr{S}'$. Assume first that σ_ℓ is a $(i+1, i+1)$-minor obtained from removing the partial derivatives of G from Σ_i. Without loss of generality, we may also assume that it is obtained by selecting the first $i + 1$ columns of Σ_i. Then, polynomials in $\mathbf{S}_\ell$

can be written as $\sigma_\ell A_{r,i+1} + \rho_{r,\ell}$ for $i+1 \leq r \leq n$ where $\rho_{r,\ell}$ has degree 0 in A_r. That implies that one can extract a diagonal matrix with σ_ℓ on the diagonal from jac($\mathbf{S}_\ell$) which, of course, has maximal rank over $\mathcal{O}(\sigma_\ell)$.
When σ_ℓ is obtained by removing one of the line A_r (e.g. A_i) a more involved but similar conclusion can be made. Since we work over the complementary of $\mathscr{S}'$, there exists $0 \leq r \leq n$ such that the X_r-coordinate of x is not 0. Extracting the submatrix of jac($\mathbf{S}_\ell$) corresponding to the partial derivatives with respect to the coefficients of G of the monomials X_r^D and $X_s X_r^{D-1}$ yields a diagonal matrix with a power of the X_r-coordinate of x multiplied by σ_ℓ on the diagonal. These are non-zero over $\mathcal{O}(\sigma_\ell) \setminus \mathscr{S}'$.
The rank property of the truncated Jacobian matrix of $\mathbf{S}_\ell$ is an immediate consequence of the above discussion. Details on the proof of the specialization property of the atlas $(\mathbf{S}_\ell, \sigma_\ell)$ are left to the reader; we mention that it is a direct consequence of specialization properties of minors with polynomial entries and Lemma 7. □

4.3 A map and its regularity at the origin

Let m_j, m'_k and $\mathbf{H}_{j,k}$ be the polynomials introduced in the paragraph on local equations for $\mathcal{N}_V$ and σ_ℓ, $\mathbf{S}_\ell$ be the $(i+1,i+1)$-minor and $(i+2,i+2)$-minors of Σ introduced in the paragraph on local equations of $S_i(g,a)$. Consider the Zariski open set $\mathscr{U}_{j,k,\ell} \subset \mathbb{C}^n \times \mathbb{C}^n \times \mathbb{C}^N \times \mathbb{C}^{ni}$ defined by

$m_j m'_k \neq 0, \quad (X_0,\ldots,X_n) \neq \mathbf{0} \quad (Y_0,\ldots,Y_n) \neq \mathbf{0}, \quad \sigma_\ell \neq 0$

and the inequations defining the complement $\mathscr{S}'$. We define now the following map:

$$\boldsymbol{\phi}_{j,k,\ell} : z \in \mathscr{U}_{j,k,\ell} \to (\mathbf{H}_{j,k}(z), \mathbf{S}_\ell(z)).$$

Observe that $\boldsymbol{\phi}_{j,k,\ell}^{-1}(\mathbf{0}) \subset \mathcal{N}_V \cap \mathscr{S}_i$.

LEMMA 10. *The map $\boldsymbol{\phi}_{j,k,\ell}$ is regular at* $\mathbf{0}$.

PROOF. Since j,k and ℓ are fixed in the sequel, we omit them as subscripts. Observe that jac($\mathbf{H},\mathbf{S}$) has the following shape

$$\mathbf{J}_{\boldsymbol{\phi}} = \begin{bmatrix} \mathrm{jac}_{\mathbf{X}}(\mathbf{H}) & 0 \\ \mathrm{jac}_{\mathbf{X}}(\mathbf{S}) & \Delta \end{bmatrix}$$

where the last columns correspond to the partial derivates with respect to the entries of $A_1,\ldots,A_i$ and G. By Lemma 8, ($\mathbf{H}_{j,k}$, $m_j m'_k$) satisfies properties $\mathsf{P}_1, \mathsf{P}_2$ and P_3. This implies that it has maximal rank at any point in $\boldsymbol{\phi}^{-1}(\mathbf{0}) \subset \mathscr{U}$. By Lemma 9, Δ has maximal rank at any point of $\boldsymbol{\phi}^{-1}(\mathbf{0})$. We deduce that $\mathbf{J}_{\boldsymbol{\phi}}$ has maximal rank at any point of $\boldsymbol{\phi}^{-1}(\mathbf{0})$ and our conclusion follows. □

In the sequel, for $(g,a) \in \mathbb{C}^N \times \mathbb{C}^{(n+1)i}$, we denote by $\boldsymbol{\phi}_{j,k,\ell}^{(g,a)}$ the restricted map $(x,y) \to \boldsymbol{\phi}_{j,k,\ell}(x,y,g,a)$. Applying Thom's weak transversality Theorem (see [33, Sec 4.2]) to $\boldsymbol{\phi}_{j,k,\ell}$ shows that there exists a non-empty Zariski open set $\mathscr{O}'''_{j,k,\ell} \subset \mathbb{C}^N \times \mathbb{C}^{(n+1)i}$ such that for all $(g,a) \in \mathscr{O}'''_{j,k,\ell}$, the restricted map $\boldsymbol{\phi}_{j,k,\ell}^{(g,a)}$ is regular at $\mathbf{0}$. Letting $\mathscr{O}'''$ be the intersection of all these non-empty Zariski open sets $\mathscr{O}'''_{j,k,\ell}$ leads to the following result.

LEMMA 11. *There exists a non-empty Zariski open set $\mathscr{O}''' \subset \mathbb{C}^N \times \mathbb{C}^{(n+1)i}$ such that for any (j,k,ℓ) and $(g,a) \in \mathscr{O}'$, the restricted map $\boldsymbol{\phi}_{j,k,\ell}^{(g,a)}$ is regular at* $\mathbf{0}$.

4.4 Transversality of the intersection

Let $\mathscr{O}$ be the intersection of the non-empty Zariski open sets $\mathscr{O}''$ and $\mathscr{O}'''$ defined in Lemma 9 and Lemma 11. Take $(g,a) \in \mathscr{O}$ and $Z_{(g,a)}$ be the Zariski closure of $\bigcup_{j,k,\ell} {\boldsymbol{\phi}_{j,k,\ell}^{(g,a)}}^{-1}(\mathbf{0})$. Recall that we need to prove the transversality of $\mathcal{N}_V \cap S_i(g,a)$ at any point outside $\mathscr{X} \cup \mathscr{Y}$. Let $\boldsymbol{\alpha}_1 = (\mathbf{H}_{j,k}, m_j m'_k)$ be the atlas of $(\mathcal{N}_V, \mathrm{sing}(\mathcal{N}_V))$ defined in Lemma 8 and $\boldsymbol{\alpha}_2 = (\mathbf{S}_\ell, \sigma_\ell)$ be the atlas of $(S_i(g,a), \mathrm{sing}(S_i(g,a)))$ defined in Lemma 9. We start by proving that the Zariski closure of $\mathcal{N}_V \cap S_i(g,a) \setminus (\mathscr{X} \cup \mathscr{Y})$ equals $Z_{g,a}$. The inclusion $Z_{(g,a)} \subset \mathcal{N}_V \cap S_i(g,a) \setminus (\mathscr{X} \cup \mathscr{Y})$ is immediate since all points in ${\boldsymbol{\phi}_{j,k,\ell}^{(g,a)}}^{-1}(\mathbf{0}) \subset Z(\mathbf{H}_{j,k}, \mathbf{S}_{k,\ell}) \cap \mathcal{O}(m_j m'_k \sigma_\ell)$ and $Z(\mathbf{H}_{j,k}, \mathbf{S}_{k,\ell}) \cap \mathcal{O}(m_j m'_k \sigma_\ell) = \mathcal{N}_V \cap S_i(g,a) \cap \mathcal{O}(m_j m'_k \sigma_\ell)$ (property P_2). We prove now the reverse inclusion. It is sufficient to prove that for any irreducible component Z of the Zariski closure of $\mathcal{N}_V \cap S_i(g,a) \setminus (\mathscr{X} \cup \mathscr{Y})$, there exists a triple (j,k,ℓ) and a Zariski closed subset $F \subsetneq Z$ such that $Z \setminus F \subset {\boldsymbol{\phi}_{j,k,\ell}^{(g,a)}}^{-1}(\mathbf{0})$. Since Z is an irreducible component of the Zariski closure of $\mathcal{N}_V \cap S_i(g,a) \setminus (\mathscr{X} \cup \mathscr{Y})$, there exists $(x,y) \in Z$ such that $(x,y) \notin \mathscr{X} \cup \mathscr{Y}$. Let $F = Z \cap (\mathscr{X} \cup \mathscr{Y})$. Now, take $(x,y) \in Z \setminus F$. By property P_4 applied to $\boldsymbol{\alpha}_1$, that implies that there exists j and k such that $x \in Z(\mathbf{H}_{j,k}) \cap \mathcal{O}(m_j m'_k)$. Besides, $(y_0,\ldots,y_n) \neq \mathbf{0}$ since $(x,y) \notin F$. This latter property implies that there exists ℓ such that $\sigma_\ell(x,y) \neq 0$. Finally, we have established that $(Z \setminus F) \cap \mathcal{O}(m_j m'_k \sigma_\ell)$ is not empty for some (j,k,ℓ). Property P_2 applied to $\boldsymbol{\alpha}_1$ and $\boldsymbol{\alpha}_2$ imply that (x,y) lies in $Z(\mathbf{H}_{j,k})$ and $Z(\mathbf{S}_\ell)$. We deduce that $(x,y) \in {\boldsymbol{\phi}_{j,k,\ell}^{(g,a)}}^{-1}(\mathbf{0})$ which implies that $Z \setminus F \subset {\boldsymbol{\phi}_{j,k,\ell}^{(g,a)}}^{-1}(\mathbf{0})$ as requested.

Property (T_1). Consider an irreducible component Z of the Zariski closure of $\mathcal{N}_V \cap S_i(g,a) \setminus (\mathscr{X} \cup \mathscr{Y})$. The above discussion implies that Z is an irreducible component of $Z_{(g,a)}$ and that there exists j,k,ℓ such that $Z \cap \mathcal{O}(m_j m'_k \sigma_\ell)$ is not empty.

Property (T_2). Recall that $(g,a) \in \mathscr{O}'$ and let Z be an irreducible component of $\mathcal{N}_V \cap S_i(g,a)$. We already proved that Z there exists (j,k,ℓ) such that $Z \cap \mathcal{O}(m_j m'_k \sigma_\ell)$ is not empty and meets ${\boldsymbol{\phi}_{j,k,\ell}^{(g,a)}}^{-1}(\mathbf{0})$. By Lemma 11, the restricted map $\boldsymbol{\phi}_{j,k,\ell}^{(g,a)}$ is regular at $\mathbf{0}$. Then, the jacobian matrix associated to $\mathbf{H}_{j,k}, \mathbf{S}_\ell$ has maximal rank at any point of $Z \cap {\boldsymbol{\phi}_{j,k,\ell}^{(g,a)}}^{-1}(\mathbf{0})$, which concludes the proof.

5. NON-GENERIC FUNCTION

We show in this section that the bounds in Theorem 1 hold under milder conditions than the genericity of the coefficients of g. Consider a d-equidimensional algebraic set $V \subset \mathbb{C}^n$ whose projective closure is smooth, a set of generators $f_1,\ldots,f_p$ of $I(V)$, and $g \in \mathbb{Q}[X_1,\ldots,X_n]$ of degree D. Let $a \in \mathbb{C}^{ni}$, $g \in \mathbb{Q}[X_1,\ldots,X_n]$ and $I_{\mathsf{crit}}(g,a)$ be the ideal generated by $f_1,\ldots,f_p$ and the $(n-d+i+1)$-minors of the matrix

$$\begin{bmatrix} \text{———} & \mathrm{jac}(\mathbf{f}) & \text{———} \\ \partial g/\partial X_1 & \cdots & \partial g/\partial X_n \\ \text{———} & a_1 & \text{———} \\ & \vdots & \\ \text{———} & a_i & \text{———} \end{bmatrix}.$$

PROPOSITION 12. *Let $i \in \{0,\ldots,d\}$ and $a \in \mathbb{C}^{ni}$. Assume that the ideal $I_{\mathsf{crit}}(g,a)$ is radical and $W(g,a)$ is empty or $(i-1)$ equidimensional. Then there exists a non-empty Zariski open subset $\mathscr{O} \subset \mathbb{C}^{in}$ such that the following holds. For any $a = (a_1,\ldots,a_i) \in \mathscr{O}$, the degree of $W((g,\mathbf{a}),V)$ is bounded above by the bounds in Theorem 1.*

LEMMA 13. *Let $Q \in \mathbb{C}[T_1,\ldots,T_\ell]$ be a nonzero multivariate polynomial, and $(t_1,\ldots,t_\ell) \in \mathbb{C}^\ell$ be such that $Q(t_1,\ldots,t_\ell) = 0$. Then there exist univariate polynomials $u_1,\ldots,u_\ell \in \mathbb{C}[\mathfrak{e}]$ such that for all $i \in \{1,\ldots,\ell\}$, $u_i(0) = t_i$ and $Q(u_1(\mathfrak{e}),\ldots,u_\ell(\mathfrak{e})) \in \mathbb{C}[\mathfrak{e}]$ is not identically zero.*

PROOF. We prove the existence of $u_1,\ldots,u_\ell$ of the form $u_i(\mathfrak{e}) = t_i + s_i\mathfrak{e}$, where $s_i \in \mathbb{C}$ for all $i \in \{1,\ldots,\ell\}$. Let $\mathbf{t}$ and $\mathbf{s}$ be shorthands for $(t_1,\ldots,t_\ell)$ and $(s_1,\ldots,s_\ell)$. Using Taylor's expansion, we write $Q(\mathbf{t}+\mathfrak{e}\mathbf{s}) = \mathfrak{e}\partial Q(\mathbf{t})(\mathbf{s}) + \mathfrak{e}^2\partial^2 Q(\mathbf{t})(\mathbf{s},\mathbf{s})/2 + \ldots + \mathfrak{e}^{\deg(Q)}\partial^{\deg(Q)} Q(\mathbf{t})(\mathbf{s},\ldots,\mathbf{s})/\deg(Q)!$. Since $Q \neq 0$, at least one of its derivatives is not zero at $\mathbf{t}$. Let k be the smallest integer such that $\mathbf{u} \mapsto \partial^k Q(\mathbf{t})(\mathbf{u}, \ldots, \mathbf{u})$ is not the zero map. Finally, let $\mathbf{s}$ be such that $\partial^k Q(\mathbf{t})(\mathbf{s}, \ldots, \mathbf{s}) \neq 0$. Hence, we have $Q(\mathbf{t} + \mathfrak{e}\mathbf{s}) - \mathfrak{e}^k \partial^k Q(\mathbf{t})(\mathbf{s}, \ldots, \mathbf{s})/k! = O(|\mathfrak{e}^{k+1}|)$. Consequently, $Q(\mathbf{t} + \mathfrak{e}\mathbf{s})$ cannot be identically zero, as this would imply $\mathfrak{e}^k = O(|\mathfrak{e}^{k+1}|)$. □

PROOF OF PROPOSITION 12. The proof is a classical deformation argument similar to the one used in [26]. Further we assume that $W(g, a)$ is not empty (else the result is immediate). By Theorem 1, there exists a polynomial Q in $N + ni = \binom{n+D}{n} + ni$ variables whose zero-set encode the pairs (g, a) for which the bounds are not satisfied. By Lemma 13, there exists $(\mathfrak{g}, \mathfrak{a}) \in \mathbb{Q}[\mathfrak{e}][X_1, \ldots, X_n] \times \mathbb{Q}[\mathfrak{e}]^{ni}$ such that their evaluation at $\mathfrak{e} = 0$ is (g, a) and the evaluation of Q at $(\mathfrak{g}, \mathfrak{a})$ (seen as an element in $\mathbb{Q}[\mathfrak{e}]^{N+ni}$) is nonzero. For $\varepsilon \in \mathbb{C}$, we let $(g_\varepsilon, a_\varepsilon)$ denote the evaluation of $\mathfrak{g}$ and $\mathfrak{a}$ at $\mathfrak{e} = \varepsilon$. For $i \in \{1, \ldots, d\}$, the set of affine spaces in $\mathbb{C}^n$ of codimension $i-1$ can be identified with a dense open subset of the Grassmaniann of $(n-i+2)$-dimensional vector spaces in $\mathbb{C}^{n+1}$. Since $W((g, a), V)$ is $(i-1)$-equidimensional, there exists a dense open subset $\mathscr{O}$ of this Grassmanian such that for any E in $\mathscr{O}$, the intersection $W((g, a), V) \cap E$ is transverse, finite and its cardinality equals the degree of $W((g, \mathbf{a}_i), V)$. Let $\mathbf{x} \in \mathbb{C}^n$ be a point in this intersection. Let $v_1, \ldots, v_n \in \mathbb{C}[X_1, \ldots, X_n, \mathfrak{e}]$ be polynomials satisfying the following assumptions: $v_1, \ldots, v_n$ is a regular sequence, for every $\varepsilon \in \mathbb{C}$ their evaluations at $\mathfrak{e} = \varepsilon$ vanish on $W((g_\varepsilon, a_\varepsilon), V) \cap E$, and the jacobian matrix $\mathrm{jac}(v_1(X_1, \ldots, X_n, 0), \ldots, v_n(X_1, \ldots, X_n, 0))$ is invertible at $\mathbf{x}$ (since $I_{\mathsf{crit}}(g, a)$ is radical). In order to obtain such polynomials, we consider n generic linear combinations of the equations defining $W((\mathfrak{g}, \mathfrak{a}), V) \cap E$. Then the holomorphic implicit mapping theorem [24, Thm. 8.6] states that for $\mathbf{x}_0 \in W((g, a), V) \cap E$ there exist open neighborhoods (for the Euclidean topology) $0 \in U_1 \subset \mathbb{C}$, $\mathbf{x}_0 \in U_2$ such that there is a holomorphic map $\varepsilon \mapsto \{\mathbf{x} \in U_2 \mid v_1(\mathbf{x}, \varepsilon) = \cdots = v_n(\mathbf{x}, \varepsilon) = 0\}$ on U_1. In particular this map is continuous, which implies that for $\varepsilon \in \mathbb{C}$ with sufficiently small complex modulus, the cardinality of $W((g_\varepsilon, a_\varepsilon), V) \cap E$ is bounded below by the degree of $W((g, a), V)$. Since this is true for any E in the Zariski dense open subset $\mathscr{O}$ of affine subsets, the cardinality of $W((g_\varepsilon, a_\varepsilon), V) \cap E$ equals its degree. Finally, as Q is not identically zero on the coefficients of $(\mathfrak{g}, \mathfrak{a})$, for ε_0 with sufficiently small modulus, the evaluation of Q at the coefficients of $(g_{\varepsilon_0}, a_{\varepsilon_0})$ is nonzero. Consequently, the bounds in Theorem 1 hold for $W((g_{\varepsilon_0}, a_{\varepsilon_0}), V)$ and hence they also hold for $W((g, a), V)$. □

6. ALGORITHMS

Terminology and computational model. In this section, we consider *bounded error probabilistic algorithms*. These algorithms are probabilistic random-access stored-program machines whose probability of success is bounded from above by an *a priori* bound. It is the same computational model as in [17]. Complexity bounds count the number of arithmetic operations $(+, -, \times, /)$ in $\mathbb{Q}$.

A lifting fiber is a data structure giving an exact representation of an equidimensional algebraic set. We recall below its definition and we refer to [17, Sec. 3.4] for more details.

DEFINITION 14. *[17, Def. 4] Let $V \subset \mathbb{C}^n$ be a d-equidimensional variety defined over $\mathbb{Q}$* (i.e. $Z_{\mathbb{C}}(I_{\mathbb{Q}}(V)) = V$). *A* lifting fiber *for V is a tuple $\mathscr{L} = (\mathbf{G}, M, \mathbf{z}, u, Q, \mathbf{v})$:*

- *A* lifting system $\mathbf{H} = (h_1, \ldots, h_{n-d}) \in \mathbb{Q}[X_1, \ldots, X_n]$, *such that $h_1, \ldots, h_{n-d}$ is a reduced regular sequence and $V \subset Z(\mathbf{H})$.*
- *A $n \times n$ invertible matrix M with entries in $\mathbb{Q}$ such that the coordinates $Y = M^{-1}X$ are in* Noether position *w.r.t. V;*
- *A* rational lifting point $\mathbf{z} = (z_1, \ldots, z_d) \in \mathbb{Q}^d$*;*
- *A* primitive element $u : \mathbb{C}^n \to \mathbb{C}$, *which is a linear form with rational coefficients having distinct values at all points of the finite set $V^{(\mathbf{z})} = V \cap \{Y_1 - z_1 = \cdots = Y_d - z_d = 0\} \subset \mathbb{C}^n$;*
- *A* polynomial $Q \in \mathbb{Q}[T]$ *of minimal degree vanishing at all points of $u(V^{(\mathbf{z})})$;*
- univariate polynomials $\mathbf{v} = (v_{d+1}, \ldots, v_n) \in \mathbb{Q}[T]^{n-d}$ *of degree less than* $\deg(Q)$ *such that*

$$\begin{gathered} Y_1 - z_1 = \cdots = Y_d - z_d = 0 \\ Y_{d+1} - v_{d+1}(T) = \cdots = Y_n - v_n(T) = 0, Q(T) = 0 \end{gathered}$$

is a rational parametrization of $V^{(\mathbf{z})}$ by the roots of Q.

The sequence $(M, u, Q, \mathbf{v})$ is called a geometric resolution *of V.*

Computing a lifting fiber can be achieved in a probabilistic way with the Kronecker solver [11]. We assume that we know a probabilistic algorithm POLARVAR which takes as input $d \in \mathbb{N}$, a lifting fiber of a d-equidimensional variety $V \subset \mathbb{C}^n$ and a sequence $\mathbf{a} = (a_1, \ldots, a_d) \in \mathbb{Q}^{d \times n}$; it returns a geometric resolution of the 0-dimensional polar variety $W(\mathbf{a}_1, V)$ or "fail". We use also the routine CHANGEPRIMITIVEELEMENT [17, Algo. 6].

In [2], the authors propose an algorithm which takes as input a reduced regular sequence $f_1, \ldots, f_{n-d}$ defining a d-equidimensional algebraic set $V \subset \mathbb{C}^n$, a matrix $\mathbf{F}$ whose entries are multivariate polynomials, and a sequence $a = (a_1 \ldots, a_d)$ of vectors in $\mathbb{Q}^n$. It returns lifting fibers for the associated *degeneracy loci*. If $\mathbf{F}$ turns out to be the jacobian matrix of the regular sequence defining the variety, then these degeneracy loci are the classical polar varieties $W(a, V)$, see [2, Section 5.1]. This algorithm works in two steps: it computes first a lifting fiber for V; then, from this lifting fiber and from the matrix a, it computes lifting fibers for the degeneracy loci. In the case of polar varieties, the complexity of the second step is bounded by $L(nD_{\max})^{O(1)}\delta^2$, where δ is the maximum of the degrees of the polar varieties $W(\mathbf{a}_i, V)$ (where $\mathbf{a}_i = (a_1, \ldots, a_i)$), $D_{\max}$ is the maximum of the degrees of $f_1, \ldots, f_{n-d}$, and L is the size of an essentially division-free straight line program for evaluating $f_1, \ldots, f_{n-d}$.

Let $a = (a_1, \ldots, a_d)$ be a sequence of d vectors in $\mathbb{Q}^n$. We construct another sequence $a' = (e_{n+1}, a'_1, \ldots, a'_d)$ of vectors in $\mathbb{Q}^{n+1}$ defined by the $(d+1) \times (n+1)$ coefficient matrix

$$A' = \left[\begin{array}{ccc|c} & \mathbf{0} & & 1 \\ \hline \text{——} & a_1 & \text{——} & \\ \vdots & \vdots & \vdots & \mathbf{0} \\ \text{——} & a_d & \text{——} & \end{array}\right].$$

LEMMA 15. *Let $\Pi_n : \mathbb{C}^{n+1} \to \mathbb{C}^n$ be the projection on the n first coordinates, and $f_1, \ldots, f_p \in \mathbb{Q}[X_1, \ldots, X_n]$ be polynomials defining a reduced smooth d-equidimensional variety and $g \in \mathbb{Q}[X_1, \ldots, X_n]$ be a polynomial. Then for any $\mathbf{a} \in \mathbb{Q}^{d \times n}$ and for $i \in \{0, \ldots, d\}$, the modified polar variety $W((g, a), Z(f_1, \ldots, f_p))$ equals $\Pi_n(W(a'_{i+1}, Z(f_1, \ldots, f_p, g - X_{n+1})))$.*

PROOF. Set $V = Z(f_1, \ldots, f_p) \subset \mathbb{C}^n$ and $V' = Z(f_1, \ldots, f_p, g - X_{n+1}) \subset \mathbb{C}^{n+1}$. Direct computations show that if V is smooth, then so is V'. The modified polar variety $W((g, \mathbf{a}_i), V)$ is defined by the set of points in V at which

$$\operatorname{rank} \begin{bmatrix} \text{——} & \mathrm{jac}(\mathbf{f}) & \text{——} \\ \text{——} & \nabla g & \text{——} \\ \text{——} & a_1 & \text{——} \\ \vdots & \vdots & \vdots \\ \text{——} & a_1 & \text{——} \end{bmatrix} \leq n - d + i.$$

Direct computations show that the corresponding matrix for $W(\mathbf{a}'_i, V')$ has the same rank at any point $(x, g(x))$ where $x \in V$. □

Algorithm 1: CRITPOINTS

Input :

- A lifting fiber $(\mathbf{H}, M, \mathbf{z}, u, Q, \mathbf{v})$ for a smooth d-equidimensional variety $V \subset \mathbb{C}^n$
- $g \in \mathbb{Q}[X_1, \ldots, X_n]$ and $a = (a_1, \ldots, a_d) \in \mathbb{Q}^{d \times n}$
- A primitive element u_{crit} for $W(\mathbf{a}_1, V)$

$M' \leftarrow \left[\begin{array}{c|c} M & \mathbf{0} \\ \hline \mathbf{0} & 1 \end{array}\right]$;

$\mathscr{L}' \leftarrow (\mathbf{H} \cup \{g - X_{n+1}\}, M', (z_1, \ldots, z_n, g(z_1, \ldots, z_n)), u, Q, (v_1, \ldots, v_n, g \circ (v_1(T), \ldots, v_n(T)) \bmod Q(T)))$;

$a' \leftarrow$ sequence of rows of $\left[\begin{array}{ccc|c} & \mathbf{0} & & 1 \\ \hline \text{———} & a_1 & \text{———} & \\ \vdots & \vdots & \vdots & \mathbf{0} \\ \text{———} & a_d & \text{———} & \end{array}\right]$;

$\mathscr{L}^{(2)} \leftarrow$ POLARVAR$(d, \mathscr{L}', a')$ or return "fail";

$(\mathbf{H}', M^{(2)}, \mathbf{z}', u_{\text{crit}}, Q', \mathbf{v}') \leftarrow$ CHANGEPRIMITIVEELEMENT$(\mathscr{L}^{(2)}, u_{\text{crit}} \circ M^{(2)})$;

$\mathbf{v}^{(2)} \leftarrow (M^{(2)})^{-1} \cdot (v_1', \ldots, v_{n+1}')^T$;

return $(\mathsf{Id}_n, u_{\text{crit}} \circ (M^{(2)})^{-1}, Q', (v_1', \ldots, v_n'))$;

THEOREM 16. *Let $\mathscr{L} = (\mathbf{H}, M, \mathbf{z}, u, Q, \mathbf{v})$ be a lifting fiber for a d-equidimensional algebraic set V, $g \in \mathbb{Q}[X_1, \ldots, X_n]$ be a polynomial of degree $D \geq 2$ and $a \in \mathbb{C}^{ni}$. Assume that V, g and a satisfy the same assumptions as in Proposition 12. Let $D_{\max}$ be the maximum of the degrees of $h_1, \ldots, h_{n-d}, g$, (where $\mathbf{H} = (h_1, \ldots, h_{n-d})$) and u be a primitive element for $W(g, V)$. Assume that the evaluation map $x \mapsto (h_1(x), \ldots, h_{n-d}(x), g(x))$ is represented by an essentially division-free straight-line program of size L. Algorithm 1 with input $(\mathscr{L}, \mathbf{a}, u)$ computes a geometric resolution of the set $W(g, V)$ or it returns "fail". Using the algorithm in [2] for* POLARVAR, *it requires at most $(nD_{\max})^{O(1)}\widetilde{O}(L\Delta^2)$ operations in $\mathbb{Q}$, where $\Delta = \sum_{j=0}^{d} \delta_{j+1}(V)(D-1)^{j-i}$.*

PROOF. We prove first the correctness of the algorithm. Note that $\mathscr{L}'$ computed during Algorithm 1 is a lifting fiber for $V' = \{(x, g(x)) \mid x \in V\}$. Assuming that POLARVAR returns a lifting fiber for $W(\mathbf{a}_1', V')$, Lemma 15 shows that the output of POLARVAR is a lifting fiber of the pairs $(x, g(x))$ for $x \in W(g, V)$. The last steps compute a geometric resolution of the projection on the n first coordinates, which is $W(g, V)$. We prove now the complexity statement. The first step of Algorithm 1 does not cost any arithmetic operations. The second step requires $\widetilde{O}(L \deg(V))$ operations in $\mathbb{Q}$ for the modular composition using quasi-linear algorithms for multiplication and reduction. The evaluation of g costs L operations. The cost of the computation of $\mathbf{a}'$ is negligible. By [2, Thm. 18], the call to POLARVAR requires $L(pnd)^{O(1)}\delta'^2$, where δ' is the maximum of the degrees of the polar varieties of V'. By Lemma 15, the projection of $W(\mathbf{a}_1', V')$ on the n first coordinates is $W(g, V)$. By Theorem 1, Proposition 12 and since $\deg(g) \geq 2$, we have $\deg(W(g, V)) \leq \Delta$. Changing the primitive element costs $\widetilde{O}(n\Delta^2)$ by [17, Lemma 6]. Finally, the linear algebra computations in the last step cost $O(n^2\Delta)$ operations in $\mathbb{Q}$. Summing all these complexities proves the complexity statement. $\square$

7. REFERENCES

[1] B. Bank, M. Giusti, J. Heintz, M. S. El Din, and E. Schost. On the geometry of polar varieties. *Applicable Algebra in Engineering, Communication and Computing*, 21(1):33–83, 2010.

[2] B. Bank, M. Giusti, J. Heintz, G. Lecerf, G. Matera, and P. Solernó. Degeneracy loci and polynomial equation solving. *Foundations of Computational Mathematics*, 15(1):159–184, 2013.

[3] B. Bank, M. Giusti, J. Heintz, and G.-M. Mbakop. Polar varieties and efficient real equation solving: the hypersurface case. *Journal of Complexity*, 13(1):5–27, 1997.

[4] B. Bank, M. Giusti, J. Heintz, and L. M. Pardo. Generalized polar varieties: Geometry and algorithms. *Journal of complexity*, 21(4):377–412, 2005.

[5] I. Bannwarth and M. S. El Din. Probabilistic algorithm for computing the dimension of real algebraic sets. In *Proceedings of ISSAC 2015*. ACM, 2015.

[6] S. Basu, R. Pollack, and M.-F. Roy. *Algorithms in real algebraic geometry*. Springer-Verlag, 2006.

[7] S. Basu and M.-F. Roy. Divide and conquer roadmap for algebraic sets. *Discrete & Computational Geometry*, 52(2):278–343, 2014.

[8] S. Basu, M.-F. Roy, M. Safey El Din, and E. Schost. A baby step–giant step roadmap algorithm for general algebraic sets. *Foundations of Computational Mathematics*, 14(6):1117–1172, 2014.

[9] F. Catanese, S. Hoşten, A. Khetan, and B. Sturmfels. The maximum likelihood degree. *American Journal of Mathematics*, pages 671–697, 2006.

[10] J. Draisma, E. Horobet, G. Ottaviani, B. Sturmfels, and R. R. Thomas. The Euclidean distance degree of an algebraic variety. *Foundations of Computational Mathematics*, pages 1–51, 2015.

[11] C. Durvye and G. Lecerf. A concise proof of the Kronecker polynomial system solver from scratch. *Expositiones Mathematicae*, 26(2):101–139, 2008.

[12] D. Eisenbud. *Commutative Algebra: with a view toward algebraic geometry*, volume 150. Springer Science & Business Media, 2013.

[13] D. Eisenbud and J. Harris. All that intersection theory in algebraic geometry. 2013.

[14] J.-C. Faugère, M. Safey El Din, and P.-J. Spaenlehauer. Critical points and Gröbner bases: the unmixed case. In *Proceedings of ISSAC 2012*, pages 162–169. ACM, 2012.

[15] J.-C. Faugère, M. Safey El Din, and P.-J. Spaenlehauer. On the complexity of the generalized MinRank problem. *Journal of Symbolic Computation*, 55:30–58, 2013.

[16] W. Fulton. *Intersection theory*, volume 2. Springer, 2012.

[17] M. Giusti, G. Lecerf, and B. Salvy. A Gröbner free alternative for polynomial system solving. *Journal of Complexity*, 17(1):154–211, 2001.

[18] A. Greuet and M. Safey El Din. Deciding reachability of the infimum of a multivariate polynomial. In *Proc. of ISSAC 2011*, pages 131–138. ACM, 2011.

[19] A. Greuet and M. Safey El Din. Probabilistic algorithm for polynomial optimization over a real algebraic set. *SIAM Journal on Optimization*, 24(3):1313–1343, 2014.

[20] D. Y. Grigor'ev and N. Vorobjov. Solving systems of polynomial inequalities in subexponential time. *Journal of symbolic computation*, 5(1):37–64, 1988.

[21] J. Heintz, M.-F. Roy, and P. Solernó. Description of the connected components of a semialgebraic set in single exponential time. *Discrete & Computational Geometry*, 11(1):121–140, 1994.

[22] A. Holme. The geometric and numerical properties of duality in projective algebraic geometry. *Manuscripta Mathematica*, 61(2):145–162, 1988.

[23] H. Hong and M. Safey El Din. Variant quantifier elimination. *Journal of Symbolic Computation*, 47(7):883–901, 2012.

[24] L. Kaup and B. Kaup. *Holomorphic functions of several variables: an introduction to the fundamental theory*, volume 3. Walter de Gruyter, 1983.

[25] E. Miller and B. Sturmfels. *Combinatorial commutative algebra*, volume 227. Springer Science & Business Media, 2005.

[26] J. Nie and K. Ranestad. Algebraic degree of polynomial optimization. *SIAM Journal on Optimization*, 20(1):485–502, 2009.

[27] D. Northcott. Semi-regular rings and semi-regular ideals. *The Quarterly Journal of Mathematics*, 11(1):81–104, 1960.

[28] R. Piene. Polar classes of singular varieties. *Annales Scientifiques de l'Ecole Normale Superieure*, 11(2):247–276, 1978.

[29] J. Renegar. On the computational complexity and geometry of the first-order theory of the reals. *Journal of symbolic computation*, 13(3):255–299, 1992.

[30] M. Safey El Din. Computing the global optimum of a multivariate polynomial over the reals. In *Proc. of ISSAC 2008*, pages 71–78. ACM, 2008.

[31] M. Safey El Din and É. Schost. Polar varieties and computation of one point in each connected component of a smooth real algebraic set. In *Proceedings of ISSAC 2003*, pages 224–231. ACM, 2003.

[32] M. Safey El Din and É. Schost. A baby steps/giant steps probabilistic algorithm for computing roadmaps in smooth bounded real hypersurface. *Discrete & Computational Geometry*, 45(1):181–220, 2011.

[33] M. Safey El Din and É. Schost. A nearly optimal algorithm for deciding connectivity queries in smooth and bounded real algebraic sets. *arXiv preprint arXiv:1307.7836*, 2013.

[34] I. R. Shafarevich and K. A. Hirsch. *Basic algebraic geometry*, volume 1. Springer, 1977.

[35] P.-J. Spaenlehauer. On the complexity of computing critical points with Gröbner bases. *SIAM Journal on Optimization*, 24(3):1382–1401, 2014.

[36] B. L. Van der Waerden. On Hilbert's function, series of composition of ideals and a generalization of the theorem of Bezout. In *Proc. Roy. Acad. Amsterdam*, volume 31, pages 749–770, 1929.

[37] B. L. Van der Waerden. On varieties in multiple-projective spaces. *Indagationes Mathematicae (Proceedings)*, 81(1):303 – 312, 1978.

Fast Fourier Orthogonalization

Léo Ducas*
CWI, Cryptology Group
Amsterdam, The Netherlands
ducas@cwi.nl

Thomas Prest†
Thales Communications & Security
Gennevilliers, France
thomas.prest@thalesgroup.com

ABSTRACT

The classical fast Fourier transform (FFT) allows to compute in quasi-linear time the product of two polynomials, in the *circular convolution ring* $\mathbb{R}[x]/(x^d - 1)$ — a task that naively requires quadratic time. Equivalently, it allows to accelerate matrix-vector products when the matrix is *circulant*.

In this work, we discover that the ideas of the FFT can be applied to speed up the orthogonalization process of matrices with circulant blocks of size $d \times d$. We show that, when d is composite, it is possible to proceed to the orthogonalization in an inductive way —up to an appropriate re-indexation of rows and columns. This leads to a structured Gram-Schmidt decomposition. In turn, this structured Gram-Schmidt decomposition accelerates a cornerstone lattice algorithm: the nearest plane algorithm. The complexity of both algorithms may be brought down to $\Theta(d \log d)$.

Our results easily extend to *cyclotomic rings*, and can be adapted to Gaussian samplers. This finds applications in lattice-based cryptography, improving the performances of trapdoor functions.

Keywords. Fast Fourier transform, Gram-Schmidt orthogonalization, nearest plane algorithm, lattice algorithms, lattice trapdoor functions.

1. INTRODUCTION

When operations involving linear algebra are to be performed over structured matrices, a natural problem is to accelerate them by exploiting the structure. The most classical example is the fast Fourier transform [2, 8], which allows to perform matrix-vector multiplication in quasilinear time when the matrix is circulant. This is achieved by exploiting the isomorphism between the ring of $d \times d$ circulant matrices and the *circular convolution ring* $\mathcal{R}_d = \mathbb{R}[x]/(x^d - 1)$.

A widely studied and more involved question is matrix decomposition [19] for structured matrices, in particular Gram-Schmidt orthgonalization (GSO). In this work, we are interested in the GSO of *circulant matrices*, and more generally of matrices with circulant blocks. Our main motivation is to accelerate lattice algorithms for lattices that admit a basis with circulant blocks. This use case allows a helpful extra degree of freedom: one may permute rows and columns of the lattice basis since this leaves the generated lattice unchanged —up to an isometry.

As we will show, a proper re-indexation of these matrices highlights an inductive structure, with a fast Fourier flavor. This leads to accelerations of the orthogonalization process —and of the related nearest plane algorithm— down to quasilinear time and space.

The Nearest Plane Algorithm, Lattices and Cryptography

The nearest plane algorithm [1] is a central algorithm over lattices. It allows, after precomputation of the GSO and using a quadratic number of real operations, to find a relatively close point in a lattice to an arbitrary target. It is a core subroutine of LLL [12], and can be used for error correction over analogical noisy channels. It has also found applications in lattice-based cryptography as a decryption algorithm, and a randomized variant (called discrete Gaussian sampling) [11, 5] provides secure trapdoor functions based on lattice problems. This leads to cryptosystems (attribute-based encryption) with fine-grained access control, as [17, 6] to name a few.

Given a basis $\mathbf{B}$ of a lattice $L \subset \mathbb{R}^d$ and a target vector $\mathbf{c}$, the nearest plane algorithm finds a lattice point somewhat close to $\mathbf{c}$. The result belongs to a fundamental domain centered in $\mathbf{c}$, whose shape is the cuboid defined by $\tilde{\mathbf{B}}$, the GSO of $\mathbf{B}$ (see Figure 1). This algorithm performs $\Theta(d^2)$ real operations. The GSO itself is required as a precomputation.

Structured lattices in cryptography.

When it comes to practical lattice-based cryptography, a quadratic cost in the dimension is rather prohibitive considering the lattices at hand have dimensions ranging in the hundreds, or even thousands. For efficiency purposes, many cryptosystems (such as [10, 14, 15] to name a few) chose to rely on lattices with some algebraic structure, improving time and memory requirements to quasilinear in the dimension.

*This work has been supported by a grant from CWI from budget for public-private-partnerships and in part by a grant from NXP Semiconductors. Part of this work was also supported by an NWO Free Competition Grant.

†Part of this work was done when the author was at the École Normale Supérieure, Paris. This work was partially funded by the European Union H2020 SAFEcrypto project (grant no. 644729).

ISSAC '16, July 19 - 22, 2016, Waterloo, ON, Canada

ISBN 978-1-4503-4380-0/16/07...$15.00

DOI: http://dx.doi.org/10.1145/2930889.2930923

This is sometimes referred as lattice-based cryptography in the *ring setting*. Technically, the chosen rings typically are *cyclotomic rings*, but those are closely related to the *convolution rings* discussed so far. The core of this optimization is the fast Fourier transform (FFT) [2, 4, 8, 18] allowing fast multiplication of polynomials. But this improvement did not apply in the case of the nearest plane algorithm or its randomized variant [11, 5]: naïve GSO do not take the algebraic structure into account.

One possible work-around [9, 21] consist of using the round-off algorithm [1] instead of the nearest-plane algorithm. However, this simpler algorithm outputs further vectors, both in the average and worst cases, weakening those cryptosystems.

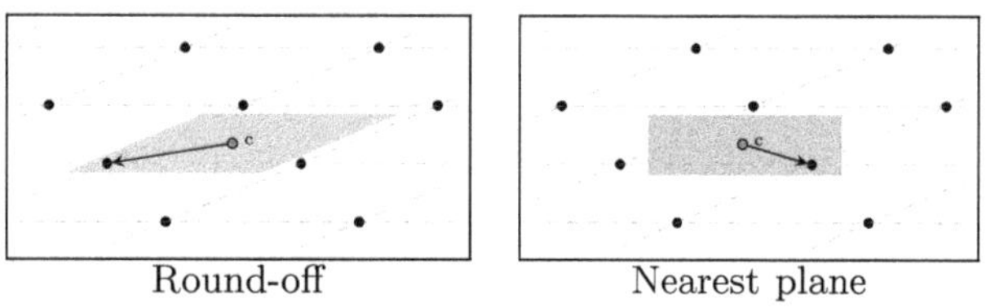

Figure 1: Round-off and nearest plane algorithms, and their associated fundamental domains.

Our contribution

In this work, we discover new algorithms, obtained by crossing Cooley-Tukey's [2] fast Fourier transform algorithm together with the orthogonalization and nearest plane algorithms (not exactly the GSO, but the closely related LDL* decomposition). Precisely, we show that, up to a re-indexation of rows and columns, the orthogonalization of matrices composed of $d \times d$-circulant blocks can be done in time $\Theta(d \log d)$ when the prime factors of d are bounded. Our algorithm produces the LDL* decomposition in a special compact format, requiring $\Theta(d \log d)$ complex numbers to represent.

From this compact representation, the nearest plane algorithm can also be performed using $\Theta(d \log d)$ real operations.[1] As a demonstration of the simplicity of our algorithms, we propose an implementation in `python` for $d \times d$-circulant matrices, when d is a power of 2.

Computational model and Parallelism.

Our algorithms and their complexity are described for Random Access Machines with unitary arithmetic operations on *real numbers*, i.e. we do not study the issue related to floating-point approximations and numerical stability.

Regarding parallelism, we note that our Fast-Fourier LDL* algorithm is almost fully parallelizable: viewed as an arithmetic circuit on real numbers, it has depth $O(\log(n))$ and width $O(n)$. This is unfortunately not the case of the Nearest Plane algorithm nor our Fast-Fourier variant, for which the n rounding steps are inherently sequential.

Techniques.

At the core of our techniques is the realization that representing elements of the convolution ring $\mathcal{R}_d = \mathbb{R}[x]/(x^d - 1)$ as circulant matrices is not the appropriate choice. To allow an induction similar to Cooley-Tukey's FFT, our representation must follow the *tower of rings* $\mathbb{R} \subset \mathcal{R}_{d_1} \subset \cdots \subset \mathcal{R}_{d_{i-1}} \subset \mathcal{R}_d$, for some chain of divisors $1|d_1| \ldots |d_{i-1}|d$.

Such a representation is obtained by applying the (mixed-radix) digit-reversal order to the indexation of the rows and column of the circulant blocks, as pictured in Figure 2.

We show that this alternative indexation allows to represent the matrix $\mathbf{L}$ of the GSO in a factorized form: a product of $\Theta(\log d)$ (sparse) structured matrices, each of which can be stored in space $O(d)$. An example is given in Figure 3.

Once this hidden structure is unveiled (Theorem 1), the algorithmic implications follow quite naturally: one first easily derive an algorithm in time $O(n \log^2 n)$ —matching previous and more general results [20]— but noting that the splitting step may be performed directly in the Fourier domain allows us to save another $\log n$ factor. For easier algorithmic manipulations, the factorization of $\mathbf{L}$ is represented using a tree.

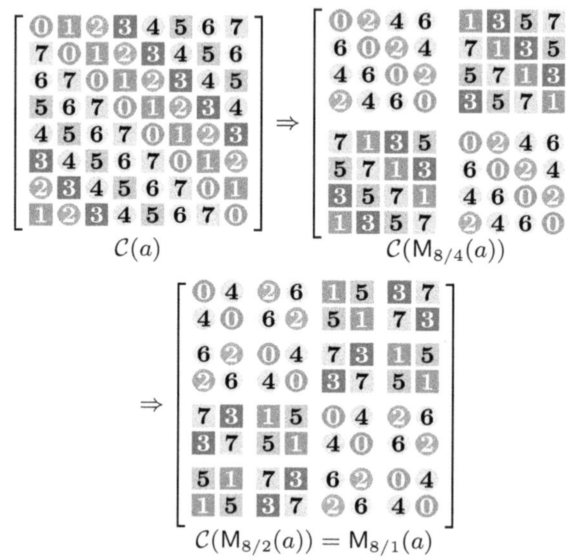

Figure 2: Re-indexing the transformation matrix of $f \in \mathcal{R}_8 \mapsto fx$ $(a = 0 + x + 2x^2 + \cdots + 7x^7 \in \mathcal{R}_8)$ **.**

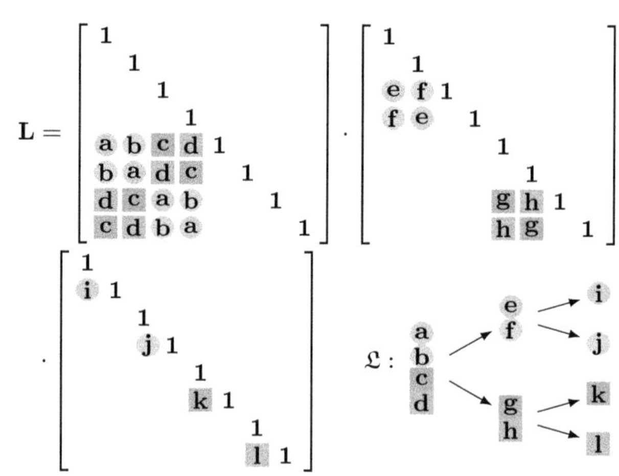

Figure 3: Factorization of L in the LDL* decomposition of $\mathsf{M}_{8/1}(a)$, and its tree representation $\mathfrak{L}$.

[1] If the number $n \times m$ of $d \times d$ circulant blocks is not constant, they contribute a factor $O(n^3)$ to the runtime of the fast-Fourier LDL* algorithm, $O(n^2)$ to its output size, and $O(n^2)$ to the run-time of the fast-Fourier nearest plane algorithm.

Related Works.

There exist many works related to the orthogonalization of structured bases. For Toeplitz matrices, Sweet [22] introduced an algorithm faster than the naive orthogonalization by a linear factor. Gragg [7] has shown that for Krylov bases – which are bases of the form $\{\mathbf{b}, r(\mathbf{b}), ..., r^{d-1}(\mathbf{b})\}$ –, the Levinson recursion [13, 3] allows, when r is an isometric operator, to perform orthogonalization in time $\Theta(d^2)$ instead of $\Theta(d^3)$.

There also exists superfast (running time $O(n \log^2 n)$) algorithms for the orthogonalization of Toeplitz-like matrices, for example by Olshevsky and Pan [20], and those are already based on a structure-preserving induction. In this light, one may interpret our result as a Fourier-compatible version of these superfast algorithms.

The question of improving the nearest-plane algorithm for structured matrices seems less studied. As far as we know, the state of the art consist of a single result [16], applying the Levinson recursion [13] to reduce by a linear factor its *space* complexity. Alternatively, a work-around of lesser quality was proposed for the NTRU signature scheme [9, 21].

Outline.

Section 2 introduces the mathematical tools that we will use through this paper. Section 3 presents our main result, namely the existence of a compact, factorized representation for the GSO and LDL* decomposition, and gives a fast Fourier flavored algorithm for computing it in this form. This compact LDL* decomposition is further exploited in Section 4, which presents a nearest plane algorithm that also has an FFT flavor. In the full version of our article[2], we propose the proofs, the extension of our results to cyclotomic rings, and a `python` code fragment. The full prototype implementation in `python` —for d a power of 2— is also available online.[3]

2. PRELIMINARIES

For any ring $\mathcal{R}$, $\mathcal{R}[x]$ will denote the ring of univariate polynomials over $\mathcal{R}$. Scalars (which includes elements of $\mathcal{R}$) will usually be noted in plain letters (such as a, b), vectors will be noted in bold letters (such as $\mathbf{a}, \mathbf{b}$) and matrices will be noted in capital bold letters (such as $\mathbf{A}, \mathbf{B}$). Vectors are mostly in row notation, and as a consequence vector-matrix products are done in this order unless stated otherwise. $(a_1, \ldots, a_n)$ denotes the row vector formed of the a_i's, whereas $[\mathbf{a}_1, \ldots, \mathbf{a}_n]$ denotes the matrix whose rows are the $\mathbf{a}_i$'s. $\mathbb{N}$ denotes the set of non-negative integers, and $\mathbb{N}^*$ the set $\mathbb{N}\backslash\{0\}$. For $i, j \in \mathbb{Z}$, $[\![i, j]\!]$ will denote the set $\{i, i+1, \ldots, j-1, j\}$.

2.1 The Convolution Ring $\mathcal{R}_d$

DEFINITION 1. *For any $d \in \mathbb{N}^*$, let $\mathcal{R}_d$ denote the ring $\mathbb{R}[x]/(x^d - 1)$, also known as circular convolution ring, or simply convolution ring.*

When d is highly composite, elementary operations in $\mathcal{R}_d$ can be performed in time $\Theta(d \log d)$ using the fast Fourier transform [2].

We equip the ring $\mathcal{R}_d$ with a conjugation operation as well as an inner product, making it an Hermitian inner product space. The definitions that we give also encompass other types of rings that are used in the full version of this article.

DEFINITION 2. *Let $h \in \mathbb{R}[x]$ be a monic polynomial with distinct roots over $\mathbb{C}$, $\mathcal{R} \triangleq \mathbb{R}[x]/(h(x))$ and a, b be arbitrary elements of $\mathcal{R}$.*

- *We note $a^\star$ and call (Hermitian) adjoint of a the unique element of $\mathcal{R}$ such that for any root ζ of h, $a^\star(\zeta) = \overline{a(\zeta)}$, where $\bar{\cdot}$ is the usual complex conjugation over $\mathbb{C}$.*
- *The inner product over $\mathcal{R}$ is $\langle a, b\rangle \triangleq \sum_{h(\zeta)=0} a(\zeta) \cdot \overline{b(\zeta)}$, and the associated norm is $\|a\| \triangleq \sqrt{\langle a, a\rangle}$.*

In the particular case of convolution rings, one can check that if $a(x) = \sum_{i=0}^{d-1} a_i x^i \in \mathcal{R}_d$, then

$$a^\star(x) = a(1/x) \bmod (x^d - 1) = a_0 + \sum_{i=1}^{d-1} a_i x^{d-i}.$$

The (Hermitian) adjoint $\mathbf{B}^\star$ of a matrix $\mathbf{B} \in \mathcal{R}^{n \times m}$ is the transpose of the coefficient-wise adjoint of $\mathbf{B}$.

While the inner product $\langle \cdot, \cdot \rangle$ (resp. the associated norm $\|\cdot\|$) is not to be mistaken with the canonical coefficient-wise dot product $\langle \cdot, \cdot \rangle_2$ (resp. the associated norm $\|\cdot\|_2$), they are closely related. One can easily check that for any $f = \sum_{i \in \mathbb{Z}_d} f_i x^i \in \mathcal{R}_d$, the vector $(f(\zeta))_{\{\zeta^d=1\}}$ can be obtained from the coefficient vector $(f_i)_{0 \leqslant i < d}$ by multiplying it by the Vandermonde matrix $\mathbf{V}_d = (\zeta_d^{ij})_{0 \leqslant i,j < d}$, where ζ_d denotes an arbitrary d-th primitive root of unity. The matrix $\mathbf{V}_d$ satisfies $\mathbf{V}_d \mathbf{V}_d^\star = d \cdot \mathbf{I}_d$ and as an immediate consequence: $\langle f, g \rangle = d \cdot \langle f, g \rangle_2$.

DEFINITION 3. *Let $m \geqslant n$ and $\mathbf{B} = \{\mathbf{b}_1, \ldots, \mathbf{b}_n\} \in \mathcal{R}^{n \times m}$. We say that $\mathbf{B}$ is full-rank (or is a basis) if for any linear combination $\sum_{1 \leqslant i \leqslant n} a_i \mathbf{b}_i$ with $a_i \in \mathcal{R}$, we have the equivalence $(\sum_i a_i \mathbf{b}_i = \mathbf{0}) \iff (\forall i, a_i = 0)$.*

We note that since $\mathcal{R}$ is generally not an integral domain, a set formed of a single nonzero vector is not necessarily full-rank. In the rest of the paper, a basis will either denote a set of independent vectors $\{\mathbf{b}_1, \ldots \mathbf{b}_n\} \in (\mathcal{R}^m)^n$, or the full-rank matrix $\mathbf{B} \in \mathcal{R}^{n \times m}$ whose rows are the $\mathbf{b}_i$'s.

2.2 The GSO and LDL* Decomposition

In this section, $\mathcal{R} = \mathbb{R}[x]/(h(x))$ as in Definition 2. We first recall a few standard definitions. A matrix $\mathbf{L} \in \mathcal{R}^{n \times n}$ is unit lower triangular if it is lower triangular and has only 1's on its diagonal.

We say that a self-adjoint matrix $\mathbf{G} \in \mathcal{R}^{n \times n}$ is full-rank Gram (or FRG) if there exist $m \geqslant n$ and a full-rank matrix $\mathbf{B} \in \mathcal{R}^{n \times m}$ such that $\mathbf{G} = \mathbf{B}\mathbf{B}^\star$. This generalizes the notion of positive definiteness for symmetric real matrices.

We now recall the GSO and LDL* decomposition. The GSO decomposes any full-rank matrix as the product of a unit lower triangular matrix and an orthogonal matrix.

PROPOSITION 1. *Let $\mathbf{B} \in \mathcal{R}^{n \times m}$ be a full-rank matrix. $\mathbf{B}$ can be uniquely decomposed as*

$$\mathbf{B} = \mathbf{L} \cdot \tilde{\mathbf{B}}, \qquad (1)$$

where $\mathbf{L}$ is unit lower triangular, and the rows of $\tilde{\mathbf{B}}$ are pairwise orthogonal.

[2]https://eprint.iacr.org/2015/1014

[3]https://github.com/lducas/ffo.py

When $\mathcal{R}$ is replaced by $\mathbb{R}$ or a number field, Proposition 1 is standard. In our case, a proof can be found in the full version of this article.

The LDL* decomposition writes any positive definite matrix as a product $\mathbf{LDL}^\star$, where $\mathbf{L} \in \mathcal{R}^{n\times n}$ is unit lower triangular with 1's on the diagonal, and $\mathbf{D} \in \mathcal{R}^{n\times n}$ is diagonal. It is related to the GSO as for a basis $\mathbf{B}$, there exists a unique GSO $\mathbf{B} = \mathbf{L}\cdot\tilde{\mathbf{B}}$ and for an FRG matrix $\mathbf{G}$, there exists a unique LDL* decomposition $\mathbf{G} = \mathbf{LDL}^\star$. If $\mathbf{G} = \mathbf{BB}^\star$, then $\mathbf{G} = \mathbf{L}\cdot(\tilde{\mathbf{B}}\tilde{\mathbf{B}}^\star)\cdot\mathbf{L}^\star$ is a valid LDL* decomposition of $\mathbf{G}$. As both decompositions are unique, the matrices $\mathbf{L}$ in both cases are actually the same. In a nutshell:

$$\begin{aligned} & \mathbf{L}\cdot\tilde{\mathbf{B}} \text{ is the GSO of } \mathbf{B} \\ \Leftrightarrow\ & \mathbf{L}\cdot(\tilde{\mathbf{B}}\tilde{\mathbf{B}}^\star)\cdot\mathbf{L}^\star \text{ is the LDL}^\star \text{ decomposition of } (\mathbf{BB}^\star). \end{aligned}$$

Algorithm 1 $\mathsf{LDL}^\star_{\mathcal{R}}(\mathbf{G})$

Require: A full-rank Gram matrix $\mathbf{G} = (G_{ij}) \in \mathcal{R}^{n\times n}$.
Ensure: The decomposition $\mathbf{G} = \mathbf{LDL}^\star$ over $\mathcal{R}$, where $\mathbf{L}$ is unit lower triangular and $\mathbf{D}$ is diagonal.

```
L, D ← 0^{n×n}
for i from 1 to n do
    L_ii ← 1
    D_i ← G_ii − Σ_{j<i} L_ij L*_ij D_j
    for j from 1 to i − 1 do
        L_ij ← (1/D_j) (G_ij − Σ_{k<j} L_ik L*_jk D_k)
    end for
end for
return ((L_ij), Diag(D_i))
```

Algorithm 1 computes the LDL* decomposition. When $\mathcal{R}$ is replaced by $\mathbb{R}$, the decomposition is noted LDL* rather than LDL* and it is well-known that it terminates without encountering divisions by 0 . In our case, we prove that it terminates correctly in the full version of this article.

2.3 Babai's Nearest Plane Algorithm

The nearest plane algorithm allows to find a lattice close to an arbitrary target in the ambient vector space. Precisely, it ensures that the difference between the target and the output lies in the fundamental parallelepiped spanned by the GSO $\tilde{\mathbf{B}}$ of a given lattice basis $\mathbf{B}$, as depicted on Figure 1.

DEFINITION 4. *Let $\mathbf{B} = \{\mathbf{b}_1, \ldots, \mathbf{b}_n\}$ be a real basis. We call fundamental parallelepiped generated by $\mathbf{B}$ and note $\mathcal{P}(\mathbf{B})$ the set* $\sum_{1\leqslant j\leqslant n} \left[-\frac{1}{2}, \frac{1}{2}\right]\mathbf{b}_j = \left[-\frac{1}{2}, \frac{1}{2}\right]^n \cdot \mathbf{B}$.

Algorithm 2 $\mathsf{NP}_{\mathbb{R}}(\mathbf{t}, \mathbf{L})$

Require: The decomposition $\mathbf{B} = \mathbf{L}\cdot\tilde{\mathbf{B}}$ of $\mathbf{B} \in \mathbb{R}^{n\times m}$, a vector $\mathbf{t} \in \mathbb{R}^n$
Ensure: A vector $\mathbf{z} \in \mathbb{Z}^n$ such that $(\mathbf{t} - \mathbf{z})\mathbf{B} \in \mathcal{P}(\tilde{\mathbf{B}})$

```
z ← 0
for j = n, ..., 1 do
    t̄_j ← t_j + Σ_{i>j} (t_i − z_i) L_ij
    z_j ← ⌊t̄_j⌉
end for
return z
```

PROPOSITION 2 (FROM [1, 12]). *Algorithm 2 outputs an integer vector $\mathbf{z}$ ($\mathbf{zB} \in \mathcal{L}(\mathbf{B})$) such that $(\mathbf{t} - \mathbf{z})\mathbf{B} \in \mathcal{P}(\tilde{\mathbf{B}})$.*

2.4 Coefficient Vectors and Circulant Matrices

DEFINITION 5. *We define linear maps $c : \mathcal{R}_d^m \to \mathbb{R}^{dm}$ and $\mathcal{C} : \mathcal{R}_d^{n\times m} \to \mathbb{R}^{dn\times dm}$ as follows. For any $a = \sum_{i\in\mathbb{Z}_d} a_i x^i \in \mathcal{R}_d$ where each $a_i \in \mathbb{R}$:*

1. *The coefficient vector of a is $c(a) = (a_0, \ldots, a_{d-1})$.*
2. *The circulant matrix of a is*

$$\mathcal{C}(a) \triangleq \begin{bmatrix} a_0 & a_1 & \cdots & a_{d-1} \\ a_{d-1} & a_0 & \cdots & a_{d-2} \\ \ddots & \ddots & \ddots & \ddots \\ a_1 & a_2 & \cdots & a_0 \end{bmatrix} = \begin{bmatrix} c(a) \\ c(xa) \\ \vdots \\ c(x^{d-1}a) \end{bmatrix} \in \mathbb{R}^{d\times d}.$$

3. *c and $\mathcal{C}$ generalize to vectors and matrices in a coefficient-wise manner.*

PROPOSITION 3. *The maps c and $\mathcal{C}$ satisfy the following properties:*

1. *$\mathcal{C}$ is an injective algebra morphism. In particular, $\mathcal{C}(a)\mathcal{C}(b) = \mathcal{C}(ab)$.*
2. *$c(a)\mathcal{C}(b) = c(ab)$.*
3. *$\mathcal{C}(a)^\star = \mathcal{C}(a^\star)$.*

Proposition 3, item 2 illustrates the following fact: the maps c and $\mathcal{C}$ are complementary. Indeed, if we consider the ordered $\mathbb{R}$-basis $\mathbf{B} = \{1, x, \ldots, x^{d-1}\}$ of $\mathcal{R}_d$, then c is the map that writes any $a \in \mathcal{R}_d$ as its unique decomposition according to $\mathbf{B}$. Similarly, for the same basis, $\mathcal{C}(a)$ is the transformation matrix of the injective map $f \in \mathcal{R}_d \mapsto fa$. This is the intrinsic reason that makes Proposition 3, item 2 true.

In Section 2.5, we will define maps V, M which will be complementary in the same way as $c, \mathcal{C}$ are.

2.5 Linearization Operators

In this section, we introduce two partial linearization operators, a vectorial one denoted by $\mathsf{V}_{d/d'}$ (or V), and a matricial one denoted by $\mathsf{M}_{d/d'}$ (or M).

They are very similar to $c, \mathcal{C}$. Indeed, for any $d'|d$ and $a \in \mathcal{R}_d$, $\mathsf{V}_{d/d'}(a)$ will write a as a vector of the $\mathcal{R}_{d'}$-module $\mathcal{R}_{d'}^{d/d'}$, and $\mathsf{M}_{d/d'}(a)$ will be the matrix associated to the injective map $f \in \mathcal{R}_d \mapsto fa$. They are in fact generalizations of the maps from Section 2.4:

1. $\mathcal{R}_d$ may not only be seen as a d-dimensional $\mathbb{R}$-vector space, but also as a d/d'-dimensional $\mathcal{R}_{d'}$-module for any $d'|d$.
2. When writing $\mathcal{R}_d$ as a d-dimensional $\mathbb{R}$-vector space, we will not use $\{1, x, \ldots, x^{d-1}\}$ as our canonical basis, but a permutation of this basis

DEFINITION 6. *Let $d \in \mathbb{N}^*$ be a product of h (not necessarily distinct) primes. Let $\mathrm{gpd}(d)$ denote the greatest proper divisor of d. When clear from context, we also note h the number of prime divisors of d (counted with multiplicity), $d_h \triangleq d$ and for $i \in [\![1, h]\!]$, $d_{i-1}\,\mathrm{gpd}(d_i)$ and $k_i \triangleq d_i/d_{i-1}$, so that $1 = d_0|d_1|\ldots|d_h = d$ and $\prod_{j\leqslant i} k_j = d_i$.*

The d_i's defined in Definition 6 form a tower of proper divisors of d. For any composite d, there exist multiple towers of proper divisors: per example , $1|6$, $1|2|6$ and $1|3|6$ for $d = 6$. In this paper, each time we mention a tower of proper divisors of d it will refer to the unique one induced by Definition 6 (e.g. for $d = 6$, that tower is $1|3|6$).

Definition 7. *Let $d, d' \in \mathbb{N}^*$ such that d' is in the tower of proper divisors of d, and let $k = d/d'$. We denote by x the indeterminate of the polynomial ring $\mathcal{R}_d = \mathbb{R}[x]/(x^d - 1)$ and by $y = x^k$ the indeterminate of $\mathcal{R}_{d'} = \mathbb{R}[y]/(y^{d'} - 1)$. We define the partial linearization $\mathsf{V}_{d/d'} : \mathcal{R}_d^m \to \mathcal{R}_{d'}^{km}$ recursively as follows:*

1. *For $d = d' = 1$, $\mathsf{V}_{d/d'}$ is the identity.*
2. *For $d' = \mathrm{gpd}(d)$ and a single element $a \in \mathcal{R}_d$, let $a = \sum_{i \in \mathbb{Z}_k} x^i a_i(y)$ where $a_i \in \mathcal{R}_{d'}$ for each i. Then*
$$\mathsf{V}_{d/d'}(a) \triangleq (a_0, \dots, a_{k-1}).$$
In other words, $\mathsf{V}_{d/d'}(a) \in \mathcal{R}_{d'}^k$ is the row vector whose coefficients are the $(a_i)_{i \in \mathbb{Z}_k}$.
3. *For a vector $\mathbf{v} \in \mathcal{R}_d^m$, $\mathsf{V}_{d/d'}(\mathbf{v}) \in \mathcal{R}_{d'}^{km}$ is the component-wise applications of $\mathsf{V}_{d/d'}$.*
4. *For $d''|d'|d$ and any vector $\mathbf{v} \in \mathcal{R}_d^m$,*
$$\mathsf{V}_{d/d''}(\mathbf{v}) \triangleq \mathsf{V}_{d'/d''} \circ \mathsf{V}_{d/d'}(\mathbf{v}) \in \mathcal{R}_{d''}^{(d/d'')m}.$$

When d is clear from context, we simply note $\mathsf{V}_{d/d'} = \mathsf{V}_{/d'}$.

Interpretation.

In practice, an element $a \in \mathcal{R}_d$ is represented by a vector of d real elements corresponding to the d coefficients of a. In this context, the operator V simply permutes coefficients. As highlighted by Figure 4, when $d = 2^h$ is a power of two, $\mathsf{V}_{d/1}$ permutes the coefficients according to the bit-reversal order[4], which appears in the radix-2 fast Fourier transform (FFT). More generally, one can show that for an arbitrary d, $\mathsf{V}_{d/1}$ permutes the coefficient according to the general mixed-radix digit reversal order, which appears in the mixed-radix Cooley-Tukey FFT [2].

$$\underset{c(a)}{\mathbf{0\ 1\ 2\ 3\ 4\ 5\ 6\ 7}} \Rightarrow \underset{c(\mathsf{V}_{/4}(a))}{\mathbf{0\ 2\ 4\ 6\quad 1\ 3\ 5\ 7}}$$
$$\Rightarrow \underset{c(\mathsf{V}_{/2}(a)) = \mathsf{V}_{/1}(a)}{\mathbf{0\ 4\quad 2\ 6\quad 1\ 5\quad 3\ 7}}$$

Figure 4: Partial vectorial linearizations.

We now move to the matrix representation M compatible with V.

Definition 8. *Following the notations of Definition 7, we define the operator $\mathsf{M}_{d/d'} : \mathcal{R}_d^{n \times m} \to \mathcal{R}_{d'}^{kn \times km}$ as follows:*

1. *For $d = d' = 1$, $\mathsf{M}_{d/d'}$ is the identity.*
2. *For $d' = \mathrm{gpd}(d), k = d/d'$ and a single element $a = \sum_{i \in \mathbb{Z}_k} x^i a_i(y)$ where each $a_i \in \mathcal{R}_{d'}$, $\mathsf{M}_{d/d'}(a)$ is the following matrix of $\in \mathcal{R}_{d'}^{k \times k}$:*
$$\begin{bmatrix} a_0 & a_1 & \cdots & a_{k-1} \\ ya_{k-1} & a_0 & \cdots & a_{k-2} \\ \ddots & \ddots & \ddots & \ddots \\ ya_1 & ya_2 & \dots & a_0 \end{bmatrix} = \begin{bmatrix} \mathsf{V}_{d/d'}(a) \\ \mathsf{V}_{d/d'}(x^k a) \\ \vdots \\ \mathsf{V}_{d/d'}(x^{(d'-1)k} a) \end{bmatrix}.$$
In particular, if d is prime, then $\mathsf{M}_{d/1}(a) \in \mathbb{R}^{d \times d}$ is exactly the circulant matrix $\mathcal{C}(a)$.
3. *For a vector $\mathbf{v} \in \mathcal{R}_d^m$ or a matrix $\mathbf{B} \in \mathcal{R}_d^{n \times m}$, $\mathsf{M}_{d/d'}(\mathbf{v}) \in \mathcal{R}_{d'}^{k \times km}$ and $\mathsf{M}_{d/d'}(\mathbf{B}) \in \mathcal{R}_{d'}^{kn \times km}$ are the component-wise applications of $\mathsf{M}_{d/d'}$.*
4. *For $d''|d'|d$ and any element $a \in \mathcal{R}_d$,*
$$\mathsf{M}_{d/d''}(a) \triangleq \mathsf{M}_{d'/d''} \circ \mathsf{M}_{d/d'}(a) \in \mathcal{R}_{d''}^{(d/d'') \times (d/d'')}.$$

When d is clear from context, we simply note $\mathsf{M}_{d/d'} = \mathsf{M}_{/d'}$.

Interpretation.

As for the operator V, the steps of applying M are depicted in Section 1 Figure 2. The linearization $\mathsf{M}_{d/d'}(a)$ writes the transformation matrix of the map $f \in \mathcal{R}_d \mapsto fa$ using the same basis as the partial linearization $\mathsf{V}_{d/d'}$. As a result, both operators are compatible: $\forall a, b \in \mathcal{R}_d, \mathsf{V}_{d/d'}(ab) = \mathsf{V}_{d/d'}(a) \cdot \mathsf{M}_{d/d'}(b)$. More properties follows.

Proposition 4. *Let $d \in \mathbb{N}^*$, a, b (resp. $\mathbf{a}, \mathbf{b}$, resp. $\mathbf{A}, \mathbf{B}$) be arbitrary scalars (resp. vectors, resp. matrices) over $\mathcal{R}_d$, and $d'|d$. To be concise, we note $\mathsf{V} \triangleq \mathsf{V}_{d/d'}$ and $\mathsf{M} \triangleq \mathsf{M}_{d/d'}$. The maps V and M satisfy the following properties:*

1. *M is an injective algebra morphism, and in particular:*
$$\mathsf{M}(\mathbf{A} \cdot \mathbf{B}) = \mathsf{M}(\mathbf{A}) \cdot \mathsf{M}(\mathbf{B}).$$
2. *V is an injective linear map.*
3. *$\mathsf{V}(ab) = \mathsf{V}(a) \cdot \mathsf{M}(b)$.*
4. *V is an isometry:*
$$\langle \mathsf{V}(\mathbf{a}), \mathsf{V}(\mathbf{b}) \rangle_2 = \langle \mathbf{a}, \mathbf{b} \rangle_2.$$
5. *$\mathbf{B}$ is full-rank if and only if $\mathsf{M}(\mathbf{B})$ is full-rank.*

The proofs are rather straightforward to check from the definitions, and can be found in the full version of this article.

Computing V and M in the Fourier Domain.

The operators V and M that we defined can be computed very efficiently when an element $a \in \mathcal{R}_d$ is represented by its coefficients but also when represented in the *Fourier domain*. In the first case, it is obvious that they can both be performed in time $\Theta(d)$ as they (symbolically) permute coefficients of a.

If a is represented in FFT form —that is, by the vector $(a(\zeta_d^i))_{i \in \mathbb{Z}_d}$ in $\mathbb{C}^d$— then computing $\mathsf{V}_{d/d'}(a)$ and $\mathsf{M}_{d/d'}(a)$ in FFT form can naively be done in time $\Theta(d \log d)$ by computing its inverse FFT, permuting its coefficients, and computing d/d' FFT's over $\mathcal{R}_{d'}$. However, it can be done in time $\Theta(d)$, as it is a single step – also known as *butterfly* – of the original fast Fourier transform. This is formalized in Lemma 1, a reformulation of a simple lemma that is at the heart of Cooley and Tukey's FFT.

Lemma 1 ([2], adapted). *Let $d \geqslant 2, d' = \mathrm{gpd}(d)$ and $k = d/d'$. Let $\mathsf{V} \triangleq \mathsf{V}_{d/d'}, \mathsf{M} \triangleq \mathsf{M}_{d/d'}$. For any $a \in \mathcal{R}_d$ (resp. $\mathbf{a} \in \mathsf{V}(\mathcal{R}_d)$, resp. $\mathbf{A} \in \mathsf{M}(\mathcal{R}_d)$):*

- *$\mathsf{V}(a)$, $\mathsf{V}^{-1}(\mathbf{a})$, $\mathsf{M}^{-1}(\mathbf{A})$ can be computed in FFT form in time $\Theta(kd)$.*
- *$\mathsf{M}(a)$ can be computed in FFT form in time $\Theta(k^2 d)$.*

Proof. Let $a \in \mathcal{R}_d$ be uniquely written $a = \sum_{i \in \mathbb{Z}_k} x^i a_i(x^k)$, where each $a_i \in \mathcal{R}_{d'}$. Cooley and Tukey show in [2] (equations 7, 8) that we can switch from the FFT of a to the FFT of all the a_i's (and conversely) in time $\Theta(kd)$. As the a_i's are the coefficients of $\mathsf{V}(a)$ and $\mathsf{M}(a)$, the result follows. □

In Sections 3 and 4, we will use the operators V and M to speed up the orthogonalization and nearest plane algorithms. The core idea is that these operators allow to "batch" orthogonalization operations, resulting in a $\Theta(d/\log(d))$ speedup.

[4]https://oeis.org/A030109

3. FAST FOURIER LDL DECOMPOSITION

This section presents our main result. We present the existence of a compact representation in Section 3.1, and then derive a fast algorithm to compute it in Section 3.2.

3.1 A Compact LDL* Decomposition

THEOREM 1. *Let $d \in \mathbb{N}$ and $1 = d_0|d_1|\dots|d_h = d$ be a tower of proper divisors of d. Let $\mathbf{b} \in \mathcal{R}_d^m$ such that $\mathsf{M}_{d/1}(\mathbf{b})$ is full-rank. There exists a GSO of $\mathsf{M}_{d/1}(\mathbf{b})$ as follows:*

$$\mathsf{M}_{d/1}(\mathbf{b}) = \left(\prod_{i=0}^{h-1} \mathsf{M}_{d_i/1}(\mathbf{L}_i)\right) \cdot \tilde{\mathbf{B}}_0$$

where $\tilde{\mathbf{B}}_0 \in \mathbb{R}^{d\times dm}$ is orthogonal, and each $\mathbf{L}_i \in \mathcal{R}_{d_i}^{(d/d_i)\times(d/d_i)}$ is a block-diagonal matrix with unit lower triangular matrices of $\mathcal{R}_{d_i}^{(d_{i+1}/d_i)\times(d_{i+1}/d_i)}$ as its d/d_{i+1} diagonal blocks.[5]

As an example, the matrix $\mathbf{L}$ of the GSO of $\mathsf{M}_{8/1}(a)$ for some $a \in \mathcal{R}_8$ is depicted in Section 1 Figure 3.

PROOF. If d is prime, the theorem is trivial as it is exactly the GSO. We suppose that d is composite and that the theorem is true for any $\mathcal{R}_i$ with $i < d$. By Proposition 4, item 5, the matrix $\mathbf{B}_{h-1} \triangleq \mathsf{M}_{d/d_{h-1}}(\mathbf{b})$ is full-rank too. Using the classical GSO, we can therefore decompose it as $\mathbf{B}_{h-1} = \mathbf{L}_{h-1}\tilde{\mathbf{B}}$, where $\mathbf{L}_{h-1} \in \mathcal{R}_{d_{h-1}}^{k_h\times k_h}, \tilde{\mathbf{B}} \in \mathcal{R}_{d_{h-1}}^{k_h\times mk_h}$ and $k_h \triangleq d/\operatorname{gpd}(d)$. $\mathbf{L}_{h-1}$ is unit lower triangular and $\tilde{\mathbf{B}}$ is orthogonal. Noting $\tilde{\mathbf{B}} = [\mathbf{b}_1, \dots, \mathbf{b}_{k_h}]$, all the $\mathbf{b}_j$'s are pairwise orthogonal and each $\mathsf{M}_{/1}(\mathbf{b}_j)$ is full-rank. By inductive hypothesis, they can be decomposed as follows:

$$\forall j \in [\![1, k_h]\!], \mathsf{M}_{d_{h-1}/1}(\mathbf{b}_j) = \left(\prod_{i=0}^{h-2} \mathsf{M}_{d_i/1}(\mathbf{L}_{i,j})\right) \cdot \tilde{\mathbf{B}}_j, \quad (2)$$

where each $\tilde{\mathbf{B}}_j \in \mathbb{R}^{d_{h-1}\times md_{h-1}}$ is full-rank orthogonal and for $i < h-1$, each $\mathbf{L}_{i,j} \in \mathcal{R}_{d_i}^{(d_{h-1}/d_i)\times(d_{h-1}/d_i)}$ is a block-diagonal matrix with unit lower triangular matrices of $\mathcal{R}_{d_i}^{(d_{i+1}/d_i)\times(d_{i+1}/d_i)}$ as its d_{h-1}/d_{i+1} diagonal blocks. To be concise, we now note $\mathsf{M} \triangleq \mathsf{M}_{d_{h-1}/1}$ and $\mathsf{V} \triangleq \mathsf{V}_{d_{h-1}/1}$. We have:

$$\begin{aligned}
\mathsf{M}_{d/1}(\mathbf{b}) &= \mathsf{M}(\mathbf{L}_{h-1}) \cdot \mathsf{M}(\tilde{\mathbf{B}}_{h-1}) \\
&= \mathsf{M}(\mathbf{L}_{h-1}) \cdot \mathsf{M}[\mathbf{b}_1, \dots, \mathbf{b}_{k_h}] \\
&= \mathsf{M}(\mathbf{L}_{h-1}) \cdot [\mathsf{M}(\mathbf{b}_1), \dots, \mathsf{M}(\mathbf{b}_{k_h})] \\
&= \mathsf{M}(\mathbf{L}_{h-1}) \cdot \operatorname{Diag}\left(\prod_{i=0}^{h-2} \mathsf{M}_{d_i/1}(\mathbf{L}_{i,j})\right) \cdot \tilde{\mathbf{B}}_0 \\
&= \mathsf{M}(\mathbf{L}_{h-1}) \cdot \left(\prod_{i=0}^{h-2} \mathsf{M}_{d_i/1}(\mathbf{L}_i)\right) \cdot \tilde{\mathbf{B}}_0 \\
&= \left(\prod_{i=0}^{h-1} \mathsf{M}_{d_i/1}(\mathbf{L}_i)\right) \cdot \tilde{\mathbf{B}}_0,
\end{aligned}$$

where $\tilde{\mathbf{B}}_0 = [\tilde{\mathbf{B}}_1, \dots, \tilde{\mathbf{B}}_{k_h}]$. The first equality simply uses the fact that M is a ring homomorphism (Proposition 4, item 1). The second and third ones are immediate from the definitions. The fourth one uses the inductive hypothesis (equation 2) on each $\mathbf{b}_j$ and take $\tilde{\mathbf{B}}_0 \triangleq [\tilde{\mathbf{B}}_1, \dots, \tilde{\mathbf{B}}_{k_h}]$. In the fifth equality, we take $\mathbf{L}_i \triangleq \operatorname{Diag}(\mathbf{L}_{i,1}, \dots, \mathbf{L}_{i,k_h})$ and just need to check that $\tilde{\mathbf{B}}_0$ and $\mathbf{L}$ are as stated by the theorem:

- Since each $\mathbf{L}_{i,j}$ is block diagonal with d_{h-1}/d_{i+1} unit lower triangular diagonal blocks, $\mathbf{L}_i$ is block diagonal with $k_h(d_{h-1}/d_{i+1}) = d/d_{i+1}$ unit lower triangular diagonal blocks.
- We also need to show that $\tilde{\mathbf{B}}_0$ is orthogonal. Each submatrix $\tilde{\mathbf{B}}_j$ of $\tilde{\mathbf{B}}_0$ is the orthogonalization of $\mathsf{M}(\mathbf{b}_j)$ by induction hypothesis. Therefore, for two distinct rows $\mathbf{u}, \mathbf{v}$ of $\tilde{\mathbf{B}}_0$:
  - If they belong to the same submatrix $\tilde{\mathbf{B}}_j$, they are orthogonal by induction hypothesis.
  - Suppose they belong to different submatrices: $\mathbf{u} \in \tilde{\mathbf{B}}_j, \mathbf{v} \in \tilde{\mathbf{B}}_\ell$ and $j \neq \ell$. Then $\mathbf{u}$ (resp. $\mathbf{v}$) is a linear combination of rows of $\mathsf{M}(\mathbf{b}_j)$ (resp. $\mathsf{M}(\mathbf{b}_\ell)$): $\mathbf{v} = \mathbf{a}_j \cdot \mathsf{M}(\mathbf{b}_j)$ and $\mathbf{v} = \mathbf{a}_\ell \cdot \mathsf{M}(\mathbf{b}_j)$ for some $\mathbf{a}_j, \mathbf{a}_\ell$ in $\mathbb{R}^{d_{h-1}}$. Noting $a_j = \mathsf{V}^{-1}(\mathbf{a}_j)$ and $a_\ell = \mathsf{V}^{-1}(\mathbf{a}_\ell)$:

    $$\begin{aligned}
    \langle \mathbf{u}, \mathbf{v} \rangle_2 &= \langle \mathsf{V}(a_j)\mathsf{M}(\mathbf{b}_j), \mathsf{V}(a_\ell)\mathsf{M}(\mathbf{b}_\ell) \rangle_2 \\
    &= \langle \mathsf{V}(a_j\mathbf{b}_j), \mathsf{V}(a_\ell\mathbf{b}_\ell) \rangle_2 \\
    &= \langle a_j\mathbf{b}_j, a_\ell\mathbf{b}_\ell \rangle_2 = 0
    \end{aligned}$$

    Where the second equality comes from Proposition 4, item 3, the third one from the fact that V is a scaled isometry (Proposition 4, item 4) and the fourth one from $\mathbf{b}_j, \mathbf{b}_\ell$ being orthogonal.

Therefore $\tilde{\mathbf{B}}_0$ is orthogonal. □

The theorem we stated gives the GSO of $\mathsf{M}_{d/1}(\mathbf{b})$ for a vector $\mathbf{b} \in \mathcal{R}_d^m$, but can be easily generalized from a vector $\mathbf{b}$ to a matrix $\mathbf{B}$, and also yields a compact LDL* decomposition.

COROLLARY 1. *Let $d \in \mathbb{N}$ and $1 = d_0|d_1|\dots|d_h = d$ be a tower of proper divisors of d. Let $\mathbf{B} \in \mathcal{R}_d^{n\times m}$ be a full-rank matrix. There exist $h+1$ matrices $(\mathbf{L}_i)_{0\leqslant i\leqslant h}$ such that:*

- *$\mathbf{L}_h \in \mathcal{R}_d^{n\times n}$ is unit lower triangular.*
- *For each $i < h$, $\mathbf{L}_i \in \mathcal{R}_{d_i}^{n(d/d_i)\times n(d/d_i)}$ is a block-diagonal matrix whose $n(d/d_{i+1})$ diagonal blocks are unit lower triangular matrices of $\mathcal{R}_{d_i}^{(d_{i+1}/d_i)\times(d_{i+1}/d_i)}$.*

Furthermore, if we note $\mathbf{L} = \left(\prod_{i=0}^{h} \mathsf{M}_{d_i/1}(\mathbf{L}_i)\right)$ and $\tilde{\mathbf{B}}_0 \triangleq \mathbf{L}^{-1} \cdot \mathsf{M}_{d/1}(\mathbf{B})$, then:

1. *The GSO of $\mathsf{M}_{d/1}(\mathbf{B})$ is $\mathsf{M}_{d/1}(\mathbf{B}) = \mathbf{L} \cdot \tilde{\mathbf{B}}_0$.*
2. *The LDL* decomposition of $\mathsf{M}_{d/1}(\mathbf{BB}^\star)$ is*

$$\mathsf{M}_{d/1}(\mathbf{B}) = \mathbf{L} \cdot (\tilde{\mathbf{B}}_0\tilde{\mathbf{B}}_0^t) \cdot \mathbf{L}^t.$$

PROOF. We have $\mathbf{B} = \mathbf{L}_h\mathbf{B}'$, where $\mathbf{L}_h$ is given by either the GSO or LDL* decomposition algorithm. $\mathbf{B}' = \{\mathbf{b}'_1, \dots, \mathbf{b}'_n\}$ is orthogonal. Applying Theorem 1 to each row vector $\mathbf{b}'_j$ of $\mathbf{B}'$ yields n decompositions $(\mathbf{L}_{i,j})_{0\leqslant i<h}$ and n orthogonal matrices $\tilde{\mathbf{B}}_j$, each spanning the same space as $\mathbf{B}_j \triangleq \mathsf{M}_{d/1}(\mathbf{b}'_j)$. Taking $\mathbf{L}_i \triangleq \operatorname{Diag}(\mathbf{L}_{i,j})$ and $\tilde{\mathbf{B}}_0 \triangleq [\tilde{\mathbf{B}}_1, \dots, \tilde{\mathbf{B}}_n]$ yields the GSO.

The LDL* decomposition is then given "for free" by its equivalence with the GSO, and indeed, one can check that since $\tilde{\mathbf{B}}_0$ is orthogonal, $\tilde{\mathbf{B}}_0\tilde{\mathbf{B}}_0^t$ is diagonal. □

Theorem 1 and Corollary 1 state that for any full-rank matrix $\mathbf{B} \in \mathcal{R}_d^{n\times m}$, the $\mathbf{L}$ matrix in the GSO (resp. LDL* decomposition) of $\mathsf{M}_{d/1}(\mathbf{B})$ (resp. $\mathsf{M}_{d/1}(\mathbf{BB}^\star)$) can be represented in a factorized form, where each of the factors $\mathbf{L}_i$ is a sparse, block-diagonal matrix.

[5]Indexed products are to be read $\prod_{i=0}^{k} \alpha_i = \alpha_k\alpha_{k-1}\cdots\alpha_0$.

3.2 A Fast Algorithm for the Compact LDL* Decomposition

Theorem 1 and Corollary 1 are constructive: more precisely, their proofs give a fast algorithm for computing a compact factorized form of $\mathbf{L}$ quickly. Algorithm 3 computes a compact LDL* decomposition in the form of the tree $\mathfrak{L}$, which nodes are labeled by structured matrices of various sizes. We note that this decomposition depends of the tower of proper divisors chosen. Algorithm 3 uses the unique one induced by Definition 6.

Algorithm 3 $\mathsf{ffLDL}^\star_{\mathcal{R}_d}(\mathbf{G})$

Require: A full-rank Gram matrix $\mathbf{G} \in \mathcal{R}_d^{n\times n}$
Ensure: The compact LDL* decomposition of $\mathbf{G}$ in FFT form

1: $(\mathbf{L}, \mathbf{D}) \leftarrow \mathsf{LDL}^\star_{\mathcal{R}_d}(\mathbf{G})$
2: **if** $d = 1$ **then**
3:    **return** $(\mathbf{L}, \mathbf{D})$
4: **end if**
5: $d' \leftarrow \mathrm{gpd}(d)$
6: **for** $i = 1, \ldots, n$ **do**
7:    $\mathfrak{L}_i \leftarrow \mathsf{ffLDL}^\star_{\mathcal{R}_{d'}}(\mathsf{M}_{d/d'}(\mathbf{D}_{ii}))$
8: **end for**
9: **return** $(\mathbf{L}, (\mathfrak{L}_i)_{1\leqslant i\leqslant n})$

Algorithm 3 computes a "fast Fourier LDL*", instead of the "fast Fourier GSO" hinted at in the proof of Corollary 1. The reason why we favor this approach is because it allows a complexity gain. This gain can already be observed in the classic versions of the aforementioned algorithms. Indeed, consider the $\mathbf{L}$ in the GSO of $\mathbf{B} \in \mathcal{R}_d^{2\times m}$, which is exactly the $\mathbf{L}$ in the LDL* decomposition of $\mathbf{BB}^\star \in \mathcal{R}_d^{2\times 2}$. Computing it with the LDL* algorithm is then $\Theta(m)$ times faster than with the Gram-Schmidt process. The same phenomenon happens with their recursive variants.

Lemma 2. *Let $d \in \mathbb{N}$ and $1 = d_0|d_1|\ldots|d_h = d$ be the tower of proper divisors of d given by the successive* gpd*'s, and for $i \in [\![1, h]\!]$, let $k_i \triangleq d_i/d_{i-1}$. Let $\mathbf{G} \in \mathcal{R}_d^{n\times n}$ be a full-rank Gram matrix. Then Algorithm 3 computes the LDL* decomposition tree of $\mathbf{G}$ in FFT form in time*

$$\Theta(n^2 d \log d) + \Theta(n^3 d) + \Theta(nd) \sum_{1\leqslant i\leqslant h} k_i^2.$$

In particular, if all the k_i are bounded by a small constant k, then the complexity of Algorithm 3 is upper bounded by $\Theta(n^3 d + n^2 d \log d)$.

The proof of Lemma 2 can be found in the full version of this article. We note that Algorithm 3 is parallelizable to up to d processes: step 1 relies on operations on polynomials which are parallelizable and all the iterations of step 7 are independent.

4. FAST FOURIER NEAREST PLANE

In this section, we show how to exploit further the compact form of the LDL* decomposition to have a fast Fourier variant of the nearest plane algorithm. It outputs vectors of the same quality (*ie* as close to the target vector) as its classical iterative counterpart Algorithm 2, but runs $\tilde{\Theta}(d)$ times faster.

Definition 9. *Let $\mathcal{Z}_d$ denote the ring $\mathbb{Z}[x]/(x^d - 1)$ of elements of $\mathcal{R}_d$ with integer coefficients.*

Algorithm 4 $\mathsf{ffNP}_{\mathcal{R}_d}(\mathbf{t}, \mathfrak{L})$

Require: $\mathbf{t} \in \mathcal{R}_d^n$, a precomputed tree $\mathfrak{L}$, (implicitly) a matrix $\mathbf{B} \in \mathcal{R}_d^{n\times m}$ such that $\mathfrak{L}$ is the compact LDL* decomposition tree of $\mathbf{BB}^\star$.
Ensure: $\mathbf{z} \in \mathcal{Z}_d^n$ such that $\mathsf{V}((\mathbf{z}-\mathbf{t})\mathbf{B}) \in \mathcal{P}(\tilde{\mathbf{B}}_0)$, where $\tilde{\mathbf{B}}_0$ is the orthogonalization of $\mathsf{M}(\mathbf{B})$.

if $d = 1$ **then**
   $(\mathbf{L}, \mathbf{D}) \leftarrow \mathfrak{L}$
   return $\mathsf{NP}_{\mathbb{R}}(\mathbf{L}, \mathbf{t})$
end if
$(\mathbf{L}, (\mathfrak{L}_i)_{1\leqslant j\leqslant n}) \leftarrow \mathfrak{L}$
$d' \leftarrow \mathrm{gpd}(d)$
for $j = n, \ldots, 1$ **do**
   $\bar{\mathbf{t}}_j \leftarrow \mathbf{t}_j + \sum_{i>j}(\mathbf{t}_i - \mathbf{z}_i)L_{ij}$
   $\mathbf{z}_j \leftarrow \mathsf{V}^{-1}_{d/d'}\left[\mathsf{ffNP}_{\mathcal{R}_{d'}}(\mathsf{V}_{d/d'}(\bar{\mathbf{t}}_j), \mathfrak{L}_j)\right]$
end for
return $\mathbf{z} = (\mathbf{z}_i, \ldots, \mathbf{z}_n)$

Lemma 3. *Let $\mathbf{B} = \{\mathbf{b}_1, \ldots, \mathbf{b}_n\} \in \mathcal{R}_d^{n\times m}$ and $\tilde{\mathbf{B}} = \{\tilde{\mathbf{b}}_1, \ldots, \tilde{\mathbf{b}}_n\}$ be its Gram-Schmidt orthogonalization in $\mathcal{R}_d$. The vectors $\mathbf{z}$ and $\bar{\mathbf{t}} = (\bar{\mathbf{t}}_1, \ldots, \bar{\mathbf{t}}_n)$ in Algorithm 4 satisfy*

$$(\mathbf{z} - \mathbf{t}) \cdot \mathbf{B} = (\mathbf{z} - \bar{\mathbf{t}}) \cdot \tilde{\mathbf{B}}.$$

Proof. We recall that for each $i \in [\![1, n]\!]$, $\tilde{\mathbf{b}}_i = \mathbf{b}_i - \sum_{j<i} L_{ij}\tilde{\mathbf{b}}_j$. We have:

$$\begin{aligned}
(\mathbf{z} - \bar{\mathbf{t}}) \cdot \tilde{\mathbf{B}} &= \textstyle\sum_{1\leqslant j\leqslant n}(\mathbf{z}_j - \bar{\mathbf{t}}_j)\tilde{\mathbf{b}}_j \\
&= \textstyle\sum_{1\leqslant j\leqslant n}\left[(\mathbf{z}_j - \mathbf{t}_j) + \sum_{i>j} L_{ij}(\mathbf{z}_i - \mathbf{t}_i)\right]\tilde{\mathbf{b}}_j \\
&= \textstyle\sum_{1\leqslant i\leqslant j\leqslant n}(\mathbf{z}_i - \mathbf{t}_i)L_{ij}\tilde{\mathbf{b}}_j \\
&= \textstyle\sum_{1\leqslant i\leqslant n}(\mathbf{z}_i - \mathbf{t}_i)\mathbf{b}_i \\
&= (\mathbf{z} - \mathbf{t}) \cdot \mathbf{B}.
\end{aligned} \tag{3}$$

The first and last equalities are trivial, the second one replaces the $\bar{\mathbf{t}}_j$'s by their definitions, the third one just simplifies the sum and the fourth one is another way of saying that $\mathbf{L} \cdot \tilde{\mathbf{B}} = \mathbf{B}$. □

Theorem 2. *Let $\mathsf{M} \triangleq \mathsf{M}_{d/1}$ and $\mathsf{V} \triangleq \mathsf{V}_{d/1}$. Algorithm 4 outputs $\mathbf{z} \in \mathcal{Z}^n$ such that $\mathsf{V}((\mathbf{z}-\mathbf{t})\mathbf{B}) \in \mathcal{P}(\tilde{\mathbf{B}}_0)$, where $\tilde{\mathbf{B}}_0$ is the orthogonalization of $\mathsf{M}(\mathbf{B})$ over $\mathbb{R}$.*

Proof. The result is trivially true if $d = 1$. We prove it in the general case. By definition, each subtree $\mathfrak{L}_j$ is the LDL* decomposition tree of $\mathsf{M}_{d/\mathrm{gpd}(d)}(\tilde{\mathbf{b}}_j)$. By induction hypothesis, we therefore know that $\mathsf{V}((\mathbf{z}_j - \bar{\mathbf{t}}_j)\tilde{\mathbf{b}}_j) \in \mathcal{P}(\tilde{\mathbf{B}}_j)$, where $\tilde{\mathbf{B}}_j$ is the orthogonalization of $\mathbf{B}_j \triangleq \mathsf{M}(\tilde{\mathbf{b}}_j)$. From Lemma 3, we have

$$(\mathbf{z} - \mathbf{t})\mathbf{B} = \sum_{j=1,\ldots,n} (\mathbf{z}_j - \bar{\mathbf{t}}_j) \cdot \tilde{\mathbf{b}}_j,$$

so $\mathsf{V}((\mathbf{z}-\mathbf{t})\mathbf{B}) \in \mathcal{P}([\tilde{\mathbf{B}}_1, \ldots, \tilde{\mathbf{B}}_n])$. Now, from the proof of Corollary 1, we know that $\tilde{\mathbf{B}}_0 = [\tilde{\mathbf{B}}_1, \ldots, \tilde{\mathbf{B}}_n]$ is actually the orthogonalization of $\mathsf{M}(\mathbf{B})$, which concludes the proof. □

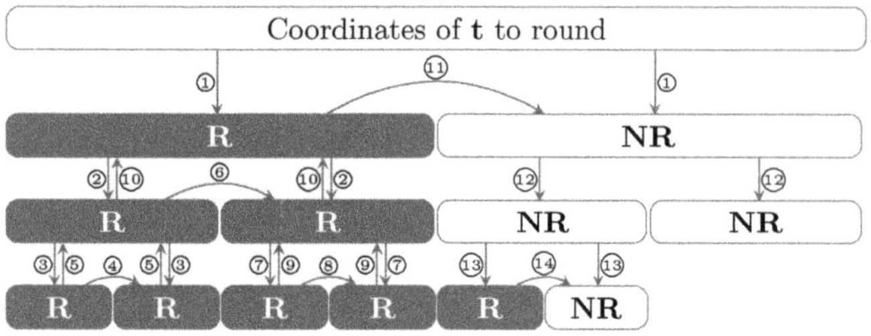

An ongoing execution of Algorithm 4 for a single $t \in \mathcal{R}_8$.

1. Arrows are labeled in their order of execution. Downward ($\downarrow \downarrow$) (resp. upward ($\uparrow \uparrow$)) arrows correspond to computing $\mathsf{V}_{d/d'}(\bar{\mathbf{t}}_j)$ (resp. $\mathsf{V}^{-1}_{d/d'}(\ldots)$) at step 9. Transverse ($\curvearrowright$) arrows correspond to step 8.

2. Cells labeled with **R** (as in **R**ounded) correspond to already completed subcalls of Algorithm 4, as opposed to those labeled with **NR** (as in **N**ot **R**ounded).

Figure 5: High-level execution of the fast Fourier nearest plane algorithm

Unlike the fast Fourier transform, Algorithm 4 is not fully parallelizable, due to step 8 ($\curvearrowright$ arrows in Figure 5). However, its complexity in d is $\Theta(d \log d)$: informally, this is because each arrow $\downarrow, \uparrow$ or $\curvearrowright$ has a linear complexity in the size of the cells it connects. A more precise statement follows.

Lemma 4. *Let $d \in \mathbb{N}$ and $1 = d_0 | d_1 | \ldots | d_h = d$ be be the tower of proper divisors of d given by the successive* gpds, *and for $i \in [\![1, h]\!]$, let $k_i \triangleq d_i / d_{i-1}$. Let $\mathbf{B} \in \mathcal{R}_d^{n \times m}$ and $\mathfrak{L}$ be its LDL* decomposition tree. The complexity of Algorithm 4 is given by:*

$$\Theta(nd \log d) + \Theta(n^2 d) + \Theta(nd) \sum_{1 \leqslant i \leqslant h} k_i^2 .$$

In particular, if all the k_i are bounded by a constant, then the complexity of Algorithm 4 is $\Theta(n^2 d + nd \log d)$.

The proof of Lemma 4 can be found in the full version of this article.

Acknowledgements

The authors would like to thank the anonymous reviewers of ISSAC and EUROCRYPT for their diligent comments, significantly contributing to improve the presentation of this article.

5. REFERENCES

[1] Babai, L. On Lovász' lattice reduction and the nearest lattice point problem. *Combinatorica 6*, 1 (1986), 1–13. Preliminary version in STACS 1985.

[2] Cooley, J. W., and Tukey, J. W. An algorithm for the machine calculation of complex Fourier series. *Mathematics of Computation 19*, 90 (1965), 297–301.

[3] Durbin, J. The fitting of time-series models. *Review of the International Statistical Institute 28*, 3 (1960), pp. 233–244.

[4] Gentleman, W. M., and Sande, G. Fast Fourier transforms: for fun and profit. In *Proceedings of the November 7-10, 1966, fall joint computer conference* (1966), ACM, pp. 563–578.

[5] Gentry, C., Peikert, C., and Vaikuntanathan, V. Trapdoors for hard lattices and new cryptographic constructions. In *STOC (2008)*.

[6] Gorbunov, S., Vaikuntanathan, V., and Wee, H. Attribute-based encryption for circuits. In *45th ACM STOC* (June 2013), D. Boneh, T. Roughgarden, and J. Feigenbaum, Eds., ACM Press, pp. 545–554.

[7] Gragg, W. B. Positive definite toeplitz matrices, the arnoldi process for isometric operators, and gaussian quadrature on the unit circle. *Journal of Computational and Applied Mathematics 46*, 1-2 (1993), 183 – 198.

[8] Heideman, M. T., Johnson, D. H., and Burrus, C. S. Gauss and the history of the fast Fourier transform. *ASSP Magazine, IEEE 1*, 4 (1984), 14–21.

[9] Hoffstein, J., Howgrave-Graham, N., Pipher, J., Silverman, J. H., and Whyte, W. NTRUSIGN: Digital signatures using the NTRU lattice. In *CT-RSA (2003)*.

[10] Hoffstein, J., Pipher, J., and Silverman, J. H. NTRU: A ring-based public key cryptosystem. In *ANTS* (1998), pp. 267–288.

[11] Klein, P. N. Finding the closest lattice vector when it's unusually close. In *SODA* (2000), pp. 937–941.

[12] Lenstra, A. K., Lenstra, Jr., H. W., and Lovász, L. Factoring polynomials with rational coefficients. *Mathematische Annalen 261*, 4 (December 1982), 515–534.

[13] Levinson, N. The Wiener RMS (root mean square) error criterion in filter design and prediction. *J. Math. Phys. Mass. Inst. Tech. 25* (1947), 261–278.

[14] Lyubashevsky, V., Micciancio, D., Peikert, C., and Rosen, A. SWIFFT: A modest proposal for FFT hashing. In *FSE (2008)*.

[15] Lyubashevsky, V., Peikert, C., and Regev, O. On ideal lattices and learning with errors over rings. In *EUROCRYPT* (2010), pp. 1–23.

[16] Lyubashevsky, V., and Prest, T. Quadratic time, linear space algorithms for Gram-Schmidt orthogonalization and Gaussian sampling in structured lattices. In *EUROCRYPT 2015*.

[17] Micciancio, D., and Peikert, C. Trapdoors for lattices: Simpler, tighter, faster, smaller. In *EUROCRYPT (2012)*.

[18] Nussbaumer, H. J. *Fast Fourier transform and convolution algorithms*, vol. 2. Springer Science & Business Media, 2012.

[19] Olshevsky, V. *Fast Algorithms for Structured Matrices: Theory and Applications*, vol. 323. American Mathematical Soc., 2003.

[20] Olshevsky, V., and Pan, V. Y. A unified superfast algorithm for boundary rational tangential interpolation problems and for inversion and factorization of dense structured matrices. In *FOCS (1998)*.

[21] Peikert, C. An efficient and parallel Gaussian sampler for lattices. In *CRYPTO* (2010), pp. 80–97.

[22] Sweet, D. R. Fast toeplitz orthogonalization. *Numerische Mathematik 43*, 1 (1984), 1–21.

Linear Time Interactive Certificates for the Minimal Polynomial and the Determinant of a Sparse Matrix

Jean-Guillaume Dumas
Univ. Grenoble Alpes
Laboratoire LJK, CNRS, umr 5224
51, av. des Mathématiques,
F38041 Grenoble, France
jean-guillaume.dumas@imag.fr

Erich Kaltofen
Department of Mathematics
North Carolina State University
Raleigh, NC 27695-8205, USA
kaltofen@math.ncsu.edu
www.kaltofen.us

Emmanuel Thomé
Caramba – Inria Nancy
Inria, CNRS (Loria), Univ. Lorraine
615, rue du jardin botanique
54600 Villers-lès-Nancy, France
emmanuel.thome@inria.fr

Gilles Villard
CNRS, U. Lyon, Laboratoire LIP
(CNRS, ENSL, Inria, UCBL)
46, allée d'Italie, F69364 Lyon
Cedex 07, France
gilles.villard@ens-lyon.fr

ABSTRACT

Computational problem certificates are additional data structures for each output, which can be used by a—possibly randomized—verification algorithm that proves the correctness of each output. In this paper, we give an algorithm that computes a certificate for the minimal polynomial of sparse or structured $n \times n$ matrices over an abstract field, of sufficiently large cardinality, whose Monte Carlo verification complexity requires a single matrix-vector multiplication and a linear number of extra field operations. We also propose a novel preconditioner that ensures irreducibility of the characteristic polynomial of the generically preconditioned matrix. This preconditioner takes linear time to be applied and uses only two random entries. We then combine these two techniques to give algorithms that compute certificates for the determinant, and thus for the characteristic polynomial, whose Monte Carlo verification complexity is therefore also linear.

1. INTRODUCTION

We consider a square sparse or structured matrix $A \in \mathbb{F}^{n\times n}$, where $\mathbb{F}$ is an exact field. By sparse or structured we mean that multiplying a vector by A requires fewer operations than a dense matrix-vector multiplication. The arithmetic cost to apply A is denoted by $\mu(A)$ which thus satisfies $\mu(A) \leq n(2n-1)$ (n^2 multiplications and $n(n-1)$ additions).

For such sparse matrices, Wiedemann's algorithm, together with some preconditioning [3], provides means to compute the rank, the minimal polynomial or the characteristic polynomial of sparse matrices, via the computation of the minimal polynomial of its associated sequence projected at random values [29].

ISSAC '16, July 19 - 22, 2016, Waterloo, ON, Canada

ISBN 978-1-4503-4380-0/16/07... $15.00

DOI: http://dx.doi.org/10.1145/2930889.2930908

The novelty of this paper is to provide an algorithm that computes a certificate for the minimal polynomial of sparse matrices. The Monte Carlo verification complexity of our certificate is linear in the input size and this certificate is composed of the minimal polynomial itself, of three other polynomials and of a vector.

The verification procedure used throughout this paper is that of *interactive certificates* with the taxonomy of [9]. Indeed, we consider a *Prover*, nicknamed *Peggy*, who will perform a computation and provide additional data structures. We also consider a *Verifier*, nicknamed *Victor*, who will check the validity of the result, faster than by just recomputing it. By *certificates* for a problem that is given by input/output specifications, we mean, as in [19, 20], *an input-dependent data structure and an algorithm that computes from that input and its certificate the specified output, and that has lower computational complexity than any known algorithm that does the same when only receiving the input. Correctness of the data structure is not assumed but validated by the algorithm.* By *interactive certificate*, we mean interactive proofs, similar to $\sum$-protocols (as in [6]) were the Prover submits a *Commitment*, that is some result of a computation; the Verifier answers by a *Challenge*, usually some uniformly sampled random values; the Prover then answers with a *Response*, that the Verifier can use to convince himself of the validity of the commitment. Several *rounds* of challenge/response might be necessary for Victor to be fully convinced. Such proof systems are said to be *complete* if the probability that a true statement is rejected by the Verifier can be made arbitrarily small; and *sound* if the probability that a false statement is accepted by the Verifier can be made arbitrarily small. In practice it is sufficient that those probability are < 1, as the protocols can always be run several times. Some of our certificates will also be *perfectly complete*, that is a true statement is never rejected by the Verifier.

All our certificates can be simulated non-interactively by Fiat-Shamir heuristic [11]: uniformly sampled random values produced by Victor are replaced by hashes of the input and of previous messages in the protocol. Complexities are preserved, as producing cryptographically strong pseudo-random bits by a cryptographic hash function (e.g., like the extendable output functions of the SHA-3 family defined in [2, 23]), is linear in the size of both its input and output. More precisely, we will need $O(n\log(n))$ cryptographically strong random bits for the minimal polynomial certificate of Figure 3, and only $O(\log(n))$ for the determinant, Figures 4 and 5.

There may be two main ways to design such certificates. On the one hand, efficient protocols can be designed for delegating computational tasks. In recent years, generic protocols have been designed for circuits with polylogarithmic depth [15, 26]. The resulting protocols are interactive and their cost for the Verifier is usually only roughly proportional to the input size. They however can produce a non negligible overhead for the Prover and are restricted to certain classes of circuits. Variants with an amortized cost for the Verifier can also be designed, see for instance [24], quite often using relatively costly homomorphic routines. We here however want the Verifier to run faster than the Prover, so we discard amortized models where the Verifier is allowed to do a large amount of precomputations, that can be amortized only if, say, the same matrix is repeatedly used [4, 14].

On the other hand, dedicated certificates (data structures and algorithms that are publicly verifiable a posteriori, without interaction) have also been developed, e.g., for dense exact linear algebra [13, 20, 12]. There the certificate constitutes a proof of correctness of a result, not of a computation, and can thus also stand an independent, computation error-correcting verification. The obtained certificates are problem-specific, but try to reduce as much as possible the overhead for the Prover, while preserving a fast verification procedure. In the current paper we give new problem-specific certificate with fast verification and negligible overhead for the Prover.

In exact linear algebra, the simplest problem with an optimal certificate is the linear system solution, LINSOLVE: for a matrix A and a vector b, checking that x is actually a solution is done by one multiplication of x by A. The cost of this check is similar to that of just enumerating all the non-zero coefficients of A. Thus certifying a linear system is reduced to multiplying a matrix by a vector: LINSOLVE$\prec$MATVECMULT. More precisely, by A$\prec$B, we mean that there exists certificates for A that use certificates for B whose verification times are essentially similar: $\text{Verif}(A) = \text{Verif}(B)^{1+o(1)}$. In [9], two reductions have been made: first, that the rank can be certified via certificates for linear systems; second, that the characteristic polynomial can be certified via certificates for the determinant: CHARPOLY$\prec$DET and RANK$\prec$LINSOLVE. The verification procedure for the rank is essentially optimal, it requires two matrix-vector products and $n^{1+o(1)}$ additional operations; while the verification of the characteristic polynomial after verification of a determinant is simply linear. No reduction, however, was given for the determinant. We bridge this gap in this paper. Indeed, we show here that the computation of the minimal polynomial can be checked in linear time by a single matrix-vector multiplication: MINPOLY$\prec$MATVECMULT. Then we use Wiedemann's reduction of the determinant to the minimal polynomial, DET$\prec$MINPOLY, [29, 17], and propose a more efficient preconditioning for the same reduction.

This paper comes with a companion paper [8] that solve similar problems but with different techniques. We nonetheless believe that they are of independent interest, as shown by the following comparison of their salient differences: that

- The paper [8] gives certificates for the Wiedemann sequence, while we here directly certify its minimal polynomial;
- Complexities for the Verifier time and the extra communications are linear here while they are increased by $(\log n)^{\Omega(1)}$ in [8];
- The verification in [8] requires a black box for the transposed matrix;
- The certificates here are interactive while in [8], one of the certificates is, up to our knowledge, the only known non-interactive protocol for the determinant with Prover complexity $n^{1.5+o(1)}$.

The paper is organized as follows. We first present in Section 2 a new multiplicative preconditioner that allows to check the determinant as a quotient of minors. In Section 3 we define Wiedemann's projected Krylov sequence and propose a Monte Carlo certificate for the minimal polynomial of this sequence in Section 4. We apply this with random projections in Section 5, which provides a certificate for the minimal polynomial of the matrix. In Section 6, we see that with a diagonal preconditioning, we obtain another certificate for the determinant. In Section 7, we then combine this idea with the preconditioner of Section 2 to obtain a more efficient certificate for the determinant. This can be combined with the characteristic polynomial reduction of [9], in order to provide also a linear time certificate for the characteristic polynomial of sparse or structured matrices.

2. A SIMPLE INTERACTIVE CERTIFICATE FOR DETERMINANT

We first present a new multiplicative preconditioner that enables the Prover to compute our simple certificate, which is based on the characteristic matrix of the companion matrix of the polynomial $z^n + \sigma$ (see (1) below).

LEMMA 1.

$$\textit{Let } \Gamma(\sigma,\tau) = \begin{bmatrix} \tau & -1 & 0 & \dots & 0 \\ 0 & \tau & -1 & \ddots & \vdots \\ \vdots & 0 & \ddots & \ddots & 0 \\ 0 & & \ddots & \tau & -1 \\ \sigma & 0 & \dots & 0 & \tau \end{bmatrix} \in \mathbb{F}[\sigma,\tau]^{n\times n}, \quad (1)$$

where τ and σ are variables. If $A \in \mathbb{F}^{n\times n}$ is non-singular, then $\det(\lambda I_n - A\,\Gamma(\sigma,\tau))$ is irreducible in $\mathbb{F}(\sigma,\tau)[\lambda]$.

PROOF. We observe that for $\Gamma(\sigma,\tau)$ in (1) we have $\det(\Gamma(\sigma,\tau)) = \tau^n + \sigma$, which is an irreducible polynomial in the bivariate polynomial domain $\mathbb{F}[\sigma,\tau]$. Next we consider the characteristic polynomial of $B(\sigma,\tau) = A\,\Gamma(\sigma,\tau)$, namely

$$\begin{aligned} c^{B(\sigma,\tau)}(\lambda) &= \det(\lambda I_n - B(\sigma,\tau)) \\ &= \lambda^n + c_{n-1}(\sigma,\tau)\lambda^{n-1} + \cdots \\ &\quad + c_1(\sigma,\tau)\lambda \underbrace{\pm \overbrace{\det(A)}^{\in\mathbb{F} \text{ and } \neq 0}(\tau^n+\sigma)}_{c_0(\sigma,\tau)}. \end{aligned} \quad (2)$$

We shall argue that the polynomial $c^{B(\sigma,\tau)}(\lambda)$ in (2) above is irreducible in $\mathbb{F}(\sigma,\tau)[\lambda]$. Because $B(\sigma,\tau)$ has linear forms in τ and σ as entries, $\deg_\tau(c_i) \le n - i$ in (2). We now suppose that

$$g(\lambda,\sigma,\tau)\; h(\lambda,\sigma,\tau) = c^{B(\sigma,\tau)}(\lambda) \quad (3)$$

is a non-trivial factorization in $\mathbb{F}[\lambda,\sigma,\tau]$. Then one of the degree-0 coefficients in λ of either g or h, which are $g(0,\sigma,\tau)$ or $h(0,\sigma,\tau)$, is a scalar multiple of $\tau^n + \sigma$ because $c_0(\sigma,\tau) = \pm\det(A)(\tau^n + \sigma) \neq 0$ (we assumed that A is non-singular) is irreducible in $\mathbb{F}[\sigma,\tau]$. Suppose $g(0,\sigma,\tau)$ is a scalar multiple of $\tau^n + \sigma$ and consequently $h(0,\sigma,\tau) \in \mathbb{F}$. Then $\deg_\tau(g) = n$ and therefore $\deg_\tau(h) = 0$, which means by (3) that h must divide all coefficients of the powers of τ in $c^{B(\sigma,\tau)}(\lambda)$ in (2). However, the term τ^n only occurs in $c_0(\sigma,\tau)$ and has coefficient $\pm\det(A)$ which is a non-zero field element, and therefore $h \in \mathbb{F}$, too. Note that $c^{B(\sigma,\tau)}(\lambda)$ has leading coefficient 1 in λ and therefore no non-trivial factor in $\mathbb{F}[\sigma,\tau]$

(one says it is primitive over $\mathbb{F}[\sigma, \tau]$). Then, by Gauss's Lemma, any factorization of $c^{B(\sigma,\tau)}(\lambda)$ in $\mathbb{F}(\sigma,\tau)[\lambda]$ can be rewritten as a factorization in $\mathbb{F}[\sigma,\tau][\lambda]$, and there is no no-trivial one, so the polynomial must be irreducible also in $\mathbb{F}(\sigma,\tau)[\lambda]$. □

The Prover must convince the Verifier that $\Delta = \det(A)$. Here is the 2 round interactive protocol. We allow a matrix A with $\det(A) = 0$ in which case the Prover may not be able to provide the same certificate for the determinant, but, with high probability, she cannot cheat the Verifier. The Prover can certify $\det(A) = 0$ by a vector $w \in \mathbb{F}^n$ with $w \neq 0^n$ and $Aw = 0^n$, which the Verifier can check. The matrix A is public.

Prover	*Communication*	*Verifier*
1. $B = A\,\Gamma(t,s)$ $t, s \in \mathbb{F}$ with $t^n + s \neq 0$,	$\xrightarrow{t,s}$	Checks $t^n + s \neq 0$,
2. $c^B(\lambda) = \det(\lambda I_n - B)$,	$\xrightarrow{c^B}$	
3. $C = [b_{i,j}]_{1\le i,j\le n-1}$, $c^C(\lambda) = \det(\lambda I_{n-1} - C)$, $t, s \in \mathbb{F}$ also with $\mathrm{GCD}(c^B, c^C) = 1$.	$\xrightarrow{c^C}$	Checks $\mathrm{GCD}(c^B(\lambda), c^C(\lambda)) = 1$
4.	$\xleftarrow{r_1}$	$r_1 \in S \subseteq \mathbb{F}$ random with $c^B(r_1) \neq 0$.
5. Computes w such that $(r_1 I_n - B)w = e_n = \begin{bmatrix}0\\ \vdots\\ 0\\ 1\end{bmatrix}$	$\xrightarrow{w}$	Checks $(r_1 I_n - B)w = e_n$, $w_n = c^C(r_1)/c^B(r_1)$.
6.		Returns $\det(A) = \dfrac{c^B(0)}{t^n + s}$.

Figure 1: A simple sparse determinant protocol

The interactive protocol is given in Figure 1. First we show it is complete, namely that if A is non-singular the Prover can choose $s, t \in \mathbb{F}$ such that $\mathrm{GCD}(c^B(\lambda), c^C(\lambda)) = 1$, provided $\mathbb{F}$ has sufficiently many elements. If A is singular, the Prover may not be able to do so, in which case she can communicate that $\det(A) = 0$ and a non-zero vector $w \in \mathbb{F}^n$, $w \neq 0^n$, with $Aw = 0^n$.

Let $c^{B(\sigma,\tau)}(\lambda) = \det(\lambda I_n - A\Gamma(\sigma,\tau))$, where $\Gamma(\sigma,\tau)$ is in (1), and let $C(\sigma,\tau) = [(B(\sigma,\tau))_{i,j}]_{1\le i,j\le n-1} \in \mathbb{F}[\sigma,\tau]^{(n-1)\times(n-1)}$. We have the non-zero Sylvester resultant

$$\rho(\sigma,\tau) = \mathrm{Res}_\lambda(c^{B(\sigma,\tau)}(\lambda), \det(\lambda I_{n-1} - C(\sigma,\tau))) \neq 0$$

because any non-trivial GCD in $\mathbb{F}(\sigma,\tau)[\lambda]$ would have to divide $c^{B(\sigma,\tau)}(\lambda)$, which is irreducible by Lemma 1. The Prover chooses t, s such that $\rho(t,s) \neq 0$, which for sufficiently large fields is possible by random selection. Note that $c^B(\lambda)$ for such choices of t, s may no longer be irreducible, but that the resultant of c^B and c^C is equal to $\rho(t,s) \neq 0$ (all polynomials have leading coefficient 1 in λ), hence $\mathrm{GCD}(c^B, c^C) = 1$.

The difficulty in certificates by interaction is the proof of soundness, that is, that the Verifier detects a dishonest Prover with high probability. Suppose that the Prover commits $H(\lambda) \neq c^B(\lambda)$ in place of $c^B(\lambda)$ and/or $h(\lambda) \neq c^C(\lambda)$ in place of $c^C(\lambda)$, with $\deg(H) = n$ and $\deg(h) = n-1$ and both H and h with leading coefficient 1 in λ. The Prover might have chosen t, s such that $\mathrm{GCD}(c^B(\lambda), c^C(\lambda)) \neq 1$. Or she may have been unable to compute such t, s in the case when A is singular, and communicated the false H and h instead of presenting a linear column relation w as a certificate of singularity. In any case, because $h(\lambda)/H(\lambda)$ is a reduced fraction of polynomials with leading coefficient 1 and because $c^B(\lambda)$ and $c^C(\lambda)$ also have leading coefficient 1, we must have $h(\lambda)/H(\lambda) \neq c^C(\lambda)/c^B(\lambda)$, or equivalently $h(\lambda)c^B(\lambda) - H(\lambda)c^C(\lambda) \neq 0$.

The Verifier with probability

$$\ge 1 - \frac{\deg(c^B(hc^B - Hc^C))}{|S| - n} \ge 1 - \frac{3n-2}{|S|-n}$$

chooses an r_1 such that and $c^B(r_1) \neq 0$ and $(hc^B - Hc^C)(r_1) \neq 0$, both of which $\Longrightarrow c^C(r_1)/c^B(r_1) \neq h(r_1)/H(r_1)$. The element r_1 satisfies $H(r_1) \neq 0$, hence the $-n$ in the denominator, roots of H are eliminated from selection set S. Note that $\deg(hc^B - Hc^C) \le 2n-2$ because the leading terms λ^{2n-1} of both products cancel.

Suppose now that r_1 is chosen with those properties. Then $\det(r_1 I_n - B) = c^B(r_1) \neq 0$, and by Cramer's rule

$$w_n = \frac{\det(r_1 I_{n-1} - C)}{\det(r_1 I_n - B)} = \frac{c^C(r_1)}{c^B(r_1)} \neq \frac{h(r_1)}{H(r_1)} \tag{4}$$

and the Verifier's last check fails. Therefore, if the last check also succeeds, with probability $\ge 1 - (3n-2)/(|S| - n)$ we have $H = c^B$ and the Verifier has the correct determinant. Therefore the protocol is sound with high probability.

We do not fully analyze how fast the Prover could compute t, s, c^B, c^C, and w, in a modified protocol using additional preconditioners, as we will use the full Wiedemann technology for sparse and black box matrices in more efficient protocols below, which we have derived from Figure 1. The Verifier in Figure 1 checks a polynomial GCD, chooses a random field element, computes a matrix-times-vector product, and performs some arithmetic, which for a sparse A constitutes work more or less proportional to the input size. Again, below we will improve the Verifier complexity, for instance make the GCD verification $O(n)$. The GCD = 1 property of Step 3 will remain the fundamental ingredient for the soundness of our protocols.

3. THE WIEDEMANN SEQUENCE

Let $A \in \mathbb{F}^{n\times n}$ and $u, v \in \mathbb{F}^n$. The infinite sequence

$$(a_0, a_1, a_2, \ldots, a_i, \ldots) \text{ with } a_0 {=} u^T v, a_i {=} u^T A^i v \text{ for } i{\ge}1, \tag{5}$$

is due to D. Wiedemann [29]. The sequence is linearly generated by the scalar minimal generating polynomial $f_v^{A,u}(\lambda) \in \mathbb{F}[\lambda]$, which is a factor of the minimal polynomial of the matrix A, the latter of which we denote by $f^A(\lambda)$. Both f^A and $f_v^{A,u}$ are defined as monic polynomials, that is, have leading coefficient equal to 1.

THEOREM 2. *Let $S \subseteq \mathbb{F}$ be of finite cardinality, which we denote by $|S| < \infty$, and let $u, v \in S^n$ be uniformly randomly sampled. Then the probability that $f_v^{A,u} = f^A$ is at least* $(1 - \deg(f^A)/|S|)^2 > 1 - 2n/|S|$ (cf. [16, Theorem 5]).

We now define the residue for the linear generator $f_v^{A,u}$.

DEFINITION 3. *Let $G_u^{A,v}(\lambda) = \sum_{i\ge 0} a_i \lambda^{-1-i} \in \mathbb{F}[[\lambda^{-1}]]$ be the generating function of the Wiedemann sequence (5). Then we define the residue $\rho_u^{A,v}(\lambda) = f_u^{A,v}(\lambda) G_u^{A,v}(\lambda) \in \mathbb{F}[\lambda]$.*

LEMMA 4. *The residue $\rho_u^{A,v}$ in Definition 3 satisfies:*

$$\mathrm{GCD}(\rho_u^{A,v}(\lambda), f_u^{A,v}(\lambda)) = 1$$

PROOF. The field of quotients of the ring of power series in λ^{-1} is denoted by $\mathbb{F}((\lambda^{-1}))$, the ring of extended power series in λ^{-1}, whose elements can be represented as $\sum_{i\le k} c_i \lambda^i$ for $c_i \in \mathbb{F}$ and $k \in \mathbb{Z}$. The residue $\rho_u^{A,v}(\lambda)$ is computed in $\mathbb{F}((\lambda^{-1}))$, but because

$f_u^{A,v}(\lambda)$ is a linear generator for $(a_i)_{i\geq 0}$, $\rho_u^{A,v}(\lambda)$ is a polynomial in $\mathbb{F}[\lambda]$ with $\deg(\rho_u^{A,v}) < \deg(f_u^{A,v})$. If the greatest common divisor $g(\lambda) = \mathrm{GCD}(\rho_u^{A,v}(\lambda), f_u^{A,v}(\lambda))$ is not trivial, then the equation $\rho_u^{A,v}/g = (f_u^{A,v}/g)G_u^{A,v}$ yields $f_u^{A,v}/g$ as a linear generator for $(a_i)_{i\geq 0}$ of lower degree than the degree of $f_u^{A,v}$, which violates the minimality of the linear generator $f_u^{A,v}$. □

4. A CERTIFICATE FOR THE LINEAR GENERATOR

We give the 2-rounds interactive protocol in Figure 2. The Prover must convince the Verifier that $f_u^{A,v}$ is indeed the Wiedemann generator for $(u^T A^i v)_{i\geq 0}$. The matrix A and vectors u, v are public.

Prover	*Communication*	*Verifier*
1. $H(\lambda) = f_u^{A,v}(\lambda)$, $h(\lambda) = \rho_u^{A,v}(\lambda)$.	$\xrightarrow{H,h}$	
2. $\phi, \psi \in \mathbb{F}[\lambda]$ with $\phi f_u^{A,v} + \psi \rho_u^{A,v} = 1$, $\deg(\phi) \leq \deg(\rho_u^{A,v}) - 1$, $\deg(\psi) \leq \deg(f_u^{A,v}) - 1$.	$\xrightarrow{\phi,\psi}$	
3.		Random $r_0 \in S \subseteq \mathbb{F}$. Checks $\mathrm{GCD}(H(\lambda), h(\lambda)) = 1$ by $\phi(r_0)H(r_0) + \psi(r_0)h(r_0) \stackrel{?}{=} 1$.
	$\xleftarrow{r_1}$	Random $r_1 \in S \subseteq \mathbb{F}$.
4. Computes w such that $(r_1 I_n - A)w = v$.	$\xrightarrow{w}$	Checks $(r_1 I_n - A)w \stackrel{?}{=} v$ and $(u^T w)H(r_1) \stackrel{?}{=} h(r_1)$. Returns $f_u^{A,v}(\lambda) = H(\lambda)$.

Figure 2: Certificate for $f_u^{A,v}$

In Step 4 Peggy may not be able to produce a vector w when $r_1 I_n - A$ is singular. However, she may instead convince Victor that the random choice of r_1 has led to a "failure". We investigate the case where the linear system is inconsistent more precisely. Let $f^{A,v}(\lambda)$ denote the minimal linear generator of the Krylov sequences of vectors $(A^i v)_{i\geq 0}$. We have that the minimal polynomial f^A of A is a multiple of $f^{A,v}$. Suppose now that $f^{A,v}(r_1) = 0$ and let $\lambda_2, \ldots, \lambda_m$ be the remaining roots of $f^{A,v}$ in the algebraic closure of $\mathbb{F}$. We obtain from $f^{A,v}(A)v = 0^n$ that $0^n = (\prod_{j=2}^m (A - \lambda_j I_n))(A - r_1 I_n)w = (\prod_{j=2}^m (A - \lambda_j I_n))(-v)$, in violation that $f^{A,v}(A)v$ constitutes the first linear dependence of the Krylov vectors $(A^i v)_{i\geq 0}$. Conversely, if $f^{A,v}(r_1) \neq 0$ then the system $(r_1 I - A)w = v$ is consistent with $w = (1/f^{A,v}(r_1))\, \vec{\rho}^{A,v}(r_1)$ (see (6) multiplied by $\lambda I_n - A$ in the soundness proof below). We just proved that the linear system $(r_1 I_n - A)$ is inconsistent with v if and only if $f^{A,v}(r_1) = 0$ (hence in particular $r_1 I_n - A$ is singular). Peggy could provide a non-zero vector in the right nullspace of $r_1 I_n - A$ as a proof that Victor has communicated a bad r_1. Since one can have $f_u^{A,v}(r_1) \neq 0$ when $f^{A,v}(r_1) = 0$ Victor cannot test the choice of r_1 before sending it even if the communicated $f_u^{A,v}$ is correct.

Given the above, the protocol is *perfectly complete*: if the values $(f_u^{A,v}, \rho_u^{A,v})$ and the system solution $w = (1/f^{A,v}(r_1))\, \vec{\rho}^{A,v}(r_1)$ communicated by the Prover are correct, the Verifier always accepts $f_u^{A,v}$. In case that the system $(r_1 I_n - A)w = v$ is inconsistent, the Prover could communicate a Farkas certificate of inconsistency $\bar{w}$ with $\bar{w}^T(r_1 I_n - A) = 0$ and $\bar{w}^T v \neq 0$. When a Farkas certificate of inconsistency is sent, the Verifier then accepts the "correct" output that the choice of r_1 has led to "failure."

In Figure 2 we allow inconsistent systems to remain uncertified for two reasons: 1. A Farkas certificate requires additional work for the Prover, possibly needing a transposed matrix times vector procedure for a black box matrix A. 2. Monte Carlo algorithms are always fast and do not fail. Their output is correct with probability $\geq$ a given bound. Our certificates indeed have Monte Carlo randomized verification algorithms, that is, as we will prove below, the interactive protocol does not fail via system inconsistency in Step 4 and, when all checks succeed, the first pair of polynomials communicated is $f_u^{A,v}$ and $\rho_u^{A,v}$ with probability $\geq (1 - (2n-2)/|S|) \times (1 - (3n-1)/|S|)$.

Proof of soundness: Now suppose that the Prover commits $H(\lambda)$ in place of $f_u^{A,v}(\lambda)$ and/or $h(\lambda)$ in place of $\rho_u^{A,v}(\lambda)$, with $n \geq \deg(H) > \deg(h)$ and $h/H \neq \rho_u^{A,v}/f_u^{A,v}$. The Verifier with probability

$$\begin{aligned} &\geq 1 - (\deg(\phi H + \psi h))\,/|S| \\ &\geq 1 - (\max\{\deg(H) + \deg(\phi), \deg(h) + \deg(\psi)\})\,/|S| \\ &\geq 1 - (2n-2)\,/|S| \end{aligned}$$

exposes that $(\phi H + \psi h)(r_0) \neq 1$. Suppose now that the Verifier's check succeeds and that actually $\mathrm{GCD}(H, h) = 1$. The Verifier with probability

$$\begin{aligned} &\geq 1 - \left(\deg(f^A(H\rho_u^{A,v} - h f_u^{A,v}))\right)/|S| \\ &\geq 1 - (3n-1)\,/|S| \end{aligned}$$

chooses an r_1 such that $f^A(r_1) \neq 0$ (that is, $r_1 I_n - A$ is non-singular) and $(H\rho_u^{A,v} - h f_u^{A,v})(r_1) \neq 0$. The latter rewrites as $h(r_1) \neq H(r_1)\rho_u^{A,v}(r_1)/f_u^{A,v}(r_1)$. Note that $f^A(r_1) \neq 0 \Rightarrow f_u^{A,v}(r_1) \neq 0$. Suppose now that r_1 is chosen with those properties. As in the proof of Lemma 4 we can define

$$\begin{aligned} G^{A,v}(\lambda) &= \sum_{i\geq 0} \lambda^{-(i+1)}(A^i v) \in \mathbb{F}^n[[\lambda^{-1}]], \\ \vec{\rho}^{A,v}(\lambda) &= f^{A,v}(\lambda)\, G^{A,v}(\lambda) \in \mathbb{F}^n[\lambda]. \end{aligned}$$

We have $(\lambda I_n - A)\, G^{A,v}(\lambda) = v$ and

$$(\lambda I_n - A)^{-1} v = \frac{1}{f^{A,v}(\lambda)}\, \vec{\rho}^{A,v}(\lambda). \qquad (6)$$

Furthermore, $(u^T \vec{\rho}^{A,v})/f^{A,v} = \rho_u^{A,v}/f_u^{A,v}$, where the left-hand side is not necessarily a reduced fraction. Thus, $u^T w\, H(r_1) = u^T(r_1 I_n - A)^{-1} v\, H(r_1) = (\rho_u^{A,v}/f_u^{A,v})(r_1) \cdot H(r_1) \neq h(r_1)$, and the Verifier's last check fails; one can compare with (4), which has $u = v = e_n$ and $f_u^{B,v} = c^B$. Therefore, if the last check also succeeds, with probability $\geq (1 - (2n-2)/|S|)(1 - (3n-1)/|S|)$ we have $\mathrm{GCD}(H, h) = 1$ and $h/H = \rho_u^{A,v}/f_u^{A,v}$.

About the certificate complexity: Excluding the input matrix A and the output minimal polynomial $f_u^{A,v}$, the certificate in Figure 2 comprises $\rho_u^{A,v}$, monic of degree strictly less than n; then ϕ, ψ, of degree respectively less than $n-2$ and $n-1$; and finally w, a vector of $\mathbb{F}^n$. The extra communications for the certificate are thus less than $4n$ field elements. For the time complexity, evaluating ϕ, f, ψ, ρ, f and ρ requires less than $6(2n)$ field operations, Aw is one matrix-vector, of cost $\mu(A)$, and checking $(r_1 I_n - A)w$ (either for a solution, or as a non-zero vector in the right nullspace) requires an additional $2n$ operations, like $u^T w$. The multiplication of the vector by $f_u^{A,v}(r_1)$ requires finally n more multiplications in the field. We have thus proven Theorem 5 thereafter.

THEOREM 5. *If the size of the field is* $\geq 3n$, *the protocol in Figure 2 is sound and complete. The associated certificate requires less than* $4n$ *extra field elements and is verifiable in less than* $\mu(A) + 17n$ *field operations.*

Note that, with slightly larger fields, one can further reduce the complexity for the Verifier.

COROLLARY 6. *If the size of the field is* $\geq 5n - 2$, *there exists a sound and perfectly complete protocol for certifying* $f_u^{A,v}$, *whose associated certificate requires less than* $4n$ *extra field elements and is verifiable in less than* $\mu(A) + 13n$ *field operations.*

PROOF. For the complexity improvement, it suffices to chose $r_0 = r_1$. Then the last evaluations of $f_u^{A,v}(r_1)$ and $\rho_u^{A,v}(r_1)$ are already computed by the GCD check. Now r_0 must be such that $f^A(H\rho_u^{A,v} - hf_u^{A,v})(\phi H + \psi h - 1)\,(r_0) \neq 0$, but the latter is of degree $\deg(f^A) + \max\{\deg(H) + \deg(\phi), \deg(h) + \deg(\psi)\} + \max\{\deg(H) + \deg(\rho_u^{A,v}), \deg(h) + \deg(f_u^{A,v})\} \leq 3n - 1 + 2n - 2$. Furthermore, the analysis in the beginning of this section shows that the protocol of Figure 2 can be extended to be *perfectly* complete. □

REMARK 7 (CERTIFICATE OVER SMALL FIELDS). For the certificates of this paper to be sound, the underlying field cannot be too small: $\Omega(n)$ for the minimal polynomial certificates, $\Omega(n^2)$ for the following determinant or characteristic polynomial certificates. If the field is smaller, then a classical technique is to embed it in an extension of adequate size. Arithmetic operations in this extension field $L \supset \mathbb{F}$ of degree $O(\log n)$ will then cost $\log(n)^{1+o(1)}$ operations in the base field, but with $s \geq \log_2(1/\epsilon)$ matrix A times vectors $\in \mathbb{F}^n$ operations, that is over the base field, an incorrect w is exposed with probability $\geq 1{-}1/2^s \geq 1{-}\epsilon$ for any constant $\epsilon > 0$.

We give the idea for $\mathbb{F}{=}\mathbb{Z}_2$ and $L{=}\mathbb{Z}_2[\theta]/(\chi(\theta))$ where χ is an irreducible polynomial in $\mathbb{Z}_2[\theta]$ with $\deg(\chi){=}k{+}1{=}O(\log n)$. The Prover returns $w{=}w^{[0]}{+}\theta w^{[1]}{+}\cdots{+}\theta^k w^{[k]}$ with $w^{[\kappa]}{\in}\mathbb{Z}_2^n$. For $v^{[0]}{+}\theta v^{[1]}{+}\cdots{+}\theta^k v^{[k]} = v{-}r_1 w$ with $v^{[\kappa]} \in \mathbb{Z}_2^n$ we must have $-Aw^{[\kappa]}{=}v^{[\kappa]}$ for all κ. Suppose that the Prover has sent a w that violates j of the equations, namely, $-Aw^{[\ell_i]}{=}y^{[\ell_i]}{\neq}v^{[\ell_i]}$ for $1 \leq i \leq j$. Then $|\{(c_1,\dots,c_j){\in}\mathbb{Z}_2^j \mid \sum_{i=1}^{j} c_i y^{[\ell_i]}{\neq}\sum_{i=1}^{j} c_i v^{[\ell_i]}\}| \geq 2^{j-1}$. The inequality is immediate for $j{=}1, 2$. For $j \geq 3$ one gets for each $\sum_{i=1}^{j-2} c_i y^{[\ell_i]}{=}\sum_{i=1}^{j-2} c_i v^{[\ell_i]}$ the two unequal linear combinations for $c_{j-1}{=}1, c_j{=}0$ and $c_{j-1}{=}0, c_j{=}1$; one also gets for each $\sum_{i=1}^{j-2} c_i y^{[\ell_i]}{\neq}\sum_{i=1}^{j-2} c_i v^{[\ell_i]}$ the unequal linear combination for $c_{j-1}{=}c_j{=}0$; a second unequal combination is either for $c_{j-1} = 1$, $c_j = 0$ or $c_{j-1}{=}c_j{=}1$, because not both can be equal at the same time. Therefore $|\{(c_0,\dots,c_k){\in}\mathbb{Z}_2^{k+1} \mid -A(\sum_{i=0}^{k} c_i w^{[i]}) \neq (\sum_{i=0}^{k} c_i v^{[i]})\ \}| \geq 2^k$ which shows that checking a random linear combination over $\mathbb{Z}_2$ exposes an incorrect w with probability $\geq 1/2$. The cost for the Verifier is thus $O(\mu(A)) + n^{1+o(1)}$ operations in $\mathbb{Z}_2$.

Complexity for the Prover: Theorem 5 places no requirement on how the Prover computes the required commitments. Coppersmith's block Wiedemann method [5], for instance, can be used.

THEOREM 8. *If the size of the field is* $> 3n$ *then the Prover can produce the certificate in Figure 2 in no more than* $(1 + o(1))n$ *multiplications of* A *times a vector in* $\mathbb{F}^n$ *and* $n^{2+o(1)}$ *additional operations in* $\mathbb{F}$, *using* $n^{1+o(1)}$ *auxiliary storage for elements in* $\mathbb{F}$.

PROOF. The Berlekamp-Massey algorithm can be applied on the sequence $(a_i)_{i\geq 0} = (u^T A^i v)_{i\geq 0}$ to recover $f_u^{A,v}$. However that requires (at most) $2n$ terms to be computed [29], and hence more multiplications of A times a vector than requested in the statement. Following [16, Sec. 7], the number of applications of A can be minimized using Coppersmith's block Wiedemann algorithm [5] with a special choice of parameters. We consider integers p and q (the blocking factors) such that $q = o(p)$, $p = n^{o(1)}$, and $1/q = o(1)$. For example, we may choose $p = (\log n)^2$ and $q = \log n$.

For the block Wiedemann algorithm we first take random $\mathcal{U}_0 \in \mathbb{F}^{n\times(p-1)}$ and $\mathcal{V}_0 \in \mathbb{F}^{n\times(q-1)}$ with entries sampled from $S \subseteq \mathbb{F}$, and construct $\mathcal{U} = [u, \mathcal{U}_0] \in \mathbb{F}^{n\times p}$ and $\mathcal{V} = [v, \mathcal{V}_0] \in \mathbb{F}^{n\times q}$. With $d_l = \lceil n/(p-1)\rceil$ and $d_r = \lceil n/(q-1)\rceil$, the rank of the block Hankel matrix $\mathsf{Hk}_{d_l,d_r}(A, \mathcal{U}_0, \mathcal{V}_0)$ in [18, (2.4)] is maximal with high probability, and equal to the dimension of the Krylov space $\mathcal{K}_{A,\mathcal{V}_0}$ (using $q \leq p$). Since the degree of the q-th (resp. the p-th) highest degree invariant factor of $\lambda - A$ has degree less than d_r (resp. d_l), less than d_r (resp. d_l) first Krylov iterates $(A^i v)_{i\geq 0}$ (resp. $(u^T A^i)_{i\geq 0}$) suffice for completing any basis of $\mathcal{K}_{A,\mathcal{V}_0}$ into a basis of $\mathcal{K}_{A,\mathcal{V}}$. (resp. $\mathcal{K}_{A,\mathcal{U}_0}$ and $\mathcal{K}_{A,\mathcal{U}}$). Therefore the rank of $\mathsf{Hk}_{d_l,d_r}(A, \mathcal{U}, \mathcal{V})$ must be maximal and equal to $\dim \mathcal{K}_{A,\mathcal{V}}$.

The determinant of a submatrix of $\mathsf{Hk}_{d_l,d_r}(A, \mathcal{U}, \mathcal{V})$ with maximal rank has degree at most $2n$ in the entries of $\mathcal{U}_0$ and $\mathcal{V}_0$. Using arguments analogous to those in [27, sec. 9.2] or [18, Sec. 3.2], by the DeMillo-Lipton/Schwartz/Zippel Lemma [7, 30, 25], we obtain that:

$$\operatorname{Prob}\left(\operatorname{rank} \mathsf{Hk}_{d_l,d_r}(A, \mathcal{U}, \mathcal{V}) = \dim \mathcal{K}_{A,\mathcal{V}}\right) \geq 1 - 2n/|S|. \quad (7)$$

If S contains sufficiently many elements, it follows [27, 18] that it is sufficient to compute the sequence of $p \times q$ matrices $\mathcal{A}_i = \mathcal{U}^T A^i \mathcal{V}$ up to $L = d_l + d_r$ terms, which can be achieved with $qL = n(1 + o(1))$ multiplications of A times a vector, and $n^{2+o(1)}$ additional operations in $\mathbb{F}$. Let

$$\mathcal{G}_{\mathcal{U}}^{A,\mathcal{V}}(\lambda) = \sum_{i\geq 0} \mathcal{A}_i \lambda^{-1-i} = \sum_{i\geq 0} \mathcal{U}^T A^i \mathcal{V} \lambda^{-1-i} \in \mathbb{F}^{p\times q}[[\lambda^{-1}]]$$

be the generating function for the block Wiedemann sequence. One can then compute a rational fraction description of $\mathcal{G}_{\mathcal{U}}^{A,\mathcal{V}}$, in the form of a pair of matrices $\mathcal{F}(\lambda) \in \mathbb{F}^{q\times q}[\lambda]$ and $\mathcal{R}(\lambda) \in \mathbb{F}^{p\times q}[\lambda]$ with degree $d_r = o(n)$, so that $\mathcal{F}$ is a minimal matrix generator for $(\mathcal{A}_i)_{i\geq 0}$, and

$$\mathcal{G}_{\mathcal{U}}^{A,\mathcal{V}}(\lambda)\mathcal{F}(\lambda) = \mathcal{R}(\lambda) \in \mathbb{F}^{p\times q}[\lambda].$$

The matrices $\mathcal{F}$ and $\mathcal{R}$ can be computed in time soft-linear in n [1], and since the dimensions are in $n^{o(1)}$, the matrix fraction $\mathcal{R}(\lambda) \times \mathcal{F}(\lambda)^{-1}$ is also obtained in soft-linear time. Any of the entries of this matrix fraction is a rational fraction description of a sequence corresponding to two chosen vectors among the blocking vectors. In particular, from the entry (1,1), Peggy obtains the rational fraction description $\rho_u^{A,v}/f_u^{A,v}$ of $(a_i)_{i\geq 0}$. The computation of ϕ and ψ follows via an extended Euclidean algorithm applied on $f_u^{A,v}$ and $\rho_u^{A,v}$.

A small variation of the above scheme solves the inhomogenous linear system in Step 4. Let $B = r_1 I_n - A$. With high probability, Victor chooses a r_1 such that $f^A(r_1) \neq 0$, hence B is non-singular. Together with (7) this gives the requirement $3n{+}1$ for the field size.

We have that $\mathcal{F}' = \mathcal{F}(r_1 - \lambda)$ is a minimal matrix generator for the sequence of $p \times q$ matrices $(\mathcal{U}^T B^i \mathcal{V})_{i\geq 0}$ (computing $\mathcal{F}'$ is a soft-linear operation). Since B is non-singular we have $\det \mathcal{F}'(0) \neq 0$. With column operations on $\mathcal{F}'$, we can arrange so that one column becomes $[f_0, 0, \dots, 0]^T$ with $f_0 \neq 0$. $\mathcal{V}$ times the latter being $f_0.v$, following the inhomogeneous case in [5, Sec. 8], this suffices to solve the linear system $Bw = v$, using $d_r = o(n)$ more matrix-vector multiplications and $n^{2+o(1)}$ operations in $\mathbb{F}$. □

5. A CERTIFICATE FOR THE MINIMAL POLYNOMIAL

With random vectors u and v, we address the certification of the minimal polynomial f^A. Indeed, using Wiedemann's study [29, Sec. VI] or the alternative approach in [17, 16], we know that for random u and v, $f_u^{A,v}$ is equal to f^A with high probability (see Theorem 2). This is shown in Figure 3.

Prover	*Communication*	*Verifier*
1.	$\xleftarrow{u,v}$	Random $u, v \in S^n \subseteq \mathbb{F}^n$.
	Figure 2	
2.	$\xrightarrow{H, h, \phi, \psi}$	
3.	$\xleftarrow{r_1}$	
4.	$\xrightarrow{w}$	Checks $H \stackrel{?}{=} f_u^{A,v}$, w.h.p.
5.		Returns $f^A = f_u^{A,v}$, w.h.p.

Figure 3: Certificate for f^A with random projections

PROPOSITION 9. *The protocol in Figure 3 is sound and complete.*

PROOF. First, the protocol is complete. Indeed, the result is correct means that $H = f^A$. Thus, if $f^A = f_u^{A,v}$, then completeness is guaranteed by the completeness in Theorem 5. Otherwise, H is a proper multiple of $f_u^{A,v}$ and $H = f^A \neq f_u^{A,v}$. If u, v are randomly chosen by Victor, this happens only with low probability, thanks to Theorem 2.

Second, for the soundness, if the result is incorrect, then $H \neq f^A$. If also $H \neq f_u^{A,v}$, then similarly, H will make the certificate of Figure 2 fail with high probability, by the soundness in Theorem 5. Otherwise, $H = f_u^{A,v} \neq f^A$, but if u, v are randomly chosen by Victor, this happens only with low probability, thanks to Theorem 2. □

COROLLARY 10. *If the size of the field is $\geq 5n-2$, there exists a sound and perfectly complete protocol for certifying f^A, whose associated certificate requires less than $8n$ extra field elements and is verifiable in less than $2\mu(A) + 26n$ field operations.*

PROOF. We add some work for the Prover, and double the certificate. First Peggy has to detect that the projections given by Victor reveal only a proper factor of the minimal polynomial. Second she needs to prove to Victor that he was wrong. For this, Peggy:

- Computes the minimal polynomial f^A of the matrix and the minimal polynomial $f_u^{A,v}$.
- If $f^A \neq f_u^{A,v}$, Peggy searches for projections $(\hat{u}, \hat{v})$, such that $\deg(f_{\hat{u}}^{A,\hat{v}}) > \deg(f_u^{A,v})$.
- Peggy then starts two certificates of Figure 2, one for (u, v), one for $(\hat{u}, \hat{v})$.

In case of success of the latter two certificates, Victor is convinced that both $f_u^{A,v}$ and $f_{\hat{u}}^{A,\hat{v}}$ are correct. But as the latter polynomial has a degree strictly larger than the former, he is also convinced that his projections can not reveal f^A. Complexities are given by applying Corollary 6 twice. □

REMARK 11 (CERTIFICATE FOR THE RANK). If A is non-singular, the certificate of [9, Figure 2] can be used to certify non-singularity: for any random vector b proposed by Victor, Peggy can solve the system $Aw = b$ and return w as a certificate. Now, if A is singular, a similar idea as for the minimal polynomial can be used to certify the rank: precondition the matrix A into a modified matrix B whose minimal polynomial is $f(x)x$ and characteristic polynomial is $f(x)x^k$, where $f(0) \neq 0$. As a consequence $\text{rank}(A) = n - k$. For instance, if A is symmetric, such a PRECONDCYCNIL preconditioner can be a non-singular diagonal matrix D if the field is sufficiently large [3, Theorem 4.3]. Otherwise, $A^T D_2 A$ is symmetric, with D_2 another diagonal matrix. Then the minimal polynomial certificate can be applied to $B = DA^T D_2 AD$ [10]. Comparing with the certificate for the rank in [9, Corollary 3], this new certificate saves a logarithmic factor in the verification time, but requires the field to be larger (from $\Omega(n)$ to $\Omega(n^2)$).

6. CERTIFICATE FOR THE DETERMINANT WITH DIAGONAL PRECONDITIONING

First of all, if A is singular, Peggy may not be able to produce the desired certificate. In which case she can communicate that $\det(A) = 0$ and produce a non-zero vector in the kernel: $w \in \mathbb{F}^n$, $w \neq 0^n$, with $Aw = 0^n$.

We thus suppose in the following that A is non-singular.

The idea of [29, Theorem 2] is to precondition the initial invertible matrix A into a modified matrix B whose characteristic polynomial is square-free, and whose determinant is an easily computable modification of that of A. For instance, such a PRECONDCYC preconditioner can be a non-singular diagonal matrix D if the field is sufficiently large [3, Theorem 4.2]:

$$\text{Prob}\left(\deg\left(f^{DA}\right) = n\right) \geq 1 - \frac{n(n-1)}{2|S|} \tag{8}$$

To certify the determinant, it is thus sufficient for Peggy to chose a non-singular diagonal matrix D and two vectors u, v such that $\deg(f_u^{DA,v}) = n$ and then to use the minimal polynomial certificate for $f_u^{DA,v}$, as shown on Figure 4.

Prover	*Communication*	*Verifier*
1. Form $B = DA$ with $D \in S^n \subseteq \mathbb{F}^{*n}$ and $u, v \in S^n$, s.t. $\deg(f_u^{B,v}) = n$.	$\xrightarrow{D,u,v}$	
	Figure 2	
2.	$\xrightarrow{H, h, \phi, \psi}$	Checks:
3.	$\xleftarrow{r_1}$	$\deg(H) \stackrel{?}{=} n$,
4.	$\xrightarrow{w}$	$H \stackrel{?}{=} f_u^{B,v}$, w.h.p.
5.		Returns $\frac{f_u^{B,v}(0)}{\det(D)}$.

Figure 4: Determinant certificate with Diagonal preconditioning for a non-singular matrix

REMARK 12. Note that in the minimal polynomial sub-routine of Figure 4, Peggy can actually choose D, u, v, since the check on the degree of $f_u^{B,v}$ prevents bad choices for D, u, v. Victor could also select them himself, the overall volume of communications would be unchanged, but he would have to perform more work, namely selecting $3n + 2$ random elements instead of just 1.

THEOREM 13. *If the size of the field is $\geq \max\{\frac{1}{2}n^2 - \frac{1}{2}n, 5n - 2\}$, the protocol for the determinant of a non-singular matrix in Figure 4 is sound and complete. The associated certificate requires less than $8n$ extra field elements and is verifiable in less than*

$\mu(A)+15n$ field operations. If the size of the field is $\geq n^2+n+5$, with high probability the Prover can produce it with no more than 2 minimal polynomial computations, and 1 system solving.

PROOF. First, if the Prover is honest, H is correctly checked to be $f_u^{B,v}$, as the minimal polynomial is complete. Then, by definition, $f_u^{B,v}$ is a factor of the characteristic polynomial of B. But if its degree is n, then it is the characteristic polynomial. Therefore its unit coefficient is the determinant of B and the certificate of Figure 4 is complete.

Second, for the soundness. If $H \neq f_u^{B,v}$, then the minimal polynomial certificate will most probably fail, by the soundness of the minimal polynomial certificate, as $|S| \geq (5n-2)$, from Corollary 6. Otherwise, the degree check enforces that $f_u^{B,v}$ is the characteristic polynomial.

Now, for the complexity, with respect to the minimal polynomial certificate and Theorem 5, this certificate requires an extra diagonal matrix D. As $u, v, f_u^{B,v}$ are not input/output anymore, the extra communications grow from $4n$ field elements to $8n$. The verification procedure is similar except that verifying a linear system solution with B requires $n+\mu(A)$ operations and that $det(D)$ has to be computed, hence the supplementary $2n$ field operations. Finally, for the Prover, in order to find suitable vectors and diagonal matrices, Peggy can select them randomly in S^n and try $f_u^{DA,v}$ until $\deg(f_u^{DA,v})=n$. It will succeed with the joint probabilities of Theorem 2 and Equation (8). For $n \geq 2$, as soon as $|S| \geq n^2+n+5$, the lower bound of the probability of success $(1-n(n-1)/(2|S|))(1-2n/|S|)$ is higher than $1/2$ and the expected number of trials for the Prover is less than 2. □

Note that the certificate (as well as that of next section) can be made perfectly complete, by using the perfectly complete certificate for the minimal polynomial of Corollary 10.

7. DETERMINANT WITH GAMMA PRECONDITIONING

In order to compute the determinant via a minimal polynomial, the diagonal preconditioning ensures that it is equal to the characteristic polynomial, as the latter is square-free with factors of degree 1. With the preconditioning of Section 2, we can differently ensure that the characteristic polynomial is irreducible. It has the same effect, that it equals the minimal polynomial, but it also enforces that it has no smaller degree factors. Therefore, for any non-zero u and v, as a non-singular matrix is non-zero, the only possibility for $f_u^{A,v}$ is to be of degree n. Thus, we can give in Figure 5 an improved certificate. It chooses pre-determined vectors u and v to be as simple as possible: the canonical vector $e_1=[1,0,\ldots,0]^T$.

THEOREM 14. *If the size of the field is $\geq \max\{n^2-n, 5n-2\}$, the protocol for the determinant of a non-singular matrix in Figure 5 is sound and complete. The associated certificate requires less than $5n$ extra field elements and is verifiable in less than $\mu(A)+13n+o(n)$ field operations. If the size of the field is $\geq 2n^2-2n$, with high probability the Prover can produce it with no more than 2 minimal polynomial computations, and 1 system solving.*

PROOF. Completeness is given by the same argument as for Theorem 13. It is similar for the soundness, provided that $H_n(s,t)\neq 0$ implies that $\deg(f_{e_1}^{B,e_1})=n$.

Therefore, let $C^{B(\sigma,\tau)}(\lambda) = \det(\lambda I_n - A\,\Gamma(\sigma,\tau))$, where $\Gamma(\sigma,\tau)$ is in (1). Then, for $e_1=[1,0,\ldots,0]^T$ the first canonical vector, let $G_1^{B(\sigma,\tau)}(\lambda) = e_1^T(\lambda I_n - A)^{-1}e_1$, and let $\rho_1^{(\sigma,\tau)}(\lambda) = C^{B(\sigma,\tau)}(\lambda)G_1^{B(\sigma,\tau)}(\lambda)$.

Prover	*Communication*	*Verifier*
1. Form $B = A\,\Gamma(s,t)$ with $s,t \in \mathbb{F}$ s.t. $\Gamma(s,t)$ non-singular ($\Leftrightarrow t^n+s\neq 0$) and $H_n(s,t)\neq 0$. (see (1) and (9))	$\xrightarrow{s,t}$	Checks $t^n+s\neq 0$.
	Figure 2	
2.	$\xrightarrow{H,h,\phi,\psi}$	Checks:
3.	$\xleftarrow{r_1}$	$\deg(H) \stackrel{?}{==} n$,
4.	$\xrightarrow{w}$	$H \stackrel{?}{==} f_{e_1}^{B,e_1}$, w.h.p.
5.		Returns $\dfrac{f_{e_1}^{B,e_1}(0)}{t^n+s}$.

Figure 5: Determinant certificate with Gamma preconditioning for a non-singular matrix

As $C^{B(\sigma,\tau)}$ is monic and $e_1^Te_1=1$, then $G_1^{B(\sigma,\tau)}$ and $\rho_1^{(\sigma,\tau)}$ are not identically zero. Further, $C^{B(\sigma,\tau)}$ is irreducible by Lemma 1 but the minimal polynomial for the projected sequence must divide C^B. Therefore the sequence has C^B for minimal polynomial. Now, this sequence is denoted by $(s_i(\sigma,\tau)) = (e_1^TB(\sigma,\tau)^ie_1)$, and let $H_n(\sigma,\tau)\in\mathbb{F}(\sigma,\tau)^{n\times n}$:

$$H_n(\sigma,\tau) = \begin{bmatrix} s_0(\sigma,\tau) & s_1(\sigma,\tau) & \ldots & s_{n-1}(\sigma,\tau) \\ s_1(\sigma,\tau) & s_2(\sigma,\tau) & \ldots & s_n(\sigma,\tau) \\ \vdots & & \ddots & \vdots \\ s_{n-1}(\sigma,\tau) & s_n(\sigma,\tau) & \ldots & s_{2n-2}(\sigma,\tau) \end{bmatrix}. \quad (9)$$

Since the minimal polynomial of the sequence is of degree n, $H_n(\sigma,\tau)$ is non-singular [18, Eq. (2.6)]. Thus, any s,t with $\det(H_n(s,t))\neq 0$ will yield $f_{e_1}^{B(s,t),e_1} = C^{B(s,t)}$. Now for the complexities:

- The volume of communication is reduced, from $8n$ to $5n$.
- With respect to Theorem 13, the cost for Victor is slightly improved: an application by D replaced by an application by $\Gamma(s,t)$, a dot-product with u replaced by one with e_1, and n operations for $\det(D)$ are replaced by less than $2\lceil\log_2(n)\rceil+1$ to compute t^n+s. The overall verification cost thus decreases from $\mu(A)+15n+o(n)$ to $\mu(A)+13n+o(n)$;
- For Peggy, applying the diagonal scaling costs n per iteration, while applying $\Gamma(s,t)$ costs $2n$ operations per iteration; but applying a random u^T costs about $2n$ operations per iteration, while applying e_1^T is just selecting the first coefficient, so her cost is slightly improved. Then, too choose such s,t, Peggy can try uniformly sampled elements in S, and see whether $\deg(f_{e_1}^{B(s,t),e_1})=n$. Since $\deg(\Gamma(\sigma,\tau))=1$, we have that $\deg(s_i(\sigma,\tau))\leq i$ and $\deg(\det(H_n(\sigma,\tau)))\leq n(n-1)$. Hence, by the DeMillo-Lipton/Schwartz/Zippel Lemma

$$\text{Prob}\left(\det(H_n(s,t))\neq 0\right) \geq 1-\frac{n(n-1)}{|S|}. \quad (10)$$

As soon as $|S|\geq 2n(n-1)$, the probability of success for Peggy is thus larger than $1/2$ and the expected number of trials is less than 2. □

We gather the differences between the protocols of Figure 4 and 5 in Table 1. The two certificate differ mostly only in the preconditioning. But this allows to gain a lot of randomization: the number of random field elements per try to sample for Peggy is reduced

Certificates for the determinant of sparse matrices		
Preconditioner	$\S 6 : D$	$\S 7 : \Gamma(t, s)$
Verifier	$\mu(A) + 15n + o(n)$	$\mu(A) + 13n + o(n)$
Communications	$8n$	$5n$
Random elements	$3n + 2$	3
Prover	$\text{MinPoly}(n) + \text{LinSys}(n)$	
Field size	$\geq \frac{1}{2}(n^2 - n)$	$\geq n^2 - n$

Table 1: Summary of the complexity bounds of the certificates presented in this paper for the determinant of sparse matrices (n is the dimension, $\mu(A)$ bounds the cost of one matrix-vector product, $\text{MinPoly}(n)$ (resp. $\text{LinSys}(n)$) is the cost of computing the minimal polynomial of a sequence (resp. of solving a linear system).

from $3n$ to only 2. As the size of the set is $\Omega(n^2)$, this reduces the number of random bits from $O(n \log(n))$ to $O(\log(n))$.

REMARK 15 (CERTIFICATE FOR THE CHARACTERISTIC POLYNOMIAL). The certificate for the determinant can be combined with the characteristic polynomial reduction of [9, Figure 1]. As this reduction is linear for Victor, this then provides now also a *linear* time verification procedure for the characteristic polynomial:

1. Peggy sends c^A as the characteristic polynomial;
2. Victor now sends back a random point $r \in S \subseteq \mathbb{F}$;
3. Peggy and Victor enter a determinant certificate for $rI - A$;
4. Once convinced, Victor checks that $\det(rI - A) \stackrel{?}{=} c^A(r)$.

For a random $r \in S$, in the determinant sub-certificate, $rI - A$ will be non-singular if $c^A(r) \neq 0$, hence with probability $\geq 1 - n/|S|$. Then $\det(rI - A)$ is certified using the certificate of Figure 5.

Best known algorithms for computing the characteristic polynomial, using either quadratic space and fast matrix multiplication or linear space [28], have cost $O(n^{2+\alpha})$ for some $\alpha > 0$. The characteristic polynomial with $\mu(A) = O(n)$ is thus an example of a problem whose worst-case complexity bound is super-quadratic in the verification cost $O(n)$.

8. REFERENCES

[1] B. Beckerman and G. Labahn. A uniform approach for the fast computation of matrix-type Padé approximants. *SIAM Journal on Matrix Analysis and Applications*, 15(3):804–823, July 1994.

[2] G. Bertoni, J. Daemen, M. Peeters, and G. Assche. Sponge-based pseudo-random number generators. In S. Mangard and F.-X. Standaert, editors, *CHES 2010*, pages 33–47. Springer, 2010.

[3] L. Chen, W. Eberly, E. L. Kaltofen, B. D. Saunders, W. J. Turner, and G. Villard. Efficient matrix preconditioners for black box linear algebra. *Linear Algebra Appl.*, 343-344:119–146, 2002. www.math.ncsu.edu/ kaltofen/bibliography/02/CEKSTV02.pdf.

[4] K.-M. Chung, Y. T. Kalai, and S. P. Vadhan. Improved delegation of computation using fully homomorphic encryption. In T. Rabin, editor, *CRYPTO 2010*, volume 6223 of *Lecture Notes in Computer Science*, pages 483–501. Springer, 2010.

[5] D. Coppersmith. Solving homogeneous linear equations over GF(2) via block Wiedemann algorithm. *Mathematics of Computation*, 62(205):333–350, Jan. 1994.

[6] R. J. F. Cramer. *Modular Design Of Secure Yet Practical Cryptographic Protocols*. PhD thesis, U. van Amsterdam, Jan. 1997.

[7] R. A. DeMillo and R. J. Lipton. A probabilistic remark on algebraic program testing. *Inf. Process. Letters*, 7(4):193–195, June 1978.

[8] J.-G. Dumas, E. Kaltofen, and E. Thomé. Certificates for the verification of Wiedemann's Krylov sequence. Technical report, arXiv:, Jan. 2016. arxiv.org/abs/1507.01083.

[9] J.-G. Dumas and E. L. Kaltofen. Essentially optimal interactive certificates in linear algebra. In K. Nabeshima, editor, *ISSAC'2014*, pages 146–153. ACM Press, New York, July 2014. www.math.ncsu.edu/ kaltofen/bibliography/14/DuKa14.pdf.

[10] W. Eberly and E. Kaltofen. On randomized Lanczos algorithms. In Küchlin [21], pages 176–183. www.math.ncsu.edu/ kaltofen/bibliography/97/EbKa97.pdf.

[11] A. Fiat and A. Shamir. How to prove yourself: Practical solutions to identification and signature problems. In A. M. Odlyzko, editor, *Advances in Cryptology - CRYPTO'86*, volume 263 of *Lecture Notes in Computer Science*, pages 186–194. Springer, 11–15 Aug. 1986.

[12] D. Fiore and R. Gennaro. Publicly verifiable delegation of large polynomials and matrix computations, with applications. In *ACM CCS '12*, pages 501–512, New York, NY, USA, 2012. ACM.

[13] R. Freivalds. Fast probabilistic algorithms. In J. Bečvář, editor, *Mathematical Foundations of Computer Science 1979*, volume 74 of *Lecture Notes in Computer Science*, pages 57–69, Olomouc, Czechoslovakia, Sept. 1979. Springer.

[14] C. Gentry, J. Groth, Y. Ishai, C. Peikert, A. Sahai, and A. Smith. Using fully homomorphic hybrid encryption to minimize non-interative zero-knowledge proofs. *Journal of Cryptology*, pages 1–24, 2014.

[15] S. Goldwasser, Y. T. Kalai, and G. N. Rothblum. Delegating computation: interactive proofs for muggles. In C. Dwork, editor, *STOC'2008*, pages 113–122. ACM Press, May 2008.

[16] E. Kaltofen. Analysis of Coppersmith's block Wiedemann algorithm for the parallel solution of sparse linear systems. *Mathematics of Computation*, 64(210):777–806, Apr. 1995. www.math.ncsu.edu/ kaltofen/bibliography/95/Ka95_mathcomp.pdf.

[17] E. Kaltofen and V. Pan. Processor efficient parallel solution of linear systems over an abstract field. In *ACM SPAA '91*, pages 180–191, New York, N.Y., 1991. ACM Press. www.math.ncsu.edu/ kaltofen/bibliography/91/KaPa91.pdf.

[18] E. Kaltofen and G. Villard. On the complexity of computing determinants. *Computational Complexity*, 13(3):91–130, 2005. www.math.ncsu.edu/ kaltofen/bibliography/04/KaVi04_2697263.pdf.

[19] E. L. Kaltofen, B. Li, Z. Yang, and L. Zhi. Exact certification in global polynomial optimization via sums-of-squares of rational functions with rational coefficients. *Journal of Symbolic Computation*, 47(1):1–15, Jan. 2012. www.math.ncsu.edu/ kaltofen/bibliography/09/KLYZ09.pdf.

[20] E. L. Kaltofen, M. Nehring, and B. D. Saunders. Quadratic-time certificates in linear algebra. In A. Leykin, editor, *ISSAC'2011*, pages 171–176. ACM Press, New York, June 2011. www.math.ncsu.edu/ kaltofen/bibliography/11/KNS11.pdf.

[21] W. W. Küchlin, editor. *ISSAC'97*. ACM Press, New York, July 1997.

[22] E. W. Ng, editor. *EUROSAM '79, International Symposium on Symbolic and Algebraic Computation, Marseille, France, June 1979, Proceedings*, volume 72 of *Lecture Notes in Computer Science*. Springer, 1979.

[23] NIST. *FIPS Publication 202: SHA-3 Standard: Permutation-Based Hash and Extendable-Output Functions*, Aug. 2015.

[24] B. Parno, J. Howell, C. Gentry, and M. Raykova. Pinocchio: Nearly practical verifiable computation. In *IEEE SP '13*, pages 238–252, Washington, DC, USA, 2013. IEEE Computer Society.

[25] J. T. Schwartz. Probabilistic algorithms for verification of polynomial identities. In Ng [22], pages 200–215.

[26] J. Thaler. Time-optimal interactive proofs for circuit evaluation. In R. Canetti and J. A. Garay, editors, *CRYPTO '13*, volume 8043 of *Lecture Notes in Computer Science*, pages 71–89. Springer, 2013.

[27] G. Villard. Further analysis of Coppersmith's block Wiedemann algorithm for the solution of sparse linear systems. In Küchlin [21], pages 32–39. perso.ens-lyon.fr/gilles.villard/BIBLIOGRAPHIE/PDF/issac97.pdf.

[28] G. Villard. Computing the Frobenius normal form of a sparse matrix. In *CASC'00*, pages 395–407. Springer, 2000. perso.ens-lyon.fr/gilles.villard/BIBLIOGRAPHIE/PDF/casc.pdf.

[29] D. H. Wiedemann. Solving sparse linear equations over finite fields. *IEEE Transactions on Information Theory*, 32(1):54–62, Jan. 1986.

[30] R. Zippel. Probabilistic algorithms for sparse polynomials. In Ng [22], pages 216–226.

Selecting Algorithms for Black Box Matrices

Checking for Matrix Properties That Can Simplify Computations

Wayne Eberly
Department of Computer Science
University of Calgary
eberly@ucalgary.ca

ABSTRACT

Processes to automate the selection of appropriate algorithms for various matrix computations are described. In particular, processes to check for, and certify, various matrix properties of black-box matrices are presented. These include sparsity patterns and structural properties that allow "superfast" algorithms to be used in place of black-box algorithms. Matrix properties that hold generically, and allow the use of matrix preconditioning to be reduced or eliminated, can also be checked for and certified — notably including in the small-field case, where this presently has the greatest impact on the efficiency of the computation.

1. INTRODUCTION

Krylov-based "black box" algorithms for matrix computations have been used for significant applications in computation number theory. They also form a significant part of the C++ template library LinBox for high-performance matrix computations. These are notable, in part, because of their versatility: Any matrix representation that allows the input matrix (or, for some algorithms, its transpose) to be multiplied by a vector can be supported.

Considerably more efficient algorithms can be used instead if the input matrix is sparse, with nonzero entries limited to specific locations, or satisfies one of various structural properties. As described, for example, by Golub and van Loan [6], Gaussian Elimination can be used quite efficiently to solve banded systems of linear equations. As described by Pan [7], various classes of matrices (including Toeplitz-like and Hankel-like matrices) have various displacement structures that can be used to reduce system solving for these matrices to polynomial arithmetic. Under these circumstances, assistance in selecting algorithms to be employed might of help as the community of users of systems like LinBox grows and non-expert users should be better supported.

Sections 2–4 of this report therefore concern attempts to detect and certify matrix properties to facilitate algorithm selection. The preliminary results given here establish that band matrices and matrices with low displacement rank — including Toeplitz-like and Hankel-like matrices — are easily detected and certified. Furthermore, it is possible to convert matrix representations, in order to allow superfast algorithms to be applied, when such matrices are discovered. As black-box algorithms have been developed several matrix properties have been identified that hold generically and that be exploited — generally by eliminating "matrix preconditioning" — to simplify or accelerate computations without sacrificing reliability. In particular, the cost of system solving can be reduced if the input matrix has a small number of nontrivial nilpotent blocks in its Jordan normal form. Simpler algorithms to compute the rank or characteristic polynomial of a matrix can be applied if the input matrix has a small number of nontrivial invariant factors. Sections 5–7 concern the detection and certification of these properties. A technique of Villard [8] is adapted, for the small-field case, to efficiently check for these properties at a cost linear in that needed to apply Wiedemann's algorithm to compute the minimal polynomial of a matrix. Interactive protocols, of the type recently described by Dumas and Kaltofen [1] are also provided.

Of course, many randomized black box algorithms are Las Vegas, so that one can simply execute algorithms without preconditioning, in hopes that desirable matrix properties are satisfied or that one "gets lucky." The above results may nevertheless be of interest if one considers exchanges between a service provider and client involving the cost of a service that is to be provided: One would hope here that the cost to the service provider (or "prover") would not exceed the lower cost to carry out a computation without preconditioning, while the cost to the client (or "verifier') would be significantly lower than that. Furthermore, a process to certify that preconditioning is necessary would also be of interest. Protocols to certify this are also given.

The expected (and, in a few cases, worst-case) costs established to detect and certify these properties, and for their verification, are as shown in Table 1. In each case, the indicated cost is the number of field operations required for a black-box matrix $A \in \mathsf{F}^{n\times n}$; $\mu \leq n(2n+1)$ is the number of operations required to multiply either A or A^T by a given vector $v \in \mathsf{F}^{n\times 1}$. It is also assumed that $\mu \geq n$. $\mathcal{M}(n)$ is the number of operations in F required for arithmetic in an extension E of F with logarithmic degree, so that $\mathcal{M}(n) \in O(\log_2 n \log_2 \log_2 n \log_2 \log_2 \log_2 n)$. The "communication" reports the number of elements of the ground field F (plus, in some cases, bits) that must be communicated between a prover and a verifier — excluding the initial cost

ISSAC '16, July 19-22, 2016, Waterloo, ON, Canada

DOI: http://dx.doi.org/10.1145/2930889.2930894

Property	Detection/Certification	Verification	Communication
Band Matrix	$\Theta(\mu k)$	$\Theta(nk+\mu)$	$\Theta(nk)$
Low Displacement Rank	$\Theta(nk^2+\mu k\log n)$	$\Theta(nk+n\log_2 n+\mu)$	$\Theta(nk+n\log_2 n)$
Few Nontrivial Nilpotent Blocks	$\Theta(n^2k+\mu n)$	$\Theta(nk+\mu)$	$\Theta(nk)$
Many Nontrivial Nilpotent Blocks	$\Theta(n^2k+\mu n)$	$\Theta(nk+\mu)$	$\Theta(nk)$
Few Nontrivial Invariant Factors	$\Theta(n^2\mathcal{M}(n)+n^2k\log_2 n+\mu n\log_2 n)$	$\Theta(n\mathcal{M}(n)+nk+\mu)$	$\Theta(nk+n\log_2 n)$
Many Nontrivial Invariant Factors	$\Theta(n^2\mathcal{M}(n)+n^2k\log_2 n+\mu n\log_2 n)$	$\Theta(n\mathcal{M}(n)+nk+\mu)$	$\Theta(nk+n\log_2 n)$

Table 1: Summary of Results

to communicate a black box matrix $A \in \mathsf{F}^{n\times n}$, parameter k and error tolerance ϵ. In typical applications one might expect k to be significantly smaller than n — indeed, polylogarithmic. The cost to check for band structure or low displacement rank, and return the information needed for superfast algorithms to be applied when they can, is significantly dominated by the cost to use a black box algorithm to complete a computation instead, in this case.

A proof of one key claim — Theorem 5.2 — has been omitted. This can be proved using a rather lengthly combinatorial argument. The complete proof is available in a longer version of this report [4].

2. BAND STRUCTURE

Let $A \in \mathsf{F}^{n\times n}$ and let k be a positive constant. Let us say that A is a ***band matrix*** with ***band width*** k if the entry $a_{i,j}$ of A in row i and column j is equal to 0 whenever $1 \le i,j \le n$ and $|i-j| > k$. Golub and van Loan [6] describe efficient algorithms, based on Gaussian Elimination, for computations on such matrices.

As shown below the detection and certification of a black-box matrix that is a band matrix, and conversion to a representation allowing other algorithms to be used, is surprisingly easy. Indeed, this is included, in part, to provide a very simple first example.

The objective of this section is to prove the following.

THEOREM 2.1. *It is possible to check whether a matrix $A \in \mathsf{F}^{n\times n}$ is a band matrix, with band width k, by selecting n values uniformly and independently from a finite subset S of F and by performing $\Theta(\mu k)$ arithmetic operations over F. If A is, indeed, a band matrix, then this is confirmed with certainty. Otherwise the probability that A is mistaken for a band matrix is at most $1/|S|$.*

A certificate with size $\Theta(nk)$ — which also allows algorithms for band matrix computations to be applied to A — can be supplied when A is a band matrix. This certificate can be verified by selecting n entries uniformly and independently from a set S, as above, and using $\Theta(nk+\mu)$ arithmetic operations over F. Once again if A is, indeed, a band matrix and the certificate is correct, then it is accepted with certainty. If the certificate it is incorrect then it is accepted with probability at most $1/|S|$.

2.1 Detection and Certification

Let $K = 2k+1$ and, for $1 \le i \le K$, let $\alpha_{K,i} \in \mathsf{F}^{n\times 1}$ such that, for $1 \le j \le n$, the jth entry of $\alpha_{K,i}$ is equal to one if $j \equiv i \bmod k$ and is zero otherwise. If A has band width k then no two (or more) of columns $i, i+K, i+2K, \dots$ of A have nonzero entries in the same row. The nonzero entries of these columns can therefore simply be read off as entries of the vector $A \cdot \alpha_{K,i}$ — and all of the nonzero entries of A can be read off the nonzero entries of each of the vectors $A\cdot\alpha_{K,1}, A\cdot\alpha_{K,2}, \dots, A\cdot\alpha_{K,K}$. Consequently, $K = 2k+1$ multiplications of A by vectors suffice for the prover to produce a representation of A as a band matrix with band width k if it indeed has this structure.

Of course, this should not be delivered to a verifier without being checked. It is possible that there is no band matrix $\widehat{A} \in \mathsf{F}^{n\times n}$, with band width k, such that $A\alpha_{K,i} = \widehat{A}\alpha_{K,i}$ for $1 \le i \le K$ — for it may be necessary for a matrix to have off-band entries in some of columns $k+1, k+2, \dots, K$ or $n-K, n-K+1, \dots, n-k-1$ in order for it to satisfy these equations — and one should stop here if this is the case.

Otherwise the band matrix $\widehat{A}$ that satisfies these conditions is unique and it suffices to check that $A = \widehat{A}$. An application of the test of Frievalds [5] suffices to check this: A vector $x \in \mathsf{F}^{n\times 1}$, whose entries are chosen uniformly and independently from a finite subset S of F, should be selected by the prover, and it should be checked whether $Ax = \widehat{A}x$. If this is not the case then $A \ne \widehat{A}$ and, once again, one should stop.

On the other hand, it is easily checked that if $A \ne \widehat{A}$, and x is chosen as above, then the probability that $Ax = \widehat{A}x$ is at most $1/|S|$ — so that, provided that S is sufficiently large, the prover should deliver a certificate so that a verification stage can proceed.

2.2 Verification

The certificate provided to the verifier, at this point, should simply be a representation of A as a band matrix — presumably provided as an $n \times (2k+1)$ array reporting the entries within the bands of A.

This can be verified using an independent repetition of the Frievalds test described above.

Since the product of a band matrix $A \in \mathsf{F}^{k\times k}$ (with band width k) and a vector $x \in \mathsf{F}^{n\times 1}$ can be computed using $\Theta(nk)$ field operations and zero tests, Theorem 2.1 is now immediate — assuming, again, that $\mu \ge n$.

3. LOW MATRIX RANK

The following is less general than the protocol of Dumas and Kaltofen [1] to certify matrix rank and, therefore, inferior in at least one significant respect. However, it can be used in the special case needed here: One is certifying that the rank of $A \in \mathsf{F}^{n\times n}$ is at most k, when k is significantly smaller than n. It also includes the construction of an alternative representation of A as needed to support the claims in Section 4.

Suppose now that $A \in \mathsf{F}^{n\times n}$ has positive rank $r \le k$. Then there exist permutation matrices $P, Q \in \mathsf{F}^{n\times n}$, matrices $L \in \mathsf{F}^{(n-r)\times r}$ and $R \in \mathsf{F}^{r\times(n-r)}$, and a nonsingular matrix $C \in$

$\mathsf{F}^{r\times r}$, such that

$$A = P \times \begin{bmatrix} I_r \\ L \end{bmatrix} \times C \times \begin{bmatrix} I_r & R \end{bmatrix} \times Q. \qquad (3.1)$$

The objective of this section is to establish the following.

LEMMA 3.1. *It is possible to check whether a matrix $A \in \mathsf{F}^{n\times n}$ has rank at most k, by selecting $\Theta(nk)$ values uniformly and independently from a finite subset S of F and performing $(nk^2 + \mu k \log n)$ arithmetic operations in F and $\Theta(n \log_2 n)$ operations on bits. This process fails with probability at most $(\min(r,k)+1)/|S|$, where r is the rank of A, and only by returning an estimate of the rank of A that is too low.*

If A has rank at most k then a decomposition of A, as shown at line (3.1), can be computed at the above cost and returned as a certificate. This certificate can be verified by choosing n values uniformly and independently from a finite subset S of F and performing $\Theta(nk+\mu)$ arithmetic operations in F and $\Theta(n \log_2 n)$ operations on bits. If the certificate is correct then it is accepted with certainty. Otherwise it is accepted with probability at most $1/|S|$.

3.1 Detection and Certification

Since the rank of A cannot exceed that of C, no decomposition as shown at line (3.1) can exist unless the rank of A is at most k. A prover can check for this condition by attempting to construct the matrices included in this decomposition, along with C^{-1}.

Let $0 \le \ell \le k$ and suppose indices $i_1, i_2, \dots, i_\ell$ of rows and $j_1, j_2, \dots, j_\ell$ of columns of an $\ell\times\ell$ nonsingular submatrix C_ℓ of A have been computed, along with the matrix C_ℓ^{-1}.

If $\ell = 0$ then the prover should begin by generating n values uniformly and independently from a finite subset S of F and using these as the entries of a vector $x \in \mathsf{F}^{n\times 1}$. If A is nonzero then $Ax \ne 0$ with probability $1 - 1/|S|$ — so that (if $|S|$ is sufficiently large) the prover may conclude that the rank of A is zero, if $Ax = 0$, and proceed to delivery of a certificate.

Otherwise x should be used to locate a nonzero column of A. Suppose that x has h nonzero entries. Set $x_1, x_2 \in \mathsf{F}^{m\times 1}$ such that x_1 has $\lceil h/2\rceil$ nonzero entries, x_2 has $\lfloor h/2 \rfloor$ nonzero entries, and $x = x_1 + x_2$. One should check whether $Ax_1 = 0$ — replacing x with x_1 if this is not the case, and replacing x with x_2 otherwise, since $Ax_2 = Ax \ne 0$ in this second case. Iterating this process at most $\lceil \log_2 n\rceil$ times, a vector $x \in \mathsf{F}^{n\times 1}$ such that $Ax \ne 0$, and x has a single nonzero entry in some position j_1, is obtained — establishing that the j_1^{th} column of A is nonzero. This column has now been computed, as Ax, and i_1 can be chosen to be any integer such that $1 \le i_1 \le n$ and the entry α of A in row i_1 and column j_1 is nonzero — so that

$$C_1 = \begin{bmatrix}\alpha\end{bmatrix} \quad \text{and} \quad C_1^{-1} = \begin{bmatrix}\alpha^{-1}\end{bmatrix}.$$

If $\ell > 0$ then the prover should begin, once again, by forming the vector x as described above. The prover should continue by computing the matrix-vector product $v = Ax$, and setting $y \in \mathsf{F}^{\ell\times 1}$ to be the vector such that, for $1 \le h \le \ell$, the entry of y in position h is the entry of v in position i_h.

The vector $z = C_\ell^{-1} y \in \mathsf{F}^{\ell\times 1}$ should next be computed. Let $w \in \mathsf{F}^{n\times 1}$ be the vector such that, for $1 \le h \le \ell$, the entry of w in position j_h is the entry of z in position h, and such that all other entries of w are zero. Finally, set $u = v - A\cdot w$ — noting that v is in the space spanned by columns $j_1, j_2, \dots, j_\ell$ of A if and only if $u = 0$.

If the rank of A is equal to ℓ then u must always be equal to zero; u is nonzero with probability at least $1 - 1/|S|$ otherwise. Consequently if $u = 0$ then the prover should proceed with the completion of a certificate, as described below.

Otherwise, if x has h nonzero entries then one should once again set $x_1, x_2 \in \mathsf{F}^{n\times 1}$ such that x_1 has $\lceil h/2\rceil$ entries, x_2 has $\lfloor h/2\rfloor$ entries, and $x = x_1 + x_2$. The above process should be applied to x_1 (instead of x) to check whether Ax_1 is in the space spanned by columns $j_1, j_2, \dots, j_\ell$ of A — replacing x with x_1 if this is not the case, and replacing x with x_2 otherwise. Iterating this process at most $\lceil\log_2 n\rceil$ times one eventually obtains a vector $x \in \mathsf{F}^{n\times 1}$ such that Ax is not in the space spanned by columns $j_1, j_2, \dots, j_\ell$ of A and x has a single nonzero entry in some position $j_{\ell+1}$. This establishes that the $j_{\ell+1}^{\text{th}}$ column of A is not in the space spanned by columns $j_1, j_2, \dots, j_\ell$ — and that columns $j_1, j_2, \dots, j_{\ell+1}$ of A are linearly independent.

One should next compute the vector $u \in \mathsf{F}^{n\times 1}$, as described above, corresponding to the final choice of the vector x — so that $u \ne 0$. It suffices to choose $i_{\ell+1}$ such that $1 \le i_{\ell+1} \le n$ and the $i_{\ell+1}^{\text{th}}$ entry of u is nonzero in order to ensure that the submatrix $C_{\ell+1}$ of A, including entries in rows $i_1, i_2, \dots, i_{\ell+1}$ and columns $j_1, j_2, \dots, j_{\ell+1}$, is nonsingular.

Note next that

$$C_{\ell+1} = \begin{bmatrix} C_\ell & s \\ t & \alpha \end{bmatrix}$$

for vectors $s \in \mathsf{F}^{\ell\times 1}$ and $t \in \mathsf{F}^{1\times \ell}$, and for some value $\alpha \in \mathsf{F}$. Since C_ℓ is nonsingular,

$$C_{\ell+1} = \begin{bmatrix} I_\ell & 0 \\ tC_\ell^{-1} & 1 \end{bmatrix} \cdot \begin{bmatrix} C_\ell & 0 \\ 0 & \beta \end{bmatrix} \cdot \begin{bmatrix} I_\ell & C_\ell^{-1}s \\ 0 & 1 \end{bmatrix}$$

where $\beta = \alpha - tC_\ell^{-1}s$. Now $\beta \ne 0$, since $C_{\ell+1}$ is also nonsingular, and

$$\begin{aligned} C_{\ell+1}^{-1} &= \begin{bmatrix} I_\ell & -C_\ell^{-1}s \\ 0 & 1 \end{bmatrix} \cdot \begin{bmatrix} C_\ell^{-1} & 0 \\ 0 & \beta^{-1} \end{bmatrix} \cdot \begin{bmatrix} I_\ell & 0 \\ -tC_\ell^{-1} & 1 \end{bmatrix} \\ &= \begin{bmatrix} C_\ell^{-1} + (C_\ell^{-1}s)\cdot(\beta^{-1}tC_\ell^{-1}) & -C_\ell^{-1}s\beta^{-1} \\ -\beta^{-1}tC_\ell^{-1} & \beta^{-1} \end{bmatrix}. \end{aligned}$$

Since $C_\ell^{-1}s \in \mathsf{F}^{\ell\times 1}$ and $\beta^{-1}tC_\ell^{-1} \in \mathsf{F}^{1\times\ell}$, this expression for $C_{\ell+1}^{-1}$ can be used to compute the entries of $C_{\ell+1}^{-1}$ using $\Theta(\ell^2)$ operations in F. The value ℓ can now be incremented and the above process repeated.

If this process is iterated until $\ell = k+1$, then the rank of A is greater than k and one can stop. Otherwise the rank $r \le k$ of A has been obtained, along with the matrix $C = C_r \in \mathsf{F}^{r\times r}$ shown at line (3.1), and the indices of the rows and columns of this matrix in A.

The permutation matrices P and Q, shown at line (3.1), can each be concisely represented as an integer array, with length n, whose i^{th} entry is the index of the nonzero entry in row i of the permutation matrix. Since the first r entries of this representation of Q are the indices $j_1, j_2, \dots, j_r$, it is not difficult to compute this representation of Q using $O(n)$ operations on integers whose binary representations have length $O(\log n)$: The only operations required are the initialization of these arrays, comparisons of integers and assignments of values. If a first array is initially sorted and a second integer array is used to maintain the locations of each of $1, 2, \dots, n$ in the initial array then one can reorder

$1, 2, \ldots, n$ in order to obtain this representation of Q using $O(r)$ exchanges of values in this array. The second of these arrays then provides a corresponding representation of Q^T. Since the initial entries of a representation of P^T are the indices $i_1, i_2, \ldots, i_r$, a representation of P^T and P can be computed in the same way using $O(n)$ operations on integers with length in $O(\log n)$ as well.

It remains only to notice that if $A_L \in \mathsf{F}^{n\times r}$ is the matrix including columns $j_1, j_2, \ldots, j_r$ of A, and $A_R \in \mathsf{F}^{r\times n}$ is the matrix including rows $i_1, i_2, \ldots, i_r$ of A, then

$$\begin{bmatrix} I_r \\ L \end{bmatrix} = P^T \cdot A_L \cdot C^{-1} \qquad \text{and} \qquad \begin{bmatrix} I_r & R \end{bmatrix} = C^{-1} \cdot A_R \cdot Q^T.$$

Since C^{-1} has already been computed, L and R can be computed using $O(nr^2)$ additional arithmetic operations in F and $\Theta(n \log_2 n)$ operations on bits.

A consideration of the above confirms that $\Theta(nk^2 + k\mu \log n)$ arithmetic operations in F and $\Theta(n \log_2 n)$ operations on bits have been used, in the worst case, to check whether the rank of A is at most k, and to compute the rank and the decomposition at line (3.1) if this is the case. This process can only fail due to unlucky choices of the randomly selected vectors $x \in \mathsf{F}^{n\times 1}$, described above. Since each selection fails with probability at most $1/|S|$ and at most $\min(r, k) + 1$ such vectors must be selected if A has rank r, the total probability of failure is at most $(r+1)/|S|$ if $r \le k$ and at most $(k+1)/|S|$ otherwise.

3.2 Verification

Once again, it suffices to apply the Frievalds test to verify that A is the zero matrix, if the reported rank is zero, or that the decomposition of A, shown at line (3.1), is correct otherwise. An examination of this decomposition confirms that this test can be carried out at the cost stated in the above lemma.

4. LOW DISPLACEMENT RANK

For $\alpha \in \mathsf{F}$, the $n \times n$ ***α-circulant matrix Z_α*** is the matrix

$$Z_f = \begin{bmatrix} 0 & & & & \alpha \\ 1 & 0 & & & \\ & 1 & & & \\ & & \ddots & & \\ & & & 0 & \\ & & & 1 & 0 \end{bmatrix} \in \mathsf{F}^{n\times n}$$

whose entry in row $i+1$ and column i is 1 for $1 \le i \le n-1$, whose entry in row 1 and column n is α, and all of whose other entries are zero. Consider the following linear operators on matrices in $\mathsf{F}^{n\times n}$:

- $\varphi_T(A) = Z_1 \cdot A - A \cdot Z_0$.
- $\varphi_H(A) = Z_1 \cdot A - A \cdot Z_0^T$.
- $\varphi_{TH}(A) = (Z_0 + Z_0^T) \cdot A - A \cdot (Z_0 + Z_0^T)$.

A matrix $A \in \mathsf{F}^{n\times n}$ is ***Toeplitz-like*** (respectively, ***Hankel-like***, and ***Toeplitz+Hankel-like***) if the rank of the matrix $\varphi_T(A)$ (respectively, $\varphi_H(A)$, and $\varphi_{TH}(A)$) is small relative to n. The matrix $\varphi_T(A)$ (respectively, $\varphi_H(A)$ or $\varphi_{TH}(A)$) is called the ***operator matrix*** and rank of this matrix is said to be the ***displacement rank*** of A. As described, for example, by Pan [7], a variety of matrix computations have "superfast algorithms" if the displacement rank of a matrix is low. Indeed, if the displacement rank is polylogarithmic in n then the worst-case running times of these algorithms are generally within a polylogarithmic factor of linear in n. A black box for multiplication of $\varphi_T(A)$ ($\varphi_H(A)$ or $\varphi_{TH}(A)$) by a vector is trivially obtained by applying a black box for multiplication of A by a vector, twice, and performing $O(n)$ additional operations in F. The following, is therefore, immediate from Lemma 3.1.

THEOREM 4.1. *One can check whether a matrix $A \in \mathsf{F}^{n\times n}$ is Toeplitz-like, Hankel-like, or Toeplitz+Hankel-like, with displacement rank at most k, and return a representation of the operator matrix of A allowing a superfast algorithm to be applied to A if this is the case.*
The cost to check for these properties, produce and return the above representation of the operator matrix, and verify it — and the probabilities and types of failures of these processes — are as described in Lemma 3.1 for the detection, certification and verification of a matrix with low rank.

5. ADDITIVE CONDITIONERS

Recall that the ***invariant factors*** of a matrix $A \in \mathsf{F}^{n\times n}$ are monic polynomials $\varphi_1, \varphi_2, \ldots, \varphi_m \in \mathsf{F}[z]$, each with positive degree, such that φ_i is divisible by φ_{i+1} for $1 \le i \le m-1$ and such that A is similar to a block diagonal matrix with the companion matrices of the polynomials $\varphi_1, \varphi_2, \ldots, \varphi_m$ as its blocks. In this case φ_1 is the minimal polynomial of A. An invariant factor φ_i is a ***nontrivial invariant factor*** if $\varphi_i \ne z$ — for its companion matrix is different from the 1×1 zero matrix in this case. Additional (trivial) "invariant factors "' $\varphi_i = 1$ will occasionally be added, below, to simplify technical statements.

The number of invariant factors divisible by z^2 is of interest because this is the same as the number of "nontrivial nilpotent blocks" (companion matrices of polynomials z^j for $j \ge 2$) in a Jordan normal form for A.

A technique of Villard [8], developed to provide a black box algorithm for computation of the Frobenius normal form, leads to an efficient interactive protocol to bound the number of nontrivial nilpotent blocks. In combination with a recent protocol of Dumas, Kaltofen, Thomé and Villard [2] to certify of the minimal polynomial of a matrix, this leads to an efficient protocol to bound the number of nontrivial invariant factors of a matrix as well.

In particular, the following result of Villard [8, Lemma 1] is of use here.

THEOREM 5.1 (VILLARD [8]). *Let $A, B \in \mathsf{F}^{n\times n}$ such that the rank of B is at most k. If $s_1, s_2, \ldots s_n$ are the invariant factors of A and $\sigma_1, \sigma_2, \ldots, \sigma_n$ are the invariant factors of $A+B$ then s_i is divisible by σ_{i+k} in $\mathsf{F}[z]$ for $1 \le i \le n-k$.*

Villard also provided a result — [8, Theorem 2] — which is of use to confirm that A *does* not have k or more nontrivial nilpotent blocks, or nontrivial invariant factors, when F is sufficiently large. The following result complements Villard's result by allowing this to be checked for, when k is small, and when F is a very small finite field — the case where "preconditioning" is generally most complicated and expensive, so that the assurance that preconditioning can be avoided might be of greatest interest.

THEOREM 5.2. *Let $A \in \mathsf{F}^{n\times n}$ where F is a finite field with size q. Let $B = V \cdot U$ where $U \in \mathsf{F}^{k\times n}$, $V \in \mathsf{F}^{n\times k}$, and the* *entries of U and V are selected uniformly and independently from* F.

(a) *If A has at most k nontrivial nilpotent blocks then the minimal polynomial of $A+B$ is not divisible by z^2 with probability at least*

$$\rho_1(q) = \left(1 - \frac{2q^{-2}}{q-1}\right) \cdot (1-q^{-1})^4.$$

(b) *If A has at most k nontrivial invariant factors and $f \in \mathsf{F}[z]$ is an irreducible polynomial with degree d such that $f \neq z$, then the probability that f does not divide the minimal polynomial of $A + B$ is at least*

$$\rho_2(q) = \left(1 - \frac{2q^{-2}}{q-1}\right) \cdot (1-q^{-1})^3$$

if $d = 1$, and at least

$$\begin{aligned}\rho_3(q,d) &= \left(1 - \frac{q^{-d}}{q^d-1}\right)^3 \cdot (1-q^{-d})^3 \\ &\geq \left(1 - \frac{1}{q^d-1}\right)^3 \geq 1 - \frac{3}{q^d-1}\end{aligned}$$

if $d \geq 2$.

A complete proof of Theorem 5.2 can be found in [4]. The matrix B, mentioned here, may be viewed as an ***additive preconditioner'*** being applied to A.

6. NONTRIVIAL NILPOTENT BLOCKS

Recall that a nilpotent block in the Jordan form of a matrix $A \in \mathsf{F}^{n\times n}$ is ***nontrivial*** if has order at least two — so that the minimal polynomial of this block is z^j for $j \geq 2$. The purpose of this section is to establish the following.

THEOREM 6.1. *It is possible to decide whether a matrix $A \in \mathsf{F}^{n\times n}$ has at most k nontrivial nilpotent blocks, in such a way that the incorrect decision is reached with probability at most ϵ for any positive constant ϵ. The cost to do so includes the selection of $\Theta(nk)$ values uniformly and independently from F and $\Theta(n^2k + \mu n)$ arithmetic operations in F.*
It is also possible both to certify that A has at most k nontrivial nilpotent blocks and to certify that A has more than k nontrivial nilpotent blocks. In both cases the verifier is guaranteed to accept if the prover's information is correct. The verifier accepts with probability at most ϵ if the prover's information is incorrect.
For both protocols, the expected cost for the prover to complete the protocol is dominated by the worst-case cost for the initial decision stage, as given above. The cost for the verifier, when confirming that A has at most k nontrivial nilpotent blocks, includes the selection of $\Theta(n)$ values, uniformly and independently from F, and $\Theta(nk + \mu)$ arithmetic operations in F. The cost for the verifier, when confirming that A has more than k nontrivial nilpotent blocks, includes the selection of $\Theta(nk)$ values, uniformly and independently from F, and $\Theta(nk + \mu)$ arithmetic operations in F.

6.1 Detection

Let $\sigma(2) = 22$, $\sigma(3) = 4$, $\sigma(4) = \sigma(5) = 2$, $\sigma(q) = 1$ when $7 \leq q \leq 13$ and $\sigma(q) = 2$ when $q \geq 16$. It is easily checked that if $\rho(q)$ is as given in Theorem 5.2, for every prime power q, then $(1-\rho(q))^{\sigma(q)} \leq 1/2$ when $2 \leq q \leq 13$ and $(1-\rho(q))^{\sigma(q)} \leq q^{-1}$ when $q \geq 16$.
In order to check whether a black-box matrix $A \in \mathsf{F}^{n\times n}$ has at most k nontrivial invariant factors, when $\mathsf{F} = \mathsf{F}_q$, and to ensure that the probability of an incorrect decision is at most a positive constant ϵ, the prover should select τ pairs of matrices $U_i \in \mathsf{F}^{k\times n}$ and $V_i \in \mathsf{F}^{n\times k}$, for $1 \leq i \leq \tau$, by choosing the entries of these matrices uniformly and independently from F — where $\tau = \lceil \log_2(2\cdot\epsilon^{-1})\rceil \cdot \sigma(q)$ if $2 \leq q \leq 13$ and $\tau = \lceil \log_q(2\cdot\epsilon^{-1})\rceil \cdot \sigma(q)$ if $q \geq 16$.
Suppose first that A has more than k nilpotent blocks, so that the $k+1^{\text{st}}$ invariant factor of A is divisible by z^2. Then it follows by Theorem 5.1, above, that the minimal polynomial of $A + V_i \cdot U_i$ is divisible by z^2 for all i.
For every such matrix it is easily checked, in this case, that if $u_{i,j}, v_{i,j} \in \mathsf{F}^{n\times 1}$ are chosen uniformly and independently from $\mathsf{F}^{n\times 1}$ then the minimal polynomial of the linearly recurrent sequence

$$u_{i,j}^T v_{i,j}, u_{i,j}^T(A + V_i \cdot U_i)v_{i,j}, u_{i,j}^T(A + V_i \cdot U_i)^2 v_{i,j}, \ldots \quad (6.1)$$

is also divisible by z^2 with probability at least $(1-1/q)^2$ — which is equal to $1/4$ if $q = 2$, and greater than $1 - 2/q$ if $q \geq 3$. Consequently, if $\lambda = \lceil \log_{4/3}(2\cdot\tau\cdot\epsilon^{-1})\rceil$ when $q = 2$, and $\lambda = \lceil \log_{q/2}(2\cdot\tau\cdot\epsilon^{-1})\rceil$ when $q \geq 3$, and pairs of vectors $u_{i,j}$ and $v_{i,j}$ are chosen uniformly and independently from $\mathsf{F}^{n\times 1}$, for $1 \leq i \leq \tau$ and $1 \leq j \leq \lambda$, then, for each i, the probability there is no integer j such that $1 \leq j \leq \lambda$, and the minimal polynomial of the linear recurrence at line (6.1) is divisible by z^2, is at most $\epsilon/(2\tau)$. The probability that it has not been confirmed that the minimal polynomial of $A + V_i \cdot U_i$ is divisible by z^2, for all i such that $1 \leq i \leq \tau$, is therefore certainly at most $\epsilon/2 < \epsilon$ in this case.
It follows that — for fixed q and ϵ — the number of applications of Wiedemann's algorithm needed to compute the minimal polynomials of sequences as above and confirm the above condition, with the desired reliability, is a constant.
On the other hand, a straightforward calculation (involving τ, as given above) and an application of Theorem 5.2(a) establishes that if A has at most k nontrivial factors then this process fails — because the minimal polynomial of every matrix $A + V_i \cdot U_i$, such that $1 \leq i \leq \tau$, is divisible by z^2 —with probability at most $\epsilon/2$.
One should again try to compute the minimal polynomial of each matrix $A + V_i \cdot U_i$ by computing the minimal polynomials of linearly recurrent sequences of the form shown at line (6.1) for λ uniformly and independently pairs of vectors $u_{i,j}, v_{i,j} \in F^{n\times 1}$. If $1 \leq i \leq \tau$ and the minimal polynomial of $A + V_iU_i$ is not divisible by z^2, then the minimal polynomial of the linear recurrent sequence shown at line (6.1) is not divisible by z^2, either, for any j that $1 \leq j \leq \lambda$. On the other hand, it follows by the above analysis that there will exist an integer j such that $1 \leq j \leq \lambda$ and the minimal polynomial of the above linearly recurrent sequence is divisible by z^2, for every integer i such that $1 \leq i \leq \tau$ and the minimal polynomial of $A + V_i \cdot U_i$ is divisible by z^2, with probability at least $1 - \epsilon/2$. In this case a pair of matrices $U \in \mathsf{F}^{k\times n}$ and $V \in \mathsf{F}^{n\times k}$, such that the minimal polynomial of $A + V \cdot U$ is not divisible by z^2, can be selected by choosing any one of the pairs of matrices U_i and V_i that have not been eliminated using the above process. The probability that either this case has not been correctly identified, or a pair of matrices U and V as described above has not been correctly selected, is at most ϵ.

Since the cost to multiply $A + V \cdot U$ by a vector $v \in \mathsf{F}^{n\times 1}$, includes the cost, μ, to multiply A by a vector, along with $\Theta(nk)$ additional operations, it is straightforward to modify the analysis of Wiedemann's algorithm in order to conclude that the cost of the above process includes the uniform and independent selection of $\Theta(nk)$ values from F, along with $\Theta(n^2k + \mu n)$ arithmetic operations in F, as claimed.

6.2 Few Nilpotent Blocks: Certification and Verification

If the prover has determined that A has at most k nontrivial nilpotent blocks, as described above, then the prover should ***commit*** by sending matrices $U \in \mathsf{F}^{k\times n}$ and $V \in \mathsf{F}^{n\times k}$, such that the minimal polynomial of $A + V \cdot U$ is not divisible by z^2, to the verifier: These have now been obtained.

It is easily checked, by consideration of a rational Jordan form, that if the minimal polynomial of a matrix $B \in \mathsf{F}^{n\times n}$ is not divisible by z^2, then a system $Bx = b$ is consistent (for a given vector $b \in \mathsf{F}^{n\times 1}$), if and only if the system $B^2x = b$ is consistent as well. On the other hand, if the minimal polynomial of B is divisible by z^2 and a vector $c \in \mathsf{F}^{n\times n}$ is selected uniformly and independently, then the probability that the system $B^2x = Bc$ is consistent is at most $|\mathsf{F}|^{-1}$.

The verifier may therefore form a ***challenge*** by selecting $\gamma = \lceil \log_q \epsilon^{-1} \rceil$ vectors $c_1, c_2, \dots, c_\gamma$ uniformly and independently from $\mathsf{F}^{n\times 1}$ (for $q = |\mathsf{F}|$), computing $b_i = (A + V \cdot U)c_i$ for $1 \le i \le \gamma$, and sending $b_1, b_2, \dots, b_\gamma$ to the prover.

The prover should compute vectors $x_1, x_2, \dots, x_\gamma \in \mathsf{F}^{n\times 1}$ such that $(A + V \cdot U)^2 x_i = b_i$ (possibly by applying Wiedemann's algorithm twice, for each i) and send these to the verifier. Finally, the verifier should check whether the required equalities are satisfied — ***accepting*** if they are, and ***rejecting*** otherwise.

If the prover's information is correct then the verifier accepts with certainty; otherwise the verifier accepts, incorrectly, with probability at most ϵ. The cost to the prover, to complete this protocol, is dominated by the cost of the "detection" stage described above. Since the verifier must only choose $\Theta(n)$ values uniformly and independently from F and multiply a constant number of vectors by $A+V\cdot U$, the number of operations used by the verifier is as claimed.

6.3 Many Nilpotent Blocks: Certification and Verification

If the prover has determined, instead, that A has more than k nontrivial nilpotent blocks, then the prover should ***commit*** by advising the verifier of this.

The verifier should then select matrices $U_i \in \mathsf{F}^{k\times n}$ and $V_i \in \mathsf{F}^{n\times k}$ for $1 \le i \le \tau$, for τ as above, by selecting the entries of these matrices uniformly and independently from F. These matrices should then be sent to the prover as a ***challenge***.

In ***response*** the prover should return vectors $x_i \in \mathsf{F}^{n\times 1}$ such that $(A + V_i \cdot U_i)x_i \ne 0 = (A + V_i \cdot U_i)^2 x_i$ for $1 \le i \le \tau$. The verifier should then ***accept*** if these conditions are all satisfied and ***reject*** otherwise.

Once again, Theorem 5.1 can be used to establish that this protocol is perfectly complete — the verifier accepts with certainty if the prover's information is correct. Theorem 5.2 and a straightforward calculation establishes that it is also sound: If the prover's information is incorrect then the probability that the verifier accepts is at most ϵ.

In order to see that the additional cost for the prover is low, recall that the ***minimal polynomial*** of a matrix $B \in \mathsf{F}^{n\times n}$ and vector $v \in \mathsf{F}^{n\times 1}$ is the monic polynomial $g \in \mathsf{F}[z]$ with least degree such that $g(B)v = 0$. Wiedemann's algorithm can be used to compute the minimal polynomial of $A+V_i\cdot U_i$ and a vector v, as the least common multiple of a number of linearly recurrent sequences as shown at line (6.1), with $v = v_{i,j}$ and uniform and independent choices of the vector $u_{i,j}$. A small number of choices of $u_{i,j}$ suffice to ensure that the minimal polynomial of $(A + V_i \cdot U_i)v$ has been discovered with high probability. Furthermore, if vectors $v_{i,j} \in \mathsf{F}^{n\times 1}$ are chosen uniformly and independently from $\mathsf{F}^{n\times 1}$, for $j = 1, 2, \dots,$, and the minimal polynomial of $A+V_i\cdot U_i$ is divisible by z^2, then the expected number of vectors $v_{i,j}$ that must be considered, before a vector $v = v_{i,j}$ is found such that the minimal polynomial of $A + V_i \cdot U_i$ and v is also divisible by z^2, is at most two.

Suppose now that a vector $v \in \mathsf{F}^{n\times 1}$ has been discovered and it has been confirmed that the minimal polynomial of $A + V_i \cdot U_i$ and v is z^2g for some polynomial $g \in \mathsf{F}[z]$. It suffices to compute and return the vector $x_i = g(A + V_i)v$ in order to satisfy the requirements given above.

The expected cost for the prover to complete this protocol is, once again, dominated by the worst-case cost of the "detection" stage. The cost for the verifier includes the selection of $\Theta(nk)$ values uniformly and independently from F and a constant number of multiplications of $A + V_i \cdot U_i$ by vectors, for matrices $U_i \in \mathsf{F}^{k\times n}$ and $V_i \in \mathsf{F}^{n\times k}$ — establishing the above claim.

7. NONTRIVIAL INVARIANT FACTORS

The purpose of this section is to establish the following.

THEOREM 7.1. *One can decide whether a matrix $A \in \mathsf{F}^{n\times n}$ has at most k nontrivial invariant factors, such that the incorrect decision is made with probability at most ϵ for any positive constant ϵ. The expected cost of this includes the selection of $\Theta(nk)$ values uniformly and independently from F and $\Theta(n^2k + \mu n)$ arithmetic operations in F.*

It is also possible both to certify that A has at most k nontrivial invariant factors and to certify that A has more than k nontrivial invariant factors. In both cases the verifier is guaranteed to accept if the prover's information is correct. The verifier accepts with probability at most ϵ if the prover's information is incorrect.

For both protocols, the expected cost for the prover to complete the protocol is in $O(n^2\mathcal{M}(n) + n^2k\log_2 n + \mu n\log_2 n)$, where $\mathcal{M}(n)$ is the number of operations in F required for an arithmetic operation in a extension E with degree in $O(\log_2 n)$ over F. When certifying that A has at most k nontrivial invariant factors, the verifier selects $O(n\log_2 n)$ values uniformly and independently from F and performs $\Theta(n\mathcal{M}(n) + nk + \mu)$ arithmetic operations in F. When certifying that A has more than k nontrivial invariant factors the verifier selects $O(n\log_2 n + nk)$ values uniformly and independently from F and performs $O(n\mathcal{M}(n) + nk + \mu)$ arithmetic operations in F.

7.1 Detection

The $k + 1^{\text{st}}$ invariant factor φ_{k+1} of A is divisible by z^2 if and only if A has more than k nontrivial nilpotent blocks. The process described in Subsection 6.1 should be applied to check this, with parameters chosen to ensure that the probability of failure is at most $\epsilon/2$.

If φ_{k+1} is not divisible by z^2 then a pair of matrices $U_0 \in \mathsf{F}^{k\times n}$ and $V_0 \in \mathsf{F}^{n\times k}$ have been found such that the minimal polynomial $f_0 \in \mathsf{F}[z]$ of $A + V_0 \cdot U_0$ is not divisible by z^2 — and f_0 has been correctly computed with probability at least $1 - \epsilon/2$ as well. The detection stage should proceed with an attempt to compute a factor $\chi \neq z$ of φ_{k+1} with positive degree, along with a certificate of this factor — or to determine that no such factor exists.

Suppose first that $q = |\mathsf{F}| = 2$. In this case a straightforward variant of the protocol described in Subsection 6.1 can be used either to conclude either that φ_{k+1} is divisible by $z+1$ or to obtain matrices $U_1 \in \mathsf{F}^{k\times n}$ and $V_1 \in \mathsf{F}^{n\times k}$ such that the minimal polynomial $f_1 \in \mathsf{F}[z]$ of $A+V_1 \cdot U_1$ is not divisible by $z+1$. Suppose that this is carried out in such a way that the probability of failure is at most $\epsilon/6$ — so that U_1, V_1 and f_1 have also been obtained with probability at least $1 - \epsilon/6$ as well in the second case.

If it has been determined that φ_{k+1} is not divisible by $z+1$, then a variant of the above protocol should be applied, once again, either to conclude that φ_{k+1} is divisible by z^2+z+1 (the only monic irreducible polynomial in $\mathsf{F}[z]$ with degree two) or to obtain matrices $U_2 \in \mathsf{F}^{k\times n}$ and $V_2 \in \mathsf{F}^{n\times k}$ such that the minimal polynomial $f_2 \in \mathsf{F}[x]$ of $A + V_2 \cdot U_2$ is not divisible by z^2+z+1. Suppose, as above, that this is carried out in such a way that the probability of failure (including failure to compute U_2, V_2 and f_2) is at most $\epsilon/6$.

Suppose, now, that it has been determined that φ_{k+1} is not divisible by z^2+z+1 either. Suppose that an additional three pairs of matrices $U_i \in \mathsf{F}^{k\times n}$ and $V_i \in \mathsf{F}^{n\times k}$ are selected uniformly and independently,for $3 \leq i \leq 5$. Then, since $1 - \rho_3(2, d) \leq 3/(2^d - 1)$ for $d \geq 4$, there are only two monic irreducible polynomials in $\mathsf{F}[z]$ with degree three, while there are at most $q^d/d = 2^d/d$ monic irreducible polynomials with degree d in $\mathsf{F}[z]$ when $d \geq 4$, it can be shown that if f_ii the minimal polynomial of $A + V_i \cdot U_i$, for $3 \leq i \leq 5$, then the probability that $\gcd(f_3, f_4, f_5)$ has a monic irreducible factor, with degree at least three, that is not also a factor of φ_{k+1}, is at most $\frac{1}{4}$.

Consequently if one chooses matrices $U_i \in \mathsf{F}^{k\times n}$ and $V_i \in \mathsf{F}^{n\times k}$ uniformly and independently, for $3 \leq i \leq \tau+2$, instead, where $\tau = 3\lceil\log_4(12\epsilon^{-1}\rceil$, and f_i is the minimal polynomial of $A + V_i \cdot U_i$ for all such i, then $\gcd(f_3, f_4, \dots, f_{\tau+2})/\varphi_{k+1}$ has an irreducible factor, with degree at most three, that is not also a divisor of φ_{k+1}, with probability at most $\epsilon/12$.

As discussed in Subsection 6.1, it is possible to ensure that each of the above minimal polynomials f_i of $A = V_i \cdot U_i$ is computed in such a way that the probability of failure here is also at most $\epsilon/12$, by computing the minimal polynomials of $\Theta(\log_2(\epsilon^{-1}))$ linearly recurrent sequences as shown at line (6.1). At this point, either a divisor of φ_{k+1} with positive degree that is different from z has been identified, or matrices $U_i \in \mathsf{F}^{k\times n}$, $V_i \in \mathsf{F}^{n\times k}$, and the minimal polynomials $f_i \in \mathsf{F}[z]$ of $A + V_i \cdot U_i$ have been identified, for $0 \leq i \leq \tau + 2 = 6\lceil\log_2(12\epsilon^{-1})\rceil + 2 \in \Theta(\log_2(\epsilon^{-1}))$, such that $\gcd(f_0, f_1, \dots, f_{\tau+2}) = \varphi_{k+1} \in \{1, z\}$. The probability of failure of this process is at most ϵ, and (for fixed ϵ) the prover has selected $\Theta(nk)$ values uniformly and independently from F, and performed $\Theta(n^2k + \mu n)$ arithmetic operations in F.

A similar analysis establishes that if $|\mathsf{F}| = q = 3$ then if $U_i \in \mathsf{F}^{k\times n}$ and $V_i \in \mathsf{F}^{n\times k}$ are chosen uniformly and independently, and $f_i \in \mathsf{F}[z]$ is the minimal polynomial of $A+V_i \cdot U_i$, for $1 \leq i \leq 5$, then $\psi = \gcd(f_1, f_2, \dots, f_6)/\varphi_{k+1}$ has an irreducible factor that is not also a factor of φ_{k+1} with probability at most 1/2. If one chooses $5\lceil\log_2(4\epsilon^{-1})\rceil$ pairs of matrices $U_i \in \mathsf{F}^{k\times n}$ and $V \in \mathsf{F}^{n\times k}$ uniformly and independently, and $f_i \in \mathsf{F}[z]$ is the minimal polynomial of $A + V_i \cdot U_i$ for all such i, then the probability that $\gcd(f_1, f_2, \dots, f_{\lceil\log_2(4\epsilon^{-1})\rceil})$ has an irreducible factor that is not also a factor of φ_{k+1} is at most $\epsilon/4$. A computation of $\Theta(\log_2(\epsilon^{-1}))$ minimal polynomials of linearly recurrent sequences, as shown at line (6.1), suffices to establish that all minimal polynomials f_i are correctly computed with probability at most $1-\epsilon/4$, as needed to obtain a similar process whose failure probability is also at most ϵ and that has the same asymptotic cost.

Similar combinatorial arguments, and applications of Theorem 5.2(b), establish similar results when $q = |\mathsf{F}| \geq 4$: If $q = 4$ or $q = 5$ then the process described for the case $q = 3$ can be applied, except that the multiplicative constant "5," included above, can be reduced to "4". This constant can be reduced to 3 when $7 \leq q \leq 13$, and it can be reduced to 2 when $q \geq 16$.

Additional information is useful if it has been decided that $\varphi_{k+1} \in \{1, z\}$. First, it is useful to have a pair of vectors $u_i, v_i \in \mathsf{F}^{n\times 1}$, such that the minimal polynomial of the linearly recurrent sequence

$$u_i^T v_i, u_i^T(A + V_i \cdot U_i)v_i, u_i^T(A + V_i \cdot U_i)^2 v_i, \dots \tag{7.1}$$

is equal to the minimal polynomial f_i of $A + V_i \cdot U_i$, for all i as above. These vectors can be generated as f_i is being computed, with an expected cost dominated by the cost to complete the above process — see, for example, Eberly [3] for details.

If it has been determined that A has at most k nontrivial invariant factors, so that $c+1$ pairs of matrices $U_i \in \mathsf{F}^{k\times n}$ and $V_I \in \mathsf{F}^{n\times k}$, and corresponding minimal polynomials $f_i \in \mathsf{F}[z]$ have been accumulated, such that $\gcd(f_0, f_1, \dots, f_c) = \varphi_{k+1} \in \{1, z\}$, then it will also be useful to compute matrices $g_0, g_1, \dots, g_c \in \mathsf{F}[z]$ such that

$$g_0 f_0 + g_1 f_1 + \cdots + g_c f_c = \varphi_{k+1}. \tag{7.2}$$

Since c, for any field size q, the extended Euclidean algorithm can be applied to compute these polynomials, such that each polynomial g_i has degree in $O(n)$, at a cost that is dominated by the cost of the rest of this process.

7.2 Few Invariant Factors: Certification and Verification

In order to ***commit*** that $A \in \mathsf{F}^{n\times n}$ has at most k invariant factors, the prover should send a sequence of $\widehat{\tau} \in \Theta(\log_2(\epsilon^{-1}))$ pairs of matrices $U_i \in \mathsf{F}^{k\times n}$ and $V_i \in \mathsf{F}^{n\times k}$, for $0 \leq i \leq \widehat{\tau} - 1$, along with

- the minimal polynomial $f_i \in \mathsf{F}[z]$ of $A + V_i \cdot U_i$,
- vectors $u_i, v_i \in \mathsf{F}^{n\times 1}$ such that f_i is also the minimal polynomial of the linearly recurrent sequence shown at line (7.1), and
- polynomials $g_i \in \mathsf{F}[z]$, for $0 \leq i \leq \widehat{\tau} - 1$, each with degree in $O(n)$, such that the equation at line (7.2) is also satisfied, where $\varphi_{k+1} \in \{1, z\}$.

Dumas, Kaltofen, Thomé and Villard [2] are primarily concerned with certification of the minimal polynomial of a matrix over a large field, namely a field F such that $|\mathsf{F}| \in \Omega(n)$. However their observations about small field computations can be extended, in a straightforward way, to establish the following.

Theorem 7.2 (Dumas, et. al.). *It is possible for a prover to compute the minimal polynomial of a given matrix $A \in \mathsf{F}^{n\times n}$ and certify it using an interactive protocol that is perfectly complete and sound: An incorrect minimal polynomial is accepted with probability at most ϵ for any desired positive constant ϵ. The prover selects $\Theta(n \log_2 n)$ values uniformly and independently from F and performs $\Theta(n^2\mathcal{M}(n)+\mu n \log_2 n)$ additional operations in F while participating in this process, where $\mathcal{M}(n)$ is the number of operations in F required for an arithmetic operation in a field extension whose degree over F is logarithmic in n. The verifier selects $O(n \log_2 n)$ values uniformly and independently from F and performs $O(n\mathcal{M}(n) + \mu)$ additional operations in F.*

With that noted, it suffices to verify the information provided by the prover by participating in the protocol of Dumas, Kaltofen, Thomé and Villard to certify the minimal polynomial f_i of $A + V_i \cdot U_i$ for $0 \leq i \leq \widehat{\tau} - 1$. If one wishes to ensure that the total probability of failure is at most ϵ then the protocol should be applied to ensure that no incorrect minimal polynomial is accepted with probability at most $\epsilon/\widehat{\tau}$. If any of these is rejected then the verifier should reject here too. Otherwise the verifier should check that $\sum_{i=0}^{\widehat{\tau}-1} g_i f_i \in \{1, \lambda\}$ — accepting if this is the case, and rejecting otherwise.
Perfect completeness and soundness of this protocol are easily established. The costs for the prover and verifier, given in Theorem 7.1, follow from the fact that the cost to multiply $A + V_i\dot{U}_i$ by a vector is in $\Theta(\mu + nk)$.

7.3 Many Invariant Factors: Certification and Verification

In this case, the prover has detected a factor $\chi \in \mathsf{F}[z]$ of φ_{k+1} that is different from 1 or z; the prover should now ***commit*** to this protocol by sending χ to the verifier. The verifier should choose matrices $U_i \in \mathsf{F}^{k\times n}$ and $V_i \in \mathsf{F}^{n\times k}$ uniformly and independently, for $0 \leq i \leq \widetilde{\tau}-1$, where $\widetilde{\tau} = \lceil \log_2(2\epsilon^{-1})\rceil$ and send these to the prover as a ***challenge***.
As a ***response*** the prover should return vectors $u_i, v_i \in \mathsf{F}^{n\times 1}$ such that the minimal polynomial of the linear recurrence at line (7.1) is χ, for $0 \leq i \leq \widetilde{\tau} - 1$. The prover and verifier should apply the protocol of Dumas, Kaltofen, Thomé and Villard once again, in order to confirm this — ensuring that any incorrect pair of vectors is accepted with probability at most $\epsilon/(2\widetilde{\tau})$, so that the total probability of failure is at most ϵ, once again.
The verifier can generate the above vectors by generating vectors $\widetilde{u}_i, \widetilde{v}_i \in \mathsf{F}^{n\times 1}$ such that the linearly recurrent sequence generated by $A+V_i \cdot U_i$, $\widetilde{u}_i$ and $\widetilde{v}_i$ is the same as the minimal polynomial f_i of $A+V_i \cdot U_i$, and setting $u_i = \widetilde{u}_i$ and $v_i = (f_i/\chi)(A+V_i \cdot U_i)\widetilde{v}_i$, for $0 \leq i \leq \widetilde{\tau}-1$. Arguments given above can now be applied, once again, to establish that the costs for the prover and verifier to complete this protocol are as in Theorem 7.1.

8. ADDITIONAL PROBLEMS

Additional properties allowing other "superfast" algorithms to be used might also be efficiently detected. For example, one might be able to detect some cases when ***nested dissection*** can be applied. The detection of ***Vandermonde-like*** and ***Cauchy-like*** matrices might be of interest — and also might be more challenging than that of detecting Toeplitz-like matrices: The operator matrices for Vandermonde-like and Cauchy-like matrices are defined using diagonal matrices whose entries can vary, and one would need to discover these diagonal matrices as part of a detection process.
This report has focussed on the case where k is extremely small. However, various "superfast" algorithms would still be superior to a black box algorithm for larger k — for example, for $k \leq \sqrt{n}$. Detection and conversion protocols that are effective, for larger k, might therefore be of interest. Protocols such that the parameter k is not selected by a client (or verifier), but is instead discovered by the service provider (or prover), can be generally be obtained by modifying the protocols in this report in a straightforward way. Finally, black box algorithms are also used for various integer matrix computations, including computations involving the ***Smith form*** of a matrices. Protocols to decide and certify whether the number of nontrivial elementary divisors of a given integer matrix would therefore be of interest.

9. REFERENCES

[1] J.-G. Dumas and E. Kaltofen. Essentially optimal interactive certificates in linear algebra. In *Proceedings, 2014 International Symposium on Symbolic and Algebraic Computation (ISSAC '14)*, pages 146–153. ACM Press, 2014.

[2] J.-G. Dumas, E. Kaltofen, E. Thomé, and G. Villard. Linear time interactive certificates for the minimal polynomial and determinant of a sparse matrix. In these proceedings.

[3] W. Eberly. Black box Frobenius decompositions over small fields. In *Proceedings, 2000 International Symposium on Symbolic and Algebraic Computation (ISSAC 2000)*, pages 106–113. ACM Press, 2000.

[4] W. Eberly. Selecting algorithms for black box matrices: Checking for matrix properties that can simplify computations. Technical Report 2016-1085-04, Department of Computer Science, University of Calgary, 2016.

[5] R. Frievalds. Fast probabilistic algorithms. In *Mathematical Foundations of Computer Science 1979*, volume 74 of *Lecture Notes in Computer Science*, pages 57–69. Springer-Verlag, 1979.

[6] G. H. Golub and C. F. Van Loan. *Matrix Computations.* Johns Hopkins University Press, fourth edition, 2012.

[7] V. Y. Pan. *Structured Matrices and Polynomials: Unified Superfast Algorithms.* Birkhäuser, 2001.

[8] G. Villard. Computing the Frobenius normal form of a sparse matrix. In *Computer Algebra in Scientific Computing (CACS 2000)*, pages 395–407. Springer, 2000.

On the Bit Complexity of Solving Bilinear Polynomial Systems

Ioannis Z. Emiris
Dept Informatics & Telecoms
University of Athens, Greece;
ATHENA Research Center
Maroussi, Greece
emiris@di.uoa.gr

Angelos Mantzaflaris
RICAM, Austrian Academy of Sciences
Altenberger Str. 69, 4040
Linz, Austria
angelos.mantzaflaris@oeaw.ac.at

Elias Tsigaridas
Sorbonne Universités, UPMC
Univ Paris 06, CNRS, INRIA,
Laboratoire d'Informatique de Paris 6 (LIP6), Équipe PolSys,
4 place Jussieu, 75252 Paris
Cedex 05, France
elias.tsigaridas@inria.fr

ABSTRACT

We bound the Boolean complexity of computing isolating hyperboxes for all complex roots of systems of bilinear polynomials. The resultant of such systems admits a family of determinantal Sylvester-type formulas, which we make explicit by means of homological complexes. The computation of the determinant of the resultant matrix is a bottleneck for the overall complexity. We exploit the quasi-Toeplitz structure to reduce the problem to efficient matrix-vector products, corresponding to multivariate polynomial multiplication. For zero-dimensional systems, we arrive at a primitive element and a rational univariate representation of the roots. The overall bit complexity of our probabilistic algorithm is $\widetilde{\mathcal{O}}_B(n^4 D^4 + n^2 D^4 \tau)$, where n is the number of variables, D equals the bilinear Bézout bound, and τ is the maximum coefficient bitsize. Finally, a careful infinitesimal symbolic perturbation of the system allows us to treat degenerate and positive dimensional systems, thus making our algorithms and complexity analysis applicable to the general case.

CCS Concepts

•**Computing methodologies** → *Symbolic calculus algorithms;*

Keywords

bilinear polynomial, polynomial system solving, separation bounds, DMM, resultant matrix

1. INTRODUCTION

Efficient algorithms for solving of polynomial systems is one of the most active areas of research in computational algebra. Its importance stems from the fact that, using polynomial systems, we can model many problems in various research disciplines. We focus on efficient algorithms for solving bilinear polynomial systems. Such systems are common in various applications, for example in cryptography [21, 30], coding theory [37], real algebraic geometry [42], and game theory [15]. We derive explicit Boolean complexity estimates for isolating all the roots of bilinear polynomial systems without assumptions on the input.

Bilinear systems. Let $S_1(d) = \mathbb{R}[x_1, \ldots, x_{n_1}]_d$, $S_2(d) = \mathbb{R}[y_1, \ldots, y_{n_1}]_d$ and $n = n_1 + n_2$. The space of polynomials of bidegree (d_1, d_2) is denoted by $S(d_1, d_2) = S_1(d_1) \otimes S_2(d_2)$. We consider a square system $f_1, \ldots, f_n$ of n polynomials $f_k \in S(1,1)$. We call these polynomials $(n_1, n_2)-$bilinear, that is, they are homogeneous of degree 1 with respect to each of the sets of (affine) variables $\{x_1, \ldots, x_{n_1}\}$ and $\{y_1, \ldots, y_{n_2}\}$. We aim to isolate all complex roots of the system

$$(\Sigma): \; f_1(\mathbf{x}, \mathbf{y}) = \cdots = f_n(\mathbf{x}, \mathbf{y}) = 0, \qquad (1)$$

where $\mathbf{x} = (x_1, \ldots, x_{n_1})$, $\mathbf{y} = (y_1, \ldots, y_{n_2})$. Each polynomial is written in matrix form as $f_k(\mathbf{x}, \mathbf{y}) = (1, \mathbf{x}) A_k (1, \mathbf{y})^\top$, where $A_k \in \mathbb{Z}^{(n_1+1)\times(n_2+1)}$, $1 \le k \le n$ are coefficient matrices.

Assuming for the moment that this system is zero-dimensional, the number of roots in $\mathbb{P}^{n_1} \times \mathbb{P}^{n_2}$ equals the bilinear Bézout bound

$$D = D(n_1, n_2) := \binom{n_1 + n_2}{n_1} = \binom{n_1 + n_2}{n_2}. \qquad (2)$$

This number is the mixed volume of the system, and, even in case of infinitely many roots, it is equal to the degree of the variety [15]. This quantity appears frequently in the complexity of our algorithms. By Stirling's formula and by assuming the worst case $n_1 \approx n_2$, we can estimate that $D \sim \frac{4^n}{\sqrt{\pi n}}$. However, if we consider $\min(n_1, n_2) = q$, with q constant, then $D \sim n^q$, i.e. polynomial in the number of variables.

EXAMPLE 1.1. *Consider the $(1,2)-$bilinear, square system*

$$\begin{aligned} f_1 &= b_0 + b_1 y_2 + b_2 y_1 + b_3 x_1 + b_4 x_1 y_2 + b_5 x_1 y_1 \\ &= 1 + y_2 + y_1 + x_1 + 2x_1 y_2 + 2x_1 y_1 \\ f_2 &= c_0 + c_1 y_2 + c_2 y_1 + c_3 x_1 + c_4 x_1 y_2 + c_5 x_1 y_1 \\ &= 1 + y_2 + 2y_1 + 2x_1 + x_1 y_2 + x_1 y_1 \\ f_3 &= d_0 + d_1 y_2 + d_2 y_1 + d_3 x_1 + d_4 x_1 y_2 + d_5 x_1 y_1 \\ &= 2 + y_2 + 2y_1 + x_1 + 2x_1 y_2 + 2x_1 y_1 \end{aligned}$$

with variable groups $\{x_1\}$ and $\{y_1, y_2\}$. The number of roots of the system in $\mathbb{P}^1 \times \mathbb{P}^2$ is $D(1,2) = 3$. These are the two affine points $(x_1; y_1, y_2) = (\pm\frac{\sqrt{3}}{3}; -1, 2 \mp \sqrt{3})$ plus the root $(x_0, x_1; y_0, y_1, y_2) = (0, 1; 0, -1, 1)$ at infinity.

ISSAC '16, July 19-22, 2016, Waterloo, ON, Canada
© 2016 ACM. ISBN 978-1-4503-4380-0/16/07...$15.00
DOI: http://dx.doi.org/10.1145/2930889.2930919

Previous Work. Systems homogeneous in distinct groups of variables were firstly discussed by Sylvester [46]. Moreover, Muir [36] and McCoy [34] gave the first expressions of the resultant of such forms as the determinant of a matrix. Sturmfels and Zelevinski [45] first discovered Sylvester-type formulas for unmixed (having the same support), multigraded systems. These formulas can be seen as certain choices of a Weyman complex of modules [48, 49]. Indeed, several classical resultant matrices can be discovered via such complexes [50], including the projective resultant [12]. The discovery of new resultant formulas coming from these homological constructions was fully explored in [14, 16], where combinatorial bounds were established for possible determinantal complexes, which allowed for an implementation discovering all such complexes. These works extended the study of resultant formulas from Sylvester-type matrices to Bézout-type and hybrid matrices. Interestingly, hybrid resultant matrices are made up from Bézout-type, Sylvester-type blocks (and toric Jacobians). Similar maps have been identified between the terms of Tate resolutions as well [10]. It turns out that for bilinear systems, the most appealing of determinantal formulas are available; these are optimal, pure Sylvester formulas, that are quite analogous to the classical Sylvester matrix of two homogeneous polynomials in one variable.

In [22], see also [44], the problem of computing the roots of bilinear systems is tackled by means of Gröbner bases. They present a modification of the F5 algorithm that avoids all reductions to zero. For generic bilinear systems the complexity of computing the Gröbner basis is $\mathcal{O}(\binom{n+n_1+1}{n_1+1}^{\omega})$ arithmetic operations, where $n_1 \leq n_2$ and ω is the exponent of matrix multiplication. To isolate the roots we need to convert the basis to a shape form. The bit complexity of such an approach w.r.t. the degree bound is not straightforward. Moreover, this arithmetic bound does not hold, when the systems are not generic or if they are not 0-dimensional. In this regard, our results are not directly comparable with [22]. Our approach is "orthogonal". It uses (a variant of) u-resultant based on the determinantal resultant matrices that we describe in Sec. 2.2. This step is fundamental for estimating bit complexity of the whole process. The arithmetic complexity of our approach is $\widetilde{\mathcal{O}}(D^3)$. To the best of knowledge, our result is the first one regarding the bit complexity of solving (i.e. computing the isolated roots) of any bilinear polynomial system, without regularity or any other assumptions on the dimension of the zero locus. We employ the primitive element representation (PER) of the roots Canny [7] and the rational univariate representation (RUR) [2, 5, 41]; for an improved version of RUR in the bivariate case we refer to [6]. A Gröbner free alternative for solving polynomial systems is explored in [25]. Our references, with respect to polynomial system solving algorithm is by no means exhaustive.

If we use the data-structure of straight-line programs there are also efficient algorithms to compute the multihomogeneous resultants, cf. [29]. For efficient algorithms for computing general resultant matrices we refer to [9, 17, 18]. For general algorithms for computing the determinant we refer to [31] and references therein.

Outline. We characterize all possible Sylvester-type formulas for the resultant of a (n_1, n_2)-bilinear system of equations. We give explicit algorithms to construct the three possible resultant matrices, which are *optimal*, in the sense that there are no extraneous factors involved (Sec. 2). We adapt the approach of Canny [7] to represent the roots using the primitive element and the rational univariate representation [2, 41] (Sec. 3) for bilinear systems, and we bound the height of the corresponding u-resultant (Sec. 3.1). We provide explicit bounds for the separation of the roots (Sec. 3.2) that depend on the bilinear Bézout bound. We present explicit bit complexity bounds for isolating all the roots of a system of bilinear polynomials (Thm. 4.1). Our algorithm runs in $\widetilde{\mathcal{O}}_B(n^2 n_1 n_2 D^4 \lg(D) + n^2 D^4 \tau)$. We also tackle the cases where the system is overdetermined (Sec. 4.2), has roots at infinity, or is positive-dimensional (Sec. 4.3). If one of the groups of unknowns has a constant number of elements, our bounds are polynomial in the number of variables.

2. SYLVESTER-TYPE FORMULAS FOR THE BILINEAR RESULTANT

In this section we describe three determinantal Sylvester formulas for the resultant of bilinear systems. Sylvester type formulas refer to matrices where the entries are single coefficients of the input polynomials (possibly with a sign change). This kind of expressions are very convenient for both the analysis and the implementation of resultant methods, since the matrix entries have known bitsize and are computable in constant time.

First, let us define the bilinear resultant in $\mathbb{P}^{n_1} \times \mathbb{P}^{n_2}$. Given a sequence $f_0, \dots, f_n$ of (n_1, n_2)−bilinear forms with variables $\mathbf{x}$ and $\mathbf{y}$ (as in Sect. 1) with symbolic coefficients, their resultant $R(f_0, \dots, f_n)$ is a multihomogeneous polynomial in $\mathbb{Z}[S(1,1)^{n+1}]$, i.e., in the coefficients of the polynomials, with degree w.r.t. (the coefficients of) f_k equal to the Bézout bound

$$\deg_{f_k} R(f_0, \dots, f_n) = D(n_1, n_2)\ ,\ k = 0, \dots, n\,.$$

The total degree of the resultant is $(n+1)D(n_1, n_2)$ and vanishes if and only if the polynomials have a common root in $\mathbb{P}^{n_1} \times \mathbb{P}^{n_2}$. That is, this resultant is an instance of the sparse resultant [23], where the toric variety is $\mathbb{P}^{n_1} \times \mathbb{P}^{n_2}$; the resultant is unique up to integer constants. Our aim is to obtain square matrices, with entries coefficients of the polynomials f_k, whose determinant is equal to their resultant, i.e. determinantal Sylvester-type formulas.

2.1 The Weyman resultant complex

In this section we recall some tools from representation theory, which will help us arrive at the bilinear resultant matrices. The bigraded resultant polynomial can be computed as the determinant of the Weyman complex [48], which arises by applying the, so called, geometric technique of [49] to the incidence variety of $f_0, \dots, f_n$ and generalizes the Cayley-Koszul complex [23]. Note that the classical Koszul complex cannot be used to derive resultant matrices in the bigraded case (cf. [43]).

For any $(m_1, m_2) \in \mathbb{Z}^2$ and $f_0, \dots, f_n \in S(1,1)$, Weyman's construction is a complex $K_\bullet = K_\bullet(m_1, m_2)$ of finite dimensional vector spaces:

$$0 \to K_{n+1} \to \cdots \to K_1 \xrightarrow{\varphi} K_0 \to \cdots \to K_{-n} \to 0\,, \quad (3)$$

where the terms are defined as $K_\nu = \oplus_{p=0}^{n} K_{\nu,p}$ with

$$K_{\nu,p} = \left(H^{a_1}_{n_1}(m_1 - p) \otimes H^{a_2}_{n_2}(m_2 - p)\right)^{\binom{n+1}{p}} \quad (4)$$

with $a_1 + a_2 = p - \nu, \nu = n+1, \dots, -n$, and $H^a_{n_i}(b), b \in \mathbb{Z}$ is the a−th cohomology group of $\mathbb{P}^{n_i}$ with coefficients in the sheaf $\mathscr{O}(b)$ [26]. These terms depend solely on n_1, n_2 and m_1, m_2. The maps between the terms (e.g. φ) depend polynomially on the coefficients of $f_0, \dots, f_n$. This construction appeared in [48] and a detailed presentation is given in [49].

The crucial property of the complex (3) is that its determinant is equal to (a power of) $R(f_0, \dots, f_n)$. The determinant of the complex is, in principle, a rational expression involving the determinants of the maps in the complex, and is usually not given as the determinant of a single matrix. However, when the complex has only two non-zero terms (for specific integers m_1, m_2), then we obtain the resultant as the determinant of the square matrix expressing the map φ at the non-zero part of the complex. We call such complexes and the induced square matrix expressions *determinantal*. The determinantal complexes are of the form

$$0 \to \bigoplus_{p=0}^{n+1} K_{1,p} \xrightarrow{\varphi} \bigoplus_{p=0}^{n+1} K_{0,p} \to 0 \, . \tag{5}$$

The linear map φ is an epimorphism if and only if the complex is exact or, equivalently, the polynomials do not have a common root in $\mathbb{P}^{n_1} \times \mathbb{P}^{n_2}$. Moreover, if n_1, n_2 are fixed, the possible values of (m_1, m_2) which lead to determinantal complexes is a finite set [14, 16]. Each non-zero cohomology group in (4) is identified by a (dual) vector space of polynomials:

$$H^a_{n_i}(b) \cong \begin{cases} S_i(b) & , a = 0 \text{ and } b \geq 0 \\ S_i^*(-b - n_i - 1) & , a = n_i \text{ and } b < -n_i \\ 0 & , \text{otherwise.} \end{cases} \tag{6}$$

Here $S_i^*(d)$ denotes the dual space of $S_i(d)$, i.e. the space of linear functionals $\lambda : S_i(d) \to \mathbb{R}$. This space is isomorphic to (evaluations of) polynomials in formal partial derivatives, e.g. $S_1^*(d) \cong \mathbb{R}[\partial_{x_1}, \ldots, \partial_{x_{n_1}}]_d$, see [32, 33] and references therein.

This identification allows us to choose bases and to express the maps φ between the modules of (5) as a square matrix depending on the coefficients of $f_0, \ldots, f_n$.

EXAMPLE 2.1. *The resultant of three $(1,1)$–bilinear forms, i.e. $n_1 = n_2 = 1$ corresponds to the determinantal complex $K_\bullet(2, 1)$, i.e. $(m_1, m_2) = (2, 1)$. Using (6), the complex (5) becomes $K_{1,1} \xrightarrow{\varphi} K_{0,0}$, i.e. it implies the existence of a map $\varphi : S(1, 0)^3 \to S(2, 1)$ whose determinant equals the resultant. This resultant matrix is depicted in [14, Sect. 7.1].*

All classically known resultant formulas can be obtained as the determinant of a map φ in (5), for particular integers $(m_1, m_2) \in \mathbb{Z}^2$. Moreover, the existence of a determinantal complex implies a determinantal formula for the resultant.

2.2 Determinantal Sylvester formulas

In this section we identify all determinantal Sylvester complexes for (n_1, n_2)–bilinear systems. These formulas are obtained if and only if the non-zero terms in (5) are

$$0 \to K_{1,p+1} \xrightarrow{\varphi} K_{0,p} \to 0 \tag{7}$$

for some $p \in \{0, \ldots, n\}$ (cf. [50]). General such formulas for multilinear systems are identified in [14, 16, 45, 50]. We specialize these results to bilinear systems in the following lemma.

LEMMA 2.2. *There exist three determinantal Sylvester maps ϕ_1, ϕ_2, ϕ_3 for the (n_1, n_2)-bilinear forms $f_0, \ldots, f_n$, up to dual pairs. These are*

(i) $\phi_1 : S(0, n_1)^{n+1} \to S(1, n_1 + 1)$, which is given as

$$(g_0, g_1, \ldots, g_n) \mapsto \sum\nolimits_{k=0}^{n} g_k f_k \ , \ g_k \in S_2(n_1) \, . \tag{8}$$

(ii) $\phi_2 : S(n_2, 0)^{n+1} \to S(n_2 + 1, 1)$ defined the same way as (8), with $g_k \in S_1(n_2)$.

(iii) $\phi_3 : S_1^*(1)^{\binom{n+1}{n_1+1}} \to S_2(1)^{\binom{n+1}{n_1}}$ with

$$(\lambda_1, \lambda_2, \ldots, \lambda_r) \mapsto (q_1, q_2, \ldots, q_s) \tag{9}$$

where $r = \binom{n+1}{n_2}$, $s = \binom{n+1}{n_1}$ and

$$q_j = \sum\nolimits_{k=0, k \notin J_j}^{n} (-1)^\sigma \lambda_\mu f_k \ , \ j = 1, \ldots, s$$

where $J_j \subset \{0, \ldots, n\}, |J_j| = n_1$ denotes the combination with lexicographic index j, $\mu = \mu(j, k)$ is the lexicographic index of the $(n_1 + 1)$-combination $J_j \cup \{k\}$ of $\{0, \ldots, n\}$, $\sigma = \sigma(j, k) = |\{t \in J_j : t < k\}|$ and $\lambda_\mu \in S_1^*(1)$, $\mu = 1, \ldots, r$.

Moreover, these are the only Sylvester maps arising from complex (3).

PROOF. The formulas (i) and (ii) are depicted in [45] for the multilinear case. They correspond to the choices $(m_1, m_2) = (1, n_1 + 1)$ and $(m_1, m_2) = (n_2 + 1, 1)$ of degree vectors in (3), respectively. They have the form of a classical Sylvester map, expressing multiplication by f_k's. The third formula is found in [48] and corresponds to the degree vector $(m_1, m_2) = (-1, n_1 + 1)$. The map expresses a linear combination of applications of dual functionals $w_0 \mathbf{1} + \sum_i w_i \partial_{x_i}$ to the f_k's [16].

For any of the three determinantal degree vectors (m_1, m_2) listed above, the vector $(n_2 - m_1, n_1 - m_2)$ is also determinantal. Due to Serre duality, this additional vector yields the transpose of the matrix corresponding to (m_1, m_2).

For the uniqueness, we look at all possible complexes of the form (7). A case by case analysis shows that the possible Sylvester maps arise from the values $p = 0$, $p = n_1$, $p = n_2$, or $p = n$, due to (6). Using (4) we obtain the complexes $K_\bullet(1, n_1 + 1)$, $K_\bullet(n_2 + 1, 1)$, $K_\bullet(-1, n_1 + 1)$ as well as their duals $K_\bullet(n_2 - 1, -1)$, $K_\bullet(-1, n_1 - 1)$, $K_\bullet(n_2 + 1, -1)$, all corresponding to the listed maps (i–iii). □

Let us remark that the dual (or adjoint) Sylvester map of (i) is a map $\Phi_1 : S^*(1, n_1 + 1) \to S_2^*(n_1)^{(n+1)}$, with

$$\lambda \mapsto (f_0 \cdot \lambda, \, f_1 \cdot \lambda, \, \ldots, \, f_n \cdot \lambda) \, , \ \lambda \in S^*(1, n_1 + 1) \, , \tag{10}$$

where the functionals $f_k \cdot \lambda$ are defined as $g \mapsto \lambda(g f_k)$.

EXAMPLE 2.3. *We demonstrate these Sylvester-type resultant matrices. Consider the $(1,2)$–bilinear system of Example 1.1, augmented by an extra polynomial f_0*

$$f_0 = a_0 + a_1 y_2 + a_2 y_1 + a_3 x_1 + a_4 x_1 y_2 + a_5 x_1 y_1 \, . \tag{11}$$

The set $f_0, \ldots, f_3$ is an overdetermined system of equations. The resultant has degree $\deg R(f_0, \ldots, f_3) = 4\, D(1, 2) = 12$, so this will be the dimension of the Sylvester-type matrices.

The maps (i) and (ii) of Lemma 2.2 are quite similar to the classical Macaulay map but also take into account the special bihomogeneous structure of the system. We have

$$\phi_1 : S(0, 1)^4 \to S(1, 2) \, ,$$

which yields the following (transposed) matrix

$$\begin{array}{c} \\ f_0 \\ y_1 f_0 \\ y_2 f_0 \\ f_1 \\ y_1 f_1 \\ y_2 f_1 \\ f_2 \\ y_1 f_2 \\ y_2 f_2 \\ f_3 \\ y_1 f_3 \\ y_2 f_3 \end{array} \begin{array}{c} \begin{array}{cccccccccccc} 1 & y_2 & y_2^2 & y_1 & y_1 y_2 & y_1^2 & x_1 & x_1 y_2 & x_1 y_2^2 & x_1 y_1 & x_1 y_1 y_2 & x_1 y_1^2 \end{array} \\ \left[\begin{array}{cccccccccccc} a_0 & a_1 & 0 & a_2 & 0 & 0 & a_3 & a_4 & 0 & a_5 & 0 & 0 \\ 0 & 0 & 0 & a_0 & a_1 & a_2 & 0 & 0 & 0 & a_3 & a_4 & a_5 \\ 0 & a_0 & a_1 & 0 & a_2 & 0 & 0 & a_3 & a_4 & 0 & a_5 & 0 \\ b_0 & b_1 & 0 & b_2 & 0 & 0 & b_3 & b_4 & 0 & b_5 & 0 & 0 \\ 0 & 0 & 0 & b_0 & b_1 & b_2 & 0 & 0 & 0 & b_3 & b_4 & b_5 \\ 0 & b_0 & b_1 & 0 & b_2 & 0 & 0 & b_3 & b_4 & 0 & b_5 & 0 \\ c_0 & c_1 & 0 & c_2 & 0 & 0 & c_3 & c_4 & 0 & c_5 & 0 & 0 \\ 0 & 0 & 0 & c_0 & c_1 & c_2 & 0 & 0 & 0 & c_3 & c_4 & c_5 \\ 0 & c_0 & c_1 & 0 & c_2 & 0 & 0 & c_3 & c_4 & 0 & c_5 & 0 \\ d_0 & d_1 & 0 & d_2 & 0 & 0 & d_3 & d_4 & 0 & d_5 & 0 & 0 \\ 0 & 0 & 0 & d_0 & d_1 & d_2 & 0 & 0 & 0 & d_3 & d_4 & d_5 \\ 0 & d_0 & d_1 & 0 & d_2 & 0 & 0 & d_3 & d_4 & 0 & d_5 & 0 \end{array} \right] \end{array} .$$

This matrix expresses the polynomial multiplication (8) with $g_k \in S_2(1)$, $k = 0, \ldots, n$. It has block structure $(n + 1) \times 1$ and each quasi-Toeplitz block is of size $D \times (n + 1)D$. From (ii) we obtain

$$\phi_2 : S(2, 0)^4 \to S(3, 1)$$

which implies a matrix of the same block structure as above:

$$
\begin{array}{c|cccccccccccc}
 & 1 & y_2 & y_1 & x_1 & x_1y_2 & x_1y_1 & x_1^2 & x_1^2y_2 & x_1^2y_1 & x_1^3 & x_1^3y_2 & x_1^3y_1 \\
\hline
f_0 & a_0 & a_1 & a_2 & a_3 & a_4 & a_5 & 0 & 0 & 0 & 0 & 0 & 0 \\
x_1f_0 & 0 & 0 & 0 & a_0 & a_1 & a_2 & a_3 & a_4 & a_5 & 0 & 0 & 0 \\
x_1^2f_0 & 0 & 0 & 0 & 0 & 0 & 0 & a_0 & a_1 & a_2 & a_3 & a_4 & a_5 \\
f_1 & b_0 & b_1 & b_2 & b_3 & b_4 & b_5 & 0 & 0 & 0 & 0 & 0 & 0 \\
x_1f_1 & 0 & 0 & 0 & b_0 & b_1 & b_2 & b_3 & b_4 & b_5 & 0 & 0 & 0 \\
x_1^2f_1 & 0 & 0 & 0 & 0 & 0 & 0 & b_0 & b_1 & b_2 & b_3 & b_4 & b_5 \\
f_2 & c_0 & c_1 & c_2 & c_3 & c_4 & c_5 & 0 & 0 & 0 & 0 & 0 & 0 \\
x_1f_2 & 0 & 0 & 0 & c_0 & c_1 & c_2 & c_3 & c_4 & c_5 & 0 & 0 & 0 \\
x_1^2f_2 & 0 & 0 & 0 & 0 & 0 & 0 & c_0 & c_1 & c_2 & c_3 & c_4 & c_5 \\
f_3 & d_0 & d_1 & d_2 & d_3 & d_4 & d_5 & 0 & 0 & 0 & 0 & 0 & 0 \\
x_1f_3 & 0 & 0 & 0 & d_0 & d_1 & d_2 & d_3 & d_4 & d_5 & 0 & 0 & 0 \\
x_1^2f_3 & 0 & 0 & 0 & 0 & 0 & 0 & d_0 & d_1 & d_2 & d_3 & d_4 & d_5
\end{array}.
$$

The multiplication map which is expressed here is again as (8) but with $g_k \in S_1(2)$, $k = 0, \ldots, n$.

Finally, the map in (iii)

$$\phi_3 \,:\, S_1^*(1)^6 \to S_2(1)^4$$

is given by the Koszul-type formula

$$(\lambda_1, \ldots, \lambda_6) \mapsto \begin{pmatrix} -\lambda_1 f_1 - \lambda_2 f_2 - \lambda_3 f_3 \\ \lambda_1 f_0 - \lambda_4 f_2 - \lambda_5 f_3 \\ \lambda_2 f_0 + \lambda_4 f_3 - \lambda_6 f_3 \\ \lambda_3 f_0 + \lambda_5 f_1 + \lambda_6 f_2 \end{pmatrix}^{\top},$$

with dual functionals $\lambda_i \in S_1^*(1)$ of the form $w_0\mathbf{1} + w_1\partial_{x_1}$. Note that $\mathbf{1} f_k$ picks the constant term of f_k, regarded as a form in $S_1(1)$. We arrive at the (transposed) matrix:

$$
\begin{array}{c|cccccccccccc}
 & 1 & y_2 & y_1 & 1 & y_2 & y_1 & 1 & y_2 & y_1 & 1 & y_2 & y_1 \\
\hline
\mathbf{1} & -b_0 & -b_1 & -b_2 & a_0 & a_1 & a_2 & 0 & 0 & 0 & 0 & 0 & 0 \\
\partial_{x_1} & -b_3 & -b_4 & -b_5 & a_3 & a_4 & a_5 & 0 & 0 & 0 & 0 & 0 & 0 \\
\mathbf{1} & -c_0 & -c_1 & -c_2 & 0 & 0 & 0 & a_0 & a_1 & a_2 & 0 & 0 & 0 \\
\partial_{x_1} & -c_3 & -c_4 & -c_5 & 0 & 0 & 0 & a_3 & a_4 & a_5 & 0 & 0 & 0 \\
\mathbf{1} & -d_0 & -d_1 & -d_2 & 0 & 0 & 0 & 0 & 0 & 0 & a_0 & a_1 & a_2 \\
\partial_{x_1} & -d_3 & -d_4 & -d_5 & 0 & 0 & 0 & 0 & 0 & 0 & a_3 & a_4 & a_5 \\
\mathbf{1} & 0 & 0 & 0 & -c_0 & -c_1 & -c_2 & b_0 & b_1 & b_2 & 0 & 0 & 0 \\
\partial_{x_1} & 0 & 0 & 0 & -c_3 & -c_4 & -c_5 & b_3 & b_4 & b_5 & 0 & 0 & 0 \\
\mathbf{1} & 0 & 0 & 0 & -d_0 & -d_1 & -d_2 & 0 & 0 & 0 & b_0 & b_1 & b_2 \\
\partial_{x_1} & 0 & 0 & 0 & -d_3 & -d_4 & -d_5 & 0 & 0 & 0 & b_3 & b_4 & b_5 \\
\mathbf{1} & 0 & 0 & 0 & 0 & 0 & 0 & -d_0 & -d_1 & -d_2 & c_0 & c_1 & c_2 \\
\partial_{x_1} & 0 & 0 & 0 & 0 & 0 & 0 & -d_3 & -d_4 & -d_5 & c_3 & c_4 & c_5
\end{array}.
$$

This resultant matrix has block structure $\binom{n+1}{n_2} \times \binom{n+1}{n_1}$ and each block has size $(n_1 + 1) \times (n_2 + 1)$.

The three above matrices all have the same determinant, which is a homogeneous polynomial of degree 12 in $\mathbb{Z}[a_0, \ldots, d_5]$ and, additionally, it is homogeneous of degree 3 in each of the variable sets $\{a_0, \ldots, a_5\}$, $\{b_0, \ldots, b_5\}$, $\{c_0, \ldots, c_5\}$, $\{d_0, \ldots, d_5\}$. This polynomial is $R(f_0, \ldots, f_3)$.

3. REPRESENTATION OF THE ROOTS

We represent the roots of the system as rational function of univariate polynomials, evaluated at the roots of a univariate polynomial. We employ the primitive element representation (PER) [7] and the rational univariate representation (RUR) [2, 5, 41]. In RUR the denominator is the same for all the rational functions; it is the derivative of the square-free part of a factor of the resultant. We start by introducing some notation. For a (multivariate) polynomial f with integer coefficients, we denote by $\mathtt{H}(f)$ the height (largest absolute value) of its coefficients, and by $\mathfrak{h}(f) = \lg(\mathtt{H}(f))$ the maximum bitsize of its coefficients. For a univariate polynomial g, $\mathtt{lc}(g)$ denotes its leading coefficient.

Consider a square system $f_1, \ldots, f_n$ of n bilinear polynomials as in Eq. (1). We add the polynomial

$$f_0(\mathbf{x}, \mathbf{y}) = u_{0,0} + \sum_{i=1}^{n_1} u_{i,0} x_i + \sum_{j=1}^{n_2} u_{0,j} y_j + \sum_{i=1}^{n_1}\sum_{j=1}^{n_2} u_{i,j} x_i y_j\,,$$

where the $u_{i,j}$ are parameters, to obtain the overconstrained system

$$(\Sigma_0) :\; f_0(\mathbf{x}, \mathbf{y}) = f_1(\mathbf{x}, \mathbf{y}) = \cdots = f_n(\mathbf{x}, \mathbf{y}) = 0. \quad (12)$$

We can compute the resultant of (Σ_0) as the determinant of any of the matrices presented in the previous section.

The PER. We follow Canny's approach [7] but instead of using a linear polynomial f_0, we use a bilinear one. This corresponds to the "trick" of hiding a variable. Another reason for choosing such a polynomial is that if all the $n + 1$ polynomials have the same support, then the determinant of the resultant matrices presented in the previous section gives exactly the resultant. A different choice for f_0 might yield a determinant equal to a multiple of the resultant. In this case we would have need to treat this extraneous factor.

The resultant $R(f_0)$ of the system (Σ_0) is a polynomial; it is a product of factors of the form

$$\sum\nolimits_{i=0}^{n_1} \sum\nolimits_{j=0}^{n_2} u_{i,j} \alpha_{k,i} \beta_{k,j}\,.$$

We choose $(n_1 + 1)(n_2 + 1) - 1$ constants and we set $r(z) = R(-z, c_{1,0}, \ldots, c_{0,1}, \ldots, c_{1,1}, \ldots, c_{n_1,n_2})$, where z is a new variable. With this substitution the factors of R corresponding to roots at infinity become constants. The other factors of R are of the form

$$z\,\alpha_{k,0}\beta_{k,0} - \sum\nolimits_{i=1}^{n_1} c_{i,0}\alpha_{k,i}\beta_{k,0} - \sum\nolimits_{j=1}^{n_2} c_{0,j}\alpha_{k,0}\beta_{k,j} - \sum\nolimits_{i=1}^{n_1}\sum\nolimits_{j=1}^{n_2} c_{i,j}\alpha_{k,i}\beta_{k,j}.$$

We may assume, without loss of generality, that $\alpha_{k,0} = \beta_{k,0} = 1$ for the roots that are not at infinity. In this way the roots of r, which we denote as ζ_m, are

$$\zeta_m = \sum_{i=1}^{n_1} c_{i,0}\alpha_{m,i} + \sum_{j=1}^{n_2} c_{0,j}\beta_{m,j} + \sum_{i=1}^{n_1}\sum_{j=1}^{n_2} c_{i,j}\alpha_{m,i}\beta_{m,j}, \quad (13)$$

where m runs over the roots of the system. By abuse of notation, we also denote by r the square-free part of r. With this notation $r(z) = \mathtt{lc}(r)\prod_m (z - \zeta_m)$, where m runs over all the distinct roots of r, and

$$r'(z) = \mathtt{lc}(r) \sum\nolimits_m \prod\nolimits_{\nu \neq m} (z - \zeta_m). \quad (14)$$

For the PER of the x coordinates of the solutions of the bilinear system, we consider the polynomials $\hat{a}_k^+(z)$ and $\hat{a}_k^-(z)$ where

$$\hat{a}_k^{\pm}(z) = R(-z, c_{1,0}, \ldots, (c_{k,0} \pm 1), \ldots, c_{n_1,0}, c_{0,1}, \ldots, c_{0,n_2}, c_{1,1}, \ldots, c_{n_1,n_2}), \quad (15)$$

for $1 \leq k \leq n_1$. That is, we consider a pair of polynomials for each of the x variables. Let $a_k^{\pm}$ be the corresponding square-free parts of $\hat{a}_k^{\pm}$, respectively. The roots of $a_k^{\pm}(z)$ are $\zeta_m \pm \alpha_{m,k}$ and so we have the factorization

$$a_k^{\pm}(z) = \mathtt{lc}(a_k^{\pm}) \prod_m (z - \zeta_m \mp \alpha_{m,k}).$$

Consider the polynomial $a_k^+(2\theta - z)$. It holds

$$a_k^+(2\theta - z) = \mathtt{lc}(a_k^+) \prod_\nu (z - 2\theta + \zeta_\nu + \alpha_{\nu,k}).$$

The resultant w.r.t. z of $a_k^-(z)$ and $a_k^+(2\theta - z)$, where θ is a new parameter, is

$$\begin{aligned} \mathtt{res}(a_k^-(z), a_k^+(2\theta - z)) &= \prod_m a_k^+(2\theta - \zeta_m + a_{m,k}) \\ &= \prod_m \prod_\nu (\zeta_m - \alpha_{m,k} - 2\theta + \zeta_\nu + \alpha_{\nu,k}). \end{aligned} \quad (16)$$

If $\theta = \zeta_l$, then the polynomials $a_k^-(z)$ and $a_k^+(2\theta - z)$ have a common root if and only if

$$\zeta_m - \alpha_{m,k} - 2\zeta_l + \zeta_\nu + \alpha_{\nu,k} = 0, \tag{17}$$

and then the resultant is 0. Eq. (17) holds for sure if $m = l = \nu$. However, there might be "bad" choices of the constants $c_{i,j}$ that result in spurious roots for different tuples of roots of the system. We will characterize these "bad" values in Sec. 3.1. When these values are avoided, we refer to the resulting f_0 as a *separating polynomial*.

Assuming that there are no spurious roots, we consider $a_k^-(z)$ and $a_k^+(2\theta - z)$ as a bivariate polynomial system. Its solutions are described by univariate polynomials $s_{k,0}$ and $s_{k,1}$ of degree $\mathcal{O}(D^2)$ [35, Thm. 1] as $s_{k,0}(\theta) = 0$ and $z = s_{k,1}(\theta)/s'_{k,0}(\theta)$. We notice from Eq. (16) that 2θ, and so the roots of $s_{k,0}(\theta)$, encode all the possible sums of the roots of $a_k^-(z)$ and $a_k^+(z)$. Hence, r divides $s_{k,0}$, since when $m = \nu$ in (16), then $\theta = \zeta_m$, which are exactly the roots of r, see (13). Therefore, for θ such that $r(\theta) = 0$, the polynomials $a_k^-(z)$ and $a_k^+(2\theta - z)$ have a common root, say $\zeta_\ell - \alpha_{\ell,k}$, which is described as $s_{k,1}(\theta)/s'_{k,0}(\theta)$. Thus, the PER for the k-th x-coordinate is

$$r_k(z) = z - \frac{s_{k,1}(z)}{s'_{k,0}(z)} = \frac{z\, s'_{k,0}(z) - s_{k,1}(z)}{s'_{k,0}(z)} = \frac{\widetilde{s}_{k,1}(z)}{s'_{k,0}(z)}, \tag{18}$$

where z runs over all the roots of r. In addition the polynomials r and $s'_{k,0}$ are relative prime, and so we can compute the inverse of $s'_{k,0}$ modulo r. Thus, we can express $r_k(z)$ as a $r_k(z) = p_k(z) \mod r(z)$, for a polynomial $p_k = \widetilde{s}_{k,1}\,(s'_{k,0})^{-1}$.

The RUR. To compute the RUR we slightly modify the approach in [2], see also [11, 41], to fit our needs. Consider $\hat{f}_{0,k}(\mathbf{x}, \mathbf{y}) = f_0(\mathbf{x}, \mathbf{y}) + \mu\, x_k$, where μ is a new variable, for $1 \le k \le n_1$, and f_0, as in PER, is a bilinear separating polynomial, that forces the roots at infinity to be constants that multiply the resultant. An explicit construction of f_0 is in Sec. 3.1. We replace f_0 with $\hat{f}_{0,k}$ in (Σ_0) to obtain a new system $(\Sigma_{0,k})$. We substitute $u_{0,0} = -z$ in f_0. Let $g_k \in (\mathbb{Z}[\mu])[z]$ be (the square-free part of) the resultant of $(\Sigma_{0,k})$ after we eliminate $\mathbf{x}$ and $\mathbf{y}$. It holds $\deg(g_k) = \mathcal{O}(D)$, and $g_k(z) = \mathtt{lc}(g_k) \prod_m (z - \zeta_m - \mu\, \alpha_{m,k})$, and

$$\tfrac{\partial}{\partial \mu} g_k = -\mathtt{lc}(g_k) \sum\nolimits_m \alpha_{m,k} \prod\nolimits_{\nu \ne m} (z - \zeta_m - \mu\, \alpha_{\nu,k}),$$

where m runs over all the distinct roots the system.. If we set $\mu = 0$ to the previous expression, we get

$$-s_k(z) = \mathtt{lc}(g_k) \sum\nolimits_m \alpha_{m,k} \prod\nolimits_{\nu \ne m} (z - \zeta_m).$$

If we combine it with Eq. (14) then we obtain the representation

$$x_k = -\frac{\mathtt{lc}(r)\, s_k(z)}{\mathtt{lc}(g_k)\, r'(z)} \tag{19}$$

for the k-th x-coordinate of the roots of the system. We can obtain a similar representation for y-coordinates.

To recover the y-coordinates of the solutions, we consider the polynomials $\hat{b}_\ell^+(z)$ and $\hat{b}_\ell^-(z)$ where

$$\hat{b}_\ell^\pm(z) = R(-z, c_{1,0}, \ldots, c_{n_1,0}, c_{0,1}, \ldots, (c_{0,\ell} \pm 1), \ldots, c_{0,n_2}, \\ c_{1,1}, \ldots, c_{n_1,n_2})$$

for $1 \le \ell \le n_2$. We work similarly and we obtain a representation $-\mathtt{lc}(r) q_k(z)/(\mathtt{lc}(g_k)\, r'(z))$, for $1 \le k \le n_2$, for the y-coordinates. In total, we have to perform this procedure $n = n_1 + n_2$ times to obtain a representation for all the coordinates.

LEMMA 3.1. *Let the polynomials of the system (Σ_0) in Eq. (12) have integer coefficients. Let the resultant of the (n_1, n_2)–bilinear system be of degree D and bitsize $\mathcal{O}(L)$. The representation of the roots using Eq. (18) consists of polynomials of degree $\mathcal{O}(D^2)$ and bitsize $\widetilde{\mathcal{O}}(D^2 + DL)$. The representation of the roots using Eq. (19) consists of polynomials of degree $\mathcal{O}(D)$ and bitsize $\widetilde{\mathcal{O}}(D + L)$. We compute them in $\widetilde{\mathcal{O}}_B(n(D^4 + D^3 L))$, with a Monte Carlo algorithm for Eq. (18) and deterministically for Eq. (19), whenever a separating polynomial f_0 is known.*

PROOF. The resultant is univariate polynomial in z. Let r be its square-free part; then $\deg(r) = \mathcal{O}(D)$ and $\mathfrak{h}(r) = \mathcal{O}(D + L)$. The same bounds holds for $a_k^\pm$, since they are also computed as determinants of the resultant matrices. With these bounds the complexity of PER is a direct consequence of [35, Thm. 1].

For Eq. (18) we proceed as follows. We pick a prime, $\mathtt{p}$, of bitsize $\widetilde{\mathcal{O}}(D^2 + DL)$, and we perform all the computations in the ring $(\mathbb{Z}/\mathbb{Z}_{\mathtt{p}})[z]/r(z)$. Then, in this ring, we compute a representation of the common root of $a_k^-(z)$ and $a_k^+(2\theta - z)$, $\frac{s_{k,1}(z)}{s_{k,0}(z)}$, by exploiting their first subresultant polynomial. For this we use fast subresultant algorithms [1, 47]. Next, we compute the inverse of $s_{k,0}$, and finally the representation $r_k(z) = p_k(z) \mod r(z)$, for $p_k = \widetilde{s}_{k,1}\,(s_{k,0})^{-1}$. In total we perform $\widetilde{\mathcal{O}}(D)$ operations in the ring. Each operation costs $\widetilde{\mathcal{O}}_B(D(D^2 + DL)) = \widetilde{\mathcal{O}}_B(D^3 + D^2 L)$, and so the overall cost is $\widetilde{\mathcal{O}}_B(D^4 + D^3 L)$ [1].

For the RUR, Eq. (19), we need to compute g_k, its square-free part, its derivative w.r.t. μ, and finally s_k. As g_k is also a determinant of a resultant matrix, it holds $\mathfrak{h}(g_k) = \widetilde{\mathcal{O}}(L)$, and so $\mathfrak{h}(s_k) = \widetilde{\mathcal{O}}(D + L)$. Moreover, $\deg(s_k) = \mathcal{O}(D)$. To compute s_k we notice that $\mathtt{lc}(r) s_k = \mathtt{lc}(g_k)\, r'\, p_k \mod r$; an operation that costs $\widetilde{\mathcal{O}}(D)$. So the overall cost is $\widetilde{\mathcal{O}}_B(n(D^4 + D^3 L))$ as we have to compute the representation for all the coordinates. □

3.1 "Bad" values for $c_{i,j}$ and the height of f_0

Following Sec. 3, we choose a bilinear f_0 to add to (Σ) and we obtain the system (Σ_0), Eq. (12), of the form

$$f_0(\mathbf{x}, \mathbf{y}) = -z + \sum_{i=1}^{n_1} c_{i,0} x_i + \sum_{j=1}^{n_2} c_{0,j} y_j + \sum_{i=1}^{n_1} \sum_{j=1}^{n_2} c_{i,j} x_i y_j\,,$$

where $c_{i,j} \in \mathbb{Z}$ are constants to be specified in the sequel, and z is a new parameter. There are values of $c_{i,j}$ that make our algorithm fail. The goal of this section is to identify these "bad" values. Moreover, We also estimate the height of the coefficients of f_0.

Assume that D bounds the affine as well as the projective isolated roots of the system, see Eq. (2). First, we replace each $c_{i,j}$ with a power of t, where t is a new indeterminate. In this way, the evaluation of f_0 at each solution of the system, say $(\alpha_{k,0}, \ldots, \alpha_{k,n_1}, \beta_{k,0}, \ldots, \beta_{k,n_2})$, results a polynomial in t

$$f_{0,k} = -\sum\nolimits_{i=0}^{n_1} \sum\nolimits_{j=0}^{n_2} t^{i(n_2+1)+j} \alpha_{k,i} \beta_{k,j}, \tag{20}$$

that has degree $n_1 n_2 + n_1 + n_2$. With this substitution, it suffices to choose a constant for t.

Our goal is to compute the values of t that cause spurious roots to appear. The first class of "bad" choices for t, and hence for the constants $c_{i,j}$, are due to (isolated) roots of the system at projective infinity. These roots might force $f_{0,k}$, and hence $r(z)$, to vanish identically. Recall that by our choice of f_0, the roots at infinity evaluate to constants and thus they multiply the resultant. Therefore, if these constants are zero, then they make the resultant to vanish identically.

For a root at infinity we may have $\alpha_{k,0} = 0$, or $\beta_{k,0} = 0$, or $\alpha_{k,0} = \beta_{k,0} = 0$, for some k. We can forget the last case as it is contained in the first two. In each of the first two cases, $f_{0,k}$ is a polynomial in t of degree $\le n_1 n_2 + n_1 + n_2 \le 2 n_1 n_2$. The product of these two polynomials is a polynomial of degree $\le 4 n_1 n_2$, in t. As there are at most D isolated roots at infinity, then each of them gives rise to a polynomial in t, as in Eq. (20), and the product of all these polynomials is a polynomial of degree at most $4 n_1 n_2 D$. In a similar way, we obtain such a polynomial when we consider the computation of the polynomials $a_k^{\pm}$ and $b_k^{\pm}$. There are $2n_1$ and $2n_2$ such polynomials, respectively, each of degree at most $4 n_1 n_2 D$ in t. Now we consider the product of all these polynomials. We obtain a polynomial in t of degree $\le 8 n_1 n_2 (n_1 + n_2) D = 8 n_1 n_2 n D$. The roots of this polynomial describe all the first class of "bad" values of t, hence of the constants $c_{i,j}$. Any value for t which does not nullify this polynomial ensures that $r(z)$, $a_k^{\pm}$, and $b_k^{\pm}$ do not vanish identically, even in the presence of isolated roots of (Σ) at infinity.

The second class of "bad" values for t are those that force Eq. (17) to vanish for distinct indices m, l, and ν. After substituting each $c_{i,j}$ by a suitable power of t, Eq. (17) becomes a polynomial in t of degree $\le 2 n_1 n_2$. We have one such polynomial for each triple of roots ζ_m, ζ_l, and ζ_ν, see Eq. (13), and for all possible k. Therefore, there are $\binom{D}{3} n_1$ plus $\binom{D}{3} n_2$ polynomials that correspond to "bad" values for the x and y coordinates, respectively. The product of all of them results a polynomial of degree at most $2 n n_1 n_2 D^3$.

Finally, we consider the product of the two polynomials that correspond to the two classes of "bad" values for the constants. This is a polynomial in t of degree at most $2 n_1 n_2 n D^3 + 8 n_1 n_2 n D \le 10 n_1 n_2 n D^3$. Hence, if we consider the integers in the interval $I = [0,\, 10 n_1 n_2 n D^3]$ there is at least one, say $t_0 \in I$, that it is not a root of this polynomial. This integer implies a safe choice of the values $c_{i,j}$. Obviously, $|t_0| = \mathtt{H}(t_0) \le 10 n_1 n_2 n D^3$.

Substituting $t = t_0$ in $f_{0,k}$, we obtain $c_{i,j}$ and f_0 such that

$$\mathtt{H}(f_0) \le (10 n_1 n_2 n D^3)^{n_1 n_2 + n}$$

and so $\mathfrak{h}(f_0) = \mathcal{O}(n_1 n_2 \lg(n_1 n_2) + n_1 n_2 \lg(D))$.

LEMMA 3.2. $\mathfrak{h}(f_0) = \mathcal{O}(n_1 n_2 \lg(n_1 n_2) + n_1 n_2 \lg(D))$.

The previous analysis and the derived bound allows us to introduce a probabilistic version for computing f_0. Using the Schwartz-Zippel lemma, if we choose t_0 from an interval that contains $c\, 10 n_1 n_2 n D^3$ integers, for a constant $c \in \mathbb{N}$, then the probability to obtain a "bad" f_0 is $1/c$. By repeated applications we can amplify this probability.

3.2 Separation and representation bounds

Separation bounds are bounds on the minimum distance between two isolated roots of a polynomial system. We use DMM bound [19, 20], which is an output sensitive aggregate version to estimate the separation bound of a system of bilinear polynomials.

We assume that $f_i \in \mathbb{Z}[\mathbf{x}, \mathbf{y}]$ and $\mathfrak{h}(f_i) \le \tau$. Then $\mathfrak{h}(f_0) = \sigma = \mathcal{O}(n_1 n_2 \lg(n_1 n_2) + n_1 n_2 \lg(D))$ (Lem. 3.2). By Lem. 2.2, we know exactly the form of the resultant for bilinear systems. In particular, it is homogeneous of degree D in the coefficients of each f_i. It has the form

$$r(z) = \cdots + \varrho_i\, z^i\, \mathbf{c}_i^{D-i} \mathbf{a}_{1,i}^D \mathbf{a}_{2,i}^D \cdots \mathbf{a}_{n,i}^D + \ldots, \qquad (21)$$

where $\varrho_i \in \mathbb{Z}$, $\mathbf{a}_{k,i}^D$ denotes a monomial in coefficients of f_k with total degree D, and $\mathbf{c}_i^{D-i}$ denotes a monomial in the coefficients of f_0 of total degree $D - i$. The degree of r, with respect to z, is D and corresponds to the number of solutions of the system. It is nonzero because we have assumed that the system has only isolated solutions, even at infinity. We bound $|\varrho_i| \le (n+1)^{2(n+1)D}$ using the fact the Newton polytopes of f_k are product of simplices. Following [19, 20] we get $\mathfrak{h}(r) = \mathcal{O}(nD\lg(nD) + D\sigma + nD\tau)$, that expands to

$$\begin{aligned} \mathfrak{h}(r) &= \mathcal{O}(nD\lg(nD) + n_1 n_2 D \lg(n_1 n_2 D) + nD\tau) \\ &= \widetilde{\mathcal{O}}(n_1 n_2 D \lg(D) + nD\tau). \end{aligned} \qquad (22)$$

The same bounds hold for $\hat{a}_k^{\pm}$, $\hat{b}_\ell^{\pm}$ and r', and this L that appears in Lem. 3.1. Therefore, for the representation of the roots, of Eq. (19) we have that $\deg(s_k) = \mathcal{O}(D)$ and

$$\mathfrak{h}(s_k) = \widetilde{\mathcal{O}}(n_1 n_2 D \lg(D) + nD\tau). \qquad (23)$$

If Δ_i is the separation bound of the i-th isolated root of (Σ), then using DMM [20, Cor. 10],

$$-\lg \prod\nolimits_i \Delta_i = \mathcal{O}(nD^2 \lg(nD) + nD^2\tau). \qquad (24)$$

Moreover, for any root of the system it holds

$$2^{-\mathcal{O}(nD\lg(n) + nD\tau)} \le |\alpha_{k,i}|, |\beta_{\ell,j}| \le 2^{\mathcal{O}(nD\lg(n) + nD\tau)}, \quad (25)$$

where $1 \le i \le n_1$ and $1 \le j \le n_2$.

4. THE COMPLEXITY OF SOLVING

In this section we establish the bit complexity of the algorithm to compute isolating hyperboxes for all the roots of the system.

4.1 Square systems of dimension 0

First, we consider the complexity of computing the determinant of the first resultant matrix, say M, of Sec. 2.2, when it is a scalar matrix. The dimension of the matrix is $(n+1)D \times (n+1)D$. We use Wiedemann's algorithm, following the approach in [9]. The arithmetic complexity is dominated by the cost of performing $(n+1)D$ applications of matrix-vector products Mb, for a vector b.

Lem. 2.2 implies that $b^\top M$ corresponds to $(n+1)$ polynomial multiplications. Each involves two polynomials: one of bidegree (1,1) and one of degree n_1 with n_2 variables (the case of the first resultant matrix), or of degree n_2 in n_1 variables (the case of the first resultant matrix). The output has $O(D)$ terms, and the cost to compute it is $\widetilde{\mathcal{O}}_B(D)$. Using Tellegen's principle [4] we obtain, at almost the same cost, an algorithm for Mb. Thus, the determinant computation costs $\widetilde{\mathcal{O}}(nD^2)$ arithmetic operations. Similar results hold for the other two resultant matrices.

It is worth to mention that for the third matrix we can exploit directly its block structure and we can avoid to use polynomial multiplication. This is so due to its construction using differentials. In this way we can compute the matrix-vector product using $\mathcal{O}(n \min(n_1, n_2)^2 D)$ operations.

Computing r requires the determinant of a (resultant) matrix depending on one parameter z; this is done using interpolation. Recall that r has degree $\mathcal{O}(D)$ and $\mathfrak{h}(r) = \widetilde{\mathcal{O}}(n_1 n_2 D \lg(D) + nD\tau)$. We need to perform $\mathcal{O}(D)$ scalar determinant evaluations; each reduces to D times $(n+1)$ polynomial multiplications. We assume the polynomials have the worst possible bitsize, that is $\widetilde{\mathcal{O}}(n_1 n_2 D \lg(D) + nD\tau)$. The cost of each multiplication is $\widetilde{\mathcal{O}}_B(n_1 n_2 D^2 \lg(D) + nD^2\tau)$, using a probabilistic [3, Thm. 7.1] or a worst case [28, Cor. 21] algorithm. Thus, the total cost for computing the polynomial r is $\widetilde{\mathcal{O}}_B(n\, n_1 n_2 D^4 \lg(D) + n^2 D^4 \tau)$.

To compute the representation of the roots of Eq. (19) we need to compute $a_k^{\pm}(z)$, $b_\ell^{\pm}$, and $s_k(z)$. The cost of computing $a_k^{\pm}(z)$ is the same as that for computing r. Since there are n coordinates, the cost for computing all $a_k^{\pm}(z)$ and $b_k^{\pm}(z)$ is $\widetilde{\mathcal{O}}_B(n^2 n_1 n_2 D^4 \lg(D) + n^3 D^4 \tau)$. Following Lem. 3.1, the degree of s_k's is $\mathcal{O}(D)$ and their bitsize is $\widetilde{\mathcal{O}}(n^2 D + n_1 n_2 D \lg(D) + nD\tau)$. The cost to construct them is $\widetilde{\mathcal{O}}_B(n^3 D^4 + n n_1 n_2 D^4 \lg(D) + n^2 D^4 \tau)$.

Next, we isolate all the complex roots of r, with cost bounded by $\widetilde{\mathcal{O}}_B(D^2\mathfrak{h}(r)) = \widetilde{\mathcal{O}}_B(D^3(n_1n_2\lg(D) + n\tau))$ [38]. We obtain isolating boxes for the complex roots of r. Then, we refine the roots up to accuracy $2^{-\lambda}$ in $\widetilde{\mathcal{O}}_B(D^2\mathfrak{h}(r) + D\lambda)$ [39]. We perform all the computations with λ bits of accuracy. We need to determine the value for λ such that the evaluation of the RUR, see Eq. (19), at the approximations of the roots of r results to disjoint hyperboxes for the roots of the system.

After refinement, for every root γ_i of r, we have an interval $[\gamma_i]$, such that its width is less than $2^{-\lambda}$; that is $\mathtt{wid}([\gamma_i]) \leq 2^{-\lambda}$. For each coordinate k, using interval or multiprecision floating point arithmetic, we evaluate Eq. (19), at $[\gamma_i]$. In this way we obtain intervals, $I_{k,i}$ for all the possible values of the k-th coordinates, where $I_{k,i} = -\frac{\mathtt{lc}(r)\, s_k([\gamma_i])}{\mathtt{lc}(g)\, r'([\gamma_i])}$. Using Horner's rule for the evaluation [27, Sec. 5.1] we have $\mathtt{wid}(s_k([\gamma_i])) \leq c_{2D}\, \overline{s}_k(|\gamma_i|)$. The constant c_{2D}, under the mild assumption that the precision used to perform the computations is bigger than $\lg(n)$, is $c_{2D} \leq 5D\,2^{-\lambda} = 2^{-\lambda+\mathcal{O}(\lg(D))}$. The polynomial $\overline{s}_k$ is s_k but with its coefficients replaced by their absolute value. Thus,

$$\overline{s}_k(|\gamma_i|) \leq (D+1)\,\mathtt{H}(s_k)\max\{1, |\gamma_i|^D\} .$$

We bound $|\gamma_i|$ using Eq. (25). A similar bound holds for $r'([\gamma_i])$. Putting everything together we have

$$\mathtt{wid}(I_{k,i}) \leq 2^{-\lambda+\widetilde{\mathcal{O}}(n_1n_2D\lg(D)+nD^2\tau)} .$$

For these intervals to be disjoint it suffices that $\mathtt{wid}(I_{k,i}) \leq 2^{-\lg\prod_i \Delta_i}$ holds. Hence, we choose a proper constant λ such that

$$\mathtt{wid}(I_{k,i}) \leq 2^{-\lambda+\widetilde{\mathcal{O}}(n_1n_2D\lg(D)+nD^2\tau)} \leq 2^{-\lg\prod_i \Delta_i},$$

which results the following bound $\lambda > \mathcal{O}(nD^2\lg(D) + nD^2\tau)$ on the precision. To actually obtain the isolating boxes for the roots we evaluate s_k and r' at the isolating boxes of the roots of r using an approximate multipoint evaluation algorithm in $\widetilde{\mathcal{O}}_B(nD^3\tau + D\lambda)$ [40, Lemma 21]. The previous discussion leads to the theorem.

THEOREM 4.1. *There is a probabilistic algorithm for isolating the roots of a 0-dimensional system of (n_1, n_2)-bilinear polynomials with integer coefficients of maximum bitsize τ, in $\widetilde{\mathcal{O}}_B(n^2n_1n_2D^4\lg(D) + n^2D^4\tau)$, where $n = n_1 + n_2$ and D is the bilinear Bézout bound of Eq. (2).*

We would have obtained the same complexity results if we had used the PER, Eq. (18), representation of the roots. In this case λ would have been $\lambda > \mathcal{O}(nD^3\lg(D) + nD^3\tau)$.

4.2 Overdetermined systems of dimension 0

Assume that the input consists of more than n bilinear polynomials, say p, that is $f_1, \dots, f_p$, which possess a finite number of (biprojective) roots. First, we have to make the system square, using the technique from [24], by considering n random linear combinations of the input polynomials, that is $h_k = \sum_{i=1}^{p} r_i f_i$, for $1 \leq k \leq n$, where r_i are random integers. The bitsize of the polynomials of this new, square system is asymptotically the same, up to logarithmic factors. We refer to [20] for details. Then, we solve the system using Thm. 4.1. We obtain a representation for the roots of the new system. The bounds of the representation and the complexity of computing it are the same as in the previous section. However, the procedure to construct a square system might introduce additional isolated points. Thus, not all isolated roots of the new system correspond to roots of the original one. Equivalently, not all the roots of the resultant, $r(z)$, correspond to roots of the original system. To identify the roots of interest we proceed as follows. We substitute the RUR of the x and y coordinates in f_k, for $1 \leq k \leq p$. That is

$$f_k\left(\frac{-\mathtt{lc}(r)\, s_1}{\mathtt{lc}(g_1)\, r'}, \dots, \frac{-\mathtt{lc}(r)\, s_{n_1}}{\mathtt{lc}(g_{n_1})\, r'}, \frac{-\mathtt{lc}(r)\, q_1}{\mathtt{lc}(h_1)\, r'}, \dots, \frac{-\mathtt{lc}(r)\, q_{n_2}}{\mathtt{lc}(h_{n_2})\, r'}\right) .$$

In this way we obtain a rational function in z, say $\frac{f_{k,0}(z)}{f_{k,1}(z)}$. Let σ be the bitsize of the polynomials in RUR. We can compute this rational function in $\widetilde{\mathcal{O}}_B(n(n + n_1n_2)D\sigma)$ [40]. It holds that $\deg(f_{k,0}) = \deg(f_{k,1}) = \mathcal{O}(D)$ and $\mathfrak{h}(f_{k,0}) = \widetilde{\mathcal{O}}(n\sigma)$. To determine which are the roots of the new system that correspond to roots of the original system, it suffices to compute the $\gcd(r, f_{1,0}, \dots, f_{p,0})$. This corresponds to, at most, p computations of GCD's of two polynomials of degree $\mathcal{O}(D)$ and bitsize $\widetilde{\mathcal{O}}(n\sigma)$. The cost for each GCD computation is $\widetilde{\mathcal{O}}_B(nD^2\sigma)$ [47], and so the total cost is $\widetilde{\mathcal{O}}_B(pnD^2\sigma)$. If we substitute $\sigma = \widetilde{\mathcal{O}}(n_1n_2D\lg(D) + nD\tau)$, then we obtain the bound $\widetilde{\mathcal{O}}_B(p(nn_1n_2D^3\lg(D) + n^2D^3\tau))$. If we use a probabilistic algorithm for the GCD of $p+1$ polynomials using one GCD operation [47], then we can eliminate the factor p.

4.3 Positive dimensional systems

The resultant computation and thus the algorithm of Thm. 4.1 fails when the system is not zero-dimensional, including the case of excess components at infinity. This section handles this situation by an infinitesimal symbolic perturbation of the given polynomials.

The resultant may vanish identically for random choices of the coefficients of f_0 (where f_0 as in Sect. 3.1), if there are infinitely many roots of the system $f_0 = f_1 = \cdots = f_n = 0$ (projective or affine). This case is not covered by the "bad" values of Sect. 3.1, which are derived under the assumption of finitely many solutions in $\mathbb{P}^{n_1} \times \mathbb{P}^{n_2}$ for the input equations $f_1, \dots, f_n$. Note that there are no extraneous factors coming from the determinantal matrix expressions of our resultant, therefore there is no other possibility of an identically zero determinant.

To compute the roots in these cases we consider the general approach of generalized characteristic polynomial of [8]. In particular, we apply the perturbation scheme for sparse systems of [13]. Assume a square $(n_1, n_2)-$bilinear system $p_1, \dots, p_n$ that has a non-zero resultant. This happens for any choice of n polynomials $p_1, \dots, p_n$ with finitely many roots in $\mathbb{P}^{n_1} \times \mathbb{P}^{n_2}$, and a generic polynomial f_0. In particular we consider random coefficients for a set of monomials per equation that appear on a (permuted) diagonal of the matrix, and zero elsewhere. Then $R(f_0, p_1, \dots, p_n) \neq 0$ implies that the matrices in Lem. 2.2 are non-singular.

We assume that a given polynomial system $f_1, \dots, f_n$ has an infinite number of solutions. Now consider the perturbed system $\tilde{f}_k = f_k + \varepsilon p_k$, $k = 1, \dots, n$ augmented by f_0. The polynomial $C(\varepsilon) := R(\tilde{f}_0, \dots, \tilde{f}_n)$ has degree equal to nD w.r.t. ε. By [13, Prop. 3.4] its leading coefficient is equal to $R(f_0, p_1, \dots, p_n)$, therefore non-zero. Therefore, if we regard $C(\varepsilon)$ as a univariate polynomial in ε, there exists a non-zero trailing coefficient, which is a polynomial in the coefficients of f_0. This trailing term of $C(\varepsilon)$ has the same property as the unperturbed resultant in the zero-dimensional case. That is, the coefficient of the ε-power factors as a product of linear forms, and the coefficients of the linear forms provide us with one point per connected component of the solution set of $f_1, \dots, f_n$. The complexity of computing the trailing non-vanishing coefficient is the complexity of the zero-dimensional case multiplied by the degree, say d, with respect to ε, of this term, as we can perform the computations $\mod \varepsilon^d$.

EXAMPLE 4.2. *Consider the $(1,2)-$bilinear, square system $f_1 = 1 + 2y_2 + 2y_1 + x_1 + 2x_1y_2 + 2x_1y_1$, $f_2 = 1 + 2y_2 + y_1 + 2x_1 + 2x_1y_2 + 2x_1y_1$, $f_3 = 1 + 2y_2 + 2y_1 + x_1 + 2x_1y_2 + 2x_1y_1$. The system has infinitely many roots, which are $(x_1; y_1, y_2) = (-1; -1, \rho)$, $(x_1; y_1, y_2) = (-\frac{1}{2} - \sigma; -\frac{1}{2} - \sigma, \sigma)$, for any $\rho, \sigma \in \mathbb{R}$ plus the root $(x_0, x_1; y_0, y_1, y_2) = (0, 1; 0, -1, 1)$ at infinity. We perturb the system by ε; for this example, perturbing one linear term per equation is sufficient. Let $\tilde{f}_1 = f_1 + \varepsilon x_1$ and $\tilde{f}_{1+j} =$*

$f_{1+j} + \varepsilon y_j$, $j = 1, 2$. *Adding the polynomial* f_0 *as in Example 2.3, we obtain the resultant* $R(f_0, \ldots, f_3) = q_0\varepsilon^6 + q_1\varepsilon^7 + q_2\varepsilon^8$, *where* q_0, q_1, q_2 *depend on the coefficients of* f_0. *The (factored) coefficient of the trailing term* $q_0\varepsilon^6$ *is:*

$$q_0(a_0, \ldots, a_5) = -32(a_4 - a_5)(a_0 - a_1 - a_2 - a_3 + a_4 + a_5)$$
$$(a_0 - \frac{1}{4}a_1 - \frac{1}{4}a_2 - \frac{1}{4}a_3 + \frac{1}{16}a_4 + \frac{1}{16}a_5),$$

which corresponds to the root at infinity plus one point on each component, namely $\rho = -1$ *and* $\sigma = -\frac{1}{4}$.

Acknowledgments: The authors are grateful to the reviewers for their careful reading and corrections they brought the original draft. ET is partially supported by ANR-11-BS02-0013 HPAC project and an FP7 Marie Curie Career Integration Grant.

References

[1] C. J. Accettella, G. M. D. Corso, and G. Manzini. Inversion of two level circulant matrices over $\mathbb{Z}_p$. *Lin. Alg. Appl.*, 366:5 – 23, 2003.

[2] M. E. Alonso, E. Becker, M.-F. Roy, and T. Wörmann. Algorithms in algebraic geometry and applications. chapter Zeros, Multiplicities, and Idempotents for Zero-dimensional Systems, pages 1–15. 1996.

[3] A. Arnold and D. S. Roche. Output-sensitive algorithms for sumset and sparse polynomial multiplication. In *Proc. ISSAC*, pages 29–36, 2015.

[4] A. Bostan, G. Lecerf, and E. Schost. Tellegen's principle into practice. In *Proc. ISSAC*, pages 37–44, 2003. ISBN 1-58113-641-2.

[5] A. Bostan, B. Salvy, and É. Schost. Fast algorithms for zero-dimensional polynomial systems using duality. *Applicable Algebra in Engineering, Communication and Computing*, 14(4):239–272, 2003.

[6] Y. Bouzidi, S. Lazard, G. Moroz, M. Pouget, F. Rouillier, and M. Sagraloff. Improved algorithms for solving bivariate systems via Rational Univariate Representations. Tech. report, Inria, June 2015.

[7] J. Canny. Some algebraic and geometric computations in PSPACE. In *Proc. 20th STOC*, pages 460–467. ACM, 1988.

[8] J. Canny. Generalised characteristic polynomials. *JSC*, 9(3):241–250, 1990.

[9] J. F. Canny, E. Kaltofen, and L. Yagati. Solving systems of nonlinear polynomial equations faster. In *Proc. ISSAC*, pages 121–128, 1989.

[10] D. Cox and E. Materov. Tate resolutions for Segre embeddings. *Algebra & Number Theory*, 2(5):523–550, 2008.

[11] X. Dahan and E. Schost. Sharp estimates for triangular sets. In *Proc. ACM ISSAC*, pages 103–110, 2004. ISBN 1-58113-827-X.

[12] C. D'Andrea and A. Dickenstein. Explicit formulas for the multivariate resultant. *J. Pure and Applied Algebra*, 164(1-2):59–86, 2001.

[13] C. D'Andrea and I. Emiris. Computing sparse projection operators. *Contemporary Mathematics*, 286:121–140, 2001.

[14] A. Dickenstein and I. Z. Emiris. Multihomogeneous resultant formulae by means of complexes. *JSC*, 36(3):317–342, 2003.

[15] I. Emiris and R. Vidunas. Root counts of semi-mixed systems, and an application to counting Nash equilibria. In *Proc. ACM ISSAC*, pages 154–161, Kobe, Japan, 2014. ACM Press.

[16] I. Z. Emiris and A. Mantzaflaris. Multihomogeneous resultant formulae for systems with scaled support. *JSC*, 47(7):820–842, 2012.

[17] I. Z. Emiris and V. Y. Pan. Symbolic and Numeric Methods for Exploiting Structure in Constructing Resultant Matrices. *JSC*, 33(4): 393–413, Apr. 2002.

[18] I. Z. Emiris and V. Y. Pan. Improved algorithms for computing determinants and resultants. *J. of Complexity*, 21(1):43–71, Feb. 2005.

[19] I. Z. Emiris, B. Mourrain, and E. P. Tsigaridas. The DMM bound: Multivariate (aggregate) separation bounds. In *Proc. ACM ISSAC*, pages 243–250, 2010.

[20] I. Z. Emiris, B. Mourrain, and E. Tsigaridas. Separation bounds for polynomial systems. Technical report, INRIA, Dec. 2015.

[21] J.-C. Faugere, F. Levy-Dit-Vehel, and L. Perret. Cryptanalysis of minrank. In *Advances in Cryptology*, pages 280–296. Springer, 2008.

[22] J.-C. Faugère, M. Safey El Din, and P.-J. Spaenlehauer. Gröbner bases of bihomogeneous ideals generated by polynomials of bidegree (1,1): Algorithms and complexity. *JSC*, 46:406–437, 2011.

[23] I. Gelfand, M. Kapranov, and A. Zelevinsky. *Discriminants, Resultants and Multidimensional Determinants*. Birkhäuser, Boston, 1994.

[24] M. Giusti and J. Heintz. La détermination des points isolés et de la dimension d'une variété algébrique peut se faire en temps polynomial. In *Proc. Int. Meeting on Commutative Algebra, Cortona*, 1993.

[25] M. Giusti, G. Lecerf, and B. Salvy. A Gröbner free alternative for polynomial system solving. *J. of Complexity*, 17(1):154–211, 2001.

[26] R. Hartshorne. *Algebraic Geometry*. Springer, New York, 1977.

[27] N. J. Higham. *Accuracy and stability of numerical algorithms*. Society for Industrial and Applied Mathematics, Philadelphia, 2002.

[28] J. v. d. Hoeven and G. Lecerf. On the bit-complexity of sparse polynomial multiplication. *JSC*, 50:227–254, 2013.

[29] G. Jeronimo and J. Sabia. Computing multihomogeneous resultants using straight-line programs. *JSC*, 42(1–2):218–235, 2007.

[30] A. Joux. A new index calculus algorithm with complexity $L(1/4 + o(1))$ in small characteristic. In *Selected Areas in Cryptography–SAC 2013*, pages 355–379. Springer, 2014.

[31] E. Kaltofen and G. Villard. On the complexity of computing determinants. *Computational Complexity*, 13(3-4):91–130, 2005.

[32] A. Mantzaflaris and B. Mourrain. Deflation and certified isolation of singular zeros of polynomial systems. In *Proc. ACM ISSAC*, pages 249–256, 2011.

[33] A. Mantzaflaris and B. Mourrain. Singular zeros of polynomial systems. In T. Dokken and G. Muntingh, editors, *Advances in Shapes, Geometry, and Algebra*, volume 10 of *Geometry and Computing*, pages 77–103. Springer, 2014.

[34] N. McCoy. On the resultant of a system of forms homogeneous in each of several sets of variables. *Trans. AMS*, 35(1):215–233, 1933.

[35] E. Mehrabi and E. Schost. A softly optimal monte carlo algorithm for solving bivariate polynomial systems over the integers. *J. of Complexity*, 34:78 – 128, 2016.

[36] T. Muir. The resultant of a set of lineo-linear equations. *Proc. Royal Soc. of South Africa*, 2(1):373–380, 1910.

[37] A. V. Ourivski and T. Johansson. New technique for decoding codes in the rank metric and its cryptography applications. *Problems of Information Transmission*, 38(3):237–246, 2002.

[38] V. Y. Pan. Univariate polynomials: Nearly optimal algorithms for numerical factorization and root-finding. *JSC*, 33(5):701 – 733, 2002.

[39] V. Y. Pan and E. Tsigaridas. Accelerated Approximation of the Complex Roots and Factors of a Univariate Polynomial. *Theoretical Computer Science*, 2015. (To appear).

[40] V. Y. Pan and E. Tsigaridas. Nearly optimal computations with structured matrices. *Theoretical Computer Science*, 2015. (To appear).

[41] F. Rouillier. Solving zero-dimensional systems through the rational univariate representation. *Applicable Algebra in Engineering, Communication and Computing*, 9(5):433–461, 1999.

[42] M. Safey El Din and É. Schost. Polar varieties and computation of one point in each connected component of a smooth real algebraic set. In *Proc. ACM ISSAC*, pages 224–231, 2003.

[43] H. Schenck, D. Cox, and A. Dickenstein. A case study in bigraded commutative algebra. *Syzygies & Hilbert Functions*, 254:67–112, 2007.

[44] P.-J. Spaenlehauer. *Solving multi-homogeneous and determinantal systems: algorithms, complexity, applications*. Thesis, Université Pierre et Marie Curie (Univ. Paris 6), Oct. 2012.

[45] B. Sturmfels and A. Zelevinsky. Multigraded resultants of Sylvester type. *J. Algebra*, 163(1):115–127, 1994.

[46] J. Sylvester. On the degree and weight of the resultant of a multipartite system of equations. *Proc. Royal Soc. of London*, 12:674–676, 1862.

[47] J. von zur Gathen and J. Gerhard. *Modern computer algebra*. Cambridge University Press, 3rd edition, 2013.

[48] J. Weyman. Calculating discriminants by higher direct images. *Trans. of AMS*, 343(1):367–389, 1994.

[49] J. Weyman. *Cohomology of Vector Bundles and Syzygies*. Cambridge Univ. Press, 2003. [Cambridge Tracts in Mathematics 149].

[50] J. Weyman and A. Zelevinsky. Determinantal formulas for multigraded resultants. *J. Alg. Geom.*, 3(4):569–597, 1994.

Computing Small Certificates of Inconsistency of Quadratic Fewnomial Systems

Jean-Charles Faugère
Sorbonne Universités, UPMC
Univ Paris 06, CNRS , INRIA
Laboratoire d'Informatique de Paris 6 (LIP6), Équipe PolSys
4 place Jussieu, 75252 Paris Cedex 05, France
jean-charles.faugere@inria.fr

Pierre-Jean Spaenlehauer
Inria, CNRS
Université de Lorraine
Nancy, France
pierre-jean.spaenlehauer@inria.fr

Jules Svartz
Min. de l'Éducation Nationale
Lycée Masséna
Sorbonne Universités, UPMC
Univ Paris 06, CNRS , INRIA
Laboratoire d'Informatique de Paris 6 (LIP6), Équipe PolSys
4 place Jussieu, 75252 Paris Cedex 05, France
jsvartz@ens-cachan.fr

ABSTRACT

Bézout's theorem states that dense generic systems of n multivariate quadratic equations in n variables have 2^n solutions over algebraically closed fields. When only a small subset $\mathbf{M}$ of monomials appear in the equations (*fewnomial systems*), the number of solutions may decrease dramatically. We focus in this work on subsets of quadratic monomials $\mathbf{M}$ such that generic systems with support $\mathbf{M}$ do not admit any solution at all. For these systems, Hilbert's Nullstellensatz ensures the existence of algebraic certificates of inconsistency. However, up to our knowledge all known bounds on the sizes of such certificates —including those which take into account the Newton polytopes of the polynomials— are exponential in n. Our main results show that if the inequality $2|\mathbf{M}|-2n \leq \sqrt{1+8\nu}-1$ holds for a quadratic fewnomial system – where ν is the matching number of a graph associated with $\mathbf{M}$, and $|\mathbf{M}|$ is the cardinality of $\mathbf{M}$ – then there exists generically a certificate of inconsistency of linear size (measured as the number of coefficients in the ground field $\mathbb{K}$). Moreover this certificate can be computed within a polynomial number of arithmetic operations. Next, we evaluate how often this inequality holds, and we give evidence that the probability that the inequality is satisfied depends strongly on the number of squares. More precisely, we show that if $\mathbf{M}$ is picked uniformly at random among the subsets of $n+k+1$ quadratic monomials containing at least $\Omega(n^{1/2+\varepsilon})$ squares, then the probability that the inequality holds tends to 1 as n grows. Interestingly, this phenomenon is related with the matching number of random graphs in the Erdös-Renyi model. Finally, we provide experimental results showing that certificates in inconsistency can be computed for systems with more than 10000 variables and equations.

Keywords

Fewnomials, effective Nullstellensatz, random graphs, polynomial system solving

ISSAC '16, July 19-22, 2016, Waterloo, ON, Canada

DOI: http://dx.doi.org/10.1145/2930889.2930927

1. INTRODUCTION

Context and problem statement. Identifying classes of structured polynomial systems and designing dedicated algorithms to solve them is a central theme in computer algebra and in computational algebraic geometry, due to the wide range of applications where such systems appear. We investigate quadratic systems involving a small number of monomials (*quadratic fewnomial systems*). Let $\mathbb{K}$ be a field, $\overline{\mathbb{K}}$ its algebraic closure and $\mathbf{M}$ be a finite subset of monomials of degree at most two in a polynomial ring $\mathbb{K}[X_1, \ldots, X_n]$. Suppose also that the constant 1 belongs to $\mathbf{M}$, and let $\mathcal{L}_\mathbf{M}$ be the $\mathbb{K}$-linear space of polynomials in $\mathbb{K}[X_1, \ldots, X_n]$ spanned by $\mathbf{M}$.

A classical question is to bound the number of solutions in $\overline{\mathbb{K}}^n$ of a system $f_1(X_1, \ldots, X_n) = \cdots = f_n(X_1, \ldots, X_n) = 0$, where all polynomials lie in $\mathcal{L}_\mathbf{M}$ and have generic coefficients. When the exponent vectors of the monomials in $\mathbf{M}$ are the points with integer coordinates in a lattice polytope, Kushnirenko's theorem states that the number of toric solutions (*i.e.* solutions whose all coordinates are nonzero) is bounded by the normalized volume of the polytope [24]. A variant of this theorem indicates that such generic polynomial systems do not admit any solution if the dimension of the $\mathbb{Q}$-linear space generated by the exponent vectors of the monomials in $\mathbf{M}$ does not equal n.

Solving a polynomial system and deciding if it has any solution in $\overline{\mathbb{K}}^n$ are two closely related questions. One classical method to produce a certificate that a polynomial system does not have any solution is to provide an algebraic relation via Hilbert's Nullstellensatz:

> **Problem 1 - Effective fewnomial Nullstellensatz.** Given a system $(f_1, \ldots, f_m) \in \mathcal{L}_\mathbf{M}^m$ such that $f_1(X) = \cdots = f_m(X) = 0$ has no solution in $\overline{\mathbb{K}}^n$, compute $h_1, \ldots h_m \in \mathbb{K}[X_1, \ldots, X_n]$ such that $\sum_{i=1}^m f_i h_i = 1$.

Bounding the sizes of the polynomials h_i is a crucial question to estimate the complexity of this problem. In this paper, the notion of size that we use is the number of coefficients in $\mathbb{K}$ required to describe the polynomials $h_1, \ldots, h_m$.

On the other hand, the specification of "solving a polynomial system" depends on the context. If the number of solutions in the algebraic closure $\overline{\mathbb{K}}$ is finite, one way to represent them symbolically is to provide a rational parametrization of their coordinates by the roots of a univariate polynomial. For the sake of simplicity, we consider only the problem of computing a univariate polynomial whose roots parametrize the set of solutions:

> **Problem 2 - Partial 0-dimensional fewnomial system solving.** Given a polynomial system $f_1 = \cdots = f_m = 0$ with support $\mathbf{M}$ that have finitely-many solutions in $\overline{\mathbb{K}}^n$ and a monomial $\mu \in \mathbf{M}$, compute a univariate polynomial $P_\mu \in \mathbb{K}[\mu]$ which vanishes at all the solutions of the system.

Hence, the roots of the univariate polynomial P_μ contain the images of the solutions of the input multivariate system via the monomial map $(X_1, \ldots, X_n) \mapsto \mu$.

Related works. Sparse elimination theory for solving systems with special monomial structures have been developed since the 80s [33]. Several lines of work have been initiated during this period. When the exponent vectors of the monomials occurring in the polynomials of the system are the lattice points in a lattice polytope, connections with convex and toric geometry have been established and dedicated solving methods have been designed: homotopy continuation methods [18, 35], resultants [33, 6], Gröbner bases [34, 13], etc. One important theme of these developments is to relate algebraic structures with combinatorial properties of convex bodies. In particular, Kushnirenko and Bernshtein's theorems [24, 2] provide bounds on the number of isolated toric solutions in terms of the Newton polytopes of the input polynomials. Another line of work have been initiated by Khovanskii in the 80s on fewnomial systems [19]. The main theme in this setting is to relate the algebraic and algorithmic complexity of several problems to the number of monomials occurring in the equations. For instance, a classical and challenging question is to bound the number of real solutions in the positive orthant, see *e.g.* [19, 30, 3, 4, 20, 21] for results on this topic. Bounding the size of a certificate of inconsistency of a polynomial system via the Nullstellensatz is a classical problem. Up to our knowledge, all known upper bounds on the size of such certificates are exponential in the number of variables n; moreover, examples by Masser and Philippon and by Lazard and Mora show that one cannot hope for better bounds in the worst case. A classical bound is given by Kollar [22]: if the maximal degree of the input inconsistent system $f_1, \ldots, f_m$ is D, then there exist $h_1, \ldots, h_m$ such that $\sum_{i=1}^m f_i\, h_i = 1$ and the degrees of the h_i are bounded by $n \min(n, m) D^{\min(n,m)} + \min(n, m) D$. This bound is general and does not require any further assumption. It was later improved to $\deg(f_i h_i) \leq \max(3, D)^n$ [14]. When there is no solution at infinity, the degrees of the polynomials h_i are bounded by $(D-1)n$ [25, 5]: the number of coefficients in dense polynomials of this degree is still exponential in n. For general polynomial systems, it would be surprising that certificates of inconsistency with size polynomial in the input size exist, as this would imply $NP = coNP$. Estimates taking into account the bitsize of the coefficients that appear in the certificate in terms of the bitsize of the coefficients of the input system are provided by *Arithmetic Nullstellensätze*, see *e.g.* [23] and references within. Two milestones on the sparse effective Nullstellensatz are the bounds in [6] and [31]: these bounds provide certificates of size bounded by a quantity which depends on the Newton polytopes of the input polynomials. However, their size is exponential in the size of the input, and these bounds do not take into account the sparsity of the support inside its Newton polytope. One of the main difficulty to generalize these techniques to fewnomial quadratic systems is the fact that the proofs rely on algebraic properties (normality, Cohen-Macaulay algebras) that hold for semigroup algebras generated by lattice points in normal polytopes, but not for semigroup algebras generated by a scattered set of monomials.

Other models of sparse systems have also been investigated. For instance, systems where each quadratic equation involves a small subset of variables have been investigated in [29] and [7]. Connections between combinatorial properties of graphs and polynomial systems is a classical topic which has been investigated from several viewpoints. For instance, square-free monomial ideals have many combinatorial properties and can be seen as the *edge ideals* of graphs, see *e.g.* [15, 17]. Connections between the regularity of the edge ideal of a graph and its matching number and co-chordal cover number are shown in [36]. Cohen-Macaulay criteria for such ideals are investigated in [16, 10].

Bounds on the size of certificate of inconsistency of polynomial systems are a important ingredient in algebraic proof complexity, see *e.g.* the Nullstellensatz proof system [1] and related works [8].

Main results. An open question is whether there exist certificates of inconsistency of polynomial size for general fewnomial systems involving $n + k + 1$ monomials in n variables. The goal of this work is to investigate this question in the case of quadratic polynomials. We present an explicit criterion which identifies subsets $\mathbf{M}$ of monomials of degree at most 2 such that systems of n equations in n variables with support $\mathbf{M}$ and generic coefficients do not have any solution, and such that there exists a sparse certificate $\sum_{i=1}^n f_i h_i = 1$, where all polynomials $h_1, \ldots, h_n$ lie in $\mathcal{L}_{\mathbf{M}}$. Therefore, the number of coefficients in $\mathbb{K}$ required to represent the certificate is the same as that of the input system. Moreover, when $\mathbf{M}$ is such a subset, we propose a method which computes such $h_1, \ldots, h_n$ within a polynomial number of arithmetic operations.

More precisely, we model the set $\mathbf{M}$ by a graph G on $n+1$ vertices, where each edge represents a nonconstant square-free monomial in $\mathbf{M}$. The constant 1 and the squares in $\mathbf{M}$ are distinguished with loops in the graph (the precise construction is described in Section 3). Let $\nu(\mathbf{M})$ denote the *matching number* (*i.e.* the maximum cardinality of a matching) of the subgraph of vertices in G with a loop.

THEOREM 1.1. *If $m \geq |\mathbf{M}| - \frac{\sqrt{1+8\nu(\mathbf{M})}-1}{2}$, then a generic system $(f_1, \ldots, f_m) \in \mathcal{L}_{\mathbf{M}}^m$ has no solution in $\overline{\mathbb{K}}^n$. Moreover, there exists $(h_1, \ldots, h_m)$ solving Problem 1 s.t. all h_i lie in $\mathcal{L}_{\mathbf{M}}$ and they can be computed within $O\left(m^\omega \binom{|\mathbf{M}|+1}{2}^\omega\right)$ operations in $\mathbb{K}$, where ω is a feasible exponent for matrix multiplication ($\omega < 2.37286$ with Le Gall's algorithm [26]).*

We would like to emphasize that the inequality $m \geq |\mathbf{M}| - \frac{\sqrt{1+8\nu(\mathbf{M})}-1}{2}$ can be checked in polynomial time, since the matching number of a graph can be computed in polynomial time with Edmonds' algorithm [11].

Next, we relate how often the assumptions of Theorem 1.1 hold with the number of squares in the support $\mathbf{M}$. If the subset of square monomials and the subset of square-free monomials in $\mathbf{M}$ are chosen at random, and the cardinality of $\mathbf{M}$ is $n+k+1$ and the number of squares is larger than $\Omega(n^{1/2+\varepsilon})$ for some $\varepsilon > 0$, then the assumptions of Theorem 1.1 hold with large probability, leading to the following statement:

THEOREM 1.2. *Let k be a fixed integer, $a_n, b_n \in \mathbb{N}$ be such $a_n + b_n = n+k+1$, and $\mathbf{M}$ be a subset of monomials of degree at most 2 in $\mathbb{K}[X_1, \ldots, X_n]$ distributed uniformly at random among those that contain the constant 1, a_n nonsquare monomials, and $b_n - 1$ non-constant square monomials. Assume further that $b_n = \Omega(n^{1/2+\varepsilon})$, for $\varepsilon > 0$. Then the probability that the assumptions of Theorem 1.1 with $m = n$ are satisfied for $\mathbf{M}$ tends towards 1 as n grows.*

The cornerstones of the proof of this theorem rely on properties of random graphs in the Erdös-Renyi model. Experiments suggest that this result is sharp: when there are at most $O(n^{1/2})$ square monomials in $\mathbf{M}$, we observe experimentally that the probability of having a certificate in $\mathcal{L}_{\mathbf{M}}^m$ seems to converge to a non-zero value smaller than 1 as n grows. This is also the case when the support is chosen uniformly at random (the expected number of squares is $O(1)$). We propose a conjecture stating that the limit probability is nonzero in that case.

We also study a limit case: when $|\mathbf{M}| = n + k + 1$ and all the squares are in $\mathbf{M}$. The generic number of solutions in this setting is given by the Bézout's theorem: it equals 2^n. We shall see that with probability tending to 1, these solutions can be compactly represented as the orbits of 2^{2k+2} points under an action of $(\mathbb{Z}/2\mathbb{Z})^{n-2k-2}$. Computing these solutions amounts to solving a system of $2k + 2$ equations in $2k + 2$ variables: the time complexity of this task does not depend on n. A direct consequence is that computing a compact representation of the solutions of such systems require a number of operations in $\mathbb{K}$ which is polynomial in n, even though their number of solutions is exponential in n. This suggests that the number of solutions in the algebraic closure, which is often used to measure the complexity of solving polynomial systems, might in some cases greatly overestimate the complexity for fewnomial systems. Another open issue is to extend this work to the non quadratic case.

Finally, we show experimental results obtained with our proof-of-concept implementation. They show that certificates of inconsistency can be computed for quadratic fewnomial systems with more than 10000 variables and equations when there are sufficiently many squares in the monomial support. Moreover, we also observe some unexpected behaviors which raise new questions about fewnomial systems. For instance, as n grows, there seems to be a phase transition in the probability of having a small certificate of inconsistency. Moreover, in the case where there are few squares in the fewnomial system (this case is not covered by the theoretical analysis), there seems to be a non-zero probability that a fewnomial system has a small certificate of inconsistency. These phenomenons remain to be explained.

Organization of the paper. Section 2 introduces notation and states preliminary results. The core result of the paper is proved in Section 3, establishing a connection between the matching number and the existence of a small certificate of inconsistency. Section 4 is devoted to a probabilistic analysis of the matching number of some random graphs in the Erdös-Renyi model. Section 5 investigates some families of fewnomial systems where all squares appear in the equations. Finally, we report experimental results in Section 6 and state a conjecture for quadratic fewnomial systems involving few square monomials.

2. NOTATION AND PRELIMINARIES

Notation. Throughout this paper, $\mathbb{K}$ denotes a field of odd characteristic. Its algebraic closure is denoted by $\overline{\mathbb{K}}$. If $X_1, \dots, X_n$ are variables, and $\alpha \in \mathbb{N}^n$, then the shorthand X^α stands for the monomial $X_1^{\alpha_1} \dots X_n^{\alpha_n}$. The symbol $\mathbf{M}$ denotes a finite subset of monomials in $\mathbb{K}[X_1, \dots, X_n]$ containing the constant 1. For any $i \in \mathbb{N}$, $\mathbf{M}^i$ denotes the subset of all products of i monomials in $\mathbf{M}$. Its cardinality is denoted by $|\mathbf{M}^i|$. By convention, $|\mathbf{M}^0| = 1$. By slight abuse of notation, we call *dimension* of an ideal I in a ring R the Krull dimension of the quotient ring R/I.

Complexity model. Complexity bounds in this paper count the number of operations $\{+, -, \times, \div\}$ in the field $\mathbb{K}$. It is not our goal to take into account the bitsize of the coefficients in $\mathbb{K}$. Hence, we count each arithmetic operation with unit cost. We do not take into account operations on monomials. The notion of size that we use for polynomial systems is the number of coefficients in $\mathbb{K}$ required to represent them. Note that if $\mathbb{K}$ is a finite field, then the bitsizes of the elements in $\mathbb{K}$ are bounded, and hence the bit complexity is the same as the arithmetic complexity. Given partial functions g, h from a set I to $\mathbb{N}$, we use the following classical Landau notation: $f = O(g)$ means that f/g is bounded above by a constant, $f = \Omega(g)$ is equivalent to $g = O(f)$, and $f = \Theta(g)$ means that $f = O(g)$ and $g = O(f)$.

Genericity. Let $\mathcal{L}_{\mathbf{M}}$ denote the $\mathbb{K}$-linear space spanned by $\mathbf{M}$. It has dimension $|\mathbf{M}|$. We say that a property holds for a generic system $(f_1, \dots, f_m) \in \mathcal{L}_{\mathbf{M}}^m$ if there exists a dense Zariski open subset $\mathcal{O}$ of $\mathcal{L}_{\mathbf{M}}^m$ s.t. this property holds for any system in $\mathcal{O}$.

Semigroup algebras. The main algebraic structure that we consider are *semigroup algebras* (also called *toric rings*): if $\mathbf{M} \subset \mathbb{K}[X_1, \dots, X_n]$ is a finite subset of monomials containing 1, we let $\mathbb{K}[\mathbf{M}]$ denote the subalgebra of $\mathbb{K}[X_1, \dots, X_n]$ generated by $\mathbf{M}$. We do not make any assumption on the Krull dimension of the ring $\mathbb{K}[\mathbf{M}]$. Semigroup algebras which are domains are the coordinate rings of affine toric varieties [9]. We refer to [28, Ch. 7] for a more detailed presentation. By slight abuse of notation, we call variety of a system $f_1, \dots, f_m \in \mathbb{K}[\mathbf{M}]$ the variety in $\overline{\mathbb{K}}^n$ associated to the ideal $\langle f_1, \dots, f_n \rangle \subset \mathbb{K}[X_1, \dots, X_n]$.

The following proposition is a variant of the weak Nullstellensatz for the total coordinate ring of projective toric varieties (see *e.g.* [9, Prop. 5.2.6]).

PROPOSITION 2.1. *The variety associated with a system $f_1, \dots, f_m \in \mathbb{K}[\mathbf{M}]$ is empty if and only if there exist $h_1, \dots, h_m \in \mathbb{K}[\mathbf{M}]$ such that $\sum_{i=1}^m f_i\, h_i = 1$.*

PROOF. the ring $\mathbb{K}[\mathbf{M}]$ is isomorphic to $\mathbb{K}[X]/I_M$, where I_M is a toric ideal generated by binomials $b_1, \dots, b_\ell$. Let $\widetilde{f_1}, \dots, \widetilde{f_m}$ be the images of $f_1, \dots, f_m$ by the isomorphism. Using the Nullstellensatz on the system $\widetilde{f_1}, \dots, \widetilde{f_m}, b_1, \dots, b_\ell$ in $\mathbb{K}[X]$ and pulling it back to $\mathbb{K}[\mathbf{M}]$ proves the proposition. □

Proposition 2.1 indicates that we can look for polynomial relations in $\mathbb{K}[\mathbf{M}]$ instead of the whole algebra $\mathbb{K}[X]$. Although narrowing the search for the certificate in $\mathbb{K}[\mathbf{M}]$ instead of $\mathbb{K}[X]$ constrains the problem, we shall see that this approach enables us to find efficiently small certificates. This leads to the following variant of Problem 1:

> **Problem 3 - Effective fewnomial Nullstellensatz in $\mathbb{K}[\mathbf{M}]$.** Given a system $f_1, \dots, f_m \in \mathbb{K}[\mathbf{M}]$ and such that $f_1(X) = \dots = f_m(X) = 0$ has no solution in $\overline{\mathbb{K}}^n$, compute $h_1, \dots, h_m \in \mathbb{K}[\mathbf{M}]$ such that $\sum_{i=1}^m f_i\, h_i = 1$.

3. MONOMIALS AND SUPPORT GRAPHS

In this section, we show a connection between graphs and properties of $\mathbb{K}[\mathbf{M}]$. In particular, we focus on quadratic relations between monomials in $\mathbf{M}$, *i.e.* at $\mathbb{K}$-linear relations in the vector space spanned by $\mathbf{M}^2$. We start by adding a new variable X_0 and by considering the homogenized support $\mathbf{M}^h = \{X_0^{2-\deg(\mu)}\mu\}_{\mu\in\mathbf{M}}$. We associate with $\mathbf{M}$ a simple labeled undirected graph G on $S = \{0, \dots, n\}$ whose edges are $E = \{(i, j) \mid X_i X_j \in \mathbf{M}^h, i \neq j\}$. Their is a loop at a vertex i iff $X_i^2 \in \mathbf{M}^h$.

EXAMPLE 3.1. *Let* $\mathbf{M} = \{1, X_1^2, X_2^2, X_3^2, X_3, X_4, X_1X_2, X_2X_3, X_3X_4\}$. *The following picture represents the graph G; squares in $\mathbf{M}^h$ are indicated by a loop.*

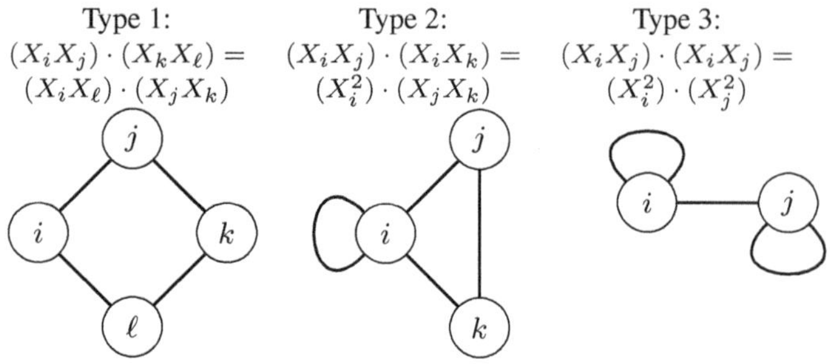

Figure 1: The three types of quadratic relations

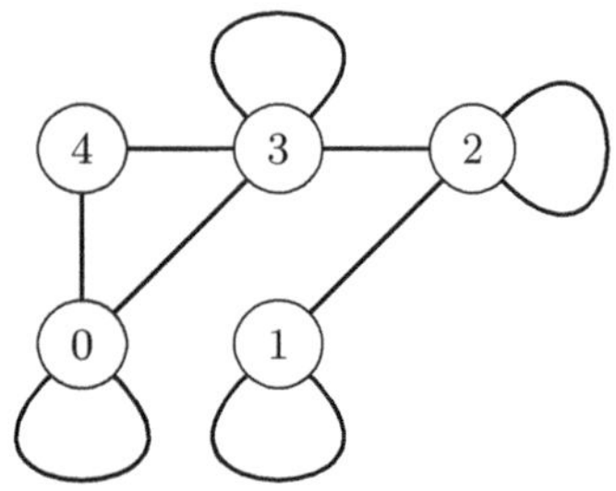

Quadratic relations between elements of $\mathbf{M}$ are of the form $\mu_1\,\mu_2 = \mu_3\,\mu_4$ for (not necessarily distinct) monomials $\mu_1, \mu_2, \mu_3, \mu_4 \in \mathbf{M}$. For the quadratic supports $\mathbf{M}$ that we consider in this paper, these quadratic relations come in three flavors that appear as subgraphs of G and are described in Figure 1. The next proposition shows how the cardinality of $\mathbf{M}^2$ can be computed from the number of quadratic relations and the number of 4-cliques in G. We recall that a 4-clique is a subgraph on 4 vertices such that every pair of vertices is linked by an edge.

PROPOSITION 3.2. *The cardinality of* $\mathbf{M}^2$ *equals* $\binom{|\mathbf{M}|+1}{2} - \lambda(G) + \mathrm{clique}_4(G)$, *where* $\lambda(G)$ *is the number of subgraphs of* G *isomorphic to any of the three graphs in Figure 1 and* $\mathrm{clique}_4(G)$ *is the number of 4-cliques in* G.

Proof. We can form $\binom{|\mathbf{M}|+1}{2}$ products of two (non-necessarily distinct) elements in $\mathbf{M}$. However, some of these products are counted several times because of the quadratic relations between elements in $\mathbf{M}$. This is corrected by the terms $-\lambda(G) + \mathrm{clique}_4(G)$; we detail below the possible cases:

- If $\mu = X_iX_jX_kX_\ell$ is a product of four distinct variables, then μ can be obtained from $\mathbf{M}$ by three different products, since $\mu = (X_iX_j)(X_kX_\ell) = (X_iX_k)(X_jX_\ell) = (X_iX_\ell)(X_jX_k)$. Depending on the number of pairs of such edges that lie in the graph, the monomial μ is counted one, two or three times in $\binom{|\mathbf{M}|+1}{2}$.
  If there is only one way to obtain μ (for example if (X_iX_j) and (X_kX_ℓ) are the only monomials in $\mathbf{M}$ whose products are μ), then the subgraph associated with the vertices $\{X_i, X_j, X_k, X_\ell\}$ is neither of type 1 nor a 4-clique. Hence, μ is counted only one time.
  If there are two ways to obtain μ, then the subgraph associated with the vertices $\{X_i, X_j, X_k, X_\ell\}$ is of type 1 but not a 4-clique. Hence, μ is counted twice in $\binom{|\mathbf{M}|+1}{2}$ but this is corrected by the term $\lambda(G)$.
  If all the three products are possible, then the subgraph associated with the vertices $\{X_i, X_j, X_k, X_\ell\}$ contains three subgraphs of type 1, and is also a 4-clique. Therefore μ is counted 3 times in $\binom{|\mathbf{M}|+1}{2}$, removed 3 times in $\lambda(G)$ and counted once in $\mathrm{clique}_4(G)$.
- If $\mu = X_i^2X_jX_k$ is a monomial involving three distinct variables, then μ is counted twice in $\binom{|\mathbf{M}|+1}{2}$ if and only the subgraph associated with the vertices $\{X_i, X_j, X_k\}$ is of type 2. In this case one contribution is removed by the term $\lambda(G)$, hence μ is counted one time.
- Similarly, monomials $\mu = X_i^2X_j^2$ are counted once or twice in the formula $\binom{|\mathbf{M}|+1}{2}$: if it is counted twice (*i.e.* when $X_iX_j, X_i^2, X_j^2 \in \mathbf{M}$), then the subgraph associated with $\{X_i, X_j\}$ is of type 3. □

Notation. For a graph G associated with a set of monomials $\mathbf{M}$, let G' be the subgraph of squares (*i.e.* the subgraph of vertices with a loop).

DEFINITION 3.3. *A* matching *(also called independent edge set) of* G' *is a set of edges of* G' *without common vertices. We let* $\nu(\mathbf{M})$ *denote the* matching number *of* G', i.e. *the maximum cardinality of a matching of* G'.

The matching number of a graph can be computed in polynomial time by Edmonds's algorithm [11]. We refer to [27] for more details on matching theory. We state now the main result of this section, which connects the matching number of the graph G' to the existence of a small certificate of inconsistency:

THEOREM 3.4. *Let* $(f_1, \ldots, f_m) \in \mathcal{L}_{\mathbf{M}}^m$ *be a system with generic coefficients. If* $m \geq |\mathbf{M}| - \frac{\sqrt{1+8\nu(\mathbf{M})}-1}{2}$, *then there exist polynomials* $h_1, \ldots, h_m \in \mathcal{L}_{\mathbf{M}}$ *such that* $\sum_{i=1}^m f_ih_i = 1$.

The proof of this theorem is postponed to the end of the section. It is actually not surprising that systems satisfying the assumptions of Theorem 3.4 do not have any solution, since the dimension of the $\mathbb{Q}$-vector space generated by the exponent vectors in $\mathbf{M}$ is upper bounded by $|\mathbf{M}| - \nu(\mathbf{M})$: each edge (i, j) in G' means that $X_i^2, X_j^2, X_iX_j \in \mathbf{M}$ and the exponent vectors of these three monomials are linearly dependent over $\mathbb{Q}$. The main point of Theorem 3.4 is that, under the condition on $\nu(\mathbf{M})$, the polynomials $(h_1, \ldots, h_m)$ for the effective Nullstellensatz can be searched in $\mathcal{L}_{\mathbf{M}}$. This allows to obtain to get small certificates of inconsistency:

COROLLARY 3.5. *With the notation and under the assumptions of Theorem 3.4, there is an explicit algorithm which solves Problem 1 within* $O\left(m|\mathbf{M}|\left(\binom{|\mathbf{M}|+1}{2} - \lambda(G) + \mathrm{clique}_4(G)\right)^{\omega-1}\right)$ *arithmetic operations, where* ω *is a feasible exponent for matrix multiplication* ($\omega < 2.37286$ *with Le Gall's algorithm [26]). This complexity is polynomial in the number of coefficients* $m|\mathbf{M}|$ *of the input system.*

PROOF. According to Theorem 3.4, there exist polynomials $h_1, \ldots, h_m$ with support $\mathbf{M}$ s.t. $\sum_i h_if_i = 1$, by decomposing the polynomials h_i in the monomial basis there exists a relation

$$\sum_i \sum_{\mu\in\mathbf{M}} \alpha_{\mu,i}\,\mu f_i = 1$$

where $\alpha_{\mu,i} \in \mathbb{K}$. Let $V \subset \mathsf{Span}_{\mathbb{K}}(\mathbf{M}^2)$ be the linear space generated by the products $\{\mu\, f_i\}_{\mu\in\mathbf{M}, i\in\{1,\ldots,m\}}$. Consequently, computing the polynomials h_i amounts to solving a linear system over $\mathbb{K}$ with $m\,|\mathbf{M}|$ unknowns and $|\mathbf{M}^2|$ equations. Solving it requires $O(m|\mathbf{M}|\cdot|\mathbf{M}^2|^{\omega-1})$ operations in $\mathbb{K}$ [32, Prop. 2.11]. Proposition 3.2 concludes the proof. □

The sequel of this section is devoted to this proof of Theorem 3.4. The squareroot involved in the formula is a consequence of the following lemma, as the maximal value of p for which $n \geq \binom{n-p+1}{2}$.

LEMMA 3.6. *There exist linear forms $\ell_1, \ldots, \ell_p \in \mathbb{K}[X_1, \ldots, X_n]$ such that the ideal*

$$I = \langle X_1^2, \ldots, X_n^2, \ell_1(X_1, \ldots, X_n), \ldots, \ell_p(X_1, \ldots, X_n)\rangle$$

contains all monomials of degree 2 iff $p \geq n - \frac{\sqrt{1+8n}-1}{2}$.

PROOF. The vector space of $(n-p)$-variate quadratic forms has dimension $\binom{n-p+1}{2}$. From the inequality $p \geq n - \frac{\sqrt{1+8n}-1}{2}$, we obtain $n \geq \binom{n-p+1}{2}$. This inequality and the fact that any quadratic form can be written as a linear combination of squares of linear forms (since $\mathrm{char}(\mathbb{K}) \neq 2$), implies that there exist $\ell'_1, \ldots, \ell'_n$ such that their squares ${\ell'_1}^2, \ldots, {\ell'_n}^2$ generate the space of $(n-p)$-variate quadratic forms. Then the dimension of the linear space generated by $\ell'_1, \ldots, \ell'_n$ is necessarily maximal and equals $n-p$. Up to permuting the indices, we assume also that $\ell'_1, \ldots, \ell'_{n-p}$ are linearly independent. Hence the ideal $I' = \langle \ell'_1(X_1, \ldots, X_{n-p})^2, \ldots, \ell'_n(X_1, \ldots, X_{n-p})^2, X_{n-p+1}, \ldots, X_n\rangle$ contains all monomials of degree 2. We rewrite I' as
$I' = \langle \ell''_1(X_1, \ldots, X_n)^2, \ldots, \ell''_n(X_1, \ldots, X_n)^2, X_{n-p+1}, \ldots, X_n\rangle$,

$$\begin{cases} \ell''_i(X_1, \ldots, X_n) = \ell'_i(X_1, \ldots, X_{n-p}) \text{ if } 1 \leq i \leq n-p \\ \ell''_i(X_1, \ldots, X_n) = X_i - \ell'_i(X_1, \ldots, X_{n-p}) \text{ otherwise.} \end{cases}$$

Note that the linear forms $\ell''_1, \ldots, \ell''_n$ are linearly independent by construction. We consider the automorphism θ of $\mathbb{K}[X_1, \ldots, X_n]$ defined by $\theta(X_i) = \ell''_i(X_1, \ldots, X_n)$, and we set $\ell_i(X_1, \ldots, X_n) = \theta^{-1}(X_{n-p+i})$ for $i \in \{1, \ldots, p\}$. Therefore I is the inverse image of I' by θ and hence contains all the monomials of degree 2.

It remains to prove the converse statement, *i.e.* that $p < n - \frac{\sqrt{1+8n}-1}{2}$ implies that there do not exist such linear forms $\ell_1, \ldots, \ell_p$. This is achieved by a similar argument: if such linear forms existed, then there would exist a set of n generators of the vector space of $(n-p)$-variate quadratic forms. This is not possible if $p < n - \frac{\sqrt{1+8n}-1}{2}$ since this vector space has dimension $\binom{n-p+1}{2}$. □

We can now prove the main theorem of this section:

PROOF OF THEOREM 3.4. We prove a homogeneous version of Theorem 3.4: let $f_1^{(h)}, \ldots, f_m^{(h)} \in \mathcal{L}_{\mathbf{M}}^h \subset \mathbb{K}[X_0, \ldots, X_n]$ be the homogenization of the generic system $f_1, \ldots, f_m$. We shall show that any monomial in $(\mathbf{M}^h)^2$ (see the definition of $\mathbf{M}^h$ at the beginning of this section) belongs to the ideal $\langle f_1^{(h)}, \ldots, f_m^{(h)}\rangle \subset \mathbb{K}[\mathbf{M}^h]$. This will imply that there exist $h_1^{(h)}, \ldots, h_m^{(h)} \in \mathbb{K}[\mathbf{M}^h]$ such that $\sum_{i=1}^m f_i^{(h)} h_i^{(h)} = X_0^4 \in (\mathbf{M}^h)^2$. Setting $X_0 = 1$ in this equation yields the desired relation.

First, we prove the existence of one system $f_1^{(h)}, \ldots, f_m^{(h)}$ such that all monomials of $(\mathbf{M}^h)^2$ appear in the ideal $\langle f_1^{(h)}, \ldots, f_m^{(h)}\rangle$. Throughout this proof, we let $A = \{\{a_1, b_1\}, \ldots, \{a_{\nu(\mathbf{M})}, b_{\nu(\mathbf{M})}\}\} \subset \{0, \ldots, n\}^2$ denote a matching of G' of maximum cardinality. We construct a system from A whose polynomials are:

1. all the monomials in $\mathbf{M}^h$ of the form X_iX_j with $i \neq j$;
2. all the monomials in $\mathbf{M}^h$ of the form X_i^2 with i not appearing in A;
3. for each $i \in \{1, \ldots, \nu(\mathbf{M})\}$, the polynomial $X_{a_i}^2 - X_{b_i}^2$;
4. the polynomials $\ell_1(X_{a_1}^2, \ldots, X_{a_{\nu(\mathbf{M})}}^2), \ldots, \ell_p(X_{a_1}^2, \ldots, X_{a_{\nu(\mathbf{M})}}^2)$, where the $\nu(\mathbf{M})$-variate linear forms $\ell_1, \ldots, \ell_p$ are obtained by replacing n by $\nu(\mathbf{M})$ in Lemma 3.6.

This is a system of $|\mathbf{M}| - \left\lfloor \frac{\sqrt{1+8\nu(\mathbf{M})}-1}{2} \right\rfloor$ polynomials, generating an ideal $I \subset \mathbb{K}[\mathbf{M}^h]$. We claim that all monomials in $(\mathbf{M}^h)^2$ are in the ideal of $\mathbb{K}[\mathbf{M}^h]$ generated by these polynomials:

- every monomial in $(\mathbf{M}^h)^2$ involving at least 3 different variables belongs necessarily to the ideal generated by the monomials X_iX_j with $i \neq j$; the same holds for monomials of the form $X_i^3X_j$ with $i \neq j$;
- next, we look at monomials of the form X_i^4. If i does not appear in A, then by construction X_i^2 is in the ideal. If i is in A, then there exists j such that $i = a_j$ or $i = b_j$. Noticing that $X_{a_j}^4 = X_{a_j}^2(X_{a_j}^2 - X_{b_j}^2) - (X_{a_j}X_{b_j})^2$ or $X_{b_j}^4 = X_{b_j}^2(X_{a_j}^2 - X_{b_j}^2) - (X_{a_j}X_{b_j})^2$ shows that $X_i^4 \in I$.
- finally, we focus on monomials of the form $X_i^2X_j^2$. If i or j do not appear in A, then either X_i^2 or X_j^2 belongs to I. If both i and j appear in A then Lemma 3.6 tells us that $X_i^2X_j^2$ belongs to the ideal generated by $\langle X_{a_1}^4, \ldots, X_{a_{\nu(\mathbf{M})}}^4, \ell_1(X_{a_1}^2, \ldots, X_{a_{\nu(\mathbf{M})}}^2), \ldots, \ell_p(X_{a_1}^2, \ldots, X_{a_{\nu(\mathbf{M})}}^2), X_{a_1}^2 - X_{b_1}^2, \ldots, X_{a_{\nu(\mathbf{M})}}^2 - X_{b_{\nu(\mathbf{M})}}^2\rangle$.

So far, we have proven that there exists at least one system such that Theorem 3.4 is correct. It remains to prove that this is true for a generic system. To this end, we note that all monomials in $(\mathbf{M}^h)^2$ belongs to $\langle f_1^{(h)}, \ldots, f_m^{(h)}\rangle \subset \mathbb{K}[\mathbf{M}^h]$ if and only if $\mathsf{Span}_{\mathbb{K}}(\{\mu f_i^{(h)}\}_{\mu \in \mathbf{M}^h, i \in \{1,\ldots,m\}}) = \mathsf{Span}_{\mathbb{K}}((\mathbf{M}^h)^2)$. This is an open condition given by the non-vanishing of a product of minors of the matrix recording the coefficients of $\{\mu f_i^{(h)}\}_{\mu \in \mathbf{M}, i \in \{1,\ldots,m\}}$. Consequently, there exists a Zariski open subset $\mathcal{O} \subset \mathbb{K}[\mathbf{M}^h]^m$ such that Theorem 3.4 holds. This open subset $\mathcal{O}$ is non-empty by the construction above. The proof is concluded by noticing that any non-empty open subset is dense in the Zariski topology. □

4. RANDOM SUPPORT GRAPHS

In this section, we assume that the support $\mathbf{M}$ is randomly generated and we estimate the probability that the assumptions of Theorem 3.4 are satisfied. Roughly speaking, the aim of this section is to show that the conditions of Theorem 3.4 hold with large probability if n is large enough and if there are sufficiently many squares in $\mathbf{M}$. Let us consider the following variant of the Erdös-Rényi random graph model: for $n \in \mathbb{N}$, we set two probabilities $p_n, q_n \in [0, 1]$, and we consider a sequence of random supports $(\mathbf{M}_n)_{n \in \mathbb{N}}$ where

- $\mathbf{M}_n$ is a subset of quadratic monomials of $\mathbb{K}[X_0, \ldots, X_n]$;
- each square X_i^2 appears in $\mathbf{M}_n$ independently with probability q_n;
- each monomial of the form X_iX_j with $i \neq j$ appears independently with probability p_n.

The goal is to estimate in which cases the random variable $\nu(\mathbf{M}_n)$ grows sufficiently quickly so that the assumptions of Theorem 3.4 are satisfied asymptotically with large probability. In order to estimate $\nu(\mathbf{M}_n)$, we first forget the meaning of the graph in terms of monomials and count the number of isolated edges in a random graph G in this variant of the Erdös-Renyi model.

PROPOSITION 4.1. *Let G be a random simple graph on $n+1$ vertices. Each vertex has a loop with probability $q \in [0, 1]$ and an edge between any two vertices appear with probability $p \in [0, 1]$. Let G' be the subgraph obtained by restricting G to the vertices with a loop and $\mathcal{E}$ be the random variable counting the number of isolated edges in G'. Then $\mathcal{E}$ has expected value and variance*

$$\mathbb{E}(\mathcal{E}) = \binom{n+1}{2} q^2 p (1 - q(1-(1-p)^2))^{n-1},$$
$$\mathrm{Var}(\mathcal{E}) = \mathbb{E}(\mathcal{E}) - \mathbb{E}(\mathcal{E})^2 + 6\binom{n+1}{4} q^4 p^2 (1-p)^4 (1-q(1-(1-p)^4))^{n-3}. \tag{4.1}$$

PROOF. For each possible edge e between two vertices $i \neq j$, we denote by X_e the random variable taking the value 1 if e is an isolated edge of G', and 0 otherwise. The probability that i and j appear as vertices with loops in G is q^2. Hence, the probability that the edge e lies in G' is $q^2 p$. Moreover, for a given vertex $k \neq i, j$, the probability that k appears in G' and at least one of the edges (i,k) and (j,k) belong to G is $q(1-(1-p)^2)$. There are $n-1$ other vertices than i and j in G, hence X_e follows a Bernoulli law of parameter $q^2 p(1-q(1-(1-p)^2))^{n-1}$. It follows that

$$\mathbb{E}(\mathcal{E}) = \sum_e \mathbb{E}(X_e) = \binom{n+1}{2} q^2 p (1-q(1-(1-p)^2))^{n-1}$$

The computation of the variance can be done similarly. □

We now apply the previous proposition in the case where p and q depends on n, and analyze the convergence of $\mathbb{E}(\mathcal{E})$ and $\mathrm{Var}(\mathcal{E})$ as n grows to infinity.

COROLLARY 4.2. *Let $p_n = \Theta(n^{-1})$ and $q_n = \Theta(n^{\beta})$. With the notation of Proposition 4.1, if $-1/2 < \beta < 0$ then $\mathbb{E}(\mathcal{E}) = \Theta(n^{2\beta+1})$ and $\mathrm{Var}(\mathcal{E}) = \Theta(n^{2\beta+1})$.*

PROOF. First, note that $\log\left[(1-q_n(1-(1-p_n)^2))^{n-1}\right] = -2np_nq_n + O(n^{-1})$ since $\beta < 0$. This shows that $\mathbb{E}(\mathcal{E}) = \frac{q_n^2 p_n n^2}{2} e^{-2np_nq_n}(1+O(n^{-1}))$. The claim on the asymptotic behavior of $\mathbb{E}(\mathcal{E})$ follows from $e^{-2np_nq_n} = \Theta(1)$. Next, let λ denote the last summand in Eq. (4.1), namely $\lambda = \mathrm{Var}(\mathcal{E}) - \mathbb{E}(\mathcal{E}) + \mathbb{E}(\mathcal{E})^2$. The asymptotic behavior of λ can be obtained by a similar analysis:

$$\log\left[(1-q_n(1-(1-p_n)^4))^{n-3}\right] = -4np_nq_n + O(n^{-1}),$$

hence $\lambda = \frac{q_n^4 p_n^2 n^4}{4} e^{-4np_nq_n}(1+O(n^{-1}))$. Notice that $\mathbb{E}(\mathcal{E})^2 = \frac{q_n^4 p_n^2 n^4}{4} e^{-4np_nq_n}(1+O(n^{-1}))$. Consequently, $\mathbb{E}(\mathcal{E})^2 - \lambda = O(n^{4\beta+1})$, since $e^{-4np_nq_n} = \Theta(1)$. Finally, putting all the estimates together, we obtain $\mathrm{Var}(\mathcal{E}) = \Theta(n^{2\beta+1}) + O(n^{4\beta+1}) = \Theta(n^{2\beta+1})$ since $\beta < 0$. □

Finally, we relate the distribution of $\mathcal{E}$ with the probability that the assumptions of Theorem 3.4 hold for fewnomial systems with $|\mathbf{M}| = n+k+1$. If one wants that $\mathbb{E}(|\mathbf{M}_n|) = n+k+1$ for some fixed k and that the expected number of squares is $(n+1)^{1/2+\varepsilon}$, then one has to choose $q_n = (n+1)^{-1/2+\varepsilon}$ and $p_n = (n+k+1-(n+1)q_n)/\binom{n+1}{2}$. The asymptotic expected behavior of the matching number in that case is described by the following statement:

LEMMA 4.3. *Let $\mathbf{M}_n$ be a sequence of random supports where each square monomial appears with probability q_n, and each square-free monomial appears with probability p_n. If $p_n = \Theta(n^{-1})$ and $q_n = \Omega(n^{-1/2+\varepsilon})$, with $0 < \varepsilon < 1/2$, then for any $\ell \in \mathbb{N}$, $\mathbf{P}(\nu(\mathbf{M}_n) \geq \ell)$ tends towards 1 as n grows.*

PROOF. Chebyshev's inequality implies that

$$\mathbf{P}(\mathcal{E} \leq \mathbb{E}(\mathcal{E})/2) \leq \mathbf{P}(|\mathcal{E} - \mathbb{E}(\mathcal{E})| \geq \mathbb{E}(\mathcal{E})/2) \leq \frac{4\,\mathrm{Var}(\mathcal{E})}{\mathbb{E}(\mathcal{E})^2} = O\left(n^{-2(-1/2+\varepsilon)-1}\right) = O\left(n^{-2\varepsilon}\right).$$

Next, notice that $\mathbb{E}(\mathcal{E})/2 = \Theta(n^{2\varepsilon})$ by Corollary 4.2. Also, note that $\mathcal{E} \leq \nu(\mathbf{M}_n)$, so that for n sufficiently large, we have $\mathbf{P}(\nu(\mathbf{M}_n) \leq n^{\varepsilon}) \leq \mathbf{P}(\mathcal{E} \leq n^{2\varepsilon}) = O(n^{-2\varepsilon})$, which tends towards 0 as n grows. □

Next, we show that these estimates also hold for a different model of random monomial supports. For $n \in \mathbb{N}$ and two integers $a, b \in \mathbb{N}$, we consider the random sets $\mathbf{U}_{n,a,b}$ of quadratic monomials in $\mathbb{K}[X_0, \ldots, X_n]$ distributed uniformly at random among those that contain a non-squares and b squares.

THEOREM 4.4. *Let k be a fixed integer, $a_n, b_n \in \mathbb{N}$ be such $a_n + b_n = n+k+1$, and $\mathbf{U}_{n,a_n,b_n}$ be a subset of quadratic monomials in $\mathbb{K}[X_0, \ldots, X_n]$ distributed uniformly at random among those that contain a_n non-square monomials and b_n squares. Assume further that $b_n = \Omega(n^{1/2+\varepsilon})$, for $\varepsilon > 0$. Then the probability that the assumptions of Theorem 3.4 with $m = n$ are satisfied for $\mathbf{U}_{n,a_n,b_n}$ tends towards 1 as n grows.*

PROOF. The proof of this theorem is technical and is similar to the classical techniques to prove properties of random graphs in the Erdös-Renyi models [12]. Details are left to the reader. □

Theorem 1.2 is a direct consequence of Theorem 4.4 and is obtained by dehomogenization.

5. SYSTEMS WITH ALL THE SQUARES

Next, we investigate the special case of fewnomial systems where all the squares X_i^2 belong to $\mathbf{M}$. This corresponds to a limit case of Theorem 4.4: $\varepsilon = 1/2$. In this setting, the Newton polytopes of the polynomials are the same as those of dense quadratic polynomials, hence these systems have generically 2^n solutions in $\overline{\mathbb{K}}^n$. In the sequel of this section, $\mathbf{M}$ is a set of monomials of degree at most 2 in $\mathbb{K}[X_1, \ldots, X_n]$, of cardinality $n+k+1$, and which contains the constant 1 and all the squares X_i^2. We also assume that $n > 2k$.

We let ℓ denote the number of variables X_i which appear in a square-free monomial in $\mathbf{M}$. Hence $\ell \leq 2k$. For a 0-dimensional system $(f_1, \ldots, f_n) \in \mathcal{L}_{\mathbf{M}}^n$, we let S denote the $n \times (n-\ell)$ matrix which contains the coefficients of the squares X_i^2 such that X_i does not appear in a square-free monomial in $\mathbf{M}$.

PROPOSITION 5.1. *Let $(f_1, \ldots, f_n) \in \mathcal{L}_{\mathbf{M}}^n$ be a 0-dimensional system with support $\mathbf{M}$. Then the system $f_1 = \cdots = f_n = 0$ has at most 2^n solutions in $\overline{\mathbb{K}}^n$. If the matrix S has full rank, then the solutions are the orbits of at most 2^{ℓ} points under the action of $(\mathbb{Z}/2\mathbb{Z})^{n-\ell}$ given by*

$$\chi: \begin{array}{ccc} (\mathbb{Z}/2\mathbb{Z})^{n-\ell} \times \overline{\mathbb{K}}^n & \to & \overline{\mathbb{K}}^n \\ (\mathbf{e}_i, (a_1, \ldots, a_n)) & \mapsto & (a_1, \ldots, -a_{i_j}, \ldots, a_n) \end{array},$$

where the set $\{i_j\}$ is the set of indices such that X_{i_j} does not appear in a square-free monomial in $\mathbf{M}$.

PROOF. Up to a permutation of the indices, we can assume w.l.o.g. that $X_1, \ldots, X_{n-\ell}$ are the variables that does not appear in a square-free monomial in $\mathbf{M}$. Since the matrix S is full-rank, we perform Gaussian elimination to remove the squares $X_{i_j}^2$ which do not belong to an edge of the graph. This provides us with an equivalent system of the form

$$\begin{cases} X_1^2 - g_1(X_{n-\ell+1}, \ldots, X_n) = 0 \\ \vdots \\ X_{n-\ell}^2 - g_{n-\ell}(X_{n-\ell+1}, \ldots, X_n) = 0 \\ h_1(X_{n-\ell+1}, \ldots, X_n) = \cdots = h_\ell(X_{n-\ell+1}, \ldots, X_n) = 0. \end{cases}$$

We end up with a system $(h_1, \ldots, h_\ell)$ of dense homogeneous polynomials in ℓ variables. Note that ℓ is bounded by $2k$, which does not depend on n. Consequently, this system can be solved within a constant number of operations as n grows. By Bézout theorem, this system has at most 2^ℓ solutions. Finally, if $(a_{n-\ell+1}, \ldots, a_n)$ is a solution of $h_1 = \cdots = h_\ell = 0$, then $(\pm\sqrt{g_1(a_{n-\ell+1}, \ldots, a_n)}, \ldots, \pm\sqrt{g_{n-\ell}(a_{n-\ell+1}, \ldots, a_n)}, a_{n-\ell+1}, \ldots, a_n)$ is a solution of the input system. Moreover, all solutions are of this form. □

Therefore, even though the number of solutions of such systems depends exponentially on n, they can be conveniently represented. Moreover, we show next that computing this representation can be achieved within a number of operations in $\mathbb{K}$ which is polynomial in n:

COROLLARY 5.2. *Let $(f_1, \ldots, f_n) \in \mathcal{L}_{\mathbf{M}}^n$ be polynomials with support $\mathbf{M}$ satisfying the above assumptions ($|\mathbf{M}| = n+k+1$, all squares are in $\mathbf{M}$, S has full-rank) and μ be a square-free monomial. For fixed k, Problem 2 with input $(f_1, \ldots, f_n)$ and μ can be solved within $O(n^\omega)$ arithmetic operations as n grows, where ω is a feasible exponent for matrix multiplication.*

PROOF. With the same notations as in the proof of Proposition 5.1, and by noticing that $\langle h_1, \ldots, h_\ell\rangle \cap \mathbb{K}[\mu] = \langle f_1, \ldots, f_n\rangle \cap \mathbb{K}[\mu]$, solving Problem 2 with input $(h_1, \ldots, h_\ell)$ and μ yields a solution to Problem 2 with input $(f_1, \ldots, f_n)$ and μ. Solving Problem 2 with input $h_1, \ldots, h_\ell$ can be achieved within a time complexity which does not depend on n. Consequently, the only complexity that depends on n is the cost of computing the polynomials $h_1, \ldots, h_\ell$. This is done by linear algebra, within $O(n^\omega)$ operations in $\mathbb{K}$. □

6. EXPERIMENTAL RESULTS

In this section, we describe experimental results, validating the theoretical results and illustrating their practical relevance. In particular, our prototype implementation of the algorithm in the proof of Corollary 3.5 is able to compute Nullstellensatz' certificates of inconsistency for systems of 30000 equations and 30000 unknowns generated from the uniform model in Theorem 4.4. This may be compared to the practical timings for solving the same problem with dense generic quadratic systems, where 20 unknowns is already a difficult challenge due to the exponential size of the certificates.

Experimental setting. $\mathbb{K}$ is the finite field GF(65521). The experimental procedure depends on parameters n, k and β:

- generate a random support $\mathbf{M}$ of $n+k+1$ monomials of degree at most 2, containing 1 and $\lfloor n^\beta \rfloor$ squares. The subsets of square monomials and non-square monomials are respectively chosen uniformly at random;
- generate a random system of n equations with support $\mathbf{M}$, where all the coefficients are chosen uniformly at random in $\mathbb{K}$;
- return "success" if our implementation returns a relation $1 = \sum_{i=1}^n h_i f_i$, with $h_i \in \mathcal{L}_{\mathbf{M}}$, else return "failure".

By Theorem 4.4, for any choice of parameters $k \in \mathbb{N}$ and $0.5 < \beta < 1$, the probability that "success" is returned should tend towards 1 as n grows.

First, we study the dependence of the asymptotic behavior on the choice of β. To this end, we fix $k = 1$ and we look at the experimental probability of success as n grows. Experimental results are reported in Figure 2. The results are in accordance with Theorem 4.4: when $\beta > 0.5$, the probability that such systems have no solution and that there exists a Nullstellensatz certificate in $\mathcal{L}_{\mathbf{M}}$ seems to tend to 1 as n grows. We also observe that the convergence

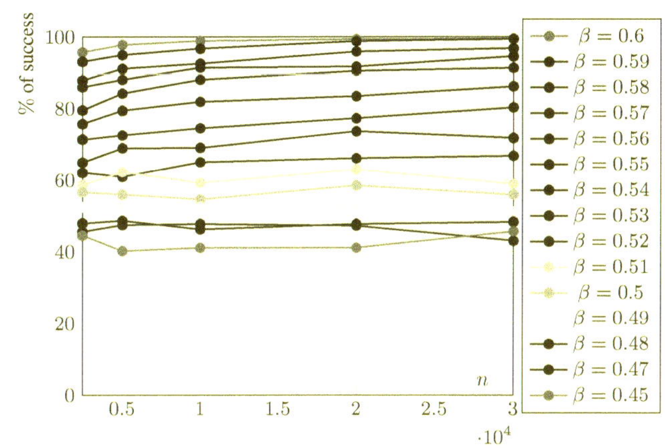

Figure 2: $k = 2$ fixed, n grows, several value of β. Every point is an average over 1000 tests. The relative positions of the curves follow the values of β.

seems to depend strongly on β: when β becomes close to the limit value 0.5, the speed of convergence seems to decrease. Next, we focus on the dependency on k. We fix $\beta = 0.9$ and let n grow for different values of k. Experiments are reported in Figure 3. Finally, we look at quadratic supports $\mathbf{M}$ of cardinality $n+k+1$ generated uniformly at random without any constraint on the number of squares. This case is not covered by the analysis of this paper and experiments show a different behavior: the probability of success of the algorithm does not seem to tend to 1 as n grows, contrary to the case $\beta > 0.5$. However, this probability seems to converges to a nonzero value.

CONJECTURE 6.1. *Let $k \in \mathbb{N}$ be a fixed integer. For $n \in \mathbb{N}$, let $\mathbf{M}_n$ be a random subset of monomials in n variables of degree at most 2, uniformly distributed among those of cardinality $n+k+1$ that contain 1. Let $f_1, \ldots, f_n \in \mathcal{L}_{\mathbf{M}}$ be a system with support $\mathbf{M}$ and generic coefficients. Then the probability that there exist $h_1, \ldots, h_n \in \mathcal{L}_{\mathbf{M}}$ such that $\sum_{i=1}^n f_i h_i = 1$ tends to a nonzero value as n grows.*

Finally, we report in Figure 4 on experiments about the efficiency our prototype implementation for computing Nullstellensatz certificates. The experiments were conducted on a Mac Retina 2.8Ghz Intel Core i7, and linear algebra computations were performed with `Magma V2.20-3`. We see in these experiments that systems with several thousands of variables can be handled in a few seconds. The algorithm works in two steps: first we reduce the quadratic system with linear algebra (the complexity of this step is independent of β and is represented by the dashed curve); then, the matrix in degree 4 (multiplying all the reduced polynomials by all the monomials in $\mathbf{M}$) is constructed and reduced. The time of this second step depends on β and is indicated by the plain curves. Therefore, these graphs seem to indicate that the cost of computing certificates of inconsistency for these systems is approximately twice the time of computing the row echelon form of a dense $n \times n$ matrix.

7. REFERENCES

[1] P. Beame, R. Impagliazzo, J. Krajíček, T. Pitassi, and P. Pudlák. Lower bounds on Hilbert's Nullstellensatz and propositional proofs. In *Foundations of Computer Science, 1994 Proceedings., 35th Annual Symposium on*, pages 794–806. IEEE, 1994.

[2] D. Bernshtein. The number of roots of a system of equations. *Functional Analysis and its Applications*, 9(3):183–185, 1975.

[3] B. Bertrand, F. Bihan, and F. Sottile. Polynomial systems with few real zeroes. *Mathematische Zeitschrift*, 253(2):361–385, 2006.

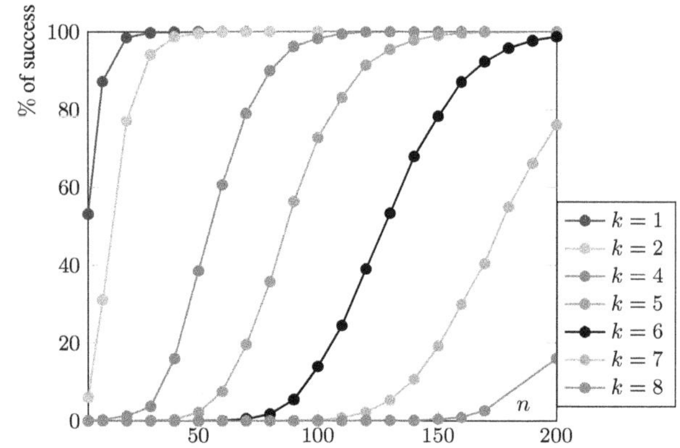

Figure 3: $\beta = 0.9$ fixed, n grows, several value of k. Every point is an average over 10000 tests.

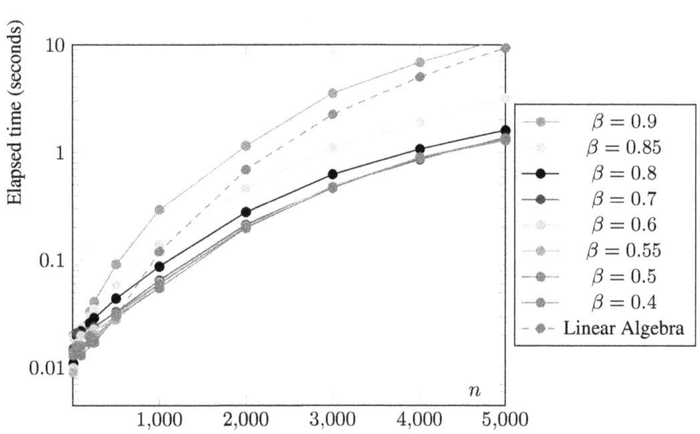

Figure 4: Timings for the computation of the certificate of inconsistency, $k = 2$.

[4] F. Bihan and F. Sottile. New fewnomial upper bounds from Gale dual polynomial systems. *Moscow mathematical journal*, 7(3):387–407, 2007.

[5] W. D. Brownawell. Bounds for the degrees in the Nullstellensatz. *Annals of Mathematics*, pages 577–591, 1987.

[6] J. Canny and I. Emiris. A subdivision-based algorithm for the sparse resultant. *Journal of the ACM*, 47(3):417–451, 2000.

[7] D. Cifuentes and P. Parrilo. Exploiting chordal structure in polynomial ideals: a Gröbner bases approach. *arXiv*, abs/1411.1745, 2014.

[8] M. Clegg, J. Edmonds, and R. Impagliazzo. Using the Groebner basis algorithm to find proofs of unsatisfiability. In *Proceedings of the twenty-eighth annual ACM symposium on Theory of computing*, pages 174–183. ACM, 1996.

[9] D. A. Cox, J. B. Little, and H. K. Schenck. *Toric varieties*. AMS, 2011.

[10] M. Crupi, G. Rinaldo, and N. Terai. Cohen-macaulay edge ideal whose height is half of the number of vertices. *Nagoya Mathematical Journal*, 201:117–131, 2011.

[11] J. Edmonds. Paths, trees, and flowers. *Canadian Journal of mathematics*, 17(3):449–467, 1965.

[12] P. Erdös and A. Rényi. On the evolution of random graphs. *Publ. Math. Inst. Hung. Acad. Sci*, 5:17–61, 1960.

[13] J.-C. Faugère, P.-J. Spaenlehauer, and J. Svartz. Sparse Gröbner bases: the unmixed case. In *Proceedings of ISSAC 2014*, 2014.

[14] N. Fitchas and A. Galligo. Nullstellensatz effectif et conjecture de Serre (théorème de Quillen-Suslin) pour le calcul formel. *Mathematische Nachrichten*, 149(1):231–253, 1990.

[15] R. Fröberg. On Stanley-Reisner rings. *Banach Center Publications*, 26(2):57–70, 1990.

[16] J. Herzog and T. Hibi. Distributive lattices, bipartite graphs and alexander duality. *Journal of Algebraic Combinatorics*, 22(3):289–302, 2005.

[17] J. Herzog, T. Hibi, and X. Zheng. Monomial ideals whose powers have a linear resolution. *Mathematica Scandinavica*, 95(1):23–32, 2004.

[18] B. Huber and B. Sturmfels. A polyhedral method for solving sparse polynomial systems. *Mathematics of Computation*, 64(212):1541–1555, 1995.

[19] A. Khovanskii. On a class of systems of transcendental equations. *Soviet Mathematics Doklady*, 22(3):762–765, 1980.

[20] P. Koiran, N. Portier, and S. Tavenas. On the intersection of a sparse curve and a low-degree curve: A polynomial version of the lost theorem. *Discrete and Computational Geometry*, 53(1):48–63, 2015.

[21] P. Koiran, N. Portier, S. Tavenas, and S. Thomassé. A τ-conjecture for newton polygons. *Foundations of Computational Mathematics*, pages 1–13, 2014.

[22] J. Kollár. Sharp effective Nullstellensatz. *Journal of the American Mathematical Society*, 1(4):963–975, 1988.

[23] T. Krick, L. M. Pardo, M. Sombra, et al. Sharp estimates for the arithmetic Nullstellensatz. *Duke Mathematical Journal*, 109(3):521–598, 2001.

[24] A. G. Kushnirenko. Newton polytopes and the Bezout theorem. *Functional Analysis and its Applications*, 10(3):233–235, 1976.

[25] D. Lazard. Algèbre linéaire sur $k[x_1, \ldots, x_n]$ et élimination. *Bull. Soc. Math. France*, 105:165–190, 1977.

[26] F. Le Gall. Powers of tensors and fast matrix multiplication. In *Proceedings of ISSAC'14*, 2014.

[27] L. Lovász and M. D. Plummer. *Matching theory*. AMS, 1986.

[28] E. Miller and B. Sturmfels. *Combinatorial commutative algebra*, volume 227. Springer Verlag, 2005.

[29] I. Semaev. On solving sparse algebraic equations over finite fields. *Designs, Codes and Crypto.*, 49(1-3):47–60, 2008.

[30] M. Shub and S. Smale. On the intractability of Hilbert's Nullstellensatz and an algebraic version of "P= NP". *Duke Mathematical Journal*, 81(1):47–54, 1996.

[31] M. Sombra. A sparse effective Nullstellensatz. *Advances in Applied Mathematics*, 22(2):271–295, 1999.

[32] A. Storjohann. Algorithms for matrix canonical forms. *Ph.D. thesis*, 2000.

[33] B. Sturmfels. Sparse elimination theory. In *Proceedings of Computational Algebraic Geometry and Commutative Algebra*, pages 377–396. Cambridge Univ. Press, 1991.

[34] B. Sturmfels. *Gröbner bases and convex polytopes*. AMS, 1996.

[35] J. Verschelde, P. Verlinden, and R. Cools. Homotopies exploiting Newton polytopes for solving sparse polynomial systems. *SIAM Journal on Numerical Analysis*, 31(3):915–930, 1994.

[36] R. Woodroofe. Matchings, coverings, and Castelnuovo-Mumford regularity. *J. of Comm. Algebra*, 2:287–304, 2014.

Computer Assisted Proof for Apwenian Sequences

Hao Fu*
Institute for Interdisciplinary Information Sciences
Tsinghua University
Beijing 100084 P.R.China
fu-h13@mails.tsinghua.edu.cn

Guo-Niu HAN
Institut de Recherche Mathématique Avancée
Université de Strasbourg et CNRS
7 rue René Descartes
67084 Strasbourg France
guoniu.han@unistra.fr

ABSTRACT

An infinite ± 1-sequence is called *Apwenian* if its Hankel determinant of order n divided by 2^{n-1} is an odd number for every positive integer n. In 1998, Allouche, Peyrière, Wen and Wen discovered and proved that the Thue–Morse sequence is an Apwenian sequence by direct determinant manipulations. Recently, Bugeaud and Han re-proved the latter result by means of an appropriate combinatorial method. By significantly improving the combinatorial method, we find several new Apwenian sequences with Computer Assistance. This research has application in Number Theory to determining the irrationality exponents of some transcendental numbers.

CCS Concepts

•**Computing methodologies** → Symbolic calculus algorithms;

Keywords

Hankel determinant, Thue–Morse sequence, Apwenian sequence, permutation, computer assisted proof

1. INTRODUCTION

For each infinite sequence $\mathbf{c} = (c_k)_{k\geq 0}$ and each nonnegative integer n the *Hankel determinant* of order n of the sequence $\mathbf{c}$ is defined by

$$H_n(\mathbf{c}) := \begin{vmatrix} c_0 & c_1 & \cdots & c_{n-1} \\ c_1 & c_2 & \cdots & c_n \\ \vdots & \vdots & \ddots & \vdots \\ c_{n-1} & c_n & \cdots & c_{2n-2} \end{vmatrix}. \tag{1}$$

*The first author was supported by the National Basic Research Program of China Grant 2011CBA00300, 2011CBA00301, the National Natural Science Foundation of China Grant 61033001, 61361136003.

ISSAC '16, July 19 - 22, 2016, Waterloo, ON, Canada

ISBN 978-1-4503-4380-0/16/07...$15.00

DOI: http://dx.doi.org/10.1145/2930889.2930891

We also speak of the Hankel determinants of the power series $\tilde{\mathbf{c}}(x) = \sum_{k\geq 0} c_k x^k$ and write $H_n(\tilde{\mathbf{c}}(x)) = H_n(\mathbf{c})$. The Hankel determinants are widely studied in Mathematics and, in several cases, can be evaluated by basic determinant manipulation, LU-decomposition, or Jacobi continued fraction (see, e.g., [12, 13, 7]). However, the Hankel determinants studied in the present paper apparently have no closed-form expressions, and require additional efforts to obtain specific arithmetical properties.

An infinite ± 1-sequence $\mathbf{c} = (c_k)_{k\geq 0}$ is called *Apwenian*[1] if its Hankel determinant of order n divided by 2^{n-1} is an odd number, i.e., $H_n(\mathbf{c})/2^{n-1} \equiv 1 \pmod 2$, for all positive integers n. The corresponding generating function or the power series $\tilde{\mathbf{c}}(x)$ is also said to be *Apwenian*. Recall that the *Thue–Morse sequence*, denoted by

$$\mathbf{e} = (e_k)_{k\geq 0} = (1, -1, -1, 1, -1, 1, 1, -1, -1, 1, 1, -1 \ldots),$$

is a special ± 1-sequence, defined by the generating function

$$\tilde{\mathbf{e}}(x) = \sum_{k=0}^{\infty} e_k x^k = \prod_{k=0}^{\infty} (1 - x^{2^k}), \tag{2}$$

or equivalently, by the recurrence relations

$$e_0 = 1, \quad e_{2k} = e_k \text{ and } e_{2k+1} = -e_k \text{ for } k \geq 0. \tag{3}$$

The Thue–Morse sequence is also called *Prouhet–Thue–Morse sequence*. For other equivalent definitions and properties related to the sequence, see [3, 2]. In 1998, Allouche, Peyrière, Wen and Wen established a congruence relation concerning the Hankel determinants of the Thue–Morse sequence [1].

Theorem 1.1 (APWW). *The Thue–Morse sequence on $\{1, -1\}$ is Apwenian.*

Theorem 1.1 has an important application in Number Theory. As a consequence of Theorem 1.1, all the Hankel determinants of the Thue–Morse sequence are nonzero. This property allowed Bugeaud [4] to prove that the irrationality exponents of the Thue–Morse–Mahler numbers are exactly 2.

The goal of the paper is to find more Apwenian sequences. Let d be a positive integer and $\mathbf{v} = (v_0, v_1, v_2, \ldots, v_{d-1})$ a finite ± 1-sequence of length d such that $v_0 = 1$. The generating polynomial of $\mathbf{v}$ is denoted by $\tilde{\mathbf{v}}(x) = \sum_{i=0}^{d-1} v_i x^i$. It is clear that the following power series

$$\Phi(\tilde{\mathbf{v}}(x)) = \prod_{k=0}^{\infty} \tilde{\mathbf{v}}(x^{d^k}) \tag{4}$$

[1]We use the term "*Apwenian*" to honor the four authors Allouche, Peyrière, Wen and Wen for their seminal paper [1].

defines a ± 1-sequence, whose n-th term is equal to

$$f_n = \prod_{i=1}^{d-1} v_i^{\#_i(n)},$$

where $\#_i(n)$ denotes the number of occurrences of the digit i in the base-d representation of n. Thus, the power series displayed in (2) is equal to $\Phi(1-x)$. Our main result is stated next.

THEOREM 1.2. *The following power series are all Apwenian:*

$$\begin{aligned}
F_2(x) &= \Phi(1-x), \\
F_3(x) &= \Phi(1-x-x^2), \\
F_5(x) &= \Phi(1-x-x^2-x^3+x^4), \\
F_{11}(x) &= \Phi(1-x-x^2+x^3-x^4+x^5+x^6+x^7 \\
&\qquad +x^8-x^9-x^{10}), \\
F_{13}(x) &= \Phi(1-x-x^2+x^3-x^4-x^5-x^6-x^7 \\
&\qquad -x^8+x^9-x^{10}-x^{11}+x^{12}), \\
F_{17a}(x) &= \Phi(1-x-x^2+x^3-x^4+x^5+x^6+x^7+x^8+x^9 \\
&\qquad +x^{10}+x^{11}-x^{12}+x^{13}-x^{14}-x^{15}+x^{16}), \\
F_{17b}(x) &= \Phi(1-x-x^2-x^3+x^4+x^5-x^6+x^7+x^8+x^9 \\
&\qquad -x^{10}+x^{11}+x^{12}-x^{13}-x^{14}-x^{15}+x^{16}).
\end{aligned}$$

Remarks. Let us make some useful comments about the above theorem.

1. The fact that the generating function $F_2(x)$ for the Thue–Morse sequence is Apwenian has already been proved in [1].

2. By using the Jacobi continued fraction expansion of a power series $F(x)$, we know that $H_n(F(x)) = H_n(F(-x))$ when d is an odd integer. See, for example, [12, 7, 9, 10]. Hence, Theorem 1.2 implies that $F_3(-x) = \Phi(1+x-x^2)$, $F_5(-x) = \Phi(1+x-x^2+x^3+x^4)$, etc. are all Apwenian.

3. There is no F_7 in Theorem 1.2, but two F_{17} (we mean F_{17a} and F_{17b}).

4. For each positive integer j we have

$$\Phi(\tilde{v}(x)) = \Phi(\prod_{k=0}^{j} \tilde{v}(x^{d^k})).$$

Consequently, $\Phi(1-x-x^2+x^3)$ is Apwenian since it is equal to $\Phi(1-x)$.

5. By exhaustive search, the list $F_2, F_3, \ldots, F_{17b}$ of Theorem 1.2 together with the transformation of Remark 2 yields a complete list of Apwenian sequences for prime integer d.

Actually, Theorem 1.1 has three proofs. The original proof of Theorem 1.1 is based on determinant manipulation by using the so-called *sudoku method* [1, 11]. The second one is a combinatorial proof derived by Bugeaud and Han [5]. The third proof is very short and makes use of Jacobi continued fraction algebra [10]. Unfortunately, the method developed in the short proof cannot be used for proving our main theorem, because the underlying Jacobi continued fractions are not ultimately periodic [10, 9]. However, another analogous result for the sequence $F_3(x)$ when dealing with modulo 3 (instead of modulo 2) is established using the short method, as stated in the next theorem [9].

THEOREM 1.3. *For every positive integer n the Hankel determinant $H_n(F_3(x))$ of the sequence $F_3(x)$ satisfies the following relation*

$$H_n(F_3(x)) \equiv \begin{cases} 1 \pmod 3 & \text{if } n \equiv 1,2 \pmod 4; \\ 2 \pmod 3 & \text{if } n \equiv 3,0 \pmod 4. \end{cases} \tag{5}$$

Combining Theorems 1.2 and 1.3 yields the following result.

COROLLARY 1.4. *For every positive integer n the Hankel determinant $H_n(F_3(x))$ verifies the following relation*

$$\frac{H_n(F_3(x))}{2^{n-1}} \equiv \begin{cases} 1 \pmod 6 & \text{if } n \equiv 0,1 \pmod 4; \\ 5 \pmod 6 & \text{if } n \equiv 2,3 \pmod 4. \end{cases} \tag{6}$$

In the following table we reproduce the first few values of the Hankel determinants of the sequence $F_3(x)$ for illustrating Theorems 1.2, 1.3 and Corollary 1.4.

n	1	2	3	4	5	6	7	8	9
$H_n(\mathbf{f})$	1	-2	-4	8	16	-32	-64	128	4864
$H_n(\mathbf{f}) \pmod 3$	1	1	2	2	1	1	2	2	1
$H_n(\mathbf{f})/2^{n-1}$	1	-1	-1	1	1	-1	-1	1	19
$\frac{H_n(\mathbf{f})}{2^{n-1}} \pmod 2$	1	1	1	1	1	1	1	1	1
$\frac{H_n(\mathbf{f})}{2^{n-1}} \pmod 6$	1	5	5	1	1	5	5	1	1

Recently, Bugeaud and Han re-proved Theorem 1.1 by means of an appropriate combinatorial method [5]. The latter method has been significantly upgraded to prove that $F_3(x), F_5(x), \ldots$ are Apwenian. As can be seen, in Section 3 Step 2, a family of cases (called *types*) is considered for proving the various recurrence relations. Roughly speaking, the types are indexed by words $s_0 s_1 s_2 \cdots s_d$ of length $d+1$ over a d-letter alphabet. Comparing to the original combinatorial method, the upgrading does not provide a shorter proof; however, it involves a systematic proof *by exhaustion* that only consists of checking all the types. The proof of Theorem 1.2 is then achieved with *Computer Assistance.*

In practice, the number of types is very large. For example, as described in [8] for the study of $F_{11}(x)$, there are 2274558 types! Fortunately, the set of permutations of each type can be decomposed into the Cartesian product of so-called *atoms* (see Substep 3(d) in the sequel), and moreover, the cardinality of each atom can be rapidly evaluated by a sequence of tests (see Definition 4.1 and Table 2).

PROBLEM 1.5. *Is the following power series Apwenian:*

$$\begin{aligned}
F_{19}(x) &= \Phi(1-x-x^2-x^3+x^4-x^5+x^6-x^7-x^8+x^9 \\
&\quad +x^{10}-x^{11}-x^{12}-x^{13}-x^{14}-x^{15}+x^{16}-x^{17}-x^{18})?
\end{aligned}$$

Find a fast computer assisted proof for Theorem 1.2 to answer the above question.

For proving that $F_{17a}(x)$ is Apwenian, our C program has taken about one week by using 24 CPU cores. No hope for $F_{19}(x)$.

Problem 1.6. *Find a human proof of Theorem 1.2 without computer assistance.*

Problem 1.7. *Characterize all the finite* ± 1*-sequences* $\mathbf{v}$ *such that* $\Phi(\tilde{\mathbf{v}}(x))$ *is Apwenian.*

As an application of Theorem 1.2 in Number Theory, the irrationality exponents of $F_5(1/b)$, $F_{11}(1/b)$, $F_{17a}(1/b)$, $F_{17b}(1/b)$ are proved to be equal to 2 (see [6]).

2. PROOF OF THEOREM 1.2

Let d be a positive integer and $\mathbf{v} = (v_0, v_1, v_2, \ldots, v_{d-1})$ be a finite ± 1-sequence of length d with $v_0 = 1$. Let $\mathbf{f} = (f_k)_{k\geq 0}$ be the ± 1-sequence defined by the following generating function

$$\tilde{\mathbf{f}}(x) = \Phi(\tilde{\mathbf{v}}(x)) = \prod_{k=0}^{\infty} \tilde{\mathbf{v}}(x^{d^k}), \tag{7}$$

where $\tilde{\mathbf{v}}(x) = \sum_{i=0}^{d-1} v_i x^i$. The above power series satisfies the following functional equation

$$\tilde{\mathbf{f}}(x) = \tilde{\mathbf{v}}(x) \prod_{k=1}^{\infty} \tilde{\mathbf{v}}\left(x^{d^k}\right) = \tilde{\mathbf{v}}(x)\tilde{\mathbf{f}}(x^d). \tag{8}$$

The sequence $\mathbf{f}$ can also be defined by the recurrence relations

$$f_0 = 1, \quad f_{dn+i} = v_i f_n \quad \text{for } n \geq 0 \text{ and } 0 \leq i \leq d-1. \tag{9}$$

We divide the set $\{1, 2, \ldots, d-1\}$ into two disjoint subsets

$$P = \{1 \leq i \leq d-1 \mid v_{i-1} \neq v_i\},$$
$$Q = \{1 \leq i \leq d-1 \mid v_{i-1} = v_i\}.$$

Two disjoint infinite sets of integers J and K play an important role in the proof of Theorem 1.2.

Definition 2.1. *If* $v_{d-1} = -1$*, define*

$$J = \{(dn+p)d^{2k} - 1 \mid n, k \in \mathbb{N}, p \in P\}$$
$$\bigcup \{(dn+q)d^{2k+1} - 1 \mid n, k \in \mathbb{N}, q \in Q\},$$
$$K = \{(dn+q)d^{2k} - 1 \mid n, k \in \mathbb{N}, q \in Q\}$$
$$\bigcup \{(dn+p)d^{2k+1} - 1 \mid n, k \in \mathbb{N}, p \in P\}.$$

If $v_{d-1} = 1$*, define*

$$J = \{(dn+p)d^{k} - 1 \mid n, k \in \mathbb{N}, p \in P\},$$
$$K = \{(dn+q)d^{k} - 1 \mid n, k \in \mathbb{N}, q \in Q\}.$$

From the above definition it is easy to see that $\mathbb{N} = J \cup K$ and following lemma.

Lemma 2.1. *For each* $t \geq 0$ *the integer* $\delta_t := |(f_t - f_{t+1})/2|$ *is equal to 1 if and only if* t *is in* J.

Let $\mathfrak{S}_m = \mathfrak{S}_{\{0,1,\ldots,m-1\}}$ be the set of all permutations on $\{0, 1, \ldots, m-1\}$. The following theorem which was proved in [5] may be viewed as the combinatorial interpretation of Theorem 1.2.

Theorem 2.2 ([5]). *Let* $\mathbf{v}$ *be a* ± 1*-sequence of length* d *with* $v_0 = 1$*. The sequence* $\mathbf{f}$ *and the set* J *associated with* $\mathbf{v}$ *are defined by* (7) *and Definition 2.1 respectively. Then, the sequence* $\mathbf{f}$ *is Apwenian if, and only if, the number of permutations* $\sigma \in \mathfrak{S}_m$ *such that* $i + \sigma(i) \in J$ *for* $i = 0, 1, \ldots, m-2$ *(no constraint on* $m - 1 + \sigma(m-1) \in \mathbb{N}$*) is an odd integer for every integer* $m \geq 1$.

For proving that the sequence $\mathbf{f}$ is Apwenian by means of Theorem 2.2, it is convenient to introduce the following notations.

Definition 2.2. *For* $m \geq \ell \geq 0$ *let* $\mathfrak{J}_{m,\ell}$ *(resp.* $\mathfrak{K}_{m,\ell}$*) be the set of all permutations* $\sigma = \sigma_0\sigma_1\cdots\sigma_{m-1} \in \mathfrak{S}_m$ *such that* $i+\sigma_i \in J$ *(resp.* $i+\sigma_i \in K$*) for* $i \in \{0, 1, \ldots, m-1\}\setminus\{\ell\}$*. Let* $n \geq 1$*; for simplicity, write:*

$$j_{m,\ell} := \#\mathfrak{J}_{m,\ell}, \qquad k_{m,\ell} := \#\mathfrak{K}_{m,\ell},$$
$$X_n := \sum_{i=0}^{n-1} j_{n,i}, \qquad Y_n := j_{n,n}, \qquad Z_n := j_{n,n-1},$$
$$U_n := \sum_{i=0}^{n-1} k_{n,i}, \qquad V_n := k_{n,n}, \qquad W_n := k_{n,n-1},$$
$$T_n := X_n + X_nY_n + Y_n,$$
$$R_n := U_n + U_nV_n + V_n.$$

Notice that if $\ell = m$, then $\{0, 1, \ldots, m-1\}\setminus\{\ell\} = \{0, 1, \ldots, m-1\}$, so that $j_{m,m}$ (resp. $k_{m,m}$) is the number of permutations $\sigma \in \mathfrak{S}_m$ such that $i + \sigma(i) \in J$ (resp. $\in K$) for all i.

By Theorem 2.2 and Definition 2.2 the sequence $\mathbf{f}$ is Apwenian if and only if $Z_n \equiv 1 \pmod 2$. In Section 4 we describe an algorithm enabling us to *find* and also *prove* a list of recurrence relations between $X_n, Y_n, Z_n, U_n, V_n, W_n$. Then, it is routine to check whether $Z_n \equiv 1 \pmod 2$ or not. Our program `Apwen.py` is an implementation of the latter algorithm in Python.

We now produce the proof of Theorem 1.2 by means of the program `Apwen.py`. Since $F_2(x)$ has been proved to be Apwenian in [1], only the three power series $F_3(x), F_5(x)$ and $F_{11}(x)$ require our attention. We can also prove that $F_{13}(x), F_{17a}(x), F_{17b}(x)$ are Apwenian in the same manner. However, the full proofs are lengthy and are not reproduced in the paper.

Consider $F_3(x)$. Take $\mathbf{v} = (1, -1, -1)$ with $d = 3$ and $v_{d-1} = -1$. Then, the corresponding infinite ± 1-sequence $\mathbf{f}$ is equal to $F_3(x)$. We have $P = \{1\}$, $Q = \{2\}$ and

$$J = \{(3n+1)3^{2k} - 1 \mid n, k \in \mathbb{N}\}$$
$$\cup \{(3n+2)3^{2k+1} - 1 \mid n, k \in \mathbb{N}\}$$
$$= \{0, 3, 5, 6, 8, 9, 12, 14, 15, 18, \ldots\},$$
$$K = \{(3n+2)3^{2k} - 1 \mid n, k \in \mathbb{N}\}$$
$$\cup \{(3n+1)3^{2k+1} - 1 \mid n, k \in \mathbb{N}\}$$
$$= \{1, 2, 4, 7, 10, 11, 13, 16, 17, \ldots\} = \mathbb{N} \setminus J.$$

By enumerating a list of 24 *types* of permutations (see Section 3), the program `Apwen.py` finds and proves the following recurrences.

Lemma 2.3. *For each* $n \geq 1$ *we have*

$$X_{3n+0} \equiv U_n, \qquad Y_{3n+0} \equiv U_n + V_n,$$
$$X_{3n+1} \equiv W_{n+1}(U_n + V_n), \qquad Y_{3n+1} \equiv W_{n+1}V_n,$$
$$X_{3n+2} \equiv W_{n+1}(U_{n+1} + V_{n+1}), \qquad Y_{3n+2} \equiv W_{n+1}V_{n+1},$$
$$Z_{3n+0} \equiv W_n(U_n + U_nV_n + V_n),$$
$$Z_{3n+1} \equiv W_{n+1}(U_n + U_nV_n + V_n),$$
$$Z_{3n+2} \equiv W_{n+1}.$$

As explained in Section 3, the above relations express X, Y, Z in terms of U, V, W since $v_{d-1} = -1$. By exchanging the values of P and Q, J and K, the program `Apwen.py` yields other relations which express U, V, W in terms of X, Y, Z by enumerating a list of 26 types of permutations.

LEMMA 2.4. *For each $n \geq 1$ we have*

$$U_{3n+0} \equiv X_n, \qquad V_{3n+0} \equiv X_n + Y_n,$$
$$U_{3n+1} \equiv Z_{n+1}Y_n, \qquad V_{3n+1} \equiv Z_{n+1}X_n,$$
$$U_{3n+2} \equiv Z_{n+1}Y_{n+1}, \qquad V_{3n+2} \equiv Z_{n+1}X_{n+1},$$
$$W_{3n+0} \equiv Z_n(X_n + X_nY_n + Y_n),$$
$$W_{3n+1} \equiv Z_{n+1}(X_n + X_nY_n + Y_n),$$
$$W_{3n+2} \equiv Z_{n+1}.$$

From Lemmas 2.3 and 2.4 we obtain the following "simplified" recurrence relations based on some elementary calculations.

COROLLARY 2.5. *For each positive integer n we have*

$$Z_{3n+0} \equiv W_nR_n, \qquad W_{3n+0} \equiv Z_nT_n,$$
$$Z_{3n+1} \equiv W_{n+1}R_n, \qquad W_{3n+1} \equiv Z_{n+1}T_n,$$
$$Z_{3n+2} \equiv W_{n+1}, \qquad W_{3n+2} \equiv Z_{n+1},$$
$$T_{3n+0} \equiv R_n, \qquad R_{3n+0} \equiv T_n,$$
$$T_{3n+1} \equiv W_{n+1}R_n, \qquad R_{3n+1} \equiv Z_{n+1}T_n,$$
$$T_{3n+2} \equiv W_{n+1}R_{n+1}, \qquad R_{3n+2} \equiv Z_{n+1}T_{n+1}.$$

Since $Z_1 = 1, T_1 = 3, W_1 = 1, R_1 = 1, Z_2 = 1, T_2 = 1, W_2 = 1$ and $R_2 = 7$, Corollary 2.5 yields $Z_m \equiv T_m \equiv W_m \equiv R_m \equiv 1 \pmod 2$ for every positive integer m by induction. Hence, $F_3(x)$ is Apwenian.

Duo to space constraints, we defer the proofs for $F_5(x)$ and $F_{11}(x)$ to the full version.

3. ALGORITHM FOR FINDING THE RECURRENCES

Keep the same *notations* as in Section 2. We will show how to *find* and also *prove* a list of recurrence relations between the quantities $X_n, Y_n, Z_n, U_n, V_n, W_n$. The set $\mathbb{N}$ of nonnegative integers is partitioned into d disjoint subsets $A_0, A_1, \ldots, A_{d-1}$ according to the value modulo d:

$$A_i = \{dn + i \mid n \in \mathbb{N}\} \quad (i = 0, 1, \ldots, d-1). \tag{10}$$

For an infinite set S let $S|_m$ be the set composed of the m smallest integers in S. Let $\beta : \mathbb{N} \to \mathbb{N}$ denote the transformation $k \mapsto \lfloor \frac{k}{d} \rfloor$. In other words,

$$\beta(k) = (k - i)/d \qquad \text{if } k \in A_i. \tag{11}$$

For simplicity, write

$$\bar{J} = \begin{cases} J & \text{if } v_{d-1} = 1, \\ K & \text{if } v_{d-1} = -1, \end{cases} \quad \text{and} \quad \bar{K} = \begin{cases} K & \text{if } v_{d-1} = 1, \\ J & \text{if } v_{d-1} = -1. \end{cases}$$

Then $\bar{\mathfrak{J}}_{m,\ell}, \bar{X}_n, \bar{Y}_n, \bar{Z}_n$ mean $\mathfrak{J}_{m,\ell}, X_n, Y_n, Z_n$ (resp. $\mathfrak{K}_{m,\ell}$, U_n, V_n, W_n) if $v_{d-1} = 1$ (resp. $v_{d-1} = -1$). It is not hard to verify the following lemma.

LEMMA 3.1. *For each $p \in P$ and $q \in Q$ we have*
(i). $A_{p-1} \subset J$ and $A_{q-1} \subset K$;
(ii). $A_{q-1} \cap J = \emptyset$ and $A_{p-1} \cap K = \emptyset$;
(iii). $\beta(A_{d-1} \cap J) = \bar{J}$ and $\beta(A_{d-1} \cap K) = \bar{K}$.

Let $i, j \in [0, d-1]$ and $x \in A_i, y \in A_j$. For determining the condition of i and j such that the sum $x + y$ belongs to J or K, there are three cases to be considered.
(S1) If $i + j + 1 \pmod d \in P$, then, $x + y \in J$;
(S2) If $i + j + 1 \pmod d \in Q$, then, $x + y \in K$;
(S3) If $i + j + 1 \pmod d = 0$, then, $x + y \in A_{d-1}$. In this case, the sum $x + y$ may belong to J or K.

Let $m \geq \ell \geq 0$. We want to enumerate the permutations in $\mathfrak{J}_{m,\ell}$ modulo 2. Each permutation $\sigma = \sigma_0\sigma_1 \cdots \sigma_{m-1} \in \mathfrak{S}_m$ may be written as the *two-line representation*

$$\begin{pmatrix} 0 & 1 & 2 & \cdots & m-1 \\ \sigma_0 & \sigma_1 & \sigma_2 & \cdots & \sigma_{m-1} \end{pmatrix}.$$

The columns $\binom{i}{\sigma_i}$ are called *bi-letters*. Let $\{a_0, a_1, \ldots, a_{d-1}\}$ be an alphabet of d letters. For each $\sigma \in \mathfrak{J}_{m,\ell}$ a bi-letter $\binom{i}{\sigma_i}$ in σ is said to be of (*normal*) *form* $\binom{a_j}{a_k}$ (resp. *specific form* $\binom{\ell}{a_k}$) if $i \neq \ell$ and $(i, \sigma_i) \in A_j \times A_k$ (resp. $i = \ell$ and $\sigma_i \in A_k$). To count the permutations from $\mathfrak{J}_{m,\ell}$ modulo 2, we proceed in several steps. In most cases the calculations are illustrated with $d = 5$.

Step 1. Occurrences of bi-letters. Since we want to enumerate permutations modulo 2, we can delete suitable pairs of the permutations and the result will not be changed. Let $i \in \mathbb{N}|_d$, if a permutation $\sigma \in \mathfrak{J}_{m,\ell}$ contains more than two bi-letters of form $\binom{a_i}{a_j}$ such that $i+j+1 \pmod d \in P$, select the first two such bi-letters $\binom{i_1}{j_1}$ and $\binom{i_2}{j_2}$. We define another permutation τ obtained from σ by exchanging j_1 and j_2 in the bottom line. This procedure is reversible. By (S1), it is easy to verify that τ is also in $\mathfrak{J}_{m,\ell}$, so that we can delete the pair σ and τ. Then, there only remain the permutations containing 0 or 1 bi-letter of form $\binom{a_i}{a_j}$ such that $i + j + 1 \pmod d \in P$.

Let $\mathfrak{J}'_{m,\ell}$ be the set of permutations $\sigma \in \mathfrak{J}_{m,\ell}$ which, for each $i \in \mathbb{N}|_d$, contains 0 or 1 bi-letter of form $\binom{a_i}{a_j}$ such that $i + j + 1 \pmod d \in P$. We have $j_{m,\ell} = \#\mathfrak{J}_{m,\ell} \equiv \#\mathfrak{J}'_{m,\ell} \pmod 2$. By (S2), each permutation $\sigma \in \mathfrak{J}'_{m,\ell}$ does not contain any bi-letter of form $\binom{a_i}{a_j}$ such that $i+j+1 \pmod d \in Q$. Thus, most of the bi-letters are of form $\binom{a_i}{a_{d-i-1}}$. In conclusion, the number of occurrences of each form is summarized in Table 1. A bi-letter of form $\binom{a_i}{a_j}$ such that $i+j+1 \pmod d \in P$ is said to be *unsociable*. A bi-letter of form $\binom{a_j}{a_{d-j-1}}$ is said to be *friendly*. By Table 1, each permutation in $\mathfrak{J}'_{m,\ell}$ contains only a few unsociable bi-letters.

form	total times
$\{\binom{a_k}{a_j} \mid k + j + 1 \pmod d \in Q\}$	0
$\{\binom{a_i}{a_j} \mid i + j + 1 \pmod d \in P\} \quad \forall i \in \mathbb{N}\|_d$	0, 1
$\{\binom{a_j}{a_{d-j-1}} \mid j \in \mathbb{N}\|_d\}$	0, 1, 2, 3, ...
$\{\binom{\ell}{a_j} \mid j \in \mathbb{N}\|_d\} \quad (\ell = m)$	0
$\{\binom{\ell}{a_j} \mid j \in \mathbb{N}\|_d\} \quad (0 \leq \ell \leq m-1)$	1

Table 1: Number of occurrences of bi-letters

Step 2. Form and type. The two-line representation of a permutation can be seen as a word of bi-letters. In fact, the order of the bi-letters does not matter. Let $m \geq 2d$. The *form* $f(\sigma)$ of a permutation $\sigma \in \mathfrak{J}'_{m,\ell}$ is obtained from σ by replacing each bi-letter of σ by its (normal or specific) form. From Table 1, the form $f(\sigma)$ of a permutation $\sigma \in \mathfrak{J}'_{m,\ell}$ is

$$\left(\begin{array}{ccc|ccc|c|ccc} a_0 & \cdot & a_0\ a_0 & a_1 & \cdot & a_1\ a_1 & \cdots & a_{d-1} & \cdot & a_{d-1}\ a_{d-1} \\ a_{d-1} & \cdot & a_{d-1}\ s_0 & a_{d-2} & \cdot & a_{d-2}\ s_1 & \cdots & a_0 & \cdot & a_0\ s_{d-1} \end{array}\right),$$

for $\ell = m$, or

$$\left(\begin{array}{ccc|cc|c|ccc|c} a_0 & \cdot & a_0\ a_0 & a_1 & \cdots & \cdots & a_{d-1} & \cdot & a_{d-1}\ a_{d-1} & \ell \\ a_{d-1} & \cdot & a_{d-1}\ s_0 & \cdot & \cdots & \cdots & a_0 & \cdot & a_0\ s_{d-1} & s_d \end{array}\right),$$

for $0 \le \ell \le m-1$, where

$$\begin{cases} s_i \in \{a_j \mid i+j+1 \pmod d \in P \cup \{0\}\},\ (i<d) \\ s_d \in \{a_0, a_1, \ldots, a_{d-1}\}. \end{cases} \tag{12}$$

Consequently, it can be characterized by a word $t(\sigma) = s_0 s_1 \ldots s_{d-1}$ or $s_0 s_1 \ldots s_{d-1} s_d$, of length d or $d+1$ respectively. The word $t(\sigma)$ is called the *type* of the permutation σ. We classify the permutations from the set $\mathfrak{J}'_{m,\ell}$ according to the type $t = s_0 s_1 \ldots s_{d-1}$ (resp. $t = s_0 s_1 \ldots s_{d-1} s_d$) by defining

$$\mathfrak{J}^t_{m,\ell} = \{\sigma \in \mathfrak{J}'_{m,\ell} \mid t(\sigma) = t\}. \tag{13}$$

Hence,

$$j_{m,\ell} \equiv \sum_t \#\mathfrak{J}^t_{m,\ell} \pmod 2. \tag{14}$$

Some types do not have any contribution for counting the permutations modulo 2, as stated in the following two lemmas.

LEMMA 3.2. *Let $\ell = m$ and $t = s_0 s_1 s_2 \ldots s_{d-1}$ (resp. $\ell \in \mathbb{N}|_m$ and $t = s_0 s_1 s_2 \ldots s_{d-1} s_d$). If there are $i < j \in [0, d-1]$ (resp. $i < j \in [0, d]$), such that $s_i = s_j$, $s_i \neq a_{d-i-1}$ and $s_j \neq a_{d-j-1}$, then*

$$\#\mathfrak{J}^t_{m,\ell} \equiv 0 \pmod 2. \tag{15}$$

PROOF. If $\mathfrak{J}^t_{m,\ell} = \emptyset$, then (15) holds. Otherwise, each permutation $\sigma \in \mathfrak{J}^t_{m,\ell}$ has two bi-letters $\binom{i_1}{i_2}$ and $\binom{j_1}{j_2}$ of forms $\binom{a_i}{a_k}$ and $\binom{a_j}{a_k}$, respectively, where $a_k = s_i = s_j$. We define another permutation τ obtains from σ by exchanging i_2 and j_2 in the bottom line. This procedure is reversible. By Lemma 3.1(i) or Table 1, it is easy to verify that τ is also in $\mathfrak{J}^t_{m,\ell}$. Thus, the transformation $\sigma \leftrightarrow \tau$ is an *involution* on $\mathfrak{J}^t_{m,\ell}$. Hence, $\#\mathfrak{J}^t_{m,\ell} \equiv 0 \pmod 2$. □

LEMMA 3.3. *Let $\ell \in \mathbb{N}|_m$ and $t = s_0 s_1 s_2 \ldots s_d$. If there is $i \in \mathbb{N}|_m$ such that $s_i \neq a_{d-i-1}$, then*

$$\sum_{\ell \in \mathbb{N}|_m \cap A_i} \#\mathfrak{J}^t_{m,\ell} \equiv 0 \pmod 2. \tag{16}$$

PROOF. For any $\ell \in \mathbb{N}|_m \cap A_i$, each permutation $\sigma \in \mathfrak{J}^t_{m,\ell}$ contains two bi-letters $\binom{i_1}{i_2}$ and $\binom{\ell}{\sigma_\ell}$ of forms $\binom{a_i}{a_j}$ and $\binom{\ell}{a_k}$, respectively. We define another permutation τ by exchanging i_2 and σ_ℓ in the bottom line. This procedure is reversible. By Lemma 3.1(i) it is easy to verify that $\tau \in \mathfrak{J}^t_{m,\ell'}$, where $\ell' = i_1 \in \mathbb{N}|_m \cap A_i$. Thus, the transformation $\sigma \leftrightarrow \tau$ is an *involution* on $\sum_{\ell \in \mathbb{N}|_m \cap A_i} \mathfrak{J}^t_{m,\ell}$. Hence, (16) holds. □

Let $m = dn + h$ ($n \ge 2$, $h \in \mathbb{N}|_d$), $k \in \mathbb{N}|_d$ and

$$\begin{cases} \mathfrak{P}_Y(m;t) & := \mathfrak{J}^t_{m,m}, \\ \mathfrak{P}_Z(m;t) & := \mathfrak{J}^t_{m,m-1}, \\ \mathfrak{P}_X(m;t,k) & := \sum_{\ell \in \mathbb{N}|_m \cap A_k} \mathfrak{J}^t_{m,\ell}. \end{cases} \tag{17}$$

From Definition 2.2, we have

$$\begin{cases} Y_{dn+h} & := \sum_t \#\mathfrak{P}_Y(dn+h;t) \\ Z_{dn+h} & := \sum_t \#\mathfrak{P}_Z(dn+h;t) \\ X_{dn+h} & :\equiv \sum_t \sum_{k \in \mathbb{N}|_d} \#\mathfrak{P}_X(dn+h;t,k). \end{cases} \tag{18}$$

By using relation (18), the recurrence relations listed in Lemmas 2.3 and 2.4, can be generated by Algorithm 1. The procedure `EvalAtoms(P,t, h,k)` appearing in Algorithm 1 evaluates the cardinality of the set $\mathfrak{P} := \mathfrak{P}_Y, \mathfrak{P}_Z$ or $\mathfrak{P}_X$ for each type t, and will be discussed in Section 4 (see Algorithm 2). Actually, Algorithm 1 delivers a recurrence relation because the output of `EvalAtoms(P,t,h,k)` is an algebra expression in terms of $X_n, X_{n+1}, Y_n, Y_{n+1}, Z_n, Z_{n+1}$.

Algorithm 1 Finding the recurrences

```
for P in ['PX', 'PY', 'PZ']:
  for h in range(d):
    Val=0
    for k in range(d) if P=='PX' else range(1):
      for t in PossibleTypes(P,h,k):
        Val=Val+EvalAtoms(P,t,h,k)
    print P,h,k,Val
```

Step 3. Counting permutations. Throughout this step we fix $m = dn + h$ ($h \in \mathbb{N}|_d$). Counting permutations from $\mathfrak{J}^t_{m,\ell}$ is lengthy; it is made in several substeps. We illustrate the entire calculations by means of four well-selected examples, using some *compressed and intuitive notation.* Then, we explain the maining of this compressed notation mean in full detail. The examples are given for $d = 5$. We write A, B, C, D, E instead of A_0, A_1, A_2, A_3, A_4 and a, b, c, d, e instead of a_0, a_1, a_2, a_3, a_4, respectively.

EXAMPLE 3.1. *Consider $m = \ell = 5n + 1$ and the type 'adbca' which satisfies condition (12). We have*

$$\begin{aligned} &\mathfrak{J}^{adbca}_{5n+1,5n+1} \\ &\stackrel{w}{=} \left(\begin{array}{cccc|ccc|ccc|ccc|ccc} 0 & \tilde{5} & 10 & 15 & 1 & 6 & 11 & 2 & \tilde{7} & 12 & \tilde{3} & 8 & 13 & 4 & 9 & 14 \\ e & a & e & e & d & d & d & c & b & c & c & b & b & a & a & a \end{array}\right) \\ &\stackrel{a}{=} \left(\begin{array}{cccc|ccc|ccc|ccc|cccc} 0 & \tilde{5} & 10 & 15 & 1 & 6 & 11 & 2 & \tilde{7} & 12 & \tilde{3} & 8 & 13 & 4 & 9 & 14 & 19 \\ e & a & e & e & d & d & d & c & b & c & c & b & b & a & a & a & \underline{19} \end{array}\right) \\ &\stackrel{e}{=} \left(\begin{array}{cccc|ccc|ccc|ccc|cccc} 0 & \tilde{5} & 10 & 15 & 1 & 6 & 11 & 2 & \tilde{7} & 12 & \tilde{3} & 8 & 13 & 4 & 9 & 14 & 19 \\ e & \underline{19} & e & e & d & d & d & c & \underline{c} & c & \underline{b} & b & b & a & a & a & \underline{a} \end{array}\right) \\ &\stackrel{d}{=} \begin{pmatrix} 0 & \tilde{5} & 10 & 15 \\ e & \underline{19} & e & e \end{pmatrix} \begin{pmatrix} 1 & 6 & 11 \\ d & d & d \end{pmatrix} \begin{pmatrix} 2 & \tilde{7} & 12 \\ c & \underline{c} & c \end{pmatrix} \begin{pmatrix} \tilde{3} & 8 & 13 \\ \underline{b} & b & b \end{pmatrix} \begin{pmatrix} 4 & 9 & 14 & 19 \\ a & a & a & \underline{a} \end{pmatrix} \\ &\stackrel{b}{=} Z_{n+1} \times Y_n \times X_n \times X_n \times Z_{n+1}. \end{aligned}$$

EXAMPLE 3.2. *Consider $m = 5n + 2$, $\ell = 5n + 1$ and the type 'dcbbaa' which satisfies condition (12). We have*

$$\begin{aligned} &\mathfrak{J}^{dcbbaa}_{5n+2,5n+1} \\ &\stackrel{w}{=} \left(\begin{array}{cccc|cccc|ccc|ccc|ccc} 0 & \tilde{5} & 10 & 15 & \tilde{1} & 6 & 11 & 16 & 2 & \tilde{7} & 12 & 3 & 8 & 13 & 4 & 9 & 14 \\ e & d & e & e & c & d & d & \underline{a} & c & b & c & b & b & b & a & a & a \end{array}\right) \end{aligned}$$

$$\overset{a}{=}\left(\begin{array}{cccc|cccc|ccc|cccc|cccc} 0 & \tilde{5} & 10 & 15 & \tilde{1} & 6 & 11 & 16 & 2 & \tilde{7} & 12 & 3 & 8 & 13 & 18 & 4 & 9 & 14 & 19 \\ e & d & e & e & c & d & d & \underline{a} & c & b & c & b & b & b & \underline{18} & a & a & a & \underline{19} \end{array}\right)$$

$$\overset{e}{=}\left(\begin{array}{cccc|cccc|ccc|cccc|cccc} 0 & \tilde{5} & 10 & 15 & \tilde{1} & 6 & 11 & 16 & 2 & \tilde{7} & 12 & 3 & 8 & 13 & 18 & 4 & 9 & 14 & 19 \\ e & \underline{19} & e & e & \underline{d} & d & d & \underline{18} & c & \underline{c} & c & b & b & b & \underline{b} & a & a & a & \underline{a} \end{array}\right)$$

$$\overset{d}{=}\begin{pmatrix} 0 & \tilde{5} & 10 & 15 \\ e & \underline{19} & e & e \end{pmatrix}\begin{pmatrix} \tilde{1} & 6 & 11 & 16 \\ \underline{d} & d & d & \underline{18} \end{pmatrix}\begin{pmatrix} 2 & \tilde{7} & 12 \\ c & \underline{c} & c \end{pmatrix}\begin{pmatrix} 3 & 8 & 13 & 18 \\ b & b & b & \underline{b} \end{pmatrix}\begin{pmatrix} 4 & 9 & 14 & 19 \\ a & a & a & \underline{a} \end{pmatrix}$$

$$\overset{b}{=} Z_{n+1} \times X_n \times X_n \times Z_{n+1} \times Z_{n+1}.$$

EXAMPLE 3.3. *Consider $m = 5n + 4$, $\ell \in C|_{n+1}$ and the type 'adcbac' which satisfies condition* (12). *We have*

$$\sum_{\ell \in C|_{n+1}} \mathfrak{J}^{adcbac}_{5n+4,\ell}$$

$$\overset{w}{=}\left(\begin{array}{cccc|cccc|cccc|cccc|ccc} 0 & \tilde{5} & 10 & 15 & 1 & 6 & 11 & 16 & 2 & \tilde{7} & 12 & 17 & 3 & 8 & 13 & 18 & 4 & 9 & 14 \\ e & a & e & e & d & d & d & d & c & \underline{c} & c & c & b & b & b & b & a & a & a \end{array}\right)$$

$$\overset{a}{=}\left(\begin{array}{cccc|cccc|cccc|cccc|cccc} 0 & \tilde{5} & 10 & 15 & 1 & 6 & 11 & 16 & 2 & \tilde{7} & 12 & 17 & 3 & 8 & 13 & 18 & 4 & 9 & 14 & 19 \\ e & a & e & e & d & d & d & d & c & \underline{c} & c & c & b & b & b & b & a & a & a & \underline{19} \end{array}\right)$$

$$\overset{e}{=}\left(\begin{array}{cccc|cccc|cccc|cccc|cccc} 0 & \tilde{5} & 10 & 15 & 1 & 6 & 11 & 16 & 2 & \tilde{7} & 12 & 17 & 3 & 8 & 13 & 18 & 4 & 9 & 14 & 19 \\ e & \underline{19} & e & e & d & d & d & d & c & \underline{c} & c & c & b & b & b & b & a & a & a & \underline{a} \end{array}\right)$$

$$\overset{d}{=}\begin{pmatrix} 0 & \tilde{5} & 10 & 15 \\ e & \underline{19} & e & e \end{pmatrix}\begin{pmatrix} 1 & 6 & 11 & 16 \\ d & d & d & d \end{pmatrix}\begin{pmatrix} 2 & \tilde{7} & 12 & 17 \\ c & \underline{c} & c & c \end{pmatrix}\begin{pmatrix} 3 & 8 & 13 & 18 \\ b & b & b & b \end{pmatrix}\begin{pmatrix} 4 & 9 & 14 & 19 \\ a & a & a & \underline{a} \end{pmatrix}$$

$$\overset{b}{=} Z_{n+1} \times Y_{n+1} \times X_{n+1} \times Y_{n+1} \times Z_{n+1}.$$

EXAMPLE 3.4. *Consider $m = 5n+1$, $\ell = 5n$ and the type 'edcaab' which satisfies condition* (12). *We have*

$$\mathfrak{J}^{edcaab}_{5n+1,5n}$$

$$\overset{w}{=}\left(\begin{array}{cccc|ccc|ccc|ccc|ccc} 0 & 5 & 10 & 15 & 1 & 6 & 11 & 2 & 7 & 12 & \tilde{3} & 8 & 13 & 4 & 9 & 14 \\ e & e & e & \underline{b} & d & d & d & c & c & c & a & b & b & a & a & a \end{array}\right)$$

$$\overset{a}{=}\left(\begin{array}{cccc|ccc|ccc|ccc|cccc} 0 & 5 & 10 & 15 & 1 & 6 & 11 & 2 & 7 & 12 & \tilde{3} & 8 & 13 & 4 & 9 & 14 & 19 \\ e & e & e & \underline{b} & d & d & d & c & c & c & a & b & b & a & a & a & \underline{19} \end{array}\right)$$

$$\overset{e}{=}\left(\begin{array}{cccc|ccc|ccc|ccc|cccc} 0 & 5 & 10 & 15 & 1 & 6 & 11 & 2 & 7 & 12 & \tilde{3} & 8 & 13 & 4 & 9 & 14 & 19 \\ e & e & e & \underline{19} & d & d & d & c & c & c & \underline{b} & b & b & a & a & a & \underline{a} \end{array}\right)$$

$$\overset{d}{=}\begin{pmatrix} 0 & 5 & 10 & 15 \\ e & e & e & \underline{19} \end{pmatrix}\begin{pmatrix} 1 & 6 & 11 \\ d & d & d \end{pmatrix}\begin{pmatrix} 2 & 7 & 12 \\ c & c & c \end{pmatrix}\begin{pmatrix} \tilde{3} & 8 & 13 \\ \underline{b} & b & b \end{pmatrix}\begin{pmatrix} 4 & 9 & 14 & 19 \\ a & a & a & \underline{a} \end{pmatrix}$$

$$\overset{b}{=} Y_n \times Y_n \times Y_n \times X_n \times Z_{n+1}.$$

Notation 1. In the above compressed writing, the letter w, a, e, d, b over the symbol " $=$ " means that the equality is obtained by substep 3(w), 3(a), 3(e), 3(d), 3(b) respectively.

Notation 2. In the compressed writing the integer n is represented by the explicit value 3. Hence, the second block in the first equality in Example 3.1 has the following meaning:

$$\left|\begin{matrix} 1 & 6 & 11 \\ d & d & d \end{matrix}\right| := \left|\begin{matrix} 1 & 6 & 11 & 16 & \cdots & 5n-4 \\ d & d & d & d & \cdots & d \end{matrix}\right|.$$

Also, the added bi-letter $\binom{19}{19}$ (see Substep 3(a)) in the second equality in Example 3.1 means $\binom{5n+4}{\underline{5n+4}}$.

Substep 3(w). Rewrite the set. For each permutation σ from $\mathfrak{J}^t_{m,\ell}$, we reorder the bi-letters of σ such that $\binom{i}{\sigma_i}$ is on the left of $\binom{j}{\sigma_j}$ if $i \mod d < j \mod d$, or if $i \equiv j \mod d$ and $i < j$. Then, we replace each letter $y \in a_k$ in the bottom line by a_k. To facilitate readability, vertical bars are inserted between the bi-letters $\binom{i}{\sigma_i}$ and $\binom{j}{\sigma_j}$ such that $i \not\equiv j \pmod d$. We get a biword w, denoted by $\rho(\sigma) = w$, called *shape* of σ.

Applying this operation to the following permutation $\sigma \in \mathfrak{J}^{adbca}_{5n+1,5n+1}$ considered in Example 3.1

$$\sigma = \begin{pmatrix} 0 & 1 & 2 & 3 & 4 & 5 & 6 & 7 & 8 & 9 & 10 & 11 & 12 & 13 & 14 & 15 \\ 4 & 3 & 2 & 7 & 15 & 0 & 13 & 1 & 11 & 10 & 14 & 8 & 12 & 6 & 5 & 9 \end{pmatrix}, \qquad (19)$$

we get the shape $\rho(\sigma) = w$, where

$$w = \left(\begin{array}{cccc|ccc|ccc|ccc|ccc} 0 & 5 & 10 & 15 & 1 & 6 & 11 & 2 & 7 & 12 & 3 & 8 & 13 & 4 & 9 & 14 \\ e & a & e & e & d & d & d & c & b & c & c & b & b & a & a & a \end{array}\right). \qquad (20)$$

Notation 3. In the compressed writing, the above shape w also represents the set $\rho^{-1}(w)$ of all the permutations σ such that $\rho(\sigma) = w$.

Each permutation $\sigma \in \mathfrak{J}^{adbca}_{5n+1,5n+1}$ contains exactly three unsociable bi-letters of form $\binom{a}{a}$, $\binom{c}{b}$, $\binom{d}{c}$, denoted by $\binom{i_0}{j_0}$, $\binom{i_1}{j_1}$, $\binom{i_2}{j_2}$, respectively. So that, for example, in the block

$$\left|\begin{matrix} 2 & 7 & 12 \\ c & b & c \end{matrix}\right|$$

there is exactly one letter 'b' in the bottom line. All other letters are 'c'. However, the position of the letter 'b' is not fixed. The shape of another permutation may contain the block

$$\left|\begin{matrix} 2 & 7 & 12 \\ b & c & c \end{matrix}\right| \quad \text{or} \quad \left|\begin{matrix} 2 & 7 & 12 \\ c & c & b \end{matrix}\right|.$$

Notation 4. The underlined bi-letters $\binom{i}{\underline{a_j}}$ in the shape of a permutation σ means that there is no constraint $i+\sigma_i \in J$ for the corresponding bi-letters $\binom{i}{\sigma_i}$ of σ. All other bi-letters of σ must satisfy the latter constraint.

In the first equality of each calculation, there is no underlined bi-letter if $m = \ell$ (Example 3.1) or exactly one underlined bi-letter if $0 \le \ell \le m-1$ (Examples 3.2 and 3.3). In the latter case, the underscore sign indicates the position of ℓ.

Notation 5. The shape w, with a tilde sign ˜ over a bi-letter $\binom{\tilde{i}}{a_j}$, represents the sum of all shapes w' which are obtained from w by moving the letter a_j, including the underscore sign if it is underlined, to other non-underlined position in the block. For example, we write (see Example 3.1)

$$\left|\begin{matrix} 2 & \tilde{7} & 12 \\ c & b & c \end{matrix}\right| := \left|\begin{matrix} 2 & 7 & 12 \\ b & c & c \end{matrix}\right| + \left|\begin{matrix} 2 & 7 & 12 \\ c & b & c \end{matrix}\right| + \left|\begin{matrix} 2 & 7 & 12 \\ c & c & b \end{matrix}\right|,$$

and (see Example 3.2)

$$\left|\begin{matrix} \tilde{1} & 6 & 11 & 16 \\ c & d & d & \underline{a} \end{matrix}\right| := \left|\begin{matrix} 1 & 6 & 11 & 16 \\ c & d & d & \underline{a} \end{matrix}\right| + \left|\begin{matrix} 1 & 6 & 11 & 16 \\ d & c & d & \underline{a} \end{matrix}\right| + \left|\begin{matrix} 1 & 6 & 11 & 16 \\ d & d & c & \underline{a} \end{matrix}\right|,$$

$$\left|\begin{matrix} \tilde{1} & 6 & 11 & 16 \\ \underline{d} & d & d & \underline{18} \end{matrix}\right| := \left|\begin{matrix} 1 & 6 & 11 & 16 \\ \underline{d} & d & d & \underline{18} \end{matrix}\right| + \left|\begin{matrix} 1 & 6 & 11 & 16 \\ d & \underline{d} & d & \underline{18} \end{matrix}\right| + \left|\begin{matrix} 1 & 6 & 11 & 16 \\ d & d & \underline{d} & \underline{18} \end{matrix}\right|.$$

Notice that there is at most one tilde in each block by Lemma 3.3

Substep 3(a). Add bi-letters. For each $\sigma \in \mathfrak{J}^t_{dn+h,\ell}$, we add all bi-letters $\binom{i}{i}$ such that $\max\{dn+h, dn+d-h\} \le i \le dn+d-1$. Thus, the number of occurrences of a_j in the bottom row becomes the same as the number of occurrences of a_{d-j-1} for any $j \in \mathbb{N}|_d$.

For instance, the bottom row of the right-hand side of $\overset{w}{=}$ in Example 3.1 contains $4 \times a, 3 \times b, 3 \times c, 3 \times d, 3 \times e$. By adding the bi-letter $\binom{19}{19}$ to the shape the number of occurrences of a in the bottom row becomes the same as the number of occurrences of e (since 19 is also an 'e'). The added bi-letter in the shape is still represented by $\binom{19}{\underline{19}}$, instead of $\binom{19}{e}$. Notice that it is underlined (see Notation 4).

Substep 3(e). Exchange. Consider all the bi-letters of the permutation σ, which are unsocial, or which were added in Substep 3(a), or still which have the specific form $\binom{\ell}{\underline{a_k}}$ with $0 \le \ell \le m-1$. Exchange the bottom letters of those bi-letters in such a way that all the bi-letters will become friendly. In most of the cases, each block contains zero or one bad bi-letter. The only exception is the block containing the specific form $\binom{\ell}{\underline{a_k}}$ with $\ell = m-1$, and another unsocial bi-letter $\binom{i}{a_j}$. In such a case we put the appropriate *explicit letter*, which was added in Substep 3(a), under the letter ℓ when the exchange was made. The whole procedure is reversible.

In Examples 3.1 and 3.2, the exchanges of the bad bi-letters are realized respectively as follows:

$$\begin{pmatrix} \cdots & \tilde{5} & \tilde{7} & \tilde{3} & 19 & \cdots \\ & a & b & c & \underline{19} & \end{pmatrix} \qquad \mapsto \qquad \begin{pmatrix} \cdots & \tilde{5} & \tilde{7} & \tilde{3} & 19 & \cdots \\ & \underline{19} & \underline{c} & \underline{b} & \underline{a} & \end{pmatrix}$$

$$\begin{pmatrix} \cdots & \tilde{5} & \tilde{1} & 16 & \tilde{7} & 18 & 19 & \cdots \\ & d & c & \underline{a} & b & \underline{18} & \underline{19} & \end{pmatrix} \qquad \mapsto \qquad \begin{pmatrix} \cdots & \tilde{5} & \tilde{1} & 16 & \tilde{7} & 18 & 19 & \cdots \\ & \underline{19} & \underline{d} & \underline{18} & \underline{c} & \underline{b} & \underline{a} & \end{pmatrix}$$

In the second example, the block $\left| \begin{smallmatrix} \tilde{1} & 16 \\ c & \underline{a} \end{smallmatrix} \right|$ contains two bad bi-letters. We put the *explicit letter* 18 instead of the symbol 'd' under the letter $\ell = 16$.

Substep 3(d). Decomposition. After Substep 3(e) Exchange, the set $\mathfrak{J}^{t}_{dn+h,\ell}$ is decomposed, in a natural way, into the Cartesian product of d sets of biwords, which are called *atoms* in the sequel.

Substep 3(b). Beta transformation. The cardinalities of the atoms can be derived by means of the transformation β defined in (11). Applying the transformation β to each letter in the top and bottom rows of each element, we can get a new permutation. We defer more details to the full version.

4. ALGORITHM FOR EVALUATING THE ATOMS

Keep the same notations as in Section 3, in particular, $m = dn + h$ ($h \in \mathbb{N}|_d$). For each numerical type t, numerical integers $h, k < d$, and *symbolic* integer n, the cardinality of the set $\mathfrak{P} := \mathfrak{P}_Y(m;t), \mathfrak{P}_Z(m;t)$ or $\mathfrak{P}_X(m;t,k)$ is evaluated by the substeps 3(w), 3(a), 3(e), 3(d), 3(b), which are fully described in Section 3. As a consequence, the latter cardinality is equal to the products of d factors (see Examples 3.1–3.4) corresponding to the d atoms respectively. The evaluation yields an algebra expression in terms of $X_n, X_{n+1}, Y_n, Y_{n+1}, Z_n, Z_{n+1}$. In this section, we show that the substeps in Step 3 can be combined into one super-step. In fact, each factor can be evaluated directly by using a prefabricated dictionary.

DEFINITION 4.1. *Let $i \in \mathbb{N}|_d$ be a fixed integer. We define several parameters depending on i, k, d, m, t, where $t = s_0 s_1 \ldots s_{d-1}$ (if $\mathfrak{P} = \mathfrak{P}_Y$) or $s_0 s_1 \ldots s_{d-1} s_d$ (if $\mathfrak{P} = \mathfrak{P}_X$ or $\mathfrak{P}_Z$):*

$$\eta_0 = \begin{cases} 1, & \text{if } i+1 \le h, \\ 0, & \text{otherwise}; \end{cases} \qquad \eta_1 = \begin{cases} 1, & \text{if } d-i \le h, \\ 0, & \text{otherwise}; \end{cases}$$

$$\eta_2 = \begin{cases} 1, & \text{if } s_i = a_{d-i-1}, \\ 0, & \text{otherwise}; \end{cases}$$

$$\eta_3 = \begin{cases} 1, & \text{if } \mathfrak{P} \ne \mathfrak{P}_Y \text{ and } s_d = a_{d-i-1}, \\ 0, & \text{otherwise}. \end{cases}$$

$$\nu = \begin{cases} \text{'}Z\text{'}, & \text{if } \mathfrak{P} = \mathfrak{P}_Z \text{ and } m-1 \in A_i, \\ \text{'}X\text{'}, & \text{if } \mathfrak{P} = \mathfrak{P}_X \text{ and } k = i, \\ \text{'}G\text{'}, & \text{otherwise}; \end{cases}$$

$$\mu_i = \begin{cases} \Psi_Z(\eta_0, \eta_1, \eta_2, \eta_3), & \text{if } \nu = \text{'}Z\text{'}, \\ \Psi_X(\eta_0, \eta_1, \eta_2, \eta_3), & \text{if } \nu = \text{'}X\text{'}, \\ \Psi_G(\eta_0, \eta_1, \eta_2), & \text{if } \nu = \text{'}G\text{'}, \end{cases}$$

where the explicit values of the functions Ψ_Z, Ψ_X, Ψ_G are given in Table 2.

η	000	001	010	011	100	101	110	111
$\Psi_G(\eta)$	$\bar{X}_n$	$\bar{Y}_n$	0	$\bar{Z}_{n+1}$	$\bar{Z}_{n+1}$	0	$\bar{X}_{n+1}$	$\bar{Y}_{n+1}$
η	0000	0010	0100	0110	1000	1010	1100	1110
$\Psi_Z(\eta)$	0	$\bar{Z}_n$	0	0	$\bar{X}_n$	$\bar{Y}_n$	0	$\bar{Z}_{n+1}$
η	0001	0011	0101	0111	1001	1011	1101	1111
$\Psi_Z(\eta)$	0	$\bar{Z}_n$	0	0	$\bar{X}_n$	0	0	$\bar{Z}_{n+1}$
η	0000	0010	0100	0110	1000	1010	1100	1110
$\Psi_X(\eta)$	0	$\bar{X}_n$	0	0	0	$\bar{Z}_{n+1}$	0	$\bar{X}_{n+1}$
η	0001	0011	0101	0111	1001	1011	1101	1111
$\Psi_X(\eta)$	0	$\bar{X}_n$	0	0	0	0	0	$\bar{X}_{n+1}$

Table 2: Explicit values of the functions Ψ_Z, Ψ_X, Ψ_G

Notice that each permutation contains $n+\eta_0$ (resp. $n+\eta_1$) letters in A_i (resp. in A_{d-i-1}).

EXAMPLE 4.1. *Consider $\mathfrak{P} = \mathfrak{J}^{adbca}_{5n+1,5n+1}$, studied in Example 3.1. In this case, $d = 5, m = 5n+1, h = 1, \ell = m = 5n+1, t = s_0 s_1 s_2 s_3 s_4 =$ 'adbca'. For $i = 1$ we have $\eta_0 = 0, \eta_1 = 0, \eta_2 = 1$. Hence, $\mu_1 = \Psi_G(0,0,1) = \bar{Y}_n$.*

EXAMPLE 4.2. *Consider $\mathfrak{P} = \mathfrak{J}^{dcbbaa}_{5n+2,5n+1}$, studied in Example 3.2. In this case, $d = 5, m = 5n+2, h = 2, \ell = m-1 = 5n+1 \in A_1, t = s_0 s_1 s_2 s_3 s_4 =$ 'dcbbaa'. For $i = 1$ we have $\eta_0 = 1, \eta_1 = 0, \eta_2 = 0, \eta_3 = 0$. So that $\mu_1 = \Psi_Z(1,0,0,0) = \bar{X}_n$.*

EXAMPLE 4.3. *Consider $\mathfrak{P} = \sum_{\ell \in C|_{n+1}} \mathfrak{J}^{adcbac}_{5n+4,\ell}$, studied in Example 3.3. In this case, $d = 5, m = 5n+4, h = 4, \ell \in A_2, t = s_0 s_1 s_2 s_3 s_4 =$ 'adcbac'. For $i = 2$ we have $\eta_0 = 1$, $\eta_1 = 1, \eta_2 = 1, \eta_3 = 1$ and $\mu_2 = \Psi_X(1,1,1,1) = \bar{X}_{n+1}$.*

THEOREM 4.1. *With the above notation, the cardinality of the set $\mathfrak{P} := \mathfrak{P}_Y, \mathfrak{P}_Z, \mathfrak{P}_X$ is equal to*

$$\#\mathfrak{P} = \mu_0 \times \mu_1 \times \mu_2 \times \cdots \times \mu_{d-1}. \tag{21}$$

For example, the set $\mathfrak{P} = \sum_{\ell \in C|_{n+1}} \mathfrak{J}^{adcbac}_{5n+4,\ell}$, studied in Example 3.3, is evaluated by means of Theorem 4.1 as follows:

$$\begin{aligned} &\sum_{\ell \in C|_{n+1}} \mathfrak{J}^{adcbac}_{5n+4,\ell} \\ &= \mu_0\, \mu_1\, \mu_2\, \mu_3\, \mu_4 \\ &= \Phi_G(1,0,0)\, \Phi_G(1,1,1)\, \Psi_X(1,1,1,1)\, \Psi_G(1,1,1)\, \Phi_G(0,1,1) \\ &= Z_{n+1}\, Y_{n+1}\, X_{n+1}\, Y_{n+1}\, Z_{n+1}. \end{aligned}$$

By Theorem 4.1, the procedure `EvalAtoms(P,t,h,k)` figured in Algorithm 1, which evaluates the cardinality of the set $\mathfrak{P} := \mathfrak{P}_Y$, $\mathfrak{P}_Z$ or $\mathfrak{P}_X$ for each type t, is described in Algorithm 2.

Algorithm 2 Evaluating the atoms

```
def EvalAtoms(P,t,h,k):
  Prod=1
  for i in Ch:
    nu='G'
    if P=='PZ' and i==(h+d-1)%d: nu='Z'
    if P=='PX' and i==k:  nu='X'
    eta=(i+1<=h, d-i<=h, t[i]==d-i-1)
    if nu=='X' or nu=='Z': eta=eta+(t[d]==d-i-1,)
    Prod=Prod*Psi(nu, eta)
  return Prod
```

Proof of Theorem 4.1. When we speak of *case*, we refer to a tuple (ν = 'G', η_0, η_1, η_2), (ν = 'Z', $\eta_0, \eta_1, \eta_2, \eta_3$) or ($\nu$ = 'X', $\eta_0, \eta_1, \eta_2, \eta_3$), which depends on $i, k, d, m, t, \mathfrak{P}$ by Definition 4.1. The case is reproduced without non-significant symbols. For example, we write $X1000$ for the case ('X', 1, 0, 0, 0).

In fact, the cases $G101, Z1011, X1011$ do not appear in product (21) and can take any value, in particular, zero. In the cases $X1000$ and $X1001$, we have $\#\mathfrak{P} = 0$ by Lemma 3.3, so that Identity (21) is true. In the cases ('G', 0, 1, 0) and (ν, η) for

$$\begin{aligned} \nu &= \text{'}Z\text{'}, \text{'}X\text{'}; \\ \eta &= (0,0,0,0),(0,1,0,0),(0,1,1,0),(1,1,0,0), \\ &\quad (0,0,0,1),(0,1,0,1),(0,1,1,1),(1,1,0,1), \end{aligned}$$

Lemma 3.2 implies that $\#\mathfrak{P} = 0$. Hence, Identity (21) is true. All other cases are proved as follows.

The evaluations of product (21) are explained in Section 3, see Examples 3.1–3.4. The factors $\mu_0, \mu_1, \ldots, \mu_{d-1}$ are obtained at the same time by proceeding with the substeps 3(w), 3(a), 3(e), 3(d), 3(b). In fact, we can evaluate each sole factor μ_i without keeping in mind the others. For this purpose, we extract all bi-letters such that either their top letter are in A_i or their bottom letter are a_{d-i-1} in the first two substeps 3(w) and 3(a).

Again, consider $i = 1$ and $\mathfrak{P} = \mathfrak{J}^{dcbbaa}_{5n+2,5n+1}$. We extract all bi-letters such that either their top letter are in $\{1, 6, 11, 16, \ldots\}$ or their bottom letter are d in the first two substeps 3(w) and 3(a) of Example 3.2. We have

$$\mathfrak{J}^{dcbbaa}_{5n+2,5n+1} \overset{w}{=} \left(\begin{array}{c|cccc|c|c|c} \tilde{5} & \tilde{1} & 6 & 11 & 16 & ? & ? & ? \\ d & c & d & d & \underline{a} & & & \end{array}\right) \overset{a}{=} \left(\begin{array}{c|cccc|c|c|c} \tilde{5} & \tilde{1} & 6 & 11 & 16 & ? & 18 & ? \\ d & c & d & d & \underline{a} & & \underline{18} & \end{array}\right),$$

and

$$\mathfrak{J}^{dcbbaa}_{5n+2,5n+1} \overset{e}{=} \left(\begin{array}{c|cccc|c|c|c} \tilde{5} & \tilde{1} & 6 & 11 & 16 & ? & 18 & ? \\ \underline{19} & \underline{d} & d & d & \underline{18} & & \underline{b} & \end{array}\right) \overset{d}{=} ?\begin{pmatrix} \tilde{1} & 6 & 11 & 16 \\ \underline{d} & d & d & \underline{18} \end{pmatrix} ? \overset{b}{=} ?X_n?.$$

It means that $\mu_1 = X_n = \bar{X}_n$. On the other hand, the case corresponds to the tuple ('Z', 1, 0, 0, 0) that takes the value $\bar{X}_n$, as shown in Example 4.2. Then we can verify Table 2 one by one by hand (see full version for more detail). □

5. IMPLEMENTATION AND OUTPUTS

Our program `Apwen.py` is an implementation of Algorithms 1 and 2 in `Python`. [2] The proof that F_{13} is Apwenian takes 11 hours by using the program `Apwen.py` on a modern personal computer. For proving that F_{17a} and F_{17b} are Apwenian, it was necessary to rewrite the program in the `C` language with some optimizations. The running times of the two programs are reproduced in the following table:

f	F_3	F_5	F_{11}	F_{13}	F_{17a}, F_{17b}	F_{19}
`Python`	$< 1s$	$< 1s$	$11m$	$11h$	∞	∞
`C`	$< 1s$	$< 1s$	$16s$	$29m$	7 days × 24 CPUs	∞

6. REFERENCES

[1] J.-P. Allouche, J. Peyrière, Z.-X. Wen, and Z.-Y. Wen. Hankel determinants of the Thue–Morse sequence. *Ann. Inst. Fourier, Grenoble*, 48:1–27, 1998.

[2] J.-P. Allouche and J. Shallit. The ubiquitous prouhet-thue-morse sequence. In *Sequences and their applications*, pages 1–16. Springer, 1999.

[3] J.-P. Allouche and J. Shallit. *Automatic sequences: Theory, applications, generalizations*. Cambridge University Press, Cambridge, 2003.

[4] Y. Bugeaud. On the rational approximation to the Thue-Morse-Mahler numbers. *Ann. Inst. Fourier (Grenoble)*, 61(5):2065–2076 (2012), 2011.

[5] Y. Bugeaud and G.-N. Han. A combinatorial proof of the non-vanishing of Hankel determinants of the Thue-Morse sequence. *Electron. J. Combin.*, 21(3):Paper 3.26, 17, 2014.

[6] Y. Bugeaud, G.-N. Han, W. Z.-Y., and Y. J.-Y. Hankel determinants, Padé approximations, and irrationality exponents. *International Mathematics Research Notices (IMRN)*, 5:1467–1496, 2016.

[7] P. Flajolet. Combinatorial aspects of continued fractions. *Discrete Math.*, 32(2):125–161, 1980.

[8] H. Fu and G.-N. Han. Computer assisted proof for apwenian sequences related to Hankel determinants. *arXiv*, 1601.04370, 2016.

[9] G.-N. Han. Hankel continued fraction and its applications. *arXiv:1406.1593*, 2014.

[10] G.-N. Han. Hankel determinant calculus for the Thue-Morse and related sequences. *J. Number Theory*, 147:374–395, 2015.

[11] G.-N. Han and W. Wu. Evaluations of the hankel determinants of a thue–morse-like sequence. *International Journal of Number Theory*, 11(06):1887–1904, 2015.

[12] C. Krattenthaler. Advanced determinant calculus. *Sém. Lothar. Combin.*, 42:Art. B42q, 67 pp., 1999. `http://www.mat.univie.ac.at/~slc/`.

[13] C. Krattenthaler. Advanced determinant calculus: a complement. *Linear Algebra Appl.*, 411:68–166, 2005.

[2] A extended version of this paper, the program `Apwen.py` and its outputs are available at `www-irma.u-strasbg.fr/~guoniu/papers/p93apwen/`

Bounds for Orders of Derivatives in Differential Elimination Algorithms

Richard Gustavson
CUNY Graduate Center
Ph.D. Program in Mathematics
365 Fifth Avenue
New York, NY 10016, USA
rgustavson@gradcenter.cuny.edu

Alexey Ovchinnikov
CUNY Queens College
Department of Mathematics
65-30 Kissena Blvd
Queens, NY 11367-1597, USA
aovchinnikov@qc.cuny.edu

Gleb Pogudin
Moscow State University
Department of Mechanics and Mathematics
Moscow, 119991, Russia
pogudin.gleb@gmail.com

ABSTRACT

We compute an upper bound for the orders of derivatives in the Rosenfeld-Gröbner algorithm. This algorithm computes a regular decomposition of a radical differential ideal in the ring of differential polynomials over a differential field of characteristic zero with an arbitrary number of commuting derivations. This decomposition can then be used to test for membership in the given radical differential ideal. In particular, this algorithm allows us to determine whether a system of polynomial PDEs is consistent.

Previously, the only known order upper bound was given by Golubitsky, Kondratieva, Moreno Maza, and Ovchinnikov for the case of a single derivation. We achieve our bound by associating to the algorithm antichain sequences whose lengths can be bounded using the results of León Sánchez and Ovchinnikov.

CCS Concepts

•Computing methodologies → Symbolic and algebraic algorithms; Algebraic algorithms;

Keywords

Polynomial differential equations; differential elimination algorithms; computational complexity

1. INTRODUCTION

The Rosenfeld-Gröbner algorithm is a fundamental algorithm in the algebraic theory of differential equations. This algorithm, which first appeared in [1, 2], takes as its input a finite set F of differential polynomials and outputs a representation of the radical differential ideal generated by F as a finite intersection of regular differential ideals. The Rosenfeld-Gröbner algorithm has many applications; for example, it can be used to test membership in a radical differential ideal, and, in conjunction with the differential Nullstellensatz, can be used to test the consistency of a system of polynomial differential equations. See [6] for a history of the development of the Rosenfeld-Gröbner algorithm and similar decomposition algorithms.

The Rosenfeld-Gröbner algorithm has been implemented in MAPLE as a part of the `DifferentialAlgebra` package. In order to determine the complexity of the algorithm, we need to (among other things) find an upper bound on the orders of derivatives that appear in all intermediate steps and in the output of the algorithm. The first step in answering this question was completed in [6], in which an upper bound in the case of a single derivation and any ranking on the set of derivatives was found. If there are n differential indeterminates and the order of the original system is h, the authors showed that an upper bound on the orders of the output of the Rosenfeld-Gröbner algorithm is $h(n-1)!$.

In this paper, we extend this result by finding an upper bound for the orders of derivatives that appear in the intermediate steps and in the output of the Rosenfeld-Gröbner algorithm in the case of an arbitrary number of commuting derivations and an orderly ranking on the derivatives. Our result depends on studying lengths of antichain sequences in the set $\mathbb{Z}^m_{\geqslant 0} \times \{1, \ldots, n\}$ equipped with a specific partial order. This analysis began in [12] and continued in [1, 11].

We show that an upper bound for the orders of derivatives in the intermediate steps and in the output of the Rosenfeld-Gröbner algorithm is given by hf_{L+1}, where h is the order of our input system of differential equations, $\{f_0, f_1, f_2, \ldots\}$ is the Fibonacci sequence $\{0, 1, 1, 2, 3, 5, \ldots\}$, and L is the maximal possible length of a certain antichain sequence (that depends solely on h, the number of derivations, and the number of differential indeterminates). Note that this is different from the upper bounds for the effective differential Nullstellensatz [3, 8], which are higher and also depend on the degree of the given system of differential equations.

The paper is organized as follows. In Section 2, we present the background material from differential algebra that is necessary to understand the Rosenfeld-Gröbner algorithm. In Section 3, we describe this algorithm as it is presented in [9], as well as two necessary auxiliary algorithms. In Section 4, we prove our main result on the upper bound. In Section 5, we calculate the upper bound for specific values using the results of [11]. In Section 6, we give an example showing that the lower bound for the orders of derivatives in the Rosenfeld-Gröbner algorithm is at least double-exponential in the number of derivations.

ISSAC '16, July 19-22, 2016, Waterloo, ON, Canada
© 2016 ACM. ISBN 978-1-4503-4380-0/16/07...$15.00
DOI: http://dx.doi.org/10.1145/2930889.2930922

2. BACKGROUND ON DIFFERENTIAL ALGEBRA

In this section, we present background material from differential algebra that is pertinent to the Rosenfeld-Gröbner algorithm. For a more in-depth discussion, we turn the reader to [9, 10].

Definition 1. A *differential ring* is a commutative ring R with a collection of m commuting derivations $\Delta = \{\partial_1, \ldots, \partial_m\}$ on R.

Definition 2. An ideal I of a differential ring is a *differential ideal* if $\delta a \in I$ for all $a \in I$ and $\delta \in \Delta$.

For a set $A \subseteq R$, we let (A), $\sqrt{(A)}$, $[A]$, and $\{A\}$ denote the smallest ideal, radical ideal, differential ideal, and radical differential ideal containing A, respectively. If $\mathbb{Q} \subseteq R$, then $\{A\} = \sqrt{[A]}$.

Remark 1. In this paper, as usual, we also use the braces $\{a_1, a_2, \ldots\}$ to denote the set containing the elements $a_1, a_2, \ldots$. Even though this notation conflicts with the above notation for radical differential ideals (used here for historical reasons), it will be clear from the context which of the two objects we mean in each particular situation.

In this paper, $\mathbf{k}$ is a differential field of characteristic zero with m commuting derivations. The set of derivative operators is denoted by

$$\Theta := \left\{\partial_1^{i_1} \cdots \partial_m^{i_m} : i_j \in \mathbb{Z}_{\geqslant 0}, 1 \leqslant j \leqslant m\right\}.$$

For $Y = \{y_1, \ldots, y_n\}$ a set of n *differential indeterminates*, the set of derivatives of Y is

$$\Theta Y := \{\theta y : \theta \in \Theta, y \in Y\}.$$

Then the ring of *differential polynomials* over $\mathbf{k}$ is defined to be

$$\mathbf{k}\{Y\} = \mathbf{k}\{y_1, \ldots, y_n\} := \mathbf{k}[\theta y : \theta y \in \Theta Y].$$

We can naturally extend the derivations $\partial_1, \ldots, \partial_m$ to the ring $\mathbf{k}\{Y\}$ by defining

$$\partial_j \left(\partial_1^{i_1} \cdots \partial_m^{i_m} y_k\right) := \partial_1^{i_1} \cdots \partial_j^{i_j+1} \cdots \partial_m^{i_m} y_k.$$

For any $\theta = \partial_1^{i_1} \cdots \partial_m^{i_m} \in \Theta$, we define the *order* of θ to be

$$\mathrm{ord}(\theta) := i_1 + \cdots + i_m.$$

For any derivative $u = \theta y \in \Theta Y$, we define

$$\mathrm{ord}(u) := \mathrm{ord}(\theta).$$

For a differential polynomial $f \in \mathbf{k}\{Y\} \setminus \mathbf{k}$, we define the order of f to be the maximum order of all derivatives that appear in f. For any finite set $A \subseteq \mathbf{k}\{Y\} \setminus \mathbf{k}$, we set

$$\mathcal{H}(A) := \max\{\mathrm{ord}(f) : f \in A\}. \qquad (1)$$

Definition 3. An *orderly ranking* on the set ΘY is a total order $<$ satisfying the following three additional properties: for all $u, v \in \Theta Y$ and all $\theta \in \Theta$, $\theta \neq \mathrm{id}$,

1. $u < \theta u$
2. if $u < v$, then $\theta u < \theta v$
3. if $\mathrm{ord}(u) < \mathrm{ord}(v)$, then $u < v$.

For a derivative $u \in \Theta Y$, we let $(\Theta Y)_{<u}$ (respectively, $(\Theta Y)_{\leqslant u}$) be the collection of all derivatives $v \in \Theta Y$ with $v < u$ (respectively, $v \leqslant u$).

From now on, we fix an orderly ranking.

Definition 4. Let $f \in \mathbf{k}\{Y\} \setminus \mathbf{k}$.

- The derivative $u \in \Theta Y$ of highest rank appearing in f is called the *leader* of f, denoted $\mathrm{lead}(f)$.
- If we write f as a univariate polynomial in $\mathrm{lead}(f)$, the leading coefficient is called the *initial* of f, denoted $\mathrm{init}(f)$.
- If we apply any derivative $\delta \in \Delta$ to f, the leader of δf is $\delta(\mathrm{lead}(f))$, and the initial of δf is called the *separant* of f, denoted $\mathrm{sep}(f)$.

Given a set $A \subseteq \mathbf{k}\{Y\} \setminus \mathbf{k}$, we will denote the set of leaders of A by $\mathfrak{L}(A)$, the set of initials of A by I_A, and the set of separants of A by S_A; we then let $H_A = I_A \cup S_A$ be the set of initials and separants of A. For any derivative $u \in \Theta Y$, we let $A_{<u}$ (respectively, $A_{\leqslant u}$) be the elements of A with leader $< u$ (respectively, $\leqslant u$), that is,

$$A_{<u} := A \cap \mathbf{k}[(\Theta Y)_{<u}] \quad \text{and} \quad A_{\leqslant u} := A \cap \mathbf{k}[(\Theta Y)_{\leqslant u}].$$

We can similarly define $(\Theta A)_{<u}$ and $(\Theta A)_{\leqslant u}$, where

$$\Theta A := \{\theta f : \theta \in \Theta, f \in A\}.$$

Given $f \in \mathbf{k}\{Y\} \setminus \mathbf{k}$ such that $\deg_{\mathrm{lead}(f)}(f) = d$, we define the *rank* of f to be

$$\mathrm{rank}(f) := \mathrm{lead}(f)^d.$$

The orderly ranking $<$ on ΘY determines a pre-order (that is, a relation satisfying all of the properties of an order, except for the property that $a \leqslant b$ and $b \leqslant a$ imply that $a = b$) on $\mathbf{k}\{Y\} \setminus \mathbf{k}$, as follows.

Definition 5. Given $f_1, f_2 \in \mathbf{k}\{Y\} \setminus \mathbf{k}$ such that $\deg_{\mathrm{lead}(f_1)}(f_1) = d_1$ and $\deg_{\mathrm{lead}(f_2)}(f_2) = d_2$, we say that

$$\mathrm{rank}(f_1) < \mathrm{rank}(f_2)$$

if $\mathrm{lead}(f_1) < \mathrm{lead}(f_2)$ or if $\mathrm{lead}(f_1) = \mathrm{lead}(f_2)$ and $d_1 < d_2$.

Definition 6. A differential polynomial f is *partially reduced* with respect to another differential polynomial g if no proper derivative of $\mathrm{lead}(g)$ appears in f, and f is *reduced* with respect to g if, in addition,

$$\deg_{\mathrm{lead}(g)}(f) < \deg_{\mathrm{lead}(g)}(g).$$

A differential polynomial is then (partially) reduced with respect to a set $A \subseteq \mathbf{k}\{Y\} \setminus \mathbf{k}$ if it is (partially) reduced with respect to every element of A.

Definition 7. For a set $A \subseteq \mathbf{k}\{Y\} \setminus \mathbf{k}$, we say that A is:

- *autoreduced* if every element of A is reduced with respect to every other element.
- *weak d-triangular* if $\mathfrak{L}(A)$ is autoreduced.
- *d-triangular* if A is weak d-triangular and every element of A is partially reduced with respect to every other element.

Note that every autoreduced set is d-triangular. Every weak d-triangular set (and thus every d-triangular and autoreduced set) is finite (see [9, Proposition 3.9]). Since the set of leaders of a weak d-triangular set A is autoreduced, distinct elements of A must have distinct leaders. If $u \in \Theta Y$ is the leader of some element of a weak d-triangular set A, we let A_u denote this element.

Definition 8. We define a pre-order on the collection of all weak d-triangular sets, which we also call *rank*, as follows. Given two weak d-triangular sets $A = \{A_1, \ldots, A_r\}$ and $B = \{B_1, \ldots, B_s\}$, in each case arranged in increasing rank, we say that $\operatorname{rank}(A) < \operatorname{rank}(B)$ if either:

- there exists a $k \leqslant \min(r, s)$ such that $\operatorname{rank}(A_i) = \operatorname{rank}(B_i)$ for all $1 \leqslant i < k$ and $\operatorname{rank}(A_k) < \operatorname{rank}(B_k)$, or
- $r > s$ and $\operatorname{rank}(A_i) = \operatorname{rank}(B_i)$ for all $1 \leqslant i \leqslant s$.

We also say that $\operatorname{rank}(A) = \operatorname{rank}(B)$ if $r = s$ and $\operatorname{rank}(A_i) = \operatorname{rank}(B_i)$ for all $1 \leqslant i \leqslant r$.

We can restrict this ranking to the collection of all d-triangular sets or the collection of all autoreduced sets.

Definition 9. A *characteristic set* of a differential ideal I is an autoreduced set $C \subseteq I$ of minimal rank among all autoreduced subsets of I.

Given a finite set $S \subseteq \mathbf{k}\{Y\}$, denote by S^∞ the multiplicative set containing 1 and generated by S. For an ideal $I \subseteq \mathbf{k}\{Y\}$, we define the *colon ideal* to be

$$I : S^\infty := \{a \in \mathbf{k}\{Y\} : \exists s \in S^\infty \text{ with } sa \in I\}.$$

If I is a differential ideal, then $I : S^\infty$ is also a differential ideal (see [10, Chapter I, Section 2]).

Definition 10. Given a differential polynomial $f \in \mathbf{k}\{Y\}$ and a weak d-triangular set $A \subseteq \mathbf{k}\{Y\}$, a *differential partial remainder* f_1 and a *differential remainder* f_2 of f with respect to A are differential polynomials such that there exist $s \in S_A^\infty$ and $h \in H_A^\infty$ such that $sf \equiv f_1 \mod [A]$ and $hf \equiv f_2 \mod [A]$, with f_1 partially reduced with respect to A and f_2 reduced with respect to A.

We denote a differential partial remainder of f with respect to A by $\text{pd-red}(f, A)$ and a differential remainder of f with respect to A by $\text{d-red}(f, A)$. There are algorithms to compute $\text{pd-red}(f, A)$ and $\text{d-red}(f, A)$ for any f and A (see [9, Algorithm 3.12 & Algorithm 3.13]). These algorithms have the property that

$$\operatorname{rank}(\text{pd-red}(f, A)),\ \operatorname{rank}(\text{d-red}(f, A)) \leqslant \operatorname{rank}(f);$$

since we have an orderly ranking, this implies that

$$\operatorname{ord}(\text{pd-red}(f, A)),\ \operatorname{ord}(\text{d-red}(f, A)) \leqslant \operatorname{ord}(f).$$

Definition 11. Two derivatives $u, v \in \Theta Y$ are said to have a *common derivative* if there exist $\phi, \psi \in \Theta$ such that $\phi u = \psi v$. Note this is the case precisely when $u = \theta_1 y$ and $v = \theta_2 y$ for some $y \in Y$ and $\theta_1, \theta_2 \in \Theta$.

Definition 12. If $u = \partial_1^{i_1} \cdots \partial_m^{i_m} y$ and $v = \partial_1^{j_1} \cdots \partial_m^{j_m} y$ for some $y \in Y$, we define the *least common derivative* of u and v, denoted $\operatorname{lcd}(u, v)$, to be

$$\operatorname{lcd}(u, v) = \partial_1^{\max(i_1, j_1)} \cdots \partial_m^{\max(i_m, j_m)} y.$$

Definition 13. For $f, g \in \mathbf{k}\{Y\} \setminus \mathbf{k}$, we define the Δ-*polynomial* of f and g, denoted $\Delta(f, g)$, as follows. If $\operatorname{lead}(f)$ and $\operatorname{lead}(g)$ have no common derivatives, set $\Delta(f, g) = 0$. Otherwise, let $\phi, \psi \in \Theta$ be such that

$$\operatorname{lcd}(\operatorname{lead}(f), \operatorname{lead}(g)) = \phi(\operatorname{lead}(f)) = \psi(\operatorname{lead}(g)),$$

and define

$$\Delta(f, g) := \operatorname{sep}(g)\phi(f) - \operatorname{sep}(f)\psi(g).$$

Definition 14. A pair (A, H) is called a *regular differential system* if the following four conditions hold:

- A is a d-triangular set
- H is a set of differential polynomials that are all partially reduced with respect to A
- $S_A \subseteq H^\infty$
- for all $f, g \in A$,
$$\Delta(f, g) \in ((\Theta A)_{<u}) : H^\infty,$$
where $u = \operatorname{lcd}(\operatorname{lead}(f), \operatorname{lead}(g))$.

Definition 15. Any ideal of the form $[A] : H^\infty$, where (A, H) is a regular differential system, is called a *regular differential ideal*.

Every regular differential ideal is a radical differential ideal (see [9, Theorem 4.12]).

Definition 16. Given a radical differential ideal $I \subseteq \mathbf{k}\{Y\}$, a *regular decomposition* of I is a finite collection of regular differential systems $\{(A_1, H_1), \ldots, (A_r, H_r)\}$ such that

$$I = \bigcap_{i=1}^{r} [A_i] : H_i^\infty.$$

Due to the Rosenfeld-Gröbner algorithm, every radical differential ideal in $\mathbf{k}\{Y\}$ has a regular decomposition.

Definition 17. A d-triangular set C is called a *differential regular chain* if it is a characteristic set of $[C] : H_C^\infty$; in this case, we call $[C] : H_C^\infty$ a *characterizable differential ideal.*

Definition 18. A *characteristic decomposition* of a radical differential ideal $I \subseteq \mathbf{k}\{Y\}$ is a representation of I as an intersection of characterizable differential ideals.

As we will recall in Section 3, every radical differential ideal also has a characteristic decomposition.

3. ROSENFELD-GRÖBNER ALGORITHM

Below we reproduce the Rosenfeld-Gröbner algorithm from [9, Section 6]. This algorithm relies on two others, called auto-partial-reduce and update, which we also include. We need to include these two auxiliary algorithms because, in Section 4, we will study their effect on the growth of the orders of derivatives in the Rosenfeld-Gröbner algorithm.

The Rosenfeld-Gröbner algorithm takes as its input two finite subsets $F, K \in \mathbf{k}\{Y\}$ and outputs a finite set $\mathcal{A}$ of regular differential systems such that

$$\{F\} : K^\infty = \bigcap_{(A,H)\in\mathcal{A}} [A] : H^\infty, \tag{2}$$

where $\mathcal{A} = \varnothing$ if $1 \in \{F\} : K^\infty$.

If we have a decomposition of $\{F\} : K^\infty$ as in (2), we can compute, using only algebraic operations, a decomposition of the form

$$\{F\} : K^\infty = \bigcap_{C\in\mathcal{C}} [C] : H_C^\infty, \tag{3}$$

where $\mathcal{C}$ is finite and each $C \in \mathcal{C}$ is a differential regular chain (see [9, Algorithm 7.1 & Algorithm 7.2]). This means that an upper bound on $\bigcup_{(A,H)\in\mathcal{A}} \mathcal{H}(A \cup H)$ from (2) will also be an upper bound on $\bigcup_{C\in\mathcal{C}} \mathcal{H}(C)$ from (3).

The Rosenfeld-Gröbner algorithm has many immediate applications. For example, if $K = \{1\}$, then $\{F\} : K^\infty = \{F\}$, so in this case, the Rosenfeld-Gröbner algorithm computes a regular decomposition of $\{F\}$, which then also gives us a characteristic decomposition of $\{F\}$ by the discussion in the previous paragraph.

The *weak differential Nullstellensatz* says that a system of polynomial differential equations $F = 0$ is consistent (that is, has a solution in some differential field extension of $\mathbf{k}$) if and only if $1 \notin [F]$ (see [10, Chapter IV, Section 2]). Thus, since Rosenfeld-Gröbner$(F, K) = \varnothing$ if and only if $1 \in \{F\} : K^\infty$, we see that $F = 0$ is consistent if and only if Rosenfeld-Gröbner$(F, \{1\}) \neq \varnothing$.

More generally, the Rosenfeld-Gröbner algorithm and its extension for computing a characteristic decomposition of a radical differential ideal allow us to test for membership in a radical differential ideal, as follows. Suppose we have computed a characteristic decomposition

$$\{F\} = \bigcap_{C\in\mathcal{C}} [C] : H_C^\infty.$$

Now, a differential polynomial $f \in \mathbf{k}\{Y\}$ is contained in $\{F\}$ if and only if $f \in [C] : H_C^\infty$ for all $C \in \mathcal{C}$; this latter case is true if and only if d-red$(f, C) = 0$, which can be tested using [9, Algorithm 3.13].

The Rosenfeld-Gröbner algorithm and its two auxiliary algorithms auto-partial-reduce and update rely on the following tuples of differential polynomials:

Definition 19. A *Rosenfeld-Gröbner quadruple* (or *RG-quadruple*) is a 4-tuple (G, D, A, H) of finite subsets of $\mathbf{k}\{Y\}$ such that:

- A is a weak d-triangular set
- $H_A \subseteq H$
- D is a set of Δ-polynomials
- for all $f, g \in A$, either $\Delta(f, g) = 0$ or $\Delta(f, g) \in D$ or

$$\Delta(f, g) \in (\Theta(A \cup G)_{<u}) : H_u^\infty,$$

where $u = \mathrm{lcd}(\mathrm{lead}(f), \mathrm{lead}(g))$ and

$$H_u = H_{A_{<u}} \cup (H \setminus H_A) \cap \mathbf{k}[(\Theta Y)_{<u}].$$

Remark 2. The RG-quadruple that is output by the update algorithm satisfies additional properties that we do not list, as they are not important for our analysis. For more information, we refer the reader to [9, Algorithm 6.10]

Algorithm: Rosenfeld-Gröbner, [9, Algorithm 6.11]

Data: F, K finite subsets of $\mathbf{k}\{Y\}$

Result: A set $\mathcal{A}$ of regular differential systems such that:

- $\mathcal{A}$ is empty if it has been detected that $1 \in \{F\} : K^\infty$
- $\{F\} : K^\infty = \bigcap_{(A,H)\in\mathcal{A}} [A] : H^\infty$ otherwise

```
S := {(F, ∅, ∅, K)};
A := ∅;
while S ≠ ∅ do
    (G, D, A, H) := an element of S;
    S̄ = S \ (G, D, A, H);
    if G ∪ D = ∅ then
        A := A ∪ auto-partial-reduce(A, H);
    else
        p := an element of G ∪ D;
        Ḡ, D̄ := G \ {p}, D \ {p};
        p̄ := d-red(p, A);
        if p̄ = 0 then
            S̄ := S̄ ∪ {(Ḡ, D̄, A, H)};
        else
            if p̄ ∉ k then
                p̄_i := p̄ − init(p̄) rank(p̄)
                p̄_s := deg_lead(p̄)(p̄)p̄ − lead(p̄) sep(p̄);
                S̄ := S̄ ∪ {update(Ḡ, D̄, A, H, p̄), (G ∪
                {p̄_s, sep(p̄)}, D̄, A, H ∪ {init(p̄)}), (Ḡ ∪
                {p̄_i, init(p̄)}, D̄, A, H)};
            end
        end
    end
    S := S̄;
end
return A;
```

Algorithm: auto-partial-reduce, [9, Algorithm 6.8]

Data: Two finite subsets A, H of $\mathbf{k}\{Y\}$ such that $(\varnothing, \varnothing, A, H)$ is an RG-quadruple

Result:

- The empty set if it is detected that $1 \in [A] : H^\infty$
- Otherwise, a set with a single regular differential system (B, K) with $\mathfrak{L}(A) = \mathfrak{L}(B)$, $H_B \subseteq K$, and $[A] : H^\infty = [B] : K^\infty$

```
B := ∅;
for u ∈ 𝔏(A) increasingly do
    b := pd-red(A_u, B);
    if rank(b) = rank(A_u) then
        B := B ∪ {b};
    else
        return (∅);
    end
end
K := H_B ∪ {pd-red(p, B) : p ∈ H \ H_A};
if 0 ∈ K then
    return (∅);
else
    return {(B, K)};
end
```

Algorithm: update, [9, Algorithm 6.10]

Data:

- A 4-tuple (G, D, A, H) of finite subsets of $\mathbf{k}\{Y\}$
- A differential polynomial p reduced with respect to A such that $(G \cup \{p\}, D, A, H)$ is an RG-quadruple

Result: A new RG-quadruple $(\bar{G}, \bar{D}, \bar{A}, \bar{H})$
$u := \mathrm{lead}(p)$;
$G_A := \{a \in A \mid \mathrm{lead}(a) \in \Theta u\}$;
$\bar{A} := A \setminus G_A$;
$\bar{G} := G \cup G_A$;
$\bar{D} := D \cup \{\Delta(p, a) \mid a \in \bar{A}\} \setminus \{0\}$;
$\bar{H} := H \cup \{\mathrm{sep}(p), \mathrm{init}(p)\}$;
return $(\bar{G}, \bar{D}, \bar{A} \cup \{p\}, \bar{H})$;

4. ORDER UPPER BOUND

Given finite subsets $F, K \subseteq \mathbf{k}\{Y\}$, let $h = \mathcal{H}(F \cup K)$ (see (1)). Our goal is to find an upper bound for

$$\mathcal{H}\left(\bigcup_{(A,H)\in\mathcal{A}} (A \cup H)\right),$$

where $\mathcal{A} = \text{Rosenfeld-Gröbner}(F, K)$, in terms of h, m (the number of derivations), and n (the number of differential indeterminates).

We approach this problem as follows. Every $(A, H) \in \mathcal{A}$ is formed by applying the algorithm auto-partial-reduce to a 4-tuple $(\varnothing, \varnothing, A', H') \in \mathcal{S}$. Thus, it suffices:

- to bound how auto-partial-reduce increases the order of a collection of differential polynomials (it turns out to not increase the order), and
- to bound $\mathcal{H}(G \cup D \cup A \cup H)$ for all (G, D, A, H) added to $\mathcal{S}$ throughout the course of the Rosenfeld-Gröbner algorithm.

We accomplish the latter by determining when the order of a tuple (G, D, A, H) added to $\mathcal{S}$ is larger than the orders of the previous elements of $\mathcal{S}$ and bounding $\mathcal{H}(G \cup D \cup A \cup H)$ in this instance, and then bounding the number of times we can add such elements to $\mathcal{S}$.

There is a sequence $\{(G_i, D_i, A_i, H_i)\}_{i=0}^N$ corresponding to each regular differential system (A, H) in the output of the Rosenfeld-Gröbner algorithm, where $N = N_{(A,H)}$, such that $(G_{i+1}, D_{i+1}, A_{i+1}, H_{i+1})$ is obtained from (G_i, D_i, A_i, H_i) during the while loop, $(G_0, D_0, A_0, H_0) = (F, \varnothing, \varnothing, K)$, and $(A, H) = \text{auto-partial-reduce}(A_N, H_N)$.

We begin with an auxiliary result, which is an analogue of the *first* property from [7, Section 5.1].

LEMMA 1. *For every $f \in A_i$ and $i < j$, there exists $g \in A_j$ such that* $\mathrm{lead}(f) \in \Theta\,\mathrm{lead}(g)$. *In particular, if p is reduced with respect to A_j, then p is also reduced with respect to A_i for all $i < j$.*

PROOF. It is sufficient to consider the case $j = i + 1$. If $(G_{i+1}, D_{i+1}, A_{i+1}, H_{i+1})$ was obtained from (G_i, D_i, A_i, H_i) without applying the update operation, then $A_i = A_{i+1}$. Otherwise, either $f \in A_i \setminus G_{A_i}$ (we use the notation from the update algorithm), or $f \in G_{A_i}$. In the former case, $f \in A_{i+1}$ as well, so we can set $g = f$. In the latter case, $\mathrm{lead}(f) \in \Theta\,\mathrm{lead}(p)$, so we can set $g = p$. □

We define a partial order $\preccurlyeq$ on the set of derivatives ΘY as follows. For $u, v \in \Theta Y$, we say that $u \preccurlyeq v$ if there exists $\theta \in \Theta$ such that $\theta u = v$. Note that this implies that u and v are both derivatives of the same $y \in Y$.

Definition 20. An *antichain sequence* in ΘY is a sequence of elements $S = \{s_1, s_2, \dots\} \subseteq \Theta Y$ that are pairwise incomparable in this partial order.

Given a sequence $\{(G_i, D_i, A_i, H_i)\}_{i=0}^N$ as above (where $N = N_{(A,H)}$ for some regular differential system (A, H) in the output of the Rosenfeld-Gröbner algorithm), we will construct an antichain sequence $S = \{s_1, s_2, \dots\} \subseteq \Theta Y$ inductively going along the sequence $\{(G_i, D_i, A_i, H_i)\}$.

Suppose $S_{j-1} = \{s_1, \dots, s_{j-1}\}$ has been constructed after considering $(G_0, D_0, A_0, H_0), \dots, (G_{i-1}, D_{i-1}, A_{i-1}, H_{i-1})$, where $S_0 = \varnothing$. A 4-tuple (G_i, D_i, A_i, H_i) can be obtained from the tuple $(G_{i-1}, D_{i-1}, A_{i-1}, H_{i-1})$ in two ways:

1. We did not perform the update operation. In this case, we do not append a new element to S.
2. We performed update with respect to some differential polynomial p. If there exists $s_k \in S_{j-1}$ such that $\mathrm{lead}(p) \preccurlyeq s_k$, we do not append a new element to S_{j-1}. Otherwise, we let $s_j = \mathrm{lead}(p)$ and define $S_j = \{s_1, \dots, s_j\}$. In the latter case, we set $k_j = i$.

We also set $k_0 = 0$.

THEOREM 1. *The sequence $\{s_j\}$ is an antichain sequence in ΘY and, for all $j \geqslant 1$,*

$$\mathrm{ord}(s_j) \leqslant hf_j,$$

where $\{f_j\}$ is the Fibonacci sequence.

PROOF. Let $i < j$. Assume that $s_j \succcurlyeq s_i$. Then, p is not reduced with respect to A_{k_i}, which contradicts Lemma 1. On the other hand, the case $s_j \preccurlyeq s_i$ is impossible by the construction of the sequence, so $\{s_j\}$ is an antichain sequence.

We denote by anti-k_i the maximal $j \in \mathbb{Z}_{\geqslant 0}$ such that $k_j \leqslant i$. For all $i \geqslant 0$, let us set $j = \text{anti-}k_i$ and prove by induction on i that

1. $\mathcal{H}\left(\bigcup_{t=0}^{i}(G_t \cup D_t \cup H_t)\right) \leqslant hf_{j+1}$;
2. $\mathcal{H}\left(\bigcup_{t=0}^{i} A_t\right) \leqslant hf_j$;
3. For all distinct elements of $\bigcup_{t=0}^{i} A_t$, the orders of the least common derivatives of their leaders do not exceed hf_{j+1}.

In the base case $i = 0 = k_0$, we have

$$\mathcal{H}(G_0 \cup D_0 \cup H_0) = h = hf_1$$

and

$$\mathcal{H}(A_0) = \mathcal{H}(\varnothing) = 0 = hf_0.$$

There are two distinct cases for $i + 1$:

1. Case $i + 1 < k_{j+1}$ (so we have anti-$k_{i+1} = j$). Then, $(G_{i+1}, D_{i+1}, A_{i+1}, H_{i+1})$ was obtained from (G_i, D_i, A_i, H_i) in one of the following ways:

(a) We did not perform the update operation. In this case, $A_{i+1} = A_i$ and

$$\mathcal{H}(G_{i+1} \cup D_{i+1} \cup H_{i+1}) \leqslant \mathcal{H}(G_i \cup D_i \cup H_i).$$

(b) We performed the update operation with respect to a differential polynomial p such that $\operatorname{lead}(f) \in \Theta \operatorname{lead}(p)$ for some $f \in \bigcup_{t=0}^{i} A_t$. In this case,

$$\mathcal{H}(A_{i+1}) \leqslant \mathcal{H}\left(\bigcup_{t=0}^{i} A_t\right).$$

Then, for all $g \in A_t$ $(t \leqslant i)$,

$$\operatorname{ord}(\Delta(p,g)) \leqslant \operatorname{ord}(\operatorname{lcd}(\operatorname{lead}(g), \operatorname{lead}(f))),$$

which is bounded by hf_{j+1} due to the third inductive hypothesis. Since $D_{i+1} \setminus D_i$ consists of some of these polynomials, $G_{i+1} \setminus G_i \subseteq A_i$, and $H_{i+1} \setminus H_i = \{\operatorname{sep}(p), \operatorname{init}(p)\}$, then

$$\mathcal{H}(G_{i+1} \cup D_{i+1} \cup H_{i+1}) \leqslant \mathcal{H}(G_i \cup D_i \cup H_i).$$

2. Case $i+1 = k_{j+1}$ (so now anti-$k_{i+1} = j+1$). We performed the update operation with respect to a differential polynomial p, which is a result of reduction of some $\tilde{p} \in G_i \cup D_i$ with respect to A_i. Then

$$\mathcal{H}(A_{i+1}) \leqslant \max(\mathcal{H}(A_i), \operatorname{ord}(p)) \leqslant hf_{j+1}.$$

Moreover, for every $g \in \bigcup_{t=0}^{i} A_t$,

$$\operatorname{ord}(\operatorname{lcd}(\operatorname{lead}(g), \operatorname{lead}(p))) \leqslant hf_j + hf_{j+1} = hf_{j+2}.$$

Since $D_{i+1} \setminus D_i$ consists of some of these polynomials, $G_{i+1} \setminus G_i \subseteq A_i$, and $H_{i+1} \setminus H_i = \{\operatorname{sep}(p), \operatorname{init}(p)\}$, we have

$$\mathcal{H}(G_{i+1} \cup D_{i+1} \cup H_{i+1}) \leqslant \max(\mathcal{H}(G_i \cup D_i \cup H_i), hf_{j+2}) = hf_{j+2}.$$

Since $\operatorname{ord}(s_j) \leqslant \mathcal{H}(A_{k_j}) \leqslant hf_j$, this completes the proof. □

Let $\mathfrak{n} = \{1, \ldots, n\}$. The set of derivatives ΘY is in one-to-one correspondence with the set $\mathbb{Z}_{\geqslant 0}^m \times \mathfrak{n}$ by associating $\partial_1^{i_1} \cdots \partial_m^{i_m} y_k \in \Theta Y$ to $((i_1, \ldots, i_m), k) \in \mathbb{Z}_{\geqslant 0}^m \times \mathfrak{n}$. We define the *degree* of an element of $\mathbb{Z}_{\geqslant 0}^m \times \mathfrak{n}$ to be the order of its corresponding element of ΘY.

Under this correspondence, the partial order $\preccurlyeq$ on ΘY determines a partial order $\preccurlyeq$ on $\mathbb{Z}_{\geqslant 0}^m \times \mathfrak{n}$ by saying $((i_1, \ldots, i_m), k) \preccurlyeq ((j_1, \ldots, j_m), l)$ if and only if $k = l$ and $i_r \leqslant j_r$ for all $1 \leqslant r \leqslant m$. Thus there is a one-to-one correspondence between the set of antichain sequences of ΘY and the set of antichain sequences of $\mathbb{Z}_{\geqslant 0}^m \times \mathfrak{n}$. Every antichain sequence of $\mathbb{Z}_{\geqslant 0}^m \times \mathfrak{n}$ (and thus of ΘY) is finite; see [12, Lemma 4.4].

Given an increasing function $f : \mathbb{Z}_{>0} \to \mathbb{Z}_{\geqslant 0}$, we say that *f bounds the degree growth* of an antichain sequence $S = \{s_1, \ldots, s_k\} \subseteq \mathbb{Z}_{\geqslant 0}^m \times \mathfrak{n}$ if $\deg(s_i) \leqslant f(i)$ for all $1 \leqslant i \leqslant k$. In [12, Lemma 4.9], it is shown that there is an upper bound on the length of an antichain sequence of $\mathbb{Z}_{\geqslant 0}^m \times \mathfrak{n}$ with degree growth bounded by f, and this upper bound depends solely on m, n, and f. We let $\mathfrak{L}_{f,m}^n$ be the maximal length of an antichain sequence of $\mathbb{Z}_{\geqslant 0}^m \times \mathfrak{n}$ with degree growth bounded by f.

Theorem 2. *Let $F, K \subseteq \mathbf{k}\{Y\}$ be finite subsets with $h = \mathcal{H}(F \cup K)$, let $\mathcal{A} = $ Rosenfeld-Gröbner(F, K), and let $L = \mathfrak{L}_{f,m}^n$, where $f(i) = hf_i$ with $\{f_i\}$ the Fibonacci sequence. Then*

$$\mathcal{H}\left(\bigcup_{(A,H) \in \mathcal{A}} (A \cup H)\right) \leqslant hf_{L+1}.$$

Proof. Since $\operatorname{ord}(\text{pd-red}(p, B)) \leqslant \operatorname{ord}(p)$ for any $p \in \mathbf{k}\{Y\}$ and weak d-triangular set B, this means that

$$\mathcal{H}(B \cup K) \leqslant \mathcal{H}(A \cup H),$$

where $\{(B, K)\} = $ auto-partial-reduced(A, H). Hence, it suffices to bound $\mathcal{H}(G \cup D \cup A \cup H)$ whenever the tuple (G, D, A, H) is added to $\mathcal{S}$ in the Rosenfeld-Gröbner algorithm.

By Theorem 1 and the correspondence between antichain sequences of ΘY and $\mathbb{Z}_{\geqslant 0}^m \times \mathfrak{n}$, we obtain an antichain sequence of $\mathbb{Z}_{\geqslant 0}^m \times \mathfrak{n}$ of degree growth bounded by $f(i)$, so the length of this sequence (and thus the sequence from Theorem 1) is at most L.

In the proof of Theorem 1, it is shown that for all $i \leqslant N$, for $j :=$ anti-k_i, we have

$$\mathcal{H}\left(\bigcup_{t=1}^{i} (G_t \cup D_t \cup A_t \cup H_t)\right) \leqslant hf_{j+1}.$$

Since the largest possible j is the length of the antichain sequence (and this j is equal to anti-k_N), for every (G_i, D_i, A_i, H_i), we have

$$\mathcal{H}(G_i \cup D_i \cup A_i \cup H_i) \leqslant hf_{L+1}.$$

Since every (G, D, A, H) added to $\mathcal{S}$ is equal to (G_i, D_i, A_i, H_i) for some i, this completes the proof. □

5. SPECIFIC VALUES

In order to apply Theorem 2, we need to be able to effectively compute $\mathfrak{L}_{f,m}^n$. [12] only proves the existence of this number, without an analysis of how to construct it. [4] constructs an upper bound for $m = 1, 2$. The first analysis for the case of arbitrary m appears in [11].

Let $f : \mathbb{Z}_{>0} \to \mathbb{Z}_{\geqslant 0}$ be an increasing function. Let us define a function $\Psi_{f,m} : \mathbb{Z}_{>0} \times \mathbb{Z}_{\geqslant 0}^m \to \mathbb{Z}_{\geqslant 0}$ by the following relations:

$$\Psi_{f,m}(i, (0, \ldots, 0, u_m)) = i,$$

$$\Psi_{f,m}(i-1, (u_1, \ldots, u_r, 0, \ldots, 0, u_m)) = \Psi_{f,m}(i, (u_1, \ldots, u_r - 1, f(i) - f(i-1) + u_m + 1, 0, \ldots, 0))$$

if $r < m-1, u_r > 0$, and

$$\Psi_{f,m}(i-1, (u_1, \ldots, u_m)) = \Psi_{f,m}(i, (u_1, \ldots, u_{m-1} - 1, f(i) - f(i-1) + u_m + 1))$$

if $u_{m-1} > 0$.

Proposition 1 ([11, Corollary 3.10]). *The maximal length of an antichain sequence in $\mathbb{Z}_{\geqslant 0}^m$ with degree growth bounded by f does not exceed*

$$\Psi_{f,m}(1, (f(1), 0, \ldots, 0)).$$

Let us also define the sequence $\psi_0, \psi_1, \ldots$ by the relations $\psi_0 = 0$ and

$$\psi_{i+1} = \Psi_{f_i,m}(1, (f_i(1), 0, \ldots, 0)) + \psi_i,$$

where $f_i(x) = f(x + \psi_i)$.

Proposition 2 ([11, Corollary 3.14]). *The maximal length of an antichain sequence in $\mathbb{Z}^m_{\geqslant 0} \times \mathfrak{n}$ with degree growth bounded by f does not exceed ψ_n.*

Now, let us apply this technique to the function $f(i) = hf_i$. We then have, by Theorem 2, that an upper bound on the orders of the output of the Rosenfeld-Gröbner algorithm will be $f(\mathfrak{L}^n_{f,m} + 1)$. In general, we cannot construct a formula for $\mathfrak{L}^n_{f,m}$ for arbitrary h, m, n that improves upon the one given in Proposition 2; however, we can compute $\mathfrak{L}^n_{f,m}$ for some specific values of h, m, n.

1. Assume that $n = 1$ and $m = 2$. Then, the maximal length of an antichain sequence does not exceed $h + 1$. In this case, the orders of the resulting polynomials are bounded by the single-exponential estimate, coming from the standard formula for the Fibonacci numbers,

$$hf_{h+2} = \frac{h}{\sqrt{5}}\left(\left(\frac{1+\sqrt{5}}{2}\right)^{h+2} - \left(\frac{1-\sqrt{5}}{2}\right)^{h+2}\right).$$

This results in the following table:

h	1	2	3	4	5	6	7
hf_{h+2}	2	6	15	32	65	126	238

2. Assume that $m = 2$ and n is arbitrary. Then, the maximal length of an antichain sequence does not exceed b_n, where b_n satisfies $b_1 = h + 1$ and $b_{n+1} = hf_{b_n+1} + b_n + 1$, which results in the following table:

n	h	b_n	hf_{b_n+1}
2	1	5	8
2	2	10	178
2	3	20	32,838
2	4	38	252, 983, 944
2	5	72	$\leq 10^{16}$
3	1	14	610
3	2	189	$\leq 10^{40}$
3	3	32,859	$\leq 10^{6868}$

3. Assume that $m = 3$ and $n = 1$. We can construct the maximal length antichain sequence of $\mathbb{Z}^3_{\geqslant 0}$ using the methods of [11], resulting in the following sequence:

$$(h,0,0), (h-1,1,0), (h-1,0,h+1), (h-2,2h+2,0), \ldots,$$
$$(h-2,0,hf_{2h+6}-(h-2)), \ldots, (h-i, hf_{c_{i-1}+1}-(h-i), 0), \ldots,$$
$$(h-i, 0, hf_{c_i}-(h-i)), \ldots, (0, hf_{c_{h-1}+1}, 0), \ldots, (0, 0, hf_{c_h}),$$

where the sequence c_i is given by $c_0 = 1$ and for $1 \leqslant i \leqslant h$,

$$c_i = c_{i-1} + 1 + hf_{c_{i-1}+1} - (h - i).$$

As a result, we see that the maximal length of an antichain sequence is equal to c_h.

Below is a table of some maximal lengths $\mathfrak{L}^n_{f,m}$ and orders $f(\mathfrak{L}^n_{f,m} + 1)$, where $f(i) = hf_i$, for $m = 3$, 4, and 5:

m	n	h	length$\leqslant$	order$\leqslant$
3	1	1	3	3
3	1	2	10	178
3	1	3	712	10^{150}
3	2	1	433,494,480	$10^{90,594,990}$
4	1	1	5	8
5	1	1	20	10,946

6. ORDER LOWER BOUND

This section gives a lower bound for the orders of the output of the Rosenfeld-Gröbner algorithm, coming from the lower bound for degrees of elements of a Gröbner basis from [11]. To be specific, we show that for m, h sufficiently large, there is a collection of r differential polynomials $F \subseteq \mathbf{k}\{y\}$ of order at most h, where $\mathbf{k}$ is equipped with m derivations, $r \sim m/2$, and $\mathbf{k}$ is constant with respect to all of the derivations, such that if $\mathcal{A} = \text{Rosenfeld-Gröbner}(F, \{1\})$, then

$$\mathcal{H}\left(\bigcup_{(A,H)\in\mathcal{A}} (A \cup H)\right) \geqslant h^{2^r}. \qquad (4)$$

The arguments presented here are standard, and we include them for completeness. We first note the following standard fact about differential ideals generated by linear differential polynomials.

Proposition 3. *Suppose $F, K \subseteq \boldsymbol{k}\{Y\}$ are composed of linear differential polynomials. Then the output of Rosenfeld-Gröbner(F, K) is either empty or consists of a single regular differential system (A, H) with A and H both composed of linear differential polynomials.*

Suppose now we apply the Rosenfeld-Gröbner algorithm to $(F, \{1\})$, where F consists of linear differential polynomials, in order to obtain a regular decomposition of $\{F\}$. Since every element of F is linear, $[F]$ is a prime differential ideal, so by Proposition 3, we have

$$[F] = \{F\} = [A] : H^\infty$$

for some regular differential system (A, H), with A and H both composed of linear differential polynomials. Since every element of A is linear, after simply performing scalar multiplications and addition, A can be transformed to an autoreduced set $\bar{A}$ without affecting the leaders and orders of elements of A. Since (A, H) is a regular differential system, $\bar{A}$ is a characteristic set of $[F]$. As a result, it suffices to find a lower bound on the orders of elements of linear characteristic sets in $\mathbf{k}\{Y\}$.

There is a well-studied one-to-one correspondence between polynomials in $\mathbf{k}[x_1, \ldots, x_m]$ and homogeneous linear differential polynomials in $\mathbf{k}\{y\}$ with m derivations and $\mathbf{k}$ a field of constants via

$$\sum c_{i_1,\ldots,i_m} x_1^{i_1} \cdots x_m^{i_m} \leftrightarrow \sum c_{i_1,\ldots,i_m} \partial_1^{i_1} \cdots \partial_m^{i_m} y. \qquad (5)$$

Any orderly ranking on Θy then determines a graded monomial order on $\mathbf{k}[x_1, \ldots, x_m]$.

Given a polynomial $f \in \mathbf{k}[x_1, \ldots, x_m]$, let $\tilde{f} \in \mathbf{k}\{y\}$ be its corresponding differential polynomial under (5). By the discussion above, if we have a collection of polynomials $f_1, \ldots, f_r \in \mathbf{k}[x_1, \ldots, x_m]$, we can construct a characteristic set $C = \{C_1, \ldots, C_s\}$ of $[\tilde{f}_1, \ldots, \tilde{f}_r] \subseteq \mathbf{k}\{y\}$ consisting of homogeneous linear differential polynomials, and so each $C_i \in \mathbf{k}\{y\}$ is in fact equal to $\tilde{g}_i$ for some $g_i \in \mathbf{k}[x_1, \ldots, x_m]$.

PROPOSITION 4 (CF. [13, PAGE 352],[5]).
With the notation above, $\{g_1, \ldots, g_s\} \subseteq \mathbf{k}[x_1, \ldots, x_m]$ *is a Gröbner basis of the ideal* $I = (f_1, \ldots, f_r)$.

By Proposition 4, we can thus find a lower bound for the orders of the output of the Rosenfeld-Gröbner algorithm via a lower bound for the degrees of elements of a Gröbner basis, as we do in the following example.

Example 1. This example demonstrates the lower bound (4) for the orders of the output of the Rosenfeld-Gröbner algorithm. In [14, Section 8], for m, h sufficiently large, a collection of m algebraic polynomials $f_1, \ldots, f_r$ of degree at most h in m algebraic indeterminates, with $r \sim m/2$, is constructed such that any Gröbner basis of $(f_1, \ldots, f_r)$ with respect to a graded monomial order has an element of degree at least h^{2^r}.

As a result of the previous discussion, we have a collection of differential polynomials $F = \tilde{f}_1, \ldots, \tilde{f}_r \in \mathbf{k}\{y\}$ of order h with m derivations such that any linear characteristic set of $[\tilde{f}_1, \ldots, \tilde{f}_r]$ will contain a differential polynomial of order at least h^{2^r}. Since in this case $\{(A, H)\} =$ Rosenfeld-Gröbner$(F, \{1\})$ can be transformed into a linear characteristic set without affecting the orders of the elements, this means that

$$\mathcal{H}(A \cup H) \geqslant h^{2^r}.$$

Acknowledgments

This work was supported by NSF grant CCF-0952591. We are grateful to the referees for their helpful comments and suggestions.

References

[1] F. Boulier, D. Lazard, F. Ollivier, and M. Petitot. Representation for the radical of a finitely generated differential ideal. In *ISSAC'95: Proceedings of the 1995 international symposium on Symbolic and algebraic computation*, pages 158–166, New York, NY, USA, 1995. ACM Press. URL http://dx.doi.org/10.1145/220346.220367.

[2] F. Boulier, D. Lazard, F. Ollivier, and M. Petitot. Computing representations for radicals of finitely generated differential ideals. *Applicable Algebra in Engineering, Communication and Computing*, 20(1):73–121, 2009. URL http://dx.doi.org/10.1007/s00200-009-0091-7.

[3] L. D'Alfonso, G. Jeronimo, and P. Solernó. Effective differential Nullstellensatz for ordinary DAE systems with constant coefficients. *Journal of Complexity*, 30 (5):588–603, 2014. URL http://dx.doi.org/10.1016/j.jco.2014.01.001.

[4] J. Freitag and O. León Sánchez. Effective uniform bounds in partial differential fields. *Advances in Mathematics*, 288:308–336, 2016. URL http://dx.doi.org/10.1016/j.aim.2015.10.013.

[5] V. Gerdt. Involutive algorithms for computing Gröbner bases. In *Computational commutative and non-commutative algebraic geometry*, volume 196 of *NATO Science Series III: Computer and Systems Sciences*. IOS, Amsterdam, 2005. URL http://arxiv.org/abs/math/0501111.

[6] O. Golubitsky, M. Kondratieva, M. Moreno Maza, and A. Ovchinnikov. A bound for Rosenfeld-Gröbner algorithm. *Journal of Symbolic Computation*, 43(8):582–610, 2008. URL http://dx.doi.org/10.1016/j.jsc.2007.12.002.

[7] O. Golubitsky, M. Kondratieva, A. Ovchinnikov, and A. Szanto. A bound for orders in differential Nullstellensatz. *Journal of Algebra*, 322(11):3852–3877, 2009. URL http://dx.doi.org/10.1016/j.jalgebra.2009.05.032.

[8] R. Gustavson, M. Kondratieva, and A. Ovchinnikov. New effective differential Nullstellensatz. *Advances in Mathematics*, 290:1138–1158, 2016. URL http://dx.doi.org/10.1016/j.aim.2015.12.021.

[9] E. Hubert. Notes on triangular sets and triangulation-decomposition algorithms II: Differential systems. In U. Langer and F. Winkler, editors, *Symbolic and Numerical Scientific Computations*, volume 2630 of *Lecture Notes in Computer Science*, pages 40–87. Springer, 2003. URL http://dx.doi.org/10.1007/3-540-45084-X_2.

[10] E. R. Kolchin. *Differential algebra and algebraic groups*. Academic Press, New York, 1973. Pure and Applied Mathematics, Vol. 54.

[11] O. León Sánchez and A. Ovchinnikov. On bounds for the effective differential Nullstellensatz. *Journal of Algebra*, 449:1–21, 2016. URL http://dx.doi.org/10.1016/j.jalgebra.2015.10.009.

[12] D. Pierce. Fields with several commuting derivations. *Journal of Symbolic Logic*, 79(1):1–19, 2014. URL http://dx.doi.org/10.1017/jsl.2013.19.

[13] W. T. Wu. On the construction of Groebner basis of a polynomial ideal based on Riquier-Janet theory. In D. Wang and Z. Zheng, editors, *Differential Equations with Symbolic Computation*, Trends in Mathematics, pages 351–368. Birkhäuser Verlag, 2005. URL http://dx.doi.org/10.1007/3-7643-7429-2_20.

[14] C. Yap. A new lower bound construction for commutative Thue systems with applications. *Journal of Symbolic Computation*, 12:1–27, 1991. URL http://dx.doi.org/10.1016/S0747-7171(08)80138-1.

Numerical Sparsity Determination and Early Termination*

Zhiwei Hao
Key Laboratory of Mathematics Mechanization, AMSS
Beijing 100190, China
haozhiwei@mmrc.iss.ac.cn

Erich L. Kaltofen
Dept. of Mathematics, NCSU
Raleigh, North Carolina
27695-8205, USA
kaltofen@math.ncsu.edu
http://www.kaltofen.us

Lihong Zhi
Key Laboratory of Mathematics Mechanization, AMSS
Beijing 100190, China
lzhi@mmrc.iss.ac.cn
http://www.mmrc.iss.ac.cn/~lzhi/

ABSTRACT

Ankur Moitra in his paper at STOC 2015 has given an in-depth analysis of how oversampling improves the conditioning of the arising Prony systems for sparse interpolation and signal recovery from numeric data. Moitra assumes that oversampling is done for a number of samples beyond the actual sparsity of the polynomial/signal. We give an algorithm that can be used to compute the sparsity and estimate the minimal number of samples needed in numerical sparse interpolation. The early termination strategy of polynomial interpolation has been incorporated in the algorithm: by oversampling at a small number of extra sample points we can diagnose that the sparsity has not been reached.

Our algorithm still has to make a guess, the number ζ of oversamples, and we show by example that if ζ is guessed too small, premature termination can occur, but our criterion is numerically more accurate than that by Kaltofen, Lee and Yang (Proc. SNC 2011, ACM [12]), but not as efficiently computable. For heuristic justification one has available the multivariate early termination theorem by Kaltofen and Lee (JSC vol. 36(3–4) 2003 [11]) for exact arithmetic, and the numeric Schwartz-Zippel Lemma by Kaltofen, Yang and Zhi (Proc. SNC 2007, ACM [13]). A main contribution here is a modified proof of the Theorem by Kaltofen and Lee that permits starting the sequence at the point $(1, \ldots, 1)$, for scalar fields of characteristic $\neq 2$ (in characteristic 2 counter-examples are given).

Keywords

Hankel matrix, Vandermonde matrix, sparse polynomial interpolation, condition number, early termination, sparse signal processing

1. INTRODUCTION

The sparse interpolation problem has been studied and widely used in many different areas of science and engineering since the work of Prony (1795). The classical Prony's method aims to solve the exponential interpolation problem

$$f(x) = \sum_{j=1}^{t} c_j \exp(d_j 2\pi \mathrm{i} x),$$

where the frequencies $d_i \in [0, 1)$. By sampling f at $f(0), \ldots, f(2t-1)$ and solving a Hankel linear system to compute the term locator polynomial whose roots are $= \exp(d_j 2\pi\mathrm{i}), 1 \leq j \leq t$. The amplitude coefficients c_j can be computed by solving a Vandermonde linear system. With highly accurate big floating point precision, Prony's method is straightforward to implement.

When there is inaccuracy (noise) in the measurements, both the Hankel matrix and Vandermonde matrix appearing in Prony's method can have exponentially large condition numbers [2, 9]. Moreover, as shown by Moitra in [17, Theorems 2.3, 3.1] there is a sharp phase transition for the condition number of the Vandermonde matrix and the minimum number of samples needed, the place of which essentially depending on the minimum separation in the presence of noise. In Moitra's algorithm [17, Algorithm 1], both the sparsity and the minimal number of samples are input as known values. However, without knowing the structure of sparsity, it is unclear how to estimate the condition number of the Vandermonde matrix and determine the minimal measurements needed. The arising Hankel matrix H_m can only be used to bound the conditioning of the Vandermonde matrix after m reaches the sparsity t (see (26), i.e., V_m has full column rank). As shown by Example 1.1, an arising Hankel matrix can be nearly-singular before m reaches t for unluckily chosen samples. Therefore, a well-conditioned Vandermonde matrix may correspond to a nearly-singular Hankel matrix when $m \leq t$. That phenomenon motivates us to investigate how to reliably determine the number of terms t of f and how many number of measurements are minimally needed in the entire process of numerical sparse interpolation with unknown sparsity.

In exact arithmetic, the early termination strategy [11] has been introduced as a means to determine the number of terms t: one terminates the interpolation algorithm after consecutively encountering singular Hankel matrices ζ times for a pre-chosen threshold $\zeta \geq 1$. It has been shown in [11] that with a high probability that grows with ζ, one does not stop before the sparsity is reached. However, in numerical cases, as we have explained above, the Hankel matrices could be extremely ill-conditioned, and one may not be able to detect the number of terms by observing the

*This research was supported in part by the National Science Foundation under Grant CCF-1421128 (Kaltofen) and by the National Natural Science Foundation of China under Grants 11571350 (Zhi).

ISSAC '16, July 19 - 22, 2016, Waterloo, ON, Canada

© 2016 ACM. ISBN 978-1-4503-4380-0/16/07...$15.00

DOI: http://dx.doi.org/10.1145/2930889.2930924

first several nearly-singular Hankel matrices. Based on the precise quantitative bounds given in [17], we present a lower bound on the t-th singular value $\sigma_t(H_m)$ of the m-th arising Hankel matrix H_m and an upper bound on the ratio of $\sigma_1(H_m)/\sigma_t(H_m)$, which give us the criterion (24), which computes the sparsity t of f by checking whether the first t singular values of all Hankel matrices $H_m, H_{m+1}, \dots, H_{m+\zeta-1}$ are larger than $1-\epsilon$ and the remaining singular values are less than ϵ and none lie in between. We show by experiments that the criterion is quite tolerant to noise in the samples. In particular, in Example 4.1 from [2] we can avoid premature termination by a moderately large number ζ (≥ 6) of oversamples.

Finally, in Section 4.1 we prove the Early Termination Theorem [11, Theorem 4] for the (unshifted)-sequence starting at the point $(1, \dots, 1)$ for coefficient fields of characteristic $\neq 2$ (see Theorem 4.1) and give counterexamples for characteristic $= 2$, which resolves an open question in [11].

2. PRELIMINARIES

We consider the polynomial version of Prony's method with coefficients from an arbitrary field K. Let $f \in \mathsf{K}[x]$, where

$$f = \sum_{i=1}^{t} c_i x^{e_i},\ c_i \neq 0,$$

and K is an arbitrary field. p is a prime number larger than $\deg(f)$. Let $a_i = f(\omega^i)$ where ω is selected as a random p-th root of unity. Let H_m be the Hankel matrix defined by the sequence of $a_0, \dots, a_{2m-2}$:

$$H_m = \begin{bmatrix} a_0 & \cdots & a_{m-1} \\ a_1 & \cdots & a_m \\ \vdots & \vdots & \vdots \\ a_{m-1} & \cdots & a_{2m-2} \end{bmatrix}. \quad (1)$$

We have the following well-known decomposition of H_m:

$$H_m = V_m \cdot D \cdot V_m^{\mathrm{T}}, \quad (2)$$

where V_m is the $m \times t$ Vandermonde matrix:

$$V_m = \begin{bmatrix} 1 & \cdots & 1 \\ \omega^{e_1} & \cdots & \omega^{e_t} \\ \vdots & \vdots & \vdots \\ \omega^{e_1(m-1)} & \cdots & \omega^{e_t(m-1)} \end{bmatrix} \quad (3)$$

and D is a $t \times t$ diagonal matrix:

$$D = \begin{bmatrix} c_1 & & \\ & \ddots & \\ & & c_t \end{bmatrix}. \quad (4)$$

By V_m^{T} we denote the transpose of the Vandermonde matrix V_m.

In exact arithmetic, the early termination strategy can determine the number of terms with high probability, i.e., with high probability, all $j \times j$ leading principle minors of H_t are non-singular for $2 \leq j \leq t$. Moreover, H_j must be singular for all $j > t$. Hence the number of terms is detected as follows: for $j = 2, 3, \dots$, the first time H_j becomes singular is when $j = t+1$. Strictly speaking, one needs that the characteristic of the field is $\neq 2$ and our new Theorem 4.1 (see Section 4.1 for more detail). It is known that the Hankel matrices can become extremely ill-conditioned: [12] investigates how to estimate the spectral norm of the inverse of a Hankel matrix H_t and how to employ several randomization ideas of [9] for heuristically achieving a relatively well-conditioned Hankel matrix H_t. Then one can detect the number of terms by observing a sharp increase in the condition number of H_{t+1}.

Oversampling is another popular method to improve the conditioning of the Hankel matrix [6]. There are many exciting new results on sparse signal recovering from noisy data, see [4, 5, 15, 17] and the references there. Especially, in [17], Ankur Moitra provides an explicit formula to estimate the condition number of the Vandermonde matrix provided that $m > (1/\Delta) + 1$, where Δ is the minimum separation of the evaluated terms in f. Moreover, a lower bound of the condition number of V_m was also given to show that in the noisy case, if $m = (1-\epsilon)/\Delta$ there is a pair of t point sources x and x', each with separation Δ, which allow only exponentially small noise to tell them apart. Such extreme ill-posedness has also been illustrated in [5] based on the work of David Slepian [18].

In the following, we will show how to apply quantitative bounds for singular values of Hankel matrices and the early termination strategy for the unshifted case in order to determine the sparsity of the polynomial f in the presence of noise.

3. NUMERIC SPARSITY DETERMINATION

We extend Theorem 2.3 in [17] to give a lower bound on the t-th singular value of H_m for $m > \frac{1}{\Delta}+1$, which provides us a new criterion to estimate the number of terms of f by checking whether the singular values of oversampled Hankel matrices are separated into those $> 1-\epsilon$ and those $< \epsilon$ and none lie in between. In this section K is specialized as the complex field.

Definition 3.1 (see [5]). *Let $\mathcal{B}$ be the unit circle obtained by identifying the endpoints on $[0,1]$. For a family of points $B \subset \mathcal{B}$, the minimal separation is defined as the closest distance between any two elements from B:*

$$\Delta(B) = \inf_{(b,b') \in B : b \neq b'} |b - b'|, \quad (5)$$

where $|b-b'|$ is the wrap-around distance. That is the length of the minor arc between b and b' divided by 2π.

Let

$$\omega = e^{2\pi i j/p},\ 0 \leq j < p, \quad (6)$$

where the integer j can be chosen randomly or fixed. Let

$$\Delta = \Delta(\omega^{e_1}, \dots, \omega^{e_t}).$$

It is clear that

$$1 + \frac{1}{\Delta} > t.$$

The following theorem has been proved in [17].

Theorem 3.1. *Let $\sigma_1 \geq \sigma_2 \geq \cdots \geq \sigma_t$ be singular values of V_m, provided $m > 1 + \frac{1}{\Delta}$, we have*

$$m - 1 + \frac{1}{\Delta} \geq \sigma_1^2 \geq \sigma_2^2 \geq \cdots \geq \sigma_t^2 \geq m - 1 - \frac{1}{\Delta}. \quad (7)$$

The condition number κ of V_m satisfies

$$\kappa^2 \leq \frac{m + 1/\Delta - 1}{m - 1/\Delta - 1}. \quad (8)$$

The upper and lower bounds given in (7) and (8) can be used to bound $\sigma_t(H_m)$ and $\sigma_1(H_m)$ for $m > 1 + \frac{1}{\Delta}$. First, let us see how to bound $\sigma_t(H_m)$ by the t-th singular value $\sigma_t(V_m)$ of V_m.

Lemma 3.2. *For $m \geqslant t$, we have*

$$\sigma_t(H_m) \geq \sigma_t^2(V_m) \cdot \min_{1 \leq i \leq t} |c_i|. \tag{9}$$

Proof. Rewrite $H_m = V_m \cdot D^{\frac{1}{2}} \cdot D^{\frac{1}{2}} \cdot V_m^{\mathrm{T}}$ and set

$$W_m = V_m \cdot D^{\frac{1}{2}} \in \mathbb{C}^{m \times t}.$$

If $\omega^{e_i} \neq \omega^{e_j}$ for $i \neq j$, and $m \geq t$, then $V_m \in \mathbb{C}^{m \times t}$ has full column rank t. Moreover, since $c_i \neq 0$, the diagonal matrix $D \in \mathbb{C}^{t \times t}$ is invertible. Hence we have

$$\operatorname{rank}(H_m) = \operatorname{rank}(D) = \operatorname{rank}(W_m) = \operatorname{rank}(V_m) = t.$$

Claim 3.3. $\sigma_t(H_m) \geqslant \sigma_t^2(W_m)$.

Indeed, let $W_m = U \cdot \Sigma \cdot V$ be the singular value decomposition of W_m, where $U \in \mathbb{C}^{m \times m}$, $\Sigma \in \mathbb{C}^{m \times t}$, $V \in \mathbb{C}^{t \times t}$. Denote by $W_m^{\dagger}$ the Moore-Penrose pseudoinverse of W_m, which has been proved to be unique [10], and $W_m^{\dagger} = V^H \cdot \Sigma^{\dagger} \cdot U^H$, where V^H and U^H represent the Hermitian transpose of the matrix V and U respectively and $\Sigma^{\dagger}$ is constructed by substituting the non-zero items in Σ by their inverse. It is clear that

$$H_m^{\dagger} = (W_m \cdot W_m^{\mathrm{T}})^{\dagger} = (W_m^{\mathrm{T}})^{\dagger} \cdot W_m^{\dagger}, \tag{10}$$

see [19]. This indicates that:

$$\sigma_1(H_m^{\dagger}) \leqslant \sigma_1((W_m^{\mathrm{T}})^{\dagger}) \cdot \sigma_1(W_m^{\dagger}) = \sigma_1^2(W_m^{\dagger}). \tag{11}$$

By noticing that:

$$\sigma_1(H_m^{\dagger}) = \frac{1}{\sigma_t(H_m)}, \sigma_1(W_m^{\dagger}) = \frac{1}{\sigma_t(W_m)}, \tag{12}$$

we obtain Claim 3.3.

Now we consider the t-th singular value of W_m. According to the property of singular values, we have

$$\sigma_t(W_m) = \min_{\operatorname{rank}(A) < t} \|W_m - A\|_2. \tag{13}$$

Let A_0 be a minimizer in (13), then $A_0 \cdot D^{-\frac{1}{2}}$ is of rank smaller than t. Therefore, we have:

$$\begin{aligned}
\sigma_t(V_m) &= \min_{\operatorname{rank}(B) < t} \|V_m - B\|_2, \\
&\leq \|V_m - A_0 \cdot D^{-\frac{1}{2}}\|_2 \\
&= \|(V_m \cdot D^{\frac{1}{2}} - A_0) \cdot D^{-\frac{1}{2}}\|_2 \\
&\leq \|W_m - A_0\|_2 \cdot \|D^{-\frac{1}{2}}\|_2 \\
&= \sigma_t(W_m) \cdot \|D^{-\frac{1}{2}}\|_2.
\end{aligned}$$

By noticing that $\frac{1}{\|D^{-1/2}\|_2^2} = \min_{1 \leq i \leq t} |c_i|$, we have

$$\sigma_t^2(W_m) \geq \sigma_t^2(V_m) \cdot \min_{1 \leq i \leq t} |c_i|. \tag{14}$$

Combining with Claim 3.3, we complete the proof. □

Remark 3.1. It should be noted that $\sigma_t(H_t) = \sigma_t^2(W_t)$ when W_t is a real matrix. Otherwise, we may have $\sigma_t(H_t) > \sigma_t^2(W_t)$. For instance, suppose:

$$V_2 = \begin{bmatrix} 1 & 1 \\ 1 & 2 \end{bmatrix}, D = \begin{bmatrix} -1 & 0 \\ 0 & 2 \end{bmatrix}, \tag{15}$$

then

$$H_2 = \begin{bmatrix} 1 & 3 \\ 3 & 7 \end{bmatrix}, W_2 = \begin{bmatrix} \mathrm{i} & \sqrt{2} \\ \mathrm{i} & 2\sqrt{2} \end{bmatrix}, \tag{16}$$

therefore

$$\sigma_2(H_2) = 0.243 > \sigma_2^2(W_2) = 0.169. \square \tag{17}$$

Remark 3.2. Lemma 3.2 is only correct for $m \geq t$. For $m < t$, there exists a well-conditioned Vandermonde matrix V_m which corresponds to a singular Hankel matrix $H_m = V_m \cdot D \cdot V_m^{\mathrm{T}}$, see Example 1.1. □

Theorem 3.4. *For given f and ω, when $m > 1 + \frac{1}{\Delta}$, we have*

$$\sigma_t(H_m) \geq \left(m - 1 - \frac{1}{\Delta}\right) \cdot \min_{1 \leq i \leq t} |c_i|, \tag{18}$$

and

$$\frac{\sigma_1(H_m)}{\sigma_t(H_m)} \leq \frac{m - 1 + \frac{1}{\Delta}}{m - 1 - \frac{1}{\Delta}} \cdot \frac{\max_{1 \leq i \leq t} |c_i|}{\min_{1 \leq i \leq t} |c_i|}. \tag{19}$$

Proof. When $m > 1 + \frac{1}{\Delta}$, according to Theorem 3.1,

$$m - 1 + \frac{1}{\Delta} \geq \sigma_1^2(V_m) \geq \sigma_t^2(V_m) \geq m - 1 - \frac{1}{\Delta}. \tag{20}$$

When $m > 1 + \frac{1}{\Delta} \geq t$, by (9), we have

$$\sigma_t(H_m) \geq \sigma_t^2(V_m) \cdot \min_{1 \leq i \leq t} |c_i| \geq \left(m - 1 - \frac{1}{\Delta}\right) \cdot \min_{1 \leq i \leq t} |c_i|.$$

On the other hand, $\sigma_1(H_m)$ is the 2-norm of H_m, we have

$$\begin{aligned}
\sigma_1(H_m) &\leq \sigma_1(V_m) \cdot \sigma_1(D) \cdot \sigma_1(V_m^{\mathrm{T}}) \\
&= \sigma_1^2(V_m) \cdot \max_{1 \leq i \leq t} |c_i| \\
&\leq \left(m - 1 + \frac{1}{\Delta}\right) \cdot \max_{1 \leq i \leq t} |c_i|.
\end{aligned}$$

Therefore we can derive (19). □

Theorem 3.4 gives us an estimation on how many evaluations we need to get a Hankel matrix with the t-th singular value larger than or equal to 1.

Theorem 3.5. *When m satisfies*

$$m \geq 1 + \frac{1}{\Delta} + \max_{1 \leq i \leq t} \frac{1}{|c_i|}, \tag{21}$$

we have $\sigma_t(H_m) \geq 1$.

Proof. According to Theorem 3.4, when $m \geq 1 + \frac{1}{\Delta}$, we have

$$\sigma_t(H_m) \geq \left(m - 1 - \frac{1}{\Delta}\right) \cdot \min_{1 \leq i \leq t} |c_i|.$$

Therefore, if m satisfies (21), then

$$\sigma_t(H_m) \geq \max_{1 \leq i \leq t} \frac{1}{|c_i|} \cdot \min_{1 \leq i \leq t} |c_i| = 1. \quad \square$$

The following perturbation theorem about the singular values can be found in [20, 16].

Theorem 3.6. *Let $\sigma_j(A)$ be the j-th singular value of A. Let E be a small perturbation matrix. For $1 \leq i \leq \dim(A)$, we have*

$$|\sigma_i(A + E) - \sigma_i(A)| \leq \|E\|_2. \tag{22}$$

Remark 3.3. In the noise-free case, for $m \geq t+1$, we have

$$\sigma_j(H_m) = 0, \; t+1 \leq j \leq m.$$

Therefore, according to Theorem 3.6, we have

$$|\sigma_j(H_m + E)| \leq \|E\|_2 \overset{\text{def}}{=} \epsilon. \tag{23}$$

The constant 1 in Theorem 3.5 can be an arbitrary number $\tau > 2\epsilon$, and we can always separate the singular values of $H_m + E$ into two groups; $\sigma_j(H_m + E) \geq \tau - \|E\|_2 > \epsilon$ for $j \leq t$ and $\sigma_j(H_m + E) \leq \epsilon$ for $j > t$. However, choosing $\tau = 1$ means the Hankel matrix H_m is far from being of rank $t-1$. □

Theorem 3.5 and inequality (23) provide us a robust criterion to detect the sparsity t in the numeric case when no premature termination occurs.

Before we state the main algorithm for detecting the sparsity t, we introduce some quantities first.

- m: size of the current Hankel matrix;
- ϵ: error bound for Hankel matrices;
- $n_{\sigma \geq 1-\epsilon}$: the number of the singular values of H_{m-1} that are larger than or equal to $1-\epsilon$;
- $n_{\sigma \leq \epsilon}$: the number of the singular values of H_{m-1} that are smaller than or equal to ϵ;
- ζ: the algorithm will be terminated if the condition

$$\begin{cases} n_{\sigma \geq 1-\epsilon}(H_{m+i}) = n_{\sigma \geq 1-\epsilon}(H_{m-1}), \\ n_{\sigma \leq \epsilon}(H_{m+i}) = m + i - n_{\sigma \geq 1-\epsilon}(H_{m-1}), \end{cases} \tag{24}$$

is satisfied for any i with $0 \leq i \leq \zeta - 1$.

Algorithm 1 Sparsity determination

Input:
$f(x)$: a univariate black box polynomial;
ζ: a positive integer, the threshold for early termination;
ϵ: an error bound for Hankel matrices.
Output:
t: the sparsity of $f(x)$.
Estimate a prime upper bound p of $\deg(f)$.
For a randomly chosen integer $j \in [1, p-1]$, set $\omega \leftarrow e^{2\pi i j/p}$, $n_{\sigma \geq 1-\epsilon} \leftarrow 0$, $n_{\sigma \leq \epsilon} \leftarrow 0$, $k \leftarrow 0$, $m \leftarrow 1$, $H_1 \leftarrow f(1)$.
while $k < \zeta$ **do**
  Compute the singular values of H_m;
  $l_1 \leftarrow$ the number of singular values larger than $1-\epsilon$;
  $l_2 \leftarrow$ the number of singular values smaller than ϵ.
  if $l_1 + l_2 = m$ and $l_1 = n_{\sigma \geq 1-\epsilon}$ **then**
    $k \leftarrow k+1$.
  else
    $k \leftarrow 0$.
  end if
  $n_{\sigma \geq 1-\epsilon} \leftarrow l_1$, $n_{\sigma \leq \epsilon} \leftarrow l_2$, $m \leftarrow m+1$.
  Update H_m by evaluating $f(x)$ at ω^{2m-3} and ω^{2m-2}.
end while
$t \leftarrow n_{\sigma \geq 1-\epsilon}$.

Theorem 3.7. *Suppose the errors in Hankel matrices are bounded by ϵ. The algorithm terminates when m satisfies*

$$m \geq 1 + \frac{1}{\Delta} + \max_{1 \leq i \leq t} \frac{1}{|c_i|} + (\zeta - 1). \tag{25}$$

With high probability, Algorithm 1 returns the number of terms t in f.

Proof. According to Theorem 3.5, when m satisfies

$$m \geq 1 + \frac{1}{\Delta} + \max_{1 \leq i \leq t} \frac{1}{|c_i|},$$

$\sigma_t(H_m)$ will be at least 1. Moreover, according to Theorem 3.6, we have

$$|\sigma_t(H_m + E)| \geq |\sigma_t(H_m)| - \|E\|_2 \geq 1 - \epsilon.$$

For $m \geq t+1$, we have

$$\sigma_j(H_m) = 0, \; t+1 \leq j \leq m.$$

According to Theorem 3.6 and inequality (23), for $j = t+1, \ldots, m$, we have

$$|\sigma_j(H_m + E)| \leq \|E\|_2 \leq \epsilon.$$

Hence the condition (24) will be satisfied ζ times.

A heuristic probabilistic analysis for Algorithm 1 returning the number of terms t in f will be given in Section 4.1. □

Remark 3.4. Since the minimum number of measurements given in (25) depends on $\min_{1 \leq i \leq t} |c_i|$, if the minimum value is much smaller than 1, then we need a large number of evaluations to bound the singular value $\sigma_t(H_m)$ from 1. In this case, the inequality (19) may give us a better criterion to stop the algorithm. □

The following theorem shows that the t-th singular value of the Vandermonde matrix V_m is bounded below by the t-th singular value of H_m too.

Theorem 3.8. *For $m \geqslant t$, we have*

$$\sigma_t(V_m) \geq \frac{\sigma_t(H_m)}{2m \max_{1 \leq i \leq t} |c_i|}. \tag{26}$$

Proof. Suppose $V_m = U \cdot \Sigma \cdot V$ is the singular value decomposition of V_m, where $\Sigma \in \mathbb{C}^{m \times t}$, $U \in \mathbb{C}^{m \times m}$, $V \in \mathbb{C}^{t \times t}$. We have

$$\begin{aligned} \sigma_t(V_m) &= \min_{\operatorname{rank}(B) < t} \|V_m - B\|_2, \\ &= \|V_m - \bar{V}_m\|_2, \end{aligned}$$

where

$$\bar{V}_m = U \cdot \operatorname{diag}(\sigma_1(V_m), \ldots, \sigma_{t-1}(V_m), 0) \cdot V.$$

Hence, we have:

$$\begin{aligned} \sigma_t(H_m) &= \min_{\operatorname{rank}(A) < t} \|V_m D V_m^{\mathrm{T}} - A\|_2 \\ &\leq \|V_m D V_m^{\mathrm{T}} - \bar{V}_m D \bar{V}_m^{\mathrm{T}}\|_2 \\ &= \|V_m D V_m^{\mathrm{T}} - V_m D \bar{V}_m^{\mathrm{T}} + V_m D \bar{V}_m^{\mathrm{T}} - \bar{V}_m D \bar{V}_m^{\mathrm{T}}\| \\ &\leq \|V_m D (V_m^{\mathrm{T}} - \bar{V}_m^{\mathrm{T}})\|_2 + \|(V_m - \bar{V}_m) D \bar{V}_m^{\mathrm{T}}\|_2 \\ &\leq \sigma_t(V_m) \|V_m\|_2 \|D\|_2 + \sigma_t(V_m) \|\bar{V}_m\|_2 \|D\|_2 \\ &\leq 2\sigma_t(V_m) \|V_m\|_2 \|D\|_2 \\ &\leq 2m \max_{1 \leq i \leq t} |c_i| \sigma_t(V_m). \quad \square \end{aligned}$$

The minimum number of measurements given in (25) depends also on the minimum separation Δ. In [9], several randomization strategies are proposed to enlarge the minimum separation. The following theorem extends results in [9, Theorem 4.3].

Theorem 3.9. *Suppose p is a prime number and $p > \deg(f)$. For a uniformly and randomly chosen integer j with $0 < j < p$ in (6), with probability at least $1 - \frac{1}{2k}$, we have*

$$\Delta > \frac{1}{2kt^2}, \ \forall k \in \mathbb{Z}_{>0}. \tag{27}$$

Proof. We extend the proof in [9, Theorem 4.3]. Assume $e_u > e_v$ for $u < v$, by Definition 3.1, we have

$$\Delta = \frac{1}{p} \cdot \min_{1 \le u < v \le t} \min\{\delta_{u,v}, p - \delta_{u,v}\}, \tag{28}$$

where

$$\delta_{u,v} = e_u \cdot j - e_v \cdot j \mod p.$$

There are at most $\binom{t}{2} \le \frac{t^2}{2}$ distinct values of $(e_u - e_v) \mod p$. For any $k \in \mathbb{Z}_{>0}$, let

$$l = \frac{p}{2kt^2}, \tag{29}$$

then for all

$$c \in \{1, \ldots, \lfloor l \rfloor\} \cup \{p - \lfloor l \rfloor + 1, \ldots, p\},$$

where the floor function $\lfloor l \rfloor$ denotes the largest integer $\le l$, there is only one $j \in \mathbb{Z}_p$ such that

$$\delta_{u,v} = c.$$

Indeed, as p is a prime number larger than $\deg(f)$, $[e_u - e_v]$ is invertible in $\mathbb{Z}_p$, which indicates

$$j = (e_u - e_v)^{-1} \cdot c \mod p,$$

Therefore for any given e_u and e_v, there are $2 \cdot \lfloor l \rfloor$ values of j such that

$$\min\{\delta_{u,v}, p - \delta_{u,v}\} \le l. \tag{30}$$

There are totally at most $(t^2/2) \cdot 2 \cdot \lfloor l \rfloor$ values of j, such that (30) is satisfied by some $\delta_{u,v}$. Therefore with probability

$$\le \frac{t^2}{2} \cdot 2 \cdot \lfloor l \rfloor \cdot \frac{1}{p} \le \frac{t^2}{2} \cdot 2l \cdot \frac{1}{p} = \frac{1}{2k},$$

we can have $\Delta \le \frac{\lfloor l \rfloor}{p} \le \frac{l}{p} \le \frac{1}{2kt^2}$, by (28) and (29). □

Example 3.1. Let $f = 2x^{109} - 5x^{59} + x^{58} + 2x^{47} + 3x^{35}$ and set $\zeta = 5$.

1. Set $\omega = e^{2\pi i/119}$, and assume the evaluation error in H_m is bounded by $\epsilon = 0.05$. The wrap-around distance is

   $$\Delta(\omega^{109}, \ldots, \omega^{35}) = \frac{1}{119}.$$

   When m becomes larger than 16, there are always 5 singular values of H_m that are larger than 1 and all other singular values of H_m are less than 0.05. Therefore the algorithm will stop after $21 = 16 + 5$ steps and return $t = 5$.

   We have $\frac{\sigma_1(H_4)}{\sigma_4(H_4)} \approx 48.7$, $\frac{\sigma_1(H_5)}{\sigma_5(H_5)} \approx 4387$. Therefore, if we use the sharp increase in the condition number of H_m to detect the sparsity, we may mistakenly take $t = 4$.

   We also notice that our algorithm can terminate much earlier than the worst case bound $\frac{1}{\Delta} + 1 = 120$ to detect the sparsity and get a well-conditioned Vandermonde matrix (the condition number of V_{16} is 8.6).

2. We take a random rotation of ω, for instance, set $\omega = e^{2\pi i \cdot 9/119}$. The minimal separation increases and the wrap-around distance is

   $$\Delta(\omega^{109}, \ldots, \omega^{35}) \approx 1/13.$$

   The termination of the algorithm is made 8 steps earlier, i.e., the condition (24) will be satisfied at $m = 8$. □

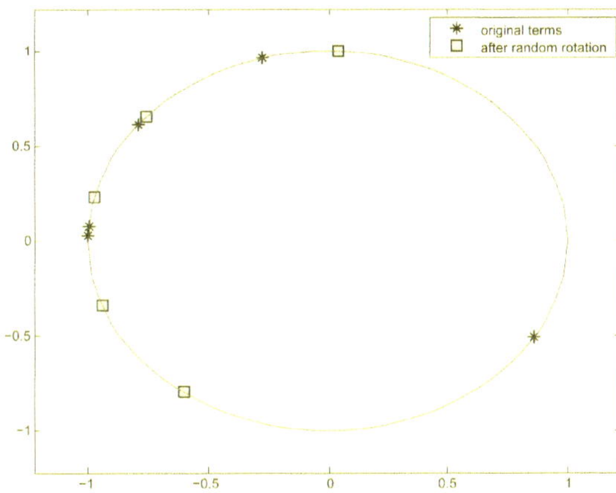

Figure 1: Terms in Example 3.1

4. EARLY TERMINATION STRATEGIES

It should be noted that Algorithm 1 may terminate before m reaches the number of terms t in f.

Example 4.1. [2] Let $f = \sum_{j=1}^{t} c_j x^{e_j}$, where $t = 61$, $c_j = 1$ for $j = 1, \ldots, t$,

$$e_j = \begin{cases} 2(j-1) & j = 1, \ldots, 41, \\ 63 + 2(j-42) & j = 42, \ldots, 51, \\ 1 + 2(j-52) & j = 52, \ldots, 61. \end{cases}$$

Figure 2 shows all terms in f evaluating at $\omega = e^{2\pi i/82}$.

1. The smallest singular value of the Hankel matrix H_m is less than 10^{-11} for any m larger than 23. It is an example used in [2] to show that the Hankel matrices can have exponentially large condition numbers.

2. For m from 37 to 41, the first 22 singular values of H_m are larger than 1, and the rest singular values of H_m are smaller than 10^{-10}. Therefore if we set $\zeta \le 5$, $\epsilon = 10^{-10}$, according to the criterion (24), the algorithm will terminate wrongly and return $t = 22$. However, if we continue to $m = 42$, the Hankel matrix H_{42} has 23 singular values larger than 1, which does not satisfy the criterion (24).

3. For this example, we have

   $$\Delta(\omega^{e_1}, \ldots, \omega^{e_t}) = \frac{1}{82}.$$

   For any $m \ge 76$, the first 61 singular values of H_m are larger than 1 while the remaining singular values are smaller than 10^{-13}. Therefore, Algorithm 1 will return $t = 61$ successfully if we set $\zeta > 5$ or $\epsilon = 10^{-13}$.

4. It is noted that the Vandermonde matrices V_m are well-conditioned for $1 \le m \le 41$, with condition numbers being about 1.41. The condition number of V_m increases to $1.9 \cdot 10^9$ when m reaches 61, and then decreases to 1.976 for m going from 62 to 81.

In the following, we will show that with high probability, the algorithm will not terminate before it reaches the sparsity t.

4.1 Kaltofen-Lee Early Termination Revisited

For exact coefficient fields, the probabilistic analysis that checking termination conditions with high probability prevents a sparsity computation where t is smaller than the

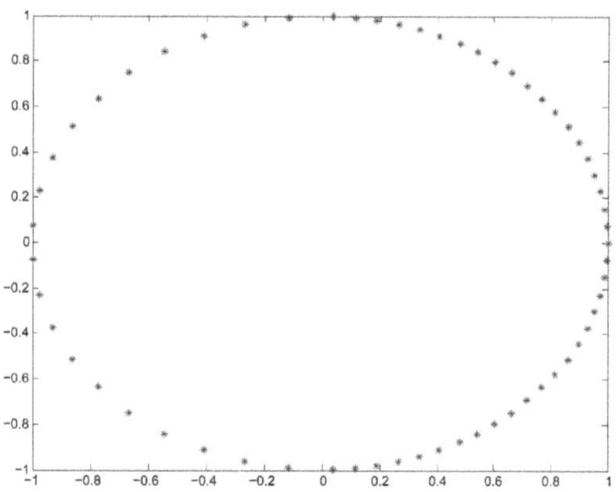

Figure 2: Terms in Example 4.1.

actual sparsity is due to [11]. The randomized algorithm in [11] is said to terminate early because the number of evaluations is $2t+1$ with high probability, which is the minimum number of evaluations necessary without knowing the sparsity t on input. The setting by Kaltofen and Lee is the multivariate polynomial version by Ben-Or and Tiwari [3] of Prony's algorithm with coefficients from an arbitrary field K. Let

$$f(x_1,\ldots,x_n)=\sum_{j=1}^{t} c_j\, x_1^{e_{j,1}}\cdots x_n^{e_{j,n}}, c_j\in\mathsf{K}, c_j\neq 0 \quad (31)$$

be a t-sparse polynomial in $\mathsf{K}[x_1,\ldots,x_n]$, let

$$\left.\begin{array}{l}\alpha_i=f(x_1^i,\ldots,x_n^i)\in\mathsf{K}[x_1,\ldots,x_n], i=1,2,3,\ldots\\ \alpha_0=c_1+\cdots+c_t\end{array}\right\} \quad (32)$$

be the evaluations of f at the i-th powers of a generic point with the j-th component being the variable x_j, and let

$$H_m(h_1,\ldots,h_{2m-1})=\begin{bmatrix} h_1 & h_2 & \ldots & h_m\\ h_2 & h_3 & \cdot^{\cdot^{\cdot}} & h_{m+1}\\ h_3 & h_4 & \cdot^{\cdot^{\cdot}} & h_{m+2}\\ \vdots & \vdots & \cdot^{\cdot^{\cdot}} & \vdots\\ h_m & h_{m+1} & \ldots & h_{2m-1}\end{bmatrix} \quad (33)$$

be an $m\times m$ Hankel matrix formed by the entries h_1, …, h_{2m-1}. Theorem 4 in [11] states that

$$\forall m, 1\le m\le t\colon \det(H_m(\alpha_1,\ldots,\alpha_{2m-1}))\neq 0.$$

One always has $\det(H_{m'}(\alpha_1,\ldots,\alpha_{2m'-1}))=0$ for all $m'\ge t+1$. Thus, by the DeMillo-Lipton/Schwartz/Zippel Lemma, by substituting field elements $\omega_j\in S\subseteq\mathsf{K}$ that are uniformly and randomly chosen from the finite set S one has with probability

$$\ge 1-\Bigl(t^3+\frac{3}{2}t^2+\frac{1}{2}t\Bigr)\deg(f)\,\frac{1}{3\,|S|} \quad (34)$$

($|S|$ denoting the number of elements in S) that the determinants of $H_m(a_1,\ldots,a_{2m-1})\neq 0$ for $a_i=\alpha_i(\omega_1,\ldots,\omega_n)$ and all m with $1\le m\le t$ [11, Theorem 5]. Therefore, the first singular Hankel matrix that appears has with high probability dimension $(t+1)\times(t+1)$, yielding the sparsity t. The entire sequence of determinants $(\det(H_m(a_1,\ldots,a_{2m-1}))_{1\le m\le t+1}$ can be computed one after another from the sequence $a_1,a_2,a_3,\ldots$ by the fraction-free Berlekamp/Massey Algorithm [7, 14] in a total of $O(t^2)$ arithmetic operations. We recall that in our numerical Algorithm 1 above the termination criterion is that singular values are separated into those $>1-\epsilon$ and those $<\epsilon$ and none in between in a matrix $H_{m+\zeta}$ that has 2ζ additional evaluations for each m.

Our univariate algorithm with floating point arithmetic above and the multivariate Ben-Or and Tiwari Algorithm with exact scalar arithmetic start the sequence at $(\omega_1^0,\ldots,\omega_n^0)=(1,1,\ldots,1)$, in which case $H_1(\alpha_0)=c_1+\cdots+c_t$ can be $=0$. If the coefficient field K has characteristic $=2$, then for $c_1=\cdots=c_t=1$ one has for all m with $0\le m\le t-1$ and $t-m$ an odd integer that $\det(H_m(\alpha_0,\ldots,\alpha_{2m-2}))=0$ (see Appendix Section 6). That fact shows that the shift in [11] starting at α_1 is necessary to have all H_m with $m\ge 2$ non-singular, for coefficient fields of characteristic $=2$.

It also follows from the Proof of Theorem 4 in [11] (see (46) below) that for coefficient fields K of any characteristic we have

$$\forall m, 1{\le}m{\le}t-1\colon \left\{\begin{array}{l}\det(H_m(\alpha_0,\ldots,\alpha_{2m-2})){\neq}0\\ \text{and/or}\\ \det(H_{m+1}(\alpha_0,\ldots,\alpha_{2m})){\neq}0.\end{array}\right\} \quad (35)$$

Therefore, if one stops when one has encountered $\zeta=2$ consecutive singular Hankel matrices, the upper bound on the probability of premature failure can be reduced at the cost of 2 additional evaluations.

For coefficient fields K of characteristic $\neq 2$ we can improve Theorem 4 in [11] unconditionally, giving a positive answer to the question raised in Footnote 2 in [11, Proof of Theorem 4].

Theorem 4.1. *Let K be a field of characteristic $\neq 2$, let α_i be as in (32) and let H_m be as in (33). Then*

$$\left.\begin{array}{l}\det(H_1(\alpha_0))=c_1+\cdots+c_t,\\ \det(H_m(\alpha_0,\ldots,\alpha_{2m-2}))\neq 0 \text{ for all } 2\le m\le t.\end{array}\right\} \quad (36)$$

Proof. Our proof gives a finer analysis of the term structure in the expansion of the formula for $\det(H_m(\alpha_0,\ldots,\alpha_{2m-2}))$ given in [11, cf. Equ. (9)] (see also (2) above). Let $J=\{1,2,\ldots,t\}$, let

$$F(y_1,\ldots,y_t)=\sum_{\{j_1,\ldots,j_m\}\subseteq J} c_{j_1}\cdots c_{j_m}\prod_{1\le v<u\le m}(y_{j_u}-y_{j_v})^2 \in\mathsf{K}[y_1,\ldots,y_t], \quad (37)$$

and let $\beta_j=x_1^{e_{j,1}}\cdots x_n^{e_{j,n}}$ be the j-th term in (31). Then we have

$$\det(H_m(\alpha_0,\ldots,\alpha_{2m-2}))=F(\beta_1,\ldots,\beta_t). \quad (38)$$

There are $\binom{t}{m}$ summands in (37) and each product in (37) has $\binom{m}{2}$ squared factors.

We will use admissible total term orders on both $\mathsf{K}[x_1,\ldots,x_n]$ for the terms in $F(\beta_1,\ldots,\beta_t)$ and on $\mathsf{K}[y_1,\ldots,y_t]$ for the terms in $F(y_1,\ldots,y_t)$ and denote them by $\succeq_x$ and $\succeq_y$, respectively. We write $\succ_x$ and $\succ_y$ when the terms are strictly in order, that is, in order and not equal. The term orders can be pure lexicographical term orders. Note that all terms in F in (37), if $F\neq 0$, have total degree $2\binom{m}{2}=m(m-1)$ in $y_1,\ldots,y_t$. We order the terms β_j in f in (31) as

$$\beta_1\succ_x\beta_2\succ_x\ldots\succ_x\beta_t \quad (39)$$

and the variables y_j as

$$y_1\succ_y y_2\succ_y\cdots\succ_y y_t. \quad (40)$$

The leading term with respect to the term order $\succeq_Y$ among all terms in all products $\prod_{1\le v<u\le m}(y_{j_u}-y_{j_v})^2$ in (37) is

$$M_1 = y_1^{2m-2} y_2^{2m-4} \cdots y_{m-2}^4 y_{m-1}^2 \in \mathsf{K}[y_1,\ldots,y_t], \qquad (41)$$

which we will prove below. We shall consider a third, partial order $\sqsupseteq_Y$ on the terms $\in \mathsf{K}[y_1,\ldots,y_t]$ of F:

Definition 4.1. *Let $M \in \mathsf{K}[y_1,\ldots,y_t]$ be a term of degree $D = m(m-1)$. By $\mathrm{vlist}(M)$ we denote the list of factors that are variables in order sorted with respect to (40):*

$$\mathrm{vlist}(M) \overset{\text{def}}{=} [\underbrace{y_{j_1},\ldots,y_{j_1}}_{e_1\ \textit{times}},\ldots,\underbrace{y_{j_k},\ldots,y_{j_k}}_{e_k\ \textit{times}}]$$
$$\textit{for } M = y_{j_1}^{e_1}\cdots y_{j_k}^{e_k}, e_1\ge 1,\ldots,e_k\ge 1, j_1<j_2<\cdots<j_k.$$

By $\mathrm{vlist}(M)[\ell]$ we denote the ℓ-th component in the list, which is a variable y_η, $j_1 \le \eta \le j_k$. Now let M' be another term in $\mathsf{K}[y_1,\ldots,y_t]$ of degree D. We define

$$M \sqsupseteq_Y M'$$
$$\overset{\text{def}}{\iff} \forall \ell, 1\le\ell\le D\colon \eta\le\eta' \textit{ for } \left\{\begin{array}{l} y_\eta = \mathrm{vlist}(M)[\ell], \\ y_{\eta'} = \mathrm{vlist}(M')[\ell] \end{array}\right\}$$
$$\iff \forall \ell, 1\le\ell\le D\colon \mathrm{vlist}(M)[\ell] \succeq_Y \mathrm{vlist}(M')[\ell]. \qquad (42)$$

We write $M \sqsupset_Y M' \overset{\text{def}}{\iff} M \sqsupseteq_Y M'$ and $M \ne M'$, which means that in (42) $\mathrm{vlist}(M)[\ell] \succ_Y \mathrm{vlist}(M')[\ell]$ for at least one index ℓ. We have

$$M \not\sqsupseteq_Y M'$$
$$\iff \exists \ell, 1\le\ell\le D : \mathrm{vlist}(M')[\ell] \succ_Y \mathrm{vlist}(M)[\ell]. \qquad (43)$$

Note that $\sqsupset_Y$ is a (strict) partial order: for $M = y_1^4 y_3^2$ and $M' = y_1^2 y_2^4 \ne M$ we have both $M \not\sqsupseteq_Y M'$ and $M' \not\sqsupseteq_Y M$. We first claim that

$$M \sqsupset_Y M' \Longrightarrow M(\beta_1,\ldots,\beta_t) \succ_X M'(\beta_1,\ldots\beta_t). \qquad (44)$$

The strict order (44) of the evaluated terms is a consequence of the (39), (40), definition (42) and the admissibility property of $\succeq_X$: for terms β, β', γ, γ' in $\mathsf{K}[x_1,\ldots,x_n]$ we have $\beta \succeq_X \beta'$ and $\gamma \succeq_X \gamma' \Longrightarrow \beta\gamma \succeq_X \beta'\gamma'$ with $\beta\gamma \succ_X \beta'\gamma'$ if $\beta \succ_X \beta'$ and/or $\gamma \succ_X \gamma'$.

Now let $M \in \mathsf{K}[y_1,\ldots,y_t]$ be any term in any of the products $\prod_{1\le v<u\le m}(y_{j_u}-y_{j_v})^2$ in (37). For the term M_1 in (41) we have

$$M_1 \sqsupseteq_Y M \text{ for all such terms } M. \qquad (45)$$

The reason is the following: for $\mu = 1,2,\ldots,m-1$, the largest position index $\ell_\mu^{[\max]}$ that y_μ can reach in $\mathrm{vlist}(M)$ is $\ell_\mu^{[\max]} = 2(m-1)+2(m-2)+\cdots+2(m-\mu)$, because the maximum total degree in $y_1,\ldots,y_\mu$ in M is $= \ell_\mu^{[\max]}$: there are least $2\binom{m-\mu}{2} = (m-\mu)(m-\mu-1)$ factors $(y_{j_u}-y_{j_v})$ with $j_u > \mu$ and $j_v > \mu$ whose variables contribute to M a total degree $\ge (m-\mu)(m-\mu-1)$, so the maximum total degree in $y_1,\ldots,y_\mu$ is $\le m(m-1)-(m-\mu)(m-\mu-1) = \ell_\mu^{[\max]}$. Those maxima are achieved for all μ in $\mathrm{vlist}(M_1)$. In particular, y_μ appears first at position $\ell_{\mu-1}^{[\max]}+1$ in $\mathrm{vlist}(M_1)$. Suppose now that $M_1 \not\sqsupseteq_Y M \iff$ there exists an ℓ with $1\le\ell\le D$ and $\mathrm{vlist}(M)[\ell] \succ_Y \mathrm{vlist}(M_1)[\ell]$ (see (42)), meaning $\mu' \le \mu-1$ for $y_{\mu'} = \mathrm{vlist}(M)[\ell]$ and $y_\mu = \mathrm{vlist}(M_1)[\ell]$. For y_μ in $\mathrm{vlist}(M_1)$ we have $\ell > \ell_{\mu-1}^{[\max]}$. This means that $y_{\mu'}$ is in a position $> \ell_{\mu-1}^{[\max]}$ in $\mathrm{vlist}(M)$, for which $\mu' \le \mu-1$ is too small to be reachable, which proves (45).

From (44) and (45) we conclude that for all $M \ne M_1$ we have $M_1(\beta_1,\ldots,\beta_t) \succ_X M(\beta_1,\ldots,\beta_t)$, which in [11, 1] was argued directly. Our argument here is more detailed and will be used again below. Next we observe that the term M_1 in (41) occurs in (37) precisely in the products $\prod_{1\le v<u\le m}(y_{j_u}-y_{j_v})^2$ for all $\{j_1,\ldots,j_m\} = \{1,\ldots,m-1,\tau\}$ with $\tau = m, m+1,\ldots,t$. Therefore we have the expansion

$$F(\beta_1,\ldots,\beta_t) = c_1\cdots c_{m-1}\Big(\sum_{\tau=m}^{t} c_\tau\Big)\, M_1(\beta_1,\ldots,\beta_t)$$
$$+ \text{ lower order terms in } x_1,\ldots,x_n.$$

Thus we conclude from (38) and $c_j \ne 0$ that

$$\Big(\sum_{\tau=m}^{t} c_\tau\Big) \ne 0 \Longrightarrow \det(H_m(\alpha_0,\ldots,\alpha_{2m-2})) \ne 0 \qquad (46)$$

(see [1, Remark 4.2]). Two consecutive sums $\sum_{\tau=m}^t c_\tau$ and $\sum_{\tau=m+1}^t c_\tau$ cannot both be $= 0$, for then $c_m = 0$, which implies (35) above.

Now suppose that $(\sum_{\tau=m}^t c_\tau) = 0$ for $2 \le m \le t$. We then consider the second highest term with respect to the order $\succ_Y$ in the expansion of (37), namely,

$$M_2 = y_1^{2m-2} y_2^{2m-4} \cdots y_{m-2}^4 y_{m-1} y_m \in \mathsf{K}[y_1,\ldots,y_t]. \qquad (47)$$

The term has variables $y_1,\ldots,y_m$ and therefore occurs in only one product, namely, $\prod_{1\le v<u\le m}(y_{j_u}-y_{j_v})^2$ with $\{j_1,\ldots,j_m\} = \{1,\ldots,m\}$, and there with coefficient -2, and thus in (37) has a coefficient $-2c_1\cdots c_m$. We shall prove that $(\sum_{\tau=m}^t c_\tau) = 0$ implies that the term $M_2(\beta_1,\ldots,\beta_t) \in \mathsf{K}[x_1,\ldots,x_n]$ in the expansion of (38) has the same coefficient.

By (44), all terms $M \in \mathsf{K}[y_1,\ldots,y_t]$ in (37) with $M_2 \sqsupset_Y M$ have $M_2(\beta_1,\ldots,\beta_t) \succ_X M(\beta_1,\ldots,\beta_t)$ and therefore cannot additively contribute to the coefficient of $M_2(\beta_1,\ldots,\beta_t)$ in the expansion (38). All remaining terms satisfy $M_2 \not\sqsupseteq_Y M$ (M_1 is such a term). Now let M be a term in (37) with $M_2 \not\sqsupseteq_Y M$. We have for all ℓ with $1 \le \ell \le D-1$ that $\mathrm{vlist}(M_2)[\ell] = \mathrm{vlist}(M_1)[\ell] \succeq_Y \mathrm{vlist}(M)[\ell]$, the latter being true by (45). Therefore, $M_2 \not\sqsupseteq_Y M$ implies that $\mathrm{vlist}(M)[D] = y_{m-1}$, because no y_μ with $\mu \le m-2$ can reach position $D > \ell_{m-2}^{[\max]} \ge \ell_\mu^{[\max]}$ and we must by (43) have $\mathrm{vlist}(M)[D] \succ_Y \mathrm{vlist}(M_2)[D] = y_m$.

We finally show that all terms M with $M_2 \not\sqsupseteq_Y M$ have a coefficient $= 0$ in (37). In the previous paragraph we have shown that $\mathrm{vlist}(M)[D] = y_{m-1}$. We claim that M can only occur in products $\prod_{1\le v<u\le m}(y_{j_u}-y_{j_v})^2$ with $\{j_1,\ldots,j_m\} = \{1,\ldots,m-1,\tau\}$ and $m \le \tau \le t$. For suppose the set $\{j_1,\ldots,j_m\}$ contains two τ, τ' with $m \le \tau \le t$ and $\tau < \tau' \le t$. Then the product $\prod_{1\le v<u\le m}(y_{j_u}-y_{j_v})^2$ has a factor $(y_\tau - y_{\tau'})^2$, so the total degree in the variables $y_1,\ldots,y_{m-1}$ of each term M in the expansion of that product is $< m(m-1)$, which implies that y_{m-1} cannot reach position D in $\mathrm{vlist}(M)$. Now suppose that a term M with $M_2 \not\sqsupseteq_Y M$ occurs in a product $\prod_{1\le v<u\le m}(y_{j_u}-y_{j_v})^2$ with $\{j_1,\ldots,j_m\} = \{1,\ldots,m-1,\tau\}$ for at least one τ with $m \le \tau \le t$ (otherwise it cannot occur in the full expansion of (37) at all). Then M occurs in those products for all τ with $m \le \tau \le t$, there

with the same coefficient a_M (by setting $y_\tau = 0$ in all products) and therefore in the expansion of (37) with coefficient $a_M c_1 \cdots c_{m-1}(\sum_{\tau=m}^{t} c_\tau) = 0$, the "$= 0$" by our assumption that $(\sum_{\tau=m}^{t} c_\tau) = 0$.

Therefore, the only non-zero scalar coefficient for the term $M_2(\beta_1, \ldots, \beta_t)$ in (38) can come from M_2 in (37), which as argued above has a coefficient $-2c_1 \cdots c_m$, which is $\neq 0$ because $c_j \neq 0$ and the the field is of characteristic $\neq 2$. We conclude that for all m and t with $2 \leq m \leq t$ we have $(\sum_{\tau=m}^{t} c_\tau) = 0 \implies \det(H_m(\alpha_0, \ldots, \alpha_{2m-2})) \neq 0$, which together with (46) proves Theorem 4.1. □

Theorem 4.1 yields a slightly better estimate on the early termination success probability than (34) for fields of characteristic $\neq 2$, namely,

$$\geq 1 - (t^3 - t + 3)\deg(f)\frac{1}{3|S|} \tag{48}$$

after $2t+1$ evaluations. The estimate (48) includes testing if $a_1 = f(\omega_1, \ldots, \omega_n)$ is $= 0$ first, in which case f is with high probability the zero polynomial ($t = 0$). If the test fails, our algorithm computes $a_0 = f(1, \ldots, 1)$ and $a_2 = f(\omega_1^2, \ldots, \omega_n^2)$ and tests $\det(H_2(a_0, a_1, a_2)) = 0$ next. We do this so that the comparison to (34) is proper, where the zero polynomial is returned after a single evaluation by terminating at $\det(H_1(a_1)) = 0$, as does ours now.

Remark 4.1. Theorem 4.1 remains valid if some $e_{j,\nu}$ in (31) are negative integers. Then $f \in \mathsf{K}[x_1, x_1^{-1}, \ldots, x_n, x_n^{-1}]$, the ring of Laurent polynomials in $x_1, \ldots, x_n$. In our probability estimate (48) with $0 \notin S$ one then can use

$$\deg(f) = \max_{1\leq j\leq t}(\textstyle\sum_{\nu=1}^{n} e_{j,\nu}) - \sum_{1\leq\nu\leq n} \min_{1\leq j\leq t}(e_{j,\nu}).$$

Note that for a regular polynomial f that notion of degree is actually smaller than the total degree of f if a variable x_ν divides f. □

Acknowledgement: The ideas of this paper were originally conceived at the Fields Institute in Toronto during our stay during the Major Program in Computer Algebra. We also thank Wen-Shin Lee for her helpful comments.

5. REFERENCES

[1] A. Arnold and E. L. Kaltofen. Error-correcting sparse interpolation in the Chebyshev basis. In *ISSAC'15 Proc. 2015 ACM Internat. Symp. Symbolic Algebraic Comput.*, pages 21–28, New York, N. Y., 2015. ACM. URL: http://www.math.ncsu.edu/~kaltofen/bibliography/15/ArKa15.pdf.

[2] B. Beckermann, G. Golub, and G. Labahn. On the numerical condition of a generalized hankel eigenvalue problem. *Numerische Mathematik*, 106(1):41–68, 2007.

[3] M. Ben-Or and P. Tiwari. A deterministic algorithm for sparse multivariate polynomial interpolation. In *Proc. Twentieth Annual ACM Symp. Theory Comput.*, pages 301–309, New York, N.Y., 1988. ACM Press.

[4] E. J. Candès and C. Fernandez-Granda. Super-resolution from noisy data. *Journal of Fourier Analysis and Applications*, 19(6):1229–1254, 2013.

[5] E. J. Candés and C. Fernandez-Granda. Towards a mathematical theory of super-resolution. *Communications on Pure and Applied Mathematics*, 67(6):906–956, 2014.

[6] A. Cuyt and W.-s. Lee. Sparse interpolation and rational approximation. *Contemporary Mathematics, American Mathematical Society*, 2015.

[7] M. Giesbrecht, E. Kaltofen, and W.-s. Lee. Algorithms for computing the sparsest shifts for polynomials via the Berlekamp/Massey algorithm. In T. Mora, editor, *Proc. 2002 Internat. Symp. Symbolic Algebraic Comput. (ISSAC'02)*, pages 101–108, New York, N. Y., 2002. ACM Press. Journal version in [8]. URL: http://www.math.ncsu.edu/~kaltofen/bibliography/02/GKL02.pdf.

[8] M. Giesbrecht, E. Kaltofen, and W.-s. Lee. Algorithms for computing sparsest shifts of polynomials in power, Chebychev, and Pochhammer bases. *J. Symbolic Comput.*, 36(3–4):401–424, 2003. URL: http://www.math.ncsu.edu/~kaltofen/bibliography/03/GKL03.pdf.

[9] M. Giesbrecht, G. Labahn, and W.-s. Lee. Symbolic-numeric sparse interpolation of multivariate polynomials. *Journal of Symbolic Computation*, 44(8):943 – 959, 2009.

[10] G. H. Golub and C. F. Van Loan. *Matrix Computations*. Johns Hopkins University Press, Baltimore, MD, USA, 1996.

[11] E. Kaltofen and W.-s. Lee. Early termination in sparse interpolation algorithms. *J. Symbolic Comput.*, 36(3–4):365–400, 2003. URL: http://www.math.ncsu.edu/~kaltofen/bibliography/03/KL03.pdf.

[12] E. Kaltofen, W.-s. Lee, and Z. Yang. Fast estimates of Hankel matrix condition numbers and numeric sparse interpolation. In M. Moreno Maza, editor, *SNC'11 Proc. 2011 Internat. Workshop on Symbolic-Numeric Comput.*, pages 130–136, New York, N. Y., June 2011. ACM. URL: http://www.math.ncsu.edu/~kaltofen/bibliography/11/KLY11.pdf.

[13] E. Kaltofen, Z. Yang, and L. Zhi. On probabilistic analysis of randomization in hybrid symbolic-numeric algorithms. In J. Verschelde and S. M. Watt, editors, *SNC'07 Proc. 2007 Internat. Workshop on Symbolic-Numeric Comput.*, pages 11–17, New York, N. Y., 2007. ACM Press. URL: http://www.math.ncsu.edu/~kaltofen/bibliography/07/KYZ07.pdf.

[14] E. Kaltofen and G. Yuhasz. A fraction free matrix Berlekamp/Massey algorithm. *Linear Algebra and Applications*, 439(9):2515–2526, Nov. 2013. URL: http://www.math.ncsu.edu/~kaltofen/bibliography/08/KaYu08.pdf.

[15] W. Liao and A. Fannjiang. MUSIC for single-snapshot spectral estimation: Stability and super-resolution. *Applied and Computational Harmonic Analysis*, 40(1):33 – 67, 2016.

[16] L. Mirsky. Symmetric gauge functions and unitarily invariant norms. *The Quarterly Journal of Mathematics*, 11(1):50–59, 1960.

[17] A. Moitra. Super-resolution, extremal functions and the condition number of vandermonde matrices. In *Proceedings of the Forty-Seventh Annual ACM on Symposium on Theory of Computing*, STOC '15, pages 821–830, New York, NY, USA, 2015. ACM.

[18] D. Slepian. Prolate spheroidal wave functions, Fourier analysis, and uncertainty— V: The discrete case. *Bell System Technical Journal*, 57(5):1371–1430, 1978.

[19] J. Stoer and R. Bulirsch. *Introduction to Numerical Analysis (3rd ed.)*. Springer-Verlag New York, 2002.

[20] H. Weyl. Das asymptotische Verteilungsgesetz der Eigenwerte linearer partieller Differentialgleichungen (mit einer Anwendung auf die Theorie der Hohlraumstrahlung). *Mathematische Annalen*, 71(4):441–479, 1912.

6. APPENDIX: CHARACTERISTIC = 2

If the coefficient field K has characteristic $= 2$, $c_1 = \cdots = c_t = 1$ and $t - m$ is an odd number, then

$$\prod_{1\leq v<u\leq m} (\beta_{j_v} - \beta_{j_u})^2 = \prod_{1\leq v<u\leq m} (\beta_{j_v}^2 - \beta_{j_u}^2), \tag{49}$$

which can be viewed as the determinant of the Vandermonde matrix V generated by $\beta_{j_1}^2, \ldots, \beta_{j_m}^2$. Then each term in the expansion of (49) must be a product of elements selected from every column of V. Therefore by (37) and (38), each term in $\det(H_m(\alpha_0, \ldots, \alpha_{2m-2}))$ has the form $M = \beta_{j_1}^{2m-2} \cdot \beta_{j_2}^{2m-4} \cdots \beta_{j_{m-1}}^2$. Let $S = \{1, \ldots, t\} \setminus \{j_1, \ldots, j_{m-1}\}$, then the coefficient of M is $c_{j_1} \cdots c_{j_{m-1}} \cdot \sum_{j_m\in S} c_{j_m} = 0$for S having an even number of elements. Therefore, we have $\det(H_m(\alpha_0, \ldots, \alpha_{2m-2})) = 0$. □

Fast Polynomial Multiplication over $\mathbb{F}_{2^{60}}$

David Harvey
School of Mathematics and Statistics
University of New South Wales
Sydney NSW 2052, Australia
d.harvey@unsw.edu.au

Joris van der Hoeven, Grégoire Lecerf
CNRS, Laboratoire d'informatique
École polytechnique
91128 Palaiseau Cedex, France
{vdhoeven,lecerf}@lix.polytechnique.fr

ABSTRACT

Can post-Schönhage–Strassen multiplication algorithms be competitive in practice for large input sizes? So far, the GMP library still outperforms all implementations of the recent, asymptotically more efficient algorithms for integer multiplication by Fürer, De–Kurur–Saha–Saptharishi, and ourselves. In this paper, we show how central ideas of our recent asymptotically fast algorithms turn out to be of practical interest for multiplication of polynomials over finite fields of characteristic two. Our Mathemagix implementation is based on the automatic generation of assembly codelets. It outperforms existing implementations in large degree, especially for polynomial matrix multiplication over finite fields.

CCS Concepts

•Mathematics of computing → Mathematical software performance; Computations in finite fields;

Keywords

Finite fields; Polynomial multiplication; Mathemagix

1. INTRODUCTION

Let $\mathbb{F}_{2^k}$ denote the finite field with 2^k elements. In this article we are interested in multiplying polynomials in $\mathbb{F}_{2^k}[x]$. This is a very basic and classical problem in complexity theory, with major applications to number theory, cryptography and error correcting codes.

1.1 Motivation

Let $\mathsf{M}_{2^k}(n)$ denote the bit complexity of multiplying two polynomials of degree $<n$ in $\mathbb{F}_{2^k}[x]$. Until recently, the best asymptotic bound for this complexity was $\mathsf{M}_{2^k}(n) = O(k\ n \log(k\ n) \log \log(k\ n))$, using a triadic version [32] of the classical Schönhage–Strassen algorithm [33].

ISSAC '16, July 19 - 22, 2016, Waterloo, ON, Canada

In [20], we improved this bound to $\mathsf{M}_{2^k}(n) = O(k\ n \log(k\ n)\ 8^{\log^*(kn)})$, where $\log^* x = \min \{i \in \mathbb{N} | \log \circ \overset{i\times}{\cdots} \circ \log x \leqslant 1\}$. The factor $8^{\log^*(kn)}$ increases so slowly that it is impossible to observe the asymptotic behavior of our algorithm in practice. Despite this, the present paper demonstrates that some of the new techniques introduced in [20, 21] can indeed lead to more efficient implementations.

One of the main reasons behind the observed acceleration is that [20] contains a natural analogue for the *three primes FFT* approach to multiplying integers [30]. For a single multiplication, this kind of algorithm is more or less as efficient as the Schönhage–Strassen algorithm: the FFTs involve more expensive arithmetic, but the inner products are faster. On recent architectures, the three primes approach for integer multiplication generally has performance superior to that of Schönhage–Strassen due to its cache efficiency [25].

The compactness of the transformed representations also makes the three primes approach very useful for linear algebra. Accordingly, the implementation described in this paper is very efficient for matrix products over $\mathbb{F}_{2^k}[x]$. This is beneficial for many applications such as half gcds, polynomial factorization, geometric error correcting codes, polynomial system solving, etc.

1.2 Related work and our contributions

Nowadays the Schönhage–Strassen algorithm is widely used in practice for multiplying large integers [18] and polynomials [4, 19]. For integers, it was the asymptotically fastest known until Fürer's algorithm [11, 12] with cost $n \log n\ K^{\log^* n}$, for input bit sizes n, where $K > 1$ is some constant (an optimized version [21] yields the explicit value $K = 16$). However, no-one has yet demonstrated a practical implementation for sizes supported by current technology. The implementation of the modular variant proposed in [7] has even been discussed in detail in [28]: their conclusion is that the break-even point seems to be beyond astronomical sizes.

In [20, 21] we developed a unified alternative strategy for both integers and polynomials. Roughly speaking, products are performed *via discrete Fourier transforms* (DFTs) that are split into smaller ones. Small transforms then reduce to smaller products. When these smaller products are still large enough, the algorithm is used recursively. Since the input size decreases logarithmically between recursive calls, there is of course just one such recursive call in practice. Our implementation was guided by these ideas, but, in the end, only a few ingredients were retained. In fact, we do not recurse at all; we handle the smaller subproducts directly over $\mathbb{F}_{2^{60}}$ with the Karatsuba algorithm.

For polynomials over finite fields, one key ingredient of [20] is the construction of suitable finite fields: we need the cardinality of their multiplicative groups to have sufficiently many small prime factors. A remarkable example is $\mathbb{F}_{2^{60}}$, outlined at the end of [20], for which we have:

$$2^{60}-1=3^2\cdot 5^2\cdot 7\cdot 11\cdot 13\cdot 31\cdot 41\cdot 61\cdot 151\cdot 331\cdot 1321.$$

Section 3 contains our first contribution: a detailed optimized implementation of DFTs over $\mathbb{F}_{2^{60}}$. We propose several original tricks to make it highly competitive on processors featuring *carry-less products*. For DFTs of small prime sizes we appeal to seminal techniques due to Rader [31] and Winograd [36]. Then the *prime-factor algorithm*, also called Good–Thomas [17, 35], is used in medium sizes, while the Cooley–Tukey algorithm [5] serves for large sizes.

In Section 4, we focus on other finite fields $\mathbb{F}_{2^k}$. When k is a divisor of 60, we design efficient embeddings into $\mathbb{F}_{2^{60}}$, and compare to the use of Kronecker segmentation and padding. For values of k up to 59, we propose a new algorithm to reduce computations to $\mathbb{F}_{2^{60}}$, in the vein of the three prime FFT technique. This constitutes our second contribution.

The practical performance of our implementation is reported in Section 5. We compare to the optimized reference library GF2X, developed by Brent, Gaudry, Thomé and Zimmermann [4], which assembles Karatsuba, Toom–Cook and the triadic Schönhage–Strassen algorithms with automatically tuned thresholds. The high performance of our implementation is of course a major outcome of this paper.

For detailed references on asymptotically fast algorithms to univariate polynomials over $\mathbb{F}_{2^k}$ and some applications, we refer the reader to [4, 20, 21]. The present article does not formally rely on [20]. In the next section we recall and slightly adapt classical results, and present our implementation framework. Our use of *codelets* for small and moderate sizes of DFT is customary in other high performance software, such as FFTW3 and SPIRAL [10, 29].

2. PRELIMINARIES

This section gathers classical building blocks used by our DFT algorithm. We also describe our implementation framework. If a and b are elements of a Euclidean domain, then a quo b and a rem b respectively represent the related quotient and remainder in the division of a by b, so that $a=(a \operatorname{quo} b)\, b+(a \operatorname{rem} b)$ holds.

2.1 Discrete Fourier transforms

Let $n_1, \ldots, n_d$ be positive integers, let $v=(n_1, \ldots, n_d)$, $n=n_1\cdots n_d$, and $i\in\{0,\ldots,n-1\}$. The *v-expansion* of i is the sequence of integers $i_0,\ldots,i_{d-1}$ such that $0\leqslant i_j<n_{j+1}$ and

$$i=i_{d-1}+i_{d-2}\,n_d+i_{d-3}\,n_{d-1}\,n_d+\cdots+i_0\,n_2\cdots n_d.$$

The *v-mirror*, written $[i]_v$, of i relative to v, is the integer defined by the following reverse expansion:

$$[i]_v=i_0+i_1\,n_1+\cdots+i_{d-2}\,n_1\cdots n_{d-2}+i_{d-1}\,n_1\cdots n_{d-1}.$$

Let $\mathbb{K}$ be a commutative field, and let $\omega\in\mathbb{K}$ be a primitive n-th root of unity, which means that $\omega^n=1$, and $\omega^j\neq 1$ for all $j\in\{1,\ldots,n-1\}$. The *discrete Fourier transform* (with respect to ω) of an n-tuple $(a_0, \ldots, a_{n-1})\in\mathbb{K}^n$ is the n-tuple $(\hat{a}_0,\ldots,\hat{a}_{n-1})\in\mathbb{K}^n$ given by $\hat{a}_i=\sum_{j=0}^{n-1}\omega^{ij}a_j$. In other words we have $\hat{a}_i=A(\omega^i)$, where $A(x)=\sum_{j=0}^{n-1}a_j\,x^j$. For efficiency reasons, in this article, we compute the $\hat{a}_i$ in the v-mirror order, where v corresponds to a certain ordering of the prime factors of n, counted with multiplicities, that will be optimized later. We shall use the following notation:

$$\mathrm{DFT}_{\omega,v}(a)=(\hat{a}_{[0]_v},\ldots,\hat{a}_{[n-1]_v}).$$

Let $1\leqslant h<d$, and let us split $v=(n_1,\ldots,n_d)$ into $v_1=(n_1,\ldots,n_h)$ and $v_2=(n_{h+1}, \ldots, n_d)$. We recall the *Cooley–Tukey algorithm* [5] in the present setting: it decomposes $\mathrm{DFT}_{\omega,v}$ into $\mathrm{DFT}_{\omega^{m_2},v_1}$ and $\mathrm{DFT}_{\omega^{m_1},v_2}$, where $m_1=n_1\cdots n_h$ and $m_2=n_{h+1}\cdots n_d$.

Algorithm 1 (In-place Cooley–Tukey algorithm)

Input. $v=(n_1, \ldots, n_d)$, $h\in\{1, \ldots, d-1\}$, an n-th primitive root of unity ω, and $a=(a_0,\ldots,a_{n-1})\in\mathbb{K}^n$.

Output. $\mathrm{DFT}_{\omega,v}(a)$, stored in a.

1. For $j\in\{0,\ldots,m_2-1\}$ do
   Let $b=(a_j, a_{j+m_2},\ldots,a_{j+(m_1-1)m_2})$
   Compute $c=\mathrm{DFT}_{\omega^{m_2},v_1}(b)$
   Replace a_{j+im_2} by c_i for all $i\in\{0,\ldots,m_1-1\}$
2. For $i\in\{0,\ldots,m_1-1\}$ and $j\in\{0,\ldots,m_2-1\}$ do
   Replace a_{j+im_2} by $a_{j+im_2}\omega^{[i]_{v_1}j}$
3. For $i\in\{0,\ldots,m_1-1\}$ do
   Let $b=(a_{im_2}, a_{im_2+1},\ldots,a_{im_2+m_2-1})$
   Compute $c=\mathrm{DFT}_{\omega^{m_1},v_2}(b)$
   Replace a_{j+im_2} by c_j for all $j\in\{0,\ldots,m_2-1\}$

PROPOSITION 1. *Algorithm 1 is correct.*

PROOF. Let α, β, γ be the successive values of the vector a at the end of steps 1, 2, and 3. We have $\alpha_{j+im_2}=\sum_{k=0}^{m_1-1}a_{j+km_2}\,\omega^{km_2[i]_{v_1}}$, $\beta_{j+im_2}=\alpha_{j+im_2}\,\omega^{[i]_{v_1}j}$, and $\gamma_{j+im_2}=\sum_{l=0}^{m_2-1}\beta_{l+im_2}\,\omega^{lm_1[j]_{v_2}}$. It follows that $\gamma_{j+im_2}=\sum_{l=0}^{m_2-1}\sum_{k=0}^{m_1-1}a_{l+km_2}\,\omega^{km_2[i]_{v_1}}\,\omega^{[i]_{v_1}l}\,\omega^{lm_1[j]_{v_2}}=\sum_{l=0}^{m_2-1}\sum_{k=0}^{m_1-1}a_{l+km_2}\,\omega^{(km_2+l)[i]_{v_1}+lm_1[j]_{v_2}}$. The conclusion follows from $[j+i\,m_2]_v=[i]_{v_1}+m_1\,[j]_{v_2}$, which implies $(l+k\,m_2)\,[i]_{v_1}+l\,m_1\,[j]_{v_2}\equiv[j+i\,m_2]_v\,(l+k\,m_2) \bmod n$. □

Notice that the order of the output depends on v, but not on h. If the input vector is stored in a contiguous segment of memory, then the first step of Algorithm 1 may be seen as an $m_1\times m_2$ matrix transposition, followed by m_2 in-place DFTs of size m_1 on contiguous data. Then the transposition is inverted. The constants $\omega^{[i]_{v_1}j}$ in step 2 are often called *twiddle factors*. Transpositions affect the performance of the strided DFTs when input sizes do not fit in the last level cache memory of the processor.

For better locality, the multiplications by twiddle factors in step 2 are actually merged into step 3, and all the necessary primitive roots and fixed multiplicands (including the twiddle factors) are pre-computed once, and cached in memory. We finally notice that the inverse DFT can be computed straightforwardly by inverting Algorithm 1.

In addition to the Cooley–Tukey algorithm we shall also use the method attributed to *Good* and *Thomas* [17, 35], and that saves all the multiplications by the twiddle factors. First it requires the n_i to be pairwise coprime, and second, input and output data must be re-indexed. The rest is identical to Algorithm 1—see [8], for instance, for complete formulas. With $\mathbb{F}_{2^{60}}$, the condition on the n_i fails only when two n_i are 3 or 5. In such a case, it is sufficient to replace v by a new vector where the two occurrences of 3 (resp. of 5) are replaced by 9 (resp. by 25), and to modify the re-indexing accordingly. In sizes 9 and 25, we build codelets upon the Cooley–Tukey formulas. A specific codelet for $n = (3\ 5)^2$ might further improve performance, but we did not implement this yet. We hardcoded the re-indexing into codelets, and we restrict to using the Good–Thomas algorithm up to sizes that fit into the cache memory. We shall discuss later the relative performance between these two DFT algorithms.

2.2 Rader reduction

When the recurrence of the Cooley–Tukey algorithm ends with a DFT of prime size n, then we may use Rader's algorithm [31] to reduce such a DFT to a cyclic polynomial product by a fixed multiplicand.

In fact, let $\mu = n-1$, let γ be a generator of the multiplicative group of $\mathbb{Z}/n\,\mathbb{Z}$, and let η be its modular inverse. We let $B(x) = \sum_{i=0}^{\mu-1} a_{\gamma^i \operatorname{rem} n}\, x^i$ and $W(x) = \sum_{i=0}^{\mu-1} \omega^{\eta^i \operatorname{rem} n}\, x^i$, and we compute $C(x) = B(x)\, W(x) \operatorname{rem} (x^\mu - 1)$. The coefficient c_i of x^i in $C(x)$ equals $\sum_{j=1}^{n-1} a_j\, \omega^{(\eta^i j) \operatorname{rem} n}$. Consequently we have $\mathrm{DFT}_{\omega,n}(a) = (\sum_{j=0}^{n-1} a_j,\ a_0 + c_{\sigma(1)-1},\ \ldots,\ a_0 + c_{\sigma(\mu)-1})$, where σ is the permutation of $\{1, \ldots, \mu\}$ defined by $\sigma(\eta^i \operatorname{rem} \mu) = i$. In this way, the DFT of a reduces to one cyclic product of size μ, by the fixed multiplicand W.

Remark. Bluestein reduction [2] allows for the conversion of DFTs into cyclic products even when n is not prime. In [20], this is crucially used for controlling the size n of recursive DFTs. This suggests that Bluestein reduction might be useful in practice for DFTs of small composite orders, say $n \leqslant 50$. For DFTs over $\mathbb{F}_{2^{60}}$, this turns out to be wrong: so far, the strategies to be described in Section 3 are more efficient.

2.3 Implementation framework

Throughout this article, we consider a platform equipped with an INTEL(R) CORE(TM) i7-4770 CPU at 3.40 GHz and 8 GB of 1600 MHz DDR3 memory, which features AVX2 and CLMUL technologies (family number 6 and model number 0x3C). The platform runs the JESSIE GNU DEBIAN operating system with a 64 bit LINUX kernel version 3.14. Care has been taken to avoid *CPU throttling* and *Turbo Boost* issues while measuring timings. We compiled with GCC [15] version 4.9.2.

In order to efficiently and easily benefit from AVX and CLMUL instruction sets, we decided to implement the lowest level of our DFTs directly in assembly code. In fact there is no standard way to take full advantage of these technologies within languages such as C and C++, where current SIMD types are not even *bona fide*. It is true that programming *via intrinsics* [26] is a reasonable compromise, but there remain a certain number of technical pitfalls such as memory alignment, register allocation, and instruction latency management.

For our convenience we developed *dynamic compilation* features (also known as *just in time* compilation) from scratch, dedicated to high performance computing within MATHEMAGIX (`http://www.mathemagix.org`). It is only used to tune assembly code for DFTs of orders a few thousands. Our implementation in the RUNTIME library partially supports the x86, SSE, and AVX instruction sets for the AMD64 *application binary interface*—missing instructions can be added easily. This of course suits most personal computers and computation clusters.

The efficiency of an SSE or AVX instruction is not easy to determine. It depends on the types of its arguments, and is usually measured in terms of latency and throughput. In ideal conditions, the *latency* is the number of CPU clock cycles needed to make the result of an instruction available to another instruction; the *reciprocal throughput*, sometimes called *issue latency*, is the (fractional) number of cycles needed to actually perform the computation—for brevity, we drop "reciprocal". For detailed definitions we refer the reader to [26], and also to [9] for useful additional comments.

In this article, we shall only use AVX-128 instructions, and 128-bit registers are denoted `xmm0`,..., `xmm15` (our code is thus compatible with the previous generation of processors). A 128-bit register may be seen as a vector of two 64-bit integers, that are said to be *packed* in it. We provide unfamiliar readers with typical examples for our aforementioned processor, with cost estimates, and using the INTEL syntax, where the destination is the first argument of instructions:

- `vmovq` loads/stores 64-bits integers from/to memory. `vmovdqu` loads/stores packed 64-bits integers not necessary aligned to 256-bit boundaries. `vmovdqa` is similar to `vmovdqu` when data is aligned on a 256-bit boundary; it is also used for moving data between registers. Latencies of these instructions are between 1 and 4, and throughputs vary between 0.3 and 1.
- `vpand`, `vpor`, and `vpxor` respectively correspond to bitwise "and", "or" and "xor" operations. Latencies are 1 and throughputs are 0.33 or 0.5.
- `vpsllq` and `vpsrlq` respectively perform left and right logical shifts on 64-bit packed integers, with latency 1 or 2, and throughput 1. We shall also use `vpunpckhqdq xmm1, xmm2, xmm3/m128` to unpack and interleave in `xmm1` the 64-bit integers from the high half of `xmm2` and `xmm3/m128`, with latency and throughput 1. Here, `xmm1`, `xmm2`, and `xmm3` do not mean that the instruction only acts on these specific registers: instead, the indices 1, 2, and 3 actually refer to argument positions. In addition, the notation `xmm3/m128` means that the third argument may be either a register or an address pointing to 128-bit data to be read from the memory.
- `vpclmulqdq xmm1, xmm2, xmm3/m128, imm8` carry-less multiplies two 64-bit integers, selected from `xmm2` and `xmm3/m128` according to the constant integer `imm8`, and stores the result into `xmm1`. The value 0 for `imm8` means that the multiplicands are the 64-bit integers from the low half of `xmm2` and `xmm3/m128`. Mathematically speaking, this corresponds to multiplying two polynomials in $\mathbb{F}_2[x]$ of degrees <64, which are packed into integers: such a polynomial is thus represented by a 64-bit integer, whose i-th bit corresponds to the coefficient of degree i. This instruction has latency 7 and throughput 2. This high latency constitutes an important issue when optimizing the assembly code. This will be discussed later.

3. DFTs OVER $\mathbb{F}_{2^{60}}$

In order to perform DFTs efficiently, we are interested in finite fields $\mathbb{F}_{2^k}$ such that $2^k - 1$ admits many small prime factors. This is typically the case [20] when k admits many small prime factors itself. Our favorite example is $k=60$, also because 60 is only slightly smaller than the bit size 64 of registers on modern architectures.

Using the eight smallest prime divisors of $2^{60}-1$ allows us to perform DFTs up to size $3^2 \cdot 5^2 \cdot 7 \cdot 11 \cdot 13 \cdot 31 \cdot 41 \cdot 61 = 17461919475$, which is sufficiently large for most of the applications. We thus begin with building DFTs in size 3, 5, 7, 11, 13, 31, 41, 61, and then combine them using the Good–Thomas and Cooley–Tukey algorithms.

3.1 Basic arithmetic in $\mathbb{F}_{2^{60}}$

The other key advantage of $k=60$ is the following defining polynomial $P(z) = (z^{61}-1)/(z-1) \in \mathbb{F}_2[z]$. Elements of $\mathbb{F}_{2^{60}}$ will thus be seen as polynomials in $\mathbb{F}_2[z]$ modulo P.

For multiplying a and b in $\mathbb{F}_{2^{60}}$, we perform the product $\tilde{a}\,\tilde{b}$ of the preimage polynomials, so that the preimage $\tilde{c}$ of $c = a\,b$ may be obtained as follows

$$\tilde{c} = ((\tilde{a}\,\tilde{b}) \operatorname{rem} (z^{61}-1)) \operatorname{rem} P.$$

The remainder by $z^{61}-1$ may be performed efficiently by using bit shifts and bitwise xor. The final division by P corresponds to a single conditional subtraction of P.

In order to decrease the reduction cost, we allow an even more redundant representation satisfying the minimal requirement that data sizes are $\leqslant 64$ bits. If $\tilde{a}, \tilde{b} \in \mathbb{F}_2[z]$ have degrees <64, then $\tilde{c} = \tilde{a}\,\tilde{b}$ may be reduced in-place by $z^{64}-z^3$, using the following macro, where xmm1 denotes any auxiliary register, and xmm0 represents a register different from xmm1 that contains $\tilde{c}$:

```
vpunpckhqdq xmm1, xmm0, xmm0
vpsllq xmm1, xmm1, 3
vpxor xmm0, xmm0, xmm1
```

In input xmm0 contains the 128-bit packed polynomial, and its 64-bit reduction is stored in its low half in output. Let us mention from here that our implementation does not yet fully exploit vector instructions of the SIMD unit. In fact we only use the 64-bit low half of the 128-bit registers, except for DFTs of small orders as explained in the next paragraphs.

3.2 DFTs of small prime orders

In size $n=3$, it is classical that a DFT needs only one product and one reduction: $\mathrm{DFT}_{\omega,(3)}(a) = (a_0+a_1+a_2, a_0+(a_1+a_2)\,\omega+a_2, a_0+a_1+(a_1+a_2)\,\omega)$. This strategy generalizes to larger n as follows, *via* the Rader reduction of Section 2.2, that involves a product of the form

$$C(x) = \left(\sum_{i=0}^{\mu-1} b_i\,x^i\right)\left(\sum_{i=0}^{\mu-1} w_i\,x^i\right) \operatorname{rem} (x^\mu - 1). \qquad (1)$$

The coefficient c_i of degree i of C satisfies:

$$c_i = \sum_{\substack{(k+l) \operatorname{rem} \mu = i \\ k<l}} (b_k+b_l)\,(w_k+w_l) + \sum_{k=0}^{\mu-1} b_k\,w_k. \qquad (2)$$

This amounts to $\mu + \mu\,(\mu-1)/2$ products, μ^2 sums (even less if the $w_k + w_l$ are pre-computed), and μ reductions.

We handcrafted these formulas in registers for $n=3, 5, 7$. Products are computed by vpclmulqdq. They are not reduced immediately. Instead we perform bitwise arithmetic on 128-bit registers, so that reductions to 64-bit integers are postponed to the end. The following table counts instructions of each type. Precomputed constants are mostly read from memory and not stored in registers. The last column *cycles* contains the number of CPU clock cycles, measured with the CPU instruction rdtsc, when running the DFT code in-place on contiguous data already present in the level 1 cache memory.

n	clmul	shift	xor	move	cycles
3	1	2	7	6	19
5	10	8	22	10	37
7	21	12	45	14	58

For $n \geqslant 11$, these computations do not fit into the 16 registers, and using auxiliary memory introduces unwanted overhead. This is why we prefer to use the method described in the next subsection.

3.3 DFTs of larger prime orders

For larger DFTs we still use the Rader reduction (1) but it is worth using Karatsuba's method instead of formula (2). Let $\eta = \mu \operatorname{quo} 2$, and let $\delta_\mu = 1$ if μ is odd and 0 otherwise. We decompose $B(x) = B_0(x) + x^\eta\,B_1(x) + \delta_\mu\,b_{\mu-1}\,x^{\mu-1}$, and $W(x) = W_0(x) + x^\eta\,W_1(x) + \delta_\mu\,w_{\mu-1}\,x^{\mu-1}$, where B_0, B_1, W_0, W_1 have degrees $\leqslant \eta - 1$. Then $B(x)\,W(x)$ may be computed as $C_0(x) + x^\eta\,C_1(x) + x^{2\eta}\,C_2(x) + \delta_\mu\,(b_{\mu-1}\,W(x) + w_{\mu-1}\,B(x))$, where $C_0(x) = B_0(x)\,W_0(x)$, $C_2(x) = B_1(x)\,W_1(x)$, and $C_1(x) = (B_0(x)+B_1(x))\,(W_0(x)+W_1(x)) - C_0(x) - C_2(x)$ are obtained by the Karatsuba algorithm.

If μ is odd, then during the recursive calls for C_0, C_1, C_2, we collect $b_i\,w_i$, for $0 \leqslant i < 2\,\eta$. Then we compute $b_{\mu-1}\,w_{\mu-1}$, so that the needed $b_{\mu-1}\,w_i + w_{\mu-1}\,b_i$ are obtained as $(b_{\mu-1}+b_i)\,(w_{\mu-1}+w_i) - b_{\mu-1}\,w_{\mu-1} - b_i\,w_i$.

During the recursive calls, reductions of products are discarded, and sums are performed over 128 bits. The total number of reductions at the end thus equals μ. We use these formulas for $n = 11, 13, 31, 41, 61$. For $n = 5, 7$ this approach leads to fewer products than with the previous method, but the number of sums and moves is higher, as reported in the following table:

n	clmul	shift	xor	move	cycles
5	9	8	34	52	63
7	18	12	76	83	83
11	42	20	184	120	220
13	54	24	244	239	450
31	270	60	1300	971	2300
41	378	80	1798	1156	3000
61	810	120	3988	2927	7300

For readability only the two most significant figures are reported in column *cycles*. The measurements typically vary by up to about 10%. It might be possible to further improve these timings by polishing register allocation, decreasing temporary memory, reducing latency effects, or even by trying other strategies [1, 3].

3.4 DFTs of composite orders

As long as the input data and the pre-computed constants fit into the level 3 cache of the processor (in our case, 8 MB), we may simply unfold Algorithm 1: we do not transpose-copy data in step 1, but rather implement DFT codelets of small prime orders, with suitable input and output strides. For instance, in size $n = 3 \cdot 5$, we perform five in-place DFTs of order 3 with stride 5, namely on (a_0, a_5, a_{10}), (a_1, a_6, a_{11}), ..., (a_4, a_9, a_{14}), then we multiply by those twiddle factors not equal to 1, and finally, we do three in-place DFTs of size 5 and stride 1. In order to minimize the effect of the latency of `vpclmulqdq`, carry-less products by twiddle factors and reductions may be organized in groups of 8, so that the result of each product is available when arriving at its corresponding reduction instructions. More precisely, if `rdi` contains the current address to entries in a, and `rsi` the current address to the twiddle factors, then 8 entry-wise products are performed as follows:

```
vmovq xmm0, [rdi+8*0]
vmovq xmm1, [rdi+8*1]
  ...
vmovq xmm7, [rdi+8*7]
vpclmulqdq xmm0, xmm0, [rsi+8*0], 0
vpclmulqdq xmm1, xmm1, [rsi+8*1], 0
  ...
vpclmulqdq xmm7, xmm7, [rsi+8*7], 0
```

Then the contents of xmm0,...,xmm7 are reduced in sequence modulo $z^{64} - z^3$, and finally the results are stored into memory.

Up to sizes $n < 10\,000$ made from primes $\leqslant 41$, we generated executable codes for the Cooley–Tukey algorithm, and measured timings for all the possible orderings v. This revealed that increasing orders, namely $n_1 \leqslant n_2 \leqslant \cdots \leqslant n_d$, yield the best performances. In size $n = 3 \cdot 5 \cdot 7 \cdot 11 = 1155$, one transform takes 44000 CPU cycles, among which 9000 are spent in multiplications by twiddle factors. We implemented the Good–Thomas algorithm in the same way as for Cooley–Tukey, and concluded that it is always faster when data fit into the cache memory. When $n = 1155$, this leads to only 38000 cycles for one transform, for which carry-less products contribute 40%.

For each size $m < 10000$, we then deduced the smallest DFT size $n \geqslant m$, together with the best ordering, leading to the fastest calculation *via* the Good–Thomas algorithm. The graph in Figure 1 represents the number of CPU cycles in terms of m obtained in this way. Thanks to the variety of prime orders, the staircase effect is softer than with the classical FFT.

For sizes n larger than a few thousands, using internal DFTs of prime size with large strides is of course a bad idea in terms of memory management. The classical technique, going back to [16], and now known as the *4-step* or *6-step* FFT in the literature, consists in decomposing n into $m_1\, m_2$ such that m_1 and m_2 are of order of magnitude $\sqrt{n}$. In the context of Algorithm 1, with $v = (n_1, \ldots, n_d)$, and $n = n_1 \cdots n_d$, we need to determine $h \in \{1, \ldots, d\}$ such that $m_1 = n_1 \cdots n_h$ and $m_2 = n_{h+1} \cdots n_d$ are the closest to $\sqrt{n}$.

As previously mentioned, for large values of m_1, m_2, step 1 of Algorithm 1 decomposes into the transposition of a $m_1 \times m_2$ matrix (in column representation), followed by m_2 in-place DFTs of size m_1 on contiguous data. Then the transposition is performed backward. In the classical case of the FFT, m_1 and m_2 are powers of two that satisfy $m_1 = m_2$ or $m_1 = 2\, m_2$, and efficient cache-friendly and cache-oblivious solutions are known to transpose such $m_2 \times m_2$ matrices in-place with AVX2 instructions. Unfortunately, we were not able to do so in our present situation. Consequently we simply transpose rows in groups of 4 into a fixed temporary buffer of size $4\, m_2$. Then we may perform 4 DFTs of size m_2 on contiguous data, and finally transpose backward. The threshold for our 4-step DFTs has been estimated in the neighborhood of 7000.

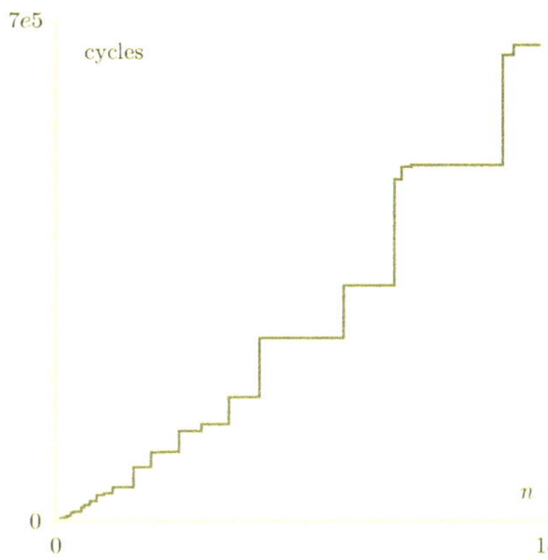

Figure 1. Timings for DFT over $\mathbb{F}_{2^{60}}$, in CPU cycles.

4. OTHER GROUND FIELDS

Usually, fast polynomial multiplication over $\mathbb{F}_2$ is used as the basic building block for other fast polynomial arithmetic over finite fields in characteristic two. It is natural to ask whether we may use our fast multiplication over $\mathbb{F}_{2^{60}}$ as the basic building block. Above all, this requires an efficient way to reduce multiplications in $\mathbb{F}_{2^k}[x]$ with $k \neq 60$ to multiplications in $\mathbb{F}_{2^{60}}[x]$. The optimal algorithms vary greatly with k. In this section, we discuss various possible strategies. Timings are reported for some of them in the next section. In the following paragraphs, $a, b \in \mathbb{F}_{2^k}[x]$ represent the two polynomials of degrees $<d$ to be multiplied, and $P_k \in \mathbb{F}_2[z]$ is the defining polynomial of $\mathbb{F}_{2^k}$ over $\mathbb{F}_2$.

4.1 Lifting and Kronecker segmentation

Case when $k = 1$. In order to multiply two packed polynomials in $\mathbb{F}_2[x]$, we use standard *Kronecker segmentation* and cut the input polynomials into slices of 30 bits. More precisely, we set $m = \lceil d/30 \rceil$, $A(y, x) = \sum_{i=0}^{m-1} \sum_{j=0}^{29} a_{30i+j}\, x^j\, y^i$ and $B(y, x) = \sum_{i=0}^{m-1} \sum_{j=0}^{29} b_{30i+j}\, x^j\, y^i$, so that $a(x) = A(x^{30}, x)$ and $b(x) = B(x^{30}, x)$. The product $c = a\, b$ then satisfies $c(x) = C(x^{30}, x)$, where $C = A\, B$. We are thus led to multiply A by B in $\mathbb{F}_{2^{60}}[x]$ by reinterpreting y as the generator of $\mathbb{F}_{2^{60}}$. In terms of the input size, this method admits a constant overhead factor of roughly 2. In fact, when considering algorithms with asymptotically softly linear cost, comparing relative input sizes gives a relevant approximation of the relative costs.

General strategies. It is well known that one can handle any value of k by reduction to the case $k = 1$. Basically, $\mathbb{F}_{2^k}$ is seen as $\mathbb{F}_2[z] / (P_k(z))$, and a product in $\mathbb{F}_{2^k}[x]$ is lifted to one product in degree $<d$ in $\mathbb{F}_2[z][x]$, with coefficients of degrees $<k$ in z, followed by $2\,d - 1$ divisions by $P_k(z)$. Then, the *Kronecker substitution* [14, Chapter 8] reduces the computation of one such product in $\mathbb{F}_2[z][x]$, said in *bi-degree* $<(k, d)$, to one product in $\mathbb{F}_2[x]$ in degree $<(2\,k - 1)\,d$. In total, we obtain a general strategy to reduce one product in degree $<d$ in $\mathbb{F}_{2^k}$ to one product in $\mathbb{F}_{2^{60}}[x]$ in degree $\leqslant \lceil ((2\,k-1)\,d)/30 \rceil$, plus $O(d\, \mathsf{M}_{2^k}(1))$ bit operations. Roughly speaking, this approach increases input bit sizes by a factor at most 4 in general, but only 3 when $k = 2$.

Instead of Kronecker substitution, we may alternatively use classical *evaluation/interpolation schemes* [23, Section 2]. Informally speaking, a multiplication in $\mathbb{F}_{2^k}[x]$ in degree $<d$ is still regarded as a multiplication of $\tilde{a}$ and $\tilde{b}$ in $\mathbb{F}_2[z][x]$ of bi-degrees $<(k, d)$, but we "specialize" the variable z at sufficiently many "points" in a suitable ring $\mathbb{A}$, then perform products in $\mathbb{A}[x]$ of degrees $<d$, and finally we "interpolate" the coefficients of $\tilde{a}\,\tilde{b}$.

The classical Karatsuba transform is such a scheme. For instance, if $k = 2$ then $\alpha(z) = \alpha_0 + \alpha_1 z$ is sent to $(\alpha_0, \alpha_0 + \alpha_1, \alpha_1)$, which corresponds to the projective evaluation at $(0, 1, \infty)$. The size overhead of this reduction is 3, but its advantage to the preceding general strategy is the splitting of the initial product into smaller independent products. The Karatsuba transform can be iterated, and even Toom–Cook transforms of [3] might be used to handle small values of k.

Another standard evaluation scheme concerns the case when k is sufficiently large. Each coefficient $\alpha(z)$ of $\tilde{a}$, $\tilde{b}$ is "evaluated" *via* one DFT of size $n \geqslant \lceil (2\,k - 1) / 30 \rceil$ applied to the Kronecker segmentation of $\alpha(z)$ into slices of 30 bits seen in $\mathbb{F}_{2^{60}}[y]$. Then we perform n products in $\mathbb{F}_{2^{60}}[x]$ in degree $<d$, and "interpolate" the output coefficients by means of inverse DFTs. Asymptotically, the size overhead is again 4.

The rest of this section is devoted to other reduction strategies involving a size growth less than 4 in various particular cases.

4.2 Field embedding

Case when $k \mid 60$. When $k \geqslant 2$ and $k \mid 60$, which corresponds to $k = 2, 3, 4, 5, 6, 10, 12, 15, 20, 30$, we may embed $\mathbb{F}_{2^k}$ into $\mathbb{F}_{2^{60}}$, by regarding $\mathbb{F}_{2^{60}}$ as a field extension of $\mathbb{F}_{2^k}$. The input polynomials are now cut into slices of degrees $<m$ with $m = \lfloor (60/k + 1)/2 \rfloor$. The overhead of this method is asymptotically $60 / (m\,k) \leqslant 2$. If $k = 4, 12, 20$, then $60 / k$ is odd, $m = (60 / k + 1) / 2$, and the overhead is <2. In particular it is only $3/2$ for $k = 20$.

Let Q be an irreducible factor of P in $\mathbb{F}_{2^k}[x]$, of degree $60/k$. Elements of $\mathbb{F}_{2^{60}}$ can thus be represented by polynomials of degrees $<60 / k$ in $\mathbb{F}_{2^k}[y]$, modulo Q, *via* the following isomorphism $\Phi: \mathbb{F}_2[z, y] / (P_k(z), \check{Q}(z, y)) \rightarrow \mathbb{F}_2[z] / (P(z))$, where $\check{Q}(z, y)$ represents the canonical preimage of Q in $\mathbb{F}_2[z, y]$. Let $f(z, y)$ be a polynomial of bi-degree $<(k, m)$ representing an element of $\mathbb{F}_{2^k}[y]$, obtained as a slice of a or b. The image $\Phi(f)$ can be obtained as $f(\Phi(z), \Phi(y))$. Consequently, if we pre-compute $\Phi(z^j\,y^i)$ for all $j < k$ and $i < m$, then deducing $\Phi(f)$ requires 59 sums in $\mathbb{F}_2[z] / (P(z))$.

The number of sums may be decreased by using larger look-up tables. Let $b_0, \ldots, b_{59}$ represent the basis $z^j\,y^i$ for $j < k$ and $i < m$, whatever the order is. Then all the $\{\Phi(\sum_{j=0}^{5} \beta_{6i+j}\,b_{6i+j}) | \, (\beta_{6i}, \ldots, \beta_{6i+5}) \in \mathbb{F}_2^6\}$ for $0 \leqslant i < 10$ can be stored in 10 look-up tables of size 64, which allows $\Phi(f)$ to be computed using 9 sums. Of course the cost for reordering and packing bits of elements of $\mathbb{F}_{2^k}[y]$ must be taken into account, and sizes of look-up tables must be carefully adjusted in terms of k. The details are omitted.

Conversely, let $g \in \mathbb{F}_2[z] / (P(z))$. We wish to compute $\Phi^{-1}(g)$. As for direct images of Φ, we may pre-compute $\Phi^{-1}(z^i)$ for all $i < 60$ and reduce the computation of $\Phi^{-1}(g)$ to 59 sums in $\mathbb{F}[z, y] / (P_k(z), \check{Q}(z, y))$. Larger look-up tables can again help to reduce the number of sums.

Let us mention that the use of look-up tables cannot benefit from SIMD technologies. On the current platform this is not yet a problem: fully vectorized arithmetic in $\mathbb{F}_{2^{60}}[z, y] / (P_k(z), \check{Q}(z, y))$ would also require SIMD versions of carry-less multiplication which are not available at present.

Case when $\gcd(60, k) \geqslant 2$. We may combine the previous strategies when k is not coprime with 60. Let $t = \gcd(60, k)$. We rewrite elements of $\mathbb{F}_{2^k}[x]$ into polynomials in $\mathbb{F}_{2^t}[y][x]$ of bi-degrees $<(k / t, d)$, and then use the Kronecker substitution to reduce to one product in $\mathbb{F}_{2^t}[x]$ in degree $(2\,k / t - 1)\,d$. For example, when $60 \mid k$, elements of $\mathbb{F}_{2^k}$ may be represented by polynomials in $\mathbb{F}_{2^{60}}[y]$. We are thus led to multiplying polynomials in $\mathbb{F}_{2^{60}}[y][x]$ in bi-degree $<(k / 60, d)$, which yields an overhead of 2. Another favorable case is when $20 \mid k$, yielding an overhead of 3.

4.3 Double-lifting

When $k \leqslant 30$, we may of course directly lift products in $\mathbb{F}_{2^k}[x]$ to products in $\mathbb{F}_2[z][x]$ of output degree in z at most 58. The latter products may thus be computed as products in $\mathbb{F}_{2^{60}}[x]$. This strategy has an overhead of $60 / k$, so it outperforms the general strategies for $k \geqslant 16$.

For $31 \leqslant k \leqslant 59$, we lift products to $\mathbb{F}_2[z][x]$ and multiply in $(\mathbb{F}_2[z] / (P(z)))[x]$ and $(\mathbb{F}_2[z] / (P(z+1)))[x]$. We then perform Chinese remaindering to deduce the product modulo $P(z)\,P(z+1)$. Multiplying A and B in $(\mathbb{F}[z] / (P(z+1)))[x]$ may be obtained as $(A(z+1, x)\,B(z+1, x) \operatorname{rem} P(z))(z+1)$. In this way all relies on the same DFT routines over $\mathbb{F}_{2^{60}}$.

If $\alpha(z) \in \mathbb{F}_2[z]$ has degree $<l$, with l a power of 2, we decompose $\alpha(z) = \alpha_0(z) + z^{l/2}\,\alpha_1(z)$ with α_0 and α_1 of degrees $<l / 2$, then $\alpha(z + 1)$ is obtained efficiently by the following induction:

$$\begin{aligned} \alpha(z+1) &= \alpha_0(z+1) + (z+1)^{l/2}\,\alpha_1(z+1) \qquad (3) \\ &= \alpha_0(z+1) + \alpha_1(z+1) + z^{l/2}\,\alpha_1(z+1). \end{aligned}$$

Chinese remaindering can also be done efficiently. Let $U(z) = z^2 + 1$ be the inverse of $P(z + 1)$ modulo $P(z)$. Residues $\gamma_0(z) \bmod P(z)$ and $\gamma_1(z) \bmod P(z+1)$ then lift into $\gamma_1(z) + (U(z)\,(\gamma_0(z) - \gamma_1(z)) \operatorname{rem} P(z))\,P(z+1)$ modulo $P(z)\,P(z + 1)$. Since $\deg \gamma_i \leqslant 58$, this formula involves only one carry-less product. Asymptotically, the overhead of this method is $2 < 120 / k < 4$.

On our platform, formula (3) may be implemented in degree <64 as follows. Assume that `xmm0` contains `101010...10`, `xmm1` contains `11001100...1100`, `xmm2` contains `11110000...11110000`, ..., and `xmm5` is filled with `11...1100...00`. Then, using `xmm15` for input and output, we simply do

```
vpand xmm14, xmm15, xmm0
vpsrlq xmm14, xmm14, 1
vpxor xmm15, xmm14, xmm15
vpand xmm14, xmm15, xmm1
vpsrlq xmm14, xmm14, 2
vpxor xmm15, xmm14, xmm15
...
vpand xmm14, xmm15, xmm5
vpsrlq xmm14, xmm14, 32
vpxor xmm15, xmm14, xmm15
```

4.4 The Crandall–Fagin reduction

For "lucky" $60 < k < 2^{30}$ such that $(x^{k+1} - 1) / (x - 1)$ is irreducible over $\mathbb{F}_2$, multiplication in $\mathbb{F}_{2^k}$ reduces to cyclic multiplication over $\mathbb{F}_2$ of length $k + 1$. Using our adaptation [20] of Crandall–Fagin's algorithm [6], multiplying two polynomials of degrees $<d$ in $\mathbb{F}_{2^k}[x]$ therefore reduces to one product in $(\mathbb{F}_{2^{60}}[y]/(y^m-1))[x]$ in degree $<d$, where m is the first integer such that $\lceil (k+1)/m \rceil \leqslant 30$. The asymptotic overhead of this method is ≈ 2. This strategy generalizes to the case when P_k divides $x^{k+r}-1$, with $r \ll k$.

For various $k > 60$, the polynomial $(x^{k+1}-1)/(x-1)$ factors into r irreducible polynomials of degree k/r. In that case, we may use the previous strategy to reduce r products in $\mathbb{F}_{2^{k/r}}[x]$ to multiplications in $\mathbb{F}_{2^{60}}[x]$, using r different defining polynomials of $\mathbb{F}_{2^{k/r}}$. Asymptotically, the overhead reaches again ≈ 2, although working with different defining polynomials of $\mathbb{F}_{2^{k/r}}$ probably involves another non trivial overhead in practice. Again, the strategy generalizes to the case when $(x^{k+1}-1)/(x-1)$ admits r irreducible factors of degree $k/r-\delta$ with $\delta \ll k/r$.

5. TIMINGS

Our polynomial products are implemented in the JUSTINLINE library of MATHEMAGIX. The source code is freely available from revision 10434 of our SVN server (`http://gforge.inria.fr/projects/mmx/`). Sources for DFTs over $\mathbb{F}_{2^{60}}$ are in the file `dft_f2_60_amd64_avx_clmul.mmx`. Those for our polynomial products in $\mathbb{F}_{2^k}[x]$ are in `polynomial_f2k_amd64_avx_clmul.mmx`. Let us recall here that MATHEMAGIX functions can also be easily exported to C++ [24]. We use version 1.1 of the GF2X library, tuned to our platform during installation. The top level function, named `gf2x_mul`, multiplies packed polynomials in $\mathbb{F}_2[x]$, and makes use of the carry-less product instruction. Triadic variants of the Schönhage–Strassen algorithm start to be used from degree $64 \cdot 6485$. GF2X can be used from versions $\geqslant 5.5$ of the NTL library [34], that uses Kronecker substitution to multiply in $\mathbb{F}_{2^k}[x]$. Consequently, we do not need to compare to NTL. We also compare to FLINT 2.5.2, tuned according to §13 of the documentation.

5.1 $\mathbb{F}_2[x]$ and $\mathbb{F}_{2^{60}}[x]$

Table 1 displays timings for multiplying polynomials of degrees $<d$ in $\mathbb{F}_{2^{60}}[x]$. The row "us" concerns the natural product *via* DFTs, the other row is the running time of `gf2x_mul` used to multiply polynomials in $\mathbb{F}_2[x]$ built from Kronecker substitution.

In Table 2, we report on timings for multiplying polynomials of degrees $<d$ in $\mathbb{F}_2[x]$. The row "us" concerns our DFT based implementation *via* Kronecker segmentation, as recalled in Section 4.1. The row GF2X is the running time for the direct call to `gf2x_mul`. The row FLINT concerns the performance of the function `nmod_poly_mul`, which reduces to products in $\mathbb{Z}[x]$ *via* Kronecker substitution. Since the packed representation is not implemented, we could not obtain timings until the end. This comparison is not intended to be fair, but rather to show unfamiliar readers why dedicated algorithms for $\mathbb{F}_2[x]$ may be worth it.

In both cases, our DFT based products turn out to be more efficient than the triadic version of the Schönhage–Strassen of GF2X, for large degrees. One major advantage of the DFT based approach concerns linear algebra. Instead of multiplying $r \times r$ matrices over $\mathbb{F}_{2^{60}}[x]$ naively in time $O(r^3 \mathsf{M}_{2^{60}}(d))$, we compute the $3r^2$ DFTs and $\approx 2d$ products of $r \times r$ matrices over $\mathbb{F}_{2^{60}}$, in time $O(r^2 \mathsf{M}_{2^{60}}(d) + r^3 d)$. Matrix multiplication over $\mathbb{F}_{2^k}[x]$ is reduced to matrix multiplication over $\mathbb{F}_{2^{60}}[x]$ using similar techniques as in Section 4. Timings for matrices over $\mathbb{F}_2[x]$, reported in Table 3, confirm the practical gain.

$\log_2 d$	16	17	18	19	20	21
us	13	28	52	140	290	640
GF2X	79	160	400	800	1600	3500

Table 1. Products in degree $<d$ in $\mathbb{F}_{2^{60}}[x]$, in milliseconds.

$\log_2 d/64$	16	17	18	19	20	21
us	29	70	170	300	730	1300
GF2X	39	89	190	490	900	2100
FLINT	840	2200	4400	11000	...	

Table 2. Products in degree $<d$ in $\mathbb{F}_2[x]$, in milliseconds.

r	1	2	4	8	16	32
us	29	120	500	2200	9800	48000
GF2X	39	320	2500	20000	160000	1300000

Table 3. Products of $r \times r$ matrices over $\mathbb{F}_2[x]$, in degree $<64 \cdot 2^{16}$, in milliseconds.

5.2 $\mathbb{F}_4[x]$ and $\mathbb{F}_{2^{59}}[x]$

Table 4 displays timings for multiplying polynomials of degrees $<d$ in $\mathbb{F}_{2^{59}}[x]$. The row "us" concerns the *double-lifting* strategy of Section 4.3. The next row is the running time of `gf2x_mul` used to multiply polynomials in $\mathbb{F}_2[x]$ built from Kronecker substitution. As expected, timings for GF2X are similar to those of Table 1, and the overhead with respect to $\mathbb{F}_{2^{60}}$ is close to 2. Overall, our implementation is about twice as fast than *via* GF2X.

Table 5 finally concerns our implementation of the strategy from Section 4.2 for products in degree $<d$ in $\mathbb{F}_4[x]$. As expected, timings are similar to those of Table 2 when input sizes are the same. We compare to the sole time needed by `gf2x_mul` used as follows: we rewrite the product in $\mathbb{F}_4[x]$ into a product in $\mathbb{F}_2[x][y]/(y^2+y+1)$, which then reduces to 3 products in $\mathbb{F}_2[x]$ in degrees $\leqslant d/2$ thanks to Karatsuba's formula.

$\log_2 d$	16	17	18	19	20	21
us	28	58	110	290	600	1300
GF2X	76	160	400	790	1600	3400

Table 4. Products in degree $<d$ in $\mathbb{F}_{2^{59}}[x]$, in milliseconds.

$\log_2 d/32$	16	17	18	19	20	21
us	30	73	170	310	750	1400
GF2X	54	120	270	570	1500	2700

Table 5. Products in degree $<d$ in $\mathbb{F}_{2^2}[x]$, in milliseconds.

6. CONCLUSION

We are pleased to observe that key ideas from [20, 21] turn out to be of practical interest even for polynomials in $\mathbb{F}_{2^k}[x]$ of medium sizes. Besides Schönhage–Strassen-type algorithms, other strategies such as the *additive Fourier transform* have been developed for $\mathbb{F}_{2^k}[x]$ [13, 27], and it would be worth experimenting them carefully in practice.

After the present article was submitted, P. Zimmermann pointed us to significant improvements in the development version of GF2X. Indeed, we could observe an average speedup of 34% with respect to the timings of Table 2, which thereby become similar to ours. For large sizes ($\log_2 d/64 \geqslant$

21), our code remains 16% faster. Let us mention a few plans for future improvements. Vectorizing our code should lead to a significant speed-up (let us mention that GF2X—especially the development version—benefits from vector optimizations from the compiler). More precisely, in our implementation of multiplication in $\mathbb{F}_2[x]$, we noticed that only one third of the time is spent in carry-less products. This is the main bottleneck for a vectorized version of our code, since the `vpclmulqdq` instruction that is used for such multiplications does not admit a genuine vectorized counterpart over 256-bit registers. Another potential improvement concerns the graph from Figure 1. We expect that it can be further smoothed by adapting the truncated Fourier transform algorithm [22]. We are also investigating further accelerations of DFTs of prime orders in Section 3.3. For instance, for $n = 7$ and $\mu = 6$, we might exploit the factorization $z^6 - 1 = (z+1)^2 (z^2 + z + 1)^2$ in order to compute cyclic products using Chinese remaindering. In the longer run, we finally expect the approach in this paper to be generalizable to finite fields of higher characteristic $3, 5, 7, 11, \ldots$

7. REFERENCES

[1] S. Ballet and J. Pieltant. On the tensor rank of multiplication in any extension of $\mathbb{F}_2$. *J. Complexity*, 27(2):230–245, 2011.

[2] L. I. Bluestein. A linear filtering approach to the computation of discrete Fourier transform. *IEEE Trans. Audio Electroacoust.*, 18(4):451–455, 1970.

[3] M. Bodrato. Towards optimal Toom-Cook multiplication for univariate and multivariate polynomials in characteristic 2 and 0. In C. Carlet and B. Sunar, editors, *Arithmetic of Finite Fields*, volume 4547 of *Lect. Notes Comput. Sci.*, pages 116–133. Springer Berlin Heidelberg, 2007.

[4] R. P. Brent, P. Gaudry, E. Thomé, and P. Zimmermann. Faster multiplication in GF(2)[x]. In A. van der Poorten and A. Stein, editors, *Algorithmic Number Theory*, volume 5011 of *Lect. Notes Comput. Sci.*, pages 153–166. Springer Berlin Heidelberg, 2008.

[5] J. W. Cooley and J. W. Tukey. An algorithm for the machine calculation of complex Fourier series. *Math. Computat.*, 19:297–301, 1965.

[6] R. Crandall and B. Fagin. Discrete weighted transforms and large-integer arithmetic. *Math. Comp.*, 62(205):305–324, 1994.

[7] A. De, P. P. Kurur, C. Saha, and R. Saptharishi. Fast integer multiplication using modular arithmetic. *SIAM J. Comput.*, 42(2):685–699, 2013.

[8] P. Duhamel and M. Vetterli. Fast Fourier transforms: A tutorial review and a state of the art. *Signal Processing*, 19(4):259–299, 1990.

[9] A. Fog. *Instruction tables. Lists of instruction latencies, throughputs and micro-operation breakdowns for Intel, AMD and VIA CPUs*. Number 4 in Optimization manuals. `http://www.agner.org`, Technical University of Denmark, 1996–2016.

[10] M. Frigo and S. G. Johnson. The design and implementation of FFTW3. *Proc. IEEE*, 93(2):216–231, 2005.

[11] M. Fürer. Faster integer multiplication. In *Proceedings of the Thirty-Ninth ACM Symposium on Theory of Computing, STOC 2007*, pages 57–66, New York, NY, USA, 2007. ACM Press.

[12] M. Fürer. Faster integer multiplication. *SIAM J. Comp.*, 39(3):979–1005, 2009.

[13] S. Gao and T. Mateer. Additive fast Fourier transforms over finite fields. *IEEE Trans. Inform. Theory*, 56(12):6265–6272, 2010.

[14] J. von zur Gathen and J. Gerhard. *Modern computer algebra*. Cambridge University Press, second edition, 2003.

[15] GCC, the GNU Compiler Collection. Software available at `http://gcc.gnu.org`, from 1987.

[16] W. M. Gentleman and G. Sande. Fast Fourier transforms: For fun and profit. In *Proceedings of the November 7-10, 1966, Fall Joint Computer Conference*, AFIPS '66 (Fall), pages 563–578. ACM Press, 1966.

[17] I. J. Good. The interaction algorithm and practical Fourier analysis. *J. R. Stat. Soc. Ser. B*, 20(2):361–372, 1958.

[18] T. Granlund et al. GMP, the GNU multiple precision arithmetic library. `http://gmplib.org`, from 1991.

[19] W. Hart et al. FLINT: Fast Library for Number Theory. `http://www.flintlib.org`, from 2008.

[20] D. Harvey, J. van der Hoeven, and G. Lecerf. Faster polynomial multiplication over finite fields. `http://arxiv.org/abs/1407.3361`, 2014.

[21] D. Harvey, J. van der Hoeven, and G. Lecerf. Even faster integer multiplication. *J. Complexity*, 2016. `http://dx.doi.org/10.1016/j.jco.2016.03.001`.

[22] J. van der Hoeven. The truncated Fourier transform and applications. In J. Schicho, editor, *Proceedings of the 2004 International Symposium on Symbolic and Algebraic Computation*, ISSAC '04, pages 290–296. ACM Press, 2004.

[23] J. van der Hoeven. Newton's method and FFT trading. *J. Symbolic Comput.*, 45(8):857–878, 2010.

[24] J. van der Hoeven and G. Lecerf. Interfacing Mathemagix with C++. In M. Monagan, G. Cooperman, and M. Giesbrecht, editors, *Proceedings of the 2013 ACM on International Symposium on Symbolic and Algebraic Computation*, ISSAC '13, pages 363–370. ACM Press, 2013.

[25] J. van der Hoeven, G. Lecerf, and G. Quintin. Modular SIMD arithmetic in Mathemagix. `http://hal.archives-ouvertes.fr/hal-01022383`, 2014.

[26] Intel Corporation, 2200 Mission College Blvd., Santa Clara, CA 95052-8119, USA. *Intel (R) Architecture Instruction Set Extensions Programming Reference*, 2015. Ref. 319433-023, `http://software.intel.com`.

[27] Sian-Jheng Lin, Wei-Ho Chung, and S. Yunghsiang Han. Novel polynomial basis and its application to Reed-Solomon erasure codes. In *2014 IEEE 55th Annual Symposium on Foundations of Computer Science (FOCS)*, pages 316–325. IEEE, 2014.

[28] C. Lüders. Implementation of the DKSS algorithm for multiplication of large numbers. In *Proceedings of the 2015 ACM on International Symposium on Symbolic and Algebraic Computation*, ISSAC '15, pages 267–274. ACM Press, 2015.

[29] L. Meng and J. Johnson. High performance implementation of the TFT. In K. Nabeshima, editor, *Proceedings of the 39th International Symposium on Symbolic and Algebraic Computation*, ISSAC '14, pages 328–334. ACM, 2014.

[30] J. M. Pollard. The fast Fourier transform in a finite field. *Math. Comp.*, 25(114):365–374, 1971.

[31] C. M. Rader. Discrete Fourier transforms when the number of data samples is prime. *Proc. IEEE*, 56(6):1107–1108, 1968.

[32] A. Schönhage. Schnelle Multiplikation von Polynomen über Körpern der Charakteristik 2. *Acta Infor.*, 7(4):395–398, 1977.

[33] A. Schönhage and V. Strassen. Schnelle Multiplikation großer Zahlen. *Computing*, 7:281–292, 1971.

[34] V. Shoup. *NTL: A Library for doing Number Theory*, 2015. Software, version 9.6.2. `http://www.shoup.net`.

[35] L. H. Thomas. Using a computer to solve problems in physics. In W. F. Freiberger and W. Prager, editors, *Applications of digital computers*, pages 42–57. Boston, Ginn, 1963.

[36] S. Winograd. On computing the discrete Fourier transform. *Math. Comp.*, 32:175–199, 1978.

A Factorization Algorithm for G-Algebras and Applications

Albert Heinle
David R. Cheriton School of Computer Science
University of Waterloo
200 University Avenue West
Waterloo, ON N2L 3G1, Canada
aheinle@uwaterloo.ca

Viktor Levandovskyy
Lehrstuhl B für Mathematik
RWTH Aachen University
Pontdriesch 16
52062 Aachen, Germany
levandov@math.rwth-aachen.de

ABSTRACT

It has been recently discovered by Bell, Heinle and Levandovskyy that a large class of algebras, including the ubiquitous G-algebras, are finite factorization domains (FFD for short).

Utilizing this result, we contribute an algorithm to find all distinct factorizations of a given element $f \in \mathcal{G}$, where $\mathcal{G}$ is any G-algebra, with minor assumptions on the underlying field.

Moreover, the property of being an FFD, in combination with the factorization algorithm, enables us to propose an analogous description of the factorized Gröbner basis algorithm for G-algebras. This algorithm is useful for various applications, e.g. in analysis of solution spaces of systems of linear partial functional equations with polynomial coefficients, coming from $\mathcal{G}$. Additionally, it is possible to include inequality constraints for ideals in the input.

Keywords

G-Algebras, Gröbner Bases, Factorization

1. INTRODUCTION

Notations: Throughout the paper we denote by $\mathbb{K}$ a field. In the algorithmic part we will assume $\mathbb{K}$ to be a computable field. $\mathbb{N}_0 = \mathbb{N} \cup \{0\}$ is the set of natural numbers including zero. For a $\mathbb{K}$-algebra R we denote by $U(R)$ the group of invertible (unit) elements of R, which is nonabelian in general. For $f \in R$ we denote by Rf the left ideal, generated by f. The main focus in this paper lies in so called G-algebras, which are defined as follows.

Definition 1. *For $n \in \mathbb{N}$ and $1 \le i < j \le n$ consider the units $c_{ij} \in \mathbb{K}^*$ and polynomials $d_{ij} \in \mathbb{K}[x_1, \ldots, x_n]$. Suppose, that there exists a monomial total well-ordering $\prec$ on $\mathbb{K}[x_1, \ldots, x_n]$, such that for any $1 \le i < j \le n$ either $d_{ij} = 0$ or the leading monomial of d_{ij} is smaller than $x_i x_j$ with respect to $\prec$. The $\mathbb{K}$-algebra $A := \mathbb{K}\langle x_1, \ldots, x_n \mid \{x_j x_i = c_{ij} x_i x_j + d_{ij} \colon 1 \le i < j \le n\}\rangle$ is called a G-algebra, if $\{x_1^{\alpha_1} \cdot \ldots \cdot x_n^{\alpha_n} : \alpha_i \in \mathbb{N}_0\}$ is a $\mathbb{K}$-basis of A.*

ISSAC '16, July 19–22, 2016, Waterloo, ON, Canada.

DOI: http://dx.doi.org/0.1145/2930889.2930906

G-algebras [1, 22] are also known as algebras of solvable type [20, 23] and as PBW algebras [4, 5]. G-algebras are Noetherian domains of finite global, Krull and Gel'fand-Kirillov dimensions.

We assume that the reader is familiar with the basic terminology in the area of Gröbner bases, both in the commutative as well as in the non-commutative case. We recommend [3, 5, 22] as literature on this topic.

Recall, that $r \in R \setminus \{0\}$ is called **irreducible**, if in any factorization $r = ab$ either $a \in U(R)$ or $b \in U(R)$ holds. Otherwise, we call r reducible.

Definition 2 (cf. [2]). *Let A be a (not necessarily commutative) domain. We say that A is a finite factorization domain (FFD, for short), if every nonzero, non-unit element of A has at least one factorization into irreducible elements and there are at most finitely many distinct factorizations into irreducible elements up to multiplication of the irreducible factors by central units in A.*

2. MOTIVATION AND APPLICATIONS

Problem 1. *Let A be a finite factorization domain and a $\mathbb{K}$-algebra. Given $f \in A \setminus (U(A) \cup \{0\})$, compute all its factorizations of the form $f = c \cdot f_1 \cdots f_n$, where $c \in U(A)$ and $f_i \in A \setminus U(A)$ are irreducible.*

This paper is devoted in part to the algorithmic solution of Problem 1 for a broad class of G-algebras. With this algorithm one can approach a number of important problems, which we discuss in detail.

Let A be a $\mathbb{K}$-algebra and $0 \neq L \subset A$ a finitely generated left ideal.

Problem 2. *Compute a proper left ideal $N \supsetneq L$.*

Unfortunately, it is not known in general, whether the problem of left maximality of a given ideal with respect to inclusion is decidable. Therefore we are interested in the local negative form of it. Namely, if Problem 2 can be solved, then L is not left maximal. Moreover, for any N as above, we have a surjection from A/L to its proper factor-module A/N, in other words the exact sequence of left A-modules

$$0 \to N/L \to A/L \to A/N \to 0$$

which contributes to the knowledge of the structure of A/L.

Suppose that $f \in A \setminus \{0\}, f \notin L$ has finitely many factorizations $f = g_i h_i$ up to multiplication by central units, where $i \in I, |I| < \infty$ and $g_i, h_i \notin U(A)$. We do not require that g_i or h_i are irreducible. Suppose, that $L \subsetneq L + Af \subsetneq A$. Then $L + Af \subseteq \bigcap_{i \in I}(L + Ah_i)$, hence there is a natural surjective homomorphism of left A-modules

$$\frac{A}{L+Af} \to \frac{A}{\bigcap_{i\in I}(L+Ah_i)} \to 0$$

Relations with solution spaces: Let $\mathcal{F}$ be a left A-module, which one may think about as the *space of solutions* for A-modules. Suppose, that a left A-module M is finitely presented by an $n \times m$ matrix P. Then $\mathrm{Sol}_A(P, \mathcal{F}) = \{f \in \mathcal{F}^{m \times 1} : Pf = 0\}$, that is the set of solutions to a linear functional system, given by P, depends not on a particular P but on M. Therefore from now on we denote $\mathrm{Sol}(M, \mathcal{F}) := \mathrm{Sol}_A(P, \mathcal{F})$, where P is some presentation matrix for M. By the Noether-Malgrange isomorphism [27], there is an isomorphism of $\mathbb{K}$-vector spaces $\mathrm{Sol}(M, \mathcal{F})$ and $\mathrm{Hom}_A(M, \mathcal{F})$, where the latter is also a right $\mathrm{End}_A(M)$-module.

In this way, after applying $\mathrm{Sol}(-, \mathcal{F}) = \mathrm{Hom}_A(-, \mathcal{F})$ to our above natural surjection, we obtain the below natural injective map of $\mathbb{K}$-vector spaces:

$$0 \to \mathrm{Sol}\left(\frac{A}{\bigcap_{i\in I}(L+Ah_i)}, \mathcal{F}\right) \to \mathrm{Sol}\left(\frac{A}{L+Af}, \mathcal{F}\right).$$

Thus it allows us to identify a subspace of the space of solutions of $A/(L + Af)$.

Note, that the following version of the left Chinese remainder theorem for modules holds:

THEOREM 1. *Let A be a $\mathbb{K}$-algebra, I a finite set of indices and $\{L_i : i \in I\}$ a set of left ideals in A. Consider the homomorphism*

$$A/\bigcap_{i\in I} L_i \xrightarrow{\phi} \bigoplus_{i\in I} A/L_i, \quad a + \bigcap_{i\in I} L_i \mapsto (a + L_1, \dots, a + L_{|I|}).$$

Then the following holds

1) *ϕ is injective*
2) *if for all $i, j \in I, i \neq j$, we have $L_i + L_j = A$, then ϕ is surjective.*

Of course, one can assume that the L_i are proper nonzero ideals.

In the second item of Theorem 1 one says that the collection $\{L_i : i \in I\}$ is **left comaximal**. Then ϕ is an isomorphism and one has a finite direct sum decomposition of the module $A/\bigcap_{i\in I} L_i$. Hence, there is a direct sum decomposition of the solution spaces

$$\mathrm{Sol}\left(A/\bigcap_{i\in I} L_i, \mathcal{F}\right) = \mathrm{Sol}\left(\bigoplus_{i\in I} A/L_i, \mathcal{F}\right) = \bigoplus_{i\in I} \mathrm{Sol}\left(A/L_i, \mathcal{F}\right).$$

Notice that the left hand side can be a direct sum even if condition 2 from Theorem 1 is not satisfied (see Example 3).

Another application: Let A be a domain and $S \subset A$ be a multiplicatively closed Ore set. By Ore's Theorem, the localization $S^{-1}A$ exists and there is an injective homomorphism $A \to S^{-1}A$ [5].

A left ideal $L \subset A$ is called **left S-closed** if $L^S = L$, where $L^S := \{a \in A \mid \exists s \in S \; sa \in L\} \supseteq L$ is the **S-closure of** L. There is another characterization of S-closedness: $L^S = \ker(A \to S^{-1}(A/L))$, where the latter homomorphism of A-modules is $a \mapsto 1^{-1}a + S^{-1}L$. Then L^S/L is the S-torsion submodule of A/L and A/L^S has no S-torsion.

PROBLEM 3. *Given $S \subset A$ an Ore set and $L \subset A$, give an algorithm to compute L^S.*

For a general S, it is unknown, whether L^S is computable. If A is the nth Weyl algebra, $S = \mathbb{K}[x_1, \dots, x_n] \setminus \{0\}$ and $L \subset A$ has finite holonomic rank, then there is an algorithm [29, 28, 30] to compute L^S (known as the **Weyl closure of** L).

The factorization can be used in the process of computing L^S as follows. Let A be an FFD. Given $\ell \in L$, one computes finitely many factorizations $\ell = a_i b_i, i \in I$ for some finite indexing set I. Then let $J := \{j \in I \mid (a_j, b_j) \in S \times L\}$. If $J \neq \emptyset$, one has $L + \{Ab_j : j \in J\} \subseteq L^S$. In such a way one obtains an approximation to L^S. Note, that $L^S = A$ if and only if $L \cap S \neq \emptyset$.

3. HOW TO FACTOR IN G-ALGEBRAS

3.1 General Algorithm

In a recent publication [2, Theorem 1.3], it was proven that each G-algebra $\mathcal{G}$ is a finite factorization domain.

In the same paper, an outline was given how one could find all possible factorizations of an element in $\mathcal{G}$. In this section, we will provide a thorough description of an algorithm to find all possible factorizations of an element in a G-algebra $\mathcal{G}$, up to multiplication by central units.

For this, we need to make a further assumption on our field $\mathbb{K}$, which holds for most practical choices of $\mathbb{K}$.

Assumption: There exists an algorithm to determine if a polynomial p in $\mathbb{K}[x]$ has roots in $\mathbb{K}$. If p has roots in $\mathbb{K}$, then this algorithm can produce all $\mathbb{K}$-roots of p.

Recall, that $\{x^\alpha = x_1^{\alpha_1} \cdot \ldots \cdot x_n^{\alpha_n} : \alpha \in \mathbb{N}_0^n\}$ is a $\mathbb{K}$-basis of $\mathcal{G}$. With respect to an admissible monomial ordering $\prec$ on $\mathcal{G}$ we can uniquely write every $g \in \mathcal{G} \setminus \{0\}$ as $g = c_\alpha x^\alpha + t_g$ with $c_\alpha \in \mathbb{K} \setminus \{0\}$. Moreover, either $t_g = 0$ or $x^\beta \prec x^\alpha$ for any summand $c_\beta x^\beta$, $c_\beta \neq 0$ of t_g. Then $\mathrm{lm}(g) = x^\alpha$ is the *leading monomial* of g and $\mathrm{lc}(g) = c_\alpha$ is the *leading coefficient* of g. Finally, the *leading term* $\mathrm{lt}(g)$ of g is defined as $\mathrm{lt}(g) := \mathrm{lc}(g) \cdot \mathrm{lm}(g)$. A polynomial $g \neq 0$ with $\mathrm{lc}(g) = 1$ is called *monic*.

It is important to recall [22], that $\mathrm{lm}(x^\alpha \cdot x^\beta) = x^{\alpha+\beta}$ holds $\forall \alpha, \beta \in \mathbb{N}_0^n$ in a G-algebra.

PROOF OF ALGORITHM 1. Let us begin with discussing the termination. The set M in line 2 is finite, as it is a permutation of a finite product of the variables in $\mathcal{G}$. Since $\mathcal{G}$ is a G-algebra, the set of total well-orderings on it, satisfying Definition 1, is nonempty. By [4, Theorem 2.3], in this set there is a weighted degree total ordering, say $\prec_w$ with strictly positive weights. Without loss of generality let us assume this is the ordering we are working with. Thus for any monomial there are only finitely many monomials which are smaller with respect to $\prec_w$. In particular, this applies to $\mathrm{lm}(a)$ and $\mathrm{lm}(b)$ in line 5. Assume there are $k, l \in \mathbb{N}_0$, such that there are exactly k monomials smaller than $\mathrm{lm}(a)$, and l monomials smaller than $\mathrm{lm}(b)$. Hence, we assume that a

Algorithm 1 Factoring an element g in a G-algebra $\mathcal{G}$

Input: $g \in \mathcal{G} \setminus \mathbb{K}$.
Output: $\{(g_1, \ldots, g_m) \mid m \in \mathbb{N}, g_i \in \mathcal{G} \setminus \mathbb{K}$ for $i \in \{1, \ldots, m\}, g_1 \cdots g_m = g\}$ (up to multiplication of each factor by a central unit).
Assumption: An admissible monomial ordering $\prec$ on $\mathcal{G}$ is fixed and g is monic with respect to it.

1: $R := \{\}$
2:
$$M := \{(p_1, \ldots, p_\nu) \mid \nu \in \mathbb{N}, p_i \in \{x_1, \ldots, x_n\}, \\ \operatorname{lm}(p_1 \cdot \ldots \cdot p_\nu) = \operatorname{lm}(g)\}$$
3: **for** $(p_1, \ldots, p_\nu) \in M$ **do**
4: **for** $i := 1$ **to** $\nu - 1$ **do**
5: Set up an ansatz for the $\mathbb{K}$-coefficients of $a \cdot b = g$ with $\operatorname{lm}(a) = p_1 \cdots p_i$, $\operatorname{lm}(b) = p_{i+1} \cdots p_\nu$, $\operatorname{lc}(a) = 1$ and $\operatorname{lc}(b) = \operatorname{lc}(p_1 \cdots p_\nu)^{-1}$.
6: $F :=$ the reduced Gröbner basis w.r.t. an elimination ordering of the ideal generated by the coefficients of $a \cdot b - g$.
7: **if** $F \neq \{1\}$ **then**
8: $V :=$ Variety of $\langle F \rangle$ in an affine space over $\mathbb{K}$.
9: $R := R \cup \{(a, b) \mid a, b \in \mathcal{G}, a \cdot b = g$, where the coefficients of a, b are given by $v \in V\}$
10: **end if**
11: **end for**
12: **end for**
13: **if** $R = \{\}$ **then**
14: **return** $\{(\mathrm{g})\}$
15: **else**
16: Recursively factor a and b for each $(a, b) \in R$.
17: **end if**
18: **return** R

and b have the form

$$a = \sum_{i=0}^{k} a_i \cdot m_a^{(i)}, \quad b = \sum_{i=0}^{l} b_i \cdot m_b^{(i)},$$

where $m_a^{(0)}, \ldots, m_a^{(k-1)}$ are the monomials smaller than $m_a^{(k)} := \operatorname{lm}(a)$, $m_b^{(0)}, \ldots, m_b^{(l-1)}$ are the monomials smaller than $m_b^{(l)} := \operatorname{lm}(b)$, and $a_0, \ldots, a_k, b_0, \ldots, b_l \in \mathbb{K}$. We can set without loss of generality $a_k := 1$ and $b_l := \operatorname{lc}(p_1 \cdots p_\nu)^{-1}$ in line 5.

Now, we can symbolicly compute

$$ab - g = \left(\sum_{i=0}^{k} a_i \cdot m_a^{(i)}\right) \cdot \left(\sum_{i=0}^{l} b_i \cdot m_b^{(i)}\right) - g.$$

The coefficients of the different products $m_a^{(i)} \cdot m_b^{(j)}$, $i, j \in \mathbb{N}_0$, in $ab - g$ are elements in the commutative polynomial ring $S := \mathbb{K}[a_0, \ldots, a_{k-1}, b_0, \ldots, b_{l-1}]$. The set C of these coefficients generates an ideal $\langle C \rangle \lhd S$. This ideal is zero-dimensional, since if $\langle C \rangle$ was not zero-dimensional, the variety $\tilde{V} \subset \overline{\mathbb{K}}^{l+k}$ over the algebraic closure of $\mathbb{K} \subset \overline{\mathbb{K}}$ of $\langle C \rangle$ would be an infinite set. As each element in V represents a distinct factorization of g, we obtain infinitely many factorizations of g, contradicting that $\mathcal{G}$ is an FFD, independent of the choice of the underlying field.

Since we have established that $\langle C \rangle$ is zero-dimensional, the variety $V \subset \mathbb{K}^{l+k}$ will be a finite set. Thus, the set R in line 9 will also be finite. The recursive call will terminate, since in each step we either discover that we cannot refine our factorization any more, or we split a given factor into two factors of strictly smaller degrees.

For the correctness discussion of our algorithm, we need to show that we can calculate the variety V in line 8.

Our assumption above states that we can find all $\mathbb{K}$-roots of a univariate polynomial. Since $\langle C \rangle$ is zero-dimensional, according to [21, 25], there exists a method to compute a finite set of triangular systems $T_1, \ldots, T_\kappa$, $\kappa \in \mathbb{N}$, in S, such that V is the union of the varieties of these triangular systems. These T_i for $i \in \{1, \ldots, \kappa\}$ are Gröbner bases of the respective ideals $\langle T_i \rangle$ with respect to the lexicographic ordering, and have the property that for any variable $x \in \{a_0, \ldots, a_{k-1}, b_0, \ldots, b_{l-1}\}$, there exists $t \in \mathbb{N}_0$, such that $x^t = \operatorname{lm}(f)$ for $f \in T_i$. Hence, there is at least one univariate polynomial contained in each T_i. Using our assumption, we can calculate the $\mathbb{K}$-roots of this polynomial, if it has any. By backwards substitution, we obtain the entire $\mathbb{K}$-variety of the ideal generated by each T_i, and hence we obtain V. □

EXAMPLE 1. *Let us consider the universal enveloping algebra $U(\mathrm{sl}_2)$ of sl_2 [12], represented by*

$$\mathbb{K}\langle e, f, h \mid fe = ef - h, he = eh + 2e, hf = fh - 2f\rangle.$$

In $U(\mathrm{sl}_2)$, we want to factorize the element

$$p := e^3 f + e^2 f^2 - e^3 + e^2 f + 2ef^2 - 3e^2 h - 2efh - 8e^2 \\ + ef + f^2 - 4eh - 2fh - 7e + f - h.$$

We fix the degree lexicographic ordering on $U(\mathrm{sl}_2)$, i.e. the leading term of p is $e^3 f$.

Therefore the set M in line 2 is given as

$$M := \{(e, e, e, f), (e, e, f, e), (e, f, e, e), (f, e, e, e)\}.$$

When choosing (e, e, e, f), for $i = 1$ one can prudently set up the ansatz

$$p = a \cdot b = (e + a_2 f + a_1 h + a_0) \cdot \\ (e^2 f + b_{12} ef^2 + b_{11} e^2 h + b_{10} efh + b_9 f^2 h + b_8 e^2 + b_7 ef \\ + b_6 f^2 + b_5 eh + b_4 fh + b_3 e + b_2 f + b_1 h + b_0).$$

When calculating the variety of the ideal in $\mathbb{K}[a_0, a_1, a_2, b_0, \ldots, b_{12}]$, generated by the coefficients of $ab - p$, one obtains one solution, which corresponds to the factorization

$$p = (e + 1) \cdot (e^2 f + ef^2 - 3eh - 2fh - e^2 + f^2 - 7e + f - h).$$

By picking (e, e, f, e) for $i = 3$ and setting up an ansatz, one obtains two more factorizations, namely

$$p = (e^2 f + 2ef - 2eh - e^2 - 4e + f - 2h - 3) \cdot (e + f)$$

and

$$p = (e^2 f + ef^2 - 2eh - e^2 + f^2 - 3e - f - 2h) \cdot (e + 1).$$

All the other combinations either produce the same factorizations or none.

When recursively calling the algorithm for each factor in the found factorizations, we discover that the first two factorizations have a reducible factor. In the end, one obtains the following two distinct factorizations of p into irreducible *factors:*

$$p = (e^2f + ef^2 - 2eh - e^2 + f^2 - 3e - f - 2h) \cdot (e+1)$$
$$= (e+1) \cdot (ef - e + f - 2h - 3) \cdot (e+f).$$

3.2 Implementation

We have developed an experimental implementation of Algorithm 1 in the computer algebra system SINGULAR:PLURAL [17]. We will make it available as part of `ncfactor.lib`. Our newly implemented procedures factorize elements in any G-algebra, whose ground field is $\mathbb{F}(q_1, \ldots, q_n)$, where $\mathbb{F}$ is either $\mathbb{Q}$ or a finite prime field and q_i are transcendental over $\mathbb{F}$.

We designed the software in a modular way, so that during runtime our function checks if a more efficient factorization algorithm is available for the specific given G-algebra and/or input polynomial. If this is the case, the input is re-directed to this function. In this way, the user can call the general function to factor elements in any one of the supported G-algebras, and runs the available optimized algorithms, where possible, without calling them individually.

3.3 Possible Improvements

Algorithm 1 solves the problem of finding all possible factorizations of an element in a G-algebra, but it will not be very efficient in general. This is not only due to the complexity of the necessary calculation of a Gröbner basis [24], but also the size of the set M is a bottleneck. In [13, 14], an algorithm for factoring elements in the nth Weyl algebra is presented, which is similar to Algorithm 1. The main difference is that the $\mathbb{Z}^n$-graded structure is utilized. There, the homogeneous polynomials of degree zero form a $\mathbb{K}$-algebra $A_n^{(0)}$, which is isomorphic to a commutative multivariate polynomial ring. The set of homogeneous polynomials of degree $z \in \mathbb{Z}^n \setminus \{0^n\}$ has the structure of a cyclic $A_n^{(0)}$-bimodule. Hence, factorization of homogeneous polynomials with respect to the $\mathbb{Z}^n$-grading reduces to factoring commutative polynomials with minor additional combinatorial steps. An inhomogeneous polynomial f has now the highest graded part $\alpha(f)$ and the lowest graded part $\omega(f)$, both of them rather polynomials than monomials. Hence $\alpha(f), \omega(f)$ have potentially smaller numbers of different factorizations than the permutations of the leading term collected in M in Algorithm 1. Indeed, it suffices to consider firstly factorizations into two polynomials, and for each candidate pair an ansatz is made for the graded terms between the highest and the lowest graded parts. This means, that the set M has smaller size in general when using this technique. Additionally, this approach takes the lowest graded part into account, which allows to eliminate certain invalid cases beforehand. The performance increase is reflected by the benchmarks presented in [13, 19].

Hence, for practical implementations of Algorithm 1, one should examine each possible G-algebra separately and take advantage of potential extra structure, like the presence of nontrivial $\mathbb{Z}^n$-grading or an isomorphism to an algebra with this structure.

We will conclude this section by summarizing the conditions that can lead to an improved version of Algorithm 1. Let A be a $\mathbb{K}$-algebra, which possesses a nontrivial (i.e. not all weight vectors are zero) $\mathbb{Z}^n$-(multi)grading. Then one can infer the following additional information:

1. For $z \in \mathbb{Z}^n$, $A_z := \{a \in A : \deg(a) = z\} \cup \{0\}$ is a $\mathbb{K}$-vector space. Moreover, $\oplus_z A_z = A$ and $A_i A_j \subseteq A_{i+j}$ for all $i, j \in \mathbb{Z}^n$.
2. A_{0^n}, the graded part of degree zero, is a $\mathbb{K}$-algebra itself (since $A_{0^n} A_{0^n} \subseteq A_{0^n}$).
3. For $z \in \mathbb{Z}^n \setminus \{0^n\}$, the z-th graded part A_z is an A_{0^n}-bimodule (since $A_{0^n} A_z, A_z A_{0^n} \subseteq A_z$).

In order to be useful for factorizing, this grading should have the following properties:

4. The graded part of degree zero, A_{0^n}, which is a $\mathbb{K}$-algebra, is additionally an FFD with "easy" factorization, preferably a commutative polynomial ring. Furthermore, for keeping the set M in Algorithm 1 small, it would be desirable if in A_{0^n} a randomly chosen polynomial is irreducible with high probability.
5. The irreducible elements in A_{0^n}, that are reducible in A, can be identified and factorized in an efficient manner. Preferably, one has a finite number of monic elements of such type.
6. For $z \in \mathbb{Z}^n \setminus \{0^n\}$, the z-th graded part A_z is a finitely generated A_{0^n}-bimodule, preferably a cyclic bimodule.

Then Algorithm 1 can be modified along the lines of algorithms from [13, 14], which we have also sketched above. Let us illustrate this approach by a concrete example.

EXAMPLE 2. *As in Example 1, let $A = U(\mathrm{sl}_2)$, that is*

$$A = \mathbb{K}\langle e, f, h \mid fe = ef - h, he = eh + 2e, hf = fh - 2f\rangle.$$

At first, let us determine which gradings are possible. Let w_e, w_f and w_h be the weights of the variables, not all zero. The two last relations of A imply that $w_h = 0$, and the first one implies $w_e + w_f = w_h = 0$, that is $w_f = -w_e$. Hence a $\mathbb{Z}$-grading $(w_e, w_f, w_h) = (1, -1, 0)$ is enough for our purposes, since $A_0 = \mathbb{K}[ef, h]$ is commutative and the z-th graded part is a cyclic A_0-bimodule, generated by e^z if $z > 0$ and by $f^{|z|}$ otherwise. This property guarantees, that $\forall r \in \mathbb{K}[ef, h]$ and $\forall z \in \mathbb{N}$ there exists $q_1, q_2 \in \mathbb{K}[ef, h]$, such that $re^z = e^z q_1$ and $e^z r = q_2 e^z$ and the same holds for the multiplication by f^z. Note, that $\deg(q_i) = \deg(r)$.

We claim that the only monic irreducible elements in A_0, which are reducible in A, are given by ef and $ef - h$. The proof to this claim is similar to the one for [14, Lemma 2.4], which we outline here: Let p be an irreducible element in A_0, which reduces into $p = \varphi \cdot \psi$ in A, where $\varphi, \psi \in A \setminus \mathbb{K}$ are monic. Since A is a domain, the factors φ, ψ are homogeneous with $\deg(\varphi) = k$ and $\deg(\psi) = -k$ for some $k \in \mathbb{Z}$. If $|k| > 1$ or $k = 0$, p would be reducible in A_0, which violates our assumption. Hence only $k = 1$ is possible. If any of φ or ψ would have a non-trivial A_0 factor, we would obtain again that p is reducible in A_0. This leaves as only options $p = ef$ or $p = fe = ef - h$, as claimed. Thus, we have shown that irreducible elements in A_0, which are reducible in A, can be easily identified and factored.

Now consider the same polynomial p as in Example 1. With respect to the $(1, -1, 0)$-grading it decomposes into the following graded parts: $\alpha(p) = -e^3$, $\omega(p) = f^2$ (as we see, in this case we have monomials in graded parts, while in general rather polynomials appear) and the intermediate parts are

$$\underbrace{e^3f - 3e^2h - 8e^2}_{\text{deg:2}} + \underbrace{e^2f - 4eh - 7e}_{\text{deg:1}} +$$

$$+\underbrace{e^2f^2-2efh+ef-h}_{\text{deg:0}}+\underbrace{2ef^2-2fh+f}_{\text{deg:}-1}.$$

Among the factorizations of $\alpha(p)=-e^3$ *and* $\omega(p)=f^2$ *into two factors, consider the case* $(-e^2)\cdot e$ *and* $f\cdot f$. *Thus, we are looking for* $a,b\in A$ *with* $\alpha(a)=e^2,\omega(a)=f$ *and* $\alpha(b)=e,\omega(b)=f$ *and* $p=ab$ *holds. In* b *we have only one possible intermediate graded part* $b_0(ef,h)$, *namely of degree 0 since* $\deg(\alpha(b))=1$ *and* $\deg(\omega(b))=-1$. *In* a *we have to specify the parts of degrees 1 resp. 0, that is* $a_1(ef,h)\cdot e$ *resp.* $a_0(ef,h)$. *After the multiplication, we obtain the following graded decomposition of intermediate graded terms of ab:*

$$\underbrace{-e^2b_0+a_1e^2}_{\text{deg:2}}+\underbrace{a_1eb_0+a_0e-e^2f}_{\text{deg:1}}+$$

$$+\underbrace{a_1ef+a_0b_0+ef-h}_{\text{deg:0}}+\underbrace{fb_0+a_0f}_{\text{deg:}-1}.$$

By fixing the maximal possible degree of $a_0,a_1,b_0\in\mathbb{K}[ef,h]$, *we can create and solve a system of equations which the coefficients of* a_0,a_1,b_0 *have to satisfy. In this example an ansatz in terms of* $1,h,ef$, *i.e. 9 unknown coefficients, leads to the system of 18 at most quadratic equations, which leads to the unique solution:* $b_0(ef,h)=0$, $a_0(ef,h)=2ef-2h-3$ *and* $a_1(ef,h)=ef-h-2$. *Substituting the polynomials, we arrive at the following factorization with polynomials sorted according to the grading:*

$$p=(-e^2+e^2f-2eh-4e+2ef-2h-3+f)\cdot(e+f)$$

This is already known to us from the Example 1. In an analogous way one can address other factorizations. Note, that in the ansatz we made, significantly less variables for unknown coefficients and a system of less equations of smaller total degree were used, compared to the general Algorithm.

4. THE FACTORIZED GRÖBNER BASIS ALGORITHM FOR G-ALGEBRAS

In what follows, by *ideal* we always mean a left ideal (unless otherwise specified).

The factorized Gröbner approach has been studied extensively for the commutative case [9, 8, 10, 15, 16], and implementations are e.g. provided in the computer algebra systems SINGULAR [11] and REDUCE [18].

The key idea is to split a Gröbner basis computation into smaller pieces with respect to the degrees of their generators. The union of the varieties of the ideals generated by these smaller pieces equals the variety of the initial system.

In the commutative case, there is also a way to constrain the solution space. One can provide an extra set of elements, that should not be reducible by the computed Gröbner bases. In this way, one excludes certain unwanted solutions, which is useful in practice. On the other hand, with this method one can work with semi-algebraic systems, that is systems of equations and inequalities, describing the difference of two given varieties.

The search for varieties in the commutative case translates to the search for solutions in the non-commutative case: All G-algebras are finite factorization domains and a general factorization algorithm via Algorithm 1 is given. Many of them are abstractions of algebras of operators, and one is interested to find common solutions of certain sets of operators, written as polynomials. Right hand factors of elements correspond to partial solutions, and hence a split similar to the commutative case is helpful in recovering partial solutions. Motivated by this observation, we generalize the factorized Gröbner basis algorithm to the G-algebra case in this section. The version of the algorithm without constraints computes, from a given ideal B, a finite collection of ideals $\{B_i : i\in I\}$ such that $B\subseteq\bigcap_{i\in I}B_i=:\widehat{B}$ holds. Note, that in the commutative case one has the equality of the radicals of B and of $\widehat{B}$ and thus the decomposition of the corresponding algebraic varieties into a union. In the non-commutative case, a nontrivial output means that at least one of the B_i is different from B. Then, even if $B\subsetneq\widehat{B}$, such output provides a solution to Problem 2 and provides moreover a decomposition of $\widehat{B}$ via an intersection of ideals. This can be seen as a certain analogue to the primary decomposition of ideals in the commutative case. With the help of this data we obtain more information on the space of solutions of the original system, cf. the description around Theorem 1 above. Moreover, our algorithm allows to introduce constraints, similar to the methods in the commutative case, which has a somewhat different meaning in our setting, the investigation of which is a future work.

EXAMPLE 3. *In the commutative case, one has the property that the radical of the input ideal will be equal to the intersection of the radicals of all ideals computed by the factorized Gröbner basis algorithm.*

Here we present an example, showing that this does not hold in general for G-algebras. Consider

$$\begin{aligned}p=&(x^6+2x^4-3x^2)\partial^2-(4x^5-4x^4-12x^2-12x)\partial\\&+(6x^4-12x^3-6x^2-24x-12)\in A_1.\end{aligned}$$

This polynomial appears in [29, Example 5.7] and has two different factorizations, namely

$$\begin{aligned}p=&(x^4\partial-x^3\partial-3x^3+3x^2\partial+6x^2-3x\partial-3x+12)\cdot\\&(x^2\partial+x\partial-3x-1)\\=&(x^4\partial+x^3\partial-4x^3+3x^2\partial-3x^2+3x\partial-6x-3)\cdot\\&(x^2\partial-x\partial-2x+4).\end{aligned}$$

A reduced Gröbner basis of $\langle x^2\partial+x\partial-3x-1\rangle\cap\langle x^2\partial-x\partial-2x+4\rangle$, *computed with* SINGULAR:PLURAL *[17], is given by*

$$\begin{aligned}\{&3x^5\partial^2+2x^4\partial^3-x^4\partial^2-12x^4\partial+x^3\partial^2-2x^2\partial^3+16x^3\partial\\&+9x^2\partial^2+18x^3+4x^2\partial+4x\partial^2-42x^2-4x\partial-12x-12,\\&2x^4\partial^4-2x^4\partial^3+11x^4\partial^2+12x^3\partial^3-2x^2\partial^4-2x^3\partial^2\\&+10x^2\partial^3-44x^3\partial-17x^2\partial^2+64x^2\partial+12x\partial^2+66x^2\\&+52x\partial+4\partial^2-168x-16\partial-60\}.\end{aligned}$$

Hence, one main difference will be that we do not claim that the union of all solutions of our smaller pieces in the factorizing Gröbner basis algorithm will always be equal to all common solutions of the initial set of polynomials. In general, we will only find a subset of all solutions using our method. However, in this example, the space of holomorphic solutions of the differential equation associated to p in fact coincides with the union of the solution spaces of the two generators of the intersection stated above.

DEFINITION 3. *Let* B,C *be finite subsets in* $\mathcal{G}$. *We call the tuple* (B,C) *a* ***constrained Gröbner tuple****, if* B *is a*

Algorithm 2 Factorized Gröbner bases Algorithm for G-Algebras (FGBG)

Input: $B := \{f_1, \ldots, f_k\} \subset \mathcal{G}$, $C := \{g_1, \ldots, g_l\} \subset \mathcal{G}$.
Output: $R := \{(\tilde{B}, \tilde{C}) \mid$
$(\tilde{B}, \tilde{C})$ is factorized constrained Gröbner tuple$\}$ with
$\langle B \rangle \subseteq \bigcap_{(\tilde{B},\tilde{C}) \in R} \langle \tilde{B} \rangle$
Assumption: All elements in B and C are monic.

1: **for** $i = 1$ **to** k **do**
2:   **if** f_i is reducible **then**
3:     $M := \{(f_i^{(1)}, f_i^{(2)} \mid f_i^{(1)}, f_i^{(2)} \in \mathcal{G} \setminus \mathbb{K}, \mathrm{lc}(f_i^{(1)}) = \mathrm{lc}(f_i^{(2)}) = 1, f_i^{(1)} \cdot f_i^{(2)} = f_i, f_i^{(1)}$ is irreducible$\}$
4:     **if** there exists $(a, b), (\tilde{a}, \tilde{b}) \in M$ with $\tilde{a} \neq a$ **then**
5:       **return**

$$\bigcup_{(a,b) \in M} \mathrm{FGBG}\left((B \setminus \{f_i\}) \cup \{b\}, C \cup \bigcup_{\substack{(\tilde{a},\tilde{b}) \in M \\ b \neq \tilde{b}}} \{\tilde{b}\} \right)$$

6:     **end if**
7:   **end if**
8: **end for**
9: $P := \{(f_i, f_j) \mid i, j \in \{1, \ldots, k\}, i < j\}$
10: **while** $P \neq \emptyset$ **do**
11:   Pick $(f, g) \in P$
12:   $P := P \setminus \{(f, g)\}$
13:   $s :=$ S-polynomial of f and g
14:   $h := \mathrm{NF}(s, B)$
15:   **if** $h \neq 0$ **then**
16:     **if** h is reducible **then**
17:       **return** $\mathrm{FGBG}(B \cup \{h\}, C)$
18:     **end if**
19:     $P := P \cup \{(h, f) \mid f \in B\}$
20:     $B := B \cup \{h\}$
21:   **end if**
22:   **if** there exists $i \in \{1, \ldots, l\}$ with $\mathrm{NF}(g_i, B) = 0$ **then**
23:     **return** $\emptyset$
24:   **end if**
25: **end while**
26: **return** $\{(B, C)\}$

Gröbner basis of $\langle B \rangle$, *and* $\mathrm{NF}(g, B) \neq 0$ *for every* $g \in C$. *We call a constrained Gröbner tuple* ***factorized****, if every* $f \in B$ *is either irreducible or has a unique irreducible left divisor.*

It is possible to strengthen the assumptions on a factorized constrained Gröbner tuple by only allowing completely irreducible elements in B, which might be preferable depending on the concrete problem. However, in our application, we allow elements with only one factorization. In this way, we increase the number of solutions we can find for a certain system $B \subset \mathcal{G}$ by using our generalized factorized Gröbner basis algorithm. This methodology also appears in the context of semifirs, where the concept of so called block factorizations or cleavages has been introduced to study the reducibility of a principal ideal [7, Chapter 3.5].

Proof of Algorithm 2. We will first discuss the termination aspect of Algorithm 2. Since M, as calculated in line 3, is of finite cardinality, the existence check in line 4 can be done in a finite number of steps. Line 5 consists of a finite number of recursive calls to FGBG. The algorithm reaches this line if there is an element f in B, which is reducible and has a non-unique irreducible left divisor. In each recursive call, the algorithm is called with an altered version of the set B, where f is being replaced in B by $b \in \mathcal{G}$, where b is chosen such that there exists an irreducible a in $\mathcal{G}$ with $f = ab$. Therefore, after a finite depth of recursion, FGBG will be called with a set B containing elements that are either irreducible or have a unique irreducible left divisor. We can make this assumption on B when FGBG reaches line 9. Lines 10–25 describe the Buchberger algorithm to compute a Gröbner basis, with two differences:

1. If the normal form h of an S-polynomial with respect to B is not 0, we check h for reducibility. If h is reducible, we call FGBG recursively, adding h to B.
2. We check the system for consistency, i.e. if there is an element in C that reduces with respect to B, we return the empty set.

Each recursive call will terminate, since we add an element to B that will reduce an S-polynomial to zero, which could not be reduced to zero before.

For the correctness discussion, one observes that lines 1–8 serve the purpose to split the computation based on the reducibility of the elements in the initial set B. If an element $f \in B$ factorizes in more than one way, we recursively call FGBG with $(B \setminus \{f\}) \cup \{b\}$ as the generator set for each maximal right hand factor b of f. Hence, the left ideal generated by $(B \setminus \{f\}) \cup \{b\}$ will contain $\langle B \rangle$, and thus $\langle B \rangle$ will be contained in the intersection of all of them, as required.

As already mentioned in the termination discussion, lines 10–25 describe the Buchberger algorithm. After computing an S-polynomial h, we check for its reducibility. If there is more than one maximal right factor r of h, we call FGBG recursively and add h to our set B. Here, we have again a guarantee that the left ideal generated by B is a subset of the left ideal generated by $B \cup \{h\}$.

The additional constraints that we impose on each recursive call enable us to minimize our computations, but do not violate the subset property. In the end, it is ensured that in all computed constrained Gröbner tuples $(\tilde{B}, \tilde{C})$, no element in C lies in the left ideal generated by $\tilde{B}$. $\square$

Example 4. *Let us execute FGBG on an example. Let*

$$B := \{\partial^4 + x\partial^2 - 2\partial^3 - 2x\partial + \partial^2 + x + 2\partial - 2,$$
$$x\partial^3 + x^2\partial - x\partial^2 + \partial^3 - x^2 + x\partial - 2\partial^2 - x + 1\}$$

be a subset of the first Weyl algebra A_1. *We assume that* $C := \{\partial - 1\}$, *and that our ordering is the degree reverse lexicographic one with* $\partial > x$. *This example is taken from the* Singular:Plural *manual [17] (and it is a Gröbner basis for the left ideal* $\langle \partial^2 + x \rangle \cap \langle \partial - 1 \rangle$; *hence we would expect the output with our chosen* C *to be* $\langle \partial^2 + x \rangle$). *Each element factors separately as*

$$\begin{aligned} f_1 :=& \partial^4 + x\partial^2 - 2\partial^3 - 2x\partial + \partial^2 + x + 2\partial - 2 \\ =& (\partial^3 + x\partial - \partial^2 - x + 2) \cdot (\partial - 1) \\ =& (\partial - 1) \cdot (\partial^3 + x\partial - \partial^2 - x + 1), \end{aligned}$$

respectively

$$\begin{aligned} f_2 :=& x\partial^3 + x^2\partial - x\partial^2 + \partial^3 - x^2 + x\partial - 2\partial^2 - x + 1 \\ =& (x\partial^2 + x^2 + \partial^2 + x - \partial - 1) \cdot (\partial - 1) \\ =& (x\partial - x + \partial - 2) \cdot (\partial^2 + x). \end{aligned}$$

Hence, in line 5, FGBG will return two recursive calls of itself, namely

- $\mathrm{FGBG}(\{\partial - 1, f_2\}, \{\partial - 1, \partial^3 + x\partial - \partial^2 - x + 1\})$
- $\mathrm{FGBG}(\{\partial^3 + x\partial - \partial^2 - x + 1, f_2\}, C)$

The first call will not produce anything, as C contains $\partial - 1$, which also appears in the generator list. Hence, we ignore this call.

The new element $b_1 := \partial^3 + x\partial - \partial^2 - x + 1$ has only one possible factorization. Therefore, we consider now the factorizations of f_2. This leads again in line 5 to two recursive calls:

- $\mathrm{FGBG}(\{b_1, \partial - 1\}, \{\partial - 1, \partial^2 + x\})$
- $\mathrm{FGBG}(\{b_1, \partial^2 + x\}, C)$

As above, the first recursive call will not return anything. Thus, we are left with $(\{b_1, \partial^2 + x\}, C)$ to proceed on line 9.

The normal form of the S-polynomial of b_1 and $\partial^2 + x$ is equal to zero. Further, the normal form of b_1, with respect to $\langle \partial^2 + x \rangle$, is equal to zero, i.e. $\partial^2 + x$ is a right divisor of b_1. Hence, we can omit b_1 and our complete Gröbner basis is given by $\{\partial^2 + x\}$. Since $\mathrm{NF}(\partial - 1, \langle \partial^2 + x \rangle) \neq 0$, our algorithm returns $\{(\{\partial^2 + x\}, C)\}$ as final output.

If we would have $C = \emptyset$ in this example, the output of our algorithm – omitting details – will be

$$\{(\{\partial - 1\}, \{b_1\}), (\{\partial^2 + x\}, \{\partial - 1\})\},$$

i.e. we recover $\langle B \rangle = \langle \partial^2 + x \rangle \cap \langle \partial - 1 \rangle$ in this case.

REMARK 1. *One can also insert an early termination criterion inside Algorithm 2, namely after at least one factorized constrained Gröbner tuple has been found. This is in the commutative case motivated by the fact that in practice users are often not interested in all the elements in a variety but would be content with at least one. For example, the computer algebra system* REDUCE *can be instructed to stop after finding one factorized Gröbner basis (see [18]). In the non-commutative case, we can only hope for partial solutions in general, but a mechanism to stop a computation once at least one is found is also desirable.*

5. CONCLUSIONS

An algorithm for factoring elements in G-algebras, where the underlying field $\mathbb{K}$ has the property that we are able to extract all possible $\mathbb{K}$-roots of any polynomial in $\mathbb{K}[x]$, has been shown (Algorithm 1).

This algorithm and the FFD-property of G-algebras enable us to propose a generalization of the factorized Gröbner basis algorithm for G-algebras (Algorithm 2).

A future work would be to identify improvements to Algorithm 1 for practically interesting G-algebras. This has been studied e.g. for partial q-differential, differential and difference operators in [13, 14], where the $\mathbb{Z}^n$ graded structure resp. a certain embedding has been utilized. In the meantime, we have implemented the unimproved version in the SINGULAR:PLURAL library `ncfactor.lib`. This update will be made available shortly. Our implementation identifies beforehand if an improved method is already included in `ncfactor.lib` for a specific algebra and, if this is the case, re-directs the input there. This modular design allows us to update the function once an improved algorithm is available for a certain G-algebra. The use of the function stays the same after such an update.

The class of algebras being FFD's according to [2] is much bigger than G-algebras. Since the termination of a factorization procedure over all these algebras is already provided by [2], this opens the possibility to design factorization algorithms over a very general class of finitely presented algebras. It would be interesting to study the applicability of our factorization methods to such algebras and, in particular, to free associative algebras. The factorization in the latter algebras has partially been studied in [6, 26].

Regarding Algorithm 2, we see two interesting future research directions. First, the further characterization of the connection between the solution space of a polynomial system $B \subset \mathcal{G}$ and the union of the solution spaces of the output of Algorithm 2 when called with B. Especially, it would be interesting to identify properties of $\mathcal{G}$ and B, under which both spaces coincide. Second, given the output of Algorithm 2 for a set of generators B, one can study what information can be derived about the ideal structure of $\langle B \rangle$.

An implementation of Algorithm 2 would also be of practical interest, which the authors intend to provide in the near future.

6. ACKNOWLEDGMENTS

We thank Eugene Zima, Jason P. Bell and Mark Giesbrecht for insightful discussions we had with them. We are grateful to Wolfram Koepf for the information on internals of REDUCE. Finally, we thank the anonymous referees for their valuable comments.

7. REFERENCES

[1] J. Apel. Gröbnerbasen in nichtkommutativen Algebren und ihre Anwendung. *Dissertation, Universität Leipzig*, 1988.

[2] J. P. Bell, A. Heinle, and V. Levandovskyy. On noncommutative finite factorization domains. *To Appear in the Transactions of the American Mathematical Society; arXiv preprint arXiv:1410.6178*, 2014.

[3] B. Buchberger. Introduction to Gröbner Bases. In *Gröbner Bases and Applications*, pages 3–31. Berlin: Springer, 1997.

[4] J. Bueso, J. Gómez-Torrecillas, and F. Lobillo. Re-filtering and exactness of the Gelfand-Kirillov dimension. *Bull. Sci. Math.*, 125(8):689–715, 2001.

[5] J. Bueso, J. Gómez-Torrecillas, and A. Verschoren. *Algorithmic methods in non-commutative algebra. Applications to quantum groups.* Dordrecht: Kluwer Academic Publishers, 2003.

[6] F. Caruso. Factorization of non-commutative polynomials. *arXiv preprint arXiv:1002.3180*, 2010.

[7] P. M. Cohn. *Free ideal rings and localization in general rings*, volume 3. Cambridge University Press, 2006.

[8] S. R. Czapor. Solving algebraic equations: combining Buchberger's algorithm with multivariate

factorization. *Journal of Symbolic Computation*, 7(1):49–53, 1989.

[9] S. R. Czapor. Solving algebraic equations via Buchberger's algorithm. In *Eurocal'87*, pages 260–269. Springer, 1989.

[10] J. H. Davenport. Looking at a set of equations. *Technical report, School of Mathematical Sciences, The University of Bath.*, 1987.

[11] W. Decker, G.-M. Greuel, G. Pfister, and H. Schönemann. SINGULAR 4-0-2 — A computer algebra system for polynomial computations. http://www.singular.uni-kl.de, 2015.

[12] J. Dixmier. *Enveloping algebras*, volume 14. Newnes, 1977.

[13] M. Giesbrecht, A. Heinle, and V. Levandovskyy. Factoring linear differential operators in n variables. In *Proceedings of the 39th International Symposium on Symbolic and Algebraic Computation*, pages 194–201. ACM, 2014.

[14] M. Giesbrecht, A. Heinle, and V. Levandovskyy. Factoring linear partial differential operators in n variables. *Journal of Symbolic Computation*, 75:127–148, 2016.

[15] H.-G. Gräbe. On factorized Gröbner bases. In *Computer algebra in science and engineering, pages 77–89. World Scientific.* Citeseer, 1995.

[16] H.-G. Gräbe. *Triangular systems and factorized Gröbner bases.* Springer, 1995.

[17] G.-M. Greuel, V. Levandovskyy, A. Motsak, and H. Schönemann. PLURAL. A SINGULAR 4.0 Subsystem for Computations with Non-commutative Polynomial Algebras. *Centre for Computer Algebra, TU Kaiserslautern.* http://www.singular.uni-kl.de, 2015.

[18] A. Hearn. Reduce user's manual, version 3.8 (2004). http://www.reduce-algebra.com/docs/reduce.pdf

[19] A. Heinle and V. Levandovskyy. Factorization of $\mathbb{Z}$-homogeneous polynomials in the first (q)-Weyl algebra. *arXiv preprint arXiv:1302.5674*, 2013. vfill

[20] A. Kandri-Rody and V. Weispfenning. Non-commutative Gröbner bases in algebras of solvable type. 9(1):1–26, 1990.

[21] D. Lazard. Solving zero-dimensional algebraic systems. *Journal of symbolic computation*, 13(2):117–131, 1992.

[22] V. Levandovskyy. Non-commutative computer algebra for polynomial algebras: Gröbner bases, applications and implementation. *Doctoral Thesis, Universität Kaiserslautern*, 2005. https://kluedo.ub.uni-kl.de/files/1670/diss-web.pdf

[23] H. Li. *Noncommutative Gröbner bases and filtered-graded transfer.* Springer, 2002.

[24] E. W. Mayr and A. R. Meyer. The complexity of the word problems for commutative semigroups and polynomial ideals. *Advances in mathematics*, 46(3):305–329, 1982.

[25] H. M. Möller. On decomposing systems of polynomial equations with finitely many solutions. *Applicable Algebra in Engineering, Communication and Computing*, 4(4):217–230, 1993.

[26] K. Mori and S. Iida. Factorization of noncommutative polynomials. *Transactions of Information Processing Society of Japan*, 34(11):2431–2442, 1993.

[27] W. M. Seiler. *Involution. The formal theory of differential equations and its applications in computer algebra.* Algorithms and Computation in Mathematics 24. Berlin:Springer, 2010.

[28] H. Tsai. *Algorithms for algebraic analysis.* PhD thesis, University of California at Berkeley, 2000.

[29] H. Tsai. Weyl closure of a linear differential operator. *Journal of Symbolic Computation*, 29:747–775, 2000.

[30] H. Tsai. Algorithms for associated primes, Weyl closure, and local cohomology of D-modules. *Local cohomology and its applications (Guanajuato, 1999)*, 226:169–194, 2001.

A Fast Parallel Sparse Polynomial GCD Algorithm

Jiaxiong Hu and Michael Monagan
Department of Mathematics, Simon Fraser University
Burnaby, British Columbia, V5A 1S6, Canada
jha107@sfu.ca and mmonagan@sfu.ca

ABSTRACT

We present a parallel GCD algorithm for sparse multivariate polynomials with integer coefficients. The algorithm combines a Kronecker substitution with a Ben-Or/Tiwari sparse interpolation modulo a smooth prime to determine the support of the GCD. We have implemented our algorithm in Cilk C. We compare it with Maple and Magma's implementations of Zippel's GCD algorithm.

1. INTRODUCTION

Let A and B be two polynomials in $\mathbb{Z}[x_0, x_1, \ldots, x_n]$. In this paper we present a sparse modular GCD algorithm for computing $G = \gcd(A, B)$ the greatest common divisor of A and B. We will compare our algorithm with Zippel's sparse GCD algorithm from [25]. Zippel's algorithm is the main GCD algorithm currently used by Maple, Magma and Mathematica.

Let $A = G\bar{A} = \sum_{i=0}^{dA} a_i x_0^i$, $B = G\bar{B} = \sum_{i=0}^{dB} b_i x_0^i$ and $G = \sum_{i=0}^{dG} c_i x_0^i$ where a_i, b_i and c_i are in $\mathbb{Z}[x_1, \ldots, x_n]$. We will assume $\gcd(a_i) = 1$ and $\gcd(b_i) = 1$, that is, the contents have already been computed and divided out.

Let $\#A$ denote the number of terms in A and let $\mathrm{Supp}(A)$ denote the set of monomials appearing in A.

Let $\mathrm{LC}(A)$ denote the leading coefficient of A taken in x_0. Let $\Gamma = \gcd(LC(A), LC(B)) = \gcd(a_{dA}, b_{dB})$. Since $LC(G)|LC(A)$ and $\mathrm{LC}(G)|LC(B)$ it must be that $\mathrm{LC}(G)|\Gamma$ thus $\Gamma = LC(G)\Delta$ for some polynomial $\Delta \in \mathbb{Z}[x_1, \ldots, x_n]$.

EXAMPLE 1. *If* $G = x_1x_0^2 + x_2x_0 + 3$, $\bar{A} = (x_2 - x_1)x_0 + x_2$ *and* $\bar{B} = (x_2 - x_1)x_0 + x_1 + 2$ *we have* $\#G = 3$, $\mathrm{LC}(G) = x_1$, $\Gamma = x_1(x_2 - x_1)$, $\Delta = x_2 - x_1$ *and* $\mathrm{Supp}(G) = \{x_1x_0^2, x_2x_0, 1\}$.

We provide an overview of the GCD algorithm. Let $H = \Delta \times G$ and $h_i = \Delta \times c_i$ so that $H = \sum_{i=0}^{dG} h_i x_0^i$. Our algorithm will compute H not G. After computing H it must then compute $\gcd(h_i)$ which is Δ and divide H by Δ to obtain G. We compute H modulo a sequence of primes $p_1, p_2, \ldots$, and recover the integer coefficients of H using Chinese remaindering. The use of Chinese remaindering is standard. Details may be found in [4, 8]. Let H_1 be the result of computing $H \mod p_1$. For the remaining primes we use the sparse interpolation approach of Zippel [25] which assumes $\mathrm{Supp}(H_1) = \mathrm{Supp}(H)$. From now on we focus on the computation of $H \mod p_1$.

To compute $H \bmod p$ the algorithm will pick a sequence of points $\beta_1, \beta_2, \ldots$ from $\mathbb{Z}_p^n$, compute monic images

$$g_j = \gcd(A(x_0, \beta_j), B(x_0, \beta_j)) \in \mathbb{Z}_p[x_0]$$

of G, in parallel, then multiply g_j by the scalar $\Gamma(\beta_j) \in \mathbb{Z}_p$. Because the scaled image $\Gamma(\beta_j) \times g_j(x_0)$ is an image of a polynomial, H, we can use polynomial interpolation to interpolate each coefficient $h_i(x_1, \ldots, x_n)$ of H from the coefficients of the scaled images.

Let $t = \max_{i=0}^{dG} \#h_i$. The parameter t measures the sparsity of H. Let $d = \max_{i=1}^{n} \deg_{x_i} H$ and $D = \max_{i=0}^{dG} \deg h_i$. The cost of sparse polynomial interpolation algorithms is determined mainly by the number of points $\beta_1, \beta_2, \ldots$ needed and also the size of the prime p needed. These all depend on t, d and D. Table 1 below presents data for several sparse interpolation algorithms.

To get a sense for how large the prime needs to be for the different algorithms we include data in Table 1 for the following **benchmark problem:** Let $G, \bar{A}, \bar{B}$ have nine variables ($n = 8$), degree $d = 20$ in each variable, and total degree $D = 60$ (to better reflect real problems). Let G have 10,000 terms with $t = 1000$. Let $\bar{A}$ and $\bar{B}$ have 100 terms so that $A = G\bar{A}$ and $B = G\bar{B}$ have about one million terms.

	#points	size of p	benchmark
Zippel [1979]	$O(ndt)$	$p > 2nd^2t^2$	$= 6.4 \times 10^9$
BenOr/Tiwari [1988]	$O(t)$	$p > p_n^D$	$= 5.3 \times 10^{77}$
Monagan/Javadi [2010]	$O(nt)$	$p > nDt^2$	$= 4.8 \times 10^8$
Discrete Logs	$O(t)$	$p > (d+1)^n$	$= 3.7 \times 10^{10}$

Table 1: Some sparse interpolation algorithms

Notes: the figure $O(ndt)$ for Zippel's algorithm is for the worst case. The average case (for random inputs) is $O(dt)$ points. Also, Kaltofen and Lee showed in [14] how to modify Zippel's algorithm so that it will work for primes much smaller than $2nd^2t^2$.

The primary disadvantage of the Ben-Or/Tiwari algorithm is the size of the prime. In [12] Javadi and Monagan modify the Ben-Or/Tiwari algorithm to work for a prime of size $O(nDt^2)$ but using $O(nt)$ points.

The discrete logs method, first proposed by Murao and Fujise [19], is a modification of the Ben-Or/Tiwari algorithm which computes discrete logarithms in the cyclic group $\mathbb{Z}_p^*$.

ISSAC '16, July 19-22, 2016, Waterloo, ON, Canada

DOI: http://dx.doi.org/10.1145/2930889.2930903

We use this method. We give details for it in Section 1.2. The advantage over the Ben-Or/Tiwari algorithm is that the prime size is $O(n \log d)$ bits instead of $O(D \log n)$ bits.

In the GCD algorithm, not all evaluation points can be used. If $\gcd(\bar{A}(x_0, \beta_j), \bar{B}(x_0, \beta_j)) \neq 1$ then β_j is said to be *unlucky* and the image g_j cannot be used to interpolate H. In Zippel's algorithm, where the β_j are chosen at random from $\mathbb{Z}_p^n$, unlucky β_j, once identified, can simply be skipped. This is not the case for the evaluation point sequences used by the Ben-Or/Tiwari algorithm and the discrete logs method. In Section 1.4, we modify these point sequences to handle unlucky evaluation points.

Our modification for the discrete logarithm sequence increases the size of p which negates some of its advantage. This led us to consider using a Kronecker substitution on $x_1, x_2, \ldots, x_n$ to map the GCD computation into a bivariate computation in $\mathbb{Z}_p[x_0, y]$. Some Kronecker substitutions result in all evaluation points being unlucky so they cannot be used. We call these Kronecker substitutions *unlucky*. In Section 2 we show (Theorem 1) that there are only finitely many of them and how to detect them quickly so that a larger Kronecker substitution may be tried.

If a Kronecker substitution is not unlucky there can still be many unlucky evaluation points because the degree in y of the resulting polynomials is exponential in n. This prompted us to investigate the distribution of the unlucky evaluation points. Our next contribution (Theorem 2) is a result for the expected number of unlucky evaluations.

In Section 3 we assemble a Monte-Carlo GCD algorithm which chooses p and computes $H \bmod p$. We have implemented our algorithm in C and parallelized it using Cilk C. We did this initially for 31 bit primes then for 63 bit primes. The first timing results revealed that almost all the time (over 95%) was spent in evaluating $A(x_0, \beta_j)$ and $B(x_0, \beta_j)$. We describe an improvement for evaluation and how we parallelized it.

In Section 4 we compare our new algorithm with the C implementations of Zippel's algorithm in Maple and Magma. The timing results are very promising. For our benchmark problem, Maple takes 62,520 seconds, Magma dies with an internal error, and our new algorithm takes 4.47 seconds on 16 cores. We conclude by discussing some ideas for reducing the number of evaluation points and the size of p.

The proofs in the paper make use of the Schwartz-Zippel Lemma and properties of the Sylvester resultant. We state these results here for later use.

LEMMA 1. *Let F be a field and A and B be polynomials in $F[x_0, x_1, \ldots, x_n]$ with positive degree in x_0. Let $R = \mathrm{res}_{x_0}(A, B)$ denote the Sylvester resultant of A and B. Then*

(i) R is a polynomial in $F[x_1, \ldots, x_n]$ and
(ii) $\deg R \leq \deg A \deg B$ (Bezout bound).

If $\alpha \in F^n$ satisfies $\deg_{x_0} A(x_0, \alpha) = \deg_{x_0}(A)$ and $\deg_{x_0} B(x_0, \alpha) = \deg_{x_0}(B)$ then
(iii) $\gcd(A(x_0, \alpha), B(x_0, \alpha)) \neq 1$
$\iff \mathrm{res}_{x_0}(A(x_0, \alpha), B(x_0, \alpha)) = 0$ *and*
(iv) $\mathrm{res}_{x_0}(A(x_0, \alpha), B(x_0, \alpha)) = R(\alpha)$.

Proofs may be found in Ch. 3 and Ch. 6 of [5]. Note that the degree condition on α means that the dimension of Sylvester's matrix for A and B in x_0 is the same as for $A(x_0, \alpha)$ and $B(x_0, \alpha)$ which proves *(iv)*.

LEMMA 2. *(Schwartz-Zippel [22, 25]). Let F be a field and $f \in F[x_1, x_2, \ldots, x_n]$ be non-zero with total degree d and let $S \subset F$. If β is chosen at random from S^n then* $\mathrm{Prob}[f(\beta) = 0] \leq \frac{d}{|S|}$. *In particular, if $F = \mathbb{Z}_p$ and $S = \mathbb{Z}_p$ then* $\mathrm{Prob}[f(\beta) = 0] \leq \frac{d}{p}$.

1.1 Ben-Or Tiwari Sparse Interpolation

Let $C(x_1, \ldots, x_n) = \sum_{i=1}^t a_i M_i$ where $a_i \in \mathbb{Z}$ and M_i are monomials in $(x_1, \ldots, x_n)$. In our context, C represents one of the coefficients of $H = \Delta G$ we wish to interpolate. Let $D = \deg C$ and let $d = \max_{i=1}^n \deg_{x_i} C$ and let p_n denote the n'th prime. Let

$$v_j = C(2^j, 3^j, 5^j, \ldots, p_n^j) \text{ for } j = 0, 1, \ldots, 2t-1.$$

The Ben-Or/Tiwari sparse interpolation algorithm [3] interpolates $C(x_1, x_2, \ldots, x_n)$ from the $2t$ points v_j. Let $m_i = M_i(2, 3, 5, \ldots, p_n) \in \mathbb{Z}$ and let $\lambda(z) = \prod_{i=1}^t (z - m_i) \in \mathbb{Z}[z]$. The algorithm proceeds in 4 steps.

1 Compute $\lambda(z)$ from v_j using the Berlekamp-Massey algorithm [16] or the Euclidean algorithm [2, 24].

2 Compute the integer roots m_i of $\lambda(z)$.

3 Factor the integers m_i using trial division by $2, 3, \ldots, p_n$ from which we obtain M_i. For example, for $n = 3$, if $m_i = 45000 = 2^3 3^2 5^4$ then $M_i = {x_1}^3 {x_2}^2 {x_3}^4$.

4 Solve the following $t \times t$ linear system $Va = b$ for the unknown coefficients a_i in $C(x_1, \ldots, x_n)$.

$$\begin{bmatrix} 1 & 1 & \ldots & 1 \\ m_1 & m_2 & \ldots & m_t \\ {m_1}^2 & {m_2}^2 & \ldots & {m_t}^2 \\ \vdots & \vdots & \vdots & \vdots \\ {m_1}^{t-1} & {m_2}^{t-1} & \ldots & m_t^{t-1} \end{bmatrix} \begin{bmatrix} a_1 \\ a_2 \\ a_3 \\ \vdots \\ a_t \end{bmatrix} = \begin{bmatrix} v_0 \\ v_1 \\ v_2 \\ \vdots \\ v_{t-1} \end{bmatrix}$$

The matrix V above is a transposed Vandermonde matrix. The linear system $Va = b$ can be solved in $O(t^2)$ arithmetic operations (see [26]). Note, the master polynomial $P(Z)$ in [26] is $\lambda(z)$.

Notice that the largest integer in $\lambda(z)$ is the constant term $\Pi_{i=1}^t m_i$ which is of size $O(tn \log D)$ bits. Moreover, in [13], Kaltofen, Lakshman and Wiley noticed a severe expression swell occurs if either the Berlekamp-Massey algorithm or the Euclidean algorithm is used to compute $\lambda(z)$ over $\mathbb{Q}$. For our purposes, because we want to interpolate H modulo a prime p, we run steps 1,2, and 4 modulo p. Provided $p > \max_{i=1}^t m_i \leq p_n^D$ the integers $m_i \bmod p$ remain unique. The roots of $\lambda(z) \in \mathbb{Z}_p[z]$ can be found using Rabin's algorithm [21] which has classical complexity $O(t^2 \log p)$.

In practice, t is not known in advance so the algorithm needs to be modified to also determine t. For p sufficiently large, if we compute $\lambda(z)$ after $j = 2, 4, 6, \ldots$ points, we will see $\deg \lambda(z) = 1, 2, 3, \ldots, t-1, t, t, t, \ldots$ with high probability. Thus we simply wait until the degree of $\lambda(z)$ does not change. This is first discussed by Kaltofen, Lee and Lobo in [14]. We will return to this in Section 3.1.

Let $M(t)$ denote the cost of multiplying two polynomials of degree t in $\mathbb{Z}_p[t]$. The fast Euclidean algorithm can be used to accelerate Step 1. It has complexity $O(M(t) \log t)$. See Ch. 11 of [7]. Computing the roots of $\lambda(z)$ in Step 2 can be done in $O(M(t) \log t \log p)$. See Ch 14 of [7]. Step 4 may be done in $O(M(t) \log t)$ using fast interpolation. See Ch 10 of [7].

1.2 Ben-Or/Tiwari with discrete logarithms

The discrete logarithm method modifies the Ben-Or/Tiwari algorithm so that the prime needed is a little larger than $(d+1)^n$ thus of size is $O(n \log d)$ bits instead of $O(D \log n)$. Murao and Fujise [19] were the first to use this method. Some practical aspects of it are discussed by van der Hoven and Lecerf in [11]. We explain how the method works.

To interpolate $C(x_1, \ldots, x_n)$ we first pick a prime p of the form $p = q_1 q_2 q_3 \ldots q_n + 1$ satisfying $q_i > \deg_{x_i} C$ and $\gcd(q_i, q_j) = 1$. Finding such primes is not difficult and we omit presenting an explicit algorithm here.

Next we pick a random primitive element $\alpha \in \mathbb{Z}_p$ which we can do using the partial factorization $p - 1 = q_1 q_2 \ldots q_n$ (see [23]). We set $\omega_i = \alpha^{(p-1)/q_i}$ so that $\omega_i^{q_i} = 1$ and replace the evaluation points $(2^j, 3^j, \ldots, p_n^j)$ with $(\omega_1^j, \omega_2^j, \ldots, \omega_n^j)$. After Step 1 we factor $\lambda(z)$ in $\mathbb{Z}_p[z]$ to determine the m_i. If $M_i = \prod_{k=1}^n x_k^{d_k}$ we have $m_i = \prod_{k=1}^n \omega_k^{d_k}$. To compute d_k in Step 3 we compute the discrete logarithm $x := \log_\alpha m_i$, that is, solve $\alpha^x \equiv m_i \pmod p$ for $0 \le x < p - 1$. We have

$$x = \log_\alpha m_i = \log_\alpha \prod_{k=1}^n \omega_k^{d_k} = \sum_{k=1}^n d_k \frac{p-1}{q_k}. \qquad (1)$$

Taking (1) mod q_k we obtain $d_k = x[(p-1)/q_k]^{-1} \mod q_k$. Step 4 remains unchanged.

For $p = q_1 q_2 \ldots q_n + 1$, a discrete logarithm can be computed in $O(\sum_{i=1}^n \sqrt{q_i})$ multiplications in $\mathbb{Z}_p$ using the Pohlig-Helman algorithm. See [20, 23]. Since the $q_i \sim d$ this leads to an $O(n\sqrt{d})$ cost. Kaltofen showed in [15] that this can be made polynomial in $\log d$ and n if one uses a Kronecker substitution to reduce multivariate interpolation to a univariate interpolation and uses a prime $p > (d+1)^n$ of the form $p = 2^k s + 1$ with s small.

1.3 Bad and Unlucky Evaluation Points

Let A and B be non constant polynomials in $\mathbb{Z}[x_0, \ldots, x_n]$ with $G = \gcd(A, B)$ and let $\bar{A} = A/G$ and $\bar{B} = B/G$. Let p be prime such that $LC(A)LC(B) \mod p \neq 0$.

Definition 1. *Let $\alpha \in \mathbb{Z}_p^n$ and let $g_\alpha(x) = \gcd(\bar{A}(x, \alpha), \bar{B}(x, \alpha))$. We say α is* bad *if $LC(A)(\alpha) = 0$ or $LC(B)(\alpha) = 0$ and α is* unlucky *if $\deg g_\alpha(x) > 0$.*

Example 2. *Let $G = (x_1 - 16)x_0 + 1$, $\bar{A} = x_0^2 + 1$ and $\bar{B} = x_0^2 + (x_1 - 1)(x_2 - 9)x_0 + 1$. Then $LC(A) = LC(B) = x_1 - 16$ so $\{(16, \beta) : \beta \in \mathbb{Z}_p\}$ are bad and $\{(1, \beta) : \beta \in \mathbb{Z}_p\}$ and $\{(\beta, 9) : \beta \in \mathbb{Z}_p\}$ are unlucky.*

The algorithm cannot reconstruct G using the image $g_\alpha(x) = \gcd(A(x, \alpha), B(x, \alpha))$ if α is unlucky. Brown's idea in [4] to detect unlucky α is based on the following Lemma.

Lemma 3. *Let α and g_α be as above and $h_\alpha = G(x, \alpha)$ mod p. If α is not bad then $h_\alpha | g_\alpha$ and $\deg_x g_\alpha \ge \deg_x G$.*

For a proof of Lemma 3 see Lemma 7.3 of [8]. Brown only uses α which are not bad and the images $g_\alpha(x)$ of least degree to interpolate G. The following Lemma implies if the prime p is large then unlucky evaluations points are rare.

Lemma 4. $\text{Prob}[\begin{smallmatrix}\alpha \text{ is bad} \\ \text{or unlucky}\end{smallmatrix}] \le \frac{\deg A \deg B + \deg A + \deg B}{p - \deg A - \deg B}$.

Proof: $\text{Prob}[\alpha \text{ is bad}] = \text{Prob}[\text{ LC}(A)(\alpha)\text{LC}(B)(\alpha) = 0 \text{ }] \le \frac{\deg(\text{LC}(A))}{p} + \frac{\deg(\text{LC}(B))}{p} \le \frac{\deg A + \deg B}{p}$. To determine $\text{Prob}[\alpha \text{ is unlucky} \mid \alpha \text{ is not bad}]$ we have α is unlucky

$$\begin{aligned} \iff &\quad \gcd(\bar{A}(x, \alpha), \bar{B}(x, \alpha)) \neq 1 \text{ (by definition)} \\ \iff &\quad \text{res}_x(\bar{A}(x, \alpha), \bar{B}(x, \alpha)) = 0 \text{ (by Lemma 1)} \\ \iff &\quad R(\alpha) = 0 \text{ where } R = \text{res}_{x_0}(\bar{A}, \bar{B}) \text{ (by Lemma 1).} \end{aligned}$$

Hence $\text{Prob}[\alpha \text{ is unlucky} \mid \alpha \text{ is not bad}] \le \frac{\deg R}{p - \deg A - \deg B}$ (by Schwartz-Zippel). Now the $\text{Prob}[\alpha \text{ is bad or unlucky}] \le \text{Prob}[\alpha \text{ is bad}] + \text{Prob}[\alpha \text{ is unlucky} \mid \alpha \text{ is not bad}] \le \frac{\deg A + \deg B}{p} + \frac{\deg R}{p - \deg A - \deg B} \le \frac{\deg R + \deg A + \deg B}{p - \deg A - \deg B}$ which by Lemma 1 is $\le \frac{\deg A \deg B + \deg A + \deg B}{p - \deg A - \deg B}$.

The following algorithm applies Lemma 3 to compute a lower bound d for $\deg_{x_i} G$. Note, later in the paper when we use Algorithm DegreeBound, if it happens that $d > \deg_{x_i} G$ (α is unlucky) then this won't affect the correctness of our algorithm, only the efficiency.

Algorithm DegreeBound(A,B,i)

Input: Non-zero $A, B \in \mathbb{Z}[x_0, x_1, \ldots, x_n]$ and an integer i satisfying $0 \le i \le n$.

Output: $d \ge \deg_{x_i}(G)$ where $G = \gcd(A, B)$.

1 Set $LA = \text{LC}(A, x_i)$ and $LB = \text{LC}(B, x_i)$. So $LA, LB \in \mathbb{Z}[x_0, \ldots, x_{i-1}, x_{i+1}, \ldots, x_n]$.

2 Pick a prime $p \gg \deg A \deg B$ such that $LA \mod p \neq 0$ and $LB \mod p \neq 0$.

3 Pick $\alpha = (\alpha_0, \ldots, \alpha_{i-1}, \alpha_{i+1}, \ldots, \alpha_n) \in \mathbb{Z}_p^n$ at random until $LA(\alpha)LB(\alpha) \neq 0$.

4 Compute $a = A(\alpha_0, \ldots, \alpha_{i-1}, x_i, \alpha_{i+1}, \ldots, \alpha_n)$ and $b = B(\alpha_0, \ldots, \alpha_{i-1}, x_i, \alpha_{i+1}, \ldots, \alpha_n)$.

5 Compute $g = \gcd(a, b)$ in $\mathbb{Z}_p[x_i]$ using the Euclidean algorithm and output $d = \deg_{x_i} g$.

1.4 Unlucky evaluations in Ben-Or/Tiwari

Consider again Example 2 where $G = (x_1 - 16)x_0 + 1$, $\bar{A} = x_0^2 + 1$ and $\bar{B} = x_0^2 + (x_1 - 1)(x_2 - 9)x_0 + 1$. For the Ben-Or/Tiwari points $\alpha_j = (2^j, 3^j)$ for $0 \le j < 2t$ observe that $\alpha_0 = (1, 1)$ and $\alpha_2 = (4, 9)$ are unlucky and $\alpha_4 = (16, 81)$ is bad. Since none of these points can be used to interpolate G we need to modify the Ben-Or/Tiwari point sequence. For the GCD problem, we want random evaluation points to avoid bad and unlucky points. The following fix works.

Pick the first $s > 0$ such that $2^s > p$ so that $(2^s, 3^s, \ldots, p_n^s)$ mod p is not fixed and use $\alpha_j = (2^j, 3^j, \ldots, p_n^j)$ for $s \le j < s + 2t$. Steps 1,2 and 3 work as before. To solve the *shifted* transposed Vandermonde system $Wc = u$

$$\begin{bmatrix} m_1^s & m_2^s & \ldots & m_t^s \\ m_1^{s+1} & m_2^{s+1} & \ldots & m_t^{s+1} \\ \vdots & \vdots & \vdots & \vdots \\ m_1^{s+t-1} & m_2^{s+t-1} & \ldots & m_t^{s+t-1} \end{bmatrix} \begin{bmatrix} c_1 \\ c_2 \\ \vdots \\ c_t \end{bmatrix} = \begin{bmatrix} v_s \\ v_{s+1} \\ \vdots \\ v_{s+t-1} \end{bmatrix}$$

we first solve the transposed Vandermonde system $Vb = u$

$$\begin{bmatrix} 1 & 1 & \ldots & 1 \\ m_1 & m_2 & \ldots & m_t \\ \vdots & \vdots & \vdots & \vdots \\ m_1^{t-1} & m_2^{t-1} & \ldots & m_t^{t-1} \end{bmatrix} \begin{bmatrix} b_1 \\ b_2 \\ \vdots \\ b_t \end{bmatrix} = \begin{bmatrix} v_s \\ v_{s+1} \\ \vdots \\ v_{s+t-1} \end{bmatrix}$$

as before to obtain $b = V^{-1}u$. Observe that the matrix $W = DV$ where D is the t by t diagonal matrix with $D_{i,i} = m_i^s$. To solve $Wc = u$ we have

$$(DV)c = u \Longrightarrow c = (V^{-1}D^{-1})u = D^{-1}(V^{-1}u) = D^{-1}b$$

Thus $c_i = u m_i^{-s}$ and we can solve $Wc = u$ in $O(t^2 + t \log s)$ multiplications.

Referring again to Example 2, if we use the discrete logarithm evaluation points $\alpha_j = (\omega_1^j, \omega_2^j)$ for $0 \le j < 2t$ then $\alpha_0 = (1,1)$ is unlucky and also, since $\omega_1^{q_1} = 1$, all $\alpha_{q_1}, \alpha_{2q_1}, \alpha_{3q_1}, \ldots$ are unlucky. Shifting the sequence to start at $j = 1$ and picking $q_i > 2t$ is problematic because for the GCD problem, t may be larger than $\max \#a_i, \#b_i$, or smaller; there is no way to know in advance. This difficulty led us to consider using a Kronecker substitution.

2. KRONECKER SUBSTITUTIONS

We propose to use a Kronecker substitution to map a multivariate polynomial GCD problem in $\mathbb{Z}[x_0, x_1, \ldots, x_n]$ into a bivariate GCD problem in $\mathbb{Z}[x, y]$. After making the Kronecker substitution, we need to interpolate $H(x, y) = \Delta(x, y)G(x, y)$ where $\deg_y H(x, y)$ will be exponential in n. To make discrete logarithms in $\mathbb{Z}_p$ feasible, we follow Kaltofen [15] and pick $p = 2^k s + 1 > \deg_y H(x, y)$ with s small.

DEFINITION 2. *Let D be an integral domain and let f be a polynomial in $D[x_0, x_1, \ldots, x_n]$. Let $r \in \mathbb{Z}^{n-1}$ with $r_i > 0$. Let $K_r : D[x_0, x_1, \ldots, x_n] \to D[x, y]$ be the Kronecker substitution $K_r(f) = f(x, y, y^{r_1}, y^{r_1 r_2}, \ldots, y^{r_1 r_2 \cdots r_{n-1}})$.*

Let $d_i = \deg_{x_i} f$ be the partial degrees of f for $1 \le i \le n$. Observe that K_r is invertible if $r_i > d_i$ for $1 \le i \le n-1$. Not all such Kronecker substitutions can be used, however, for the GCD problem. We consider an example.

EXAMPLE 3. *Consider the following GCD problem*

$$G = x + y + z, \quad \bar{A} = x^3 - yz, \quad \bar{B} = x^2 - y^2$$

in $\mathbb{Z}[x, y, z]$. Since $\deg_y G = 1$ the Kronecker substitution $K_r(G) = G(x, y, y^2)$ is invertible. But $\gcd(K_r(\bar{A}), K_r(\bar{B}))$ $= \gcd(\bar{A}(x, y, y^2), \bar{B}(x, y, y^2)) = \gcd(x^3 - y^3, x^2 - y^2) = x - y$. If we proceed to interpolate the $\gcd(K_r(A), K_r(B))$ we will obtain $(x - y)K_r(G)$ in expanded form from which and we cannot recover G.

We call such a Kronecker substitution unlucky. Theorem 1 below tells us that the number of unlucky Kronecker substitutions is finite. To detect them we will also avoid bad Kronecker substitutions in an analogous way Brown did to detect unlucky evaluation points.

DEFINITION 3. *Let K_r be a Kronecker substitution. We say K_r is* bad *if $\deg_x K_r(A) < \deg_{x_0} A$ or $\deg_x K_r(B) < \deg_{x_0} B$ and K_r is* unlucky *if $\deg_x \gcd(K_r(\bar{A}), K_r(\bar{B})) > 0$.*

LEMMA 5. *Let $f \in \mathbb{Z}[x_1, \ldots, x_n]$ be non-zero and $d_i \ge 0$ for $1 \le i \le n$. Let X be the number of Kronecker substitutions from the sequence $r_k = [d_1 + k, d_2 + k, \ldots, d_{n-1} + k]$ for $k = 1, 2, 3, \ldots$ for which $K_r(f) = 0$. Then $X \le (n-1)\sqrt{2 \deg f}$.*

Proof: $K_r(f) = 0 \iff f(y, y^{r_1}, y^{r_1 r_2}, \ldots, y^{r_1 r_2 \cdots r_{n-1}}) = 0$
$\iff f \bmod \langle x_1 - y, x_2 - y^{r_1}, \ldots, x_n - y^{r_1 r_2 \cdots r_{n-1}} \rangle = 0$
$\iff f \bmod \langle x_2 - x_1^{r_1}, x_3 - x_2^{r_2}, \ldots, x_n - x_{n-1}^{r_{n-1}} \rangle = 0.$

Thus X is the number ideals $I = \langle x_2 - x_1^{r_1}, \ldots, x_n - x_{n-1}^{r_{n-1}} \rangle$ for which $f \bmod I = 0$ with $r_i = d_i + 1, d_i + 2, \ldots$. We prove that $X \le (n-1)\sqrt{2 \deg f}$ by induction on n.

If $n = 1$ then I is empty so $f \bmod I = f$ and hence $X = 0$ and the Lemma holds. For $n = 2$ we have $f(x_1, x_2) \bmod \langle x_2 - x_1^{r_1} \rangle = 0 \implies x_2 - x_1^{r_1} | f$. Now X is maximal when $d_1 = 0$ and $r_1 = 1, 2, 3, \ldots$. We have

$$\sum_{r_1=1}^{X} r_1 \le \deg f \Longrightarrow X(X+1)/2 \le \deg f \Longrightarrow X < \sqrt{2 \deg f}.$$

For $n > 2$ we proceed as follows. Either $x_n - x_{n-1}^{r_{n-1}} | f$ or it doesn't. If not then the polynomial $S = f(x_1, \ldots, x_{n-1}, x_{n-1}^{r_{n-1}})$ is non-zero. For the sub-case $x_n - x_{n-1}^{r_{n-1}} | f$ we obtain at most $\sqrt{2 \deg f}$ such factors of f using the previous argument. For the case $S \ne 0$ we have

$$S \bmod I = 0 \iff S \bmod \langle x_2 - x_1^{r_1}, \ldots, x_{n-2} - x_{n-1}^{r_{n-2}} \rangle = 0$$

Notice that $\deg_{x_i} S = \deg_{x_i} f$ for $1 \le i \le n-2$. Hence, by induction on n, $X < (n-2)\sqrt{2 \deg f}$ for this case. Adding the number of unlucky Kronecker substitutions for both cases yields $X \le (n-1)\sqrt{2 \deg f}$. □

THEOREM 1. *Let $A, B \in \mathbb{Z}[x_0, x_1, \ldots, x_n]$ be non-zero, $G = \gcd(A, B)$, $\bar{A} = A/G$ and $B = \bar{B}/G$. Let $d_i \ge \deg_{x_i} G$. Let X be the number of bad and unlucky Kronecker substitutions K_{r_k} from the sequence $r_k = [d_1 + k, d_2 + k, \ldots, d_{n-1} + k]$ for $k = 1, 2, 3, \ldots$. Then*

$$X \le \sqrt{2}(n-1)\left[\sqrt{\deg A} + \sqrt{\deg B} + \sqrt{\deg A \deg B}\right].$$

Proof Let $LA = \mathrm{LC}(A)$ and $LB = \mathrm{LC}(B)$ be the leading coefficients of A and B in x_0. Then K_r is bad $\iff K_r(LA) = 0$ or $K_r(LB) = 0$. Applying Lemma 5, the number of bad Kronecker substitutions is at most

$$(n-1)(\sqrt{2 \deg LA} + \sqrt{2 \deg LB}) \le (n-1)(\sqrt{2 \deg A} + \sqrt{2 \deg B}).$$

Now let $R = \mathrm{res}_{x_0}(\bar{A}, \bar{B})$. We will assume K_r is not bad.

$$\begin{aligned} K_r \text{ is unlucky} &\iff \deg_x(\gcd(K_r(\bar{A}), K_r(\bar{B})) > 0 \\ &\iff \mathrm{res}_x(K_r(\bar{A}), K_r(\bar{B})) = 0 \\ &\iff K_r(\mathrm{res}_x(\bar{A}, \bar{B})) = 0 \\ &\iff K_r(R) = 0 \ \ (K_r \text{ is not bad}). \end{aligned}$$

By Lemma 5, the number of unlucky Kronecker substitutions $\le (n-1)\sqrt{2 \deg R} \le (n-1)\sqrt{2 \deg A \deg B}$ by Lemma 1. Adding the two contributions proves the theorem. □

In algorithm PGCD below, we identify an unlucky substitution as follows. After computing the first two monic images $g_1(x)$ and $g_2(x)$ in step 9 if both $\deg_x g_1 > d_0$ and $\deg_x g_2 > d_0$ then with high probability K_r is unlucky so we try the next Kronecker substitution $r = [r_1 + 1, r_2 + 1, \ldots, r_{n-1} + 1]$.

It is still not obvious that a Kronecker substitution that is not unlucky can be used because it can create a content in y of exponential degree. The following example shows how we recover $H = \Delta G$ when this happens.

EXAMPLE 4. *Consider the following GCD problem*

$$G = wx^2 + zy, \quad \bar{A} = ywx + z, \quad \bar{B} = yzx + w$$

in $\mathbb{Z}[x, y, z, w]$. We have $\Gamma = wy$ and $\Delta = y$. For $K(f) = f(x, y, y^3, y^9)$ we have $\gcd(K(A), K(B)) = K(G)\gcd(y^{10}x + y^3, y^4 x + y^9) = (y^9 x^2 + y^4)y^3 = y^7(y^5 x^2 + 1)$.

One must not try to compute $\gcd(K(A), K(B))$ because the degree of the content of $\gcd(K(A), K(B))$ (y^7 in our example) can be exponential in n the number of variables and we cannot compute this efficiently using the Euclidean algorithm. The crucial observation is that if we compute **monic** images $g_j = \gcd(K(A)(x, \alpha^j), K(B)(x, \alpha^j))$ any content is divided out, and when we scale by $K(\Gamma)(\alpha^j)$ and interpolate y in $K(H)$ using sparse interpolation, we recover any content. We obtain $K(H) = K(\Delta)K(G) = y^{10}x^2 + y^5$, then invert K to obtain $H = (yw)x^2 + (y^2z)$.

2.1 Unlucky evaluation points

Even if the Kronecker substitution is not unlucky, after applying it to input polynomials A and B, because the degree in y may be very large, the number of bad and unlucky evaluation points may be very large.

EXAMPLE 5. *Consider the following GCD problem*

$$G = x_0 + x_1^d + x_2^d + \cdots + x_n^d,$$
$$\bar{A} = x_0 + x_1 + \cdots + x_{n-1} + x_n, \text{ and}$$
$$\bar{B} = x_0 + x_1 + \cdots + x_{n-1} + 1.$$

Using $r = [d+1, d+1, \ldots, d+1]$ we need $p > (d+1)^n$. But $R = \mathrm{res}_{x_0}(\bar{A}, \bar{B}) = 1 - x_n$ and $K_r(R) = 1 - y^{r_1 r_2 \cdots r_{n-1}} = 1 - y^{(d+1)^{n-1}}$ which means there could be as many as $(d+1)^{n-1}$ unlucky evaluation points, that is, one in $d+1$.

To guarantee that we avoid unlucky evaluation points with high probability we would need to pick $p \gg \deg_y K_r(R)$ which could be much larger than what is needed to interpolate $K_r(H)$. But this upper bound based on the resultant is a worst case. This lead us to investigate what the expected number of unlucky evaluation points is. We ran an experiment. We computed all monic quadratic and cubic bivariate polynomials over small finite fields $\mathbb{F}_q$ of size $q = 2, 3, 4, 5, 7, 8, 11$ and counted the number of unlucky evaluation points to find the following result.

THEOREM 2. *Let $\mathbb{F}_q$ be a finite field with q elements and $f = x^l + \sum_{i=0}^{l-1}(\sum_{j=0}^{d_i} a_{ij}y^j)x^i$ and $g = x^m + \sum_{i=0}^{m-1}(\sum_{j=0}^{e_i} b_{ij}y^j)x^i$ with $l \geq 1$, $m \geq 1$, and $a_{ij}, b_{ij} \in \mathbb{F}_q$. Let $X = |\{\alpha \in \mathbb{F}_q : \gcd(f(x,\alpha), g(x,\alpha)) \neq 1\}|$ be a random variable over all choices $a_{ij}, b_{ij} \in \mathbb{F}_q$. So $0 \leq X \leq q$ and for f and g not coprime in $\mathbb{F}_q[x,y]$ we have $X = q$. If $d_i \geq 0$ and $e_i \geq 0$ then $\mathrm{E}[X] = 1$.*

Proof: Let $C(y) = \sum_{i=0}^{d} c_i y^i$ with $d \geq 0$ and $c_i \in \mathbb{F}_q$ and fix $\beta \in \mathbb{F}_q$. Consider the evaluation map $C_\beta : \mathbb{F}_q^{d+1} \to \mathbb{F}_q$ given by $C_\beta(c_0, \ldots, c_d) = \sum_{i=0}^{d} c_i \beta^i$. We claim that C is balanced, that is, C maps q^d inputs to each element of $\mathbb{F}_q$. It follows that $f(x, \beta)$ is also balanced, that is, over all choices for $a_{i,j}$ each monic polynomial in $\mathbb{F}_q[x]$ of degree n is obtained equally often. Similarly for $g(x, \beta)$.

Recall that two univariate polynomials a, b in $\mathbb{F}_q[x]$ with degree $\deg a > 0$ and $\deg b > 0$ are coprime with probability $1 - 1/q$ (see Ch 11 of Mullen and Panario [18]). This is also true under the restriction that they are monic. Therefore $f(x, \beta)$ and $g(x, \beta)$ are coprime with probability $1 - 1/q$. Since we have q choices for β we obtain

$$E[X] = \sum_{\beta \in \mathbb{F}_q} \mathrm{Prob}[\gcd(A(x,\beta), B(x,\beta)) \neq 1] = q(1 - (1 - \frac{1}{q})) = 1.$$

Proof of claim. Since $B = \{1, y - \beta, (y-\beta)^2, \ldots, (y-\beta)^d\}$ is a basis for polynomials of degree d we can write each $C(y) = \sum_{i=0}^{d} c_i y^i$ as $C(y) = u_0 + \sum_{i=1}^{d} u_i (y - \beta)^i$ for a unique choice of $u_0, u_1, \ldots, u_d \in \mathbb{F}_q$. Since $C(\beta) = u_0$ it follows that all q^d choices for $u_1, \ldots, u_d$ result in $C(\beta) = u_0$ hence C is balanced. □

That $E[X] = 1$ was a surprise to us. We thought $E[X]$ would have a logarithmic dependence on $\deg f$ and $\deg g$. In light of Theorem 2, when picking $p > \deg_y(K_r(H))$ we will ignore the unlucky evaluation points, and, should the algorithm encounter unlucky evaluations, restart the algorithm with a larger prime.

3. GCD ALGORITHM

Algorithm PGCD(A,B,Γ)

Input $A = a_l x_0^l + \ldots + a_0$, and $B = b_m x_0^m + \ldots + b_0$ with $a_i, b_i \in \mathbb{Z}[x_1, \ldots x_n]$ and $\Gamma \in \mathbb{Z}[x_1, \ldots, x_n]$ satisfying $\gcd(a_i) = 1$ (A is primitive) and $\gcd(b_i) = 1$ (B is primitive) and $\Gamma = \gcd(a_l, b_m) = LC(G) \times \Delta$ where $G = \gcd(A, B)$.

Output A prime p and polynomial $H \in \mathbb{Z}_p[x_0, x_1, \ldots, x_n]$ satisfying $H = \Delta \times G \bmod p$ with probability at least $1 - \frac{\deg A \deg B + \min(\deg A, \deg B)}{p - \deg A - \deg B}$.

1 Compute $d_i = DegreeBound(A, B, i)$ for $0 \leq i \leq n-1$. Set $r_i = 1 + \min(\deg_{x_i} A, \deg_{x_i} B, d_i + \deg_{x_i} \Gamma)$ for $1 \leq i \leq n-1$.

Kronecker-substitution:

2 Let $Y = (y, y^{r_1}, y^{r_1 r_2}, \ldots, y^{r_1 r_2 \cdots r_{n-1}})$ be the Kronecker substitution. Set $K(A) = A(x, Y)$, $K(B) = B(x, Y)$ and $K(\Gamma) = \Gamma(Y)$.

3 If $\deg_x K(A) < \deg_{x_0} A$ or $\deg_x K(B) < \deg_{x_0} B$ then this Kronecker substitution is bad. Set $r_i = r_i + 1$ for $1 \leq i \leq n-1$ and **goto** Kronecker-substitution.

Pick-a-Prime:

4 Pick a new prime $p > 2\Pi_{i=1}^n r_i$ of the form $p = 2^k q + 1$ with q small.

5 If $\deg_x(K(A) \bmod p) < \deg_x A$ or $\deg_x(K(B) \bmod p) < \deg_x B$ then the prime is bad so **goto** Pick-a-Prime.

6 Set shift $s = 1$ and $j = 0$ and compute a random generator α for $\mathbb{Z}_p^*$.

Next-image:

7 Set $j = j + 1$. If $j = p - 1$ then we've run out of evaluation points. This could happen if one of the coefficients h_i of H is dense. **Goto** Pick-a-Prime and increase the length of p by 10 bits.

8 Compute $a_i = K(A)(x, \alpha^j)$ and $b_i = K(B)(x, \alpha^j)$. If $\deg_x a_i < \deg_{x_0} A$ or $\deg_x b_i < \deg_{x_0} B$ then α_j is bad so set $s = j$ and **goto** Next-image.

9 Compute $g_j = \gcd(a_i, b_i)$ in $\mathbb{Z}_p[x]$ using the Euclidean algorithm.

10 **Case** $\deg g_j < d_0$: (the degree bound d_0 is wrong) Set $d_0 = \deg g_j$, $s = j$ and **goto** Next-image.

11 **Case** $\deg g_j > d_0$: (α^j is unlucky)

11a If this happens for $j = s$ and $j = s + 1$ then the Kronecker substitution is very probably unlucky so set $r_i = r_i + 1$ for $1 \leq i \leq n - 1$ and **goto** Kronecker-substitution.

11b If this is the 2nd unlucky evaluation then **goto** Pick-a-Prime and double the length of p. Otherwise set $s = j$ and **goto** Next-image.

12 **Case** $\deg g_j = d_0$: (we have a new image)

12a Scale the image: Set $g_j = K(\Gamma)(\alpha^j)g_j$. If $s - j$ is even then **goto** compute-next-image – we need at least two new images for the next step.

12b Run the Berlekamp-Massey algorithm on the coefficients of the images $g_s, g_{s+1}, \ldots, g_{s+j}$ to obtain $\lambda_i(z)$ for $0 \leq i \leq d_0$. If any $\lambda_i(z)$ changed from the previous step **goto** Next-image.

12c Compute the roots of each $\lambda_i(z)$. If any $\lambda_i(z)$ has fewer than $\deg \lambda_i(z)$ distinct roots **goto** Next-image.

12d Complete the sparse interpolation to obtain polynomials $h_i(y) \in \mathbb{Z}_p[y]$. Note, s is the shift used for the shifted transposed Vandermonde systems. Set $H(x, y) := \sum_{i=0}^{d_0} h_i(y)x^i$ which we hope is equal to $\Delta(Y)G(x, Y)$.

12e Invert the Kronecker substitution to obtain H. If $\deg_{x_i} H > \min(\deg_{x_i} A, \deg_{x_i} B, d_i + \deg_{x_i} \Gamma)$ for any $1 \leq i \leq n$ then $H \neq \Delta G$ so **goto** Next-image.

12f **Probabilistic check:** Pick $\beta \in \mathbb{Z}_p^n$ at random until $\deg A(x_0, \beta) = \deg_{x_0} A$ and $\deg B(x_0, \beta) = \deg_{x_0} B$. Compute $g_\beta = \gcd(A(x_0, \beta), B(x_0, \beta))$. If $H(x_0, \beta) = \Gamma(\beta)g_\beta$ then **output** (p, H). Otherwise either t_i is wrong for some i or $d_0 > \deg_{x_0} G$ or β is unlucky. In all cases continue **goto** Next-image.

To prove the claim on the output (p, H) let $H = \sum_{i=0}^{d_0} h_i x_0^i$ and let $G = \sum_{i=0}^{dG} c_i x_0^i$. We will bound the probability that algorithm PGCD outputs $H \neq \Delta G \mod p$. Notice that if PGCD outputs H it must be that $\deg_{x_0} H = d_0 = \deg_{x_0} g_\beta$. Now either $d_0 > dG$ or $d_0 = dG$. If $d_0 > dG$ then H is wrong. Now $d_0 > dG \Rightarrow \beta$ is unlucky thus $\text{Prob}[d_0 > dG] \leq \text{Prob}[\beta \text{ is unlucky}]$ which is at most $\frac{\deg A \deg B}{p - \deg A - \deg B}$. If $d_0 = dG$ then H is output iff $h_i(\beta) = \Delta(\beta)c_i(\beta) \mod p$ for $0 \leq i \leq d_0$. Let $f_i = h_i - \Delta c_i \mod p$. $H \neq \Delta G$ implies $f_i \neq 0$ for at least one i, say $i = j$. The Schwartz-Zippel lemma implies $\text{Prob}[f_j(\beta) = 0] \leq \frac{\deg f_i}{p - \deg A - \deg B}$. Now the degree condition on $\deg_{x_i} H$ means the total degree $\deg f_i \leq \min(\deg A, \deg B)$ thus $\text{Prob}[f_j(\beta) = 0] \leq \frac{\min(\deg A, \deg B)}{p - \deg A - \deg B}$. Adding both probabilities $\text{Prob}[H \neq \Delta G \mod p] \leq \frac{\min(\deg A, \deg B)}{p - \deg A - \deg B} + \frac{\deg A \deg B}{p - \deg A - \deg B}$ and the result follows.

We are not able to say what the expected running time of the algorithm is. If we were to choose $p > At^B$ for suitably chosen constants A and B, then such an analysis should be possible. But since we do not have a bound for t other than $t < (d+1)^n$, this would lead to a significantly larger prime.

3.1 Determining t

Algorithm PGCD assumes in step 12b that if none of the $\lambda_i(z)$ changed then $(j - s + 1)/2 = t$ but it could be that $(j - s + 1)/2 < t$. Let $V_r = (v_0, v_1, \ldots, v_{2r-1})$ be a sequence where $r \geq 1$. The Berlekamp-Massey algorithm (BMA) with input V_r computes a feedback polynomial $c(z)$ which is the reciprocal of $\lambda(z)$ if $r = t$. In PGCD, we determine the t by computing $c(z)$s on the input sequence V_r for $r = 1, 2, 3, \ldots$. If a $c(z)$ remains unchanged from the input V_k to the input V_{k+1}, then we conclude that this $c(z)$ is *stable* which implies that the last two consecutive discrepancies are both zero, see [16, 14] for a definition of the discrepancy. However, it is possible that the degree of $c(z)$ on the input V_{k+2} might increase again. In [14], Kaltofen, Lee and Lobo proved (Theorem 3) that the BMA encounters the first zero discrepancy after $2t$ points with probability at least

$$1 - \frac{t(t+1)(2t+1)\deg(C)}{6|S|}$$

where S is the set of all possible evaluation points. Here is an example where we encounter a zero discrepancy before $2t$ points. Consider

$$f(y) = y^7 + 60y^6 + 40y^5 + 48y^4 + 23y^3 + 45y^2 + 75y + 55$$

over $\mathbb{Z}_{101}$ with generator $\alpha = 93$. Since f has 8 terms, 16 points are required to determine the correct $\lambda(z)$ and two more for confirmation. We compute $f(\alpha^j)$ for $0 \leq j \leq 17$ and obtain $V_9 = (44, 95, 5, 51, 2, 72, 47, 44, 21, 59, 53, 29, 71, 39, 2, 27, 100, 20)$. We run the BMA on input V_r for $1 \leq r \leq 9$ and obtain feedback polynomials in the following table.

r	Output $c(z)$
1	$69z + 1$
2	$24z^2 + 59z + 1$
3	$24z^2 + 59z + 1$
4	$24z^2 + 59z + 1$
5	$70z^7 + 42z^6 + 6z^3 + 64z^2 + 34z + 1$
6	$70z^7 + 42z^6 + 25z^5 + 87z^4 + 16z^3 + 20z^2 + 34z + 1$
7	$z^7 + 67z^6 + 95z^5 + 2z^4 + 16z^3 + 20z^2 + 34z + 1$
8	$31z^8 + 61z^7 + 91z^6 + 84z^5 + 15z^4 + 7z^3 + 35z^2 + 79z + 1$
9	$31z^8 + 61z^7 + 91z^6 + 84z^5 + 15z^4 + 7z^3 + 35z^2 + 79z + 1$

The ninth call of the BMA confirms that the feedback polynomial returned by the eighth call is the desired one. But, by our design, the algorithm terminates at the third call because the feedback polynomial remains unchanged from the second call. It also remains unchanged for V_4. In this case, $\lambda(z) = z^2 c(1/z) = z^2 + 59z + 24$ has roots 56 and 87 which correspond to monomials y^4 and y^{20} since $\alpha^4 = 56$ and $\alpha^{20} = 87$.

The example shows that we may encounter a stable feedback polynomial too early. Furthermore, the recovered monomials may have degree higher than the degree of the input polynomial $f(y)$. Algorithm PGCD must check H for monomials of too high degree in step 12e for the degree argument in the proof of the claim to be valid.

3.2 Evaluation

Let $A, B \in \mathbb{Z}_p[x_0, x_1, \ldots, x_n]$, $s = \#A + \#B$, and $d = \max_{i=1}^n d_i$ where $d_i = \max(\deg_{x_i} A, \deg_{x_i} B)$. If we use a Kronecker substitution $K(A) = A(x, y, y^{r_1}, \ldots, y^{r_1 r_2 \cdots r_{n-1}})$ with $r_i = d_i + 1$, then $\deg_y K(A) < (d+1)^n$. Thus we can evaluate the s monomials in $K(A)(x, y)$ and $K(B)(x, y)$ at $y = \alpha^k$ in $O(sn \log d)$ multiplications. Instead we first compute $\beta_1 = \alpha^k$ and $\beta_{i+1} = \beta_i^{r_i}$ for $i = 1, 3, \ldots, n-2$ then precompute n tables of powers $1, \beta_i, \beta_i^2, \ldots, \beta_i^{d_i}$ for $1 \leq i \leq n$ using at most nd multiplications. Now, for each term in

A and B of the form $cx_0^{e_0}x_1^{e_1}\dots x_n^{e_n}$ we compute $c\times\beta_1^{e_1}\times\dots\times\beta_n^{e_n}$ using the tables in n multiplications. Hence we can evaluate $K(A)(x,\alpha^k)$ and $K(B)(x,\alpha^k)$ in at most $nd+ns$ multiplications. Thus for T evaluation points $\alpha,\alpha^2,\dots,\alpha^T$, the evaluation cost is $O(ndT+nsT)$ multiplications.

When we first implemented algorithm PGCD we noticed that often well over 95% of the time was spent evaluating the input polynomials A and B at the points α^k. This happens when $\#G\ll\#A+\#B$. The following method uses the fact that for a monomial $M_i(x_1,x_2,\dots,x_n)$

$$M_i(\beta_1^k,\beta_2^k,\dots,\beta_n^k) = M_i(\beta_1,\beta_2,\dots,\beta_n)^k$$

to reduce the total evaluation cost from $O(ndT+nsT)$ multiplications to $O(nd+ns+sT)$. Note, no sorting on x_0 is needed in step 4b if the monomials in the input A are are sorted on x_0.

Algorithm Evaluate.

Input $A=\sum_{i=1}^m c_i x_0^{e_i} M_i(x_1,\dots,x_n)\in\mathbb{Z}_p[x_0,\dots,x_n]$, $T>0$, $\beta_1,\beta_2,\dots,\beta_n\in\mathbb{Z}_p$, and integers $d_1,d_2,\dots,d_n$ with $d_i\geq\deg_{x_i}A$.

Output $A(x_0,\beta_1^k,\dots,\beta_n^k)$ for $1\leq k\leq T$.

1 Create the vector $C=[c_1,c_2,\dots,c_m]\in\mathbb{Z}_p^m$.
2 Compute $[\beta_i^j : j=0,1,\dots,d_i]$ for $1\leq i\leq n$.
3 Compute $\Gamma=[M_i(\beta_1,\beta_2,\dots,\beta_n):1\leq i\leq m]$.
4 For $k=1,2,\dots,T$ do
  4a Compute the vector $C:=[C_i\times\Gamma_i$ for $1\leq i\leq m]$.
  4b Assemble $\sum_{i=1}^m C_i x_0^{e_i}=A(x_0,\beta_1^k,\dots,\beta_n^k)$.

Even with this improvement evaluation still takes most of the time so we must parallelize it. Each evaluation of A could be parallelized in blocks of size m/N for N cores. In Cilk C, this is only effective, however, if the blocks are large enough (at least 50,000) so that the time for each block is much larger than the time it takes Cilk to create a task. For this reason, it is necessary to also parallelize on k. To parallelize on k for N cores, we multiply the previous N values of C in parallel by the vector

$$\Gamma_N=[M_i(\beta_1,\beta_2,\dots,\beta_n)^N : 1\leq i\leq m]$$

Because most of the time is still in evaluation, we are presently implementing the asymptotically fast method of van der Hoven and Lecerf [10] and attempting to parallelize it. For our evaluation problem it has complexity $O(nd+ns+s\log^2 T)$ which is better than our $O(nd+ns+sT)$ method for large T.

4. BENCHMARKS

We have implemented algorithm PGCD for 31, 63 and 127 bit primes in Cilk C. For 127 bit primes we use the 128 bit signed integer type `__int128_t` supported by the gcc compiler. We parallelized evaluation (see Section 3.2) and we interpolate the coefficients $h_i(y)$ in parallel in step 12e. To assess how good it is, we have compared it with the serial implementations of Zippel's algorithm in Maple 2015 and Magma 2.21. For Maple we were able to determine the time spent computing G modulo the first prime only in Zippel's algorithm. It is over 90% of the total GCD time. For Magma we could not do this so the Magma timings are for the entire GCD computation over $\mathbb{Z}$.

All timings were made on the gaby server in the CECM at Simon Fraser University. This machine has two Intel Xeon E-2660 8 core CPUs running at 3.0 GHz on one core and 2.2 GHz on 8 cores. Thus the maximum parallel speedup is a factor of $16\times 2.2/3.0=11.7$.

For our first benchmark (see Table 2) we created polynomials $G,\bar{A}$ and $\bar{B}$ in 6 variables ($n=5$) and 9 variables ($n=8$) of degree at most d in each variable. We generated $100d$ random terms for G and 100 random terms for $\bar{A}$ and $\bar{B}$. The integer coefficients of $G,\bar{A},\bar{B}$ were generated at random from $[0,2^{31}-1]$. The monomials in $G,\bar{A}$ and $\bar{B}$ were generated using random exponents from $[0,d-1]$ for each variable. For G we included monomials $1,x_0^d,x_1^d,\dots,x_6^d$ so that G is monic in all variables and $\Gamma=1$. Our GCD code used the 62 bit prime $p=29\times 2^{57}+1$. Maple used the 32 bit prime $2^{32}-5$ for the first image in Zippel's algorithm.

			New GCD algorithm		Zippel's algorithm	
n	d	t	1 core (eval)	16 cores	Maple	Magma
5	10	114	0.62s (68%)	0.091s (6.8x)	48.04s	6.97s
5	20	122	1.32s (69%)	0.155s (8.5x)	185.70s	318.22s
5	50	121	3.48s (69%)	0.326s (10.7x)	1525.80s	$>10^4s$
5	100	102	7.08s (69%)	0.657s (10.8x)	6018.23s	$>10^4s$
5	200	125	14.64s (71%)	1.287s (11.4x)	NA	NA
5	500	135	38.79s (71%)	3.397s (11.4x)	NA	NA
8	5	89	0.27s (61%)	0.065s (4.2x)	30.87s	2.39s
8	10	110	0.63s (65%)	0.098s (6.4x)	138.41s	6.15s
8	20	114	1.35s (66%)	0.163s (8.3x)	664.33s	63.49s
8	50	113	3.52s (66%)	0.336s (10.5x)	6390.22s	1226.77s
8	100	121	7.43s (68%)	0.645s (11.5x)	NA	NA

Table 2: Timings (seconds) for GCD problems.

In Table 2 column d is the maximum degree of the terms of $G,\bar{A},\bar{B}$ in each variable, column t is the maximum number of terms of the coefficients of G and column eval is the %age of the time spent evaluating the inputs, that is computing $K(A)(x_0,\alpha^j)$ and $K(B)(x_0,\alpha^j)$ for $j=1,2,\dots,T$. The parallel speedup on 16 cores is shown in parens.

Our second benchmark (see Table 3) is for 9 variables where the degree of $G,\bar{A},\bar{B}$ is at most 20 in each variable. The terms are generated at random as before but restricted to have total degree at most 60. The middle row is our benchmark problem from Section 1.

		New GCD algorithm		Zippel's algorithm	
$\#G$	$\#A$	1 core (eval)	16 cores	Maple	Magma
10^3	10^5	0.66s (68%)	0.100s (6.6x)	341.9s	63.55s
10^3	10^6	5.66s (90%)	0.717s (9.4x)	5553.5s	FAIL
10^4	10^6	48.44s (87%)	4.474s (10.2x)	62520.1s	FAIL
10^3	10^7	52.102 (92%)	4.591s (11.3x)	NA	NA
10^4	10^7	428.96s (98%)	37.43s (11.5x)	NA	NA

Table 3: Timings (seconds) for 9 variable GCDs

Tables 2 and 3 show that most of the time is in evaluation. They show a parallel speedup approaching the maximum of 11.7 on this machine. There was a parallel bottleneck in how we computed the $\lambda_i(z)$ polynomials that limited parallel speedup to 10 on these benchmarks. For N cores, after generating a new batch of N images we used the Euclidean algorithm for Step 12b which is quadratic in the number of images j computed so far. To address this we now use an incremental version of the Berlekamp-Massey algorithm which is $O(Nj)$.

In comparing the new algorithm with Maple's implementation of Zippel's algorithm, for $n = 8, d = 50$ in Table 2 we achieve a speedup of a factor of $1815 = 6390.22/3.52$ on 1 core. Since Zippel's algorithm uses $O(dt)$ points and our Ben-Or/Tiwari algorithm uses $2t + O(1)$ points, we get a factor of $O(d)$ speedup because of this.

Our improved evaluation gives us a another factor of n speedup over Maple's implementation of Zippel's algorithm. Another factor is the cost of multiplication in $\mathbb{Z}_p$. The reader should realize that the running time of algorithm PGCD is proportional to the cost of multiplication in $\mathbb{Z}_p$. Maple is using `% p` to divide in C which generates a hardware division instruction which is much more expensive than a multiplication. We are using Roman Pearce's implementation of Möller and Granlund [17] which reduces division by p to two multiplications plus other cheap operations.

5. CONCLUSION AND FINAL REMARKS

We have shown that a Kronecker substitution can be used to reduce a multivariate GCD computation to bivariate by using a discrete logs Ben-Or/Tiwari point sequence. Our parallel implementation is fast and practical. Several questions remain. The Ben-Or/Tiwari method requires $2t+O(1)$ points. Can we use fewer points? Can we do anything when $\#\Delta > 1$ which increases t? For polynomials in more variables or higher degree algorithm PGCD may need a prime p larger than 127 bits. Can we do anything to reduce the size of the prime needed?

Algorithm PGCD interpolates H from univariate images in $\mathbb{Z}_p[x_0]$. If instead we interpolate H from bivariate images in $\mathbb{Z}_p[x_0, x_1]$, this will likely reduce both t and $\#\Delta$. For our benchmark problem this reduces t by a factor of 9 and the cost of the bivariate GCD computations in $\mathbb{Z}_p[x_0, x_1]$, if computed with Brown's dense GCD algorithm [4], would remain negligible compared with the cost of evaluating A and B. Although we have not implemented this we estimate a speedup of a factor of 6 on 16 cores.

We cite the methods of Garg and Schost [6], Giesbrecht and Roche [9] and Arnold, Giesbrecht and Roche [1] which can use a smaller prime and would also use fewer than $2t + O(1)$ evaluations. These methods compute $a_i = K_r(A)(x, y)$, $b_i = K_r(B)(x, y)$ and $g_i = \gcd(a_i, b_i)$ all mod $\langle p, y^{q_i} - 1\rangle$ for several primes q_i and recover the exponents of y in $K_r(H)$ using Chinese remaindering. The algorithms differ in the size of q_i and how they avoid or recover from exponent collisions. It is not clear whether this approach can work for the GCD problem as these methods assume a division free evaluation but computing g_i requires division and $y = 1$ may be bad or unlucky. They also require $q_i \gg t$ which means computing g_i will be expensive for large t.

In contrast, the earlier method of Murao and Fujise in [19], which also uses Chinese remaindering on the exponents, should work. Another approach is to try to compress the Kronecker substitution. We are considering the idea suggested by van der Hoven in [11].

6. REFERENCES

[1] A. Arnold, M. Giesbrecht and D. Roche. Faster Sparse Multivariate Polynomial Interpolation of Straight-Line Programs. `arXiv:1412.4088`[cs.SC], December 2014.

[2] N. B. Atti, G. M. Diaz-Toca, and H. Lombardi. The Berlekamp-Massey algorithm revisited. AAECC **17** pp. 75–82, 2006.

[3] M. Ben-Or and P. Tiwari. A deterministic algorithm for sparse multivariate polynomial interpolation. In *Proc. of STOC '20*, ACM Press, pp. 301–309, 1988.

[4] W. S. Brown. On Euclid's Algorithm and the Computation of Polynomial Greatest Common Divisors. *J. ACM* **18**:478–504, 1971.

[5] D. Cox, J. Little, D. O'Shea. *Ideals, Varities and Algorithms*. Springer-Verlag, 1991.

[6] Sanchit Garg and Eric Schost. Interpolation of polynomials given by straight-line programs. *J. Theor. Comp. Sci.*, **410**:2659–2662, June 2009.

[7] J. von zur Gathen and J. Gerhard. *Modern Computer Algebra*. Cambridge University Press, UK, 1999.

[8] K. O. Geddes, S. R. Czapor, and G. Labahn. *Algorithms for Computer Algebra*. Kluwer, 1992.

[9] Mark Giesbrecht and Daniel S. Roche. Diversification improves interpolation. In *Proc. ISSAC 2011*, ACM Press, pp. 123–130, 2011.

[10] Joris van der Hoven and Grégoire Lecerf. On the bit complexity of sparse polynomial multiplication. *J. Symb. Cmpt.* **50**:227–254, 2013.

[11] Joris van der Hoven and Grégoire Lecerf. Sparse polynomial interpolation in practice. *CCA* **48**:187–191, September 2015.

[12] Mahdi Javadi and Michael Monagan. Parallel Sparse Polynomial Interpolation over Finite Fields. In *Proc. of PASCO 2010*, ACM Press, pp. 160–168, 2010.

[13] E. Kaltofen, Y.N. Lakshman and J-M. Wiley. Modular Rational Sparse Multivariate Interpolation Algorithm. In *Proc. ISSAC 1990*, pp. 135-139, ACM Press, 1990.

[14] E. Kaltofen, W. Lee, and A. Lobo. Early Termination in Ben-Or/Tiwari Sparse Interpolation and a Hybrid of Zippel's algorithm. In *Proc. ISSAC 2000*, ACM Press, pp. 192−201, 2000.

[15] E. Kaltofen. Fifteen years after DSC and WLSS2. In *Proc. of PASCO 2010*, ACM Press, pp. 10–17, 2010.

[16] J. L. Massey. Shift-register synthesis and BCH decoding. *IEEE Trans. on Information Theory*, 15:122–127, 1969.

[17] Niels Möller and Torbjorn Granlund. Improved division by invariant integers. *IEEE Trans. on Computers*, **60**:165–175, 2011.

[18] Gary Mullen and Daniel Panario. *Handbook of Finite Fields*. CRC Press, 2013.

[19] Hirokazu Murao and Tetsuro Fujise. Modular Algorithm for Sparse Multivariate Polynomial Interpolation and its Parallel Implementation. *J. Symb. Cmpt.* **21**:377–396, 1996.

[20] S. Pohlig and M. Hellman. An improved algorithm for computing logarithms over GF(p) and its cryptographic significance. *IEEE Trans. on Information Theory*, **24**:106–110, 1978.

[21] Michael Rabin. Probabilistic algorithms in finite fields. *SIAM J. Comput*, **9**:273–280, 1979.

[22] Jack Schwartz. Fast probabilistic algorithms for verification of polynomial identities. *J. ACM*, **27**:701–717, 1980.

[23] Douglas Stinson. *Cryptography, Theory and Practice*, Chapman and Hall, 2006.

[24] Y. Sugiyama, M. Kashara, S. Hirashawa and T. Namekawa. A Method for Solving Key Equation for Decoding Goppa Codes. *Information and Control* **27**:87–99, 1975.

[25] Richard Zippel. Probabilistic algorithms for sparse polynomials. In *Proc. of EUROSAM '79*, pp. 216–226. Springer-Verlag, 1979.

[26] Richard Zippel. Interpolating Polynomials from their Values. *J. Symb Cmpt.* **9**:375–403, 1990.

New Bounds for Hypergeometric Creative Telescoping*

Hui Huang[1,2]

[1]KLMM, AMSS, Chinese Academy of Sciences, Beijing 100190, (China)

[2]Institute for Algebra, Johannes Kepler University, Linz A-4040, (Austria)

huanghui@amss.ac.cn

ABSTRACT

Based on a modified version of Abramov-Petkovšek reduction, a new algorithm to compute minimal telescopers for bivariate hypergeometric terms was developed last year. We investigate further in this paper and present a new argument for the termination of this algorithm, which provides an independent proof of the existence of telescopers and even enables us to derive lower as well as upper bounds for the order of telescopers for hypergeometric terms. Compared to the known bounds in the literature, our bounds are sometimes better, and never worse than the known ones.

Categories and Subject Descriptors

I.1.2 [**Computing Methodologies**]: Symbolic and Algebraic Manipulation—*Algebraic Algorithms*

General Terms

Algorithms, Theory

Keywords

Modified Abramov-Petkovšek reduction, Hypergeometric term, Telescoper, Order bound

1. INTRODUCTION

This paper is about creative telescoping for hypergeometric terms. A *hypergeometric term* is an expression $f_{x,y}$ in, say, two variables x, y such that the two shift quotients $f_{x+1,y}/f_{x,y}$ and $f_{x,y+1}/f_{x,y}$ can be expressed as rational functions in x and y. The prototypical example of a hypergeometric term is the binomial coefficient $f_{x,y} = \binom{x}{y}$. Creative telescoping is the main tool for simplifying definite sums of hypergeometric terms. The task consists in finding some nonzero recurrence operator L and another hypergeometric term $g_{x,y}$ such that $L \cdot f_{x,y} = g_{x,y+1} - g_{x,y}$. It is required that the operator L does not contain y or the shift operator σ_y, i.e., it must have the form $L = e_0 + e_1\sigma_x + \cdots + e_\rho\sigma_x^\rho$ for some $e_0, \ldots, e_\rho$ that only depend on x.

If L and $g_{x,y}$ are as above, we say that L is a *telescoper* for $f_{x,y}$, and $g_{x,y}$ is a *certificate* for L. Once a telescoper for $f_{x,y}$ is known, we can extract useful information about definite sums such as $F_x = \sum_{y=0}^{x} f_{x,y}$ from L. See [13, 14] for further information. These references also contain classical algorithms for computing telescopers and certificates for given hypergeometric terms. During the past 25 years, the technique of creative telescoping has been generalized and refined in various ways [12, 6, 7, 8, 9, 10, 11]. The latest trend in this development are so-called reduction-based algorithms, first presented in [7]. One of their features is that they can find a telescoper for a given term f without also computing the corresponding certificate. This is interesting because a certificate is not always needed, and it is typically much larger (and thus computationally more expensive) than the telescoper, so we may not want to compute it if we don't have to.

Reduction-based algorithms have been first developed in the differential case, for various cases [7, 8, 9, 11]. The basic idea, formulated for the shift case, is as follows. Let $\mathcal{C}$ be a field of characteristic zero. Suppose we know a function $\mathrm{red}_y(\cdot)$, called *reduction*, with the property that for all f in the domain under consideration, say $\mathbb{D}$, containing $\mathcal{C}(x, y)$, there exists a g in the same domain such that $f - \mathrm{red}_y(f) = \sigma_y(g) - g$, i.e., the difference $f - \mathrm{red}_y(f)$ is a summable term. We call $\mathrm{red}_y(f)$ a *remainder* of f with respect to the reduction $\mathrm{red}_y(\cdot)$. Then in order to find a telescoper for f, we can compute $\mathrm{red}_y(f), \mathrm{red}_y(\sigma_x(f)), \mathrm{red}_y(\sigma_x^2(f)), \ldots$ until we find a linear dependence over the field $\mathcal{C}(x)$. If such a dependence is found, say $e_0\,\mathrm{red}_y(f) + \cdots + e_\rho\,\mathrm{red}_y(\sigma_x^\rho(f)) = 0$ for some $e_0, \ldots, e_\rho$ in $\mathcal{C}(x)$, then $e_0 + \cdots + e_\rho\sigma_x^\rho$ is a telescoper for f.

In order to show that this method terminates, one possible approach is to show that the $\mathcal{C}(x)$-vector space spanned by $\mathrm{red}_y(f), \mathrm{red}_y(\sigma_x(f)), \mathrm{red}_y(\sigma_x^2(f)), \ldots$ for $f \in \mathbb{D}$ has a finite dimension. Then, as soon as ρ exceeds this dimension, we can be sure that a telescoper will be found. This approach was taken in [8, 9, 11]. As a nice side result, this approach provides an independent proof of the existence of telescopers, and even a bound on their order. In the paper from last year [10], the authors used a different approach. Instead of showing that the remainders form a finite-dimensional vector space, they showed that for every summable term f, we have

*H. Huang was supported by the Austrian Science Fund (FWF) grant W1214-13, three NSFC grants (91118001, 60821002/F02, 11501552) and a 973 project (2011CB302401).

ISSAC'16, July 19 - 22 2016, Waterloo, ON, Canada.

ACM 978-1-4503-4380-0/16/07 ...$15.00.

DOI: http://dx.doi.org/10.1145/2930889.2930893.

$\text{red}_y(f) = 0$. This also ensures that the method terminates (assuming that we already know for other reasons that a telescoper exists), and in fact that it will find the smallest possible telescoper, but it does not provide a bound on its order.

This discrepancy in the approaches for the differential case and the shift case is unpleasant. It is not clear why the shift case should require a different argument. The goal of the present paper is to show that it does not. We will continue the development of last year's theory to a point where we can also show that the remainders belong to a finite-dimensional vector space. As a result, we obtain new bounds for the order of telescopers for hypergeometric terms. We obtain lower as well as upper bounds. We do not find exactly the same bounds that are already in the literature [12, 2]. Comparing our bounds to the known bounds, it appears that for "generic" input, the values often agree (of course, because the known bounds are already generically sharp). However, there are some special examples in which our bounds are better than the known bounds. On the other hand, our bounds are never worse than the old bounds.

2. PRELIMINARIES

Using the same notations as in [10], we let $\mathbb{F}$ be a field of characteristic zero, and $\mathbb{F}(y)$ be the field of rational functions in y over $\mathbb{F}$. Let σ_y be the automorphism that maps $r(y)$ to $r(y+1)$ for every $r \in \mathbb{F}(y)$. The pair $(\mathbb{F}(y), \sigma_y)$ is called a difference field. A difference ring extension of $(\mathbb{F}(y), \sigma_y)$ is a ring $\mathbb{D}$ containing $\mathbb{F}(y)$ together with a distinguished endomorphism $\sigma_y \colon \mathbb{D} \to \mathbb{D}$ whose restriction to $\mathbb{F}(y)$ agrees with the automorphism defined before. An element $c \in \mathbb{D}$ is called a constant if $\sigma_y(c) = c$. We denote by $\deg_y(p)$ the degree of a nonzero polynomial $p \in \mathbb{F}[y]$.

Definition 2.1. *Let $\mathbb{D}$ be a difference ring extension of $\mathbb{F}(y)$. A nonzero element $T \in \mathbb{D}$ is called a* hypergeometric term *over $\mathbb{F}(y)$ if $\sigma_y(T) = rT$ for some $r \in \mathbb{F}(y)$. We call r the* shift quotient *of T w.r.t. y.*

A univariate hypergeometric term T is called *hypergeometric summable* if there exists another hypergeometric term G s.t. $T = \Delta_y(G)$, where Δ_y denotes the difference of σ_y and the identity map. We abbreviate "hypergeometric summable" as "summable" in this paper.

Recall [3, §1] that a nonzero polynomial in $\mathbb{F}[y]$ is said to be *shift-free* if no two distinct roots differ by an integer. A nonzero rational function in $\mathbb{F}(y)$ is said to be *shift-reduced* if its numerator is co-prime with any shift of its denominator.

According to [3, 5], for a given hypergeometric term T there always exists a rational function $S \in \mathbb{F}(y)$ and another hypergeometric term H whose shift quotient is shift-reduced, s.t. $T = SH$. This is called a *multiplicative decomposition* of T. We call the shift quotient $K = \sigma_y(H)/H$ a *kernel* of T and S the corresponding *shell*.

Based on Abramov and Petkovšek's work in [3, 5], the authors of [10] presented a modified version of Abramov-Petkovšek reduction, which determines summability without solving any auxiliary difference equations. To describe it concisely, we first recall some terminology.

Let T be a hypergeometric term whose kernel is K and the corresponding shell is S. Then $T = SH$, where H is a hypergeometric term whose shift quotient is K. Write $K = u/v$, where u, v are polynomials in $\mathbb{F}[y]$ with $\gcd(u, v) = 1$.

Definition 2.2. *A nonzero polynomial p in $\mathbb{F}[y]$ is said to be* strongly prime *with K if $\gcd\left(p, \sigma_y^{-i}(u)\right) = \gcd\left(p, \sigma_y^{i}(v)\right) = 1$ for all $i \geq 0$.*

Now define the $\mathbb{F}$-linear map ϕ_K from $\mathbb{F}[y]$ to itself by sending p to $u\sigma_y(p) - vp$ for all $p \in \mathbb{F}[y]$. We call ϕ_K the *map for polynomial reduction w.r.t. K*. Let

$$\mathbb{W}_K = \text{span}\{y^\ell \mid \ell \in \mathbb{N}, \ell \neq \deg_y(p) \text{ for all } p \in \text{im}(\phi_K)\}.$$

Then $\mathbb{F}[y] = \text{im}(\phi_K) \oplus \mathbb{W}_K$, and thus we call $\mathbb{W}_K$ the *standard complement of* $\text{im}(\phi_K)$.

Definition 2.3. *Let f be a rational function in $\mathbb{F}(y)$. Another rational function r in $\mathbb{F}(y)$ is called a* (discrete) residual form *of f w.r.t. K if there exists $g \in \mathbb{F}(y)$ and a, b, q in $\mathbb{F}[y]$ s.t.*

$$f = K\sigma_y(g) - g + r \quad \text{and} \quad r = \frac{a}{b} + \frac{q}{v},$$

where $\deg_y(a) < \deg_y(b)$, $\gcd(a, b) = 1$, b is shift-free and strongly prime with K, and q belongs to $\mathbb{W}_K$. For brevity, we just say that r is a residual form *w.r.t. K if f is clear from the context. We call b the* significant denominator *of r.*

The modified Abramov-Petkovšek reduction [10, Theorem 4.8] can be stated as follows.

Theorem 2.4. *With the notations given above, the modified version of the Abramov-Petkovšek reduction computes a rational function g in $\mathbb{F}(y)$ and a residual form r w.r.t. K, such that*

$$T = \Delta_y(gH) + rH. \tag{1}$$

Moreover, T is summable if and only if $r = 0$.

3. PROPERTIES OF RESIDUAL FORMS

In this section, we will explore important properties of residual forms, which enables us to derive nontrivial relationship among remainders in Section 5.

Unlike the differential case, a rational function may have more than one residual form in shift case. However, these residual forms are related to each other in some way. Before describing it, let us recall some technology.

Recall [5, §2] that polynomials $p_1, p_2 \in \mathbb{F}[y]$ are said to be *shift-equivalent* (w.r.t. y) if $p_1 = \sigma_y^\ell(p_2)$ for some $\ell \in \mathbb{Z}$, denoted by $p_1 \sim_y p_2$. It is an equivalence relation.

Let f be a rational function in $\mathbb{F}(y)$. We call the rational function pair $(K, S) \in \mathbb{F}(y)^2$ a *rational normal form (RNF)* of f if $f = K \cdot \sigma_y(S)/S$ and K is shift-reduced. By [5, Theorem 1], every rational function has at least one RNF. Let T be a hypergeometric term over $\mathbb{F}(y)$. It is not hard to see that $(K, S) \in \mathbb{F}(y)^2$ is an RNF of $\sigma_y(T)/T$ if and only if K and S are a kernel and the corresponding shell of T.

Definition 3.1. *Two shift-free polynomials $p, q \in \mathbb{F}[y]$ are called* shift-related *(w.r.t. y), denoted by $p \approx_y q$, if for any nontrivial monic irreducible factor f of p, there exists a unique monic irreducible factor g of q with the same multiplicity as f in p s.t. $f \sim_y g$, and vice versa.*

One can show that $\approx_y$ is an equivalence relation.

Proposition 3.2. *Let K be a shift-reduced rational function in $\mathbb{F}(y)$. Assume that $r_1, r_2 \in \mathbb{F}(y)$ are both residual forms of the same rational function in $\mathbb{F}(y)$ w.r.t. K. Then the significant denominators of r_1 and r_2 are shift-related to each other.*

Proof. Assume that r_1, r_2 are of the forms

$$r_1 = \frac{a_1}{b_1} + \frac{q_1}{v} \quad \text{and} \quad r_2 = \frac{a_2}{b_2} + \frac{q_2}{v},$$

where $a_i, b_i \in \mathbb{F}[y]$, $\deg(a_i) < \deg(b_i)$, $\gcd(a_i, b_i) = 1$, b_i is shift-free and strongly prime with K, $q_i \in \mathbb{W}_K$ for $i = 1, 2$, and v is the denominator of K. Since r_1, r_2 are both residual forms of the same rational function, there exists $g \in \mathbb{F}(y)$ s.t.

$$r_2 = K\sigma_y(g) - g + r_1.$$

It follows that

$$\frac{a_2 v}{b_2} = u\sigma_y(g) - v(g) + (q_1 - q_2) + \frac{a_1 v}{b_1}. \tag{2}$$

Let $f \in \mathbb{F}[y]$ be a nontrivial monic irreducible factor of b_1 with multiplicity $\alpha > 0$. If f^α divides b_2, then we are done. Otherwise, let g_d be the denominator of g. Then f^α divides g_d or $\sigma_y(g_d)$ as $\gcd(b_1, a_1 v) = 1$. If f^α divides g_d, let

$$m = \max\{\ell \in \mathbb{Z} \mid \sigma_y^\ell(f)^\alpha \text{ divides } g_d\}.$$

Then $m \geq 0$ and $\sigma_y^{m+1}(f)^\alpha \mid \sigma_y(g_d)$. Since b_1 is strongly prime with K, $\gcd(\sigma_y^{m+1}(f)^\alpha, u) = 1$. Apparently, neither b_1 nor g_d is divisible by $\sigma_y^{m+1}(f)^\alpha$ as b_1 is shift-free and m is maximal. Hence (2) implies $\sigma_y^{m+1}(f)^\alpha$ is the required factor of b_2. Similarly, we can show that $\sigma_y^m(f)^\alpha$ with

$$m = \min\{\ell \in \mathbb{Z} \mid \sigma_y^\ell(f)^\alpha \text{ divides } g_d\} \leq -1,$$

is the required factor of b_2, if f^α divides $\sigma_y(g_d)$.

In summary, there always exists a monic irreducible factor of b_2 with multiplicity at least α s.t. it is shift-equivalent to f. Due to the shift-freeness of b_2, this factor is unique. Conversely, the proof proceeds in a similar way as above. According to the definition, $b_1 \approx_y b_2$. □

Given a hypergeometric term, it is readily seen that the above proposition reveals the relationship between two residual forms w.r.t. the same kernel. To study the case with different kernels, we need to develop two lemmas.

Lemma 3.3. *Let (K, S) be an RNF of a rational function f in $\mathbb{F}(y)$ and r be a residual form of S w.r.t. K. Write*

$$K = \frac{u}{v} \quad \textit{with } u, v \in \mathbb{F}[y] \textit{ and } \gcd(u, v) = 1.$$

Assume that $p \in \mathbb{F}[y]$ is a nontrivial monic irreducible factor of v with multiplicity $\alpha > 0$. Then

$$(K', S') = \left(\frac{u}{v'\sigma_y(p)^\alpha}, p^\alpha S\right)$$

is an RNF of f, in which $v' = v/p^\alpha$. Moreover, there exists a residual form r' of S' w.r.t. K' whose significant denominator is equal to that of r.

Proof. Since K is shift-reduced, so is K'. Then the first assertion follows by noticing

$$K\frac{\sigma_y(S)}{S} = \frac{u}{v'p^\alpha}\frac{\sigma_y(S)}{S} = \frac{u}{v'\sigma_y(p)^\alpha}\frac{\sigma_y(p^\alpha S)}{p^\alpha S} = K'\frac{\sigma_y(S')}{S'}.$$

Let r be of the form $r = a/b + q/v$ where $a, b \in \mathbb{F}[y]$, $\deg(a) < \deg(b)$, $\gcd(a, b) = 1$, b is shift-free and strongly prime with K, and $q \in \mathbb{W}_K$. Then there exists $g \in \mathbb{F}(y)$ s.t.

$$S = K\sigma_y(g) - g + \frac{a}{b} + \frac{q}{v'p^\alpha},$$

which implies that

$$\begin{aligned} S' = p^\alpha S &= p^\alpha K\sigma_y(g) - p^\alpha g + \frac{ap^\alpha}{b} + \frac{q}{v'} \\ &= \frac{u}{v'\sigma_y(p)^\alpha}\sigma_y(p^\alpha g) - p^\alpha g + \frac{ap^\alpha}{b} + \frac{q\sigma_y(p)^\alpha}{v'\sigma_y(p)^\alpha} \\ &= K'\sigma_y(p^\alpha g) - p^\alpha g + \frac{ap^\alpha}{b} + \frac{q\sigma_y(p)^\alpha}{v'\sigma_y(p)^\alpha} \end{aligned}$$

Since b is strongly prime with K and $\gcd(a, b) = 1$, we have $\gcd(ap^\alpha, b) = 1$. According to Lemma 4.2 and Remark 4.3 in [10], there exist $g' \in \mathbb{F}(y), a', q' \in \mathbb{F}[y]$ with $\deg_y(a') < \deg_y(b)$ and $\gcd(a', b) = 1$, and $q' \in \mathbb{W}_{K'}$ s.t.

$$S' = K'\sigma_y(g') - g' + \left(\frac{a'}{b} + \frac{q'}{v'\sigma_y(p)^\alpha}\right).$$

Note that b is strongly prime with K, so b is also strongly prime with K'. By the shift-freeness of b,

$$\frac{a'}{b} + \frac{q'}{v'\sigma_y(p)^\alpha}$$

is a residual form of S' w.r.t. K'. The lemma follows. □

Lemma 3.4. *Let (K, S) be an RNF of a rational function f in $\mathbb{F}(y)$ and r be a residual form of S w.r.t. K. Write*

$$K = \frac{u}{v} \quad \textit{with } u, v \in \mathbb{F}[y] \textit{ and } \gcd(u, v) = 1.$$

Assume that $p \in \mathbb{F}[y]$ is a nontrivial monic irreducible factor of u with multiplicity $\alpha > 0$. Then

$$(K', S') = \left(\frac{u'\sigma_y^{-1}(p)^\alpha}{v}, \sigma_y^{-1}(p)^\alpha S\right)$$

is an RNF of f, in which $u' = u/p^\alpha$. Moreover, there exists a residual form r' of S' w.r.t. K' whose significant denominator is equal to that of r.

Proof. Similar to Lemma 3.3. □

Proposition 3.5. *Let (K, S) be an RNF of a rational function f in $\mathbb{F}(y)$ and r be a residual form of S w.r.t. K. Then there exists another RNF $(\tilde{K}, \tilde{S})$ of f such that*

1. *$\tilde{K}$ has shift-free numerator and shift-free denominator;*
2. *there exists a residual form $\tilde{r}$ of $\tilde{S}$ w.r.t. $\tilde{K}$ whose significant denominator is equal to that of r.*

Proof. Let $K = u/v$ with $u, v \in \mathbb{F}[y]$ and $\gcd(u, v) = 1$, and b be the significant denominator of r.

Assume that v is not shift-free. Then there exist two nontrivial monic irreducible factors p and $\sigma_y^m(p)$ ($m > 0$) of v with multiplicity $\alpha > 0$ and $\beta > 0$, respectively. W.L.O.G., suppose further that $\sigma_y^\ell(p)$ is not a factor of v for all $\ell < 0$ and $\ell > m$. By Lemma 3.3, f has an RNF (K', S'), in which K' has a denominator $v' = \tilde{v}\sigma_y(p)^\alpha$, where $\tilde{v} = v/p^\alpha$, and the numerator remains to be u. Moreover, there exists a residual form of S' w.r.t. K' whose significant denominator is b. If $m = 1$, $\sigma_y(p)$ is an irreducible factor of v' with multiplicity $\alpha + \beta$. Otherwise, it is an irreducible factor of v' with multiplicity α. More importantly, $\sigma_y^\ell(p)$ is not a factor of v' for all $\ell < 1$. Iteratively using the argument, we arrive at an RNF of f such that $\sigma_y^m(p)$ divides the denominator of the new kernel with certain multiplicity but $\sigma_y^i(p)$ does not whenever $i \neq m$. Moreover, there exists a residual form of the new shell with respect to the new kernel whose significant denominator is equal to b. Applying the same argument to each irreducible factor, we can obtain an RNF of f whose kernel has a shift-free denominator and whose shell has a residual form with significant denominator b.

With Lemma 3.4, one can obtain an RNF of f whose kernel has a shift free numerator whose shell has a residual form with significant denominator b. □

A nonzero rational function is said to be *shift-free* if it is shift-reduced and its denominator and numerator are both shift-free. The main result is given below.

Proposition 3.6. *Let (K, S) and (K', S') be two RNF's of a rational function f in $\mathbb{F}(y)$, r and r' be residual forms of S (w.r.t. K) and S' (w.r.t. K'), respectively. Then the significant denominators of r and r' are shift-related.*

Proof. Let b and b' be the significant denominators of r and r', respectively. By the above proposition, there exist two RNF's $(\tilde{K}, \tilde{S})$ and $(\tilde{K}', \tilde{S}')$ of f such that their kernels are shift-free and their shells have residual forms whose significant denominators are b and b', respectively.

According to [5, Theorem 2], the respective denominators $\tilde{v}$ and $\tilde{v}'$ of $\tilde{K}$ and $\tilde{K}'$ are shift-related. Thus, for a nontrivial monic irreducible factor p of $\tilde{v}$ with multiplicity $\alpha > 0$, there exists a unique factor $\sigma_y^{\ell}(p)$ of $\tilde{v}'$ with the same multiplicity. W.L.O.G., we may assume $\ell \leq 0$. Otherwise, we can switch the roles of $(\tilde{K}, \tilde{S})$ and $(\tilde{K}', \tilde{S}')$. If $\ell < 0$, a repeated use of Lemma 3.3 leads to a new RNF $(\tilde{K}'', \tilde{S}'')$ from $(\tilde{K}', \tilde{S}')$ such that $\tilde{K}''$ is shift-free, p is a factor of the denominator of $\tilde{K}''$ with the same multiplicity.

Applying the above argument to each irreducible factor and using Lemma 3.4 for numerators in the same fashion, we can obtain two new RNF's whose kernels are equal and whose shells have respective residual forms with significant denominators b and b'. It follows that b and b' are shift-related by Proposition 3.2. □

4. TELESCOPING VIA REDUCTIONS

We now translate terminology concerning univariate hypergeometric terms to bivariate ones. Let $\mathcal{C}$ be a field of characteristic zero, and $\mathcal{C}(x, y)$ be the field of rational functions in x and y over $\mathcal{C}$. Let σ_x, σ_y be the shift operators w.r.t. x and y, respectively, defined by,

$$\sigma_x(f(x, y)) = f(x+1, y) \text{ and } \sigma_y(f(x, y)) = f(x, y+1),$$

for any f in $\mathcal{C}(x, y)$. Then the pair $(\mathcal{C}(x, y), \{\sigma_x, \sigma_y\})$ forms a partial difference field.

Definition 4.1. *Let $\mathbb{D}$ be a partial difference ring extension of $\mathcal{C}(x, y)$. A nonzero element $T \in \mathbb{D}$ is called a* hypergeometric term *over $\mathcal{C}(x, y)$ if there exist $f, g \in \mathcal{C}(x, y)$ s.t. $\sigma_x(T) = fT$ and $\sigma_y(T) = gT$. We call f and g the x-shift quotient and y-shift quotient of T, respectively.*

An irreducible polynomial p in $\mathcal{C}[x, y]$ is called *integer-linear* over $\mathcal{C}$ if there exists a univariate polynomial $P \in \mathcal{C}[z]$ and two integers λ, μ s.t. $p = P(\lambda x + \mu y)$. A polynomial in $\mathcal{C}[x, y]$ is called *integer-linear* over $\mathcal{C}$ if all its irreducible factors are integer-linear. A rational function in $\mathcal{C}(x, y)$ is called *integer-linear* over $\mathcal{C}$ if its denominator and numerator are both integer-linear.

Let $\mathcal{C}(x)\langle S_x \rangle$ be the ring of linear recurrence operators in x, in which the commutation rule is that $S_x r = \sigma_x(r) S_x$ for all $r \in \mathcal{C}(x)$. The application of an operator $L = \sum_{i=0}^{\rho} e_i S_x^i \in \mathcal{C}(x)\langle S_x \rangle$ to a hypergeometric term T is defined as $L(T) = \sum_{i=0}^{\rho} e_i \sigma_x^i(T)$.

Given a hypergeometric term T over $\mathcal{C}(x, y)$, the computational problem of creative telescoping is to construct a nonzero operator $L \in \mathcal{C}(x)\langle S_x \rangle$ s.t.

$$L(T) = \Delta_y(G),$$

for some hypergeometric term G. We call L a *telescoper* for T w.r.t. y and G a *certificate* for L. To avoid unnecessary duplication, we make a convention.

Convention 4.2. *Let T be a hypergeometric term over $\mathcal{C}(x, y)$ with a multiplicative decomposition SH, where S is in $\mathcal{C}(x, y)$ and H is a hypergeometric term whose y-shift quotient K is shift-reduced w.r.t. y. By [4, Theorem 8], we know K is integer-linear over $\mathcal{C}$. Write $K = u/v$ where $u, v \in \mathcal{C}(x)[y]$ and* $\gcd(u, v) = 1$.

For hypergeometric terms, telescopers do not always exist. Abramov presented a criterion for determining the existence of telescopers in [1, Theorem 10]. With Convention 4.2, applying the modified Abramov-Petkovšek reduction to T w.r.t. y yields (1). By Abramov's criterion, T has a telescoper if and only if the significant denominator of r in (1) is integer-linear over $\mathcal{C}$. Based on this criterion and the modified reduction, the authors of [10] developed a reduction-based telescoping algorithm, named ReductionCT, which either finds a minimal telescoper for T, or proves that no telescoper exists. The key advantage of this algorithm is that it separates the computation of telescopers from that of certificates. This is desirable in the typical situation where we are only interested in the telescopers and their size is much smaller than that of certificates.

When the existence of telescopers for T is guaranteed, we summarize below the idea of the algorithm ReductionCT.

We begin by fixing the order of a telescoper for T, say ρ, and then look for a telescoper of that order. If none exists, we look for one of the next higher order. We make an ansatz

$$L = e_0 + e_1 S_x + \cdots + e_\rho S_x^\rho$$

with undetermined coefficients $e_0, \ldots, e_\rho \in \mathcal{C}(x)$. For i from 0 to ρ, iteratively applying the modified reduction to $\sigma_x^i(T)$ and manipulating the resulting residual forms according to Theorem 5.6 in [10] lead to

$$\sigma_x^i(T) = \Delta_y(g_i H) + \left(\frac{a_i}{b_i} + \frac{q_i}{v}\right) H, \tag{3}$$

where $g_i \in \mathcal{C}(x, y)$, $a_i, b_i \in \mathcal{C}(x)[y]$ with $\deg_y(a_i) < \deg_y(b_i)$, $\gcd(a_i, b_i) = 1$, b_i is shift-free w.r.t. y and strongly prime with K, and q_i belongs to $\mathbb{W}_K$. Moreover, the least common multiple B_ρ of $b_0, \ldots, b_\rho$ is shift-free w.r.t. y. Let

$$A_\rho = \sum_{i=0}^{\rho} e_i a_i \frac{B_\rho}{b_i} \quad \text{and} \quad Q_\rho = \sum_{i=0}^{\rho} e_i q_i.$$

Then $\deg_y(A_\rho) < \deg_y(B_\rho)$, B_ρ is shift-free w.r.t. y and strongly prime with K. Moreover, $\mathbb{W}_K$ is a linear space over $\mathcal{C}(x)$, so Q is in $\mathbb{W}_K$. A direct calculation shows that

$$L(T) = \Delta_y\left(\sum_{i=0}^{\rho} e_i g_i H\right) + \left(\frac{A_\rho}{B_\rho} + \frac{Q_\rho}{v}\right) H.$$

According to Theorem 2.4, $L(T)$ is summable w.r.t. y if and only if $A_\rho/B_\rho + Q_\rho/v = 0$. Equivalently, L is a telescoper for T if and only if the linear system

$$\begin{cases} A_\rho = e_0 a_0 \frac{B_\rho}{b_0} + e_1 a_1 \frac{B_\rho}{b_1} + \cdots + e_\rho a_\rho \frac{B_\rho}{b_\rho} = 0 \\ Q_\rho = e_0 q_0 + e_1 q_1 + \cdots + e_\rho q_\rho = 0 \end{cases} \tag{4}$$

has a nontrivial solution in $\mathcal{C}(x)^{\rho+1}$. A linear dependence among these residual forms $\{a_i/b_i + q_i/v\}_{i=0}^{\rho}$, for minimal ρ, gives rise to a minimal telescoper for T.

The termination of the algorithm ReductionCT is guaranteed by Abramov's criterion, see Theorem 6.3 in [10] for more details. However, instead of using Abramov's criterion, one could prove the algorithm ReductionCT terminates by showing that the residual forms $\{a_i/b_i + q_i/v\}_{i\geq 0}$ from (3) form a finite-dimensional vector space over $\mathcal{C}(x)$. This is exactly what we are going to do in the next section.

5. FINITE-DIMENSIONAL REMAINDERS

In this section, we will show that some sequence of $\{b_i\}_{i\geq 0}$ satisfying (3) has a common multiple B, provided that T has a telescoper. Moreover, B is shift-free and strongly prime with K. The existence of this common multiple implies that the corresponding $\{a_i/b_i + q_i/v\}_{i\geq 0}$ from (3) span a finite-dimensional vector space over $\mathcal{C}(x)$, and lead to upper and lower bounds on the order of minimal telescopers. To this end, we need some preparations.

5.1 Shift-homogeneous decomposition

Recall [3] that irreducible polynomials p, q in $\mathcal{C}[x,y]$ are said to be *shift-equivalent* w.r.t. x, y, denoted by $p \sim_{x,y} q$, if there exist two integers m, n such that $q = \sigma_x^m \sigma_y^n(p)$. Clearly $\sim_{x,y}$ is an equivalence relation. Choosing the pure lexicographic order $x \prec y$, we say a polynomial is *monic* if its highest term has coefficient 1. A rational function is said to be *shift-homogeneous* if all non-constant monic irreducible factors of its denominator and numerator belong to the same shift-equivalence class.

By grouping together the factors in the same shift-equivalence class, every rational function $r \in \mathcal{C}(x,y)$ can be decomposed into the form

$$r = c\, r_1 \ldots r_s \tag{5}$$

where $c \in \mathcal{C}$, $s \in \mathbb{N}$, each r_i is a shift-homogeneous rational function, and any two non-constant monic irreducible factors of r_i and r_j are pairwise shift-inequivalent whenever $i \neq j$. We call (5) a *shift-homogeneous decomposition* of r. The shift-homogeneous decomposition is unique up to the order of the factors and multiplication by nonzero constants.

Let $p \in \mathcal{C}[x,y]$ be an irreducible integer-linear polynomial. Then $p = P(\lambda x + \mu y)$ for $P \in \mathcal{C}[z]$ and $\lambda, \mu \in \mathbb{Z}$. W.L.O.G., we further assume that $\mu \geq 0$ and $\gcd(\lambda, \mu) = 1$. By Bézout's relation, there exist unique integers α, β with $|\alpha| < |\mu|$ and $|\beta| < |\lambda|$ such that $\alpha\lambda + \beta\mu = 1$. Define $\delta^{(\lambda,\mu)}$ to be $\sigma_x^\alpha \sigma_y^\beta$. For brevity, we just write δ if (λ, μ) is clear from the context. Note that $\delta(P(z)) = P(z+1)$ with $z = \lambda x + \mu y$, which allows us to treat integer-linear polynomials as univariate ones. For a Laurent polynomial $\xi = \sum_{i=\ell}^{\rho} m_i \delta^i$ in $\mathbb{Z}[\delta, \delta^{-1}]$ with $\ell, \rho, m_i \in \mathbb{Z}$ and $\ell \leq \rho$, define

$$p^\xi = \delta^\ell(p^{m_\ell})\delta^{\ell+1}(p^{m_{\ell+1}}) \cdots \delta^\rho(p^{m_\rho}).$$

It is readily seen that for any two irreducible integer-linear polynomials $p, q \in \mathcal{C}[x,y]$ of the forms $p = P(\lambda_1 x + \mu_1 y)$ and $q = Q(\lambda_2 x + \mu_2 y)$ with $P, Q \in \mathcal{C}[z]$, $\lambda_1, \mu_1, \lambda_2, \mu_2 \in \mathbb{Z}$, $\mu_1, \mu_2 \geq 0$ and $\gcd(\lambda_1, \mu_1) = \gcd(\lambda_2, \mu_2) = 1$, we have $p \sim_{x,y} q$ if and only if $\lambda_1 = \lambda_2$, $\mu_1 = \mu_2$ and $q = p^{\delta^k}$ for some integer k, in which $\delta = \delta^{(\lambda_1,\mu_1)} = \delta^{(\lambda_2,\mu_2)}$.

Adapt from (5), every integer-linear rational function r in $\mathcal{C}(x,y)$ admits the following decomposition

$$r = c_r\, h_1^{\xi_1} \cdots h_s^{\xi_s} \tag{6}$$

where $c_r \in \mathcal{C}$, $s \in \mathbb{N}$, each $h_i \in \mathcal{C}[x,y]$ is irreducible, monic and integer-linear over $\mathcal{C}$, and then $h_i = P_i(\lambda_i x + \mu_i y)$ for $P_i \in \mathcal{C}[z]$, $\lambda_i, \mu_i \in \mathbb{Z}$ with $\mu_i \geq 0$, $\gcd(\lambda_i, \mu_i) = 1$, and $\xi_i \in \mathbb{Z}[\delta^{(\lambda_i,\mu_i)}, (\delta^{(\lambda_i,\mu_i)})^{-1}]$. Moreover, $h_i \nsim_{x,y} h_j$ whenever $i \neq j$. W.L.O.G., we further assume that ξ_i belongs to $\mathbb{Z}[\delta^{(\lambda_i,\mu_i)}]$.

5.2 Relationship among remainders

With Proposition 3.6, we can describe an inherent relationship among any residual forms $\{a_i/b_i + q_i/v\}_{i\geq 0}$ satisfying (3).

Lemma 5.1. *With Convention 4.2, let r be a residual form of S w.r.t. K. Then $\sigma_x(K)$ and $\sigma_x(S)$ are a kernel and the corresponding shell of $\sigma_x(T)$ w.r.t. y. Moreover, $\sigma_x(r)$ is a residual form of $\sigma_x(S)$ w.r.t. $\sigma_x(K)$.*

Proof. According to Convention 4.2, $\sigma_x(T) = \sigma_x(S)\sigma_x(H)$ and $\sigma_x(K)$ is the y-shift quotient of $\sigma_x(H)$. To prove the first assertion, one needs to show that $\sigma_x(K)$ is shift-reduced w.r.t. y, which can be proven by observing that, for any two polynomials $p_1, p_2 \in \mathcal{C}(x)[y]$, $\gcd(\sigma_x(p_1), \sigma_x(p_2)) = 1$ if and only if $\gcd(p_1, p_2) = 1$. Let $r = a/b + q/v$, where a, b, q belong to $\mathcal{C}(x)[y]$, $\deg_y(a) < \deg_y(b)$, $\gcd(a,b) = 1$, b is shift-free and strongly prime with K, and $q \in \mathbb{W}_K$. Clearly, we have $\deg_y(\sigma_x(a)) < \deg_y(\sigma_x(b))$ and $\gcd(\sigma_x(a), \sigma_x(b)) = 1$. The shift-freeness and strong primeness w.r.t. $\sigma_x(K)$ of $\sigma_x(b)$ easily follows by the above observation.

Note that $\sigma_x \circ \deg_y = \deg_y \circ \sigma_x$ and $\sigma_x \circ \mathrm{lc}_y = \mathrm{lc}_y \circ \sigma_x$, where $\mathrm{lc}_y(p)$ is the leading coefficient of a polynomial p in $\mathcal{C}(x)[y]$. So the standard complements $\mathbb{W}_K$ and $\mathbb{W}_{\sigma_x(K)}$ for polynomial reduction have the same echelon basis according to the case study in [10, §4.2]. It follows from $q \in \mathbb{W}_K$ that $\sigma_x(q) \in \mathbb{W}_{\sigma_x(K)}$. Accordingly, $\sigma_x(r)$ is a residual form of $\sigma_x(S)$ w.r.t. $\sigma_x(K)$. □

Proposition 5.2. *With Convention 4.2, for every nonnegative integer i, assume that $\sigma_x^i(T)$ can be decomposed into (3), where $g_i \in \mathcal{C}(x,y)$, $a_i, b_i \in \mathcal{C}(x)[y]$ with $\deg_y(a_i) < \deg_y(b_i)$, $\gcd(a_i, b_i) = 1$, b_i shift-free w.r.t. y and strongly prime with K, and q_i belongs to $\mathbb{W}_K$. Then $b_i \approx_y \sigma_x^i(b_0)$.*

Proof. It suffices to show $b_1 \approx_y \sigma_x(b_0)$. The rest follows by a direct induction on i.

Applying σ_x to both sides of (3) with $i = 0$ gives

$$\sigma_x(T) = \sigma_x(\Delta_y(g_0 H)) + \sigma_x\left(\frac{a_0}{b_0} + \frac{q_0}{v}\right)\sigma_x(H)$$

$$= \Delta_y(\sigma_x(g_0 H)) + \left(\frac{\sigma_x(a_0)}{\sigma_x(b_0)} + \frac{\sigma_x(q_0)}{\sigma_x(v)}\right)\sigma_x(H)$$

It follows from Lemma 5.1 that $(\sigma_x(K), \sigma_x(S))$ is an RNF of the y-shift quotient of $\sigma_x(T)$, and $\sigma_x(a_0)/\sigma_x(b_0) + \sigma_x(q_0)/\sigma_x(v)$ is a residual form of $\sigma_x(S)$ w.r.t. $\sigma_x(K)$. Let $N = \sigma_x(H)/H$. Then $(K, \sigma_x(S)N)$ is also an RNF of the y-shift quotient of $\sigma_x(T)$. By (3) with $i = 1$, $a_1/b_1 + q_1/v$

is a residual form of $\sigma_x(S)N$ w.r.t. K. By Proposition 3.6, we have $\sigma_x(b_0) \approx_y b_1$. □

The following lemma says that, with Convention 4.2, for any polynomial f in $\mathcal{C}(x)[y]$, there always exists $g \in \mathcal{C}(x)[y]$ s.t. $f \approx_y g$ and g is strongly prime with K.

Lemma 5.3. *With Convention 4.2, assume that p is an irreducible polynomial in $\mathcal{C}(x)[y]$. Then there exists an integer m s.t. $\sigma_y^m(p)$ is strongly prime with K.*

Proof. It suffices to consider the following three cases according to the definition of strong primeness.

Case 1. p is strongly prime with K. Then the lemma follows by letting $m = 0$.

Case 2. There exists an integer $k \geq 0$ s.t. $\sigma_y^k(p) \mid u$. Then for every integer ℓ, we have $\gcd(\sigma_y^\ell(p), v) = 1$, since K is shift-reduced w.r.t. y. Let

$$m = \max\{i \in \mathbb{N} \mid \sigma_y^i(p) \mid u\} + 1.$$

One can see that $\sigma_y^m(p)$ is strongly prime with K.

Case 3. There exists an integer $k \leq 0$ s.t. $\sigma_y^k(p) \mid v$. Then for every integer ℓ, we have $\gcd(\sigma_y^\ell(p), u) = 1$, since K is shift-reduced w.r.t. y. Let

$$m = \min\{i \in \mathbb{N} \mid \sigma_y^i(p) \mid v\} - 1.$$

One can see that $\sigma_y^m(p)$ is strongly prime with K.

The lemma follows. □

The following proposition computes a common multiple of some sequence $\{b_i\}_{i \geq 0}$ satisfying (3), provided that b_0 is integer-linear.

Proposition 5.4. *With Convention 4.2, assume that*

$$T = \Delta_y(gH) + \left(\frac{a}{b} + \frac{q}{v}\right) H, \tag{7}$$

where $g \in \mathcal{C}(x,y)$, $a, b \in \mathcal{C}(x)[y]$, $\deg_y(a) < \deg_y(b)$, $\gcd(a,b) = 1$, b is shift-free w.r.t. y and strongly prime with K, and $q \in \mathbb{W}_K$. Further assume b is integer-linear. Then there exists a polynomial $B \in \mathcal{C}(x)[y]$ with B shift-free w.r.t. y and strongly prime with K s.t. $b \mid B$, and for every nonnegative integer $i \geq 0$, $\sigma_x^i(T)$ can be decomposed into

$$\sigma_x^i(T) = \Delta_y(g_i H) + \left(\frac{a_i}{B} + \frac{q_i}{v}\right) H, \tag{8}$$

where $g_i \in \mathcal{C}(x,y)$, $a_i \in \mathcal{C}(x)[y]$ with $\deg_y(a_i) < \deg_y(B)$ and $q_i \in \mathbb{W}_K$.

Proof. When $b \in \mathcal{C}(x)$. By the modified Abramov-Petkovšek reduction, (3) holds for every $i > 0$. Then $b_i \in \mathcal{C}(x)$ by Proposition 5.2. The proposition follows by letting $B = 1$. Assume that $b \notin \mathcal{C}(x)$. Since b is integer-linear, by (6),

$$b = c_b \cdot h_1^{\xi_1} \cdots h_t^{\xi_t} \tag{9}$$

where $c_b \in \mathcal{C}(x)$, $t \in \mathbb{N}$, each h_j is a monic irreducible integer-linear polynomial of the form $h_j = P_j(\lambda_j x + \mu_j y)$ for $P_j \in \mathcal{C}[z]$, $\lambda_j, \mu_j \in \mathbb{Z}$, $\mu_j > 0$ and $\gcd(\lambda_j, \mu_j) = 1$, and ξ_j belongs to $\mathbb{N}[\delta^{(\lambda_j,\mu_j)}]$ for $1 \leq j \leq t$. Moreover, $h_j \not\sim_{x,y} h_k$ whenever $j \neq k$. Due to the primeness of h_j and the partial fraction decomposition of a/b, it suffices to prove the local case, that is, $c_b = t = 1$ and

$$b = P(\lambda x + \mu y)^{\sum_{i=0}^{s} c_i \delta^i},$$

where $P \in \mathcal{C}[z]$, $s, c_i \in \mathbb{N}$, $\lambda, \mu \in \mathbb{Z}$, $\mu > 0$ and $\delta = \delta^{(\lambda,\mu)}$. Note that for every $i \in \mathbb{N}$, there are unique integers j, k_j with $0 \leq j \leq \mu - 1$ s.t. $i = \mu k_j + j$. Let $c_j' = c_{\mu k_j + j}$. Since b is shift-free w.r.t. y, we have

$$b = \prod_{j=0}^{\mu-1} P(\lambda x + \mu y + j)^{c_j' \sigma_y^{k_j}}.$$

For every $0 \leq j \leq \mu - 1$, set ℓ_j to be k_j if $m_j \neq 0$, or some integer otherwise with $P(\lambda x + \mu y + j)^{\sigma_y^{\ell_j}}$ strongly prime with K by Lemma 5.3. Let $m = \max_{0 \leq j \leq \mu-1}\{c_j'\}$ and

$$B = \prod_{j=0}^{\mu-1} P(\lambda x + \mu y + j)^{m \sigma_y^{\ell_j}}. \tag{10}$$

Since $\ell_j = k_j$ when $m_j \neq 0$, every irreducible factor of b divides B and thus $b \mid B$ by the maximum of m. B is shift-free w.r.t. y since $0 \leq j \leq \mu - 1$. Moreover, B is strongly prime with K by the choice of ℓ_j.

It remains to show that (8) holds for every nonnegative integer i. To prove this, we first show $\sigma_x(B) \approx_y B$. By (10),

$$B \approx_y \prod_{j=0}^{\mu-1} P(\lambda x + \mu y + j)^m,$$

which establishes that

$$\sigma_x(B) \approx_y \prod_{j=0}^{\mu-1} P(\lambda x + \mu y + j + \lambda)^m.$$

One sees that there is a unique integer $0 \leq k \leq \mu - 1$ s.t.

$$P(\lambda x + \mu y + j + \lambda) \sim_y P(\lambda x + \mu y + k).$$

Conversely, for any $0 \leq k \leq \mu - 1$, there exists a unique integer $0 \leq j \leq \mu - 1$ s.t. the above equivalence holds. Thus

$$\sigma_x(B) \approx_y \prod_{k=0}^{\mu-1} P(\lambda x + \mu y + k)^m \approx_y B.$$

For $i = 0$, letting $a_0 = aB/b$ and $q_0 = q$ gives (8). For every $i > 0$, $\sigma_x^i(B) \approx_y \sigma_x^{i-1}(B)$ since $\sigma_x(B) \approx_y B$ and then $\sigma_x^i(B) \approx_y B$. By the modified Abramov-Petkovšek reduction, (3) holds for every $i \geq 0$, in which $b_0 = b$. According to Proposition 5.2, $b_i \approx_y \sigma_x^i(b_0)$. It follows from $b \mid B$ that $\sigma_x^i(b) \mid \sigma_x^i(B)$. Consequently, we have

$$b_i \approx_y \sigma_x^i(b) \mid \sigma_x^i(B) \approx_y B.$$

Thus there is $\tilde{b}_i \in \mathcal{C}(x)[y]$ dividing B so that $\tilde{b}_i \approx_y b_i$. Moreover, $\tilde{b}_i$ is strongly prime with K as B is. It follows from Theorem 5.6 in [10] that there exist $\tilde{g}_i \in \mathcal{C}(x,y)$, $\tilde{a}_i \in \mathcal{C}(x)[y]$ with $\deg_y(\tilde{a}_i) < \deg_y(\tilde{b}_i)$ and $\tilde{q}_i \in \mathbb{W}_K$ such that $\sigma_x^i(T) = \Delta_y(\tilde{g}_i H) + (\tilde{a}_i/\tilde{b}_i + \tilde{q}_i/v)H$. The assertion follows by noticing

$$\sigma_x^i(T) = \Delta_y(\tilde{g}_i H) + \left(\frac{\tilde{a}_i B/\tilde{b}_i}{B} + \frac{\tilde{q}_i}{v}\right) H.$$

□

Under the assumptions and notations of Proposition 5.4, applying the modified Abramov-Petkovšek reduction to T w.r.t. y yields (1). By Proposition 3.2 and Proposition 3.6, the significant denominator of r in (1) is shift-related to b w.r.t. y. Thus the shift-equivalence classes represented by $h_j\,(1 \le j \le t)$ in (9) are independent of the choice of b. Therefore, the degree of B w.r.t. y is fixed once a hypergeometric term T is given, although the form of B depends on the choice of b.

5.3 Upper and lower bounds

Now we show that Proposition 5.4 implies some residual forms $\{a_i/b_i + q_i/v\}_{i\ge 0}$ satisfying (3) form a finite-dimensional vector space over $\mathcal{C}(x)$, and then derive the order bounds for minimal telescopers.

Theorem 5.5. *With the assumptions and notations introduced in Proposition 5.4, the order of a minimal telescoper for T is no more than*

$$\max\{\deg_y(u), \deg_y(v)\} - [\![\deg_y(v-u) \le \deg_y(u) - 1]\!] + \sum_{j=1}^{t} \mu_j m_j \deg(P_j),$$

where m_j is the maximum coefficient of ξ_j for $1 \le j \le t$, and $[\![\varphi]\!]$ equals 1 if φ is true, otherwise it is 0.

Proof. Let $L = \sum_{i=0}^{\rho} e_i S_x^i$ with $\rho \in \mathbb{N}$, $e_0, \ldots, e_\rho \in \mathcal{C}(x)$, not all zero, be a minimal telescoper for T w.r.t. y. By Proposition 5.4, (8) holds for every $0 \le i \le \rho$. Then by the arguments in Section 4, the linear system (4), in which $b_i = B_\rho = B$ for $1 \le i \le \rho$, of equations for the variables $\{e_0, \ldots, e_\rho\}$ has a nontrivial solution in $\mathcal{C}(x)^{\rho+1}$. Since $Q_\rho \in \mathbb{W}_K$, the number of terms w.r.t. y in Q_ρ is no more than $\dim_{\mathcal{C}(x)}(\mathbb{W}_K)$, which is bounded by

$$\max\{\deg_y(u), \deg_y(v)\} - [\![\deg_y(v-u) \le \deg_y(u) - 1]\!]$$

according to Proposition 4.7 in [10]. Note that The solutions of the system (4) are in one-to-one correspondence with the telescopers for T. Comparing coefficients of like powers of y of the linear system (4) yields at most $\deg_y(A_\rho) + \dim_{\mathcal{C}(x)} \mathbb{W}_K + 1$ equations. Hence this system has nontrivial solutions whenever $\rho > \deg_y(A_\rho) + \dim_{\mathcal{C}(x)} \mathbb{W}_K$. It implies that the order of a minimal telescoper for T is no more than $\deg_y(A_\rho) + \dim_{\mathcal{C}(x)} \mathbb{W}_K + 1$. The theorem follows by applying $\deg_y(A_\rho) < \deg_y(B) = \sum_{j=1}^{t} \mu_j m_j \deg_y(P_j)$. □

In addition, we can further obtain a lower bound for the order of telescopers for T.

Theorem 5.6. *With the assumptions of Proposition 5.4, further assume that T is not summable w.r.t. y. Then the order of a telescoper for T is at least*

$$\max_{\substack{p \mid b,\ \text{multi.}\alpha \\ \text{irred. \& monic} \\ \deg_y(p) > 0}} \min\left\{\rho \in \mathbb{N}\setminus\{0\} : \begin{array}{l} \sigma_y^{\ell}(p)^{\alpha} \mid \sigma_x^{\rho}(b) \\ \textit{for some } \ell \in \mathbb{Z} \end{array}\right\}.$$

Proof. Let $L = \sum_{i=0}^{\rho} e_i S_x^i$ with $\rho \in \mathbb{N}$, $e_0, \ldots, e_\rho \in \mathcal{C}(x)$, not all zero, be a minimal telescoper for T. Then $\rho \ge 1$ as T is not summable. By the modified Abramov-Petkovšek reduction, we have (3) holds for $0 \le i \le \rho$, in which $b_0 = b$. Note that L is a minimal telescoper, so $e_0 \ne 0$ and

$$e_0 \frac{a_0}{b_0} + e_1 \frac{a_1}{b_1} + \cdots + e_\rho \frac{a_\rho}{b_\rho} = 0$$

by the system (4). By partial fraction decomposition, for any monic irreducible factor p of b_0 with $\deg_y(p) > 0$ and multiplicity $\alpha > 0$, there exists an integer i with $1 \le i \le \rho$ so that p^α is also a factor of b_i. According to Proposition 5.2, $b_i \approx_y \sigma_x^i(b_0)$. Thus there is a factor p' of $\sigma_x^i(b_0)$ with multiplicity at least α s.t. $p' \sim_y p$. Let i_p be the minimal one with this property. Then the assertion follows by the fact that for each factor p of $b_0 = b$, there exist no telescopers for T of order less than i_p. □

With the upper and lower bounds, one may try to analyze the complexity of the algorithm ReductionCT from [10] and further improve it by adding them into the procedures. Instead of doing so, in the rest of this paper, we are going to compare our bounds to the known ones in the literature.

6. COMPARISON OF BOUNDS

Upper and lower bounds for the order of telescopers for hypergeometric terms have been studied in [12] and [2], respectively. In this section, we are going to review these known bounds and then compare them to our bounds.

6.1 Apagodu-Zeilberger upper bound

Let T be a *proper* hypergeometric term over $\mathcal{C}(x, y)$, that is it can be written in the form

$$T = p w^x z^y \prod_{i=1}^{m} \frac{(\alpha_i x + \alpha_i' y + \alpha_i'' - 1)!(\beta_i x - \beta_i' y + \beta_i'' - 1)!}{(\mu_i x + \mu_i' y + \mu_i'' - 1)!(\nu_i x - \nu_i' y + \nu_i'' - 1)!}, \tag{11}$$

where $p \in \mathcal{C}[x, y]$, $m \in \mathbb{N}$ is fixed, $\alpha_i, \alpha_i', \beta_i, \beta_i', \mu_i, \mu_i', \nu_i, \nu_i'$ are non-negative integers and $w, z, \alpha_i'', \beta_i'', \mu_i'', \nu_i'' \in \mathcal{C}$. Further assume that there exist no integers i, j with $1 \le i, j \le m$ s.t.

$$\begin{aligned} &\{\alpha_i = \mu_j \ \ \& \ \ \alpha_i' = \mu_j' \ \ \& \ \ \alpha_i'' - \mu_j'' \in \mathbb{N}\} \\ \text{or } &\{\beta_i = \nu_j \ \ \& \ \ \beta_i' = \nu_j' \ \ \& \ \ \beta_i'' - \nu_j'' \in \mathbb{N}\}. \end{aligned}$$

We refer this as the *generic* situation. Then Apagodu and Zeiberger [12] stated that the order of a minimal telescoper for T is bounded by

$$B_{AZ} = \max\left\{\sum_{i=1}^{m}(\alpha_i' + \nu_i'), \sum_{i=1}^{m}(\beta_i' + \mu_i')\right\}.$$

We now show that B_{AZ} given above is at least the order bound on minimal telescopers for T obtained from Theorem 5.5. Reordering the factorial terms in (11) if necessary, let $\mathcal{S}$ be the maximal set of integers i with $1 \le i \le m$ satisfying

$$\begin{aligned} &\{\alpha_i = \mu_i \ \ \& \ \ \alpha_i' = \mu_i' \ \ \& \ \ \mu_i'' - \alpha_i'' \in \mathbb{N}\} \\ \text{or } &\{\beta_i = \nu_i \ \ \& \ \ \beta_i' = \nu_i' \ \ \& \ \ \nu_i'' - \beta_i'' \in \mathbb{N}\}. \end{aligned}$$

Rewrite T as

$$r w^x z^y \prod_{\substack{i=1 \\ i \notin \mathcal{S}}}^{m} \frac{(\alpha_i x + \alpha_i' y + \alpha_i'' - 1)!(\beta_i x - \beta_i' y + \beta_i'' - 1)!}{(\mu_i x + \mu_i' y + \mu_i'' - 1)!(\nu_i x - \nu_i' y + \nu_i'' - 1)!},$$

where $r \in \mathcal{C}(x, y)$. For $q \in \mathcal{C}[x, y]$, and $m \in \mathbb{N}$, let

$$q^{\overline{m}} = q(q+1)(q+2)\cdots(q+m-1)$$

with the convention $q^{\overline{0}} = 1$. It can be calculated that the kernel and shell of the shift quotient $\sigma_y(T)/T$ are

$$K = z \prod_i \frac{(\alpha_i x + \alpha_i' y + \alpha_i'')^{\overline{\alpha_i'}}(\nu_i x - \nu_i' y + \nu_i'' - \mu_i)^{\overline{\nu_i'}}}{(\mu_i x + \mu_i' y + \mu_i'')^{\overline{\mu_i'}}(\beta_i x - \beta_i' y + \beta_i'' - \beta_i')^{\overline{\beta_i'}}},$$

where the product runs over all i from 1 to m s.t. $i \notin \mathcal{S}$, $\alpha_i', \beta_i' > 0$ and $\mu_i', \nu_i' > 0$, and $S = r$, respectively. Let $K = u/v$ with $\gcd(u,v) = 1$. Note that K is proper, a straightforward calculation implies

$$\deg_y(u) = \sum_{i=1, i\notin\mathcal{S}}^{m} (\alpha_i' + \nu_i') \text{ and } \deg_y(v) = \sum_{i=1, i\notin\mathcal{S}}^{m} (\beta_i' + \mu_i').$$

Applying the modified Abramov-Petkovšek reduction to T w.r.t. y yields (7), in which b is integer-linear. Since b comes from the shift-free part of the denominator of r, it factors into integer-linear polynomials of degree 1 which are shift-equivalent to either $(\mu_i x + \mu_i' y + \mu_i'')$ or $(\beta_i x - \beta_i' y + \beta_i'')$ w.r.t. x, y for some $i \in \mathcal{S}$. Note that each i in $\mathcal{S}$ increases the multiplicities of the corresponding integer-linear factors in b by at most 1. Hence, the bound given in Theorem 5.5 is no more than

$$\max\{\deg_y(u), \deg_y(v)\} - [\![\deg_y(v-u) \le \deg_y(u) - 1]\!] + \sum_{i=1, i\in\mathcal{S}}^{m} (\beta_i' + \mu_i'),$$

which is exactly equal to $B_{AZ} - [\![\deg_y(v-u) \le \deg_y(u) - 1]\!]$ since $\sum_{i=1, i\in\mathcal{S}}^{m} (\alpha_i' + \nu_i') = \sum_{i=1, i\in\mathcal{S}}^{m} (\beta_i' + \mu_i')$.

In general, i.e., when we have the generic situation, the order bound in Theorem 5.5 is almost the same as B_{AZ}. However, our bound may be much tighter in some special examples.

Example 6.1. *Consider a rational function*

$$T = \frac{\alpha^2 y^2 + \alpha^2 y - \alpha\beta y + 2\alpha x y + x^2}{(x + \alpha y + \alpha)(x + \alpha y)(x + \beta y)},$$

where α, β are positive integers and $\alpha \neq \beta$. Rewriting T into the proper form yields $B_{AZ} = \alpha + \beta$. On the other hand, the kernel of $\sigma_y(T)/T$ is 1 since T is a rational function. By the modified Abramov-Petkovšek reduction, $b = x + \beta y$ in (7). According to Theorem 5.5, a minimal telescoper for T has order no more than β, which is indeed the real order of minimal telescopers for T.

Remark 6.2. *Only with [1, Theorem 10], the upper order bound on minimal telescopers derived in [12] can be also applied to non-proper hypergeometric terms. On the other hand, Theorem 5.5 can be applied to any hypergeometric term provided that its telescopers exist.*

6.2 Abramov-Le lower bound

With Convention 4.2, assume that T has the initial reduction (7), in which b is integer-linear. Define $H' = H/v$. A direct calculation leads to $\sigma_y(H')/H' = u/\sigma_y(v)$, which is again shift-reduced w.r.t. y. Let $d' \in \mathcal{C}(x)[y]$ be the denominator of $\sigma_x(H')/H'$. Then the algorithm LowerBound in [2] asserts that the order of telescopers for T is at least

$$B_{AL} = \max_{\substack{p \mid b \\ \text{irred. \& monic} \\ \deg_y(p) > 0}} \min \left\{ \rho \in \mathbb{N} \setminus \{0\} : \begin{array}{c} \sigma_y^{\ell}(p) \mid \sigma_x^{\rho}(b) \\ \text{or} \\ \sigma_y^{\ell}(p) \mid \sigma_x^{\rho-1}(d') \\ \text{for some } \ell \in \mathbb{Z} \end{array} \right\}$$

Comparing to B_{AL}, it is obvious that the lower bound given by Theorem 5.6 can be better but not worse than B_{AL}.

Example 6.3. *Consider a hypergeometric term*

$$T = \frac{1}{(x - \alpha y - \alpha)(x - \alpha y - 2)!},$$

where $\alpha \in \mathbb{Z}$ and $\alpha \geq 2$. By the algorithm LowerBound*, a telescoper for T has order at least 2. On the other hand, a telescoper for T has order at least α by Theorem 5.6. In fact, α is exactly the order of minimal telescopers for T.*

7. ACKNOWLEDGEMENT

I am very grateful to my advisors Manuel Kauers and Ziming Li for their helpful discussions and valuable comments. I also would like to thank Shaoshi Chen for his suggestions and support. Besides, I wish to express my gratitude to anonymous referees for many useful suggestions.

8. REFERENCES

[1] S. A. Abramov. When does Zeilberger's algorithm succeed? *Adv. in Appl. Math.*, 30(3):424–441, 2003.

[2] S. A. Abramov and H. Le. On the order of the recurrence produced by the method of creative telescoping. *Discrete Math.*, 298(1–3):2–17, 2005.

[3] S. A. Abramov and M. Petkovšek. Minimal decomposition of indefinite hypergeometric sums. In *Proc. of ISSAC'01*, pp. 7–14, 2001.

[4] S. A. Abramov and M. Petkovšek. Proof of a conjecture of Wilf and Zeilberger. *Preprint Series of the Institute of Mathematics, Physics and Mechanics*, University of Ljubljana, vol. 39, 2001.

[5] S. A. Abramov and M. Petkovšek. Rational normal forms and minimal decompositions of hypergeometric terms. *J. Symbolic Comput.*, 33(5):521–543, 2002.

[6] M. Apagodu and D. Zeilberger. Multi-variable Zeilberger and Almkvist-Zeilberger algorithms and the sharpening of Wilf-Zeilberger theory. *Adv. in Appl. Math.*, 37(2):139–152, 2006.

[7] A. Bostan, S. Chen, F. Chyzak, and Z. Li. Complexity of creative telescoping for bivariate rational functions. In *Proc. of ISSAC '10*, pp. 203–210, 2010.

[8] A. Bostan, S. Chen, F. Chyzak, Z. Li, and G. Xin. Hermite reduction and creative telescoping for hyperexponential functions. In *Proc. of ISSAC'13*, pp. 77–84, 2013.

[9] A. Bostan, P. Lairez, and B. Salvy. Creative telescoping for rational functions using the Griffith-Dwork method. In *Proc. of ISSAC'13*, pp. 93–100, 2013.

[10] S. Chen, H. Huang, M. Kauers, and Z. Li. A modified Abramov-Petkovšek reduction and creative telescoping for hypergeometric terms. In *Proc. of ISSAC'15*, pp. 117–124, 2015.

[11] S. Chen, M. Kauers, and C. Koutschan. Reduction-based creative telescoping for algebraic functions. To appear in *Proc. of ISSAC'16*, 2016.

[12] M. Mohammed and D. Zeilberger. Sharp upper bounds for the orders of the recurrences output by the Zeilberger and q-Zeilberger algorithms. *J. Symbolic Comput.*, 39(2):201–207, 2005.

[13] M. Petkovšek, H. S. Wilf, and Doron Zeilberger. $A = B$. A K Peters Ltd., Wellesley, MA, 1996.

[14] D. Zeilberger. The method of creative telescoping. *J. Symbolic Comput.*, 11:195–204, 1991.

Constructing Small Generating Sets for the Multiplicative Groups of Algebras over Finite Fields

Ming-Deh Huang
Department of Computer Science
University of Southern California
Los Angeles, CA 90089
mdhuang@usc.edu

Lian Liu
Department of Computer Science
University of Southern California
Los Angeles, CA 90089
lianliu@usc.edu

ABSTRACT

We consider computational problems concerning algebras over finite fields. In particular, we propose an algorithm for finding a small generating set for the multiplicative group of $\mathbb{F}_p[x]/F$, where p is a prime number and $F \in \mathbb{F}_p[x]$ is an arbitrary polynomial. Based on this result, a new set of expander graphs can be explicitly constructed. In addition, we present algorithms for basis construction and decomposition of a given element with respect to the basis.

CCS Concepts

•Theory of computation → Expander graphs and randomness extractors; •Computing methodologies → Algebraic algorithms; •Mathematics of computing → Spectra of graphs;

Keywords

computational algebra; generating sets; character sums; expander graphs

1. INTRODUCTION

In computational algebra, it is often desired to find small generating sets for given groups. This problem has many applications. For example, in the index calculus method for solving the discrete logarithm problem over the multiplicative groups of finite fields, one is interested in finding a reasonably small generating set over which enough relations can be found [2, 11]. Generating sets are also involved in explicit construction of expander graphs [4, 13]. Informally, expander graphs are graphs with strong expansion properties. They have been applied in many areas including computational complexity theory, coding theory and communication networks [6, 9].

In this paper we are interested in finding small generating sets for the multiplicative groups of algebras of the form $B := \mathbb{F}_p[x]/F$, where p is a prime number and $F \in \mathbb{F}_p[x]$ is an arbitrary polynomial.

ISSAC '16, July 19 - 22, 2016, Waterloo, ON, Canada

ISBN 978-1-4503-4380-0/16/07...$15.00

DOI: http://dx.doi.org/10.1145/2930889.2930921

When F is irreducible of degree d, a fundamental result of Chung [4] states that if $\sqrt{p} > d-1$, then the set $x+\mathbb{F}_p := \{x+t : t \in \mathbb{F}_p\}$ forms a generating set for $\mathbb{F}_q^\times \simeq (\mathbb{F}_p[x]/F)^\times$, where $q := p^d$. In addition, the *Cayley graphs* built on $\mathbb{F}_q^\times$ with the generating set $x+\mathbb{F}_p$, with $q = p^d$ and $\sqrt{p} > d-1$, form a set of expander graphs.

A goal of this paper is to generalize Chung's results [4] to the general case of $B := \mathbb{F}_p[x]/F$ where F is not necessarily irreducible. In Section 3.1, we present algorithms for finding different types of generating sets for $B^\times$. We also show that they offer more flexibility for expander graph construction.

Another issue discussed in this paper is the construction of a basis for $B^\times$ and the decomposition of elements in $B^\times$ with respect to the basis. In the special case where F is irreducible, the problem of finding a basis for $B^\times := (\mathbb{F}_p[x]/F)^\times$ is also called finding a *primitive element* for the finite field $\mathbb{F}_p[x]/F$, which is known to be hard in general [10]. In fact, it is an important open problem which has not yet been fully settled. However, there are existing algorithms for solving its relaxations or special cases under certain assumptions. For example, in [18] and its extensions [15], the author showed that for certain (p, d) pairs, elements of high order can be constructed using Gauss periods. And in [3, 10, 16], the authors addressed the special case of finding primitive elements in finite fields of small characteristics. The decomposition problem in this special case is better known as the *discrete logarithm* problem, which is a classic hard problem that has been extensively studied. Recent breakthroughs include Gologlu et. al. [8] and Joux [11], both of which compute discrete logarithms in finite fields of small characteristics faster than previously known under certain heuristics.

In Section 3.2, we analyze the structure of $B^\times$. We propose algorithms for finding a basis for $B^\times$ as well as decomposing elements with respect to this basis when p is relatively large. Both algorithms require an existing primitive element or discrete logarithm algorithm as their subroutine.

One of the goals of designing these algorithms is to validate the generating sets we proposed in Section 3.1. Since these algorithms enable us to test whether a given set of elements generates $B^\times$, we would be able to see whether or not our theoretically proven generating sets are actually larger than necessary. Our experimental results in Section 4 suggest that a square-root number of elements in our generating sets might already be sufficient to generate the entire group. However further investigation is required to determine whether this is indeed the case.

2. PRELIMINARIES

2.1 Character Sums

A *character* of a group G is a group homomorphism $\chi : G \to \mathbb{C}^*$. Clearly, sending all elements to 1 yields a character, which is called a *trivial character*, while all other characters are said to be *nontrivial*. We use $X(G)$ to denote the set of all distinct characters of G, and let $\tilde{X}(G)$ denote the set of all nontrivial characters of G. When G is a finite abelian group, we have $|X(G)| = |G|$, and the following fundamental property is known (see [9], Proposition 8.5):

PROPOSITION 1. *Assume a fixed order $g_1, \ldots, g_{|G|} \in G$ on the elements of G, then $\{(\chi(g_1), \ldots, \chi(g_{|G|}))|\chi \in X\}$ form a orthogonal basis for $\mathbb{C}^n$, where $n = |G|$.*

Character sums have been extensively studied in the past decades [5, 12, 14]. In particular, Weil's estimate [20] and its generalizations are important to our approach.

PROPOSITION 2. *Let B be an arbitrary finite n-dimensional commutative $\mathbb{F}_q$-algebra and x be an element of B. If χ is a character of the multiplicative group $B^\times$ (extended by zero to all of B) which is non-trivial on $\mathbb{F}_q[x]$, then*

$$\left|\sum_{t\in\mathbb{F}_q} \chi(t-x)\right| \leq (n-1)\sqrt{q}$$

Proposition 2 was initially conjectured by Katz in [12]. Subsequently, Lenstra observed in his unpublished notes ("Multiplicative groups generated by linear expression") that the proposition actually follows as a consequence of Weil's character sum estimate [20]. We refer readers to [19] (Corollary 2.2) for details of this proposition.

2.2 Expanders and Cayley Graphs

Informally speaking, *expander graphs* (abbr. *expanders*) are sparse graphs which are well-connected. Intuitively, every small subset of vertices has a relatively large neighborhood. The expansion of a k-regular graph (or k-regular directed graph) Γ can be measured by its *spectral gap*, which is defined as $k - \lambda$, where λ is the second largest eigenvalue (in absolute value) of the adjacency matrix of Γ [9]. We say Γ is an *(n, k, γ)-expander* if it is a k-regular graph (or k-regular directed graph) with n vertices and its spectral gap is at least γ. In this paper, we would simply call Γ an *expander* if the parameters n, k, γ are clear from the context.

Cayley graphs have been used as a general technique for expander graph construction [4, 6, 9, 19]. Let G be a finite abelian group and $S \subseteq G$ be a subset of elements, the *Cayley graph* induced by G and S, denoted by $\Gamma(G, S)$, is the directed graph with vertex set G and for all $g, h \in G$, there is an directed edge $g \to h$ if and only if $sg = h$ for some $s \in S$. For simplicity, we say $\Gamma(G, S)$ is a Cayley graph over G. By construction, Cayley graphs are *$|S|$-regular directed graphs*, meaning that all vertices have the same in-degree and out-degree, both equaling $|S|$. In addition, S is a generating set of G if and only if $\Gamma(G, S)$ is strongly connected, or in other words, $\Gamma(G, S)$ has a finite diameter. Chung [4] showed that the diameter of a directed graph is related to the eigenvalues of its adjacency matrix:

PROPOSITION 3. *If a directed regular graph Γ with n vertices has out-degree k and the eigenvectors of its adjacency matrix M form an orthogonal basis, then*

$$\mathrm{diam}(\Gamma) \leq \left\lceil \frac{\log(n-1)}{\log(\frac{k}{\lambda})} \right\rceil$$

where λ is the second largest eigenvalue (in absolute value) of M.

It is worth mentioning that a recent work by Shparlinski [17] showed that in the special case where Γ is a Cayley graph over $\mathbb{F}_q^\times$ induced by certain types of generating sets, this diameter bound can be improved.

A natural question to ask is what are the eigenvalues of a Cayley graph. It is easy to verify that the eigenvalues can be expressed as character sums (see [4, 9]):

PROPOSITION 4. *Let M be the adjacency matrix of $\Gamma(G, S)$. Assume the rows and columns are both indexed by $g_1, \ldots, g_{|G|}$, then the eigenvectors of M are $\{(\chi(g_1), \ldots, \chi(g_{|G|}))|\chi \in X(G)\}$ corresponding to eigenvalues $\{\sum_{s\in S} \chi(s)|\chi \in X(G)\}$.*

Combining Propositions 1, 3 and 4, we can see that S generates G if $|\sum_{s\in S} \chi(S)| < |S|$ for all nontrivial characters in $X(G)$. In expander graph construction, on one hand, we want the resulting graph, $\Gamma(G, S)$ to be sparse, so a small cardinality of S is desired. On the other hand, the spectral gap $\gamma = |S| - \lambda = |S| - \max_{\chi\in\tilde{X}(G)} |\sum_{s\in S} \chi(s)|$ should be large in order to guarantee a "large" expansion. In this paper, our goal is to find such a small generating set S for $B^\times$ so that the resulting Cayley graph $\Gamma(B^\times, S)$ is provably an expander.

3. ALGORITHMS

3.1 Generating Sets and Expander Graphs

Given the standard factorization of $F = \prod_{i=1}^m f_i^{e_i}$ where for all $1 \leq i \leq m$, f_i is irreducible, by Chinese Remainder Theorem, we have the isomorphism

$$\psi : \bigoplus_{i=1}^{m} (\mathbb{F}_p[x]/f_i^{e_i})^\times \xrightarrow{\sim} (\mathbb{F}_p[x]/F)^\times \qquad (1)$$

where ψ can be computed using standard Chinese Remainder Theorem algorithms. We may first consider a simplified problem of finding a small generating set for each component on the left-hand side before handling the general case. Let $v_{i,s}^m \in \bigoplus_{i=1}^m A_i^\times$ where $A_i := \mathbb{F}_p[x]/f_i^{e_i}$ denote an m-dimensional vector with s in the i-th entry and zeros elsewhere. That is,

$$v_{i,s}^m := \underbrace{0 \oplus \ldots \oplus 0}_{i-1} \oplus s \oplus \underbrace{0 \oplus \ldots \oplus 0}_{m-i}.$$

Suppose a generating set S_i for $A_i^\times$ is given for all $1 \leq i \leq m$, then clearly, $\{\psi(v_{i,s}^m)|1 \leq i \leq m, s \in S_i\}$ would be a generating set for $B^\times$. Therefore, in Sections 3.1.1, 3.1.2 and 3.1.3, we will focus our discussion on finding a small generating set for the multiplicative groups of algebras $A := \mathbb{F}_p[x]/f^e$, where $f \in \mathbb{F}_p[x]$ stands for an irreducible polynomial of degree $d \geq 1$, and $e \geq 1$ is an integer. Note that we will use A as the abbreviation for $\mathbb{F}_p[x]/f^e$. When $e = 1$, we are done, since $x + \mathbb{F}_p$ is a generating set for $A^\times$, which directly follows from Chung [4]. Therefore, in Sections 3.1.1, 3.1.2 and 3.1.3, we will assume $e > 1$.

3.1.1 Regarding A as an $\mathbb{F}_p$-algebra

Observe that A can be naturally regarded as an $\mathbb{F}_p$-algebra. Based on this observation, we obtain the first type of small generating sets for $A^\times$, as stated in Theorem 1.

THEOREM 1. *If $\sqrt{p} > de - 1$, then $(\mathbb{F}_p - x) \cap A^\times$ is a generating set for $A^\times$. Furthermore, every element in $A^\times$ can be written as $\prod_{i=1}^{t} (a_i - x)$ where $a_i \in \mathbb{F}_p$ with*

$$t < 2de + 1 + \frac{4de \log(de-1)}{\log p - 2\log(de-1)}$$

PROOF. A is an $\mathbb{F}_p$-algebra having dimension de, by Proposition 2, for all nontrivial character χ of $A^\times$ (extended by zero to all of A),

$$\left| \sum_{t \in \mathbb{F}_p} \chi(t - x) \right| \le (de-1)\sqrt{p}. \tag{2}$$

The rest of the proof follows from Propositions 3 and 4. □

THEOREM 2. *If $\sqrt{p} > de - 1$, then $\Gamma(A^\times, S)$ is an expander, where $S = (\mathbb{F}_p - x) \cap A^\times$.*

PROOF. The spectral gap γ satisfies

$$\gamma = p - \max_{\chi \in \hat{X}(A^\times)} \left| \sum_{t \in \mathbb{F}_p} \chi(t - x) \right| \ge p - (de-1)\sqrt{p} > 0 \tag{3}$$

where the first inequality follows from Equation (2). □

3.1.2 Regarding A as an $\mathbb{F}_q$-algebra

Theorem 1 requires $\sqrt{p} > de - 1$, which could be too strict a requirement on p. In situations where p is small, we would like to look for other types of generating sets. We define $q := p^d$ and $\mathbb{F}_q := \mathbb{F}_p[x]/f$. Notice that by enlarging the ground field from $\mathbb{F}_p$ to $\mathbb{F}_q$, A can actually be regarded as an $\mathbb{F}_q$-algebra. In order to see this, we will begin with a few lemmas.

LEMMA 1. *Let $a \in A$ be written in the form $a = \sum_{i=0}^{e-1} a_i f^i$ with each $a_i \in A$ having degree less than d. Then $a \in A^\times$ if and only if $a_0 \ne 0 \pmod f$.*

PROOF. For sufficiency, since $a \in A^\times$, there is an inverse element $b = \sum_{i=0}^{e-1} b_i f^i$ such that $ab = 1$. That is,

$$\begin{aligned}\left(\sum_{i=0}^{e-1} a_i f^i\right)\left(\sum_{i=0}^{e-1} b_i f^i\right) &= a_0b_0 + (a_0b_1 + a_1b_0)f + \dots \\ &= 1 \pmod{f^e},\end{aligned} \tag{4}$$

so $a_0b_0 = 1 \pmod f \Rightarrow a_0 \ne 0 \pmod f$.

For necessity, suppose $a_0 \ne 0 \pmod f$, then it suffices to show the existence of $b = a^{-1}$. Assume that $b = \sum_{i=0}^{e-1} b_i f^i$ ($\deg b_i < d$ for all i), taking the product

$$\begin{aligned}\left(\sum_{i=0}^{e-1} a_i f^i\right)\left(\sum_{i=0}^{e-1} b_i f^i\right) &= a_0b_0 + (a_0b_1 + a_1b_0)f + \dots \\ &= c_0 + c_1 f + \dots .\end{aligned} \tag{5}$$

Since $a_0 \ne 0 \pmod f$, there is b_0 such that $a_0b_0 = 1 \pmod f$ and $b_0 \ne 0 \pmod f$. Given b_0, b_1 is uniquely determined by the linear equation $a_0b_1 + a_1b_0 = 0 \pmod f$ over $\mathbb{F}_q$. In general, each b_i $(1 \le i \le e-1)$ is uniquely determined by the linear equation $c_i = 0 \pmod f$ over $\mathbb{F}_q$ for $b_0, \dots, b_{i-1}$ values that have been determined in previous steps. Therefore, there is a unique b such that $ab = 1 \pmod f$, and thus $a \in A^\times$. □

LEMMA 2. *For each $a_0 \in \mathbb{F}_q^\times$, there exists a unique $a \in A^\times$ which can be written as $a = \sum_{i=0}^{e-1} a_i f^i$, where each $a_i \in A$ has degree less than d, and $a^{q-1} = 1 \pmod{f^e}$.*

PROOF. Since $a_0 \in \mathbb{F}_q^\times$, $a \in A^\times$ by Lemma 1. Write $a = \sum_{i=0}^{e-1} a_i f^i$, with each $a_i \in A$ has degree less than d. We want $a^{q-1} = 1 \pmod{f^e}$, so we need

$$\begin{aligned}a^{q-1} &= \left(\sum_{i=0}^{e-1} a_i f^i\right)^{q-1} \\ &= a_0^{q-1} + (q-1)\, a_0^{q-2} a_1 f + \dots \\ &= 1 \pmod{f^e}.\end{aligned} \tag{6}$$

From Equation (6), we get

$$a_0^{q-1} + (q-1)\, a_0^{q-2} a_1 f = 1 \pmod{f^2}. \tag{7}$$

Because $a_0^{q-1} = 1 \pmod f$, we know there is some $A_0 \in A$ with $\deg A_0 < d$ such that

$$a_0^{q-1} = 1 + A_0 f \pmod{f^2}. \tag{8}$$

Combining Equations (7) and (8), we see that a_1 is uniquely determined by the linear equation

$$A_0 + (q-1)\, a_0^{q-2} a_1 = 0 \pmod f \tag{9}$$

over $\mathbb{F}_q$. Inductively, assume $a_0, a_1, \dots, a_{k-1}$ are uniquely determined. In order to guarantee $a^{q-1} = 1 \pmod{f^e}$, we need

$$\begin{aligned}&\left(\sum_{i=0}^{e-1} a_i f^i\right)^{q-1} \\ &= \left(\sum_{i=0}^{k-1} a_i f^i + a_k f^k + \sum_{i=k+1}^{e-1} a_i f^i\right)^{q-1} \pmod{f^{k+1}} \\ &= \left(\sum_{i=0}^{k-1} a_i f^i + a_k f^k\right)^{q-1} \pmod{f^{k+1}} \\ &= \left(\sum_{i=0}^{k-1} a_i f^i\right)^{q-1} + (q-1)\left(\sum_{i=0}^{k-1} a_i f^i\right)^{q-2} a_k f^k \pmod{f^{k+1}} \\ &= 1 \pmod{f^{k+1}}.\end{aligned} \tag{10}$$

By induction, the first term can be written as

$$\left(\sum_{i=0}^{k-1} a_i f^i\right)^{q-1} = 1 + A_{k-1} f^k \tag{11}$$

for some $A_{k-1} \in A$ where $\deg A_{k-1} < d$. Then a_k is uniquely determined by the linear equation

$$A_{k-1} + (q-1)\left(\sum_{i=0}^{k-1} a_i f^i\right)^{q-2} a_k = 0 \pmod f \tag{12}$$

over $\mathbb{F}_q$. That completes the proof. □

Lemma 2 yields a well-defined function $\pi : \mathbb{F}_q^\times \to A^\times$, which can be extended to all of $\mathbb{F}_q$ by forcing $\pi(0) = 0$. We proved that π is essentially an embedding of $\mathbb{F}_q$ into A.

Lemma 3. *Let $\pi : \mathbb{F}_q^\times \to A$ be the function where for all $a_0 \in \mathbb{F}_q$,*

$$\pi(a_0) = \begin{cases} 0 & , \textit{if } a_0 = 0 \\ a = \sum_{i=0}^{e-1} a_i f^i \in A \textit{ s.t. } a^{q-1} = 1 & , \textit{otherwise} \end{cases}$$

then $\pi(\mathbb{F}_q) \simeq \mathbb{F}_q$ as fields.

Proof. First of all, we enforce $\pi(0) = 0$, and we also have $\pi(1) = 1$. Assume $a_0, b_0 \in \mathbb{F}_q$, and that they can be written as $\pi(a_0) = \sum_{i=0}^{e-1} a_i f^i$, $\pi(b_0) = \sum_{i=0}^{e-1} b_i f^i$. We start by showing $\pi(a_0 b_0) = \pi(a_0)\pi(b_0)$. When $a_0 = 0$ or $b_0 = 0$, this is obvious. Otherwise, notice that the first term of both sides are $a_0 b_0$, and we have

$$(\pi(a_0)\pi(b_0))^{q-1} = \pi(a_0)^{q-1}\pi(b_0)^{q-1} = 1. \quad (13)$$

By Lemma 2 , $\pi(a_0 b_0) = \pi(a_0)\pi(b_0)$. Next, we verify $\pi(a_0^{-1}) = \pi(a_0)^{-1}$ for all $a_0 \neq 0$. Since $a_0^{q-1} = 1$, $a_0^{-1} = a_0^{q-2}$. Therefore,

$$\pi(a_0^{-1}) = \pi(a_0^{q-2}) = \pi(a_0)^{q-2}. \quad (14)$$

Since $\pi(a_0)^{q-1} = 1$, $\pi(a_0)^{q-2} = \pi(a_0)^{-1}$. Now it remains to show $\pi(a_0 + b_0) = \pi(a_0) + \pi(b_0)$. If $a_0 = 0$ or $b_0 = 0$, this is obvious. Otherwise, since the first term of both sides is $a_0 + b_0$, by Lemma 2, it suffices to show $(\pi(a_0) + \pi(b_0))^{q-1} = 1$. Denote the set $T = \{a \in A : a^{q-1} = 1\}$ and the set $T' = \{a \in A : a^q = a\} = T \cup \{0\}$. Since A is a ring of characteristic p,

$$(\pi(a_0) + \pi(b_0))^q = \pi(a_0)^q + \pi(b_0)^q = \pi(a_0) + \pi(b_0). \quad (15)$$

That is, $\pi(a_0) + \pi(b_0) \in T'$, and hence either $\pi(a_0) + \pi(b_0) \in T$ or $\pi(a_0) + \pi(b_0) = 0$. In the first case, we are done; in the latter case, $a_0 = -b_0$, so we also have $\pi(a_0 + b_0) = \pi(0) = 0 = \pi(a_0) + \pi(b_0)$. □

The proofs for Lemmas 1, 2 and 3 actually describes an algorithm for computing the embedding of $\mathbb{F}_q$ into A, and the pseudo code is shown in Algorithm 1. Taking p, f, e and a polynomial $a_0 \in \mathbb{F}_p[x]$ with degree less than d as input, the algorithm computes $a \in \mathbb{F}_p[x]$ that corresponds to $\pi(a_0)$ in $\mathbb{F}_p[x]/f^e$. We comment that in Line 8, by inverse, we mean finding the inverse element in $\mathbb{F}_q$.

Algorithm 1 Embed(a_0, p, f, e)

1: **if** $a_0 = 0$ **then**
2:     **return** 0
3: **else**
4:     $d := \deg f$, $q := p^d$
5:     $a := a_0$
6:     **for** $k = 1, \ldots, e-1$ **do**
7:         $A_{k-1} := ((a^{q-1} \mod f^{k+1}) - 1)/f^k$
8:         $a_k := ((q-1)(a^{q-2} \mod f))^{-1}(-A_{k-1})$
9:         $a := a + a_k f^k$
10:     **end for**
11:     **return** a
12: **end if**

Lemma 4. *A is a $\mathbb{F}_q$-algebra of dimension e.*

Proof. A is an $\mathbb{F}_q$-algebra through the embedding π, in the sense that the action of $b \in \mathbb{F}_q$ on A is such that for all $a \in A$, $b \cdot a := \pi(b)a$ where the product in the right hand side is the one in A. □

Theorem 3. *If $\sqrt{q} \geq e-1$, then the set $(\pi(\mathbb{F}_q) - x) \cap A^\times$ is a generating set for $A^\times$. Furthermore, every element of $A^\times$ can be written as $\prod_{i=1}^{t} (\pi(a_i) - x)$ where $a_i \in \mathbb{F}_q$ and*

$$t < 2e + 1 + \frac{4e \log(e-1)}{d \log p - 2\log(e-1)}.$$

Proof. By Lemma 4, A can be regarded as a $\mathbb{F}_q$-algebra of dimension e. By Proposition 2, for all nontrivial character χ of $A^\times$ (extended by zero to all of A),

$$\left| \sum_{t \in \mathbb{F}_q} \chi(\pi(t) - x) \right| \leq (e-1)\sqrt{q}. \quad (16)$$

The rest of the proof follows from Propositions 3 and 4. □

Theorem 4. *If $\sqrt{q} > e-1$, then $\Gamma(A^\times, S)$ is an expander, where $S = (\pi(\mathbb{F}_q) - x) \cap A^\times$.*

Proof. The spectral gap γ satisfies

$$\gamma = q - \max_{\chi \in \tilde{X}(A^\times)} \left| \sum_{t \in \mathbb{F}_q} \chi(\pi(t) - x) \right| \geq q - (e-1)\sqrt{q} > 0 \quad (17)$$

where the first inequality follows from Equation (16). □

3.1.3 Finding small generating sets

Theorem 3 sets a relatively mild restriction on p, which only needs $\sqrt{q} > e-1$, but this generating set is of size q, which might be more than necessary in many cases. Only a small fraction of this set might already be sufficient to generate the group. Besides, in terms of expander graphs construction, the resulting graphs might be dense. Thus, in this section, we go one step further to find generating sets of smaller sizes.

Let $K \subset \mathbb{F}_q$ be a subfield of size p^c, where $c|d$. We have

Theorem 5. *If K is a subfield of $\mathbb{F}_q$ of size p^c and $p^{c/2} > (de/c) - 1$, then $(\pi(K) - x) \cap A^\times$ is a generating set for $A^\times$. Furthermore, every element of $A^\times$ can be written as $\prod_{i=1}^{t} (\pi(a_i) - x)$, where $a_i \in K$ and*

$$t < 2\frac{de}{c} + 1 + \frac{4\frac{de}{c}\log(\frac{de}{c} - 1)}{\frac{d}{c}\log p - 2\log(\frac{de}{c} - 1)}.$$

Proof. By Lemma 4, A can be regarded as a K-algebra of dimension de/c. By Proposition 2, for all nontrivial character χ of $A^\times$ (extended by zero to all of A),

$$\left| \sum_{t \in K} \chi(\pi(t) - x) \right| \leq \left(\frac{de}{c} - 1\right) p^{c/2}. \quad (18)$$

The rest of the proof follows from Propositions 3 and 4. □

Theorem 6. *Let $K \subset \mathbb{F}_{p^d}$ be a subfield of $\mathbb{F}_q$ of size p^c where $c|d$. If $p^{c/2} > (de/c) - 1$, then $\Gamma(A^\times, S)$ is an expander, where $S = (\pi(K) - x) \cap A^\times$.*

Proof. The spectral gap γ satisfies

$$\begin{aligned} \gamma &= p^c - \max_{\chi \in \tilde{X}(A^\times)} \left| \sum_{t \in K} \chi(\pi(t) - x) \right| \\ &\geq p^c - \left(\frac{de}{c} - 1\right) p^{c/2} > 0 \end{aligned} \quad (19)$$

where the first inequality follows from Equation (18). □

Algorithm 2 Genset(p, f, e)

```
1: Let d := deg f, factorize d (if not provided)
2: Find c such that c|d and p^{c/2} > (de/c) − 1
3: Let φ : F_{p^c} ↪ F_p[x]/f a finite field homomorphism
4: return (Embed(φ(F_{p^c})) − x) ∩ A^×
```

Based on the above discussion, we present the pseudo code of our algorithm for finding a small generating set for $A^\times$, as shown in Algorithm 2. It takes p, f and e as input, and the output will be the small subset $S \subset A$, and $\Gamma(A^\times, S)$ is provably an expander. Notice that Line 3 in this pseudo code is used to find a subfield of $\mathbb{F}_q$ of size p^c, which is available in some algebraic programming languages [1, 7], and thus we omit the details.

A downside of this construction is that when d has few divisors, for example, d is a prime number, then $c = 1$ and $c = d$ are the only two options. On the other extreme, when d has abundant divisors, we may be able to construct better generating sets. For example, in expander graph construction, one may want to choose a perfect power as the value for d, say $d = b^n$ for some small number b. In this scenario, we have

COROLLARY 1. *If p and e are fixed and $d = b^n$ is a perfect power, where b fixed. Then Algorithm 2 returns a generating set of $A^\times$ of size $p^{O(\log d)}$.*

PROOF. Notice that $c \geq 2\log_p d + 2$ would be sufficient for the condition of Theorem 5, $p^{c/2} > (de/c) - 1$, to hold. Let $m_0 \in \mathbb{R}$ be such that $b^{m_0} = 2\log_p d + 2$. Write $c = b^m$, so we have $m = \lceil m_0 \rceil \leq m_0 + 1$. Thus, $c \leq 2b(\log_p d + 1) = O(\log d)$. □

3.1.4 Extending to the general case

In Sections 3.1.1, 3.1.2 and 3.1.3, we consider algebras of the form $A := \mathbb{F}_p[x]/f^e$. In this section, we are going to extend existing results to the more general case, where the algebra is of the form $B := \mathbb{F}_p[x]/F$, where $F \in \mathbb{F}_p[x]$ is an arbitrary polynomial. At the beginning of Section 3.1, we have seen the overall idea of our algorithm: with Algorithm 2, we generate a small generating set for each component; the union of these sets are then "pulled back" to $B^\times$ via the Chinese Remainder Theorem isomorphism ψ to get our final generating set for $B^\times$. It is straightforward to show that the resulting set obtained by this method forms a generating set for $B^\times$. In the rest of this paper, we will assume $F = \prod_{i=1}^m f_i^{e_i}$ where each $f_i \in \mathbb{F}_p[x]$ is an irreducible polynomial of degree d_i. We will also use the abbreviation $A_i := \mathbb{F}_p[x]/f_i^{e_i}$ in our analysis.

THEOREM 7. *Let K_i be a subfield of $\mathbb{F}_p[x]/f_i$ of size p^{c_i}, and π_i be an embedding of K_i into A_i. If $p^{c_i/2} > (d_i e_i/c_i) - 1$ for all $1 \leq i \leq m$, then $\{\psi(v_{i,s}^m) | s \in (\pi_i(K_i) - x) \cap A_i^\times, 1 \leq i \leq m\}$ is a generating set for $B^\times$.*

PROOF. By Theorem 5, each $\pi_i(K_i) - x$ is a generating set for the component $A_i^\times$, so their union $\bigcup_{i=1}^m \pi_i(K_i) - x$ generates $\bigoplus_{i=1}^m A_i^\times$. Since ψ is an isomorphism, we can see the claim. □

The pseudo code is shown in Algorithm 3. Taking p and F as its input, Algorithm 3 finds a small generating set having the form described in Theorem 7 for $B^\times$.

Algorithm 3 FinalGenset(p, F)

```
Factorize F into F = ∏_{i=1}^m f_i^{e_i} (if not provided), where
  each f_i is an irreducible polynomial of degree d_i
Let ψ : ⊕_{i=1}^m (F_p[x]/f_i^{e_i})^× ~→ (F_p[x]/F)^× be the C.R.T
  isomorphism
S := ∅
for i = 1, ..., m do
    S_i := Genset(p, f_i, e_i)
    for each s ∈ S_i do
        S := S ∪ {ψ(v_{i,s}^m)}
    end for
end for
return S
```

COROLLARY 2. *If p is fixed and for all $1 \leq i \leq m$, e_i is fixed and $d_i = b_i^{n_i}$ is a perfect power, where b_i is fixed, then Algorithm 3 returns a generating set of $B^\times$ of size $\sum_{i=1}^m p^{O(\log d_i)}$.*

PROOF. This can be seen by applying Corollary 1 to each component $A_i^\times$. □

Now it only remains to show that graphs of the form $\Gamma(B^\times, S)$, where S is found by Algorithm 3, are a set of expanders.

THEOREM 8. *Let K_i is a subfield of $\mathbb{F}_p[x]/f_i$ of size p^{c_i}, and π_i be an embedding of K_i into A_i. If $p^{c_i/2} > (d_i e_i/c_i) - 1$ for all $1 \leq i \leq m$, then $\Gamma(B^\times, S)$ where $S := \{\psi(v_{i,s}^m) | i \in (\pi_i(K_i) - x) \cap A_i^\times, 1 \leq i \leq m\}$ is an expander.*

PROOF. Define $S_i := \pi_i(K_i) - x$, $1 \leq i \leq m$. Since $B^\times \simeq \bigoplus_{i=1}^m A_i^\times$, for all $\chi \in \tilde{X}(B^\times)$, there exists $\chi_i \in \tilde{X}(A_i^\times)$ $(1 \leq i \leq m)$ such that

$$\forall b \simeq \bigoplus_{i=1}^m b_i \in B^\times : \chi(b) = \prod_{i=1}^m \chi_i(b_i). \tag{20}$$

Consider an arbitrary character $\chi \in \tilde{X}(B^\times)$, and assume $\chi_1 \in \tilde{X}(A_1^\times), \ldots, \chi_m \in \tilde{X}(A_m^\times)$ are the characters that satisfy Equation (20). For all elements $b \in B^\times$ of the form $b \simeq v_{i,s}^m$, all but the i-th coordinate are zeros, so

$$\chi(\psi(v_{i,s}^m)) = \chi_i(s) \prod_{j \neq i} \chi_j(0) = \chi_i(s). \tag{21}$$

Combining Equation (21) with Proposition 2, we obtain

$$\begin{aligned} \left|\sum_{s \in S} \chi(s)\right| &= \left|\sum_{i=1}^m \sum_{s \in \{\psi(v_{i,s}^m) | s \in S_i\}} \chi(s)\right| \\ &= \left|\sum_{i=1}^m \sum_{s \in S_i} \chi_i(s)\right| \leq \sum_{i=1}^m \left|\sum_{s \in S_i} \chi_i(s)\right| \\ &\leq \sum_{i=1}^m \left(\frac{d_i e_i}{c_i} - 1\right) p^{c_i/2}. \end{aligned} \tag{22}$$

Given that $p^{c_i/2} > (d_i e_i/c_i) - 1$ for all $1 \leq i \leq m$, the spectral gap γ of the Cayley graph satisfies

$$\begin{aligned}\gamma &\geq \sum_{i=1}^{m} |S_i| - \max_{\chi \in \tilde{X}(B^\times)} \left| \sum_{s \in S} \chi(s) \right| \\ &\geq \sum_{i=1}^{m} p^{c_i} - \sum_{i=1}^{m} \left(\frac{d_i e_i}{c_i} - 1 \right) p^{c_i/2} \\ &> 0.\end{aligned} \tag{23}$$

□

3.2 Basis and Decomposition

3.2.1 Building a basis

In order to find a basis for $B^\times$, we first decide the structure of the group, so that the size of a basis can be determined. As we have already seen from Equation (1), $B^\times$ can first be decomposed into $\bigoplus_{i=1}^{m} A_i^\times$ (recall that $A_i := \mathbb{F}_p[x]/f_i^{e_i}$). Therefore, it only remains to find out the decomposition of the group $A^\times := \mathbb{F}_p[x]/f^e$, with f and e defined the same as in Section 3.1. We observe that if $p \geq e$, $A^\times$ can be decomposed as shown in Lemma 5 below.

LEMMA 5. *If $p \geq e$, then*

$$A^\times \simeq \mathbb{Z}/(p^d - 1)\mathbb{Z} \oplus \left(\bigoplus_{d(e-1)} \mathbb{Z}/p\mathbb{Z} \right).$$

PROOF. Consider the map $\varphi : A^\times \to (\mathbb{F}_p[x]/f)^\times$ where for each $a \in A^\times$, $\varphi(a) = a \pmod f$. Clearly, φ is an onto function. We can see that the kernel of the map is precisely

$$\ker\varphi = \{1+bf : b \in A \text{ where } 0 \leq \deg b \leq d(e-1)-1\}. \tag{24}$$

For every $1+bf \in \ker\varphi$, since A as a ring has characteristic p, its p-th power is given by

$$(1+bf)^p = 1 + b^p f^p \pmod{f^e}. \tag{25}$$

Given the condition that $p \geq e$, we have

$$1 + b^p f^p = 1 \pmod{f^e}. \tag{26}$$

So, by the structure theorem of finite abelian groups, we have

$$\ker\varphi \simeq \bigoplus_{d(e-1)} \mathbb{Z}/p\mathbb{Z}. \tag{27}$$

In addition, notice that $|\ker\varphi| = p^{d(e-1)}$, which is relatively prime to $|\mathrm{im}\varphi| = p^d - 1$. It follows that $A^\times$ is isomorphic to their direct product, as desired. □

THEOREM 9. *If $p \geq \max_{i=1}^{m} e_i$, then*

$$B^\times \simeq \bigoplus_{i=1}^{m} \left(\mathbb{Z}/(p^{d_i} - 1)\mathbb{Z} \oplus \bigoplus_{d_i(e_i-1)} \mathbb{Z}/p\mathbb{Z} \right).$$

PROOF. It follows from Lemma 5 and Equation (1). □

Theorem 9 holds if and only if $p \geq \max_{i=1}^{m} e_i$, and thus our basis construction and decomposition algorithms will only deal with this situation. Assuming this condition, it suffices to find a basis for the group $A^\times$. From the proof for Lemma 5, we can see that

$$A^\times = \pi(\mathbb{F}_q^\times) \times \ker\varphi, \tag{28}$$

and as we have seen in Lemma 5, $\pi(\mathbb{F}_q^\times) \simeq \mathbb{Z}/(q-1)\mathbb{Z}$ and $\ker\varphi \simeq \bigoplus_{d(e-1)} \mathbb{Z}/p\mathbb{Z}$.

For the former component $\pi(\mathbb{F}_q^\times)$, we will simply use an existing algorithm such as [10] to find a generator.

We then consider the latter component $\ker\varphi$. Let K_j $(1 \leq j \leq e)$ denote the subset of $A^\times$ of the form $\{1 + hf^j \bmod f^e : h \in \mathbb{F}_p[x]\}$. By definition, $K_1 = \ker\varphi$ and $K_e = \{1\}$. One may verify that each K_j is actually a subgroup of $\ker\varphi$. Consider the following filtration of subgroups:

$$K_1 \supsetneq K_2 \supsetneq \ldots \supsetneq K_e.$$

We have

LEMMA 6. *For each $1 \leq j \leq e-1$,*

$$K_j/K_{j+1} = \prod_{k=0}^{d-1} \langle 1 + x^k f^j \rangle \simeq \bigoplus_{k=0}^{d-1} \mathbb{Z}/p\mathbb{Z}$$

PROOF. Consider the map $K_j \to \mathbb{F}_p[x]/f$ sending $1+hf^j$ to $h \bmod f$ for all $1+hf^j \in K_j$ with $\deg h < d$. It is easy to verify that this is a group homomorphism with K_{j+1} as the kernel. Therefore, we have

$$K_j/K_{j+1} \simeq \mathbb{F}_p[x]/f \simeq \bigoplus_{k=0}^{d-1} \mathbb{Z}/p\mathbb{Z}, \tag{29}$$

whereby $1+hf^j$ is mapped to $\bigoplus_{k=0}^{d-1} h_k$ if h is written in the form $h = \sum_{k=0}^{d-1} h_k x^k$. Under this isomorphism, the basis $\{x^k \bmod f | k = 0, ..., d-1\}$ for $\mathbb{F}_p[x]/f$ corresponds to the basis $\{1 + x^k f^j | k = 0, ..., d-1\}$ for K_j/K_{j+1}. □

LEMMA 7. *The set of polynomials $\{1 + x^k f^j | 0 \leq k \leq d-1, 1 \leq j \leq e-1\}$ forms a basis for $\ker\varphi$.*

PROOF. Clearly, this set contains $d(e-1)$ elements, which is the right size. So it suffices to show it is a generating set for $\ker\varphi$. Given any element $k_j \in K_j$, we first write it into the form $k_j = 1 + \sum_{t=j}^{e-1} h_t f^t$, where each h_t has degree less than d. Under the isomorphism between K_j/K_{j+1} and $\mathbb{F}_p[x]/f$ in the proof of Lemma 6, we see that k_j, $1 + h_j f^j$, and $\prod_{k=0}^{d-1} (1 + x^k f^j)^{h_{j,k}}$ are all in the same class in K_j/K_{j+1} assuming h_j is written in the form $h_j = \sum_{k=0}^{d-1} h_{j,k} x^k$. By Lemma 6, the class of k_j modulo K_{j+1} is mapped to $\bigoplus_{k=0}^{d-1} h_{j,k}$. That is,

$$k_j = \left(\prod_{k=0}^{d-1} (1 + x^k f^j)^{h_{j,k}} \right) k_{j+1}, \tag{30}$$

where $k_{j+1} \in K_{j+1}$ is uniquely determined. Therefore, any element $k_1 = 1 + \sum_{t=1}^{e-1} h_t f^t \in K_1 = \ker\varphi$ can be decomposed recursively via Equation (30) for all $1 \leq i \leq e-1$, so k_1 can be written as a product of elements from the set. □

Therefore, if $p \geq e$, then we can use $Z := \{\pi(g)\} \cup \{1 + x^k f^j | 0 \leq k \leq d-1, 1 \leq j \leq e-1\}$ as a basis for $A^\times$, where g is a generator for $(\mathbb{F}_p[x]/f)^\times$. This observation can be quickly extended to the general case $B^\times$.

THEOREM 10. *Let g_i be a generator of $(\mathbb{F}_p[x]/f_i)^\times$ and π_i be the embedding map from $\mathbb{F}_p[x]/f_i$ into A_i. If $p \geq \max_{i=1}^{m} e_i$, then the set $Z := \bigcup_{i=1}^{m} \{\psi(v_{i,z}^m) | z \in Z_i\}$ forms a basis for $B^\times$, where for all $1 \leq i \leq m$, $Z_i := \pi_i(g_i) \cup \{1 + x^k f^j | 0 \leq k \leq d-1, 1 \leq j \leq e-1\}$.*

PROOF. By Lemma 5 and Lemma 7, each Z_i is a basis for $A_i^\times$. And $B^\times \simeq \bigoplus_{i=1}^m A_i^\times$. The union $\bigcup_{i=1}^m \{v_{i,z}^m | z \in Z_i\}$ forms a basis for the right-hand side. □

Based on Theorem 10, we developed Algorithm 4. Given the input p and F, if $p \geq \max_{i=1}^m e_i$, it outputs a basis for $B^\times$; otherwise, it reports failure in finding a basis.

Algorithm 4 Basis(p, F)

Factorize F into $F = \prod_{i=1}^m f_i^{e_i}$ (if not provided), where each f_i is an irreducible polynomial of degree d_i
if $p \geq \max_{i=1}^m e_i$ **then**
  $Z := \emptyset$
  for $i = 1, \ldots, m$ **do**
    Find a generator g for $(\mathbb{F}_p[x]/f_i)^\times$ using existing algorithms such as [10]
    $z := \text{Embed}(g, p, f_i, e_i)$
    $Z := Z \cup \{\psi(v_{i,z}^m)\}$
    for all $0 \leq j \leq d-1$ and all $1 \leq k \leq e$ **do**
      $Z := Z \cup \{\psi(v_{i,1+x^j f^k}^m)\}$
    end for
  end for
else
  return unknown
end if

3.2.2 *Decomposition*

In the proof for Theorem 7, we have seen an outline of our algorithm for decomposition. The pseudo code for this algorithm is shown in Algorithm 5. Given an element $b \in \mathbb{F}_p[x]$ corresponding to an element in $B^\times$, the algorithm either outputs its coordinates $\bigoplus_{i=1}^m (b_{i,0} \oplus \bigoplus_{j=1}^{d_i(e_i-1)} b_{i,j})$ with respect to Theorem 9 (if $p \geq \max_{i=1}^m e_i$), or claims a failure in decomposition. We comment that in Line 6 and 13, the inverse element is found in $A_i^\times$.

Algorithm 5 Decomposition(p, F, b)

1: Factorize F into $F = \prod_{i=1}^m f_i^{e_i}$ (if not provided), where each f_i is an irreducible polynomial of degree d_i
2: **if** $p \geq \max_{i=1}^m e_i$ **then**
3:   **for** i=1,..., m **do**
4:     $a := b \mod f_i^{e_i}$
5:     $\eta := \text{Embed}(a \mod f_i, p, f_i, e_i)$
6:     $\kappa := \eta^{-1} a$
7:     $b_{i,0}$:= discrete-log of $a \mod f$ in $(\mathbb{F}_p[x]/f_i)^\times$
8:     **for** $j = 1, \ldots, e-1$ **do**
9:       $h_j := (\kappa \mod f^{j+1} - 1)/f^j$, and assume $h_j = \sum_{k=0}^{d-1} h_{j,k} x^k$
10:       **for** $k = 0, \ldots, d-1$ **do**
11:         $b_{i,j,k} := h_{j,k}$
12:       **end for**
13:       $\kappa := (\prod_{k=0}^{d-1}(1 + x^k f^j)^{h_{j,k}})^{-1} \kappa$
14:     **end for**
15:   **end for**
16:   **return** $\bigoplus_{i=1}^m (b_{i,0} \oplus \bigoplus_{j=1}^{e-1} \bigoplus_{k=0}^{d-1} b_{i,j,k})$
17: **else**
18:   **return** unknown
19: **end if**

4. EXPERIMENTS

An important question about the generating sets we presented in Section 3.1 is whether they are too large to be practical. That is, a small subset of our generating sets may be sufficient to generate the group. Therefore, we ran experiments to see whether the size of the generating sets we presented can be substantially reduced in practice, where a practically optimal generating set is constructed by drawing random subsets from our original construction. To some extent, we can infer from the results whether the restrictions in Theorems 1, 3 and 5 can be significantly weakened in practice.

Our programs are implemented in Sage [7]. For simplicity, we only run experiments on algebras of the form $A := \mathbb{F}_p[x]/f^e$, where $f \in \mathbb{F}_p[x]$ is irreducible of degree d. We compare the sizes of three types of generating sets for $A^\times$. The first type, having the form $\pi(\mathbb{F}_q) - x$, corresponds to Theorem 3. It's size equals $q := p^d$. The second type of generating sets are of the form $\pi(K) - x$ corresponding to Theorem 5, where $K \subset \mathbb{F}_q$ is a subfield of size p^c. The third type of generating sets are constructed by adding random elements of $\pi(K) - x$ to the empty set one by one, until it generates $A^\times$. We write its size as p^b where $b \in \mathbb{R}$. Clearly, we have the relationship $b \leq c \leq d$.

Our first experiment compares the growth of c and d. In this experiment, we set $p = 7$, $e = 5$ and $d = 2^1, 2^2, 2^3, \ldots$. The result is shown in Figure 1. From Figure 1 we see that when d is a perfect power, c grows linearly with $\log d$, as stated in Corollary 1.

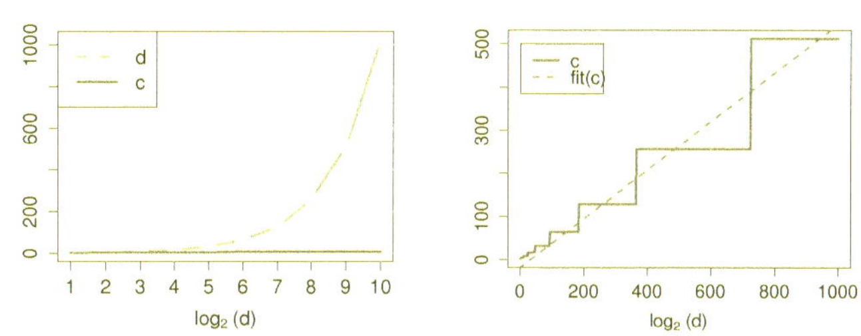

(a) Comparison of c and d (b) The growth of c with d

Figure 1: The growth of c and d

In the second set of experiments, we compare b and c with different choices of parameters. We first set $e = 4$ and $d = 2^1, 2^2, 2^3, \ldots$ and we increase p from 5 to 11. From Figure 2, we observe a logarithmic growth from both b and c against d, and $c \approx 2b$. Also, we can see that when p increases, the growth rate of b and c decreases.

The third set of experiments studies the effect of e while fixing the value of $p = 7$, and the results are shown in Figure 3. From this experiment, we see that when e increases, the growth rate of both b and c increases.

From the experimental results shown in Figure 2 and 3, we observe that $c \approx 2b$, which implies that a square root number of random elements from $\pi(K) - x$ might already be sufficient as a generating set. This may imply that sparser expander graphs can possibly be constructed over the multiplicative groups of finite algebras. How to find such subsets that can be used for expander graph construction remains an open problem.

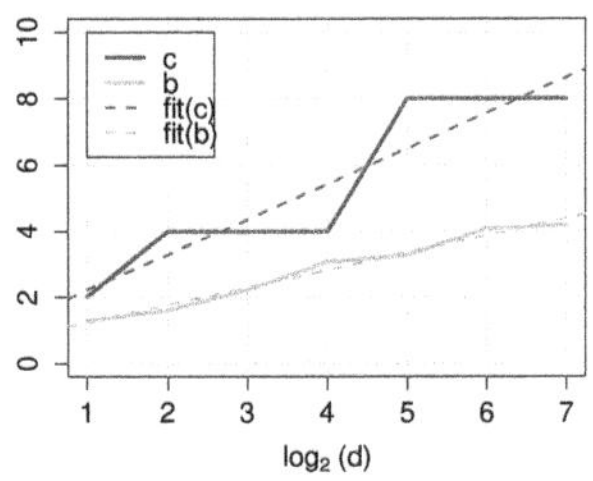

(a) $p = 5, e = 4$

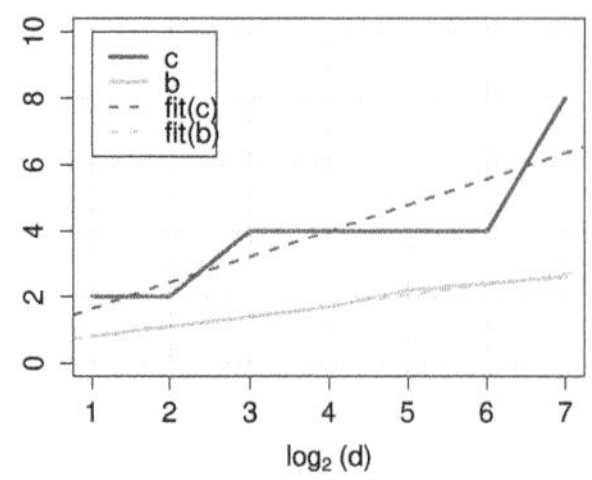

(b) $p = 11, e = 4$

Figure 2: The effect of p

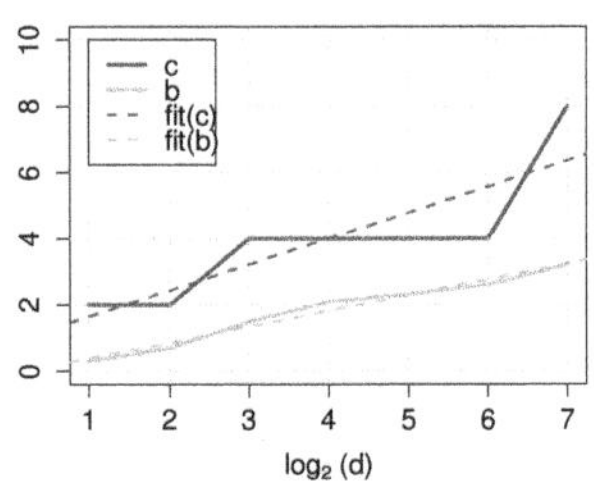

(a) $p = 7, e = 3$

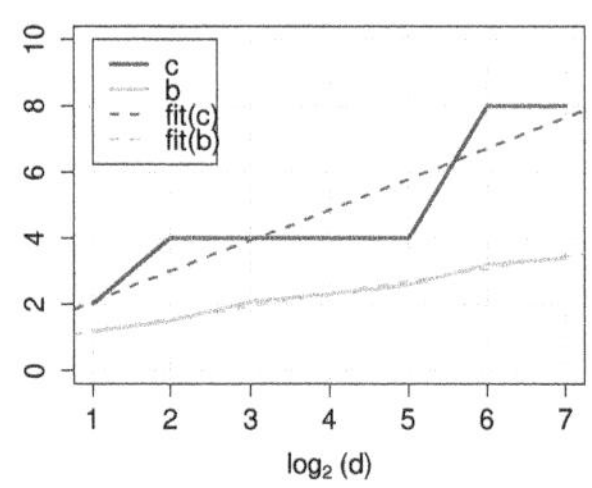

(b) $p = 7, e = 5$

Figure 3: The effect of e

5. CONCLUSION

In this paper, we generalize Chung's [4] to the case of $\mathbb{F}_p[x]/F$ where $F \in \mathbb{F}_p[x]$ is not necessarily irreducible. We present algorithms for finding different types of small generating sets for $B^\times$ which can be applied to explicit construction of expander graphs. We also propose algorithms for finding a basis for $B^\times$ and decomposing elements with respect to this basis.

From our experiments, we observe that a square root number of elements in the generating set we found are usually sufficient to generate the whole group. How to find these elements and use them for expander graph construction remains an open problem. In addition, basis construction and decomposition for $B^\times$ when p is small will be another future work.

6. ACKNOWLEDGMENTS

We would like to thank the anonymous reviewers for pointing out several errors and typos in the initial submission of this paper.

7. REFERENCES

[1] Finite field morphisms. http://doc.sagemath.org/html/en/reference/finite_rings/sage/rings/finite_rings/hom_finite_field.html.

[2] L. M. Adleman and M.-D. A. Huang. Function field sieve method for discrete logarithms over finite fields. *Information and Computation*, 151(1-2):5–16, 1999.

[3] A. Bhowmick and T. H. LÃł. On primitive elements in finite fields of low characteristic. *Finite Fields and Their Applications*, 35:64 – 77, 2015.

[4] F. R. K. Chung. Diameters and eigenvalues. *American Mathematical Society*, 2(2):187–196, 1989.

[5] F. R. K. Chung. Several generalizations of weil sums. *J. Number Theory*, 49:95–106, 1994.

[6] F. R. K. Chung. *Spectral Graph Theory*. American Mathematical Society, 1997.

[7] T. S. Developers. *Sage Mathematics Software (Version 7.1)*, 2016. `http://www.sagemath.org`.

[8] F. Göloğlu, R. Granger, G. McGuire, and J. Zumbrägel. *Advances in Cryptology – CRYPTO 2013: 33rd Annual Cryptology Conference, Santa Barbara, CA, USA, August 18-22, 2013. Proceedings, Part II*, pages 109–128. Springer Berlin Heidelberg, Berlin, Heidelberg, 2013.

[9] S. Hoory, N. Linial, and A. Wigderson. Expander graphs and their applications. *BULL. AMER. MATH. SOC.*, 43(4):439–561, 2006.

[10] M. Huang and A. K. Narayanan. Finding primitive elements in finite fields of small characteristic. *CoRR*, abs/1304.1206, 2013.

[11] A. Joux. A new index calculus algorithm with complexity $l(1/4 + o(1))$ in very small characteristic. Cryptology ePrint Archive, Report 2013/095, 2013.

[12] N. M. Katz. An estimate for character sums. *Journal of the American Mathematical Society*, 2(2):pp. 197–200, 1989.

[13] M. Lu, D. Wan, L.-P. Wang, and X.-D. Zhang. Algebraic cayley graphs over finite fields. *Finite Fields and Their Applications*, 28:43 – 56, 2014.

[14] G. L. Mullen and D. Panario. *Handbook of Finite Fields*. Chapman & Hall/CRC, 1st edition, 2013.

[15] R. Popovych. Elements of high order in finite fields of the form. *Finite Fields and Their Applications*, 19(1):86–92, 2013.

[16] V. Shoup. Searching for primitive roots in finite fields. *Mathematics of Computation*, 58(197):369–380, 1992.

[17] I. E. Shparlinski. Cayley graphs generated by small degree polynomials over finite fields. *SIAM Journal on Discrete Mathematics*, 29(1):376–381, 2015.

[18] J. von zur Gathen and I. Shparlinski. Orders of gauss periods in finite fields. *Applicable Algebra in Engineering, Communication and Computing*, 9(1):15–24.

[19] D. Wan. Generators and irreducible polynomials over finite fields. *Mathematics of Computation*, 66:1195–1212, 1997.

[20] A. Weil. *Basic number theory*. Grundlehren der mathematischen Wissenschaften. Springer-Verlag, 1974.

Fast Computation of Minimal Interpolation Bases in Popov Form for Arbitrary Shifts

Claude-Pierre Jeannerod
Inria, Université de Lyon
Laboratoire LIP (CNRS, Inria, ENSL, UCBL)
claude-pierre.jeannerod@ens-lyon.fr

Vincent Neiger
ENS de Lyon, Université de Lyon
Laboratoire LIP (CNRS, Inria, ENSL, UCBL)
vincent.neiger@ens-lyon.fr

Éric Schost
University of Waterloo
David R. Cheriton School of Computer Science
eschost@uwaterloo.ca

Gilles Villard
CNRS, Université de Lyon
Laboratoire LIP (CNRS, Inria, ENSL, UCBL)
gilles.villard@ens-lyon.fr

ABSTRACT

We compute minimal bases of solutions for a general interpolation problem, which encompasses Hermite-Padé approximation and constrained multivariate interpolation, and has applications in coding theory and security.

This problem asks to find univariate polynomial relations between m vectors of size σ; these relations should have small degree with respect to an input degree shift. For an arbitrary shift, we propose an algorithm for the computation of an interpolation basis in shifted Popov normal form with a cost of $\mathcal{O}^{\sim}(m^{\omega-1}\sigma)$ field operations, where ω is the exponent of matrix multiplication and the notation $\mathcal{O}^{\sim}(\cdot)$ indicates that logarithmic terms are omitted.

Earlier works, in the case of Hermite-Padé approximation [34] and in the general interpolation case [18], compute non-normalized bases. Since for arbitrary shifts such bases may have size $\Theta(m^2\sigma)$, the cost bound $\mathcal{O}^{\sim}(m^{\omega-1}\sigma)$ was feasible only with restrictive assumptions on the shift that ensure small output sizes. The question of handling arbitrary shifts with the same complexity bound was left open.

To obtain the target cost for any shift, we strengthen the properties of the output bases, and of those obtained during the course of the algorithm: all the bases are computed in shifted Popov form, whose size is always $\mathcal{O}(m\sigma)$. Then, we design a divide-and-conquer scheme. We recursively reduce the initial interpolation problem to sub-problems with more convenient shifts by first computing information on the degrees of the intermediate bases.

Keywords

M-Padé approximation; Hermite-Padé approximation; order basis; polynomial matrix; shifted Popov form.

ISSAC'16, July 19–22, 2016, Waterloo, ON, Canada

ISBN 978-1-4503-4380-0/16/07...$15.00

DOI: http://dx.doi.org/10.1145/2930889.2930928

1. INTRODUCTION

1.1 Problem and main result

We focus on the following interpolation problem from [31, 2]. For a field $\mathbb{K}$ and some positive integer σ, we have as input m vectors $\mathbf{e}_1, \ldots, \mathbf{e}_m$ in $\mathbb{K}^{1\times\sigma}$, seen as the rows of a matrix $\mathbf{E} \in \mathbb{K}^{m\times\sigma}$. We also have a *multiplication matrix* $\mathbf{J} \in \mathbb{K}^{\sigma\times\sigma}$ which specifies the multiplication of vectors $\mathbf{e} \in \mathbb{K}^{1\times\sigma}$ by polynomials $p \in \mathbb{K}[X]$ as $p \cdot \mathbf{e} = \mathbf{e}\,p(\mathbf{J})$. Then, we want to find $\mathbb{K}[X]$-linear relations between these vectors, that is, some $\mathbf{p} = (p_1, \ldots, p_m) \in \mathbb{K}[X]^m$ such that $\mathbf{p} \cdot \mathbf{E} = p_1 \cdot \mathbf{e}_1 + \cdots + p_m \cdot \mathbf{e}_m = 0$. Such a $\mathbf{p}$ is called an *interpolant for* $(\mathbf{E}, \mathbf{J})$.

Hereafter, the matrix $\mathbf{J}$ is in Jordan canonical form: this assumption is satisfied in many interesting applications, as explained below. The notion of interpolant we consider is directly related to the one introduced in [31, 2]. Suppose that $\mathbf{J}$ has n Jordan blocks of dimensions $\sigma_1 \times \sigma_1, \ldots, \sigma_n \times \sigma_n$ and with respective eigenvalues $x_1, \ldots, x_n$; in particular, $\sigma = \sigma_1 + \cdots + \sigma_n$. Then, one may identify $\mathbb{K}^\sigma$ with

$$\mathfrak{F} = \mathbb{K}[X]/(X^{\sigma_1}) \times \cdots \times \mathbb{K}[X]/(X^{\sigma_n}),$$

by mapping any $\mathbf{f} = (f_1, \ldots, f_n)$ in $\mathfrak{F}$ to the vector $\mathbf{e} \in \mathbb{K}^\sigma$ made from the concatenation of the coefficient vectors of $f_1, \ldots, f_n$. Over $\mathfrak{F}$, the $\mathbb{K}[X]$-module structure on $\mathbb{K}^\sigma$ given by $p \cdot \mathbf{e} = \mathbf{e}\,p(\mathbf{J})$ becomes

$$p \cdot \mathbf{f} = (p(X + x_1)f_1 \bmod X^{\sigma_1}, \ldots, p(X + x_n)f_n \bmod X^{\sigma_n}).$$

Now, if $(\mathbf{e}_1, \ldots, \mathbf{e}_m) \in \mathbb{K}^{m\times\sigma}$ is associated to $(\mathbf{f}_1, \ldots, \mathbf{f}_m) \in \mathfrak{F}^m$, with $\mathbf{f}_i = (f_{i,1}, \ldots, f_{i,n})$ and $f_{i,j}$ in $\mathbb{K}[X]/(X^{\sigma_j})$ for all i, j, the relation $p_1 \cdot \mathbf{e}_1 + \cdots + p_m \cdot \mathbf{e}_m = 0$ means that for all j in $\{1, \ldots, n\}$, we have

$$p_1(X + x_j)f_{1,j} + \cdots + p_m(X + x_j)f_{m,j} = 0 \bmod X^{\sigma_j};$$

applying a translation by $-x_j$, this is equivalent to

$$p_1 f_{1,j}(X - x_j) + \cdots + p_m f_{m,j}(X - x_j) = 0 \bmod (X - x_j)^{\sigma_j}.$$

Thus, in terms of vector M-Padé approximation as in [31, 2], $(p_1, \ldots, p_m)$ is an interpolant for $(\mathbf{f}_1, \ldots, \mathbf{f}_m)$, $x_1, \ldots, x_n$, and $\sigma_1, \ldots, \sigma_n$.

The set of all interpolants for $(\mathbf{E}, \mathbf{J})$ is a free $\mathbb{K}[X]$-module of rank m. We are interested in computing a basis of this module, represented as a matrix in $\mathbb{K}[X]^{m\times m}$ and called an *interpolation basis for* $(\mathbf{E}, \mathbf{J})$. Its rows are interpolants for $(\mathbf{E}, \mathbf{J})$, and any interpolant for $(\mathbf{E}, \mathbf{J})$ can be written as a unique $\mathbb{K}[X]$-linear combination of its rows.

Besides, we look for interpolants that have some type of minimal degree. Following [31, 34], for a nonzero $\mathbf{p} = [p_1, \ldots, p_m] \in \mathbb{K}[X]^{1\times m}$ and a *shift* $\mathbf{s} = (s_1, \ldots, s_m) \in \mathbb{Z}^m$, we define the $\mathbf{s}$-*degree* of $\mathbf{p}$ as $\max_{1\leqslant j\leqslant m}(\deg(p_j)+s_j)$. Up to a change of sign, this notion of $\mathbf{s}$-degree is equivalent to the one in [3] and to the notion of *defect* from [1, Definition 3.1].

Then, the $\mathbf{s}$-*row degree* of a matrix $\mathbf{P} \in \mathbb{K}[X]^{k\times m}$ of rank k is the tuple $\mathrm{rdeg}_{\mathbf{s}}(\mathbf{P}) = (d_1, \ldots, d_k) \in \mathbb{Z}^k$ with d_i the $\mathbf{s}$-degree of the i-th row of $\mathbf{P}$. The $\mathbf{s}$-*leading matrix* of $\mathbf{P} = [p_{ij}]_{i,j}$ is the matrix in $\mathbb{K}^{k\times m}$ whose entry (i, j) is the coefficient of degree $d_i - s_j$ of p_{ij}. Then, $\mathbf{P}$ is $\mathbf{s}$-*reduced* if its $\mathbf{s}$-leading matrix has rank k; see [3].

Our aim is to compute an $\mathbf{s}$-*minimal* interpolation basis for $(\mathbf{E}, \mathbf{J})$, that is, one which is $\mathbf{s}$-reduced: equivalently, it is an interpolation basis whose $\mathbf{s}$-row degree, once written in nondecreasing order, is lexicographically minimal. This corresponds to Problem 1 below. In particular, an interpolant of minimal degree can be read off from an $\mathbf{s}$-minimal interpolation basis for the *uniform* shift $\mathbf{s} = \mathbf{0}$.

PROBLEM 1 (MINIMAL INTERPOLATION BASIS).
Input:

- *the base field* $\mathbb{K}$,
- *the dimensions* m *and* σ,
- *a matrix* $\mathbf{E} \in \mathbb{K}^{m\times\sigma}$,
- *a Jordan matrix* $\mathbf{J} \in \mathbb{K}^{\sigma\times\sigma}$,
- *a shift* $\mathbf{s} \in \mathbb{Z}^m$.

Output: *an* $\mathbf{s}$-*minimal interpolation basis for* $(\mathbf{E}, \mathbf{J})$.

A well-known particular case of this problem is Hermite-Padé approximation, that is, the computation of *order bases* (or σ-bases, or minimal approximant bases), where $\mathbf{J}$ has only eigenvalue 0. Previous work on this case includes [1, 14, 30, 34] with algorithms focusing on $\mathbf{J}$ with n blocks of identical size σ/n. For a shift $\mathbf{s} \in \mathbb{N}^m$ with nonnegative entries, we write $|\mathbf{s}|$ for the sum of its entries. Then, in this context, the cost bound $\mathcal{O}\tilde{}(m^{\omega-1}\sigma)$ has been obtained under each of the following assumptions:

(H_1) $\max(\mathbf{s}) - \min(\mathbf{s}) \in \mathcal{O}(\sigma/m)$ in [34, Theorem 5.3] and more generally $|\mathbf{s} - \min(\mathbf{s})| \in \mathcal{O}(\sigma)$ in [33, Section 4.1];

(H_2) $|\max(\mathbf{s}) - \mathbf{s}| \in \mathcal{O}(\sigma)$ in [34, Theorem 6.14].

These assumptions imply in particular that any $\mathbf{s}$-minimal basis has size in $\mathcal{O}(m\sigma)$, where by *size* we mean the number of field elements used to represent the matrix.

An interesting example of a shift not covered by (H_1) or (H_2) is $\mathbf{h} = (0, \sigma, 2\sigma, \ldots, (m-1)\sigma)$ which is related to the Hermite form [3, Lemma 2.6]. In general, as detailed in Appendix A, one may assume without loss of generality that $\min(\mathbf{s}) = 0$, $\max(\mathbf{s}) \in \mathcal{O}(m\sigma)$, and $|\mathbf{s}| \in \mathcal{O}(m^2\sigma)$.

There are also applications of Problem 1 to multivariate interpolation, where $\mathbf{J}$ is not nilpotent anymore, and for which we have neither (H_1) nor (H_2), as we will see in Subsection 1.3. It was left as an open problem in [34, Section 7] to obtain algorithms with cost bound $\mathcal{O}\tilde{}(m^{\omega-1}\sigma)$ for such matrices $\mathbf{J}$ and for arbitrary shifts. In this paper, we solve this open problem.

An immediate challenge is that for an arbitrary shift $\mathbf{s}$, the size of an $\mathbf{s}$-minimal interpolation basis may be beyond our target cost: we show this in Appendix B with an example of Hermite-Padé approximation. Our answer is to compute a basis in $\mathbf{s}$-*Popov form*: among its many interesting features, it can be represented using at most $m(\sigma+1)$ elements from $\mathbb{K}$, and it is canonical: for every nonsingular $\mathbf{A} \in \mathbb{K}[X]^{m\times m}$ and $\mathbf{s} \in \mathbb{Z}^m$, there is a unique matrix $\mathbf{P}$ in $\mathbf{s}$-Popov form which is left-unimodularly equivalent to $\mathbf{A}$. We use the definition from [2, Section 7], phrased using the notion of pivot [19, Section 6.7.2].

DEFINITION 1.1 (PIVOT OF A ROW). *Let* $\mathbf{p} = [p_j]_j \in \mathbb{K}[X]^{1\times m}$ *be a nonzero row vector and let* $\mathbf{s} \in \mathbb{Z}^m$. *The* $\mathbf{s}$-pivot index *of* $\mathbf{p}$ *is the largest index* $j \in \{1, \ldots, m\}$ *such that* $\mathrm{rdeg}_{\mathbf{s}}(\mathbf{p}) = \deg(p_j) + s_j$*; then,* p_j *and* $\deg(p_j)$ *are called the* $\mathbf{s}$-pivot entry *and the* $\mathbf{s}$-pivot degree *of* $\mathbf{p}$.

DEFINITION 1.2 (POPOV FORM). *Let* $\mathbf{P} \in \mathbb{K}[X]^{m\times m}$ *be nonsingular and let* $\mathbf{s} \in \mathbb{Z}^m$. *Then,* $\mathbf{P}$ *is said to be in* $\mathbf{s}$-Popov form *if its* $\mathbf{s}$-*pivot entries are monic and on its diagonal, and if in each column of* $\mathbf{P}$ *the nonpivot entries have degree less than the pivot entry.*

We call $\mathbf{s}$-*Popov interpolation basis for* $(\mathbf{E}, \mathbf{J})$ the unique interpolation basis for $(\mathbf{E}, \mathbf{J})$ which is in $\mathbf{s}$-Popov form; in particular, it is an $\mathbf{s}$-minimal one. For small values of σ, namely $\sigma \in \mathcal{O}(m)$, we gave in [18, Section 7] an algorithm which computes the $\mathbf{s}$-Popov interpolation basis in $\mathcal{O}\tilde{}(\sigma^{\omega-1}m)$ operations for an arbitrary $\mathbf{s}$ [18, Theorem 1.4]. Hence, in what follows, we focus on the case $m \in \mathcal{O}(\sigma)$.

We use the convenient assumption that $\mathbf{J}$ is given to us as a list of eigenvalues and block sizes:

$$\mathbf{J} = ((x_1, \sigma_{1,1}), \ldots, (x_1, \sigma_{1,r_1}), \ldots, (x_t, \sigma_{t,1}), \ldots, (x_t, \sigma_{t,r_t})),$$

for some pairwise distinct eigenvalues $x_1, \ldots, x_t$, with $r_1 \geqslant \cdots \geqslant r_t$ and $\sigma_{i,1} \geqslant \cdots \geqslant \sigma_{i,r_i}$ for all i; we say that this representation is *standard*.

THEOREM 1.3. *Assuming that* $\mathbf{J} \in \mathbb{K}^{\sigma\times\sigma}$ *is a Jordan matrix given by a standard representation, there is a deterministic algorithm which solves Problem 1 using*

$$\mathcal{O}(m^{\omega-1}\mathsf{M}(\sigma)\log(\sigma)\log(\sigma/m)^2) \qquad \text{if } \omega > 2,$$
$$\mathcal{O}(m\mathsf{M}(\sigma)\log(\sigma)\log(\sigma/m)^2\log(m)^3) \qquad \text{if } \omega = 2$$

operations in $\mathbb{K}$ *and returns the* $\mathbf{s}$-*Popov interpolation basis for* $(\mathbf{E}, \mathbf{J})$.

In this result, $\mathsf{M}(\cdot)$ is such that polynomials of degree at most d in $\mathbb{K}[X]$ can be multiplied using $\mathsf{M}(d)$ operations in $\mathbb{K}$, and $\mathsf{M}(\cdot)$ satisfies the super-linearity properties of [13, Chapter 8]. It follows from [8] that $\mathsf{M}(d)$ can be taken in $\mathcal{O}(d\log(d)\log(\log(d)))$. The exponent ω is so that we can multiply $m \times m$ matrices in $\mathcal{O}(m^\omega)$ ring operations on any ring, the best known bound being $\omega < 2.38$ [11, 22].

Compared to our work in [18], our algorithm here has two key new features:

- it supports arbitrary shifts with a cost $\mathcal{O}\tilde{}(m^{\omega-1}\sigma)$;
- it computes the basis in $\mathbf{s}$-Popov form.

To the best of our knowledge, no algorithm for Problem 1 with cost $\mathcal{O}\tilde{}(m^{\omega-1}\sigma)$ was known previously for *arbitrary* shifts, even for the specific case of order basis computation.

If $\mathbf{J}$ is given as an arbitrary list $((x_1, \sigma_1), \ldots, (x_n, \sigma_n))$, we can reorder it (and permute the columns of $\mathbf{E}$ accordingly) to obtain an equivalent standard representation in time $\mathcal{O}(\mathsf{M}(\sigma)\log(\sigma)^3)$ [5, Proposition 12]; if $\mathbb{K}$ is equipped with an order, and if we assume that comparisons take unit time, this can of course be done in time $\mathcal{O}(\sigma\log(\sigma))$.

1.2 Overview of our approach

Several previous algorithms for order basis computation, such as those in [1, 14], follow a divide-and-conquer scheme inspired by the Knuth-Schönhage-Moenck algorithm [20, 29, 23] This paper builds on our previous work in [18], where we extended this recursive approach to more general interpolation problems. However, the main algorithm in [18] does not handle an arbitrary shift $\mathbf{s}$ with a satisfactory complexity; here, we use it as a black box, after showing how to reduce the problem to a new one with suitable shift.

Let $\mathbf{E}$, $\mathbf{J}$, and $\mathbf{s}$ be our input, and write $\mathbf{J}^{(1)}$ and $\mathbf{J}^{(2)}$ for the $\sigma/2\times\sigma/2$ leading and trailing principal submatrices of $\mathbf{J}$. First, compute an $\mathbf{s}$-minimal interpolation basis $\mathbf{P}^{(1)}$ for $\mathbf{J}^{(1)}$ and the first $\sigma/2$ columns of $\mathbf{E}$; then, compute the last $\sigma/2$ columns $\mathbf{E}^{(2)}$ of the *residual* $\mathbf{P}^{(1)}\cdot\mathbf{E}$; then, compute a $\mathbf{t}$-minimal interpolation basis $\mathbf{P}^{(2)}$ for $(\mathbf{E}^{(2)},\mathbf{J}^{(2)})$ with $\mathbf{t}=\mathrm{rdeg}_{\mathbf{s}}(\mathbf{P}^{(1)})$; finally, return the matrix product $\mathbf{P}^{(2)}\mathbf{P}^{(1)}$.

This approach allows to solve Problem 1 using $\mathcal{O}^{\sim}(m^\omega\sigma)$ operations in $\mathbb{K}$. In the case of Hermite-Padé approximation, this is the divide-and-conquer algorithm in [1]. Besides, an $\mathbf{s}$-minimal basis computed by this method has degree at most σ and thus size in $\mathcal{O}(m^2\sigma)$, and there are indeed instances of Problem 1 for which this size reaches $\Theta(m^2\sigma)$. In Appendix B, we show such an instance for the algorithm in [1], in the case of Hermite-Padé approximation.

It is known that the average degree of the rows of any $\mathbf{s}$-minimal interpolation basis is at most $(\sigma+\xi)/m$, where $\xi=|\mathbf{s}-\min(\mathbf{s})|$ [31, Theorem 4.1]. In [18], focusing on the case where ξ is small compared to σ, and preserving such a property in recursive calls via changes of shifts, we obtained the cost bound

$$\mathcal{O}(m^{\omega-1}\mathsf{M}(\sigma)\log(\sigma)\log(\sigma/m)+m^{\omega-1}\mathsf{M}(\xi)\log(\xi/m)) \quad (1)$$

to solve Problem 1; this cost is for $\omega>2$, and a similar one holds for $\omega=2$, both being in $\mathcal{O}^{\sim}(m^{\omega-1}(\sigma+\xi))$. The fundamental reason for this kind of improvement over $\mathcal{O}^{\sim}(m^\omega\sigma)$, already seen with [34], is that one controls the average row degree of the bases $\mathbf{P}^{(2)}$ and $\mathbf{P}^{(1)}$, *and* of their product $\mathbf{P}^{(2)}\mathbf{P}^{(1)}$.

This result is $\mathcal{O}^{\sim}(m^{\omega-1}\sigma)$ for ξ in $\mathcal{O}(\sigma)$. The main difficulty to extend it to any shift $\mathbf{s}$ is to control the size of the computed bases: the Hermite-Padé example pointed out above corresponds to $\xi=\Theta(m\sigma)$ and leads to an output of size $\Theta(m^2\sigma)$ for the algorithm of [18] as well.

The key ingredient to control this size is to work with bases in $\mathbf{s}$-Popov form: for any $\mathbf{s}$, the $\mathbf{s}$-Popov interpolation basis $\mathbf{P}$ for $(\mathbf{E},\mathbf{J})$ has average *column* degree at most σ/m and size at most $m(\sigma+1)$, as detailed in Section 2.

Now, suppose that we have computed recursively the bases $\mathbf{P}^{(2)}$ and $\mathbf{P}^{(1)}$ in $\mathbf{s}$- and $\mathbf{t}$-Popov form; we want to output the $\mathbf{s}$-Popov form $\mathbf{P}$ of $\mathbf{P}^{(2)}\mathbf{P}^{(1)}$. In general, this product is not normalized and may have size $\Theta(m^2\sigma)$: its computation is beyond our target cost. Thus, one main idea is that we will *not* rely on polynomial matrix multiplication to combine the bases obtained recursively; instead, we use a minimal interpolation basis computation for a shift that has good properties as explained below.

An important remark is that if we know *a priori* the column degree $\boldsymbol{\delta}$ of $\mathbf{P}$, then the problem becomes easier. This idea was already used in algorithms for the Hermite form $\mathbf{H}$ of a polynomial matrix [15, 33], which first compute the column degree $\boldsymbol{\delta}$ of $\mathbf{H}$, and then obtain $\mathbf{H}$ as a submatrix of some minimal nullspace basis for a shift involving $-\boldsymbol{\delta}$.

In Section 4, we study the problem of computing the $\mathbf{s}$-Popov interpolation basis $\mathbf{P}$ for $(\mathbf{E},\mathbf{J})$ having its column degree $\boldsymbol{\delta}$ as an additional input. We show that this reduces to the computation of a $\mathbf{d}$-minimal interpolation basis $\mathbf{R}$ with the specific shift $\mathbf{d}=-\boldsymbol{\delta}$. The properties of this shift $\mathbf{d}$ allow us first to compute $\mathbf{R}$ in $\mathcal{O}^{\sim}(m^{\omega-1}\sigma)$ operations using the partial linearization framework from [30, Section 3] and the minimal interpolation basis algorithm in [18, Section 3], and second to easily retrieve $\mathbf{P}$ from $\mathbf{R}$.

Still, in general we do not know $\boldsymbol{\delta}$. We will thus compute it, relying on a variation of the divide-and-conquer strategy at the beginning of this subsection. We stop the recursion as soon as $\sigma\leqslant m$, in which case we do not need $\boldsymbol{\delta}$ to achieve efficiency: the algorithm from [18, Section 7] computes the $\mathbf{s}$-Popov interpolation basis in $\mathcal{O}^{\sim}(\sigma^{\omega-1}m)$ operations for any $\mathbf{s}$ [18, Theorem 1.4]. Then, we show in Section 3 that from $\mathbf{P}^{(1)}$ and $\mathbf{P}^{(2)}$ computed recursively *in shifted Popov form*, we can obtain $\boldsymbol{\delta}$ for free. Finally, instead of considering $\mathbf{P}^{(2)}\mathbf{P}^{(1)}$, we use the knowledge of $\boldsymbol{\delta}$ to compute the basis $\mathbf{P}$ from scratch as explained in the previous paragraph.

This summarizes our main algorithm, which is presented in Section 2.

1.3 Previous work and applications

As a particular case of Problem 1, when all the eigenvalues of $\mathbf{J}$ are zero, we obtain the following complexity result about *order basis* computation [34, Definition 2.2].

THEOREM 1.4. *Let $m,n\in\mathbb{Z}_{>0}$, let $(\sigma_1,\ldots,\sigma_n)\in\mathbb{Z}^n_{>0}$, let $\mathbf{s}\in\mathbb{Z}^m$, and let $\mathbf{F}\in\mathbb{K}[X]^{m\times n}$ with its j-th column $\mathbf{F}_{*,j}$ of degree less than σ_j. The unique basis $\mathbf{P}\in\mathbb{K}[X]^{m\times m}$ in $\mathbf{s}$-Popov form of the $\mathbb{K}[X]$-module of approximants*

$$\{\mathbf{p}\in\mathbb{K}[X]^{1\times m}\mid \mathbf{p}\mathbf{F}_{*,j}=0 \bmod X^{\sigma_j} \text{ for each } j\}$$

can be computed deterministically using

$$\mathcal{O}(m^{\omega-1}\mathsf{M}(\sigma)\log(\sigma)\log(\sigma/m)^2) \qquad \text{if } \omega>2,$$

$$\mathcal{O}(m\mathsf{M}(\sigma)\log(\sigma)\log(\sigma/m)^2\log(m)^3) \qquad \text{if } \omega=2$$

operations in $\mathbb{K}$, where $\sigma=\sigma_1+\cdots+\sigma_n$.

Previous work on this problem includes [1, 14, 30, 34, 18], mostly with identical orders $\sigma_1=\cdots=\sigma_n$; an interesting particular case is Hermite-Padé approximation with $n=1$. To simplify matters, for all our comparisons, we consider $\omega>2$. For order basis computation with $\sigma_1=\cdots=\sigma_n$ and $n\leqslant m$, the cost bound $\mathcal{O}(m^\omega\mathsf{M}(\sigma/m)\log(\sigma/n))$ was achieved in [34] under either of the assumptions (H_1) and (H_2) on the shift. Still, the corresponding algorithm returns a basis $\mathbf{P}$ which is only $\mathbf{s}$-reduced, and because both the shift $\mathbf{s}$ and the degrees in $\mathbf{P}$ may be unbalanced, one cannot directly rely on the fastest known normalization algorithm [28] to compute the $\mathbf{s}$-Popov form of $\mathbf{P}$ within the target cost.

Another application of Problem 1 is a multivariate interpolation problem that arises for example in the first step of algorithms for the list-decoding of Parvaresh-Vardy codes [26] and of folded Reed-Solomon codes [16], as well as in robust Private Information Retrieval [12]. The bivariate case corresponds to the interpolation steps of Kötter and Vardy's soft-decoding [21] and Guruswami and Sudan's list-decoding [17] algorithms for Reed-Solomon codes.

Given a set of points in $\mathbb{K}^{r+1}$ and associated multiplicities, this problem asks to find a multivariate polynomial $Q(X, Y_1, \ldots, Y_r)$ such that: (*a*) Q has prescribed exponents for the Y variables, so that the problem can be linearized with respect to Y, leaving us with a linear algebra problem over $\mathbb{K}[X]$; (*b*) Q vanishes at all the given points with their multiplicities, inducing a structure of $\mathbb{K}[X]$-module on the set of solutions; (*c*) Q has some type of minimal weighted degree, which can be seen as the minimality of the shifted degree of the vector over $\mathbb{K}[X]$ that represents Q.

Following the coding theory context [17, 26], given a point $(x, y) \in \mathbb{K}\times\mathbb{K}^r$ and a set of exponents $\mu \subset \mathbb{N}^{r+1}$, we say that the polynomial $Q(X, Y) \in \mathbb{K}[X, Y_1, \ldots, Y_r]$ *vanishes at* (x, y) *with multiplicity support* μ if the shifted polynomial $Q(X + x, Y + y)$ has no monomial with exponent in μ. We will only consider supports that are *stable under division*, meaning that if $(\gamma_0, \gamma_1, \ldots, \gamma_r)$ is in μ, then any $(\gamma_0', \gamma_1', \ldots, \gamma_r')$ with $\gamma_j' \leqslant \gamma_j$ for all j is also in μ.

Now, given a set of exponents $\Gamma \subset \mathbb{N}^r$, we represent $Q(X, Y) = \sum_{\gamma\in\Gamma} p_\gamma Y^\gamma$ as the row $\mathbf{p} = [p_\gamma]_{\gamma\in\Gamma} \in \mathbb{K}[X]^{1\times m}$ where m is the cardinality of Γ. Again, we assume that the exponent set Γ is stable under division; then, the set of solutions is a free $\mathbb{K}[X]$-module of rank m. In the mentioned applications, we typically have $\Gamma = \{(\gamma_1, \ldots, \gamma_r) \in \mathbb{N}^r \mid \gamma_1 + \cdots + \gamma_r \leqslant \ell\}$ for an integer ℓ called the *list-size parameter*.

Besides, we are given some weights $\mathbf{w} = (w_1, \ldots, w_r) \in \mathbb{N}^r$ on the variables $Y = Y_1, \ldots, Y_r$, and we are looking for $Q(X, Y)$ which has minimal $\mathbf{w}$-weighted degree, which is the degree in X of the polynomial

$$Q(X, X^{w_1} Y_1, \ldots, X^{w_r} Y_r) = \sum_{\gamma\in\Gamma} p_\gamma X^{\gamma_1 w_1+\cdots+\gamma_r w_r} Y_1^{\gamma_1} \cdots Y_r^{\gamma_r}.$$

This is exactly requiring that the $\mathbf{s}$-degree of $\mathbf{p} = [p_\gamma]_\gamma$ be minimal, for $\mathbf{s} = [\gamma_1 w_1 + \cdots + \gamma_r w_r]_\gamma$. We note that it is sometimes important, for example in [12], to return a whole $\mathbf{s}$-minimal interpolation basis and not only one interpolant of small $\mathbf{s}$-degree.

PROBLEM 2 (MULTIVARIATE INTERPOLATION).
Input:

- *number of Y variables $r > 0$,*
- *set $\Gamma \subset \mathbb{N}^r$ of cardinality m, stable under division,*
- *pairwise distinct points $\{(x_k, y_k) \in \mathbb{K} \times \mathbb{K}^r\}_{1\leqslant k\leqslant p}$,*
- *supports $\{\mu_k \subset \mathbb{N}^{r+1}\}_{1\leqslant k\leqslant p}$, stable under division,*
- *a shift $\mathbf{s} \in \mathbb{Z}^m$.*

Output: *a matrix $\mathbf{P} \in \mathbb{K}[X]^{m\times m}$ such that*

- *the rows of $\mathbf{P}$ form a basis of the $\mathbb{K}[X]$-module*

$$\left\{\mathbf{p} = [p_\gamma]_{\gamma\in\Gamma} \in \mathbb{K}[X]^{1\times m} \;\middle|\; \sum_{\gamma\in\Gamma} p_\gamma(X) Y^\gamma \text{ vanishes at } (x_k, y_k) \text{ with support } \mu_k \text{ for } 1 \leqslant k \leqslant p\right\},$$

- *$\mathbf{P}$ is $\mathbf{s}$-reduced.*

For more details about the reduction from Problem 2 to Problem 1, explaining how to build the input matrices $(\mathbf{E}, \mathbf{J})$ with $\mathbf{J}$ a Jordan matrix in standard representation, we refer the reader to [18, Subsection 2.4]. In particular, the dimension σ is the sum of the cardinalities of the multiplicity supports. In the mentioned applications to coding theory, we have $m = \binom{r+\ell}{r}$ where ℓ is the list-size parameter; and σ is the so-called *cost* in the soft-decoding context [21, Section III], that is, the number of linear equations when linearizing the problem over $\mathbb{K}$. As a consequence of Theorem 1.3, we obtain the following complexity result.

THEOREM 1.5. *Let $\sigma = \sum_{1\leqslant k\leqslant p} \#\mu_k$. There is a deterministic algorithm which solves Problem 2 using*

$$\mathcal{O}(m^{\omega-1}\mathsf{M}(\sigma)\log(\sigma)\log(\sigma/m)^2) \qquad \text{if } \omega > 2,$$
$$\mathcal{O}(m\mathsf{M}(\sigma)\log(\sigma)\log(\sigma/m)^2\log(m)^3) \qquad \text{if } \omega = 2$$

operations in $\mathbb{K}$, and returns the unique basis of solutions which is in $\mathbf{s}$-Popov form.

Under the assumption that the x_k are pairwise distinct, the cost bound $\mathcal{O}(m^{\omega-1}\mathsf{M}(\sigma)\log(\sigma)^2)$ was achieved for an arbitrary shift using fast structured linear algebra [9, Theorems 1 and 2], following work by [25, 27, 32]. However, the corresponding algorithm is randomized and returns only one interpolant of small $\mathbf{s}$-degree. For a broader overview of previous work on this problem, we refer the reader to the introductive sections of [4, 9] and to [18, Section 2].

The term $\mathcal{O}(m^{\omega-1}\mathsf{M}(\xi)\log(\xi/m))$ reported in (1) for the cost of the algorithm of [18] can be neglected if $\xi \in \mathcal{O}(\sigma)$; this is for instance satisfied in the context of bivariate interpolation for soft- or list-decoding of Reed-Solomon codes [18, Sections 2.5 and 2.6]. However, we do not have this bound on ξ in the list-decoding of Parvaresh-Vardy codes and folded Reed-Solomon codes and in Private Information Retrieval. Thus, in these cases our algorithm achieves the best known cost bound, improving upon [7, 6, 10, 12, 18].

2. FAST POPOV INTERPOLATION BASIS

In this section, we present our main result, Algorithm 1. It relies on three subroutines; two of them are from [18], while the third is a key new ingredient, detailed in Section 4.

- LINEARIZATIONMIB [18, Algorithm 9] solves the base case $\sigma \leqslant m$ using linear algebra over $\mathbb{K}$. The inputs are $\mathbf{E}$, $\mathbf{J}$, $\mathbf{s}$, as well as an integer for which we can take the first power of two greater than or equal to σ.
- COMPUTERESIDUALS [18, Algorithm 5] (with an additional pre-processing detailed at the end of Section 4) computes the residual $\mathbf{P}^{(1)}\cdot\mathbf{E}$ from the first basis $\mathbf{P}^{(1)}$ obtained recursively.
- KNOWNMINDEGMIB, detailed in Section 4, computes the $\mathbf{s}$-Popov interpolation basis when one knows *a priori* the $\mathbf{s}$-minimal degree of $(\mathbf{E}, \mathbf{J})$ (see below).

In what follows, by $\mathbf{s}$-*minimal degree of* $(\mathbf{E}, \mathbf{J})$ we mean the tuple of degrees of the diagonal entries of the $\mathbf{s}$-Popov interpolation basis $\mathbf{P}$ for $(\mathbf{E}, \mathbf{J})$. Because $\mathbf{P}$ is in $\mathbf{s}$-Popov form, this is also the column degree of $\mathbf{P}$, and the sum of these degrees is $\deg(\det(\mathbf{P}))$. As a consequence, using Theorem 4.1 in [31] (or following the lines of [19] and [2]) we obtain the following lemma, which implies in particular that the size of $\mathbf{P}$ is at most $m(\sigma + 1)$.

Lemma 2.1. *Let* $\mathbf{E} \in \mathbb{K}^{m\times\sigma}$, $\mathbf{J} \in \mathbb{K}^{\sigma\times\sigma}$, $\mathbf{s} \in \mathbb{Z}^m$, *and let* $(\delta_1, \ldots, \delta_m)$ *be the* **s**-*minimal degree of* $(\mathbf{E}, \mathbf{J})$. *Then, we have* $\delta_1 + \cdots + \delta_m \leqslant \sigma$.

Algorithm 1. PopovMIB

Input:

- *a matrix* $\mathbf{E} \in \mathbb{K}^{m\times\sigma}$,
- *a Jordan matrix* $\mathbf{J} \in \mathbb{K}^{\sigma\times\sigma}$ *in standard representation,*
- *a shift* $\mathbf{s} \in \mathbb{Z}^m$.

Output:

- *the* **s**-*Popov interpolation basis* $\mathbf{P}$ *for* $(\mathbf{E}, \mathbf{J})$,
- *the* **s**-*minimal degree* $\boldsymbol{\delta} = (\delta_1, \ldots, \delta_m)$ *of* $(\mathbf{E}, \mathbf{J})$.

1. *If* $\sigma \leqslant m$, *return* LinearizationMIB$(\mathbf{E}, \mathbf{J}, \mathbf{s}, 2^{\lceil \log_2(\sigma)\rceil})$

2. *Else*

a. $\mathbf{E}^{(1)} \leftarrow$ *first* $\lceil \sigma/2 \rceil$ *columns of* $\mathbf{E}$

b. $(\mathbf{P}^{(1)}, \boldsymbol{\delta}^{(1)}) \leftarrow$ PopovMIB$(\mathbf{E}^{(1)}, \mathbf{J}^{(1)}, \mathbf{s})$

c. $\mathbf{E}^{(2)} \leftarrow$ *last* $\lfloor \sigma/2 \rfloor$ *columns of* $\mathbf{P}^{(1)} \cdot \mathbf{E} =$ ComputeResiduals$(\mathbf{J}, \mathbf{P}^{(1)}, \mathbf{E})$

d. $(\mathbf{P}^{(2)}, \boldsymbol{\delta}^{(2)}) \leftarrow$ PopovMIB$(\mathbf{E}^{(2)}, \mathbf{J}^{(2)}, \mathbf{s} + \boldsymbol{\delta}^{(1)})$

e. $\mathbf{P} \leftarrow$ KnownMinDegMIB$(\mathbf{E}, \mathbf{J}, \mathbf{s}, \boldsymbol{\delta}^{(1)} + \boldsymbol{\delta}^{(2)})$

f. *Return* $(\mathbf{P}, \boldsymbol{\delta}^{(1)} + \boldsymbol{\delta}^{(2)})$

Taking for granted the results in the next sections, we now prove our main theorem.

Proof of Theorem 1.3. For the case $\sigma \leqslant m$, the correctness and the cost bound of Algorithm 1 both follow from [18, Theorem 1.4]: it uses $\mathcal{O}(\sigma^{\omega-1}m + \sigma^\omega \log(\sigma))$ operations (with an extra $\log(\sigma)$ factor if $\omega = 2$).

Now, we consider the case $\sigma > m$. Using the notation in the algorithm, assume that $\mathbf{P}^{(1)}$ is the **s**-Popov interpolation basis for $(\mathbf{E}^{(1)}, \mathbf{J}^{(1)})$, and $\mathbf{P}^{(2)}$ is the **t**-Popov interpolation basis for $(\mathbf{E}^{(2)}, \mathbf{J}^{(2)})$, where $\mathbf{t} = \mathbf{s} + \boldsymbol{\delta}^{(1)} = \mathrm{rdeg}_{\mathbf{s}}(\mathbf{P}^{(1)})$, and $\boldsymbol{\delta}^{(1)}$ and $\boldsymbol{\delta}^{(2)}$ are the **s**- and $\mathbf{s} + \boldsymbol{\delta}^{(1)}$-minimal degrees of $(\mathbf{E}^{(1)}, \mathbf{J}^{(1)})$ and $(\mathbf{E}^{(2)}, \mathbf{J}^{(2)})$, respectively.

We claim that $\mathbf{P}^{(2)}\mathbf{P}^{(1)}$ is **s**-reduced: this will be proved in Lemma 3.2. Let us then prove that $\mathbf{P}^{(2)}\mathbf{P}^{(1)}$ is an interpolation basis for $(\mathbf{E}, \mathbf{J})$. Let $\mathbf{p} \in \mathbb{K}[X]^{1\times m}$ be an interpolant for $(\mathbf{E}, \mathbf{J})$. Since $\mathbf{J}$ is upper triangular, $\mathbf{p}$ is in particular an interpolant for $(\mathbf{E}^{(1)}, \mathbf{J}^{(1)})$, so there exists $\mathbf{v} \in \mathbb{K}[X]^{1\times m}$ such that $\mathbf{p} = \mathbf{v}\mathbf{P}^{(1)}$. Besides, we have $\mathbf{P}^{(1)} \cdot \mathbf{E} = [0|\mathbf{E}^{(2)}]$, so that $0 = \mathbf{p} \cdot \mathbf{E} = \mathbf{v}\mathbf{P}^{(1)} \cdot \mathbf{E} = [0|\mathbf{v} \cdot \mathbf{E}^{(2)}]$, and thus $\mathbf{v} \cdot \mathbf{E}^{(2)} = 0$. Then, there exists $\mathbf{w} \in \mathbb{K}[X]^{1\times m}$ such that $\mathbf{v} = \mathbf{w}\mathbf{P}^{(2)}$, which gives $\mathbf{p} = \mathbf{w}\mathbf{P}^{(2)}\mathbf{P}^{(1)}$.

In particular, the **s**-Popov interpolation basis for $(\mathbf{E}, \mathbf{J})$ is the **s**-Popov form of $\mathbf{P}^{(2)}\mathbf{P}^{(1)}$. Thus, Lemma 3.2 combined with Lemma 3.3 will show that the **s**-minimal degree of $(\mathbf{E}, \mathbf{J})$ is $\boldsymbol{\delta}^{(1)} + \boldsymbol{\delta}^{(2)}$. As a result, Proposition 4.3 states that Step **2.e** correctly computes the **s**-Popov interpolation basis for $(\mathbf{E}, \mathbf{J})$.

Concerning the cost bound, the recursion stops when $\sigma \leqslant m$, and thus the algorithm uses $\mathcal{O}(m^\omega \log(m))$ operations (with an extra $\log(m)$ factor if $\omega = 2$). The depth of the recursion is $\mathcal{O}(\log(\sigma/m))$; we have two recursive calls in dimensions $m \times \sigma/2$, and two calls to subroutines with cost bounds given in Corollary 4.5 and Proposition 4.3, respectively. The conclusion follows from the super-linearity properties of $\mathsf{M}(\cdot)$. $\square$

3. OBTAINING THE MINIMAL DEGREE FROM RECURSIVE CALLS

In this section, we show that the **s**-minimal degree of $(\mathbf{E}, \mathbf{J})$ can be deduced for free from two bases computed recursively as in Algorithm 1. To do this, we actually prove a slightly more general result about the degrees of the **s**-pivot entries of so-called weak Popov matrix forms [24].

Definition 3.1 (Weak Popov form, pivot degree). *Let* $\mathbf{P} \in \mathbb{K}[X]^{m\times m}$ *be nonsingular and let* $\mathbf{s} \in \mathbb{Z}^m$. *Then,* $\mathbf{P}$ *is said to be in* **s**-weak Popov form *if the* **s**-*pivot indices of its rows are pairwise distinct;* $\mathbf{P}$ *is said to be in* **s**-diagonal weak Popov form *if its* **s**-*pivot entries are on its diagonal.*

If $\mathbf{P}$ *is in* **s**-*weak Popov form, the* **s**-pivot degree *of* $\mathbf{P}$ *is the tuple* $(\delta_1, \ldots, \delta_m)$ *where for* $j \in \{1, \ldots, m\}$, δ_j *is the* **s**-*pivot degree of the row of* $\mathbf{P}$ *which has* **s**-*pivot index* j.

We recall from Section 1 that for $\mathbf{P} \in \mathbb{K}[X]^{k\times m}$, its **s**-leading matrix $\mathrm{lm}_{\mathbf{s}}(\mathbf{P}) \in \mathbb{K}^{k\times m}$ is formed by the coefficients of degree 0 of $\mathbf{X}^{-\mathbf{d}}\,\mathbf{P}\mathbf{X}^{\mathbf{s}}$, where $\mathbf{d} = \mathrm{rdeg}_{\mathbf{s}}(\mathbf{P})$ and $\mathbf{X}^{\mathbf{s}}$ stands for the diagonal matrix with entries $X^{s_1}, \ldots, X^{s_m}$. Then, a nonsingular $\mathbf{P} \in \mathbb{K}[X]^{m\times m}$ is in **s**-diagonal weak Popov form with **s**-pivot degree $\boldsymbol{\delta}$ if and only if $\mathrm{lm}_{\mathbf{s}}(\mathbf{P})$ is lower triangular and invertible and $\mathrm{rdeg}_{\mathbf{s}}(\mathbf{P}) = \mathbf{s} + \boldsymbol{\delta}$.

For example, at all stages of the algorithms in [31, 1, 18] for Problem 1 (as well as [14] if avoiding row permutations at the base case of the recursion), the computed bases are in shifted diagonal weak Popov form. This is due to the compatibility of this form with matrix multiplication, as stated in the next lemma.

Lemma 3.2. *Let* $\mathbf{s} \in \mathbb{Z}^m$, $\mathbf{P}^{(1)} \in \mathbb{K}[X]^{m\times m}$ *in* **s**-*diagonal weak Popov form with* **s**-*pivot degree* $\boldsymbol{\delta}^{(1)}$, $\mathbf{t} = \mathbf{s} + \boldsymbol{\delta}^{(1)} = \mathrm{rdeg}_{\mathbf{s}}(\mathbf{P}^{(1)})$, *and* $\mathbf{P}^{(2)} \in \mathbb{K}[X]^{m\times m}$ *in* **t**-*diagonal weak Popov form with* **t**-*pivot degree* $\boldsymbol{\delta}^{(2)}$. *Then,* $\mathbf{P}^{(2)}\mathbf{P}^{(1)}$ *is in* **s**-*diagonal weak Popov form with* **s**-*pivot degree* $\boldsymbol{\delta}^{(1)} + \boldsymbol{\delta}^{(2)}$.

Proof. By the predictable-degree property [19, Theorem 6.3-13] we have $\mathrm{rdeg}_{\mathbf{s}}(\mathbf{P}^{(2)}\mathbf{P}^{(1)}) = \mathrm{rdeg}_{\mathbf{t}}(\mathbf{P}^{(2)}) = \mathbf{t} + \boldsymbol{\delta}^{(2)} = \mathbf{s} + \boldsymbol{\delta}^{(1)} + \boldsymbol{\delta}^{(2)}$. The result follows since $\mathrm{lm}_{\mathbf{s}}(\mathbf{P}^{(2)}\mathbf{P}^{(1)}) = \mathrm{lm}_{\mathbf{t}}(\mathbf{P}^{(2)})\mathrm{lm}_{\mathbf{s}}(\mathbf{P}^{(1)})$ is lower triangular and invertible. $\square$

For matrices in **s**-Popov form, the **s**-pivot degree coincides with the column degree: in particular, the **s**-minimal degree of $(\mathbf{E}, \mathbf{J})$ is the **s**-pivot degree of the **s**-Popov interpolation basis for $(\mathbf{E}, \mathbf{J})$. With the notation of Algorithm 1, the previous lemma proves that the **s**-pivot degree of $\mathbf{P}^{(2)}\mathbf{P}^{(1)}$ is $\boldsymbol{\delta}^{(1)} + \boldsymbol{\delta}^{(2)}$. In the rest of this section, we prove that the **s**-Popov form of $\mathbf{P}^{(2)}\mathbf{P}^{(1)}$ has the same **s**-pivot degree as $\mathbf{P}^{(2)}\mathbf{P}^{(1)}$. Consequently, the **s**-minimal degree of $(\mathbf{E}, \mathbf{J})$ is $\boldsymbol{\delta}^{(1)} + \boldsymbol{\delta}^{(2)}$ and thus can be found from $\mathbf{P}^{(2)}$ and $\mathbf{P}^{(1)}$ without computing their product.

It is known that left-unimodularly equivalent **s**-reduced matrices have the same **s**-row degree up to permutation [19, Lemma 6.3-14]. Here, we prove that the **s**-pivot degree is invariant among left-unimodularly equivalent matrices in **s**-weak Popov form.

LEMMA 3.3. *Let* $\mathbf{s} \in \mathbb{Z}^m$ *and let* $\mathbf{P}$ *and* $\mathbf{Q}$ *in* $\mathbb{K}[X]^{m \times m}$ *be two left-unimodularly equivalent nonsingular polynomial matrices in* $\mathbf{s}$*-weak Popov form. Then* $\mathbf{P}$ *and* $\mathbf{Q}$ *have the same* $\mathbf{s}$*-pivot degree.*

PROOF. Since row permutations preserve both the $\mathbf{s}$-pivot degrees and left-unimodular equivalence, we can assume that $\mathbf{P}$ and $\mathbf{Q}$ are in $\mathbf{s}$-diagonal weak Popov form. The $\mathbf{s}$-pivot degrees of $\mathbf{P}$ and $\mathbf{Q}$ are then $\mathrm{rdeg}_{\mathbf{s}}(\mathbf{P}) - \mathbf{s}$ and $\mathrm{rdeg}_{\mathbf{s}}(\mathbf{Q}) - \mathbf{s}$, and it remains to check that $\mathrm{rdeg}_{\mathbf{s}}(\mathbf{P}) = \mathrm{rdeg}_{\mathbf{s}}(\mathbf{Q})$.

For any nonsingular $\mathbf{W} \in \mathbb{K}[X]^{m \times m}$ in $\mathbf{s}$-weak Popov form we have $|\mathrm{rdeg}_{\mathbf{s}}(\mathbf{W})| = \deg(\det(\mathbf{W})) + |\mathbf{s}|$ [19, Section 6.3.2]. Thus, if $\mathbf{W}$ is furthermore comprised entirely of rows in the $\mathbb{K}[X]$-row space of $\mathbf{P}$ (that is, $\mathbf{W}$ is a left multiple of $\mathbf{P}$) then we must have $|\mathrm{rdeg}_{\mathbf{s}}(\mathbf{W})| \geqslant |\mathrm{rdeg}_{\mathbf{s}}(\mathbf{P})|$.

To arrive at a contradiction, suppose there exists a row index i such that the $\mathbf{s}$-degree of $\mathbf{P}_{i,*}$ differs from that of $\mathbf{Q}_{i,*}$ and without loss of generality assume that the s-degree of $\mathbf{Q}_{i,*}$ is strictly less than that of $\mathbf{P}_{i,*}$. Then the matrix $\mathbf{W}$ obtained from $\mathbf{P}$ by replacing the i-th row of $\mathbf{P}$ with $\mathbf{Q}_{i,*}$ is in $\mathbf{s}$-diagonal weak Popov form. This is a contradiction, since $|\mathrm{rdeg}_{\mathbf{s}}(\mathbf{W})| < |\mathrm{rdeg}_{\mathbf{s}}(\mathbf{P})|$ and $\mathbf{Q}_{i,*}$ is in the $\mathbb{K}[X]$-row space of $\mathbf{P}$ for $\mathbf{Q}$ is left-unimodularly equivalent to $\mathbf{P}$. □

In particular, any nonsingular matrix in $\mathbf{s}$-weak Popov form has the same $\mathbf{s}$-pivot degree as its $\mathbf{s}$-Popov form, which proves our point about the $\mathbf{s}$-Popov form of $\mathbf{P}^{(2)}\mathbf{P}^{(1)}$.

4. COMPUTING INTERPOLATION BASES WITH KNOWN MINIMAL DEGREE

In this section, we propose an efficient algorithm for computing the $\mathbf{s}$-Popov interpolation basis $\mathbf{P}$ for $(\mathbf{E}, \mathbf{J})$ when the $\mathbf{s}$-minimal degree $\boldsymbol{\delta}$ of $(\mathbf{E}, \mathbf{J})$ is known *a priori*.

First, we show that the shift $\mathbf{d} = -\boldsymbol{\delta}$ leads to the same $\mathbf{d}$-Popov interpolation basis $\mathbf{P}$ as the initial shift $\mathbf{s}$. Then, we prove that $\mathbf{P}$ can be easily recovered from any interpolation basis which is simply $\mathbf{d}$-reduced. The following lemma extends [28, Lemmas 15 and 17] to the case of any shift $\mathbf{s}$.

LEMMA 4.1. *Let* $\mathbf{s} \in \mathbb{Z}^m$*, and let* $\mathbf{P} \in \mathbb{K}[X]^{m \times m}$ *be in* $\mathbf{s}$*-Popov form with column degree* $\boldsymbol{\delta} = (\delta_1, \ldots, \delta_m)$*. Then* $\mathbf{P}$ *is also in* $\mathbf{d}$*-Popov form for* $\mathbf{d} = (-\delta_1, \ldots, -\delta_m)$*, and we have* $\mathrm{rdeg}_{\mathbf{d}}(\mathbf{P}) = (0, \ldots, 0)$*. In particular, for any matrix* $\mathbf{R} \in \mathbb{K}[X]^{m \times m}$ *which is unimodularly equivalent to* $\mathbf{P}$ *and* $\mathbf{d}$*-reduced,* $\mathbf{R}$ *has column degree* $\boldsymbol{\delta}$*, and* $\mathbf{P} = \mathrm{lm}_{\mathbf{d}}(\mathbf{R})^{-1}\mathbf{R}$*.*

PROOF. Let us denote $\mathbf{P} = [p_{ij}]_{i,j}$, and let $i \in \{1, \ldots, m\}$. Since $\mathbf{P}$ is in $\mathbf{s}$-Popov form, it is enough to prove that the $\mathbf{d}$-pivot entries of the rows of $\mathbf{P}$ are on its diagonal. We have $\deg(p_{ij}) < \deg(p_{jj}) = \delta_j$ for all $j \neq i$, and $\deg(p_{ii}) = \delta_i$. Then, the i-th row of $\mathbf{P}$ has $\mathbf{d}$-pivot index i and $\mathbf{d}$-degree 0. Thus $\mathbf{P}$ is in $\mathbf{d}$-Popov form with $\mathbf{d}$-row degree $(0, \ldots, 0)$.

Now, let $\mathbf{R}$ be a $\mathbf{d}$-reduced matrix left-unimodularly equivalent to $\mathbf{P}$. Then, $\mathrm{rdeg}_{\mathbf{d}}(\mathbf{R}) = \mathrm{rdeg}_{\mathbf{d}}(\mathbf{P}) = (0, \ldots, 0)$, so that we can write $\mathbf{R} = \mathrm{lm}_{\mathbf{d}}(\mathbf{R})\mathbf{X}^{\boldsymbol{\delta}} + \mathbf{Q}$ with the j-th column of $\mathbf{Q}$ of degree less than δ_j. In particular, since $\mathrm{lm}_{\mathbf{d}}(\mathbf{R})$ is invertible, the column degree of $\mathbf{R}$ is $\boldsymbol{\delta}$. Besides, we obtain $\mathrm{lm}_{\mathbf{d}}(\mathbf{R})^{-1}\mathbf{R} = \mathbf{X}^{\boldsymbol{\delta}} + \mathrm{lm}_{\mathbf{d}}(\mathbf{R})^{-1}\mathbf{Q}$, and the j-th column of $\mathrm{lm}_{\mathbf{d}}(\mathbf{R})^{-1}\mathbf{Q}$ has degree less than δ_j. Thus $\mathrm{lm}_{\mathbf{d}}(\mathbf{R})^{-1}\mathbf{R}$ is in $\mathbf{d}$-Popov form and unimodularly equivalent to $\mathbf{P}$, hence equal to $\mathbf{P}$. □

In particular, if $\boldsymbol{\delta}$ is the $\mathbf{s}$-minimal degree of $(\mathbf{E}, \mathbf{J})$ and $\mathbf{d} = -\boldsymbol{\delta}$, any $\mathbf{d}$-minimal interpolation basis $\mathbf{R}$ for $(\mathbf{E}, \mathbf{J})$ has size at most $m^2 + m|\boldsymbol{\delta}|$, which for $\sigma \geqslant m$ is in $\mathcal{O}(m\sigma)$. Still, the algorithm in [18] cannot directly be used to compute such an $\mathbf{R}$ efficiently, because $|\mathbf{d} - \min(\mathbf{d})|$ can be as large as $\Theta(m\sigma)$, for example when $\boldsymbol{\delta} = (\sigma, 0, \ldots, 0)$; in this case, this algorithm uses $\mathcal{O}\tilde{~}(m^\omega \sigma)$ operations.

By Lemma 2.1, however, $\mathbf{d} = -\boldsymbol{\delta}$ satisfies $|\max(\mathbf{d}) - \mathbf{d}| \leqslant \sigma$. For this type of unbalanced shift, a solution in $\mathcal{O}\tilde{~}(m^{\omega-1}\sigma)$ already exists in the particular case of order basis computation [34, Section 6], building upon the partial linearization technique in [30, Section 3]. Here, we adopt a similar approach, taking advantage of the *a priori* knowledge of the column degree of the output matrix.

LEMMA 4.2. *Let* $\mathbf{E} \in \mathbb{K}^{m \times \sigma}$*,* $\mathbf{J} \in \mathbb{K}^{\sigma \times \sigma}$*, and* $\mathbf{s} \in \mathbb{Z}^m$*, and let* $\boldsymbol{\delta} = (\delta_1, \ldots, \delta_m)$ *denote the* $\mathbf{s}$*-minimal degree of* $(\mathbf{E}, \mathbf{J})$*.*

Then, let $\delta = \lceil \sigma/m \rceil \geqslant 1$*, and for* $i \in \{1, \ldots, m\}$ *write* $\delta_i = (\alpha_i - 1)\delta + \beta_i$ *with* $\alpha_i = \lceil \delta_i/\delta \rceil$ *and* $1 \leqslant \beta_i \leqslant \delta$ *if* $\delta_i > 0$*, and with* $\alpha_i = 1$ *and* $\beta_i = 0$ *if* $\delta_i = 0$*. Let* $\overline{m} = \alpha_1 + \cdots + \alpha_m$*. Then, define* $\overline{\boldsymbol{\delta}} \in \mathbb{N}^{\overline{m}}$ *as*

$$\overline{\boldsymbol{\delta}} = (\underbrace{\delta, \ldots, \delta, \beta_1}_{\alpha_1}, \ldots, \underbrace{\delta, \ldots, \delta, \beta_m}_{\alpha_m}) \tag{2}$$

and the expansion-compression matrix $\mathcal{E} \in \mathbb{K}[X]^{\overline{m} \times m}$ *as*

$$\mathcal{E} = \begin{bmatrix} 1 & & \\ X^\delta & & \\ \vdots & & \\ X^{(\alpha_1-1)\delta} & & \\ & \ddots & \\ & & 1 \\ & & X^\delta \\ & & \vdots \\ & & X^{(\alpha_m-1)\delta} \end{bmatrix}. \tag{3}$$

Let further $\mathbf{d} = -\overline{\boldsymbol{\delta}} \in \mathbb{Z}^{\overline{m}}$ *and* $\mathbf{R} \in \mathbb{K}[X]^{\overline{m} \times \overline{m}}$ *be a* $\mathbf{d}$*-minimal interpolation basis for* $(\mathcal{E} \cdot \mathbf{E}, \mathbf{J})$*. Then, the* $\mathbf{s}$*-Popov interpolation basis for* $(\mathbf{E}, \mathbf{J})$ *is the submatrix of* $\mathrm{lm}_{\mathbf{d}}(\mathbf{R})^{-1}\mathbf{R}\mathcal{E}$ *formed by its rows at indices* $\alpha_1 + \cdots + \alpha_i$ *for* $1 \leqslant i \leqslant m$*.*

PROOF. Let $\mathbf{P}$ denote the $\mathbf{s}$-Popov interpolation basis for $(\mathbf{E}, \mathbf{J})$; $\mathbf{P}$ has column degree $\boldsymbol{\delta}$. First, we partially linearize the columns of $\mathbf{P}$ in degree δ to obtain $\widetilde{\mathbf{P}} \in \mathbb{K}[X]^{m \times \overline{m}}$; more precisely, $\widetilde{\mathbf{P}}$ is a matrix of degree at most δ and such that $\mathbf{P} = \widetilde{\mathbf{P}}\mathcal{E}$. Then, we define $\overline{\mathbf{P}} \in \mathbb{K}[X]^{\overline{m} \times \overline{m}}$ as follows:

- for $1 \leqslant i \leqslant m$, the row $\alpha_1 + \cdots + \alpha_i$ of $\overline{\mathbf{P}}$ is the row i of $\widetilde{\mathbf{P}}$;
- for $0 \leqslant i \leqslant m - 1$ and $1 \leqslant j \leqslant \alpha_{i+1} - 1$, the row $\alpha_1 + \cdots + \alpha_i + j$ of $\overline{\mathbf{P}}$ is the row $[0, \cdots, 0, X^\delta, -1, 0, \cdots, 0] \in \mathbb{K}[X]^{1 \times \overline{m}}$ with the entry X^δ at column index $\alpha_1 + \cdots + \alpha_i + j$.

Since $\mathbf{P}$ is in $\mathbf{s}$-Popov form with column degree $\boldsymbol{\delta}$, it is in $-\boldsymbol{\delta}$-Popov form by Lemma 4.1. Then, one can check that $\overline{\mathbf{P}}$ is in $\mathbf{d}$-Popov form and has $\mathbf{d}$-row degree $(0, \ldots, 0)$.

By construction, every row of $\overline{\mathbf{P}}$ is an interpolant for $(\mathcal{E} \cdot \mathbf{E}, \mathbf{J})$. In particular, since $\mathbf{R}$ is an interpolation basis for $(\mathcal{E} \cdot \mathbf{E}, \mathbf{J})$, there is a matrix $\mathbf{U} \in \mathbb{K}[X]^{\overline{m} \times \overline{m}}$ such that $\overline{\mathbf{P}} = \mathbf{U}\mathbf{R}$. Besides, there exists no interpolant $\overline{\mathbf{p}} \in \mathbb{K}[X]^{1 \times \overline{m}}$ for $(\mathcal{E} \cdot \mathbf{E}, \mathbf{J})$ which has $\mathbf{d}$-degree less than 0: otherwise, $\overline{\mathbf{p}}\mathcal{E}$ would be an interpolant for $(\mathbf{E}, \mathbf{J})$, and it is easily checked that it would have $-\boldsymbol{\delta}$-degree less than 0, which is impossible.

Thus every row of $\mathbf{R}$ has $\mathbf{d}$-degree at least 0, and the predictable degree property [19, Theorem 6.3.13] shows that $\mathbf{U}$ is a constant matrix, and therefore unimodular. Then, $\overline{\mathbf{P}}$ is an interpolation basis for $(\mathcal{E} \cdot \mathbf{E}, \mathbf{J})$, and since it is in $\mathbf{d}$-Popov form, by Lemma 4.1 we obtain that $\overline{\mathbf{P}} = \mathrm{lm}_{\mathbf{d}}(\mathbf{R})^{-1}\mathbf{R}$. The conclusion follows. □

Then, it remains to prove that such a basis $\mathbf{R}$ can be computed efficiently using the algorithm MinimalInterpolationBasis in [18]; this leads to Algorithm 2.

Algorithm 2. KnownMinDegMIB

Input:

- *a matrix* $\mathbf{E} \in \mathbb{K}^{m \times \sigma}$ *with* $\sigma \geqslant m > 0$,
- *a Jordan matrix* $\mathbf{J} \in \mathbb{K}^{\sigma \times \sigma}$ *in standard representation,*
- *a shift* $\mathbf{s} \in \mathbb{Z}^m$,
- $\boldsymbol{\delta} = (\delta_1, \ldots, \delta_m) \in \mathbb{N}^m$ *the* $\mathbf{s}$*-minimal degree of* $(\mathbf{E}, \mathbf{J})$.

Output: *the* $\mathbf{s}$*-Popov interpolation basis* $\mathbf{P}$ *for* $(\mathbf{E}, \mathbf{J})$.

1. $\delta \leftarrow \lceil \sigma/m \rceil$, $\alpha_i \leftarrow \max(1, \lceil \delta_i/\delta \rceil)$ *for* $1 \leqslant i \leqslant m$, $\overline{m} \leftarrow \alpha_1 + \cdots + \alpha_m$
2. *Let* $\overline{\boldsymbol{\delta}} \in \mathbb{N}^{\overline{m}}$ *as in* (2) *and* $\mathbf{d} \leftarrow -\overline{\boldsymbol{\delta}} \in \mathbb{N}^{\overline{m}}$
3. *Let* $\mathcal{E} \in \mathbb{K}[X]^{\overline{m} \times m}$ *as in* (3) *and* $\overline{\mathbf{E}} \leftarrow \mathcal{E} \cdot \mathbf{E}$
4. $\mathbf{R} \leftarrow$ MinimalInterpolationBasis$(\overline{\mathbf{E}}, \mathbf{J}, \mathbf{d} + (\delta, \ldots, \delta))$
5. $\overline{\mathbf{P}} \leftarrow \mathrm{lm}_{\mathbf{d}}(\mathbf{R})^{-1}\mathbf{R}$
6. *Return the submatrix of* $\overline{\mathbf{P}}\mathcal{E}$ *formed by the rows at indices* $\alpha_1 + \cdots + \alpha_i$ *for* $1 \leqslant i \leqslant m$

Proposition 4.3. *Assuming that* $\mathbf{J} \in \mathbb{K}^{\sigma \times \sigma}$ *is a Jordan matrix given by a standard representation, and assuming we have the* $\mathbf{s}$*-minimal degree of* $(\mathbf{E}, \mathbf{J})$ *as an additional input, there is a deterministic algorithm* KnownMinDegMIB *which solves Problem 1 using*

$$\mathcal{O}(m^{\omega-1}\mathsf{M}(\sigma)\log(\sigma)\log(\sigma/m)) \qquad \text{if } \omega > 2,$$
$$\mathcal{O}(m\mathsf{M}(\sigma)\log(\sigma)\log(\sigma/m)\log(m)^3) \qquad \text{if } \omega = 2$$

operations in $\mathbb{K}$.

Proof. We focus on the case $\sigma \geqslant m$; otherwise, a better cost bound can be achieved even without knowing $\boldsymbol{\delta}$ [18, Theorem 1.4]. The correctness of Algorithm 2 follows from Lemma 4.2. We remark that it uses $\mathbf{d} + (\delta, \ldots, \delta)$ rather than $\mathbf{d}$ because the minimal interpolation basis algorithm in [18] requires the input shift to have non-negative entries. Since adding a constant to every entry of $\mathbf{d}$ does not change the notion of $\mathbf{d}$-reducedness, the basis $\mathbf{R}$ obtained at Step 4 is a $\mathbf{d}$-minimal interpolation basis for $(\mathbf{E}, \mathbf{J})$.

Concerning the cost bound, we will show that it is dominated by the time spent in Step 4. First, we prove that $|\mathbf{d} - \min(\mathbf{d})| \in \mathcal{O}(\sigma)$, so that the cost of Step 4 follows from [18, Theorem 1.5]. We have $\alpha_i \leqslant 1 + \delta_i/\delta \leqslant 1 + m\delta_i/\sigma$ for all i. Thus, $\overline{m} = \alpha_1 + \cdots + \alpha_m \leqslant m + \sum_{1 \leqslant i \leqslant m} m\delta_i/\sigma \leqslant 2m$ thanks to Lemma 2.1. Then, since all entries of $\mathbf{d}$ are in $\{-\delta, \ldots, 0\}$, we obtain $|\mathbf{d} - \min(\mathbf{d})| \leqslant \overline{m}\delta \leqslant 2m(1 + \sigma/m) \leqslant 4\sigma$.

Step 3 can be done in $\mathcal{O}(m\mathsf{M}(\sigma)\log(\sigma))$ operations according to Lemma 4.4 below.

Lemma 4.1 proves that the sum of the column degrees of $\mathbf{R}$ is $|\overline{\boldsymbol{\delta}}| = |\boldsymbol{\delta}| \leqslant \sigma$. Then, the product in Step 5 can be done in $\mathcal{O}(m^{\omega-1}\sigma)$ operations, by first linearizing the columns of $\mathbf{R}$ into a $\overline{m} \times \overline{m} + |\boldsymbol{\delta}|$ matrix over $\mathbb{K}$, then left-multiplying this matrix by $\mathrm{lm}_{\mathbf{d}}(\mathbf{R})^{-1}$ (itself computed using $\mathcal{O}(m^{\omega})$ operations), and finally performing the inverse linearization.

Because of the degrees in $\overline{\mathbf{P}}$ and the definition of $\mathcal{E}$, the output in Step 6 can be formed without using any arithmetic operation. □

The efficient computation of $\mathcal{E} \cdot \mathbf{E}$ can be done with the algorithm for computing residuals in [18, Section 6].

Lemma 4.4. *The product* $\mathcal{E} \cdot \mathbf{E}$ *at Step 3 of Algorithm 2 can be computed using* $\mathcal{O}(m\mathsf{M}(\sigma)\log(\sigma))$ *operations in* $\mathbb{K}$.

Proof. The product $\mathcal{E} \cdot \mathbf{E}$ has $\overline{m}$ rows, with $\overline{m} \leqslant 2m$ as above. Besides, by definition of $\mathcal{E}$, each row of $\mathcal{E} \cdot \mathbf{E}$ is a product of the form $X^{i\delta} \cdot \mathbf{E}_{j,*}$, where $0 \leqslant i \leqslant m$, $1 \leqslant j \leqslant m$, and $\mathbf{E}_{j,*}$ denotes the row j of $\mathbf{E}$. In particular, $i\delta \leqslant 2\sigma$: then, according to [18, Proposition 6.1], each of these $\overline{m}$ products can be performed using $\mathcal{O}(\mathsf{M}(\sigma)\log(\sigma))$ operations in $\mathbb{K}$. □

This lemma and the partial linearization technique can also be used to compute the residual at Step 2.c of Algorithm 1, that is, a product of the form $\mathbf{P} \cdot \mathbf{E}$ with the sum of the column degrees of $\mathbf{P}$ bounded by σ. First, we expand the high-degree columns of $\mathbf{P}$ to obtain $\overline{\mathbf{P}} \in \mathbb{K}[X]^{m \times \overline{m}}$ of degree less than $\lceil \sigma/m \rceil$ such that $\mathbf{P} = \overline{\mathbf{P}}\mathcal{E}$; then, we compute $\overline{\mathbf{E}} = \mathcal{E} \cdot \mathbf{E}$; and finally we rely on the algorithm in [18, Proposition 6.1] to compute $\overline{\mathbf{P}} \cdot \overline{\mathbf{E}} = \mathbf{P} \cdot \mathbf{E}$ efficiently.

Corollary 4.5. *Let* $\mathbf{E} \in \mathbb{K}^{m \times \sigma}$ *with* $\sigma \geqslant m$, *and let* $\mathbf{J} \in \mathbb{K}^{\sigma \times \sigma}$ *be a Jordan matrix given by a standard representation. Let* $\mathbf{P} \in \mathbb{K}[X]^{m \times m}$ *with column degree* $(\delta_1, \ldots, \delta_m)$ *such that* $\delta_1 + \cdots + \delta_m \leqslant \sigma$. *Then, the product* $\mathbf{P} \cdot \mathbf{E}$ *can be computed using* $\mathcal{O}(m^{\omega-1}\mathsf{M}(\sigma)\log(\sigma))$ *operations in* $\mathbb{K}$.

Acknowledgments. We thank B. Beckermann and G. Labahn for their valuable comments, as well as an anonymous referee for suggesting a shorter proof of Lemma 3.3. C.-P. Jeannerod and G. Villard were partly supported by the ANR project HPAC (ANR 11 BS02 013). V. Neiger was supported by the international mobility grants Explo'ra Doc from *Région Rhône-Alpes*, *PALSE*, and *Mitacs Globalink - Inria*. É. Schost was supported by NSERC.

5. REFERENCES

[1] B. Beckermann and G. Labahn. A uniform approach for the fast computation of matrix-type Padé approximants. *SIAM J. Matrix Anal. Appl.*, 15(3):804–823, 1994.

[2] B. Beckermann and G. Labahn. Fraction-free computation of matrix rational interpolants and matrix gcds. *SIAM J. Matrix Anal. Appl.*, 22(1):114–144, 2000.

[3] B. Beckermann, G. Labahn, and G. Villard. Normal forms for general polynomial matrices. *J. Symbolic Comput.*, 41(6):708–737, 2006.

[4] P. Beelen and K. Brander. Key equations for list decoding of Reed-Solomon codes and how to solve them. *J. Symbolic Comput.*, 45(7):773–786, 2010.

[5] A. Bostan, C.-P. Jeannerod, and É. Schost. Solving structured linear systems with large displacement rank. *Theor. Comput. Sci.*, 407(1-3):155–181, 2008.

[6] K. Brander. *Interpolation and List Decoding of Algebraic Codes.* PhD thesis, Technical University of Denmark, 2010.

[7] P. Busse. *Multivariate List Decoding of Evaluation Codes with a Gröbner Basis Perspective.* PhD thesis, University of Kentucky, 2008.

[8] D. G. Cantor and E. Kaltofen. On fast multiplication of polynomials over arbitrary algebras. *Acta Inform.*, 28(7):693–701, 1991.

[9] M. Chowdhury, C.-P. Jeannerod, V. Neiger, É. Schost, and G. Villard. Faster algorithms for multivariate interpolation with multiplicities and simultaneous polynomial approximations. *IEEE Trans. Inf. Theory*, 61(5):2370–2387, 2015.

[10] H. Cohn and N. Heninger. Approximate common divisors via lattices. In *Tenth Algorithmic Number Theory Symposium*, pages 271–293. Mathematical Sciences Publishers (MSP), 2012-2013.

[11] D. Coppersmith and S. Winograd. Matrix multiplication via arithmetic progressions. *J. Symbolic Comput.*, 9(3):251–280, 1990.

[12] C. Devet, I. Goldberg, and N. Heninger. Optimally robust private information retrieval. In *USENIX Security 12*, pages 269–283. USENIX, 2012.

[13] J. von zur Gathen and J. Gerhard. *Modern Computer Algebra (third edition).* Cambridge University Press, 2013.

[14] P. Giorgi, C.-P. Jeannerod, and G. Villard. On the complexity of polynomial matrix computations. In *ISSAC'03*, pages 135–142. ACM, 2003.

[15] S. Gupta and A. Storjohann. Computing Hermite forms of polynomial matrices. In *ISSAC'11*, pages 155–162. ACM, 2011.

[16] V. Guruswami and A. Rudra. Explicit codes achieving list decoding capacity: Error-correction with optimal redundancy. *IEEE Trans. Inf. Theory*, 54(1):135–150, 2008.

[17] V. Guruswami and M. Sudan. Improved decoding of Reed-Solomon and algebraic-geometry codes. *IEEE Trans. Inf. Theory*, 45(6):1757–1767, 1999.

[18] C.-P. Jeannerod, V. Neiger, É. Schost, and G. Villard. Computing minimal interpolation bases. HAL Open archive - https://hal.inria.fr/hal-01241781, 2015.

[19] T. Kailath. *Linear Systems.* Prentice-Hall, 1980.

[20] D. E. Knuth. The analysis of algorithms. In *Congrès int. Math., Nice, France*, volume 3, pages 269–274, 1970.

[21] R. Koetter and A. Vardy. Algebraic soft-decision decoding of Reed-Solomon codes. *IEEE Trans. Inf. Theory*, 49(11):2809–2825, 2003.

[22] F. Le Gall. Powers of tensors and fast matrix multiplication. In *ISSAC'14*, pages 296–303. ACM, 2014.

[23] R. T. Moenck. Fast computation of GCDs. In *Proc. 5th ACM Symp. Theory Comp.*, pages 142–151, 1973.

[24] T. Mulders and A. Storjohann. On lattice reduction for polynomial matrices. *J. Symbolic Comput.*, 35:377–401, 2003.

[25] V. Olshevsky and M. A. Shokrollahi. A displacement approach to efficient decoding of algebraic-geometric codes. In *STOC'99*, pages 235–244. ACM, 1999.

[26] F. Parvaresh and A. Vardy. Correcting errors beyond the Guruswami-Sudan radius in polynomial time. In *FOCS'05*, pages 285–294. IEEE, 2005.

[27] R. M. Roth and G. Ruckenstein. Efficient decoding of Reed-Solomon codes beyond half the minimum distance. *IEEE Trans. Inf. Theory*, 46(1):246–257, 2000.

[28] S. Sarkar and A. Storjohann. Normalization of row reduced matrices. In *ISSAC'11*, pages 297–304. ACM, 2011.

[29] A. Schönhage. Schnelle Berechnung von Kettenbruchentwicklungen. *Acta Inform.*, 1:139–144, 1971.

[30] A. Storjohann. Notes on computing minimal approximant bases. In *Dagstuhl Seminar Proceedings*, 2006.

[31] M. Van Barel and A. Bultheel. A general module theoretic framework for vector M-Padé and matrix rational interpolation. *Numer. Algorithms*, 3:451–462, 1992.

[32] A. Zeh, C. Gentner, and D. Augot. An interpolation procedure for list decoding Reed-Solomon codes based on generalized key equations. *IEEE Trans. Inf. Theory*, 57(9):5946–5959, 2011.

[33] W. Zhou. *Fast Order Basis and Kernel Basis Computation and Related Problems.* PhD thesis, University of Waterloo, 2012.

[34] W. Zhou and G. Labahn. Efficient algorithms for order basis computation. *J. Symbolic Comput.*, 47(7):793–819, 2012.

APPENDIX

A. REDUCING THE ENTRIES OF THE SHIFT

Let $\mathbf{A} \in \mathbb{K}[X]^{m\times m}$ be nonsingular, let $\mathbf{s} \in \mathbb{Z}^m$, and consider $\sigma \in \mathbb{N}$ such that $\sigma > \deg(\det(\mathbf{A}))$. Here, we show how to construct a shift $\mathbf{t} \in \mathbb{N}^m$ such that

- the $\mathbf{s}$-Popov form $\mathbf{P}$ of $\mathbf{A}$ is also in $\mathbf{t}$-Popov form;
- $\min(\mathbf{t}) = 0$, $\max(\mathbf{t}) \leqslant (m-1)\sigma$, and $|\mathbf{t}| \leqslant m^2\sigma/2$.

We write $\hat{\mathbf{s}} = (s_{\pi(1)}, \ldots, s_{\pi(m)})$ where π is a permutation of $\{1,\ldots,m\}$ such that $\hat{\mathbf{s}}$ is non-decreasing. Then, we define $\hat{\mathbf{t}} = (\hat{t}_1,\ldots,\hat{t}_m)$ by $\hat{t}_1 = 0$ and, for $2 \leqslant i \leqslant m$,

$$\hat{t}_i - \hat{t}_{i-1} = \begin{cases} \sigma & \text{if } \hat{s}_i - \hat{s}_{i-1} \geqslant \sigma, \\ \hat{s}_i - \hat{s}_{i-1} & \text{otherwise.} \end{cases}$$

Let $\mathbf{t} = (\hat{t}_{\pi^{-1}(1)}, \ldots, \hat{t}_{\pi^{-1}(m)})$. Since the diagonal entries of $\mathbf{P}$ have degree at most $\deg(\det(\mathbf{A})) < \sigma$, we obtain that $\mathbf{P}$ is in $\mathbf{t}$-diagonal weak Popov form and thus in $\mathbf{t}$-Popov form.

B. EXAMPLE OF ORDER BASIS WITH SIZE BEYOND OUR TARGET COST

We focus on a Hermite-Padé approximation problem with input $\mathbf{F}$ of dimensions $2m \times 1$ as below, order σ with $\sigma \geqslant m$, and shift $\mathbf{s} = (0,\ldots,0,\sigma,\ldots,\sigma) \in \mathbb{N}^{2m}$ with m entries 0 and m entries σ.

Let f be a polynomial in X with nonzero constant coefficient, and let $f_1,\ldots,f_m$ be generic polynomials in X of degree less than σ. Then, we consider the following input with all entries truncated modulo X^σ:

$$\mathbf{F} = [f, f+Xf, X(f+Xf), \cdots, X^{m-2}(f+Xf), f_1, \cdots, f_m]^{\mathsf{T}}.$$

After m steps, the iterative algorithm in [1] has computed an $\mathbf{s}$-minimal basis $\mathbf{P}^{(m)}$ of approximants for $\mathbf{F}$ and order m, which is such that $\mathbf{t} = \mathrm{rdeg}_{\mathbf{s}}(\mathbf{P}^{(m)}) = (1,\ldots,1,\sigma,\ldots,\sigma)$ and $\mathbf{P}^{(m)}\mathbf{F} = [0,\cdots,0,X^m f, X^m g_1, \cdots, X^m g_m]^{\mathsf{T}} \bmod X^\sigma$, for some polynomials $g_1,\ldots,g_m$.

Now we finish the process up to order σ. Since the coefficient of degree m of $X^m f$ is nonzero and because of the specific shift $\mathbf{t}$, the obtained $\mathbf{s}$-minimal basis $\mathbf{P}$ of approximants for $\mathbf{F}$ has degree profile

$$\mathbf{P} = \begin{bmatrix} [1] & [0] & & & & & \\ \vdots & \ddots & \ddots & & & & \\ [1] & \cdots & [1] & [0] & & & \\ [d+1] & \cdots & [d+1] & [d+1] & & & \\ [d] & \cdots & [d] & [d] & [0] & & \\ \vdots & \cdots & \vdots & \vdots & & \ddots & \\ [d] & \cdots & [d] & [d] & & & [0] \end{bmatrix},$$

where $d = \sigma - m$, $[i]$ denotes an entry of degree i, the entries left blank correspond to the zero polynomial, and the entries $[d+1]$ are on the m-th row. In particular, $\mathbf{P}$ has size $\Theta(m^2\sigma)$.

Computing Real Roots of Real Polynomials ...
... and now For Real!

Alexander Kobel
Max-Planck-Institut
für Informatik
Universität des Saarlandes
Campus E1 4
66123 Saarbrücken, Germany
alexander.kobel
@mpi-inf.mpg.de

Fabrice Rouillier
INRIA Paris
Institut de Mathématiques de
Jussieu Paris Rive Gauche
CNRS UMR 7586
Université P. & M. Curie
4 place Jussieu 75252 Paris
Cedex 05, France
Fabrice.Rouillier@inria.fr

Michael Sagraloff
Max-Planck-Institut
für Informatik
Campus E1 4
66123 Saarbrücken, Germany
michael.sagraloff
@mpi-inf.mpg.de

ABSTRACT

Very recent work introduces an asymptotically fast subdivision algorithm, denoted ANEWDSC, for isolating the real roots of a univariate real polynomial. The method combines Descartes' Rule of Signs to test intervals for the existence of roots, Newton iteration to speed up convergence against clusters of roots, and approximate computation to decrease the required precision. It achieves record bounds on the worst-case complexity for the considered problem, matching the complexity of Pan's method for computing all complex roots and improving upon the complexity of other subdivision methods by several magnitudes.

In the article at hand, we report on an implementation of ANEWDSC on top of the RS root isolator. RS is a highly efficient realization of the classical Descartes method and currently serves as the default real root solver in Maple. We describe crucial design changes within ANEWDSC and RS that led to a high-performance implementation without harming the theoretical complexity of the underlying algorithm.

With an excerpt of our collection of benchmarks, available at http://anewdsc.mpi-inf.mpg.de/, we illustrate that the theoretical gain in performance of ANEWDSC over other subdivision methods also transfers into practice. These experiments also show that our new implementation outperforms both RS and mature competitors by magnitudes for notoriously hard instances with clustered roots. For all other instances, we avoid almost any overhead by integrating additional optimizations and heuristics.

Keywords

real roots; univariate polynomials; root finding; root isolation; Newton's method; Descartes method; approximate arithmetic; certified computation

ISSAC '16, July 19–22, 2016, Waterloo, ON, Canada.

ISBN 978-1-4503-4380-0/16/07...$15.00
DOI: 10.1145/2930889.2930937

1. INTRODUCTION

Computing the real roots of a univariate polynomial is one of the fundamental tasks in numerics and computer algebra, and numerous methods have been proposed to solve this problem. The leading general-purpose solvers in practice are based on subdivision algorithms that rely on Descartes' Rule of Signs to test for the existence of roots in a certain interval.

The computation for an input polynomial $P \in \mathbb{R}[x]$ can be considered as a binary tree where each node corresponds to an interval $I = (a, b)$ and a polynomial $P_I = (x+1)^n P(\frac{ax+b}{x+1})$. The number v_I of sign changes in the coefficient sequence of P_I then exceeds the number of roots contained in I by an even non-negative number. In the original algorithm [2], the two children of a node are obtained by a simple bisection on the interval and relative transformations on the polynomials, which yields the polynomial P_I. A node is a leaf if $v_I = 0$ or $v_I = 1$; in the first case, I contains no root, whereas, in the latter case, the interval is isolating for a real root. Considerable efforts have been taken to improve the worst-case complexity of different variants of the Descartes method, and to provide efficient implementations: different traversal orders of the subdivision tree to optimize the memory usage [10], the use of interval arithmetic [8], new strategies to optimize the main transformations [16], extensions to polynomials with approximate coefficients [11, 5], and many others.

Nevertheless, most formulations suffer from at least one of the following two deficiencies: First, the subdivision strategies only achieve *linear* convergence against the roots. In presence of clusters, those approaches require a large number of subdivisions to separate the roots. Second, the algorithms are designed for exact arithmetic on the coefficients of P. An unguarded choice of the subdivision points can impose an unnecessarily large precision demand when such an approach is translated literally to arbitrary precision dyadic numbers. Even worse, completeness is not guaranteed for polynomials whose coefficients can only be approximated. For example, consider the polynomial $P(x) = \pi x^2 - (\pi + e)x + e$ with roots at (exactly) 1 and $e/\pi \approx 0.865$, and assume that its coefficients are given as an oracle for arbitrarily good dyadic approximations. In this setting, $P(1) = 0$ cannot be decided without resorting to a symbolic simplification of the input, which is beyond the means of the root isolation method. Likewise, the number of sign variations on the intervals $(1 - \epsilon, 1)$ and $(1, 1 + \epsilon)$ for any ϵ cannot be determined with approximate arithmetic. Thus, once an interval is split at $x = 1$, a straight-forward algorithm will request better and better approximations of P from the oracle, but will not terminate.

Both shortcomings have been resolved in [19]: The proposed algorithm ANEWDSC combines the bisection strategy with Newton iteration to achieve *quadratic* convergence against clusters. Thus, long chains of intervals I with the same v_I are compressed to only logarithmic length (compared to the length when considering bisection only). In addition, intervals are split at *admissible points,* where the polynomial takes a (relatively) large absolute value. This allows the precision demand of the computation to be kept small, improving by an order of magnitude over previous approaches. Due to the exclusive use of approximate arithmetic, the method also applies to (square-free) polynomials with arbitrary real coefficients. Both the number of subdivision steps and the precision demand is optimal up to polylogarithmic factors, and the bound on its bit complexity is comparable to the record bound [12] that is implied by an algorithm based on Pan's near-optimal method [14] for approximate polynomial factorization. We provide more specific bounds in Section 2.

Unfortunately, asymptotically fast algorithms are often extremely hard to be implemented or do not exhibit their theoretical performance in practice. The contribution of this paper is to show that, for the problem of real root computation, we can bridge this gap between theory and practice. We report on an implementation of ANEWDSC on top of the Descartes-based real root finder inside the RS library. It preserves the key features of RS, which are a close-to-optimal memory consumption and the intensive use of adaptive multiprecision interval arithmetic [15].

We present our design changes both to RS and within ANEWDSC that make it possible to achieve significant performance gains on hard instances on the one hand and proven complexity guarantees on the other hand without sacrificing efficiency for small or intrinsically easy instances. The analysis is supported by benchmark results that show that ANEWDSC can defy the leading general-purpose solvers for real roots in their special domains, and outperforms the existing implementations on notoriously hard instances.

2. THE DESCARTES METHOD AND THE ANEWDSC ALGORITHM

We briefly review the classical Descartes method [2] as well as the algorithm ANEWDSC as introduced in [19]. Given an interval $\mathcal{I} = (a_0, b_0) \subset \mathbb{R}$ and a polynomial

$$P(x) = p_n x^n + p_{n-1}x^{n-1} + \cdots + p_1 x + p_0 \in \mathbb{R}[x], \quad (1)$$

the Descartes method recursively subdivides $\mathcal{I}$ into equally sized intervals until each subinterval $I = (a, b) \subset \mathcal{I}$ has either been shown to contain no root or exactly one root of P. In order to test an interval for the existence of a root of P, a coordinate transformation $x \mapsto \frac{ax+b}{x+1}$ is considered, which maps $\mathbb{R}^+$ one-to-one onto the interval I. Then, Descartes' Rule of Signs applied to the polynomial

$$P_I(x) := \sum_{i=0}^{n} p_{I,i}x^i := (x+1)^n \cdot P\Big(\frac{ax+b}{x+1}\Big) \quad (2)$$

states that the number of sign changes $v_I := \mathrm{var}(P, I) := \mathrm{var}(P_I)$ in the coefficient sequence of P_I exceeds the number m_I of roots (counted with multiplicity) of P in I by a non-negative even integer. In other words, $m_I \le v_I$ and $m_I \equiv v_I \mod 2$. In each step of the recursion within the Descartes method, the number v_I is computed. If $v_I = 0$, the interval I is discarded. If $v_I = 1$, I is stored as isolating. Intervals with $v_I > 1$ are further subdivided into two equally sized subintervals. In addition, it is checked whether the subdivision point, that is the midpoint $m(I) = \frac{a+b}{2}$ of I, is a root of P.

Algorithm 1: Classical Descartes Method

INPUT: A polynomial P as in (1) and an interval $\mathcal{I}$.

REPORTS: Disjoint isolating intervals for all roots of P in $\mathcal{I}$.

- Initialize the list of active intervals to $\mathcal{A} := \{\mathcal{I}\}$.
- While $\mathcal{A} \neq \emptyset$:
  - ▷ Remove an arbitrary $I = (a, b)$ from $\mathcal{A}$.
  - ▷ If $v_I = 0$, discard I and continue.
  - ▷ If $v_I = 1$, report I and continue.
  - ▷ Otherwise, add $(a, m(I))$ and $(m(I), b)$ to $\mathcal{A}$. If $P(m(I)) = 0$, additionally report $\{m(I)\}$.

If the polynomial P contains only simple roots in $\mathcal{I}$, the Descartes method yields isolating intervals for all these roots; otherwise, it converges towards the roots, but does not terminate. If $\mathcal{I}$ is chosen large enough to contain all real roots, and all these roots are simple, the algorithm isolates all real roots of P. The proof for termination relies on the well known One- and Two-Circle Theorems [4, 13], which provide lower bounds on the width $w(I)$ of any produced interval I.

Regarding the worst-case complexity of the above algorithm, we focus, only for simplicity, on the so-called *benchmark problem* of computing all real roots of a square-free polynomial P of degree n with *integer* coefficients of absolute value less than 2^τ. Nevertheless, we aim to stress the fact that, for polynomials with arbitrary real coefficients, more general bounds are known [18, 19], which are expressed in terms of the separations and the absolute values of the roots of P, thus being more adaptive and meaningful.

We denote by $\mathcal{T}$ the subdivision tree whose nodes are the intervals I considered by the algorithm. The function $\mathrm{var}(\cdot)$ is sign diminishing, that is, for any disjoint subintervals I_1 and I_2 of I, we have $v_{I_1} + v_{I_2} \le v_I$; e.g. see [4] for a proof. This implies that $\mathcal{T}$ has width at most $2n$, while the lower bound on the width of the produced intervals implies that its height is in $O(\tau + \log \sigma_P^{-1})$, where σ_P is the minimum root separation of P. Since $\log \sigma_P^{-1} = \tilde{O}(n\tau)$, the bound $\tilde{O}(n^2\tau)$ on the total size of $\mathcal{T}$ follows.[1] A more refined argument [6, 4], which takes into account the fact that $\sum_{i=1}^{n} \log \sigma_P(z_i)^{-1} = \tilde{O}(n\tau)$, even shows that $|\mathcal{T}| = \tilde{O}(n\tau)$. The coefficients of the polynomials P_I have bitsize bounded by $\tilde{O}(n^2\tau)$, hence the precision demand for exactly computing P_I is also bounded by $\tilde{O}(n^2\tau)$. This yields the bound $\tilde{O}(n^3\tau)$ for the bit complexity of computing P_I, even when using asymptotically fast methods for polynomial arithmetic. We conclude that the cost of the classical Descartes method is bounded by $\tilde{O}(n^4\tau^2)$ bit operations. This matches the bound achieved by many other popular subdivision algorithms for real root computation such as the continued fraction (CF) method [1, 20], the Bolzano method [21], or the Sturm method [3]. We remark that the $\tilde{O}(n^4\tau^2)$ upper bound on the bit complexity is actually tight for the latter algorithms; see [6, 1, 3].

The main strengths of the Descartes method are its simplicity and the fact that the subdivision tree size and running time adapt to the separation of the roots [6, 4, 18]. On well-conditioned inputs, the performance is significantly better

[1] The tilde denotes that we omit polylogarithmic factors in n or τ.

than indicated by the worst-case bounds. Indeed, we observe that, for many polynomials (e.g. random polynomials), the size of the tree is only logarithmic in n, in which case the precision demand does not exceed $\tilde{O}(\tau + n)$. In such cases, the bit complexity is by several magnitudes smaller than the worst case bound. However, despite its good behavior for many instances, the method has two major shortcomings.

First, in order to determine the sign of the coefficients of P_I as well as the sign of P at the midpoint of I, exact arithmetic is assumed. If the coefficients of P are integer or rational, this is feasible, at the expensive of a precision that exceeds the actual demand by one order of magnitude; see Table 1 and [18, 19] for more details. However, if the coefficients of P can only be approximated (e.g trigonometric expressions), then computing the sign of the coefficients of P_I is impossible in general. Another shortcoming is that the classical subdivision strategies only achieve linear convergence against the roots. For some inputs, this is not critical as the separations of the roots are large and the subdivision tree has small height. However, if roots appear in clusters, numerous subdivision steps have to be performed in order to separate distinct roots from each other, and there exist polynomials[2] for which the Descartes method produces a sequence of intervals I_j of length $\Omega(n\tau)$ with identical v_{I_j}.

subdivision rule and model of computation	subdivision tree size	precision demand	overall bit complexity
bisection, exact over $\mathbb{Z}/\mathbb{Q}$	$\tilde{O}(n\tau)$	$\tilde{O}(n^2\tau)$	$\tilde{O}(n^4\tau^2)$
bisection, approximate	$\tilde{O}(n\tau)$	$\tilde{O}(n\tau)$	$\tilde{O}(n^3\tau^2)$
Newton, exact over $\mathbb{Z}/\mathbb{Q}$	$\tilde{O}(n)$	$\tilde{O}(n^2\tau)^*$	$\tilde{O}(n^3\tau)$
Newton, approximate	$\tilde{O}(n)$	$\tilde{O}(n\tau)^\dagger$	$\tilde{O}(n^3 + n^2\tau)$

All mentioned bounds are tight for certain classes of inputs.
*Amortized precision demand over the entire tree is only $\tilde{O}(n\tau)$.
†Amortized precision demand over the entire tree is only $\tilde{O}(n+\tau)$.

Table 1: worst-case complexity of variants of Descartes methods for polynomials in $\mathbb{Z}[x]$ with degree n and bitsize τ

In [19], the algorithm ANewDsc[3] has been introduced. It uses approximate arithmetic and an accelerated subdivision strategy based on Newton's iteration to address both of the aforementioned shortcomings. We sketch the main ideas to an extent as needed in the discussion of its implementation. At some points, we simplified the presentation at the cost of mathematical rigor by skipping some rather technical details. In contrast, our implementation takes into account all details, thus being certified and complete.

ANewDsc is similar to the classical Descartes method in the sense that it recursively subdivides a given interval $\mathcal{I}$ and that it uses a predicate based on Descartes' Rule of Signs to test for roots. However, it is tailored to rely solely on approximate computation. For this, ANewDsc uses the so called "01-Test",[4] that can be evaluated using approximate arithmetic only. Similar to the original Descartes test, a call of the predicate on an interval I returns a value $t_I \in \{0, 1, *\}$ with the following guarantees: If $t_I = 0$, then I contains no root of P; if $t_I = 1$, then I isolates a simple root of P; and if $t_I = *$, no conclusion shall be drawn about the number of roots of P in I. We remark that the 01-Test is stronger than the classical sign variation test in the sense that $v_I = 0$ (or 1) implies that the 01-Test returns 0 (or 1), too.

Algorithm 2: Find Admissible Point

INPUT: Polynomial P as in (1) and a multipoint $m[\epsilon; N]$.

OUTPUT: Admissible point $m^* \in m[\epsilon; N]$.

- For $\rho = 2, 4, 8, \ldots$:
  - ▷ For all $m_i \in m[\epsilon; N]$, compute approximations $\tilde{v}_i$ of $v_i := P(m_i)$ with $|\tilde{v}_i - v_i| < 2^{-\rho}$.
  - ▷ Determine a point $m_{i_0} = m_i$ that maximizes $|\tilde{v}_i|$.
  - ▷ If $|\tilde{v}_{i_0}| > 2^{-\rho+2}$, return $m^* := m_{i_0}$.

The precision demand of the 01-Test on (a, b) is bounded by $\tilde{O}(n + n\log|a| + n\log|b| + \log|P(a)|^{-1} + \log|P(b)|^{-1} + \log\|P\|_\infty))$ bits.[5] Hence, we strive to choose boundary points a and b where the value of $|P|$ is not too small. This is realized by an additional layer on the subdivision scheme. Instead of choosing a fixed subdivision point m (in the classical method, the midpoint $m(I)$ of an interval I) in each step, ANewDsc chooses a nearby, so-called *admissible point* m^*, where $|P|$ becomes large. More precisely, for a point m, a positive integer N with $N \geq n$, and a positive value ϵ, we call a point

$$m^* \in m[\epsilon; N] := \{m_i := m + i \cdot \epsilon \text{ for } i = -\lceil \tfrac{N}{2} \rceil, \ldots, \lceil \tfrac{N}{2} \rceil\}$$

admissible with respect to the multipoint $m[\epsilon; N]$ *(or just admissible)* if $|P(m^*)| \geq \frac{1}{4} \cdot \max_i |P(m_i)|$. Algorithm 2 computes such a point using only approximate arithmetic.[6] Indeed, since $m[\epsilon; N]$ contains at least one point that has distance $\epsilon/2$ or more to all roots of P, we have $\max_i |P(m_i)| > 0$, and thus the algorithm terminates with a precision ρ that is bounded by $2 \cdot (1 + \log\max(1, (\max_i |P(m_i)|)^{-1}))$.

In [19], we always choose $N = n$. Using approximate multipoint evaluation [9], this guarantees that the cost for the approximate evaluations of P at all points m_i does not considerably exceed the cost for the evaluation at only one point. In addition, in each step, ϵ is chosen small enough (e.g., $\epsilon \approx w(I)/4$ in a bisection step with $m = m(I)$) such that the size and the structure of the subdivision tree induced by ANewDsc does not change (in the worst case) when passing from an admissible point $m^* \in m[\epsilon; N]$ to an arbitrary point in the interval $[m - \lceil \frac{N}{2} \rceil \epsilon, m + \lceil \frac{N}{2} \rceil \epsilon]$. In fact, choosing m^* to be admissible only affects the needed precision demand in each iteration but not the size of the subdivision tree.

For simplicity, we will not further specify ϵ (nor N) throughout the following considerations and just assume that ϵ is chosen small enough; for details, see [19]. In this context, we just say that a point m^* is *admissible for* m. With a suitable choice of the parameters, subdivision on admissible points reduces the worst-case precision demand of the Descartes method to $\tilde{O}(n\tau)$ in the integer setting, improving upon the classical approach by one order of magnitude. Besides, it allows to process inputs where the coefficients can only be approximated as we avoid splitting on roots *without* verifying that P is zero at any point.

[2]As an example, consider the Mignotte-like polynomials from Table 2 having two real roots with pairwise distance $2^{-\Omega(n\tau)}$.

[3]The algorithm is an approximate arithmetic variant of the algorithm NewDsc from [17], which exclusively uses exact arithmetic. The acronym ANewDsc should be read as "A New Descartes" or, alternatively, as "Approximate Arithmetic Newton-Descartes."

[4]The 01-Test is split into two separate subroutines. Both are modified variants of the classical sign variation tests, where it is checked whether $\text{var}(P, J) = 0$ or $\text{var}(P, J) = 1$ for some intervals J. For details and proofs regarding the 01-Test, we refer the reader to [19, Sec. 2.4].

[5]We remark that the precise bound on the precision demand is slightly more complicated; see [19, Sec. 2.4] for details.

[6]Note that in [19, p. 54], there is a typo in the Admissible Point algorithm: *repeat ... until* (loop (2)) should read *repeat ... while*. However, the proof of [19, Thm. 5 (b)] uses the correct statement.

In order to overcome the second shortcoming of the Descartes method, ANewDsc combines bisection with Newton iteration. For this, it uses a trial and error approach, called "Newton-Test", to speed up convergence towards clusters of roots. In each iteration, the Newton-Test aims to replace an interval $I = (a, b)$ by some sub-interval $I' = (a', b') \subset I$ of width $w(I') \approx w(I)/N_I$ such that I' contains all roots of P in I. Here, N_I denotes a parameter that corresponds to the actual speed of convergence. Initially, N_I is set to 4. If the Newton step succeeds, we define $N_{I'} := N_I^2$. In case of failure, we fall back to bisection, that is, I is subdivided into two (almost) equally-sized subintervals I_ℓ and I_r, and we define $N_{I_\ell} := N_{I_r} := \max(4, \sqrt{N_I})$. In [19, Sec. 3.2], it has been shown that the Newton step succeeds under guarantee if there exists a sufficiently small cluster $\mathcal{C}$ of roots of P that is centered at some point in I and is sufficiently well-separated from the remaining roots of P.

The method runs in three steps. In the first step, it estimates the multiplicity k of such a cluster.[7] Then, in the second step, it performs a corresponding Newton iteration to obtain a λ with $|\lambda - z_i| < w(I)/2N_I$ for each root $z_i \in \mathcal{C}$. Finally, the method aims to validate the approximation λ of the cluster $\mathcal{C}$. For this, we apply the 01-Test to the intervals (a, a') and (b, b'), where $I' = (a', b') \subset I$ is an interval of width $w(I') \approx w(I)/N_I$ centered at λ. If the latter test yields the value 0 for both intervals (a, a') and (b, b'), it follows that I' contains all roots that are contained in I, in which case we say that the Newton-Test succeeds. Notice that, even in case of success, we may not conclude that there exists a cluster of k roots, however, we may conclude that I may be replaced by I' without discarding any root.

It should further be mentioned that the Newton-Test also integrates a so-called Boundary-Test, which, by default, always checks whether one of the two intervals $(a, a+w(I)/N_I)$ or $(b - w(I)/N_I, b)$ contains all roots that are contained in I. Again, for this, the 01-Test is applied to $(a + w(I)/N_I, b)$ and $(a, b - w(I)/N_I)$, respectively; see Algorithm 4 and [19, Sec. 3.2] for more details.

In [19], the bit complexity bit complexity as well as the bounds on the number of iterations and the precision demand of ANewDsc are stated in terms of the degree of P and values that exclusively depend on the roots z_i of the polynomial, such as the product of the absolute values of all roots beyond the unit disk or the product of the pairwise distances between any two roots. Those bounds are both more adaptive to the intrinsic complexity of the problem and apply for inputs with approximable coefficients. For brevity, we only restrict to the benchmark problem here: The length of a sequence of intervals I_j with invariant $\operatorname{var}(P, I_j)$ is now upper bounded by $\tilde{O}(\log(n\tau))$ compared to $\tilde{O}(n\tau)$ for the classical Descartes method. This is due to the fact that the Newton-Test succeeds and achieves quadratic convergence for all but $\tilde{O}(\log(n\tau))$ intervals. As a consequence, the overall size of the subdivision tree is bounded by $O(v_{\mathcal{I}} \cdot \log(n\tau)) = O(n \log(n\tau))$, which is near-optimal; see also [19, Theorems 27–29]. The bit complexity of the algorithm is bounded by $\tilde{O}(n^3 + n^2\tau)$, which is by three magnitudes better than the bound for the Descartes method (also see Table 1) and comparable to the best bound known [12, 7] for the benchmark problem as achieved by an algorithm based on Pan's near-optimal method [14] for approximate polynomial factorization. The bound is obtained by an amortized analysis of the cost at each node in the subdivision tree. The cost for processing a certain interval I is related to the maximum of all products $\max_{z_i} \sigma_P(z_i) \cdot |P'(z_i)|$, where the z_i's range over all roots in the one-circle region of I. In the worst-case, the cost at a node is of size $\tilde{O}(n^2\tau)$, whereas, in average, it is of size $\tilde{O}(n(n + \tau))$. The precision demand is upper bounded by $\tilde{O}(n\tau)$ in the worst case and of size $\tilde{O}(n + \tau)$ in average.

[7]Algorithm 3 only computes some rational value $\tilde{k}$. Under the assumption that a cluster $\mathcal{C}$ as above exists, we have $k \approx \tilde{k}$ and, in particular, k equals the integer that is closest to $\tilde{k}$.

Algorithm 3: Newton-Test

INPUT: A polynomial P as in (1), an interval $I = (a, b)$, and an $N_I \in \mathbb{N}$ of the form $N_I = 2^{2^l}$ with $l \in \mathbb{N}_{\geq 1}$.

OUTPUT: FALSE or an interval $I' \subset I$, with $\frac{N_I w(I')}{w(I)} \in [\frac{1}{8}, 1]$, that contains all roots of P in I.

- For $j \in \{1, 2, 3\}$, let $\xi_j := a + \frac{j}{4} \cdot w(I)$, compute admissible points ξ_j^* for ξ_j and the Newton correction terms $v_j := P(\xi_j^*)/P'(\xi_j^*)$.
- For all pairs $i, j \in \{1, 2, 3\}$ with $i < j$:
  - ▷ Compute approximations $\tilde{\lambda}_{i,j}$ of $\lambda_{i,j} := \xi_i^* + \tilde{k} \cdot v_i$, where $\tilde{k} := (\xi_j^* - \xi_i^*)/(v_i - v_j)$, with $|\tilde{\lambda}_{i,j} - \lambda_{i,j}| \leq 1/32N_I$.
  - ▷ If $\tilde{\lambda}_{i,j} \notin [a, b]$, discard (i, j). Otherwise, define $\ell_{i,j} := \lfloor(\tilde{\lambda}_{i,j} - a) \cdot 4N_I/w(I)\rfloor \in \{0, \ldots, 4N_I\}$, $a_{i,j} := a + \max\{0, \ell_{i,j} - 1\} \cdot w(I)/4N_I$, and $b_{i,j} := a + \min\{4N_I, \ell_{i,j} + 2\} \cdot w(I)/4N_I$. If $a_{i,j} = a$, set $a_{i,j}^* := a$, and if $b_{i,j} = b$, set $b_{i,j}^* := b$. Otherwise, compute admissible points $a_{i,j}^*$ and $b_{i,j}^*$ for $a_{i,j}$ and $b_{i,j}$.
  - ▷ If the 01-Test returns 0 for both intervals $(a, a_{i,j}^*)$ and $(b_{i,j}^*, b)$, return $I' = (a_{i,j}^*, b_{i,j}^*)$. Otherwise, discard the pair (i, j).
- *Boundary test:* If all pairs have been discarded, compute admissible points m_ℓ^* and m_r^* for $m_\ell := a + w(I)/2N_I$ and $m_r := b - w(I)/2N_I$.
  - ▷ If the 01-Test yields 0 for (m_ℓ^*, b), return (a, m_ℓ^*).
  - ▷ If the 01-Test yields 0 for (a, m_r^*), return (m_r^*, b).
  - ▷ Otherwise, return FALSE.

This is a simplified version of Newton- and Boundary-Test from [19]. For the sake of a concise presentation, some technical details (e.g. concerning the precision management) are omitted.

3. IMPLEMENTING ANewDsc INSIDE RS

The RS library contains a generic framework [16] that allows to instantiate several variants of the Descartes method. The choices include several bisection variants as well as continued fraction-based subdivision. The default configuration, which we will denote as "RS" throughout the following considerations, achieves its high efficiency by a careful low-level implementation of the bottleneck subroutines as well as a few sophisticated and—at that time—innovative design choices.

RS uses a hybrid arithmetic strategy. Starting with a low precision (of 63 bits), all predicates are evaluated in interval arithmetic using MPFI [15]. Whenever a predicate cannot be conclusively decided within the working precision, the computation is interrupted and later resumed with a higher precision. When it is conceivable that exact arithmetic is less costly than interval arithmetic at high precision, a heuristic can trigger exact computation; this facilitates further optimizations like (virtual) deflation of exact dyadic roots.

Algorithm 4: ANEWDSC

INPUT: A polynomial P as in (1) and an interval $\mathcal{I}$.

REPORTS: Disjoint isolating intervals for all roots of P in $\mathcal{I}$.

- Initialize the list of active intervals to $\mathcal{A} := \{(\mathcal{I}, 4)\}$.
- While $\mathcal{A} \neq \emptyset$:
  - ▷ Remove an arbitrary (I, N_I) with $I = (a, b)$ from $\mathcal{A}$.
  - ▷ If the 01-Test on I returns 0, discard I and continue.
  - ▷ If the 01-Test on I returns 1, report I and continue.
  - ▷ Otherwise: *Quadratic (or Newton) step*
    If the Newton-Test on P and (I, N_I) returns an interval I', add (I', N_I^2) to $\mathcal{A}$ and continue.
  - ▷ Otherwise: *Linear (or bisection) step*
    Compute an admissible point m^* for $m(I)$ and add $(I', N_{I'})$ and $(I'', N_{I''})$ to $\mathcal{A}$, where $I' = (a, m^*)$, $I'' = (m^*, b)$, and $N_{I'} := N_{I''} := \max(4, \sqrt{N_I})$.

The realization of the sign variation test in RS is adapted to this interval setting: While we work with exact polynomials $f = \sum f_i x^i$ in theory, the computations are executed on coefficient-wise interval approximations $[f] = \sum [f]_i x^i$ of f such that $f_i \in [f]_i$ for all i. In particular, the value of $\operatorname{var}(f)$ is replaced by a (super-)set $\operatorname{var}([f]) = \{v^-, \ldots, v^+\}$ of possible sign variations for the family of polynomials in $[f]$, that is, $\operatorname{var}(g) \in \operatorname{var}([f])$ for all $g \in [f]$. In this model, a sign variation test for a polynomial $[f]$ succeeds if and only if $\operatorname{var}([f]) = \{0\}$, $\operatorname{var}([f]) = \{1\}$, or $0, 1 \notin \operatorname{var}([f])$. Otherwise, the accuracy is not sufficient to decide the branching strategy for the current interval, and the precision is increased. We keep this classical test as a filter in ANEWDSC; if it does not succeed, we call the full 01-Test, which again uses the interval sign variation computation as a primitive.

Another crucial difference between RS and the previous variants of the Descartes method is the traversal of the subdivision tree. In Collins' and Akritas' [2] formulation, the subdivision tree is explored in a depth-first search strategy. This traversal allows to obtain some of the intermediate polynomials with comparatively little computational effort from previous results, but comes at the expense of storing a potentially very long list of active nodes. On the other hand, Krandick's variant [8] with breadth-first traversal is more memory-efficient, but requires more expensive arithmetic operations; see [16, Sec. 3]. The trade-off which proved optimal for RS was a depth-first search traversal in a near-constant-memory variant, oblivious of intermediate results. To keep the arithmetic cost of the algorithm close to the optimum for bisection methods, RS uses specifically tailored subroutines for reconstructing the discarded intermediate polynomials. They are supplemented by a custom garbage collector that ensures that only an insignificant amount of time is spent for memory management. For details of those design choices, we refer to the original description of RS [16, Sec. 4].

RS is a promising basis for an implementation of ANEWDSC due to its high performance as a general-purpose solver and the availability in Maple. Also, the extensive use of interval arithmetic offers the flexibility to design a numerical root solver for polynomials with irrational coefficients that can be approximated arbitrarily well. However, to combine the theoretical improvements of the new algorithm with the long-evolved insights for a practical realization, modifications are required on both ends. In this section, we will describe the most crucial design decisions in this light.

3.1 Changes over the theoretical ANEWDSC

Random sampling of pseudo-admissible points.

A tight analysis of the theoretical worst-case bit complexity of any variant of the Descartes method heavily relies on asymptotically fast algorithms for polynomial arithmetic. However, in practice, many asymptotically fast methods are only effective for inputs larger than a threshold that is well beyond what can realistically be handled with state-of-the-art solvers. Until now, careful implementations of the naive algorithms are more efficient except for artificial counterexamples.

The most prominent places where such tools are used in ANEWDSC are the basis transformations from (1) to (2) (so-called *Taylor shifts*) and the approximate multipoint evaluations within the admissible point selections. With the advanced methods, both subroutines require only a near-linear number of arithmetic operations in the coefficient ring, compared to quadratically many for naive approaches. The Taylor shifts are intrinsic to any Descartes method (although we will discuss a partial remedy for some situations at the end of Section 3.2). But the multipoint evaluations in the "Admissible Point" routine can be avoided: In our initial description of ANEWDSC, we choose an admissible point $m^* \in \mathbf{m} := m[\epsilon; n]$ such that $|P(m^*)| \geq \frac{1}{4} \cdot \max_{m_i \in \mathbf{m}} |P(m_i)|$. For our implementation, we propose to consider the multipoint $\mathbf{M} := m[\frac{\epsilon}{2^\lambda}; n \cdot 2^\lambda]$ instead, which spans the same range as $\mathbf{m}$ (i.e. the extremal points in $\mathbf{m}$ and $\mathbf{M}$ define the same interval $[m - \lceil \frac{n}{2} \rceil \epsilon, m + \lceil \frac{n}{2} \rceil \epsilon])$ but contains 2^λ times as many points as $\mathbf{m}$. Here, λ is a positive integer of size $O(\log n)$. However, instead of choosing an admissible point in $\mathbf{M}$ we choose a so-called *pseudo-admissible point*, where P is only required to take an absolute value that is related to the current working precision. For this, we randomly sample a point m_j from $\mathbf{M}$ and compute an approximation $\tilde{v}_j$ of $v_j = P(m_j)$ (via interval arithmetic) with $|\tilde{v}_j - v_j| < 2^{-\rho}$. If $|\tilde{v}_j| > 2^{-\rho+2}$, we keep m_j. Otherwise, we double the precision ρ and choose a new sample point; see also Algorithm 5.

Algorithm 5: Find Pseudo-Admissible Point

INPUT: A polynomial $P(x)$ as in (1) and a multipoint $\mathbf{M} := m[\frac{\epsilon}{2^\lambda}; 2^\lambda n]$ with $\lambda \in \mathbb{N}_{\geq 2}$ and $\lambda = O(\log n)$.

OUTPUT: A point $m' \in \mathbf{M}$ with value $P(m') \neq 0$.

- For $\rho = 63, 127, 255, \ldots$:
  - ▷ Pick a random m_j among the points in $\mathbf{M}$.
  - ▷ Compute an approximation $\tilde{v}_j$ of $v_j = P(m_j)$ with $|\tilde{v}_j - v_j| < 2^{-\rho}$ (using interval arithmetic).
  - ▷ If $|\tilde{v}'| > 2^{-\rho+2}$, return $m' := m_j$.

The following lemma guarantees that, with high probability, we choose a point $m' \in \mathbf{M}$ for which $|P(m')|$ is not much smaller than $\max_{m_i \in \mathbf{m}} |P(m_i)|$.

LEMMA 1. *Algorithm 5 returns a point* $m' \in \mathbf{M}$ *such that*

$$\log |P(m')| = 2^k \cdot O(n \log n + \log \max(1, (\max_{m_i \in \mathbf{m}} |P(m_i)|)^{-1}))$$

with probability $1 - 2^{-k\lambda} \geq 1 - 2^{-k}$.

PROOF. Let $\mathbf{M}^* \subset \mathbf{M}$ denote the subset consisting of all points in $\mathbf{M}$ whose distance to all roots of P is at least $\epsilon \cdot 2^{-\lambda}$. Let $\bar{m} \in \mathbf{m}$ be a point with $|P(\bar{m})| = \max_{m_i \in \mathbf{m}} |P(m_i)|$, and define $\rho_0 := \lceil \log \max(1, |P(\bar{m})|^{-1}) \rceil$. For any complex root z of P and any point $m_j \in \mathbf{M}^*$, we have $\frac{|\bar{m} - z|}{|m_j - z|} > \frac{1}{1 + n 2^\lambda} > 2^{-\lambda - 1 - \log n}$ and, thus, $\frac{|P(m_j)|}{|P(\bar{m})|} > 2^{-n(\lambda + 1 + \log n)}$.

Now suppose that, in a certain iteration of Algorithm 5, we have $\rho \geq \rho_0 + n(\lambda + 1 + \log n) + 2$. Then, it holds that $2^{-\rho+2} < |P(m_j)|$ for all $m_j \in \mathbf{M}^*$; hence, the algorithm terminates if we pick such an m_j. Since $\mathbf{M}^*$ contains at least $2^\lambda(n+1) - 2n$ points, the probability of choosing a point from $\mathbf{M}^*$ is at least $1 - 2^{-(\lambda-1)}$. Hence, with probability $1 - 2^{-k(\lambda-1)}$, we terminate with a ρ of size $2^k \cdot O(n \log n + \log \max(1, (\max_{m_i \in \mathbf{m}} |P(m_i)|)^{-1}))$. □

Our analysis shows that, in expectation, there might be an increase in precision by an additive term of size $O(n \log n)$ when choosing a pseudo-admissible point instead of an admissible point; in practice, we observe that the increase in precision is entirely negligible. We further remark that the complexity bounds as derived in [19] are not affected, since a term of size $\tilde{O}(n)$ already appears in the bound on the precision demand of the 01-Test. Yet, our implementation only models the theoretical result in a Las-Vegas setting due to the random choice of a pseudo-admissible point.

Heuristics to delay invocations of the Newton step.

The asymptotic cost of the calls to the Newton-Test is dominated by the Taylor shift which is part of the sign-variation test for any interval. However, in practice there is a noticeable impact of unsuccessful Newton-Tests on the performance due to the expensive 01-Tests for the siblings $(a, a^*_{i,j})$ and $(b^*_{i,j}, b)$ of the candidate intervals $(a^*_{i,j}, b^*_{i,j})$. Thus, we strive for calling the Newton-Test only if it will succeed with high likelihood; vice versa, in the generic situation of well-distributed roots without any distinguished root clusters, as little computation time as possible should be wasted.

We say that a linear step on an interval I to I' and I'' leads to a *proper split* if $\operatorname{var}(P, I')$ and $\operatorname{var}(P, I'')$ are both non-zero. In this case, Obreshkoff's One-circle theorem [4, 13] asserts that there is at least one root in the neighborhood of I'' that is not part of a potential cluster within I', and the symmetric argument holds for I''. There are two explanations for such a situation: If the goal on the convergence speed was too optimistic (that is, the value of N_I was set too high), the candidate interval in the Newton-Test might not comprise the entire cluster of roots. In this case, a success of the Newton step on I' and I'' with a coarser resolution $N_{I'} = N_{I''} = \sqrt{N_I}$ is not entirely unlikely. However, if $N_I = 4$ was already at the minimum, the roots near I' and I'' are well-separated compared to the resolution N_I, and an immediate success of the Newton-Test would be an unexpected artifact.

We installed a heuristic to distinguish those situations and inhibit Newton-Tests in the latter case. For each node I in the subdivision tree, we keep track of the distance to its closest ancestor J with $N_J = 4$ that lead to a proper split. If this distance is smaller than $\log n$, we immediately process I with bisection[8] and keep $N_I = 4$. On intervals with well-separated roots where we never achieve nor profit from quadratic convergence, this strategy renders it likely that there is never even an attempt to call a Newton-Test, and the overhead of ANEWDSC compared to the variant ADSC without the Newton-Test is almost zero. On the other hand, the size of the subdivision tree is increased by at most a factor of size $O(\log n)$, and thus stays soft-linear in n and polylogarithmic in τ in the worst case.

[8]In the terminology of [19], *proper splits* occur on a subset of the *special nodes* of the subdivision tree, and we allow paths of $\lceil \log n \rceil$ many *ordinary nodes* before further Newton-Tests.

3.2 Changes over the classical RS

Full caching instead of constant-memory version.

The default instantiations of RS use a near-constant-memory strategy. None of the intermediate local polynomials are cached, but are computed from the previously considered node. In general, this means that larger round-off errors are accumulated, and expensive recomputation from scratch is potentially required more often. Yet, performance comparisons show a clear benefit of this approach due to the drastically reduced costs for memory management and RS' sophisticated way of performing incremental computations between adjacent nodes in the subdivision tree [16, Sec. 4].

However, the fast transformations rely on certain structural properties of the subdivision tree: in a pure bisection algorithm, all emerging intervals are of the form $(\frac{c}{2^e}, \frac{c+1}{2^e})$ for some integers c and e. In this setting and with the strong specification of the traversal order of the tree, a good portion of the arithmetic operations for Taylor shifts can be achieved by cheap bitshift and addition operations. In contrast, a general Taylor shift requires noticeably more expensive multiplications of arbitrary precision interval values.

These relations between the intervals are lost when Newton steps are performed or the canonical dyadic subdivision points need to be replaced by (pseudo-)admissible points. Furthermore, optimizations such as the delayed Newton calls are incompatible with strategies that keep only one interval in memory at a time, because the behavior of the algorithm on some interval is no longer independent of the neighborhood: whether a quadratic convergence step is pursued becomes conditional on the outcome of the 01-Test on its sibling.

Fortunately, using the Newton technique, long chains of intervals with a unique descendant in the bisection tree are compressed to only logarithmic height, thus shrinking the entire tree by an order of magnitude in the worst-case and even two orders of magnitude for some special instances (e.g. sparse polynomials with clustered roots such as Mignotte polynomials). In this light, the impact of the constant-memory strategy is much less pronounced, and it is advisable to switch back to the naive approach of caching all intermediate results. We stress that, without the Newton iteration, the memory consumption in a depth-first traversal would be prohibitive for particular examples with strongly clustered, ill-separated roots such as Mignotte polynomials.

Degree truncation through partial Taylor shifts.

We can consider any univariate polynomial $P(x)$ as a function $P(x) = p_n \cdot \prod_{j=1}^{n}(x - z_j)$ in its (not necessarily distinct) complex roots z_j. When the domain of interest is restricted to a small region in the complex plane, say, a disk $D \subset \mathbb{C}$, the relative influence of each root z_j on P scales with the distance of z_j to the points $x \in D$. If there are only $k \ll n$ roots in D and all other roots are well-separated from D, the distance to the remote roots is almost stable for all $x \in D$, and $P|_D$ is dominated by the roots in D.

In this situation, the local behavior of P is captured in its partial Taylor expansion around a point within D up to the k-th term. Hence, an approximation of P by its truncated Taylor expansion might suffice for computing isolating intervals for the real roots. We consider this approach whenever a Newton step succeeds and suggests the existence of a well-separated cluster of $k \ll n$ roots around an interval I. We remark that the multiplicity guess $k := \operatorname{round}(\tilde{k})$ is already computed within the Newton-Test. To ensure correctness, we conservatively take into account the truncation error as the interval evaluation of the Lagrangian remainder term.

More precisely, whenever the inclusion-exclusion-predicates of ANewDsc call for sign variation tests on some P_I, we work on an approximation for the intermediate polynomial $Q_I := \sum_{i=0}^{n} q_{I,i}x^i := P(a+(b-a)x)$ on $I=(a,b)$,

$$\tilde{Q}_I(x) = \sum_{i=0}^{k-1} q_{I,i}x^i + [r]_{I,k}x^k, \quad [r]_{I,k} \supset \frac{P^{(k)}(I)}{k!},$$

where the coefficient $[r]_{I,k}$ of the Lagrangian remainder is evaluated on the entire interval I in conservative interval arithmetic. The root exclusion test on the truncated polynomial remains almost identical; however, we modify the certificate for inclusion of a single root.

LEMMA 2. *Let P be a polynomial as in (1) and $I=(a,b)$ and $\tilde{Q}_I$ be as above. Define $\tilde{G}_I := (x+1)^k\ \tilde{Q}_I((x+1)^{-1})$ and $\tilde{H}_I := (x+1)^{k-1}\ \tilde{Q}_I'((x+1)^{-1})$.*

1. *If $\tilde{v}_I := \operatorname{var}(\tilde{G}_I) = \{0\}$, then P has no root in I.*[9]
2. *If $\tilde{v}_I = \{1\}$ and, additionally, $\tilde{v}_I' := \operatorname{var}(\tilde{H}_I) = \{0\}$, then P has exactly one simple real root in I.*

PROOF. We consider the polynomials $\tilde{Q}_I$, $\tilde{G}_I$ and $\tilde{H}_I$ simultaneously as polynomials with interval coefficients and as the set of exact polynomials with coefficients contained in the intervals. Assume that $\tilde{v}_I = 0$, but P has a root $\xi = a + \lambda(b-a) \in I$. By the Lagrange representation of the truncation error in Taylor's theorem, there exists a $\xi \in I$ such that the polynomial $F_I(x) := \sum_{i=0}^{k-1} q_{I,i}x^i + \frac{P^{(k)}(\xi)}{k!}x^k$ of degree k has a root at λ. Hence, Descartes' Rule of Signs asserts $\operatorname{var}((x+1)^k F_I((x+1)^{-1})) > 0$. Since $F_I \in \tilde{Q}_I$, it follows that $(x+1)^k F_I((x+1)^{-1}) \in \tilde{G}_I$ because the transformations in interval arithmetic overestimate the possible values. This contradicts the assumption that $\tilde{v}_I = 0$.

For the second part, an analogous argument on the derivative shows that P is strictly increasing or strictly decreasing on I if $\tilde{v}' = \{0\}$. Since $\tilde{v}_I = \{1\}$, we know that P takes values of different sign at the endpoints of I; hence, P has exactly one root in I. □

If a 01-Test in the processing of a node is unsuccessful, we usually double the working precision. However, if the local polynomials are only partial Taylor expansions, the source of the loss in accuracy may also stem from the truncation. Hence, before increasing the working precision, we gradually double the multiplicity guess k until we eventually compute the full polynomial. This approach guarantees that, in the worst case, after $\log n$ steps the heuristic falls back to the theoretical model. Hence, even if the heuristic is unsuccessful, the complexity increases at most by a factor of $\log n$.

We observe that partial Taylor shifts give a tremendous speedup for polynomials with tight clusters of low multiplicity. In such situations, we can consider the technique as a partial substitute for the current deficiency of asymptotically fast Taylor shifts. For instances with clusters consisting of constantly many roots, the expected speedup is linear in n: if the heuristic applies, the local polynomials on each active region in the subdivision tree have to computed up to only constantly many coefficients of the Taylor series. This prediction is accurately reflected in the benchmarks.

[9]Recall that var(·), called on an interval polynomial, returns a (super-)set of the possible numbers of sign variations; see the remarks about the use of interval arithmetic in RS in Section 3.

4. EXPERIMENTS

We present and discuss a short excerpt of our extensive benchmark suite; the entire collection is available online at http://anewdsc.mpi-inf.mpg.de/. The objective is to illustrate that the integration of ANewDsc into RS entails very small overheads for instances with well-distributed roots and shallow subdivision trees, but huge performance gains in challenging situations with clustered roots.

The classical RS serves as a baseline in a configuration similar to the one used in Maple, but without some crucial optimizations to improve comparability. In particular, we disabled the hardware floating-point phase, which is not yet supported for ANewDsc, as well as the heuristic for switching to exact arithmetic that can improve performance, but destroys the guarantees on the expected precision demand. Besides the full-fledged ANewDsc (denoted as AND in the tables), we also list the intermediate variant ADsc. It includes subdivision on pseudo-admissible points and full caching, but neither Newton iterations nor degree truncation.

We compare to three well-established competitors:

MPSolve (named MPS in the tables) is the leading complex root solver. It is known to keep up with the most efficient real root isolators even though it solves a more general problem. Given our more modest goals, we restrict the region of interest to the real line, and call MPSolve in its latest version 3.1.5 with `unisolve -au -Gi -SR -Dr -Of -j1 -o1048576`.

CF denotes the *continued fraction*-based variant of the Descartes method available in *Mathematica* 10. We bypass the high-level interface of the computer algebra system via `System'Private'RealRoots` to eliminate the effect of preprocessing stages that are applied by the usual `RootIntervals` call (e.g. the detection and special handling of sparse polynomials or simplifications for even or odd polynomials).

Finally, we compare against Carl Witty's variant of Eigenwillig's bitstream Descartes method in Bernstein basis [5], which constitutes the default real root isolator in the *Sage* 7.0 open-source computer algebra system. We invoke the algorithm in the optimized variant for 64-bit architectures with `real_roots (f, skip_squarefree=True, wordsize=64)`.

All instances are passed as dense integer polynomials, filtered in a preprocessing stage to factor out side effects of optimizations unrelated to the solver. It involves the trivial algebraic simplification of even and odd polynomials, verification of square-freeness and reduction to the primitive part. The values in the tables are runtimes in seconds, measured on a single run on the same machine. Degree and coefficient bitsize are denoted by n and τ.

Polynomials of Mignotte type are classical benchmark instances. Their ill-separated pair of roots at approximately $2^{-\tau/2} \pm 2^{-n\tau/2}$ forces a huge subdivision depth in bisection approaches. This behavior is mitigated by the quadratic convergence in ANewDsc: The subdivision tree size shrinks from approximately 33500 nodes for RS and ADsc to a mere 47 for ANewDsc for $(n,\tau) = (129, 512)$, and even an instance with $\tau = 2^{16}$ leads to a tree with only 65 nodes. For such instances, CF presumably exhibits an almost optimal subdivision tree due to the rational center of the cluster; however, the performance is spoiled by the use of exact arithmetic. The class of nested Mignotte polynomials, shown around an irrational center in Table 3, shows the robustness of ANewDsc both to the higher multiplicity 20 and the irrational center of the cluster.

n	τ	MPS	CF	Sage	RS	ADsc	AND
257	14	0.7	0.1	1.6	7.6	7.7	0.1
513	14	2.9	0.2	2.4	87.6	89.1	0.2
1025	14	13.8	1.1	4.8	>600	>600	0.7
2049	14	78.5	7.2	12.8			2.9
4097	14	486.3	67.6	85.8			11.2
8193	14	>600	224.3	>600			43.2
16385	14		>600				188.1
129	128	1.2	0.3	0.5	26.2	25.1	0.1
129	512	5.9	3.8	3.9	378.5	293.8	0.4
129	2048	43.4	78.4	>600	>600	>600	3.3
129	8192	274.7	>600				20.8
129	32768	>600					96.8
129	131072						503.0

Table 2: Mignotte: $x^n - ((2^{\tau/2} - 1)x - 1)^2$

n	τ	MPS	CF	Sage	RS	ADsc	AND
260	140	2.7	1.0	1.9	1.6	1.7	0.4
516	140	9.5	21.6	3.3	18.0	18.0	0.8
1028	140	67.8	565.0	>600	230.3	232.4	7.1
2052	140	283.6	>600		>600	>600	13.1
4100	140	>600					88.4
8196	140						394.0
260	160	3.1	1.4	0.3	2.2	2.3	0.9
260	640	5.8	14.9	*call*	20.8	19.2	0.9
260	2560	33.7	222.6	*stack*	301.2	254.0	3.7
260	10240	248.0	>600	*over-*	>600	>600	31.4
260	40960	>600		*flow*			341.2

Table 3: nested Mignotte: $\prod_{i=1}^{4} (x^{n/4} - ((2^{\tau/8} - 1)x^2 - 1)^{2i})$

n	τ	MPS	CF	Sage	RS	ADsc	AND
1024	1024	2.5	0.3	4.1	0.6	0.6	0.5
2048	1024	9.8	0.9	8.4	1.6	1.7	1.7
4096	1024	37.5	2.7	29.1	3.8	3.7	3.5
8192	1024	159.4	22.1	183.5	36.0	36.3	36.5
16384	1024	578.9	376.6	>600	275.1	280.9	279.0

Table 4: dense with uniformly random coefficients in $(-2^\tau, 2^\tau) \cap \mathbb{Z}$

n	τ	MPS	CF	Sage	RS	ADsc	AND
256	506	4.7	34.1	1.6	18.2	19.1	1.1
512	762	25.9	456.9	3.7	107.7	110.4	3.0
1024	1274	207.5	>600	22.5	>600	>600	23.6
2048	2296	>600		>600			132.2
4096	4343						596.6

Table 5: clustered: $f^2 - 1$ for $f = \sum_i a_i \binom{n}{i}^{1/2} x^i / \sqrt{i+1}$ with a_i drawn from a normal Gaussian distribution, rounded to $\mathbb{Z}[x]$

Random polynomials have a low number ($\Theta(\log n)$) of well-separated real roots; they require only low precision for the isolation and induce flat subdivision trees. Hence, we can expect no gain from the improvements in ANewDsc. On the other hand, the experiments confirm that the enhancements incur almost no additional cost. We observe similar overheads of low constant factors compared to RS on other classes of polynomials with well-distributed roots, such as Wilkinson polynomials with evenly spaced real roots, different classes of orthogonal polynomials, or resultants of random bivariate polynomials that arise in projection-based polynomial system solving and the topology analysis of real algebraic curves.

Finally, polynomials with normal Gaussian-distributed coefficients have, in expectation, significantly more real roots ($\Theta(\sqrt{n})$). By squaring and perturbing such inputs, we construct benchmark instances with many clusters of multiplicity two. We find that ANewDsc quickly detects the clusters, succeeds in the Newton steps, and computes the appropriate number of terms in the partial Taylor shifts.

The benchmarks are performed on polynomials with exact integer coefficients. Nevertheless, we emphasize that ANewDsc can process inputs with arbitrary approximable, possibly irrational coefficients. We observe that the performance is unaffected if, for example, the coefficients of the random instances (Tables 4 and 5) are drawn from a continuous distribution, or the coefficients of the Mignotte-like polynomials are irrational numbers of comparable magnitude.

Acknowledgments. We thank Maplesoft for their support in the development of RS, Leonardo Robol (Katholieke Universiteit Leuven) for his help and support on running the development version of MPSolve and Adam Strzebonski (Wolfram Research) for his instructions on how to control the behavior of Mathematica's `RootIntervals` function.

5. REFERENCES

[1] G. E. Collins. Continued fraction real root isolation using the Hong bound. *JSC*, 2014.

[2] G. E. Collins & A. G. Akritas. Polynomial real root isolation using Descartes' Rule of Signs. In *SYMSAC*, pp. 272–275, 1976.

[3] Z. Du, V. Sharma & C. K. Yap. Amortized Bounds for Root Isolation via Sturm Sequences. In *SNC*, pp. 113–129, 2007.

[4] A. Eigenwillig. *Real Root Isolation for Exact and Approximate Polynomials Using Descartes' Rule of Signs.* PhD thesis, Saarland University, 2008.

[5] A. Eigenwillig et al. A Descartes algorithm for polynomials with bit-stream coefficients. In *CASC*, pp. 138–149, 2005.

[6] A. Eigenwillig, V. Sharma & C. K. Yap. Almost tight complexity bounds for the Descartes method. In *ISSAC*, pp. 151–158, 2006.

[7] I. Z. Emiris, V. Y. Pan & E. P. Tsigaridas. Algebraic algorithms. In *Computing Handbook: Computer Science and Software Engineering*, ch. 10, pp. 1–30. CRC, 3rd ed., 2014.

[8] J. R. Johnson & W. Krandick. Polynomial real root isolation using approximate arithmetic. In *ISSAC*, pp. 225–232, 1997.

[9] A. Kobel & M. Sagraloff. On the complexity of computing with planar algebraic curves. *J. Compl.*, 31(2):206–236, 2015.

[10] W. Krandick. Isolierung reeller Nullstellen von Polynomen. In J. Herzberger, editor, *Wissenschaftliches Rechnen*, pp. 105–154. Akademie Verlag, Berlin, 1995.

[11] K. Mehlhorn & M. Sagraloff. A deterministic Descartes algorithm for real polynomials. *JSC*, 46(1):70–90, 2011.

[12] K. Mehlhorn, M. Sagraloff & P. Wang. From approximate factorization to root isolation with application to cylindrical algebraic decomposition. *JSC*, 66:34–69, 2015.

[13] N. Obreshkoff. *Zeros of Polynomials.* Marina Drinov, Sofia, 2003. Translation of the Bulgarian original.

[14] V. Y. Pan. Univariate polynomials: Nearly optimal algorithms for numerical factorization and root-finding. *JSC*, 33(5):701–733, 2002.

[15] N. Revol & F. Rouillier. Motivations for an arbitrary precision interval arithmetic and the MPFI library. *Reliable Computing*, 11(4):275–290, 2005.

[16] F. Rouillier & P. Zimmermann. Efficient isolation of [a] polynomial's real roots. *JCAM*, 162:33–50, 2004.

[17] M. Sagraloff. When Newton meets Descartes: A simple and fast algorithm to isolate the real roots of a polynomial. In *ISSAC*, pp. 297–304, 2012.

[18] M. Sagraloff. On the complexity of the Descartes method when using approximate arithmetic. *JSC*, 65(0):79–110, 2014.

[19] M. Sagraloff & K. Mehlhorn. Computing real roots of real polynomials. *JSC*, 73:46–86, 2016.

[20] E. P. Tsigaridas. Improved bounds for the CF algorithm. *TCS*, 479:120–126, 2013.

[21] C. K. Yap & M. Sagraloff. A simple but exact and efficient algorithm for complex root isolation. In *ISSAC*, pp. 353–360, 2011.

Equivariant Gröbner Bases of Symmetric Toric Ideals

Robert Krone
Queen's University, Kingston, Ontario.
rk71@queensu.ca

ABSTRACT

It has been shown previously that a large class of monomial maps equivariant under the action of an infinite symmetric group have finitely generated kernels up to the symmetric action. We prove that these symmetric toric ideals also have finite Gröbner bases up to symmetry for certain monomial orders. An algorithm is presented for computing equivariant Gröbner bases that terminates whenever a finite basis exists, improving on previous algorithms that only guaranteed termination in rings Noetherian up to symmetry. This algorithm can be used to compute equivariant Gröbner bases of the above toric ideals, given the monomial map.

1. INTRODUCTION

Kernels of monomial maps between polynomial rings (i.e. toric ideals) can be used to describe certain statistical models [DS+98]. Often these maps coming from statistics have symmetry under the action of large symmetric groups, which has led to the study of toric ideals invariant under $\mathfrak{S}_\infty$-action. In various cases of interest these symmetric toric ideals were proved to be generated by the orbits of a finite number of binomials, even as they live in non-Noetherian rings e.g. [AT05][HS12].

A negative result [DO06] demonstrated monomial maps with kernels not finitely generated up to symmetry. However in the case that the target ring has variables with at most one index running to infinity, [DEKL15] proved finite generation up to symmetry of the kernel always holds, generalizing the previous finite generation results. This work left open many computational questions around efficiently finding generating sets up to symmetry of these ideal. In some simple cases [KKL14] gave formulas for small generating sets.

The approach we take in this paper to computing generators is through Gröbner bases. We prove that the symmetric toric ideals considered in [DEKL15] also have finite equivariant Gröbner bases, at least for specifically chosen monomial orders. The question of whether finite Gröbner bases exist for all appropriate orders remains open. Additionally we present an algorithm for computing equivariant Gröbner bases that has guaranteed termination as long as a finite Gröbner basis exists. Although this algorithm concept has been used previously, it has not appeared before in the literature. Previously presented algorithms guaranteed termination only in rings that are Noetherian up to symmetry, while many of the rings we work with fail this criterion. This newly presented algorithm can compute a Gröbner basis of a symmetric toric ideal, given a description of the monomial map that defines it.

ISSAC '16, July 19-22, 2016, Waterloo, ON, Canada

DOI: http://dx.doi.org/10.1145/2930889.2930902

2. PRELIMINARIES

Let R be a graded commutative K-algebra equipped with a left action of monoid Π. We mainly consider the case where R has the structure of a monoid algebra, that is for some abelian monoid M, the elements of R consist of formal sums of elements of M with coefficients in K. A common example of a graded monoid algebra is a polynomial ring $R = K[X]$ with variables from the set X each with positive degree. In this case M is the free abelian monoid generated by X, which we will denote by $[X]$. To make notation consistent with the polynomial case, we will denote the monoid algebra of M over K by KM. We will also refer to elements of M as "monomials" in analogy to the polynomial case. Additionally the action of Π on $R = KM$ will typically be induced by a Π-action on M by monoid homomorphisms.

Our particular focus in this paper is when Π is $\mathfrak{S}_\infty$ or certain related monoids. Here $\mathfrak{S}_\infty$ will be defined as the group of all permutations of $\mathbb{N}$ that fix all but a finite number of elements, $\mathfrak{S}_\infty := \bigcup_n \mathfrak{S}_n$.

Example 2.1. Let $R = K[x_1, x_2, x_3, \ldots]$ with $\mathfrak{S}_\infty$ acting on R by permuting the variables, so that $\sigma x_i = x_{\sigma(i)}$.

Definition 2.2. An ideal $I \subseteq R$ is a Π-*invariant ideal* if $\sigma I \subseteq I$ for all $\sigma \in \Pi$.

The ring R is both an R-module and a Π-module, and there is a ring $R * \Pi$ which captures both of these actions, and which will be referred to as the *twisted monoid ring* of Π with coefficients in R. The elements of $R * \Pi$ are of the form $\sum_{\sigma \in \Pi} f_\sigma \cdot \sigma$ with each $f_\sigma \in R$ and only a finite number non-zero. The additive structure is the same as the usual monoid ring, but multiplication is "twisted" in that

$$(f \cdot \sigma)(g \cdot \tau) = f\sigma(g) \cdot \sigma\tau$$

where $\sigma(g)$ denotes the element of R obtained by acting on g by σ.

R is a $R * \Pi$-module, and the definition of Π-invariant ideals can be restated as $R * \Pi$-submodules of R.

When $R = KM$ with Π acting on M, then we can define monoid $M * \Pi$ whose elements are pairs in $M \times \Pi$ with monoid operation

$$(m, \sigma)(n, \tau) = (m\sigma(n), \sigma\tau).$$

There is a left action of $M * \Pi$ on M and the elements of $M * \Pi$ are the "monomials" of $R * \Pi$.

Some authors call a functor from category $\mathcal{C}$ to the category of commutative K-algebras (or K-modules) a *$\mathcal{C}$-algebra* (or *$\mathcal{C}$-module* respectively) [CEF12]. The monoid Π can be considered as a category with single object x. Algebra R with left Π-action encodes the same data as a Π-algebra F with $R = F(x)$. We will therefore refer to R as a Π-algebra, and a Π-invariant ideal is an ideal that is a Π-submodule of R.

Definition 2.3. A Π-invariant ideal $I \subseteq R$ is *Π-finitely generated* if there is a finite set $F \subseteq I$ such that the Π-orbits of the elements of F generate I. Ring R is called *Π-Noetherian* if every Π-invariant ideal in R is Π-finitely generated.

If a Π-invariant ideal I is generated by the Π-orbits of a set F, we will write

$$I = \langle F \rangle_\Pi.$$

Such a set F generates I as an $R * \Pi$-module.

A Π-algebra is Π-finitely generated if it is generated as an algebra by the Π-orbits of a finite set.

Example 2.4. Continuing Example 2.1 in which $R = K[x_1, x_2, x_3, \ldots]$, the ideal $\mathfrak{m} = \langle x_1, x_2, x_3, \ldots \rangle$ is a $\mathfrak{S}_\infty$-invariant ideal. Moreover, it is $\mathfrak{S}_\infty$-finitely generated because $\mathfrak{m} = \langle x_1 \rangle_{\mathfrak{S}_\infty}$. Also R is a $\mathfrak{S}_\infty$-finitely generated K-algebra with generator x_1.

Definition 2.5. Let R be a $\mathfrak{S}_\infty$-algebra. For $f \in R$, the *width* of f is the smallest integer n such that for every $\sigma \in \mathfrak{S}_\infty$ that fixes $\{1, \ldots, n\}$, σ also fixes f. The width of f is denoted $w(f)$. If no such integer n exists, then $w(f) = \infty$. For a set $F \subseteq R$, its width is $w(F) := \sup_{f \in F}\{w(f)\}$.

$\mathfrak{S}_\infty$-algebra R has the *finite width property* if every element of R has finite width. The tools described in this paper generally apply only to such algebras, so from here forward every $\mathfrak{S}_\infty$-algebra is assumed to have the finite width property. For a $\mathfrak{S}_\infty$-invariant ideal $I \subseteq R$ and an integer n we can define the nth truncation of I as

$$I_n := \{f \in I \mid w(f) \leq n\}.$$

The set I_n is naturally a $\mathfrak{S}_n$-invariant ideal of R_n. An equivalent statement of the finite width property is that R is equal to the direct limit of its truncations. If I is $\mathfrak{S}_\infty$-finitely generated, then there is sufficiently large $n \in \mathbb{N}$ such that $I = \langle I_n \rangle_{\mathfrak{S}_\infty}$.

The definition of width also applies to $\Pi = \mathrm{Inc}(\mathbb{N})$, the monoid of strictly increasing functions, which is introduced below.

Definition 2.6. Given $R = KM$ with Π acting on M, there is a natural quasi-order $|_\Pi$ on M called the *Π-divisibility quasi-order* defined by $a|_\Pi b$ if there exists $\sigma \in \Pi$ such that σa divides b. Equivalently $a|_\Pi b$ if $b \in \langle a \rangle_\Pi$.

Recall that a monomial order on $R = KM$ is a total order $\leq$ on M that is a well-order, and that respects multiplication, meaning if $a \leq b$ then $ac \leq bc$ for all $c \in M$.

Definition 2.7. A monomial order $\leq$ on $R = KM$ *respects* Π if whenever $a \leq b$ then $\sigma a \leq \sigma b$ for all $\sigma \in \Pi$.

Therefore order $\leq$ is a Π respecting monomial order on R if $\leq$ is a total well-order on M that respects the action of $M * \Pi$. Now we have the tools to describe the Π-equivariant version of Gröbner bases.

Definition 2.8. Let $R = KM$ be a monoid ring with Π action on M, and let $\leq$ be a Π respecting monomial order. Given a Π-invariant ideal $I \subseteq R$, a *Π-equivariant Gröbner basis* of I is a set $G \subseteq I$ such that the Π orbits of G form a Gröbner basis of I,

$$\langle \mathrm{in}_\leq \Pi G \rangle = \mathrm{in}_\leq I.$$

We require $\leq$ to be a Π respecting order because it is equivalent to the condition that

$$\mathrm{in}_\leq \sigma f = \sigma \, \mathrm{in}_\leq f$$

for all $f \in R$ and $\sigma \in \Pi$. Therefore with such an order

$$\langle \mathrm{in}_\leq G \rangle_\Pi = \langle \mathrm{in}_\leq \Pi G \rangle = \mathrm{in}_\leq I.$$

This also implies that $\mathrm{in}_\leq I$ is a Π-invariant ideal. Note that since the Π orbits of G are a Gröbner basis of I, we have $\langle G \rangle_\Pi = I$.

Proposition 2.9 (Remark 2.1 of [BD11])**.** *Let Π be a group which acts non-trivially on M. Then KM has no Π respecting monomial orders.*

Proof. Suppose that $\leq$ is a Π respecting order and choose $\sigma \in \Pi$ and $m \in M$ such that $m \neq \sigma m$. If $m > \sigma m$ then $\sigma^n m > \sigma^{n+1} m$ for all n so

$$m > \sigma m > \sigma^2 m > \cdots$$

is an infinite descending chain of monomials, contradicting the fact that $\leq$ is a well-order. If $m < \sigma m$ then $m > \sigma^{-1} m > \sigma^{-2} m > \cdots$ is an infinite descending chain. □

In particular this means that R with non-trivial $\mathfrak{S}_\infty$ action has no $\mathfrak{S}_\infty$ respecting monomial orders. As in prior work such as [AH07], this problem is handled by introducing a related monoid $\mathrm{Inc}(\mathbb{N})$ to replace $\mathfrak{S}_\infty$ which allows for monomial orders but is somehow large enough compared to $\mathfrak{S}_\infty$ not to break properties like finite generation.

Define the *monoid of strictly increasing functions* as

$$\mathrm{Inc}(\mathbb{N}) := \{\rho : \mathbb{N} \to \mathbb{N} \mid \text{ for all } a < b, \rho(a) < \rho(b)\}.$$

For any $\mathfrak{S}_\infty$-algebra R, there is a natural action of $\mathrm{Inc}(\mathbb{N})$ on R as follows. Fixing $f \in R$, for any $\sigma \in \mathfrak{S}_\infty$ the value of σf depends only on the restriction $\sigma|_{[w(f)]}$ considering σ as a function $\mathbb{N} \to \mathbb{N}$. For any $\rho \in \mathrm{Inc}(\mathbb{N})$ there exists $\sigma \in \mathfrak{S}_\infty$ such that $\sigma|_{[w(f)]} = \rho|_{[w(f)]}$ and define $\rho f = \sigma f$. It can be checked that this gives a well-defined action of $\mathrm{Inc}(\mathbb{N})$ on R.

It immediately follows from the definition of the action that $\mathrm{Inc}(\mathbb{N}) f \subseteq \mathfrak{S}_\infty f$. Despite the fact that $\mathrm{Inc}(\mathbb{N})$ is not a submonoid of $\mathfrak{S}_\infty$, it behaves like one in terms of its action on R. An injective map $\sigma|_{[w(f)]} : [w(f)] \to \mathbb{N}$ can always be factored into $\rho' \circ \tau$ with $\tau \in \mathfrak{S}_{w(f)}$ and $\rho' : [w(f)] \to \mathbb{N}$ a strictly increasing function. The map ρ' can be extended to some $\rho \in \mathrm{Inc}(\mathbb{N})$, and then $\sigma f = \rho(\tau f)$. Thus

$$\mathfrak{S}_\infty f = \bigcup_{\tau \in \mathfrak{S}_{w(f)}} \mathrm{Inc}(\mathbb{N})(\tau f).$$

This fact that the $\mathfrak{S}_\infty$-orbit of any f is a finite union of $\mathrm{Inc}(\mathbb{N})$-orbits implies the following statements.

Proposition 2.10. *Let R be a $\mathfrak{S}_\infty$-algebra with the finite width property and let $I \subseteq R$ be a $\mathfrak{S}_\infty$-invariant ideal.*

- *I is $\mathrm{Inc}(\mathbb{N})$-invariant.*
- *I is $\mathfrak{S}_\infty$-finitely generated if and only if I is $\mathrm{Inc}(\mathbb{N})$-finitely generated.*
- *If R is $\mathrm{Inc}(\mathbb{N})$-Noetherian then R is $\mathfrak{S}_\infty$-Noetherian.*

When computing Gröbner bases of $\mathfrak{S}_\infty$-invariant ideals we will work with the $\mathrm{Inc}(\mathbb{N})$ action instead. If G is an $\mathrm{Inc}(\mathbb{N})$-equivariant Gröbner basis for $\mathfrak{S}_\infty$-invariant ideal I, then the $\mathfrak{S}_\infty$-orbits of G also form a Gröbner basis of I. Generally the rings we are interested in will have $\mathrm{Inc}(\mathbb{N})$ respecting monomial orders.

Example 2.11. Let $R = K[x_1, x_2, \ldots]$ with $\mathrm{Inc}(\mathbb{N})$-action defined by $\rho \cdot x_i = x_{\rho(i)}$. The lexicographic order $\leq$ on the monomials of R with $x_1 < x_2 < x_3 < \cdots$ is a $\mathrm{Inc}(\mathbb{N})$ respecting monomial order. This is the only possible lexicographic order on R that respects $\mathrm{Inc}(\mathbb{N})$. There are also a graded lexicographic and a graded reverse lexicographic order on R that respect $\mathrm{Inc}(\mathbb{N})$. There is no $\mathrm{Inc}(\mathbb{N})$ respecting monomial order on R that is defined by a single weight vector in $\mathbb{R}^{\mathbb{N}}$.

It is an open question to characterize all possible $\mathrm{Inc}(\mathbb{N})$ respecting monomial orders on a given ring KM with $\mathrm{Inc}(\mathbb{N})$ action. We can make the following statement about such orders.

Proposition 2.12. *If $\leq$ is a Π respecting monomial order on KM, then $\leq$ refines the Π-divisibility quasi-order $|_\Pi$.*

Proof. Suppose a and b are monomials with $a|_\Pi b$, so there is some pair $\sigma \in \Pi$, $c \in M$ such that $c\sigma a = b$. From the proof of Proposition 2.9 we see that $a \leq \sigma a$. Since $1 \leq c$ and $\leq$ respects multiplication, $\sigma a \leq c\sigma a = b$. □

An implication of this proposition is that if KM has a Π respecting monomial order then the Π-divisibility quasi-order must be a partial order, meaning it has the anti-symmetry property: if $a|_\Pi b$ and $b|_\Pi a$ then $a = b$.

If R is Π-Noetherian with a Π respecting monomial order, then any Π-invariant ideal $I \subseteq R$ will have a finite Π-equivariant Gröbner basis. This follows from the fact that $\mathrm{in}_\leq I$ is Π-finitely generated. We recount two prior results that give examples of $\mathrm{Inc}(\mathbb{N})$-Noetherian rings, and will be directly relevant to the remainder of this paper.

Theorem 2.13 (Theorem 1.1 of [HS12]). *Let $X = \{x_{ij} \mid i \in [k], j \in \mathbb{N}\}$, and let $\mathfrak{S}_\infty$ act on $[X]$ by permuting the second index, $\sigma x_{ij} = x_{i\sigma(j)}$ for $\sigma \in \mathfrak{S}_\infty$. Then $K[X]$ is $\mathrm{Inc}(\mathbb{N})$-Noetherian.*

Theorem 2.14 (Theorem 1.1 of [DEKL15]). *Let $K[Y]$ be a $\mathfrak{S}_\infty$-finitely generated $\mathfrak{S}_\infty$-algebra with the finite width property, and with $\mathfrak{S}_\infty$ action on variable set Y. For $K[X]$ defined as in Theorem 2.13, let ϕ be a $\mathfrak{S}_\infty$-equivariant monomial map*

$$\phi : K[Y] \to K[X].$$

Then

- *$\ker \phi$ is $\mathrm{Inc}(\mathbb{N})$-finitely generated,*
- *$\mathrm{im}\, \phi$ is $\mathrm{Inc}(\mathbb{N})$-Noetherian.*

The conditions on ring $K[Y]$ in Theorem 2.14 are quite general and Hillar and Sullivant [HS12] prove that such rings are generally not $\mathfrak{S}_\infty$-Noetherian. They show that Noetherianity fails for the example $K[Y]$ where $Y = \{y_{ij} \mid i, j \in \mathbb{N}\}$ with $\sigma y_{ij} = y_{\sigma(i)\sigma(j)}$ for $\sigma \in \mathfrak{S}_\infty$.

When R is not Π-Noetherian, we do not know in general if a Π-finitely generated ideal $I \subseteq R$ has a finite Π-equivariant Gröbner basis, or if so, for which monomial orders. However we will prove in Section 4 that the $\mathfrak{S}_\infty$-invariant toric ideal $\ker \phi$ as in Theorem 2.14 does have finite $\mathrm{Inc}(\mathbb{N})$-equivariant Gröbner bases for specifically chosen monomial orders. This will allow an algorithm to compute such a Gröbner basis of $\ker \phi$, given the map ϕ.

3. EQUIVARIANT BUCHBERGER ALGORITHM

3.1 Description of the algorithm

An equivariant adaptation of Buchberger's algorithm was proposed in [AH07] and formalized in [BD11] and [DEKL15].

Let $R = KM$ with Π acting on M, and let $\leq$ be a Π respecting monomial order. For $G \subseteq R$, a *Π-normal form* of f with respect to G denoted $\mathrm{NF}_{\Pi G}(f)$ is the result of repeated reductions of f by elements of ΠG until no more reductions are possible.

The equivariant Buchberger algorithm departs from the conventional Buchberger algorithm only at the step of adding new S-pairs to the list S. This departure is described after, along with a definition of $O_{f,g}$ and the "finite S-pair condition."

Algorithm 3.1 (Brouwer–Draisma [BD11]). $G = \mathrm{Buchberger}(F)$

Require: F is a finite set of elements in $R = KM$ with Π acting on M and satisfying the finite S-pair condition.

Ensure: G is Π-equivariant Gröbner basis of $\langle F \rangle_\Pi$.

$G \leftarrow F$
$S \leftarrow \bigcup_{f,g \in G} O_{f,g}$
while $S \neq \emptyset$ **do**
  pick $(h_1, h_2) \in S$
  $S \leftarrow S \setminus \{(h_1, h_2)\}$
  $h \leftarrow \mathrm{NF}_{\Pi G}(h_1 - \frac{\mathrm{LC}(h_1)}{\mathrm{LC}(h_2)} h_2)$
  if $h \neq 0$ **then**
    $G \leftarrow G \cup \{h\}$
    $S \leftarrow S \cup \left(\bigcup_{g \in G} O_{g,h}\right)$
  end if
end while

Given $f, g \in R$ define

$$\mathcal{S}_{f,g} :=$$
$$\{(m_1 f, m_2 g) \mid m_1, m_2 \in M * \Pi \text{ s.t. } \mathrm{in}_{\leq} m_1 f = \mathrm{in}_{\leq} m_2 g\}.$$

This set is closed under the diagonal action of $M * \Pi$ making $\mathcal{S}_{f,g}$ a $M * \Pi$-set. A set $G \subseteq R$ satisfies the *equivariant Buchberger criterion* if for all $(h_1, h_2) \in \bigcup_{f,g \in G} \mathcal{S}_{f,g}$,

$$\mathrm{NF}_{\Pi G}(\mathrm{LC}(h_2)h_1 - \mathrm{LC}(h_1)h_2) = 0.$$

The set G is a Π-equivariant Gröbner basis of $\langle G \rangle_\Pi$ if and only if it satisfies the equivariant Buchberger criterion. The proof of this fact follows by applying the usual Buchberger criterion to the set ΠG (see Theorem 2.5 of [BD11]).

For each pair $f, g \in G$, it is sufficient to check the equivariant Buchberger criterion on a $M * \Pi$ generating set of $\mathcal{S}_{f,g}$, which we denote $O_{f,g}$.

Definition 3.2. A Π-algebra $R = KM$ has the *finite S-pair condition* if for any $f, g \in R$, the set $\mathcal{S}_{f,g}$ is finitely generated as a $M * \Pi$-set. In [BD11] this condition is referred to as "EGB4."

If R fails the finite S-pair condition then we cannot apply the equivariant Buchberger algorithm. When Π is trivial and R is a polynomial ring (the setting of the conventional Buchberger algorithm), $\mathcal{S}_{f,g}$ is generated by a single pair

$$\left(\frac{\mathrm{lcm}(\mathrm{in}_{\leq} f, \mathrm{in}_{\leq} g)}{\mathrm{in}_{\leq}(f)} f, \frac{\mathrm{lcm}(\mathrm{in}_{\leq} f, \mathrm{in}_{\leq} g)}{\mathrm{in}_{\leq}(g)} g \right).$$

This generator is called the "S-pair" of f, g. Therefore R in this case satisfies the finite S-pair condition, and the equivariant Buchberger algorithm specializes to the conventional Buchberger algorithm.

Proposition 3.3. *If $\mathfrak{S}_\infty$-algebra R is a polynomial ring with the finite width condition, then R has the finite S-pair condition.*

This is a simple generalization of Lemma 3.4 of [BD11].

Proof. Fix $f, g \in R$. Since R is a polynomial ring, for fixed $\sigma_1, \sigma_2 \in \mathrm{Inc}(\mathbb{N})$, all elements of $\mathcal{S}_{f,g}$ of the form $(m_1\sigma_1 f, m_2\sigma_2 g)$ with $m_1, m_2 \in M$ are monomial multiples of the usual S-pair of $\sigma_1 f, \sigma_2 g$,

$$\left(\frac{m}{\mathrm{in}_{\leq} \sigma_1 f} \sigma_1 f, \ \frac{m}{\mathrm{in}_{\leq} \sigma_2 g} \sigma_2 g \right)$$

where $m = \mathrm{lcm}(\mathrm{in}_{\leq} \sigma_1 f, \mathrm{in}_{\leq} \sigma_2 g)$.

Any $f, g \in R$ have finite width so $\sigma_1 f$ depends only on $\sigma_1|_{[w(f)]}$, and similarly for $\sigma_2 g$. In fact we can always factor the pair as

$$(\sigma_1 f, \sigma_2 g) = \tau(\rho_1 f, \rho_2 g)$$

for some $\tau \in \mathrm{Inc}(\mathbb{N})$, while $\rho_1 : [w(f)] \to [w(f) + w(g)]$ and $\rho_2 : [w(g)] \to [w(f) + w(g)]$ are strictly increasing functions. Here ρ_1 and ρ_2 are chosen to "interlace" the variables of f and g in the same way as σ_1, σ_2. (To consider ρ_1, ρ_2 as elements of $\mathrm{Inc}(\mathbb{N})$, take any choice of extensions to maps on $\mathbb{N}$.)

Then $\mathcal{S}_{f,g}$ is generated by the finite set of pairs of the form

$$\left(\frac{m}{\mathrm{in}_{\leq} \rho_1 f} \rho_1 f, \ \frac{m}{\mathrm{in}_{\leq} \rho_2 g} \rho_2 g \right)$$

with $\rho_1 : [w(f)] \to [w(f) + w(g)]$ and $\rho_2 : [w(g)] \to [w(f) + w(g)]$ where $m = \mathrm{lcm}(\mathrm{in}_{\leq} \rho_1 f, \mathrm{in}_{\leq} \rho_2 g)$. □

We note that Algorithm 3.1 is guaranteed to terminate when R is Π-Noetherian. Without Noetherianity, a finite Gröbner basis might not exist, and when it does it is not known in general if the equivariant Buchberger algorithm will terminate.

3.2 A terminating $\mathrm{Inc}(\mathbb{N})$-equivariant Gröbner basis algorithm

The algorithm concept in this section has been used implicitly before in computations by Jan Draisma, Anton Leykin and perhaps others, but does not appear in the literature (at least to the knowledge of the author) so it is given a presentation here.

Let $R = KM$ with $\mathrm{Inc}(\mathbb{N})$ action on M, R satisfying the finite S-pair condition, and with each truncation R_n a Noetherian ring. (These conditions are satisfied for example when R is $\mathrm{Inc}(\mathbb{N})$-finitely generated polynomial ring, as in Theorem 2.14.) Let $I \subseteq R$ be a $\mathrm{Inc}(\mathbb{N})$-invariant ideal which is $\mathrm{Inc}(\mathbb{N})$-generated by finite set F, and moreover has finite $\mathrm{Inc}(\mathbb{N})$-equivariant Gröbner basis G. Define the *generator truncation* of I to be $\tilde{I}_{F,n} := \langle \mathrm{Inc}(\mathbb{N})F \cap R_n \rangle \cap R_n$. Note that $\tilde{I}_{F,n} \subseteq I_n$ but in general equality does not hold. For $f \in I$ define $w_F(f)$ to be the minimum value of n for which $f \in \tilde{I}_{F,n}$.

The truncated EGB algorithm again takes finite generating set F as its input. For each successive $n \geq w(F)$, compute a set G_n such that $\mathrm{Inc}(\mathbb{N})G_n \cap R_n$ is a Gröbner basis for $\tilde{I}_{F,n}$. Then check if G_n is a $\mathrm{Inc}(\mathbb{N})$-equivariant Gröbner basis of I using the equivariant Buchberger criterion, and if so return G_n.

Algorithm 3.4. $G = \mathrm{TruncatedEGB}(F)$

Require: F is a finite set of elements in $R = KM$ with $\mathrm{Inc}(\mathbb{N})$ acting on M, R satisfies the finite S-pair conditions, and each R_n is Noetherian.

Ensure: G is a $\mathrm{Inc}(\mathbb{N})$-equivariant Gröbner basis of $I := \langle F \rangle_{\mathrm{Inc}(\mathbb{N})}$.

$G \leftarrow F$
$n \leftarrow w(F)$
while G not a $\mathrm{Inc}(\mathbb{N})$-equivariant Gröbner basis of I **do**
  $G \leftarrow$ Gröbner basis of $\tilde{I}_{F,n}$
  $n \leftarrow n + 1$
end while

proof of termination. For each n, let G_n denote the value of G after that step. Computing G_n is a finite process since it takes place in R_n which is Noetherian. G_n is a finite set and so it has a finite number of S-pairs to be checked. Therefore testing whether G_n is a $\mathrm{Inc}(\mathbb{N})$-equivariant Gröbner basis is finite. It remains to be proved that G_n is a $\mathrm{Inc}(\mathbb{N})$-equivariant Gröbner basis for some value of n. If H is a $\mathrm{Inc}(\mathbb{N})$-equivariant Gröbner basis of I, for any $h \in H$ we have $h \in \tilde{I}_{F,n}$ for all $n \geq w_F(h)$, so $\mathrm{in}_{\leq}(h) \in \mathrm{in}_{\leq}(\tilde{I}_{F,n})$. Therefore there is some element $g \in G_n$ with $\mathrm{in}_{\leq}(g)|_{\mathrm{Inc}(\mathbb{N})} \mathrm{in}_{\leq}(h)$. For $n = \max_{h \in H} w_F(h)$, the initial ideal $\langle \mathrm{in}_{\leq}(G_n) \rangle_{\mathrm{Inc}(\mathbb{N})}$ contains $\langle \mathrm{in}_{\leq}(H) \rangle_{\mathrm{Inc}(\mathbb{N})}$ and so G_n is a $\mathrm{Inc}(\mathbb{N})$-equivariant Gröbner basis of I. □

In practice, G_n can be computed either using a traditional Gröbner basis algorithm on input $\mathrm{Inc}(\mathbb{N})F \cap R_n$, or using an equivariant Buchberger algorithm on input F with the following two caveats:

- consider only S-pairs $(m_1 f, m_2 g)$ with $m_1 f$ and $m_2 g$ both having width $\leq n$,
- perform only reductions such that the outcome has width $\leq n$.

Moreover we do not need to restart the algorithm from scratch for each n. Instead $G_{n-1} \cup F$ can be used as the input for the nth step instead of F.

If $\leq$ is a width order (a monomial order such that $w(a) < w(b)$ implies $a < b$), the second condition is satisfied automatically since reductions cannot increase the width. Therefore the normal form of a given S-pair does not depend on n and only needs to be computed once. As a result we can use Algorithm 3.1, queuing S-pairs by width so that the smallest width S-pairs are considered first. The algorithm terminates once the queue is empty. A separate check for whether G_n is a $\mathrm{Inc}(\mathbb{N})$-equivariant Gröbner basis for I is not needed since this is equivalent to reducing all S-pairs in the queue.

For width orders, the stopping criterion in Algorithm 3.4 can be rephrased as follows.

Proposition 3.5. *For $I = \langle F \rangle_{\mathrm{Inc}(\mathbb{N})}$, let $\leq$ be a width order and G_n be a Gröbner basis of $\tilde{I}_{F,n}$ with $n \geq w(F)$. Then G_n is a $\mathrm{Inc}(\mathbb{N})$-equivariant Gröbner basis of I if and only if $\mathrm{Inc}(\mathbb{N})G_n \cap R_{2n}$ is a Gröbner basis of its ideal.*

Proof. If G_n is not an equivariant Gröbner basis of I then there is an S-pair that does not reduce to zero. From the proof of Proposition 3.3, every such S-pairs is a pair in $\mathrm{Inc}(\mathbb{N})G_n \cap R_{2n}$. Therefore $\mathrm{Inc}(\mathbb{N})G_n \cap R_{2n}$ fails Buchberger's criterion. Conversely if G_n is an equivariant Gröbner basis of I, then $\mathrm{Inc}(\mathbb{N})G_n$ is a Gröbner basis of I. Since $\leq$ is a width order, the elements that reduce polynomials in I_{2n} must be in $\mathrm{Inc}(\mathbb{N})G_n \cap R_{2n}$, so $\mathrm{Inc}(\mathbb{N})G_n \cap R_{2n}$ is a Gröbner basis of I_{2n}. □

In fact the above $2n$ can be reduced to $2n-1$ because the S-pairs in width $2n$ have no variables in common between the two polynomials. Such S-pairs always reduce to zero.

4. SYMMETRIC GRÖBNER BASES OF TORIC IDEALS

The previous section an algorithm was given that is capable of computing a n $\mathrm{Inc}(\mathbb{N})$-equivariant Gröbner basis of an ideal in a ring of the form $K[Y]$ with $\mathrm{Inc}(\mathbb{N})$ action on Y and Y having a finite number of orbits, with guaranteed termination *if* a finite Gröbner basis for the ideal exists. In this section we prove that any $\mathfrak{S}_\infty$-invariant toric ideal $\ker \phi$ of form in Theorem 2.14 has a finite Gröbner basis with respect to a particularly chosen monomial order. We then show that a Gröbner basis can be computed given the monomial map ϕ, using elimination.

4.1 Existence of equivariant Gröbner bases of toric ideals

As in Theorem 2.14, let $K[Y]$ be a $\mathfrak{S}_\infty$-finitely generated polynomial ring with $\mathfrak{S}_\infty$ action on the variable set Y. Let $X = \{x_{i,j} \mid i \in [\ell], j \in \mathbb{N}\}$ with $\mathfrak{S}_\infty$ acting on the second index of each $x_{i,j}$. Let $\phi : K[Y] \to K[X]$ be a $\mathfrak{S}_\infty$-equivariant monomial map.

Theorem 4.1. *$\ker \phi$ has a finite $\mathrm{Inc}(\mathbb{N})$-equivariant Gröbner basis H with respect to a $\mathrm{Inc}(\mathbb{N})$ respecting monomial order $\leq$ that can be constructed based on ϕ.*

A key strategy to studying ϕ used in [DEKL15] was working with a certain factorization of the map, and we make use of this strategy here as well.

Let N be the number of $\mathfrak{S}_\infty$-orbits in Y, and for the pth orbit choose a representative y_p with minimum width and let $k_p = w(y_p)$. Define a new variable set

$$Y' := \{y'_{p,(\alpha_1,\ldots,\alpha_{k_p})} \mid p \in [N],\ \alpha_1, \ldots, \alpha_{k_p} \in \mathbb{N} \text{ distinct } \} \tag{4.1}$$

with $\mathfrak{S}_\infty$ action on Y' by

$$\sigma y'_{p,(\alpha_1,\ldots,\alpha_{k_p})} = y'_{p,(\sigma(\alpha_1),\ldots,\sigma(\alpha_{k_p}))}.$$

Y' has the same number of $\mathfrak{S}_\infty$-orbits as Y and minimal-width orbit representatives with the same widths, but Y' has a standard form we will take advantage of. There is a surjective $\mathfrak{S}_\infty$-equivariant map $\theta : Y' \to Y$ defined by $y'_{p,(1,\ldots,k_p)} \mapsto y_p$, and this map extends to $\mathfrak{S}_\infty$-equivariant monomial map $\theta : K[Y'] \to K[Y]$.

Define variable set

$$Z := \{z_{p,i,j} \mid p \in [N], i \in [k_p], j \in \mathbb{N}\}$$

with $\mathfrak{S}_\infty$ action on the last index $\sigma z_{p,i,j} = z_{p,i,\sigma(j)}$. Define $\mathfrak{S}_\infty$-equivariant monomial map $\pi : K[Y'] \to K[Z]$ by

$$\pi : y'_{p,(\alpha_1,\ldots,\alpha_{k_p})} \mapsto \prod_{i \in [k_p]} z_{p,i,\alpha_i}.$$

Note that this map π depends only on the values of $k_1, \ldots, k_p$. The important fact is that $\phi \circ \theta$ factors through the map π, so there is a $\mathfrak{S}_\infty$-equivariant monomial map $\psi : K[Z] \to K[X]$ that makes the following diagram commute.

$$\begin{array}{ccc} K[Y'] & \xrightarrow{\pi} & K[Z] \\ \downarrow \theta & & \downarrow \psi \\ K[Y] & \xrightarrow{\phi} & K[X] \end{array}$$

Proposition 4.2. *If $G \subseteq K[Y']$ is a $\mathrm{Inc}(\mathbb{N})$-equivariant Gröbner basis of $\ker(\phi \circ \theta)$ for $\mathrm{Inc}(\mathbb{N})$ respecting monomial order $\leq'$, then $\theta(G) \subseteq K[Y]$ is a $\mathrm{Inc}(\mathbb{N})$-equivariant Gröbner basis of $\ker \phi$ for a $\mathrm{Inc}(\mathbb{N})$ respecting monomial order $\leq$ determined by $\leq'$.*

Proof. Let $\nu : K[Y] \to K[Y']$ be the right-inverse map of θ defined on variables $y \in Y$ by letting $\nu(y)$ be the $\leq'$-minimal variable in $\theta^{-1}(y)$. Define order $\leq$ on $[Y]$ by letting $a \leq b$ if and only if $\nu(a) \leq' \nu(b)$. It is clear that $\leq$ is a total well-order on $[Y]$, and it respects multiplication because ν is a homomorphism. To prove that $\leq$ respects $\mathrm{Inc}(\mathbb{N})$, it is sufficient to show that ν in $\mathrm{Inc}(\mathbb{N})$-equivariant, i.e. for any $\rho \in \mathrm{Inc}(\mathbb{N})$ and $a \in [Y]$ that $\rho\nu(a) = \nu(\rho a)$.

Because θ is $\mathrm{Inc}(\mathbb{N})$-equivariant, $\rho\nu(a)$ and $\nu(\rho a)$ are in the same fiber of θ and so $\nu(\rho a) \leq' \rho\nu(a)$. On the other hand, there exists $\sigma \in \mathfrak{S}_\infty$ such that $\sigma\rho$ and $\rho\sigma$ are the identity on $[w(\rho a)]$ and then $\sigma\nu(\rho a) \in \theta^{-1}(a)$. This implies $\nu(a) \leq' \sigma\nu(\rho a)$. Applying ρ to both gives $\rho\nu(a) \leq' \rho\sigma\nu(\rho a) = \nu(\rho a)$.

To show $\theta(G)$ is a Gröbner basis, let f be any non-zero polynomial in $\ker \phi$. There is $g \in \mathrm{Inc}(\mathbb{N})G$ that reduces $\nu(f)$ because $\nu(f)$ is in $\ker(\phi \circ \theta)$. Since $\mathrm{in}_{\leq'} g$ divides $\mathrm{in}_{\leq'} \nu(f)$ which is minimal in its fiber, $\mathrm{in}_{\leq'} g$ is a product of minimal variables so it is also minimal in its fiber. Because $\mathrm{in}_{\leq'} g$ is larger than the other monomials in g, it is certainly larger than the minimal representatives of the fibers of those monomials. Therefore $\text{in}_\leq(\theta(g)) = \theta(\text{in}_{\leq'} g)$ and so $\theta(g) \in \text{Inc}(\mathbb{N})\theta(G)$ reduces f. □

The above proposition implies that to prove Theorem 4.1 it is sufficient to prove it for maps of the form $\psi \circ \pi : K[Y'] \to K[X]$. Therefore we can assume without loss of generality that $Y = Y'$ and ϕ factors as

$$K[Y] \xrightarrow{\pi} K[Z] \xrightarrow{\psi} K[X].$$

We now construct the monomial order $\leq$ on $K[Y]$ for which we will prove the existence of a finite equivariant Gröbner basis. Let $\mathcal{M}$ denote the monoid of monomials $\pi[Y] \subseteq [Z]$, called a *matching monoid.* Choose an $\text{Inc}(\mathbb{N})$ respecting monomial order $\leq_1$ on $K\mathcal{M}$ and an $\text{Inc}(\mathbb{N})$ respecting reverse lexicographic order $\leq_2$ on $K[Y]$. Let $\leq$ be the monomial order on $K[Y]$ defined by $a < b$ if $\pi(a) <_1 \pi(b)$ or $\pi(a) = \pi(b)$ and $a <_2 b$.

We will first prove the existence of a finite $\text{Inc}(\mathbb{N})$-equivariant Gröbner basis of $\ker \pi$ for order $\leq$. The following proposition will allow us to do so by bounding the degree of a Gröbner basis.

Proposition 4.3. *Let $F \subset K[Y]$ be a set of binomials with degree bounded by d. Then F is contained in a finite number of* $\text{Inc}(\mathbb{N})$*-orbits.*

Proof. Let k be the maximum size of the index supports of variables in Y. The index support of a polynomial is the union of the index supports of its variables, so a binomial of degree $\leq d$ has index support size bounded by $2kd$. Any $f \in F$ has in its $\mathfrak{S}_\infty$-orbit a binomial of width $\leq 2kd$. There are only a finite number of pairs of monomials in $K[Y]_{2kd}$ with degree $\leq d$. Therefore F is contained in a finite number of $\mathfrak{S}_\infty$-orbits, and every $\mathfrak{S}_\infty$-orbit is the union of a finite number of $\text{Inc}(\mathbb{N})$-orbits. □

We also require the following useful characterization of the matching monoid $\mathcal{M}$. Any monomial in $[Z]$ can be expressed as z^A with $A := (A_1, \ldots, A_p)$ where each A_p is a k_p by infinite matrix.

Lemma 4.4 (Proposition 3.1 of [DEKL15]). *Monomial $z^A \in [Z]$ is in $\mathcal{M}$ if and only if for each $p = 1, \ldots, N$ there is integer $d_p \geq 0$ such that all row sums of A_p are equal to d_p and all column sums are $\leq d_p$.*

A consequence is that for $z^A, z^B \in \mathcal{M}$, z^A divides z^B in $\mathcal{M}$ (meaning there is a quotient $z^C \in \mathcal{M}$) if and only if $A \leq B$ entry-wise and for each $p = 1, \ldots, N$ every column sum of $B_p - A_p$ is bounded by $d'_p - d_p$ where d'_p and d_p are the row sums of B_p and A_p respectively.

Proposition 4.5. *The kernel of π has a Gröbner basis for order $\leq$ consisting of binomials of degree at most $2\max_p k_p - 1$.*

The argument of the following proof is due to Jan Draisma, originally used to show a degree bound on generators of $\ker \pi$. We adapt it to Gröbner bases.

Proof. Given monomial $v \in [Y]$, let u be the minimal monomial with $\pi(u) = \pi(v)$, i.e. the standard monomial of $\ker \pi$ in the equivalence class of v. It suffices to show that there exists a chain $v = v_0 > v_1 > \ldots > v_t = u$ such that $\pi(v_s) = \pi(u)$ for all s and $(v_s - v_{s+1})/\gcd(v_s, v_{s+1})$ has degree at most $2\max_p k_p - 1$. We first consider the case $N = 1$ and drop the index p for simplicity of notation.

Proceed by induction on the degree of v. Suppose v and u have a variable y_J in common. By the induction hypothesis there is a chain from v/y_J to u/y_J satisfying the desired conditions, since u/y_J is also a standard monomial. Multiplying by y_J gives a chain from v to u.

Assume then that v and u have no variables in common. Let $z^A = \pi(v) = \pi(u)$. Let y_J be the smallest variable in u and $z^B = \pi(y_J)$. The matrix B has k non-zero entries and row sums equal to 1. Since $A \geq B$, monomial v has a divisor v' of degree $e \leq k$ such that $\pi(v') =: z^{A'}$ and $A' \geq B$. The row sums of A' are equal to e and let S be the set of indices for which the column sum of A' is also equal to e. Abusing notation let J also denote the set of column indices where B is non-zero. By Lemma 4.4, z^B divides $z^{A'}$ in $\mathcal{M}$ if and only if S is contained in J, because then all column sums of $A' - B$ will be $\leq e - 1$. The column indices $S \setminus J$ are the obstacles to divisibility, but there are few of them. The total entry sum of A' is ek, and the columns of J make a non-trivial contribution to the sum, so then $|S \setminus J| < k$.

For each $j \in S \setminus J$, the jth column sum of A is strictly less than $\deg u$ because y_J does not contribute. Therefore v also has a variable y_{L_j} with j not among the entries of L_j. Let w be the product of the set of variables of the form y_{L_j} for some $j \in S \setminus J$ and let $v'' = v'w$. Letting $z^{A''} = \pi(v'')$, the set of indices for which the column sum of A'' is equal to $\deg v''$ is contained in J. Therefore $A'' - B$ has all column sums $\leq \deg v'' - 1$ and so $z^{A''-B} \in \mathcal{M}$. Choose any monomial $v''_1 \in \pi^{-1}(z^{A'-B})$, and let $v_1 = v\frac{v''_1 y_J}{v''}$. By construction, $\pi(v_1) = \pi(v)$ and v_1 shares the variable y_J with u. Note that since $u < v$ and $\leq$ is reverse lexicographic on each fiber of π, every variable in v is larger than y_J, so $v > v_1$ as well. Since v_1 and u share a variable, by the induction hypothesis there is a chain from v_1 to u satisfying the desired conditions. The degree of $(v - v_1)/\gcd(v, v_1)$ is bounded by $\deg v''$ which is $\leq 2k - 1$.

For the case $N > 1$ group v and u by their variable orbits as $v = v_1 \cdots v_N$ and $u = u_1 \cdots u_N$. By the above, each v_p can be reduced to u_p with reductions by Gröbner basis elements of degree $\leq 2\max_p k_p - 1$. Applying these reductions in sequence brings v to u. □

Let F denote such a finite $\text{Inc}(\mathbb{N})$-equivariant Gröbner basis of $\ker \pi$. We also know there exists G, a finite $\text{Inc}(\mathbb{N})$-equivariant Gröbner basis of $\ker \psi \cap \text{im}\, \pi$ with respect to $\leq_1$, because $\text{im}\, \pi$ is $\text{Inc}(\mathbb{N})$-Noetherian by Theorem 2.14. The goal is to combine F with a "lift" of G to form a Gröbner basis of $\ker \phi$, and then show that this Gröbner basis has bounded degree.

Lemma 4.6. *Let z^A, z^B be any pair of monomials in $\mathcal{M}$, and u any monomial in $\pi^{-1}(z^A)$. There exists monomial $v \in \pi^{-1}(z^B)$ such that*

$$\deg_{tot} \frac{u - v}{\gcd(u, v)} \leq 5\|A - B\|_1.$$

Proof. First we consider the case $N = 1$ and drop the index p for simplicity of notation. We will prove that u has a large factor u' such that $\pi(u') \mid z^B$ in $\mathcal{M}$. Then v can be chosen to be $v = u'v''$ where v'' is any monomial in $\pi^{-1}(z^B/\pi(u'))$. The sizes of $v'' = v/u'$ and $u'' = u/u'$ will be small.

Let $n = \deg u$ and m the degree of the monomials in $\pi^{-1}(z^B)$. Express u as the product of a sequence of variables $u = \prod_{i=1}^{n} y_{J_i}$, and let u_j denote the partial product $u_j = \prod_{i=1}^{j} y_{J_i}$. Let A_j be the exponent matrix of $\pi(u_j)$ noting that $A_n = A$. For any exponent matrix C, $C_{+\ell}$ will denote the ℓth column sum of C. We will throw out variables y_{J_i} which cause obstructions to $\pi(u)$ dividing z^B. Let L be the set of all $j \in [n]$ such that none of the following is true.

(1) $j > m$,

(2) the index sequence $J_j = (\alpha_1, \ldots, \alpha_k)$ has an element α_i such that $(A_j)_{i,\alpha_i} > B_{i,\alpha_i}$,

(3) there exists ℓ not in the index sequence J_j such that $j - (A_j)_{+\ell} > m - B_{+\ell}$.

As j increases, $(A_j)_{i,\ell}$ increases exactly for y_{J_j} such that ℓ is the ith index of J_j, and $j - (A_j)_{+\ell}$ increases exactly when ℓ does not appear in J_j. Let $u' := \prod_{i \in L} y_{J_i}$ and A' be the exponent matrix of $\pi(u')$. Forbidding case (2) ensures that no entry $A'_{i,\ell}$ exceeds entry $B_{i,\ell}$, so $A' \leq B$. Forbidding case (3) keeps $\deg(u') - A'_{+\ell}$ from ever exceeding $m - B_{+\ell}$ for all columns ℓ. Thus the column sums of $z^B/\pi(u')$ are $\leq m - \deg(u')$ so by Lemma 4.4 $z^B/\pi(u')$ is in $\mathcal{M}$.

We will give a lower bound on $|L| = \deg(u')$ by bounding the number of values $j \in [n]$ that satisfy each case above.

Case (1): The number of values of $j \in [n]$ with $j > m$ is bounded by $|n - m|$.

Case (2): The number of values of $j \in [n]$ satisfying condition (2) is bounded by

$$\sum_{i,\ell} |A_{i,\ell} - B_{i,\ell}| = \|A - B\|_1.$$

Case (3): Here we consider j satisfying condition (3) only for $j \leq m$. Let $n' = \min(m, n)$. The number of such values of j is bounded by

$$\sum_{\ell} \max\{0, B_{+\ell} - (A_{n'})_{+\ell}\} + n' - m \leq \|A_{n'} - B\|_1$$

$$\leq \|A - B\|_1 + \|A_{n'} - A\|_1 \leq \|A - B\|_1 + k|n - m|.$$

The sum of all entries in A is kn and for B is km which shows that $k|n - m| \leq \|A - B\|_1$. Therefore

$$\deg(u'') = n - |L| \leq (3 + 1/k)\|A - B\|_1,$$

$$\deg(v'') = m - |L| \leq n - |L| + |n - m| \leq (3 + 2/k)\|A - B\|_1.$$

So then

$$\deg \frac{u - v}{\gcd(u, v)} \leq \deg(u'' - v'') \leq (3 + 2/k)\|A - B\|_1$$

$$\leq 5\|A - B\|_1.$$

For $N > 1$, for each $p \in [N]$ construct $v_p \in \pi^{-1}(y^{B_p})$ such that $\deg_p \frac{u_p - v_p}{\gcd(u_p, v_p)} \leq 5\|A_p - B_p\|_1$. Then take $v = v_1 \cdots v_N$. □

With some additional care, the factor 5 in the bound could be significantly improved.

Let C be the maximum value of $\|A - B\|_1$ over all binomials $z^A - z^B$ in G. Let $\mathcal{G}$ be the set of all binomials f in $K[Y]$ such that $\pi(f) = \sigma w g$ for some $\sigma \in \mathrm{Inc}(\mathbb{N})$, $w \in \mathcal{M}$ and $g \in G$, and such that $\deg_{tot} f \leq 5C$. In other words $\mathcal{G}$ consists of all lifts of elements of $\mathrm{Inc}(\mathbb{N})G$ of bounded degree. Finally let $\mathcal{H} = \mathrm{Inc}(\mathbb{N})F \cup \mathcal{G}$.

Proposition 4.7. *$\mathcal{H}$ is a Gröbner basis of $\ker \phi$ with respect to $\leq$.*

Proof. It's clear that $\mathcal{H} \subseteq \ker \phi$. We will show that any $u \in [Y]$ which is not a standard monomial of $\ker \pi$ can be reduced by $\mathcal{H}$.

First consider the case that πu is not a standard monomial of $\ker \psi$. There is a binomial $g \in G$ which reduces πu, which we will write as $g = a - b$ with a the leading term. There is $\sigma \in \mathrm{Inc}(\mathbb{N})$, $c \in \mathcal{M}$ such that $\sigma c a = \pi u$. By Lemma 4.6 there is $v \in \pi^{-1}(\sigma c b)$ such that $\deg(u' - v') \leq 5C$ where $u' = u/\gcd(u, v)$ and $v' = v/\gcd(u, v)$. The binomial $u' - v'$ is contained in $\mathcal{H}$ and it reduces u.

Otherwise πu is a standard monomial of $\ker \psi$ but u is not a standard monomial of $\ker \phi$. Then u is reduced by some element of $\mathrm{Inc}(\mathbb{N})F$. □

By Proposition 4.3, $\mathcal{H}$ is contained in a finite number of $\mathrm{Inc}(\mathbb{N})$ orbits. Letting H be such a finite set of orbit representatives, H is a $\mathrm{Inc}(\mathbb{N})$ equivariant Gröbner basis of $\ker \phi$ with respect to the order $\leq$. This concludes the proof of Theorem 4.1. It is not known if $\ker \phi$ has finite $\mathrm{Inc}(\mathbb{N})$-equivariant Gröbner bases monomial orders other than those of the form in Theorem 4.1.

4.2 Computing equivariant Gröbner bases of toric ideals

To compute a Gröbner basis of $\ker \phi$ from the description of ϕ we first assume that $Y = Y'$ for Y' defined in 4.1. A Gröbner basis of the graph of ϕ, denoted $\Gamma_\phi \subseteq K[Y][X]$, is computed with respect to an elimination order for X. We must prove that the graph has a finite $\mathrm{Inc}(\mathbb{N})$-equivariant Gröbner basis with respect to such an elimination order. Algorithm 3.4 then provides a way to compute the Gröbner basis.

$\Gamma_\phi := \langle y - \phi(y) \mid y' \in Y' \rangle$ is itself a $\mathfrak{S}_\infty$-invariant toric ideal. It is the kernel of the monomial map $\phi' : K[Y][X] \to K[X]$ defined by $\phi'(y^A x^C) = \phi(y^A)x^C$. Factoring ϕ' in the prescribed way produces

$$K[Y][X] \xrightarrow{\pi'} K[Z][X] \xrightarrow{\psi'} K[X]$$

where $\pi'(y^A x^C) = \pi(y^A)x^C$ and $\psi'(z^B x^C) = \psi(z^B)x^C$.

The monoid order $\leq_1$ on $\mathrm{im}\,\pi$ can be extended to an order $\leq'_1$ on $\mathrm{im}\,\pi' = (\mathrm{im}\,\pi)[X]$ that eliminates X. Define $\leq'$ to be the order on $[Y][X]$ such that $y^A x^C < y^B x^D$ if $\pi(y^A)x^C <'_1 \pi(y^B)x^D$ or $\pi(y^A)x^C = \pi(y^B)x^D$ and $y^A <_2 y^B$. The restriction of $\leq'$ to $[Y]$ is the hybrid order $\leq$ constructed previously from $\leq_1$ and $\leq_2$. The order $\leq'$ eliminates $[X]$, and satisfies the hypotheses for Theorem 4.1 so there exists a finite $\mathrm{Inc}(\mathbb{N})$-equivariant Gröbner basis H for Γ_ϕ with respect to $\leq'$. Using the above algorithm, H can be explicitly computed from the $\mathrm{Inc}(\mathbb{N})$-generators of Γ_ϕ, which are

$$\{\sigma y_p - \phi(\sigma y_p) \mid p \in [N],\ \sigma \in \mathfrak{S}_{k_p}\}$$

where $y_1, \ldots, y_N$ are representatives of the $\mathfrak{S}_\infty$-orbits of Y. Then $G = H \cap K[Y]$ is a $\mathrm{Inc}(\mathbb{N})$-equivariant Gröbner basis for $\ker(\phi) = \Gamma_\phi \cap K[Y]$ for the order $\leq$.

If $Y \neq Y'$, then we can compute an equivariant Gröbner basis G for the kernel of $\phi \circ \theta : K[Y'] \to K[X]$ as above. By Proposition 4.2, $\theta(G)$ is a $\mathrm{Inc}(\mathbb{N})$-equivariant Gröbner basis for $\ker \phi$.

5. EXAMPLE

A simple example is given to illustrate the above algorithms and the connection between $\mathfrak{S}_\infty$-invariant toric ideals and algebraic statistics.

Let A and B be two discrete random variables with outcomes in the set $[N]$. Let $x_{1,i} = \Pr[A = i]$, $x_{2,i} = \Pr[B = i]$ and $y_{i,j} = \Pr[A = i \text{ and } B = j]$. Variables A and B are independent if and only if $y_{i,j} = x_{1,i}x_{2,j}$ for all $i, j \in [N]$. The independence model is the set of y values in $\mathbb{R}^{N^2}$ of this form. The ideal of polynomials vanishing on this set is $\ker(\phi_N)$ for

$$\phi_N : \mathbb{R}[y_{i,j} \mid i, j \in [N]] \to \mathbb{R}[x_{i,j} \mid i \in \{1, 2\}, j \in [N]]$$

$$y_{i,j} \mapsto x_{1,i}x_{2,j}.$$

The monomial map ϕ_N is $\mathfrak{S}_N$-equivariant where $\mathfrak{S}_N$ acts by permuting the labels in $[N]$. To study the asymptotic behavior as N gets large, we pass to $\mathfrak{S}_\infty$-equivariant map

$$\phi : \mathbb{R}[y_{i,j} \mid i, j \in \mathbb{N}] \to \mathbb{R}[x_{i,j} \mid i \in \{1, 2\}, j \in \mathbb{N}]$$

$$y_{i,j} \mapsto x_{1,i}x_{2,j}.$$

The variable set Y consists of two $\mathfrak{S}_\infty$-orbits, $\{y_{i,j} \mid i \neq j\}$ and $\{y_{i,i}\}$. Here $Y = Y'$ so we need not consider a quotient map θ. The graph Γ_ϕ has three Inc($\mathbb{N}$)-generators,

$$F = \{y_{1,2} - x_{1,1}x_{2,2}, y_{2,1} - x_{1,2}x_{2,1}, y_{1,1} - x_{1,1}x_{2,1}\}.$$

Choose a monomial order $\leq$ that eliminates the X variables and satisfies the hypotheses for Theorem 4.1. Because $w(F) = 2$, we compute a Gröbner basis G_n of $(\widetilde{\Gamma_\phi})_{F,n}$ for each successive $n \geq 2$.

The sets G_2 and G_3 fail the equivariant Buchberger's criterion, but G_4 succeeds.

$$G = G_4 \cap \mathbb{R}[Y] =$$

$$\mathfrak{S}_4\{y_{1,2}y_{3,4} - y_{1,4}y_{3,2}, y_{1,1}y_{2,3} - y_{1,3}y_{2,1}, y_{1,1}y_{2,2} - y_{1,2}y_{2,1}\}.$$

Considering $\mathbb{R}[Y]$ as the coordinate ring of infinite by infinite matrices, the independence model is the variety of rank 1 matrices. The $\mathfrak{S}_\infty$-orbits of G form all 2×2 minors, which indeed generate the polynomials that vanish on rank 1 matrices.

6. REFERENCES

[AH07] Matthias Aschenbrenner and Christopher Hillar. Finite generation of symmetric ideals. *Transactions of the American Mathematical Society*, 359(11):5171–5192, 2007.

[AT05] Satoshi Aoki and Akimichi Takemura. Markov chain Monte Carlo exact tests for incomplete two-way contingency table. *Journal of Statistical Computation and Simulation*, 75(10):787–812, 2005.

[BD11] Andries E. Brouwer and Jan Draisma. Equivariant Gröbner bases and the two-factor model. *Math. Comput.*, 80:1123–1133, 2011.

[CEF12] Thomas Church, Jordan S Ellenberg, and Benson Farb. Fi-modules: a new approach to stability for sn-representations. *arXiv preprint arXiv:1204.4533*, 2012.

[DEKL15] Jan Draisma, Rob H Eggermont, Robert Krone, and Anton Leykin. Noetherianity for infinite-dimensional toric varieties. *Algebra & Number Theory*, 9(8):1857–1880, 2015.

[DO06] Jesús A. De Loera and Shmuel Onn. Markov bases of three-way tables are arbitrarily complicated. *Journal of Symbolic Computation*, 41:173–181, 2006.

[DS+98] Persi Diaconis, Bernd Sturmfels, et al. Algebraic algorithms for sampling from conditional distributions. *The Annals of statistics*, 26(1):363–397, 1998.

[HS12] Christopher J. Hillar and Seth Sullivant. Finite groebner bases in infinite dimensional polynomial rings and applications. *Advances in Mathematics*, 229(1):1–25, 2012.

[KKL14] Thomas Kahle, Robert Krone, and Anton Leykin. Equivariant lattice generators and markov bases. In *International Symposium on Symbolic and Algebraic Computation*, 2014.

On p-adic Differential Equations with Separation of Variables

Pierre Lairez[*]
Technische Universität
Berlin, Germany
pierre@lairez.fr

Tristan Vaccon
JSPS-Rikkyo University
Tokyo, Japan
vaccon@rikkyo.ac.jp

ABSTRACT

Several algorithms in computer algebra involve the computation of a power series solution of a given ordinary differential equation. Over finite fields, the problem is often lifted in an approximate p-adic setting to be well-posed. This raises precision concerns: how much precision do we need on the input to compute the output accurately? In the case of ordinary differential equations with separation of variables, we make use of the recent technique of differential precision to obtain optimal bounds on the stability of the Newton iteration. The results apply, for example, to algorithms for manipulating algebraic numbers over finite fields, for computing isogenies between elliptic curves or for deterministically finding roots of polynomials in finite fields. The new bounds lead to significant speedups in practice.

CCS Concepts

•Computing methodologies → Algebraic algorithms; *Number theory algorithms;* **•Mathematics of computing → Ordinary differential equations;**

Keywords

Ordinary differential equation; p-adic numbers; Newton iteration; numerical stability; differential precision

1. INTRODUCTION

We study, in a p-adic context, the loss of precision occuring during the computation of a power series solution of a certain class of differential equations. We use the method of differential precision that relies on a first-order analysis.

1.1 The p-adic context

Let $\mathbb{Z}_p$ be the ring of p-adic integer, for a given prime p, and $\mathbb{Q}_p$ its field of fractions. The p-adic valuation on $\mathbb{Q}_p$ is denoted v_p, and the p-adic norm is defined by $|a| = p^{-v_p(a)}$, for $a \in \mathbb{Q}_p$. For $a \in \mathbb{Q}_p$ and ε a positive real number, let $a + O(\varepsilon)$ denote the set of all $b \in \mathbb{Q}_p$ such that $|a - b| \leqslant \varepsilon$. For $a, b \in \mathbb{Z}_p$, we have $a = b + O(\varepsilon)$ if and only if $a \equiv b \pmod{p^{-\lfloor \log_p \varepsilon \rfloor}}$.

A computer can handle p-adic numbers given with bounded precision: a p-adic number a is approximately represented by a rational number a' and a radius ε such that $a \in a' + O(\varepsilon)$. This leads to a *ball arithmetic* over $\mathbb{Q}_p$. The ultrametric nature of $\mathbb{Q}_p$ makes ball arithmetic particularly convenient since errors do not propagate when adding two numbers:

$$(a + O(\varepsilon)) + (b + O(\eta)) = a + b + O(\max(\varepsilon, \eta)),$$

or multiplying them:

$$(a + O(\varepsilon))\,(b + O(\eta)) = ab + O(\max(\eta\,|a|\,, \varepsilon\,|b|)),$$

or dividing them:

$$\frac{a + O(\varepsilon)}{b + O(\eta)} = \frac{a}{b} + O(\max(\eta\,|a|\,|b|^{-2}\,, \varepsilon\,|b|^{-1})).$$

These formulae are optimal: the equalities are set equalities and not only left-to-right inclusions. When considering an algorithm performing additions, multiplications and divisions over p-adic numbers, it is possible to track the precision during all the intermediate steps. Thus, it is possible to run the algorithm on inputs given approximately as balls, and to return the result as a ball with the guarantee that whatever the *exact* values of the input are, the *exact* result lies in the ball returned. However, even if for every single operation the formulae above give the optimal precision of the result, the optimality does not compose. This is the well-known *dependency problem.* It is a major obstacle to the application of ball arithmetic over $\mathbb{Q}_p$, in the same way as it constricts interval arithmetic over $\mathbb{R}$.

For example, let us consider the computation of the determinant of a matrix with p-adic integer coefficients, given at precision ε. Since the determinant is an integral polynomial function of the coefficients, the determinant is also known at precision at least ε. However, if it is computed through a Gaussian elimination, and if at some point of the computation, one of the pivots has a positive valuation, then basic precision tracking will indicate that the result is only correct at precision less than ε. The *intrinsic* loss of precision is null, or even negative (Caruso, Roe, and Vaccon 2015), while the *algorithmic* loss, that depend on the algorithm, may be positive.

Caruso, Roe, and Vaccon (2014) have shown, in a p-adic setting, how to use first order analysis to obtain rigorous and optimal precision bounds on both the intrinsic and the

[*]Partially funded by the DFG grant BU 1371/2-2.

ISSAC '16, July 19–22, 2016, Waterloo, ON, Canada
© 2016 ACM. ISBN 978-1-4503-4380-0/16/07…$15.00
DOI: http://dx.doi.org/10.1145/2930889.2930912

algorithmic loss of precision. The method relies on the following fact:

LEMMA 1 (Caruso, Roe, and Vaccon 2014). *Let $\varphi : \mathbb{Q}_p^n \to \mathbb{Q}_p^m$ be a differentiable map and let $x \in \mathbb{Q}_p^n$. If the differential $\mathrm{d}_x\varphi$ at x is surjective, then $\varphi(x+B) = \varphi(x) + \mathrm{d}_x\varphi(B)$ for any zero-centered small enough ball B.*

In other words, if the precision on the input x is B, then the precision on the output $\varphi(x)$ is $\mathrm{d}_x\varphi(B)$; this is the inclusion of $\varphi(x+B)$ in $\varphi(x)+\mathrm{d}_x\varphi(B)$. And conversely, every pertubation of $\varphi(x)$ up to $\mathrm{d}_x\varphi(B)$ comes from a pertubation from the input x up to B; this is the converse inclusion of $\varphi(x)+\mathrm{d}_x\varphi(B)$ in $\varphi(x+B)$. What *small enough* is can be expressed in terms of the norms of the higher differentials of φ at x, in the case that φ is analytic at x.

1.2 Main result

We study here the computation of a power series with p-adic coefficients solution of a given first-order ordinary differential equation with separation of variables. Let g and h be power series in $\mathbb{Z}_p[\![t]\!]$ such that $h(0) = 1$ and $g(0) \neq 0$. We consider the following differential equation:

$$y' = g \cdot h(y), \quad y(0) = 0. \tag{E}$$

It has a unique solution $y \in \mathbb{Q}_p[\![t]\!]$. We make the assumption that this solution has integer coefficients, that is $y \in \mathbb{Z}_p[\![t]\!]$. Given the n first coefficients of g and h, at bounded precision, how far can we approximate y? At which computational cost?

The case of a general initial condition $y(0) = c$ reduces to the equation above by changing $h(t)$ in $h(t+c)$. In particular, the linear equation $y' = g \cdot y$, with $y(0) = 1$ can be written $z' = g \cdot (1+z)$, with $z(0) = 0$, thanks to the transformation $z = y - 1$. Nevertheless, the initial condition $y(0) = 0$ ensures that the composition $h(y)$ is well defined when h is a general power series.

DEFINITION. For ε a positive real number and n a positive integer, an *approximation modulo (p^κ, t^n)* of a power series $f = \sum_{i\geqslant 0} a_i t^i \in \mathbb{Z}_p[\![t]\!]$ is a power series $\bar{f} = \sum_{i\geqslant 0} b_i t^i \in \mathbb{Z}_p[\![t]\!]$ such that $a_i = b_i \pmod{p^\kappa}$ for all $i < n$.

The complexity of computing y depends on the complexity of the power series multiplication and the composition $h(f)$ for a general power series f. Let $M_\mathbb{Z}(p^\lambda, n)$ the number of bit operations required to compute the product of two polynomials of degree n with coefficients in $\mathbb{Z}/p^\lambda\mathbb{Z}$. Let $C_h(p^\lambda, n)$, the number of bit operations needed to compute an approximation modulo (p^λ, t^n) of $h(f)$ given an approximation modulo (p^λ, t^n) of a power series $f \in \mathbb{Z}_p[\![t]\!]$. We assume that $C_h(p^\lambda, 2n) \geqslant 2C_h(p^\lambda, n)$. In the general case, Kedlaya and Umans (2011) proved the quasi-optimal bound $C_h(p^\lambda, n) = O\big((n\lambda \log p)^{1+o(1)}\big)$. In practice, h is given as a procedure that computes the composition $h(f)$ modulo (p^λ, t^n) for any $f \in \mathbb{Z}_p[\![t]\!]$ given modulo (p^λ, t^n). This composition is easy to compute in most applications: h is often a rational function of small degree or a radical of such a rational function so that $C_h(p^\lambda, n) = O(M_\mathbb{Z}(p^\lambda, n))$. We may regard h as known with infinite precision, but the computations depends only on a suitable approximation of h.

Our main result is then the following:

THEOREM 2. *Let $n > 0$, $\kappa > 0$ (or $\kappa > 1$ if $p = 2$) and let $\lambda = \kappa + \lfloor \log_p n \rfloor$. One can compute an approximation modulo (p^κ, t^{n+1}) of the solution y of* (E) *given approximations modulo (p^λ, t^n) of g and h, using $O\left(M_\mathbb{Z}(p^\lambda, n) + C_h(p^\lambda, n)\right)$ bit operations.*

This result was already known in the linear case: Bostan et al. (2005) gave the first proof and then Grenet, Hoeven, and Lecerf (2015) gave a simpler one. In the non-linear case, Lercier and Sirvent (2008) obtained a weaker bound: they showed that an approximation modulo (p^κ, t^n) can be computed from approximations modulo $(p^{\kappa+O(\log(n)^2)}, t^n)$ of g and h. A preliminary version of the present work appeared in Vaccon's PhD thesis (Vaccon 2015). Naturally, the result also holds over unramified extensions of $\mathbb{Q}_p$, see §2.

1.3 Applications

1.3.1 Newton sums

The problem studied by Bostan et al. (2005) is the recovery of a polynomial given its Newton sums. Let $f \in \mathbb{Z}_p[t]$ be a monic polynomial of degree d, and let ν_n be the nth Newton sum of f: if $\alpha_1, \ldots, \alpha_d$ are the roots of f in $\overline{\mathbb{Q}_p}$, then ν_n is the sum $\alpha_1^n + \cdots + \alpha_d^n$, it is an element of $\mathbb{Z}_p$. How can we recover f given Newton sums $\nu_0, \ldots, \nu_d$? Let g be the polynomial $x^d f(1/x)$, and H_f be the generating function $H_f(t) = \sum_{n\geqslant 0} \nu_{n+1} t^n$. Then $g' = -H_f g$, so that g is a solution of a first-order linear differential equation (Schönhage 1993). Therefore, knowing an approximation modulo (p^κ, t^d) of H_f makes it possible to recover each coefficient of g (and hence f) modulo $p^{\kappa - \lfloor \log_p n \rfloor}$.

An interesting application is the computation over $\mathbb{F}_p$ of composed products; composed sums can be treated similarly (Bostan et al. 2005). Let f and g be monic polynomials of $\mathbb{F}_p[t]$ of degree d and e respectively, with associated roots $(\alpha_i)_{1\leqslant 1\leqslant d}$ and $(\beta_j)_{1\leqslant j\leqslant e}$ in $\overline{\mathbb{F}_p}$. We define the composed product of f and g to be

$$f \otimes g = \prod_{i,j}(t - \alpha_i\beta_j) = \underset{y}{res}(y^d f(t/y), g(y)),$$

this is a polynomial in $\mathbb{F}_p[t]$ of degree de. Then $H_{f\otimes g}$ is the coefficient-wise product of the two power series H_f and H_g (also known as the Hadamard product). This gives a strategy to compute efficiently $f \otimes g$. Firsty, arbitrarily lift f and g as polynomials in $\mathbb{Z}_p[t]$, denoted $\bar{f}$ and $\bar{g}$. The composed product $\bar{f} \otimes \bar{g}$ is a polynomial in $\mathbb{Z}_p[t]$ and equals $f \otimes g$ modulo p. Secondly, compute approximations modulo (p^κ, t^{de}) of $H_{\bar{f}}$ and $H_{\bar{g}}$, with $\kappa = 1 + \lfloor \log_p(de) \rfloor$, and, with a coefficient-wise product, an approximation modulo (p^κ, t^{de}) of $H_{\bar{f}\otimes\bar{g}}$. Thirdly, compute an approximation modulo (p, t^{de+1}) of $\bar{f}\otimes\bar{g}$ using Theorem 2, and deduce the value of $f \otimes g$.

Another application of this procedure to root finding in finite fields is developed by Grenet, Hoeven, and Lecerf (2015). Our work does not improve the complexity given by Bostan et al. (2005), in the case of a linear equation, but it gives a simpler proof that generalizes to nonlinear differential equations.

1.3.2 Isogeny computation

To compute normalized isogenies between elliptic curves, Bostan et al. (2008) and Lercier and Sirvent (2008) studied the differential equation

$$y'^2 = g \cdot h(y), \tag{1}$$

where g and h are series in $\mathbb{Z}_p[\![t]\!]$. In their context, this differential equation is known to admit a solution in $\mathbb{Z}_p[\![t]\!]$. Like the previous example, it comes from a lift of a problem over $\mathbb{F}_p$. This equation rewrites equivalently as $y' = \sqrt{g}\sqrt{h(y)}$, and, when $p \neq 2$, the series $\sqrt{g}$ and $\sqrt{h}$ are still in $\mathbb{Z}_p[\![t]\!]$, so we can apply Theorem 2. The study of this equation when $p = 2$ is still an open problem.

In order to compute an approximation of y modulo (p, t^{n+1}), we obtain that it is enough to have approximations of g and h modulo $(p^{1+\lfloor \log_p n \rfloor}, t^n)$. This improves upon the result of Lercier and Sirvent (2008) which requires approximations modulo $(p^{O(\log(n)^2)}, t^n)$.

Acknowledgements

We are grateful to Alin Bostan, Xavier Caruso, Luca De Feo, Reynald Lercier, Éric Schost and Kazuhiro Yokoyama for fruitful discussions.

2. THE ALGORITHM

We may consider the more general setting of an unramified finite extension K of $\mathbb{Q}_p$. This is useful, for example, for the computation of isogenies. Let $\mathcal{O}_K$ denote the ring of integers of K. For example, we may naturally consider $K = \mathbb{Q}_p$ and $\mathcal{O}_K = \mathbb{Z}_p$.

Let $h \in \mathcal{O}_K[\![t]\!]$, a power series with integer coefficients, with $h(0) = 1$. For $g \in K[\![t]\!]$, let $Y(g)$ be the unique $y \in K[\![t]\!]$ such that $y(0) = 0$ and $y' = g \cdot h(y)$. Existence and uniqueness are clear because the differential equation rewrites equivalently into a well posed recurrence relation on the coefficients of y.

For $g \in K[\![t]\!]$, let N_g denote the Newton operator:

$$N_g(u) = u - h(u) \int \left(\frac{u'}{h(u)} - g \right),$$

where $\int f$, for $f \in K[\![t]\!]$, denotes the unique power series $F \in K[\![t]\!]$ such that $F' = f$ and $F(0) = 0$.

Proposition 3. *Let $g, u \in K[\![t]\!]$ be formal power series, and let $n > 0$. If $u = Y(g) \pmod{t^n}$ then*

$$N_g(u) = Y(g) \pmod{t^{2n}}.$$

Proof. Let $e = u'/h(u) - g$. Since $u = Y(g) \pmod{t^n}$, we have $e = 0 \pmod{t^{n-1}}$ and $\int e = 0 \pmod{t^n}$. With $v = N_g(u)$, we compute

$$v' - g\,h(v) = u' - u'h'(u) \textstyle\int e - h(u)e - g\,h(v).$$

Then, the first-order expansion of $h(v)$ at $h(u)$ gives

$$h(v) = h(u) - h'(u)h(u) \textstyle\int e \mod t^{2n},$$

and, using the equality $u' = h(u)e + g\,h(u)$, we obtain

$$v' - g\,h(v) = -e\,h(u)h'(u) \textstyle\int e = 0 \mod t^{2n-1}.$$

This implies that $v = Y(g) \pmod{t^{2n}}$. □

The iteration of the Newton operator leads to Algorithm 1. In an exact setting, the correctness of this procedure would be clear, thanks to Proposition 3. In a p-adic setting, where the coefficients of the power series g and h are known with finite precision only, what can be obtained with Newton iteration is not clear because the operation $\int$ involves divisions.

Let us begin with a quick analysis of Algorithm 1. On input (g, h, n), it performs a recursive call and computes $u = \text{DSol}(g, h, m)$, with $m = \lceil \frac{n-1}{2} \rceil$. Let us assume that u is an approximation modulo (p^κ, t^{m+1}) of $Y(g)$, for some $\kappa > 0$.

Algorithm 1. The Newton iteration to solve a first-order differential equation.

Input. g and $h \in \mathcal{O}_K[\![t]\!]$ given modulo (p^λ, t^n) — that is, given as polynomials of degree less than n with coefficients in $\mathcal{O}_K/p^\lambda\mathcal{O}_K$.

Output. A power series $u \in \mathcal{O}_K[\![t]\!]$ given modulo (p^λ, t^{n+1}).

Specification. If $Y(g) \pmod{t^{n+1}}$ has integer coefficients and if $\lambda \geqslant \kappa + \lfloor \log_p n \rfloor$, then u is an approximation of $Y(g)$ modulo (p^κ, t^{n+1}).

```
function DSol(g, h, n)
    if n = 0 then
        return 0 (mod t)
    else
        u ← DSol(g, h, ⌈(n−1)/2⌉)
        return N_g(u) (mod t^(n+1))
                        ▷ Compute at fixed precision λ.
```

Then $N_g(u)$ is an approximation modulo $(p^{\kappa - \lfloor \log_p n \rfloor}, t^{n+1})$: Indeed, the computation of $N_g(u)$ involves divisions by the integers from 2 to n on distinct coefficients, so the loss of precision is at most the maximum valuation of these integers, which is $\lfloor \log_p n \rfloor$. Thus, if we define $\mu(0) = 0$ and $\mu(n) = \lfloor \log_p n \rfloor + \mu(\lceil \frac{n-1}{2} \rceil)$, we obtain that $\text{DSol}(g, h, n)$ is an approximation modulo $(p^{\lambda - \mu(n)}, t^{n+1})$ of $Y(g)$. We can check that $\mu(n) = O(\log(n)^2)$. Theorem 5 improves on that analysis and shows that the precision of the result is at least $\lambda - \lfloor \log_p n \rfloor$ and matches the intrinsic loss of precision.

We assume the *fixed precision model* for computing with p-adic numbers: at precision λ, it amounts to work over the ring $\mathcal{O}_K/p^\lambda\mathcal{O}_K$. When a division a/b arises, with the approximation of a and $b \in \mathcal{O}_K$ given in $\mathcal{O}_K/p^\lambda\mathcal{O}_K$, three cases may arise:

- $v_p(b) = 0$, in which case b is invertible in $\mathcal{O}_K/p^\lambda\mathcal{O}_K$ and the division is well defined.
- $v_p(a) \geqslant v_p(b) > 0$, in which case a/b is in $\mathcal{O}_K$ but its approximation in $\mathcal{O}_K/p^\lambda\mathcal{O}_K$ is not fully determined by the approximations of a and b, so a/b is arbitrarily defined in this model to be the class in $\mathcal{O}_K/p^\lambda\mathcal{O}_K$ of the smallest integer $c \geqslant 0$ such that $a = bc \pmod{p^\lambda}$.
- $v_p(a) < v_p(b)$, in which case a/b is not an integer and an error is raised.

The main argument for the correctness of Algorithm 1 is the following proposition, proved in Section 3.

Proposition 4. *Let $n > 0$ and $\kappa > 0$ (or $\kappa > 1$ if $p = 2$) be integers, and let $g \in \mathcal{O}_K[\![t]\!]$ such that $Y(g) \pmod{t^{n+1}}$ has integer coefficients. For any $y \in K[\![t]\!]$ the following are equivalent:*

1. *$y = Y(\bar{g}) \pmod{t^{n+1}}$ for some power series $\bar{g} \in \mathcal{O}_K[\![t]\!]$ such that $\int(\bar{g} - g) = 0 \pmod{p^\kappa}$;*
2. *$y = Y(g) \pmod{p^\kappa, t^{n+1}}$.*

Theorem 5. *Algorithm 1 is correct: if $\kappa > 0$ (or $\kappa > 1$ if $p = 2$) and $\lambda \geqslant \lfloor \log_p n \rfloor + \kappa$, then for all $g \in \mathcal{O}_K[\![t]\!]$ such that $Y(g)$ has integer coefficients, the output of the procedure $\text{DSol}(g, h, n)$ equals $Y(g) \pmod{p^\kappa, t^{n+1}}$.*

Moreover, it performs $\mathcal{O}\left(M_{\mathcal{O}_K}(p^\lambda, n) + C_h(p^\lambda, n)\right)$ bit operations, where $M_{\mathcal{O}_K}(p^\lambda, n)$ is the cost of computing the product of two polynomials of degree n with coefficients in $\mathcal{O}_K/p^\lambda\mathcal{O}_K$.

Proof. We proceed by induction on n. The case $n = 0$ is trivial, so let us assume that $n > 0$. Let $g \in \mathcal{O}_K[\![t]\!]$ such that $Y(g)$ has integer coefficients, let $m = \lceil \frac{n-1}{2} \rceil$ and let $u \in K[\![t]\!]$ be the output of DSOL(g, h, m). By induction hypothesis, $u = Y(g) \pmod{p^\kappa, t^{m+1}}$. (In particular u has integer coefficients.) By Proposition 4, this implies that $y = Y(\bar{g}) \pmod{t^{m+1}}$ for some $\bar{g} \in \mathcal{O}_K[\![t]\!]$ such that $\int(g-\bar{g}) \pmod{p^\kappa}$. Proposition 3 gives that $Y(\bar{g}) = N_{\bar{g}}(u) \pmod{t^{n+1}}$ and Proposition 4 gives further that $Y(\bar{g}) = Y(g) \pmod{p^\kappa, t^{n+1}}$. We check that $N_g(u) = N_{\bar{g}}(u) - h(u)\int(g-\bar{g})$ and since $h(u)$ has integer coefficients, this implies that $N_g(u) = Y(g) \pmod{p^\kappa, t^{n+1}}$.

We now relate $N_g(u)$ to the output of the procedure DSOL(g, h, n). Let $e = u'/h(u) - g$. By definition, the output is $N_g(u) = u - h(u)\int e$, computed over $\mathcal{O}_K/p^\lambda\mathcal{O}_K$, in the fixed precision model. Let E be the primitive $\int e \pmod{t^{n+1}}$ computed in this model, so that the output is exactly $u - h(u)E$. Clearly $E = \int e + \int \eta \pmod{t^{n+1}}$ for some $\eta = 0 \pmod{p^\lambda}$ that reflects the indeterminacies in the divisions. Since $\lambda \geqslant \lfloor \log_p n \rfloor + \kappa$, $\int \eta = 0 \pmod{p^\kappa}$ and thus, the output $N_g(u) + \int \eta$ equals $Y(g) \pmod{p^\kappa, t^{n+1}}$. This concludes the proof of correctness.

Concerning the complexity, the last iteration involves a composition by h with cost $C_h(p^\lambda, n)$, a few multiplications with cost $M_{\mathcal{O}_K}(p^\lambda, n)$ and an inversion $1/h(u)$ with cost $\mathcal{O}\left(M_{\mathcal{O}_K}(p^\lambda, n)\right)$ too with a Newton iteration (Kung 1974). With the assumption that the cost of an iteration is greater than twice the cost of the previous one, it is well known that the cost of a Newton algorithm is dominated by the cost of the last iteration, which gives the result. □

The condition $\lambda \geqslant \lfloor \log_p n \rfloor + \kappa$ cannot be improved further: it matches the *intrinsic* loss of precision. This is shown, for example, by the differential equation $y' = at^{b-1}$, with $a \in K$, whose solution is $\frac{a}{b}t^b$. If we take $b = p^{\lfloor \log_p n \rfloor}$ and if a is known at precision λ then y is known at precision no more than $\lambda - \lfloor \log_p n \rfloor$.

3. DIFFERENTIAL PRECISION

We apply the method of Caruso, Roe, and Vaccon (2014) to study the loss in precision in the resolution of the differential equation (E) and give a proof of Proposition 4.

Let $n > 0$ and let E and F denote respectively the two n-dimensional K-vector spaces $K[\![t]\!]/(t^n)$ and $tK[\![t]\!]/(t^{n+1})$. Let $\mathcal{Y}$ be the polynomial map

$$\begin{aligned} \mathcal{Y} : E &\longrightarrow F \\ [u] &\longmapsto [Y(u)], \end{aligned}$$

which is well defined because the $n+1$ first coefficients of $Y(u)$ depend only on the n first coefficients of u. Let $g \in \mathcal{O}_K[\![t]\!]$ be such that $\mathcal{Y}(g)$ has integer coefficients in the monomial basis. Let $\mathrm{d}\mathcal{Y}$ denote the first differential of $\mathcal{Y}$: for any $g \in E$, $\mathrm{d}_g\mathcal{Y}$ is a linear map $E \to F$. Let $d^k\mathcal{Y}$ denote the higher differentials: for any $g \in E$, $\mathrm{d}_g^k\mathcal{Y}$ is a multilinear map $E^k \to F$.

LEMMA 6. *For any $w \in E$, $\mathrm{d}\mathcal{Y}(w) = h(\mathcal{Y})\int w$. Moreover, for any $k \geqslant 1$, there exists a polynomial $P_k \in \mathbb{Z}[u_0, \ldots, u_{k-1}]$ such that for any $w_1, \ldots, w_k \in E$,*

$$\mathrm{d}^k\mathcal{Y}(w_1, \ldots, w_k) = P_k\left(h(\mathcal{Y}), h'(\mathcal{Y}), \ldots, h^{(k-1)}(\mathcal{Y})\right) \prod_{i=1}^{k} \int w_i. \quad (2)$$

Proof. Differentiating with respect to g the defining relation $\mathcal{Y}(g)' = g \cdot h(\mathcal{Y}(g)) \pmod{t^n}$ leads to

$$[\mathrm{d}_g\mathcal{Y}(w)]' = w \cdot h(\mathcal{Y}(g)) + g \cdot h'(\mathcal{Y}(g)) \cdot \mathrm{d}_g\mathcal{Y}(w),$$

which is a first-order inhomogeneous linear differential equation in $\mathrm{d}_g\mathcal{Y}(w)$. The initial condition $\mathrm{d}_g\mathcal{Y}(w)(0) = 0$ determines a unique solution, namely $h(\mathcal{Y}(g))\int w$.

The second claim follows by induction. Equation (2) holds for $k = 1$ with $P_1 = u_0$; differentiating it leads to the recurrence relation

$$P_{k+1}(u_0, \ldots, u_k) = u_0 \sum_{i=0}^{k-1} \frac{\partial P}{\partial u_i} u_{i+1}. \qquad \square$$

The space F is endowed with the maximum norm in the monomial basis, denoted by $\|\cdot\|_F$. In particular, an element u of F has integer coefficients if and only if $\|u\|_F \leqslant 1$. The space E is endowed with the norm

$$\|u\|_E \stackrel{\text{def}}{=} \left\|\int u\right\|_F.$$

Let $\|\mathrm{d}_g^k\mathcal{Y}\|$ denote the operator norm of $\mathrm{d}_g^k\mathcal{Y}$, that is

$$\|\mathrm{d}_g^k\mathcal{Y}\| = \sup\left\{\|\mathrm{d}_g^k\mathcal{Y}(w_1, \ldots, w_k)\|_F \;\middle|\; \|\int w_i\|_F \leqslant 1\right\}. \quad (3)$$

LEMMA 7. *$\|\mathrm{d}_g^k\mathcal{Y}\| \leqslant 1$, for any $k \geqslant 1$.*

Proof. Since h and $\mathcal{Y}(g)$ have integer coefficients, this follows easily from Lemma 6 and Equation (3). □

PROPOSITION 8. *For any $\varepsilon \leqslant \frac{1}{p}$ (or $\varepsilon \leqslant \frac{1}{4}$ for $p = 2$),*

$$\mathcal{Y}(g + B_\varepsilon) = \mathcal{Y}(g) + \mathrm{d}_g\mathcal{Y}(B_\varepsilon),$$

where $B_\varepsilon = \{w \in E \;:\; \|w\|_E \leqslant \varepsilon\}$.

Proof. We apply the result of Caruso, Roe, and Vaccon (2014, Corollary 3.16). Using their notations, we can use $C = 1$ because the closed ball of radius 1 in F (that is the set of elements with integer coefficients) is included in $\mathrm{d}_g\mathcal{Y}(B_1)$: Indeed for any $u \in F$ we have $\mathrm{d}_g\mathcal{Y}\left((u/\mathcal{Y}(g))'\right) = u$, and if $\|u\|_F \leqslant 1$ then $\|(u/\mathcal{Y}(g))'\|_E = \|(u/\mathcal{Y}(g))\|_F \leqslant 1$, because u and $\mathcal{Y}(g)$ have integer coefficients.

For $k \geqslant 2$, let M_k denote $\|\frac{1}{k!}\mathrm{d}_g^k\mathcal{Y}\|$. By Lemma 7, this is simply $|\frac{1}{k!}|$. Corollary 3.16 (ibid.), with $\rho = 1$ in their notations, implies that $\mathcal{Y}(g + B_\varepsilon) = \mathcal{Y}(g) + \mathrm{d}_g\mathcal{Y}(B_\varepsilon)$ as long as ε satisfies

$$\varepsilon < \exp\left(\inf_{k \geqslant 2} \frac{-\log M_k}{k-1}\right) = \inf_{k \geqslant 2} p^{-\frac{v_p(k!)}{k-1}}.$$

Let A denote the right-hand side. Legendre's formula for the p-adic valuation of $k!$ shows that $v_p(k!) \leqslant \frac{k}{p-1}$. Therefore $A \geqslant p^{-2/(p-1)}$. For $p \geqslant 5$, this bound gives $A > \frac{1}{p}$, which proves the claim. For $p = 3$, we have

$$A \geqslant \min\left(3^{-v_3(2!)}, \inf_{k \geqslant 3} 3^{-\frac{v_3(k!)}{k-1}}\right) \geqslant \min\left(1, 3^{-\frac{3}{4}}\right) > 3^{-1},$$

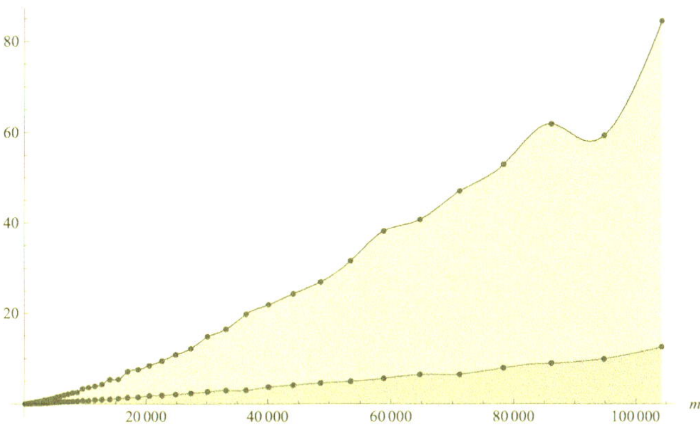

Figure 1. Timings in seconds, measured on a laptop, of Algorithm 1 run at precision λ_{old} (upper curve) and λ_{new} (lower curve) in order to compute an approximation modulo $(5, t^{4m+1})$ of the solution of Equation (4).

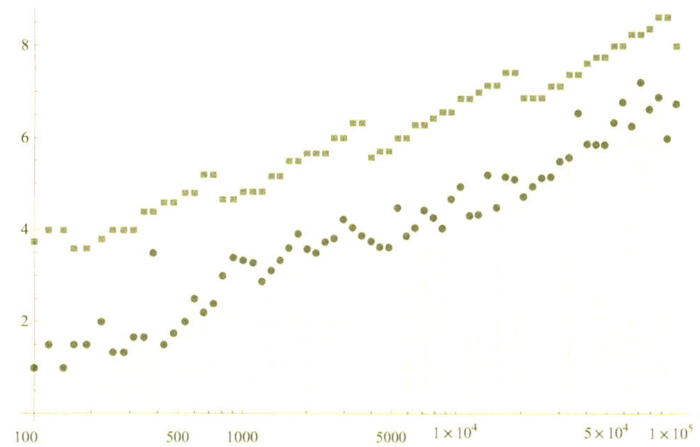

Figure 2. Practical speedup obtained with the new precision analysis compared with the theoretical improvement (m-axis in logarithmic scale).
(■) ratio $\lambda_{\text{old}}/\lambda_{\text{new}}$; (•) actual speedup.

and for $p = 2$, we have

$$A \geqslant \min\left(2^{-v_2(2!)}, \inf_{k\geqslant 3} 2^{-\frac{v_2(k!)}{k-1}}\right) \geqslant \min\left(2^{-1}, 2^{-\frac{3}{2}}\right) > 2^{-2},$$

which concludes the proof. □

Proof of Proposition 4. Let $\varepsilon = p^{-\kappa}$. The norm of an element $v \in F$ is given by $p^{-\lambda}$ where λ is the largest integer such that $v = 0 \pmod{p^\lambda}$. Since $h(\mathcal{Y}(g))$ is invertible modulo (p^λ, t^{n+1}), for any $\lambda > 0$, this shows that $\|v\|_F = \|h(\mathcal{Y}(g))v\|_F$ for any $v \in F$. Therefore, with Lemma 6 and the definition of the norms,

$$\mathrm{d}_g\mathcal{Y}(B_\varepsilon) = \{v \in F \mid v = 0 \mod p^\kappa\}.$$

Moreover, $B_\varepsilon = \left\{u \in E \mid \int u = 0 \mod p^\kappa\right\}$, and Proposition 4 now appears as a rewording of Proposition 8. □

4. EXPERIMENTS

Let us consider the differential equation

$$y' = \sqrt{\frac{1 + \frac{1}{4}m^2y^2 + m^6y^6}{1 + \frac{1}{4}t^2 + t^6}}, \quad y(0) = 0, \tag{4}$$

inspired from algorithms for computing isogenies (Bostan et al. 2008; Lercier and Sirvent 2008). Using an implementation in Magma (Bosma, Cannon, and Playoust 1997) of Algorithm 1, we computed the power series expansion of $y \pmod{5, t^{4m+1}}$ for several m. We compared (Figure 1) the CPU time spent on the computation when using on the one hand the precision $\lambda_{\text{new}} = 1 + \lfloor \log_5(4m) \rfloor$, following Theorem 5, and using on the other hand the precision $\lambda_{\text{old}} = 1 + \mu(4m) = \mathcal{O}(\log(m)^2)$ found by a straightforward precision analysis — see the discussion in §2 for the definition of μ. For example, with $m = 104281$, we compute $\lambda_{\text{old}} = 72$ and $\lambda_{\text{new}} = 9$. The number of arithmetic operations performed does not depend on the precision λ, only on m, but the number of bit operations does since the base ring for the computation is $\mathbb{Z}/5^\lambda\mathbb{Z}$. Thus, the expected speedup is $\lambda_{\text{old}}/\lambda_{\text{new}}$, which is close to what we observed (Figure 2). The implementation is available at

https://gist.github.com/lairez/d648b0d7b5392d0fef71.

References

W. Bosma, J. Cannon, and C. Playoust (1997). "The Magma algebra system. I. The user language". In: *J. Symbolic Comput.* 24.3-4, pp. 235–265. DOI: 10.1006/jsco.1996.0125.

A. Bostan, L. González-Vega, H. Perdry, and É. Schost (2005). "From Newton sums to coefficients: complexity issues in characteristic p". In: *Proc. of MEGA*. Ed. by A. Dickenstein, P. Gianni, and T. Recio. Porto Conte, Italy.

A. Bostan, F. Morain, B. Salvy, and É. Schost (2008). "Fast algorithms for computing isogenies between elliptic curves". In: *Math. Comput.* 77.263, pp. 1755–1778. DOI: 10.1090/S0025-5718-08-02066-8.

X. Caruso, D. Roe, and T. Vaccon (2014). "Tracking p-adic precision". In: *LMS J. Comput. Math.* 17.suppl. A, pp. 274–294. DOI: 10.1112/S1461157014000357.

— (2015). "p-Adic Stability In Linear Algebra". In: *Proc. of ISSAC*. Bath, United Kingdom. ACM, pp. 101–108. DOI: 10.1145/2755996.2756655.

B. Grenet, J. van der Hoeven, and G. Lecerf (2015). "Deterministic root finding over finite fields using Graeffe transforms". In: *Appl. Algebra Engrg. Comm. Comput.* DOI: 10.1007/s00200-015-0280-5.

K. S. Kedlaya and C. Umans (2011). "Fast polynomial factorization and modular composition". In: *SIAM J. Comput.* 40.6, pp. 1767–1802. DOI: 10.1137/08073408X.

H. T. Kung (1974). "On computing reciprocals of power series". In: *Numer. Math.* 22, pp. 341–348.

R. Lercier and T. Sirvent (2008). "On Elkies subgroups of ℓ-torsion points in elliptic curves defined over a finite field". In: *J. Théor. Nombres Bordeaux* 20, pp. 783–797.

A. Schönhage (1993). "Fast parallel computation of characteristic polynomials by Leverrier's power sum method adapted to fields of finite characteristic". In: *Automata, languages and programming (Lund, 1993)*. Vol. 700. LNCS. Berlin: Springer, pp. 410–417. DOI: 10.1007/3-540-56939-1_90.

T. Vaccon (2015). "Précision p-adique. Applications en calcul formel, théorie des nombres et cryptographie". PhD thesis. Université de Rennes I.

Positive Root Isolation for Poly-Powers

Jing-Cao Li
Department of Computer Science and Technology
East China Normal University, Shanghai, China
ecnujcli@126.com

Cheng-Chao Huang
Institute of Systems Science
East China Normal University, Shanghai, China
ecnucchuang@126.com

Ming Xu
Department of Computer Science and Technology
East China Normal University, Shanghai, China
mxu@cs.ecnu.edu.cn

Zhi-Bin Li
Institute of Systems Science
East China Normal University, Shanghai, China
lizb@cs.ecnu.edu.cn

ABSTRACT

We consider a class of univariate real functions—poly-powers—that extend integer exponents to real algebraic exponents for polynomials. Our purpose is to isolate positive roots of such a function into disjoint intervals, which can be further easily computed up to any desired precision. To this end, we first classify poly-powers into simple and non-simple ones, depending on the number of linearly independent exponents. For the former, we present a complete isolation method based on Gelfond–Schneider theorem. For the latter, the completeness depends on Schanuel's conjecture. Finally experiential results demonstrate the effectivity of the proposed method.

Keywords

real root isolation; generalized polynomial; transcendental number; interval arithmetic

1. INTRODUCTION

Solving nonlinear equation captures a central position in Computer Algebra with extremely wide applications to many fields, such as physics, economics, control theory and systems biology. The foundation of equation-solving is to locate real roots of univariate functions. Since those roots are not rational (even not algebraic) in general, one can only expect to isolate them into disjoint intervals, which can be easily refined to any desired precision for further use.

Polynomials are the principal objects for real root isolation. The early work can date back to 17th century. Isaac Newton proposed a numerical iteration method for solving $\mathbb{R}$-polynomial equations [15]. The iterative values could approach real roots at quadratic convergence rate, which depended on the choosing of starting points. Later, a large number of modifications were proposed and applied to solve nonlinear equations and systems. With the hypothesis of differentiability, Smale improved Newton's method by deducing consequences from data at a single point [19]. This point of view had valuable features for computation. Newton's method could further solve the general polynomial system, provided the computational precision satisfied a bound polynomial in some parameters [9]. For another, Dedieu and Yakoubsohn presented the exclusion algorithm [10] for efficiently isolating real roots of $\mathbb{R}$-polynomials. However, due to the hardness of sign-determination of constants [17], one cannot always distinguish between a root of multiplicity k and a cluster of k roots for $\mathbb{R}$-polynomials. To be more complete, Yap *et al.* exploited soft sign-determination that asked whether $\alpha > 0$ or $\alpha < 0$, but not $\alpha = 0$, and then established the first exact algorithm for analyzing root clusters of complex analytic functions [27]. To avoid missing of multiple real roots and numerical errors, algebraic methods were designed to overcome these shortages. For instance, Collins and his coauthors respectively presented the differentiation method [6] and another one based on the sign rule of Descartes [5] for $\mathbb{Q}$-polynomials. These methods became rather popular as well as numerical ones.

Motivated by the profound Tarski's problem [23]—deciding the theory $\mathrm{T}(\mathbb{R}; <, =; +, \cdot, \exp; 0, 1)$, many efforts had been put in the study of exponential functions. In [16], Richardson investigated the structure of real roots of exponential polynomials, elements of $\mathbb{Q}[x, \mathrm{e}^x]$. Later Achatz *et al.* proposed the first complete real root isolation algorithm for such functions [1]. Its rationale was the differentiation method, and its completeness was ensured by Lindemann's theorem [18]. Meantime, Strzeboński studied the real root isolation of exp-log functions and tame elementary functions, respectively, in [20, 21]. But the completeness of the procedure depended on Schanuel's conjecture [2]. Recently, these methods had been developed as decision procedure [14], cylindrical decomposition [22], and quantifier elimination [24] for certain multivariate formulas.

In this paper, we study a class of the generalized polynomials, named poly-powers, closely related to polynomials and exponential polynomials (to be specified below). It has the normal form

$$f(x) = \beta_0 + \beta_1 x^{\alpha_1} + \cdots + \beta_n x^{\alpha_n}, \qquad (1)$$

where α_i $(1 \le i \le n)$ and β_i $(0 \le i \le n)$ are $\mathbb{R}_{\mathrm{alg}}$-numbers with $0 < \alpha_1 < \cdots < \alpha_n$ and $n > 0$. For convenience, we assume w. l. o. g. that the poly-power we study has a nonzero constant term, viz. $\beta_0 \neq 0$ in $f(x)$.

ISSAC '16, July 19–22, 2016, Waterloo, ON, Canada.
© 2016 ACM. ISBN 978-1-4503-4380-0/16/07...$15.00
DOI: http://dx.doi.org/10.1145/2930889.2930909

Our purpose is to isolate positive roots of poly-powers. First of all, we perform factorization to simplify the input poly-power. To this end, we have to find a linearly independent base of its coefficients and exponents. Based on that, we get a multivariate polynomial representation of the input poly-power and thus perform the factorization. The union of positive roots of irreducible factors consists of those of the input poly-power. More importantly, factorization can help us classify poly-powers into simple and non-simple ones, depending on the number of linearly independent exponents in an irreducible poly-power. Then we propose the positive root isolation algorithm for irreducible poly-powers by bisection and interval estimate. The whole procedure is established on algebraic manipulation, and hence is absolutely exact. The completeness is ensured by Gelfond–Schneider theorem for simple poly-powers, and by Schanuel's conjecture for non-simple ones. Finally we implement the proposed method with the MAPLE platform to demonstrate the effectivity.

Related work. The functions similar to poly-powers are *generalized polynomials* in [3] and *multiple power sums* in [25] that both extend integer exponents to real exponents for polynomials. Specifically, it has the form $b_0x^{a_0}+b_1x^{a_1}+\cdots+b_nx^{a_n}$ with $a_i, b_i \in \mathbb{R}$ $(0 \le i \le n)$, which is slightly more expressive than poly-powers. In [3], Bak *et al.* used generalized polynomials to estimate the convergence rate of functions in the spaces $\mathcal{L}_p[0,1]$ and $\mathcal{C}[0,1]$. In 2005, Coste *et al.* proved the generalized Budan–Fourier theorem to count the number of complex roots of multiple power sums [7]. Xu *et al.* reproved the generalized Budan–Fourier theorem to count the number of positive roots, and gave the upper and the lower bounds of all positive roots. Note that the set of computable (real) numbers $\mathcal{R}$, including real algebraic numbers $\mathbb{R}_{\rm alg}$, is only a countable subset of real numbers $\mathbb{R}$. So we restrict those exponents into $\mathbb{R}_{\rm alg}$-numbers to rigorously ensure the computability.

From another point of view, the poly-power is closely related to the exponential polynomial

$$\beta_0(t) + \beta_1(t)\mathrm{e}^{\alpha_1 t} + \cdots + \beta_n(t)\mathrm{e}^{\alpha_n t}, \tag{2}$$

where all α_i are $\mathbb{R}_{\rm alg}$-numbers and $\beta_i(t)$ are $\mathbb{R}_{\rm alg}$-polynomials. It subsumes the poly-power, because the latter can be immediately obtained by substituting of $x = \mathrm{e}^t$ and restricting all $\beta_i(t)$ to $\mathbb{R}_{\rm alg}$-numbers. Under Schanuel's conjecture, Chonev *et al.* gave a procedure to decide whether the above exponential polynomial has a real root in an appointed interval (see Subsection 2.1 of [4]). However, they only concerned the existence of real roots, rather than the real root isolation.

Organization. In Section 2 we decompose the poly-power into simpler ones. Then we present the isolation method in Section 3, and implement it in Section 4. Finally Section 5 is the conclusion.

2. DECOMPOSITION

In this section, we aim to decompose the input poly-power into simpler ones that preserve positive roots. Naturally one may relate it to factorization. However, since the exponents in a poly-power are generally $\mathbb{R}_{\rm alg}$-numbers (unlike integers in a polynomial), there is no direct way to do the factorization. To resolve it, we first find a $\mathbb{Z}$-linearly independent base which spans all exponents. Based on that, the poly-power can be transformed to an equivalent multivariate polynomial relation among independent powers, which is easy to be factorized. These irreducible factors would be simpler poly-powers. Thus we complete the decomposition of the input poly-power.

Let $\mathcal{A}$ denote the field extension (over $\mathbb{Q}$) generated by all $\mathbb{R}_{\rm alg}$-numbers $\alpha_1, \ldots, \alpha_n; \beta_0, \ldots, \beta_n$ appearing in the poly-power. (In fact, it suffices to require that $\mathcal{A}$ is generated by $\beta_0, \ldots, \beta_n$ for the purpose of this section. But it will bring much convenience in later if $\mathcal{A}$ is generated by $\alpha_1, \ldots, \alpha_n; \beta_0, \ldots, \beta_n$.) We expect to obtain a $\mathbb{Z}$-linearly independent base $\{v_1, \ldots, v_\ell\}$ of them, which fortunately can be completed by the following algorithm.

Algorithm 1 Computing a Simple Extension over $\mathbb{Q}$ [13]

$$(\mu; p_1, \ldots, p_n) \Leftarrow \mathsf{Simple}(\mu_1, \ldots, \mu_n)$$

Input: Each μ_i is a $\mathbb{R}_{\rm alg}$-number, equipped with minimal polynomial ρ_i and isolation interval $\mathcal{I}_i$.

Output: μ is a $\mathbb{R}_{\rm alg}$-number, equipped with minimal polynomial ρ and isolation interval $\mathcal{I}$, such that $\mu_i = p_i(\mu) \in \mathbb{Z}[\mu]$ with $\deg(p_i) < \deg(\rho)$.

By invoking Algorithm 1 with $\mathsf{Simple}(\alpha_1, \ldots, \alpha_n, \beta_0, \ldots, \beta_n)$, we can obtain a simple extension representation $\mathbb{Q}(\mu)$ for $\mathcal{A}$, viz. $\mathbb{Q}(\mu) = \mathbb{Q}(\alpha_1, \ldots, \alpha_n, \beta_0, \ldots, \beta_n)$. Then the $\mathbb{R}_{\rm alg}$-numbers $1, \mu, \ldots, \mu^{l-1}$, where $l = \deg(\rho)$, must be $\mathbb{Z}$-linearly independent. (Otherwise μ could be defined by a polynomial with degree less than l, which contradicts that ρ is the minimal polynomial of μ.) So we have the representation

$$\begin{bmatrix} \alpha_1 \\ \vdots \\ \alpha_n \end{bmatrix} = \begin{bmatrix} p_{1,0} & p_{1,1} & \cdots & p_{1,l-1} \\ \vdots & \vdots & \ddots & \vdots \\ p_{n,0} & p_{n,1} & \cdots & p_{n,l-1} \end{bmatrix} \begin{bmatrix} 1 \\ \mu \\ \vdots \\ \mu^{l-1} \end{bmatrix}, \tag{3}$$

where all $p_{i,0}, p_{i,1}, \ldots, p_{i,l-1}$ are taken from coefficients of $\mathbb{Z}$-polynomials $\alpha_i = p_i(\mu) = p_{i,0} + p_{i,1}\mu + \cdots + p_{i,l-1}\mu^{l-1}$ $(0 \le i \le n)$. Note that there may still exist linear dependence between column vectors $(p_{1,j}, \ldots, p_{n,j})^{\rm T}$ $(0 \le j \le l-1)$. It implies that the size of the base $\{1, \mu, \ldots, \mu^{l-1}\}$ could be reduced by linearly combining base elements, provided that the coefficient matrix has rank less than l. After reduction, we obtain a $\mathbb{Z}$-linearly independent base $\{\nu_1, \ldots, \nu_\ell\}$, satisfying:

$$\begin{bmatrix} \alpha_1 \\ \vdots \\ \alpha_n \end{bmatrix} = \begin{bmatrix} q_{1,1} & \cdots & q_{1,\ell} \\ \vdots & \ddots & \vdots \\ q_{n,1} & \cdots & q_{n,\ell} \end{bmatrix} \begin{bmatrix} \nu_1 \\ \vdots \\ \nu_\ell \end{bmatrix}, \tag{4}$$

where $q_{i,j} \in \mathbb{Z}$, $\gcd(q_{1,j}, \ldots, q_{n,j}) = 1$ and the coefficient matrix has the full rank ℓ. Furthermore, we can fix the $\mathbb{Z}$-linearly independent base $\{v_1, \ldots, v_\ell\}$, satisfying:

$$\begin{bmatrix} \alpha_1 \\ \vdots \\ \alpha_n \end{bmatrix} = \begin{bmatrix} r_{1,1} & \cdots & r_{1,\ell} \\ \vdots & \ddots & \vdots \\ r_{n,1} & \cdots & r_{n,\ell} \end{bmatrix} \begin{bmatrix} v_1 \\ \vdots \\ v_\ell \end{bmatrix}, \tag{5}$$

where $v_i \in \mathbb{R}^+_{\rm alg}$, $r_{i,j} \in \mathbb{Z}^+$, $\gcd(r_{1,j}, \ldots, r_{n,j}) = 1$, and the coefficient matrix has the full rank ℓ, since $\alpha_1, \ldots, \alpha_n$ are positive.

Now the poly-power $f(x)$ can be represented as an element of the ring $\mathcal{A}[x^{v_1}, \ldots, x^{v_\ell}]$ with a nonzero constant term. We call by *associated* polynomial $g(x^{v_1}, \ldots, x^{v_\ell})$ the aforementioned polynomial representation of $f(x)$. Note that $\mathcal{A}[x^{\upsilon_1}, \ldots, x^{\upsilon_\ell}]$ is a unique factorization domain, the decomposition of $f(x)$ corresponds to the factorization of $g(x^{\upsilon_1}, \ldots, x^{\upsilon_\ell})$, which has been well implemented in existing materials, e. g. [13]. A poly-power is said to be *irreducible* if its associated polynomial is irreducible.

EXAMPLE 2.1. *Consider the poly-power*

$$\begin{aligned} f(x) = 20 &- \tfrac{20}{3}x + 15x^{\sqrt{3}} + \tfrac{9}{4}x^2 - (4\sqrt{5} + \tfrac{5}{2})x^{\sqrt{3}+1} \\ &- 4x^{3\sqrt{2}-1} + \tfrac{45}{16}x^{2\sqrt{3}} + \tfrac{4\sqrt{5}}{3}x^{\sqrt{3}+2} + (\tfrac{4\sqrt{3}}{5} + \tfrac{2}{3})x^{3\sqrt{2}} \\ &- 3\sqrt{5}x^{2\sqrt{3}+1} - \tfrac{\sqrt{5}}{9}x^{\sqrt{3}+3} - \tfrac{3}{2}x^{\sqrt{3}+3\sqrt{2}-1} - \tfrac{4\sqrt{3}}{15}x^{3\sqrt{2}+1} \\ &+ \tfrac{\sqrt{5}}{2}x^{2\sqrt{3}+2} + (\tfrac{3\sqrt{3}}{5} + \tfrac{4\sqrt{5}}{5})x^{\sqrt{3}+3\sqrt{2}} - \tfrac{9\sqrt{5}}{16}x^{3\sqrt{3}+1} \\ &+ \tfrac{\sqrt{3}}{45}x^{3\sqrt{2}+2} + \tfrac{1}{5}x^{6\sqrt{2}-2} - (\tfrac{\sqrt{3}}{10} + \tfrac{2\sqrt{5}}{15})x^{\sqrt{3}+3\sqrt{2}+1} \\ &- \tfrac{4\sqrt{3}}{25}x^{6\sqrt{2}-1} + (\tfrac{9\sqrt{3}}{80} + \tfrac{3\sqrt{5}}{10})x^{2\sqrt{3}+3\sqrt{2}} + \tfrac{2\sqrt{3}}{75}x^{6\sqrt{2}} \\ &- (\tfrac{3\sqrt{3}}{5} + \tfrac{\sqrt{5}}{25})x^{6\sqrt{2}+\sqrt{3}-1} + \tfrac{\sqrt{3}}{125}x^{9\sqrt{2}-2}. \end{aligned}$$

Applying the above method to the exponents in $f(x)$, we get a $\mathbb{Z}$-linearly independent base

$$\{\nu_1, \nu_2, \nu_3\} = \{1, \sqrt{2}, \sqrt{3}\},$$

by which all exponents can be $\mathbb{Z}$-linearly expressed. Namely, $f(x)$ is equivalent to an element of the local ring $\mathcal{A}[x^{\nu_1}, x^{-\nu_1}, x^{\nu_2}, x^{-\nu_2}, x^{\nu_3}, x^{-\nu_3}]$, where $\mathcal{A}$ is the field extension generated by all exponents and coefficients in $f(x)$.

Note that there are some exponents linearly expressed by $\{\nu_1, \nu_2, \nu_3\}$ with negative coefficients, like the exponent $9\sqrt{2}-2 = 9\nu_2 - 2\nu_1$ in the last term. It implies that $f(x)$ cannot have a polynomial representation using the base $\{\nu_1, \nu_2, \nu_3\}$. Fortunately, we can always find another $\mathbb{Z}$-linearly independent base by ***difference substitution*** *[26], saying*

$$\{\upsilon_1, \upsilon_2, \upsilon_3\} = \{1, \sqrt{2} - 1, \sqrt{3} - \sqrt{2}\}, \quad (6)$$

by which all exponents are $\mathbb{Z}^+$-linearly expressed. Now $f(x)$ is equivalent to an element $g(x^{\upsilon_1}, x^{\upsilon_2}, x^{\upsilon_3})$ of the ring $\mathcal{A}[x^{\upsilon_1}, x^{\upsilon_2}, x^{\upsilon_3}]$. The latter is the associate polynomial of $f(x)$.

Finally, we have the factorization

$$g(x^{\upsilon_1}, x^{\upsilon_2}, x^{\upsilon_3}) = \varphi_1 \cdot \varphi_2^2,$$

where $\varphi_1 = 5 - \sqrt{5}x^{\upsilon_3}x^{\upsilon_2}(x^{\upsilon_1})^2 + \frac{\sqrt{3}}{5}(x^{\upsilon_2})^3(x^{\upsilon_1})^3$ and $\varphi_2 = -2 + \frac{1}{3}x^{\upsilon_1} - \frac{3}{4}x^{\upsilon_3}x^{\upsilon_2}x^{\upsilon_1} + \frac{1}{5}(x^{\upsilon_2})^3(x^{\upsilon_1})^2$ are irreducible poly-powers over $\mathcal{A}[x^{\upsilon_1}, x^{\upsilon_2}, x^{\upsilon_3}]$. In other words, we obtain two irreducible poly-powers

$$\begin{aligned} \varphi_1 &= 5 - \sqrt{5}x^{\sqrt{3}+1} + \tfrac{\sqrt{3}}{5}x^{3\sqrt{2}}, \\ \varphi_2 &= -2 + \tfrac{1}{3}x - \tfrac{3}{4}x^{\sqrt{3}} + \tfrac{1}{5}x^{3\sqrt{2}-1}. \end{aligned}$$

whose positive roots are exactly the original poly-power $f(x)$'s (see Figure 1).

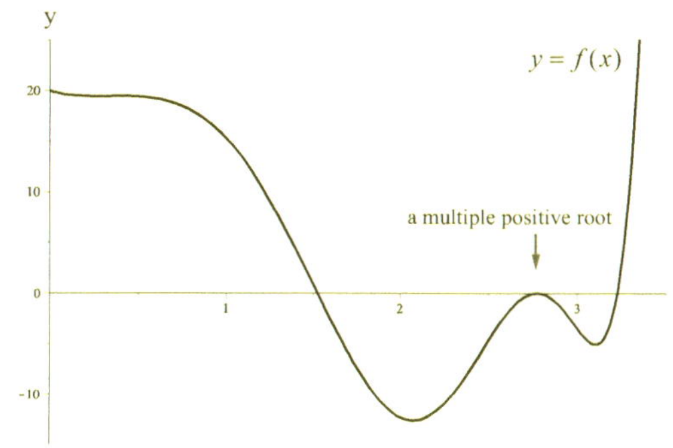

(a) The original poly-power

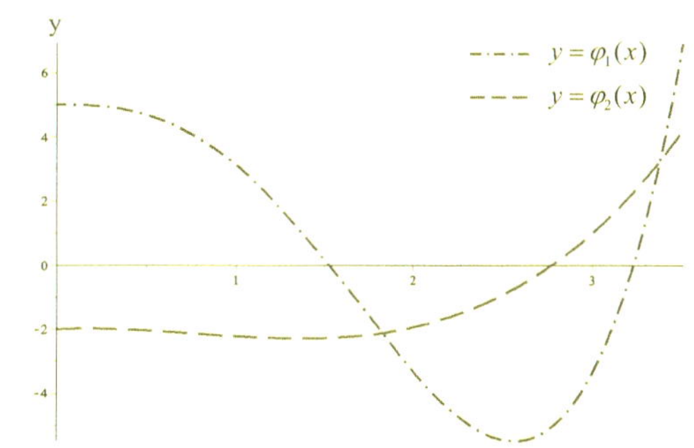

(b) Two irreducible poly-powers

Figure 1: Decomposition

3. POSITIVE ROOT ISOLATION

In this section we aim to:

1. isolate positive roots for the irreducible poly-power whose associated polynomial has at most two variables;
2. isolate positive roots for the irreducible poly-power whose associated polynomial has at least three variables;
3. isolate positive roots for the reducible poly-power.

We apply number-theoretic results to rule out multiple positive roots. Based on that and interval arithmetic, we will give two criteria respectively to check whether an interval contains exactly one positive root or none. After checking sufficiently precise subintervals, we could eventually obtain the complete list of isolation intervals for all positive roots.

3.1 Simple Case

Here we present the positive root isolation algorithm for an irreducible poly-power equivalent to a bivariate associated polynomial. That function is called the simple poly-power, an element of $\mathcal{A}[x^{\upsilon_1}, x^{\upsilon_2}]$. When the associated polynomial is univariate in $y = x^{\upsilon_1}$, the positive root isolation for the poly-power $f(x)$ would amount to that for the univariate polynomial $g(y)$, which can be plainly solved.

Let φ be an element of $\mathcal{A}[x^{\upsilon_1}, x^{\upsilon_2}]$. It can be rewritten as an element of $\mathcal{A}[y, y^{\upsilon}]$ with the substitution of $y = x^{\upsilon_1}$ and $\upsilon = \upsilon_2/\upsilon_1$, which is a simple poly-power too. Clearly, υ is irrational. Thus we can w. l. o. g. focus only on the positive root isolation for $\varphi \in \mathcal{A}[y, y^{\upsilon}]$ in this subsection.

We first recall a classic number-theoretic result that:

THEOREM 3.1 (GELFOND–SCHNEIDER (1934), SEE [18]). *The numbers β^{α} are transcendental for all algebraic numbers $\beta \in \mathbb{A} \setminus \{0, 1\}$ and all irrational algebraic numbers $\alpha \in \mathbb{A}$.*

LEMMA 3.1. *Let φ be an irreducible element of $\mathcal{A}[y, y^{\upsilon}]$ with positive degree in y^{υ}. Then φ has no $\mathbb{R}^+_{\mathrm{alg}}$-root with the only possible exception for $y = 1$.*

The proof is similar to that of Theorem 3.5 of [1], but makes use of Theorem 3.1.

LEMMA 3.2. *Let φ be an irreducible element of $\mathcal{A}[y, y^{\upsilon}]$ with positive degree in y^{υ}. Then φ has no multiple positive root with the only possible exception for $y = 1$.*

PROOF. (The proof is similar to that of Theorem 2.7 of [1], but makes use of Theorem 3.1. To be self-contained, we will give the proof below.)

Let the *strictly 1-shifted derivative* (*shifted derivative* for short, see Definition 1 of [11]) of φ be defined as

$$\psi = y \cdot \varphi'. \tag{7}$$

Obviously, ψ shares the same positive roots with φ', and shares the same exponents with φ. Furthermore it can be easily verified that ψ is an element of $\mathcal{A}[y, y^{\upsilon}]$ since $\mathcal{A}$ is the field extension generated by $\alpha_1, \ldots, \alpha_n; \beta_0, \ldots, \beta_n$, and φ, ψ are co-prime since φ is irreducible and ψ has less terms than φ. Assume that y_0 is a multiple positive root of φ, viz. $\varphi = 0$ and $\psi = 0$ simultaneously hold at $y = y_0$. After applying Sylvester's resultant to eliminate y polynomially in φ and ψ, the result would be a nonzero element of $\mathcal{A}[y^{\upsilon}]$ that is zero at $y = y_0$. It implies that y_0^{υ} is algebraic by Corollary 4 of [13], so is y_0. Finally we have $y_0 = 1$ by Theorem 3.1, since υ is irrational. $\square$

This lemma indicates that all positive roots (except 1) of φ are simple. It also implies that the shifted derivative ψ is nonzero at any positive root (except 1) of φ, and even in a sufficiently small neighbor of a positive root of φ. So we utilize the following criteria to determine whether an interval contains exactly one positive root or none.

CRITERION 3.1. *A poly-power φ has exactly one positive root in the interval $\mathcal{I}$ excluding 1 if the under-approximation (subset) of its range includes zero and the over-approximation (superset) of the range of its shifted derivative ψ excludes zero, i. e., $0 \in \mathrm{Rg}^{-}(\varphi, \mathcal{I})$ and $0 \notin \mathrm{Rg}^{+}(\psi, \mathcal{I})$.*

CRITERION 3.2. *A poly-power φ has no positive root in the interval $\mathcal{I}$ if the over-approximation of its range excludes zero, i. e., $0 \notin \mathrm{Rg}^{+}(\varphi, \mathcal{I})$.*

The correctness of the two above criteria is straightforward. Then we turn to algorithmically construct those approximations using the fact that all algebraic numbers are computable. The standard encoding of algebraic numbers is using minimal polynomials and isolation intervals that can offer numerical approximations of any precision. In fact, Thom's lemma [8] gives another encoding of algebraic numbers, but it cannot directly offer numerical approximation. So we adopt the former one in the paper.

In what follows, we will construct the over-approximation $\mathrm{Rg}^{+}(f, \mathcal{I})$ of the range of a poly-power $f(x)$ on a rational interval $\mathcal{I} = (a, b) \subset (0, 1) \cup (1, +\infty)$. To get a safe approximation, we introduce the **interval arithmetic** rule: for $a > 1$, $a^{(\underline{\alpha}, \overline{\alpha})} = (a^{\underline{\alpha}}, a^{\overline{\alpha}})$ and $(a, b)^{(\underline{\alpha}, \overline{\alpha})} = (a^{\underline{\alpha}}, b^{\overline{\alpha}})$, where $(\underline{\alpha}, \overline{\alpha})$ is a rational interval approximation of α; for $a < 1$, $a^{(\underline{\alpha}, \overline{\alpha})} = (a^{\overline{\alpha}}, a^{\underline{\alpha}})$ and $(a, b)^{(\underline{\alpha}, \overline{\alpha})} = (a^{\overline{\alpha}}, b^{\underline{\alpha}})$; and others are standard. For convenience, we denote by (α) the approximation $(\underline{\alpha}, \overline{\alpha})$. Assume w. l. o. g. that $f(x)$ is expressed in the form (1). Then, using interval arithmetic, we can obtain the over-approximation

$$\mathrm{Rg}^{+}(f, \mathcal{I}) = \beta_0 + \beta_1 \cdot \mathcal{I}^{(\alpha_1)} + \cdots + \beta_n \cdot \mathcal{I}^{(\alpha_n)}. \tag{8}$$

On the other hand, to get an under-approximation $\mathrm{Rg}^{-}(f, \mathcal{I})$, we first assume $f(a) \neq f(b)$. Otherwise we can replace a with a slightly shifted $a + \epsilon \in \mathcal{I}$, satisfying $f(a + \epsilon) \neq f(b)$. Then, we can get two estimation intervals V_{left} and V_{right} respectively for the values $f(x)$ at endpoints of $\mathcal{I}$:

$$V_{\mathrm{left}} = \beta_0 + \beta_1 \cdot a^{(\alpha_1)} + \cdots + \beta_n \cdot a^{(\alpha_n)},$$
$$V_{\mathrm{right}} = \beta_0 + \beta_1 \cdot b^{(\alpha_1)} + \cdots + \beta_n \cdot b^{(\alpha_n)}.$$

Moreover, V_{left} and V_{right} would be sparable, when (α_i) $(1 \leq i \leq n)$ are sufficiently precise. Finally, we can get an under-approximation

$$\mathrm{Rg}^{-}(f, \mathcal{I}) = \begin{cases} (\sup V_{\mathrm{left}}, \inf V_{\mathrm{right}}) \\ \qquad \text{if } \sup V_{\mathrm{left}} < \inf V_{\mathrm{right}}, \\ (\sup V_{\mathrm{right}}, \inf V_{\mathrm{left}}) \\ \qquad \text{if } \sup V_{\mathrm{right}} < \inf V_{\mathrm{left}}. \end{cases} \tag{9}$$

Thus we can obtain the over-approximations $\mathrm{Rg}^{+}(\varphi, \mathcal{I})$, $\mathrm{Rg}^{+}(\psi, \mathcal{I})$ and the under-approximation $\mathrm{Rg}^{-}(\varphi, \mathcal{I})$ of the range of the poly-powers φ, ψ on the interval $\mathcal{I}$. Those approximations are algebraic, and could be easily refined as rational intervals within any predefined error, provided that the length of $\mathcal{I}$ is sufficiently small and υ is sufficiently approached.

EXAMPLE 3.1. *Consider the poly-power $\varphi_1 = 5 - \sqrt{5}x^{\sqrt{3}+1} + \frac{\sqrt{3}}{5}x^{3\sqrt{2}}$ in Example 2.1. Its shifted derivative is*

$$\psi_1 = -(\sqrt{15} + \sqrt{5})x^{\sqrt{3}+1} + \tfrac{3\sqrt{6}}{5}x^{3\sqrt{2}}.$$

Here we will estimate the ranges of φ_1 and ψ_1 on the intervals $(\frac{45}{32}, \frac{103}{64})$ and $(1, \frac{45}{32})$, and thereby infer the number of positive roots of φ_1 in them.

On the interval $\mathcal{I}' = (\frac{45}{32}, \frac{103}{64})$, using the interval estimates of algebraic numbers $(\sqrt{2}) = (\frac{181}{128}, \frac{91}{64})$, $(\sqrt{3}) = (\frac{113511}{65536}, \frac{14189}{8192})$ and $(\sqrt{5}) = (\frac{285}{128}, \frac{573}{256})$, we can compute

$$\begin{aligned} &\mathrm{Rg}^{+}(\varphi_1, \mathcal{I}') \\ &= 5 - (\sqrt{5}) \cdot \left(\tfrac{45}{32}, \tfrac{103}{64}\right)^{(\sqrt{3})+1} + \tfrac{(\sqrt{3})}{5} \cdot \left(\tfrac{45}{32}, \tfrac{103}{64}\right)^{3\cdot(\sqrt{2})} \\ &\subset \Big(5 - \tfrac{573}{256} \cdot \left(\tfrac{103}{64}\right)^{\frac{22381}{8192}} + \tfrac{113511}{327680} \cdot \left(\tfrac{45}{32}\right)^{\frac{543}{128}}, \\ &\qquad 5 - \tfrac{285}{128} \cdot \left(\tfrac{45}{32}\right)^{\frac{179047}{65536}} + \tfrac{14189}{40960} \cdot \left(\tfrac{103}{64}\right)^{\frac{273}{64}} \Big) \\ &\subset (-1.75, 1.99). \end{aligned}$$

Note that interval estimates of algebraic numbers can be easily offered to any desired precision. In fact, the above ones suffice in our examples. Furthermore, we can obtain two estimation intervals V_{left} and V_{right} respectively for the values of φ_1 at endpoints of $\mathcal{I}'$:

$$\begin{aligned} V_{\mathrm{left}} &= 5 - (\sqrt{5}) \cdot \left(\tfrac{45}{32}\right)^{(\sqrt{3})+1} + \tfrac{(\sqrt{3})}{5} \cdot \left(\tfrac{45}{32}\right)^{3\cdot(\sqrt{2})} \\ &\subset \Big(5 - \tfrac{573}{256} \cdot \left(\tfrac{45}{32}\right)^{\frac{22381}{8192}} + \tfrac{113511}{327680} \cdot \left(\tfrac{45}{32}\right)^{\frac{543}{128}}, \\ &\qquad 5 - \tfrac{285}{128} \cdot \left(\tfrac{45}{32}\right)^{\frac{179047}{65536}} + \tfrac{14189}{40960} \cdot \left(\tfrac{45}{32}\right)^{\frac{273}{64}} \Big) \\ &\subset (0.80, 0.84), \\ V_{\mathrm{right}} &= 5 - (\sqrt{5}) \cdot \left(\tfrac{103}{64}\right)^{(\sqrt{3})+1} + \tfrac{(\sqrt{3})}{5} \cdot \left(\tfrac{103}{64}\right)^{3\cdot(\sqrt{2})} \\ &\subset \Big(5 - \tfrac{573}{256} \cdot \left(\tfrac{103}{64}\right)^{\frac{22381}{8192}} + \tfrac{113511}{327680} \cdot \left(\tfrac{103}{64}\right)^{\frac{543}{128}}, \\ &\qquad 5 - \tfrac{285}{128} \cdot \left(\tfrac{103}{64}\right)^{\frac{179047}{65536}} + \tfrac{14189}{40960} \cdot \left(\tfrac{103}{64}\right)^{\frac{273}{64}} \Big) \\ &\subset (-0.61, -0.52). \end{aligned}$$

As $\sup V_{\text{right}} < \inf V_{\text{left}}$*, we have*

$$\mathrm{Rg}^-(\varphi_1, \mathcal{I}') = (\sup V_{\text{right}}, \inf V_{\text{left}}) \supset (-0.52, 0.80).$$

Similarly, we calculate

$$\mathrm{Rg}^+(\psi_1, \mathcal{I}') \subset (-16.20, -4.18).$$

It is clear that $0 \in \mathrm{Rg}^-(\varphi_1, \mathcal{I}')$ *and* $0 \notin \mathrm{Rg}^+(\psi_1, \mathcal{I}')$*. Applying Criterion 3.1, we can know that* φ_1 *has exactly one positive root in the interval* $(\frac{45}{32}, \frac{103}{64})$*.*

For the interval $\mathcal{I}'' = (1, \frac{45}{32})$*, we have*

$$\mathrm{Rg}^+(\varphi_1, \mathcal{I}'') \subset (-14.06, 0.25),$$
$$\mathrm{Rg}^-(\varphi_1, \mathcal{I}'') \supset (0.84, 3.10).$$

Neither Criterion 3.1 nor Criterion 3.2 is applicable. Then we have to bisect $\mathcal{I}''$ *to decide whether* $\mathcal{I}''$ *contains positive roots or none. On the subintervals* $(1, \frac{77}{64})$ *and* $(\frac{77}{64}, \frac{45}{32})$*, we have*

$$\mathrm{Rg}^+(\varphi_1, (1, \tfrac{77}{64})) \subset (1.63, 3.54),$$
$$\mathrm{Rg}^+(\varphi_1, (\tfrac{77}{64}, \tfrac{45}{32})) \subset (0.07, 2.80).$$

Obviously, $0 \notin \mathrm{Rg}^+(\varphi_1, (1, \frac{77}{64})) \cup \mathrm{Rg}^+(\varphi_1, (\frac{77}{64}, \frac{45}{32}))$*. Applying Criterion 3.2, we can know that* φ_1 *has no positive root in the interval* $(1, \frac{45}{32})$*.*

Now we are ready to state the isolation algorithm (see Algorithm 2). Its rationale is that for a positive rational interval $\mathcal{I}$ excluding 1, we can bisect it and recursively tackle each subinterval, until one of the two criteria is applicable. Note that, to ensure termination, the approximation (v) of v should be dynamically refined in the running time.

Algorithm 2 The positive root isolation for $\mathcal{A}[y, y^v]$

$$\{\mathcal{I}_1, \ldots, \mathcal{I}_n\} \Leftarrow \mathsf{Isolate}(\varphi, \mathcal{I})$$

Input: $\varphi \in \mathcal{A}[y, y^v]$ is a simple poly-power with positive degree in y^v, which is defined on the rational interval $\mathcal{I} = (a, b) \subset (0, 1) \cup (1, +\infty)$.

Output: $\mathcal{I}_1, \ldots, \mathcal{I}_n$ are finitely many disjoint intervals, such that each contains exactly one positive root of φ in $\mathcal{I}$, and together contain all.

```
let ψ = x · φ' be the shifted derivative of φ;
compute Rg+(φ,I), Rg−(φ,I) and Rg+(ψ,I);
if Criterion 3.1 holds then
    return I;
else if Criterion 3.2 holds then
    return ∅;
else
    Isolate(φ, (a, (a+b)/2));
    Isolate(φ, ((a+b)/2, b));
end if
```

Correctness. We first note that those midpoints $\frac{a+b}{2}$ cannot be any positive root of φ by Lemma 3.1, since they are rational ($\neq 1$). So splitting (a, b) into $(a, \frac{a+b}{2})$ and $(\frac{a+b}{2}, b)$ would not miss any positive root. Second, multiple roots of φ are ruled out by Lemma 3.2. Then we know that all positive roots of φ in (a, b) are simple. Since φ is analytic on $(0, +\infty)$ (i.e., it is infinitely differentiable and is converged by its Taylor expansion), we can infer that φ has finitely many positive roots. Therefore, they would be isolated sooner or later by bisection, provided that the power function is sufficiently approached, which is guaranteed by the computability of algebraic numbers.

Example 3.2. *Consider the irreducible* poly-power $\varphi_1 = 5 - \sqrt{5}x^{\sqrt{3}+1} + \frac{\sqrt{3}}{5}x^{3\sqrt{2}}$ *in Example 2.1 again. Using the base* $\{1, \sqrt{2} - 1, \sqrt{3} - \sqrt{2}\}$*, the associated polynomial of* φ_1 *is trivariate. However, we note that* φ_1 *has exactly two nonconstant terms. So it can be rewritten as a bivariate associated polynomial under the base* $\{\sqrt{2}, \sqrt{3} + 1\}$*, which can be solved by Algorithm 2.*

By invoking Algorithm 2 with $\mathsf{Isolate}(\varphi_1, (1, \frac{15}{2}))$*, we first get its shifted derivative* ψ_1 *as shown in Example 3.1. Then we compute the approximations* $\mathrm{Rg}^+(\varphi_1, \mathcal{I})$*,* $\mathrm{Rg}^-(\varphi_1, \mathcal{I})$ *and* $\mathrm{Rg}^+(\psi_1, \mathcal{I})$*, where* $\mathcal{I}$ *is initialized with* $(1, \frac{15}{2})$*. Once Criterion 3.1 or Criterion 3.2 holds, we get an immediate return. Otherwise we bisect the interval and recursively invoke Algorithm 2 on subintervals. The final computational results are shown in Table 1, where '+' means* $\inf \mathrm{Rg}^+ > 0$*, '−' means* $\sup \mathrm{Rg}^+ < 0$ *and '*$\star$*' means the interval contains exactly one positive root. The first three records in Table 1 have been verified in Example 3.1.*

Interval	$\pm/\star$	Interval	$\pm/\star$	Interval	$\pm/\star$
$(1, \frac{77}{64})$	$+$	$(\frac{349}{128}, \frac{181}{64})$	$-$	$(\frac{1695}{512}, \frac{427}{128})$	$+$
$(\frac{77}{64}, \frac{45}{32})$	$+$	$(\frac{181}{64}, \frac{375}{128})$	$-$	$(\frac{427}{128}, \frac{1721}{512})$	$+$
$(\frac{45}{32}, \frac{103}{64})$	$\star$	$(\frac{375}{128}, \frac{763}{256})$	$-$	$(\frac{1721}{512}, \frac{867}{256})$	$+$
$(\frac{103}{64}, \frac{425}{256})$	$-$	$(\frac{763}{256}, \frac{97}{32})$	$-$	$(\frac{867}{256}, \frac{55}{16})$	$+$
$(\frac{425}{256}, \frac{219}{128})$	$-$	$(\frac{97}{32}, \frac{207}{64})$	$\star$	$(\frac{55}{16}, \frac{893}{256})$	$+$
$(\frac{219}{128}, \frac{29}{16})$	$-$	$(\frac{207}{64}, \frac{13261}{4096})$	$+$	$(\frac{893}{256}, \frac{453}{128})$	$+$
$(\frac{29}{16}, \frac{245}{128})$	$-$	$(\frac{13261}{4096}, \frac{6637}{2048})$	$+$	$(\frac{453}{128}, \frac{233}{64})$	$+$
$(\frac{245}{128}, \frac{129}{64})$	$-$	$(\frac{6637}{2048}, \frac{13287}{4096})$	$+$	$(\frac{233}{64}, \frac{479}{128})$	$+$
$(\frac{129}{64}, \frac{271}{128})$	$-$	$(\frac{13287}{4096}, \frac{3325}{1024})$	$+$	$(\frac{479}{128}, \frac{123}{32})$	$+$
$(\frac{271}{128}, \frac{71}{32})$	$-$	$(\frac{3325}{1024}, \frac{6663}{2048})$	$+$	$(\frac{123}{32}, \frac{259}{64})$	$+$
$(\frac{71}{32}, \frac{297}{128})$	$-$	$(\frac{6663}{2048}, \frac{1669}{512})$	$+$	$(\frac{259}{64}, \frac{17}{4})$	$+$
$(\frac{297}{128}, \frac{155}{64})$	$-$	$(\frac{1669}{512}, \frac{3351}{1024})$	$+$	$(\frac{17}{4}, \frac{149}{32})$	$+$
$(\frac{155}{64}, \frac{323}{128})$	$-$	$(\frac{3351}{1024}, \frac{841}{256})$	$+$	$(\frac{149}{32}, \frac{81}{16})$	$+$
$(\frac{323}{128}, \frac{21}{8})$	$-$	$(\frac{841}{256}, \frac{3377}{1024})$	$+$	$(\frac{81}{16}, \frac{47}{8})$	$+$
$(\frac{21}{8}, \frac{349}{128})$	$-$	$(\frac{3377}{1024}, \frac{1695}{512})$	$+$	$(\frac{47}{8}, \frac{15}{2})$	$+$

Table 1: Positive Root Isolation for φ_1

Finally, we obtain that φ_1 *has two positive roots, which lies in* $(\frac{45}{32}, \frac{103}{64})$ *and* $(\frac{97}{32}, \frac{207}{64})$ *respectively.*

The remaining problem is to find the upper and the lower bounds for all positive roots of a poly-power. We refer to the following result.

Lemma 3.3 (Corollary 12 of [25]). *For a* poly-power $f(x)$ *in the form (1), the number*

$$U = \max\left(1, \left(\sum_{i=0}^{n-1} \left|\frac{\beta_i}{\beta_n}\right|\right)^{\frac{1}{\tau}}\right) \quad \textit{with } \tau = \alpha_n - \alpha_{n-1}$$

is an upper bound for its positive roots.

The lower bound L for all positive roots of the aforementioned $f(x)$ can be similarly obtained, since it is exactly the reciprocal of the upper bound for all positive roots of $x^{\alpha_n} \cdot f(\frac{1}{x})$, another poly-power.

EXAMPLE 3.3. *Consider the two irreducible poly-powers* $\varphi_1 = 5 - \sqrt{5}x^{\sqrt{3}+1} + \frac{\sqrt{3}}{5}x^{3\sqrt{2}}$ *and* $\varphi_2 = -2 + \frac{1}{3}x - \frac{3}{4}x^{\sqrt{3}} + \frac{1}{5}x^{3\sqrt{2}-1}$ *in Example 2.1. For* φ_1*, we can compute an upper bound* $U = \frac{15}{2}$ *for its positive roots, since*

$$\max\left(1, \tfrac{5}{\sqrt{3}}\left(\sqrt{5}+5\right)^{\frac{1}{3\sqrt{2}-\sqrt{3}-1}}\right)$$

$$< \max\left(1, \tfrac{5\cdot 65536}{113511}\left(\tfrac{573}{256}+5\right)^{\frac{1}{\frac{3\cdot 181}{128}-\frac{14189}{8192}-1}}\right) < \frac{15}{2}.$$

Correspondingly, we can compute a lower bound $L = 1$ *as the reciprocal of*

$$\max\left(1, \tfrac{1}{5}\left(\sqrt{5}+\tfrac{\sqrt{3}}{5}\right)^{\frac{1}{\sqrt{3}+1}}\right) = 1,$$

which is an upper bound for all positive roots of

$$x^{3\sqrt{2}} \cdot \varphi_1(\tfrac{1}{x}) = \tfrac{\sqrt{3}}{5} - \sqrt{5}x^{3\sqrt{2}-\sqrt{3}-1} + 5x^{3\sqrt{2}}.$$

We thereby know that all positive roots of φ_1 *have been isolated in Example 3.2. Similarly, we obtain that all positive roots of* φ_2 *are bounded by* $(1, \frac{13}{2})$.

REMARK 3.1. *In Algorithm 2, the values of* φ *are expected to be nonzero at any endpoints of* $\mathcal{I}$*, and then we can get sign-invariant approximations of the ranges of* $\varphi(\mathcal{I})$*. Obviously,* $\varphi(L)$ *and* $\varphi(U)$ *are nonzero by the definition of the upper and the lower bounds of positive roots. If* $\varphi(1) \neq 0$*, Algorithm 2 still works for* $(L, 1)$ *and* $(1, U)$*, because all positive roots of* φ *are simple then. Otherwise we have to find a rational number* $\epsilon > 0$ *such that* φ *has no positive root in the neighbor* $\delta(1; \epsilon) = (1-\epsilon, 1) \cup (1, 1+\epsilon)$*. Specifically, the constant* ϵ *can be chosen as any positive number less than*

$$\min\left(\frac{\varphi^{(K)}(1)}{\sup\limits_{y\in[1-\theta,1+\theta]} |\varphi^{(K+1)}(y)|}, \theta\right),$$

where K *is the minimal positive integer, satisfying the* K*th derivative* $\varphi^{(K)}(1) \neq 0$*, for any* $\theta > 0$.

Thereby, we can isolate all positive roots of a simple poly-power φ by invoking Algorithm 2 with $\mathsf{Isolate}(\varphi, (L, 1))$ and $\mathsf{Isolate}(\varphi, (1, U))$ for $\varphi(1) \neq 0$ (and with $\mathsf{Isolate}(\varphi, (L, 1-\epsilon))$ and $\mathsf{Isolate}(\varphi, (1+\epsilon, U))$ otherwise). It completes the positive root isolation for simple poly-powers.

3.2 Non-simple Case

Here we present the positive root isolation algorithm for the general poly-power φ, whose associated polynomial is allowed to be a product of irreducible factors with arbitrarily many variables. Specifically, we have to isolate positive roots of an irreducible poly-power whose associated polynomial has more than two variables, and isolate those of a reducible poly-power. We will reuse Algorithm 2 here. The only gap to be filled is showing that φ would have no multiple positive root. We solve it by another number-theoretic result:

CONJECTURE 3.1 (SCHANUEL (1960S), SEE [2]). *Let* $\lambda_1, \ldots, \lambda_m$ *be* $\mathbb{Z}$*-linearly independent complex numbers. Then the field extension*

$$\mathbb{Q}(\lambda_1, e^{\lambda_1}, \ldots, \lambda_m, e^{\lambda_m}) : \mathbb{Q}$$

has transcendence degree at least m.

By Conjecture 3.1 Chonev *et al.* proved a significant result on common roots in a recent work:

LEMMA 3.4 (PROPOSITION 3 OF [4]). *Let* $\{\upsilon_1, \ldots, \upsilon_m\}$ *and* $\{\omega_1, \ldots, \omega_n\}$ *be two* $\mathbb{Z}$*-linearly independent sets of* $\mathbb{R}_{\text{alg}}$*-numbers, and* ϕ_1, ϕ_2 *two co-prime elements of* $\mathbb{A}[t, e^{t\upsilon_1}, \ldots, e^{t\upsilon_m}, e^{\imath t\omega_1}, \ldots, e^{\imath t\omega_n}]$*. Then* ϕ_1 *and* ϕ_2 *have no nonzero common real root.*

COROLLARY 3.1. *Let* $\upsilon_1, \ldots, \upsilon_m$ *be* $\mathbb{Z}$*-linearly independent* $\mathbb{R}_{\text{alg}}$*-numbers, and* φ_1, φ_2 *two co-prime elements of* $\mathcal{A}[x^{\upsilon_1}, \ldots, x^{\upsilon_m}]$*. Then* φ_1 *and* φ_2 *have no common positive root with the only possible exception for* $x = 1$.

It follows immediately from Lemma 3.4 with the substitution of $x = e^t$ $(1 \leq i \leq m)$.

COROLLARY 3.2. *Let* $\upsilon_1, \ldots, \upsilon_m$ *be* $\mathbb{Z}$*-linearly independent* $\mathbb{R}_{\text{alg}}$*-numbers, and* φ *an irreducible element of* $\mathcal{A}[x^{\upsilon_1}, \ldots, x^{\upsilon_m}]$*. Then* φ *has no multiple positive root with the only possible exception for* $x = 1$.

It follows from Lemma 3.4 with the substitution of $x = e^t$ $(1 \leq i \leq m)$ and the fact that φ and its shifted derivative ψ are co-prime. This corollary entails that an irreducible poly-power has no multiple positive root (except 1). Hence, under Conjecture 3.1, Algorithm 2 still works for the irreducible poly-power whose associated polynomial has more than two variables.

EXAMPLE 3.4. *Consider the irreducible poly-power* $\varphi_2 = -2 + \frac{1}{3}x - \frac{3}{4}x^{\sqrt{3}} + \frac{1}{5}x^{3\sqrt{2}-1}$ *in Example 2.1. Its associated polynomial is trivariate. Under Conjecture 3.1, however, we can isolate its positive roots by Algorithm 2.*

We invoke Algorithm 2 with $\mathsf{Isolate}(\varphi_2, (1, \frac{13}{2}))$*, as* $(1, \frac{13}{2})$ *is the bound of positive roots of* φ_2 *shown in Example 3.3. The computational procedure is similar to Example 3.2, and the final computational result is shown in Table 2.*

Interval	$\pm/\star$	Interval	$\pm/\star$	Interval	$\pm/\star$
$(1, \frac{27}{16})$	$-$	$(\frac{19}{8}, \frac{49}{16})$	$\star$	$(\frac{15}{4}, \frac{41}{8})$	$+$
$(\frac{27}{16}, \frac{65}{32})$	$-$	$(\frac{49}{16}, \frac{109}{32})$	$+$	$(\frac{41}{8}, \frac{13}{2})$	$+$
$(\frac{65}{32}, \frac{19}{8})$	$-$	$(\frac{109}{32}, \frac{15}{4})$	$+$		

Table 2: Positive Root Isolation for φ_2

Finally, we obtain that φ_2 *has exactly one positive root, which lies in* $(\frac{19}{8}, \frac{49}{16})$.

On the other hand, Corollary 3.1 entails that two distinct irreducible poly-powers have no common positive root (except 1). Hence a square-free poly-power must have no multiple positive root (except 1). We can repeatedly bisect isolation intervals for positive roots of distinct irreducible poly-powers, until all of them become clearly disjoint. It completes our positive isolation procedure, in which the termination depends on Conjecture 3.1.

EXAMPLE 3.5. *Combining Example 3.2 with Example 3.4, we have that* φ_1 *has two positive roots in* $\mathcal{I}_1 = (\frac{45}{32}, \frac{103}{64})$ *and* $\mathcal{I}_2 = (\frac{97}{32}, \frac{207}{64})$ *respectively, and* φ_2 *has one in* $\mathcal{I}_3 = (\frac{19}{8}, \frac{49}{16})$.

Note that two distinct irreducible poly-powers have no common positive root (except 1) under Conjecture 3.1. So we *know that $f(x) = \varphi_1 \cdot \varphi_2^2$ has three distinct positive roots in those intervals. However, the isolation intervals $\mathcal{I}_2$ and $\mathcal{I}_3$ are not disjoint, viz. $\mathcal{I}_2 \cap \mathcal{I}_3 \neq \emptyset$. In other words, $\mathcal{I}_2$ and $\mathcal{I}_3$ are not precise enough to distinguish two distinct roots of $f(x)$. Thus, we proceed to bisect $\mathcal{I}_2$ and $\mathcal{I}_3$ repeatedly, until the resulting isolation intervals $\hat{\mathcal{I}}_2 = (\frac{401}{128}, \frac{207}{64})$ and $\hat{\mathcal{I}}_3 = (\frac{87}{32}, \frac{49}{16})$ become disjoint.*

Finally, we have that $f(x)$ has totally three distinct positive roots respectively in the interval $\mathcal{I}_1, \hat{\mathcal{I}}_3, \hat{\mathcal{I}}_2$, among which the one in $\hat{\mathcal{I}}_3$ has multiplicity 2 (see Figure 2).

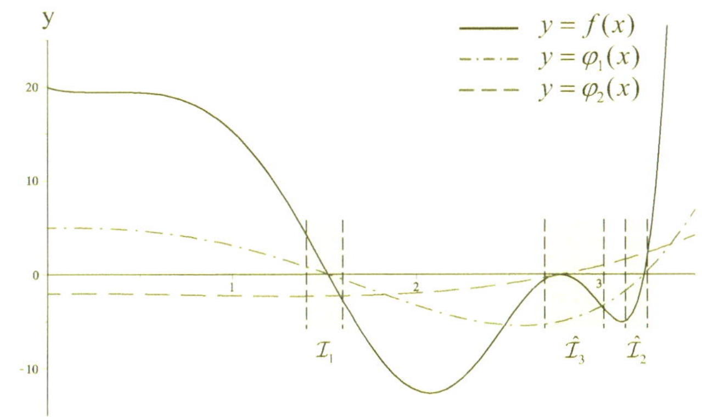

Figure 2: The Isolation Intervals for $f(x)$

4. EXPERIMENTS

This section will demonstrate the effectivity of the proposed method for isolating positive roots of poly-powers. The prototype of our method has been implemented with the MAPLE platform (see Figure 3).

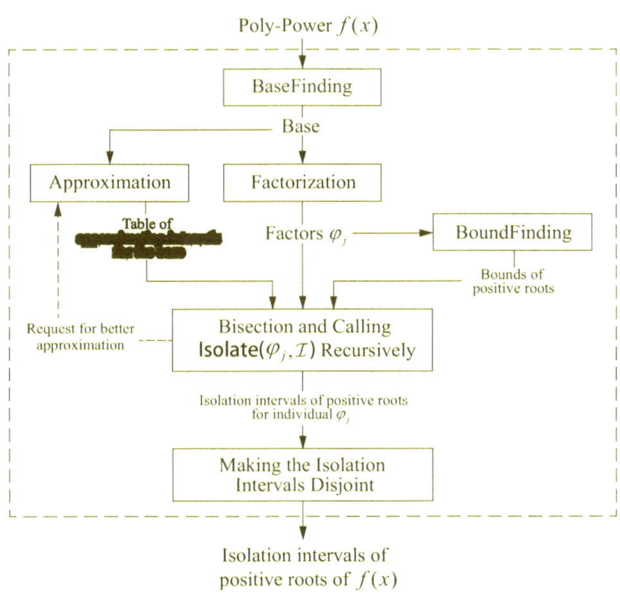

Figure 3: The Implementation Prototype

The experiments have been run on a 64-bit Windows computer with a 2.20 GHz Intel Core i7 processor and 16 GB of RAMs. For an input poly-power we first factorize it by Algorithm 1. The factorization has been well implemented with existing tools. So our experiments only focus on the irreducible poly-powers to demonstrate the effectivity of the positive root isolation algorithm. We experiment with irreducible poly-powers of i) different numbers of terms and ii) sizes of base (listed below).

$$f_1(x) = 5 - \sqrt{5}x^{\sqrt{3}+1} + \frac{\sqrt{3}}{5}x^{3\sqrt{2}},$$
$$f_2(x) = -2 + \frac{1}{3}x - \frac{3}{4}x^{\sqrt{3}} + \frac{1}{5}x^{3\sqrt{2}-1},$$
$$f_3(x) = 1 + x^2 - 5x^{\sqrt{7}} + \frac{1}{2}x^{3\sqrt{7}+1},$$
$$f_4(x) = 2 - 5x^{\sqrt{7}} - x^{\sqrt{3}+\sqrt{7}} + \frac{1}{2}x^{3\sqrt{2}+1},$$
$$f_5(x) = -2 + 2\sqrt{7}x - 3x^{\sqrt{7}} - x^{\sqrt{3}+\sqrt{7}} + \frac{1}{2}x^{3\sqrt{2}+1},$$
$$f_6(x) = -1 - 60x^{\sqrt{\sqrt{7}+1}} + 22\sqrt{7}x^{\sqrt{3}} + x^{2\sqrt[3]{7}} + x^{3\sqrt[5]{4}},$$
$$f_7(x) = -1 - x^{\sqrt[7]{3}} + 40\sqrt{2}x^{\sqrt{3}} - 60x^{\sqrt{\sqrt{7}+1}} + x^{\sqrt{7}} + x^{2\sqrt[3]{7}} + \frac{7}{2}x^{3\sqrt[5]{4}} - x^5,$$
$$f_8(x) = 10 - x^{\sqrt[7]{3}} + 40\sqrt{2}x^{\sqrt{3}} - 60x^{\sqrt{\sqrt{7}+1}} + x^{\sqrt{7}} + x^{2\sqrt[3]{7}} + \frac{7}{2}x^{3\sqrt[5]{4}} - 2x^5,$$
$$f_9(x) = -\frac{1}{10} + 5\sqrt{2}x^{\sqrt{3}} - x^{\frac{6}{7}\sqrt{2}} + 2x^{\sqrt{2}+\frac{1}{2}} - 20x^{\sqrt{7}} + 2x^{2\sqrt{3}} + 7x^{2\sqrt{2}+1} + \frac{7}{2}x^{\sqrt{2}+\sqrt{3}+1} - 2x^5 + \frac{5}{7}x^{3\sqrt{3}},$$
$$f_{10}(x) = 20 - x^{\sqrt[7]{3}} + \sqrt{2}x^{\sqrt{3}} + 2x^{\sqrt{\sqrt{7}+1}} - 20x^{\sqrt{7}} + 2x^{2\sqrt[3]{6}} + x^{2\sqrt[3]{7}} + \frac{7}{2}x^{3\sqrt[5]{4}} - 3x^5 + 2x^{3\sqrt{3}}.$$

The experimental results are summarized in Table 3, in which the columns give:

- the time (in seconds) for isolating positive roots of the input poly-power (Time),
- the number of terms of the input poly-power (Terms),
- the size of the base for exponents and coefficients (Base),
- the number of distinct positive roots (Roots),
- the maximal recursion depth of Isolate (Depth).

They suggest that our method can isolate positive roots of poly-powers in the level of seconds. Furthermore, we can see that the time consumption on the isolation procedure is mainly correlated with the maximal recursion depth and with the number of distinct positive roots. In other words, most of the computation amount is caused by bisecting the intervals and computing the approximations of the ranges of the poly-powers and their shifted derivatives.

No.	Time	Terms	Base	Roots	Depth
1	0.522	3	4	2	10
2	0.181	4	3	1	9
3	0.693	4	2	2	10
4	0.726	4	4	2	10
5	1.834	5	4	3	16
6	2.48	5	6	3	18
7	2.98	8	8	4	20
8	0.317	8	8	1	10
9	4.12	10	4	5	22
10	0.451	10	9	2	9

Table 3: Experimental Results

A pretreatment. Note that the rational approximations for $\mathbb{R}_{\text{alg}}$-elements in the base (5) will be repeatedly used for constructing the approximations (8) and (9). Therefore it is profitable to store those approximations of many different precision once in a table as a pretreatment (see the bolded label in Figure 3). Based on that, we can conveniently compute those Rg^+ and Rg^- by looking up that table. Roughly speaking, this pretreatment would save up to 90% of the total computation amount for the aforementioned examples. Anyway, we would require better approximations when they are not good enough in the running time.

5. CONCLUSION

In this paper, we presented a method to isolate positive roots of poly-powers. It is complete for simple poly-powers, and is "conditionally" complete (refer to Schanuel's conjecture) for non-simple ones. Thereby we made full use of a number-theoretic roadmap from the solvability to its known frontier. For further work, we are interested in the minimum distance estimation of distinct positive roots of poly-powers, which would yield another isolation method. Besides, a potential application of our work lies in the reachability problem for linear dynamical systems and systems biology, such as nutrient flow in an aquarium [12].

6. ACKNOWLEDGMENTS

The authors thank Zhenbing Zeng for his insightful suggestions on this work. The authors are also grateful to the reviewers whose careful comments helped us to improve the accurateness. This work is partially supported by NSFC (Nos. 11401218 & 11435005), SRFDP (No. 20130076120010), and the Open Project of Shanghai Key Laboratory of Trustworthy Computing (No. 07dz22304201403).

7. REFERENCES

[1] M. Achatz, S. McCallum, and V. Weispfenning. Deciding polynomial–exponential problems. In J. R. Sendra and L. González-Vega, editors, *Proc. ISSAC 2008*, pages 215–222, New York, 2008. ACM Press.

[2] J. Ax. On Schanuel's conjectures. *Annals of Mathematics*, 93(2):252–268, 1971.

[3] J. Bak, D. Leviatan, D. Newman, and J. Tzimbalario. Generalized polynomial approximation. *Israel Journal of Mathematics*, 15(4):337–349, 1973.

[4] V. Chonev, J. Ouaknine, and J. Worrell. On the Skolem problem for continuous linear dynamical systems. In *Proc. ICALP 2016*, 2016. to appear.

[5] G. E. Collins and A. G. Akritas. Polynomial real root isolation using Descarte's rule of signs. In *Proc. SYMSAC 1976*, pages 272–275, New York, 1976. ACM Press.

[6] G. E. Collins and R. Loos. Polynomial real root isolation by differentiation. In *Proc. SYMSAC 1976*, pages 15–25, New York, 1976. ACM Press.

[7] M. Coste, T. Lajous-Loaeza, H. Lombardic, and M.-F. Roy. Generalized Budan–Fourier theorem and virtual roots. *Journal of Complexity*, 21(4):479–486, 2005.

[8] M. Coste and M. F. Roy. Thom's lemma, the coding of real algebraic numbers and the computation of the topology of semi-algebraic sets. *Journal of Symbolic Computation*, 5(1–2):121–129, 1988.

[9] F. Cucker and S. Smale. Complexity estimates depending on condition and round-off error. *Journal of the ACM*, 46(1):113–184, 1999.

[10] J.-P. Dedieu and J.-C. Yakoubsohn. Computing the real roots of a polynomial by the exclusion algorithm. *Numerical Algorithms*, 4(1):1–24, 1993.

[11] A. Gupta, P. Kamath, N. Kayal, and R. Saptharishi. Approaching the chasm at depth four. In *Proc. CCC 2013*, pages 65–73, Los Alamitos, CA, 2013. IEEE Computer Society.

[12] G. B. Gustafson. *Systems of Differential Equations*. 1998. available at `www.math.utah.edu/~gustafso/s2013/2250/systemsExamplesTheory2008.pdf`.

[13] R. Loos. Computing in algebraic extensions. In B. Buchberger, G. E. Collins, and R. Loos, editors, *Computer Algebra: Symbolic and Algebraic Computation, 2nd Edition*, pages 173–187, Berlin, 1983. Springer.

[14] S. McCallum and V. Weispfenning. Deciding polynomial-transcendental problems. *Journal of Symbolic Computation*, 47(1):16–31, 2012.

[15] I. Newton. *De analysi per aequationes numero terminorum infinitas*. William Jones, London, 1711.

[16] D. Richardson. Towards computing non algebraic cylindrical decompositions. In S. M. Watt, editor, *Proc. ISSAC 1991*, pages 247–255, New York, 1991. ACM Press.

[17] D. Richardson. How to recognize zero. *Journal of Symbolic Computation*, 24(6):627–645, 1997.

[18] C. L. Siegel. *Transcendental Numbers*. Princeton University Press, Princeton, NJ, 1949.

[19] S. Smale. Newton's method estimates from data at one point. In R. E. Ewing, K. I. Gross, and C. F. Martin, editors, *The Merging of Disciplines: New Directions in Pure, Applied, and Computational Mathematics*, pages 185–196, Berlin, 1986. Springer.

[20] A. Strzeboński. Real root isolation for exp–log functions. In J. R. Sendra and L. González-Vega, editors, *Proc. ISSAC 2008*, pages 303–313, New York, 2008. ACM Press.

[21] A. Strzeboński. Real root isolation for tame elementary functions. In J. R. Johnson, H. Park, and E. Kaltofen, editors, *Proc. ISSAC 2009*, pages 341–350, New York, 2009. ACM Press.

[22] A. Strzeboński. Cylindrical decomposition for systems transcendental in the first variable. *Journal of Symbolic Computation*, 46(11):1284–1290, 2011.

[23] A. Tarski. *A Decision Method for Elementary Algebra and Geometry*. University of California Press, Berkeley, 2 edition, 1951.

[24] M. Xu, Z.-B. Li, and L. Yang. Quantifier elimination for a class of exponential polynomial formulas. *Journal of Symbolic Computation*, 68(1):146–168, 2015.

[25] M. Xu, C. Mu, Z. Zeng, and Z.-B. Li. A heuristic approach to positive root isolation for multiple power sums. *Journal of Universal Computer Science*, 16(14):1912–1926, 2010.

[26] L. Yang. Solving harder problems with lesser mathematics. In *Proc. 10th Asian Technology Conference in Mathematics*, pages 37–46, Blacksburg, 2005. ATCM Inc.

[27] C. Yap, M. Sagraloff, and V. Sharma. Analytic root clustering: A complete algorithm using soft zero tests. In P. Bonizzoni, V. Brattka, and B. Löwe, editors, *Proc. CiE 2013*, LNCS 7921, pages 433–444, Berlin, 2013. Springer.

Symbolic-Numeric Tools for Analytic Combinatorics in Several Variables

Stephen Melczer
University of Waterloo
& LIP (U. Lyon, CNRS, ENS Lyon, UCBL)
Waterloo, ON, Canada
smelczer@uwaterloo.ca

Bruno Salvy
Inria
LIP (U. Lyon, CNRS, ENS Lyon, UCBL)
Lyon, France
Bruno.Salvy@inria.fr

ABSTRACT

Analytic combinatorics studies the asymptotic behavior of sequences through the analytic properties of their generating functions. This article provides effective algorithms required for the study of analytic combinatorics in several variables, together with their complexity analyses. Given a multivariate rational function we show how to compute its smooth isolated critical points, with respect to a polynomial map encoding asymptotic behaviour, in complexity singly exponential in the degree of its denominator. We introduce a numerical Kronecker representation for solutions of polynomial systems with rational coefficients and show that it can be used to decide several properties (0 coordinate, equal coordinates, sign conditions for real solutions, and vanishing of a polynomial) in good bit complexity. Among the critical points, those that are minimal—a property governed by inequalities on the moduli of the coordinates—typically determine the dominant asymptotics of the diagonal coefficient sequence. When the Taylor expansion at the origin has all non-negative coefficients (known as the 'combinatorial case') and under regularity conditions, we utilize this Kronecker representation to determine probabilistically the minimal critical points in complexity singly exponential in the degree of the denominator, with good control over the exponent in the bit complexity estimate. Generically in the combinatorial case, this allows one to automatically and rigorously determine asymptotics for the diagonal coefficient sequence. Examples obtained with a preliminary implementation show the wide applicability of this approach.

Keywords

Analytic Combinatorics in Several Variables, Kronecker Representation, Symbolic-Numeric Algorithms

1. INTRODUCTION

The starting point of analytic combinatorics is an integral representation for the Taylor coefficients of a function analytic at the origin: if

$$F(z_1,\dots,z_n) = \sum_{k_1,\dots,k_n} c_{k_1,\dots,k_n} z_1^{k_1}\cdots z_n^{k_n},$$

then $$c_{k_1,\dots,k_n} = \frac{1}{(2\pi i)^n}\int_T F(z_1,\dots,z_n)\frac{dz_1\cdots dz_n}{z_1^{k_1+1}\cdots z_n^{k_n+1}},$$

where T is a torus around the origin defined by $z_i = r_i e^{2\pi i\theta_i}$ for sufficiently small $r_1,\dots,r_n$. Of special interest is the sequence of *diagonal* coefficients

$$A_k := c_{k,\dots,k} = \frac{1}{(2\pi i)^n}\int_T F(z_1,\dots,z_n)\frac{dz_1\cdots dz_n}{(z_1\cdots z_n)^{k+1}}. \quad (1)$$

The principle of analytic combinatorics is to study this integral by deforming the contour T in such a way that it avoids the singularities of the integrand and tends to *critical points* where the integral concentrates as $k\to\infty$. A variety of techniques for analytic functions in one variable ($n=1$) are presented in the book by Flajolet and Sedgewick [10]. More recently, Pemantle and Wilson have given analogous tools in the more involved multivariate situation [21].

Our aim in this work is to launch the study of analytic combinatorics in several variables from the point of view of computer algebra and complexity, in the case when $F(\mathbf{z})$ is a rational function[1] $G(\mathbf{z})/H(\mathbf{z}) \in \mathbb{Q}(\mathbf{z})$.

Example 1. The sequence $A_k = \sum_{i=0}^{k}\binom{k}{i}^2\binom{k+i}{i}^2$ of Apéry numbers is, like all multiple binomial sums, the diagonal of a rational function [3]; in this case, their generating function is the diagonal of $1/H(a,b,c,z)$ where

$$H(a,b,c,z) = 1 - z(1+a)(1+b)(1+c)(abc+bc+b+c+1).$$

With this rational input, our algorithm produces automatically the asymptotic behaviour

$$A_k = \frac{(17+12\sqrt{2})^k}{k^{3/2}}\cdot\frac{\sqrt{34+24\sqrt{2}}}{8\pi^{3/2}}(1+O(1/k)). \quad (2)$$

See Example 3 below for details. In general, it is not possible to provide such an explicit closed form for the quantities involved in the asymptotic behaviour. The output will then be a combination of an exact symbolic representation and a precise numerical estimate:

$$A_k = (33.97056274\dots)^k k^{-3/2}(.2200437670\dots + O(1/k)).$$

Example 2. The kth coefficient A_k of the diagonal of the rational function

$$F(x,y) := \frac{1-x^3y^6+x^3y^4+x^2y^4+x^2y^3}{1-x-y+x^2y^3-x^3y^3-x^4y^4-x^3y^6+x^4y^6},$$

[1] We use boldface letters for n-tuples: $\mathbf{z} = (z_1,\dots,z_n)$, $\mathbf{k} = (k_1,\dots,k_n)$, $\mathbf{z}^{\mathbf{k}} = z_1^{k_1}\cdots z_n^{k_n}$, $\mathbf{z}^k = (z_1\cdots z_n)^k$, ...

ISSAC '16, July 19 - 22, 2016, Waterloo, ON, Canada

ACM ISBN 978-1-4503-4380-0/16/07...$15.00.

DOI: http://dx.doi.org/10.1145/2930889.2930913

is the number of binary words with k zeroes and k ones that do not contain 10101101 or 1110101 [20, §5.3]. Here the numerical output of our algorithm has the same form,

$$A_k = (.6029459856\ldots)(3.910193204\ldots)^k k^{-1/2}(1 + O(1/k))$$

with its symbolic form

$$A_k = \frac{u^{-k}}{\sqrt{k\pi}} A(u)\sqrt{B(u)}(1 + O(1/k)), \quad P(u) = 0,$$

for explicit polynomials P, A, B in $\mathbb{Z}[u]$ of degree at most 20 and $u \approx 0.2557418388$ approximating a specific root of P.

The method described by Pemantle and Wilson can be summarized as follows:

(i) *Locate the critical points* of the map $\phi : (\mathbf{z}) \mapsto z_1 \cdots z_n$ on the algebraic set $\mathcal{V}(H) := \{\mathbf{z} \mid H(\mathbf{z}) = 0\}$. Assuming $\mathcal{V}(H)$ is a smooth manifold, the critical points are defined by the family of equations given by $H = 0$ and the vanishing of the set of maximal minors of the Jacobian matrix of $[H, \phi]$. Since we also need to avoid the algebraic set $\mathcal{V}(\phi) := \{\mathbf{z} \mid \phi(\mathbf{z}) = 0\}$, this system is equivalent to the vanishing of

$$\left(H, z_1\frac{\partial H}{\partial z_1} - \lambda, \ldots, z_n\frac{\partial H}{\partial z_n} - \lambda\right) \tag{3}$$

after introducing a Lagrange multiplier λ.

(ii) *Filter out* those critical points that do not contribute to the asymptotic behavior of (1). In particular, keep only those critical points that can be reached by deformation of the contour T outside of $\mathcal{V}(H) \cup \mathcal{V}(\phi)$.

(iii) *Compute the local behavior* of F at the contributing critical points.

(iv) *Transfer* into the asymptotic behavior of the integral.

The theory, as it has developed, has shown on one hand how difficult analyzing the integral (1) in full generality can be while at the same time detailing large classes of problems to which systematic techniques apply. Although the methods developed by Pemantle and Wilson are quite explicit, their arguments often rely on some human intervention, typically in the filtering step, which can be quite involved.

Our Contributions. This work gives, to our knowledge, the first completely automatic treatment and complexity analysis for the asymptotic enumeration of a large class of multivariate problems.

From a computer algebra perspective the critical points are simply the solutions of the polynomial system (3), but the process of filtering the critical points involves deciding inequalities of moduli, which relies on techniques that are typically more expensive. Our approach is to combine robust numerical evaluation techniques and exact polynomial representations with a tight control over the degree and the bit size of the coefficients.

We make generic regularity assumptions which result in zero dimensional polynomial systems. The solutions of the system are given by a Kronecker representation (also known as a rational univariate representation) which consists of a square-free univariate polynomial $P(u)$ and a parametrization of the coordinates of the form $Q(u)/P'(u)$. The size of the integer coefficients appearing in these polynomials obey known bounds. Using this tool we define a *numerical Kronecker representation*, where the roots of P are evaluated numerically with sufficient precision to determine which (if any) of the coordinates are 0 or equal between two or more solutions, and to determine their sign in the case of real solutions. We show that, under regularity assumptions, such a representation can be computed in good complexity (Theorem 3.12). More precisely, if a system of n polynomials of degree at most d and integer coefficients of height (bit size) at most h in n variables forms a reduced regular sequence, then the numerical Kronecker representation can be computed in $\tilde{O}(hd^{3n})$ bit operations by a probabilistic algorithm. Since generically the number of solutions is d^n, this can be seen as polynomial complexity in a natural size of the problem. More precise estimates taking into account the complexity of evaluation of the polynomial system (hence for instance its sparseness) can also be given. The idea of using such a representation in order to reduce numerical computations to the resolution of univariate polynomials is not new. However, to the best of our knowledge, the connection between the good properties of the Kronecker representation in terms of bit size and the fast and precise algorithms operating on univariate polynomials has not been made before, except in the case of bivariate systems [4, 15].

Previous work. DeVries et al. [7] gave an algorithm going from $F(x, y)$ to diagonal asymptotics in the bivariate case assuming that the critical points are isolated. Raichev [22] developed a Sage package which computes the asymptotic contribution of a non-degenerate critical point on the border of the domain of convergence at which $\mathcal{V}(H)$ is smooth or the transverse intersection of smooth algebraic varieties, however the users of this package must know *a priori* that the critical points they examine are the ones which contribute to dominant asymptotics (under stronger hypotheses than we require this can be used to give rigorous asymptotics). Neither of these works provides a complexity analysis.

Another approach to the asymptotic behaviour of the integral (1) is to compute a differential equation for the generating function of the diagonal by creative telescoping. This equation is Fuchsian, so that the possible behaviour of the generating function at its dominant singularity is known and a list of possible asymptotic behaviours for the coefficients can be deduced. However, the constant factor in front of these asymptotic behaviours is not provided by this method, which does not even let one decide whether this coefficient is zero. This approach has good complexity [2] and can be combined with the present work in order to provide full asymptotic expansions of the coefficients efficiently.

Concerning polynomial systems, the literature is vast [19]. Our work is in the filiation of works by Giusti, Heintz, Pardo and collaborators [11, 12, 16, 25] on the use of the Kronecker representation in complex or real geometry, going far beyond the simple systems we consider here. Relevant works using the alternate denomination rational univariate representation [23, 1] also exploit numerical evaluation and tight bounds on the distance between solutions [8]. These bounds are comparable to ours when expressed in terms of d^n, but they exploit more information on the input, such as mixed volume, that we do not take into account at this stage.

Notation for complexity estimates. We start with $H \in \mathbb{Z}[\mathbf{z}]$ of degree d where $\mathbf{z} = (z_1, \ldots, z_n)$. In all complexity estimates, $d \geqslant 2$ is assumed and $D := d^n$.

For f and g two functions defined and positive over $(\mathbb{N}^\star)^m$, the notation $f(a_1, \ldots, a_m) = O(g(a_1, \ldots, a_m))$ is used in complexity estimates when there exists a constant K such that $f(a_1, \ldots, a_m) \leq Kg(a_1, \ldots, a_m)$ in this domain.

The sizes and complexity of our operations grow like D^c, where c is an exponent that we want to bound tightly. We make use of the usual $\tilde{O}$ notation to avoid technical discussions on the subexponential terms. By definition, $f = \tilde{O}(g)$ when $f = O(g \log^k g)$ for some $k \geq 0$. For instance, $O(nD) = \tilde{O}(D)$ since we assume $d \geqslant 2$.

Plan. This article is structured as follows. We first give a brief summary of the work of Pemantle and Wilson that we use. Next, we present our symbolic-numeric tools in Section 3. This is then applied in Section 4 to the computation of the contributing critical points in the combinatorial case. We conclude with a few experiments using a preliminary implementation in Maple.

2. ANALYTIC COMBINATORICS IN SEVERAL VARIABLES

We gather here the main results we need from the book of Pemantle and Wilson [21], to which we refer for more information. Note that their results are often more general than what is presented below, allowing meromorphic functions instead of just rational ones, and asymptotics of coefficient sequences along rays other than the main diagonal.

Given a rational function $F(\mathbf{z}) = G(\mathbf{z})/H(\mathbf{z}) \in \mathbb{Q}(\mathbf{z})$ with $G, H \in \mathbb{Q}[\mathbf{z}]$ co-prime, whose Taylor expansion at the origin has non-empty domain of convergence $\mathcal{D}$, our aim is to compute the asymptotic behavior of the integral (1) giving the kth coefficient of its diagonal, as k tends to infinity.

Critical Points. A critical point is, by definition, a point satisfying Eq. (3). A critical point $\boldsymbol{\zeta}$ is called *minimal* when it belongs to the boundary $\partial\mathcal{D}$. It is *smooth* when $\nabla H(\boldsymbol{\zeta}) \neq \mathbf{0}$ and *non-degenerate* when the Hessian of the map $\phi\,|_{\mathcal{V}(H)}$ is not singular at $\boldsymbol{\zeta}$. Note that smoothness and non-degeneracy are generic properties.

Informally, the torus T in Eq. (1) can be deformed to be arbitrarily close to a minimal critical point inside of the domain of analyticity of the integrand without changing the value of the integral. Next, if the critical point is smooth, a local analysis amounts to computing a residue, reducing to an integral over $\mathcal{V}(H)$. If, moreover, the point is non-degenerate then a saddle-point analysis can be performed.

More precisely, when $\boldsymbol{\zeta}$ is smooth we may assume, without loss of generality, that $\partial H/\partial z_n(\boldsymbol{\zeta}) \neq 0$ so the implicit function theorem gives an analytic function $g(z_1, \ldots, z_{n-1})$ parameterizing z_n on an open neighborhood of $\boldsymbol{\zeta}$ in $\mathcal{V}(H)$. Writing $\hat{\mathbf{z}} = (z_1, \ldots, z_{n-1})$, extending the contour to absorb the pole and then taking a residue at $z_n = g(\hat{\mathbf{z}})$, the integrand of (1) becomes

$$\frac{-G(\hat{\mathbf{z}}, g(\hat{\mathbf{z}}))}{\frac{\partial H}{\partial z_n}(\hat{\mathbf{z}}, g(\hat{\mathbf{z}}))} \frac{d\hat{\mathbf{z}}}{\phi(\hat{\mathbf{z}}, g(\hat{\mathbf{z}}))^{k+1}},$$

which is then analyzed locally on $\mathcal{V}(H)$ in the neighborhood of $\hat{\mathbf{z}} = \hat{\boldsymbol{\zeta}}$. Define $\psi(\hat{\mathbf{z}}) := \phi(\hat{\mathbf{z}}, g(\hat{\mathbf{z}}))$. Observe that $\psi(\hat{\boldsymbol{\zeta}}) = \phi(\boldsymbol{\zeta}) = \boldsymbol{\zeta}^{\mathbf{1}}$ and that the critical point equations are equivalent to $\nabla\psi(\hat{\boldsymbol{\zeta}}) = 0$. A Taylor expansion then gives

$$\psi(\hat{\mathbf{z}}) := \phi(\boldsymbol{\zeta}) + \frac{1}{2}(\hat{\mathbf{z}} - \hat{\boldsymbol{\zeta}})^t \cdot \mathcal{H}(\boldsymbol{\zeta}) \cdot (\hat{\mathbf{z}} - \hat{\boldsymbol{\zeta}}) + O(|\hat{\mathbf{z}} - \hat{\boldsymbol{\zeta}}|^3),$$

where $\mathcal{H}$ is the Hessian matrix of ψ, and the integrand is asymptotically equivalent to

$$\frac{-G(\boldsymbol{\zeta})}{\frac{\partial H}{\partial z_n}(\boldsymbol{\zeta})\phi(\boldsymbol{\zeta})^{k+1}} \exp\left(-\frac{k+1}{2\phi(\boldsymbol{\zeta})}(\hat{\mathbf{z}} - \hat{\boldsymbol{\zeta}})^t \cdot \mathcal{H}(\boldsymbol{\zeta}) \cdot (\hat{\mathbf{z}} - \hat{\boldsymbol{\zeta}})\right).$$

If $\boldsymbol{\zeta}$ is non-degenerate, this is precisely the setting for the saddle-point method, leading to the following result.

Lemma 2.1. *[21, Th. 9.2.7, Cor. 9.2.9] Suppose $F(\mathbf{z})$ has a smooth, minimal, non-degenerate critical point at $\boldsymbol{\zeta}$ and that $E_{\boldsymbol{\zeta}} := \mathcal{V} \cap \{\mathbf{z} : |z_i| \leq |\zeta_i|, 1 \leq i \leq n\} = \{\boldsymbol{\zeta}\}$. Then the diagonal coefficients A_k behave like*

$$\boldsymbol{\zeta}^{-k} k^{\frac{1-n}{2}} \left(\frac{(2\pi)^{(1-n)/2}}{\sqrt{\boldsymbol{\zeta}^{3-n}|\mathcal{H}(\boldsymbol{\zeta})|/\zeta_n^2}} \frac{-G(\boldsymbol{\zeta})}{\zeta_n \frac{\partial H}{\partial z_n}(\boldsymbol{\zeta})} + O\left(\frac{1}{k}\right)\right), \quad (4)$$

where $|\mathcal{H}|$ is the determinant of the Hessian of ψ above. When $E_{\boldsymbol{\zeta}}$ contains a finite number of non-degenerate minimal critical points, one simply sums up the contributions given by each point. The branch of the square-root $\sqrt{|\mathcal{H}(\boldsymbol{\zeta})|}$ is determined by taking the product of the principal branch square-roots of the eigenvalues of the Hessian $\mathcal{H}(\boldsymbol{\zeta})$.

If $G(\boldsymbol{\zeta}) = 0$ then the leading term in Eq. (4) will vanish. One can often determine dominant behaviour by calculating more terms of the asymptotic expansion [21, Cor. 13.3.3].

Simplifying Assumptions. Following Lemma 2.1 we make the following assumptions throughout the rest of the article:

(A1) The map $|\phi| : \overline{\mathcal{D}} \to \mathbb{R}$ achieves its supremum at a unique point in $\overline{\mathcal{D}}$ (see [21, Def. 8.1.4]);
(A2) $\mathcal{V}(H)$ is smooth (H and its partial derivatives do not simultaneously vanish);
(A3) all critical points of ϕ are non-degenerate.

Note that (A3) implies that there are a finite number of critical points, as any non-degenerate critical point is isolated. In Section 4 we make an additional algebraic assumption (A) on an ideal encoding the critical points. This assumption is slightly stronger than requiring a finite number of critical points, but is necessary for our precise complexity results.

The text of Pemantle and Wilson [21] always assumes (A1) and that ϕ admits a critical point in $\mathbb{C}^n$. Although it includes results when there are no critical points on $\partial\mathcal{D}$, they do not yield explicit asymptotic formulas in the same automatic manner as the minimal critical point case. The results there rely on isolated critical points, and all explicit general asymptotic results in dimension $n > 2$ need non-degenerate critical points. Chapters 10 and 11 develop the theory when $\mathcal{V}(H)$ is not smooth; extending the results of this work to cover non-smooth cases is ongoing work.

Combinatorial Case. The geometric situation becomes much simpler when the coefficients $a_{\mathbf{k}}$ of the generating function are nonnegative, which is known as the *combinatorial* case. When this occurs, absolute convergence leads to the following analogue of Pringsheim's theorem.

Lemma 2.2. *[21, Prop. 8.4.3] If $a_{\mathbf{k}} \geq 0$ for all but a finite set of values then*

- *ϕ admits a minimal critical point unless the supremum of $|\phi|$ is not achieved on $\overline{\mathcal{D}}$;*
- *under (A2), if ϕ admits a minimal critical point then it admits one with all positive coordinates; if ϕ admits two minimal critical points with positive coordinates then it admits an infinite number of them.*

3. SYMBOLIC-NUMERIC TOOLKIT

3.1 Polynomials and their roots

Our algorithms reduce all computations to manipulations of univariate or bivariate polynomials. We use several algorithms and classical bounds which we recall here.

Height. The *height* $h(P)$ of a polynomial $P \in \mathbb{Z}[\mathbf{z}]$ is the maximum of 0 and the logarithms in base 2 of the absolute values of the coefficients of P. Thus $h(P)$ gives a bound on the bit size of the coefficients. (Note that some authors define the height as the exponential of this one.) The height satisfies the following well-known inequalities.

Lemma 3.1. *For $P_1, \dots, P_k, P, Q \in \mathbb{Z}[z]$,*

$$h(P_1 + \cdots + P_k) \leqslant \max_i h(P_i) + \log_2 k,$$

$$h(P_1 \cdots P_k) \leqslant \sum_i h(P_i) + \sum_{i=1}^{k-1} \deg P_i,$$

$$h(P) \leqslant \deg P + h(PQ) + \log_2 \sqrt{\deg(PQ) + 1}.$$

The first two are direct consequences of the definition; the last one is Mignotte's bound [18].

Bounds on roots of polynomials. The following useful bounds are classical.

Lemma 3.2. *[18] Let $A \in \mathbb{Z}[T]$ be a polynomial of degree $d \geqslant 2$ and height h. If $A(\alpha) = 0$, then*

- *if $\alpha \neq 0$, then $1/(2^h + 1) \leq |\alpha| \leq 2^h + 1$;*
- *if $A(\beta) = 0$ and $\alpha \neq \beta$, then $|\alpha - \beta| \geq d^{-(d+2)/2} \|A\|^{1-d}$;*
- *if $Q(\alpha) \neq 0$ for $Q \in \mathbb{Z}[T]$, then*

$$|Q(\alpha)| \geq ((d+1)2^{h(Q)})^{-d+1} 2^{-h \deg Q};$$

- *if A is square-free then $|A'(\alpha)| \geqslant d^{-d} \|A\|^{-2d+1}$,*

where $\|A\|$ is the 2-norm of the vector of coefficients, easily bounded by $2^h \sqrt{d+1}$.

Bounds on resultants and gcds.

Lemma 3.3. *For P and Q in $\mathbb{Z}[U]$ of height at most h and degree at most d, $\gcd(P, Q)$ has height $\tilde{O}(d + h)$ and can be computed in $\tilde{O}(d^2 + dh)$ bit operations.*

For P and Q in $\mathbb{Z}[T, U]$, let

$$\delta = \deg_U P \deg_T Q + \deg_U Q \deg_T P$$

$$\eta = h(P) \deg_U Q + h(Q) \deg_U P + \log((\deg_U P + \deg_U Q)!),$$

then $\deg \mathrm{Res}_U(P, Q) \leq \delta$, $h(\mathrm{Res}_U(P, Q)) \leq \eta$.

Proof. The height of the gcd is given by Lemma 3.1 and the univariate complexity is well known [26, Cor. 11.17]. The bounds for the resultant follow from a direct expansion of the determinant of the Sylvester matrix for $\mathrm{Res}_U(P, Q)$ using Lemma 3.1 again. □

Algorithms for roots of polynomials.

Lemma 3.4. *[24],[17],[15, Th. 10] For a square-free $A \in \mathbb{Z}[T]$ of degree d and height h,*

- *isolating intervals (resp. disks) of radius less than $2^{-\kappa}$ for all real (resp. complex) roots of A can be computed in $\tilde{O}(d^3 + d^2 h + d\kappa)$ bit operations;*
- *for real (resp. complex) t, computing real (resp. complex) a_t such that $|A(t) - a_t| < 2^{-\ell}$ can be achieved in $\tilde{O}(d(h + \ell + d \log \max(1, |t|)))$ bit operations given $\tilde{O}(h + \ell + d \log \max(1, |t|))$ bits of t;*
- *simultaneously computing such approximations at points $t_1, \dots, t_N$ with $N = O(d)$ can be achieved within the same bound with $|t|$ replaced by $\max |t_i|$.*

Corollary 3.5. *Given a polynomial $A \in \mathbb{Z}[T]$ as above, isolating intervals (or disks) of radius less than $2^{-O(d(h+d))}$ for its real (or complex) roots and a factor $P \in \mathbb{Z}[T]$ of A, then selecting which real (or complex) roots of A are roots of P can be achieved in $\tilde{O}(d^3 + d^2 h)$ bit operations.*

Proof. By Lemma 3.1, the height of P is bounded by $\deg P + h + \log_2 \sqrt{d+1}$. Then the previous lemma gives isolating intervals or disks for the roots of P in $\tilde{O}(d^3 + d^2 h + d\kappa)$ bit operations and the separation bound of Lemma 3.2 shows that $\kappa = O(d(h + d))$ is sufficient to associate a unique isolating disk or interval to each root of A. □

Grouping Roots by Modulus. Unlike the good separation bound given in Lemma 3.2 between distinct complex roots of a polynomial, which decreases like 2^{-hd}, the best separation bound for the moduli of roots that we know of [13, Th. 1] gives an order of 2^{-hd^3}, which is not sufficient for our purposes. Grouping roots by identical modulus can be done with the following instead.

Lemma 3.6. *For $A \in \mathbb{Z}[T]$ of degree $d \geq 2$ and height h, if $A(\alpha) = 0$ and $A(|\alpha|) \neq 0$, then*

$$A(|\alpha|) A(-|\alpha|) \geq ((d^2 + 1) 2^{2h})^{-d^2+1} 2^{-2d^2(h + \log d)}.$$

Proof. The Graeffe polynomial $G(T) := A(\sqrt{T}) A(-\sqrt{T})$ has degree d, height at most $2h$ and its positive real roots are the square of the real roots of A. By Lemma 3.3, the resultant $R(u) = \mathrm{Res}_T(A(T), T^d A(u/T))$ has degree at most d^2 and height bounded by $2hd + 2d \log d$. It vanishes at the products $\alpha\beta$ of roots of A and in particular at the square $|\alpha|^2 = \alpha\bar{\alpha}$. The conclusion follows directly from the third statement of Lemma 3.2. □

Corollary 3.7. *With the same notation, if $0 < r_1 \leq \cdots \leq r_k$ are the real positive roots of A then all roots of A of modulus exactly $r_1, \dots, r_k$ can be computed, with isolating disks of radius $2^{-\tilde{O}(hd^2)}$, in $\tilde{O}(hd^3)$ bit operations.*

Proof. By Lemmas 3.2 and 3.4, we can determine all complex roots α of A to $\tilde{O}(hd^2)$ bits and decide which are real and positive in $\tilde{O}(hd^3)$ bit operations. Furthermore, Lemma 3.2 implies that each $|\alpha|$ is bounded by $2^{O(h)}$ so that evaluating A simultaneously at the moduli of all the roots and their negatives at precision $\tilde{O}(hd^2)$ also costs $\tilde{O}(hd^3)$ bit operations. When $A(|\alpha|)A(-|\alpha|)$ is smaller than the bound of Lemma 3.6, then $A(|\alpha|) = 0$ and $|\alpha|$ can be identified with one of the real roots of A since it is known to a larger precision than the separation bound from Lemma 3.2. □

In practice, one would first compute roots only at precision $\tilde{O}(hd)$, in $\tilde{O}(hd^2)$ bit operations, and then check whether any of the nonreal roots has a modulus that could equal one of the real positive roots in view of its isolating interval. Only those roots need to be refined to higher precision (say, by Newton iteration) before invoking Lemma 3.6.

3.2 Numerical Kronecker Representation

In the next section we locate the dominant critical points using a combination of rigorous numerical evaluations, via Lemma 3.4, and algorithms for polynomial systems, for which we require precise bounds on degrees and heights. Our basic data-structure is a Kronecker representation. We now develop the required bounds and algorithms.

Kronecker Representation. Let $\mathbf{f} = (f_1, \dots, f_n)$ and g be polynomials in $\mathbb{Q}[\mathbf{z}]$. Assume that $\mathbf{f}$ forms a *reduced regular sequence* in $\mathbb{C} \setminus \mathcal{V}(g)$. This means that for $i = 1, \dots, n-1$, the saturation $\mathcal{I}_i$ with respect to g of the ideal generated by $(f_1, \dots, f_{i-1})$ is radical and f_i is not a zero divisor modulo $\mathcal{I}_i$. A consequence is that the system $f_1 = \cdots = f_n$ with

$g \neq 0$ has finitely many solutions. A *Kronecker representation* of these solutions is a system:

$$P(u) = 0, \qquad \begin{cases} P'(u)z_1 - Q_1(u) & = 0, \\ & \vdots \\ P'(u)z_n - Q_n(u) & = 0, \end{cases} \tag{5}$$

where $u = \sum_{i=1}^{n} \lambda_i z_i$ is a linear form in the z_i's with integer coefficients that takes a different value at each distinct solution $\mathbf{z}$ of the system, P is a square-free polynomial in $\mathbb{Z}[u]$ and $Q_1, \ldots, Q_n$ are in $\mathbb{Z}[u]$ of degree bounded by that of P.

It is often convenient to consider the polynomials $f_1, \ldots, f_n$, g of degree at most d as given by a straight-line program (a program using only assignments, constants and arithmetic operations [5]) which evaluates them simultaneously at any $\mathbf{z}$ using at most L arithmetic operations. A pessimistic bound on L is obtained by considering $n+1$ dense polynomials in n variables, leading to $L = \tilde{O}(D)$. (Recall that $D = d^n$.)

The main properties of the Kronecker representation, summarizing results due to Giusti, Heintz, Lecerf, Pardo, Schost and collaborators, are as follows.

Proposition 3.8. *Let $f_1, \ldots, f_n, g$ be polynomials in $\mathbb{Z}[\mathbf{z}]$ of degree at most d and height at most h, given by a straight-line program of size at most L and integers of height $\tilde{O}(h)$, such that $\mathbf{f}$ forms a reduced regular sequence in $\mathbb{C}^n \setminus \mathcal{V}(g)$. Then a Kronecker representation of the solutions to $f_1 = \cdots = f_n = 0$ where $g \neq 0$ of the form (5) exists, where the coefficients of the linear form u are bounded by $O(D^2)$, the degree of P (and each Q_i) is bounded by D and the heights of P and the Q_i are bounded by $\tilde{O}(hD)$. It can be computed by a probabilistic algorithm in $\tilde{O}(hLD^2) = \tilde{O}(hD^3)$ bit operations.*

The probabilistic aspects are harmless in practice; we refer to the literature for a discussion of bounds on the probability of error and probabilistic checks [12, §2.1],[25, §15.6].

Proof. By Bézout's bound the system has at most D solutions. Thus a generic linear form separates these solutions if the product of the $\binom{D}{2}$ differences of its evaluations at its solutions is nonzero. This is a polynomial of degree $\binom{D}{2}$ in the coefficients of the linear form and the conclusion on its height follows from the Zippel-Schwarz lemma [26, Lem. 6.44]. The algorithm and its arithmetic complexity of $\tilde{O}(LD^2)$ are given by Giusti *et alii* [12]. The bound on the height of the coefficients is due to Schost [25, Th. 12]. A modular computation can be performed using a prime of length $\tilde{O}(\log(hD^2))$ [25, Prop. 44, Cor. 4] and computing such a prime is not expensive [26, Th. 18.10]. The bit complexity of that stage follows by multiplying this logarithm by the arithmetic complexity, and the modular result is Newton lifted to $\mathbb{Z}$ in $\tilde{O}(hLD^2)$ bit operations [12, Th. 2], dominating the complexity. ☐

Reduction. The analogue of Gröbner base reduction takes the following form, which controls the height of the result.

Lemma 3.9. *With the same hypotheses, given a polynomial $q \in \mathbb{Z}[\mathbf{z}]$ of degree at most d and height bounded by h, there exists a parameterization $P'(u) - TQ_q(u)$ of the values taken by q on the solutions of (5), of degree smaller than D and height in $\tilde{O}(hD)$. Moreover, there exists a polynomial $\Phi_q \in \mathbb{Z}[T]$ of degree at most D and height $\tilde{O}(hD^2)$ that vanishes at the values taken by q on the solutions. Given a straight-line program of evaluation complexity $\ell = \tilde{O}(D)$, Q_q can be computed in $\tilde{O}(\ell hD^2)$ bit operations, and Φ_q in $\tilde{O}(hD^2(D + \ell))$ bit operations. If q is linear, the height of Φ_q is $\tilde{O}(hD)$ and the complexity of finding Φ_q and Q_q drops to $\tilde{O}(hD^2)$.*

Proof. Consider the extended system $(f_1, \ldots, f_n, t - q)$ for a new variable t. As $t - q$ is linear and monic in t, the number of solutions is unchanged and the separating linear form u for the original system is still separating for the new system. The degree and height of Q_q follow from Proposition 3.8.

The computation of the polynomial $P'(u) - TQ_q(u)$ parameterizing the values of q at the solutions can be obtained in $\tilde{O}(\ell D)$ arithmetic (not bit) operations by expanding $q(Q_1(u)/P'(u), \ldots, Q_n(u)/P'(u))$ as a power series at precision $2D$ and multiplying by $P'(u)$. The bit complexity is obtained by Hensel lifting [12].

By Lemma 3.3, the height of the resultant of $P(u)$ and $P'(u) - TQ_q(u)$ is $\tilde{O}(hD^2)$ and by Lemma 3.1 this is also a bound on the height of its factors, in particular the minimal polynomial of multiplication by Q_q/P' in $\mathbb{Q}[u]/P(u)$. In the case when q has degree 1, the key point is that the bound on the height of the polynomial Φ_q is governed by bounds on the height of the variety defined by Eq. (5) [16, 6, 25]. This variety has dimension 0, degree bounded by D and height at most $\tilde{O}(hD)$, which implies that its image by an affine q also has height of that order [16, Prop. 2.4].

The polynomial Φ_q can then be computed by modular computation modulo sufficiently many primes and Chinese remaindering using the efficient minimal polynomial algorithm of Kedlaya and Umans [14, §8.4]. ☐

In most of our uses, the existence of the polynomial Φ with such bounds is important but we do not need it explicitly.

Numerical Kronecker Representation. We now combine the results of Lemma 3.1 and Proposition 3.8. Since the linear form u of the Kronecker representation is a linear form in the z_i with integer coefficients, it takes a real value when the coordinates of a solution do, and conversely. Thus the real roots of P are in one-to-one correspondence with the real solutions of the system.

A *numerical Kronecker representation* of the real (resp. complex) roots of a system is given by a Kronecker representation and isolating intervals (resp. disks) for the roots of the polynomial P. Selecting the solutions of the system having a particular property then means selecting the isolating intervals (resp. disks) of the corresponding roots of P.

Lemma 3.10. *With the same hypotheses as Proposition 3.8, a numerical Kronecker representation of the real (resp. complex) solutions with isolating intervals (resp. disks) of radius $2^{-\kappa}$ can be computed in $\tilde{O}(D(hD^2 + \kappa))$ bit operations.*

Proof. Combine the bounds on P from Proposition 3.8 and the results summarized in Lemma 3.1. ☐

Zero coordinates and sign. The numerical Kronecker representation allows for *exact* symbolic-numeric computation. We begin with zero testing of coordinates: as P is square-free, its derivative is not 0 at its roots and thus detecting whether a coordinate of a point parameterized by a root α of P is 0 reduces to detecting whether the polynomial Q_i vanishes at α. To do this one can compute the gcd of P and Q_i and then identify their common roots, working numerically with sufficient precision.

Lemma 3.11. *With the same hypotheses as Proposition 3.8 detecting the coordinates of solutions that are exactly 0 can be performed in $\tilde{O}(hD^3)$ bit operations, and so can computing the sign of the coordinates of real solutions.*

Proof. By Lemma 3.3, the gcd of P and Q_i has height $\tilde{O}(hD)$ and can be computed in $\tilde{O}(hD^2)$ bit operations. Corollary 3.5 and Lemma 3.10 then show that $\tilde{O}(hD^3)$ bit operations are sufficient to compute the roots of P cancelling Q_i

at a sufficient precision $\kappa = \tilde{O}(hD^2)$. Evaluating P' and the Q_i at the same precision then gives the sign of the non-zero coordinates of real solutions by Lemma 3.2. □

Numerical evaluation of the solutions. In summary, we have obtained the following result.

Theorem 3.12. *With the same hypotheses as Proposition 3.8, computing isolating intervals (resp. disks) of radius $2^{-\kappa}$ for all coordinates of all real (resp. complex) solutions of the system, recognizing the zero coordinates and computing the signs of the coordinates of the real solutions can be performed in a total of $\tilde{O}(D(hD^2 + \kappa))$ bit operations.*

Proof. The precision on the roots of P needed to decide that a coordinate is not zero and find the sign of the coordinates of real solutions is $\tilde{O}(hD^2)$ bits, as shown in the proof of Lemma 3.11. For any $\kappa \geq 0$, computing the roots of P to precision $2^{-\kappa-\tilde{O}(hD^2)}$ is sufficient to evaluate the coordinates up to precision $2^{-\kappa}$. By Lemma 3.4, this numerical resolution of P is achieved in $\tilde{O}(D(hD^2+\kappa))$ bit operations and the simultaneous evaluation of P' and the Q_i to this precision again obeys that complexity bound. □

Equal coordinates. Deciding equality can also be done exactly, again within the same complexity bound. This amounts to detecting an index i and two distinct roots of P giving the same values to Q_i/P'.

Lemma 3.13. *With the same hypotheses as Proposition 3.8, detecting which solutions have an identical coordinate can be performed in $\tilde{O}(hD^3)$ bit operations.*

Proof. By Lemma 3.9, there exists a polynomial $\Phi_i(T) \in \mathbb{Z}[T]$ that cancels the values of $Q_i(u)/P'(u) \bmod P(u)$ and has degree at most D and height $\tilde{O}(hD)$. Thus, by Lemma 3.2, the distance between distinct values of Q_i/P' at solutions cannot be smaller than $2^{-\tilde{O}(hD^2)}$. By Lemma 3.2, $\log|1/P'(v)| = \tilde{O}(hD^2)$ at the roots v of P, so knowing $Q_i(v)$ and $P'(v)$ to $\tilde{O}(hD^2)$ bits is sufficient to obtain $Q_i(v)/P'(v)$ to $\tilde{O}(hD^2)$ bits. By Lemma 3.4, computing Q_i and P' at all real (resp. complex) roots of P with that precision can be achieved in $\tilde{O}(hD^3)$ bit operations given the roots of P at precision $\kappa = \tilde{O}(hD^2)$, which is also computable in that complexity. Adding the costs of this computation for each Q_i does not change the $\tilde{O}$ complexity estimate. □

4. CONTRIBUTING CRITICAL POINTS

We now apply this machinery to the computation of minimal critical points in analytic combinatorics.

4.1 Computation of the Critical Points

The critical points of the map $\phi : (\mathbf{z}) \mapsto z_1 \cdots z_n$ are computed from System (3). We make the following assumption:

(A) *System (3) is a reduced regular sequence in $\mathbb{C}^{n+1} \setminus \mathcal{V}(\lambda)$.*

As $\lambda = z_j H_{z_j}$ for each $j = 1, \ldots, n$ the condition $z_j \neq 0$ follows from $\lambda \neq 0$. Furthermore, a non-smooth point of the variety is marked by the simultaneous vanishing of all the partial derivatives, so that by removing $\mathcal{V}(\lambda)$ we are only considering the smooth critical points.

Lemma 4.1. *Under assumption (A), a Kronecker representation of the solutions of System (3) completed by the equation $T - \phi(\mathbf{z})$ is of the form (5), with two more parameterizations $P'(u) - \lambda Q_\lambda(u)$, and $P'(u) - TQ_\phi(u)$; the polynomial P and the Q_i, Q_λ and Q_ϕ have degree at most D and height $\tilde{O}(hD)$. The Kronecker representation can be computed in $\tilde{O}(hD^3)$ bit operations; an accompanying numerical Kronecker representation in $\tilde{O}(hD^3)$ bit operations.*

Proof. Under assumption (A), the system formed by H and the $n-1$ polynomials $z_i H_{z_i} - z_n H_{z_n}$ for $i = 1, \ldots, n-1$ satisfies the hypotheses of Proposition 3.8, giving the desired degree, height and complexity bounds for the z_i variables. The polynomials Q_λ and Q_ϕ are obtained by Lemma 3.9 and the numerical Kronecker representation from Theorem 3.12. □

4.2 The Minimal Positive Critical Point

In the combinatorial case, by absolute convergence, minimality of a point $\boldsymbol{\zeta}$ with positive coordinates means that the line segment from the origin to $\boldsymbol{\zeta}$ does not intersect $\mathcal{V}(H)$. Furthermore, by Lemma 2.2 if there are a finite number of critical points then there is a unique minimal critical point whose coordinates are positive real numbers.

Thus, the question of minimality can be restated as finding the critical point with positive coordinates $\boldsymbol{\zeta}$ such that the polynomial $H(t\zeta_1, \ldots, t\zeta_n)$ has no roots in the interval $(0, 1)$. This in turn is equivalent to the absence of a root of the polynomial $A(u, t) = P'(u)^d H(tz(u))$ in the interval $(0, 1)$ when u is evaluated at the root of P corresponding to $\boldsymbol{\zeta}$. We could not find a way to exploit Sturm sequences without increasing the exponent of D in the complexity to at least 4. Instead, we compute a Kronecker representation for System (3) enriched with the equation $H(tz_1, \ldots, tz_n)$ for a new variable t and gather the critical points as above.

Lemma 4.2. *Suppose assumptions (A1)–(A3) and (A) are satisfied, and that G/H is combinatorial. Let $\boldsymbol{\zeta}$ be the unique minimal critical point with positive real coordinates. Then one can find isolating intervals of width less than $2^{-\kappa}$ for each coordinate of $\boldsymbol{\zeta}$ using a probabilistic algorithm running in $\tilde{O}(h(dD)^3 + D\kappa)$ bit operations.*

Proof. Since System (3) has finitely many solutions, so does the one with $H(tz_1, \ldots, tz_n)$ added in. The linear form used in (5) may not separate the solutions anymore as multiple values of t correspond to one previous solution, so we use a new linear form involving t as well, which we denote v to avoid confusion. The results of Proposition 3.8 show the existence of a Kronecker representation with a square-free univariate polynomial $\tilde{P}(v) = 0$ and parameterizations of the form $\tilde{P}'(v)z_i - \tilde{Q}_i(v) = 0$ for i in $\{1, \ldots, n, \lambda, T, t\}$, with $\tilde{P}, \tilde{Q}_i$ of degree at most dD and all heights bounded by $\tilde{O}(hdD)$. It can be computed in $\tilde{O}(h(dD)^3)$ bit operations.

By construction, the solutions of the original system are recovered when $t = 1$, so $\tilde{P}'(v) - \tilde{Q}_t(v)$ has a gcd with $\tilde{P}$ corresponding to the (at most D) critical points. This gcd can be computed in $\tilde{O}(hd^2D^2)$ bit operations [26, Cor. 11.11]. By Corollary 3.5, we can recover the roots of P corresponding to solutions of the original system in $\tilde{O}(h(dD)^3)$ bit operations. Theorem 3.12 allows us to compute the signs of t and $1-t$ on the other roots in $\tilde{O}(h(dD)^3)$ bit operations. □

4.3 Critical Points on the Same Torus

Next, Lemma 2.1 shows that the other critical points lying on the same torus (i.e., having the same coordinate-wise modulus) may contribute to the dominant term of the asymptotic behavior. In the combinatorial case, we can again make use of the numerical Kronecker representation to obtain them in good complexity, although this is a more expensive operations than the previous ones.

Proposition 4.3. *Suppose assumptions (A1)–(A3) and (A) are satisfied, and that G/H is combinatorial. Then isolating disks of radius less than $2^{-\kappa}$ can be computed for each coordinate of* all *minimal critical points by a probabilistic algorithm running in $\tilde{O}(D(hD^3+\kappa))$ bit operations.*

Proof. Let $\boldsymbol{\zeta}$ be the unique minimal critical point with positive real coordinates. By Lemma 3.9, the minimal polynomials $M_1, \ldots, M_n$ of the z_i coordinates have degree at most D, height $\tilde{O}(hD)$ and can all be computed in $\tilde{O}(hD^2)$ bit operations. As ζ_i is a real positive root of M_i for $i = 1, \ldots, n$, by Lemma 3.6, if $|\sigma_i| = \zeta_i$ then $M_i(\sigma_i) = 0$, which can be detected by evaluating $M(|\sigma_i|)M(-|\sigma_i|)$ with $\tilde{O}(hD^3)$ bits of precision. By Theorem 3.12 with $\kappa = \tilde{O}(hD^3)$, this can be achieved in $\tilde{O}(hD^4)$ bit operations, which is also the cost for evaluating the M_i simultaneously at the roots of P. □

This is the most costly operation we use, but in many cases it is sufficient to check whether $\phi(\mathbf{z})$ takes different values at each critical point. As the polynomial $T - \phi(\mathbf{z})$ is part of the original system, this can be checked in $\tilde{O}(hD^3)$ bit operations by Lemma 3.13. When two critical points give the same value to ϕ, then the test above is used.

4.4 Degenerate Critical Points

Simple but tedious multivariate calculus shows that the (i, j) entry of the Hessian matrix $\mathcal{H}$ of Lemma 2.1 is

$$\frac{\phi(\boldsymbol{\zeta})}{\lambda\zeta_i\zeta_j}(U_{i,n}+U_{j,n}-U_{i,j}-U_{n,n}-\lambda), \quad U_{k,\ell} := \zeta_k\zeta_\ell\frac{\partial^2 H}{\partial z_k \partial z_\ell}(\boldsymbol{\zeta}),$$

when $i \neq j$ and the formula for a diagonal element is the same with the term $-\lambda$ replaced by -2λ.

Thus by multilinearity, the determinant is of the form $\phi(\boldsymbol{\zeta})^{n-3}\zeta_n^2/\lambda^{n-1}$ times the determinant of a matrix of polynomials of degree at most d and height $O(h + \log d)$. The prefactor is not 0 in view of our hypotheses and will cancel out other factors in the final formula from Lemma 2.1. By Lemma 3.9 each entry of the remaining determinant reduces to a polynomial in u of degree smaller than D and height $\tilde{O}(hD)$, divided by $P'(u)$ that can be taken out of the determinant to yield a leading factor of $P'(u)^{1-n}$. The remaining determinant is a polynomial of degree smaller than nD and height $\tilde{O}(hD)$ that can be computed by evaluation-interpolation in $\tilde{O}(hD^2)$ bit operations. By Lemma 3.4, it can be evaluated at the roots of P with error smaller than $2^{-\kappa}$ in $\tilde{O}(D(hD^2+\kappa))$ bit operations given $\tilde{O}(hD^2+\kappa)$ bits of the roots of P. In summary, we have proved the following.

Lemma 4.4. *Under assumption (A), the degeneracy of the critical points can be tested in $\tilde{O}(hD^3)$ bit operations; the determinant of the Hessian of Lemma 2.1 can be computed with error less than $2^{-\kappa}$ in $\tilde{O}(D(hD^2+\kappa))$ bit operations.*

4.5 Dominant Asymptotics

Once the minimal critical points have been obtained, the computation is completed by evaluating the formula from Lemma 2.1. The following theorem is a direct consequence of the previous lemmas. To lighten notation we assume that $G(\mathbf{z})$ has height $O(h)$ and degree $O(d)$.

Theorem 4.5. *Suppose assumptions (A1)–(A3) and (A) hold, and $F(\mathbf{z})$ is combinatorial. If $F(\mathbf{z})$ admits a single minimal critical point $\boldsymbol{\zeta}$ then*

$$A_k = \left(T^{-k} \cdot k^{(1-n)/2} \cdot (2\pi)^{(1-n)/2}\right)(C + O(1/k)),$$

where T and C are algebraic constants. Isolating disks for T and C of radius less than $2^{-\kappa}$ can be obtained by a probabilistic algorithm in $\tilde{O}(h(dD)^3 + D\kappa)$ bit operations.

If $F(\mathbf{z})$ admits more than one minimal critical point then this can be detected in $\tilde{O}(hD^4)$ bit operations; each has a value of T with the same modulus, and A_k is asymptotically equal to the sum of the contributions of each point, obtained within the same complexity as above.

Note that all the steps of the algorithm have a complexity bound of $\tilde{O}(h(dD)^3)$ bit operations except for the test that critical points lie on the same torus, for which easy filters are available in practice (see Example 4). If $G(\boldsymbol{\zeta}) = 0$, then one can usually find dominant asymptotics by taking further terms of the relevant Taylor expansions at $\boldsymbol{\zeta}$.

5. EXPERIMENTS

We list here several examples highlighting the above techniques and detail some of the steps taken by our implementation. Note that while the theoretical bounds were obtained using an algorithm that computes the Kronecker representation directly [12], our preliminary implementation relies on a fast implementation of Gröbner bases [9][2]. Although our theoretical bounds do not include explicit constants, in practice one has the actual polynomials that arise in the computation and can therefore calculate the accuracy needed to perform the operations of the numerical Kronecker method.

Example 3. We first detail the computations in the case of Apéry's sequence from Example 1. The polynomial $H(a, b, c, z) = 1 - z(1 + a)(1 + b)(1 + c)(abc + bc + b + c + 1)$ of degree 7 defines a smooth variety, and each term in the power series expansion of $1/H$ is non-negative. A Kronecker representation of the solutions of the system

$$aH_a - \lambda, bH_b - \lambda, cH_c - \lambda, zH_z - \lambda, T - abcz, H(a, b, c, z)$$

with the linear form $u = T$ (before using a random linear form, we try a few simple ones that, if they do separate the solutions, lead to smaller integers) is $u^2 - 34u + 1 = 0$,

$$a = \frac{2u - 82}{2u - 34}, b = c = \frac{24}{2u - 34}, z = \frac{-164u + 4}{2u - 34}, T = u. \quad (6)$$

Thus, there are two (real) critical points and a simple numerical evaluation shows that the only one with positive coordinates corresponds to $u = 17 - 12\sqrt{2}$.

Next, we prove automatically that there is no intersection of $\mathcal{V}(H)$ with the segment from 0 to that critical point. The linear form T does not separate the solutions of the system with $H(ta, tb, tc, tz)$ replacing H, but the linear form $u = T + t$ does. It leads to a Kronecker representation with polynomial $\tilde{P}(u)$ of degree 14, with a factor of degree 2 that corresponds to the critical points and is recovered by taking the gcd of P with $P' - Q_t$. The other factor has four real roots, but none of them gives a value of t in $(0, 1)$.

Since both critical points are real, it is easily checked numerically that they do not lie on the same torus. Then, the evaluation of the asymptotic behaviour using Eq. (6) gives

$$\frac{u^{-k}}{\pi^{3/2}k^{3/2}}\frac{\sqrt{3462 - 102u}}{48}(1 + O(1/k)).$$

[2]The code and Maple worksheets for these examples are available at http://diagasympt.gforge.inria.fr.

Finally, injecting $u = 17-12\sqrt{2}$ gives the result from Eq. (2).

Example 4. [20, §5.3] We give more details on Example 2. By its combinatorial origin, the rational function F is combinatorial and one can check that its denominator defines a smooth variety. The linear form $u = T$ is separating. The Kronecker representation gives a polynomial P of degree 21 and a parameterization $P'(u)x - Q_1(u) = P'(u)y - Q_2(u) = 0$, with Q_1 and Q_2 of degree 20 in u with largest coefficient about 2500. As with most examples here it exhibits the nice behaviour of the Kronecker representation with respect to the sizes of the integers [23]: if we used the representation $x = \tilde{Q}_1(u)$ with polynomial $\tilde{Q}_1$, then $\tilde{Q}_1$ has rational coefficients whose largest numerator is about 10^{20}.

There are 3 real positive roots of P, which are candidates for the minimal critical point with positive coordinates (that only the positive roots are relevant is due to our choice of linear form). Of these, two give points (x, y) with positive coordinates: $u_1 \approx 0.255$ and $u_2 \approx 2.792$. We can prove that u_1 is minimal by adding the equation $H(tx, ty) = 0$ to our system and getting the new Kronecker representation; using a Gröbner Basis computation takes too long, but one can use a subresultant calculation to compute the new Kronecker representation in under a minute on modern laptops.

Next, in this example, in order to check that the critical point given by u_1 is the only critical point on its torus it is sufficient to evaluate numerically the parameterization of T at the roots of P. This gives a cheap filter that eliminates many cases and avoids the more costly computation of Lemma 3.6. A further simplification here is that since $T = u$, it is sufficient to compare the moduli of the complex roots of P with u_1 and it is found that indeed, there are no other critical point on the torus. Lemma 2.1 then gives the asymptotics displayed in Example 2.

Example 5. The rational function

$$F(x, y) = \frac{1}{(1-x-y)(20-x-40y)-1},$$

has a smooth denominator and is combinatorial (factor $(1-x-y)$ out of the denominator). The Kronecker computation finds two critical points with positive coordinates: $(x_1, y_1) \approx (0.548, 0.309)$ and $(x_2, y_2) \approx (9.997, 0.252)$. Since $x_1 < x_2$ and $y_1 > y_2$, just by examining the critical points we cannot determine which is the critical minimal point. Adding the polynomial $H(tx, ty)$ to the system shows that there is a point with approximate coordinates $(0.092x_2, 0.092y_2)$ in $\mathcal{V}$, so that x_1 is the minimal critical point. To three decimal places the diagonal asymptotics have the form

$$A_k = (5.88\ldots)^k k^{-1/2}(0.054\ldots) \cdot (1 + O(1/k)).$$

6. CONCLUSION

This is only the beginning. The numerical Kronecker representation seems to be an interesting (and useful) tool. The next step will be to extend these results by removing some of the regularity constraints on which it relies.

In terms of analytic combinatorics our results give the first known complexity bounds. Much work remains to be done to extend to asymptotics off the main diagonal, to degenerate or non-smooth cases, to relax the regularity conditions and to see whether the non-combinatorial case can also be brought into the same (singly exponential) complexity class.

Acknowledgments. The authors thank É. Schost for help with some results in his thesis. This work has been supported in part by FastRelax ANR-14-CE25-0018-01, NSERC, the French Ministry of Foreign Affairs, and the France Canada Research Fund.

7. REFERENCES

[1] S. Basu, R. Pollack, and M.-F. Roy. *Algorithms in real algebraic geometry*. Springer-Verlag, Berlin, 2006.

[2] A. Bostan, P. Lairez, and B. Salvy. Creative telescoping for rational functions using the Griffiths-Dwork method. In *ISSAC '13*, pages 93–100. ACM Press, 2013.

[3] A. Bostan, P. Lairez, and B. Salvy. Multiple binomial sums. AriXiv 1510.07487, 2015.

[4] Y. Bouzidi, S. Lazard, M. Pouget, and F. Rouillier. Separating linear forms and rational univariate representations of bivariate systems. *J. Symbolic Comput.*, 68(1):84–119, 2015.

[5] P. Bürgisser, M. Clausen, and M. A. Shokrollahi. *Algebraic complexity theory*, volume 315 of *Grundlehren der Mathematischen Wissenschaften*. Springer-Verlag, 1997.

[6] X. Dahan and E. Schost. Sharp estimates for triangular sets. In *ISSAC '04*, pages 103–110. ACM Press, 2004.

[7] T. DeVries, J. van der Hoeven, and R. Pemantle. Automatic asymptotics for coefficients of smooth, bivariate rational functions. *Online J. Anal. Comb.*, 6 : 24 pg, 2011.

[8] I. Z. Emiris, B. Mourrain, and E. P. Tsigaridas. The DMM bound: multivariate (aggregate) separation bounds. In *ISSAC 2010*, pages 243–250. ACM, New York, 2010.

[9] J.-C. Faugère. FGb: A Library for Computing Gröbner Bases. In *ICMS 2010*, *LNCS* v. 6327, 84–87. Springer, 2010.

[10] P. Flajolet and R. Sedgewick. *Analytic Combinatorics*. Cambridge University Press, 2009.

[11] M. Giusti, J. Heintz, J. E. Morais, J. Morgenstern, and L. M. Pardo. Straight-line programs in geometric elimination theory. *J. Pure Appl. Algebra*, 124(1-3):101–146, 1998.

[12] M. Giusti, G. Lecerf, and B. Salvy. A Gröbner free alternative for polynomial system solving. *J.Complexity*, 17(1):154–211, 2001.

[13] X. Gourdon and B. Salvy. Effective asymptotics of linear recurrences with rational coefficients. *Discr. Math.*, 153(1–3):145–163, 1996.

[14] K. S. Kedlaya and C. Umans. Fast polynomial factorization and modular composition. *SIAM J. Comput.*, 40(6):1767–1802, 2011.

[15] A. Kobel and M. Sagraloff. On the complexity of computing with planar algebraic curves. *J. Complexity*, 31(2):206–236, 2015.

[16] T. Krick, L. M. Pardo, and M. Sombra. Sharp estimates for the arithmetic Nullstellensatz. *Duke Math. J.*, 109(3):521–598, 2001.

[17] K. Mehlhorn, M. Sagraloff, and P. Wang. From approximate factorization to root isolation with application to cylindrical algebraic decomposition. *J. Symbolic Comput.*, 66:34–69, 2015.

[18] M. Mignotte. *Mathematics for Computer Algebra*. Springer New York, 1992.

[19] T. Mora. *Solving polynomial equation systems I–IV. Encyclopedia of Mathematics and its Applications.* Cambridge University Press, 2003–2016.

[20] R. Pemantle and M. C. Wilson. Twenty combinatorial examples of asymptotics derived from multivariate generating functions. *SIAM Review*, 50:199–272, 2008.

[21] R. Pemantle and M. C. Wilson. *Analytic Combinatorics in Several Variables*. Cambridge University Press, 2013.

[22] A. Raichev. amgf documentation – release 0.8. https://github.com/araichev/amgf, 2012.

[23] F. Rouillier. Solving zero-dimensional systems through the rational univariate representation. *Appl. Algebra Engrg. Comm. Comput.*, 9(5):433–461, 1999.

[24] M. Sagraloff and K. Mehlhorn. Computing real roots of real polynomials. *J. Symbolic Comput.*, 73:46–86, 2016.

[25] É. Schost. *Sur la résolution des systèmes polynomiaux à paramètres*. PhD thesis, École polytechnique, 2001.

[26] J. von zur Gathen and J. Gerhard. *Modern computer algebra*. Cambridge University Press, 2003.

A Fast Algorithm for Computing the Truncated Resultant

Guillaume Moroz
Inria Nancy Grand Est
guillaume.moroz@inria.fr

Éric Schost
University of Waterloo
eschost@uwaterloo.ca

ABSTRACT

Let P and Q be two polynomials in $\mathbb{K}[x, y]$ with degree at most d, where $\mathbb{K}$ is a field. Denoting by $R \in \mathbb{K}[x]$ the resultant of P and Q with respect to y, we present an algorithm to compute $R \bmod x^k$ in $\mathcal{O}\tilde{~}(kd)$ arithmetic operations in $\mathbb{K}$, where the $\mathcal{O}\tilde{~}$ notation indicates that we omit polylogarithmic factors. This is an improvement over state-of-the-art algorithms that require to compute R in $\mathcal{O}\tilde{~}(d^3)$ operations before computing its first k coefficients.

1. INTRODUCTION

Computing the resultant of two polynomials is an ubiquitous question in symbolic computation, with applications to polynomial system solving [17], computational topology [18, 2, 12, 7, 8, 5, 22, 6], Galois theory [28, 24, 1, 23], computations with algebraic numbers [4], etc.

From the complexity viewpoint, this question admits a satisfactory answer in the simplest case of polynomials P, Q with coefficients in a field $\mathbb{K}$. Euclid's algorithm can be adapted to compute the resultant R of P and Q in time $\mathcal{O}(d^2)$, assuming arithmetic operations in $\mathbb{K}$ are counted at unit cost (a thorough discussion of resultant algorithms based on Euclid's algorithm is in [14]). Using fast polynomial multiplication and divide-and-conquer techniques, the Knuth-Schönhage half-gcd algorithm [21, 27] allows one to compute R in time $\mathcal{O}\tilde{~}(d)$. This is optimal, up to logarithmic factors, since the input has size $\Theta(d)$.

However, no such quasi-linear result is known in the important case of bivariate polynomials over $\mathbb{K}$, or in the very similar case of univariate polynomial with integer coefficients (in which case one would be interested in bit complexity estimates). In the former situation, suppose we consider two polynomials P and Q in $\mathbb{K}[x, y]$, with degree at most d, and we want to compute their resultant R with respect to y, so that R is in $\mathbb{K}[x]$. The polynomial R has degree at most d^2, so both input and output can be represented using $\Theta(d^2)$ elements in $\mathbb{K}$. However, the best known algorithms to compute R take $\mathcal{O}\tilde{~}(d^3)$ operations in $\mathbb{K}$, either by means of evaluation / interpolation techniques, or in a direct manner [26].

ISSAC '16, July 19 - 22, 2016, Waterloo, ON, Canada

ISBN 978-1-4503-4380-0/16/07...$15.00

DOI: http://dx.doi.org/10.1145/2930889.2930931

In this paper, we are interested in the computation of the resultant R of such bivariate polynomials *truncated at order* k, that is of $R \bmod x^k$ for some given parameter k. This kind of question appears for instance in the algorithms of [17, 23], where we want two terms in the expansion, so that $k = 2$. A related example, in a slightly more involved setting, involves the evaluation of the second derivative of some subresultants, for input polynomials in $\mathbb{K}[x, y, z]$ [19].

Of course, one could simply compute R itself and truncate it afterwards; however, it seems wasteful to compute all d^2 terms of R, incurring a cost of $\mathcal{O}\tilde{~}(d^3)$, before discarding many of them. Now, for all but finitely many values a in $\mathbb{K}$, it is possible to compute $R \bmod (x - a)^k$ using $\mathcal{O}\tilde{~}(dk)$ operations in $\mathbb{K}$: indeed, as soon as the nonzero subresultants of P and Q do not vanish at a, we can run the Knuth-Schönhage algorithm with coefficients truncated modulo $(x - a)^k$, without attempting to invert an element that would vanish at a. The running time claimed above then follows from the fact that arithmetic operations in $\mathbb{K}[x]/(x - a)^k$ can be done using $\mathcal{O}\tilde{~}(k)$ operations in $\mathbb{K}$ (for such standard complexity results, our reference is [13]).

If however we cannot choose the expansion point, as is the case here, there is no guarantee that all divisions remain feasible in $\mathbb{K}[x]/\langle x^k \rangle$; attempting to divide by an element of positive valuation would entail a loss of x-adic precision.

An obvious solution is to use a *division-free* algorithm over $\mathbb{K}[x]/\langle x^k \rangle$ (by contrast, so-called fraction-free algorithms often require the base ring to be a domain). The best result we are aware of is due to Kaltofen and Villard [20], with a cost of $\mathcal{O}(d^{2.698})$ ring operations to compute the determinant of a matrix of size d over any ring, and thus $\mathcal{O}\tilde{~}(d^{2.698}k)$ operations in $\mathbb{K}$ to solve our problem.

In [10], Caruso studies the phenomenon of loss of precision in the iterative version of the subresultant algorithm. He shows that on average, if the base field is finite, this loss of precision grows linearly with the degree of the inputs. In that same reference, he also shows how to modify this algorithm to reduce the loss of precision, resulting in a cost of $\mathcal{O}\tilde{~}(d^2(k + \delta))$ operations in $\mathbb{K}$, where δ is the maximum of the x-adic valuations of the non-zero leading subresultants of the input polynomials (under the assumption that these leading subresultants all have valuation less than $k/2$). When $\mathbb{K}$ is finite, the expected value of δ is $\mathcal{O}(\log(d))$, so that the average running time becomes $\mathcal{O}\tilde{~}(d^2k)$.

Our main result is a complexity estimate for the computation of $R \bmod x^k$, using the Knuth-Schönhage divide-and-conquer algorithm. We show that we can compute $R \bmod x^k$ using $\tilde{\mathcal{O}}(dk)$ base field operations, when $\mathbb{K}$ has characteristic zero, or at least k.

We proceed in three steps. First, we compute cofactors U, V and an integer t such that $UV + PQ = x^t \bmod x^{t+1}$ holds in $\mathcal{R}_k = \mathbb{K}[x,y]/\langle x^k\rangle$; this is done in Section 3 by a suitable adaptation of the half-gcd algorithm. From this equality, we will able to deduce a first-order linear differential equation satisfied by the resultant R (Section 5). Solving this differential equation is straightforward, once an initial condition is known; Section 4 shows how to compute the first non-zero term in the resultant.

2. PRELIMINARIES

To a polynomial P of $\mathcal{R}_k$, we associate a valuation $v(P)$ defined as the smallest exponent on x in the monomials of P for P non-zero; by convention, $v(0) = k$. By Gauss' Lemma, for any polynomials P and Q in $\mathcal{R}_k$, we have $v(PQ) = v(P) + v(Q)$ if the sum is less than k (otherwise, $PQ = 0$). In all the algorithms of the paper, a polynomial P of $\mathcal{R}_k$ is represented by the monomial $x^{v(P)}$ and the polynomial $P/x^{v(P)}$ of valuation 0. We do not take into account the boolean cost of exponent manipulations, in the sense that we assume that we can add two valuations in constant time. We define the valuation $v(P,Q)$ of a pair of polynomials $(P,Q) \in \mathcal{R}_k^2$ as the minimum of the valuations of P and Q. We let $\mathcal{S}_k \subset \mathcal{R}_k^2$ be the set of all pairs of polynomials (P,Q) with $v(P) < v(Q)$, to which we adjoin $(0,0)$.

For $n \in \mathbb{N}$, we define Π_n as the function from $\mathcal{R}_k$ to itself, and by extension from $\mathcal{S}_k$ to itself, such that:

$$\Pi_n(P) = P \operatorname{rem}_x x^{v(P)+n}$$
$$\Pi_n(P,Q) = (P \operatorname{rem}_x x^{v(P,Q)+n}, Q \operatorname{rem}_x x^{v(P,Q)+n});$$

if $v(P)+n \geq k$ in this definition, we simply replace it by k. We denote by $\mathcal{U}(\mathcal{R}_k)$ the set of invertible elements of $\mathcal{R}_k$; they are exactly the polynomials P such that $v(P) = 0$ and $\Pi_1(P) \in \mathbb{K}$.

We call *degree* of an element of $\mathbb{K}[x]/\langle x^k\rangle$ the degree of its canonical lift to $\mathbb{K}[x]$. We will often write expressions of the form $Q = P/x^{v(P)}$, for some P in $\mathcal{R}_k$. Such a quotient is not unique; we remove ambiguities by requiring that all coefficients of Q have degree in x less than $k - v(P)$.

If P is a polynomial in $\mathcal{R}_k$, then $[x^i]P \in \mathbb{K}[y]$ is the coefficient of x^i in it. Then, we say that P is *normal* if $\deg_y([x^{v(P)}]P) > \deg_y([x^i]P)$ for all $i > v(P)$. Equivalently, this is the case if the leading coefficient of P has the form $cx^{v(P)}$, for some non-zero c in $\mathbb{K}$.

Being normal is a useful property. For instance, it allows us to define quotient and remainder in a Euclidean division in many cases: if $P \in \mathcal{R}_k$ is normal and $Q \in \mathcal{R}_k$ has valuation at least $v(P)$, there exist U and R in $\mathcal{R}_k$ with $\deg(R) < \deg(P)$, and such that $Q = UP + R$; U is uniquely defined modulo $x^{k-v(P)}$, whereas R is unique. We will write $Q \operatorname{div}_y P$ for the unique quotient U with degree in x less than $k - v(P)$, and $R = Q \operatorname{rem}_y P$.

The following normalization property will be essential for our algorithms. Below, $\mathsf{M}(n)$ is a bound on the number of arithmetic operations in $\mathbb{K}$ for computing the product of two polynomials f, g in $\mathbb{K}[x]$ of degree at most n; we assume that M satisfies the super-linearity conditions of [13, Chapter 8]. Using the Cantor-Kaltofen algorithm [9], we can take $\mathsf{M}(n)$ in $\mathcal{O}(n \log(n) \log\log(n))$. Using Kronecker's substitution as in [15], multiplication or Euclidean division in degree d in $\mathcal{R}_k$ can then be done in $\mathcal{O}(\mathsf{M}(kd))$ operations in $\mathbb{K}$.

Lemma 1 (Normalization). *For P non-zero in $\mathcal{R}_k$, there exist polynomials U and T in $\mathcal{R}_k$ such that T is normal, U is a unit, with $\Pi_1(U) = 1$, and $P = UT$.*

The polynomial T is unique, whereas U is uniquely defined modulo $x^{k-v(P)}$. Moreover, if P has degree d, for $n \leq k - v(P)$, given $\Pi_n(P)$, $\Pi_n(U)$ and $\Pi_n(T)$ can be computed using $\mathcal{O}(\mathsf{M}(dn))$ operations in $\mathbb{K}$.

Proof. Up to dividing P by $x^{v(P)}$, we may assume that P has valuation 0. Then, uniqueness and the corresponding algorithm are from Algorithm Q in [25]; the cost analysis is a straightforward extension of that given for Hensel step in [13, Chapter 15] using Kronecker substitution for the arithmetic operations. Once the result is known for $P/x^{v(P)}$, we recover our claim by multiplying T by $x^{v(P)}$. □

Given P in $\mathcal{R}_k$, we denote by respectively $\mathrm{Lc}(P)$ and $N(P)$ the unique U and T that satisfy the above conditions, with U having degree in x less than $k - v(P)$; these two polynomials have degree in y at most d, and $v(N(P)) = v(P)$. We also define $\mathrm{Lc}_n(P) = \Pi_n(\mathrm{Lc}(P))$ and $N_n(P) = \Pi_n(N(P))$; by the previous lemma, if P has degree d, for any n, $\mathrm{Lc}_n(P)$ and $N_n(P)$ can be computed in time $\mathcal{O}(\mathsf{M}(dn))$.

Using this result, we can reduce the problem of computing the resultant of two polynomials in $\mathcal{R}_k$ to the problem of computing the resultant of two normal polynomials.

Lemma 2. *Let P and Q be in $\mathcal{R}_k$ of degrees in y at most d. Then there exist four monic polynomials A, B, C, D in $\mathcal{R}_k$, with degrees at most d, and u in $\mathbb{K}[x]/\langle x^k\rangle$ such that $\mathrm{Res}(P,Q) = u\,\mathrm{Res}(A,B)\,\mathrm{Res}(C,D)$. Moreover, A, B, C, D, u can be computed in time $\mathcal{O}(\mathsf{M}(dk))$.*

Proof. By the multiplicative property of the resultant, $\mathrm{Res}(P,Q) = \mathrm{Res}(\mathrm{Lc}(P),Q)\,\mathrm{Res}(N(P),Q)$. Let d_c, d_n, d_Q be the degrees in y of $\mathrm{Lc}(P), N(P)$ and Q respectively.

Taking the reciprocal polynomial of $\mathrm{Lc}(P)$ and Q changes at most the sign of their resultant. Let us thus define $\tilde{P} = y^{d_c}\mathrm{Lc}(P)(1/y)$ and $\tilde{Q} = y^{d_Q}Q(1/y)$ and let $c_0 \in \mathbb{K}[x]/\langle x^k\rangle$ be the leading coefficient of $\tilde{P}$. By construction, c_0 is a unit, so we can define $A = \tilde{P}/c_0 \in \mathcal{R}_k$, and we have $\mathrm{Res}(\mathrm{Lc}(P),Q) = (-1)^{d_c d_Q} c_0{}^{d_Q}\,\mathrm{Res}(A,\tilde{Q})$, where A is monic in y. Let R be the remainder of the Euclidean division of $\tilde{Q}$ by A and let $B = R + A$; since A is monic, $\mathrm{Res}(A,\tilde{Q}) = \mathrm{Res}(A,B)$.

Similarly, because $N(P)$ is normal, we can write it as $N(P) = n_0 C$, where $n_0 \in \mathbb{K}[x]/\langle x^k\rangle$ is its leading coefficient and C is monic in y; then, we have $\mathrm{Res}(N(P),Q) = n_0{}^{d_Q}\,\mathrm{Res}(C,Q)$. Defining as above $D = (Q \operatorname{rem}_y C) + C$, we deduce $\mathrm{Res}(N(P),Q) = n_0{}^{d_Q}\,\mathrm{Res}(C,D)$, and finally

$$\mathrm{Res}(P,Q) = (-1)^{d_c d_Q}(c_0 n_0)^{d_Q}\,\mathrm{Res}(A,B)\,\mathrm{Res}(C,D).$$

A is monic of degree at most d, since $\mathrm{Lc}(P)$, has degree at most d. The remainder R has degree less than the degree of A, so that $B = R + A$ is monic of the same degree as A. The same holds for C and D.

In terms of complexity, after computing $\mathrm{Lc}(P)$ and $N(P)$, all other operations are $\mathcal{O}(d)$ inversions or multiplications of power series in $\mathbb{K}[x]/\langle x^k\rangle$, and $\mathcal{O}(1)$ Euclidean divisions by monic polynomials of degree at most d in $\mathcal{R}_k$. Their total cost is $\mathcal{O}(\mathsf{M}(dk))$ operations in $\mathbb{K}$. □

3. COMPUTING PSEUDO INVERSES

In this section, we show that given two polynomials P, Q in $\mathcal{R}_k$, we can compute a matrix $\mathbf{M} = \left(\begin{smallmatrix} U & V \\ X & Y \end{smallmatrix}\right) \in \mathscr{M}_2(\mathcal{R}_k)$ such that $UP + VQ$ is of the form $x^t \bmod x^{t+1}$, for some integer t; we call U and V *pseudo-inverses* of P and Q.

To simplify notation, for $s = (P, Q)$ and $\mathbf{M}$ as above, we simply write $\mathbf{M} \cdot s$ for the matrix-vector product $\mathbf{M}\left(\begin{smallmatrix} P \\ Q \end{smallmatrix}\right)$.

3.1 The pseudo-division operator $\mathcal{Q}$

In this subsection, we define an operator $\mathcal{Q} : \mathcal{S}_k \to \mathcal{S}_k$ and study its properties. For $s = (0, 0)$, we define $\mathcal{Q}(s) = \mathrm{Id}$; otherwise, the construction involves three stages.

For a non-zero pair of polynomials $s = (P, Q)$ in $\mathcal{S}_k$, define

$$\eta(s) := v(Q \text{ rem}_y N(P)) - v(P).$$

This is well-defined, as $N(P)$ has the same valuation as P.

LEMMA 3. *For an integer n and s in $\mathcal{S}_k$, given $\Pi_n(s)$, we can compute $\min(\eta(s), n)$ using $\mathcal{O}(\mathsf{M}(dn))$ operations in $\mathbb{K}$.*

PROOF. We start by dividing both P and Q by $x^{v(P)}$; this does not involve any arithmetic operation. We can then compute the normalization $N_n(P)/x^{v(P)}$, and do the Euclidean division of $Q/x^{v(P)}$ by this polynomial, using coefficients taken modulo x^n, both in time $\mathcal{O}(\mathsf{M}(dn))$. The valuation of the remainder is precisely $\min(\eta(s), n)$. □

The next lemma shows a more intrinsic characterization of η. We denote by $\sigma_0 : \mathcal{R}_k \to \mathbb{K}[y]$ the evaluation morphism that sends x to 0.

LEMMA 4. *For any integer $t \geq 0$, with $J_t(s) = \langle P, Q \rangle : x^{v(s)+t}$ and $I_t(s) = \sigma_0(J_t(s))$, we have*

$$\begin{cases} I_t(s) = I_0(s) \text{ if } 0 \leq t < \eta(s) \\ I_t(s) \supsetneq I_0(s) \text{ if } t \geq \eta(s). \end{cases}$$

PROOF. For $t \geq v(s)$, we have $I_0(s) \subset I_t(s)$. Then, let $Q' = Q \text{ rem}_y N(P)$. If $0 \leq t < \eta(s)$ let W be such that $x^{v(s)+t}W = UP + VQ' \in \langle P, Q \rangle$. Since $x^{v(s)+\eta(s)}$ divides Q' and $t + 1 \leq \eta(s)$ we have $x^{v(s)+t}W = UP \mod x^{v(s)+t+1}$, so x^t divides U and $x^{v(s)}W = U'P \mod x^{v(s)+1}$. Thus $I_t(s) \subset I_0(s)$ and $I_t(s) = I_0(s)$. If $t \geq \eta(s)$, $I_t(s)$ contains the residue class of the remainder of $\Pi_1(Q)/x^{v(Q)}$ by $\Pi_1(P)/x^{v(P)}$, that is a non-zero polynomial of degree less than $\deg_y(\Pi_1(P))$, and is not included in $I_0(s)$. □

For $s = (P, Q)$ as above, perform a Euclidean division of Q by the normal polynomial $N_{\eta(s)}(P)$, and define the matrix

$$\mathbf{D}_s := \begin{pmatrix} x^{\eta(s)} & 0 \\ -\left(Q \text{ div}_y N_{\eta(s)}(P)\right) \text{ rem}_x x^{\eta(s)} & \mathrm{Lc}_{\eta(s)}(P) \end{pmatrix}.$$

Then, the polynomial $\tilde{Q}$ defined by

$$\mathbf{D}_s \cdot \begin{pmatrix} P \\ Q \end{pmatrix} = \begin{pmatrix} x^{\eta(s)}P \\ \tilde{Q} \end{pmatrix}$$

has valuation $v(P) + \eta(s)$ and we have the inequality $\deg_y(\Pi_1(\tilde{Q})) < \deg_y(\Pi_1(P))$.

Given $P, Q \in \mathbb{K}[y]$ of degree at most d, and denoting by G their monic gcd, there exists an invertible matrix $\mathbf{G}_{(P,Q)}$ with entries in $\mathbb{K}[y]$ of degree less than d such that

$$\mathbf{G}_{(P,Q)} \cdot \begin{pmatrix} P \\ Q \end{pmatrix} = \begin{pmatrix} G \\ 0 \end{pmatrix}.$$

If $Q = 0$ then $G_{(P,Q)}$ is the identity matrix. By extension, for $s = (P, Q) \in \mathcal{R}_k^2$ with $v(P) = v(Q)$, we define $\mathbf{G}_s$ as $\mathbf{G}_{(\Pi_1(P)/x^{v(P)}, \Pi_1(Q)/x^{v(Q)})}$. By construction, the entries $(\tilde{P}, \tilde{Q})$ of $\mathbf{G}_s \cdot s$ satisfy $v(\tilde{P}) < v(\tilde{Q})$, or $\tilde{P} = \tilde{Q} = 0$; in other words, the pair $\mathbf{G}_s \cdot s$ belongs to $\mathcal{S}_k$.

For a pair $s = (P, Q)$ in $\mathcal{S}_k$ with $P \neq 0$ we define $\mathbf{N}_s$ by

$$\mathbf{N}_s = \begin{pmatrix} \mathrm{Lc}(P)^{-1} & 0 \\ -\mathrm{Lc}(P)^{-1}(Q \text{ div}_y N(P)) & 1 \end{pmatrix}.$$

If $P = 0$, set $\mathbf{N}_s = \mathrm{Id}$. Else, $v(Q) > v(P)$ and there exists a matrix $\mathbf{R}$ such that $\mathbf{N}_s = \mathrm{Id} + x\mathbf{R}$; then, $\mathbf{N}_s$ is invertible.

LEMMA 5. *For $s = (P, Q) \in \mathcal{S}_k^2$, define*

$$\mathcal{Q}(s) := \mathbf{N}_{\mathbf{G}_{\mathbf{D}_s \cdot s} \cdot \mathbf{D}_s \cdot s} \cdot \mathbf{G}_{\mathbf{D}_s \cdot s} \cdot \mathbf{D}_s.$$

Then,

1. *$\mathcal{Q}(s) \cdot s$ is in $\mathcal{S}_k$;*
2. *the following equality between ideals holds:*
$$\langle \mathcal{Q}(s) \cdot s \rangle = \langle s \rangle \cap \left\langle x^{v(s)+\eta(s)} \right\rangle;$$
3. *$\Pi_1(\mathcal{Q}(s) \cdot s) = \left(\begin{smallmatrix} x^{v(s)+\eta(s)}G \\ 0 \end{smallmatrix}\right)$, where G is the gcd of $\Pi_1(P)/x^{v(s)}$ and $\Pi_1(\tilde{Q})/x^{v(s)+\eta(s)}$;*
4. *$\mathcal{Q}(s) \cdot s$ and $\mathcal{Q}(s') \cdot s'$ generate the same ideal, for any pair s' that generates the same ideal as s;*
5. *the entries of $\mathcal{Q}(s) \cdot s$ have degree less than $\deg_y(\Pi_1(P))$.*

For $s = (P, Q) \in \mathcal{S}_k$, where P and Q have degree at most d, given $\Pi_n(s)$ for some $n \geq \eta(s)$, $\Pi_{n-\eta(s)}(\mathcal{Q}(s) \cdot s)$ can be computed using $\mathcal{O}(\mathsf{M}(dn) + \mathsf{M}(d)\log(d))$ operations in $\mathbb{K}$.

PROOF. We saw just above the lemma that $\mathbf{G}_{\mathbf{D}_s \cdot s} \cdot (\mathbf{D}_s \cdot s)$ belongs to $\mathcal{S}_k$. Since applying the matrix $\mathbf{N}_{\mathbf{G}_{\mathbf{D}_s \cdot s} \cdot \mathbf{D}_s \cdot s}$ to this vector does not change the valuations of its entries, we deduce that $\mathcal{Q}(s) \cdot s$ is in $\mathcal{S}_k$.

In order to prove the relation $\langle \mathcal{Q}(s) \cdot s \rangle = \langle s \rangle \cap \langle x^{v(s)+\eta(s)} \rangle$, it is sufficient to prove that $\langle \mathbf{D}_s \cdot s \rangle = \langle s \rangle \cap \langle x^{v(s)+\eta(s)} \rangle$, since the matrices $\mathbf{N}_{\mathbf{G}_{\mathbf{D}_s \cdot s} \cdot \mathbf{D}_s \cdot s}$ and $\mathbf{G}_{\mathbf{D}_s \cdot s}$ are invertible over $\mathcal{R}_k$. The two polynomials in the vector $\mathbf{D}_s \cdot s = (x^{\eta(s)}P, \tilde{Q})$ are divisible by $x^{v(P)+\eta(s)}$, thus $\langle \mathbf{D}_s \cdot s \rangle \subset \langle s \rangle \cap \langle x^{v(P)+\eta(s)} \rangle$. For the other inclusion, let W be a polynomial in $\langle s \rangle \cap \langle x^{v(P)+\eta(s)} \rangle$. Since we have $s = \langle P, Q \rangle = \langle P, \tilde{Q} \rangle$, we can write $W = UP + V\tilde{Q}$, for some U, V in $\mathcal{R}_k$. On the other hand, we know that $x^{v(P)+\eta(s)}$ divides W, and since it also divides $\tilde{Q}$, it divides UP. This implies that $x^{\eta(s)}$ divides U, which means that W is in $\langle \mathbf{D}_s \cdot s \rangle$. This allows us to conclude for the equality of ideals, noting that $v(s) = v(P)$.

The third point comes from the fact that the matrix $\mathbf{N}_{\mathbf{G}_{\mathbf{D}_s \cdot s} \cdot \mathbf{D}_s \cdot s}$ can be written $\mathrm{Id} + x\mathbf{R}$, so that $\Pi_1(\mathcal{Q}(s) \cdot s) = \Pi_1(\mathbf{G}_{\mathbf{D}_s \cdot s} \cdot \mathbf{D}_s \cdot s) = \left(\begin{smallmatrix} x^{v(s)+\eta(s)}G \\ 0 \end{smallmatrix}\right)$.

If s and s' generate the same ideal, $\eta(s) = \eta(s')$ (Lemma 4); using the second item, this proves point 4.

The degree property follows from the fact that in the pair $(A, B) = \mathcal{Q}(s) \cdot s$, A is normal of degree $\deg_y(G) < \deg_y(\Pi_1(P))$, and B is a remainder modulo $N(A)$.

Computing $\mathbf{D}_s$ can be done in time $\mathcal{O}(\mathsf{M}(d\eta(s)))$ using Lemma 1 to compute $N_{\eta(s)}(P)$ and $\mathrm{Lc}_{\eta(s)}(P)$ in time $\mathcal{O}(\mathsf{M}(d\eta(s)))$. The matrix-vector product that gives $\tilde{Q}$ is done in degree n in x and d in y, in time $\mathcal{O}(\mathsf{M}(dn))$. Then, we saw that $\Pi_1(\tilde{Q})$ has degree less than d, so computing $\mathbf{G}_{\mathbf{D}_s \cdot s}$ is an extended gcd calculation in $\mathbb{K}[y]$ that can be done in time $\mathcal{O}(\mathsf{M}(d)\log(d))$. Applying $\mathbf{G}_{\mathbf{D}_s \cdot s}$ to $\mathbf{D}_s \cdot s$ takes $\mathcal{O}(n\mathsf{M}(d))$, and results in a matrix of degree $\mathcal{O}(d)$ in y. Finally, applying $\mathbf{N}_{\mathbf{G}_{\mathbf{D}_s \cdot s} \cdot \mathbf{D}_s \cdot s}$ to $\mathbf{G}_{\mathbf{D}_s \cdot s} \cdot \mathbf{D}_s \cdot s$ is again a normalization at precision n along with arithmetic operations that can all be done in time $\mathcal{O}(\mathsf{M}(dn))$. □

3.2 An extension of the half-gcd

Our goal is now to iterate the pseudo-division $\mathcal{Q}(s)$ until we reach an integer t such that $\langle s \rangle \cap \langle x^t \rangle = \langle x^t \rangle$. We use a divide-and-conquer algorithm, inspired by the half-gcd algorithm. If we applied this idea directly, the increase in degree in y of the transition matrices would prevent us from getting a softly linear bound in the degree of the input; we will thus work modulo an equivalence relation, to control the size of the intermediate polynomials.

Consider the following equivalence relation on $\mathcal{S}_k$: for any two pairs (P, Q) and (P', Q') in $\mathcal{S}_k$, we say that $(P, Q) \sim (P', Q')$ if and only if the ideals they generate are the same. In particular, this implies that $v(P, Q) = v(P', Q')$ and that $\Pi_1(P)$ and $\Pi_1(P')$ are equal up to a constant.

Let further $\mathcal{H}, \mathcal{H}'$ be two functions from $\mathcal{S}_k$ to $\mathscr{M}_2(\mathcal{R}_k)$. Extending the equivalence property to the set of functions, we say that $\mathcal{H}$ and $\mathcal{H}'$ are equivalent if for all $s \in \mathcal{S}_k$ we have $\mathcal{H}(s) \cdot s \sim \mathcal{H}'(s) \cdot s$. We still write in this case $\mathcal{H} \sim \mathcal{H}'$.

DEFINITION 1 (EUCLIDEAN FUNCTION). *We say that* $\mathcal{H} : \mathcal{S}_k \to \mathscr{M}_2(\mathcal{R}_k)$ *is* Euclidean *if:*

- *for all* $s, s' \in \mathcal{S}_k$, *if* $s \sim s'$, *then* $\mathcal{H}(s) \cdot s \sim \mathcal{H}(s') \cdot s'$
- *for all* $s \in \mathcal{S}_k$, *if* s *is non-zero,* $v(\mathcal{H}(s) \cdot s) > v(s)$.

We denote $v(\mathcal{H}(s).s) - v(s)$ *by* $\eta_{\mathcal{H}}(s)$, *and we say that* $\mathcal{H}$ *is* online *if for all* $s \in \mathcal{S}_k$:

- $\eta_{\mathcal{H}}(\Pi_i(s)) \geq i$ *for all* $i \leq \eta_{\mathcal{H}}(s)$
- $\mathcal{H}(s) \cdot s \sim \mathcal{H}(\Pi_i(s)) \cdot s$ *for all* $i \geq \eta_{\mathcal{H}}(s) + 1$.

LEMMA 6. *The function $\mathcal{Q}$ introduced in Lemma 5 is an online Euclidean function.*

PROOF. The first point was proved in Lemma 5. Now, let $s = (P, Q)$ be a non-zero element of $\mathcal{S}_k$. By construction, we have $v(\mathcal{Q}(s) \cdot s) = v(s) + \eta(s)$. In particular, $\eta(s) = v(Q \text{ rem}_y N(P)) - v(P) \geq v(Q) - v(P) > 0$. Thus, $\mathcal{Q}$ is a Euclidean function.

To prove that $\mathcal{Q}$ is online, notice that $\mathcal{Q}(s \text{ rem}_x x^{v(s)+i}) \text{ rem}_x x^i = \mathcal{Q}(s) \text{ rem}_x x^i$. In particular for $i \leq \eta_{\mathcal{Q}}(s)$, $\mathcal{Q}(\Pi_i(s)) \cdot \Pi_i(s)$ is given by

$$\left(\mathcal{Q}(s) \text{ rem}_x x^i\right) \cdot \left(s \text{ rem}_x x^{v(s)+i}\right) \bmod x^{v(s)+i}$$
$$= \mathcal{Q}(s) \cdot s \quad \bmod x^{v(s)+i} = (0,0) \quad \bmod x^{v(s)+i},$$

so that $\eta_{\mathcal{Q}}(\Pi_i(s)) \geq i$.

If $i > \eta(s)$, we prove that there exists a matrix $\mathbf{R}$ such that $\mathcal{Q}(\Pi_i(s)) = (\mathrm{Id} + x\mathbf{R}) \cdot \mathcal{Q}(s)$. Indeed, if that holds, $(\mathrm{Id} + x\mathbf{R})$ is an invertible matrix over $\mathcal{R}_k$, so that $\langle \mathcal{Q}(\Pi_i(s)) \cdot s \rangle = \langle \mathcal{Q}(s) \cdot s \rangle$. Moreover $\Pi_1(\mathcal{Q}(\Pi_i(s)) \cdot s) = \Pi_1(\mathcal{Q}(s) \cdot s)$, which will be sufficient to conclude. Let $\mathbf{M} = \mathbf{G}_{\mathbf{D}_s \cdot s} \cdot \mathbf{D}_s$. If $i > \eta(s)$, we note by construction that $\mathbf{M} \text{ rem}_x x^i = \mathbf{M}$. Moreover there exists a matrix $\mathbf{R}$ such that $\mathbf{N}_{\mathbf{M} \cdot s} \text{ rem}_x x^i = (\mathrm{Id} + x\mathbf{R}) \cdot \mathbf{N}_{\mathbf{M} \cdot s}$, so that $\mathcal{Q}(\Pi_i(s)) = (\mathrm{Id} + x\mathbf{R}) \cdot \mathcal{Q}(s)$. □

Let s be an element of $\mathcal{S}_k$ and define by recurrence the following sequence of elements of $\mathscr{M}_2(\mathcal{R}_k)$:

$$\begin{cases} \mathbf{Q}_0 & = & \mathrm{Id} \\ \mathbf{Q}_{n+1} & = & \mathcal{Q}(\mathbf{Q}_n \cdot s) \cdot \mathbf{Q}_n. \end{cases} \tag{1}$$

For s in $\mathcal{S}_k$, the sequence $(v(\mathbf{Q}_i \cdot s))_{i \in \mathbb{N}}$ is increasing, until it reaches $v(\mathbf{Q}_i \cdot s) = k$. Thus given an integer n, we can define the function $\mathcal{Q}_n$ from $\mathcal{S}_k$ to $\mathscr{M}_2(\mathcal{R}_k)$ by

$$\mathcal{Q}_n : \mathcal{S}_k \to \mathscr{M}_2(\mathcal{R}_k)$$
$$s \mapsto \mathbf{Q}_{i_0}, \; i_0 = \max\{i \in \mathbb{N} \mid v(\mathbf{Q}_i \cdot s) - v(s) \leq n\}$$

for s non-zero; for $s = (0, 0)$, we set $\mathcal{Q}_n(s) = \mathrm{Id}$. In particular, for any s, $\mathcal{Q}_0(s) = \mathrm{Id}$ (since for s non-zero, $\mathbf{Q}_1 \cdot s = \mathcal{Q}(s) \cdot s$ has valuation greater than that of s).

LEMMA 7. *For $n \geq 0$, if $s \sim s'$ in $\mathcal{S}_k$ then $\mathcal{Q}_n(s) \cdot s \sim \mathcal{Q}_n(s') \cdot s'$. Moreover, let j be the minimal integer such that $I_j(s) = I_n(s)$; then, $\langle \mathcal{Q}_n(s) \cdot s \rangle = \langle s \rangle \cap \langle x^{v(s)+j} \rangle$.*

PROOF. We use a recurrence on n. For $n = 0$, it is clear that $\mathcal{Q}_0$ satisfies the desired properties. Then, given $n \geq 1$ and $s \sim s'$ two equivalent elements of $\mathcal{S}_k$ we know by recurrence assumption that $t := \mathcal{Q}_{n-1}(s) \cdot s \sim t' := \mathcal{Q}_{n-1}(s') \cdot s'$.

If $v(\mathcal{Q}(t) \cdot t) > v(s) + n$, then $v(\mathcal{Q}(t') \cdot t') > v(s') + n$ and $\mathcal{Q}_n(s) = \mathcal{Q}_{n-1}(s)$ and $\mathcal{Q}_n(s') = \mathcal{Q}_{n-1}(s')$, so that $\mathcal{Q}_n(s) \cdot s \sim \mathcal{Q}_n(s') \cdot s'$. Moreover, in this case, let j be the minimal integer such that $I_j(s) = I_{n-1}(s)$. For all $\ell < \eta(t)$ we have $I_\ell(t) = I_0(t)$. In particular, $\ell := n - (v(t) - v(s)) < \eta(t)$, and $I_\ell(t) = I_n(s)$ and $I_0(t) = I_{n-1}(s)$. Hence, $\langle \mathcal{Q}_n(s) \cdot s \rangle = \langle s \rangle \cap \langle x^{v(s)+j} \rangle$ and j is the smallest integer such that $I_n(s) = I_{n-1}(s) = I_j(s)$.

Otherwise, $v(s) + n - 1 < v(\mathcal{Q}(t) \cdot t) \leq v(s) + n$, so that $v(\mathcal{Q}(t) \cdot t) = v(s) + n$. Then $v(\mathcal{Q}(t') \cdot t') = v(s') + n$. Thus $\mathcal{Q}_n(s) = \mathcal{Q}(t) \cdot \mathcal{Q}_{n-1}(s)$ and $\mathcal{Q}_n(s') = \mathcal{Q}(t') \cdot \mathcal{Q}_{n-1}(s')$. Since $\mathcal{Q}$ is a Euclidean function, $\mathcal{Q}(t) \cdot t \sim \mathcal{Q}(t') \cdot t'$ and this leads to $\mathcal{Q}_n(s) \cdot s \sim \mathcal{Q}_n(s') \cdot s'$. Moreover, let ℓ be the smallest integer such that $I_\ell(t) \neq I_0(t)$. We have $\langle \mathcal{Q}(t) \cdot t \rangle = \langle t \rangle \cap \langle x^{v(t)+\ell} \rangle$. According to Lemma 4 we have $\ell = \eta(t) = v(s) + n - v(t)$. In particular $n = v(t) + \ell - v(s)$, and we have $I_n(s) = I_\ell(t)$ and for all $i < n$ we have $I_i(s) \neq I_n(s)$. Thus, n is the smallest integer j such that $I_j(s) = I_n(s)$ and $\langle \mathcal{Q}_n(s) \cdot s) \rangle = \langle \mathcal{Q}(t) \cdot t \rangle = \langle t \rangle \cap \langle x^{v(t)+\eta(t)} \rangle$. Since $\langle t \rangle = \langle \mathcal{Q}_{n-1}(s) \cdot s \rangle = \langle s \rangle \cap \langle x^{v(s)+i} \rangle$ for some $i \leq n-1$, this leads to $\langle \mathcal{Q}_n(s) \cdot s) \rangle = \langle s \rangle \cap \langle x^{v(s)+n} \rangle$. □

Our goal is to compute efficiently a mapping equivalent to $\mathcal{Q}_n$. To this effect, we introduce in Algorithm 1 a generalized version of the half-gcd algorithm [13, p. 320]. In order to control the degree in y of the intermediate elements in Algorithm 1, we use a function $\varphi_{s,n} : \mathscr{M}_2(\mathcal{R}_k) \to \mathscr{M}_2(\mathcal{R}_k)$, that depends on an element $s \in \mathcal{S}_k$ and an integer n.

Let $s = (P, Q)$ be a pair of polynomials in $\mathcal{S}_k$, n be an integer, and let $\mathbf{M} = \left(\begin{smallmatrix} A & B \\ C & D \end{smallmatrix}\right)$ be a matrix of $\mathscr{M}_2(\mathcal{R}_k)$. If $Q = 0$ or $v(\mathbf{M} \cdot s) = v(s)$ then we let $\varphi_{s,n}(\mathbf{M}) = \mathrm{Id}$. Otherwise, neither P nor Q are zero and we define $\varphi_{s,n}(\mathbf{M})$ as the remainder of

$$\begin{pmatrix} L_Q(L_P A \text{ rem}_y N_u(Q)) & L_P(L_Q B \text{ rem}_y N_u(P)) \\ L_Q(L_P C \text{ rem}_y N_u(Q)) & L_P(L_Q D \text{ rem}_y N_u(P)) \end{pmatrix}$$

by x^{n+1}, where L_P, L_Q are $\mathrm{Lc}(P), \mathrm{Lc}(Q)$ and $N_u(P), N_u(Q)$ are two polynomials with constant leading coefficients such that $N(P) = x^{v(P)} N_u(P)$ and $N(Q) = x^{v(Q)} N_u(Q)$.

LEMMA 8 (SIZE CONTROL). *Let $s \in \mathcal{S}_k$ and assume $\mathbf{M} \cdot s$ is also in $\mathcal{S}_k$. If $\mathbf{M} \cdot s \sim \mathcal{Q}_n(s) \cdot s$, let $j = v(\mathbf{M} \cdot s) - v(s)$. Then $\varphi_{s,j}(\mathbf{M}) \cdot s \in \mathcal{S}_k$ and $\varphi_{s,j}(\mathbf{M}) \cdot s \sim \mathbf{M} \cdot s$.*

Moreover the degree in y of the entries in $\varphi_{s,j}(\mathbf{M})$ are bounded by $d_Q - 1$ for the first column and $d_P - 1$ for the second one, with $d_P = \deg_y(P)$ and $d_Q = \deg_y(Q)$.

PROOF. The degree bound follows from $\deg(L_P) + \deg(N_u(P)) = d_P$, and similarly for Q. If $Q = 0$ or $v(\mathbf{M} \cdot s) = v(s)$ then $\mathcal{Q}_n(s) = \mathrm{Id}$ for all $0 \leq n < k$, and $\varphi_{s,j}(\mathbf{M}) = \mathrm{Id} = \mathcal{Q}_n(s)$.

Now let $s = (P, Q)$ a pair in $\mathcal{S}_k$ with $Q \neq 0$ and $v(\mathbf{M} \cdot s) > v(s)$ and let $\binom{G}{H} = \mathbf{M} \cdot \binom{P}{Q}$. By assumption, $\langle G, H \rangle = \langle P, Q \rangle \cap \langle x^{v(s)+j} \rangle$. Moreover, $\Pi_1(G, H) = (\Pi_1(G), 0)$ and Lemma 5 shows that $\deg_y(\Pi_1(G)) < d_P$.

Assume first that P and Q are normal. In this case, $L_P = L_Q = 1$ and we have

$$\varphi_{s,j}(\mathbf{M}) \cdot \begin{pmatrix} P \\ Q \end{pmatrix} = \begin{pmatrix} G + K N_u(P) N_u(Q) + L x^{j+1} \\ H + M N_u(P) N_u(Q) + N x^{j+1} \end{pmatrix},$$

where K, M are polynomials of $\mathcal{R}_k$ and L, N are in $\langle P, Q \rangle$, so that $v(L) \geq v(s)$ and $v(N) \geq v(s)$. In this case we also know that the degrees of $G + K N_u(P) N_u(Q) + L x^{j+1}$ and $H + M N_u(P) N_u(Q) + N x^{j+1}$ are lower than $d_P + d_Q$. On the other hand, $G \operatorname{rem}_x x^{v(s)+j+1}$ has a degree in y less than d_P and $H \operatorname{rem}_x x^{v(s)+j+1} = 0$. Also, $L x^{j+1} \operatorname{rem}_x x^{v(s)+j+1} = N x^{j+1} \operatorname{rem}_x x^{v(s)+j+1} = 0$. Hence, K and M have a valuation greater than or equal to $v(s) + j + 1$ and $K N_u(P) N_u(Q)$ and $M N_u(P) N_u(Q)$ are in $\langle x^{j+1} P \rangle$.

Thus $\varphi_{s,j}(\mathbf{M}) \cdot \binom{P}{Q} = \begin{pmatrix} G+G' \\ H+H' \end{pmatrix}$, where G' and H' are two polynomials of $\langle x^{j+1} P, x^{j+1} Q \rangle$. In particular, by assumption this implies that G' and H' belongs to the ideal $\langle xG, xH \rangle$. Thus there is an invertible matrix that sends $\binom{G}{H}$ to $\begin{pmatrix} G+G' \\ H+H' \end{pmatrix}$ and $\langle G, H \rangle = \langle G + G', H + H' \rangle$ and $\Pi_1(G + G', H + H') = \Pi_1(G, H)$. In particular $\varphi_{s,j}(\mathbf{M}) \cdot s \in \mathcal{S}_k$.

If P and Q are not normal, let $\mathbf{L}$ be the matrix $\begin{pmatrix} L_P & 0 \\ 0 & L_Q \end{pmatrix}$. In this case, $\mathbf{M} \cdot s = \mathbf{M} \cdot \mathbf{L} \cdot \begin{pmatrix} N(P) \\ N(Q) \end{pmatrix}$. Hence, using the first part of the proof on $N(s) = (N(P), N(Q))$, we have

$$\varphi_{N(s),j}(\mathbf{M} \cdot \mathbf{L}) \cdot \mathbf{L}^{-1} \cdot s = \varphi_{N(s),j}(\mathbf{M} \cdot \mathbf{L}) \cdot \begin{pmatrix} N(P) \\ N(Q) \end{pmatrix}$$
$$\sim \mathbf{M} \cdot \mathbf{L} \cdot \begin{pmatrix} N(P) \\ N(Q) \end{pmatrix} \sim \mathbf{M} \cdot s.$$

Then, $\varphi_{s,j}(\mathbf{M}) = \varphi_{N(s),j}(\mathbf{M} \cdot \mathbf{L}) \cdot \left(\det(\mathbf{L})\mathbf{L}^{-1}\right) \mod x^{j+1}$. In particular, using the same argument as above, this implies that $\varphi_{s,j}(\mathbf{M}) \cdot s = \varphi_{N(s),j}(\mathbf{M} \cdot \mathbf{L}) \cdot \left(\det(\mathbf{L})\mathbf{L}^{-1}\right) \cdot s \mod \langle xG, xH \rangle$. Finally, we can factor out $\det(\mathbf{L})$ and since it is invertible, this implies that $\det(\mathbf{L}) \varphi_{N(s),j}(\mathbf{M} \cdot \mathbf{L}) \cdot \mathbf{L}^{-1} \cdot s$ generates the ideal $\langle G, H \rangle$. Finaly, using tthe same argument as above, this leads to $\varphi_{s,j}(\mathbf{M}) \cdot s \sim \mathbf{M} \cdot s$. □

LEMMA 9 (GENERALIZED HALF-GCD). *For $n \in \mathbb{N}$, denote by $\mathcal{H}(n, .) : s \mapsto \mathcal{H}(n, s)$ the function computed by Algorithm 1. Then, $\mathcal{H}(n, .) \sim \mathcal{Q}_n$.*

PROOF. We prove by recurrence on n that $\mathcal{H}(n, .) \sim \mathcal{Q}_n$. For $n = 0$, and for any $s \in \mathcal{S}_k$, we have by construction $\mathcal{H}(0, s) = \mathrm{Id}$. On the other hand, we saw that for all s, $\mathcal{Q}_0(s) = \mathrm{Id}$, so our claim holds. Now assume that $\mathcal{H}(i, .) \sim \mathcal{Q}_i$ for $0 \leq i < n$; we prove that the equivalence holds for n. Let $n_0 = \lfloor \frac{n}{2} \rfloor, n_1 = n - \left(v(\tilde{t}) - v(\tilde{s})\right)$.

Algorithm 1 Generalized version of the half-gcd

```
function GENERICHALFGCD(n, s)
    s̃ ← Π_{n+1}(s)
    if n = 0 or s̃ = (0, 0) then
        return Id
    end if
    R ← GENERICHALFGCD(⌊n/2⌋, s̃)
    n′ ← n − (v(R · s̃) − v(s̃))
    ũ ← Π_{n′+1}(R · s̃)
    η ← min(η(ũ), n′ + 1)
    if η > n′ then
        return R
    end if
    t̃ ← Π_{n′−η+1}(Q(ũ) · ũ)
    S ← GENERICHALFGCD(n − (v(t̃) − v(s̃)), t̃)
    M ← φ_{s̃, v(S·t̃)−v(s̃)}(S · Q(ũ) · R)
    return M
end function
```

For any s, s', if $\Pi_{n+1}(s) = \Pi_{n+1}(s')$, then $\mathcal{H}(n, s) = \mathcal{H}(n, s')$, since then $\tilde{s} = \tilde{s}'$. In particular, with the notation of the algorithm, $\Pi_{n_0+1}(s) = \Pi_{n_0+1}(\tilde{s})$, which implies that $\mathcal{H}(n_0, \tilde{s}) = \mathcal{H}(n_0, s)$. Hence, by recurrence assumption, we get that $\mathbf{R} \cdot s = \mathcal{H}(n_0, s) \cdot s \sim \mathcal{Q}_{n_0}(s) \cdot s$.

The definition of $\mathcal{Q}_{n_0}$ implies that $v(\mathcal{Q}_{n_0}(s) \cdot s) - v(s) \leq \lfloor n/2 \rfloor$, and by the claim above, we get that $v(\mathbf{R} \cdot s) - v(s) \leq \lfloor n/2 \rfloor$. This implies that $v(\mathbf{R} \cdot s) = v(\mathbf{R} \cdot \tilde{s})$, and, since $n' = n - (v(\mathbf{R} \cdot \tilde{s}) - v(\tilde{s}))$, that $\Pi_{n'+1}(\mathbf{R} \cdot s) = \Pi_{n'+1}(\mathbf{R} \cdot \tilde{s}) = \tilde{u}$.

To continue, we distinguish two cases. If $\eta(\mathbf{R} \cdot s) \geq n' + 1$ then the first part of $\mathcal{Q}$ being online shows that $\eta(\Pi_{n'+1}(\mathbf{R} \cdot s)) = \eta(\tilde{u}) \geq n' + 1$. Hence, in this case, the algorithm returns $\mathbf{R}$. On the other hand, we will prove that in this case, $\mathcal{Q}_n(s) = \mathcal{Q}_{n_0}(s)$; one this is established, this implies that $\mathcal{Q}_n(s) \cdot s \sim \mathbf{R} \cdot s$, so our correctness claim holds in this case. Indeed, $\eta(\mathbf{R} \cdot s) = \eta(\mathcal{Q}_{n_0}(s) \cdot s)$ (in view of the equivalence written above, and of Lemma 4), which can be rewritten as $v(\mathcal{Q}(\mathcal{Q}_{n_0}(s) \cdot s) \cdot \mathcal{Q}_{n_0}(s) \cdot s) - v(\mathcal{Q}_{n_0}(s) \cdot s)$. On the other hand, $n' = n - (v(\mathbf{R} \cdot \tilde{s}) - v(\tilde{s}))$ gives $n' = n - v(\mathcal{Q}_{n_0}(s) \cdot s) + v(s)$. Hence, $\eta(\mathbf{R} \cdot s) \geq n' + 1$ means that

$$v(\mathcal{Q}(\mathcal{Q}_{n_0}(s) \cdot s) \cdot \mathcal{Q}_{n_0}(s) \cdot s) - v(s) \geq n + 1,$$

which precisely implies that $\mathcal{Q}_{n_0}(s) = \mathcal{Q}_n(s)$.

If $n' + 1 > \eta(\mathbf{R} \cdot s)$, $\mathcal{Q}$ being online leads to the equivalence $\mathcal{Q}(\tilde{u}) \cdot \mathbf{R} \cdot s \sim \mathcal{Q}(\mathbf{R} \cdot s) \cdot \mathbf{R} \cdot s$. We claim that the right-hand side has valuation $v(\tilde{t}) = v(\mathcal{Q}(\tilde{u}) \cdot \tilde{u})$. Indeed, the proof of Lemma 6 establishes the existence of a matrix $\mathbf{K}$ such that $\mathcal{Q}(\tilde{u}) = (\mathrm{Id} + \mathbf{K})\mathcal{Q}(\mathbf{R} \cdot s)$; this implies that $v(\mathcal{Q}(\tilde{u}) \cdot \tilde{u}) = v(\mathcal{Q}(\mathbf{R} \cdot s) \cdot \tilde{u})$. On the other hand, the inequality $n' + 1 > \eta(\mathbf{R} \cdot s)$ also implies that $v(\mathcal{Q}(\mathbf{R} \cdot s) \cdot \tilde{u})$ and $v(\mathcal{Q}(\mathbf{R} \cdot s) \cdot \mathbf{R} \cdot s)$ are the same, which proves our claim.

Using $\mathbf{R} \cdot s \sim \mathcal{Q}_{n_0}(s) \cdot s$, and $\mathcal{Q}$ being Euclidean, we get $\mathcal{Q}(\mathbf{R} \cdot s) \cdot \mathbf{R} \cdot s \sim \mathcal{Q}(\mathcal{Q}_{n_0}(s) \cdot s) \cdot \mathcal{Q}_{n_0}(s) \cdot s$. We claim that the right-hand side is equivalent to $\mathcal{Q}_{n-n_1}(s)$, which will prove $\mathcal{Q}(\tilde{u}) \cdot \mathbf{R} \cdot s \sim \mathcal{Q}_{n-n_1}(s) \cdot s$. Indeed, by definition, $\mathcal{Q}_{n-n_1}(s)$ is the last element in the sequence $(\mathbf{Q}_i \cdot s)$ from (1) having valuation at most $v(\tilde{t})$. On the other hand, the previous paragraph proves that $\mathcal{Q}(\mathcal{Q}_{n_0}(s) \cdot s) \cdot \mathcal{Q}_{n_0}(s) \cdot s$, which belongs to the sequence $(\mathbf{Q}_i \cdot s)$, has valuation $v(\tilde{t})$; this is enough to conclude, since the valuations $v(\mathbf{Q}_i \cdot s)$ increase.

Then $\mathbf{S} = \mathcal{H}(n_1, \tilde{t})$; by recurrence assumption, $\mathcal{H}(n_1, .) \sim \mathcal{Q}_{n_1}$. Moreover, $\tilde{t} = \Pi_{n_1+1}(\mathcal{Q}(\tilde{u}) \cdot \tilde{u}) = \Pi_{n_1+1}(\mathcal{Q}(\tilde{u}) \cdot \mathbf{R} \cdot s)$, and by construction $\mathcal{H}(n_1, \tilde{t}) = \mathcal{H}(n_1, \mathcal{Q}(\tilde{u}) \cdot \mathbf{R} \cdot s)$, so that

$$\mathbf{S} \cdot \mathcal{Q}(\tilde{u}) \cdot \mathbf{R} \cdot s \sim \mathcal{Q}_{n_1}(\mathcal{Q}(\tilde{u}) \cdot \mathbf{R} \cdot s) \cdot \mathcal{Q}(\tilde{u}) \cdot \mathbf{R} \cdot s$$
$$\sim \mathcal{Q}_{n_1}(\mathcal{Q}_{n-n_1}(s)) \cdot \mathcal{Q}_{n-n_1}(s) \cdot s.$$

The definition of the sequence $(\mathcal{Q}_n)$ implies that the latter expression is equivalent to $\mathcal{Q}_n(s) \cdot s$.

Finally, since the function $\varphi_{s,n}$ satisfies $\varphi_{s,n}(\mathbf{S} \cdot \mathcal{Q}(\tilde{u}) \cdot \mathbf{R}) \cdot s \sim \mathbf{S} \cdot \mathcal{Q}(\tilde{u}) \cdot \mathbf{R} \cdot s$, we conclude that $\mathcal{H}(n, .) \sim \mathcal{Q}_n$. □

LEMMA 10. *Let $s = (P, Q)$ be in $\mathcal{S}_k$, of degrees at most d. For $n > 0$, Algorithm 1 computes $\mathcal{H}(n, s)$ in time $\mathcal{O}(\mathsf{M}(dn)\log(n) + \mathsf{M}(d)n\log(d))$.*

PROOF. For $n = 0$, for any s, computing $\mathcal{H}(0, s)$ takes constant time. For a higher value of n, remark that the recursive calls are made with arguments n_0, n_1 that are at most $\lfloor \frac{n}{2} \rfloor$: this is clear for n_0; for $n_1 = n - (v(\tilde{t}) - v(\tilde{s}))$, this is because $v(\tilde{t}) - v(\tilde{s}) = v(\mathcal{Q}(\tilde{u}) \cdot u) - v(\tilde{s})$ must be greater than $\lfloor n/2 \rfloor$, by definition of $\mathcal{Q}_{n_0}$.

The matrix $\mathbf{R}$ has entries of degree at most d (because $\tilde{s}$ does), so computing $\tilde{u}$ takes time $\mathcal{O}(\mathsf{M}(dn))$, and its entries have degree $\mathcal{O}(d)$. More precisely, we saw in the proof of the previous lemma that $\mathbf{R} \cdot s \sim \mathcal{Q}_{n_0}(s) \cdot s$. Because $\mathcal{Q}_{n_0}$ is obtained by iterating $\mathcal{Q}$, the last item in Lemma 5 shows that the first entry of $\mathcal{Q}_{n_0}(s) \cdot s$ has degree less than d; as pointed out before, this implies the same property for $\mathbf{R} \cdot s$, and thus for $\tilde{u}$ (which is a truncation of it).

Computing η takes time $\mathcal{O}(\mathsf{M}(dn))$ by Lemma 3, and the same holds for $\tilde{t}$ by Lemma 5, up to an extra term $\mathcal{O}(\mathsf{M}(d)\log(d))$. In addition, that lemma shows that the entries of $\tilde{t}$ have degree less than that of the first entry of $\tilde{u}$, and thus less than d.

After the last recursive call, it remains to compute $\mathbf{M}$. We first compute $\mathbf{Q}_1 = \mathcal{Q}(\tilde{u}) \mod (N_u(P), x^\ell)$ and $\mathbf{Q}_2 = \mathcal{Q}(\tilde{u}) \mod (N_u(Q), x^\ell)$, where $\ell = v(\mathbf{S} \cdot \tilde{t}) - v(\tilde{s}) \leq n$. This can be done in time $\mathcal{O}(\mathsf{M}(dn))$: $\mathcal{Q}(\tilde{u})$ is a product of three matrices, called $\mathbf{G}, \mathbf{D}, \mathbf{N}$ in Subsection 3.1. The first two have polynomial entries of degree at most d, and can be computed in time $\mathcal{O}(\mathsf{M}(dn))$; the last one involves a denominator of the form $\mathrm{Lc}(U)^{-1}$, for some polynomial U of degree at most d. The inverse of $\mathrm{Lc}(U)$ may have degree $\Omega(dk)$, but one can directly compute it modulo $N_u(P)$ or $N_u(Q)$ using Newton iteration on x in time $\mathcal{O}(\mathsf{M}(dn))$.

Then we compute $\mathbf{M}_1 = \varphi_{\tilde{s},\ell}(\mathbf{S} \cdot \mathbf{Q}_1 \cdot \mathbf{R})$ and $\mathbf{M}_2 = \varphi_{\tilde{s},\ell}(\mathbf{S} \cdot \mathbf{Q}_2 \cdot \mathbf{R})$ and we let $\mathbf{M}$ be the concatenation of the first column of $\mathbf{M}_2$ and the second column of $\mathbf{M}_1$. Thus $\mathbf{M}$ can be computed in time $\mathcal{O}(\mathsf{M}(dn))$.

Overall, the time spent on input (n, s) is $\mathcal{O}(\mathsf{M}(dn) + \mathsf{M}(d)\log(d))$, plus two recursive calls with parameter at most $\lfloor n/2 \rfloor$, in degree at most d. The total is thus $\mathcal{O}(\mathsf{M}(dn)\log(n) + \mathsf{M}(d)n\log(d))$. □

3.3 Computing pseudo-inverses

Given two polynomials P and Q in $\mathcal{R}_k$, we will use Algorithm 1 to compute U and V such that $UP + VQ = x^t \mod x^{t+1}$, where t is the smallest integer such that $\langle P, Q \rangle \cap \langle x^t \rangle = \langle x^t \rangle$. In particular, the valuation of the resultant of P and Q is greater than or equal to t.

COROLLARY 1. *Assume that $P, Q \in \mathcal{R}_k$ have degree at most d, and let t be the minimal integer such that $\langle P, Q \rangle \cap \langle x^t \rangle = \langle x^t \rangle$. It is possible to compute in time $\mathcal{O}(\mathsf{M}(dt)\log(t) + \mathsf{M}(d)t\log(d))$ two polynomials $U, V \in \mathcal{R}_k$ such that $UP + VQ = x^t \mod x^{t+1}$, with $\deg_y(U) < \deg_y(Q)$ and $\deg_y(V) < \deg_y(P)$.*

PROOF. Without loss of generality, assume that $v(P) \leq v(Q)$. Suppose first that we actually have $v(P) < v(Q)$, and define $s = (P, Q) \in \mathcal{S}_k$. In the following we let $t' = t - v(s)$.

In particular we have $I_{t'}(s) = \langle 1 \rangle$ and since for all $i < t'$, $I_i(s) \subsetneq I_{t'}(s)$, the properties of $\mathcal{Q}_{t'}$ given in Lemma 7 ensure that $\mathcal{Q}_{t'}(s) \cdot s = \langle s \rangle \cap \langle x^t \rangle = \langle x^t \rangle$. Moreover, for any integer $i \geq t'$, we have $\mathcal{Q}_i(s) = \mathcal{Q}_{t'}(s)$. Thus, by the equivalence property of $\mathcal{H}$ given in Lemma 9, we have for any $i \geq t'$:

$$\mathcal{H}(i, s) \cdot s = \begin{pmatrix} x^t(a + xW) \\ x^{t+1}H \end{pmatrix},$$

where $s = (P, Q)$ and W, H are in $\mathcal{R}_k$ and a is a non-zero constant. Thus it is enough to compute $\mathcal{H}(i, s)$ for any $i \geq t'$ to recover U and V from the first row of the matrix $\mathcal{H}(i, s)$. On the other hand for any $i < t'$, the first coordinate of $\Pi_1(\mathcal{H}(i, s) \cdot s)$ has a degree greater or equal to 1. Thus we can apply Algorithm 1 to the input $(2^i, s)$, for i from 1 to $\lceil \log k \rceil$ until the first polynomial of $\Pi_1(\mathcal{H}(2^i, s) \cdot s)$ has degree 0 in y. We will find $2^{i_0} \geq t'$ while calling $\mathcal{H}$ at most $\lceil \log t' \rceil$ times, and this will allow us to conclude.

Suppose now that $v(P) = v(Q)$, let $s = (P, Q)$ and $s' = \mathbf{G}_s \cdot s$, where $\mathbf{G}$ is the gcd matrix defined in Subsection 3.1. Then s' satisfies the assumptions of the previous paragraph, we can compute polynomials U', V' such that $U'P' + V'Q' = x^t \mod x^{t+1}$, with $s' = (P', Q')$. Remark that the value of t is indeed the minimal possible one for s as well, since $\mathbf{G}$ is a unit; note also that the degrees of P', Q' are $\mathcal{O}(d)$, and thus so are those of U' and V'.

Multiplying U', V' by $\mathbf{G}$, we obtain polynomials U'', V'' of degree $\mathcal{O}(d)$ such that $U''P + V''Q = x^t \mod x^{t+1}$. Then, define $U = L_Q(L_P U'' \mod N_u(Q))$ and $V = L_P(L_Q V'' \mod N_u(P))$, with $L_P, L_Q, N_u(P), N_u(Q)$ defined as in Lemma 8. These polynomials have prescribed degrees, can be computed modulo x^{t+1} in time $\mathcal{O}(\mathsf{M}(dt))$, and the same proof as in Lemma 8 shows that $UP + VQ = x^t \mod x^{t+1}$. □

4. THE FIRST NON-ZERO COEFFICIENT

Before computing the first k coefficients of the resultant $R(x) \in \mathbb{K}[x]/\langle x^k \rangle$ of two polynomials $P, Q \in \mathcal{R}_k$, we focus on computing the first non-zero coefficient of R. The following lemma will allow us to compute it by recurrence.

LEMMA 11. *Let $M, N \in \mathcal{R}_k$ and $U \in \mathcal{U}(\mathcal{R}_k)$ and an integer $t \leq k$ be such that $MP + NQ = x^t U$ with $\deg_y(N) < \deg_y(P)$, and such that P and N are normal and $\Pi_1(U) = 1$. Furthermore, assume that $v(P) = v(N) = 0$.*

Denote by d_P, d_Q, d_M, d_N the degrees in y of P, Q, M, N respectively, by $p_0 \in \mathbb{K}$ the coefficient of y^{d_P} in P, and by $n_0 \in \mathbb{K}$ the coefficient of y^{d_N} in N. Then, there exists V unit in $\mathbb{K}[x]/\langle x^k \rangle$, with $\Pi_1(V) = 1$, such that:

$$\mathrm{Res}\,(P, Q) = x^{t(d_P - d_N)}(-1)^{d_N d_P} \frac{p_0^{d_N + d_Q}}{n_0^{d_M + d_P}} V \,\mathrm{Res}\,(N, M).$$

PROOF. By the multiplication rules of the resultant,

$$\mathrm{Res}\,(P, N)\,\mathrm{Res}\,(P, Q) = \mathrm{Res}\,(P, NQ)$$
$$\mathrm{Res}\,(N, P)\,\mathrm{Res}\,(N, M) = \mathrm{Res}\,(N, MP)$$

Replacing in the first equality NQ by $NQ + MP = x^t U$, we get $\mathrm{Res}\,(P, NQ) = p_0^{d_N + d_Q - d_U}\,\mathrm{Res}\,(P, x^t U)$ (see for example [16, 11]). Finally, $\mathrm{Res}\,(P, x^t U) = x^{t d_P}\,\mathrm{Res}\,(P, U)$. Then since P is normal of valuation zero and $\Pi_1(U) = 1$, there exists $W = 1 + x\tilde{W} \in \mathbb{K}[x]/\langle x^k \rangle$ such that $\mathrm{Res}\,(P, U) = p_0^{d_U} W$.

Applying these arguments to $\mathrm{Res}\,(N, MP)$, we conclude:

$$\mathrm{Res}\,(P,N)\,\mathrm{Res}\,(P,Q) = p_0^{d_N+d_Q} x^{td_P} W$$
$$\mathrm{Res}\,(N,P)\,\mathrm{Res}\,(N,M) = n_0^{d_M+d_P} x^{td_N} W'$$

Note that the symmetry formula for the resultant implies that $\mathrm{Res}\,(P,N) = (-1)^{d_P d_N}\,\mathrm{Res}\,(N,P)$. Then dividing the two equalities, we recover the desired result. □

LEMMA 12 (FIRST NON-ZERO COEFFICIENT). *Let d be a bound on the degrees in y of P and Q. One can determine whether $R = \mathrm{Res}\,(P,Q)$ vanishes in $\mathbb{K}[x]/\langle x^k\rangle$, and if not compute its first non-zero coefficient and its valuation in $\mathcal{O}(\mathsf{M}(dk)\log(k) + \mathsf{M}(d)k\log(d))$ arithmetic operations.*

PROOF. Lemma 2 allows us to reduce to the case where P and Q are normal polynomials; the cost of this reduction is $\mathcal{O}(\mathsf{M}(dk))$. Starting from normal P and Q, we prove the result by induction; the proof actually only uses the fact that one polynomial, say P, is normal. We use an integer argument τ, which gives us a (strict) upper bound on the valuation of the resultant; initially, it is set to k.

Dividing by powers of x, we can assume that $v(P) = v(Q) = 0$; the upper bound τ remains valid. We then compute the resultant of $\Pi_1(P)$ and $\Pi_1(Q)$ in $\mathbb{K}[y]$, in time $\mathcal{O}(\mathsf{M}(d)\log(d))$. If it is non-zero, we are done.

Else, let t be the smallest integer such that $\langle P,Q\rangle \cap \langle x^t\rangle = \langle x^t\rangle$; hence, $t \le \tau$, but we also have $t > 0$. Define function $F(d,n) = \mathsf{M}(dn)\log(n) + \mathsf{M}(d)n\log(d)$. Using Corollary 1, we see that there exists a universal constant c_1 such that we can compute in $c_1 F(d,t)$ operations two polynomials U and V in $\mathcal{R}_k$ of degree less than d such that $UP + VQ = x^t W$ with $W \in \mathcal{U}(\mathcal{R}_k)$, with more precisely $\deg_y(U) < \deg_y(P)$. Since t is minimal, this implies $v(U,V) = 0$ and since $v(P) = 0$, this implies that $v(V) = 0$.

If $t = \tau$, we are done. Else, let $A = \Pi_{t+1}(\mathrm{Lc}(V))$, $N = \Pi_{t+1}(N_u(V))$ and $M = \Pi_{t+1}\left(U/A \text{ rem}_y\ N_u(Q)\right)$. Since A is a unit, these definitions imply the equality $MP + NQ = x^t(1 + xY) + ZN_u(Q)P$, for some polynomials Y and Z. The degree of the left-hand side is less than $\deg_y(P) + \deg_y(Q)$, whereas $N_u(Q)P$ is monic of degree $\deg_y(P)+\deg_y(Q)$. Hence, the previous equality shows that $ZN_u(Q)P$ vanishes modulo x^{t+1}. The assumptions of Lemma 11 are satisfied; we can thus do a recursive call on N and M, with upper bound $\tau - t$, from which we can recover our output using the formula in that lemma.

In terms of complexity, all calculations giving A, N, M can be done in $c_2\mathsf{M}(dt)$ operations (the only non-trivial point is the computation of $1/A \text{ rem}_y\ N_u(Q)$, which is done by Newton iteration on x). Hence, the runtime $G(d,\tau)$ satisfies $G(d,\tau) \le c_0\mathsf{M}(d)\log(d) + c_1F(d,t) + c_2\mathsf{M}(dt) + G(d,\tau - t)$. Using the super-linearity of F in t and of M, and the definition of F, we deduce the overall cost $G(d,k) = \mathcal{O}(F(d,k))$. □

5. A DIFFERENTIAL EQUATION

Let P and Q be in $\mathbb{K}[x,y]$, and let $R \in \mathbb{K}[x]$ be their resultant with respect to y. We now prove our main result:

THEOREM 1. *If P and Q have degree at most d and $\mathbb{K}$ has characteristic zero, or at least k, one can compute $R \text{ rem}_x\ x^k$ using $\mathcal{O}(\mathsf{M}(dk)\log(k) + \mathsf{M}(d)k\log(d))$ operations in $\mathbb{K}$.*

First reduction: If the degree in x of P or Q is greater than or equal to k, let $P_k = P \text{ rem}_x\ x^k$ and $Q_k \text{ rem}_x\ x^k$ and let d_P, d_Q be the degrees in y of P and Q respectively. Then,

$$\mathrm{Res}_{\,d_P,d_Q}(P_k, Q_k) = \mathrm{Res}\,(P,Q) \mod x^k,$$

where Res_{d_P,d_Q} denotes the determinant of the Sylvester matrix associated to the degrees (d_P, d_Q). If both leading coefficients of P and Q have a valuation less than k, then $\mathrm{Res}_{d_P,d_Q}(P_k,Q_k) = \mathrm{Res}(P_k,Q_k)$. If both leading coefficients have a valuation greater than or equal to k then $\mathrm{Res}(P,Q) = 0 \bmod x^k$. Finally, if only the leading coefficient of say Q has a valuation greater or equal to k, then we have $\mathrm{Res}_{\,d_P,d_Q}(P_k,Q_k) = p_0^{d_Q - \deg_y(Q_k)}\,\mathrm{Res}\,(P_k,Q_k)$, where p_0 is the leading coefficient of P in y. Thus, in any case, we can recover the resultant of P and Q modulo x^k from that of P_k and Q_k, in a time that fits in our runtime bound.

Second reduction: Assume that P and Q have degree at most d in y, with coefficients of degree less than k. Using Lemma 2, in time $\mathcal{O}(\mathsf{M}(dk))$, we can reduce the problem of computing $\mathrm{Res}\,(P,Q) \text{ rem}_x\ x^k$ to a similar problem with P and Q both monic in y, reduced modulo x^k, and with no degree increase in y (that lemma proves the existence of suitable polynomials in $\mathcal{R}_k$, so we take their canonical lifts to $\mathbb{K}[x,y]$). Hence, below, we suppose we are in this case.

With the results of the previous section, we can test if $R = \mathrm{Res}\,(P,Q)$ vanishes modulo x^k, and if not, find its valuation $\mu \le k$ and the coefficient c of x^μ, in time $\mathcal{O}(\mathsf{M}(dk)\log k + \mathsf{M}(d)k\log d)$. We thus assume that $R \text{ rem}_x\ x^k$ is non-zero, as otherwise we are done. The key to our algorithm is the following differential equation satisfied by R over $\mathbb{K}(x)[y]$; below, we write $d_P = \deg_y(P)$ and $d_Q = \deg_y(Q)$.

LEMMA 13. *The following equality holds:*

$$\frac{dR}{dx} = R\left(\mathrm{coeff}\left(\frac{1}{P}\frac{dP}{dx}\frac{dQ}{dy} \text{ rem}_y\ Q, y^{d_Q-1}\right)\right.$$
$$\left. + \,\mathrm{coeff}\left(\frac{1}{Q}\frac{dQ}{dx}\frac{dP}{dy} \text{ rem}_y\ P, y^{d_P-1}\right)\right).$$

PROOF. Let $\mathbf{A}$ be the Sylvester matrix of P and Q with respect to the variable y, so that $R = \det(\mathbf{A})$. Since $R \text{ rem}_x\ x^k$ is non-zero, $\mathbf{A}$ is a unit over $\mathbb{K}(x)$.

Differentiating this equality with respect to x, we obtain $\frac{dR}{dx} = R\,\mathrm{trace}\left(\mathbf{A}^{-1}\frac{d\mathbf{A}}{dx}\right)$. Since $\mathbf{A}$ is the matrix of the mapping $(F,G) \mapsto FP + GQ$ (in the canonical monomial bases), $\frac{d\mathbf{A}}{dx}$ represents $(F,G) \mapsto F\frac{dP}{dx} + G\frac{dQ}{dx}$, in the same bases. Similarly, the inverse $\mathbf{A}^{-1}$ represents the mapping $S \mapsto (S/P \text{ rem}_y\ Q, S/Q \text{ rem}_y\ P)$. Due to the block structure of the matrix $\mathbf{A}^{-1}\frac{d\mathbf{A}}{dx}$, its trace is the trace of the block-diagonal operator

$$(F,G) \mapsto \left(F\frac{1}{P}\frac{dP}{dx} \text{ rem}_y\ Q,\ G\frac{1}{Q}\frac{dQ}{dx} \text{ rem}_y\ P\right).$$

This mapping being block-diagonal, its trace is the sum of the traces of its two components, $F \mapsto F\frac{1}{P}\frac{dP}{dx} \text{ rem}_y\ Q$ and $G \mapsto G\frac{1}{Q}\frac{dQ}{dx} \text{ rem}_y\ P$. To conclude, remark that these traces are respectively $\mathrm{coeff}\left(\frac{1}{P}\frac{dP}{dx}\frac{dQ}{dy} \text{ rem}_y\ Q, y^{d_Q-1}\right)$ and $\mathrm{coeff}\left(\frac{1}{Q}\frac{dQ}{dx}\frac{dP}{dy} \text{ rem}_y\ P, y^{d_P-1}\right)$. □

Using Corollary 1, we can compute in time $\mathcal{O}(\mathsf{M}(dk)\log(k) + \mathsf{M}(d)k\log(d))$ we know two cofactors U and V in $\mathbb{K}[x,y]$, of degree less than k in x such that $\deg(U,y) < d_Q$, $\deg(V,y) < d_P$ and

$UP + VQ = x^t \bmod x^{t+1}$, with t chosen minimal, so that $t \leq \mu$. Then, $t \leq k$, since otherwise $R = 0 \mod x^k$.

From this, we deduce U', V' with the same degree constraints on y and degree less than $2t + k - 1$ in x, such that

$$U'P + V'Q = x^t \bmod x^{2t+k-1}:$$

compute W such that $UP+VQ = x^t(1+xW) \mod x^{2t+k-1}$, then the inverses A (resp. B) of $1+xW$ modulo $\langle Q, x^{2t+k-1}\rangle$ (resp. modulo $\langle P, x^{2t+k-1}\rangle$), and let $U' = UA \text{ rem}_y\, Q$ and $V' = VB \text{ rem}_y\, P$. The only non-trivial point is the inversions, which are done by Newton iteration with respect to x; overall, the cost of this step is $\mathcal{O}(\mathsf{M}(dk))$.

The defining equality for U' and V' can be rewritten as

$$U'P + V'Q = x^t(1 + x^{t+k-1}S),$$

for some S in $\mathbb{K}[x, y]$. Their degree constraints then show that the inverse of P modulo Q is $U'/(x^t(1 + x^{t+k-1}S)) \text{ rem}_y\, Q$; similarly, the inverse of Q modulo P is $V'/(x^t(1 + x^{t+k-1}S)) \text{ rem}_y\, P$. This further implies that $x^t \frac{dR}{dx}$ is equal to

$$R\left(\text{coeff}\left(\frac{U'}{1 + x^{t+k-1}S}\frac{dP}{dx}\frac{dQ}{dy} \text{ rem}_y\, Q, y^{d_Q - 1}\right)\right.$$
$$\left. + \text{coeff}\left(\frac{V'}{1 + x^{t+k-1}S}\frac{dQ}{dx}\frac{dP}{dy} \text{ rem}_y\, P, y^{d_P - 1}\right)\right).$$

Taking this equality modulo x^{t+k-1}, we obtain a relation of the form $x^t \frac{dR}{dx} = RF \bmod x^{t+k-1}$, with

$$F = \text{coeff}\left(U'\frac{dP}{dx}\frac{dQ}{dy} \text{ rem}_y\, Q, y^{d_Q-1}\right)$$
$$+ \text{coeff}\left(V'\frac{dQ}{dx}\frac{dP}{dy} \text{ rem}_y\, P, y^{d_P-1}\right) \bmod x^{t+k-1}.$$

Because P and Q are both monic in y, once U' and V' are known, we can compute F using $\mathcal{O}(\mathsf{M}((t + k)d))$ operations in $\mathbb{K}$, which is $\mathcal{O}(\mathsf{M}(kd))$.

Recall that R is has the form $cx^\mu + \cdots$, for some $\mu < k$, so that $\frac{dR}{dx}$ has the form $\mu c x^{\mu-1} + \cdots$. Thus, the Laurent series $\frac{1}{R}\frac{dR}{dx}$ has valuation at least -1, so that F has valuation at least $t - 1$. Dividing by x^{t-1} on both sides, we obtain $x\frac{dR}{dx} = R\tilde{F} \bmod x^k$, with $\tilde{F} = F/x^{t-1}$. From now on, let us assume that the characteristic p of the base field is at least equal to k, or zero. Then, this relation determines $R \bmod x^k$ up to a constant factor, and knowing the initial condition c allows us to deduce $R \bmod x^k$ unambiguously. Given $\tilde{F}$, this is done by means of [3, Theorem 2], which allows us to compute $R \bmod x^k$ in $\mathcal{O}(\mathsf{M}(k))$ operations in $\mathbb{K}$. Summing all the costs seen so far concludes the proof of our theorem.

Acknowledgements. The authors sincerely thank the reviewers for their careful reading and suggestions. Moroz is supported by project Singcast (ANR-13-JS02-0006); Schost is supported by NSERC.

6. REFERENCES

[1] P. Aubry and A. Valibouze. Using Galois ideals for computing relative resolvents. *J. Symb. Comp.*, 30(6):635–651, 2000.

[2] E. Berberich, P. Emeliyanenko, and M. Sagraloff. An elimination method for solving bivariate polynomial systems: Eliminating the usual drawbacks. In *ALENEX*, pages 35–47. SIAM, 2011.

[3] A. Bostan, M. F. I. Chowdhury, R. Lebreton, B. Salvy, and É. Schost. Power series solutions of singular (q)-differential equations. In *ISSAC'12*, pages 107–114. ACM, 2012.

[4] A. Bostan, P. Flajolet, B. Salvy, and É. Schost. Fast computation of special resultants. *Journal of Symbolic Computation*, 41(1):1–29, 2006.

[5] Y. Bouzidi, S. Lazard, G. Moroz, M. Pouget, and F. Rouillier. Improved algorithm for computing separating linear forms for bivariate systems. In *ISSAC'14*, pages 75–82. ACM, 2014.

[6] Y. Bouzidi, S. Lazard, G. Moroz, M. Pouget, F. Rouillier, and M. Sagraloff. Improved algorithms for solving bivariate systems via Rational Univariate Representations. Research report, Inria, 2015.

[7] Y. Bouzidi, S. Lazard, M. Pouget, and F. Rouillier. Rational univariate representations of bivariate systems and applications. In *ISSAC'13*, pages 109–116. ACM, 2013.

[8] Y. Bouzidi, S. Lazard, M. Pouget, and F. Rouillier. Separating linear forms for bivariate systems. In *ISSAC'13*, pages 117–124. ACM, 2013.

[9] D. G. Cantor and E. Kaltofen. On fast multiplication of polynomials over arbitrary algebras. *Acta Informatica*, 28(7):693–701, 1991.

[10] X. Caruso. Resultants and subresultants of p-adic polynomials. abs/1507.06502, 2015.

[11] D. Cox, J. Little, and D. O'Shea. *Using algebraic geometry*. Graduate Texts in Mathematics. Springer-Verlag, 1998.

[12] P. Emeliyanenko and M. Sagraloff. On the complexity of solving a bivariate polynomial system. In *ISSAC'12*, pages 154–161. ACM, 2012.

[13] J. von zur Gathen and J. Gerhard. *Modern Computer Algebra*. Cambridge University Press, third edition, 2013.

[14] J. von zur Gathen and T. Lücking. Subresultants revisited. *Theoretical Computer Science*, 297(1–3):199–239, 2003.

[15] J. von zur Gathen and V. Shoup. Computing Frobenius maps and factoring polynomials. *Computational Complexity*, 2(3):187–224, 1992.

[16] I. Gelfand, M. Kapranov, and A. Zelevinsky. *Discriminants, Resultants, and Multidimensional Determinants*. Modern Birkhäuser Classics. Birkhäuser Boston, 2008.

[17] M. Giusti, G. Lecerf, and B. Salvy. A Gröbner free alternative for polynomial system solving. *J. Complexity*, 17(2):154–211, 2001.

[18] L. González-Vega and M. E. Kahoui. An improved upper complexity bound for the topology computation of a real algebraic plane curve. *J. Complexity*, 12(4):527 – 544, 1996.

[19] R. Imbach, G. Moroz, and M. Pouget. Numeric certified algorithm for the topology of resultant and discriminant curves. abs/1412.3290, 2014.

[20] E. Kaltofen and G. Villard. On the complexity of computing determinants. *Comput. Complexity*, 13(3-4):91–130, 2004.

[21] D. E. Knuth. The analysis of algorithms. In *Congrès int. Math., Nice, France*, volume 3, pages 269–274, 1970.

[22] A. Kobel and M. Sagraloff. On the complexity of computing with planar algebraic curves. *Journal of Complexity*, 31(2):206–236, 2015.

[23] R. Lebreton and É. Schost. Algorithms for the universal decomposition algebra. In *ISSAC'12*, pages 234–241. ACM, 2012.

[24] F. Lehobey. Resolvent computations by resultants without extraneous powers. In *ISSAC'97*, pages 85–92. ACM, 1997.

[25] D. R. Musser. Multivariate polynomial factorization. *J. Assoc. Comput. Mach.*, 22:291–308, 1975.

[26] D. Reischert. Asymptotically fast computation of subresultants. In *ISSAC'97*, pages 233–240. ACM, 1997.

[27] A. Schönhage. Schnelle Berechnung von Kettenbruchentwicklungen. *Acta Inform.*, 1:139–144, 1971.

[28] L. Soicher. The computation of Galois groups. Master's thesis, Concordia University, 1981.

Comprehensive Gröbner Systems in Rings of Differential Operators, Holonomic D-modules and B-functions

Katsusuke Nabeshima
Graduate School of Science and Technology,
Tokushima University,
2-1 Minamijosanjima,
Tokushima, JAPAN
nabeshima@tokushima-u.ac.jp

Katsuyoshi Ohara
Faculty of Mathematics and Physics,
Kanazawa University,
Kakuma-machi,
Kanazawa, JAPAN
ohara@se.kanazawa-u.ac.jp

Shinichi Tajima
Graduate School of Pure and Applied Sciences,
University of Tsukuba,
1-1-1 Tennoudai,
Tsukuba, JAPAN
tajima@math.tsukuba.ac.jp

ABSTRACT

An algorithm for computing comprehensive Gröbner systems (CGS) is introduced in rings of linear partial differential operators. Their applications to b-functions are considered. The resulting algorithm designed for a wide use of computing comprehensive Gröbner systems can be used to compute all the roots of b-functions and relevant holonomic D-modules. Furthermore, with our implementation, effective methods are illustrated for computing holonomic D-modules associated with hypersurface singularities. It is shown that the proposed algorithm is full of versatility.

Categories and Subject Descriptors

I.1.2 [**Computing Methodologies**]: Symbolic and Algebraic Manipulation

Keywords

b-functions, holonomic D-modules, comprehensive Gröbner systems, hypersurface singularities

1. INTRODUCTION

The concept of comprehensive Gröbner bases and comprehensive Gröbner systems (CGS) were introduced by Weispfenning [33] to study parametric polynomial systems. After that CGS has been known as one of important tools to analyze parametric systems.

In this paper we introduce an algorithm for computing CGS in rings of partial differential operators, its applications to b-functions and their implementation.

First, we consider in Section 3 how to compute CGS in rings of partial differential operators. Recently, based on Kalkbrener's results [6], effective algorithms have been published in [8, 17] for computing CGS in a commutative polynomial ring. By adapting the Kalkbrener's results, we extend these algorithms for computing CGS to the case of rings of partial differential operators and to a special class of Poincaré-Birkhoff-Witt algebras, a non-commutative ring.

ISSAC '16, July 19-22, 2016, Waterloo, ON, Canada

© 2016 ACM. ISBN 978-1-4503-4380-0/16/07...$15.00

DOI: http://dx.doi.org/10.1145/2930889.2930918

Second, we discuss in Section 4 some applications of the CGS, together with our implementation, to b-functions (or Bernstein-Sato polynomials) of parametric polynomials and relevant holonomic D-modules.

The b-function of a hypersurface is an important object with numerous applications. The explicit calculation of b-functions is of major interest. Actually, after a breakthrough that was given by T. Oaku [23] in 1997, several ways of computing b-functions have been published, for instance in [1, 2, 13, 19, 18, 24, 25, 32]. It is observed recently in [30, 31] that D-modules relevant to b-functions can be used to extract a lot of information on singularities (for instance, characteristic variety and monodromy) which can not be obtained from b-functions. Based on these observations, we develop methods for computing holonomic systems of D-modules associated with roots of a b-function. We show that the resulting algorithm for computing CGS in rings of partial differential operators can be applied to compute all the roots of b-functions and holonomic D-modules associated with these roots. Furthermore, we show that it is also possible, by using the algorithm, to compute holonomic D-modules associated with a given subset of (candidates of) roots of the b-function of f and the holonomic D-modules supported on the variety defined by a primary component of the primary ideal decomposition of the ideal generated by $f, \frac{\partial f}{\partial x_1}, \frac{\partial f}{\partial x_2}, \dots, \frac{\partial f}{\partial x_n}$, where $f \in \mathbb{C}[x_1, x_2, \dots, x_n]$. We will see that the algorithm for computing CGS has a high degree of versatility.

In this paper we also consider, in the context of comprehensive Gröbner systems, a method of computing the annihilating ideal of f^s for the case where the given f is a polynomial with parameters. We introduce algorithms of computing the annihilator and the roots of b-functions for such parametric cases. The key idea is the use of a special class of parametric Poincaré-Birkhoff-Witt algebras as an extension of Briançon-Maisonobe's method.

All algorithms and methods in this paper have been implemented in the computer algebra system Risa/Asir [20]. Currently, our implementation is in the following URL.

http://www-math.ias.tokushima-u.ac.jp/~nabesima/softwares.html

Soon, it will be included in a package of OpenXM [26].

As far as we know only our implementation has functions for computing CGS in rings of partial differential operators (except for our previous implementation [16]), parametric annihilating ideal of f^s and b-functions of a parametric polynomial f.

2. PRELIMINARY

Let K be a field of characteristic zero, $\bar{K}$ an algebraic closure of K. The set of natural numbers $\mathbb{N}$ includes zero. $\mathbb{C}$ is the field of complex numbers.

Let $K\langle x, \partial_x\rangle$ denote the Weyl algebra, the ring of linear partial differential operators with coefficients in K, where $x = (x_1, \ldots, x_n)$, $\partial_x = (\partial_1, \ldots, \partial_n)$, $\partial_i = \frac{\partial}{\partial x_i}$ with relations $x_i x_j = x_j x_i$, $\partial_i \partial_j = \partial_j \partial_i$, $\partial_j x_i = x_i \partial_j$ $(i \neq j)$ and $\partial_i x_i = x_i \partial_i + 1$.

Let $u = (u_1, \ldots, u_m)$ be variables such that $u \cap x = \emptyset$, $K[u]\langle x, \partial_x\rangle$ a ring of partial differential operators with coefficients in a polynomial ring $K[u]$, $K\langle u, x, \partial_x\rangle$ a ring of differential operators with coefficients in K. Symbols $\mathrm{pp}(x, \partial_x)$, $\mathrm{pp}(u)$ and $\mathrm{pp}(u, x, \partial_x)$ are the sets of power products of $x \cup \partial_x$, u and $u \cup x \cup \partial_x$.

Throughout the paper we assume that a partial differential operator in $K\langle x, \partial_x\rangle$ (or $K[u]\langle x, \partial_x\rangle$), is always represented in the *canonical form* that is each power product of a partial differential operator is written as $x_1^{\alpha_1} x_2^{\alpha_2} \cdots x_n^{\alpha_n} \partial_1^{\beta_1} \partial_2^{\beta_2} \cdots \partial_n^{\beta_n}$ where $\alpha_1, \alpha_2, \ldots, \alpha_n, \beta_1, \beta_2, \ldots, \beta_n \in \mathbb{N}$.

We have the following natural K-vector space isomorphism $\Psi : K\langle u, x, \partial_x\rangle \to K[u, x, \xi]$ $(u^\alpha x^\beta \partial_x^\gamma \to u^\alpha x^\beta \xi^\gamma)$ where $K[u, x, \xi]$ is a commutative polynomial ring, $\xi = (\xi_1, \ldots, \xi_n)$ and $\partial_1, \partial_2, \ldots, \partial_n$ correspond to $\xi_1, \xi_2, \ldots, \xi_n$. We also use the same notation as $\Psi : K[u]\langle x, \partial_x\rangle \to K[u][x, \xi]$ $(u^\alpha x^\beta \partial_x^\gamma \to u^\alpha x^\beta \xi^\gamma)$. For example, let $p = 2u_1u_2x_1^2\partial_1 + u_2x_1^2\partial_1 + x_1 \in \mathbb{C}\langle u_1, u_2, x_1, \partial_1\rangle$. Then $\Psi(p) = 2u_1u_2x_1^2\xi_1 + u_2x_1^2\xi_1 + x_1 \in \mathbb{C}[u_1, u_2, x_1, \xi_1]$. For all $i \in \{1, \ldots, n\}$, the inverse map Ψ^{-1} is defined as changing symbols ξ_i into ∂_i.

Fix a term ordering $\succ$ on $\mathrm{pp}(u, x, \partial_x)$ (corresponds $\mathrm{pp}(u, x, \xi)$). Let $p \in K\langle u, x, \partial_x\rangle$. Then, $\mathrm{lpp}(p)$, $\mathrm{lm}(p)$ and $\mathrm{lc}(p)$ denote as the leading power product, leading coefficient and leading monomial of $\Psi(p)$ in $K[u, x, \xi]$. Furthermore, for a subset P in $K\langle u, x, \partial_x\rangle$, we define $\mathrm{lpp}(P) := \{\mathrm{lpp}(p) | p \in P\}$, $\mathrm{lc}(P) := \{\mathrm{lc}(p) | p \in P\}$ and $\mathrm{lm}(P) := \{\mathrm{lm}(p) |\ p \in P\}$.

Let $p' \in K[u]\langle x, \partial_x\rangle$. Then, $\mathrm{lpp}_{\{x,\partial_x\}}(p')$, $\mathrm{lc}_{\{x,\partial_x\}}(p')$ and $\mathrm{lm}_{\{x,\partial_x\}}(p')$ denote as the leading power product, leading coefficient and leading monomial of $\Psi(p')$ in $K[u][x, \xi]$. Furthermore, for $P' \subset K[u]\langle x, \partial_x\rangle$, we define $\mathrm{lpp}_{\{x,\partial_x\}}(P') = \{\mathrm{lpp}_{\{x,\partial_x\}}(p') |\ p' \in P'\}$, $\mathrm{lc}_{\{x,\partial_x\}}(P') = \{\mathrm{lc}_{\{x,\partial_x\}}(p') |\ p' \in P'\}$ and $\mathrm{lm}_{\{x,\partial_x\}}(P') = \{\mathrm{lm}_{\{x,\partial_x\}}(p') | p' \in P'\}$.

Note that for $f, g \in K\langle u, x, \partial_x\rangle$ (or $K[u]\langle x, \partial_x\rangle$), $\mathrm{lm}(fg) = \mathrm{lm}(f)\,\mathrm{lm}(g)$ (or $\mathrm{lm}_{\{x,\partial_x\}}(fg) = \mathrm{lm}_{\{x,\partial_x\}}(f)\,\mathrm{lm}_{\{x,\partial_x\}}(g)$).

For example, let $p = 2u_1u_2x_1^2\partial_1 + u_2x_1^2\partial_1 + x_1$ where $\partial_1 = \frac{\partial}{\partial x_1}$. If $p \in \mathbb{C}\langle u_1, u_2, x_1, \partial_1\rangle$ and $\succ$ is the lexicographic term ordering on $\mathrm{pp}(u_1, u_2, x_1, \partial_1)$ s.t. $x_1 \succ \partial_1 \succ u_1 \succ u_2$ (corresponding to $x_1 \succ \xi_1 \succ u_1 \succ u_2$), then $\mathrm{lpp}(p) = u_1u_2x_1^2\xi_1$, $\mathrm{lc}(p) = 2$ and $\mathrm{lm}(p) = 2u_1u_2x_1^2\xi_1$. If $p \in \mathbb{C}[u_1, u_2]\langle x_1, \partial_1\rangle$ and $\succ$ is the lexicographic term ordering on $\mathrm{pp}(x_1, \partial_1)$ s.t. $x_1 \succ \partial_1$ (corresponding to $x_1 \succ \xi_1$), then $\mathrm{lpp}_{\{x_1,\partial_1\}}(p) = u_1u_2x_1^2\xi_1$, $\mathrm{lc}_{\{x_1,\partial_x\}}(p) = 2$ and $\mathrm{lm}_{\{x_1,\partial_1\}}(p) = 2u_1u_2x_1^2\xi_1$.

For every $\bar{a} \in \bar{K}^m$, we define the canonical specialization homomorphism $\sigma_{\bar{a}} : K[u]\langle x, \partial_x\rangle \to \bar{K}\langle x, \partial_x\rangle$ as a map that substitutes u by $\bar{a}$ in a partial differential operator $p(u, x, \partial_x) \in K[u]\langle x, \partial_x\rangle$. The image under $\sigma_{\bar{a}}$ of an ideal $I \subset K[u]\langle x, \partial_x\rangle$ is denoted by $\sigma_{\bar{a}}(I) := \{\sigma_{\bar{a}}(p) | p \in I\} \subseteq \bar{K}\langle x, \partial_x\rangle$.

For instance, let $p = 2u_1u_2x_1^2\partial_1 + u_2x_1^2\partial_1 + x_1$ in $\mathbb{C}[u_1, u_2]\langle x_1, \partial_1\rangle$ and $(-2, 1), (0, \frac{1}{2}) \in \mathbb{C}^2$. Then, by substituting values $(-2, 1), (0, \frac{1}{2})$ into (u_1, u_2), we get $\sigma_{(-2,1)}(p) = -4x_1^2\partial_1 + x_1^2\partial_1 + x_1$ and $\sigma_{(0,\frac{1}{2})}(p) = \frac{1}{2}x_1^2\partial_1 + x_1$.

For $g_1, \ldots, g_r \in K[u]$, $\mathbb{V}(g_1, \ldots, g_r) \subseteq \bar{K}^m$ denotes the affine variety of $g_1, \ldots, g_r$, i.e., $\mathbb{V}(g_1, \ldots, g_r) := \{\bar{a} \in \bar{K}^m | g_1(\bar{a}) = \cdots = g_r(\bar{a}) = 0\}$, $\mathbb{V}(0) = \bar{K}^m$ (or $\mathbb{V}(\emptyset) = \bar{K}^m$) and $\mathbb{V}(1) = \emptyset$. We call an algebraically constructible set of a form $\mathbb{V}(g_1, \ldots, g_r) \backslash \mathbb{V}(g'_1, \ldots, g'_{r'}) \subseteq \bar{K}^m$ with $g_1, \ldots, g_r, g'_1, \ldots, g'_{r'} \in K[u]$, a *stratum*. (Notation $\mathbb{A}_1, \mathbb{A}_2, \ldots, \mathbb{A}_\ell$ are frequently used to represent strata.)

Let $p_1, \ldots, p_r \in K[u]\langle x, \partial_x\rangle$ (or $K\langle u, x, \partial_x\rangle$). Then, the left ideal generated by $p_1, \ldots, p_r$ is written as $Id(p_1, \ldots, p_r)$.

DEFINITION 1. *Fix a term ordering on* $\mathrm{pp}(u, x, \partial_x)$. *Let* $p_1, .., p_r \in K\langle u, x, \partial_x\rangle$ *and* $G = \{g_1, .., g_r\} \subset Id(p_1, .., p_r) \subset K\langle u, x, \partial_x\rangle$. *Then, G is a Gröbner basis of* $Id(p_1, \ldots, p_r)$ *if G satisfies* $Id(\mathrm{lm}(I)) = Id(\mathrm{lm}(g_1), \ldots, \mathrm{lm}(g_r))$.

There exist algorithms and implementations to compute Gröbner bases in $K\langle u, x, \partial_x\rangle$. A definition of Gröbner bases in $K[u]\langle x, \partial_x\rangle$ is the following.

DEFINITION 2. *Fix a term ordering on* $\mathrm{pp}(x, \partial_x)$. *Let* $p_1, .., p_r \in K[u]\langle x, \partial_x\rangle$ *and* $G = \{g_1, .., g_r\} \subset Id(p_1, .., p_r) \subset K[u]\langle x, \partial_x\rangle$. *Then, G is a Gröbner basis of* $Id(p_1, \ldots, p_r)$ *if G satisfies* $Id(\mathrm{lm}_{\{x,\partial_x\}}(I)) = Id(\mathrm{lm}_{\{x,\partial_x\}}(g_1), .., \mathrm{lm}_{\{x,\partial_x\}}(g_r))$.

An algorithm for computing a Gröbner basis of a given ideal in $K[u]\langle x, \partial_x\rangle$ is Algorithm 1.

Note that two symbols $K\langle u, x, \partial_x, [\partial t, s]\rangle$ and $K[u]\langle x, \partial_x, [\partial t, s]\rangle$ that are enclosed in parentheses in Algorithm 1 designate a special class of parametric Poincaré-Birkhoff-Witt algebras. The topics concerning parametric Poincaré-Birkhoff-Witt algebras will be discussed in section 4.5. We will come back here to see how to compute Gröbner basis of a given ideal in $K[u]\langle x, \partial_x, [\partial t, s]\rangle$.

Algorithm 1. GB

Specification:GB($\{p_1, \ldots, p_r\}, \succ$)
Computing a Gröbner basis of $Id(p_1, \ldots, p_r)$ w.r.t. $\succ$ in $K[u]\langle x, \partial_x\rangle$ (or $K[u]\langle x, \partial_x, [\partial t, s]\rangle$).
Input: $p_1, \ldots, p_r \in K[u]\langle x, \partial_x\rangle$ (or $K[u]\langle x, \partial_x, [\partial t, s]\rangle$),
$\succ$: a term ordering on $\mathrm{pp}(x, \partial_x)$ (or $\mathrm{pp}(x, \partial_x, \partial t, s)$).
Output: G: a Gröbner basis of $Id(p_1, \ldots, p_r)$ w.r.t. $\succ$ in $K[u]\langle x, \partial_x\rangle$ (or $K[u]\langle x, \partial_x, [\partial t, s]\rangle$).

1. Consider $p_1, \ldots, p_r$ as elements of $K\langle u, x, \partial_x\rangle$ (or $K\langle u, x, \partial_x, [\partial t, s]\rangle$).
2. Compute the reduced Gröbner basis G of $Id(p_1, \ldots, p_r)$ w.r.t. a block term order $\succ_b$ s.t. $\{x, \partial_x\} \gg \{u\}$ on $\mathrm{pp}(u, x, \partial_x)$, in $K\langle u, x, \partial_x\rangle$ (or $\{x, \partial_x, \partial t, s\} \gg \{u\}$ on $\mathrm{pp}(u, x, \partial_x, \partial t, s)$, in $K\langle u, x, \partial_x, [\partial t, s]\rangle$).
3. Consider G as a set of $K[u]\langle x, \partial_x\rangle$ (or $K[u]\langle x, \partial_x, [\partial t, s]\rangle$).

THEOREM 3. *Algorithm 1 (*GB*) outputs a Gröbner basis of* $Id(p_1, \ldots, p_r)$ *w.r.t.* $\succ$ *in* $K[u]\langle x, \partial_x\rangle$.

PROOF. We show that for all $f \in Id(p_1, \ldots, p_r) \subset K[u]\langle x, \partial_x\rangle$, $\mathrm{lm}_{\{x,\partial_x\}}(f)$ is in $Id(\mathrm{lm}_{\{x,\partial_x\}}(G))$. Suppose that $G = \{g_1, \ldots, g_\ell\}$. Since f can be regard as an element of $K\langle u, x, \partial_x\rangle$ and $G \subset K\langle u, x, \partial_x\rangle$, f can be written as $f = h_1g_1 + \cdots + h_\ell g_\ell$ s.t. $\mathrm{lm}(h) \succ_b \mathrm{lm}(h_1g_1) \succ_b \cdots \succ_b \mathrm{lm}(h_\ell g_\ell)$ where $h_1, \ldots, h_\ell \in K[u, x, \partial_x]$ and $\succ_b$ is the block order. As $\succ_b$ is the block order, we have $\mathrm{lm}(f) \succ \mathrm{lm}(h_1g_1) \succ \cdots \succ \mathrm{lm}(h_\ell g_\ell)$, too. W.l.o.g., $h_1g_1, \ldots, h_kg_k$ have the same leading power product $\mathrm{lpp}_{\{x,\partial_x\}}(h)$ where $k \leq \ell$. That is,

$\mathrm{lm}_{\{x,\partial_x\}}(f) = \mathrm{lm}_{\{x,\partial_x\}}(h_1g_1) + \cdots + \mathrm{lm}_{\{x,\partial_x\}}(h_kg_k)$. Since $\mathrm{lm}_{\{x,\partial_x\}}(h_ig_i) = \mathrm{lm}_{\{x,\partial_x\}}(h_i)\,\mathrm{lm}_{\{x,\partial_x\}}(g_i)$, $\mathrm{lm}_{\{x,\partial_x\}}(f) = \mathrm{lm}_{\{x,\partial_x\}}(h_1)\,\mathrm{lm}_{\{x,\partial_x\}}(g_1) + \cdots + \mathrm{lm}_{\{x,\partial_x\}}(h_k)\,\mathrm{lm}_{\{x,\partial_x\}}(g_k)$ holds. Therefore, $\mathrm{lm}_{\{x,\partial_x\}}(f)$ is in $Id(\mathrm{lm}_{\{x,\partial_x\}}(G))$ w.r.t. $\succ$. □

3. CGS

Here we introduce an algorithm for computing comprehensive Gröbner systems in rings of partial differential operators.

Weispfenning introduced, studied and constructed comprehensive Gröbner systems for parametric ideals in commutative polynomial rings in 1992 [33]. After that, several researchers have published different algorithms for computing comprehensive Gröbner systems in commutative polynomial rings [8, 15, 16, 17]. In this section, we generalize some of these algorithms to the case of rings of partial differential operators.

To the best of our knowledge, there is currently, in the rings of partial differential operators, only one implementation of comprehensive Gröbner systems. The implementation and algorithm have been given in the Ph.D. Thesis [16] of the first author of the present paper, which has not been published in any journal.

By making use of an extended version of the theory of stability of Gröbner bases of ideals under specializations (Kalkbrener's results [6]), we improve here the previous algorithms and implementation of [16].

Definition 4 (CGS). *Fix a term ordering on* $\mathrm{pp}(x,\partial_x)$. *Let* P *be a subset of* $K[u]\langle x,\partial_x\rangle$, $\mathbb{A}_1,\dots,\mathbb{A}_\ell$ *strata in* K^m *and let* $G_1,\dots,G_\ell$ *be subsets in* $K[u]\langle x,\partial_x\rangle$. *A finite set* $\mathcal{G} = \{(\mathbb{A}_1,G_1),\dots,(\mathbb{A}_\ell,G_\ell)\}$ *of pairs is called a comprehensive Gröbner system (CGS) on* $\mathbb{A}_1\cup\cdots\cup\mathbb{A}_\ell$ *for* P *if for all* $a\in\mathbb{A}_i$, $\sigma_a(G_i)$ *is a Gröbner basis of* $Id(\sigma_a(P))$ *in* $K\langle x,\partial_x\rangle$ *for each* $i=1,\dots,\ell$. *We call a pair* $(\mathbb{A}_i,G_i)$ *segment of* $\mathcal{G}$. *We simply say* $\mathcal{G}$ *is a comprehensive Gröbner system for* P *if* $\mathbb{A}_1\cup\cdots\cup\mathbb{A}_\ell = K^m$.

In order to introduce the core theorem, we need the following definition.

Definition 5. *Fix a term ordering on* $\mathrm{pp}(x,\partial_x)$. *Let* P *be a subset in* $K[u]\langle x,\partial_x\rangle$. *A set* $\{m_1,..,m_\ell\}\subseteq \mathrm{lpp}_{\{x,\partial_x\}}(P)$ *is said to be the minimal basis of* $\mathrm{lpp}_{\{x,\partial_x\}}(P)$ *if no* m_i *in the set divides another* m_j *for* $i\neq j$ *where* $i,j\in\{1,\dots,\ell\}$. *The minimal basis of* $\mathrm{lpp}_{\{x,\partial_x\}}(P)$ *is written as* $\mathrm{MBlpp}(P)$.

The next theorem tells us the stability in $K[u]\langle x,\partial_x\rangle$ of Gröbner bases under the specialization homomorphism. This is an extension of Theorem 3 of [17].

Theorem 6. *Let* G *be a Gröbner basis of an ideal* $I\subseteq K[u]\langle x,\partial_x\rangle$ *w.r.t. a term ordering* $\succ$ *on* $\mathrm{pp}(x,\partial_x)$. $E := G\cap K[u]$, $G' := G\backslash E$, *and* $\mathrm{MBlpp}(G') = \{m_1,\dots,m_\ell\}$. *Suppose that* $G_i = \{f\in G' \mid \mathrm{lpp}_{\{x,\partial_x\}}(f) = m_i\}$ *for each* $i\in\{1,\dots,\ell\}$. *Then, for all* $\bar a\in\mathbb{V}(E)\backslash(\mathbb{V}(\mathrm{lc}_{\{x,\partial_x\}}(G_1))\cup\mathbb{V}(\mathrm{lc}_{\{x,\partial_x\}}(G_2))\cup\cdots\cup\mathbb{V}(\mathrm{lc}_{\{x,\partial_x\}}(G_\ell)))$, $\sigma_{\bar a}(G_1\cup G_2\cup\cdots\cup G_\ell)$ *is a Gröbner basis of* $\sigma_{\bar a}(I)$ *w.r.t.* $\succ$ *in* $K\langle x,\partial_x\rangle$.

Proof. For all $\bar a\in\mathbb{V}(E)\backslash(\mathbb{V}(\mathrm{lc}_{\{x,\partial_x\}}(G_1))\cup\mathbb{V}(\mathrm{lc}_{\{x,\partial_x\}}(G_2))\cup\cdots\cup\mathbb{V}(\mathrm{lc}_{\{x,\partial_x\}}(G_\ell)))$, there exists $p_i\in G_i$ s.t. $\sigma_{\bar a}(\mathrm{lm}_{\{x,\partial_x\}}(p_i))\neq 0$ for each $i\in\{1,..,\ell\}$. Suppose that $G=\{g_1,\dots,g_r\}$ and $P=\{p_1,\dots,p_\ell\}$. Then, clearly $P\subseteq G$ and $\mathrm{MBlpp}(P) = \mathrm{MBlpp}(G\backslash E) = \{m_1,\dots,m_\ell\}$. We prove the following claim.

Claim
For all $\bar a\in\mathbb{V}(E)\backslash(\mathbb{V}(\mathrm{lc}_{\{x,\partial_x\}}(G_1))\cup\mathbb{V}(\mathrm{lc}_{\{x,\partial_x\}}(G_2))\cup\cdots\cup\mathbb{V}(\mathrm{lc}_{\{x,\partial_x\}}(G_\ell)))$, $\sigma_{\bar a}(\mathrm{lm}_{\{x,\partial_x\}}(I)) = \mathrm{lm}_{\{x,\partial_x\}}(\sigma_{\bar a}(I))$.

Proof of the claim: It is obvious that $\sigma_{\bar a}(\mathrm{lm}_{\{x,\partial_x\}}(I))\subset \mathrm{lm}_{\{x,\partial_x\}}(\sigma_{\bar a}(I))$. We show the reverse inclusion. As G is a Gröbner basis of I w.r.t. $\succ$ in $K[u]\langle x,\partial_x\rangle$, it is enough to show that
$\langle\sigma_a(\mathrm{lm}_{\{x,\partial_x\}}(g_1)),\dots,\sigma_a(\mathrm{lm}_{\{x,\partial_x\}}(g_r))\rangle\supset \mathrm{lm}_{\{x,\partial_x\}}(\sigma_a(I))$.

Let $f\in I$ with $\sigma_a(f)\neq 0$. It suffices to show

"there exists g_j s.t. $\sigma_a(\mathrm{lm}_{\{x,\partial_x\}}(g_j))$ divides $\mathrm{lm}_{\{x,\partial_x\}}(\sigma_a(f))$ and $\sigma_a(\mathrm{lc}_{\{x,\partial_x\}}(g_j))\neq 0$ where $j\in\{1,\dots,r\}$." $(*)$

We do the proof by induction on $\succ$.
(Induction basis:) Let $\mathrm{lpp}_{\{x,\partial_x\}}(f)$ be the smallest element in $\mathrm{lpp}_{\{x,\partial_x\}}(I)$ w.r.t. $\succ$. If $\sigma_a(\mathrm{lc}_{\{x,\partial_x\}}(f))\neq 0$, then $\mathrm{lc}_{\{x,\partial_x\}}(\sigma_a(f)) = \sigma_a(\mathrm{lc}_{\{x,\partial_x\}}(f))$. Thus, $\mathrm{lpp}_{\{x,\partial_x\}}(\sigma_a(f)) = \mathrm{lpp}_{\{x,\partial_x\}}(f)$ is divisible by some elements of $\{\mathrm{lpp}_{\{x,\partial_x\}}(g_1),\dots,\mathrm{lpp}_{\{x,\partial_x\}}(g_r)\}$, namely, there exists g_j s.t. $\sigma_a(\mathrm{lm}_{\{x,\partial_x\}}(g_j))$ divides $\mathrm{lm}_{\{x,\partial_x\}}(\sigma_a(f))$ and $\sigma_a(\mathrm{lc}_{\{x,\partial_x\}}(g_j))\neq 0$ where $j\in\{1,\dots,r\}$.

We assume that $\sigma_a(\mathrm{lc}_{\{x,\partial_x\}}(f)) = 0$. Since $f\in I$, there exists $p\in P$ s.t. $\mathrm{lpp}_{\{x,\partial_x\}}(p)\mid \mathrm{lpp}_{\{x,\partial_x\}}(f)$ and $\sigma_a(\mathrm{lc}_{\{x,\partial_x\}}(p))\neq 0$. Then, for the p, defining

$$f' = \mathrm{lc}_{\{x,\partial_x\}}(p)f - \mathrm{lc}_{\{x,\partial_x\}}(f)\cdot\Psi^{-1}\left(\frac{\mathrm{lpp}_{\{x,\partial_x\}}(f)}{\mathrm{lpp}_{\{x,\partial_x\}}(p)}\right)p,$$

we obtain that $\mathrm{lpp}_{\{x,\partial_x\}}(f)\succ \mathrm{lpp}_{\{x,\partial_x\}}(f')$, $f'\in I$ and $\mathrm{lpp}_{\{x,\partial_x\}}(\sigma_a(f')) = \mathrm{lpp}_{\{x,\partial_x\}}(\sigma_a(f))$. Since $\mathrm{lpp}_{\{x,\partial_x\}}(f)$ is the smallest element in $\mathrm{lpp}_{\{x,\partial_x\}}(I)$, f' must be 0. As $\sigma_a(f)\neq 0$, this is a contradiction. Therefore, if $\sigma_a(f)\neq 0$, then we always have $\sigma_a(\mathrm{lc}_{\{x,\partial_x\}}(f))\neq 0$.
(Induction step:) We assume that $(*)$ holds for partial differential operators whose leading power products are smaller than $\mathrm{lpp}_{\{x,\partial_x\}}(f)$ w.r.t. $\succ$. If $\sigma_a(\mathrm{lc}_{\{x,\partial_x\}}(f))\neq 0$, then $\mathrm{lc}_{\{x,\partial_x\}}(\sigma_a(f)) = \sigma_a(\mathrm{lc}_{\{x,\partial_x\}}(f))$. Thus, $\mathrm{lpp}_{\{x,\partial_x\}}(\sigma_a(f)) = \mathrm{lpp}_{\{x,\partial_x\}}(f)$ is divisible by some element of $\{\mathrm{lpp}_{\{x,\partial_x\}}(g_1),\dots,\mathrm{lpp}_{\{x,\partial_x\}}(g_r)\}$.

We assume that $\sigma_a(\mathrm{lc}_{\{x,\partial_x\}}(f)) = 0$. Since $f\in I$, there exists $p\in P$ s.t. $\mathrm{lpp}_{\{x,\partial_x\}}(p)\mid \mathrm{lpp}_{\{x,\partial_x\}}(f)$ and $\sigma_a(\mathrm{lc}_{\{x,\partial_x\}}(p))\neq 0$. Then, for the P, defining

$$f' = \mathrm{lc}_{\{x,\partial_x\}}(p)f - \mathrm{lc}_{\{x,\partial_x\}}(f)\cdot\Psi^{-1}\left(\frac{\mathrm{lpp}_{\{x,\partial_x\}}(f)}{\mathrm{lpp}_{\{x,\partial_x\}}(p)}\right)p,$$

we get $\mathrm{lpp}_{\{x,\partial_x\}}(\sigma_a(f')) = \mathrm{lpp}_{\{x,\partial_x\}}(\sigma_a(f))$ and $\mathrm{lpp}_{\{x,\partial_x\}}(f)\succ \mathrm{lpp}_{\{x,\partial_x\}}(f')$. Thus, by the induction hypothesis, $\mathrm{lpp}_{\{x,\partial_x\}}(\sigma_a(f'))$ is divisible by some elements of $\{\mathrm{lpp}_{\{x,\partial_x\}}(g_1),\dots,\mathrm{lpp}_{\{x,\partial_x\}}(g_r)\}$. That is, $\mathrm{lpp}_{\{x,\partial_x\}}(\sigma_a(f))$ is also divisible by them. Therefore, $(*)$ holds. □

By the claim,

$$\begin{aligned}\mathrm{lm}_{\{x,\partial_x\}}(\sigma_{\bar a}(I)) &= Id(\sigma_{\bar a}(\mathrm{lm}_{\{x,\partial_x\}}(g_1)),\dots,\sigma_{\bar a}(\mathrm{lm}_{\{x,\partial_x\}}(g_r)))\\ &= Id(\mathrm{MBlpp}(G\backslash E))\\ &= Id(\mathrm{MBlpp}(G_1\cup G_2\cup\cdots\cup G_\ell))\\ &= Id(\sigma_{\bar a}(\mathrm{lm}_{\{x,\partial_x\}}(G_1\cup G_2\cup\cdots\cup G_\ell)))\end{aligned}$$

in $K\langle x,\partial_x\rangle$. As $G_1\cup G_2\cup\cdots\cup G_\ell\subset I\subset K[u]\langle x,\partial_x\rangle$, it is obvious that $\sigma_{\bar a}(G_1\cup G_2\cup\cdots\cup G_\ell)\subset\sigma_{\bar a}(I)\subset K\langle x,\partial_x\rangle$. Therefore, $\sigma_{\bar a}(G_1\cup G_2\cup\cdots\cup G_\ell)$ is a Gröbner basis of $\sigma_{\bar a}(I)$ w.r.t. $\succ$ in $K\langle x,\partial_x\rangle$. □

In order to construct an effective algorithm for computing systems of partial differential equations and b-functions, the next corollary that is essentially the same as Kapur-Sun-Wang's theorem [8], is much more convenient than Theorem 6.

COROLLARY 7. *Using the same notation as in Theorem 6, let* $g_i \in G_i$ *and* $h_i = \mathrm{lc}_{\{x,\partial_x\}}(g_i)$ *for each* $i \in \{1,\ldots,\ell\}$. *Then, for all* $\bar{a} \in \mathbb{V}(E)\setminus\mathbb{V}(h_1h_2\cdots h_\ell)$, $\sigma_{\bar{a}}(\{g_1,g_2,\ldots,g_\ell\})$ *is a minimal Gröbner basis of* $\sigma_{\bar{a}}(I)$ *w.r.t.* $\succ$ *in* $\bar{K}\langle x,\partial_x\rangle$.

PROOF. As $\mathbb{V}(E)\setminus\mathbb{V}(h_1h_2\cdots h_\ell) \subseteq \mathbb{V}(E)\setminus(\mathbb{V}(\mathrm{lc}_{\{x,\partial_x\}}(G_1)) \cup \mathbb{V}(\mathrm{lc}_{\{x,\partial_x\}}(G_2)) \cup\cdots\cup \mathbb{V}(\mathrm{lc}_{\{x,\partial_x\}}(G_\ell)))$, by Theorem 6 $Id(\sigma_{\bar{a}}(\mathrm{lm}_{\{x,\partial_x\}}(\{g_1,g_2,\ldots,g_\ell\}))) = Id(\sigma_{\bar{a}}(\mathrm{lm}_{\{x,\partial_x\}}(G_1\cup G_2 \cup\cdots\cup G_\ell)))$. Therefore, $\sigma_{\bar{a}}(\{g_1,g_2,\ldots,g_\ell\})$ is a Gröbner basis of $\sigma_{\bar{a}}(I)$ w.r.t. $\succ$ in $\bar{K}\langle x,\partial_x\rangle$. As no $\mathrm{lpp}(\sigma_{\bar{a}}(g_i))$ in the set $\mathrm{lpp}(\{\sigma_{\bar{a}}(g_1),\sigma_{\bar{a}}(g_2),\ldots,\sigma_{\bar{a}}(g_\ell)\})$ divides another $\mathrm{lpp}(\sigma_{\bar{a}}(g_j))$ for $i\neq j$ where $i,j\in\{1,\ldots,\ell\}$, it is minimal. □

We are ready to introduce an algorithm for computing CGS, based on Corollary 7. The proof of the correctness follows from [8] and the termination follows from [29]. By the same reason as Algorithm 1, the symbol $K[u]\langle x,\partial_x,[\partial t,s]\rangle$ is enclosed in parentheses of the algorithm, too.

Algorithm 2 CGS

Specification: CGS($E,N,P,\succ$)
Computing a CGS of $Id(P)$ w.r.t. $\succ$ on $\mathbb{V}(E)\setminus\mathbb{V}(N)$.
Input: E: a subset of $K[u]$, N: a subset of $K[u]$,
 P: a subset of $K[u]\langle x,\partial_x\rangle$ (or $K[u]\langle x,\partial_x,[\partial t,s]\rangle$),
 $\succ$: a term ordering on $\mathrm{pp}(x,\partial_x)$ (or $\mathrm{pp}(x,\partial_x,\partial t,s)$).
Output: $\mathcal{G}$: a CGS of P w.r.t. $\succ$ on $\mathbb{V}(E)\setminus\mathbb{V}(N)$.
BEGIN
$\mathcal{G}\leftarrow\emptyset$;
if $\mathbb{V}(E)\setminus\mathbb{V}(N)=\emptyset$ **then** return $\mathcal{G}$; **end-if**
$G\leftarrow$GB($P\cup E,\succ$);
if $1\in G$ **then**
 $\mathcal{G}\leftarrow\mathcal{G}\cup\{(\mathbb{V}(E)\setminus\mathbb{V}(N),\{1\})\}$; return $\mathcal{G}$;
end-if
$G'\leftarrow G\setminus((G\cap K[u])\cap Id(E))$;
$\{m_1,\ldots,m_\ell\}\leftarrow \mathrm{MBlpp}(G')$; $h\leftarrow 1$;
for each $i=1$ **to** ℓ **do**
 $g_i\leftarrow$ take g_i from G' s.t. $\mathrm{lpp}_{\{x,\partial_x\}}(g_i)=m_i$;
 $h\leftarrow \mathrm{lc}_{\{x,\partial_x\}}(g_i)\cdot h$;
end-for
$h_1^{\alpha_1}h_2^{\alpha_2}\cdots h_r^{\alpha_r}\leftarrow$ factorization(h); $(*)$
/* h_i is an irreducible factor, $\alpha_i\in\mathbb{N}$,
 for each $i\in\{1,\ldots,r\}$. $h=h_1^{\alpha_1}h_2^{\alpha_2}\cdots h_r^{\alpha_r}$ */
if $(\mathbb{V}(E)\setminus\mathbb{V}(N))\setminus\mathbb{V}(h_1h_2\cdots h_r))\neq\emptyset$ **then**
 $\mathcal{G}\leftarrow\mathcal{G}\cup\{(E,N\wedge\{h_1h_2\cdots h_r\},\{g_1,g_2,\ldots,g_\ell\})\}$;
end-if
$\mathcal{G}\leftarrow\mathcal{G}\cup$ CGS $(E\cup\{h_1\},N,G',\succ)\cup$
 CGS$(E\cup\{h_2\},N\wedge\{h_1\},G',\succ)\cup$
 CGS$(E\cup\{h_3\},N\wedge\{h_1h_2\},G',\succ)\cup$
 $\cdots\cup$ CGS$(E\cup\{h_\ell\},N\wedge\{h_1h_2\cdots h_{\ell-1}\},G',\succ)$;
return $\mathcal{G}$;
END
(Note that for $A,B\subset K[u]$, $A\wedge B=\{pq|\ p\in A,q\in B\}$.)

Remark: The function factorization(h) computes the factorization of h in $K[u]$ that is one of optimizations. We will return to the part $(*)$ for b-functions in Section 4, again. In order to keep the presentation simple, we have deliberately avoided tricks and optimizations. The techniques in [8, 15, 16, 17, 29] are applicable to obtain small and nice outputs of CGS. In fact, our implementation incorporate these optimizations.

THEOREM 8. *Algorithm 2 (*CGS*) outputs a CGS of P on* $\mathbb{V}(E)\setminus\mathbb{V}(N)$ *and terminates.*

PROOF. By Corollary 7, $(\mathbb{V}(E)\setminus\mathbb{V}(N\wedge\{h_1h_2\cdots h_r\},\{g_1,\ldots,g_\ell\})$ is a segment of the **CGS**. We show the termination. It suffices to show that the algorithm only creates finite branches. In each call of CGS, the number of elements in $\mathrm{MBlpp}(G')$ is finite. Since $\mathrm{lc}_{\{x,\partial_x\}}(g_i)\in K[u]$ for some $g_i\in G$, where G is a reduced Gröbner basis for $Id(P\cup E)\subset K\langle u,x,\partial_x\rangle$ and $\mathrm{lc}_{\{x,\partial_x\}}(g_i)\notin\langle E\rangle\subset K[u]$, as otherwise, $g\in G$ can be simplified further by the Gröbner basis of $\langle E\rangle$. In the next recursive call of CGS, the input $E\cup\{h_j\}$ whose ideal is strictly larger than $\langle E\rangle$ from the previous call of CGS. Therefore, each branch terminates after finite steps. □

Algorithm 2 has been implemented in the computer algebra system Risa/Asir. The following function is available in our implementation.

• `newcgsw1(P,U,[V,D],Ord)`
This function computes a CGS of `P` w.r.t. a term ordering `Ord`. `U` is a list of parameters, `V` is a list of variables and `D` is a list of the partial differential operators w.r.t. the variables in `V`.

Let $F=\{x^2\partial_y+2x\partial_x^2+ax\partial_x^2, xy\partial_x^2+by, y^2\partial_x+by^2\}\subset\mathbb{C}[a,b]\langle x,y,\partial_x,\partial_y\rangle$ and $\succ$ the lexicographic term ordering s.t. $x\succ y\succ\partial_x\succ\partial_y$ where $\partial_x=\frac{\partial}{\partial x},\partial_y=\frac{\partial}{\partial y}$.
The function newcgsw1 outputs a CGS of F w.r.t. $\succ$ as follows.

```
[2503] newcgsw1([x^2*dy+2*x*dx^2+a*x*dx^2,x*y*dx^2+b*y,y^
2*dx+b*y^2],[a,b],[[x,y],[dx,dy]],2);
[[b],[b,a^2+4*a+4]]
[dy*a+2*dy,dx*a+2*dx]

[[b,a+2],[1]]
[dy^2*y+2*dy,dx*y,dy*y^2,dy*x^2,dx*x^2-2*dy*y*x]

[[a+2],[b,a+2]]
[b*y,b*x^2]

[[0],[b*a+2*b]]
[1]
```

This output means that a CGS of F w.r.t. $\succ$ is
$\{(\mathbb{V}(b)\setminus\mathbb{V}(b,a^2+4a+4),\{a\partial_y+2\partial_y,a\partial_x+2\partial_x\}),$
$(\mathbb{V}(b,a+2),\{y\partial_y^2+2\partial_y,y\partial_x,y^2\partial_y,x^2\partial_y,x^2\partial_x-2xy\partial_y\}),$
$(\mathbb{V}(a+2)\setminus\mathbb{V}(b,a+2),\{by,bx^2\}),\ (\mathbb{C}^2\setminus\mathbb{V}(ba+2b),\{1\})\}$.
Notice that, due to the specification of the computer algebra system Risa/Asir, the outputs `dy*y^2`, `dx*x^2` and `dy*y*x` above mean partial differential operators of the form $y^2\partial_y$, $x^2\partial_x$ and $xy\partial_y$.
Now we can compute a CGS in rings of partial differential operators.

4. APPLICATIONS TO B-FUNCTIONS AND HOLONOMIC D-MODULES

Here we present various applications of CGS to b-functions and holonomic D-modules.
Let f be a non-constant polynomial in $\mathbb{C}[x]$. Then, the annihilating ideal of f^s is

$$\mathrm{Ann}(f^s):=\{p\in\mathbb{C}\langle s,x,\partial_x\rangle\mid pf^s=0\}$$

where s is an indeterminate. We consider three left ideals $\mathrm{Ann}(f^s)$, $\mathrm{Ann}(f^s)+Id(f)$ and $\mathrm{Ann}(f^s)+Id(f)+J_f$ where $J_f=Id(\frac{\partial f}{\partial x_1},\frac{\partial f}{\partial x_2},\ldots,\frac{\partial f}{\partial x_n})$. These left ideals define the following three D-modules $\mathbb{C}\langle s,x,\partial_x\rangle/\mathrm{Ann}(f^s)$,

$\mathbb{C}\langle s, x, \partial_x\rangle/(\mathrm{Ann}(f^s) + Id(f))$ and $\mathbb{C}\langle s, x, \partial_x\rangle/(\mathrm{Ann}(f^s) + Id(f) + J_f)$.

The global b-function or the Bernstein-Sato polynomial of f is defined as the monic generator $b_f(s)$ of

$$(\mathrm{Ann}(f^s) + Id(f)) \cap \mathbb{C}[s].$$

It is known that the b-function of f always has $s+1$ as a factor and has a form $(s+1)\tilde{b}_f(s)$, where $\tilde{b}_f(s) \in \mathbb{C}[s]$. The polynomial $\tilde{b}_f(s)$ is called the reduced b-function of f.

There exists several algorithms and implementations to compute a basis of the ideal $\mathrm{Ann}(f^s)$, and the b-function $b_f(s)$. The computer algebra systems Macaulay 2[5], SINGULAR[4] and Risa/Asir, for example, have functions for computing them.

In this section we introduce how the algorithm CGS works for b-functions and holonomic D-modules associated with hypersurface singularities. Moreover, we present algorithms for computing parametric annihilating ideals of f^s and parametric b-functions. We will see that CGS provides a lot of information of hypersurface singularities of f.

We have implemented all methods and algorithms which are presented in this article, in the computer algebra system Risa/Asir. The following three Risa/Asir functions will be used in the illustration of applications of CGS.

- ann(F)

This function returns a basis of the annihilating ideal of $\mathtt{F}^s$.

- diff(F,x)

This function returns $\frac{\partial \mathtt{F}}{\partial x}$ where F is a polynomial and x is a variable.

- append([$a_1, a_2, \ldots, a_{r_1}$],[$b_1, b_2, \ldots, b_{r_2}$])

This function maps a pair of lists ([$a_1, a_2, \ldots, a_{r_1}$],[$b_1, b_2, \ldots, b_{r_2}$]) to a list [$a_1, a_2, \ldots, a_{r_1}, b_1, b_2, \ldots, b_{r_2}$].

In subsections 4.1, 4.2, 4.3 and 4.4, we fix the notation f as a polynomial in $\mathbb{C}[x]$ and the notation H as a basis of the ideal $\mathrm{Ann}(f^s)$. In subsections 4.5 and 4.6, we will treat a parametric polynomial f in $\mathbb{C}[u][x]$.

4.1 Application 1

Let us regard s as a parameter and compute a CGS of $H \cup \{f\}$ in $\mathbb{C}[s]\langle x, \partial_x\rangle$. The procedure is the following method.

Method 1
Step 1: Commute a basis H of the ideal $\mathrm{Ann}(f^s)$.
Step 2: Compute a CGS of $H \cup \{f\}$.

For example, let us consider $f = x^2 + y^3 \in \mathbb{C}[x, y]$. Then, a CGS of $H \cup \{f\}$ w.r.t. $\succ$ is the following, where $\succ$ is the total degree lexicographic term ordering s.t. $x \succ y \succ \frac{\partial}{\partial x} \succ \frac{\partial}{\partial y}$.

```
[2504] F=x^2+y^3$
[2505] L=append([F],ann(F))$
[2506] newcgsw1(L,[s],[[x,y],[dx,dy]],1);
[[s+1],[1]]
[3*dx*x+2*dy*y+6,2*dy*x-3*dx*y^2,x^2+y^3]

[[6*s+5],[1]]
[y,x]

[[6*s+7],[1]]
[x,dy*y+2,y^2]

[[0],[36*s^3+108*s^2+107*s+35]]
[1]
```

This output means;
if $s = -1$, then $\{3x\frac{\partial}{\partial x} + 2y\frac{\partial}{\partial y} + 6, 2x\frac{\partial}{\partial y} - 3y^2\frac{\partial}{\partial x}, x^2 + y^3\}$ is a Gröbner basis of $Id(\mathtt{L})$ in $\mathbb{C}\langle x, y, \frac{\partial}{\partial x}, \frac{\partial}{\partial y}\rangle$,
if $s = -\frac{5}{6}$, then $\{x, y\}$ is a Gröbner basis w.r.t $\succ$ of $Id(\mathtt{L})$,
if $s = -\frac{7}{6}$, then $\{x, y\frac{\partial}{\partial y} + 2, y^2\}$ is a Gröbner basis of $Id(\mathtt{L})$,
if $36s^3 + 108s^2 + 107s + 35 \neq 0$, then $\{1\}$ is a Gröbner basis of $Id(\mathtt{L})$.

Let us consider the b-function $b_f(s) = (s+1)(s+\frac{5}{6})(s+\frac{7}{6})$ of $f = x^2 + y^3$. As $36b_f(s) = 36s^3 + 108s^2 + 107s + 35$, the b-function appears in the output as the last stratum [[0],[36*s^3+108*s^2+107*s+35]]. The roots of $b_f(s)$ also appear in the other strata above.

This is NOT a strange coincidence. We have the following theorem.

THEOREM 9. *Method 1 always outputs $\sqrt{b_f(s)}$ and all roots of the $b_f(s) = 0$ as strata where $\sqrt{b_f(s)}$ is the square-free polynomial of $b_f(s)$.*

PROOF. The function newcgsw1 executes Algorithm 2. In Algorithm 2, first we have to compute the reduced Gröbner basis G of $Id(H \cup \{f\})$ w.r.t. a block term ordering s.t. $\{x, \partial_x\} \gg s$ in $\mathbb{C}\langle s, x, \partial_x\rangle$. ($E = \{0\}$ and $N = \{1\}$.) As the generator of $(\mathrm{Ann}(f^s) + Id(f)) \cap \mathbb{C}[s]$ is the b-function of f and G is the reduced Gröbner basis w.r.t. the block term ordering, hence $b_f(s) \in G \cap \mathbb{C}[s]$. Thus, since $\mathrm{MBlpp}(G) = \{1\}$, $(\mathbb{C} \setminus \mathbb{V}(\sqrt{b_f(s)}), \{b_f(s)\})$ is a segment of the CGS. Look at $(*)$ in Algorithm 2. The rationality of the roots of $b_f(s)$ has been shown by [10]. Hence, $b_f(s)$ can be factorized into linear factors over the field of rational numbers, and we can easily compute the factorization of $b_f(s)$. Therefore, all roots of the b-function appear as strata. □

4.2 Application 2

Let us consider the Jacobian ideal $Id(\frac{\partial f}{\partial x_1}, \frac{\partial f}{\partial x_2}, \ldots, \frac{\partial f}{\partial x_n})$ of f and compute a CGS of $(\mathrm{Ann}(f^s) + Id(f, \frac{\partial f}{\partial x_1}, \frac{\partial f}{\partial x_2}, \ldots, \frac{\partial f}{\partial x_n})$ in $\mathbb{C}[s]\langle x, \partial_x\rangle$ where $f \in \mathbb{C}[x]$. That is, the procedure is the following method.

Method 2
Step 1: Compute a basis H of the ideal $\mathrm{Ann}(f^s)$.
Step 2: Compute a CGS of $H \cup \{f, \frac{\partial f}{\partial x_1}, \frac{\partial f}{\partial x_2}, \ldots, \frac{\partial f}{\partial x_n}\}$.

We borrow from [35] the following theorem.

THEOREM 10. *Let $\gamma \in \mathbb{Q}$ and $J_f = Id(\frac{\partial f}{\partial x_1}, \ldots, \frac{\partial f}{\partial x_n})$. Set*

$$M_{(\gamma, f)} = \mathbb{C}\langle s, x, \partial_x\rangle/(\mathrm{Ann}(f^s) + Id(f) + J_f + Id(s - \gamma)).$$

Then, if $\tilde{b}_f(\gamma) \neq 0$, then $M_{(\gamma,f)} = \{0\}$, and if $\tilde{b}_f(\gamma) = 0$, then $M_{(\gamma,f)}$ is a holonomic D-module and $supp(M_{(\gamma,f)}) \subseteq Sing(S)$ where $supp(M_{(\gamma,f)})$ is the support of $M_{(\gamma,f)}$ and $Sing(S)$ is the singular locus of the hypersurface $S = \{x \in \mathbb{C}^n \mid f(x) = 0\}$, i.e., $Sing(S) = \mathbb{V}\left(f, \frac{\partial f}{\partial x_1}, \frac{\partial f}{\partial x_2}, \ldots, \frac{\partial f}{\partial x_n}\right)$.

By this theorem, we have the following corollary.

COROLLARY 11. *Method 2 outputs $\sqrt{\tilde{b}_f(s)}$, all roots of $\tilde{b}_f(s)$ and presentations holonomic D-modules $M_{(\gamma,f)}$ where γ is a root of $\tilde{b}_f(s)$.*

PROOF. The existence of $\tilde{b}_f(s)$ in $Id(H \cup \{f, \frac{\partial f}{\partial x_1}, \ldots, \frac{\partial f}{\partial x_n})$ has been shown in [35]. The rest of the proof is the same as Theorem 9. □

4.3 Application 3

Remember that Algorithm 2 has four arguments E, N, P, and $\succ$. We can compute a CGS of P on $\mathbb{V}(E)\setminus\mathbb{V}(N)$. That is, we can impose conditions on parameters by specifying the sets E and N.

> **Method 3**
> Step 1: Compute a basis H of the ideal $\mathrm{Ann}(f^s)$.
> Step 2: Execute `CGS`$(E, N, H \cup \{f, \frac{\partial f}{\partial x_1}, \ldots, \frac{\partial f}{\partial x_n}\}, \succ)$.

The following function is available in our implementation.

- `sup_cgsw([E,N],P,U,[V,D],Ord)`

This function executes Algorithm 2 and computes a CGS of `P` w.r.t. a term ordering `Ord` on $\mathbb{V}$(`E`)$\setminus\mathbb{V}$(`N`). The lists `U,V,D` and a term ordering `Ord` are same as the arguments of the function `newcgsw1`.

Let us consider $f = x^2 + xy^2 \in \mathbb{C}[x, y]$. Then, a CGS of $H \cup \{f, \frac{\partial f}{\partial x}, \frac{\partial f}{\partial y}\}$ w.r.t. $\succ$ on $\mathbb{V}((6s+5)(3s+3)(s-2))$, is the following, where $\succ$ is the total degree lexicographic term ordering s.t. $x \succ y \succ \frac{\partial}{\partial x} \succ \frac{\partial}{\partial y}$. (That is, i.e., $E = \{(6s+5)(3s+3)(s-2)\}$ and $N = \{1\}$.)

```
[2513] F=x^2+x*y^2$
[2514] L=append(ann(F),[F,diff(F,x),diff(F,y)])$
[2515] sup_cgsw([[(6*s+5)*(3*s+3)*(s-2)],[1]],L,[s],[[x,y]
,[dx,dy]],1);
[[-s+2],[1]]
[1]

[[s+1],[1]]
[x,dy*y+3,y^3]

[[-6*s-5],[1]]
[y^2,-dy*y-2,x]
```

This output says that $s = 2$ is not a root of $b_f(s) = 0$.

The next example is a CGS of $H \cup \{f, \frac{\partial f}{\partial x}, \frac{\partial f}{\partial y}\}$ w.r.t. $\succ$ on $\mathbb{C}\setminus\mathbb{V}((6s+5)(3s+3)(s-2))$, i.e., $E = \{0\}$ and $N = \{(6s+5)(3s+3)(s-2)\}$.

```
[2516] sup_cgsw([[0],[(s+1)*(3*4+1)*(6*s+7)]],L,[s],[[x,y]
,[dx,dy]],1);
[[3*s+4],[1]]
[-dy*x+y^2,-3*dx*x-dy*y-8,x^2,3*dx*y^2+dy^2*y+6*dy,2*x+y^
3,y^2*x,-dy^2*y^2-8*dy*y-10,(-12*dy*dx+dy^4)*y-24*dx+8*dy
^3]

[[6*s+5],[1]]
[x,-dy*y-2,y^2]

[[0],[8424*s^6+54756*s^5+147654*s^4+211419*s^3+169520*s^2
+72163*s+12740]]
[1]
```

4.4 Application 4

Let Q be a primary component of the primary ideal decomposition of $Id(f, \frac{\partial f}{\partial x_1}, \ldots, \frac{\partial f}{\partial x_n})$. `newcgs1` computes holonomic D-modules supported on $\mathbb{V}(Q)$ as follows.

> **Method 4**
> Step 1: Compute a basis H of the ideal $\mathrm{Ann}(f^s)$.
> Step 2: Compute a primary component Q of the primary ideal decomposition of $Id(f, \frac{\partial f}{\partial x_1}, \frac{\partial f}{\partial x_2}, \ldots, \frac{\partial f}{\partial x_n})$.
> Step 3: Compute a CGS of $Q \cup H$.

Let us consider $f = x^3y^2 - z^5 \in \mathbb{C}[x, y, z]$. Then, the primary ideal decomposition of the ideal $Id(f, \frac{\partial f}{\partial x}, \frac{\partial f}{\partial y}, \frac{\partial f}{\partial z})$ is $Id(f, \frac{\partial f}{\partial x}, \frac{\partial f}{\partial y}, \frac{\partial f}{\partial z}) = Id(y, z^4) \cap Id(x^2, z^4) \cap Id(x^3, y^2, z^4)$.

We take the primary component $\{y, z^4\}$ and compute a CGS of $\{y, z^4\} \cup H$. Then, we get holonomic D-modules supported on $\mathbb{V}(y, z^4)$.

```
[2517] F=x^3*y^2-z^5$
[2518] L=append([y,z^4],ann(F))$
[2519] newcgsw1(L,[s],[[x,y,z],[dx,dy,dz]],0);
[[10*s+7],[1]]
[z,y,-2*dx*x-3]

[[10*s+9],[1]]
[y,dz*z+2,-2*dx*x-3,z^2]

[[10*s+11],[1]]
[y,dz*z+3,-2*dx*x-3,z^3]

[[10*s+13],[1]]
[y,dz*z+4,-2*dx*x-3,z^4]

[[0],[10000*s^4+40000*s^3+59000*s^2+38000*s+9009]]
[1]
```

4.5 Parametric annihilating ideal

Here we consider as Application 5 an algorithm for computing a parametric annihilating ideal of f^s, and we introduce an algorithm for computing bases of a parametric annihilating ideal of f^s.

Before describing the algorithm, we recall the approach of Briançon-Maisonobe [2] for computing a basis of $\mathrm{Ann}(f^s)$ where f is a non-constant and non-parametric polynomial in $\mathbb{C}[x]$.

Consider $\mathbb{C}\langle \partial t, s\rangle$ with relations

$$\partial t \cdot s = s\partial t + \partial t$$

and let $\mathbb{C}\langle x, \partial_x, [\partial t, s]\rangle$ denote the Poincaré-Birkhoff-Witt algebra $\mathbb{C}\langle x, \partial_x\rangle \otimes_{\mathbb{C}} \mathbb{C}\langle \partial t, s\rangle$ with relations $x_i s = s x_i, \partial_i s = s\partial_i, x_i\partial t = \partial t x_i, \partial_i\partial t = \partial t\partial_i, \partial t s = s\partial t + \partial t, x_i x_j = x_j x_i, \partial_i\partial_j = \partial_j\partial_i, \partial_j x_i = x_i\partial_j$ $(i \neq j)$ and $\partial_i x_i = x_i\partial_i + 1$. Moreover, consider the following left ideal in $\mathbb{C}\langle x, \partial_x, [\partial t, s]\rangle$:

$$I = Id(f\partial t + s, \frac{\partial}{\partial x_1} + \partial t\frac{\partial f}{\partial x_1}, \frac{\partial}{\partial x_2} + \partial t\frac{\partial f}{\partial x_2}, \ldots, \frac{\partial}{\partial x_n} + \partial t\frac{\partial f}{\partial x_n}).$$

Briançon and Maisonobe proved in [2] that $\mathrm{Ann}(f^s) = I \cap \mathbb{C}\langle s, x, \partial_x\rangle$ and hence the latter can be computed via the Gröbner basis w.r.t. an elimination ordering for $\{\partial t\}$. There exist algorithms and implementations to compute Gröbner bases in $\mathbb{C}\langle x, \partial_x, [\partial t, s]\rangle$ [3, 7, 11, 27].

We turn to parametric cases. Let $\mathbb{C}[u]\langle x, \partial_x, [\partial t, s]\rangle$ denote the Poincaré-Birkhoff-Witt algebra with coefficients in the polynomial ring $\mathbb{C}[u]$ and $f \in \mathbb{C}[u][x]$. Suppose that $P = \{f\partial t + s, \frac{\partial}{\partial x_1} + \partial t\frac{\partial f}{\partial x_1}, \frac{\partial}{\partial x_2} + \partial t\frac{\partial f}{\partial x_2}, \ldots, \frac{\partial}{\partial x_n} + \partial t\frac{\partial f}{\partial x_n}\}$. Then, the definition of Gröbner basis of $Id(P)$ in $\mathbb{C}[u]\langle x, \partial_x, [\partial t, s]\rangle$, is the same as Definition 2, and one can also compute the Gröbner basis by Algorithm 1. Moreover, we can generalize Theorem 6 and Corollary 7 to $\mathbb{C}\langle x, \partial_x, [\partial t, s]\rangle$ by changing the subscript $\{x, \partial_x\}$ into $\{x, \partial_x, \partial t, s\}$ in the theorem and in the proof. Consequently, we can also compute in $\mathbb{C}[u]\langle x, \partial_x, [\partial t, s]\rangle$ a comprehensive Gröbner system of P by Algorithm 2.

Now, we generalize Briançon-Maisonobe's method for computing a basis of $\mathrm{Ann}(f^s)$ to parametric cases. The correctness and termination follow from `CGS` and Briançon-Maisonobe's method.

Algorithm 3 ParaAnn

Specification: ParaAnn(f)
Computing a parametric annihilating ideal of f^s.
Input: $f \in \mathbb{C}[u][x]$.
Output: $\mathcal{B} = \{(E_1, N_1, B_1), (E_2, N_2, B_2), \ldots, (E_\ell, N_\ell, B_\ell)\}$: For all $\bar{a} \in \mathbb{V}(E_i) \setminus \mathbb{V}(N_i)$, $\sigma_a(B_i)$ is a basis of $\mathrm{Ann}(\sigma_a(f)^s)$, for each $i \in \{1, \ldots, \ell\}$.
BEGIN
$\mathcal{B} \leftarrow \emptyset$;
$P \leftarrow \{f\partial t + s, \frac{\partial}{\partial x_1} + \partial t\frac{\partial f}{\partial x_1}, \frac{\partial}{\partial x_2} + \partial t\frac{\partial f}{\partial x_2}, \ldots, \frac{\partial}{\partial x_n} + \partial t\frac{\partial f}{\partial x_n}\}$;
$\succ_{\partial t} \leftarrow$ an elimination ordering for $\{\partial t\}$;
$\mathcal{G} \leftarrow$CGS($\{0\}, \{1\}, P, \succ_{\partial t}$) in $\mathbb{C}[u]\langle x, \partial_x, [\partial t, s]\rangle$;
while $\mathcal{G} \neq \emptyset$ **do**
  select (E, N, G) from $\mathcal{G}$; $\mathcal{G} \leftarrow \mathcal{G} \setminus \{(E, N, G)\}$;
  $\mathcal{B} \leftarrow \mathcal{B} \cup \{(E, N, G \cap \mathbb{C}\langle s, x, \partial_x\rangle)\}$;
end-while
return $\mathcal{B}$;
END

The following function is available in our implementation.

- para_ann(F,U,V)

This function executes Algorithm 3 and computes parametric annihilating ideal of F^s for a given polynomial F with parameters. The lists U, V are same as the arguments of the function newcgsw1.

There's a procedure annfsParamBM of the computer algebra system SINGULAR's dmod.lib(http://www.singular.uni-kl.de/Manual/latest/sing_597.htm) which computes the generic annihilator as well as the description of exceptional variety.

4.6 B-functions of a parametric polynomial

Here we introduce an algorithm for computing b-functions of a parametric polynomial and its implementation. As the b-function $b_f(s)$ is the generator of $(\mathrm{Ann}(f^s) + Id(f)) \cap \mathbb{C}[s]$, the algorithm for computing b-functions of a parametric polynomial, can be naturally constructed by combining the algorithm ParaAnn (computing a parametric annihilating ideal) and CGS (computing CGS).

Algorithm 4 ParaBF

Specification: ParaBF(f)
Computing b-functions of a parametric polynomial f.
Input: $f \in \mathbb{C}[u][x]$.
Output: $\mathcal{P} = \{(\mathbb{A}_1, b_1(s)), (\mathbb{A}_2, b_2(s)), \ldots, (\mathbb{A}_\ell, b_\ell(s))\}$: If parameters u belong to $\mathbb{A}_i$, then $b_i(s)$ is the b-function of f where $i \in \{1, \ldots, \ell\}$.
BEGIN
$\mathcal{P} \leftarrow \emptyset$; $\mathcal{B} \leftarrow$ParaAnn(f);
while $\mathcal{B} \neq \emptyset$ **do**
  select (E, N, B) from $\mathcal{B}$; $\mathcal{B} \leftarrow \mathcal{B} \setminus \{(E, N, B)\}$;
  $\mathcal{G} \leftarrow$CGS($E, N, B \cup \{f\}$) ;
  while $\mathcal{G} \neq \emptyset$ **do**
    select (E', N', G) from $\mathcal{G}$; $\mathcal{G} \leftarrow \mathcal{G} \setminus \{(E', N', G)\}$;
    $\mathcal{P} \leftarrow \mathcal{P} \cup \{(\mathbb{V}(E') \setminus \mathbb{V}(N'), G \cap \mathbb{C}[s])\}$;
  end-while
end-while
return $\mathcal{P}$;
END

The following function is available in our implementation.

- cgs_bf(P,U,V)

This function executes Algorithm 4 and computes b-functions of a parametric polynomial F. The lists U and V are same as the arguments of the function newcgsw1.

Let $f = x^3 + xy^2 + ay^3 \in \mathbb{C}[a][x, y]$. Then, our program outputs the following as b-functions of f.

```
[2520] cgs_bf(x^3+x*y^2+a*y^3,[a],[x,y]);
[[27*a^2+4],[1]]
[[s+1,2],[2*s+1,1]]

[[a],[1]]
[[s+1,2],[3*s+2,1],[3*s+4,1]]

[[0],[27*a^3+4*a]]
[[s+1,2],[3*s+2,1],[3*s+4,1]]
```

This output means:
if $27a^2 + 4 = 0$, then $b_f(s) = (s + 1)^2(2s + 1)$,
if $a = 0$, then $b_f(s) = (s + 1)^2(3s + 2)(3s + 4)$, and
if $27a^3 + 4a \neq 0$, then $b_f(s) = (s + 1)^2(3s + 2)(3s + 4)$.

From this output, we see that if $a = \pm\sqrt{-\frac{4}{27}}$, then the b-function changes drastically, namely, the properties of the hypersurface singularity is different from the other values of the parameters. The function cgs_bf gives us such a useful information.

The next example $f = x^2 + xy^3 + ay^3 + by^4 \in \mathbb{C}[a, b][x, y]$ has two parameters a and b.

```
[2521] cgs_bf(x^2+x*y^3+a*y^3+b*y^4,[a,b],[x,y]);
[[b],[a,b]]
[[s+1,1],[6*s+5,1],[6*s+7,1]]

[[a],[a,b]]
[[s+1,2],[4*s+3,1],[4*s+5,1]]

[[a,b],[1]]
[[s+1,2],[3*s+2,1],[3*s+4,1],[6*s+5,1],[6*s+7,1]]

[[27*a^2-16*b^3],[a,b]]
[[s+1,2],[6*s+5,1],[6*s+7,1]]

[[0],[27*b*a^3-16*b^4*a]]
[[s+1,1],[6*s+5,1],[6*s+7,1]]
```

Table 1 represents the meaning of the output above.

stratum	$b_f(s)$
$\mathbb{V}(b) \setminus \mathbb{V}(a, b)$	$(s + 1)(6s + 5)(6s + 7)$
$\mathbb{V}(a) \setminus \mathbb{V}(a, b)$	$(s + 1)^2(4s + 3)(4s + 5)$
$\mathbb{V}(a, b)$	$(s + 1)^2(3s + 2)(3s + 4)$ $\times(6s + 5)(6s + 7)$
$\mathbb{V}(27a^2 - 16b^3) \setminus \mathbb{V}(a, b)$	$(s + 1)^2(6s + 5)(6s + 7)$
$\mathbb{C}^2 \setminus \mathbb{V}(27ba^3 - 16b^4a)$	$(s + 1)(6s + 5)(6s + 7)$

Table 1: A list of b-functions of $x^2 + xy^3 + ay^3 + by^4$

5. CONCLUSIONS AND REMARKS

We have presented six applications of the algorithm CGS and CGS. The algorithm CGS works powerfully as follows:

1. outputting holonomic D-modules associated with roots of the b-function (or the reduced b-function) of f by inputting $H \cup \{f\}$ or $H \cup \{f, \frac{\partial f}{\partial x_1}, \ldots, \frac{\partial f}{\partial x_n}\}$,
2. outputting holonomic D-modules supported on $\mathbb{V}(Q)$ by inputting $H \cup Q$ where Q is a primary component of the primary ideal decomposition of $Id(f, \frac{\partial f}{\partial x_1}, \ldots, \frac{\partial f}{\partial x_n})$,

3. outputting various information of hypersurface singularities by arranging the input's arguments, without applying special techniques.

Therefore, the algorithm CGS has versatility. Other existing algorithms on b-functions do not have these properties.

We have also introduced two algorithms for computing a parametric annihilating ideal of f^s and b-functions of a parametric polynomial f, both are based on the CGS theory. The algorithms give us useful information of hypersurface singularities, and are useful to analyze deformations of hypersurface singularities.

We have implemented all algorithms of this paper in the computer algebra system Risa/Asir and published it.

Finally, let us give a remark. If the equation $b_f(s) = 0$ has multiple roots, then the structures of systems of partial differential equations of $\mathrm{Ann}(f^s) + Id(f)$ (or $\mathrm{Ann}(f^s) + Id(f, \frac{\partial f}{\partial x_1}, \ldots, \frac{\partial f}{\partial x_n})$) associated with the roots, depend on the multiplicity, like eigenvalue problems. However, it is easy to improve and enhance the algorithm CGS for the generalization (multiplicity). This will be reported elsewhere.

Acknowledgments
This work has been partly supported by JSPS Grant-in-Aid for Young Scientists (B) (No.15K17513) and Grant-in-Aid for Scientific Research (C) (No. 15KT0102, 15K04891).

6. REFERENCES

[1] D. Andres, V. Levandovskyy and J. Martín-Morales, Principal intersection and Bernstein-Sato polynomial of an affine variety. *Proc. ISSAC2009*, pages 231–238. ACM, 2009.

[2] J. Briançon and P. Maisonobe, Remarques sur l'idéal de Bernstein associé à des polynômes. prépublication Univ. Nice-Sophia Antipolis, n° 650, Mai, 2002.

[3] J. Bueso, J. Castro, J. Gómez-Torrecillas and J. Lobillo, An introduction to effective calculus in quantum groups. *Rings, Hopf Algebras and Brauer Groups. Lecture Note in Pure and Applied Mathematics*, **197**, pages 55–83, Marcel-Dekker, New York, 1998.

[4] W. Decker, G.-M. Greuel, G. Pfister and H. Schönemann, SINGULAR 4-0-2 A computer algebra system for polynomial computations. 2015. http://www.singular.uni-kl.de

[5] D. Grayson and M. Stilman, MACAULAY 2: a software system for algebraic geometry. http://www.math.uiuc.edu/Macaulay2

[6] M. Kalkbrener, On the stability of Gröbner bases under specializations. *J. Symb. Comp.*, **24**, pages 51–58, 1997.

[7] A. Kandri-Rody and V. Weispfenning, Noncommutative Gröbner bases in algebras of solvable type. *J. Symb. Comp.*, **9**, pages 1–26, 1990.

[8] D. Kapur, Y. Sun and D. Wang, A new algorithm for computing comprehensive Gröbner systems. *Proc. ISSAC2010*, pages 29–36. ACM, 2010.

[9] M. Kashiwara, On the maximally overdetermined system of linear differential equations. *Publ. Res. Inst. Math. Sci.*, **10**, pages 563–579. 1974-1975.

[10] M. Kashiwara, B-functions and holonomic systems: Rationality of roots of b-functions. *Invent. Math.*, **38**, pages 33–53. 1976.

[11] V. Levandovskyy, Non-commutative computer algebra for polynomial algebras: Gröbner bases, applications and implementation. Doctoral Thesis, Universität Kaiserslautern (Germany), 2005. https://kluedo.ub.uni-kl.de/files/1670/diss-web.pdf

[12] V. Levandovskyy and J. Martín-Morales, Computational D-module theory with SINGULAR, comparison with other systems and two new algorithms. *Proc. ISSAC2008*, pages 173–180. ACM, 2008.

[13] V. Levandovskyy and J. Martín-Morales, Algorithms for checking rational roots of b-functions and their applications. *J. Algebra*, **352**, pages 408–429. 2012.

[14] A. Leykin, Constructibility of the set of polynomials with a fixed Bernstein-Sato polynomial: an algorithmic approach *J. Symb. Comp.*, **32**, pages 663–675. 2001.

[15] A. Montes and M. Wibmer, Gröbner bases for polynomial systems with parameters. *J. Symb. Comp.*, **45**, pages 1391–1425, 2010.

[16] K. Nabeshima, Comprehensive Gröbner bases in various domains. Doctoral Thesis, Johannes Kepler Universität Linz (Austria), 2007. http://www.risc.jku.at/publications/download/risc_3116/Nabeshima_thesis.pdf

[17] K. Nabeshima, Stability conditions of monomial bases and comprehensive Gröbner systems. *Proc. CASC2012, LNCS*, **7442**, pages 248–259, Springer, 2012.

[18] K. Nishiyama and M. Noro, Stratification associated with local b-functions. *J. Symb. Comp.*, **45**, pages 462–480. 2010.

[19] M. Noro, An efficient modular algorithm for computing the global b-function. *Proc. Mathematical Software*, pages 147–157, World Scientific, 2002.

[20] M. Noro and T. Takeshima, Risa/Asir- A computer algebra system. *Proc. ISSAC1992*, pages 387–396, ACM, 1992. http://www.math.kobe-u.ac.jp/Asir/asir.html

[21] T. Oaku and T. Shimoyama, A Gröbner basis method for modules over rings of differential operators, *J. Symb. Comp.*, **18**, pages 223–248. 1994.

[22] T. Oaku, Computation of the characteristic variety and the singular locus of a system of differential equations with polynomial coefficients, *Japan J. Indust. Appl. Math.*, **11**, pages 485–497. 1994.

[23] T. Oaku, An algorithm of computing b-functions. *Duke Math. J.*, **87**, pages 115–132. 1997.

[24] T. Oaku, Algorithms for b-functions, restrictions, and algebraic local cohomology groups of D-modules. *Adv. Appl. Math.*, **19**, pages 61–105. 1997.

[25] T. Oaku, Algorithms for the b-function and D-modules associated with a polynomial. *J. Pure Appl. Algebra*, **117** and **118**, pages 495–518. 1997.

[26] OpenXM committers, OpenXM, a project to integrate mathematical software systems. 1998-2016. http://www.openxm.org

[27] M. García Román and S. García Román, Gröbner bases and syzygies on bimodules over PBW algebras. *J. Symb. Comp.*, **40**, pages 1039–1052. 2005.

[28] C. Sabbah, Introduction to the theory of D-modules. Lecture Notes, Nankai, 2011. http://www.math.polytechnique.fr/cmat/sabbah/sabbah_nankai110705.pdf

[29] A. Suzuki and Y. Sato, A simple algorithm to compute comprehensive Gröbner bases using Gröbner bases. *Proc. ISSAC2006*, pages 326–331, ACM, 2006.

[30] S. Tajima, On b-functions and algebraic local cohomology classes attached to hypersurface with line singularities. *RIMS Kôkyûroku Bessatsu*, **52**, pages 174–191. 2014.

[31] S. Tajima and Y. Umeta, Computing structures of holonomic D-modules associated with a simple line singularity. To appear in *RIMS Kôkyûroku Bessatsu*.

[32] J. Ucha and F. Castro-Jiménez, On the computation of Bernstein-Sato ideals. *J. Symb. Comp.*, **37**, pages 629–639. 2004.

[33] V. Weispfenning, Comprehensive Gröbner bases. *J. Symb. Comp.*, **14**, pages 1–29. 1992.

[34] T. Yano, On the holonomic system of f^s and b-functions. *Publ. RIMS*, **12**, pages 469–480. 1978.

[35] T. Yano, On the theory of b-functions. *Publ. RIMS*, **14**, pages 111–202. 1978.

Solving Rank-Constrained Semidefinite Programs in Exact Arithmetic

Simone Naldi
Fields Institute for Research
in Mathematical Sciences
222 College Street, M5T 3J1
Toronto, Ontario, Canada
simone.naldi@tu-dortmund.de

ABSTRACT

We consider the problem of minimizing a linear function over an affine section of the cone of positive semidefinite matrices, with the additional constraint that the feasible matrix has prescribed rank. When the rank constraint is active, this is a non-convex optimization problem, otherwise it is a semidefinite program. Both find numerous applications especially in systems control theory and combinatorial optimization, but even in more general contexts such as polynomial optimization or real algebra. While numerical algorithms exist for solving this problem, such as interior-point or Newton-like algorithms, in this paper we propose an approach based on symbolic computation. We design an exact algorithm for solving rank-constrained semidefinite programs, whose complexity is essentially quadratic on natural degree bounds associated to the given optimization problem: for subfamilies of the problem where the size of the feasible matrix is fixed, the complexity is polynomial in the number of variables. The algorithm works under assumptions on the input data: we prove that these assumptions are generically satisfied. We also implement it in Maple and discuss practical experiments.

Keywords

Semidefinite programming; LMI; rank constraints; exact algorithms; polynomial optimization; spectrahedra; sums of squares

1. INTRODUCTION

1.1 Problem statement

Let $x = (x_1, \ldots, x_n)$ denote a vector of unknowns. We consider the standard semidefinite programming problem with additional rank constraints, as follows:

$$(\mathrm{SDP})_r \qquad \begin{aligned} &\inf_{x \in \mathbb{R}^n} \ \ell_c(x) \\ &s.t. \ A(x) \succeq 0, \ \ \operatorname{rank} A(x) \leq r \end{aligned} \tag{1}$$

Here $\ell_c(x) = c^T x$, $c \in \mathbb{Q}^n$, $A(x) = A_0 + x_1 A_1 + \cdots + x_n A_n$ is a symmetric linear matrix with $A_i \in \mathbb{S}_m(\mathbb{Q})$ (the set of symmetric matrices of size m with entries in $\mathbb{Q}$), and r is an integer, $0 \leq r \leq m$. The formula $A(x) \succeq 0$ means that $A(x)$ is positive semidefinite (*i.e.*, all its eigenvalues are nonnegative) and is called a linear matrix inequality (LMI). Remark that for $r = m$ this is the standard semidefinite programming problem since the rank constraint is inactive. Moreover, when $c = 0$ (*i.e.*, c is the zero vector), $(\mathrm{SDP})_r$ is a rank-constrained LMI. In the whole paper, we refer to $(\mathrm{SDP})_r$ as a rank-constrained semidefinite program with parameters (m, n, r).

The feasible set $\{x \in \mathbb{R}^n : A(x) \succeq 0\}$ of $(\mathrm{SDP})_m$ is denoted by $\mathscr{S}$, and is called a spectrahedron in the convex algebraic geometry literature, or equivalently LMI-set. It is a convex basic semialgebraic set. Conversely, for $r < m$, $(\mathrm{SDP})_r$ is no more a convex optimization problem, in general. Indeed, denoted by $\mathscr{D}_r = \{x \in \mathbb{C}^n : \operatorname{rank} A(x) \leq r\}$ the determinantal variety associated to $A(x)$ of maximal rank r, the feasible set of $(\mathrm{SDP})_r$ is exactly $\mathscr{S} \cap \mathscr{D}_r \cap \mathbb{R}^n = \mathscr{S} \cap \mathscr{D}_r$.

The purpose of this paper is to design an exact algorithm for solving problem $(\mathrm{SDP})_r$. By exact, we mean that, with rational input data $(c, A_0, A_1, \ldots, A_n) \in \mathbb{Q}^n \times \mathbb{S}_m^{n+1}(\mathbb{Q})$ the output of the algorithm is either an empty list, or a finite set S encoded by a rational parametrization [29]. This is the exact algebraic representation encoded by a vector $Q = (q, q_0, q_1, \ldots, q_n) \subset \mathbb{Q}[t]$ such that q_0, q are coprime and:

$$S = \left\{ \left(\frac{q_1(t)}{q_0(t)}, \ldots, \frac{q_n(t)}{q_0(t)} \right) : q(t) = 0 \right\}. \tag{2}$$

When S is not empty, the degree of q is the algebraic degree of every element in S. When the output is not the empty list, the set S which is returned contains at least one minimizer x^* of $(\mathrm{SDP})_r$. Under general assumptions on input data, which are highlighted and discussed below, the strategy to reach our main goal is twofold:

- we prove that the *semialgebraic* optimization problem $(\mathrm{SDP})_r$ can be reduced to a (*finite*) *sequence* of *algebraic* optimization problems, that is, whose feasible set is real algebraic;
- we adapt previous techniques to design *exact algorithms* for solving the reduced algebraic optimization problems.

The coordinates of a minimizer can be approximated by intervals of arbitrary size of rational numbers, by isolating the real solutions of the univariate equation $q(t) = 0$. For complexity estimates of the real root isolation problem *cf.* [26]: these strongly depend on the degree of the polynomial q, to which we refer as the *output degree* of our algorithm.

Once the output is returned, one can compute the list of minimizers by sorting the set S with respect to the value of the objective function $\ell_c(x)$, and deleting the solutions lying out of the feasible set $\mathscr{S} \cap \mathscr{D}_r$: hence, our goal is also to give a bound for the maximal size of the output set S.

ISSAC '16, July 19-22, 2016, Waterloo, ON, Canada
© 2016 ACM. ISBN 978-1-4503-4380-0/16/07...$15.00
DOI: http://dx.doi.org/10.1145/2930889.2930925

1.2 Motivations and previous work

Several problems in optimization are naturally modeled by (rank-constrained) semidefinite programming, SDP for short [1, 3]. Given $f, f_1, \ldots, f_s \in \mathbb{R}[x]$, the general polynomial optimization problem $\inf\{f(x) : \forall i\, f_i(x) \geq 0\}$ can be reduced to a sequence of semidefinite programs of increasing size (*cf.* Lasserre [20], Parrilo [27]). Since this sequence is almost always finite [23], lots of efforts have been made in order to develop efficient algorithms for SDP. Moreover, LMI and SDP conditions frequently appear in systems control theory [2]. Finding low-rank positive semidefinite matrices also concerns the completion problem for some classes of matrices in combinatorics [21]. Finally, an independent application of SDP-based techniques, but highly related to the polynomial optimization problem, is that of checking nonnegativity of multivariate polynomials. Indeed, deciding whether a given $f \in \mathbb{R}[x_1, \ldots, x_k]$ is a sum of squares of at most r polynomials (hence, nonnegative) is equivalent to a rank-constrained semidefinite program (see Section 6.2 and, *e.g.*, [28]).

The ellipsoid method [11] gives an iterative algorithm for solving any convex optimization problem, whose number of iterations is polynomial in the input parameters with fixed precision (*e.g.*, see [1]), even though it is proved to be inefficient in practice. On the other hand, the extension of Karmakar's interior-point method beyond linear programming [22] yields efficient algorithms for computing floating point approximations of a solution, implemented in several solvers such as SeDuMi, SOSTOOLS *etc.* However, these algorithms cannot, in general, manage additional determinantal conditions or non-convexity. Moreover, SDP relaxations of hard combinatorial optimization problems (as the max-cut [10]) usually discard such algebraic constraints, since they break desirable convexity properties. Moreover, interior-point algorithms cannot certify the emptiness of the feasible set or the reaching of solutions of a given rank, and can often suffer of numerical round-off errors. Remark, here, that if the standard SDP problem $(\text{SDP})_m$ has a solution x^* of rank r, then x^* is also a solution of the non-convex problem $(\text{SDP})_r$ (the viceversa is false, in general). Finally, one cannot extract information about the algebraic degree [24] of the solution with numerical methods.

In [25], Newton-like "tangent and lift" and projection methods for approximating a point at the intersection of a linear space and a manifold are proposed: the authors use this approach for solving rank constrained LMI but, in general, without guarantees of convergence, and with the request of a starting feasible point. Henrion, Safey El Din and the author proposed in [15] an exact algorithm for LMI, via suitable variants of the critical point method. This algorithm, implemented in the Maple library SPECTRA [16], has a runtime essentially quadratic on a multilinear Bézout bound on the output degree, and polynomial in n when m is fixed. This last property is shared with the algorithm in [19], which, however, cannot be used in practice, since it strongly relies on quantifier elimination techniques. The algorithm in [9] is also exact, but cannot manage semialgebraic constraints and has regularity assumptions on the input, which are not satisfied in our case. The related problem of computing witness points on determinantal algebraic sets has been addressed and solved in [12, 13, 14].

1.3 General notation

If $f = \{f_1, \ldots, f_s\} \subset \mathbb{Q}[x]$, we denote by $\mathsf{Z}(f)$ the set of complex solutions of $f_1 = 0, \ldots, f_s = 0$, called a complex algebraic set. We also consider real solutions of polynomial equations, that is the real algebraic set $\mathsf{Z}_{\mathbb{R}}(f)$. If $S \subset \mathbb{C}^n$, the ideal of polynomials vanishing on S is denoted by $\mathsf{I}(S)$. An ideal $I \subset \mathbb{R}[x]$ is called radical if it equals its radical $\sqrt{I} = \{f \in \mathbb{R}[x] : \exists s \in \mathbb{N}, f^s \in I\}$. An ideal of type $\mathsf{I}(S)$ is always a radical ideal. By Hilbert's Nullstellensatz, one has $\mathsf{I}(\mathsf{Z}(I)) = \sqrt{I}$. The Jacobian matrix of partial derivatives of $\{f_1, \ldots, f_s\}$ is denoted by $Df = (\frac{\partial f_i}{\partial x_j})_{i,j}$.

An algebraic set $V \subset \mathbb{C}^n$ is called irreducible if it is not the union of two proper algebraic subsets; otherwise it is the finite union of irreducible algebraic sets $V = V_1 \cup \cdots \cup V_s$, called the irreducible components. The dimension of V is the Krull dimension of its coordinate ring $\mathbb{C}[x]/\mathsf{I}(V)$. If the V_i in the previous decomposition have the same dimension d, then V is equidimensional of dimension d. Let $V \subset \mathbb{C}^n$ be equidimensional of co-dimension c, and let $\mathsf{I}(V) = \langle f_1, \ldots, f_s \rangle$. We say that V is smooth if its singular locus, that is the algebraic set defined by $f = (f_1, \ldots, f_s)$ and by the $c \times c$ minors of Df, is empty. A set $\mathscr{E} = \mathsf{Z}(I) \setminus \mathsf{Z}(J)$ is called locally closed, and its dimension is the dimension of its Zariski closure $\mathsf{Z}(\mathsf{I}(\mathscr{E}))$.

If V is equidimensional and smooth, and if $g \colon \mathbb{C}^n \to \mathbb{C}^m$ is an algebraic map, the critical points of the restriction of g to V are denoted by $\text{crit}\,(g, V)$, and defined by $f = (f_1, \ldots, f_s)$ and by the $c+m$ minors of $D(f, g)$. Equivalently, a point $x \in V$ is critical for g on V if and only if the differential map $dg \colon T_x V \to \mathbb{C}^m$ is not surjective (where $T_x V$ is the Zariski tangent space of V at x, *cf.* [31, Sec. 2.1.2]). The elements of $g(\text{crit}\,(g, V))$ are the critical values, and the elements of $\mathbb{C}^m \setminus g(\text{crit}\,(g, V))$ are the regular values of the restriction of g to V.

Let $S \subset \mathbb{R}^n$ be any set, and let $f \colon \mathbb{R}^n \to \mathbb{R}$ be a continuous function with respect to the Euclidean topology of $\mathbb{R}^n$ and $\mathbb{R}$. A point $x^* \in S$ is a local minimizer of f on S, if there exists an Euclidean open set $U \subset \mathbb{R}^n$ such that $x^* \in U$ and $f(x^*) \leq f(x)$ for every $x \in U \cap S$. A point $x^* \in S$ is a minimizer of f on S if $f(x^*) \leq f(x)$ for every $x \in S$. In particular, if $C \subset S$ is a connected component of S, every minimizer of f on C is a local minimizer of f on S.

We finally recall the notation introduced previously. We consider $m \times m$ symmetric matrices $A_0, A_1, \ldots, A_n \in \mathbb{S}_m(\mathbb{Q})$, and a linear matrix $A(x) = A_0 + x_1 A_1 + \cdots + x_n A_n$. The convex set $\mathscr{S} = \{x \in \mathbb{R}^n : A(x) \succeq 0\}$ is called a spectrahedron. The integer $r \in \mathbb{N}$ will denote the maximal admissible rank in (1). Given an integer $p \in \mathbb{N}$, with $0 \leq p \leq r$, we denote by $\mathscr{D}_p = \{x \in \mathbb{C}^n : \text{rank} A(x) \leq p\}$ the determinantal variety of maximal rank p generated by $A(x)$.

1.4 Outline of main results

We consider the rank-constrained semidefinite programming problem (1), encoded by rational data $(c, A) \in \mathbb{Q}^n \times \mathbb{S}_m^{n+1}(\mathbb{Q})$, and by the integer r related to the rank constraint. Our paper can be divided into two parts.

In the first part (Sections 2 and 3) we prove geometrical properties of problem $(\text{SDP})_r$. In Section 2.1, we represent the algebraic sets $\mathscr{D}_p, p = 0, \ldots, r$, as projections of incidence varieties defined by bilinear equations, and in Proposition 1 we prove that the latter sets are generically smooth and equidimensional. The solutions of $(\text{SDP})_r$ are also local minimizers of ℓ_c on $\mathscr{D}_p \cap \mathbb{R}^n$ (this is proved in Theorem 4) and are obtained as the projection of critical points of the same map restricted to the incidence varieties (Lemma 2), which are finitely many (Proposition 3). As an outcome, we prove that a *generic* rank-constrained semidefinite program admits finitely many minimizers (Corollary 6).

The second part hosts the formal description of an algorithm for solving $(\text{SDP})_r$ (Section 4) and its correctness (Theorem 7). A complexity analysis is then performed in Section 5, with explicit bounds on the size of the output set S (*cf.* (2)) computed in Proposition 8. We finally discuss the results of numerical tests performed via a first implementation of our algorithm in Section 6.

2. PRELIMINARIES

2.1 Representation via incidence varieties

The algebraic set $\mathscr{D}_p$ will not be represented as the vanishing locus of the $(p+1)\times(p+1)$ minors of $A(x)$, mainly by two reasons. The first is that computing determinants is a difficult task. Even if this first issue could be avoided by some precomputation, the singularities of determinantal varieties appear generically. We are going to represent $\mathscr{D}_p$ as the projection of a more regular algebraic set, reviewing a classical construction.

Let V be a vector space of dimension d and let $\mathbb{G}(e,d)$ be the Grassmannian of linear subspaces of dimension e of V, with $e \leq d$. Fixed a basis of V, a point $L = \mathrm{span}(v_1,\ldots,v_e) \in \mathbb{G}(e,d)$ is represented by the $d\times e$ matrix whose columns are $v_1,\ldots,v_e$. With this in mind, we consider linear subspaces of $\mathbb{C}^m$ to model rank defects in $A(x)$.

Let $A(x) \in \mathbb{S}_m^{n+1}(\mathbb{Q})$, and let $p,r \in \mathbb{N}$, with $0 \leq p \leq r \leq m$. We denote by $Y(y) = (y_{i,j})$ a $m\times(m-p)$ matrix with unknowns entries. Then, for $x^* \in \mathbb{C}^n$, $A(x^*)$ has rank at most p, if and only if there is $y^* \in \mathbb{C}^{m(m-p)}$ such that $A(x^*)Y(y^*) = 0$, with $\mathrm{rank}\, Y(y^*) = m-p$. Moreover, one can suppose that one of the maximal minors of $Y(y^*)$ is the identity matrix I_{m-p} (*cf.* for example [8, Sec. 2]).

For $\iota \subset \{1,\ldots,m\}$ with $\#\iota = m-p$, we denote by Y_ι the maximal minor of $Y(y)$ whose rows are indexed by ι. We deduce that $\mathscr{D}_p$ is the image under the projection $\pi_n \colon \mathbb{C}^n \times \mathbb{C}^{m(m-p)} \to \mathbb{C}^n$ of the algebraic set

$$\mathscr{V}_p = \bigcup_{\substack{\iota \subset \{1,\ldots,m\} \\ \#\iota = m-p}} \mathscr{V}_{p,\iota}$$

where $\mathscr{V}_{p,\iota} = \{(x,y) \in \mathbb{C}^n \times \mathbb{C}^{m(m-p)} : A(x)Y(y) = 0, Y_\iota = \mathrm{I}_{m-p}\}$. We call the sets $\mathscr{V}_{p,\iota}$ *incidence varieties* for $\mathscr{D}_p$. We denote by $f(A,\iota)$ (often simply by f) the polynomial system defining $\mathscr{V}_{p,\iota}$. We prove the following Proposition on the regularity of $\mathscr{V}_{p,\iota}$.

Proposition 1 *Let $\iota \subset \{1,\ldots,m\}$ with $\#\iota = m-p$.*

1. *There is a subsystem $f_{red} \subset f(A,\iota)$ of cardinality $\#f_{red} = m(m-p)+\binom{m-p+1}{2}$ such that $\mathrm{Z}(f_{red}) = \mathrm{Z}(f(A,\iota)) = \mathscr{V}_{p,\iota}$.*
2. *There is a non-empty Zariski open set $\mathscr{A} \subset \mathbb{S}_m^{n+1}(\mathbb{C})$ such that, if $A \in \mathscr{A} \cap \mathbb{S}_m^{n+1}(\mathbb{Q})$, $\mathscr{V}_{p,\iota}$ is either empty or smooth and equidimensional of co-dimension $m(m-p)+\binom{m-p+1}{2}$, and f generates a radical ideal.*

PROOF. We start with Point 1. Suppose without loss of generality that $\iota = \{1,\ldots,m-p\}$, and denote by $g_{i,j}$ the $(i,j)-$th entry of the matrix $A(x)Y(y)$ where Y_ι has been substituted by I_{m-p}. The system f_{red} is defined as follows: $f_{red} = (g_{i,j} \text{ for } i \geq j, Y_\iota - \mathrm{I}_{m-p})$. We prove now that $\mathrm{Z}(f_{red}) = \mathrm{Z}(f(A,\iota))$. If $a_{i,j}$ is the $(i,j)-$th entry of A, for $i<j$ one has that $g_{i,j} - g_{j,i} = \sum_{\ell=m-p+1}^{m} a_{i,\ell}y_{\ell,j} - a_{j,\ell}y_{\ell,i}$, since A is symmetric. Using the polynomial relations $g_{k,\ell} = 0$ for $k > m-p$ one can solve for $a_{i,\ell}$ and $a_{j,\ell}$, and deduce

$$\begin{aligned} g_{i,j} - g_{j,i} &\equiv \\ &\equiv \sum_{\ell=m-p+1}^{m} \left(-\sum_{t=m-p+1}^{m} a_{\ell,t}y_{t,i}y_{\ell,j} + \sum_{t=m-p+1}^{m} a_{\ell,t}y_{t,j}y_{\ell,i} \right) \\ &\equiv \sum_{\ell,t=m-p+1}^{m} a_{\ell,t}\left(-y_{t,i}y_{\ell,j} + y_{t,j}y_{\ell,i}\right) \equiv 0 \end{aligned}$$

modulo $\langle g_{k,\ell}, k > m-p \rangle$. This proves Point 1.

We now give the proof of Point 2. We denote by φ the polynomial map : $\mathbb{C}^{n+m(m-p)} \times \mathbb{S}_m^{n+1}(\mathbb{C}) \to \mathbb{C}^{m(m-p)+\binom{m-p+1}{2}}$ sending (x,y,A) to $f_{red}(x,y,A)$, and let φ_A denote the section map $\varphi_A(x,y) = \varphi(x,y,A)$. Hence $\varphi_A^{-1}(0) = \mathscr{V}_{p,\iota}$. If $\varphi^{-1}(0) = \emptyset$, then for all $A \in \mathbb{S}_m^{n+1}(\mathbb{C})$, $\varphi_A^{-1}(0) = \mathscr{V}_{p,\iota} = \emptyset$, and we conclude defining $\mathscr{A} = \mathbb{S}_m^{n+1}(\mathbb{C})$.

If $\varphi^{-1}(0) \neq \emptyset$, we prove below that 0 is a regular value of φ. We deduce by Thom's Weak Transversality Theorem [30, Sec.4.2] that there exists a non-empty Zariski open set $\mathscr{A}_\iota \subset \mathbb{S}_m^{n+1}(\mathbb{C})$ such that for $A \in \mathscr{A}_\iota$, 0 is a regular value of φ_A. We finally deduce by the Jacobian Criterion [4, Th.16.19] that for $A \in \mathscr{A}_\iota$, $\mathscr{V}_{p,\iota}$ is smooth and equidimensional of co-dimension $m(m-p)+\binom{m-p+1}{2}$, and that the ideal generated by f_{red} is radical. We conclude defining $\mathscr{A} = \cap_\iota \mathscr{A}_\iota$.

Now we only have to prove that 0 is a regular value of φ. Let $D\varphi$ be the Jacobian matrix of φ. We denote by $a_{\ell,i,j}$ the variable representing the $(i,j)-$th entry of A. We consider the derivatives of elements in f_{red} with respect to:

- the variables $\eta = \{a_{0,i,j} : i \leq m-p \text{ or } j \leq m-p\}$;
- the variables $y_{i,j}$ with $i \in \iota$.

Let $(x,y,A) \in \varphi^{-1}(0)$. The submatrix of $D\varphi(x,y,A)$ containing such derivatives, contains the following non-singular blocks: the derivatives of $A(x)Y(y)$ w.r.t. elements in η, that is a unit block $\mathrm{I}_{(m-p)(m+p+1)/2}$; the derivatives of $Y_\iota - \mathrm{I}_{m-p}$, that is a unit block $\mathrm{I}_{(m-r)^2}$. These two blocks are orthogonal, and we deduce that $D\varphi$ is full rank at the point (x,y,A). Since (x,y,A) is arbitrary in $\varphi^{-1}(0)$, we conclude that 0 is a regular value of φ. □

2.2 Critical points

In this section we consider polynomial systems encoding the local minimizers of the linear function $\ell_c(x) \colon \mathbb{R}^n \to \mathbb{R}$ in (1) restricted to the determinantal variety $\mathscr{D}_p \cap \mathbb{R}^n$, with $0 \leq p \leq r$. We denote by L_c the map $L_c \colon \mathbb{R}^{n+m(m-p)} \to \mathbb{R}$ sending (x,y) to $c^T x$, that is $L_c = \ell_c \circ \pi_n$, with $\pi_n \colon \mathbb{R}^{n+m(m-p)} \to \mathbb{R}^n$, $\pi_n(x,y) = x$. With analogy to the description of $\mathscr{D}_p$ via incidence varieties of the previous section, we consider the set $\mathrm{crit}(\ell_c, \mathscr{V}_{p,\iota} \cap \mathbb{R}^{n+m(m-p)})$ of critical points of the restriction of L_c to $\mathscr{V}_{p,\iota} \cap \mathbb{R}^{n+m(m-p)}$.

Lemma 2 *Let $\mathscr{A} \subset \mathbb{S}_m^{n+1}(\mathbb{C})$ be the Zariski open set given in Proposition 1, and let $A \in \mathscr{A}$. The set of local minimizers of ℓ_c on $\mathscr{D}_p \cap \mathbb{R}^n$ is contained in the image of the union of the sets $\mathrm{crit}(L_c, \mathscr{V}_{p,\iota})$, for $\iota \subset \{1,\ldots,m\}$, with $\#\iota = m-p$, via the projection map $\pi_n(x,y) = x$.*

PROOF. Let $\tilde{x} \in \mathbb{R}^n$ be a local minimizer of ℓ_c on $\mathscr{D}_p \cap \mathbb{R}^n$, and let $C_{\tilde{x}} \subset \mathscr{D}_p \cap \mathbb{R}^n$ be the connected component containing x. Let $t = \ell_c(\tilde{x})$. Then $\ell_c(x) \geq t$ for all $x \in U \cap C_{\tilde{x}}$, for some U connected open set. By definition of $\mathscr{V}_p$, and since $\tilde{x} \in \mathscr{D}_p$, there exists $\iota \subset \{1,\ldots,m-p\}$ and $\tilde{y} \in \mathbb{R}^{m(m-p)}$ such that $(\tilde{x},\tilde{y}) \in \mathscr{V}_{p,\iota}$. Let $C_{(\tilde{x},\tilde{y})}$ be the connected component of $\mathscr{V}_{p,\iota} \cap \mathbb{R}^{n+m(m-p)}$ containing $(\tilde{x},\tilde{y})$. We claim (and prove below) that $(\tilde{x},\tilde{y})$ is a minimizer of L_c on $\pi_n^{-1}(U) \cap C_{(\tilde{x},\tilde{y})}$, hence local minimizer on $\pi_n^{-1}(U) \cap \mathscr{V}_{p,\iota}$. We deduce that $t = \ell_c(\tilde{x}) = L_c(\tilde{x},\tilde{y})$ lies in the boundary of $L_c(\pi_n^{-1}(U) \cap C_{\tilde{x},\tilde{y}})$. In particular, the differential map of L_c at x is not surjective: because $A \in \mathscr{A}$, then $\mathscr{V}_{p,\iota}$ is smooth and equidimensional, and hence $(\tilde{x},\tilde{y}) \in \mathrm{crit}(L_c, \mathscr{V}_{p,\iota} \cap \mathbb{R}^{m(m-p)})$.

Recall that $L_c(\tilde{x},\tilde{y}) = \ell_c(\tilde{x}) = t$, and suppose that there is $(x,y) \in \pi_n^{-1}(U) \cap C_{(\tilde{x},\tilde{y})}$ such that $L_c(x,y) < t$. There exists a continuous semialgebraic map $\tau \colon [0,1] \to C_{(\tilde{x},\tilde{y})}$ such that $\tau(0) = (\tilde{x},\tilde{y})$ and $\tau(1) = (x,y)$. We deduce that $\pi_n \circ \tau$ is also continuous and semialgebraic (since π_n is). Since $\pi_n \circ \tau(0) = \tilde{x}$ and $\pi_n \circ \tau(1) = x$, one gets $x \in U \cap C_{\tilde{x}}$. Then $\ell_c(x) = L_c(x,y) < t = \ell_c(\tilde{x})$ contradicts the hypothesis that $\tilde{x}$ is a local minimizer of ℓ_c on $C_{\tilde{x}}$. □

Lemma 2 states that the minimizers of ℓ_c on $\mathscr{D}_p \cap \mathbb{R}^n$ are obtained as the projection on the first n variables of the critical points of L_c over the lifted incidence variety $\mathscr{V}_p \cap \mathbb{R}^{n+m(m-p)}$. We are now going to prove that such critical points are generically finite. Let us suppose that $A \in \mathscr{A}$ (see Proposition 1), and let $c \in \mathbb{Q}^n$. We also fix a subset $\iota \subset \{1,\ldots,m\}$ of cardinality $\#\iota = m-p$.

We have denoted, in Section 2.1, by $f \subset \mathbb{Q}[x,y]$ the polynomial system defining $\mathscr{V}_{p,\iota}$, constituted by the entries of $A(x)Y(y)$ and of $Y_\iota - \mathrm{I}_{m-p}$. By Proposition 1, we deduce that f_{red}, and hence f, generates a radical ideal and defines a smooth equidimensional algebraic set of co-dimension $m(m-p)+\binom{m-p+1}{2}$. The set $\mathrm{crit}(L_c, \mathscr{V}_{p,\iota})$ is hence defined (modulo eliminating the Lagrange multipliers) by the following polynomial system:

$$\mathrm{lag}(\iota): \qquad f=0; \quad (g,h) = z' \begin{bmatrix} Df \\ DL_c \end{bmatrix} = 0, \qquad (3)$$

where $z = (z_1,\ldots,z_{(2m-p)(m-p)},1)$ is the vector of Lagrange multipliers: these are the classical first-order optimality conditions. In the previous notation, the vector g (resp. h) is of size n (resp. $m(m-p)$). For the sake of brevity, we say that a point $(x,y,z) \in \mathsf{Z}(\mathrm{lag}(\iota))$ has rank p, if $\mathrm{rank} A(x) = p$.

Our next goal in this section is to prove the following Proposition. It states that if the linear function ℓ_c in Problem (1) is generic, the points $x^* \in \mathscr{D}_p \cap \mathbb{R}^n$, such that $\mathrm{rank} A(x^*) = p$, that correspond to critical points (x^*, y^*) of the restriction of L_c to $\mathscr{V}_p \cap \mathbb{R}^{n+m(m-p)}$, are finitely many.

Proposition 3 *Let $\mathscr{A} \subset \mathbb{S}_m^{n+1}(\mathbb{C})$ be the Zariski open set defined by Proposition 1, and let $A \in \mathscr{A} \cap \mathbb{S}_m^{n+1}(\mathbb{Q})$. There exists a non-empty Zariski open set $\mathscr{C} \subset \mathbb{C}^n$ such that, for $c \in \mathscr{C} \cap \mathbb{Q}^n$, for every $p = 0,\ldots,r$, and for every $\iota \subset \{1,\ldots,m\}$ such that $\#\iota = m-p$, the projection of the solutions of the system lag(ι) of rank p over the x−space is a finite set.*

In order to prove Proposition 3, we use the local description of determinantal varieties as developed in [12, Sec. 4.1] and in [13, Sec. 5.1]. This is briefly recalled below. Suppose that $x \in \mathscr{D}_p \cap \mathbb{R}^n$, with $\mathrm{rank} A(x) = p$, and that the upper-left $p \times p$ submatrix N of $A(x)$ is non-singular (at least one of the $p \times p$ submatrices of $A(x)$ is non-singular). That is

$$A(x) = \begin{bmatrix} N & Q \\ P & R \end{bmatrix} \qquad (4)$$

and $\det N \neq 0$. Suppose also w.l.o.g. that $\iota = \{1,\ldots,m-p\}$. By [12, Sec.4.1] or [14, Lemma 13], the local equations of $\mathscr{V}_{p,\iota}$ over x are given by

$$\begin{bmatrix} \mathrm{I}_p & N^{-1}Q \\ 0 & \Sigma(N) \end{bmatrix} Y(y) = 0 \qquad \text{and} \qquad Y_\iota - \mathrm{I}_{m-p} = 0, \qquad (5)$$

where $\Sigma(N) = R - PN^{-1}Q$ is the Schur complement of $A(x)$ at N, well defined since N is not singular: these are elements of the local ring $\mathbb{Q}[x,y]_{\det N}$ at $I = \langle \det N \rangle$. Let $Y^{(1)}$ (resp. $Y^{(2)}$) be the matrix obtained by isolating the first p rows (resp. last $m-p$ rows) from $Y(y)$. Let U_ι be such that $U_\iota Y(y) = Y_\iota$, and let $U_\iota = U_\iota^{(1)} | U_\iota^{(2)}$ be the corresponding column subdivision of U_ι. Then (5) imply $\mathrm{I}_{m-p} = U_\iota^{(1)} Y^{(1)} + U_\iota^{(2)} Y^{(2)} = (U_\iota^{(2)} - U_\iota^{(1)} N^{-1} Q) Y^{(2)}$ and hence that both $Y^{(2)}$ and $U_\iota^{(2)} - U_\iota^{(1)} N^{-1} Q$ are invertible (in the local ring $\mathbb{Q}[x]_{\det N}$). We deduce the following equivalent form of the previous equations:

$$\tilde{f}: \qquad \begin{array}{l} Y^{(1)} + N^{-1} Q Y^{(2)} = 0, \quad \Sigma(N) = 0, \\ Y^{(2)} - (U_\iota^{(2)} - U_\iota^{(1)} N^{-1} Q)^{-1} = 0, \end{array} \qquad (6)$$

denoted by $\tilde{f}$. Up to reordering its entries, the Jacobian matrix of $\tilde{f}$ is

$$D\tilde{f} = \begin{bmatrix} D_x[\Sigma(N)]_{i,j} & 0_{(m-p)^2 \times m(m-p)} & \\ \star & \mathrm{I}_{p(m-p)} & \star \\ & 0 & \mathrm{I}_{(m-p)^2} \end{bmatrix}.$$

If $A \in \mathscr{A}$, by Proposition 1 the rank of $D\tilde{f}$ equals $\#f_{red} = m(m-r) + \binom{m-r+1}{2}$ at every $x \in \mathsf{Z}(\tilde{f})$. Similarly, we localize the Lagrange system lag(ι) (*cf.* (3)) by defining:

$$(\tilde{g}, \tilde{h}) = z' \begin{bmatrix} D\tilde{f} \\ DL_c \end{bmatrix}.$$

By the structure of $D\tilde{f}$, one gets $\tilde{h}_i = z_{(m-p)^2+i}$, for $i = 1,\ldots,m(m-p)$, and hence one can substitute $z_{(m-p)^2+i} = 0, i = 1,\ldots,m(m-p)$, in $(\tilde{f}, \tilde{g})$.

PROOF OF PROPOSITION 3. Let $d = m(m-p) + \binom{m-p+1}{2}$ and $e = \binom{m-p}{2}$ so that $d + e = (2m-p)(m-p) = \#z$. First, we claim that there exists a non-empty Zariski open set $\mathscr{C}_N \subset \mathbb{C}^n$ such that if $c \in \mathscr{C}_N \cap \mathbb{Q}^n$ the Jacobian matrix of the local system $(\tilde{f}, \tilde{g}, \tilde{h})$ has maximal possible rank. Here N refers to the upper left $p \times p$ submatrix of A as above. We conclude by defining $\mathscr{C} = \cap_N \mathscr{C}_N$ (where N runs over the family of $p \times p$ submatrices of A), which is non-empty and Zariski open.

The proof is similar to that of Point 2 of Proposition 1 and hence we only sketch it. Let

$$\begin{array}{rccc} \varphi: & \mathbb{C}^{n+d+e+m(m-p)} \times \mathbb{C}^n & \longrightarrow & \mathbb{C}^{n+d+e+m(m-p)} \\ & (x,y,z,c) & \longmapsto & (\tilde{f}, \tilde{g}, \tilde{h})(x,y,z,c). \end{array}$$

Then the Jacobian matrix of $(\tilde{f}, \tilde{g}, \tilde{h})$ is $D\varphi$ as a polynomial map. We prove that 0 is a regular value of φ, and apply Thom's Weak Transversality Theorem [30, Sec.4.2] as in the proof of Proposition 1. Let $(x,y,z,c) \in \varphi^{-1}(0)$ (if it does not exist, define $\mathscr{C}_N = \mathbb{C}^n$). Since polynomials in $\tilde{f}$ only depend on x and y, then $D\tilde{f}$ is a submatrix of $D\varphi$ and the columns corresponding to the derivatives with respect to z of $\tilde{f}$ are zero. Hence the rank of $D\varphi$ is at most $n+d+m(m-r)$ since $D\tilde{f}$ has e rank defects by Proposition 1 (recall that $A \in \mathscr{A}$). A $(n+d+m(m-p)) \times (n+d+m(m-p))$ full-rank submatrix of $D\varphi$ at (x,y,z,c) is given by: the derivatives with respect to: (1) x, y, (2) $c_1,\ldots,c_n$, and (3) $z_{(m-p)^2+i}, i = 1,\ldots,m(m-p)$.

Now, we can conclude the proof. Let $c \in \mathscr{C} = \cap_N \mathscr{C}_N$ (previously defined). From the previous claim, we deduce that the locally closed set $\mathscr{E} = \mathsf{Z}(\mathrm{lag}(\iota)) \cap \{(x,y,z) : \mathrm{rank} A(x) = p\}$ is empty or equidimensional of dimension e. Let

$$\begin{array}{rccc} \pi: & \mathbb{C}^{n+m(m-p)+d+e} & \longrightarrow & \mathbb{C}^n \\ & (x,y,z) & \longmapsto & x \end{array}$$

be the projection over the x−space, and $x^* \in \pi(\mathscr{E})$. In particular $\mathrm{rank} A(x^*) = p$, and there is a unique $y^* \in \mathbb{C}^{m(m-p)}$ such that $f(x^*, y^*) = 0$. We deduce that $\pi^{-1}(x^*)$ is isomorphic to the linear space defined by

$$\left\{ (z_1,\ldots,z_{d+e}) : (z_1,\ldots,z_{d+e}) Df = (c', 0) \right\}.$$

Since the rank of Df is d, $\pi^{-1}(x^*)$ is a linear space of dimension e, and by the Theorem on the Dimension of Fibers [31, Sect. 6.3, Theorem 7] $\pi_x(\mathscr{E})$ has dimension 0. □

3. FROM SEMI-ALGEBRAIC TO ALGEBRAIC OPTIMIZATION

In order to prove that our algorithm is correct, we present in this section the main geometric result of this work. By the independent interest of the results of this section, we need to introduce, first, some notation.

Given $c \in \mathbb{Q}^n$ and $A \in \mathbb{S}_m^{n+1}(\mathbb{Q})$, for $0 \leq r \leq m$, we have denoted by $\mathscr{F}_r(A,c)$ the (possibly empty or infinite) set of minimizers of ℓ_c on $\mathscr{S} \cap \mathscr{D}_r$. By simplicity, we also call $\mathscr{F}_r(A,c)$ the set of minimizers of $(\text{SDP})_r$. When $r = m$, $\mathscr{F}_m(A,c)$ is the convex optimal face of the spectrahedron $\mathscr{S}$ in direction c. Indeed, since every face of a spectrahedron is exposed, it is exactly defined as the set of minimizers of some semidefinite program $(\text{SDP})_m$. We denote by

$$\mathscr{R}_r(A,c) = \left\{ p : 0 \leq p \leq r, \exists x \in \mathscr{F}_r(A,c), \operatorname{rank} A(x) = p \right\}$$

the rank profile of $\mathscr{F}_r(A,c)$. Clearly, $\mathscr{F}_r(A,c) \neq \emptyset$ if and only if $\mathscr{R}_r(A,c) \neq \emptyset$. This is our main theorem in this section.

Theorem 4 *Suppose that $\mathscr{F}_r(A,c) \neq \emptyset$, and let $p \in \mathscr{R}_r(A,c)$. For $x^* \in \mathscr{F}_r(A,c)$ such that $\operatorname{rank} A(x^*) = p$, then x^* is a local minimizer of ℓ_c on $\mathscr{D}_p \cap \mathbb{R}^n$.*

PROOF. Suppose that x^* is as in the hypothesis. We denote by $C^* \subset \mathscr{D}_p \cap \mathbb{R}^n$ the connected component of $\mathscr{D}_p \cap \mathbb{R}^n$ containing x^*. Hence there are three possible (non mutually exclusive) cases, that we analyze below. Recall that $p \leq r$, hence $\mathscr{D}_p \subset \mathscr{D}_r$.

First case: $C^* \subset \mathscr{S}$. Hence $C^* \subset \mathscr{S} \cap \mathscr{D}_p \subset \mathscr{S} \cap \mathscr{D}_r$. Since $\mathscr{S} \cap \mathscr{D}_r$ is the feasible set of $(\text{SDP})_r$ and x^* is a minimizer of $(\text{SDP})_r$, hence x^* is a minimizer of ℓ_c on C^*. Hence it is a local minimizer of ℓ_c on $\mathscr{D}_p \cap \mathbb{R}^n$, as claimed.

Second case: There exists an open set $U \subset \mathbb{R}^n$ such that $x^* \in U$ and $U \cap (\mathscr{D}_{m-1} \setminus \mathscr{S}) = \emptyset$. This means that U intersects $\mathscr{D}_{m-1} \cap \mathbb{R}^n$ only at positive semidefinite matrices, and $U \cap \mathscr{S}$ is an open subset of $\mathscr{S}$ containing x^*. We deduce that x^* is a minimizer of ℓ_c on $U \cap \mathscr{D}_p \subset U \cap \mathscr{S}$, hence a local minimizer of ℓ_c on $\mathscr{D}_p \cap \mathbb{R}^n$.

Third case: $C^* \not\subset \mathscr{S}$, and for all $U \subset \mathbb{R}^n$ open set, such that $x^* \in U$, then $U \cap (\mathscr{D}_{m-1} \setminus \mathscr{S}) \neq \emptyset$. We prove below that such a situation cannot occur. Indeed, one first deduces that, for all U as above, $U \cap (\mathscr{D}_p \setminus \mathscr{S}) \neq \emptyset$ since $C^* \not\subset \mathscr{S}$. For a positive integer $d \in \mathbb{N}$, we denote by $B(x^*, 1/d)$ the open ball with center x^* and radius $1/d$, that is $B(x^*, 1/d) = \{x \in \mathbb{R}^n : \|x - x^*\| < 1/d\}$, where $\|x\|$ is the Euclidean norm of x. By hypothesis, for all $d \in \mathbb{N}$ there exists $x(d) \in B(x^*, 1/d) \cap \mathscr{D}_p$ such that $A(x(d)) \not\succeq 0$. Hence $x(d) \to x^*$ when $d \to \infty$. Denoting by $e_1(x) \leq e_2(x) \leq \cdots \leq e_m(x)$ the ordered eigenvalues of $A(x)$, one deduces that, for all $d \in \mathbb{N}$, $e_1(x(d)) < 0$ and hence $e_{m-p+1}(x(d)) \leq 0$ (since the matrix $A(x(d))$ has at least $m-p$ null eigenvalues). In particular $e_{m-p+1}(x(d)) \to e_{m-p+1}(x^*) \leq 0$ when $d \to \infty$. Since $x^* \in \mathscr{S}$, then $e_1(x^*) = \cdots = e_{m-p}(x^*) = e_{m-p+1}(x^*) = 0$, and the rank of $A(x^*)$ is at most $p-1$, which contradicts the hypotheses. □

We prove two corollaries of Theorem 4 and of previous results, which are worth to be made explicit and highlighted.

Corollary 5 *Let $x^* \in \mathscr{F}_r(A,c)$ satisfy the following property: for all Euclidean open sets $U \subset \mathbb{R}^n$ containing x^*, U contains a matrix with a negative eigenvalue. Then, if $p = \operatorname{rank} A(x^*)$, the connected component $C^* \subset \mathscr{D}_p \cap \mathbb{R}^n$ containing x^* is contained in $\mathscr{S}$.*

PROOF. We apply *mutatis mutandis* the argument of the Third case in the proof of Theorem 4, without the hypothesis that $C^* \not\subset \mathscr{S}$. Hence we conclude that necessarily $C^* \subset \mathscr{S}$. □

The second corollary gives a finiteness theorem for the set of solutions of a generic rank constrained semidefinite program (1).

Corollary 6 *Let $\mathscr{A} \subset \mathbb{S}_m^{n+1}(\mathbb{C})$ and $\mathscr{C} \subset \mathbb{C}^n$ be the Zariski open sets defined respectively in Proposition 1 and 3. If $A \in \mathscr{A} \cap \mathbb{S}_m^{n+1}(\mathbb{Q})$ and $c \in \mathscr{C} \cap \mathbb{Q}^n$, the set $\mathscr{F}_r(A,c)$ of minimizers of the rank-constrained semidefinite program $(SDP)_r$ is finite.*

PROOF. Remark that $\mathscr{F}_r(A,c)$ is the union of sets $B_p \subset \mathscr{F}_r(A,c)$, for $p \in \mathscr{R}_r(A,c)$, corresponding to minimizers of rank p, that is $\mathscr{F}_r(A,c) = \cup_{p \in \mathscr{R}_r(A,c)} B_p$. We prove that B_p is finite for all $p \in \mathscr{R}_r(A,c)$.

Let $x^* \in B_p$. By Theorem 4, x^* is a local minimizer of ℓ_c on $\mathscr{D}_p \cap \mathbb{R}^n$. Since $A \in \mathscr{A}$, by Lemma 2 B_p is included in the union of the projections of the sets of critical points of L_c on $\mathscr{V}_{p,\iota}$, for $\iota \subset \{1,\ldots,m\}, \#\iota = m-p$. Since $c \in \mathscr{C}$, and since $\operatorname{rank} A(x^*) = p$, by Proposition 3 B_p is the projection of a finite set, hence finite. □

4. THE ALGORITHM

The main algorithm described in this work is called SOLVESDP.

4.1 Description

We first describe the main subroutines of SOLVESDP.

CheckReg. With input $A \in \mathbb{S}_m^{n+1}(\mathbb{Q})$ and $p \leq r$, it returns `true` if for all $\iota \subset \{1,\ldots,m\}$, with $\#\iota = m-p$, the set $\mathscr{V}_{p,\iota}$ is smooth and equidimensional; otherwise, it returns `false`.

Optimize. With input A, c and p, it returns the vector of ideals $(\operatorname{lag}(\iota_1), \ldots, \operatorname{lag}(\iota_{\binom{m}{p}})) \subset \mathbb{Q}[x,y,z]$, where $\iota_j \subset \{1,\ldots,m\}$, with $\#\iota_j = m-p$, $j = 1,\ldots,\binom{m}{p}$. The set $\cup_j \mathsf{Z}(\operatorname{lag}(\iota_j))$ encodes the union of the critical points of L_c restricted to the components $\mathscr{V}_{p,\iota}$ of $\mathscr{V}_p$.

Project. With input the output of Optimize, it substitutes each ideal $\operatorname{lag}(\iota_j)$ with the elimination ideal $I_{\iota_j} = \operatorname{lag}(\iota_j) \cap \mathbb{Q}[x]$, for $j = 1,\ldots,\binom{m}{p}$, returning $I = (I_{\iota_j}, i = 1,\ldots,\binom{m}{p})$.

We recall the definition of rational parametrization of a finite set $S \subset \mathbb{R}^n$: this is given by a vector $Q = (q, q_0, q_1, \ldots, q_n) \subset \mathbb{Q}[t]$ such that S admits a representation (2). We need to define two routines performing operations on rational parametrizations of finite sets.

RatPar. Given a zero-dimensional ideal $I_{\iota_j} \subset \mathbb{Q}[x]$, it returns a rational parametrization $Q = (q, q_0, q_1, \ldots, q_n) \subset \mathbb{Q}[t]$ of I_{ι_j}. If I_{ι_j} is not zero-dimensional, it returns an error message.

Union. Given rational parametrizations $Q_1, Q_2 \subset \mathbb{Q}[t]$ encoding two finite sets $V_1, V_2 \subset \mathbb{C}^n$, it returns a rational parametrization $Q \subset \mathbb{Q}[t]$ encoding $V_1 \cup V_2$.

The following is the formal procedure of SOLVESDP. We offer below a more explicit description of the algorithm for the sake of clarity.

Algorithm 1 SolveSDP

procedure SOLVESDP(A, c, r)
  $Q \leftarrow [\,]$
  for $p = 0, \ldots, r$ **do**
    if CheckReg(A, p) = `false` **then return** error
    $I \leftarrow$ Project(Optimize(A, c, p))
    for $j = 1, \ldots, \binom{m}{p}$ **do**
      $Q_{\iota_j} \leftarrow$ RatPar(I_{ι_j})
      $Q \leftarrow$ Union(Q, Q_{ι_j})
  return Q

The input is a triple (A, c, r), where $A \in \mathbb{S}_m^{n+1}(\mathbb{Q})$ is $(n+1)$−tuple of symmetric matrices with rational coefficients, $c \in \mathbb{Q}^n$ defines the linear function ℓ_c in (1) and r is the maximum admissible rank. For every value of p from 0 to r, the algorithm checks whether the regularity assumption on the incidence varieties $\mathscr{V}_{p,\iota}, \iota \subset \{1,\ldots,m\}$, for $\#\iota = m-p$, holds. If this is the case, it computes rational parametrizations Q_ι of the Lagrange systems encoding the critical points of the map L_c, on the components $\mathscr{V}_{p,\iota}$ of the incidence variety $\mathscr{V}_p$. The output is a rational parametrization Q encoding the union of the finite sets defined by the Q_ι's.

4.2 Correctness

We prove in this section that SOLVESDP is correct. Our proof relies on intermediate results already stated and proved in the previous sections.

Theorem 7 *Let $\mathscr{A} \subset \mathbb{S}_m^{n+1}(\mathbb{C})$ and $\mathscr{C} \subset \mathbb{C}^n$ be the Zariski open sets defined respectively by Proposition 1 and 3. Let $A \in \mathscr{A} \cap \mathbb{S}_m^{n+1}(\mathbb{Q})$, $c \in \mathscr{C} \cap \mathbb{Q}^n$ and $0 \leq r \leq m$. Then the output of* SOLVESDP *is a rational parametrization of a finite set containing all minimizers of (SDP)$_r$.*

PROOF. Let (A, c, r) be the input of SOLVESDP, and let $x^* \in \mathbb{R}^n$ be a solution of (SDP)$_r$. Let $p = \text{rank}A(x^*)$. By Theorem 4, x^* is a local minimizer of ℓ_c on $\mathscr{D}_p \cap \mathbb{R}^n$. Let us denote by S the image of the union of sets $\text{crit}\,(L_c, \mathscr{V}_{p,\iota}), \iota \subset \{1,\ldots,m\}, \#\iota = m-p$ under the projection $\pi_n(x,y) = x$, namely

$$S = \pi_n\left(\bigcup_{\#\iota=m-p} \text{crit}\,(L_c, \mathscr{V}_{p,\iota})\right).$$

Lemma 2 implies that $x^* \in S$. Since $A \in \mathscr{A}$, by Proposition 1 $\mathscr{V}_{p,\iota}$ is smooth and equidimensional of dimension $m(m-p) + \binom{m-p+1}{2}$. Hence, for all $\iota \subset \{1,\ldots,m\}$, with $\#\iota = m-p$, the set $\text{crit}\,(L_c, \mathscr{V}_{p,\iota} \cap \mathbb{R}^{n+m(m-p)})$ is defined by the Lagrange system $\text{lag}(\iota)$ introduced in (3). We conclude that there exists ι as above, and $y^* \in \mathbb{C}^{n+m(m-p)}$ and $z^* \in \mathbb{C}^{(2m-p)(m-p)+1}$ such that (x^*, y^*, z^*) is a solution of $\text{lag}(\iota)$ of rank p (indeed, by hypothesis $\text{rank}A(x^*) = p$). By Proposition 3, the solutions of rank p of $\text{lag}(\iota)$ are finitely many.

Hence, respectively, the subroutines Optimize, Project and RatPar compute a rational parametrization $Q_\iota = (q^{(\iota)}, q_0^{(\iota)}, \ldots, q_n^{(\iota)}) \subset \mathbb{Q}[t]$ such that there exists $t^* \in \mathbb{R}$ such that

$$x^* = (q_1^{(\iota)}(t^*)/q_0^{(\iota)}(t^*), \ldots, q_n^{(\iota)}(t^*)/q_0^{(\iota)}(t^*)).$$

Then the output Q is a rational parametrization containing x^*. By the genericity of x^* among the solutions of (SDP)$_r$, we conclude. □

5. COMPLEXITY ANALYSIS

5.1 Degree bounds for the output representation

The output of SOLVESDP is a rational univariate parametrization $Q = (q, q_0, q_1, \ldots, q_n) \subset \mathbb{Q}[t]$. To recover the coordinates of the minimizers of Problem (1), one can perform real root isolation on the univariate polynomial q. Hence we are interested in bounding the degree of q, which is done by the following Proposition.

Proposition 8 *Let $Q = (q, q_0, q_1, \ldots, q_n) \subset \mathbb{Q}[t]$ be the rational parametrization returned by* SOLVESDP. *Then*

$$\deg q \leq \sum_{p=0}^{r} \binom{m}{p} \theta(m,n,p),$$

where

$$\theta(m,n,p) = \sum_k \binom{c_p}{n-k} \binom{n-1}{k+c_p-1-p(m-p)} \binom{p(m-p)}{k},$$

with $c_p = (m-p)(m+p+1)/2$.

PROOF. We first prove that θ gives a bound on the degree of the ideal generated by $\text{lag}(\iota)$, that is on the degree of the partial rational parametrization Q_ι. Since Q encodes the union of all algebraic sets defined by the Q_ι's, and since the previous degree does not depend on ι, we conclude by adding all such bounds (each one multiplied by $\binom{m}{p}$, the number of subset ι of cardinality $m-p$). This relies on an equivalent construction of $\text{lag}(\iota)$ which is given below.

Given $p \in \{0,\ldots,r\}$, we fix a subset $\iota \subset \{1,\ldots,m\}$ with $\#\iota = m-p$. We exploit the multilinearity of the polynomial system f defining the incidence variety $\mathscr{V}_{p,\iota}$. First, we eliminate variables $y_{i,j}$, with $i \in \iota$, by substituting $Y_\iota = \text{I}_{m-p}$; we also eliminate polynomials $Y_\iota - \text{I}_{m-p}$ in f_{red} (*cf.* Proposition 1). One obtains a polynomial system $\widetilde{f}$ of cardinality $c_p := (m-p)(m+p+1)/2$. Moreover, by construction, $\widetilde{f}$ is constituted by c_p polynomials of bi-degree at most $(1,1)$ with respect to the groups of variables x and

$$\bar{y} := (y_{i,j} : i \notin \iota). \tag{7}$$

We also suppose without loss of generality that the linear map ℓ_c in Problem (1) defines the projection over x_1, that is that $c = (1,0,\ldots,0)$. Hence, the system $\text{lag}(\iota)$ is equivalent to the following. We consider the c_p elements in $\widetilde{f}$. Let $D\widetilde{f}$ be the Jacobian matrix of $\widetilde{f}$ w.r.t. variables $x, \bar{y}$, and let D_1 be the matrix obtained by eliminating the first column from $D\widetilde{f}$. The critical points of the projection over x_1 restricted to $\mathsf{Z}(\widetilde{f})$ are then defined by $\widetilde{f} = 0$ and by $z' D_1 = 0$, where

$$\bar{z} := (z_1, \ldots, z_{c_p - 1}, 1) \tag{8}$$

is a non-zero vector of $c_p - 1$ Lagrange multipliers.

Hence $\text{lag}(\iota)$ is equivalent to a polynomial system of

- c_p equations of bi-degree at most $(1,1,0)$ w.r.t. $x, \bar{y}, \bar{z}$;
- $n-1$ equations of bi-degree at most $(0,1,1)$ w.r.t. $x, \bar{y}, \bar{z}$;
- $p(m-p)$ equations of bi-degree at most $(1,0,1)$ w.r.t. $x, \bar{y}, \bar{z}$.

We call this new polynomial system $\widetilde{\text{lag}(\iota)}$. By the Multilinear Bézout Theorem (*cf.* for example [30, Prop. 11.1.1]) the degree of $\widetilde{\text{lag}(\iota)}$ is bounded above by the coefficient of $s_x^n s_y^{p(m-p)} s_z^{c_p-1}$ in

$$(s_x + s_y)^{c_p} (s_y + s_z)^{n-1} (s_x + s_z)^{p(m-p)},$$

which is exactly $\theta(m,n,p)$. □

5.2 Bounds on the arithmetic operations

Our goal in this section is to bound the number of arithmetic operations over $\mathbb{Q}$ performed by the main subroutine of SOLVESDP, which is the computation of the rational parametrization Q_ι done by RatPar. Before that, we give bounds for the complexity of routines Project and Union. Let $\widetilde{\text{lag}(\iota)} \subset \mathbb{Q}[x, \bar{y}, \bar{z}]$ (*cf.* (7) and (8)) be the equivalent Lagrange system built in the proof of Proposition 8, and $\theta = \theta(m,n,p)$ be the bound on the degree of $\widetilde{\text{lag}(\iota)}$. From [30, Chapter 10], one gets the following estimates:

- by [30, Lemma 10.1.5], Project can be performed with at most $n^2\theta(m,n,p)^2$ arithmetic operations;
- by [30, Lemma 10.1.3], Union can be performed with at most $n(\sum_{s=0}^{p} \binom{m}{s} \theta(m,n,s))^2$ arithmetic operations.

We now turn to the complexity of RatPar. Our complexity model is the symbolic homotopy algorithm for computing rational parametrization in [17]. This is a probabilistic exact algorithm for solving zero-dimensional systems via rational parametrizations, exploiting their sparsity. It allows to express the arithmetic complexity of RatPar as a function of geometric invariants of the system $\widetilde{\mathrm{lag}(\iota)}$ (mainly of its degree, which is bounded by $\theta(m,n,p)$, *cf.* Proposition 8).

We briefly recall the construction of the homotopy curve in [17]. This is similar to [13, Sec.4]. Let t be a new variable, and recall that $\widetilde{\mathrm{lag}(\iota)}$ contains quadratic polynomials with bilinear structure with respect to the three groups of variables $x, \bar{y}, \bar{z}$. Let $g \subset \mathbb{Q}[x, \bar{y}, \bar{z}]$ be a new polynomial system such that: (1) $\#g = \#\widetilde{\mathrm{lag}(\iota)}$, (2) the i–th entry of g is a polynomial with the same monomial structure as the i–th entry of $\widetilde{\mathrm{lag}(\iota)}$, and (3) the solutions of g are finitely many and known. Since $\widetilde{\mathrm{lag}(\iota)}$ is bilinear in $x, \bar{y}, \bar{z}$, the system g can be obtained by considering suitable products of linear forms in, respectively, x, $\bar{y}$ and $\bar{z}$. The algorithm in [17] builds the homotopy curve $\mathsf{Z}(h)$ defined by

$$h = t\widetilde{\mathrm{lag}(\iota)} + (1-t)g \subset \mathbb{Q}[x, \bar{y}, \bar{z}, t].$$

The proof of the following lemma is technical and we omit it.

Lemma 9 *Let $\theta(m,n,p)$ be the bound on the degree of $\mathsf{Z}(\widetilde{\mathrm{lag}(\iota)})$ computed in Proposition 8. The degree of the homotopy curve $\mathsf{Z}(h)$ is in*

$$\mathscr{O}((n + c_p + p(m-p)) \min\{n, c_p\} \theta(m,n,p)).$$

The degree of $\mathsf{Z}(\widetilde{\mathrm{lag}(\iota)})$ and of the homotopy curve $\mathsf{Z}(h)$ are the main ingredients of the complexity bound for the algorithm [17], which is given by [17, Prop. 6.1]. We use this complexity bound in our estimate. Indeed, let us denote by

$$\Delta_{xy} = \{1, x_i, y_j, x_i y_j : i = 1, \ldots, n, j = 1, \ldots, p(m-p)\}$$
$$\Delta_{yz} = \{1, y_j, z_k, y_j z_k : j = 1, \ldots, p(m-p), k = 1 \ldots, c_p - 1\}$$
$$\Delta_{xz} = \{1, x_i, z_k, x_i z_k : i = 1, \ldots, n, k = 1, \ldots, c_p - 1\}$$

the supports of polynomials in $\widetilde{\mathrm{lag}(\iota)}$. To state our complexity result for SolveSDP, we suppose that all the regularity assumptions on $A(x)$ are satisfied. We avoid in particular to consider the control subroutine CheckReg in our complexity analysis.

Theorem 10 *Suppose that $A \in \mathscr{A}$ (defined in Proposition 1). Then* SolveSDP *runs within*

$$\mathscr{O}\left(\sum_{p=0}^{r} \binom{m}{p} (npc_p(m-p))^5 \theta(m,n,p)^2\right)$$

arithmetic operations over $\mathbb{Q}$, where $c_p = (m-p)(m+p+1)/2$.

Proof. Complexity bounds for subroutines Project and Union have been computed earlier in Section 5.2.

By [17, Prop.6.1], one can compute a rational parametrization of $\widetilde{\mathrm{lag}(\iota)}$ within $\mathscr{O}((\tilde{n}^2 N \log \Delta + \tilde{n}^{\omega+1}) e e')$ where: $\tilde{n} = n + p(m-p) + c_p - 1$ is the number of variables in $\widetilde{\mathrm{lag}(\iota)}$; $N = c_p \#\Delta_{xy} + (n-1)\#\Delta_{yz} + p(m-p)\#\Delta_{xz} \in \mathscr{O}(npc_p(m-p))$; $\Delta = \max\{\|q\| : q \in \Delta_{xy} \cup \Delta_{yz} \cup \Delta_{xz}\} \leq \tilde{n}$; finally e is the degree of $\mathsf{Z}(\widetilde{\mathrm{lag}(\iota)})$ and e' the degree of $\mathsf{Z}(h)$, and ω is the exponent of matrix multiplication. Applying bounds computed in Proposition 8 and Lemma 9, and since $\tilde{n} \leq N$ and $\omega \leq 3$, we conclude that RatPar runs within $\mathscr{O}(N^5 \theta(m,n,p)^2)$ arithmetic operations. We conclude by recalling that for every $p = 0, \ldots, r$, the routine RatPar runs $\binom{m}{p}$ times. □

6. EXPERIMENTS

We present results of our tests on a Maple implementation of the algorithm SolveSDP. We integrate this implementation in the Maple library SPECTRA [16] since the main goal of this library is to contain symbolic algorithms for semidefinite programming and related problems. A beta version of SPECTRA can be freely downloaded from the following web page:

http://homepages.laas.fr/snaldi/software.html

The rational parametrizations are computed using Gröbner bases via the Maple implementation of Faugère's software FGb [5], exploiting the multilinearity of Lagrange systems already exhibited in Section 5.1 (*cf.* [6] for a tailored algorithm). The regularity assumptions on the input (A, c) are also checked by testing the emptiness of complex algebraic sets, hence performing Gröbner bases computations.

In Section 6.1 we use SolveSDP to solve generic rank-constrained semidefinite programs, giving details of timings and output degrees of our implementations. In Section 6.2 we consider an application of our results for computing certificates of nonnegativity for univariate polynomials.

6.1 Random SDP

In this test, we draw $(n+1)$–tuples of random $m \times m$ symmetric linear matrices $A_0, A_1, \ldots, A_n$ with rational coefficients. The numerators and denominators of the rational entries are generated with respect to the uniform distribution in a given interval (in our case, in $\mathbb{Z} \cap [-10^3, 10^3]$). We also draw random linear forms $\ell_c = c^T x$, and we consider different rank-constrained semidefinite programs.

As explained in Section 4, the most costly routine in SolveSDP is the computation of rational parametrizations of the Lagrange systems $\mathrm{lag}(\iota)$ defined in (3), namely Step 7 in the formal description in Section 4.1. We report in Table 1 on timings (column SolveSDP) and output degrees (column Deg) relative to the computation of the rational parametrization of a single Lagrange system. Ideally, we recall that to get the total time for SolveSDP one should take the sum of these timings for $p = 0, \ldots, r$ weighted by $\binom{m}{p}$ (similarly to the complexity bound in Theorem 10).

(m,n,p)	SolveSDP	Deg	(m,n,p)	SolveSDP	Deg
(3,3,2)	11 s	4	(5,3,3)	3 s	20
(4,3,2)	2 s	10	(5,4,3)	1592 s	90
(4,4,2)	9 s	30	(5,5,3)	16809 s	207
(4,5,2)	29 s	42	(5,2,4)	7 s	20
(4,6,2)	71 s	30	(5,3,4)	42 s	40
(4,7,2)	103 s	10	(5,4,4)	42 s	40
(4,3,3)	10 s	16	(5,5,4)	858 s	16
(4,4,3)	21 s	8	(6,6,3)	704 s	112
(5,7,2)	25856 s	140	(6,3,5)	591 s	80

Table 1: Optimization over $\mathscr{D}_p \cap \mathbb{R}^n$

We remark that our implementation is able to tackle from small to medium-size input semidefinite programs and different rank constraints. As an example, for $(m,n,p) = (5,7,2)$ one should compute the critical points of a general linear form over the algebraic set defined by $\binom{5}{3}\binom{5}{3} = 100$ polynomials of degree 3 in 7 variables, which is unreachable by the state-of-the-art algorithms: our implementation computes a rational parametrization of degree 140 after seven hours. Further, when the size m is fixed, the cost in terms of computation seems to reflect suitably both the growth of output degree and of the number of variables n.

Moreover, it is worth to highlight that the entries of column Deg coincide exactly with the *algebraic degree of SDP* with parameters

(m,n,p), as computed in [24, Table 2]. This fact is not obvious since our algorithm builds intermediate incidence varieties whose degree is typically larger than the degree of the determinantal varieties: hence one could *a priori* expect the degree of the output representation to be larger than the expected degree (which si computed in [24]). Even though the estimate of the output degree in Proposition 8 does not depend explicitly on formulas in [24], but only on multilinear bounds, this fact is remarkable and represents a guarantee of optimality of our method.

6.2 Minimal Sum-Of-Squares certificates

In this final section, we consider an interesting application of rank-constrained semidefinite programming. Let $x = (x_1, \dots, x_k)$ and let $f \in \mathbb{R}[x]_{2d}$ be a homogeneous polynomial of degree $2d$, for $d \geq 1$. Let $b = \{\prod_i x_i^{j_i}\}_{\sum_i j_i = d}$ be the monomial basis of $\mathbb{R}[x]_d$. The sum-of-squares (SOS) decompositions of f are parametrized by the so-called *Gram spectrahedron* of f:

$$\mathscr{G}(f) = \{X \in \mathbb{S}_{\binom{k+d-1}{d}}(\mathbb{R}) : X \succeq 0,\, f = b^T X b\},$$

and any $X \in \mathscr{G}(f)$ is called a *Gram matrix* for f. *cf.* [28]. Remark here that the constraint $f = b^T X b$ is linear in the entries of X. If $f = f_1^2 + \cdots + f_r^2$, we say that f has a SOS decomposition *of length* r. We deduce that deciding whether f has a SOS decomposition of length at most r is equivalent to the following rank-constrained semidefinite program:

$$f = b^T X b \qquad X \succeq 0 \qquad \operatorname{rank} X \leq r.$$

We have generated nonnegative polynomials by taking sums of squares of random homogeneous polynomials of degree d. Applying SOLVESDP to this subfamily of problem $(\text{SDP})_r$, we have been able to handle example with $k \leq 3$ and $2d \leq 6$, corresponding to Gram matrices of size 10. We believe that this is due to the particular sparsity of these linear matrices.

7. FINAL REMARKS

This paper addresses a fundamental problem in computational real algebraic geometry, that is rank-constrained semidefinite programming. Our algorithm is able to return an exact algebraic representation of all minimizers, with explicit bounds on its output degree and whose complexity is essentially quadratic on the mentioned degree bound. The algorithm works under assumptions on the input, which are proved to be generically satisfied. This is done by exploiting the determinantal structure of this optimization problem, and by reducing it to linear optimization over determinantal varieties. This reduction step allows to manage (non-convex) additional rank constraints. To the best of our knowledge, this is the first exact algorithm for solving $(\text{SDP})_r$.

8. REFERENCES

[1] M. F. Anjos, J. B. Lasserre (editors). Handbook of semidefinite, conic and polynomial optimization. Int. Series in Operational Research and Management Science. V.166, Springer, NY, 2012.

[2] S. Boyd, L. El Ghaoui, E. Feron and V. Balakrishnan. Linear matrix inequalities in system and control theory. Studies in Applied Mathematics 15. SIAM, Philadelphia, 1994.

[3] S. Boyd, L. Vandenberghe. Semidefinite programming. SIAM Review, 38(1):49–95, 1996.

[4] D. Eisenbud. Commutative algebra with a view toward algebraic geometry. Springer-Verlag, New York, 1995.

[5] J.-C. Faugère. FGB: a library for computing Gröbner bases. In Mathematical Software–ICMS 2010, pp. 84–87, Springer, 2010.

[6] J.-C. Faugère, C. Mou. Fast algorithm for change of ordering of zero-dimensional Gröbner bases with sparse multiplication matrices. Proceedings of ISSAC 2011, pp. 115–122, San Jose, USA.

[7] J.-C. Faugère, P. Gianni, D. Lazard, T. Mora. Efficient computation of zero-dimensional Gröbner bases by change of ordering. Journal of Symbolic Computation, 16(4):329–344, 1993.

[8] J.C. Faugère, M. Safey El Din, P.J. Spaenlehauer. Computing loci of rank defects of linear matrices using Grobner bases and Applications to Cryptology. Proceedings of ISSAC 2010, Munich.

[9] A. Greuet, M. Safey El Din. Probabilistic algorithm for the global optimization of a polynomial over a real algebraic set. SIAM J. Opt., 24(3):1313–1343, 2014.

[10] M. X. Goemans, D. Williamson. Improved approximation algorithms for maximum cuts and satisfiability problems using semidefinite programming. J. of the ACM 42:1115–1145, 1995.

[11] M. Grötschel, L. Lovász, A. Schrijver. Geometric algorithms and combinatorial optimization. Springer, Berlin, 1988.

[12] D. Henrion, S. Naldi, M. Safey El Din. Real root finding for determinants of linear matrices. Journal of Symbolic Computation, 74:205–238, 2016.

[13] D. Henrion, S. Naldi, M. Safey El Din. Real root finding for rank defects in linear Hankel matrices. Proceedings of ISSAC 2015, Bath, UK, 221–228, 2015.

[14] D. Henrion, S. Naldi, M. Safey El Din. Real root finding for low rank linear matrices. hal-01159210,v.1, June 2015.

[15] D. Henrion, S. Naldi, M. Safey El Din. Exact algorithms for linear matrix inequalities. hal-01184320,v.1, August 2015.

[16] D. Henrion, S. Naldi, M. Safey El Din. SPECTRA: Semidefinite Programming solved Exactly with Computation Tools of Real Algebra. Software documentation, 2015. Web page: http://homepages.laas.fr/snaldi/software.html.

[17] G. Jeronimo, G. Matera, P. Solernò, A. Waissbein. Deformation techniques for sparse systems. Foundations of Computational Mathematics, 9(1):1–50, 2009.

[18] E. Kaltofen, B. Li, Z. Yang, L. Zhi. Exact certification of global optimality of approximate factorizations via rationalizing sums-of-squares with floating point scalars. ISSAC 2008, 155-163.

[19] L. Khachiyan and L. Porkolab. On the complexity of semidefinite programs. J. Global Optim., 10:351–365, 1997.

[20] J.B. Lasserre. Global optimization with polynomials and the problem of moments. SIAM J. Opt., 11(3):796–817, 2001.

[21] M. Laurent, M. E. Nagy, A. Varvitsiotis. Complexity of the positive semidefinite matrix completion problem with a rank constraint. Discrete Geometry and Optimization. In Fields Institute Communications, K. Bezdek, A. Deza and Y. Ye (eds), Springer, (69)105–120, 2013.

[22] Y. Nesterov and A. Nemirovsky. Interior-point polynomial algorithms in convex programming. Studies in Applied Mathematics 13. SIAM, Philadelphia, 1994.

[23] J. Nie. Optimality conditions and finite convergence of Lasserre's hierarchy. Mathematical Programming, Ser. A, 146:97-121, 2014.

[24] J. Nie, K. Ranestad, B. Sturmfels. The algebraic degree of semidefinite programming. Mathematical Programming, Ser. A,122:379–405, 2010.

[25] R. Orsi, U. Helmke, and J. B. Moore. A Newton-like method for solving rank constrained linear matrix inequalities. Automatica, 42(11):1875-1882, 2006.

[26] V. Pan, E. Tsigaridas. Nearly optimal refinement of real roots of a univariate polynomial. hal-01105263, 2014.

[27] P. Parrilo. Semidefinite programming relaxations for semialgebraic problems. Mathematical Programming Ser.B 96(2):293–320, 2003.

[28] V. Powers, T. Woermann. An algorithm for sums of squares of real polynomials. J. Pure and Appl. Alg. 127:99–104, 1998.

[29] F. Rouillier. Solving zero-dimensional systems through the rational univariate representation. J. of Applicable Algebra in Engineering, Communication and Computing. 9(5):433–461, 1999.

[30] M. Safey El Din, É. Schost. A nearly optimal algorithm for deciding connectivity queries in smooth and bounded real algebraic sets. Preprint arXiv:1307.7836, 2013.

[31] I. Shafarevich. Basic algebraic geometry 1. Springer, Berlin, 1977.

Fast Computation of Shifted Popov Forms of Polynomial Matrices via Systems of Modular Polynomial Equations

Vincent Neiger
ENS de Lyon
Laboratoire LIP, CNRS, Inria, UCBL, U. Lyon
vincent.neiger@ens-lyon.fr

ABSTRACT

We give a Las Vegas algorithm which computes the shifted Popov form of an $m \times m$ nonsingular polynomial matrix of degree d in expected $\widetilde{\mathcal{O}}(m^\omega d)$ field operations, where ω is the exponent of matrix multiplication and $\widetilde{\mathcal{O}}(\cdot)$ indicates that logarithmic factors are omitted. This is the first algorithm in $\widetilde{\mathcal{O}}(m^\omega d)$ for shifted row reduction with arbitrary shifts.

Using partial linearization, we reduce the problem to the case $d \leqslant \lceil \sigma/m \rceil$ where σ is the generic determinant bound, with σ/m bounded from above by both the average row degree and the average column degree of the matrix. The cost above becomes $\widetilde{\mathcal{O}}(m^\omega \lceil \sigma/m \rceil)$, improving upon the cost of the fastest previously known algorithm for row reduction, which is deterministic.

Our algorithm first builds a system of modular equations whose solution set is the row space of the input matrix, and then finds the basis in shifted Popov form of this set. We give a deterministic algorithm for this second step supporting arbitrary moduli in $\widetilde{\mathcal{O}}(m^{\omega-1}\sigma)$ field operations, where m is the number of unknowns and σ is the sum of the degrees of the moduli. This extends previous results with the same cost bound in the specific cases of order basis computation and M-Padé approximation, in which the moduli are products of known linear factors.

Keywords

Shifted Popov form; polynomial matrices; row reduction; Hermite form; system of modular equations.

1. INTRODUCTION

In this paper, we consider two problems of linear algebra over the ring $\mathbb{K}[X]$ of univariate polynomials, for some field $\mathbb{K}$: computing the shifted Popov form of a matrix, and solving systems of modular equations.

1.1 Shifted Popov form

A polynomial matrix $\mathbf{P}$ is row reduced [22, Section 6.3.2] if its rows have some type of minimal degree (we give precise definitions below). Besides, if $\mathbf{P}$ satisfies an additional normalization property, then it is said to be in Popov form [22, Section 6.7.2]. Given a matrix $\mathbf{A}$, the efficient computation of a (row) reduced form of $\mathbf{A}$ and of the Popov form of $\mathbf{A}$ has received a lot of attention recently [14, 28, 16].

In many applications one rather considers the degrees of the rows of $\mathbf{P}$ shifted by some integers which specify degree weights on the columns of $\mathbf{P}$, for example in list-decoding algorithms [2, 7], robust Private Information Retrieval [12], and more generally in polynomial versions of the Coppersmith method [9, 10]. A well-known specific shifted Popov form is the Hermite form; there has been recent progress on its fast computation [17, 15, 35]. The case of an arbitrary shift has been studied in [6].

For a *shift* $\mathbf{s} = (s_1, \ldots, s_n) \in \mathbb{Z}^n$, the $\mathbf{s}$-*degree* of $\mathbf{p} = [p_1, \ldots, p_n] \in \mathbb{K}[X]^{1 \times n}$ is $\max_{1 \leqslant j \leqslant n}(\deg(p_j) + s_j)$; the $\mathbf{s}$-*row degree* of $\mathbf{P} \in \mathbb{K}[X]^{m \times n}$ is $\mathrm{rdeg}_{\mathbf{s}}(\mathbf{P}) = (d_1, \ldots, d_m)$ with d_i the $\mathbf{s}$-degree of the i-th row of $\mathbf{P}$. Then, the $\mathbf{s}$-*leading matrix* of $\mathbf{P} = [p_{i,j}]_{ij}$ is the matrix $\mathrm{lm}_{\mathbf{s}}(\mathbf{P}) \in \mathbb{K}^{m \times n}$ whose entry (i, j) is the coefficient of degree $d_i - s_j$ of $p_{i,j}$.

Now, we assume that $m \leqslant n$ and $\mathbf{P}$ has full rank. Then, $\mathbf{P}$ is said to be $\mathbf{s}$-*reduced* [22, 6] if $\mathrm{lm}_{\mathbf{s}}(\mathbf{P})$ has full rank. For a full rank $\mathbf{A} \in \mathbb{K}[X]^{m \times n}$, an $\mathbf{s}$-*reduced form of* $\mathbf{A}$ is an $\mathbf{s}$-reduced matrix $\mathbf{P}$ whose row space is the same as that of $\mathbf{A}$; by row space we mean the $\mathbb{K}[X]$-module generated by the rows of the matrix. Equivalently, $\mathbf{P}$ is left-unimodularly equivalent to $\mathbf{A}$ and the tuple $\mathrm{rdeg}_{\mathbf{s}}(\mathbf{P})$ sorted in nondecreasing order is lexicographically minimal among the $\mathbf{s}$-row degrees of all matrices left-unimodularly equivalent to $\mathbf{A}$.

Specific $\mathbf{s}$-reduced matrices are those in $\mathbf{s}$-*Popov form* [22, 5, 6], as defined below. One interesting property is that the $\mathbf{s}$-Popov form is canonical: there is a unique $\mathbf{s}$-reduced form of $\mathbf{A}$ which is in $\mathbf{s}$-Popov form, called the $\mathbf{s}$-*Popov form of* $\mathbf{A}$.

Definition 1.1 (Pivot). *Let $\mathbf{p} = [p_j]_j \in \mathbb{K}[X]^{1 \times n}$ be nonzero and let $\mathbf{s} \in \mathbb{Z}^n$. The* $\mathbf{s}$-pivot index *of $\mathbf{p}$ is the largest index j such that $\mathrm{rdeg}_{\mathbf{s}}(\mathbf{p}) = \deg(p_j) + s_j$. Then we call p_j and $\deg(p_j)$ the* $\mathbf{s}$-pivot entry *and the* $\mathbf{s}$-pivot degree *of $\mathbf{p}$.*

We remark that adding a constant to the entries of $\mathbf{s}$ does not change the notion of $\mathbf{s}$-pivot. For example, we will sometimes assume $\min(\mathbf{s}) = 0$ without loss of generality.

Definition 1.2 (Shifted Popov form). *Let $m \leqslant n$, let $\mathbf{P} \in \mathbb{K}[X]^{m \times n}$ be full rank, and let $\mathbf{s} \in \mathbb{Z}^n$. Then, $\mathbf{P}$ is said to be in* $\mathbf{s}$-Popov form *if the $\mathbf{s}$-pivot indices of its rows are strictly increasing, the corresponding $\mathbf{s}$-pivot entries are monic, and in each column of $\mathbf{P}$ which contains a pivot the nonpivot entries have degree less than the pivot entry.*

In this case, the $\mathbf{s}$-pivot degree *of $\mathbf{P}$ is $\boldsymbol{\delta} = (\delta_1, \ldots, \delta_m) \in \mathbb{N}^m$, with δ_i the $\mathbf{s}$-pivot degree of the i-th row of $\mathbf{P}$.*

ISSAC'16, July 19–22, 2016, Waterloo, ON, Canada

ISBN 978-1-4503-4380-0/16/07…$15.00

DOI: http://dx.doi.org/10.1145/2930889.2930936

Here, although we will encounter Popov forms of rectangular matrices in intermediate nullspace computations, our main focus is on computing shifted Popov forms of *square nonsingular matrices*. For the general case, studied in [6], a fast solution would require further developments. A square matrix in $\mathbf{s}$-Popov form has its $\mathbf{s}$-pivot entries on the diagonal, and its $\mathbf{s}$-pivot degree is the tuple of degrees of its diagonal entries and coincides with its column degree.

> PROBLEM 1 (SHIFTED POPOV NORMAL FORM).
> Input: *the base field* $\mathbb{K}$, *a nonsingular matrix* $\mathbf{A} \in \mathbb{K}[X]^{m\times m}$, *a shift* $\mathbf{s} \in \mathbb{Z}^m$.
> Output: *the* $\mathbf{s}$*-Popov form of* $\mathbf{A}$.

Two well-known specific cases are the Popov form [27, 22] for the *uniform* shift $\mathbf{s} = \mathbf{0}$, and the Hermite form [19, 22] for the shift $\mathbf{h} = (0, \delta, 2\delta, \ldots, (m-1)\delta) \in \mathbb{N}^m$ with $\delta = m \deg(\mathbf{A})$ [6, Lemma 2.6]. For a broader perspective on shifted reduced forms, we refer the reader to [6].

For such problems involving $m \times m$ matrices of degree d, one often wishes to obtain a cost bound similar to that of polynomial matrix multiplication in the same dimensions: $\widetilde{\mathcal{O}}(m^\omega d)$ operations in $\mathbb{K}$. Here, ω is so that we can multiply $m \times m$ matrices over a commutative ring in $\mathcal{O}(m^\omega)$ operations in that ring, the best known bound being $\omega < 2.38$ [11, 25]. For example, one can compute $\mathbf{0}$-reduced [14, 16], $\mathbf{0}$-Popov [28], and Hermite [15, 35] forms of $m \times m$ nonsingular matrices of degree d in $\widetilde{\mathcal{O}}(m^\omega d)$ field operations.

Nevertheless, d may be significantly larger than the average degree of the entries of the matrix, in which case the cost $\widetilde{\mathcal{O}}(m^\omega d)$ seems unsatisfactory. Recently, for the computation of order bases [30, 34], nullspace bases [36], interpolation bases [20, 21], and matrix inversion [37], fast algorithms do take into account some types of average degrees of the matrices rather than their degree. Here, in particular, we achieve a similar improvement for the computation of shifted Popov forms of a matrix.

Given $\mathbf{A} = [a_{i,j}]_{ij} \in \mathbb{K}[X]^{m\times m}$, we denote by $\sigma(\mathbf{A})$ the *generic bound for* $\deg(\det(\mathbf{A}))$ [16, Section 6], that is,

$$\sigma(\mathbf{A}) = \max_{\pi \in S_m} \sum_{1 \leqslant i \leqslant m} \overline{\deg}(a_{i,\pi_i}) \qquad (1)$$

where S_m is the set of permutations of $\{1, \ldots, m\}$, and $\overline{\deg}(p)$ is defined over $\mathbb{K}[X]$ as $\overline{\deg}(0) = 0$ and $\overline{\deg}(p) = \deg(p)$ for $p \neq 0$. We have $\deg(\det(\mathbf{A})) \leqslant \sigma(\mathbf{A}) \leqslant m \deg(\mathbf{A})$, and $\sigma(\mathbf{A}) \leqslant \min(|\mathrm{rdeg}(\mathbf{A})|, |\mathrm{cdeg}(\mathbf{A})|)$ with $|\mathrm{rdeg}(\mathbf{A})|$ and $|\mathrm{cdeg}(\mathbf{A})|$ the sums of the row and column degrees of $\mathbf{A}$. We note that $\sigma(\mathbf{A})$ can be substantially smaller than $|\mathrm{rdeg}(\mathbf{A})|$ and $|\mathrm{cdeg}(\mathbf{A})|$, for example if $\mathbf{A}$ has one row and one column of uniformly large degree and other entries of low degree.

THEOREM 1.3. *There is a Las Vegas randomized algorithm which solves Problem 1 in expected* $\widetilde{\mathcal{O}}(m^\omega \lceil \sigma(\mathbf{A})/m \rceil) \subseteq \widetilde{\mathcal{O}}(m^\omega \deg(\mathbf{A}))$ *field operations.*

The ceiling function indicates that the cost is $\widetilde{\mathcal{O}}(m^\omega)$ when $\sigma(\mathbf{A})$ is small compared to m, in which case $\mathbf{A}$ has mostly constant entries. Here we are mainly interested in the case $m \in \mathcal{O}(\sigma(\mathbf{A}))$: the cost bound may be written $\widetilde{\mathcal{O}}(m^{\omega-1}\sigma(\mathbf{A}))$ and is both in $\widetilde{\mathcal{O}}(m^{\omega-1}|\mathrm{rdeg}(\mathbf{A})|)$ and $\widetilde{\mathcal{O}}(m^{\omega-1}|\mathrm{cdeg}(\mathbf{A})|)$.

Previous work on fast algorithms related to Problem 1 is summarized in Table 1. The fastest known algorithm for the $\mathbf{0}$-Popov form is deterministic and has cost $\widetilde{\mathcal{O}}(m^\omega d)$ with $d = \deg(\mathbf{A})$; it first computes a $\mathbf{0}$-reduced form of $\mathbf{A}$ [16], and then its $\mathbf{0}$-Popov form via normalization [28]. Obtaining the Hermite form in $\widetilde{\mathcal{O}}(m^\omega d)$ was first achieved by a probabilistic algorithm in [15], and then deterministically in [35].

Ref.	Problem	Cost bound	
[18]	Hermite form	$\widetilde{\mathcal{O}}(m^4 d)$	
[31]	Hermite form	$\widetilde{\mathcal{O}}(m^{\omega+1} d)$	
[33]	Popov & Hermite forms	$\widetilde{\mathcal{O}}(m^{\omega+1} d + (md)^\omega)$	
[1, 2]	weak Popov form	$\widetilde{\mathcal{O}}(m^{\omega+1} d)$	
[26]	Popov & Hermite forms	$\mathcal{O}(m^3 d^2)$	
[14]	$\mathbf{0}$-reduction	$\widetilde{\mathcal{O}}(m^\omega d)$	$\star$
[28]	Popov form of $\mathbf{0}$-reduced	$\widetilde{\mathcal{O}}(m^\omega d)$	
[17]	Hermite form	$\widetilde{\mathcal{O}}(m^\omega d)$	$\star$
[16]	$\mathbf{0}$-reduction	$\widetilde{\mathcal{O}}(m^\omega d)$	
[35]	Hermite form	$\widetilde{\mathcal{O}}(m^\omega d)$	
[16]+[28]	$\mathbf{s}$-Popov form for any $\mathbf{s}$	$\widetilde{\mathcal{O}}(m^\omega (d+\mu))$	
Here	$\mathbf{s}$-Popov form for any $\mathbf{s}$	$\widetilde{\mathcal{O}}(m^\omega \lceil \sigma(\mathbf{A})/m \rceil)$	$\star$

Table 1: Fast algorithms for shifted reduction problems ($d = \deg(\mathbf{A})$; $\star$ = probabilistic; $\mu = \max(\mathbf{s}) - \min(\mathbf{s})$).

For an arbitrary $\mathbf{s}$, the algorithm in [6] is fraction-free and uses a number of operations that is, depending on $\mathbf{s}$, at least quintic in m and quadratic in $\deg(\mathbf{A})$.

When $\mathbf{s}$ is not uniform there is a folklore solution based on the fact that $\mathbf{Q}$ is in $\mathbf{s}$-Popov form if and only if $\mathbf{QD}$ is in $\mathbf{0}$-Popov form, with $\mathbf{D} = \mathrm{diag}(X^{s_1}, \ldots, X^{s_m})$ and assuming $\mathbf{s} \geqslant 0$. Then, this solution computes the $\mathbf{0}$-Popov form $\mathbf{P}$ of $\mathbf{AD}$ using [16, 28] and returns $\mathbf{PD}^{-1}$. This approach uses $\widetilde{\mathcal{O}}(m^\omega(d+\mu))$ operations where $\mu = \max(\mathbf{s}) - \min(\mathbf{s})$, which is not satisfactory when μ is large. For example, its cost for computing the Hermite form is $\widetilde{\mathcal{O}}(m^{\omega+2} d)$. This is the worst case since one can assume without loss of generality that $\mu \in \mathcal{O}(m \deg(\det(\mathbf{A}))) \subseteq \mathcal{O}(m^2 d)$ [21, Appendix A].

Here we obtain, to the best of our knowledge, the best known cost bound $\widetilde{\mathcal{O}}(m^\omega \lceil \sigma(\mathbf{A})/m \rceil) \subseteq \widetilde{\mathcal{O}}(m^\omega d)$ for an arbitrary shift $\mathbf{s}$. This removes the dependency in μ, which means in some cases a speedup by a factor m^2. Besides, this is also an improvement for both specific cases $\mathbf{s} = \mathbf{0}$ and $\mathbf{s} = \mathbf{h}$ when $\mathbf{A}$ has unbalanced degrees.

One of the main difficulties in row reduction algorithms is to control the size of the manipulated matrices, that is, the number of coefficients from $\mathbb{K}$ needed for their dense representation. A major issue when dealing with arbitrary shifts is that the size of an $\mathbf{s}$-reduced form of $\mathbf{A}$ may be beyond our target cost. This is a further motivation for focusing on the computation of the $\mathbf{s}$-Popov form of $\mathbf{A}$: by definition, the sum of its column degrees is $\deg(\det(\mathbf{A}))$, and therefore its size is at most $m^2 + m \deg(\det(\mathbf{A}))$, independently of $\mathbf{s}$.

Consider for example $\mathbf{A} = \left[\begin{smallmatrix} \mathbf{B}_1 & \mathbf{0} \\ \mathbf{0} & \mathbf{B}_2 \end{smallmatrix}\right]$ for any $\mathbf{0}$-reduced $\mathbf{B}_1$ and $\mathbf{B}_2$ in $\mathbb{K}[X]^{m\times m}$. Then, taking $\mathbf{s} = (0, \ldots, 0, d, \ldots, d)$ with $d > 0$, $\left[\begin{smallmatrix} \mathbf{B}_1 & \mathbf{0} \\ \mathbf{C} & \mathbf{B}_2 \end{smallmatrix}\right]$ is an $\mathbf{s}$-reduced form of $\mathbf{A}$ for any $\mathbf{C} \in \mathbb{K}[X]^{m\times m}$ with $\deg(\mathbf{C}) \leqslant d$; for some $\mathbf{C}$ it has size $\Theta(m^2 d)$, with d arbitrary large independently of $\deg(\mathbf{A})$.

Furthermore, the size of the unimodular transformation leading from $\mathbf{A}$ to $\mathbf{P}$ may be beyond the target cost, which is why fast algorithms for $\mathbf{0}$-reduction and Hermite form do not directly perform unimodular transformations on $\mathbf{A}$ to reduce the degrees of its entries. Instead, they proceed in two steps: first, they work on $\mathbf{A}$ to find some equations which describe its row space, and then they find a basis of solutions to these equations in $\mathbf{0}$-reduced form or Hermite form. We will follow a similar two-step strategy for an arbitrary shift.

It seems that some new ingredient is needed, since for both $\mathbf{s} = \mathbf{0}$ and $\mathbf{s} = \mathbf{h}$ the fastest algorithms use shift-specific properties at some point of the process: namely, the facts that a $\mathbf{0}$-reduced form of $\mathbf{A}$ has degree at most $\deg(\mathbf{A})$ and that the Hermite form of $\mathbf{A}$ is triangular.

As in [17], we first compute the Smith form $\mathbf{S}$ of $\mathbf{A}$ and partial information on a right unimodular transformation $\mathbf{V}$; this is where the probabilistic aspect comes from. This gives a description of the row space of $\mathbf{A}$ as the set of row vectors $\mathbf{p} \in \mathbb{K}[X]^{1\times m}$ such that $\mathbf{pV} = \mathbf{qS}$ for some $\mathbf{q} \in \mathbb{K}[X]^{1\times m}$. Since $\mathbf{S}$ is diagonal, this can be seen as a system of modular equations: the second step is the fast computation of a basis of solutions in $\mathbf{s}$-Popov form, which is our new ingredient.

1.2 Systems of modular equations

Hereafter, $\mathbb{K}[X]_{\neq 0}$ denotes the set of nonzero polynomials. We fix some moduli $\mathfrak{M} = (\mathfrak{m}_1, \ldots, \mathfrak{m}_n) \in \mathbb{K}[X]^n_{\neq 0}$, and for $\mathbf{A}, \mathbf{B} \in \mathbb{K}[X]^{m\times n}$ we write $\mathbf{A} = \mathbf{B} \bmod \mathfrak{M}$ if there exists $\mathbf{Q} \in \mathbb{K}[X]^{m\times n}$ such that $\mathbf{A} = \mathbf{B} + \mathbf{Q}\,\mathrm{diag}(\mathfrak{M})$. Given $\mathbf{F} \in \mathbb{K}[X]^{m\times n}$ specifying the equations, we call *solution for* $(\mathfrak{M}, \mathbf{F})$ any $\mathbf{p} \in \mathbb{K}[X]^{1\times m}$ such that $\mathbf{pF} = 0 \bmod \mathfrak{M}$.

The set of all such $\mathbf{p}$ is a $\mathbb{K}[X]$-submodule of $\mathbb{K}[X]^{1\times m}$ which contains $\mathrm{lcm}(\mathfrak{m}_1, \ldots, \mathfrak{m}_n)\mathbb{K}[X]^{1\times m}$, and is thus free of rank m [24, p. 146]. Then, we represent any basis of this module as the rows of a matrix $\mathbf{P} \in \mathbb{K}[X]^{m\times m}$, called a *solution basis for* $(\mathfrak{M}, \mathbf{F})$. Here, for example for the application to Problem 1, we are interested in such bases that are $\mathbf{s}$-reduced, in which case $\mathbf{P}$ is said to be an $\mathbf{s}$*-minimal solution basis for* $(\mathfrak{M}, \mathbf{F})$. The unique such basis which is in $\mathbf{s}$-Popov form is called the $\mathbf{s}$*-Popov solution basis for* $(\mathfrak{M}, \mathbf{F})$.

> PROBLEM 2 (MINIMAL SOLUTION BASIS).
> Input: *the base field* $\mathbb{K}$, *moduli* $\mathfrak{M} = (\mathfrak{m}_1, \ldots, \mathfrak{m}_n) \in \mathbb{K}[X]^n_{\neq 0}$, *a matrix* $\mathbf{F} \in \mathbb{K}[X]^{m\times n}$ *such that* $\deg(\mathbf{F}_{*,j}) < \deg(\mathfrak{m}_j)$, *a shift* $\mathbf{s} \in \mathbb{Z}^m$.
> Output: *an* $\mathbf{s}$*-minimal solution basis for* $(\mathfrak{M}, \mathbf{F})$.

Well-known specific cases of this problem are *Hermite-Padé approximation* with a single equation modulo some power of X, and *M-Padé approximation* [3, 32] with moduli that are products of known linear factors. Moreover, an $\mathbf{s}$*-order basis for* $\mathbf{F}$ *and* $(\sigma_1, \ldots, \sigma_n)$ [34] is an $\mathbf{s}$-minimal solution basis for $(\mathfrak{M}, \mathbf{F})$ with $\mathfrak{M} = (X^{\sigma_1}, \ldots, X^{\sigma_n})$.

An overview of fast algorithms for Problem 2 is given in Table 2. For M-Padé approximation, and thus in particular for order basis computation, there is an algorithm to compute the $\mathbf{s}$-Popov solution basis using $\widetilde{\mathcal{O}}(m^{\omega-1}\sigma)$ operations, with $\sigma = \deg(\mathfrak{m}_1) + \cdots + \deg(\mathfrak{m}_n)$ [21]. Here, for $n \in \mathcal{O}(m)$, we extend this result to arbitrary moduli.

THEOREM 1.4. *Assuming* $n \in \mathcal{O}(m)$, *there is a deterministic algorithm which solves Problem 2 using* $\widetilde{\mathcal{O}}(m^{\omega-1}\sigma)$ *field operations, with* $\sigma = \deg(\mathfrak{m}_1) + \cdots + \deg(\mathfrak{m}_n)$, *and returns the* $\mathbf{s}$*-Popov solution basis for* $(\mathfrak{M}, \mathbf{F})$.

We note that Problem 2 is a minimal interpolation basis problem [5, 20] when the so-called *multiplication matrix* $\mathbf{M}$ is block diagonal with companion blocks. Indeed, $\mathbf{p}$ is a solution for $(\mathfrak{M}, \mathbf{F})$ if and only if $\mathbf{p}$ is an *interpolant for* $(\mathbf{E}, \mathbf{M})$ [20, Definition 1.1], where $\mathbf{E} \in \mathbb{K}^{m\times\sigma}$ is the concatenation of the coefficient vectors of the columns of $\mathbf{F}$ and $\mathbf{M} \in \mathbb{K}^{\sigma\times\sigma}$ is $\mathrm{diag}(\mathbf{M}_1, \ldots, \mathbf{M}_n)$ with $\mathbf{M}_j$ the companion matrix associated with $\mathfrak{m}_j$. In this context, the multiplication $\mathbf{p} \cdot \mathbf{E}$ defined by $\mathbf{M}$ as in [5, 20] precisely corresponds to $\mathbf{pF} \bmod \mathfrak{M}$.

In particular, Theorem 1.4 follows from [20, Theorem 1.4] when $\sigma \in \mathcal{O}(m)$. If some of the moduli have small degree, we use this result for base cases of our recursive algorithm.

Ref.	Cost bound	Moduli	Particularities
[3, 32]	$\mathcal{O}(m^2\sigma^2)$	split	
[4]	$\mathcal{O}(m\sigma^2)$	$\mathfrak{m}_j = X^{\sigma/n}$	partial basis
[4]	$\widetilde{\mathcal{O}}(m^\omega\sigma)$	$\mathfrak{m}_j = X^{\sigma/n}$	
[14]	$\widetilde{\mathcal{O}}(m^\omega\sigma/n)$	$\mathfrak{m}_j = X^{\sigma/n}$	
[30]	$\widetilde{\mathcal{O}}(m^\omega\lceil\sigma/m\rceil)$	$\mathfrak{m}_j = X^{\sigma/n}$	partial basis, $\lvert\mathbf{s}\rvert \leqslant \sigma$
[34]	$\widetilde{\mathcal{O}}(m^\omega\lceil\sigma/m\rceil)$	$\mathfrak{m}_j = X^{\sigma/n}$	$\lvert\mathbf{s}\rvert \leqslant \sigma$
[8]	$\widetilde{\mathcal{O}}(m^{\omega-1}\sigma)$, probabilistic	any	returns a single small degree solution
[20]	$\widetilde{\mathcal{O}}(m^{\omega-1}\sigma)$	split	$\lvert\mathbf{s}\rvert \leqslant \sigma$
[20]	$\widetilde{\mathcal{O}}(m\sigma^{\omega-1})$	any	$\mathbf{s}$-Popov, $\sigma \in \mathcal{O}(m)$
[21]	$\widetilde{\mathcal{O}}(m^{\omega-1}\sigma)$	split	$\mathbf{s}$-Popov
Here	$\widetilde{\mathcal{O}}(m^{\omega-1}\sigma)$	any	$\mathbf{s}$-Popov

Table 2: Fast algorithms for Problem 2 ($n \in \mathcal{O}(m)$; *partial basis* = returns small degree rows of an $\mathbf{s}$-minimal solution basis; *split* = product of known linear factors**).**

In the case of M-Padé approximation, knowing the moduli as products of linear factors leads to rewriting the problem as a minimal interpolation basis computation with $\mathbf{M}$ in Jordan form [5, 20]. Since $\mathbf{M}$ is upper triangular, one can then rely on recurrence relations to solve the problem iteratively [3, 32, 4, 5]. The fast algorithms in [4, 14, 34, 20, 21], beyond the techniques used to achieve efficiency, are essentially divide-and-conquer versions of this iterative solution and are thus based on the same recurrence relations.

However, for arbitrary moduli the matrix $\mathbf{M}$ is not triangular and there is no such recurrence in general. Then, a natural idea is to relate solution bases to nullspace bases: Problem 2 asks to find $\mathbf{P}$ such that there is some quotient $\mathbf{Q}$ with $[\mathbf{P}|\mathbf{Q}]\mathbf{N} = \mathbf{0}$ for $\mathbf{N} = [\mathbf{F}^\mathsf{T}| -\mathrm{diag}(\mathfrak{M})]^\mathsf{T}$. More precisely, $[\mathbf{P}|\mathbf{Q}]$ can be obtained as a $\mathbf{u}$-minimal nullspace basis of $\mathbf{N}$ for the shift $\mathbf{u} = (\mathbf{s} - \min(\mathbf{s}), \mathbf{0}) \in \mathbb{N}^{m+n}$.

Using recent ingredients from [17, 21] outlined in the next paragraphs, the main remaining difficulty is to deal with this nullspace problem when $n = 1$. Here, we give a $\widetilde{\mathcal{O}}(m^{\omega-1}\sigma)$ algorithm to solve it using its specific properties: $\mathbf{N}$ is the column $[\mathbf{F}^\mathsf{T}|\mathfrak{m}_1]^\mathsf{T}$ with $\deg(\mathbf{F}) < \deg(\mathfrak{m}_1) = \sigma$, and the last entry of $\mathbf{u}$ is $\min(\mathbf{u})$. First, when $\max(\mathbf{u}) \in \mathcal{O}(\sigma)$ we show that $[\mathbf{P}|\mathbf{Q}]$ can be efficiently obtained as a submatrix of the $\mathbf{u}$-Popov order basis for $\mathbf{N}$ and order $\mathcal{O}(\sigma)$. Then, when $\max(\mathbf{u})$ is large compared to σ and assuming $\mathbf{u}$ is sorted non-decreasingly, $\mathbf{P}$ has a lower block triangular shape. We show how this shape can be revealed, along with the $\mathbf{s}$-pivot degree of $\mathbf{P}$, using a divide-and-conquer approach which splits $\mathbf{u}$ into two shifts of amplitude about $\max(\mathbf{u})/2$.

Then, for $n \geqslant 1$ we use a divide-and-conquer approach on n which is classical in such contexts: two solution bases $\mathbf{P}^{(1)}$ and $\mathbf{P}^{(2)}$ are computed recursively in shifted Popov form and are multiplied together to obtain the $\mathbf{s}$-minimal solution basis $\mathbf{P}^{(2)}\mathbf{P}^{(1)}$ for $(\mathfrak{M}, \mathbf{F})$. However this product is usually not in $\mathbf{s}$-Popov form and may have size beyond our target cost. Thus, as in [21], instead of computing $\mathbf{P}^{(2)}\mathbf{P}^{(1)}$, we use $\mathbf{P}^{(2)}$ and $\mathbf{P}^{(1)}$ to deduce the $\mathbf{s}$-pivot degree of $\mathbf{P}$.

In both recursions above, we focus on finding the $\mathbf{s}$-pivot degree of $\mathbf{P}$. Using ideas and results from [17, 21], we show that this knowledge about the degrees in $\mathbf{P}$ allows us to complete the computation of $\mathbf{P}$ within the target cost.

2. FAST COMPUTATION OF THE SHIFTED POPOV SOLUTION BASIS

Hereafter, we call **s**-*minimal degree of* $(\mathfrak{M}, \mathbf{F})$ the **s**-pivot degree $\boldsymbol{\delta}$ of the **s**-Popov solution basis for $(\mathfrak{M}, \mathbf{F})$; $\boldsymbol{\delta}$ coincides with the column degree of this basis. A central result for the cost analysis is that $|\boldsymbol{\delta}| = \delta_1 + \cdots + \delta_m$ is at most $\sigma = \deg(\mathfrak{m}_1) + \cdots + \deg(\mathfrak{m}_n)$. This is classical for M-Padé approximation [32, Theorem 4.1] and holds for minimal interpolation bases in general (see for example [20, Lemma 7.17]).

2.1 Solution bases from nullspace bases and fast algorithm for known minimal degree

This subsection summarizes and slightly extends results from [17, Section 3]. We first show that the **s**-Popov solution basis for $(\mathfrak{M}, \mathbf{F})$ is the principal $m \times m$ submatrix of the **u**-Popov nullspace basis of $[\mathbf{F}^\mathsf{T} | \operatorname{diag}(\mathfrak{M})]^\mathsf{T}$ for some $\mathbf{u} \in \mathbb{Z}^{m+n}$.

Lemma 2.1. *Let* $\mathfrak{M} = (\mathfrak{m}_1, \ldots, \mathfrak{m}_n) \in \mathbb{K}[X]^n_{\neq 0}$, $\mathbf{s} \in \mathbb{Z}^m$, $\mathbf{F} \in \mathbb{K}[X]^{m \times n}$ *with* $\deg(\mathbf{F}_{*,j}) < \deg(\mathfrak{m}_j)$, $\mathbf{P} \in \mathbb{K}[X]^{m \times m}$, *and* $\mathbf{w} \in \mathbb{Z}^n$ *be such that* $\max(\mathbf{w}) \leqslant \min(\mathbf{s})$. *Then,* $\mathbf{P}$ *is the* **s***-Popov solution basis for* $(\mathfrak{M}, \mathbf{F})$ *if and only if* $[\mathbf{P}|\mathbf{Q}]$ *is the* **u***-Popov nullspace basis of* $[\mathbf{F}^\mathsf{T} | \operatorname{diag}(\mathfrak{M})]^\mathsf{T}$ *for some* $\mathbf{Q} \in \mathbb{K}[X]^{m \times n}$ *and* $\mathbf{u} = (\mathbf{s}, \mathbf{w}) \in \mathbb{Z}^{m+n}$. *In this case,* $\deg(\mathbf{Q}) < \deg(\mathbf{P})$ *and* $[\mathbf{P}|\mathbf{Q}]$ *has* **s***-pivot index* $(1, 2, \ldots, m)$.

Proof. Let $\mathbf{N} = [\mathbf{F}^\mathsf{T} | \operatorname{diag}(\mathfrak{M})]^\mathsf{T}$. It is easily verified that $\mathbf{P}$ is a solution basis for $(\mathfrak{M}, \mathbf{F})$ if and only if there is some $\mathbf{Q} \in \mathbb{K}[X]^{m \times n}$ such that $[\mathbf{P}|\mathbf{Q}]$ is a nullspace basis of $\mathbf{N}$.

Now, having $\deg(\mathbf{F}_{*,j}) < \deg(\mathfrak{m}_j)$ implies that any $[\mathbf{p}|\mathbf{q}] \in \mathbb{K}[X]^{1 \times (m+n)}$ in the nullspace of $\mathbf{N}$ satisfies $\deg(\mathbf{q}) < \deg(\mathbf{p})$, and since $\max(\mathbf{w}) \leqslant \min(\mathbf{s})$ we get $\operatorname{rdeg}_\mathbf{w}(\mathbf{q}) < \operatorname{rdeg}_\mathbf{s}(\mathbf{p})$. In particular, for any matrix $[\mathbf{P}|\mathbf{Q}] \in \mathbb{K}[X]^{m \times (m+n)}$ such that $[\mathbf{P}|\mathbf{Q}]\mathbf{N} = 0$, we have $\operatorname{lm}_\mathbf{u}([\mathbf{P}|\mathbf{Q}]) = [\operatorname{lm}_\mathbf{s}(\mathbf{P})|\mathbf{0}]$. This implies that $\mathbf{P}$ is in **s**-Popov form if and only if $[\mathbf{P}|\mathbf{Q}]$ is in **u**-Popov form with **s**-pivot index $(1, \ldots, m)$. □

We now show that, when we have *a priori* knowledge about the **s**-pivot entries of a **s**-Popov nullspace basis, it can be computed efficiently via an **s**-Popov order basis.

Lemma 2.2. *Let* $\mathbf{s} \in \mathbb{Z}^{m+n}$ *and let* $\mathbf{N} \in \mathbb{K}[X]^{(m+n) \times n}$ *be of full rank. Let* $\mathbf{B} \in \mathbb{K}[X]^{m \times (m+n)}$ *be the* **s***-Popov nullspace basis for* $\mathbf{N}$, $(\pi_1, \ldots, \pi_m)$ *be its* **s***-pivot index,* $(\delta_1, \ldots, \delta_m)$ *be its* **s***-pivot degree, and* $\delta \geqslant \deg(\mathbf{B})$ *be a degree bound. Then, let* $\mathbf{u} = (u_1, \ldots, u_{m+n}) \in \mathbb{Z}^{m+n}_{\leqslant 0}$ *with*

$$u_j = \begin{cases} -\delta - 1 & \text{if } j \notin \{\pi_1, \ldots, \pi_m\}, \\ -\delta_i & \text{if } j = \pi_i. \end{cases}$$

Writing $(\sigma_1, \ldots, \sigma_n)$ *for the column degree of* $\mathbf{N}$, *let* $\tau_j = \sigma_j + \delta + 1$ *for* $1 \leqslant j \leqslant n$ *and let* $\mathbf{A}$ *be the* **u***-Popov order basis for* $\mathbf{N}$ *and* $(\tau_1, \ldots, \tau_n)$. *Then,* $\mathbf{B}$ *is the submatrix of* $\mathbf{A}$ *formed by its rows at indices* $\{\pi_1, \ldots, \pi_m\}$.

Proof. First, $\mathbf{B}$ is in **u**-Popov form with $\operatorname{rdeg}_\mathbf{u}(\mathbf{B}) = \mathbf{0}$. Define $\mathbf{C} \in \mathbb{K}[X]^{(m+n) \times (m+n)}$ whose i-th row is $\mathbf{B}_{j,*}$ if $i = \pi_j$ and $\mathbf{A}_{i,*}$ if $i \notin \{\pi_1, \ldots, \pi_m\}$: we want to prove $\mathbf{C} = \mathbf{A}$.

Let $\mathbf{p} = [p_j]_j \in \mathbb{K}[X]^{1 \times (m+n)}$ be a row of $\mathbf{A}$, and assume $\operatorname{rdeg}_\mathbf{u}(\mathbf{p}) < 0$. This means $\deg(p_j) < -u_j$ for all j, so that $\deg(\mathbf{p}) < \max(-\mathbf{u}) = \delta + 1$. Then, for all $1 \leqslant j \leqslant n$ we have $\deg(\mathbf{p}\mathbf{N}_{*,j}) < \sigma_j + \delta + 1 = \tau_j$, and from $\mathbf{p}\mathbf{N}_{*,j} = 0 \bmod X^{\tau_j}$ we obtain $\mathbf{p}\mathbf{N}_{*,j} = 0$, which is absurd by minimality of $\mathbf{B}$. As a result, $\operatorname{rdeg}_\mathbf{u}(\mathbf{A}) \geqslant \mathbf{0} = \operatorname{rdeg}_\mathbf{u}(\mathbf{B})$ componentwise.

Besides, $\mathbf{C}\mathbf{F} = 0 \bmod (X^{\tau_1}, \ldots, X^{\tau_n})$ and since $\mathbf{C}$ has its **u**-pivot entries on the diagonal, it is **u**-reduced: by minimality of $\mathbf{A}$, we obtain $\operatorname{rdeg}_\mathbf{u}(\mathbf{A}) = \operatorname{rdeg}_\mathbf{u}(\mathbf{C})$. Then, it is easily verified that $\mathbf{C}$ is in **u**-Popov form, hence $\mathbf{C} = \mathbf{A}$. □

In particular, computing the **s**-Popov nullspace basis $\mathbf{B}$, when its **s**-pivot index, its **s**-pivot degree, and $\delta \geqslant \deg(\mathbf{B})$ are known, can be done in $\widetilde{\mathcal{O}}(m^{\omega-1}(\sigma + n\delta))$ with $\sigma = \sigma_1 + \cdots + \sigma_n$ using the order basis algorithm in [21].

As for Problem 2, with Lemma 2.1 this gives an algorithm for computing $\mathbf{P}$ *and* the quotients $\mathbf{Q} = -\mathbf{P}\mathbf{F}/\operatorname{diag}(\mathfrak{M})$ when we know *a priori* the **s**-minimal degree $\boldsymbol{\delta}$ of $(\mathfrak{M}, \mathbf{F})$. Here, we would choose $\delta = \max(\boldsymbol{\delta}) \geqslant \deg([\mathbf{P}|\mathbf{Q}])$: in some cases $\delta = \Theta(\sigma)$ and this has cost bound $\widetilde{\mathcal{O}}(m^{\omega-1}(\sigma + n\sigma))$, which exceeds our target $\widetilde{\mathcal{O}}(m^{\omega-1}\sigma)$. An issue is that $\mathbf{Q}$ has size $\mathcal{O}(mn\sigma)$ when $\mathbf{P}$ has columns of large degree; yet here we are not interested in $\mathbf{Q}$. This can be solved using partial linearization to expand the columns of large degree in $\mathbf{P}$ into more columns of smaller degree as in the next result, which holds in general for interpolation bases [21, Lemma 4.2].

Lemma 2.3. *Let* $\mathfrak{M} \in \mathbb{K}[X]^n_{\neq 0}$ *with entries having degrees* $(\sigma_1, \ldots, \sigma_n)$. *Let* $\mathbf{F} \in \mathbb{K}[X]^{m \times n}$ *and* $\mathbf{s} \in \mathbb{Z}^m$. *Furthermore, let* $\boldsymbol{\delta} = (\delta_1, \ldots, \delta_m)$ *denote the* **s***-minimal degree of* $(\mathfrak{M}, \mathbf{F})$.

Writing $\sigma = \sigma_1 + \cdots + \sigma_n$, *let* $\delta = \lceil \sigma/m \rceil \geqslant 1$, *and for* $i \in \{1, \ldots, m\}$ *write* $\delta_i = (\alpha_i - 1)\delta + \beta_i$ *with* $\alpha_i \geqslant 1$ *and* $0 \leqslant \beta_i < \delta$, *and let* $\widetilde{m} = \alpha_1 + \cdots + \alpha_m$. *Define* $\widetilde{\boldsymbol{\delta}} \in \mathbb{N}^{\widetilde{m}}$ *as*

$$\widetilde{\boldsymbol{\delta}} = (\underbrace{\delta, \ldots, \delta, \beta_1}_{\alpha_1}, \ldots, \underbrace{\delta, \ldots, \delta, \beta_m}_{\alpha_m}) \tag{2}$$

and the expansion-compression matrix $\mathcal{E} \in \mathbb{K}[X]^{\widetilde{m} \times m}$ *as*

$$\mathcal{E} = \begin{bmatrix} 1 & & \\ X^\delta & & \\ \vdots & & \\ X^{(\alpha_1-1)\delta} & & \\ & \ddots & \\ & & 1 \\ & & X^\delta \\ & & \vdots \\ & & X^{(\alpha_m-1)\delta} \end{bmatrix}. \tag{3}$$

Let $\mathbf{d} = -\widetilde{\boldsymbol{\delta}} \in \mathbb{Z}^{\widetilde{m}}$ *and* $\mathbf{P} \in \mathbb{K}[X]^{\widetilde{m} \times \widetilde{m}}$ *be the* **d***-Popov solution basis for* $(\mathfrak{M}, \mathcal{E}\mathbf{F} \bmod \mathfrak{M})$. *Then,* $\mathbf{P}$ *has* **d***-pivot degree* $\widetilde{\boldsymbol{\delta}}$ *and the* **s***-Popov solution basis for* $(\mathfrak{M}, \mathbf{F})$ *is the submatrix of* $\mathbf{P}\mathcal{E}$ *formed by its rows at indices* $\{\alpha_1 + \cdots + \alpha_i, 1 \leqslant i \leqslant m\}$.

This leads to Algorithm 1, which solves Problem 2 efficiently when the **s**-minimal degree $\boldsymbol{\delta}$ is known *a priori*.

Algorithm 1 (KnownDegPolModSys).
Input: polynomials $\mathfrak{M} = (\mathfrak{m}_1, \ldots, \mathfrak{m}_n) \in \mathbb{K}[X]^n_{\neq 0}$, a matrix $\mathbf{F} \in \mathbb{K}[X]^{m \times n}$ with $\deg(\mathbf{F}_{*,j}) < \deg(\mathfrak{m}_j)$, a shift $\mathbf{s} \in \mathbb{Z}^m$, $\boldsymbol{\delta} = (\delta_1, \ldots, \delta_m)$ the **s**-minimal degree of $(\mathfrak{M}, \mathbf{F})$.
Output: the **s**-Popov solution basis for $(\mathfrak{M}, \mathbf{F})$.

1. $\delta \leftarrow \lceil (\deg(\mathfrak{m}_1) + \cdots + \deg(\mathfrak{m}_n))/m \rceil$, $\alpha_i \leftarrow \lfloor \delta_i/\delta \rfloor + 1$ for $1 \leqslant i \leqslant m$, $\widetilde{m} \leftarrow \alpha_1 + \cdots + \alpha_m$, $\widetilde{\boldsymbol{\delta}}$ as in (2), $\mathcal{E}$ as in (3), $\widetilde{\mathbf{F}} \leftarrow \mathcal{E}\mathbf{F} \bmod \mathfrak{M}$
2. $\mathbf{u} \leftarrow (-\widetilde{\boldsymbol{\delta}}, -\delta - 1, \ldots, -\delta - 1) \in \mathbb{Z}^{\widetilde{m}+n}$ $\boldsymbol{\tau} \leftarrow (\deg(\mathfrak{m}_j) + \delta + 1)_{1 \leqslant j \leqslant n}$
3. $\widetilde{\mathbf{P}} \leftarrow$ the **u**-Popov order basis for $[\widetilde{\mathbf{F}}^\mathsf{T} | \operatorname{diag}(\mathfrak{M})]^\mathsf{T}$ and $\boldsymbol{\tau}$ $\mathbf{P} \leftarrow$ the principal $\widetilde{m} \times \widetilde{m}$ submatrix of $\widetilde{\mathbf{P}}$
4. Return the submatrix of $\mathbf{P}\mathcal{E}$ formed by the rows at indices $\alpha_1 + \cdots + \alpha_i$ for $1 \leqslant i \leqslant m$

Proposition 2.4. *Algorithm* KnownDegPolModSys *is correct. Writing* $\sigma = \deg(\mathfrak{m}_1) + \cdots + \deg(\mathfrak{m}_n)$ *and assuming* $\sigma \geqslant m \geqslant n$, *it uses* $\widetilde{\mathcal{O}}(m^{\omega-1}\sigma)$ *operations in* $\mathbb{K}$.

Proof. By Lemmas 2.3 and 2.1, since $\min(-\widetilde{\boldsymbol{\delta}}) > -\delta - 1$ and $\mathbf{u} = (-\widetilde{\boldsymbol{\delta}}, -\delta - 1, \ldots, -\delta - 1)$, the $-\widetilde{\boldsymbol{\delta}}$-Popov solution basis for $(\mathfrak{M},\widetilde{\mathbf{F}})$ is the principal $\widetilde{m}\times\widetilde{m}$ submatrix of the $\mathbf{u}$-Popov nullspace basis $\mathbf{B}$ for $[\widetilde{\mathbf{F}}^{\mathsf{T}}|\operatorname{diag}(\mathfrak{M})]^{\mathsf{T}}$, and $\mathbf{B}$ has $\mathbf{u}$-pivot index $\{1,\ldots,\widetilde{m}\}$, $\mathbf{u}$-pivot degree $\widetilde{\boldsymbol{\delta}}$, and $\deg(\mathbf{B})\leqslant\delta$. Then, by Lemma 2.2, $\mathbf{B}$ is formed by the first $\widetilde{m}$ rows of $\widetilde{\mathbf{P}}$ at Step **3**, hence $\mathbf{P}$ is the $\mathbf{d}$-Popov solution basis for $(\mathfrak{M},\mathbf{F})$. The correctness then follows from Lemma 2.3.

Since $|\boldsymbol{\delta}|\leqslant\sigma$, $\mathcal{E}$ has $\widetilde{m}\leqslant 2m$ rows and $\mathcal{E}\mathbf{F} \bmod \mathfrak{M}$ can be computed in $\widetilde{\mathcal{O}}(m\sigma)$ operations using fast polynomial division [13]. The cost bound of Step **3** follows from [21, Theorem 1.4] since $\tau_1+\cdots+\tau_n=\sigma+n(1+\lceil\sigma/m\rceil)\in\mathcal{O}(\sigma)$. □

2.2 The case of one equation

We now present our main new ingredients, focusing on the case $n=1$. First, we show that when the shift $\mathbf{s}$ has a small *amplitude* $\operatorname{amp}(\mathbf{s})=\max(\mathbf{s})-\min(\mathbf{s})$, one can solve Problem 2 via an order basis computation at small order.

Lemma 2.5. *Let $\mathfrak{m}\in\mathbb{K}[X]_{\neq 0}$, $\mathbf{s}\in\mathbb{Z}^m$, and $\mathbf{F}\in\mathbb{K}[X]^{m\times 1}$ with $\deg(\mathbf{F})<\deg(\mathfrak{m})=\sigma$. Then, for any $\tau\geqslant\operatorname{amp}(\mathbf{s})+2\sigma$, the $\mathbf{s}$-Popov solution basis for $(\mathfrak{m},\mathbf{F})$ is the principal $m\times m$ submatrix of the $\mathbf{u}$-Popov order basis for $[\mathbf{F}^{\mathsf{T}}|\mathfrak{m}]^{\mathsf{T}}$ and τ, with $\mathbf{u}=(\mathbf{s},\min(\mathbf{s}))\in\mathbb{Z}^{m+1}$.*

Proof. Let $\mathbf{A}=\left[\begin{smallmatrix}\mathbf{P}&\mathbf{q}\\\mathbf{p}&q\end{smallmatrix}\right]$ denote the $\mathbf{u}$-Popov order basis for $[\mathbf{F}^{\mathsf{T}}|\mathfrak{m}]^{\mathsf{T}}$ and τ, where $\mathbf{P}\in\mathbb{K}[X]^{m\times m}$ and $q\in\mathbb{K}[X]$. Consider $\mathbf{B}=[\bar{\mathbf{P}}|\bar{\mathbf{q}}]$ the $\mathbf{u}$-Popov nullspace basis of $[\mathbf{F}^{\mathsf{T}}|\mathfrak{m}]^{\mathsf{T}}$: thanks to Lemma 2.1, it is enough to prove that $\mathbf{B}=[\mathbf{P}|\mathbf{q}]$.

First, we have $\operatorname{rdeg}(\mathbf{p})\leqslant\deg(q)$ by choice of $\mathbf{u}$, so that $q\mathfrak{m}\neq 0$ implies $\deg(\mathbf{pF}+q\mathfrak{m})=\deg(q)+\sigma$. Since $\mathbf{pF}+q\mathfrak{m}=0 \bmod X^{\tau}$, this gives $\deg(q)+\sigma\geqslant\tau$. This also shows that the $\mathbf{u}$-pivot entries of $\mathbf{B}$ are located in $\bar{\mathbf{P}}$.

Then, since the sum of the $\mathbf{u}$-pivot degrees of $\mathbf{A}$ is at most τ, the sum of the $\mathbf{s}$-pivot degrees of $\mathbf{P}$ is at most σ; with $[\mathbf{P}|\mathbf{q}]$ in $\mathbf{u}$-Popov form, this gives $\deg(\mathbf{q})<\sigma+\operatorname{amp}(\mathbf{s})\leqslant\tau-\sigma$. We obtain $\deg(\mathbf{PF}+\mathbf{q}\mathfrak{m})<\tau$, so that $\mathbf{PF}+\mathbf{q}\mathfrak{m}=0$. Thus, the minimality of $\mathbf{B}$ and $\mathbf{A}$ gives the conclusion. □

When $\operatorname{amp}(\mathbf{s})\in\mathcal{O}(\sigma)$, this gives a fast solution to our problem. In what follows, we present a divide-and-conquer approach on $\operatorname{amp}(\mathbf{s})$, with base case $\operatorname{amp}(\mathbf{s})\in\mathcal{O}(\sigma)$.

We first give an overview, assuming $\mathbf{s}$ is non-decreasing. A key ingredient is that when $\operatorname{amp}(\mathbf{s})$ is large compared to σ, then $\mathbf{P}$ has a lower block triangular shape, since it is in $\mathbf{s}$-Popov form with sum of $\mathbf{s}$-pivot degrees $|\boldsymbol{\delta}|\leqslant\sigma$. Typically, if $s_{i+1}-s_i\geqslant\sigma$ for some i then $\mathbf{P}=\left[\begin{smallmatrix}\mathbf{P}^{(1)}&\mathbf{0}\\ *&\mathbf{P}^{(2)}\end{smallmatrix}\right]$ with $\mathbf{P}^{(1)}\in\mathbb{K}[X]^{i\times i}$. Even though the block sizes are unknown in general, we show that they can be revealed efficiently along with $\boldsymbol{\delta}$ by a divide-and-conquer algorithm, as follows.

First, we use a recursive call with the first j entries $\mathbf{s}^{(0)}$ of $\mathbf{s}$ and $\mathbf{F}^{(0)}$ of $\mathbf{F}$, where j is such that $\operatorname{amp}(\mathbf{s}^{(0)})$ is about half of $\operatorname{amp}(\mathbf{s})$. This reveals the first $i\leqslant j$ entries $\boldsymbol{\delta}^{(1)}$ of $\boldsymbol{\delta}$ and the first i rows $[\mathbf{P}^{(1)}|\mathbf{0}]$ of $\mathbf{P}$, with $\mathbf{P}^{(1)}\in\mathbb{K}[X]^{i\times i}$. A central point is that $\operatorname{amp}(\mathbf{s}^{(2)})$ is about half of $\operatorname{amp}(\mathbf{s})$ as well, where $\mathbf{s}^{(2)}$ is the tail of $\mathbf{s}$ starting at the entry $i+1$.

Then, knowing the degrees $\boldsymbol{\delta}^{(1)}$ allows us to set up an order basis computation that yields a *residual*, that is, a column $\mathbf{G}\in\mathbb{K}[X]^{(m-i)\times 1}$ and a modulus $\mathfrak{n}$ such that we can continue the computation of $\mathbf{P}$ using a second recursive call, which consists in computing the $\mathbf{s}^{(2)}$-Popov solution basis for $(\mathfrak{n},\mathbf{G})$. From these two calls we obtain $\boldsymbol{\delta}$, and then we recover $\mathbf{P}$ using Algorithm 1.

Now we present the details. We fix $\mathbf{F}\in\mathbb{K}[X]^{m\times 1}$, $\mathfrak{m}\in\mathbb{K}[X]_{\neq 0}$ with $\sigma=\deg(\mathfrak{m})>\deg(\mathbf{F})$, $\mathbf{s}\in\mathbb{Z}^m$, $\mathbf{P}$ the $\mathbf{s}$-Popov solution basis for $(\mathfrak{m},\mathbf{F})$, and $\boldsymbol{\delta}$ its $\mathbf{s}$-pivot degree. In what follows, $\boldsymbol{\pi}^{\mathbf{s}}=(\pi_1,\ldots,\pi_m)$ is any permutation of $\{1,\ldots,m\}$ such that $(s_{\pi_1},\ldots,s_{\pi_m})$ is non-decreasing.

Then, for $\mathbf{t}=(t_1,\ldots,t_m)\in\mathbb{Z}^m$ we write $\mathbf{t}_{[i:j]}$ for the subtuple of $\mathbf{t}$ formed by its entries at indices $\{\pi_i,\ldots,\pi_j\}$, and for a matrix $\mathbf{M}\in\mathbb{K}[X]^{m\times m}$ we write $\mathbf{M}_{[i:j,k:l]}$ for the submatrix of $\mathbf{M}$ formed by its rows at indices $\{\pi_i,\pi_{i+1},\ldots,\pi_j\}$ and columns at indices $\{\pi_k,\pi_{k+1},\ldots,\pi_l\}$. The main ideas in this subsection can be understood by focusing on the case of a non-decreasing $\mathbf{s}$, taking $\pi_i=i$ for all i: then we have $\mathbf{t}_{[i:j]}=(t_i,t_{i+1},\ldots,t_j)$ and $\mathbf{M}_{[i:j,k:l]}=(\mathbf{M}_{u,v})_{i\leqslant u\leqslant j,k\leqslant v\leqslant l}$.

We now introduce the notion of splitting index, which will help us to locate zero blocks in $\mathbf{P}$.

Definition 2.6 (Splitting index). *Let $\mathbf{d}\in\mathbb{N}^m$, $\mathbf{t}\in\mathbb{Z}^m$ and $\boldsymbol{\pi}^{\mathbf{t}}=(\mu_i)_i$. Then, $i\in\{1,\ldots,m-1\}$ is a* splitting index *for $(\mathbf{d},\mathbf{t})$ if $d_{\mu_j}+t_{\mu_j}-t_{\mu_{i+1}}<0$ for all $j\in\{1,\ldots,i\}$.*

In particular, if i is a splitting index for $(\boldsymbol{\delta},\mathbf{s})$, then we have $[\mathbf{P}_{[:i,:i]}|\mathbf{P}_{[:i,i+1:]}]=[\mathbf{P}_{[:i,:i]}|\mathbf{0}]$. Our algorithm first looks for such a splitting index, and then uses $\mathbf{P}_{[:i,i+1:]}=\mathbf{0}$ to split the problem into two subproblems of dimensions i and $m-i$.

To find a splitting index, we rely on the following property: if $(\mathbf{d},\mathbf{t})$ does not admit a splitting index, then $|\mathbf{d}|>\operatorname{amp}(\mathbf{t})$. This allows us to partition $\mathbf{s}$ into ℓ subtuples which all contain a splitting index, as follows.

Given $\alpha\in\mathbb{Z}_{>0}$ we let $\ell=1+\lfloor\operatorname{amp}(\mathbf{s})/\alpha\rfloor$ and we consider the subtuples $\mathbf{s}_1,\ldots,\mathbf{s}_\ell$ of $\mathbf{s}$ where $\mathbf{s}_k$ consists of the entries of $\mathbf{s}$ in $\{\min(\mathbf{s})+(k-1)\alpha,\ldots,\min(\mathbf{s})+k\alpha-1\}$; this gives a subroutine $\textsc{Partition}(\mathbf{s},\alpha)=(\mathbf{s}_1,\ldots,\mathbf{s}_\ell)$. Now we take $\alpha\geqslant 2\sigma$ and we assume $s_{\pi_{i+1}}-s_{\pi_i}\leqslant\sigma$ for $1\leqslant i<m$ without loss of generality [21, Appendix A]. Then, for $1\leqslant k<\ell$, since $|\boldsymbol{\delta}|\leqslant\sigma$ and $\operatorname{amp}(\mathbf{t})\geqslant\sigma$ with $\mathbf{t}=(\mathbf{s}_k,\min(\mathbf{s}_{k+1}))$, by the above remark $\mathbf{s}_k$ contains a splitting index for $(\boldsymbol{\delta},\mathbf{s})$.

Still, we do not know in advance which entries of $\mathbf{s}_k$ correspond to splitting indices for $(\boldsymbol{\delta},\mathbf{s})$. Thus we recursively compute the $\mathbf{s}$-Popov solution basis $\mathbf{P}^{(0)}$ for $\mathbf{s}_1,\ldots,\mathbf{s}_{\ell/2}$, and we are now going to prove that this gives us a splitting index which divides the computation into two subproblems, the first of which has been already solved by computing $\mathbf{P}^{(0)}$.

Lemma 2.7. *Let $j\in\{2,\ldots,m\}$, $\mathbf{s}^{(0)}=\mathbf{s}_{[:j]}$, $\mathbf{P}^{(0)}$ be the $\mathbf{s}^{(0)}$-Popov solution basis for $(\mathfrak{m},\mathbf{F}_{[:j]})$, and $\boldsymbol{\delta}^{(0)}$ be its $\mathbf{s}^{(0)}$-pivot degree. Suppose that there is a splitting index $i\leqslant j$ for $(\boldsymbol{\delta}^{(0)},\mathbf{s}^{(0)})$. Let $\mathbf{P}^{(1)}\in\mathbb{K}[X]^{i\times i}$ be the $\mathbf{s}^{(1)}$-Popov solution basis for $(\mathfrak{m},\mathbf{F}_{[:i]})$ with $\mathbf{s}^{(1)}=\mathbf{s}_{[:i]}$, and let $\boldsymbol{\delta}^{(1)}$ be its $\mathbf{s}^{(1)}$-pivot degree. Then i is a splitting index for $(\boldsymbol{\delta},\mathbf{s})$ and $\mathbf{P}_{[:i,:i]}=\mathbf{P}^{(1)}=\mathbf{P}^{(0)}_{[:i,:i]}$, hence $\boldsymbol{\delta}_{[:i]}=\boldsymbol{\delta}^{(1)}=\boldsymbol{\delta}^{(0)}_{[:i]}$ (where $\mathbf{P}^{(0)}$ and $\boldsymbol{\delta}^{(0)}$ are indexed by $\{\pi_1,\ldots,\pi_j\}$ sorted increasingly).*

Proof. Since i is a splitting index for $(\boldsymbol{\delta}^{(0)},\mathbf{s}^{(0)})$ we have $[\mathbf{P}^{(0)}_{[:i,:i]}|\mathbf{P}^{(0)}_{[:i,i+1:]}]=[\mathbf{Q}|\mathbf{0}]$ for some $\mathbf{Q}\in\mathbb{K}[X]^{i\times i}$. Now, for any $\mathbf{B}\in\mathbb{K}[X]^{m\times m}$ with $[\mathbf{B}_{[:i,:i]}|\mathbf{B}_{[:i,i+1:]}]=[\mathbf{P}^{(1)}|\mathbf{0}]$, $\mathbf{B}_{[i,:]}$ is in $\mathbf{s}$-Popov form with its rows being solutions for $(\mathfrak{M},\mathbf{F})$. Then, by minimality of $\mathbf{P}$, $\mathbf{P}_{[:i,:]}$ has $\mathbf{s}$-pivot degree at most $\boldsymbol{\delta}^{(1)}$ componentwise, so that i is also a splitting index for $(\boldsymbol{\delta},\mathbf{s})$, and in particular $[\mathbf{P}_{[:i,:i]}|\mathbf{P}_{[:i,i+1:]}]=[\mathbf{R}|\mathbf{0}]$ for some $\mathbf{R}\in\mathbb{K}[X]^{i\times i}$. It remains to prove that $\mathbf{Q}=\mathbf{R}=\mathbf{P}^{(1)}$.

Since $\mathbf{RF}_{[:i]}=0 \bmod \mathfrak{m}$ and $\mathbf{R}=\mathbf{P}_{[:i,:i]}$ is in $\mathbf{s}^{(1)}$-Popov form, proving that all solutions $\mathbf{p}\in\mathbb{K}[X]^{1\times i}$ for $(\mathfrak{m},\mathbf{F}_{[:i]})$ are in the row space of $\mathbf{R}$ is enough to obtain $\mathbf{R}=\mathbf{P}^{(1)}$. Since $\mathbf{q}\in\mathbb{K}[X]^{1\times m}$ defined by $[\mathbf{q}_{[:i]}|\mathbf{q}_{[i+1:]}]=[\mathbf{p}|\mathbf{0}]$ is a solution for $(\mathfrak{m},\mathbf{F})$, $\mathbf{q}=\boldsymbol{\lambda}\mathbf{P}$ for some $\boldsymbol{\lambda}\in\mathbb{K}[X]^{1\times m}$. Now $\mathbf{P}$ is nonsingular, thus $\mathbf{P}_{[:i,i+1:]}=\mathbf{0}$ implies that $[\boldsymbol{\lambda}_{[:i]}|\boldsymbol{\lambda}_{[i+1:]}]=$

$[\boldsymbol{\mu}|\mathbf{0}]$ with $\boldsymbol{\mu} \in \mathbb{K}[X]^{1\times i}$, hence $\mathbf{p} = \mathbf{q}_{[:i]} = \boldsymbol{\lambda}_{[:i]}\mathbf{P}_{[:i,:i]} + \boldsymbol{\lambda}_{[i+1:]}\mathbf{P}_{[i+1:,:i]} = \boldsymbol{\mu}\mathbf{Q}$. Similar arguments give $\mathbf{Q} = \mathbf{P}^{(1)}$. □

The next two lemmas show that knowing $\boldsymbol{\delta}^{(1)}$, which is $\boldsymbol{\delta}_{[:i]}$, allows us to compute a so-called *residual* $(\mathfrak{n}, \mathbf{G})$ from which we can complete the computation of $\boldsymbol{\delta}$ and $\mathbf{P}$.

LEMMA 2.8. *Let $\mathbf{s}^{(2)} = \mathbf{s}_{[i+1:]}$, $\mathbf{d} = -\boldsymbol{\delta}^{(1)} + \min(\mathbf{s}^{(2)}) - 2\sigma \in \mathbb{Z}^i$, $\mathbf{v} \in \mathbb{Z}^m$ be such that $[\mathbf{v}_{[:i]}|\mathbf{v}_{[i+1:]}] = [\mathbf{d}|\mathbf{s}^{(2)}]$, and $\mathbf{u} = (\mathbf{v}, \min(\mathbf{d})) \in \mathbb{Z}^{m+1}$. Let $\left[\begin{smallmatrix}\mathbf{A} & \mathbf{q}\\ \mathbf{p} & q\end{smallmatrix}\right]$ be the $\mathbf{u}$-Popov order basis for $[\mathbf{F}^\mathsf{T}|\mathfrak{m}]^\mathsf{T}$ and 2σ, where $\mathbf{A} \in \mathbb{K}[X]^{m\times m}$ and $q \in \mathbb{K}[X]$. Then we have $\deg(q) \geqslant \sigma$, $\mathbf{A}_{[:i,i+1:]} = \mathbf{0}$, $\mathbf{p}_{[i+1:]} = \mathbf{0}$, and $[\mathbf{A}_{[:i,:i]}|\mathbf{q}_{[:i]}] = [\mathbf{P}^{(1)}|\mathbf{q}^{(1)}]$ with $\mathbf{q}^{(1)} = -\mathbf{P}^{(1)}\mathbf{F}_{[:i]}/\mathfrak{m}$.*

PROOF. Since $\mathbf{u} = (\mathbf{v}, \min(\mathbf{v}))$ we have $\deg(\mathbf{p}) \leqslant \deg(q)$, and since $\deg(\mathbf{F}) < \deg(\mathfrak{m})$ the degree of $\mathbf{pF}+q\mathfrak{m}$ is $\deg(q)+\sigma$; then $\mathbf{pF}+q\mathfrak{m} = 0 \bmod X^{2\sigma}$ implies $\deg(q)+\sigma \geqslant 2\sigma$. Now, since $\mathbf{A}$ is in $\mathbf{v}$-Popov form and $\deg(\mathbf{A}) \leqslant 2\sigma - \deg(q) < 2\sigma$, from $\min(\mathbf{s}^{(2)}) \geqslant \max(\mathbf{d})+2\sigma$ we get $\mathbf{A}_{[:i,i+1:]} = \mathbf{0}$. Besides, $\mathbf{p}_{[i+1:]} = \mathbf{0}$ since either $\deg(q) < 2\sigma$ and then $\min(\mathbf{s}^{(2)}) > \min(\mathbf{d})+\deg(q)$, or $\mathbf{A}$ is the identity matrix and then $\mathbf{p} = \mathbf{0}$.

Furthermore, by Lemma 2.1 $[\mathbf{P}^{(1)}|\mathbf{q}^{(1)}]$ is the $(\mathbf{d}, \min(\mathbf{d}))$-Popov nullspace basis for $[\mathbf{F}_{[:i]}^\mathsf{T}|\mathfrak{m}]^\mathsf{T}$, with $(\mathbf{d}, \min(\mathbf{d}))$-pivot index $\{1, \ldots, i\}$, $(\mathbf{d}, \min(\mathbf{d}))$-pivot degree $\boldsymbol{\delta}^{(1)}$ and degree at most $\max(\boldsymbol{\delta}^{(1)})$. Then, as in the proof of Lemma 2.2, one can show that $[\mathbf{A}_{[:i,:i]}|\mathbf{q}_{[:i]}] = [\mathbf{P}^{(1)}|\mathbf{q}^{(1)}]$. □

Thus, up to row and column permutations this order basis is $\left[\begin{smallmatrix}\mathbf{P}^{(1)} & \mathbf{0} & \mathbf{q}^{(1)}\\ * & \mathbf{P}^{(2)} & *\\ * & \mathbf{0} & q\end{smallmatrix}\right]$ with $\mathbf{P}^{(2)} = \mathbf{A}_{[i+1:,i+1:]} \in \mathbb{K}[X]^{(m-i)\times(m-i)}$ in $\mathbf{s}^{(2)}$-Popov form; let $\boldsymbol{\delta}^{(2)}$ denote its $\mathbf{s}^{(2)}$-pivot degree.

LEMMA 2.9. *Let $\mathfrak{n} = X^{-2\sigma}(\mathbf{p}_{[i+1:]}\mathbf{F}_{[i+1:]} + q\mathfrak{m}) \in \mathbb{K}[X]$ and $\mathbf{G} = X^{-2\sigma}(\mathbf{A}_{[i+1:,:]}\mathbf{F} + \mathbf{q}_{[i+1:]}\mathfrak{m}) \in \mathbb{K}[X]^{(m-i)\times 1}$. Then, $\deg(\mathbf{G}) < \deg(\mathfrak{n}) \leqslant \sigma - |\boldsymbol{\delta}^{(1)}| - |\boldsymbol{\delta}^{(2)}|$. Let $\mathbf{P}^{(3)}$ be the $\mathbf{t}$-Popov solution basis for $(\mathfrak{n}, \mathbf{G})$ with $\mathbf{t} = \mathrm{rdeg}_{\mathbf{s}^{(2)}}(\mathbf{P}^{(2)})$ and $\boldsymbol{\delta}^{(3)}$ be its $\mathbf{t}$-pivot degree. Then, $(\boldsymbol{\delta}_{[:i]}, \boldsymbol{\delta}_{[i+1:]}) = (\boldsymbol{\delta}^{(1)}, \boldsymbol{\delta}^{(2)} + \boldsymbol{\delta}^{(3)})$.*

PROOF. The sum $|\boldsymbol{\delta}^{(1)}| + |\boldsymbol{\delta}^{(2)}| + \deg(q)$ of the $\mathbf{u}$-pivot degrees of $\left[\begin{smallmatrix}\mathbf{A} & \mathbf{q}\\ \mathbf{p} & q\end{smallmatrix}\right]$ is at most the order 2σ. Thus, we have $\deg(\mathfrak{n}) = \deg(q) - \sigma \leqslant \sigma - |\boldsymbol{\delta}^{(1)}| - |\boldsymbol{\delta}^{(2)}|$, $\deg(\mathbf{A}_{[i+1:,:i]}) < |\boldsymbol{\delta}^{(1)}| \leqslant \sigma$, $\deg(\mathbf{A}_{[i+1:,i+1:]}) \leqslant |\boldsymbol{\delta}^{(2)}| \leqslant \sigma$, and $\deg(\mathbf{q}_{[i+1:]}) < \deg(q)$. This implies $\deg(\mathbf{G}) < \deg(q) - \sigma = \deg(\mathfrak{n})$.

Let $\mathbf{q}^{(3)} = -\mathbf{P}^{(3)}\mathbf{G}/\mathfrak{n}$ and $t = \mathrm{rdeg}_{\mathbf{u}}([\mathbf{p}|q]) = \deg(q) + \min(\mathbf{d}) \leqslant \min(\mathbf{s}^{(2)}) \leqslant \min(\mathbf{t})$. By Lemma 2.1, $[\mathbf{P}^{(3)}|\mathbf{q}^{(3)}]$ is the $(\mathbf{t}, t)$-Popov nullspace basis for $[\mathbf{G}^\mathsf{T}|\mathfrak{n}]^\mathsf{T}$. Defining $\mathbf{B} \in \mathbb{K}[X]^{m\times m}$ and $\mathbf{c} \in \mathbb{K}[X]^{m\times 1}$ by $\left[\begin{smallmatrix}\mathbf{B}_{[:i,:i]} & \mathbf{B}_{[:i,i+1:]} & \mathbf{c}_{[:i]}\\ \mathbf{B}_{[i+1:,:i]} & \mathbf{B}_{[i+1:,i+1:]} & \mathbf{c}_{[i+1:]}\end{smallmatrix}\right] = \left[\begin{smallmatrix}\mathbf{I} & \mathbf{0} & \mathbf{0}\\ \mathbf{0} & \mathbf{P}^{(3)} & \mathbf{q}^{(3)}\end{smallmatrix}\right]$, then $[\mathbf{B}\ \mathbf{c}]\left[\begin{smallmatrix}\mathbf{A} & \mathbf{q}\\ \mathbf{p} & q\end{smallmatrix}\right]$ is a $\mathbf{u}$-minimal nullspace basis of $[\mathbf{F}^\mathsf{T}|\mathfrak{m}]^\mathsf{T}$ [36, Theorem 3.9]. Thus Lemma 2.1 implies that $\bar{\mathbf{P}} = [\mathbf{B}\ \mathbf{c}]\left[\begin{smallmatrix}\mathbf{A}\\ \mathbf{p}\end{smallmatrix}\right]$ is a $\mathbf{v}$-minimal solution basis for $(\mathfrak{m}, \mathbf{F})$.

It is easily checked that $\mathbf{P}$ is in $\mathbf{v}$-Popov form, so that the $\mathbf{v}$-Popov form of $\bar{\mathbf{P}}$ is $\mathbf{P}$ and its $\mathbf{v}$-pivot degree is $\boldsymbol{\delta}$. Besides $\left[\begin{smallmatrix}\bar{\mathbf{P}}_{[:i,:i]} & \bar{\mathbf{P}}_{[:i,i+1:]}\\ \bar{\mathbf{P}}_{[i+1:,:i]} & \bar{\mathbf{P}}_{[i+1:,i+1:]}\end{smallmatrix}\right] = \left[\begin{smallmatrix}\mathbf{P}^{(1)} & \mathbf{0}\\ \mathbf{P}^{(3)}\mathbf{A}_{2,1}+\mathbf{q}^{(3)}\mathbf{A}_{3,1} & \mathbf{P}^{(3)}\mathbf{P}^{(2)}\end{smallmatrix}\right]$, so that $(\boldsymbol{\delta}_{[:i]}, \boldsymbol{\delta}_{[i+1:]}) = (\boldsymbol{\delta}^{(1)}, \boldsymbol{\delta}^{(2)} + \boldsymbol{\delta}^{(3)})$ [21, Section 3]. □

This results in Algorithm 2. It takes as input α which dictates the amplitude of the subtuples that partition $\mathbf{s}$; as mentioned above, the initial call can be made with $\alpha = 2\sigma$.

PROPOSITION 2.10. *Algorithm* POLMODSYSONE *is correct and uses $\widetilde{\mathcal{O}}(m^{\omega-1}\sigma)$ operations in $\mathbb{K}$.*

PROOF. The correctness follows from the results in this subsection. By [21, Theorem 1.4], each leaf of the recursion at Step **1.a** in dimension m uses $\widetilde{\mathcal{O}}(m^{\omega-1}\alpha)$ operations.

ALGORITHM 2 (POLMODSYSONE).

Input: a polynomial $\mathfrak{m} \in \mathbb{K}[X]_{\neq 0}$ of degree σ, a column $\mathbf{F} \in \mathbb{K}[X]^{m\times 1}$ with $\deg(\mathbf{F}) < \deg(\mathfrak{m})$, a shift $\mathbf{s} \in \mathbb{Z}^m$, a parameter $\alpha \in \mathbb{Z}_{>0}$ with $\alpha \geqslant 2\sigma$.

Output: the $\mathbf{s}$-Popov solution basis for $(\mathfrak{m}, \mathbf{F})$ and the $\mathbf{s}$-minimal degree $\boldsymbol{\delta}$ of $(\mathfrak{m}, \mathbf{F})$.

1. If $\mathrm{amp}(\mathbf{s}) \leqslant 2\alpha$:
  a. $\mathbf{A} \leftarrow$ the $(\mathbf{s}, \min(\mathbf{s}))$-Popov order basis for $[\mathbf{F}^\mathsf{T}|\mathfrak{m}]^\mathsf{T}$ and $2\alpha + 2\sigma$; return the principal $m\times m$ submatrix of $\mathbf{A}$ and the degrees of its diagonal entries

2. Else: /* $\ell = 1 + \lfloor \mathrm{amp}(\mathbf{s})/\alpha \rfloor \geqslant 3$ */
  a. $(\mathbf{s}_1, \ldots, \mathbf{s}_\ell) \leftarrow$ PARTITION$(\mathbf{s}, \alpha)$,
  $j \leftarrow$ sum of the lengths of $\mathbf{s}_1, \ldots, \mathbf{s}_{\lceil \ell/2\rceil}$, $\mathbf{s}^{(0)} \leftarrow \mathbf{s}_{[:j]}$,
  $(\mathbf{P}^{(0)}, \boldsymbol{\delta}^{(0)}) \leftarrow$ POLMODSYSONE$(\mathfrak{m}, \mathbf{F}_{[:j]}, \mathbf{s}^{(0)}, \alpha)$
  b. $i \leftarrow$ the largest splitting index for $(\boldsymbol{\delta}^{(0)}, \mathbf{s}^{(0)})$, $\boldsymbol{\delta}^{(1)} \leftarrow \boldsymbol{\delta}^{(0)}_{[:i]}$, $\mathbf{s}^{(2)} \leftarrow \mathbf{s}_{[i+1:]}$, $\mathbf{d} = -\boldsymbol{\delta}^{(1)} + \min(\mathbf{s}^{(2)}) - 2\sigma$, $\mathbf{v} \in \mathbb{Z}^m$ with $[\mathbf{v}_{[:i]}|\mathbf{v}_{[i+1:]}] \leftarrow [\mathbf{d}|\mathbf{s}^{(2)}]$, $\mathbf{u} = (\mathbf{v}, \min(\mathbf{d}))$
  c. $\left[\begin{smallmatrix}\mathbf{A} & \mathbf{q}\\ \mathbf{p} & q\end{smallmatrix}\right] \leftarrow \mathbf{u}$-Popov order basis for $[\mathbf{F}^\mathsf{T}|\mathfrak{m}]^\mathsf{T}$ and 2σ,
  $\boldsymbol{\delta}^{(2)} \leftarrow$ the $\mathbf{s}^{(2)}$-pivot degree of $\mathbf{A}_{[i+1:,i+1:]}$
  $\mathbf{G} \leftarrow X^{-2\sigma}(\mathbf{A}_{[i+1:,:]}\mathbf{F} + \mathbf{q}_{[i+1:]}\mathfrak{m})$,
  $\mathfrak{n} \leftarrow X^{-2\sigma}(\mathbf{p}_{[i+1:]}\mathbf{F}_{[i+1:]} + q\mathfrak{m})$.
  d. $\mathbf{t} \leftarrow \mathbf{s}^{(2)} + \boldsymbol{\delta}^{(2)} = \mathrm{rdeg}_{\mathbf{s}^{(2)}}(\mathbf{A}_{[i+1:,i+1:]})$,
  $(\mathbf{P}^{(3)}, \boldsymbol{\delta}^{(3)}) \leftarrow$ POLMODSYSONE$(\mathfrak{n}, \mathbf{G}, \mathbf{t}, \alpha)$
  e. $\boldsymbol{\delta} \in \mathbb{N}^m$ with $(\boldsymbol{\delta}_{[:i]}, \boldsymbol{\delta}_{[i+1:]}) \leftarrow (\boldsymbol{\delta}^{(1)}, \boldsymbol{\delta}^{(2)} + \boldsymbol{\delta}^{(3)})$
  $\mathbf{P} \leftarrow$ KNOWNDEGPOLMODSYS$(\mathfrak{m}, \mathbf{F}, \mathbf{s}, \boldsymbol{\delta})$
  f. Return $(\mathbf{P}, \boldsymbol{\delta})$

Running the algorithm with initial input $\alpha = 2\sigma$, the recursive tree has depth $\mathcal{O}(\log(\ell)) = \mathcal{O}(\log(1 + \mathrm{amp}(\mathbf{s})/2\sigma))$, with $\mathrm{amp}(\mathbf{s})/2\sigma \in \mathcal{O}(m^2)$ [21, Appendix A]. All recursive calls are for a modulus of degree $\sigma < \alpha$. The order basis computation at Step **2.c** uses $\widetilde{\mathcal{O}}(m^{\omega-1}\sigma)$ operations; the computation of $\mathbf{G}$ and $\mathfrak{n}$ at Step **2.c** can be done in time $\widetilde{\mathcal{O}}(m^{\omega-1}\sigma)$ using partial linearization as in Lemma 2.11 below; Step **2.e** uses $\widetilde{\mathcal{O}}(m^{\omega-1}\sigma)$ operations by Proposition 2.4.

On a given level of the tree, the sum of the dimensions of the column vector in input of each sub-problem is in $\mathcal{O}(m)$. Since $a^{\omega-1} + b^{\omega-1} \leqslant (a+b)^{\omega-1}$ for all $a, b > 0$, each level of the tree uses a total of $\widetilde{\mathcal{O}}(m^{\omega-1}\alpha)$ operations. □

2.3 Fast divide-and-conquer algorithm

Now that we have an efficient algorithm for $n = 1$, our main algorithm uses a divide-and-conquer approach on n. Similarly to [21, Algorithm 1], from the two bases obtained recursively we first deduce the $\mathbf{s}$-minimal degree $\boldsymbol{\delta}$, and then we use this knowledge to compute $\mathbf{P}$ with Algorithm 1. When $\sigma = \deg(\mathfrak{m}_1) + \cdots + \deg(\mathfrak{m}_n) \in \mathcal{O}(m)$, we rely on the algorithm LINEARIZATIONMIB in [20, Algorithm 9].

The computation of the so-called *residual* at Step **3.c** can be done efficiently using partial linearization, as follows.

LEMMA 2.11. *Let $\mathfrak{M} = (\mathfrak{m}_j)_j \in \mathbb{K}[X]^n_{\neq 0}$, $\mathbf{P} \in \mathbb{K}[X]^{m\times m}$, $\mathbf{F} \in \mathbb{K}[X]^{m\times n}$ with $m \geqslant n$ and $\deg(\mathbf{F}_{*,j}) < \sigma_j = \deg(\mathfrak{m}_j)$, and let $\sigma \geqslant m$ such that $\sigma \geqslant \sigma_1 + \cdots + \sigma_n$ and $|\mathrm{cdeg}(\mathbf{P})| \leqslant \sigma$. Then $\mathbf{PF} \bmod \mathfrak{M}$ can be computed in $\widetilde{\mathcal{O}}(m^{\omega-1}\sigma)$ operations.*

PROOF. Using notation from Lemma 2.3, we let $\widetilde{\mathbf{P}} \in \mathbb{K}[X]^{m\times\widetilde{m}}$ such that $\mathbf{P} = \widetilde{\mathbf{P}}\mathcal{E}$ and $\deg(\widetilde{\mathbf{P}}) < \lceil|\mathrm{cdeg}(\mathbf{P})|/m\rceil$. As above, $\widetilde{\mathbf{F}} = \mathcal{E}\mathbf{F} \bmod \mathfrak{M}$ can be computed in time $\widetilde{\mathcal{O}}(m\sigma)$. Here we want to compute $\mathbf{PF} \bmod \mathfrak{M} = \widetilde{\mathbf{P}}\,\widetilde{\mathbf{F}} \bmod \mathfrak{M}$.

ALGORITHM 3 (POLMODSYS).

Input: polynomials $\mathfrak{M} = (\mathfrak{m}_1, \ldots, \mathfrak{m}_n) \in \mathbb{K}[X]^n_{\neq 0}$, a matrix $\mathbf{F} \in \mathbb{K}[X]^{m\times n}$ with $\deg(\mathbf{F}_{*,j}) < \deg(\mathfrak{m}_j)$, a shift $\mathbf{s} \in \mathbb{Z}^m$.

Output: the $\mathbf{s}$-Popov solution basis for $(\mathfrak{M}, \mathbf{F})$ and the $\mathbf{s}$-minimal degree $\boldsymbol{\delta}$ of $(\mathfrak{M}, \mathbf{F})$.

1. If $\sigma = \deg(\mathfrak{m}_1) + \cdots + \deg(\mathfrak{m}_n) \leqslant m$:

a. Build $\mathbf{E} \in \mathbb{K}^{m\times\sigma}$ and $\mathbf{M} \in \mathbb{K}^{\sigma\times\sigma}$ as in Section 1.2

b. Return LINEARIZATIONMIB($\mathbf{E}, \mathbf{M}, \mathbf{s}, 2^{\lceil \log_2(\sigma)\rceil}$)

2. Else if $n = 1$: Return POLMODSYSONE($\mathfrak{m}_1, \mathbf{F}, \mathbf{s}, 2\sigma$)

3. Else:

a. $\mathfrak{M}^{(1)}, \mathbf{F}^{(1)} \leftarrow (\mathfrak{m}_1, \ldots, \mathfrak{m}_{\lfloor n/2\rfloor}), \mathbf{F}_{*,1\ldots\lfloor n/2\rfloor}$
$\mathfrak{M}^{(2)}, \mathbf{F}^{(2)} \leftarrow (\mathfrak{m}_{\lfloor n/2\rfloor+1}, \ldots, \mathfrak{m}_n), \mathbf{F}_{*,\lfloor n/2\rfloor+1\ldots n}$

b. $\mathbf{P}^{(1)}, \boldsymbol{\delta}^{(1)} \leftarrow$ POLMODSYS($\mathfrak{M}^{(1)}, \mathbf{F}^{(1)}, \mathbf{s}$)

c. $\mathbf{R} \leftarrow \mathbf{P}^{(1)}\mathbf{F}^{(2)} \bmod \mathfrak{M}^{(2)}$

d. $\mathbf{P}^{(2)}, \boldsymbol{\delta}^{(2)} \leftarrow$ POLMODSYS($\mathfrak{M}^{(2)}, \mathbf{R}, \mathrm{rdeg}_{\mathbf{s}}(\mathbf{P}^{(1)})$)

e. $\mathbf{P} \leftarrow$ KNOWNDEGPOLMODSYS($\mathfrak{M}, \mathbf{F}, \mathbf{s}, \boldsymbol{\delta}^{(1)} + \boldsymbol{\delta}^{(2)}$)

f. Return $(\mathbf{P}, \boldsymbol{\delta}^{(1)} + \boldsymbol{\delta}^{(2)})$

We have $\deg(\widetilde{\mathbf{P}}) \leqslant \lceil \sigma/m \rceil \leqslant 2\sigma/m$. Since $|\mathrm{cdeg}(\widetilde{\mathbf{F}})| < \sigma$ and $n \leqslant m \leqslant \widetilde{m} \leqslant 2m$, $\widetilde{\mathbf{F}}$ can be partially linearized into $\mathcal{O}(m)$ columns of degree $\mathcal{O}(\sigma/m)$. Then, $\widetilde{\mathbf{P}}\,\widetilde{\mathbf{F}}$ is computed in $\widetilde{\mathcal{O}}(m^{\omega-1}\sigma)$ operations. The j-th column of $\widetilde{\mathbf{P}}\,\widetilde{\mathbf{F}}$ has $\widetilde{m} \leqslant 2m$ rows and degree less than $\sigma_j + 2\sigma/m$: it can be reduced modulo $\mathfrak{m}_j$ in $\widetilde{\mathcal{O}}(\sigma + m\sigma_j)$ operations [13, Chapter 9]; summing over $1 \leqslant j \leqslant n$ with $n \leqslant m$, this is in $\widetilde{\mathcal{O}}(m\sigma)$. □

PROOF OF THEOREM 1.4. The correctness and the cost $\widetilde{\mathcal{O}}(m^{\omega-1}\sigma)$ for Steps **1** and **2** of Algorithm 3 follow from [20, Theorem 1.4] and Proposition 2.10. With the costs of Steps **3.c** and **3.e** given in Proposition 2.4 and Lemma 2.11, we obtain the announced cost bound.

Now, using notation in Step **3**, suppose $\mathbf{P}^{(1)}$ and $\mathbf{P}^{(2)}$ are the $\mathbf{s}$- and $\mathrm{rdeg}_{\mathbf{s}}(\mathbf{P}^{(1)})$-Popov solution bases for $(\mathfrak{M}^{(1)}, \mathbf{F}^{(1)})$ and $(\mathfrak{M}^{(2)}, \mathbf{R})$. Then $\mathbf{P}^{(2)}\mathbf{P}^{(1)}$ is a solution basis for $(\mathfrak{M}, \mathbf{F})$: if $\mathbf{p}$ is a solution for $(\mathfrak{M}, \mathbf{F})$, it is one for $(\mathfrak{M}^{(1)}, \mathbf{F}^{(1)})$ and thus $\mathbf{p} = \boldsymbol{\lambda}\mathbf{P}^{(1)}$ for some $\boldsymbol{\lambda}$, and it is one for $(\mathfrak{M}^{(2)}, \mathbf{F}^{(2)})$ so that $\mathbf{p}\mathbf{F}^{(2)} = \boldsymbol{\lambda}\mathbf{P}^{(1)}\mathbf{F}^{(2)} = \boldsymbol{\lambda}\mathbf{R} = \mathbf{0} \bmod \mathfrak{M}^{(2)}$ and thus $\boldsymbol{\lambda} = \boldsymbol{\mu}\mathbf{P}^{(2)}$ for some $\boldsymbol{\mu}$; then $\mathbf{p} = \boldsymbol{\mu}\mathbf{P}^{(2)}\mathbf{P}^{(1)}$.

Then $\mathbf{P}^{(2)}\mathbf{P}^{(1)}$ is an $\mathbf{s}$-minimal solution basis for $(\mathfrak{M}, \mathbf{F})$ and its $\mathbf{s}$-Popov form has $\mathbf{s}$-pivot degree $\boldsymbol{\delta}^{(1)} + \boldsymbol{\delta}^{(2)}$ [21, Section 3]. The correctness follows from Proposition 2.4. □

3. FAST COMPUTATION OF THE SHIFTED POPOV FORM OF A MATRIX

3.1 Fast shifted Popov form algorithm

Our fast method for computing the $\mathbf{s}$-Popov form of a nonsingular $\mathbf{A} \in \mathbb{K}[X]^{m\times m}$ uses two steps, as follows.

1. Compute the Smith form of $\mathbf{A}$, giving the moduli $\mathfrak{M}$, and a corresponding right unimodular transformation, giving the equations $\mathbf{F}$, so that $\mathbf{A}$ is a solution basis for $(\mathfrak{M}, \mathbf{F})$.
2. Find the $\mathbf{s}$-Popov solution basis for $(\mathfrak{M}, \mathbf{F})$.

We first show the correctness of this approach.

LEMMA 3.1. *Let $\mathbf{A} \in \mathbb{K}[X]^{m\times m}$ be nonsingular and $\mathbf{S} = \mathbf{UAV}$ be the Smith form of $\mathbf{A}$ with $\mathbf{U}$ and $\mathbf{V}$ unimodular. Let $\mathfrak{M} \in \mathbb{K}[X]^m_{\neq 0}$ and $\mathbf{F} \in \mathbb{K}[X]^{m\times m}$ be such that $\mathbf{S} = \mathrm{diag}(\mathfrak{M})$ and $\mathbf{F} = \mathbf{V} \bmod \mathfrak{M}$. Then $\mathbf{A}$ is a solution basis for $(\mathfrak{M}, \mathbf{F})$.*

PROOF. Let $\mathbf{p} \in \mathbb{K}[X]^{1\times m}$. If $\mathbf{p}$ is in the row space of $\mathbf{A}$ then $\mathbf{p}$ is a solution for $(\mathfrak{M}, \mathbf{F})$ since $\mathbf{AV} = \mathbf{U}^{-1}\mathbf{S}$ with $\mathbf{U}^{-1}$ over $\mathbb{K}[X]$. Now if $\mathbf{pF} = 0 \bmod \mathfrak{M}$, then $\mathbf{pV} = \mathbf{qS}$ for some $\mathbf{q}$ and $\mathbf{p} = \mathbf{qUA}$ is in the row space of $\mathbf{A}$. □

Concerning the cost of Step **1**, such $\mathfrak{M}$ and $\mathbf{F}$ can be obtained in expected $\widetilde{\mathcal{O}}(m^\omega \deg(\mathbf{A}))$ operations, by computing

1.a $\mathbf{R}$ a row reduced form of $\mathbf{A}$ [16, Theorem 18],

1.b $\mathrm{diag}(\mathfrak{M})$ the Smith form of $\mathbf{R}$ [29, Algorithm 12],

1.c $(*, \mathbf{F})$ a reduced Smith transform for $\mathbf{R}$ [15, Figure 3.2];

as in [15, Figure 6.1], Steps **1.b** and **1.c** should be performed in conjunction with the preconditioning techniques detailed in [23]. One may take for $\mathfrak{M}$ only the nontrivial Smith factors, and for $\mathbf{F}$ only the nonzero columns of the transform.

The product of the moduli in $\mathfrak{M}$ is $\det(\mathbf{A})$ so that the sum of their degrees is $\deg(\det(\mathbf{A}))$. Then, according to Theorem 1.4, Step **2** of the algorithm outlined above costs $\widetilde{\mathcal{O}}(m^{\omega-1}\deg(\det(\mathbf{A})))$ operations. Thus this algorithm solves Problem 1 in expected $\widetilde{\mathcal{O}}(m^\omega \deg(\mathbf{A}))$ field operations.

3.2 Reducing to almost uniform degrees

In this subsection, we use the partial linearization techniques from [16, Section 6] to prove the following result.

PROPOSITION 3.2. *Let $\mathbf{A} \in \mathbb{K}[X]^{m\times m}$ be nonsingular and let $\mathbf{s} \in \mathbb{Z}^m$. With no field operation, one can build a nonsingular $\widetilde{\mathbf{A}} \in \mathbb{K}[X]^{\widetilde{m}\times\widetilde{m}}$ and a shift $\mathbf{u} \in \mathbb{Z}^{\widetilde{m}}$ such that $\widetilde{m} \leqslant 3m$, $\deg(\widetilde{\mathbf{A}}) \leqslant \lceil \sigma(\mathbf{A})/m \rceil$, and the $\mathbf{s}$-Popov form of $\mathbf{A}$ is the principal $m\times m$ submatrix of the $\mathbf{u}$-Popov form of $\widetilde{\mathbf{A}}$.*

With the algorithm in the previous subsection, this implies Theorem 1.3. In the specific case of Hermite form computation, for which there is a deterministic algorithm with cost bound $\widetilde{\mathcal{O}}(m^\omega \deg(\mathbf{A}))$ [35], one can verify that this leads to a *deterministic* algorithm using $\widetilde{\mathcal{O}}(m^\omega \lceil \sigma(\mathbf{A})/m\rceil)$ operations. (However, for $\mathbf{s} = \mathbf{0}$ this does not give a $\widetilde{\mathcal{O}}(m^\omega \lceil \sigma(\mathbf{A})/m\rceil)$ *deterministic* algorithm for the Popov form using [16, 28], since the corresponding $\mathbf{u}$ is $(\mathbf{0}, t, \ldots, t)$ with $t \geqslant \deg(\mathbf{A})$.)

DEFINITION 3.3 (COLUMN PARTIAL LINEARIZATION). *Let $\mathbf{A} \in \mathbb{K}[X]^{m\times m}$ and $\boldsymbol{\delta} = (\delta_i)_i \in \mathbb{N}^m$. Then let $\delta = 1 + \lfloor(\delta_1 + \cdots + \delta_m)/m\rfloor$, let $\alpha_i \geqslant 1$ and $0 \leqslant \beta_i < \delta$ be such that $\delta_i = (\alpha_i - 1)\delta + \beta_i$ for $1 \leqslant i \leqslant m$, let $\widetilde{m} = \alpha_1 + \cdots + \alpha_m$, and let $\mathcal{E} = [\mathbf{I}|\mathbf{E}^\mathsf{T}]^\mathsf{T} \in \mathbb{K}[X]^{\widetilde{m}\times m}$ be the expansion-compression matrix with $\mathbf{I}$ the identity matrix and*

$$\mathbf{E} = \begin{bmatrix} X^{\delta} & & \\ \vdots & & \\ X^{(\alpha_1-1)\delta} & & \\ & \ddots & \\ & & X^{\delta} \\ & & \vdots \\ & & X^{(\alpha_m-1)\delta} \end{bmatrix}. \qquad (4)$$

The column partial linearization *$\mathcal{L}^{c}_{\boldsymbol{\delta}}(\mathbf{A}) \in \mathbb{K}[X]^{\widetilde{m}\times\widetilde{m}}$ of $\mathbf{A}$ is defined as follows:*

- *the first m rows of $\mathcal{L}^{c}_{\boldsymbol{\delta}}(\mathbf{A})$ form the unique matrix $\widetilde{\mathbf{A}} \in \mathbb{K}[X]^{m\times\widetilde{m}}$ such that $\mathbf{A} = \widetilde{\mathbf{A}}\mathcal{E}$ and $\widetilde{\mathbf{A}}$ has all columns of degree less than δ except possibly those at indices $m + (\alpha_1 - 1) + \cdots + (\alpha_i - 1)$ for $1 \leqslant i \leqslant m$,*
- *for $1 \leqslant i \leqslant m$, the row $m + (\alpha_1 - 1) + \cdots + (\alpha_{i-1} - 1) + 1$ of $\mathcal{L}^{c}_{\boldsymbol{\delta}}(\mathbf{A})$ is $[0, \ldots, 0, -X^\delta, 0, \ldots, 0, 1, 0, \ldots, 0]$ where $-X^\delta$ is at index i and 1 is on the diagonal,*

- *for* $1 \leqslant i \leqslant m$ *and* $2 \leqslant j \leqslant \alpha_i - 1$, *the row* $m+(\alpha_1-1)+\cdots+(\alpha_{i-1}-1)+j$ *of* $\mathcal{L}^{\mathrm{c}}_{\boldsymbol{\delta}}(\mathbf{A})$ *is* $[0,\ldots,0,-X^{\delta},1,0,\ldots,0]$ *where* 1 *is on the diagonal.*

Defining the *row partial linearization* $\mathcal{L}^{\mathrm{r}}_{\boldsymbol{\delta}}(\mathbf{A})$ of $\mathbf{A}$ similarly, both linearizations are related by $\mathcal{L}^{\mathrm{r}}_{\boldsymbol{\delta}}(\mathbf{A}) = \mathcal{L}^{\mathrm{c}}_{\boldsymbol{\delta}}(\mathbf{A}^{\mathsf{T}})^{\mathsf{T}}$.

Now we show that for a well-chosen $\mathbf{u}$, one can directly read the $\mathbf{s}$-Popov form of $\mathbf{A}$ as a submatrix of the $\mathbf{u}$-Popov form of $\mathcal{L}^{\mathrm{r}}_{\boldsymbol{\delta}}(\mathbf{A})$ (resp. $\mathcal{L}^{\mathrm{c}}_{\boldsymbol{\delta}}(\mathbf{A})$).

LEMMA 3.4. *Let* $\mathbf{A} \in \mathbb{K}[X]^{m\times m}$ *be nonsingular,* $\mathbf{s} \in \mathbb{Z}^m$, $\mathbf{P}$ *be the* $\mathbf{s}$*-Popov form of* $\mathbf{A}$, *and* $\boldsymbol{\delta} \in \mathbb{N}^m$. *We have that:*

(i) if $\widetilde{m}$ *is the dimension of* $\mathcal{L}^{\mathrm{r}}_{\boldsymbol{\delta}}(\mathbf{A})$ *and* $\mathbf{u} = (\mathbf{s}, t, \ldots, t)$ *is in* $\mathbb{Z}^{\widetilde{m}}$ *with* $t \geqslant \max(\mathbf{s}) + \deg(\mathbf{P})$, *then the* $\mathbf{u}$*-Popov form of* $\mathcal{L}^{\mathrm{r}}_{\boldsymbol{\delta}}(\mathbf{A})$ *is* $\begin{bmatrix}\mathbf{P} & \mathbf{0}\\ * & \mathbf{I}\end{bmatrix}$;

(ii) if $\widetilde{m}$ *is the dimension of* $\mathcal{L}^{\mathrm{c}}_{\boldsymbol{\delta}}(\mathbf{A})$, $\mathbf{E}$ *is as in (4), and* $\mathbf{u} = (\mathbf{s}, \mathbf{t}) \in \mathbb{Z}^{\widetilde{m}}$ *for any* $\mathbf{t} \in \mathbb{Z}^{\widetilde{m}-m}$, *then the* $\mathbf{u}$*-Popov form of* $\mathcal{L}^{\mathrm{c}}_{\boldsymbol{\delta}}(\mathbf{A}) \begin{bmatrix}\mathbf{I} & \mathbf{0}\\ \mathbf{E} & \mathbf{I}\end{bmatrix}$ *is* $\begin{bmatrix}\mathbf{P} & \mathbf{0}\\ \mathbf{0} & \mathbf{I}\end{bmatrix}$;

(iii) if $\widetilde{m}$ *is the dimension of* $\mathcal{L}^{\mathrm{c}}_{\boldsymbol{\delta}}(\mathbf{A})$ *and* $\mathbf{u} = (\mathbf{s}, t, \ldots, t)$ *is in* $\mathbb{Z}^{\widetilde{m}}$ *with* $t \geqslant \max(\mathbf{s}) + \deg(\mathbf{P})$, *then the* $\mathbf{u}$*-Popov form of* $\mathcal{L}^{\mathrm{c}}_{\boldsymbol{\delta}}(\mathbf{A})$ *is* $\begin{bmatrix}\mathbf{P} & \mathbf{0}\\ * & \mathbf{I}\end{bmatrix}$.

PROOF. *(i)* $\mathcal{L}^{\mathrm{r}}_{\boldsymbol{\delta}}(\mathbf{A})$ is left-unimodularly equivalent to $[\begin{smallmatrix}\mathbf{A} & \mathbf{0}\\ \mathbf{B} & \mathbf{I}\end{smallmatrix}]$ for some $\mathbf{B} \in \mathbb{K}[X]^{(\widetilde{m}-m)\times m}$ [16, Theorem 10 (i)]. Then, let $\mathbf{R}$ be the remainder of $\mathbf{B}$ modulo $\mathbf{P}$, that is, the unique matrix in $\mathbb{K}[X]^{(\widetilde{m}-m)\times m}$ which has column degree bounded by the column degree of $\mathbf{P}$ componentwise and such that $\mathbf{R} = \mathbf{B} + \mathbf{QP}$ for some matrix $\mathbf{Q}$ (see for example [22, Theorem 6.3-15], noting that $\mathbf{P}$ is $\mathbf{0}$-column reduced).

Let $\mathbf{W}$ denote the unimodular matrix such that $\mathbf{P} = \mathbf{WA}$. Then, $[\begin{smallmatrix}\mathbf{W} & \mathbf{0}\\ \mathbf{QW} & \mathbf{I}\end{smallmatrix}][\begin{smallmatrix}\mathbf{A} & \mathbf{0}\\ \mathbf{B} & \mathbf{I}\end{smallmatrix}] = [\begin{smallmatrix}\mathbf{P} & \mathbf{0}\\ \mathbf{R} & \mathbf{I}\end{smallmatrix}]$ is left-unimodularly equivalent to $\mathcal{L}^{\mathrm{r}}_{\boldsymbol{\delta}}(\mathbf{A})$. Besides, since $\deg(\mathbf{R}) < \deg(\mathbf{P})$, we have that $[\begin{smallmatrix}\mathbf{P} & \mathbf{0}\\ \mathbf{R} & \mathbf{I}\end{smallmatrix}]$ is in $\mathbf{u}$-Popov form by choice of t.

(ii) The matrix $[\begin{smallmatrix}\mathbf{P} & \mathbf{0}\\ \mathbf{0} & \mathbf{I}\end{smallmatrix}]$ is obviously in $\mathbf{u}$-Popov form: it remains to prove that it is left-unimodularly equivalent to $\mathcal{L}^{\mathrm{c}}_{\boldsymbol{\delta}}(\mathbf{A})[\begin{smallmatrix}\mathbf{I} & \mathbf{0}\\ \mathbf{E} & \mathbf{I}\end{smallmatrix}]$. Let $\mathbf{T}$ denote the trailing principal submatrix $\mathbf{T} = \mathcal{L}^{\mathrm{c}}_{\boldsymbol{\delta}}(\mathbf{A})_{m+1\ldots\widetilde{m},m+1\ldots\widetilde{m}}$, and let $\mathbf{W}$ be the unimodular matrix such that $\mathbf{WP} = \mathbf{A}$. Then, $\mathbf{T}$ is unit lower triangular, thus unimodular, and by construction of $\mathcal{L}^{\mathrm{c}}_{\boldsymbol{\delta}}(\mathbf{A})$, for some matrix $\mathbf{B}$ we have $\mathcal{L}^{\mathrm{c}}_{\boldsymbol{\delta}}(\mathbf{A})[\begin{smallmatrix}\mathbf{I} & \mathbf{0}\\ \mathbf{E} & \mathbf{I}\end{smallmatrix}] = [\begin{smallmatrix}\mathbf{A} & \mathbf{B}\\ \mathbf{0} & \mathbf{T}\end{smallmatrix}] = [\begin{smallmatrix}\mathbf{W} & \mathbf{B}\\ \mathbf{0} & \mathbf{T}\end{smallmatrix}][\begin{smallmatrix}\mathbf{P} & \mathbf{0}\\ \mathbf{0} & \mathbf{I}\end{smallmatrix}]$.

(iii) From *(ii)*, $\mathcal{L}^{\mathrm{c}}_{\boldsymbol{\delta}}(\mathbf{A})$ is left-unimodularly equivalent to $[\begin{smallmatrix}\mathbf{P} & \mathbf{0}\\ \mathbf{0} & \mathbf{I}\end{smallmatrix}][\begin{smallmatrix}\mathbf{I} & \mathbf{0}\\ -\mathbf{E} & \mathbf{I}\end{smallmatrix}] = [\begin{smallmatrix}\mathbf{P} & \mathbf{0}\\ -\mathbf{E} & \mathbf{I}\end{smallmatrix}]$. Using arguments in the proof of *(i)* above, by choice of t the $\mathbf{u}$-Popov form of $[\begin{smallmatrix}\mathbf{P} & \mathbf{0}\\ -\mathbf{E} & \mathbf{I}\end{smallmatrix}]$ is $[\begin{smallmatrix}\mathbf{P} & \mathbf{0}\\ \mathbf{R} & \mathbf{I}\end{smallmatrix}]$ with $\mathbf{R}$ the remainder of $-\mathbf{E}$ modulo $\mathbf{P}$. □

In the usual case where $\deg(\mathbf{P})$ is not known *a priori*, one may choose t using the inequality $\deg(\mathbf{P}) \leqslant \deg(\det(\mathbf{P})) = \deg(\det(\mathbf{A})) \leqslant m\deg(\mathbf{A})$.

This result implies Proposition 3.2 thanks to the following remark from [16]. Let π_1, π_2 be permutation matrices such that $\mathbf{B} = \pi_1\mathbf{A}\pi_2 = [b_{i,j}]_{ij}$ satisfies $\deg(b_{i,i}) \geqslant \deg(b_{j,k})$ for all $j,k \geqslant i$ and $1 \leqslant i \leqslant m$. Defining $\mathbf{d} = (d_i)_i \in \mathbb{N}^m$ by $d_i = \overline{\deg}(b_{i,i}) = \begin{cases}\deg(b_{i,i}) & \text{if } b_{i,i} \neq 0\\ 0 & \text{otherwise}\end{cases}$, we have $d_1+\cdots+d_m \leqslant \sigma(\mathbf{A})$ by definition of $\sigma(\mathbf{A})$ in (1). Let $\boldsymbol{\delta} = \pi_1^{-1}\mathbf{d}$, where $\mathbf{d}$ is seen as a column vector, and $\boldsymbol{\gamma} = \mathrm{cdeg}(\mathcal{L}^{\mathrm{r}}_{\boldsymbol{\delta}}(\mathbf{A}))$. Then the matrix $\widetilde{\mathbf{A}} = \mathcal{L}^{\mathrm{c}}_{\boldsymbol{\gamma}}(\mathcal{L}^{\mathrm{r}}_{\boldsymbol{\delta}}(\mathbf{A}))$ is $\widetilde{m}\times\widetilde{m}$ with $\widetilde{m} < 3m$, and we have $\deg(\widetilde{\mathbf{A}}) \leqslant \lceil \sigma(\mathbf{A})/m \rceil$ [16, Corollary 3]. Lemma 3.4 further shows that the $\mathbf{s}$-Popov form of $\mathbf{A}$ is the principal $m \times m$ submatrix of the $\mathbf{u}$-Popov form of $\widetilde{\mathbf{A}}$, for the shift $\mathbf{u} = (\mathbf{s}, t, \ldots, t) \in \mathbb{Z}^{\widetilde{m}}$ with $t = \max(\mathbf{s}) + m\deg(\mathbf{A})$.

Acknowledgements. The author sincerely thanks the anonymous reviewers for their careful reading and detailed comments, which were very helpful for preparing the final version of this paper. He also thanks C.-P. Jeannerod, G. Labahn, É. Schost, A. Storjohann, and G. Villard for their interesting and useful comments. The author gratefully acknowledges financial support provided through the international mobility grants *Explo'ra Doc from Région Rhône-Alpes*, *PALSE*, and *Mitacs Globalink - Inria*.

4. REFERENCES

[1] M. Alekhnovich. Linear Diophantine equations over polynomials and soft decoding of Reed-Solomon codes. In *FOCS'02*, pages 439–448. IEEE, 2002.

[2] M. Alekhnovich. Linear Diophantine equations over polynomials and soft decoding of Reed-Solomon codes. *IEEE Trans. Inf. Theory*, 51(7):2257–2265, July 2005.

[3] B. Beckermann. A reliable method for computing M-Padé approximants on arbitrary staircases. *J. Comput. Appl. Math.*, 40(1):19–42, 1992.

[4] B. Beckermann and G. Labahn. A uniform approach for the fast computation of matrix-type Padé approximants. *SIAM J. Matrix Anal. Appl.*, 15(3):804–823, July 1994.

[5] B. Beckermann and G. Labahn. Fraction-free computation of matrix rational interpolants and matrix gcds. *SIAM J. Matrix Anal. Appl.*, 22(1):114–144, 2000.

[6] B. Beckermann, G. Labahn, and G. Villard. Normal forms for general polynomial matrices. *J. Symbolic Comput.*, 41(6):708–737, 2006.

[7] P. Busse. *Multivariate List Decoding of Evaluation Codes with a Gröbner Basis Perspective*. PhD thesis, University of Kentucky, 2008.

[8] M. Chowdhury, C.-P. Jeannerod, V. Neiger, É. Schost, and G. Villard. Faster algorithms for multivariate interpolation with multiplicities and simultaneous polynomial approximations. *IEEE Trans. Inf. Theory*, 61(5):2370–2387, 2015.

[9] H. Cohn and N. Heninger. Approximate common divisors via lattices. In *Tenth Algorithmic Number Theory Symposium*, pages 271–293. Mathematical Sciences Publishers (MSP), 2012-2013.

[10] H. Cohn and N. Heninger. Ideal forms of Coppersmith's theorem and Guruswami-Sudan list decoding. *Advances in Mathematics of Communications*, 9(3):311–339, 2015.

[11] D. Coppersmith and S. Winograd. Matrix multiplication via arithmetic progressions. *J. Symbolic Comput.*, 9(3):251–280, 1990.

[12] C. Devet, I. Goldberg, and N. Heninger. Optimally robust private information retrieval. Cryptology ePrint Archive, Report 2012/083, 2012.

[13] J. von zur Gathen and J. Gerhard. *Modern Computer Algebra (third edition)*. Cambridge University Press, 2013.

[14] P. Giorgi, C.-P. Jeannerod, and G. Villard. On the complexity of polynomial matrix computations. In *ISSAC'03*, pages 135–142. ACM, 2003.

[15] S. Gupta. Hermite forms of polynomial matrices. Master's thesis, University of Waterloo, 2011.

[16] S. Gupta, S. Sarkar, A. Storjohann, and J. Valeriote. Triangular x-basis decompositions and derandomization of linear algebra algorithms over $K[x]$. *J. Symbolic Comput.*, 47(4):422–453, 2012.

[17] S. Gupta and A. Storjohann. Computing Hermite forms of polynomial matrices. ISSAC'11, pages 155–162. ACM, 2011.

[18] J. L. Hafner and K. McCurley. Asymptotically fast triangularization of matrices over rings. *SIAM Journal on Computing*, 20(6):1068–1083, 1991.

[19] C. Hermite. Sur l'introduction des variables continues dans la théorie des nombres. *Journal für die reine und angewandte Mathematik*, 41:191–216, 1851.

[20] C.-P. Jeannerod, V. Neiger, É. Schost, and G. Villard. Computing minimal interpolation bases. HAL Open archive - https://hal.inria.fr/hal-01241781, 2015.

[21] C.-P. Jeannerod, V. Neiger, É. Schost, and G. Villard. Fast computation of minimal interpolation bases in Popov form for arbitrary shifts. HAL Open archive - https://hal.inria.fr/hal-01265983, 2016.

[22] T. Kailath. *Linear Systems*. Prentice-Hall, 1980.

[23] E. Kaltofen, M.S. Krishnamoorthy, and D. Saunders. Parallel algorithms for matrix normal forms. *Linear Algebra Appl.*, 136:189–208, 1990.

[24] S. Lang. *Algebra (Revised Third Edition)*. Springer-Verlag New-York Inc., 2002.

[25] F. Le Gall. Powers of tensors and fast matrix multiplication. In *ISSAC'14*, pages 296–303. ACM, 2014.

[26] T. Mulders and A. Storjohann. On lattice reduction for polynomial matrices. *J. Symbolic Comput.*, 35:377–401, 2003.

[27] V. M. Popov. Invariant description of linear, time-invariant controllable systems. *SIAM Journal on Control*, 10(2):252–264, 1972.

[28] S. Sarkar and A. Storjohann. Normalization of row reduced matrices. In *ISSAC'11*, pages 297–304. ACM, 2011.

[29] A. Storjohann. High-order lifting and integrality certification. *J. Symbolic Comput.*, 36(3-4):613–648, 2003.

[30] A. Storjohann. Notes on computing minimal approximant bases. In *Dagstuhl Seminar Proceedings*, 2006.

[31] A. Storjohann and G. Labahn. Asymptotically fast computation of Hermite normal forms of integer matrices. ISSAC'96, pages 259–266. ACM, 1996.

[32] M. Van Barel and A. Bultheel. A general module theoretic framework for vector M-Padé and matrix rational interpolation. *Numer. Algorithms*, 3:451–462, 1992.

[33] G. Villard. Computing Popov and Hermite forms of polynomial matrices. ISSAC'96, pages 250–258. ACM, 1996.

[34] W. Zhou and G. Labahn. Efficient algorithms for order basis computation. *J. Symbolic Comput.*, 47(7):793–819, 2012.

[35] W. Zhou and G. Labahn. A fast, deterministic algorithm for computing a Hermite normal form of a polynomial matrix. arXiv e-Print archive - http://arxiv.org/abs/1602.02049, 2016.

[36] W. Zhou, G. Labahn, and A. Storjohann. Computing minimal nullspace bases. In *ISSAC'12*, pages 366–373. ACM, 2012.

[37] W. Zhou, G. Labahn, and A. Storjohann. A deterministic algorithm for inverting a polynomial matrix. *J. Complexity*, 31(2):162–173, 2015.

Faster LLL-type Reduction of Lattice Bases

Arnold Neumaier
Universität Wien, Austria
Fakultät für Mathematik
Arnold.Neumaier@univie.ac.at

Damien Stehlé
ENS de Lyon, France
Laboratoire LIP
(U. Lyon, CNRS, ENSL, INRIA, UCBL)
damien.stehle@ens-lyon.fr

ABSTRACT

We describe an asymptotically fast variant of the LLL lattice reduction algorithm. It takes as input a basis $\mathbf{B} \in \mathbb{Z}^{n\times n}$ and returns a (reduced) basis $\mathbf{C}$ of the Euclidean lattice L spanned by $\mathbf{B}$, whose first vector satisfies $\|\mathbf{c}_1\| \leq (1+c)(4/3)^{(n-1)/4}(\det L)^{1/n}$ for any fixed $c > 0$. It terminates within $O(n^{4+\varepsilon}\beta^{1+\varepsilon})$ bit operations for any $\varepsilon > 0$, with $\beta = \log \max_i \|\mathbf{b}_i\|$. It does rely on fast integer arithmetic but does not make use of fast matrix multiplication.

Keywords

Lattice reduction; LLL; blocking

1. INTRODUCTION

A Euclidean lattice is a set $L = \mathbf{B}\mathbb{Z}^n$ of all integer linear combinations of the columns of a full column rank matrix $\mathbf{B} \in \mathbb{R}^{m\times n}$. In this setup, the columns $\mathbf{b}_i$ of $\mathbf{B}$ are said to form a basis of the lattice. Any lattice of dimension $n \geq 2$ admits infinitely many lattice bases and two basis matrices $\mathbf{B}, \mathbf{C}$ span the same lattice if and only if there exists $\mathbf{U} \in \mathbb{Z}^{n\times n}$ of determinant ± 1 such that $\mathbf{B} = \mathbf{CU}$. Such a matrix $\mathbf{U}$ is said unimodular. Note that this implies that the lattice determinant $\det L = \sqrt{\det(\mathbf{B}^T\mathbf{B})}$ does not depend on the choice of the basis $\mathbf{B}$ of L.

Many interesting computational problems can be reduced to finding a basis $\mathbf{C}$ of a lattice L consisting of short vectors, from an arbitrary input basis $\mathbf{B}$ of L (see, e.g., [12]). This task, called lattice reduction, comes in different flavors. The most standard variant is LLL reduction [6], as it can be performed in polynomial time (if the input basis $\mathbf{B}$ is integral) and provides reasonable output guarantees. In particular, the first vector of a LLL-reduced basis $\mathbf{C}$ satisfies:

$$\|\mathbf{c}_1\| \leq \alpha^{(n-1)/4}(\det L)^{1/n}, \tag{1}$$

where α can be any constant greater than $4/3$.

Assume now that the input basis $\mathbf{B}$ is integral. Let $\beta = \log \max_i \|\mathbf{b}_i\|$. Observe that we may assume that $\beta \geq \Omega(n)$, as else (1) is already reached by the input basis $\mathbf{B}$. For the sake of simplicity, we further assume that $m = n$. The original LLL algorithm terminates within $O(n^5\beta^{2+\varepsilon})$ bit operations [6, 4], where $\varepsilon > 0$ is arbitrary. The $\widetilde{L}^1$ algorithm [13] produces bases satisfying (1) in time $O(n^{5+\varepsilon}\beta^{1+\varepsilon})$. If $\beta = O(n^c)$ for some $c < 2 - 1/(5-\omega) \approx 1.619$, then $\widetilde{L}^1$ is outperformed by Storjohann's algorithm [18], whose run time is $O(n^{3+1/(5-\omega)+\varepsilon}\beta^{2+\varepsilon})$. Here $\omega < 2.373$ refers to the matrix multiplication exponent.

ISSAC '16, July 19–22, 2016, Waterloo, ON, Canada

ISBN 978-1-4503-4380-0/16/07...$15.00

DOI: http://dx.doi.org/10.1145/2930889.2930917

OUR RESULT. We present an algorithm that takes as input a basis matrix $\mathbf{B} \in \mathbb{Z}^{n\times n}$ of an arbitrary integer lattice L and returns a basis matrix $\mathbf{C}$ of L whose first vector satisfies

$$\|\mathbf{c}_1\| \leq (1+c)(4/3)^{(n-1)/4}(\det L)^{1/n}. \tag{1a}$$

Here $c > 0$ is an algorithm parameter that can be set arbitrarily close to 0 (and can even tend to 0). The algorithm terminates within $O(n^{4+\varepsilon}\beta^{1+\varepsilon})$ bit operations, for any $\varepsilon > 0$. Note that (1a) is a little stronger than (1). Further, the cost increase when $c > 0$ gets lower is quite limited. The algorithm is not only the (asymptotically) fastest known today, but is also arguably simpler than those of [13, 18]: it does not rely on basis roundings as [13] or fast matrix multiplication as [18].

TECHNIQUES. A classical approach to decrease the cost dependency of LLL-type algorithms with respect to n is to rely on blocking techniques. This was first proposed by Schönhage [15] and further investigated in [18, 5]. We use a recursive blocking technique inspired from that of [5]: the Gram-Schmidt orthogonalisation (GSO) of the basis is split into large blocks such that consecutive diagonal blocks overlap by half, and the reduction algorithm makes recursive calls on these blocks. Unfortunately, the algorithm of [5] suffers from several drawbacks. First, the guaranteed output quality is worse than (1): the first output vector is only known to satisfy $\|\mathbf{c}_1\| \leq 2^{O(n\log n)}(\det L)^{1/n}$. Second, its cost bound $O(n^{3+\varepsilon}\beta^{2+\varepsilon})$ is (more than) quadratic in β: this is because there are $\Omega(\beta)$ recursion leaves, and the cost of each one is $\Omega(\beta)$.

We overcome both limitations by changing the strategy used at each recursion level for selecting the inputs to the recursive calls. Instead of a local (LLL-like) strategy consisting in choosing the first (or an arbitrary) block for which some progress can be made, we use a "rolling pin" strategy *à la* Block-Korkin-Zolotarev [14, 3]: BKZ reduces the blocks by increasing value of their starting index, and repeats such a "rolling pin tour" sufficiently many times for the basis to be reduced. This global strategy allows to avoid spending time making little local progress on the GSO and instead ensuring some significant global progress at every tour. More concretely, it was shown in [3] that $O(\log\beta)$ block calls suffice for a fixed value of n, rather than $O(\beta)$, to obtain bases that are well reduced. Note that BKZ was introduced in a different context: it aims at finding much shorter lattice vectors than guaranteed by (1), by using for each block an HKZ-reduction algorithm such as the one from [8]. The cost of BKZ grows as $2^{O(s)}(n\beta)^{O(1)}$, if s denotes the block-size. The convergence analysis from [3] can be adapted to recursive blocking for LLL-type reduction (rather than non-recursive calls to an HKZ-reduction). We adapt the simpler analysis by Neumaier in [10] of the SDBKZ variant of BKZ recently proposed by Micciancio and Walter [9]. The fact we obtain (1a) rather than (1) is a side-product of using a global ("rolling pin") strategy. This phenomenon was already noted in [3].

Our "rolling pin" strategy differs from that of BKZ in two ways. First, our blocks overlap by half (like [5]), instead of $s-1$ dimensions out of s, in order to decrease the cost dependence in n. Note that considering blocks overlapping by half was also considered in [1], in the context of finding much shorter vectors than provided by (1). Second, the "rolling pin tours" proceed backwards (from the end of the diagonal to the start) rather than forwards, in order to prove that the first vector of the output basis satisfies (1a). Note that for block-size $s=2$, the BKZ and SDBKZ algorithms produce short bases satisfying (1a), but the analyses from [3, 10] lead to a run-time bound of $O(n^{6+\varepsilon}\beta^{1+\varepsilon})$.

EXTENSIONS. The algorithm also works for rational input matrices $\mathbf{B}\in\mathbb{Q}^{n\times n}$. If β denotes the maximum over all entries of $\mathbf{B}$ of the sum of the bit-sizes of the numerator and denominator, then the cost can be bounded as $O(n^{5+\varepsilon}\beta^{1+\varepsilon})$. If the input matrix has real entries, then it may be rounded and our algorithm can be used to compute a reducing unimodular transformation. We refer the reader to [2] for a sufficient bound on the rounding precision to guarantee reducedness of the final basis.

The algorithm may be adapted to take as input the Gram matrix $\mathbf{B}^T\mathbf{B}$ rather than the basis matrix $\mathbf{B}$. If $\mathbf{B}^T\mathbf{B}$ is integral, then the time bound $O(n^{4+\varepsilon}\beta^{1+\varepsilon})$ still applies, and the algorithm returns an equivalent Gram matrix $\mathbf{C}^T\mathbf{C}=\mathbf{U}^T\mathbf{C}^T\mathbf{C}\mathbf{U}$ and the associated unimodular transformation $\mathbf{U}\in\mathbb{Z}^{n\times n}$ such that $\|\mathbf{c}_1\|$ is bounded as in (1a). If $\mathbf{B}\in\mathbb{Z}^{m\times n}$ is not square, one may first compute $\mathbf{B}^T\mathbf{B}\in\mathbb{Z}^{n\times n}$, run the latter algorithm on $\mathbf{B}^T\mathbf{B}$ and apply to $\mathbf{B}$ every unimodular operation made. This results in an algorithm whose run time is $O(mn^{\omega+\varepsilon}\beta^{1+\varepsilon}+n^{4+\varepsilon}\beta^{1+\varepsilon})$.

2. REMINDERS

In this section, we give the background that is necessary for presenting our algorithm. We refer to [7, 12] for introductions on lattices and to the LLL lattice reduction algorithm.

MAGNITUDES OF REDUCING MATRICES. Assume $\mathbf{B},\mathbf{C}\in\mathbb{Q}^{n\times n}$ are two basis matrices of the same lattice. Let $\mathbf{U}=\mathbf{B}^{-1}\mathbf{C}$. As mentioned above, matrix $\mathbf{U}$ is integral and has determinant ± 1. We may bound the magnitude of every entry of $\mathbf{U}$ as

$$\max_{i,j}|u_{i,j}|\leq(\max_i\|\mathbf{b}_i\|)^{n-1}(\max_i\|\mathbf{c}_i\|)/|\det\mathbf{B}|. \qquad (2)$$

Note that if $\mathbf{B}$ is integral, then the latter is bounded from above by $(\max_i\|\mathbf{b}_i\|)^{n-1}(\max_i\|\mathbf{c}_i\|)$.

Lattice reduction aims at finding $\mathbf{U}$ such that $\mathbf{BU}$ has nice properties, such as (1). In our algorithm, such a matrix will be computed by progressively updating a $\mathbf{U}$ initially set to $\mathbf{Id}$. We will use the latter bound to update $\mathbf{U}$ modulo a large integer during the execution of our algorithm: this is to master the arithmetic cost of updating $\mathbf{U}$, while making sure that the final value of $\mathbf{U}$ is correct as it is guaranteed to be smaller than half that modulus. Note that to use such a bound, we need to possess an a priori bound on the norms of the columns of the output matrix $\mathbf{C}=\mathbf{BU}$. As proved in Subsection 3.1, we have an a priori bound $\max_i\|\mathbf{c}_i\|\leq\sqrt{n}\max_i\|\mathbf{b}_i\|$.

GRAM-SCHMIDT ORTHOGONALISATION. Let $(\mathbf{b}_1|\ldots|\mathbf{b}_n)\in\mathbb{Z}^{n\times n}$ be non-singular. We recall that the Gram-Schmidt orthogonalisation (GSO) $(\mathbf{b}_1^*|\ldots|\mathbf{b}_n^*)\in\mathbb{Q}^{n\times n}$ is defined as follows (for $1\leq j<i\leq n$):

$$\mathbf{b}_i^*:=\mathbf{b}_i-\sum_{j<i}\mu_{i,j}\mathbf{b}_j^*,\quad\text{with}\quad\mu_{i,j}:=\frac{\langle\mathbf{b}_i,\mathbf{b}_j^*\rangle}{\|\mathbf{b}_j^*\|^2}.$$

Our algorithm will work on $\mathbf{B}=(\mathbf{b}_1|\ldots|\mathbf{b}_n)$ only implicitly, by instead manipulating the pair $(\mathbf{d},\mathbf{M})\in\mathbb{Q}^n\times\mathbb{Q}^{n\times n}$ with $\mathbf{d}:=(\|\mathbf{b}_i^*\|^2)_{i\leq n}$ and $m_{i,j}=\mu_{i,j}$ if $j<i$ and $m_{i,j}=0$ otherwise. We call this pair the GSO coefficients of $\mathbf{B}$.

We recall that the numerators and denominators of the GSO coefficients $(\mathbf{d},\mathbf{M})$ are of magnitudes bounded from above by

$$\begin{aligned}&\big(\max_{i\leq n}\det\left((\mathbf{b}_1|\ldots|\mathbf{b}_i)^T(\mathbf{b}_1|\ldots|\mathbf{b}_i)\right)\big)\big(\max_i\|\mathbf{b}_i\|^2\big)\\&=\big(\max_{i\leq n}\prod_{j\leq i}d_j\big)\big(\max_i(d_i+\sum_{j<i}d_jm_{i,j}^2)\big)\end{aligned}\qquad(3)$$

(see, e.g., [6, Proof of (1.26)]). Applying a transformation matrix $\mathbf{U}$ on $\mathbf{B}$ incurs an update of the GSO coefficients which can be computed from $\mathbf{U}$ and the GSO coefficients only. Further, when this transformation corresponds to a swap of two consecutive columns of $\mathbf{B}$ or the subtraction of an integer multiple of column to another column, the update of the GSO may be performed on $O(n)$ arithmetic operations.

SIZE-REDUCTION. A basis matrix $\mathbf{B}$ is said size-reduced if its GSO coefficients satisfy $|\mu_{i,j}|\leq 1/2$ for all $i>j$. A size-reduction algorithm is described in [6, Eq. (21)]: for a given index i, it makes all $|\mu_{i,j}|$'s smaller or equal to $1/2$ by adding to $\mathbf{b}_i$ appropriate integer multiples of $\mathbf{b}_j$ for $j<i$. Using this algorithm for $i=2,3,\ldots,n$ leads to a size-reduction algorithm for basis matrices. For a given column, the algorithm performs $O(n^2)$ arithmetic operations on rational numbers whose numerators and denominators stay bounded from above by

$$2^n\left(\max_{i\leq n}\prod_{j\leq i}d_j\right)\left(\max_i d_i+\sum_{j<i}d_jm_{i,j}^2\right),\qquad(4)$$

where $(\mathbf{d},\mathbf{M})$ are the GSO coefficients of $\mathbf{B}$ (see [6, Proof of (1.26)]). Size-reduction can be performed using and updating the GSO coefficients only. The unimodular transformation obtained by size-reducing a column has $O(n)$ nontrivial coefficients which are easily obtained during the execution of the algorithm.

REDUCTION OF 2-DIMENSIONAL LATTICES. Schönhage's algorithm [16] takes as input the GSO coefficients of a basis $\mathbf{B} \in \mathbb{Q}^{2\times 2}$ and returns a unimodular $\mathbf{U} \in \mathbb{Z}^{2\times 2}$ such that matrix $\mathbf{C} = \mathbf{BU}$ has smallest possible $\|\mathbf{c}_1\|$. This implies, by Minkowski's theorem, that $\|\mathbf{c}_1\| \leq (4/3)^{1/4}|\det \mathbf{B}|^{1/2}$. Its run time is $O(\mathcal{M}(k)\log k)$, where k denotes the (total) bit-size of the input GSO coefficients, and $\mathcal{M}(\ell)$ denotes the time required to multiply two ℓ-bit long integers.

We observe that Yap's algorithm [19] allows one to reduce 2-dimensional lattice bases in quasi-linear time. We use Schönhage's algorithm instead as we have GSO coefficients as inputs rather than a basis matrix.

3. THE ALGORITHM(S)

Algorithm `Reduce`, presented in Figure 1, is our main algorithm. However, the complexity gain over previous works stems from `RecursiveReduce`, described in Figure 2, which `Reduce` may call several times. Algorithm `Reduce` is needed as `RecursiveReduce` works only in specific dimensions, because of its recursive nature. If the dimension n of the input of `Reduce` is one of those specific dimensions, then `Reduce` may call `RecursiveReduce` only once. Else, the number of calls to `Reduce` is $(n\beta)^{o(1)}$.

The sequence of specific dimensions is driven by the correctness and cost analyses of `RecursiveReduce`. It is defined recursively: the base case is $n_1 = 2$, and, for $k \geq 2$, we define n_k as the largest multiple of n_{k-1} that is $\leq \sqrt{2}^{4-k} L^{k(k-1)/4}$. Here $L = O(\log(n\beta/\eta))$, where $\eta > 0$ is an algorithm parameter that drives the strength of the reduction (the smaller $\eta > 0$, the more reduced). We refer to Lemma 9 for the precise definition of L. Note that each n_k is even, and, assuming that L is sufficiently large, we have $n_k \in [\sqrt{2}^{3-k} L^{k(k-1)/4}, \sqrt{2}^{4-k} L^{k(k-1)/4}]$ for all k. As a result, the number of recursion levels r of `RecursiveReduce` satisfies

$$r = O(\sqrt{\log n/\log L}) = O(\sqrt{\log n/\log\log(n\beta/\eta)}).$$

Algorithms `Reduce` and `RecursiveReduce` use the GSO coefficients to define the lower-dimensional inputs of the recursive calls. Given the GSO $(\mathbf{d}, \mathbf{M}) \in \mathbb{Q}^n \times \mathbb{Q}^{n\times n}$, we define the GSO block of starting index $t+1$ and dimension s as $(\mathbf{d}', \mathbf{M}') \in \mathbb{Q}^s \times \mathbb{Q}^{s\times s}$, with $d'_i = d_{t+i}$ for $1 \leq i \leq s$ and $m'_{i,j} = m_{t+i,t+j}$ for $1 \leq i,j \leq s$. Note that $(\mathbf{d}', \mathbf{M}')$ are exactly the GSO coefficients of the vectors $\mathbf{b}_{t+1}^{(t)}, \ldots, \mathbf{b}_{t+s}^{(t)}$ obtained by projecting $\mathbf{b}_{t+1}, \ldots, \mathbf{b}_{t+s}$ orthogonally to the span of $\mathbf{b}_1, \ldots, \mathbf{b}_t$.

A call to `RecursiveReduce` on $(\mathbf{d}', \mathbf{M}')$ provides an s-dimensional unimodular matrix $\mathbf{U}'$ that reduces the basis $\mathbf{b}_{t+1}^{(t)}, \ldots, \mathbf{b}_{t+s}^{(t)}$. This matrix may be extended into an n-dimensional matrix $\mathbf{U}''$ so that when applied on the matrix $\mathbf{B}$ corresponding to $(\mathbf{d}, \mathbf{M})$, it does not change columns $\mathbf{b}_i$ for $i \leq t$ and $i > t+s$, and modifies vectors $\mathbf{b}_{t+1}, \ldots, \mathbf{b}_{t+s}$ exactly by applying $\mathbf{U}'$ to them. This is the purpose of Step 9 of `Reduce` and Step 6 of `RecursiveReduce`. The transformation may be applied to $(\mathbf{d}, \mathbf{M})$ directly. This may modify d_i for $i \in [t+1, t+s]$, and $m_{i,j}$ for $i \in [t+1, t+s]$ and $j > i$, and for $j \in [t+1, t+s]$ and $i < j$. Updating $(\mathbf{d}, \mathbf{M})$ costs $O(ns^2)$ arithmetic operations. This is performed at Step 10 of `Reduce` and Step 8 of `RecursiveReduce`.

In `Reduce`, the first four steps are meant to prepare the actual computation. `Reduce` calls `RecursiveReduce` on n_r-dimensional GSO blocks, with starting indices $k = 0, \ldots, n - n_r$. Note that the blocks overlap by $n_r - 1$ dimensions. `Reduce` may be viewed as BKZ with block-size n_r and calls to HKZ reduction within the blocks replaced by calls to `RecursiveReduce`. The analysis from [3] could be adapted from BKZ to `RecursiveReduce`. We chose to adapt the analysis of SDBKZ from [10], as it is more compact (see Section 5).

Inputs: A basis matrix $\mathbf{B} \in \mathbb{Z}^{n\times n}$ of a lattice L.
A reduction parameter $\eta \in (0, 1]$.
Output: A reduced basis matrix of L.

1. Let n_r be the largest specific dimension that is $\leq n$.
2. Compute the GSO coefficients $(\mathbf{d}, \mathbf{M})$ of $\mathbf{B}$.
3. Size-reduce $\mathbf{B}$ while updating $(\mathbf{d}, \mathbf{M})$ accordingly.
4. Define $\overline{\beta} = 2 + \lceil \log_2(\sqrt{n}(\max_{i\leq n}\|\mathbf{b}_i\|)^n)\rceil$.
5. Repeat the following $(n/n_r)^2\lceil \ln(\overline{\beta}/\eta)\rceil$ times, unless $n = n_r$, in which case once suffices.
6. For $k = 0$ to $n - n_r$, do:
7. Let $(\mathbf{d}', \mathbf{M}')$ be the GSO block of starting index $k+1$ and dimension n_r.
8. Call `RecursiveReduce` on inputs $(\mathbf{d}', \mathbf{M}')$, η, $\overline{\beta}$. Let $\mathbf{U} \in \mathbb{Z}^{n_r\times n_r}$ be the output.
9. Let $\mathbf{U}' \in \mathbb{Z}^{n\times n}$ be the identity matrix, except that $u'_{i,j} = u_{i-k,j-k}$ for $i,j \in [k+1, k+n_r]$.
10. Replace $\mathbf{B}$ by $\mathbf{BU}'$, updating $(\mathbf{d}, \mathbf{M})$ accordingly.
11. Size-reduce $\mathbf{B}$, updating $(\mathbf{d}, \mathbf{M})$ accordingly.
12. Return $\mathbf{B}$.

Figure 1: Algorithm `Reduce`.

Inputs: GSO coefficients $(\mathbf{d}, \mathbf{M}) \in \mathbb{Q}^n \times \mathbb{Q}^{n\times n}$.
A reduction parameter $\eta \in (0, 1]$ and $\overline{\beta} \in \mathbb{Z}$.
Output: A unimodular matrix $\mathbf{U} \in \mathbb{Z}^{n\times n}$.

1. If $n = 2$, return the output of Schönhage's algorithm.
2. Let $\mathbf{U} = \mathbf{Id}$.
Repeat the following $(2n_r/n_{r-1})^2\lceil \ln(8\overline{\beta}/\eta)\rceil$ times.
3. For k from $2(n_r/n_{r-1} - 1)$ down to 0, do:
4. Let $(\mathbf{d}', \mathbf{M}')$ be the GSO block of starting index $t + 1 = kn_{r-1}/2 + 1$ and dimension n_{r-1}.
5. Call `RecursiveReduce` on inputs $(\mathbf{d}', \mathbf{M}')$, η, $\overline{\beta}$. Let $\mathbf{U}' \in \mathbb{Z}^{n_{r-1}\times n_{r-1}}$ be the output.
6. Let $\mathbf{U}'' \in \mathbb{Z}^{n_r\times n_r}$ be the identity matrix, except that $u''_{i,j} = u'_{i-t,j-t}$ for $i,j \in [t+1, t+n_{r-1}]$.
7. $\mathbf{U} := \mathbf{UU}'' \bmod 2^{\overline{\beta}}$.
8. Update $(\mathbf{d}, \mathbf{M})$ according to transformation $\mathbf{U}''$.
9. Size-reduce $(\mathbf{d}, \mathbf{M})$ from indices $t+1$ to $t + n_{r-1}$, and update $\mathbf{U}$ modulo $2^{\overline{\beta}}$ accordingly.
10. Return $\mathbf{U}$.

Figure 2: Algorithm `RecursiveReduce`.

In `RecursiveReduce`, the input n_r-dimensional GSO is split into $2n_r/n_{r-1} - 1$ blocks of dimension n_{r-1} and starting indices $kn_{r-1}/2 + 1$ for $k = 0, 1, \ldots, 2(n_r/n_{r-1} - 1)$. Note that these blocks overlap by half. The n_r-dimensional call makes backwards sweeps of recursive calls on these blocks: it considers each block by decreasing value of k, and when it reaches $k = 0$, it starts a new tour with $k = 2(n_r/n_{r-1} - 1)$. The number of tours $(2n_r/n_{r-1})^2\lceil \log_2(8\overline{\beta}/\eta)\rceil$ is dictated by the convergence towards reduced bases analysis of the successive-backwards-sweeps strategy (see Section 4). Moving backwards rather than forwards is important for proving (1a): indeed, at the end, the block corresponding to

$k = 0$ is recursively reduced, and so is its first sub-block, and so is its first sub-sub-block, etc. The leaves of the recursion correspond to reductions of 2-dimensional lattice bases. These are performed using Schönhage's algorithm.

THEOREM 1. *Let $c > 0$. Given as input a basis matrix $\mathbf{B} \in \mathbb{Z}^{n\times n}$ of a lattice L and parameters $\eta = c/(3n)$, r and $(n_i)_{i\le r}$, Algorithm* `Reduce` *returns a basis* $\mathbf{C}$ *of* L *which is size-reduced and satisfies:*

$$\|\mathbf{c}_1\| \le (1+c)\left(4/3\right)^{(n-1)/4}(\det L)^{1/n}.$$

THEOREM 2. *Given $\mathbf{B} \in \mathbb{Z}^{n\times n}$ and $\eta = \Omega(1/n^2)$ as inputs, Algorithm* `Reduce` *terminates within*

$$O\left(kn^3\mathcal{M}(n\beta)\right) \text{ bit operations,}$$

with $\beta := \log \max_i \|\mathbf{b}_i\|$ and

$$k := 2^{O\left(\sqrt{(\log n)(\log\log(n\beta))}\right)}\log^2(n\beta).$$

As k is $(n\beta)^{o(1)}$, the latter cost bound is $\le O(n^{4+\varepsilon}\beta^{1+\varepsilon})$ for all $\varepsilon > 0$.

3.1 Elementary properties

We start with a few basic observations. The first one states that the algorithms are invariant under scaling of $\mathbf{d}$.

LEMMA 1. *Consider two distinct inputs $(\mathbf{d},\mathbf{M})$, $(\mathbf{d}',\mathbf{M}')$ of* `RecursiveReduce` *(with all other inputs identical). Let $\mathbf{U}$ and $\mathbf{U}'$ be the respective outputs. Assume $\mathbf{M} = \mathbf{M}'$ and that there exists $t > 0$ such that $\mathbf{d}' = t\mathbf{d}$. Then $\mathbf{U} = \mathbf{U}'$. The same property holds for* `Reduce`.

The following lemma is useful to bound the bit-sizes of all rationals occurring during the algorithm, and also the magnitude of the output unimodular matrix $\mathbf{U}$.

LEMMA 2. *During the execution of* `Reduce`*, the only operation that may change the value of $\max_i d_i$ is an execution of Schönhage's algorithm. Further, the value of this quantity after such an execution of Schönhage's algorithm cannot be larger than its value before this execution of Schönhage's algorithm.*

PROOF. When considering basis $\mathbf{B}$, the only basis/GSO operations that are performed during the execution of `Reduce` are either a replacement of some basis vector $\mathbf{b}_i$ by $\mathbf{b}_i + \sum_{j<i} x_j\mathbf{b}_j$, or an execution of Schönhage's algorithm on vectors $\mathbf{b}_i$ and $\mathbf{b}_{i+1}$ orthogonalized against $\mathbf{b}_1,\ldots,\mathbf{b}_{i-1}$. Only executions of Schönhage's algorithm can change $\mathbf{d}$.

As Schönhage's algorithm applied to 2-dimensional $(\mathbf{d},\mathbf{M})$ produces a $(\mathbf{d}',\mathbf{M}')$ with smallest d_1', we must have $d_1' \le d_1 \le \max(d_1,d_2)$. Further, Pythagoras' theorem and the fact that we use integer transformations imply that $d_1' \ge \min(d_1,d_2)$. Now, note that $d_1'd_2' = d_1d_2$ (the determinant is preserved), which implies that $\min(d_1,d_2) \le d_2' \le \max(d_1,d_2)$. Hence we have $\max(d_1,d_2) \le \max(d_1',d_2')$. □

By combining Lemma 2 and the discussion at the start of Section 2, we obtain the following.

LEMMA 3. *The matrix $\mathbf{U}$ returned at the end of the execution of* `RecursiveReduce` *is exactly the unimodular matrix that is the product of all unimodular matrices that have been successively applied to the GSO coefficients.*

PROOF. The only source of discrepancy between the output matrix $\mathbf{U}$ and the product of all unimodular matrices that have been successively applied to the GSO coefficients is the update of $\mathbf{U}$ modulo $2^{\overline{\beta}}$ at Steps 7 and 9. Let $\mathbf{B}$ and $\mathbf{C}$ respectively denote the bases corresponding to the input GSO coefficients, and to the final value of the GSO coefficients. We want to show that $\mathbf{U} = \mathbf{C}^{-1}\mathbf{B}$. For this, it suffices to show that each coefficient of $\mathbf{C}^{-1}\mathbf{B}$ has magnitude $< 2^{\overline{\beta}-1}$ so that reductions modulo $2^{\overline{\beta}}$ in the process of computing $\mathbf{U}$ have no impact on the output.

By Lemma 2 and the fact that $\mathbf{C}$ is size-reduced, we have that $\|\mathbf{c}_i\| \le \sqrt{n}\max_j\|\mathbf{b}_j^*\| \le \sqrt{n}\max_j\|\mathbf{b}_j\|$ for all $i \le n$. By (2), this implies that each coefficient of $\mathbf{C}^{-1}\mathbf{B}$ has magnitude $\le \sqrt{n}(\max_j\|\mathbf{b}_j\|)^n$. This is $< 2^{\overline{\beta}-1}$, by design of $\overline{\beta}$. □

The latter result implies that `Reduce` indeed returns a basis of the input lattice. Together with Section 2, it also implies that all rationals and integers that occur during the execution of the algorithm have bit-sizes $O(n\beta)$. The cost of `Reduce` can hence be bounded by the number of arithmetic operations multiplied by $O(\mathcal{M}(n\beta))$.

4. CORRECTNESS OF `RECURSIVEREDUCE`

This section is devoted to proving Theorem 1 for `RecursiveReduce`. The main proof component is the analysis of the convergence towards reduced bases of the repeated backwards sweeps of recursive calls.

4.1 Convergence of `RecursiveReduce`

Suppose we are at a certain recursion level r. Algorithm `RecursiveReduce` reduces the n_r-dimensional basis by making recursive calls in dimension n_{r-1}. These are grouped in tours, and each tour consists in recursive calls on GSO blocks with starting indices $1 + kn_{r-1}/2$ for k from $2(n_r/n_{r-1} - 1)$ down to 0.

We define α_r as the maximum, over all input n_r-dimensional GSO coefficients $(\mathbf{d},\mathbf{M})$, of the quantity

$$\Big(\prod_{i=1}^{n_r/2} d_i'\Big)^2/(\prod_{i=1}^{n_r} d_i'), \tag{5}$$

where $(\mathbf{d}',\mathbf{M}')$ are the GSO coefficients at the end of the execution of `RecursiveReduce`. This quantity measures how small the first half of the GSO coefficients are, relative to the second half. As seen in Section 2, we have $\alpha_1 \le 4/3$.

The following lemma, inspired from [10, Sec. 3.3], quantifies the progress made during a tour.

LEMMA 4. *Let $\mathbf{d}$ and $\mathbf{d}'$ respectively denote the values of the GSO coefficients at the start and the end of an iteration of the loop starting at Step 3 of* `RecursiveReduce`*. We define (for $1 \le k \le \ell$)*

$$g_k := \ln \prod_{i\le kn_{r-1}/2} d_i, \quad g_k' := \ln \prod_{i\le kn_{r-1}/2} d_i',$$

with $\ell = 2n_r/n_{r-1}$. We further define:

$$\begin{aligned} \mu &:= \max_{k<\ell}\frac{1}{\ell-k}\left(\frac{g_k}{k} - \frac{g_\ell}{\ell}\right), \\ \mu' &:= \max_{k<\ell}\frac{1}{\ell-k}\left(\frac{g_k'}{k} - \frac{g_\ell'}{\ell}\right), \\ \mu^* &:= \frac{\ln\alpha_{r-1}}{2}. \end{aligned}$$

Then we have

$$\mu' \leq \mu^* \quad or \quad \mu' \leq \mu^* + (1 - \frac{1}{\ell^2})(\mu - \mu^*).$$

This results states that across tours, the sequence of successive μ's lies below an affine dynamical system. Convergence is geometric: every ℓ^2 tours, the quantity $\mu - \mu^*$ either becomes negative, or it decreases by a constant factor. Note that the result is qualitatively similar to those of [3, 10] for dimension $\ell := 2n_r/n_{r-1}$ and "block size" 2.

PROOF. By dividing each d_i by $(\prod_{j\leq n} d_j)^{1/n}$, we see that we may assume without loss of generality that $g_\ell = g'_\ell = 0$ (by Lemma 1). Further, we define $g_0 = g'_0 = 0$.

Because of the backward ordering of the recursive calls during a tour, and thanks to (5), we have, for $k = \ell - 1$ down to $k = 1$:

$$2(g'_k - g_{k-1}) - (g'_{k+1} - g_{k-1}) \leq \ln \alpha_{r-1}.$$

This may be rewritten as

$$g'_k \leq \frac{1}{2}(g'_{k+1} + g_{k-1}) + \mu^*. \tag{6}$$

Assume first that $\mu \leq \mu^*$. We prove by induction on $k = \ell$ down to $k = 1$ that $g'_k \leq (\ell - k)k\mu^*$, which implies that $\mu' \leq \mu^*$. The case $k = \ell$ follows by preservation of the determinant. We now assume that $k < \ell$. Then, by induction and (6), we have

$$\begin{aligned} g'_k &\leq \frac{1}{2}((\ell-k-1)(k+1) + (\ell-k+1)(k-1))\mu^* + \mu^* \\ &= (\ell-k)k\mu^*. \end{aligned}$$

We now assume that $\mu > \mu^*$. We prove by induction on $k = \ell$ down to $k = 1$ that

$$g'_k \leq (\ell-k)k\Big(\mu^* + (1 - \frac{1}{\ell^2})(\mu - \mu^*)\Big).$$

The case $k = \ell$ follows by preservation of the determinant. We now assume that $k < \ell$. Let $q := (\ell - (k-1))(k-1)/2$. Then $(\ell - (k+1))(k+1) = 2((\ell-k)k - 1 - q)$ and $(\ell - (k-1))(k-1) = 2q$. Hence, by induction and (6), we have:

$$\begin{aligned} g'_k &\leq ((\ell-k)k - 1 - q)\Big(\mu^* + (1 - \frac{1}{\ell^2})(\mu - \mu^*)\Big) + q\mu + \mu^* \\ &= (q + (1 - \frac{1}{\ell^2})((\ell-k)k - 1 - q))(\mu - \mu^*) + (\ell-k)k\mu^*. \end{aligned}$$

Now, observe that $q \leq \ell^2 - 1$, hence $q/(1+q) \leq (\ell^2-1)/\ell^2 = 1 - 1/\ell^2$. This gives (using the positivity of $\mu - \mu^*$):

$$g'_k \leq (1 - \frac{1}{\ell^2})(\ell-k)k(\mu - \mu^*) + (\ell-k)k\mu^*,$$

which completes the proof. □

We now use Lemma 4 to show that at the end of the $\ell^2\lceil\ln(8\overline{\beta}/\eta)\rceil$ tours, the basis is quite close to being reduced.

LEMMA 5. *At the end of the execution of* `RecursiveReduce`, *we have:*

$$\max_{k<\ell} \frac{1}{\ell - k}\left(\frac{g_k}{k} - \frac{g_\ell}{\ell}\right) \leq \frac{\ln \alpha_{r-1}}{2} + \frac{\eta}{8}.$$

PROOF. Let μ and μ' respectively denote the values of $\max_{k<\ell} \frac{1}{\ell-k}(\frac{g_k}{k} - \frac{g_\ell}{\ell})$ at the start and at the end of the execution of `RecursiveReduce`. By Lemma 4, we have that $\mu' \leq (\ln \alpha_{r-1})/2$ or:

$$\begin{aligned} \mu' - \frac{\ln \alpha_{r-1}}{2} &\leq (1 - \frac{1}{\ell^2})^{\ell^2\lceil\ln(8\overline{\beta}/\eta)\rceil}(\mu - \frac{\ln \alpha_{r-1}}{2}) \\ &\leq \exp(-\lceil\ln(8\overline{\beta}/\eta)\rceil)\mu \\ &\leq \frac{\eta}{8}\frac{\mu}{\overline{\beta}}. \end{aligned}$$

Thanks to Lemma 2, we know that $\mu \leq \overline{\beta}$ and hence we obtain that $\mu' \leq \frac{\ln \alpha_{r-1}}{2} + \frac{\eta}{8}$. □

4.2 Proof of Theorem 1 for `RecursiveReduce`

Thanks to Lemma 3, it only remains to prove the bound on $\|\mathbf{c}_1\|$ of the output basis $\mathbf{C}$ of `RecursiveReduce`. For this, we use the results from the previous subsection on the convergence of `RecursiveReduce`.

LEMMA 6. *For all $r \geq 1$, we have $\alpha_r \leq ((4/3)e^{2\eta})^{n_r^2/4}$.*

PROOF. By Lemma 5 with $k = \ell/2$, we have (using the same notations as above):

$$\frac{2}{\ell^2}(2g_{\ell/2} - g_\ell) \leq \mu' \leq \frac{\ln \alpha_{r-1}}{2} + \frac{\eta}{8}.$$

We obtain (using the fact that $\ln \alpha_r$ is the largest possible value for $2g_{\ell/2} - g_\ell$)

$$\ln \alpha_r \leq \frac{\ell^2}{2}\Big(\frac{\ln \alpha_{r-1}}{2} + \frac{\eta}{8}\Big) = \frac{n_r^2}{n_{r-1}^2}\Big(\ln \alpha_{r-1} + \frac{\eta}{4}\Big).$$

We can then derive

$$\begin{aligned} \frac{1}{n_r^2}\ln \alpha_r &\leq \frac{1}{n_{r-1}^2}\Big(\ln \alpha_{r-1} + \frac{\eta}{4}\Big) \\ &\leq \frac{1}{n_{r-2}^2}\Big(\ln \alpha_{r-2} + \frac{\eta}{4}\Big) + \frac{1}{n_{r-1}^2}\frac{\eta}{4} \\ &\leq \ldots \\ &\leq \frac{1}{4}\ln \alpha_1 + \frac{\eta}{4}\sum_{i\leq r}\frac{1}{n_i^2}. \end{aligned}$$

The result follows by bounding α_1 by $4/3$ and $\sum_{i\leq r} 1/n_i^2$ by $\pi^2/6$. □

By Lemma 5 (with $k = 2$) and Lemma 6, we have, letting $\mathbf{d}'$ denote the values of the GSO coefficients at the end of the execution of `RecursiveReduce`:

$$\begin{aligned} \prod_{i=1}^{n_{r-1}} d'_i &\leq \Big((4/3)e^{2\eta}\Big)^{\frac{n_{r-1}^2}{4}(\frac{2n_r}{n_{r-1}}-2)}(e^{\frac{\eta}{4}})^{\frac{2n_r}{n_{r-1}}-2}\Big(\prod_{i=1}^{n_r} d'_i\Big)^{\frac{n_{r-1}}{n_r}} \\ &\leq \Big((4/3)e^{4\eta}\Big)^{\frac{n_{r-1}}{2}(n_r - n_{r-1})}\Big(\prod_{i=1}^{n_r} d'_i\Big)^{\frac{n_{r-1}}{n_r}}. \end{aligned}$$

By raising to the power or $1/n_{r-1}$, we obtain:

$$\Big(\prod_{i=1}^{n_{r-1}} d'_i\Big)^{\frac{1}{n_{r-1}}} \leq \Big((4/3)^{1/2}e^{2\eta}\Big)^{n_r - n_{r-1}}\Big(\prod_{i=1}^{n_r} d'_i\Big)^{\frac{1}{n_r}}.$$

By applying the latter to all values of r, we obtain:

$$\Big(d'_1 d'_2\Big)^{\frac{1}{2}} \leq \Big((4/3)^{1/2}e^{2\eta}\Big)^{n_r - 2}\Big(\prod_{i=1}^{n_r} d'_i\Big)^{\frac{1}{n_r}}.$$

Now, as the first two output vectors are reduced (by correctness of Schönhage's algorithm), we obtain:

$$d'_1 \le \left((4/3)^{1/2} e^{2\eta}\right)^{n_r-1} \left(\prod_{i=1}^{n_r} d'_i\right)^{\frac{1}{n_r}}. \quad (7)$$

To complete the proof of Theorem 1 for `RecursiveReduce`, note that for $\eta = c/(3n_r)$, we have $e^{\eta(n_r-1)} \le 1+c$.

5. CORRECTNESS OF REDUCE

We now extend the correctness of `RecursiveReduce` to that of `Reduce`. This is direct when $n = n_r$, as in that case `Reduce` makes a single call to `RecursiveReduce`. In the rest of this section, we assume that $n > n_r$. Then `Reduce` calls `RecursiveReduce` many times, in a BKZ fashion. The convergence analysis is adapted from [10].

The convergence analysis does not need to consider the inner workings of `RecursiveReduce`: it only relies on the fact that if $(\mathbf{d}', \mathbf{M}')$ are the GSO coefficients at the end of the execution of `RecursiveReduce`, then we have, by (7):

$$(d'_1)^{n_r} / (\prod_{i=1}^{n_r} d'_i) \le \overline{\alpha}_1^{(n_r-1)n_r}, \quad (8)$$

with $\overline{\alpha}_1 = (4/3)^{1/2} e^{2\eta}$.

LEMMA 7. *Let* $\mathbf{d}$ *and* $\mathbf{d}'$ *respectively denote the values of the GSO coefficients at the start and the end of an iteration of the loop starting at Step 6 of* `Reduce`. *We define (for* $1 \le k \le n$*)*

$$\overline{g}_k := \ln \prod_{i \le k} d_i, \quad \overline{g}'_k := \ln \prod_{i \le k} d'_i.$$

We further define:

$$\overline{\mu} := \max_{k \le n-n_r+1} \frac{1}{n-k}\left(\frac{\overline{g}_k}{k} - \frac{\overline{g}_n}{n}\right),$$
$$\overline{\mu}' := \max_{k \le n-n_r+1} \frac{1}{n-k}\left(\frac{\overline{g}'_k}{k} - \frac{\overline{g}'_n}{n}\right),$$
$$\overline{\mu}^* := \ln \overline{\alpha}_1.$$

Then we have

$$\overline{\mu}' \le \overline{\mu}^* \quad or \quad \overline{\mu}' \le \overline{\mu}^* + (1-a)(\overline{\mu} - \overline{\mu}^*),$$

with $a = \frac{n_r-1}{n-1}$ *if* $n_r \ge n/2$ *and* $a = \frac{n_r^2-n_r}{n^2/4+n_r^2-n_r}$ *otherwise. Note that in both cases we have* $a \ge n_r^2/n^2$.

PROOF. Without loss of generality, we assume that that $\overline{g}_n = \overline{g}'_n = 0$. Further, we define $\overline{g}_0 = \overline{g}'_0 = 0$.

Because of the forward ordering of the calls to `RecursiveReduce` during a tour, and thanks to (8), we have, for $k = 1$ to $k = n - n_r + 1$:

$$\overline{g}'_k - \overline{g}'_{k-1} \le (n_r - 1)\overline{\mu}^* + \frac{1}{n_r}(\overline{g}_{k+n_r-1} - \overline{g}'_{k-1}).$$

This may be rewritten as

$$\overline{g}'_k \le \frac{1}{n_r}\overline{g}_{k+n_r-1} + (1 - \frac{1}{n_r})\overline{g}'_{k-1} + (n_r-1)\overline{\mu}^*. \quad (9)$$

Assume first that $\overline{\mu} \le \overline{\mu}^*$. We prove by induction on k that $\overline{g}'_k \le (n-k)k\overline{\mu}^*$, which implies that $\overline{\mu}' \le \overline{\mu}^*$. The case $k = 0$ follows from $\overline{g}'_0 = 0$. We now assume that $k > 0$. Then, by induction and (9), we have (grouping the multiples of $1/n_r$ together):

$$\overline{g}'_k \le ((n-k+1)(k-1) + (n - n_r - 2k + 2) + (n_r - 1))\overline{\mu}^*$$
$$= (n-k)k\overline{\mu}^*.$$

We now assume that $\overline{\mu} > \overline{\mu}^*$. We prove by induction on k that

$$\overline{g}'_k \le (n-k)k\left(\overline{\mu}^* + (1-a)(\overline{\mu} - \overline{\mu}^*)\right).$$

The case $k = 0$ follows from $\overline{g}'_0 = 0$. We now assume that $k > 0$. By induction and (9), we have:

$$\overline{g}'_k \le (n_r - 1)\overline{\mu}^* + \frac{1}{n_r}(n - k - n_r + 1)(k + n_r - 1)\overline{\mu}$$
$$+ (1 - \frac{1}{n_r})(n-k+1)(k-1)\left(\overline{\mu}^* + (1-a)(\overline{\mu} - \overline{\mu}^*)\right)$$
$$= \frac{X}{n_r}(\overline{\mu} - \overline{\mu}^*) + (n-k)k\overline{\mu}^*,$$

with

$$X = (n-k-n_r+1)(k+n_r-1) + (n_r-1)(n-k+1)(k-1)(1-a).$$

Since $\overline{\mu} - \overline{\mu}^* > 0$, it suffices to prove that for all k, we have $X \le n_r(n-k)k(1-a)$. By subtracting the latter from X and differentiating with respect to k, we obtain that the inequality is the strongest for $k = 1$ when $n_r \ge n/2$ and for $k = n/2 - n_r + 1$ otherwise. The fact that $a \le (n_r-1)/(n-1)$ allows to handle the first case, whereas $a \le (n_r^2 - n_r)/(n^2/4 + n_r^2 - n_r)$ allows to handle the second one. This completes the proof. □

Lemma 7 may be used to show that after $O(n^2/n_r^2)$ tours, the basis is quite close to being reduced.

LEMMA 8. *At the end of the execution of* `Reduce`*, we have:*

$$\max_{k \le n-n_r+1} \frac{1}{n-k}\left(\frac{\overline{g}_k}{k} - \frac{\overline{g}_n}{n}\right) \le \ln \overline{\alpha}_1 + \eta.$$

PROOF. Let $\overline{\mu}$ and $\overline{\mu}'$ respectively denote the values of $\max_{k \le n-n_r+1} \frac{1}{n-k}(\frac{\overline{g}_k}{k} - \frac{\overline{g}_n}{n})$ at the start and at the end of the execution of `Reduce`. By Lemma 7, we have that $\overline{\mu}' \le \ln \overline{\alpha}_1$ or:

$$\overline{\mu}' - \ln \overline{\alpha}_1 \le (1 - \frac{n_r^2}{n^2})^{(n/n_r)^2 \lceil \ln(\overline{\beta}/\eta) \rceil}(\overline{\mu} - \ln \overline{\alpha}_1).$$

Once may proceed exactly as in the proof of Lemma 5 to show that the latter is $\le \ln \overline{\alpha}_1 + \eta$. □

To prove Theorem 1, we instantiate Lemma 8 with $k = 1$. This gives, using the definition of $\overline{\alpha}_1$:

$$d'_1 \le \left((4/3)^{1/2} e^{3\eta}\right)^{n-1} \left(\prod_{i=1}^{n} d'_i\right)^{1/n},$$

where $\mathbf{d}'$ denotes the values of the GSO coefficients at the end of the execution of `Reduce`. To complete the proof of Theorem 1, note that for $\eta = c/(3n)$, we have $e^{3\eta(n-1)/2} \le 1 + c$.

6. COST ANALYSIS

This section is devoted to proving Theorem 2. We first bound the bit-sizes of all integers and rationals occurring during the executions of `Reduce` and `RecursiveReduce`.

By Lemma 2, we know that the quantity $\max_i d_i$ cannot increase. Therefore, the integer $2^{\overline{\beta}}$ is always larger than the bound (3) for any basis during the execution of the algorithm, except possibly during Steps 3, 10 and 11 of `Reduce` and Steps 8 and 9 of `RecursiveReduce`. During these steps, the bound (4) is $\leq 2^{n+\overline{\beta}}$. This implies that all GSO coefficients appearing during the execution of `Reduce` and those of `RecursiveReduce` have bit-sizes $O(n+\overline{\beta})$, which is itself $O(n\beta)$. Finally, by construction, all (integer) entries of unimodular transformations are manipulated modulo $2^{\overline{\beta}}$.

Overall, each arithmetic operation occurring during the execution involves $O(\mathcal{M}(n\beta))$ bit operations.

The following lemma provides a recursive cost bound. The result follows from [16] for $r=1$. It follows from Subsection 4.2 and inspection of algorithm `RecursiveReduce` for $r>1$.

LEMMA 9. *We consider the execution of* `RecursiveReduce` *given as inputs* $\overline{\beta}, \eta$ *and any* n_r*-dimensional GSO coefficients* $(\mathbf{d}, \mathbf{M})$ *of a basis* $\mathbf{B}$ *with* $n_r \log \|\mathbf{B}\| \leq \overline{\beta}$. *Let* C_r *denote the maximum number of bit operations performed during the execution, over all possible* $(\mathbf{d}, \mathbf{M})$. *Then, we have, for some absolute constant* $K>0$,

$$C_1 \leq K\mathcal{M}(\overline{\beta})\log(\overline{\beta}),$$

and, for $r>1$,

$$C_r \leq \frac{n_r^3}{n_{r-1}^3} L\left(C_{r-1} + n_{r-1} n_r^2 \mathcal{M}(\overline{\beta})\right),$$

with $L = K\ln(8\overline{\beta}/\eta)$.

Now, we define $T_r := C_r/(n_r^3 L\mathcal{M}(\overline{\beta}))$. From Lemma 9, we have $T_1 \leq 1$ and, for $r>1$,

$$T_r \leq LT_{r-1} + \frac{n_r^2}{n_{r-1}^2}.$$

By design of the sequence of specific dimensions $(n_k)_{k\geq 1}$, we have:

$$T_r \leq \exp\left(O(\sqrt{(\log n)(\log L)})\right).$$

Therefore:

$$C_r \leq \exp\left(O(\sqrt{(\log n)(\log\log(n\beta))})\right)\log(n\beta) n_r^3 \mathcal{M}(n\beta).$$

During the execution of `Reduce`, algorithm `RecursiveReduce` is called $O((n^2/n_r^2)\log(n\beta))$ times. The cost of `Reduce` is hence bounded by:

$$O\left(\frac{n^2}{n_r^2}\log(n\beta)\Big(C_r + n^3\mathcal{M}(n\beta)\Big)\right).$$

By choice of r, we have

$$\frac{n}{n_r} \leq \exp\left(O(\sqrt{(\log n)(\log\log(n\beta))})\right).$$

This allows us to complete the proof of Theorem 2.

7. CONCLUSION

We have presented and analyzed the asymptotically fastest LLL-type reduction algorithm known so far. The dominating component of the cost stems from the leaves of the recursion, which correspond to 2-dimensional lattices. As a consequence, using fast matrix multiplication and Storjohann's weak size-reduction (see [18, Lemma 13]) in the naive way only affects lower order terms, and hence does not allow us to lower the complexity upper bound.

We did not implement the algorithm as – for dimensions of practical interest – it is very unlikely to be competitive with the L^2 algorithm from [11]. Indeed, the (arithmetic) term $\mathcal{M}(n\beta)$ of our complexity bound will asymptotically be reached from above, whereas the complexity bound $O(n^3\mathcal{M}(n)(n+\beta)\beta)$ of L^2 is experimentally pessimistic (see [17]).

Acknowledgments

The authors thank Paul Kirchner and Gilles Villard for interesting discussions. The second author was supported by the ERC Starting Grant ERC-2013-StG-335086-LATTAC.

8. REFERENCES

[1] N. Gama, N. Howgrave-Graham, H. Koy, and P. Q. Nguyen. Rankin's Constant and Blockwise Lattice Reduction. In *Proc. of CRYPTO*, volume 4117 of *LNCS*, pages 112–130. Springer, 2006.

[2] Saruchi, I. Morel, D. Stehlé, and G. Villard. LLL reducing with the most significant bits. In *Proc. of ISSAC*, pages 367–374. ACM, 2014.

[3] G. Hanrot, X. Pujol, and D. Stehlé. Analyzing blockwise lattice algorithms using dynamical systems. In *Proc. of CRYPTO*, volume 6841 of *LNCS*, pages 447–464. Springer, 2011.

[4] E. Kaltofen. On the complexity of finding short vectors in integer lattices. In *Proc. of EUROCAL'83*, volume 162 of *LNCS*, pages 236–244. Springer, 1983.

[5] H. Koy and C.-P. Schnorr. Segment LLL-reduction of lattice bases. In *Proc. of CALC*, volume 2146 of *LNCS*, pages 67–80. Springer, 2001.

[6] A. K. Lenstra, H. W. Lenstra, Jr., and L. Lovász. Factoring polynomials with rational coefficients. *Math. Ann*, 261:515–534, 1982.

[7] L. Lovász. *An Algorithmic Theory of Numbers, Graphs and Convexity*. SIAM, 1986. CBMS-NSF Regional Conference Series in Applied Mathematics.

[8] D. Micciancio and P. Voulgaris. A deterministic single exponential time algorithm for most lattice problems based on Voronoi cell computations. In *Proc. of STOC*, pages 351–358. ACM, 2010.

[9] D. Micciancio and M. Walter. Practical, predictable lattice basis reduction. In *Proc. of EUROCRYPT*, volume 9665 of *LNCS*, page 1123. Springer, 2016.

[10] A. Neumaier. Bounding basis reduction properties. *IACR Cryptology ePrint Archive*, 2016:4, 2016.

[11] P. Q. Nguyen and D. Stehlé. An LLL algorithm with quadratic complexity. *SIAM J. Comput*, 39(3):874–903, 2009.

[12] P. Q. Nguyen and B. Vallée. *The LLL Algorithm: Survey and Applications*. Information Security and Cryptography. Springer, 2009.

[13] A. Novocin, D. Stehlé, and G. Villard. An LLL-reduction algorithm with quasi-linear time complexity. In *Proc. of STOC*, pages 403–412. ACM, 2011.

[14] C.-P. Schnorr and M. Euchner. Lattice basis reduction: improved practical algorithms and solving

subset sum problems. *Mathematics of Programming*, 66:181–199, 1994.

[15] A. Schönhage. Factorization of univariate integer polynomials by Diophantine approximation and improved basis reduction algorithm. In *Proc. of ICALP*, volume 172 of *LNCS*, pages 436–447. Springer, 1984.

[16] A. Schönhage. Fast reduction and composition of binary quadratic forms. In *Proc. of ISSAC*, pages 128–133. ACM, 1991.

[17] D. Stehlé. *Floating-Point LLL: Theoretical and Practical Aspects*. 2010. Chapter of [12].

[18] A. Storjohann. Faster algorithms for integer lattice basis reduction. Technical report, ETH Zürich, 1996.

[19] C. K. Yap. Fast unimodular reduction: planar integer lattices. In *Proc. of FOCS*, pages 437–446. IEEE Computer Society Press, 1992.

System of Partial Differential Equations for the Hypergeometric Function ${}_1F_1$ of a Matrix Argument on Diagonal Regions

Masayuki Noro
Department of Mathematics, Rikkyo University
3-34-1 Nishi-Ikebukuro, Toshima-ku, Tokyo, 171-8501 Japan
noro@rikkyo.ac.jp

ABSTRACT

The hypergeometric function ${}_1F_1$ of a matrix argument Y is a symmetric entire function in the eigenvalues $y_1, \ldots, y_m$ of Y. It appears in the distribution function of the largest eigenvalue of a Wishart matrix and its numerical evaluation is important in multivariate distribution theory. Hashiguchi et al. (J. Multivariate Analysis, 2013) proposed an efficient algorithm for evaluating the matrix ${}_1F_1$ by the holonomic gradient method (HGM). The algorithm is based on the system of partial differential equations (PDEs) satisfied by the matrix ${}_1F_1$ given by Muirhead (Ann. Math. Statist., 1970) and it cannot be applied to the diagonal cases, i.e. the cases where several y_i's are equal because the system of PDEs has singularities on the diagonal region. Hashiguchi et al. derived an ordinary differential equation (ODE) satisfied by ${}_1F_1(y, y)$ in the bivariate case from some relations which are obtained by applying l'Hôpital rule to the system of PDEs for ${}_1F_1(y_1, y_2)$. In this paper we generalize this approach for computing systems of PDEs satisfied by the matrix ${}_1F_1$ for various diagonalization patterns. We show that the existence of a system of PDEs for a diagonalized ${}_1F_1$ is reduced to the non-singularity of the matrices systematically derived from the diagonalization pattern. By checking the non-singularity numerically, we show that there exists a system of PDEs for a diagonalized ${}_1F_1$ if the size of each diagonal block ≤ 36. We have computed an ODE for ${}_1F_1(y, \ldots, y)$ up to $m = 22$. We made a test implementation of HGM for diagonal cases and we show some numerical results.

Keywords

Partial differential equations; Statistics; Hypergeometric function; Wishart distribution; Gröbner basis

1. INTRODUCTION

Let Y be an $m \times m$ symmetric matrix with eigenvalues $y_1, \ldots, y_m$. Let $\kappa = (k_1, \ldots, k_\ell) \vdash k$ ($k_1 \geq \ldots \geq k_\ell$) be a partition of k s.t. $\ell \leq m$. $\mathcal{C}_\kappa(Y)$ is the zonal polynomial corresponding to κ (see [9]). $\mathcal{C}_\kappa(Y)$ is a homogeneous symmetric polynomial of degree k in $y_1, \ldots, y_m$. The zonal polynomials are determined by the following properties:

1. The leading term of $\mathcal{C}_\kappa(Y)$ with respect to the lexicographic order is $y_1^{k_1} \cdots y_\ell^{k_\ell}$,
2. $\mathcal{C}_\kappa(Y)$ is an eigenfunction of the differential operator
$$\Delta_Y = \sum_{i=1}^m y_i^2 \frac{\partial^2}{\partial y_i^2} + \sum_{i=1}^m \sum_{\substack{j=1 \\ j \neq i}}^m \frac{y_i^2}{y_i - y_j} \frac{\partial}{\partial y_i},$$
3. $\mathrm{tr}(Y)^k = (y_1 + \cdots + y_m)^k = \sum_{\kappa=(k_1,\ldots,k_\ell) \vdash k, \ell \leq m} \mathcal{C}_\kappa(Y)$.

The hypergeometric function ${}_1F_1$ of a matrix argument Y is defined by

$$ {}_1F_1(a; c; Y) = \sum_{k=0}^{\infty} \sum_{\kappa=(k_1,\ldots,k_\ell) \vdash k, \ell \leq m} \frac{(a)_\kappa}{(c)_\kappa} \frac{\mathcal{C}_\kappa(Y)}{k!}, \quad (1)$$

where the Pochhammer symbol $(a)_\kappa$ is defined by

$$(a)_\kappa = \prod_{i=1}^{\ell} (a - \frac{i-1}{2})_{k_i}, \quad (a)_{k_i} = \prod_{j=1}^{k_i} (a + j - 1) \quad ((a)_0 = 1).$$

Let X be an $n \times m$ matrix whose rows are independent $N_m(0, \Sigma)$ vectors, where $N_m(0, \Sigma)$ is the m-variate normal distribution with mean 0 and covariance matrix Σ. Then $W = X^T X$ is called a Wishart matrix and W is said to have the Wishart distribution with n degrees of freedom and covariance matrix Σ. We note that Σ is a real symmetric matrix. Let ℓ_1 be the largest eigenvalue of a Wishart matrix. According to [4] the cumulative distribution function $\Pr[\ell_1 < t|\Sigma]$ is given by

$$C \exp(-\frac{t}{2} \mathrm{tr} \Sigma^{-1}) t^{\frac{1}{2}nm} {}_1F_1(\frac{m+1}{2}; \frac{n+m+1}{2}; \frac{t}{2}\Sigma^{-1}), \quad (2)$$

$$C = \frac{\Gamma_m(\frac{m+1}{2})}{2^{\frac{1}{2}nm} (\det \Sigma)^{\frac{1}{2}n} \Gamma_m(\frac{n+m+1}{2})},$$

$$\Gamma_m(a) = \pi^{\frac{1}{4}m(m-1)} \prod_{i=1}^m \Gamma(a - \frac{i-1}{2}).$$

Throughout this paper we write $F = {}_1F_1$. In [7] Muirhead showed that F satisfies a system of partial differential equations

$$P_i F = 0 \quad (i = 1, \ldots, m), \quad (3)$$

ISSAC '16, July 19 - 22, 2016, Waterloo, ON, Canada

ISBN 978-1-4503-4380-0/16/07...$15.00
DOI: http://dx.doi.org/10.1145/2930889.2930905

$$P_i = \partial_i^2 + (\frac{c}{y_i} - 1)\partial_i + \frac{1}{2}\sum_{j=1, j\neq i}^{m}(\frac{1}{y_i - y_j} - \frac{1}{y_i})(\partial_i - \partial_j) - \frac{a}{y_i}. \quad (4)$$

He also showed that F is the unique solution of (3) provided that F is symmetric in $y_1, \ldots, y_m$ and holomorphic at the origin.

Since F is expressed as an infinite series (1), it is possible to compute numerically the values of F by using (1). Koev-Edelman [5] proposed an efficient algorithm for computing zonal polynomials. But the computation of zonal polynomials of large degrees is still hard because of the combinatorial explosion. Furthermore the convergence of F is slow if the arguments are large ([8], [3]). By the holonomic gradient method (HGM) [10] we can evaluate a function if a system of PDEs satisfied by the function is known. It is considered as a generalization of the well-known method that converts an n-th order ODE to an n-dimensional system of first order ODEs. In [4] an algorithm for evaluating F by HGM is described. The paper shows the performance of the implementation and it is good both in the speed and the accuracy if the number of variables m is not so large, e.g. $m = 10$. However there remains one open problem. Since (4) has singularities on the diagonal region

$$\{(y_1, \ldots, y_m) \mid y_i = 0 \text{ or } y_i = y_j \text{ for some } i, j (i \neq j)\},$$

we cannot apply HGM for computing the values of F on the diagonal region. In order to treat such cases we have to derive a system of PDEs on the diagonal region. In [4] a third order ODE satisfied by $f(y) = F(y, y)$ in the case of $m = 2$ is derived by the following procedure.

1. $f'(y)$, $f''(y)$, $f'''(y)$ are represented in terms of $\partial_1^i \partial_2^j F(y, y)$.
2. A number of relations among $f^{(k)}(y)$ and $\partial_1^i \partial_2^j F(y, y)$ are computed by applying l'Hôpital rule to (3) and their derivatives.
3. $\partial_1^i \partial_2^j F(y, y)$ are eliminated to obtain a relation of $f(y)$, $f'(y)$, $f''(y)$, $f'''(y)$.

The paper concludes that a "by-hand" calculation by this method is tedious and is infeasible. In [4] a method based on the restriction algorithm for holonomic D-modules are also tried but the attempt was failed already for $m = 4$. In fact Kondo [6] showed that the left D-ideal generated by $y_i \prod_{j\neq i}(y_i - y_j)P_i$'s is not holonomic for $m = 4$. In this paper we show that the former method can be generalized for computing a system of PDEs for various patterns of diagonalizations of variables. The applicability of our new method is determined by the non-singularity of matrices obtained by applying l'Hôpital rule systematically to (3) and their derivatives. We show that there exists a system of PDEs for a diagonalized ${}_1F_1$ if the size of each diagonal block ≤ 36. We have computed an ODE for ${}_1F_1(y, \ldots, y)$ up to $m = 22$. We implement HGM based on our method for computing systems of PDEs on the diagonal region in Risa/Asir [12] and and we show some numerical results.

2. RECURSIVE REDUCTION OF THE SYSTEM OF PDES

In this section we give an algorithm for deriving systems of PDEs satisfied by ${}_1F_1$ for various diagonalization patterns.

We set

$$F(y_1, \ldots, y_m) = {}_1F_1(a; c; Y), \quad Y = \mathrm{diag}(y_1, \ldots, y_m).$$

2.1 One diagonal block case

We first consider the case where the diagonalization is given by $y_k = \cdots = y_1$ and $y_1, y_{k+1}, \ldots, y_m$ are distinct. We set

$$z = (y_{k+1}, \ldots, y_m), \quad \partial_z = (\partial_{k+1}, \ldots, \partial_m).$$

For a function $g(y_1, \ldots, y_m)$, we define $\phi(g)(y_1, z)$ as

$$g|_{y_k=\ldots=y_1} = g(y_1, \ldots, y_1, z).$$

We set $f(y_1, z) = \phi(F)(y_1, z)$. We derive a partial differential equation for f from $P_1 F = 0$.

For a partition α we write $\alpha = (n_1^{s_1}, \ldots, n_\ell^{s_\ell})$ if

$$\alpha = (n_1, \ldots, n_1, n_2, \ldots, n_2, \ldots, n_\ell, \ldots, n_\ell)$$

for $n_1 > n_2 > \cdots > n_\ell > 0$ and each n_j appears s_j times. First of all we give a formula for expressing $\partial_1^i f(y_1, z)$ in terms of $\phi(\partial^\alpha F)$'s.

LEMMA 2.1.

$$\partial_1^i f(y_1, z) = \sum_{\alpha=(n_1^{s_1}, \ldots, n_\ell^{s_\ell})\vdash i, \ell\leq k} q_\alpha \phi(\partial^\alpha F),$$

$$q_\alpha = \frac{i!}{(n_1!)^{s_1}\cdots(n_\ell!)^{s_\ell}} \cdot \frac{k!}{s_1!\cdots s_\ell!(k - (s_1 + \cdots + s_\ell))!}. \quad (5)$$

PROOF. Since $\partial_1^i f(y_1, z) = \phi((\partial_1 + \cdots + \partial_k)^i F)$

$$\partial_1^i f(y_1, z) = \sum_{n_1+\cdots+n_k=i} \frac{i!}{n_1!\cdots n_k!}\phi(\partial_1^{n_1}\cdots\partial_k^{n_k} F). \quad (6)$$

The symmetry of ${}_1F_1$ implies

$$\phi(\partial_1^{n_{\sigma(1)}}\cdots\partial_k^{n_{\sigma(k)}} F) = \phi(\partial_1^{n_1}\cdots\partial_k^{n_k} F) \quad (7)$$

for any $\sigma \in S_k$, where S_k is the symmetric group on $\{1, \ldots, k\}$. Then we have

$$\partial_1^i f(y_1, z) = \sum_{\alpha=(n_1, \ldots, n_k)\vdash i} \frac{i!}{n_1!\cdots n_k!} c_\alpha \phi(\partial^\alpha F), \quad (8)$$

where $c_\alpha = \#\{(n_1, \ldots, n_k) \mid \text{there exists } \sigma \in S_k \text{ s.t. } (n_{\sigma(1)}, \ldots, n_{\sigma(k)}) = \alpha\}$. If $\alpha = (n_1^{s_1}, \ldots, n_\ell^{s_\ell})$ for $n_1 > \cdots > n_\ell > 0$, then

$$\begin{aligned} c_\alpha &= \#\{(U_1, \ldots, U_\ell) \mid U_p \subset \{1, \ldots, k\}, \\ &\quad \#U_p = s_p\ (1 \leq p \leq \ell), U_p \cap U_q = \emptyset\ (1 \leq p, q \leq \ell)\} \\ &= \frac{k!}{s_1!(k - s_1)!} \cdot \frac{(k - s_1)!}{s_2!(k - s_1 - s_2)!} \\ &\quad \cdots \frac{(k - s_1 - \cdots - s_{\ell-1})!}{s_\ell!(k - s_1 - \cdots - s_\ell)!} \\ &= \frac{k!}{s_1!\cdots s_\ell!(k - (s_1 + \cdots + s_\ell))!}. \end{aligned}$$

□

For $\alpha = (n_1, n_2, \ldots, n_k) \vdash i$ with $n_1 \geq 2$ we set $\alpha^- = (n_1 - 2, n_2, \ldots, n_k)$. Then $P_1 F = 0$ implies

$$\partial^{\alpha^-} P_1 F = \partial^\alpha F + \frac{1}{2}\partial^{\alpha^-}\sum_{j=2}^{k}\frac{\partial_1 F - \partial_j F}{y_1 - y_j} + (\partial^{\alpha^-} \circ R)F = 0, \quad (9)$$

$$R = (\frac{c}{y_1} - 1)\partial_1 + \frac{1}{2}\sum_{j=k+1}^{m} \frac{1}{y_1 - y_j}(\partial_1 - \partial_j)$$
$$-\frac{1}{2}\sum_{j=2}^{m} \frac{1}{y_1}(\partial_1 - \partial_j) - \frac{a}{y_1}.$$

Since the terms in (9) except for $\partial^{\alpha^-}\frac{\partial_1 F - \partial_j F}{y_1 - y_j}$ do not have $y_1 - y_j$ $(j \le k)$ in their denominators, these terms converge as $y_j \to y_1$. Therefore $\lim_{y_j \to y_1} \partial^{\alpha^-}\frac{\partial_1 F - \partial_j F}{y_1 - y_j}$ also exists.

LEMMA 2.2 (L'HÔPITAL RULE). *If a function $g(z)$ is holomorphic at $z = a$ and $\lim_{z\to a} \frac{g(z)}{(z-a)^s}$ exists, then*

$$\lim_{z\to a} \frac{g(z)}{(z-a)^s} = \frac{g^{(s)}(a)}{s!}. \tag{10}$$

PROOF. Let $g(z) = \sum_{i=0}^{\infty} \frac{g^{(i)}(a)}{i!}(z-a)^i$ be the Taylor expansion of $g(z)$ at $z = a$. Then

$$\frac{g(z)}{(z-a)^s} = \frac{g(a)}{(z-a)^s} + \cdots + \frac{g^{(s)}(a)}{s!} + \sum_{i=1}^{\infty} \frac{g^{(i+s)}(a)}{(i+s)!}(z-a)^i.$$

Since $\lim_{z\to a} \frac{g(z)}{(z-a)^s}$ exists, $\lim_{z\to a}(z-a)^i \cdot \frac{g(z)}{(z-a)^s} = 0$ for all $i \ge 1$, which implies $g(a) = 0$, $g'(a) = 0$, $\ldots$ $g^{(s-1)}(a) = 0$ and finally we have (10). □

LEMMA 2.3.

$$\sum_{\ell=0}^{n} (-1)^\ell \frac{1}{k+\ell+1}\binom{n}{\ell} = \frac{n!k!}{(n+k+1)!}$$

PROOF. $x^k(1-x)^n = \sum_{\ell=0}^{n}\binom{n}{\ell}(-1)^\ell x^{k+\ell}$ implies

$$\sum_{\ell=0}^{n}(-1)^\ell \frac{1}{k+\ell+1}\binom{n}{\ell} = \int_0^1 x^k(1-x)^n dx = \frac{k!n!}{(k+n+\ell)!}.$$

□

For $\beta = (n_1, \ldots, n_m)$ we set

$$s_j(\beta) = (0, n_2, \ldots, n_{j-1}, 0, n_{j+1}, \ldots, n_m).$$

PROPOSITION 2.4. *Suppose that $g(y_1, \ldots, y_m)$ is holomorphic at $y_j = y_1$. If $\lim_{y_j\to y_1} \partial^\beta \frac{g(y_1,\ldots,y_m)}{y_1 - y_j}$ exists for $\beta = (n_1, \ldots, n_m)$ then*

$$\lim_{y_j\to y_1} \partial^\beta \frac{g(y_1,\ldots,y_m)}{y_1 - y_j}$$
$$= -\sum_{i=0}^{n_1} \frac{n_1!n_j!}{(n_1-i)!(n_j+i+1)!}(\partial_1^{n_1-i}\partial_j^{n_j+i+1}\partial^{s_j(\beta)}g)|_{y_j=y_1}.$$

PROOF. By applying the Leibniz rule we have

$$\partial^\beta \frac{g}{y_1 - y_j}$$
$$= \sum_{k=0}^{n_1}\sum_{\ell=0}^{n_j}\binom{n_1}{k}\binom{n_j}{\ell}\frac{(-1)^k(k+\ell)!}{(y_1-y_j)^{k+\ell+1}}\partial_1^{n_1-k}\partial_j^{n_j-\ell}\partial^{s_j(\beta)}g$$
$$= \frac{h}{(y_1-y_j)^{n_1+n_j+1}},$$

$$h = \sum_{k=0}^{n_1}\sum_{\ell=0}^{n_j}\binom{n_1}{k}\binom{n_j}{\ell}(-1)^k(k+\ell)!(y_1-y_j)^{n_1+n_k-k-\ell}$$
$$\times \partial_1^{n_1-k}\partial_j^{n_j-l}\partial^{s_j(\beta)}g.$$

By Lemma 2.2

$$\lim_{y_j\to y_1}\frac{h}{(y_1-y_j)^{n_1+n_j+1}} = \frac{(-1)^{n_1+n_j+1}\partial_j^{n_1+n_j+1}h|_{y_j=y_1}}{(n_1+n_j+1)!}.$$

By the Leibniz rule again

$$\partial_j^{n_1+n_j+1}h$$
$$= \sum_{k=0}^{n_1}\sum_{\ell=0}^{n_j}\binom{n_1}{k}\binom{n_j}{\ell}(-1)^k(k+\ell)!$$
$$\times \sum_{p=0}^{n_1+n_j+1}\binom{n_1+n_j+1}{p}\partial_j^p(y_1-y_j)^{n_1+n_j-k-\ell}$$
$$\times \partial_j^{n_1+n_j+1-p}\partial_1^{n_1-k}\partial_j^{n_j-\ell}\partial^{s_j(\beta)}g.$$

When computing $\partial_j^{n_1+n_j+1}h|_{y_j=y_1}$ only the terms for $p = n_1 + n_j - k - \ell$ remain and

$$\partial_j^{n_1+n_j+1}h|_{y_j=y_1} = \sum_{k=0}^{n_1}\sum_{\ell=0}^{n_j}\binom{n_1}{k}\binom{n_j}{\ell}(-1)^{n_1+n_j-\ell}$$
$$\times (k+\ell)!\binom{n_1+n_j+1}{n_1+n_j-k-\ell}(n_1+n_j-k-\ell)!$$
$$\times \partial_1^{n_1-k}\partial_j^{n_j+k+1}\partial^{s_j(\beta)}g.$$

Thus we have

$$\lim_{y_j\to y_1}\partial^\beta\frac{g(y_1,\ldots,y_m)}{y_1-y_j}$$
$$= \sum_{k=0}^{n_1}\binom{n_1}{k}\left(\sum_{\ell=0}^{n_j}\frac{(-1)^{\ell+1}}{k+\ell+1}\binom{n_j}{\ell}\right)\partial_1^{n_1-k}\partial_j^{n_j+k+1}\partial^{s_j(\beta)}g$$
$$= \sum_{k=0}^{n_1}\binom{n_1}{k}\frac{-n_j!k!}{(n_j+k+1)!}\partial_1^{n_1-k}\partial_j^{n_j+k+1}\partial^{s_j(\beta)}g$$
$$= -\sum_{k=0}^{n_1}\frac{n_1!n_j!}{(n_1-k)!(n_j+k+1)!}\partial_1^{n_1-k}\partial_j^{n_j+k+1}\partial^{s_j(\beta)}g$$

by Lemma 2.3. □

COROLLARY 2.5. *For $\alpha = (n_1, \ldots, n_m)$ $(n_1 \ge 2)$*

$$\lim_{y_j\to y_1}\partial^{\alpha^-}\frac{\partial_1 F - \partial_j F}{y_1 - y_j}$$
$$= -\frac{1}{n_j+1}(\partial_1^{n_1-1}\partial_j^{n_j+1}\partial^{s_j(\alpha)}F)|_{y_j=y_1}$$
$$+ \sum_{i=2}^{n_1}\frac{(n_1-2)!n_j!(n_j-n_1+2i)}{(n_1-i)!(n_j+i)!}(\partial_1^{n_1-i}\partial_j^{n_j+i}\partial^{s_j(\alpha)}F)|_{y_j=y_1}.$$

For a positive integer s $(s \le k+1)$ we set

$$B_s = \{\alpha = (n_1, \ldots, n_k) \mid \alpha \vdash s\} = \{\alpha_1^{(s)}, \ldots, \alpha_{b_s}^{(s)}\},$$

where $b_s = \#B_s$ and $\alpha_{b_s}^{(s)} = (1^s)$ for $s \le k$.

THEOREM 2.6. *For each* $\alpha_i^{(s)} = (n_1, \dots, n_k) \in B_s$ *such that* $n_1 \ge 2$ *there exists a relation*

$$\sum_{\ell=1}^{b_s} u_{i\ell}^{(s)} \phi(\partial^{\alpha_\ell} F) = \sum_{\gamma \in B_t, t \le s-1} v_{i\gamma}^{(s)}(y_1, z, \partial_z)\phi(\partial^\gamma F), \quad (11)$$

where $u_{i\ell}^{(s)} \in \mathbb{Q}$, $v_{i\gamma}^{(s)}(y_1, z, \partial_z) \in \mathbb{Q}(y_1, z)\langle \partial_z \rangle$, $\mathrm{ord}(v_{i\gamma}^{(s)}) \le 1$ *and* $\mathrm{ord}(v_{i\gamma}^{(s)}) + |\gamma| \le s - 1$.

PROOF. From (9) and Corollary 2.5 we have

$$\phi(\partial^{\alpha_i^{(s)}} F) + \frac{1}{2}\sum_{j=2}^{k}\sum_{\ell=1}^{n_1} c_\ell \phi(\partial_1^{n_1-\ell}\partial_j^{n_j+\ell}\partial^{s_j(\alpha_i^{(s)})}F)$$

$$= - \lim_{y_2 \to y_1, \dots, y_k \to y_1} (\partial^{\alpha^-} \circ R)F, \quad (12)$$

$$c_\ell = \begin{cases} -\frac{1}{n_j+1} & (\ell = 1) \\ \frac{(n_1-2)!n_j!(n_j-n_1+2\ell)}{(n_1-\ell)!(n_j+\ell)!} & (\ell = 2, \dots, n_1) \end{cases}$$

Since $\mathrm{ord}(\partial_1^{n_1-\ell}\partial_j^{n_j+\ell}\partial^{s_j(\alpha)}) = s$, each $\phi(\partial_1^{n_1-\ell}\partial_j^{n_j+\ell}\partial^{s_j(\alpha)}F)$ in (12) is equal to $\phi(\partial^\alpha F)$ for some $\alpha \in B_s$. Thus the left hand side of (12) can be written as $\sum_{\ell=1}^{b_s} u_{i\ell}^{(s)}\phi(\partial^{\alpha_\ell}F)$ for some $u_{i\ell}^{(s)} \in \mathbb{Q}$. We compute $\lim_{y_2 \to y_1, \dots, y_k \to y_1} (\partial^{\alpha^-} \circ R)F$. We set

$$r_\ell(y_1, \partial_1) = \partial_1^\ell \circ \frac{1}{y_1} = \sum_{i=0}^{\ell} \frac{(-1)^i i!}{y_1^{i+1}}\partial_1^{\ell-i}.$$

Then $\partial_1^\ell \circ \frac{1}{y_1 - y_j} = r_\ell(y_1 - y_j, \partial_1)$ and

$$\begin{aligned} \partial^{\alpha^-} \circ R &= (cr_{n_1-2}(y_1, \partial_1)\partial_1 - \partial_1^{n_1-1} - ar_{n_1-2}(y_1, \partial_1))\partial^{\alpha'} \\ &+ \frac{1}{2}\sum_{j=k+1}^{m} r_{n_1-2}(y_1 - y_j, \partial_1)(\partial_1 - \partial_j)\partial^{\alpha'} \\ &- \frac{1}{2}\sum_{j=2}^{m} r_{n_1-2}(y_1, \partial_1)(\partial_1 - \partial_j)\partial^{\alpha'}, \end{aligned}$$

where $\alpha' = (0, n_2, \dots, n_k)$. R does not contain $y_1 - y_2, \dots, y_1 - y_k$ in its denominators and we have $\lim_{y_2 \to y_1, \dots, y_k \to y_1} (\partial^{\alpha^-} \circ R)F = \phi((\partial^{\alpha^-} \circ R)F)$. By $\phi(\partial_j \partial^\gamma F) = \partial_j \phi(\partial^\gamma F)$ for $j = k+1, \dots, m$ and (7), the right hand side of (12) can be written as

$$\sum_\gamma v_{i\gamma}^{(s)}(y_1, z, \partial_z)\phi(\partial^\gamma F),$$

where γ is a partition.

$$\mathrm{ord}\, r_{n_1-2}(y_1, \partial_1), \mathrm{ord}\, r_{n_1-2}(y_1 - y_j, \partial_1) \le n_1 - 2$$

implies $|\gamma| \le s - 1$. Thus $\gamma \in B_t$ for some $t \le s - 1$. $\mathrm{ord}(\partial^{\alpha^-} \circ R) \le s - 1$ implies $\mathrm{ord}(v_{i\gamma}^{(s)}) + |\gamma| \le s - 1$. □

COROLLARY 2.7. *We set* $U_s = (\phi(\partial^{\alpha_i^{(s)}}F))_{i=1,\dots,b_s}^T$ *and define a* $b_s \times b_s$ *matrix* $C_s = (c_{ij}^{(s)})$ *and a column vector* $V_s = (v_i^{(s)})_{i=1,\dots,b_s}^T$ *as follows:*

- $s = k+1$
  $c_{ij}^{(k+1)} = u_{ij}^{(k+1)} (1 \le i, j \le b_{k+1})$,
  $v_i^{(k+1)} =$ *the right hand side of (11)* $(1 \le i \le b_{k+1})$
- $1 \le s \le k$

$$c_{ij}^{(s)} = \begin{cases} u_{ij}^{(s)} & (1 \le i \le b_s - 1, 1 \le j \le b_s) \\ q_{\alpha_j^{(s)}} & (i = b_s, q_\alpha \text{ is given in (5)}) \end{cases}$$

$$v_i^{(s)} = \begin{cases} \text{the right hand side of (11)} & (1 \le i \le b_s - 1) \\ \partial_1^s f(y_1, z) & (i = b_s). \end{cases}$$

Then $C_s U_s = V_s$ $(1 \le s \le k+1)$.

DEFINITION 2.8. $C_1, \dots, C_{k+1}$ *in Corollary 2.7 are called the rewriting matrices for the block size* k.

REMARK 2.9. *The rewriting matrices for the block size* k *are constructed from* $\sum_{j=2}^{k} \frac{\partial_1 F - \partial_j F}{y_1 - y_j}$ *and they do not depend on the total number of variables.*

THEOREM 2.10. *If the rewriting matrices for the block size* k *are all non-singular, then there exists an operator* $P \in \mathbb{Q}(y_1, z)\langle \partial_z \rangle$

$$P = \partial_1^{k+1} + d_1(y_1, z, \partial_z)\partial_1^k + \dots + d_{k+1}(y_1, z, \partial_z) \quad (13)$$

such that $Pf(y_1, z) = 0$, $\mathrm{ord}(P - \partial_1^{k+1}) \le k$.

PROOF. Let $C_1, \dots, C_{k+1}$ be the rewriting matrices for the block size k. If they are all non-singular, then we have

$$U_s = C_s^{-1}V_s \quad (1 \le s \le k+1).$$

Since each element of $C_s^{-1}V_s$ is written in a form

$$c\partial_1^s f(y_1, z) + \sum_{\gamma \in B_t, t \le s-1} v_\gamma(y_1, z, \partial_z)\phi(\partial^\gamma F),$$

where $v_\gamma \in \mathbb{Q}(y_1, z)\langle \partial_z \rangle$ and $c \in \mathbb{Q}$, each element of U_{k+1} is eventually expressed as a $\mathbb{Q}(y_1, z)\langle \partial_z \rangle$-linear combination of $\partial_1^t f(y_1, z)$. We substitute U_{k+1} into

$$\partial_1^{k+1} f(y_1, z) = \sum_{\alpha = (n_1^{s_1}, \dots, n_\ell^{s_\ell}) \vdash k+1} q_\alpha \phi(\partial^\alpha F),$$

then we obtain the desired relation $Pf(y_1, z) = 0$. $\mathrm{ord}(P - \partial_1^{k+1}) \le k$ follows from the fact $\mathrm{ord}(v_\gamma) + |\gamma| \le s - 1$ in (13). □

2.2 General case

We consider the case where there are several diagonal blocks. Suppose that $\{y_1, \dots, y_m\}$ is a disjoint union of $Y_1, \dots, Y_\ell$, $\#Y_i = m_i$ $(i = 1, \dots, \ell)$. We assume $y_t \in Y_t$ $(t = 1, \dots, \ell)$ for simplicity. We set $y = (y_j \mid y_j \in Y_1)$. For a function $g(y_1, \dots, y_m)$, we define $\psi(g)(y_1, y_2, \dots, y_\ell)$ and $\psi_1(g)(y, y_2, \dots, y_\ell)$ as the restrictions of g to

$$\{(y_1, \dots, y_m) \mid y_j = y_t \text{ for all } y_j \in Y_t, t = 1, \dots, \ell\}$$

and

$$\{(y_1, \dots, y_m) \mid y_j = y_t \text{ for all } y_j \in Y_t, t = 2, \dots, \ell\}.$$

respectively.

LEMMA 2.11. $\psi_1(F)$ *satisfies* $\hat{P}_1\psi_1(F) = 0$, *where*

$$\hat{P}_1 = \partial_1^2 + (\frac{c}{y_1} - 1)\partial_1 + \frac{1}{2}\sum_{\substack{y_j \in Y_1 \\ y_j \ne y_1}} (\frac{1}{y_1 - y_j} - \frac{1}{y_1})(\partial_1 - \partial_j)$$

$$+ \frac{1}{2}\sum_{j=2}^{\ell}(\frac{1}{y_1 - y_j} - \frac{1}{y_1})(m_j\partial_1 - \partial_j) - \frac{a}{y_1}. \quad (14)$$

PROOF. Since P_1 does not contain $y_i - y_j$ $(y_i, y_j \in Y_t, t = 2, \ldots, \ell)$, $P_1 F = 0$ implies $\psi_1(P_1 F) = 0$. Thus we have

$$\begin{aligned}\psi_1(P_1 F) &= \partial_1^2 \psi_1(F) + (\frac{c}{y_1} - 1)\partial_1 \psi_1(F) - \frac{a}{y_1}\psi_1(F) \\ &+ \frac{1}{2}\sum_{\substack{y_j \in Y_1 \\ y_j \neq y_1}} (\frac{1}{y_1 - y_j} - \frac{1}{y_1})(\partial_1 - \partial_j)\psi_1(F) \\ &+ \frac{1}{2}\sum_{t=2}^{\ell} \psi_1(S_t F) = 0,\end{aligned}$$

where $S_t = \sum_{y_j \in Y_t} (\frac{1}{y_1 - y_j} - \frac{1}{y_1})(\partial_1 - \partial_j)$. Then

$$\begin{aligned}\psi_1(S_t F) &= \sum_{y_j \in Y_t} (\frac{1}{y_1 - y_t} - \frac{1}{y_1})(\partial_1 - \partial_j)\psi_1(F) \\ &= (\frac{1}{y_1 - y_t} - \frac{1}{y_1})(m_t \partial_1 \psi_1(F) - \sum_{y_j \in Y_t} \psi_1(\partial_j F)) \\ &= (\frac{1}{y_1 - y_t} - \frac{1}{y_1})(m_t \partial_1 \psi_1(F) - \partial_t \psi_1(F))\end{aligned}$$

implies $\hat{P}_1 \psi_1(F) = 0$. □

For computing an operator P s.t. $P\psi(F) = 0$, we apply the procedure in 2.1 to the equation (14). The form of $\hat{P}_1$ differs from P_1 only in the coefficients of the second summation in (14). Since $y_1 - y_j$ $(y_j \in Y_1)$ does not appear in this term, it only contributes to the right hand side in (12) and the parts containing $y_1 - y_j$ $(y_j \in Y_1)$ in P_1 and $\hat{P}_1$ are the same. This implies that we obtain the same rewriting matrices as those obtained in the case of one diagonal block (see Remark 2.9). Let $\prec$ be a graded term order in the ring of differential operators $D_\ell = \mathbb{Q}(a, c)(y_1, \ldots, y_\ell)\langle \partial_1, \ldots, \partial_\ell \rangle$.

THEOREM 2.12. *If Algorithm 1 outputs a set of differential operators $Q_1 \ldots, Q_\ell \in D_\ell$ then they satisfy*

$$Q_1 \psi(F) = \cdots = Q_\ell \psi(F) = 0 \qquad (15)$$

and $\mathrm{in}_\prec(Q_i) = \partial_i^{m_i + 1}$ $(i = 1, \ldots, \ell)$.

PROOF. Theorem 2.10 implies $Q_i \psi(F) = 0$ and $\mathrm{in}_\prec(Q_i) = \partial_i^{m_i}$. □

REMARK 2.13. *1. From our experiments we conjecture that the output of Algorithm 1 forms a Gröbner basis in D_ℓ with respect to the term order $\prec$.*

2. Even if the output of Algorithm 1 is a Gröbner basis, it may not be reduced. Thus we have to inter-reduce it to obtain the reduced Gröbner basis.

As an example, we give the result in the case $y_1 = y_2$ for an arbitrary m.

Algorithm 1 Restriction to a diagonal region

Input : $Y_1, \ldots, Y_\ell \subset Y = \{y_1, \ldots, y_m\}$, $Y = Y_1 \cup \cdots \cup Y_\ell$
$Y_i \cap Y_j = \emptyset\, (i \neq j), \#Y_i = m_i, y_i \in Y_i\, (i = 1, \ldots, m)$
Output : Operators $Q_1, \ldots, Q_\ell \in D_\ell$
s.t. $Q_1 \psi(F) = \cdots = Q_\ell \psi(F) = 0$
or *failure* if some rewriting matrix is singular.

for $t = 1$ to ℓ **do**

$$\begin{aligned}R^{(t)} &\leftarrow (\frac{c}{y_t} - 1)\partial_t + \frac{1}{2}\sum_{\substack{y_j \in Y_t \\ y_j \neq y_t}} (-\frac{1}{y_t})(\partial_t - \partial_j) \\ &+ \frac{1}{2}\sum_{\substack{j = 1, \cdots, \ell \\ j \neq t}} (\frac{1}{y_t - y_j} - \frac{1}{y_t})(m_j \partial_t - \partial_j) - \frac{a}{y_t}\end{aligned}$$

$C_1, \ldots, C_{m_t + 1} \leftarrow$ the rewriting matrices for the block size m_t
if some C_i is singular **then**
return *failure*
else
Compute $Q_t = \partial_t^{m_t + 1} + \sum_{j=0}^{m_t} d_j \partial_t^j$ s.t. $Q_t \psi(F) = 0$
by applying Theorem 2.10 using $R^{(t)}$ as R in (9)
end if
end for
return $Q_1, \ldots, Q_\ell$

THEOREM 2.14. $f(y_1, y_3, \ldots, y_m) = F(y_1, y_1, y_3, \ldots, y_m)$ *satisfies* $hf = h_3 f = \cdots = h_m f = 0$, *where*

$$\begin{aligned}h &= \partial_1^3 + \left(\frac{3}{2}u + \frac{2}{y_1}\right)\partial_1^2 - 2P\partial_1 \\ &+ \left(\frac{1}{2}u\left(u + \frac{2}{y_1}\right) - \frac{4a}{y_1}\right)\partial_1 - uP - \frac{2au}{y_1}, \\ u &= \frac{2c - 2y_1 - m}{y_1} + \sum_{j=3}^{m} \frac{1}{y_1 - y_j}, \\ P &= \sum_{j=3}^{m} (\frac{1}{y_1 - y_j} - \frac{1}{y_1})\partial_j, \\ h_i &= \partial_i^2 + (\frac{c}{y_i} - 1)\partial_i + \frac{1}{2}\sum_{\substack{j = 3, \ldots, m \\ j \neq i}} (\frac{1}{y_i - y_j} - \frac{1}{y_i})(\partial_i - \partial_j) \\ &+ \frac{1}{2}(\frac{1}{y_i - y_1} - \frac{1}{y_i})(2\partial_i - \partial_1) - \frac{a}{y_i} \quad (i = 3, \ldots, m)\end{aligned}$$

PROOF. We use the notations in Section 2.1. We set $B_3 = \{\alpha_1^{(3)} = (3), \alpha_2^{(3)} = (2, 1)\}$, $B_2 = \{\alpha_1^{(2)} = (2), \alpha_2^{(2)} = (1, 1)\}$, $B_1 = \{\alpha_1^{(1)} = (1)\}$. Let C_s be the rewriting matrix for the block size 2 determined by B_s $(s = 1, 2, 3)$. Then

$$C_3 = \begin{pmatrix} \frac{5}{4} & -\frac{1}{4} \\ \frac{1}{4} & \frac{3}{4} \end{pmatrix}, C_2 = \begin{pmatrix} \frac{3}{2} & -\frac{1}{2} \\ 2 & 2 \end{pmatrix}, C_1 = (2)$$

and they are non-singular. Thus Algorithm 1 outputs a set of operators. In this case a shortcut can be applied. From C_3 we have

$$\frac{1}{4}\phi(\partial_1^3 F) + \frac{3}{4}\phi(\partial_1^2 \partial_2 F) = -(\partial_2 \circ R)F. \qquad (16)$$

We set $z = (y_3, \ldots, y_m)$. Since $\partial_1^3 f(y_1, z) = 2(\phi(\partial_1^3 F) + 3\phi(\partial_1^2\partial_2 F))$, the left hand side of (16) is equal to $\frac{1}{8}\partial_1^3 f(y_1, z)$. From C_2 we have

$$\begin{aligned}\phi(\partial_1^2 F) &= \frac{1}{8}\partial_1^3 f(y_1, z) - \frac{1}{2}\phi(RF),\\ \phi(\partial_1\partial_2 F) &= \frac{3}{8}\partial_1^3 f(y_1, z) + \frac{1}{2}\phi(RF).\end{aligned}$$

We also have $\phi(\partial_1 F) = \frac{1}{2}\partial_1 f(y_1, z)$. By substituting these into $\phi((\partial_2 \circ R)F)$ and $\phi(RF)$ we obtain the operator h. The operator h_i is obtained by Lemma 2.11. □

3. IMPLEMENTATION

3.1 Implementation of Algorithm 1

We implemented Algorithm 1 in Risa/Asir [11]. Since the differential operators $P_1, \ldots, P_m$ contain fractions in their coefficients, we have to be very careful when we execute arithmetic operations on them. In particular we have to avoid expansion of polynomial multiplication as far as possible. To realize this we developed a special package in which the coefficients are represented as a sum of fractions without reducing to a common denominator. Each fraction is a product of a numerator and $\frac{1}{(y_i-y_j)^k}$'s and $\frac{1}{y_i^k}$'s. Both of sums and products are represented as a sorted list. A fraction and a sum are considered as a monomial and a polynomial respectively. It is possible that a sum of fractions is reduced to zero. But we do not care such cases because all the computations needed in Algorithm 1 are multiplications of a matrix and a vector and substitutions. The reduction of sums of fractions are only necessary when we apply the Buchberger criterion to the set of differential operators. We note that the default algorithm implemented in a package **n_wishartd.rr** in [11] is slightly different from Algorithm 1. For reducing $\partial^\alpha F$ we search $\alpha_i \geq 2$ for $i = m, m-1, \ldots$ and use P_i instead of P_1. By this change it may happen that the modified rewriting matrix is singular. In such a case we add other relations until the matrix becomes full-rank. The reason why we made this change is that the resulting matrices tend to have smaller coefficients than the original ones. We show some results related to Algorithm 1. We executed Algorithm 1 for all diagonalization patterns when $m \leq 12$. The results are found in [11]. If a block size k in a diagonalization is large it is hard to complete the execution of Algorithm 1 because the sizes of the rewriting matrices are partition numbers and increase rapidly. However the check of the non-singularity of the rewriting matrices are rather easy. By applying the modular computation we have checked that the rewriting matrices are all non-singular up to $k = 36$.

If the number of diagonal blocks ℓ is 1, we obtain an ODE $Q^{(m)} f(y) = 0$ for $f(y) = F(y, \ldots, y)$. Currently we have computed $Q^{(m)}$ up to $m = 22$. They are of the form

$$\partial^{m+1} + \sum_{i=1}^{m} \frac{u_i(a, c, y)}{y^{m-i+1}}\partial^i + \frac{u_0(a, c, y)}{y^m},$$

where $u_i(a, c, y) \in \mathbb{Q}[a, c, y]$ and $\deg_y u_i \leq m - i + 1$ $(i = 1, \ldots, m)$, $\deg_y u_0 \leq m$.

3.2 Implementation of HGM

3.2.1 *A review of HGM*

First of all we briefly review HGM [10, 4]. We set $x = (x_1, \ldots, x_n)$ and $K = \mathbb{C}(x)$. Suppose that a function $f(x)$ satisfies a system of PDEs $P_1 f = \cdots = P_t f = 0$ for $P_1, \ldots, P_t \in R = K\langle\partial_1, \ldots, \partial_n\rangle$. We set $G = \{P_1, \ldots, P_t\}$. We also suppose that the left ideal $I = \langle G\rangle \subset R$ is zero-dimensional, that is $\dim_K R/I < \infty$ and G is the reduced Gröbner basis of I. Let $S = \{s_1 = 1, \ldots, s_d\}$ be a set of standard monomials with respect to I, where $d = \dim_K R/I$. We set $U = (s_j f \mid j = 1, \ldots, d)^T$, where s_j acts as a differential operator on the function f. For each i, j the division by G gives a relation

$$\partial_i s_j \equiv \sum_{k=1}^{d} c_{jk}^{(i)} s_k \bmod I \quad \text{for some } c_{jk}^{(i)} \in K$$

and we have

$$\frac{\partial U}{\partial x_i} = M_i(x)U, \quad M_i(x) = (c_{jk}^{(i)})_{1\leq j,k\leq d} \quad (i = 1, \ldots, n). \tag{17}$$

We call (17) the Pfaffian system. For computing $U(x^{(1)})$ $(x^{(1)} = t_1 x)$ we choose an initial point $x^{(0)} = t_0 x$ for some t_0 $(0 < t_0 < t_1)$ and set $u(t) = U(tx)$. Then $u(t)$ satisfies

$$\frac{du(t)}{dt} = \left(\sum_{i=1}^{n} x_i M_i(tx)\right) u(t), \quad u(t_0) = U(x^{(0)}). \tag{18}$$

If $U(x^{(0)})$ is given, (18) is an initial value problem of an ODE and we can numerically solve it to obtain $U(x^{(1)}) = u(t_1)$. Here we assumed that G is a Gröbner basis. In general this assumption is necessary to ensure the existence of the solution of the Pfaffian system (17).

3.2.2 *HGM for computing* $\Pr[\ell_1 < t|\Sigma]$

We apply HGM for computing $\Pr[\ell_1 < t|\Sigma]$ where a diagonal matrix Σ has repeated eigenvalues. Though our implementation theoretically accepts any diagonalization patterns, from the practical viewpoint we only deal with the case where the number of the diagonal blocks is 2. Set

$$f(x_1, x_2) = F|_{y_1=\cdots=y_k=x_1, y_{k+1}=\cdots=y_m=x_2}.$$

For $\frac{1}{2}\Sigma^{-1} = (\beta_1, \ldots, \beta_1, \beta_2, \ldots, \beta_2)$ with k β_1's and $m-k$ β_2's, set $\beta = (\beta_1, \beta_2)$. Let Q_1, Q_2 be the output of Algorithm 1 s.t.

$$Q_1 f = Q_2 f = 0 \tag{19}$$

and $\mathrm{in}(Q_1) = \partial_1^{k+1}$, $\mathrm{in}(Q_2) = \partial_2^{m-k+1}$ where $\partial_i = \partial/\partial x_i (i = 1, 2)$. In our implementation we compute the Pfaffian matrices without checking whether $G = \{Q_1, Q_2\}$ is a Gröbner basis. This is valid because we already know that there exists the solution F and it satisfies (18). Set $S = \{\partial_1^i \partial_2^j \mid 0 \leq i \leq k, 0 \leq j \leq m-k\} = \{s_1 = 1, \ldots, s_d\}$ $(d = (k+1)(m-k+1))$ and $U = (s_i f \mid i = 1, \ldots, d)^T$. Let $\partial_i U = M_i U$ $(i = 1, 2)$ be the Pfaffian system. Then

$$u(t) = C\exp(-t(k\beta_1 + (m-k)\beta_2))t^{\frac{1}{2}nm}U(t\beta)$$

satisfies an ODE

$$\frac{du}{dt} = M(t)u, \tag{20}$$

$$M(t) = (-(k\beta_1+(m-k)\beta_2)+\frac{mn}{2t})I_d+\beta_1 M_1(t\beta)+\beta_2 M_2(t\beta),$$

where I_d is the $d \times d$ identity matrix. After computing $u(t)$ by solving numerically (20) we obtain $\Pr[\ell_1 < t|\Sigma]$ as the first element of $u(t)$.

3.2.3 Computation of an initial vector $u(t_0)$

As in [4] an initial vector can be computed by using the expression (1) according to [5], but it will be hard to compute the terms in F up to a high degree. In our case we already have a system of PDEs satisfied by $f(x_1, x_2)$ and it will be efficient if we can compute the power series expansion of $f(x_1, x_2)$ from the system. In order to do this the uniqueness of the solution of the system is necessary. Though we have not yet proven it, our current implementation assumes it and simply tries to compute the series by using the system. So far the truncated power series has been always uniquely determined by the system up to a rather high total degree, e.g. 200. The degree of truncation is currently determined as the one at which the value of F given by the truncated power series becomes stable.

The selection of an optimal t_0 is practically important because it affects both the determination of the truncation degree and the step size in the subsequent ODE solving. If t_0 is small the convergence of the power series is fast but we may have to set the step size in the ODE solving very small for getting an accurate result, which makes the number of steps large and eventually makes the ODE solving very hard. In actual computations we have to heuristically determine t_0 as large as possible so that the power series converges in reasonable time.

3.2.4 Computation of Pfaffian matrices

In [4] the Pfaffian matrices are carefully computed for $I = \langle P_1, \ldots, P_m \rangle$ where P_i is given in (4), because $\dim_K R/I = 2^m$ for $K = \mathbb{C}\langle y_1, \ldots, y_m \rangle$, $R = K\langle \partial_1, \ldots, \partial_m \rangle$ and it is large if m is large. In the case $\ell = 2$, the dimension $d = (k+1)(m-k+1)$ is small compared with 2^m and we simply compute the remainder $\partial_i s_j \bmod G$ $(i = 1, 2,\ j = 1, \ldots, d)$ by the division algorithm.

3.2.5 Solving ODE

For solving (20) numerically we apply the Runge-Kutta method. Although many efficient Runge-Kutta solvers are available, we try our own implementation because some special treatments are necessary for getting both the accuracy and the efficiency. The initial vector $u(t_0)$ often has very small elements and it cannot be expressed by the double-precision floating point number. However the computation in each step in Runge-Kutta method should be done by hardware floating-point arithmetic because the necessary number of steps can be huge. Algorithm 2 is designed for satisfying these requirements. In Algorithm 2, $Update(v, t, h)$ is a procedure to compute the next vector by a Runge-Kutta method. In this algorithm a vector v is normalized in the sense that its first element is 1, expecting that all the elements of v can be represented by double-precision floating point numbers. In this case $Update(v, t, h)$ can be done by hardware floating-point arithmetic. Since the equation (20) is linear, $Update(v, t, h)$ is linear in v and $q = \prod_{i=0}^{N} q_i$ gives an approximate value of the first element of $u(t)$. The computation of q is done by MPFR library[2]. In our current implementation $Update(v, t, h)$ executes the fifth order Runge-Kutta method given by Buthcher [1]. The initial number of

Algorithm 2 Runge-Kutta iteration

Input : $t_0, t_1 \in \mathbb{R}$, $v = u(t_0) \in \mathbb{R}^d$, a step size N
Output : an approximate value of the first element of $u(t_1)$

```
q_0 ← v_1; v ← v/q_0; h ← (t_1 − t_0)/N; t ← t_0
for i = 1 to N do
    v ← Update(v, t, h); q_i ← v_1; v ← v/q_i; t ← t + h
end for
return ∏_{i=0}^{N} q_i
```

steps are set to 10^4 by default and we repeat the execution of Algorithm 2, doubling the number of steps until the values get stabilized.

3.2.6 Experiments

We implemented HGM for computing $\Pr[\ell_1 < t|\Sigma]$ in [11] and made experiments following the setting in Sheena and Takemura [13]. Let Σ be a diagonal matrix $\mathrm{diag}(\alpha, \beta, \ldots, \beta)$ of size m with $\beta \le \alpha \le 1$. We want to compute the probability

$$\Pr[\alpha \le (\chi^2_\gamma(n))^{-1}\ell_1|\Sigma] = 1 - \Pr[\alpha\chi^2_\gamma(n) > \ell_1|\Sigma],$$

where $\chi^2_\gamma(n)$ is the upper 100γ percentile of the χ^2 distribution with n degrees of freedom and l_1 is the largest eigenvalue of a Wishart matrix. In [13] the probabilities were computed by a simulation for $m = 10$, $\gamma = 0.05, 0.95$ and $\alpha = 1$. For each case, 50000 random Wishart matrices were generated and their largest eigenvalues were computed for various n's and β's. Here we try computing them by HGM and compare the results with the values in [13] to evaluate the performance of our implementation. In Table 3.2.6, 3.2.6, 3.2.6 and 3.2.6 'HGM' shows the results by HGM and 'ST' shows those by the simulation given in [13]. In an execution of HGM, Algorithm 2 is repeated by doubling the number of steps N until the first four digits get stabilized. The numbers in parentheses indicate the initial point t_0, the final number of steps and the total computing time. Timings were measured on Intel eon E5-4617, 2.90GHz. The computing time includes 4.7sec for computing the diagonalized system of equations. The tables show that both results are close to each other except for several ones and the computing times are reasonable.

n	$\chi_{0.95}(n)$	HGM (t_0, *#steps*, *time*)	ST
10	3.9403	1.0000 (1, 2×10^4, 6.8sec)	1.000
50	34.7643	1.0000 (2, 4×10^4, 6.9sec)	1.000
100	77.9295	0.9980 (10, 2×10^4, 8.4sec)	0.998
500	449.147	0.9760 (50, $2^4 \times 10^4$, 15sec)	0.976
1000	927.594	0.9691 (100, $2^6 \times 10^4$, 34sec)	0.970

Table 1: $m = 10$, $\beta = 0.5$, $\gamma = 0.95$

n	$\chi_{0.95}(n)$	HGM (t_0, *#steps*, *time*)	ST
10	3.9403	0.9539 (0.1, 2×10^4, 14sec)	0.953
50	34.7643	0.9512(0.1, $2^6 \times 10^4$, 31sec)	0.950
100	77.9295	0.9508(0.4, $2^6 \times 10^4$, 39sec)	0.950
500	449.147	0.9503 (2, $2^9 \times 10^4$, 220sec)	0.950
1000	927.594	0.9502 (4, $2^{10} \times 10^4$, 450sec)	0.951

Table 2: $m = 10$, $\beta = 0.01$, $\gamma = 0.95$

n	$\chi_{0.05}(n)$	HGM (t_0, *#steps*, *time*)	ST
10	18.307	0.4595 (1, 2×10^4, 6.6sec)	0.459
50	67.50	0.1777 (2, $2^3 \times 10^4$, 8.4sec)	0.179
100	124.34	0.1323 (10, $2^2 \times 10^4$, 9.0sec)	0.133
500	553.13	0.08263 (50, $2^5 \times 10^4$, 21sec)	0.083
1000	1074.7	0.07238 (100, $2^6 \times 10^4$, 34sec)	0.071

Table 3: $m = 10$, $\beta = 0.5$, $\gamma = 0.05$

n	$\chi_{0.05}(n)$	HGM (t_0, *#steps*, *time*)	ST
10	18.307	0.05142 (0.1, $2^2 \times 10^4$, 16sec)	0.051
50	67.50	0.05077 (0.1, $2^7 \times 10^4$, 55sec)	0.050
100	124.34	0.05058 (0.4, $2^6 \times 10^4$, 40sec)	0.051
500	553.13	0.05028 (2, $2^9 \times 10^4$, 220sec)	0.050
1000	1074.7	0.05025 (4, $2^{10} \times 10^4$, 420sec)	0.048

Table 4: $m = 10$, $\beta = 0.01$, $\gamma = 0.05$

4. CONCLUDING REMARKS

We proposed an algorithm for computing a system of PDEs satisfied by the matrix ${}_1F_1$ on the diagonal region. In this algorithm each higher order derivative of F is represented by lower order ones on the diagonal region and the derivatives with respect to the diagonal variable. Then the derivatives in the initial relation (5) are recursively rewritten and a new PDE for the diagonalized F is obtained. In this method each monomial ∂^α is reduced by P_i only once then we immediately apply l'Hôpital rule to the remainder. There are two advantages of this strategy. One is that we can compute explicitly the coefficient of derivatives after taking limit in advance, which saves the costs for applying l'Hôpital rule. The other is that the recursive reduction decreases computational costs. In fact, our first attempt was that we compute the normal form of ∂^α with respect to $\{P_1, \ldots, P_m\}$, which is proven to form a Gröbner basis in [4]. This strategy may be essentially the same as Algorithm 1, but the normal form computations are very hard and we only could obtain results up to $m = 8$.

As an application of the algorithm we implemented HGM for computing the cumulative distribution function $\Pr[\ell_1 < t|\Sigma]$. Our experiment shows that it performs well even if the eigenvalues of the covariance matrix Σ are small and t is large.

Finally we list open problems concerning our new method.

1. Non-singularity of the rewriting matrices

   We could check that the rewriting matrices are all non-singular if the block size ≤ 36, but we do not have a theoretical proof yet.

2. Gröbner basis property of the system on the diagonal region

   We conjecture that the differential operators obtained by Algorithm 1 always form a Gröbner basis. We have checked it up to $m = 9$. Even if it is not a Gröbner basis we can apply HGM because their initial terms generate a zero-dimensional monomial ideal. However it is worth proving that it is a Gröbner basis from the theoretical viewpoint.

3. Uniqueness of the power series solution of the system on the diagonal region

   We conjecture that the diagonalized F is the unique solution holomorphic at the origin but we have not yet proven it.

4. Error estimate for the result of HGM

   In our current implementation of HGM we judge the convergence of an iteration by simply checking whether the obtained values get stabilized. This method is too naive and we need some error estimate of the result of HGM.

Acknowledgments

This work was supported by JSPS KAKENHI Grant Number 15K05008. The author thanks Nobuki Takayama, Yo Sheena and Akimichi Takemura for helpful discussions.

5. REFERENCES

[1] J. C. Butcher. *Numerical Methods for Ordinary Differential Equations, 2nd edition.* John Wiley and Sons, 2008.

[2] L. Fousse, G. Hanrot, V. Lefèvre, P. Pelissier, and P. Zimmermann. MPFR: A multiple-precision binary floating-point library with correct rounding. *ACM Trans. Math. Softw*, 33:00000818, 2007.

[3] H. Hashiguchi and N. Niki. Numerical computation on distributions of the largest and the smallest latent roots of the Wishart matrix. *J. Japanese Soc. Comput. Statist.*, 19(1):45–56, 2006.

[4] H. Hashiguchi, Y. Numata, N. Takayama, and A. Takemura. Holonomic gradient method for the distribution function of the largest root of a Wishart matrix. *J. Multivariate Analysis*, 117:296–312, 2013.

[5] P. Koev and A. Edelman. The efficient evaluation of the hypergeometric function of a matrix argument. *Math. Comp.*, 75(254):833–846, 2006.

[6] T. Kondo. On a holonomic system of partial differential equations satisfied by the matrix ${}_1F_1$ (in Japanese). *Master's thesis, Kobe university*, 2013.

[7] R. J. Muirhead. System of partial differential equations for hypergeometric functions of matrix argument. *Ann. Math. Statist.*, 41:991–1001, 1970.

[8] R. J. Muirhead. Latent roots and matrix variates: a review of some asymptotic results. *Ann. Statist.*, 6(1):5–33, 1978.

[9] R. J. Muirhead. *Aspects of Multivariate Statistical Theory.* John Wiley and Sons, 1982.

[10] H. Nakayama, K. Nishiyama, M. Noro, K. Ohara, T. Sei, N. Takayama, and A. Takemura. Holonomic gradient descent and its application to the Fisher-Bingham integral. *Adv. Appl. Math.*, 47:639–658, 2011.

[11] M. Noro. a Risa/Asir package for computing PDEs for a matrix ${}_1F_1$ on diagonal regions. http://www2.rikkyo.ac.jp/web/noro/wishart.

[12] Risa/Asir developing team. Risa/Asir, a computer algebra system. http://www.math.kobe-u.ac.jp/Asir.

[13] Y. Sheena and A. Takemura. Inference on eigenvalues of Wishart distribution using asymptotics with respect to the dispersion of population eigenvalues. *The Indian J. Statist.*, 69:717–733, 2007.

Computing with Quasiseparable Matrices

Clément Pernet
Univ. Grenoble Alpes Laboratoire LIP Inria, Université de Lyon
46, Allée d'Italie, F69364 Lyon Cedex 07, France
Clement.Pernet@imag.fr

ABSTRACT

The class of quasiseparable matrices is defined by a pair of bounds, called the quasiseparable orders, on the ranks of the sub-matrices entirely located in their strictly lower and upper triangular parts. These arise naturally in applications, as e.g. the inverse of band matrices, and are widely used for they admit structured representations allowing to compute with them in time linear in the dimension. We show, in this paper, the connection between the notion of quasiseparability and the rank profile matrix invariant, presented in [Dumas & al. ISSAC'15]. This allows us to propose an algorithm computing the quasiseparable orders (r_L, r_U) in time $O(n^2 s^{\omega-2})$ where $s = \max(r_L, r_U)$ and ω the exponent of matrix multiplication. We then present two new structured representations, a binary tree of PLUQ decompositions, and the Bruhat generator, using respectively $O(ns \log \frac{n}{s})$ and $O(ns)$ field elements instead of $O(ns^2)$ for the classical generator and $O(ns \log n)$ for the hierarchically semiseparable representations. We present algorithms computing these representations in time $O(n^2 s^{\omega-2})$. These representations allow a matrix-vector product in time linear in the size of their representation. Lastly we show how to multiply two such structured matrices in time $O(n^2 s^{\omega-2})$.

1. INTRODUCTION

The inverse of a tridiagonal matrix, when it exists, is a dense matrix with the property that all sub-matrices entirely below or above its diagonal have rank at most one. This property and many generalizations of it, defining the semiseparable and quasiseparable matrices, have been extensively studied over the past 80 years. We refer to [16] and [17] for a broad bibliographic overview on the topic. In this paper, we will focus on the class of quasiseparable matrices, introduced in [8]:

Definition 1. *An $n \times n$ matrix M is (r_L, r_U)-quasiseparable if its strictly lower and upper triangular parts satisfy the following low rank structure: for all $1 \le k \le n-1$,*

$$\mathit{rank}(\mathsf{M}_{k+1..n,1..k}) \le r_L, \quad (1)$$
$$\mathit{rank}(\mathsf{M}_{1..k,k+1..n}) \le r_U. \quad (2)$$

The values r_L and r_U define the quasiseparable orders of M.

Quasiseparable matrices can be represented with fewer than n^2 coefficients, using a structured representation, called a generator. The most commonly used generator [8, 16, 17, 9, 1] for a matrix M, consists of $(n-1)$ pairs of vectors $p(i), q(i)$ of size r_L, $(n-1)$ pairs of vectors $g(i), h(i)$ of size r_U, $n-1$ matrices $a(i)$ of dimension $r_L \times r_L$, and $n-1$ matrices $b(i)$ of dimension $r_U \times r_U$ such that

$$\mathsf{M}_{i,j} = \begin{cases} p(i)^T \mathsf{a}^{>}_{ij} q(j), & 1 \le j < i \le n \\ d(i), & 1 \le i = j \le n \\ g(i)^T \mathsf{b}^{<}_{ij} h(j), & 1 \le i < j \le n \end{cases}$$

where $\mathsf{a}^{>}_{ij} = \mathsf{a}(i-1)\dots\mathsf{a}(j+1)$ for $j > i+1$, $\mathsf{a}_{j+1,j} = 1$, and $\mathsf{b}^{<}_{ij} = \mathsf{b}(i+1)\dots\mathsf{b}(i-1)$ for $i > j+1$, $b_{i,i+1} = 1$. This representation, of size $O(n(r_L^2 + r_U^2))$ makes it possible to apply a vector in $O(n(r_L^2 + r_U^2))$ field operations, multiply two quasiseparable matrices in time $O(n \max(r_L, r_U)^3)$ and also compute the inverse in time $O(n \max(r_L, r_U)^3)$ [8].

The contribution of this paper, is to make the connection between the notion of quasiseparability and a matrix invariant, the rank profile matrix, that we introduced in [6]. More precisely, we show that the PLUQ decompositions of the lower and upper triangular parts of a quasiseparable matrix, using a certain class of pivoting strategies, also have a structure ensuring that their memory footprint and the time complexity to compute them does not depend on the rank of the matrix but on the quasiseparable order (which can be arbitrarily lower). Note that we will assume throughout the paper that the PLUQ decomposition algorithms mentioned have the ability to reveal ranks. This is the case when computing with exact arithmetic (e.g. finite fields or multiprecision rationals), but not always with finite precision floating point arithmetic. In the latter context, a special care need to be taken for the pivoting of LU decompositions [10, 14], and QR or SVD decompositions are often more commonly used [2, 3]. This study is motivated by the design of new algorithms on polynomial matrices where quasiseparable matrices naturally occur, and more generally by the framework of the `LinBox` library [15] for black-box exact linear algebra.

After defining and recalling the properties of the rank profile matrix in Section 2, we propose in Section 3 an algorithm computing the quasiseparable orders (r_L, r_U) in time $O(n^2 s^{\omega-2})$ where $s = \max(r_L, r_U)$ and ω the exponent of

ISSAC '16, July 19 - 22, 2016, Waterloo, ON, Canada

ACM ISBN 978-1-4503-4380-0/16/07... $15.00

DOI: http://dx.doi.org/10.1145/2930889.2930915

matrix multiplication. We then present in Section 4 two new structured representations, a binary tree of PLUQ decompositions, and the Bruhat generator, using respectively $O(ns \log \frac{n}{s})$ and $O(ns)$ field elements instead of $O(ns^2)$ for the previously known generators. We present in Section 5 algorithms computing them in time $O(n^2 s^{\omega-2})$. These representations support a matrix-vector product in time linear in the size of their representation. Lastly we show how to multiply two such structured matrices in time $O(n^2 s^{\omega-2})$.

Throughout the paper, $\mathsf{A}_{i..j,k..l}$ will denote the sub-matrix of A of row indices between i and j and column indices between k and l. The matrix of the canonical basis, with a one at position (i,j) will be denoted by $\Delta^{(i,j)}$.

2. PRELIMINARIES

2.1 Left triangular matrices

We will make intensive use of matrices with non-zero elements only located above the main anti-diagonal. We will refer to these matrices as left triangular, to avoid any confusion with upper triangular matrices.

DEFINITION 2. *A left triangular matrix is any $m \times n$ matrix A such that $\mathsf{A}_{i,j} = 0$ for all $i > n - j$.*

The left triangular part of a matrix A, denoted by Left(A) will refer to the left triangular matrix extracted from it. We will need the following property on the left triangular part of the product of a matrix by a triangular matrix.

LEMMA 1. *Let $\mathsf{A} = \mathsf{BU}$ be an $m \times n$ matrix where U is $n \times n$ upper triangular. Then Left(A) = Left(Left(B)U).*

PROOF. Let $\bar{\mathsf{A}} = \text{Left}(\mathsf{A}), \bar{\mathsf{B}} = \text{Left}(\mathsf{B})$. For $j \le n - i$, we have $\bar{\mathsf{A}}_{i,j} = \sum_{k=1}^{n} \mathsf{B}_{i,k} \cdot \mathsf{U}_{k,j} = \sum_{k=1}^{j} \mathsf{B}_{i,k} \cdot \mathsf{U}_{k,j}$ as U is upper triangular. Now for $k \le j \le n-i$, $\mathsf{B}_{i,k} = \bar{\mathsf{B}}_{i,k}$, which proves that the left triangular part of A is that of Left(B)U. □

Applying Lemma 1 on A^T yields Lemma 2

LEMMA 2. *Let $\mathsf{A} = \mathsf{LB}$ be an $m \times n$ matrix where L is $m \times m$ lower triangular. Then Left(A) = Left(LLeft(B)).*

Lastly, we will extend the notion of quasiseparable order to left triangular matrices, in the natural way: the left quasiseparable order is the maximal rank of any leading $k \times (n-k)$ sub-matrix. When no confusion may occur, we will abuse the definition and simply call it the quasiseparable order.

2.2 The rank profile matrix

We will use a matrix invariant, introduced in [6, Theorem 1], that summarizes the information on the ranks of any leading sub-matrices of a given input matrix.

DEFINITION 3. *[6, Theorem 1] The rank profile matrix of an $m \times n$ matrix A of rank r is the unique $m \times n$ matrix $\mathcal{R}_\mathsf{A}$, with only r non-zero coefficients, all equal to one, located on distinct rows and columns such that any leading sub-matrices of $\mathcal{R}_\mathsf{A}$ has the same rank as the corresponding leading sub-matrix in A.*

This invariant can be computed in just one Gaussian elimination of the matrix A, at the cost of $O(mnr^{\omega-2})$ field operations [6], provided some conditions on the pivoting strategy being used. It is obtained from the corresponding PLUQ decomposition as the product

$$\mathcal{R}_A = \mathsf{P} \begin{bmatrix} \mathsf{I}_r & \\ & 0_{(m-r)\times(n-r)} \end{bmatrix} \mathsf{Q}.$$

We also recall in Theorem 1 an important property of such PLUQ decompositions revealing the rank profile matrix.

THEOREM 1 ([7, TH. 24], [5, TH. 1]). *Let $\mathsf{A} = \mathsf{PLUQ}$ be a PLUQ decomposition revealing the rank profile matrix of A. Then, $\mathsf{P}\begin{bmatrix}\mathsf{L} & 0_{m\times(m-r)}\end{bmatrix}\mathsf{P}^T$ is lower triangular and $\mathsf{Q}^T \begin{bmatrix} \mathsf{U} \\ 0_{(n-r)\times n} \end{bmatrix} \mathsf{Q}$ is upper triangular.*

LEMMA 3. *The rank profile matrix invariant is preserved by multiplication*

1. *to the left with an invertible lower triangular matrix,*
2. *to the right with an invertible upper triangular matrix.*

PROOF. Let $B = LA$ for an invertible lower triangular matrix L. Then $\text{rank}(B_{1..i,1..j}) = \text{rank}(L_{1..i,1..i} A_{1..i,1..j}) = \text{rank}(A_{1..i,1..j})$ for any $i \le m, j \le n$. Hence $\mathcal{R}_B = \mathcal{R}_A$. □

3. COMPUTING THE QUASISEPARABLE ORDERS

Let M be an $n \times n$ matrix of which one want to determine the quasiseparable orders (r_L, r_U). Let L and U be respectively the lower triangular part and the upper triangular part of M.

Let J_n be the unit anti-diagonal matrix. Multiplying on the left by J_n reverts the row order while multiplying on the right by J_n reverts the column order. Hence both $\mathsf{J}_n\mathsf{L}$ and $\mathsf{U}\mathsf{J}_n$ are left triangular matrices. Remark that the conditions (1) and (2) state that all leading $k \times (n-k)$ sub-matrices of $\mathsf{J}_n\mathsf{L}$ and $\mathsf{U}\mathsf{J}_n$ have rank no greater than r_L and r_U respectively. We will then use the rank profile matrix of these two left triangular matrices to find these parameters.

3.1 From a rank profile matrix

First, note that the rank profile matrix of a left triangular matrix is not necessarily left triangular. For example, the rank profile matrix of $\begin{bmatrix} 1&1&0 \\ 1&0&0 \\ 0&0&0 \end{bmatrix}$ is $\begin{bmatrix} 1&0&0 \\ 0&1&0 \\ 0&0&0 \end{bmatrix}$. However, only the left triangular part of the rank profile matrix is sufficient to compute the left quasiseparable orders.

Suppose for the moment that the left-triangular part of the rank profile matrix of a left triangular matrix is given (returned by a function LT-RPM). It remains to enumerate all leading $k \times (n-k)$ sub-matrices and find the one with the largest number of non-zero elements. Algorithm 1 shows how to compute the largest rank of all leading sub-matrices of such a matrix. Run on $\mathsf{J}_n\mathsf{L}$ and $\mathsf{U}\mathsf{J}_n$, it returns successively the quasiseparable orders r_L and r_U.

This algorithm runs in $O(n)$ provided that the rank profile matrix R is stored in a compact way, e.g. using a vector of r pairs of pivot indices $([(i_1, j_1), \ldots, (i_r, j_r)]$.

3.2 Computing the rank profile matrix of a left triangular matrix

We now deal with the missing component: computing the left triangular part of the rank profile matrix of a left triangular matrix.

Algorithm 1 QS-order

Input: A, an $n \times n$ matrix
Output: $\max\{\text{rank}(A_{1..k,1..n-k}) : 1 \le k \le n-1\}$

R $\leftarrow$ LT-RPM(A) $\triangleright$ The left triangular part of the rank profile matrix of A
rows $\leftarrow$ (False,...,False)
cols $\leftarrow$ (False,...,False)
for all (i, j) such that $R_{i,j} = 1$ **do**
  rows[i] $\leftarrow$ True
  cols[j] $\leftarrow$ True
end for
$s, r \leftarrow 0$
for $i = 1 \dots n$ **do**
  if rows[i] **then** $r \leftarrow r + 1$
  if cols[$n - i + 1$] **then** $r \leftarrow r - 1$
  $s \leftarrow \max(s, r)$
end for
return s

3.2.1 From a PLUQ decomposition

A first approach is to run any Gaussian elimination algorithm that can reveal the rank profile matrix, as described in [6]. In particular, the PLUQ decomposition algorithm of [5] computes the rank profile matrix of A in $O(n^2 r^{\omega-2})$ where $r = \text{rank}(A)$. However this estimate is pessimistic as it does not take into account the left triangular shape of the matrix. Moreover, this estimate does not depend on the left quasiseparable order s but on the rank r, which may be much higher.

REMARK 1. *The discrepancy between the rank r of a left triangular matrix and its quasiseparable order arises from the location of the pivots in its rank profile matrix. Pivots located near the top left corner of the matrix are shared by many leading sub-matrices, and are therefore likely contribute to the quasiseparable order. On the other hand, pivots near the anti-diagonal can be numerous, but do not add up to a large quasiseparable order. As an illustration, consider the two following extreme cases:*

1. *a matrix A with generic rank profile. Then the leading $r \times r$ sub-matrix of A has rank r and the quasiseparable order is $s = r$.*
2. *the matrix with $n-1$ ones right above the anti-diagonal. It has rank $r = n - 1$ but quasiseparable order 1.*

Remark 1 indicates that in the unlucky cases when $r \gg s$, the computation should reduce to instances of smaller sizes, hence a trade-off should exist between, on one hand, the discrepency between r and s, and on the other hand, the dimension n of the problems. All contributions presented in the remaining of the paper are based on such trade-offs.

3.2.2 A dedicated algorithm

In order to reach a complexity depending on s and not r, we adapt in Algorithm 2 the tile recursive algorithm of [5], so that the left triangular structure of the input matrix is preserved and can be used to reduce the amount of computation.

Algorithm 2 does not assume that the input matrix is left triangular, as it will be called recursively with arbitrary matrices, but guarantees to return the left triangular part of the rank profile matrix. While the top left quadrant A_1

Algorithm 2 LT-RPM: Left Triangular part of the Rank Profile Matrix

Input: A: an $n \times n$ matrix
Output: $\mathcal{R}$: the left triangular part of the RPM of A

if $n = 1$ **then return** [0]
Split $A = \begin{bmatrix} A_1 & A_2 \\ A_3 & \end{bmatrix}$ where A_3 is $\lfloor \frac{n}{2} \rfloor \times \lfloor \frac{n}{2} \rfloor$
Decompose $A_1 = P_1 \begin{bmatrix} L_1 \\ M_1 \end{bmatrix} \begin{bmatrix} U_1 & V_1 \end{bmatrix} Q_1$
$\mathcal{R}_1 \leftarrow P_1 \begin{bmatrix} I_{r_1} & \\ & 0 \end{bmatrix} Q_1$ where $r_1 = \text{rank}(A_1)$.
$\begin{bmatrix} B_1 \\ B_2 \end{bmatrix} \leftarrow P_1^T A_2$
$\begin{bmatrix} C_1 & C_2 \end{bmatrix} \leftarrow A_3 Q_1^T$
Here $A = \left[\begin{array}{cc|c} L_1\backslash U_1 & V_1 & B_1 \\ M_1 & 0 & B_2 \\ \hline C_1 & C_2 & \end{array}\right]$.
$D \leftarrow L_1^{-1} B_1$
$E \leftarrow C_1 U_1^{-1}$
$F \leftarrow B_2 - M_1 D$
$G \leftarrow C_2 - E V_1$
Here $A = \left[\begin{array}{cc|c} L_1\backslash U_1 & V_1 & D \\ M_1 & 0 & F \\ \hline E & G & \end{array}\right]$.
$H \leftarrow P_1 \begin{bmatrix} 0_{r_1 \times \frac{n}{2}} \\ F \end{bmatrix}$
$I \leftarrow \begin{bmatrix} 0_{r_1 \times \frac{n}{2}} & G \end{bmatrix} Q_1$
$\mathcal{R}_2 \leftarrow$ LT-RPM(H)
$\mathcal{R}_3 \leftarrow$ LT-RPM(I)
return $\mathcal{R} \leftarrow \begin{bmatrix} \mathcal{R}_1 & \mathcal{R}_2 \\ \mathcal{R}_3 & \end{bmatrix}$

is eliminated using any PLUQ decomposition algorithm revealing the rank profile matrix, the top right and bottom left quadrants are handled recursively.

THEOREM 2. *Given an $n \times n$ input matrix A with left quasiseparable order s, Algorithm 2 computes the left triangular part of the rank profile matrix of A in $O(n^2 s^{\omega-2})$.*

PROOF. First remark that

$$P_1 \begin{bmatrix} D \\ F \end{bmatrix} = \underbrace{P_1 \begin{bmatrix} L_1^{-1} & \\ -M_1 L_1^{-1} & I_{n-r_1} \end{bmatrix} P_1^T}_{L} P_1 \begin{bmatrix} B_1 \\ B_2 \end{bmatrix} = L A_2.$$

Hence

$$L \begin{bmatrix} A_1 & A_2 \end{bmatrix} = P_1 \left[\begin{array}{c|c} \begin{bmatrix} U_1 & V_1 \end{bmatrix} Q_1 & D \\ 0 & F \end{array}\right].$$

From Theorem 1, the matrix L is lower triangular and by Lemma 3 the rank profile matrix of $\begin{bmatrix} A_1 & A_2 \end{bmatrix}$ equals that of $P_1 \left[\begin{array}{c|c} \begin{bmatrix} U_1 & V_1 \end{bmatrix} Q_1 & D \\ 0 & F \end{array}\right]$. Now as U_1 is upper triangular and non-singular, this rank profile matrix is in turn that of $P_1 \left[\begin{array}{c|c} \begin{bmatrix} U_1 & V_1 \end{bmatrix} Q_1 & 0 \\ 0 & F \end{array}\right]$ and its left triangular part is $\begin{bmatrix} \mathcal{R}_1 & \mathcal{R}_2 \end{bmatrix}$.

By a similar reasoning, $\begin{bmatrix} \mathcal{R}_1 & \mathcal{R}_3 \end{bmatrix}^T$ is the left triangular part of the rank profile matrix of $\begin{bmatrix} A_1 & A_3 \end{bmatrix}^T$, which shows that the algorithm is correct.

Let s_1 be the left quasiseparable order of H and s_2 that of I. The number of field operations to run Algorithm 2 is

$$T(n, s) = \alpha r_1^{\omega-2} n^2 + T_{\text{LT-RPM}}(n/2, s_1) + T_{\text{LT-RPM}}(n/2, s_2)$$

for a positive constant α. We will prove by induction that $T(n,s) \leq 2\alpha s^{\omega-2}n^2$.

Again, since L is lower triangular, the rank profile matrix of LA_2 is that of A_2 and the quasiseparable orders of the two matrices are the same. Now H is the matrix LA_2 with some rows zeroed out, hence s_1, the quasiseparable order of H is no greater than that of A_2 which is less or equal to s. Hence $\max(r_1, s_1, s_2) \leq s$ and we obtain $T(n,s) \leq \alpha s^{\omega-2}n^2 + 4\alpha s^{\omega-2}(n/2)^2 = 2\alpha s^{\omega-2}n^2$. □

4. MORE COMPACT GENERATORS

Taking advantage of their low rank property, quasiseparable matrices can be represented by a structured representation allowing to compute efficiently with them, as for example in the context of QR or QZ elimination [9, 1].

The most commonly used generator, as described in [8, 1] and in the introduction, represents an (r_L, r_U)-quasiseparable matrix of order n by $O(n(r_L^2 + r_U^2))$ field coefficients[1].

Alternatively, hierarchically semiseparable representations (HSS) [18, 11] use numerical rank revealing factorizations of the off-diagonal blocks in a divide and conquer approach, reducing the size to $O(\max(r_L, r_U)n \log n)$ [11].

A third approach, based on Givens or unitary weights [4], performs another kind of elimination so as to compact the low rank off-diagonal blocks of the input matrix.

We propose, in this section, two alternative generators, based on an exact PLUQ decomposition revealing the rank profile matrix. The first one matches the best space complexity of the HSS representation, and improves the time complexity to compute it by a reduction to fast matrix multiplication. The second one also improves on the space complexity of HSS representation by removing the extra $\log n$ factor and shares some similarities with the unitary weight representations of [4].

First, remark that storing a PLUQ decomposition of rank r and dimension $n \times n$ uses $2rn - r^2$ coefficients: each of the L and U factor has dimension $n \times r$ or $r \times n$; the negative r^2 term comes from the lower and upper triangular shapes of L and U. Here again, the rank r can be larger than the quasiseparable order s thus storing directly a PLUQ decomposition is too expensive. But as in Remark 1, the setting where $r \gg s$ is precisely when the pivots are near the anti-diagonal, and therefore the L and U factors have an additional structure, with numerous zeros. The two proposed generators, rely on this fact.

4.1 A binary tree of PLUQ decompositions

Following the divide and conquer scheme of Algorithm 2, we propose a first generator requiring

$$O(n(r_L \log \frac{n}{r_L} + r_U \log \frac{n}{r_U})) \quad (3)$$

coefficients.

For a left triangular matrix $\mathsf{A} = \begin{bmatrix} \mathsf{A}_1 & \mathsf{A}_2 \\ \mathsf{A}_3 & \end{bmatrix}$, the sub-matrix A_1 is represented by its PLUQ decomposition $(\mathsf{P}_1, \mathsf{L}_1, \mathsf{U}_1, \mathsf{Q}_1)$, which requires $2r_1\frac{n}{2} \leq sn$ field coefficients for L_1 and U_1 and $2n$ indices for P and Q. This scheme is then recursively applied for the representation of A_2 and A_3. These matrices have quasiseparable order at most s, therefore the following recurrence relation for the size of the representation holds:

$$\begin{cases} S(n,s) = sn + 2S(n/2, s) & \text{for } s < n/2 \\ S(n,s) = \frac{n^2}{2} + 2S(n/2, n/4) & \text{for } s \geq n/2 \end{cases}$$

For $s \geq n/2$, it solves in $S(n,s) = n^2$. Then for $s < n/2$, $S(n,s) = sn + 2sn/2 + \cdots + 2^k S(n/2^k, s)$, for k such that $\frac{n}{2^k} \leq s < \frac{n}{2^{k-1}}$, which is $k = \lceil \log_2 \frac{n}{s} \rceil$. Hence $S(n,s) = sn \log_2 \frac{n}{s} + sn = O(sn \log \frac{n}{s})$. The estimate (3) is obtained by applying this generator to the upper and lower triangular parts of the (r_L, r_U)-quasiseparable matrix.

This first generator does not take fully advantage of the rank structure of the matrix: the representation of each anti-diagonal block is independent from the pivots found in the block A_1. The second generator, that will be presented in the next section adresses this issue, in order to remove the logarithmic factors in the estimate (3).

4.2 The Bruhat generator

We propose an alternative generator inspired by the generalized Bruhat decomposition [13, 12, 7]. Contrarily to the former one, it is not depending on a specific recursive cutting of the matrix.

Given a left triangular matrix A of quasiseparable order s and a PLUQ decomposition of it, revealing its rank profile matrix E, the generator consists in the three matrices

$$\mathcal{L} = \text{Left}(\mathsf{P} \begin{bmatrix} \mathsf{L} & 0 \end{bmatrix} \mathsf{Q}), \quad (4)$$

$$\mathcal{E} = \text{Left}(\mathsf{E}), \quad (5)$$

$$\mathcal{U} = \text{Left}(\mathsf{P} \begin{bmatrix} \mathsf{U} \\ 0 \end{bmatrix} \mathsf{Q}). \quad (6)$$

Lemma 4 shows that these three matrices suffice to recover the initial left triangular matrix.

LEMMA 4. $\mathsf{A} = \mathit{Left}(\mathcal{L}\mathcal{E}^T\mathcal{U})$

PROOF. $\mathsf{A} = \mathsf{P}\begin{bmatrix} \mathsf{L} & 0_{m\times(n-r)} \end{bmatrix} \mathsf{Q}\mathsf{Q}^T \begin{bmatrix} \mathsf{U} \\ 0_{(n-r)\times n} \end{bmatrix} \mathsf{Q}$. From Theorem 1, the matrix $\mathsf{Q}^T \begin{bmatrix} \mathsf{U} \\ 0 \end{bmatrix} \mathsf{Q}$ is upper triangular and the matrix $\mathsf{P}\begin{bmatrix} \mathsf{L} & 0 \end{bmatrix} \mathsf{P}^T$ is lower triangular. Applying Lemma 1 yields $\mathsf{A} = \text{Left}(\mathsf{A}) = \text{Left}(\mathcal{L}\mathsf{Q}^T \begin{bmatrix} \mathsf{U} \\ 0 \end{bmatrix} \mathsf{Q}) = \text{Left}(\mathcal{L}\mathsf{E}^T\mathsf{P} \begin{bmatrix} \mathsf{U} \\ 0 \end{bmatrix} \mathsf{Q})$, where $\mathsf{E} = \mathsf{P}\begin{bmatrix} \mathsf{I}_r & \\ & 0 \end{bmatrix}\mathsf{Q}$. Then, as $\mathcal{L}\mathsf{E}^T$ is the matrix $\mathsf{P}\begin{bmatrix} \mathsf{L} & 0 \end{bmatrix}\mathsf{P}^T$ with some coefficients zeroed out, it is lower triangular, hence applying again Lemma 2 yields

$$\mathsf{A} = \text{Left}(\mathcal{L}\mathsf{E}^T\mathcal{U}). \quad (7)$$

Consider any non-zero coefficient $e_{j,i}$ of E^T that is not in its the left triangular part, i.e. $j > n - i$. Its contribution to the product $\mathcal{L}\mathsf{E}^T$, is only of the form $\mathcal{L}_{k,j}e_{j,i}$. However the leading coefficient in column j of $\mathsf{P}\begin{bmatrix} \mathsf{L} & 0 \end{bmatrix}\mathsf{Q}$ is precisely at position (i,j). Since $i > n - j$, this means that the j-th column of $\mathcal{L}$ is all zero, and therefore $e_{i,j}$ has no contribution to the product. Hence we finally have $\mathsf{A} = \text{Left}(\mathcal{L}\mathcal{E}^T\mathcal{U})$. □

We now analyze the space required by this generator.

LEMMA 5. *Consider an $n \times n$ left triangular rank profile matrix* R *with quasiseparable order s. Then a left triangular matrix* L *all zero except at the positions of the pivots of* R *and below these pivots, does not contain more than $s(n-s)$ non-zero coefficients.*

[1]Note that the statement of $O(n(r_L + r_U))$ for the same generator in [9] is erroneous.

PROOF. Let $p(k) = \text{rank}(\mathsf{R}_{1..k,1..n-k})$. The value $p(k)$ indicates the number of non zero columns located in the $k \times n-k$ leading sub-matrix of L. Consequently the sum $\sum_{k=1}^{n-1} p(k)$ is an upper bound on the number of non-zero coefficients in L. Since $p(k) \leq s$, it is bounded by sn. More precisely, there is no more than k pivots in the first k columns and the first k rows, hence $p(k) \leq k$ and $p(n-k) \leq k$ for $k \leq s$. The bound becomes $s(s+1)+(n-2s-1)s = s(n-s)$. □

COROLLARY 1. *The generator* $(\mathcal{L}, \mathcal{E}, \mathcal{U})$ *uses* $2s(n-s)$ *field coefficients and* $O(n)$ *additional indices.*

PROOF. The leading column elements of $\mathcal{L}$ are located at the pivot positions of the left triangular rank profile matrix $\mathcal{E}$. Lemma 5 can therefore be applied to show that this matrix occupies no more than $s(n-s)$ non-zero coefficients. The same argument applies to the matrix $\mathcal{U}$. □

Figure 1 illustrates this generator on a left triangular matrix of quasiseparable order 5. As the supports of $\mathcal{L}$ and $\mathcal{U}$ are disjoint, the two matrices can be shown on the same left triangular matrix. The pivots of $\mathcal{E}$ (black) are the leading coefficients of every non-zero row of $\mathcal{U}$ and non-zero column of $\mathcal{L}$.

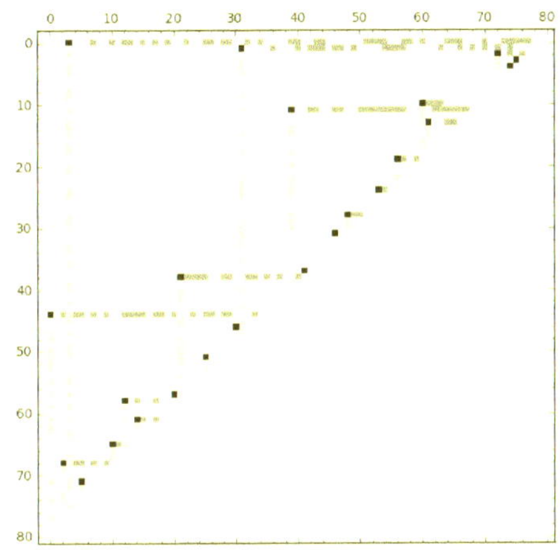

Figure 1: Support of the $\mathcal{L}$ (yellow), $\mathcal{E}$ (black) and $\mathcal{U}$ (red) matrices of the Bruhat generator for a 80×80 left triangular matrix of quasiseparable order 5.

COROLLARY 2. *Any* (r_L, r_U)*-quasiseparable matrix of dimension* $n \times n$ *can be represented by a generator using no more than* $2n(r_L + r_U) + n - 2(r_L^2 - 2r_U^2)$ *field elements.*

4.3 The compact Bruhat generator

The sparse structure of the Bruhat generator makes it not amenable to the use of fast matrix arithmetic. We therefore propose here a slight variation of it, that we will use in section 5 for fast complexity estimates. We will first describe this compact representation for the $\mathcal{L}$ factor of the Bruhat generator.

First, remark that there exists a permutation matrix $\mathcal{Q}$ moving the non-zero columns of $\mathcal{L}$ to the first r positions, sorted by increasing leading row index, i.e. such that $\mathcal{L}\mathcal{Q}$ is in column echelon form. The matrix $\mathcal{L}\mathcal{Q}$ is now compacted, but still has $r = \text{rank}(A)$ columns, which may exceed s and thus preventing to reach complexities in terms of n and s only. We will again use the argument of Lemma 5 to produce a more compact representation with only $O(ns)$ non-zero elements, stored in dense blocks. Algorithm 3 shows how to build such a representation composed of a block diagonal matrix and a block sub-diagonal matrix, where all blocks have column dimension s: $\begin{bmatrix} \mathsf{D}_1 & & & \\ \mathsf{S}_2 & \mathsf{D}_2 & & \\ & \mathsf{S}_3 & \mathsf{D}_3 & \\ & & \ddots & \ddots \\ & & \mathsf{S}_t & \mathsf{D}_t \end{bmatrix}$.

Algorithm 3 Compressing the Bruhat generator

Input: $\mathcal{L}$: the first matrix of the Bruhat generator
Output: $\mathsf{D}, \mathsf{S}, \mathsf{T}, \mathcal{Q}$: the compression of $\mathcal{L}$

1: $\mathcal{Q} \leftarrow$ a permutation s.t. $\mathcal{L}\mathcal{Q}$ is in column echelon form
2: $\mathsf{C} \leftarrow \mathcal{L}\mathcal{Q}\begin{bmatrix} \mathsf{I}_r \\ 0 \end{bmatrix}$ where $r = \text{rank}(\mathcal{L})$
3: Split C in column slices of width s.
4: $\quad \triangleright\ \mathsf{C} = \begin{bmatrix} \mathsf{C}_{11} & & & \\ \mathsf{C}_{21} & \mathsf{C}_{22} & & \\ \vdots & \vdots & \ddots & \\ \mathsf{C}_{t1} & \mathsf{C}_{t2} & \dots & \mathsf{C}_{tt} \end{bmatrix}$ where C_{ii} is $k_i \times s$.
5: $\mathsf{D} \leftarrow \text{Diag}(\mathsf{C}_{11}, \dots, \mathsf{C}_{tt})$
6: $\mathsf{C} \leftarrow \mathsf{C} - \mathsf{D} = \begin{bmatrix} 0 & & & \\ \mathsf{C}_{21} & & & \\ \vdots & \ddots & \ddots & \\ \mathsf{C}_{t1} & \dots & \mathsf{C}_{t,t-1} & 0 \end{bmatrix}$
7: $\mathsf{T} \leftarrow \mathsf{I}_n$
8: **for** $i = 3 \dots t$ **do**
9: $\quad$ **for** each non zero column j of $\begin{bmatrix} \mathsf{C}_{i,i-2} \\ \dots \\ \mathsf{C}_{t,i-2} \end{bmatrix}$ **do**
10: $\quad\quad$ Let k be a zero column of $\begin{bmatrix} \mathsf{C}_{i,i-1} \\ \dots \\ \mathsf{C}_{t,i-1} \end{bmatrix}$
11: $\quad\quad$ Move col. j in $\begin{bmatrix} \mathsf{C}_{i,i-2} \\ \vdots \\ \mathsf{C}_{t,i-2} \end{bmatrix}$ to col. k in $\begin{bmatrix} \mathsf{C}_{i,i-1} \\ \vdots \\ \mathsf{C}_{t,i-1} \end{bmatrix}$.
12: $\quad\quad \mathsf{T} \leftarrow (\mathsf{I}_n + \Delta^{(k,j)} - \Delta^{(k,k)}) \times \mathsf{T}$
13: $\quad$ **end for**
14: **end for**
15: $\mathsf{S} \leftarrow \mathsf{C} = \begin{bmatrix} 0 & & & \\ \mathsf{C}_{21} & 0 & & \\ & \ddots & \ddots & \\ & & \mathsf{C}_{t,t-1} & 0 \end{bmatrix}$
16: **Return** $(\mathsf{D}, \mathsf{S}, \mathsf{T}, \mathcal{Q})$

LEMMA 6. *Algorithm 3 computes a tuple* $(\mathsf{D}, \mathsf{S}, \mathsf{T}, \mathcal{Q})$ *where* $\mathcal{Q}$ *is a permutation matrix putting* $\mathcal{L}$ *in column echelon form,* $\mathsf{T} \in \{0,1\}^{r \times r}$, $\mathsf{D} = \text{Diag}(\mathsf{D}_1, \dots, \mathsf{D}_t)$, $\mathsf{S} = \begin{bmatrix} 0 & & \\ \mathsf{S}_2 & 0 & \\ & \ddots & \ddots \\ & & \mathsf{S}_t \end{bmatrix}$ *where each* D_i *and* S_i *is* $k_i \times s$ *for* $k_i \geq s$ *and* $\sum_{i=1}^{t} k_i = n$. *This tuple is the compact Bruhat generator for* $\mathcal{L}$ *and satisfies* $\mathcal{L} = \begin{bmatrix} \mathsf{D} + \mathsf{ST} & 0_{n \times (n-r)} \end{bmatrix} \mathcal{Q}^T$.

PROOF. First, note that for every i, the dimensions of the blocks S_i and D_i are that of the block C_{ii}. This block contains s pivots, hence $k_i \geq s$. We then prove that there always exists a zero column to pick at step 10. The loci of the possible non-zero elements in $\mathcal{L}$ are column segments below a pivot and above the anti-diagonal. From Lemma 5, these segments have the property that each row of $\mathcal{L}$ is intersected by no more than s of them. This property is preserved by column permutation, and still holds on the matrix C. In the first row of $\begin{bmatrix} \mathsf{C}_{i1} & \dots & \mathsf{C}_{ii} \end{bmatrix}$, there is a pivot located in the block C_{ii}. Hence there is at most $s-1$ such segments intersecting $\begin{bmatrix} \mathsf{C}_{i1} & \dots & \mathsf{C}_{i,i-1} \end{bmatrix}$. These $s-1$ columns can all be gathered in the block $\mathsf{C}_{i,i-1}$ of column dimension s.

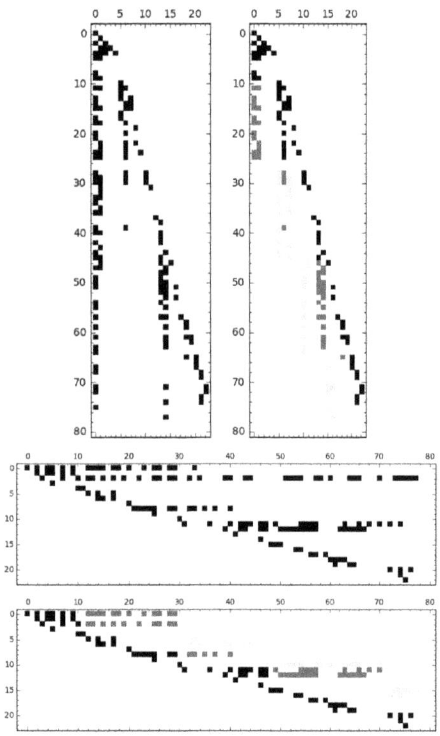

Figure 2: Support of the matrices $\mathcal{LQ}$ (left), $\mathcal{PU}$ (center) and of the corresponding compact Bruhat generator (right and bottom) for the matrix of Figure 1. In the compact Bruhat generator: D is in black and S in magenta and yellow; those rows and columns moved at step 11 of Algorithm 3 are in yellow.

There only remains to show that ST is the matrix C of step 6. For every pair of indices (j,k) selected in loop 8, right multiplication by $(\mathsf{I}_n + \Delta^{(k,j)} - \Delta^{(k,k)})$ adds up column k to column j and zeroes out column k. On matrix S, this has the effect of reverting each operation done at step 11 in the reverse order of the loop 8. □

A compact representation of $\mathcal{U}$ is obtained in Lemma 7 by running Algorithm 3 on $\mathcal{U}^T$ and transposing its output.

LEMMA 7. *There exist a tuple* $(\mathsf{D},\mathsf{S},\mathsf{T},\mathcal{P})$ *called the compact Bruhat generator for* $\mathcal{U}$ *such that* $\mathcal{P}$ *is a permutation matrix putting* $\mathcal{U}$ *in row echelon form,* $\mathsf{T} \in \{0,1\}^{r\times r}$, $\mathsf{D} = Diag(\mathsf{D}_1,\dots,\mathsf{D}_t)$, $\mathsf{S} = \begin{bmatrix} 0 & \mathsf{S}_2 & & \\ & \ddots & \ddots & \\ & & 0 & \mathsf{S}_t \end{bmatrix}$ *where each* D_i *and* S_i *is* $s \times k_i$ *for* $k_i \geq s$ *and* $\sum_{i=1}^t k_i = n$ *and* $\mathcal{U} = \mathcal{P}^T \begin{bmatrix} \mathsf{D}+\mathsf{TS} \\ 0_{(n-r)\times n}\end{bmatrix}$.

According to (7), the reconstruction of the initial matrix A, from the compact Bruhat generators, writes

$$\mathsf{A} = (\mathsf{D}_\mathcal{L} + \mathsf{S}_\mathcal{L}\mathsf{T}_\mathcal{L})\mathsf{R}(\mathsf{D}_\mathcal{U} + \mathsf{T}_\mathcal{U}\mathsf{S}_\mathcal{U}) \tag{8}$$

where R is the leading $r \times r$ sub-matrix of $\mathcal{Q}^T\mathcal{E}^T\mathcal{P}^T$. As it has full rank, it is a permutation matrix.

This factorization is a compact version of the generalized Bruhat decomposition [13, 7]: the left factor is a column echelon form, the right factor a row echelon form.

5. COST OF COMPUTING WITH THE NEW GENERATORS

5.1 Computation of the generators

5.1.1 The binary tree generators

Let $T_1(n,s)$ denote the cost of the computation of the binary tree generator for an $n \times n$ matrix of order of quasiseparability s. It satisfies the recurrence relation $T_1(n,s) = K_\omega s^{\omega-2}\left(\frac{n}{2}\right)^2 + 2T_1(n/2,s)$, which solves in

$$T(n,s) = \frac{K_\omega}{2}s^{\omega-2}n^2 \text{ with } K_\omega = \frac{2^{\omega-2}}{(2^\omega-2)(2^{\omega-2}-1)}C_\omega$$

where C_ω is the leading constant of the complexity of matrix multiplication [5].

5.1.2 The Bruhat generator

We propose in Algorithm 4 an evolution of Algorithm 2 to compute the factors of the Bruhat generator.

Algorithm 4 LT-Bruhat

Input: A: an $n \times n$ matrix
Output: $(\mathcal{L},\mathcal{E},\mathcal{U})$: a Bruhat generator for the left triangular part of A

if $n = 1$ **then return** $([0],[0],[0])$

Split $\mathsf{A} = \begin{bmatrix}\mathsf{A}_1 & \mathsf{A}_2 \\ \mathsf{A}_3 & \end{bmatrix}$ where A_3 is $\lfloor \frac{n}{2} \rfloor \times \lfloor \frac{n}{2} \rfloor$

Decompose $\mathsf{A}_1 = \mathsf{P}_1 \begin{bmatrix}\mathsf{L}_1 \\ \mathsf{M}_1\end{bmatrix} \begin{bmatrix}\mathsf{U}_1 & \mathsf{V}_1\end{bmatrix} \mathsf{Q}_1$ ▷ PLUQ(A_1)

$\mathsf{R}_1 \leftarrow \mathsf{P}_1 \begin{bmatrix}\mathsf{I}_{r_1} & \\ & 0\end{bmatrix} \mathsf{Q}_1$ where $r_1 = \text{rank}(\mathsf{A}_1)$.

$\begin{bmatrix}\mathsf{B}_1 \\ \mathsf{B}_2\end{bmatrix} \leftarrow \mathsf{P}_1{}^T\mathsf{A}_2$ ▷ PermR($\mathsf{A}_2, \mathsf{P}_1{}^T$)

$\begin{bmatrix}\mathsf{C}_1 & \mathsf{C}_2\end{bmatrix} \leftarrow \mathsf{A}_3\mathsf{Q}_1{}^T$ ▷ PermC($\mathsf{A}_3, \mathsf{Q}_1{}^T$)

Here $A = \left[\begin{array}{cc|c} \mathsf{L}_1\backslash\mathsf{U}_1 & \mathsf{V}_1 & \mathsf{B}_1 \\ \mathsf{M}_1 & 0 & \mathsf{B}_2 \\ \hline \mathsf{C}_1 & \mathsf{C}_2 & \end{array}\right]$.

$\mathsf{D} \leftarrow \mathsf{L}_1{}^{-1}\mathsf{B}_1$ ▷ TRSM($\mathsf{L}_1, \mathsf{B}_1$)

$\mathsf{E} \leftarrow \mathsf{C}_1\mathsf{U}_1{}^{-1}$ ▷ TRSM($\mathsf{C}_1, \mathsf{U}_1$)

$\mathsf{F} \leftarrow \mathsf{B}_2 - \mathsf{M}_1\mathsf{D}$ ▷ MM($\mathsf{B}_2, \mathsf{M}_1, \mathsf{D}$)

$\mathsf{G} \leftarrow \mathsf{C}_2 - \mathsf{E}\mathsf{V}_1$ ▷ MM($\mathsf{C}_2, \mathsf{E}, \mathsf{V}_1$)

Here $\mathsf{A} = \left[\begin{array}{cc|c} \mathsf{L}_1\backslash\mathsf{U}_1 & \mathsf{V}_1 & \mathsf{D} \\ \mathsf{M}_1 & 0 & \mathsf{F} \\ \hline \mathsf{E} & \mathsf{G} & \end{array}\right]$.

$\mathsf{H} \leftarrow \mathsf{P}_1 \begin{bmatrix} 0_{r_1\times\frac{n}{2}} \\ \mathsf{F}\end{bmatrix}$

$\mathsf{I} \leftarrow \begin{bmatrix} 0_{r_1\times\frac{n}{2}} & \mathsf{G}\end{bmatrix}\mathsf{Q}_1$

$(\mathcal{L}_2,\mathcal{E}_2,\mathcal{U}_2) \leftarrow$ LT-Bruhat(H)

$(\mathcal{L}_3,\mathcal{E}_3,\mathcal{U}_3) \leftarrow$ LT-Bruhat(I)

$\mathcal{L} \leftarrow \text{Left}\left(\begin{bmatrix}\mathsf{P}_1 & \\ & \mathsf{I}_{\frac{n}{2}}\end{bmatrix}\begin{bmatrix}\mathsf{L}_1 & \\ \mathsf{M}_1 & 0 \\ \mathsf{E} & 0\end{bmatrix}\begin{bmatrix}\mathsf{Q}_1 & \\ & \mathsf{I}_{\frac{n}{2}}\end{bmatrix}\right) + \begin{bmatrix} 0 & \mathcal{L}_2 \\ \mathcal{L}_3 & \end{bmatrix}$

$\mathcal{U} \leftarrow \begin{bmatrix} \mathsf{P}_1\begin{bmatrix}\mathsf{U}_1 & \mathsf{V}_1 \\ 0 & 0\end{bmatrix}\mathsf{Q}_1 & \text{Left}(\mathsf{P}_1\begin{bmatrix}\mathsf{D}\\0\end{bmatrix}) \\ 0 & 0\end{bmatrix} + \begin{bmatrix} 0 & \mathcal{U}_2 \\ \mathcal{U}_3 & \end{bmatrix}$

$\mathcal{E} \leftarrow \begin{bmatrix}\mathcal{E}_1 & \mathcal{E}_2 \\ \mathcal{E}_3 & \end{bmatrix}$

return $(\mathcal{L},\mathcal{E},\mathcal{U})$

THEOREM 3. *For any* $n \times n$ *matrix* A *with a left triangular part of quasiseparable order* s, *Algorithm 4 computes the Bruhat generator of the left triangular part of* A *in* $O(s^{\omega-2}n^2)$ *field operations.*

PROOF. The correctness of $\mathcal{E}$ is proven in Theorem 2. We will prove by induction the correctness of $\mathcal{U}$, noting that the correctness of $\mathcal{L}$ works similarly.

Let $H = P_2L_2U_2Q_2$ and $I = P_3L_3U_3Q_3$ be PLUQ decompositions of H and I revealing their rank profile matrices. Assume that Algorithm LT-Bruhat is correct in the two recursive calls 15 and 16, that is

$$\mathcal{U}_2 = \text{Left}(P_2 \begin{bmatrix} U_2 \\ 0 \end{bmatrix} Q_2), \quad \mathcal{U}_3 = \text{Left}(P_3 \begin{bmatrix} U_3 \\ 0 \end{bmatrix} Q_3),$$
$$\mathcal{L}_2 = \text{Left}(P_2 \begin{bmatrix} L_2 & 0 \end{bmatrix} Q_2), \quad \mathcal{L}_3 = \text{Left}(P_3 \begin{bmatrix} L_3 & 0 \end{bmatrix} Q_3).$$

At step 7, we have

$$\begin{bmatrix} A_1 & A_2 \\ A_3 & * \end{bmatrix} = \begin{bmatrix} P_1 & \\ & I_{\frac{n}{2}} \end{bmatrix} \left[\begin{array}{cc|c} L_1 & & \\ M_1 & I_{\frac{n}{2}-r_1} & \\ \hline E & 0 & I_{\frac{n}{2}} \end{array}\right] \times$$
$$\left[\begin{array}{cc|c} U_1 & V_1 & D \\ & 0 & F \\ \hline & G & \end{array}\right] \begin{bmatrix} Q_1 & \\ & I_{\frac{n}{2}} \end{bmatrix}$$

As the first r_1 rows of $P_1^T H$ are zeros, there exists $\bar{P}_2$ a permutation matrix and $\bar{L}_2$, a lower triangular matrix, such that $P_1^T P_2 L_2 = \begin{bmatrix} 0_{r_1 \times \frac{n}{2}} \\ \bar{P}_2 \bar{L}_2 \end{bmatrix}$. Similarly, there exsist $\bar{Q}_3$, a permutation matrix and $\bar{U}_3$, an upper triangular matrix, such that $U_3 Q_3 Q_1^T = \begin{bmatrix} 0_{\frac{n}{2} \times r_1} & \bar{U}_3 \bar{Q}_3 \end{bmatrix}$. Hence

$$\begin{bmatrix} A_1 & A_2 \\ A_3 & * \end{bmatrix} = \begin{bmatrix} P_1 & \\ & P_3 \end{bmatrix} \left[\begin{array}{cc|c} L_1 & & \\ M_1 & \bar{P}_2 \bar{L}_2 & \\ \hline P_3^T E & 0 & L_3 \end{array}\right] \times$$
$$\left[\begin{array}{cc|c} U_1 & V_1 & DQ_2^T \\ & 0 & U_2 \\ & \bar{U}_3 \bar{Q}_3 & \end{array}\right] \begin{bmatrix} Q_1 & \\ & Q_2 \end{bmatrix}$$

Setting $N_1 = \bar{P}_2^T M_1$ and $W_1 = V_1 \bar{Q}_3^T$, we have

$$\begin{bmatrix} A_1 & A_2 \\ A_3 & * \end{bmatrix} = \begin{bmatrix} P_1 \begin{bmatrix} I_{r_1} & \\ & \bar{P}_2 \end{bmatrix} & \\ & P_3 \end{bmatrix} \left[\begin{array}{ccc} L_1 & & \\ N_1 & \bar{L}_2 & \\ \hline E & 0 & L_3 \end{array}\right] \times$$
$$\left[\begin{array}{cc|c} U_1 & W_1 & DQ_2^T \\ & 0 & U_2 \\ & \bar{U}_3 & \end{array}\right] \begin{bmatrix} \begin{bmatrix} I_{r_1} & \\ & \bar{Q}_3 \end{bmatrix} Q_1 & \\ & Q_2 \end{bmatrix}.$$

A PLUQ of $\begin{bmatrix} A_1 & A_2 \\ A_3 & \end{bmatrix}$ revealing its rank profile matrix is then obtained from this decomposition by a row block cylic-shift on the second factor and a column block cyclic shift on the third factor as in [5, Algorithm 1].

Finally,

$$P \begin{bmatrix} U \\ 0 \end{bmatrix} Q = \begin{bmatrix} P_1 & \\ & I_{\frac{n}{2}} \end{bmatrix} \begin{bmatrix} U_1 & V_1 & D \\ & 0 & \bar{P}_2 U_2 Q_2 \\ & P_3 \bar{U}_3 \bar{Q}_3 & \\ 0 & 0 & 0 \end{bmatrix} \begin{bmatrix} Q_1 & \\ & I_{\frac{n}{2}} \end{bmatrix}$$
$$= \begin{bmatrix} P_1 \begin{bmatrix} U_1 & V_1 \\ 0 & 0 \end{bmatrix} Q_1 & P_1 \begin{bmatrix} D \\ 0 \end{bmatrix} \\ 0 & 0 \end{bmatrix} + \begin{bmatrix} & P_2 \begin{bmatrix} U_2 \\ 0 \end{bmatrix} Q_2 \\ P_3 \begin{bmatrix} U_3 \\ 0 \end{bmatrix} Q_3 & \end{bmatrix}.$$

Hence

$$\text{Left}(PUQ) = \begin{bmatrix} P_1 \begin{bmatrix} U_1 & V_1 \\ 0 & 0 \end{bmatrix} Q_1 & \text{Left}(P_1 \begin{bmatrix} D \\ 0 \end{bmatrix}) \\ 0 & 0 \end{bmatrix} + \begin{bmatrix} & \mathcal{U}_2 \\ \mathcal{U}_3 & \end{bmatrix}.$$

The complexity analysis is exactly that of Theorem 2. □

The computation of a compact Bruhat generator is obtained by combining Algorithm 4 with Algorithm 3.

5.2 Applying a vector

For the three generators proposed earlier, the application of a vector to the corresponding left triangular matrix takes the same amount of field operations as the number of coefficients used for its representation. This yields a cost of $O(n(r_L \log \frac{n}{r_L} + r_U \log \frac{n}{r_U}))$ field operations for multiplying a vector to an (r_L, r_U)-quasiseparable matrix using the binary tree PLUQ generator and $O(n(r_L + r_U))$ using either one of the Bruhat generator or its compact variant.

5.3 Multiplying two left-triangular matrices

5.3.1 *The binary tree PLUQ generator*

Let $T_{\text{RL}}(n, s)$ denote the cost of multiplying a dense $s \times n$ matrix by a left triangular quasiseparable matrix of order s. The natural divide and conquer algorithm yields the recurrence formula:

$$T_{\text{RL}}(n, s) = 2T_{\text{RL}}(n/2, s) + O(ns^{\omega-1}) = O(ns^{\omega-1} \log \frac{n}{s}).$$

Let $T_{\text{PL}}(n, s)$ denote the cost of multiplying a PLUQ decomposition of dimension n and rank $s \leq n/2$ with a left triangular quasiseparable matrix of order s. The product can be done in

$$T_{\text{PL}}(n, s) = T_{\text{RL}}(n, s) + O(n^2 s^{\omega-2}) = O(n^2 s^{\omega-2}).$$

Lastly, let $T_{\text{LL}}(n, s)$ denote the cost of multiplying two left-triangular matrices of quasiseparability order s. Again the natural recursive algorithm yields:

$$\begin{aligned} T_{\text{LL}}(n, s) &= 2T_{\text{LL}}(n/2, s) + 2T_{\text{PL}}(n/2, s) + O(n^2 s^{\omega-2}) \\ &= O(n^2 s^{\omega-2}) \end{aligned}$$

5.3.2 *The Bruhat generator*

Using the decomposition (8), the product of two left triangular matrices writes $A \times B = C_A R_A E_A \times C_B R_B E_B$ where $C_X = D_{\mathcal{L}_X} + S_{\mathcal{L}_X} T_{\mathcal{L}_X}$ and $E_X = D_{\mathcal{U}_X} + T_{\mathcal{U}_X} S_{\mathcal{U}_X}$ for $X \in \{A, B\}$. We will compute it using the following parenthesizing:

$$A \times B = C_A (R_A (E_A \times C_B) R_B) E_B. \quad (9)$$

The product $E_A \times C_B = (D_{\mathcal{U}_A} + T_{\mathcal{U}_A} S_{\mathcal{U}_A})(D_{\mathcal{L}_B} + S_{\mathcal{L}_B} T_{\mathcal{L}_B})$ only consists in multiplying together block diagonal or sub-diagonal matrices $n \times r_B$ or $r_A \times n$. We will describe the product of two block diagonal matrices (flat times tall); the other cases with sub-diagonal matrices work similarly.

Each term to be multiplied is decomposed in a grid of $s \times s$ tiles (except at the last row and column positions). In this grid, the non-zero blocks are non longer in a block-diagonal layout: in a flat matrix, the leading block of a block row may lie at the same block column position as the trailing block of its preceding block row, as shown in Figure 3. However, since $k_i \geq s$ for all i, no more than two

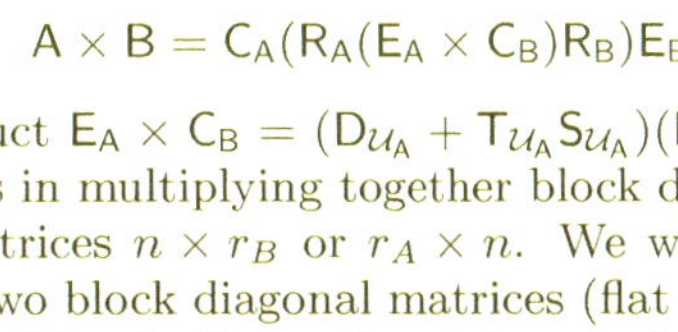

Figure 3: Aligning a block diagonal matrix (blue) on an $s \times s$ grid. Each block row of the aligned structure (red) may overlap with the previous and next block rows on at most one $s \times s$ tile on each side.

consecutive block rows of a flat matrix lie in the same block column. Consequently these terms can be decomposed as a sum of two block diagonal matrices aligned on an $s \times s$ grid. Multiplying two such matrices costs $O(s^{\omega-1}n)$ which is consequently also the cost of computing the product $\mathsf{E_A C_B}$. After left and right multiplication by the permutations $\mathsf{R_A}$ and $\mathsf{R_B}$, this $r_\mathsf{A} \times r_\mathsf{B}$ dense matrix is multiplied to the left by $\mathsf{C_A}$. This costs $O(nr_B s^{\omega-2})$. Lastly, the right multiplication by E_B of the resulting $n \times r_\mathsf{A}$ matrix costs $O(n^2 s^{\omega-2})$ which dominates the overall cost.

5.4 Multiplying two quasiseparable matrices

Decomposing each multiplicand into its upper, lower and diagonal terms, a product of two quasiseparable matrices writes $\mathsf{A} \times \mathsf{B} = (\mathsf{L_A} + \mathsf{D_A} + \mathsf{U_A})(\mathsf{L_B} + \mathsf{D_B} + \mathsf{U_B})$. Beside the scaling by diagonal matrices, all other operations involve a product between any combination of lower an upper triangular matrices, which in turn translates into products of left triangular matrices and J_n as shows in Table 1. The complexity of section 5.3 directly applies for the computation of Upper × Lower and Lower × Upper products. For the other products, a J_n factor has to be added between the $\mathsf{E_A}$ and $\mathsf{C_B}$ factors in the innermost product of (9). As reverting the row order of $\mathsf{C_B}$ does not impact the cost of computing this product, the same complexity applies here too.

×	Lower	Upper
Lower	J_n × Left × J_n × Left	J_n × Left × Left × J_n
Upper	Left × J_n × J_n × Left	Left × J_n × Left × J_n

Table 1: Reducing products of lower and upper to products of left triangular matrices.

THEOREM 4. *Mutliplying two quasiseparable matrices of order respectively* $(l_\mathsf{A}, u_\mathsf{A})$ *and* $(l_\mathsf{B}, u_\mathsf{B})$ *costs* $O(n^2 s^{\omega-2})$ *field operations where* $s = \max(l_\mathsf{A}, u_\mathsf{A}, l_\mathsf{B}, u_\mathsf{B})$, *using either one of the binary tree or the compact Bruhat generator.*

6. PERSPECTIVES

The algorithms proposed for multiplying two quasiseparable matrices output a dense $n \times n$ matrix in time $O(n^2 s^{\omega-2})$ for $s = \max(l_\mathsf{A}, u_\mathsf{A}, l_\mathsf{B}, u_\mathsf{B})$. However, the product is also a quasiseparable matrix, of order $(l_\mathsf{A} + l_\mathsf{B}, u_\mathsf{A} + u_\mathsf{B})$ [8, Theorem 4.1], which can be represented by a Bruhat generator with only $O(n(l_\mathsf{A} + l_\mathsf{B} + u_\mathsf{A} + u_\mathsf{B}))$ coefficients. A first natural question is thus to find an algorithm computing this representation from the generators of A and B in time $O(ns^{\omega-1})$.

Second, a probabilistic algorithm [7, § 7] reduces the complexity of computing the rank profile matrix to $O\tilde{}(n^2 + r^\omega)$. It is not clear whether it can be applied to compute a compact Bruhat generator in time $O\tilde{}(n^2 + \max(l_\mathsf{A}, u_\mathsf{A})^\omega)$.

Acknowledgment

We thank Paola Boito for introducing us to the field of quasiseparable matrices and two anonymous referees for pointing us to the HSS and the Givens weight representations. We acknowledge the financial support from the HPAC project (ANR 11 BS02 013) and from the OpenDreamKit Horizon 2020 European Research Infrastructures project (#676541).

References

[1] P. Boito, Y. Eidelman, and L. Gemignani. "Implicit QR for companion-like pencils". In: *Math. of Computation* 85.300 (2016), pp. 1753–1774. DOI: 10.1090/mcom/3020.

[2] T. F. Chan. "Rank revealing QR factorizations". In: *Linear Algebra and its Applications* 88 (Apr. 1987), pp. 67–82. DOI: 10.1016/0024-3795(87)90103-0.

[3] S. Chandrasekaran and I. Ipsen. "On Rank-Revealing Factorisations". In: *SIAM Journal on Matrix Analysis and Applications* 15.2 (Apr. 1994), pp. 592–622. DOI: 10.1137/S0895479891223781.

[4] S. Delvaux and M. Van Barel. "A Givens-Weight Representation for Rank Structured Matrices". In: *SIAM J. on Matrix Analysis and Applications* 29.4 (Nov. 2007), pp. 1147–1170. DOI: 10.1137/060654967.

[5] J.-G. Dumas, C. Pernet, and Z. Sultan. "Simultaneous computation of the row and column rank profiles". In: *Proc. ISSAC'13*. Ed. by M. Kauers. Boston, USA: ACM Press, 2013, pp. 181–188. DOI: 10.1145/2465506.2465517.

[6] J.-G. Dumas, C. Pernet, and Z. Sultan. "Computing the Rank Profile Matrix". In: *Proc. ISSAC'15*. Bath, UK: ACM, 2015, pp. 149–156. DOI: 10.1145/2755996.2756682.

[7] J.-G. Dumas, C. Pernet, and Z. Sultan. *Fast Computation of the Rank Profile Matrix and the Generalized Bruhat Decomposition*. Tech. rep. arXiv:1601.01798. 2015.

[8] Y. Eidelman and I. Gohberg. "On a new class of structured matrices". In: *Integral Equations and Operator Theory* 34.3 (Sept. 1999), pp. 293–324. DOI: 10.1007/BF01300581.

[9] Y. Eidelman, I. Gohberg, and V. Olshevsky. "The QR iteration method for Hermitian quasiseparable matrices of an arbitrary order". In: *Linear Algebra and its Applications* 404 (2005), pp. 305–324. DOI: 10.1016/j.laa.2005.02.037.

[10] T.-M. Hwang, W.-W. Lin, and E. K. Yang. "Rank revealing LU factorizations". In: *Linear Algebra and its Applications* 175 (Oct. 1992), pp. 115–141. DOI: 10.1016/0024-3795(92)90305-T.

[11] K. Lessel, M. Hartman, and S. Chandrasekaran. *A fast memory efficient construction algorithm for hierarchically semi-separable representations*. Tech. rep. http://scg.ece.ucsb.edu/publications/MemoryEfficientHSS.pdf. 2015.

[12] G. I. Malaschonok. "Fast generalized Bruhat decomposition". In: *CASC'10*. Vol. 6244. LNCS. Tsakhkadzor, Armenia: Springer-Verlag, 2010, pp. 194–202. DOI: 10.1007/978-3-642-15274-0_16.

[13] W. Manthey and U. Helmke. "Bruhat canonical form for linear systems". In: *Linear Algebra and its Applications* 425.2–3 (2007). Special Issue in honor of Paul Fuhrmann, pp. 261–282. DOI: 10.1016/j.laa.2007.01.022.

[14] C.-T. Pan. "On the existence and computation of rank-revealing LU factorizations". In: *Linear Algebra and its Applications*. Special Issue: Conference celebrating the 60th birthday of R. J. Plemmons 316.1–3 (Sept. 2000), pp. 199–222. DOI: 10.1016/S0024-3795(00)00120-8.

[15] The LinBox Group. *LinBox: Linear algebra over black-box matrices*. v1.4.1. http://linalg.org/. 2016.

[16] R. Vandebril, M. V. Barel, G. Golub, and N. Mastronardi. "A bibliography on semiseparable matrices". In: *CALCOLO* 42.3 (2005), pp. 249–270. DOI: 10.1007/s10092-005-0107-z.

[17] R. Vandebril, M. Van Barel, and N. Mastronardi. *Matrix computations and semiseparable matrices: linear systems*. Vol. 1. The Johns Hopkins University Press, 2007.

[18] J. Xia, S. Chandrasekaran, M. Gu, and X. S. Li. "Fast algorithms for hierarchically semiseparable matrices". In: *Numerical Linear Algebra with Applications* 17.6 (Dec. 2010), pp. 953–976. DOI: 10.1002/nla.691.

Algorithmic Operator Algebras via Normal Forms for Tensors

Jamal Hossein Poor*, Clemens G. Raab*, and Georg Regensburger*
Johann Radon Institute for Computational and Applied Mathematics (RICAM)
Austrian Academy of Sciences
4040 Linz, Austria
{jamal.hossein.poor,clemens.raab,georg.regensburger}@ricam.oeaw.ac.at

ABSTRACT

We propose a general algorithmic approach to noncommutative operator algebras generated by linear operators. Ore algebras are a well-established tool covering many cases arising in applications. However, integro-differential operators, for example, do not fit this structure. Instead of using (parametrized) Gröbner bases in noncommutative polynomial algebras as has been used so far in the literature, we use Bergman's basis-free analog in tensor algebras. This allows for a finite reduction system with unique normal forms. To have a smaller reduction system, we develop a generalization of Bergman's setting, which also makes the algorithmic verification of the confluence criterion more efficient. We provide an implementation in Mathematica and we illustrate both versions of the tensor setting using integro-differential operators as an example.

Keywords

operator algebra; tensor algebra; integro-differential operators; noncommutative Gröbner basis; reduction systems

1. INTRODUCTION

Skew polynomials are used in the literature for an algebraic and algorithmic treatment of many common operators like differential and difference operators; see e.g. [6] or the recent overview [8]. Normal forms for skew polynomials are given by the standard polynomial basis. However, normal forms for univariate integral operators are of the form $f\int g$. We show that tensor algebras and their quotients are useful for algebraic modeling of and algorithmic computations with linear operators. Tensor algebras naturally capture the multilinearity of composition of linear operators. In addition, they allow basis-free treatment of multiplication operators. Moreover, for integro-differential operators, they also cover general rings of constants which do not have to be fields.

*Supported by the Austrian Science Fund (FWF): P27229.

ISSAC '16, July 19 - 22, 2016, Waterloo, ON, Canada

ISBN 978-1-4503-4380-0/16/07...$15.00

DOI: http://dx.doi.org/10.1145/2930889.2930900

For computing in quotients of tensor algebras, we use Bergman's analog [3] of Gröbner bases, which we recall in Section 2. Obstructions for general algorithms, like deciding existence of finite Gröbner bases, are inherited from the noncommutative polynomial algebra case. In this paper, we focus on verification of confluence based on Bergman's criterion, for which we need to compute in the tensor algebra. However, for a confluent reduction system, determining normal forms reduces to a combinatorial problem on words.

In Section 3, we apply Bergman's original result to integro-differential operators in a direct way. Motivated by shortcomings of that, we develop a two-level tensor setting in Section 4. Its flexibility in modeling operator algebras allows for a smaller reduction system and makes the computation more efficient, see Section 5. In each section, we comment about the computational aspects and our implementation. The Mathematica package `TenReS` [10] together with the examples of this paper is available at:

http://gregensburger.com/software/TenReS.zip

Using differential operators, we illustrate advantages of the tensor setting over construction in noncommutative polynomial algebras. Assuming no knowledge about their normal forms, we cannot use skew polynomials here. Throughout the paper, K denotes a commutative ring with unity.

Example 1. Recall that differential operators with polynomial coefficients (Weyl algebra) over a field $F \supseteq \mathbb{Q}$ can be defined as the quotient algebra $F\langle X, D\rangle/(DX - XD - 1)$ of $F\langle X, D\rangle$. For any differential K-algebra (R, ∂) over K, we introduce for each $f \in R$ an indeterminate $\lceil f\rceil$ and consider the noncommutative polynomial algebra $K\langle(\lceil f\rceil)_{f\in R}, \partial\rangle$. If we have a K-basis of R, then we just take basis elements as generators and use basis expansion in each step. However, this would not affect the main points of the following discussion. We factor out the two-sided ideal generated by the parametrized identities

$$\lceil f\rceil\lceil g\rceil = \lceil fg\rceil \quad \text{and} \quad \partial\lceil f\rceil = \lceil f\rceil\partial + \lceil \partial f\rceil$$

for $f, g \in R$, corresponding to the composition of multiplication operators and the Leibniz rule. Computing the parametrized S-polynomial between these two identities, we obtain after some reduction steps

$$\begin{aligned} S(\partial\lceil f\rceil, \lceil f\rceil\lceil g\rceil) &= (\lceil f\rceil\partial + \lceil\partial f\rceil)\lceil g\rceil - \partial\lceil fg\rceil \\ &\to \lceil fg\rceil\partial + \lceil f\partial g\rceil + \lceil(\partial f)g\rceil - \lceil fg\rceil\partial - \lceil\partial(fg)\rceil \end{aligned}$$

for $f, g \in R$. For reducing this parametrized S-polynomial to zero, we would need the identity $\lceil\partial(fg)\rceil = \lceil(\partial f)g\rceil + \lceil f\partial g\rceil$ for $f, g \in R$, corresponding to addition and the Leibniz rule in the algebra R. However, such identities cannot directly be used for Gröbner bases in the noncommutative polynomial algebra without expansion w.r.t. a basis of R.

As mentioned above, for a basis-free treatment of the K-linear structure of R, we can use the tensor algebra on the module $R \oplus K\partial$ for differential operators. To deal with parametrized rules, one uses reduction rules defined by K-module homomorphisms. Corresponding to the two parametrized identities above, we need two homomorphisms defined by $f \otimes g \mapsto fg$ and $\partial \otimes f \mapsto f \otimes \partial + \partial f$. The S-polynomials formed from these two homomorphisms reduce to zero for all $f, g \in R$ due to the Leibniz rule in R:

$$\begin{aligned}\mathrm{S}(\partial \otimes f, f \otimes g) &= (f \otimes \partial + \partial f) \otimes g - \partial \otimes (fg) \\ &\to fg \otimes \partial + f\partial g + (\partial f)g - fg \otimes \partial - \partial(fg) = 0.\end{aligned}$$

2. GRÖBNER BASES FOR TENSORS

In this section, we introduce the setting and notions for Gröbner bases in tensor algebras following Bergman and using standard notation for reduction systems from [1]. We first outline the construction of the K-tensor algebra $K\langle M\rangle$ on a K-module M, which is a generalization of the noncommutative polynomial algebra on a set.

We denote the n-fold tensor product of M with itself over K by $M^{\otimes n} = M \otimes \ldots \otimes M$ (n factors). In particular, $M^{\otimes 1} = M$ and we interpret $M^{\otimes 0}$ as the free K-module $K\epsilon$, where ϵ denotes the empty tensor. Elements of the form $m_1 \otimes \ldots \otimes m_n \in M^{\otimes n}$ with $m_1, \ldots, m_n \in M$, are called *pure tensors* and they generate $M^{\otimes n}$ as a K-module. A K-module homomorphism from $M^{\otimes n}$, $n \geq 1$, to a K-module is uniquely determined by specifying it on the generators $m_1 \otimes \ldots \otimes m_n$, in such a way that the value is a K-multilinear function of $m_1, \ldots, m_n$. As a K-module, $K\langle M\rangle$ is defined as the direct sum $K\langle M\rangle = \bigoplus_{n=0}^{\infty} M^{\otimes n}$ with multiplication $M^{\otimes r} \times M^{\otimes s} \to M^{\otimes(r+s)}$ given by

$$(m_1 \otimes \ldots \otimes m_r, \tilde{m}_1 \otimes \ldots \otimes \tilde{m}_s) \mapsto m_1 \otimes \ldots \otimes m_r \otimes \tilde{m}_1 \otimes \ldots \otimes \tilde{m}_s,$$

which can be extended to $K\langle M\rangle$ by bilinearity. With this multiplication $K\langle M\rangle$ is a K-algebra with ϵ being its one element. Note that for a free K-module M with basis X, the K-tensor algebra $K\langle M\rangle$ is isomorphic to the noncommutative polynomial algebra $K\langle X\rangle$. It has the set of all products $x_1 \otimes \ldots \otimes x_n$ for $x_1, \ldots, x_n \in X$ as a K-module basis.

Now we are ready to introduce the setting for Gröbner bases in tensor algebras following Bergman. Let $(M_x)_{x \in X}$ be a family of K-modules indexed by a set X. The modules M_x play the role of the indeterminates in the noncommutative polynomial algebra, where one would take the free module $M_x = Kx$ generated by the indeterminate x.

We denote the free monoid on X by $\langle X\rangle$ and its one element by ϵ. The free monoid $\langle X\rangle$ can also be regarded as the word monoid over the alphabet X with ϵ as the empty word. For every word $W = x_1 \ldots x_n \in \langle X\rangle$, we denote the tensor product of the corresponding modules by

$$M_W = M_{x_1} \otimes \cdots \otimes M_{x_n}.$$

In particular, we have $M_\epsilon = K\epsilon$ for the empty word/tensor ϵ. The pure tensors $m_1 \otimes \ldots \otimes m_n \in M_W$ with $m_i \in M_{x_i}$ play the role of the monomials in the noncommutative polynomial algebra. We consider the direct sum

$$M = \bigoplus_{x \in X} M_x \qquad (1)$$

and the K-tensor algebra on M:

$$K\langle M\rangle = \bigoplus_{n=0}^{\infty} M^{\otimes n} = \bigoplus_{W \in \langle X\rangle} M_W. \qquad (2)$$

Every tensor $t \in K\langle M\rangle$ can be written as a linear combination of pure tensors. However, in contrast to linear combinations of monomials in the noncommutative polynomial algebra, this representation is not unique. Still, using module homomorphisms, one can define reductions analogous to polynomial reduction for commutative Gröbner bases.

Definition 2.1. *Let M be given by* (1)*. A* reduction rule *for $K\langle M\rangle$ is given by a pair (W, h) of a word $W \in \langle X\rangle$ and a K-module homomorphism $h\colon M_W \to K\langle M\rangle$. For a reduction rule $r = (W, h)$ and words $A, B \in \langle X\rangle$, we define a* reduction *as the K-module homomorphism*

$$h_{A,r,B}\colon K\langle M\rangle \to K\langle M\rangle$$

acting as $\mathrm{id}_A \otimes h \otimes \mathrm{id}_B$ on M_{AWB} and the identity on all other M_V with $V \in \langle X\rangle$ and $V \neq AWB$.

For a tensor $a \otimes w \otimes b \in M_{AWB}$ with $a \in M_A$, $w \in M_W$, and $b \in M_B$, the reduction $h_{A,r,B}$ is given by

$$a \otimes w \otimes b \mapsto a \otimes h(w) \otimes b.$$

So, as for polynomial reduction, we "replace" the "monomial" w by the "tail" $h(w)$ given by the homomorphism h.

Let $t \in K\langle M\rangle$. A reduction $h_{A,r,B}$ acts trivially on t, i.e. $h_{A,r,B}(t) = t$, if the summand of t in M_{AWB} is zero, see Eq. (2). A reduction rule $r = (W, h)$ *reduces* t *to* $s \in K\langle M\rangle$ if a reduction $h_{A,r,B}$ for some $A, B \in \langle X\rangle$ acts nontrivially on t and $h_{A,r,B}(t) = s$ and we write $t \to_r s$.

A *reduction system* over X for $K\langle M\rangle$ is a set Σ of reduction rules. Every reduction system Σ induces a *reduction relation* $\to_\Sigma$ on tensors by defining $t \to_\Sigma s$ for $t, s \in K\langle M\rangle$ if $t \to_r s$ for some reduction rule $r \in \Sigma$. Fixing a reduction system Σ, we say that $t \in K\langle M\rangle$ *can be reduced* to $s \in K\langle M\rangle$ by Σ if $t = s$ or there exists a finite sequence of reduction rules $r_1, \ldots, r_n$ in Σ such that

$$t \to_{r_1} t_1 \to \ldots \to_{r_{n-1}} t_{n-1} \to_{r_n} s$$

and we write $t \xrightarrow{*}_\Sigma s$. In other words, $\xrightarrow{*}_\Sigma$ denotes the reflexive transitive closure of the reduction relation $\to_\Sigma$.

The set of *irreducible words* $\langle X\rangle_{\mathrm{irr}} \subseteq \langle X\rangle$ consists of those words having no subwords from the set $\{W \mid (W, h) \in \Sigma\}$. We define the submodule of *irreducible tensors* as

$$K\langle M\rangle_{\mathrm{irr}} = \bigoplus_{W \in \langle X\rangle_{\mathrm{irr}}} M_W. \qquad (3)$$

We also need to consider partial orders on $\langle X\rangle$. A *monoid partial ordering* on $\langle X\rangle$ is a partial order $\leq$ on $\langle X\rangle$ such that $\epsilon \leq A$ and $B < \tilde{B} \Rightarrow ABC < A\tilde{B}C$ for all $A, B, \tilde{B}, C \in \langle X\rangle$. It is called *Noetherian* if there are no infinite descending chains. It is *compatible* with a reduction system Σ if for all reduction rules $(W, h) \in \Sigma$, we have

$$h(M_W) \subseteq \bigoplus_{V < W} M_V.$$

If a compatible monoid partial ordering is Noetherian, then there do not exist infinite sequences of reductions in Σ. In other words, the reduction relation $\to_\Sigma$ is *terminating* or

Noetherian. So, in that case, every $t \in K\langle M\rangle$ can be reduced in finitely many steps to an irreducible tensor

$$t \xrightarrow{*}_{\Sigma} s \in K\langle M\rangle_{\mathrm{irr}}$$

and such an s is called a *normal form* of t. In general, a tensor can have different normal forms. If $t \in K\langle M\rangle$ has a *unique normal form*, we denote it by $t\downarrow_{\Sigma}$. Note that such a unique normal form is unique as an element in $K\langle M\rangle_{\mathrm{irr}}$, but as tensor, it has several representations.

For ensuring unique normal forms for reduction systems on tensor algebras, we state below Bergman's analog of Buchberger's criterion for Gröbner bases [5]. In the context of Gröbner-Shirshov bases for various algebraic structures this is also referred to as the Composition-Diamond Lemma; see e.g. the recent survey [4] and in connection with integro-differential algebras also [7].

We study the cases when two different rules of a reduction system Σ act nontrivially on tensors in M_W for $W \in \langle X\rangle$.

Definition 2.2. *An* overlap ambiguity *is given by reduction rules* $(W,h),(\tilde{W},\tilde{h}) \in \Sigma$ *and nonempty words* $A,B,C \in \langle X\rangle$ *such that*

$$W = AB \quad \text{and} \quad \tilde{W} = BC.$$

It is called resolvable *if for all* $a \in M_A$, $b \in M_B$, *and* $c \in M_C$, *the* S-polynomial *can be reduced to zero:*

$$h(a \otimes b) \otimes c - a \otimes \tilde{h}(b \otimes c) \xrightarrow{*}_{\Sigma} 0.$$

An inclusion ambiguity *is given by distinct reduction rules* $(W,h),(\tilde{W},\tilde{h}) \in \Sigma$ *and words* $A,B,C \in \langle X\rangle$ *with* $W = B$ *and* $\tilde{W} = ABC$. *It is called* resolvable *if for all* $a \in M_A$, $b \in M_B$, *and* $c \in M_C$, *the* S-polynomial *can be reduced to zero:* $a \otimes h(b) \otimes c - \tilde{h}(a \otimes b \otimes c) \xrightarrow{*}_{\Sigma} 0$.

With slight abuse of notation, we refer to S-polynomials of an overlap or inclusion ambiguity, respectively, by

$$\mathrm{S}(A\underline{B},\underline{B}C) \quad \text{or} \quad \mathrm{S}(\underline{B},A\underline{B}C).$$

A reduction system Σ induces the two-sided ideal

$$I_\Sigma := (t - h(t) \mid (W,h) \in \Sigma \text{ and } t \in M_W) \subseteq K\langle M\rangle. \quad (4)$$

For studying operator algebras, we want to compute in the factor algebra $K\langle M\rangle/I_\Sigma$. If all ambiguities are resolvable, we can do this constructively using reductions in $K\langle M\rangle$ and the normal forms with respect to $\to_\Sigma$. This is the *confluence criterion* (condition 1. below) that we will check algorithmically, for a brief discussion see the following subsection.

Theorem 2.3. *([3]) Let* $(M_x)_{x\in X}$ *be a family of* K*-modules indexed by a set* X, *and let* $M = \bigoplus_{x\in X} M_x$. *Let* Σ *be a reduction system on* $K\langle M\rangle$ *and* $\leq$ *be a Noetherian monoid partial ordering on* $\langle X\rangle$ *that is compatible with* Σ. *Then the following are equivalent:*

1. *All ambiguities of* Σ *are resolvable.*
2. *Every* $t \in K\langle M\rangle$ *has a unique normal form* $t\downarrow_\Sigma$.
3. $K\langle M\rangle/I_\Sigma$ *and* $K\langle M\rangle_{irr}$ *are isomorphic as* K*-modules.*

If these conditions hold, then we can define a multiplication on $K\langle M\rangle_{irr}$ *by* $s \cdot t := (s \otimes t)\downarrow_\Sigma$ *so that* $K\langle M\rangle/I_\Sigma$ *and* $K\langle M\rangle_{irr}$ *are isomorphic as* K*-algebras.*

Example 2. We revisit Example 1 to study it formally in the tensor algebra setting. Let (R,∂) be a differential K-algebra. We consider the K-module $M_F = R$ of "functions" from the differential algebra R (indexed by the letter F), the free K-module $M_D = K\partial$ generated by ∂ (indexed by the letter D), and the direct sum $M = M_F \oplus M_D$. Then words over the alphabet $X = \{F,D\}$ index the direct summands of the K-tensor algebra $K\langle M\rangle$.

We interpret elements $f \in R$ as multiplication operators, ∂ as the derivation on R, and the tensor product $\otimes$ as the composition of linear operators. Hence we consider the reduction system $\Sigma = \{r_{FF}, r_{DF}\}$ with the two reduction rules

$$r_{FF} = (FF, f\otimes g \mapsto fg) \text{ and } r_{DF} = (DF, \partial\otimes f \mapsto f\otimes\partial + \partial f)$$

corresponding to the composition of multiplication operators and the Leibniz rule. Note that the K-module homomorphisms corresponding to r_{FF} and r_{DF} map $M_{FF} \to M_F$ and $M_{DF} \to M_{FD} \oplus M_F$, respectively.

So any monoid partial ordering $\leq$ on $\langle X\rangle$ with $DF > FD$ is compatible with Σ, e.g. the degree-lexicographic ordering with $D > F$. There are two overlap ambiguities. The S-polynomials of the first reduce to zero in two reduction steps:

$$\begin{aligned}\mathrm{S}(F\underline{F},\underline{F}F) &= (fg)\otimes h - f\otimes(gh)\\ &\to_{r_{FF}} fgh - f\otimes(gh) \to_{r_{FF}} fgh - fgh = 0.\end{aligned}$$

We already have seen in Example 1 that the S-polynomials $\mathrm{S}(D\underline{F},\underline{F}F)$ reduce to zero. Hence by Theorem 2.3 every $t \in K\langle M\rangle$ has a unique normal form $t\downarrow_\Sigma$ in $K\langle M\rangle_{\mathrm{irr}}$ given by

$$K\epsilon \oplus M_F \oplus M_D \oplus (M_F \otimes M_D) \oplus M_D^{\otimes 2} \oplus (M_F \otimes M_D^{\otimes 2}) \oplus \dots$$

since $\langle X\rangle_{\mathrm{irr}} = \{\epsilon, F, D, FD, D^2, FD^2, \dots\}$. In other words, $t\downarrow_\Sigma$ can be written as a K-linear combination of pure tensors of the form ϵ, f, ∂, $f\otimes\partial$, $\partial\otimes\partial$, $f\otimes\partial\otimes\partial, \dots$

2.1 Computational Aspects

Considering the algorithmic aspects of Theorem 2.3, we assume that we have a finite reduction system Σ over a finite alphabet X. Moreover, a compatible Noetherian monoid partial order has to be assumed on $\langle X\rangle$.

Generating the finite set of ambiguities is just a simple combinatorial task in the word monoid $\langle X\rangle$. Determining $\langle X\rangle_{\mathrm{irr}}$ is a purely combinatorial problem on words as well, albeit less simple. Since modules M_W are generated by pure tensors, it suffices to work with S-polynomials defined by pure tensors constructed from general elements of the basic modules M_x. The result of a reduction step, i.e. the application of a homomorphism from the reduction system, needs to be simplified in the tensor algebra. This involves application of properties of the tensor product and of identities in the modules, like the Leibniz rule in the example above. In practice, the reduction to zero often can be detected heuristically without having a canonical simplifier in the modules.

The package `TenReS` provides routines to generate all ambiguities and corresponding S-polynomials of a reduction system given by the user. It also includes routines for computing in the tensor algebra. Computations in the modules (1) and homomorphisms of reduction rules have to be implemented by the user in each concrete case.

3. INTEGRO-DIFFERENTIAL OPERATORS

Integro-differential operators were introduced in [14, 16] to study boundary problems using noncommutative polynomial algebras and a basis of the coefficient algebra; see also the survey [17]. For polynomial coefficients, also generalized Weyl algebras [2] and skew polynomials [13] have been used to study them. In this section, we apply Bergman's tensor setting presented above to the construction of normal forms for integro-differential operators (IDO) over an arbitrary integro-differential algebra. First, we recall the definition of an integro-differential algebra [17, 9].

Definition 3.1. *Let (R, ∂) be a differential algebra over K such that $1 \in R$ and $\partial R = R$. Moreover, let $\int\colon R \to R$ be an K-linear operation on R such that*

$$\partial \textstyle\int f = f \tag{5}$$

for all $f \in R$. We call $(R, \partial, \int)$ an integro-differential algebra *over K if the* evaluation $\mathrm{E}\colon R \to K$ *defined by* $\mathrm{E} := \mathrm{id} - \int\partial$ *is multiplicative, i.e. for all $f, g \in R$ we have*

$$\mathrm{E} fg = (\mathrm{E} f)\mathrm{E} g. \tag{6}$$

For the rest of this paper, we fix an arbitrary integro-differential algebra $(R, \partial, \int)$ over its ring of constants K with evaluation $\mathrm{E} = \mathrm{id} - \int\partial$. Recall from [9] that in any integro-differential algebra, we have the direct sum decomposition

$$R = K \oplus \textstyle\int R$$

into constant and non-constant "functions". We consider the corresponding K-modules

$$M_K = K \quad \text{and} \quad M_{\tilde{F}} = \textstyle\int R \tag{7}$$

(indexed by the symbols K and $\tilde{F}$). Note that the elements of M_K and $M_{\tilde{F}}$ are not interpreted as functions but as multiplication operators induced by those functions. We also consider the set

$$\Phi := \{\varphi\colon R \to K \mid \varphi \text{ is } K\text{-linear and multiplicative}\} \tag{8}$$

of all characters on R, which we refer to as multiplicative "functionals". Note that $\mathrm{E} \in \Phi$ by definition. Again, we have a direct sum decomposition $K\Phi = K\mathrm{E} \oplus K\tilde{\Phi}$ where $\tilde{\Phi} := \Phi \setminus \{\mathrm{E}\}$. For the K-linear operators ∂, $\int$, E, and $\varphi \in \tilde{\Phi}$ we consider the free modules

$$M_D = K\partial, \quad M_I = K\textstyle\int, \quad M_E = K\mathrm{E}, \quad M_{\tilde{C}} = K\tilde{\Phi} \tag{9}$$

generated by them (indexed by the symbols D, I, E, and $\tilde{C}$). Now, let

$$M = M_K \oplus M_{\tilde{F}} \oplus M_D \oplus M_I \oplus M_E \oplus M_{\tilde{C}} \tag{10}$$

and $X = \{K, \tilde{F}, D, I, E, \tilde{C}\}$. In order to compute with these operators we need to collect the identities they satisfy in form of a reduction system. To this end, we first list basic identities (like the Leibniz rule) and some of their consequences (like integration by parts) that hold in R. For all $f, g \in R$ and $\varphi, \psi \in \Phi$:

$\varphi f g = (\varphi f)\varphi g$	$\partial \int g = g$
$\psi\varphi g = (\psi 1)\varphi g$	$\int \partial g = g - \mathrm{E} g$
$\mathrm{E}\int g = 0$	$\int f \varphi g = (\int f)\varphi g$
$\partial f g = f \partial g + (\partial f) g$	$\int f \partial g = f g - \int(\partial f) g - (\mathrm{E} f)\mathrm{E} g$
$\partial \varphi g = 0$	$\int f \int g = (\int f)\int g - \int(\int f) g$

All these identities correspond to identities for operators acting on $g \in R$. Together with the properties of multiplication operators we list them in Table 1 in the form of words $W \in \langle X \rangle$ and reduction homomorphisms $h\colon M_W \to K\langle M \rangle$ defined in terms of all $f, g \in M_{\tilde{F}}$ and $\varphi, \psi \in \Phi$.

K	$1 \mapsto \epsilon$
$\tilde{F}\tilde{F}$	$f \otimes g \mapsto fg$
$E\tilde{F}, \tilde{C}\tilde{F}$	$\varphi \otimes f \mapsto (\varphi f)\varphi$
$EE, E\tilde{C}, \tilde{C}E, \tilde{C}\tilde{C}$	$\psi \otimes \varphi \mapsto (\psi 1)\varphi$
EI	$\mathrm{E} \otimes \int \mapsto 0$
$D\tilde{F}$	$\partial \otimes f \mapsto f \otimes \partial + \partial f$
$DE, D\tilde{C}$	$\partial \otimes \varphi \mapsto 0$
DI	$\partial \otimes \int \mapsto \epsilon$
$IE, I\tilde{C}$	$\int \otimes \varphi \mapsto \int 1 \otimes \varphi$
ID	$\int \otimes \partial \mapsto \epsilon - \mathrm{E}$
II	$\int \otimes \int \mapsto \int 1 \otimes \int - \int \otimes \int 1$
$I\tilde{F}E, I\tilde{F}\tilde{C}$	$\int \otimes f \otimes \varphi \mapsto \int f \otimes \varphi$
$I\tilde{F}D$	$\int \otimes f \otimes \partial \mapsto f - \int \otimes \partial f - (\mathrm{E} f)\mathrm{E}$
$I\tilde{F}I$	$\int \otimes f \otimes \int \mapsto \int f \otimes \int - \int \otimes \int f$

Table 1: Reduction rules for IDO

Definition 3.2. *Let $(R, \partial, \int)$ be an integro-differential algebra over its ring of constants K. We call*

$$R\langle \partial, \textstyle\int, \Phi \rangle := K\langle M \rangle / J$$

the algebra of integro-differential operators, *where J is the ideal induced by the reduction system obtained from Table 1.*

In order to compute in $R\langle \partial, \int, \Phi \rangle$ we want to analyze the reduction system defined by Table 1 according to Bergman's theorem above and determine normal forms of tensors.

Theorem 3.3. *Let $(R, \partial, \int)$ be an integro-differential K-algebra and let Φ be the set of multiplicative functionals as in Eq. (8). Let M be as in Eqs. (7), (9), and (10) and let the reduction system Σ be defined by Table 1.*

Then every $t \in K\langle M \rangle$ has a unique normal form $t \downarrow_\Sigma$, which is given by a K-linear combination of pure tensors

$$f \otimes \varphi \otimes \partial^{\otimes j} \quad \text{or} \quad f \otimes \varphi \otimes \textstyle\int \otimes g$$

where $j \in \mathbb{N}_0$, each of $f, g \in M_{\tilde{F}}$ and $\varphi \in \Phi$ may be absent, and $\varphi \otimes \int$ does not specialize to $\mathrm{E} \otimes \int$. Moreover,

$$R\langle \partial, \textstyle\int, \Phi \rangle \cong K\langle M \rangle_{irr}$$

as K-algebras, where the multiplication on $K\langle M \rangle_{irr}$ is defined by $s \cdot t := (s \otimes t)\downarrow_\Sigma$.

Proof. We use the alphabet $X = \{K, \tilde{F}, D, I, E, \tilde{C}\}$. For defining a Noetherian monoid partial order $\le$ on $\langle X \rangle$ that is compatible with Σ, it is sufficient to require the Noetherian monoid partial order to satisfy

$$\tilde{F}\tilde{F} > K,\ D\tilde{F} > \tilde{F}D > K,\ I\tilde{F}D > E,\ ID > E,\ I > \tilde{F}.$$

For instance, we could use a degree-lexicographic order with $I > D > \tilde{C} > E > \tilde{F} > K$ or other degree-lexicographic orders with $D > \tilde{F}$ and $I > \tilde{F}$. Then by our software package we verify that all ambiguities of Σ are resolvable, see Section 3.1. Hence by Theorem 2.3 every element of $K\langle M \rangle$ has a unique normal form and $R\langle \partial, \int, \Phi \rangle \cong K\langle M \rangle_{\mathrm{irr}}$ as K-algebras.

It remains to determine the explicit form of elements in $K\langle M \rangle_{\mathrm{irr}}$. In order to do so, we determine the set of irreducible words $\langle X \rangle_{\mathrm{irr}}$ in $\langle X \rangle$. Irreducible words containing only the letters K and $\tilde{F}$ have to avoid the subwords K and $\tilde{F}\tilde{F}$, hence only the words ϵ and $\tilde{F}$ are left. The irreducible words containing only E and $\tilde{C}$ are exactly ϵ, E, and $\tilde{C}$, since they have to avoid the subwords $EE, E\tilde{C}, \tilde{C}E, \tilde{C}\tilde{C}$. Altogether, we see that the irreducible words containing only the letters $K, \tilde{F}, E, \tilde{C}$ are given by the set

$$\{\epsilon, \tilde{F}, E, \tilde{C}, \tilde{F}E, \tilde{F}\tilde{C}\},$$

since they have to avoid the subwords $E\tilde{F}$ and $\tilde{C}\tilde{F}$. Allowing also the letter D, we have to avoid the subwords $D\tilde{F}$, DE, and $D\tilde{C}$. Therefore, we can only append D^j with $j \in \mathbb{N}_0$ to the words in the set above in order to obtain all irreducible words not containing I. Finally, we also allow the letter I. Since subwords EI and DI have to be avoided, the first I in an irreducible word can only be preceded by ϵ, $\tilde{F}$, $\tilde{C}$, or $\tilde{F}\tilde{C}$. We also have to avoid the subwords $IE, I\tilde{C}, ID, II$, so any letter immediately following I has to be $\tilde{F}$. In addition, we have to avoid the subwords $I\tilde{F}E, I\tilde{F}\tilde{C}, I\tilde{F}D, I\tilde{F}I$, so I cannot be followed by a subword of length greater than one. Altogether, the irreducible words from $\langle X\rangle_{\text{irr}}$ are of the form

$$\tilde{F}VD^j \quad \text{or} \quad \tilde{F}\tilde{C}I\tilde{F}$$

where $j \in \mathbb{N}_0$ and each of $\tilde{F}$, $\tilde{C}$, and $V \in \{E, \tilde{C}\}$ may be absent. The normal forms follow from (3). □

3.1 Computational aspects

We briefly discuss how our implementation of the verification of the confluence criterion for tensor algebras behaves on the reduction system Σ given by Table 1.

Using the package **TenReS**, we determine that there are 79 ambiguities. The corresponding S-polynomials are generated automatically from general elements of basic modules. Applying the tensor reduction rules from Σ together with identities in R, all S-polynomials are reduced to zero automatically. Here we just comment about the reduction process and refer to the example file for details.

There are 3 ambiguities for which the corresponding S-polynomials are zero anyway, for instance

$$\mathrm{S}(D\underline{E}, \underline{E}I) = 0 \otimes \textstyle\int - \partial \otimes 0 = 0.$$

The S-polynomials of 69 remaining ambiguities are reduced to zero by just applying automatically the implementation of rules from Σ and identities in R, e.g. for general $f \in M_{\tilde{F}}$:

$$\begin{aligned}\mathrm{S}(I\underline{D}, \underline{D}\tilde{F}) &= (\epsilon - \mathrm{E}) \otimes f - \textstyle\int \otimes (f \otimes \partial + \partial f) \\ &\to_{r_{E\tilde{F}}} f - (\mathrm{E}f)\mathrm{E} - \textstyle\int \otimes f \otimes \partial - \textstyle\int \otimes \partial f \to_{r_{I\tilde{F}D}} 0.\end{aligned}$$

For the remaining 7 ambiguities the program has to do more in order to reduce the S-polynomials completely to zero. This is because after some reduction steps expressions in R occur, which do not belong to any of the two submodules M_K and $M_{\tilde{F}}$ in general, and no reduction applies that acts on that term. To remedy this, these expressions then have to be split further according to $R = M_K \oplus M_{\tilde{F}}$ in order to proceed with the reduction process. We give one such instance, which first can be reduced as follows.

$$\begin{aligned}\mathrm{S}(I\tilde{F}\underline{D}, \underline{D}I) &= (f - \textstyle\int \otimes \partial f - (\mathrm{E}f)\mathrm{E}) \otimes \textstyle\int - \textstyle\int \otimes f \otimes \epsilon \\ &\to_{r_{EI}} f \otimes \textstyle\int - \textstyle\int \otimes (\partial f) \otimes \textstyle\int - \textstyle\int \otimes f\end{aligned}$$

Then there is no reduction that directly applies to any of these terms, since $\partial f \in R$ is neither in M_K nor in $M_{\tilde{F}}$ for general $f \in M_{\tilde{F}} = \int R$. So we write $f = \int c + \int g$ for appropriate $c \in M_K$ and $g \in M_{\tilde{F}}$. This replacement is done automatically in our implementation. Then the reduction process continues as usual.

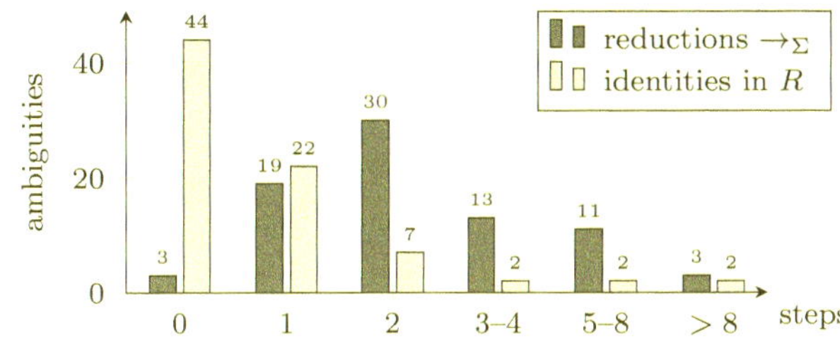

Figure 1: Histogram of computational steps used by our implementation for resolving each ambiguitiy

We collect more detailed statistics about the whole reduction process in Figure 1. For 3 ambiguities we do not need to apply reductions and for a total of 44 ambiguities no identities in R are applied in order to reduce the corresponding S-polynomial to 0. The maximal number of reductions used for one ambiguity is 12 and the maximal number of identities in R is 10, which both happens for $\mathrm{S}(I\tilde{F}\underline{D}, \underline{D}\tilde{F})$. Per ambiguity on average 2.84 reductions and 1.00 identities have been used in the computation.

Inspecting the computation more closely one sees also that many S-polynomial reductions actually are done more than once, due to the splitting (10). For instance the S-polynomials $\mathrm{S}(I\tilde{F}\underline{I}, \underline{I}E)$ and $\mathrm{S}(I\tilde{F}\underline{I}, \underline{I}\tilde{C})$ are reduced completely in the same way. Since that happens a lot for this particular reduction system we want to refine the setting in order to reduce the redundancy.

4. TWO-LEVEL TENSOR SETTING

In the example of the previous section the reduction system contained several reduction rules, where the homomorphism is defined by the same formula and the homomorphisms differ only by the choice of their domain. This leads to some redundancy in the investigation of ambiguities and S-polynomials. Sticking to the above definition of reduction systems for tensor algebras, this situation cannot be avoided.

To increase flexibility in formulating reduction systems for $K\langle M\rangle$, we generalize the setting by considering two decompositions of the K-module M at the same time, where one decomposition is a refinement of the other:

$$M = \bigoplus_{x \in X} M_x = \bigoplus_{y \in Y} M_y. \tag{11}$$

Definition 4.1. *Let $(M_x)_{x\in X}$ and $(M_y)_{y\in Y}$ be two families of K-modules indexed by sets X and Y, respectively. We call $(M_x)_{x\in X}$* a refinement *of $(M_y)_{y\in Y}$ if there exists a partition $(X_y)_{y\in Y}$ of X such that*

- *$X_y = \{y\}$ for all $y \in X \cap Y$ and*
- *$M_y = \bigoplus_{x\in X_y} M_x$ for all $y \in Y$.*

Following this definition, whenever a letter occurs in both alphabets X and Y the corresponding module is the same in both decompositions. If X_y is not a singleton, the module M_y is actually refined. We consider the *combined alphabet*

$$Z := X \cup Y.$$

For words $W = w_1 \dots w_n \in \langle Z\rangle$, we define the corresponding submodule of $K\langle M\rangle$ as before by $M_W := M_{w_1} \otimes \dots \otimes M_{w_n}$.

We define the *set of specializations* of W by replacing all its letters from $Y \setminus X$ by corresponding letters from X:

$$S(W) := \{V \in \langle X \rangle \mid |V| = n \wedge \forall i : (v_i = w_i \vee v_i \in X_{w_i})\}.$$

Remark 1. Note that for $V \in \langle X \rangle$ and $W \in \langle Z \rangle$ the modules M_V and M_W either intersect only in 0 or M_V is contained in M_W. Note further that $S(W)$ consists of all $V \in \langle X \rangle$ such that M_V is a submodule of M_W. Moreover,

$$M_W = \bigoplus_{V \in S(W)} M_V.$$

Remark 2. Reduction rules (over Z) are defined by replacing X with Z in Definition 2.1. A reduction system Σ over Z is simply a set of such reduction rules. We define the ideal I_Σ by (4), and we define the irreducible words $\langle X \rangle_{\text{irr}}$ w.r.t. Σ as the set of words from $\langle X \rangle$ containing no subwords from the set $\bigcup \{S(W) \mid (W,h) \in \Sigma\}$. Based on $\langle X \rangle_{\text{irr}}$, we define $K\langle M \rangle_{\text{irr}}$ as in (3).

Modeling an operator algebra as $K\langle M \rangle / I_\Sigma$, this two-level setting provides much more flexibility in describing the ideal by a reduction system Σ. Previously, with just one decomposition (1), $K\langle M \rangle$ was a direct sum of the modules M_W, which are the possible domains for the homomorphisms of reduction rules (over X). Now, with two decompositions (11), the sum of all M_W is not direct anymore, allowing coexistence of reduction rules (over Z) that could not be used together in a reduction system before without splitting them into several rules.

In some of the following proofs for a reduction system Σ over Z, we need the *induced reduction system* Σ_X over X:

$$\Sigma_X := \bigcup_{(W,h) \in \Sigma} \{(V, h|_{M_V}) \mid V \in S(W)\}. \tag{12}$$

From (12), it is obvious that the following lemma holds.

Lemma 4.2. *Let Σ be a reduction system over Z inducing Σ_X over X. Then the reduction relations and the irreducible words are the same for Σ and for Σ_X.*

Definition 4.3. *We call a partial order $\leq$ on $\langle Z \rangle$ consistent with $(M_x)_{x \in X}$ being a refinement of $(M_y)_{y \in Y}$ if for all words $V, W \in \langle Z \rangle$ with $V < W$ we also have $\tilde{V} < \tilde{W}$ for all specializations $\tilde{V} \in S(V)$ and $\tilde{W} \in S(W)$.*

Note that the above definition implies $\tilde{W} \not< W$ for all $\tilde{W} \in S(W)$, which can be seen by choosing $V = \tilde{W}$.

A monoid partial order $\leq$ on $\langle Z \rangle$ is *compatible* with a reduction system Σ over Z if for all $(W,h) \in \Sigma$ we have

$$h(M_W) \subseteq \sum_{\substack{V \in \langle Z \rangle \\ V < W}} M_V.$$

If in addition $\leq$ is also consistent with $(M_x)_{x \in X}$ being a refinement of $(M_y)_{y \in Y}$ then we have

$$\sum_{\substack{V \in \langle Z \rangle \\ V < W}} M_V = \bigoplus_{\substack{V \in \langle Z \rangle \\ V < W}} M_V = \bigoplus_{\substack{V \in \langle X \rangle, \tilde{W} \in S(W) \\ V < \tilde{W}}} M_V.$$

Lemma 4.4. *Let Σ be a reduction system over Z and let $\leq$ be a monoid partial order on $\langle Z \rangle$ consistent with $(M_x)_{x \in X}$ being a refinement of $(M_y)_{y \in Y}$ and compatible with Σ. Then the restricted order $\leq$ on $\langle X \rangle$ is compatible with Σ_X.*

We also generalize the notion of ambiguities to take specialization into account, see Definition 4.5. To this end, note first that for $W, \tilde{W} \in \langle Z \rangle$ having a common specialization, i.e. $S(W) \cap S(\tilde{W}) \neq \emptyset$, there exists $V \in \langle Z \rangle$ such that

$$S(V) = S(W) \cap S(\tilde{W}).$$

While the word V is not necessarily unique, the corresponding module M_V is unique and will be denoted by

$$M_{\min(W,\tilde{W})} := M_V.$$

Remark 3. The module $M_{\min(W,\tilde{W})}$ is the biggest module M_V, $V \in \langle Z \rangle$, contained in M_W and $M_{\tilde{W}}$. In fact, we even have $M_{\min(W,\tilde{W})} = M_W \cap M_{\tilde{W}}$.

Example 3. Consider disjoint sets $X = \{x_1, x_2, x_3\}$ and $Y = \{y_1, y_2\}$ with $M_{y_1} = M_{x_1}$ and $M_{y_2} = M_{x_2} \oplus M_{x_3}$. Then $Z = \{x_1, x_2, x_3, y_1, y_2\}$ and $(M_x)_{x \in X}$ is a refinement of $(M_y)_{y \in Y}$ since we have the partition $\{\{x_1\}, \{x_2, x_3\}\}$ of X. The words $W = x_1 y_2 y_2$ and $\tilde{W} = y_1 y_2 x_2$ in $\langle Z \rangle$ satisfy $S(W) \cap S(\tilde{W}) = \{x_1 x_2 x_2, x_1 x_3 x_2\} \neq \emptyset$. Both choices $V = y_1 y_2 x_2$ and $V = x_1 y_2 x_2$ satisfy $S(V) = S(W) \cap S(\tilde{W})$ and $M_V = M_{x_1} \otimes M_{y_2} \otimes M_{x_2}$. So $M_{\min(W,\tilde{W})} = M_{x_1} \otimes M_{y_2} \otimes M_{x_2}$.

Definition 4.5. *Let $(W,h), (\tilde{W}, \tilde{h}) \in \Sigma$ be two reduction rules and let $A, B_1, B_2, C \in \langle Z \rangle$ be nonempty words with*

$$W = AB_1, \quad \tilde{W} = B_2 C, \quad B_1 \neq B_2,$$
$$\text{and} \quad S(B_1) \cap S(B_2) \neq \emptyset,$$

then we call this an overlap ambiguity with specialization. *Note that $B_1 \neq B_2$ ensures that this is not an overlap ambiguity (without specialization). An overlap ambiguity with specialization is called* resolvable *if for all $a \in M_A$, $b \in M_{\min(B_1,B_2)}$, and $c \in M_C$ the* S-polynomial *can be reduced to zero:*

$$h(a \otimes b) \otimes c - a \otimes \tilde{h}(b \otimes c) \xrightarrow{*}_\Sigma 0.$$

Similarly, an inclusion ambiguity with specialization *is given by two reduction rules $(W,h), (\tilde{W}, \tilde{h}) \in \Sigma$ and words $A, B_1, B_2, C \in \langle Z \rangle$ with $W = B_1$, $\tilde{W} = AB_2C$, $B_1 \neq B_2$, and $S(B_1) \cap S(B_2) \neq \emptyset$. An inclusion ambiguity with specialization is called* resolvable *if for all $a \in M_A$, $b \in M_{\min(B_1,B_2)}$, and $c \in M_C$ the* S-polynomial *can be reduced to zero: $a \otimes h(b) \otimes c - \tilde{h}(a \otimes b \otimes c) \xrightarrow{*}_\Sigma 0$.*

Again, we use $\mathrm{S}(A\underline{B_1}, \underline{B_2}C)$ or $\mathrm{S}(\underline{B_1}, A\underline{B_2}C)$, respectively, to refer to S-polynomials of an overlap or inclusion ambiguity with specialization.

Remark 4. Note that in total there now can be 4 types of ambiguities: in addition to the two types of ambiguities (without specialization) of Definition 2.2 there are also corresponding versions with specialization as defined above.

With these definitions we can prove the following generalization of Bergman's result. In order to prove properties of the reduction system Σ, we apply Bergman's result (Theorem 2.3) to the induced reduction system Σ_X over X.

Theorem 4.6. *Let $(M_x)_{x \in X}$ and $(M_y)_{y \in Y}$ be two families of K-modules indexed by sets X and Y, respectively, such that $(M_x)_{x \in X}$ is a refinement of $(M_y)_{y \in Y}$ and let $M = \bigoplus_{x \in X} M_x$. Let Σ be a reduction system over $Z := X \cup Y$ on $K\langle M \rangle$ and $\leq$ be a Noetherian monoid partial order on $\langle Z \rangle$ consistent with $(M_x)_{x \in X}$ being a refinement of $(M_y)_{y \in Y}$ and compatible with Σ. Then the following are equivalent:*

1. *All ambiguities of* Σ *are resolvable.*

2. *Every* $t \in K\langle M\rangle$ *has a unique normal form* $t{\downarrow_\Sigma}$.

3. $K\langle M\rangle/I_\Sigma$ *and* $K\langle M\rangle_{irr}$ *are isomorphic as* K*-modules.*

If these conditions hold, then we can define a multiplication on $K\langle M\rangle_{irr}$ *by* $s \cdot t := (s \otimes t){\downarrow_\Sigma}$ *so that* $K\langle M\rangle/I_\Sigma$ *and* $K\langle M\rangle_{irr}$ *are isomorphic as* K*-algebras.*

PROOF. Lemma 4.2 shows that we can replace the reduction system Σ by its refinement Σ_X without changing the reduction relation. Consequently, also the reduction ideals and normal forms agree, i.e. $I_\Sigma = I_{\Sigma_X}$ and $t{\downarrow_\Sigma} = s \Leftrightarrow t{\downarrow_{\Sigma_X}} = s$ for all $s, t \in K\langle M\rangle$. The lemma also implies that $\langle X\rangle_{\text{irr}}$ and hence $K\langle M\rangle_{\text{irr}}$ stay the same. Furthermore, we note that every S-polynomial of Σ_X is also an S-polynomial of Σ and, conversely, every S-polynomial of Σ is a linear combination of S-polynomials of Σ_X. Hence all ambiguities of Σ are resolvable if and only if all ambiguities of Σ_X are resolvable, since $\to_\Sigma$ and $\to_{\Sigma_X}$ are the same. Finally, Lemma 4.4 implies that Σ_X and the restriction of $\leq$ to $\langle X\rangle$ satisfy the assumptions of Theorem 2.3, which concludes the proof. □

4.1 Computational Aspects

Many properties that we discussed for Bergman's tensor setting also hold for the generalization we introduced above. For instance, determining ambiguities and irreducible words is done just on the level of words.

The main computational benefit of Theorem 4.6 compared to Theorem 2.3 lies in the fact that for the confluence criterion we only need to check ambiguities of Σ over the combined alphabet Z and no computations with the induced reduction system Σ_X are needed. Computing with the induced reduction system over X instead, generally would lead to a higher number of ambiguities, since one reduction rule in Σ can give rise to many reduction rules in Σ_X. Only for determination of irreducible words we restrict to $\langle X\rangle$.

The package **TenReS** also provides routines for generating all overlap and inclusion ambiguities with specialization together with their corresponding S-polynomials. It can also generate all irreducible words up to given length.

5. AN IMPROVED REDUCTION SYSTEM

In this section, we apply the two-level version of Bergman's tensor setting to our example, the tensor algebra of integro-differential operators. First, we define two alphabets

$$X = \{K, \tilde{F}, D, I, E, \tilde{C}\} \quad \text{and} \quad Y = \{F, D, I, C\},$$

with the K-modules defined in Eqs. (7) and (9) as well as

$$M_F = M_K \oplus M_{\tilde{F}} \quad \text{and} \quad M_C = M_E \oplus M_{\tilde{C}}. \qquad (13)$$

Then the decomposition (10) is a refinement of

$$M = M_F \oplus M_D \oplus M_I \oplus M_C. \qquad (14)$$

The reduction system Σ over the combined alphabet is given by Table 2, defined in terms of all $f, g \in R$ and $\varphi, \psi \in \Phi$.

Following (12), the induced reduction system Σ_X is obtained, according to (13), by splitting rules whose words contain F or C into "smaller" rules using $X_F = \{K, \tilde{F}\}$ and $X_C = \{E, \tilde{C}\}$. For example, the reduction rule $(CF, h) \in \Sigma$ is split into the rules $(W, h|_{M_W}) \in \Sigma_X$ where $W \in S(CF) = \{EK, E\tilde{F}, \tilde{C}K, \tilde{C}\tilde{F}\}$.

FF	$f \otimes g \mapsto fg$
CF	$\varphi \otimes f \mapsto (\varphi f)\varphi$
CC	$\psi \otimes \varphi \mapsto (\psi 1)\varphi$
DF	$\partial \otimes f \mapsto f \otimes \partial + \partial f$
DC	$\partial \otimes \varphi \mapsto 0$
DI	$\partial \otimes \textstyle\int \mapsto \epsilon$
IC	$\textstyle\int \otimes \varphi \mapsto \textstyle\int 1 \otimes \varphi$
ID	$\textstyle\int \otimes \partial \mapsto \epsilon - \mathrm{E}$
II	$\textstyle\int \otimes \textstyle\int \mapsto \textstyle\int 1 \otimes \textstyle\int - \textstyle\int \otimes \textstyle\int 1$
IFC	$\textstyle\int \otimes f \otimes \varphi \mapsto \textstyle\int f \otimes \varphi$
IFD	$\textstyle\int \otimes f \otimes \partial \mapsto f - \textstyle\int \otimes \partial f - (\mathrm{E}f)\mathrm{E}$
IFI	$\textstyle\int \otimes f \otimes \textstyle\int \mapsto \textstyle\int f \otimes \textstyle\int - \textstyle\int \otimes \textstyle\int f$
K	$1 \mapsto \epsilon$
EI	$\mathrm{E} \otimes \textstyle\int \mapsto 0$

Table 2: Reduction rules for IDO on two levels

Theorem 5.1. *Let* $(R, \partial, \textstyle\int)$ *be an integro-differential* K*-algebra and let* Φ *be the set of multiplicative functionals as in Eq. (8). Let* M *be as in Eqs. (13) and (14) and let the reduction system* Σ *be defined by Table 2.*

Then every $t \in K\langle M\rangle$ *has a unique normal form of the same type as in Theorem 3.3 and, as* K*-algebras,*

$$K\langle M\rangle/I_\Sigma \cong K\langle M\rangle_{irr}.$$

PROOF. We use the alphabet $Z = X \cup Y$ where $X = \{K, \tilde{F}, D, I, E, \tilde{C}\}$ and $Y = \{F, D, I, C\}$. For defining a Noetherian monoid partial order $\leq$ on $\langle Z\rangle$ that is compatible with Σ, it is sufficient to require the order to satisfy

$$DF > FD,\ IFD > E,\ ID > E,\ I > \tilde{F}.$$

For instance, we could use a degree-lexicographic order with $I > D > C > F$ on $\langle Y\rangle$ or other degree-lexicographic orders with $D > F$ and $I > F$. We extend it to a partial monoid order on $\langle Z\rangle$ based on Definition 4.3 in order to make it consistent with $(M_x)_{x\in X}$ being a refinement of $(M_y)_{y\in Y}$. Then by our software package we verify that all ambiguities of Σ are resolvable, see Section 5.1. Hence by Theorem 4.6 every element of $K\langle M\rangle$ has a unique normal form and $K\langle M\rangle/I_\Sigma \cong K\langle M\rangle_{\text{irr}}$ as K-algebras.

It remains to determine the explicit form of elements in $K\langle M\rangle_{\text{irr}}$. To do so, we determine the set of irreducible words $\langle X\rangle_{\text{irr}}$ in $\langle X\rangle$. Note that $\tilde{\Sigma} \subset \Sigma_X$, where $\tilde{\Sigma}$ is given by Table 1. Hence the irreducible words w.r.t. Σ are among the irreducible words w.r.t. $\tilde{\Sigma}$. In the proof of Theorem 3.3 we already determined the latter to be of the form $\tilde{F}VD^j$ or $\tilde{F}\tilde{C}I\tilde{F}$, where $j \in \mathbb{N}_0$ and each of $\tilde{F}$, $\tilde{C}$, and $V \in \{E, \tilde{C}\}$ may be absent. All of them are also irreducible w.r.t. Σ since they do not contain subwords from $\{W \mid (W, h) \in \Sigma_X \setminus \tilde{\Sigma}\}$. The normal forms follow from (3). □

In order to show $R\langle \partial, \textstyle\int, \Phi\rangle = K\langle M\rangle/I_\Sigma$, we prove the following lemma.

Lemma 5.2. *Let the reduction system* $\tilde{\Sigma}$ *over* X *be given by Table 1 and let the reduction system* Σ *over* Z *be given by Table 2. Then* $I_{\tilde{\Sigma}}$ *and* I_Σ *are the same.*

PROOF. In view of Lemma 4.2, we show $I_{\tilde{\Sigma}} = I_{\Sigma_X}$, where the induced reduction system Σ_X is described immediately before Theorem 5.1. Comparing $\tilde{\Sigma}$ and Σ_X, we see that $\tilde{\Sigma} \subset \Sigma_X$, hence $I_{\tilde{\Sigma}} \subseteq I_{\Sigma_X}$. Conversely, we can verify, e.g. by the package **TenReS**, for all 10 elements $(W, h) \in \Sigma_X \setminus \tilde{\Sigma}$ that $t - h(t) \in I_{\tilde{\Sigma}}$ for all $t \in M_W$ implying $I_{\Sigma_X} \subseteq I_{\tilde{\Sigma}}$. □

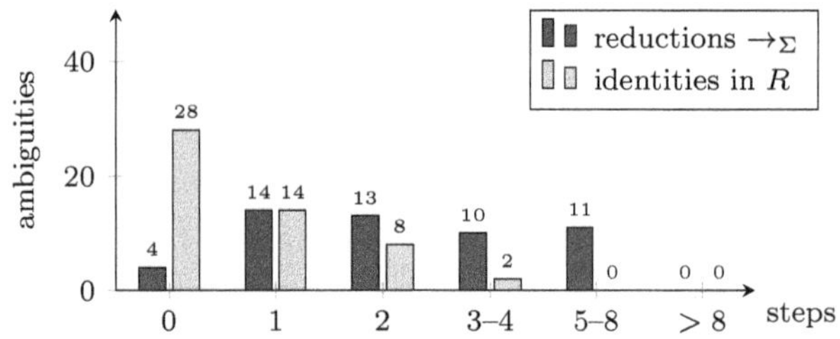

Figure 2: Histogram of computational steps used by our implementation for resolving each ambiguitiy

5.1 Computational aspects

In the following, we discuss computational details of the two-level tensor setting for integro-differential operators. Applying `TenReS` to the reduction system Σ given by Table 2, in total 52 ambiguities and corresponding S-polynomials are generated. In contrast to the computations for Table 1, we do not need to introduce any further splitting of expressions in R during reduction of the S-polynomials. For instance,

$$\mathrm{S}(IF\underline{D}, \underline{D}I) = (f - \textstyle\int \otimes \partial f - (\mathrm{E}f)\mathrm{E}) \otimes \textstyle\int - \textstyle\int \otimes f \otimes \epsilon$$
$$\to_{r_{EI}} f \otimes \textstyle\int - \textstyle\int \otimes \partial f \otimes \textstyle\int - \textstyle\int \otimes f \to_{r_{IFI}} \cdots \overset{*}{\to}_{r_K} 0.$$

There are 41 ambiguities without specialization, they only involve the first 12 reduction rules (over Y). The remaining 11 ambiguities consist of 4 overlap ambiguities with specialization and 7 inclusion ambiguities with specialization. They all involve the last two reduction rules (over X) in Table 2 and their S-polynomials are reduced to zero. For example,

$$\mathrm{S}(IF\underline{C}, \underline{E}I) = (\textstyle\int f \otimes \mathrm{E}) \otimes \textstyle\int - \textstyle\int \otimes f \otimes 0 \to_{r_{EI}} \textstyle\int f \otimes 0 = 0,$$
$$\mathrm{S}(\underline{K}, D\underline{F}) = \partial \otimes \epsilon \otimes \epsilon - 1 \otimes \partial \ \to_{r_K} \partial - \partial = 0.$$

In Figure 2 we present more detailed statistics on the whole reduction process. For 4 ambiguities, we do not need to apply any reduction, and 28 do not need identities in R. The maximal number of required reduction rules and identities from R are 8 and 4, respectively, which for instance is the case for the S-polynomial $\mathrm{S}(IF\underline{I}, \underline{I}FD)$. Per ambiguity on average 2.73 reductions and 0.73 identities have been used in the computation. So not only the number of ambiguities is less than before, but also the average effort per ambiguity has reduced.

We emphasize again that the confluence criterion of Theorem 4.6 directly works with the reduction system Σ, no computations with the induced reduction system Σ_X over X are needed. The 31 reduction rules of Σ_X would give rise to 149 overlap ambiguities and 11 inclusion ambiguities.

6. OUTLOOK

We showed that the new two-level tensor setting allows for a simpler study and a more general construction of integro-differential operators than via noncommutative polynomial algebras. So we are confident that this approach is also suitable for studying other operator algebras. Due to space limitations, we did not include our results for generalizations of integro-differential operators which contain more operators like linear substitutions, addressing the univariate case of [15], or arbitrary linear functionals. These operator algebras have applications to boundary problems and delay equations [12]. Beyond verification of confluence, we are studying an analog of Buchberger's algorithm [5] and Knuth-Bendix completion [11] for tensors, see [10] for an example.

7. REFERENCES

[1] F. Baader and T. Nipkow. *Term rewriting and all that.* Cambridge University Press, Cambridge, 1998.

[2] V. V. Bavula. The algebra of integro-differential operators on an affine line and its modules. *J. Pure Appl. Algebra*, 217:495–529, 2013.

[3] G. M. Bergman. The diamond lemma for ring theory. *Adv. in Math.*, 29:178–218, 1978.

[4] L. A. Bokut and Y. Chen. Gröbner-Shirshov bases and their calculation. *Bull. Math. Sci.*, 4:325–395, 2014.

[5] B. Buchberger. *An algorithm for finding the bases elements of the residue class ring modulo a zero dimensional polynomial ideal (German).* PhD thesis, University of Innsbruck, 1965.

[6] F. Chyzak and B. Salvy. Non-commutative elimination in Ore algebras proves multivariate identities. *J. Symbolic Comput.*, 26:187–227, 1998.

[7] X. Gao, L. Guo, and M. Rosenkranz. Free integro-differential algebras and Gröbner-Shirshov bases. *J. Algebra*, 442:354–396, 2015.

[8] J. Gómez-Torrecillas. Basic module theory over non-commutative rings with computational aspects of operator algebras. In *AADIOS 2012*, volume 8372 of *LNCS*, pages 23–82. Springer, Heidelberg, 2014. With an appendix by V. Levandovskyy.

[9] L. Guo, G. Regensburger, and M. Rosenkranz. On integro-differential algebras. *J. Pure Appl. Algebra*, 218:456–473, 2014.

[10] J. Hossein Poor, C. G. Raab, and G. Regensburger. Normal forms for operators via Gröbner bases in tensor algebras. In *Proceedings of ICMS 2016*, volume 9725 of *LNCS*. Springer, 2016. To appear.

[11] D. E. Knuth and P. B. Bendix. Simple word problems in universal algebras. In *Computational Problems in Abstract Algebra*, pages 263–297. Pergamon, Oxford, 1970.

[12] A. Quadrat. A constructive algebraic analysis approach to Artstein's reduction of linear time-delay systems. *IFAC-PapersOnLine*, 48(12):209–214, 2015.

[13] G. Regensburger, M. Rosenkranz, and J. Middeke. A skew polynomial approach to integro-differential operators. In *Proceedings of ISSAC '09*, pages 287–294, New York, NY, USA, 2009. ACM.

[14] M. Rosenkranz. A new symbolic method for solving linear two-point boundary value problems on the level of operators. *J. Symbolic Comput.*, 39:171–199, 2005.

[15] M. Rosenkranz, X. Gao, and L. Guo. An algebraic study of multivariable integration and linear substitution. 2015. arXiv:1503.01694 [math.RA].

[16] M. Rosenkranz and G. Regensburger. Solving and factoring boundary problems for linear ordinary differential equations in differential algebras. *J. Symbolic Comput.*, 43:515–544, 2008.

[17] M. Rosenkranz, G. Regensburger, L. Tec, and B. Buchberger. Symbolic analysis for boundary problems: From rewriting to parametrized Gröbner bases. In *Numerical and Symbolic Scientific Computing*, pages 273–331. Springer Vienna, 2012.

Algorithms for Simultaneous Padé Approximations

Johan Rosenkilde, né Nielsen
Technical University of Denmark
Denmark
jsrn@jsrn.dk

Arne Storjohann
University of Waterloo
Canada
astorjoh@uwaterloo.ca

ABSTRACT

We describe how to solve simultaneous Padé approximations over a power series ring $\mathsf{K}[[x]]$ for a field K using $O^{\sim}(n^{\omega-1}d)$ operations in K, where d is the sought precision and n is the number of power series to approximate. We develop two algorithms using different approaches. Both algorithms return a reduced sub-bases that generates the complete set of solutions to the input approximations problem that satisfy the given degree constraints. Our results are made possible by recent breakthroughs in fast computations of minimal approximant bases and Hermite Padé approximations.

1. INTRODUCTION

The Simultaneous Padé approximation problem concerns approximating several power series $S_1, \ldots, S_n \in \mathsf{K}[[x]]$ with rational functions $\frac{\sigma_1}{\lambda}, \ldots, \frac{\sigma_n}{\lambda}$, all sharing the same denominator λ. In other words, for some $d \in \mathbb{Z}_{\geq 0}$, we seek $\lambda \in \mathsf{K}[x]$ of low degree such that each of

$$\mathrm{rem}(\lambda S_1,\ x^d), \mathrm{rem}(\lambda S_2,\ x^d),\ \ldots,\ \mathrm{rem}(\lambda S_n,\ x^d)$$

has low degree. The study of Simultaneous Padé approximations traces back to Hermite's proof of the transcendence of e [18]. Solving Simultaneous Padé approximations has numerous applications, such as in coding theory, e.g. [13, 28]; or in distributed, reliable computation [11]. Many algorithms have been developed for this problem, see e.g. [3, 26, 27, 29] as well as the references therein. Usually one cares about the regime where $d \gg n$. Obtaining $O(nd^2)$ is classical through successive cancellation, see [4] or [13] for a Berlekamp–Massey-type variant. Using fast arithmetic, the previous best was $O^{\sim}(n^{\omega}d)$, where ω is the exponent for matrix multiplication, see Section 1.1. That can be done by computing a minimal approximant basis with e.g. [15, 16]; this approach traces back to [2, 3]. Another possibility which achieves the same complexity is fast algorithms for solving structured linear systems, e.g. [8]; see [10] for a discussion of this approach.

A common description is to require $\deg \lambda < N_0$ for some degree bound N_0, and similarly $\deg \mathrm{rem}(\lambda S_1,\ x^d) < N_i$ for $i = 1, \ldots, n$. The degree bounds could arise naturally from the application, or could be set such that a solution must exist. A natural generalisation is also to replace the x^d moduli with arbitrary $g_1, \ldots, g_n \in \mathsf{K}[x]$. Formally, for any field K:

PROBLEM 1. *Given a tuple $(\boldsymbol{S}, \boldsymbol{g}, \boldsymbol{N})$ where*

- $\boldsymbol{S} = (S_1, \ldots, S_n) \in \mathsf{K}[x]^n$ *is a sequence of polynomials,*
- $\boldsymbol{g} = (g_1, \ldots, g_n) \in \mathsf{K}[x]^n$ *is a sequence of moduli polynomials with* $\deg S_i < \deg g_i$ *for* $i = 1, \ldots, n$,
- *and* $\boldsymbol{N} = (N_0, \ldots, N_n) \in \mathbb{Z}_{\geq 0}^{n+1}$ *are degree bounds satisfying* $1 \leq N_0 \leq \max_i \deg g_i$ *and* $N_i \leq \deg g_i$ *for* $i = 1, \ldots, n$,

find, if it exists, a non-zero vector $(\lambda, \phi_1, \ldots, \phi_n)$ *such that*

1. $\lambda S_i \equiv \phi_i \mod g_i$ *for* $i = 1, \ldots, n$, *and*
2. $\deg \lambda < N_0$ *and* $\deg \phi_i < N_i$ *for* $i = 1, \ldots, n$.

We will call any vector $(\lambda, \phi_1, \ldots, \phi_n)$ as above *a solution* to a given Simultaneous Padé approximation problem. Note that if the N_i are set too low, then it might be the case that no solution exists.

EXAMPLE 2. *Consider over* $\mathbb{F}_2[x]$ *that* $g_1 = g_2 = g_3 = x^5$, *and* $\boldsymbol{S} = (S_1, S_2, S_3) = \big(x^4 + x^2 + 1,\ x^4 + 1,\ x^4 + x^3 + 1\big)$, *with degree bounds* $\boldsymbol{N} = (5, 3, 4, 5)$. *Then* $\lambda_1 = x^4 + 1$ *is a solution, since* $\deg \lambda_1 < 5$ *and*

$$\lambda_1 \boldsymbol{S} \equiv \big(x^2 + 1,\ 1,\ x^3 + 1\big) \mod x^5 \ .$$

$\lambda_2 = x^3 + x$ *is another solution, since*

$$\lambda_2 \boldsymbol{S} \equiv \big(x,\ x^3 + x,\ x^4 + x^3 + x\big) \mod x^5 \ .$$

These two solutions are linearly independent over $\mathbb{F}_2[x]$ *and span all solutions.*

Several previous algorithms for solving Problem 1 are more ambitious and produce an entire *basis* of solutions that satisfy the first output condition $\lambda S_i \equiv \phi_i \mod g_i$ for $i = 1, \ldots, n$, including solutions that do not satisfy the degree bounds stipulated by the second output condition. Our algorithms are slightly more restricted in that we only return the sub-basis that generates the set of solutions that satisfy both output requirements of Problem 1. Formally:

PROBLEM 3. *Given an instance of Problem 1, find a matrix* $A \in \mathsf{K}[x]^{* \times (n+1)}$ *such that:*

- *Each row of A is a solution to the instance.*

ISSAC '16, July 19 - 22, 2016, Waterloo, ON, Canada

ISBN 978-1-4503-4380-0/16/07...$15.00

DOI: http://dx.doi.org/10.1145/2930889.2930933

- *All solutions are in the* $\mathsf{K}[x]$*-row space of* A.
- A *is* $(-\boldsymbol{N})$*-row reduced*[1].

The last condition ensures that A is minimal, in a sense, according to the degree bounds $\boldsymbol{N}$, and that we can easily parametrise which linear combinations of the rows of A are solutions. We recall the relevant definitions and lemmas in Section 2.

We will call such a matrix A a *solution basis*. In the complexities we report here, we cannot afford to compute A explicitly. For example, if all $g_i = x^d$, the number of field elements required to explicitly write down all of the entries of A could be $\Omega(n^2 d)$. Instead, we remark that A is completely given by the problem instance as well as the first column of A, containing the λ polynomials.[2] Our algorithms will therefore represent A row-wise using the following compact representation.

Definition 4. *For a given instance of Problem 3, a* solution specification *is a tuple* $(\boldsymbol{\lambda}, \boldsymbol{\delta}) \in \mathsf{K}[x]^{k\times 1} \times \mathbb{Z}^k_{<0}$ *such that the* completion *of* $\boldsymbol{\lambda}$ *is a solution basis, and where* $\boldsymbol{\delta}$ *are the* $(-\boldsymbol{N})$*-degrees of the rows of* A.

The completion *of* $\boldsymbol{\lambda} = (\lambda_1, \dots, \lambda_k)^\top$ *is the matrix*

$$\begin{bmatrix} \lambda_1 & \operatorname{rem}(\lambda_1 S_1,\ g_1) & \dots & \operatorname{rem}(\lambda_1 S_n,\ g_n) \\ \vdots & & \ddots & \vdots \\ \lambda_k & \operatorname{rem}(\lambda_k S_1,\ g_1) & \dots & \operatorname{rem}(\lambda_k S_n,\ g_n) \end{bmatrix} .$$

Note that $\boldsymbol{\delta}$ will consist of only negative numbers, since any solution $\boldsymbol{v}$ by definition has $\deg_{-\boldsymbol{N}} \boldsymbol{v} < 0$.

Example 5. *A solution specification for the problem in Example 2 is*

$$(\boldsymbol{\lambda}, \boldsymbol{\delta}) = \left([x^4+1,\ x^3+x]^\top,\ (-1,-1)\right) .$$

The completion of this is

$$A = \begin{bmatrix} x^4+1 & x^2+1 & 1 & x^3+1 \\ x^3+x & x & x^3+x & x^4+x^3+x \end{bmatrix}$$

One can verify that A *is* $(-\boldsymbol{N})$*-row reduced.*

We present two algorithms for solving Problem 3, both with complexity $O\big(n^{\omega-1}\,\mathsf{M}(d)\,(\log d)\,(\log d/n)^2\big)$, where $d = \max_i \deg g_i$ and $\mathsf{M}(d)$ is the cost of multiplying two polynomials of degree d, see Section 1.1. They both depend crucially on recent developments that allow computing minimal approximant bases of non-square matrices faster than for the square case [19,34]. We remark that from the solution basis, one can also compute the expanded form of one or a few of the solutions in the same complexity, for instance if a single, expanded solution to the simultaneous Padé problem is needed.

Our first algorithm in Section 4 assumes $g_i = x^d$ for all i and some $d \in \mathbb{Z}_{\geq 0}$. It utilises a well-known duality between Simultaneous Padé approximations and Hermite Padé approximations, see e.g. [3]. The Hermite Padé problem is immediately solvable by fast minimal approximant basis computation. A remaining step is to efficiently compute a single row of the adjoint of a matrix in Popov form, and this is done by combining partial linearisation [16] and high-order lifting [31].

Our second algorithm in Section 5 supports arbitrary g_i. The algorithm first solves n single-sequence Padé approximations, each of $S_1, \dots, S_n$. The solution bases for two problem instances can be combined by computing the intersection of their row spaces; this is handled by a minimal approximant basis computation. A solution basis of the full Simultaneous Padé problem is then obtained by structuring intersections along a binary tree.

Before we describe our algorithms, we give some preliminary notation and definitions in Section 2, and in Section 3 we describe some of the computational tools that we employ.

Both our algorithms have been implemented in Sage v. 7.0 [30] (though asymptotically slower alternatives to the computational tools are used). The source code can be downloaded from http://jsrn.dk/code-for-articles.

1.1 Cost model

We count basic arithmetic operations in K on an algebraic RAM. We will state complexity results in terms of an exponent ω for matrix multiplication, and a function $\mathsf{M}(\cdot)$ that is a multiplication time for $\mathsf{K}[x]$ [33, Definition 8.26]. Then two $n \times n$ matrices over K can be multiplied in $O(n^\omega)$ operations in K, and two polynomials in $\mathsf{K}[x]$ of degree strictly less than d can be multiplied in $\mathsf{M}(d)$ operations in K. The best known algorithms allow $\omega < 2.38$ [12,14], and we can always take $\mathsf{M}(d) \in O(n(\log n)(\operatorname{loglog} n))$ [9]. In this paper we assume that $\omega > 2$, and that $\mathsf{M}(d)$ is super-linear while $\mathsf{M}(d) \in o(d^{\omega-1})$. The assumption $\mathsf{M}(d) \in o(d^{\omega-1})$ simply stipulates that if fast matrix multiplication techiques are used then fast polynomial multiplication should be used also: for example, $n\,\mathsf{M}(nd) \in O(n^\omega\,\mathsf{M}(d))$.

2. PRELIMINARIES

Here we gather together some definitions and results regarding row reduced bases, minimal approximant basis, and their shifted variants. For a matrix A we denote by $A_{i,j}$ the entry in row i and column j. For a matrix A over $\mathsf{K}[x]$ we denote by $\operatorname{Row}(A)$ the $\mathsf{K}[x]$-linear row space of A.

2.1 Degrees and shifted degrees

The degree of a nonzero vector $\boldsymbol{v} \in \mathsf{K}[x]^{1\times m}$ or matrix $A \in \mathsf{K}[x]^{n\times m}$ is denoted by $\deg \boldsymbol{v}$ or $\deg A$, and is the maximal degree of entries of $\boldsymbol{v}$ or A. If A has no zero rows the *row degrees* of A, denoted by $\operatorname{rowdeg} A$, is the tuple $(d_1, \dots, d_n)$ with $d_i = \deg \operatorname{row}(A, i)$.

The (row-wise) *leading matrix* of A, denoted by $\operatorname{LM}(A) \in \mathsf{K}^{n\times m}$, has $\operatorname{LM}(A)_{i,j}$ equal to the coefficient of x^{d_i} of $A_{i,j}$.

Next we recall [2,19,34] the shifted variants of the notion of degree, row degrees, and leading matrix. For a *shift* $\boldsymbol{s} = (s_1, \dots, s_n) \in \mathbb{Z}^n$, define the $n \times n$ diagonal matrix $x^{\boldsymbol{s}}$ by

$$x^{\boldsymbol{s}} := \begin{bmatrix} x^{s_1} & & \\ & \ddots & \\ & & x^{s_n} \end{bmatrix} .$$

Then the $\boldsymbol{s}$*-degree* of v, the $\boldsymbol{s}$*-row degrees* of A, and the $\boldsymbol{s}$*-leading matrix* of A, are defined by $\deg_{\boldsymbol{s}} v := \deg v x^{\boldsymbol{s}}$,

[1] The notions $(-\boldsymbol{N})$-degree, $\deg_{-\boldsymbol{N}}$ and $(-\boldsymbol{N})$-row reduced are recalled in Section 2.

[2] The restriction $N_i \leq \deg g_i$ in Problem 1 ensures that for a given λ, the only possibilities for the ϕ_i in a solution are $\operatorname{rem}(\lambda S_i,\ g_i)$. In particular, if we allowed $N_i > \deg g_i$ then $(0, \dots, 0, g_i, 0, \dots, 0)$ would be a solution which can not be directly reconstructed from its first element.

$\text{rowdeg}_{\boldsymbol{s}} A := \text{rowdeg}\, Ax^{\boldsymbol{s}}$, and $\text{LM}_{\boldsymbol{s}}(A) := \text{LM}(Ax^{\boldsymbol{s}})$. Note that we pass over the ring of Laurent polynomials only for convenience; our algorithms will only compute with polynomials. As pointed out in [19], up to negation the definition of $\boldsymbol{s}$-degree is equivalent to that used in [7] and to the notion of *defect* in [4].

For an instance $(\boldsymbol{S}, \boldsymbol{g}, \boldsymbol{N})$ of Problem 1, in the context of defining matrices, we will be using $\boldsymbol{S}$ and $\boldsymbol{g}$ as vectors, and by $\Gamma_{\boldsymbol{g}}$ denote the diagonal matrix with the entries of $\boldsymbol{g}$ on its diagonal.

2.2 Row reduced

Although row reducedness can be defined for matrices of arbitrary shape and rank, it suffices here to consider the case of matrices of full row rank. A matrix $R \in \mathsf{K}[x]^{n\times m}$ is *row reduced* if $\text{LM}(R)$ has full row rank, and *$\boldsymbol{s}$-row reduced* if $\text{LM}_{\boldsymbol{s}}(R)$ has full row rank. Every $A \in \mathsf{K}[x]^{n\times m}$ of full row rank is left equivalent to a matrix $R \in \mathsf{K}[x]^{n\times m}$ that is $\boldsymbol{s}$-row reduced. The rows of R give a basis for $\text{Row}(A)$ that is minimal in the following sense: the list of $\boldsymbol{s}$-degrees of the rows of R, when sorted in non-decreasing order, will be lexicographically minimal. An important feature of row reduced matrices is the so-called "predictable degree"-property [21, Theorem 6.3-13]: for any $\boldsymbol{v} \in \mathsf{K}[x]^{1\times n}$, we have

$$\deg_{\boldsymbol{s}}(\boldsymbol{v}R) = \max_{i=1,\ldots,n} (\deg_{\boldsymbol{s}} \text{row}(R,i) + \deg v_i) .$$

A canonical $\boldsymbol{s}$-reduced basis is provided by the $\boldsymbol{s}$-Popov form. Although an $\boldsymbol{s}$-Popov form can be defined for a matrix of arbitrary shape and rank, it suffices here to consider the case of a non-singular matrix. The following definition is equivalent to [19, Definition 1.2].

DEFINITION 6. *A non-singular matrix $R \in \mathsf{K}[x]^{n\times n}$ is in $\boldsymbol{s}$-Popov form if $\text{LM}_{\boldsymbol{s}}(R)$ is unit lower triangular and the degrees of off-diagonal entries of R are strictly less than the degree of the diagonal entry in the same column.*

2.3 Adjoints of row reduced matrices

For a non-singular matrix A recall that the adjoint of A, denoted by $\text{adj}(A)$, is equal to $(\det A)A^{-1}$, and that entry $\text{adj}(A)^{\top}_{i,j}$ is equal to $(-1)^{i+j}$ times the determinant of the $(n-1)\times(n-1)$ sub-matrix that is obtained from A by deleting row i and column j.

LEMMA 7. *Let $A \in \mathsf{K}[x]^{n\times n}$ be $\boldsymbol{s}$-row reduced. Then $\text{adj}(A)^{\top}$ is $(-\boldsymbol{s})$-row reduced with*

$$\text{rowdeg}_{(-\boldsymbol{s})}\text{adj}(A)^{\top} = (\eta - s - \eta_1, \ldots, \eta - s - \eta_n) ,$$

where $\boldsymbol{\eta} = \text{rowdeg}_{\boldsymbol{s}} A$, $\eta = \sum_i \eta_i$ and $s = \sum_i s_i$.

PROOF. Since A is $\boldsymbol{s}$-row reduced then $Ax^{\boldsymbol{s}}$ is row reduced. Note that $\text{adj}(Ax^{\boldsymbol{s}})^{\top}(Ax^{\boldsymbol{s}})^{\top} = (\det Ax^{\boldsymbol{s}})I_m$ with $\deg\det Ax^{\boldsymbol{s}} = \eta$. It follows that row i of $\text{adj}(Ax^{\boldsymbol{s}})^{\top}$ must have degree at least $\eta - \eta_i$ since η_i is the degree of column i of $(Ax^{\boldsymbol{s}})^{\top}$. However, entries in row i of $\text{adj}(Ax^{\boldsymbol{s}})^{\top}$ are minors of the matrix obtained from $Ax^{\boldsymbol{s}}$ by removing row i, hence have degree at most $\eta - \eta_i$. It follows that the (row-wise) leading coefficient matrix of $\text{adj}(Ax^{\boldsymbol{s}})^{\top}$ is non-singular, hence $\text{adj}(Ax^{\boldsymbol{s}})^{\top}$ is row reduced. Since $\text{adj}(Ax^{\boldsymbol{s}})^{\top} = (\det x^{\boldsymbol{s}})\text{adj}(A)^{\top}x^{-\boldsymbol{s}}$ we conclude that $\text{adj}(A)^{\top}$ is $(-\boldsymbol{s})$-row reduced with $\text{rowdeg}_{(-\boldsymbol{s})}\text{adj}(A) = (\eta - \eta_1 - s, \ldots, \eta - \eta_n - s)$. □

2.4 Minimal approximant bases

We recall the standard notion of minimal approximant basis, sometimes known as order basis or σ-basis [4]. For a matrix $A \in \mathsf{K}[x]^{n\times m}$ and order $d \in \mathbb{Z}_{\geq 0}$, an *order d approximant* is a vector $\boldsymbol{p} \in \mathsf{K}[x]^{1\times n}$ such that $\boldsymbol{p}A \equiv \boldsymbol{0} \bmod x^d$.

An *approximant basis of order d* is then a matrix $F \in \mathsf{K}[x]^{n\times n}$ which is a basis of all order d approximants. Such a basis always exists and has full rank n. For a shift $\boldsymbol{s} \in \mathbb{Z}^n$, F is then an *$\boldsymbol{s}$-minimal approximant basis* if it is $\boldsymbol{s}$-row reduced.

Let $\mathsf{MinBasis}(d, A, \boldsymbol{s})$ be a function that returns $(F, \boldsymbol{\delta})$, where F is an $\boldsymbol{s}$-minimal approximant basis of A of order d, and $\boldsymbol{\delta} = \text{rowdeg}_{\boldsymbol{s}} F$. The next lemma recalls a well known method of constructing minimal approximant bases recursively. Although the output of $\mathsf{MinBasis}$ may not be unique, the lemma holds for *any* $\boldsymbol{s}$-minimal approximant basis that $\mathsf{MinBasis}$ might return.

LEMMA 8. *Let $A = \left[\, A_1 \mid A_2 \,\right]$ over $\mathsf{K}[x]$. If $(F_1, \boldsymbol{\delta}_1) = \mathsf{MinBasis}(d, A_1, \boldsymbol{s})$ and $(F_2, \boldsymbol{\delta}_2) = \mathsf{MinBasis}(d, F_1 A_2, \boldsymbol{\delta}_1)$, then $F_2 F_1$ is an $\boldsymbol{s}$-minimal approximant basis of A of order d with $\boldsymbol{\delta}_2 = \text{rowdeg}_{\boldsymbol{s}} F_2 F_1$.*

Sometimes only the *negative part* of an $\boldsymbol{s}$-minimal approximant bases is required, the submatrix of the approximant bases consisting of rows with negative $\boldsymbol{s}$-degree. Let function $\mathsf{NegMinBasis}(d, A, \boldsymbol{s})$ have the same output as $\mathsf{MinBasis}$, but with F restricted to the negative part.

COROLLARY 9. *Lemma 8 still holds if $\mathsf{MinBasis}$ is replaced by $\mathsf{NegMinBasis}$, and "an $\boldsymbol{s}$-minimal" is replaced with "the negative part of an $\boldsymbol{s}$-minimal."*

Using for example the algorithm `M-Basis` of [15], it is easy to show that any order d approximant basis G for an A of column dimension m has $\det G = x^D$ for some $D \in \mathbb{Z}_{\geq 0}$ with $D \leq md$.

Many problems of $\mathsf{K}[x]$ matrices or approximations reduce to the computation of (shifted) minimal approximant bases, see e.g. [4, 15], often resulting in the best known asymptotic complexities for these problems.

2.5 Direct solving of Simultaneous Padé approximations

Let $(\boldsymbol{S}, \boldsymbol{g}, \boldsymbol{N})$ be an instance of Problem 3 of size n. We recall some known approaches for computing a solution specification using row reduction and minimal approximant basis computation.

2.5.1 Via reduced basis

Using the predictable degree property it is easy to show that if $R \in \mathsf{K}[x]^{(n+1)\times(n+1)}$ is an $(-\boldsymbol{N})$-reduced basis of

$$A = \left[\begin{array}{c|c} 1 & \boldsymbol{S} \\ \hline & \Gamma_{\boldsymbol{g}} \end{array}\right] \in \mathsf{K}[x]^{(n+1)\times(n+1)},$$

then the sub-matrix of R comprised of the rows with negative $(-\boldsymbol{N})$-degree form a solution basis. A solution specification $(\boldsymbol{\lambda}, \boldsymbol{\delta})$ is then a subvector $\boldsymbol{\lambda}$ of the first column of R, with $\boldsymbol{\delta}$ the corresponding subtuple $\boldsymbol{\delta}$ of $\text{rowdeg}_{(-\boldsymbol{N})} R$.

Mulders and Storjohann [24] gave an iterative algorithm for performing row reduction by successive cancellation; it is similar to but faster than earlier algorithms [21, 22]. Generically on input $F \in \mathsf{K}[x]^{m\times m}$ it has complexity $O(n^3(\deg F)^2)$.

Alekhnovich [1] gave what is essentially a Divide & Conquer variant of Mulders and Storjohann's algorithm, with complexity $O^{\sim}(n^{\omega+1} \deg F)$. Nielsen remarked [26] that these algorithms perform fewer iterations when applied to the matrix A above, due to its low *orthogonality defect*: $\mathrm{OD}(F) = \sum \mathrm{rowdeg} F - \deg \det F$, resulting in $O(n^2 (\deg A)^2)$ respectively $O^{\sim}(n^{\omega} \deg A)$. Nielsen also used the special shape of A to give a variant of the Mulders–Storjohann algorithm that computes coefficients in the working matrix in a lazy manner with a resulting complexity $O(n\, \mathsf{P}(\deg A))$, where $\mathsf{P}(\deg A) = (\deg A)^2$ when the g_i are all powers of x, and $\mathsf{P}(\deg A) = \mathsf{M}(\deg A) \deg A$ otherwise.

Giorgi, et al. [15] gave a reduction for performing row reduction by computing a minimal approximant basis. For the special matrix A, this essentially boils down to the approach described in the following section.

When $n = 1$, the extended Euclidean algorithm on input S_1 and g_1 can solve the approximation problem by essentially computing the reduced basis of the 2×2 matrix A: each iteration corresponds to a reduced basis for a range of possible shifts [17, 20, 32]. The complexity of this is $O(\mathsf{M}(\deg g_1) \log \deg g_1)$.

2.5.2 *Via minimal approximant basis*

First consider the special case when all $g_i = x^d$ for the same d. An approximant $\boldsymbol{v} = (\lambda, \phi_1, \ldots, \phi_n)$ of order d of

$$A = \begin{bmatrix} -\boldsymbol{S} \\ I \end{bmatrix} \in \mathsf{K}[x]^{(n+1)\times n}$$

clearly satisfies $\lambda S_i \equiv \phi_i \mod x^d$ for $i = 1, \ldots, n$; conversely, any such vector $\boldsymbol{v}$ satisfying these congruences must be an approximant of A of order d. So the negative part of a $(-\boldsymbol{N})$-minimal approximant basis of A of order d is a solution basis.

In the general case we can reduce to a minimal approximant bases computation as shown by Algorithm 1. Correctness of the algorithm follows from the following result.

THEOREM 10. *Corresponding to an instance $(\boldsymbol{S}, \boldsymbol{g}, \boldsymbol{N})$ of Problem 3 of size n, define a shift $\boldsymbol{h}$ and order d:*

- $\boldsymbol{h} := -(\boldsymbol{N} \mid N_0 - 1, \ldots, N_0 - 1) \in \mathbb{Z}^{2n+1}$
- $d := N_0 + \max_i \deg g_i - 1$

If G is the negative part of an $\boldsymbol{h}$-minimal approximant basis of

$$H = \begin{bmatrix} -\boldsymbol{S} \\ I \\ \Gamma_{\boldsymbol{g}} \end{bmatrix} \in \mathsf{K}[x]^{(2n+1)\times n}$$

of order d, then the submatrix of G comprised of the first $n+1$ columns is a solution basis to the problem instance.

PROOF. An approximant $\boldsymbol{v} = (\lambda, \phi_1, \ldots, \phi_n, q_1, \ldots, q_n)$ of order d of H clearly satisfies

$$\lambda S_i = \phi_i + q_i g_i \bmod x^d \qquad (1)$$

for $i = 1, \ldots, n$; conversely, any such vector $\boldsymbol{v}$ satisfying these congruences must be an approximant of H of order d.

Now suppose $\boldsymbol{v}$ is an order d approximant of H with negative $\boldsymbol{h}$-degree, so $\deg \lambda \leq N_0 - 1$, $\deg \phi_i \leq N_i - 1$, and $\deg q_i \leq N_0 - 2$. Since Problem 1 specifies that $\deg S_i < \deg g_i$ and $N_i \leq \deg g_i$, both λS_i and $q_i g_i$ will have degree bounded by $N_0 + \deg g_i - 2$. Since Problem 1 specifies that $N_0 \geq 1$, it follows that both the left and right hand sides of (1) have degree bounded by $N_0 + \deg g_i - 2$, which is strictly less than d. We conclude that

$$\lambda S_i = \phi_i + q_i g_i \qquad (2)$$

for $i = 1, \ldots, n$. It follows that $\boldsymbol{v}H = 0$ so $\boldsymbol{v}$ is in the left kernel of H. Moreover, restricting $\boldsymbol{v}$ to its first $n+1$ entries gives $\bar{\boldsymbol{v}} := (\lambda, \phi_1, \ldots, \phi_n)$, a solution to the simultaneous Padé problem with $\deg_{-\boldsymbol{N}} \bar{\boldsymbol{v}} = \deg_{\boldsymbol{h}} \boldsymbol{v}$. Conversely, if $\bar{\boldsymbol{v}} = (\lambda, \phi_1, \ldots, \phi_n)$ is a solution to the simultaneous Padé problem, then the extension $\boldsymbol{v} = (\lambda, \phi_1, \ldots, \phi_n, q_1, \ldots, q_n)$ with $q_i = (\lambda S_i - \phi_i)/g_i \in \mathsf{K}[x]$ for $i = 1, \ldots, n$ is an approximant of H of order d with $\deg_{\boldsymbol{h}} \boldsymbol{v} = \deg_{-\boldsymbol{N}} \bar{\boldsymbol{v}}$.

Finally, consider that a left kernel basis for H is given by

$$K = [\, K_1 \mid K_2 \,] = \left[\begin{array}{cc|c} 1 & \boldsymbol{S} & \\ & \Gamma_{\boldsymbol{g}} & -I \end{array} \right].$$

We must have $G = MK$ for some polynomial matrix M of full row rank. But then MK_1 also has full row rank with $\mathrm{rowdeg}_{-\boldsymbol{N}} MK_1 = \mathrm{rowdeg}_{\boldsymbol{h}} G$. $\square$

Algorithm 1 DirectSimPade

Input: $(\boldsymbol{S}, \boldsymbol{g}, \boldsymbol{N})$, an instance of Problem 3 of size n.
Output: $(\boldsymbol{\lambda}, \boldsymbol{\delta})$, a solution specification.

$\boldsymbol{h} \leftarrow -(\boldsymbol{N} \mid N_0 - 1, \ldots, N_0 - 1) \in \mathbb{Z}^{2n+1}$
$d \leftarrow N_0 + \max_i \deg g_i - 1$
$H = \begin{bmatrix} -\boldsymbol{S} \\ I \\ \Gamma_{\boldsymbol{g}} \end{bmatrix}$
$([\, \boldsymbol{\lambda} \mid * \,], \boldsymbol{\delta}) \leftarrow \mathsf{NegMinBasis}(d, H, \boldsymbol{h})$
return $(\boldsymbol{\lambda}, \boldsymbol{\delta})$

DirectSimPade can be performed in time $O^{\sim}(n^{\omega} \deg H) = O^{\sim}(n^{\omega} \max_i \deg g_i)$ using the minimal approximant basis algorithm by Jeannerod, et al. [19], see Section 3.

A closely related alternative to DirectSimPade is the recent algorithm by Neiger [25] for computing solutions to modular equations with general moduli g_i. This would give the complexity $O^{\sim}(n^{\omega-1} \sum_i \deg g_i) \subset O^{\sim}(n^{\omega} \max_i \deg g_i)$.

All of the above solutions ignore the sparse, simple structure of the input matrices, which is why they do not obtain the improved complexity that we do here.

3. COMPUTATIONAL TOOLS

The main computational tool we will use is the following very recent result from Jeannerod, Neiger, Schost and Villard [19] on minimal approximant basis computation.

THEOREM 11 ([19, SPECIAL CASE OF THEOREM 1.4]). *There exists an algorithm* PopovBasis$(d, A, \boldsymbol{s})$ *where the input is an order $d \in \mathbb{Z}_+$, a polynomial matrix $A \in \mathsf{K}[x]^{n\times m}$ of degree at most d, and shift $\boldsymbol{s} \in \mathbb{Z}^n$, and which returns $(F, \boldsymbol{\delta})$, where F is an $\boldsymbol{s}$-minimal approximant basis of A of order d, F is in $\boldsymbol{s}$-Popov form, and $\boldsymbol{\delta} = \mathrm{rowdeg}_{\boldsymbol{s}} F$.* PopovBasis *has complexity $O(n^{\omega-1} \mathsf{M}(\sigma) (\log \sigma) (\log \sigma/n)^2)$ operations in K, where $\sigma = md$.*

Our next result says that we can quickly compute the first row of $\mathrm{adj}(F)$ if F is a minimal approximant basis in Popov form. In particular, since F is an approximant basis $\det F = x^D$ for some $D \leq \sigma$, where $\sigma = md$ from Theorem 11.

THEOREM 12. *Let $F \in \mathsf{K}[x]^{n\times n}$ be in Popov form and with* $\det F = x^D$ *for some $D \in \mathbb{Z}_{\geq 0}$. Then the first row of* $\operatorname{adj}(F)$ *can be computed in $O(n^{\omega-1}\,\mathsf{M}(D)\,(\log D)\,(\log D/n))$ operations in* K.

PROOF. Because F is in $\boldsymbol{s}$-Popov form, D is the sum of the column degrees of F. We consider two cases: $D \geq n$ and $D < n$.

First suppose $D \geq n$. Partial linearisation [16, Corollary 2] can produce from F, with no operations in K, a new matrix $G \in \mathsf{K}[x]^{\bar{n}\times\bar{n}}$ with dimension $\bar{n} < 2n$, $\deg G \leq \lceil D/n \rceil$, $\det G = \det F$, and such that F^{-1} is equal to the principal $n \times n$ sub-matrix of G^{-1}. Let $\boldsymbol{v} \in \mathsf{K}[x]^{1\times\bar{n}}$ be the first row of $x^D I_{\bar{n}}$. Then the first row of $\operatorname{adj}(F)$ will be the first n entries of the first row of $\boldsymbol{v}G^{-1}$. High-order X-adic lifting [31, Algorithm 5] using the modulus $X = (x-1)^{\lceil D/n \rceil}$ will compute $\boldsymbol{v}G^{-1}$ in $O\big(n^{\omega}\,\mathsf{M}(\lceil D/n \rceil)\,(\log\lceil D/n \rceil)\big)$ operations in K [31, Corollary 16]. Since $D \geq n$ this cost estimate remains valid if we replace $\lceil D/n \rceil$ with D/n. Finally, from the super-linearity assumption on $\mathsf{M}(\cdot)$ we have $M(D/n) \leq (1/n)\mathsf{M}(D)$, thus matching our target cost.

Now suppose $D < n$. In this case we can not directly appeal to the partial linearisation technique since the resulting $O(n^{\omega}\lceil D/n \rceil)$ may be asymptotically larger than our target cost. But $D < n$ means that F has — possibly many — columns of degree 0; since F is in Popov form, such columns have a 1 on the matrix's diagonal and are 0 on the remaining entries. The following describes how to essentially ignore those columns. D is then greater than or equal to the number of remaining columns, thus effectuating the gain from the partial linearisation.

If $n-k$ is the number of such columns in F that means we can find a permutation matrix P such that

$$\hat{F} := PFP^{\top} = \left[\begin{array}{c|c} F_1 & \\ \hline F_2 & I_{n-k} \end{array}\right],$$

with each column of F_1 having degree strictly greater than zero. Let i be the row index of the single 1 in the first column of $P^{\top}$. Since $F^{-1} = P^{\top}\hat{F}^{-1}P$, we have

$$\operatorname{row}(\operatorname{adj}(F), 1)P^{-1} = x^D \operatorname{row}(\hat{F}^{-1}, i). \qquad (3)$$

Considering that

$$\hat{F}^{-1} = \left[\begin{array}{c|c} F_1^{-1} & \\ \hline -F_2F_1^{-1} & I_{n-k} \end{array}\right],$$

it will suffice to compute the first k entries of the vector on the right hand side of (3). If $i \leq k$ then let $\boldsymbol{v} \in \mathsf{K}[x]^{1\times k}$ be row i of $x^D I_k$. Otherwise, if $i > k$ then let $\boldsymbol{v}$ be row $i-k$ of $-x^D F_2$. Then in both cases, $\boldsymbol{v}F_1^{-1}$ will be equal to the first k entries of the vector on the right hand side of (3). Like before, high-order lifting combined with partial linearisation will compute this vector in $O\big(k^{\omega}\,\mathsf{M}(\lceil D/k \rceil)\,(\log\lceil D/k \rceil)\big)$ operations in K. Since $D \geq k$ the cost estimate remains valid if $\lceil D/k \rceil$ is replaced with D/k. $\square$

4. REDUCTION TO HERMITE PADÉ

In this section we present an algorithm for solving Problem 3 when $g_1 = \ldots = g_n = x^d$ for some $d \in \mathbb{Z}_{\geq 0}$. The algorithm is based on the well-known duality between the Simultaneous Padé problem and the Hermite Padé problem, see for example [3]. This duality, first observed in a special case [23], and then later in the general case [5], was exploited in [6] to develop algorithms for the fraction free computation of Simultaneous Padé approximation. We begin with a technical lemma that is at the heart of this duality.

LEMMA 13. *Let $\hat{A}, \hat{B} \in \mathsf{K}[x]^{(n+1)\times(n+1)}$ be as follows.*

$$\hat{A} = \left[\begin{array}{c|c} x^d & -\boldsymbol{S} \\ \hline & I \end{array}\right] \qquad \hat{B} = \left[\begin{array}{c|c} 1 & \\ \hline \boldsymbol{S}^{\top} & x^d I \end{array}\right]$$

Then $\hat{B}$ is the adjoint of $\hat{A}^{\top}$. Furthermore, $\hat{A}^{\top}$ is an approximant basis for $\hat{B}$ of order d, and $\hat{B}^{\top}$ is an approximant basis of $\hat{A}$ of order d.

PROOF. Direct computation shows that $\hat{A}^{\top}\hat{B} = x^d I_m = \det \hat{A}^{\top} I_m$, so $\hat{B}$ is the adjoint of $\hat{A}^{\top}$.

Let now G be an approximant basis of $\hat{B}$. By the above computation the row space of $\hat{A}^{\top}$ must be a subset of the row space of G. But since $G\hat{B} = (x^d I_m)R$ for some $R \in \mathsf{K}[x]^{(n+1)\times(n+1)}$, then $\det G = x^d \det R$. Thus $x^d \mid \det G$. But $\det \hat{A}^{\top} = x^d$, so the row space of $\hat{A}^{\top}$ can not be smaller than the row space of G. That is, $\hat{A}^{\top}$ is an approximant basis for B of order d. Taking the transpose through the argument shows that $\hat{B}^{\top}$ is an approximant basis of $\hat{B}$ of order d. $\square$

THEOREM 14. *Let A and B be as follows.*

$$A = \left[\begin{array}{c} -\boldsymbol{S} \\ \hline I \end{array}\right] \in \mathsf{K}[x]^{(n+1)\times(n+1)} \qquad B = \left[\begin{array}{c} 1 \\ \boldsymbol{S} \end{array}\right] \in \mathsf{K}[x]^{(n+1)\times 1}$$

If G is an $\boldsymbol{N}$-minimal approximant basis of B of order d with shift $\boldsymbol{N} \in \mathbb{Z}_{\geq 0}^{n+1}$, then $\operatorname{adj}(G^{\top})$ is a $(-\boldsymbol{N})$-minimal approximant basis of A of order d. Moreover, if $\boldsymbol{\eta} = \operatorname{rowdeg}_{\boldsymbol{N}} G$, then $\operatorname{rowdeg}_{-\boldsymbol{N}} \operatorname{adj}(G) = (\eta - N - \eta_1, \ldots, \eta - N - \eta_{n+1})$, where $\eta = \sum_i \eta_i$ and $N = \sum_i N_i$.

PROOF. Introduce $\hat{A}$ and $\hat{B}$ as in Lemma 13. Clearly G is also an $\boldsymbol{N}$-minimal approximant basis of $\hat{B}$ of order d. Likewise, $\hat{A}$ and A have the same minimal approximant bases for given order and shift.

Assume, without loss of generality, that we have scaled G such that $\det G$ is monic. Since $\hat{A}^{\top}$ is also an approximant basis for $\hat{B}$ of order d, then $\det G = \det \hat{A}^{\top} = x^d$. By definition $G\hat{B} = x^d R$ for some matrix $R \in \mathsf{K}[x]^{(n+1)\times(n+1)}$. That means

$$x^{2d}((G\hat{B})^{\top}))^{-1} = x^{2d}((x^d R)^{\top})^{-1}, \qquad \text{so}$$

$$(x^d(G^{\top})^{-1})(x^d(\hat{B}^{\top})^{-1}) = x^d(R^{\top})^{-1}, \qquad \text{that is}$$

$$\operatorname{adj}(G^{\top})\hat{A} = x^d(R^{\top})^{-1}.$$

Now $\det R = 1$ since $(x^d)^{n+1}\det R = \det(G\hat{B}) = x^{d+nd}$, so $(R^{\top})^{-1} = \operatorname{adj}(R^{\top}) \in \mathsf{K}[x]^{(n+1)\times(n+1)}$. Therefore $\operatorname{adj}(G^{\top})$ is an approximant basis of $\hat{A}$ of order d. The theorem now follows from Lemma 7 by noting that G is $\boldsymbol{N}$-row reduced. $\square$

EXAMPLE 15. *We apply Theorem 14 to the problem of Example 2 with shifts $\boldsymbol{N} = (5, 3, 4, 5)$. We have*

$$A = \begin{bmatrix} x^4+x^2+1 & x^4+1 & x^4+x^3+1 \\ 1 & & \\ & 1 & \\ & & 1 \end{bmatrix}$$

$$B = \begin{bmatrix} 1 \\ x^4+x^2+1 \\ x^4+1 \\ x^4+x^3+1 \end{bmatrix}$$

Algorithm 2 DualitySimPade

Input: $(\boldsymbol{S}, (x^d, \ldots, x^d), \boldsymbol{N})$, an instance of Problem 3 of size n.

Output: $(\boldsymbol{\lambda}, \boldsymbol{\delta})$, solution specification.

1 $B \leftarrow [1, S_1, \ldots, S_n]^T \in \mathsf{K}[x]^{(n+1)\times 1}$
2 $G \leftarrow \mathsf{PopovBasis}(d, B, \boldsymbol{N})$
3 $\boldsymbol{\eta} \leftarrow \mathrm{rowdeg}_{\boldsymbol{N}} G$
4 $\hat{\boldsymbol{\lambda}} \leftarrow$ first column of $\mathrm{adj}(G^\top)$
5 $\hat{\boldsymbol{\delta}} \leftarrow (\eta - N - \eta_1, \ldots, \eta - N - \eta_{n+1})$, where $\eta = \sum_i \eta_i$ and $N = \sum_i N_i$
6 $I \leftarrow \{i \mid \hat{\boldsymbol{\delta}}_i < 0\}$, and $k \leftarrow |I|$
7 $(\boldsymbol{\lambda},\ \boldsymbol{\delta}) \leftarrow (\hat{\boldsymbol{\lambda}}_{i\in I},\ (\hat{\boldsymbol{\delta}}_i)_{i\in I}) \in \mathsf{K}[x]^{k\times 1} \times \mathbb{Z}^k$
8 **return** $(\boldsymbol{\lambda}, \boldsymbol{\delta})$

An $\boldsymbol{N}$-minimal approximant basis to order $d = 5$ of B is

$$G = \begin{bmatrix} x & 0 & x & 0 \\ 1 & x^2+1 & 0 & 0 \\ 0 & 1 & x^2+1 & 0 \\ 0 & x & x+1 & 1 \end{bmatrix}, \textit{ and}$$

$$\mathrm{adj}(G)^\top = \begin{bmatrix} x^4+1 & x^2+1 & 1 & x^3+1 \\ x & x^3+x & x & x^4+x \\ x^3+x & x & x^3+x & x^4+x^3+x \\ 0 & 0 & 0 & x^5 \end{bmatrix}.$$

$\mathrm{adj}(G)^\top$ *can be confirmed to be an $(-\boldsymbol{N})$-minimal approximant basis of A, since $\mathrm{adj}(G)^\top A \equiv 0 \mod x^d$, and since the $(-\boldsymbol{N})$-leading coefficient matrix of $\mathrm{adj}(G)^\top$ has full rank.*

Algorithm 2 uses Theorem 14 to solve a Simultaneous Padé approximation by computing a minimal approximant basis of B in Popov form.

THEOREM 16. *Algorithm 2 is correct. The cost of the algorithm is $O(n^{\omega-1}\,\mathsf{M}(d)(\log d)(\log d/n)^2)$ operations in K.*

PROOF. Correctness follows from Theorem 14. The complexity estimate is achieved if the algorithms supporting Theorem 11 and Theorem 12 are used for the computation in lines 2 and 4, respectively. □

5. A DIVIDE & CONQUER ALGORITHM

Our second algorithm can handle the full generality of Problem 3. It works by first solving n single Padé approximations, one for each of the S_i individually, and then intersecting these solutions to form approximations of multiple S_i simultaneously. The intersection is structured in a Divide & Conquer tree, and performed by computing minimal approximant bases. Let $(\boldsymbol{S}, \boldsymbol{g}, \boldsymbol{N})$ be an instance of Problem 3 of size n.

The idea of the intersection algorithm is the following: consider that we have solution specifications for two different Simultaneous Padé problems, $(\boldsymbol{\lambda}_1, \boldsymbol{\delta}_1)$ and $(\boldsymbol{\lambda}_2, \boldsymbol{\delta}_2)$. We then compute an approximant basis G of the following matrix:

$$R = \left[\begin{array}{c|c} 1 & 1 \\ \hline -\boldsymbol{\lambda}_1 & \\ \hline & -\boldsymbol{\lambda}_2 \end{array}\right] \qquad (4)$$

G then encodes the *intersection* of the $\mathsf{K}[x]$-linear combinations of the $\boldsymbol{\lambda}_1$ with the $\mathsf{K}[x]$-linear combinations of the $\boldsymbol{\lambda}_2$: any $\lambda \in \mathsf{K}[x]$ residing in both sets of polynomials will appear as the first entry of a vector in the row space of G. We compute G as an $\boldsymbol{r}$-minimal approximant basis to high enough order, where $\boldsymbol{r}$ is selected carefully such that the $\boldsymbol{r}$-degree of any $(\lambda \mid \ldots) \in \mathrm{Row}(G)$ will equal the $(-\boldsymbol{N})$-degree of the completion of λ according to the combined Simultaneous Padé problem, whenever this degree is negative. From those rows of G with negative $\boldsymbol{r}$-degree we then get a solution specification for the combined problem.

EXAMPLE 17. *Consider again Example 2. We divide the problem into two sub-problems $\boldsymbol{S}_1 = (S_1, S_2)$, $\boldsymbol{N}_1 = (5,3,4)$, and $\boldsymbol{S}_2 = (S_3)$ and $\boldsymbol{N}_2 = (5,5)$. Note that $N_{1,0} = N_{2,0} = 5$, since this is the degree bound on the sought λ for the combined problem. The sub-problems have the following solution specifications and their completions:*

$$(\boldsymbol{\lambda}_1, \boldsymbol{\delta}_1) = ([x^4+1,\ x^3+x]^\top,\ (-1,-1))$$

$$A_1 = \begin{pmatrix} x^4+1 & x^2+1 & 1 \\ x^3+x & x & x^3+x \end{pmatrix}$$

$$(\boldsymbol{\lambda}_2, \boldsymbol{\delta}_2) = ([x^2,\ x^3+x+1]^\top,\ (-3,-2))$$

$$A_2 = \begin{pmatrix} x^2 & x^2 \\ x^3+x+1 & x+1 \end{pmatrix}$$

We construct R as in (4), and compute G, a minimal approximant basis of R of order 7 and with shifts $\boldsymbol{r} = (-5 \mid -1, -1 \mid -3, -2)$ (the G below is actually in $\boldsymbol{r}$-Popov form):

$$G = \begin{pmatrix} x^8 & 0 & 0 & 0 & 0 \\ x^3+x+1 & x^4+1 & 1 & 0 & 1 \\ x^3+x^2+x+1 & 1 & x+1 & 1 & 1 \\ x^4+x^3+x+1 & 1 & 1 & x^2 & 1 \\ x^4+1 & 1 & 0 & x+1 & x+1 \end{pmatrix}$$

G has $\boldsymbol{r}$-row degree $(3,3,0,-1,-1)$. Only rows 4 and 5 have negative $\boldsymbol{r}$-degree, and their first entries are the linearly independent solutions x^4+x^3+x+1 and x^4+1. Both solutions complete into vectors with $(-\boldsymbol{N})$-degree -1.

To prove the correctness of the above intuition, we will use Algorithm 1 (DirectSimPade). The following lemma says that to solve two simultaneous Padé approximations, one can compute a minimal approximant basis of one big matrix A constructed essentially from two of the matrices employed in DirectSimPade. Afterwards, Lemma 19 uses this to show that a minimal approximant basis of R in (4) provides the crucial information in a minimal approximant basis of A.

LEMMA 18. *Let $(\boldsymbol{S}_1, \boldsymbol{g}_1, \boldsymbol{N}_1)$ and $(\boldsymbol{S}_2, \boldsymbol{g}_2, \boldsymbol{N}_2)$ be two instances of Problem 3 of lengths n_1, n_2 respectively, and where $\boldsymbol{N}_1 = (N_0 \mid \grave{\boldsymbol{N}}_1)$ and $\boldsymbol{N}_2 = (N_0 \mid \grave{\boldsymbol{N}}_2)$. Let $\boldsymbol{S} = (\boldsymbol{S}_1 \mid \boldsymbol{S}_2)$, $\boldsymbol{g} = (\boldsymbol{g}_1 \mid \boldsymbol{g}_2)$ and $\boldsymbol{N} = (N_0 \mid \grave{\boldsymbol{N}}_1 \mid \grave{\boldsymbol{N}}_2)$ be the combined problem having length $n = n_1 + n_2$.*

Let $\boldsymbol{h}_i = (-\boldsymbol{N}_i \mid N_0 - 1 \ldots N_0 - 1) \in \mathbb{Z}^{2n_i+1}$ for $i = 1, 2$. Let $(F, \boldsymbol{\delta}) = \mathsf{NegMinBasis}(d, A, \boldsymbol{a})$, where A of dimension $(2n+3) \times (n+2)$ is given as:

$$A = [\ A_1 \mid A_2\ ] = \left[\begin{array}{cc|cc} & & 1 & 1 \\ -\boldsymbol{S}_1 & & -1 & \\ I & & & \\ \Gamma_{\boldsymbol{g}_1} & & & \\ & -\boldsymbol{S}_2 & & -1 \\ & I & & \\ & \Gamma_{\boldsymbol{g}_2} & & \end{array}\right],$$

Algorithm 3 RecursiveSimPade

Input: $(\boldsymbol{S}, \boldsymbol{g}, \boldsymbol{N})$, an instance of Problem 3 of size n.
Output: $(\boldsymbol{\lambda}, \boldsymbol{\delta})$, a solution specification.

1 **if** $n = 1$ **then**
2   **return** DirectSimPade$(\boldsymbol{S}, \boldsymbol{g}, \boldsymbol{N})$
3 **else**
4     $\boldsymbol{S}_1, \boldsymbol{g}_1 \leftarrow$ the first $\lceil n/2 \rceil$ elements of $\boldsymbol{S}, \boldsymbol{g}$
5     $\boldsymbol{S}_2, \boldsymbol{g}_2 \leftarrow$ the last $\lfloor n/2 \rfloor$ elements of $\boldsymbol{S}, \boldsymbol{g}$
6     $\boldsymbol{N}_1 \leftarrow (N_0, N_1, \ldots, N_{\lceil n/2 \rceil})$
7     $\boldsymbol{N}_2 \leftarrow (N_0, N_{\lceil n/2 \rceil + 1}, \ldots, N_n)$
8     $(\boldsymbol{\lambda}_1, \boldsymbol{\delta}_1) \leftarrow$ RecursiveSimPade$(\boldsymbol{S}_1, \boldsymbol{g}_1, \boldsymbol{N}_1)$
9     $(\boldsymbol{\lambda}_2, \boldsymbol{\delta}_2) \leftarrow$ RecursiveSimPade$(\boldsymbol{S}_2, \boldsymbol{g}_2, \boldsymbol{N}_2)$
10     $\boldsymbol{r} \leftarrow (-N_0 \mid \boldsymbol{\delta}_1 \mid \boldsymbol{\delta}_2)$
11     $d \leftarrow N_0 + \max_i \deg g_i - 1$
12     $R \leftarrow \left[\begin{array}{c|c} 1 & 1 \\ \hline -\boldsymbol{\lambda}_1 & \\ \hline & -\boldsymbol{\lambda}_2 \end{array}\right]$
13     $([\ \boldsymbol{\lambda} \mid * \ ], \boldsymbol{\delta}) \leftarrow$ NegMinBasis$(d, R, \boldsymbol{r})$
14   **return** $(\boldsymbol{\lambda}, \boldsymbol{\delta})$
15 **end if**

with $\boldsymbol{a} = (-N_0 \mid \boldsymbol{h}_1 \mid \boldsymbol{h}_2)$ *and* $d = N_0 + \max_i \deg g_i - 1$. *Then* $(\boldsymbol{\lambda}, \boldsymbol{\delta})$ *is a solution specification to* $(\boldsymbol{S}, \boldsymbol{g}, \boldsymbol{N})$, *where* $\boldsymbol{\lambda}$ *is the first column of* F.

PROOF. Note that the matrix A is right equivalent to the following matrix B:

$$B := A \begin{bmatrix} & & I & \\ & & & I \\ 1 & & S_1 & \\ & 1 & & S_2 \end{bmatrix} = \left[\begin{array}{cc|cc} 1 & 1 & -\boldsymbol{S}_1 & -\boldsymbol{S}_2 \\ -1 & & & \\ & & I & \\ & & \Gamma_{\boldsymbol{g}_1} & \\ & -1 & & \\ & & & I \\ & & & \Gamma_{\boldsymbol{g}_2} \end{array}\right].$$

Since F is an $\boldsymbol{a}$-minimal approximant of A of order d, then it will also be one for B. Let P be the permutation matrix that produces the following matrix $C := PB$:

$$C = PB = \left[\begin{array}{cc|cc} 1 & 1 & -\boldsymbol{S}_1 & -\boldsymbol{S}_2 \\ & & I & \\ & & & I \\ & & \Gamma_{\boldsymbol{g}_1} & \\ & & & \Gamma_{\boldsymbol{g}_2} \\ \hline -1 & & & \\ & -1 & & \end{array}\right] = \left[\begin{array}{cc|c} 1 & 1 & -\boldsymbol{S} \\ & & I \\ & & \Gamma_{\boldsymbol{g}} \\ \hline -1 & & \\ & -1 & \end{array}\right].$$

Define $\boldsymbol{c} := \boldsymbol{a}P^{-1}$, and note that $\boldsymbol{c} = (\boldsymbol{h} \mid -N_0, -N_0)$. Since $F =$ NegMinBasis$(d, A, \boldsymbol{a})$, then $(FP^{-1}, \boldsymbol{\delta})$ is a valid output of NegMinBasis$(d, C, \boldsymbol{c})$. Furthermore, since the first column of P is $(1, 0, \ldots, 0)$, the first column of F will be equal to the first column of FP^{-1}.

We are therefore finished if we can show that if $(F', \boldsymbol{\delta}')$ is any valid output of NegMinBasis$(d, C, \boldsymbol{c})$, then the first column of F' together with $\boldsymbol{\delta}'$ form a solution specification to $(\boldsymbol{S}, \boldsymbol{g}, \boldsymbol{N})$.

Consider therefore such an $(F', \boldsymbol{\delta}')$. By the first two columns of C, we must have $F'_{*,1} \equiv F'_{*,2n+2} \equiv F'_{*,2n+3} \bmod x^d$, where $F'_{*,i}$ denotes the i'th column of F'. Since each row of F' have negative $\boldsymbol{c}$-degree, and since $N_0 < d$, then the congruences must lift to equalities. We can therefore write $F = [G \mid F'_{*,1} \mid F'_{*,1}]$ for some $G \in \mathsf{K}[x]^{k \times (2n+1)}$ for some k, and we have $\mathrm{rowdeg}_{\boldsymbol{h}} G = \mathrm{rowdeg}_{\boldsymbol{c}} F' = \boldsymbol{\delta}'$.

By the last n columns of C, we have $GH \equiv 0 \mod x^d$, where

$$H = \begin{bmatrix} -\boldsymbol{S} \\ I \\ \Gamma_{\boldsymbol{g}} \end{bmatrix}.$$

In fact, $(G, \boldsymbol{\delta}')$ is a valid output for NegMinBasis$(d, H, \boldsymbol{h})$: for G has full row rank since F' does; G is $\boldsymbol{h}$-row reduced since F' is $\boldsymbol{c}$-row reduced; and any negative $\boldsymbol{h}$-order d approximant of H must clearly be in the span of G since F' is a negative $\boldsymbol{c}$-minimal approximant basis of C.

By the choice of d, then Theorem 10 therefore implies that the first column of G together with $\boldsymbol{\delta}'$ form a solution specification to the problem $(\boldsymbol{S}, \boldsymbol{g}, \boldsymbol{N})$. Since the first column of G is also the first column of F', this finishes the proof. □

LEMMA 19. *In the context of Lemma 18, let* $(\boldsymbol{\lambda}_1, \boldsymbol{\delta}_1)$ *and* $(\boldsymbol{\lambda}_2, \boldsymbol{\delta}_2)$ *be solution specifications to the two sub-problems, and let* $\boldsymbol{r} = (-N_0 \mid \boldsymbol{\delta}_1 \mid \boldsymbol{\delta}_2)$. *If* $([\boldsymbol{\lambda} \mid *], \boldsymbol{\delta}) =$ NegMinBasis$(d, R, \boldsymbol{r})$, *where* $\boldsymbol{\lambda}$ *is a column vector and*

$$R = \left[\begin{array}{c|c} 1 & 1 \\ \hline -\boldsymbol{\lambda}_1 & \\ \hline & -\boldsymbol{\lambda}_2 \end{array}\right],$$

then $(\boldsymbol{\lambda}, \boldsymbol{\delta})$ *is a solution specification for the combined problem.*

PROOF. We will prove the lemma by using Lemma 9 to relate valid outputs of NegMinBasis$(d, R, \boldsymbol{r})$ with valid outputs of NegMinBasis$(d, A, \boldsymbol{a})$ from Lemma 18.

For $i = 1, 2$, since $(\boldsymbol{\lambda}_i, \boldsymbol{\delta}_i)$ is a solution specification to the i'th problem, then by Theorem 10 there is some $G_i \in \mathsf{K}[x]^{k_i \times 2n_i + 1}$ whose first column is $\boldsymbol{\lambda}_i$ and such that G_i is a valid output of NegMinBasis$(d, H_i, \boldsymbol{h}_i)$, where

$$H_i = \begin{bmatrix} -\boldsymbol{S}_i \\ I \\ \Gamma_{\boldsymbol{g}_i} \end{bmatrix} \in \mathsf{K}[x]^{(2n_i+1) \times n_i},$$

and $\boldsymbol{h}_i$ is as in Lemma 18. Note now that if

$$F_1 := \begin{bmatrix} 1 & & \\ & G_1 & \\ & & G_2 \end{bmatrix} \in \mathsf{K}[x]^{(k_1+k_2+1) \times (2n_1+2n_2+3)},$$

then $(F_1, \boldsymbol{r})$ is a valid output of NegMinBasis$(d, A_1, \boldsymbol{a})$: for $\mathrm{rowdeg}_{\boldsymbol{a}} F_1$ is clearly $\boldsymbol{r}$; F_1 has full row rank and is $\boldsymbol{r}$-row reduced; and the rows of F_1 must span all $\boldsymbol{a}$-order d approximants of A_1, since the three column "parts" of F_1 correspond to the three row parts of A_1. .

Note now that $F_1 A_2 = R$. Thus by Lemma 9, if $(F_2, \boldsymbol{\delta}) =$ NegMinBasis$(d, R, \boldsymbol{r})$, then $(F_2 F_1, \boldsymbol{\delta})$ is a valid output of NegMinBasis$(d, A, \boldsymbol{a})$. Note that by the shape of F_1 then the first column $\boldsymbol{\lambda}$ of $F_2 F_1$ is the first column of F_2. Thus $\boldsymbol{\lambda}, \boldsymbol{\delta}$ are exactly as stated in the lemma, and by Lemma 18 they must be a solution specification to the combined problem. □

THEOREM 20. *Algorithm 3 is correct. The cost of the algorithm is* $O(n^{\omega-1}\,\mathsf{M}(d)(\log d)(\log d/n)^2)$, $d = \max_i \deg g_i$.

PROOF. Correctness follows from Lemma 19. For complexity, note that the choice of order in Line 11 is bounded by $2 \max_i \deg g_i$, i.e. twice the value of d of this theorem. So if $T(n)$ is the cost Algorithm 3 for given n and where the order will be bounded by $O(d)$, then we have the following recursion:

$$T(n) = \begin{cases} 2T(n/2) + P(n) & \text{if } n > 1 \\ O(\mathsf{M}(d)\log d) & \text{if } n = 1 \text{ (see Section 2.5.1)} \end{cases},$$

where $P(n)$ is the cost of line 13. Using algorithm PopovBasis for the computation of the negative part of the minimal approximant bases we can set $P(n)$ to the target cost. The recursion then implies $T(n) \in O(P(n))$. □

Acknowledgements. The authors would like to thank George Labahn for valuable discussions, and for making us aware of the Hermite–Simultaneous Padé duality. We would also like to thank Vincent Neiger for making preprints of [19] available to us. The first author would like to thank the Digiteo Foundation for funding the research visit at Waterloo, during which most of the ideas of this paper were developed.

6. REFERENCES

[1] M. Alekhnovich. Linear Diophantine Equations Over Polynomials and Soft Decoding of Reed–Solomon Codes. *IEEE Trans. Inf. Th.*, 51(7):2257–2265, 2005.

[2] M. V. Barel and A. Bultheel. A general module theoretic framework for vector M-Padé and matrix rational interpolation. *Numerical Algorithms*, 3(1):451–461, Dec. 1992.

[3] B. Beckermann and G. Labahn. A uniform approach for Hermite Padé and simultaneous Padé approximants and their matrix-type generalizations. *Numerical Algorithms*, 3(1):45–54, 1992.

[4] B. Beckermann and G. Labahn. A Uniform Approach for the Fast Computation of Matrix-Type Padé Approximants. *SIAM J. Matr. Anal. Appl.*, 15(3):804–823, July 1994.

[5] B. Beckermann and G. Labahn. Recursiveness in matrix rational interpolation problems. *J. Comp. App. Math.*, 77(1–2):5–34, Jan. 1997.

[6] B. Beckermann and G. Labahn. Fraction-Free Computation of Simultaneous Padé Approximants. In *Proc. of ISSAC*, pages 15–22, 2009.

[7] B. Beckermann, G. Labahn, and G. Villard. Normal forms for general polynomial matrices. *J. Symb. Comp.*, 41(6):708–737, 2006.

[8] A. Bostan, C.-P. Jeannerod, and E. Schost. Solving structured linear systems with large displacement rank. *Th. Comp. Sc.*, 407(1–3):155–181, Nov. 2008.

[9] D. G. Cantor and E. Kaltofen. On fast multiplication of polynomials over arbitrary algebras. *Acta Informatica*, 28(7):693–701, 1991.

[10] M. Chowdhury, C.-P. Jeannerod, V. Neiger, E. Schost, and G. Villard. Faster Algorithms for Multivariate Interpolation With Multiplicities and Simultaneous Polynomial Approximations. *IEEE Trans. Inf. Theory*, 61(5):2370–2387, May 2015.

[11] Clément Pernet. *High Performance and Reliable Algebraic Computing.* Nov. 2014. Habilitation.

[12] D. Coppersmith and S. Winograd. Matrix Multiplication via Arithmetic Progressions. *J. Symb. Comp.*, 9(3):251–280, 1990.

[13] G.-L. Feng and K. K. Tzeng. A Generalization of the Berlekamp-Massey Algorithm for Multisequence Shift-Register Synthesis with Applications to Decoding Cyclic Codes. *IEEE Trans. Inf. Theory*, 37(5):1274–1287, 1991.

[14] F. L. Gall. Powers of tensors and fast matrix multiplication. In *Proc. of ISSAC*, pages 296–303, 2014.

[15] P. Giorgi, C. Jeannerod, and G. Villard. On the Complexity of Polynomial Matrix Computations. In *Proc. of ISSAC*, pages 135–142, 2003.

[16] S. Gupta, S. Sarkar, A. Storjohann, and J. Valeriote. Triangular x-basis decompositions and derandomization of linear algebra algorithms over $\mathsf{K}[x]$. *J. Symb. Comp.*, 47(4):422–453, 2012.

[17] F. Gustavson and D. Yun. Fast algorithms for rational Hermite approximation and solution of Toeplitz systems. *IEEE Trans. Circ. Sys.*, 26(9):750–755, 1979.

[18] C. Hermite. Sur la Formule d'Interpolation de Lagrange. *J. Reine und Angewandte Math.*, 84(1):70–79, 1878.

[19] C.-P. Jeannerod, V. Neiger, E. Schost, and G. Villard. Fast computation of minimal interpolation bases in Popov form for arbitrary shifts. Submitted to ISSAC'16.

[20] J. Justesen. On the complexity of decoding Reed-Solomon codes (Corresp.). *IEEE Trans. Inf. Theory*, 22(2):237–238, Mar. 1976.

[21] T. Kailath. *Linear Systems.* Prentice-Hall, 1980.

[22] A. Lenstra. Factoring Multivariate Polynomials over Finite Fields. *J. Comp. Syst. Sc.*, 30(2):235–248, 1985.

[23] K. Mahler. Perfect systems. *Compos. Math*, 19:95–168, 1968.

[24] T. Mulders and A. Storjohann. On Lattice Reduction for Polynomial Matrices. *J. Symb. Comp.*, 35(4):377–401, 2003.

[25] V. Neiger. Fast computation of shifted Popov forms of polynomial matrices via systems of modular polynomial equations. Submitted to ISSAC'16.

[26] J. S. R. Nielsen. Generalised Multi-sequence Shift-Register Synthesis using Module Minimisation. In *Proc. of IEEE ISIT*, 2013.

[27] Z. Olesh and A. Storjohann. The vector rational function reconstruction problem. In *Proc. of WWCA*, pages 137–149, 2006.

[28] G. Schmidt, V. Sidorenko, and M. Bossert. Collaborative Decoding of Interleaved Reed–Solomon Codes and Concatenated Code Designs. *IEEE Trans. Inf. Theory*, 55(7):2991–3012, 2009.

[29] V. Sidorenko and G. Schmidt. A Linear Algebraic Approach to Multisequence Shift-Register Synthesis. *Prob. Inf. Trans.*, 47(2):149–165, 2011.

[30] W. A. Stein et al. SageMath Software. http://www.sagemath.org.

[31] A. Storjohann. High-order lifting and integrality certification. *J. Symb. Comp.*, 36(3):613–648, 2003.

[32] Y. Sugiyama, M. Kasahara, S. Hirasawa, and T. Namekawa. Further Results on Goppa Codes and their Applications to Constructing Efficient Binary Codes. *IEEE Trans. Inf. Theory*, 22(5):518–526, 1976.

[33] J. von zur Gathen and J. Gerhard. *Modern Computer Algebra.* Cambridge Univ. Press, 3rd edition, 2012.

[34] W. Zhou and G. Labahn. Efficient algorithms for order basis computation. *J. Symb. Comp.*, 47(7):793–819, 2012.

Contraction of Ore Ideals with Applications

Yi Zhang*

Institute for Algebra, Johannes Kepler University, Linz A-4040, Austria
KLMM, AMSS, Chinese Academy of Sciences, Beijing 100190, China
zhangy@amss.ac.cn

ABSTRACT

Ore operators form a common algebraic abstraction of linear ordinary differential and recurrence equations. Given an Ore operator L with polynomial coefficients in x, it generates a left ideal I in the Ore algebra over the field $\mathbf{k}(x)$ of rational functions. We present an algorithm for computing a basis of the contraction ideal of I in the Ore algebra over the ring $R[x]$ of polynomials, where R may be either $\mathbf{k}$ or a domain with $\mathbf{k}$ as its fraction field. This algorithm is based on recent work on desingularization for Ore operators by Chen, Jaroschek, Kauers and Singer. Using a basis of the contraction ideal, we compute a completely desingularized operator for L whose leading coefficient not only has minimal degree in x but also has minimal content. Completely desingularized operators have interesting applications such as certifying integer sequences and checking special cases of a conjecture of Krattenthaler.

Keywords

Ore Algebra, Desingularization, Contraction, Syzygy

1. INTRODUCTION

There are various reasons why linear differential equations are easier than non-linear ones. One is of course that the solutions of linear differential equations form a vector space over the underlying field of constants. Another important feature concerns the singularities. While for a nonlinear differential equation the location of the singularity may depend continuously on the initial value, this is not possible for linear equations. Instead, a solution f of a differential equation

$$a_0(x)f(x) + \cdots + a_r(x)f^{(r)}(x) = 0,$$

where $a_0, \ldots, a_r$ are some analytic functions, can only have singularities at points $\xi \in \mathbb{C}$ with $a_r(\xi) = 0$.

In this article, we consider the case where $a_0, \ldots, a_r$ are polynomials. In this case, a_r can have only finitely many roots. We shall also consider the case of recurrence equations

$$a_0(n)f(n) + \cdots + a_r(n)f(n+r) = 0,$$

where again there is a strong connection between the roots of a_r and the singularities of a solution.

While every singularity of a solution leaves a trace in the leading coefficient of an equation, the converse is not true. In general, the leading coefficient a_r may have roots at a point where no solution is singular. Such points are called apparent singularities, and it is sometimes of interest to identify them. One technique for doing so is called desingularization. As an example, consider the recurrence operator

$$L = (1+16n)^2\partial^2 - 32(7+16n)\partial - (1+n)(17+16n)^2,$$

which is taken from [1, Section 4.1]. Here, ∂ denotes the shift operator $f(n) \mapsto f(n+1)$. For any choice of two initial values $u_0, u_1 \in \mathbb{Q}$, there is a unique sequence $u\colon \mathbb{N} \to \mathbb{Q}$ with $u(0) = u_0$, $u(1) = u_1$ and L applied to u gives the zero sequence. A priori, it is not obvious whether or not u is actually an integer sequence, if we choose u_0, u_1 from $\mathbb{Z}$, because the calculation of the $(n+2)$nd term from the earlier terms via the recurrence encoded by L requires a division by $(1+16n)^2$, which could introduce fractions. In order to show that this division never introduces a denominator, the authors of [1] note that every solution of L is also a solution of its left multiple

$$\begin{aligned} T &= \left(\frac{64}{(17+16n)^2}\partial + \frac{(23+16n)(25+16n)}{(17+16n)^2}\right)L \\ &= 64\partial^3 + (16n+23)(16n-7)\partial^2 - (576n+928)\partial \\ &\quad -(16n+23)(16n+25)(n+1). \end{aligned}$$

The operator T has the interesting property that the factor $(1+16n)^2$ has been "removed" from the leading coefficient. This is, however, not quite enough to complete the proof, because now a denominator could still arise from the division by 64 at each calculation of a new term via T. To complete the proof, the authors show that the potential denominators introduced by $(1+16n)^2$ and by 64, respectively, are in conflict with each other, and therefore no such denominators can occur at all.

The process of obtaining the operator T from L is called desingularization, because there is a polynomial factor in the leading coefficient of L which does not appear in the leading coefficient of T. In the example above, the price to be paid for the desingularization was a new constant factor 64 which

---

*Supported by the Austrian Science Fund (FWF) grants Y464-N18, NSFC grants (91118001, 60821002/F02) and a 973 project (2011CB302401).

ISSAC'16, ISSAC '16, July 19 - 22, 2016, Waterloo, ON, Canada

ACM 978-1-4503-4380-0/16/07 ... $15.00.
DOI: http://dx.doi.org/10.1145/2930889.2930890

appears in the leading coefficient of T but not in the original leading coefficient of L. Desingularization algorithms in the literature [2, 1, 3, 7, 8] care only about the removal of polynomial factors without introducing new polynomial factors, but they do not consider the possible introduction of new constant factors. A contribution of the present paper is a desingularization algorithm which minimizes, in a sense, also any constant factors introduced during the desingularization. For example, for the operator L above, our algorithm finds the alternative desingularization

$$\begin{aligned}\tilde{T} \;=\; & \partial^3 + \left(128n^3 - 104n^2 - 11n - 3\right)\partial^2 + \\ & \left(-256n^2 + 127n + 94\right)\partial - \\ & (128n^2 + 24n - 131)(1+n)^2,\end{aligned} \qquad (1)$$

which immediately certifies the integrality of its solutions.

In more algebraic terms, we consider the following problem. Given an operator $L \in \mathbb{Z}[x][\partial]$, where $\mathbb{Z}[x][\partial]$ is an Ore algebra (see Section 2 for definitions), we consider the left ideal $\langle L\rangle = \mathbb{Q}(x)[\partial]L$ generated by L in the extended algebra $\mathbb{Q}(x)[\partial]$. The contraction of $\langle L\rangle$ to $\mathbb{Z}[x][\partial]$ is defined as $\mathrm{Cont}(L) := \langle L\rangle \cap \mathbb{Z}[x][\partial]$. This is a left ideal of $\mathbb{Z}[x][\partial]$ which contains $\mathbb{Z}[x][\partial]L$, but in general more operators. Our goal is to compute a $\mathbb{Z}[x][\partial]$-basis of $\mathrm{Cont}(L)$. In the example above, such a basis is given by $\{L, \tilde{T}\}$ (see Example 4.8). The traditional desingularization problem corresponds to computing a basis of the $\mathbb{Q}[x][\partial]$-left ideal $\langle L\rangle \cap \mathbb{Q}[x][\partial]$.

The contraction problem for Ore algebras $\mathbb{Q}[x][\partial]$ was proposed by Chyzak and Salvy [10, Section 4.3]. For the analogous problem in commutative polynomial rings, there is a standard solution via Gröbner bases [4, Section 8.7]. It reduces the contraction problem to a saturation problem. This reduction also works for the differential case, but in that case it is not so helpful because it is less obvious how to solve the saturation problem. A solution was proposed by Tsai [24], which involves homological algebra and D-modules theory. Our work is based on desingularization for Ore operators in [7, 8]. In particular, the p-removing operator in [8, Lemma 4] provides us with a key to determine contraction ideals. The algorithm developed in this paper applies to both differential and difference cases. Moreover, we compute a completely desingularized operator in a contraction ideal, which has minimal leading coefficient in terms of both degree and content.

The rest of this paper is organized as follows. In Section 2, we describe Ore polynomial rings over a principal ideal domain, and extend the notion of p-removed operators to them. The notion of desingularized operators is defined and connected with contraction ideals in Section 3. We determine a contraction ideal in Section 4, and compute completely desingularized operators in Section 5.

2. PRELIMINARIES

This section is divided into three parts. First, we describe Ore algebras that are used in the paper. Second, we extend the notion of p-removed operators in [7, 8]. At last, we make some remarks on Gröbner basis computation over a principal ideal domain.

2.1 Ore Algebra

Throughout the paper, we let R be a principal ideal domain. For instance, R can be the ring of integers or that of univariate polynomials over a field. Note that $R[x]$ is a unique factorization domain. So every nonzero polynomial f in $R[x]$ can be written as cg, where $c \in R$ and $g \in R[x]$ whose coefficients have the trivial greatest common divisor. We call c the content and g the primitive part of f. They are unique up to the units in R.

We consider the *Ore algebra* $R[x][\partial;\sigma,\delta]$, where $\sigma : R[x] \to R[x]$ is a ring automorphism that leaves the elements of R fixed, and $\delta : R[x] \to R[x]$ is a σ-derivation, *i.e.*, an R-linear map satisfying the skew Leibniz rule

$$\delta(fg) = \sigma(f)\delta(g) + \delta(f)g \quad \text{for } f, g \in R[x].$$

The addition in $R[x][\partial;\sigma,\delta]$ is coefficient-wise and the multiplication is defined by associativity via the commutation rule $\partial p = \sigma(p)\partial + \delta(p)$ for $p \in R[x]$. The ring $R[x][\partial;\sigma,\delta]$ is abbreviated as $R[x][\partial]$ when σ and δ are clear from the context.

Given $L \in R[x][\partial]$, we can uniquely write it as

$$L = \ell_r\partial^r + \ell_{r-1}\partial^{r-1} + \cdots + \ell_0$$

with $\ell_0, \ldots, \ell_r \in R[x]$ and $\ell_r \neq 0$. We call r the *order* and ℓ_r the *leading coefficient* of L. They are denoted by $\deg_\partial(L)$ and $\mathrm{lc}_\partial(L)$, respectively. Assume that $P \in R[x][\partial]$ is of order k. A repeated use of the commutation rule yields

$$\mathrm{lc}_\partial(PL) = \mathrm{lc}_\partial(P)\sigma^k(\mathrm{lc}_\partial(L)). \qquad (2)$$

For a subset S of $R[x][\partial]$, the left ideal generated by S is denoted by $R[x][\partial] \cdot S$.

Let Q_R be the quotient field of R. Then $Q_R(x)[\partial]$ is an Ore algebra containing $R[x][\partial]$. For $L \in R[x][\partial]$, we define the *contraction ideal* of L to be $Q_R(x)[\partial]L \cap R[x][\partial]$ and denote it by $\mathrm{Cont}(L)$.

2.2 Removability

We generalize some terminologies given in [7, 8] by replacing the coefficient ring $\mathbb{K}[x]$ with $R[x]$, where $\mathbb{K}$ is a field.

Definition 2.1. *Let $L \in R[x][\partial]$ with positive order, and p be a divisor of $\mathrm{lc}_\partial(L)$ in $R[x]$.*

(i) We say that p is removable *from L at order k if there exist $P \in Q_R(x)[\partial]$ with order k, and $w, v \in R[x]$ with $\gcd(p, w) = 1$ in $R[x]$ such that*

$$PL \in R[x][\partial] \quad \text{and} \quad \sigma^{-k}(\mathrm{lc}_\partial(PL)) = \frac{w}{vp}\,\mathrm{lc}_\partial(L).$$

We call P a p-removing operator *for L over $R[x]$, and PL the corresponding* p-removed operator.

(ii) p is simply called removable *from L if it is removable at order k for some $k \in \mathbb{N}$. Otherwise, p is called* non-removable *from L.*

Note that every p-removed operator lies in $\mathrm{Cont}(L)$.

Example 2.2. *In the example of Section 1, $(1 + 16n)^2$ is removable from L at order 1. And T is the corresponding $(1 + 16n)^2$-removed operator for L.*

Example 2.3. *In the differential Ore algebra $\mathbb{Z}[x][\partial]$, where $\partial x = x\partial + 1$, let $L = x(x-1)\partial - 1$. Then $(1-x)\partial^2 - 2\partial = \left(\frac{1}{x}\partial\right)L$ is an x-removed operator for L (see [8, Example 3]).*

The authors of [7] provide a convenient form of p-removing operators over $\mathbb{K}[x]$ in order to get an order bound. We derive a similar form over $R[x]$ and use it in Section 5.

Lemma 2.4. *Let $L \in R[x][\partial]$ with positive order. Assume that $p \in R[x]$ is removable from L at order k. Then there exists a p-removing operator for L over $R[x]$ in the form*

$$\frac{p_0}{\sigma^k(p)^{d_0}} + \frac{p_1}{\sigma^k(p)^{d_1}}\partial + \cdots + \frac{p_k}{\sigma^k(p)^{d_k}}\partial^k,$$

where p_i belongs to $R[x]$, $\gcd(p_i, \sigma^k(p)) = 1$ in $R[x]$ or $p_i = 0$, $i = 0, 1, \ldots, k$, and $d_k \geq 1$.

Proof. By (2) and Definition 2.1 (i), $\mathrm{lc}_\partial(P) = \sigma^k(w/(vp))$ for some w, v in $R[x]$ with $\gcd(w, p) = 1$. Then we can write a p-removing operator for L over $R[x]$ in the form

$$P = \frac{p_0}{q_0\sigma^k(p)^{d_0}} + \frac{p_1}{q_1\sigma^k(p)^{d_1}}\partial + \cdots + \frac{p_k}{q_k\sigma^k(p)^{d_k}}\partial^k,$$

where $p_i, q_i \in R[x]$, $\gcd(p_iq_i, \sigma^k(p)) = 1$ in $R[x]$ or $p_iq_i = 0$, $i = 0, \ldots, k$, $d_k \geq 1$. Let $\tilde{P} = \left(\prod_{i=0}^k q_i\right) P$, $\tilde{p}_i = p_i \left(\prod_{j=0}^k q_j\right)/q_i$, $i = 0, \ldots, k$. Then

$$\tilde{P} = \frac{\tilde{p}_0}{\sigma^k(p)^{d_0}} + \frac{\tilde{p}_1}{\sigma^k(p)^{d_1}}\partial + \cdots + \frac{\tilde{p}_k}{\sigma^k(p)^{d_k}}\partial^k,$$

where $\gcd(\tilde{p}_i, \sigma^k(p)) = 1$ in $R[x]$ or $\tilde{p}_i = 0$, $i = 0, \ldots, k$. Moreover,

$$\sigma^{-k}(\mathrm{lc}_\partial(\tilde{P}L)) = \frac{\sigma^{-k}(\tilde{p}_k)}{p^{d_k}}\,\mathrm{lc}_\partial(L).$$

By Definition 2.1, $\tilde{P}$ is a p-removing operator for L over $R[x]$ with the required form. □

2.3 Gröbner bases

In Sections 4 and 5, we will make essential use of Gröbner bases in $R[x][\partial]$. When $R = \mathbf{k}[t]$ with $\mathbf{k}$ being a field, the notion of Gröbner bases and Buchberger's algorithm are available [15]. Furthermore, the corresponding implementation is available in [16]. In our case, σ is an R-automorphism of $R[x]$, which implies that $\sigma(x) = ax + b$ where a, b are in R and a is a unit. Let $\prec$ be a term order on $\{x^i\partial^j \mid i, j \in \mathbb{N}\}$. For any non-zero operator $P \in R[x][\partial]$, we define the *head term* of P to be the highest term appearing in P with respect to $\prec$, and denote it by $\mathrm{HT}(P)$. The coefficient of $\mathrm{HT}(P)$ is called the *head coefficient* of P. Let c be the head coefficient of P with respect to $\prec$. By the commutation rule, $\partial^i P$ has head coefficient ca^i, which is associated to c, because a^i is a unit. This observation enables us to extend the notion of Gröbner bases and Buchberger's algorithm in [4, 22] to Ore case in a straightforward way. For details, see [18, 6] and [20, IV.46.13].

3. DESINGULARIZATION AND CONTRACTION

In this section, we define the notion of desingularized operators, and connect it with contraction ideals. As a matter of notation, for an operator $L \in R[x][\partial]$, we set

$$M_k(L) = \{P \in \mathrm{Cont}(L) \mid \deg_\partial(P) \leq k\}.$$

Note that $M_k(L)$ is a left $R[x]$–submodule of $\mathrm{Cont}(L)$. We call it the kth submodule of $\mathrm{Cont}(L)$. When the operator L is clear from context, $M_k(L)$ is simply denoted by M_k.

Definition 3.1. *Let $L \in R[x][\partial]$ with order $r > 0$, and*

$$\mathrm{lc}_\partial(L) = cp_1^{e_1}\cdots p_m^{e_m}, \tag{3}$$

where $c \in R$ and $p_1, \ldots, p_m \in R[x] \setminus R$ are irreducible and pairwise coprime. An operator $T \in R[x][\partial]$ of order k is called a desingularized operator for L *if $T \in \mathrm{Cont}(L)$ and*

$$\sigma^{r-k}(\mathrm{lc}_\partial(T)) = \frac{a}{bp_1^{k_1}\cdots p_m^{k_m}}\,\mathrm{lc}_\partial(L), \tag{4}$$

where $a, b \in R$ with $b \neq 0$, and $p_i^{d_i}$ is non-removable from L for each $d_i > k_i$, $i = 1 \ldots m$.

Desingularized operators always exist by [8, Lemma 4].

Lemma 3.2. *Let $L \in R[x][\partial]$ be of order $r > 0$, and $k \in \mathbb{N}$ with $k \geq r$. Assume that T is a desingularized operator for L and $\deg_\partial(T) = k$.*

(i) $\deg_x(\mathrm{lc}_\partial(T)) = \min\{\deg_x(\mathrm{lc}_\partial(Q)) \mid Q \in M_k(L) \setminus \{0\}\}$.

(ii) $\partial^i T$ is a desingularized operator for L for each $i \in \mathbb{N}$.

(iii) Set $\mathrm{lc}_\partial(T) = ag$, where $a \in R$ and $g \in R[x]$ is primitive. Then, for all $F \in \mathrm{Cont}(L)$ of order j with $j \geq k$, $\sigma^{j-k}(g)$ divides $\mathrm{lc}_\partial(F)$ in $R[x]$.

Proof. (i) Let $t = \mathrm{lc}_\partial(T)$ and

$$d = \min\{\deg_x(\mathrm{lc}_\partial(Q)) \mid Q \in M_k(L) \setminus \{0\}\}.$$

Suppose that $d < \deg_x(t)$. Then there exists $Q \in \mathrm{Cont}(L)$ with $\deg_x(\mathrm{lc}_\partial(Q)) = d$. Without loss of generality, we can assume that $\deg_\partial(Q) = k$, because the leading coefficients of Q and $\partial^i Q$ are of the same degree for all $i \in \mathbb{N}$.

By pseudo-division in $R[x]$, we have that

$$st = q\,\mathrm{lc}_\partial(Q) + h$$

for some $s \in R \setminus \{0\}$, $q, h \in R[x]$, and $h = 0$ or $\deg_x(h) < d$. If h were nonzero, then $sT - qQ$ would be a nonzero operator of order k in $\mathrm{Cont}(L)$ whose leading coefficient is of degree less than d, a contradiction. Thus, $st = q\,\mathrm{lc}_\partial(Q)$. In particular, $\deg_x(q)$ is positive, as $d < \deg_x(t)$. It follows from (4) that

$$\sigma^{r-k}(\mathrm{lc}_\partial(Q)) = \sigma^{r-k}\left(\frac{st}{q}\right) = \frac{sa}{\sigma^{r-k}(q)bp_1^{k_1}\cdots p_m^{k_m}}\,\mathrm{lc}_\partial(L),$$

which belongs to $R[x]$. Hence, $\sigma^{r-k}(q)$ divides $\mathrm{lc}_\partial(L)$ in $R[x]$. Consequently, there exists $i \in \{1 \ldots m\}$ such that p_i divides $\sigma^{r-k}(q)$ in $R[x]$. This implies that p^{k_i+1} is removable from L, a contradiction.

(ii) It is immediate from Definition 3.1.

(iii) Let $\mathrm{lc}_\partial(F) = uf$, where $u \in R$ and f is primitive in $R[x]$. By (ii), $\partial^{j-k}T$ is a desingularized operator whose leading coefficient equals $a\sigma^{j-k}(g)$. A similar argument used in the proof of the first assertion implies that

$$vf = p\sigma^{j-k}(g) \quad \text{for some } v \in R \setminus \{0\} \text{ and } p \in R[x].$$

By Gauss's Lemma in $R[x]$, $\sigma^{j-k}(g) \mid f$. □

We describe a relation between desingularized operators and contraction ideals. Let I be a left ideal in $R[x][\partial]$, and $a \in R$. The saturation of I with respect to a is defined to be

$$I : a^\infty = \left\{P \in R[x][\partial] \mid a^i P \in I \text{ for some } i \in \mathbb{N}\right\}.$$

Since a is a constant with respect to σ and δ, the saturation $I : a^\infty$ is a left ideal.

Theorem 3.3. *Let $L \in R[x][\partial]$ with order $r > 0$. Assume that T is a desingularized operator for L. Let $\text{lc}_\partial(T)=ag$, where $a \in R$ and g is primitive in $R[x]$. If k is such that $T \in M_k$ for some $k \in \mathbb{N}$, then*

$$\text{Cont}(L) = (R[x][\partial] \cdot M_k) : a^\infty.$$

Proof. By Lemma 3.2 (ii), we may assume that the order of T is equal to k. Set $J = (R[x][\partial] \cdot M_k) : a^\infty$.

First, assume that $F \in J$. Then there exists $j \in \mathbb{N}$ such that $a^j F \in R[x][\partial] \cdot M_k$. It follows that $F \in Q_R(x)[\partial]L$. Thus, $F \in \text{Cont}(L)$ by definition.

Next, note that $\text{Cont}(L) = \cup_{i=r}^{\infty} M_i$ and that $M_i \subseteq M_{i+1}$. It suffices to show $M_i \subseteq J$ for all $i \geq k$. We proceed by induction on i.

For $i = k$. $M_k \subseteq J$ by definition.

Suppose that the claim holds for i. For any $F \in M_{i+1} \backslash M_i$, $\deg_\partial(F) = i+1$. By Lemma 3.2 (iii), $\text{lc}_\partial(F) = p\sigma^{i+1-k}(g)$ for some $p \in R[x]$. Then $\text{lc}_\partial(aF) = \text{lc}_\partial(p\partial^{i+1-k}T)$. It follows that $aF - p\partial^{i+1-k}T \in M_i$. Since

$$p\partial^{i+1-k}T \in R[x][\partial] \cdot M_k \subseteq R[x][\partial] \cdot M_i,$$

we have that $aF \in R[x][\partial] \cdot M_i$. On the other hand, $M_i \subset J$ by the induction hypothesis. Thus, $aF \in R[x][\partial] \cdot J$, which is J. Accordingly, $F \in J$ by the definition of saturation. □

4. AN ALGORITHM FOR COMPUTING CONTRACTION IDEALS

First, we translate an upper bound for the order of a desingularized operator over $Q_R[x]$ to $R[x]$.

Lemma 4.1. *Let $L \in R[x][\partial]$ with order $r > 0$, and $p \in R[x]$ be a primitive polynomial and a divisor of $\text{lc}_\partial(L)$. Assume that there exists a p-removing operator for L over $Q_R[x]$. Then there exists a p-removing operator for L over $R[x]$ of the same order as the one over $Q_R[x]$.*

Proof. Assume that $P \in Q_R(x)[\partial]$ is a p-removing operator for L over $Q_R[x]$. Let P be of order k. Then PL is of the form

$$PL = \frac{a_{k+r}}{b_{k+r}}\partial^{k+r} + \cdots + \frac{a_1}{b_1}\partial + \frac{a_0}{b_0}$$

for some $a_i \in R[x], b_i \in R \setminus \{0\}$, $i = 0, \ldots, k+r$. Moreover,

$$\sigma^{-k}\left(\text{lc}_\partial(PL)\right) = \frac{w}{vp}\,\text{lc}_\partial(L),$$

where $w, v \in R[x]$ with $\gcd(w,p) = 1$.

Let $b = \text{lcm}(b_0, b_1, \ldots, b_{k+r})$ in R and $P' = bP$. Then

$$P'L \in R[x][\partial] \quad \text{and} \quad \sigma^{-k}(\text{lc}_\partial(PL)) = \frac{bw}{vp}\,\text{lc}_\partial(L).$$

Since p is primitive, we have that $\gcd(bw, p) = 1$ in $R[x]$. Thus, P' is a p-removing operator of order k. □

By the above lemma, an order bound for a p-removing operator over $Q_R[x]$ is also an order bound for a p-removing operator over $R[x]$. The former has been well-studied in the literature. Order bounds for differential operators are given in [24, Algorithm 3.4] and [13, Lemma 4.3.12]. Those for recurrence operators are given in [7, Lemma 4] and [13, Lemma 4.3.3]. The quotients of desingularized operators with the given ideal generator are p-removing operators. So we can find order bounds for them.

By Theorem 3.3, determining a contraction ideal amounts to finding a desingularized operator T and a spanning set of M_k over $R[x]$, where k is an upper bound for the order of T.

Next, we present an algorithm for constructing a spanning set for $M_k(L)$ over $R[x]$, where L is a nonzero operator in $R[x][\partial]$ and k is a positive integer. To this end, we embed M_k into the free module $R[x]^{k+1}$ over $R[x]$.

Let us recall the right-hand division in $Q_R(x)[\partial]$ (see [5, Section 3] and [21, Page 483]). For each $F, G \in Q_R(x)[\partial]$ with $G \neq 0$, there exist unique elements $Q, R \in Q_R(x)[\partial]$ with $\deg_\partial(R) < \deg_\partial(G)$ or $R = 0$ such that $F = QG + R$. We call R the *right-hand remainder* of F by G and denote it by $\text{rrem}(F, G)$.

Let $F \in R[x][\partial]$ with order k. Then $F \in M_k$ if and only if $F \in Q_R(x)[\partial]L$, which is equivalent to $\text{rrem}(F, L) = 0$. Assume that $F = z_k\partial^k + \ldots + z_0$, where $z_k, \ldots, z_0 \in R[x]$ are to be determined. Then $\text{rrem}(F, L) = 0$ gives rise to a linear system

$$(z_k, \ldots, z_0)A = \mathbf{0}, \tag{5}$$

where A is a $(k+1) \times r$ matrix over $Q_R(x)$. Clearing denominators of the elements in A, we may further assume that A is a matrix over $R[x]$. We are concerned with the solutions of (5) *over* $R[x]$. Set

$$N_k = \left\{(f_k, \ldots, f_0) \in R[x]^{k+1} \mid (f_k, \ldots, f_0)A = \mathbf{0}\right\}.$$

We call N_k the module of syzygies defined by (5). With the notation just specified, the following theorem is evident.

Theorem 4.2.

$$\begin{array}{cccc} \phi: & M_k & \longrightarrow & N_k \\ & \sum_{i=0}^{k} f_i\partial^i & \mapsto & (f_k, \ldots, f_0) \end{array}$$

is a module isomorphism over $R[x]$.

By Theorem 4.2, M_k is finitely generated over $R[x]$. To find a spanning set over of M_k over $R[x]$, it suffices to compute a spanning set of the module of syzygies defined by (5) over $R[x]$. When R is a field, we just need to solve (5) over a principal ideal domain [23, Chapter 5]. When R is the ring of integers or the ring of univariate polynomials over a field, we can use Gröbner bases of polynomials over a principal domain [14, 12]. Their implementations are available in computer algebra systems such as `Macaulay2` [12] and `Singular` [11].

We now consider how to construct a desingularized operator for L. For $k \in \mathbb{Z}^+$, we define

$$I_k = \left\{[\partial^k]P \mid P \in M_k\right\} \cup \{0\},$$

where $[\partial^k]P$ stands for the coefficient of ∂^k in P. It is clear that I_k is an ideal of $R[x]$. We call I_k the kth coefficient ideal of $\text{Cont}(L)$. By the commutation rule, $\sigma(I_k) \subset I_{k+1}$.

Lemma 4.3. *Let $L \in R[x][\partial]$ be of positive order. If the kth submodule M_k of $\text{Cont}(L)$ has a spanning set $\{B_1, \ldots, B_\ell\}$ over $R[x]$, then the kth coefficient ideal*

$$I_k = \left\langle [\partial^k]B_1, \ldots, [\partial^k]B_\ell \right\rangle.$$

Proof. Obviously, $\langle [\partial^k]B_1, \ldots, [\partial^k]B_\ell \rangle \subseteq I_k$. Let $f \in I_k$. Then $f = \text{lc}_\partial(F)$ for some $F \in M_k$ with $\deg_\partial(F) = k$. Since M_k is generated by $\{B_1, \ldots, B_\ell\}$ over $R[x]$,

$$F = h_1B_1 + \cdots + h_\ell B_\ell, \quad \text{where } h_1, \ldots, h_\ell \in R[x].$$

Thus, $f = h_1\left([\partial^k]B_1\right) + \cdots + h_\ell\left([\partial^k]B_\ell\right)$. Consequently, $f \in \langle [\partial^k]B_1, \ldots, [\partial^k]B_\ell \rangle$. □

Theorem 4.4. *Let $L \in R[x][\partial]$ be of positive order. Assume that the kth submodule M_k of $\mathrm{Cont}(L)$ contains a desingularized operator for L. Let s be a nonzero element in the kth coefficient ideal with minimal degree. Then an operator S in M_k with leading coefficient s is a desingularized operator.*

Proof. Assume that T is a desingularized operator in M_k. By Lemma 3.2 (ii), we may assume that the order of T is equal to k. Let $t = \mathrm{lc}_\partial(T)$. Then $\deg(t) = \deg(s)$ by Lemma 3.2 (i). Let u be the leading coefficient of s with respect to x and v be that of t. Then $ut - vs$ is zero. Otherwise, $uT - vS$ would be an operator of order k whose leading coefficient with respect to ∂ has degree lower than $\deg_x(t)$, a contradiction to Lemma 3.2 (i). It follows from $ut = vs$ and Definition 3.1 that S is a desingularized operator. □

Let L be an operator in $R[x][\partial]$ of positive order. We can compute a spanning set $\{B_1, \ldots, B_\ell\}$ for the kth submodule of $\mathrm{Cont}(L)$ by Theorem 4.2, where k is an upper bound on the order of a desingularized operator for L.

Set $b_i = [\partial^k]B_i$, $i = 1, \ldots, \ell$. By Lemma 4.3, the kth coefficient ideal I_k of $\mathrm{Cont}(L)$ is generated by $\{b_1, \ldots, b_\ell\}$. Let $\bar{I}_k$ be the extension ideal of I_k in $Q_R[x]$. Since $Q_R[x]$ is a principal ideal domain, we have that $\bar{I}_k = \langle s' \rangle$ for some $s' \in Q_R[x]$. Then there exist $c'_1, \ldots, c'_\ell \in Q_R[x]$ such that $c'_1 b_1 + \ldots + c'_\ell b_\ell = s'$. By clearing denominators, we can find $c_1, \ldots, c_\ell \in R[x]$ such that $c_1 b_1 + \cdots + c_\ell b_\ell = s$, where $s = cs'$ for some $c \in R$. Then s is an element in I_k with minimal degree. It follows from Theorem 4.4 that $T = c_1 B_1 + \cdots + c_\ell B_\ell$ is a desingularized operator for L with $\mathrm{lc}_\partial(T) = s$.

Let c be the content of s. By Theorem 3.3, $\mathrm{Cont}(L)$ is the saturation of $R[x][\partial] \cdot M_k$ with respect to c. Note that c is contained in the center of $R[x][\partial]$. So a basis of the saturation ideal can be computed in the same way as in the commutative case.

To this end, we need to introduce some new indeterminates. Let σ_y be the identity map of $R[x, y]$, where y is a new indeterminate. Let δ_y be the σ_y-derivation that maps everything in $R[x, y]$ to zero. Then one can extend the ring $R[x][\partial]$ to $R[x, y][\partial, \partial_y]$. Moreover, $R[y][\partial_y]$ lies in the center of the extended ring. For $r \in R$, one can define an evaluation map

$$\begin{array}{cccc} \phi_r : & R[x, y][\partial, \partial_y] & \longrightarrow & R[x][\partial] \\ & \sum_{i=0}^{\ell} \sum_{j=0}^{m} f_{ij} y^i \partial_y^j & \mapsto & \sum_{i=0}^{\ell} f_{i0} r^i, \end{array}$$

where $f_{ij} \in R[x][\partial]$. Since $R[y][\partial_y]$ is contained in the center of $R[x, y][\partial, \partial_y]$, the map ϕ_r is a ring homomorphism.

Proposition 4.5. *Let I be a left ideal of $R[x][\partial]$ and c be non-zero element in R. Assume that J is a left ideal*

$$R[x, y][\partial, \partial_y] \cdot (I \cup \{1 - cy\}),$$

Then $I : c^\infty = J \cap R[x][\partial]$.

Proof. Let $J_{x,\partial} = J \cap R[x][\partial]$. If $G \in J_{x,\partial}$, then

$$G = Q_1 P + Q_2(1 - cy) \tag{6}$$

with $Q_1, Q_2 \in R[x, y][\partial, \partial_y]$ and $P \in I$. Temporarily passing to the extended ring $Q_R[x, y][\partial, \partial_y]$ of $R[x, y][\partial]$, we may apply the evaluation homomorphism $\phi_{1/c}$ to (6) and then multiply the equation by c^d, where $d = \deg_y(Q_1)$. We thus obtain $c^d G = QP$ with Q being in $R[x][\partial]$. Consequently, $J_{x,\partial} \subset I : c^\infty$.

Conversely, let $G \in I : c^\infty$, say $c^d G \in I$. Then $G \in R[x][\partial]$ and $c^d G \in J$. Since $1 - cy$ belongs to J,

$$1 - (cy)^d = (1 + cy + (cy)^2 + \cdots + (cy)^{d-1})(1 - cy) \in J$$

Since y and c commute with every element of $R[x, y][\partial]$,

$$\left(1 - (cy)^d\right) G = G \left(1 - (cy)^d\right) \in J.$$

Again, $(cy)^d G = y^d (c^d G) \in J$ because $c^d G \in J$. It follows that $G = \left(1 - (cy)^d\right) G + (cy)^d G \in J$. Thus, $G \in J_{x,\partial}$. □

For the case $R = \mathbb{Q}[t]$, where t is an indeterminate, an implementation of a saturation ideal with respect to a constant is available in [16].

We outline our method for determining contraction ideals.

Algorithm 4.6. *Given $L \in R[x][\partial]$, where $\partial x = (x + 1)\partial$ or $\partial x = x\partial + 1$, compute a basis of $\mathrm{Cont}(L)$.*

(1) Derive an upper bound k on the order of a desingularized operator for L.

(2) Compute a spanning set of M_k over $R[x]$.

(3) Compute a desingularized operator T, and set a to be the content of $\mathrm{lc}_\partial(T)$.

(4) Compute a basis of $(R[x][\partial] \cdot M_k) : a^\infty$.

The termination of this algorithm is evident. Its correctness follows from Theorem 3.3. We assume that the commutation rule in $R[x][\partial]$ is either $\partial x = (x + 1)\partial$ or $\partial x = x\partial + 1$ in $R[x][\partial]$, because we only know order bounds for those cases. In the shift case, a bound is derived from [7, Lemma 4]. More concretely, we factor $\mathrm{lc}_\partial(L)$ and compute the maximum of the dispersions of the factors with the trailing coefficient. In the differential case, we need to follow steps 1, 2 and 3 in [24, Algorithm 3.4] to rewrite the input operator as a b-function in the algebraic extension of each factor of $\mathrm{lc}_\partial(L)$, and bound integer roots of the trailing coefficient in each b-function. In step 2, we need to solve linear systems over $R[x]$ as stated in Theorem 4.2. This can be done by Gröbner basis computation. In step 3, T is computed according to Theorem 4.4 and the extended Euclidean algorithm in $Q_R[x]$. The last step is carried out according to Proposition 4.5.

Example 4.7. *Let $\mathbb{Q}[t][n][\partial]$ be the shift Ore algebra, in which the commutation rule is $\partial n = (n + 1)\partial$. Consider*

$$L = (n - 1)(n + t)\partial + n + t + 1.$$

By [7, Lemma 4], we obtain an order bound 2 for a desingularized operator. Thus, M_2 contains a desingularized operator for L. In step 2 of Algorithm 4.6, we find that M_2 is generated by

$$\begin{aligned} T_1 &= (2 + t)n\partial^2 + (4 - n + t)\partial - 1, \\ T_2 &= (n - 1)n\partial^2 + 2(n - 1)\partial + 1, \end{aligned}$$

where T_1 is a desingularized operator, $\mathrm{lc}_\partial(T_1) = (2 + t)n$. Using Gröbner bases, $\mathrm{Cont}(L) = (\mathbb{Q}[t][n][\partial] \cdot M_2) : (2 + t)^\infty$ is generated by $\{L, T_1\}$.

Let us consider the example in Section 1.

Example 4.8. *In the shift Ore algebra* $\mathbb{Z}[n][\partial]$*, let*

$$L = (1 + 16n)^2\partial^2 - 32(7 + 16n)\partial - (1 + n)(17 + 16n)^2.$$

By [7, Lemma 4], we obtain an order bound 3 for a desingularized operator. Thus, M_3 *contains a desingularized operator for L. In step 2 of Algorithm 4.6, we find that* M_3 *is generated by* $\{L, \tilde{T}\}$*, where* $\tilde{T}$ *is given in (1). Note that* $\mathrm{lc}_\partial(\tilde{T})=1$*. Thus,* $\tilde{T}$ *is a desingularized operator. Consequently,*

$$\mathrm{Cont}(L) = (\mathbb{Z}[n][\partial] \cdot \{L, \tilde{T}\}) : 1^\infty = \mathbb{Z}[n][\partial] \cdot \{L, \tilde{T}\}.$$

Example 4.9. *Let* $\mathbb{Z}[x][\partial]$ *be the differential Ore algebra, in which the commutation rule is* $\partial x = x\partial + 1$*. Consider the operator* $L = x\partial^2 - (x + 2)\partial + 2 \in \mathbb{Z}[x][\partial]$ *in [3]. By [24, Algorithm 3.4], we obtain an order bound 4 for a desingularized operator. Thus,* M_4 *contains a desingularized operator for L. In step 2 of Algorithm 4.6, we find that* M_4 *is generated by* $\{L, \partial L, T\}$*, where* $T = \partial^4 - \partial^3$*. Note that* $\mathrm{lc}_\partial(T) = 1$*. Thus, T is a desingularized operator. Consequently,*

$$\mathrm{Cont}(L) = (\mathbb{Z}[x][\partial] \cdot \{L, \partial L, T\}) : 1^\infty = \mathbb{Z}[x][\partial] \cdot \{L, T\}.$$

5. COMPLETE DESINGULARIZATION

As seen in Section 1, the shift operator

$$L = (1 + 16n)^2\partial^2 - (224 + 512n)\partial - (1 + n)(17 + 16n)^2$$

has a desingularized operator T with leading coefficient 64. But the content of $\mathrm{lc}_\partial(L)$ is 1. The redundant content 64 has been removed by computing another desingularized operator $\tilde{T}$ in (1). This enables us to see immediately that the sequence annihilated by L is an integer sequence when its initial values are integers.

Krattenthaler proposes a conjecture in [17]: Let $(a_n)_{n\geq 0}$ and $(b_n)_{n\geq 0}$ be two P-recursive sequences over $\mathbb{Z}$ with leading coefficients n. Then $(n!a_nb_n)_{n\geq 0}$ is also a P-recursive sequence over $\mathbb{Z}$ with leading coefficient n. To test the conjecture for the two particular sequences, one may first compute an annihilator L of $(n!a_nb_n)_{n\geq 0}$, and then look for a nonzero operator in $\mathrm{Cont}(L)$ whose leading coefficient has both minimal degree and "minimal" content with respect to n. When the content is equal to 1, the conjecture is true for these sequences.

These two observations motivate us to define the notion of completely desingularized operators.

Definition 5.1. *Let* $L \in R[x][\partial]$ *with positive order, and Q a desingularized operator for L. Set c be the content of* $\mathrm{lc}_\partial(Q)$*. We call Q a* completely desingularized operator *for L if c is a divisor of the content of the leading coefficient of every desingularized operator for L.*

To see the existence of completely desingularized operators, we assume that L is of order r. For a desingularized operator T of order k, equations (3) and (4) in Definition 3.1 enable us to write

$$\sigma^{r-k}\left(\mathrm{lc}_\partial(T)\right) = c_T\, g, \tag{7}$$

where $c_T \in R$ and $g = p_1^{e_1-k_1} \cdots p_s^{e_m-k_m}$. Note that g is primitive and independent of the choice of desingularized operators.

Lemma 5.2. *Let* $L \in R[x][\partial]$ *with order* $r > 0$*. Set I to be the set consisting of zero and* c_T *given in (7) for all desingularized operators for L. Then I is an ideal of R.*

Proof. By Definition 3.1, the product of a nonzero element of R and a desingularized operator for L is also a desingularized one. So it suffices to show that I is closed under addition. Let T_1 and T_2 be two desingularized operators of orders k_1 and k_2, respectively. Assume that $k_1 \geq k_2$. By (7),

$$\sigma^{r-k_1}\left(\mathrm{lc}_\partial(T_1)\right) = c_1\, g \quad \text{and} \quad \sigma^{r-k_2}\left(\mathrm{lc}_\partial(T_2)\right) = c_2\, g.$$

If $c_1 + c_2 = 0$, then there is nothing to prove. Otherwise, a direct calculation implies that

$$\mathrm{lc}_\partial(T_1) = c_1\sigma^{k_1-r}(g) \quad \text{and} \quad \mathrm{lc}_\partial\left(\partial^{k_1-k_2}T_2\right) = c_2\sigma^{k_1-r}(g).$$

Thus, $T_1+\partial^{k_1-k_2}T_2$ has leading coefficient $(c_1+c_2)\sigma^{k_1-r}(g)$. Accordingly, $T_1 + \partial^{k_1-k_2}T_2$ is a desingularized one, which implies that $c_1 + c_2$ belongs to I. □

Since R is a principal ideal domain, I in the above lemma is generated by an element c, which corresponds to a completely desingularized operator.

The next technical lemma serves as a step-stone to construct completely desingularized operators.

Lemma 5.3. *Let* $L \in R[x][\partial]$ *with order* $r > 0$*, and* $k \geq r$*. Then* $R[x][\partial]\cdot M_k{=}R[x][\partial]\cdot M_{k+1}$ *if and only if* $\sigma(I_k){=}I_{k+1}$*.*

Proof. Assume that $\sigma(I_k) = I_{k+1}$. Since $M_k \subset M_{k+1}$, it suffices to prove that $M_{k+1} \subset R[x][\partial] \cdot M_k$.

For each $T \in M_{k+1} \setminus M_k$, we have that $\mathrm{lc}_\partial(T) \in \sigma(I_k)$. Thus, there exists $F \in M_k$ such that $\sigma(\mathrm{lc}_\partial(F)) = \mathrm{lc}_\partial(T)$. In other words, $T - \partial F \in M_k$. Consequently, $T \in R[x][\partial] \cdot M_k$.

Conversely, assume that $R[x][\partial] \cdot M_{k+1} = R[x][\partial] \cdot M_k$. It suffices to prove that $I_{k+1} \subseteq \sigma(I_k)$ because $\sigma(I_k) \subseteq I_{k+1}$ by definition. Let $\mathcal{B}$ be a spanning set of M_k over R[x]. Then $\mathcal{B}$ is also a basis of the left ideal $R[x][\partial] \cdot M_k$.

Let $\prec$ be the term order such that $x^{\ell_1}\partial^{m_1}{\prec}x^{\ell_2}\partial^{m_2}$ if either $m_1{<}m_2$ or $m_1{=}m_2$ and $\ell_1{<}\ell_2$. Since $\deg_\partial(P){\leq}k$ for each $P \in \mathcal{B}$, S-polynomials and G-polynomials formed by elements in M_k have orders no more than k [4, Definition 10.9]. By Buchberger's algorithm, there exists a Gröbner basis $\mathcal{G}$ of $R[x][\partial] \cdot \mathcal{B}$ with respect to $\prec$ such that $\deg_\partial(G) \leq k$ for each $G \in \mathcal{G}$.

For $p{\in}I_{k+1}{\setminus}\{0\}$, there exists $T \in M_{k+1} \setminus M_k$ such that $\mathrm{lc}_\partial(T){=}p$. Since $T{\in}R[x][\partial] \cdot M_{k+1}$, we have $T{\in}R[x][\partial] \cdot M_k$. It follows that T is reduced to zero by $\mathcal{G}$. Thus,

$$T = \sum_{G\in\mathcal{G}} V_G G \quad \text{with } \mathrm{HT}(V_G G) \preceq \mathrm{HT}(T). \tag{8}$$

By the choice of term order, $\deg_\partial(V_G G) \leq k + 1$. If $V_G G$ is of order $k + 1$, then $\mathrm{lc}_\partial(V_G G) = a_G\, \sigma^{k+1-d_G}(\mathrm{lc}_\partial(G))$, where a_G is in $R[x]$ and d_G is the order of G. Comparing the leading coefficients of operators in both sides of (8) and noticing $\deg_\partial(T) = k + 1$, we have

$$p = \sum_{\deg_\partial(V_G G)=k+1} a_G\, \sigma^{k+1-d_G}(\mathrm{lc}_\partial(G)).$$

It follows that

$$\sigma^{-1}(p) = \sum_{\deg_\partial(V_G G)=k+1} \sigma^{-1}(a_G)\, \sigma^{k-d_G}(\mathrm{lc}_\partial(G)). \tag{9}$$

On the other hand, $\sigma^{k-d_G}(\mathrm{lc}_\partial(G)) = \mathrm{lc}_\partial\left(\partial^{k-d_G}G\right)$ implies that $\sigma^{k-d_G}(\mathrm{lc}_\partial(G)) \in I_k$. We have that $\sigma^{-1}(p) \in I_k$ by (9). Thus, $I_{k+1} \subset \sigma(I_k)$. □

By the above lemma, $I_j = \sigma^{j-\ell}(I_\ell)$ whenever $j \geq \ell$ and $\text{Cont}(L) = R[x][\partial] \cdot M_\ell$. In this case, a basis of I_j can be obtain by shifting a basis of I_ℓ, which allows us to find a completely desingularized operator.

Theorem 5.4. *Let $L \in R[x][\partial]$ with order $r > 0$. Assume that the ℓth submodule M_ℓ of $\text{Cont}(L)$ contains a basis of $\text{Cont}(L)$. Let I_ℓ be the ℓth coefficient ideal of $\text{Cont}(L)$, and $\mathbf{G}$ a reduced Gröbner basis of I_ℓ. Let $f \in \mathbf{G}$ be of the lowest degree in x and F be the operator in $\text{Cont}(L)$ with $\text{lc}_\partial(F) = f$. Then F is a completely desingularized operator for L.*

Proof. By Lemma 5.2, $\text{Cont}(L)$ contains a completely desingularized operator S. Let $j = \deg_\partial(S)$. Then $\text{lc}_\partial(S)$ is in I_j for some $j \geq \ell$. By Lemma 5.3, $\sigma^{j-\ell}(I_\ell) = I_j$. It follows that $\sigma^{\ell-j}(\text{lc}_\partial(S))$ belongs to I_ℓ. By (7), we have

$$\sigma^{r-j}(\text{lc}_\partial(S)) = c_S\, g,$$

where $c_S \in R$ and g is a primitive polynomial in $R[x]$. A direct calculation implies that $\sigma^{\ell-j}(\text{lc}_\partial(S)) = c_S\sigma^{\ell-r}(g)$. Since $\sigma^{\ell-j}(\text{lc}_\partial(S)) \in I_\ell$, so does $c_S\sigma^{\ell-r}(g)$.

Note that F is a desingularized operator by Theorem 4.4. By (7), $\sigma^{r-\ell}(f) = c_F\, g$, where $c_F \in R$. Thus, $f = c_F\sigma^{\ell-r}(g)$.

Since $\mathbf{G}$ is a reduced Gröbner basis of I_ℓ, f is the unique polynomial in $\mathbf{G}$ with minimal degree. Moreover, $c_S\sigma^{l-r}(g)$ is of minimal degree in I_ℓ. So it can be reduced to zero by f. Thus, $c_F \mid c_S$. On the other hand, $c_S \mid c_F$ by Definition 5.1. Thus, c_S and c_F are associated to each other. Consequently, F is a completely desingularized operator for L. □

The construction in the above theorem leads to the following algorithm.

Algorithm 5.5. *Given $L \in R[x][\partial]$, where $\partial x = (x+1)\partial$ or $\partial x = x\partial + 1$, compute a completely desingularized operator for L.*

(1) Compute a basis $\mathcal{A}$ of $\text{Cont}(L)$ by Algorithm 4.6.

(2) Set ℓ to be the highest order of the elements in $\mathcal{A}$. Compute a spanning set of M_ℓ over $R[x]$.

(3) Set $\mathcal{B}' = \{B \in \mathcal{B} \mid \deg_\partial(B) = \ell\}$. Compute a reduced Gröbner basis $\mathbf{G}$ of $\langle\{\text{lc}_\partial(B) \mid B \in \mathcal{B}'\}\rangle$.

(4) Set f to be the polynomial in $\mathbf{G}$ whose degree is the lowest one in x. Tracing back to the computation of step 3, one can find $u_B \in R[x]$ such that $f = \sum_{B\in\mathcal{B}'} u_B \,\text{lc}_\partial(B)$.

(5) Output $\sum_{B\in\mathcal{B}'} u_B B$.

The termination of this algorithm is evident. Its correctness follows from Theorem 5.4.

Example 5.6. *Consider two sequences $(a_n)_{n\geq 0}$ and $(b_n)_{n\geq 0}$ satisfying the following two recurrence equations [17]*

$$na_n = a_{n-1} + a_{n-2} \quad \text{and} \quad nb_n = b_{n-1} + b_{n-5},$$

respectively. The sequence $c_n = n!a_nb_n$ has an annihilator $L \in \mathbb{Z}[n][\partial]$ with

$$\deg_\partial(L) = 10 \text{ and } \text{lc}_\partial(L) = (n+10)(n^6+47n^5+\cdots+211696).$$

In step 1 of the above algorithm, $\text{Cont}(L) = R[x][\partial] \cdot M_{14}$. In steps 2 and 3, we observe that I_{14} is generated by $n+14$. In other words, we obtain a completely desingularized operator T of order 14 with $\text{lc}_\partial(T) = n + 14$. Translating into the recurrence equations of c_n, we arrive at

$$nc_n = \alpha_1 c_{n-1} + \cdots + \alpha_{14} c_{n-14},$$

where $\alpha_i \in \mathbb{Z}[n]$, $i = 1, \ldots, 14$. This verifies Krattenthaler's conjecture for the sequences a_n and b_n.

Note that it is impossible to have a completely desingularized operator of order less than 14. In fact, for some lower orders, one can obtain

$$\begin{aligned}
\sigma^{-11}(I_{11}) &= \langle 11104n, 4n(n-466), n(n^2-34n+1336)\rangle,\\
\sigma^{-12}(I_{12}) &= \langle 4n, n(n-24)\rangle,\\
\sigma^{-13}(I_{13}) &= \langle 2n, n(n-26)\rangle.
\end{aligned}$$

They cannot produce a leading coefficient whose degree and content are both minimal.

Example 5.7. *Consider the following recurrence equations:*

$$\begin{aligned}
na_n &= (31n-6)a_{n-1} + (49n-110)a_{n-2} + (9n-225)a_{n-3},\\
nb_n &= (4n+13)b_{n-1} + (69n-122)b_{n-2} + (36n-67)b_{n-3}.
\end{aligned}$$

Let $c_n = n!a_nb_n$, which has an annihilator $L \in \mathbb{Z}[n][\partial]$ of order 10 with $\text{lc}_\partial(L)=(n+9)\alpha$, where $\alpha\in\mathbb{Z}[n]$ and $\deg_n(\alpha)=20$.

By the known algorithms for desingularization in [2, 1, 7, 8], we find that c_n satisfies the recurrence equation

$$\beta nc_n = \beta_1 c_{n-1} + \ldots + \beta_{10} c_{n-10},$$

where β is an 853-digit integer, $\beta_i \in \mathbb{Z}[n]$, $i = 1, \ldots, 10$.

On the other hand, Algorithm 5.5 finds a completely desingularized operator T for L of order 14 whose leading coefficient is $n + 14$. Translating into the recurrence equation of c_n yields $nc_n = \gamma_1 c_{n-1} + \cdots + \gamma_{14} c_{n-14}$, where $\gamma_i \in \mathbb{Z}[n]$.

Let $L \in R[x][\partial]$ with positive order and T a desingularized operator for L. Then the degree of $\text{lc}_\partial(T)$ in x is equal to

$$d = \deg_x(\text{lc}_\partial(L)) - (\deg_x(p_1)k_1 + \cdots + \deg_x(p_m)k_m),$$

where $k_1, \ldots, k_m$ are given in Definition 4.1. Hence, $\text{Cont}(L)$ cannot contain any operator whose leading coefficient has degree lower than d.

We provide a lower bound for the content of the leading coefficients of operators in $\text{Cont}(L)$ with respect to the divisibility relation on R. To this end, we write

$$L = a_k f_k(x)\partial^k + a_{k-1}f_{k-1}(x)\partial^{k-1} + \cdots + a_0 f_0(x)$$

where $a_i \in R$ and $f_i(x) \in R[x]$ is primitive, $i = 0, 1, \ldots, k$. We say that L is *R-primitive* if $\gcd(a_0, a_1, \ldots, a_k) = 1$. As an easy consequence of [9, Lemma 9.5], Gauss's lemma in the commutative case also holds for R-primitive polynomials.

Lemma 5.8. *Let P and Q be two operators in $R[x][\partial]$. If P and Q are R-primitive, so is PQ.*

Theorem 5.9. *Let $L \in R[x][\partial]$ with positive order and p be a non-unit element of R. If L is R-primitive and $p \mid \text{lc}_\partial(L)$, then p is non-removable.*

Proof. Assume that p is removable, then there exists a p-removing operator P such that $PL \in R[x][\partial]$. By Lemma 2.1, we can write

$$P = \frac{p_0}{p^{d_0}} + \frac{p_1}{p^{d_1}}\partial + \cdots + \frac{p_k}{p^{d_k}}\partial^k$$

where $p_i \in R[x]$, $\gcd(p_i, p) = 1$ in $R[x]$, $i = 0, \ldots, k$ and $d_k \geq 1$. Let $d = \max_{0\leq i\leq k} d_i$ and $P_1 = p^d P$. Then the content c of P_1 with respect to ∂ is $\gcd(p_0,\dots,p_k)$ because $\gcd(p_i,p)=1$, $i=0,\dots,k$. Let $P_1=cP_2$. Then P_2 is the primitive part of P_1. In particular, P_2 is R-primitive. Then $cP_2L=p^dPL$. Since $\gcd(c,p)=1$ and $PL\in R[x][\partial]$, p divides the content of P_2L with respect to ∂. Since p is a non-unit element of R, P_2L is not R-primitive, a contradiction to Lemma 5.8. □

Example 5.10. *The minimal annihilator of* $\binom{4n}{n}+3^n$ *is of order 2. Its leading coefficient is*

$$3(n+2)(3n+4)(3n+5)(7n+3)\left(25n^2+21n+2\right)$$

We observe that 3 *is a constant factor of the leading coefficient. By Theorem 5.9,* 3 *is non-removable.*

6. CONCLUDING REMARKS

In this paper, we determine a basis of a contraction ideal defined by an Ore operator in $R[x][\partial]$, and compute a completely desingularized operator whose leading coefficient is minimal in terms of both degree and content. A more challenging topic is to consider the corresponding problems in the multivariate case.

Our algorithms rely heavily on the computation of Gröbner bases over a principal ideal domain R. At present, the computation of Gröbner bases over R is not fully available in a computer algebra system. So the algorithms in this paper are not yet implemented. To improve their efficiency, we need to use linear algebra over R as much as possible.

7. ACKNOWLEDGEMENT

I am grateful to my supervisors Manuel Kauers and Ziming Li for initiating this research project, stimulating inspirational discussions and helping me revise the paper. I thank Shaoshi Chen and anonymous referees for valuable information on literatures.

8. REFERENCES

[1] S. A. Abramov, M. Barkatou, and M. van Hoeij. Apparent singularities of linear difference equations with polynomial coefficients. *AAECC*, 117–133, 2006.

[2] S. A. Abramov and M. van Hoeij. Desingularization of linear difference operators with polynomial coefficients. In *Proc. of ISSAC'99*, 269–275, New York, NY, USA, 1999, ACM.

[3] M. A. Barkatou and S. S. Maddah. Removing apparent singularities of systems of linear differential equations with rational function coefficients. In *Proc. of ISSAC'15*, 53–60, New York, NY, USA, 2015, ACM.

[4] T. Becker and V. Weispfenning. *Gröbner Bases, A Computational Approach to Commutative Algebra.* Springer-Verlag, New York, USA, 1993.

[5] M. Bronstein and M. Petkovšek. An introduction to pseudo-linear algebra. *Theoretical Computer Science*, 3 -33, 1996.

[6] M. Ceria and T. Mora. Buchberger-Zacharias theory of multivariate Ore extensions. Submitted to J. of Pure and Applied Algebra., 2015.

[7] S. Chen, M. Jaroschek, M. Kauers, and M. F. Singer. Desingularization explains order-degree curves for Ore operators. In *Proc. of ISSAC'13*, 157–164, New York, NY, USA, 2013, ACM.

[8] S. Chen, M. Kauers, and M. F. Singer. Desingularization of Ore operators. *J. Symb. Comput.*, 74:617–626, 2016.

[9] R. C. Churchill and Y. Zhang. Irreducibility criteria for skew polynomials. *Journal of Algebra*, 322:3797–3822, 2009.

[10] F. Chyzak and B. Salvy. Non-commutative elimination in Ore algebras proves multivariate identities. *J. Symb. Comput.* , 26:187–227, 1998.

[11] W. Decker et al. *Singular, a computer algebra system for polynomial computations.* `https://www.singular.uni-kl.de/`.

[12] D. Grayson, M. Stillman, and D. Eisenbud. Macaulay2, a software system for research in algebraic geometry. `http://www.math.uiuc.edu/Macaulay2/`.

[13] M. Jaroschek. *Removable Singularities of Ore Operators.* PhD thesis, RISC-Linz, Johannes Kepler Univ., 2013.

[14] A. Kandri-Rody and D. Kapur. Computing a Gröbner basis of a polynomial ideal over a Euclidean domain. *J. Symb. Comput.* , 6:37–57, 1988.

[15] A. Kandri-Rody and V. Weispfenning. Non-commutative Gröbner bases in algebras of solvable type. *J. Symb. Comput.* , 9:1–26, 1990.

[16] C. Koutschan. *HolonomicFunctions (User's Guide).* RISC Report Series, Johannes Kepler Univ., 2010.

[17] G. Labahn et al. Workshop on symbolic combinatorics and computational differential algebra. `http://www.fields.utoronto.ca/video-archive/event/411/2015`.

[18] Z. Li and Y. Zhang. A note on Groebner bases of Ore polynomials over a PID. `http://www.algebra.uni-linz.ac.at/people/yzhang/GB.pdf`.

[19] J. Middeke. *A computational view on normal forms of matrices of Ore polynomials.* PhD thesis, Johannes Kepler University Linz, 2011.

[20] T. Mora. *Solving Polynomial Equation Systems* Vol. IV. Cambridge University Press, 2016.

[21] Ø. Ore. Theory of non-commutative polynomials. *The Annal of Mathematics*, 34:480–508, 1933.

[22] M. Saito, B. Sturmfels, and N. Takayama. *Gröbner Deformations of Hypergeometric Differential Equations.* Springer-Verlag, New York, USA, 1999.

[23] A. Storjohann. *Algorithms for Matrix Canonical Forms.* PhD thesis, Swiss Federal Institute of Technology Zurich, 2000.

[24] H. Tsai. Weyl closure of a linear differential operator. *J. Symb. Comput.* , 29:747–775, 2000.

Author Index

www.ingramcontent.com/pod-product-compliance
Ingram Content Group UK Ltd.
Pitfield, Milton Keynes, MK11 3LW, UK
UKHW051511290926
15471UKWH00008B/1554

9 781450 343800